THE MACMILLAN VISUAL DICTIONARY: MULTILINGUAL EDITION

THE MACMILLAN VISUAL DICTIONARY: MULTILINGUAL EDITION

MACMILLAN
U.S.A.

Library of Congress Cataloging-in-Publication Data

The Macmillan visual dictionary : multilingual edition / [compiled by]
Jean-Claude Corbeil and Ariane Archambault.
p. cm.
Includes bibliographical references (p.) and index.
ISBN 0-02-578115-4
1. Picture dictionaries. 2. Dictionaries. Polyglot. I. Corbeil, Jean-Claude.
II. Archambault, Ariane.
P361. M28 1994
413'. 1—dc20 94-15016
CIP

Created and produced
by Québec/Amérique International
a division of
Éditions Québec/Amérique Inc.
425, rue Saint-Jean-Baptiste, Montréal, Québec H2Y 2Z7
Tel. : (514) 393-1450 Fax : (514) 866-2430

Printed in Canada

10 9 8 7 6 5 4 3 2 1

ENGLISH LANGUAGE EDITION

William Rosen - *Publisher*
Natalie Chapman - *Senior Editor*
Nancy Cooperman - *Associate Editor*
Camillo LoGiudice - *Production Director*
Brian Holmes - *Production Editor*

EDITORIAL STAFF FOR THE ORIGINAL EDITION

Jacques Fortin - *Publisher*
Jean-Claude Corbeil - *Editor-in-chief*
Ariane Archambault - *Assistant Editor*
François Fortin - *Illustrations Editor*
Jean-Louis Martin - *Art Director*

COMPUTER GRAPHIC ARTISTS

Jacques Perrault
Anne Tremblay
Jocelyn Gardner
Christiane Beauregard
Michel Blais
Rielle Lévesque
Marc Lalumière
Stéphane Roy
Alice Comtois
Jean-Yves Ahern
Benoît Bourdeau

COMPUTER COPYEDITING

Yves Ferland

RESEARCH EDITOR

Serge D'Amico

PAGE SETUP

Pascal Goyette
Lucie Mc Brearty
Martin Langlois

PRODUCTION

Tony O'Riley

GRAPHIC DESIGN

Emmanuel Blanc

ACKNOWLEDGMENTS

In preparing *The Macmillan Visual Dictionary: Multilingual Edition*, we have benefited from the help of numerous groups, organizations and companies, which have provided us with up-to-date technical documents. We have also received judicious advice from various specialists, colleagues, terminologists and translators. We extend a special thank-you to our initial contributors, Édith Girard, René St-Pierre, Marielle Hébert, Christiane Vachon and Anik Lapointe. In addition, we wish to express our sincere gratitude to the following individuals and organizations:

A.C. Delco
Aérospatiale (France)
Aérospatiale Canada (ACI) Inc.
Air Canada (Linguistic Policy and Services)
Amity-Leather Products Company
Animat Inc.
Archambault Musique
International Association of Lighthouse Authorities (Marie-Hélène Grillet)
Association des groupes d'astronomes amateurs (Jean-Marc Richard)
Atlas Copco
Atomic Energy of Canada Ltd. (Pierre Giguère)
Bell Canada
Bell Helicopter Textron
Bellefontaine
Benoît, Richard
Beretta
Black & Decker
Bombardier Inc.
Boutique de harnais Pépin
British Hovercraft Corporation Ltd. (Division of Westland Aerospace)
C. Plath North American Division
Caloritech Inc.
Cambridge Instruments (Canada) Inc.
CAMIF (Direction relations extérieures)
Canada Billard & Bowling Inc. (Bernard Monsec)
Canadian National (Information and Linguistic Services)
Canadian Kenworth Company
Canadian Coleman Supply Inc.
Canadian Liquid Air Ltd.
Canadian Curling Association
Canadian Coast Guard
Canadian Broadcasting Corporation (Gilles Amyot, Pierre Beaucage, Claude L'Hérault, Pierre Laroche)
Carpentier, Jean-Marc
Casavant Frères Limitée (Gilbert Lemieux)
Centre de Tissage Leclerc Inc.
Chromalox Inc.
Clerc, Redjean
Club de tir à l'arc de Montréal
Club de planeur Champlain
Collège Jean de Brébeuf (Paul-Émile Tremblay)
Collège militaire royal de Saint-Jean
Communauté urbaine de Montréal (Bureau de transport métropolitain)
Complexe sportif Claude-Robillard
Control Data Canada Ltd.
Cycles Performance
David M. Stewart Museum (Philippe Butler)
Department of National Defence of Canada (Public Relations)
Detson
Direction des constructions navales (Programmes internationaux) (France)
Distributions TTI Inc.
Energy, Mines and Resources Canada (Canada Centre for Remote Sensing)
Environment Canada (Atmospheric Environment Service, Gilles Sanscartier)
FACOM
Fédération québécoise des échecs
Fédération québécoise de tennis
Fédération québécoise de luge et bobsleigh
Fédération québécoise de canot-camping
Fédération québécoise de boxe olympique
Fédération québécoise de badminton
Fédération québécoise d'haltérophilie
Fédération québécoise d'escrime
Fédération de patinage de vitesse du Québec
Festival des Montolfières du Haut-Richelieu
Fincantieri Naval Shipbuilding Division
Fisher Scientific Ltd.
Ford New-Holland Inc.
Gadbois, Alain
GAM Pro Plongée
G.E. Astro-Space Division
G.T.E. Sylvania Canada Ltd.
General Electric Canada Inc. (Dominion Engineering Works, Mony Schinasi)
General Motors of Canada Ltd.
GIAT Industries
Government of Canada Terminology Bank
Gym Plus
Harrison (1985) Inc.
Hewitt Equipment Ltd.
Hippodrome Blue Bonnets (Robert Perez)
Honeywell Ltd.
Hortipro
Hughes Aircraft Company
Hydro-Québec (Centre de documentation, Anne Crépeau)
IBM Canada Ltd.
Imperial Oil Ltd.
Institut de recherche d'Hydro-Québec (IREQ)
International Telecommunications Satellite Organization (Intelsat)
International Civil Aviation Organization (IATA)
Jardin Botanique de Montréal
John Deere Ltd.
Johnson & Johnson Inc.
La Maison Olympique (Sylvia Doucette)
La Cordée
Le Beau Voyage
Le Coz, Jean-Pierre
Lee Valley Tools Ltd.
Leica Camera
Les Manufacturiers Draco ltée
Les Instruments de Musique Twigg Inc.
Les Équipements Chalin ltée
Les Appareils orthopédiques BBG Inc.
Leviton Manufacturing of Canada Ltd.
Liebherr-Québec
Manac Inc.
Manutan
Marcoux, Jean-Marie
Marrazza Musique
MATRA S.A.
Matra Défense (Direction de la communication)
Mazda Canada
Médiatel
Mendes Inc. (François Caron)
Michelin
MIL Tracy (Henri Vacher)
Ministère des transports du Québec (Sécurité routière, Signalisation routière)
Monette Sport Inc.
Moto Internationale
National Oceanic and Atmospheric Administration (NOAA) — National Environmental Satellite and Information Service (Frank Lepore)
National Aeronautics and Space Administration (NASA)
Nikon Canada Inc.
Northern Telecom Canada Ltd.
Office de la langue française du Québec (Chantal Robinson)
Ogilvie Mills Ltd. (Michel Ladouceur)
Olivetti Systems and Networks Canada Ltd.
Ontario Hydro
Paterson Darkroom Necessities
Petro-Canada (Calgary)
Philips Electronics Ltd. (Philips Lighting)
Philips Electronics Ltd. (Scientific and Analytical Equipment)
Pierre-Olivier Decor
Planétarium Dow (Pierre Lacombe)
Plastimo
Port of Montreal (Public Affairs)
Pratt & Whitney Canada Inc.
Quincaillerie A.C.L. Inc.
Radio-Québec
Remington Products (Canada) Inc.
Russell Rinfret
Rodriguez Cantieri navali S.p.A.
S.A. Redoute Catalogue (Relations extérieures)
Samsonite
Secretary of State of Canada (Translation Bureau)
Shell Canada
SIAL Poterie
Smith-Corona (Canada) Ltd.
SNC Defence Products Ltd.
Société Nationale des Chemins de Fer français (S.N.C.F.) (Direction de la communication)
Société de transport de la Communauté urbaine de Montréal
Spalding Canada
Spar Aerospace Ltd. (Hélène Lapierre)
St. Lawrence Seaway Authority (Normand Dodier)
Sunbeam Corporation (Canada) Ltd.
Swimming Canada
Teleglobe Canada Inc. (Roger Leblanc)
Telesat Canada (Yves Comtois)
The Coal Association of Canada
The British Petroleum Company p.l.c. (Photographic Services)
Thibault
Tideland Signal Canada Ltd.
Transport Canada (Montreal Airports, Gilbert L'Espérance, Koos R. Van der Peijl)
Ultramar Canada Inc.
United States Department of Defense (Department of the Navy, Office of Information)
Université du Québec à Montréal (Module des arts, Michel Fournier)
Université du Québec (Institut national de la recherche scientifique, Benoît Jean)
Varin, Claude
Via Rail Canada Inc.
Viala L.R. Inc. (Jean Beaudin)
Ville de Montréal (Bureau du cinéma; Service de l'habitation et du développement urbain; Service de la prévention des incendies, Robert Gilbert, Réal Audet; Service des travaux publics)
Volcano Inc.
Volkswagen Canada Inc.
Volvo Canada Ltd.
Water Ski Canada
Weider
Wild Leitz Canada ltée
Xerox Canada Inc.
Yamaha Canada Music Ltd.

T*he Macmillan Visual Dictionary: Multilingual Edition* is quite unlike other dictionaries with respect to both contents and presentation. Given its uniqueness, a few words of explanation will help you appreciate its usefulness and the quality of the information it contains. The following introduction explains how and why *The Macmillan Visual Dictionary: Multilingual Edition* differs from language dictionaries and encyclopedias. For dictionary "fans" and professional lexicographers, we have included a brief description of the principles and methods that guided us in producing the dictionary.

A PICTURE/WORD DICTIONARY

The Macmillan Visual Dictionary: Multilingual Edition closely links pictures and words.

The pictures describe and analyze today's world: the objects of everyday life, our physical environment, the animal and vegetable life that surrounds us, the communication and work techniques that are changing our lifestyles, the weapons that preoccupy us, the means of transportation that are breaking down geographical barriers, the sources of energy on which we depend, etc.

Illustrations play a specific role in our dictionary: they serve to define words, enabling dictionary users to "see" immediately the meaning of each term. Users can thus recognize the objects they are looking for and, at a single glance, find the corresponding vocabulary.

The Macmillan Visual Dictionary: Multilingual Edition provides users with the words they need to accurately name the objects that make up the world around them.

The terms in the dictionary have been carefully selected from current documents written by experts in each area. In case of doubt, the vocabulary has been studied by specialists in the corresponding field and cross-checked in encyclopedias and language dictionaries. We have taken these precautions to ensure the accuracy of each word and a high level of standardization.

A DICTIONARY FOR ONE AND ALL

The Macmillan Visual Dictionary: Multilingual Edition is aimed at all persons who participate in one way or another in contemporary civilization and, as a consequence, need to know and use a great number of technical terms from a wide range of fields.

It thus addresses the needs and curiosity of each and every one of us. It is not designed only for specialists.

The depth of analysis varies according to the subject. Rather than arbitrarily providing a uniform breakdown of each subject, the authors have acknowledged that people's degrees of knowledge differ from one field to another, and that the complexity of the topics dealt with varies widely. For example, more people are familiar with clothing and automobiles than with atomic energy or telecommunications satellites, and find the former subjects simpler than the latter. Another aspect of the same problem is that, in describing human anatomy, we are obliged to use medical terminology, even though the terms seem more complicated than those for fruits and vegetables. In addition, our world is changing: photographic vocabulary, for example, has become much more complicated due to camera automation. Similarly, although microcomputer fans are familiar with computer terminology, the field remains a mystery for much of the rest of the population.

The Macmillan Visual Dictionary: Multilingual Edition allows for these phenomena, and thus reflects the specialized vocabulary commonly used in each field.

AN EASY-TO-CONSULT DICTIONARY

People may use *The Macmillan Visual Dictionary: Multilingual Edition* in several different ways, thanks to the List of Chapters (page xxxi), the detailed table of contents (page xv), and the index (page 833).

Users may consult the dictionary:

By going from an idea to a word, if they are familiar with an object and can clearly visualize it, but cannot find or do not know the name for it. The table of contents breaks down each subject according to an easy-to-consult, stratified classification system. *The Macmillan Visual Dictionary: Multilingual Edition* is the only dictionary that allows users to find a word from its meaning.

By going from a word to an idea, if they want to check the meaning of a term. The index refers users to the illustrations, which provide the names for the individual features.

At a glance, by using the List of Chapters. The colored page edges help users find the chapters they are looking for.

For foreign language equivalents, by browsing through the book or going into depth for particular themes. The objects of the modern world are clearly identified at a glance in four languages.

For sheer pleasure, by flipping from one illustration to another, or from one word to another, for the sole purpose of enjoying the illustrations and enriching their knowledge.

A DICTIONARY WITH A DIFFERENCE

We are all familiar with several types of dictionaries and encyclopedias. It is not always easy, however, to grasp their distinguishing features. The following overview highlights the main differences between *The Macmillan Visual Dictionary: Multilingual Edition* and other reference works.

a) Language dictionaries

These dictionaries describe the meanings given by speakers to the general vocabulary of their language.

They provide two major types of information: headwords (vocabulary), and a list of the meanings of each term (dictionary entries).

The vocabulary, which comprises all of the words covered by lexicographical descriptions, constitutes the framework of the dictionary. For consultation purposes, the headwords are arranged in alphabetical order. Generally speaking, the vocabulary includes common, contemporary language, archaic words useful for understanding the texts or history of a civilization, and a certain number of widely used technical terms.

Each dictionary entry provides an itemized, semantic description of the corresponding headword. Generally, the entry indicates the part of speech for the headword, its etymology and its various meanings, as well as the word's social usage (familiar, colloquial, vulgar, etc.) according to criteria that, even today, remain somewhat "impressionistic."

In general, language dictionaries are classified according to their target users and the number of terms in the vocabulary, which, in addition to nouns, includes all other parts of speech (verbs, pronouns, adjectives, adverbs, prepositions, conjunctions, etc.). A 5,000-word dictionary is intended for children, one with 15,000 words is suitable for elementary schools and a 50,000-word dictionary covers the needs of the general public.

b) Encyclopedic dictionaries

In addition to the information included in language dictionaries, encyclopedic dictionaries provide details about the nature, functioning, and history of things, thus enabling laymen with solid general knowledge and specialists to understand the scope of a word. They devote much more space to technical terms, and reflect current scientific and technological developments. Generally speaking, pictures play an important role in illustrating the text. The size of encyclopedic dictionaries varies according to the breadth of the vocabulary, the length of the entries, the emphasis placed on proper nouns and the number of fields of specialization covered.

c) Encyclopedias

Unlike the preceding category of reference works, encyclopedias do not deal with language. They are devoted to providing scientific, technical, occasionally economic, historical and geographic descriptions. The arrangement of the entries varies, as all classification systems are valid: alphabetic, conceptual, chronological, by field of specialization, etc. The number of different encyclopedias is virtually unlimited, given the fragmentation of civilization into multiple categories. There is, however, a distinction between universal encyclopedias and specialized encyclopedias.

d) Specialized lexicons and vocabularies

These works usually address specific needs created by scientific and technological progress. They focus on ensuring efficient communication through precise, standardized terminology. They vary in all respects: the method of compilation, the authors' approach to the subject matter, the scope of the vocabulary, the number of languages, and the means of establishing equivalents in the various languages (i.e., by simple translation or by a comparison of unilingual terminologies). Specialized lexicography has become an area of intense activity. The number of works is multiplying in all sectors and in all language combinations.

e) *The Macmillan Visual Dictionary: Multilingual Edition*

The Macmillan Visual Dictionary: Multilingual Edition is a terminology-oriented dictionary. It is aimed at providing members of the general public with the specific terms they need, in their own or another language, to name the objects of daily life, and helping them grasp the meaning of words through illustrations. The Multilingual Edition is an ideal tool for both second-language and mother tongue vocabulary building. Grouped together in interlocking categories, the various elements are interdefined. The dictionary is thus organized according to chapters, subjects, specific objects, and features of these objects. Depending on a person's degree of familiarity with a given chapter, the terminology may seem simple or technical. The fundamental goal, however, is to provide non-specialists with a coherent analysis of useful, necessary vocabulary for each subject.

The Macmillan Visual Dictionary: Multilingual Edition is not an encyclopedia, for at least two reasons: rather than describing objects, it names them; in addition, it avoids listing all the objects in a given category. For example, rather than enumerating the various types of trees, it focuses on a typical representative of the category, and examines its structure and individual parts.

It may even less be considered a language dictionary: like other terminological works, it contains no written definitions and covers only nouns and, in particular, noun phrases.

Nor may it be seen as a compendium of specialized vocabularies, as it avoids terminology used only by specialists, focusing instead on more widespread terms—at the risk of being considered simplistic by experts in specific fields.

The Macmillan Visual Dictionary: Multilingual Edition is the first terminology-oriented dictionary to group together in a single volume the thousands of technical and not-so-technical terms most commonly used in our society, where science, technology, and their end products are part of everyday life.

This is the editorial policy that has guided us in creating this dictionary. Consequently, the number of words it contains does not have the same significance as for a language dictionary, for several reasons: in keeping with our editorial policy, we have deliberately chosen to limit the number of words; unlike conventional dictionaries, this work focuses exclusively on nouns, the most significant words in the language, to the exclusion of adjectives, verbs, prepositions, etc.; and finally no one is sure exactly how to count compound terms!

COMPUTER-PRODUCED ILLUSTRATIONS

The illustrations in *The Macmillan Visual Dictionary: Multilingual Edition* have been created by computer from recent documents and original photographs.

The use of computers has given the illustrations a highly realistic, almost photographic look, while allowing us to highlight the essential features corresponding to the vocabulary. The graphic precision of *The Macmillan Visual Dictionary: Multilingual Edition* is one of the main sources of its excellence as an encyclopedic and lexicographical reference tool.

In addition, thanks to computers, we have been able to improve the accuracy of the lines joining objects to their names, thus enhancing the clarity of the link between words and the things they describe.

CAREFULLY ESTABLISHED VOCABULARY

In creating *The Macmillan Visual Dictionary: Multilingual Edition*, we have used the method of systematic and comparative terminological research, which is standard practice among professionals who prepare works of this type.

This method comprises several steps, which follow one another in a logical order. The following paragraphs provide a brief description of each of these steps.

Field delimitation

First of all, on the basis of our objectives, we defined the scope and contents of the proposed work.

We began by choosing the chapters we felt it necessary to cover. We then divided each chapter into fields and sub-fields, taking care to abide by our editorial policy and avoiding overspecialization and the temptation to cover all subjects in detail. This step resulted in a working table of contents, the dictionary framework, which guided our subsequent steps and was refined as the work progressed. The detailed table of contents is the end result of this process.

Documentary research

In keeping with our production plan, we assembled pertinent documents likely to provide us with the required information about words and concepts in each subject matter.

In order of reliability, our documentary sources were as follows:

• Articles and books by experts in the various fields, written in their native language, with an acceptable degree of specialization. Translations of such texts provide revealing information about vocabulary usage, but must be used with due caution;

• Technical documents, such as national standards or the guidelines of the International Standard Organization (ISO), product instructions, technical documents provided by manufacturers, official government publications, etc.;

• Catalogs, commercial texts, advertisements from specialized magazines and major newspapers;

• Encyclopedias, encyclopedic dictionaries, and unilingual language dictionaries;

• Unilingual, bilingual, and multilingual specialized vocabularies and dictionaries. The quality and reliability of these works, however, must be carefully assessed;

• Bilingual and multilingual language dictionaries.

In all, we consulted four to five thousand references. The selected bibliography included in the dictionary indicates only the general documentary sources consulted, and does not include specialized sources.

Sifting through the documents

A terminologist went through the documents for each subject, in search of specific concepts and the words used to express them by different authors and works. Gradually, a framework was established, as the terminologist noted the use of the same term for a given concept from one source to another, or, on the contrary, the use of several terms for the same idea. In the latter case, the terminologist continued his research until he was able to form a well-documented opinion of each competing term. All of this research was recorded, with reference notes.

Creation of a multilingual terminology base

The English terminology is based on standard North American usage; the French terminology on the European French norm; and the Spanish terminology on Castilian usage. The norm for German terminology reflects the criteria used by major German publishing houses. Nothing in this dictionary is the result of translation; all languages have been prepared by renowned specialists and verified by major dictionary houses. Because of this, errors frequently found in other multilingual dictionaries based exclusively on a translation approach have been avoided.

Creation of terminological files

The preceding step enabled us to assemble all of the elements for our terminological files.

Each concept identified and defined by an illustration has been paired with the term most frequently used to describe it by the leading authors or in the most reliable sources. Where several competing terms were found in the reference material, following discussion and consensus between the terminologist and the scientific director, a single term was chosen.

Terminological variants

Frequently, several words may be used to designate virtually the same concept.

We dealt with such situations as follows:

• In some cases, a term was used by a single author or appeared only once in our documentary sources. We retained the most frequently used competing term.

• Technical terms are often compound words with or without a hyphen, or several-word expressions. This results in at least two types of terminological variants:

a) The compound technical term may be shortened by the deletion of one or more of its elements, especially where the meaning is clear in the context. The shortened expression may even become the normal term for the concept. In such cases, we retained the compound form, leaving users the freedom to abbreviate it according to the context.

b) An element of the compound term may itself have equivalents (most often synonyms from the commonly spoken language). We retained the most frequently used form.

Variants may stem from the evolution of the language, without terminological consequences. We therefore retained the most contemporary or well-known form.

TERMINOLOGICAL APPROACH

A few comments about the terminological approach, as compared to the lexicographical approach, are in order.

Language dictionaries have a long history. They are familiar reference works, used by most people since early school age, with a well-established, widely known and accepted tradition. We all know how to consult a dictionary and interpret the information it provides—or fails to provide.

Terminological dictionaries are either very recent or intended for a specialized public. There is no solid tradition to guide those who design and produce such works. Although specialists know how to interpret dictionaries pertaining to their own fields, given that they are familiar with the terminology, the same cannot be said for the layperson, who is confused by variants. Finally, whereas language dictionaries have to a certain extent established standard word usage among their users, specialized vocabularies are characterized by competing terms in new fields of specialization.

Users of a reference work such as *The Macmillan Visual Dictionary: Multilingual Edition* should take into account these elements in assessing this new type of reference tool.

JEAN-CLAUDE CORBEIL
ARIANE ARCHAMBAULT

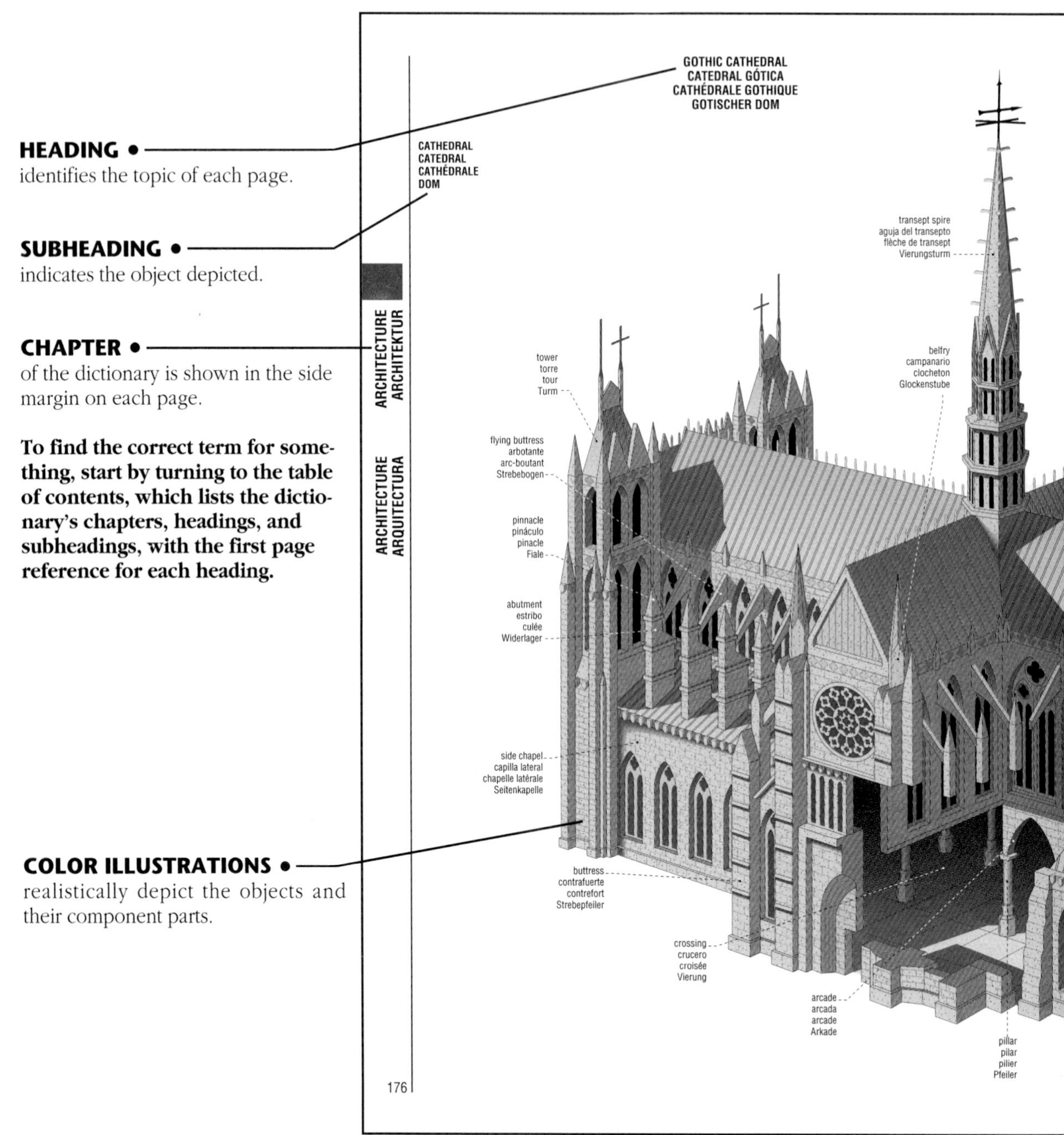
GOTHIC CATHEDRAL
CATEDRAL GÓTICA
CATHÉDRALE GOTHIQUE
GOTISCHER DOM
CATHEDRAL
CATEDRAL
CATHÉDRALE
DOM
ARCHITECTURE
ARCHITEKTUR
ARCHITECTURE
ARQUITECTURA
transept spire
aguja del transepto
flèche de transept
Vierungsturm
tower
torre
tour
Turm
belfry
campanario
clocheton
Glockenstube
flying buttress
arbotante
arc-boutant
Strebebogen
pinnacle
pináculo
pinacle
Fiale
abutment
estribo
culée
Widerlager
side chapel
capilla lateral
chapelle latérale
Seitenkapelle
buttress
contrafuerte
contrefort
Strebepfeiler
crossing
crucero
croisée
Vierung
arcade
arcada
arcade
Arkade
pillar
pilar
pilier
Pfeiler
176

HEADING •
identifies the topic of each page.

SUBHEADING •
indicates the object depicted.

CHAPTER •
of the dictionary is shown in the side margin on each page.

To find the correct term for something, start by turning to the table of contents, which lists the dictionary's chapters, headings, and subheadings, with the first page reference for each heading.

COLOR ILLUSTRATIONS •
realistically depict the objects and their component parts.

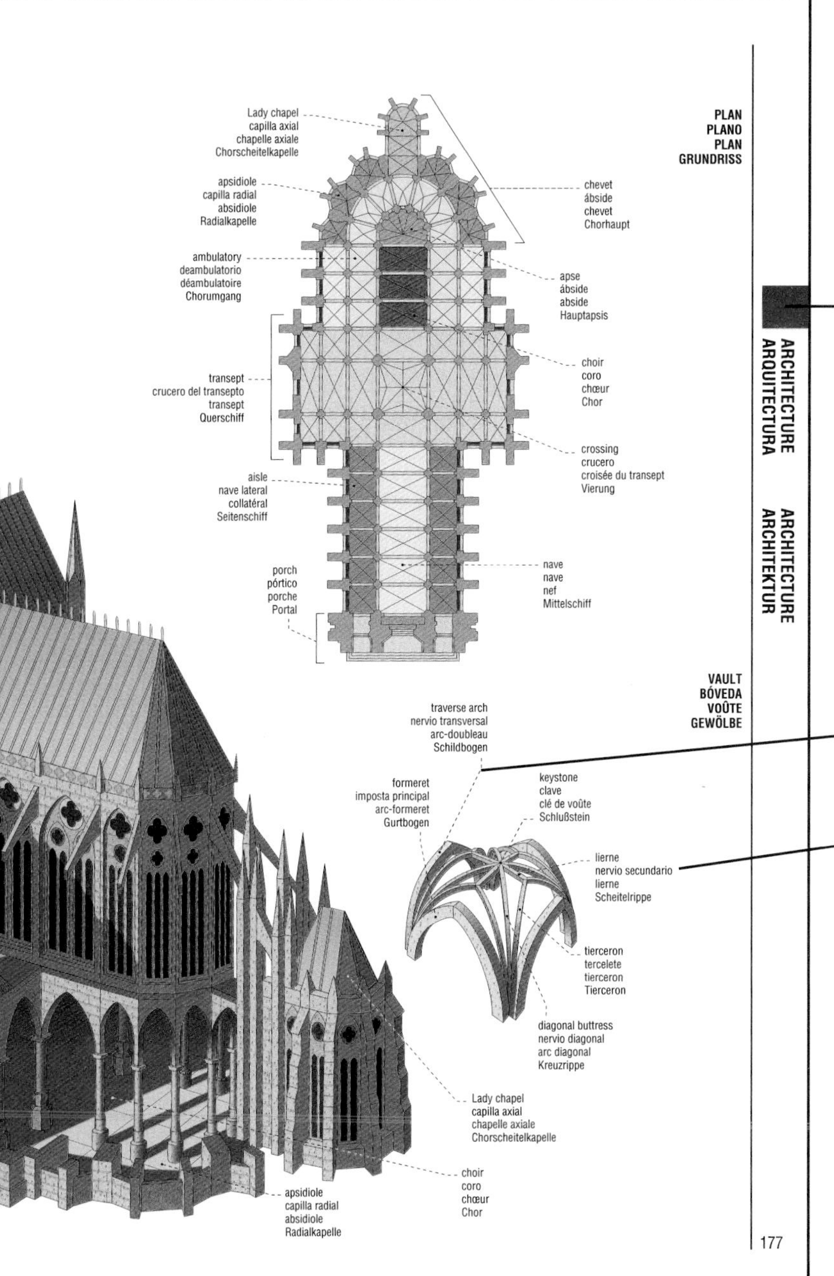
PLAN
PLANO
PLAN
GRUNDRISS
Lady chapel
capilla axial
chapelle axiale
Chorscheitelkapelle
apsidiole
capilla radial
absidiole
Radialkapelle
ambulatory
deambulatorio
déambulatoire
Chorumgang
transept
crucero del transepto
transept
Querschiff
aisle
nave lateral
collatéral
Seitenschiff
porch
pórtico
porche
Portal
chevet
ábside
chevet
Chorhaupt
apse
ábside
abside
Hauptapsis
choir
coro
chœur
Chor
crossing
crucero
croisée du transept
Vierung
nave
nave
nef
Mittelschiff
ARCHITECTURE
ARQUITECTURA
ARCHITECTURE
ARCHITEKTUR
VAULT
BÓVEDA
VOÛTE
GEWÖLBE
traverse arch
nervio transversal
arc-doubleau
Schildbogen
formeret
imposta principal
arc-formeret
Gurtbogen
keystone
clave
clé de voûte
Schlußstein
lierne
nervio secundario
lierne
Scheitelrippe
tierceron
tercelete
tierceron
Tierceron
diagonal buttress
nervio diagonal
arc diagonal
Kreuzrippe
Lady chapel
capilla axial
chapelle axiale
Chorscheitelkapelle
choir
coro
chœur
Chor
apsidiole
capilla radial
absidiole
Radialkapelle
177

• COLORED TAB
on the edge of the page corresponds to the chapter as shown in the List of Chapters. This color-coding allows you to find, at a glance, the subject you are looking for.

• DOTTED LINES
link the terms with the objects they describe.

• TERMS
are included in the index, with references to all pages on which they appear.

To see an illustration depicting a term that you know, consult the index.

SELECTED BIBLIOGRAPHY

DICTIONARIES

- *Gage Canadian Dictionary.* Toronto: Gage Publishing Limited, 1983, 1313 p.
- *The New Britannica/Webster Dictionary and Reference Guide.* Chicago, Toronto: Encyclopedia Britannica, 1981, 1505 p.
- *The Oxford English Dictionary.* Second edition. Oxford: Clarendon Press, 1989, 20 vol.
- *The Oxford Illustrated Dictionary.* Oxford: Clarendon Press, 1967, 974 p.
- *Oxford American Dictionary.* Eugene Ehrlich, et al. New York, Oxford: Oxford University Press, 1980, 816 p.
- *The Random House Dictionary of the English Language.* Second edition. New York: Random House 1983, 2059 p.
- *Webster's Encyclopedic Unabridged Dictionary of the English Language.* New York: Portland House, 1989, 2078 p.
- *Webster's Third New International Dictionary.* Springfield: Merriam-Webster, 1986, 2662 p.
- *Webster's Ninth New Collegiate Dictionary.* Springfield: Merriam-Webster, 1984, 1563 p.
- *Webster's New World Dictionary of American Language.* New York: The World Pub., 1953.

ENCYCLOPEDIAS

- *Academic American Encyclopedia.* Princeton: Arete Publishing Company, 1980, 21 vol.
- *Architectural Graphic Standards.* Eighth edition. New York: John Wiley & Sons, 1988, 854 p.
- *Chamber's Encyclopedia.* New rev. edition. London: International Learning System, 1989.
- *Collier's Encyclopedia.* New York: Macmillan Educational Company, 1984, 24 vol.
- *Compton's Encyclopedia.* Chicago: F.E. Compton Company, Division of Encyclopedia Britannica Inc., 1982, 26 vol.
- *Encyclopedia Americana.* International Edition, Danbury: Grolier, 1981, 30 vol.
- *How It Works, The Illustrated Science and Invention Encyclopedia.* New York: H.S. Stuttman, 1977, 21 vol.
- *McGraw-Hill Encyclopedia of Science & Technology.* New York: McGraw-Hill Book Company, 1982, 15 vol.
- *Merit Students Encyclopedia.* New York: Macmillan Educational Company, 1984, 20 vol.
- *New Encyclopedia Britannica.* Chicago, Toronto: Encyclopedia Britannica, 1985, 32 vol.
- *The Joy of Knowledge Encyclopedia.* London: Mitchell Beazley Encyclopedias, 1976, 7 vol.
- *The Random House Encyclopedia.* New York: Random House, 1977, 2 vol.
- *The World Book Encyclopedia.* Chicago: Field Enterprises Educational Corporation, 1973.

FRENCH AND ENGLISH DICTIONARIES

- Collins-Robert, *French-English, English-French Dictionary,* London, Glasgow, Cleveland, Toronto: Collins-Robert, 1978, 781 p.
- Dubois, Marguerite, *Dictionnaire moderne français-anglais.* Paris: Larousse, 1980, 752 p.
- Harrap's *New Standard French and English Dictionary.* Part one, French-English. London: Harrap's 1977, 2 vol. Part two, English-French. London: Harrap's 1983, 2 vol.
- Harrap's *Shorter French and English Dictionary,* London, Toronto, Willington, Sydney: Harrap's 1953, 940 p.

CONTENTS

MARITIME TRANSPORT

AIR TRANSPORT

SPACE TRANSPORT

OFFICE SUPPLIES

OFFICE AUTOMATION

MUSIC

CREATIVE LEISURE ACTIVITIES

MEASURING DEVICES

OPTICAL INSTRUMENTS

HEALTH AND SAFETY

ENERGY

HEAVY MACHINERY

WEAPONS

LIST OF CHAPTERS

ASTRONOMY
ASTRONOMÍA
ASTRONOMIE
ASTRONOMIE

CONTENTS

CELESTIAL COORDINATE SYSTEM
COORDENADAS ASTRONÓMICAS
COORDONNÉES CÉLESTES
KOORDINATENSYSTEM DER HIMMELSKUGEL

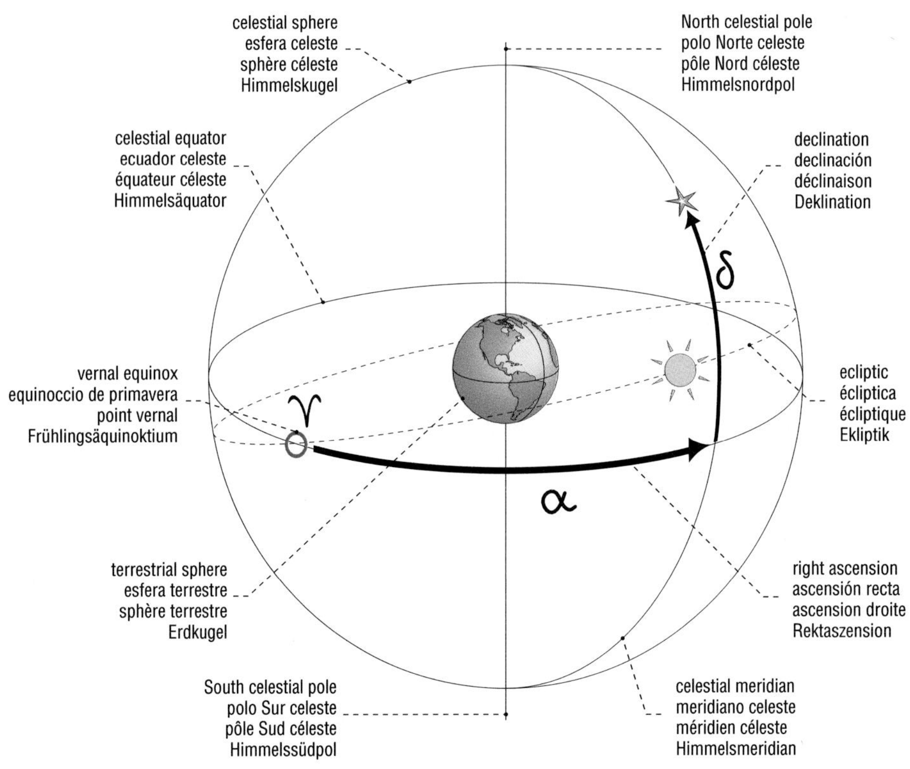

celestial sphere
esfera celeste
sphère céleste
Himmelskugel
North celestial pole
polo Norte celeste
pôle Nord céleste
Himmelsnordpol
celestial equator
ecuador celeste
équateur céleste
Himmelsäquator
declination
declinación
déclinaison
Deklination
δ
vernal equinox
equinoccio de primavera
point vernal
Frühlingsäquinoktium
ecliptic
écliptica
écliptique
Ekliptik
α
terrestrial sphere
esfera terrestre
sphère terrestre
Erdkugel
right ascension
ascensión recta
ascension droite
Rektaszension
South celestial pole
polo Sur celeste
pôle Sud céleste
Himmelssüdpol
celestial meridian
meridiano celeste
méridien céleste
Himmelsmeridian

EARTH COORDINATE SYSTEM
COORDENADAS GEOGRÁFICAS
COORDONNÉES TERRESTRES
KOORDINATENSYSTEM DER ERDKUGEL

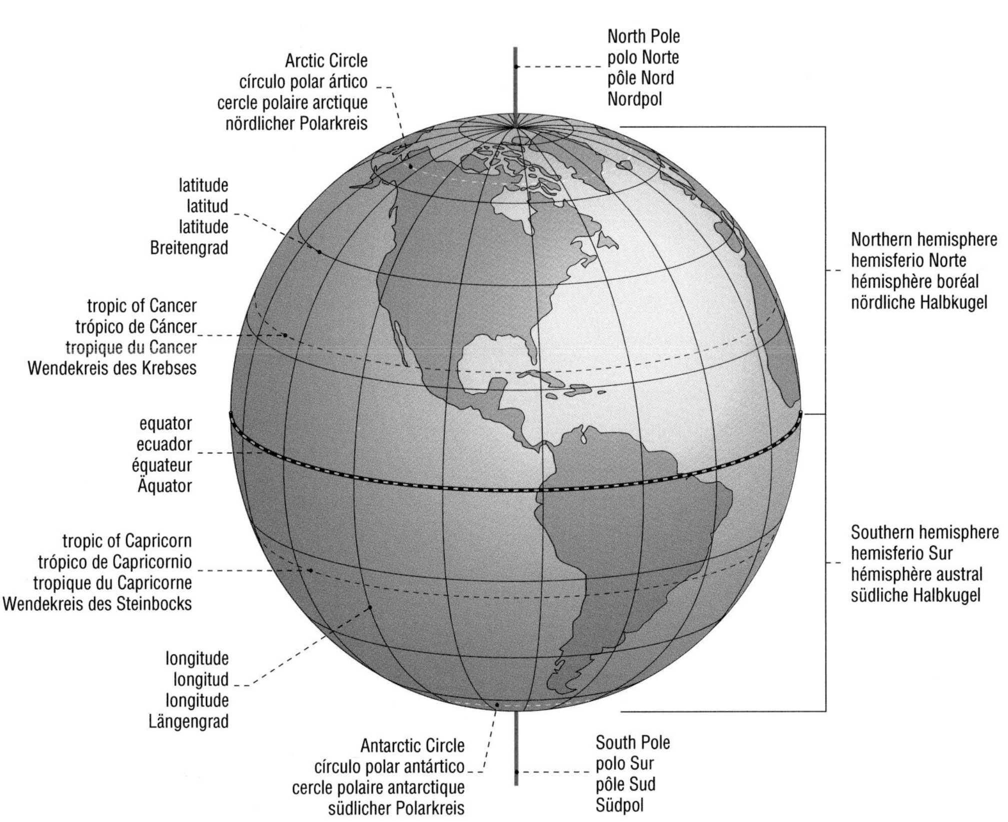

Arctic Circle
círculo polar ártico
cercle polaire arctique
nördlicher Polarkreis
North Pole
polo Norte
pôle Nord
Nordpol
latitude
latitud
latitude
Breitengrad
Northern hemisphere
hemisferio Norte
hémisphère boréal
nördliche Halbkugel
tropic of Cancer
trópico de Cáncer
tropique du Cancer
Wendekreis des Krebses
equator
ecuador
équateur
Äquator
Southern hemisphere
hemisferio Sur
hémisphère austral
südliche Halbkugel
tropic of Capricorn
trópico de Capricornio
tropique du Capricorne
Wendekreis des Steinbocks
longitude
longitud
longitude
Längengrad
Antarctic Circle
círculo polar antártico
cercle polaire antarctique
südlicher Polarkreis
South Pole
polo Sur
pôle Sud
Südpol

SOLAR SYSTEM
SISTEMA SOLAR
SYSTÈME SOLAIRE
SONNENSYSTEM

PLANETS AND MOONS
PLANETAS Y LUNAS
PLANÈTES ET SATELLITES
PLANETEN UND MONDE

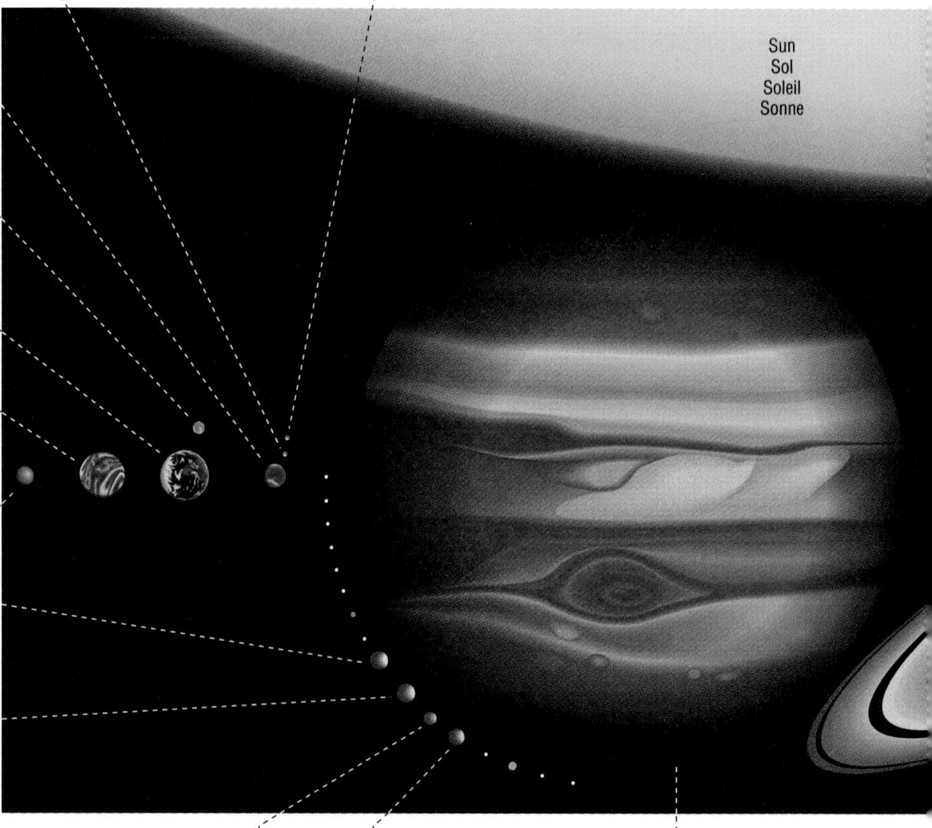

Phobos
Fobos
Phobos
Phobos

Deimos
Deimos
Deimos
Deimos

Mars
Marte
Mars
Mars ♂

Sun
Sol
Soleil
Sonne

Moon
Luna
Lune
Mond

Earth
Tierra
Terre
Erde ♁

Venus
Venus
Vénus
Venus ♀

Mercury
Mercurio
Mercure
Merkur ☿

Ganymede
Ganimedes
Ganymède
Ganymed

Callisto
Calixto
Callisto
Callisto

Europa
Europa
Europe
Europa

Io
Io
Io
Io

♃ Jupiter
Júpiter
Jupiter
Jupiter

ORBITS OF THE PLANETS
ÓRBITAS DE LOS PLANETAS
ORBITES DES PLANÈTES
UMLAUFBAHNEN DER PLANETEN

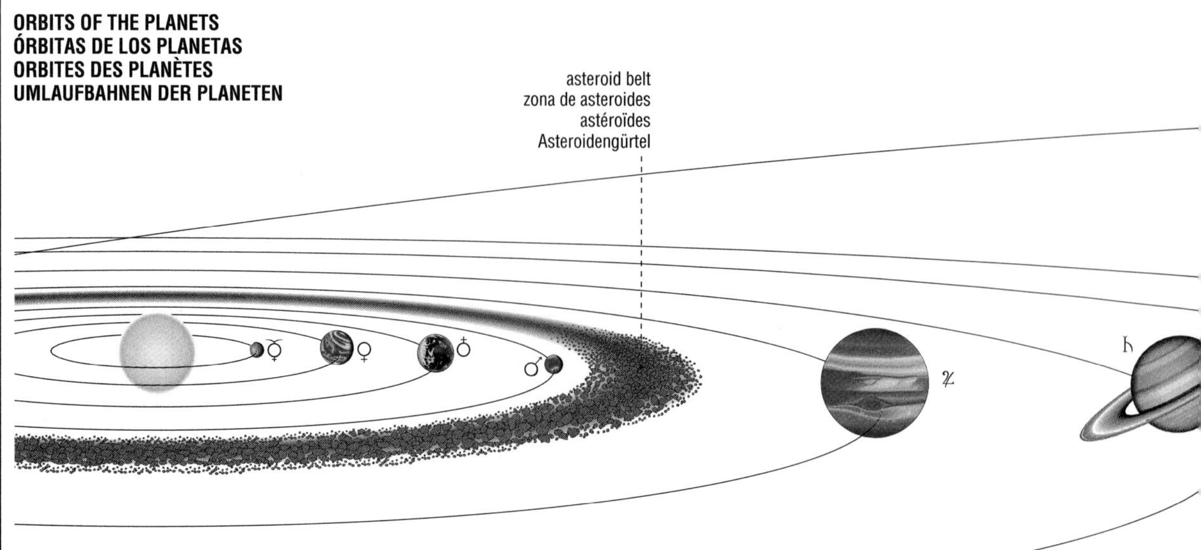
asteroid belt
zona de asteroides
astéroïdes
Asteroidengürtel

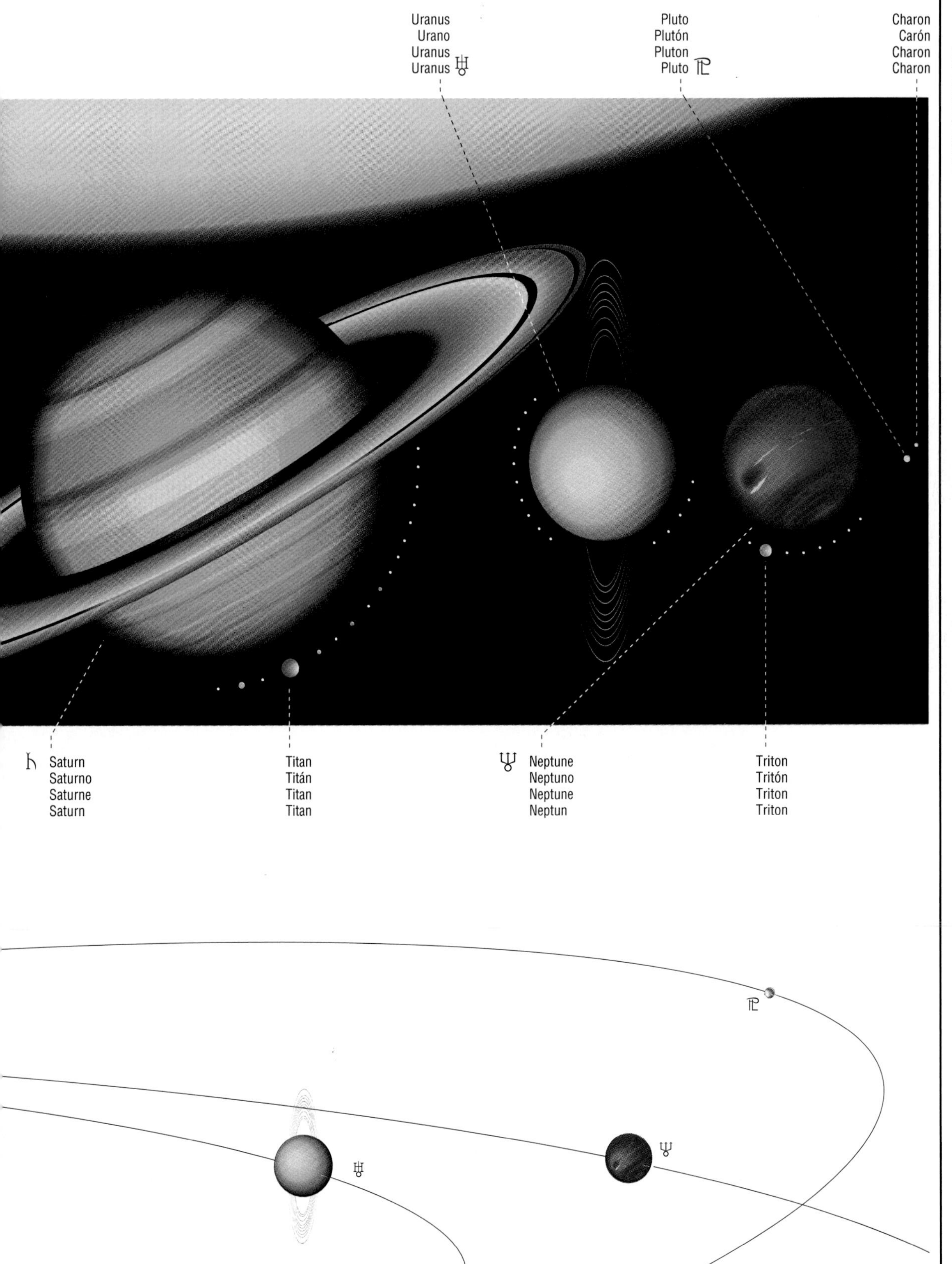
Uranus
Urano
Uranus
Uranus ♅
Pluto
Plutón
Pluton
Pluto ♇
Charon
Carón
Charon
Charon
♄ Saturn
Saturno
Saturne
Saturn
Titan
Titán
Titan
Titan
♆ Neptune
Neptuno
Neptune
Neptun
Triton
Tritón
Triton
Triton

SUN
SOL
SOLEIL
SONNE

STRUCTURE OF THE SUN
ESTRUCTURA DEL SOL
STRUCTURE DU SOLEIL
STRUKTUR DER SONNE

photosphere
fotosfera
photosphère
Photosphäre

spicules
espículas
spicule
Spikulen

chromosphere
cromosfera
chromosphère
Chromosphäre

corona
corona
couronne
Korona

convection zone
zona de convección
zone de convection
Konvektionszone

radiation zone
zona de radiación
zone de radiation
Strahlungszone

core
núcleo
noyau
Kern

flare
erupción
éruption
Flare

faculae
fáculas
facule
Fackeln

sunspot
mancha solar
tache
Sonnenfleck

filament
filamento
filament
Filament

prominence
protuberancia
protubérance
Protuberanz

granulation
granos de arroz
granulation
Granulation

PHASES OF THE MOON
FASES DE LA LUNA
PHASES DE LA LUNE
MONDPHASEN

new moon
Luna nueva
nouvelle Lune
Neumond

new crescent
creciente
premier croissant
Mondsichel (zunehmender Mond)

first quarter
cuarto creciente
premier quartier
Halbmond (erstes Viertel)

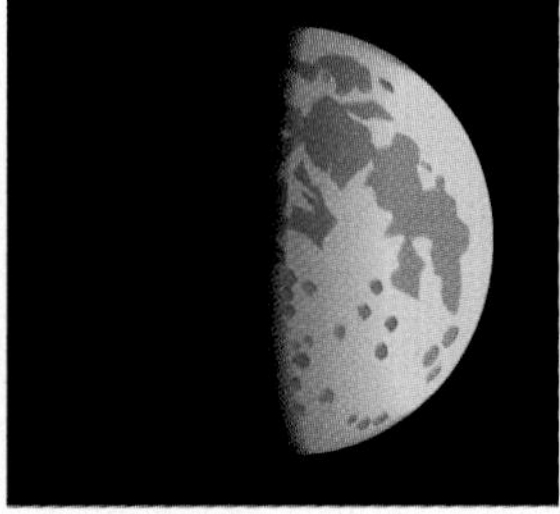

waxing gibbous
quinto octante
gibbeuse croissante
zunehmender Mond

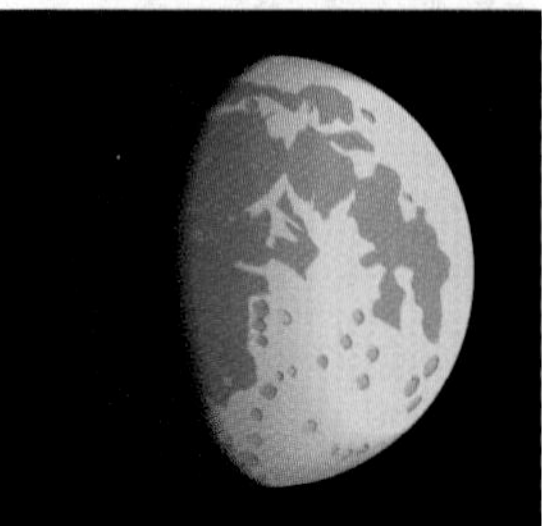

MOON
LUNA
LUNE
MOND

LUNAR FEATURES
SUPERFICIE LUNAR
RELIEF LUNAIRE
OBERFLÄCHENFORMATIONEN DES MONDES

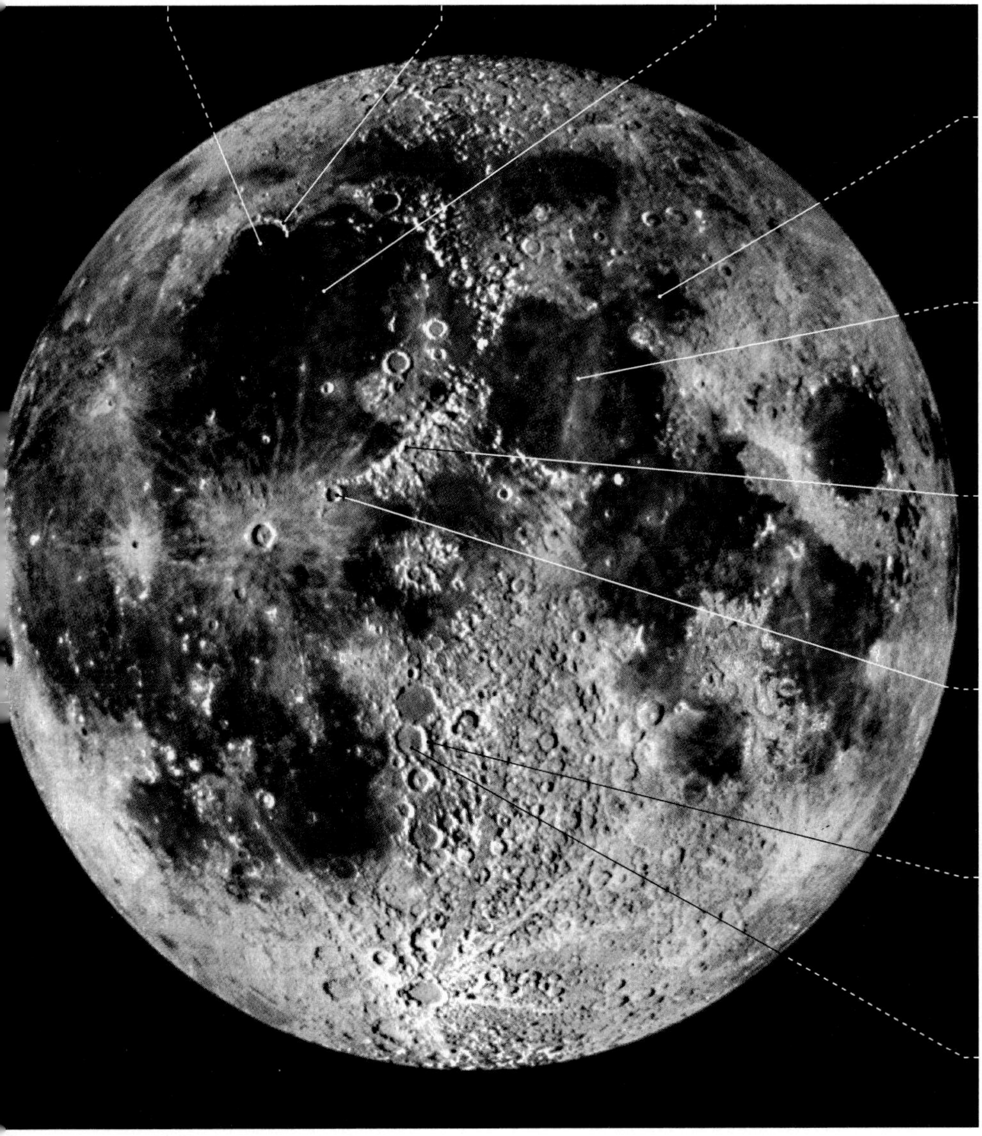

bay
bahía
baie
Bucht

cliff
risco
falaise
Felsen

ocean
océano
océan
Ozean

lake
lago
lac
See

sea
mar
mer
Meer

mountain range
cordillera
chaîne de montagnes
Bergkette

crater
cráter
cratère
Krater

wall
muro
rempart
Wand

cirque
circo
cirque
Kar

full moon
Luna llena
pleine Lune
Vollmond

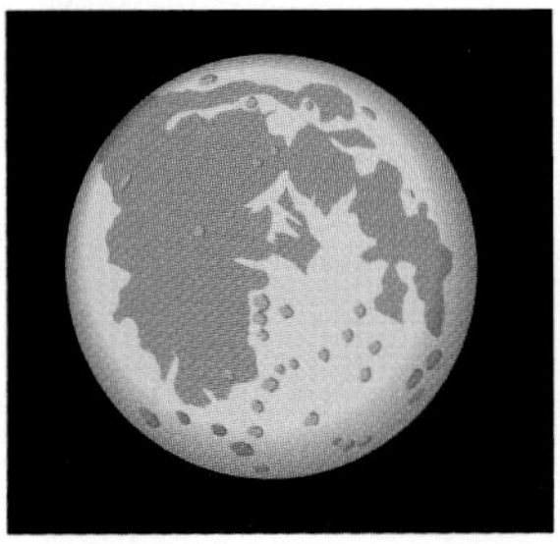

waning gibbous
tercer octante
gibbeuse décroissante
abnehmender Mond

last quarter
cuarto menguante
dernier quartier
Halbmond (letztes Viertel)

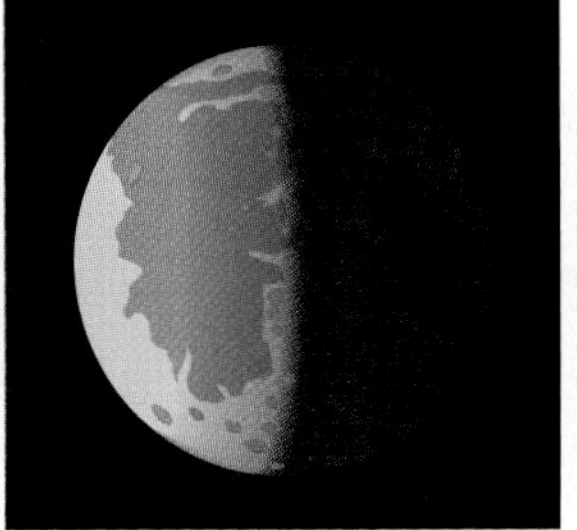

old crescent
menguante
dernier croissant
Mondsichel (abnehmender Mond)

SOLAR ECLIPSE
ECLIPSE DE SOL
ÉCLIPSE DE SOLEIL
SONNENFINSTERNIS

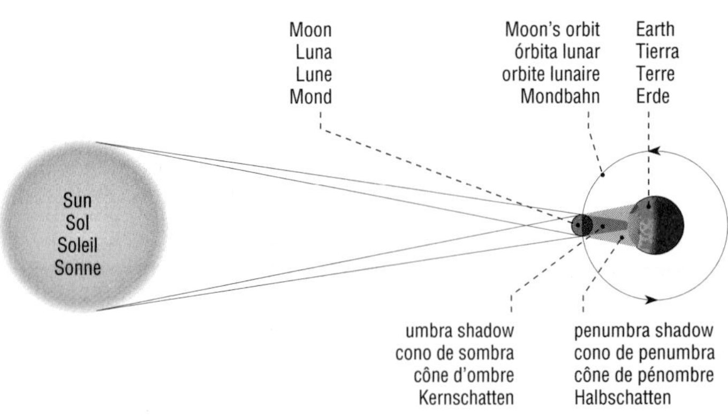
Moon
Luna
Lune
Mond
Moon's orbit
órbita lunar
orbite lunaire
Mondbahn
Earth
Tierra
Terre
Erde
Sun
Sol
Soleil
Sonne
umbra shadow
cono de sombra
cône d'ombre
Kernschatten
penumbra shadow
cono de penumbra
cône de pénombre
Halbschatten

TYPES OF ECLIPSES
TIPOS DE ECLIPSES
TYPES D'ÉCLIPSES
FINSTERNISARTEN

total eclipse
eclipse total
éclipse totale
totale Finsternis

annular eclipse
eclipse anular
éclipse annulaire
ringförmige Finsternis

partial eclipse
eclipse parcial
éclipse partielle
partielle Finsternis

LUNAR ECLIPSE
ECLIPSE DE LUNA
ÉCLIPSE DE LUNE
MONDFINSTERNIS

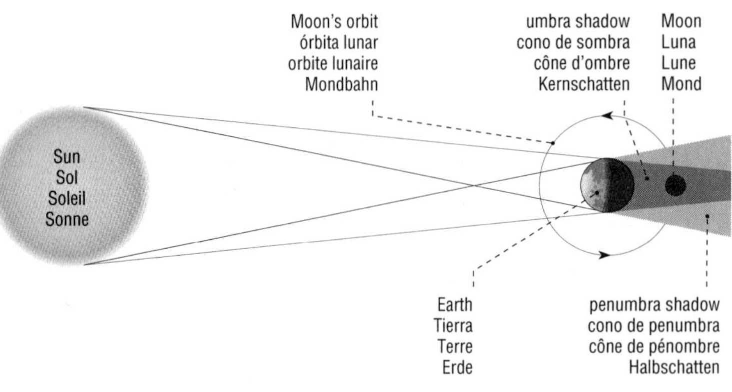
Moon's orbit
órbita lunar
orbite lunaire
Mondbahn
umbra shadow
cono de sombra
cône d'ombre
Kernschatten
Moon
Luna
Lune
Mond
Sun
Sol
Soleil
Sonne
Earth
Tierra
Terre
Erde
penumbra shadow
cono de penumbra
cône de pénombre
Halbschatten

TYPES OF ECLIPSES
TIPOS DE ECLIPSES
TYPES D'ÉCLIPSES
FINSTERNISARTEN

partial eclipse
eclipse parcial
éclipse partielle
partielle Finsternis

total eclipse
eclipse total
éclipse totale
totale Finsternis

SEASONS OF THE YEAR
ESTACIONES DEL AÑO
CYCLE DES SAISONS
JAHRESZEITEN

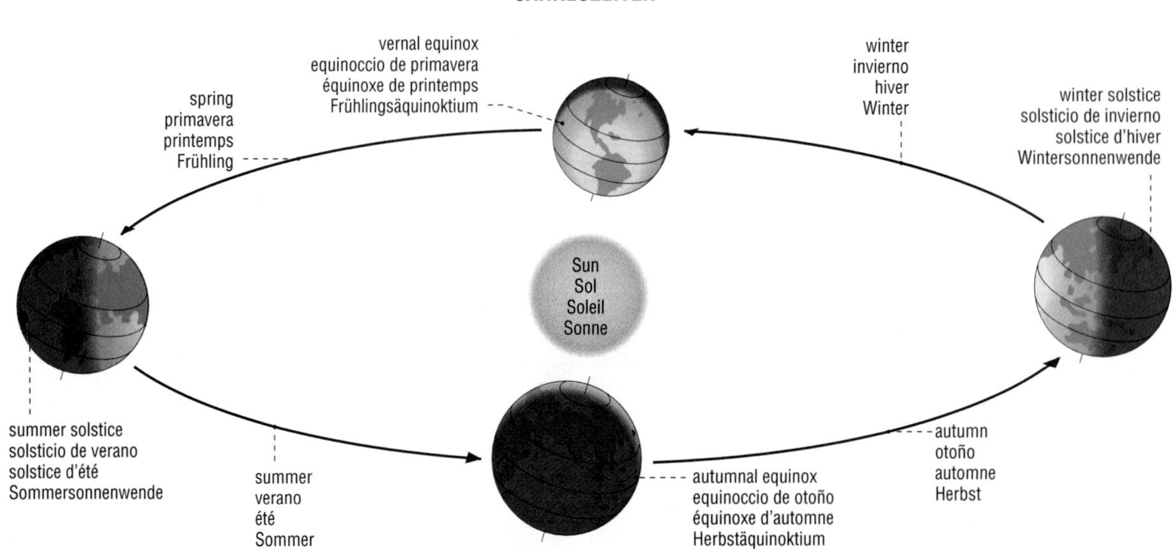
vernal equinox
equinoccio de primavera
équinoxe de printemps
Frühlingsäquinoktium
winter
invierno
hiver
Winter
spring
primavera
printemps
Frühling
winter solstice
solsticio de invierno
solstice d'hiver
Wintersonnenwende
Sun
Sol
Soleil
Sonne
summer solstice
solsticio de verano
solstice d'été
Sommersonnenwende
summer
verano
été
Sommer
autumnal equinox
equinoccio de otoño
équinoxe d'automne
Herbstäquinoktium
autumn
otoño
automne
Herbst

COMET
COMETA
COMÈTE
KOMET

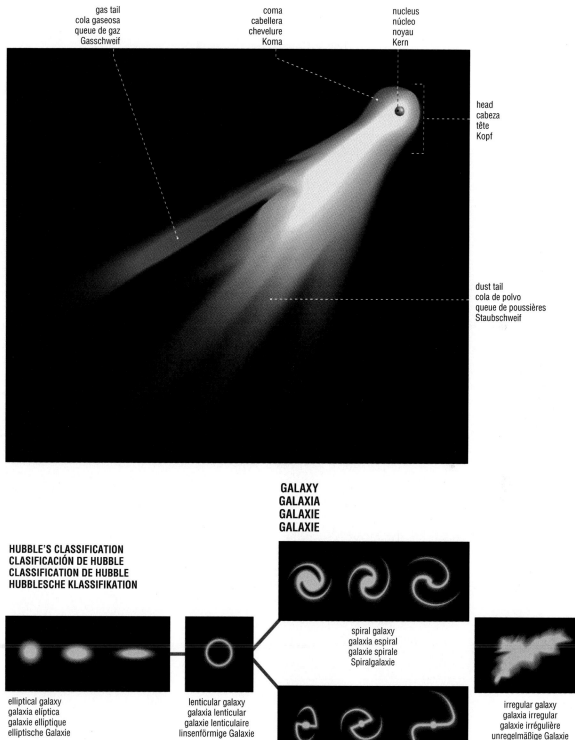

gas tail
cola gaseosa
queue de gaz
Gasschweif

coma
cabellera
chevelure
Koma

nucleus
núcleo
noyau
Kern

head
cabeza
tête
Kopf

dust tail
cola de polvo
queue de poussières
Staubschweif

GALAXY
GALAXIA
GALAXIE
GALAXIE

HUBBLE'S CLASSIFICATION
CLASIFICACIÓN DE HUBBLE
CLASSIFICATION DE HUBBLE
HUBBLESCHE KLASSIFIKATION

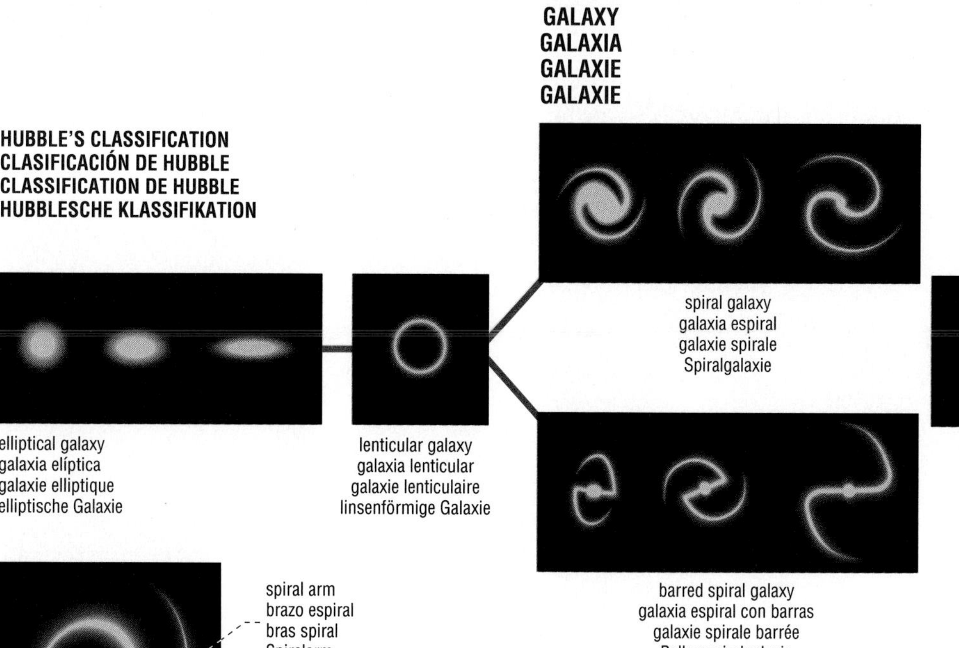

elliptical galaxy
galaxia elíptica
galaxie elliptique
elliptische Galaxie

lenticular galaxy
galaxia lenticular
galaxie lenticulaire
linsenförmige Galaxie

spiral galaxy
galaxia espiral
galaxie spirale
Spiralgalaxie

barred spiral galaxy
galaxia espiral con barras
galaxie spirale barrée
Balkenspiralgalaxie

irregular galaxy
galaxia irregular
galaxie irrégulière
unregelmäßige Galaxie

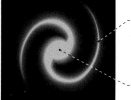

spiral arm
brazo espiral
bras spiral
Spiralarm

nucleus
núcleo
noyau galactique
Kern

CONSTELLATIONS OF THE NORTHERN HEMISPHERE
CONSTELACIONES EN EL HEMISFERIO BOREAL
CONSTELLATIONS DE L'HÉMISPHÈRE BORÉAL
KONSTELLATIONEN DER NÖRDLICHEN HALBKUGEL

1
6
3
7
4
5
8
12
9
10
11
14
16
13
15
26
25
23
24
27
22
28
34
30
31
29
33
35
32
39
40

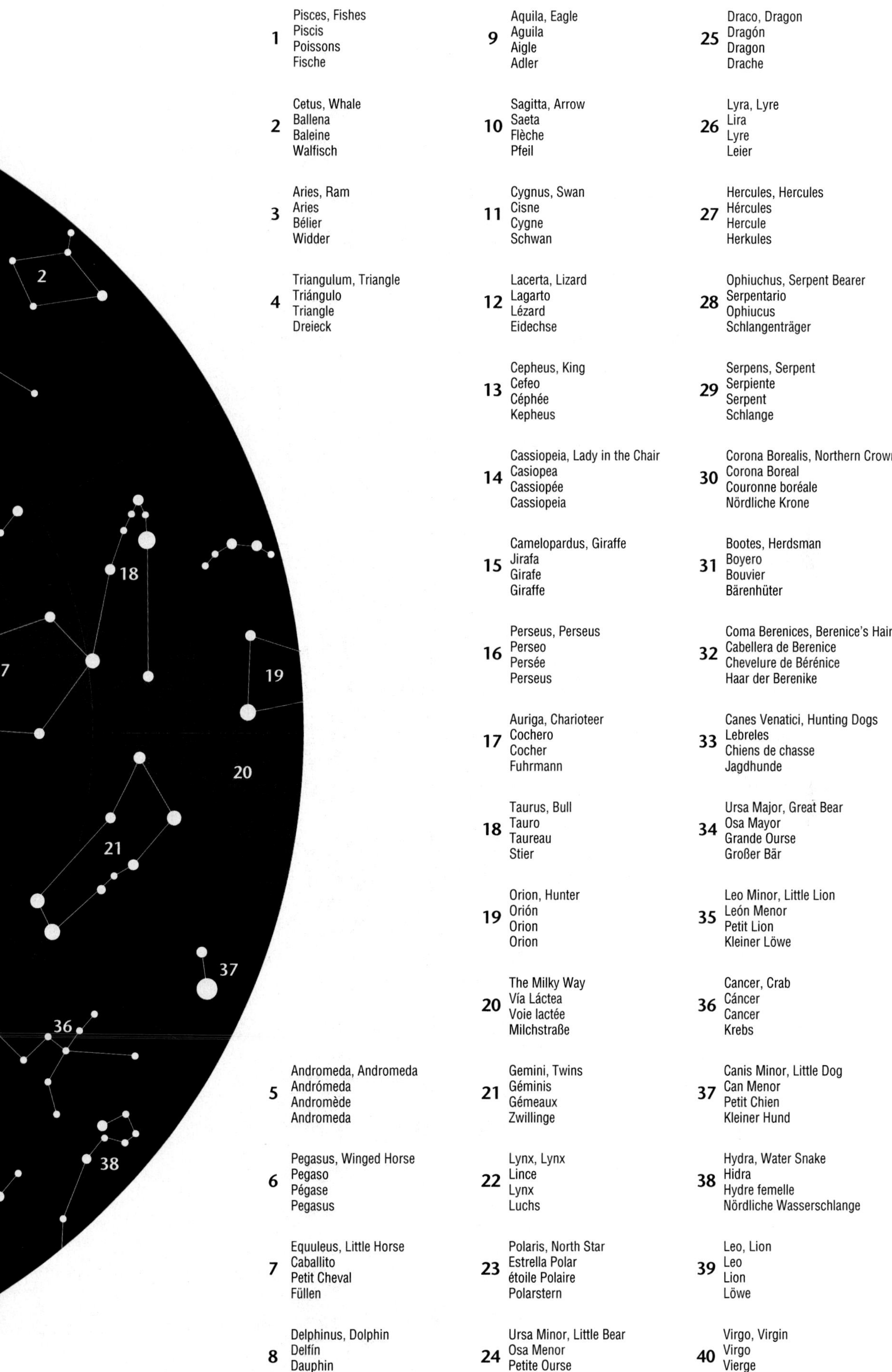
2
18
7
19
20
21
37
36
38

1
Pisces, Fishes
Piscis
Poissons
Fische

2
Cetus, Whale
Ballena
Baleine
Walfisch

3
Aries, Ram
Aries
Bélier
Widder

4
Triangulum, Triangle
Triángulo
Triangle
Dreieck

5
Andromeda, Andromeda
Andrómeda
Andromède
Andromeda

6
Pegasus, Winged Horse
Pegaso
Pégase
Pegasus

7
Equuleus, Little Horse
Caballito
Petit Cheval
Füllen

8
Delphinus, Dolphin
Delfín
Dauphin
Delphin

9
Aquila, Eagle
Aguila
Aigle
Adler

10
Sagitta, Arrow
Saeta
Flèche
Pfeil

11
Cygnus, Swan
Cisne
Cygne
Schwan

12
Lacerta, Lizard
Lagarto
Lézard
Eidechse

13
Cepheus, King
Cefeo
Céphée
Kepheus

14
Cassiopeia, Lady in the Chair
Casiopea
Cassiopée
Cassiopeia

15
Camelopardus, Giraffe
Jirafa
Girafe
Giraffe

16
Perseus, Perseus
Perseo
Persée
Perseus

17
Auriga, Charioteer
Cochero
Cocher
Fuhrmann

18
Taurus, Bull
Tauro
Taureau
Stier

19
Orion, Hunter
Orión
Orion
Orion

20
The Milky Way
Vía Láctea
Voie lactée
Milchstraße

21
Gemini, Twins
Géminis
Gémeaux
Zwillinge

22
Lynx, Lynx
Lince
Lynx
Luchs

23
Polaris, North Star
Estrella Polar
étoile Polaire
Polarstern

24
Ursa Minor, Little Bear
Osa Menor
Petite Ourse
Kleiner Bär

25
Draco, Dragon
Dragón
Dragon
Drache

26
Lyra, Lyre
Lira
Lyre
Leier

27
Hercules, Hercules
Hércules
Hercule
Herkules

28
Ophiuchus, Serpent Bearer
Serpentario
Ophiucus
Schlangenträger

29
Serpens, Serpent
Serpiente
Serpent
Schlange

30
Corona Borealis, Northern Crown
Corona Boreal
Couronne boréale
Nördliche Krone

31
Bootes, Herdsman
Boyero
Bouvier
Bärenhüter

32
Coma Berenices, Berenice's Hair
Cabellera de Berenice
Chevelure de Bérénice
Haar der Berenike

33
Canes Venatici, Hunting Dogs
Lebreles
Chiens de chasse
Jagdhunde

34
Ursa Major, Great Bear
Osa Mayor
Grande Ourse
Großer Bär

35
Leo Minor, Little Lion
León Menor
Petit Lion
Kleiner Löwe

36
Cancer, Crab
Cáncer
Cancer
Krebs

37
Canis Minor, Little Dog
Can Menor
Petit Chien
Kleiner Hund

38
Hydra, Water Snake
Hidra
Hydre femelle
Nördliche Wasserschlange

39
Leo, Lion
Leo
Lion
Löwe

40
Virgo, Virgin
Virgo
Vierge
Jungfrau

CONSTELLATIONS OF THE SOUTHERN HEMISPHERE
CONSTELACIONES DEL HEMISFERIO AUSTRAL
CONSTELLATIONS DE L'HÉMISPHÈRE AUSTRAL
KONSTELLATIONEN DER SÜDLICHEN HALBKUGEL

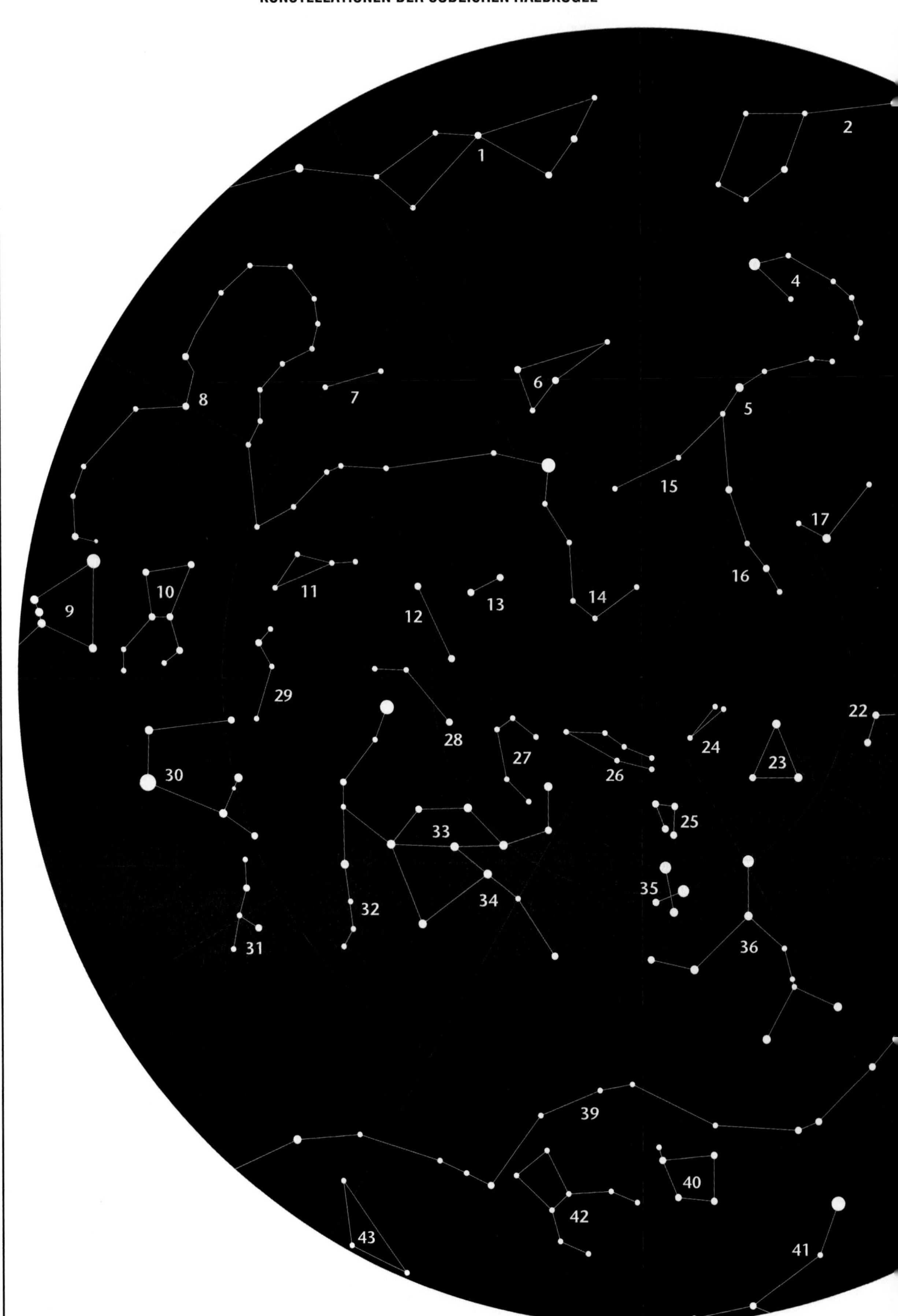
1
2
4
6
7
8
5
15
17
16
9
10
11
12
13
14
29
22
28
24
27
23
30
26
25
33
35
34
32
36
31
39
40
42
43
41

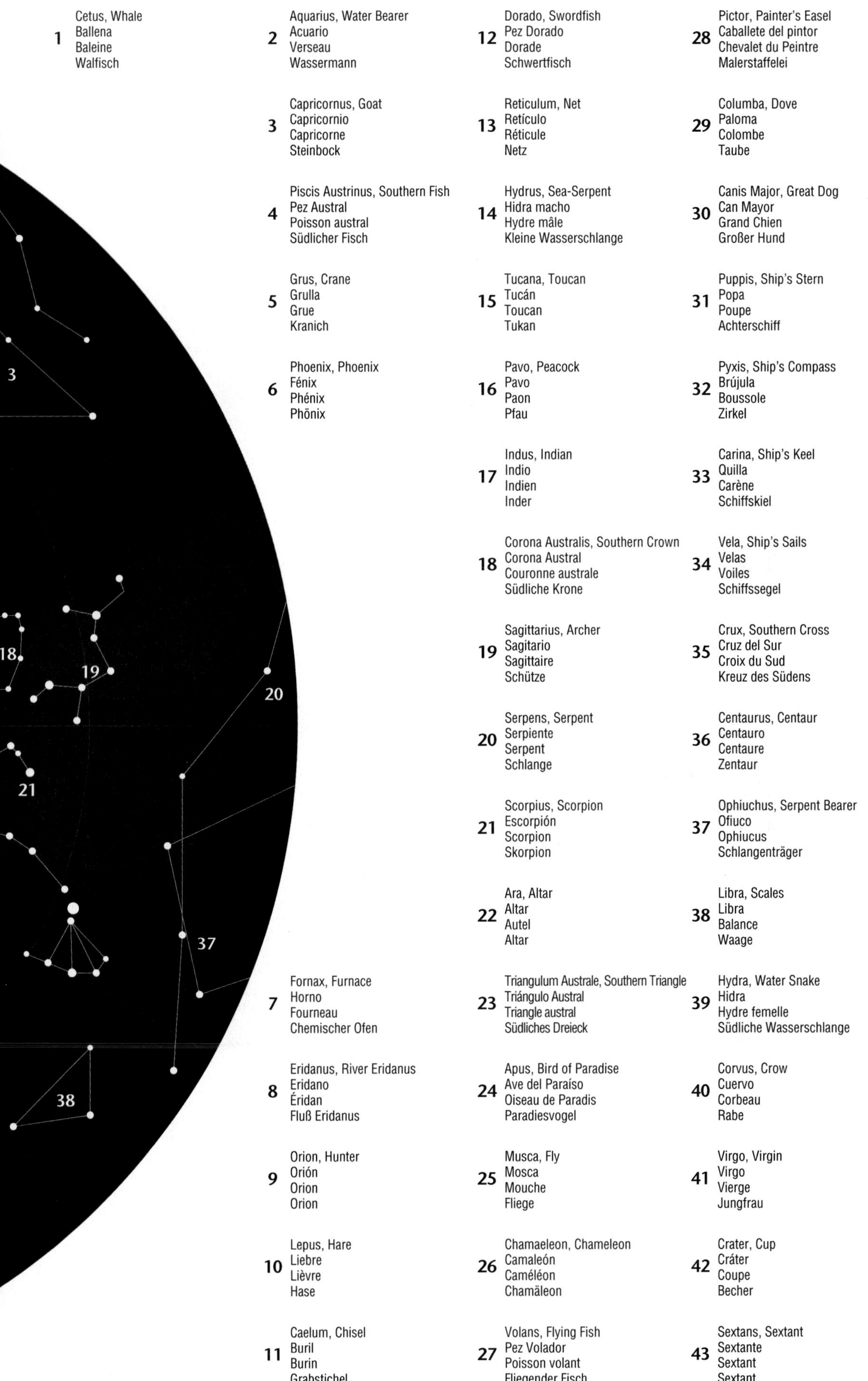
3
18
19
20
21
37
38

1 Cetus, Whale
Ballena
Baleine
Walfisch

2 Aquarius, Water Bearer
Acuario
Verseau
Wassermann

3 Capricornus, Goat
Capricornio
Capricorne
Steinbock

4 Piscis Austrinus, Southern Fish
Pez Austral
Poisson austral
Südlicher Fisch

5 Grus, Crane
Grulla
Grue
Kranich

6 Phoenix, Phoenix
Fénix
Phénix
Phönix

7 Fornax, Furnace
Horno
Fourneau
Chemischer Ofen

8 Eridanus, River Eridanus
Eridano
Éridan
Fluß Eridanus

9 Orion, Hunter
Orión
Orion
Orion

10 Lepus, Hare
Liebre
Lièvre
Hase

11 Caelum, Chisel
Buril
Burin
Grabstichel

12 Dorado, Swordfish
Pez Dorado
Dorade
Schwertfisch

13 Reticulum, Net
Retículo
Réticule
Netz

14 Hydrus, Sea-Serpent
Hidra macho
Hydre mâle
Kleine Wasserschlange

15 Tucana, Toucan
Tucán
Toucan
Tukan

16 Pavo, Peacock
Pavo
Paon
Pfau

17 Indus, Indian
Indio
Indien
Inder

18 Corona Australis, Southern Crown
Corona Austral
Couronne australe
Südliche Krone

19 Sagittarius, Archer
Sagitario
Sagittaire
Schütze

20 Serpens, Serpent
Serpiente
Serpent
Schlange

21 Scorpius, Scorpion
Escorpión
Scorpion
Skorpion

22 Ara, Altar
Altar
Autel
Altar

23 Triangulum Australe, Southern Triangle
Triángulo Austral
Triangle austral
Südliches Dreieck

24 Apus, Bird of Paradise
Ave del Paraíso
Oiseau de Paradis
Paradiesvogel

25 Musca, Fly
Mosca
Mouche
Fliege

26 Chamaeleon, Chameleon
Camaleón
Caméléon
Chamäleon

27 Volans, Flying Fish
Pez Volador
Poisson volant
Fliegender Fisch

28 Pictor, Painter's Easel
Caballete del pintor
Chevalet du Peintre
Malerstaffelei

29 Columba, Dove
Paloma
Colombe
Taube

30 Canis Major, Great Dog
Can Mayor
Grand Chien
Großer Hund

31 Puppis, Ship's Stern
Popa
Poupe
Achterschiff

32 Pyxis, Ship's Compass
Brújula
Boussole
Zirkel

33 Carina, Ship's Keel
Quilla
Carène
Schiffskiel

34 Vela, Ship's Sails
Velas
Voiles
Schiffssegel

35 Crux, Southern Cross
Cruz del Sur
Croix du Sud
Kreuz des Südens

36 Centaurus, Centaur
Centauro
Centaure
Zentaur

37 Ophiuchus, Serpent Bearer
Ofiuco
Ophiucus
Schlangenträger

38 Libra, Scales
Libra
Balance
Waage

39 Hydra, Water Snake
Hidra
Hydre femelle
Südliche Wasserschlange

40 Corvus, Crow
Cuervo
Corbeau
Rabe

41 Virgo, Virgin
Virgo
Vierge
Jungfrau

42 Crater, Cup
Cráter
Coupe
Becher

43 Sextans, Sextant
Sextante
Sextant
Sextant

ASTRONOMICAL OBSERVATORY
OBSERVATORIO ASTRONÓMICO
OBSERVATOIRE ASTRONOMIQUE
STERNWARTE

TELESCOPE
TELESCOPIO
TÉLESCOPE
TELESKOP

OBSERVATORY
OBSERVATORIO
OBSERVATOIRE
STERNWARTE

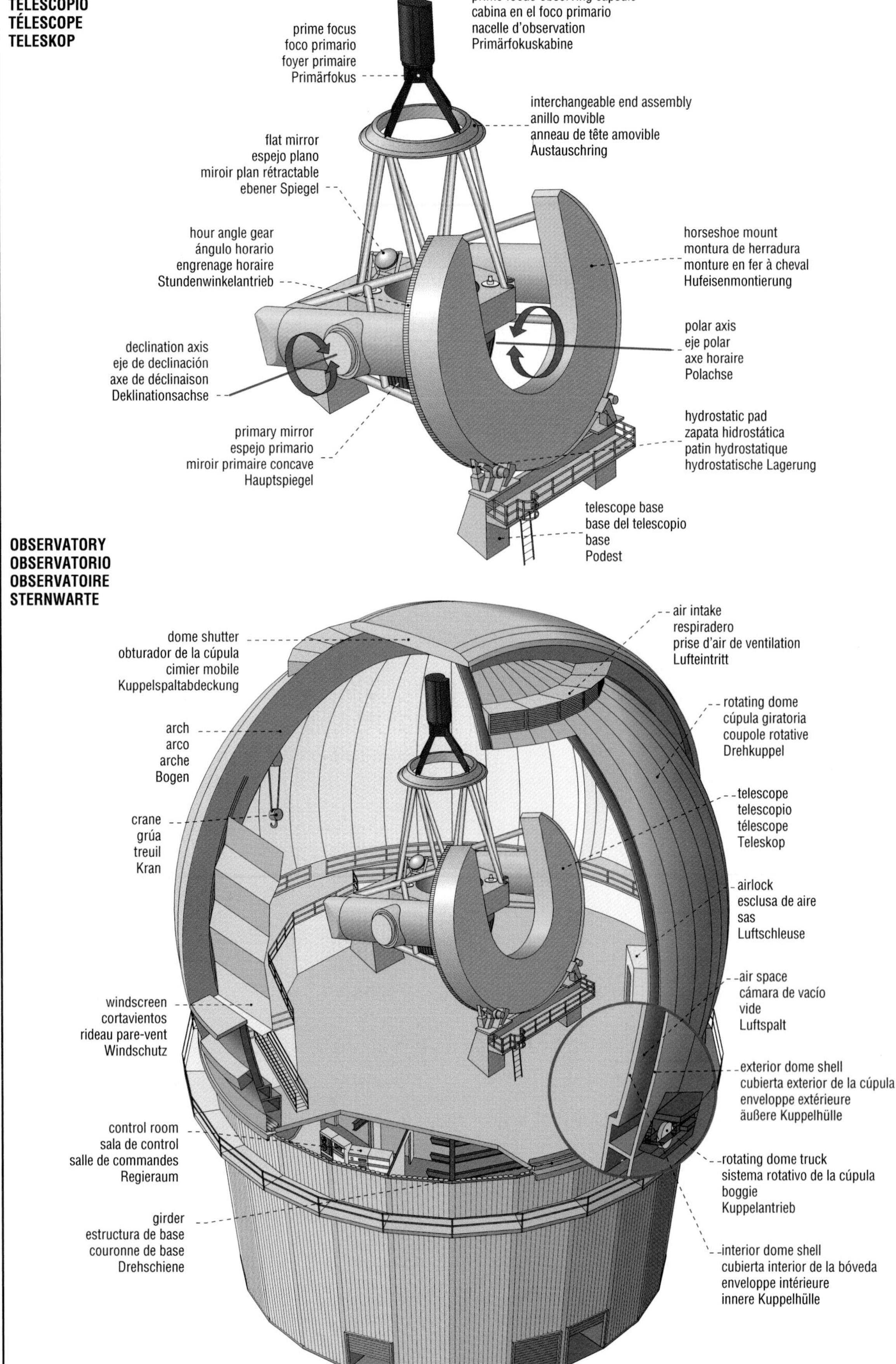
prime focus observing capsule
cabina en el foco primario
nacelle d'observation
Primärfokuskabine
prime focus
foco primario
foyer primaire
Primärfokus
interchangeable end assembly
anillo movible
anneau de tête amovible
Austauschring
flat mirror
espejo plano
miroir plan rétractable
ebener Spiegel
hour angle gear
ángulo horario
engrenage horaire
Stundenwinkelantrieb
horseshoe mount
montura de herradura
monture en fer à cheval
Hufeisenmontierung
polar axis
eje polar
axe horaire
Polachse
declination axis
eje de declinación
axe de déclinaison
Deklinationsachse
hydrostatic pad
zapata hidrostática
patin hydrostatique
hydrostatische Lagerung
primary mirror
espejo primario
miroir primaire concave
Hauptspiegel
telescope base
base del telescopio
base
Podest
dome shutter
obturador de la cúpula
cimier mobile
Kuppelspaltabdeckung
air intake
respiradero
prise d'air de ventilation
Lufteintritt
rotating dome
cúpula giratoria
coupole rotative
Drehkuppel
arch
arco
arche
Bogen
telescope
telescopio
télescope
Teleskop
crane
grúa
treuil
Kran
airlock
esclusa de aire
sas
Luftschleuse
air space
cámara de vacío
vide
Luftspalt
windscreen
cortavientos
rideau pare-vent
Windschutz
exterior dome shell
cubierta exterior de la cúpula
enveloppe extérieure
äußere Kuppelhülle
control room
sala de control
salle de commandes
Regieraum
rotating dome truck
sistema rotativo de la cúpula
boggie
Kuppelantrieb
girder
estructura de base
couronne de base
Drehschiene
interior dome shell
cubierta interior de la bóveda
enveloppe intérieure
innere Kuppelhülle

RADIO TELESCOPE
RADIOTELESCOPIO
RADIOTÉLESCOPE
RADIOTELESKOP

ALTAZIMUTH MOUNTING
MONTURA ACIMUTAL
MONTURE ALTAZIMUTALE
ALTAZIMUTALE MONTIERUNG

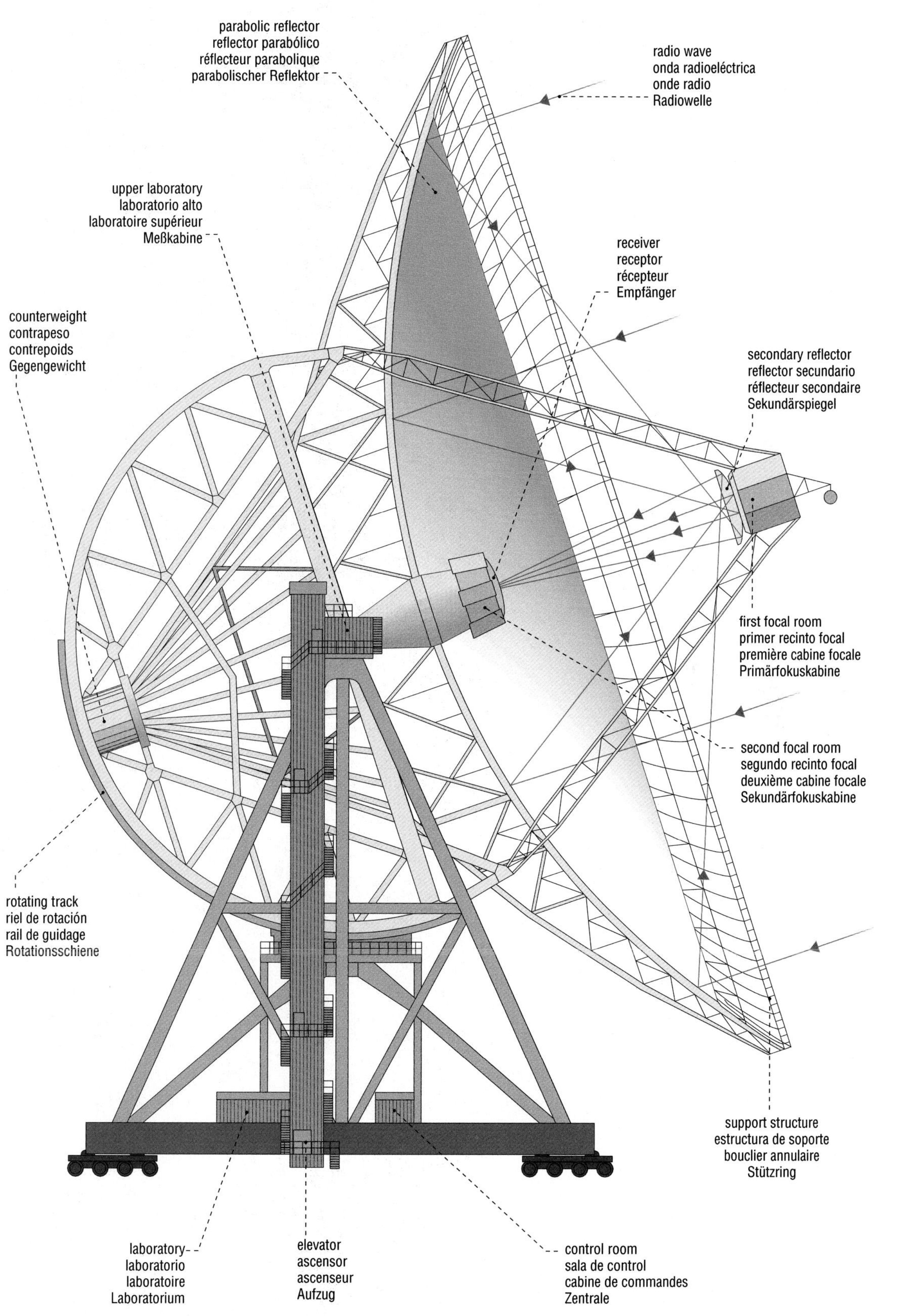
parabolic reflector
reflector parabólico
réflecteur parabolique
parabolischer Reflektor
radio wave
onda radioeléctrica
onde radio
Radiowelle
upper laboratory
laboratorio alto
laboratoire supérieur
Meßkabine
receiver
receptor
récepteur
Empfänger
counterweight
contrapeso
contrepoids
Gegengewicht
secondary reflector
reflector secundario
réflecteur secondaire
Sekundärspiegel
first focal room
primer recinto focal
première cabine focale
Primärfokuskabine
second focal room
segundo recinto focal
deuxième cabine focale
Sekundärfokuskabine
rotating track
riel de rotación
rail de guidage
Rotationsschiene
support structure
estructura de soporte
bouclier annulaire
Stützring
laboratory
laboratorio
laboratoire
Laboratorium
elevator
ascensor
ascenseur
Aufzug
control room
sala de control
cabine de commandes
Zentrale

HUBBLE SPACE TELESCOPE
TELESCOPIO ESPACIAL HUBBLE
TÉLESCOPE SPATIAL HUBBLE
HUBBLE RAUMTELESKOP

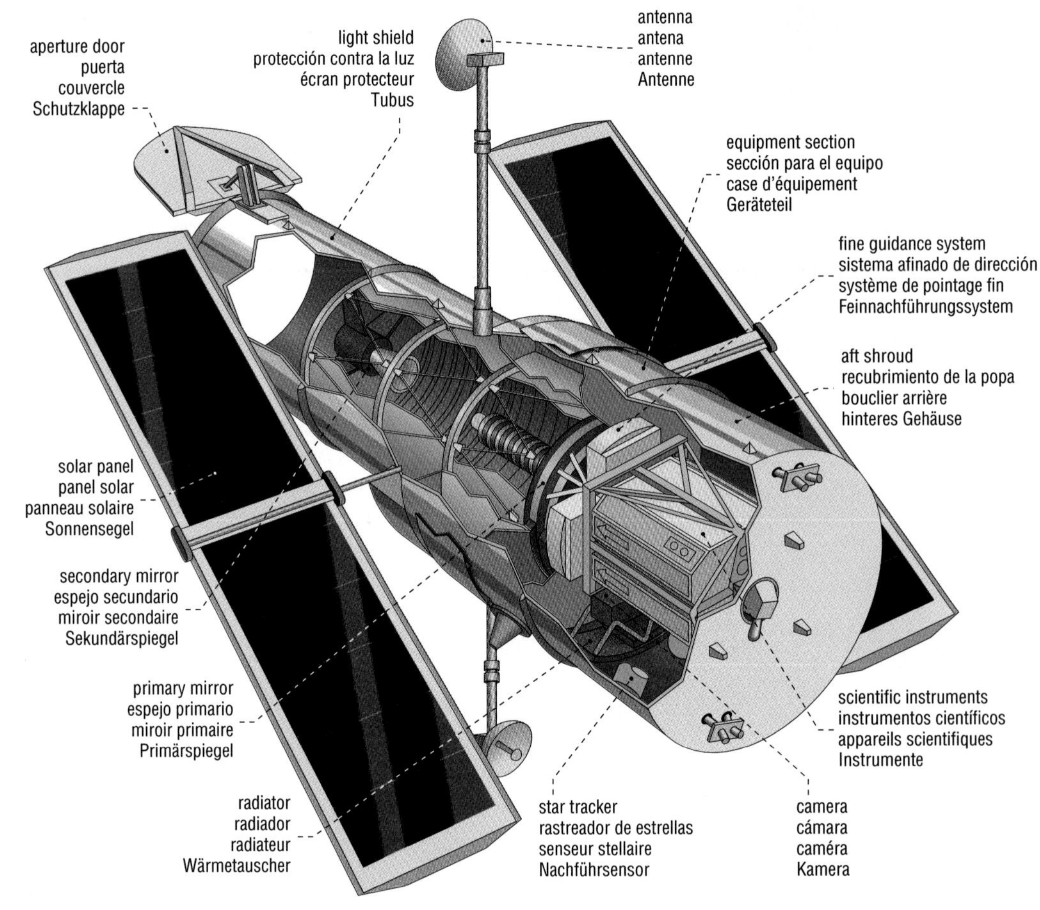
aperture door
puerta
couvercle
Schutzklappe
light shield
protección contra la luz
écran protecteur
Tubus
antenna
antena
antenne
Antenne
equipment section
sección para el equipo
case d'équipement
Geräteteil
fine guidance system
sistema afinado de dirección
système de pointage fin
Feinnachführungssystem
aft shroud
recubrimiento de la popa
bouclier arrière
hinteres Gehäuse
solar panel
panel solar
panneau solaire
Sonnensegel
secondary mirror
espejo secundario
miroir secondaire
Sekundärspiegel
primary mirror
espejo primario
miroir primaire
Primärspiegel
radiator
radiador
radiateur
Wärmetauscher
star tracker
rastreador de estrellas
senseur stellaire
Nachführsensor
camera
cámara
caméra
Kamera
scientific instruments
instrumentos científicos
appareils scientifiques
Instrumente

PLANETARIUM
PLANETARIO
PLANÉTARIUM
PLANETARIUM

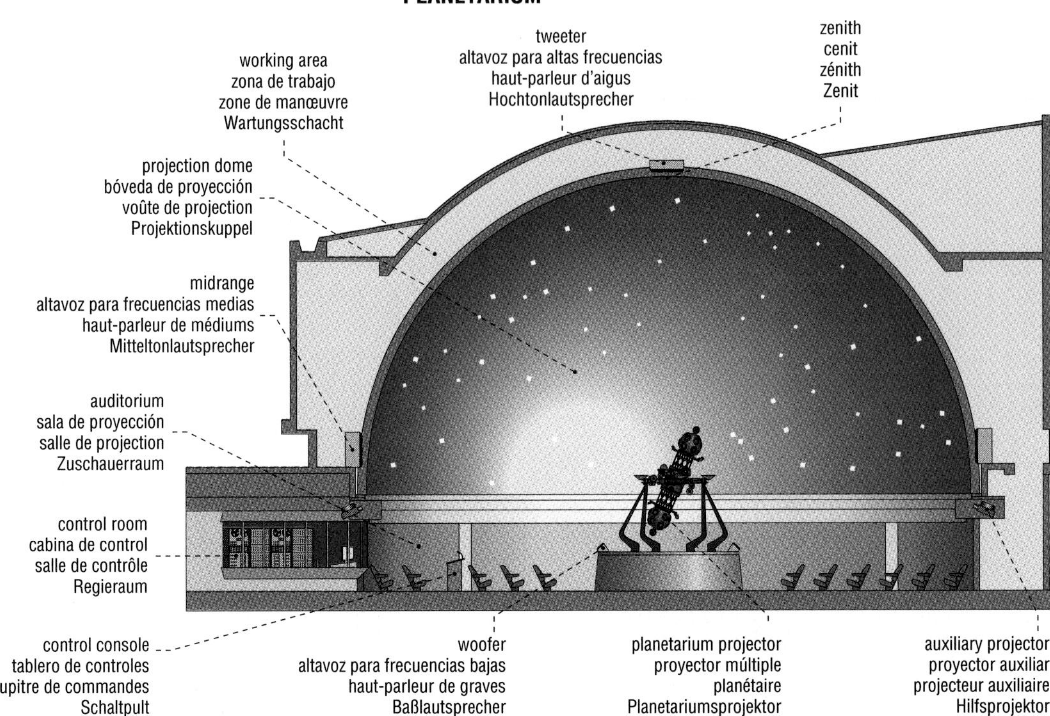
working area
zona de trabajo
zone de manœuvre
Wartungsschacht
tweeter
altavoz para altas frecuencias
haut-parleur d'aigus
Hochtonlautsprecher
zenith
cenit
zénith
Zenit
projection dome
bóveda de proyección
voûte de projection
Projektionskuppel
midrange
altavoz para frecuencias medias
haut-parleur de médiums
Mitteltonlautsprecher
auditorium
sala de proyección
salle de projection
Zuschauerraum
control room
cabina de control
salle de contrôle
Regieraum
control console
tablero de controles
pupitre de commandes
Schaltpult
woofer
altavoz para frecuencias bajas
haut-parleur de graves
Baßlautsprecher
planetarium projector
proyector múltiple
planétaire
Planetariumsprojektor
auxiliary projector
proyector auxiliar
projecteur auxiliaire
Hilfsprojektor

Wilmington
Reading
Lynnfield
Pinehurst
Burlington
Wakefield
Stoneham
Woburn
Winchester
Saugus
Melrose
Lexington
Malden
Medford
Arlington
Everett
Revere
Lynn Harbor
Somerville
Belmont
Chelsea
Waltham
Cambridge
Winth
Watertown
Newton
Boston
Boston Harbor
Brookline
Quincy Bay
Needham
Quincy
Dedham
Milton
Braintree
Islington
Norwood

CONTENTS

PROFILE OF THE EARTH'S ATMOSPHERE
CORTE DE LA ATMÓSFERA TERRESTRE
COUPE DE L'ATMOSPHÈRE TERRESTRE
PROFIL DURCH DIE ERDATMOSPHÄRE

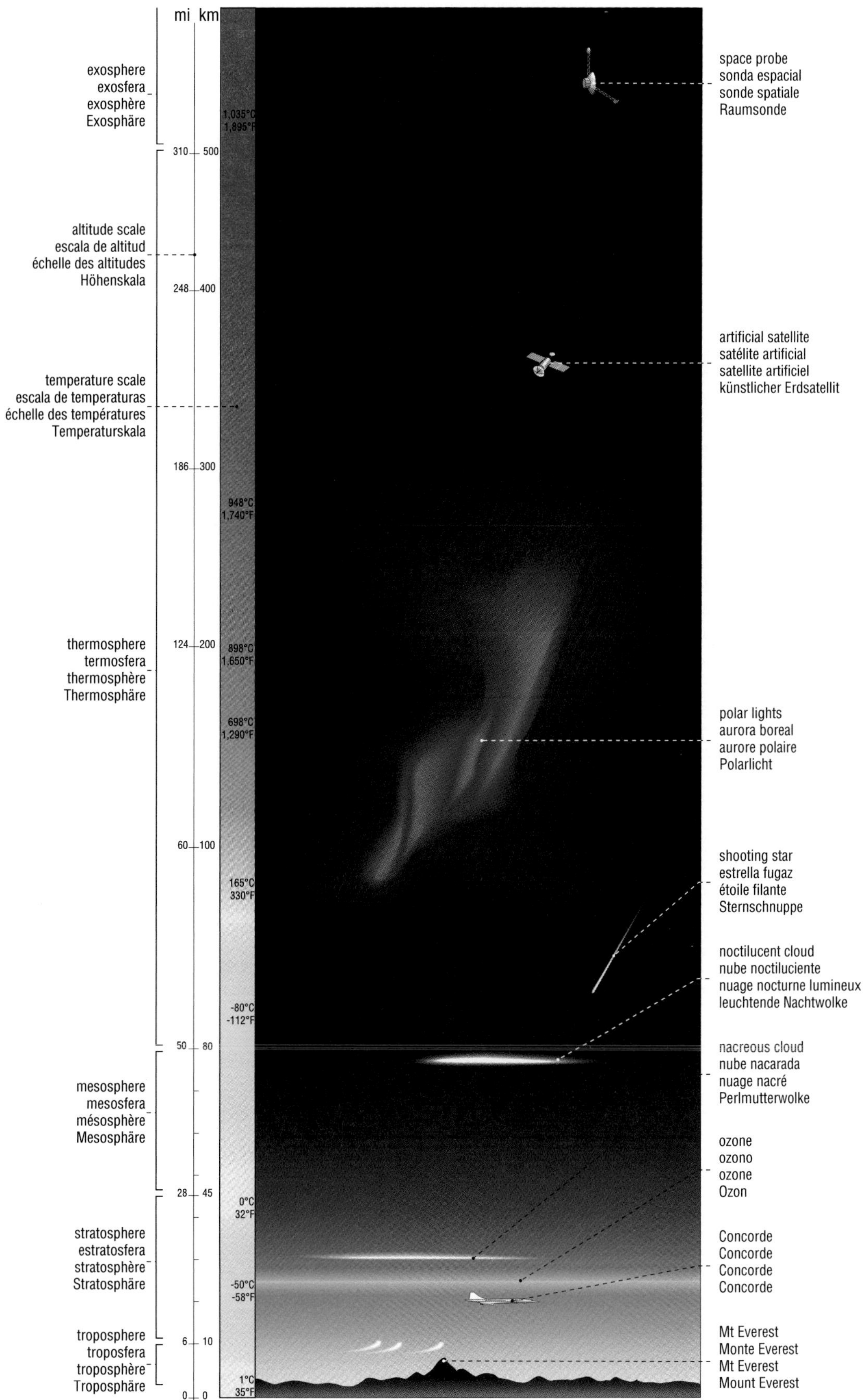
mi km
exosphere
exosfera
exosphère
Exosphäre
1,035°C
1,895°F
space probe
sonda espacial
sonde spatiale
Raumsonde
310 500
altitude scale
escala de altitud
échelle des altitudes
Höhenskala
248 400
artificial satellite
satélite artificial
satellite artificiel
künstlicher Erdsatellit
temperature scale
escala de temperaturas
échelle des températures
Temperaturskala
186 300
948°C
1,740°F
thermosphere
termosfera
thermosphère
Thermosphäre
124 200
898°C
1,650°F
698°C
1,290°F
polar lights
aurora boreal
aurore polaire
Polarlicht
60 100
165°C
330°F
shooting star
estrella fugaz
étoile filante
Sternschnuppe
noctilucent cloud
nube noctiluciente
nuage nocturne lumineux
leuchtende Nachtwolke
-80°C
-112°F
50 80
nacreous cloud
nube nacarada
nuage nacré
Perlmutterwolke
mesosphere
mesosfera
mésosphère
Mesosphäre
ozone
ozono
ozone
Ozon
28 45
0°C
32°F
stratosphere
estratosfera
stratosphère
Stratosphäre
Concorde
Concorde
Concorde
Concorde
-50°C
-58°F
troposphere
troposfera
troposphère
Troposphäre
6 10
Mt Everest
Monte Everest
Mt Everest
Mount Everest
1°C
35°F
0 0

CONFIGURATION OF THE CONTINENTS
CONFIGURACIÓN DE LOS CONTINENTES
CONFIGURATION DES CONTINENTS
KONFIGURATION DER KONTINENTE

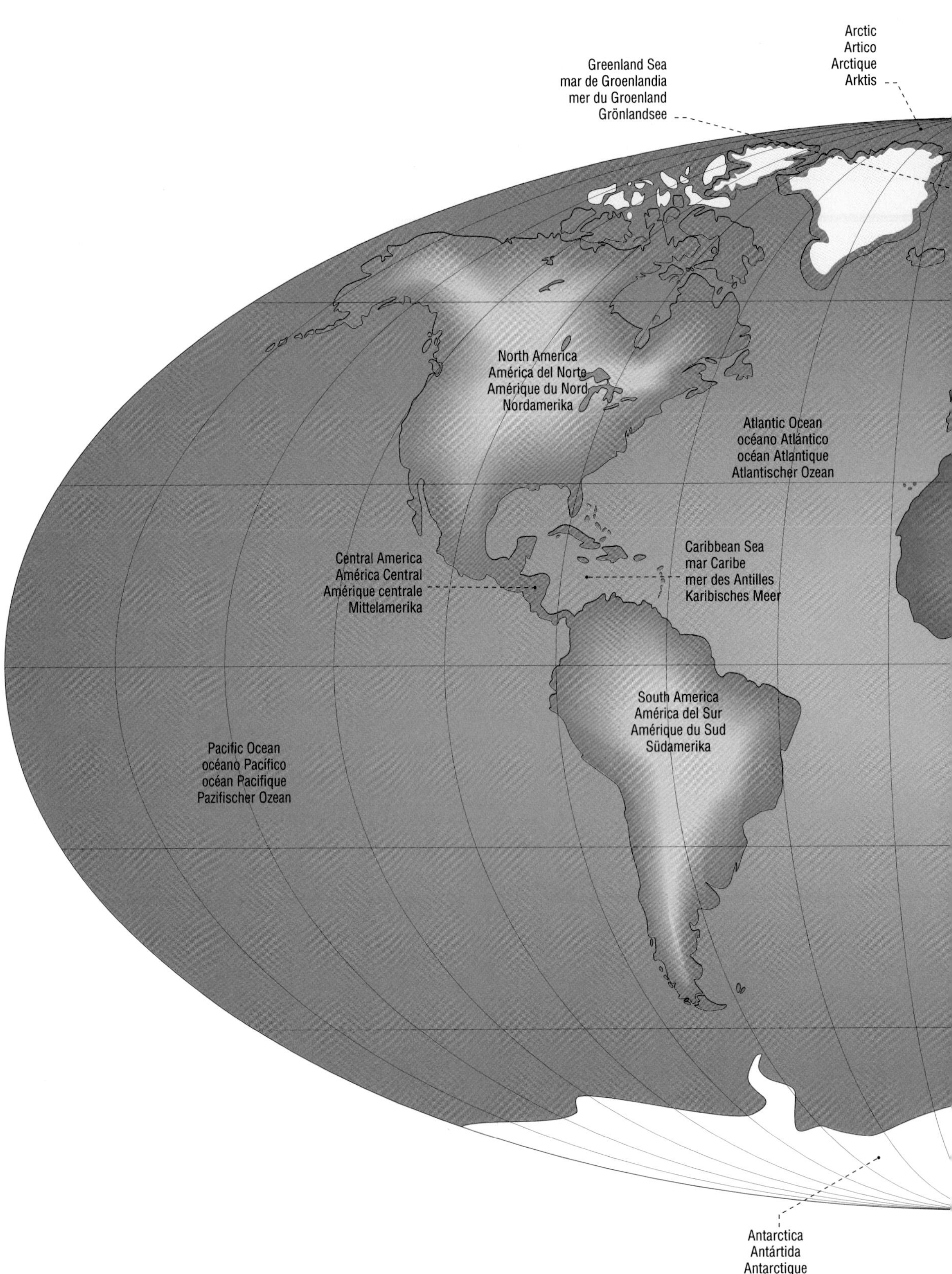
Arctic
Artico
Arctique
Arktis
Greenland Sea
mar de Groenlandia
mer du Groenland
Grönlandsee
North America
América del Norte
Amérique du Nord
Nordamerika
Atlantic Ocean
océano Atlántico
océan Atlantique
Atlantischer Ozean
Central America
América Central
Amérique centrale
Mittelamerika
Caribbean Sea
mar Caribe
mer des Antilles
Karibisches Meer
South America
América del Sur
Amérique du Sud
Südamerika
Pacific Ocean
océano Pacífico
océan Pacifique
Pazifischer Ozean
Antarctica
Antártida
Antarctique
Antarktis

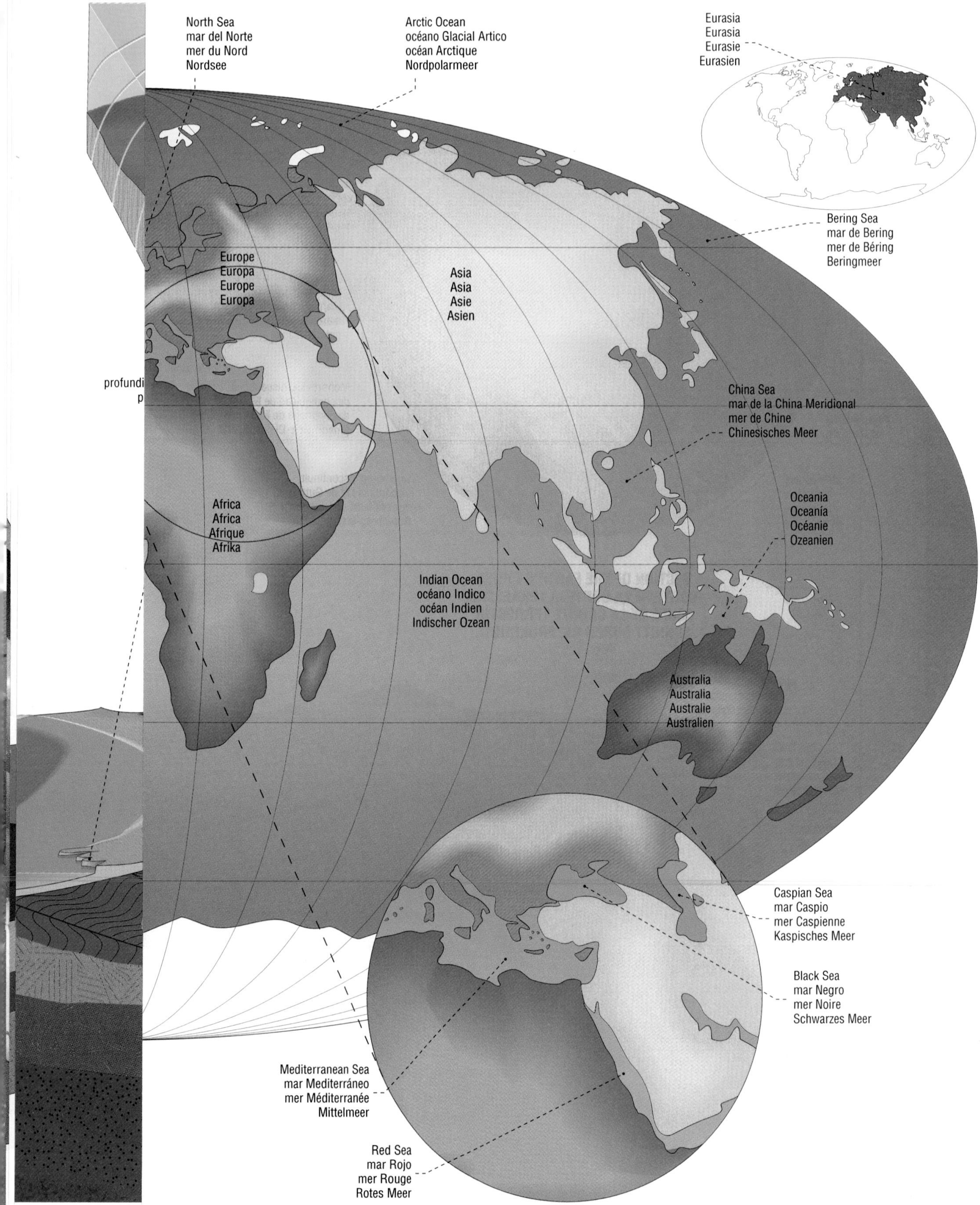

North Sea
mar del Norte
mer du Nord
Nordsee

Arctic Ocean
océano Glacial Artico
océan Arctique
Nordpolarmeer

Eurasia
Eurasia
Eurasie
Eurasien

Bering Sea
mar de Bering
mer de Béring
Beringmeer

Europe
Europa
Europe
Europa

Asia
Asia
Asie
Asien

profundi
p

China Sea
mar de la China Meridional
mer de Chine
Chinesisches Meer

Oceania
Oceanía
Océanie
Ozeanien

Africa
Africa
Afrique
Afrika

Indian Ocean
océano Indico
océan Indien
Indischer Ozean

Australia
Australia
Australie
Australien

Caspian Sea
mar Caspio
mer Caspienne
Kaspisches Meer

Black Sea
mar Negro
mer Noire
Schwarzes Meer

Mediterranean Sea
mar Mediterráneo
mer Méditerranée
Mittelmeer

Red Sea
mar Rojo
mer Rouge
Rotes Meer

POLLUTION OF FOOD ON GROUND
CONTAMINACIÓN DE ALIMENTOS EN LA TIERRA
POLLUTION DES ALIMENTS AU SOL
SCHADSTOFFBELASTUNG IM BODEN

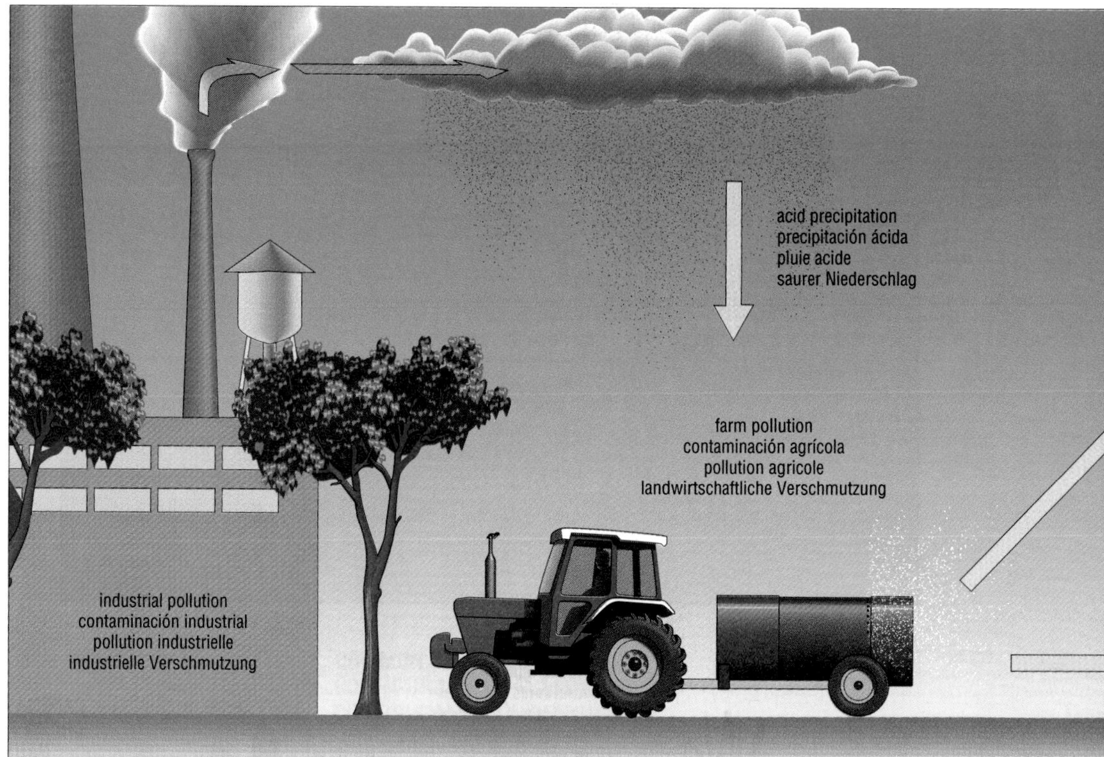
acid precipitation
precipitación ácida
pluie acide
saurer Niederschlag
farm pollution
contaminación agrícola
pollution agricole
landwirtschaftliche Verschmutzung
industrial pollution
contaminación industrial
pollution industrielle
industrielle Verschmutzung

POLLUTION OF FOOD IN WATER
CONTAMINACIÓN DE ALIMENTOS EN EL AGUA
POLLUTION DES ALIMENTS DANS L'EAU
SCHADSTOFFBELASTUNG IM WASSER

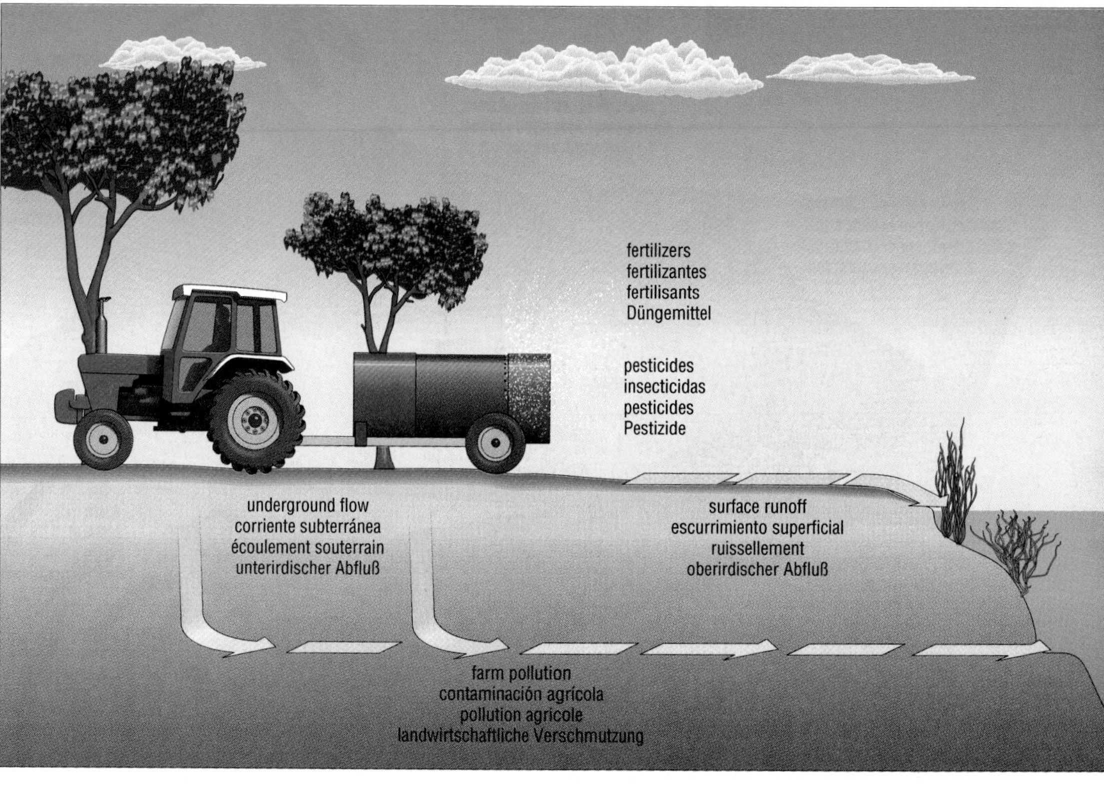
fertilizers
fertilizantes
fertilisants
Düngemittel
pesticides
insecticidas
pesticides
Pestizide
underground flow
corriente subterránea
écoulement souterrain
unterirdischer Abfluß
surface runoff
escurrimiento superficial
ruissellement
oberirdischer Abfluß
farm pollution
contaminación agrícola
pollution agricole
landwirtschaftliche Verschmutzung

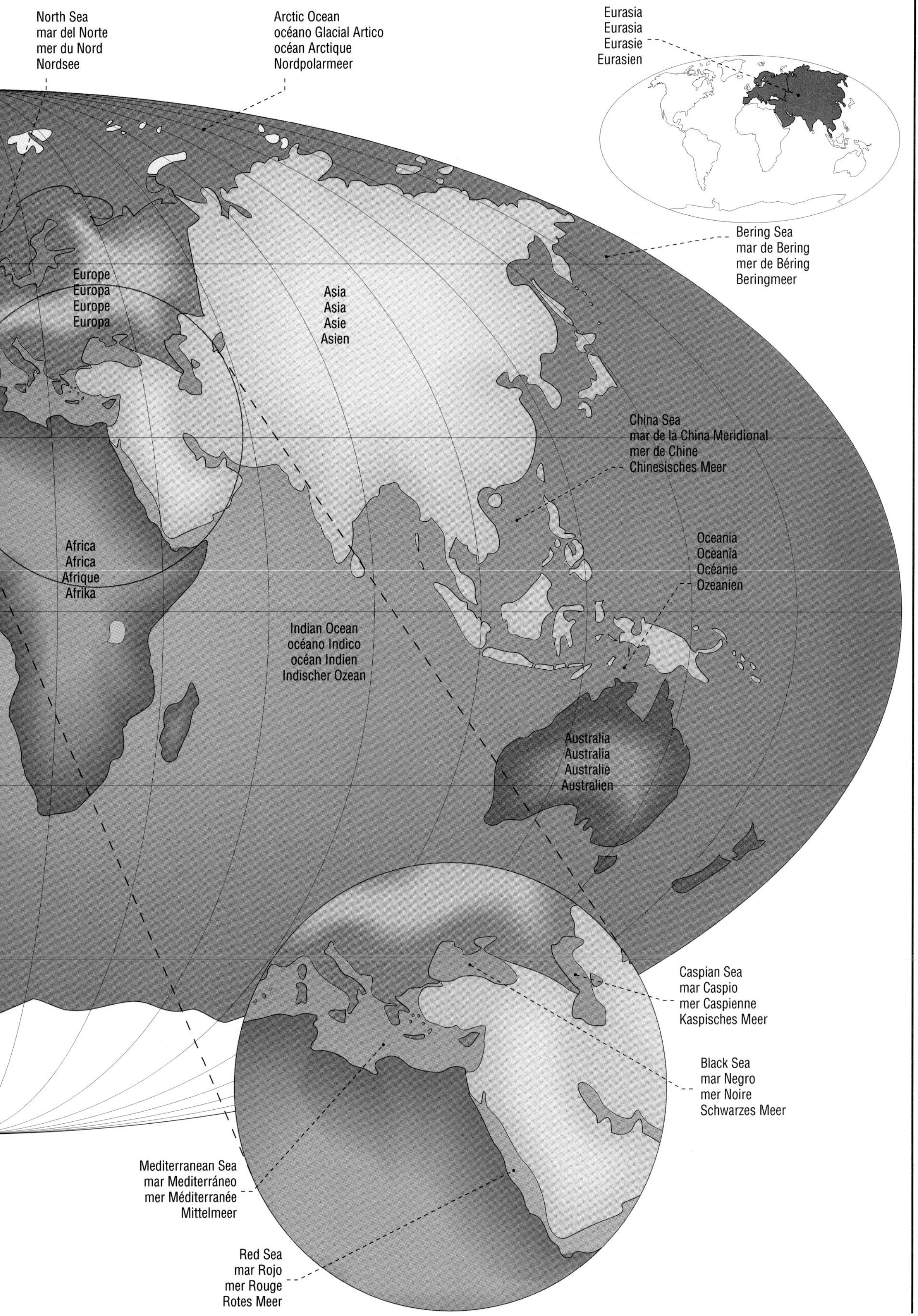
North Sea
mar del Norte
mer du Nord
Nordsee
Arctic Ocean
océano Glacial Artico
océan Arctique
Nordpolarmeer
Eurasia
Eurasia
Eurasie
Eurasien
Bering Sea
mar de Bering
mer de Béring
Beringmeer
Europe
Europa
Europe
Europa
Asia
Asia
Asie
Asien
China Sea
mar de la China Meridional
mer de Chine
Chinesisches Meer
Oceania
Oceanía
Océanie
Ozeanien
Africa
Africa
Afrique
Afrika
Indian Ocean
océano Indico
océan Indien
Indischer Ozean
Australia
Australia
Australie
Australien
Caspian Sea
mar Caspio
mer Caspienne
Kaspisches Meer
Black Sea
mar Negro
mer Noire
Schwarzes Meer
Mediterranean Sea
mar Mediterráneo
mer Méditerranée
Mittelmeer
Red Sea
mar Rojo
mer Rouge
Rotes Meer

STRUCTURE OF THE EARTH
ESTRUCTURA DE LA TIERRA
STRUCTURE DE LA TERRE
STRUKTUR DER ERDE

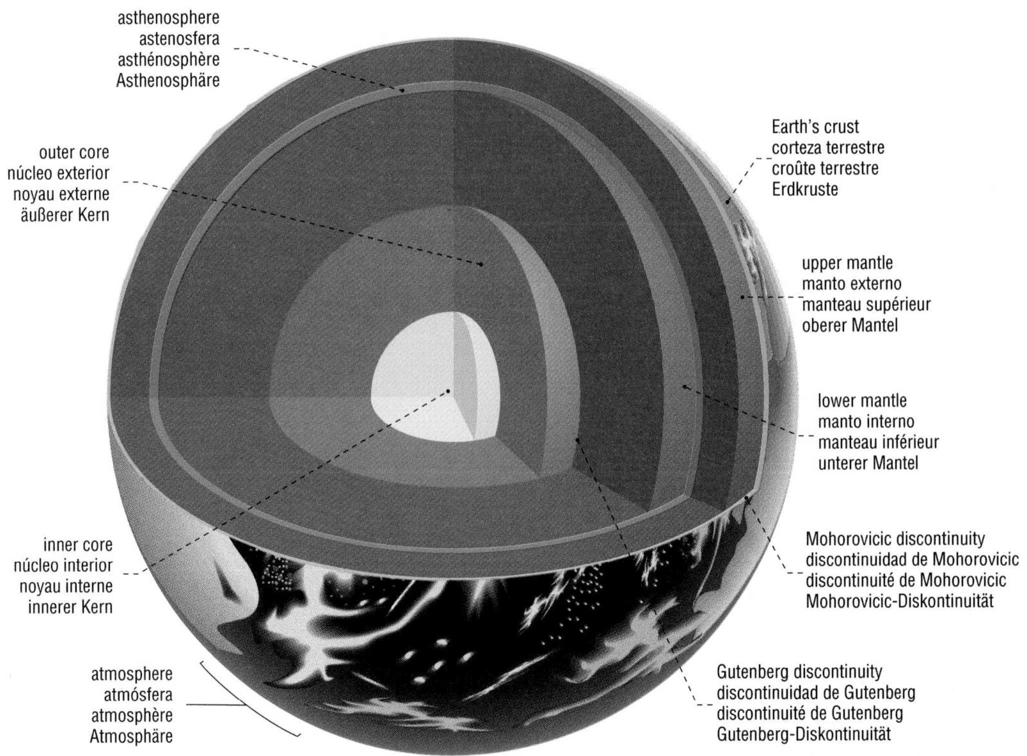
asthenosphere
astenosfera
asthénosphère
Asthenosphäre
outer core
núcleo exterior
noyau externe
äußerer Kern
Earth's crust
corteza terrestre
croûte terrestre
Erdkruste
upper mantle
manto externo
manteau supérieur
oberer Mantel
lower mantle
manto interno
manteau inférieur
unterer Mantel
inner core
núcleo interior
noyau interne
innerer Kern
Mohorovicic discontinuity
discontinuidad de Mohorovicic
discontinuité de Mohorovicic
Mohorovicic-Diskontinuität
atmosphere
atmósfera
atmosphère
Atmosphäre
Gutenberg discontinuity
discontinuidad de Gutenberg
discontinuité de Gutenberg
Gutenberg-Diskontinuität

SECTION OF THE EARTH'S CRUST
CORTE DE LA CORTEZA TERRESTRE
COUPE DE LA CROÛTE TERRESTRE
SCHNITT DURCH DIE ERDKRUSTE

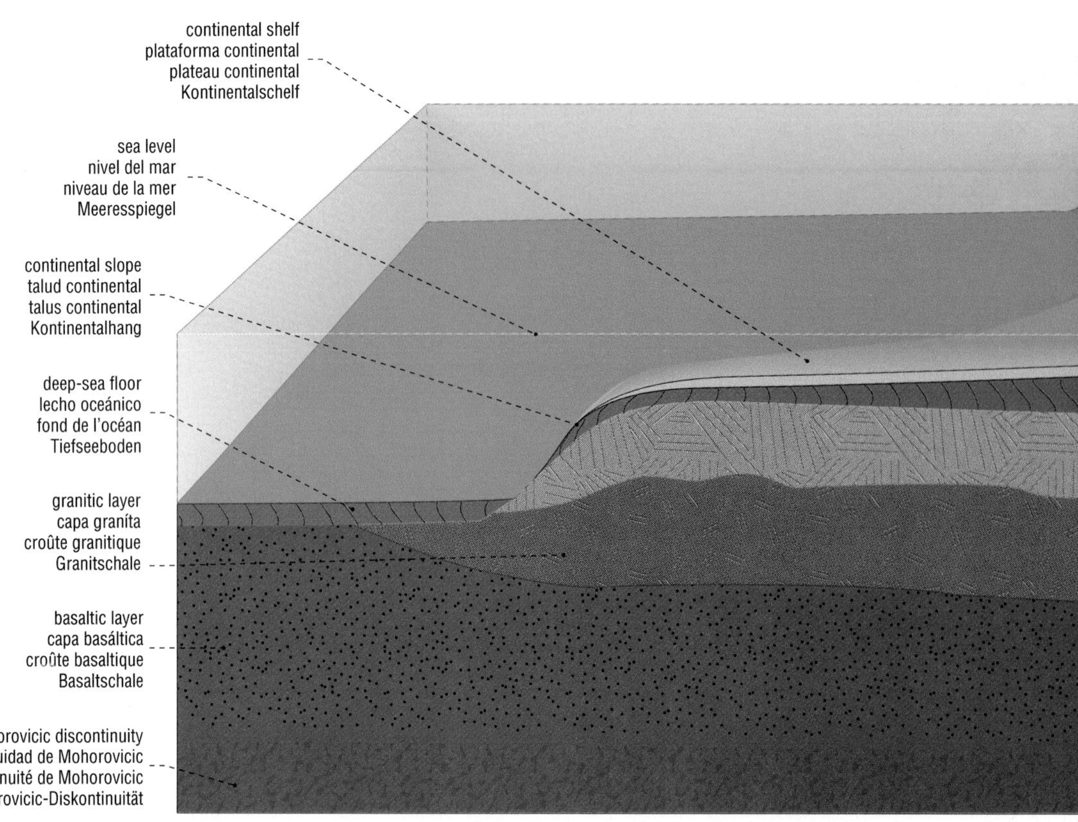
continental shelf
plataforma continental
plateau continental
Kontinentalschelf
sea level
nivel del mar
niveau de la mer
Meeresspiegel
continental slope
talud continental
talus continental
Kontinentalhang
deep-sea floor
lecho oceánico
fond de l'océan
Tiefseeboden
granitic layer
capa granita
croûte granitique
Granitschale
basaltic layer
capa basáltica
croûte basaltique
Basaltschale
Mohorovicic discontinuity
discontinuidad de Mohorovicic
discontinuité de Mohorovicic
Mohorovicic-Diskontinuität

EARTHQUAKE
TERREMOTO
SÉISME
ERDBEBEN

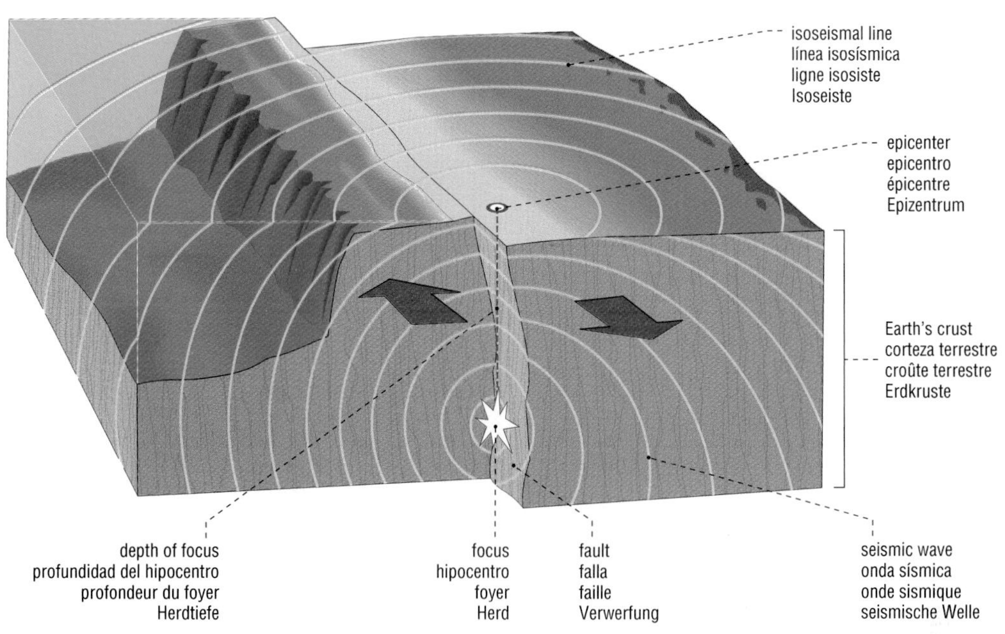
isoseismal line
línea isosísmica
ligne isosiste
Isoseiste
epicenter
epicentro
épicentre
Epizentrum
Earth's crust
corteza terrestre
croûte terrestre
Erdkruste
depth of focus
profundidad del hipocentro
profondeur du foyer
Herdtiefe
focus
hipocentro
foyer
Herd
fault
falla
faille
Verwerfung
seismic wave
onda sísmica
onde sismique
seismische Welle

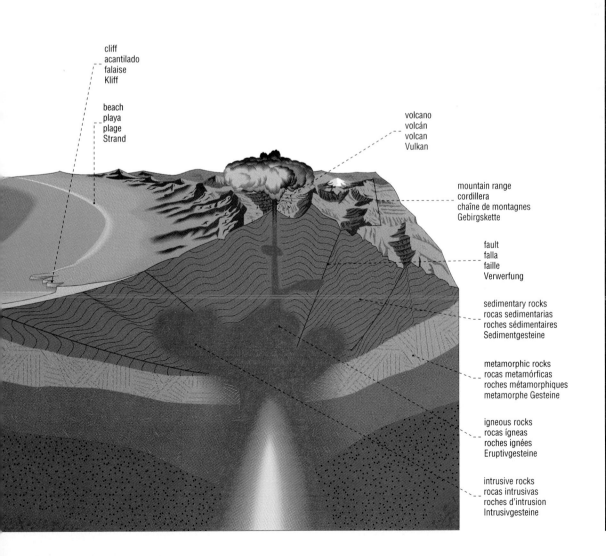

cliff
acantilado
falaise
Kliff

beach
playa
plage
Strand

volcano
volcán
volcan
Vulkan

mountain range
cordillera
chaîne de montagnes
Gebirgskette

fault
falla
faille
Verwerfung

sedimentary rocks
rocas sedimentarias
roches sédimentaires
Sedimentgesteine

metamorphic rocks
rocas metamórficas
roches métamorphiques
metamorphe Gesteine

igneous rocks
rocas ígneas
roches ignées
Eruptivgesteine

intrusive rocks
rocas intrusivas
roches d'intrusion
Intrusivgesteine

CAVE
GRUTA
GROTTE
HÖHLE

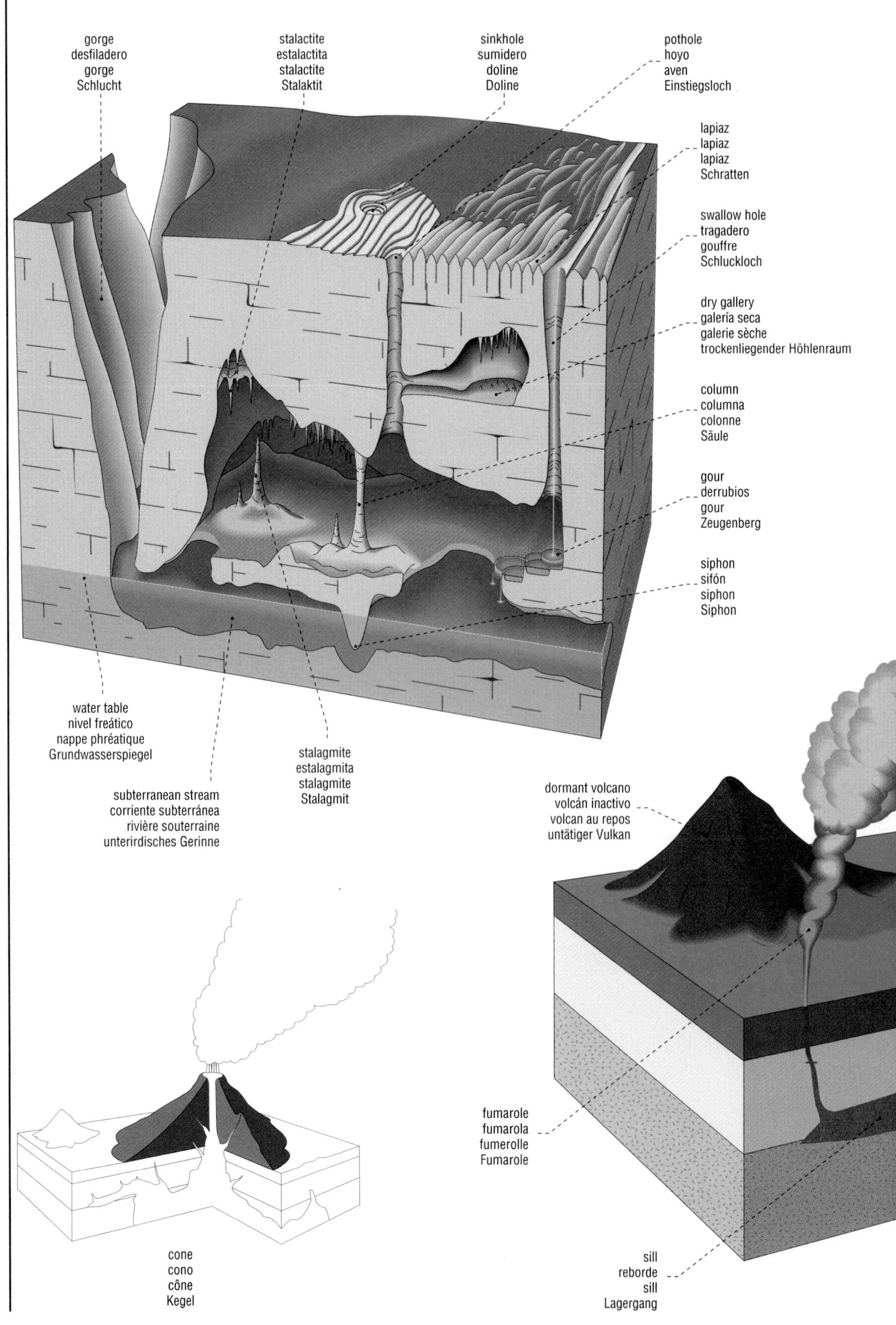
gorge
desfiladero
gorge
Schlucht
stalactite
estalactita
stalactite
Stalaktit
sinkhole
sumidero
doline
Doline
pothole
hoyo
aven
Einstiegsloch
lapiaz
lapiaz
lapiaz
Schratten
swallow hole
tragadero
gouffre
Schluckloch
dry gallery
galería seca
galerie sèche
trockenliegender Höhlenraum
column
columna
colonne
Säule
gour
derrubios
gour
Zeugenberg
siphon
sifón
siphon
Siphon
water table
nivel freático
nappe phréatique
Grundwasserspiegel
stalagmite
estalagmita
stalagmite
Stalagmit
subterranean stream
corriente subterránea
rivière souterraine
unterirdisches Gerinne
dormant volcano
volcán inactivo
volcan au repos
untätiger Vulkan
fumarole
fumarola
fumerolle
Fumarole
cone
cono
cône
Kegel
sill
reborde
sill
Lagergang

VOLCANO
VOLCÁN
VOLCAN
VULKAN

VOLCANO DURING ERUPTION
VOLCÁN EN ERUPCIÓN
VOLCAN EN ÉRUPTION
VULKAN MIT AUSBRUCHSTÄTIGKEIT

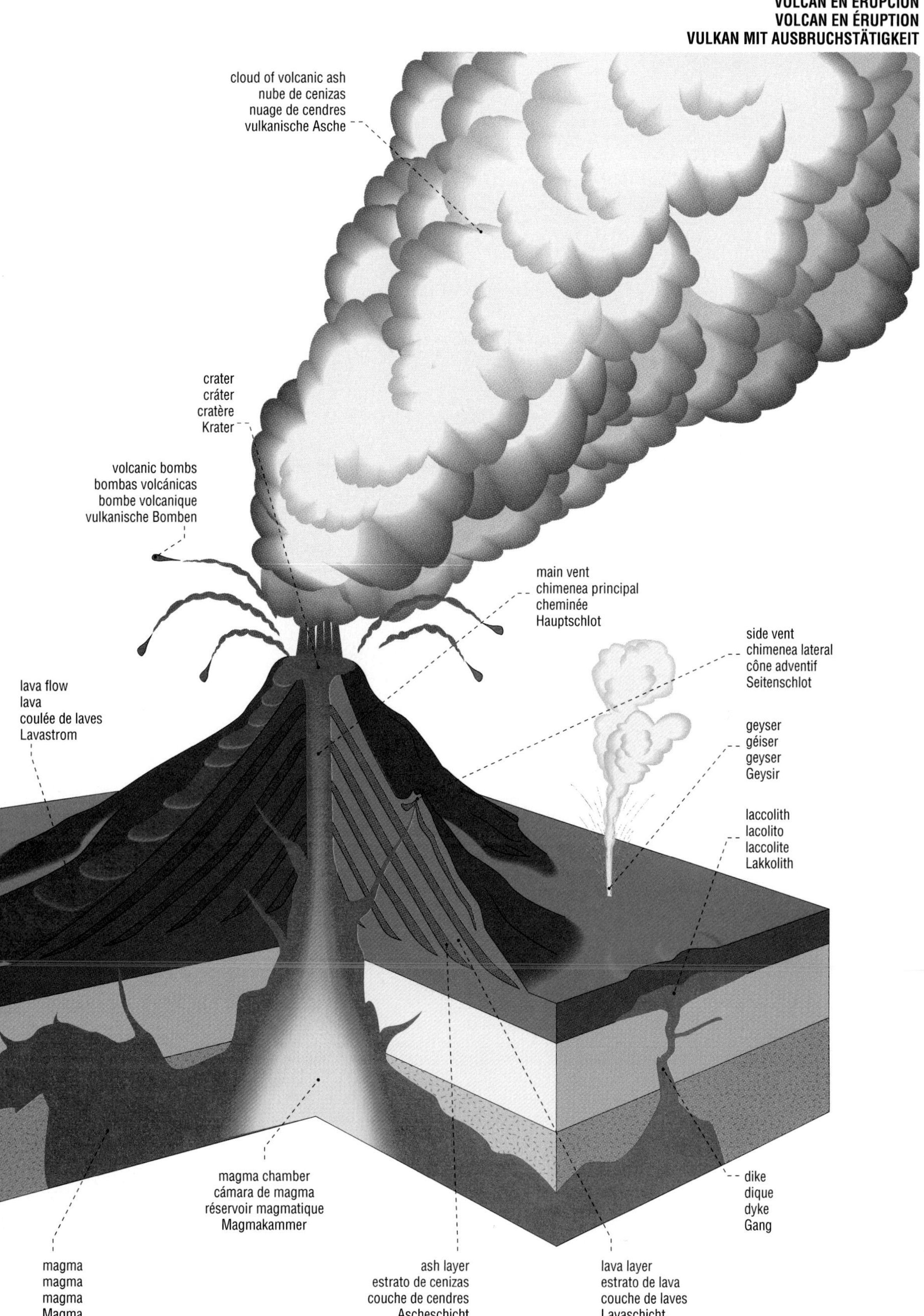
cloud of volcanic ash
nube de cenizas
nuage de cendres
vulkanische Asche
crater
cráter
cratère
Krater
volcanic bombs
bombas volcánicas
bombe volcanique
vulkanische Bomben
main vent
chimenea principal
cheminée
Hauptschlot
side vent
chimenea lateral
cône adventif
Seitenschlot
lava flow
lava
coulée de laves
Lavastrom
geyser
géiser
geyser
Geysir
laccolith
lacolito
laccolite
Lakkolith
magma chamber
cámara de magma
réservoir magmatique
Magmakammer
dike
dique
dyke
Gang
magma
magma
magma
Magma
ash layer
estrato de cenizas
couche de cendres
Ascheschicht
lava layer
estrato de lava
couche de laves
Lavaschicht

GLACIER
GLACIAR
GLACIER
GLETSCHER

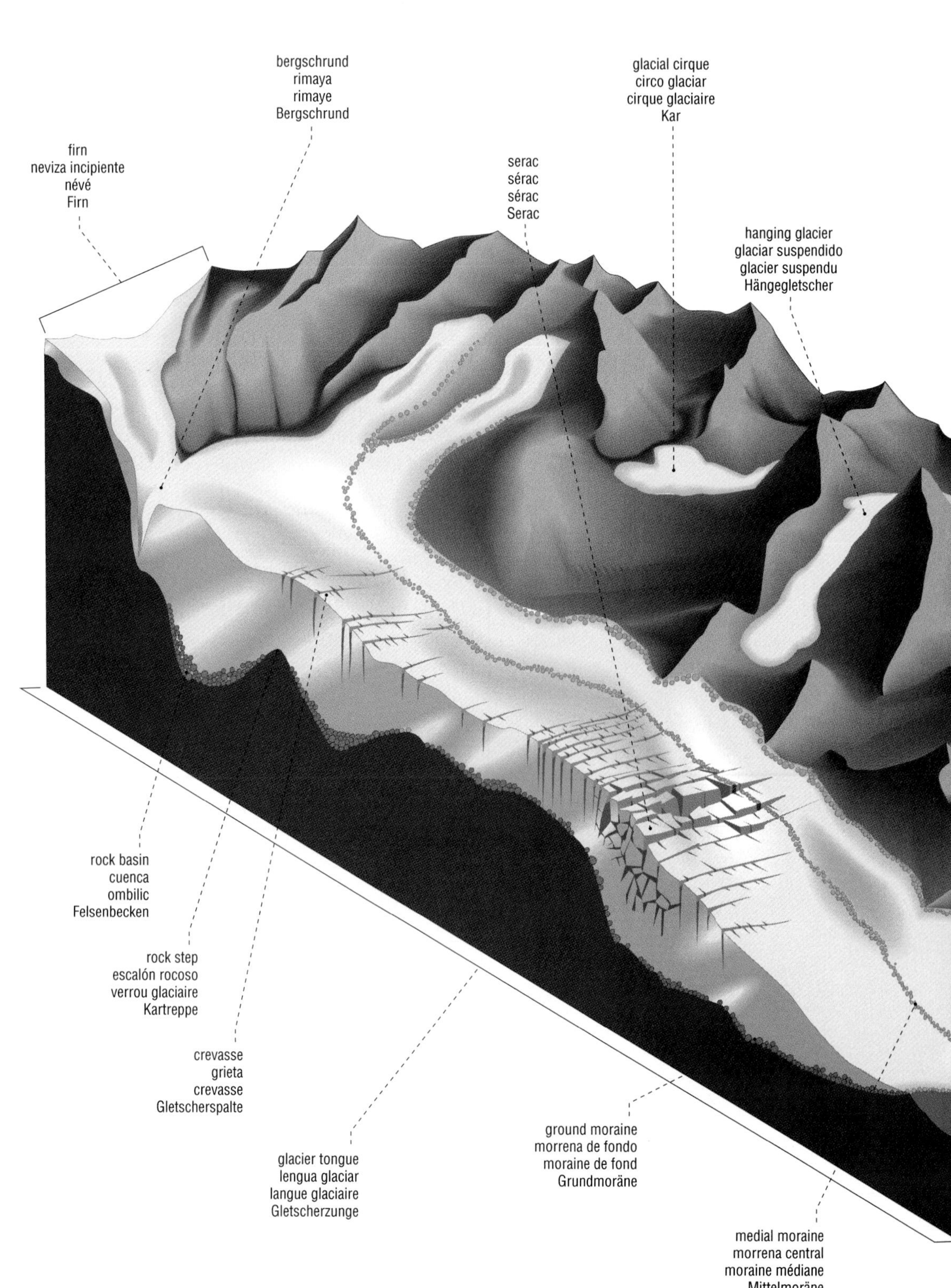
bergschrund
rimaya
rimaye
Bergschrund
glacial cirque
circo glaciar
cirque glaciaire
Kar
firn
neviza incipiente
névé
Firn
serac
sérac
sérac
Serac
hanging glacier
glaciar suspendido
glacier suspendu
Hängegletscher
rock basin
cuenca
ombilic
Felsenbecken
rock step
escalón rocoso
verrou glaciaire
Kartreppe
crevasse
grieta
crevasse
Gletscherspalte
ground moraine
morrena de fondo
moraine de fond
Grundmoräne
glacier tongue
lengua glaciar
langue glaciaire
Gletscherzunge
medial moraine
morrena central
moraine médiane
Mittelmoräne

MOUNTAIN
MONTAÑA
MONTAGNE
BERG

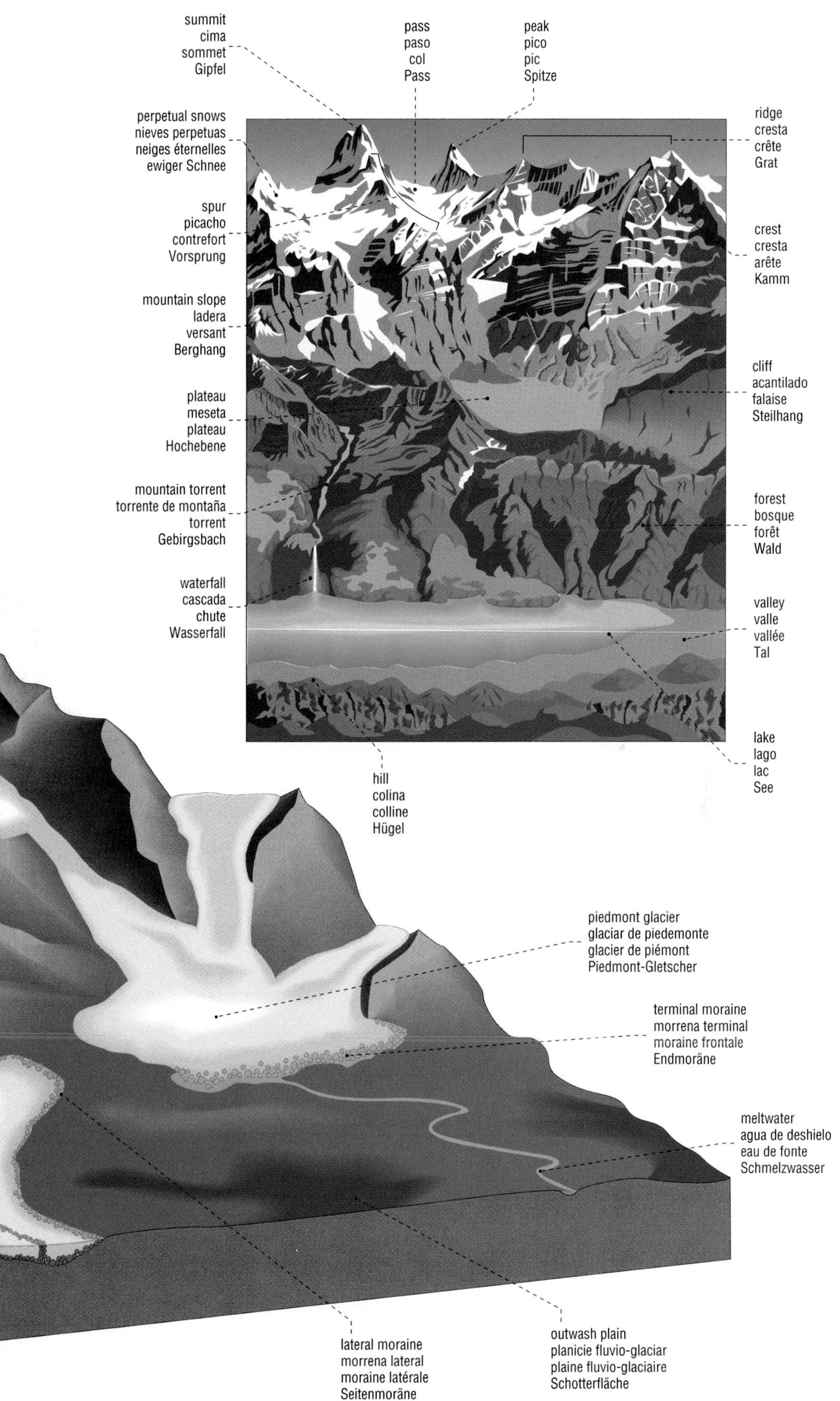
summit
cima
sommet
Gipfel
pass
paso
col
Pass
peak
pico
pic
Spitze
perpetual snows
nieves perpetuas
neiges éternelles
ewiger Schnee
ridge
cresta
crête
Grat
spur
picacho
contrefort
Vorsprung
crest
cresta
arête
Kamm
mountain slope
ladera
versant
Berghang
cliff
acantilado
falaise
Steilhang
plateau
meseta
plateau
Hochebene
mountain torrent
torrente de montaña
torrent
Gebirgsbach
forest
bosque
forêt
Wald
waterfall
cascada
chute
Wasserfall
valley
valle
vallée
Tal
lake
lago
lac
See
hill
colina
colline
Hügel
piedmont glacier
glaciar de piedemonte
glacier de piémont
Piedmont-Gletscher
terminal moraine
morrena terminal
moraine frontale
Endmoräne
meltwater
agua de deshielo
eau de fonte
Schmelzwasser
lateral moraine
morrena lateral
moraine latérale
Seitenmoräne
outwash plain
planicie fluvio-glaciar
plaine fluvio-glaciaire
Schotterfläche

OCEAN FLOOR
LECHO MARINO
FOND DE L'OCÉAN
MEERESGRUND

MID-OCEAN RIDGE
DORSAL OCEÁNICA
DORSALE MÉDIO-OCÉANIQUE
OZEANISCHER RÜCKEN

TOPOGRAPHIC FEATURES
CONFIGURACIÓN TOPOGRÁFICA
ÉLÉMENTS TOPOGRAPHIQUES
TOPOGRAPHISCHE MERKMALE

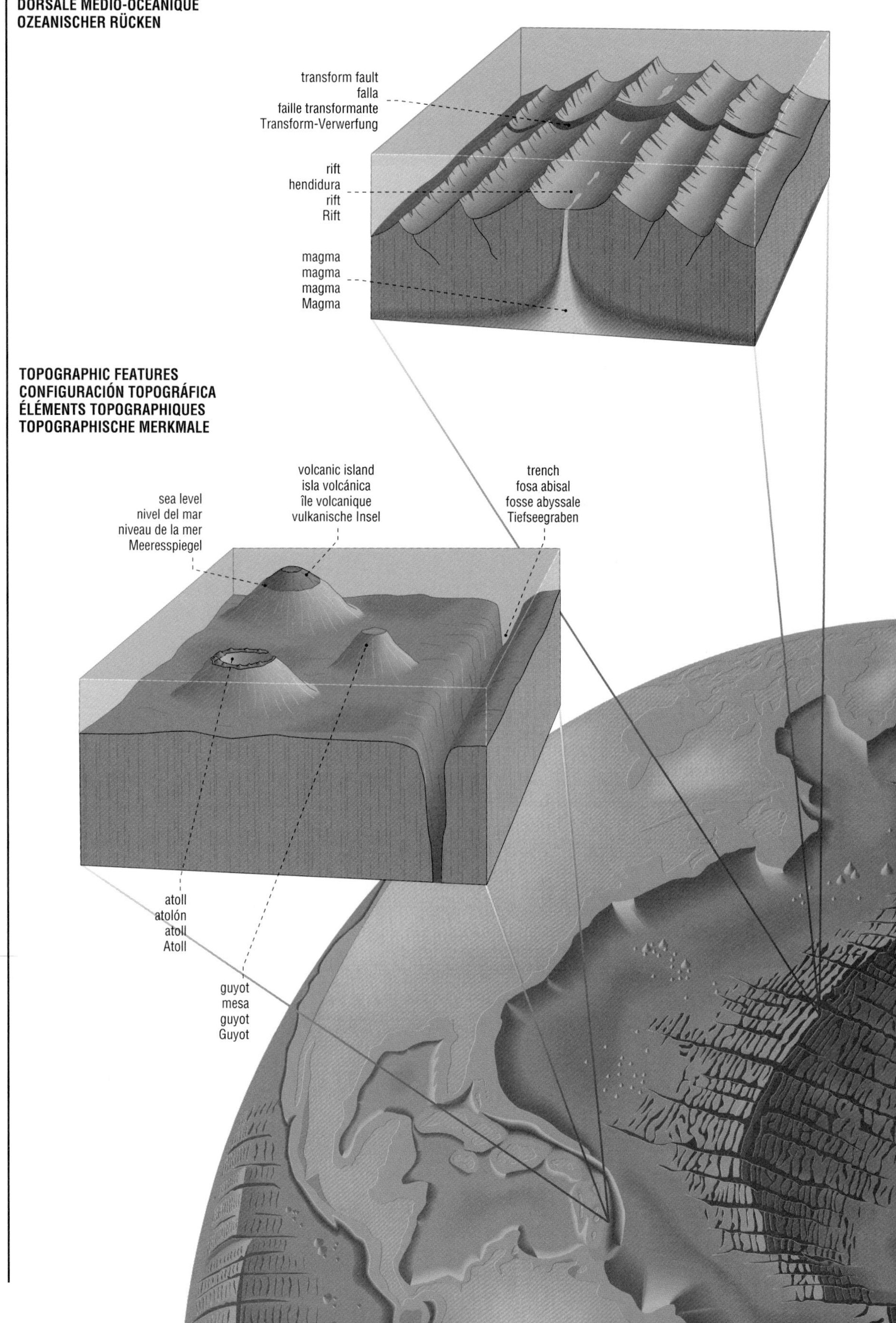
transform fault
falla
faille transformante
Transform-Verwerfung
rift
hendidura
rift
Rift
magma
magma
magma
Magma
volcanic island
isla volcánica
île volcanique
vulkanische Insel
sea level
nivel del mar
niveau de la mer
Meeresspiegel
trench
fosa abisal
fosse abyssale
Tiefseegraben
atoll
atolón
atoll
Atoll
guyot
mesa
guyot
Guyot

ABYSSAL PLAIN
LLANURA ABISAL
PLAINE ABYSSALE
TIEFSEE-EBENE

CONTINENTAL MARGIN
CUENCA OCEÁNICA
MARGE CONTINENTALE
KONTINENTALRAND

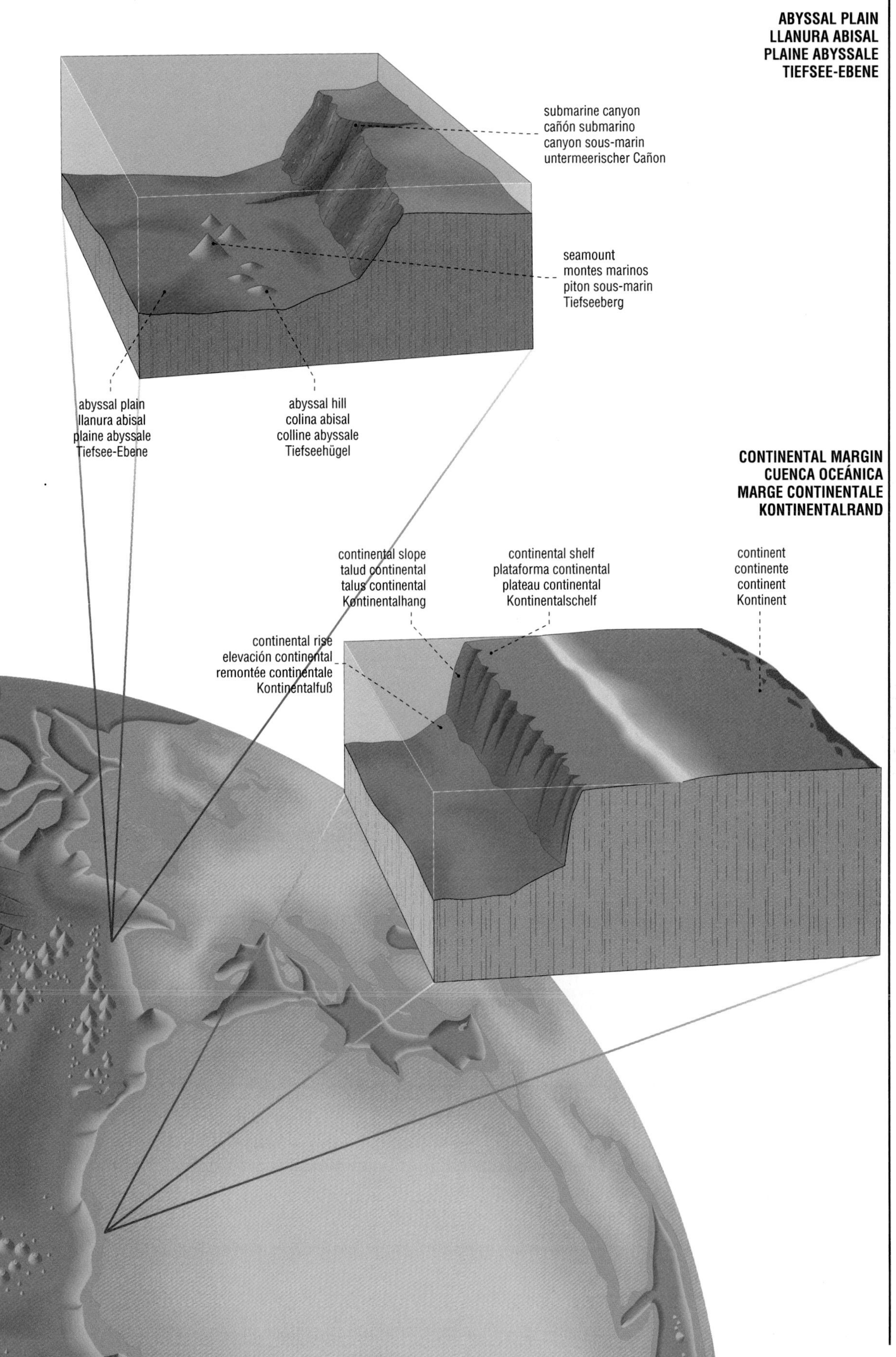
submarine canyon
cañón submarino
canyon sous-marin
untermeerischer Cañon
seamount
montes marinos
piton sous-marin
Tiefseeberg
abyssal plain
llanura abisal
plaine abyssale
Tiefsee-Ebene
abyssal hill
colina abisal
colline abyssale
Tiefseehügel
continental slope
talud continental
talus continental
Kontinentalhang
continental shelf
plataforma continental
plateau continental
Kontinentalschelf
continent
continente
continent
Kontinent
continental rise
elevación continental
remontée continentale
Kontinentalfuß

WAVE
OLA
VAGUE
WELLE

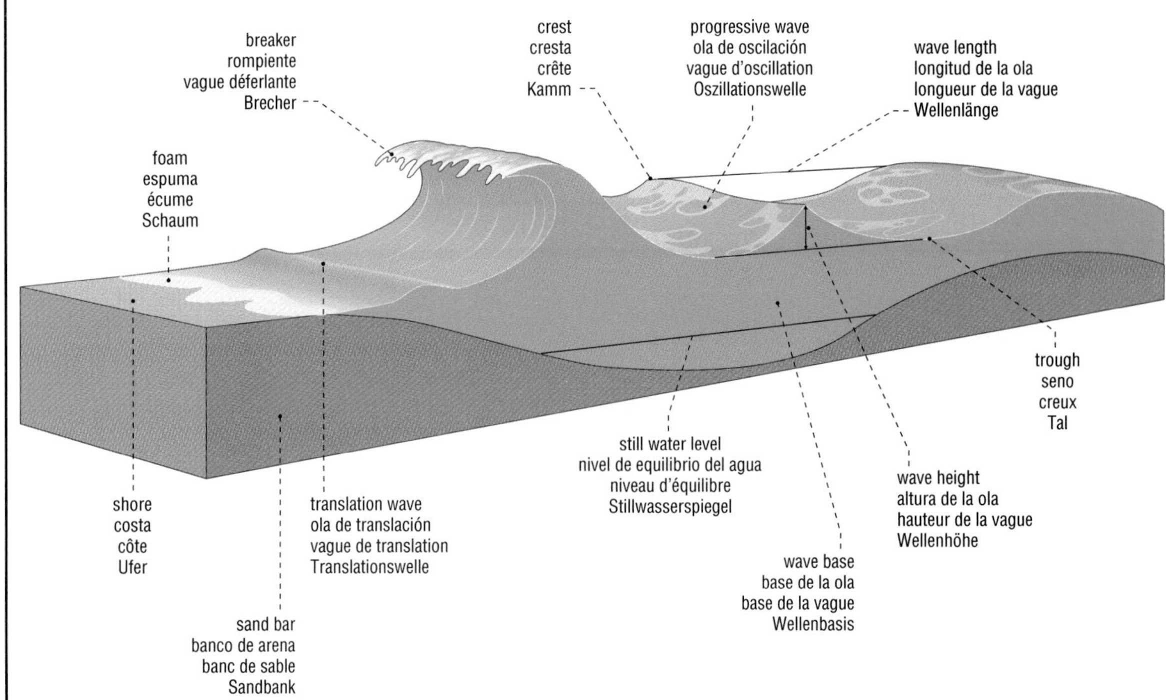
breaker
rompiente
vague déferlante
Brecher
crest
cresta
crête
Kamm
progressive wave
ola de oscilación
vague d'oscillation
Oszillationswelle
wave length
longitud de la ola
longueur de la vague
Wellenlänge
foam
espuma
écume
Schaum
trough
seno
creux
Tal
still water level
nivel de equilibrio del agua
niveau d'équilibre
Stillwasserspiegel
wave height
altura de la ola
hauteur de la vague
Wellenhöhe
shore
costa
côte
Ufer
translation wave
ola de translación
vague de translation
Translationswelle
wave base
base de la ola
base de la vague
Wellenbasis
sand bar
banco de arena
banc de sable
Sandbank

COMMON COASTAL FEATURES
CONFIGURACIÓN DEL LITORAL
CONFIGURATION DU LITTORAL
KÜSTENFORMEN

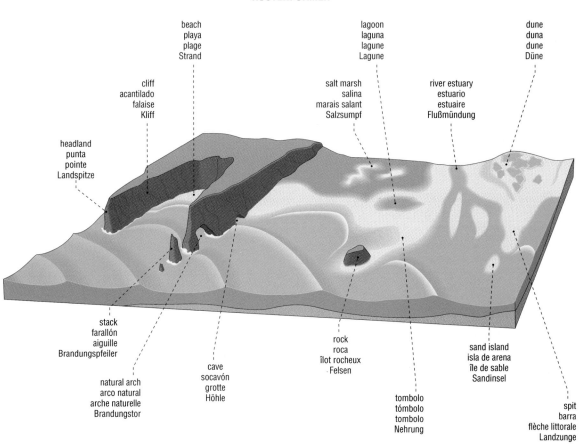

beach
playa
plage
Strand

lagoon
laguna
lagune
Lagune

dune
duna
dune
Düne

cliff
acantilado
falaise
Kliff

salt marsh
salina
marais salant
Salzsumpf

river estuary
estuario
estuaire
Flußmündung

headland
punta
pointe
Landspitze

stack
farallón
aiguille
Brandungspfeiler

rock
roca
îlot rocheux
Felsen

sand island
isla de arena
île de sable
Sandinsel

natural arch
arco natural
arche naturelle
Brandungstor

cave
socavón
grotte
Höhle

tombolo
tómbolo
tombolo
Nehrung

spit
barra
flèche littorale
Landzunge

ECOLOGY
ECOLOGÍA
ÉCOLOGIE
ÖKOLOGIE

STRUCTURE OF THE BIOSPHERE
ESTRUCTURA DE LA BIOSFERA
STRUCTURE DE LA BIOSPHÈRE
STRUKTUR DER BIOSPHÄRE

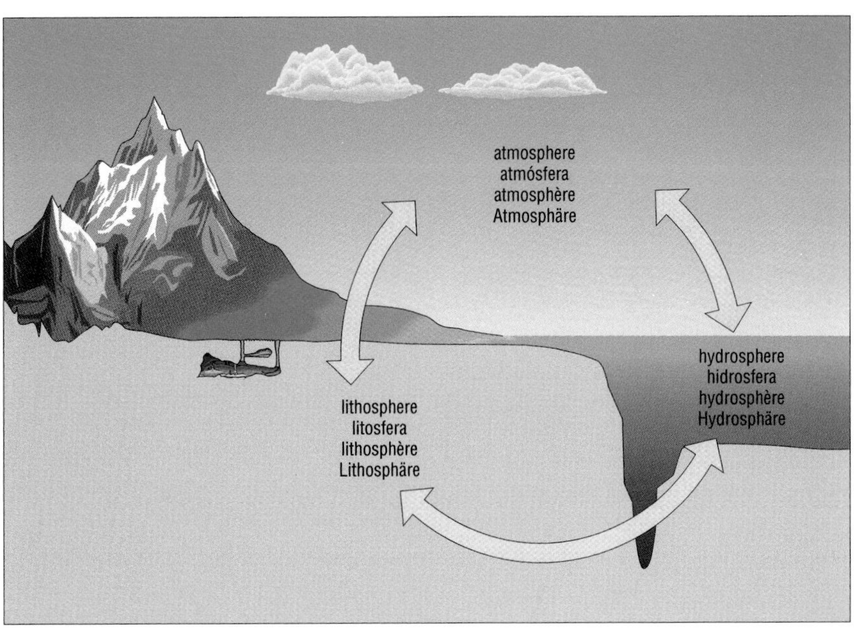
atmosphere
atmósfera
atmosphère
Atmosphäre
hydrosphere
hidrosfera
hydrosphère
Hydrosphäre
lithosphere
litosfera
lithosphère
Lithosphäre

FOOD CHAIN
CADENA ALIMENTICIA
CHAÎNE ALIMENTAIRE
NAHRUNGSKETTE

basic source of food
fuente básica de alimento
source alimentaire fondamentale
primäre Nahrungsmittelquelle

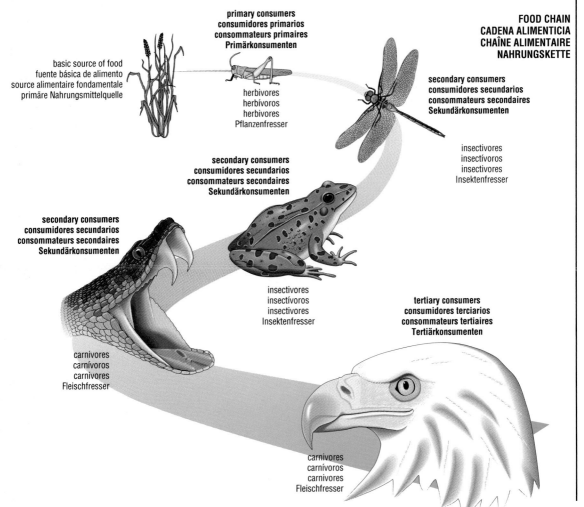

primary consumers
consumidores primarios
consommateurs primaires
Primärkonsumenten

herbivores
herbívoros
herbivores
Pflanzenfresser

secondary consumers
consumidores secundarios
consommateurs secondaires
Sekundärkonsumenten

insectivores
insectívoros
insectivores
Insektenfresser

secondary consumers
consumidores secundarios
consommateurs secondaires
Sekundärkonsumenten

insectivores
insectívoros
insectivores
Insektenfresser

secondary consumers
consumidores secundarios
consommateurs secondaires
Sekundärkonsumenten

carnivores
carnívoros
carnivores
Fleischfresser

tertiary consumers
consumidores terciarios
consommateurs tertiaires
Tertiärkonsumenten

carnivores
carnívoros
carnivores
Fleischfresser

ECOLOGY
ECOLOGÍA
ÉCOLOGIE
ÖKOLOGIE

POLLUTION OF FOOD ON GROUND
CONTAMINACIÓN DE ALIMENTOS EN LA TIERRA
POLLUTION DES ALIMENTS AU SOL
SCHADSTOFFBELASTUNG IM BODEN

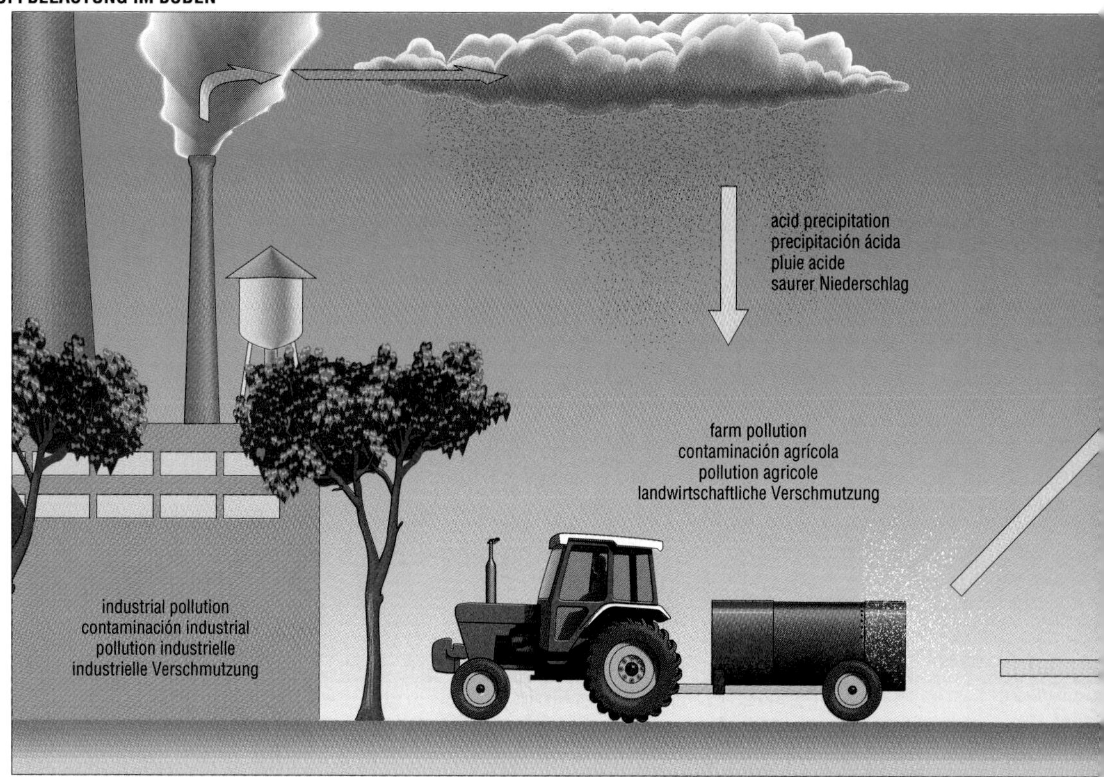
acid precipitation
precipitación ácida
pluie acide
saurer Niederschlag
farm pollution
contaminación agrícola
pollution agricole
landwirtschaftliche Verschmutzung
industrial pollution
contaminación industrial
pollution industrielle
industrielle Verschmutzung

POLLUTION OF FOOD IN WATER
CONTAMINACIÓN DE ALIMENTOS EN EL AGUA
POLLUTION DES ALIMENTS DANS L'EAU
SCHADSTOFFBELASTUNG IM WASSER

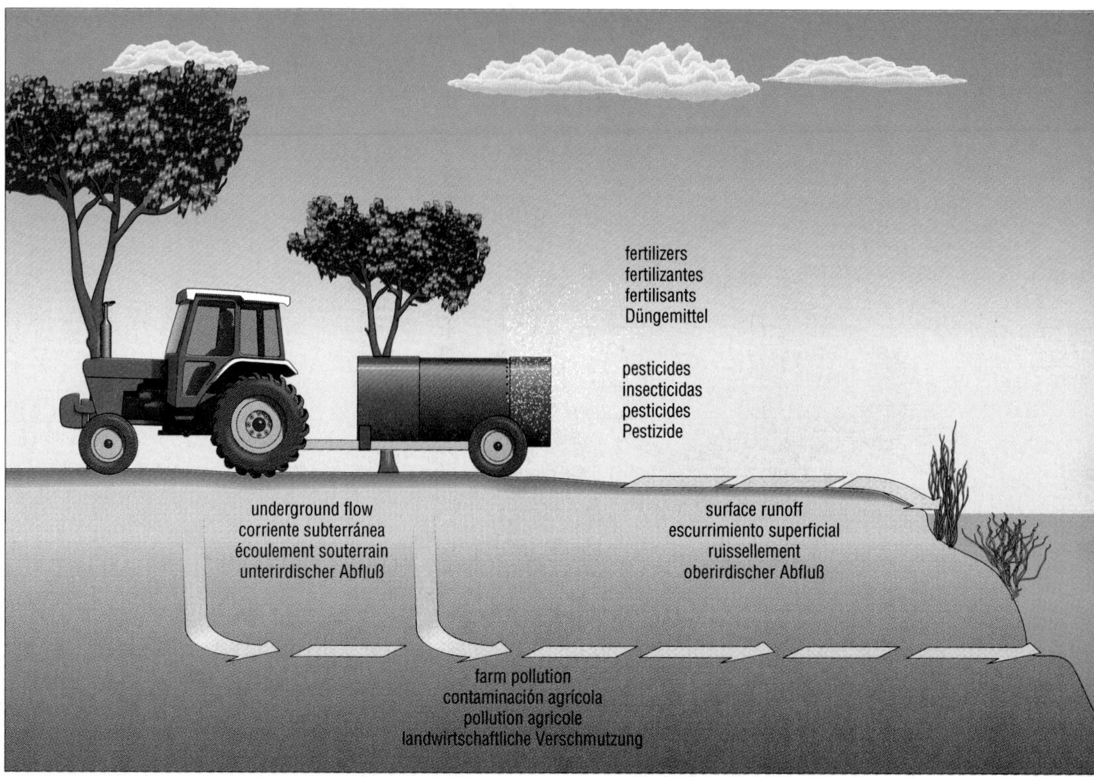
fertilizers
fertilizantes
fertilisants
Düngemittel
pesticides
insecticidas
pesticides
Pestizide
underground flow
corriente subterránea
écoulement souterrain
unterirdischer Abfluß
surface runoff
escurrimiento superficial
ruissellement
oberirdischer Abfluß
farm pollution
contaminación agrícola
pollution agricole
landwirtschaftliche Verschmutzung

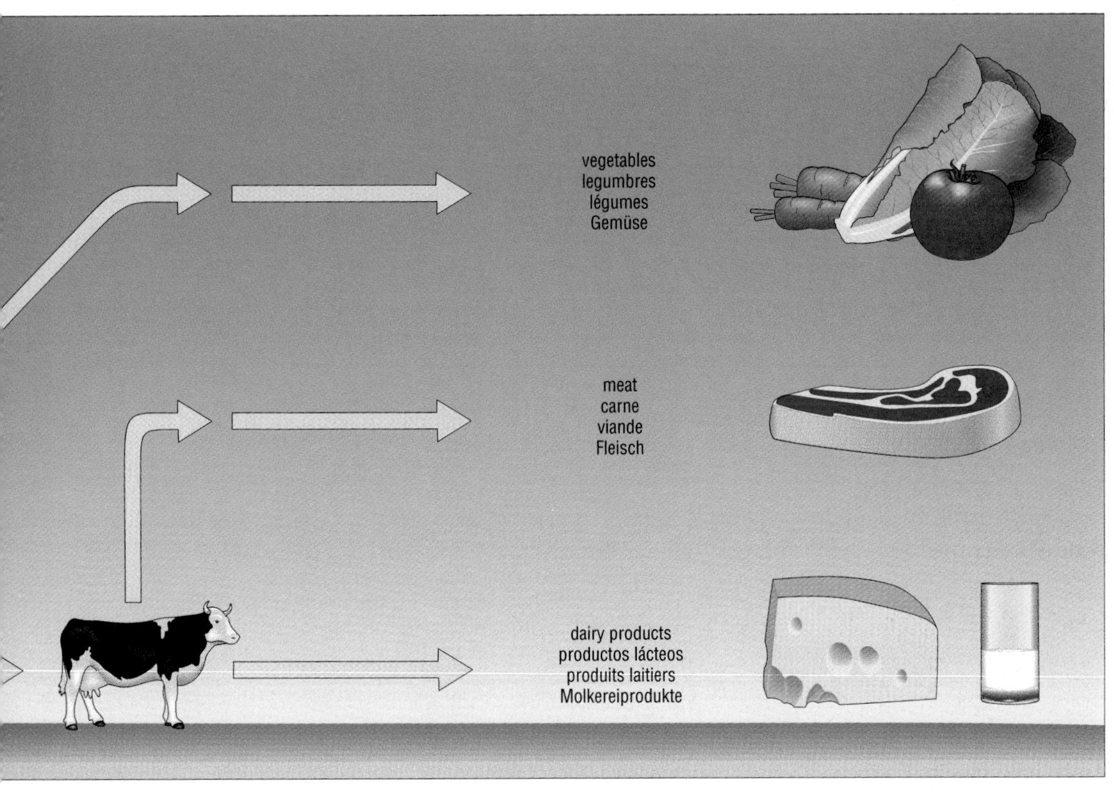
vegetables
legumbres
légumes
Gemüse
meat
carne
viande
Fleisch
dairy products
productos lácteos
produits laitiers
Molkereiprodukte

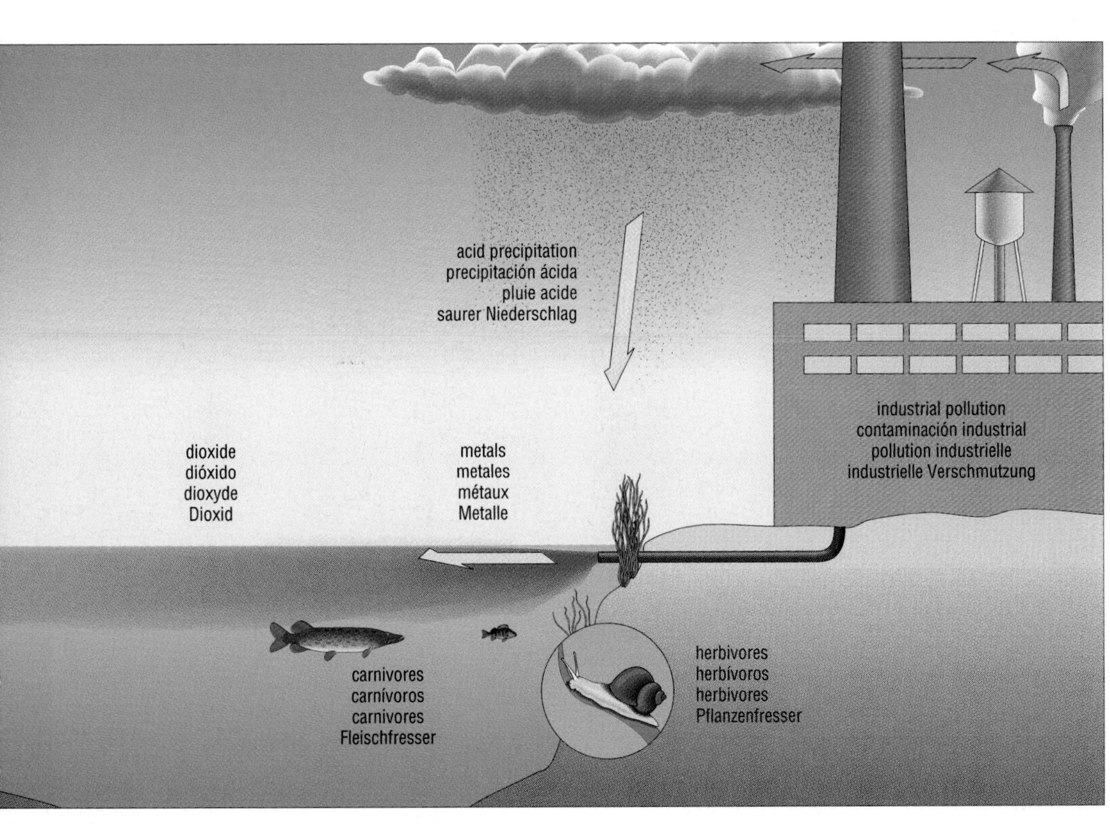
acid precipitation
precipitación ácida
pluie acide
saurer Niederschlag
industrial pollution
contaminación industrial
pollution industrielle
industrielle Verschmutzung
dioxide
dióxido
dioxyde
Dioxid
metals
metales
métaux
Metalle
carnivores
carnívoros
carnivores
Fleischfresser
herbivores
herbívoros
herbivores
Pflanzenfresser

ECOLOGY
ECOLOGÍA
ÉCOLOGIE
ÖKOLOGIE

ATMOSPHERIC POLLUTION
CONTAMINACIÓN ATMOSFÉRICA
POLLUTION DE L'AIR
ATMOSPHÄRISCHE VERSCHMUTZUNG

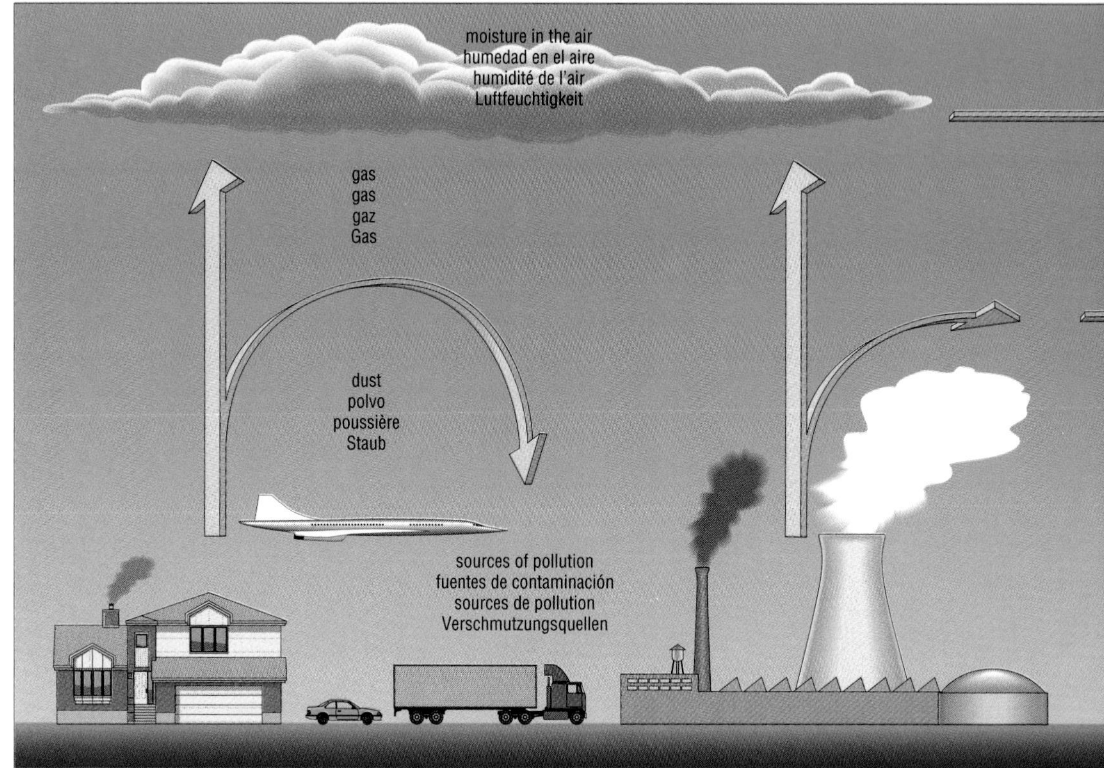
moisture in the air
humedad en el aire
humidité de l'air
Luftfeuchtigkeit
gas
gas
gaz
Gas
dust
polvo
poussière
Staub
sources of pollution
fuentes de contaminación
sources de pollution
Verschmutzungsquellen

HYDROLOGIC CYCLE
CICLO HIDROLÓGICO
CYCLE DE L'EAU
WASSERKREISLAUF

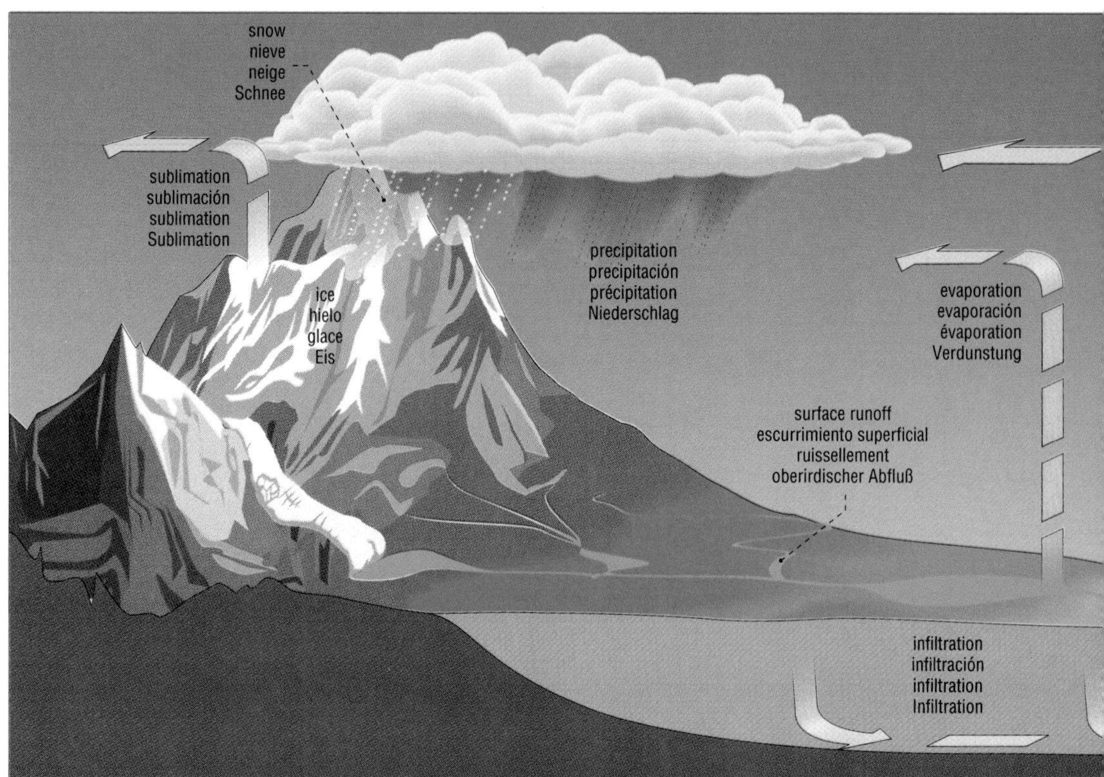
snow
nieve
neige
Schnee
sublimation
sublimación
sublimation
Sublimation
ice
hielo
glace
Eis
precipitation
precipitación
précipitation
Niederschlag
evaporation
evaporación
évaporation
Verdunstung
surface runoff
escurrimiento superficial
ruissellement
oberirdischer Abfluß
infiltration
infiltración
infiltration
Infiltration

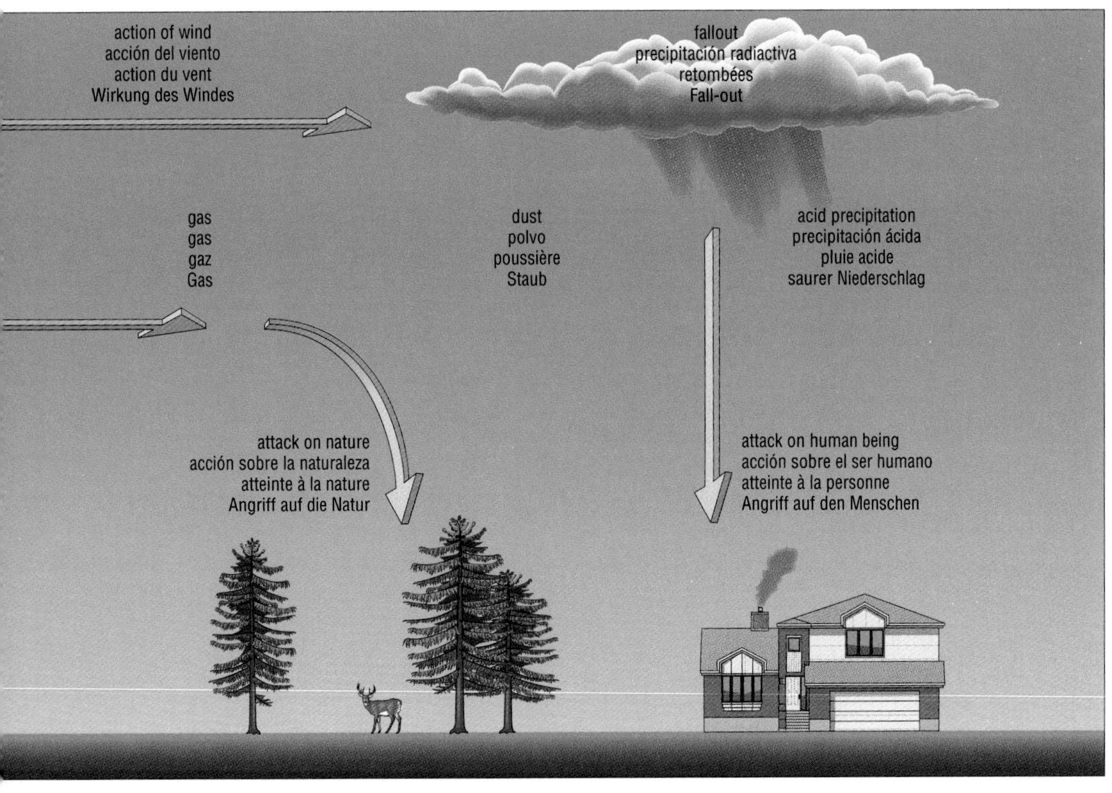
action of wind
acción del viento
action du vent
Wirkung des Windes
fallout
precipitación radiactiva
retombées
Fall-out
gas
gas
gaz
Gas
dust
polvo
poussière
Staub
acid precipitation
precipitación ácida
pluie acide
saurer Niederschlag
attack on nature
acción sobre la naturaleza
atteinte à la nature
Angriff auf die Natur
attack on human being
acción sobre el ser humano
atteinte à la personne
Angriff auf den Menschen

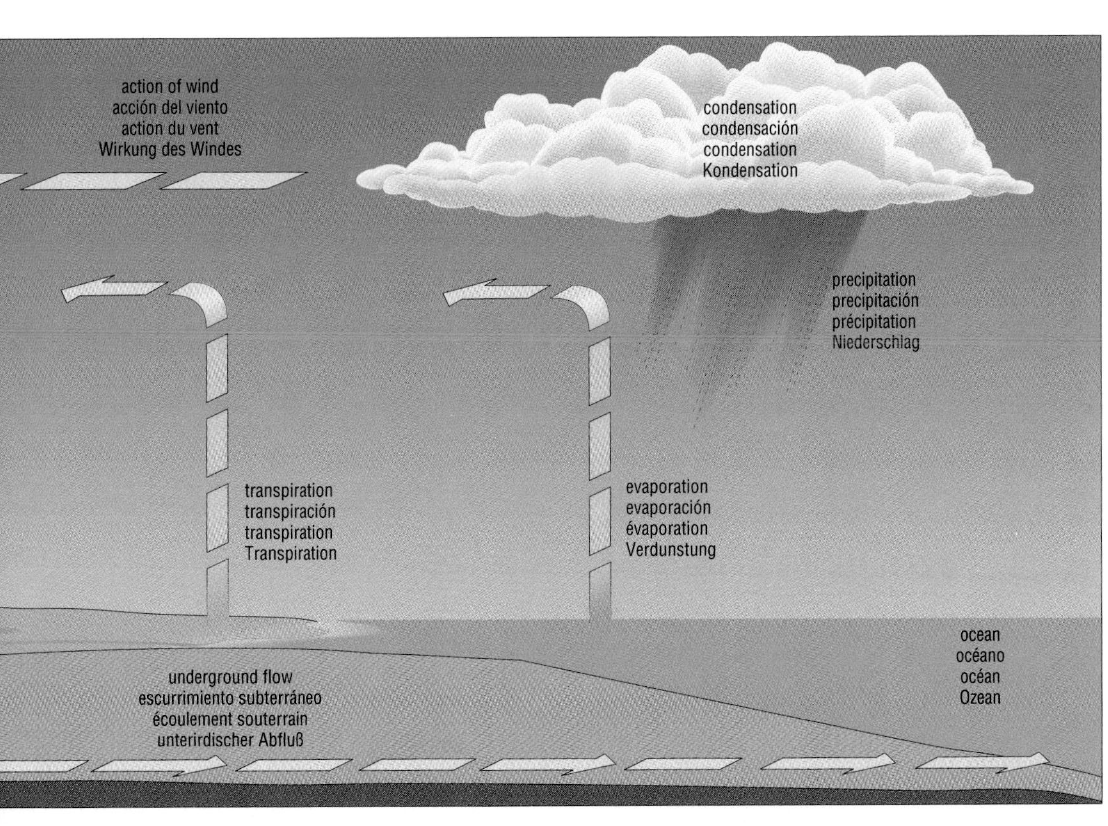
action of wind
acción del viento
action du vent
Wirkung des Windes
condensation
condensación
condensation
Kondensation
precipitation
precipitación
précipitation
Niederschlag
transpiration
transpiración
transpiration
Transpiration
evaporation
evaporación
évaporation
Verdunstung
ocean
océano
océan
Ozean
underground flow
escurrimiento subterráneo
écoulement souterrain
unterirdischer Abfluß

PRECIPITATIONS
PRECIPITACIONES
PRÉCIPITATIONS
NIEDERSCHLÄGE

STORMY SKY
CIELO TURBULENTO
CIEL D'ORAGE
STÜRMISCHER HIMMEL

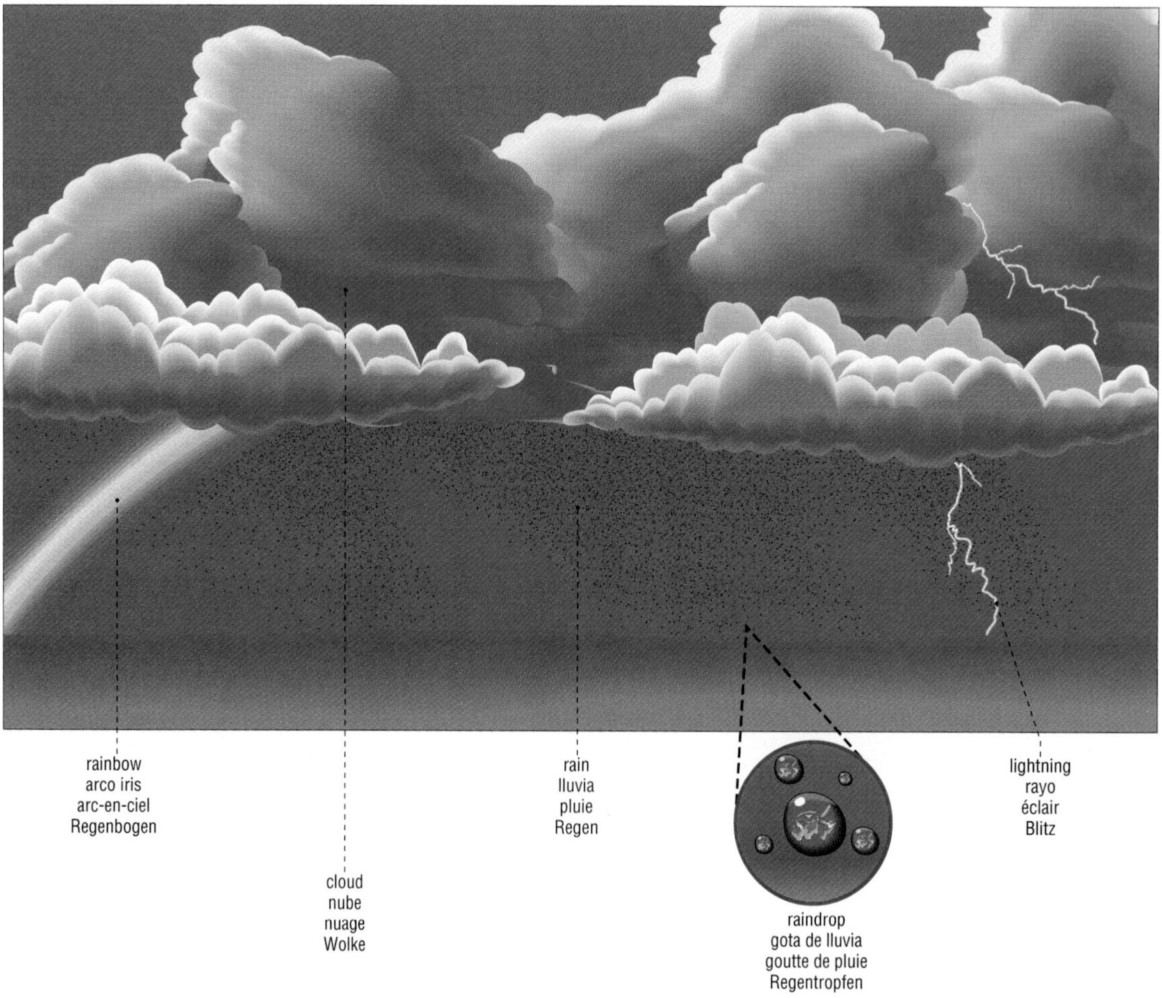

rainbow
arco iris
arc-en-ciel
Regenbogen

cloud
nube
nuage
Wolke

rain
lluvia
pluie
Regen

raindrop
gota de lluvia
goutte de pluie
Regentropfen

lightning
rayo
éclair
Blitz

CLASSIFICATION OF SNOW CRYSTALS
CLASIFICACIÓN DE LOS CRISTALES DE NIEVE
CLASSIFICATION DES CRISTAUX DE NEIGE
KLASSIFIKATION VON SCHNEEKRISTALLEN

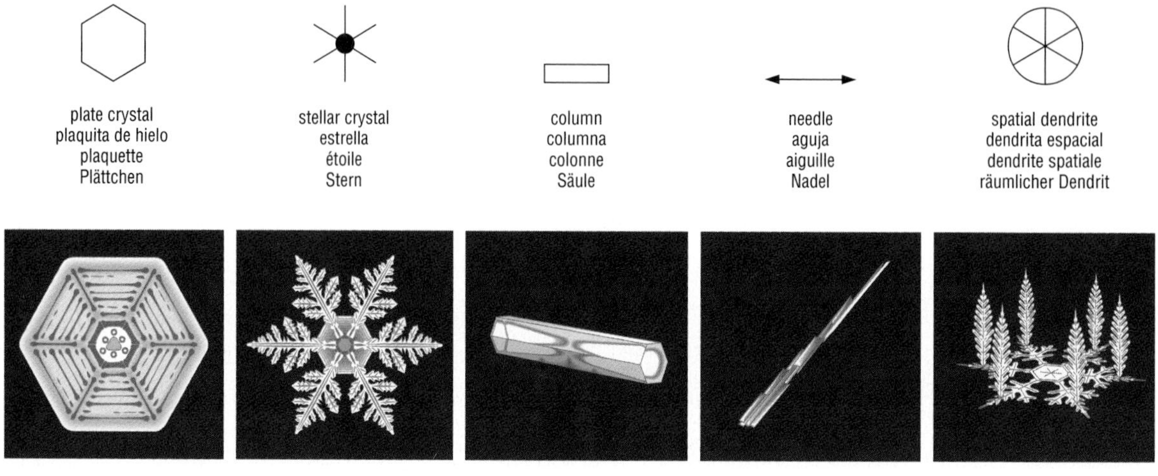

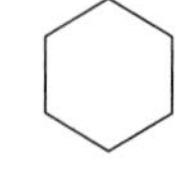

plate crystal
plaquita de hielo
plaquette
Plättchen

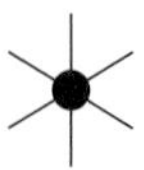

stellar crystal
estrella
étoile
Stern

column
columna
colonne
Säule

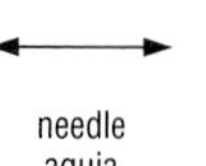

needle
aguja
aiguille
Nadel

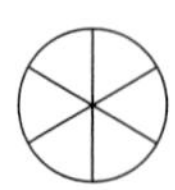

spatial dendrite
dendrita espacial
dendrite spatiale
räumlicher Dendrit

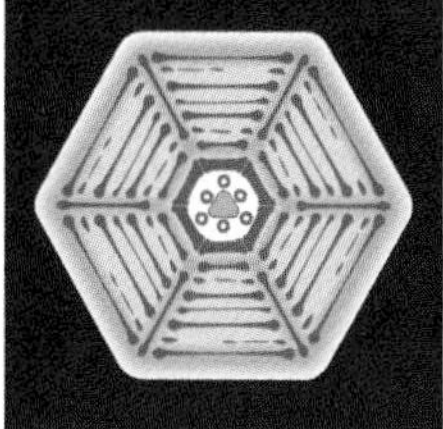

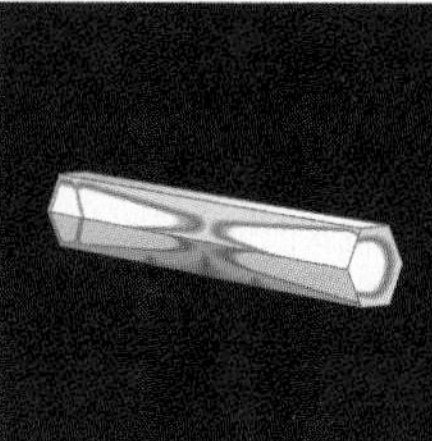

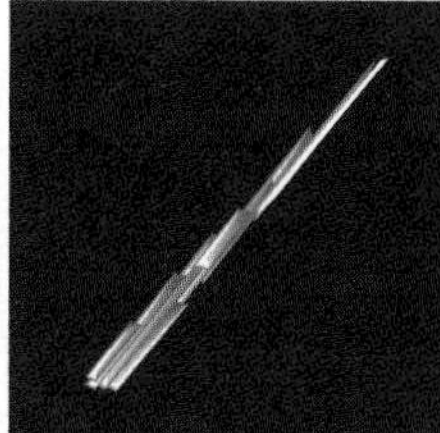

mist
neblina
brume
Dunst

fog
niebla
brouillard
Nebel

dew
rocío
rosée
Tau

frost
escarcha
verglas
Rauhreif

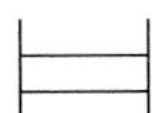
capped column
columna con capuchon
colonne avec capuchon
bedeckte Säule

irregular crystal
cristales irregulares
cristaux irréguliers
irreguläres Aggregat

snow pellet
copo de nieve
neige roulée
Reif- und Frostgraupel

sleet
cellisca
grésil
Eiskörnchen

hail
granizo
grêlon
Hagel

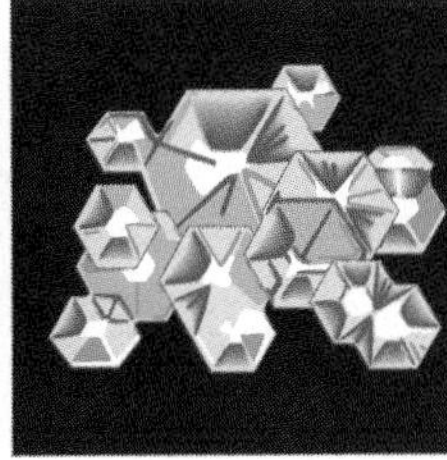
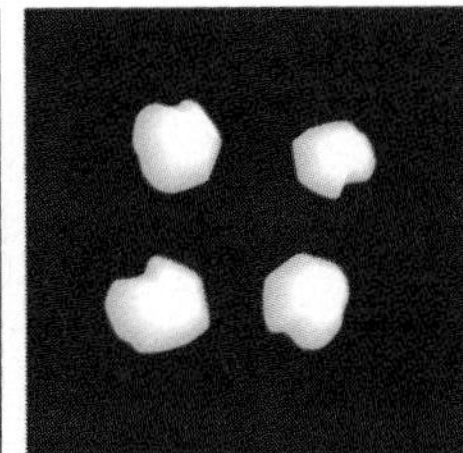
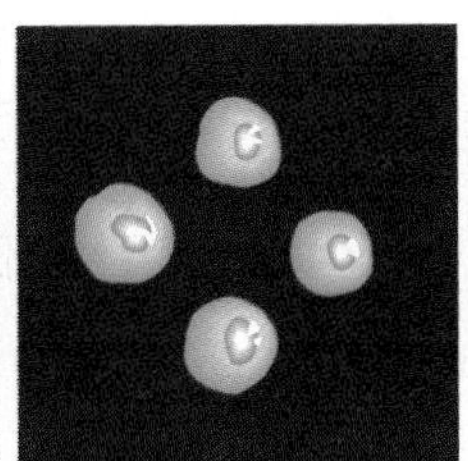
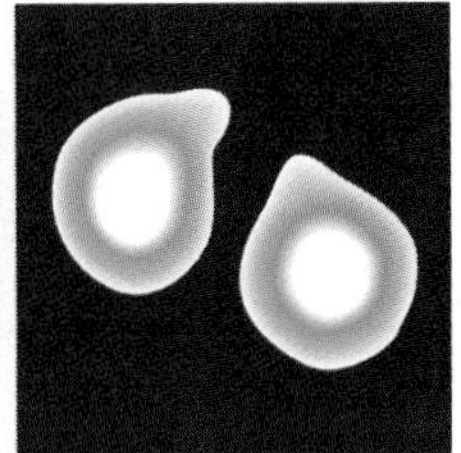

METEOROLOGY
METEOROLOGÍA
MÉTÉOROLOGIE
METEOROLOGIE

WEATHER MAP
CARTA DEL TIEMPO
CARTE MÉTÉOROLOGIQUE
WETTERKARTE

wind direction and speed
dirección y velocidad del viento
direction et force du vent
Windrichtung und -geschwindigkeit

barometric pressure
presión barométrica
pression barométrique
Luftdruck

isobar
isobara
isobare
Isobare

low pressure center
zona de baja presión
dépression
Tiefdruckgebiet

precipitation area
zona de precipitación
zone de précipitation
Niederschlagsgebiet

trough
depresión barométrica
creux barométrique
Trog

type of the air mass
masa de aire
type de la masse d'air
Luftmasse

high pressure center
zona de alta presión
anticyclone
Hochdruckgebiet

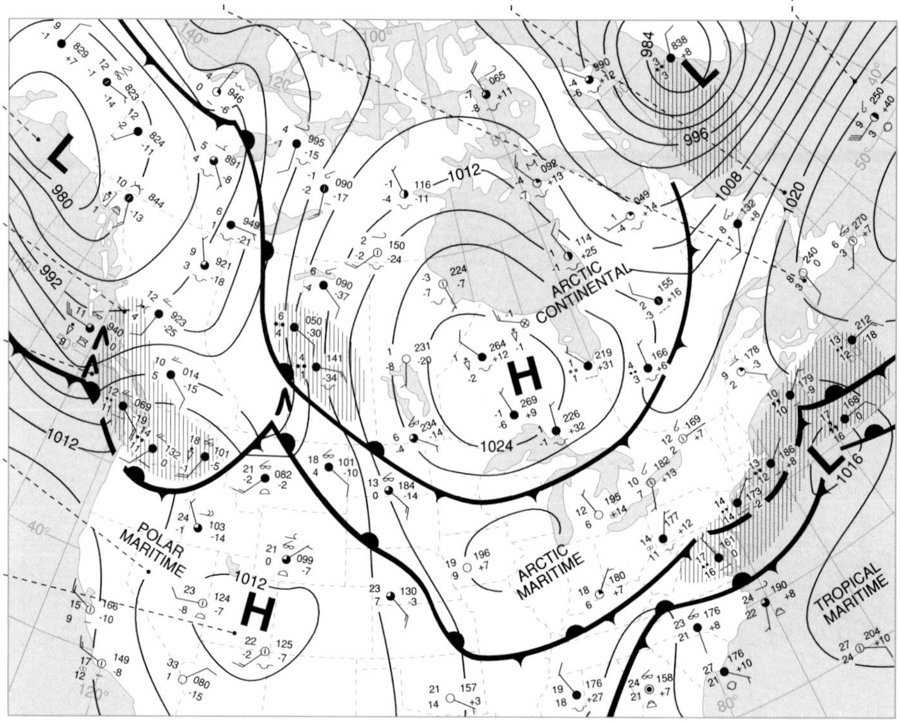

ARCTIC CONTINENTAL

POLAR MARITIME

ARCTIC MARITIME

TROPICAL MARITIME

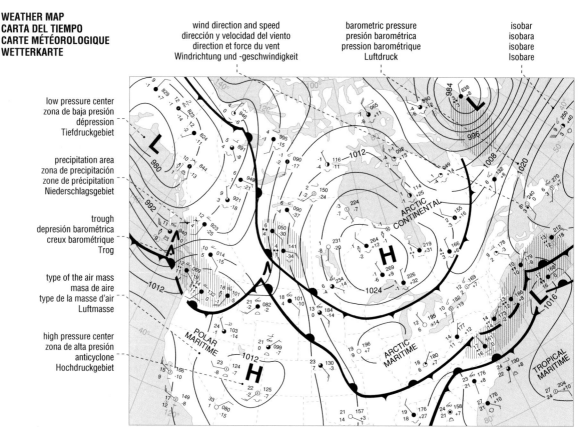

STATION MODEL
MODELO DE CLAVE
DISPOSITION DES INFORMATIONS D'UNE STATION
STATIONSMODELL

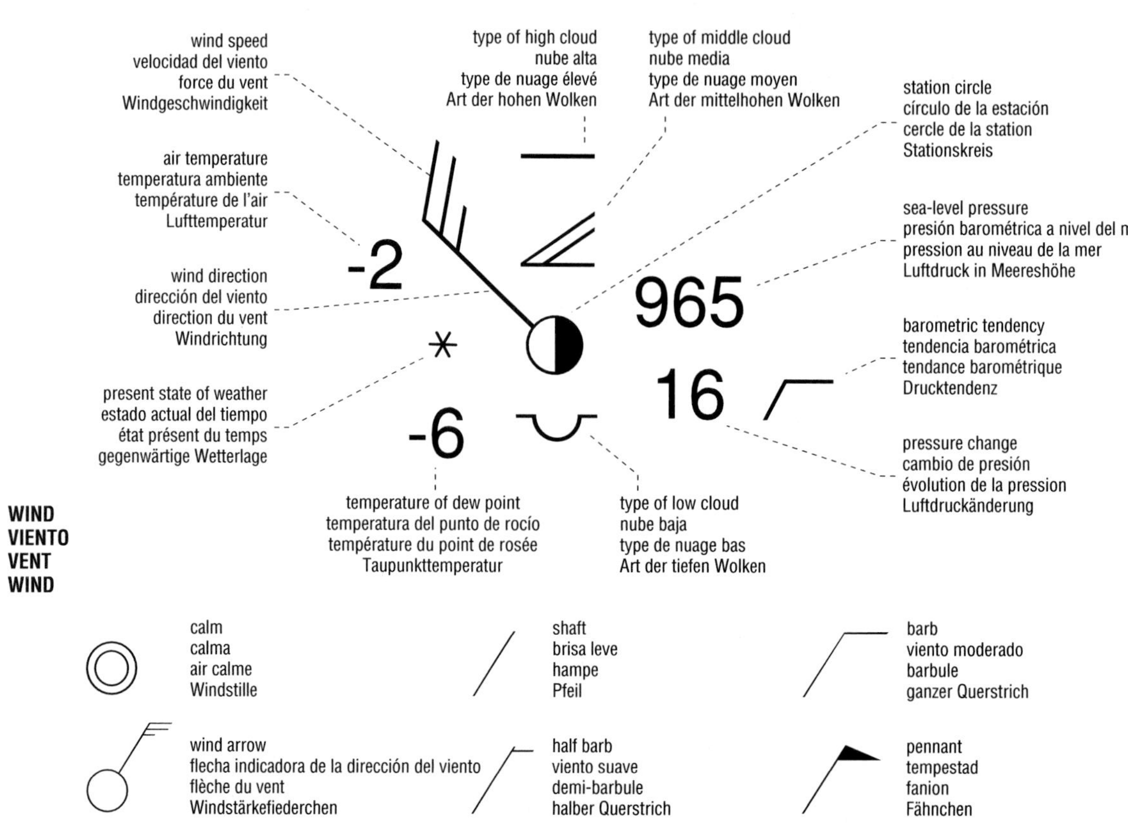
wind speed
velocidad del viento
force du vent
Windgeschwindigkeit
type of high cloud
nube alta
type de nuage élevé
Art der hohen Wolken
type of middle cloud
nube media
type de nuage moyen
Art der mittelhohen Wolken
station circle
círculo de la estación
cercle de la station
Stationskreis
air temperature
temperatura ambiente
température de l'air
Lufttemperatur
-2
sea-level pressure
presión barométrica a nivel del mar
pression au niveau de la mer
Luftdruck in Meereshöhe
965
wind direction
dirección del viento
direction du vent
Windrichtung
barometric tendency
tendencia barométrica
tendance barométrique
Drucktendenz
16
present state of weather
estado actual del tiempo
état présent du temps
gegenwärtige Wetterlage
-6
pressure change
cambio de presión
évolution de la pression
Luftdruckänderung
temperature of dew point
temperatura del punto de rocío
température du point de rosée
Taupunkttemperatur
type of low cloud
nube baja
type de nuage bas
Art der tiefen Wolken
WIND
VIENTO
VENT
WIND
calm
calma
air calme
Windstille
shaft
brisa leve
hampe
Pfeil
barb
viento moderado
barbule
ganzer Querstrich
wind arrow
flecha indicadora de la dirección del viento
flèche du vent
Windstärkefiederchen
half barb
viento suave
demi-barbule
halber Querstrich
pennant
tempestad
fanion
Fähnchen

INTERNATIONAL WEATHER SYMBOLS
SÍMBOLOS METEOROLÓGICOS INTERNACIONALES
SYMBOLES MÉTÉOROLOGIQUES INTERNATIONAUX
INTERNATIONALE WETTERSYMBOLE

FRONTS
FRENTES
FRONTS
FRONTEN

surface cold front
frente frío de superficie
front froid en surface
Kaltfront am Boden

surface warm front
frente cálido de superficie
front chaud en surface
Warmfront am Boden

occluded front
frente ocluido
front occlus
Okklusion

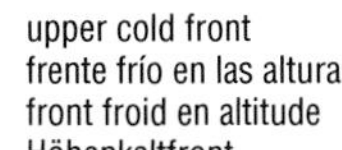
upper cold front
frente frío en las alturas
front froid en altitude
Höhenkaltfront

upper warm front
frente cálido en las alturas
front chaud en altitude
Höhenwarmfront

stationary front
frente estacionario
front stationnaire
stationäre Front

SKY COVERAGE
NUBOSIDAD
NÉBULOSITÉ
BEDECKUNGSGRAD

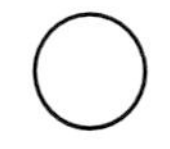
clear sky
despejado
ciel clair
wolkenloser Himmel

scattered sky
nubes dispersas
ciel à nébulosité dispersée
Himmel mit vereinzelten Wolken

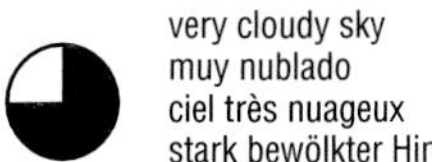
very cloudy sky
muy nublado
ciel très nuageux
stark bewölkter Himmel

overcast sky
completamente nublado
ciel couvert
bedeckter Himmel

cloudy sky
medio nublado
ciel nuageux
bewölkter Himmel

slightly covered sky
ligeramente nublado
ciel peu nuageux
heiterer Himmel

obscured sky
obscurecido por contaminación
ciel noir
nicht angebbar (z.B. wegen Nebel)

PRESENT WEATHER
FENÓMENOS ATMOSFÉRICOS
MÉTÉORES
METEORE

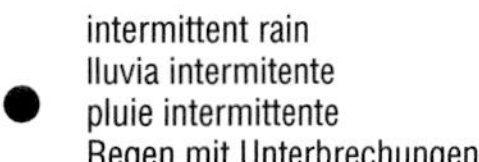
intermittent rain
lluvia intermitente
pluie intermittente
Regen mit Unterbrechungen

snow shower
chubasco de nieve
averse de neige
Schneeschauer

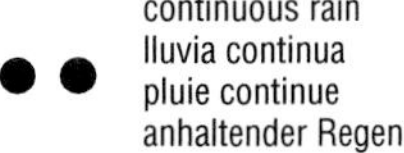
continuous rain
lluvia continua
pluie continue
anhaltender Regen

thunderstorm
tormenta
orage
Gewitter

sleet
aguanieve
grésil
Schneeregen

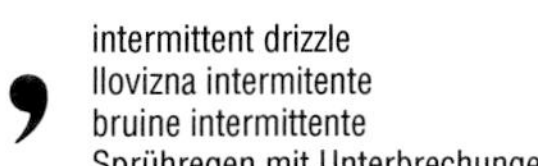
intermittent drizzle
llovizna intermitente
bruine intermittente
Sprühregen mit Unterbrechungen

heavy thunderstorm
tormenta eléctrica
orage violent
starkes Gewitter

hail shower
granizada
averse de grêle
Hagelschauer

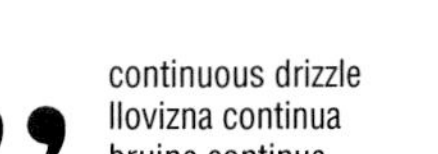
continuous drizzle
llovizna continua
bruine continue
anhaltender Sprühregen

sandstorm or dust storm
tormenta de polvo
tempête de sable ou de poussière
Sand- oder Staubsturm

squall
borrasca
grain
Bö

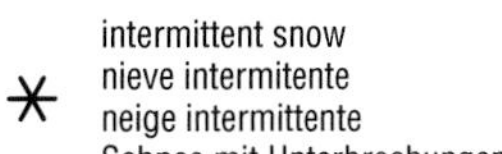
intermittent snow
nieve intermitente
neige intermittente
Schnee mit Unterbrechungen

tropical storm
tormenta tropical
tempête tropicale
tropischer Sturm

freezing rain
lluvia helada
pluie verglaçante
Eisregen

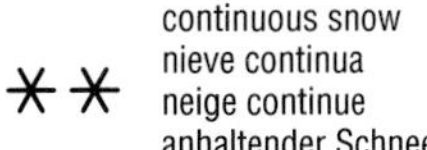
continuous snow
nieve continua
neige continue
anhaltender Schnee

hurricane
huracán
ouragan
Orkan

smoke
humo
fumée
Rauch

rain shower
chubasco
averse de pluie
Regenschauer

slight drifting snow low
acumulación baja de nieve liviana
chasse-neige faible basse
leichtes Schneetreiben

mist
neblina
brume
Dunst

heavy drifting snow low
acumulación baja de nieve pesada
chasse-neige forte basse
starkes Schneetreiben

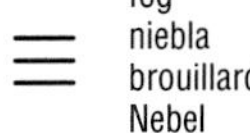
fog
niebla
brouillard
Nebel

METEOROLOGICAL MEASURING INSTRUMENTS
INSTRUMENTOS DE MEDICIÓN METEOROLÓGICA
INSTRUMENTS DE MESURE MÉTÉOROLOGIQUE
METEOROLOGISCHE MESSINSTRUMENTE

MEASURE OF SUNSHINE
MEDICIÓN DE LA LUZ SOLAR
MESURE DE L'ENSOLEILLEMENT
MESSUNG DES SONNENSCHEINS

sunshine recorder
actinómetro
héliographe
Sonnenscheinautograph

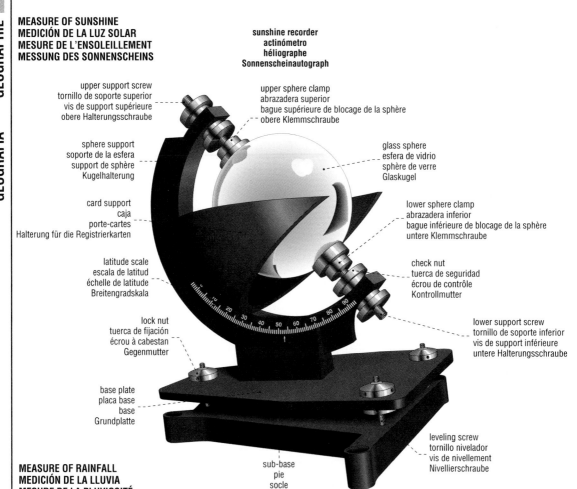

upper support screw
tornillo de soporte superior
vis de support supérieure
obere Halterungsschraube

upper sphere clamp
abrazadera superior
bague supérieure de blocage de la sphère
obere Klemmschraube

sphere support
soporte de la esfera
support de sphère
Kugelhalterung

glass sphere
esfera de vidrio
sphère de verre
Glaskugel

card support
caja
porte-cartes
Halterung für die Registrierkarten

lower sphere clamp
abrazadera inferior
bague inférieure de blocage de la sphère
untere Klemmschraube

latitude scale
escala de latitud
échelle de latitude
Breitengradskala

check nut
tuerca de seguridad
écrou de contrôle
Kontrollmutter

lock nut
tuerca de fijación
écrou à cabestan
Gegenmutter

lower support screw
tornillo de soporte inferior
vis de support inférieure
untere Halterungsschraube

base plate
placa base
base
Grundplatte

leveling screw
tornillo nivelador
vis de nivellement
Nivellierschraube

sub-base
pie
socle
Sockel

MEASURE OF RAINFALL
MEDICIÓN DE LA LLUVIA
MESURE DE LA PLUVIOSITÉ
MESSUNG DES REGENFALLS

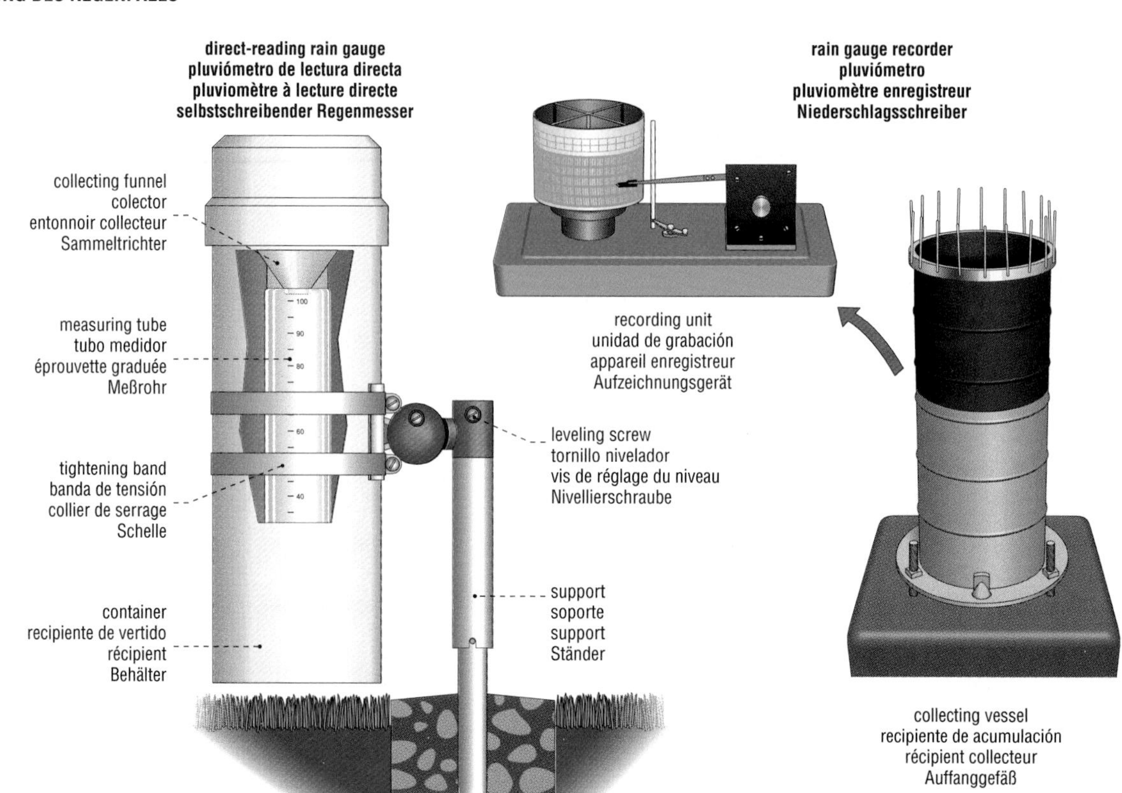
direct-reading rain gauge
pluviómetro de lectura directa
pluviomètre à lecture directe
selbstschreibender Regenmesser
collecting funnel
colector
entonnoir collecteur
Sammeltrichter
measuring tube
tubo medidor
éprouvette graduée
Meßrohr
tightening band
banda de tensión
collier de serrage
Schelle
container
recipiente de vertido
récipient
Behälter
leveling screw
tornillo nivelador
vis de réglage du niveau
Nivellierschraube
support
soporte
support
Ständer
rain gauge recorder
pluviómetro
pluviomètre enregistreur
Niederschlagsschreiber
recording unit
unidad de grabación
appareil enregistreur
Aufzeichnungsgerät
collecting vessel
recipiente de acumulación
récipient collecteur
Auffanggefäß

INSTRUMENT SHELTER
CASETA DE INSTRUMENTOS METEOROLÓGICOS
ABRI MÉTÉOROLOGIQUE
WETTERHÜTTE

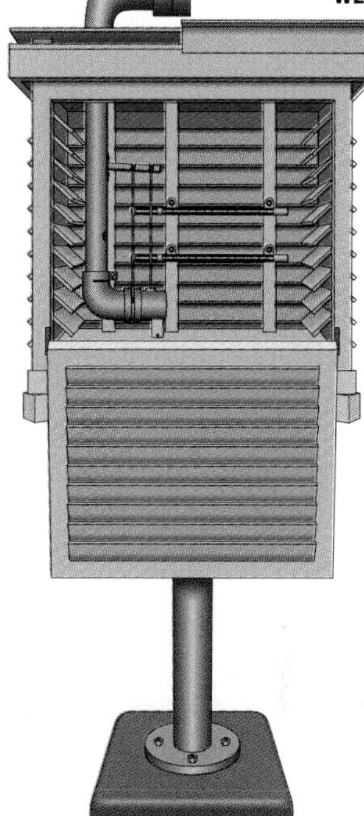

MEASURE OF TEMPERATURE
MEDICIÓN DE LA TEMPERATURA
MESURE DE LA TEMPÉRATURE
MESSUNG DER TEMPERATUR

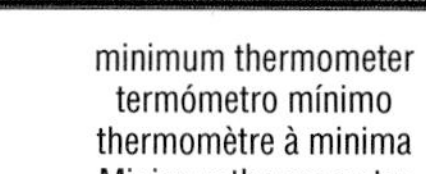

minimum thermometer
termómetro mínimo
thermomètre à minima
Minimumthermometer

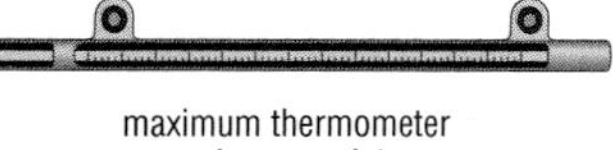

maximum thermometer
termómetro máximo
thermomètre à maxima
Maximumthermometer

MEASURE OF AIR PRESSURE
MEDICIÓN DE LA PRESIÓN DEL AIRE
MESURE DE LA PRESSION
MESSUNG DES LUFTDRUCKS

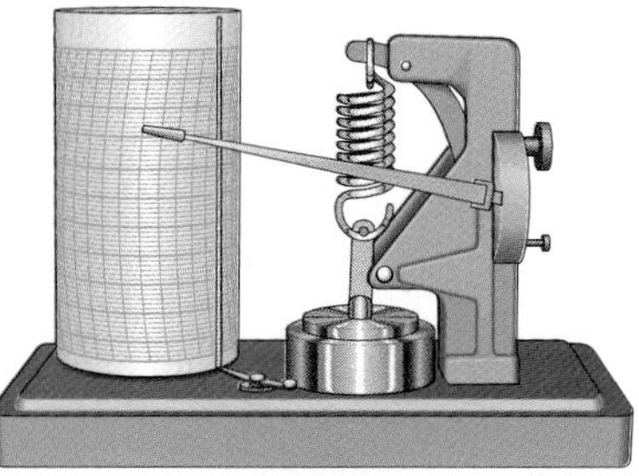

barograph
barógrafo
baromètre enregistreur
Barograph

mercury barometer
barómetro de mercurio
baromètre à mercure
Quecksilberbarometer

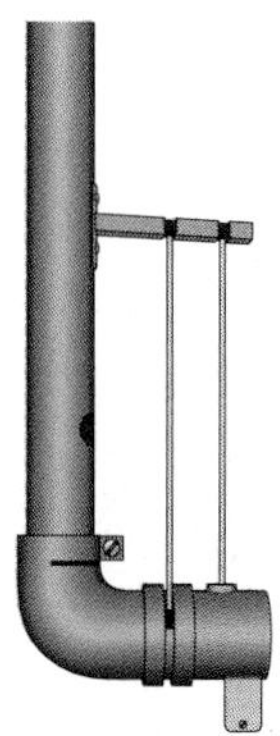

psychrometer
psicrómetro
psychromètre
Psychrometer

MEASURE OF WIND DIRECTION
MEDICIÓN DE LA DIRECCIÓN DEL VIENTO
MESURE DE LA DIRECTION DU VENT
MESSUNG DER WINDRICHTUNG

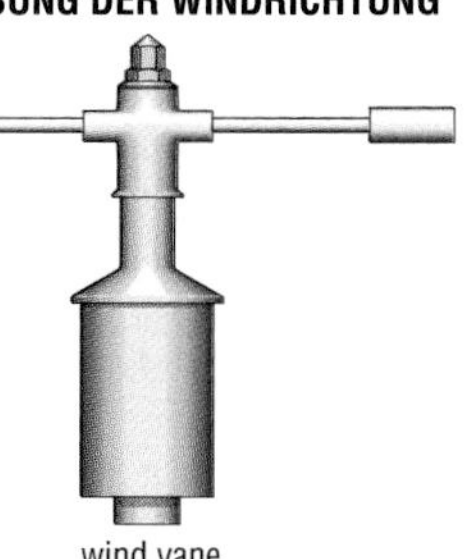

wind vane
veleta
girouette
Windfahne

MEASURE OF WIND STRENGTH
MEDICIÓN DE LA FUERZA DEL VIENTO
MESURE DE LA VITESSE DU VENT
MESSUNG DER WINDSTÄRKE

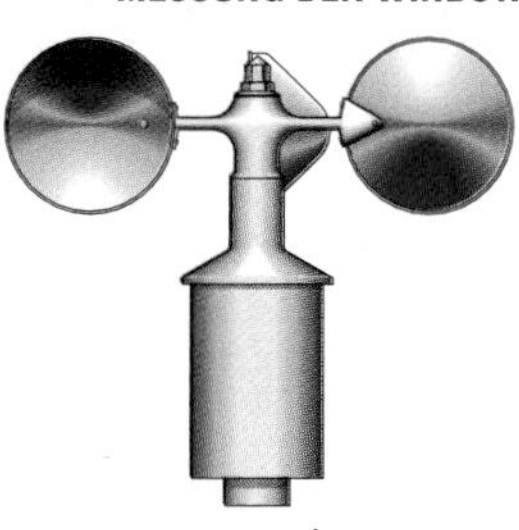

anemometer
anemómetro
anémomètre
Anemometer

MEASURE OF HUMIDITY
MEDICIÓN DE LA HUMEDAD
MESURE DE L'HUMIDITÉ
MESSUNG DER LUFTFEUCHTIGKEIT

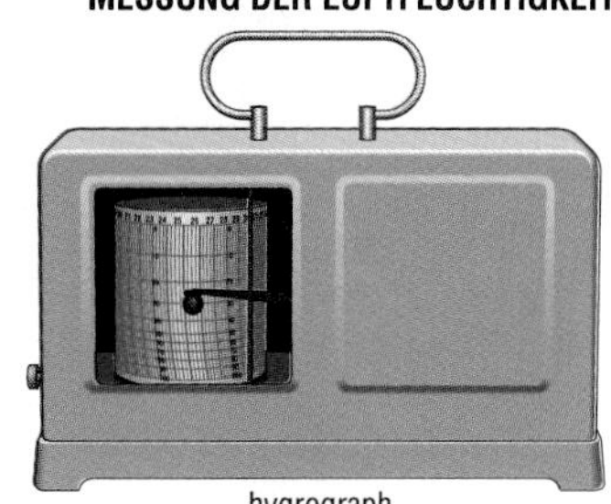

hygrograph
higrógrafo
hygromètre enregistreur
Hygrograph

MEASURE OF SNOWFALL
MEDICIÓN DE NEVADAS
MESURE DE LA NEIGE
MESSUNG DES SCHNEEFALLS

snow gauge
nivómetro
nivomètre
Schneemesser

MEASURE OF CLOUD CEILING
MEDICIÓN DE LA ALTURA DE LAS NUBES
MESURE DE LA HAUTEUR DES NUAGES
MESSUNG DER WOLKENHÖHE

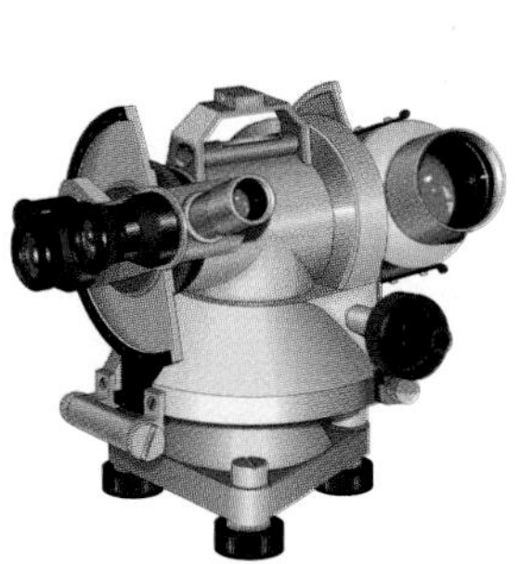

theodolite
teodolito
théodolite
Theodolit

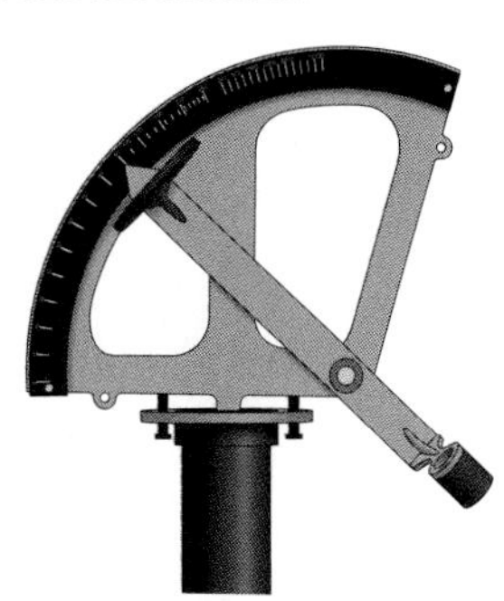

alidade
alidada
alidade
Alhidade

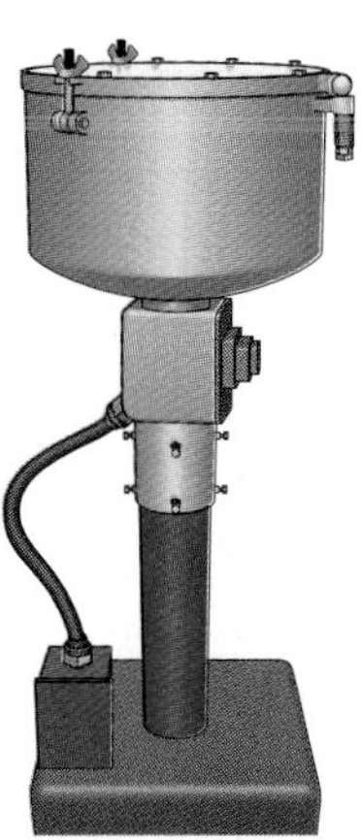

ceiling projector
proyector de altura máxima
projecteur de plafond
Wolkenhöhenmesser

WEATHER SATELLITE
SATÉLITE METEOROLÓGICO
SATELLITE MÉTÉOROLOGIQUE
WETTERSATELLIT

GEOSTATIONARY SATELLITE
SATÉLITE GEOESTACIONARIO
SATELLITE GÉOSTATIONNAIRE
GEOSTATIONÄRER SATELLIT

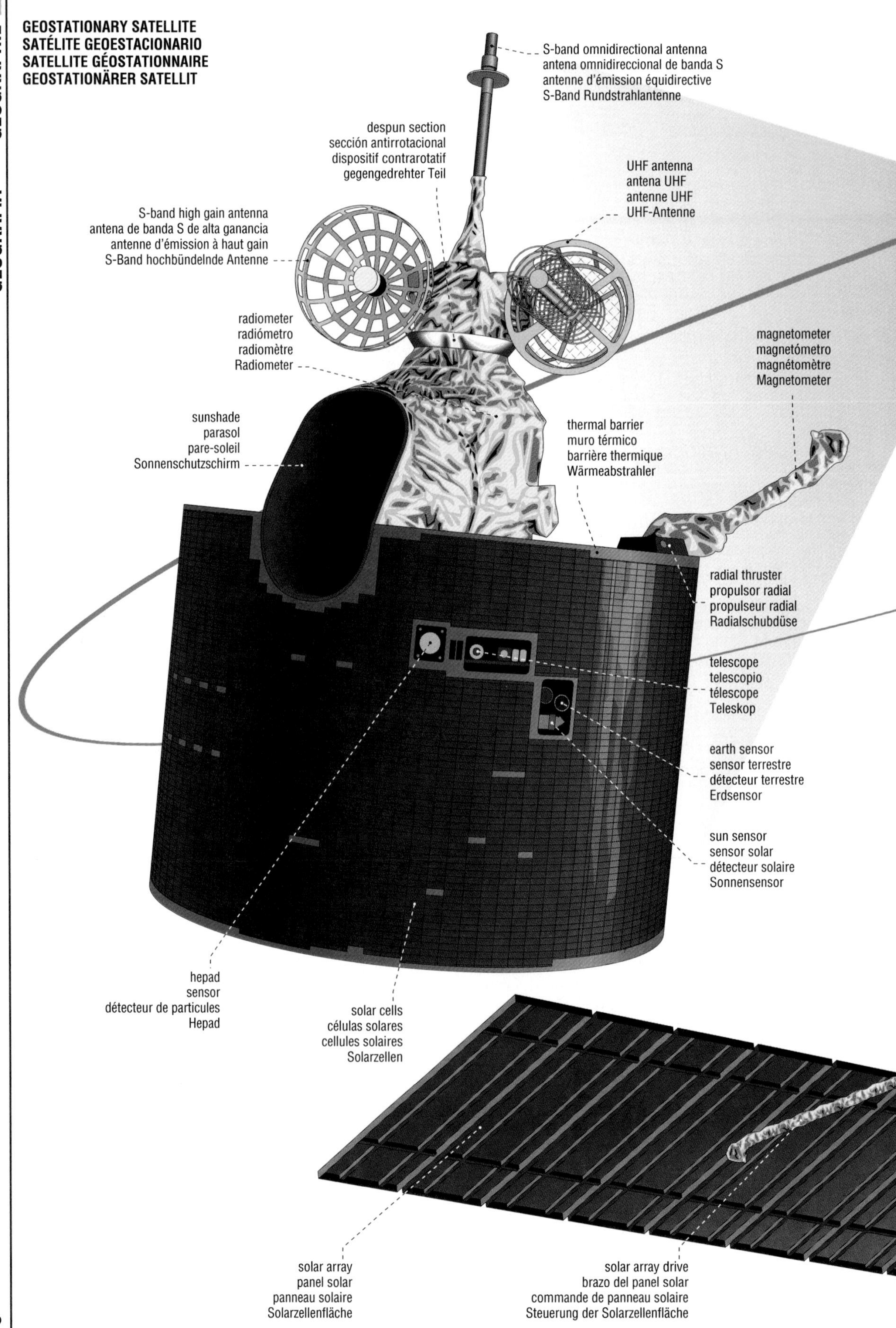
S-band omnidirectional antenna
antena omnidireccional de banda S
antenne d'émission équidirective
S-Band Rundstrahlantenne
despun section
sección antirrotacional
dispositif contrarotatif
gegengedrehter Teil
UHF antenna
antena UHF
antenne UHF
UHF-Antenne
S-band high gain antenna
antena de banda S de alta ganancia
antenne d'émission à haut gain
S-Band hochbündelnde Antenne
radiometer
radiómetro
radiomètre
Radiometer
magnetometer
magnetómetro
magnétomètre
Magnetometer
sunshade
parasol
pare-soleil
Sonnenschutzschirm
thermal barrier
muro térmico
barrière thermique
Wärmeabstrahler
radial thruster
propulsor radial
propulseur radial
Radialschubdüse
telescope
telescopio
télescope
Teleskop
earth sensor
sensor terrestre
détecteur terrestre
Erdsensor
sun sensor
sensor solar
détecteur solaire
Sonnensensor
hepad
sensor
détecteur de particules
Hepad
solar cells
células solares
cellules solaires
Solarzellen
solar array
panel solar
panneau solaire
Solarzellenfläche
solar array drive
brazo del panel solar
commande de panneau solaire
Steuerung der Solarzellenfläche

ORBIT OF THE SATELLITES
ÓRBITA DE LOS SATÉLITES
ORBITE DES SATELLITES
UMLAUFBAHN DER SATELLITEN

POLAR-ORBITING SATELLITE
SATÉLITE DE ÓRBITA POLAR
SATELLITE À DÉFILEMENT
POLARUMLAUFENDER SATELLIT

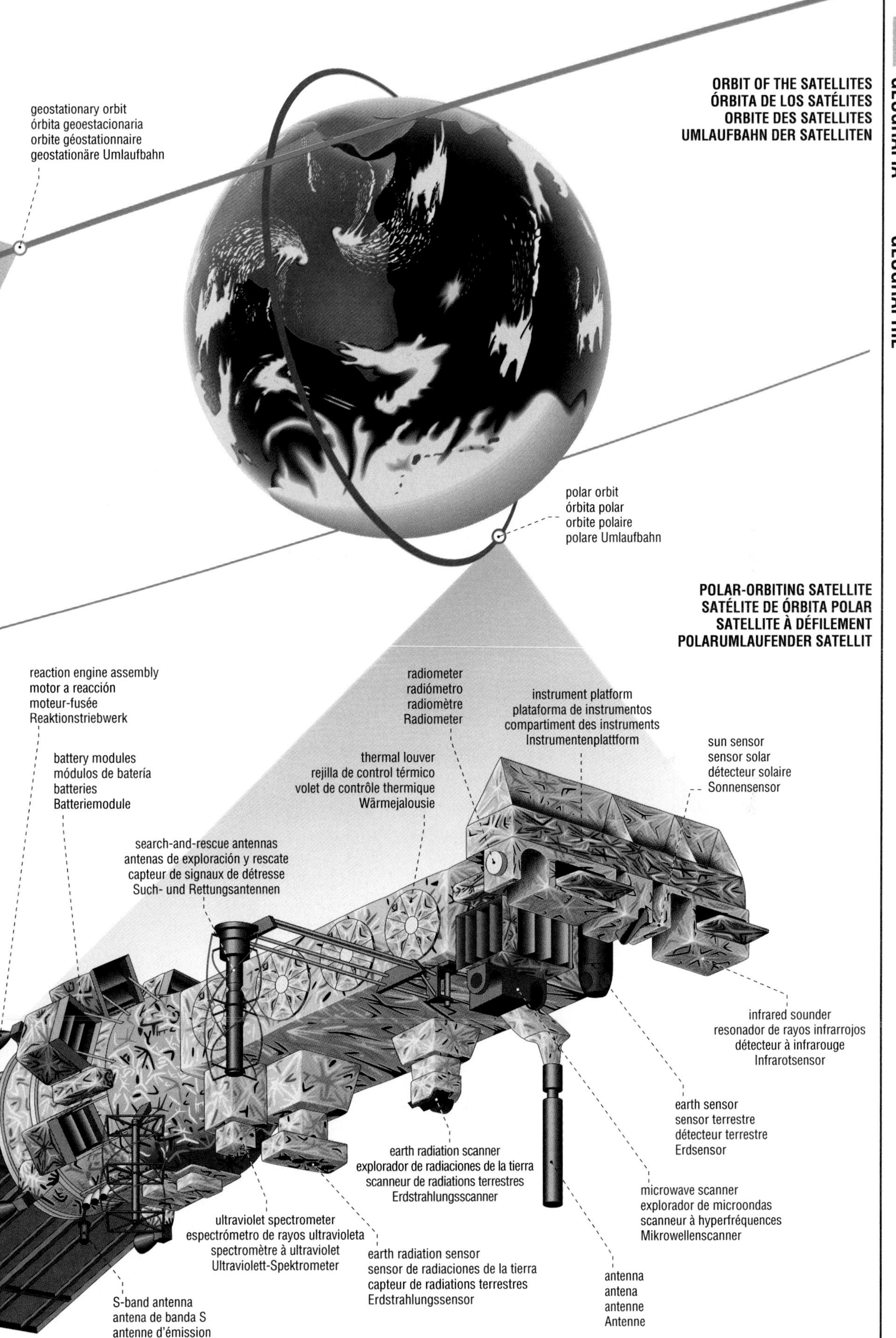
geostationary orbit
órbita geoestacionaria
orbite géostationnaire
geostationäre Umlaufbahn
polar orbit
órbita polar
orbite polaire
polare Umlaufbahn
reaction engine assembly
motor a reacción
moteur-fusée
Reaktionstriebwerk
battery modules
módulos de batería
batteries
Batteriemodule
search-and-rescue antennas
antenas de exploración y rescate
capteur de signaux de détresse
Such- und Rettungsantennen
radiometer
radiómetro
radiomètre
Radiometer
thermal louver
rejilla de control térmico
volet de contrôle thermique
Wärmejalousie
instrument platform
plataforma de instrumentos
compartiment des instruments
Instrumentenplattform
sun sensor
sensor solar
détecteur solaire
Sonnensensor
infrared sounder
resonador de rayos infrarrojos
détecteur à infrarouge
Infrarotsensor
earth sensor
sensor terrestre
détecteur terrestre
Erdsensor
earth radiation scanner
explorador de radiaciones de la tierra
scanneur de radiations terrestres
Erdstrahlungsscanner
microwave scanner
explorador de microondas
scanneur à hyperfréquences
Mikrowellenscanner
ultraviolet spectrometer
espectrómetro de rayos ultravioleta
spectromètre à ultraviolet
Ultraviolett-Spektrometer
earth radiation sensor
sensor de radiaciones de la tierra
capteur de radiations terrestres
Erdstrahlungssensor
antenna
antena
antenne
Antenne
S-band antenna
antena de banda S
antenne d'émission
S-Band Antenne

CLOUDS AND METEOROLOGICAL SYMBOLS
NUBES Y SÍMBOLOS METEOROLÓGICOS
NUAGES ET SYMBOLES MÉTÉOROLOGIQUES
WOLKEN UND METEOROLOGISCHE SYMBOLE

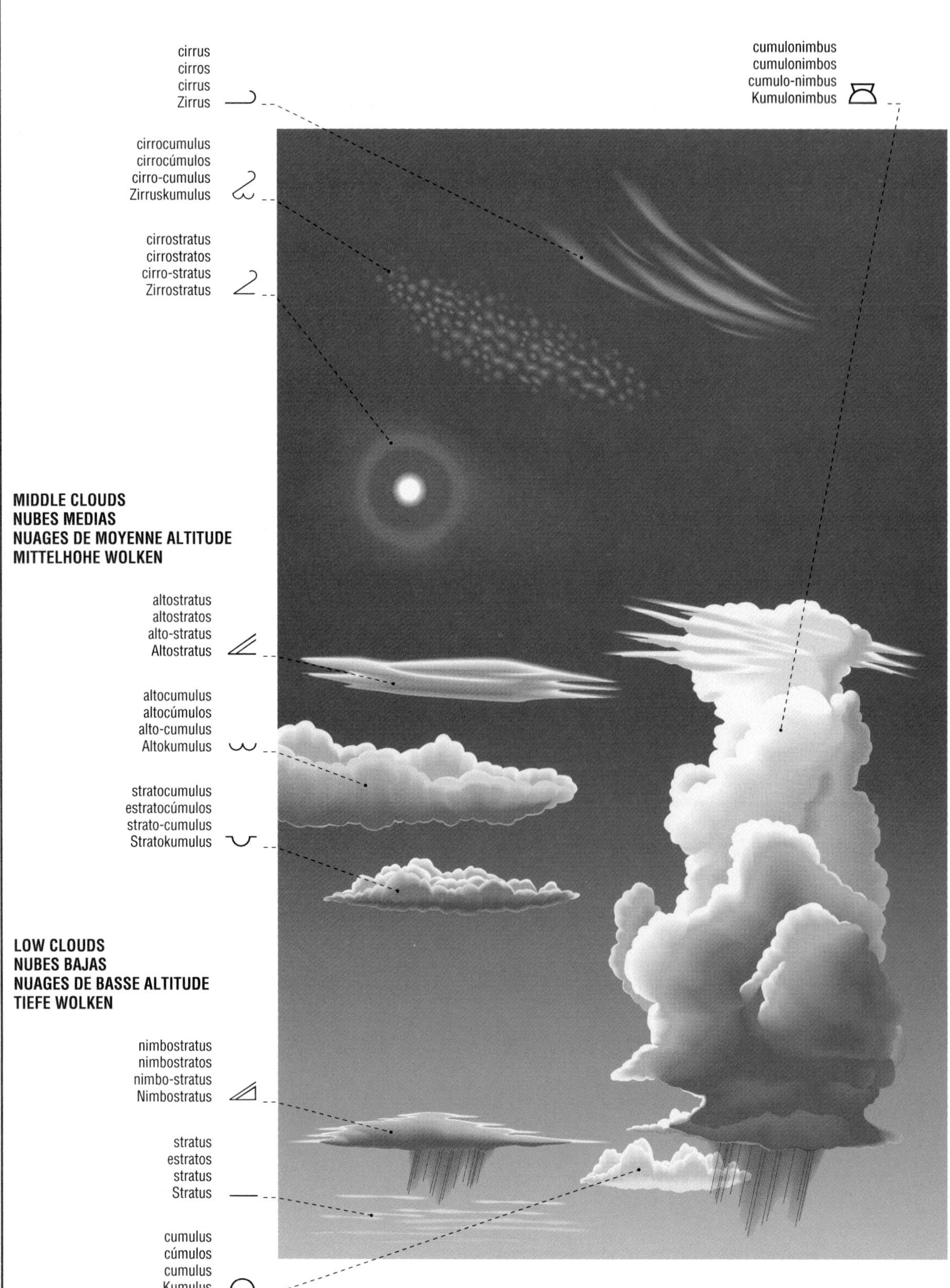
HIGH CLOUDS
NUBES ALTAS
NUAGES DE HAUTE ALTITUDE
HOHE WOLKEN
CLOUDS OF VERTICAL DEVELOPMENT
NUBES DE DESARROLLO VERTICAL
NUAGES À DÉVELOPPEMENT VERTICAL
QUELLWOLKEN
cirrus
cirros
cirrus
Zirrus
cumulonimbus
cumulonimbos
cumulo-nimbus
Kumulonimbus
cirrocumulus
cirrocúmulos
cirro-cumulus
Zirruskumulus
cirrostratus
cirrostratos
cirro-stratus
Zirrostratus
MIDDLE CLOUDS
NUBES MEDIAS
NUAGES DE MOYENNE ALTITUDE
MITTELHOHE WOLKEN
altostratus
altostratos
alto-stratus
Altostratus
altocumulus
altocúmulos
alto-cumulus
Altokumulus
stratocumulus
estratocúmulos
strato-cumulus
Stratokumulus
LOW CLOUDS
NUBES BAJAS
NUAGES DE BASSE ALTITUDE
TIEFE WOLKEN
nimbostratus
nimbostratos
nimbo-stratus
Nimbostratus
stratus
estratos
stratus
Stratus
cumulus
cúmulos
cumulus
Kumulus

CLIMATES OF THE WORLD
CLIMAS DEL MUNDO
CLIMATS DU MONDE
KLIMATE DER WELT

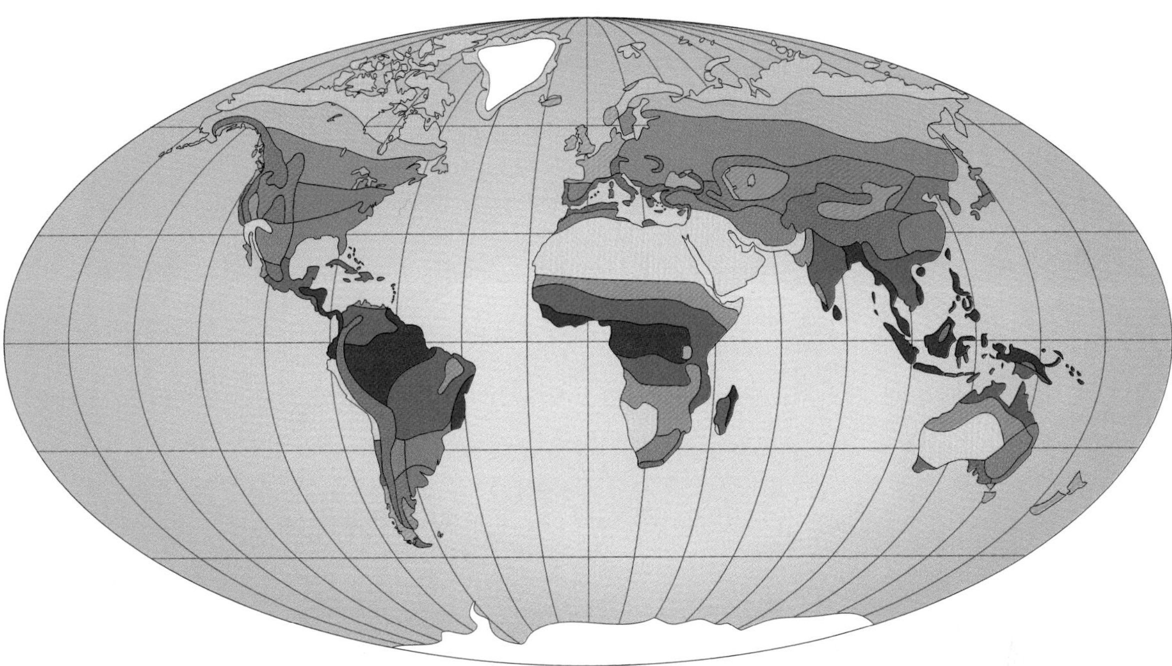

TROPICAL CLIMATES
CLIMAS TROPICALES
CLIMATS TROPICAUX
TROPISCHE KLIMATE

tropical rain forest
tropical lluvioso
forêt tropicale
tropischer Regenwald

tropical savanna
sabana
savane
tropische Savanne

steppe
estepario
steppe
Steppe

desert
desértico
désert
Wüste

CONTINENTAL CLIMATES
CLIMAS CONTINENTALES
CLIMATS CONTINENTAUX
KONTINENTALKLIMATE

dry continental - arid
continental seco-árido
continental aride
kontinental-trocken - trocken

dry continental - semiarid
continental seco-semiárido
continental semi-aride
kontinental-trocken - halbtrocken

TEMPERATE CLIMATES
CLIMAS TEMPLADOS
CLIMATS TEMPÉRÉS
GEMÄSSIGTE KLIMATE

humid - long summer
húmedo de verano largo
humide, à été long
feucht - langer Sommer

humid - short summer
húmedo de verano corto
humide, à été court
feucht - kurzer Sommer

marine
marítimo
océanique
maritim

SUBTROPICAL CLIMATES
CLIMAS SUBTROPICALES
CLIMATS SUBTROPICAUX
SUBTROPISCHE KLIMATE

Mediterranean subtropical
subtropical mediterráneo
méditerranéen
mediterrane Subtropen

humid subtropical
subtropical húmedo
subtropical humide
feuchte Subtropen

dry subtropical
subtropical seco
subtropical sec
trockene Subtropen

POLAR CLIMATES
CLIMAS POLARES
CLIMATS POLAIRES
POLARKLIMATE

polar tundra
tundra
toundra
Polartundra

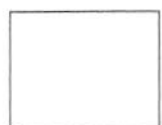
polar ice cap
hielos perpetuos
calotte glaciaire
Eiskappe

HIGHLAND CLIMATES
CLIMAS DE ALTA MONTAÑA
CLIMATS DE MONTAGNE
HOCHLANDKLIMATE

highland climates
climas de alta montaña
climats de montagne
Hochlandklimate

SUBARCTIC CLIMATES
CLIMAS SUBÁRTICOS
CLIMATS SUBARCTIQUES
SUBARKTISCHE KLIMATE

subarctic climates
climas subárticos
climats subarctiques
subarktische Klimate

DESERT
DESIERTO
DÉSERT
WÜSTE

oasis
oasis
oasis
Oase

palm grove
palmar
palmeraie
Palmenhain

mesa
otero
mésa
Tafelberg

butte
hamada
butte
Zeugenberg

rocky desert
desierto rocoso
désert de pierres
Steinwüste

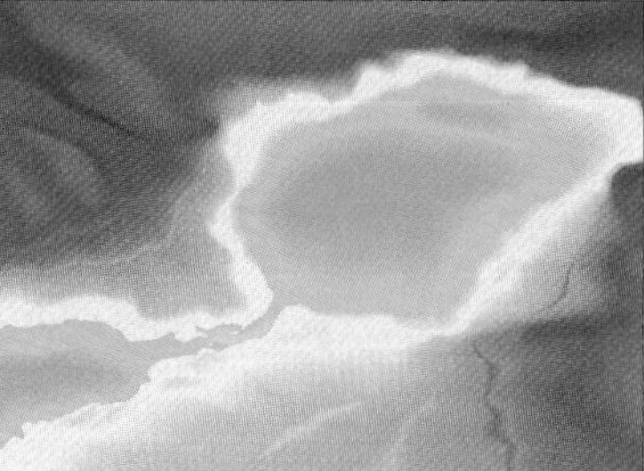

saline lake
laguna salada
lac salé
Salzsee

sandy desert
desierto arenoso
désert de sable
Sandwüste

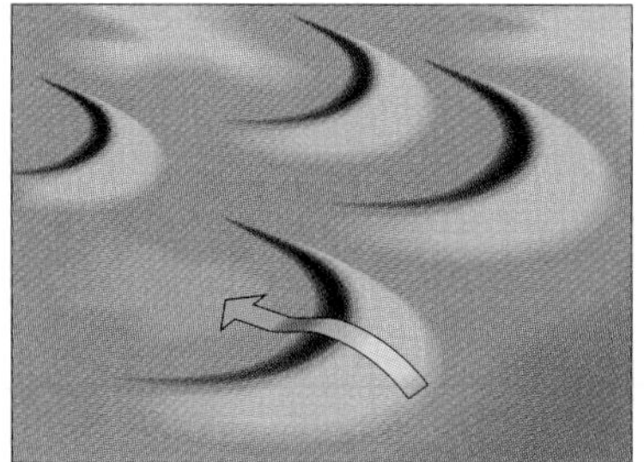

crescentic dune
barjana
dune en croissant
Sicheldüne

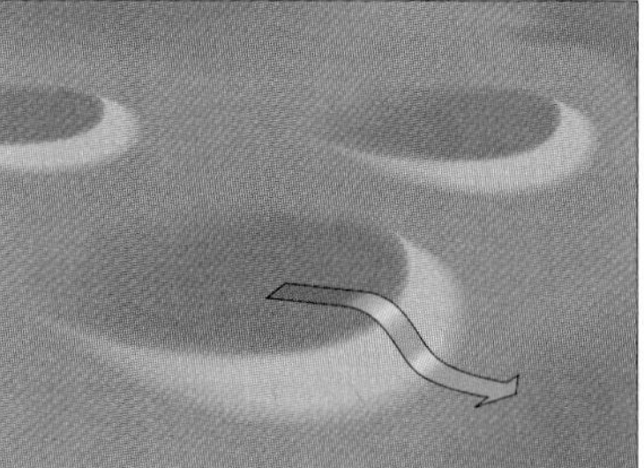

parabolic dune
duna parabólica
dune parabolique
Parabeldüne

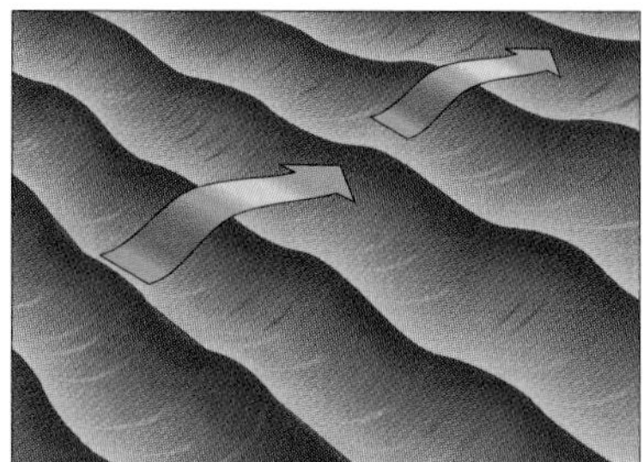

transverse dunes
dunas paralelas
dunes transversales
Querdünen

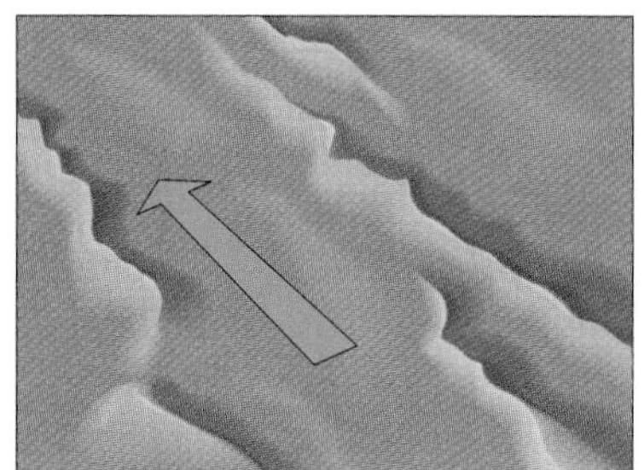

chain of dunes
cadena de dunas
cordon de dunes
Dünenzug

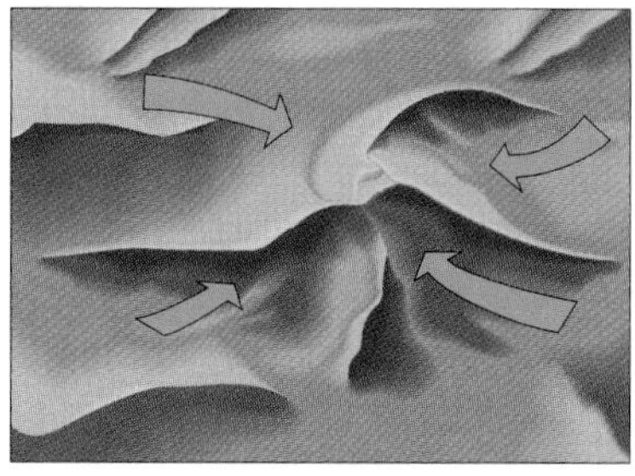

complex dune
duna compleja
dune complexe
komplexe Düne

longitudinal dunes
dunas longitudinales
dunes longitudinales
Längsdünen

CARTOGRAPHY
CARTOGRAFÍA
CARTOGRAPHIE
KARTOGRAPHIE

HEMISPHERES
HEMISFERIOS
HÉMISPHÈRES
HEMISPHÄREN

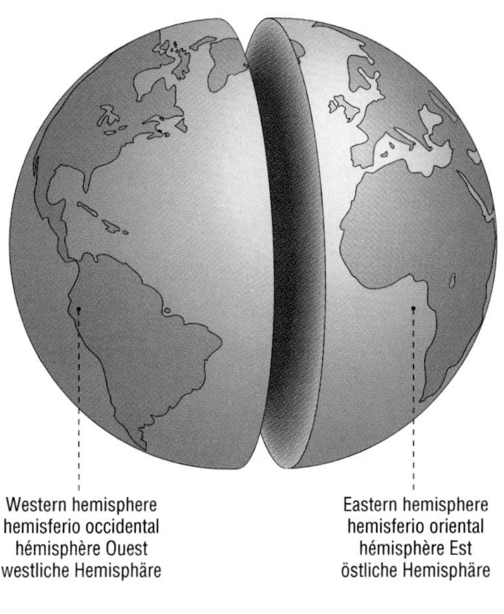
Western hemisphere
hemisferio occidental
hémisphère Ouest
westliche Hemisphäre
Eastern hemisphere
hemisferio oriental
hémisphère Est
östliche Hemisphäre

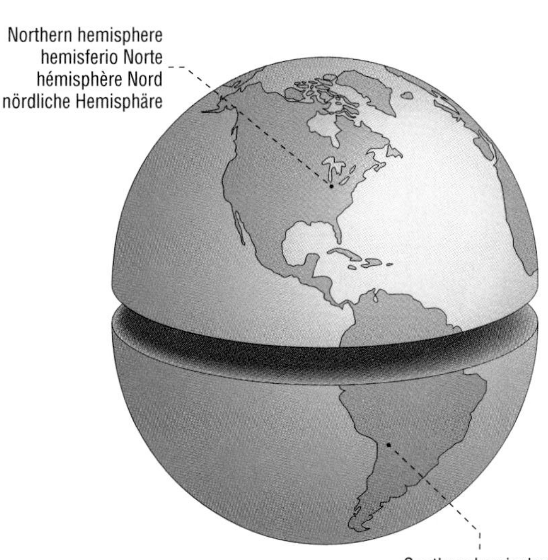
Northern hemisphere
hemisferio Norte
hémisphère Nord
nördliche Hemisphäre
Southern hemisphere
hemisferio Sur
hémisphère Sud
südliche Hemisphäre

GRID SYSTEM
SISTEMA DE REJILLA
DIVISIONS CARTOGRAPHIQUES
GRADNETZ

lines of latitude
líneas de latitud
latitude
Breitengrade

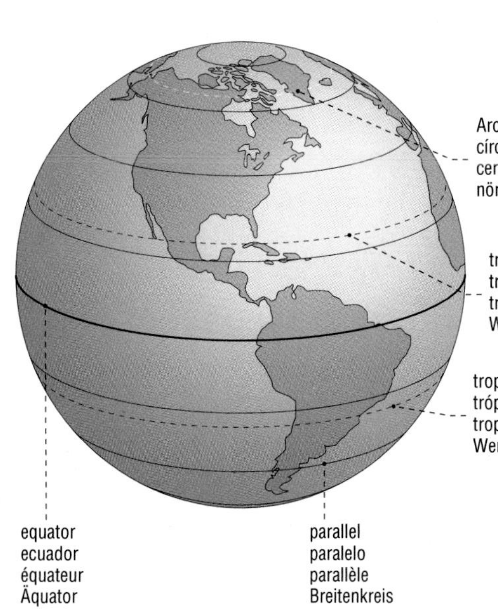
Arctic Circle
círculo polar ártico
cercle polaire arctique
nördlicher Polarkreis
tropic of Cancer
trópico de Cáncer
tropique du Cancer
Wendekreis des Krebses
tropic of Capricorn
trópico de Capricornio
tropique du Capricorne
Wendekreis des Steinbocks
equator
ecuador
équateur
Äquator
parallel
paralelo
parallèle
Breitenkreis

lines of longitude
líneas de longitud
longitude
Längengrade

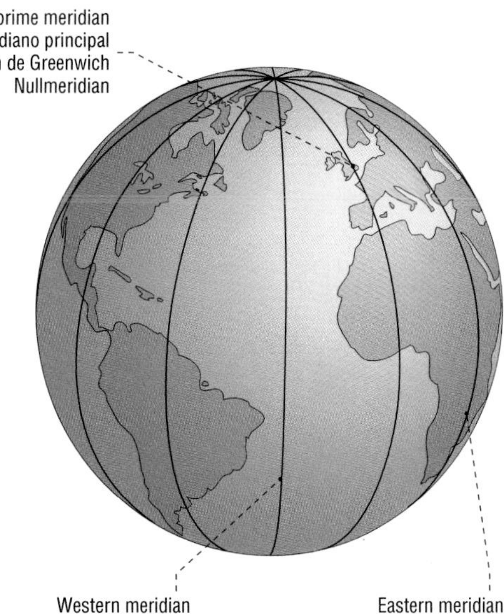
prime meridian
meridiano principal
méridien de Greenwich
Nullmeridian
Western meridian
meridiano occidental
méridien ouest
westlicher Meridian
Eastern meridian
meridiano oriental
méridien est
östlicher Meridian

REMOTE DETECTION SATELLITE
SATÉLITE DE DETECCIÓN A LARGA DISTANCIA
SATELLITE DE TÉLÉDÉTECTION
ERDERKENNUNGSGEODÄTISCHER SATELLIT

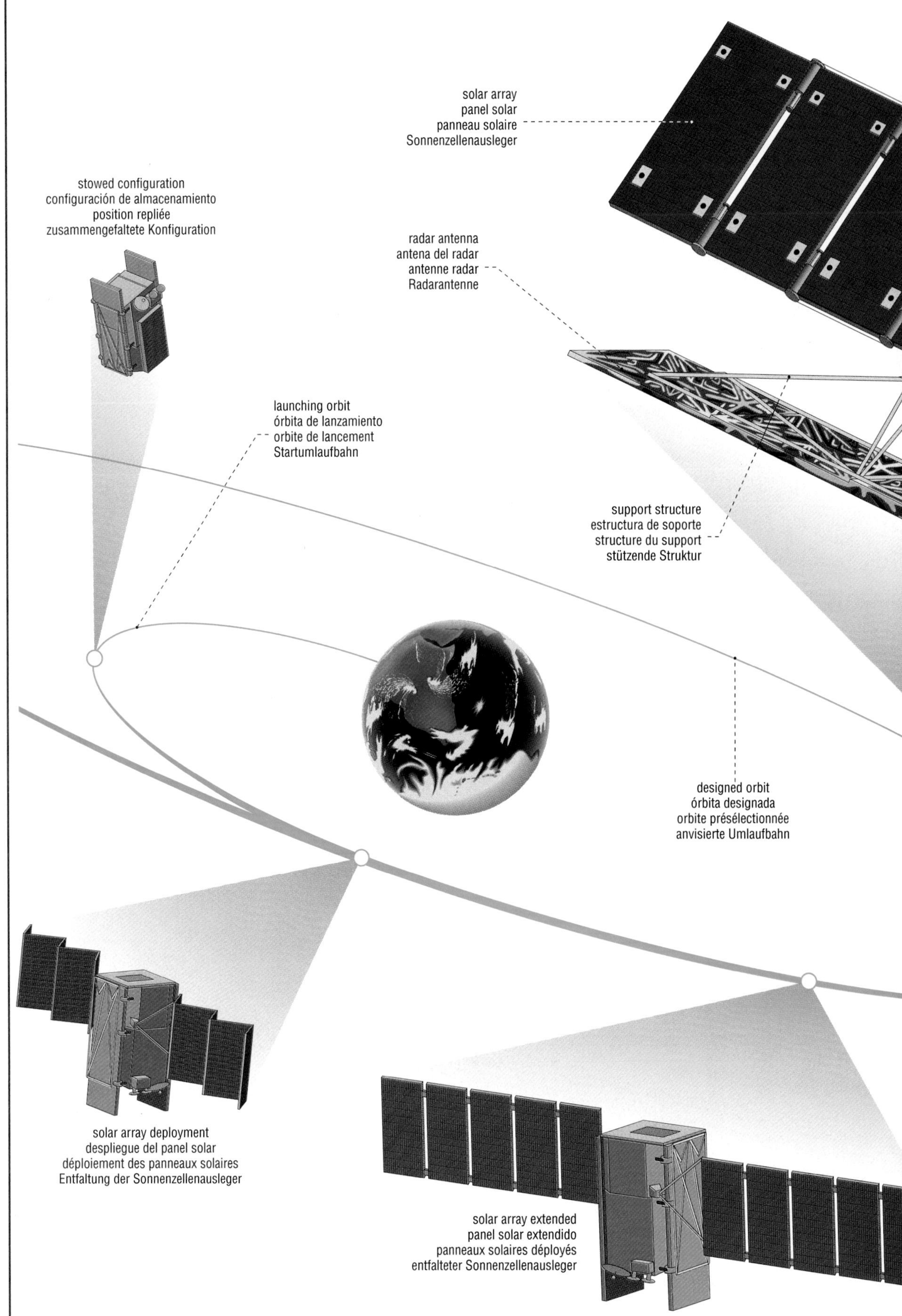
solar array
panel solar
panneau solaire
Sonnenzellenausleger
stowed configuration
configuración de almacenamiento
position repliée
zusammengefaltete Konfiguration
radar antenna
antena del radar
antenne radar
Radarantenne
launching orbit
órbita de lanzamiento
orbite de lancement
Startumlaufbahn
support structure
estructura de soporte
structure du support
stützende Struktur
designed orbit
órbita designada
orbite présélectionnée
anvisierte Umlaufbahn
solar array deployment
despliegue del panel solar
déploiement des panneaux solaires
Entfaltung der Sonnenzellenausleger
solar array extended
panel solar extendido
panneaux solaires déployés
entfalteter Sonnenzellenausleger

RADARSAT SATELLITE
SATÉLITE RADARSAT
SATELLITE RADARSAT
RADARSAT

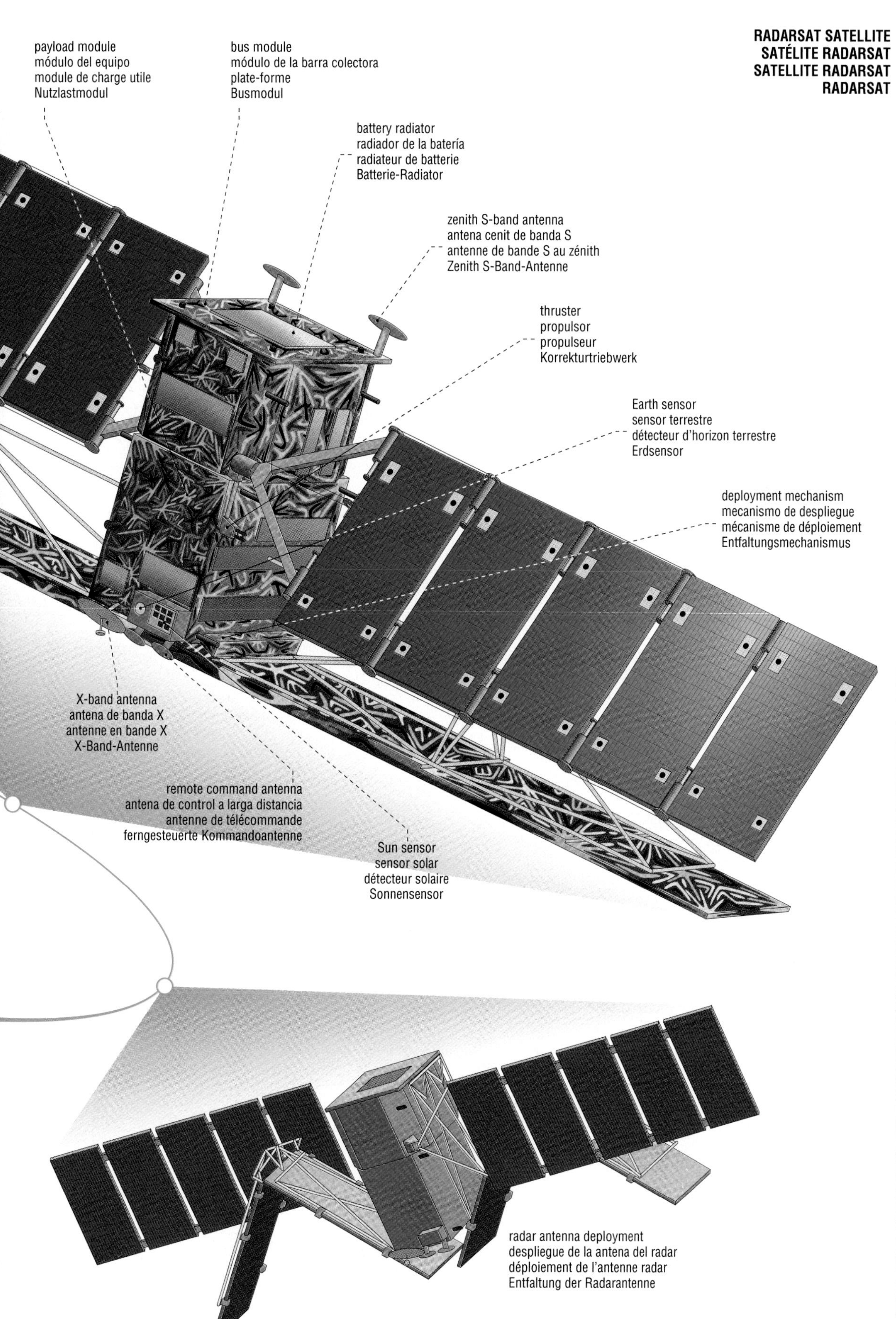
payload module
módulo del equipo
module de charge utile
Nutzlastmodul
bus module
módulo de la barra colectora
plate-forme
Busmodul
battery radiator
radiador de la batería
radiateur de batterie
Batterie-Radiator
zenith S-band antenna
antena cenit de banda S
antenne de bande S au zénith
Zenith S-Band-Antenne
thruster
propulsor
propulseur
Korrekturtriebwerk
Earth sensor
sensor terrestre
détecteur d'horizon terrestre
Erdsensor
deployment mechanism
mecanismo de despliegue
mécanisme de déploiement
Entfaltungsmechanismus
X-band antenna
antena de banda X
antenne en bande X
X-Band-Antenne
remote command antenna
antena de control a larga distancia
antenne de télécommande
ferngesteuerte Kommandoantenne
Sun sensor
sensor solar
détecteur solaire
Sonnensensor
radar antenna deployment
despliegue de la antena del radar
déploiement de l'antenne radar
Entfaltung der Radarantenne

CARTOGRAPHY
CARTOGRAFÍA
CARTOGRAPHIE
KARTOGRAPHIE

MAP PROJECTIONS
PROYECCIONES DEL MAPA
PROJECTIONS CARTOGRAPHIQUES
KARTENNETZENTWÜRFE

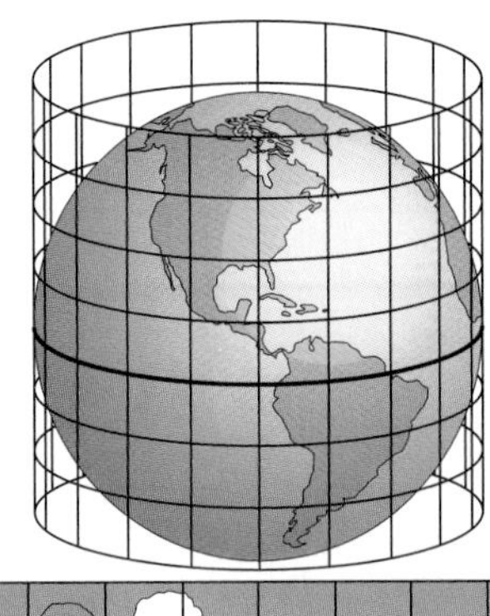

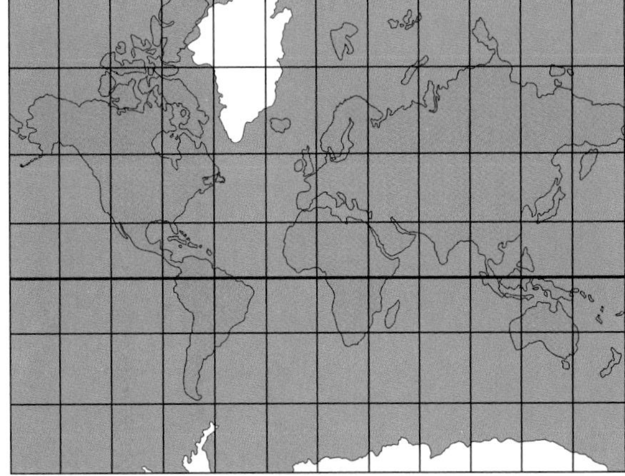

cylindrical projection
proyección cilíndrica
projection cylindrique
Zylinderprojektion

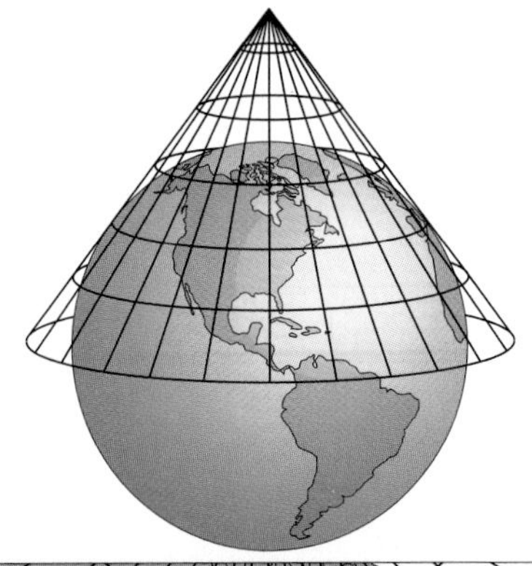

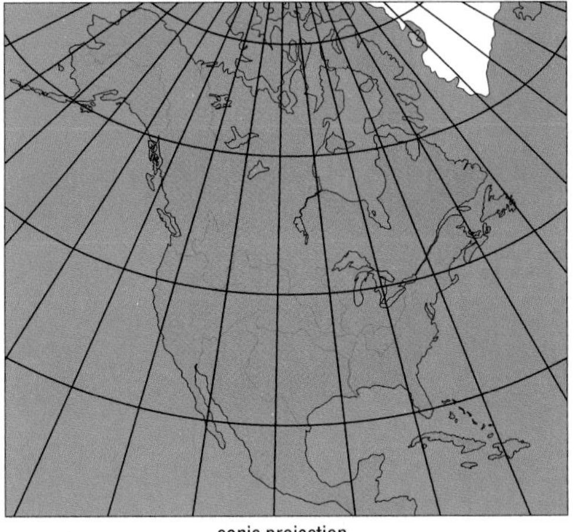

conic projection
proyección cónica
projection conique
Kegelprojektion

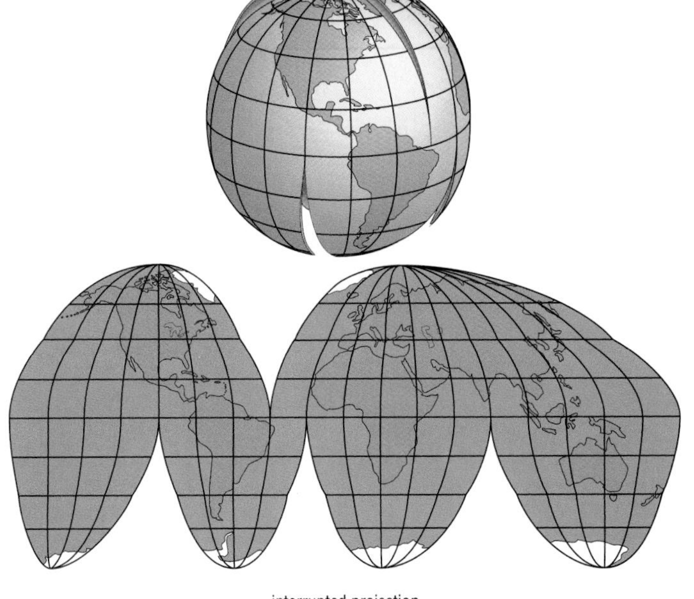

interrupted projection
proyección interrumpida
projection interrompue
zerlappte Projektion

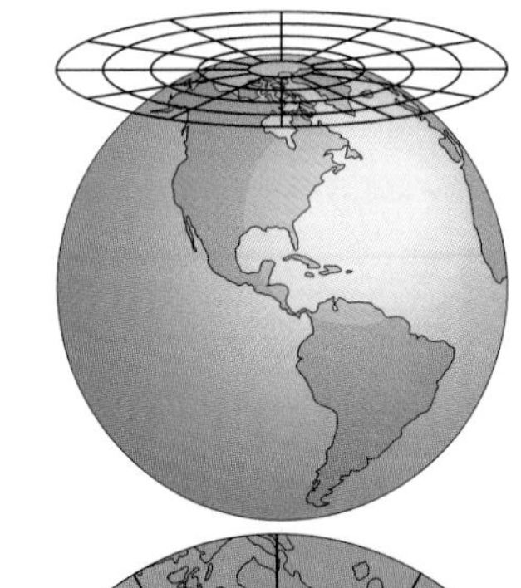

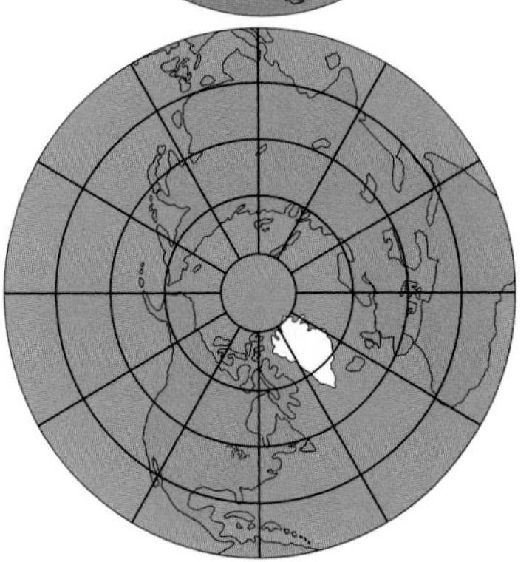

plane projection
proyección plana
projection horizontale
Azimutalprojektion

POLITICAL MAP
MAPA POLÍTICO
CARTE POLITIQUE
POLITISCHE KARTE

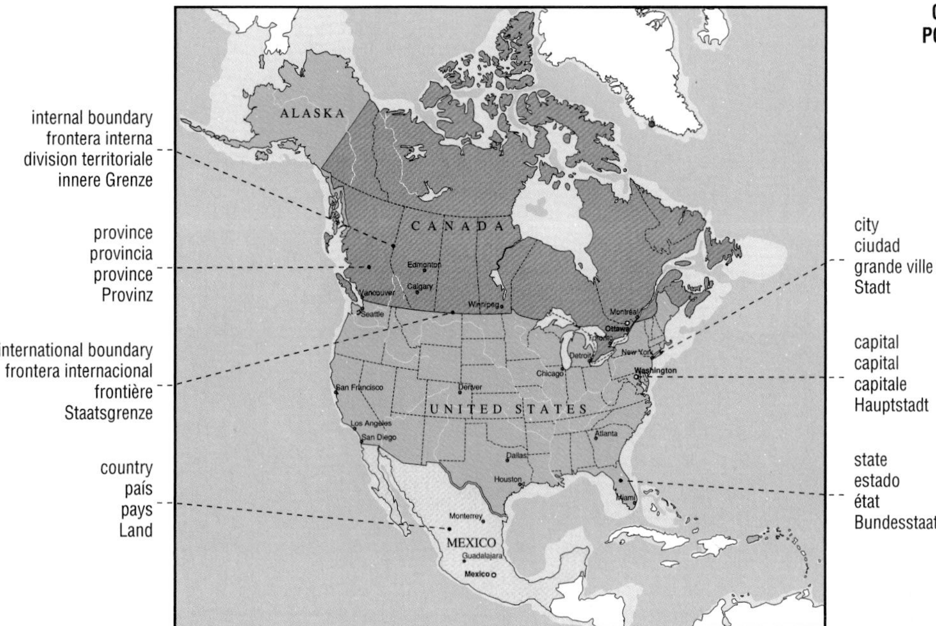
internal boundary
frontera interna
division territoriale
innere Grenze
province
provincia
province
Provinz
international boundary
frontera internacional
frontière
Staatsgrenze
country
país
pays
Land
city
ciudad
grande ville
Stadt
capital
capital
capitale
Hauptstadt
state
estado
état
Bundesstaat
ALASKA
CANADA
UNITED STATES
MEXICO
Edmonton
Calgary
Vancouver
Seattle
Winnipeg
Montréal
Ottawa
Toronto
New York
Detroit
Chicago
Washington
San Francisco
Denver
Los Angeles
San Diego
Atlanta
Dallas
Houston
Miami
Monterrey
Guadalajara
Mexico

PHYSICAL MAP
MAPA FÍSICO
CARTE PHYSIQUE
LANDSCHAFTSKARTE

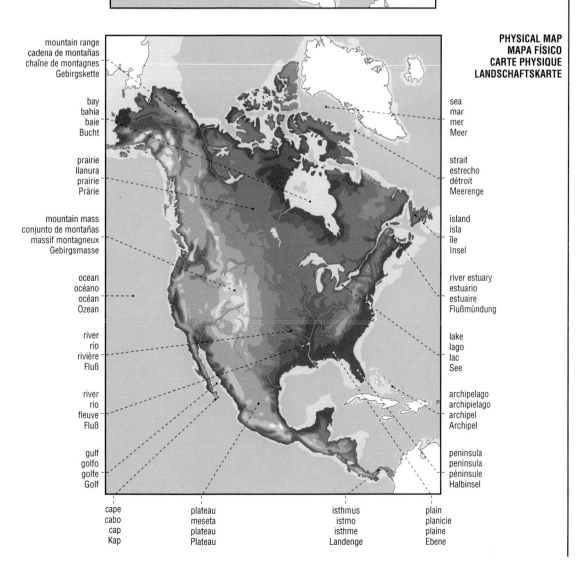

mountain range
cadena de montañas
chaîne de montagnes
Gebirgskette

bay
bahía
baie
Bucht

prairie
llanura
prairie
Prärie

mountain mass
conjunto de montañas
massif montagneux
Gebirgsmasse

ocean
océano
océan
Ozean

river
rio
rivière
Fluß

river
rio
fleuve
Fluß

gulf
golfo
golfe
Golf

sea
mar
mer
Meer

strait
estrecho
détroit
Meerenge

island
isla
île
Insel

river estuary
estuario
estuaire
Flußmündung

lake
lago
lac
See

archipelago
archipielago
archipel
Archipel

peninsula
península
péninsule
Halbinsel

cape
cabo
cap
Kap

plateau
meseta
plateau
Plateau

isthmus
istmo
isthme
Landenge

plain
planicie
plaine
Ebene

CARTOGRAPHY
CARTOGRAFÍA
CARTOGRAPHIE
KARTOGRAPHIE

URBAN MAP
MAPA URBANO
PLAN URBAIN
STADTPLAN

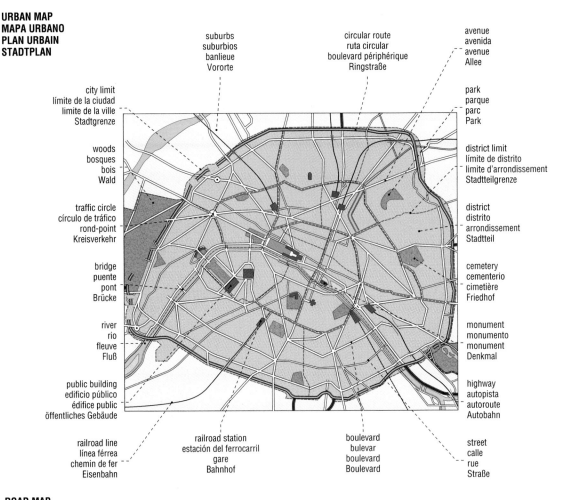

suburbs
suburbios
banlieue
Vororte

circular route
ruta circular
boulevard périphérique
Ringstraße

avenue
avenida
avenue
Allee

city limit
límite de la ciudad
limite de la ville
Stadtgrenze

park
parque
parc
Park

woods
bosques
bois
Wald

district limit
límite de distrito
limite d'arrondissement
Stadtteilgrenze

traffic circle
círculo de tráfico
rond-point
Kreisverkehr

district
distrito
arrondissement
Stadtteil

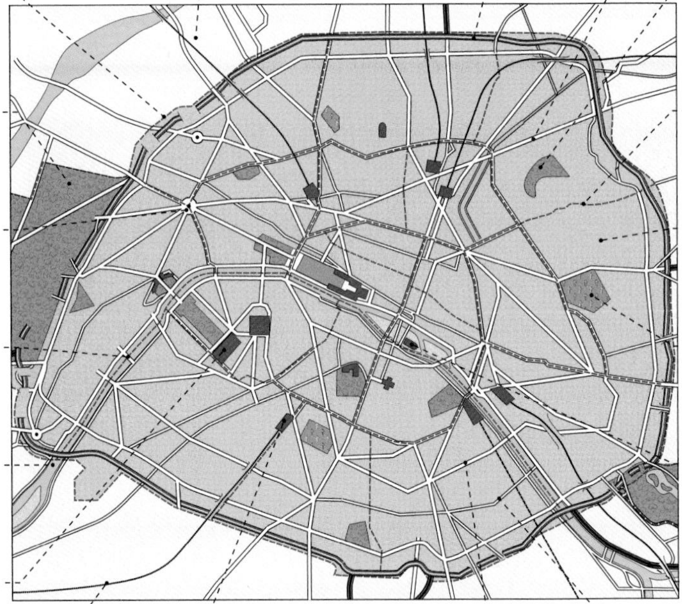

bridge
puente
pont
Brücke

cemetery
cementerio
cimetière
Friedhof

river
rio
fleuve
Fluß

monument
monumento
monument
Denkmal

public building
edificio público
édifice public
öffentliches Gebäude

highway
autopista
autoroute
Autobahn

railroad line
línea férrea
chemin de fer
Eisenbahn

railroad station
estación del ferrocarril
gare
Bahnhof

boulevard
bulevar
boulevard
Boulevard

street
calle
rue
Straße

ROAD MAP
MAPA DE CARRETERAS
CARTE ROUTIÈRE
STRASSENKARTE

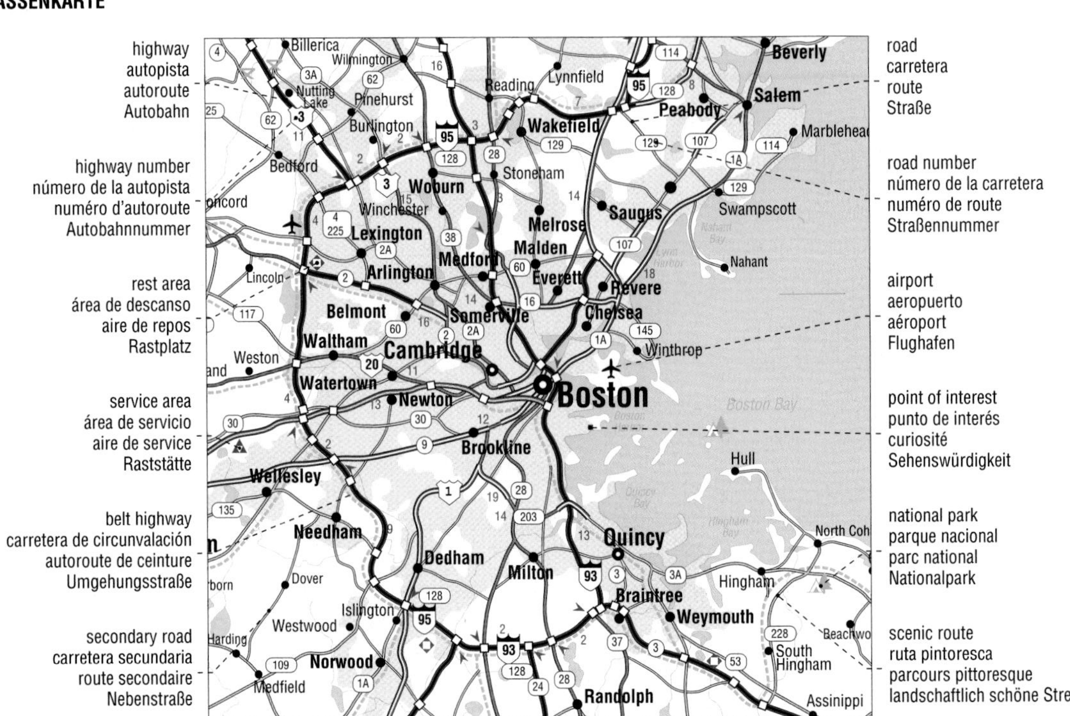
highway
autopista
autoroute
Autobahn
highway number
número de la autopista
numéro d'autoroute
Autobahnnummer
rest area
área de descanso
aire de repos
Rastplatz
service area
área de servicio
aire de service
Raststätte
belt highway
carretera de circunvalación
autoroute de ceinture
Umgehungsstraße
secondary road
carretera secundaria
route secondaire
Nebenstraße
road
carretera
route
Straße
road number
número de la carretera
numéro de route
Straßennummer
airport
aeropuerto
aéroport
Flughafen
point of interest
punto de interés
curiosité
Sehenswürdigkeit
national park
parque nacional
parc national
Nationalpark
scenic route
ruta pintoresca
parcours pittoresque
landschaftlich schöne Strecke
Billerica
Wilmington
Lynnfield
Beverly
Reading
Peabody
Salem
Pinehurst
Burlington
Wakefield
Marblehead
Bedford
Stoneham
Woburn
Swampscott
Winchester
Lexington
Melrose
Saugus
Malden
Nahant
Medford
Arlington
Everett
Revere
Lincoln
Belmont
Somerville
Chelsea
Waltham
Cambridge
Winthrop
Weston
Watertown
Boston
Boston Bay
Newton
Brookline
Hull
Wellesley
Needham
Quincy
Dedham
Milton
Dover
Hingham
Braintree
Weymouth
Islington
Westwood
South Hingham
Norwood
Medfield
Randolph
Assinippi

VEGETABLE KINGDOM
REINO VEGETAL

RÈGNE VÉGÉTAL
PFLANZENREICH

CONTENTS

MUSHROOM
HONGO
CHAMPIGNON
PILZ

STRUCTURE OF A MUSHROOM
ANATOMÍA DE UN HONGO
STRUCTURE D'UN CHAMPIGNON
AUFBAU EINES PILZES

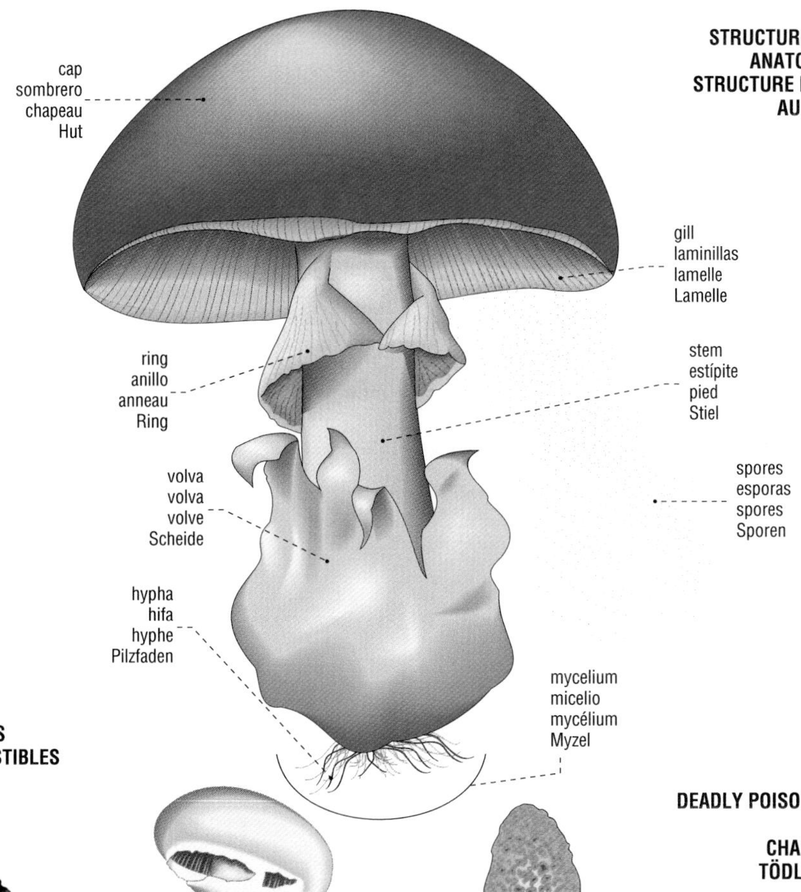
cap
sombrero
chapeau
Hut
gill
laminillas
lamelle
Lamelle
ring
anillo
anneau
Ring
stem
estípite
pied
Stiel
volva
volva
volve
Scheide
spores
esporas
spores
Sporen
hypha
hifa
hyphe
Pilzfaden
mycelium
micelio
mycélium
Myzel

EDIBLE MUSHROOMS
HONGOS COMESTIBLES
CHAMPIGNONS COMESTIBLES
SPEISEPILZE

truffle
trufa
truffe
Trüffel

cultivated mushroom
champiñón (Agaricus campestris)
champignon de couche
Zuchtchampignon

morel
morilla (Morchella esculenta)
morille
Morchel

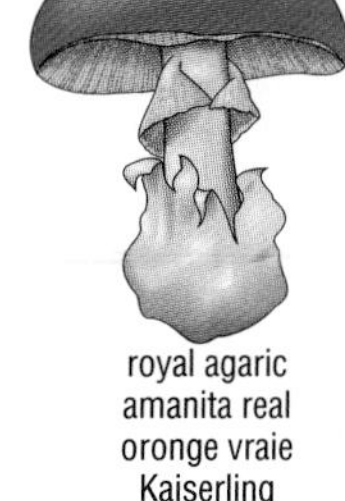
royal agaric
amanita real
oronge vraie
Kaiserling

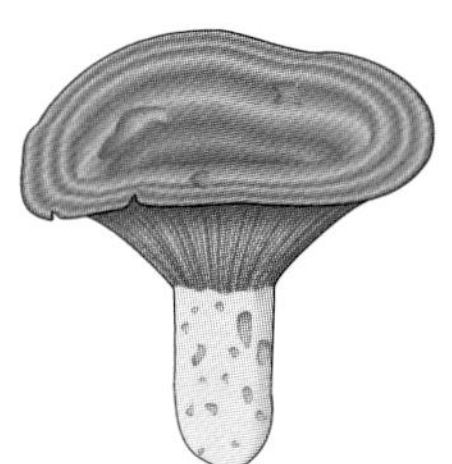
delicious lactarius
mízcalo (Lactarius deliciosus)
lactaire délicieux
echter Reizker

green russula
gorroverde
russule verdoyante
grasgrüner Täubling

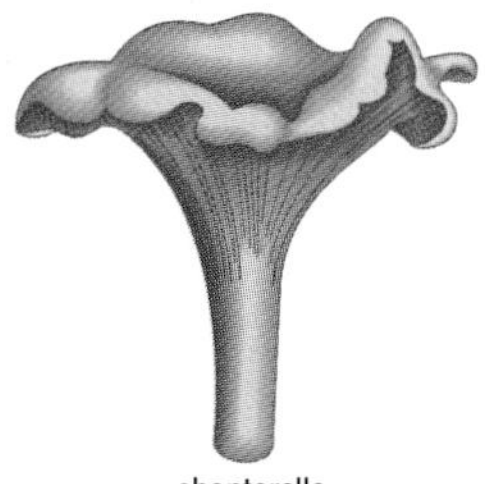
chanterelle
cantarela
chanterelle commune
Pfifferling

boletus
boleto
cèpe
Steinpilz

oyster mushroom
sabañón
pleurote en huître
Austernseitling

DEADLY POISONOUS MUSHROOM
HONGO MORTAL
CHAMPIGNON MORTEL
TÖDLICH GIFTIGER PILZ

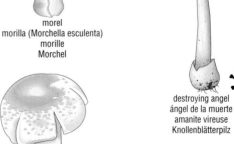

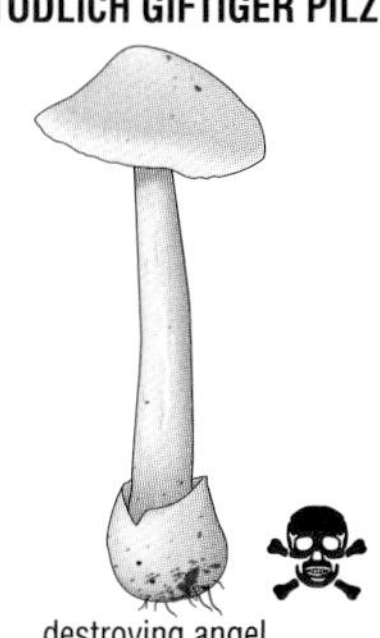
destroying angel
ángel de la muerte
amanite vireuse
Knollenblätterpilz

POISONOUS MUSHROOM
HONGO VENENOSO
CHAMPIGNON VÉNÉNEUX
GIFTPILZ

fly agaric
amanita de las moscas
fausse oronge
Fliegenpilz

TYPES OF LEAVES
LA HOJA SEGÚN SU LIMBO
TYPES DE FEUILLES
BLATTFORMEN

LEAF MARGIN
LA HOJA SEGÚN SU BORDE
BORD D'UNE FEUILLE
BLATTRAND

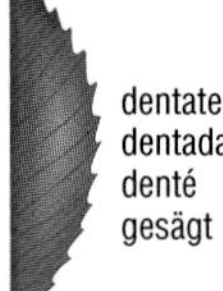

dentate
dentada
denté
gesägt

doubly dentate
bidentada
doublement denté
doppelt gesägt

crenate
festoneada
crénelé
gekerbt

ciliate
ciliada
cilié
gewimpert

entire
entera
entier
ganzrandig

lobate
lobulada
lobé
gebuchtet

COMPOUND LEAVES
HOJAS COMPUESTAS
FEUILLES COMPOSÉES
ZUSAMMENGESETZTE BLÄTTER

trifoliolate
trifoliada
trifoliée
dreizählig

palmate
palmaticompuesta
palmée
handförmig

pinnatifid
pinnatifida
pennée
fiederteilig

odd pinnate
imparipinnada
imparipennée
unpaarig gefiedert

abruptly pinnate
paripinnada
paripennée
paarig gefiedert

SIMPLE LEAVES
HOJAS SIMPLES
FEUILLES SIMPLES
EINFACHE BLÄTTER

orbiculate
orbicular
arrondie
rund

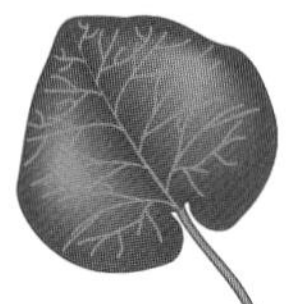

reniform
reniforme
réniforme
nierenförmig

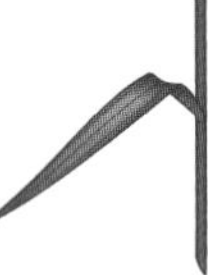

linear
aciculada
linéaire
lineal

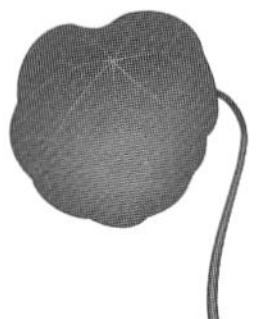

peltate
peltada
peltée
schildförmig

hastate
astada
hastée
pfeilförmig

ovate
aovada
ovoïde
eiförmig

cordate
acorazonada
cordée
herzförmig

spatulate
espatulada
spatulée
spatelförmig

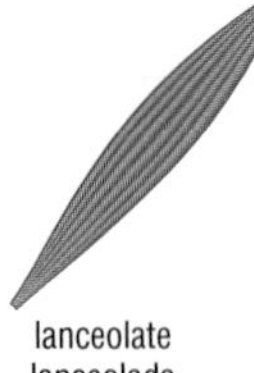

lanceolate
lanceolada
lancéolée
lanzettlich

LEAF
HOJA
FEUILLE
BLATT

stipule
estípula
stipule
Blattansatz

sheath
vaina
gaine
Blattscheide

leaf axil
axila de la hoja
point d'attache
Blattachsel

petiole
pecíolo
pétiole
Blattstiel

vein
nervadura secundaria
nervure secondaire
Blattader

midrib
nervadura principal
nervure principale
Mittelrippe

STRUCTURE OF A PLANT
ANATOMÍA DE UNA PLANTA
STRUCTURE D'UNE PLANTE
AUFBAU EINER PFLANZE

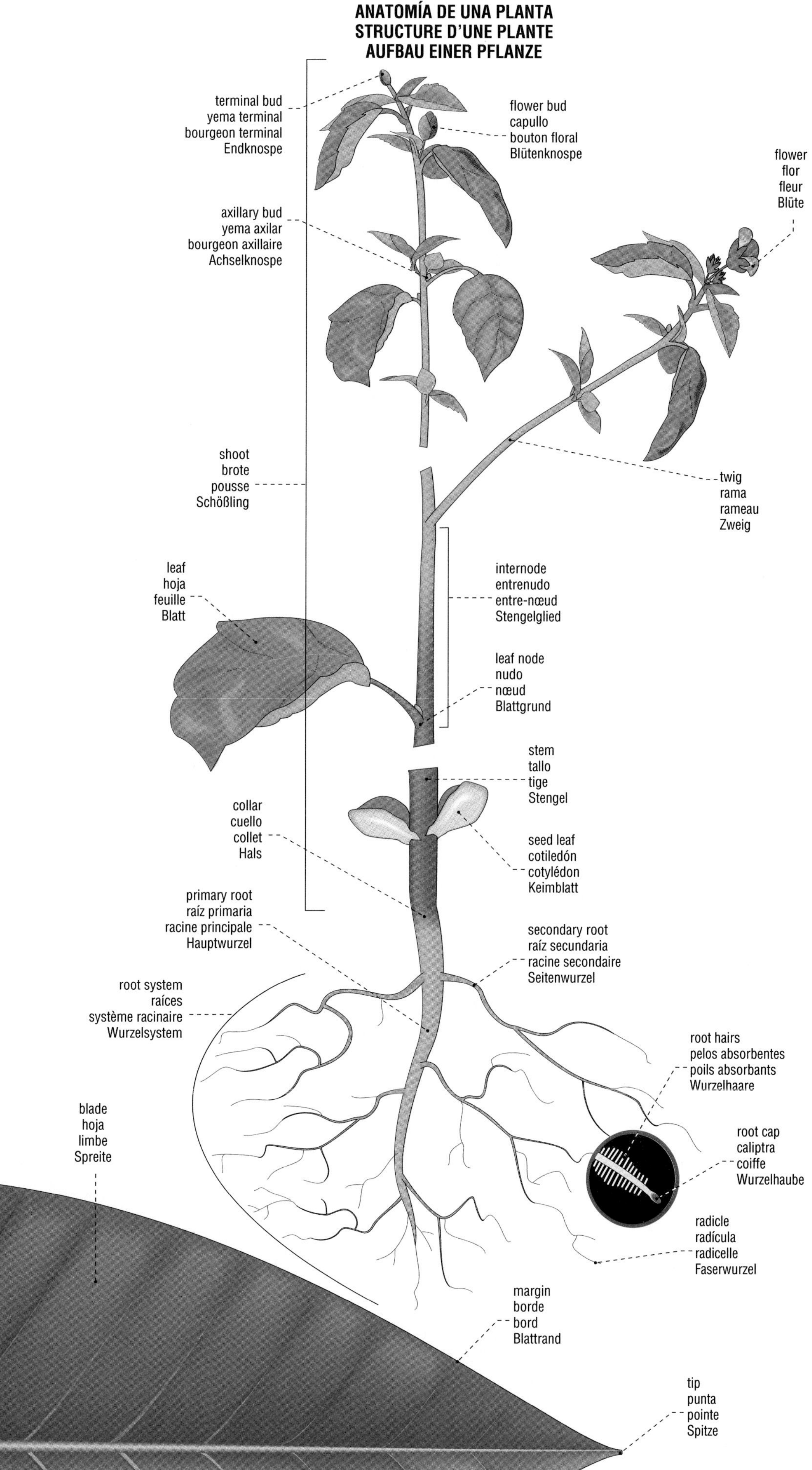
terminal bud
yema terminal
bourgeon terminal
Endknospe
flower bud
capullo
bouton floral
Blütenknospe
flower
flor
fleur
Blüte
axillary bud
yema axilar
bourgeon axillaire
Achselknospe
shoot
brote
pousse
Schößling
twig
rama
rameau
Zweig
leaf
hoja
feuille
Blatt
internode
entrenudo
entre-nœud
Stengelglied
leaf node
nudo
nœud
Blattgrund
stem
tallo
tige
Stengel
collar
cuello
collet
Hals
seed leaf
cotiledón
cotylédon
Keimblatt
primary root
raíz primaria
racine principale
Hauptwurzel
secondary root
raíz secundaria
racine secondaire
Seitenwurzel
root system
raíces
système racinaire
Wurzelsystem
root hairs
pelos absorbentes
poils absorbants
Wurzelhaare
blade
hoja
limbe
Spreite
root cap
caliptra
coiffe
Wurzelhaube
radicle
radícula
radicelle
Faserwurzel
margin
borde
bord
Blattrand
tip
punta
pointe
Spitze

CONIFER
CONÍFERA
CONIFÈRE
NADELBAUM

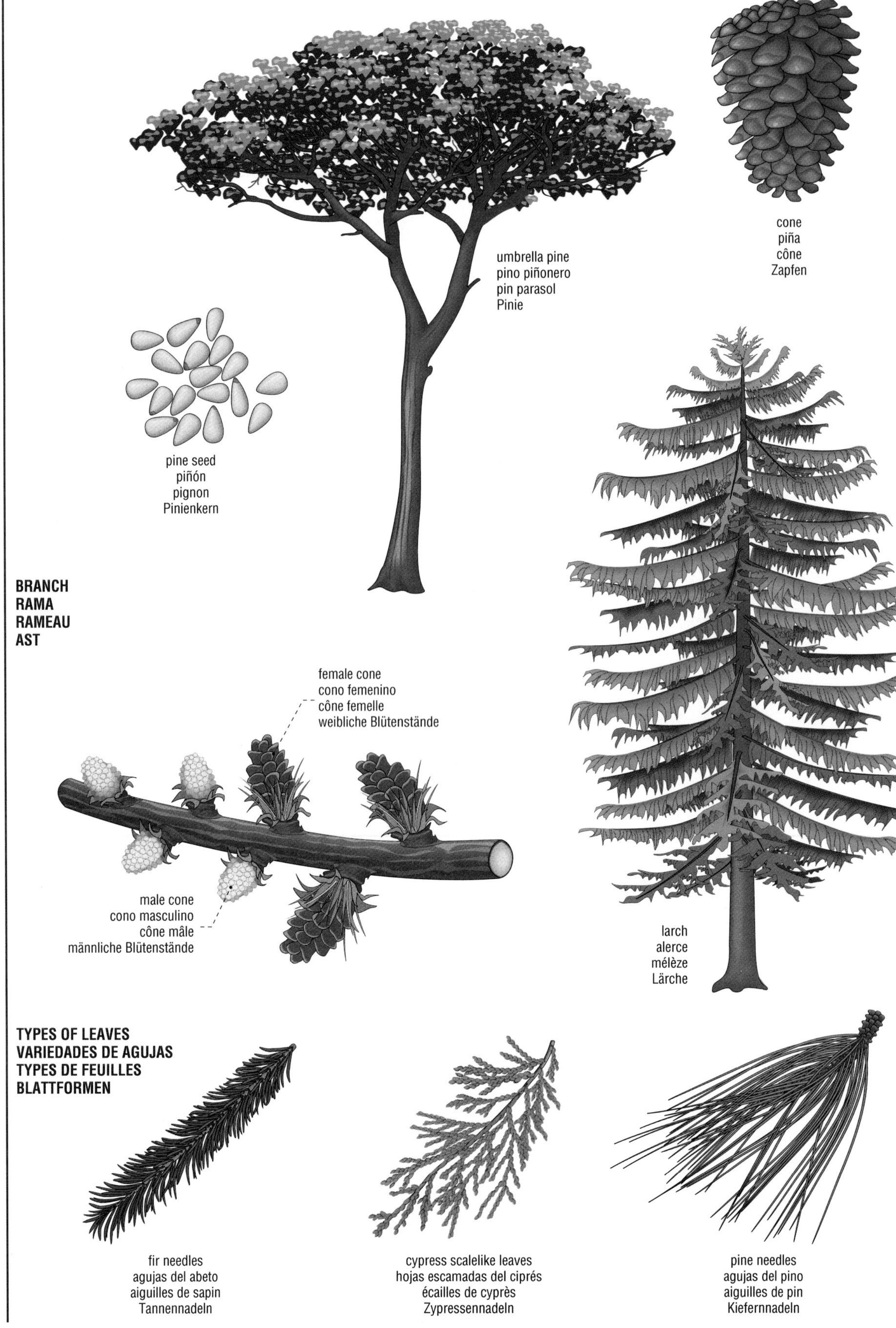
umbrella pine
pino piñonero
pin parasol
Pinie
cone
piña
cône
Zapfen
pine seed
piñón
pignon
Pinienkern
larch
alerce
mélèze
Lärche
BRANCH
RAMA
RAMEAU
AST
female cone
cono femenino
cône femelle
weibliche Blütenstände
male cone
cono masculino
cône mâle
männliche Blütenstände
TYPES OF LEAVES
VARIEDADES DE AGUJAS
TYPES DE FEUILLES
BLATTFORMEN
fir needles
agujas del abeto
aiguilles de sapin
Tannennadeln
cypress scalelike leaves
hojas escamadas del ciprés
écailles de cyprès
Zypressennadeln
pine needles
agujas del pino
aiguilles de pin
Kiefernnadeln

STRUCTURE OF A TREE
ANATOMÍA DE UN ÁRBOL
STRUCTURE D'UN ARBRE
AUFBAU EINES BAUMES

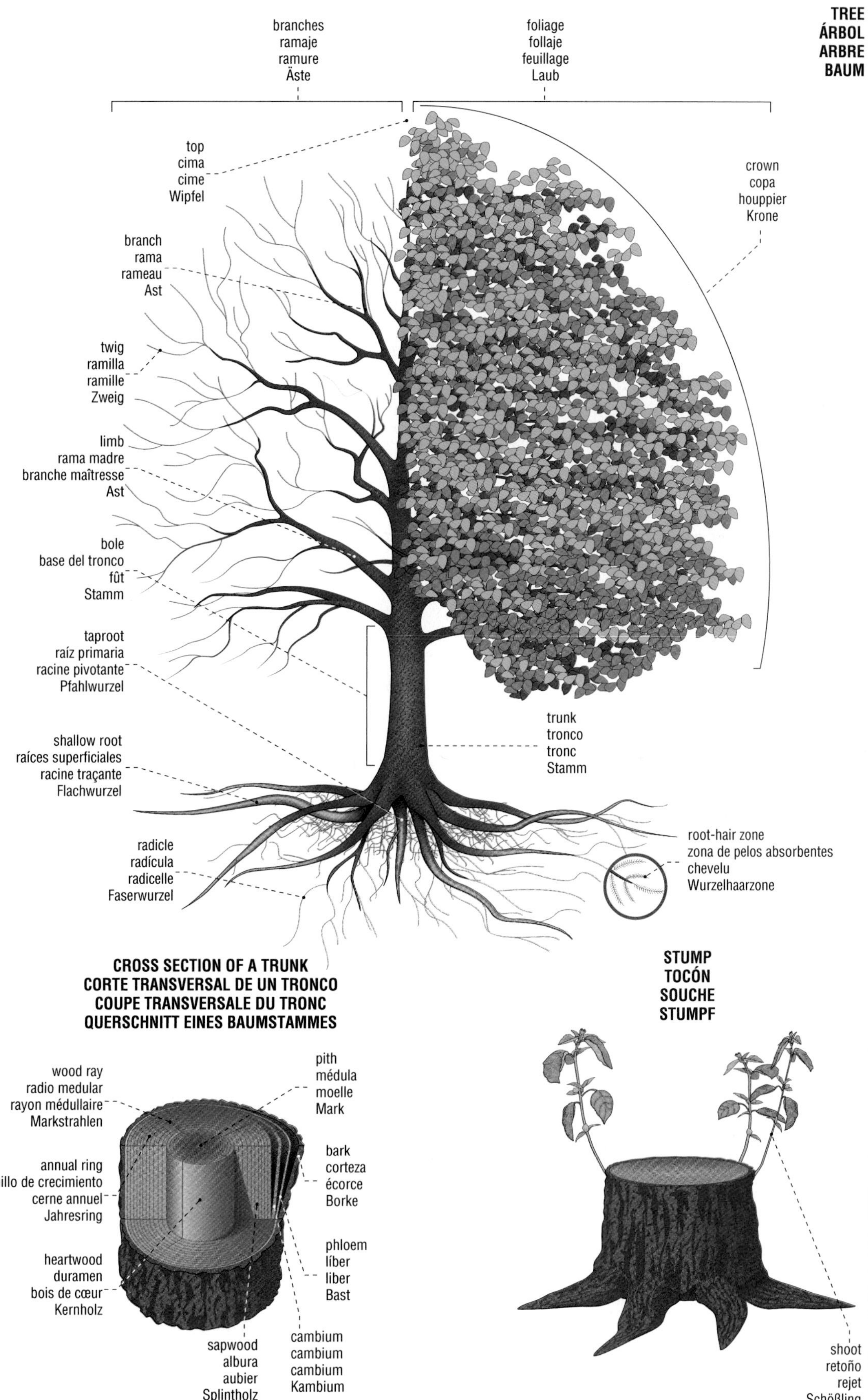
branches
ramaje
ramure
Äste
foliage
follaje
feuillage
Laub
top
cima
cime
Wipfel
crown
copa
houppier
Krone
branch
rama
rameau
Ast
twig
ramilla
ramille
Zweig
limb
rama madre
branche maîtresse
Ast
bole
base del tronco
fût
Stamm
taproot
raíz primaria
racine pivotante
Pfahlwurzel
trunk
tronco
tronc
Stamm
shallow root
raíces superficiales
racine traçante
Flachwurzel
root-hair zone
zona de pelos absorbentes
chevelu
Wurzelhaarzone
radicle
radícula
radicelle
Faserwurzel
CROSS SECTION OF A TRUNK
CORTE TRANSVERSAL DE UN TRONCO
COUPE TRANSVERSALE DU TRONC
QUERSCHNITT EINES BAUMSTAMMES
wood ray
radio medular
rayon médullaire
Markstrahlen
pith
médula
moelle
Mark
annual ring
anillo de crecimiento
cerne annuel
Jahresring
bark
corteza
écorce
Borke
heartwood
duramen
bois de cœur
Kernholz
phloem
líber
liber
Bast
sapwood
albura
aubier
Splintholz
cambium
cambium
cambium
Kambium
STUMP
TOCÓN
SOUCHE
STUMPF
shoot
retoño
rejet
Schößling

STRUCTURE OF A FLOWER
ANATOMÍA DE UNA FLOR
STRUCTURE D'UNE FLEUR
AUFBAU EINER BLÜTE

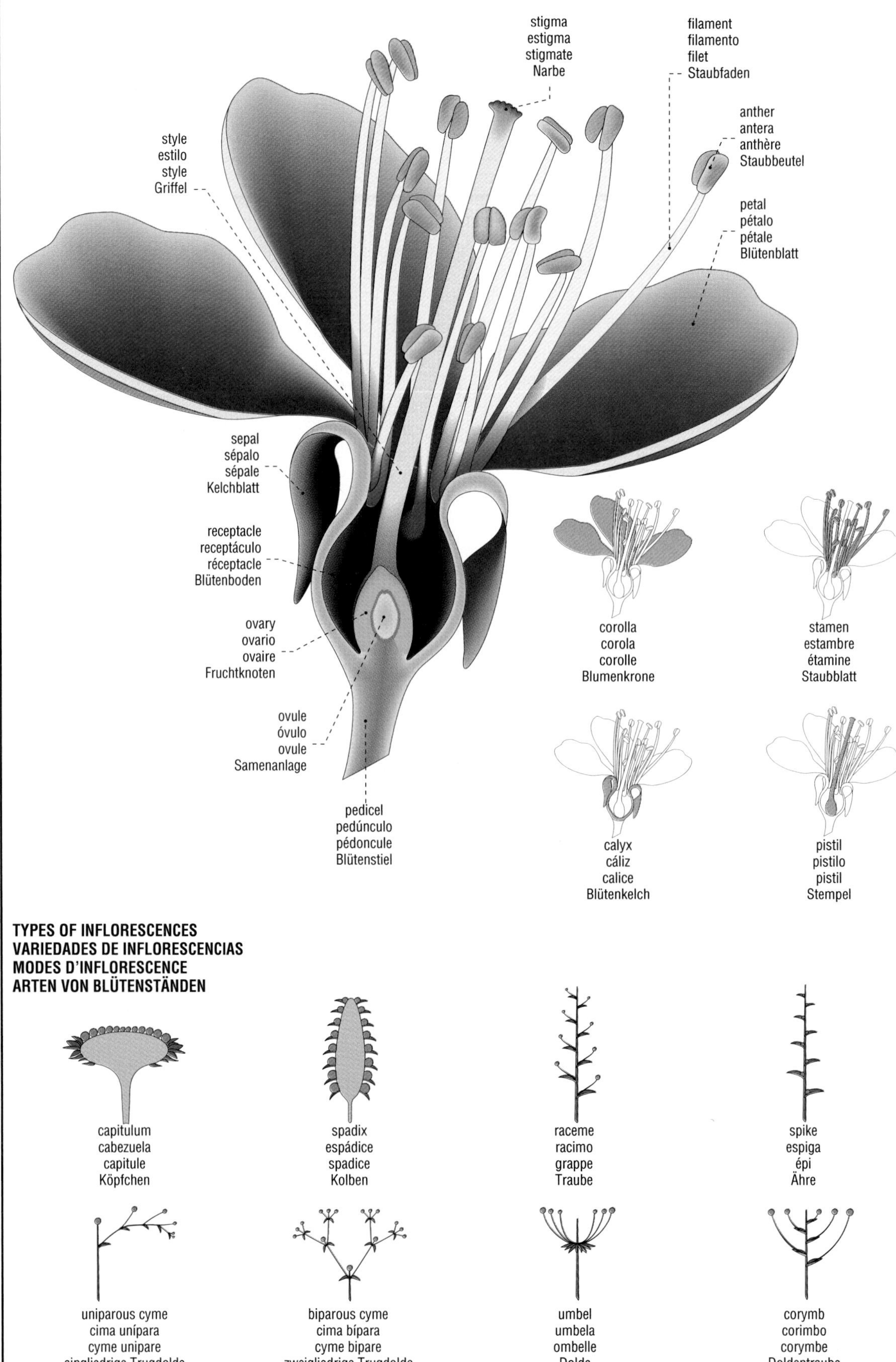
stigma
estigma
stigmate
Narbe
filament
filamento
filet
Staubfaden
anther
antera
anthère
Staubbeutel
style
estilo
style
Griffel
petal
pétalo
pétale
Blütenblatt
sepal
sépalo
sépale
Kelchblatt
receptacle
receptáculo
réceptacle
Blütenboden
ovary
ovario
ovaire
Fruchtknoten
ovule
óvulo
ovule
Samenanlage
pedicel
pedúnculo
pédoncule
Blütenstiel
corolla
corola
corolle
Blumenkrone
stamen
estambre
étamine
Staubblatt
calyx
cáliz
calice
Blütenkelch
pistil
pistilo
pistil
Stempel
TYPES OF INFLORESCENCES
VARIEDADES DE INFLORESCENCIAS
MODES D'INFLORESCENCE
ARTEN VON BLÜTENSTÄNDEN
capitulum
cabezuela
capitule
Köpfchen
spadix
espádice
spadice
Kolben
raceme
racimo
grappe
Traube
spike
espiga
épi
Ähre
uniparous cyme
cima unípara
cyme unipare
eingliedrige Trugdolde
biparous cyme
cima bípara
cyme bipare
zweigliedrige Trugdolde
umbel
umbela
ombelle
Dolde
corymb
corimbo
corymbe
Doldentraube

GRAPE
UVA
VIGNE
REBE

MATURING STEPS
ETAPAS DE LA MADURACIÓN
ÉTAPES DE MATURATION
STUFEN DER REIFE

flowering
en flor
floraison
Blüte

fruition
fructificación
nouaison
Fruchtbildung

ripening
proceso de maduración
véraison
Reifeprozeß

ripeness
maduración completa
maturité
Vollreife

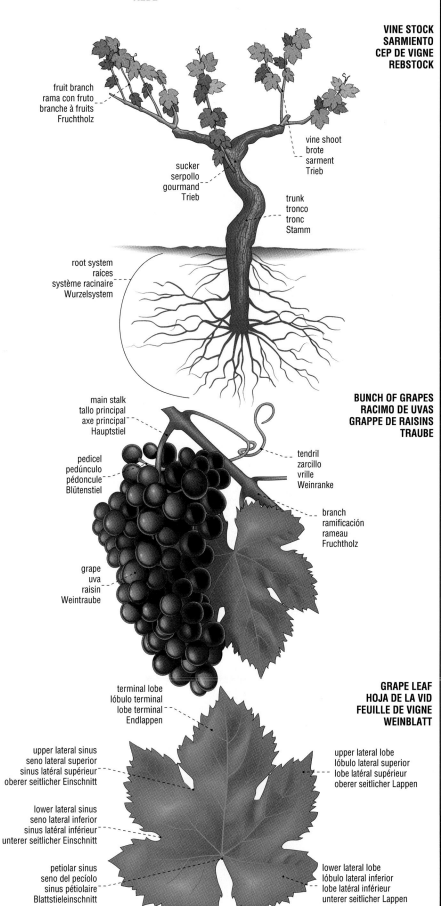

VINE STOCK
SARMIENTO
CEP DE VIGNE
REBSTOCK

fruit branch
rama con fruto
branche à fruits
Fruchtholz

vine shoot
brote
sarment
Trieb

sucker
serpollo
gourmand
Trieb

trunk
tronco
tronc
Stamm

root system
raíces
système racinaire
Wurzelsystem

BUNCH OF GRAPES
RACIMO DE UVAS
GRAPPE DE RAISINS
TRAUBE

main stalk
tallo principal
axe principal
Hauptstiel

tendril
zarcillo
vrille
Weinranke

pedicel
pedúnculo
pédoncule
Blütenstiel

branch
ramificación
rameau
Fruchtholz

grape
uva
raisin
Weintraube

GRAPE LEAF
HOJA DE LA VID
FEUILLE DE VIGNE
WEINBLATT

terminal lobe
lóbulo terminal
lobe terminal
Endlappen

upper lateral sinus
seno lateral superior
sinus latéral supérieur
oberer seitlicher Einschnitt

upper lateral lobe
lóbulo lateral superior
lobe latéral supérieur
oberer seitlicher Lappen

lower lateral sinus
seno lateral inferior
sinus latéral inférieur
unterer seitlicher Einschnitt

petiolar sinus
seno del pecíolo
sinus pétiolaire
Blattstieleinschnitt

lower lateral lobe
lóbulo lateral inferior
lobe latéral inférieur
unterer seitlicher Lappen

FLESHY FRUITS: BERRY FRUITS
FRUTOS CARNOSOS: BAYAS
FRUITS CHARNUS: BAIES
FLEISCHIGE FRÜCHTE: BEERENOBST

SECTION OF A BERRY
CORTE DE UNA BAYA
COUPE D'UNE BAIE
QUERSCHNITT EINER BEERE

GRAPE
UVA
RAISIN
WEINTRAUBE

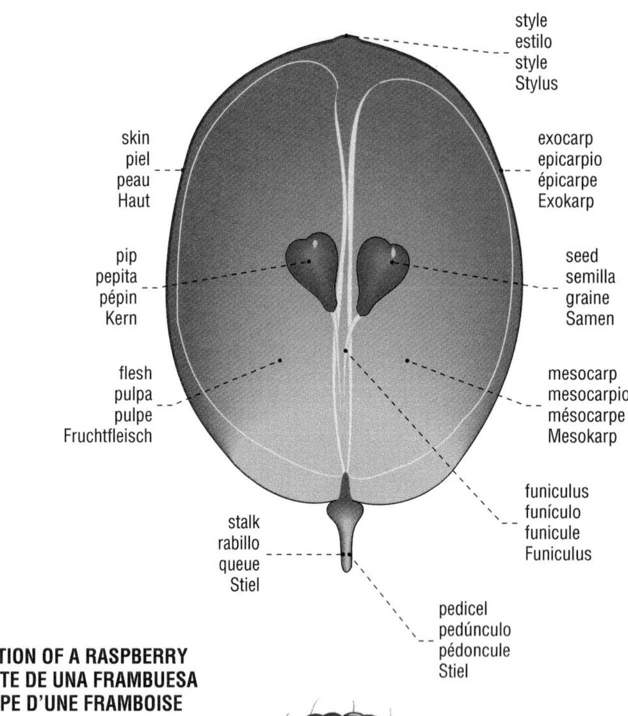
usual terms
términos familiares
termes familiers
gebräuchliche Bezeichnungen
technical terms
términos técnicos
termes techniques
wissenschaftliche Bezeichnungen
style
estilo
style
Stylus
skin
piel
peau
Haut
exocarp
epicarpio
épicarpe
Exokarp
pip
pepita
pépin
Kern
seed
semilla
graine
Samen
flesh
pulpa
pulpe
Fruchtfleisch
mesocarp
mesocarpio
mésocarpe
Mesokarp
funiculus
funículo
funicule
Funiculus
stalk
rabillo
queue
Stiel
pedicel
pedúnculo
pédoncule
Stiel

SECTION OF A RASPBERRY
CORTE DE UNA FRAMBUESA
COUPE D'UNE FRAMBOISE
QUERSCHNITT EINER HIMBEERE

seed
semilla
graine
Samen
drupelet
drupéolo
drupéole
Steinfrüchtchen
receptacle
receptáculo
réceptacle
Blütenboden
sepal
sépalo
sépale
Kelchblatt
pedicel
pedúnculo
pédoncule
Stiel

SECTION OF A STRAWBERRY
CORTE DE UNA FRESA
COUPE D'UNE FRAISE
QUERSCHNITT EINER ERDBEERE

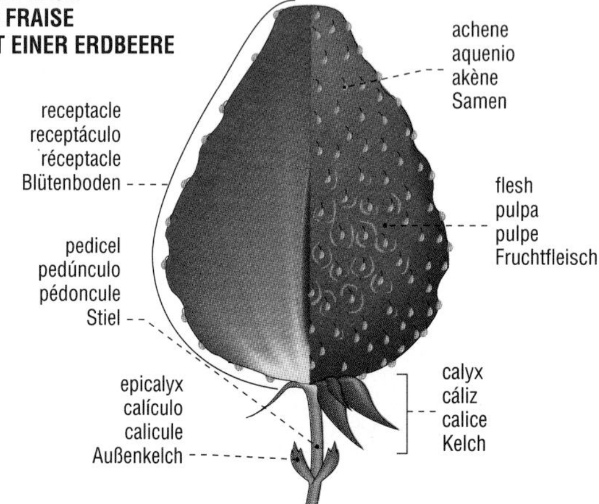
achene
aquenio
akène
Samen
receptacle
receptáculo
réceptacle
Blütenboden
flesh
pulpa
pulpe
Fruchtfleisch
pedicel
pedúnculo
pédoncule
Stiel
epicalyx
calículo
calicule
Außenkelch
calyx
cáliz
calice
Kelch

MAJOR TYPES OF BERRIES
PRINCIPALES VARIEDADES DE BAYAS
PRINCIPALES VARIÉTÉS DE BAIES
DIE WICHTIGSTEN BEERENARTEN

black currant
grosella negra
cassis
schwarze Johannisbeere

currant
grosella
groseille à grappes
Johannisbeere

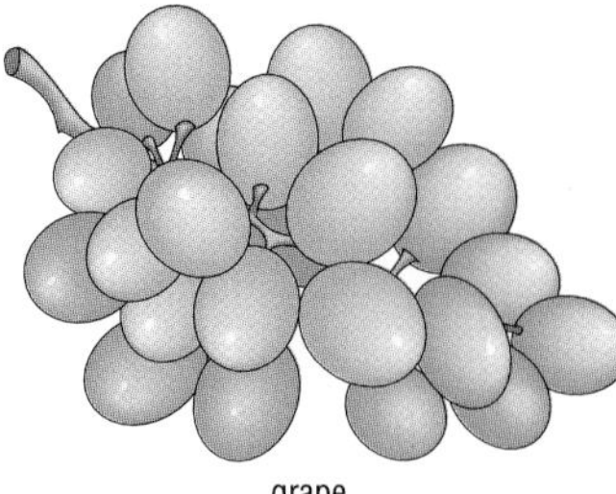
grape
uva
raisin
Weintraube

gooseberry
grosella espinosa
groseille à maquereau
Stachelbeere

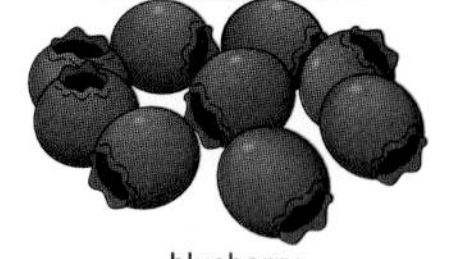
blueberry
arándano
myrtille
Heidelbeere

huckleberry
ráspano
airelle
amerikanische Heidelbeere

cranberry
arándano agrio
canneberge
Preiselbeere

STONE FLESHY FRUITS
FRUTOS CARNOSOS CON HUESO
FRUITS CHARNUS À NOYAU
STEINOBST

SECTION OF A STONE FRUIT
CORTE DE UN FRUTO CARNOSO CON HUESO
COUPE D'UN FRUIT À NOYAU
QUERSCHNITT EINER STEINFRUCHT

PEACH
MELOCOTÓN
PÊCHE
PFIRSICH

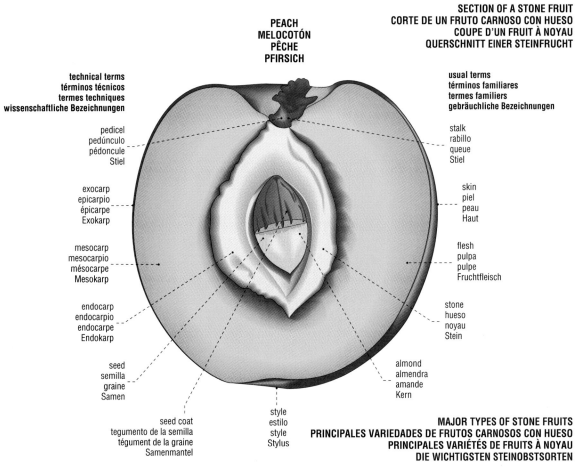

technical terms **términos técnicos** **termes techniques** **wissenschaftliche Bezeichnungen**	**usual terms** **términos familiares** **termes familiers** **gebräuchliche Bezeichnungen**
pedicel pedúnculo pédoncule Stiel	stalk rabillo queue Stiel
exocarp epicarpio épicarpe Exokarp	skin piel peau Haut
mesocarp mesocarpio mésocarpe Mesokarp	flesh pulpa pulpe Fruchtfleisch
endocarp endocarpio endocarpe Endokarp	stone hueso noyau Stein
seed semilla graine Samen	almond almendra amande Kern
seed coat tegumento de la semilla tégument de la graine Samenmantel	

style
estilo
style
Stylus

MAJOR TYPES OF STONE FRUITS
PRINCIPALES VARIEDADES DE FRUTOS CARNOSOS CON HUESO
PRINCIPALES VARIÉTÉS DE FRUITS À NOYAU
DIE WICHTIGSTEN STEINOBSTSORTEN

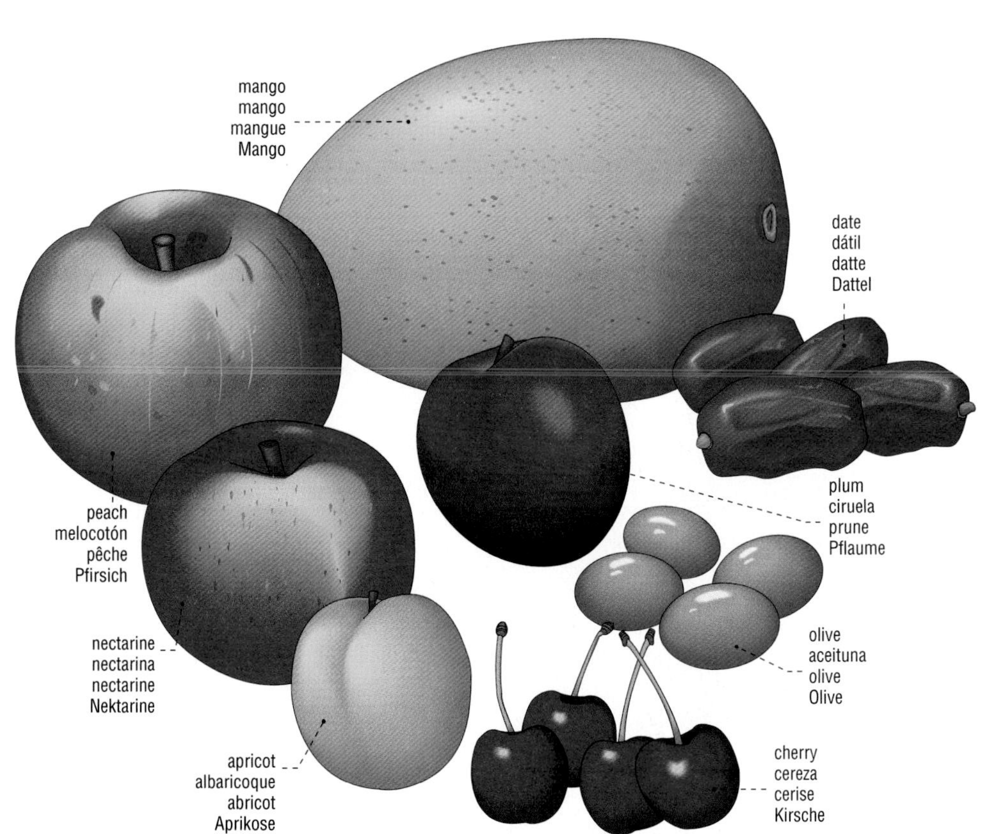
mango
mango
mangue
Mango
date
dátil
datte
Dattel
peach
melocotón
pêche
Pfirsich
plum
ciruela
prune
Pflaume
nectarine
nectarina
nectarine
Nektarine
olive
aceituna
olive
Olive
apricot
albaricoque
abricot
Aprikose
cherry
cereza
cerise
Kirsche

POME FLESHY FRUITS
FRUTOS CARNOSOS CON SEMILLAS
FRUITS CHARNUS À PÉPINS
KERNOBST

SECTION OF A POME FRUIT
CORTE DE UN FRUTO CARNOSO CON SEMILLAS
COUPE D'UN FRUIT À PÉPINS
QUERSCHNITT EINER KERNFRUCHT

MAJOR TYPES OF POME FRUITS
PRINCIPALES VARIEDADES DE FRUTOS CARNOSOS CON SEMILLAS
PRINCIPALES VARIÉTÉS DE FRUITS À PÉPINS
DIE WICHTIGSTEN KERNOBSTSORTEN

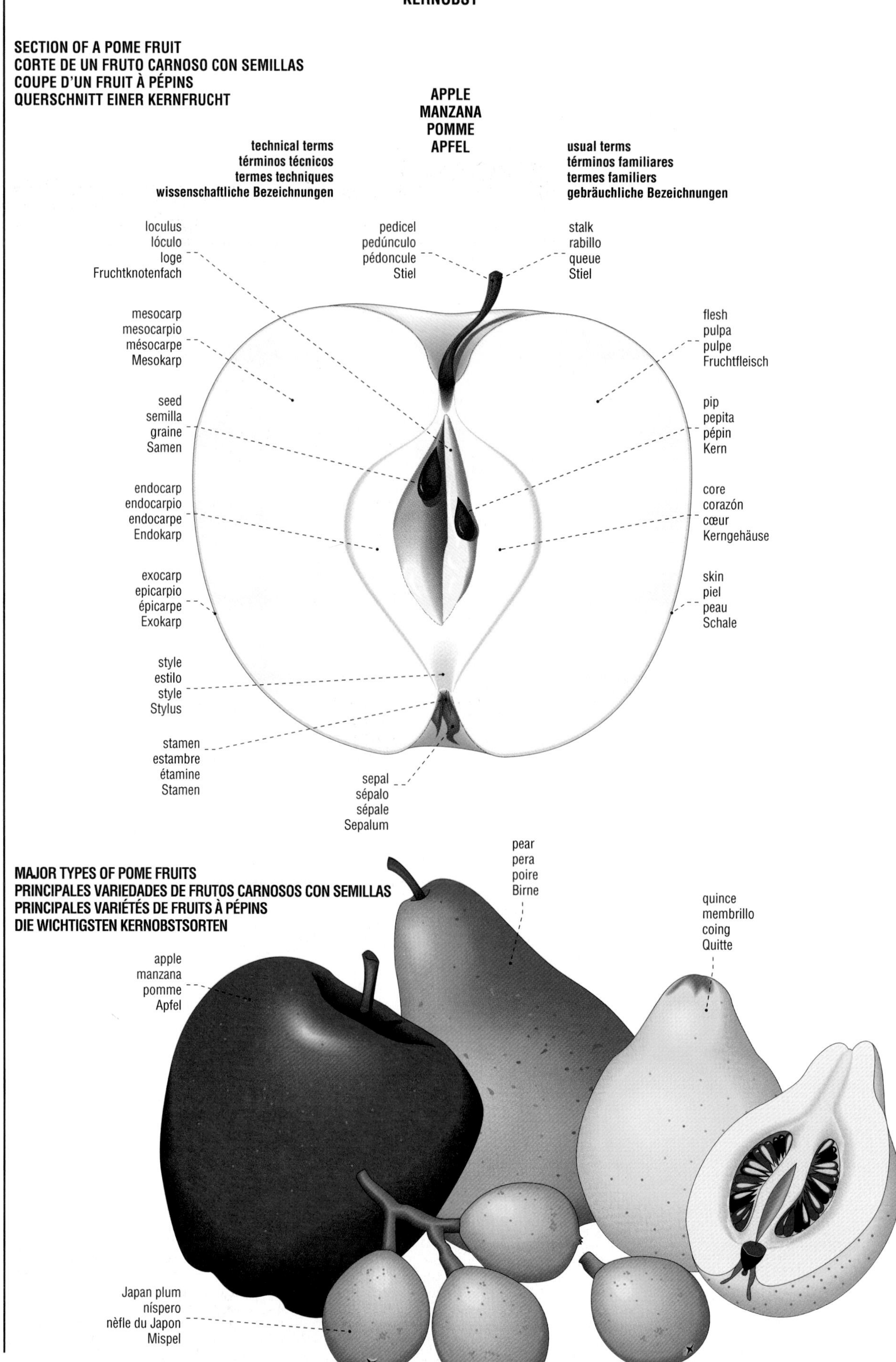
APPLE
MANZANA
POMME
APFEL
technical terms
términos técnicos
termes techniques
wissenschaftliche Bezeichnungen
usual terms
términos familiares
termes familiers
gebräuchliche Bezeichnungen
loculus
lóculo
loge
Fruchtknotenfach
pedicel
pedúnculo
pédoncule
Stiel
stalk
rabillo
queue
Stiel
mesocarp
mesocarpio
mésocarpe
Mesokarp
flesh
pulpa
pulpe
Fruchtfleisch
seed
semilla
graine
Samen
pip
pepita
pépin
Kern
endocarp
endocarpio
endocarpe
Endokarp
core
corazón
cœur
Kerngehäuse
exocarp
epicarpio
épicarpe
Exokarp
skin
piel
peau
Schale
style
estilo
style
Stylus
stamen
estambre
étamine
Stamen
sepal
sépalo
sépale
Sepalum
pear
pera
poire
Birne
quince
membrillo
coing
Quitte
apple
manzana
pomme
Apfel
Japan plum
níspero
nèfle du Japon
Mispel

FLESHY FRUITS: CITRUS FRUITS
FRUTOS CARNOSOS: CÍTRICOS
FRUITS CHARNUS: AGRUMES
FLEISCHIGE FRÜCHTE: ZITRUSFRÜCHTE

SECTION OF A CITRUS FRUIT
CORTE DE UN CÍTRICO
COUPE D'UN AGRUME
QUERSCHNITT EINER ZITRUSFRUCHT

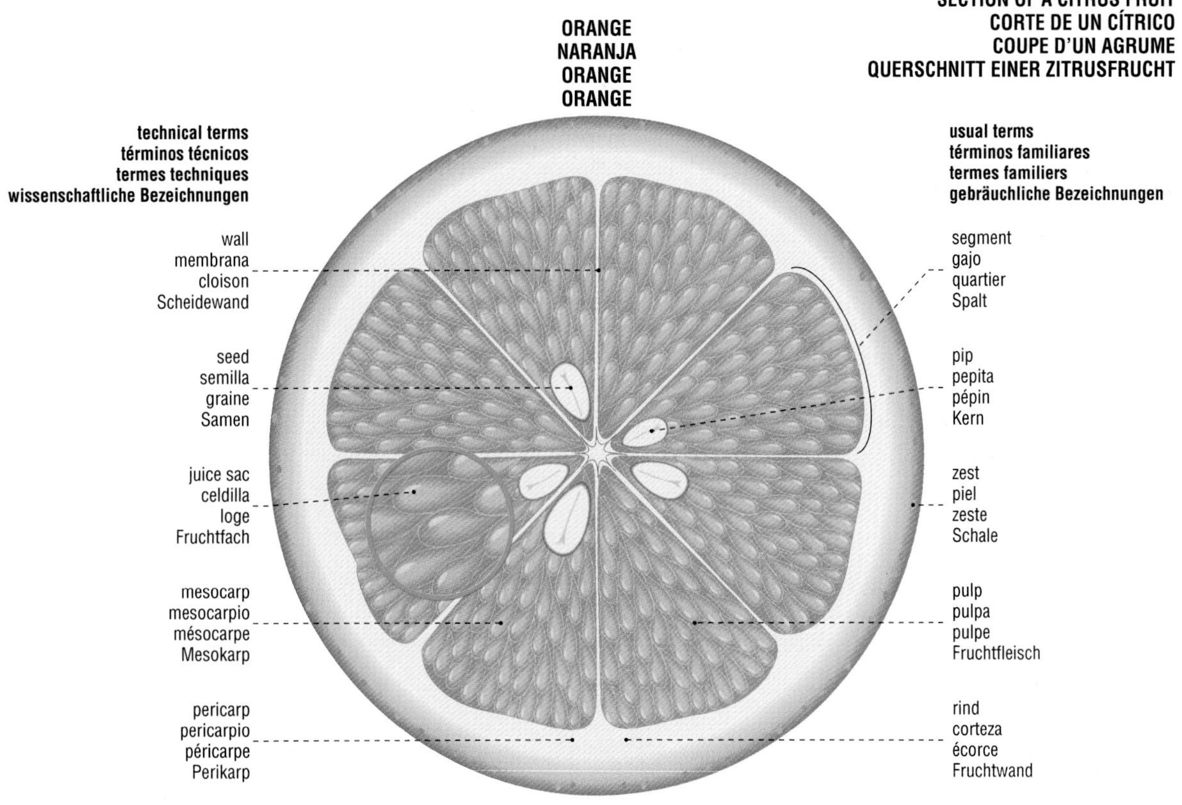
ORANGE
NARANJA
ORANGE
ORANGE
technical terms
términos técnicos
termes techniques
wissenschaftliche Bezeichnungen
usual terms
términos familiares
termes familiers
gebräuchliche Bezeichnungen
wall
membrana
cloison
Scheidewand
segment
gajo
quartier
Spalt
seed
semilla
graine
Samen
pip
pepita
pépin
Kern
juice sac
celdilla
loge
Fruchtfach
zest
piel
zeste
Schale
mesocarp
mesocarpio
mésocarpe
Mesokarp
pulp
pulpa
pulpe
Fruchtfleisch
pericarp
pericarpio
péricarpe
Perikarp
rind
corteza
écorce
Fruchtwand

MAJOR TYPES OF CITRUS FRUITS
PRINCIPALES VARIEDADES DE CÍTRICOS
PRINCIPALES VARIÉTÉS D'AGRUMES
DIE WICHTIGSTEN ZITRUSFRÜCHTE

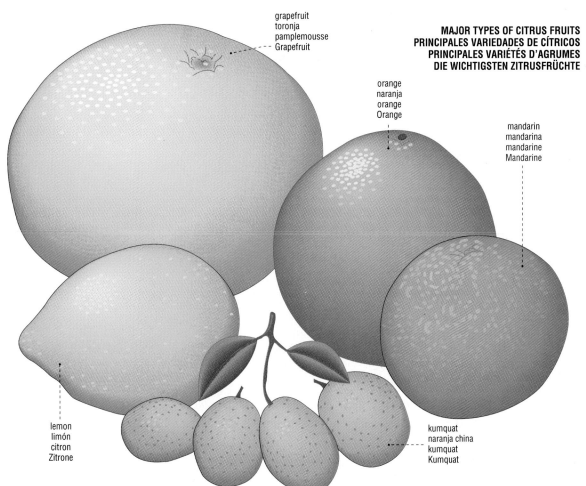

grapefruit
toronja
pamplemousse
Grapefruit

orange
naranja
orange
Orange

mandarin
mandarina
mandarine
Mandarine

lemon
limón
citron
Zitrone

kumquat
naranja china
kumquat
Kumquat

DRY FRUITS: NUTS
FRUTOS SECOS: OLEAGINOSOS
FRUITS SECS: NOIX
TROCKENFRÜCHTE: NÜSSE

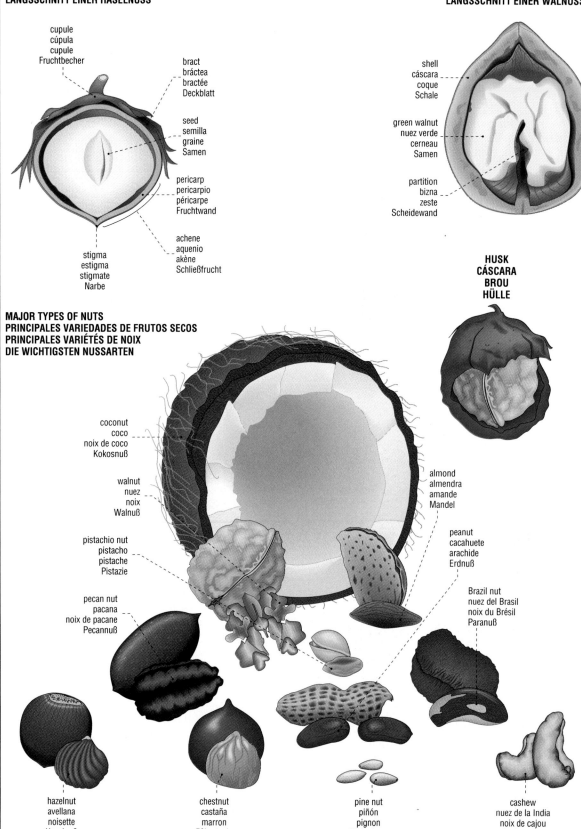

SECTION OF A HAZELNUT
CORTE DE UNA AVELLANA
COUPE D'UNE NOISETTE
LÄNGSSCHNITT EINER HASELNUSS

cupule
cúpula
cupule
Fruchtbecher

bract
bráctea
bractée
Deckblatt

seed
semilla
graine
Samen

pericarp
pericarpio
péricarpe
Fruchtwand

achene
aquenio
akène
Schließfrucht

stigma
estigma
stigmate
Narbe

SECTION OF A WALNUT
CORTE DE UNA NUEZ
COUPE D'UNE NOIX
LÄNGSSCHNITT EINER WALNUSS

shell
cáscara
coque
Schale

green walnut
nuez verde
cerneau
Samen

partition
bizna
zeste
Scheidewand

HUSK
CÁSCARA
BROU
HÜLLE

MAJOR TYPES OF NUTS
PRINCIPALES VARIEDADES DE FRUTOS SECOS
PRINCIPALES VARIÉTÉS DE NOIX
DIE WICHTIGSTEN NUSSARTEN

coconut
coco
noix de coco
Kokosnuß

walnut
nuez
noix
Walnuß

pistachio nut
pistacho
pistache
Pistazie

pecan nut
pacana
noix de pacane
Pecannuß

almond
almendra
amande
Mandel

peanut
cacahuete
arachide
Erdnuß

Brazil nut
nuez del Brasil
noix du Brésil
Paranuß

hazelnut
avellana
noisette
Haselnuß

chestnut
castaña
marron
Eßkastanie

pine nut
piñón
pignon
Pinienkern

cashew
nuez de la India
noix de cajou
Cashewkern

VARIOUS DRY FRUITS
FRUTOS SECOS: DEHISCENTES
FRUITS SECS DIVERS
VERSCHIEDENE TROCKENFRÜCHTE

SECTION OF A FOLLICLE
CORTE DE UN FOLÍCULO
COUPE D'UN FOLLICULE
QUERSCHNITT EINER FRUCHTKAPSEL

star anise
anís estrellado
anis étoilé
Sternanis

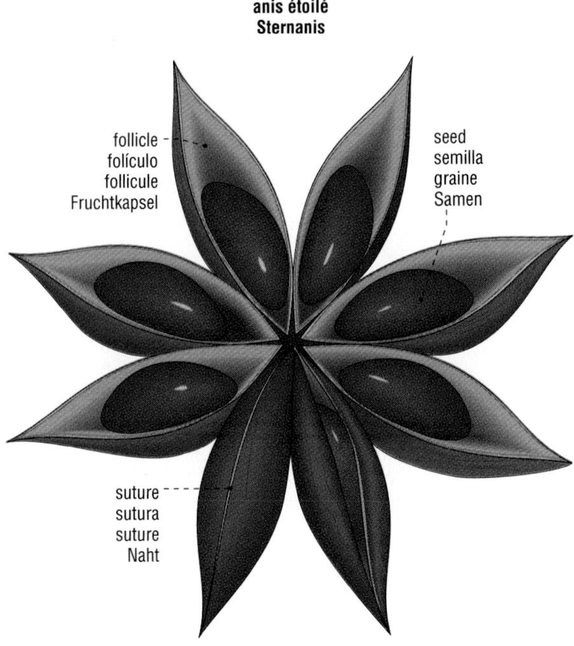
follicle
folículo
follicule
Fruchtkapsel
seed
semilla
graine
Samen
suture
sutura
suture
Naht

SECTION OF A SILIQUE
CORTE DE UNA SILICUA
COUPE D'UNE SILIQUE
LÄNGSSCHNITT EINER FRUCHTSCHOTE

mustard
mostaza
moutarde
Senf

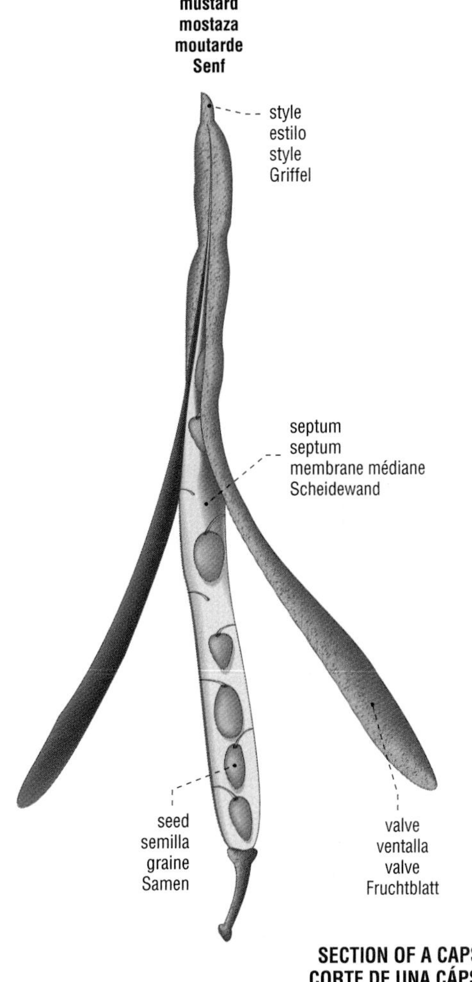
style
estilo
style
Griffel
septum
septum
membrane médiane
Scheidewand
seed
semilla
graine
Samen
valve
ventalla
valve
Fruchtblatt

SECTION OF A LEGUME
CORTE DE UNA LEGUMBRE
COUPE D'UNE GOUSSE
LÄNGSSCHNITT EINER HÜLSENFRUCHT

pea
guisante
pois
Erbsenschote

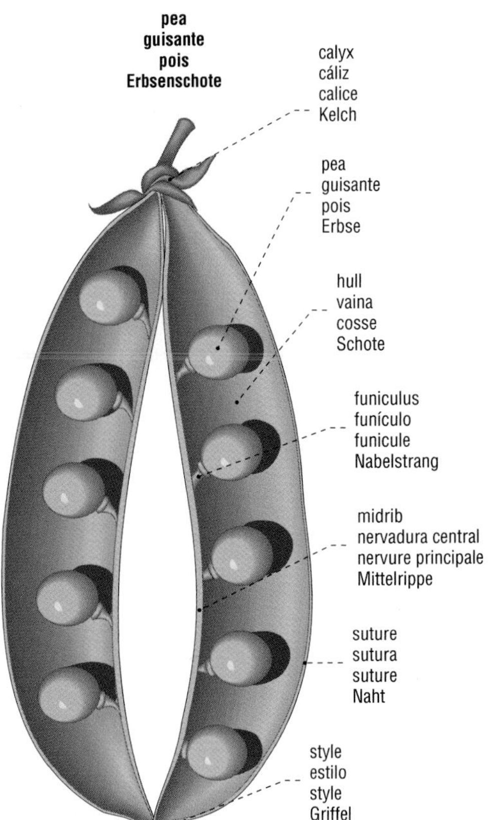
calyx
cáliz
calice
Kelch
pea
guisante
pois
Erbse
hull
vaina
cosse
Schote
funiculus
funículo
funicule
Nabelstrang
midrib
nervadura central
nervure principale
Mittelrippe
suture
sutura
suture
Naht
style
estilo
style
Griffel

SECTION OF A CAPSULE
CORTE DE UNA CÁPSULA
COUPE D'UNE CAPSULE
LÄNGSSCHNITT EINER KAPSEL

poppy
amapola
pavot
Mohn

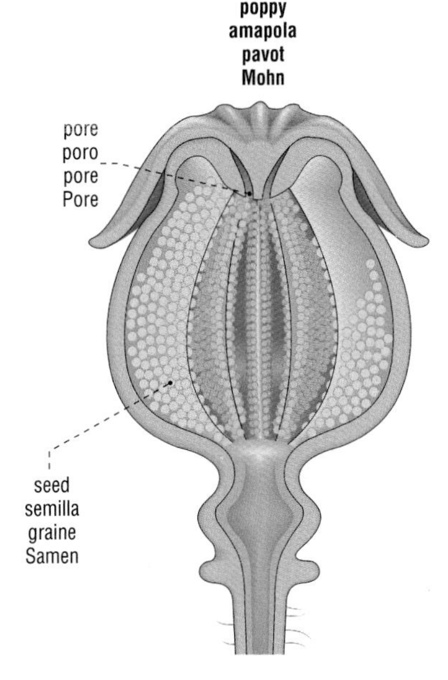
pore
poro
pore
Pore
seed
semilla
graine
Samen

TROPICAL FRUITS
FRUTAS TROPICALES
FRUITS TROPICAUX
SÜDFRÜCHTE

MAJOR TYPES OF TROPICAL FRUITS
PRINCIPALES VARIEDADES DE FRUTAS TROPICALES
PRINCIPAUX FRUITS TROPICAUX
DIE WICHTIGSTEN SÜDFRÜCHTE

litchi
litchi
litchi
Litschi
Japanese persimmon
caqui
kaki
Kaki
papaya
papaya
papaye
Papaya
kiwi
kiwi
kiwi
Kiwi
banana
plátano
banane
Banane
pomegranate
granada
grenade
Granatapfel
cherimoya
chirimoya
chérimole
Chirimoya
Indian fig
higo chumbo
figue de Barbarie
Kaktusfeige
avocado
aguacate
avocat
Avocado
guava
guayaba
goyave
Guave
pineapple
piña
ananas
Ananas

VEGETABLES
HORTALIZAS
LÉGUMES
GEMÜSE

FRUIT VEGETABLES
FRUTOS
LÉGUMES FRUITS
FRUCHTGEMÜSE

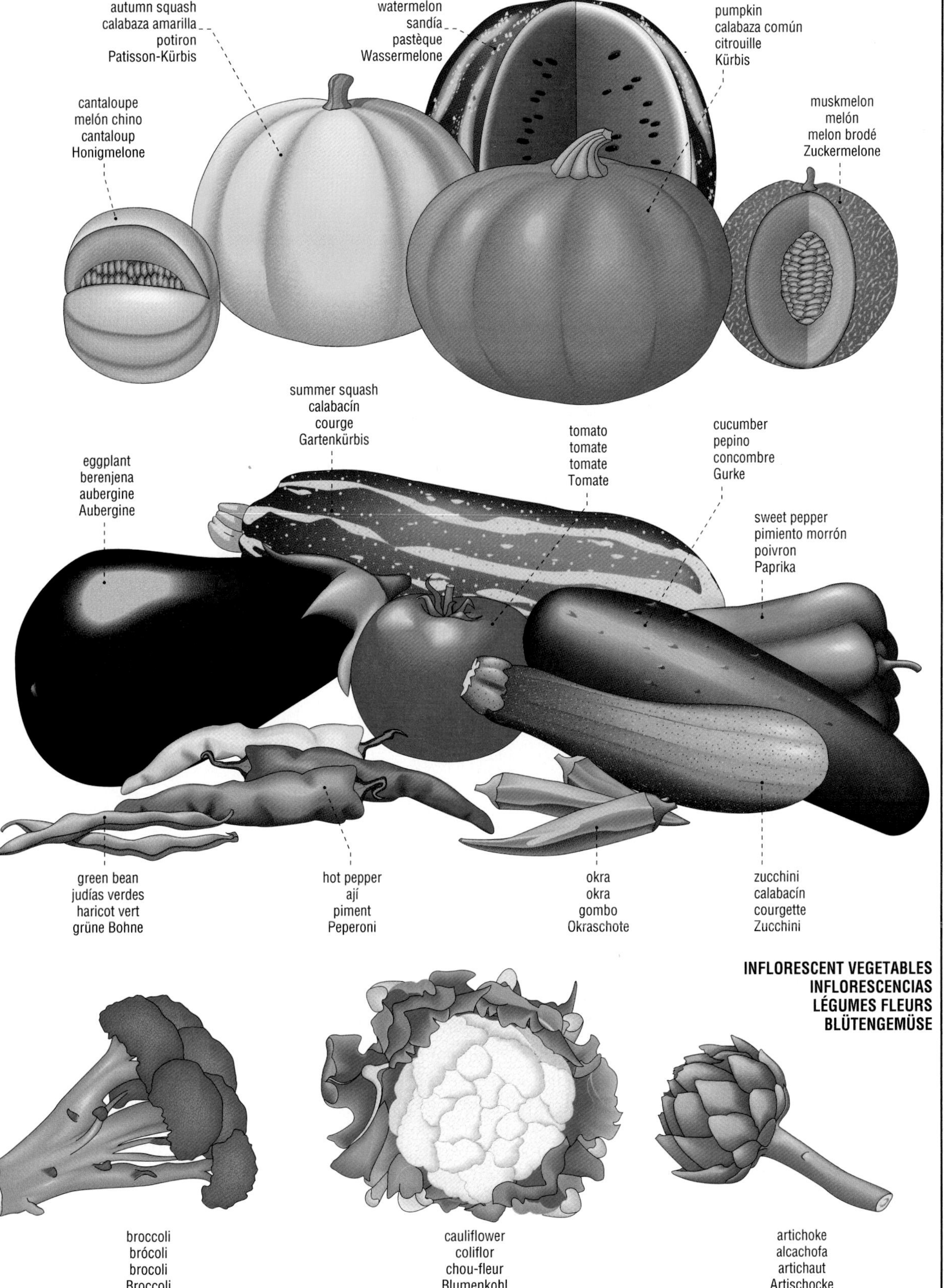
autumn squash
calabaza amarilla
potiron
Patisson-Kürbis
watermelon
sandía
pastèque
Wassermelone
pumpkin
calabaza común
citrouille
Kürbis
cantaloupe
melón chino
cantaloup
Honigmelone
muskmelon
melón
melon brodé
Zuckermelone
summer squash
calabacín
courge
Gartenkürbis
eggplant
berenjena
aubergine
Aubergine
tomato
tomate
tomate
Tomate
cucumber
pepino
concombre
Gurke
sweet pepper
pimiento morrón
poivron
Paprika
green bean
judías verdes
haricot vert
grüne Bohne
hot pepper
ají
piment
Peperoni
okra
okra
gombo
Okraschote
zucchini
calabacín
courgette
Zucchini

INFLORESCENT VEGETABLES
INFLORESCENCIAS
LÉGUMES FLEURS
BLÜTENGEMÜSE

broccoli
brócoli
brocoli
Broccoli

cauliflower
coliflor
chou-fleur
Blumenkohl

artichoke
alcachofa
artichaut
Artischocke

VEGETABLES
HORTALIZAS
LÉGUMES
GEMÜSE

SECTION OF A BULB
CORTE DE UN BULBO
COUPE D'UN BULBE
LÄNGSSCHNITT EINER ZWIEBEL

BULB VEGETABLES
BULBOS
LÉGUMES BULBES
ZWIEBELGEMÜSE

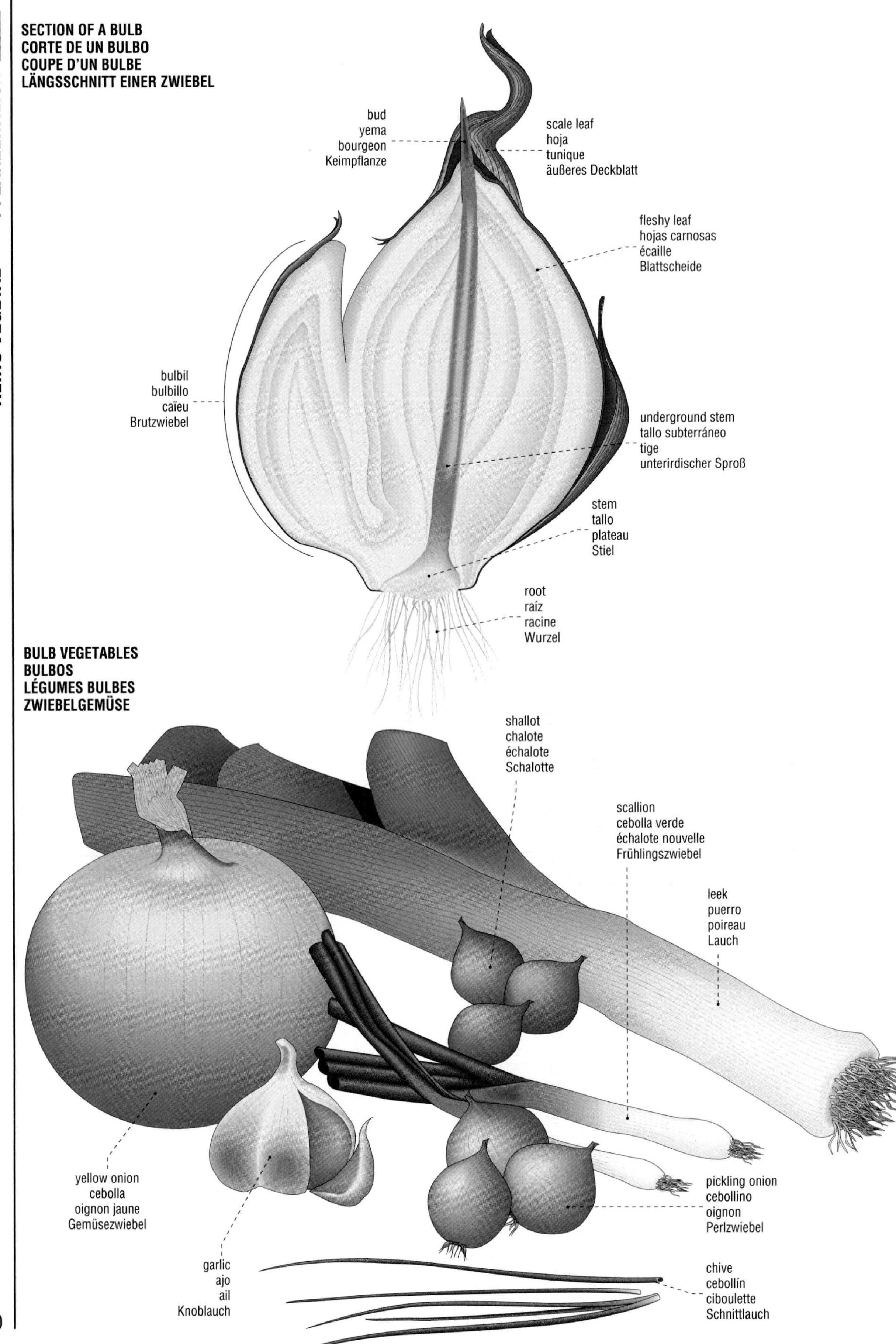
bud
yema
bourgeon
Keimpflanze
scale leaf
hoja
tunique
äußeres Deckblatt
fleshy leaf
hojas carnosas
écaille
Blattscheide
bulbil
bulbillo
caïeu
Brutzwiebel
underground stem
tallo subterráneo
tige
unterirdischer Sproß
stem
tallo
plateau
Stiel
root
raíz
racine
Wurzel
shallot
chalote
échalote
Schalotte
scallion
cebolla verde
échalote nouvelle
Frühlingszwiebel
leek
puerro
poireau
Lauch
yellow onion
cebolla
oignon jaune
Gemüsezwiebel
pickling onion
cebollino
oignon
Perlzwiebel
garlic
ajo
ail
Knoblauch
chive
cebollín
ciboulette
Schnittlauch

VEGETABLES
HORTALIZAS
LÉGUMES
GEMÜSE

TUBER VEGETABLES
TUBÉRCULOS
LÉGUMES TUBERCULES
KNOLLENGEMÜSE

ROOT VEGETABLES
RAÍCES
LÉGUMES RACINES
WURZELGEMÜSE

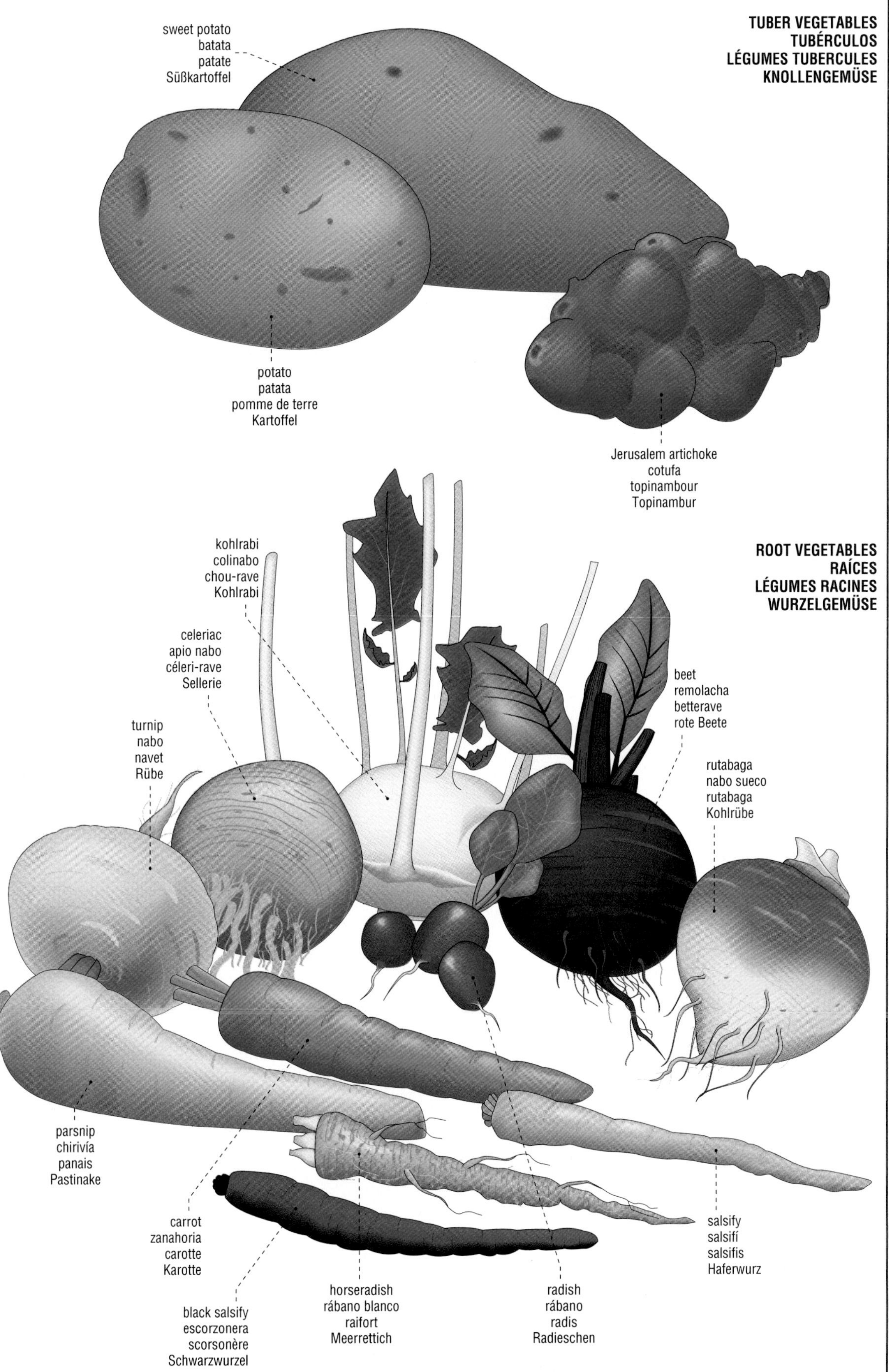
sweet potato
batata
patate
Süßkartoffel
potato
patata
pomme de terre
Kartoffel
Jerusalem artichoke
cotufa
topinambour
Topinambur
kohlrabi
colinabo
chou-rave
Kohlrabi
celeriac
apio nabo
céleri-rave
Sellerie
turnip
nabo
navet
Rübe
beet
remolacha
betterave
rote Beete
rutabaga
nabo sueco
rutabaga
Kohlrübe
parsnip
chirivía
panais
Pastinake
carrot
zanahoria
carotte
Karotte
black salsify
escorzonera
scorsonère
Schwarzwurzel
horseradish
rábano blanco
raifort
Meerrettich
radish
rábano
radis
Radieschen
salsify
salsifí
salsifis
Haferwurz

VEGETABLES
HORTALIZAS
LÉGUMES
GEMÜSE

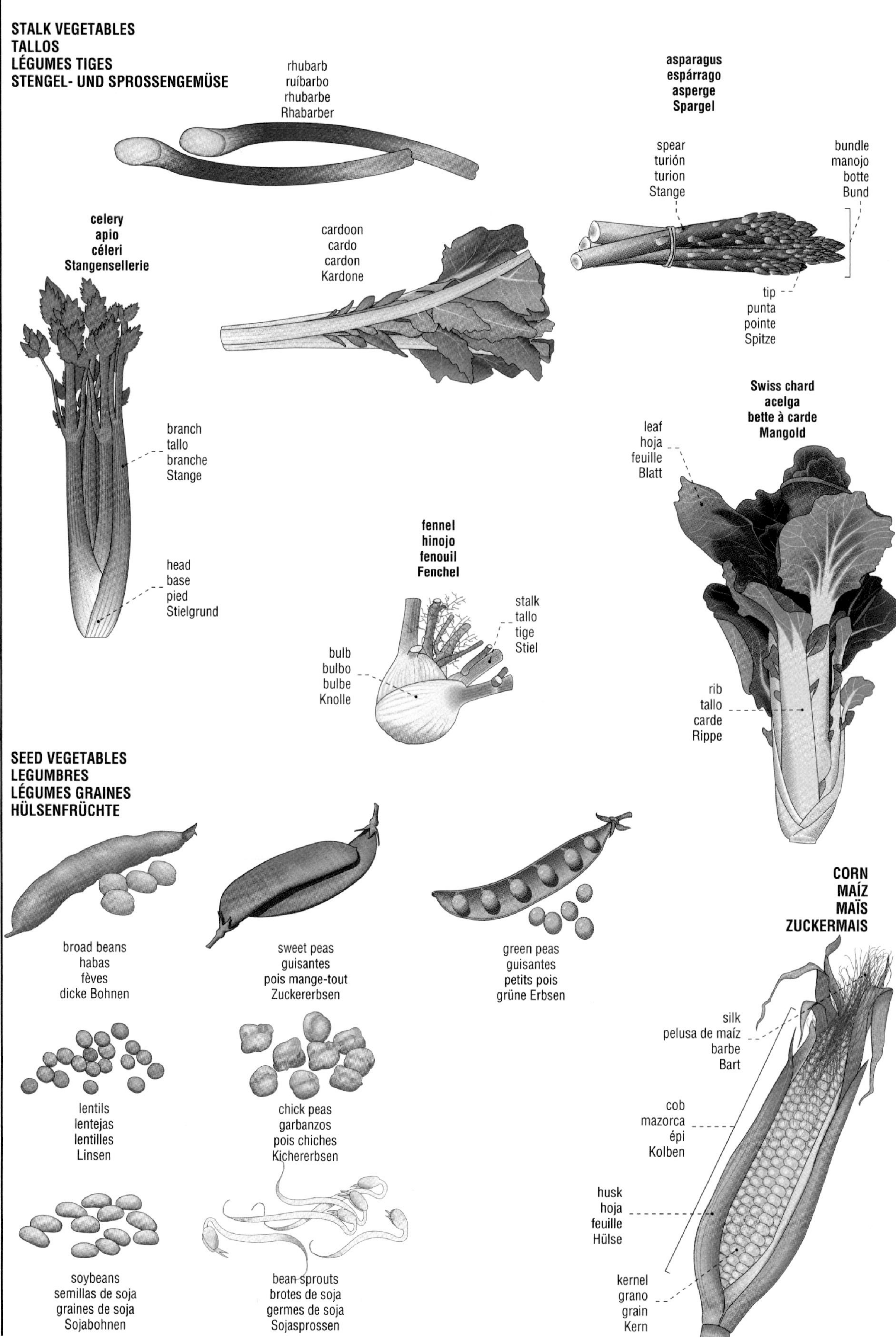
STALK VEGETABLES
TALLOS
LÉGUMES TIGES
STENGEL- UND SPROSSENGEMÜSE
rhubarb
ruíbarbo
rhubarbe
Rhabarber
asparagus
espárrago
asperge
Spargel
spear
turión
turion
Stange
bundle
manojo
botte
Bund
tip
punta
pointe
Spitze
celery
apio
céleri
Stangensellerie
cardoon
cardo
cardon
Kardone
branch
tallo
branche
Stange
head
base
pied
Stielgrund
Swiss chard
acelga
bette à carde
Mangold
leaf
hoja
feuille
Blatt
fennel
hinojo
fenouil
Fenchel
stalk
tallo
tige
Stiel
bulb
bulbo
bulbe
Knolle
rib
tallo
carde
Rippe
SEED VEGETABLES
LEGUMBRES
LÉGUMES GRAINES
HÜLSENFRÜCHTE
broad beans
habas
fèves
dicke Bohnen
sweet peas
guisantes
pois mange-tout
Zuckererbsen
green peas
guisantes
petits pois
grüne Erbsen
CORN
MAÍZ
MAÏS
ZUCKERMAIS
silk
pelusa de maíz
barbe
Bart
lentils
lentejas
lentilles
Linsen
chick peas
garbanzos
pois chiches
Kichererbsen
cob
mazorca
épi
Kolben
husk
hoja
feuille
Hülse
soybeans
semillas de soja
graines de soja
Sojabohnen
bean sprouts
brotes de soja
germes de soja
Sojasprossen
kernel
grano
grain
Kern

VEGETABLES
HORTALIZAS
LÉGUMES
GEMÜSE

LEAF VEGETABLES
VERDURAS DE HOJAS
LÉGUMES FEUILLES
BLATTGEMÜSE

corn salad
colleja
mâche
Feldsalat

watercress
berro
cresson de fontaine
Brunnenkresse

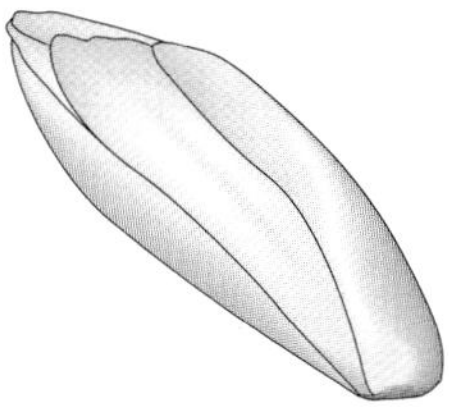

chicory
achicoria
endive
Chicorée

Brussels sprouts
coles de Bruselas
choux de Bruxelles
Rosenkohl

curled kale
col rizada
chou frisé
Grünkohl

grape leaf
hoja de parra
feuille de vigne
Weinblatt

garden sorrel
acedera
oseille
Garten-Sauerampfer

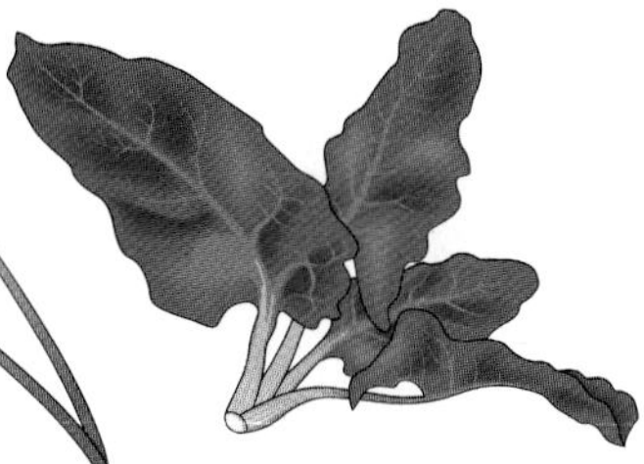

spinach
espinaca
épinard
Spinat

curled endive
escarola rizada
chicorée
krause Endivie

broad-leaved endive
escarola
scarole
glatte Endivie

romaine lettuce
lechuga romana
romaine
Romagna-Salat

dandelion
diente de león
pissenlit
Löwenzahn

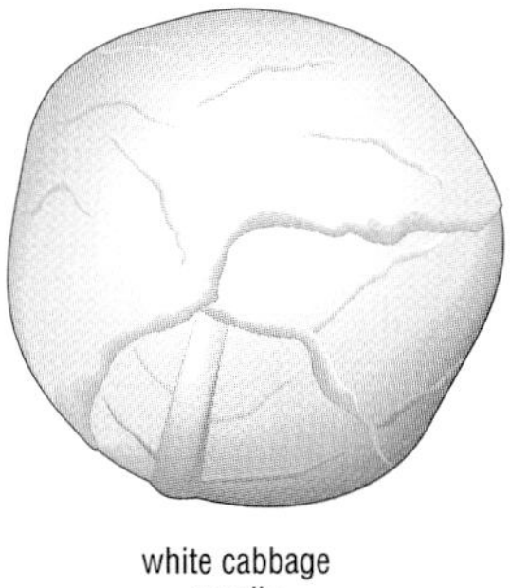

white cabbage
repollo
chou pommé blanc
Weißkohl

cabbage lettuce
lechuga francesa
laitue pommée
Kopfsalat

green cabbage
repollo verde
chou pommé vert
Kohl

Chinese cabbage
col de China
chou chinois
Chinakohl

HERBS
HIERBAS AROMÁTICAS
FINES HERBES
KRÄUTER

dill
eneldo
aneth
Dill

basil
albahaca
basilic
Basilikum

borage
borraja
bourrache
Boretsch

chervil
perifollo
cerfeuil
Kerbel

coriander
cilantro
coriandre
Koriander

tarragon
estragón
estragon
Estragon

hyssop
hisopo
hysope
Ysop

sweet bay
laurel
laurier
Lorbeer

lovage
ligústico
livèche
Liebstöckel

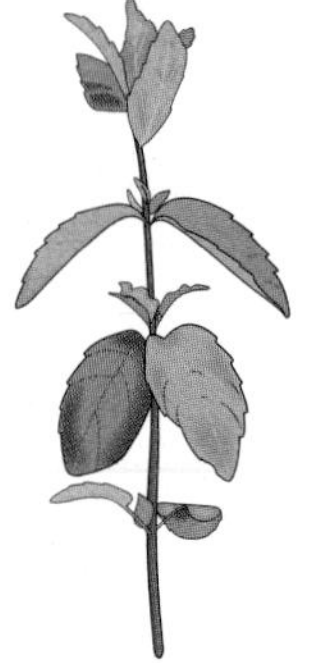
mint
hierbabuena
menthe
Minze

oregano
orégano
origan
Oregano

parsley
perejil
persil
Petersilie

rosemary
romero
romarin
Rosmarin

savory
ajedrea
sarriette
Bohnenkraut

sage
salvia
sauge
Salbei

thyme
tomillo
thym
Thymian

ANIMAL KINGDOM
RÈGNE ANIMAL
REINO ANIMAL
TIERREICH

CONTENTS

INSECTS AND SPIDER
INSECTOS Y ARAÑA
INSECTES ET ARAIGNÉE
INSEKTEN UND SPINNE

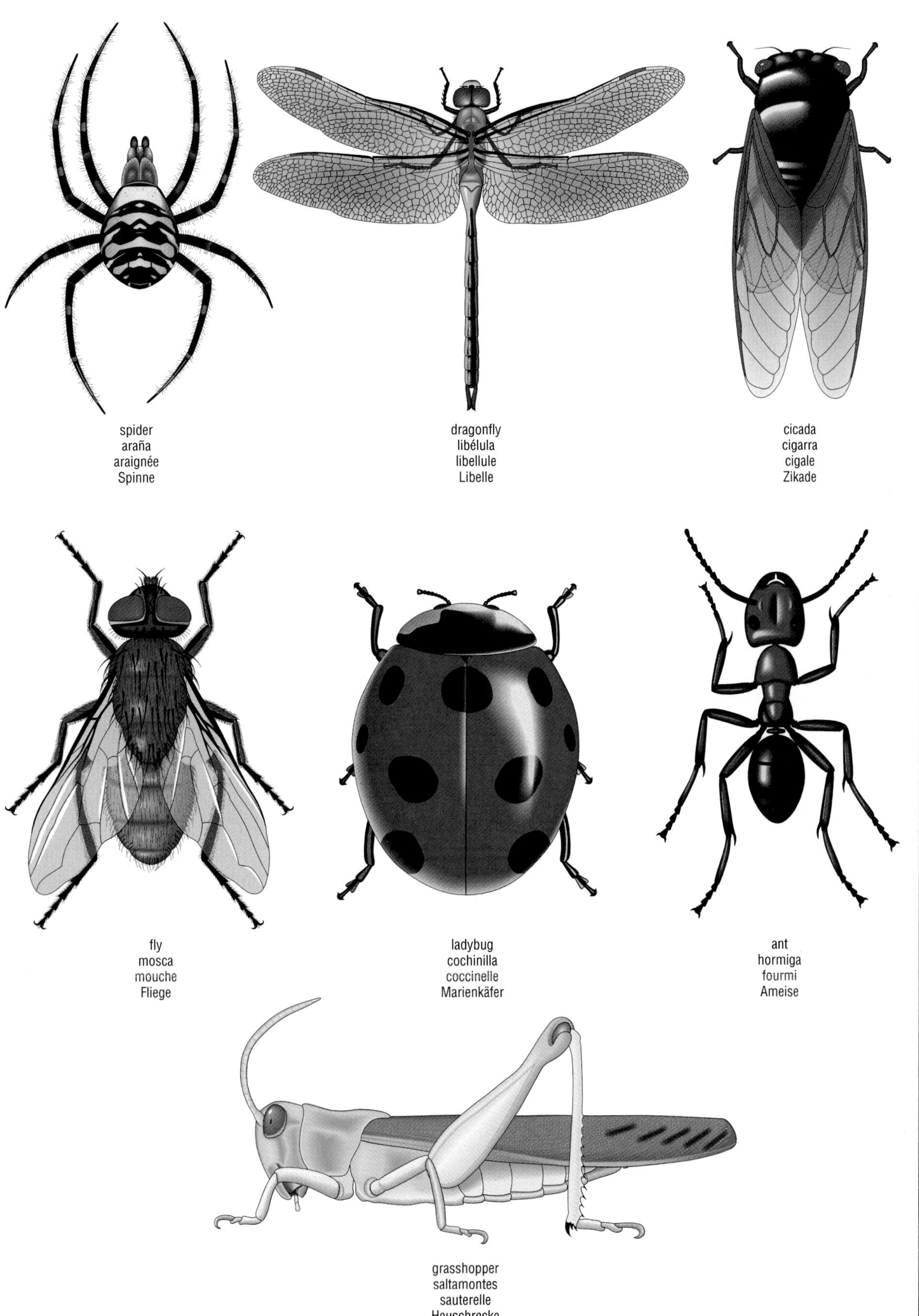

spider
araña
araignée
Spinne

dragonfly
libélula
libellule
Libelle

cicada
cigarra
cigale
Zikade

fly
mosca
mouche
Fliege

ladybug
cochinilla
coccinelle
Marienkäfer

ant
hormiga
fourmi
Ameise

grasshopper
saltamontes
sauterelle
Heuschrecke

BUTTERFLY
MARIPOSA
PAPILLON
SCHMETTERLING

CATERPILLAR
ORUGA
CHENILLE
RAUPE

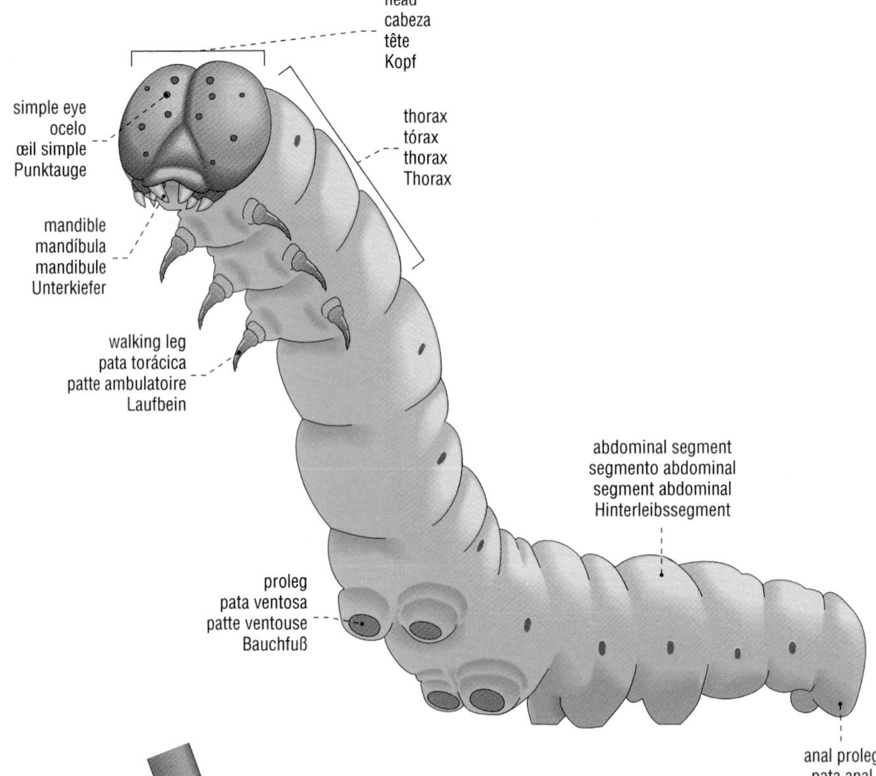
head
cabeza
tête
Kopf
simple eye
ocelo
œil simple
Punktauge
thorax
tórax
thorax
Thorax
mandible
mandíbula
mandibule
Unterkiefer
walking leg
pata torácica
patte ambulatoire
Laufbein
abdominal segment
segmento abdominal
segment abdominal
Hinterleibssegment
proleg
pata ventosa
patte ventouse
Bauchfuß
anal proleg
pata anal
patte anale
Analfuß

CHRYSALIS
CRISÁLIDA
CHRYSALIDE
PUPPE

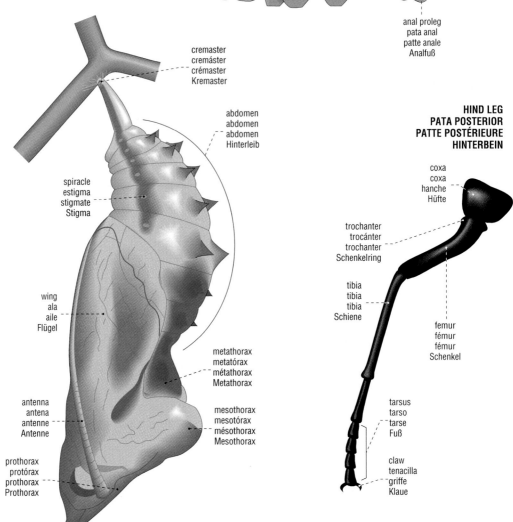

cremaster
cremáster
crémaster
Kremaster

abdomen
abdomen
abdomen
Hinterleib

spiracle
estigma
stigmate
Stigma

wing
ala
aile
Flügel

metathorax
metatórax
méthathorax
Metathorax

antenna
antena
antenne
Antenne

mesothorax
mesotórax
mésothorax
Mesothorax

prothorax
protórax
prothorax
Prothorax

HIND LEG
PATA POSTERIOR
PATTE POSTÉRIEURE
HINTERBEIN

coxa
coxa
hanche
Hüfte

trochanter
trocánter
trochanter
Schenkelring

tibia
tibia
tibia
Schiene

femur
fémur
fémur
Schenkel

tarsus
tarso
tarse
Fuß

claw
tenacilla
griffe
Klaue

BUTTERFLY
MARIPOSA
PAPILLON
SCHMETTERLING

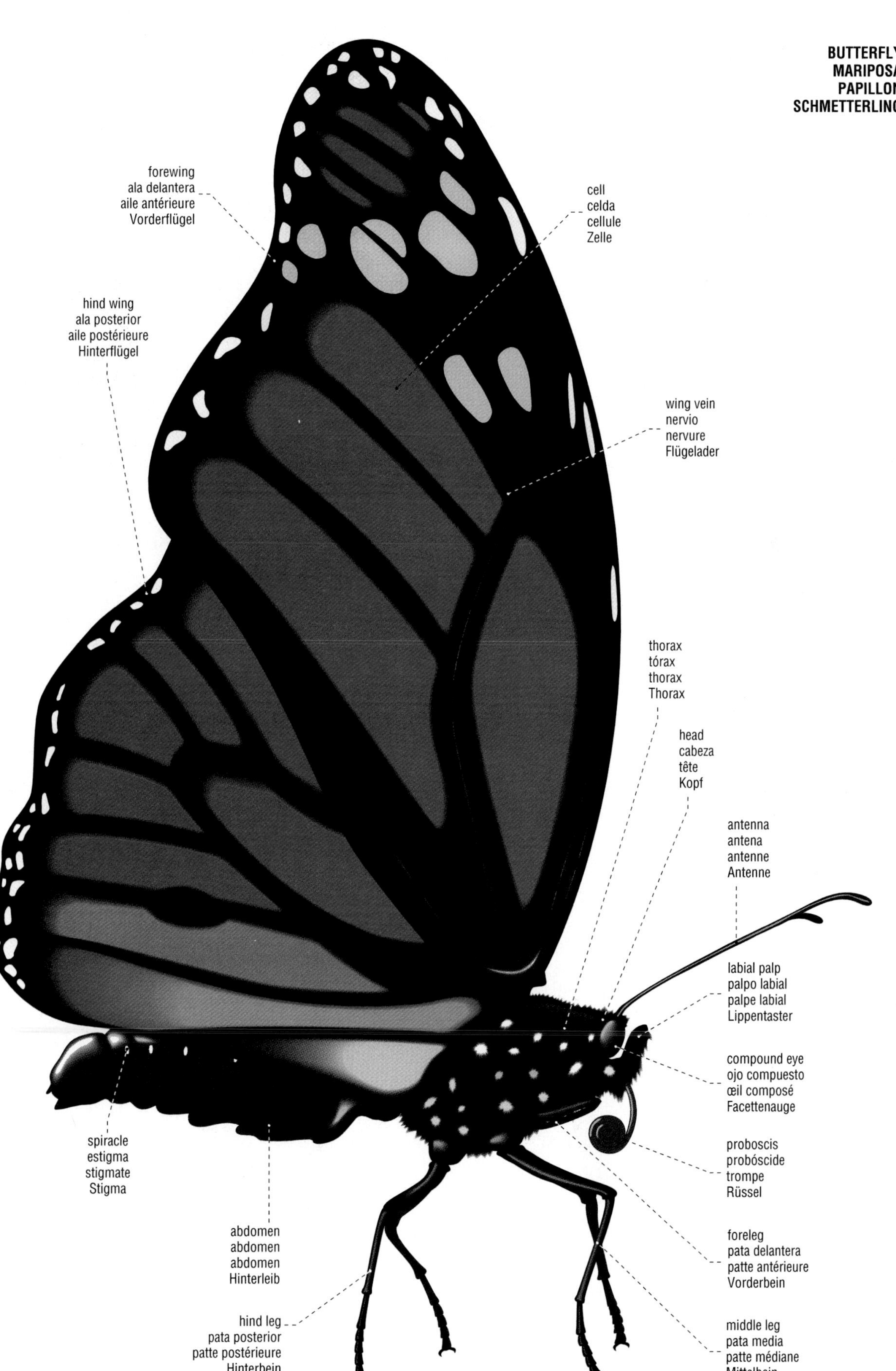
forewing
ala delantera
aile antérieure
Vorderflügel
cell
celda
cellule
Zelle
hind wing
ala posterior
aile postérieure
Hinterflügel
wing vein
nervio
nervure
Flügelader
thorax
tórax
thorax
Thorax
head
cabeza
tête
Kopf
antenna
antena
antenne
Antenne
labial palp
palpo labial
palpe labial
Lippentaster
compound eye
ojo compuesto
œil composé
Facettenauge
spiracle
estigma
stigmate
Stigma
proboscis
probóscide
trompe
Rüssel
abdomen
abdomen
abdomen
Hinterleib
foreleg
pata delantera
patte antérieure
Vorderbein
hind leg
pata posterior
patte postérieure
Hinterbein
middle leg
pata media
patte médiane
Mittelbein

HONEYBEE
ABEJA
ABEILLE
HONIGBIENE

WORKER
OBRERA
OUVRIÈRE
ARBEITERIN

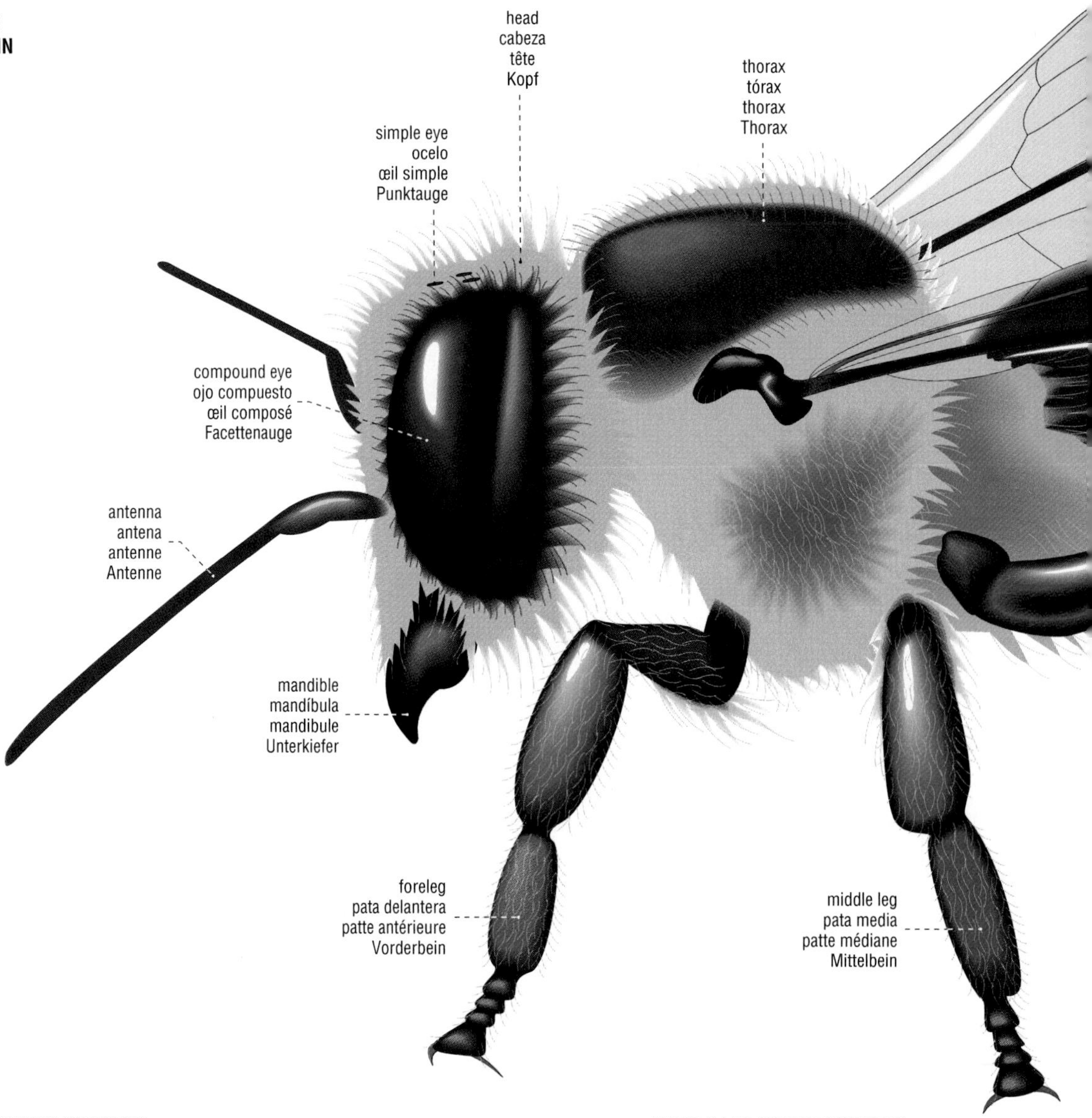

head
cabeza
tête
Kopf

thorax
tórax
thorax
Thorax

simple eye
ocelo
œil simple
Punktauge

compound eye
ojo compuesto
œil composé
Facettenauge

antenna
antena
antenne
Antenne

mandible
mandíbula
mandibule
Unterkiefer

foreleg
pata delantera
patte antérieure
Vorderbein

middle leg
pata media
patte médiane
Mittelbein

FORELEG (OUTER SURFACE)
PATA DELANTERA (SUPERFICIE EXTERIOR)
PATTE ANTÉRIEURE (FACE EXTERNE)
VORDERBEIN (AUSSENSEITE)

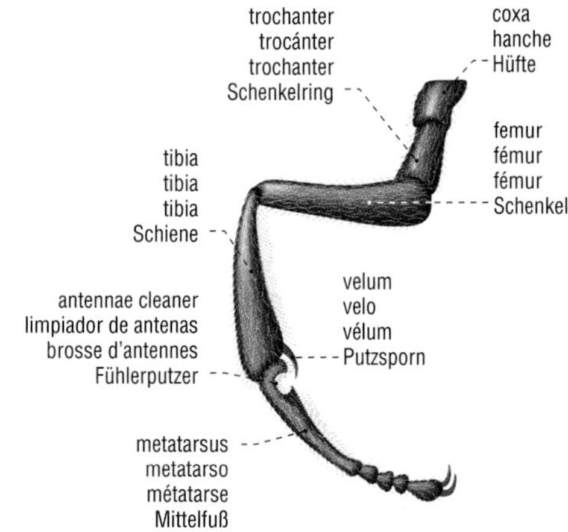
coxa
coxa
hanche
Hüfte
trochanter
trocánter
trochanter
Schenkelring
femur
fémur
fémur
Schenkel
tibia
tibia
tibia
Schiene
velum
velo
vélum
Putzsporn
antennae cleaner
limpiador de antenas
brosse d'antennes
Fühlerputzer
metatarsus
metatarso
métatarse
Mittelfuß

MIDDLE LEG (OUTER SURFACE)
PATA MEDIA (SUPERFICIE EXTERIOR)
PATTE MÉDIANE (FACE EXTERNE)
MITTELBEIN (AUSSENSEITE)

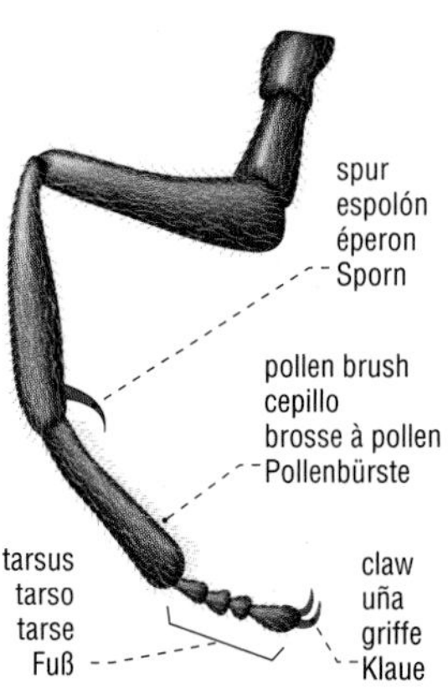
spur
espolón
éperon
Sporn
pollen brush
cepillo
brosse à pollen
Pollenbürste
tarsus
tarso
tarse
Fuß
claw
uña
griffe
Klaue

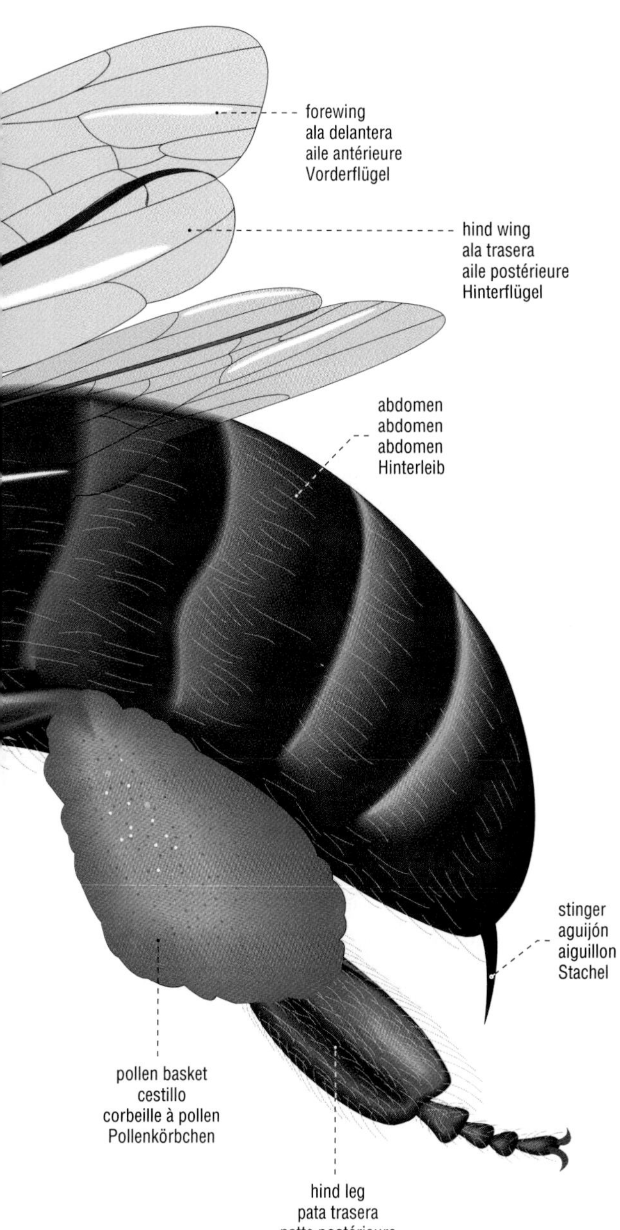
forewing
ala delantera
aile antérieure
Vorderflügel
hind wing
ala trasera
aile postérieure
Hinterflügel
abdomen
abdomen
abdomen
Hinterleib
stinger
aguijón
aiguillon
Stachel
pollen basket
cestillo
corbeille à pollen
Pollenkörbchen
hind leg
pata trasera
patte postérieure
Hinterbein

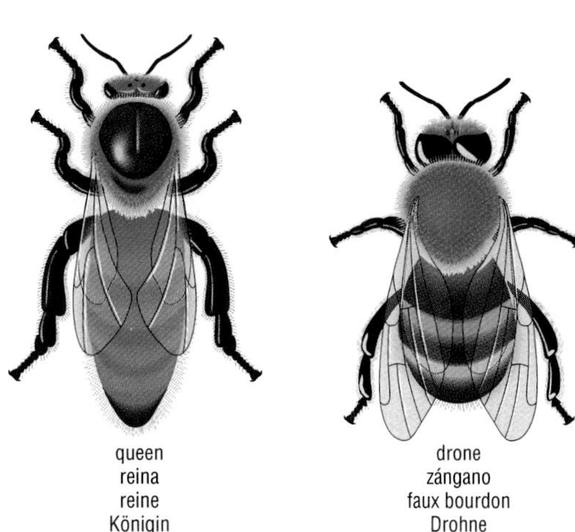
queen
reina
reine
Königin
drone
zángano
faux bourdon
Drohne

worker
obrera
ouvrière
Arbeiterin

MOUTHPARTS
APÉNDICES BUCALES
PIÈCES BUCCALES
MUNDWERKZEUGE

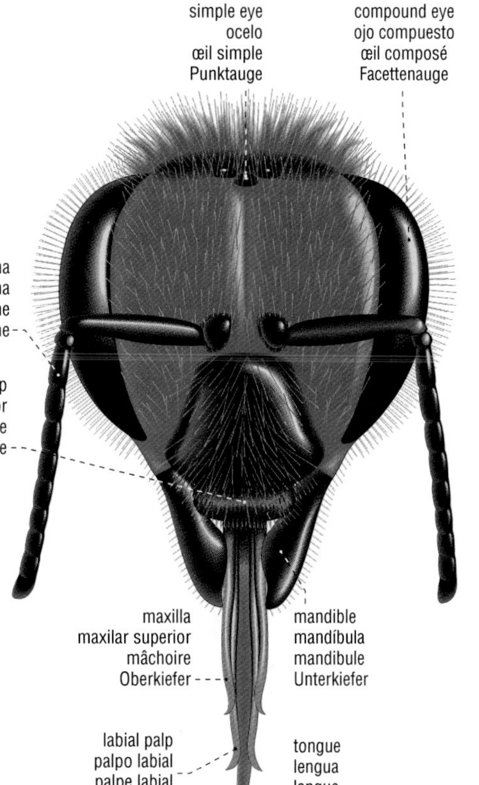
simple eye
ocelo
œil simple
Punktauge
compound eye
ojo compuesto
œil composé
Facettenauge
antenna
antena
antenne
Antenne
upper lip
labio superior
lèvre supérieure
Oberlippe
maxilla
maxilar superior
mâchoire
Oberkiefer
mandible
mandíbula
mandibule
Unterkiefer
labial palp
palpo labial
palpe labial
Lippentaster
tongue
lengua
langue
Zunge

HIND LEG (INNER SURFACE)
PATA TRASERA (SUPERFICIE INTERIOR)
PATTE POSTÉRIEURE (FACE INTERNE)
HINTERBEIN (INNENSEITE)

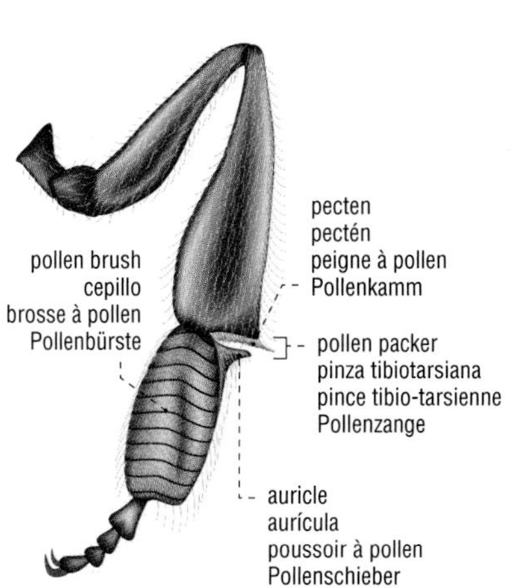
pollen brush
cepillo
brosse à pollen
Pollenbürste
pecten
pectén
peigne à pollen
Pollenkamm
pollen packer
pinza tibiotarsiana
pince tibio-tarsienne
Pollenzange
auricle
aurícula
poussoir à pollen
Pollenschieber

HONEYBEE
ABEJA DE COLMENA
ABEILLE
HONIGBIENE

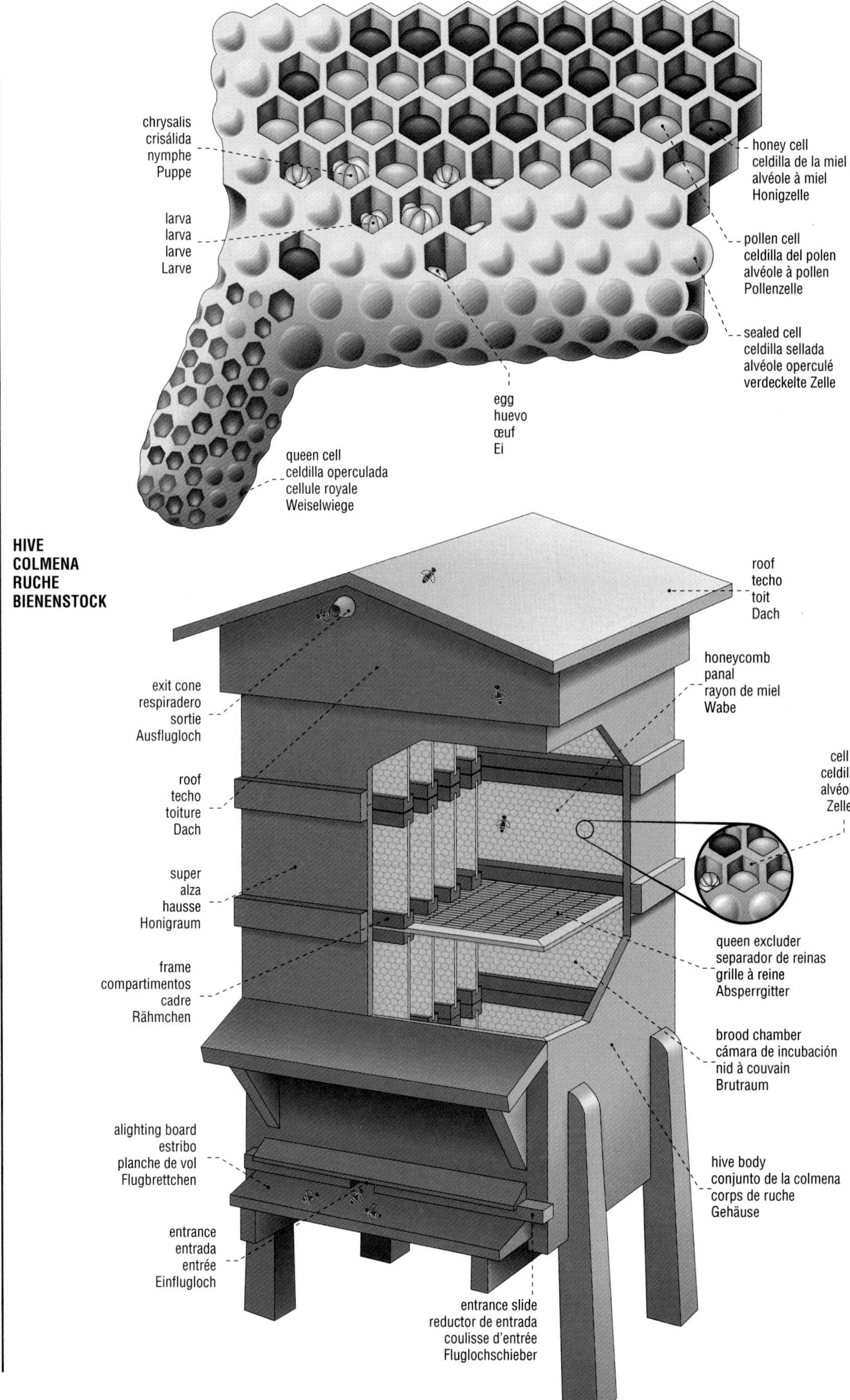
HONEYCOMB SECTION
CORTE DE UN PANAL
COUPE D'UN RAYON DE MIEL
WABENAUSSCHNITT
chrysalis
crisálida
nymphe
Puppe
larva
larva
larve
Larve
honey cell
celdilla de la miel
alvéole à miel
Honigzelle
pollen cell
celdilla del polen
alvéole à pollen
Pollenzelle
sealed cell
celdilla sellada
alvéole operculé
verdeckelte Zelle
egg
huevo
œuf
Ei
queen cell
celdilla operculada
cellule royale
Weiselwiege
HIVE
COLMENA
RUCHE
BIENENSTOCK
roof
techo
toit
Dach
honeycomb
panal
rayon de miel
Wabe
exit cone
respiradero
sortie
Ausflugloch
cell
celdilla
alvéole
Zelle
roof
techo
toiture
Dach
super
alza
hausse
Honigraum
queen excluder
separador de reinas
grille à reine
Absperrgitter
frame
compartimentos
cadre
Rähmchen
brood chamber
cámara de incubación
nid à couvain
Brutraum
alighting board
estribo
planche de vol
Flugbrettchen
hive body
conjunto de la colmena
corps de ruche
Gehäuse
entrance
entrada
entrée
Einflugloch
entrance slide
reductor de entrada
coulisse d'entrée
Fluglochschieber

GASTROPOD
MOLUSCO GASTERÓPODO
GASTÉROPODE
SCHNECKE

SNAIL
CARACOL TERRESTRE
ESCARGOT
SCHNECKE

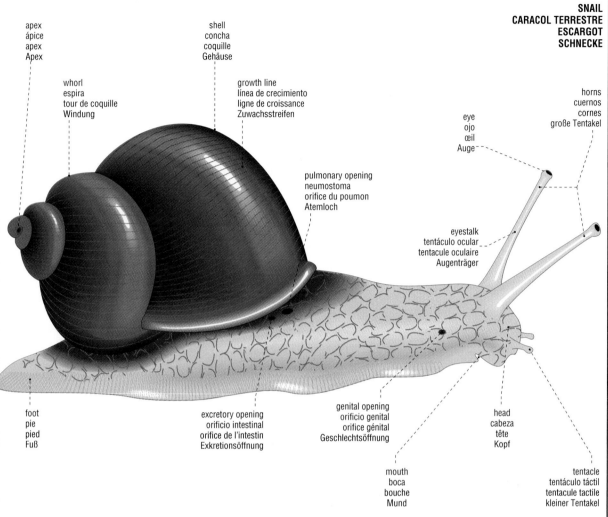

apex
ápice
apex
Apex

shell
concha
coquille
Gehäuse

whorl
espira
tour de coquille
Windung

growth line
línea de crecimiento
ligne de croissance
Zuwachsstreifen

eye
ojo
œil
Auge

horns
cuernos
cornes
große Tentakel

pulmonary opening
neumostoma
orifice du poumon
Atemloch

eyestalk
tentáculo ocular
tentacule oculaire
Augenträger

foot
pie
pied
Fuß

excretory opening
orificio intestinal
orifice de l'intestin
Exkretionsöffnung

genital opening
orificio genital
orifice génital
Geschlechtsöffnung

head
cabeza
tête
Kopf

mouth
boca
bouche
Mund

tentacle
tentáculo táctil
tentacule tactile
kleiner Tentakel

MAJOR EDIBLE GASTROPODS
GASTERÓPODOS COMESTIBLES
PRINCIPAUX GASTÉROPODES COMESTIBLES
WICHTIGSTE ESSBARE SCHNECKEN

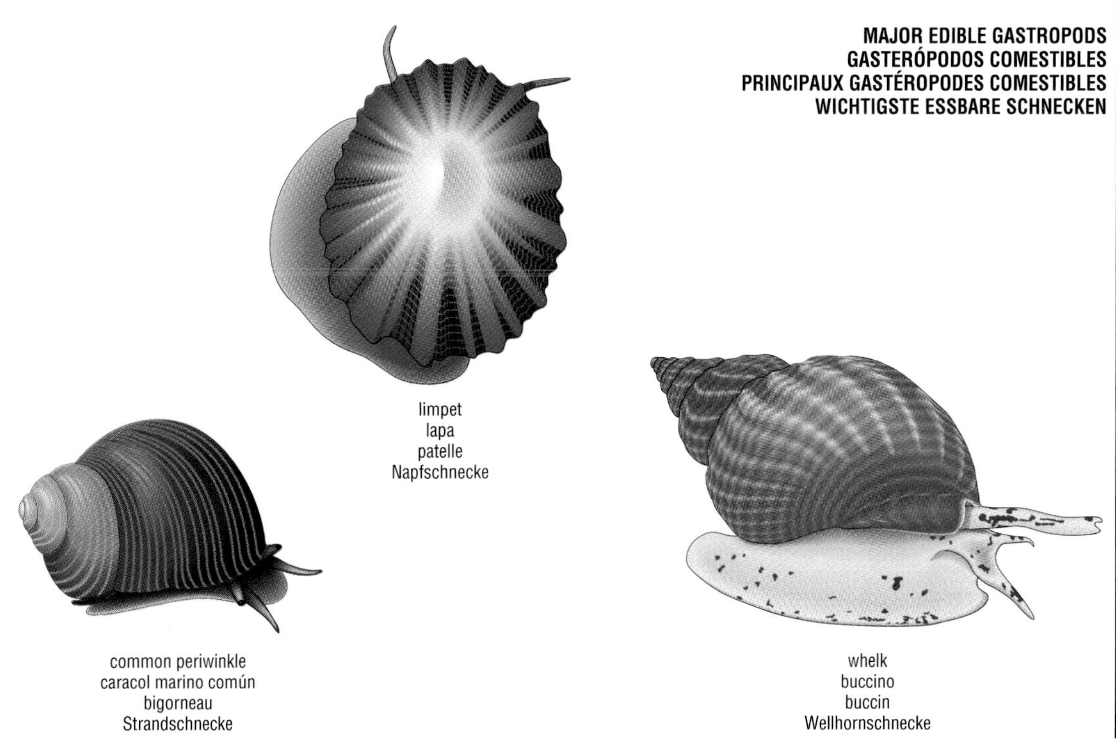

limpet
lapa
patelle
Napfschnecke

common periwinkle
caracol marino común
bigorneau
Strandschnecke

whelk
buccino
buccin
Wellhornschnecke

AMPHIBIANS
ANFIBIOS
AMPHIBIENS
AMPHIBIEN

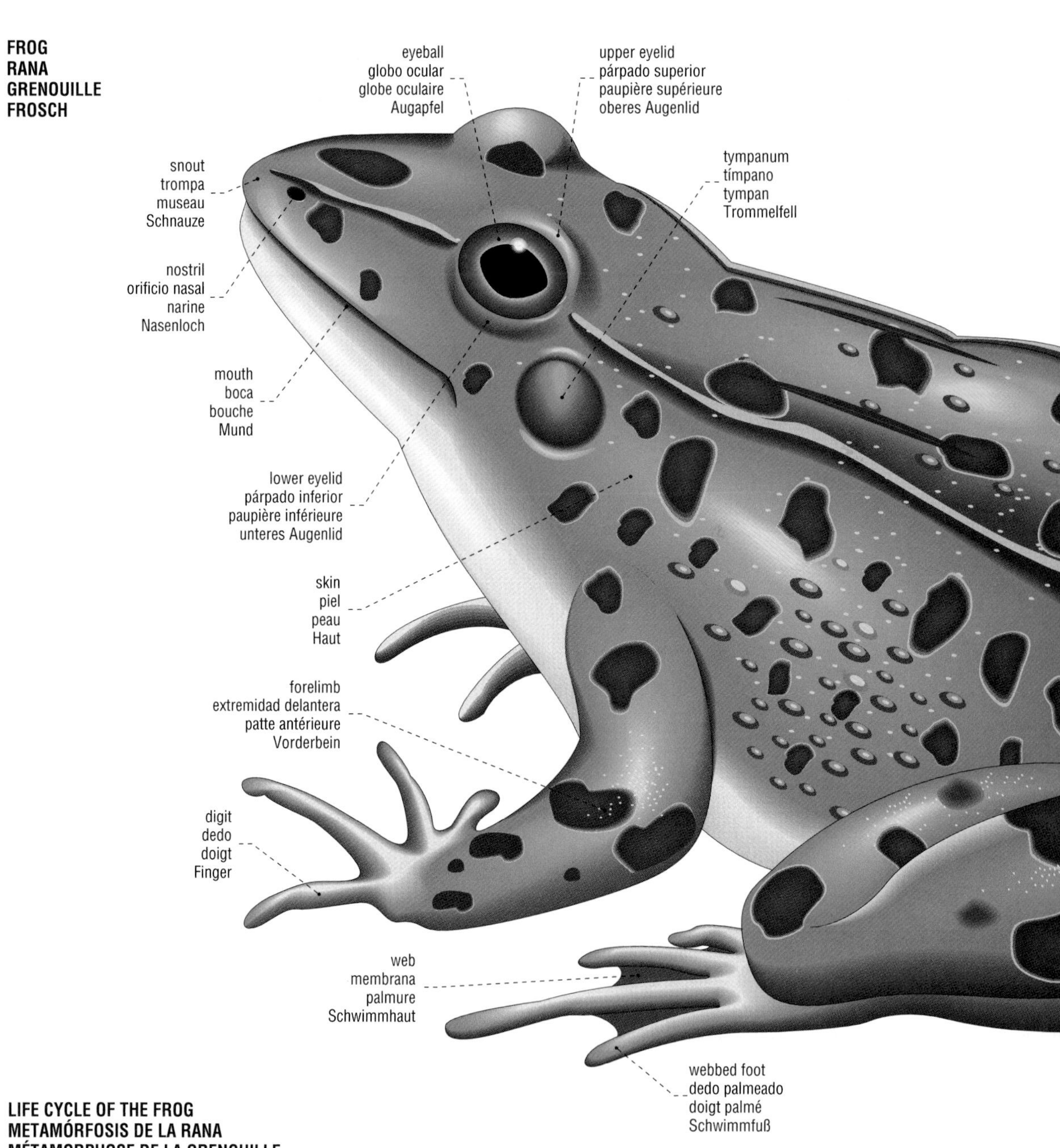
FROG
RANA
GRENOUILLE
FROSCH
eyeball
globo ocular
globe oculaire
Augapfel
upper eyelid
párpado superior
paupière supérieure
oberes Augenlid
snout
trompa
museau
Schnauze
tympanum
tímpano
tympan
Trommelfell
nostril
orificio nasal
narine
Nasenloch
mouth
boca
bouche
Mund
lower eyelid
párpado inferior
paupière inférieure
unteres Augenlid
skin
piel
peau
Haut
forelimb
extremidad delantera
patte antérieure
Vorderbein
digit
dedo
doigt
Finger
web
membrana
palmure
Schwimmhaut
webbed foot
dedo palmeado
doigt palmé
Schwimmfuß

LIFE CYCLE OF THE FROG
METAMÓRFOSIS DE LA RANA
MÉTAMORPHOSE DE LA GRENOUILLE
LEBENSZYKLUS DES FROSCHES

eggs
huevos
œufs
Eier

tadpole
renacuajo
têtard
Kaulquappe

hind limb
extremidad posterior
patte postérieure
Hinterbein

forelimb
extremidad delantera
patte antérieure
Vorderbein

external gills
branquias externas
branchies externes
äußere Kiemen

operculum
opérculo
opercule
Kiemendeckel

MAJOR AMPHIBIANS
ANFIBIOS COMUNES
PRINCIPAUX AMPHIBIENS
WICHTIGSTE AMPHIBIEN

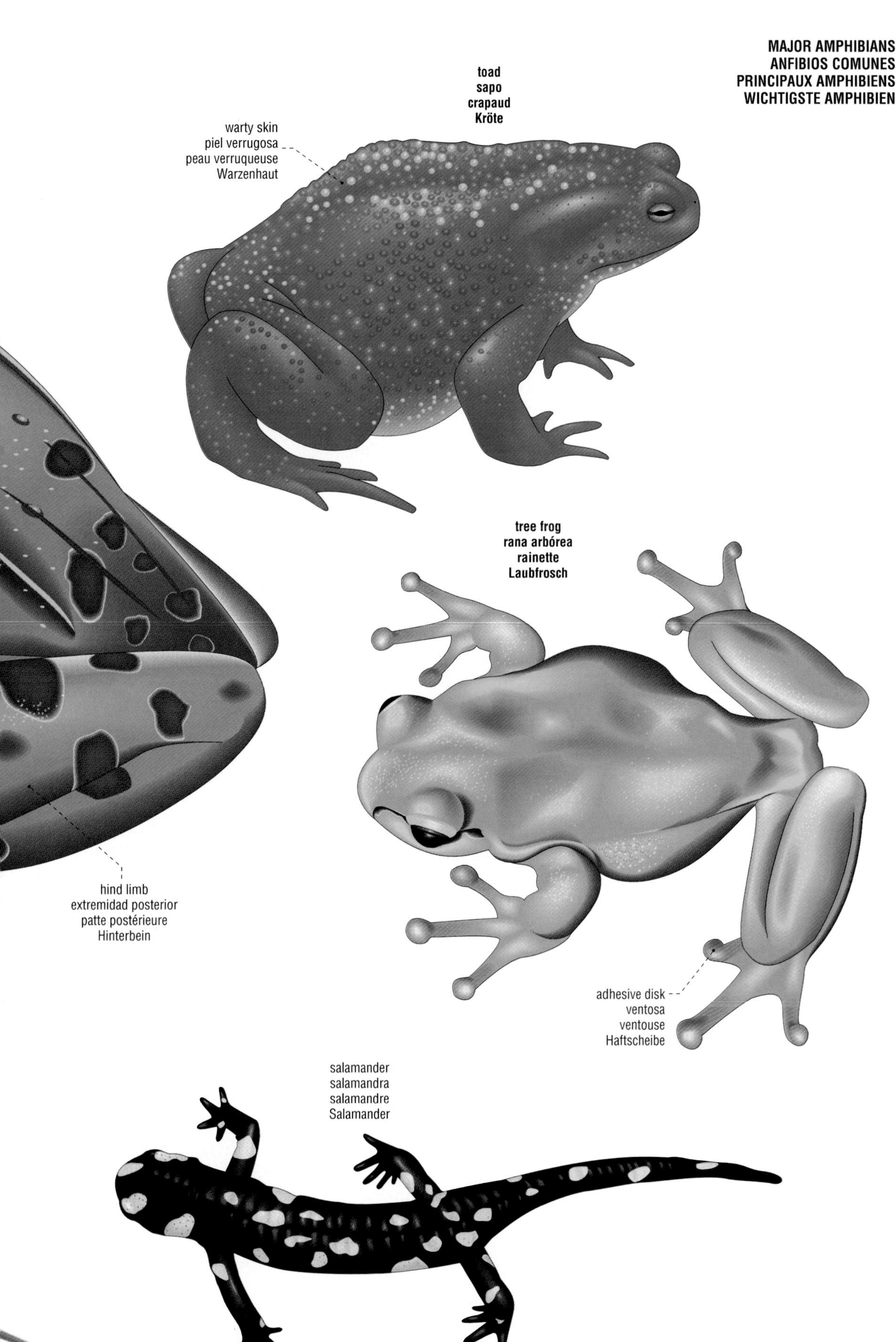
toad
sapo
crapaud
Kröte
warty skin
piel verrugosa
peau verruqueuse
Warzenhaut
tree frog
rana arbórea
rainette
Laubfrosch
hind limb
extremidad posterior
patte postérieure
Hinterbein
adhesive disk
ventosa
ventouse
Haftscheibe
salamander
salamandra
salamandre
Salamander

FISH
PEZ
POISSON
FISCH

MORPHOLOGY
MORFOLOGÍA
MORPHOLOGIE
MORPHOLOGIE

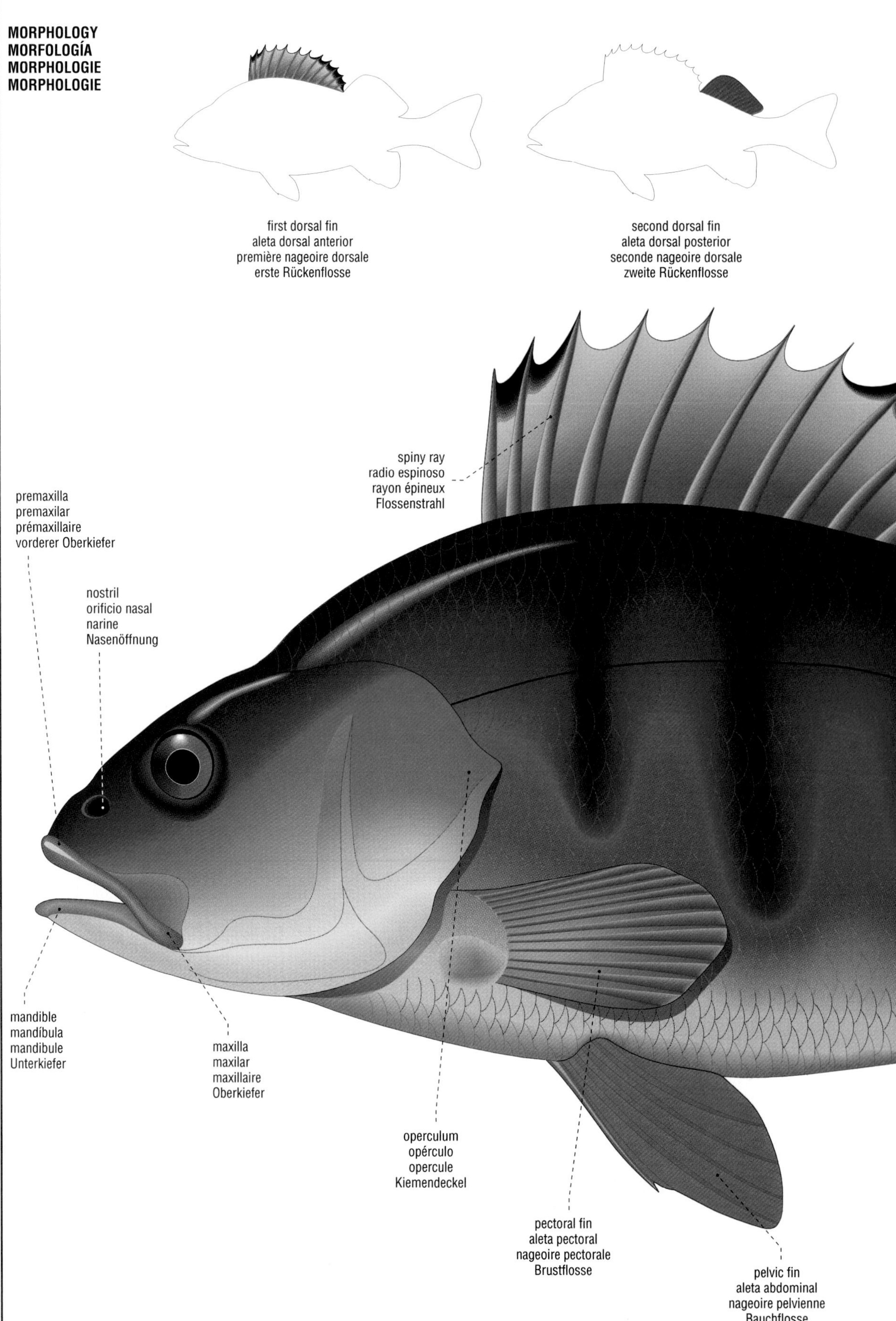
first dorsal fin
aleta dorsal anterior
première nageoire dorsale
erste Rückenflosse
second dorsal fin
aleta dorsal posterior
seconde nageoire dorsale
zweite Rückenflosse
spiny ray
radio espinoso
rayon épineux
Flossenstrahl
premaxilla
premaxilar
prémaxillaire
vorderer Oberkiefer
nostril
orificio nasal
narine
Nasenöffnung
mandible
mandíbula
mandibule
Unterkiefer
maxilla
maxilar
maxillaire
Oberkiefer
operculum
opérculo
opercule
Kiemendeckel
pectoral fin
aleta pectoral
nageoire pectorale
Brustflosse
pelvic fin
aleta abdominal
nageoire pelvienne
Bauchflosse

GILLS
BRANQUIAS
BRANCHIES
KIEMEN

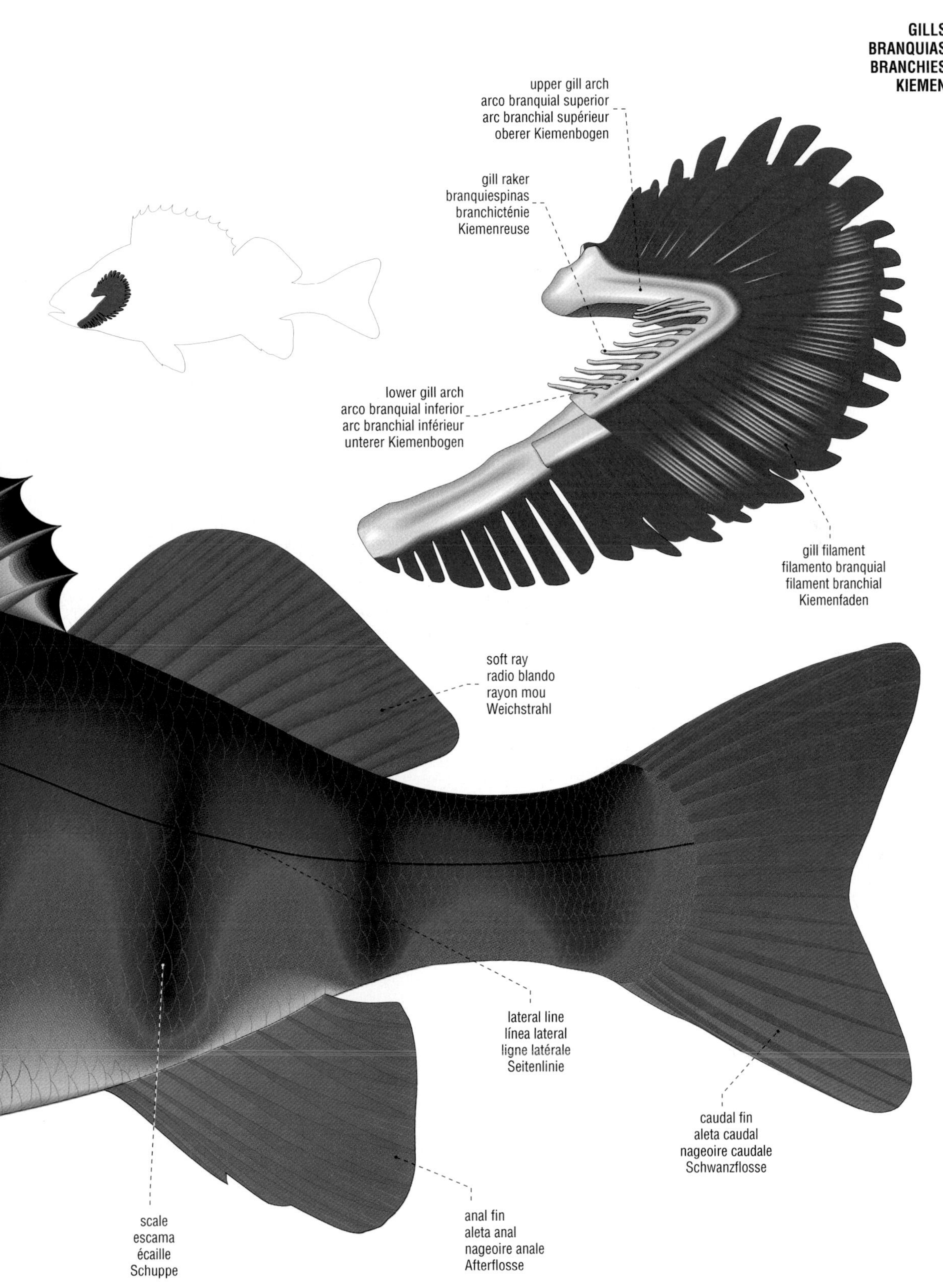
upper gill arch
arco branquial superior
arc branchial supérieur
oberer Kiemenbogen
gill raker
branquiespinas
branchicténie
Kiemenreuse
lower gill arch
arco branquial inferior
arc branchial inférieur
unterer Kiemenbogen
gill filament
filamento branquial
filament branchial
Kiemenfaden
soft ray
radio blando
rayon mou
Weichstrahl
lateral line
línea lateral
ligne latérale
Seitenlinie
caudal fin
aleta caudal
nageoire caudale
Schwanzflosse
scale
escama
écaille
Schuppe
anal fin
aleta anal
nageoire anale
Afterflosse

FISH
PEZ
POISSON
FISCH

ANATOMY
ANATOMÍA
ANATOMIE
ANATOMIE

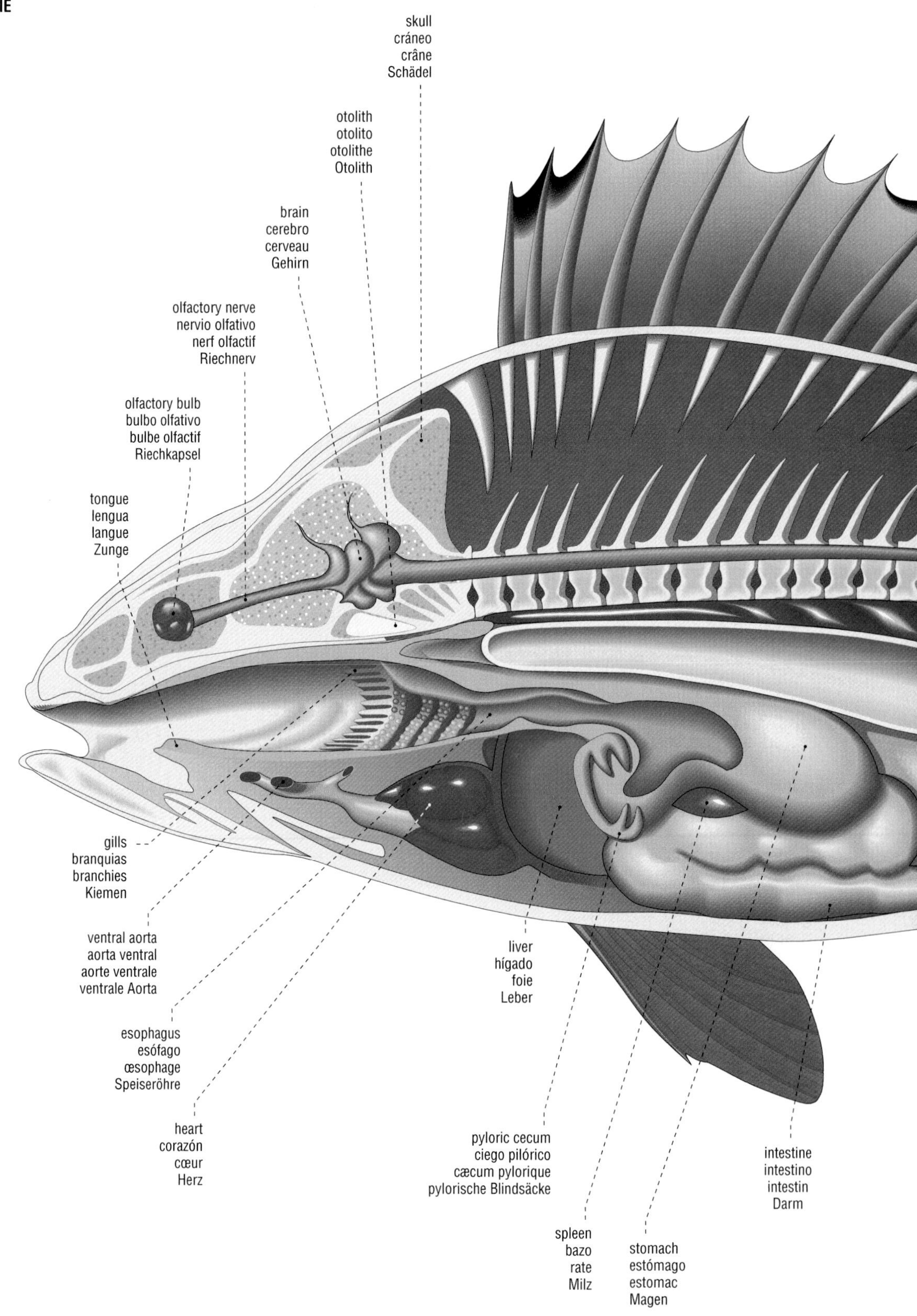
skull
cráneo
crâne
Schädel
otolith
otolito
otolithe
Otolith
brain
cerebro
cerveau
Gehirn
olfactory nerve
nervio olfativo
nerf olfactif
Riechnerv
olfactory bulb
bulbo olfativo
bulbe olfactif
Riechkapsel
tongue
lengua
langue
Zunge
gills
branquias
branchies
Kiemen
ventral aorta
aorta ventral
aorte ventrale
ventrale Aorta
esophagus
esófago
œsophage
Speiseröhre
heart
corazón
cœur
Herz
liver
hígado
foie
Leber
pyloric cecum
ciego pilórico
cæcum pylorique
pylorische Blindsäcke
spleen
bazo
rate
Milz
stomach
estómago
estomac
Magen
intestine
intestino
intestin
Darm

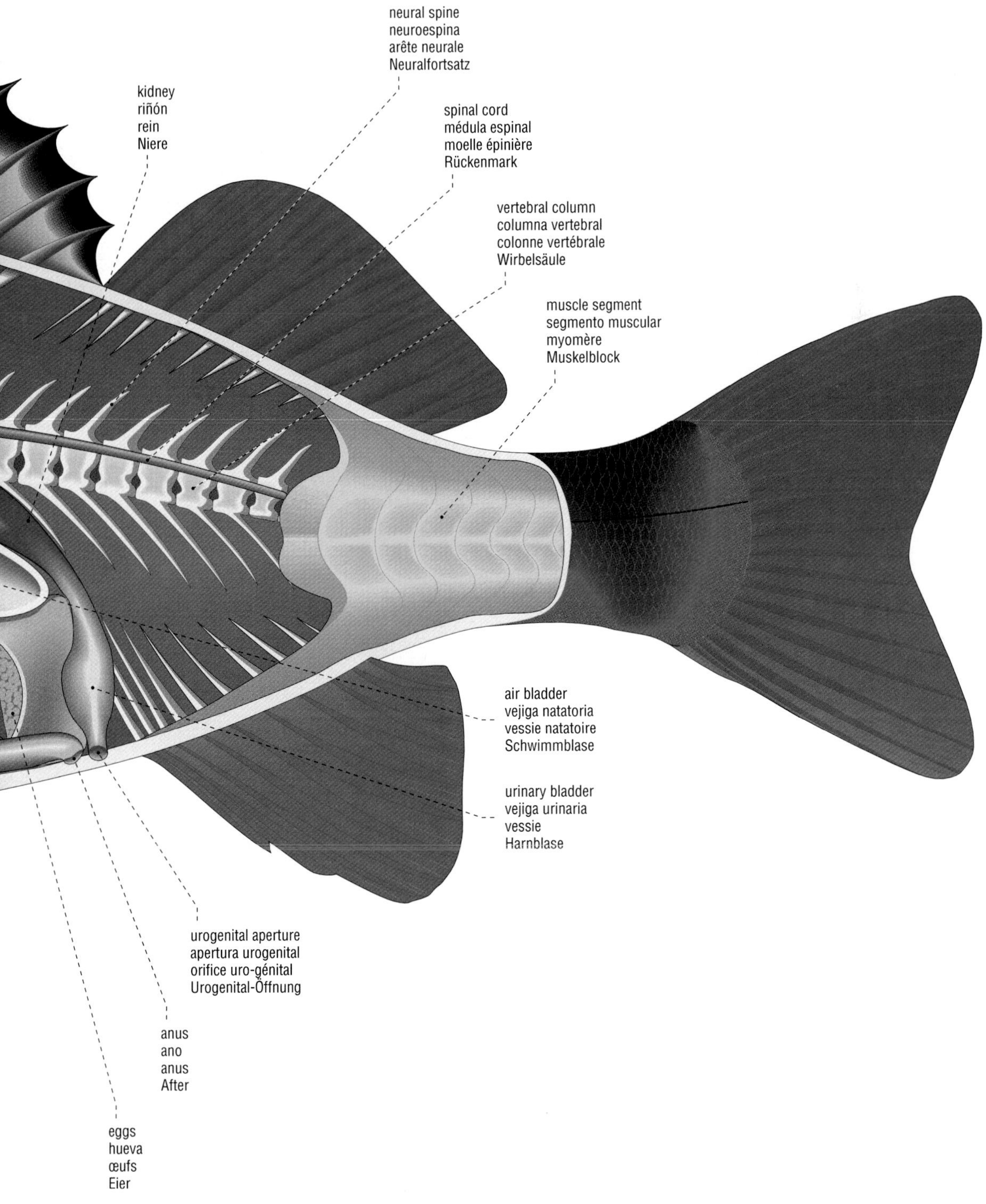
neural spine
neuroespina
arête neurale
Neuralfortsatz
kidney
riñón
rein
Niere
spinal cord
médula espinal
moelle épinière
Rückenmark
vertebral column
columna vertebral
colonne vertébrale
Wirbelsäule
muscle segment
segmento muscular
myomère
Muskelblock
air bladder
vejiga natatoria
vessie natatoire
Schwimmblase
urinary bladder
vejiga urinaria
vessie
Harnblase
urogenital aperture
apertura urogenital
orifice uro-génital
Urogenital-Öffnung
anus
ano
anus
After
eggs
hueva
œufs
Eier

CRUSTACEAN
CRUSTÁCEO
CRUSTACÉ
KREBSTIERE

LOBSTER
LANGOSTA
HOMARD
HUMMER

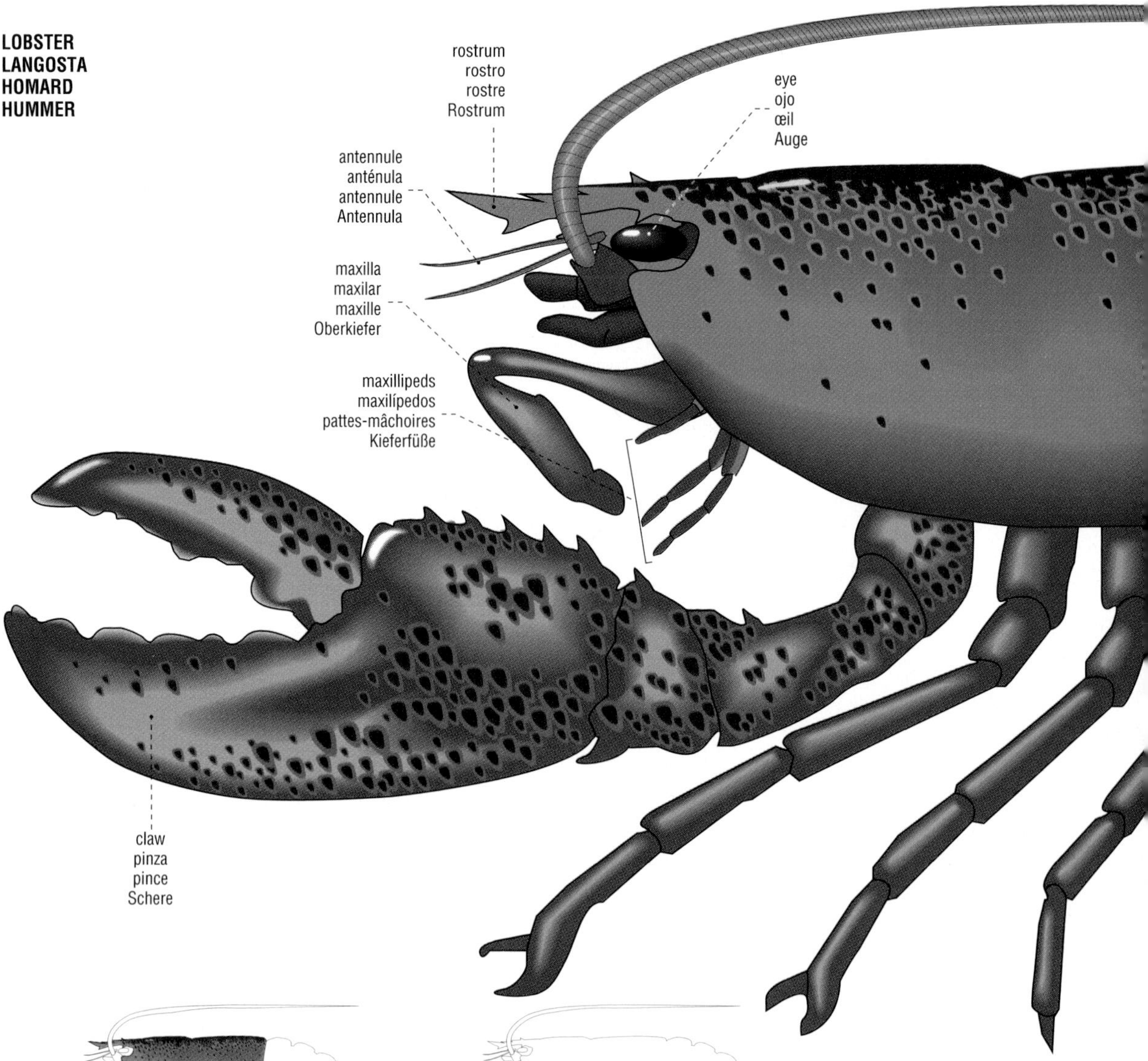

rostrum
rostro
rostre
Rostrum

eye
ojo
œil
Auge

antennule
anténula
antennule
Antennula

maxilla
maxilar
maxille
Oberkiefer

maxillipeds
maxilípedos
pattes-mâchoires
Kieferfüße

claw
pinza
pince
Schere

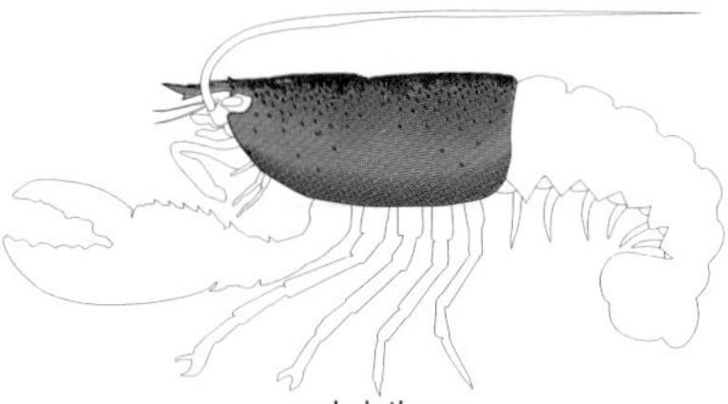

cephalothorax
cefalotórax
céphalothorax
Kopfbruststück

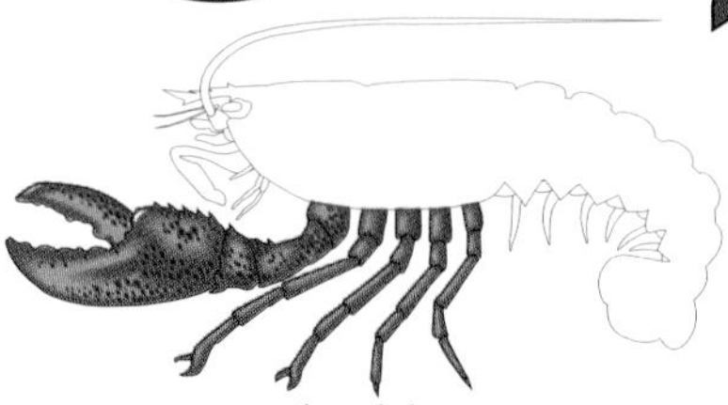

thoracic legs
apéndices torácicos
pattes thoraciques
Brustbeine

MAJOR EDIBLE CRUSTACEANS
CRUSTÁCEOS COMESTIBLES COMUNES
PRINCIPAUX CRUSTACÉS COMESTIBLES
WICHTIGSTE ESSBARE KREBSE

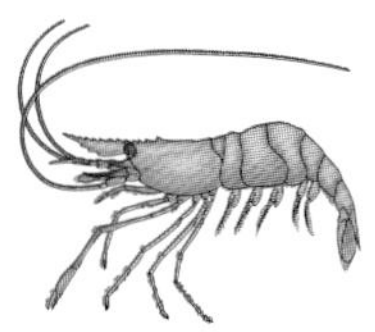

shrimp
gamba
crevette
Garnele

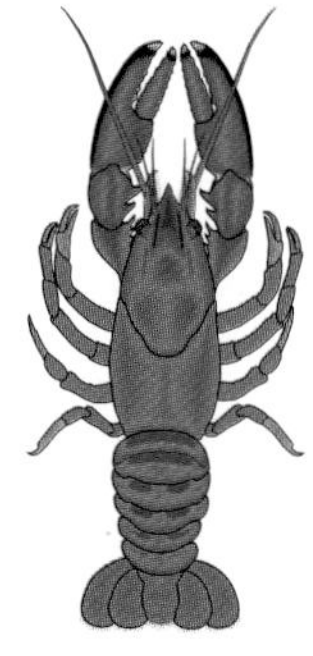

crayfish
langostino
écrevisse
Flußkrebs

crab
cangrejo
crabe
Krabbe

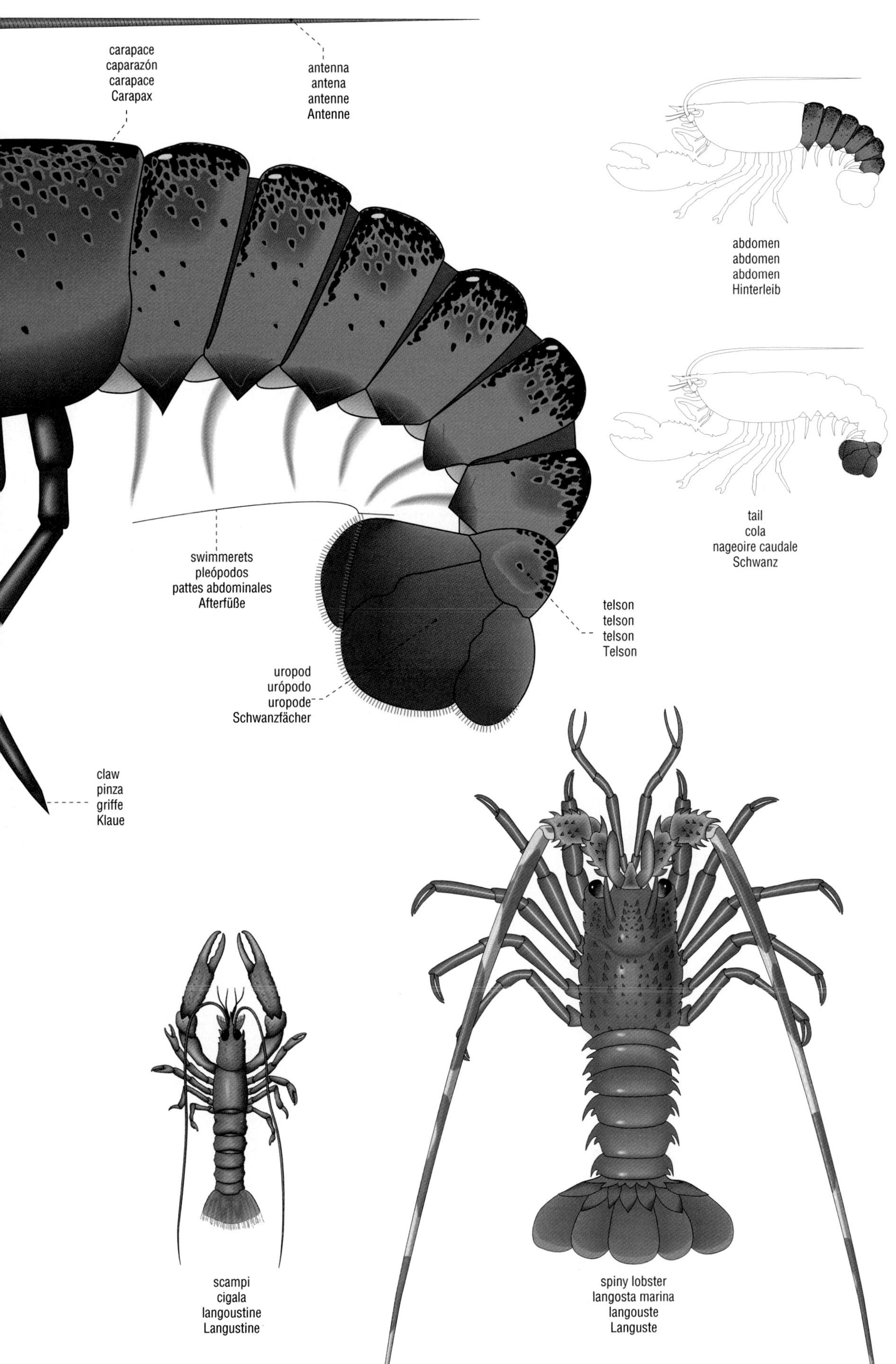
carapace
caparazón
carapace
Carapax
antenna
antena
antenne
Antenne
abdomen
abdomen
abdomen
Hinterleib
tail
cola
nageoire caudale
Schwanz
swimmerets
pleópodos
pattes abdominales
Afterfüße
telson
telson
telson
Telson
uropod
urópodo
uropode
Schwanzfächer
claw
pinza
griffe
Klaue
scampi
cigala
langoustine
Langustine
spiny lobster
langosta marina
langouste
Languste

MOLLUSK
MOLUSCO
MOLLUSQUE
WEICHTIER

OYSTER
OSTRA
HUÎTRE
AUSTER

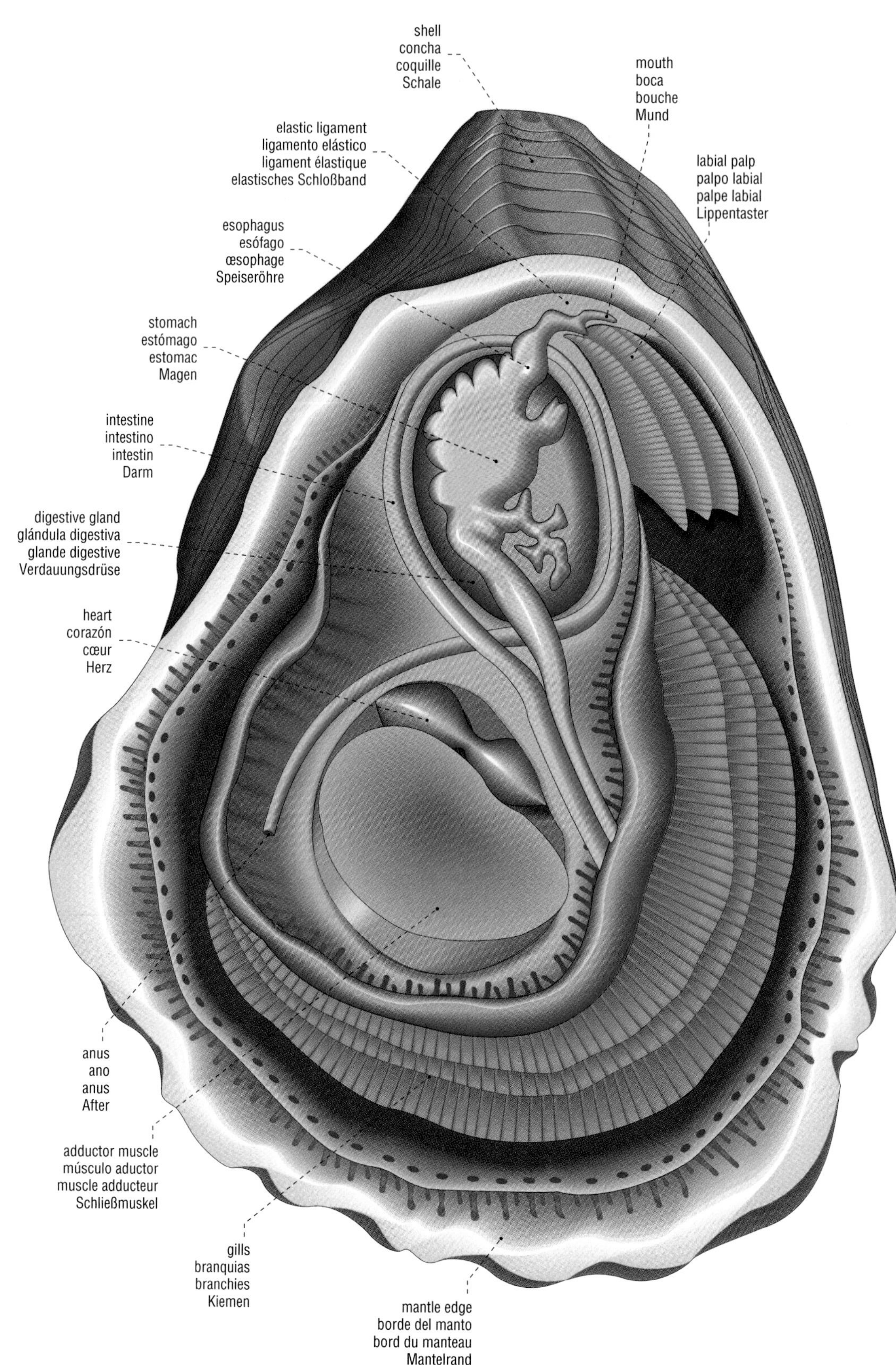
shell
concha
coquille
Schale
mouth
boca
bouche
Mund
elastic ligament
ligamento elástico
ligament élastique
elastisches Schloßband
labial palp
palpo labial
palpe labial
Lippentaster
esophagus
esófago
œsophage
Speiseröhre
stomach
estómago
estomac
Magen
intestine
intestino
intestin
Darm
digestive gland
glándula digestiva
glande digestive
Verdauungsdrüse
heart
corazón
cœur
Herz
anus
ano
anus
After
adductor muscle
músculo aductor
muscle adducteur
Schließmuskel
gills
branquias
branchies
Kiemen
mantle edge
borde del manto
bord du manteau
Mantelrand

MAJOR EDIBLE MOLLUSKS
MOLUSCOS COMESTIBLES
PRINCIPAUX MOLLUSQUES COMESTIBLES
WICHTIGSTE ESSBARE WEICHTIERE

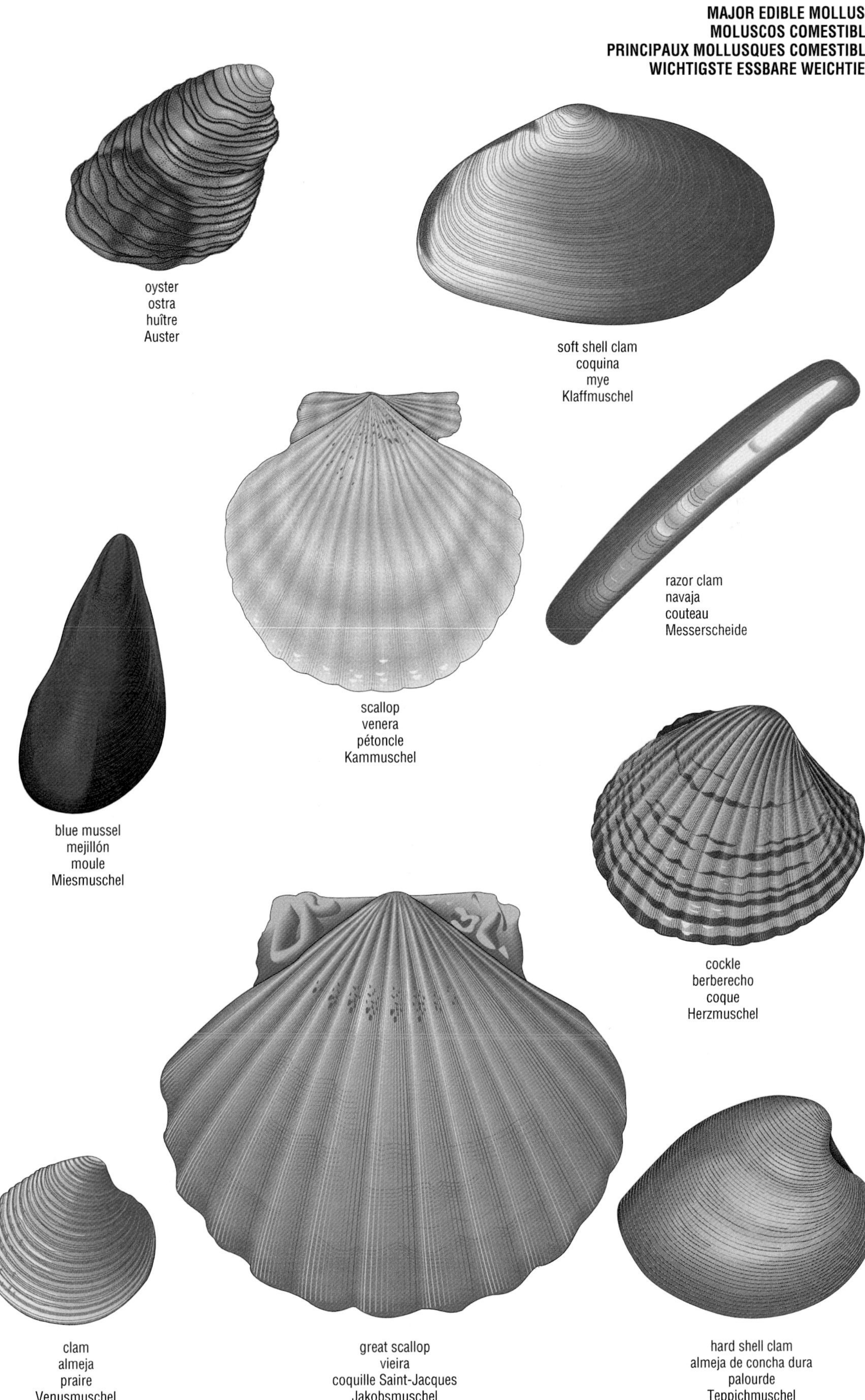
oyster
ostra
huître
Auster
soft shell clam
coquina
mye
Klaffmuschel
razor clam
navaja
couteau
Messerscheide
scallop
venera
pétoncle
Kammuschel
blue mussel
mejillón
moule
Miesmuschel
cockle
berberecho
coque
Herzmuschel
clam
almeja
praire
Venusmuschel
great scallop
vieira
coquille Saint-Jacques
Jakobsmuschel
hard shell clam
almeja de concha dura
palourde
Teppichmuschel

UNIVALVE SHELL
CONCHA UNIVALVA
COQUILLE UNIVALVE
EINKLAPPIGE SCHALE

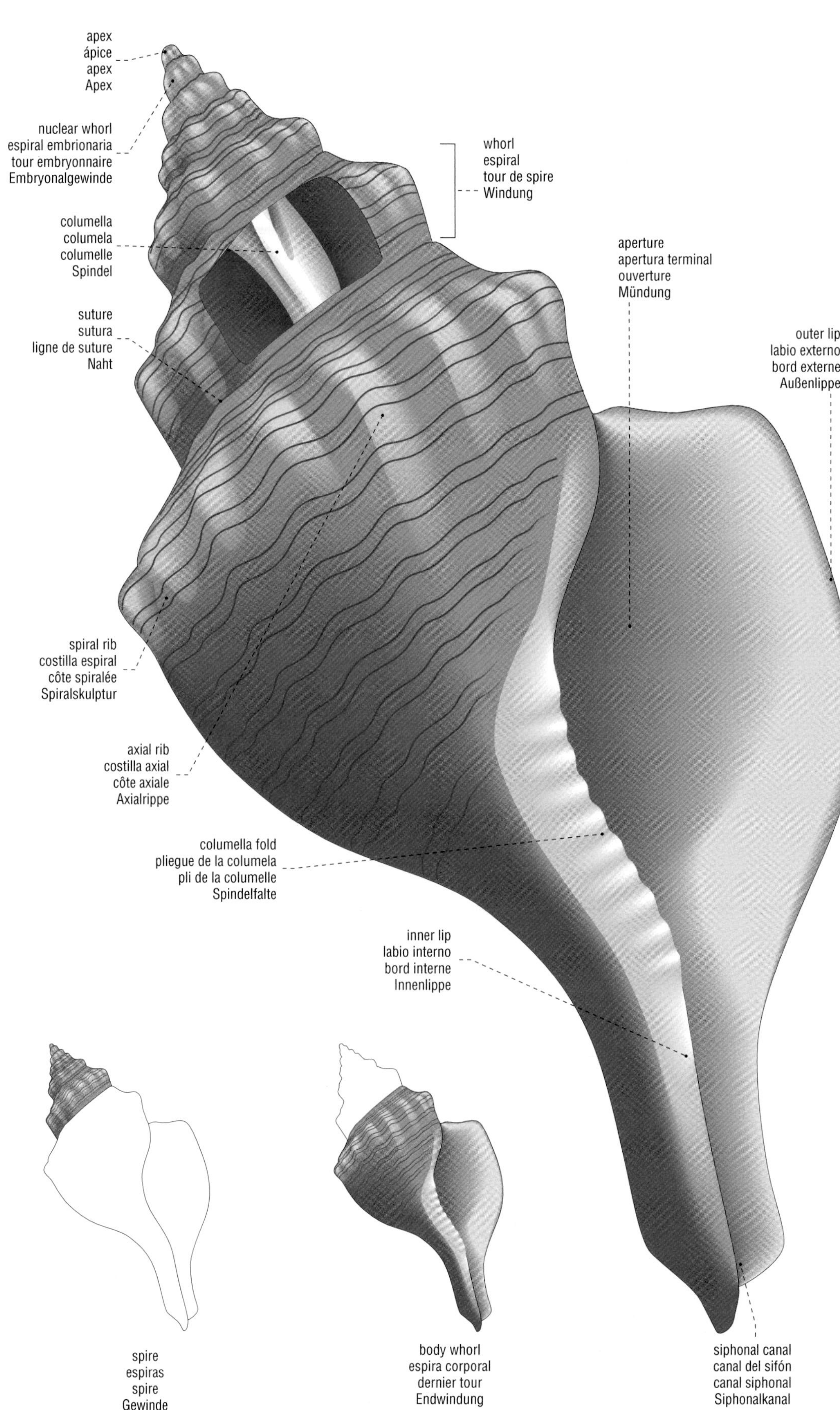
apex
ápice
apex
Apex
nuclear whorl
espiral embrionaria
tour embryonnaire
Embryonalgewinde
columella
columela
columelle
Spindel
suture
sutura
ligne de suture
Naht
whorl
espiral
tour de spire
Windung
aperture
apertura terminal
ouverture
Mündung
outer lip
labio externo
bord externe
Außenlippe
spiral rib
costilla espiral
côte spiralée
Spiralskulptur
axial rib
costilla axial
côte axiale
Axialrippe
columella fold
pliegue de la columela
pli de la columelle
Spindelfalte
inner lip
labio interno
bord interne
Innenlippe
spire
espiras
spire
Gewinde
body whorl
espira corporal
dernier tour
Endwindung
siphonal canal
canal del sifón
canal siphonal
Siphonalkanal

BIVALVE SHELL
CONCHA BIVALVA
COQUILLE BIVALVE
ZWEIKLAPPIGE SCHALE

DORSAL VIEW
VISTA DORSAL
VUE DORSALE
RÜCKANSICHT

LEFT VALVE
VALVA IZQUIERDA
VALVE GAUCHE
LINKE KLAPPE

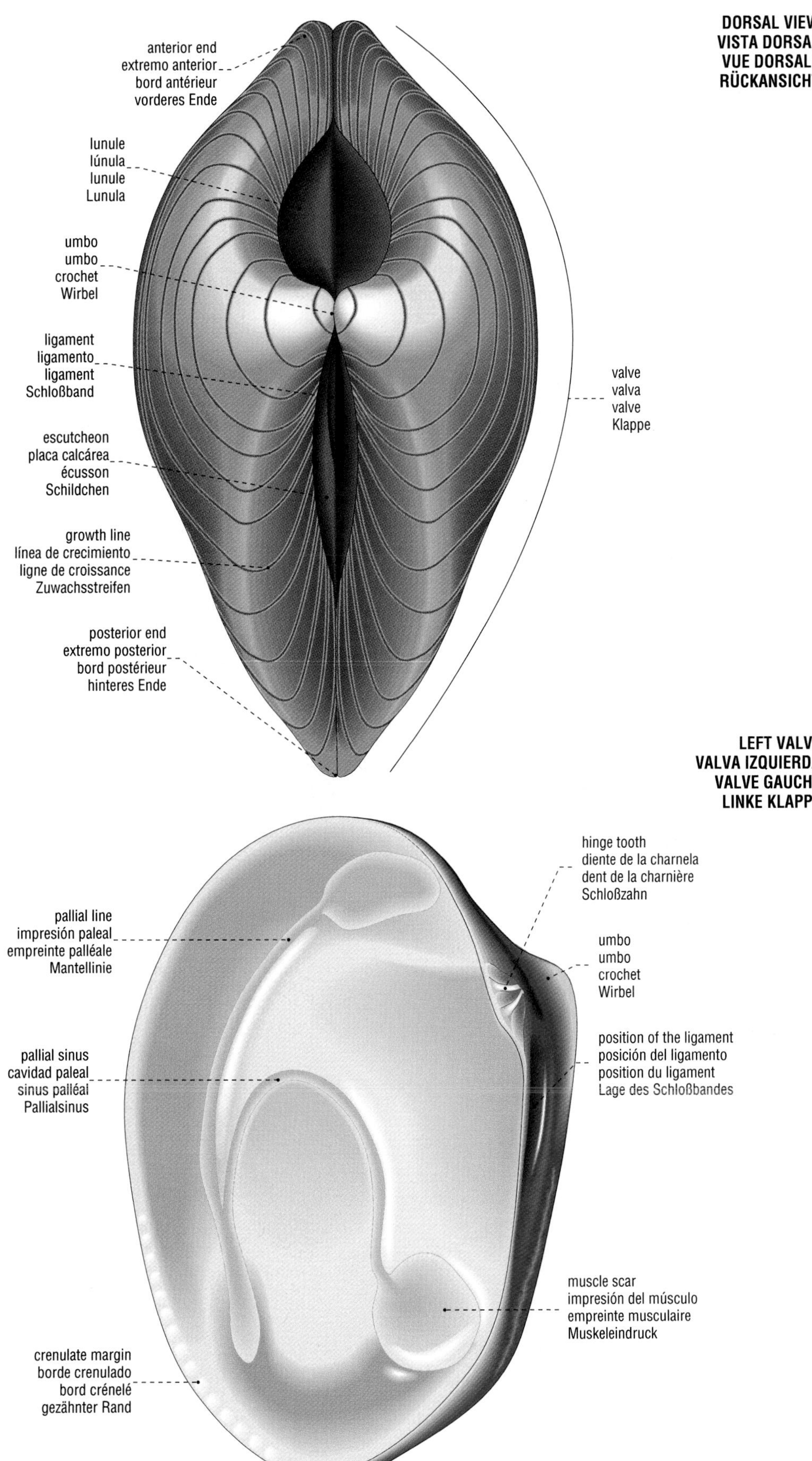
anterior end
extremo anterior
bord antérieur
vorderes Ende
lunule
lúnula
lunule
Lunula
umbo
umbo
crochet
Wirbel
ligament
ligamento
ligament
Schloßband
escutcheon
placa calcárea
écusson
Schildchen
growth line
línea de crecimiento
ligne de croissance
Zuwachsstreifen
posterior end
extremo posterior
bord postérieur
hinteres Ende
valve
valva
valve
Klappe
hinge tooth
diente de la charnela
dent de la charnière
Schloßzahn
pallial line
impresión paleal
empreinte palléale
Mantellinie
umbo
umbo
crochet
Wirbel
position of the ligament
posición del ligamento
position du ligament
Lage des Schloßbandes
pallial sinus
cavidad paleal
sinus palléal
Pallialsinus
muscle scar
impresión del músculo
empreinte musculaire
Muskeleindruck
crenulate margin
borde crenulado
bord crénelé
gezähnter Rand

REPTILE
REPTIL
REPTILE
REPTIL

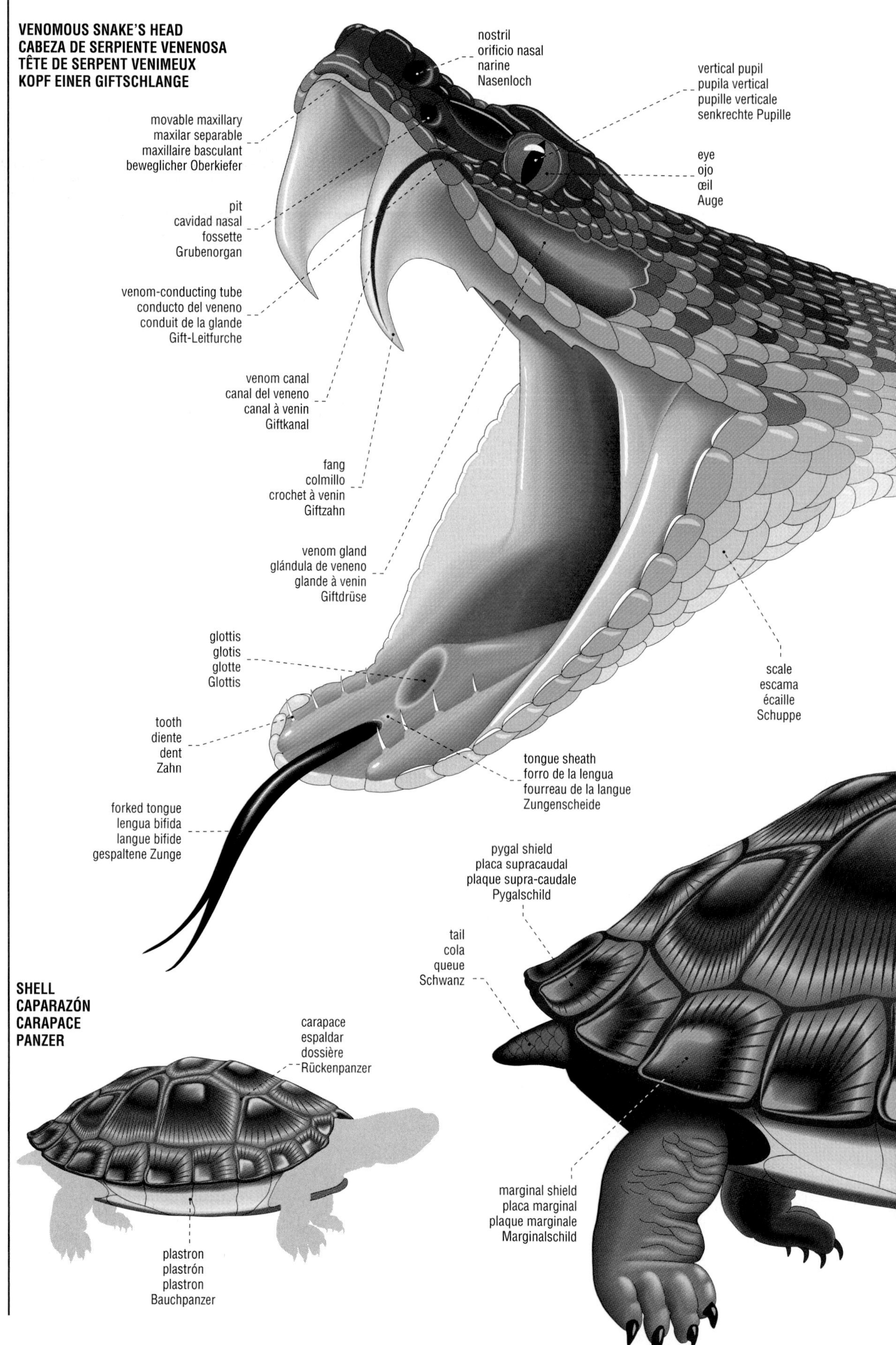
VENOMOUS SNAKE'S HEAD
CABEZA DE SERPIENTE VENENOSA
TÊTE DE SERPENT VENIMEUX
KOPF EINER GIFTSCHLANGE
nostril
orificio nasal
narine
Nasenloch
vertical pupil
pupila vertical
pupille verticale
senkrechte Pupille
movable maxillary
maxilar separable
maxillaire basculant
beweglicher Oberkiefer
eye
ojo
œil
Auge
pit
cavidad nasal
fossette
Grubenorgan
venom-conducting tube
conducto del veneno
conduit de la glande
Gift-Leitfurche
venom canal
canal del veneno
canal à venin
Giftkanal
fang
colmillo
crochet à venin
Giftzahn
venom gland
glándula de veneno
glande à venin
Giftdrüse
glottis
glotis
glotte
Glottis
scale
escama
écaille
Schuppe
tooth
diente
dent
Zahn
tongue sheath
forro de la lengua
fourreau de la langue
Zungenscheide
forked tongue
lengua bifida
langue bifide
gespaltene Zunge
pygal shield
placa supracaudal
plaque supra-caudale
Pygalschild
tail
cola
queue
Schwanz
SHELL
CAPARAZÓN
CARAPACE
PANZER
carapace
espaldar
dossière
Rückenpanzer
marginal shield
placa marginal
plaque marginale
Marginalschild
plastron
plastrón
plastron
Bauchpanzer

RATTLESNAKE
SERPIENTE DE CASCABEL
SERPENT À SONNETTES
KLAPPERSCHLANGE

TURTLE
TORTUGA
TORTUE
SCHILDKRÖTE

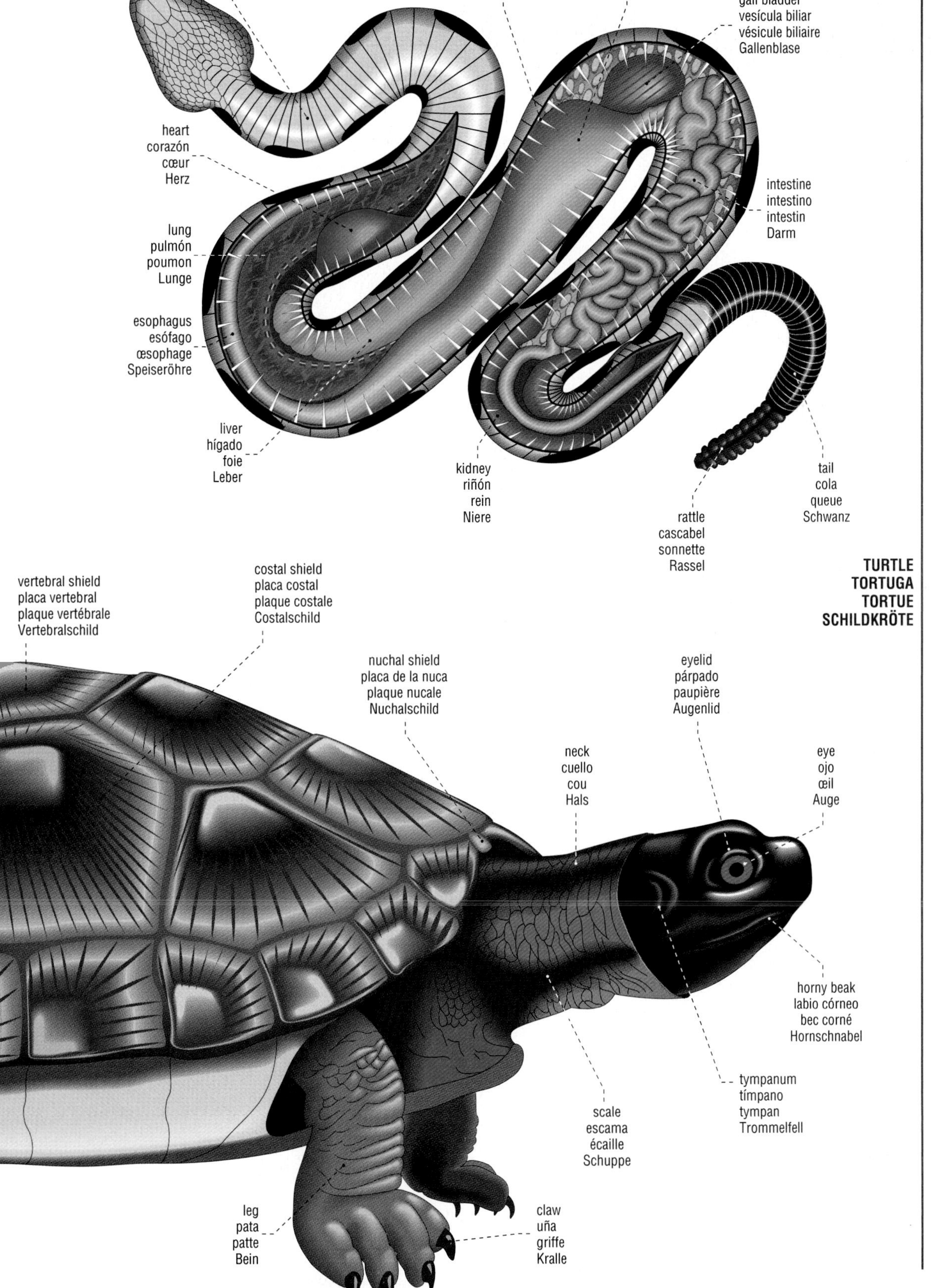
belly scale
escama ventral
écaille ventrale
Bauchschuppe
rib
costilla
côte
Rippe
stomach
estómago
estomac
Magen
gall bladder
vesícula biliar
vésicule biliaire
Gallenblase
heart
corazón
cœur
Herz
intestine
intestino
intestin
Darm
lung
pulmón
poumon
Lunge
esophagus
esófago
œsophage
Speiseröhre
liver
hígado
foie
Leber
kidney
riñón
rein
Niere
tail
cola
queue
Schwanz
rattle
cascabel
sonnette
Rassel
vertebral shield
placa vertebral
plaque vertébrale
Vertebralschild
costal shield
placa costal
plaque costale
Costalschild
nuchal shield
placa de la nuca
plaque nucale
Nuchalschild
eyelid
párpado
paupière
Augenlid
neck
cuello
cou
Hals
eye
ojo
œil
Auge
horny beak
labio córneo
bec corné
Hornschnabel
tympanum
tímpano
tympan
Trommelfell
scale
escama
écaille
Schuppe
leg
pata
patte
Bein
claw
uña
griffe
Kralle

TYPES OF JAWS
TIPOS DE MANDÍBULAS
TYPES DE MÂCHOIRES
GEBISSARTEN

BEAVER
CASTOR
CASTOR
BIBER

RODENT'S JAW
MANDÍBULA DE ROEDOR
MÂCHOIRE DE RONGEUR
NAGETIERGEBISS

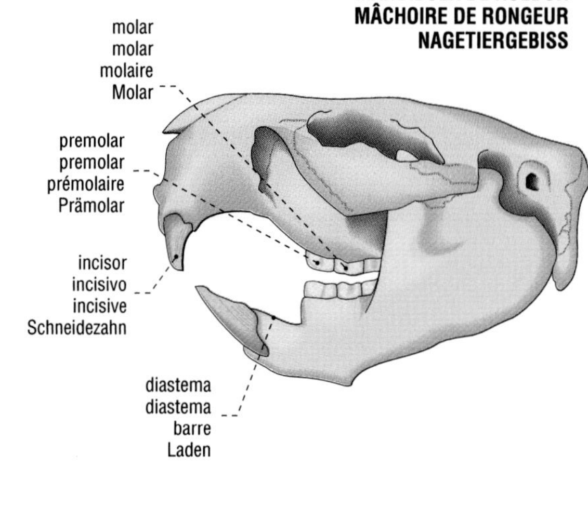
molar
molar
molaire
Molar
premolar
premolar
prémolaire
Prämolar
incisor
incisivo
incisive
Schneidezahn
diastema
diastema
barre
Laden

LION
LEÓN
LION
LÖWE

CARNIVORE'S JAW
MANDÍBULA DE CARNÍVORO
MÂCHOIRE DE CARNIVORE
FLEISCHFRESSERGEBISS

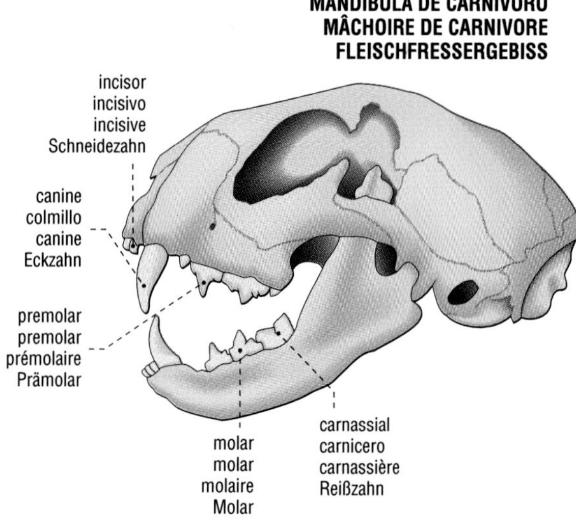
incisor
incisivo
incisive
Schneidezahn
canine
colmillo
canine
Eckzahn
premolar
premolar
prémolaire
Prämolar
molar
molar
molaire
Molar
carnassial
carnicero
carnassière
Reißzahn

HORSE
CABALLO
CHEVAL
PFERD

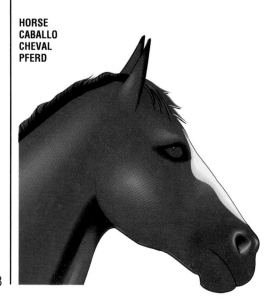

HERBIVORE'S JAW
MANDÍBULA DE HERBÍVORO
MÂCHOIRE D'HERBIVORE
PFLANZENFRESSERGEBISS

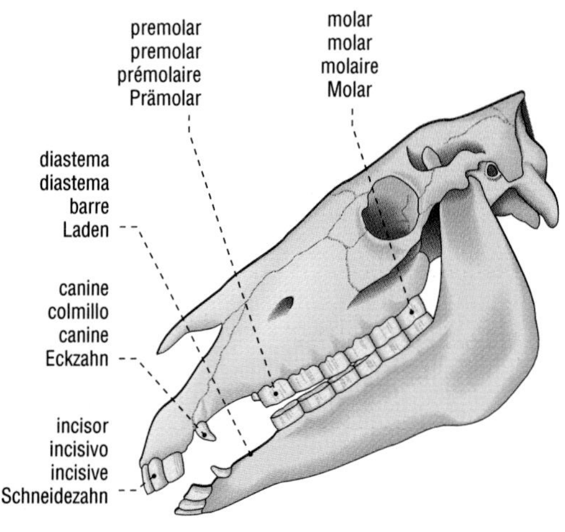
premolar
premolar
prémolaire
Prämolar
molar
molar
molaire
Molar
diastema
diastema
barre
Laden
canine
colmillo
canine
Eckzahn
incisor
incisivo
incisive
Schneidezahn

MAJOR TYPES OF HORNS
CUERNOS: TIPOS MÁS COMUNES
PRINCIPAUX TYPES DE CORNES
WICHTIGSTE HORNARTEN

horns of mouflon
cuernos de muflón
cornes de mouflon
Hörner eines Mufflons

horns of giraffe
cuernos de jirafa
cornes de girafe
Hörner einer Giraffe

horns of rhinoceros
cuernos de rinoceronte
cornes de rhinocéros
Hörner eines Nashorns

MAJOR TYPES OF TUSKS
COLMILOS: TIPOS MÁS COMUNES
PRINCIPAUX TYPES DE DÉFENSES
WICHTIGSTE STOSSZÄHNE

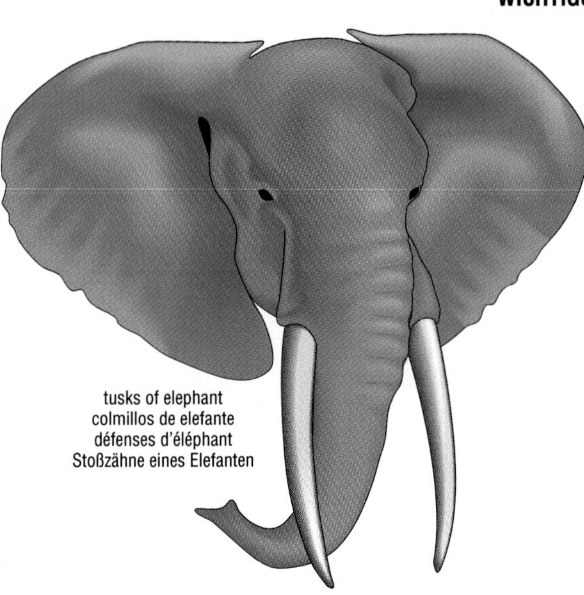

tusks of elephant
colmillos de elefante
défenses d'éléphant
Stoßzähne eines Elefanten

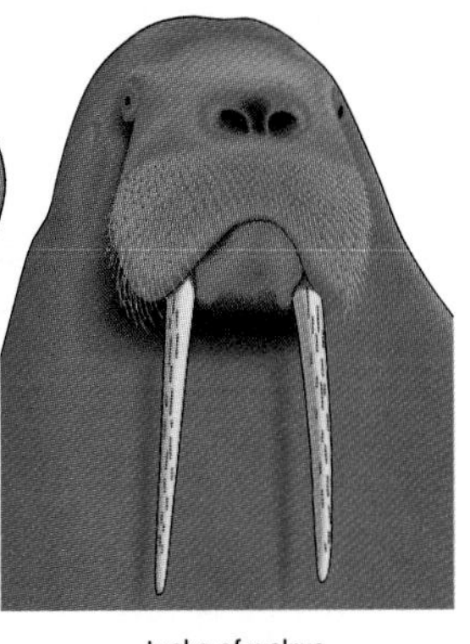

tusks of walrus
colmillos de morsa
défenses de morse
Eckzähne eines Walrosses

tusks of wart hog
colmillos de facócero
défenses de phacochère
Hauer eines Warzenschweins

TYPES OF HOOFS
PATAS DE UNGULADOS: TIPOS MÁS COMUNES
TYPES DE SABOTS
HUFARTEN

one-toe hoof
de una pezuña
sabot à 1 doigt
Ein-Zehenhuf

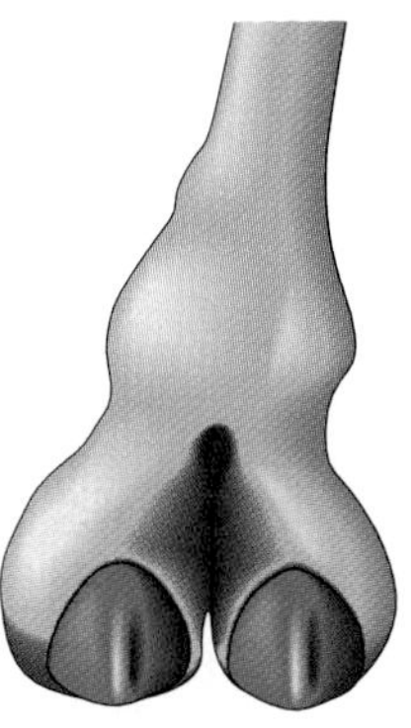

two-toed hoof
de dos pezuñas
sabot à 2 doigts
Zwei-Zehenhuf

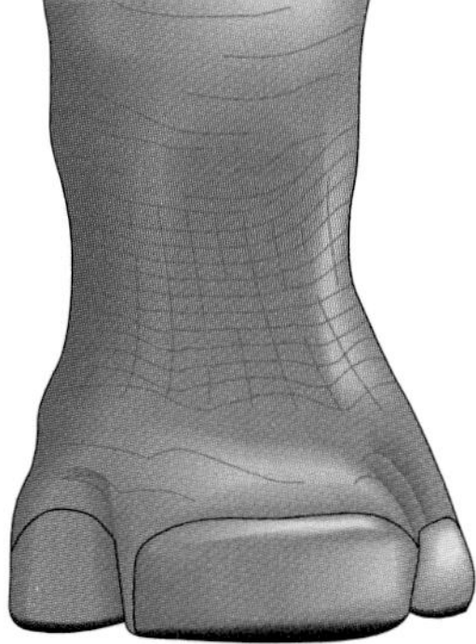

three-toed hoof
de tres pezuñas
sabot à 3 doigts
Drei-Zehenhuf

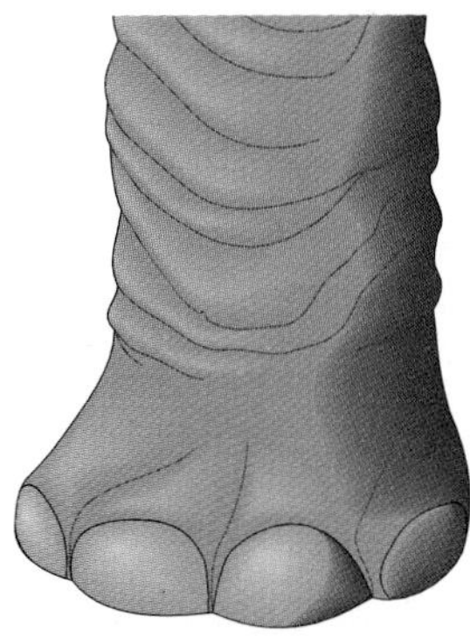

four-toed hoof
de cuatro pezuñas
sabot à 4 doigts
Vier-Zehenhuf

HORSE
CABALLO
CHEVAL
PFERD

MORPHOLOGY
MORFOLOGÍA
MORPHOLOGIE
MORPHOLOGIE

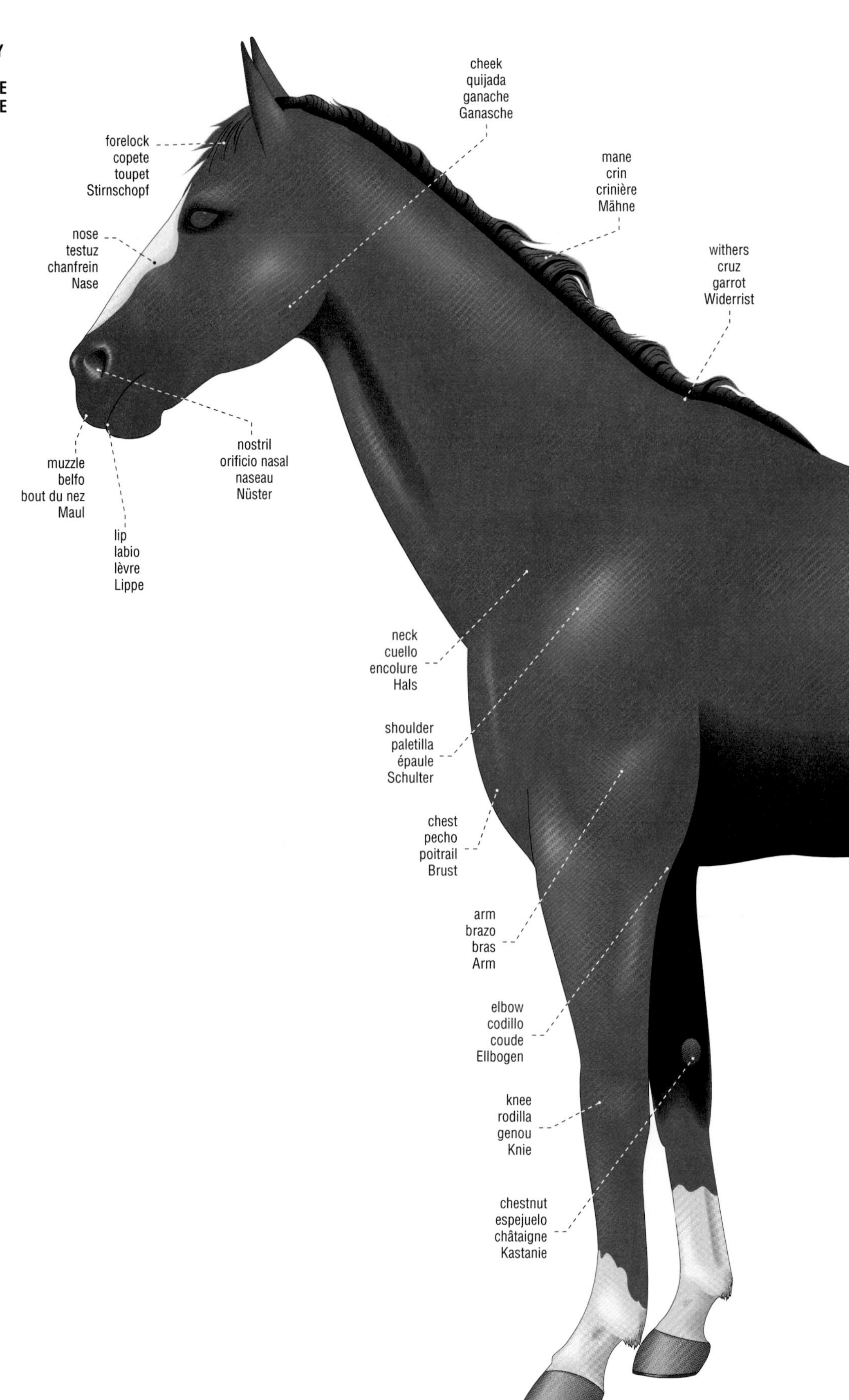
cheek
quijada
ganache
Ganasche
forelock
copete
toupet
Stirnschopf
mane
crin
crinière
Mähne
nose
testuz
chanfrein
Nase
withers
cruz
garrot
Widerrist
muzzle
belfo
bout du nez
Maul
nostril
orificio nasal
naseau
Nüster
lip
labio
lèvre
Lippe
neck
cuello
encolure
Hals
shoulder
paletilla
épaule
Schulter
chest
pecho
poitrail
Brust
arm
brazo
bras
Arm
elbow
codillo
coude
Ellbogen
knee
rodilla
genou
Knie
chestnut
espejuelo
châtaigne
Kastanie

GAITS
LOS PASOS
ALLURES
GANGARTEN

pace
el paso de andadura
amble
Paßgang

walk
el paso
pas
Schritt

trot
el trote
trot
Trab

gallop
el galope
galop
Galopp

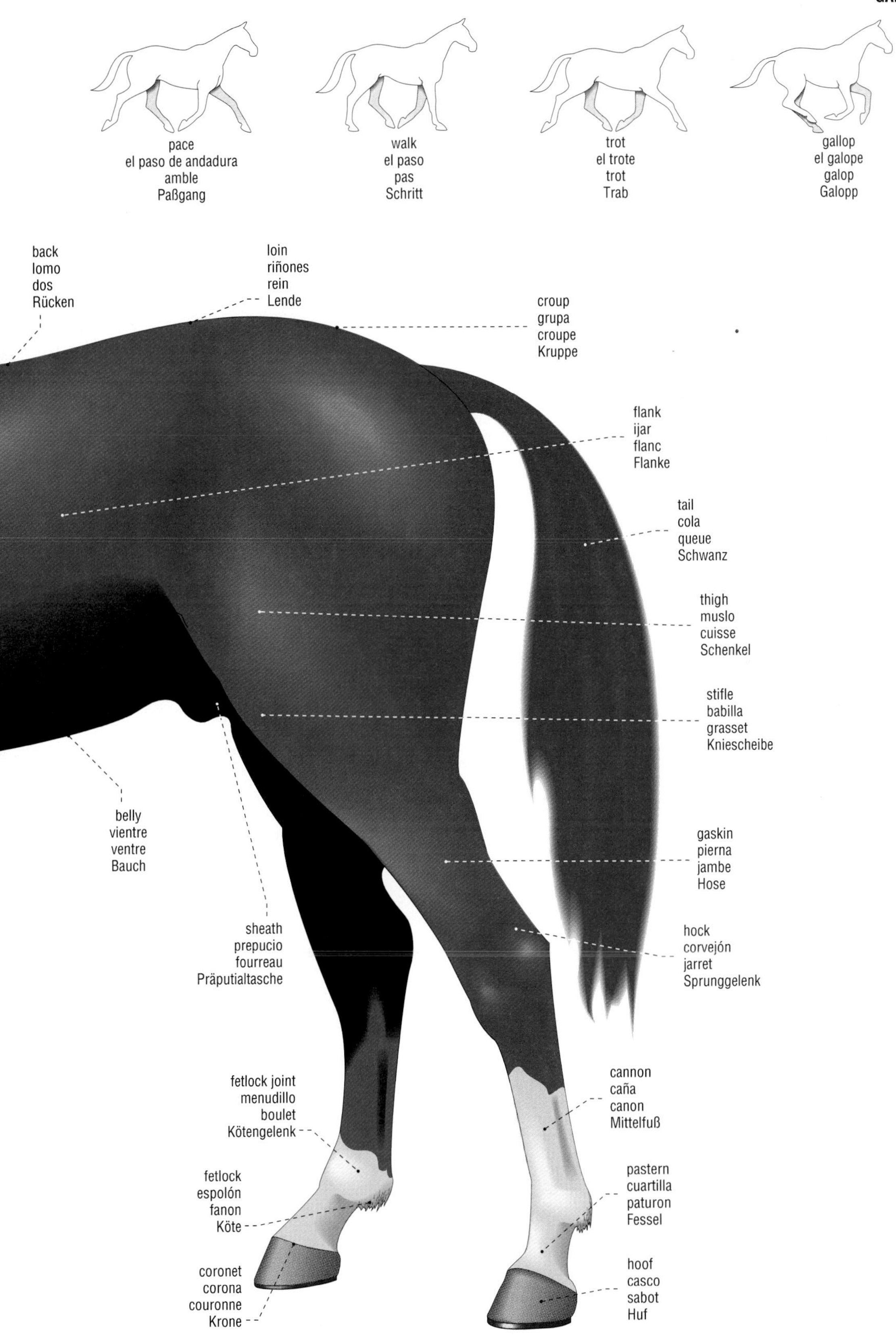
back
lomo
dos
Rücken
loin
riñones
rein
Lende
croup
grupa
croupe
Kruppe
flank
ijar
flanc
Flanke
tail
cola
queue
Schwanz
thigh
muslo
cuisse
Schenkel
stifle
babilla
grasset
Kniescheibe
belly
vientre
ventre
Bauch
gaskin
pierna
jambe
Hose
sheath
prepucio
fourreau
Präputialtasche
hock
corvejón
jarret
Sprunggelenk
fetlock joint
menudillo
boulet
Kötengelenk
cannon
caña
canon
Mittelfuß
fetlock
espolón
fanon
Köte
pastern
cuartilla
paturon
Fessel
coronet
corona
couronne
Krone
hoof
casco
sabot
Huf

HORSE
CABALLO
CHEVAL
PFERD

SKELETON
ESQUELETO
SQUELETTE
SKELETT

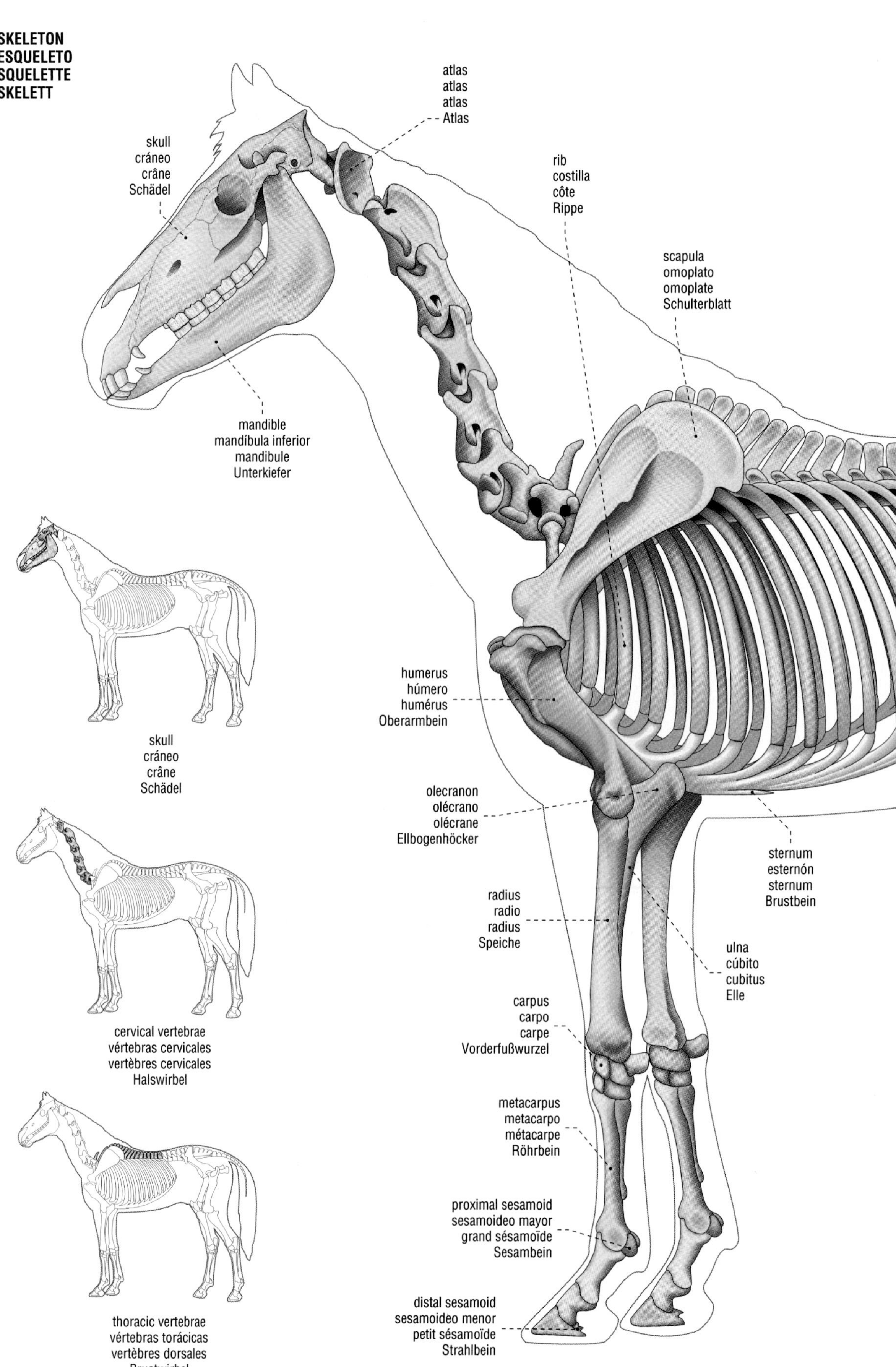
atlas
atlas
atlas
Atlas
skull
cráneo
crâne
Schädel
rib
costilla
côte
Rippe
scapula
omoplato
omoplate
Schulterblatt
mandible
mandíbula inferior
mandibule
Unterkiefer
humerus
húmero
humérus
Oberarmbein
olecranon
olécrano
olécrane
Ellbogenhöcker
sternum
esternón
sternum
Brustbein
radius
radio
radius
Speiche
ulna
cúbito
cubitus
Elle
carpus
carpo
carpe
Vorderfußwurzel
metacarpus
metacarpo
métacarpe
Röhrbein
proximal sesamoid
sesamoideo mayor
grand sésamoïde
Sesambein
distal sesamoid
sesamoideo menor
petit sésamoïde
Strahlbein
skull
cráneo
crâne
Schädel
cervical vertebrae
vértebras cervicales
vertèbres cervicales
Halswirbel
thoracic vertebrae
vértebras torácicas
vertèbres dorsales
Brustwirbel

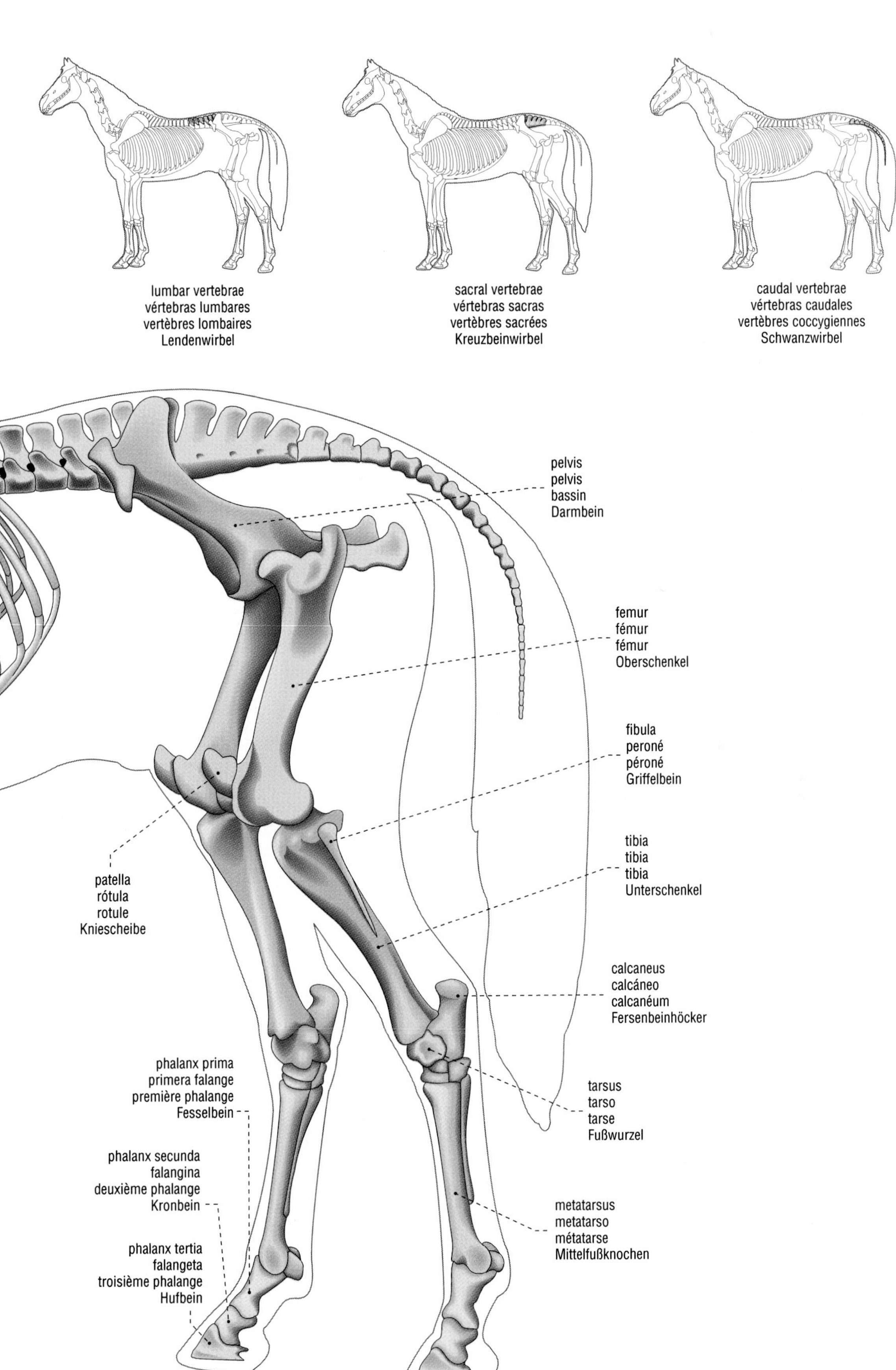
lumbar vertebrae
vértebras lumbares
vertèbres lombaires
Lendenwirbel
sacral vertebrae
vértebras sacras
vertèbres sacrées
Kreuzbeinwirbel
caudal vertebrae
vértebras caudales
vertèbres coccygiennes
Schwanzwirbel
pelvis
pelvis
bassin
Darmbein
femur
fémur
fémur
Oberschenkel
fibula
peroné
péroné
Griffelbein
tibia
tibia
tibia
Unterschenkel
patella
rótula
rotule
Kniescheibe
calcaneus
calcáneo
calcanéum
Fersenbeinhöcker
phalanx prima
primera falange
première phalange
Fesselbein
tarsus
tarso
tarse
Fußwurzel
phalanx secunda
falangina
deuxième phalange
Kronbein
metatarsus
metatarso
métatarse
Mittelfußknochen
phalanx tertia
falangeta
troisième phalange
Hufbein

HORSE
CABALLO
CHEVAL
PFERD

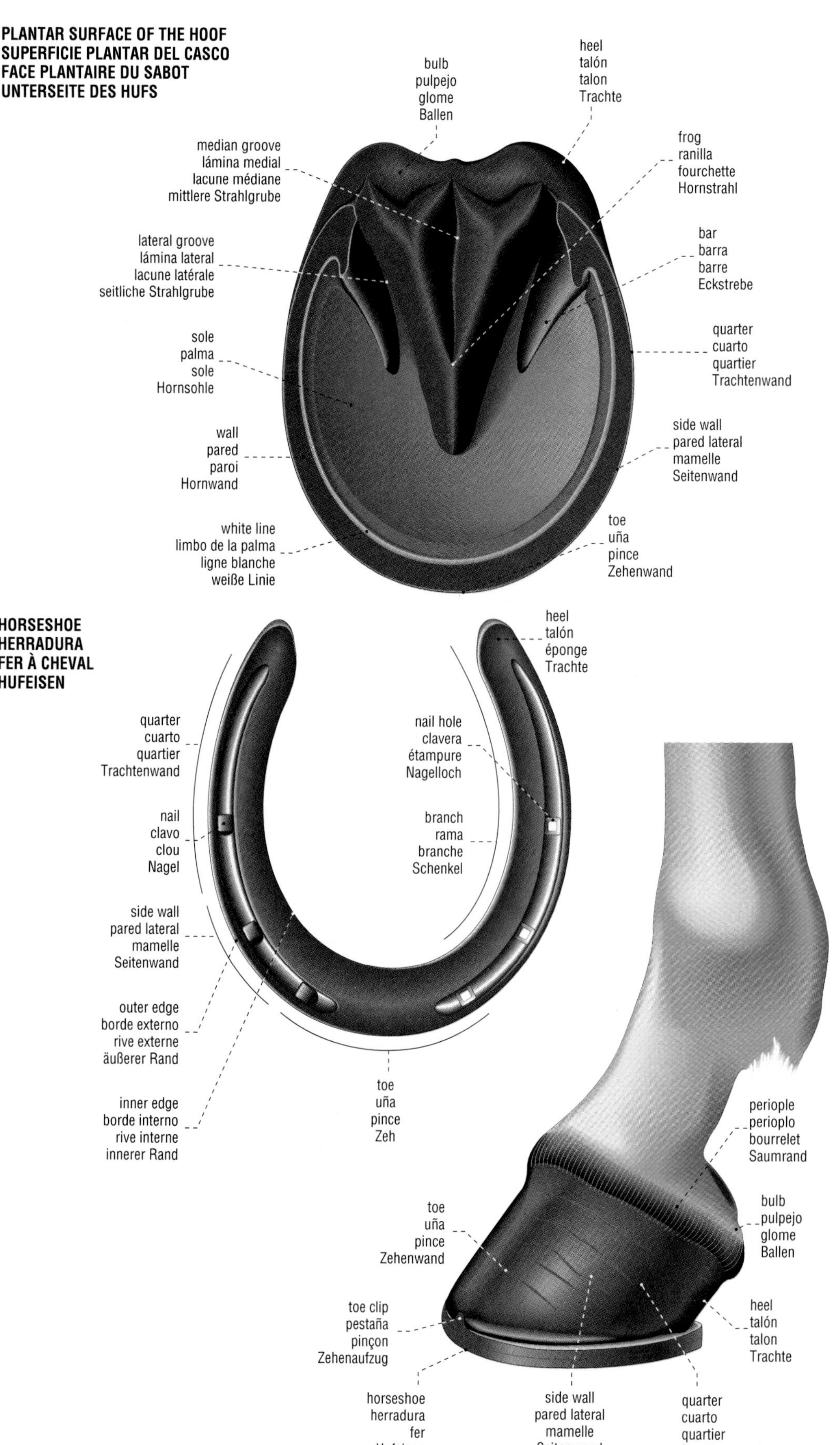
PLANTAR SURFACE OF THE HOOF
SUPERFICIE PLANTAR DEL CASCO
FACE PLANTAIRE DU SABOT
UNTERSEITE DES HUFS
bulb
pulpejo
glome
Ballen
heel
talón
talon
Trachte
median groove
lámina medial
lacune médiane
mittlere Strahlgrube
frog
ranilla
fourchette
Hornstrahl
lateral groove
lámina lateral
lacune latérale
seitliche Strahlgrube
bar
barra
barre
Eckstrebe
quarter
cuarto
quartier
Trachtenwand
sole
palma
sole
Hornsohle
wall
pared
paroi
Hornwand
side wall
pared lateral
mamelle
Seitenwand
white line
limbo de la palma
ligne blanche
weiße Linie
toe
uña
pince
Zehenwand
HORSESHOE
HERRADURA
FER À CHEVAL
HUFEISEN
heel
talón
éponge
Trachte
quarter
cuarto
quartier
Trachtenwand
nail hole
clavera
étampure
Nagelloch
nail
clavo
clou
Nagel
branch
rama
branche
Schenkel
side wall
pared lateral
mamelle
Seitenwand
outer edge
borde externo
rive externe
äußerer Rand
inner edge
borde interno
rive interne
innerer Rand
toe
uña
pince
Zeh
HOOF
CASCO
SABOT
HUF
periople
perioplo
bourrelet
Saumrand
bulb
pulpejo
glome
Ballen
toe
uña
pince
Zehenwand
toe clip
pestaña
pinçon
Zehenaufzug
heel
talón
talon
Trachte
horseshoe
herradura
fer
Hufeisen
side wall
pared lateral
mamelle
Seitenwand
quarter
cuarto
quartier
Trachtenwand

DEER FAMILY
CÉRVIDOS
CERVIDÉS
FAMILIE DER HIRSCHE

DEER ANTLERS
CORNAMENTA
BOIS DE CERF
HIRSCHGEWEIH

KINDS OF DEER
PRINCIPALES CÉRVIDOS
PRINCIPAUX CERVIDÉS
HIRSCHARTEN

fork
horquilla
enfourchure
Gabel
palm
palma
empaumure
Krone
crown tine
candil coronal
époi
Kronenende
pearl
capa córnea
perlure
Perle
royal antler
tercera
chevillure
Mittelsproß
gutter
canalón
gouttière
Furche
surroyal antler
cuarta
trochure
Wolfssproß
bay antler
baya
surandouiller
Eissproß
beam
asta
merrain
Stange
brow tine
candil frontal
andouiller de massacre
Augsproß
burr
rodete
meule
Rose
pearls
perlas
pierrures
Perlen
pedicle
muñón
pivot
Rosenstock
caribou
caribú
renne
Rentier
white-tailed deer
ciervo de Virginia
cerf de Virginie
Reh
moose
alce
élan
Elch
wapiti
wapití
cerf du Canada
Wapitihirsch

DOG
PERRO
CHIEN
HUND

MORPHOLOGY
MORFOLOGÍA
MORPHOLOGIE
MORPHOLOGIE

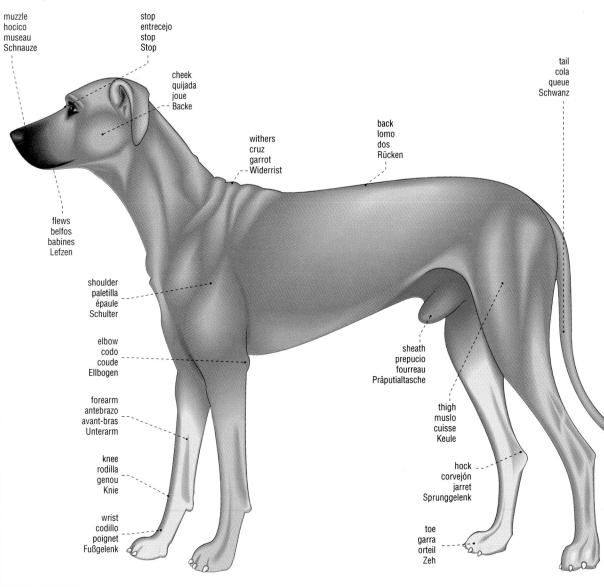

muzzle
hocico
museau
Schnauze

stop
entrecejo
stop
Stop

cheek
quijada
joue
Backe

tail
cola
queue
Schwanz

back
lomo
dos
Rücken

withers
cruz
garrot
Widerrist

flews
belfos
babines
Lefzen

shoulder
paletilla
épaule
Schulter

elbow
codo
coude
Ellbogen

sheath
prepucio
fourreau
Präputialtasche

forearm
antebrazo
avant-bras
Unterarm

thigh
muslo
cuisse
Keule

knee
rodilla
genou
Knie

hock
corvejón
jarret
Sprunggelenk

wrist
codillo
poignet
Fußgelenk

toe
garra
orteil
Zeh

DOG'S FOREPAW
PATA DELANTERA DEL PERRO
PATTE ANTÉRIEURE
VORDERPFOTE DES HUNDES

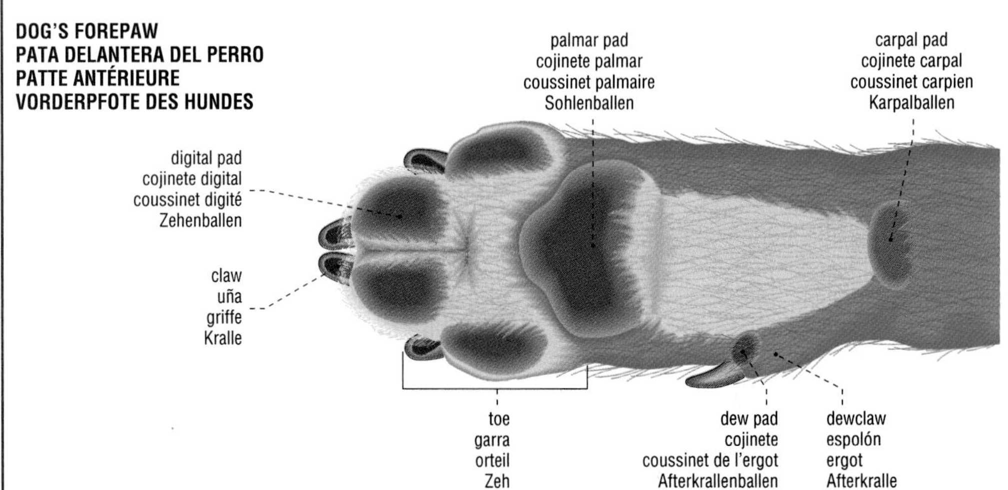
palmar pad
cojinete palmar
coussinet palmaire
Sohlenballen
carpal pad
cojinete carpal
coussinet carpien
Karpalballen
digital pad
cojinete digital
coussinet digité
Zehenballen
claw
uña
griffe
Kralle
toe
garra
orteil
Zeh
dew pad
cojinete
coussinet de l'ergot
Afterkrallenballen
dewclaw
espolón
ergot
Afterkralle

CAT
GATO DOMÉSTICO
CHAT
KATZE

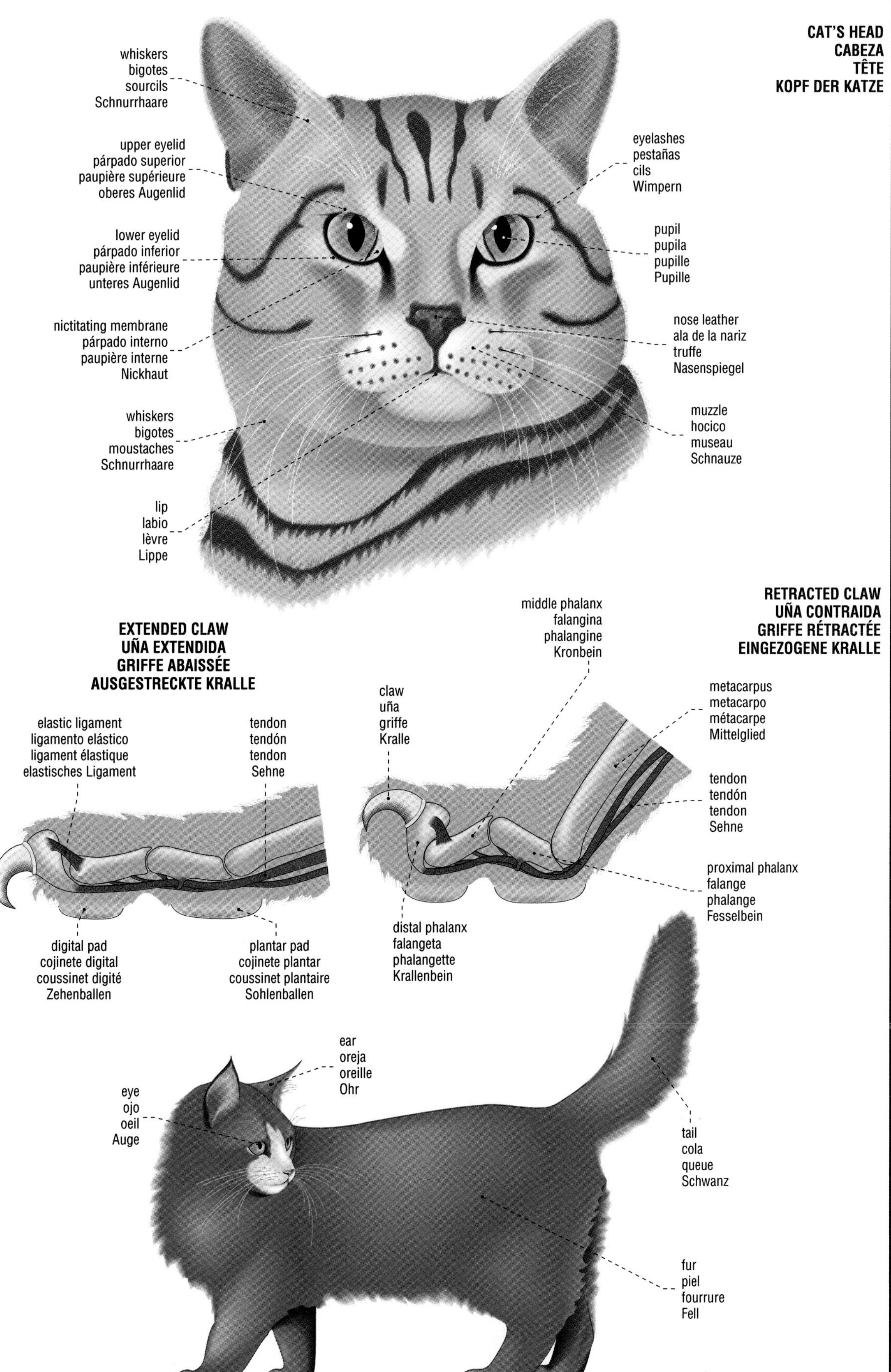
CAT'S HEAD
CABEZA
TÊTE
KOPF DER KATZE
whiskers
bigotes
sourcils
Schnurrhaare
upper eyelid
párpado superior
paupière supérieure
oberes Augenlid
lower eyelid
párpado inferior
paupière inférieure
unteres Augenlid
nictitating membrane
párpado interno
paupière interne
Nickhaut
whiskers
bigotes
moustaches
Schnurrhaare
lip
labio
lèvre
Lippe
eyelashes
pestañas
cils
Wimpern
pupil
pupila
pupille
Pupille
nose leather
ala de la nariz
truffe
Nasenspiegel
muzzle
hocico
museau
Schnauze
EXTENDED CLAW
UÑA EXTENDIDA
GRIFFE ABAISSÉE
AUSGESTRECKTE KRALLE
elastic ligament
ligamento elástico
ligament élastique
elastisches Ligament
tendon
tendón
tendon
Sehne
digital pad
cojinete digital
coussinet digité
Zehenballen
plantar pad
cojinete plantar
coussinet plantaire
Sohlenballen
middle phalanx
falangina
phalangine
Kronbein
claw
uña
griffe
Kralle
RETRACTED CLAW
UÑA CONTRAIDA
GRIFFE RÉTRACTÉE
EINGEZOGENE KRALLE
metacarpus
metacarpo
métacarpe
Mittelglied
tendon
tendón
tendon
Sehne
proximal phalanx
falange
phalange
Fesselbein
distal phalanx
falangeta
phalangette
Krallenbein
ear
oreja
oreille
Ohr
eye
ojo
oeil
Auge
tail
cola
queue
Schwanz
fur
piel
fourrure
Fell

BIRD
AVE
OISEAU
VOGEL

MORPHOLOGY
MORFOLOGÍA
MORPHOLOGIE
MORPHOLOGIE

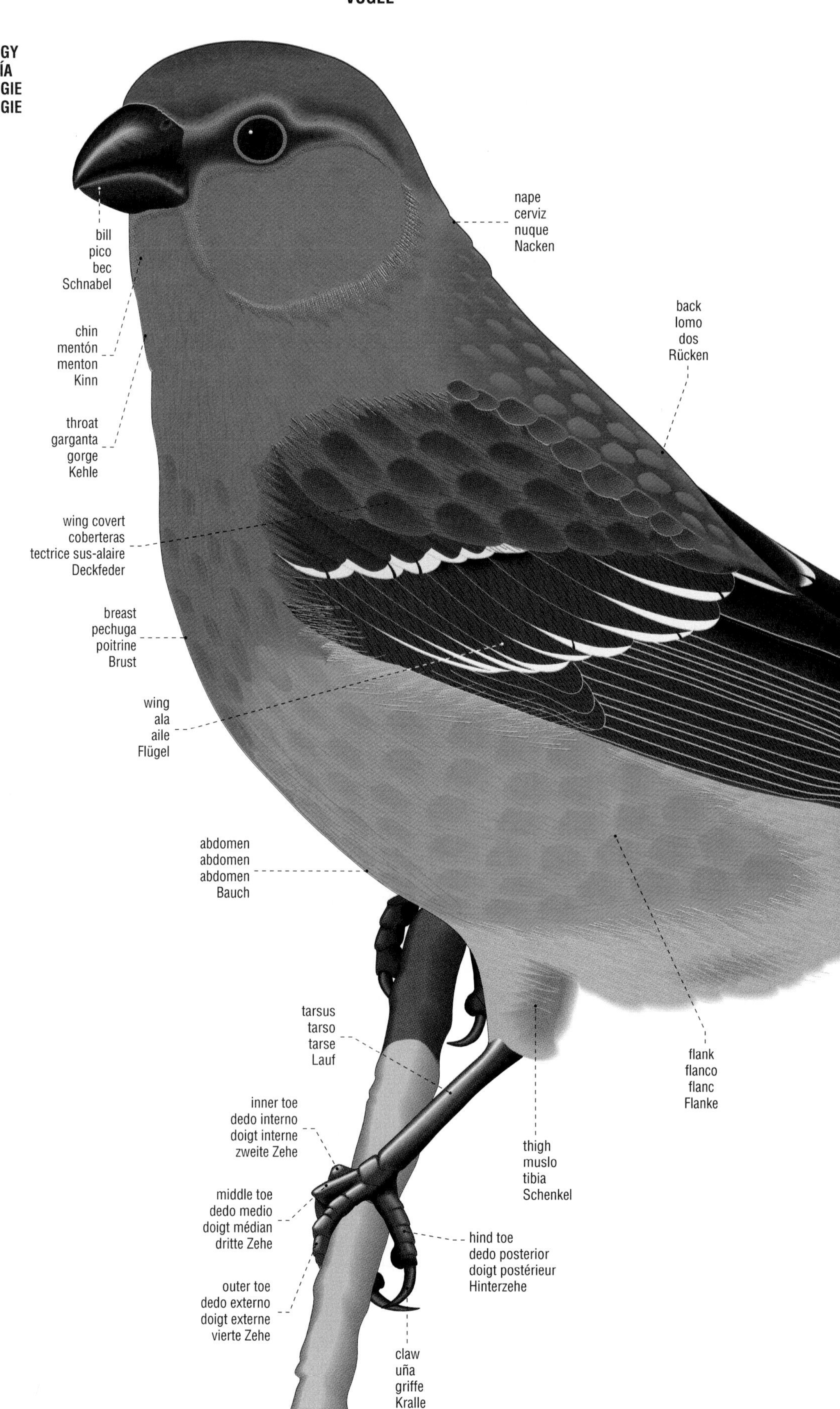
bill
pico
bec
Schnabel
chin
mentón
menton
Kinn
throat
garganta
gorge
Kehle
wing covert
coberteras
tectrice sus-alaire
Deckfeder
breast
pechuga
poitrine
Brust
wing
ala
aile
Flügel
abdomen
abdomen
abdomen
Bauch
tarsus
tarso
tarse
Lauf
inner toe
dedo interno
doigt interne
zweite Zehe
middle toe
dedo medio
doigt médian
dritte Zehe
outer toe
dedo externo
doigt externe
vierte Zehe
claw
uña
griffe
Kralle
hind toe
dedo posterior
doigt postérieur
Hinterzehe
thigh
muslo
tibia
Schenkel
flank
flanco
flanc
Flanke
back
lomo
dos
Rücken
nape
cerviz
nuque
Nacken

HEAD
CABEZA
TÊTE
KOPF

EGG
HUEVO
ŒUF
EI

forehead
frente
front
Stirn
crown
penacho
calotte
Scheitel
nostril
orificio nasal
narine
Nasenloch
eyebrow stripe
lista superciliar
raie sourcilière
Augenstreif
upper mandible
mandíbula superior
maxillaire
Oberschnabel
eye ring
anillo ocular
anneau oculaire
Augenring
auriculars
manchas auriculares
région auriculaire
Ohrdecken
lower mandible
mandíbula inferior
mandibule
Unterschnabel
lore
puente
lorum
Zügel
malar region
región malar
région malaire
Bartregion
rump
obispillo
croupion
Bürzel
tail feather
plumas timoneras
rectrice
Schwanzfeder
under tail covert
cobertera inferior de la cola
tectrice sous-caudale
Unterschwanzdecken
upper tail covert
cobertera superior de la cola
tectrice sus-caudale
Oberschwanzdecken
blastodisc
blastodisco
germe
Keimscheibe
shell
cascarón
coquille
Schale
vitelline membrane
membrana vitelina
membrane vitelline
Dotterhaut
shell membrane
membrana del cascarón
membrane coquillière
Schalenhaut
air space
cámara de aire
chambre à air
Luftkammer
chalaza
chalaza
chalaze
Hagelschnur
yolk
yema
jaune
Eigelb
albumen
albúmina
albumen
Eiweiß

BIRD
AVE
OISEAU
VOGEL

WING
ALA
AILE
FLÜGEL

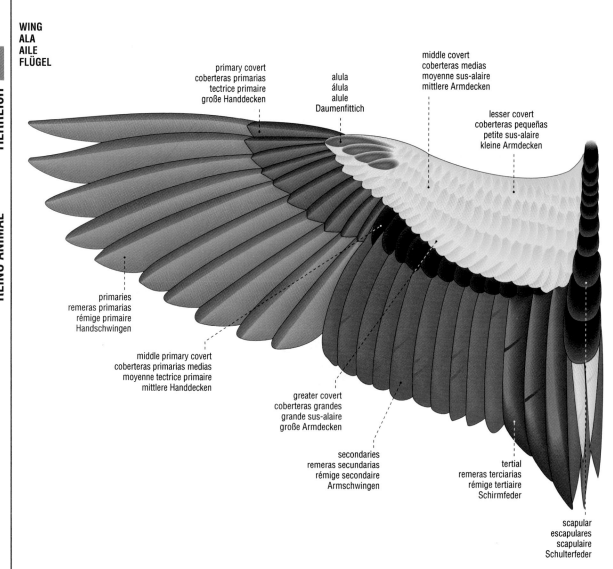

primary covert
coberteras primarias
tectrice primaire
große Handdecken

alula
álula
alule
Daumenfittich

middle covert
coberteras medias
moyenne sus-alaire
mittlere Armdecken

lesser covert
coberteras pequeñas
petite sus-alaire
kleine Armdecken

primaries
remeras primarias
rémige primaire
Handschwingen

middle primary covert
coberteras primarias medias
moyenne tectrice primaire
mittlere Handdecken

greater covert
coberteras grandes
grande sus-alaire
große Armdecken

secondaries
remeras secundarias
rémige secondaire
Armschwingen

tertial
remeras terciarias
rémige tertiaire
Schirmfeder

scapular
escapulares
scapulaire
Schulterfeder

CONTOUR FEATHER
PLUMA
PENNE
KONTURFEDER

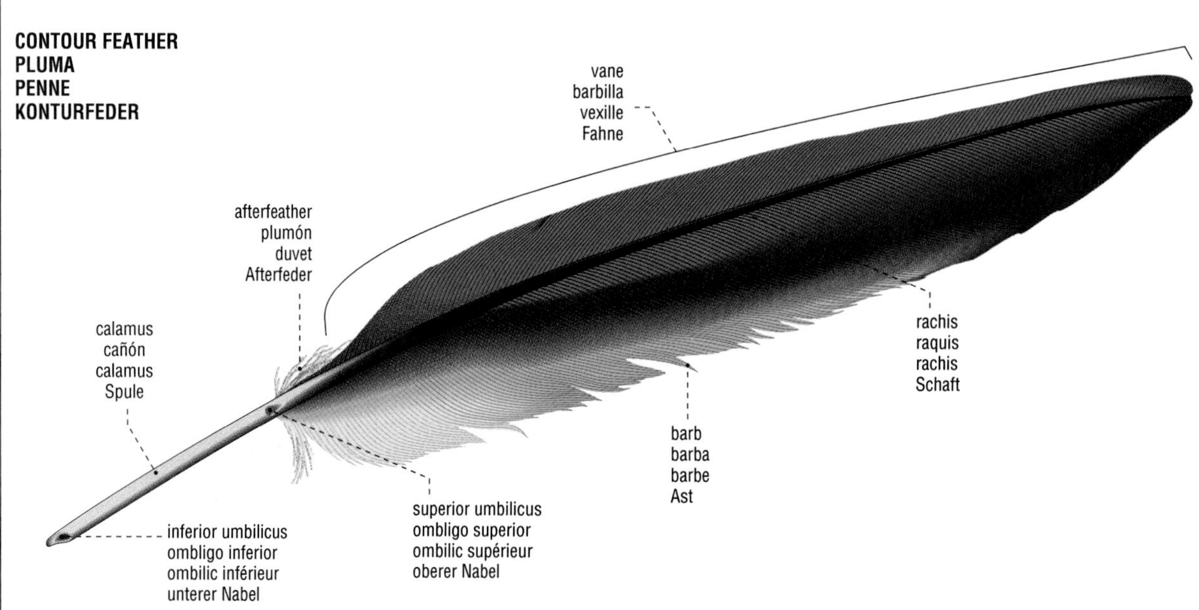
vane
barbilla
vexille
Fahne
afterfeather
plumón
duvet
Afterfeder
calamus
cañón
calamus
Spule
rachis
raquis
rachis
Schaft
barb
barba
barbe
Ast
superior umbilicus
ombligo superior
ombilic supérieur
oberer Nabel
inferior umbilicus
ombligo inferior
ombilic inférieur
unterer Nabel

PRINCIPAL TYPES OF BILLS
PRINCIPALES TIPOS DE PICOS
PRINCIPAUX TYPES DE BECS
WICHTIGSTE SCHNABELARTEN

bird of prey
ave de rapiña
oiseau de proie
Raubvogel

aquatic bird
ave acuática
oiseau aquatique
Wasservogel

wading bird
ave zancuda
oiseau échassier
Watvogel

granivorous bird
ave granívora
oiseau granivore
Körnerfresser

insectivorous bird
ave insectívora
oiseau insectivore
Insektenfresser

PRINCIPAL TYPES OF FEET
PRINCIPALES TIPOS DE PATAS
PRINCIPAUX TYPES DE PATTES
WICHTIGSTE FUSSARTEN

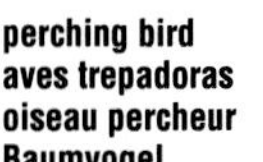

perching bird
aves trepadoras
oiseau percheur
Baumvogel

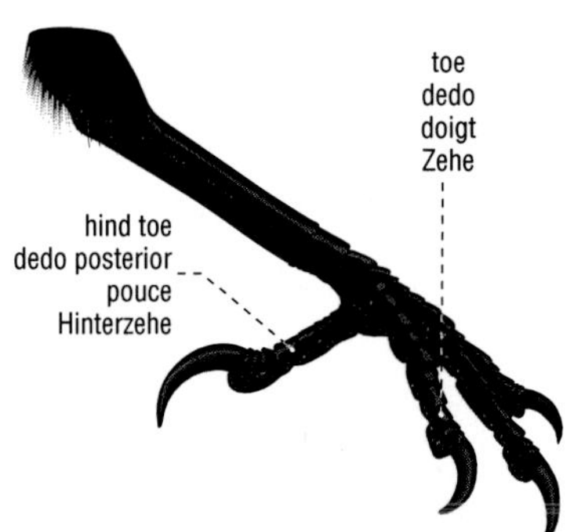
toe
dedo
doigt
Zehe
hind toe
dedo posterior
pouce
Hinterzehe

bird of prey
aves de rapiña
oiseau de proie
Raubvogel

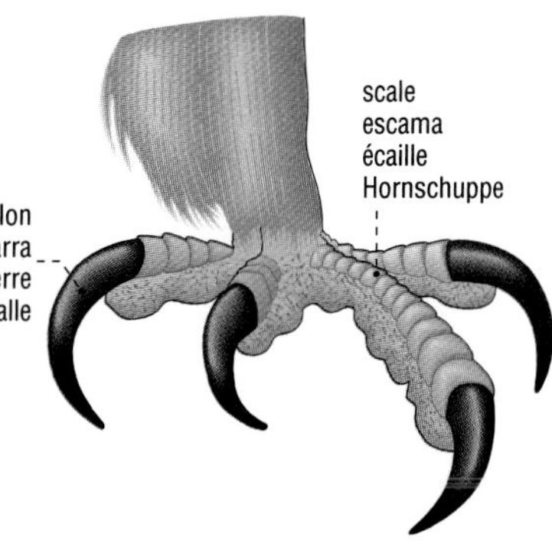
scale
escama
écaille
Hornschuppe
talon
garra
serre
Kralle

aquatic bird
aves acuáticas
oiseau aquatique
Wasservogel

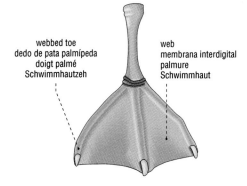

webbed toe
dedo de pata palmípeda
doigt palmé
Schwimmhautzeh

web
membrana interdigital
palmure
Schwimmhaut

aquatic bird
aves acuáticas
oiseau aquatique
Wasservogel

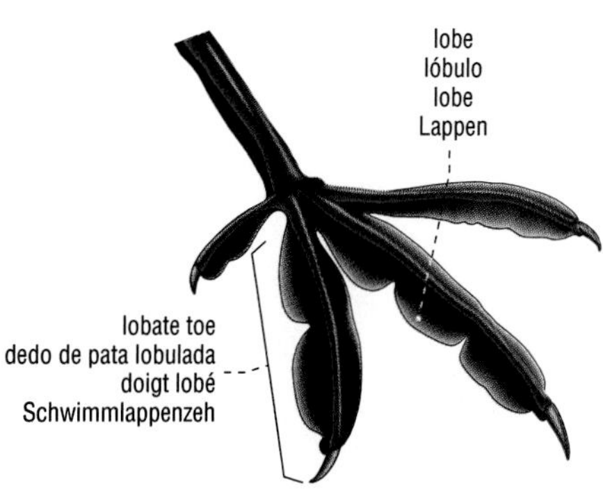
lobe
lóbulo
lobe
Lappen
lobate toe
dedo de pata lobulada
doigt lobé
Schwimmlappenzeh

BAT
MURCIÉLAGO
CHAUVE-SOURIS
FLEDERMAUS

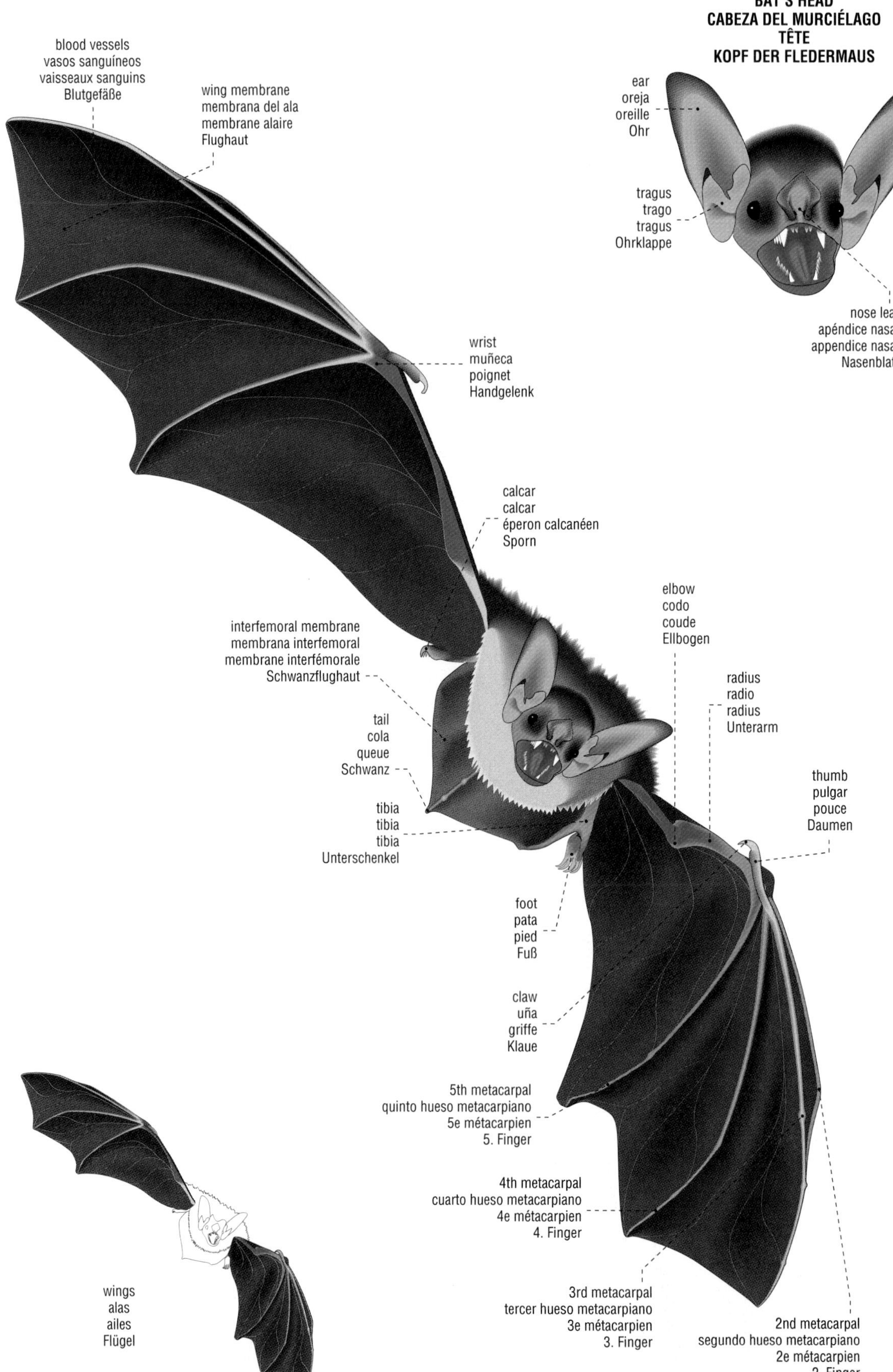
BAT'S HEAD
CABEZA DEL MURCIÉLAGO
TÊTE
KOPF DER FLEDERMAUS
blood vessels
vasos sanguíneos
vaisseaux sanguins
Blutgefäße
wing membrane
membrana del ala
membrane alaire
Flughaut
ear
oreja
oreille
Ohr
tragus
trago
tragus
Ohrklappe
nose leaf
apéndice nasal
appendice nasal
Nasenblatt
wrist
muñeca
poignet
Handgelenk
calcar
calcar
éperon calcanéen
Sporn
elbow
codo
coude
Ellbogen
interfemoral membrane
membrana interfemoral
membrane interfémorale
Schwanzflughaut
radius
radio
radius
Unterarm
tail
cola
queue
Schwanz
thumb
pulgar
pouce
Daumen
tibia
tibia
tibia
Unterschenkel
foot
pata
pied
Fuß
claw
uña
griffe
Klaue
5th metacarpal
quinto hueso metacarpiano
5e métacarpien
5. Finger
4th metacarpal
cuarto hueso metacarpiano
4e métacarpien
4. Finger
wings
alas
ailes
Flügel
3rd metacarpal
tercer hueso metacarpiano
3e métacarpien
3. Finger
2nd metacarpal
segundo hueso metacarpiano
2e métacarpien
2. Finger

HUMAN BEING ÊTRE HUMAIN
SER HUMANO MENSCH

CONTENTS

PLANT CELL
CÉLULA VEGETAL
CELLULE VÉGÉTALE
PFLANZENZELLE

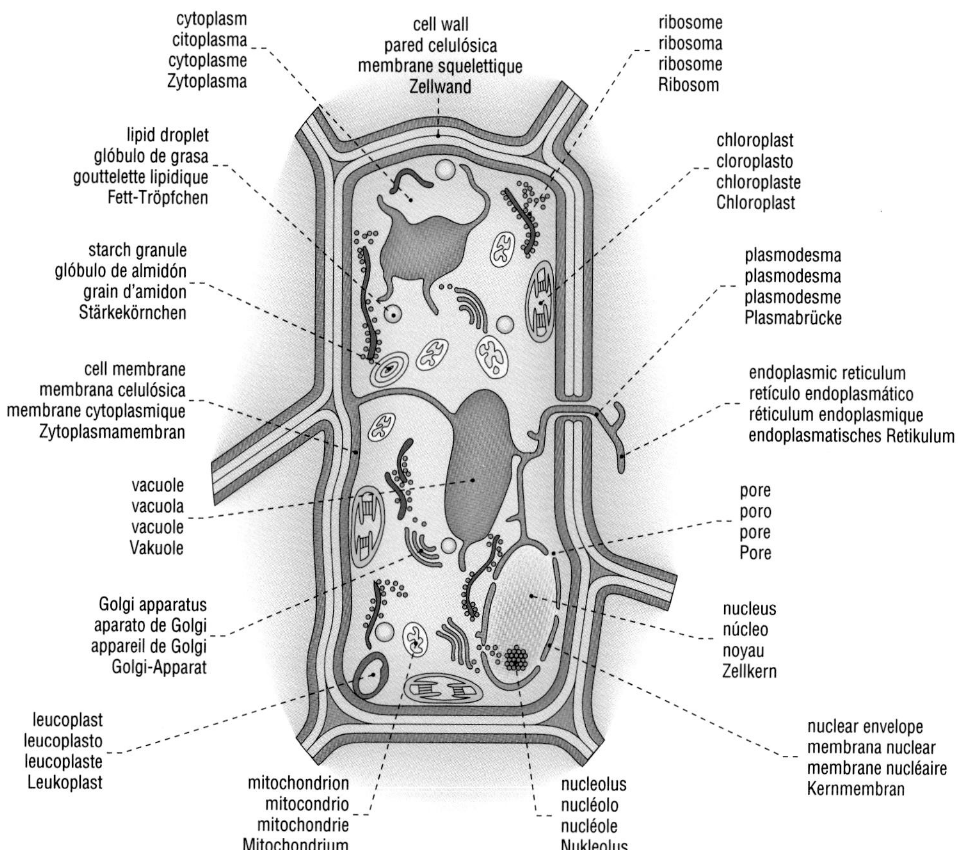
cytoplasm
citoplasma
cytoplasme
Zytoplasma
cell wall
pared celulósica
membrane squelettique
Zellwand
ribosome
ribosoma
ribosome
Ribosom
lipid droplet
glóbulo de grasa
gouttelette lipidique
Fett-Tröpfchen
chloroplast
cloroplasto
chloroplaste
Chloroplast
starch granule
glóbulo de almidón
grain d'amidon
Stärkekörnchen
plasmodesma
plasmodesma
plasmodesme
Plasmabrücke
cell membrane
membrana celulósica
membrane cytoplasmique
Zytoplasmamembran
endoplasmic reticulum
retículo endoplasmático
réticulum endoplasmique
endoplasmatisches Retikulum
vacuole
vacuola
vacuole
Vakuole
pore
poro
pore
Pore
Golgi apparatus
aparato de Golgi
appareil de Golgi
Golgi-Apparat
nucleus
núcleo
noyau
Zellkern
leucoplast
leucoplasto
leucoplaste
Leukoplast
nuclear envelope
membrana nuclear
membrane nucléaire
Kernmembran
mitochondrion
mitocondrio
mitochondrie
Mitochondrium
nucleolus
nucléolo
nucléole
Nukleolus

ANIMAL CELL
CÉLULA ANIMAL
CELLULE ANIMALE
TIERISCHE ZELLE

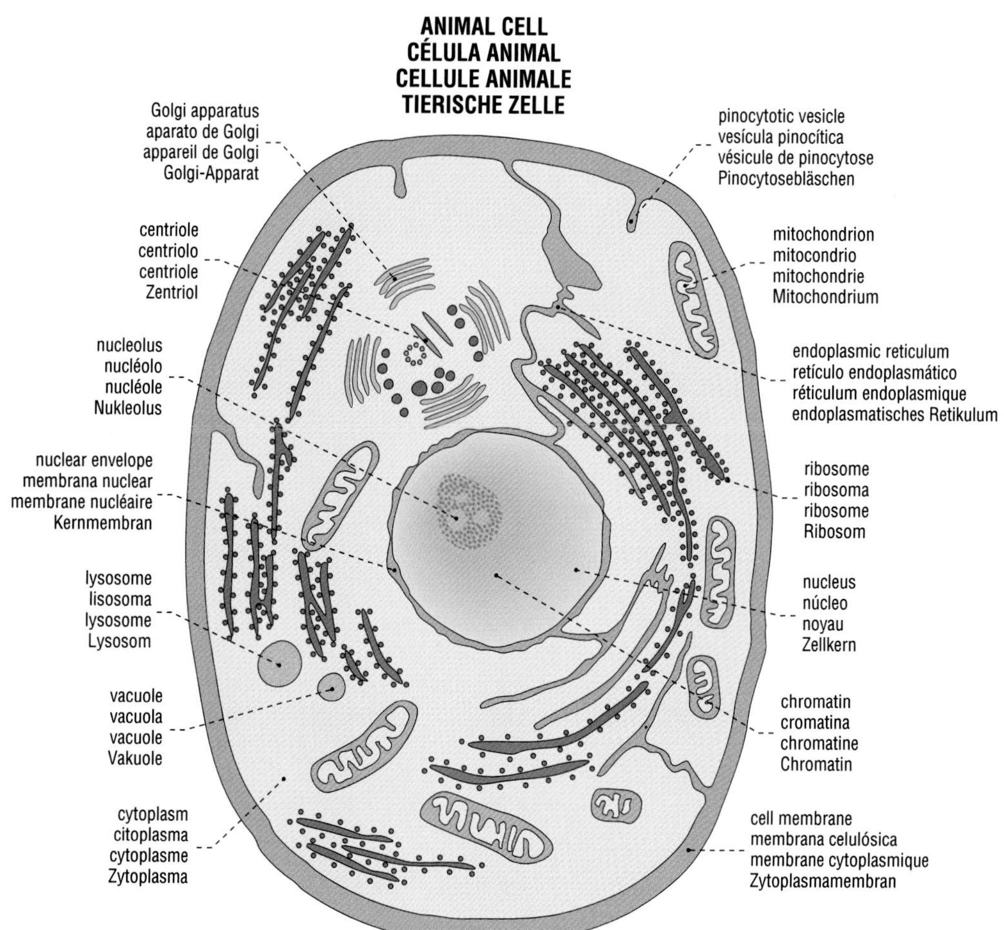
Golgi apparatus
aparato de Golgi
appareil de Golgi
Golgi-Apparat
pinocytotic vesicle
vesícula pinocítica
vésicule de pinocytose
Pinocytosebläschen
centriole
centriolo
centriole
Zentriol
mitochondrion
mitocondrio
mitochondrie
Mitochondrium
nucleolus
nucléolo
nucléole
Nukleolus
endoplasmic reticulum
retículo endoplasmático
réticulum endoplasmique
endoplasmatisches Retikulum
nuclear envelope
membrana nuclear
membrane nucléaire
Kernmembran
ribosome
ribosoma
ribosome
Ribosom
lysosome
lisosoma
lysosome
Lysosom
nucleus
núcleo
noyau
Zellkern
vacuole
vacuola
vacuole
Vakuole
chromatin
cromatina
chromatine
Chromatin
cytoplasm
citoplasma
cytoplasme
Zytoplasma
cell membrane
membrana celulósica
membrane cytoplasmique
Zytoplasmamembran

HUMAN BODY
CUERPO HUMANO
CORPS HUMAIN
MENSCHLICHER KÖRPER

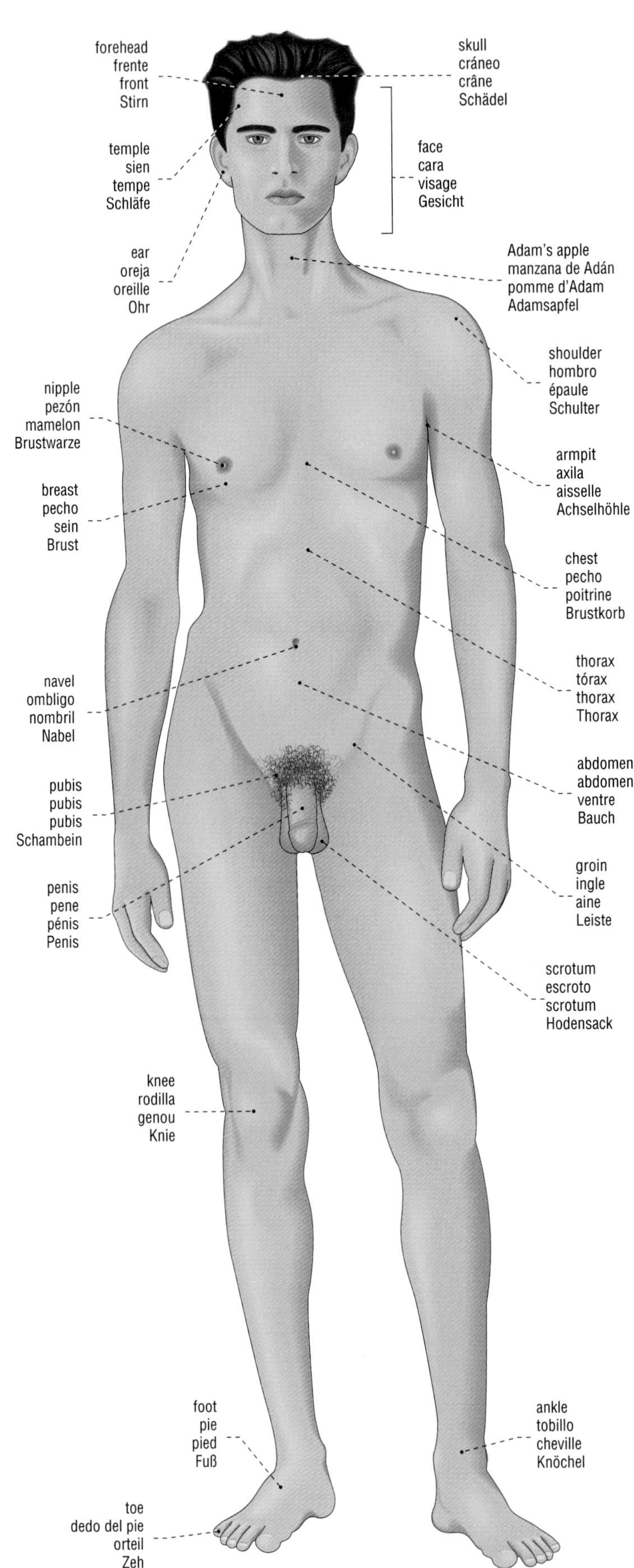
forehead
frente
front
Stirn
skull
cráneo
crâne
Schädel
temple
sien
tempe
Schläfe
face
cara
visage
Gesicht
ear
oreja
oreille
Ohr
Adam's apple
manzana de Adán
pomme d'Adam
Adamsapfel
shoulder
hombro
épaule
Schulter
nipple
pezón
mamelon
Brustwarze
armpit
axila
aisselle
Achselhöhle
breast
pecho
sein
Brust
chest
pecho
poitrine
Brustkorb
thorax
tórax
thorax
Thorax
navel
ombligo
nombril
Nabel
abdomen
abdomen
ventre
Bauch
pubis
pubis
pubis
Schambein
groin
ingle
aine
Leiste
penis
pene
pénis
Penis
scrotum
escroto
scrotum
Hodensack
knee
rodilla
genou
Knie
foot
pie
pied
Fuß
ankle
tobillo
cheville
Knöchel
toe
dedo del pie
orteil
Zeh

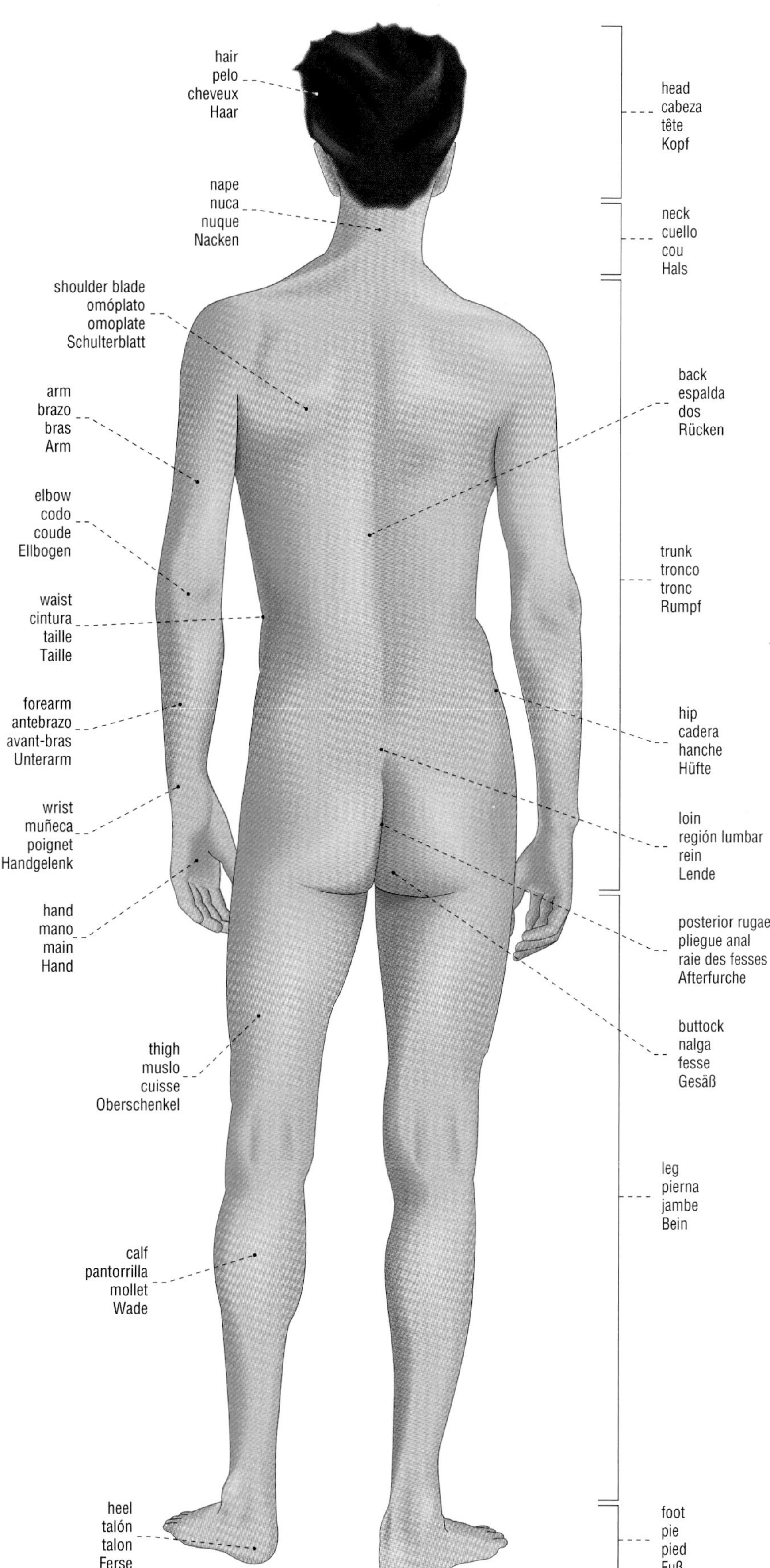
hair
pelo
cheveux
Haar
nape
nuca
nuque
Nacken
shoulder blade
omóplato
omoplate
Schulterblatt
arm
brazo
bras
Arm
elbow
codo
coude
Ellbogen
waist
cintura
taille
Taille
forearm
antebrazo
avant-bras
Unterarm
wrist
muñeca
poignet
Handgelenk
hand
mano
main
Hand
thigh
muslo
cuisse
Oberschenkel
calf
pantorrilla
mollet
Wade
heel
talón
talon
Ferse
head
cabeza
tête
Kopf
neck
cuello
cou
Hals
back
espalda
dos
Rücken
trunk
tronco
tronc
Rumpf
hip
cadera
hanche
Hüfte
loin
región lumbar
rein
Lende
posterior rugae
pliegue anal
raie des fesses
Afterfurche
buttock
nalga
fesse
Gesäß
leg
pierna
jambe
Bein
foot
pie
pied
Fuß

HUMAN BEING
SER HUMANO
ÊTRE HUMAIN
MENSCH

HUMAN BODY
CUERPO HUMANO
CORPS HUMAIN
MENSCHLICHER KÖRPER

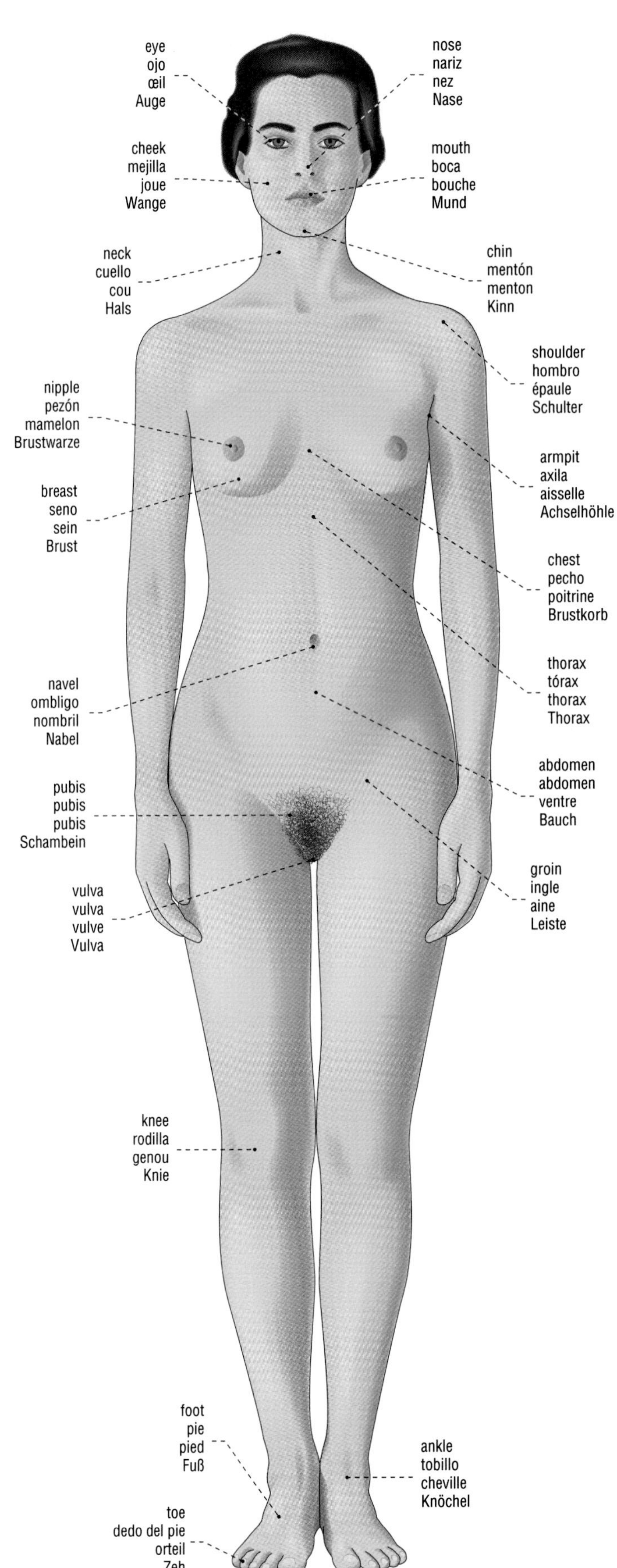

eye
ojo
œil
Auge
nose
nariz
nez
Nase
cheek
mejilla
joue
Wange
mouth
boca
bouche
Mund
neck
cuello
cou
Hals
chin
mentón
menton
Kinn
shoulder
hombro
épaule
Schulter
nipple
pezón
mamelon
Brustwarze
armpit
axila
aisselle
Achselhöhle
breast
seno
sein
Brust
chest
pecho
poitrine
Brustkorb
thorax
tórax
thorax
Thorax
navel
ombligo
nombril
Nabel
abdomen
abdomen
ventre
Bauch
pubis
pubis
pubis
Schambein
groin
ingle
aine
Leiste
vulva
vulva
vulve
Vulva
knee
rodilla
genou
Knie
foot
pie
pied
Fuß
ankle
tobillo
cheville
Knöchel
toe
dedo del pie
orteil
Zeh

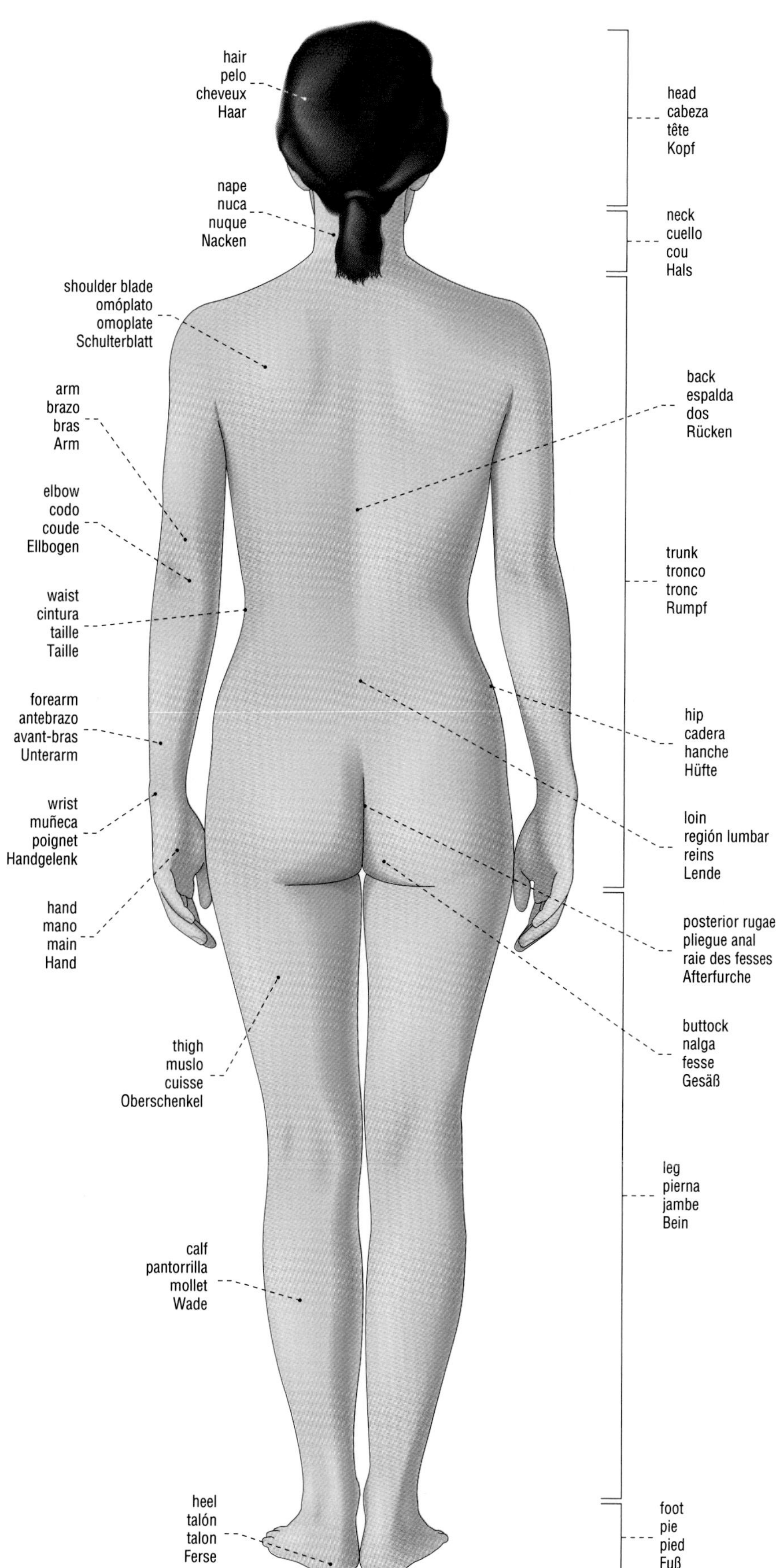
hair
pelo
cheveux
Haar
nape
nuca
nuque
Nacken
shoulder blade
omóplato
omoplate
Schulterblatt
arm
brazo
bras
Arm
elbow
codo
coude
Ellbogen
waist
cintura
taille
Taille
forearm
antebrazo
avant-bras
Unterarm
wrist
muñeca
poignet
Handgelenk
hand
mano
main
Hand
thigh
muslo
cuisse
Oberschenkel
calf
pantorrilla
mollet
Wade
heel
talón
talon
Ferse
head
cabeza
tête
Kopf
neck
cuello
cou
Hals
back
espalda
dos
Rücken
trunk
tronco
tronc
Rumpf
hip
cadera
hanche
Hüfte
loin
región lumbar
reins
Lende
posterior rugae
pliegue anal
raie des fesses
Afterfurche
buttock
nalga
fesse
Gesäß
leg
pierna
jambe
Bein
foot
pie
pied
Fuß

MUSCLES
MÚSCULOS
MUSCLES
MUSKELN

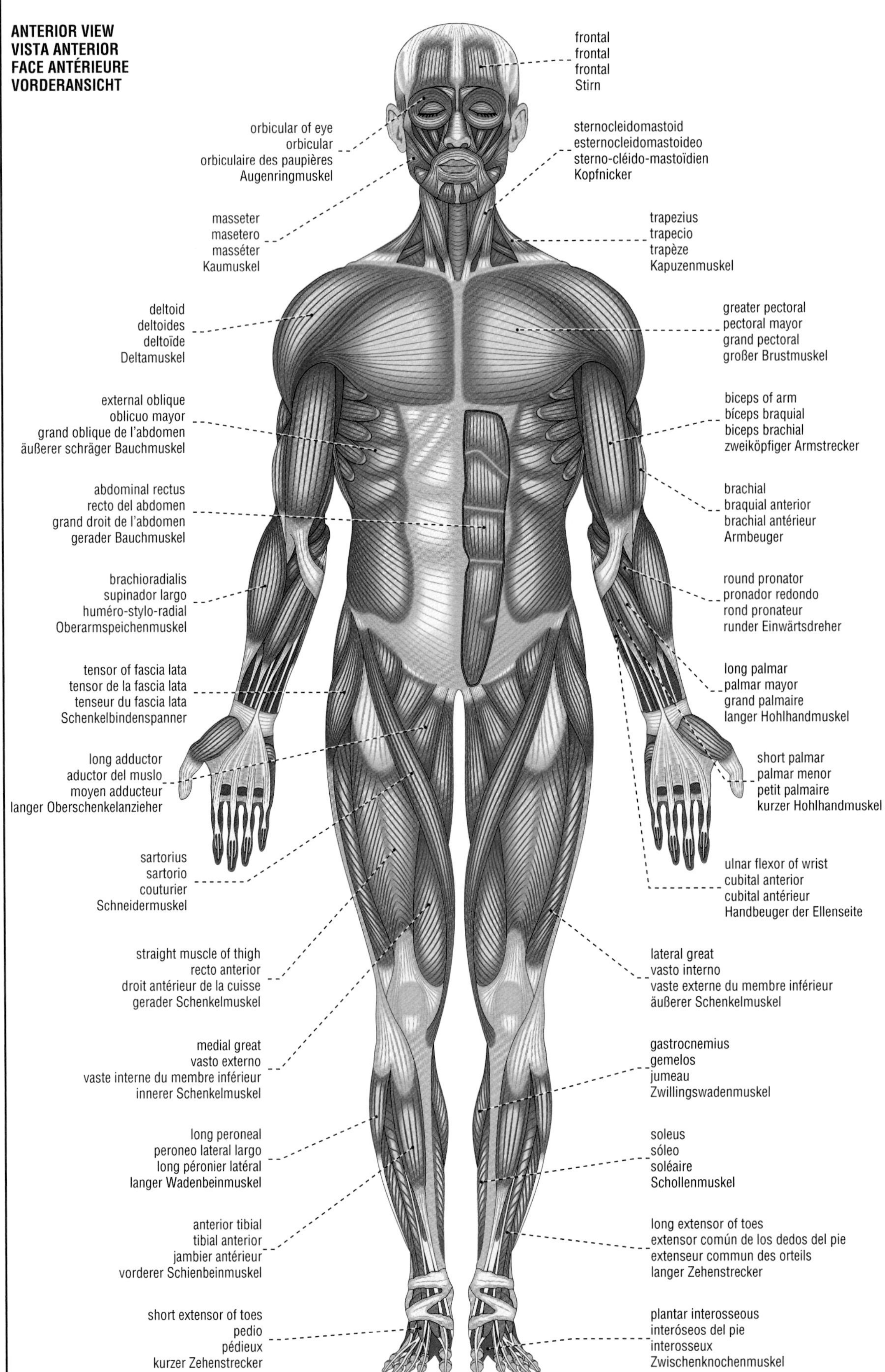
ANTERIOR VIEW
VISTA ANTERIOR
FACE ANTÉRIEURE
VORDERANSICHT
frontal
frontal
frontal
Stirn
orbicular of eye
orbicular
orbiculaire des paupières
Augenringmuskel
sternocleidomastoid
esternocleidomastoideo
sterno-cléido-mastoïdien
Kopfnicker
masseter
masetero
masséter
Kaumuskel
trapezius
trapecio
trapèze
Kapuzenmuskel
deltoid
deltoides
deltoïde
Deltamuskel
greater pectoral
pectoral mayor
grand pectoral
großer Brustmuskel
external oblique
oblicuo mayor
grand oblique de l'abdomen
äußerer schräger Bauchmuskel
biceps of arm
bíceps braquial
biceps brachial
zweiköpfiger Armstrecker
abdominal rectus
recto del abdomen
grand droit de l'abdomen
gerader Bauchmuskel
brachial
braquial anterior
brachial antérieur
Armbeuger
brachioradialis
supinador largo
huméro-stylo-radial
Oberarmspeichenmuskel
round pronator
pronador redondo
rond pronateur
runder Einwärtsdreher
tensor of fascia lata
tensor de la fascia lata
tenseur du fascia lata
Schenkelbindenspanner
long palmar
palmar mayor
grand palmaire
langer Hohlhandmuskel
long adductor
aductor del muslo
moyen adducteur
langer Oberschenkelanzieher
short palmar
palmar menor
petit palmaire
kurzer Hohlhandmuskel
sartorius
sartorio
couturier
Schneidermuskel
ulnar flexor of wrist
cubital anterior
cubital antérieur
Handbeuger der Ellenseite
straight muscle of thigh
recto anterior
droit antérieur de la cuisse
gerader Schenkelmuskel
lateral great
vasto interno
vaste externe du membre inférieur
äußerer Schenkelmuskel
medial great
vasto externo
vaste interne du membre inférieur
innerer Schenkelmuskel
gastrocnemius
gemelos
jumeau
Zwillingswadenmuskel
long peroneal
peroneo lateral largo
long péronier latéral
langer Wadenbeinmuskel
soleus
sóleo
soléaire
Schollenmuskel
anterior tibial
tibial anterior
jambier antérieur
vorderer Schienbeinmuskel
long extensor of toes
extensor común de los dedos del pie
extenseur commun des orteils
langer Zehenstrecker
short extensor of toes
pedio
pédieux
kurzer Zehenstrecker
plantar interosseous
interóseos del pie
interosseux
Zwischenknochenmuskel

POSTERIOR VIEW
VISTA POSTERIOR
FACE POSTÉRIEURE
RÜCKANSICHT

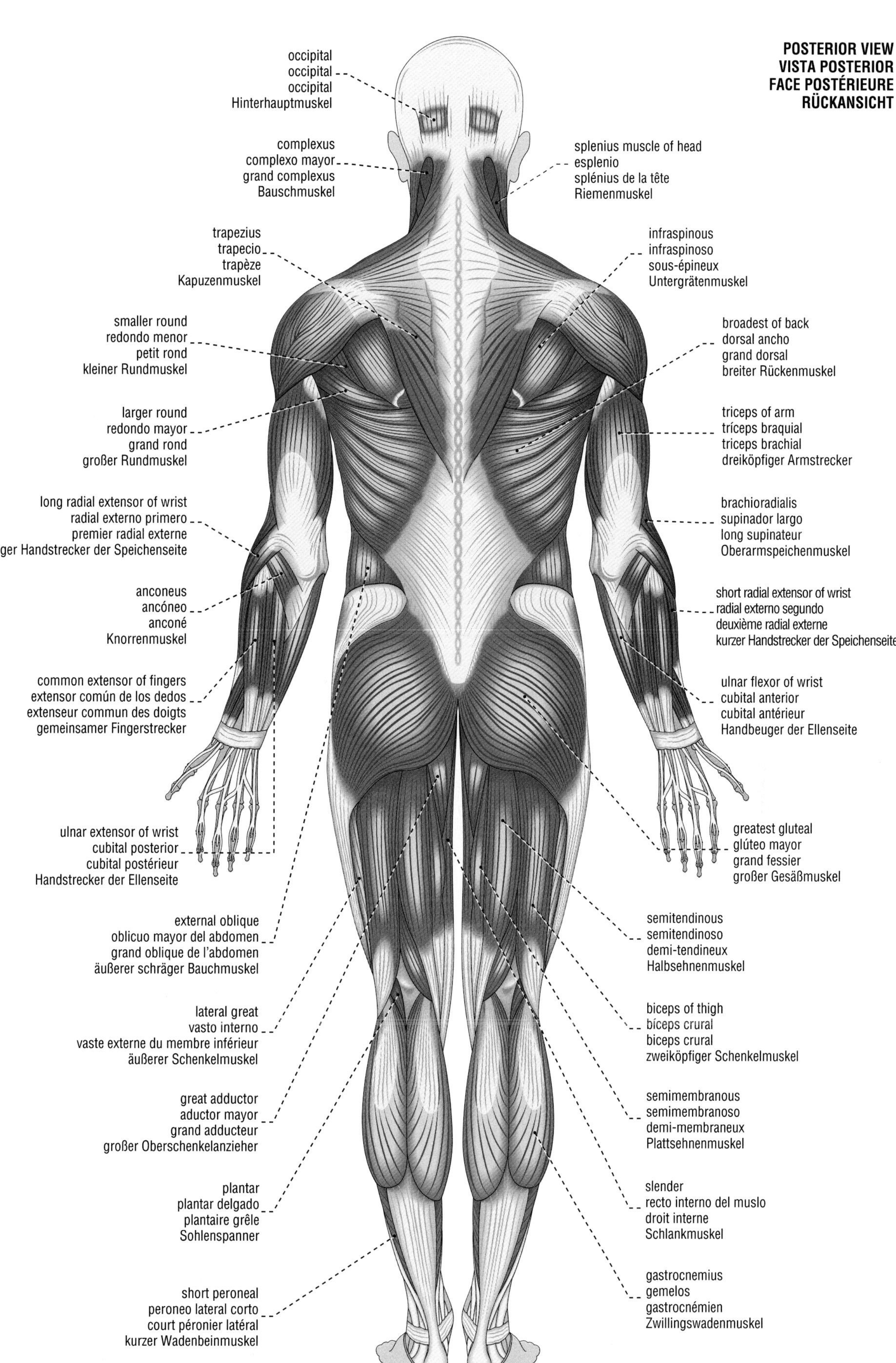

occipital
occipital
occipital
Hinterhauptmuskel
complexus
complexo mayor
grand complexus
Bauschmuskel
splenius muscle of head
esplenio
splénius de la tête
Riemenmuskel
trapezius
trapecio
trapèze
Kapuzenmuskel
infraspinous
infraspinoso
sous-épineux
Untergrätenmuskel
smaller round
redondo menor
petit rond
kleiner Rundmuskel
broadest of back
dorsal ancho
grand dorsal
breiter Rückenmuskel
larger round
redondo mayor
grand rond
großer Rundmuskel
triceps of arm
tríceps braquial
triceps brachial
dreiköpfiger Armstrecker
long radial extensor of wrist
radial externo primero
premier radial externe
langer Handstrecker der Speichenseite
brachioradialis
supinador largo
long supinateur
Oberarmspeichenmuskel
anconeus
ancóneo
anconé
Knorrenmuskel
short radial extensor of wrist
radial externo segundo
deuxième radial externe
kurzer Handstrecker der Speichenseite
common extensor of fingers
extensor común de los dedos
extenseur commun des doigts
gemeinsamer Fingerstrecker
ulnar flexor of wrist
cubital anterior
cubital antérieur
Handbeuger der Ellenseite
ulnar extensor of wrist
cubital posterior
cubital postérieur
Handstrecker der Ellenseite
greatest gluteal
glúteo mayor
grand fessier
großer Gesäßmuskel
external oblique
oblicuo mayor del abdomen
grand oblique de l'abdomen
äußerer schräger Bauchmuskel
semitendinous
semitendinoso
demi-tendineux
Halbsehnenmuskel
lateral great
vasto interno
vaste externe du membre inférieur
äußerer Schenkelmuskel
biceps of thigh
bíceps crural
biceps crural
zweiköpfiger Schenkelmuskel
great adductor
aductor mayor
grand adducteur
großer Oberschenkelanzieher
semimembranous
semimembranoso
demi-membraneux
Plattsehnenmuskel
plantar
plantar delgado
plantaire grêle
Sohlenspanner
slender
recto interno del muslo
droit interne
Schlankmuskel
short peroneal
peroneo lateral corto
court péronier latéral
kurzer Wadenbeinmuskel
gastrocnemius
gemelos
gastrocnémien
Zwillingswadenmuskel

SKELETON
ESQUELETO
SQUELETTE
SKELETT

ANTERIOR VIEW
VISTA ANTERIOR
VUE ANTÉRIEURE
VORDERANSICHT

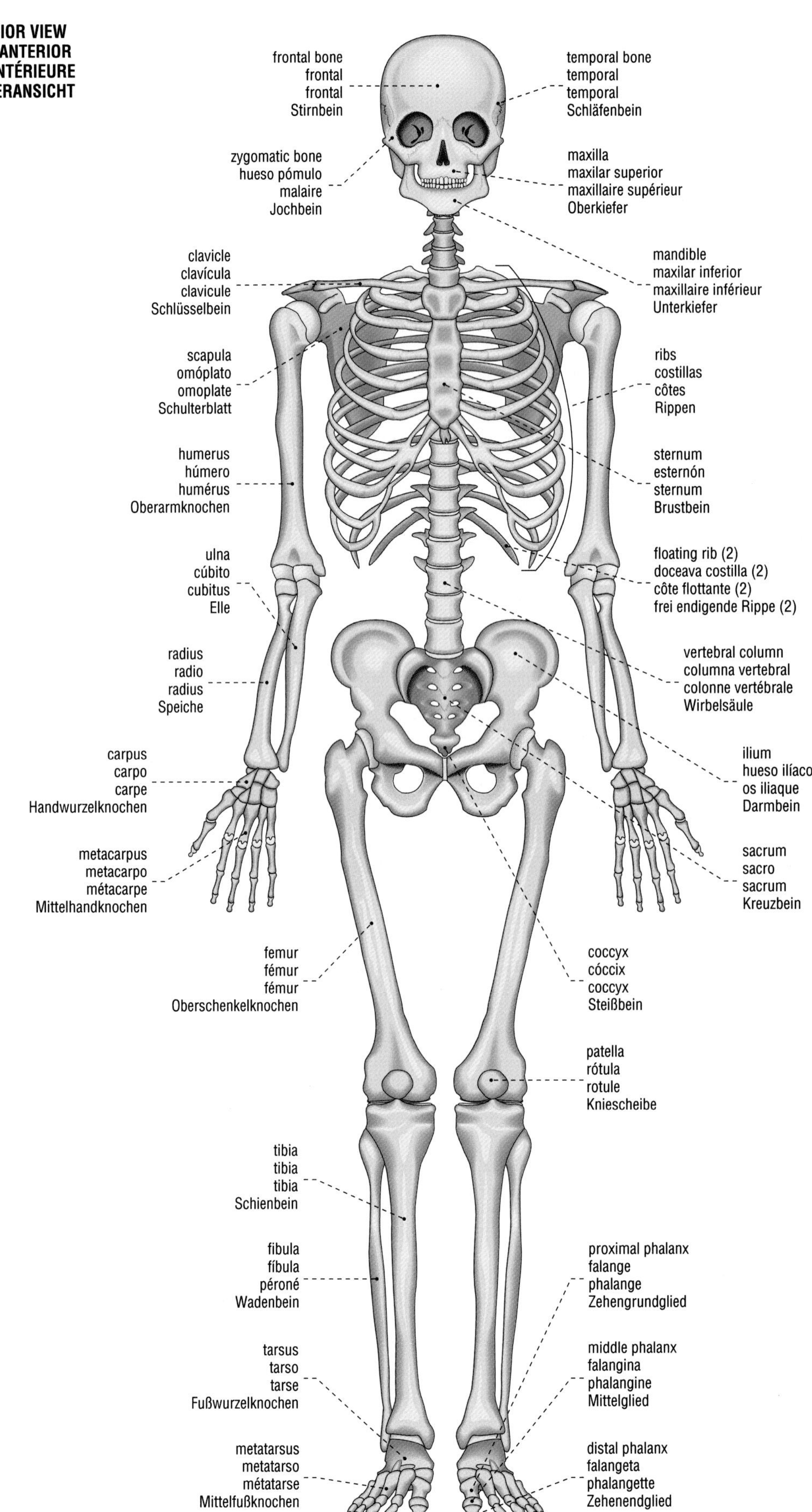
frontal bone
frontal
frontal
Stirnbein
temporal bone
temporal
temporal
Schläfenbein
zygomatic bone
hueso pómulo
malaire
Jochbein
maxilla
maxilar superior
maxillaire supérieur
Oberkiefer
clavicle
clavícula
clavicule
Schlüsselbein
mandible
maxilar inferior
maxillaire inférieur
Unterkiefer
scapula
omóplato
omoplate
Schulterblatt
ribs
costillas
côtes
Rippen
humerus
húmero
humérus
Oberarmknochen
sternum
esternón
sternum
Brustbein
ulna
cúbito
cubitus
Elle
floating rib (2)
doceava costilla (2)
côte flottante (2)
frei endigende Rippe (2)
radius
radio
radius
Speiche
vertebral column
columna vertebral
colonne vertébrale
Wirbelsäule
carpus
carpo
carpe
Handwurzelknochen
ilium
hueso ilíaco
os iliaque
Darmbein
metacarpus
metacarpo
métacarpe
Mittelhandknochen
sacrum
sacro
sacrum
Kreuzbein
femur
fémur
fémur
Oberschenkelknochen
coccyx
cóccix
coccyx
Steißbein
patella
rótula
rotule
Kniescheibe
tibia
tibia
tibia
Schienbein
fibula
fíbula
péroné
Wadenbein
proximal phalanx
falange
phalange
Zehengrundglied
tarsus
tarso
tarse
Fußwurzelknochen
middle phalanx
falangina
phalangine
Mittelglied
metatarsus
metatarso
métatarse
Mittelfußknochen
distal phalanx
falangeta
phalangette
Zehenendglied

POSTERIOR VIEW
VISTA POSTERIOR
VUE POSTÉRIEURE
RÜCKANSICHT

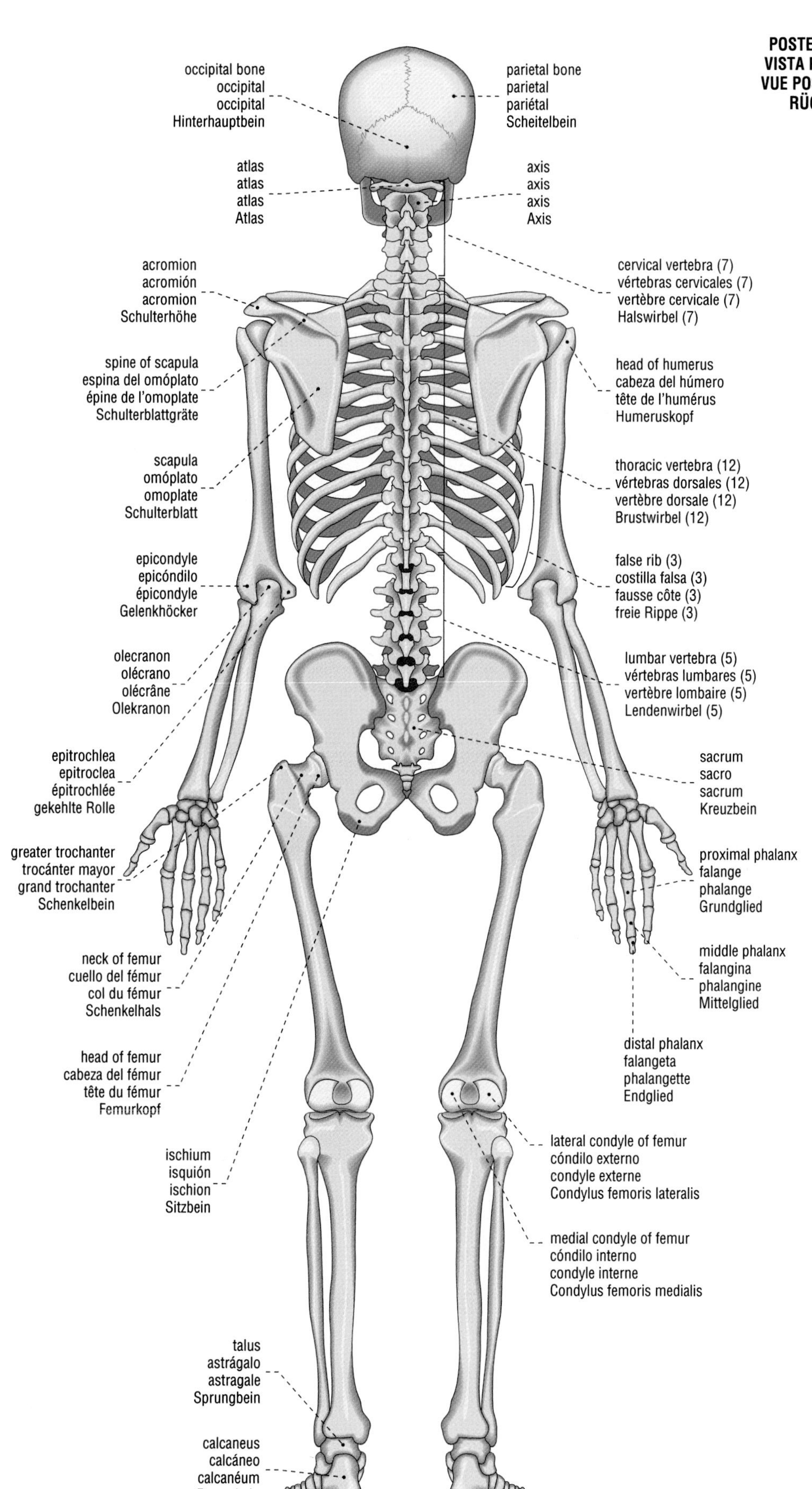
occipital bone
occipital
occipital
Hinterhauptbein
parietal bone
parietal
pariétal
Scheitelbein
atlas
atlas
atlas
Atlas
axis
axis
axis
Axis
acromion
acromión
acromion
Schulterhöhe
cervical vertebra (7)
vértebras cervicales (7)
vertèbre cervicale (7)
Halswirbel (7)
spine of scapula
espina del omóplato
épine de l'omoplate
Schulterblattgräte
head of humerus
cabeza del húmero
tête de l'humérus
Humeruskopf
scapula
omóplato
omoplate
Schulterblatt
thoracic vertebra (12)
vértebras dorsales (12)
vertèbre dorsale (12)
Brustwirbel (12)
epicondyle
epicóndilo
épicondyle
Gelenkhöcker
false rib (3)
costilla falsa (3)
fausse côte (3)
freie Rippe (3)
olecranon
olécrano
olécrâne
Olekranon
lumbar vertebra (5)
vértebras lumbares (5)
vertèbre lombaire (5)
Lendenwirbel (5)
epitrochlea
epitroclea
épitrochlée
gekehlte Rolle
sacrum
sacro
sacrum
Kreuzbein
greater trochanter
trocánter mayor
grand trochanter
Schenkelbein
proximal phalanx
falange
phalange
Grundglied
neck of femur
cuello del fémur
col du fémur
Schenkelhals
middle phalanx
falangina
phalangine
Mittelglied
head of femur
cabeza del fémur
tête du fémur
Femurkopf
distal phalanx
falangeta
phalangette
Endglied
ischium
isquión
ischion
Sitzbein
lateral condyle of femur
cóndilo externo
condyle externe
Condylus femoris lateralis
medial condyle of femur
cóndilo interno
condyle interne
Condylus femoris medialis
talus
astrágalo
astragale
Sprungbein
calcaneus
calcáneo
calcanéum
Fersenbein

BLOOD CIRCULATION
CIRCULACIÓN SANGUÍNEA
CIRCULATION SANGUINE
BLUTKREISLAUF

SCHEMA OF CIRCULATION
DIAGRAMA DE LA CIRCULACIÓN
SCHÉMA DE LA CIRCULATION
SCHEMA DES BLUTKREISLAUFS

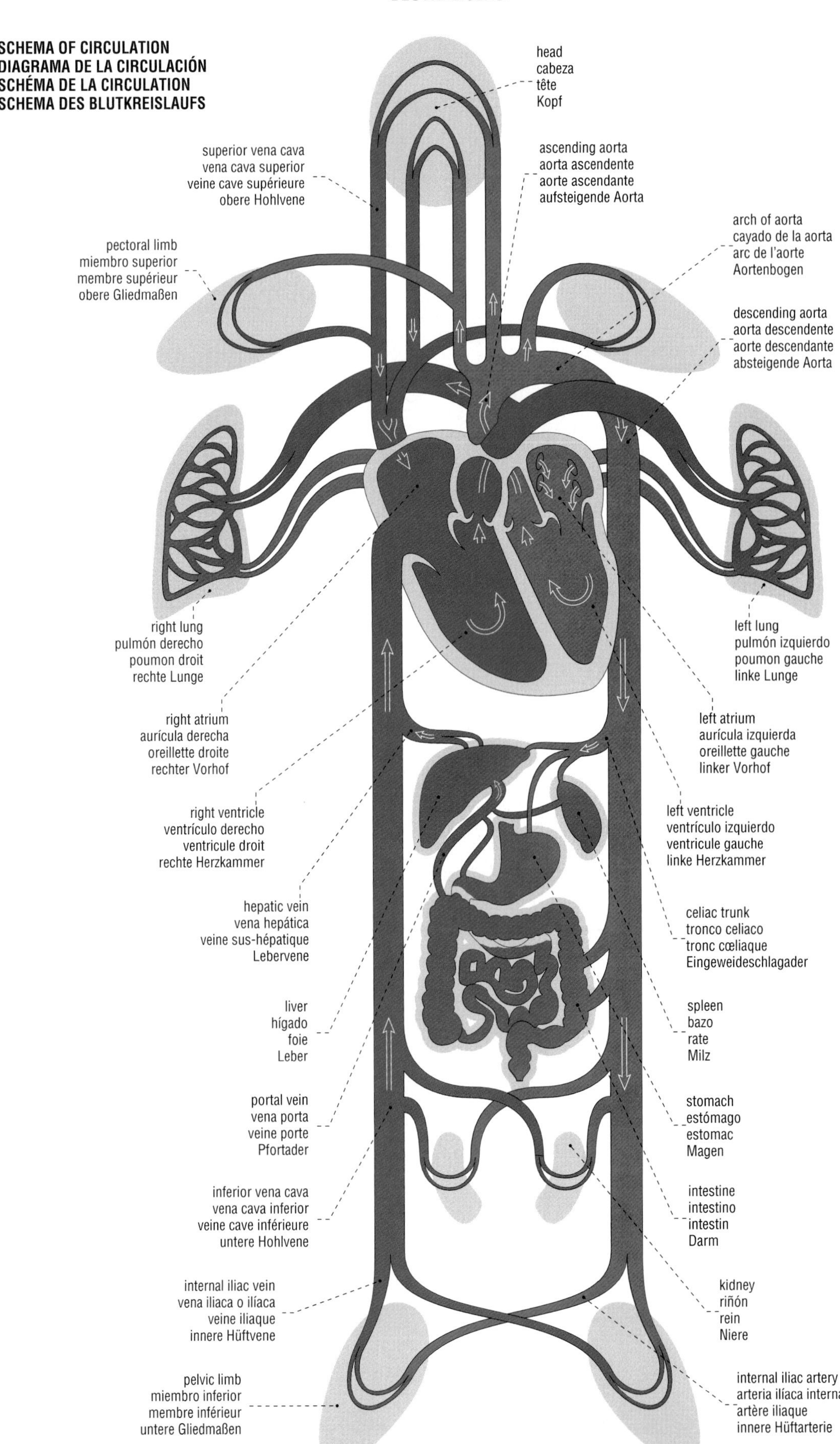
head
cabeza
tête
Kopf
superior vena cava
vena cava superior
veine cave supérieure
obere Hohlvene
ascending aorta
aorta ascendente
aorte ascendante
aufsteigende Aorta
arch of aorta
cayado de la aorta
arc de l'aorte
Aortenbogen
pectoral limb
miembro superior
membre supérieur
obere Gliedmaßen
descending aorta
aorta descendente
aorte descendante
absteigende Aorta
right lung
pulmón derecho
poumon droit
rechte Lunge
left lung
pulmón izquierdo
poumon gauche
linke Lunge
right atrium
aurícula derecha
oreillette droite
rechter Vorhof
left atrium
aurícula izquierda
oreillette gauche
linker Vorhof
right ventricle
ventrículo derecho
ventricule droit
rechte Herzkammer
left ventricle
ventrículo izquierdo
ventricule gauche
linke Herzkammer
hepatic vein
vena hepática
veine sus-hépatique
Lebervene
celiac trunk
tronco celiaco
tronc cœliaque
Eingeweideschlagader
liver
hígado
foie
Leber
spleen
bazo
rate
Milz
portal vein
vena porta
veine porte
Pfortader
stomach
estómago
estomac
Magen
inferior vena cava
vena cava inferior
veine cave inférieure
untere Hohlvene
intestine
intestino
intestin
Darm
internal iliac vein
vena iliaca o ilíaca
veine iliaque
innere Hüftvene
kidney
riñón
rein
Niere
pelvic limb
miembro inferior
membre inférieur
untere Gliedmaßen
internal iliac artery
arteria ilíaca interna
artère iliaque
innere Hüftarterie

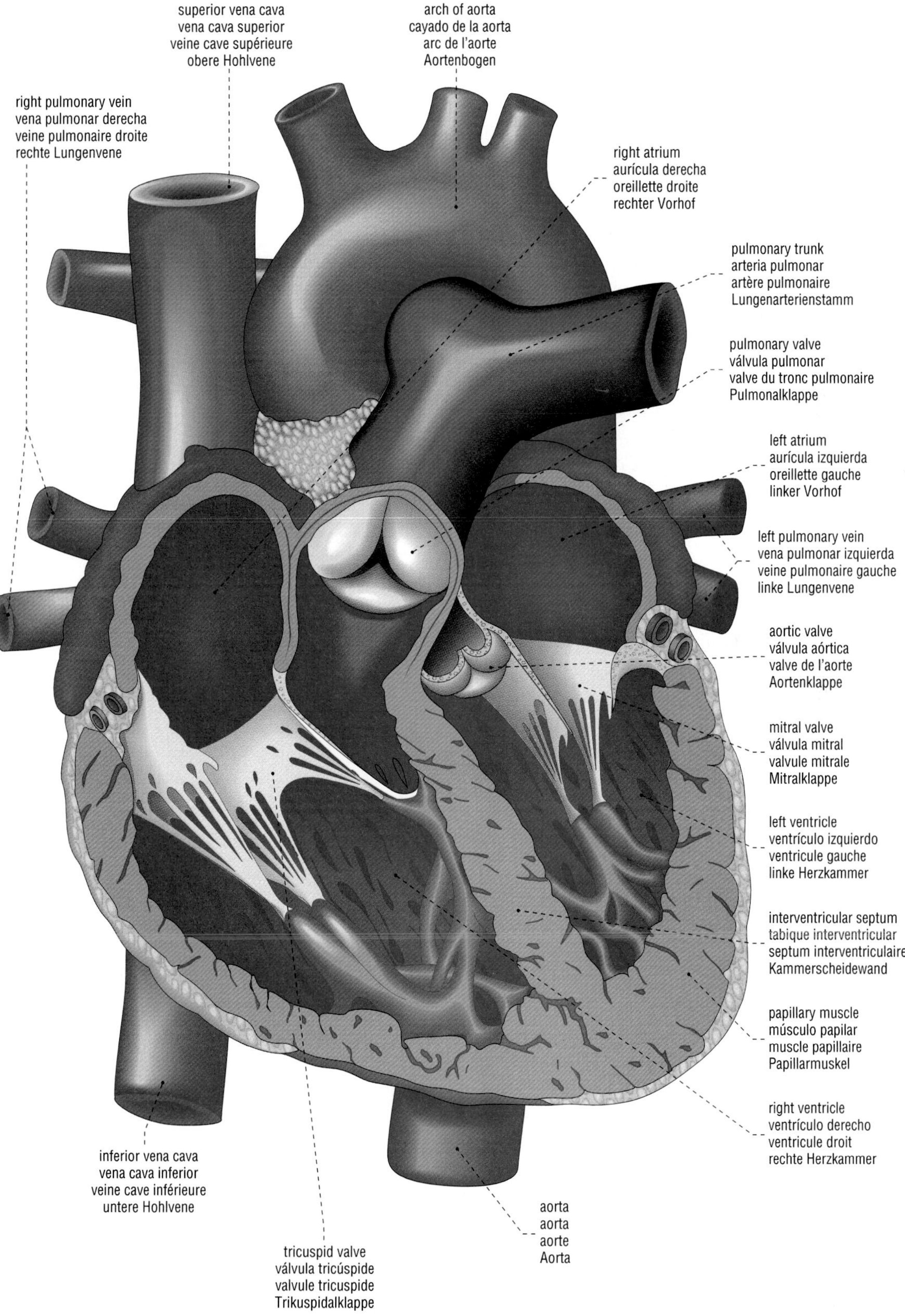
superior vena cava
vena cava superior
veine cave supérieure
obere Hohlvene
arch of aorta
cayado de la aorta
arc de l'aorte
Aortenbogen
right pulmonary vein
vena pulmonar derecha
veine pulmonaire droite
rechte Lungenvene
right atrium
aurícula derecha
oreillette droite
rechter Vorhof
pulmonary trunk
arteria pulmonar
artère pulmonaire
Lungenarterienstamm
pulmonary valve
válvula pulmonar
valve du tronc pulmonaire
Pulmonalklappe
left atrium
aurícula izquierda
oreillette gauche
linker Vorhof
left pulmonary vein
vena pulmonar izquierda
veine pulmonaire gauche
linke Lungenvene
aortic valve
válvula aórtica
valve de l'aorte
Aortenklappe
mitral valve
válvula mitral
valvule mitrale
Mitralklappe
left ventricle
ventrículo izquierdo
ventricule gauche
linke Herzkammer
interventricular septum
tabique interventricular
septum interventriculaire
Kammerscheidewand
papillary muscle
músculo papilar
muscle papillaire
Papillarmuskel
right ventricle
ventrículo derecho
ventricule droit
rechte Herzkammer
inferior vena cava
vena cava inferior
veine cave inférieure
untere Hohlvene
aorta
aorta
aorte
Aorta
tricuspid valve
válvula tricúspide
valvule tricuspide
Trikuspidalklappe

BLOOD CIRCULATION
CIRCULACIÓN SANGUÍNEA
CIRCULATION SANGUINE
BLUTKREISLAUF

PRINCIPAL VEINS AND ARTERIES
PRINCIPALES VENAS Y ARTERIAS
PRINCIPALES VEINES ET ARTÈRES
DIE WICHTIGSTEN VENEN UND ARTERIEN

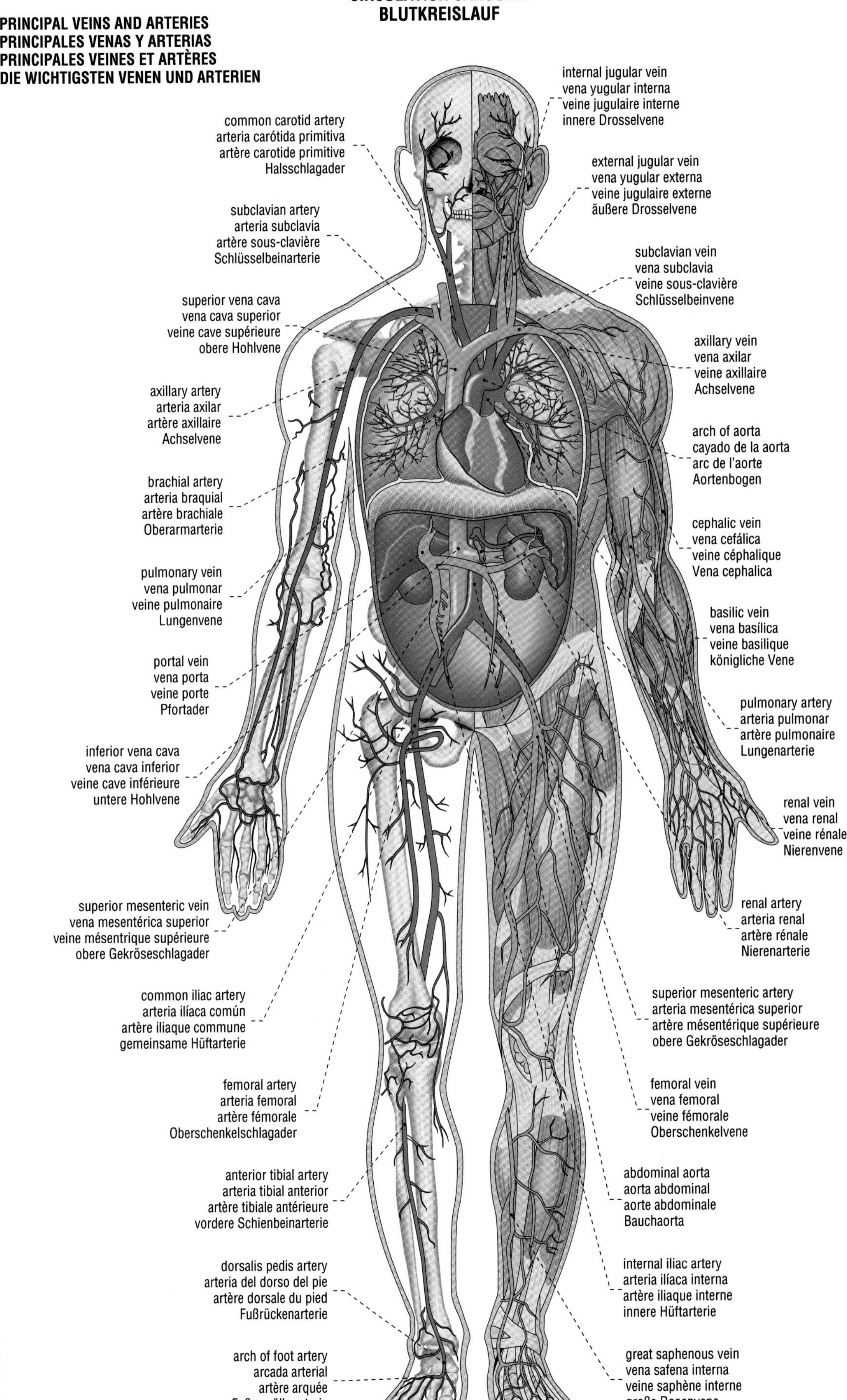
common carotid artery
arteria carótida primitiva
artère carotide primitive
Halsschlagader
subclavian artery
arteria subclavia
artère sous-clavière
Schlüsselbeinarterie
superior vena cava
vena cava superior
veine cave supérieure
obere Hohlvene
axillary artery
arteria axilar
artère axillaire
Achselvene
brachial artery
arteria braquial
artère brachiale
Oberarmarterie
pulmonary vein
vena pulmonar
veine pulmonaire
Lungenvene
portal vein
vena porta
veine porte
Pfortader
inferior vena cava
vena cava inferior
veine cave inférieure
untere Hohlvene
superior mesenteric vein
vena mesentérica superior
veine mésentrique supérieure
obere Gekröseschlagader
common iliac artery
arteria ilíaca común
artère iliaque commune
gemeinsame Hüftarterie
femoral artery
arteria femoral
artère fémorale
Oberschenkelschlagader
anterior tibial artery
arteria tibial anterior
artère tibiale antérieure
vordere Schienbeinarterie
dorsalis pedis artery
arteria del dorso del pie
artère dorsale du pied
Fußrückenarterie
arch of foot artery
arcada arterial
artère arquée
Fußgewölbearterie
internal jugular vein
vena yugular interna
veine jugulaire interne
innere Drosselvene
external jugular vein
vena yugular externa
veine jugulaire externe
äußere Drosselvene
subclavian vein
vena subclavia
veine sous-clavière
Schlüsselbeinvene
axillary vein
vena axilar
veine axillaire
Achselvene
arch of aorta
cayado de la aorta
arc de l'aorte
Aortenbogen
cephalic vein
vena cefálica
veine céphalique
Vena cephalica
basilic vein
vena basílica
veine basilique
königliche Vene
pulmonary artery
arteria pulmonar
artère pulmonaire
Lungenarterie
renal vein
vena renal
veine rénale
Nierenvene
renal artery
arteria renal
artère rénale
Nierenarterie
superior mesenteric artery
arteria mesentérica superior
artère mésentérique supérieure
obere Gekröseschlagader
femoral vein
vena femoral
veine fémorale
Oberschenkelvene
abdominal aorta
aorta abdominal
aorte abdominale
Bauchaorta
internal iliac artery
arteria ilíaca interna
artère iliaque interne
innere Hüftarterie
great saphenous vein
vena safena interna
veine saphène interne
große Rosenvene

MALE GENITAL ORGANS
ÓRGANOS GENITALES MASCULINOS
ORGANES GÉNITAUX MASCULINS
MÄNNLICHE GESCHLECHTSORGANE

SAGITTAL SECTION
CORTE SAGITAL
COUPE SAGITTALE
SAGITTALSCHNITT

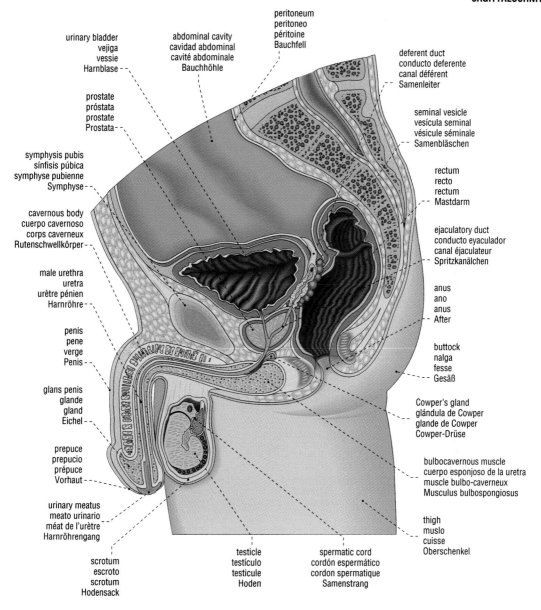

urinary bladder
vejiga
vessie
Harnblase

abdominal cavity
cavidad abdominal
cavité abdominale
Bauchhöhle

peritoneum
peritoneo
péritoine
Bauchfell

prostate
próstata
prostate
Prostata

symphysis pubis
sínfisis púbica
symphyse pubienne
Symphyse

cavernous body
cuerpo cavernoso
corps caverneux
Rutenschwellkörper

male urethra
uretra
urètre pénien
Harnröhre

penis
pene
verge
Penis

glans penis
glande
gland
Eichel

prepuce
prepucio
prépuce
Vorhaut

urinary meatus
meato urinario
méat de l'urètre
Harnröhrengang

scrotum
escroto
scrotum
Hodensack

testicle
testículo
testicule
Hoden

spermatic cord
cordón espermático
cordon spermatique
Samenstrang

deferent duct
conducto deferente
canal déférent
Samenleiter

seminal vesicle
vesícula seminal
vésicule séminale
Samenbläschen

rectum
recto
rectum
Mastdarm

ejaculatory duct
conducto eyaculador
canal éjaculateur
Spritzkanälchen

anus
ano
anus
After

buttock
nalga
fesse
Gesäß

Cowper's gland
glándula de Cowper
glande de Cowper
Cowper-Drüse

bulbocavernous muscle
cuerpo esponjoso de la uretra
muscle bulbo-caverneux
Musculus bulbospongiosus

thigh
muslo
cuisse
Oberschenkel

SPERMATOZOON
ESPERMATOZOIDE
SPERMATOZOÏDE
SPERMA

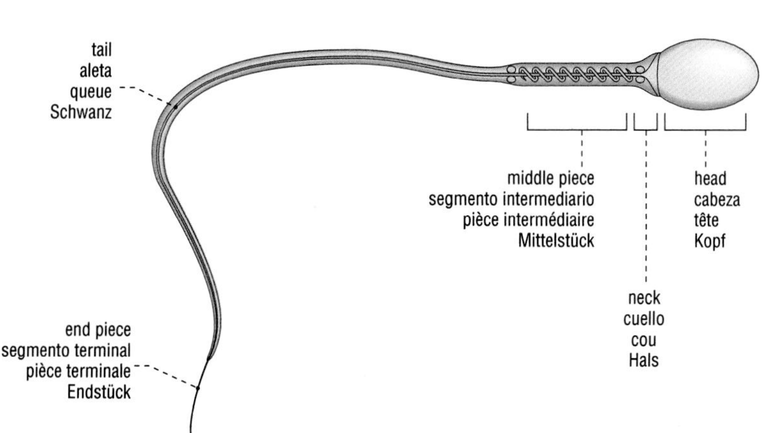
tail
aleta
queue
Schwanz
end piece
segmento terminal
pièce terminale
Endstück
middle piece
segmento intermediario
pièce intermédiaire
Mittelstück
neck
cuello
cou
Hals
head
cabeza
tête
Kopf

FEMALE GENITAL ORGANS
ÓRGANOS GENITALES FEMENINOS
ORGANES GÉNITAUX FÉMININS
WEIBLICHE GESCHLECHTSORGANE

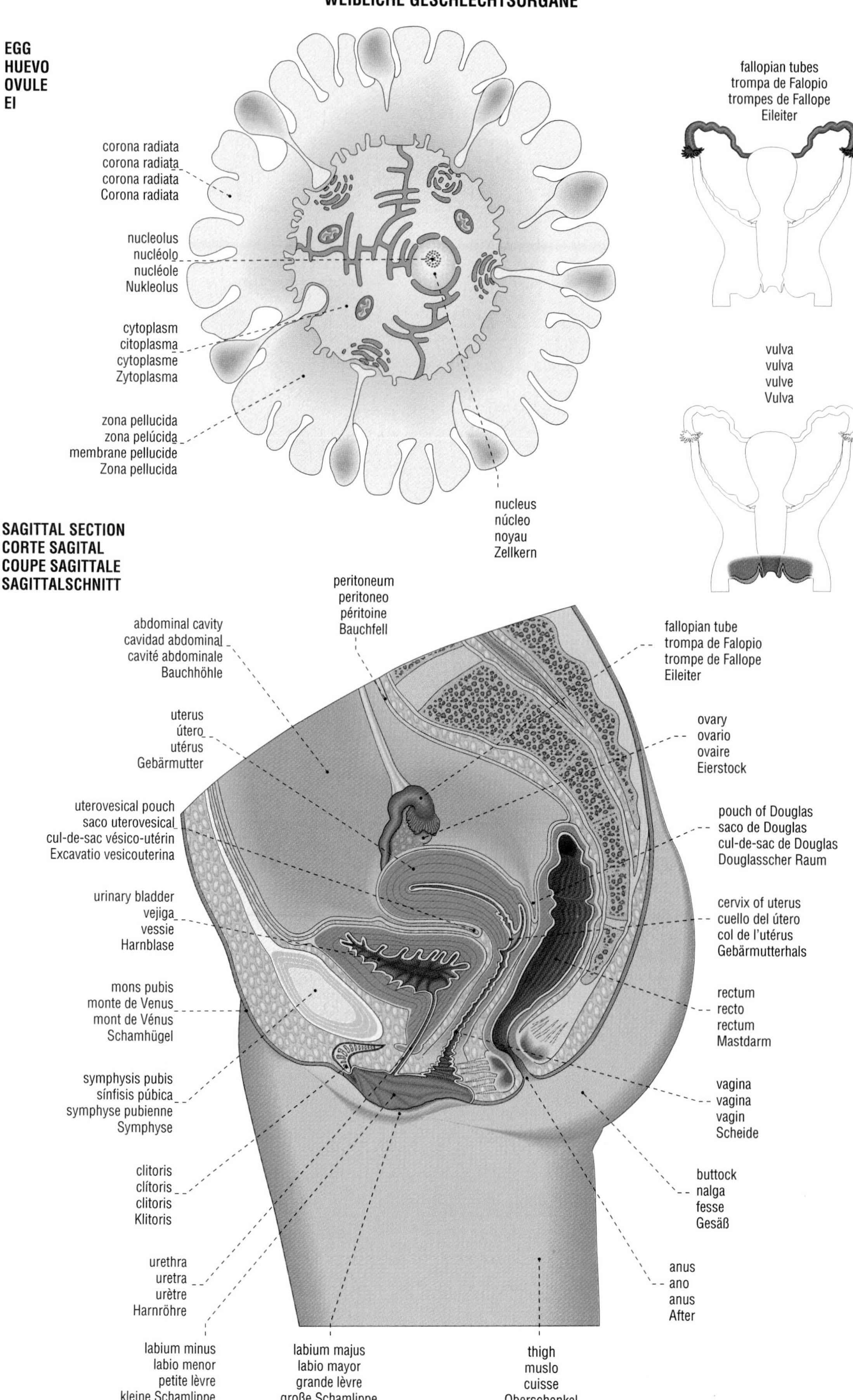
EGG
HUEVO
OVULE
EI
corona radiata
corona radiata
corona radiata
Corona radiata
nucleolus
nucléolo
nucléole
Nukleolus
cytoplasm
citoplasma
cytoplasme
Zytoplasma
zona pellucida
zona pelúcida
membrane pellucide
Zona pellucida
nucleus
núcleo
noyau
Zellkern
fallopian tubes
trompa de Falopio
trompes de Fallope
Eileiter
vulva
vulva
vulve
Vulva
SAGITTAL SECTION
CORTE SAGITAL
COUPE SAGITTALE
SAGITTALSCHNITT
peritoneum
peritoneo
péritoine
Bauchfell
abdominal cavity
cavidad abdominal
cavité abdominale
Bauchhöhle
uterus
útero
utérus
Gebärmutter
uterovesical pouch
saco uterovesical
cul-de-sac vésico-utérin
Excavatio vesicouterina
urinary bladder
vejiga
vessie
Harnblase
mons pubis
monte de Venus
mont de Vénus
Schamhügel
symphysis pubis
sínfisis púbica
symphyse pubienne
Symphyse
clitoris
clítoris
clitoris
Klitoris
urethra
uretra
urètre
Harnröhre
labium minus
labio menor
petite lèvre
kleine Schamlippe
labium majus
labio mayor
grande lèvre
große Schamlippe
thigh
muslo
cuisse
Oberschenkel
fallopian tube
trompa de Falopio
trompe de Fallope
Eileiter
ovary
ovario
ovaire
Eierstock
pouch of Douglas
saco de Douglas
cul-de-sac de Douglas
Douglasscher Raum
cervix of uterus
cuello del útero
col de l'utérus
Gebärmutterhals
rectum
recto
rectum
Mastdarm
vagina
vagina
vagin
Scheide
buttock
nalga
fesse
Gesäß
anus
ano
anus
After

FEMALE GENITAL ORGANS
ÓRGANOS GENITALES FEMENINOS
ORGANES GÉNITAUX FÉMININS
WEIBLICHE GESCHLECHTSORGANE

POSTERIOR VIEW
VISTA POSTERIOR
VUE POSTÉRIEURE
RÜCKANSICHT

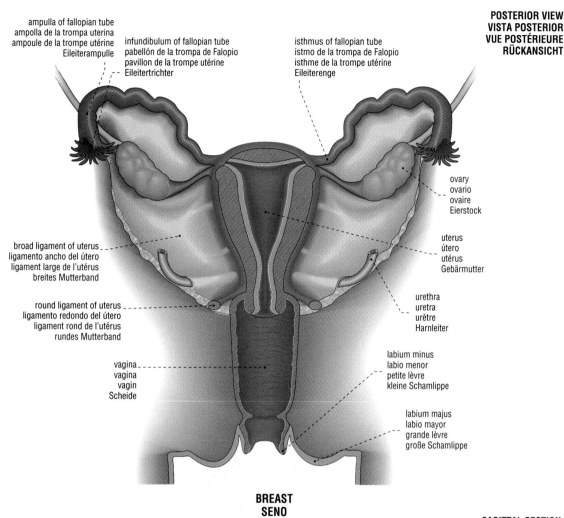

ampulla of fallopian tube
ampolla de la trompa uterina
ampoule de la trompe utérine
Eileiterampulle

infundibulum of fallopian tube
pabellón de la trompa de Falopio
pavillon de la trompe utérine
Eileitertrichter

isthmus of fallopian tube
istmo de la trompa de Falopio
isthme de la trompe utérine
Eileiterenge

ovary
ovario
ovaire
Eierstock

broad ligament of uterus
ligamento ancho del útero
ligament large de l'utérus
breites Mutterband

uterus
útero
utérus
Gebärmutter

urethra
uretra
urètre
Harnleiter

round ligament of uterus
ligamento redondo del útero
ligament rond de l'utérus
rundes Mutterband

labium minus
labio menor
petite lèvre
kleine Schamlippe

vagina
vagina
vagin
Scheide

labium majus
labio mayor
grande lèvre
große Schamlippe

BREAST
SENO
SEIN
BRUST

SAGITTAL SECTION
CORTE SAGITAL
COUPE SAGITTALE
SAGITTALSCHNITT

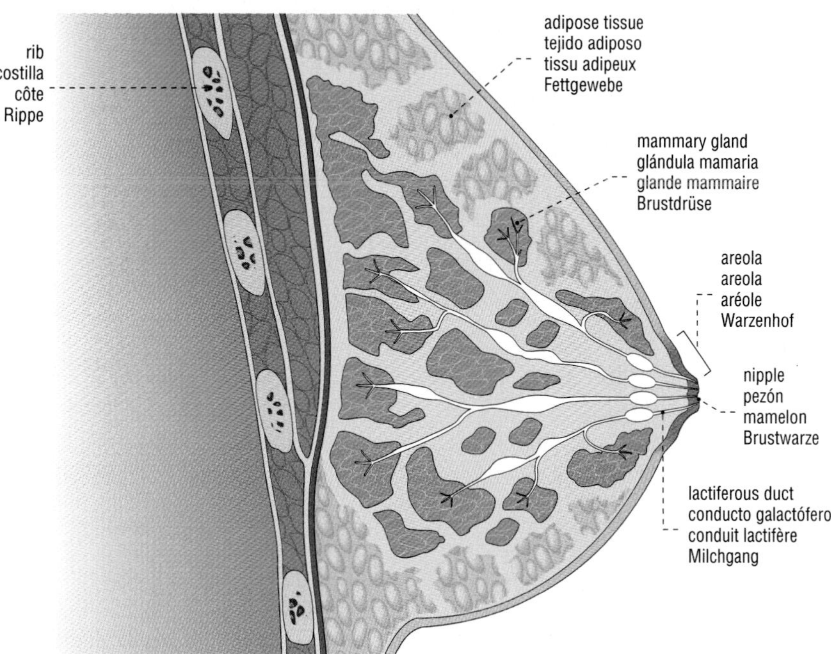
rib
costilla
côte
Rippe
adipose tissue
tejido adiposo
tissu adipeux
Fettgewebe
mammary gland
glándula mamaria
glande mammaire
Brustdrüse
areola
areola
aréole
Warzenhof
nipple
pezón
mamelon
Brustwarze
lactiferous duct
conducto galactófero
conduit lactifère
Milchgang

RESPIRATORY SYSTEM
APARATO RESPIRATORIO
APPAREIL RESPIRATOIRE
LUFTWEGE

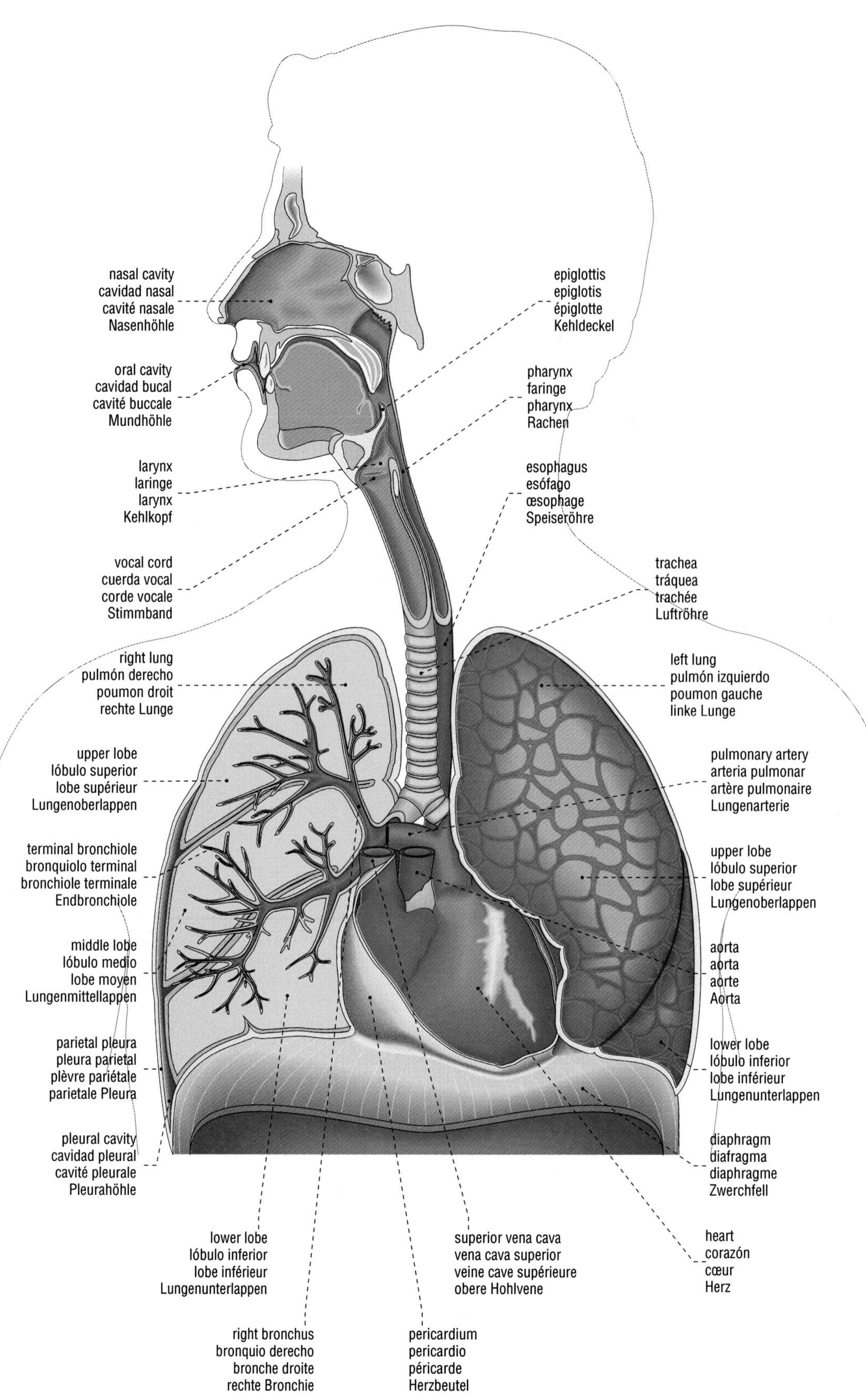
nasal cavity
cavidad nasal
cavité nasale
Nasenhöhle
oral cavity
cavidad bucal
cavité buccale
Mundhöhle
larynx
laringe
larynx
Kehlkopf
vocal cord
cuerda vocal
corde vocale
Stimmband
right lung
pulmón derecho
poumon droit
rechte Lunge
upper lobe
lóbulo superior
lobe supérieur
Lungenoberlappen
terminal bronchiole
bronquiolo terminal
bronchiole terminale
Endbronchiole
middle lobe
lóbulo medio
lobe moyen
Lungenmittellappen
parietal pleura
pleura parietal
plèvre pariétale
parietale Pleura
pleural cavity
cavidad pleural
cavité pleurale
Pleurahöhle
epiglottis
epiglotis
épiglotte
Kehldeckel
pharynx
faringe
pharynx
Rachen
esophagus
esófago
œsophage
Speiseröhre
trachea
tráquea
trachée
Luftröhre
left lung
pulmón izquierdo
poumon gauche
linke Lunge
pulmonary artery
arteria pulmonar
artère pulmonaire
Lungenarterie
upper lobe
lóbulo superior
lobe supérieur
Lungenoberlappen
aorta
aorta
aorte
Aorta
lower lobe
lóbulo inferior
lobe inférieur
Lungenunterlappen
diaphragm
diafragma
diaphragme
Zwerchfell
heart
corazón
cœur
Herz
lower lobe
lóbulo inferior
lobe inférieur
Lungenunterlappen
superior vena cava
vena cava superior
veine cave supérieure
obere Hohlvene
right bronchus
bronquio derecho
bronche droite
rechte Bronchie
pericardium
pericardio
péricarde
Herzbeutel

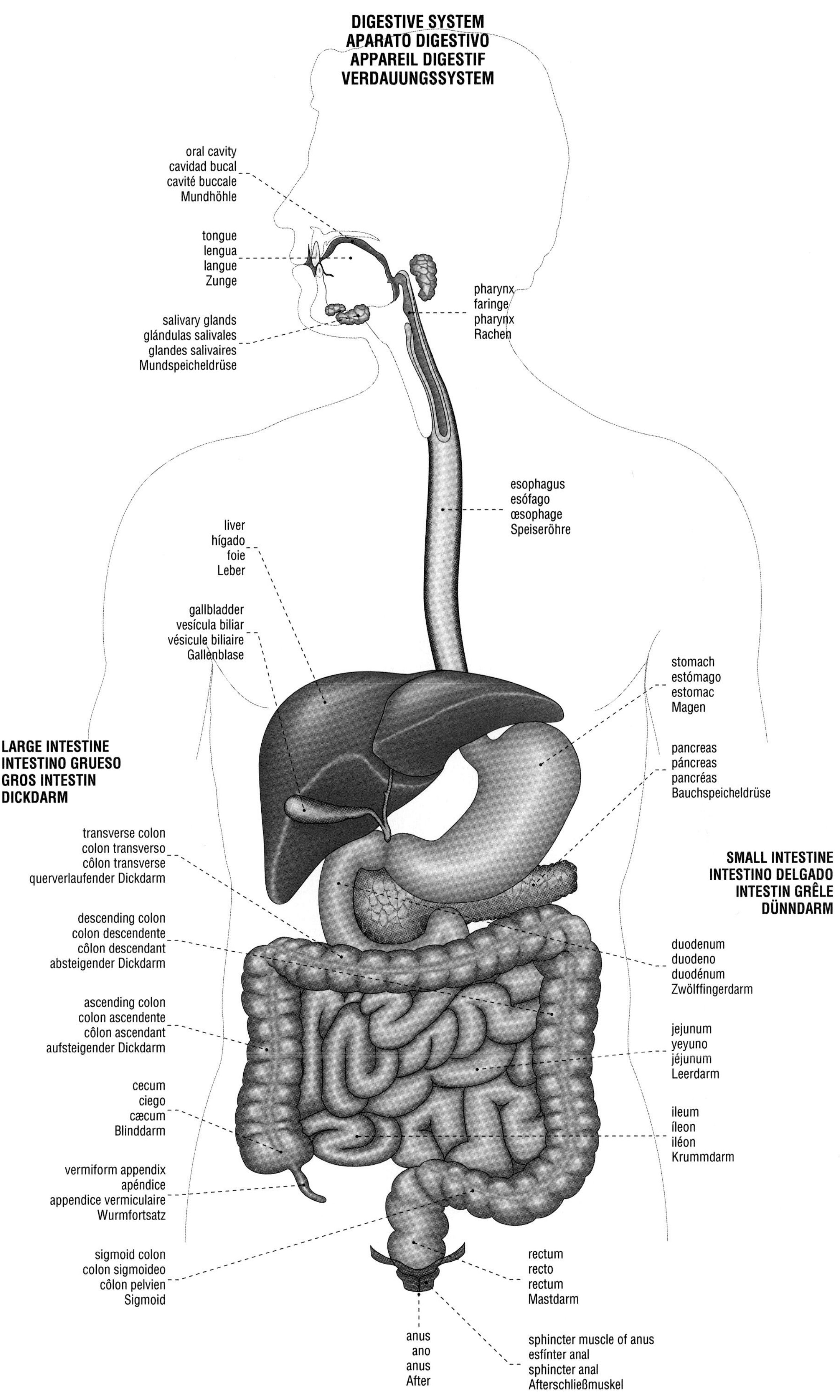
DIGESTIVE SYSTEM
APARATO DIGESTIVO
APPAREIL DIGESTIF
VERDAUUNGSSYSTEM
oral cavity
cavidad bucal
cavité buccale
Mundhöhle
tongue
lengua
langue
Zunge
salivary glands
glándulas salivales
glandes salivaires
Mundspeicheldrüse
pharynx
faringe
pharynx
Rachen
esophagus
esófago
œsophage
Speiseröhre
liver
hígado
foie
Leber
gallbladder
vesícula biliar
vésicule biliaire
Gallenblase
stomach
estómago
estomac
Magen
pancreas
páncreas
pancréas
Bauchspeicheldrüse
LARGE INTESTINE
INTESTINO GRUESO
GROS INTESTIN
DICKDARM
transverse colon
colon transverso
côlon transverse
querverlaufender Dickdarm
SMALL INTESTINE
INTESTINO DELGADO
INTESTIN GRÊLE
DÜNNDARM
descending colon
colon descendente
côlon descendant
absteigender Dickdarm
duodenum
duodeno
duodénum
Zwölffingerdarm
ascending colon
colon ascendente
côlon ascendant
aufsteigender Dickdarm
jejunum
yeyuno
jéjunum
Leerdarm
cecum
ciego
cæcum
Blinddarm
ileum
íleon
iléon
Krummdarm
vermiform appendix
apéndice
appendice vermiculaire
Wurmfortsatz
sigmoid colon
colon sigmoideo
côlon pelvien
Sigmoid
rectum
recto
rectum
Mastdarm
anus
ano
anus
After
sphincter muscle of anus
esfínter anal
sphincter anal
Afterschließmuskel

URINARY SYSTEM
APARATO URINARIO
APPAREIL URINAIRE
HARNSYSTEM

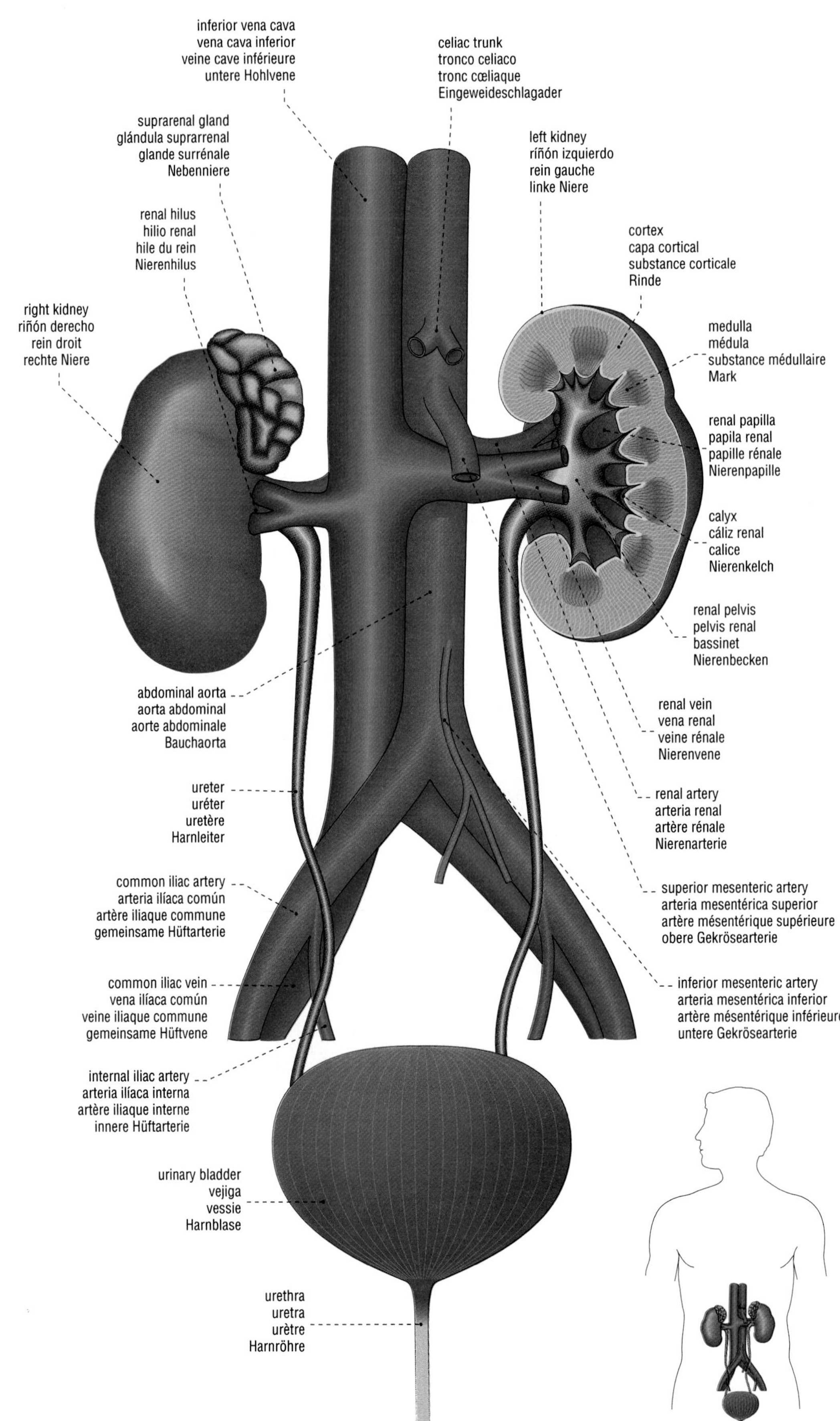
inferior vena cava
vena cava inferior
veine cave inférieure
untere Hohlvene
celiac trunk
tronco celiaco
tronc cœliaque
Eingeweideschlagader
suprarenal gland
glándula suprarrenal
glande surrénale
Nebenniere
left kidney
riñón izquierdo
rein gauche
linke Niere
renal hilus
hilio renal
hile du rein
Nierenhilus
cortex
capa cortical
substance corticale
Rinde
right kidney
riñón derecho
rein droit
rechte Niere
medulla
médula
substance médullaire
Mark
renal papilla
papila renal
papille rénale
Nierenpapille
calyx
cáliz renal
calice
Nierenkelch
renal pelvis
pelvis renal
bassinet
Nierenbecken
abdominal aorta
aorta abdominal
aorte abdominale
Bauchaorta
renal vein
vena renal
veine rénale
Nierenvene
ureter
uréter
uretère
Harnleiter
renal artery
arteria renal
artère rénale
Nierenarterie
common iliac artery
arteria ilíaca común
artère iliaque commune
gemeinsame Hüftarterie
superior mesenteric artery
arteria mesentérica superior
artère mésentérique supérieure
obere Gekrösearterie
common iliac vein
vena ilíaca común
veine iliaque commune
gemeinsame Hüftvene
inferior mesenteric artery
arteria mesentérica inferior
artère mésentérique inférieure
untere Gekrösearterie
internal iliac artery
arteria ilíaca interna
artère iliaque interne
innere Hüftarterie
urinary bladder
vejiga
vessie
Harnblase
urethra
uretra
urètre
Harnröhre

NERVOUS SYSTEM
SISTEMA NERVIOSO
SYSTÈME NERVEUX
NERVENSYSTEM

PERIPHERAL NERVOUS SYSTEM
SISTEMA NERVIOSO PERIFÉRICO
SYSTÈME NERVEUX PÉRIPHÉRIQUE
PERIPHERES NERVENSYSTEM

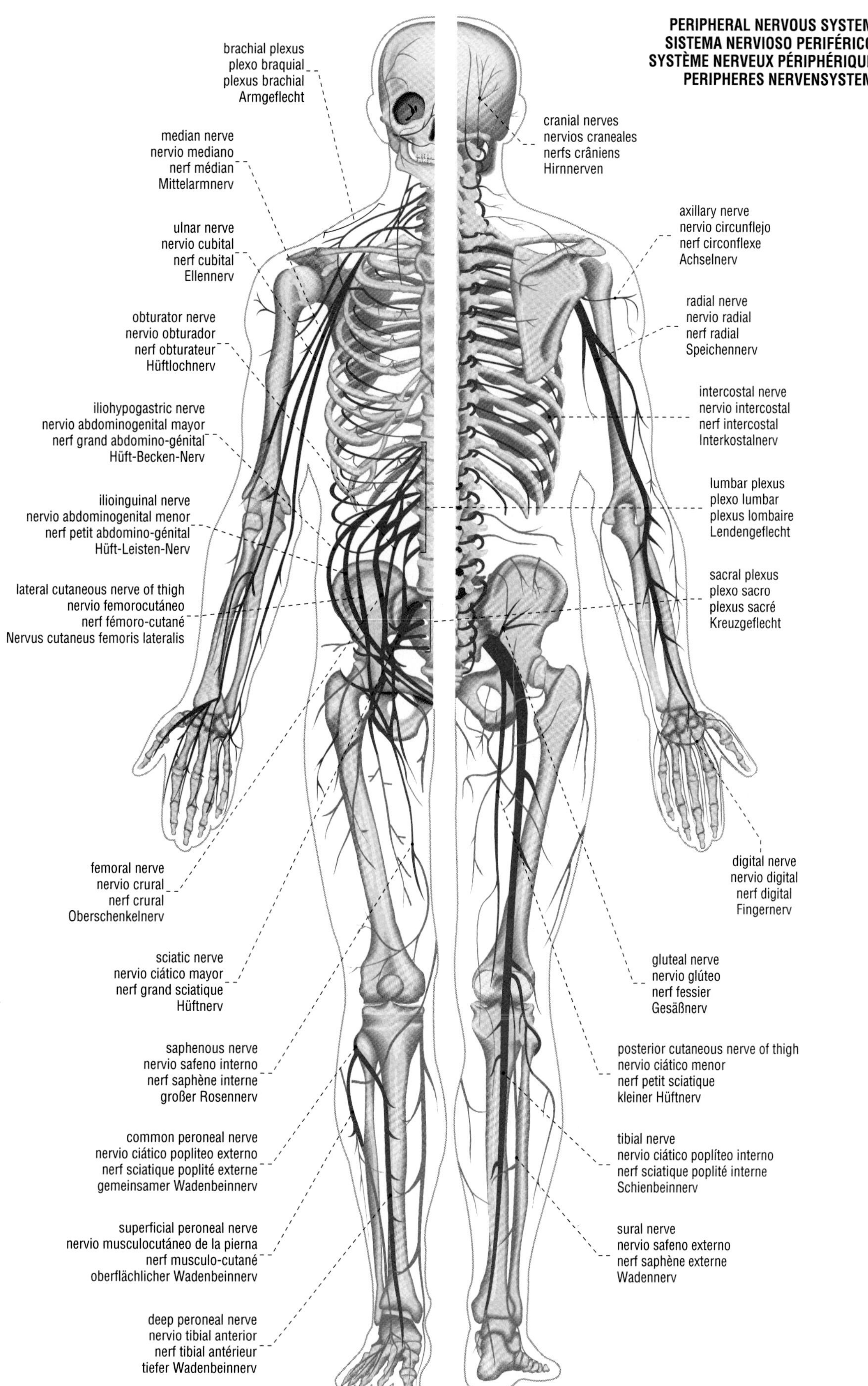

brachial plexus
plexo braquial
plexus brachial
Armgeflecht
median nerve
nervio mediano
nerf médian
Mittelarmnerv
ulnar nerve
nervio cubital
nerf cubital
Ellennerv
obturator nerve
nervio obturador
nerf obturateur
Hüftlochnerv
iliohypogastric nerve
nervio abdominogenital mayor
nerf grand abdomino-génital
Hüft-Becken-Nerv
ilioinguinal nerve
nervio abdominogenital menor
nerf petit abdomino-génital
Hüft-Leisten-Nerv
lateral cutaneous nerve of thigh
nervio femorocutáneo
nerf fémoro-cutané
Nervus cutaneus femoris lateralis
femoral nerve
nervio crural
nerf crural
Oberschenkelnerv
sciatic nerve
nervio ciático mayor
nerf grand sciatique
Hüftnerv
saphenous nerve
nervio safeno interno
nerf saphène interne
großer Rosennerv
common peroneal nerve
nervio ciático popliteo externo
nerf sciatique poplité externe
gemeinsamer Wadenbeinnerv
superficial peroneal nerve
nervio musculocutáneo de la pierna
nerf musculo-cutané
oberflächlicher Wadenbeinnerv
deep peroneal nerve
nervio tibial anterior
nerf tibial antérieur
tiefer Wadenbeinnerv
cranial nerves
nervios craneales
nerfs crâniens
Hirnnerven
axillary nerve
nervio circunflejo
nerf circonflexe
Achselnerv
radial nerve
nervio radial
nerf radial
Speichennerv
intercostal nerve
nervio intercostal
nerf intercostal
Interkostalnerv
lumbar plexus
plexo lumbar
plexus lombaire
Lendengeflecht
sacral plexus
plexo sacro
plexus sacré
Kreuzgeflecht
digital nerve
nervio digital
nerf digital
Fingernerv
gluteal nerve
nervio glúteo
nerf fessier
Gesäßnerv
posterior cutaneous nerve of thigh
nervio ciático menor
nerf petit sciatique
kleiner Hüftnerv
tibial nerve
nervio ciático poplíteo interno
nerf sciatique poplité interne
Schienbeinnerv
sural nerve
nervio safeno externo
nerf saphène externe
Wadennerv

NERVOUS SYSTEM
SISTEMA NERVIOSO
SYSTÈME NERVEUX
NERVENSYSTEM

CENTRAL NERVOUS SYSTEM
SISTEMA NERVIOSO CENTRAL
SYSTÈME NERVEUX CENTRAL
ZENTRALES NERVENSYSTEM

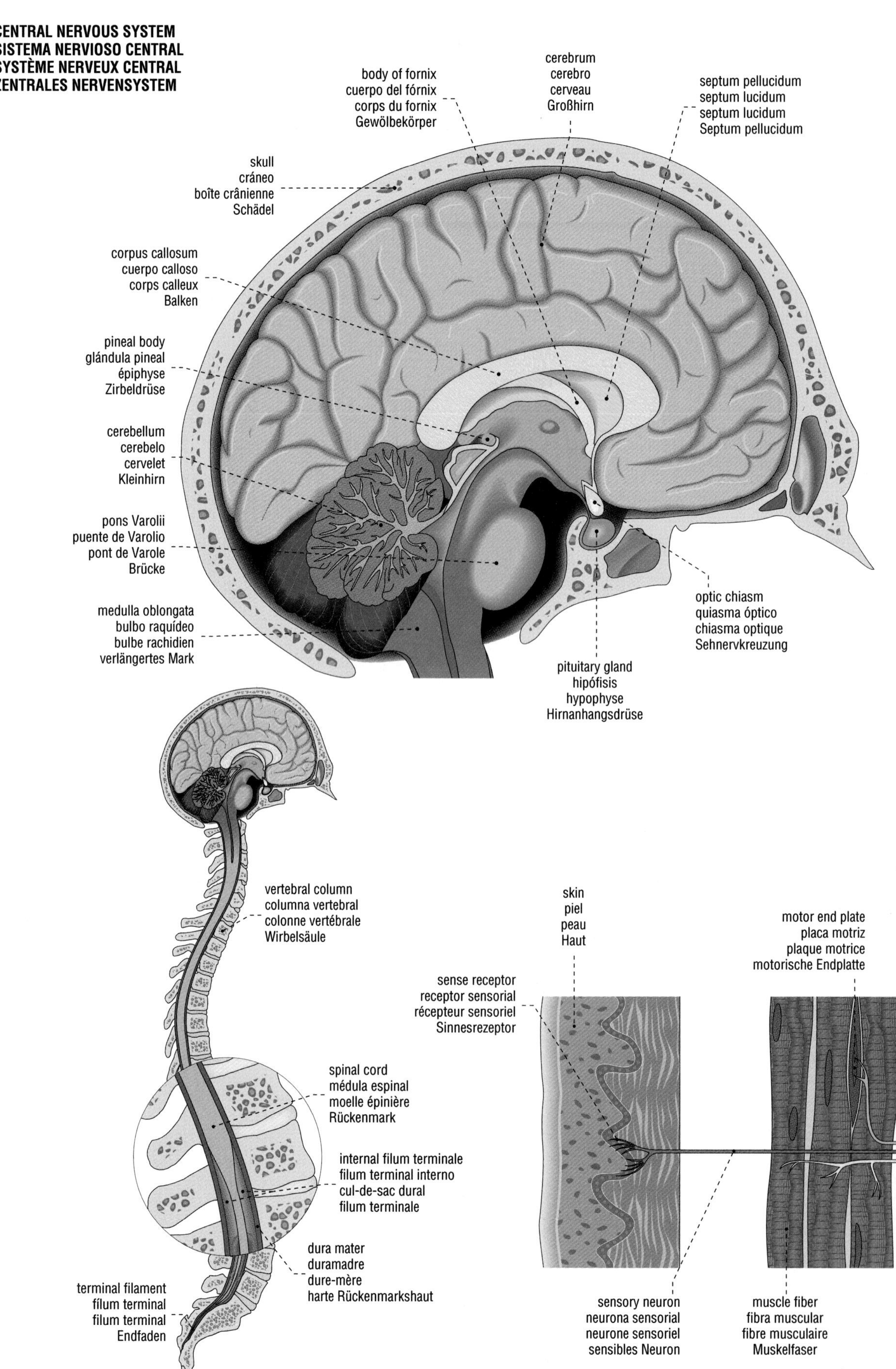
body of fornix
cuerpo del fórnix
corps du fornix
Gewölbekörper
cerebrum
cerebro
cerveau
Großhirn
septum pellucidum
septum lucidum
septum lucidum
Septum pellucidum
skull
cráneo
boîte crânienne
Schädel
corpus callosum
cuerpo calloso
corps calleux
Balken
pineal body
glándula pineal
épiphyse
Zirbeldrüse
cerebellum
cerebelo
cervelet
Kleinhirn
pons Varolii
puente de Varolio
pont de Varole
Brücke
medulla oblongata
bulbo raquídeo
bulbe rachidien
verlängertes Mark
optic chiasm
quiasma óptico
chiasma optique
Sehnervkreuzung
pituitary gland
hipófisis
hypophyse
Hirnanhangsdrüse
vertebral column
columna vertebral
colonne vertébrale
Wirbelsäule
spinal cord
médula espinal
moelle épinière
Rückenmark
internal filum terminale
filum terminal interno
cul-de-sac dural
filum terminale
dura mater
duramadre
dure-mère
harte Rückenmarkshaut
terminal filament
fílum terminal
filum terminal
Endfaden
skin
piel
peau
Haut
sense receptor
receptor sensorial
récepteur sensoriel
Sinnesrezeptor
motor end plate
placa motriz
plaque motrice
motorische Endplatte
sensory neuron
neurona sensorial
neurone sensoriel
sensibles Neuron
muscle fiber
fibra muscular
fibre musculaire
Muskelfaser

LUMBAR VERTEBRA
VÉRTEBRA LUMBAR
VERTÈBRE LOMBAIRE
LENDENWIRBEL

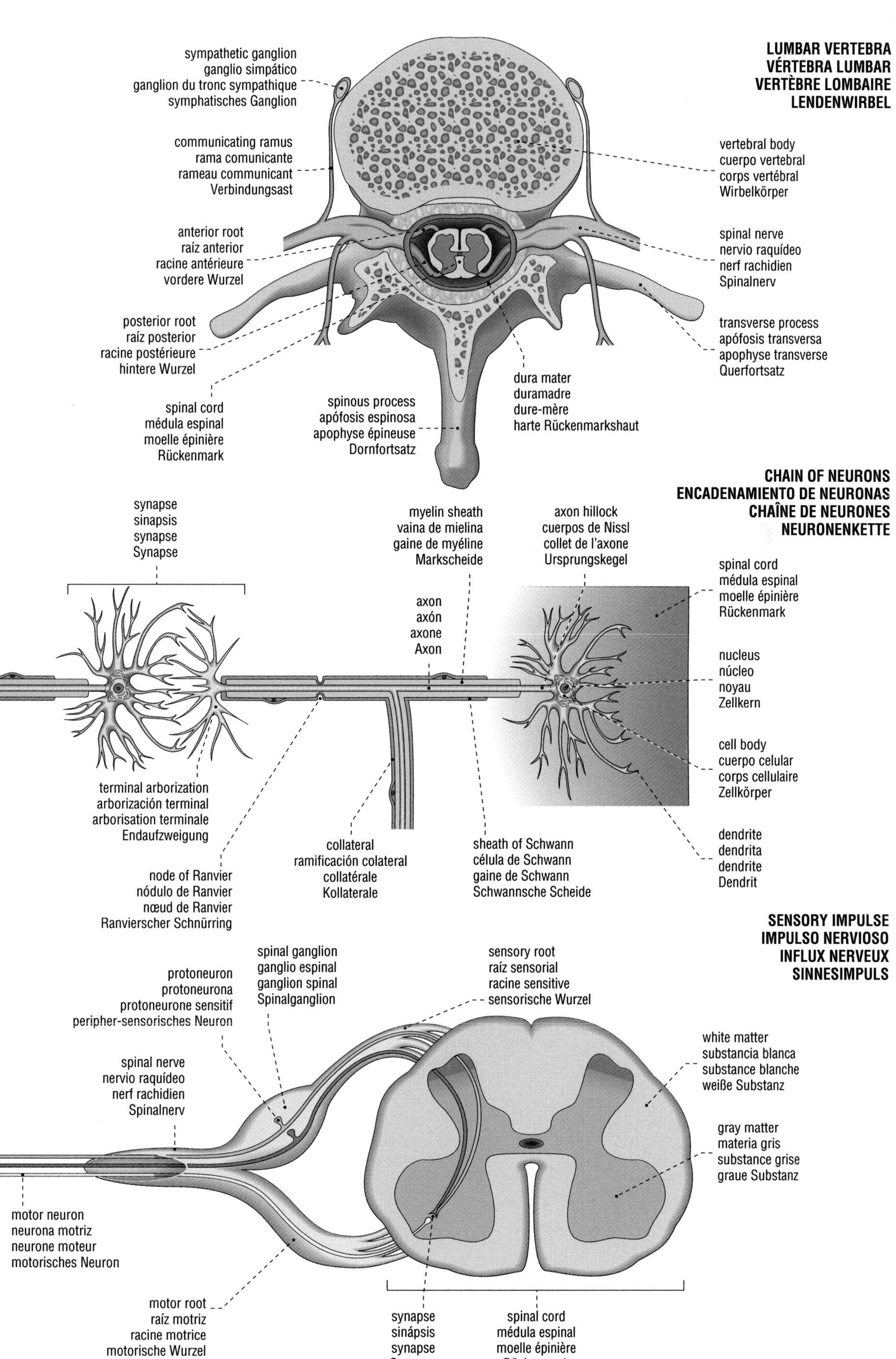
sympathetic ganglion
ganglio simpático
ganglion du tronc sympathique
symphatisches Ganglion
communicating ramus
rama comunicante
rameau communicant
Verbindungsast
anterior root
raíz anterior
racine antérieure
vordere Wurzel
posterior root
raíz posterior
racine postérieure
hintere Wurzel
spinal cord
médula espinal
moelle épinière
Rückenmark
spinous process
apófosis espinosa
apophyse épineuse
Dornfortsatz
dura mater
duramadre
dure-mère
harte Rückenmarkshaut
vertebral body
cuerpo vertebral
corps vertébral
Wirbelkörper
spinal nerve
nervio raquídeo
nerf rachidien
Spinalnerv
transverse process
apófosis transversa
apophyse transverse
Querfortsatz
synapse
sinapsis
synapse
Synapse
myelin sheath
vaina de mielina
gaine de myéline
Markscheide
axon hillock
cuerpos de Nissl
collet de l'axone
Ursprungskegel
axon
axón
axone
Axon
spinal cord
médula espinal
moelle épinière
Rückenmark
nucleus
núcleo
noyau
Zellkern
cell body
cuerpo celular
corps cellulaire
Zellkörper
dendrite
dendrita
dendrite
Dendrit
terminal arborization
arborización terminal
arborisation terminale
Endaufzweigung
collateral
ramificación colateral
collatérale
Kollaterale
sheath of Schwann
célula de Schwann
gaine de Schwann
Schwannsche Scheide
node of Ranvier
nódulo de Ranvier
nœud de Ranvier
Ranvierscher Schnürring
protoneuron
protoneurona
protoneurone sensitif
peripher-sensorisches Neuron
spinal ganglion
ganglio espinal
ganglion spinal
Spinalganglion
sensory root
raíz sensorial
racine sensitive
sensorische Wurzel
white matter
substancia blanca
substance blanche
weiße Substanz
gray matter
materia gris
substance grise
graue Substanz
spinal nerve
nervio raquídeo
nerf rachidien
Spinalnerv
motor neuron
neurona motriz
neurone moteur
motorisches Neuron
motor root
raíz motriz
racine motrice
motorische Wurzel
synapse
sinápsis
synapse
Synapse
spinal cord
médula espinal
moelle épinière
Rückenmark

CHAIN OF NEURONS
ENCADENAMIENTO DE NEURONAS
CHAÎNE DE NEURONES
NEURONENKETTE

SENSORY IMPULSE
IMPULSO NERVIOSO
INFLUX NERVEUX
SINNESIMPULS

SENSE ORGANS: TOUCH
TACTO
ORGANES DES SENS: TOUCHER
SINNESORGANE: TASTSINN

SKIN
PIEL
PEAU
HAUT

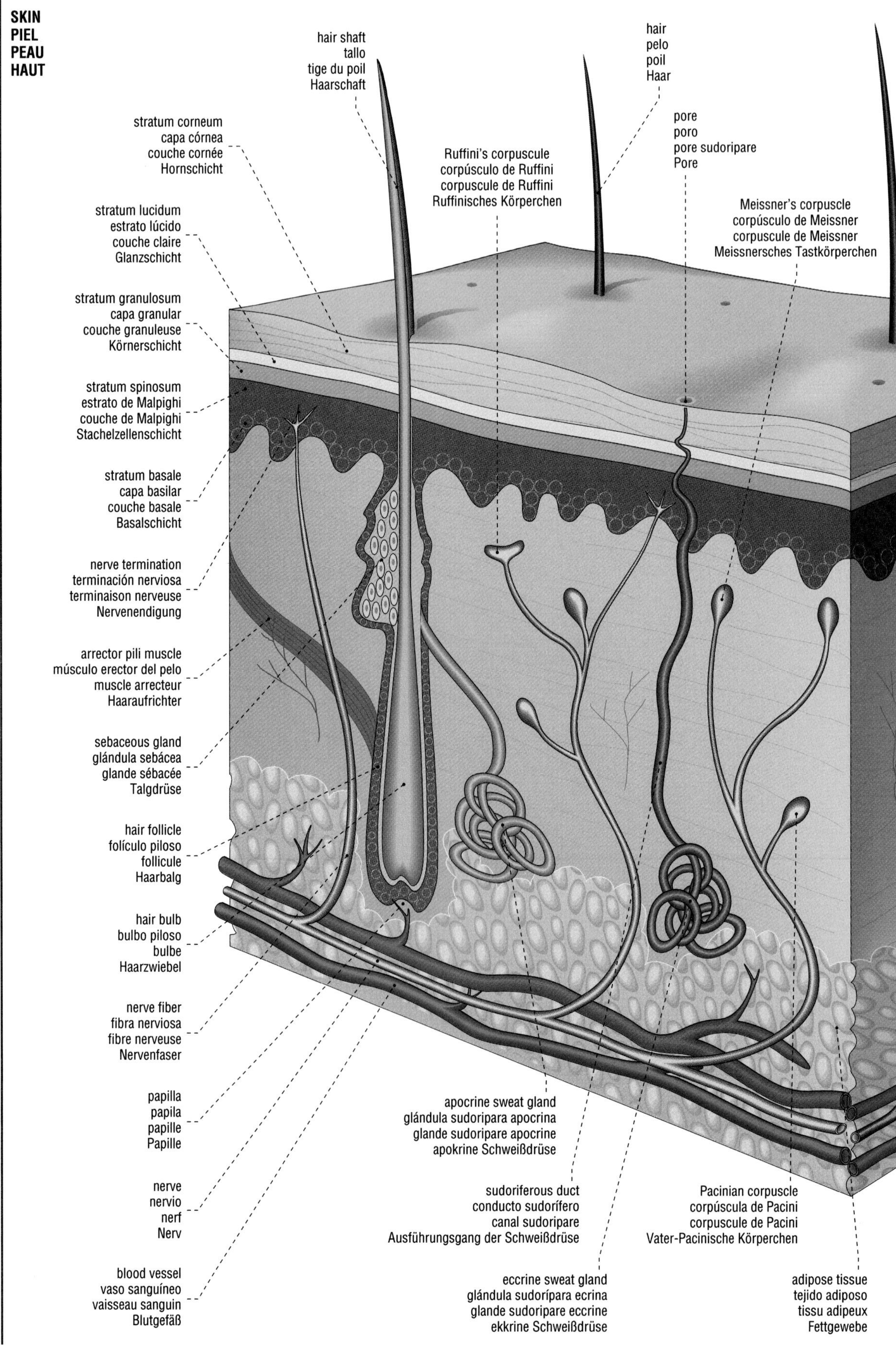
hair shaft
tallo
tige du poil
Haarschaft
hair
pelo
poil
Haar
pore
poro
pore sudoripare
Pore
stratum corneum
capa córnea
couche cornée
Hornschicht
Ruffini's corpuscule
corpúsculo de Ruffini
corpuscule de Ruffini
Ruffinisches Körperchen
Meissner's corpuscle
corpúsculo de Meissner
corpuscule de Meissner
Meissnersches Tastkörperchen
stratum lucidum
estrato lúcido
couche claire
Glanzschicht
stratum granulosum
capa granular
couche granuleuse
Körnerschicht
stratum spinosum
estrato de Malpighi
couche de Malpighi
Stachelzellenschicht
stratum basale
capa basilar
couche basale
Basalschicht
nerve termination
terminación nerviosa
terminaison nerveuse
Nervenendigung
arrector pili muscle
músculo erector del pelo
muscle arrecteur
Haaraufrichter
sebaceous gland
glándula sebácea
glande sébacée
Talgdrüse
hair follicle
folículo piloso
follicule
Haarbalg
hair bulb
bulbo piloso
bulbe
Haarzwiebel
nerve fiber
fibra nerviosa
fibre nerveuse
Nervenfaser
papilla
papila
papille
Papille
apocrine sweat gland
glándula sudorípara apocrina
glande sudoripare apocrine
apokrine Schweißdrüse
nerve
nervio
nerf
Nerv
sudoriferous duct
conducto sudorífero
canal sudoripare
Ausführungsgang der Schweißdrüse
Pacinian corpuscle
corpúscula de Pacini
corpuscule de Pacini
Vater-Pacinische Körperchen
blood vessel
vaso sanguíneo
vaisseau sanguin
Blutgefäß
eccrine sweat gland
glándula sudorípara ecrina
glande sudoripare eccrine
ekkrine Schweißdrüse
adipose tissue
tejido adiposo
tissu adipeux
Fettgewebe

FINGER
DEDO
DOIGT
FINGER

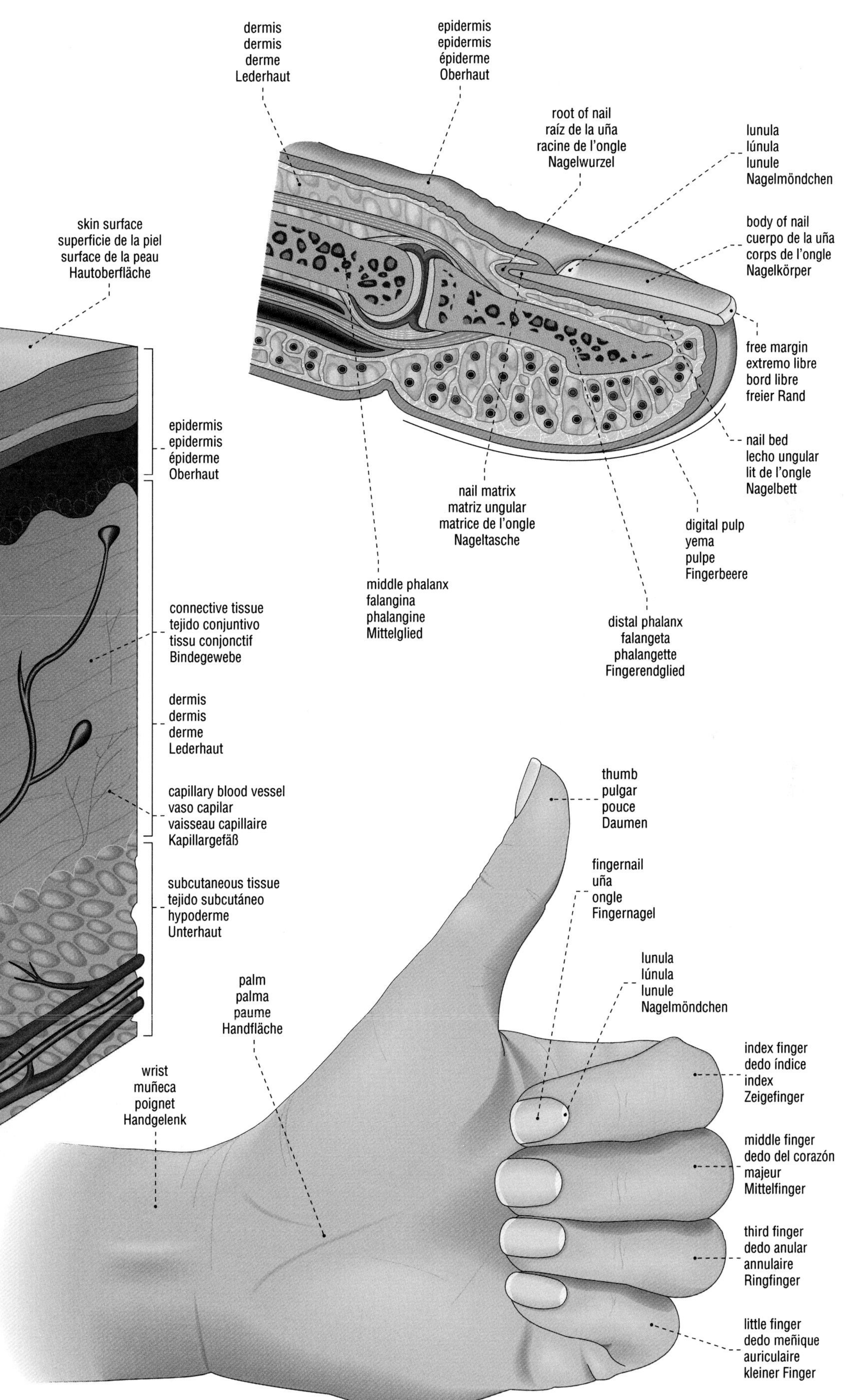
dermis
dermis
derme
Lederhaut
epidermis
epidermis
épiderme
Oberhaut
root of nail
raíz de la uña
racine de l'ongle
Nagelwurzel
lunula
lúnula
lunule
Nagelmöndchen
body of nail
cuerpo de la uña
corps de l'ongle
Nagelkörper
free margin
extremo libre
bord libre
freier Rand
nail bed
lecho ungular
lit de l'ongle
Nagelbett
digital pulp
yema
pulpe
Fingerbeere
distal phalanx
falangeta
phalangette
Fingerendglied
nail matrix
matriz ungular
matrice de l'ongle
Nageltasche
middle phalanx
falangina
phalangine
Mittelglied
skin surface
superficie de la piel
surface de la peau
Hautoberfläche
epidermis
epidermis
épiderme
Oberhaut
connective tissue
tejido conjuntivo
tissu conjonctif
Bindegewebe
dermis
dermis
derme
Lederhaut
capillary blood vessel
vaso capilar
vaisseau capillaire
Kapillargefäß
subcutaneous tissue
tejido subcutáneo
hypoderme
Unterhaut
thumb
pulgar
pouce
Daumen
fingernail
uña
ongle
Fingernagel
lunula
lúnula
lunule
Nagelmöndchen
palm
palma
paume
Handfläche
wrist
muñeca
poignet
Handgelenk
index finger
dedo índice
index
Zeigefinger
middle finger
dedo del corazón
majeur
Mittelfinger
third finger
dedo anular
annulaire
Ringfinger
little finger
dedo meñique
auriculaire
kleiner Finger

HAND
MANO
MAIN
HAND

SENSE ORGANS: HEARING
EL OÍDO
ORGANES DES SENS: OUÏE
SINNESORGANE: GEHÖR

PARTS OF THE EAR
PARTES DEL OÍDO
PARTIES DE L'OREILLE
TEILE DES OHRS

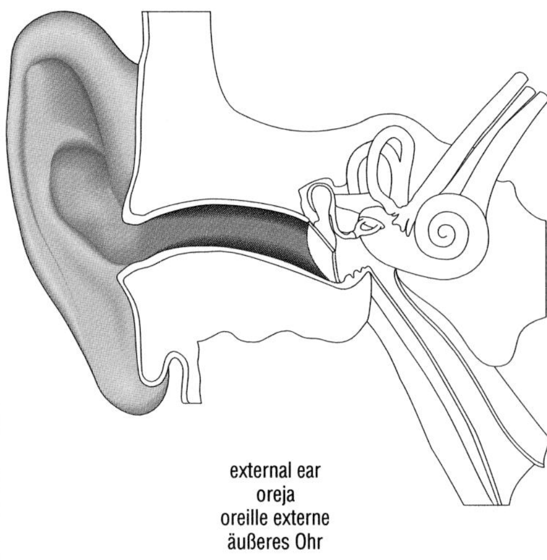

external ear
oreja
oreille externe
äußeres Ohr

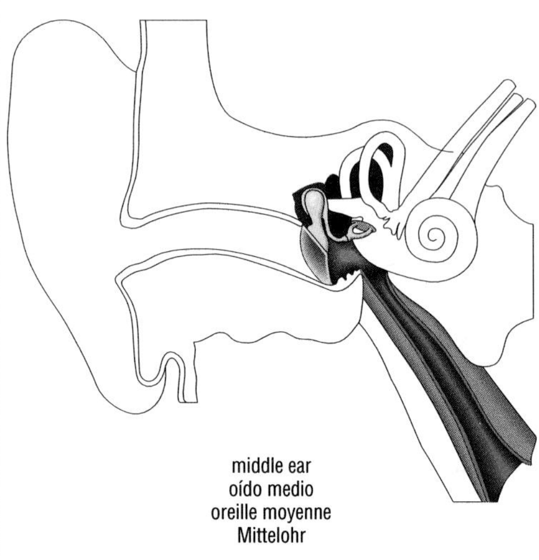

middle ear
oído medio
oreille moyenne
Mittelohr

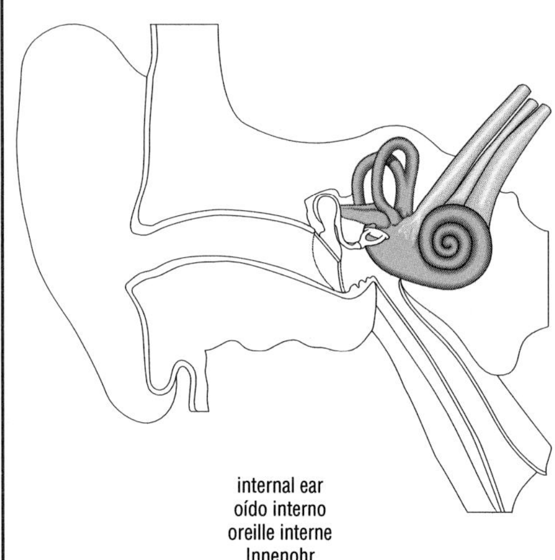

internal ear
oído interno
oreille interne
Innenohr

AUDITORY OSSICLES
HUESECILLOS AUDITIVOS
OSSELETS
GEHÖRKNÖCHELCHEN

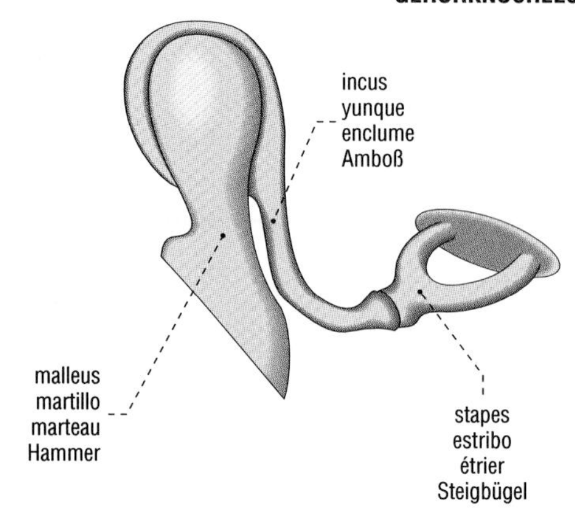
incus
yunque
enclume
Amboß
malleus
martillo
marteau
Hammer
stapes
estribo
étrier
Steigbügel

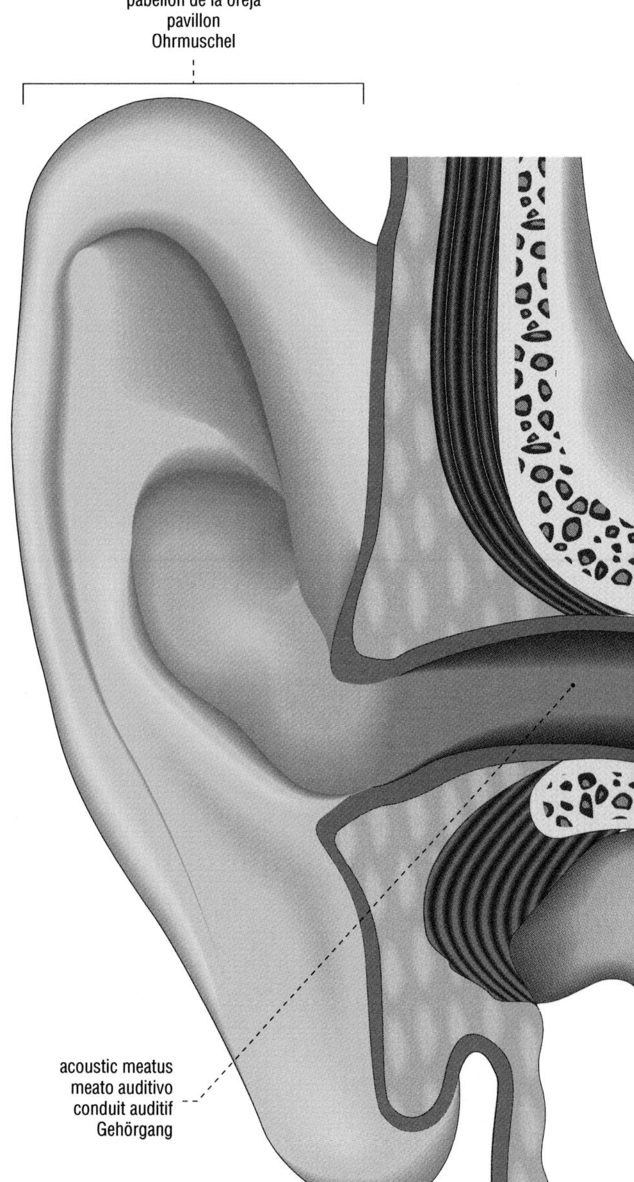
auricle
pabellón de la oreja
pavillon
Ohrmuschel
acoustic meatus
meato auditivo
conduit auditif
Gehörgang

AURICLE
PABELLÓN DE LA OREJA
PAVILLON
OHRMUSCHEL

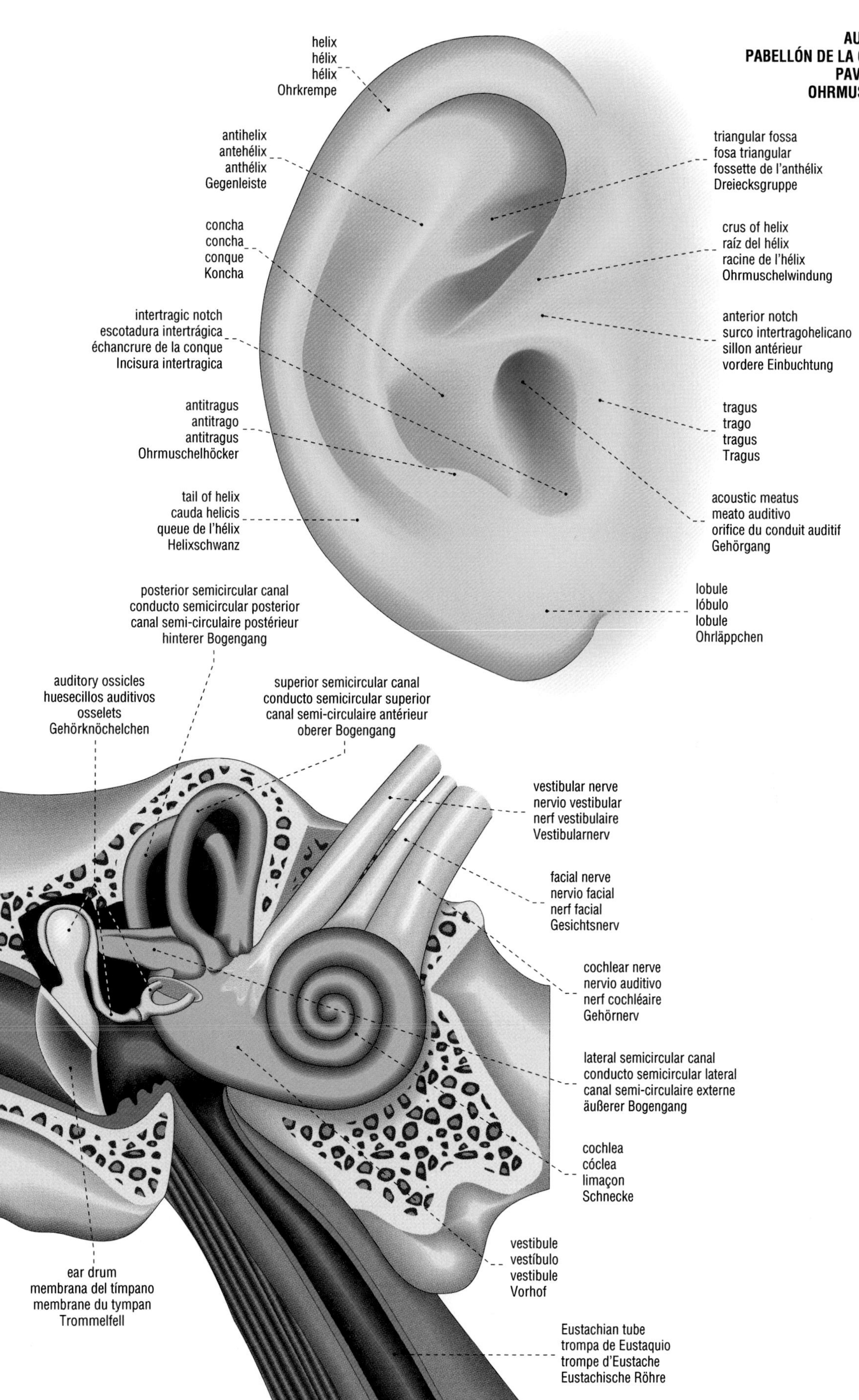
helix
hélix
hélix
Ohrkrempe
antihelix
antehélix
anthélix
Gegenleiste
concha
concha
conque
Koncha
intertragic notch
escotadura intertrágica
échancrure de la conque
Incisura intertragica
antitragus
antitrago
antitragus
Ohrmuschelhöcker
tail of helix
cauda helicis
queue de l'hélix
Helixschwanz
triangular fossa
fosa triangular
fossette de l'anthélix
Dreiecksgruppe
crus of helix
raíz del hélix
racine de l'hélix
Ohrmuschelwindung
anterior notch
surco intertragohelicano
sillon antérieur
vordere Einbuchtung
tragus
trago
tragus
Tragus
acoustic meatus
meato auditivo
orifice du conduit auditif
Gehörgang
lobule
lóbulo
lobule
Ohrläppchen
posterior semicircular canal
conducto semicircular posterior
canal semi-circulaire postérieur
hinterer Bogengang
auditory ossicles
huesecillos auditivos
osselets
Gehörknöchelchen
superior semicircular canal
conducto semicircular superior
canal semi-circulaire antérieur
oberer Bogengang
vestibular nerve
nervio vestibular
nerf vestibulaire
Vestibularnerv
facial nerve
nervio facial
nerf facial
Gesichtsnerv
cochlear nerve
nervio auditivo
nerf cochléaire
Gehörnerv
lateral semicircular canal
conducto semicircular lateral
canal semi-circulaire externe
äußerer Bogengang
cochlea
cóclea
limaçon
Schnecke
ear drum
membrana del tímpano
membrane du tympan
Trommelfell
vestibule
vestíbulo
vestibule
Vorhof
Eustachian tube
trompa de Eustaquio
trompe d'Eustache
Eustachische Röhre

SENSE ORGANS: SIGHT
LA VISTA
ORGANES DES SENS: VUE
SINNESORGANE: SEHVERMÖGEN

EYE
OJO
ŒIL
AUGE

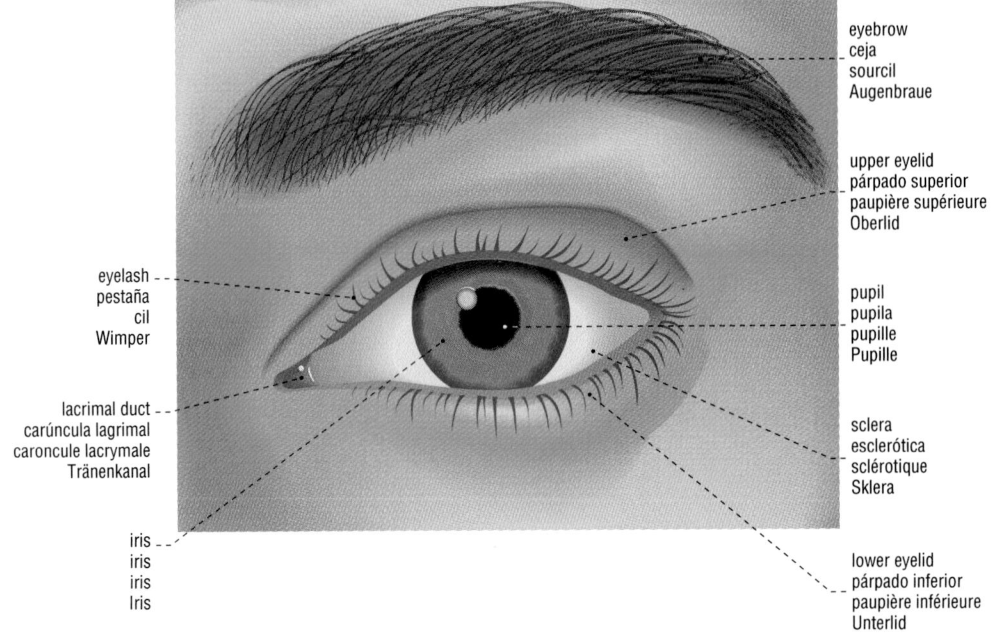
eyebrow
ceja
sourcil
Augenbraue
upper eyelid
párpado superior
paupière supérieure
Oberlid
eyelash
pestaña
cil
Wimper
pupil
pupila
pupille
Pupille
lacrimal duct
carúncula lagrimal
caroncule lacrymale
Tränenkanal
sclera
esclerótica
sclérotique
Sklera
iris
iris
iris
Iris
lower eyelid
párpado inferior
paupière inférieure
Unterlid

EYEBALL
GLOBO OCULAR
GLOBE OCULAIRE
AUGAPFEL

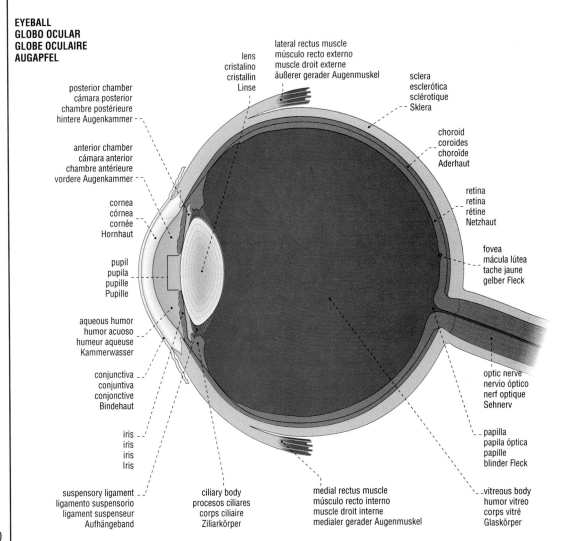

lens
cristalino
cristallin
Linse

lateral rectus muscle
músculo recto externo
muscle droit externe
äußerer gerader Augenmuskel

sclera
esclerótica
sclérotique
Sklera

posterior chamber
cámara posterior
chambre postérieure
hintere Augenkammer

choroid
coroides
choroïde
Aderhaut

anterior chamber
cámara anterior
chambre antérieure
vordere Augenkammer

retina
retina
rétine
Netzhaut

cornea
córnea
cornée
Hornhaut

fovea
mácula lútea
tache jaune
gelber Fleck

pupil
pupila
pupille
Pupille

aqueous humor
humor acuoso
humeur aqueuse
Kammerwasser

conjunctiva
conjuntiva
conjonctive
Bindehaut

optic nerve
nervio óptico
nerf optique
Sehnerv

iris
iris
iris
Iris

papilla
papila óptica
papille
blinder Fleck

suspensory ligament
ligamento suspensorio
ligament suspenseur
Aufhängeband

ciliary body
procesos ciliares
corps ciliaire
Ziliarkörper

medial rectus muscle
músculo recto interno
muscle droit interne
medialer gerader Augenmuskel

vitreous body
humor vitreo
corps vitré
Glaskörper

SENSE ORGANS: SMELL
EL OLFATO
ORGANES DES SENS: ODORAT
SINNESORGANE: GERUCHSSINN

EXTERNAL NOSE
NARIZ
PARTIES EXTERNES DU NEZ
ÄUSSERE NASE

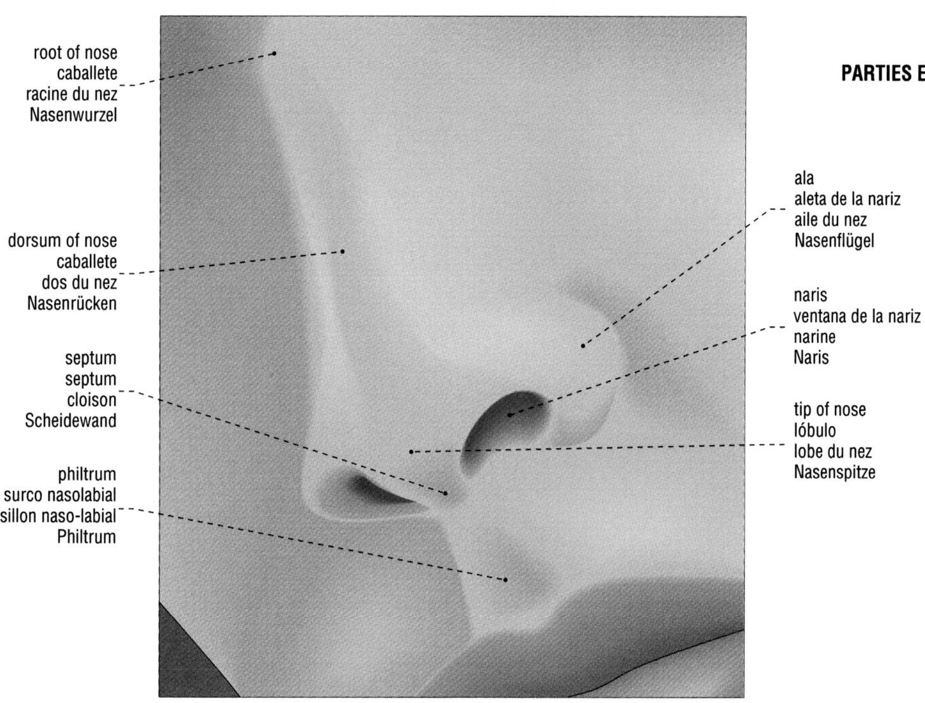
root of nose
caballete
racine du nez
Nasenwurzel
dorsum of nose
caballete
dos du nez
Nasenrücken
septum
septum
cloison
Scheidewand
philtrum
surco nasolabial
sillon naso-labial
Philtrum
ala
aleta de la nariz
aile du nez
Nasenflügel
naris
ventana de la nariz
narine
Naris
tip of nose
lóbulo
lobe du nez
Nasenspitze

NASAL FOSSAE
FOSAS NASALES
FOSSES NASALES
NASENHÖHLE

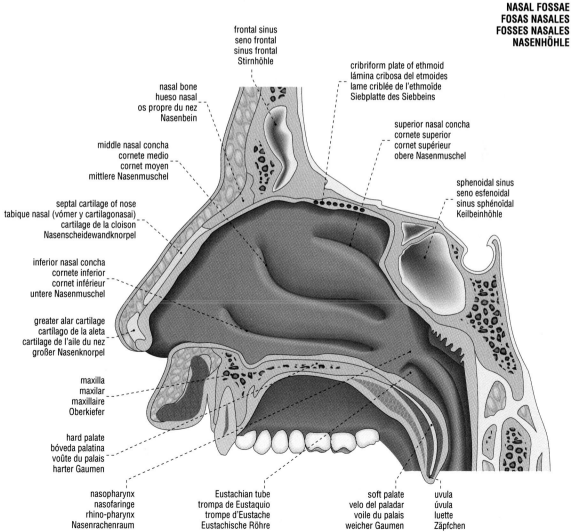

frontal sinus
seno frontal
sinus frontal
Stirnhöhle

cribriform plate of ethmoid
lámina cribosa del etmoides
lame criblée de l'ethmoïde
Siebplatte des Siebbeins

nasal bone
hueso nasal
os propre du nez
Nasenbein

superior nasal concha
cornete superior
cornet supérieur
obere Nasenmuschel

middle nasal concha
cornete medio
cornet moyen
mittlere Nasenmuschel

sphenoidal sinus
seno esfenoidal
sinus sphénoïdal
Keilbeinhöhle

septal cartilage of nose
tabique nasal (vómer y cartilagonasai)
cartilage de la cloison
Nasenscheidewandknorpel

inferior nasal concha
cornete inferior
cornet inférieur
untere Nasenmuschel

greater alar cartilage
cartílago de la aleta
cartilage de l'aile du nez
großer Nasenknorpel

maxilla
maxilar
maxillaire
Oberkiefer

hard palate
bóveda palatina
voûte du palais
harter Gaumen

nasopharynx
nasofaringe
rhino-pharynx
Nasenrachenraum

Eustachian tube
trompa de Eustaquio
trompe d'Eustache
Eustachische Röhre

soft palate
velo del paladar
voile du palais
weicher Gaumen

uvula
úvula
luette
Zäpfchen

SENSES OF SMELL AND TASTE
EL OLFATO Y EL GUSTO
SENS DE L'ODORAT ET DU GOÛT
GERUCHS- UND GESCHMACKSSINN

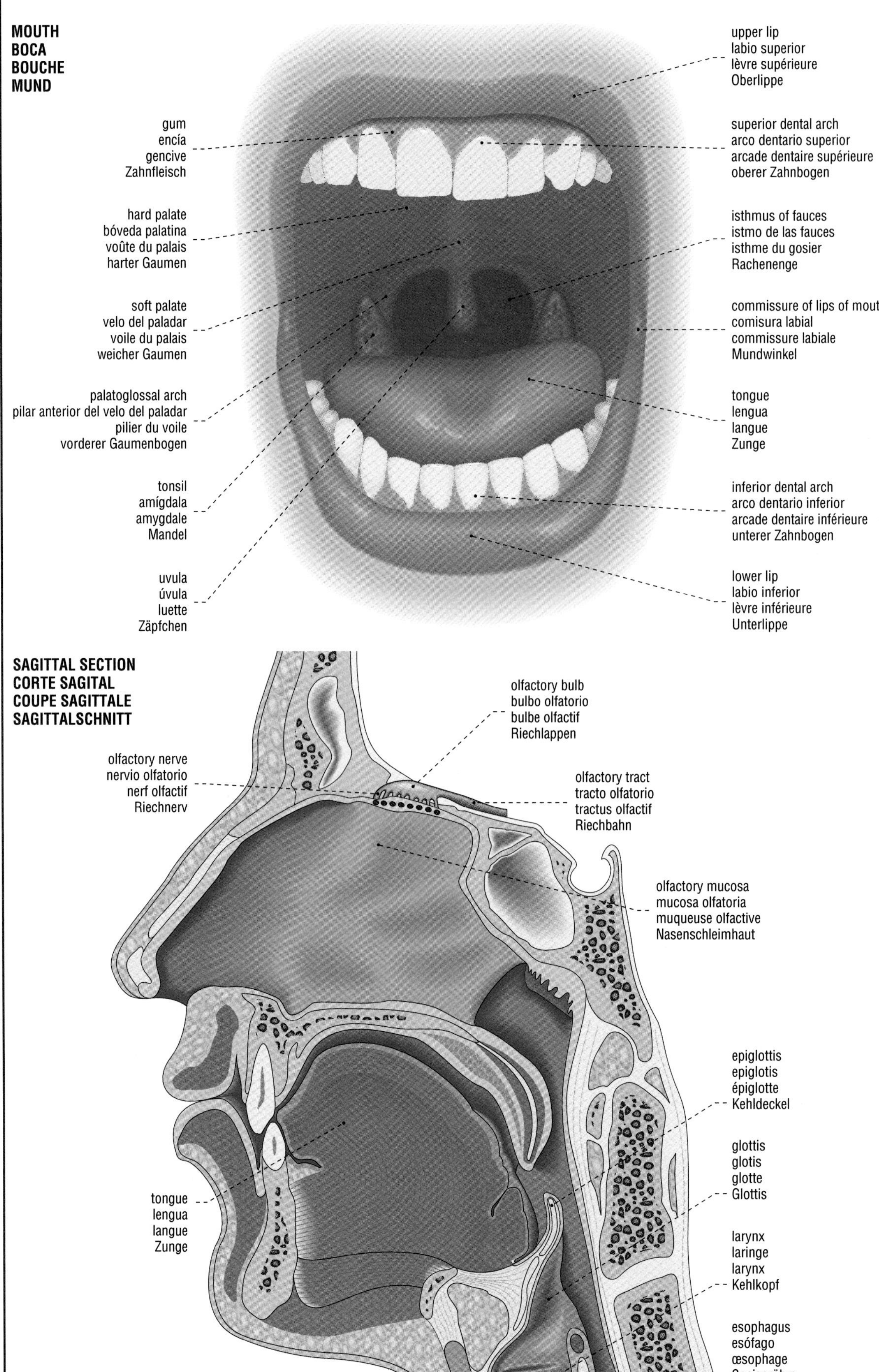
MOUTH
BOCA
BOUCHE
MUND
upper lip
labio superior
lèvre supérieure
Oberlippe
gum
encía
gencive
Zahnfleisch
superior dental arch
arco dentario superior
arcade dentaire supérieure
oberer Zahnbogen
hard palate
bóveda palatina
voûte du palais
harter Gaumen
isthmus of fauces
istmo de las fauces
isthme du gosier
Rachenenge
soft palate
velo del paladar
voile du palais
weicher Gaumen
commissure of lips of mouth
comisura labial
commissure labiale
Mundwinkel
palatoglossal arch
pilar anterior del velo del paladar
pilier du voile
vorderer Gaumenbogen
tongue
lengua
langue
Zunge
tonsil
amígdala
amygdale
Mandel
inferior dental arch
arco dentario inferior
arcade dentaire inférieure
unterer Zahnbogen
uvula
úvula
luette
Zäpfchen
lower lip
labio inferior
lèvre inférieure
Unterlippe
SAGITTAL SECTION
CORTE SAGITAL
COUPE SAGITTALE
SAGITTALSCHNITT
olfactory bulb
bulbo olfatorio
bulbe olfactif
Riechlappen
olfactory nerve
nervio olfatorio
nerf olfactif
Riechnerv
olfactory tract
tracto olfatorio
tractus olfactif
Riechbahn
olfactory mucosa
mucosa olfatoria
muqueuse olfactive
Nasenschleimhaut
epiglottis
epiglotis
épiglotte
Kehldeckel
glottis
glotis
glotte
Glottis
tongue
lengua
langue
Zunge
larynx
laringe
larynx
Kehlkopf
esophagus
esófago
œsophage
Speiseröhre

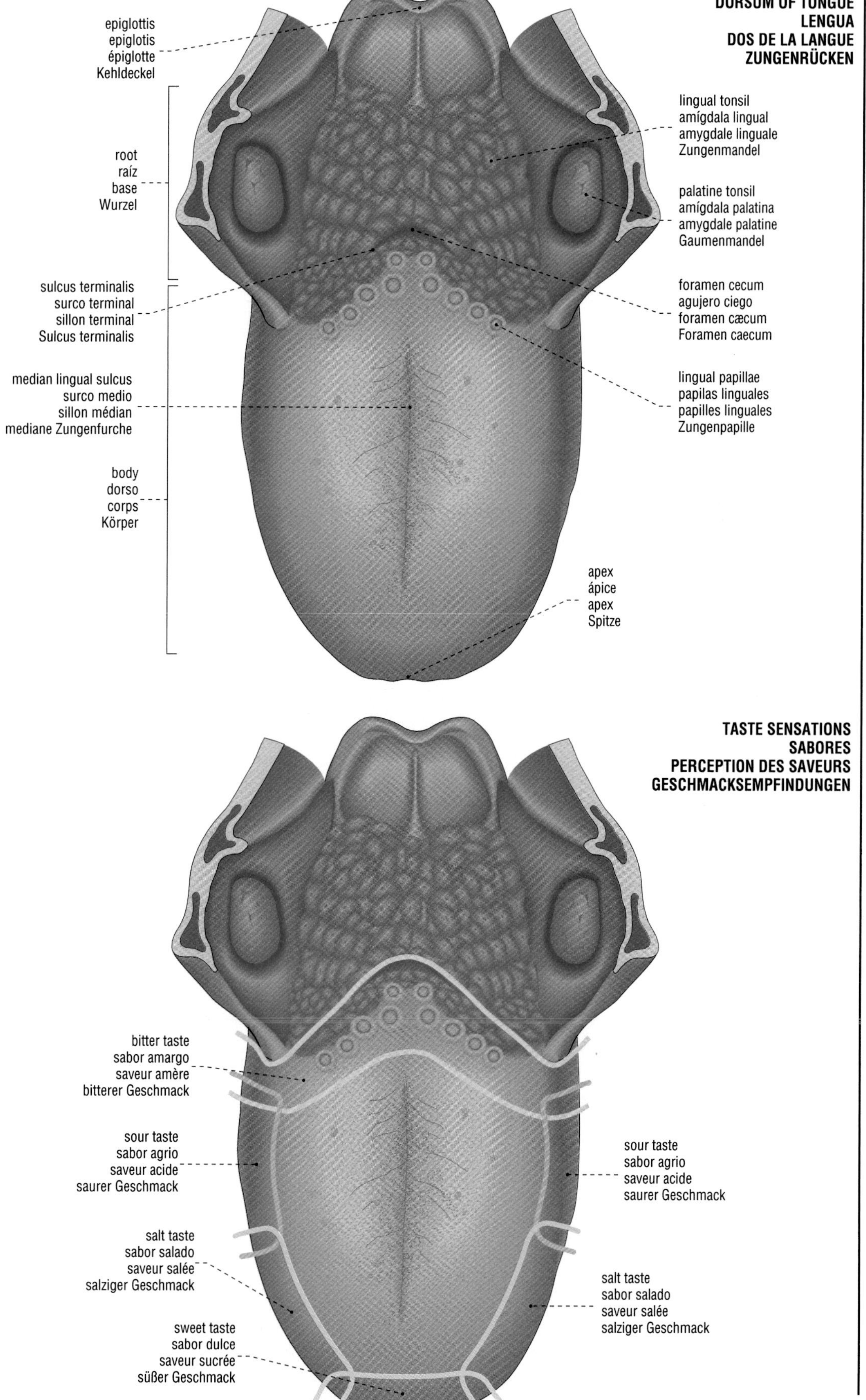
DORSUM OF TONGUE
LENGUA
DOS DE LA LANGUE
ZUNGENRÜCKEN
epiglottis
epiglotis
épiglotte
Kehldeckel
root
raíz
base
Wurzel
sulcus terminalis
surco terminal
sillon terminal
Sulcus terminalis
median lingual sulcus
surco medio
sillon médian
mediane Zungenfurche
body
dorso
corps
Körper
lingual tonsil
amígdala lingual
amygdale linguale
Zungenmandel
palatine tonsil
amígdala palatina
amygdale palatine
Gaumenmandel
foramen cecum
agujero ciego
foramen cæcum
Foramen caecum
lingual papillae
papilas linguales
papilles linguales
Zungenpapille
apex
ápice
apex
Spitze
TASTE SENSATIONS
SABORES
PERCEPTION DES SAVEURS
GESCHMACKSEMPFINDUNGEN
bitter taste
sabor amargo
saveur amère
bitterer Geschmack
sour taste
sabor agrio
saveur acide
saurer Geschmack
sour taste
sabor agrio
saveur acide
saurer Geschmack
salt taste
sabor salado
saveur salée
salziger Geschmack
salt taste
sabor salado
saveur salée
salziger Geschmack
sweet taste
sabor dulce
saveur sucrée
süßer Geschmack

TEETH
DIENTES
DENTS
ZÄHNE

HUMAN DENTURE
DENTADURA HUMANA
DENTURE HUMAINE
MENSCHLICHES GEBISS

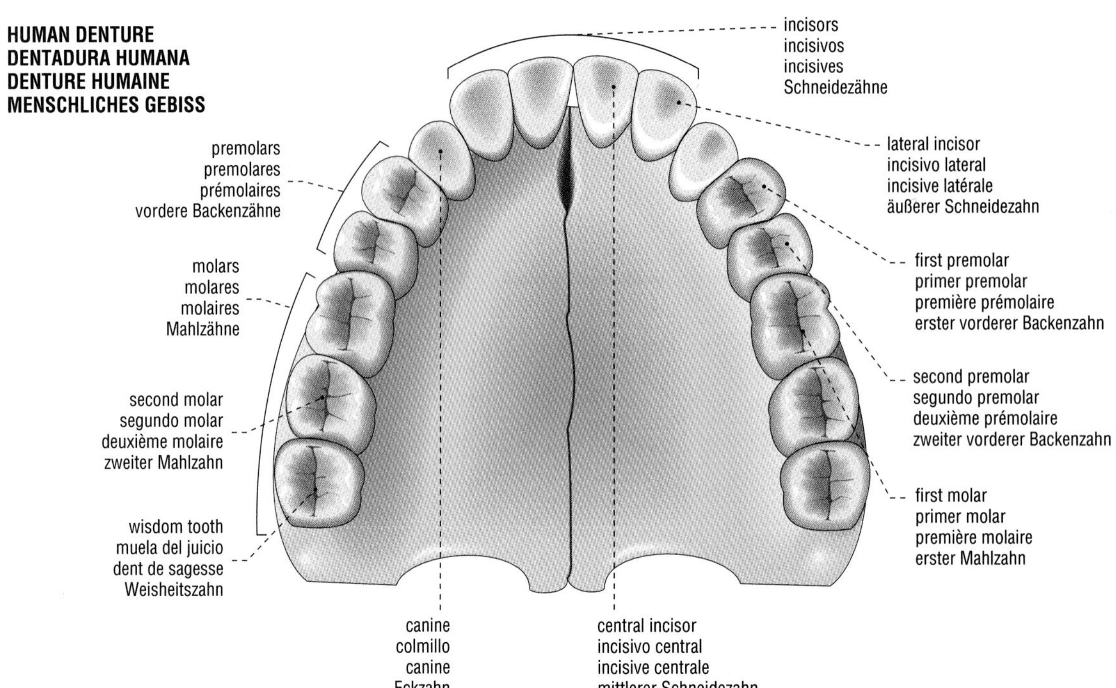
incisors
incisivos
incisives
Schneidezähne
premolars
premolares
prémolaires
vordere Backenzähne
lateral incisor
incisivo lateral
incisive latérale
äußerer Schneidezahn
molars
molares
molaires
Mahlzähne
first premolar
primer premolar
première prémolaire
erster vorderer Backenzahn
second molar
segundo molar
deuxième molaire
zweiter Mahlzahn
second premolar
segundo premolar
deuxième prémolaire
zweiter vorderer Backenzahn
first molar
primer molar
première molaire
erster Mahlzahn
wisdom tooth
muela del juicio
dent de sagesse
Weisheitszahn
canine
colmillo
canine
Eckzahn
central incisor
incisivo central
incisive centrale
mittlerer Schneidezahn

CROSS SECTION OF A MOLAR
CORTE TRANSVERSAL DE UN MOLAR
COUPE D'UNE MOLAIRE
LÄNGSSCHNITT DURCH EINEN MAHLZAHN

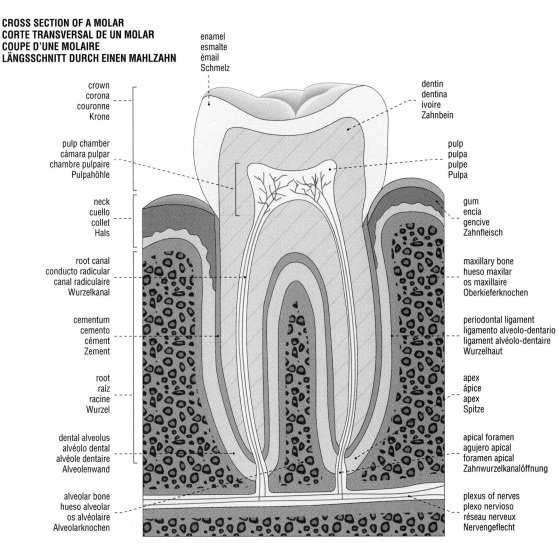

enamel
esmalte
émail
Schmelz

crown
corona
couronne
Krone

dentin
dentina
ivoire
Zahnbein

pulp chamber
cámara pulpar
chambre pulpaire
Pulpahöhle

pulp
pulpa
pulpe
Pulpa

neck
cuello
collet
Hals

gum
encía
gencive
Zahnfleisch

root canal
conducto radicular
canal radiculaire
Wurzelkanal

maxillary bone
hueso maxilar
os maxillaire
Oberkieferknochen

cementum
cemento
cément
Zement

periodontal ligament
ligamento alveolo-dentario
ligament alvéolo-dentaire
Wurzelhaut

root
raíz
racine
Wurzel

apex
ápice
apex
Spitze

dental alveolus
alvéolo dental
alvéole dentaire
Alveolenwand

apical foramen
agujero apical
foramen apical
Zahnwurzelkanalöffnung

alveolar bone
hueso alveolar
os alvéolaire
Alveolarknochen

plexus of nerves
plexo nervioso
réseau nerveux
Nervengeflecht

FARMING
FERME
AGRICULTURA
LANDWIRTSCHAFT

CONTENTS

TRACTOR
TRACTOR
TRACTEUR AGRICOLE
TRAKTOR

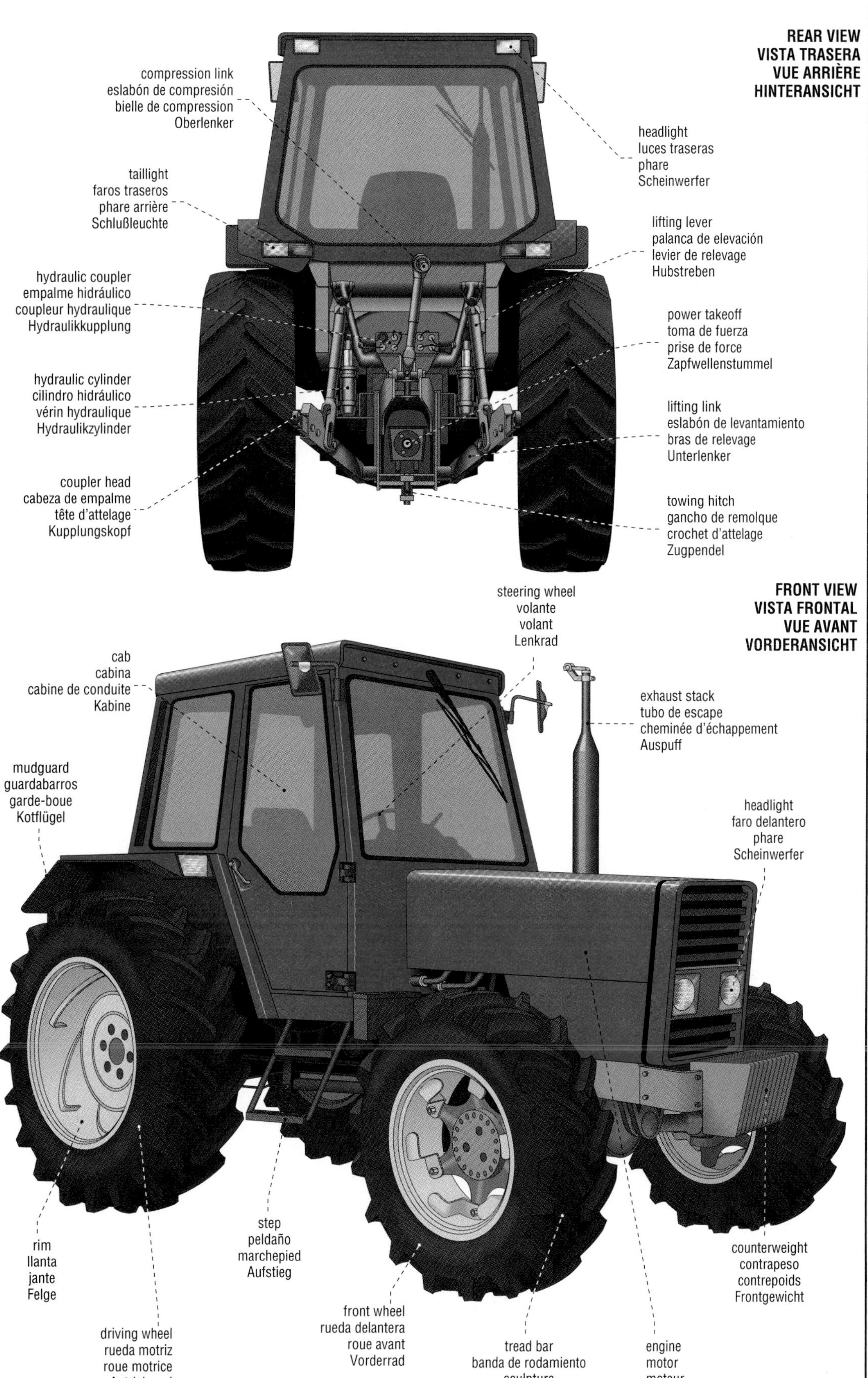
REAR VIEW
VISTA TRASERA
VUE ARRIÈRE
HINTERANSICHT
compression link
eslabón de compresión
bielle de compression
Oberlenker
headlight
luces traseras
phare
Scheinwerfer
taillight
faros traseros
phare arrière
Schlußleuchte
lifting lever
palanca de elevación
levier de relevage
Hubstreben
hydraulic coupler
empalme hidráulico
coupleur hydraulique
Hydraulikkupplung
power takeoff
toma de fuerza
prise de force
Zapfwellenstummel
hydraulic cylinder
cilindro hidráulico
vérin hydraulique
Hydraulikzylinder
lifting link
eslabón de levantamiento
bras de relevage
Unterlenker
coupler head
cabeza de empalme
tête d'attelage
Kupplungskopf
towing hitch
gancho de remolque
crochet d'attelage
Zugpendel
FRONT VIEW
VISTA FRONTAL
VUE AVANT
VORDERANSICHT
steering wheel
volante
volant
Lenkrad
cab
cabina
cabine de conduite
Kabine
exhaust stack
tubo de escape
cheminée d'échappement
Auspuff
mudguard
guardabarros
garde-boue
Kotflügel
headlight
faro delantero
phare
Scheinwerfer
rim
llanta
jante
Felge
step
peldaño
marchepied
Aufstieg
counterweight
contrapeso
contrepoids
Frontgewicht
driving wheel
rueda motriz
roue motrice
Antriebsrad
front wheel
rueda delantera
roue avant
Vorderrad
tread bar
banda de rodamiento
sculpture
Stollen
engine
motor
moteur
Motor

FARMSTEAD
GRANJA
FERME
BAUERNHOF

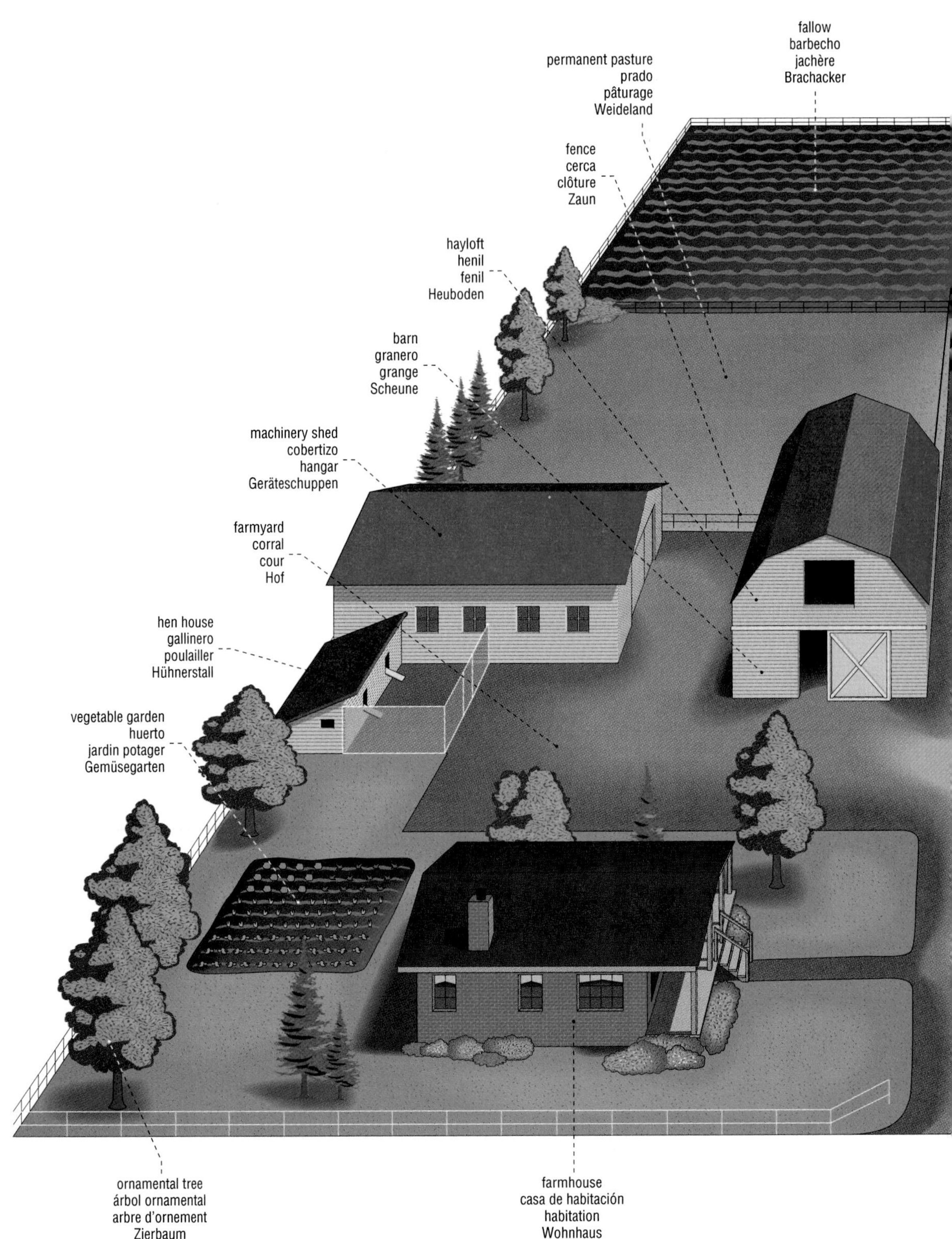
fallow
barbecho
jachère
Brachacker
permanent pasture
prado
pâturage
Weideland
fence
cerca
clôture
Zaun
hayloft
henil
fenil
Heuboden
barn
granero
grange
Scheune
machinery shed
cobertizo
hangar
Geräteschuppen
farmyard
corral
cour
Hof
hen house
gallinero
poulailler
Hühnerstall
vegetable garden
huerto
jardin potager
Gemüsegarten
ornamental tree
árbol ornamental
arbre d'ornement
Zierbaum
farmhouse
casa de habitación
habitation
Wohnhaus

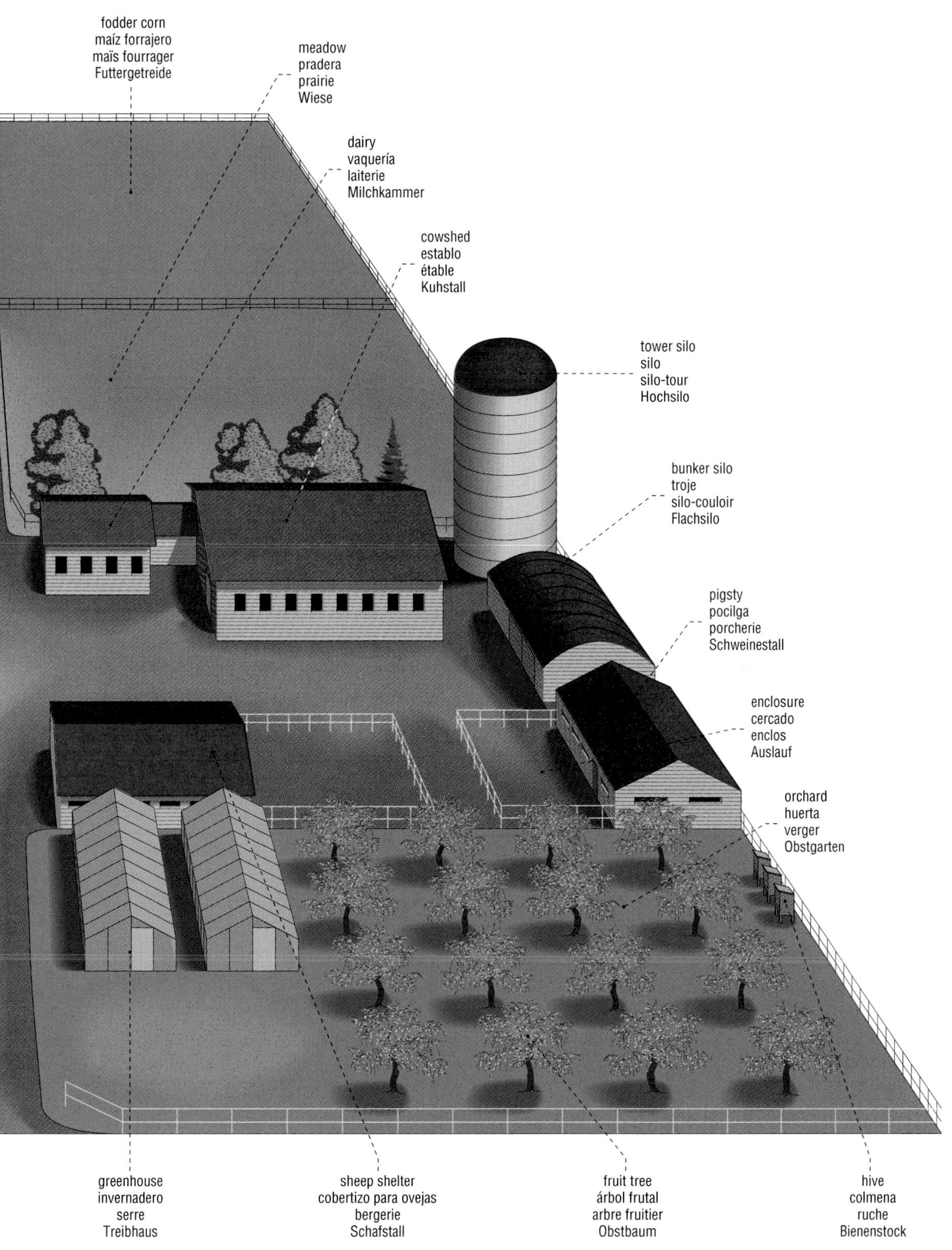
fodder corn
maíz forrajero
maïs fourrager
Futtergetreide
meadow
pradera
prairie
Wiese
dairy
vaquería
laiterie
Milchkammer
cowshed
establo
étable
Kuhstall
tower silo
silo
silo-tour
Hochsilo
bunker silo
troje
silo-couloir
Flachsilo
pigsty
pocilga
porcherie
Schweinestall
enclosure
cercado
enclos
Auslauf
orchard
huerta
verger
Obstgarten
greenhouse
invernadero
serre
Treibhaus
sheep shelter
cobertizo para ovejas
bergerie
Schafstall
fruit tree
árbol frutal
arbre fruitier
Obstbaum
hive
colmena
ruche
Bienenstock

FARM ANIMALS
ANIMALES DE LA GRANJA
ANIMAUX DE LA FERME
NUTZVIEH

hen
gallina
poule
Henne

chick
pollito
poussin
Küken

rooster
gallo
coq
Hahn

duck
pato
canard
Ente

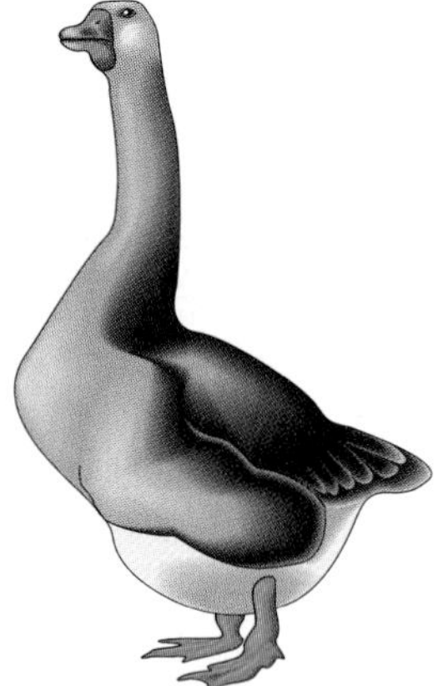

goose
ganso
oie
Gans

turkey
pavo
dindon
Truthahn

goat
cabra
chèvre
Ziege

lamb
cordero
agneau
Lamm

sheep
oveja
mouton
Schaf

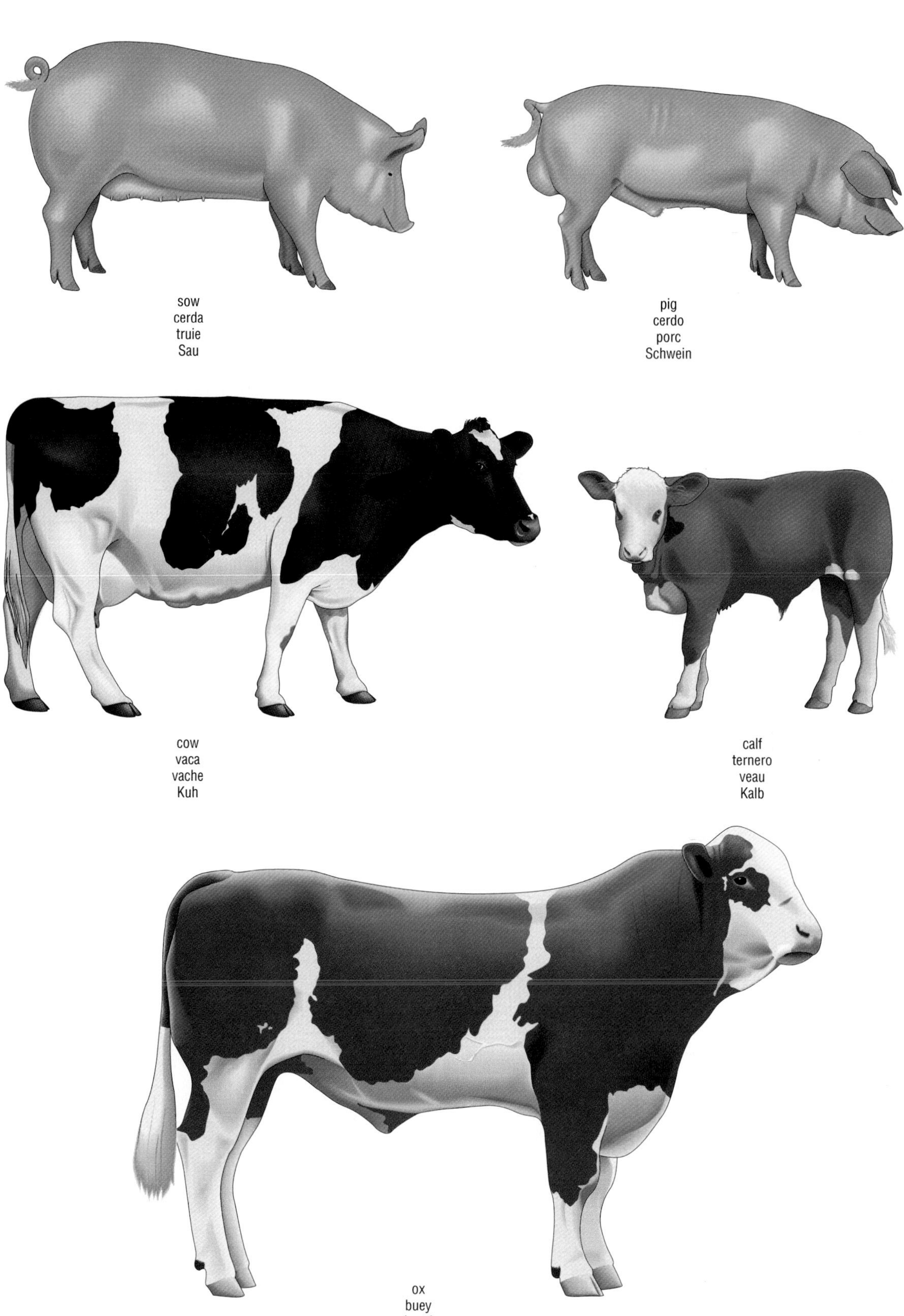
sow
cerda
truie
Sau
pig
cerdo
porc
Schwein
cow
vaca
vache
Kuh
calf
ternero
veau
Kalb
ox
buey
bœuf
Ochse

PRINCIPAL TYPES OF CEREALS
PRINCIPALES TIPOS DE CEREALES
PRINCIPALES VARIÉTÉS DE CÉRÉALES
DIE WICHTIGSTEN GETREIDESORTEN

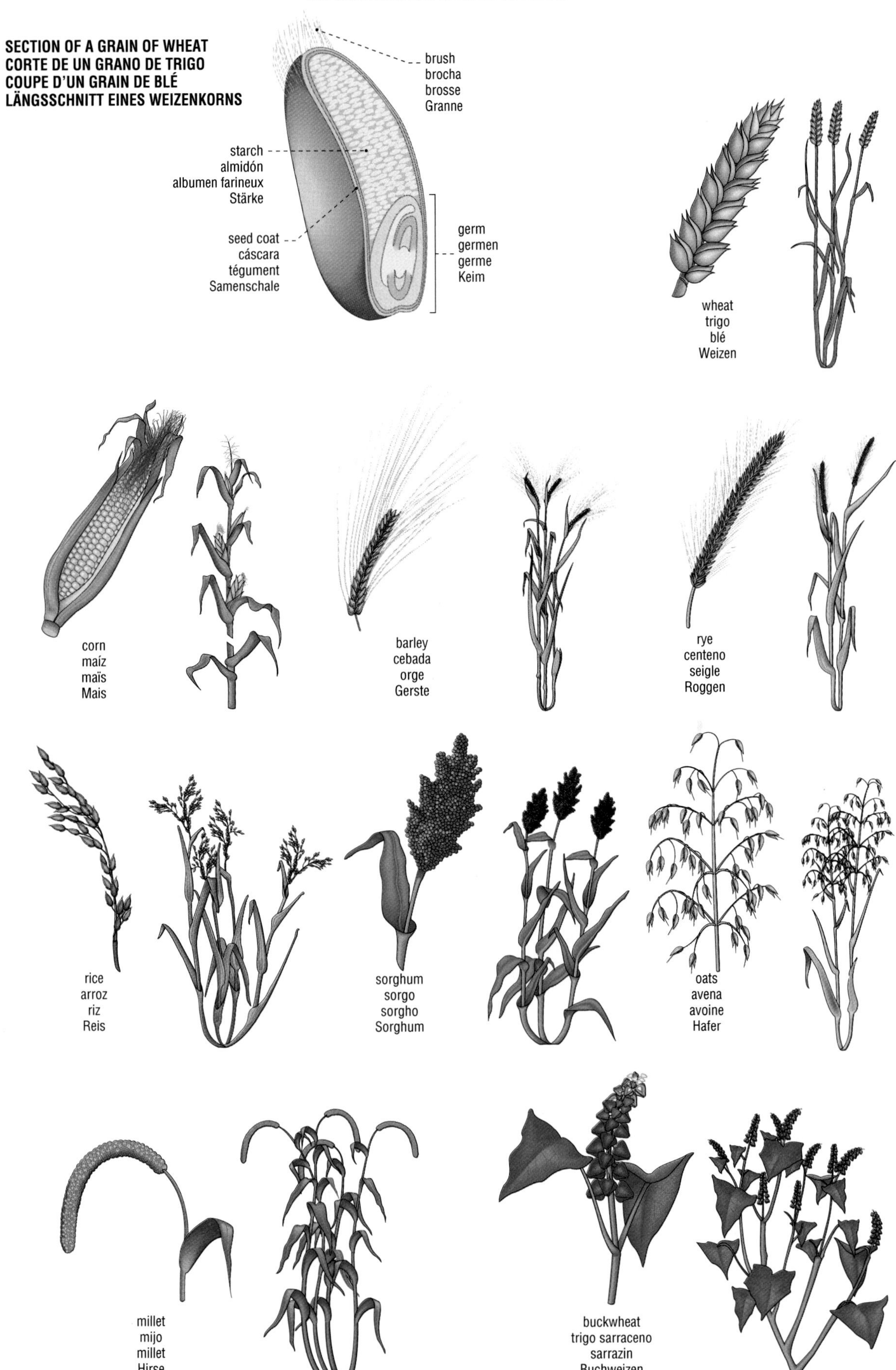
SECTION OF A GRAIN OF WHEAT
CORTE DE UN GRANO DE TRIGO
COUPE D'UN GRAIN DE BLÉ
LÄNGSSCHNITT EINES WEIZENKORNS
brush
brocha
brosse
Granne
starch
almidón
albumen farineux
Stärke
seed coat
cáscara
tégument
Samenschale
germ
germen
germe
Keim
wheat
trigo
blé
Weizen
corn
maíz
maïs
Mais
barley
cebada
orge
Gerste
rye
centeno
seigle
Roggen
rice
arroz
riz
Reis
sorghum
sorgo
sorgho
Sorghum
oats
avena
avoine
Hafer
millet
mijo
millet
Hirse
buckwheat
trigo sarraceno
sarrazin
Buchweizen

BREAD
PAN
PAIN
BROT

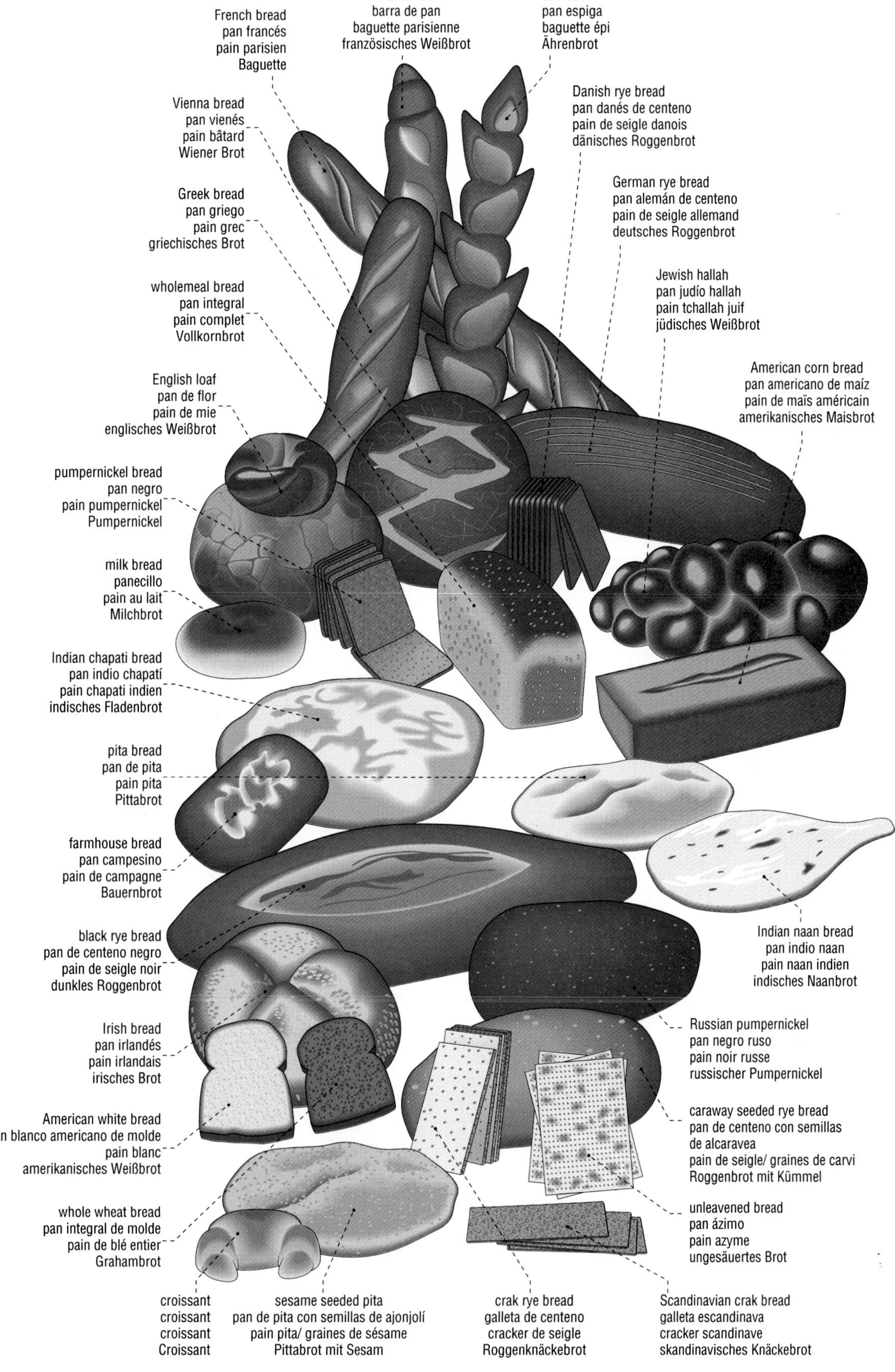
French bread
pan francés
pain parisien
Baguette
French loaf
barra de pan
baguette parisienne
französisches Weißbrot
ear loaf
pan espiga
baguette épi
Ährenbrot
Vienna bread
pan vienés
pain bâtard
Wiener Brot
Danish rye bread
pan danés de centeno
pain de seigle danois
dänisches Roggenbrot
Greek bread
pan griego
pain grec
griechisches Brot
German rye bread
pan alemán de centeno
pain de seigle allemand
deutsches Roggenbrot
wholemeal bread
pan integral
pain complet
Vollkornbrot
Jewish hallah
pan judío hallah
pain tchallah juif
jüdisches Weißbrot
English loaf
pan de flor
pain de mie
englisches Weißbrot
American corn bread
pan americano de maíz
pain de maïs américain
amerikanisches Maisbrot
pumpernickel bread
pan negro
pain pumpernickel
Pumpernickel
milk bread
panecillo
pain au lait
Milchbrot
Indian chapati bread
pan indio chapatí
pain chapati indien
indisches Fladenbrot
pita bread
pan de pita
pain pita
Pittabrot
farmhouse bread
pan campesino
pain de campagne
Bauernbrot
black rye bread
pan de centeno negro
pain de seigle noir
dunkles Roggenbrot
Indian naan bread
pan indio naan
pain naan indien
indisches Naanbrot
Irish bread
pan irlandés
pain irlandais
irisches Brot
Russian pumpernickel
pan negro ruso
pain noir russe
russischer Pumpernickel
American white bread
pan blanco americano de molde
pain blanc
amerikanisches Weißbrot
caraway seeded rye bread
pan de centeno con semillas
de alcaravea
pain de seigle/ graines de carvi
Roggenbrot mit Kümmel
whole wheat bread
pan integral de molde
pain de blé entier
Grahambrot
unleavened bread
pan ázimo
pain azyme
ungesäuertes Brot
croissant
croissant
croissant
Croissant
sesame seeded pita
pan de pita con semillas de ajonjolí
pain pita/ graines de sésame
Pittabrot mit Sesam
crak rye bread
galleta de centeno
cracker de seigle
Roggenknäckebrot
Scandinavian crak bread
galleta escandinava
cracker scandinave
skandinavisches Knäckebrot

STEPS FOR CULTIVATING SOIL
PASOS PARA EL CULTIVO DEL SUELO
ÉTAPES DE LA CULTURE DU SOL
ARBEITSVERFAHREN DER BODENBEARBEITUNG

PLOWING SOIL
ARADO
RETOURNER LA TERRE
PFLÜGEN DES BODENS

ribbing plow
arado de vertedera
charrue à soc
Beetpflug

FERTILIZING SOIL
ABONADO
FERTILISER LA TERRE
DÜNGEN DES BODENS

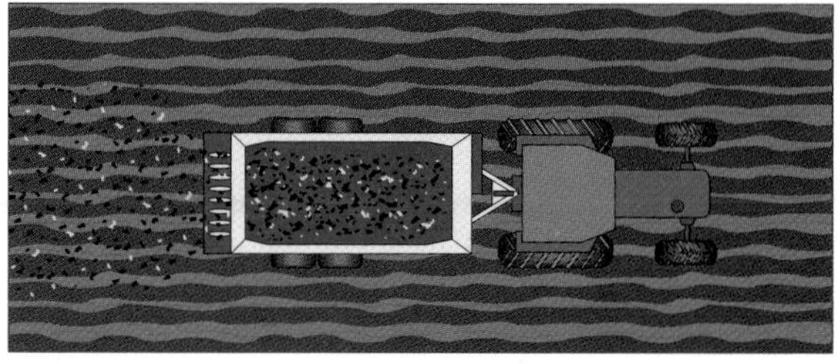

manure spreader
esparcidora de estiércol
épandeur de fumier
Dungstreuer

PULVERIZING SOIL
PULVERIZACIÓN
AMEUBLIR LA TERRE
EGGEN DES BODENS

tandem disk harrow
pulverizador de discos
pulvérisateur tandem
Scheibenegge

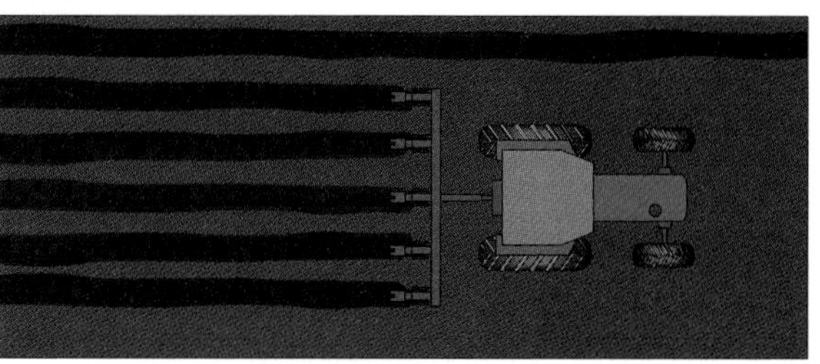

cultivator
cultivador
cultivateur
Hackrahmen

PLANTING
SIEMBRA
SEMER
SÄEN

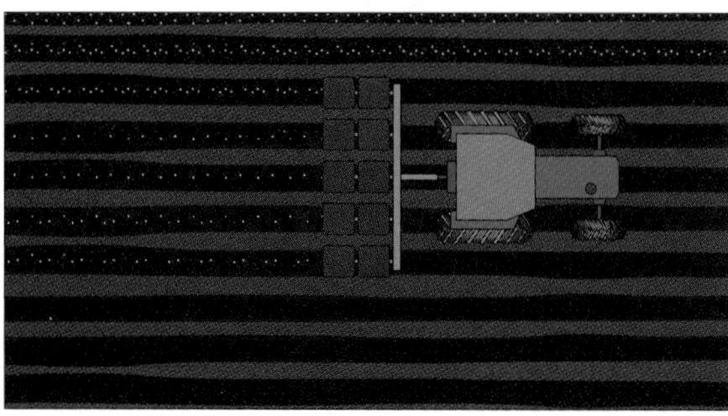

seed drill
sembradora a chorrillo
semoir en lignes
Drillmaschine

MOWING
SIEGA
FAUCHER
MÄHEN

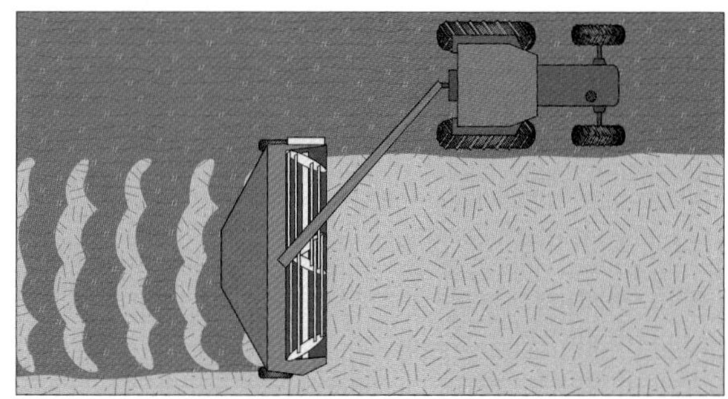

flail mower
segadora
faucheuse-conditionneuse
Anhängemähwerk

**TEDDING
HENIFICACIÓN
FANER
ZETTEN UND WENDEN**

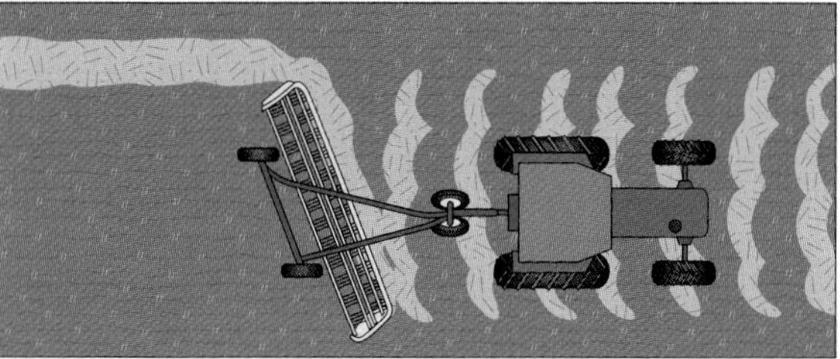

rake
rastrillo
râteau
Schubrechwender

**HARVESTING
COSECHA
RÉCOLTER
ERNTEN**

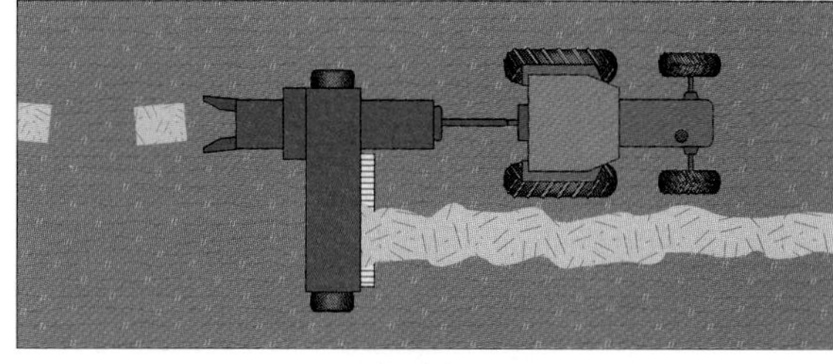

hay baler
empacadora de heno
ramasseuse-presse
Hochdruckpresse

**HARVESTING
COSECHA
RÉCOLTER
ERNTEN**

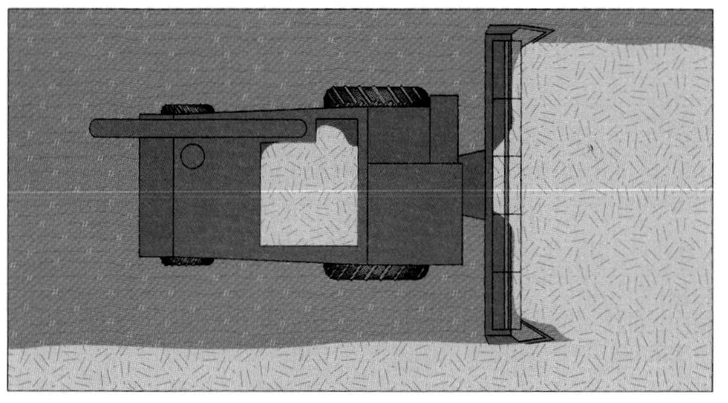

combine harvester
cosechadora trilladora
moissonneuse-batteuse
Mähdrescher

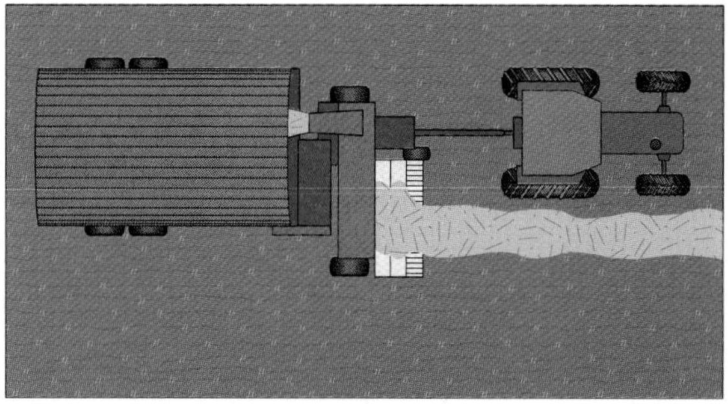

forage harvester
cosechadora de forraje
fourragère
Feldhäckseler

**ENSILING
ENSILAJE
ENSILER
SILIEREN**

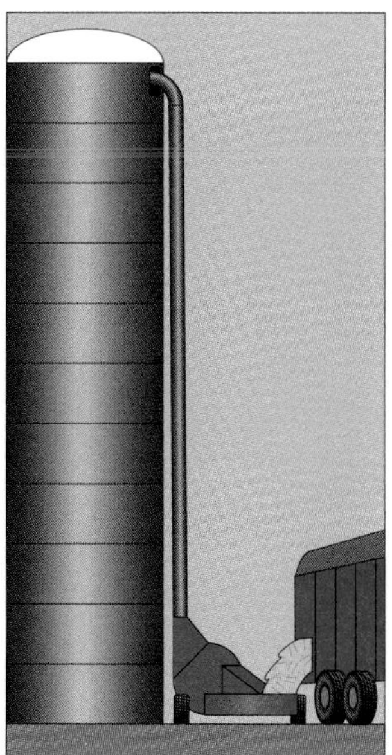

forage blower
aventador de frorraje
souffleuse de fourrage
Abladegebläse

PLOWING SOIL
ARADO
RETOURNER LA TERRE
PFLÜGEN

RIBBING PLOW
ARADO DE VERTEDERA
CHARRUE À SOC
BEETPFLUG

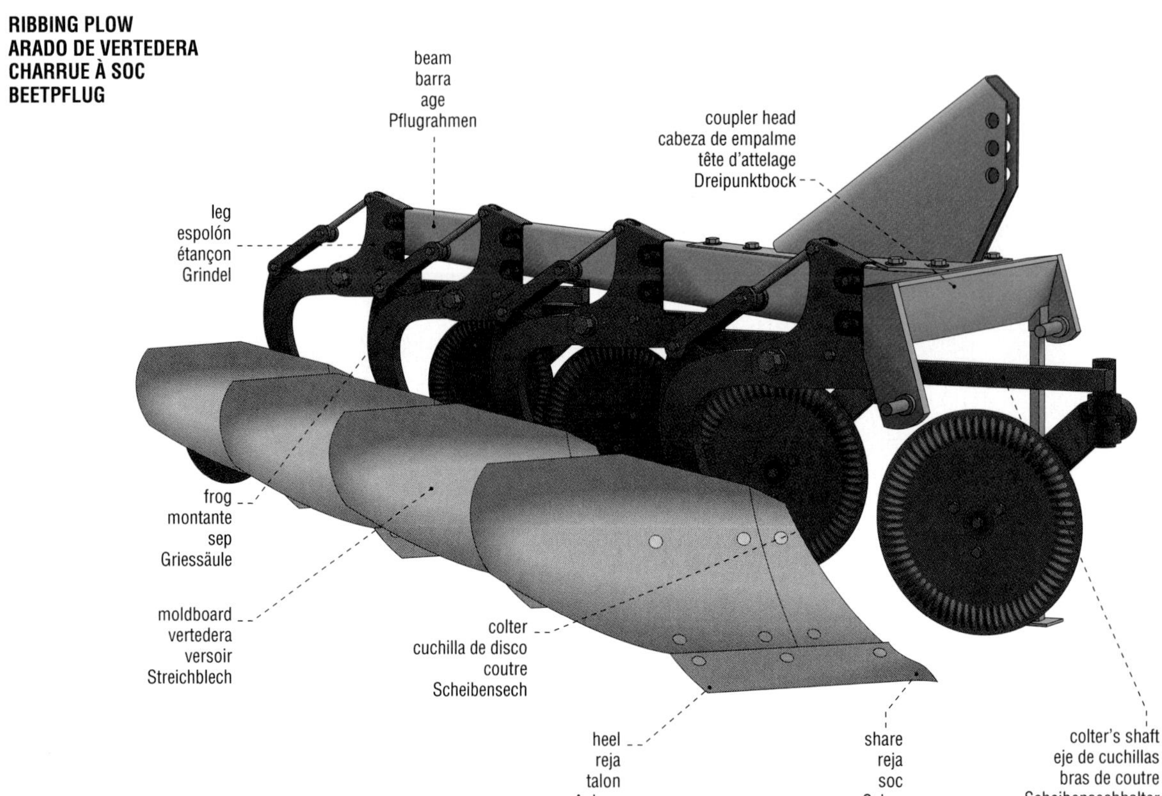
beam
barra
age
Pflugrahmen
coupler head
cabeza de empalme
tête d'attelage
Dreipunktbock
leg
espolón
étançon
Grindel
frog
montante
sep
Griessäule
moldboard
vertedera
versoir
Streichblech
colter
cuchilla de disco
coutre
Scheibensech
heel
reja
talon
Anlage
share
reja
soc
Schar
colter's shaft
eje de cuchillas
bras de coutre
Scheibensechhalter

FERTILIZING SOIL
ABONADO
FERTILISER LA TERRE
DÜNGEN

MANURE SPREADER
ESPARCIDORA DE ESTIÉRCOL
ÉPANDEUR DE FUMIER
DUNGSTREUER

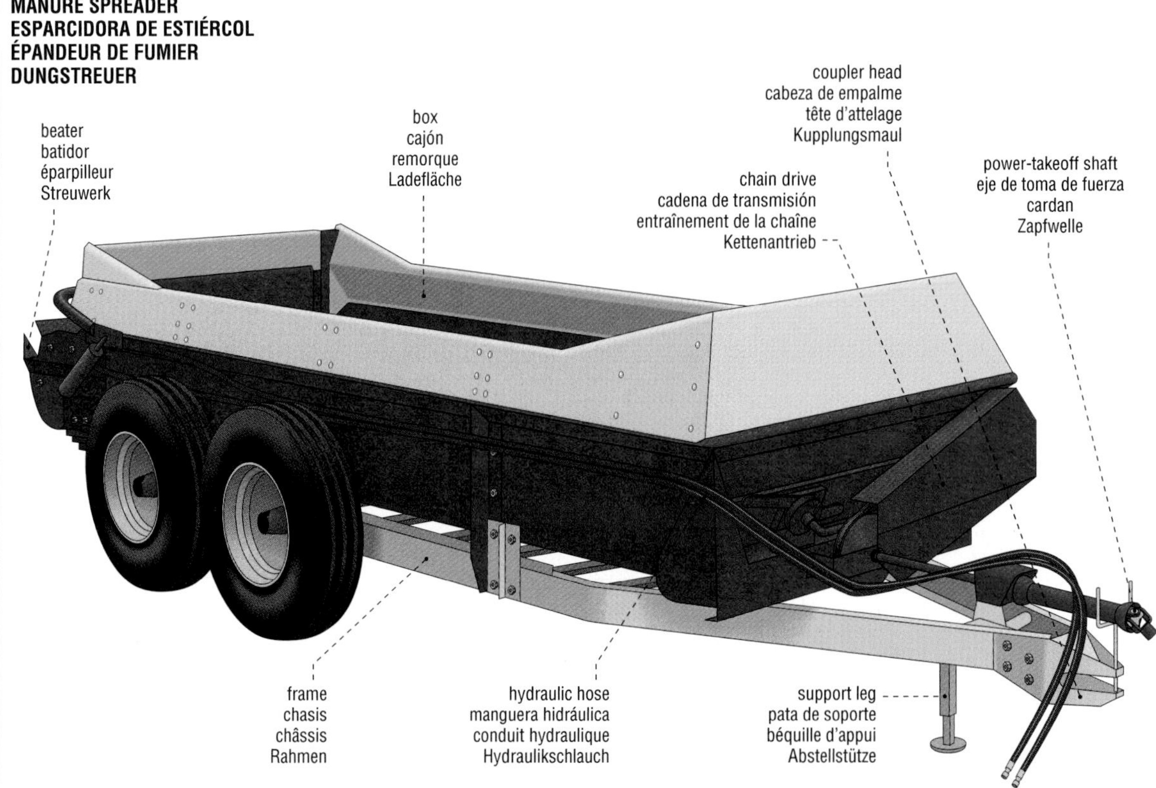
beater
batidor
éparpilleur
Streuwerk
box
cajón
remorque
Ladefläche
coupler head
cabeza de empalme
tête d'attelage
Kupplungsmaul
chain drive
cadena de transmisión
entraînement de la chaîne
Kettenantrieb
power-takeoff shaft
eje de toma de fuerza
cardan
Zapfwelle
frame
chasis
châssis
Rahmen
hydraulic hose
manguera hidráulica
conduit hydraulique
Hydraulikschlauch
support leg
pata de soporte
béquille d'appui
Abstellstütze

PULVERIZING SOIL
PULVERIZACIÓN
AMEUBLIR LA TERRE
EGGEN DES BODENS

TANDEM DISK HARROW
PULVERIZADOR DE DISCOS
PULVÉRISEUR TANDEM
SCHEIBENEGGE

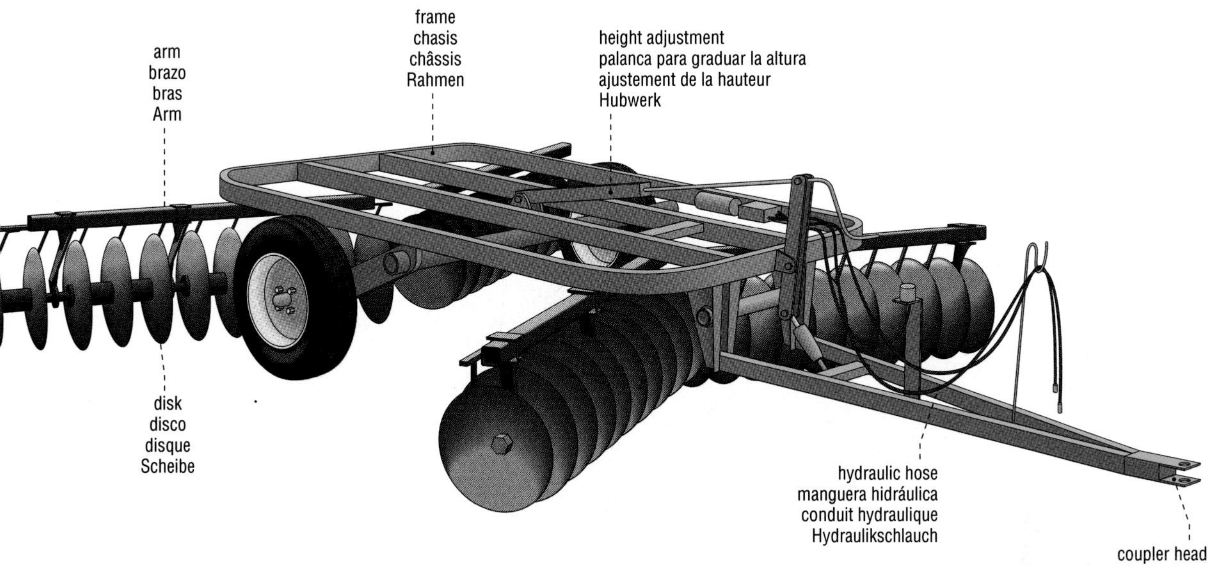
arm
brazo
bras
Arm
frame
chasis
châssis
Rahmen
height adjustment
palanca para graduar la altura
ajustement de la hauteur
Hubwerk
disk
disco
disque
Scheibe
hydraulic hose
manguera hidráulica
conduit hydraulique
Hydraulikschlauch
coupler head
cabeza de emplame
tête d'attelage
Kupplungsmaul

CULTIVATOR
CULTIVADOR
CULTIVATEUR
GRUBBER

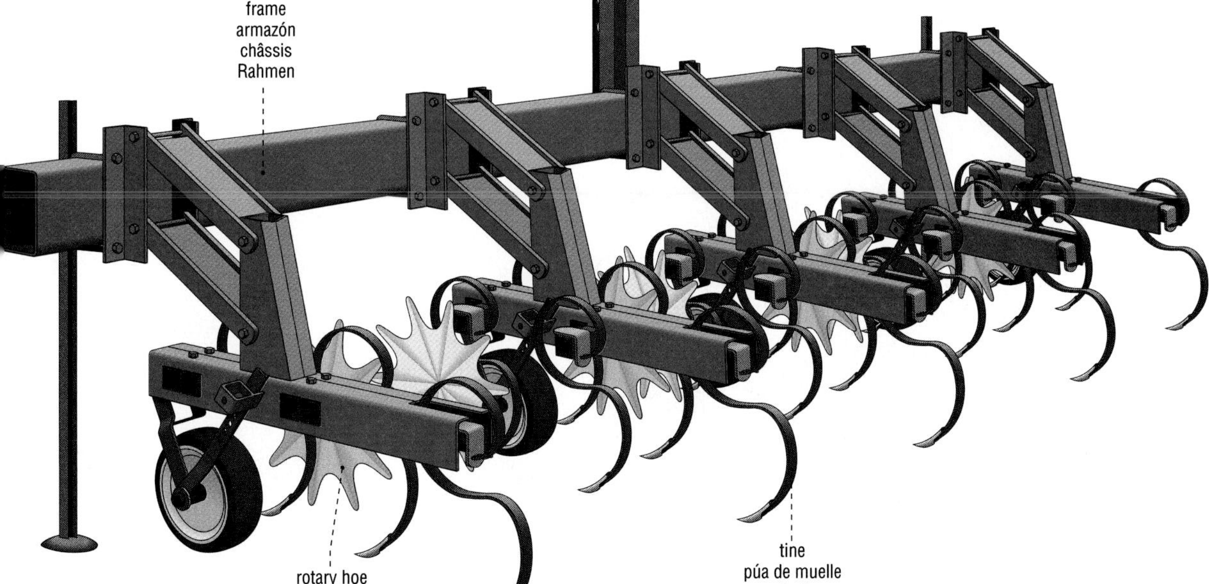

frame
armazón
châssis
Rahmen

rotary hoe
azadón rotatorio
houe rotative
Sternscheibe

tine
púa de muelle
dent
Zinke

PLANTING
SIEMBRA
SEMER
SÄEN

SEED DRILL
SEMBRADORA A CHORRILLO
SEMOIR EN LIGNES
DRILLMASCHINE

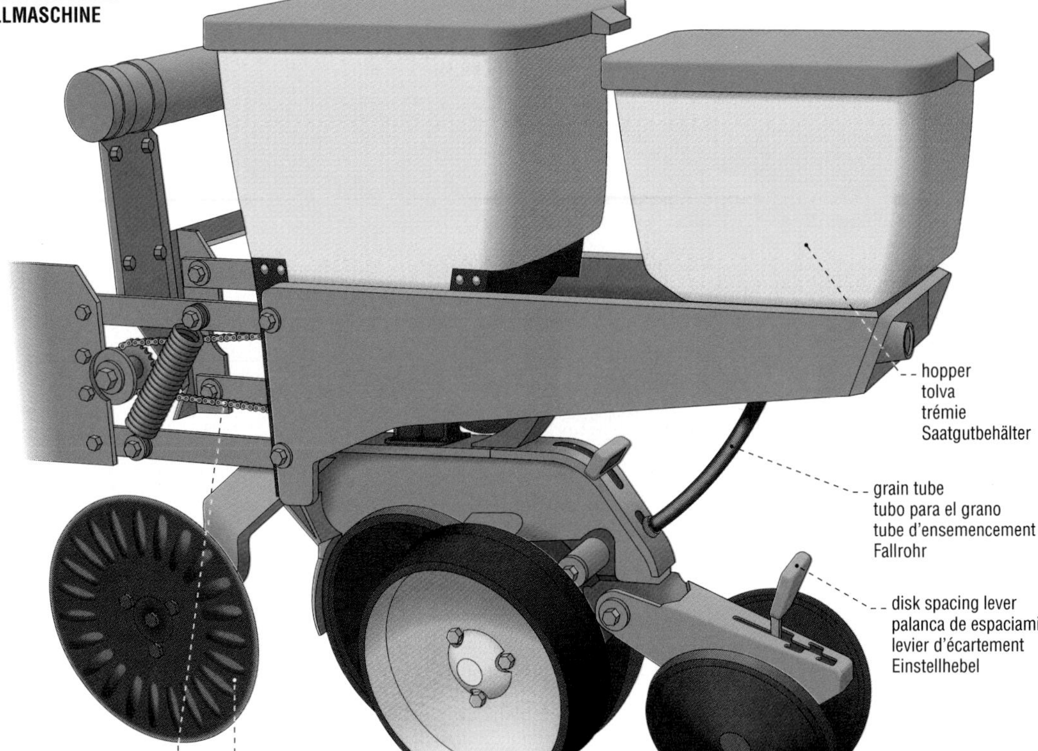

hopper
tolva
trémie
Saatgutbehälter

grain tube
tubo para el grano
tube d'ensemencement
Fallrohr

disk spacing lever
palanca de espaciamiento de los discos
levier d'écartement
Einstellhebel

chain drive
cadena de transmisión
chaîne d'entraînement
Antrieb

colter
cuchilla
coutre
Sech

press wheel
rueda compresora
roue de pression
Druckrolle

covering disk
disco tapador
disque d'enterrage
Zustreicher

MOWING
SIEGA
FAUCHER
MÄHEN

FLAIL MOWER
SEGADORA
FAUCHEUSE-CONDITIONNEUSE
ANHÄNGEMÄHWERK

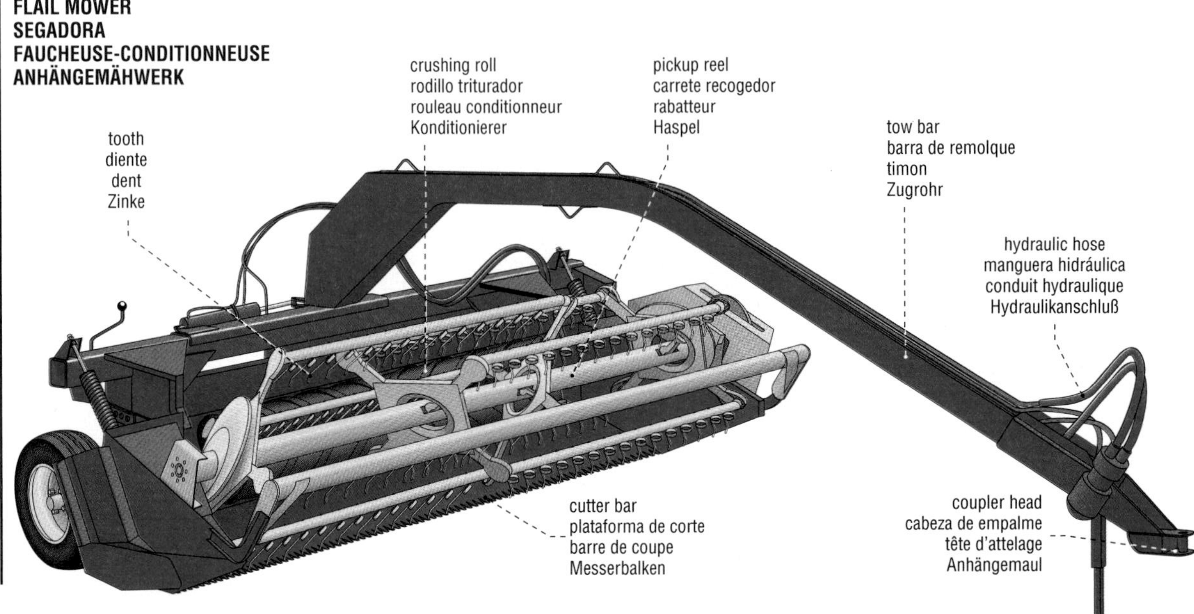
crushing roll
rodillo triturador
rouleau conditionneur
Konditionierer
pickup reel
carrete recogedor
rabatteur
Haspel
tooth
diente
dent
Zinke
tow bar
barra de remolque
timon
Zugrohr
hydraulic hose
manguera hidráulica
conduit hydraulique
Hydraulikanschluß
cutter bar
plataforma de corte
barre de coupe
Messerbalken
coupler head
cabeza de empalme
tête d'attelage
Anhängemaul

TEDDING
HENIFICACIÓN
FANER
ZETTEN UND WENDEN

RAKE
RASTRILLO
RÂTEAU
SCHUBRECHWENDER

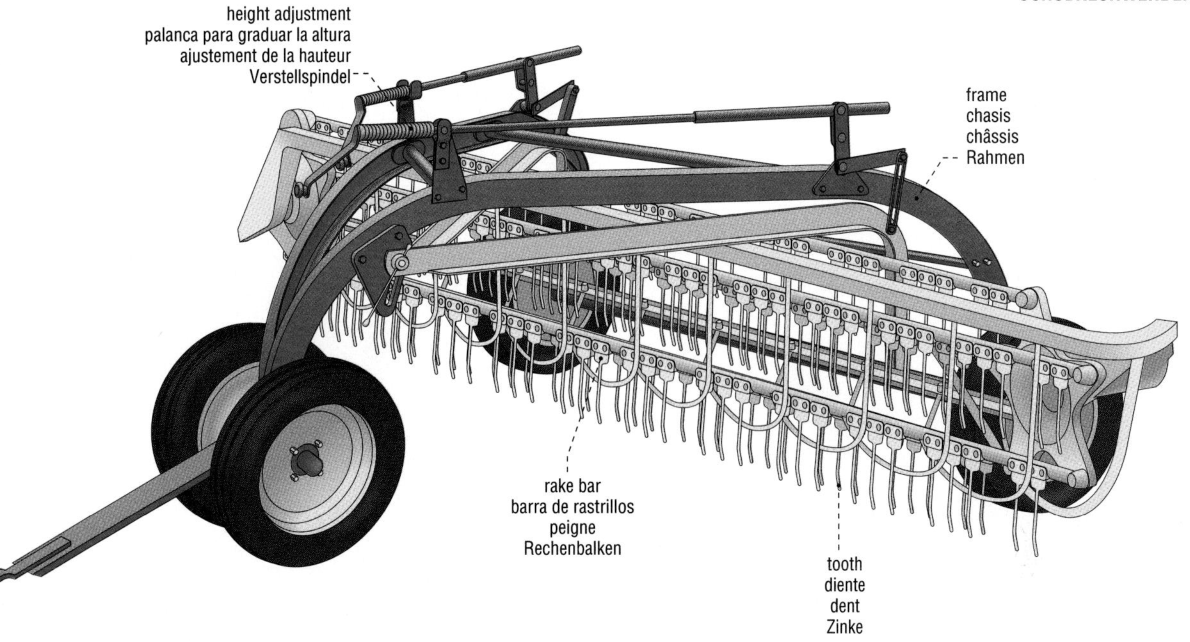
height adjustment
palanca para graduar la altura
ajustement de la hauteur
Verstellspindel
frame
chasis
châssis
Rahmen
rake bar
barra de rastrillos
peigne
Rechenbalken
tooth
diente
dent
Zinke

HARVESTING
COSECHA
RÉCOLTER
ERNTEN

HAY BALER
EMPACADORA DE HENO
RAMASSEUSE-PRESSE
HOCHDRUCKPRESSE

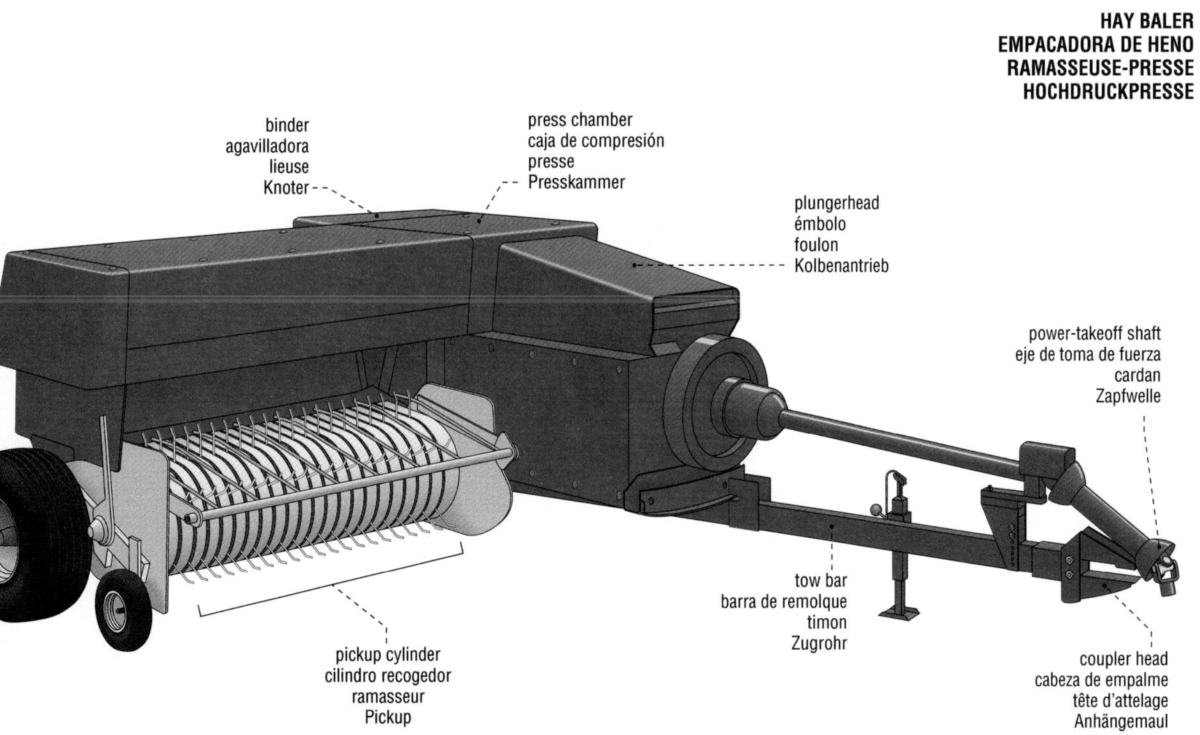
binder
agavilladora
lieuse
Knoter
press chamber
caja de compresión
presse
Presskammer
plungerhead
émbolo
foulon
Kolbenantrieb
power-takeoff shaft
eje de toma de fuerza
cardan
Zapfwelle
tow bar
barra de remolque
timon
Zugrohr
coupler head
cabeza de empalme
tête d'attelage
Anhängemaul
pickup cylinder
cilindro recogedor
ramasseur
Pickup

COMBINE HARVESTER
COSECHADORA TRILLADORA
MOISSONNEUSE-BATTEUSE
MÄHDRESCHER

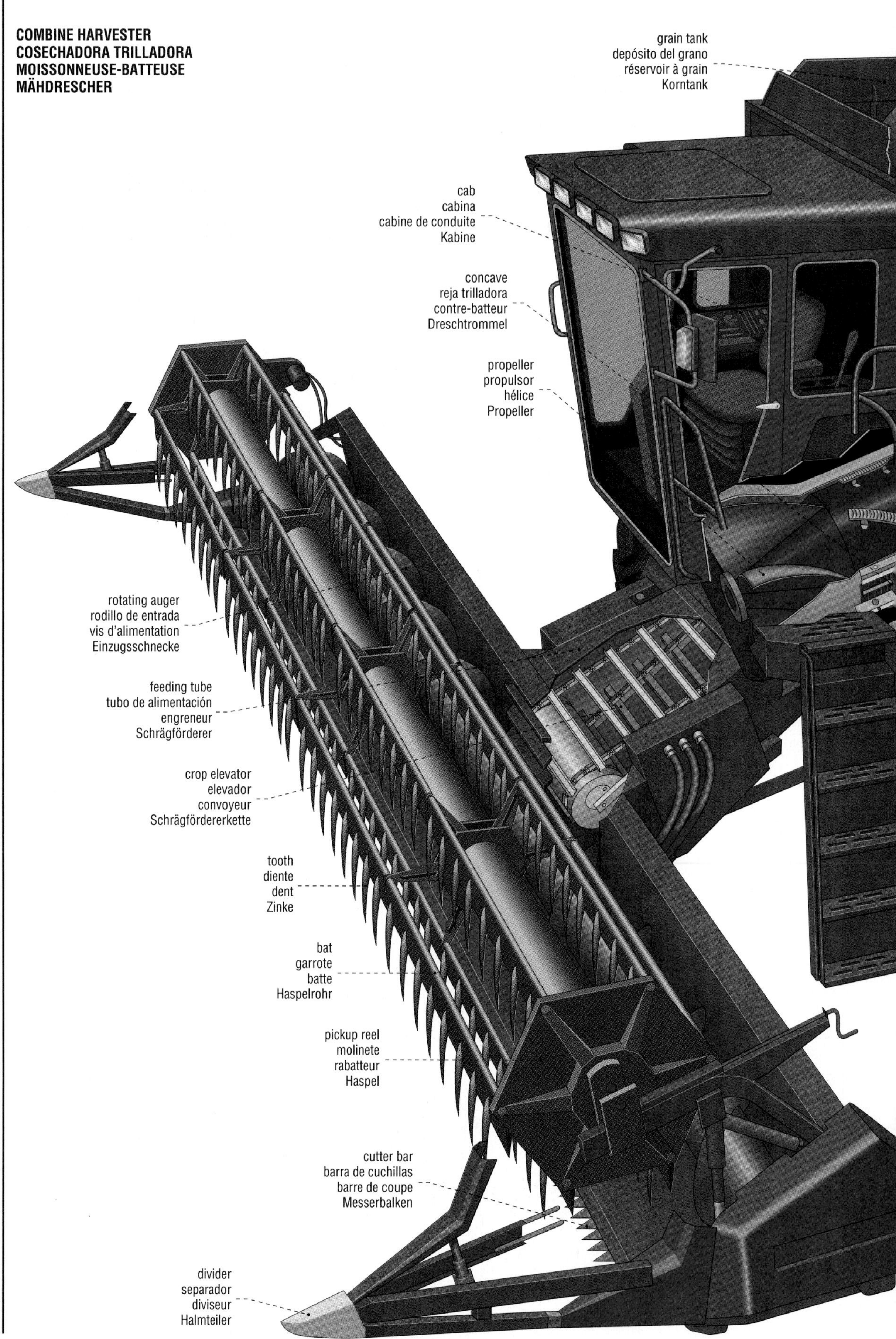
grain tank
depósito del grano
réservoir à grain
Korntank
cab
cabina
cabine de conduite
Kabine
concave
reja trilladora
contre-batteur
Dreschtrommel
propeller
propulsor
hélice
Propeller
rotating auger
rodillo de entrada
vis d'alimentation
Einzugsschnecke
feeding tube
tubo de alimentación
engreneur
Schrägförderer
crop elevator
elevador
convoyeur
Schrägfördererkette
tooth
diente
dent
Zinke
bat
garrote
batte
Haspelrohr
pickup reel
molinete
rabatteur
Haspel
cutter bar
barra de cuchillas
barre de coupe
Messerbalken
divider
separador
diviseur
Halmteiler

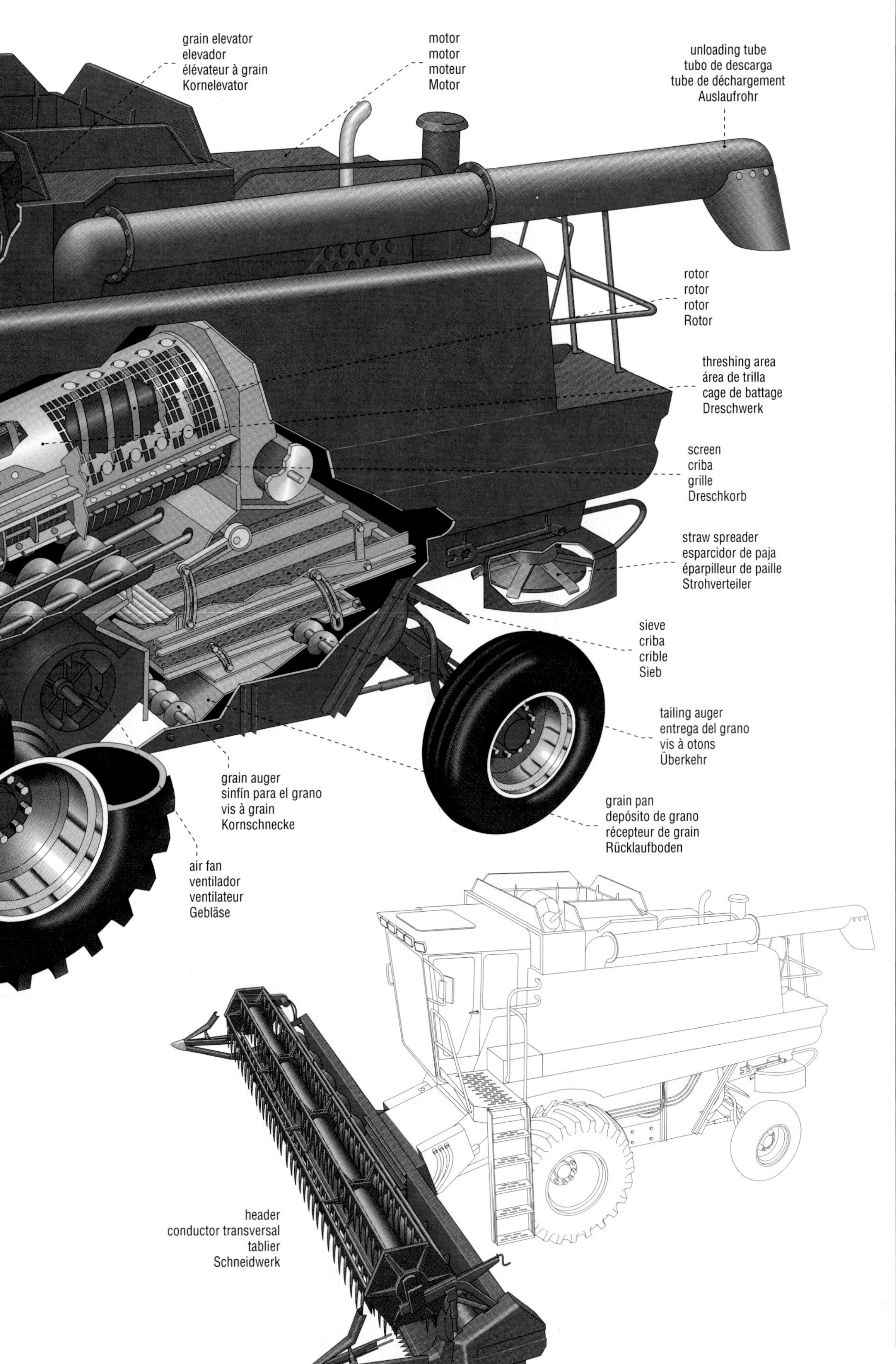
grain elevator
elevador
élévateur à grain
Kornelevator
motor
motor
moteur
Motor
unloading tube
tubo de descarga
tube de déchargement
Auslaufrohr
rotor
rotor
rotor
Rotor
threshing area
área de trilla
cage de battage
Dreschwerk
screen
criba
grille
Dreschkorb
straw spreader
esparcidor de paja
éparpilleur de paille
Strohverteiler
sieve
criba
crible
Sieb
tailing auger
entrega del grano
vis à otons
Überkehr
grain pan
depósito de grano
récepteur de grain
Rücklaufboden
grain auger
sinfín para el grano
vis à grain
Kornschnecke
air fan
ventilador
ventilateur
Gebläse
header
conductor transversal
tablier
Schneidwerk

HARVESTING
COSECHA
RÉCOLTER
ERNTEN

FORAGE HARVESTER
COSECHERA DE FORRAJE
FOURRAGÈRE
FELDHÄCKSELER

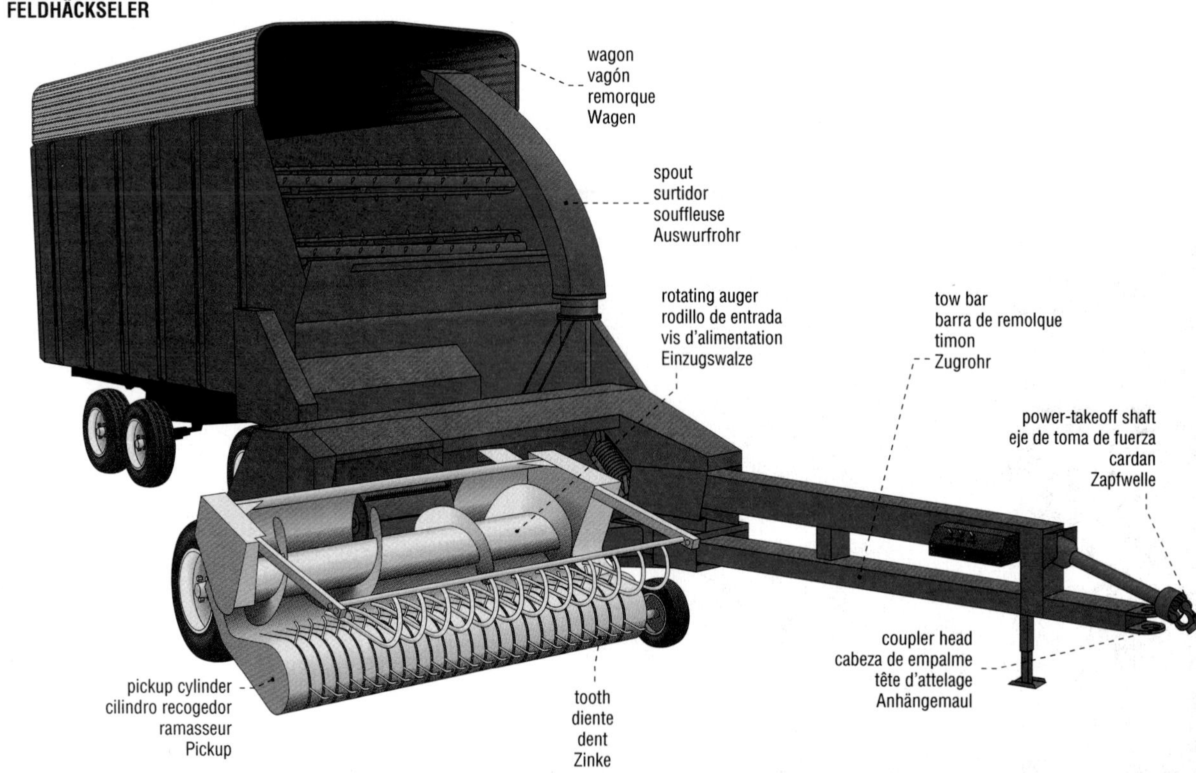
wagon
vagón
remorque
Wagen
spout
surtidor
souffleuse
Auswurfrohr
rotating auger
rodillo de entrada
vis d'alimentation
Einzugswalze
tow bar
barra de remolque
timon
Zugrohr
power-takeoff shaft
eje de toma de fuerza
cardan
Zapfwelle
coupler head
cabeza de empalme
tête d'attelage
Anhängemaul
tooth
diente
dent
Zinke
pickup cylinder
cilindro recogedor
ramasseur
Pickup

ENSILING
ENSILAJE
ENSILER
SILIEREN

FORAGE BLOWER
AVENTADOR DE FORRAJE
SOUFFLEUSE DE FOURRAGE
ABLADEGEBLÄSE

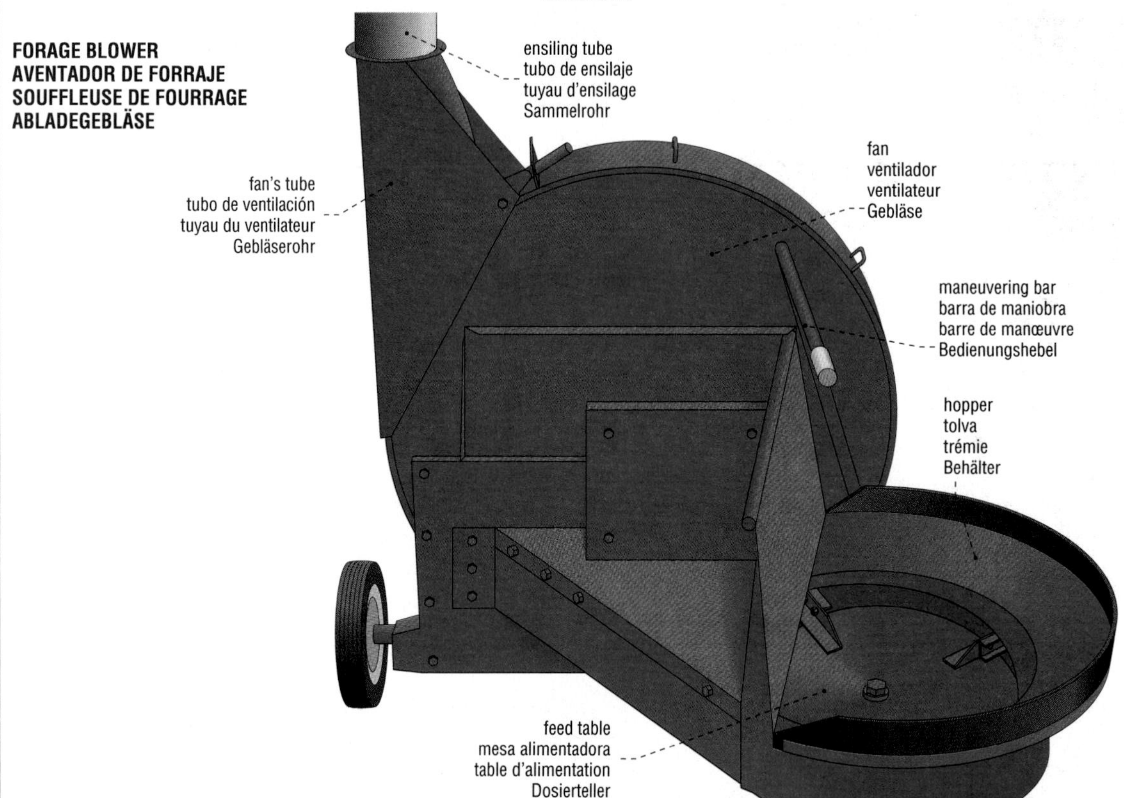
ensiling tube
tubo de ensilaje
tuyau d'ensilage
Sammelrohr
fan's tube
tubo de ventilación
tuyau du ventilateur
Gebläserohr
fan
ventilador
ventilateur
Gebläse
maneuvering bar
barra de maniobra
barre de manœuvre
Bedienungshebel
hopper
tolva
trémie
Behälter
feed table
mesa alimentadora
table d'alimentation
Dosierteller

ARCHITECTURE
ARQUITECTURA
ARCHITECTURE
ARCHITEKTUR

CONTENTS

TRADITIONAL HOUSES
VIVIENDAS TRADICIONALES
MAISONS TRADITIONNELLES
TRADITIONELLE WOHNHÄUSER

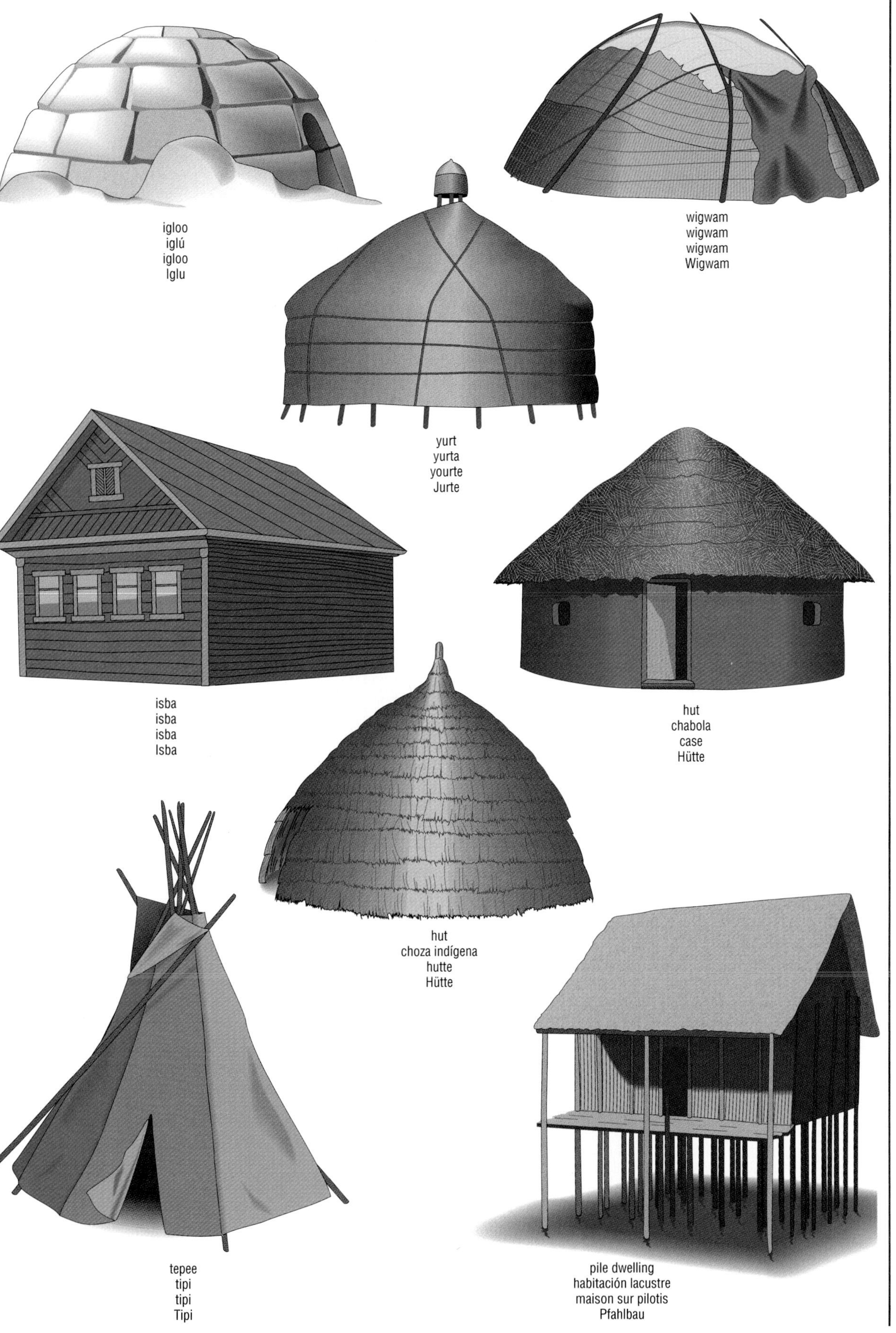

igloo
iglú
igloo
Iglu
wigwam
wigwam
wigwam
Wigwam
yurt
yurta
yourte
Jurte
isba
isba
isba
Isba
hut
chabola
case
Hütte
hut
choza indígena
hutte
Hütte
tepee
tipi
tipi
Tipi
pile dwelling
habitación lacustre
maison sur pilotis
Pfahlbau

ARCHITECTURAL STYLES
ESTILOS ARQUITECTÓNICOS
STYLES D'ARCHITECTURE
BAUSTILE

IONIC ORDER
ORDEN JÓNICO
ORDRE IONIQUE
IONISCHE SÄULENORDNUNG

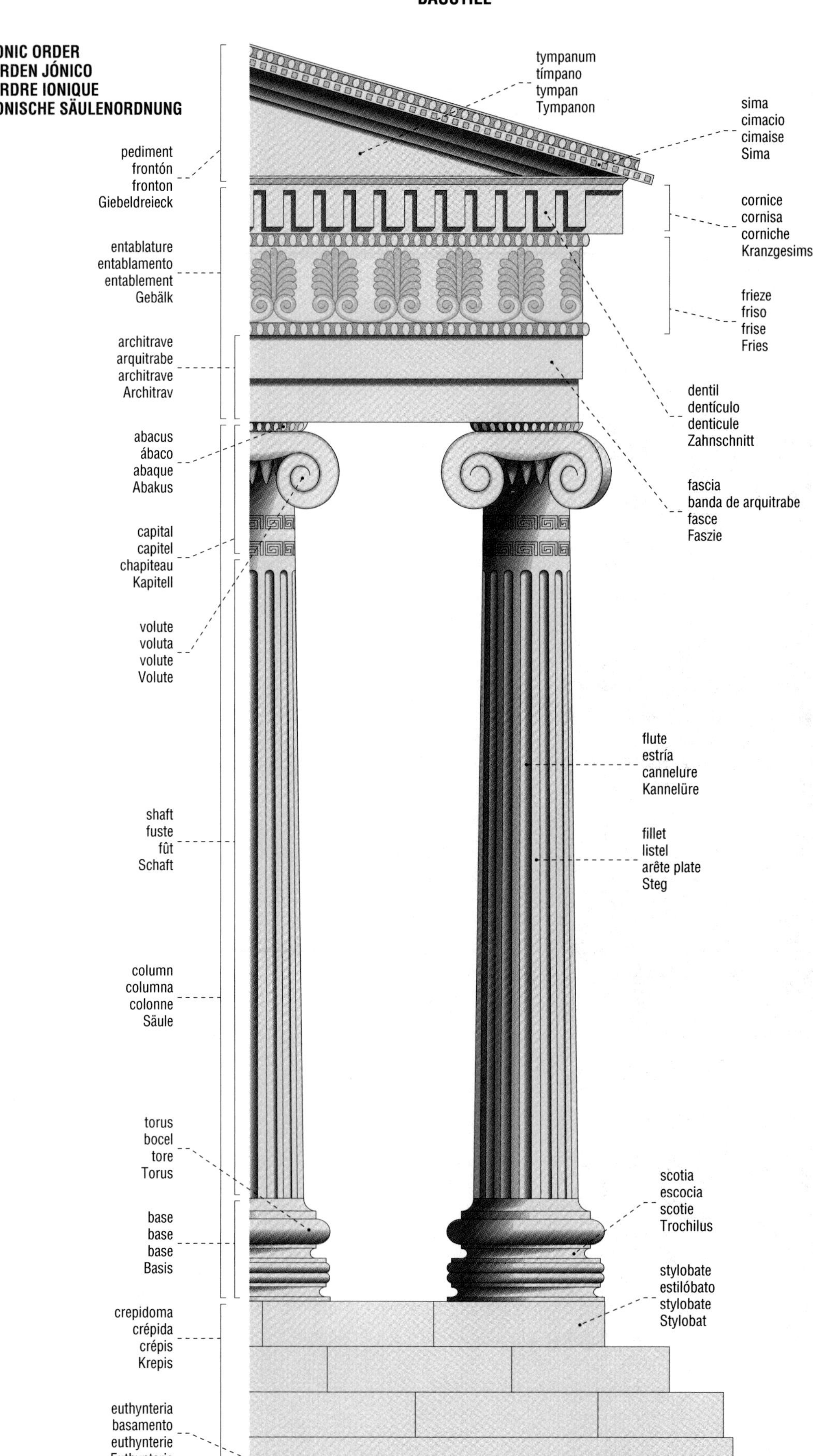
pediment
frontón
fronton
Giebeldreieck
entablature
entablamento
entablement
Gebälk
architrave
arquitrabe
architrave
Architrav
abacus
ábaco
abaque
Abakus
capital
capitel
chapiteau
Kapitell
volute
voluta
volute
Volute
shaft
fuste
fût
Schaft
column
columna
colonne
Säule
torus
bocel
tore
Torus
base
base
base
Basis
crepidoma
crépida
crépis
Krepis
euthynteria
basamento
euthynterie
Euthynterie
tympanum
tímpano
tympan
Tympanon
sima
cimacio
cimaise
Sima
cornice
cornisa
corniche
Kranzgesims
frieze
friso
frise
Fries
dentil
dentículo
denticule
Zahnschnitt
fascia
banda de arquitrabe
fasce
Faszie
flute
estría
cannelure
Kannelüre
fillet
listel
arête plate
Steg
scotia
escocia
scotie
Trochilus
stylobate
estilóbato
stylobate
Stylobat

DORIC ORDER
ORDEN DÓRICO
ORDRE DORIQUE
DORISCHE SÄULENORDNUNG

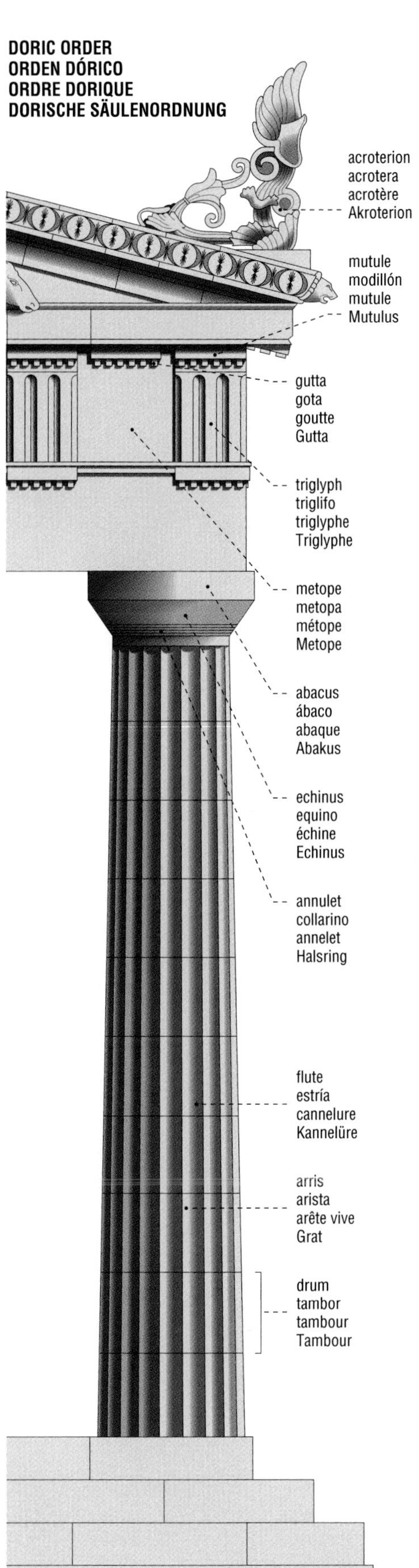
acroterion
acrotera
acrotère
Akroterion
mutule
modillón
mutule
Mutulus
gutta
gota
goutte
Gutta
triglyph
triglifo
triglyphe
Triglyphe
metope
metopa
métope
Metope
abacus
ábaco
abaque
Abakus
echinus
equino
échine
Echinus
annulet
collarino
annelet
Halsring
flute
estría
cannelure
Kannelüre
arris
arista
arête vive
Grat
drum
tambor
tambour
Tambour

CORINTHIAN ORDER
ORDEN CORINTIO
ORDRE CORINTHIEN
KORINTHISCHE SÄULENORDNUNG

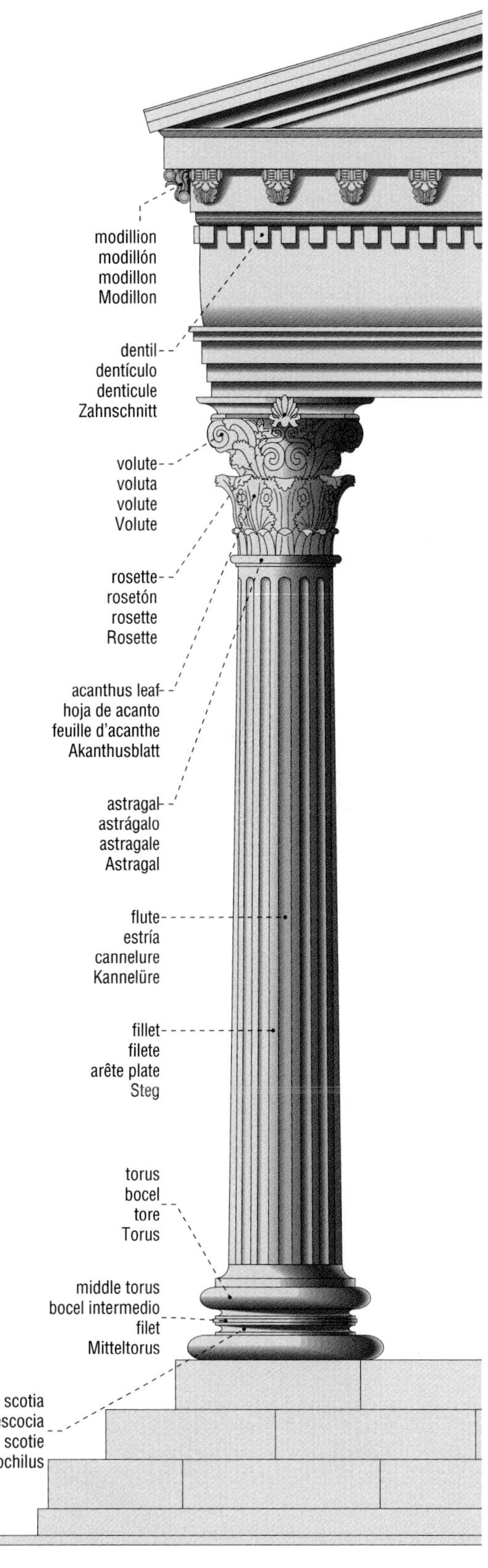
modillion
modillón
modillon
Modillon
dentil
dentículo
denticule
Zahnschnitt
volute
voluta
volute
Volute
rosette
rosetón
rosette
Rosette
acanthus leaf
hoja de acanto
feuille d'acanthe
Akanthusblatt
astragal
astrágalo
astragale
Astragal
flute
estría
cannelure
Kannelüre
fillet
filete
arête plate
Steg
torus
bocel
tore
Torus
middle torus
bocel intermedio
filet
Mitteltorus
scotia
escocia
scotie
Trochilus

GREEK TEMPLE
TEMPLO GRIEGO
TEMPLE GREC
GRIECHISCHER TEMPEL

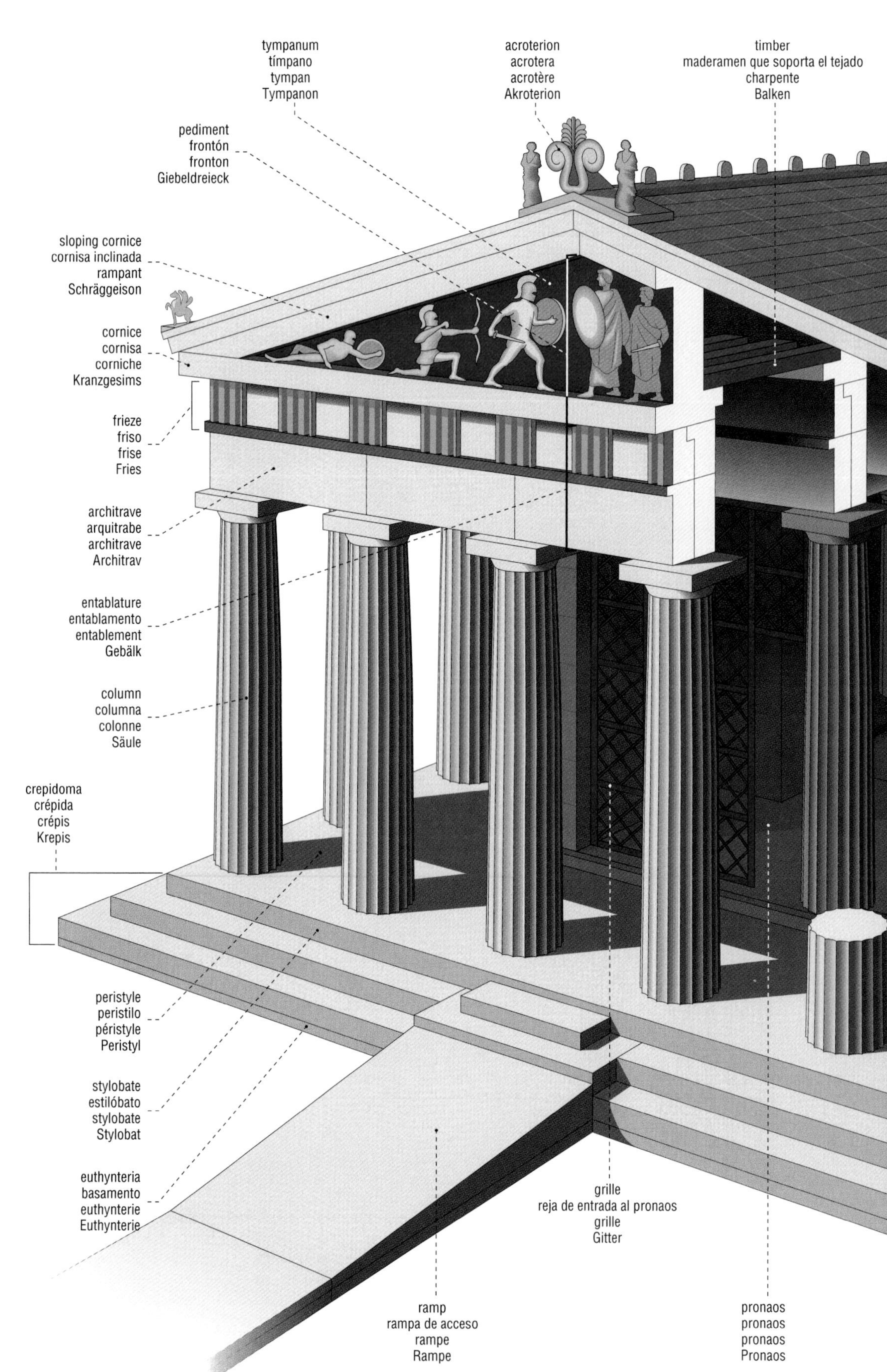

tympanum
tímpano
tympan
Tympanon
acroterion
acrotera
acrotère
Akroterion
timber
maderamen que soporta el tejado
charpente
Balken
pediment
frontón
fronton
Giebeldreieck
sloping cornice
cornisa inclinada
rampant
Schräggeison
cornice
cornisa
corniche
Kranzgesims
frieze
friso
frise
Fries
architrave
arquitrabe
architrave
Architrav
entablature
entablamento
entablement
Gebälk
column
columna
colonne
Säule
crepidoma
crépida
crépis
Krepis
peristyle
peristilo
péristyle
Peristyl
stylobate
estilóbato
stylobate
Stylobat
euthynteria
basamento
euthynterie
Euthynterie
grille
reja de entrada al pronaos
grille
Gitter
ramp
rampa de acceso
rampe
Rampe
pronaos
pronaos
pronaos
Pronaos

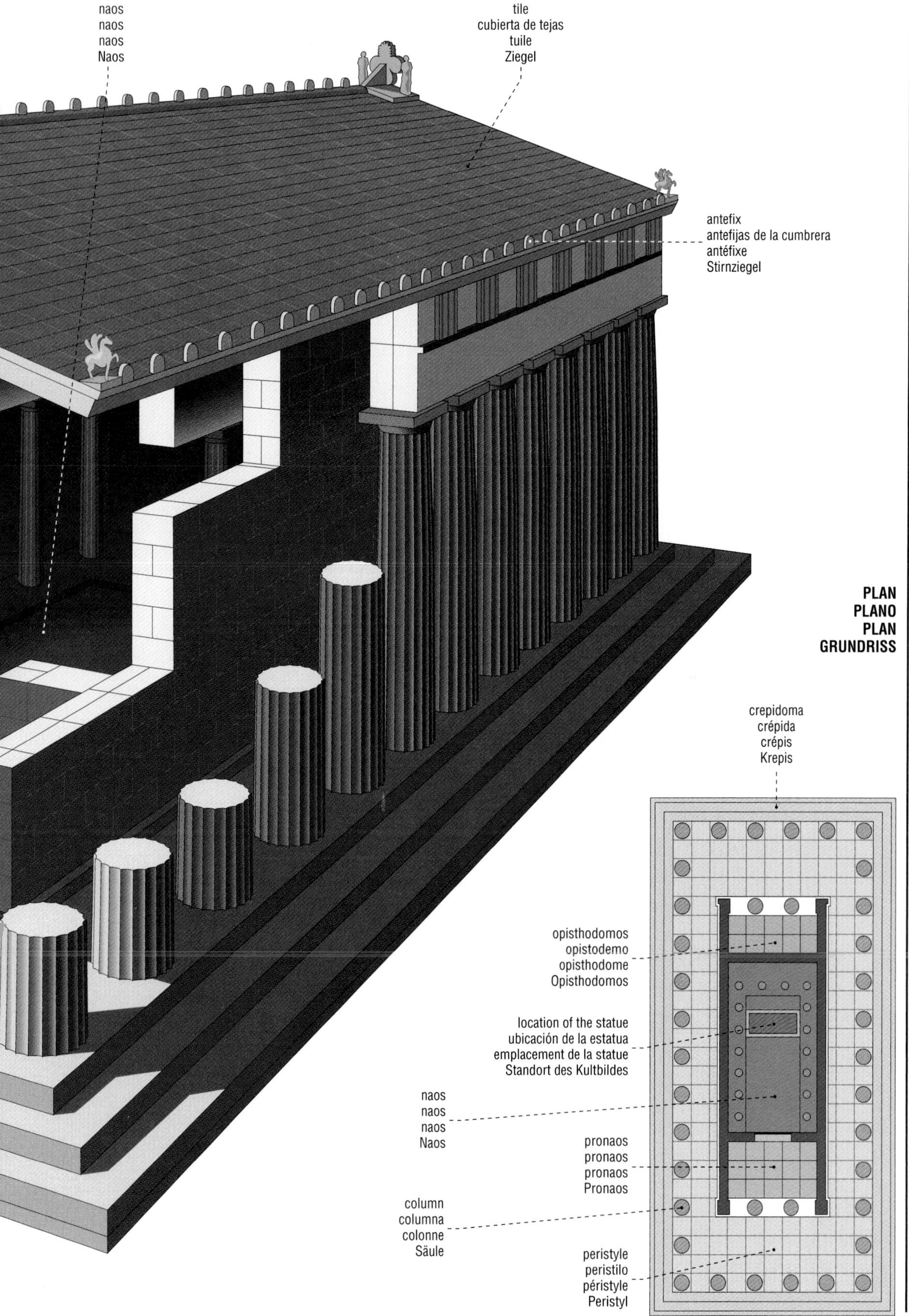
naos
naos
naos
Naos
tile
cubierta de tejas
tuile
Ziegel
antefix
antefijas de la cumbrera
antéfixe
Stirnziegel
PLAN
PLANO
PLAN
GRUNDRISS
crepidoma
crépida
crépis
Krepis
opisthodomos
opistodemo
opisthodome
Opisthodomos
location of the statue
ubicación de la estatua
emplacement de la statue
Standort des Kultbildes
naos
naos
naos
Naos
pronaos
pronaos
pronaos
Pronaos
column
columna
colonne
Säule
peristyle
peristilo
péristyle
Peristyl

ROMAN HOUSE
CASA ROMANA
MAISON ROMAINE
RÖMISCHES WOHNHAUS

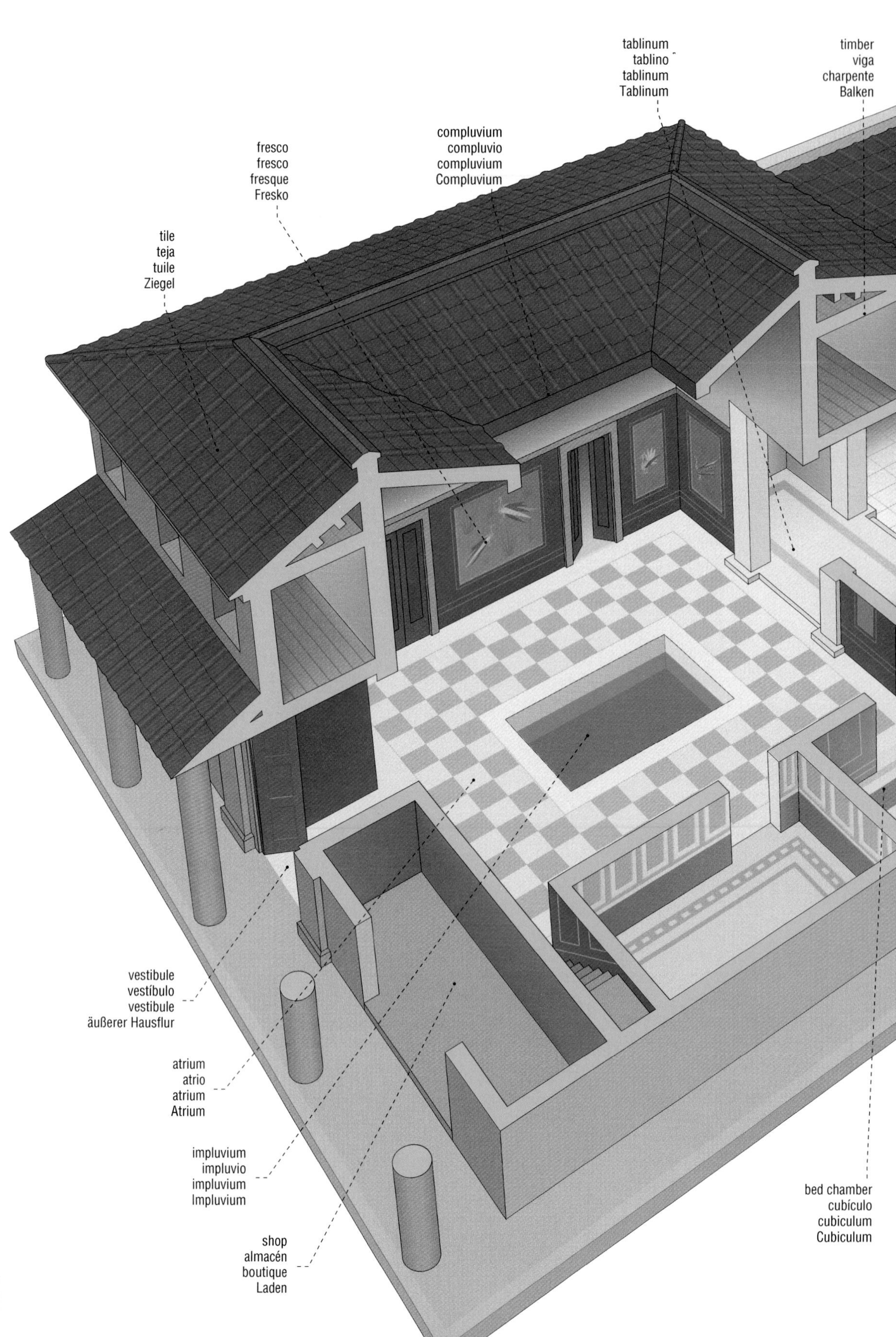
tablinum
tablino
tablinum
Tablinum
timber
viga
charpente
Balken
compluvium
compluvio
compluvium
Compluvium
fresco
fresco
fresque
Fresko
tile
teja
tuile
Ziegel
vestibule
vestíbulo
vestibule
äußerer Hausflur
atrium
atrio
atrium
Atrium
impluvium
impluvio
impluvium
Impluvium
shop
almacén
boutique
Laden
bed chamber
cubículo
cubiculum
Cubiculum

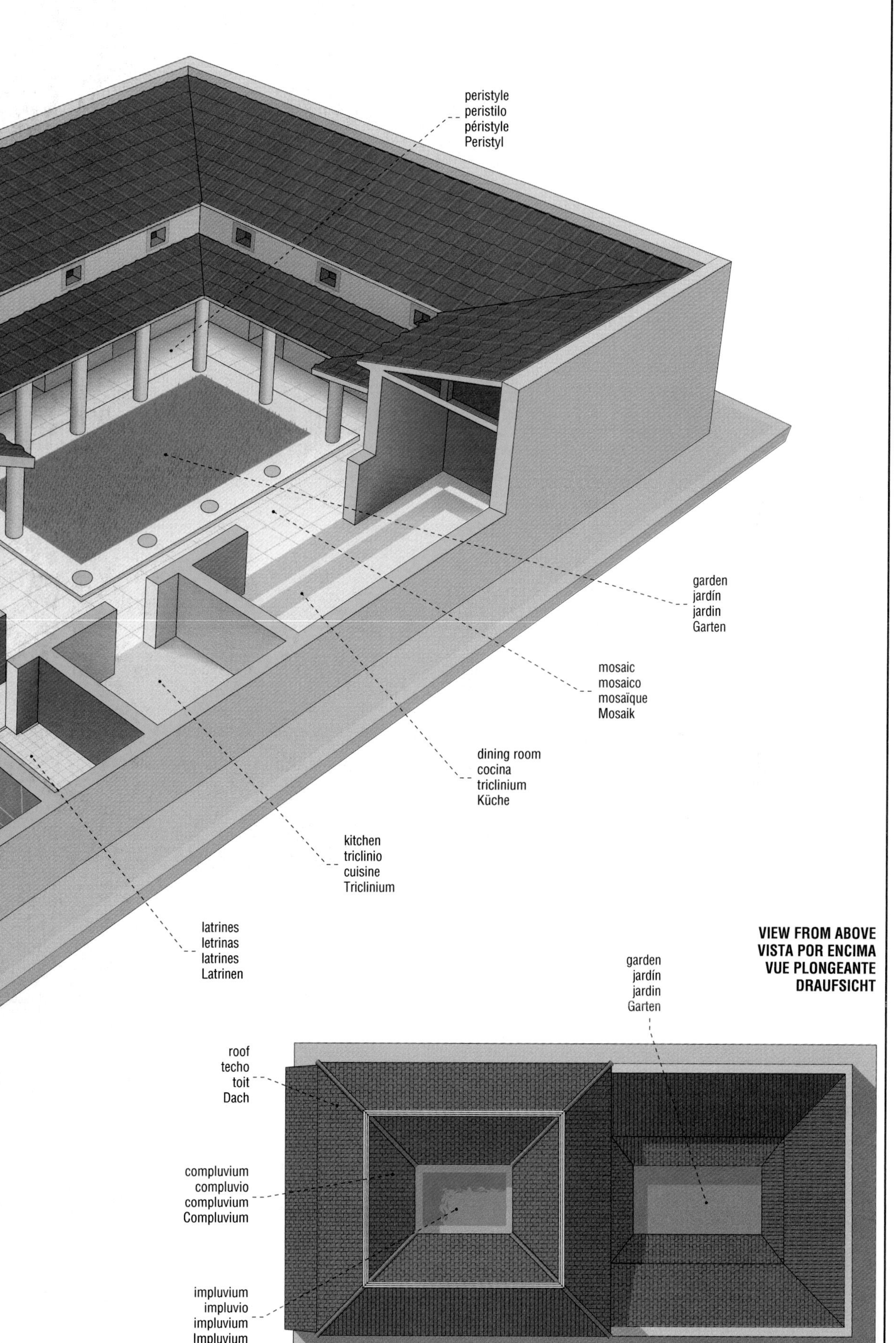
peristyle
peristilo
péristyle
Peristyl
garden
jardín
jardin
Garten
mosaic
mosaico
mosaïque
Mosaik
dining room
cocina
triclinium
Küche
kitchen
triclinio
cuisine
Triclinium
latrines
letrinas
latrines
Latrinen
VIEW FROM ABOVE
VISTA POR ENCIMA
VUE PLONGEANTE
DRAUFSICHT
garden
jardín
jardin
Garten
roof
techo
toit
Dach
compluvium
compluvio
compluvium
Compluvium
impluvium
impluvio
impluvium
Impluvium

MOSQUE
MEZQUITA
MOSQUÉE
MOSCHEE

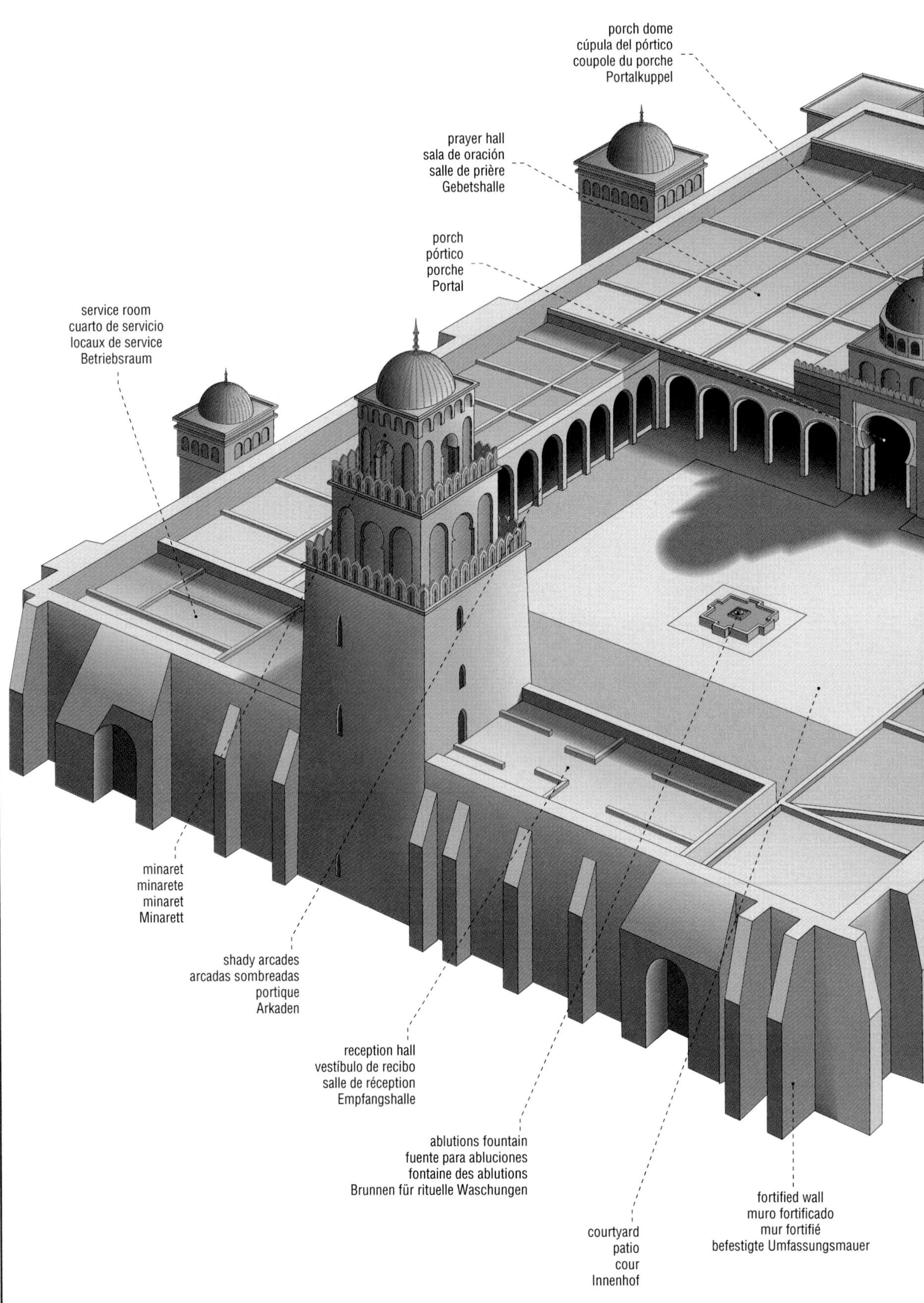
porch dome
cúpula del pórtico
coupole du porche
Portalkuppel
prayer hall
sala de oración
salle de prière
Gebetshalle
porch
pórtico
porche
Portal
service room
cuarto de servicio
locaux de service
Betriebsraum
minaret
minarete
minaret
Minarett
shady arcades
arcadas sombreadas
portique
Arkaden
reception hall
vestíbulo de recibo
salle de réception
Empfangshalle
ablutions fountain
fuente para abluciones
fontaine des ablutions
Brunnen für rituelle Waschungen
courtyard
patio
cour
Innenhof
fortified wall
muro fortificado
mur fortifié
befestigte Umfassungsmauer

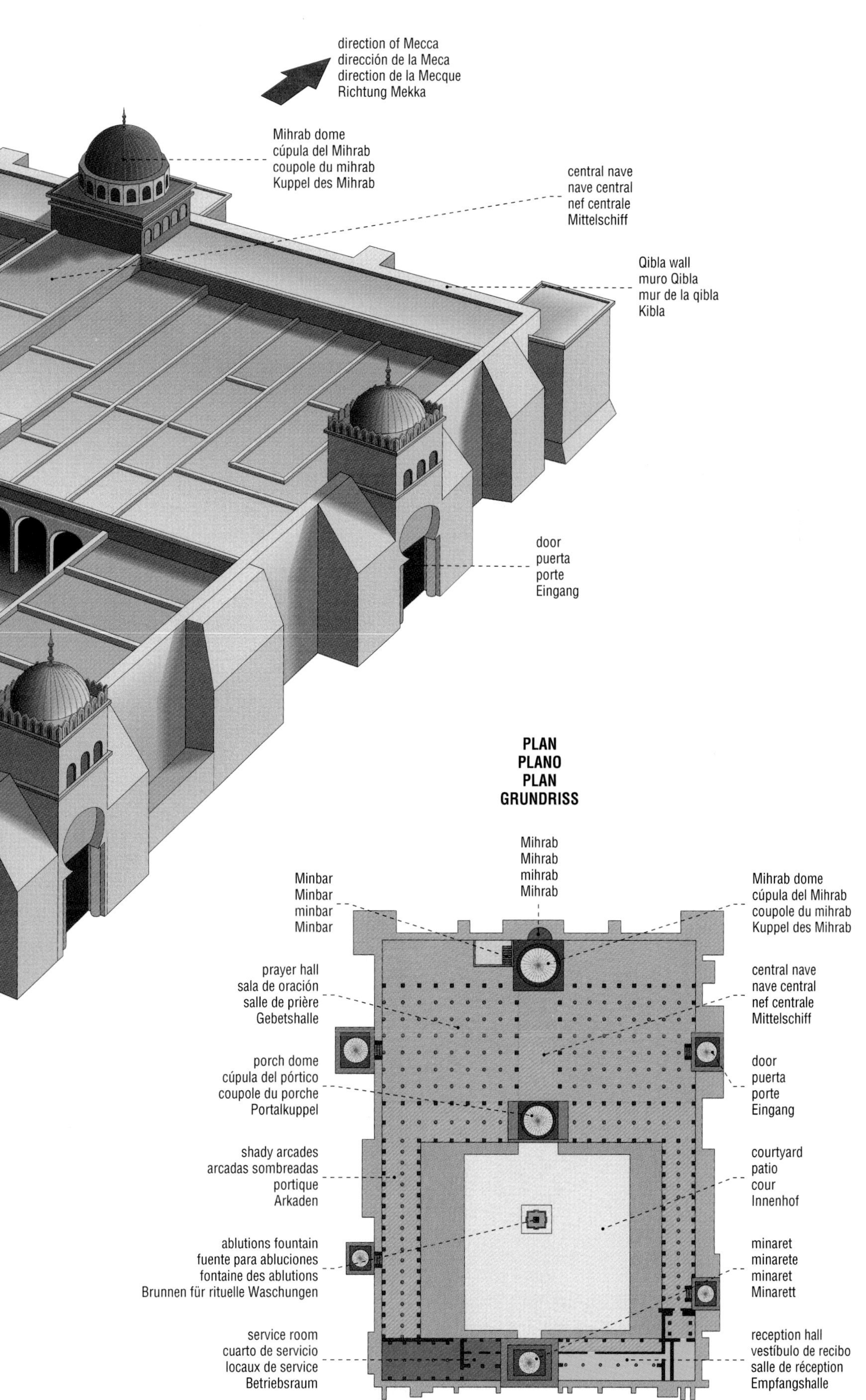

direction of Mecca
dirección de la Meca
direction de la Mecque
Richtung Mekka
Mihrab dome
cúpula del Mihrab
coupole du mihrab
Kuppel des Mihrab
central nave
nave central
nef centrale
Mittelschiff
Qibla wall
muro Qibla
mur de la qibla
Kibla
door
puerta
porte
Eingang
PLAN
PLANO
PLAN
GRUNDRISS
Mihrab
Mihrab
mihrab
Mihrab
Minbar
Minbar
minbar
Minbar
Mihrab dome
cúpula del Mihrab
coupole du mihrab
Kuppel des Mihrab
prayer hall
sala de oración
salle de prière
Gebetshalle
central nave
nave central
nef centrale
Mittelschiff
porch dome
cúpula del pórtico
coupole du porche
Portalkuppel
door
puerta
porte
Eingang
shady arcades
arcadas sombreadas
portique
Arkaden
courtyard
patio
cour
Innenhof
ablutions fountain
fuente para abluciones
fontaine des ablutions
Brunnen für rituelle Waschungen
minaret
minarete
minaret
Minarett
service room
cuarto de servicio
locaux de service
Betriebsraum
reception hall
vestíbulo de recibo
salle de réception
Empfangshalle

ARCH
ARCO
ARC
BOGEN

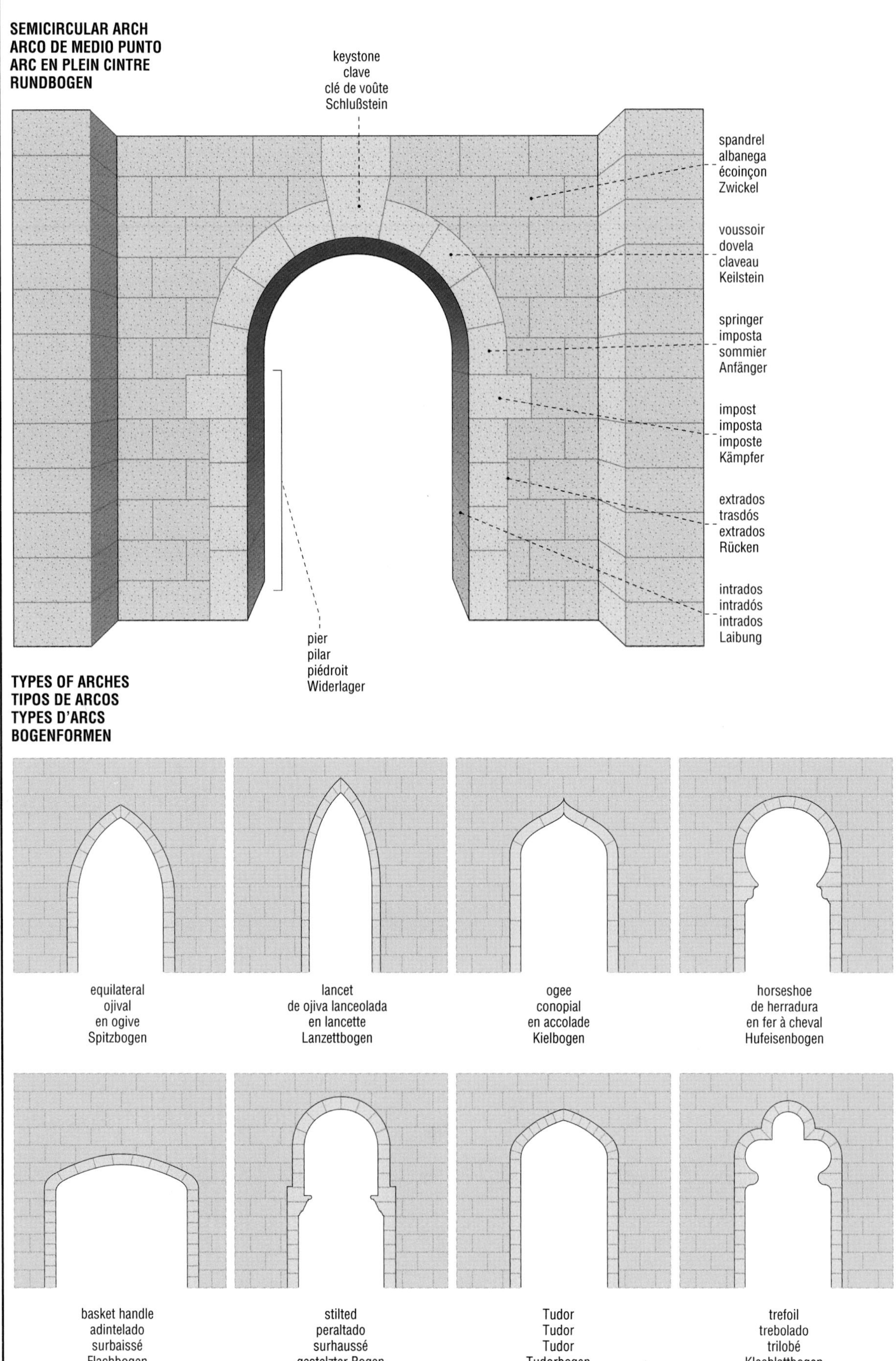
SEMICIRCULAR ARCH
ARCO DE MEDIO PUNTO
ARC EN PLEIN CINTRE
RUNDBOGEN
keystone
clave
clé de voûte
Schlußstein
spandrel
albanega
écoinçon
Zwickel
voussoir
dovela
claveau
Keilstein
springer
imposta
sommier
Anfänger
impost
imposta
imposte
Kämpfer
extrados
trasdós
extrados
Rücken
intrados
intradós
intrados
Laibung
pier
pilar
piédroit
Widerlager
TYPES OF ARCHES
TIPOS DE ARCOS
TYPES D'ARCS
BOGENFORMEN
equilateral
ojival
en ogive
Spitzbogen
lancet
de ojiva lanceolada
en lancette
Lanzettbogen
ogee
conopial
en accolade
Kielbogen
horseshoe
de herradura
en fer à cheval
Hufeisenbogen
basket handle
adintelado
surbaissé
Flachbogen
stilted
peraltado
surhaussé
gestelzter Bogen
Tudor
Tudor
Tudor
Tudorbogen
trefoil
trebolado
trilobé
Kleeblattbogen

GOTHIC CATHEDRAL
CATEDRAL GÓTICA
CATHÉDRALE GOTHIQUE
GOTHISCHER DOM

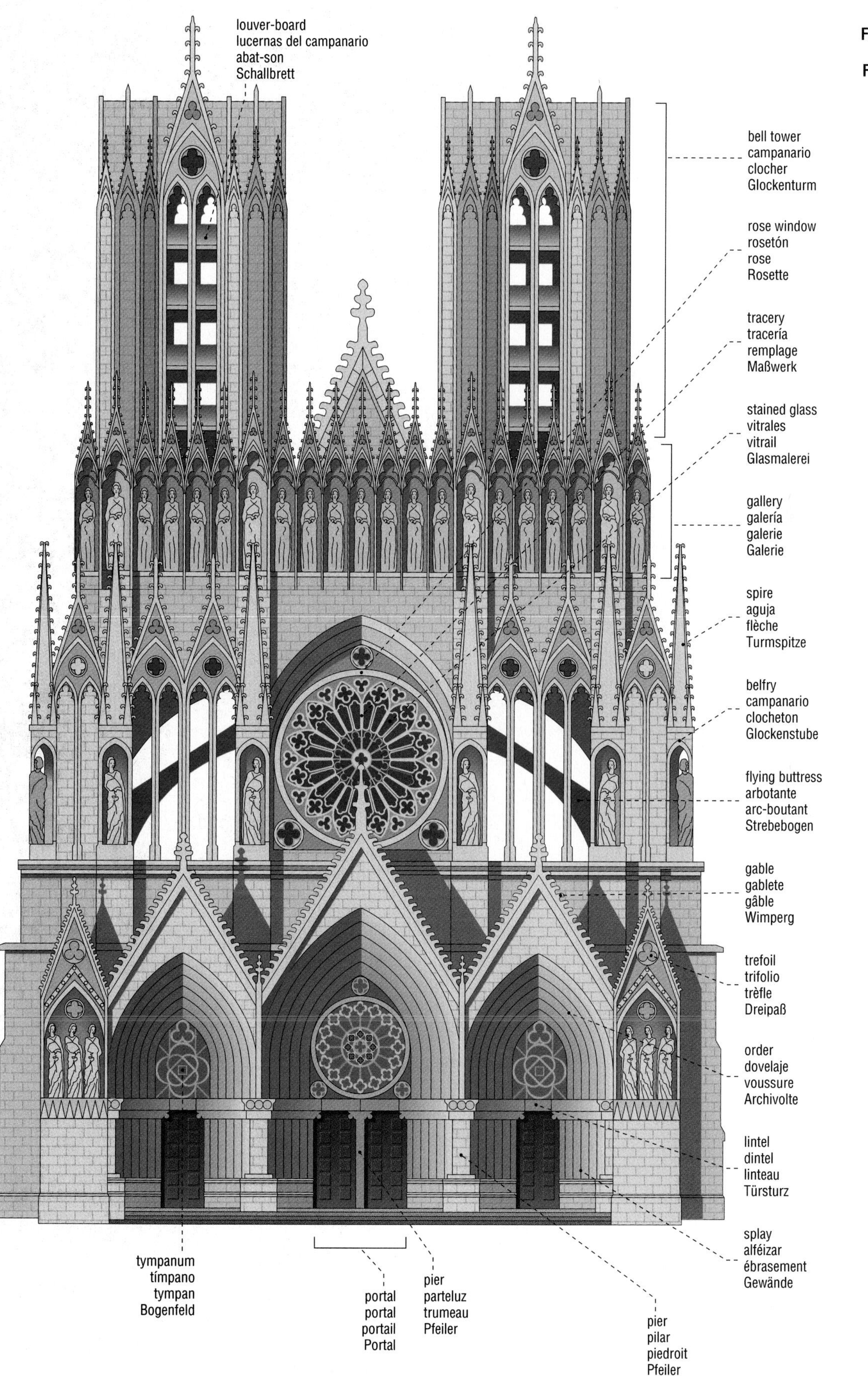
louver-board
lucernas del campanario
abat-son
Schallbrett
bell tower
campanario
clocher
Glockenturm
rose window
rosetón
rose
Rosette
tracery
tracería
remplage
Maßwerk
stained glass
vitrales
vitrail
Glasmalerei
gallery
galería
galerie
Galerie
spire
aguja
flèche
Turmspitze
belfry
campanario
clocheton
Glockenstube
flying buttress
arbotante
arc-boutant
Strebebogen
gable
gablete
gâble
Wimperg
trefoil
trifolio
trèfle
Dreipaß
order
dovelaje
voussure
Archivolte
lintel
dintel
linteau
Türsturz
splay
alféizar
ébrasement
Gewände
tympanum
tímpano
tympan
Bogenfeld
portal
portal
portail
Portal
pier
parteluz
trumeau
Pfeiler
pier
pilar
piedroit
Pfeiler

GOTHIC CATHEDRAL
CATEDRAL GÓTICA
CATHÉDRALE GOTHIQUE
GOTISCHER DOM

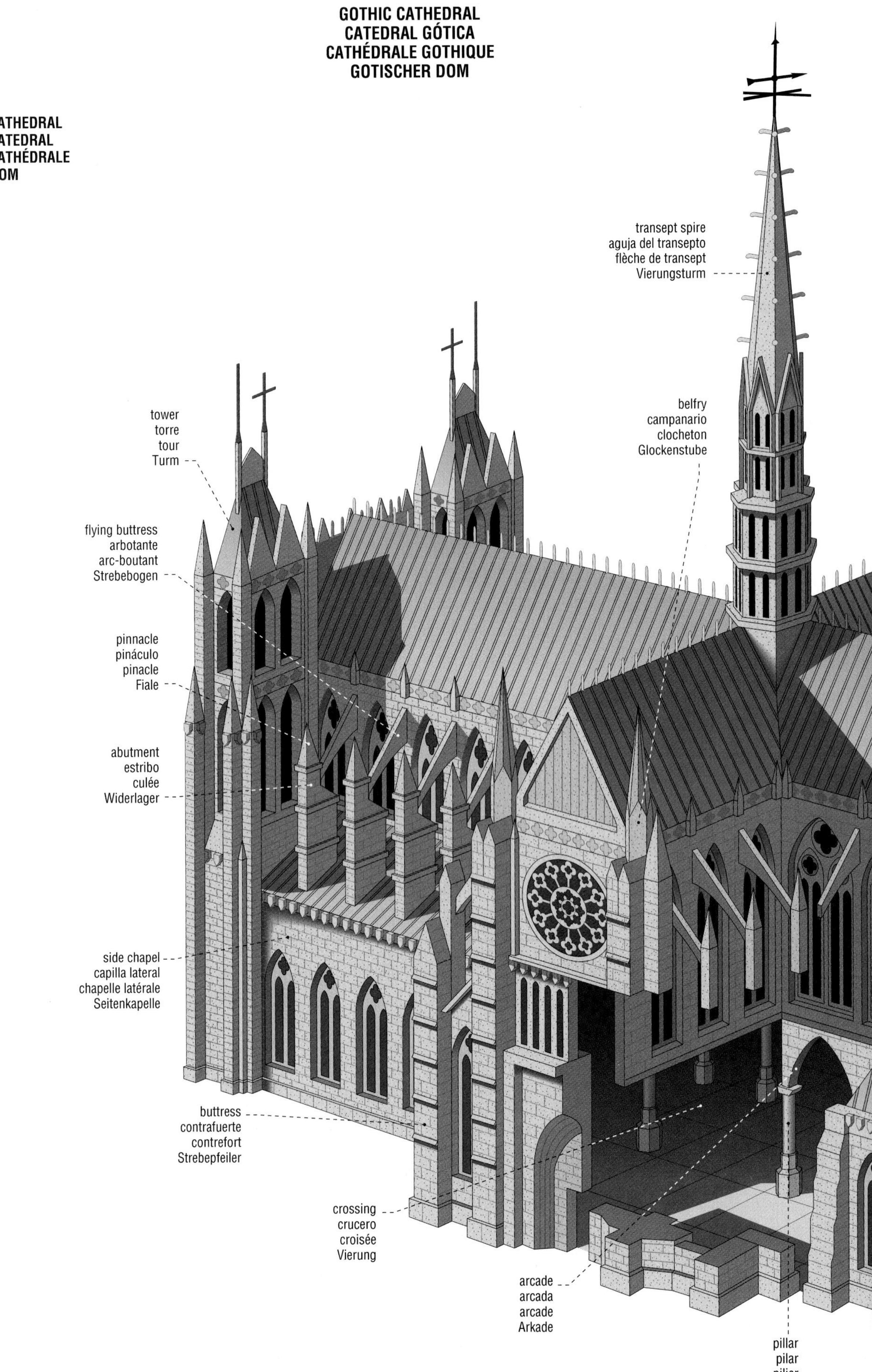
transept spire
aguja del transepto
flèche de transept
Vierungsturm
tower
torre
tour
Turm
belfry
campanario
clocheton
Glockenstube
flying buttress
arbotante
arc-boutant
Strebebogen
pinnacle
pináculo
pinacle
Fiale
abutment
estribo
culée
Widerlager
side chapel
capilla lateral
chapelle latérale
Seitenkapelle
buttress
contrafuerte
contrefort
Strebepfeiler
crossing
crucero
croisée
Vierung
arcade
arcada
arcade
Arkade
pillar
pilar
pilier
Pfeiler

PLAN
PLANO
PLAN
GRUNDRISS

VAULT
BÓVEDA
VOÛTE
GEWÖLBE

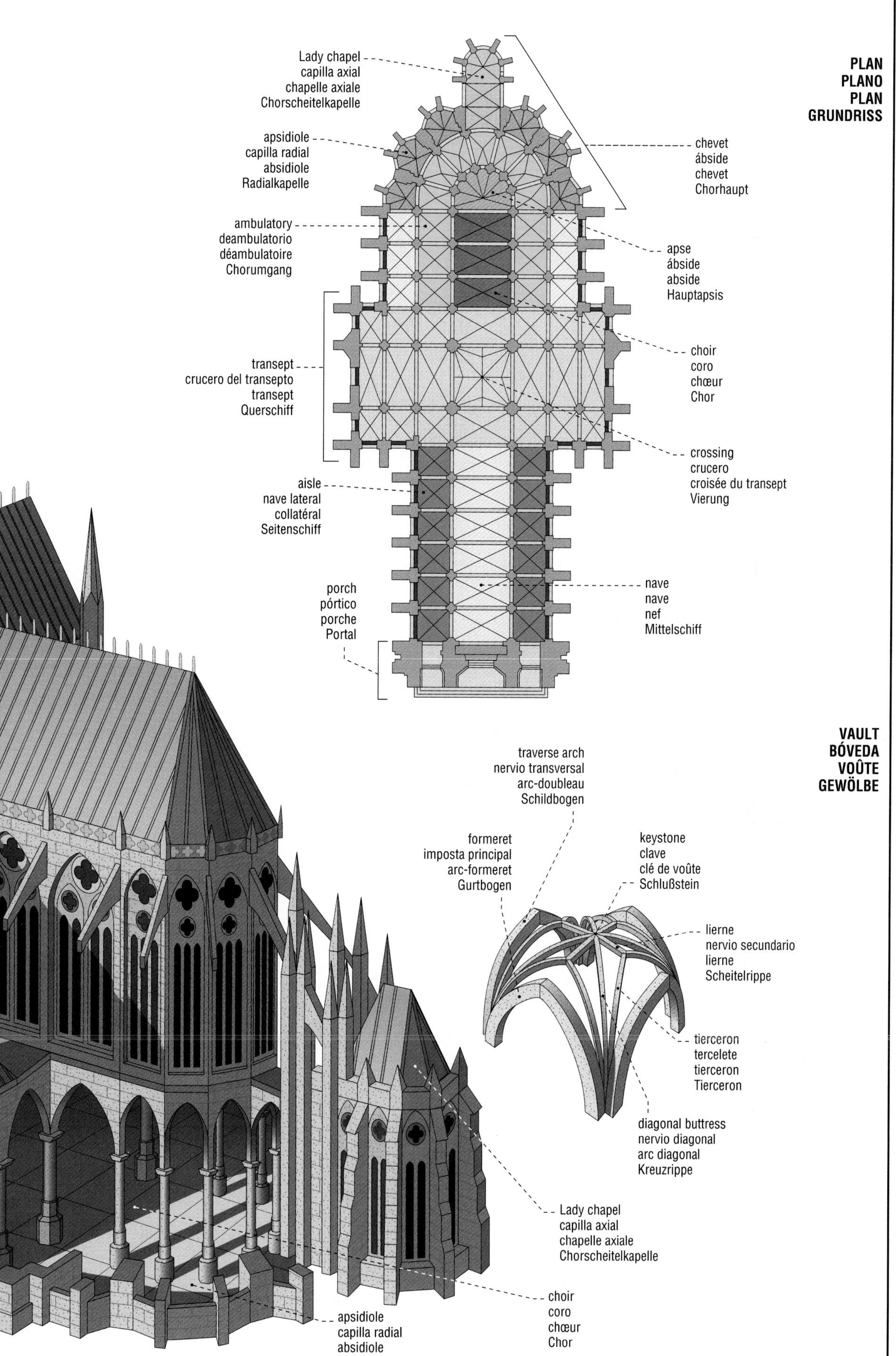
Lady chapel
capilla axial
chapelle axiale
Chorscheitelkapelle
apsidiole
capilla radial
absidiole
Radialkapelle
ambulatory
deambulatorio
déambulatoire
Chorumgang
transept
crucero del transepto
transept
Querschiff
aisle
nave lateral
collatéral
Seitenschiff
porch
pórtico
porche
Portal
chevet
ábside
chevet
Chorhaupt
apse
ábside
abside
Hauptapsis
choir
coro
chœur
Chor
crossing
crucero
croisée du transept
Vierung
nave
nave
nef
Mittelschiff
traverse arch
nervio transversal
arc-doubleau
Schildbogen
formeret
imposta principal
arc-formeret
Gurtbogen
keystone
clave
clé de voûte
Schlußstein
lierne
nervio secundario
lierne
Scheitelrippe
tierceron
tercelete
tierceron
Tierceron
diagonal buttress
nervio diagonal
arc diagonal
Kreuzrippe
Lady chapel
capilla axial
chapelle axiale
Chorscheitelkapelle
choir
coro
chœur
Chor
apsidiole
capilla radial
absidiole
Radialkapelle

VAUBAN FORTIFICATION
FORTIFICACIÓN DE VAUBAN
FORTIFICATION À LA VAUBAN
VAUBAN-FESTUNG

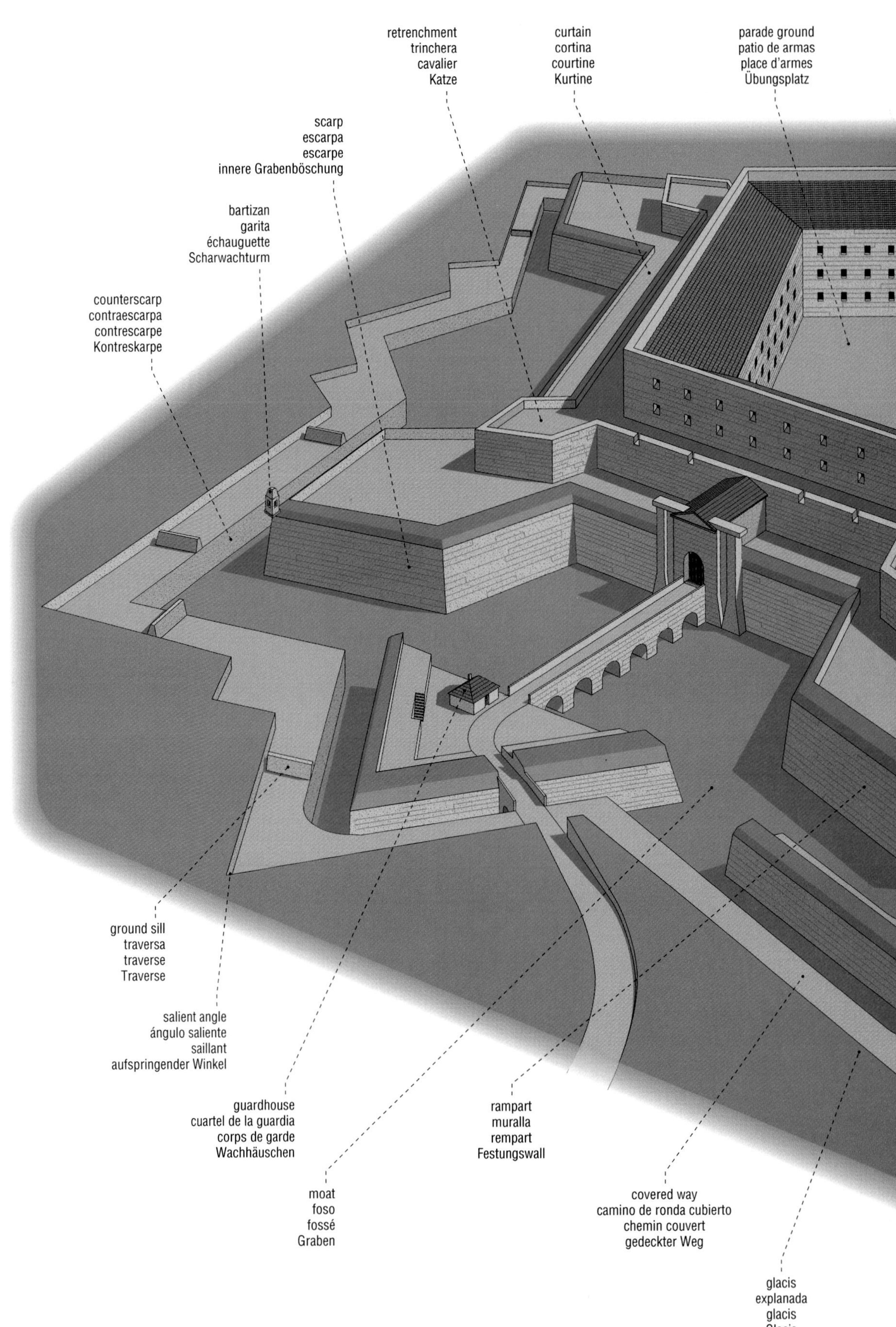
retrenchment
trinchera
cavalier
Katze
curtain
cortina
courtine
Kurtine
parade ground
patio de armas
place d'armes
Übungsplatz
scarp
escarpa
escarpe
innere Grabenböschung
bartizan
garita
échauguette
Scharwachturm
counterscarp
contraescarpa
contrescarpe
Kontreskarpe
ground sill
traversa
traverse
Traverse
salient angle
ángulo saliente
saillant
aufspringender Winkel
guardhouse
cuartel de la guardia
corps de garde
Wachhäuschen
rampart
muralla
rempart
Festungswall
moat
foso
fossé
Graben
covered way
camino de ronda cubierto
chemin couvert
gedeckter Weg
glacis
explanada
glacis
Glacis

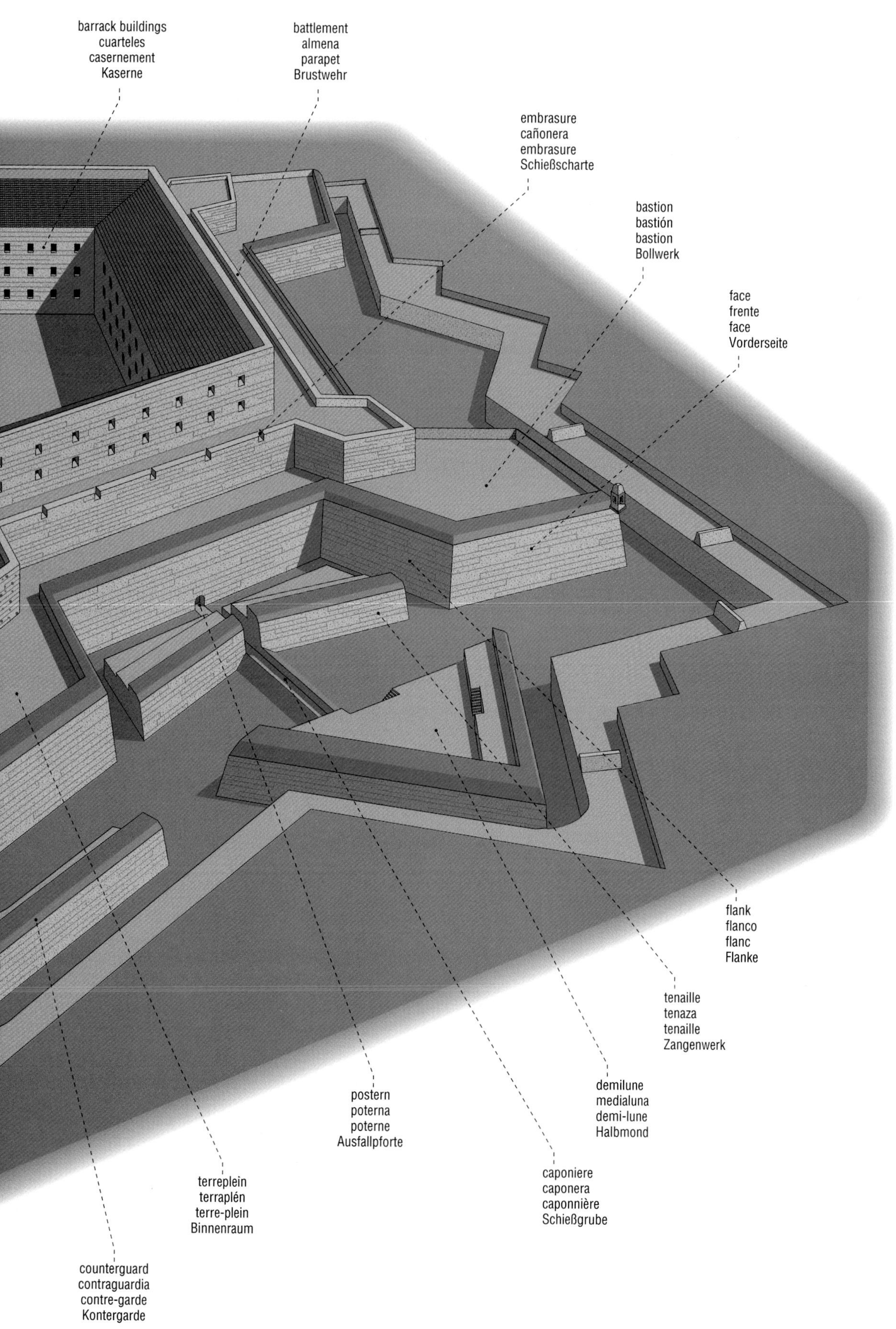
barrack buildings
cuarteles
casernement
Kaserne
battlement
almena
parapet
Brustwehr
embrasure
cañonera
embrasure
Schießscharte
bastion
bastión
bastion
Bollwerk
face
frente
face
Vorderseite
flank
flanco
flanc
Flanke
tenaille
tenaza
tenaille
Zangenwerk
demilune
medialuna
demi-lune
Halbmond
postern
poterna
poterne
Ausfallpforte
caponiere
caponera
caponnière
Schießgrube
terreplein
terraplén
terre-plein
Binnenraum
counterguard
contraguardia
contre-garde
Kontergarde

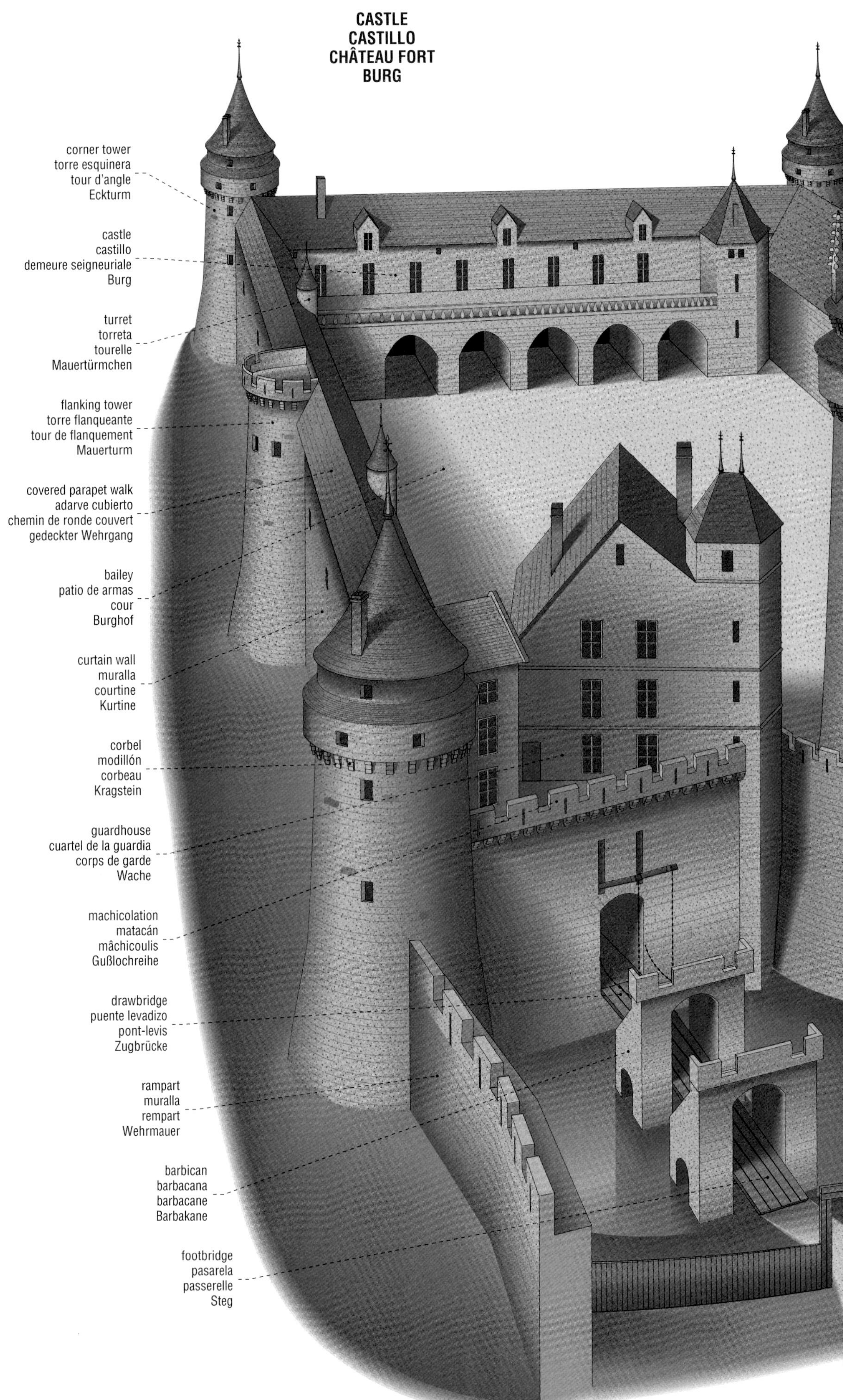
CASTLE
CASTILLO
CHÂTEAU FORT
BURG
corner tower
torre esquinera
tour d'angle
Eckturm
castle
castillo
demeure seigneuriale
Burg
turret
torreta
tourelle
Mauertürmchen
flanking tower
torre flanqueante
tour de flanquement
Mauerturm
covered parapet walk
adarve cubierto
chemin de ronde couvert
gedeckter Wehrgang
bailey
patio de armas
cour
Burghof
curtain wall
muralla
courtine
Kurtine
corbel
modillón
corbeau
Kragstein
guardhouse
cuartel de la guardia
corps de garde
Wache
machicolation
matacán
mâchicoulis
Gußlochreihe
drawbridge
puente levadizo
pont-levis
Zugbrücke
rampart
muralla
rempart
Wehrmauer
barbican
barbacana
barbacane
Barbakane
footbridge
pasarela
passerelle
Steg

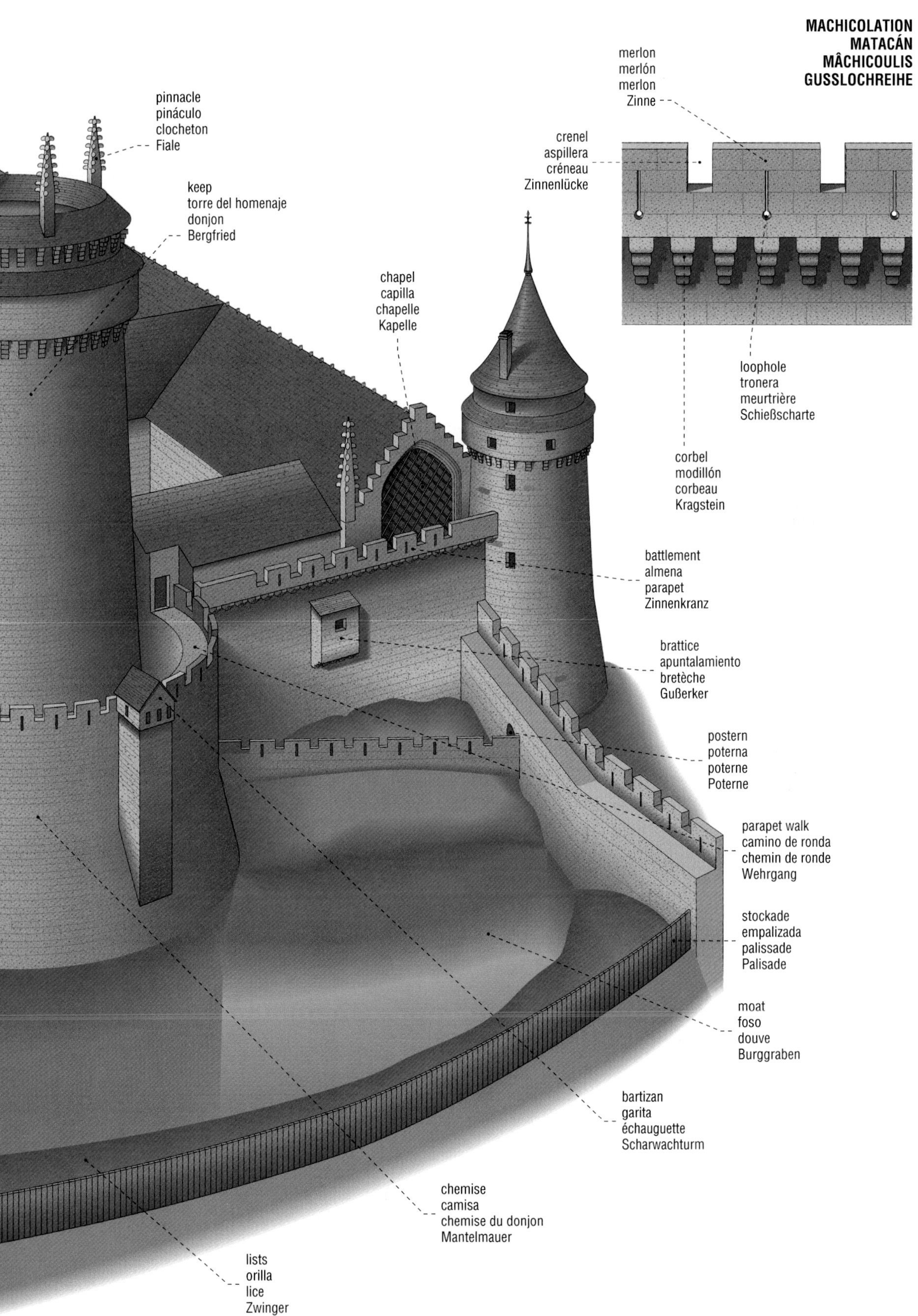
MACHICOLATION
MATACÁN
MÂCHICOULIS
GUSSLOCHREIHE
merlon
merlón
merlon
Zinne
crenel
aspillera
créneau
Zinnenlücke
loophole
tronera
meurtrière
Schießscharte
corbel
modillón
corbeau
Kragstein
pinnacle
pináculo
clocheton
Fiale
keep
torre del homenaje
donjon
Bergfried
chapel
capilla
chapelle
Kapelle
battlement
almena
parapet
Zinnenkranz
brattice
apuntalamiento
bretèche
Gußerker
postern
poterna
poterne
Poterne
parapet walk
camino de ronda
chemin de ronde
Wehrgang
stockade
empalizada
palissade
Palisade
moat
foso
douve
Burggraben
bartizan
garita
échauguette
Scharwachturm
chemise
camisa
chemise du donjon
Mantelmauer
lists
orilla
lice
Zwinger

ROOFS
TECHOS
TOITS
DÄCHER

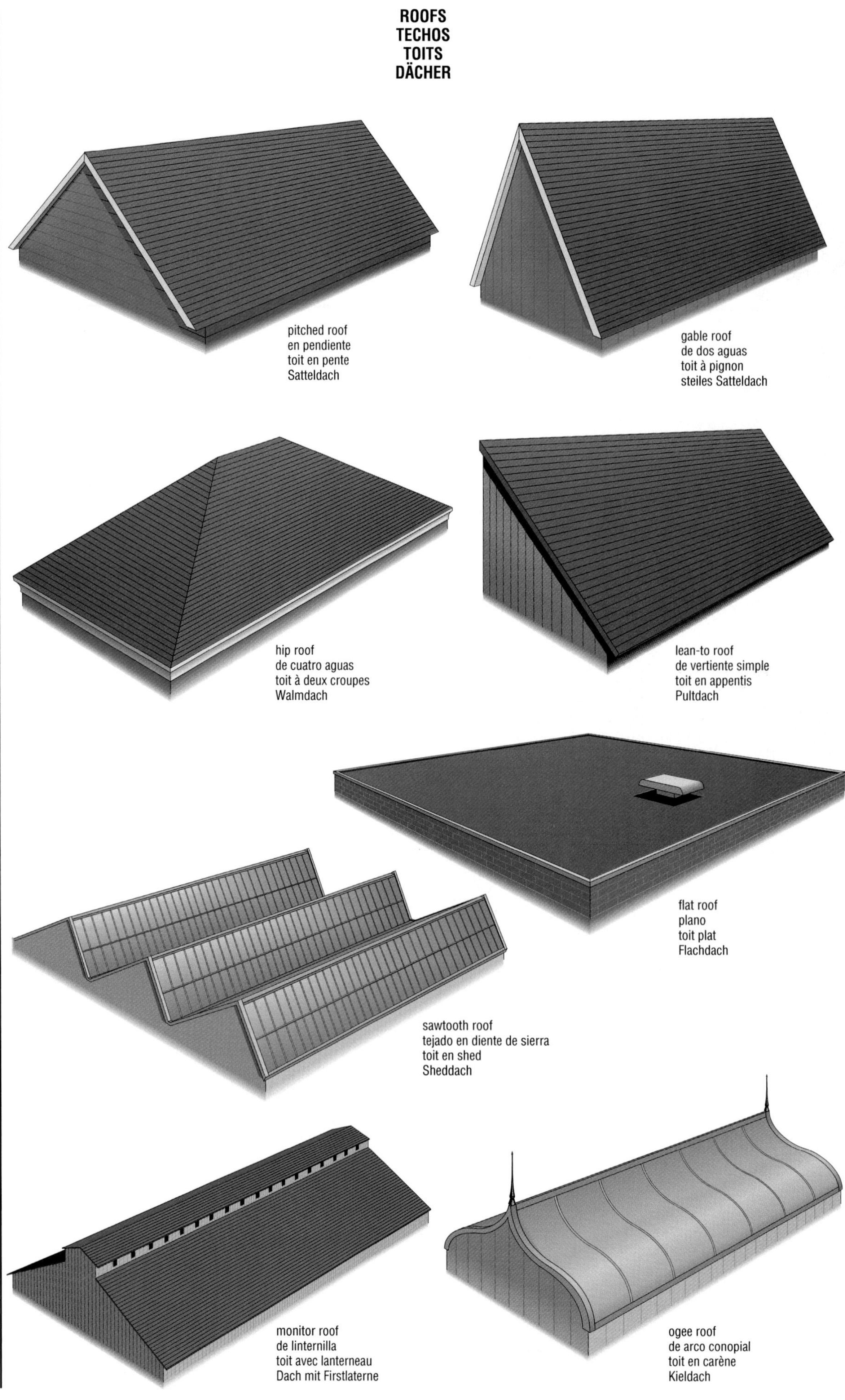
pitched roof
en pendiente
toit en pente
Satteldach
gable roof
de dos aguas
toit à pignon
steiles Satteldach
hip roof
de cuatro aguas
toit à deux croupes
Walmdach
lean-to roof
de vertiente simple
toit en appentis
Pultdach
flat roof
plano
toit plat
Flachdach
sawtooth roof
tejado en diente de sierra
toit en shed
Sheddach
monitor roof
de linternilla
toit avec lanterneau
Dach mit Firstlaterne
ogee roof
de arco conopial
toit en carène
Kieldach

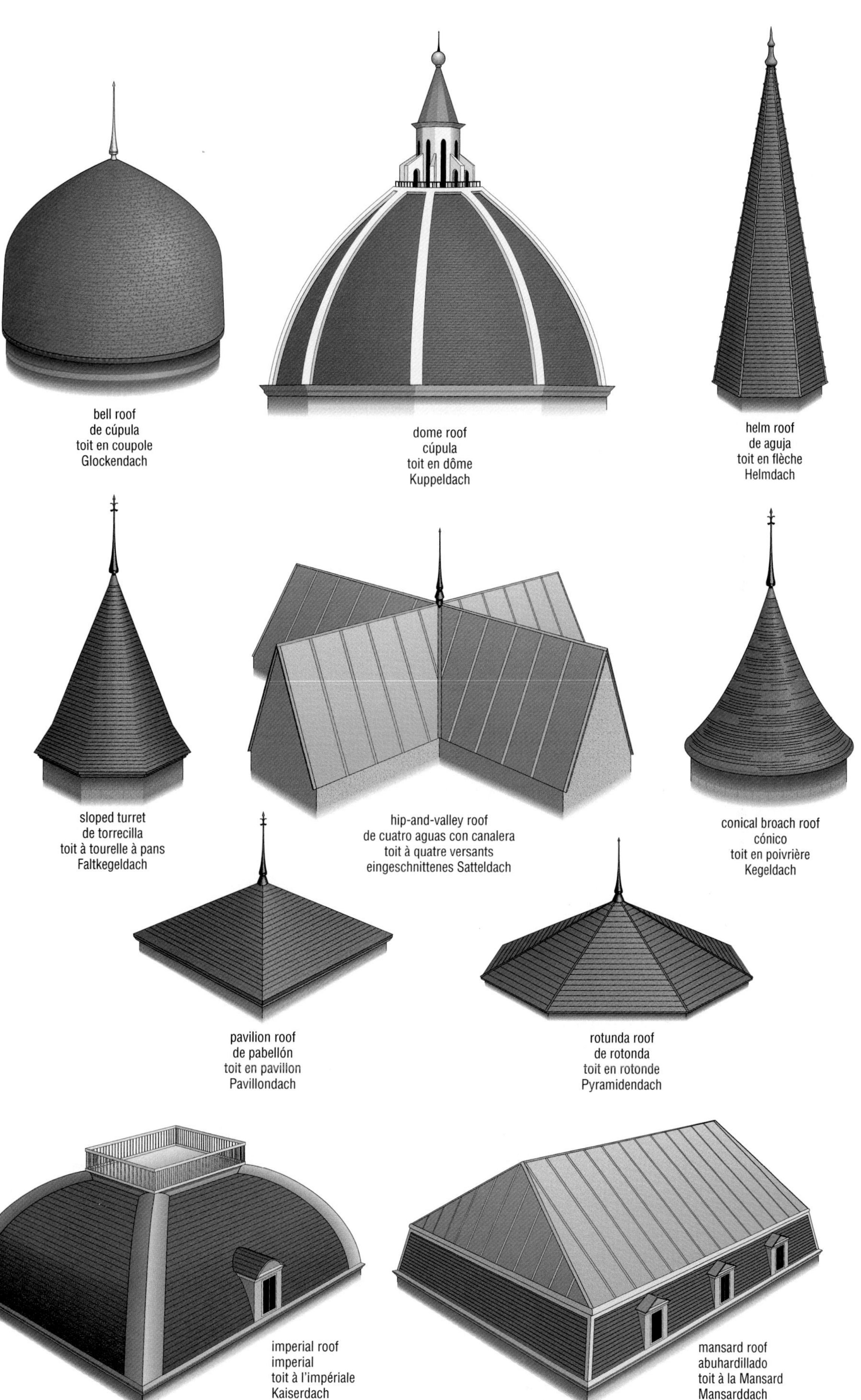
bell roof
de cúpula
toit en coupole
Glockendach
dome roof
cúpula
toit en dôme
Kuppeldach
helm roof
de aguja
toit en flèche
Helmdach
sloped turret
de torrecilla
toit à tourelle à pans
Faltkegeldach
hip-and-valley roof
de cuatro aguas con canalera
toit à quatre versants
eingeschnittenes Satteldach
conical broach roof
cónico
toit en poivrière
Kegeldach
pavilion roof
de pabellón
toit en pavillon
Pavillondach
rotunda roof
de rotonda
toit en rotonde
Pyramidendach
imperial roof
imperial
toit à l'impériale
Kaiserdach
mansard roof
abuhardillado
toit à la Mansard
Mansarddach

DOWNTOWN
CENTRO DE UNA CIUDAD
CENTRE-VILLE
CITY

park
parque
parc
Park
convention center
centro de congresos
palais des congrès
Kongreßzentrum
office tower
edificio de oficinas
tour à bureaux
Bürohochhaus
square
zona verde
espace vert
Grünanlage
cathedral
catedral
cathédrale
Kathedrale
passenger station
estación de ferrocarril
gare
Bahnhof
median strip
separador
terre-plein
Mittelstreifen
planetarium
planetario
planétarium
Planetarium
railroad
vía férrea
voie ferrée
Eisenbahn
traffic island
separador
îlot refuge
Verkehrsinsel
boulevard
avenida
boulevard
Boulevard
street
calle
rue
Straße
delivery ramp
rampa para mercancías
rampe de livraison
Auffahrt
freeway
autopista
autoroute
Autobahn

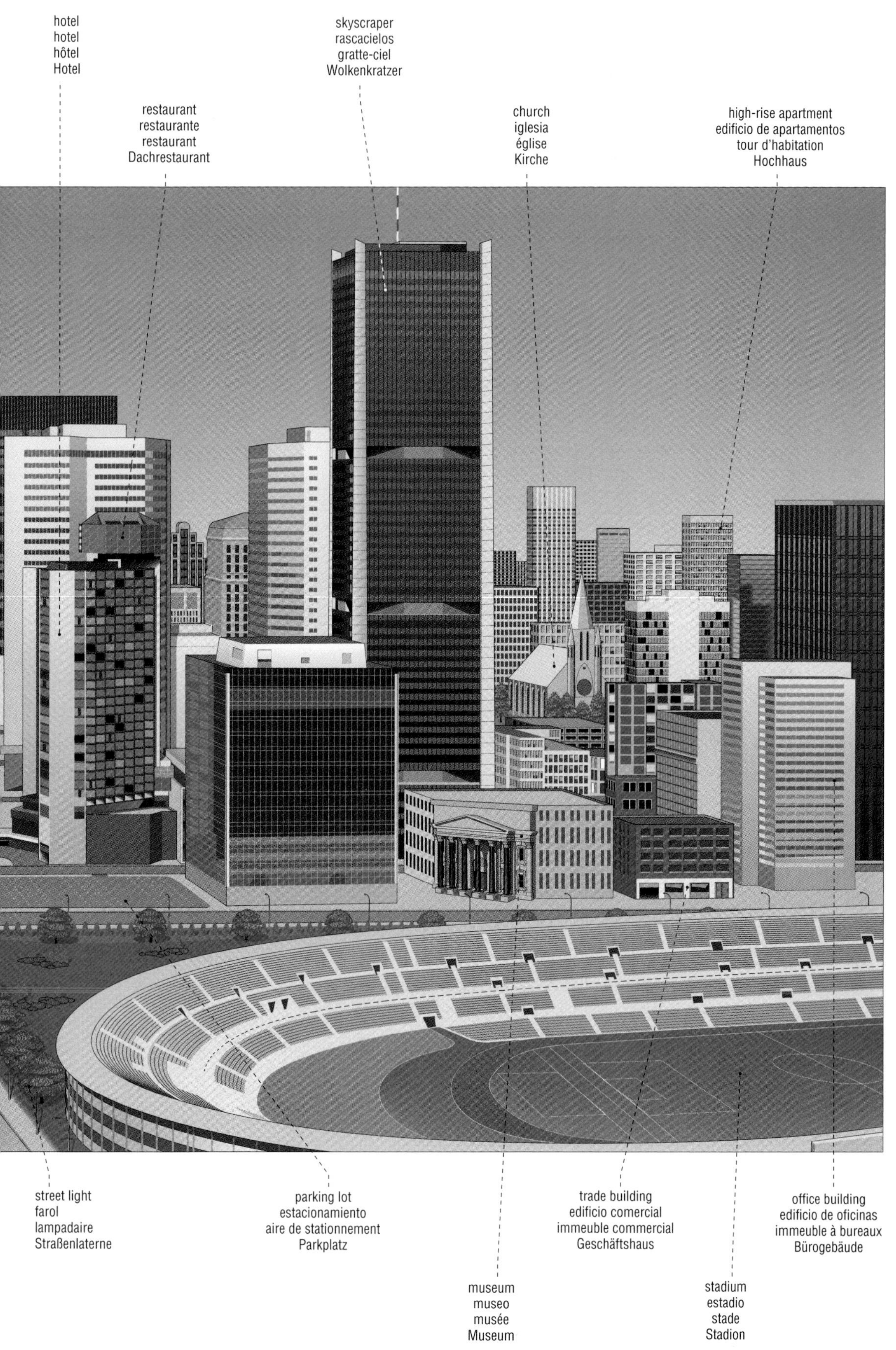
hotel
hotel
hôtel
Hotel
skyscraper
rascacielos
gratte-ciel
Wolkenkratzer
restaurant
restaurante
restaurant
Dachrestaurant
church
iglesia
église
Kirche
high-rise apartment
edificio de apartamentos
tour d'habitation
Hochhaus
street light
farol
lampadaire
Straßenlaterne
parking lot
estacionamiento
aire de stationnement
Parkplatz
trade building
edificio comercial
immeuble commercial
Geschäftshaus
office building
edificio de oficinas
immeuble à bureaux
Bürogebäude
museum
museo
musée
Museum
stadium
estadio
stade
Stadion

CROSS SECTION OF A STREET
VISTA TRANSVERSAL DE UNA CALLE
COUPE D'UNE RUE
QUERSCHNITT EINER STRASSE

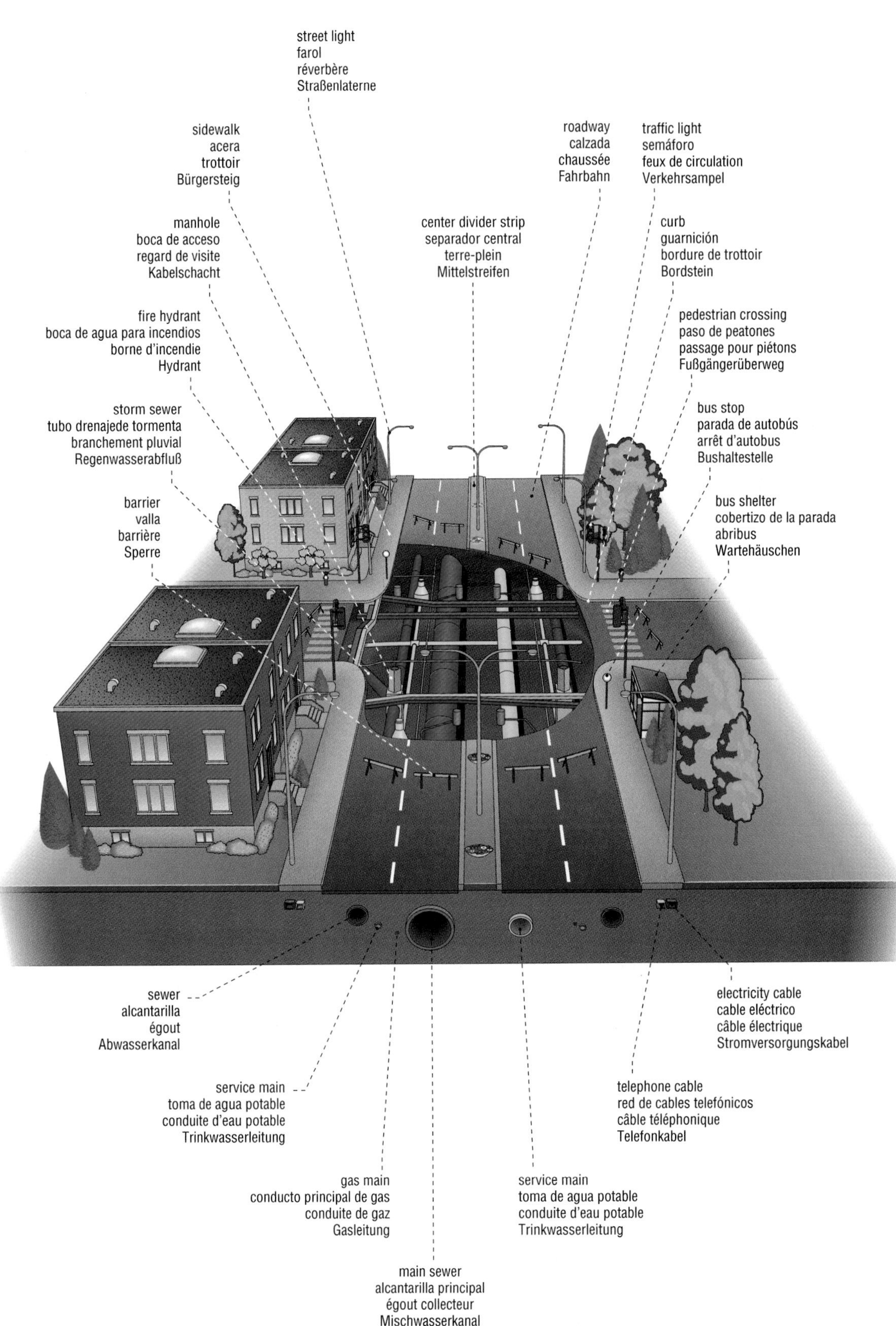
street light
farol
réverbère
Straßenlaterne
sidewalk
acera
trottoir
Bürgersteig
roadway
calzada
chaussée
Fahrbahn
traffic light
semáforo
feux de circulation
Verkehrsampel
manhole
boca de acceso
regard de visite
Kabelschacht
center divider strip
separador central
terre-plein
Mittelstreifen
curb
guarnición
bordure de trottoir
Bordstein
fire hydrant
boca de agua para incendios
borne d'incendie
Hydrant
pedestrian crossing
paso de peatones
passage pour piétons
Fußgängerüberweg
storm sewer
tubo drenajede tormenta
branchement pluvial
Regenwasserabfluß
bus stop
parada de autobús
arrêt d'autobus
Bushaltestelle
barrier
valla
barrière
Sperre
bus shelter
cobertizo de la parada
abribus
Wartehäuschen
sewer
alcantarilla
égout
Abwasserkanal
electricity cable
cable eléctrico
câble électrique
Stromversorgungskabel
service main
toma de agua potable
conduite d'eau potable
Trinkwasserleitung
telephone cable
red de cables telefónicos
câble téléphonique
Telefonkabel
gas main
conducto principal de gas
conduite de gaz
Gasleitung
service main
toma de agua potable
conduite d'eau potable
Trinkwasserleitung
main sewer
alcantarilla principal
égout collecteur
Mischwasserkanal

CITY HOUSES
VIVIENDAS URBANAS
MAISONS DE VILLE
HÄUSERFORMEN IN DER STADT

cottage
casa de campo
villa
Cottage

single-family home
casas independientes
maison individuelle
Einfamilienhaus

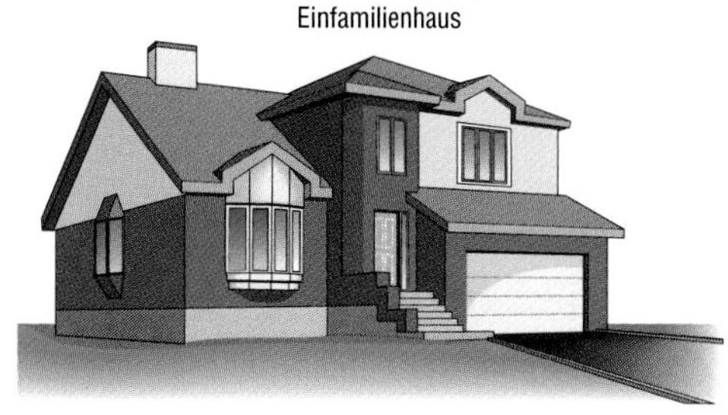

apartment building
condominios
appartements en copropriété
Eigentumswohnungen

semi-detached cottage
casas gemelas
maison individuelle jumelée
Doppelhaus

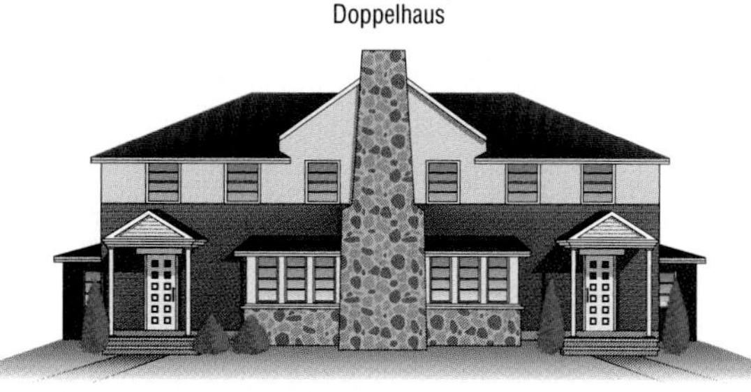

town houses
casas en serie
maisons en rangée
Reihenhaus

high-rise apartment
edificio de apartamentos
tour d'habitation
Wohnblock

THEATER
TEATRO
SALLE DE SPECTACLE
THEATER

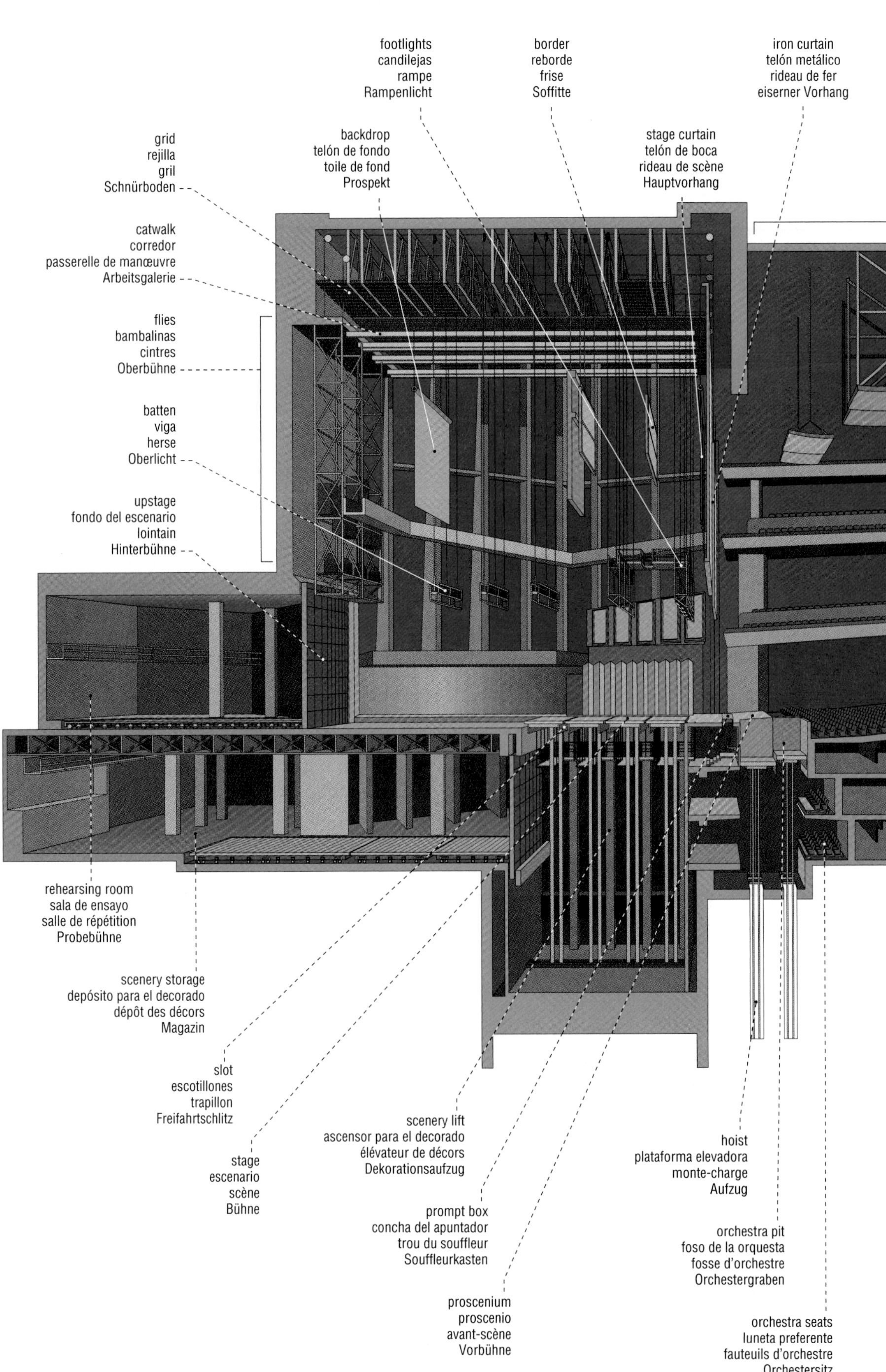
footlights
candilejas
rampe
Rampenlicht
border
reborde
frise
Soffitte
iron curtain
telón metálico
rideau de fer
eiserner Vorhang
grid
rejilla
gril
Schnürboden
backdrop
telón de fondo
toile de fond
Prospekt
stage curtain
telón de boca
rideau de scène
Hauptvorhang
catwalk
corredor
passerelle de manœuvre
Arbeitsgalerie
flies
bambalinas
cintres
Oberbühne
batten
viga
herse
Oberlicht
upstage
fondo del escenario
lointain
Hinterbühne
rehearsing room
sala de ensayo
salle de répétition
Probebühne
scenery storage
depósito para el decorado
dépôt des décors
Magazin
slot
escotillones
trapillon
Freifahrtschlitz
stage
escenario
scène
Bühne
scenery lift
ascensor para el decorado
élévateur de décors
Dekorationsaufzug
prompt box
concha del apuntador
trou du souffleur
Souffleurkasten
proscenium
proscenio
avant-scène
Vorbühne
hoist
plataforma elevadora
monte-charge
Aufzug
orchestra pit
foso de la orquesta
fosse d'orchestre
Orchestergraben
orchestra seats
luneta preferente
fauteuils d'orchestre
Orchestersitz

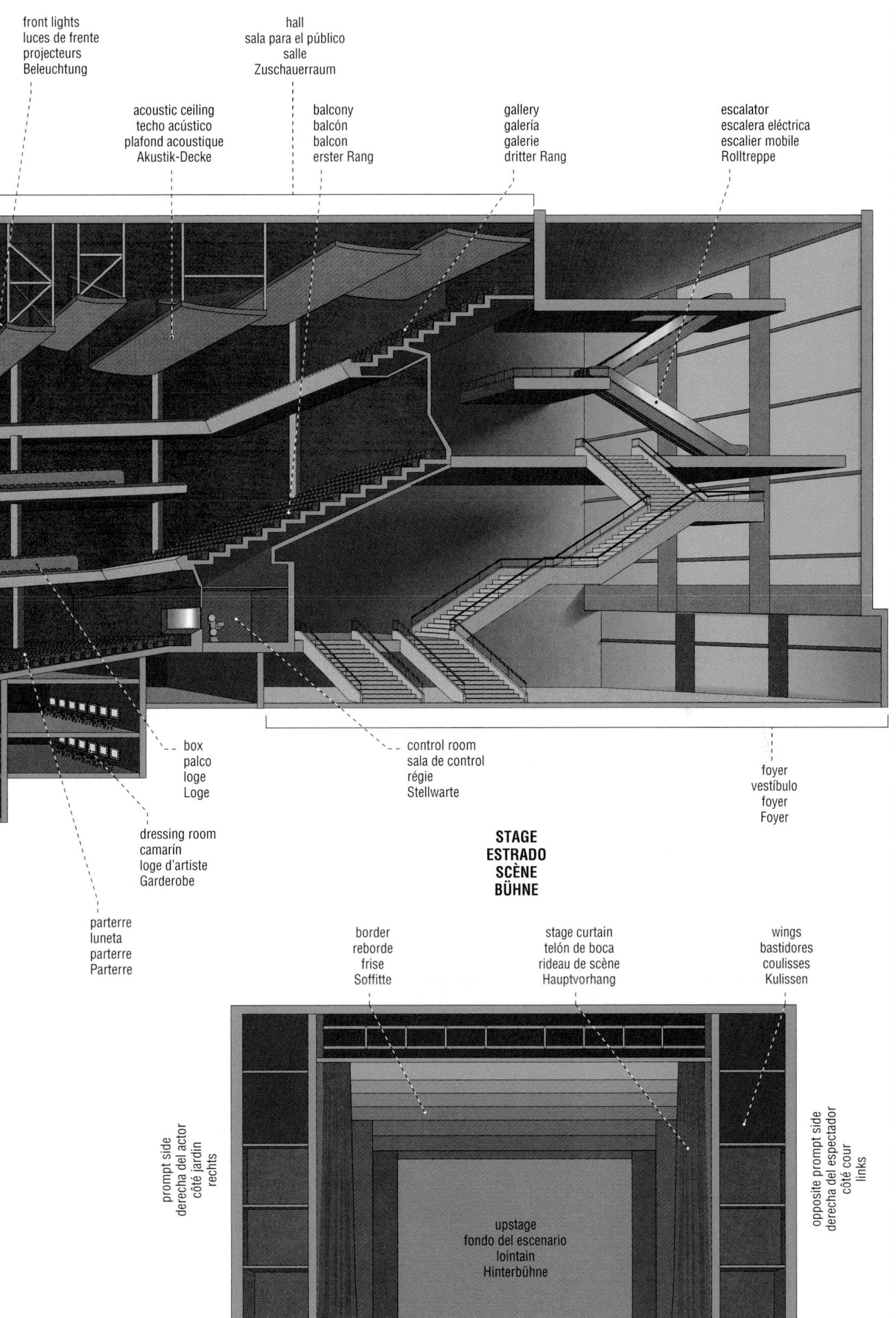
front lights
luces de frente
projecteurs
Beleuchtung
hall
sala para el público
salle
Zuschauerraum
acoustic ceiling
techo acústico
plafond acoustique
Akustik-Decke
balcony
balcón
balcon
erster Rang
gallery
galería
galerie
dritter Rang
escalator
escalera eléctrica
escalier mobile
Rolltreppe
box
palco
loge
Loge
control room
sala de control
régie
Stellwarte
foyer
vestíbulo
foyer
Foyer
dressing room
camarín
loge d'artiste
Garderobe
parterre
luneta
parterre
Parterre
STAGE
ESTRADO
SCÈNE
BÜHNE
border
reborde
frise
Soffitte
stage curtain
telón de boca
rideau de scène
Hauptvorhang
wings
bastidores
coulisses
Kulissen
prompt side
derecha del actor
côté jardin
rechts
opposite prompt side
derecha del espectador
côté cour
links
upstage
fondo del escenario
lointain
Hinterbühne

OFFICE BUILDING
EDIFICIO DE OFICINAS
ÉDIFICE À BUREAUX
BÜROGEBÄUDE

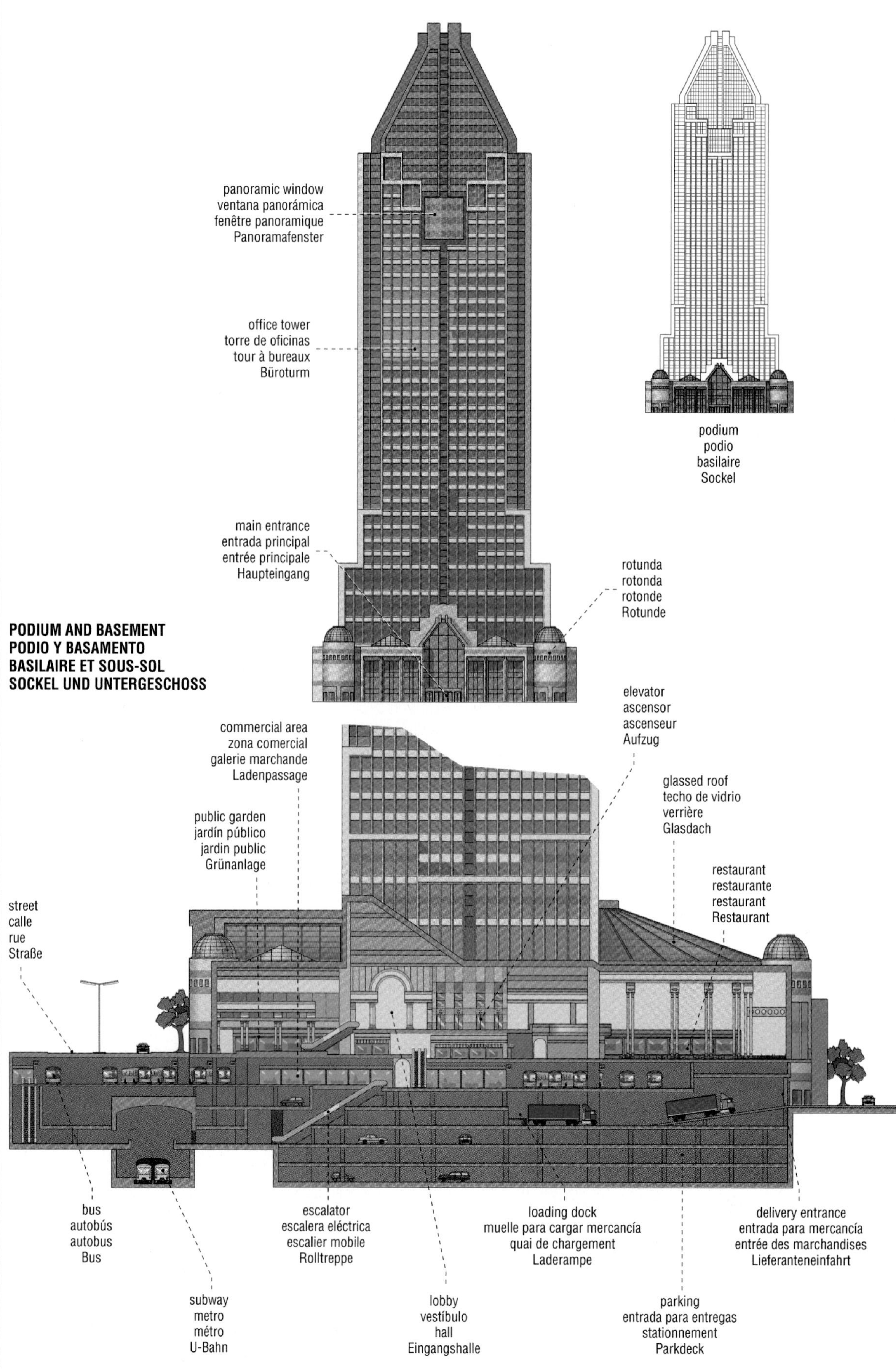
panoramic window
ventana panorámica
fenêtre panoramique
Panoramafenster
office tower
torre de oficinas
tour à bureaux
Büroturm
main entrance
entrada principal
entrée principale
Haupteingang
rotunda
rotonda
rotonde
Rotunde
podium
podio
basilaire
Sockel
PODIUM AND BASEMENT
PODIO Y BASAMENTO
BASILAIRE ET SOUS-SOL
SOCKEL UND UNTERGESCHOSS
commercial area
zona comercial
galerie marchande
Ladenpassage
elevator
ascensor
ascenseur
Aufzug
public garden
jardín público
jardin public
Grünanlage
glassed roof
techo de vidrio
verrière
Glasdach
restaurant
restaurante
restaurant
Restaurant
street
calle
rue
Straße
bus
autobús
autobus
Bus
escalator
escalera eléctrica
escalier mobile
Rolltreppe
loading dock
muelle para cargar mercancía
quai de chargement
Laderampe
delivery entrance
entrada para mercancía
entrée des marchandises
Lieferanteneinfahrt
subway
metro
métro
U-Bahn
lobby
vestíbulo
hall
Eingangshalle
parking
entrada para entregas
stationnement
Parkdeck

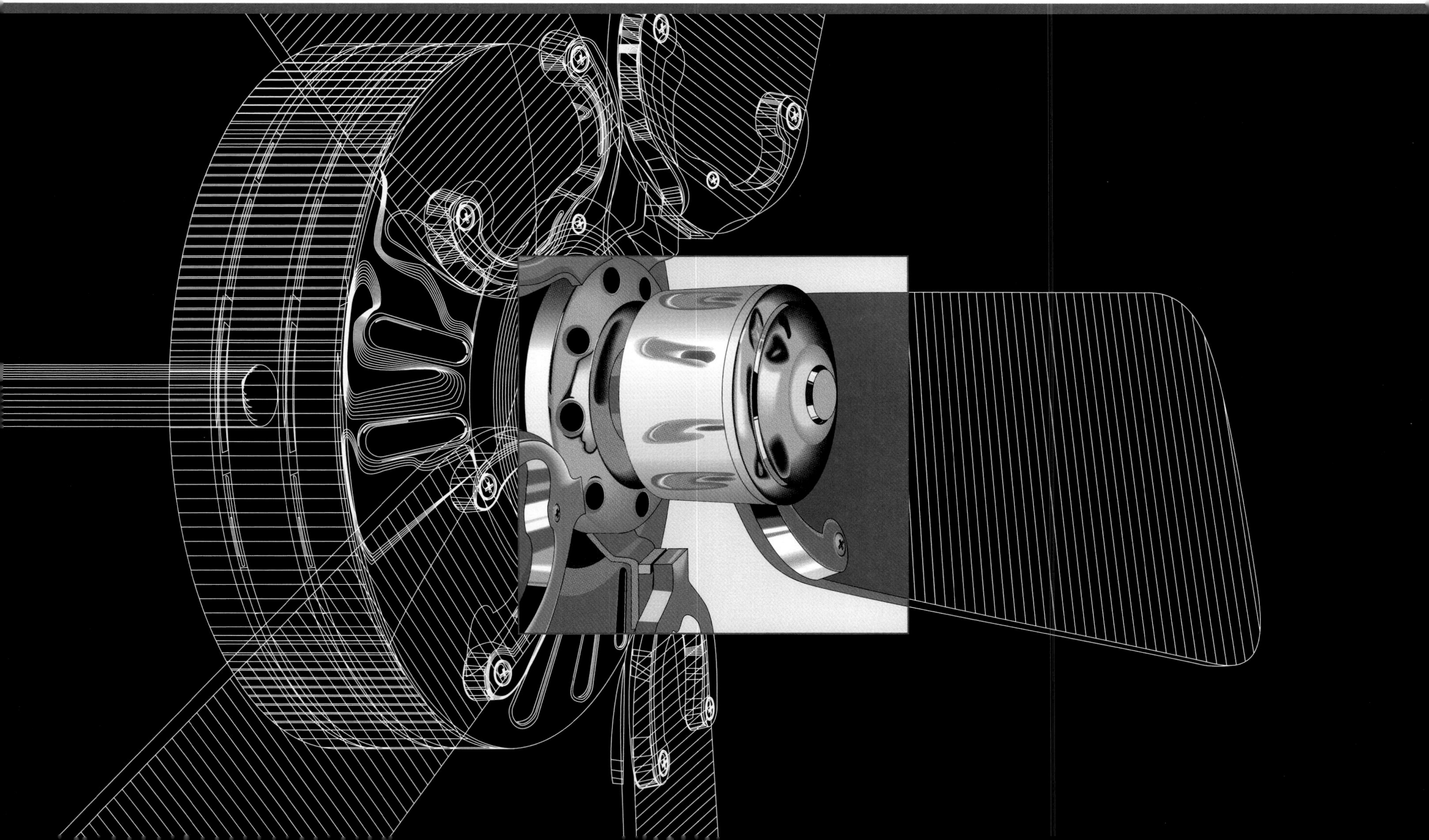

CONTENTS

BLUEPRINT READING
PLANO DE UNA CASA
LECTURE DE PLANS
GEBÄUDEPLANUNG

ELEVATION
ELEVACIÓN
ÉLEVATION
ANSICHT

SITE PLAN
PLANO DEL TERRENO
PLAN DU TERRAIN
LAGEPLAN

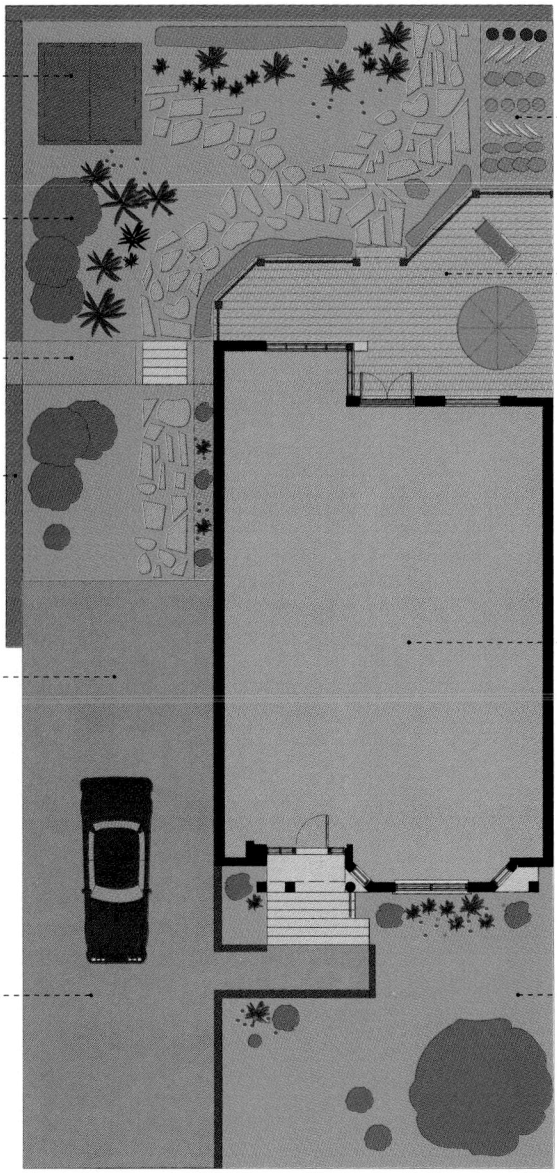

shed
cobertizo
remise
Schuppen

vegetable garden
huerto
jardin potager
Nutzgarten

pleasure garden
jardín
jardin d'agrément
Ziergarten

patio
terraza
terrasse
Terrasse

grade slope
desnivel
déclivité du terrain
Böschung

property line
lindero
limite du terrain
Grundstücksgrenze

house
casa
maison
Haus

parking
estacionamiento
stationnement
Abstellplatz

driveway
entrada del coche
allée
Zufahrt

lawn
césped
pelouse
Rasen

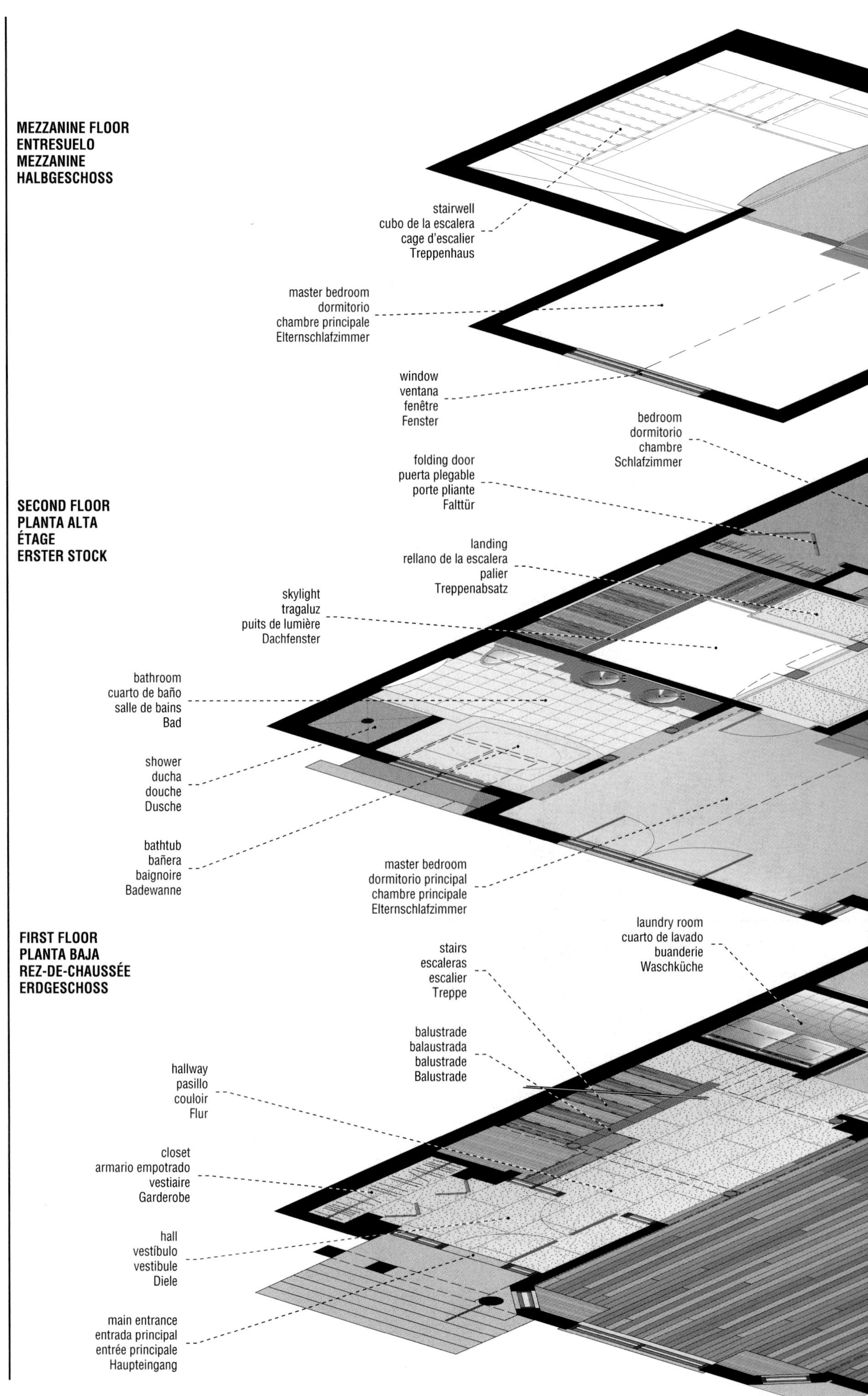
MEZZANINE FLOOR
ENTRESUELO
MEZZANINE
HALBGESCHOSS
stairwell
cubo de la escalera
cage d'escalier
Treppenhaus
master bedroom
dormitorio
chambre principale
Elternschlafzimmer
window
ventana
fenêtre
Fenster
bedroom
dormitorio
chambre
Schlafzimmer
folding door
puerta plegable
porte pliante
Falttür
SECOND FLOOR
PLANTA ALTA
ÉTAGE
ERSTER STOCK
landing
rellano de la escalera
palier
Treppenabsatz
skylight
tragaluz
puits de lumière
Dachfenster
bathroom
cuarto de baño
salle de bains
Bad
shower
ducha
douche
Dusche
bathtub
bañera
baignoire
Badewanne
master bedroom
dormitorio principal
chambre principale
Elternschlafzimmer
FIRST FLOOR
PLANTA BAJA
REZ-DE-CHAUSSÉE
ERDGESCHOSS
laundry room
cuarto de lavado
buanderie
Waschküche
stairs
escaleras
escalier
Treppe
balustrade
balaustrada
balustrade
Balustrade
hallway
pasillo
couloir
Flur
closet
armario empotrado
vestiaire
Garderobe
hall
vestíbulo
vestibule
Diele
main entrance
entrada principal
entrée principale
Haupteingang

BLUEPRINT READING
ELEMENTOS BÁSICOS DE UN PLANO
LECTURE DE PLANS
GEBÄUDEPLANUNG

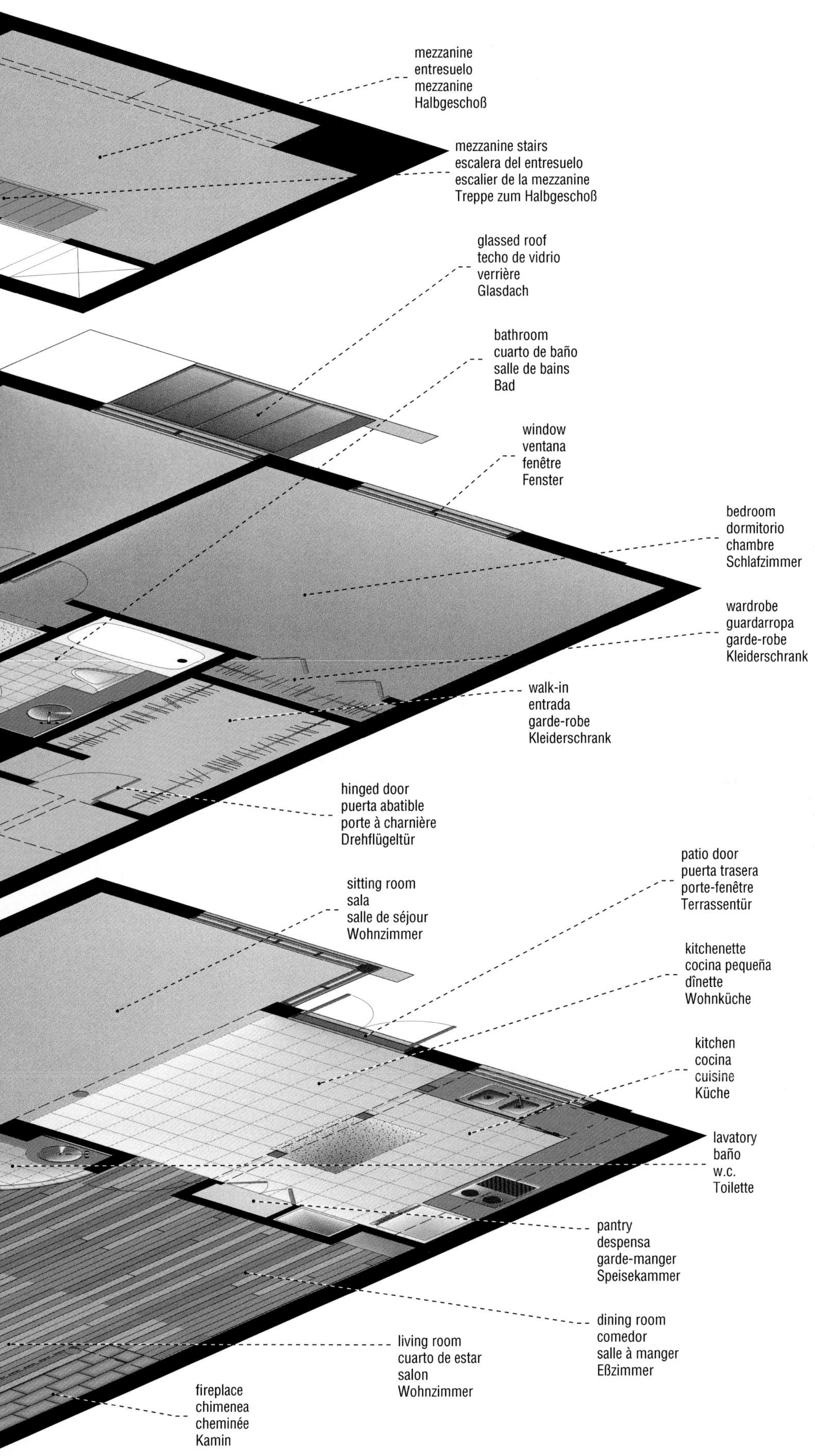

mezzanine
entresuelo
mezzanine
Halbgeschoß
mezzanine stairs
escalera del entresuelo
escalier de la mezzanine
Treppe zum Halbgeschoß
glassed roof
techo de vidrio
verrière
Glasdach
bathroom
cuarto de baño
salle de bains
Bad
window
ventana
fenêtre
Fenster
bedroom
dormitorio
chambre
Schlafzimmer
wardrobe
guardarropa
garde-robe
Kleiderschrank
walk-in
entrada
garde-robe
Kleiderschrank
hinged door
puerta abatible
porte à charnière
Drehflügeltür
sitting room
sala
salle de séjour
Wohnzimmer
patio door
puerta trasera
porte-fenêtre
Terrassentür
kitchenette
cocina pequeña
dînette
Wohnküche
kitchen
cocina
cuisine
Küche
lavatory
baño
w.c.
Toilette
pantry
despensa
garde-manger
Speisekammer
dining room
comedor
salle à manger
Eßzimmer
living room
cuarto de estar
salon
Wohnzimmer
fireplace
chimenea
cheminée
Kamin

EXTERIOR OF A HOUSE
EXTERIOR DE UNA CASA
EXTÉRIEUR D'UNE MAISON
AUSSENANSICHT EINES HAUSES

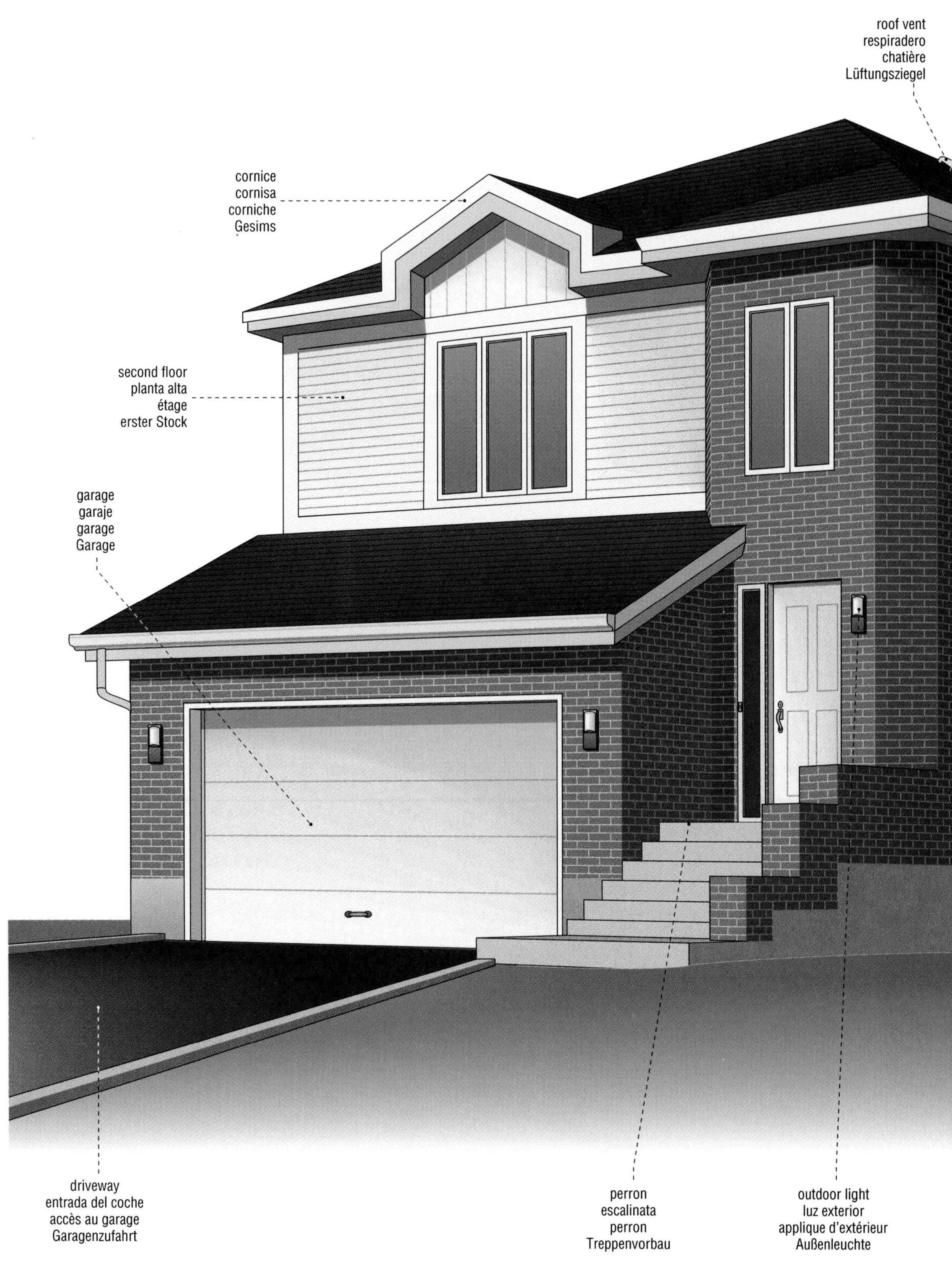
roof vent
respiradero
chatière
Lüftungsziegel
cornice
cornisa
corniche
Gesims
second floor
planta alta
étage
erster Stock
garage
garaje
garage
Garage
driveway
entrada del coche
accès au garage
Garagenzufahrt
perron
escalinata
perron
Treppenvorbau
outdoor light
luz exterior
applique d'extérieur
Außenleuchte

chimney pot
capuchón de la chimenea
mitron
Kaminaufsatz
chimney stack
cañón de chimenea
souche
Kamin
chimney
chimenea
cheminée
Schornstein
lightning rod
pararrayos
paratonnerre
Blitzableiter
roof
techo
toit
Dach
skylight
tragaluz
tabatière
Dachfenster
gable
buhardilla
pignon
Giebelseite
gable vent
respiradero
évent de pignon
Belüftungsgitter
gutter
canalón
gouttière
Dachrinne
bay window
mirador
fenêtre en baie
Erkerfenster
downspout
bajada de aguas
descente de gouttière
Regenrohr
bow window
ventanal
fenêtre en saillie
Erkerfenster
first floor
planta baja
rez-de-chaussée
Erdgeschoß
basement window
respiradero
fenêtre de sous-sol
Kellerfenster
basement
sótano
sous-sol
Keller

STRUCTURE OF A HOUSE
ESTRUCTURA DE UNA CASA
STRUCTURE D'UNE MAISON
KONSTRUKTION EINES HAUSES

FRAME
ARMAZÓN
CHARPENTE
RAHMEN

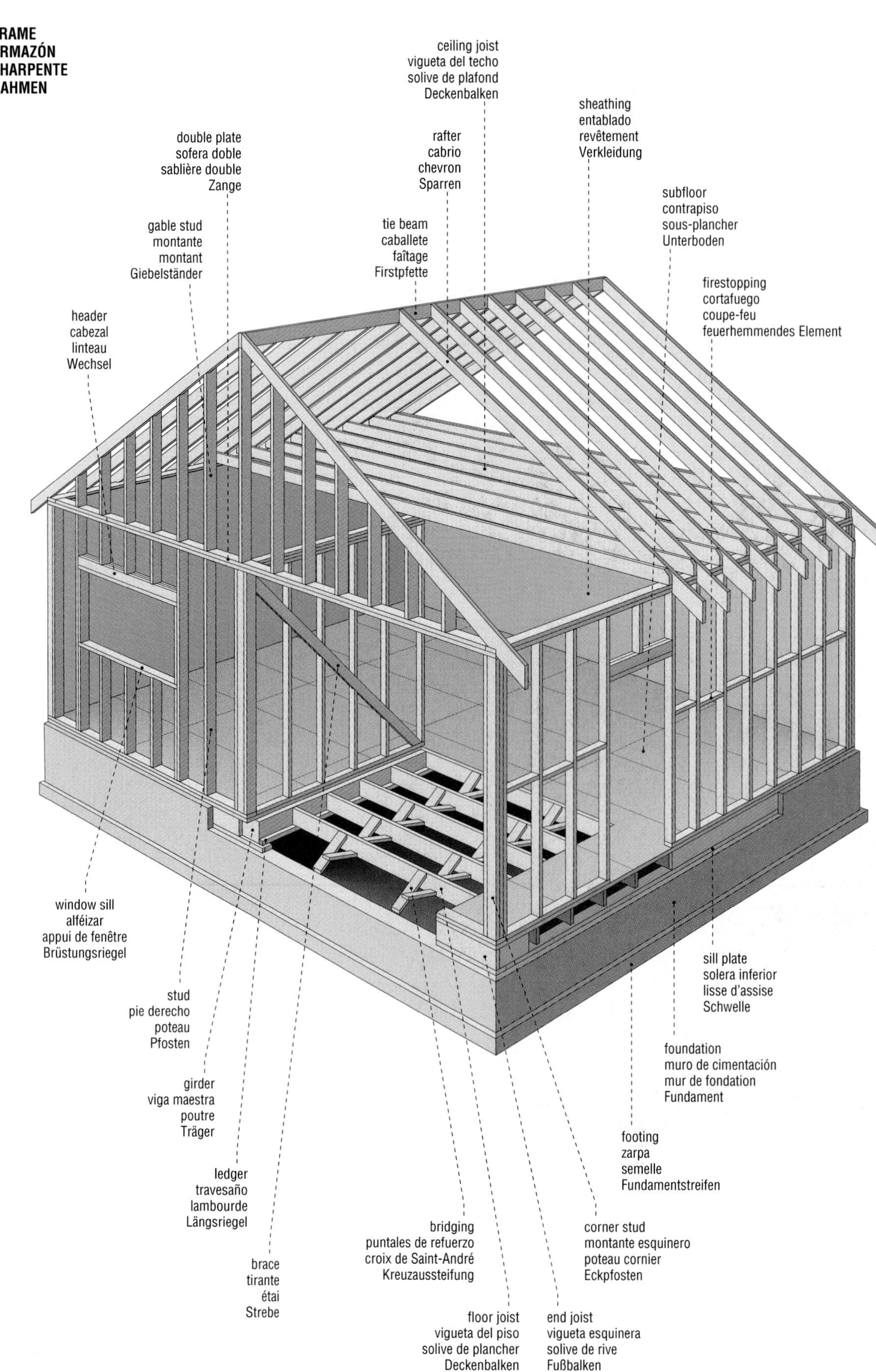
ceiling joist
vigueta del techo
solive de plafond
Deckenbalken
sheathing
entablado
revêtement
Verkleidung
double plate
sofera doble
sablière double
Zange
rafter
cabrio
chevron
Sparren
subfloor
contrapiso
sous-plancher
Unterboden
gable stud
montante
montant
Giebelständer
tie beam
caballete
faîtage
Firstpfette
firestopping
cortafuego
coupe-feu
feuerhemmendes Element
header
cabezal
linteau
Wechsel
window sill
alféizar
appui de fenêtre
Brüstungsriegel
sill plate
solera inferior
lisse d'assise
Schwelle
stud
pie derecho
poteau
Pfosten
foundation
muro de cimentación
mur de fondation
Fundament
girder
viga maestra
poutre
Träger
footing
zarpa
semelle
Fundamentstreifen
ledger
travesaño
lambourde
Längsriegel
bridging
puntales de refuerzo
croix de Saint-André
Kreuzaussteifung
corner stud
montante esquinero
poteau cornier
Eckpfosten
brace
tirante
étai
Strebe
floor joist
vigueta del piso
solive de plancher
Deckenbalken
end joist
vigueta esquinera
solive de rive
Fußbalken

ROOF TRUSS
ARMADURA DEL TECHO
FERME DE TOIT
DACHSTUHL

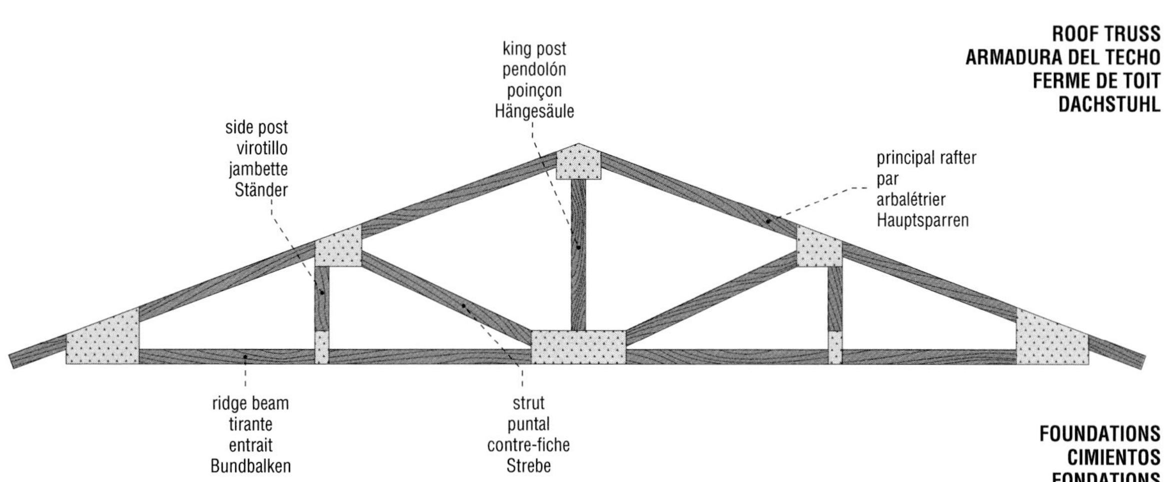
king post
pendolón
poinçon
Hängesäule
side post
virotillo
jambette
Ständer
principal rafter
par
arbalétrier
Hauptsparren
ridge beam
tirante
entrait
Bundbalken
strut
puntal
contre-fiche
Strebe

FOUNDATIONS
CIMIENTOS
FONDATIONS
FUNDAMENT

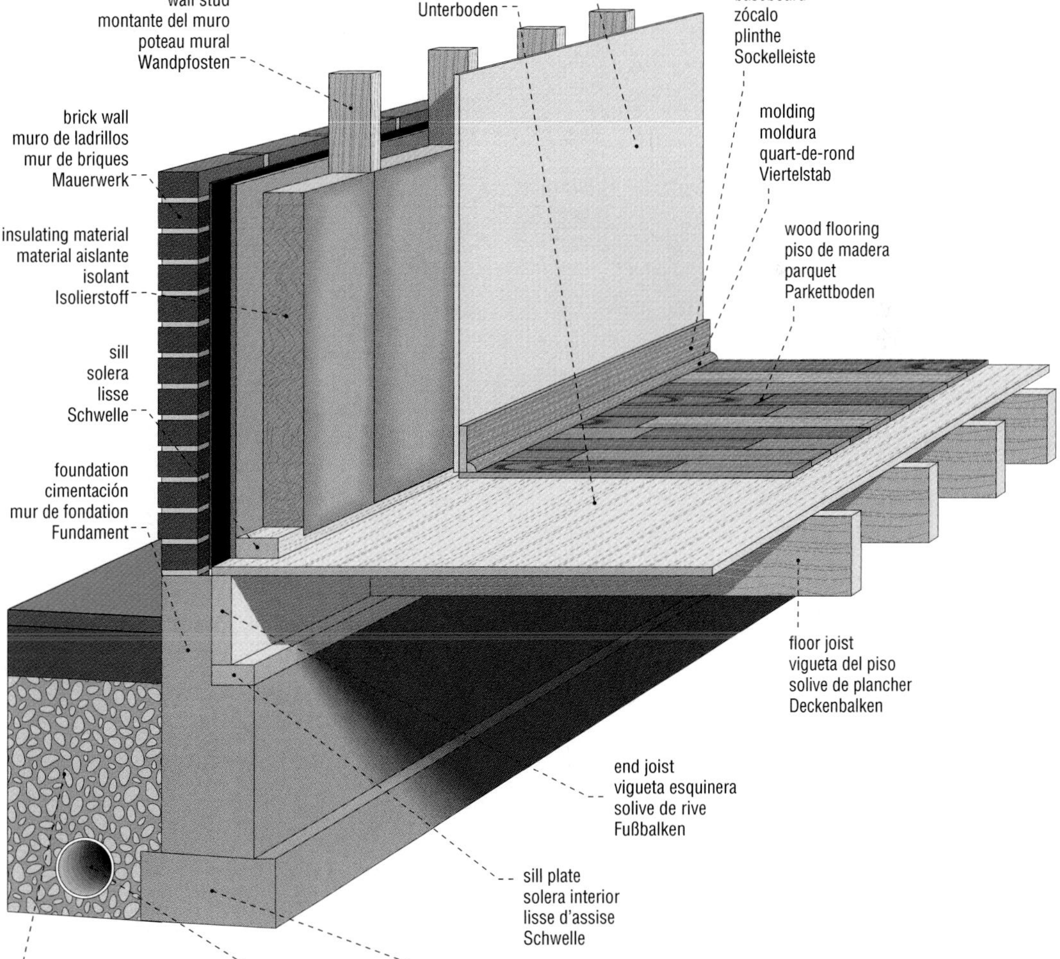

sheathing
entablado
revêtement
Innenputz

subfloor
contrapiso
sous-plancher
Unterboden

wall stud
montante del muro
poteau mural
Wandpfosten

baseboard
zócalo
plinthe
Sockelleiste

brick wall
muro de ladrillos
mur de briques
Mauerwerk

molding
moldura
quart-de-rond
Viertelstab

insulating material
material aislante
isolant
Isolierstoff

wood flooring
piso de madera
parquet
Parkettboden

sill
solera
lisse
Schwelle

foundation
cimentación
mur de fondation
Fundament

floor joist
vigueta del piso
solive de plancher
Deckenbalken

end joist
vigueta esquinera
solive de rive
Fußbalken

sill plate
solera interior
lisse d'assise
Schwelle

footing
zarpa
semelle
Fundamentstreifen

gravel
grava
gravier
Kies

drain tile
tubo de drenaje
drain
Sickerrohr

WOOD FLOORING
PISOS DE MADERA
PARQUET
PARKETTBODEN

WOOD FLOORING ON CEMENT SCREED
PARQUÉ SOBRE BASE DE CEMENTO
PARQUET SUR CHAPE DE CIMENT
PARKETTBODEN AUF ZEMENTESTRICH

WOOD FLOORING ON WOODEN STRUCTURE
ENTARIMADO SOBRE ESTRUCTURA DE MADERA
PARQUET SUR OSSATURE DE BOIS
PARKETTBODEN AUF HOLZUNTERBAU

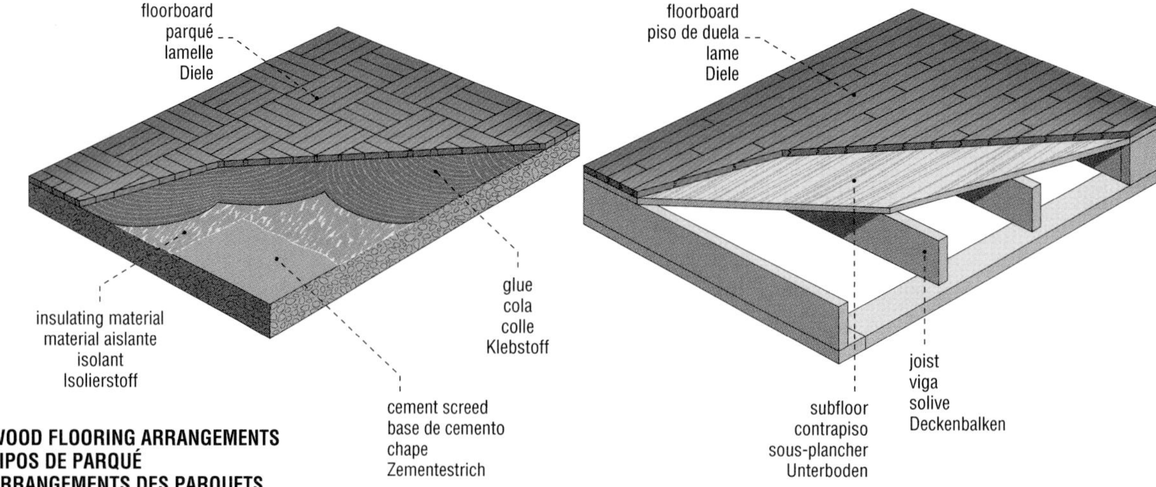
floorboard
parqué
lamelle
Diele
insulating material
material aislante
isolant
Isolierstoff
glue
cola
colle
Klebstoff
cement screed
base de cemento
chape
Zementestrich
floorboard
piso de duela
lame
Diele
subfloor
contrapiso
sous-plancher
Unterboden
joist
viga
solive
Deckenbalken

WOOD FLOORING ARRANGEMENTS
TIPOS DE PARQUÉ
ARRANGEMENTS DES PARQUETS
PARKETTMUSTER

overlay flooring
parqué sobrepuesto
parquet à coupe perdue
Stabparkett im verlorenen Verband

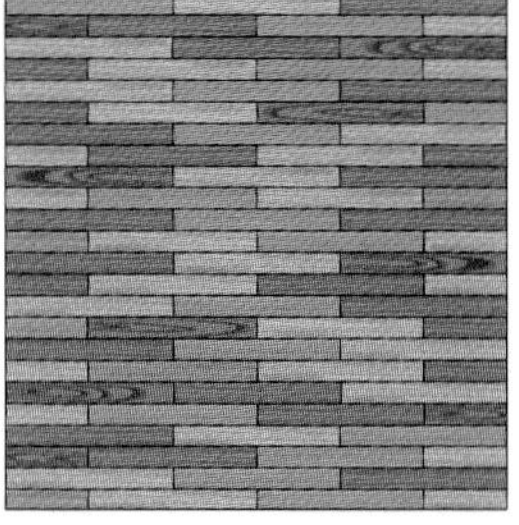

strip flooring with alternate joints
parqué alternado a la inglesa
parquet à coupe de pierre
Stabparkett

herringbone parquet
parqué espinapez
parquet à bâtons rompus
Fischgrätenparkett

herringbone pattern
espinapez
parquet en chevrons
Fischgrätenmuster

inlaid parquet
parqué entretejido
parquet mosaïque
Mosaikparkett

basket weave pattern
parqué de cestería
parquet en vannerie
Würfelmusterparkett

Arenberg parquet
parqué Arenberg
parquet d'Arenberg
Arenberg-Parkett

Chantilly parquet
parqué Chantilly
parquet Chantilly
Chantilly-Parkett

Versailles parquet
parqué Versailles
parquet Versailles
Versailles-Parkett

STAIRS
ESCALERA
ESCALIER
TREPPE

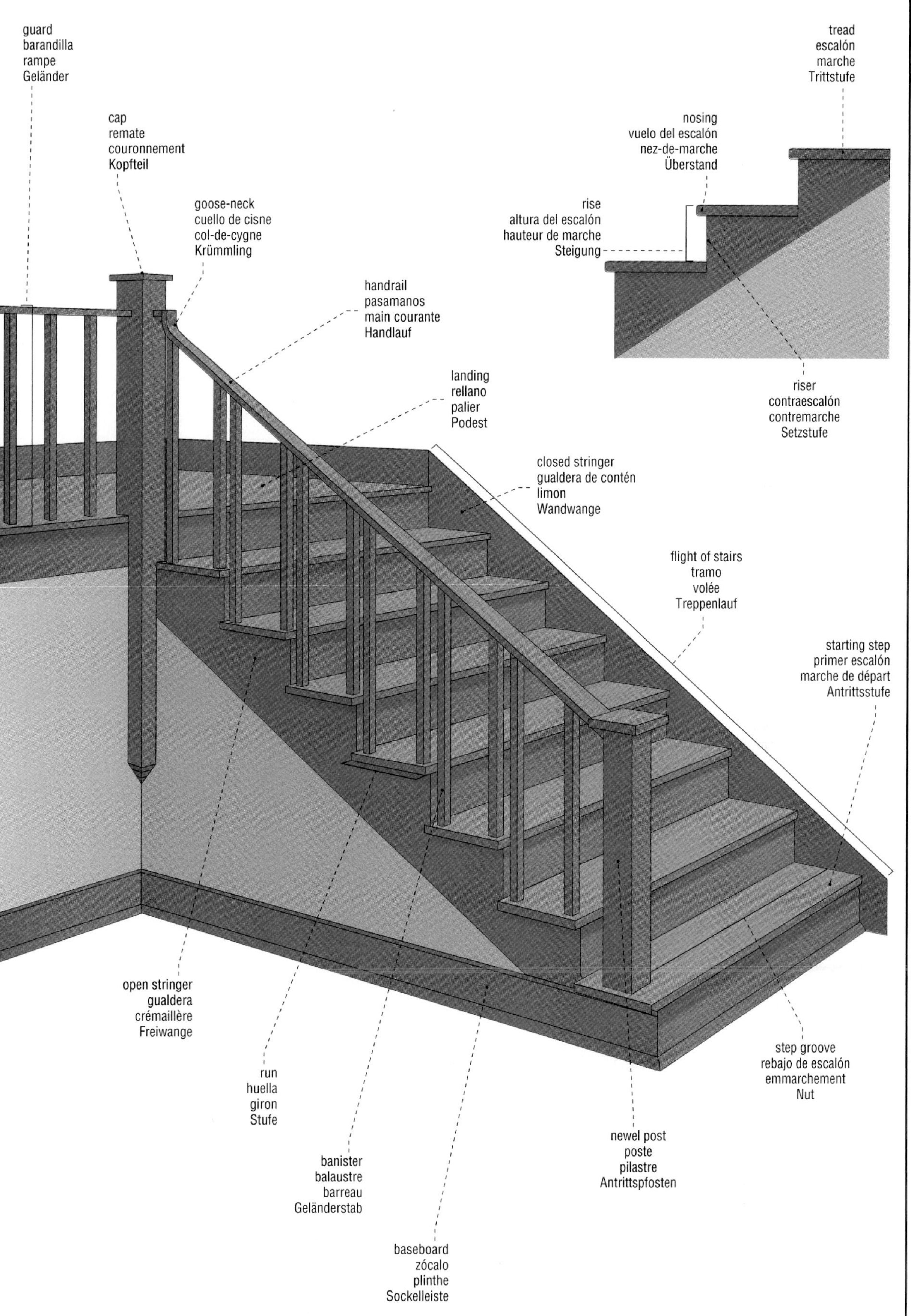
guard
barandilla
rampe
Geländer
cap
remate
couronnement
Kopfteil
goose-neck
cuello de cisne
col-de-cygne
Krümmling
handrail
pasamanos
main courante
Handlauf
landing
rellano
palier
Podest
tread
escalón
marche
Trittstufe
nosing
vuelo del escalón
nez-de-marche
Überstand
rise
altura del escalón
hauteur de marche
Steigung
riser
contraescalón
contremarche
Setzstufe
closed stringer
gualdera de contén
limon
Wandwange
flight of stairs
tramo
volée
Treppenlauf
starting step
primer escalón
marche de départ
Antrittsstufe
open stringer
gualdera
crémaillère
Freiwange
run
huella
giron
Stufe
banister
balaustre
barreau
Geländerstab
baseboard
zócalo
plinthe
Sockelleiste
newel post
poste
pilastre
Antrittspfosten
step groove
rebajo de escalón
emmarchement
Nut

DOOR
PUERTA
PORTE
TÜR

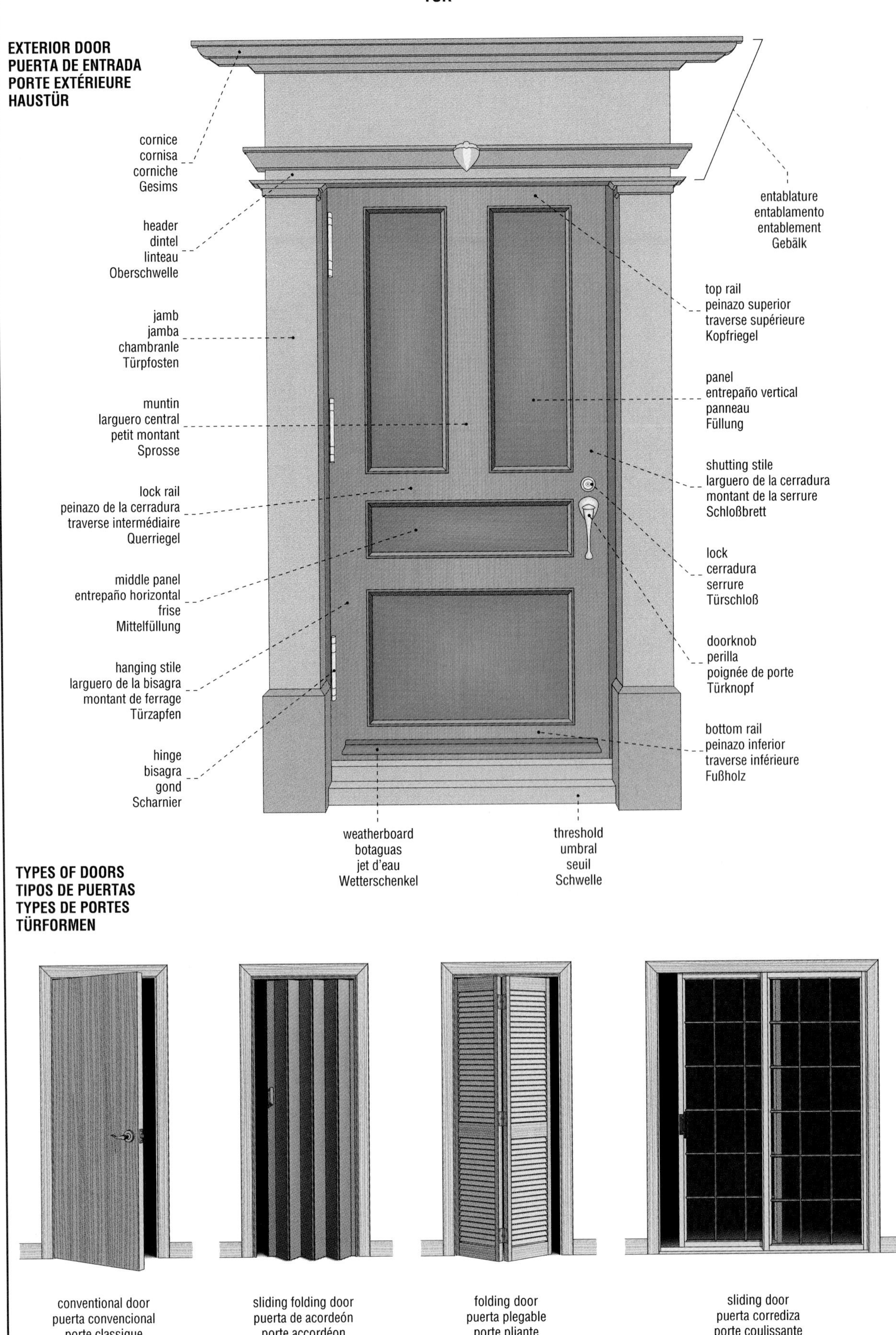
EXTERIOR DOOR
PUERTA DE ENTRADA
PORTE EXTÉRIEURE
HAUSTÜR
cornice
cornisa
corniche
Gesims
header
dintel
linteau
Oberschwelle
jamb
jamba
chambranle
Türpfosten
muntin
larguero central
petit montant
Sprosse
lock rail
peinazo de la cerradura
traverse intermédiaire
Querriegel
middle panel
entrepaño horizontal
frise
Mittelfüllung
hanging stile
larguero de la bisagra
montant de ferrage
Türzapfen
hinge
bisagra
gond
Scharnier
entablature
entablamento
entablement
Gebälk
top rail
peinazo superior
traverse supérieure
Kopfriegel
panel
entrepaño vertical
panneau
Füllung
shutting stile
larguero de la cerradura
montant de la serrure
Schloßbrett
lock
cerradura
serrure
Türschloß
doorknob
perilla
poignée de porte
Türknopf
bottom rail
peinazo inferior
traverse inférieure
Fußholz
weatherboard
botaguas
jet d'eau
Wetterschenkel
threshold
umbral
seuil
Schwelle
TYPES OF DOORS
TIPOS DE PUERTAS
TYPES DE PORTES
TÜRFORMEN
conventional door
puerta convencional
porte classique
Drehflügeltür
sliding folding door
puerta de acordeón
porte accordéon
Harmonikatür
folding door
puerta plegable
porte pliante
Falttür
sliding door
puerta corrediza
porte coulissante
Schiebetür

WINDOW
VENTANA
FENÊTRE
FENSTER

STRUCTURE
ESTRUCTURA
STRUCTURE
KONSTRUKTION

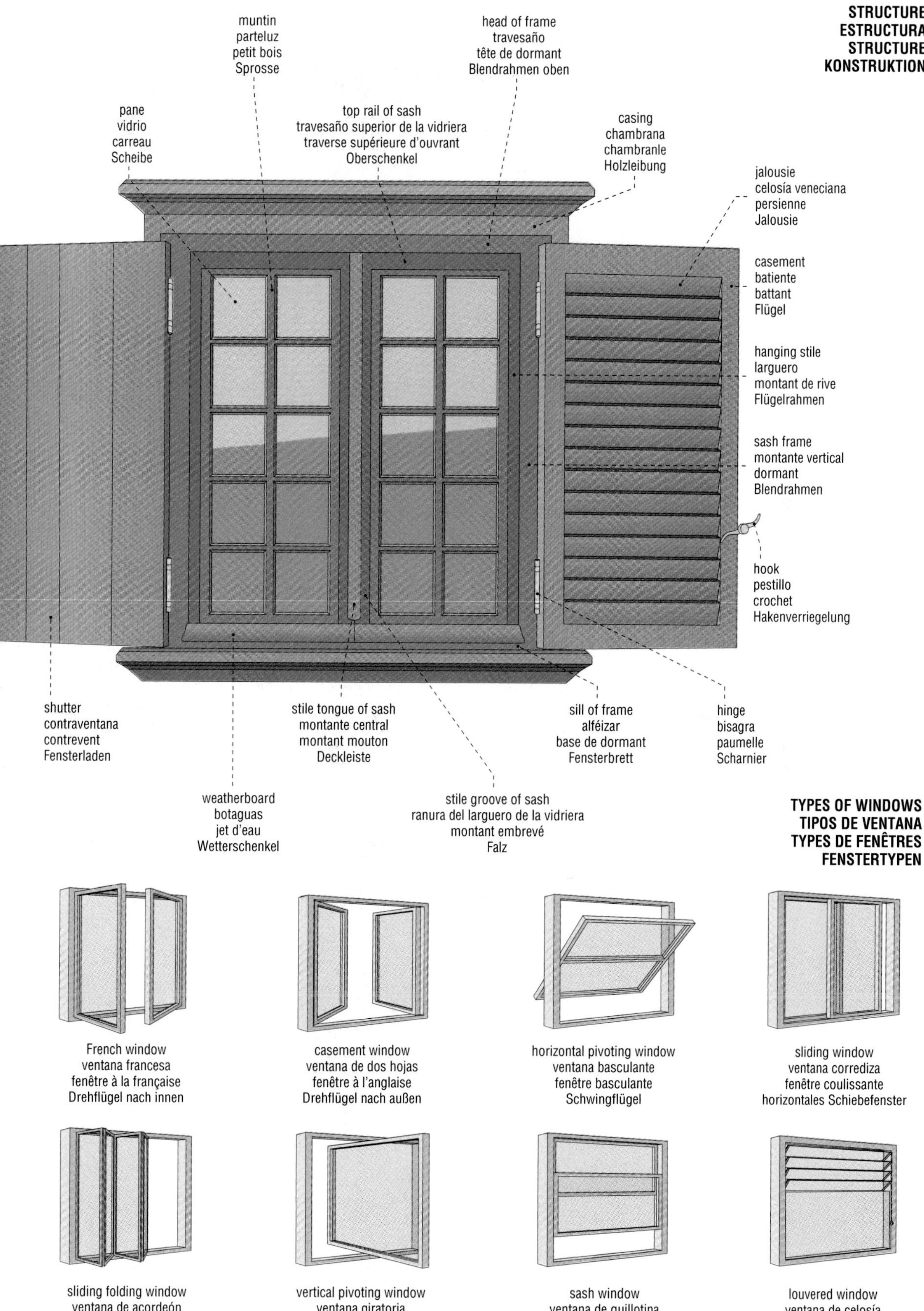
muntin
parteluz
petit bois
Sprosse
head of frame
travesaño
tête de dormant
Blendrahmen oben
pane
vidrio
carreau
Scheibe
top rail of sash
travesaño superior de la vidriera
traverse supérieure d'ouvrant
Oberschenkel
casing
chambrana
chambranle
Holzleibung
jalousie
celosía veneciana
persienne
Jalousie
casement
batiente
battant
Flügel
hanging stile
larguero
montant de rive
Flügelrahmen
sash frame
montante vertical
dormant
Blendrahmen
hook
pestillo
crochet
Hakenverriegelung
shutter
contraventana
contrevent
Fensterladen
stile tongue of sash
montante central
montant mouton
Deckleiste
sill of frame
alféizar
base de dormant
Fensterbrett
hinge
bisagra
paumelle
Scharnier
weatherboard
botaguas
jet d'eau
Wetterschenkel
stile groove of sash
ranura del larguero de la vidriera
montant embrevé
Falz

TYPES OF WINDOWS
TIPOS DE VENTANA
TYPES DE FENÊTRES
FENSTERTYPEN

French window
ventana francesa
fenêtre à la française
Drehflügel nach innen
casement window
ventana de dos hojas
fenêtre à l'anglaise
Drehflügel nach außen
horizontal pivoting window
ventana basculante
fenêtre basculante
Schwingflügel
sliding window
ventana corrediza
fenêtre coulissante
horizontales Schiebefenster
sliding folding window
ventana de acordeón
fenêtre en accordéon
Faltfenster
vertical pivoting window
ventana giratoria
fenêtre pivotante
Wendeflügel
sash window
ventana de guillotina
fenêtre à guillotine
vertikales Schiebefenster
louvered window
ventana de celosía
fenêtre à jalousies
Jalousiefenster

HEATING
CALEFACCIÓN
CHAUFFAGE
HEIZUNG

FIREPLACE
CHIMENEA
CHEMINÉE À FOYER OUVERT
KAMIN

SLOW-BURNING STOVE
ESTUFA DE LEÑA A FUEGO LENTO
POÊLE À COMBUSTION LENTE
LANGSAM BRENNENDER OFEN

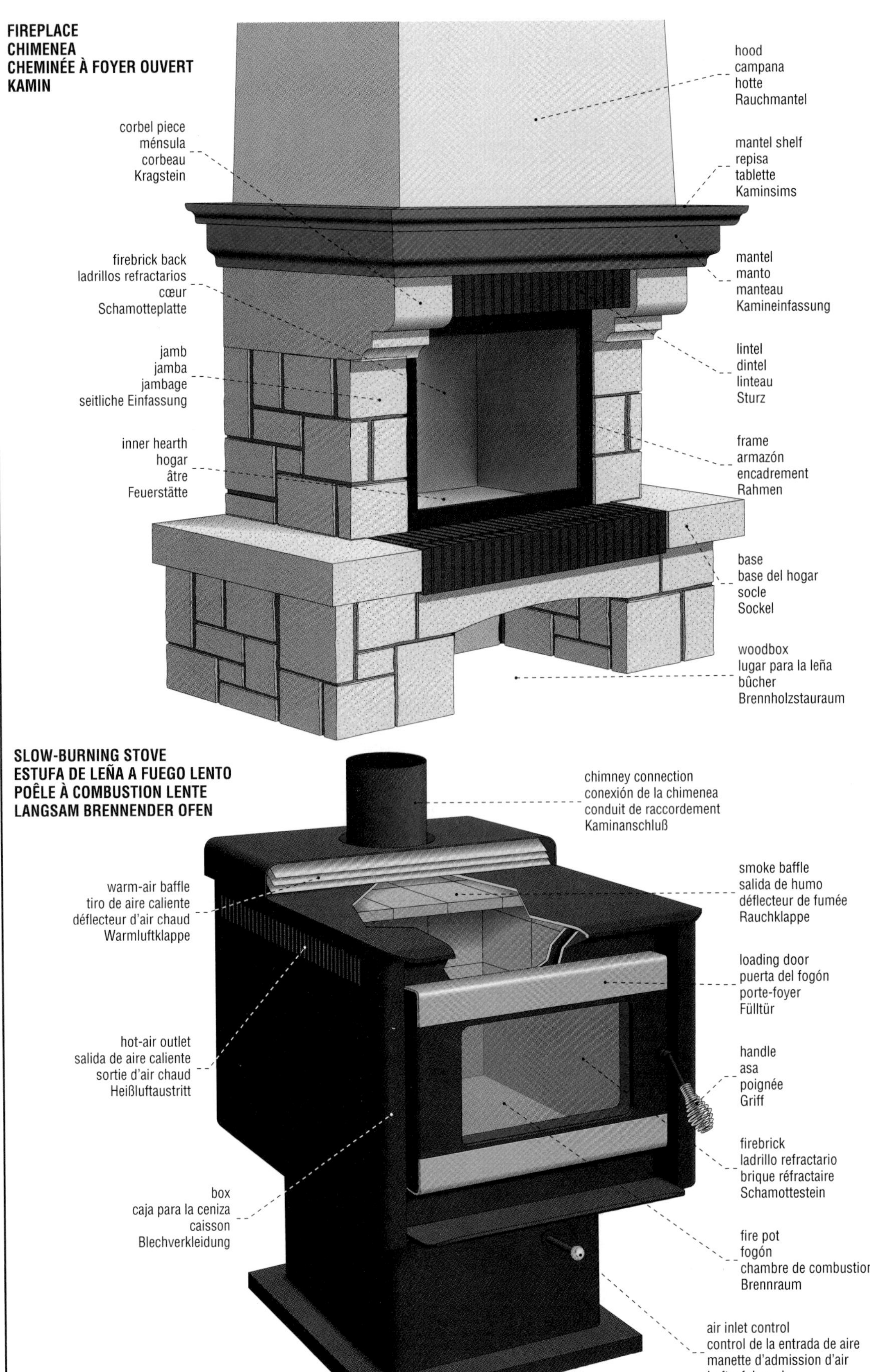
hood
campana
hotte
Rauchmantel
corbel piece
ménsula
corbeau
Kragstein
mantel shelf
repisa
tablette
Kaminsims
firebrick back
ladrillos refractarios
cœur
Schamotteplatte
mantel
manto
manteau
Kamineinfassung
jamb
jamba
jambage
seitliche Einfassung
lintel
dintel
linteau
Sturz
inner hearth
hogar
âtre
Feuerstätte
frame
armazón
encadrement
Rahmen
base
base del hogar
socle
Sockel
woodbox
lugar para la leña
bûcher
Brennholzstauraum
chimney connection
conexión de la chimenea
conduit de raccordement
Kaminanschluß
warm-air baffle
tiro de aire caliente
déflecteur d'air chaud
Warmluftklappe
smoke baffle
salida de humo
déflecteur de fumée
Rauchklappe
loading door
puerta del fogón
porte-foyer
Fülltür
hot-air outlet
salida de aire caliente
sortie d'air chaud
Heißluftaustritt
handle
asa
poignée
Griff
firebrick
ladrillo refractario
brique réfractaire
Schamottestein
box
caja para la ceniza
caisson
Blechverkleidung
fire pot
fogón
chambre de combustion
Brennraum
air inlet control
control de la entrada de aire
manette d'admission d'air
Luftzufuhrregler

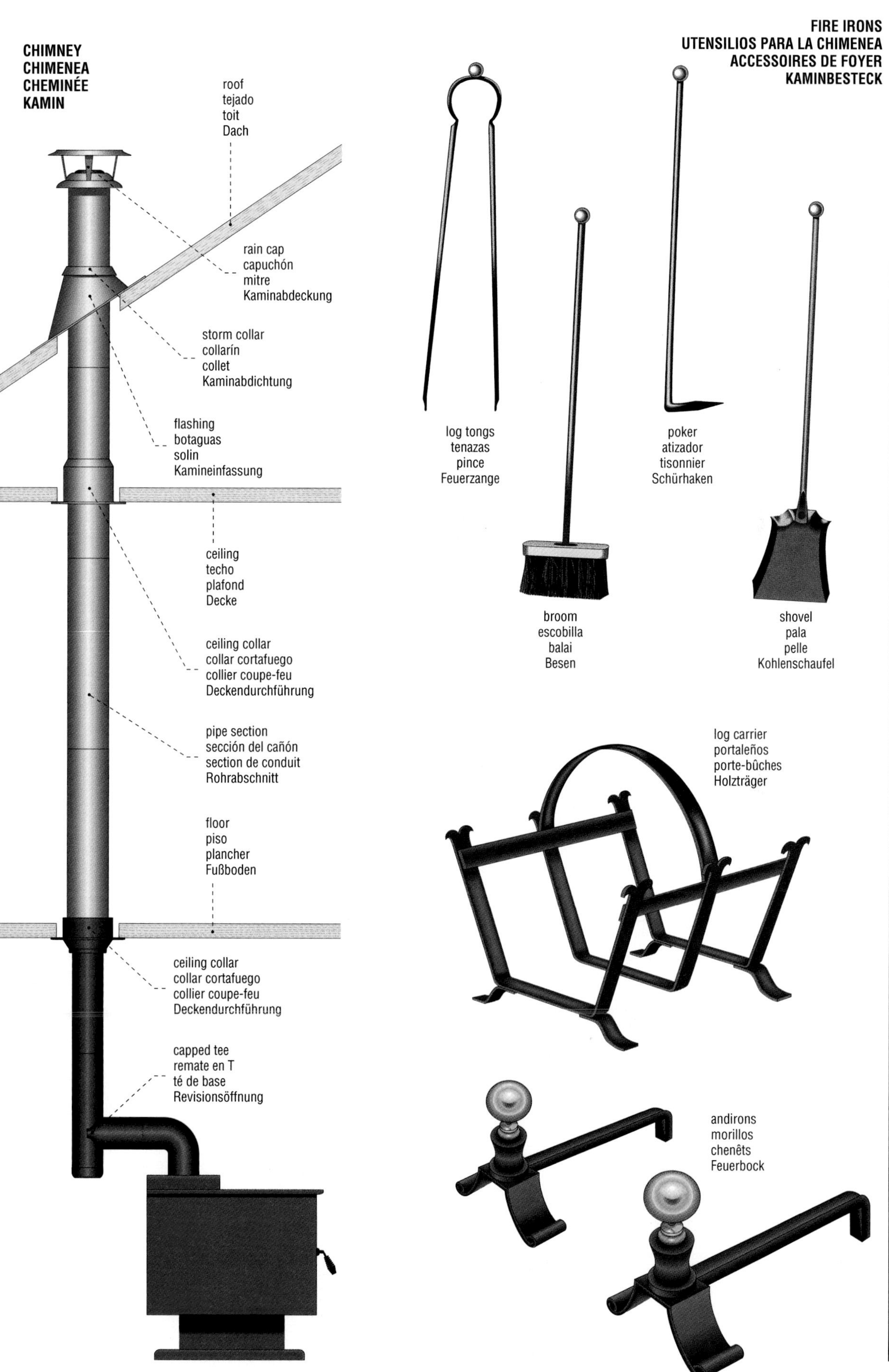
CHIMNEY
CHIMENEA
CHEMINÉE
KAMIN
roof
tejado
toit
Dach
rain cap
capuchón
mitre
Kaminabdeckung
storm collar
collarín
collet
Kaminabdichtung
flashing
botaguas
solin
Kamineinfassung
ceiling
techo
plafond
Decke
ceiling collar
collar cortafuego
collier coupe-feu
Deckendurchführung
pipe section
sección del cañón
section de conduit
Rohrabschnitt
floor
piso
plancher
Fußboden
ceiling collar
collar cortafuego
collier coupe-feu
Deckendurchführung
capped tee
remate en T
té de base
Revisionsöffnung
FIRE IRONS
UTENSILIOS PARA LA CHIMENEA
ACCESSOIRES DE FOYER
KAMINBESTECK
log tongs
tenazas
pince
Feuerzange
poker
atizador
tisonnier
Schürhaken
broom
escobilla
balai
Besen
shovel
pala
pelle
Kohlenschaufel
log carrier
portaleños
porte-bûches
Holzträger
andirons
morillos
chenêts
Feuerbock

FORCED WARM-AIR SYSTEM
SISTEMA DE AIRE CALIENTE A PRESIÓN
INSTALLATION À AIR CHAUD PULSÉ
WARMLUFTSYSTEM MIT ZWANGSUMLAUF

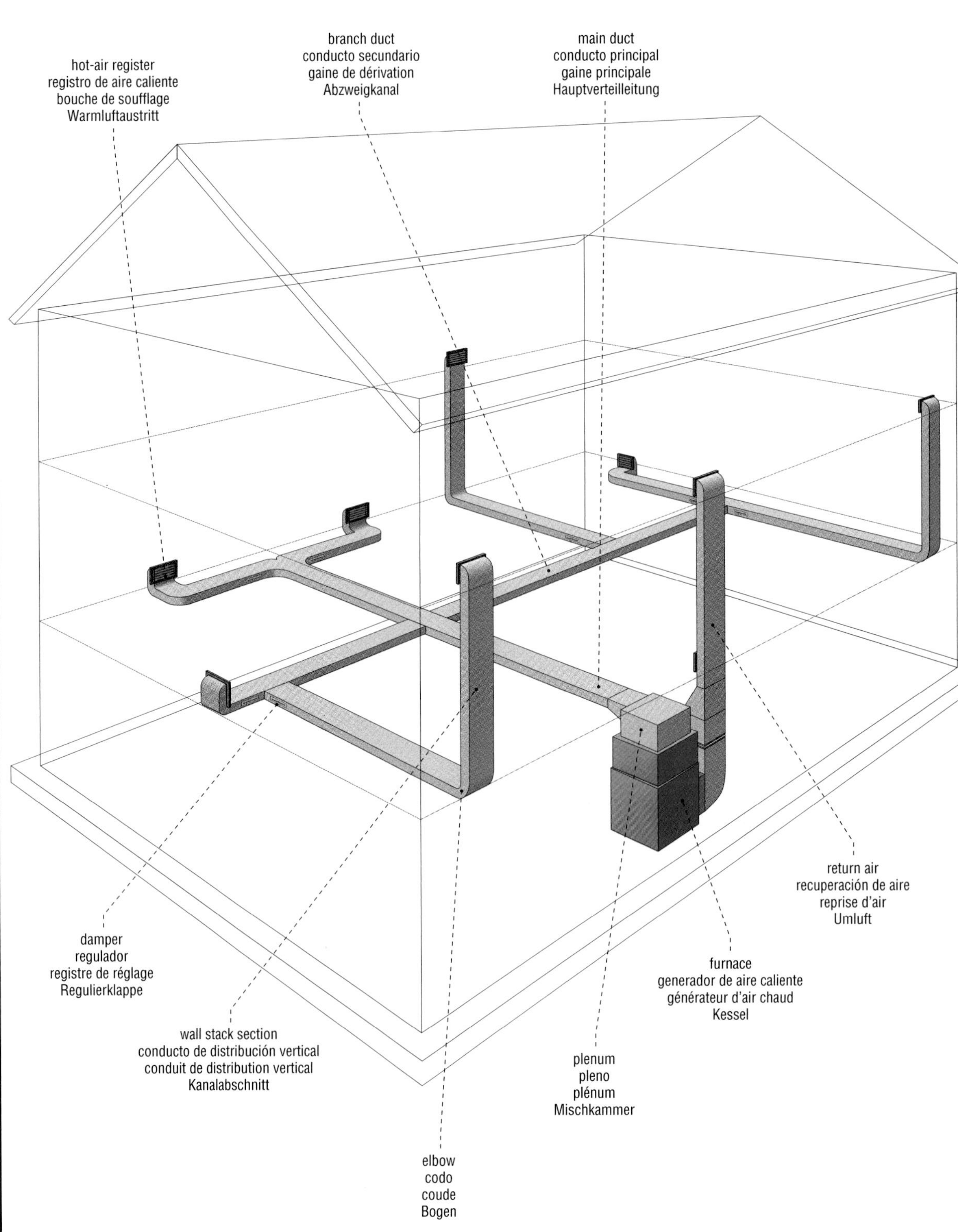
hot-air register
registro de aire caliente
bouche de soufflage
Warmluftaustritt
branch duct
conducto secundario
gaine de dérivation
Abzweigkanal
main duct
conducto principal
gaine principale
Hauptverteilleitung
return air
recuperación de aire
reprise d'air
Umluft
damper
regulador
registre de réglage
Regulierklappe
furnace
generador de aire caliente
générateur d'air chaud
Kessel
wall stack section
conducto de distribución vertical
conduit de distribution vertical
Kanalabschnitt
plenum
pleno
plénum
Mischkammer
elbow
codo
coude
Bogen

ELECTRIC FURNACE
CALEFACCIÓN ELÉCTRICA
GÉNÉRATEUR D'AIR CHAUD ÉLECTRIQUE
ELEKTRISCHER KESSEL

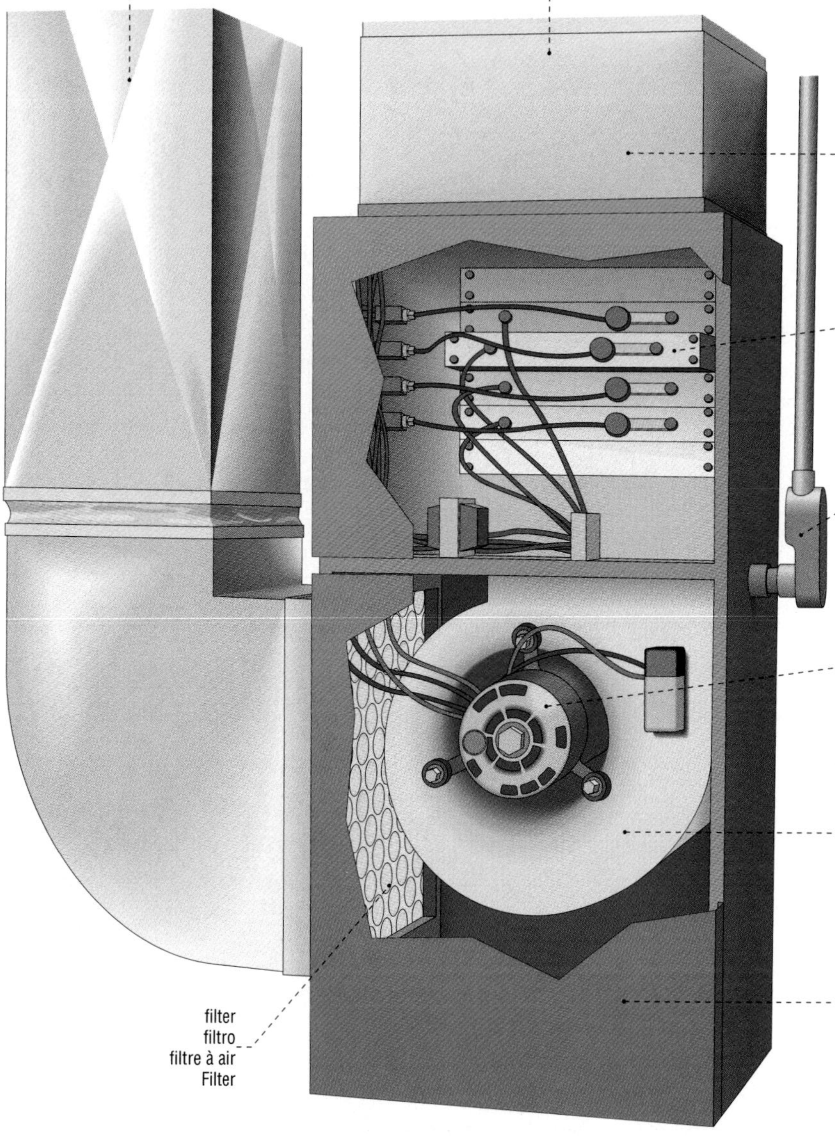

return air
recuperación de aire
reprise d'air
Umluft

hot-air outflow
salida de aire caliente
sortie d'air chaud
Warmluftaustritt

plenum
pleno
plénum
Mischkammer

heating element
elemento calorífero
élément de chauffe
Heizelement

electric connection
conexión eléctrica
entrée électrique
Stromanschluß

blower motor
motor del ventilador
moteur
Gebläsemotor

blower
ventilador
ventilateur
Gebläse

access panel
panel de acceso
panneau d'accès
Revisionstür

filter
filtro
filtre à air
Filter

TYPES OF REGISTERS
REJILLAS
TYPES DE BOUCHES
LUFTDURCHLÄSSE

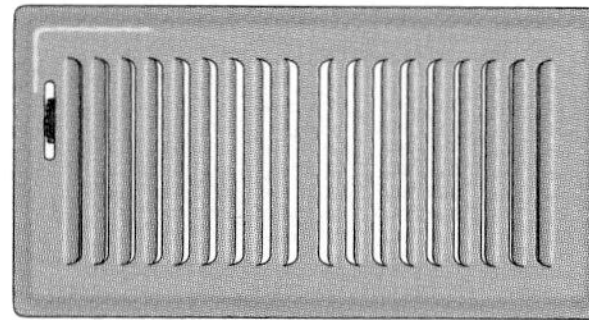

baseboard register
rejilla de piso
bouche de soufflage
Leistendurchlaß

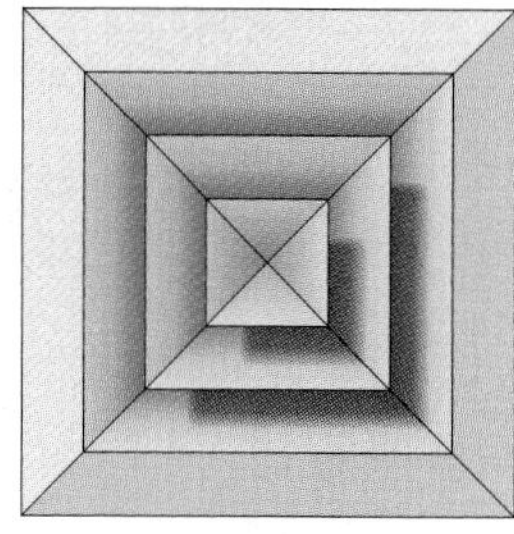

ceiling register
rejilla de techo
bouche à induction
Deckendurchlaß

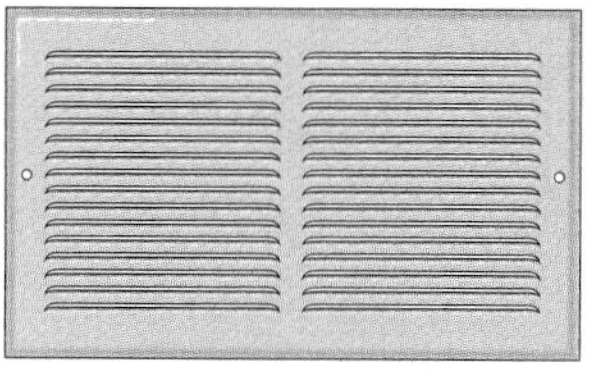

wall register
rejilla de pared
bouche d'extraction
Wanddurchlaß

HEATING
CALEFACCIÓN
CHAUFFAGE
HEIZUNG

FORCED HOT-WATER SYSTEM
SISTEMA DE AGUA CALIENTE A PRESIÓN
INSTALLATION À EAU CHAUDE
WARMWASSERHEIZUNG MIT ZWANGSUMLAUF

COLUMN RADIATOR
RADIADOR TUBULAR
RADIATEUR À COLONNES
PLATTENHEIZKÖRPER

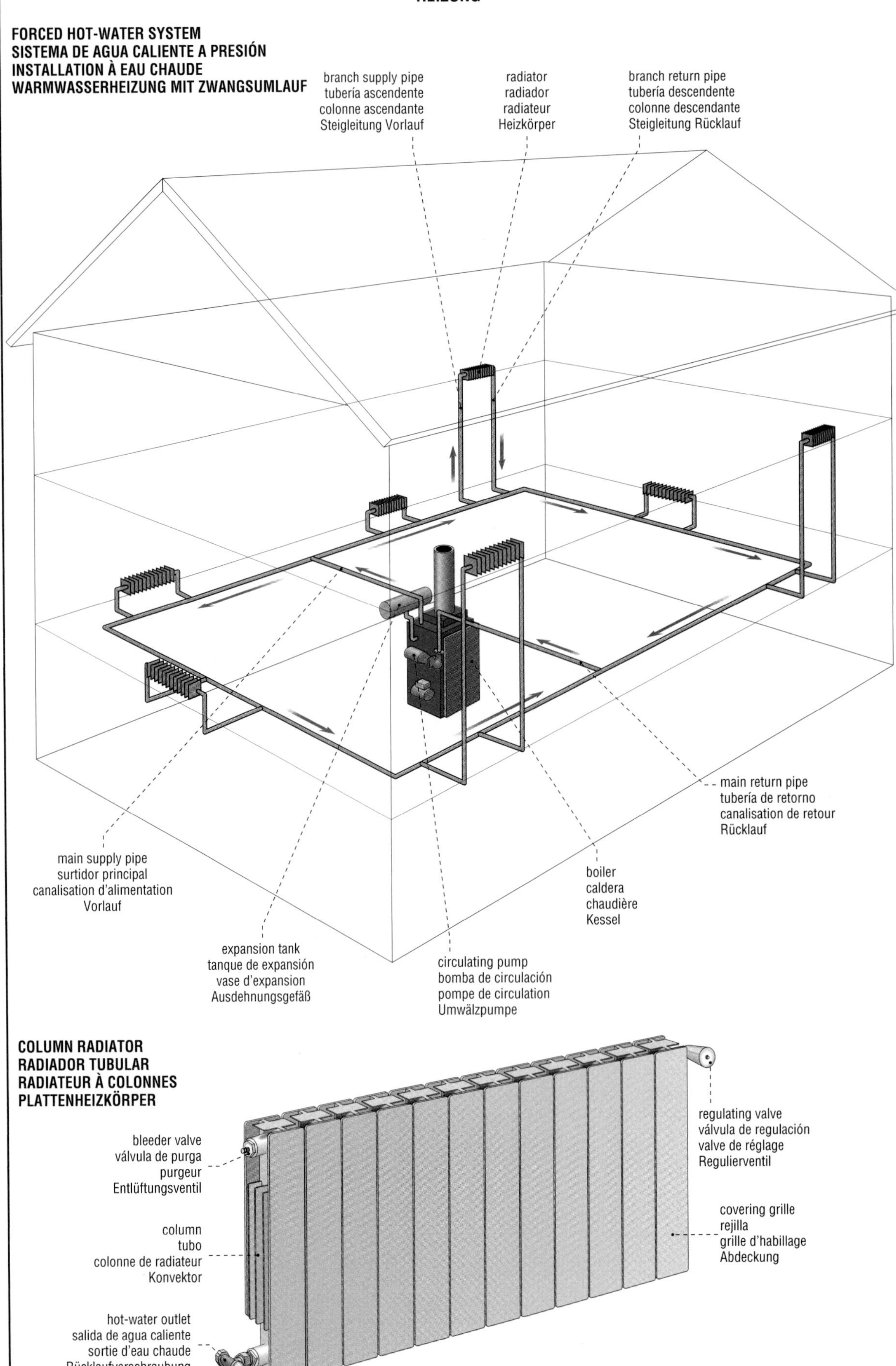
branch supply pipe
tubería ascendente
colonne ascendante
Steigleitung Vorlauf
radiator
radiador
radiateur
Heizkörper
branch return pipe
tubería descendente
colonne descendante
Steigleitung Rücklauf
main return pipe
tubería de retorno
canalisation de retour
Rücklauf
main supply pipe
surtidor principal
canalisation d'alimentation
Vorlauf
boiler
caldera
chaudière
Kessel
expansion tank
tanque de expansión
vase d'expansion
Ausdehnungsgefäß
circulating pump
bomba de circulación
pompe de circulation
Umwälzpumpe
regulating valve
válvula de regulación
valve de réglage
Regulierventil
bleeder valve
válvula de purga
purgeur
Entlüftungsventil
covering grille
rejilla
grille d'habillage
Abdeckung
column
tubo
colonne de radiateur
Konvektor
hot-water outlet
salida de agua caliente
sortie d'eau chaude
Rücklaufverschraubung

BOILER
CALDERA
CHAUDIÈRE
KESSEL

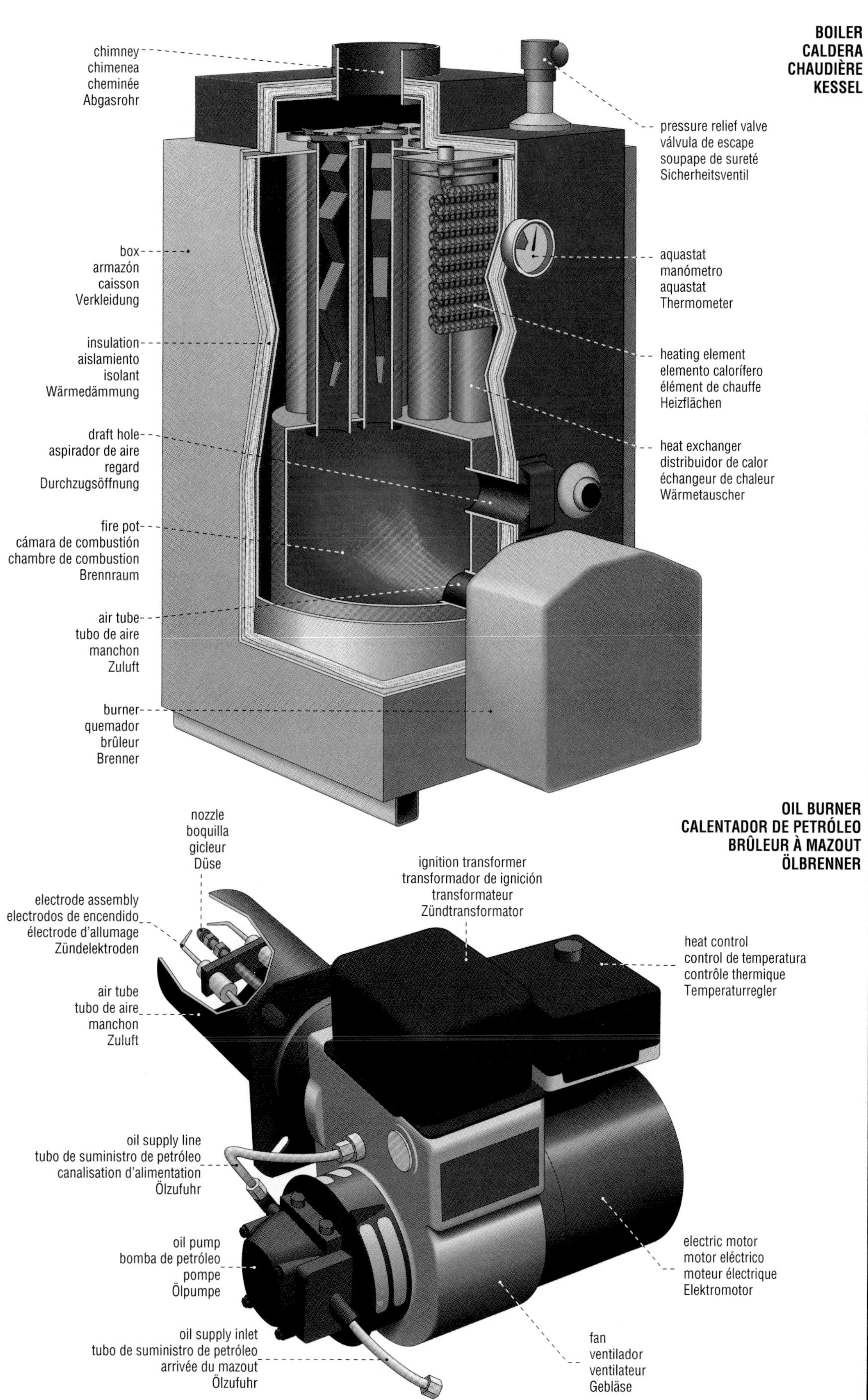
chimney
chimenea
cheminée
Abgasrohr
pressure relief valve
válvula de escape
soupape de sureté
Sicherheitsventil
box
armazón
caisson
Verkleidung
aquastat
manómetro
aquastat
Thermometer
insulation
aislamiento
isolant
Wärmedämmung
heating element
elemento calorífero
élément de chauffe
Heizflächen
draft hole
aspirador de aire
regard
Durchzugsöffnung
heat exchanger
distribuidor de calor
échangeur de chaleur
Wärmetauscher
fire pot
cámara de combustión
chambre de combustion
Brennraum
air tube
tubo de aire
manchon
Zuluft
burner
quemador
brûleur
Brenner
OIL BURNER
CALENTADOR DE PETRÓLEO
BRÛLEUR À MAZOUT
ÖLBRENNER
nozzle
boquilla
gicleur
Düse
ignition transformer
transformador de ignición
transformateur
Zündtransformator
electrode assembly
electrodos de encendido
électrode d'allumage
Zündelektroden
heat control
control de temperatura
contrôle thermique
Temperaturregler
air tube
tubo de aire
manchon
Zuluft
oil supply line
tubo de suministro de petróleo
canalisation d'alimentation
Ölzufuhr
oil pump
bomba de petróleo
pompe
Ölpumpe
electric motor
motor eléctrico
moteur électrique
Elektromotor
oil supply inlet
tubo de suministro de petróleo
arrivée du mazout
Ölzufuhr
fan
ventilador
ventilateur
Gebläse

HEATING
CALEFACCIÓN
CHAUFFAGE
HEIZUNG

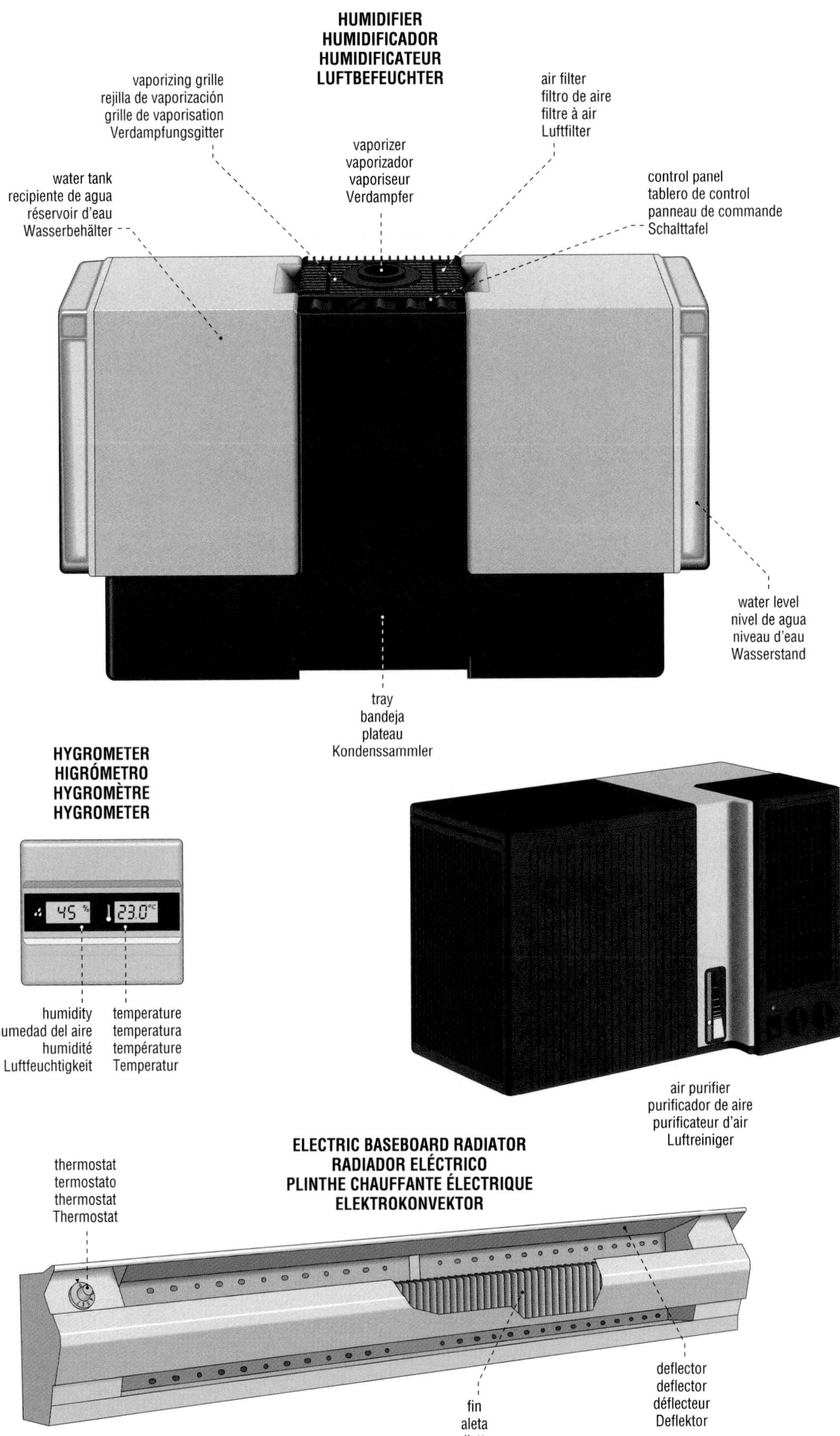
HUMIDIFIER
HUMIDIFICADOR
HUMIDIFICATEUR
LUFTBEFEUCHTER
vaporizing grille
rejilla de vaporización
grille de vaporisation
Verdampfungsgitter
air filter
filtro de aire
filtre à air
Luftfilter
vaporizer
vaporizador
vaporiseur
Verdampfer
water tank
recipiente de agua
réservoir d'eau
Wasserbehälter
control panel
tablero de control
panneau de commande
Schalttafel
water level
nivel de agua
niveau d'eau
Wasserstand
tray
bandeja
plateau
Kondenssammler
HYGROMETER
HIGRÓMETRO
HYGROMÈTRE
HYGROMETER
45 %
23.0 °C
humidity
humedad del aire
humidité
Luftfeuchtigkeit
temperature
temperatura
température
Temperatur
air purifier
purificador de aire
purificateur d'air
Luftreiniger
ELECTRIC BASEBOARD RADIATOR
RADIADOR ELÉCTRICO
PLINTHE CHAUFFANTE ÉLECTRIQUE
ELEKTROKONVEKTOR
thermostat
termostato
thermostat
Thermostat
fin
aleta
ailette
Rippe
deflector
deflector
déflecteur
Deflektor

CONVECTOR
RADIADOR DE CONVEXIÓN
CONVECTEUR
KONVEKTOR

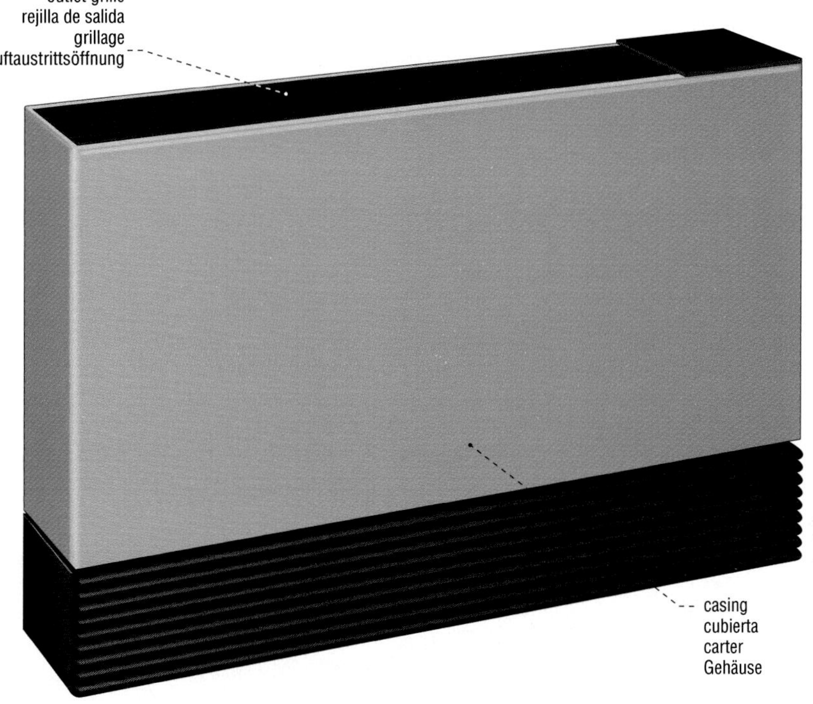

outlet grille
rejilla de salida
grillage
Luftaustrittsöffnung
casing
cubierta
carter
Gehäuse

AUXILIARY HEATING
CALEFACCIÓN AUXILIAR
CHAUFFAGE D'APPOINT
ZUSATZHEIZUNG

radiant heater
calentador eléctrico
radiateur rayonnant
Heizstrahler

oil-filled heater
calentador de aceite
radiateur bain d'huile
ölgefüllter Heizkörper

fan heater
ventilador de aire caliente
radiateur soufflant
Heizlüfter

HEAT PUMP
SISTEMA DE BOMBA DE CALOR
POMPE À CHALEUR
WÄRMEPUMPE

OUTDOOR UNIT
UNIDAD EXTERIOR
MODULE EXTÉRIEUR
ANLAGE FÜR AUSSENAUFSTELLUNG

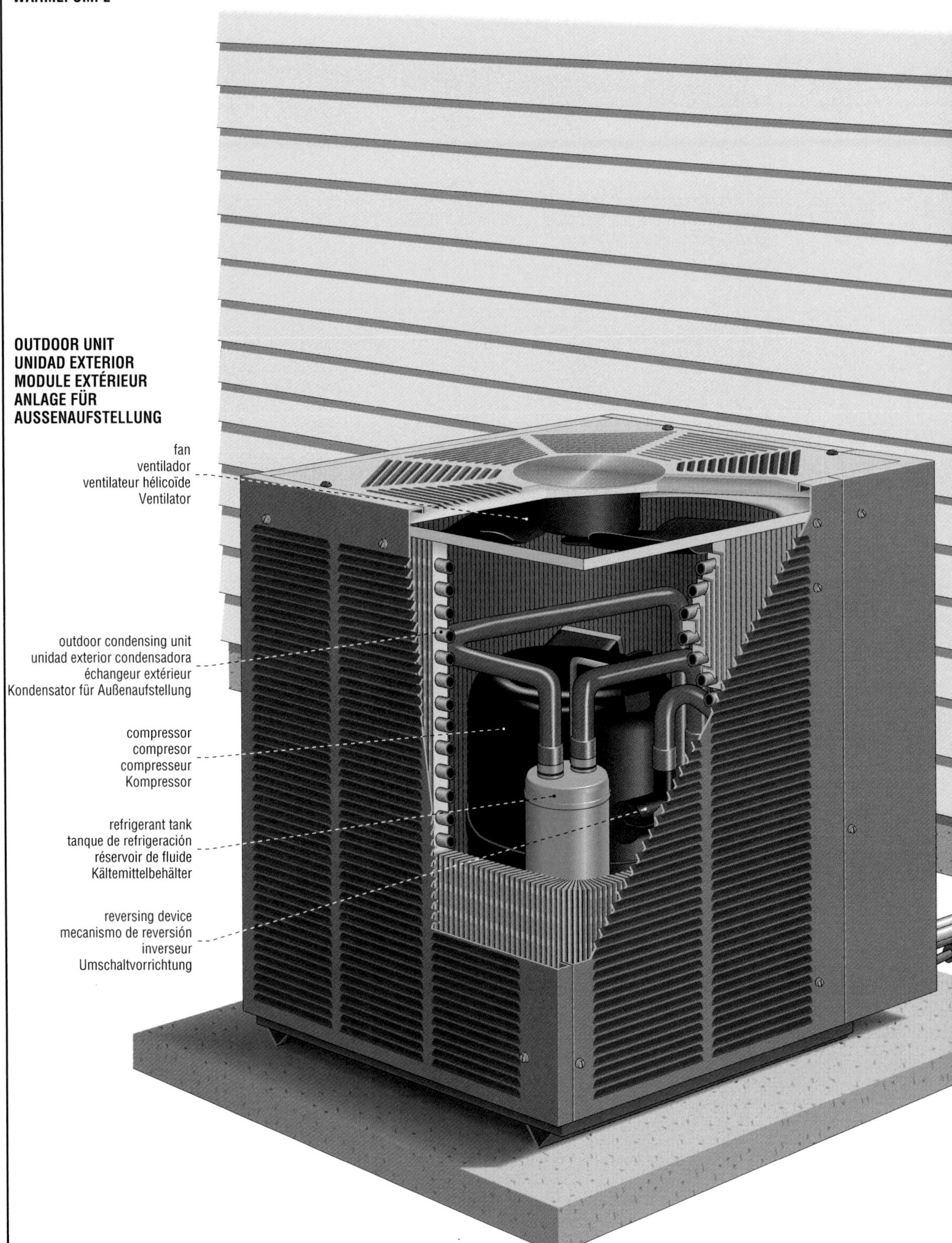
fan
ventilador
ventilateur hélicoïde
Ventilator
outdoor condensing unit
unidad exterior condensadora
échangeur extérieur
Kondensator für Außenaufstellung
compressor
compresor
compresseur
Kompressor
refrigerant tank
tanque de refrigeración
réservoir de fluide
Kältemittelbehälter
reversing device
mecanismo de reversión
inverseur
Umschaltvorrichtung

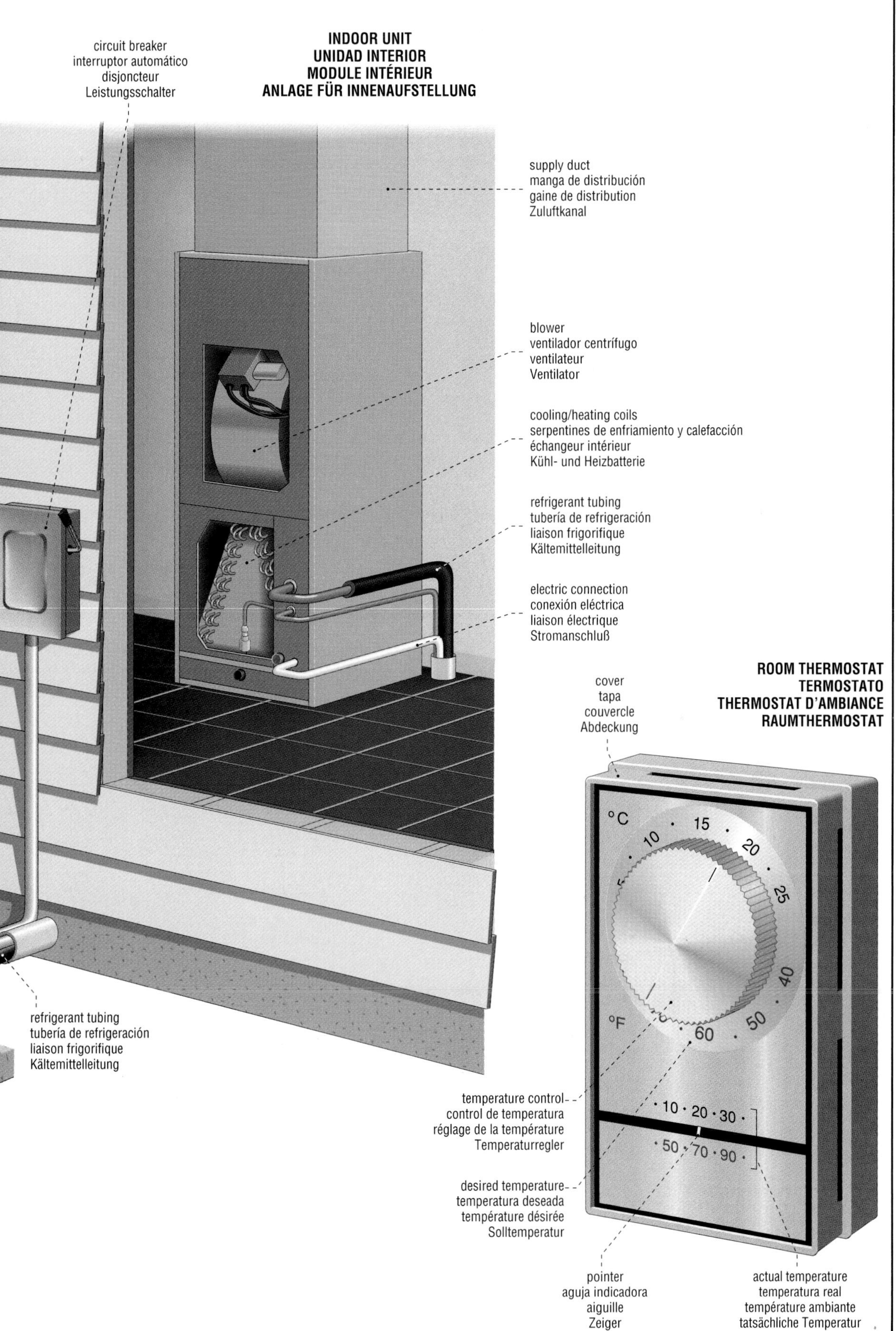
circuit breaker
interruptor automático
disjoncteur
Leistungsschalter
INDOOR UNIT
UNIDAD INTERIOR
MODULE INTÉRIEUR
ANLAGE FÜR INNENAUFSTELLUNG
supply duct
manga de distribución
gaine de distribution
Zuluftkanal
blower
ventilador centrífugo
ventilateur
Ventilator
cooling/heating coils
serpentines de enfriamiento y calefacción
échangeur intérieur
Kühl- und Heizbatterie
refrigerant tubing
tubería de refrigeración
liaison frigorifique
Kältemittelleitung
electric connection
conexión eléctrica
liaison électrique
Stromanschluß
refrigerant tubing
tubería de refrigeración
liaison frigorifique
Kältemittelleitung
ROOM THERMOSTAT
TERMOSTATO
THERMOSTAT D'AMBIANCE
RAUMTHERMOSTAT
cover
tapa
couvercle
Abdeckung
°C
10
15
20
25
40
50
60
°F
10 · 20 · 30
50 · 70 · 90
temperature control
control de temperatura
réglage de la température
Temperaturregler
desired temperature
temperatura deseada
température désirée
Solltemperatur
pointer
aguja indicadora
aiguille
Zeiger
actual temperature
temperatura real
température ambiante
tatsächliche Temperatur

AIR CONDITIONING
AIRE ACONDICIONADO
CLIMATISATION
KLIMAANLAGE

CEILING FAN
VENTILADOR DE TECHO
VENTILATEUR DE PLAFOND
DECKENVENTILATOR

rod
flecha
tige
Stange

motor
motor
moteur
Motor

blade
aspa
pale
Blatt

ROOM AIR CONDITIONER
ACONDICIONADOR DE AIRE
CLIMATISEUR DE FENÊTRE
RAUMKLIMAANLAGE

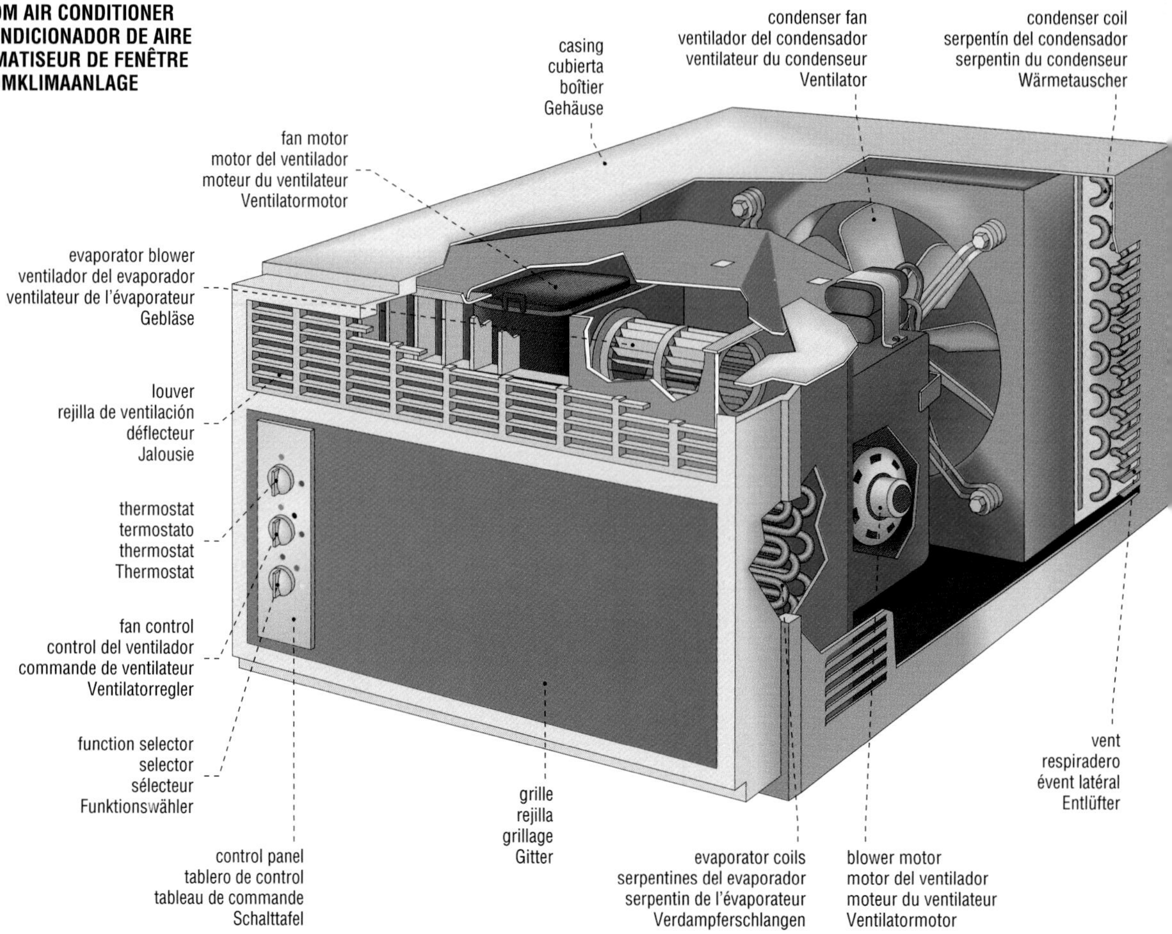

casing
cubierta
boîtier
Gehäuse

condenser fan
ventilador del condensador
ventilateur du condenseur
Ventilator

condenser coil
serpentín del condensador
serpentin du condenseur
Wärmetauscher

fan motor
motor del ventilador
moteur du ventilateur
Ventilatormotor

evaporator blower
ventilador del evaporador
ventilateur de l'évaporateur
Gebläse

louver
rejilla de ventilación
déflecteur
Jalousie

thermostat
termostato
thermostat
Thermostat

fan control
control del ventilador
commande de ventilateur
Ventilatorregler

function selector
selector
sélecteur
Funktionswähler

vent
respiradero
évent latéral
Entlüfter

control panel
tablero de control
tableau de commande
Schalttafel

grille
rejilla
grillage
Gitter

evaporator coils
serpentines del evaporador
serpentin de l'évaporateur
Verdampferschlangen

blower motor
motor del ventilador
moteur du ventilateur
Ventilatormotor

PLUMBING SYSTEM
CAÑERÍAS
CIRCUIT DE PLOMBERIE
SANITÄRINSTALLATIONSSYSTEM

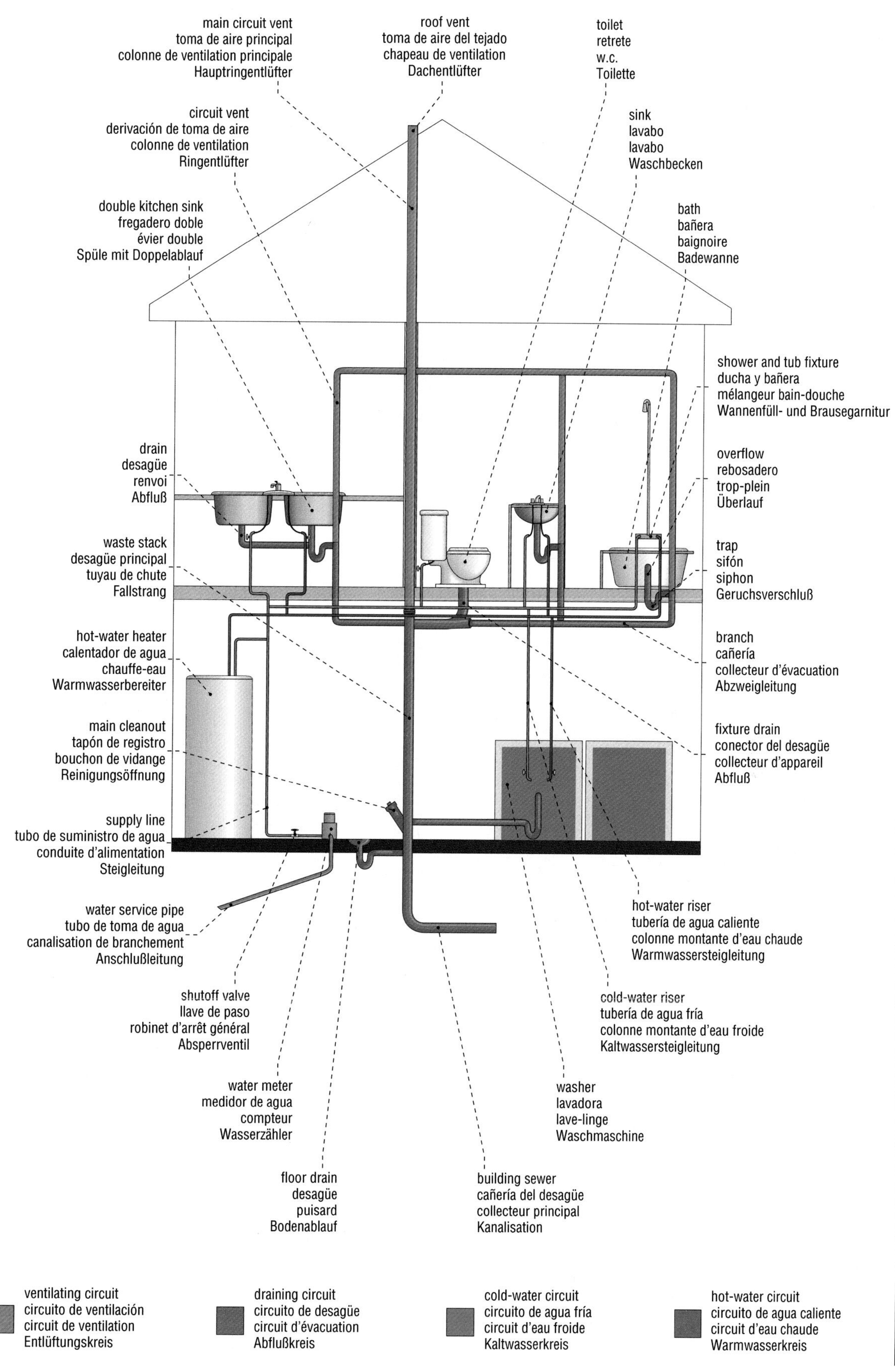
main circuit vent
toma de aire principal
colonne de ventilation principale
Hauptringentlüfter
roof vent
toma de aire del tejado
chapeau de ventilation
Dachentlüfter
toilet
retrete
w.c.
Toilette
circuit vent
derivación de toma de aire
colonne de ventilation
Ringentlüfter
sink
lavabo
lavabo
Waschbecken
double kitchen sink
fregadero doble
évier double
Spüle mit Doppelablauf
bath
bañera
baignoire
Badewanne
shower and tub fixture
ducha y bañera
mélangeur bain-douche
Wannenfüll- und Brausegarnitur
drain
desagüe
renvoi
Abfluß
overflow
rebosadero
trop-plein
Überlauf
waste stack
desagüe principal
tuyau de chute
Fallstrang
trap
sifón
siphon
Geruchsverschluß
hot-water heater
calentador de agua
chauffe-eau
Warmwasserbereiter
branch
cañería
collecteur d'évacuation
Abzweigleitung
main cleanout
tapón de registro
bouchon de vidange
Reinigungsöffnung
fixture drain
conector del desagüe
collecteur d'appareil
Abfluß
supply line
tubo de suministro de agua
conduite d'alimentation
Steigleitung
water service pipe
tubo de toma de agua
canalisation de branchement
Anschlußleitung
hot-water riser
tubería de agua caliente
colonne montante d'eau chaude
Warmwassersteigleitung
shutoff valve
llave de paso
robinet d'arrêt général
Absperrventil
cold-water riser
tubería de agua fría
colonne montante d'eau froide
Kaltwassersteigleitung
water meter
medidor de agua
compteur
Wasserzähler
washer
lavadora
lave-linge
Waschmaschine
floor drain
desagüe
puisard
Bodenablauf
building sewer
cañería del desagüe
collecteur principal
Kanalisation
ventilating circuit
circuito de ventilación
circuit de ventilation
Entlüftungskreis
draining circuit
circuito de desagüe
circuit d'évacuation
Abflußkreis
cold-water circuit
circuito de agua fría
circuit d'eau froide
Kaltwasserkreis
hot-water circuit
circuito de agua caliente
circuit d'eau chaude
Warmwasserkreis

PEDESTAL-TYPE SUMP PUMP
BOMBA TIPO PEDESTAL PARA SUMIDERO
POMPE DE PUISARD
SCHMUTZWASSERHEBEANLAGE

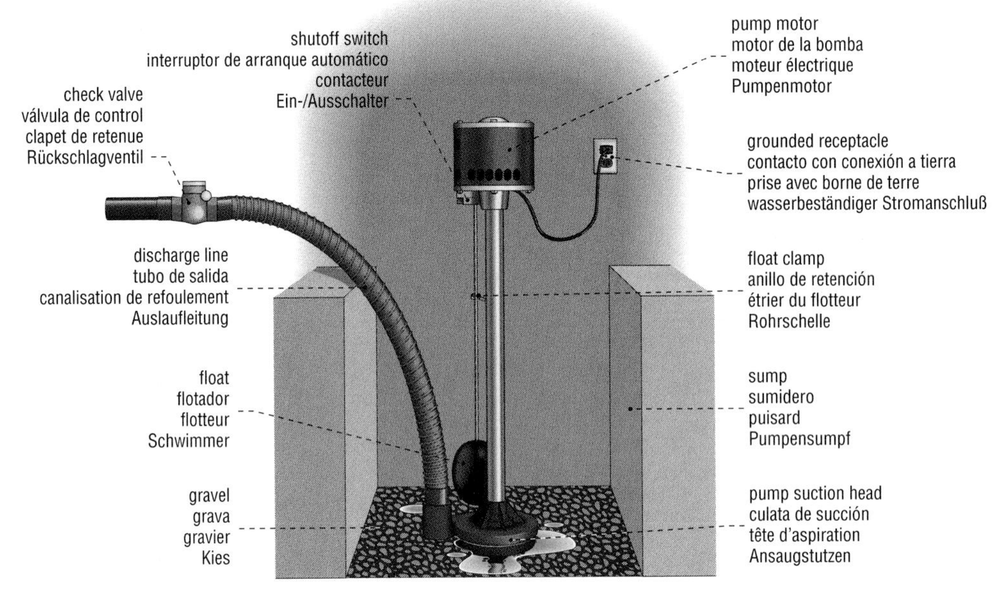
shutoff switch
interruptor de arranque automático
contacteur
Ein-/Ausschalter
pump motor
motor de la bomba
moteur électrique
Pumpenmotor
check valve
válvula de control
clapet de retenue
Rückschlagventil
grounded receptacle
contacto con conexión a tierra
prise avec borne de terre
wasserbeständiger Stromanschluß
discharge line
tubo de salida
canalisation de refoulement
Auslaufleitung
float clamp
anillo de retención
étrier du flotteur
Rohrschelle
float
flotador
flotteur
Schwimmer
sump
sumidero
puisard
Pumpensumpf
gravel
grava
gravier
Kies
pump suction head
culata de succión
tête d'aspiration
Ansaugstutzen

SEPTIC TANK
FOSA SÉPTICA
FOSSE SEPTIQUE
VERSITZGRUBE

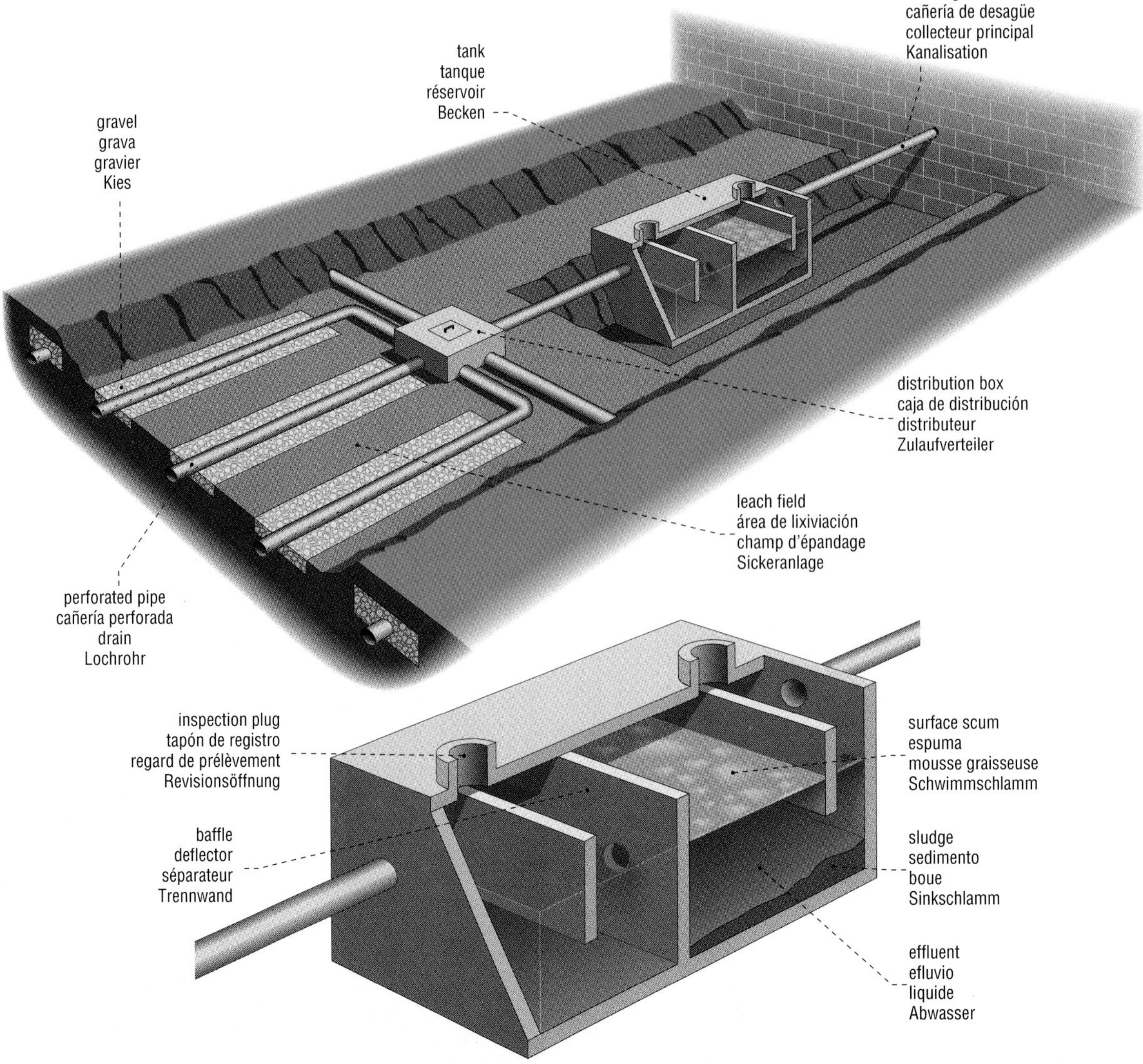

building sewer
cañería de desagüe
collecteur principal
Kanalisation

tank
tanque
réservoir
Becken

gravel
grava
gravier
Kies

distribution box
caja de distribución
distributeur
Zulaufverteiler

leach field
área de lixiviación
champ d'épandage
Sickeranlage

perforated pipe
cañería perforada
drain
Lochrohr

inspection plug
tapón de registro
regard de prélèvement
Revisionsöffnung

surface scum
espuma
mousse graisseuse
Schwimmschlamm

baffle
deflector
séparateur
Trennwand

sludge
sedimento
boue
Sinkschlamm

effluent
efluvio
liquide
Abwasser

HOUSE FURNITURE
AMEUBLEMENT DE LA MAISON
ENSERES DOMÉSTICOS
HAUSEINRICHTUNG

CONTENTS

TABLE
MESA
TABLE
TISCH

GATE-LEG TABLE
MESA DE HOJAS ABATIBLES
TABLE À ABATTANTS
KLAPPTISCH

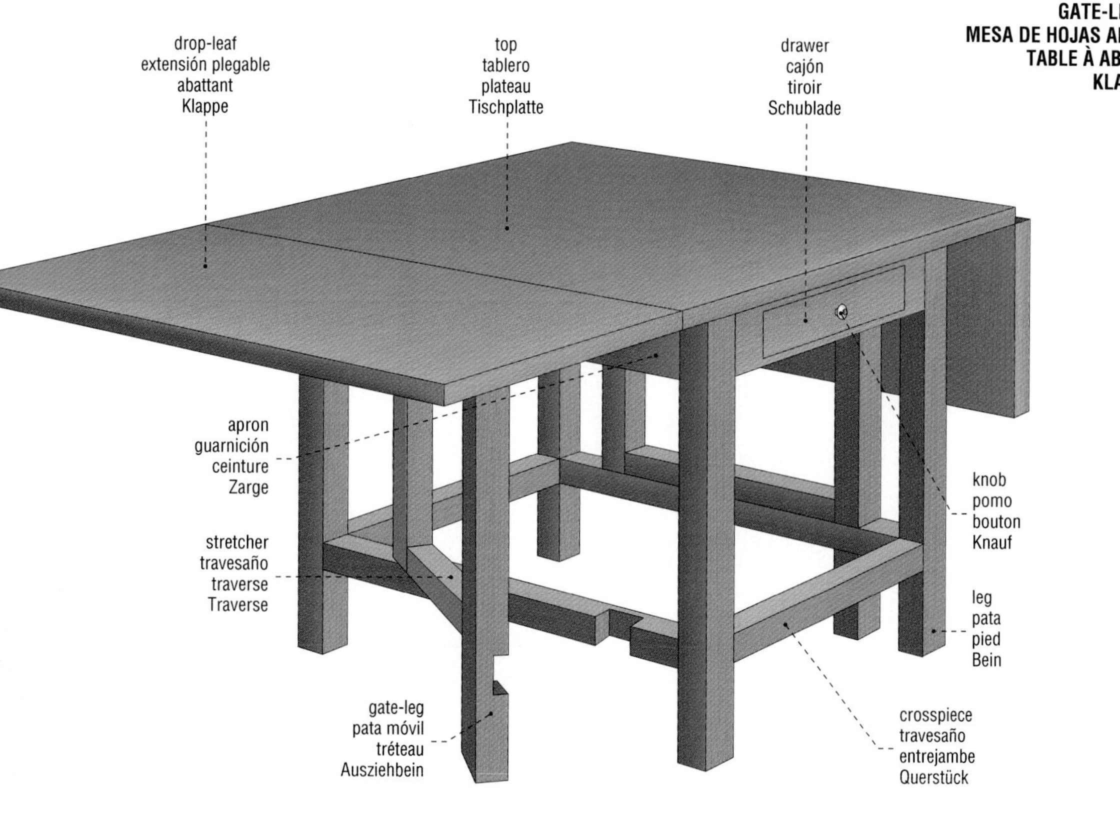
drop-leaf
extensión plegable
abattant
Klappe
top
tablero
plateau
Tischplatte
drawer
cajón
tiroir
Schublade
apron
guarnición
ceinture
Zarge
stretcher
travesaño
traverse
Traverse
knob
pomo
bouton
Knauf
leg
pata
pied
Bein
gate-leg
pata móvil
tréteau
Ausziehbein
crosspiece
travesaño
entrejambe
Querstück

TYPES OF TABLES
TIPOS DE MESAS
PRINCIPAUX TYPES DE TABLES
DIE WICHTIGSTEN TISCHTYPEN

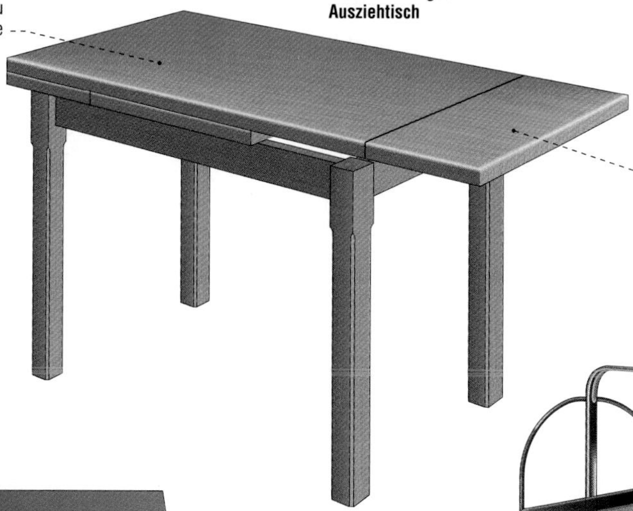

extension table
mesa plegable
table à rallonges
Ausziehtisch

top
tablero
plateau
Tischplatte

extension
extensión
rallonge
Auszug

serving cart
mesita de servicio
desserte
Servierwagen

nest of tables
juego de mesas
tables gigognes
Satztische

ARMCHAIR
SILLA DE BRAZOS
FAUTEUIL
ARMLEHNSTUHL

PARTS
PARTES
PARTIES
TEILE

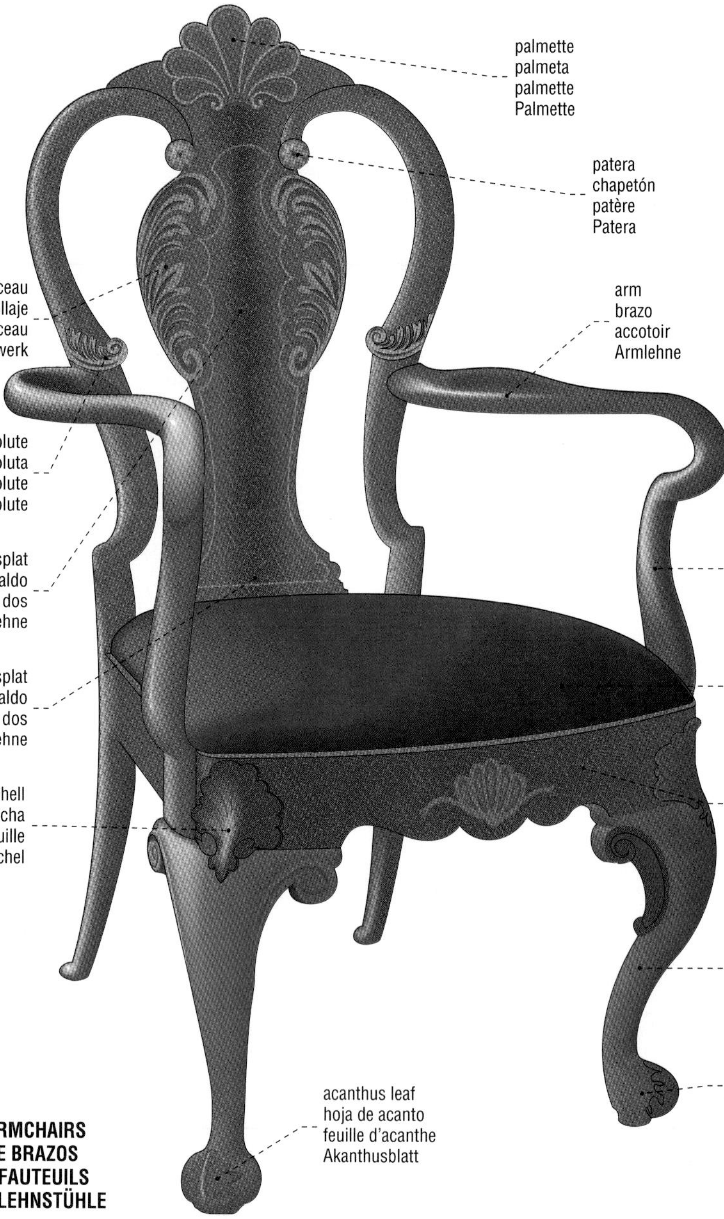

palmette
palmeta
palmette
Palmette

patera
chapetón
patère
Patera

rinceau
follaje
rinceau
Laubwerk

arm
brazo
accotoir
Armlehne

volute
voluta
volute
Volute

arm stump
soporte del brazo
console d'accotoir
Armstütze

splat
respaldo
plat de dos
Rückenlehne

base of splat
base del respaldo
embase de plat de dos
Basis der Stuhllehne

seat
asiento
siège
Sitz

cockleshell
concha
coquille
Muschel

apron
cortina
ceinture
Zarge

cabriole leg
pata curvada
pied cambré
Cabriole-Bein

scroll foot
pie de voluta
volute
Bein mit S-Kurve

acanthus leaf
hoja de acanto
feuille d'acanthe
Akanthusblatt

PRINCIPAL TYPES OF ARMCHAIRS
PRINCIPALES SILLAS DE BRAZOS
PRINCIPAUX TYPES DE FAUTEUILS
DIE WICHTIGSTEN ARMLEHNSTÜHLE

bergère
silla poltrona
bergère
Bergère

cabriolet
silla cabriolé
cabriolet
kleiner Lehnstuhl

director's chair
silla plegable de lona
fauteuil metteur en scène
Regiestuhl

sofa
sofá
canapé
Sofa

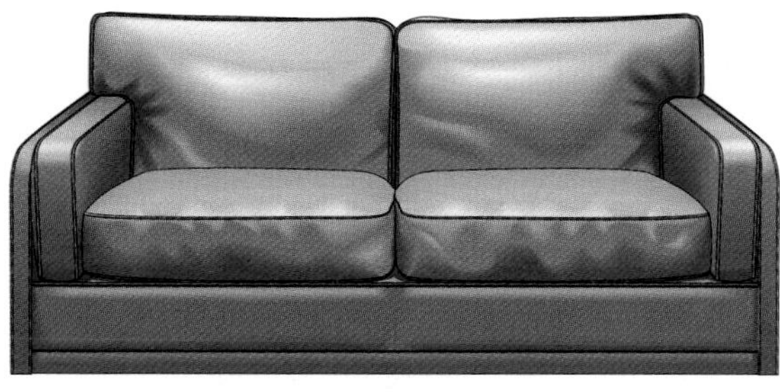

love seat
confidente
causeuse
Zweisitzer

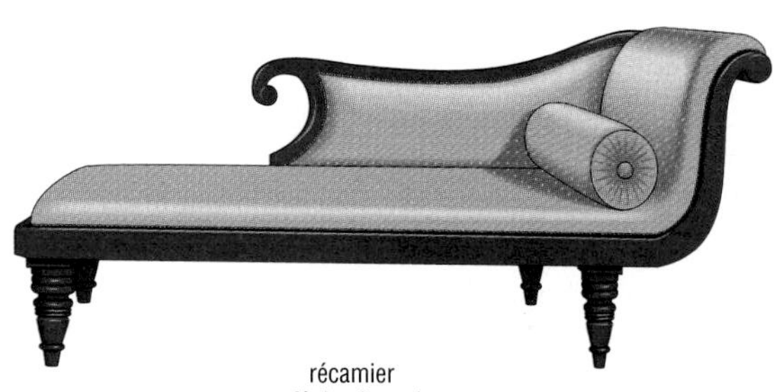

récamier
sofá tipo imperio
récamier
Récamiere

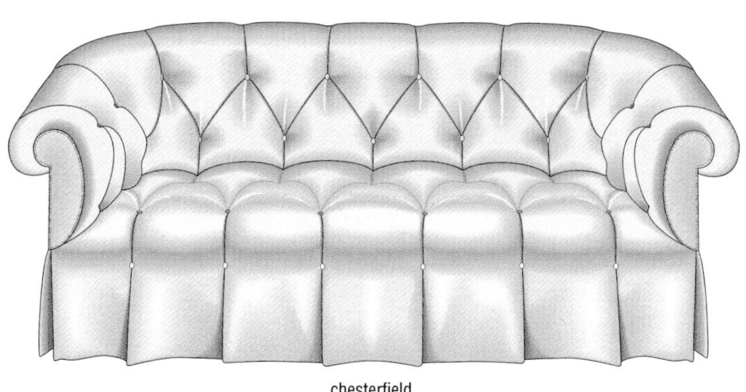

chesterfield
chesterfield
canapé capitonné
Polstersofa

méridienne
meridiana
méridienne
Kanapee

Wassily chair
silla Wassily
fauteuil Wassily
Wassily-Stuhl

rocking chair
mecedora
berceuse
Schaukelstuhl

club chair
butaca
fauteuil club
Clubsessel

SEATS
ASIENTOS
SIÈGES
SITZMÖBEL

banquette
banco
banquette
Sitzbank
ottoman
taburete
pouf
Puff
bean bag chair
silla cojín
fauteuil-sac
Sitzsack
bench
banco
banc
Bank
bar stool
taburete
tabouret-bar
Barhocker
footstool
escabel
tabouret
Hocker
step chair
banco escalera
chaise-escabeau
Tritthocker

SIDE CHAIR
SILLA SIN BRAZOS
CHAISE
STUHL

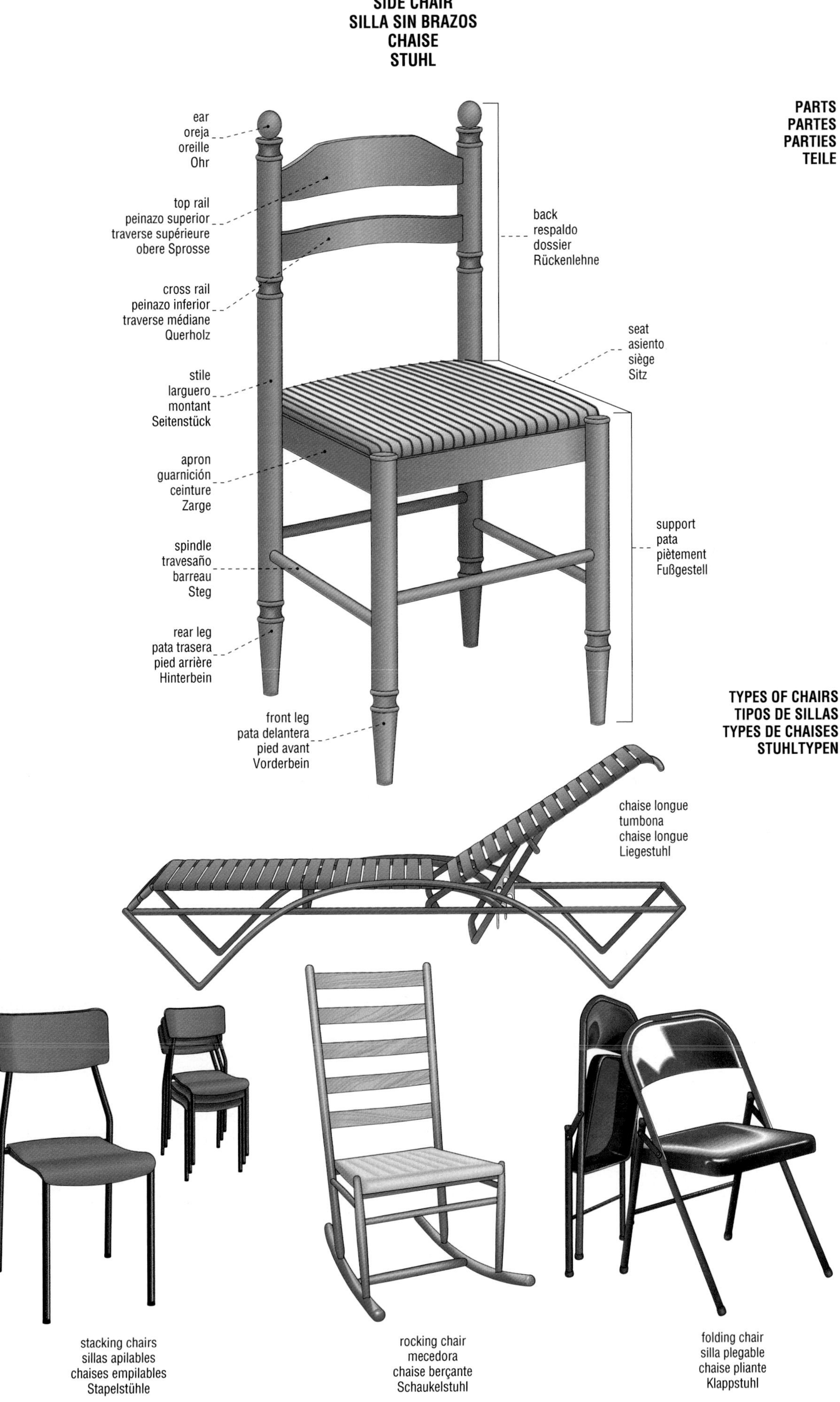
ear
oreja
oreille
Ohr
top rail
peinazo superior
traverse supérieure
obere Sprosse
cross rail
peinazo inferior
traverse médiane
Querholz
stile
larguero
montant
Seitenstück
apron
guarnición
ceinture
Zarge
spindle
travesaño
barreau
Steg
rear leg
pata trasera
pied arrière
Hinterbein
front leg
pata delantera
pied avant
Vorderbein
back
respaldo
dossier
Rückenlehne
seat
asiento
siège
Sitz
support
pata
piètement
Fußgestell
chaise longue
tumbona
chaise longue
Liegestuhl
stacking chairs
sillas apilables
chaises empilables
Stapelstühle
rocking chair
mecedora
chaise berçante
Schaukelstuhl
folding chair
silla plegable
chaise pliante
Klappstuhl

BED
CAMA
LIT
BETT

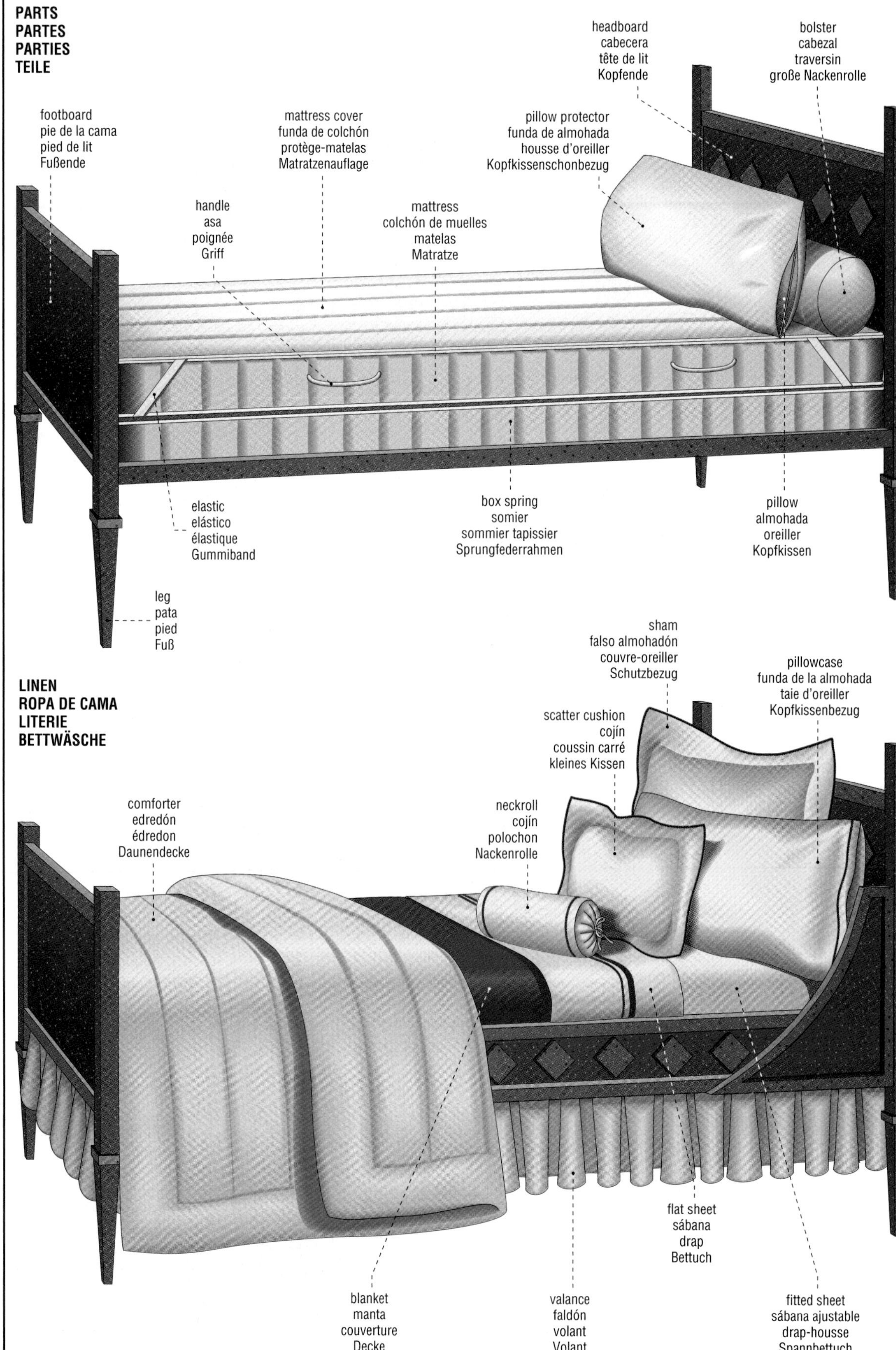
PARTS
PARTES
PARTIES
TEILE
headboard
cabecera
tête de lit
Kopfende
bolster
cabezal
traversin
große Nackenrolle
footboard
pie de la cama
pied de lit
Fußende
mattress cover
funda de colchón
protège-matelas
Matratzenauflage
pillow protector
funda de almohada
housse d'oreiller
Kopfkissenschonbezug
handle
asa
poignée
Griff
mattress
colchón de muelles
matelas
Matratze
elastic
elástico
élastique
Gummiband
box spring
somier
sommier tapissier
Sprungfederrahmen
pillow
almohada
oreiller
Kopfkissen
leg
pata
pied
Fuß
sham
falso almohadón
couvre-oreiller
Schutzbezug
pillowcase
funda de la almohada
taie d'oreiller
Kopfkissenbezug
LINEN
ROPA DE CAMA
LITERIE
BETTWÄSCHE
scatter cushion
cojín
coussin carré
kleines Kissen
comforter
edredón
édredon
Daunendecke
neckroll
cojín
polochon
Nackenrolle
flat sheet
sábana
drap
Bettuch
blanket
manta
couverture
Decke
valance
faldón
volant
Volant
fitted sheet
sábana ajustable
drap-housse
Spannbettuch

ARMOIRE
ARMARIO
ARMOIRE
KLEIDERSCHRANK

frieze
friso
frise
Fries
center post
montante central
dormant
Setzholz
cornice
cornisa
corniche
Kranzprofil
top rail
peinazo superior
traverse supérieure
obere Querleiste
door panel
entrepaño
panneau de vantail
Türfüllung
diamond point
punta de diamante
pointe de diamant
Rautenspitze
lock
cerradura
serrure
Schloß
hanging stile
larguero de la bisagra
montant de ferrage
Hängesäule
rail
peinazo
traverse
Querleiste
frame stile
larguero del marco
montant de bâti
Rahmenleiste
hinge
bisagra
gond
Scharnier
peg
espiga
cheville
Zapfen
bottom rail
peinazo inferior
traverse inférieure
untere Querleiste
foot
pata
pied
Fuß
bracket base
rodapié
soubassement
Sockelprofil
frame
armazón
bâti
Rahmen
door
puerta
vantail
Tür

STORAGE FURNITURE
ARMARIOS Y GABINETES
MEUBLES DE RANGEMENT
AUFBEWAHRUNGSMÖBEL

linen chest
baúl
coffre
Truhe

dresser
tocador
commode
Kommode

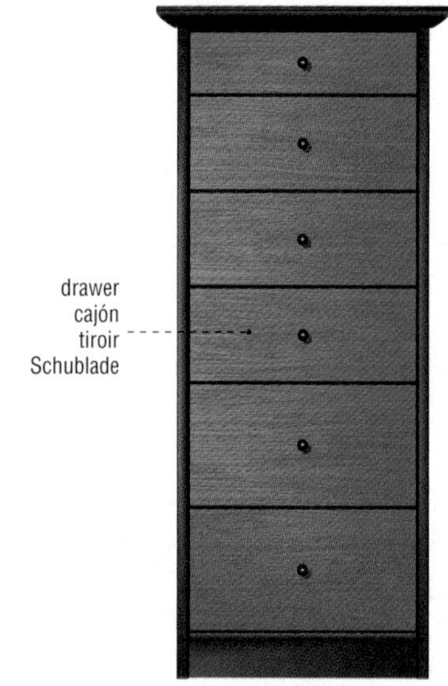
drawer
cajón
tiroir
Schublade

chiffonier
chifonier
chiffonnier
Chiffoniere

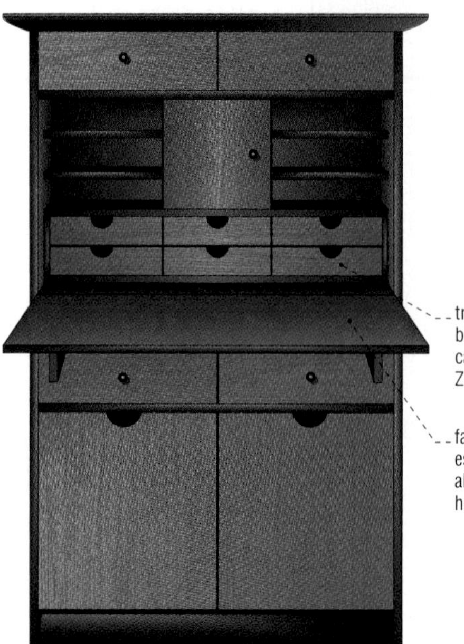
tray
batea
casier
Zugschublade
fall front
escritorio
abattant
herausklappbare Schreibplatte

secretary
bufete
secrétaire
Sekretär

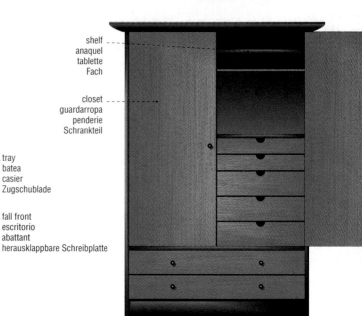

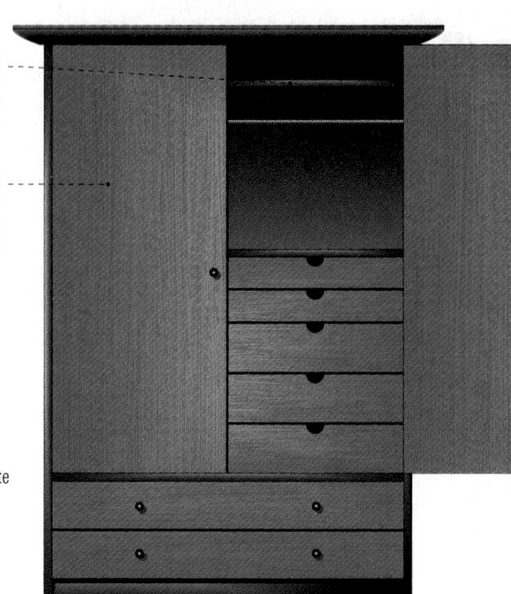
shelf
anaquel
tablette
Fach
closet
guardarropa
penderie
Schrankteil

wardrobe
ropero
armoire-penderie
Kleiderschrank

cocktail cabinet
mueble bar
bar
Cocktailbar

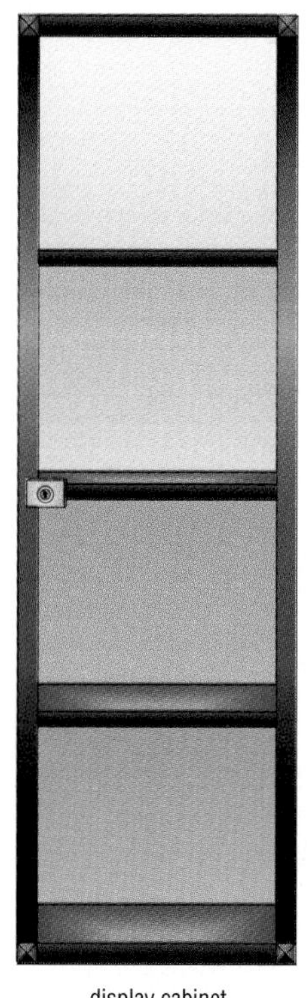

display cabinet
vitrina
vitrine
Vitrine

glass-fronted display cabinet
armario de vajilla
buffet-vaisselier
Vitrinenschrank

corner cupboard
rinconera
encoignure
Eckschrank

buffet
aparador
buffet
Büfett

WINDOW ACCESSORIES
ACCESORIOS PARA LAS VENTANAS
PARURES DE FENÊTRE
DEKORATIONEN

TYPES OF CURTAINS
TIPOS DE CORTINAS
TYPES DE RIDEAUX
GARDINENTYPEN

GLASS CURTAIN
CORTINA DE VENTANA
RIDEAU DE VITRAGE
SCHEIBENGARDINE

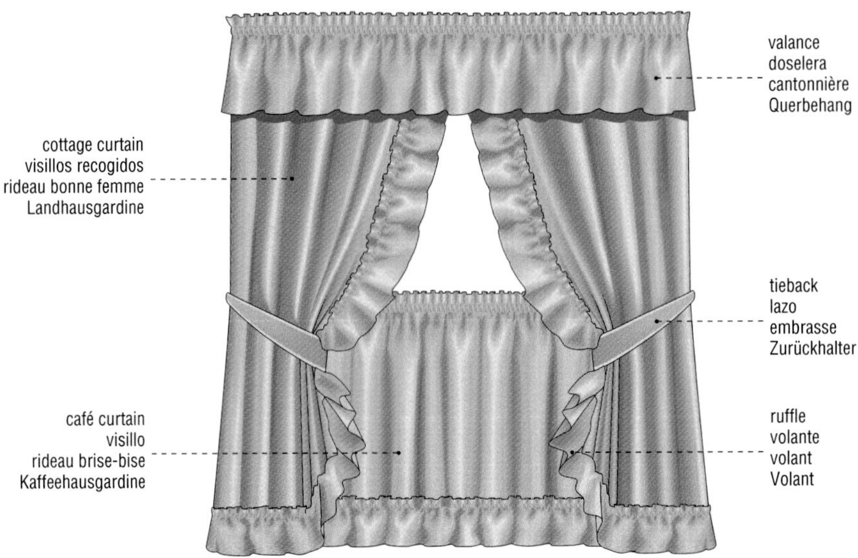
valance
doselera
cantonnière
Querbehang
cottage curtain
visillos recogidos
rideau bonne femme
Landhausgardine
tieback
lazo
embrasse
Zurückhalter
café curtain
visillo
rideau brise-bise
Kaffeehausgardine
ruffle
volante
volant
Volant

ATTACHED CURTAIN
CORTINA SUJETA DE DOBLE BARRA
RIDEAU COULISSÉ
SPANNER

LOOSE CURTAIN
CORTINA SUELTA CORREDIZA
RIDEAU FLOTTANT
LOSER VORHANG

TYPES OF PLEATS
TIPOS DE CENEFAS
TYPES DE PLIS
FALTENARTEN

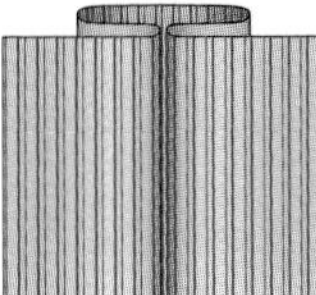

box pleat
pliegue de cajón
pli creux
Schachtelfalte

pinch pleat
pliegue de pinza
pli pincé
Kirsorfalte

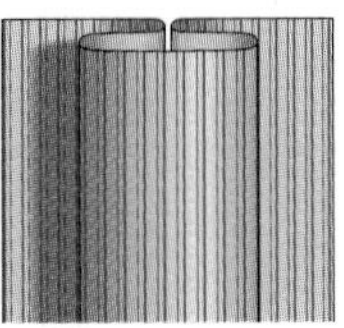

inverted pleat
pliegue de cajón invertido
pli rond
eingelegte Falte

CURTAIN
CORTINA
RIDEAU
VORHANG

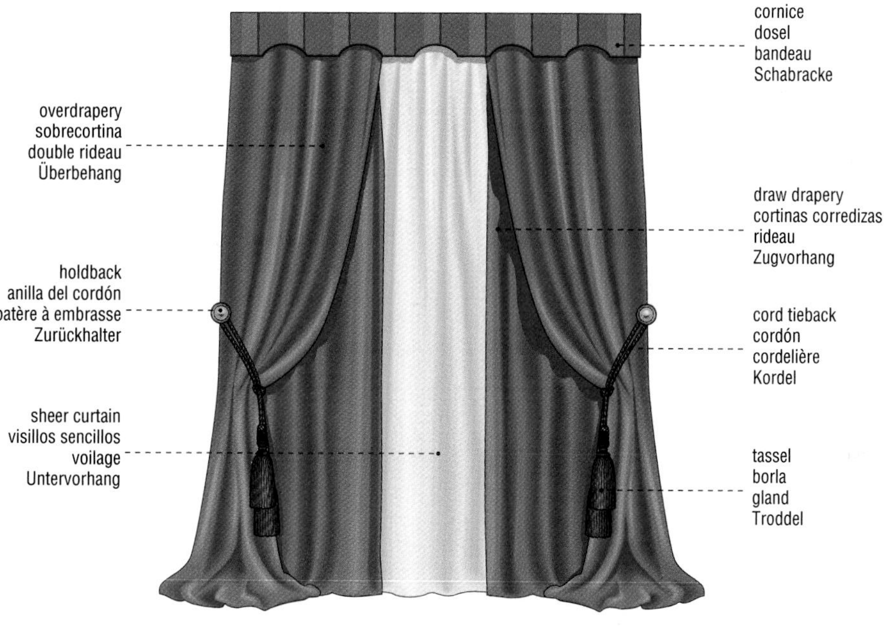
cornice
dosel
bandeau
Schabracke
overdrapery
sobrecortina
double rideau
Überbehang
draw drapery
cortinas corredizas
rideau
Zugvorhang
holdback
anilla del cordón
patère à embrasse
Zurückhalter
cord tieback
cordón
cordelière
Kordel
sheer curtain
visillos sencillos
voilage
Untervorhang
tassel
borla
gland
Troddel

BALLOON CURTAIN
CORTINA ABOMBADA
RIDEAU BALLON
BALLONVORHANG

CRISSCROSS CURTAINS
CORTINAS CRUZADAS
RIDEAUX CROISÉS
RAFFGARDINE

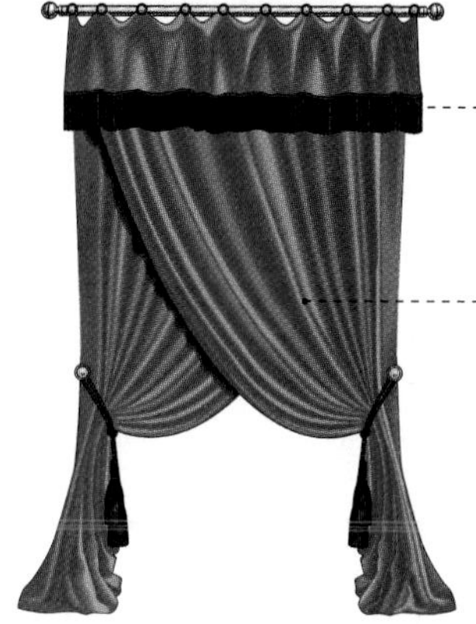
fringe trimming
cenefa con flecos
frange de passementerie
Fransen
panel
cortina
panneau
Panel

TYPES OF HEADINGS
TIPOS DE DOSELES
TYPES DE TÊTES
KÖPFCHENTYPEN

draped swag
festón colgado
cantonnière drapée
Freihand-Dekoration

pencil pleat heading
dosel plisado de canotillo
fronçage tuyauté
Bleistiftband

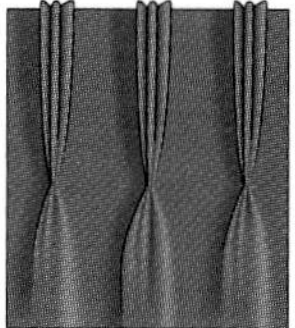

pleated heading
dosel plisado
tête plissée
Kirschband

shirred heading
dosel fruncido
tête froncée
Durchzug

WINDOW ACCESSORIES
ACCESORIOS PARA LAS VENTANAS
PARURES DE FENÊTRE
FENSTERZUBEHÖR

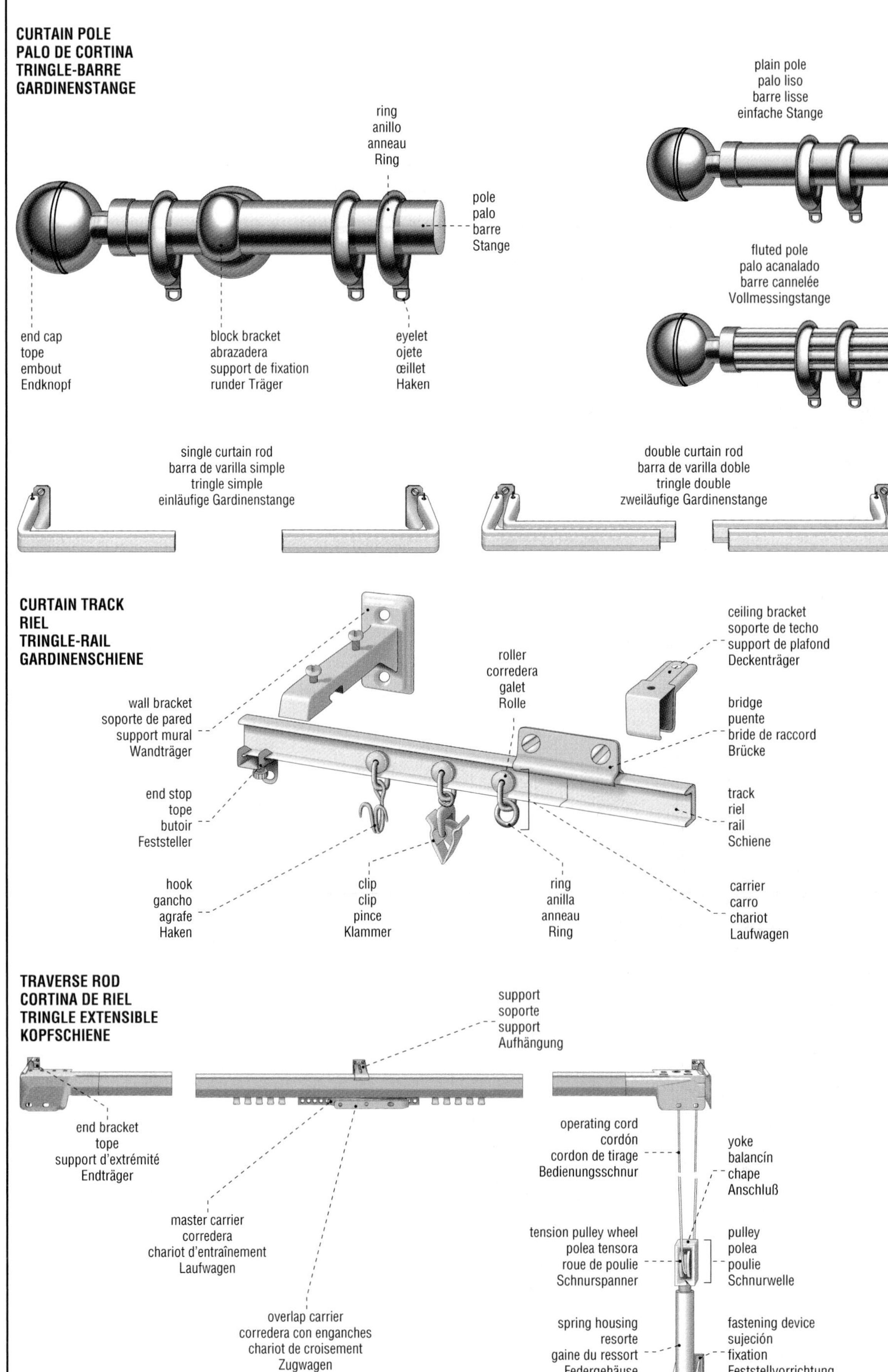
CURTAIN POLE
PALO DE CORTINA
TRINGLE-BARRE
GARDINENSTANGE
ring
anillo
anneau
Ring
pole
palo
barre
Stange
end cap
tope
embout
Endknopf
block bracket
abrazadera
support de fixation
runder Träger
eyelet
ojete
œillet
Haken
plain pole
palo liso
barre lisse
einfache Stange
fluted pole
palo acanalado
barre cannelée
Vollmessingstange
single curtain rod
barra de varilla simple
tringle simple
einläufige Gardinenstange
double curtain rod
barra de varilla doble
tringle double
zweiläufige Gardinenstange
CURTAIN TRACK
RIEL
TRINGLE-RAIL
GARDINENSCHIENE
wall bracket
soporte de pared
support mural
Wandträger
end stop
tope
butoir
Feststeller
hook
gancho
agrafe
Haken
clip
clip
pince
Klammer
roller
corredera
galet
Rolle
ring
anilla
anneau
Ring
ceiling bracket
soporte de techo
support de plafond
Deckenträger
bridge
puente
bride de raccord
Brücke
track
riel
rail
Schiene
carrier
carro
chariot
Laufwagen
TRAVERSE ROD
CORTINA DE RIEL
TRINGLE EXTENSIBLE
KOPFSCHIENE
support
soporte
support
Aufhängung
end bracket
tope
support d'extrémité
Endträger
master carrier
corredera
chariot d'entraînement
Laufwagen
overlap carrier
corredera con enganches
chariot de croisement
Zugwagen
operating cord
cordón
cordon de tirage
Bedienungsschnur
yoke
balancín
chape
Anschluß
tension pulley wheel
polea tensora
roue de poulie
Schnurspanner
pulley
polea
poulie
Schnurwelle
spring housing
resorte
gaine du ressort
Federgehäuse
fastening device
sujeción
fixation
Feststellvorrichtung

ROLLER SHADE
STORE
STORE À ENROULEMENT AUTOMATIQUE
ROLLO

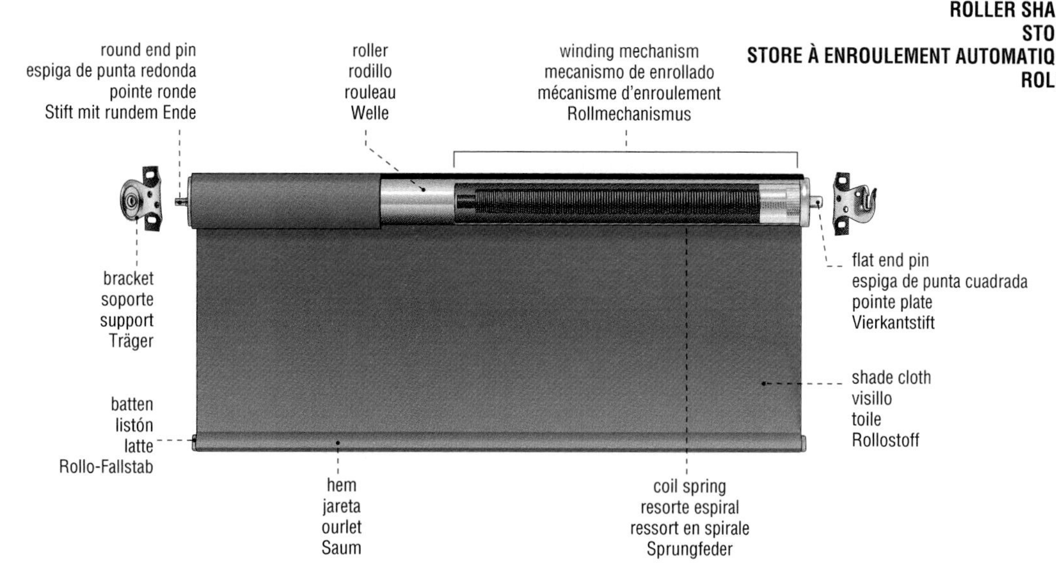

round end pin
espiga de punta redonda
pointe ronde
Stift mit rundem Ende
roller
rodillo
rouleau
Welle
winding mechanism
mecanismo de enrollado
mécanisme d'enroulement
Rollmechanismus
bracket
soporte
support
Träger
flat end pin
espiga de punta cuadrada
pointe plate
Vierkantstift
shade cloth
visillo
toile
Rollostoff
batten
listón
latte
Rollo-Fallstab
hem
jareta
ourlet
Saum
coil spring
resorte espiral
ressort en spirale
Sprungfeder

VENETIAN BLIND
PERSIANA VENECIANA
STORE VÉNITIEN
JALOUSIE

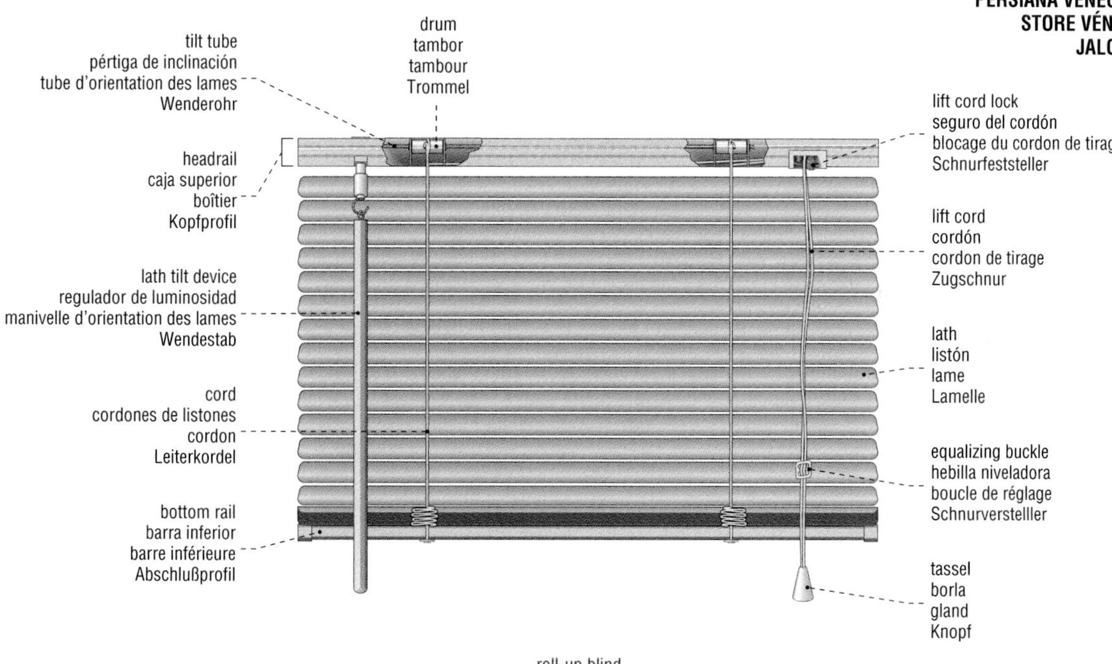

tilt tube
pértiga de inclinación
tube d'orientation des lames
Wenderohr
drum
tambor
tambour
Trommel
lift cord lock
seguro del cordón
blocage du cordon de tirage
Schnurfeststeller
headrail
caja superior
boîtier
Kopfprofil
lift cord
cordón
cordon de tirage
Zugschnur
lath tilt device
regulador de luminosidad
manivelle d'orientation des lames
Wendestab
lath
listón
lame
Lamelle
cord
cordones de listones
cordon
Leiterkordel
equalizing buckle
hebilla niveladora
boucle de réglage
Schnurverstelller
bottom rail
barra inferior
barre inférieure
Abschlußprofil
tassel
borla
gland
Knopf

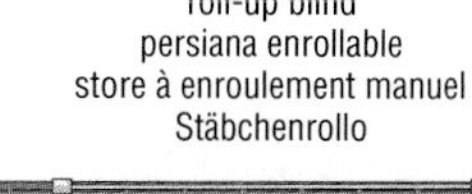

roll-up blind
persiana enrollable
store à enroulement manuel
Stäbchenrollo

roman shade
persianas romana
store bateau
Raffrollo

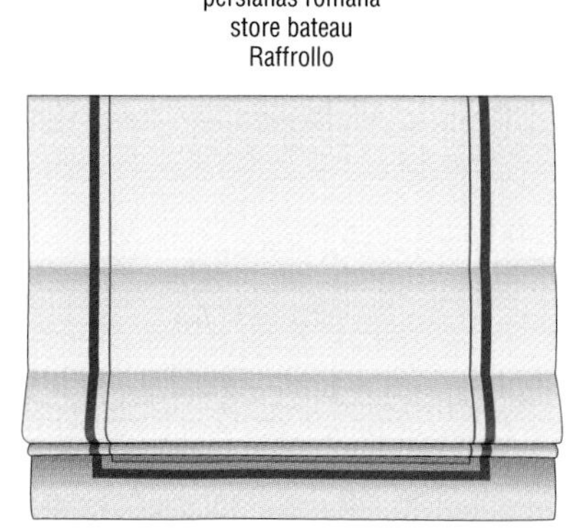

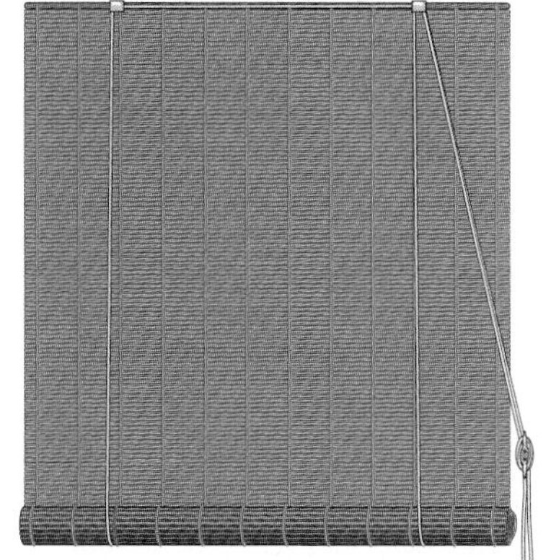

indoor shutters
postigos interiores
volets d'intérieur
Innenläden

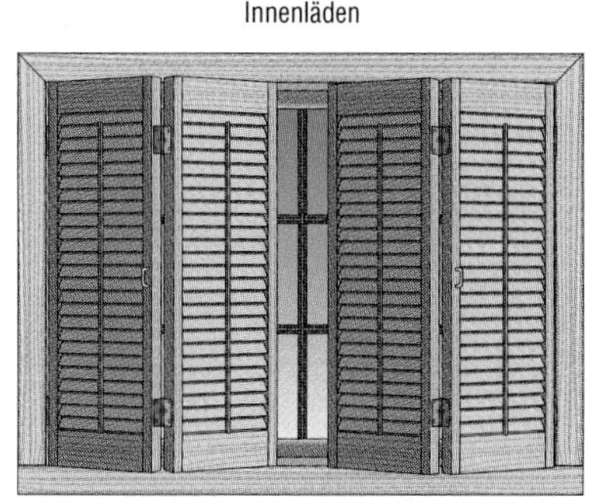

LIGHTS
LÁMPARAS
LUMINAIRES
LAMPEN

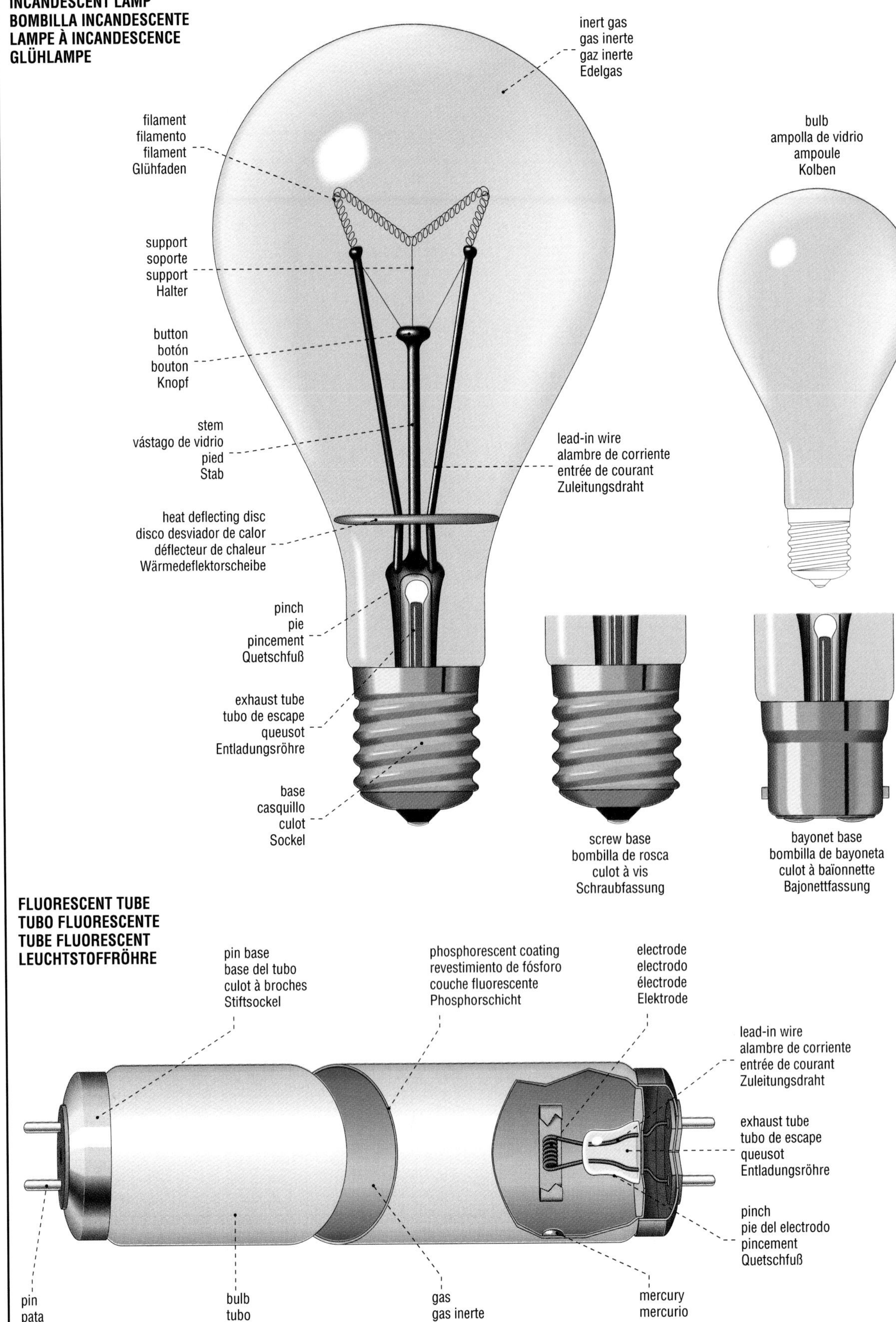
INCANDESCENT LAMP
BOMBILLA INCANDESCENTE
LAMPE À INCANDESCENCE
GLÜHLAMPE
inert gas
gas inerte
gaz inerte
Edelgas
filament
filamento
filament
Glühfaden
bulb
ampolla de vidrio
ampoule
Kolben
support
soporte
support
Halter
button
botón
bouton
Knopf
stem
vástago de vidrio
pied
Stab
lead-in wire
alambre de corriente
entrée de courant
Zuleitungsdraht
heat deflecting disc
disco desviador de calor
déflecteur de chaleur
Wärmedeflektorscheibe
pinch
pie
pincement
Quetschfuß
exhaust tube
tubo de escape
queusot
Entladungsröhre
base
casquillo
culot
Sockel
screw base
bombilla de rosca
culot à vis
Schraubfassung
bayonet base
bombilla de bayoneta
culot à baïonnette
Bajonettfassung
FLUORESCENT TUBE
TUBO FLUORESCENTE
TUBE FLUORESCENT
LEUCHTSTOFFRÖHRE
pin base
base del tubo
culot à broches
Stiftsockel
phosphorescent coating
revestimiento de fósforo
couche fluorescente
Phosphorschicht
electrode
electrodo
électrode
Elektrode
lead-in wire
alambre de corriente
entrée de courant
Zuleitungsdraht
exhaust tube
tubo de escape
queusot
Entladungsröhre
pinch
pie del electrodo
pincement
Quetschfuß
pin
pata
broche
Stift
bulb
tubo
tube
Kolben
gas
gas inerte
gaz
Gas
mercury
mercurio
mercure
Quecksilber

TUNGSTEN-HALOGEN LAMP
LÁMPARA HALÓGENA
LAMPE À HALOGÈNE
WOLFRAM-HALOGENLAMPE

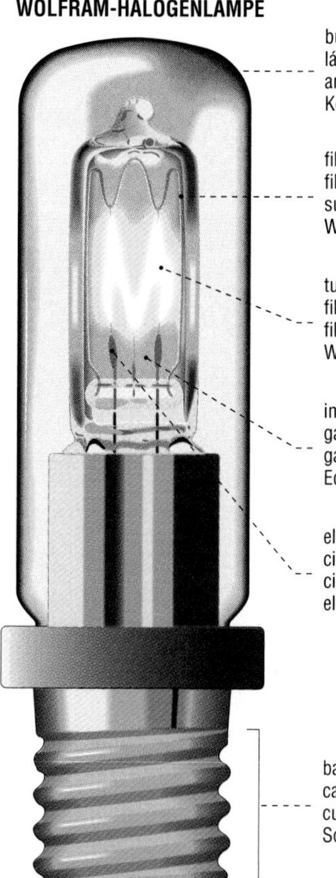

bulb
lámpara
ampoule
Kolben
filament support
filamento
support du filament
Wendelhalter
tungsten filament
filamento de tungsteno
filament de tungstène
Wolframwendel
inert gas
gas inerte
gaz inerte
Edelgas
electric circuit
circuito eléctrico
circuit électrique
elektrischer Kreislauf
base
casquillo
culot
Sockel
contact
contacto
plot
Kontakt

TUNGSTEN-HALOGEN LAMP
LÁMPARA HALÓGENA
LAMPE À HALOGÈNE
WOLFRAM-HALOGENLAMPE

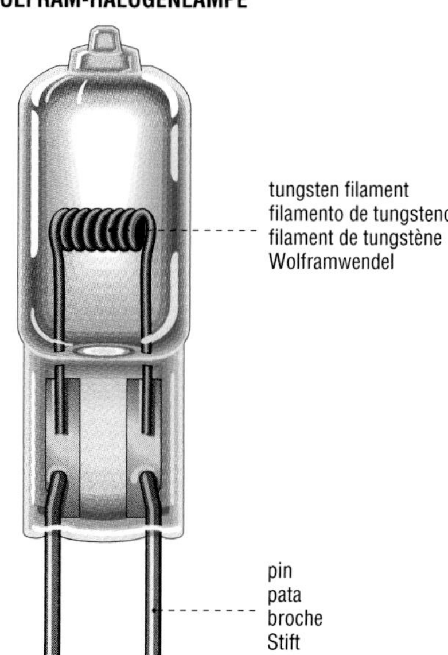

tungsten filament
filamento de tungsteno
filament de tungstène
Wolframwendel
pin
pata
broche
Stift

ENERGY SAVING BULB
BOMBILLA ECONÓMICA
LAMPE À ÉCONOMIE D'ÉNERGIE
ENERGIESPARLAMPE

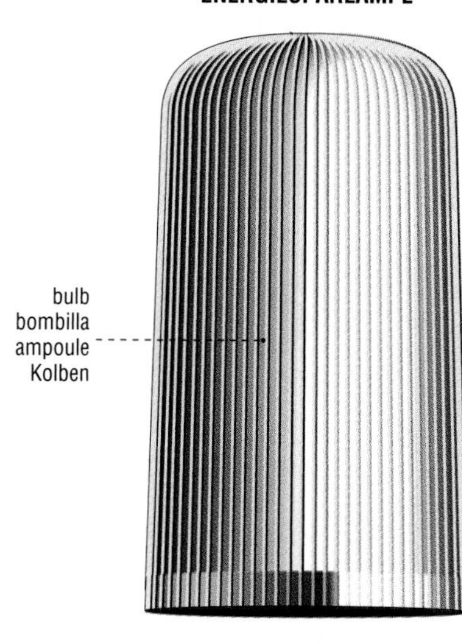

bulb
bombilla
ampoule
Kolben

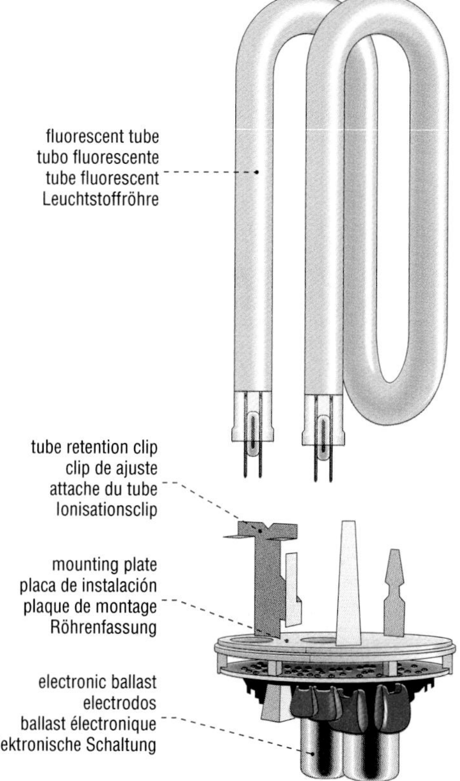

fluorescent tube
tubo fluorescente
tube fluorescent
Leuchtstoffröhre
tube retention clip
clip de ajuste
attache du tube
Ionisationsclip
mounting plate
placa de instalación
plaque de montage
Röhrenfassung
electronic ballast
electrodos
ballast électronique
elektronische Schaltung

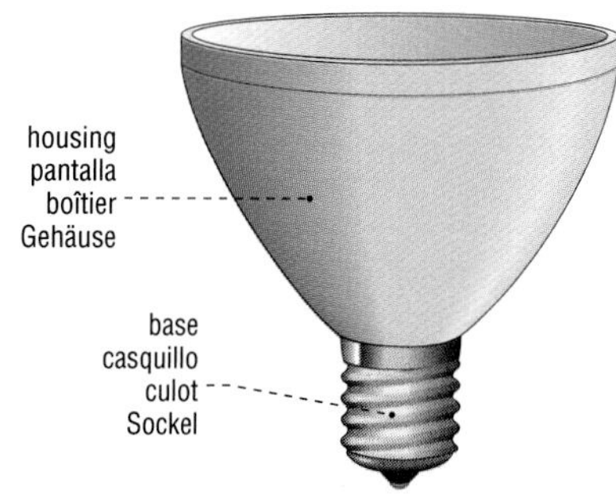

housing
pantalla
boîtier
Gehäuse
base
casquillo
culot
Sockel

LIGHTS
LÁMPARAS
LUMINAIRES
LAMPEN

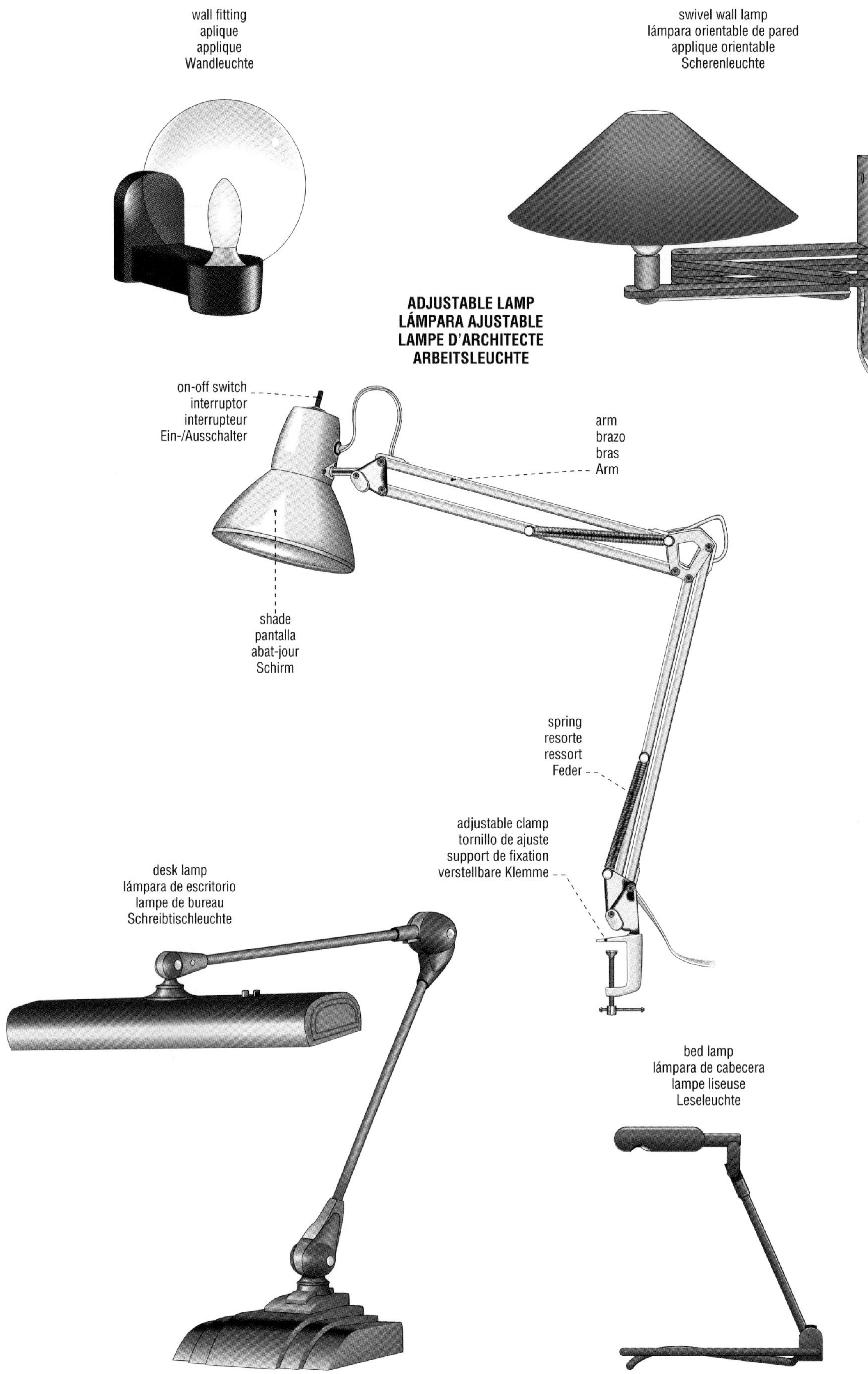
wall fitting
aplique
applique
Wandleuchte
swivel wall lamp
lámpara orientable de pared
applique orientable
Scherenleuchte
ADJUSTABLE LAMP
LÁMPARA AJUSTABLE
LAMPE D'ARCHITECTE
ARBEITSLEUCHTE
on-off switch
interruptor
interrupteur
Ein-/Ausschalter
arm
brazo
bras
Arm
shade
pantalla
abat-jour
Schirm
spring
resorte
ressort
Feder
adjustable clamp
tornillo de ajuste
support de fixation
verstellbare Klemme
desk lamp
lámpara de escritorio
lampe de bureau
Schreibtischleuchte
bed lamp
lámpara de cabecera
lampe liseuse
Leseleuchte

TRACK LIGHTING
RIEL DE ILUMINACIÓN
RAIL D'ÉCLAIRAGE
STROMSCHIENENLEUCHTE

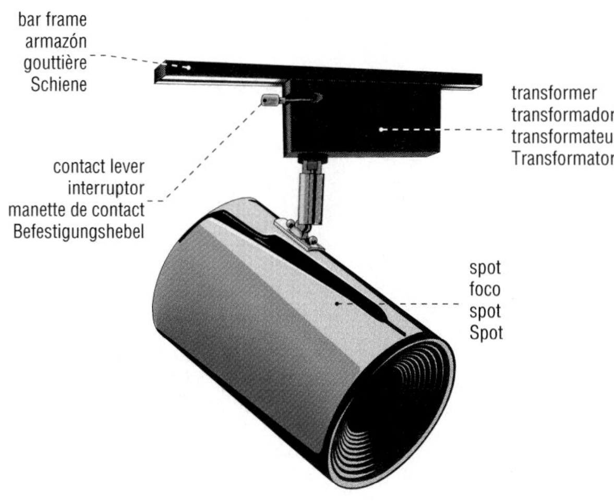
bar frame
armazón
gouttière
Schiene
contact lever
interruptor
manette de contact
Befestigungshebel
transformer
transformador
transformateur
Transformator
spot
foco
spot
Spot

post lantern
farola
lanterne de pied
Straßenlaterne

clamp spotlight
lámpara de pinza
spot à pince
Klemmspot

wall lantern
farol
lanterne murale
Wandlaterne

strip light
lámparas en serie
rampe d'éclairage
Lampenreihe

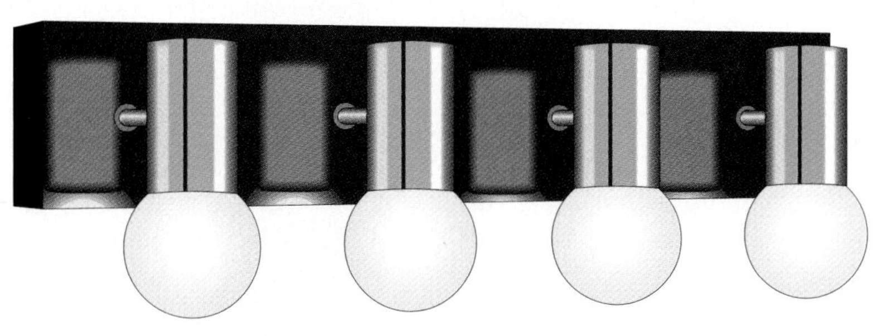

LIGHTS
LÁMPARAS
LUMINAIRES
LAMPEN

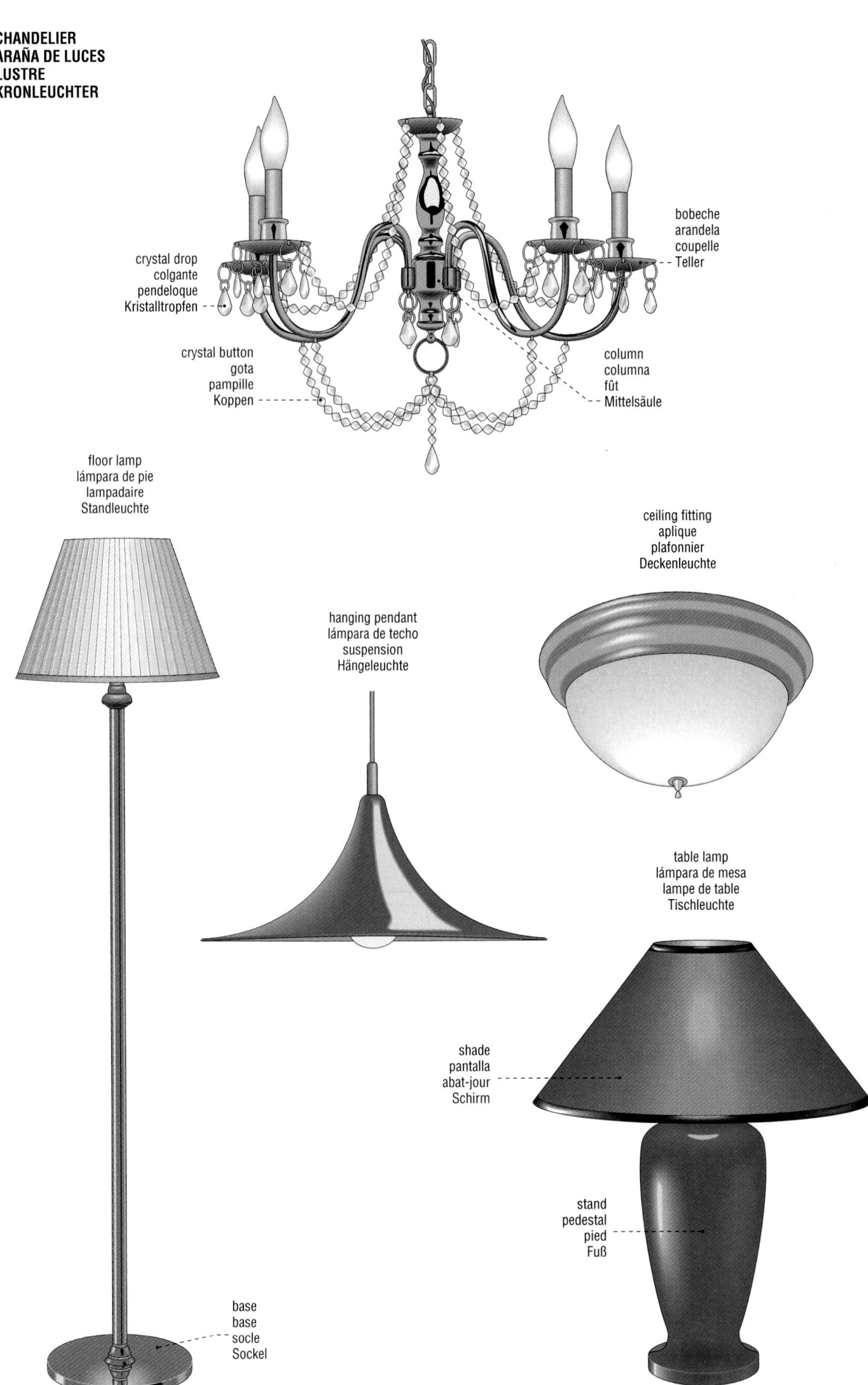
CHANDELIER
ARAÑA DE LUCES
LUSTRE
KRONLEUCHTER
bobeche
arandela
coupelle
Teller
crystal drop
colgante
pendeloque
Kristalltropfen
crystal button
gota
pampille
Koppen
column
columna
fût
Mittelsäule
floor lamp
lámpara de pie
lampadaire
Standleuchte
ceiling fitting
aplique
plafonnier
Deckenleuchte
hanging pendant
lámpara de techo
suspension
Hängeleuchte
table lamp
lámpara de mesa
lampe de table
Tischleuchte
shade
pantalla
abat-jour
Schirm
stand
pedestal
pied
Fuß
base
base
socle
Sockel

GLASSWARE
CRISTALERÍA
VERRES
GLÄSER

port glass
copa para oporto
verre à porto
Süßweinglas

sparkling wine glass
copa de cava
coupe à mousseux
Sektschale

brandy snifter
copa de coñac
verre à cognac
Kognakschwenker

liqueur glass
copa para licores
verre à liqueur
Likörglas

white wine glass
copa de vino blanco
verre à vin blanc
Weißweinglas

bordeaux glass
copa para vinos de Burdeos
verre à bordeaux
Bordeauxglas

burgundy glass
copa para vinos de Borgoña
verre à bourgogne
Burgunderglas

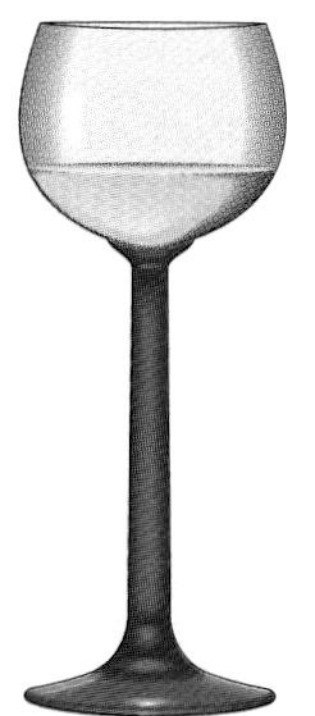
Alsace glass
copa para vino de Alsacia
verre à vin d'Alsace
Elsaßglas

old-fashioned glass
vaso corto
verre à whisky
Whiskybecher

highball glass
vaso largo
verre à gin
Longdrinkglas

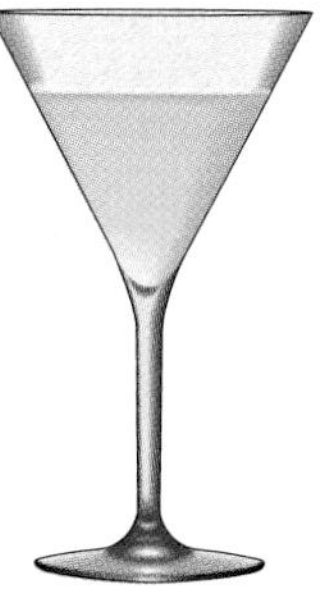
cocktail glass
copa de cóctel
verre à cocktail
Cocktailglas

water goblet
copa para agua
verre à eau
Wasserglas

decanter
garrafa
carafe
Karaffe

small decanter
garrafita
carafon
kleine Karaffe

champagne flute
copa de champaña
flûte à champagne
Sektkelch

beer mug
jarra para cerveza
chope à bière
Bierkrug

DINNERWARE
VAJILLA Y SERVICIO DE MESA
VAISSELLE
GESCHIRR

demitasse
tacita de café
tasse à café
Mokkatasse

cup
taza
tasse à thé
Tasse

coffee mug
jarra para café
chope à café
Becher

creamer
jarrito de la leche
crémier
Milchkännchen

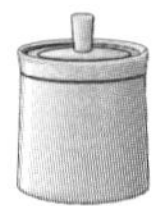

sugar bowl
azucarero
sucrier
Zuckerdose

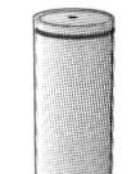

pepper shaker
pimentera
poivrière
Pfefferstreuer

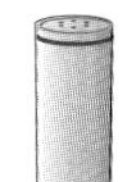

salt shaker
salero
salière
Salzstreuer

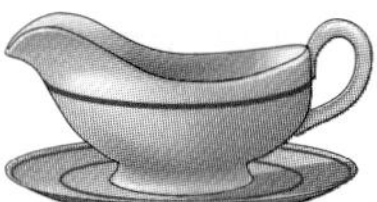

gravy boat
salsera
saucière
Sauciere

butter dish
mantequera
beurrier
Butterdose

ramekin
cuenco de queso blando
ramequin
Auflaufförmchen

soup bowl
bol para sopa
bol
Suppenschale

rim soup bowl
plato sopero
assiette creuse
Suppenteller

dinner plate
plato llano
assiette plate
flacher Teller

salad plate
plato para ensalada
assiette à salade
Salatteller

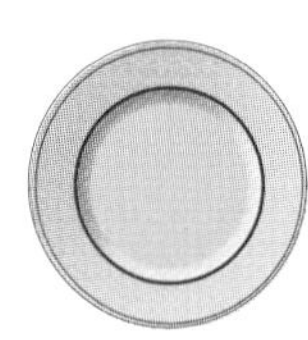

bread and butter plate
plato para pan y mantequilla
assiette à dessert
kleiner Teller

teapot
tetera
théière
Teekanne

platter
fuente de servir
plat ovale
Platte

vegetable bowl
fuente de verdura
légumier
Kartoffelschüssel

fish platter
fuente para pescado
plat à poisson
Fischplatte

hors d'oeuvre dish
bandeja para canapés
ravier
Horsd'oeuvre-Schale

water pitcher
jarra para agua
pichet
Wasserkrug

salad bowl
ensaladera
saladier
Salatschüssel

salad dish
bol para ensalada
bol à salade
Salatschale

soup tureen
sopera
soupière
Suppenterrine

SILVERWARE
CUBERTERÍA
COUVERT
SILBERBESTECK

KNIFE
CUCHILLO
COUTEAU
MESSER

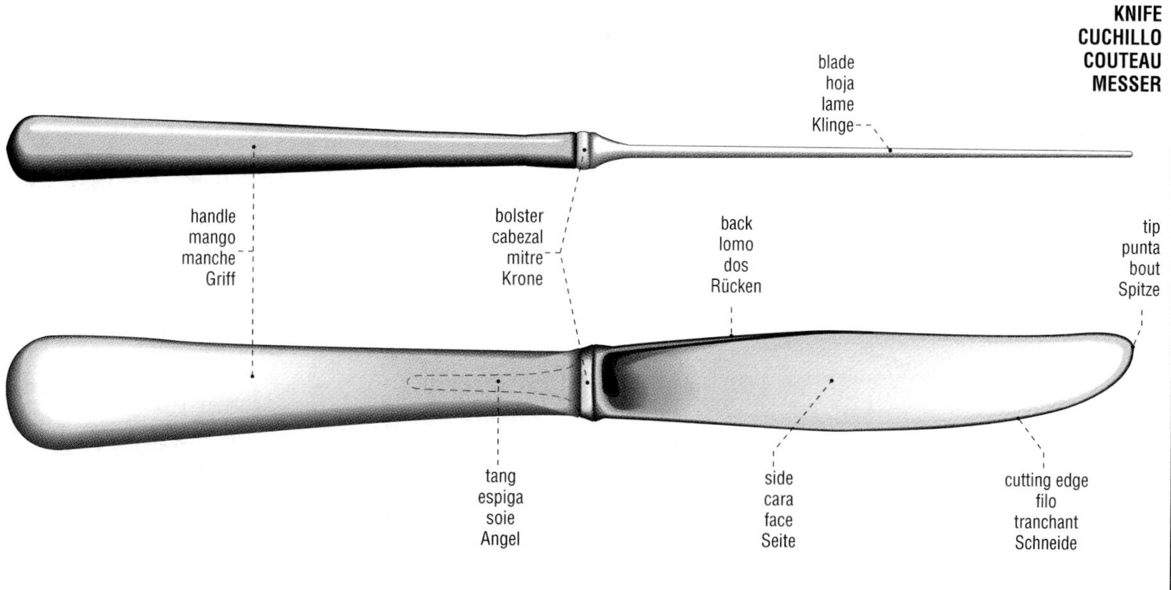
blade
hoja
lame
Klinge
handle
mango
manche
Griff
bolster
cabezal
mitre
Krone
back
lomo
dos
Rücken
tip
punta
bout
Spitze
tang
espiga
soie
Angel
side
cara
face
Seite
cutting edge
filo
tranchant
Schneide

PRINCIPAL TYPES OF KNIVES
TIPOS DE CUCHILLOS
PRINCIPAUX TYPES DE COUTEAUX
DIE WICHTIGSTEN MESSERTYPEN

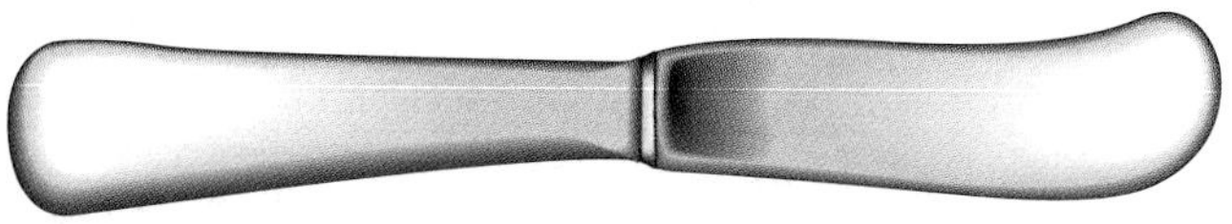

butter knife
cuchillo para mantequilla
couteau à beurre
Buttermesser

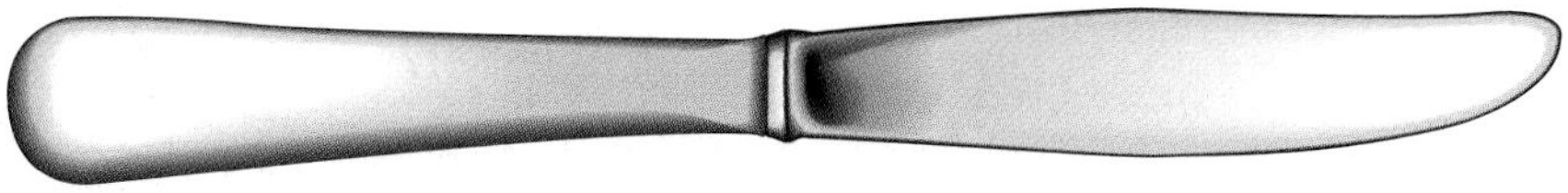

dessert knife
cuchillo para postre
couteau à dessert
Dessertmesser

fish knife
cuchillo para pescado
couteau à poisson
Fischmesser

cheese knife
cuchillo para queso
couteau à fromage
Käsemesser

dinner knife
cuchillo de mesa
couteau de table
Menümesser

steak knife
cuchillo para carne
couteau à bifteck
Steakmesser

SILVERWARE
CUBERTERÍA
COUVERT
SILBERBESTECK

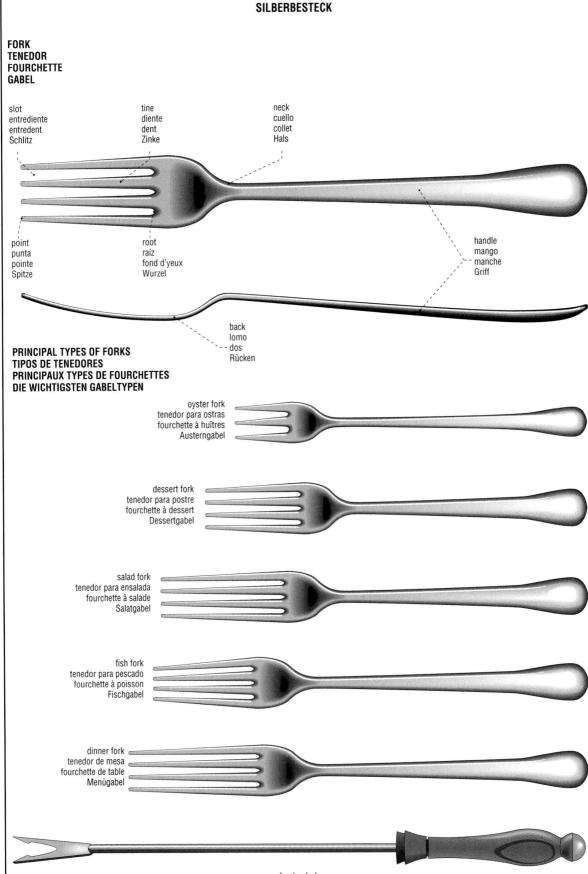

FORK
TENEDOR
FOURCHETTE
GABEL

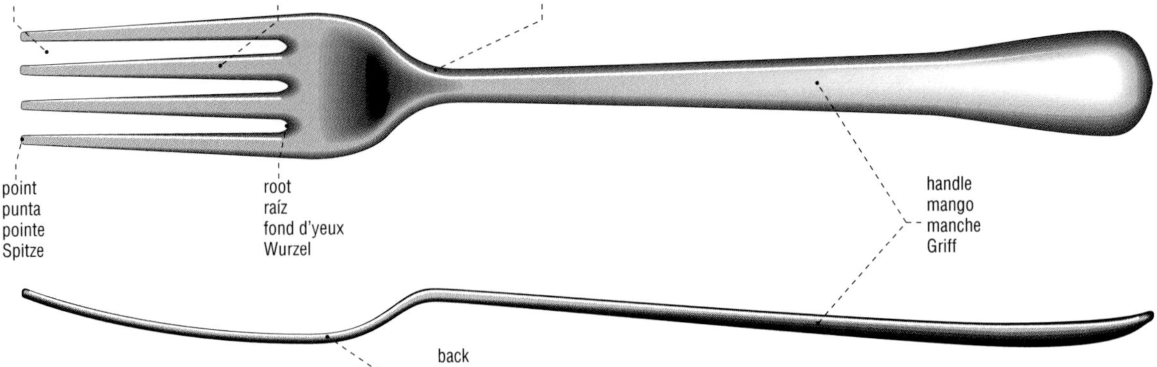

slot
entrediente
entredent
Schlitz

tine
diente
dent
Zinke

neck
cuello
collet
Hals

point
punta
pointe
Spitze

root
raíz
fond d'yeux
Wurzel

handle
mango
manche
Griff

back
lomo
dos
Rücken

PRINCIPAL TYPES OF FORKS
TIPOS DE TENEDORES
PRINCIPAUX TYPES DE FOURCHETTES
DIE WICHTIGSTEN GABELTYPEN

oyster fork
tenedor para ostras
fourchette à huîtres
Austerngabel

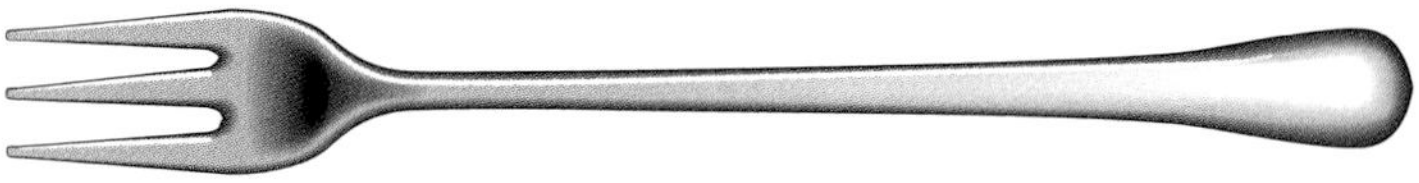

dessert fork
tenedor para postre
fourchette à dessert
Dessertgabel

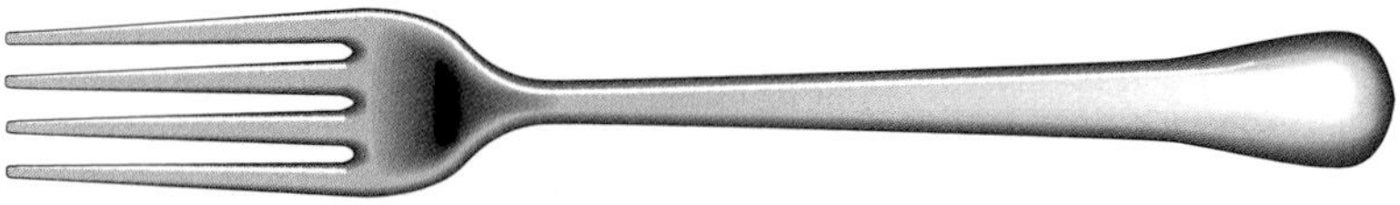

salad fork
tenedor para ensalada
fourchette à salade
Salatgabel

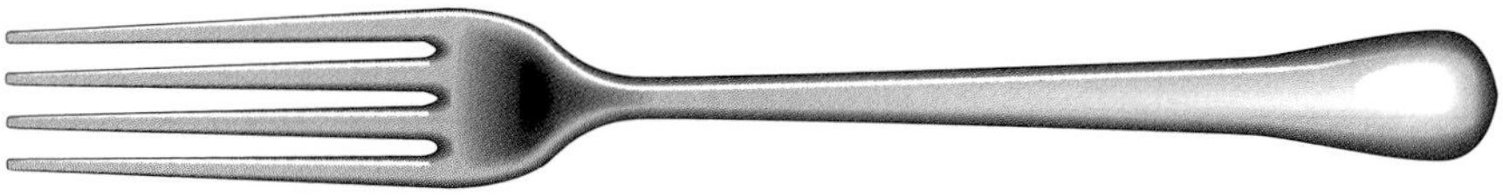

fish fork
tenedor para pescado
fourchette à poisson
Fischgabel

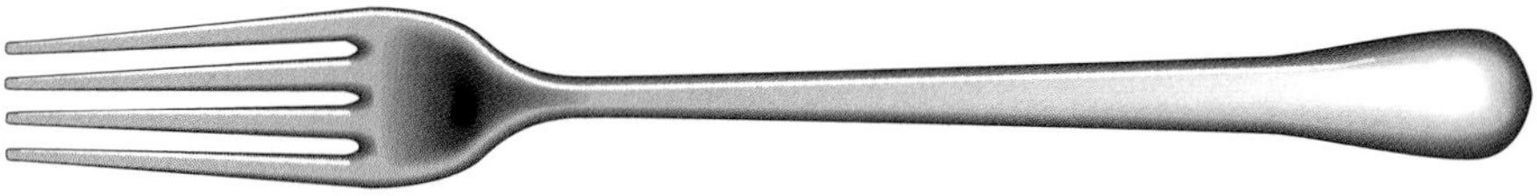

dinner fork
tenedor de mesa
fourchette de table
Menügabel

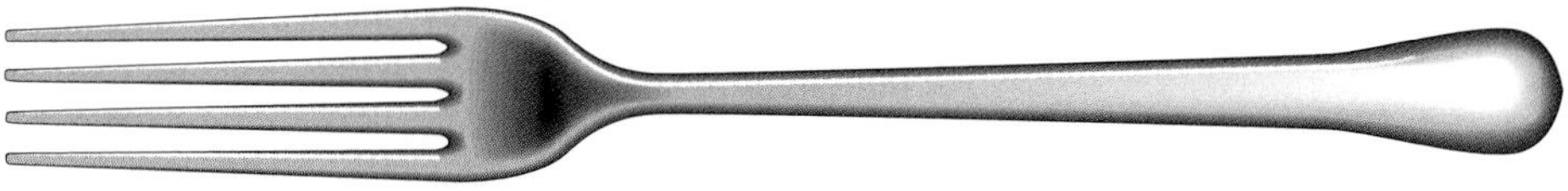

fondue fork
tenedor para fondue
fourchette à fondue
Fonduegabel

SPOON
CUCHARA
CUILLER
LÖFFEL

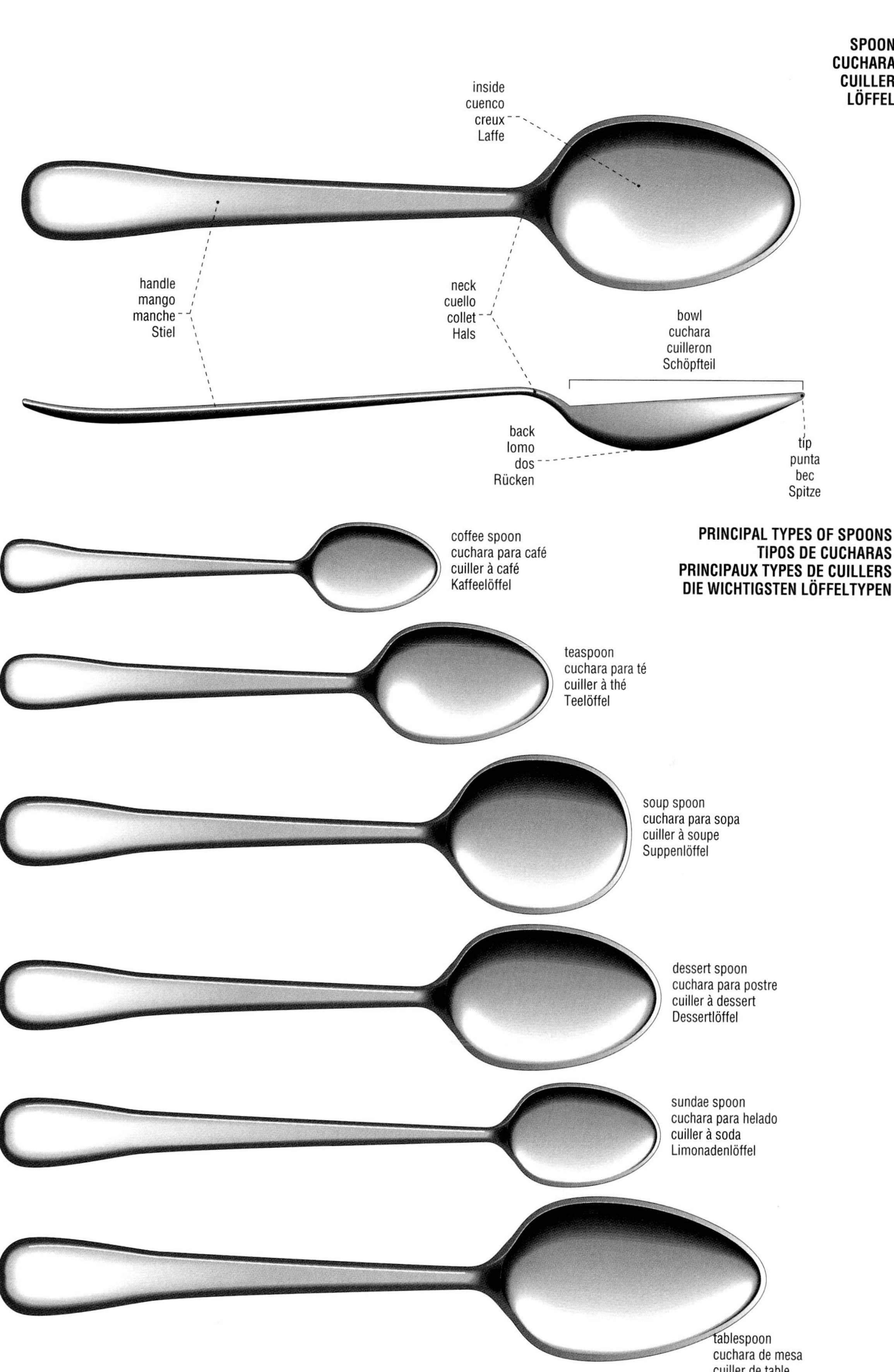
inside
cuenco
creux
Laffe
handle
mango
manche
Stiel
neck
cuello
collet
Hals
bowl
cuchara
cuilleron
Schöpfteil
back
lomo
dos
Rücken
tip
punta
bec
Spitze
coffee spoon
cuchara para café
cuiller à café
Kaffeelöffel
teaspoon
cuchara para té
cuiller à thé
Teelöffel
soup spoon
cuchara para sopa
cuiller à soupe
Suppenlöffel
dessert spoon
cuchara para postre
cuiller à dessert
Dessertlöffel
sundae spoon
cuchara para helado
cuiller à soda
Limonadenlöffel
tablespoon
cuchara de mesa
cuiller de table
Eßlöffel

PRINCIPAL TYPES OF SPOONS
TIPOS DE CUCHARAS
PRINCIPAUX TYPES DE CUILLERS
DIE WICHTIGSTEN LÖFFELTYPEN

KITCHEN UTENSILS
UTENSILIOS DE COCINA
USTENSILES DE CUISINE
KÜCHENUTENSILIEN

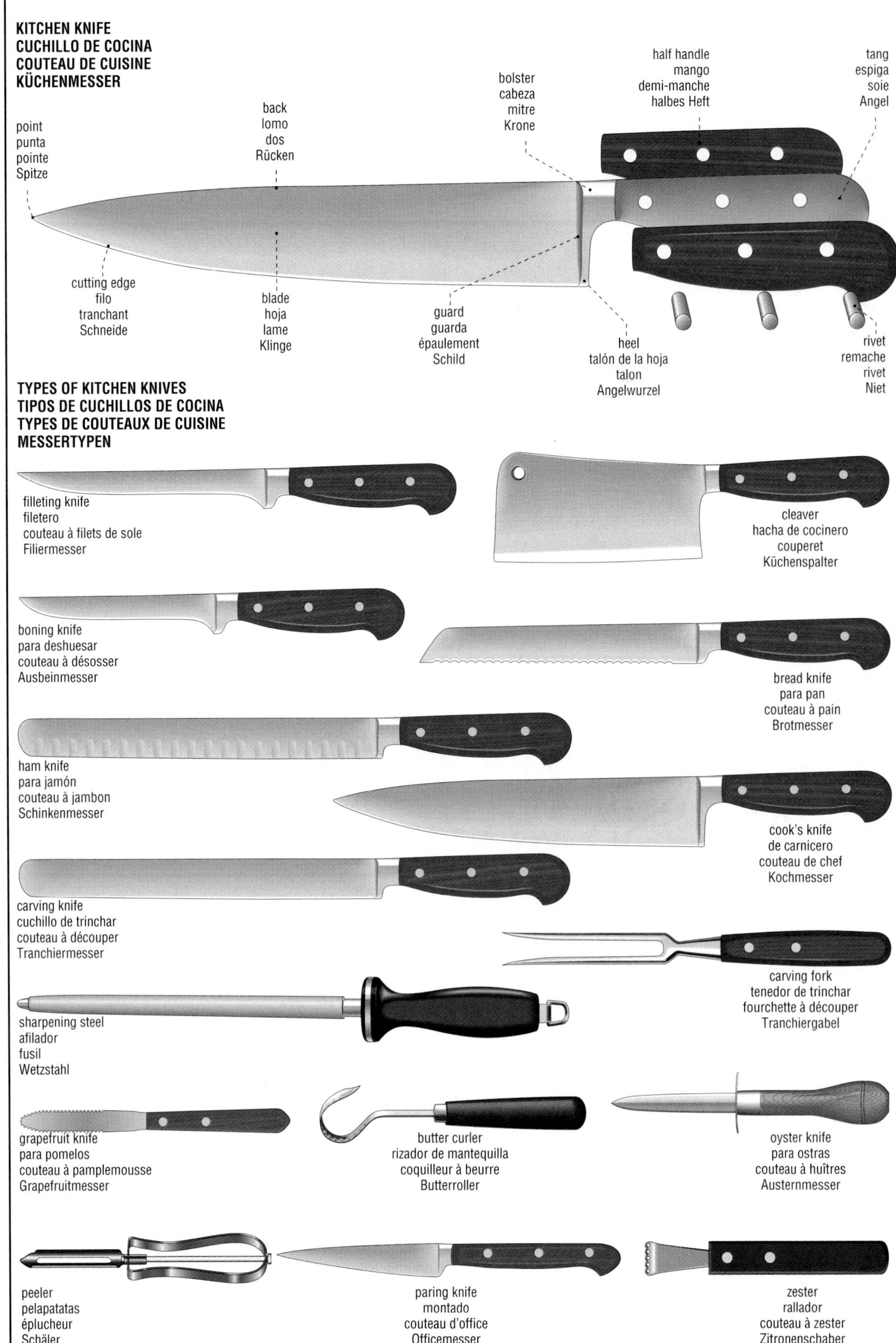
KITCHEN KNIFE
CUCHILLO DE COCINA
COUTEAU DE CUISINE
KÜCHENMESSER
point
punta
pointe
Spitze
back
lomo
dos
Rücken
bolster
cabeza
mitre
Krone
half handle
mango
demi-manche
halbes Heft
tang
espiga
soie
Angel
cutting edge
filo
tranchant
Schneide
blade
hoja
lame
Klinge
guard
guarda
épaulement
Schild
heel
talón de la hoja
talon
Angelwurzel
rivet
remache
rivet
Niet
TYPES OF KITCHEN KNIVES
TIPOS DE CUCHILLOS DE COCINA
TYPES DE COUTEAUX DE CUISINE
MESSERTYPEN
filleting knife
filetero
couteau à filets de sole
Filiermesser
cleaver
hacha de cocinero
couperet
Küchenspalter
boning knife
para deshuesar
couteau à désosser
Ausbeinmesser
bread knife
para pan
couteau à pain
Brotmesser
ham knife
para jamón
couteau à jambon
Schinkenmesser
cook's knife
de carnicero
couteau de chef
Kochmesser
carving knife
cuchillo de trinchar
couteau à découper
Tranchiermesser
carving fork
tenedor de trinchar
fourchette à découper
Tranchiergabel
sharpening steel
afilador
fusil
Wetzstahl
grapefruit knife
para pomelos
couteau à pamplemousse
Grapefruitmesser
butter curler
rizador de mantequilla
coquilleur à beurre
Butterroller
oyster knife
para ostras
couteau à huîtres
Austernmesser
peeler
pelapatatas
éplucheur
Schäler
paring knife
montado
couteau d'office
Officemesser
zester
rallador
couteau à zester
Zitronenschaber

FOR STRAINING AND DRAINING
COLADORES Y ESCURRIDORES
POUR PASSER ET ÉGOUTTER
ZUM SIEBEN UND TROCKNEN

funnel
embudo
entonnoir
Trichter

colander
escurridor
passoire
Durchschlag

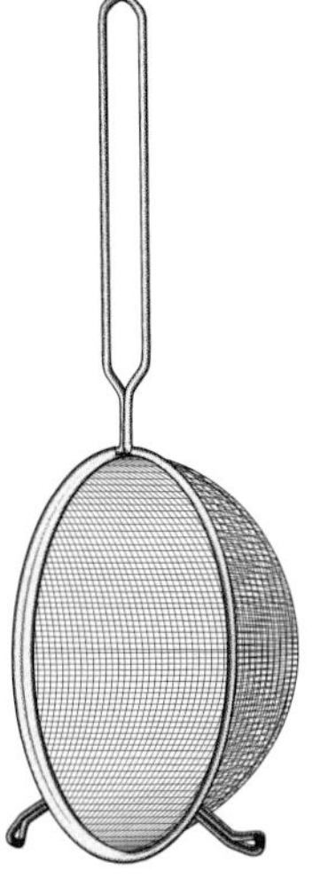

strainer
cedazo
passoire
Sieb

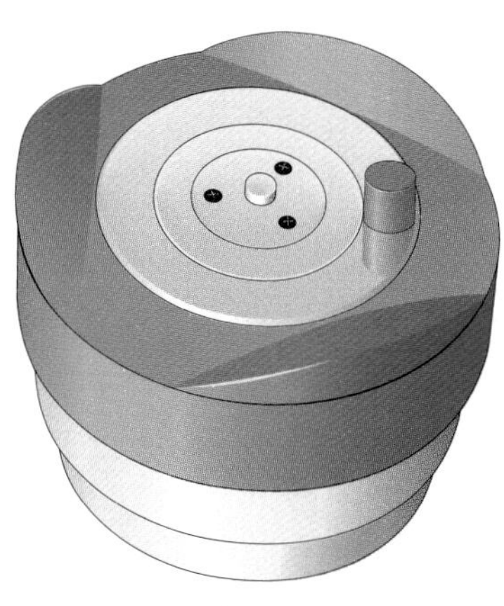

salad spinner
secadora de ensalada
essoreuse à salade
Salatschleuder

FOR GRINDING AND GRATING
PARA MOLER Y RALLAR
POUR BROYER ET RÂPER
ZUM ZERKLEINERN UND ZERREIBEN

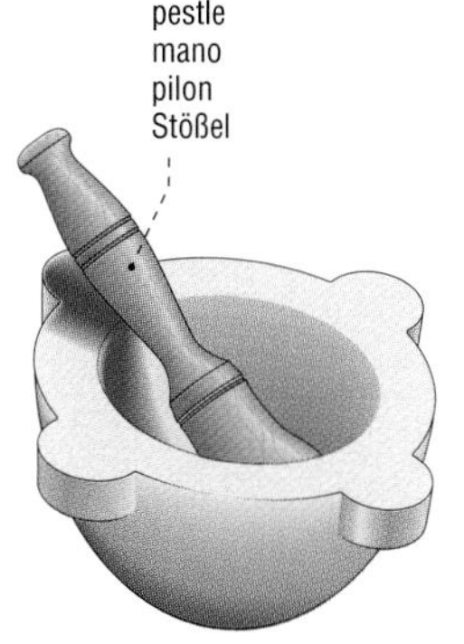
pestle
mano
pilon
Stößel

mortar
mortero
mortier
Mörser

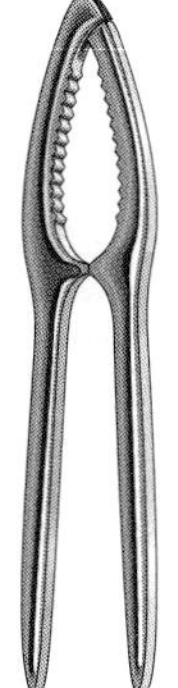

nutcracker
cascanueces
casse-noix
Nußknacker

garlic press
exprimidor de ajos
presse-ail
Knoblauchpresse

citrus juicer
exprimelimones
presse-agrumes
Zitronenpresse

meat grinder
máquina de picar carne
hachoir
Fleischwolf

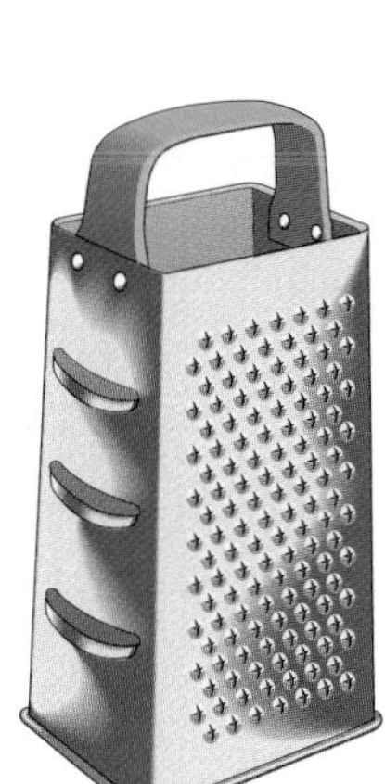

grater
rallador
râpe
Reibe

pasta maker
máquina para hacer pasta italiana
machine à faire les pâtes
Nudelmaschine

KITCHEN UTENSILS
UTENSILIOS DE COCINA
USTENSILES DE CUISINE
KÜCHENUTENSILIEN

SET OF UTENSILS
JUEGO DE UTENSILIOS
JEU D'USTENSILES
KÜCHENSET

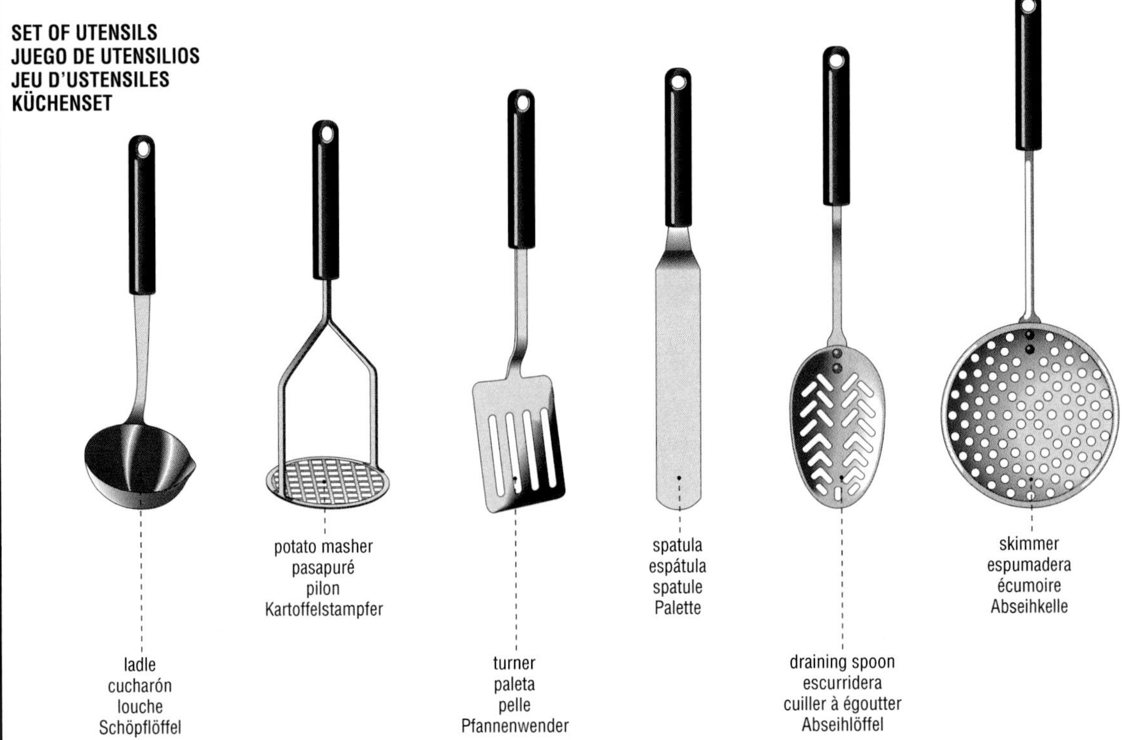

ladle
cucharón
louche
Schöpflöffel

potato masher
pasapuré
pilon
Kartoffelstampfer

turner
paleta
pelle
Pfannenwender

spatula
espátula
spatule
Palette

draining spoon
escurridera
cuiller à égoutter
Abseihlöffel

skimmer
espumadera
écumoire
Abseihkelle

FOR OPENING
UTENSILIOS PARA ABRIR Y DESCORCHAR
POUR OUVRIR
ZUM ÖFFNEN

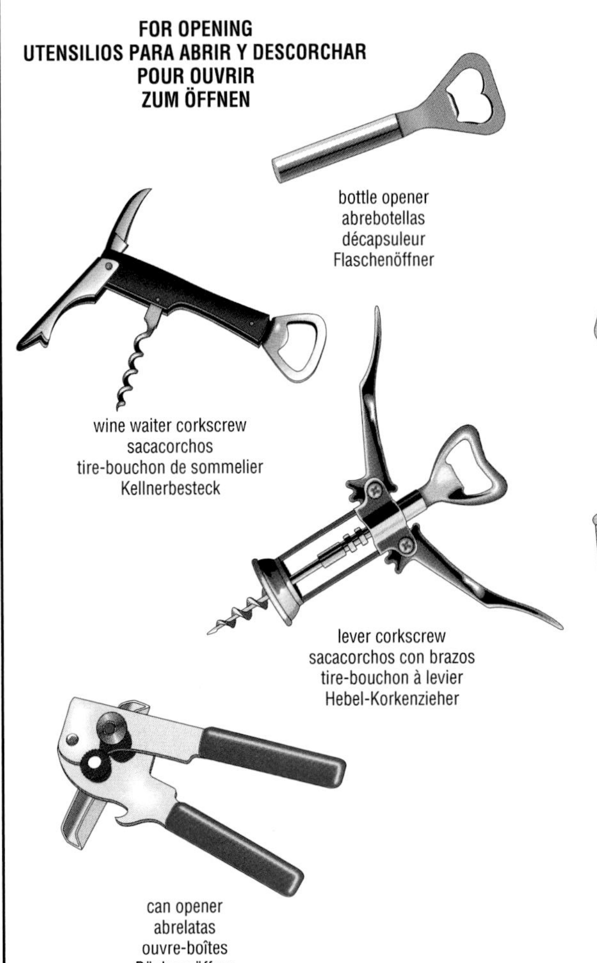

bottle opener
abrebotellas
décapsuleur
Flaschenöffner

wine waiter corkscrew
sacacorchos
tire-bouchon de sommelier
Kellnerbesteck

lever corkscrew
sacacorchos con brazos
tire-bouchon à levier
Hebel-Korkenzieher

can opener
abrelatas
ouvre-boîtes
Büchsenöffner

kitchen timer
reloj de cocina
minuteur
Küchenuhr

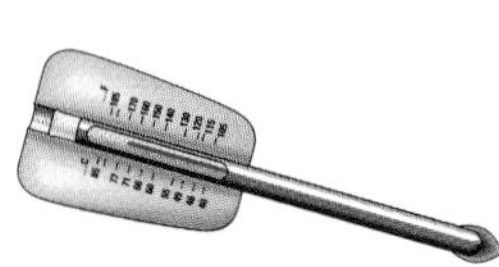

meat thermometer
termómetro para carne
thermomètre à viande
Fleischthermometer

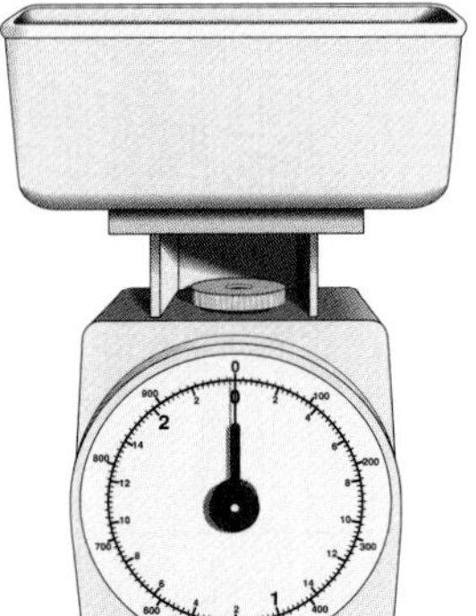

kitchen scale
báscula de cocina
balance de cuisine
Küchenwaage

FOR MEASURING
UTENSILIOS PARA MEDIR
POUR MESURER
ZUM MESSEN

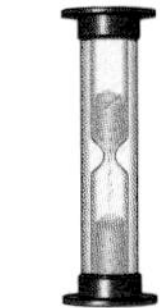

egg timer
minutero para huevos pasados por agua
sablier
Eieruhr

measuring spoons
cucharas para medir
cuillers doseuses
Meßlöffel

measuring cups
tazas para medir
mesures
Meßbecher

pastry brush
pincel de repostería
pinceau à pâtisserie
Kuchenpinsel

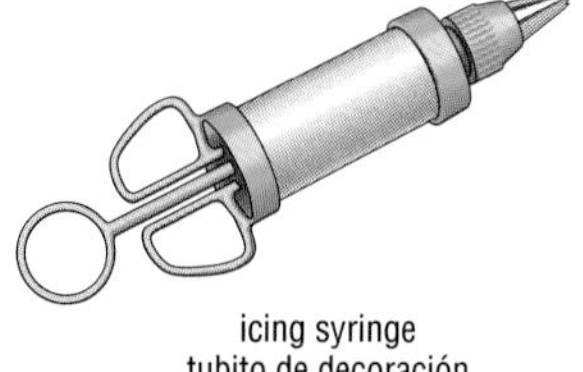

icing syringe
tubito de decoración
piston à décorer
Garnierspritze

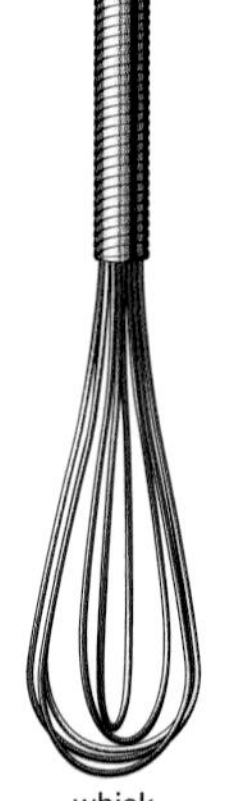

whisk
batidor
fouet
Schneebesen

egg beater
batidor mecánico
batteur à œufs
Rad-Schneeschläger

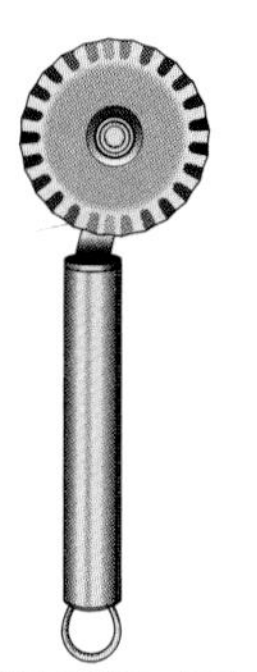

pastry cutting wheel
cortapastas
roulette de pâtissier
Kuchenrad

sifter
tamiz
tamis à farine
Mehlsieb

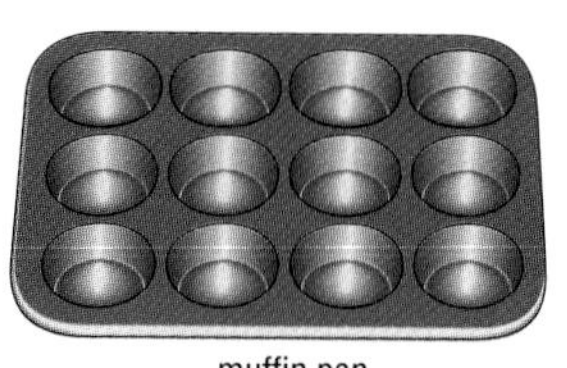

muffin pan
molde para magdalenas
moule à muffins
Mohrenkopfform

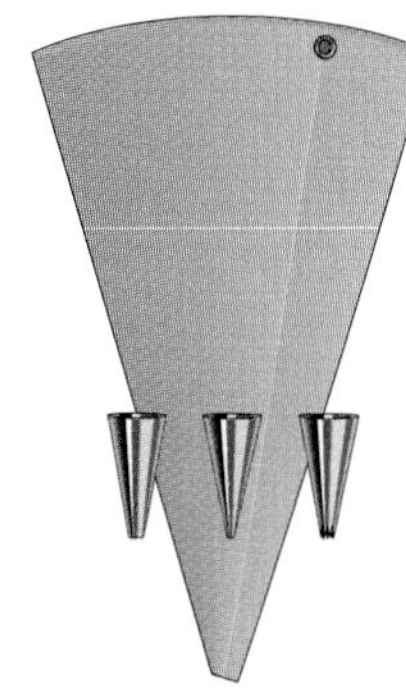

pastry bag and nozzles
manga y boquillas
poche à douilles
Spritzbeutel mit Düsen

cookie sheet
bandeja para hornear galletas
plaque à biscuits
Backblech

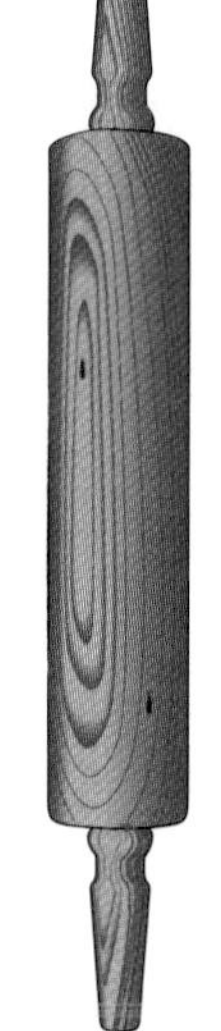

rolling pin
rodillo
rouleau à pâtisserie
Nudelholz

mixing bowls
boles para batir
bols à mélanger
Rührschüsseln

cookie cutters
moldes de pastas
emporte-pièces
Ausstechformen

removable-bottomed pan
molde redondo con muelles
moule à fond amovible
Springform

pie pan
molde para tartas
moule à tarte
flache Kuchenform

quiche plate
molde acanalado
moule à quiche
Quicheform

cake pan
molde para bizcocho
moule à gâteau
Kuchenform

KITCHEN UTENSILS
UTENSILIOS DE COCINA
USTENSILES DE CUISINE
KÜCHENUTENSILIEN

MISCELLANEOUS UTENSILS
UTENSILIOS DIVERSOS
USTENSILES DIVERS
VERSCHIEDENERLEI UTENSILIEN

stoner
deshuesador de frutas
dénoyauteur
Entsteiner

ice cream scoop
cuchara para servir helado
cuiller à glace
Eisportionierer

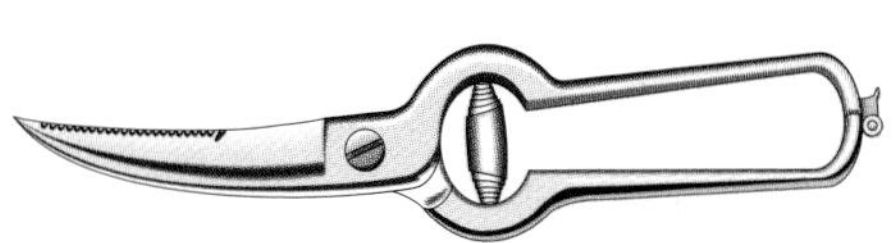
poultry shears
tijeras para aves
cisaille à volaille
Geflügelschere

spaghetti tongs
tenacillas para espagueti
pince à spaghettis
Spaghettizange

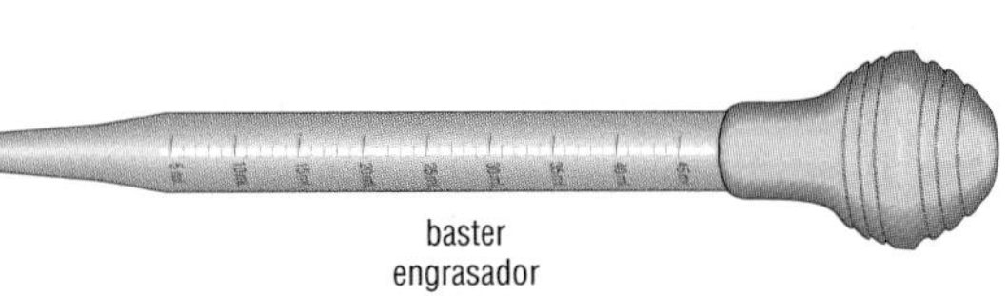
baster
engrasador
poire à jus
Fettgießer

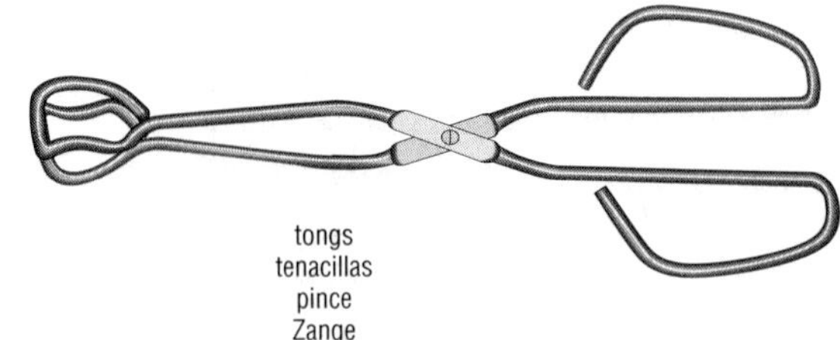
tongs
tenacillas
pince
Zange

vegetable brush
cepillo para verduras
brosse à légumes
Gemüsebürste

tea ball
esfera de té
boule à thé
Tee-Ei

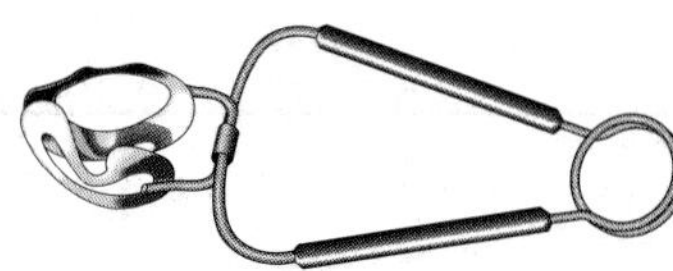
snail tongs
tenacillas para caracoles
pince à escargots
Schneckenzange

dredger
espolvoreador
saupoudreuse
Streuer

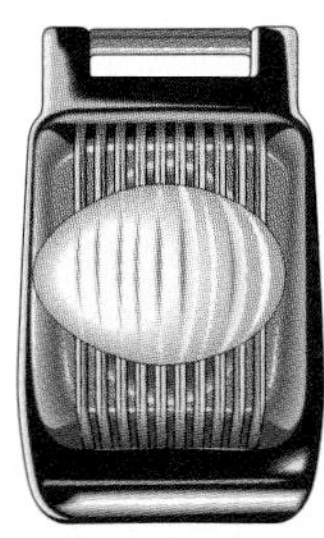
egg slicer
cortador de huevos duros
coupe-œuf
Eierschneider

snail dish
plato para caracoles
plat à escargots
Schneckenpfännchen

COFFEE MAKERS
CAFETERAS
CAFETIÈRES
KAFFEEMASCHINEN

AUTOMATIC DRIP COFFEE MAKER
CAFETERA DE FILTRO AUTOMÁTICA
CAFETIÈRE FILTRE
KAFFEEMASCHINE

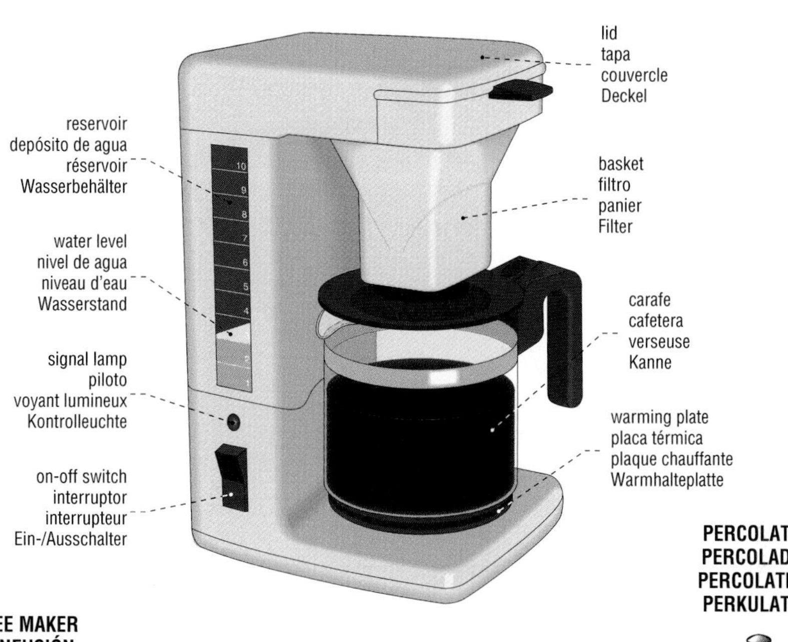
lid
tapa
couvercle
Deckel
reservoir
depósito de agua
réservoir
Wasserbehälter
basket
filtro
panier
Filter
water level
nivel de agua
niveau d'eau
Wasserstand
carafe
cafetera
verseuse
Kanne
signal lamp
piloto
voyant lumineux
Kontrolleuchte
warming plate
placa térmica
plaque chauffante
Warmhalteplatte
on-off switch
interruptor
interrupteur
Ein-/Ausschalter

VACUUM COFFEE MAKER
CAFETERA DE INFUSIÓN
CAFETIÈRE À INFUSION
VAKUUM-KAFFEEMASCHINE

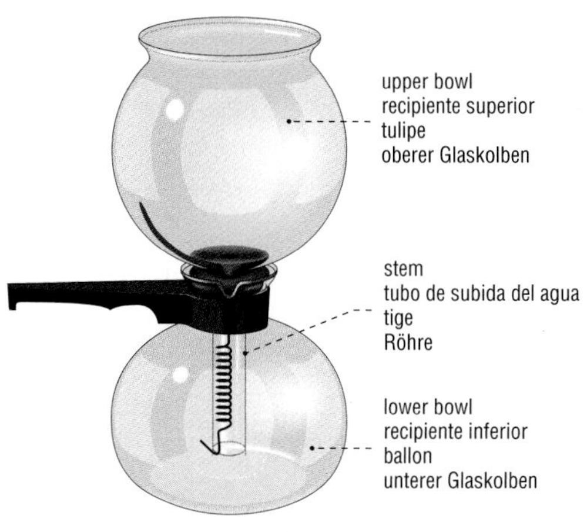
upper bowl
recipiente superior
tulipe
oberer Glaskolben
stem
tubo de subida del agua
tige
Röhre
lower bowl
recipiente inferior
ballon
unterer Glaskolben

PERCOLATOR
PERCOLADOR
PERCOLATEUR
PERKULATOR

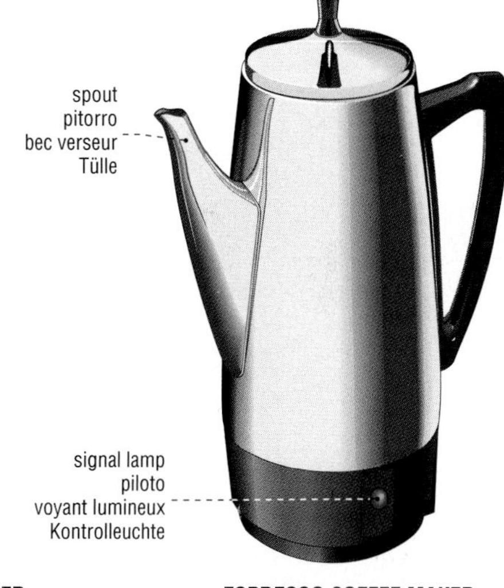
spout
pitorro
bec verseur
Tülle
signal lamp
piloto
voyant lumineux
Kontrolleuchte

PLUNGER
CAFETERA DE ÉMBOLO
CAFETIÈRE À PISTON
PRESSFILTERKANNE

NEAPOLITAN COFFEE MAKER
CAFETERA NAPOLITANA
CAFETIÈRE NAPOLITAINE
NEAPOLITANISCHE TROPFKANNE

ESPRESSO COFFEE MAKER
CAFETERA ITALIANA
CAFETIÈRE ESPRESSO
ESPRESSO-MASCHINE

COOKING UTENSILS
UTENSILIOS DE COCINA
BATTERIE DE CUISINE
KOCHGERÄTE

WOK SET
WOK
WOK
WOK-SET

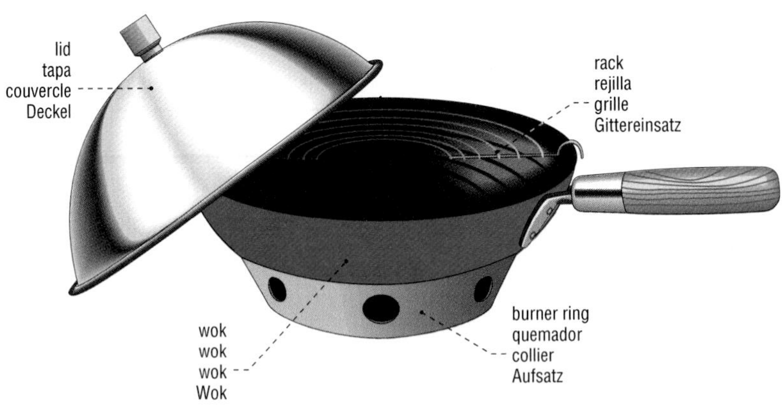
lid
tapa
couvercle
Deckel
rack
rejilla
grille
Gittereinsatz
wok
wok
wok
Wok
burner ring
quemador
collier
Aufsatz

FISH POACHER
BESUGUERA
POISSONNIÈRE
FISCHKOCHTOPF

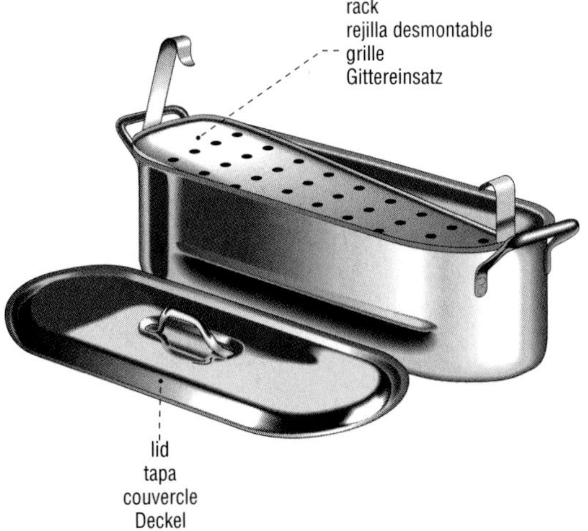
rack
rejilla desmontable
grille
Gittereinsatz
lid
tapa
couvercle
Deckel

FONDUE SET
JUEGO PARA FONDUE
SERVICE À FONDUE
FONDUE-SET

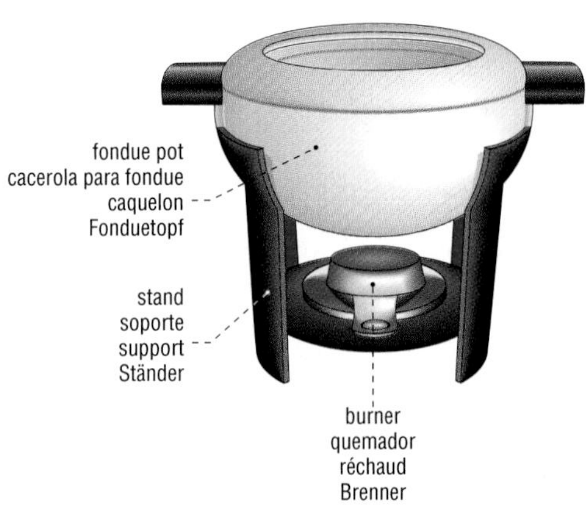
fondue pot
cacerola para fondue
caquelon
Fonduetopf
stand
soporte
support
Ständer
burner
quemador
réchaud
Brenner

PRESSURE COOKER
OLLA A PRESIÓN
AUTOCUISEUR
DAMPFKOCHTOPF

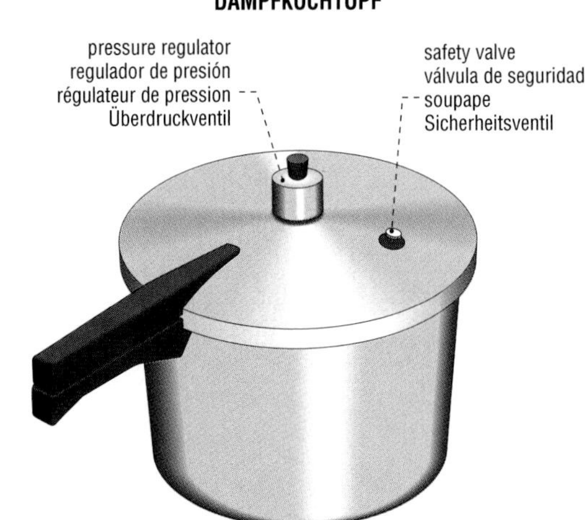
pressure regulator
regulador de presión
régulateur de pression
Überdruckventil
safety valve
válvula de seguridad
soupape
Sicherheitsventil

roasting pans
asadores
plats à four
Bräter

Dutch oven
cacerola refractaria
faitout
flacher Bratentopf

stock pot
olla
marmite
Suppentopf

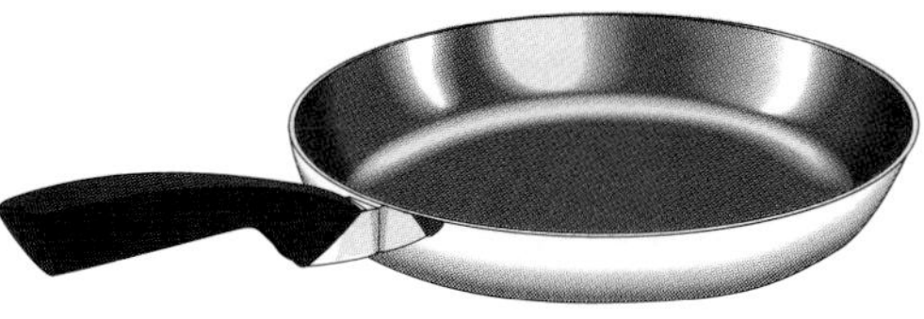

frying pan
sartén
poêle à frire
Bratpfanne

pancake pan
sartén para crepas
poêle à crêpes
Crêpe-Pfanne

couscous kettle
olla para alcuzcuz
couscoussier
Kuskustopf

egg poacher
escalfador de huevos
pocheuse
Eipochierer

sauté pan
sartén honda
sauteuse
Schmorpfanne

vegetable steamer
alcachofa para vegetales
étuveuse
Gemüsedünster

double boiler
cacerola para baño de María
bain-marie
Wasserbadtopf

saucepan
cacerola
casserole
Stielkasserolle

DOMESTIC APPLIANCES
APARATOS ELECTRODOMÉSTICOS
APPAREILS ÉLECTROMÉNAGERS
HAUSHALTSGERÄTE

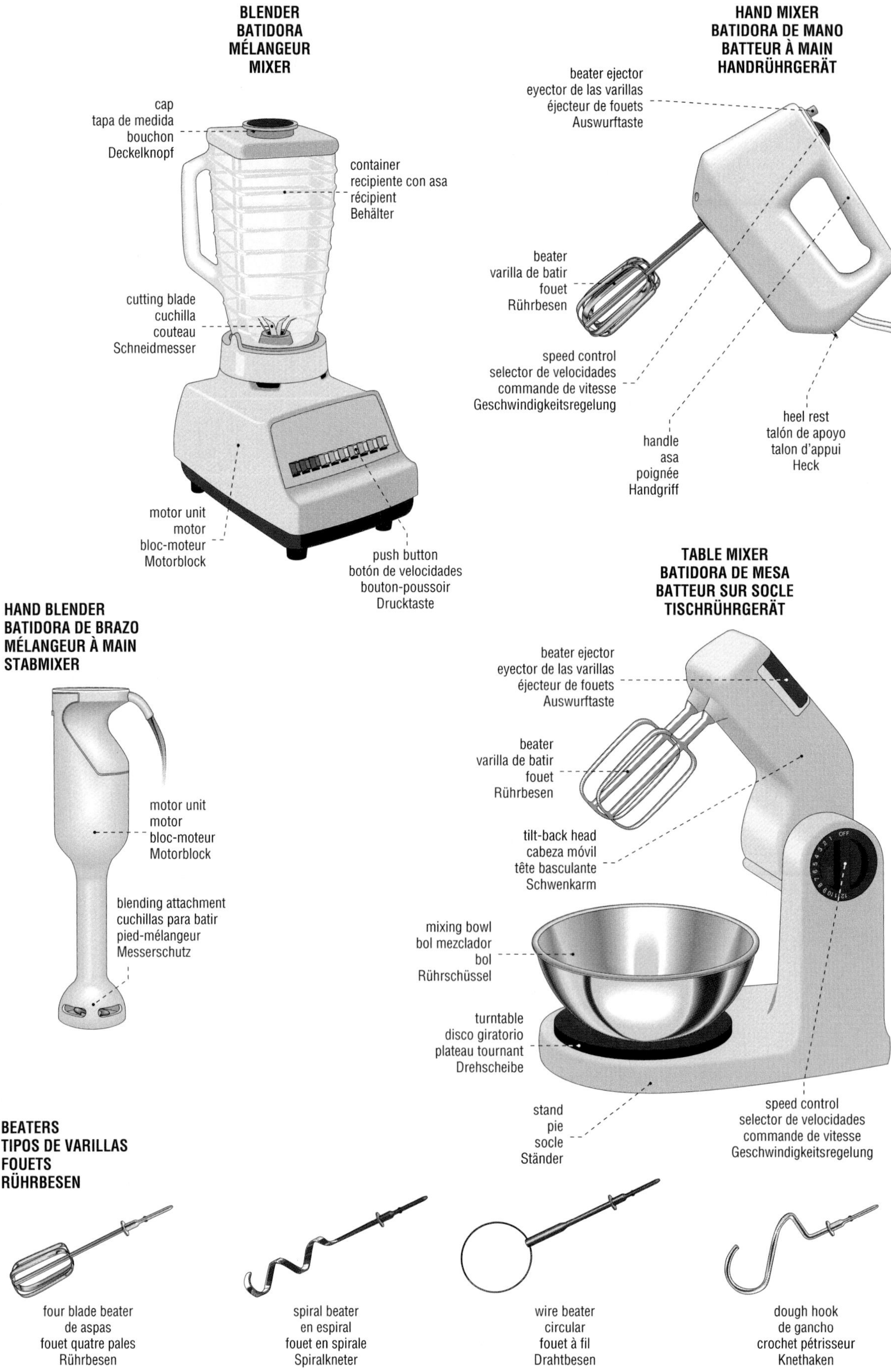

BLENDER
BATIDORA
MÉLANGEUR
MIXER
cap
tapa de medida
bouchon
Deckelknopf
container
recipiente con asa
récipient
Behälter
cutting blade
cuchilla
couteau
Schneidmesser
motor unit
motor
bloc-moteur
Motorblock
push button
botón de velocidades
bouton-poussoir
Drucktaste
HAND MIXER
BATIDORA DE MANO
BATTEUR À MAIN
HANDRÜHRGERÄT
beater ejector
eyector de las varillas
éjecteur de fouets
Auswurftaste
beater
varilla de batir
fouet
Rührbesen
speed control
selector de velocidades
commande de vitesse
Geschwindigkeitsregelung
handle
asa
poignée
Handgriff
heel rest
talón de apoyo
talon d'appui
Heck
HAND BLENDER
BATIDORA DE BRAZO
MÉLANGEUR À MAIN
STABMIXER
motor unit
motor
bloc-moteur
Motorblock
blending attachment
cuchillas para batir
pied-mélangeur
Messerschutz
TABLE MIXER
BATIDORA DE MESA
BATTEUR SUR SOCLE
TISCHRÜHRGERÄT
beater ejector
eyector de las varillas
éjecteur de fouets
Auswurftaste
beater
varilla de batir
fouet
Rührbesen
tilt-back head
cabeza móvil
tête basculante
Schwenkarm
mixing bowl
bol mezclador
bol
Rührschüssel
turntable
disco giratorio
plateau tournant
Drehscheibe
stand
pie
socle
Ständer
speed control
selector de velocidades
commande de vitesse
Geschwindigkeitsregelung
OFF

BEATERS
TIPOS DE VARILLAS
FOUETS
RÜHRBESEN

four blade beater de aspas fouet quatre pales Rührbesen	spiral beater en espiral fouet en spirale Spiralkneter	wire beater circular fouet à fil Drahtbesen	dough hook de gancho crochet pétrisseur Knethaken

FOOD PROCESSOR
ROBOT DE COCINA
ROBOT DE CUISINE
KÜCHENMASCHINE

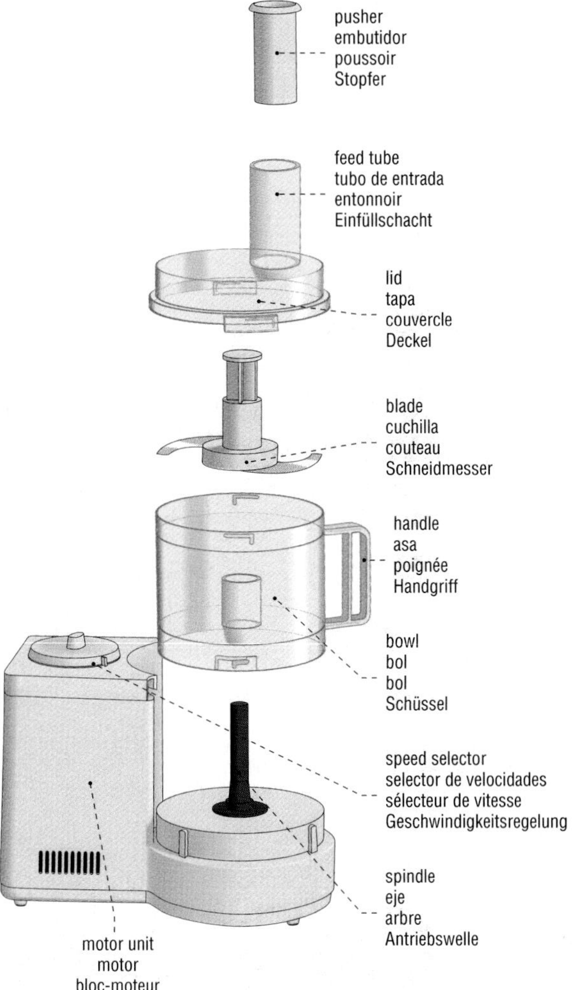

pusher
embutidor
poussoir
Stopfer
feed tube
tubo de entrada
entonnoir
Einfüllschacht
lid
tapa
couvercle
Deckel
blade
cuchilla
couteau
Schneidmesser
handle
asa
poignée
Handgriff
bowl
bol
bol
Schüssel
speed selector
selector de velocidades
sélecteur de vitesse
Geschwindigkeitsregelung
spindle
eje
arbre
Antriebswelle
motor unit
motor
bloc-moteur
Motorblock

ICE CREAM FREEZER
HELADERA
SORBETIÈRE
EISMASCHINE

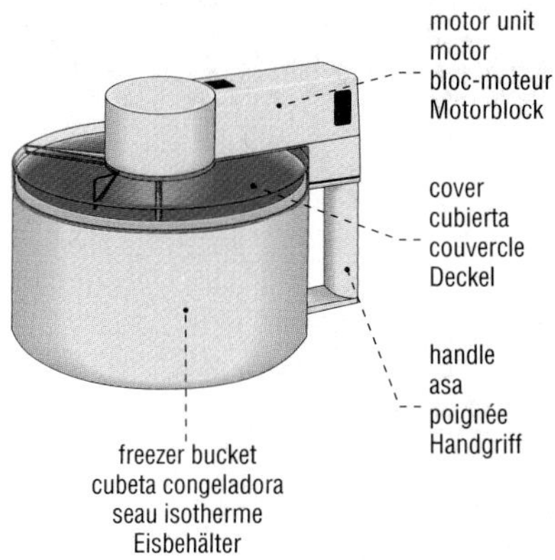

motor unit
motor
bloc-moteur
Motorblock
cover
cubierta
couvercle
Deckel
handle
asa
poignée
Handgriff
freezer bucket
cubeta congeladora
seau isotherme
Eisbehälter

DISKS
DISCO
DISQUES
SCHEIBEN

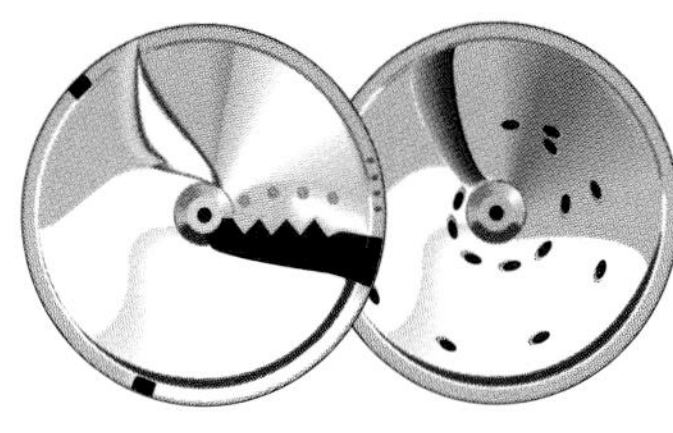

CITRUS JUICER
EXPRIMIDOR DE CÍTRICOS
PRESSE-AGRUMES
ZITRUSPRESSE

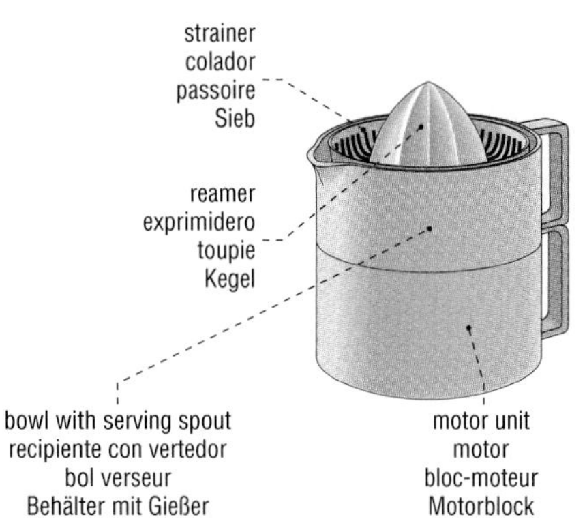

strainer
colador
passoire
Sieb
reamer
exprimidero
toupie
Kegel
bowl with serving spout
recipiente con vertedor
bol verseur
Behälter mit Gießer
motor unit
motor
bloc-moteur
Motorblock

JUICER
EXTRACTOR DE JUGOS
CENTRIFUGEUSE
ENTSAFTER

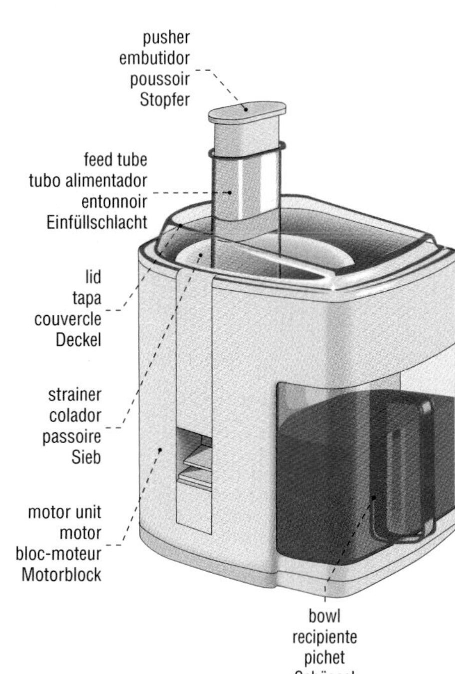

pusher
embutidor
poussoir
Stopfer
feed tube
tubo alimentador
entonnoir
Einfüllschlacht
lid
tapa
couvercle
Deckel
strainer
colador
passoire
Sieb
motor unit
motor
bloc-moteur
Motorblock
bowl
recipiente
pichet
Schüssel

DOMESTIC APPLIANCES
APARATOS ELECTRODOMÉSTICOS
APPAREILS ÉLECTROMÉNAGERS
HAUSHALTSGERÄTE

KETTLE
HERVIDOR DE SILBATO
BOUILLOIRE
WASSERKESSEL

TOASTER
TOSTADOR
GRILLE-PAIN
TOASTER

DEEP FRYER
FREIDORA
FRITEUSE
FRITEUSE

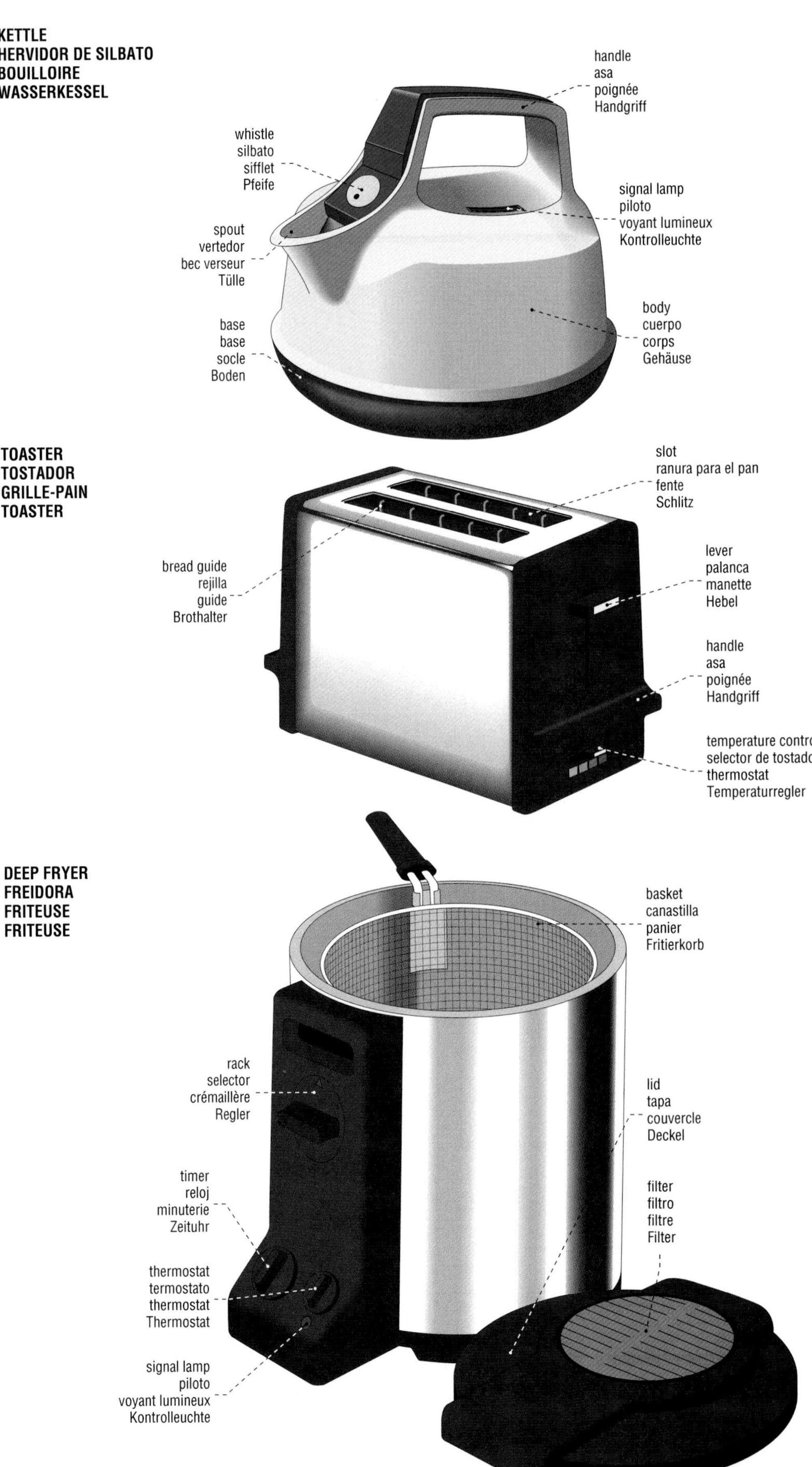
handle
asa
poignée
Handgriff
whistle
silbato
sifflet
Pfeife
signal lamp
piloto
voyant lumineux
Kontrolleuchte
spout
vertedor
bec verseur
Tülle
body
cuerpo
corps
Gehäuse
base
base
socle
Boden
slot
ranura para el pan
fente
Schlitz
lever
palanca
manette
Hebel
bread guide
rejilla
guide
Brothalter
handle
asa
poignée
Handgriff
temperature control
selector de tostado
thermostat
Temperaturregler
basket
canastilla
panier
Fritierkorb
rack
selector
crémaillère
Regler
lid
tapa
couvercle
Deckel
timer
reloj
minuterie
Zeituhr
filter
filtro
filtre
Filter
thermostat
termostato
thermostat
Thermostat
signal lamp
piloto
voyant lumineux
Kontrolleuchte

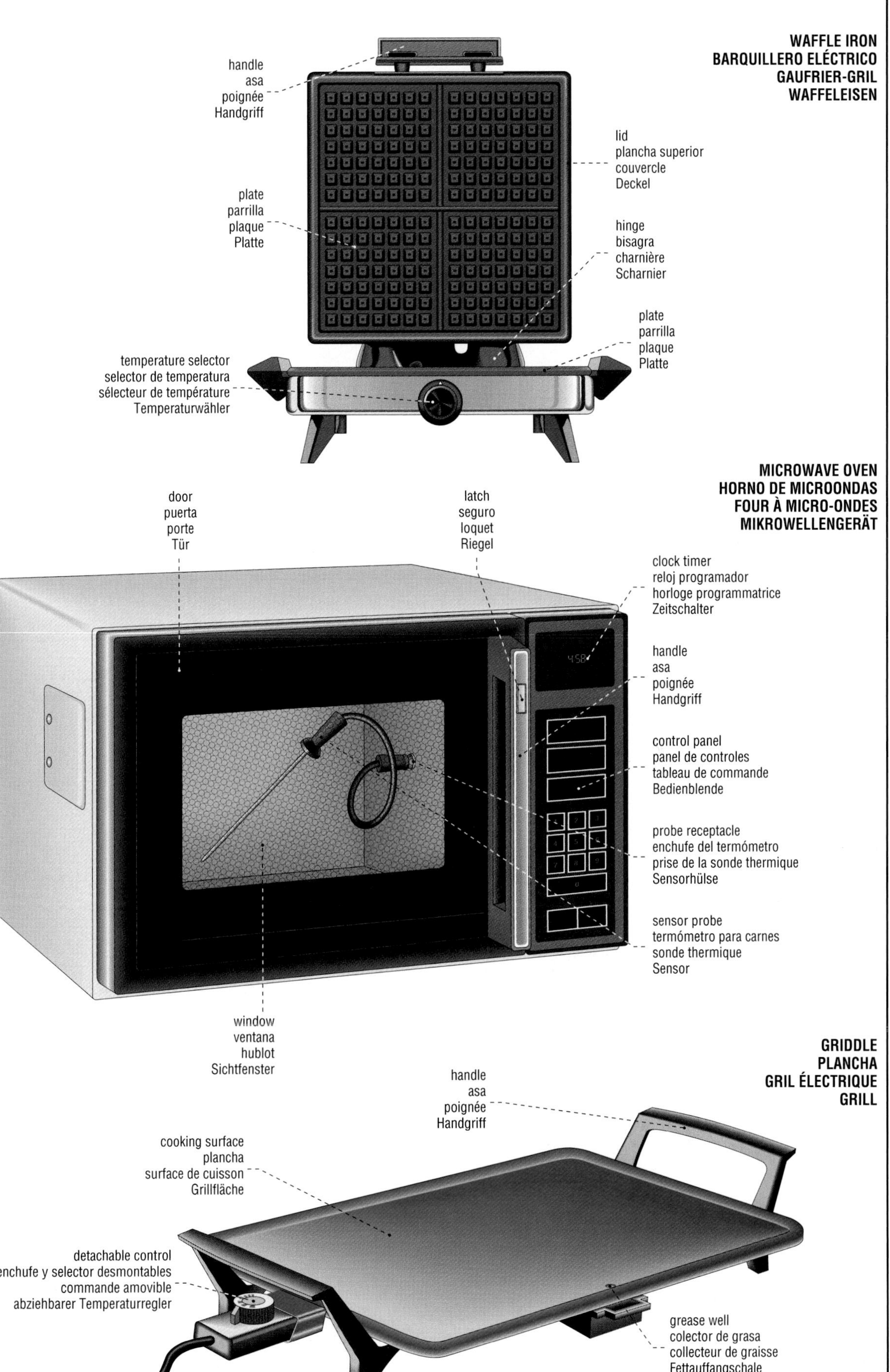
WAFFLE IRON
BARQUILLERO ELÉCTRICO
GAUFRIER-GRIL
WAFFELEISEN
handle
asa
poignée
Handgriff
lid
plancha superior
couvercle
Deckel
plate
parrilla
plaque
Platte
hinge
bisagra
charnière
Scharnier
plate
parrilla
plaque
Platte
temperature selector
selector de temperatura
sélecteur de température
Temperaturwähler
MICROWAVE OVEN
HORNO DE MICROONDAS
FOUR À MICRO-ONDES
MIKROWELLENGERÄT
door
puerta
porte
Tür
latch
seguro
loquet
Riegel
clock timer
reloj programador
horloge programmatrice
Zeitschalter
handle
asa
poignée
Handgriff
control panel
panel de controles
tableau de commande
Bedienblende
probe receptacle
enchufe del termómetro
prise de la sonde thermique
Sensorhülse
sensor probe
termómetro para carnes
sonde thermique
Sensor
window
ventana
hublot
Sichtfenster
GRIDDLE
PLANCHA
GRIL ÉLECTRIQUE
GRILL
handle
asa
poignée
Handgriff
cooking surface
plancha
surface de cuisson
Grillfläche
detachable control
enchufe y selector desmontables
commande amovible
abziehbarer Temperaturregler
grease well
colector de grasa
collecteur de graisse
Fettauffangschale

REFRIGERATOR
FRIGORÍFICO
RÉFRIGÉRATEUR
KÜHLSCHRANK

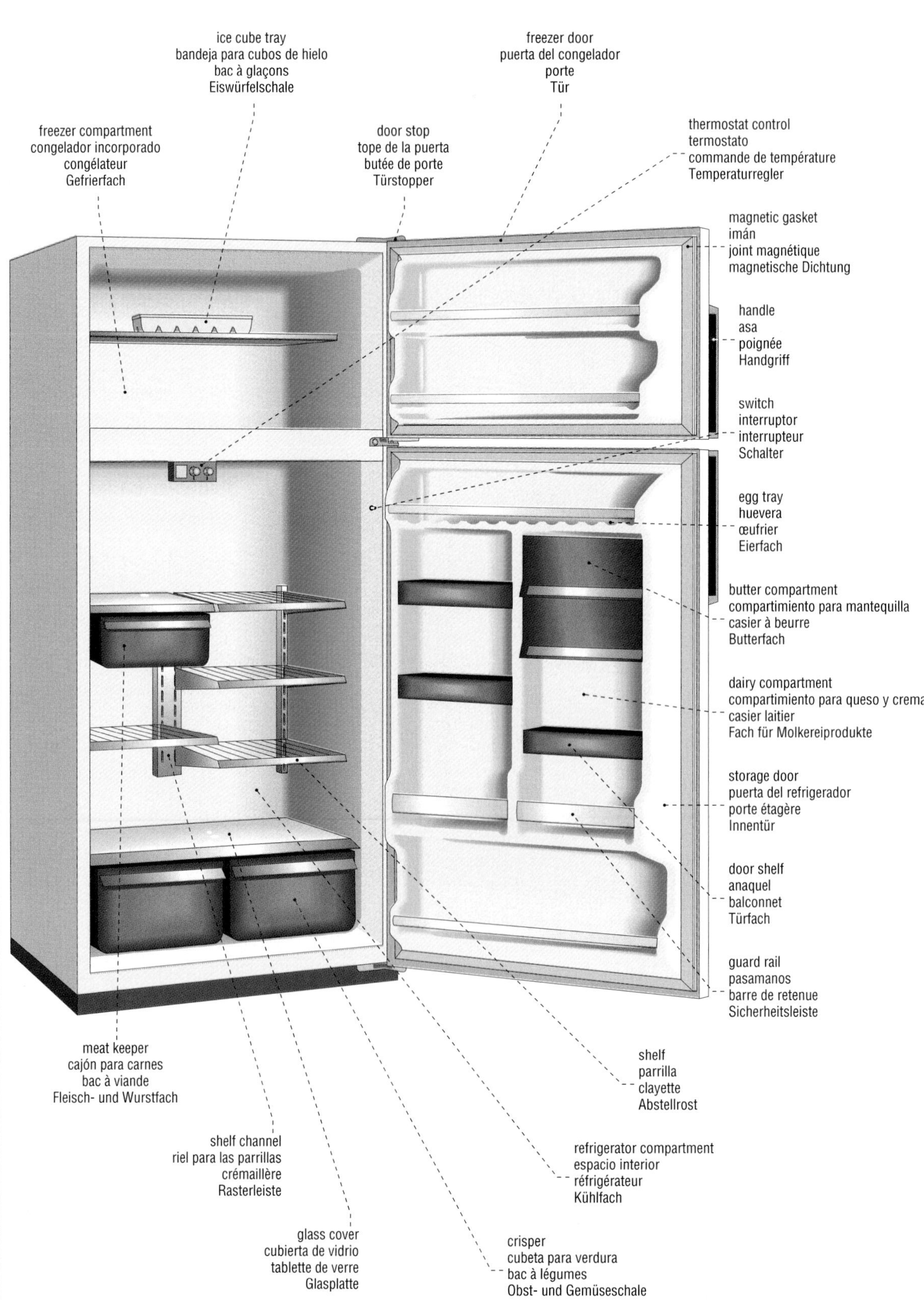
ice cube tray
bandeja para cubos de hielo
bac à glaçons
Eiswürfelschale
freezer door
puerta del congelador
porte
Tür
freezer compartment
congelador incorporado
congélateur
Gefrierfach
door stop
tope de la puerta
butée de porte
Türstopper
thermostat control
termostato
commande de température
Temperaturregler
magnetic gasket
imán
joint magnétique
magnetische Dichtung
handle
asa
poignée
Handgriff
switch
interruptor
interrupteur
Schalter
egg tray
huevera
œufrier
Eierfach
butter compartment
compartimiento para mantequilla
casier à beurre
Butterfach
dairy compartment
compartimiento para queso y crema
casier laitier
Fach für Molkereiprodukte
storage door
puerta del refrigerador
porte étagère
Innentür
door shelf
anaquel
balconnet
Türfach
guard rail
pasamanos
barre de retenue
Sicherheitsleiste
meat keeper
cajón para carnes
bac à viande
Fleisch- und Wurstfach
shelf
parrilla
clayette
Abstellrost
shelf channel
riel para las parrillas
crémaillère
Rasterleiste
refrigerator compartment
espacio interior
réfrigérateur
Kühlfach
glass cover
cubierta de vidrio
tablette de verre
Glasplatte
crisper
cubeta para verdura
bac à légumes
Obst- und Gemüseschale

RANGE HOOD
CAMPANA
HOTTE
DUNSTABZUGSHAUBE

ELECTRIC RANGE
COCINA ELÉCTRICA
CUISINIÈRE ÉLECTRIQUE
ELEKTROHERD

filter
filtro
filtre
Filter
clock timer
reloj
horloge programmatrice
Schaltuhr
oven control knob
botón del horno
réglage du four
Backofenschalter
signal lamp
piloto
voyant lumineux
Kontrolleuchte
backguard
panel de mandos
dosseret
Blende
control knob
botón de control
bouton de commande
Schalter
timed outlet
enchufe con control de tiempo
prise chronométrée
Zusatzstecker
control panel
tablero de controles
tableau de commande
Bedienblende
surface element
placa
serpentin
Kochplatte
oven
horno
four
Backofen
cooktop edge
borde
rebord
Herdkante
rack
rejilla
grille
Rost
cooktop
cubierta
surface de cuisson
Kochstelle
window
ventana
hublot
Sichtfenster
handle
asa
poignée
Griff
drawer
cajón
tiroir
Geschirrwagen
trim ring
arandela
anneau
Schutzring
drip bowl
protector
cuvette
Auffangschüssel
terminal
enchufe
borne
Anschluß
tubular element
resistencia
élément tubulaire
Heizspirale

DOMESTIC APPLIANCES
APARATOS ELECTRODOMÉSTICOS
APPAREILS ÉLECTROMÉNAGERS
HAUSHALTSGERÄTE

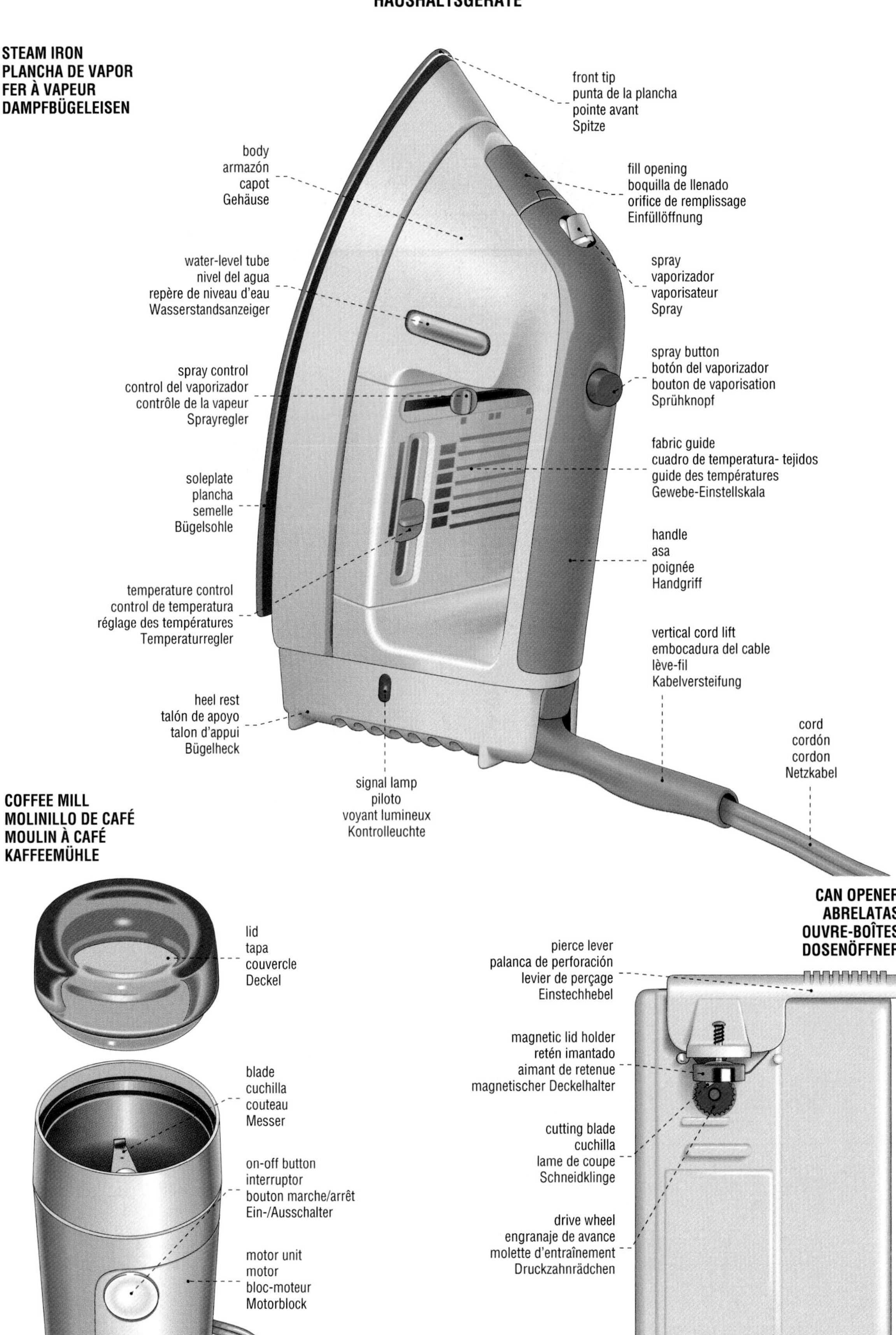
STEAM IRON
PLANCHA DE VAPOR
FER À VAPEUR
DAMPFBÜGELEISEN
front tip
punta de la plancha
pointe avant
Spitze
body
armazón
capot
Gehäuse
fill opening
boquilla de llenado
orifice de remplissage
Einfüllöffnung
water-level tube
nivel del agua
repère de niveau d'eau
Wasserstandsanzeiger
spray
vaporizador
vaporisateur
Spray
spray button
botón del vaporizador
bouton de vaporisation
Sprühknopf
spray control
control del vaporizador
contrôle de la vapeur
Sprayregler
fabric guide
cuadro de temperatura- tejidos
guide des températures
Gewebe-Einstellskala
soleplate
plancha
semelle
Bügelsohle
handle
asa
poignée
Handgriff
temperature control
control de temperatura
réglage des températures
Temperaturregler
vertical cord lift
embocadura del cable
lève-fil
Kabelversteifung
heel rest
talón de apoyo
talon d'appui
Bügelheck
cord
cordón
cordon
Netzkabel
signal lamp
piloto
voyant lumineux
Kontrolleuchte
COFFEE MILL
MOLINILLO DE CAFÉ
MOULIN À CAFÉ
KAFFEEMÜHLE
lid
tapa
couvercle
Deckel
blade
cuchilla
couteau
Messer
on-off button
interruptor
bouton marche/arrêt
Ein-/Ausschalter
motor unit
motor
bloc-moteur
Motorblock
CAN OPENER
ABRELATAS
OUVRE-BOÎTES
DOSENÖFFNER
pierce lever
palanca de perforación
levier de perçage
Einstechhebel
magnetic lid holder
retén imantado
aimant de retenue
magnetischer Deckelhalter
cutting blade
cuchilla
lame de coupe
Schneidklinge
drive wheel
engranaje de avance
molette d'entraînement
Druckzahnrädchen

DOMESTIC APPLIANCES
APARATOS ELECTRODOMÉSTICOS
APPAREILS ÉLECTROMÉNAGERS
HAUSHALTSGERÄTE

CONTROL PANEL
PANEL DE MANDOS
TABLEAU DE COMMANDE
BEDIENBLENDE

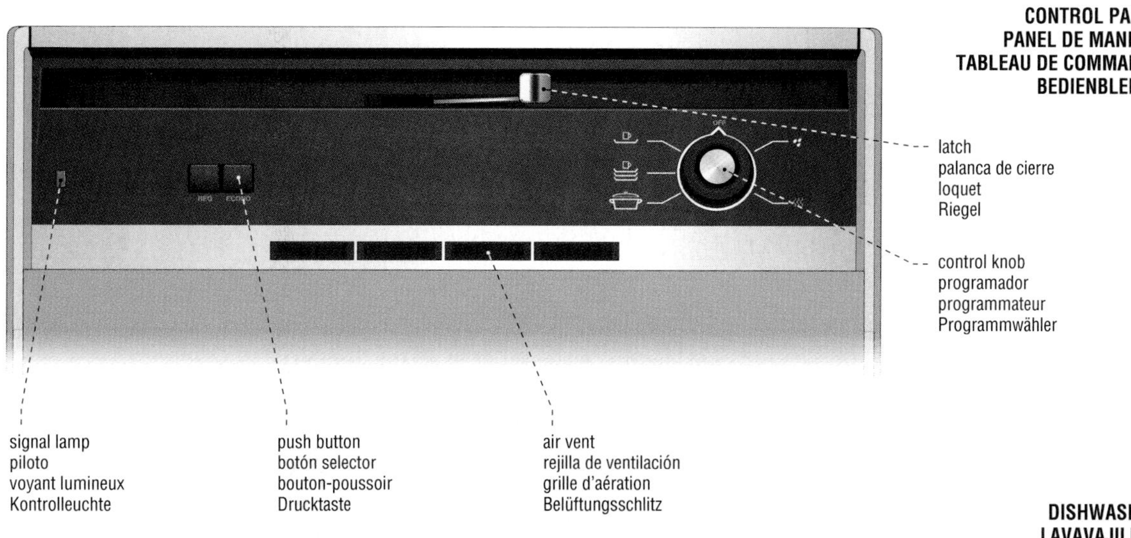
latch
palanca de cierre
loquet
Riegel
control knob
programador
programmateur
Programmwähler
signal lamp
piloto
voyant lumineux
Kontrolleuchte
push button
botón selector
bouton-poussoir
Drucktaste
air vent
rejilla de ventilación
grille d'aération
Belüftungsschlitz

DISHWASHER
LAVAVAJILLAS
LAVE-VAISSELLE
GESCHIRRSPÜLMASCHINE

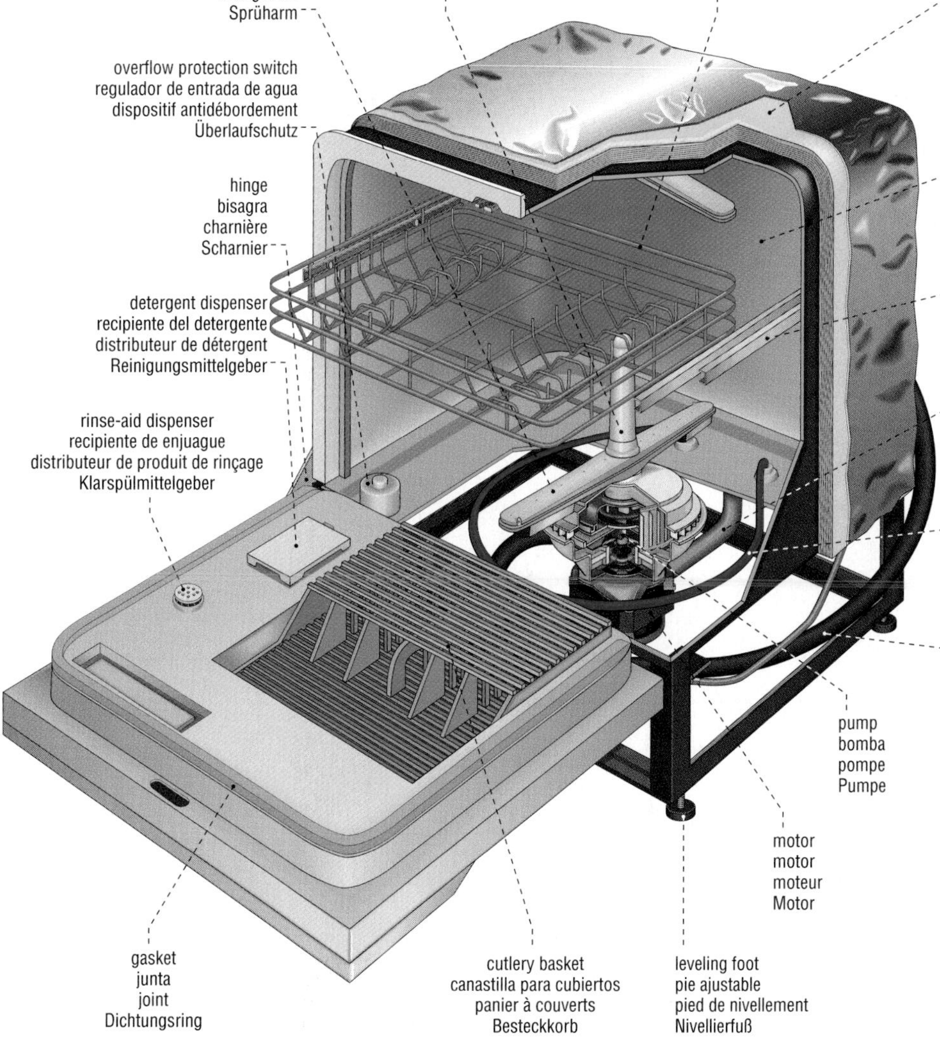

spray arm
pulverizador
bras gicleur
Sprüharm

wash tower
torrecilla de lavado
tourelle
Wascherarm

rack
canastilla
panier
Korb

insulating material
aislante
isolant
Isoliermaterial

overflow protection switch
regulador de entrada de agua
dispositif antidébordement
Überlaufschutz

tub
cubeta de lavado
cuve
Bottich

hinge
bisagra
charnière
Scharnier

slide
rail corredizo
glissière
Schiene

detergent dispenser
recipiente del detergente
distributeur de détergent
Reinigungsmittelgeber

water hose
manguera de alimentación
conduite d'eau
Wasserschlauch

rinse-aid dispenser
recipiente de enjuague
distributeur de produit de rinçage
Klarspülmittelgeber

heating element
resistencia
élément chauffant
Heizelement

drain hose
manguera de desagüe
tuyau de vidange
Ablaufschlauch

pump
bomba
pompe
Pumpe

motor
motor
moteur
Motor

gasket
junta
joint
Dichtungsring

cutlery basket
canastilla para cubiertos
panier à couverts
Besteckkorb

leveling foot
pie ajustable
pied de nivellement
Nivellierfuß

WASHER
LAVADORA
LAVE-LINGE
WASCHMASCHINE

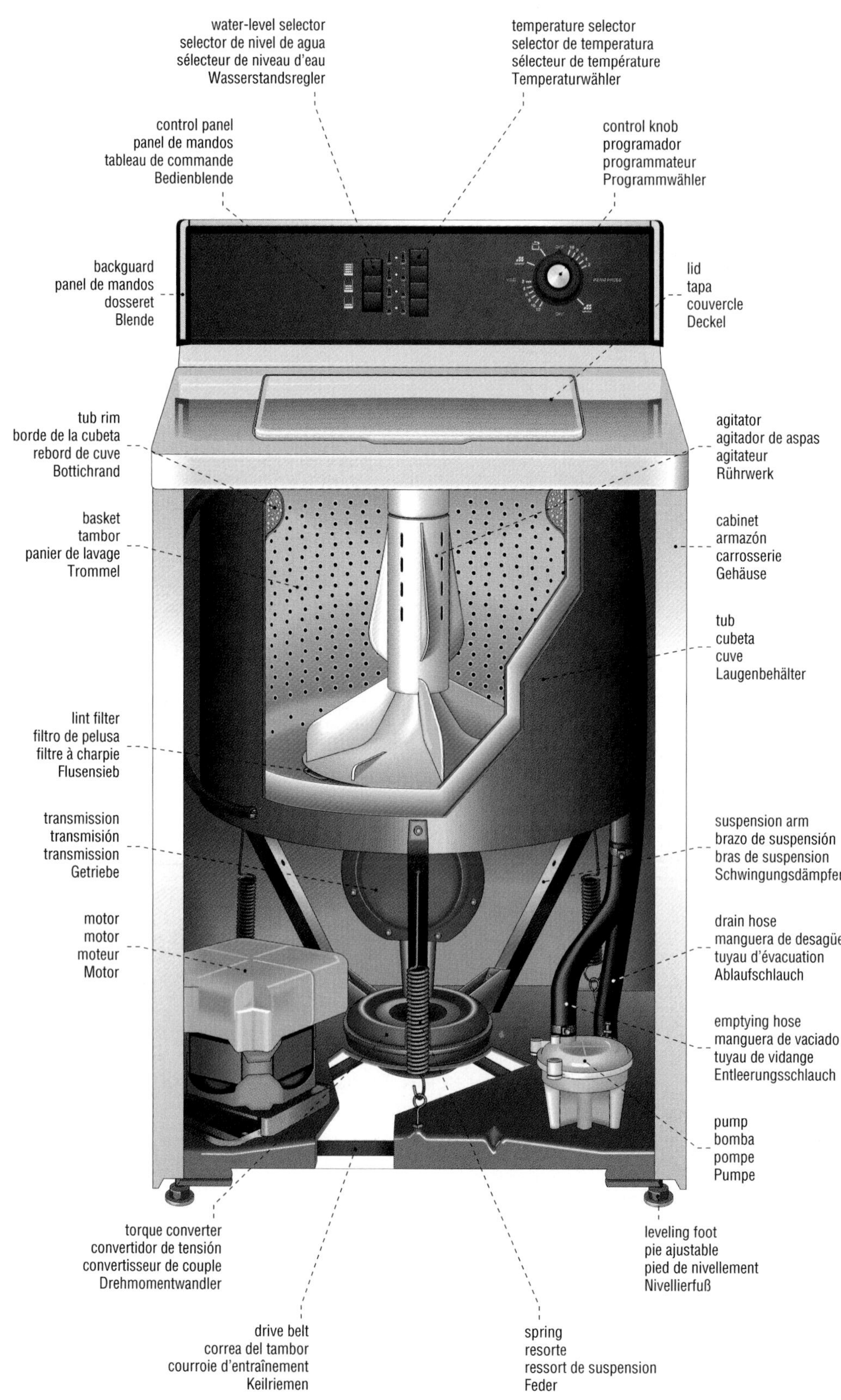
water-level selector
selector de nivel de agua
sélecteur de niveau d'eau
Wasserstandsregler
temperature selector
selector de temperatura
sélecteur de température
Temperaturwähler
control panel
panel de mandos
tableau de commande
Bedienblende
control knob
programador
programmateur
Programmwähler
backguard
panel de mandos
dosseret
Blende
lid
tapa
couvercle
Deckel
tub rim
borde de la cubeta
rebord de cuve
Bottichrand
agitator
agitador de aspas
agitateur
Rührwerk
basket
tambor
panier de lavage
Trommel
cabinet
armazón
carrosserie
Gehäuse
tub
cubeta
cuve
Laugenbehälter
lint filter
filtro de pelusa
filtre à charpie
Flusensieb
transmission
transmisión
transmission
Getriebe
suspension arm
brazo de suspensión
bras de suspension
Schwingungsdämpfer
motor
motor
moteur
Motor
drain hose
manguera de desagüe
tuyau d'évacuation
Ablaufschlauch
emptying hose
manguera de vaciado
tuyau de vidange
Entleerungsschlauch
pump
bomba
pompe
Pumpe
torque converter
convertidor de tensión
convertisseur de couple
Drehmomentwandler
leveling foot
pie ajustable
pied de nivellement
Nivellierfuß
drive belt
correa del tambor
courroie d'entraînement
Keilriemen
spring
resorte
ressort de suspension
Feder

ELECTRIC DRYER
SECADORA DE ROPA
SÈCHE-LINGE ÉLECTRIQUE
WÄSCHETROCKNER

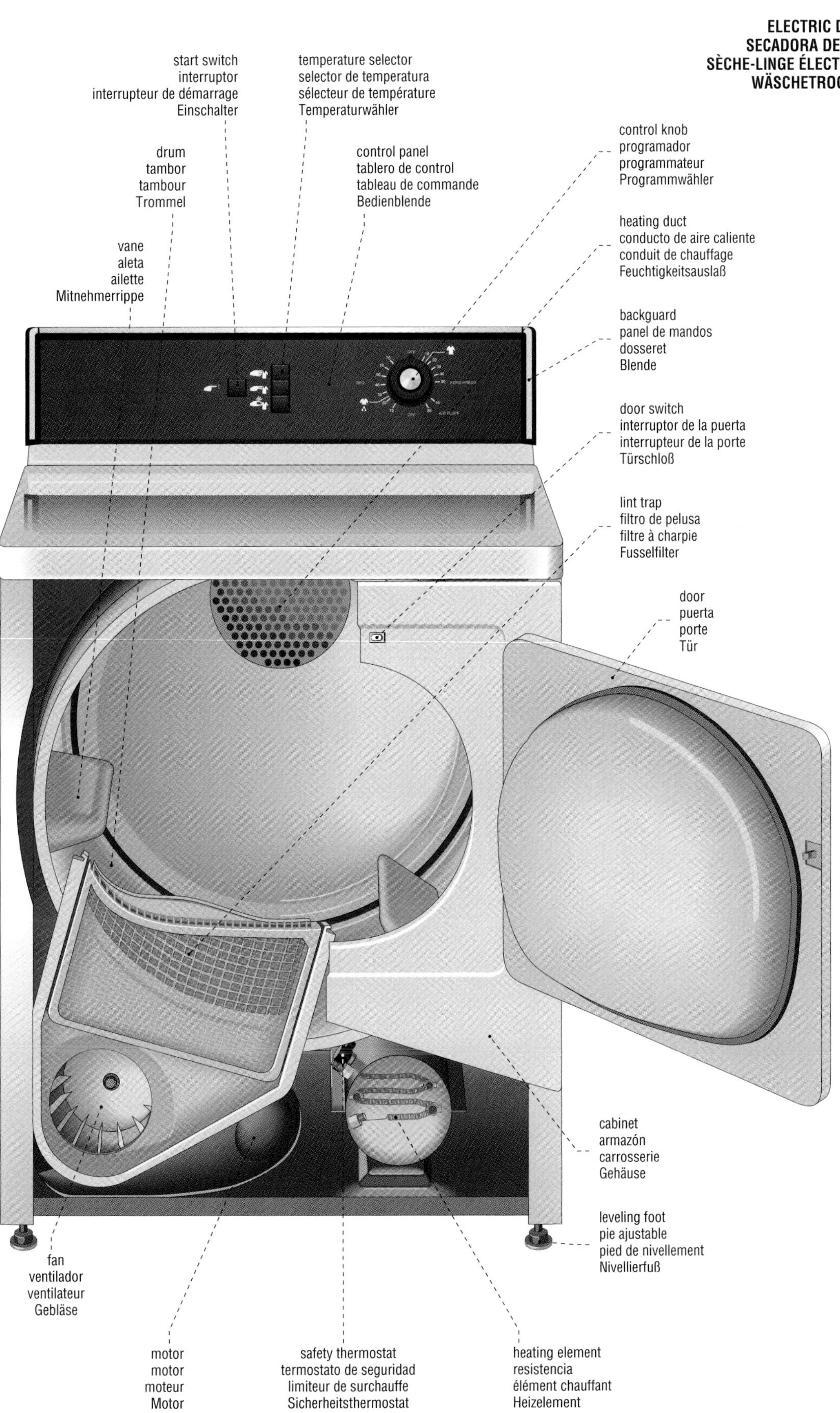

start switch
interruptor
interrupteur de démarrage
Einschalter
temperature selector
selector de temperatura
sélecteur de température
Temperaturwähler
drum
tambor
tambour
Trommel
control panel
tablero de control
tableau de commande
Bedienblende
control knob
programador
programmateur
Programmwähler
vane
aleta
ailette
Mitnehmerrippe
heating duct
conducto de aire caliente
conduit de chauffage
Feuchtigkeitsauslaß
backguard
panel de mandos
dosseret
Blende
door switch
interruptor de la puerta
interrupteur de la porte
Türschloß
lint trap
filtro de pelusa
filtre à charpie
Fusselfilter
door
puerta
porte
Tür
cabinet
armazón
carrosserie
Gehäuse
leveling foot
pie ajustable
pied de nivellement
Nivellierfuß
fan
ventilador
ventilateur
Gebläse
motor
motor
moteur
Motor
safety thermostat
termostato de seguridad
limiteur de surchauffe
Sicherheitsthermostat
heating element
resistencia
élément chauffant
Heizelement

DOMESTIC APPLIANCES
APARATOS ELECTRODOMÉSTICOS
APPAREILS ÉLECTROMÉNAGERS
HAUSHALTSGERÄTE

HAND VACUUM CLEANER
ASPIRADOR MANUAL
ASPIRATEUR À MAIN
AKKU-MINI-STAUBSAUGER

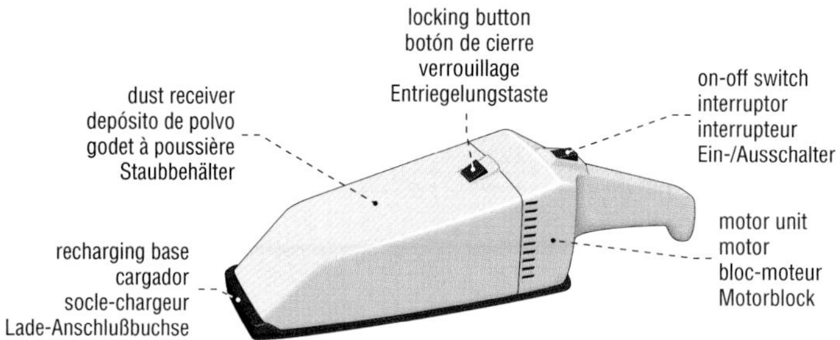
locking button
botón de cierre
verrouillage
Entriegelungstaste
dust receiver
depósito de polvo
godet à poussière
Staubbehälter
on-off switch
interruptor
interrupteur
Ein-/Ausschalter
motor unit
motor
bloc-moteur
Motorblock
recharging base
cargador
socle-chargeur
Lade-Anschlußbuchse

CANISTER VACUUM CLEANER
ASPIRADOR
ASPIRATEUR-TRAÎNEAU
KESSELSTAUBSAUGER

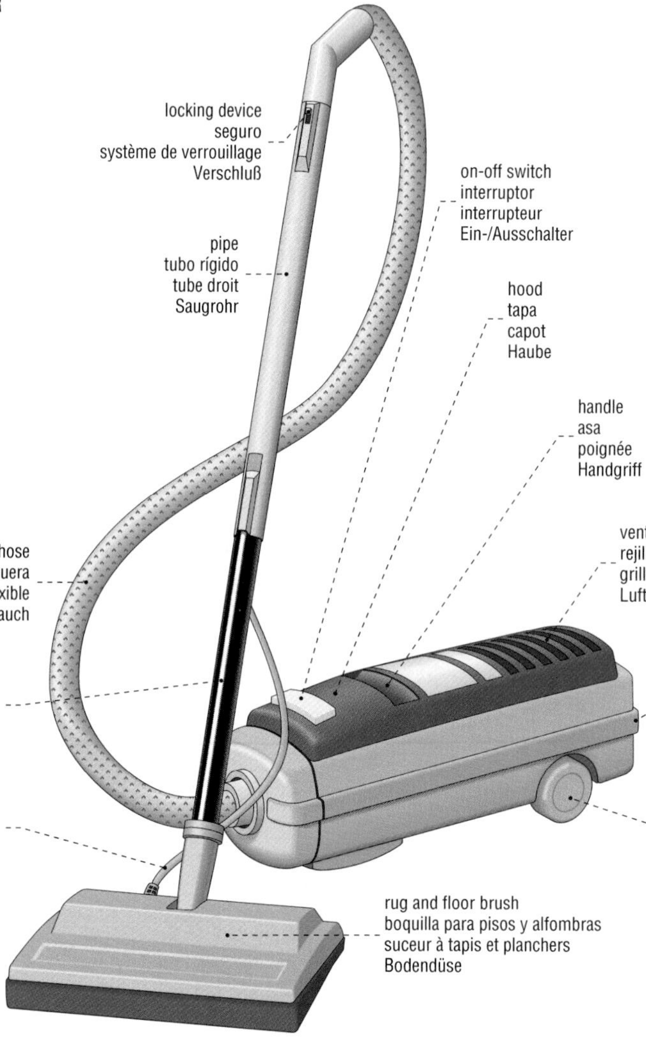

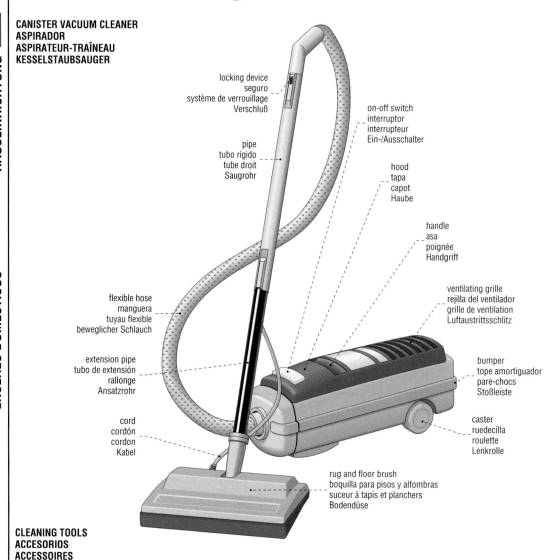

locking device
seguro
système de verrouillage
Verschluß

on-off switch
interruptor
interrupteur
Ein-/Ausschalter

pipe
tubo rígido
tube droit
Saugrohr

hood
tapa
capot
Haube

handle
asa
poignée
Handgriff

ventilating grille
rejilla del ventilador
grille de ventilation
Luftaustrittsschlitz

flexible hose
manguera
tuyau flexible
beweglicher Schlauch

extension pipe
tubo de extensión
rallonge
Ansatzrohr

bumper
tope amortiguador
pare-chocs
Stoßleiste

cord
cordón
cordon
Kabel

caster
ruedecilla
roulette
Lenkrolle

rug and floor brush
boquilla para pisos y alfombras
suceur à tapis et planchers
Bodendüse

CLEANING TOOLS
ACCESORIOS
ACCESSOIRES
SAUGZUBEHÖR

upholstery nozzle
boquilla para tapicería
suceur triangulaire à tissus
Polsterdüse

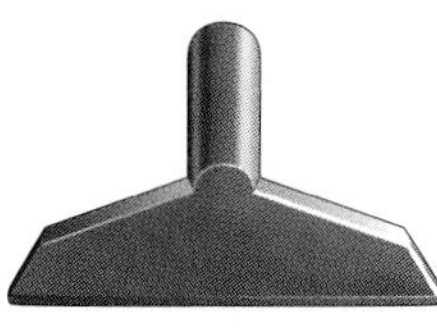

crevice tool
boquilla rinconera
suceur plat
Fugendüse

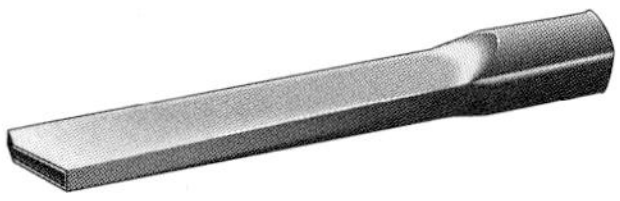

floor brush
cepillo para pisos
brosse à planchers
Bürste

dusting brush
cepillo-plumero
brosse à épousseter
Saugpinsel

GARDENING
JARDINERÍA
JARDINAGE
GARTENARBEIT

CONTENTS

PLEASURE GARDEN
JARDÍN
JARDIN D'AGRÉMENT
ZIERGARTEN

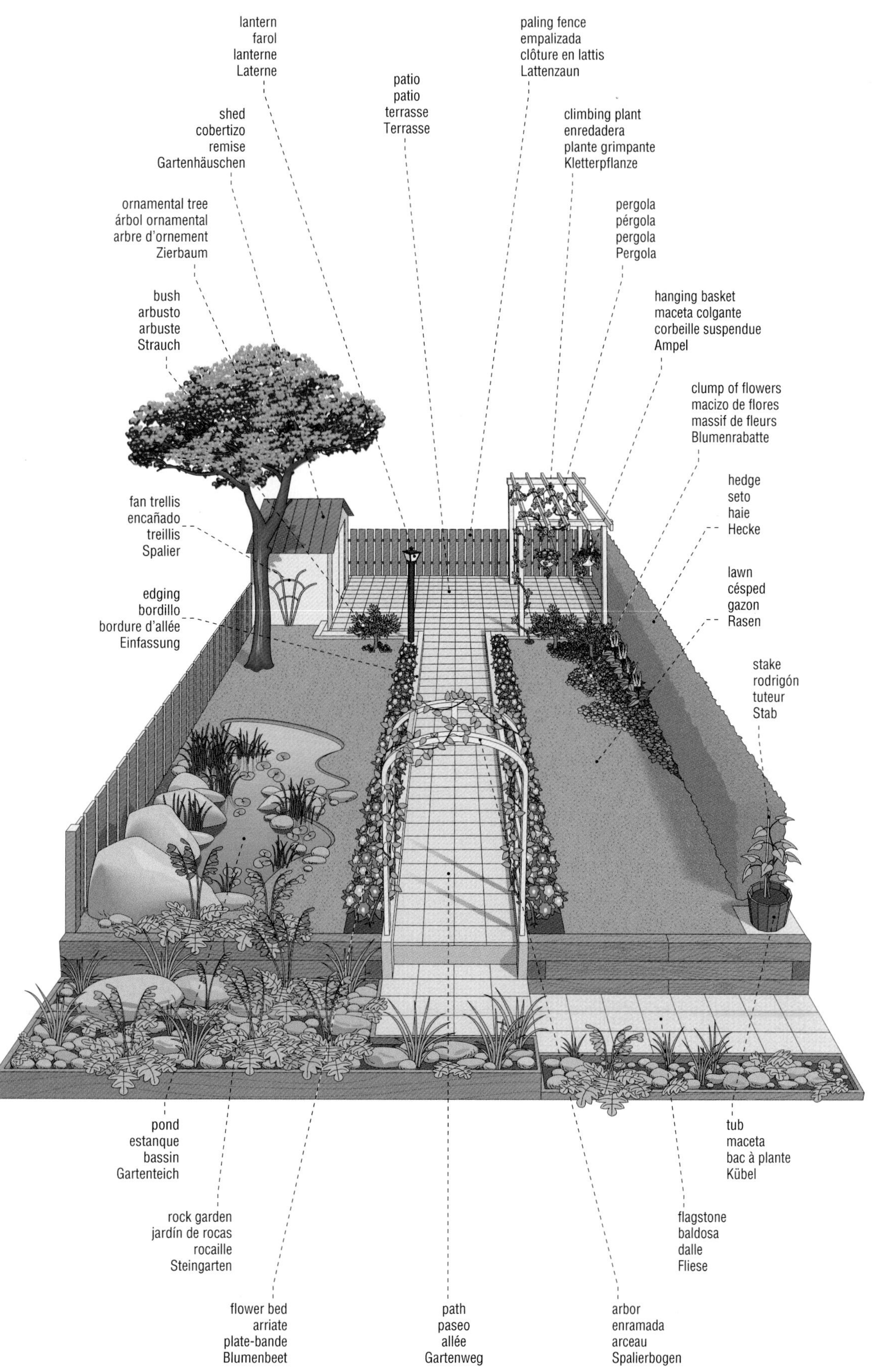

lantern
farol
lanterne
Laterne
patio
patio
terrasse
Terrasse
paling fence
empalizada
clôture en lattis
Lattenzaun
shed
cobertizo
remise
Gartenhäuschen
climbing plant
enredadera
plante grimpante
Kletterpflanze
ornamental tree
árbol ornamental
arbre d'ornement
Zierbaum
pergola
pérgola
pergola
Pergola
bush
arbusto
arbuste
Strauch
hanging basket
maceta colgante
corbeille suspendue
Ampel
clump of flowers
macizo de flores
massif de fleurs
Blumenrabatte
fan trellis
encañado
treillis
Spalier
hedge
seto
haie
Hecke
edging
bordillo
bordure d'allée
Einfassung
lawn
césped
gazon
Rasen
stake
rodrigón
tuteur
Stab
pond
estanque
bassin
Gartenteich
tub
maceta
bac à plante
Kübel
rock garden
jardín de rocas
rocaille
Steingarten
flagstone
baldosa
dalle
Fliese
flower bed
arriate
plate-bande
Blumenbeet
path
paseo
allée
Gartenweg
arbor
enramada
arceau
Spalierbogen

TOOLS AND EQUIPMENT
HERRAMIENTAS Y MÁQUINAS
OUTILLAGE
GARTENGERÄT

pistol nozzle
pistola pulverizadora
pistolet d'arrosage
Gießpistole

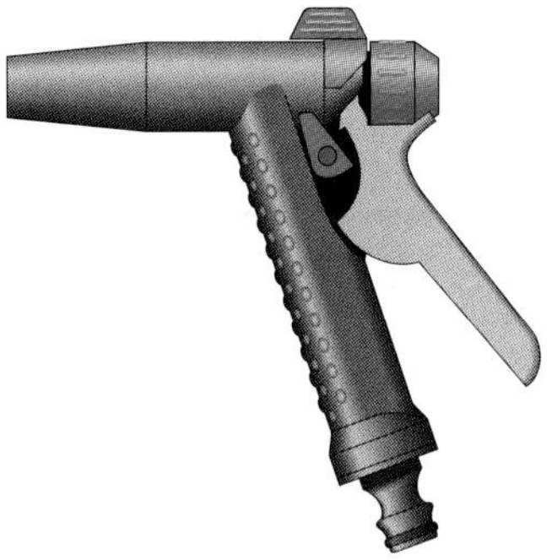

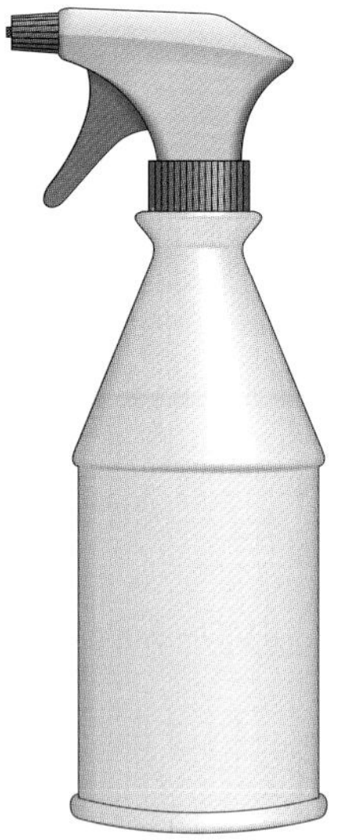

sprayer
pulverizador
vaporisateur
Sprühflasche

spray nozzle
boquilla pulverizadora
pistolet arrosoir
Gießbrause

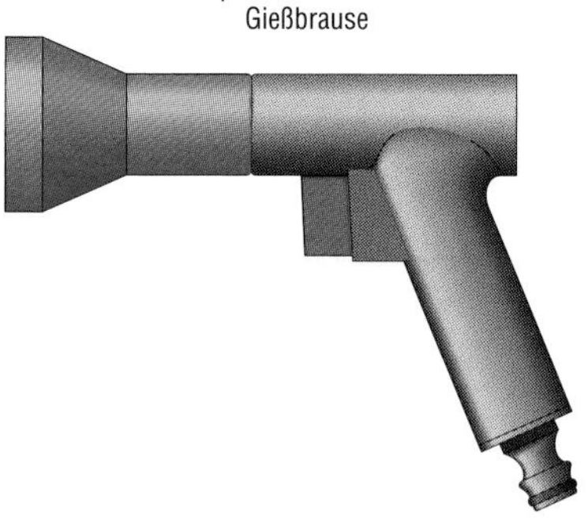

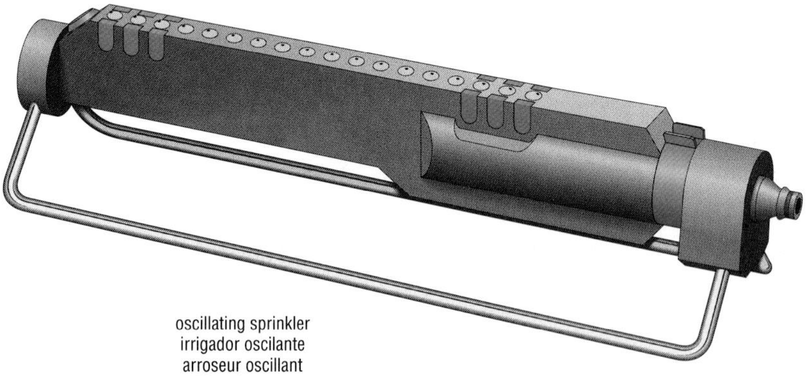

arm
brazo
bras
Drehdüse

oscillating sprinkler
irrigador oscilante
arroseur oscillant
Viereckregner

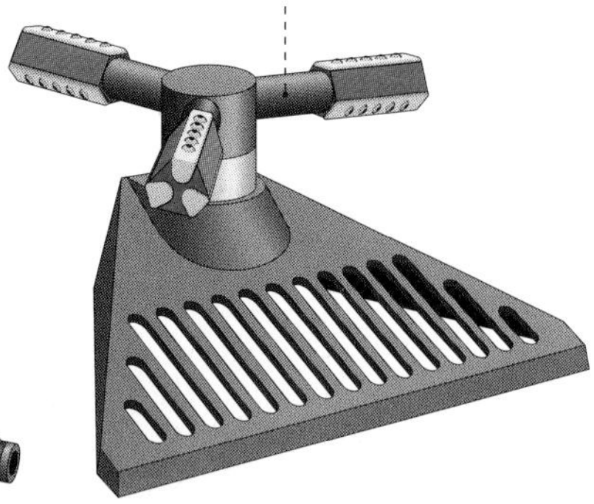

REVOLVING SPRINKLER
IRRIGADOR GIRATORIO
ARROSEUR ROTATIF
KREISREGNER

IMPULSE SPRINKLER
IRRIGADOR DE IMPULSO
ARROSEUR CANON
IMPULSREGNER

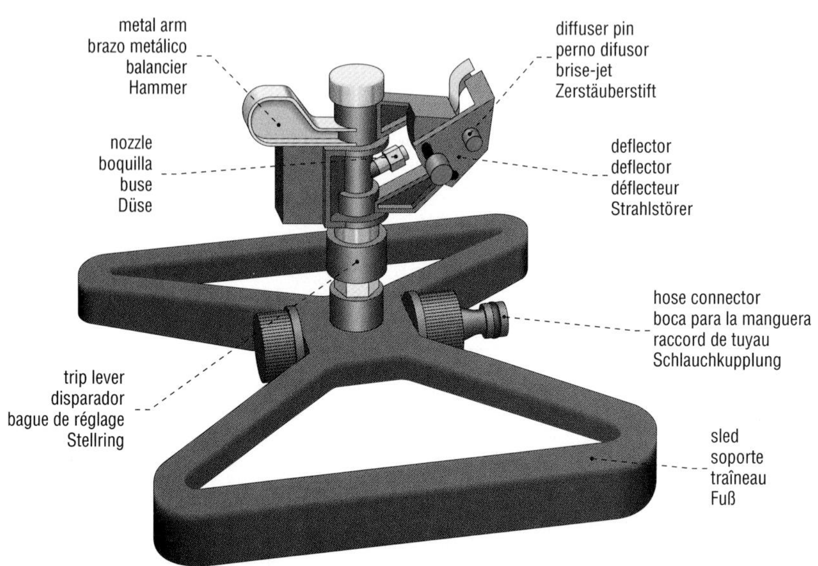
metal arm
brazo metálico
balancier
Hammer
diffuser pin
perno difusor
brise-jet
Zerstäuberstift
nozzle
boquilla
buse
Düse
deflector
deflector
déflecteur
Strahlstörer
hose connector
boca para la manguera
raccord de tuyau
Schlauchkupplung
trip lever
disparador
bague de réglage
Stellring
sled
soporte
traîneau
Fuß

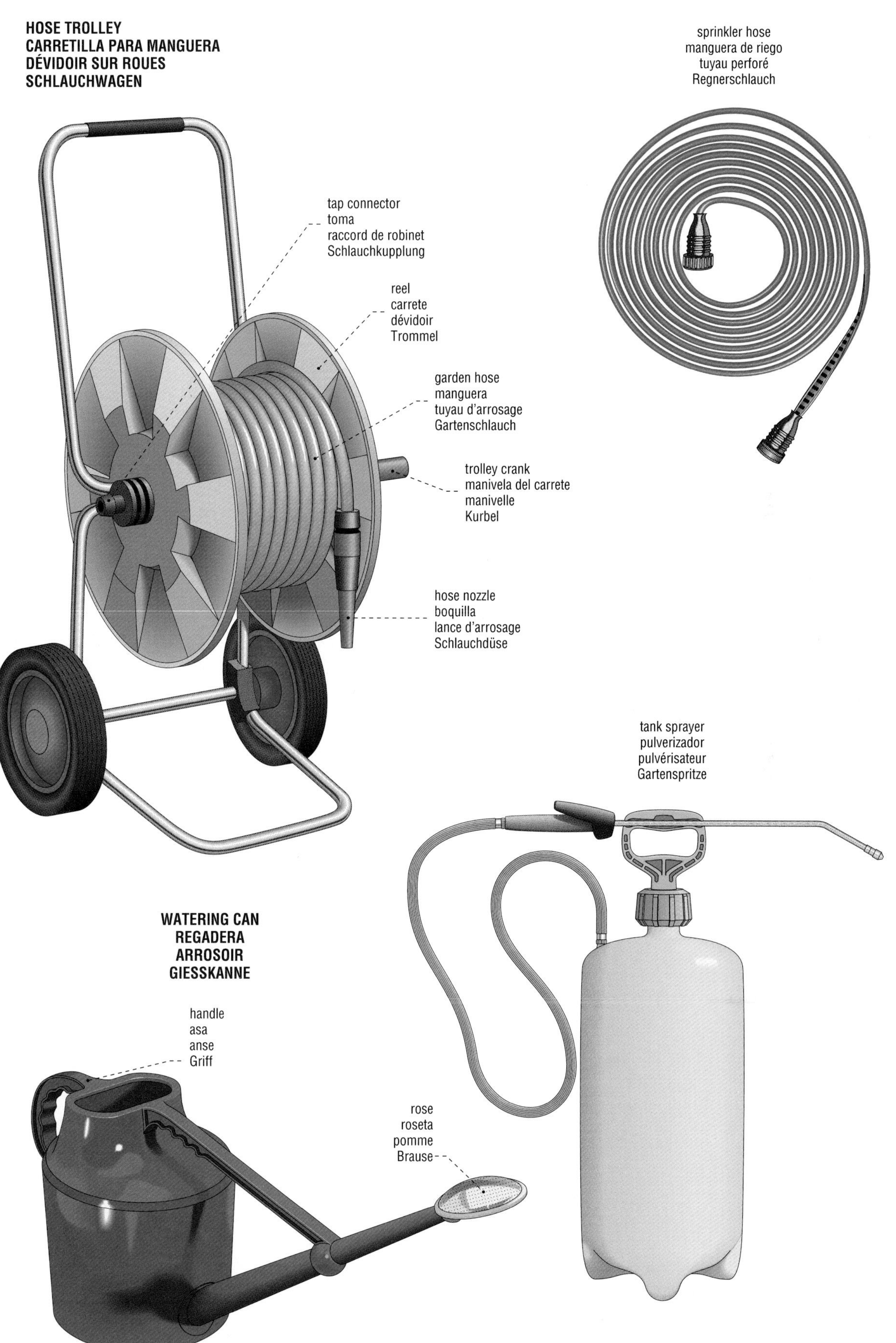
HOSE TROLLEY
CARRETILLA PARA MANGUERA
DÉVIDOIR SUR ROUES
SCHLAUCHWAGEN
tap connector
toma
raccord de robinet
Schlauchkupplung
reel
carrete
dévidoir
Trommel
garden hose
manguera
tuyau d'arrosage
Gartenschlauch
trolley crank
manivela del carrete
manivelle
Kurbel
hose nozzle
boquilla
lance d'arrosage
Schlauchdüse
sprinkler hose
manguera de riego
tuyau perforé
Regnerschlauch
tank sprayer
pulverizador
pulvérisateur
Gartenspritze
WATERING CAN
REGADERA
ARROSOIR
GIESSKANNE
handle
asa
anse
Griff
rose
roseta
pomme
Brause

TOOLS AND EQUIPMENT
HERRAMIENTAS Y MÁQUINAS
OUTILLAGE
GARTENGERÄT

shovel
pala
pelle
Grabschaufel

spade
laya
bêche
Spaten

spading fork
horca
fourche à bêcher
Grabgabel

lawn edger
cuchilla para delimitar el césped
coupe-bordures
Kantenstecher

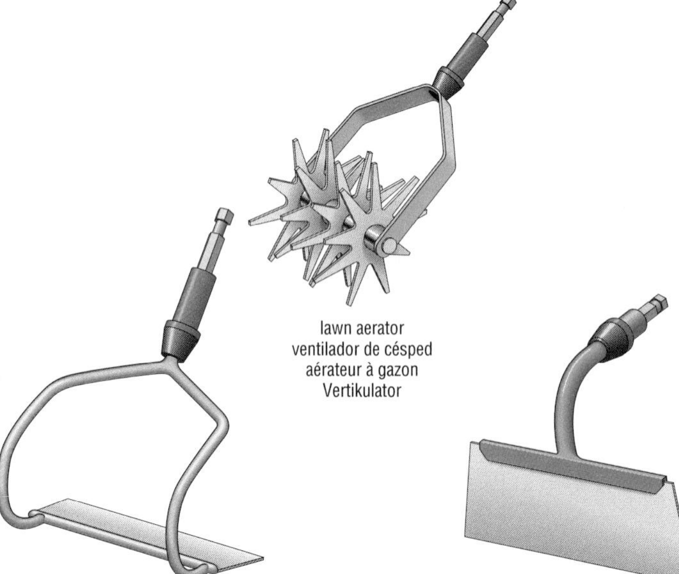

lawn aerator
ventilador de césped
aérateur à gazon
Vertikulator

scuffle hoe
azada de doble filo
ratissoire
Ziehhacke

draw hoe
azada
binette
Rübenhacke

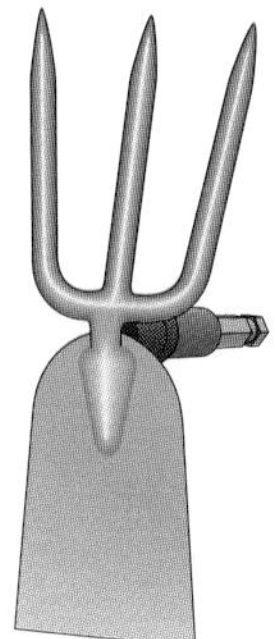

hoe-fork
almocafre
serfouette
Kombihacke

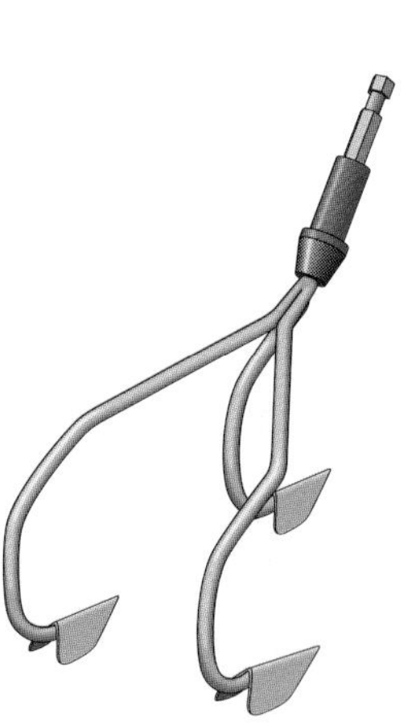

weeding hoe
escardillo
sarcloir
Handkultivator

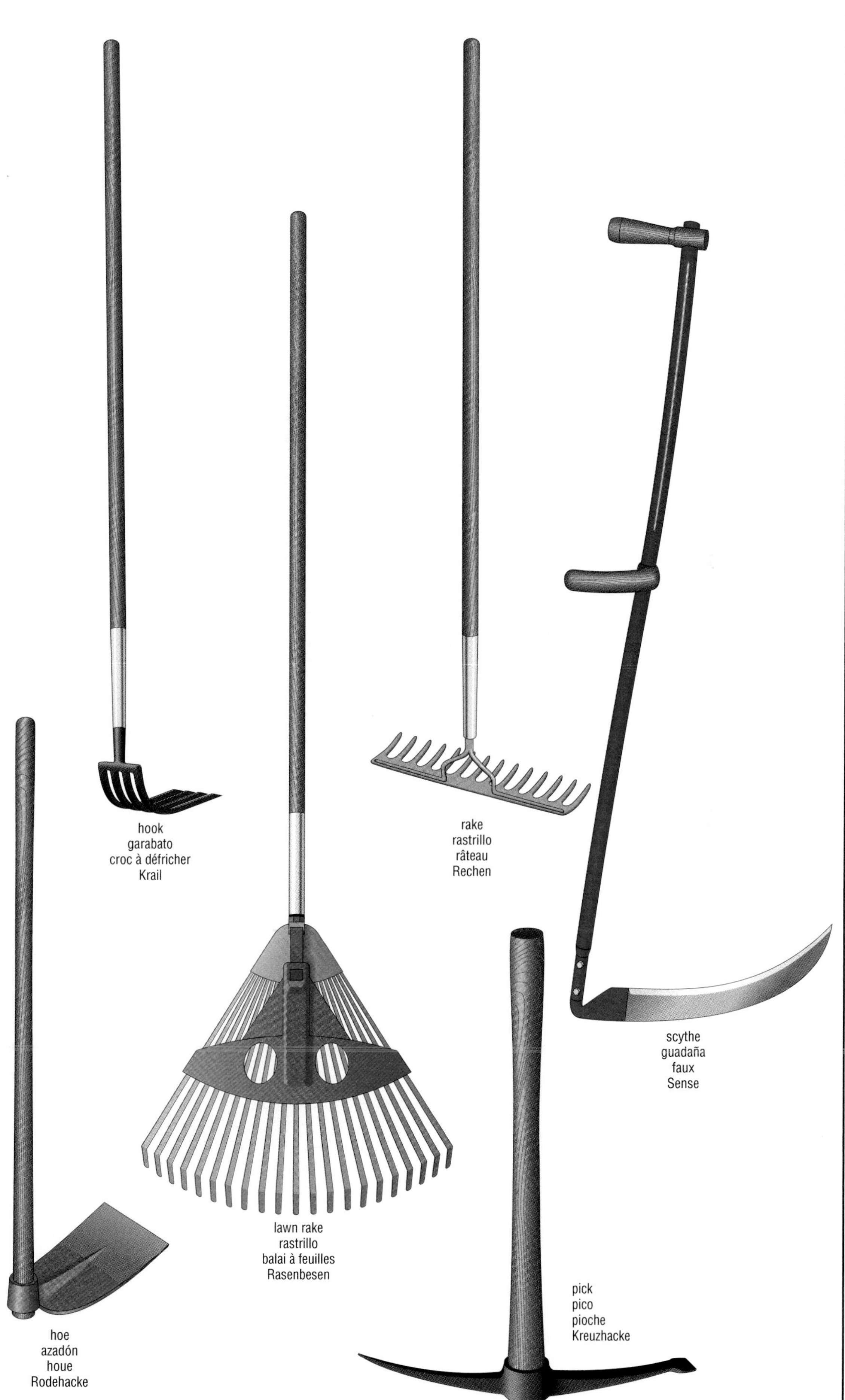
hook
garabato
croc à défricher
Krail
rake
rastrillo
râteau
Rechen
scythe
guadaña
faux
Sense
lawn rake
rastrillo
balai à feuilles
Rasenbesen
pick
pico
pioche
Kreuzhacke
hoe
azadón
houe
Rodehacke

TOOLS AND EQUIPMENT
HERRAMIENTAS Y MÁQUINAS
OUTILLAGE
GARTENGERÄT
hand fork
horquilla de mano
fourche à fleurs
Handgabel
weeder
desyerbador
tire-racine
Unkrautstecher
trowel
desplantador
transplantoir
Blumenkelle
small hand cultivator
cultivador de mano
griffe à fleurs
Kralle
seeder
sembradora de mano
semoir à main
Sähkelle
garden line
instrumento para alinear el jardín
cordeau
Pflanzschnur
dibble
plantador
plantoir
Pflanzholz
bulb dibble
plantador de bulbos
plantoir à bulbes
Pflanzlochstecher
HEDGE TRIMMER
CORTASETOS ELÉCTRICO
TAILLE-HAIES
ELEKTRISCHE HECKENSCHERE
cord
cable
cordon
Kabel
hand protector
protector
bouclier
Handschutz
trigger
gatillo
gâchette
Drückerschalter
blade
cuchilla
lame
Messer
tooth
diente
dent
Zahn
electric motor
motor eléctrico
moteur électrique
Elektromotor

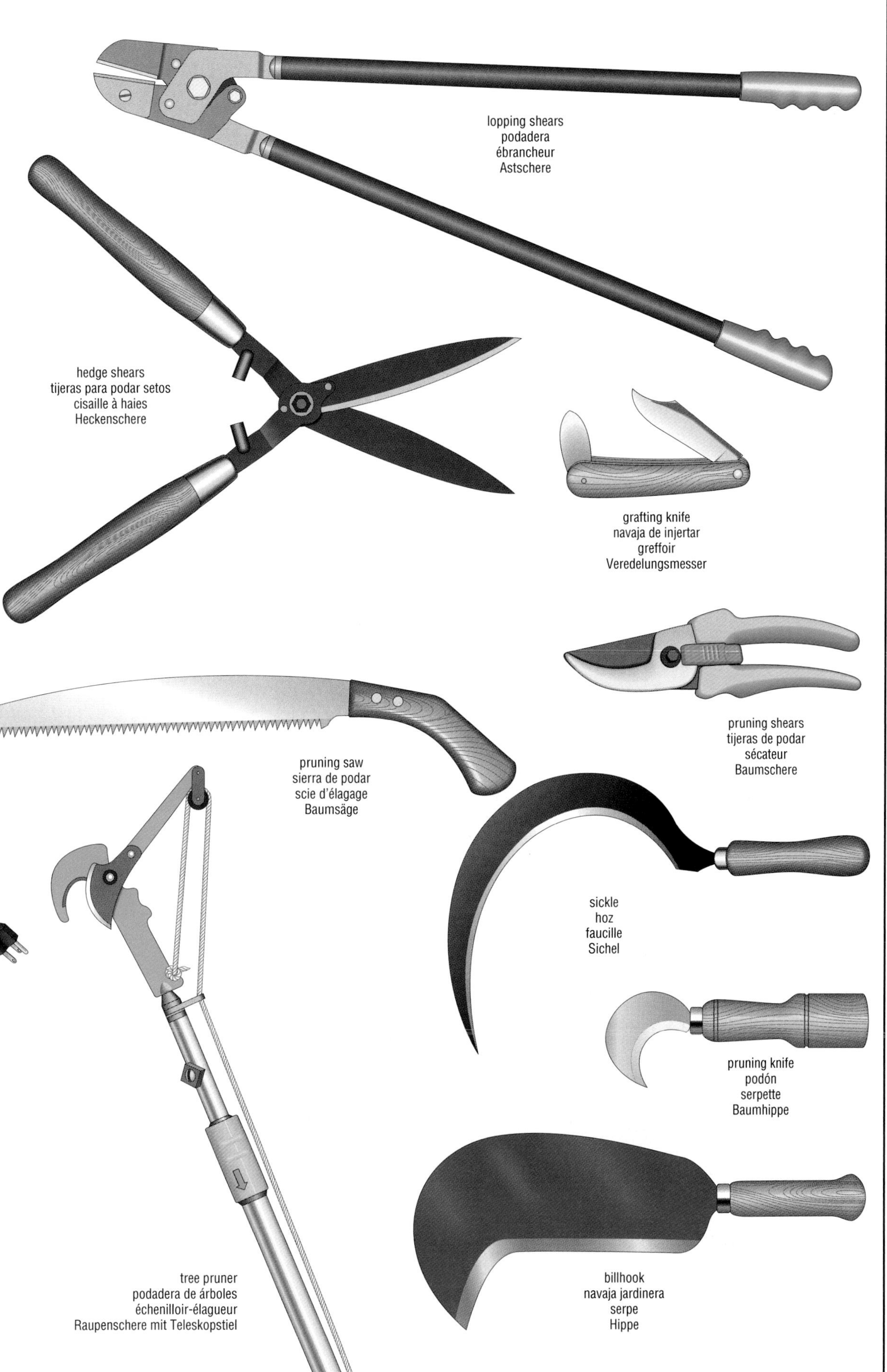
lopping shears
podadera
ébrancheur
Astschere
hedge shears
tijeras para podar setos
cisaille à haies
Heckenschere
grafting knife
navaja de injertar
greffoir
Veredelungsmesser
pruning shears
tijeras de podar
sécateur
Baumschere
pruning saw
sierra de podar
scie d'élagage
Baumsäge
sickle
hoz
faucille
Sichel
pruning knife
podón
serpette
Baumhippe
tree pruner
podadera de árboles
échenilloir-élagueur
Raupenschere mit Teleskopstiel
billhook
navaja jardinera
serpe
Hippe

TOOLS AND EQUIPMENT
HERRAMIENTAS Y MÁQUINAS
OUTILLAGE
GARTENGERÄT

spreader
esparcidora de abono
épandeur
Düngerstreuer
MOTORIZED EARTH AUGER
TALADRO DE MOTOR
TARIÈRE MOTORISÉE
ERDBOHRER
handle
manillar
mancheron
Lenkholm
control cable
cable de control
câble de commande
Gaszug
auger bit
taladro
mèche de tarière
Bohrschnecke
starting cable
cable de arranque
câble du démarreur
Starterzug
motor
motor
moteur
Motor
WHEELBARROW
CARRETILLA
BROUETTE
SCHUBKARRE
tray
caja
caisse
Mulde
handle
brazo
brancard
Griff
leg
pata
pied
Stütze
wheel
rueda
roue
Rad
roller
rodillo
rouleau
Walze

HAND MOWER
CORTACÉSPED
TONDEUSE MÉCANIQUE
HANDRASENMÄHER
blade
cuchilla
lame
Messer
cutting cylinder
cilindro de corte
cylindre de coupe
Schneidzylinder
EDGER
PODADORA DE BORDES
TAILLE-BORDURES
RASENTRIMMER
cord
cable
cordon
Kabel
electric motor
motor eléctrico
moteur électrique
Elektromotor
security casing
cubierta de seguridad
carter de sécurité
Schutzgehäuse
nylon yarn
hilo de nilón
fil de nylon
Nylonschnur
POWER MOWER
CORTACÉSPED ELÉCTRICO
TONDEUSE À MOTEUR
MOTORRASENMÄHER
handle
barra
guidon
Griff
speed control
control de velocidad
sélecteur de régime
Geschwindigkeitsregler
safety handle
palanca de seguridad
poignée de sécurité
Sicherheitsgriff
ignition key
encendido
clé de contact
Zündschlüssel
grassbox
caja para el césped
bac de ramassage
Grasfang
motor
motor
moteur
Motor
starter
motor de arranque
démarreur manuel
Anlasser
accelerator cable
cable del acelerador
câble d'accélération
Gaszug
filler cap
boca del tanque de combustible
bouchon de remplissage
Einfüllstutzen
spark plug
bujía
bougie
Zündkerze
deflector
deflector
déflecteur
Leitblech
casing
caja
carter
Gehäuse

TOOLS AND EQUIPMENT
HERRAMIENTAS Y MÁQUINAS
OUTILLAGE
GARTENGERÄT

CHAINSAW
SIERRA DE CADENA
SCIE À CHAÎNE
KETTENSÄGE

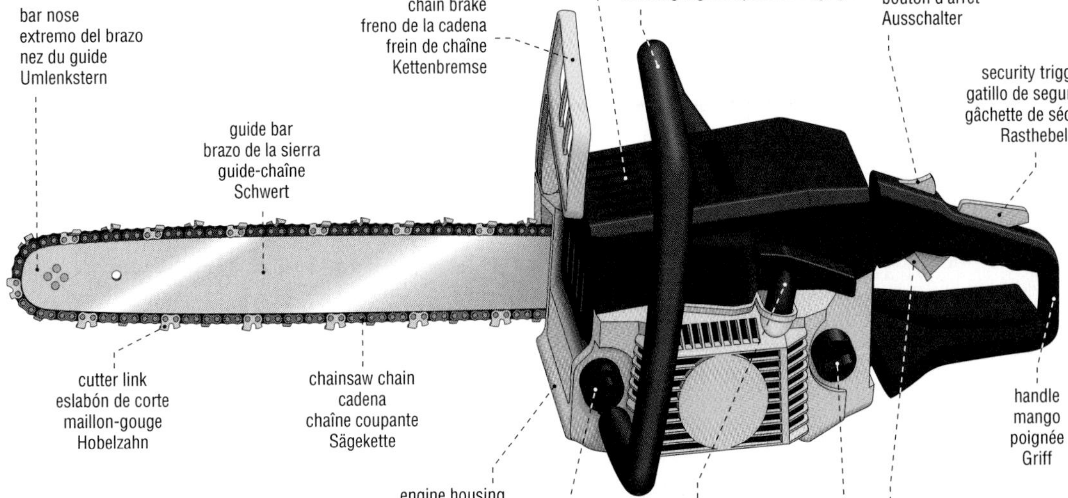

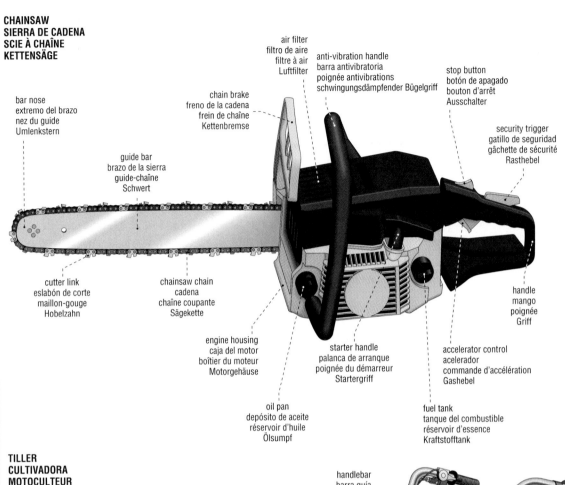

air filter
filtro de aire
filtre à air
Luftfilter
anti-vibration handle
barra antivibratoria
poignée antivibrations
schwingungsdämpfender Bügelgriff
stop button
botón de apagado
bouton d'arrêt
Ausschalter
chain brake
freno de la cadena
frein de chaîne
Kettenbremse
bar nose
extremo del brazo
nez du guide
Umlenkstern
security trigger
gatillo de seguridad
gâchette de sécurité
Rasthebel
guide bar
brazo de la sierra
guide-chaîne
Schwert
cutter link
eslabón de corte
maillon-gouge
Hobelzahn
chainsaw chain
cadena
chaîne coupante
Sägekette
handle
mango
poignée
Griff
engine housing
caja del motor
boîtier du moteur
Motorgehäuse
starter handle
palanca de arranque
poignée du démarreur
Startergriff
accelerator control
acelerador
commande d'accélération
Gashebel
oil pan
depósito de aceite
réservoir d'huile
Ölsumpf
fuel tank
tanque del combustible
réservoir d'essence
Kraftstofftank

TILLER
CULTIVADORA
MOTOCULTEUR
GARTENFRÄSE

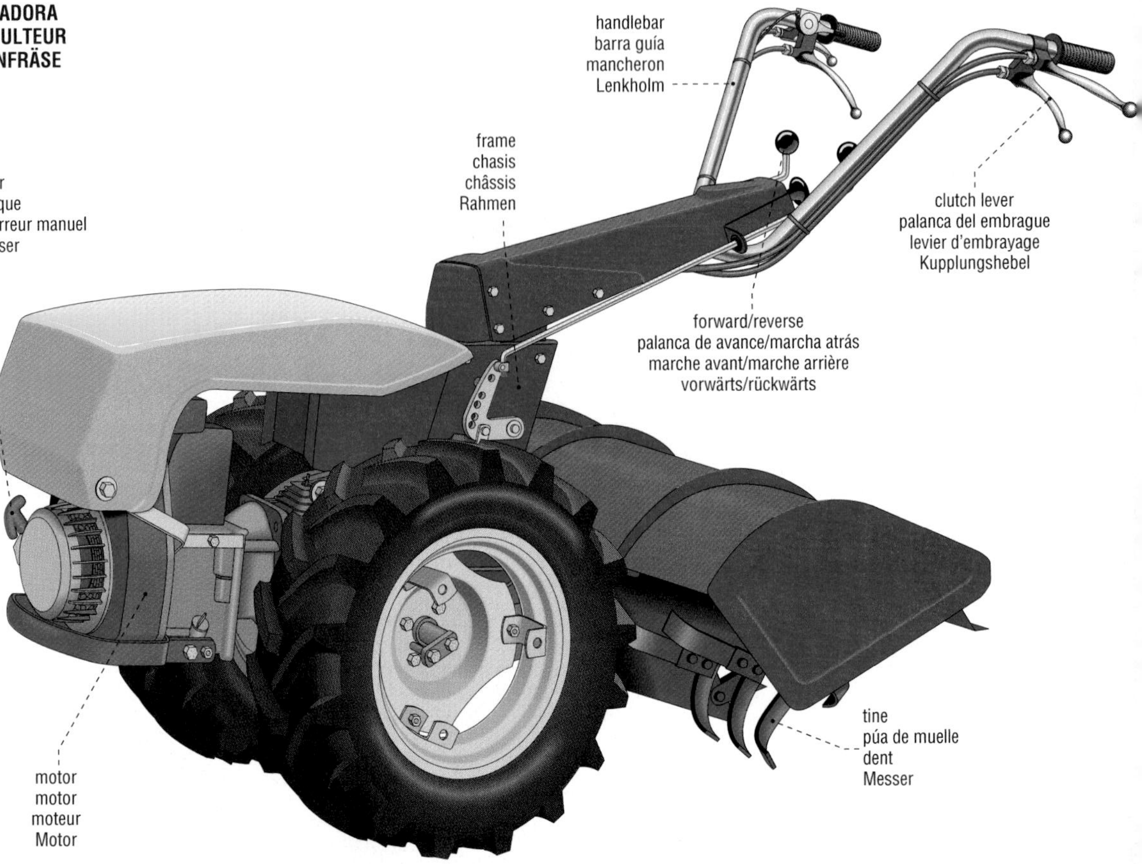

handlebar
barra guía
mancheron
Lenkholm
frame
chasis
châssis
Rahmen
starter
arranque
démarreur manuel
Anlasser
clutch lever
palanca del embrague
levier d'embrayage
Kupplungshebel
forward/reverse
palanca de avance/marcha atrás
marche avant/marche arrière
vorwärts/rückwärts
tine
púa de muelle
dent
Messer
motor
motor
moteur
Motor

DO-IT-YOURSELF
REPARACIONES CASERAS

BRICOLAGE
DO-IT-YOURSELF

CONTENTS

CARPENTRY: TOOLS
CARPINTERÍA: HERRAMIENTAS
MENUISERIE: OUTILS
SCHREINEREI: WERKZEUGE

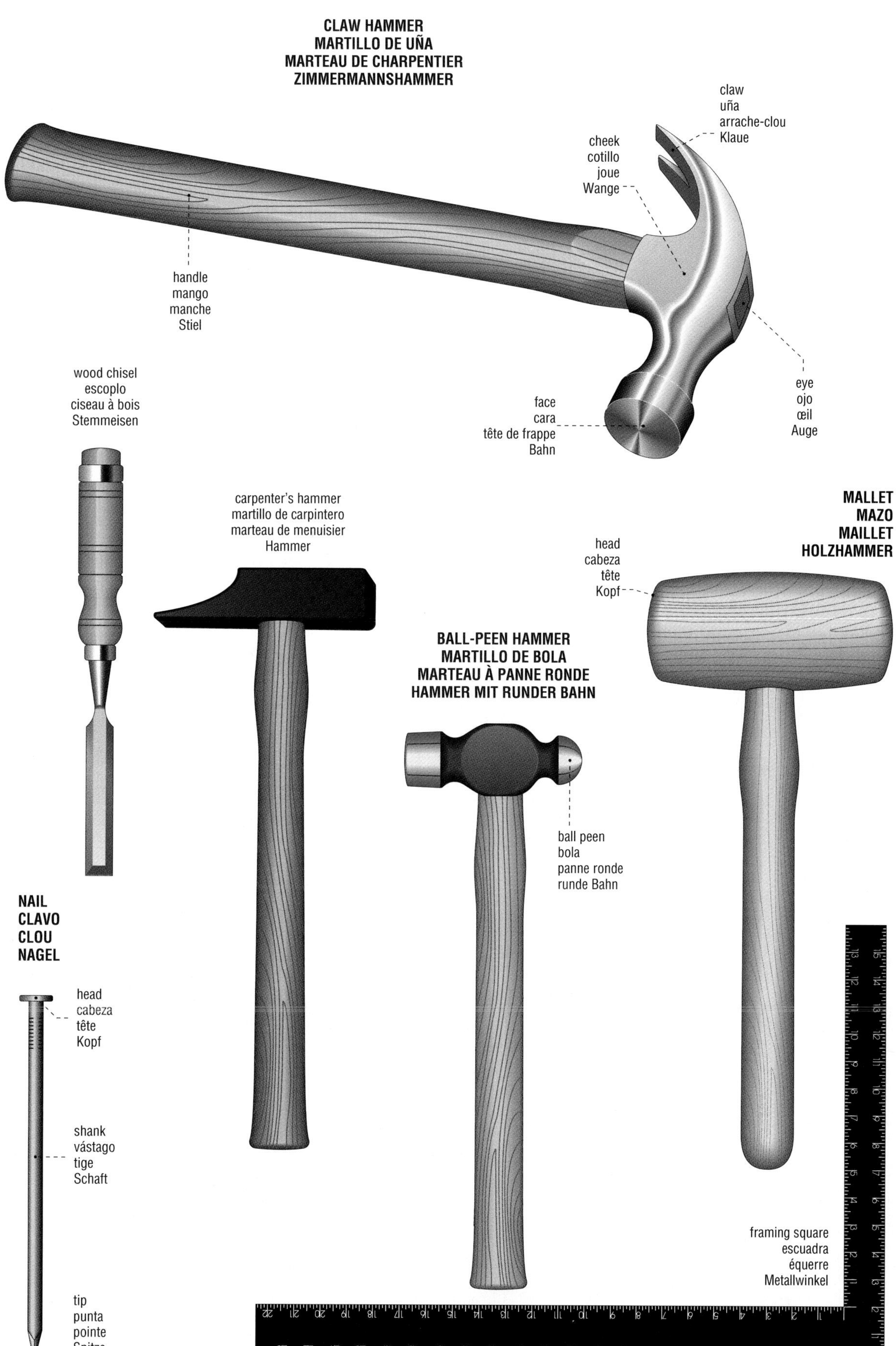
CLAW HAMMER
MARTILLO DE UÑA
MARTEAU DE CHARPENTIER
ZIMMERMANNSHAMMER
claw
uña
arrache-clou
Klaue
cheek
cotillo
joue
Wange
handle
mango
manche
Stiel
eye
ojo
œil
Auge
face
cara
tête de frappe
Bahn
wood chisel
escoplo
ciseau à bois
Stemmeisen
carpenter's hammer
martillo de carpintero
marteau de menuisier
Hammer
MALLET
MAZO
MAILLET
HOLZHAMMER
head
cabeza
tête
Kopf
BALL-PEEN HAMMER
MARTILLO DE BOLA
MARTEAU À PANNE RONDE
HAMMER MIT RUNDER BAHN
ball peen
bola
panne ronde
runde Bahn
NAIL
CLAVO
CLOU
NAGEL
head
cabeza
tête
Kopf
shank
vástago
tige
Schaft
tip
punta
pointe
Spitze
framing square
escuadra
équerre
Metallwinkel

CARPENTRY: TOOLS
CARPINTERÍA: HERRAMIENTAS
MENUISERIE: OUTILS
SCHREINEREI: WERKZEUGE

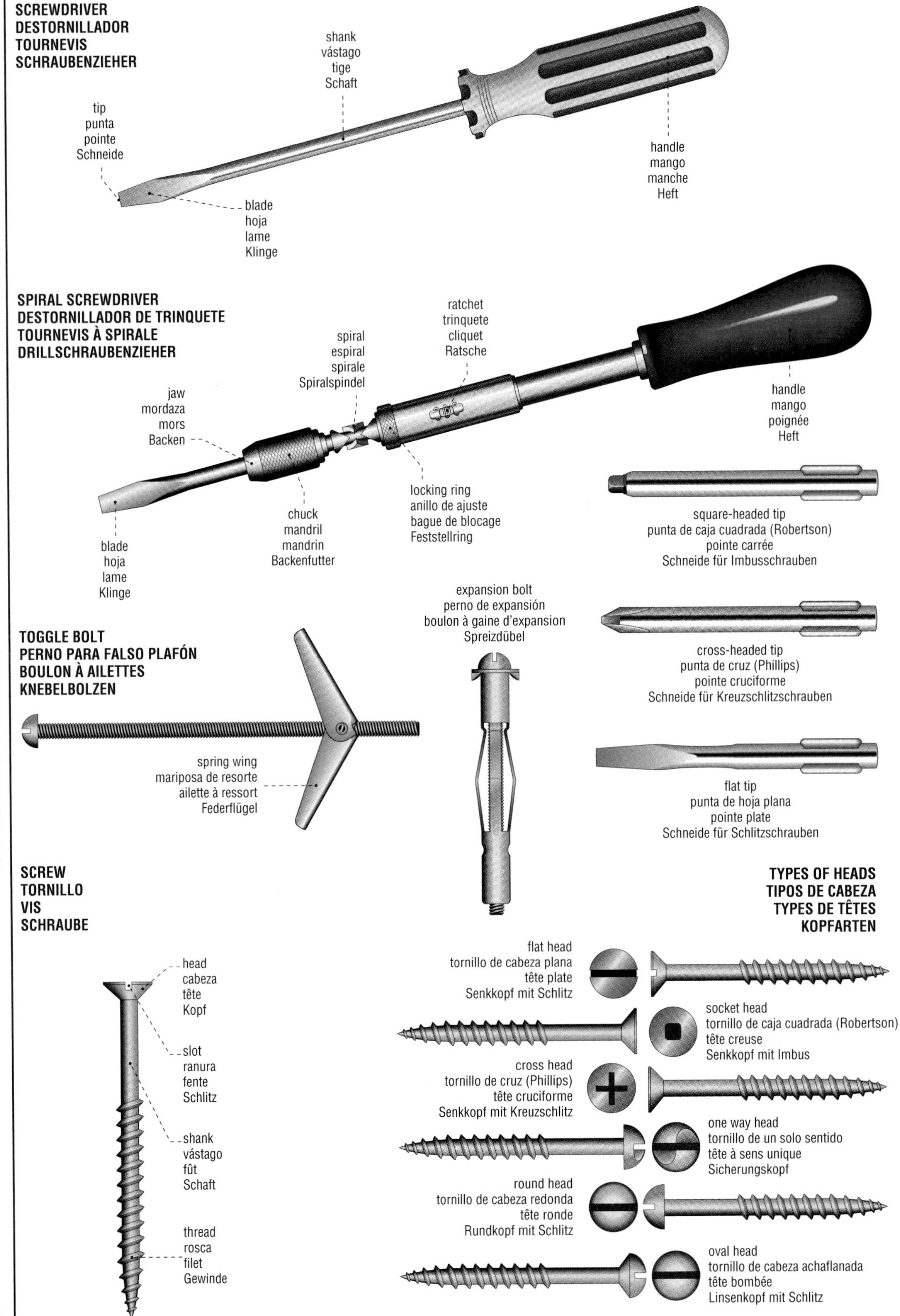

SCREWDRIVER
DESTORNILLADOR
TOURNEVIS
SCHRAUBENZIEHER
shank
vástago
tige
Schaft
tip
punta
pointe
Schneide
handle
mango
manche
Heft
blade
hoja
lame
Klinge
SPIRAL SCREWDRIVER
DESTORNILLADOR DE TRINQUETE
TOURNEVIS À SPIRALE
DRILLSCHRAUBENZIEHER
ratchet
trinquete
cliquet
Ratsche
spiral
espiral
spirale
Spiralspindel
jaw
mordaza
mors
Backen
handle
mango
poignée
Heft
locking ring
anillo de ajuste
bague de blocage
Feststellring
chuck
mandril
mandrin
Backenfutter
blade
hoja
lame
Klinge
square-headed tip
punta de caja cuadrada (Robertson)
pointe carrée
Schneide für Imbusschrauben
expansion bolt
perno de expansión
boulon à gaine d'expansion
Spreizdübel
TOGGLE BOLT
PERNO PARA FALSO PLAFÓN
BOULON À AILETTES
KNEBELBOLZEN
cross-headed tip
punta de cruz (Phillips)
pointe cruciforme
Schneide für Kreuzschlitzschrauben
spring wing
mariposa de resorte
ailette à ressort
Federflügel
flat tip
punta de hoja plana
pointe plate
Schneide für Schlitzschrauben
SCREW
TORNILLO
VIS
SCHRAUBE
TYPES OF HEADS
TIPOS DE CABEZA
TYPES DE TÊTES
KOPFARTEN
head
cabeza
tête
Kopf
flat head
tornillo de cabeza plana
tête plate
Senkkopf mit Schlitz
socket head
tornillo de caja cuadrada (Robertson)
tête creuse
Senkkopf mit Imbus
slot
ranura
fente
Schlitz
cross head
tornillo de cruz (Phillips)
tête cruciforme
Senkkopf mit Kreuzschlitz
shank
vástago
fût
Schaft
one way head
tornillo de un solo sentido
tête à sens unique
Sicherungskopf
round head
tornillo de cabeza redonda
tête ronde
Rundkopf mit Schlitz
thread
rosca
filet
Gewinde
oval head
tornillo de cabeza achaflanada
tête bombée
Linsenkopf mit Schlitz

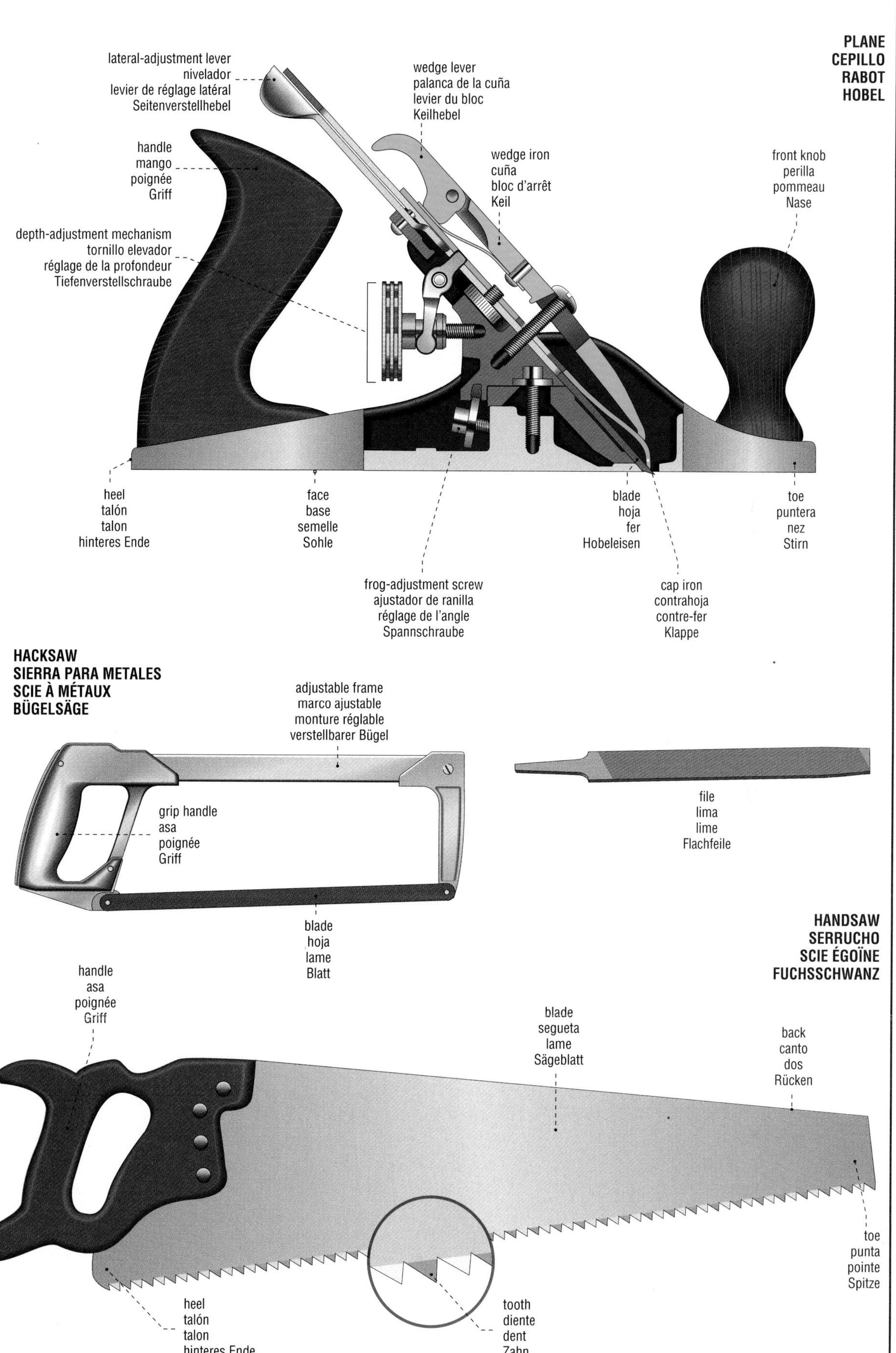
PLANE
CEPILLO
RABOT
HOBEL
lateral-adjustment lever
nivelador
levier de réglage latéral
Seitenverstellhebel
wedge lever
palanca de la cuña
levier du bloc
Keilhebel
handle
mango
poignée
Griff
wedge iron
cuña
bloc d'arrêt
Keil
front knob
perilla
pommeau
Nase
depth-adjustment mechanism
tornillo elevador
réglage de la profondeur
Tiefenverstellschraube
heel
talón
talon
hinteres Ende
face
base
semelle
Sohle
blade
hoja
fer
Hobeleisen
toe
puntera
nez
Stirn
frog-adjustment screw
ajustador de ranilla
réglage de l'angle
Spannschraube
cap iron
contrahoja
contre-fer
Klappe
HACKSAW
SIERRA PARA METALES
SCIE À MÉTAUX
BÜGELSÄGE
adjustable frame
marco ajustable
monture réglable
verstellbarer Bügel
grip handle
asa
poignée
Griff
file
lima
lime
Flachfeile
blade
hoja
lame
Blatt
HANDSAW
SERRUCHO
SCIE ÉGOÏNE
FUCHSSCHWANZ
handle
asa
poignée
Griff
blade
segueta
lame
Sägeblatt
back
canto
dos
Rücken
toe
punta
pointe
Spitze
heel
talón
talon
hinteres Ende
tooth
diente
dent
Zahn

CARPENTRY: TOOLS
CARPINTERÍA: HERRAMIENTAS
MENUISERIE: OUTILS
SCHREINEREI: WERKZEUGE

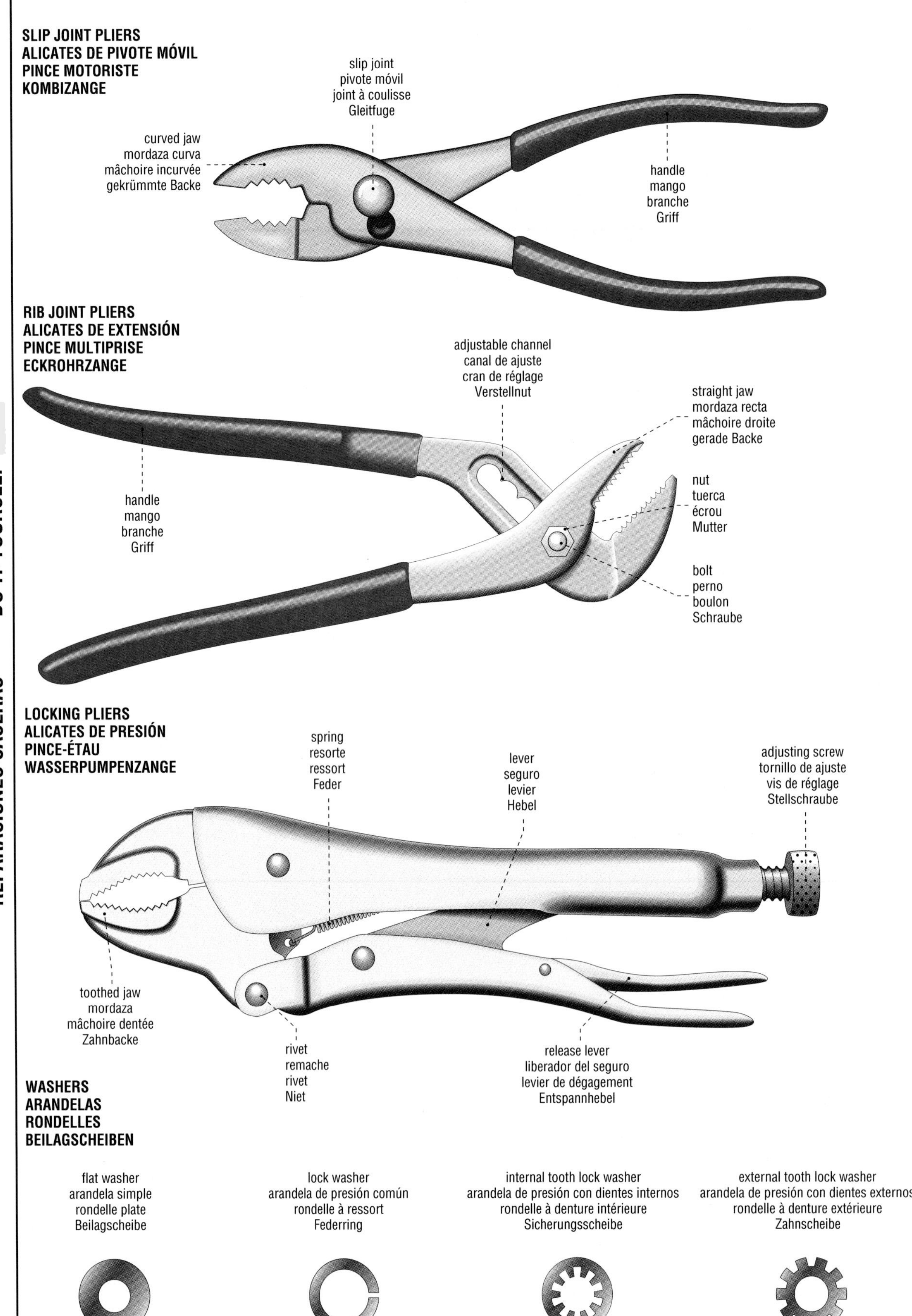
SLIP JOINT PLIERS
ALICATES DE PIVOTE MÓVIL
PINCE MOTORISTE
KOMBIZANGE
slip joint
pivote móvil
joint à coulisse
Gleitfuge
curved jaw
mordaza curva
mâchoire incurvée
gekrümmte Backe
handle
mango
branche
Griff
RIB JOINT PLIERS
ALICATES DE EXTENSIÓN
PINCE MULTIPRISE
ECKROHRZANGE
adjustable channel
canal de ajuste
cran de réglage
Verstellnut
straight jaw
mordaza recta
mâchoire droite
gerade Backe
handle
mango
branche
Griff
nut
tuerca
écrou
Mutter
bolt
perno
boulon
Schraube
LOCKING PLIERS
ALICATES DE PRESIÓN
PINCE-ÉTAU
WASSERPUMPENZANGE
spring
resorte
ressort
Feder
lever
seguro
levier
Hebel
adjusting screw
tornillo de ajuste
vis de réglage
Stellschraube
toothed jaw
mordaza
mâchoire dentée
Zahnbacke
rivet
remache
rivet
Niet
release lever
liberador del seguro
levier de dégagement
Entspannhebel
WASHERS
ARANDELAS
RONDELLES
BEILAGSCHEIBEN
flat washer
arandela simple
rondelle plate
Beilagscheibe
lock washer
arandela de presión común
rondelle à ressort
Federring
internal tooth lock washer
arandela de presión con dientes internos
rondelle à denture intérieure
Sicherungsscheibe
external tooth lock washer
arandela de presión con dientes externos
rondelle à denture extérieure
Zahnscheibe

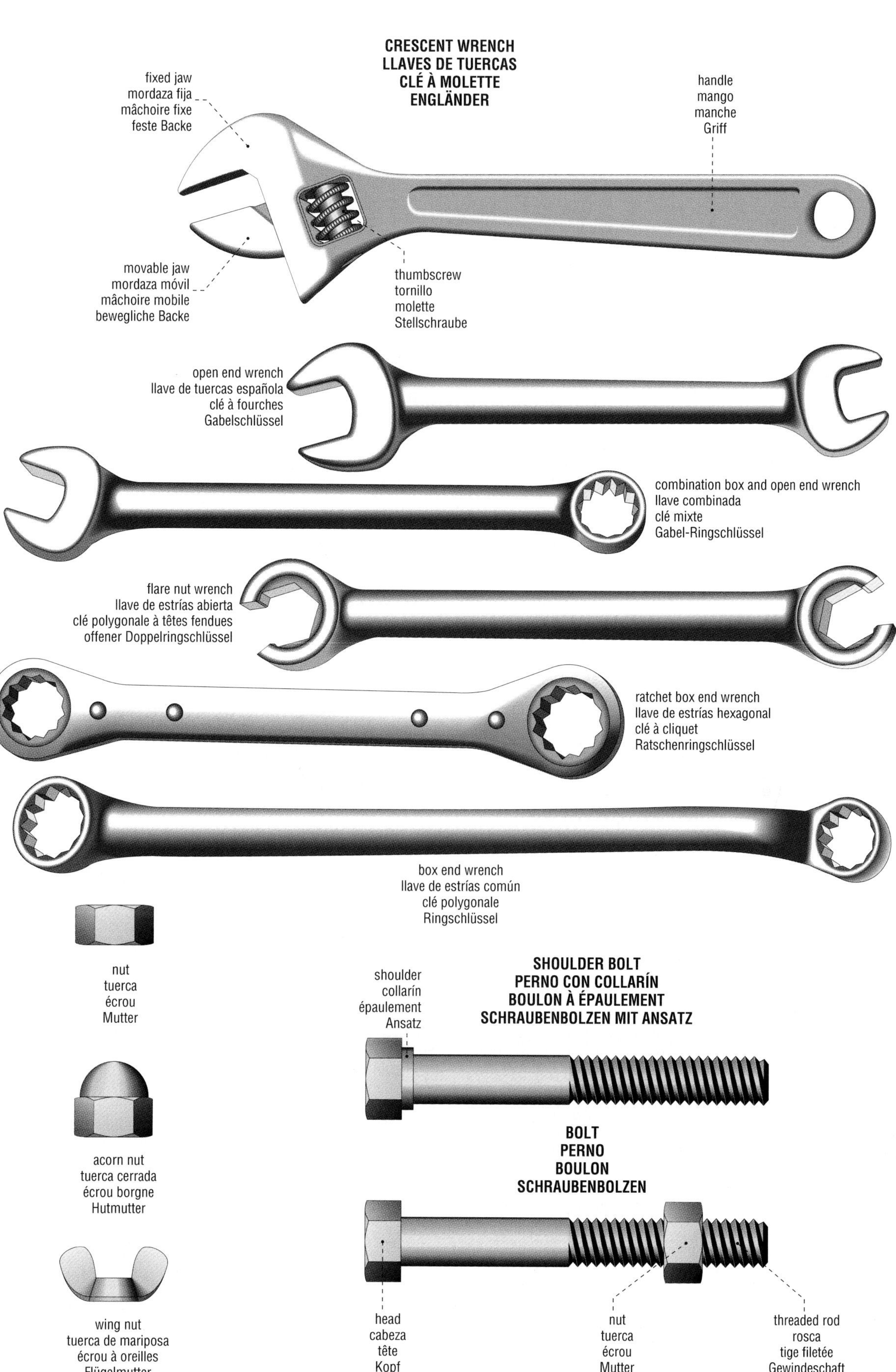
CRESCENT WRENCH
LLAVES DE TUERCAS
CLÉ À MOLETTE
ENGLÄNDER
fixed jaw
mordaza fija
mâchoire fixe
feste Backe
handle
mango
manche
Griff
movable jaw
mordaza móvil
mâchoire mobile
bewegliche Backe
thumbscrew
tornillo
molette
Stellschraube
open end wrench
llave de tuercas española
clé à fourches
Gabelschlüssel
combination box and open end wrench
llave combinada
clé mixte
Gabel-Ringschlüssel
flare nut wrench
llave de estrías abierta
clé polygonale à têtes fendues
offener Doppelringschlüssel
ratchet box end wrench
llave de estrías hexagonal
clé à cliquet
Ratschenringschlüssel
box end wrench
llave de estrías común
clé polygonale
Ringschlüssel
nut
tuerca
écrou
Mutter
acorn nut
tuerca cerrada
écrou borgne
Hutmutter
wing nut
tuerca de mariposa
écrou à oreilles
Flügelmutter
SHOULDER BOLT
PERNO CON COLLARÍN
BOULON À ÉPAULEMENT
SCHRAUBENBOLZEN MIT ANSATZ
shoulder
collarín
épaulement
Ansatz
BOLT
PERNO
BOULON
SCHRAUBENBOLZEN
head
cabeza
tête
Kopf
nut
tuerca
écrou
Mutter
threaded rod
rosca
tige filetée
Gewindeschaft

ELECTRIC DRILL
TALADRO ELÉCTRICO
PERCEUSE ÉLECTRIQUE
ELEKTRISCHE BOHRMASCHINE
name plate
placa de especificaciones
plaque signalétique
Typenschild
warning plate
placa de advertencias
plaque d'instructions
Sicherheitshinweisschild
housing
caja
boîtier
Gehäuse
switch lock
seguro del interruptor
blocage de l'interrupteur
Feststellknopf
switch
interruptor
interrupteur
Schalter
chuck
mandril
mandrin
Backenfutter
jaw
mordaza
mors
Backen
auxiliary handle
mango auxiliar
poignée auxiliaire
zusätzlicher Griff
pistol grip handle
mango
poignée-pistolet
Pistolengriff
cable sleeve
protector del cable
manchon de câble
Kabelmantel
cable
cable de corriente
câble
Kabel
plug
enchufe
fiche
Stecker
HAND DRILL
TALADRO DE MANO
CHIGNOLE
HANDBOHRER
turning handle
manivela
manivelle
Kurbel
side handle
perilla
poignée latérale
Seitengriff
main handle
mango
poignée supérieure
Hauptgriff
jaw
mordaza
mors
Backe
drive wheel
cremallera
roue d'engrenage
Stirnzahnrad
pinion
piñón
pignon
Kegelzahnrad
chuck
mandril
mandrin
Backenfutter
drill
broca
foret
Bohrer

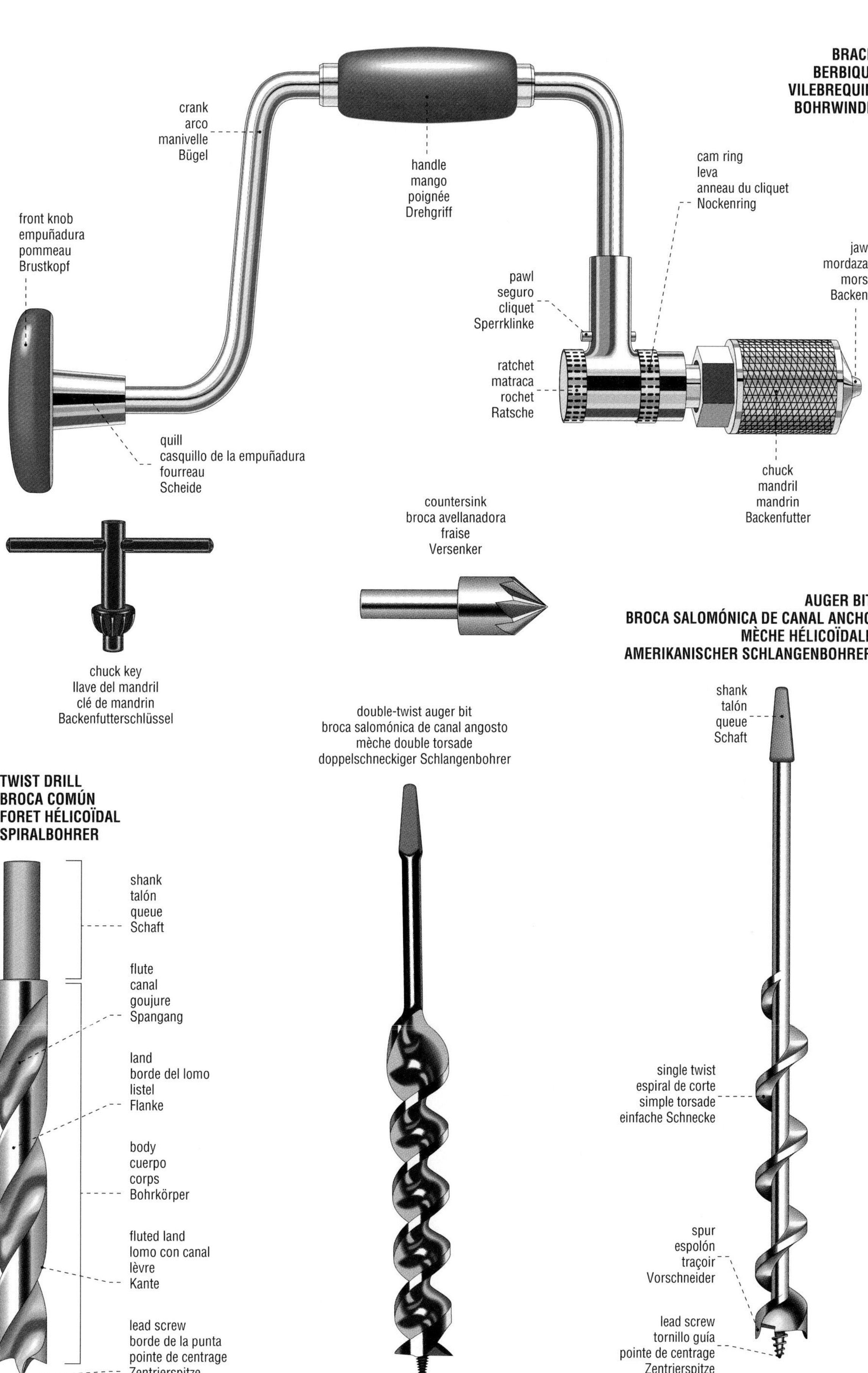
BRACE
BERBIQUÍ
VILEBREQUIN
BOHRWINDE
crank
arco
manivelle
Bügel
handle
mango
poignée
Drehgriff
cam ring
leva
anneau du cliquet
Nockenring
front knob
empuñadura
pommeau
Brustkopf
jaw
mordaza
mors
Backen
pawl
seguro
cliquet
Sperrklinke
ratchet
matraca
rochet
Ratsche
quill
casquillo de la empuñadura
fourreau
Scheide
chuck
mandril
mandrin
Backenfutter
countersink
broca avellanadora
fraise
Versenker
chuck key
llave del mandril
clé de mandrin
Backenfutterschlüssel
AUGER BIT
BROCA SALOMÓNICA DE CANAL ANCHO
MÈCHE HÉLICOÏDALE
AMERIKANISCHER SCHLANGENBOHRER
shank
talón
queue
Schaft
double-twist auger bit
broca salomónica de canal angosto
mèche double torsade
doppelschneckiger Schlangenbohrer
TWIST DRILL
BROCA COMÚN
FORET HÉLICOÏDAL
SPIRALBOHRER
shank
talón
queue
Schaft
flute
canal
goujure
Spangang
land
borde del lomo
listel
Flanke
body
cuerpo
corps
Bohrkörper
fluted land
lomo con canal
lèvre
Kante
lead screw
borde de la punta
pointe de centrage
Zentrierspitze
single twist
espiral de corte
simple torsade
einfache Schnecke
spur
espolón
traçoir
Vorschneider
lead screw
tornillo guía
pointe de centrage
Zentrierspitze

CARPENTRY: TOOLS
CARPINTERÍA: HERRAMIENTAS
MENUISERIE: OUTILS
SCHREINEREI: WERKZEUGE

C-CLAMP
PRENSA EN C
SERRE-JOINT
ZWINGE

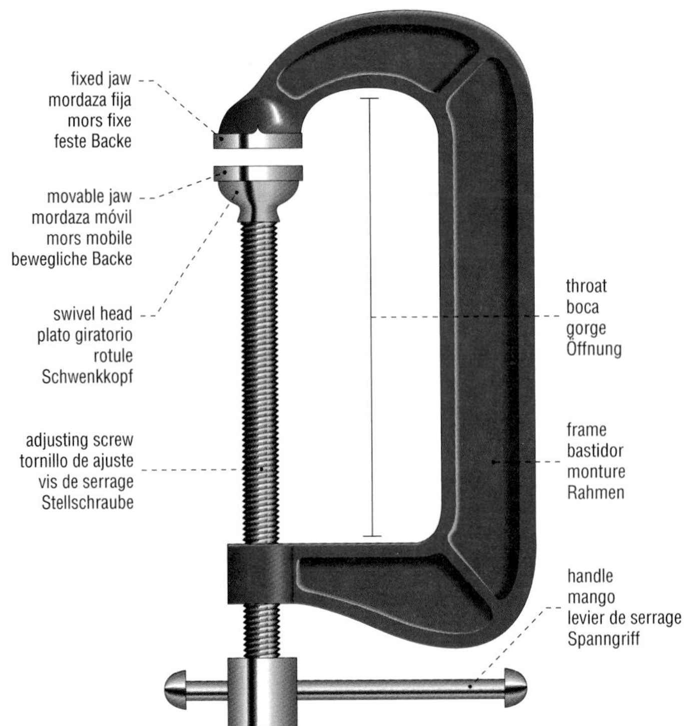
fixed jaw
mordaza fija
mors fixe
feste Backe
movable jaw
mordaza móvil
mors mobile
bewegliche Backe
swivel head
plato giratorio
rotule
Schwenkkopf
adjusting screw
tornillo de ajuste
vis de serrage
Stellschraube
throat
boca
gorge
Öffnung
frame
bastidor
monture
Rahmen
handle
mango
levier de serrage
Spanngriff

VISE
TORNO DE BANCO
ÉTAU
SCHRAUBSTOCK

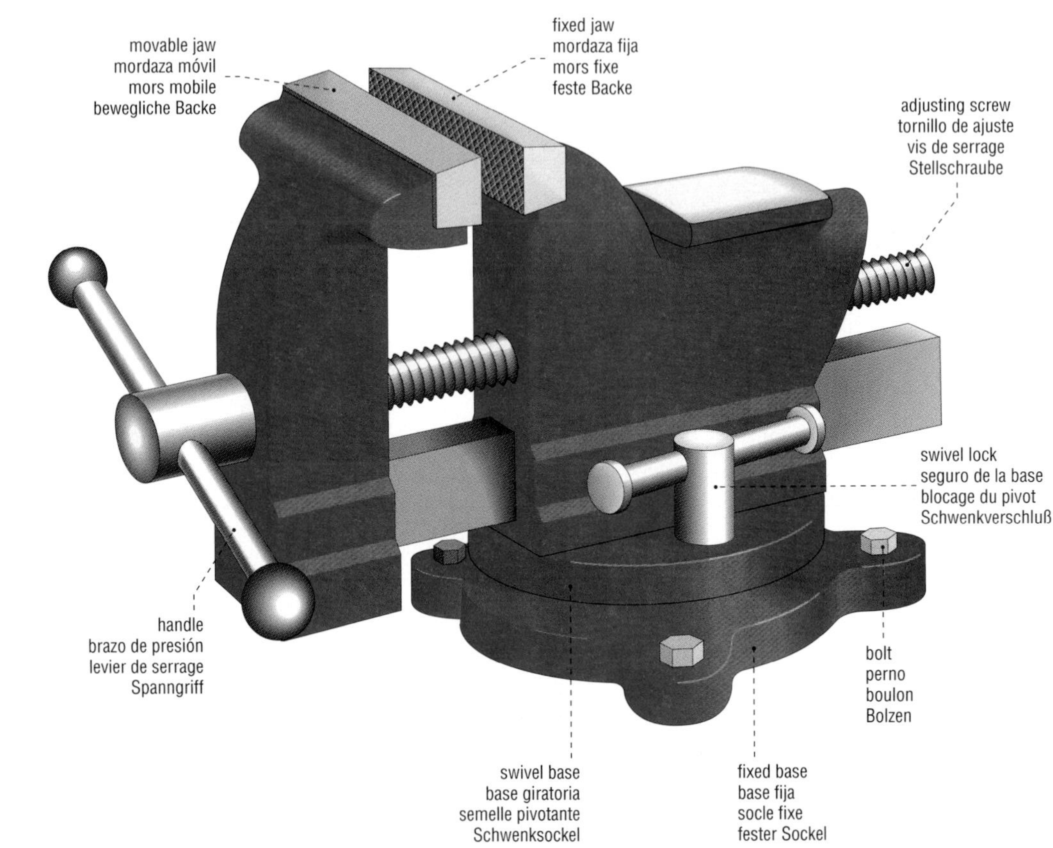
movable jaw
mordaza móvil
mors mobile
bewegliche Backe
fixed jaw
mordaza fija
mors fixe
feste Backe
adjusting screw
tornillo de ajuste
vis de serrage
Stellschraube
swivel lock
seguro de la base
blocage du pivot
Schwenkverschluß
handle
brazo de presión
levier de serrage
Spanngriff
bolt
perno
boulon
Bolzen
swivel base
base giratoria
semelle pivotante
Schwenksockel
fixed base
base fija
socle fixe
fester Sockel

ROUTER
ACANALADOR
TOUPIE
OBERFRÄSER

head
parche
tête
Kopf
motor
motor
moteur
Motor
cord sleeve
protector del cable
manchon du cordon
Kabelmantel
switch
interruptor
interrupteur
Schalter
guide handle
asa
poignée de guidage
Führungsgriff
depth adjustment
ajuste de profundidad
réglage de profondeur
Tiefeneinstellung
collet
collarín
collet
Anlaufhülse
tool holder
mordaza
porte-outil
Werkzeugfutter
base
base
base
Fuß

DRILL PRESS
TALADRO VERTICAL
PERCEUSE À COLONNE
STÄNDERBOHRMASCHINE

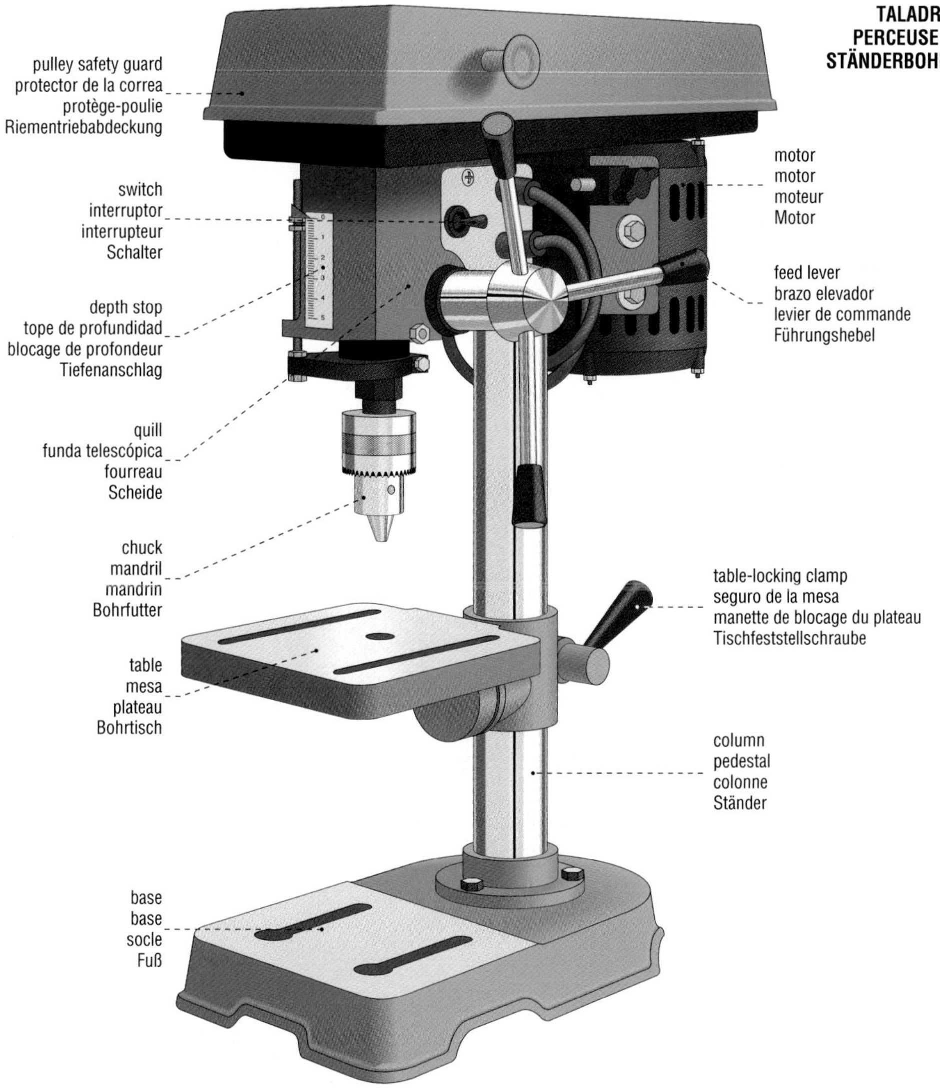

pulley safety guard
protector de la correa
protège-poulie
Riementriebabdeckung

switch
interruptor
interrupteur
Schalter

motor
motor
moteur
Motor

feed lever
brazo elevador
levier de commande
Führungshebel

depth stop
tope de profundidad
blocage de profondeur
Tiefenanschlag

quill
funda telescópica
fourreau
Scheide

chuck
mandril
mandrin
Bohrfutter

table-locking clamp
seguro de la mesa
manette de blocage du plateau
Tischfeststellschraube

table
mesa
plateau
Bohrtisch

column
pedestal
colonne
Ständer

base
base
socle
Fuß

CARPENTRY: TOOLS
CARPINTERÍA: HERRAMIENTAS
MENUISERIE: OUTILS
SCHREINEREI: WERKZEUGE

CIRCULAR SAW BLADE
DISCO
LAME DE SCIE CIRCULAIRE
KREISSÄGEBLATT

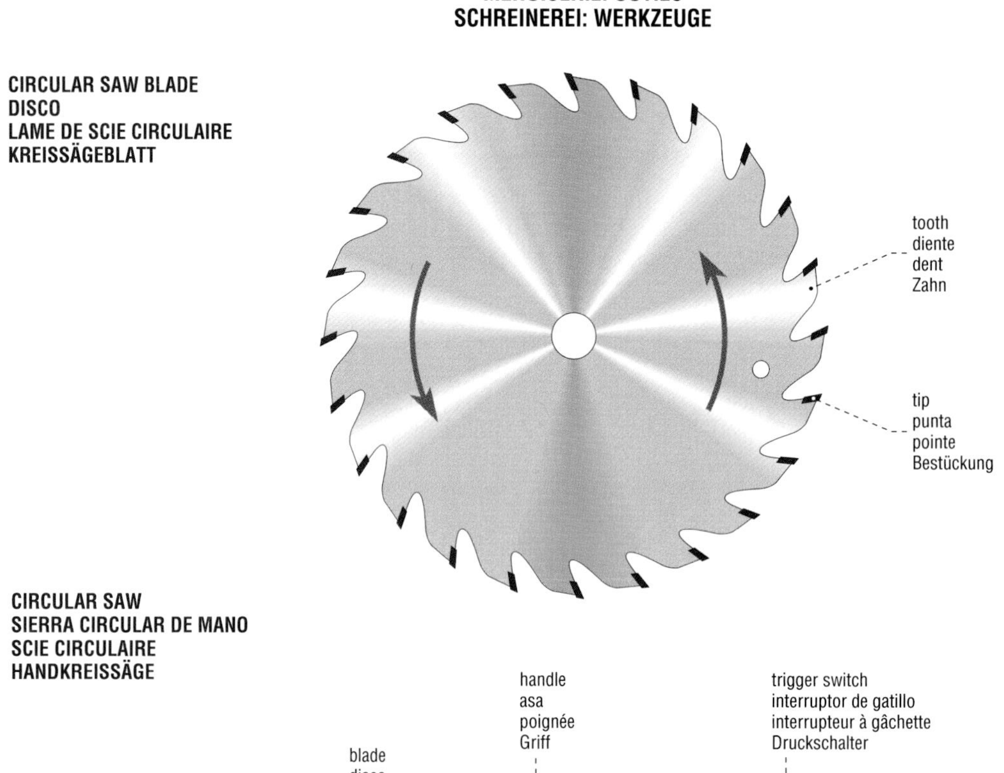
tooth
diente
dent
Zahn
tip
punta
pointe
Bestückung

CIRCULAR SAW
SIERRA CIRCULAR DE MANO
SCIE CIRCULAIRE
HANDKREISSÄGE

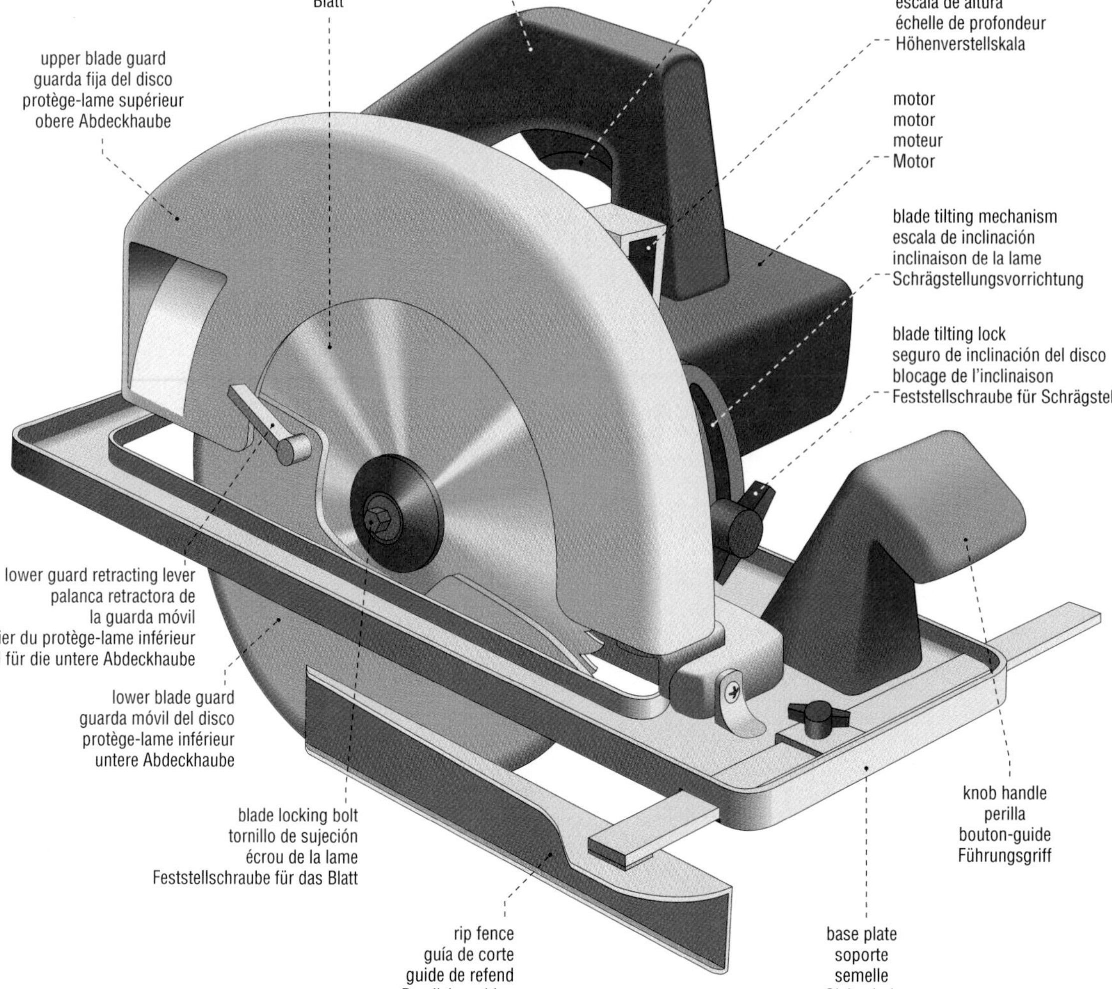

handle
asa
poignée
Griff

trigger switch
interruptor de gatillo
interrupteur à gâchette
Druckschalter

blade
disco
lame
Blatt

height adjustment scale
escala de altura
échelle de profondeur
Höhenverstellskala

upper blade guard
guarda fija del disco
protège-lame supérieur
obere Abdeckhaube

motor
motor
moteur
Motor

blade tilting mechanism
escala de inclinación
inclinaison de la lame
Schrägstellungsvorrichtung

blade tilting lock
seguro de inclinación del disco
blocage de l'inclinaison
Feststellschraube für Schrägstellung

lower guard retracting lever
palanca retractora de
la guarda móvil
levier du protège-lame inférieur
Hebel für die untere Abdeckhaube

lower blade guard
guarda móvil del disco
protège-lame inférieur
untere Abdeckhaube

knob handle
perilla
bouton-guide
Führungsgriff

blade locking bolt
tornillo de sujeción
écrou de la lame
Feststellschraube für das Blatt

rip fence
guía de corte
guide de refend
Parallelanschlag

base plate
soporte
semelle
Gleitschuh

TABLE SAW
SIERRA CIRCULAR DE MESA
PLATEAU DE SCIAGE
TISCHKREISSÄGE

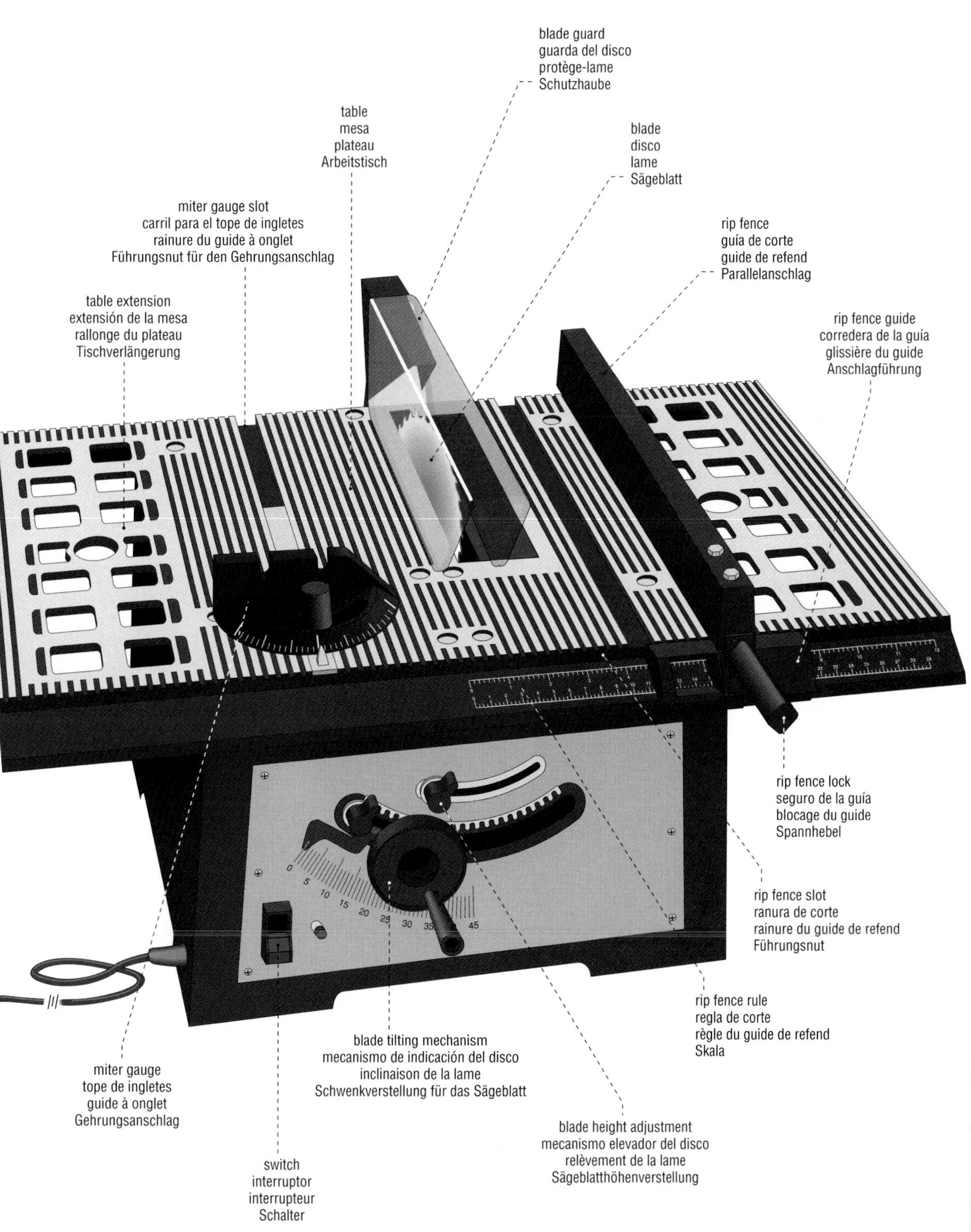
blade guard
guarda del disco
protège-lame
Schutzhaube
table
mesa
plateau
Arbeitstisch
blade
disco
lame
Sägeblatt
miter gauge slot
carril para el tope de ingletes
rainure du guide à onglet
Führungsnut für den Gehrungsanschlag
rip fence
guía de corte
guide de refend
Parallelanschlag
table extension
extensión de la mesa
rallonge du plateau
Tischverlängerung
rip fence guide
corredera de la guía
glissière du guide
Anschlagführung
rip fence lock
seguro de la guía
blocage du guide
Spannhebel
rip fence slot
ranura de corte
rainure du guide de refend
Führungsnut
rip fence rule
regla de corte
règle du guide de refend
Skala
blade tilting mechanism
mecanismo de indicación del disco
inclinaison de la lame
Schwenkverstellung für das Sägeblatt
miter gauge
tope de ingletes
guide à onglet
Gehrungsanschlag
blade height adjustment
mecanismo elevador del disco
relèvement de la lame
Sägeblatthöhenverstellung
switch
interruptor
interrupteur
Schalter

BUILDING MATERIALS
MATERIALES DE CONSTRUCCIÓN
MATÉRIAUX DE CONSTRUCTION
BAUMATERIALIEN

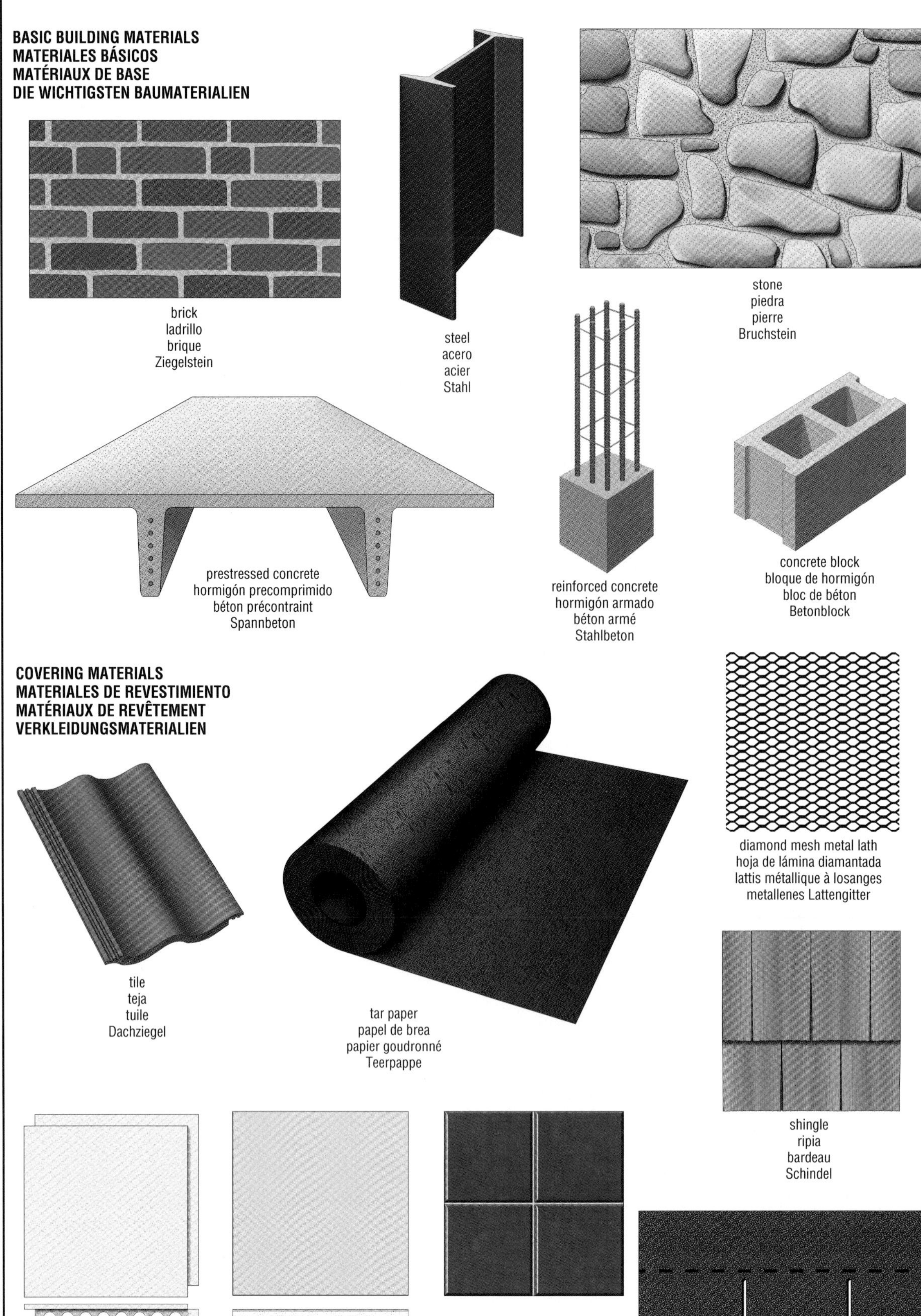

BASIC BUILDING MATERIALS
MATERIALES BÁSICOS
MATÉRIAUX DE BASE
DIE WICHTIGSTEN BAUMATERIALIEN
brick
ladrillo
brique
Ziegelstein
steel
acero
acier
Stahl
stone
piedra
pierre
Bruchstein
prestressed concrete
hormigón precomprimido
béton précontraint
Spannbeton
reinforced concrete
hormigón armado
béton armé
Stahlbeton
concrete block
bloque de hormigón
bloc de béton
Betonblock
COVERING MATERIALS
MATERIALES DE REVESTIMIENTO
MATÉRIAUX DE REVÊTEMENT
VERKLEIDUNGSMATERIALIEN
diamond mesh metal lath
hoja de lámina diamantada
lattis métallique à losanges
metallenes Lattengitter
tile
teja
tuile
Dachziegel
tar paper
papel de brea
papier goudronné
Teerpappe
shingle
ripia
bardeau
Schindel
gypsum tile
tablero de yeso
carreau de plâtre
Rigipsplatte
plain gypsum lath
hoja de yeso liso
lattis de plâtre lisse
ebene Rigipsplatte
floor tile
baldosa
carreau
Fliese
asphalt shingle
teja de asfalto
bardeau d'asphalte
Asphaltschindel

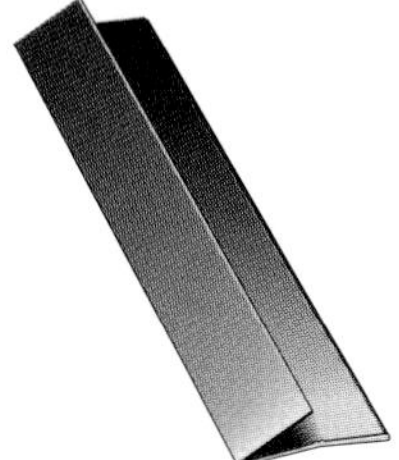

spring-metal insulation
aislante metálico
isolant de ruban métallique
Metallverbindung

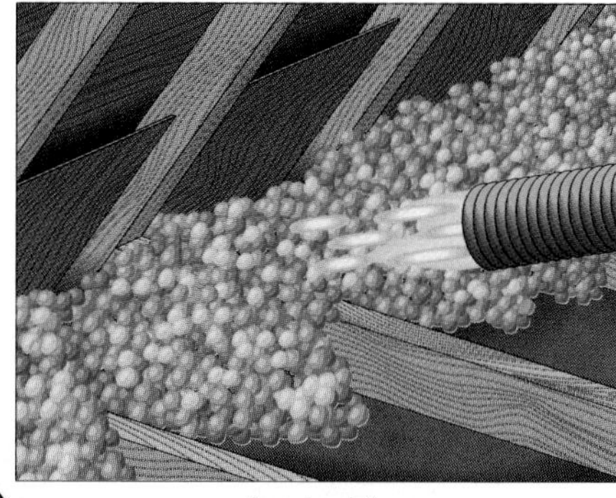

foam insulation
aislante de espuma
isolant moussé
Bauschaumisolierung

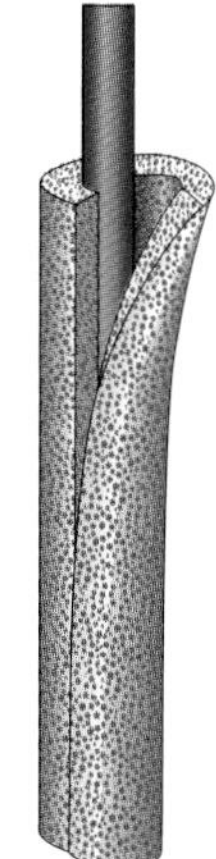

molded insulation
aislante premoldeado
isolant en coquille
geformte Rohrummantelung

foam-rubber insulation
aislante de esponja
isolant en caoutchouc-mousse
Schaumgummiisolierung

vinyl insulation
aislante vinílico
isolant en vinyle
Vinylisolierung

board insulation
tablero rígido aislante
isolant en panneau
Plattenisolierung

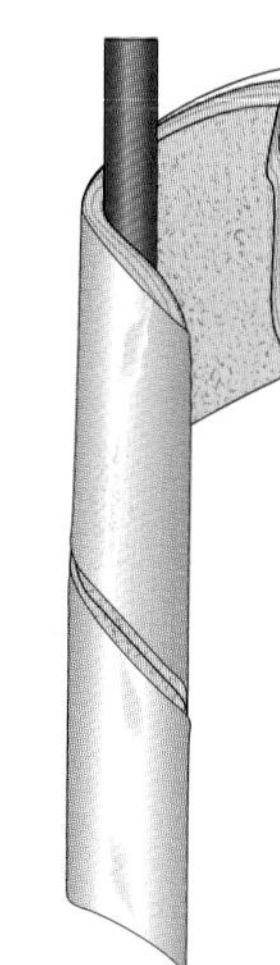

pipe-wrapping insulation
cinta aislante para tubería
isolant en ruban
Rohrummantelung

loose fill insulation
aislante a granel
isolant en vrac
Schüttungsisolierung

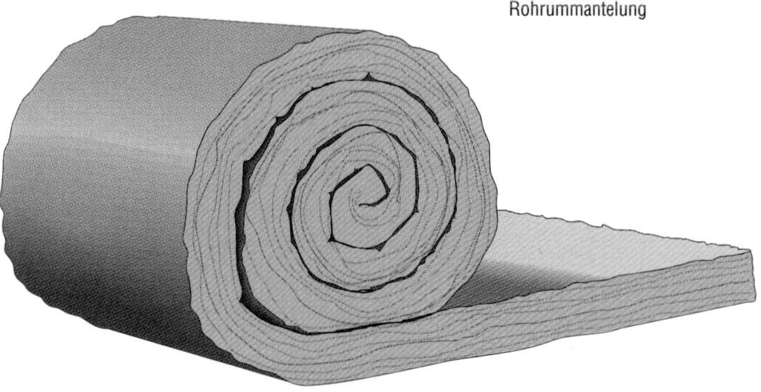

blanket insulation
rollo para recubrimiento impermeabilizante
isolant en rouleau
Mattenisolierung

BUILDING MATERIALS
MATERIALES DE CONSTRUCCIÓN
MATÉRIAUX DE CONSTRUCTION
BAUMATERIALIEN

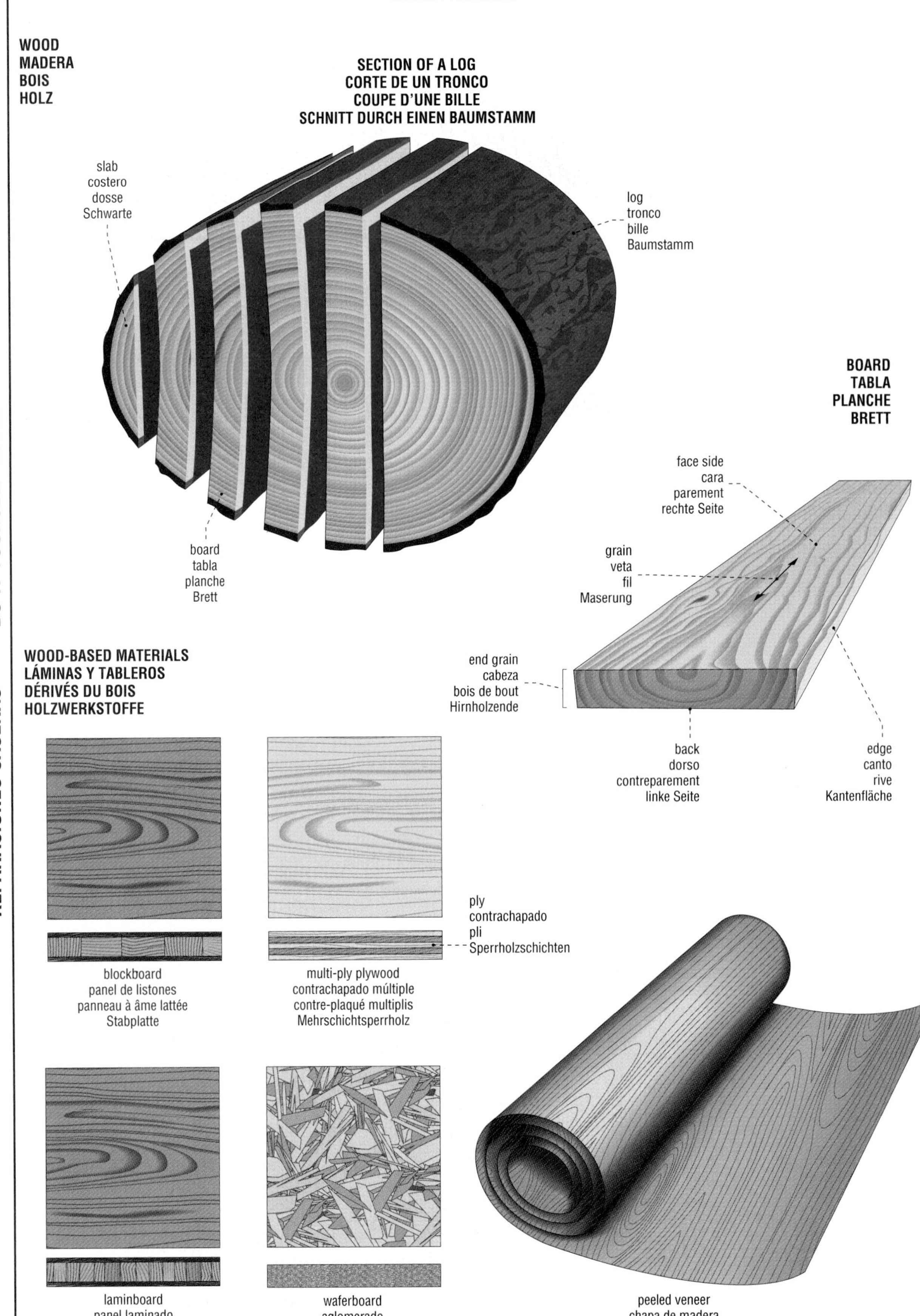

WOOD
MADERA
BOIS
HOLZ
SECTION OF A LOG
CORTE DE UN TRONCO
COUPE D'UNE BILLE
SCHNITT DURCH EINEN BAUMSTAMM
slab
costero
dosse
Schwarte
log
tronco
bille
Baumstamm
board
tabla
planche
Brett
BOARD
TABLA
PLANCHE
BRETT
face side
cara
parement
rechte Seite
grain
veta
fil
Maserung
end grain
cabeza
bois de bout
Hirnholzende
back
dorso
contreparement
linke Seite
edge
canto
rive
Kantenfläche
WOOD-BASED MATERIALS
LÁMINAS Y TABLEROS
DÉRIVÉS DU BOIS
HOLZWERKSTOFFE
ply
contrachapado
pli
Sperrholzschichten
blockboard
panel de listones
panneau à âme lattée
Stabplatte
multi-ply plywood
contrachapado múltiple
contre-plaqué multiplis
Mehrschichtsperrholz
laminboard
panel laminado
panneau à âme lamellée
Stäbchenplatte
waferboard
aglomerado
panneau de copeaux
Grobspanplatte
peeled veneer
chapa de madera
placage déroulé
Schälfurnier

WOOD-BASED MATERIALS
LÁMINAS Y TABLEROS
DÉRIVÉS DU BOIS
HOLZWERKSTOFFE

hardboard
tablero de fibra de madera
panneau de fibres
Hartfaserplatte

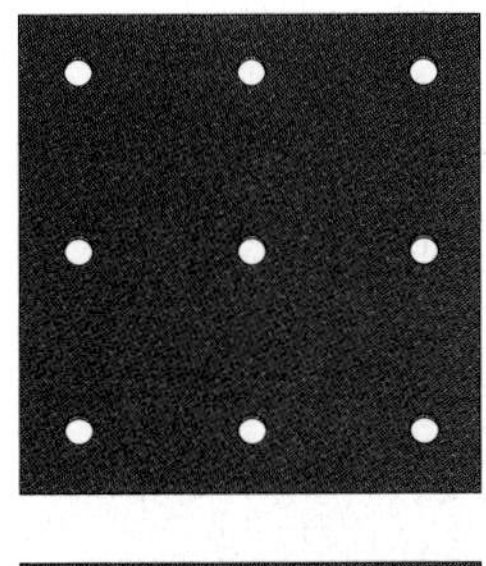

perforated hardboard
tablero de fibra de madera perforada
panneau de fibres perforé
gelochte Hartfaserplatte

plastic-laminated particle board
tablero de aglomerado con laminado de plástico
panneau de particules lamifié
kunststoffbeschichtete Hartfaserplatte

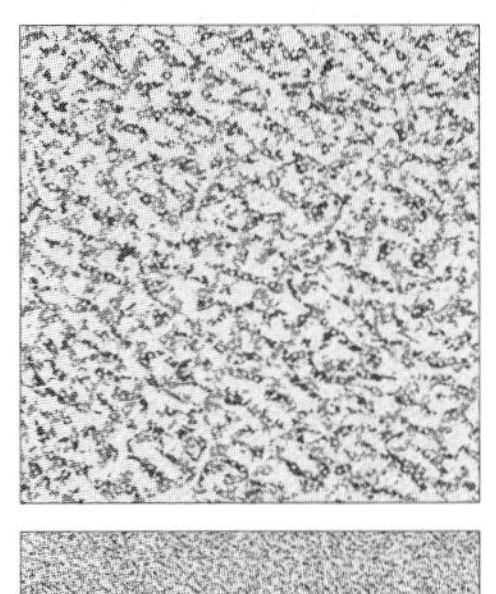

particle board
tablero de aglomerado
panneau de particules
Spanplatte

LOCK
CERRAJERÍA
SERRURE
SCHLOSS

GENERAL VIEW
VISTA GENERAL
VUE D'ENSEMBLE
ÜBERSICHT

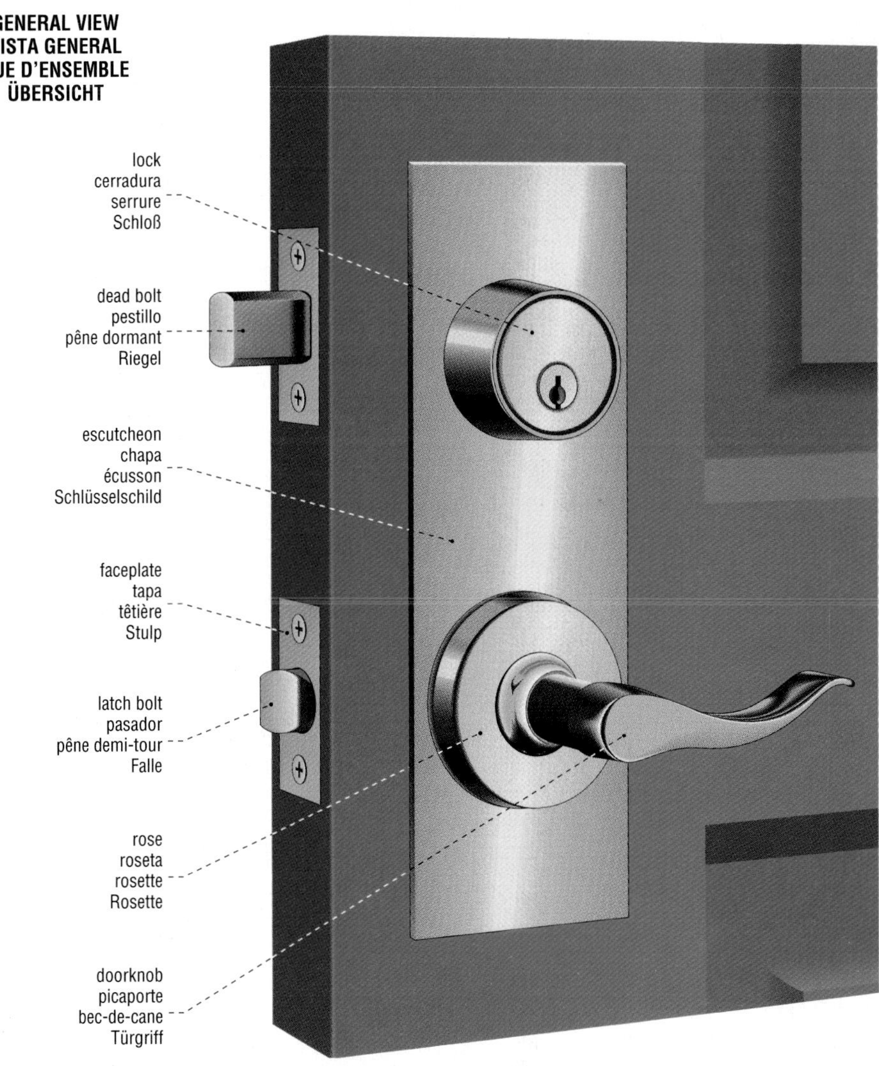
lock
cerradura
serrure
Schloß
dead bolt
pestillo
pêne dormant
Riegel
escutcheon
chapa
écusson
Schlüsselschild
faceplate
tapa
têtière
Stulp
latch bolt
pasador
pêne demi-tour
Falle
rose
roseta
rosette
Rosette
doorknob
picaporte
bec-de-cane
Türgriff

LOCK
CERRAJERÍA
SERRURE
SCHLOSS

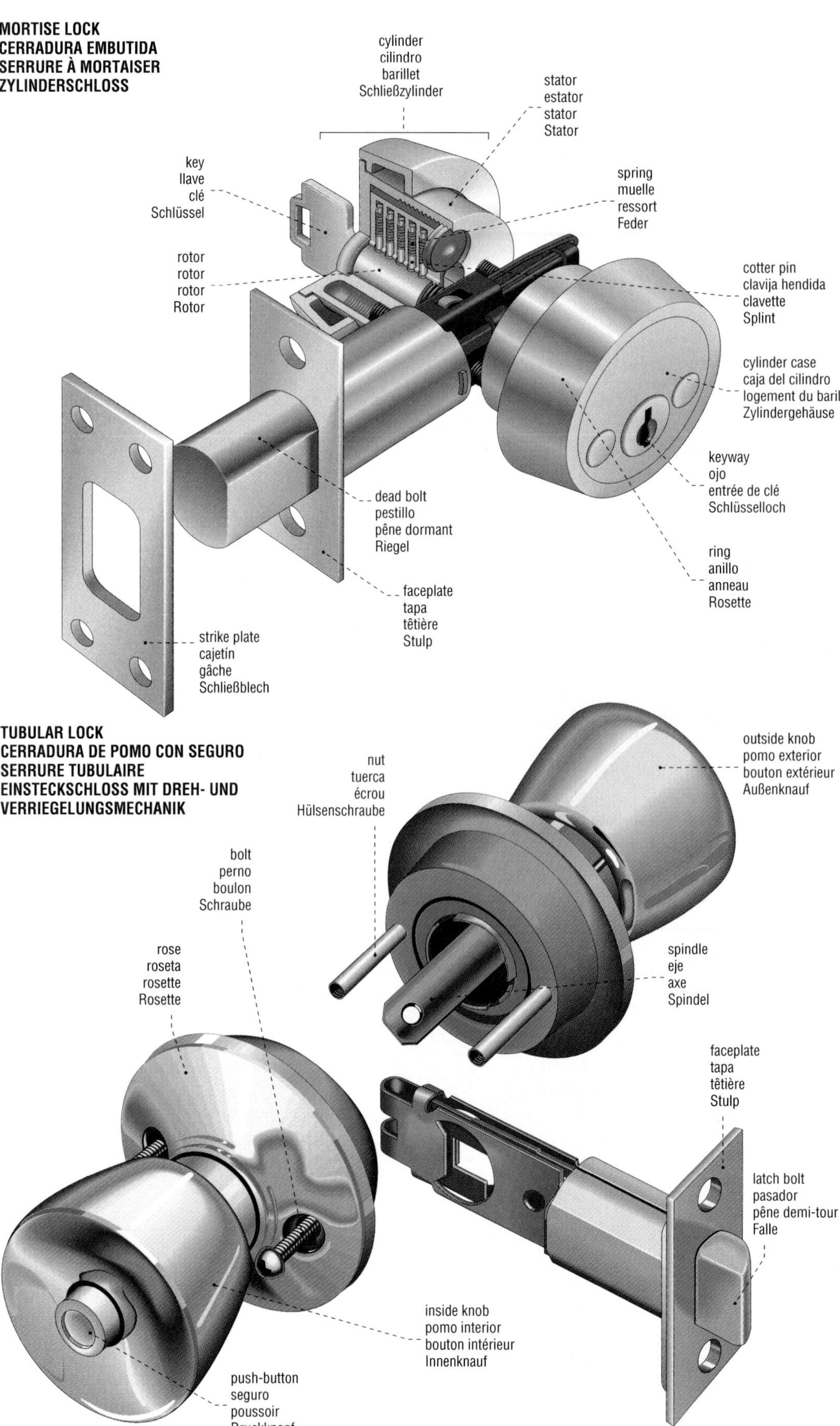

MORTISE LOCK
CERRADURA EMBUTIDA
SERRURE À MORTAISER
ZYLINDERSCHLOSS
cylinder
cilindro
barillet
Schließzylinder
stator
estator
stator
Stator
key
llave
clé
Schlüssel
spring
muelle
ressort
Feder
rotor
rotor
rotor
Rotor
cotter pin
clavija hendida
clavette
Splint
cylinder case
caja del cilindro
logement du barillet
Zylindergehäuse
keyway
ojo
entrée de clé
Schlüsselloch
dead bolt
pestillo
pêne dormant
Riegel
ring
anillo
anneau
Rosette
faceplate
tapa
têtière
Stulp
strike plate
cajetín
gâche
Schließblech
TUBULAR LOCK
CERRADURA DE POMO CON SEGURO
SERRURE TUBULAIRE
EINSTECKSCHLOSS MIT DREH- UND VERRIEGELUNGSMECHANIK
outside knob
pomo exterior
bouton extérieur
Außenknauf
nut
tuerca
écrou
Hülsenschraube
bolt
perno
boulon
Schraube
spindle
eje
axe
Spindel
rose
roseta
rosette
Rosette
faceplate
tapa
têtière
Stulp
latch bolt
pasador
pêne demi-tour
Falle
inside knob
pomo interior
bouton intérieur
Innenknauf
push-button
seguro
poussoir
Druckknopf

MASONRY
HERRAMIENTAS DE ALBAÑIL
MAÇONNERIE
MAUREREI

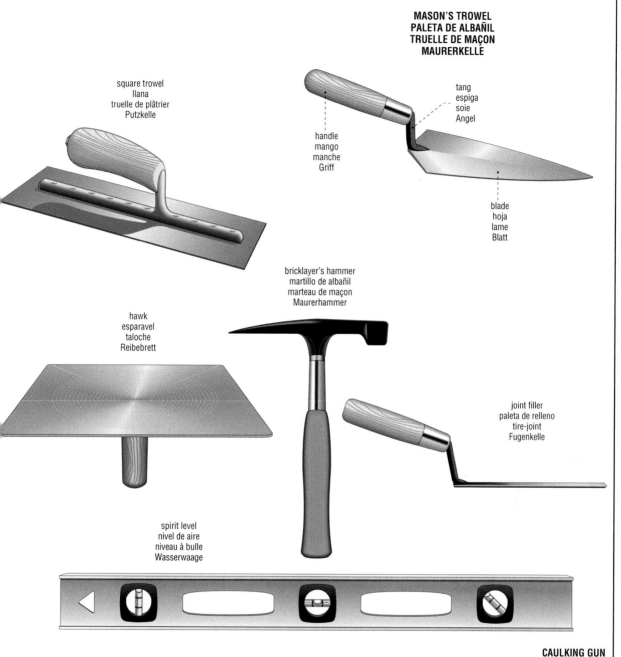

MASON'S TROWEL
PALETA DE ALBAÑIL
TRUELLE DE MAÇON
MAURERKELLE

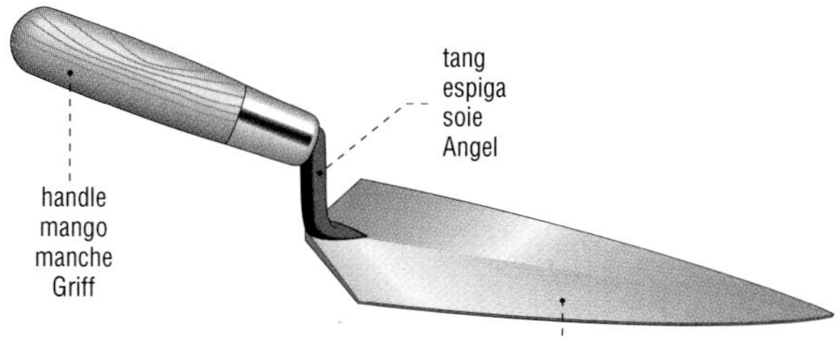

square trowel
llana
truelle de plâtrier
Putzkelle

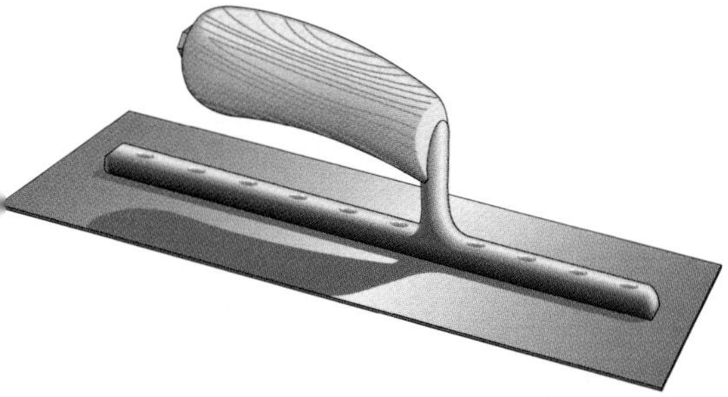

tang
espiga
soie
Angel

handle
mango
manche
Griff

blade
hoja
lame
Blatt

bricklayer's hammer
martillo de albañil
marteau de maçon
Maurerhammer

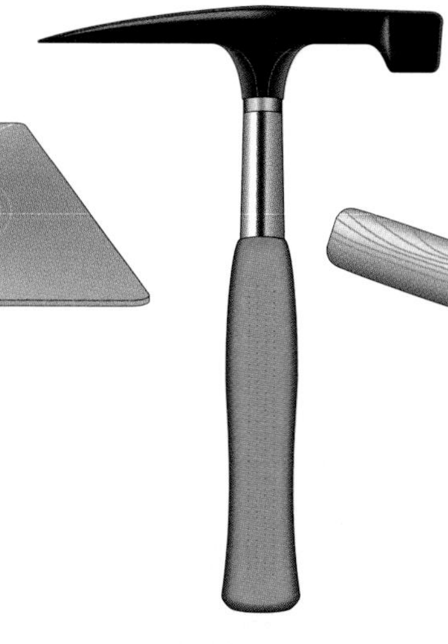

hawk
esparavel
taloche
Reibebrett

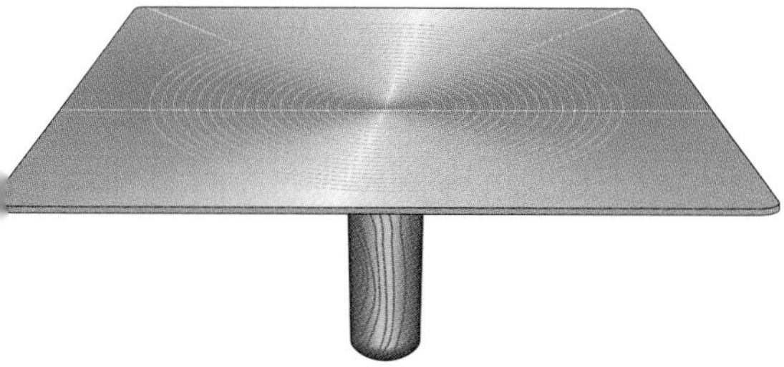

joint filler
paleta de relleno
tire-joint
Fugenkelle

spirit level
nivel de aire
niveau à bulle
Wasserwaage

CAULKING GUN
PISTOLA PARA CALAFATEO
PISTOLET À CALFEUTRER
KARTUSCHENPISTOLE

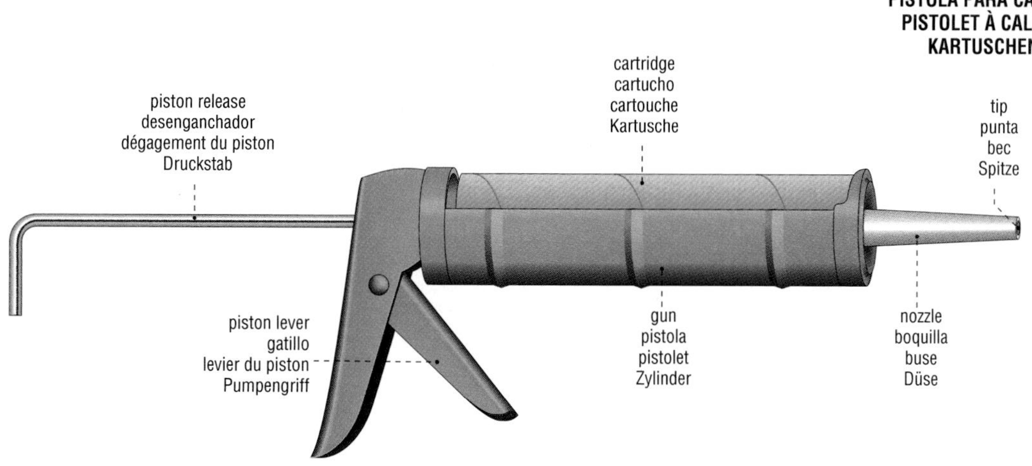
cartridge
cartucho
cartouche
Kartusche
piston release
desenganchador
dégagement du piston
Druckstab
tip
punta
bec
Spitze
piston lever
gatillo
levier du piston
Pumpengriff
gun
pistola
pistolet
Zylinder
nozzle
boquilla
buse
Düse

PLUMBING: BATHROOM
FONTANERÍA: CUARTO DE BAÑO
PLOMBERIE: SALLE DE BAINS
SANITÄRINSTALLATION: BADEZIMMER

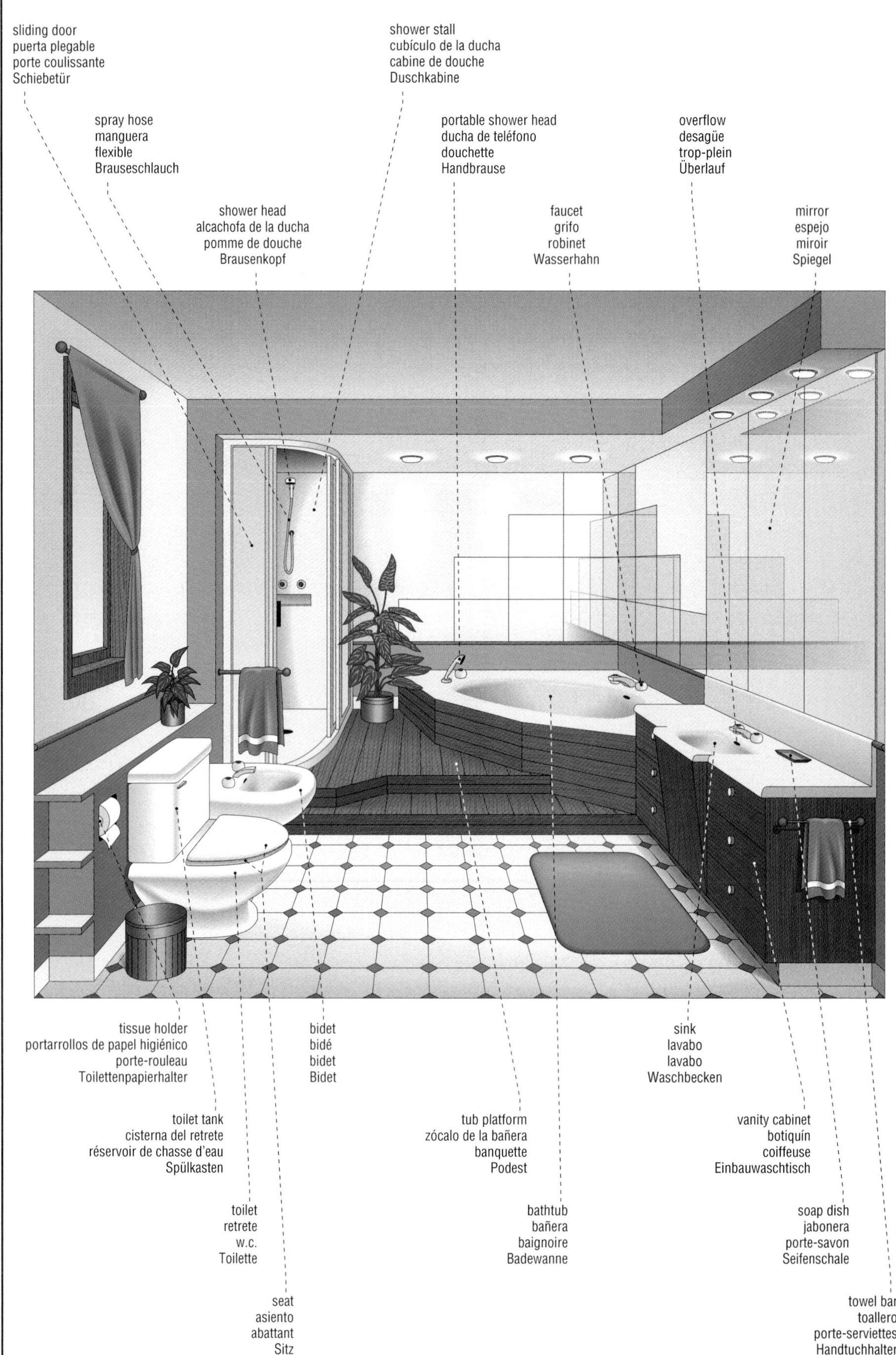
sliding door
puerta plegable
porte coulissante
Schiebetür
shower stall
cubículo de la ducha
cabine de douche
Duschkabine
spray hose
manguera
flexible
Brauseschlauch
portable shower head
ducha de teléfono
douchette
Handbrause
overflow
desagüe
trop-plein
Überlauf
shower head
alcachofa de la ducha
pomme de douche
Brausenkopf
faucet
grifo
robinet
Wasserhahn
mirror
espejo
miroir
Spiegel
tissue holder
portarrollos de papel higiénico
porte-rouleau
Toilettenpapierhalter
bidet
bidé
bidet
Bidet
sink
lavabo
lavabo
Waschbecken
toilet tank
cisterna del retrete
réservoir de chasse d'eau
Spülkasten
tub platform
zócalo de la bañera
banquette
Podest
vanity cabinet
botiquín
coiffeuse
Einbauwaschtisch
toilet
retrete
w.c.
Toilette
bathtub
bañera
baignoire
Badewanne
soap dish
jabonera
porte-savon
Seifenschale
seat
asiento
abattant
Sitz
towel bar
toallero
porte-serviettes
Handtuchhalter

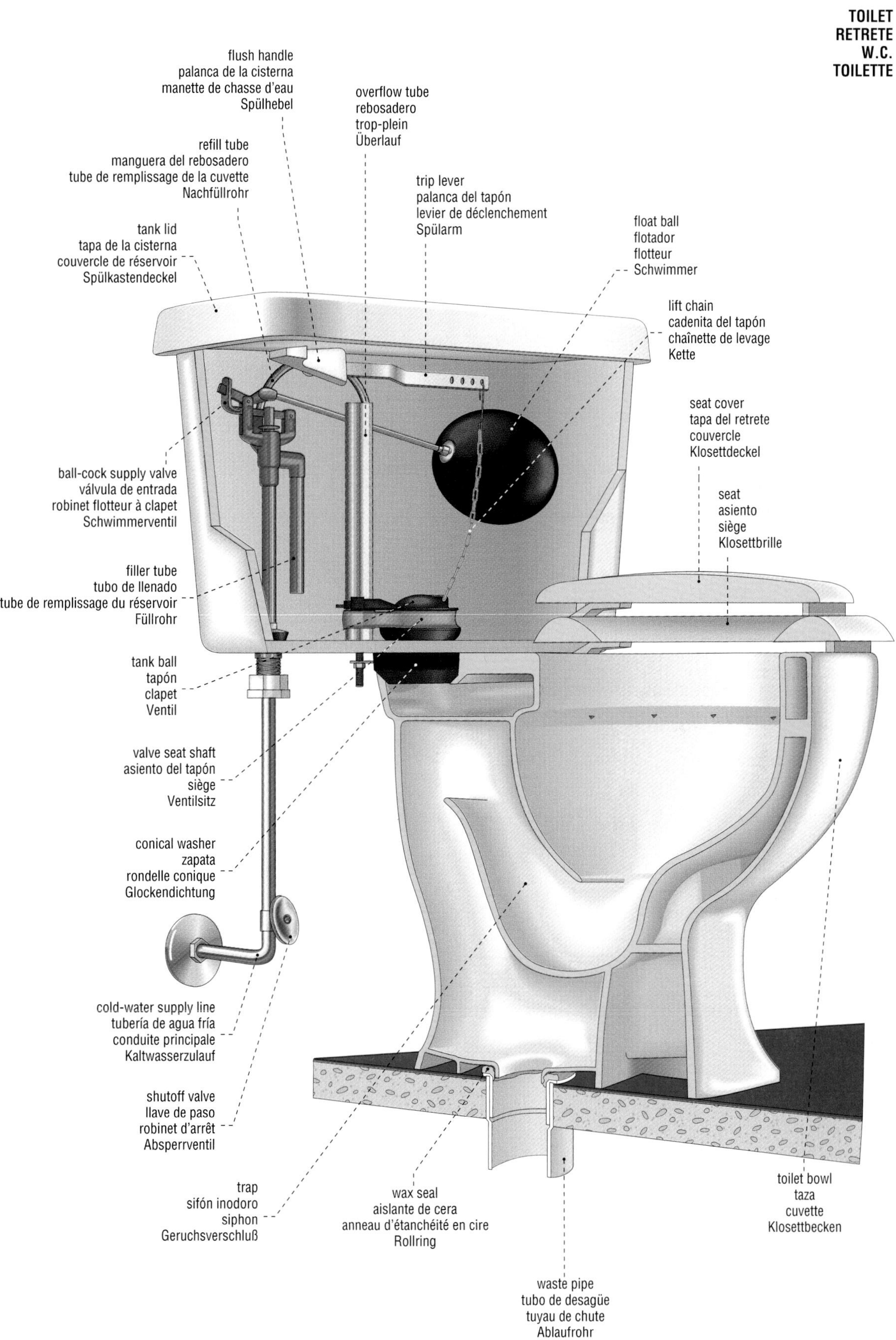
flush handle
palanca de la cisterna
manette de chasse d'eau
Spülhebel
overflow tube
rebosadero
trop-plein
Überlauf
refill tube
manguera del rebosadero
tube de remplissage de la cuvette
Nachfüllrohr
trip lever
palanca del tapón
levier de déclenchement
Spülarm
tank lid
tapa de la cisterna
couvercle de réservoir
Spülkastendeckel
float ball
flotador
flotteur
Schwimmer
lift chain
cadenita del tapón
chaînette de levage
Kette
seat cover
tapa del retrete
couvercle
Klosettdeckel
ball-cock supply valve
válvula de entrada
robinet flotteur à clapet
Schwimmerventil
seat
asiento
siège
Klosettbrille
filler tube
tubo de llenado
tube de remplissage du réservoir
Füllrohr
tank ball
tapón
clapet
Ventil
valve seat shaft
asiento del tapón
siège
Ventilsitz
conical washer
zapata
rondelle conique
Glockendichtung
cold-water supply line
tubería de agua fría
conduite principale
Kaltwasserzulauf
shutoff valve
llave de paso
robinet d'arrêt
Absperrventil
trap
sifón inodoro
siphon
Geruchsverschluß
wax seal
aislante de cera
anneau d'étanchéité en cire
Rollring
toilet bowl
taza
cuvette
Klosettbecken
waste pipe
tubo de desagüe
tuyau de chute
Ablaufrohr

PLUMBING
FONTANERÍA
PLOMBERIE
SANITÄRINSTALLATION

STEM FAUCET
GRIFO
ROBINET
WANDAUSLAUFVENTIL

BALL-TYPE FAUCET
GRIFO DE BOLA
MITIGEUR À BILLE CREUSE
MISCHBATTERIE MIT KUGELDICHTUNG

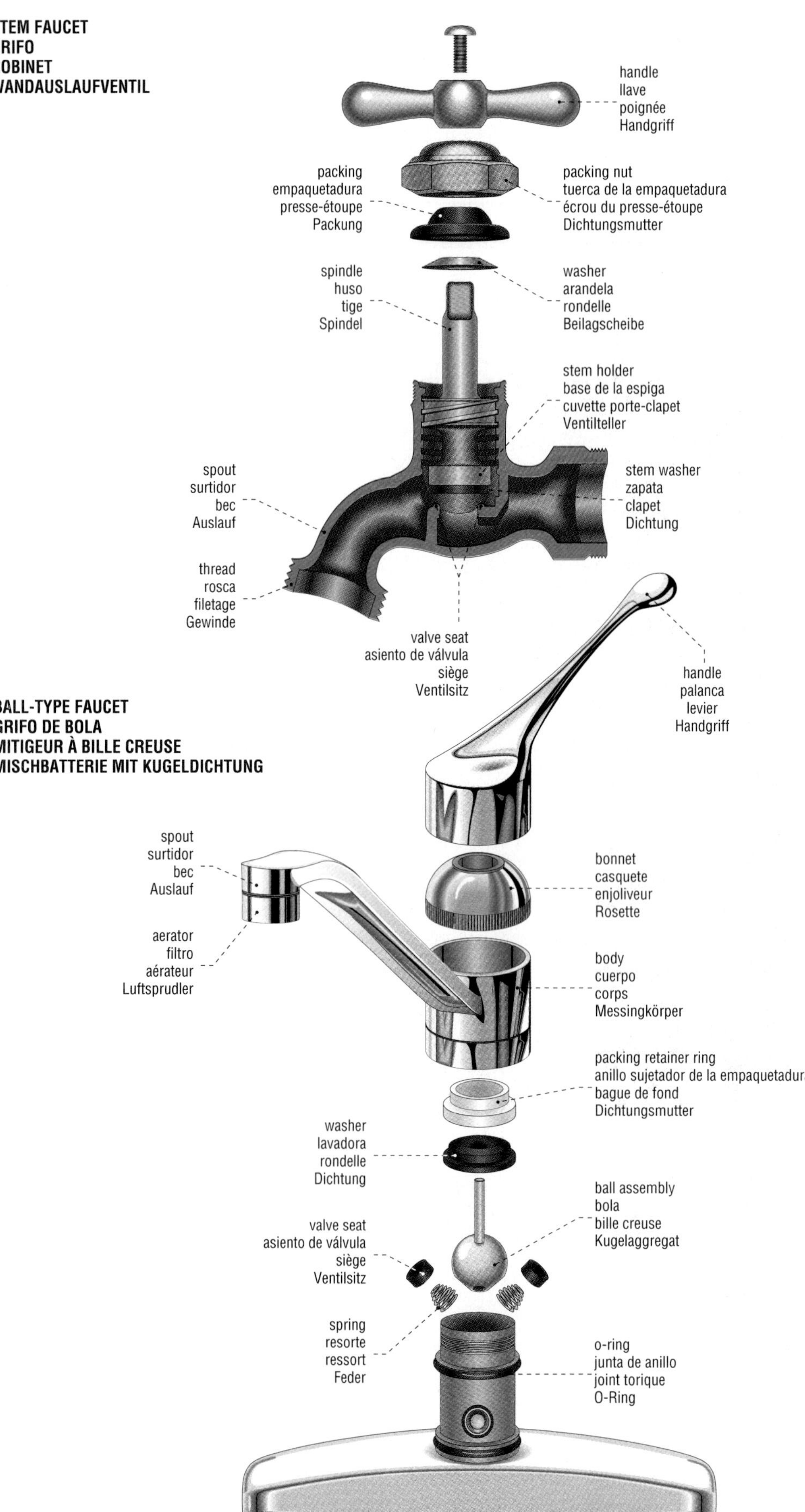
handle
llave
poignée
Handgriff
packing
empaquetadura
presse-étoupe
Packung
packing nut
tuerca de la empaquetadura
écrou du presse-étoupe
Dichtungsmutter
spindle
huso
tige
Spindel
washer
arandela
rondelle
Beilagscheibe
stem holder
base de la espiga
cuvette porte-clapet
Ventilteller
spout
surtidor
bec
Auslauf
stem washer
zapata
clapet
Dichtung
thread
rosca
filetage
Gewinde
valve seat
asiento de válvula
siège
Ventilsitz
handle
palanca
levier
Handgriff
spout
surtidor
bec
Auslauf
bonnet
casquete
enjoliveur
Rosette
aerator
filtro
aérateur
Luftsprudler
body
cuerpo
corps
Messingkörper
packing retainer ring
anillo sujetador de la empaquetadura
bague de fond
Dichtungsmutter
washer
lavadora
rondelle
Dichtung
ball assembly
bola
bille creuse
Kugelaggregat
valve seat
asiento de válvula
siège
Ventilsitz
spring
resorte
ressort
Feder
o-ring
junta de anillo
joint torique
O-Ring

DISC FAUCET
GRIFO DE DISCO
MITIGEUR À DISQUE
MISCHBATTERIE MIT KERAMIKDICHTUNG

handle
palanca
levier
Handgriff
bonnet
casquete
enjoliveur
Rosette
cylinder
cilindro
cylindre
Zylinder
seal
zapata
anneau d'étanchéité
Dichtung
spout
surtidor
bec
Auslauf
water inlet
entrada de agua
entrée d'eau
Wasserzulauf
aerator
flitro
aérateur
Luftsprudler
escutcheon
placa
applique du robinet
Messingkörper

CARTRIDGE FAUCET
GRIFO DE CARTUCHO
MITIGEUR À CARTOUCHE
MISCHBATTERIE MIT KARTUSCHENDICHTUNG

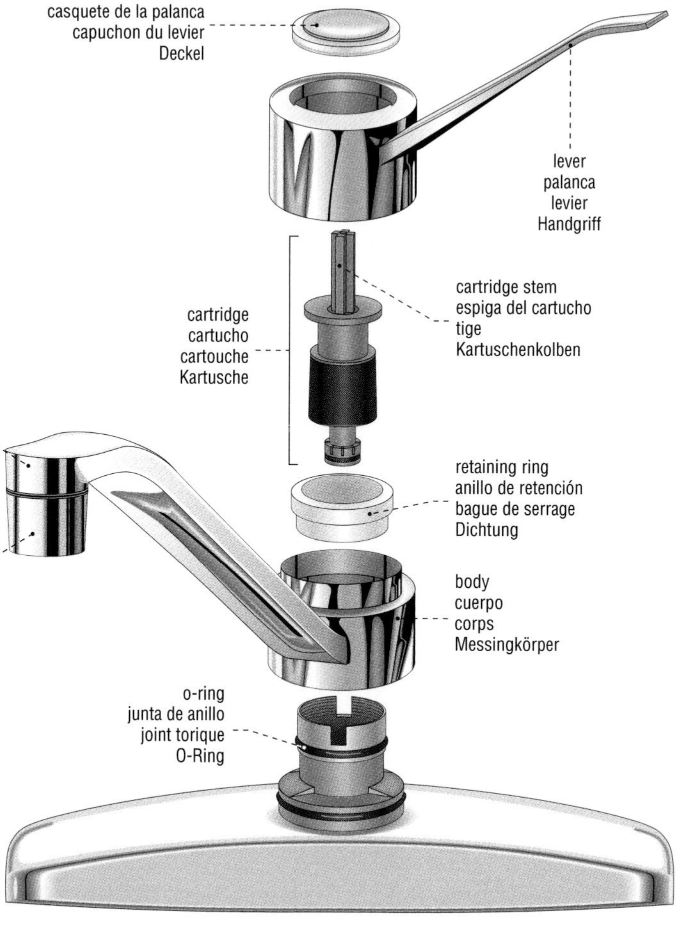

lever cover
casquete de la palanca
capuchon du levier
Deckel

lever
palanca
levier
Handgriff

cartridge stem
espiga del cartucho
tige
Kartuschenkolben

cartridge
cartucho
cartouche
Kartusche

spout
surtidor
bec
Auslauf

retaining ring
anillo de retención
bague de serrage
Dichtung

aerator
flitro
aérateur
Luftsprudler

body
cuerpo
corps
Messingkörper

o-ring
junta de anillo
joint torique
O-Ring

GARBAGE DISPOSAL SINK
FREGADERO CON TRITURADOR DE BASURA
ÉVIER-BROYEUR
SPÜLE MIT MÜLLSCHLUCKER

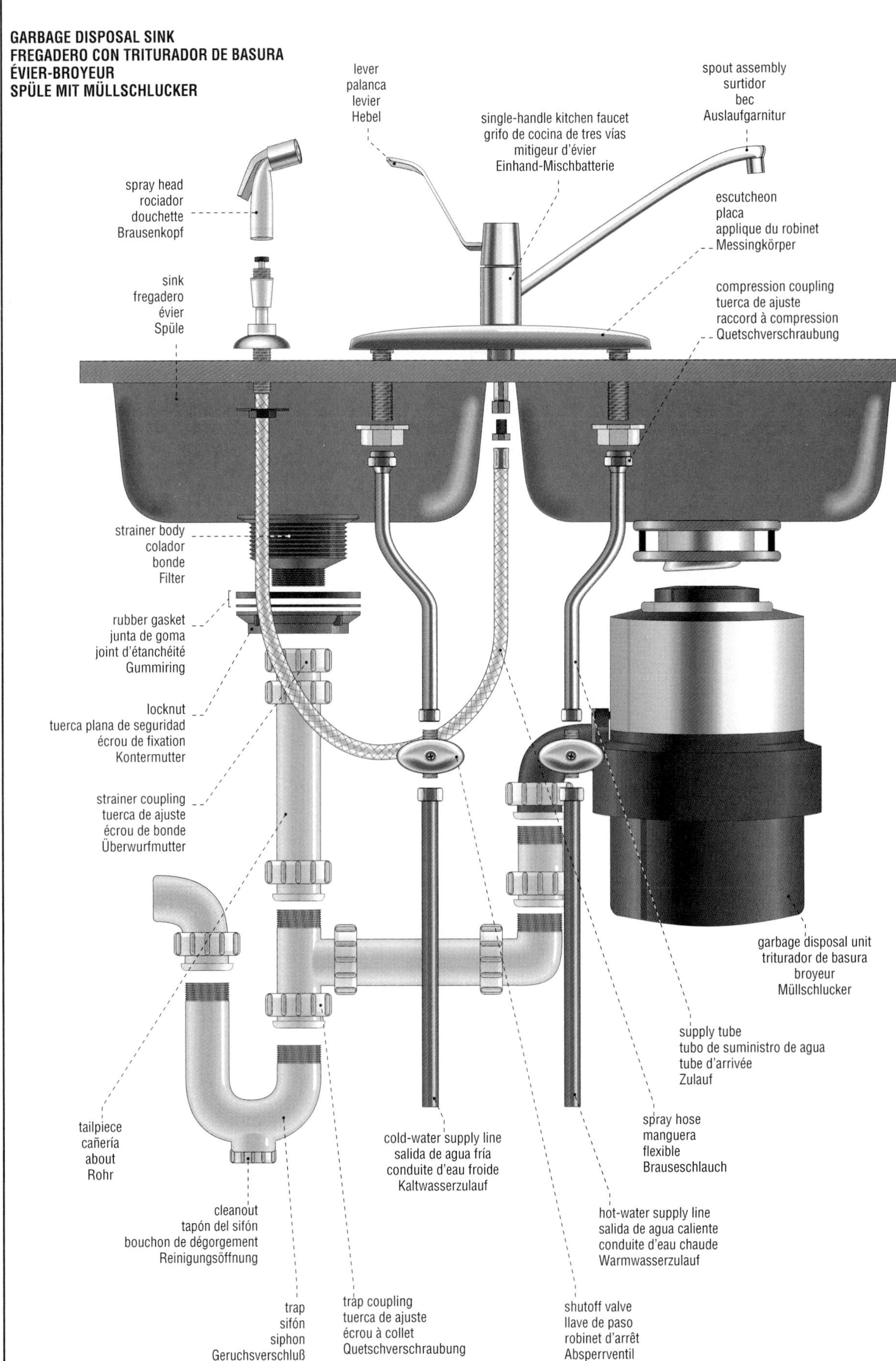
lever
palanca
levier
Hebel
spout assembly
surtidor
bec
Auslaufgarnitur
single-handle kitchen faucet
grifo de cocina de tres vías
mitigeur d'évier
Einhand-Mischbatterie
spray head
rociador
douchette
Brausenkopf
escutcheon
placa
applique du robinet
Messingkörper
sink
fregadero
évier
Spüle
compression coupling
tuerca de ajuste
raccord à compression
Quetschverschraubung
strainer body
colador
bonde
Filter
rubber gasket
junta de goma
joint d'étanchéité
Gummiring
locknut
tuerca plana de seguridad
écrou de fixation
Kontermutter
strainer coupling
tuerca de ajuste
écrou de bonde
Überwurfmutter
garbage disposal unit
triturador de basura
broyeur
Müllschlucker
supply tube
tubo de suministro de agua
tube d'arrivée
Zulauf
tailpiece
cañería
about
Rohr
cold-water supply line
salida de agua fría
conduite d'eau froide
Kaltwasserzulauf
spray hose
manguera
flexible
Brauseschlauch
cleanout
tapón del sifón
bouchon de dégorgement
Reinigungsöffnung
hot-water supply line
salida de agua caliente
conduite d'eau chaude
Warmwasserzulauf
trap
sifón
siphon
Geruchsverschluß
trap coupling
tuerca de ajuste
écrou à collet
Quetschverschraubung
shutoff valve
llave de paso
robinet d'arrêt
Absperrventil

GAS WATER-HEATER TANK
CALENTADOR DE GAS
CHAUFFE-EAU AU GAZ
GASWARMWASSERBEREITER

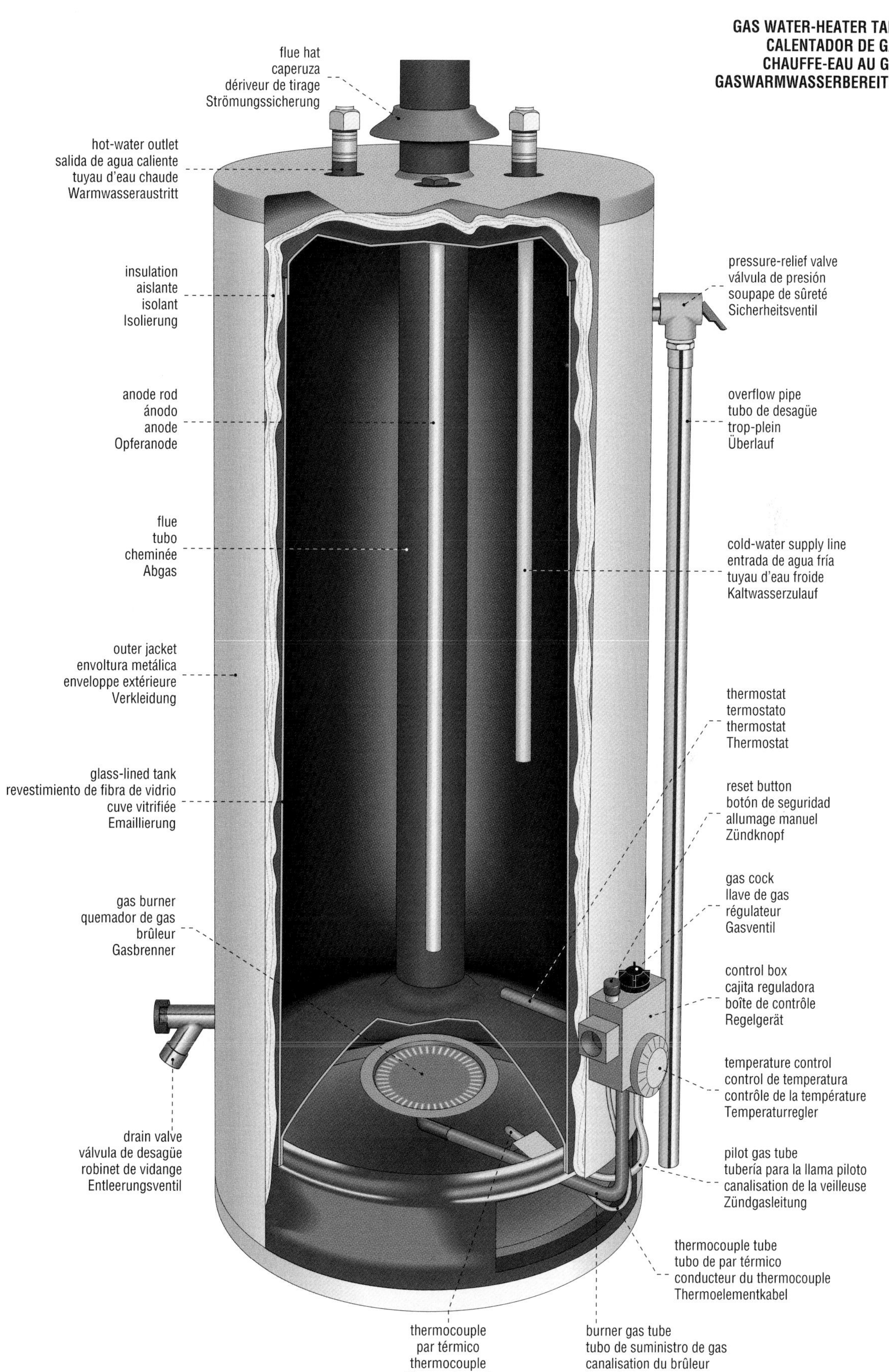
flue hat
caperuza
dériveur de tirage
Strömungssicherung
hot-water outlet
salida de agua caliente
tuyau d'eau chaude
Warmwasseraustritt
insulation
aislante
isolant
Isolierung
anode rod
ánodo
anode
Opferanode
flue
tubo
cheminée
Abgas
outer jacket
envoltura metálica
enveloppe extérieure
Verkleidung
glass-lined tank
revestimiento de fibra de vidrio
cuve vitrifiée
Emaillierung
gas burner
quemador de gas
brûleur
Gasbrenner
drain valve
válvula de desagüe
robinet de vidange
Entleerungsventil
thermocouple
par térmico
thermocouple
Thermoelement
burner gas tube
tubo de suministro de gas
canalisation du brûleur
Gasrohr
pressure-relief valve
válvula de presión
soupape de sûreté
Sicherheitsventil
overflow pipe
tubo de desagüe
trop-plein
Überlauf
cold-water supply line
entrada de agua fría
tuyau d'eau froide
Kaltwasserzulauf
thermostat
termostato
thermostat
Thermostat
reset button
botón de seguridad
allumage manuel
Zündknopf
gas cock
llave de gas
régulateur
Gasventil
control box
cajita reguladora
boîte de contrôle
Regelgerät
temperature control
control de temperatura
contrôle de la température
Temperaturregler
pilot gas tube
tubería para la llama piloto
canalisation de la veilleuse
Zündgasleitung
thermocouple tube
tubo de par térmico
conducteur du thermocouple
Thermoelementkabel

PLUMBING: EXAMPLES OF BRANCHING
FONTANERÍA: CONEXIONES
PLOMBERIE: EXEMPLES DE BRANCHEMENT
SANITÄRINSTALLATION: BEISPIELE FÜR ABZWEIGUNGEN

WASHER
LAVADORA
LAVE-LINGE
WASCHMASCHINE

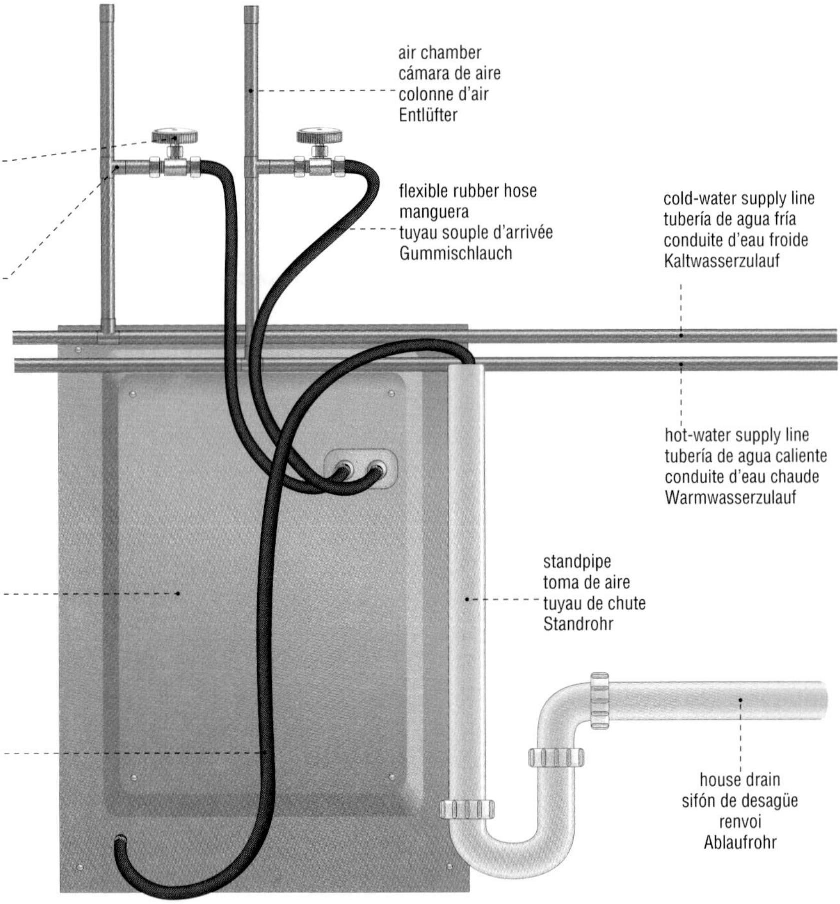

air chamber
cámara de aire
colonne d'air
Entlüfter

shutoff valve
llave de paso
robinet d'arrêt
Absperrventil

flexible rubber hose
manguera
tuyau souple d'arrivée
Gummischlauch

cold-water supply line
tubería de agua fría
conduite d'eau froide
Kaltwasserzulauf

tee
connector en T
raccord té
T-Stück

hot-water supply line
tubería de agua caliente
conduite d'eau chaude
Warmwasserzulauf

washer
lavadora
lave-linge
Waschmaschine

standpipe
toma de aire
tuyau de chute
Standrohr

drain hose
manguera de desagüe
tuyau d'évacuation
Ablaufschlauch

house drain
sifón de desagüe
renvoi
Ablaufrohr

DISHWASHER
MÁQUINA LAVAPLATOS
LAVE-VAISSELLE
GESCHIRRSPÜLMASCHINE

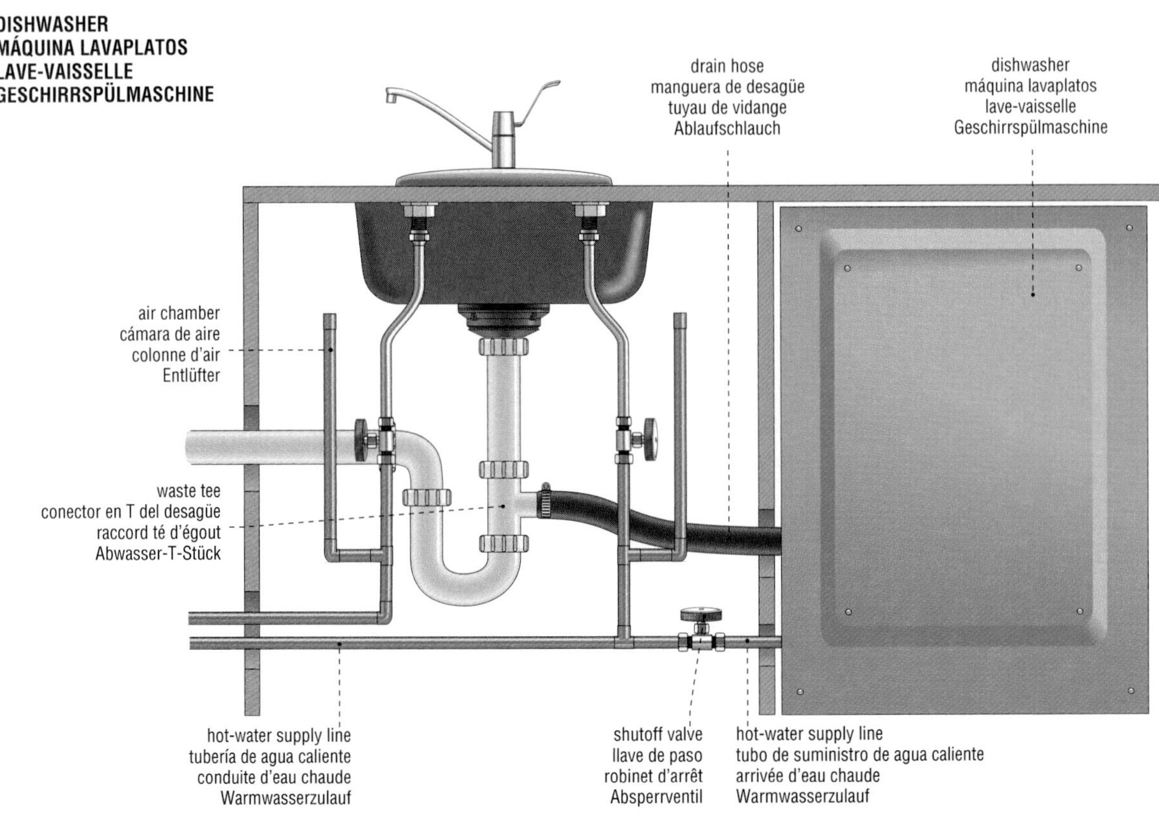
drain hose
manguera de desagüe
tuyau de vidange
Ablaufschlauch
dishwasher
máquina lavaplatos
lave-vaisselle
Geschirrspülmaschine
air chamber
cámara de aire
colonne d'air
Entlüfter
waste tee
conector en T del desagüe
raccord té d'égout
Abwasser-T-Stück
hot-water supply line
tubería de agua caliente
conduite d'eau chaude
Warmwasserzulauf
shutoff valve
llave de paso
robinet d'arrêt
Absperrventil
hot-water supply line
tubo de suministro de agua caliente
arrivée d'eau chaude
Warmwasserzulauf

PLUMBING
FONTANERÍA
PLOMBERIE
SANITÄRINSTALLATION

PLUMBING TOOLS
HERRAMIENTAS DE FONTANERO
OUTILS POUR PLOMBERIE
INSTALLATIONSWERKZEUGE

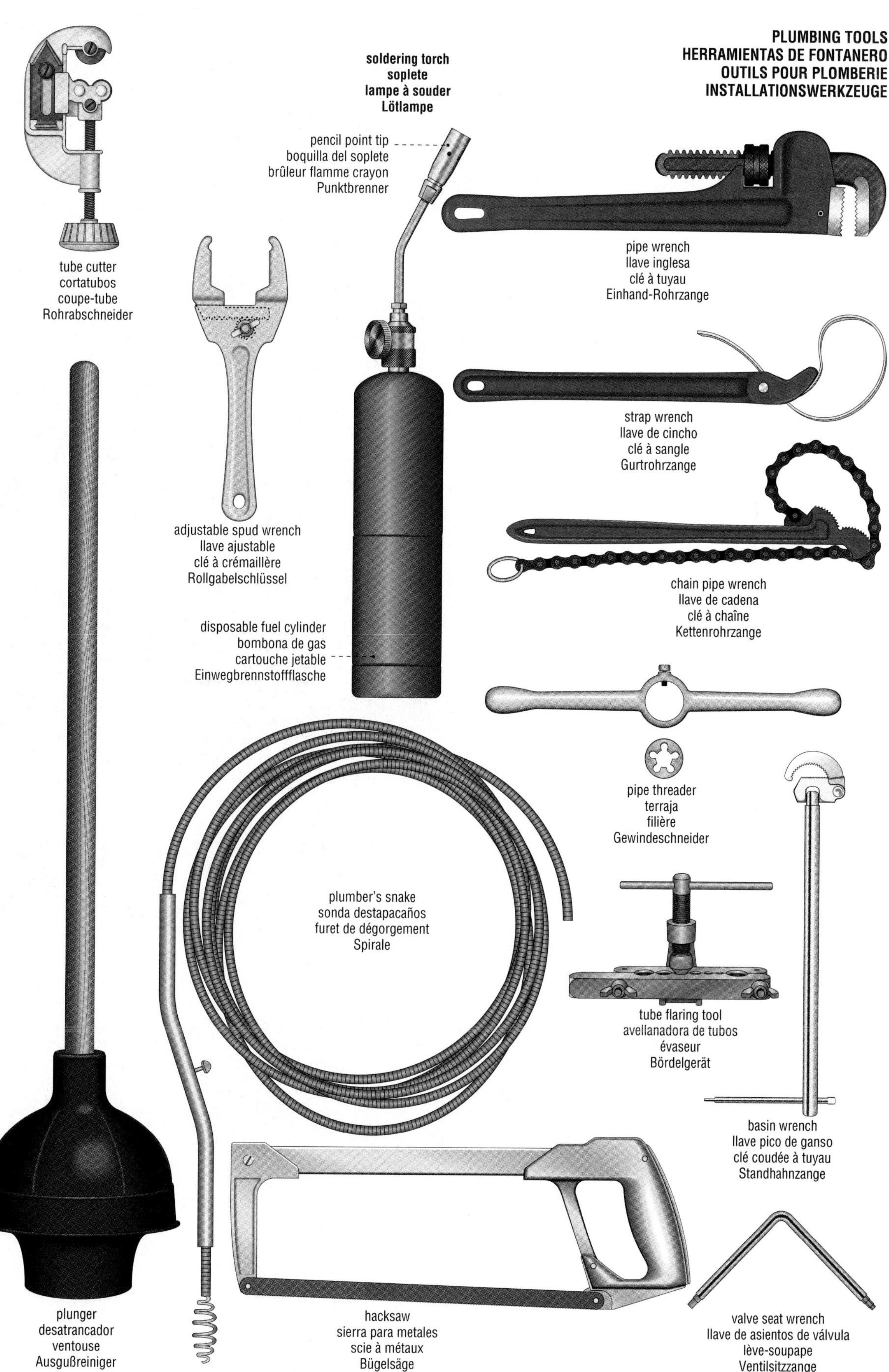
tube cutter
cortatubos
coupe-tube
Rohrabschneider
soldering torch
soplete
lampe à souder
Lötlampe
pencil point tip
boquilla del soplete
brûleur flamme crayon
Punktbrenner
pipe wrench
llave inglesa
clé à tuyau
Einhand-Rohrzange
strap wrench
llave de cincho
clé à sangle
Gurtrohrzange
adjustable spud wrench
llave ajustable
clé à crémaillère
Rollgabelschlüssel
chain pipe wrench
llave de cadena
clé à chaîne
Kettenrohrzange
disposable fuel cylinder
bombona de gas
cartouche jetable
Einwegbrennstoffflasche
pipe threader
terraja
filière
Gewindeschneider
plumber's snake
sonda destapacaños
furet de dégorgement
Spirale
tube flaring tool
avellanadora de tubos
évaseur
Bördelgerät
basin wrench
llave pico de ganso
clé coudée à tuyau
Standhahnzange
plunger
desatrancador
ventouse
Ausgußreiniger
hacksaw
sierra para metales
scie à métaux
Bügelsäge
valve seat wrench
llave de asientos de válvula
lève-soupape
Ventilsitzzange

MECHANICAL CONNECTORS
CONEXIONES MECÁNICAS
RACCORDS MÉCANIQUES
MECHANISCHE VERBINDUNGEN

compression fitting
ensamblaje por compresión
raccord à compression
Quetschverschraubung

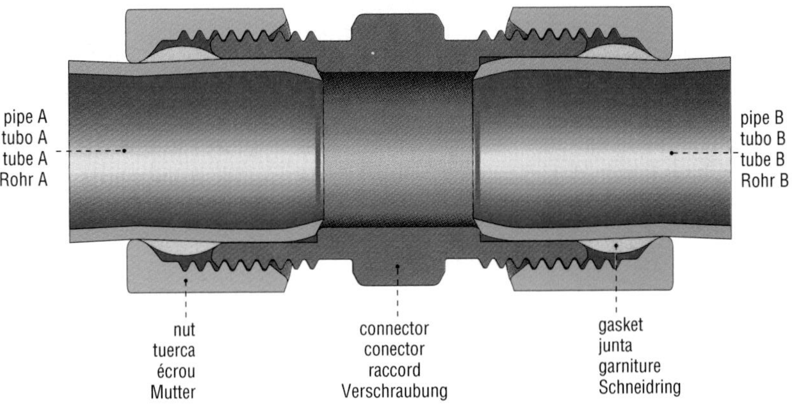
pipe A
tubo A
tube A
Rohr A
pipe B
tubo B
tube B
Rohr B
nut
tuerca
écrou
Mutter
connector
conector
raccord
Verschraubung
gasket
junta
garniture
Schneidring

flare joint
ensamblaje abocinado
raccord à collet repoussé
Bördelverbindung

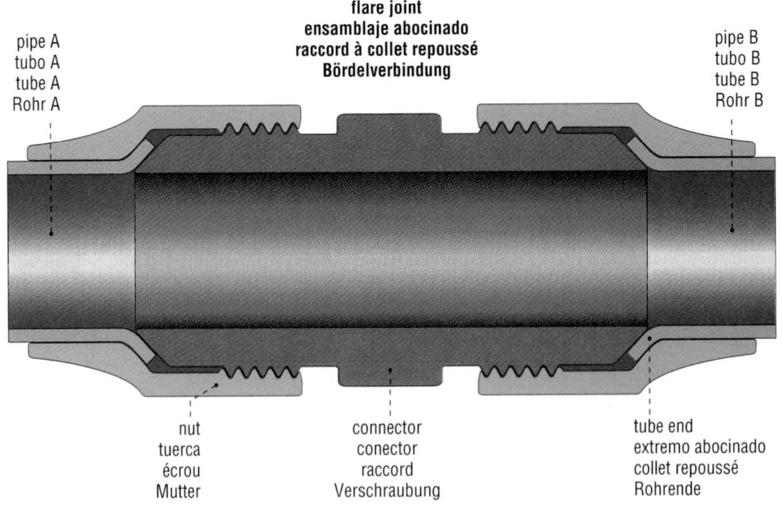
pipe A
tubo A
tube A
Rohr A
pipe B
tubo B
tube B
Rohr B
nut
tuerca
écrou
Mutter
connector
conector
raccord
Verschraubung
tube end
extremo abocinado
collet repoussé
Rohrende

union
unión
raccord union
Verschraubung

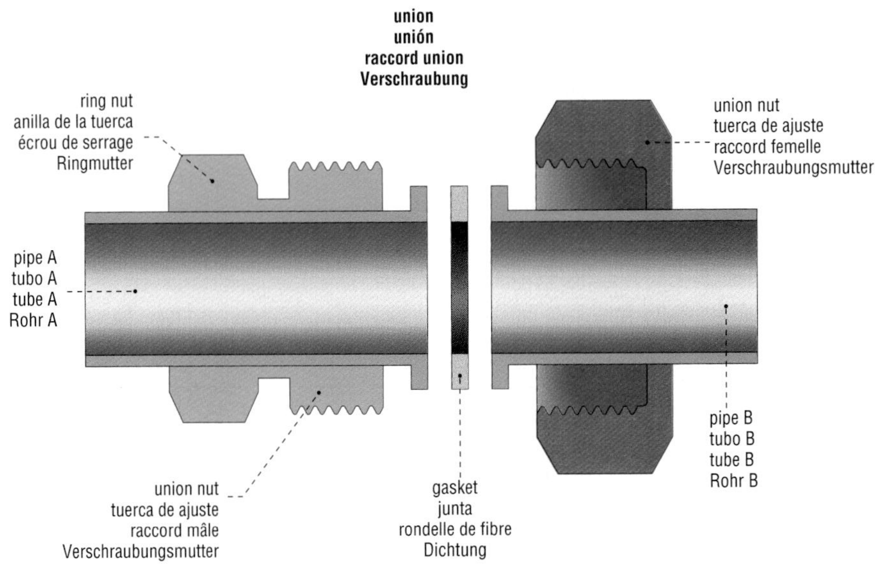
ring nut
anilla de la tuerca
écrou de serrage
Ringmutter
union nut
tuerca de ajuste
raccord femelle
Verschraubungsmutter
pipe A
tubo A
tube A
Rohr A
pipe B
tubo B
tube B
Rohr B
union nut
tuerca de ajuste
raccord mâle
Verschraubungsmutter
gasket
junta
rondelle de fibre
Dichtung

TRANSITION FITTINGS
CONEXIONES DE TRANSICIÓN
ADAPTEURS
ÜBERGÄNGE

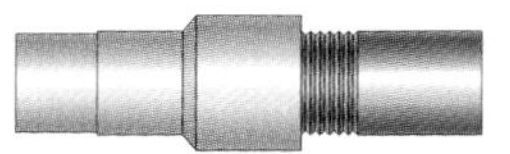
steel to plastic
de acero a plástico
plastique et acier
Stahl auf Kunststoff

copper to plastic
de cobre a plástico
plastique et cuivre
Kupfer auf Kunststoff

copper to steel
de cobre a acero
cuivre et acier
Kupfer auf Stahl

FITTINGS
CONEXIONES
RACCORDS
FITTINGS

45° elbow
codo de 45 grados
coude à 45°
Winkel 45°

elbow
codo de 90 grados
coude
Winkel

U-bend
conexión en U
coude à 180°
Doppelbogen

tee
conexión en T
té
Strömungs-T

Y-branch
conexión en Y
culotte
Abzweig 45°

offset
desviación
coude de renvoi
Etagenbogen

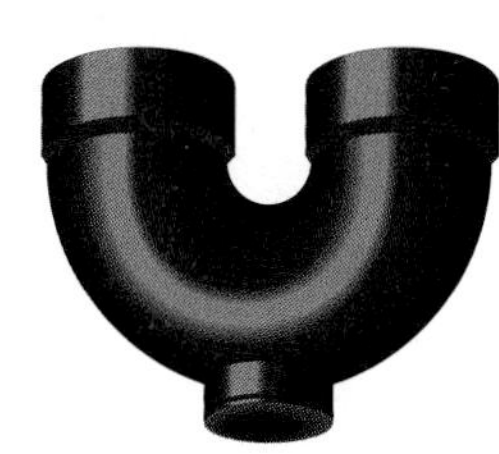
trap
sifón
siphon
Siphonwinkel

square head plug
tapón macho
bouchon mâle sans bourrelet
Vierkantstopfen

cap
tapón
bouchon femelle
Kappe

flush bushing
boquilla de reducir
réduction mâle-femelle
Muffe

nipple
boquilla
mamelon double
Nippel

reducing coupling
reductor de calibre
raccord de réduction
Reduziermuffenippel

threaded cap
tapón hembra
bouchon femelle à visser
Gewindekappe

pipe coupling
unión
manchon
Rohrverschraubung

hexagon bushing
boquilla de reducir con
cabeza hexagonal
réduction mâle-femelle hexagonale
Sechskantstopfen

LADDERS AND STEPLADDERS
ESCALERAS DE MANO
ÉCHELLES ET ESCABEAUX
LEITERN UND STEHLEITERN

STEPLADDER
ESCALERA DE TIJERA
ESCABEAU
STEHLEITER
tool shelf
bandeja para herramientas
tablette porte-outil
Arbeitsbrett
top
parte superior
plateau
Ablage
step
peldaño
marche
Tritt
brace
tirante
entretoise
Ausklapparretierung
step stool
escalerilla
tabouret-escabeau
Tritthocker
EXTENSION LADDER
ESCALERA DE EXTENSIÓN
ÉCHELLE COULISSANTE
AUSZIEHLEITER
rung
travesaño
échelon
Sprosse
side rail
larguero
montant
Holm
pulley
polea
poulie
Seilzug
locking device
broche
dispositif de blocage
Sprossenarretierung
hoisting rope
cuerda de elevación
corde de tirage
Seil
anti-slip shoe
zapata antideslizante
patin antidérapant
Anti-Rutschfuß
PLATFORM LADDER
ESCALERA DE PLATAFORMA
MARCHEPIED
TRITTLEITER
shelf
entrepaño
tablette
Ablagebrett
safety rail
barandilla
garde-corps
Sicherheitsholm
frame
armazón
piètement
Gestell
platform
plataforma
plate-forme
Plattform
step
peldaño
marche
Stufe
rubber tip
zapata de goma
embout
Gummistöpsel

straight ladder
escalera común
échelle droite
Anlegeleiter
foldaway ladder
escalera de guardilla
échelle escamotable
Dachbodenklappleiter
hook ladder
escalera de gancho
échelle à crochets
Einhängeleiter
rope ladder
escalera de cuerda
échelle de corde
Strickleiter
multi-purpose ladder
escalera para usos múltiples
échelle transformable
Mehrzweckleiter
ladder scaffold
andamio sobre ruedas
échelle d'échafaudage
Leitergerüst
fruit-picking ladder
escalera de recolección de fruta
échelle fruitière
landwirtschaftliche Nutzleiter
rolling ladder
escalera rodante
échelle roulante
Rollenleiter

PAINTING UPKEEP
HERRAMIENTAS PARA PINTAR
PEINTURE D'ENTRETIEN
MALERBEDARF

SPRAY PAINT GUN
PISTOLA DE PINTAR
PISTOLET À PEINTURE
SPRITZPISTOLE
nozzle
boquilla
buse à fluide
Düse
air cap
anillo de ajuste
bouchon d'air
Lufteinlaß
trigger
gatillo
gâchette
Druckabzug
vent hole
orificio de entrada de aire
orifice d'aération
Entlüftung
container
depósito de pintura
godet
Behälter
spreader adjustment screw
válvula de ajuste
soupape de réglage du fluide
Einstellventil für die Strahlbreite
fluid adjustment screw
regulador de fluidos
réglage du pointeau du fluide
Einstellventil für die Flüssigkeitsmenge
air valve
válvula de aire
soupape à air
Luftventil
gun body
mango
corps du pistolet
Pistolengriff
air hose connection
conexión para la manguera de aire
raccord d'arrivée d'air
Luftdruckanschluß
SCRAPER
RASPADOR
GRATTOIR
SPACHTEL
blade
hoja
lame
Blatt
knurled bolt
tornillo
bouton moleté
Niet
handle
mango
manche
Griff
BRUSH
BROCHA
PINCEAU
STREICHBÜRSTE
handle
mango
manche
Griff
ferrule
collar
virole
Stock
bristles
cerdas
soies
Borsten
PAINT ROLLER
RODILLO DE PINTOR
ROULEAU
FARBROLLER
tray
bandeja de pintura
bac
Wanne
handle
mango
poignée
Griff
roller frame
armazón
armature
Walzenbefestigung
roller cover
rodillo
manchon
Walze

SOLDERING AND WELDING
SOLDADURA
SOUDAGE
LÖTEN UND SCHWEISSEN

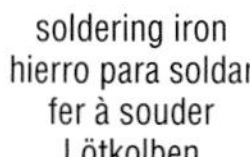
soldering iron
hierro para soldar
fer à souder
Lötkolben

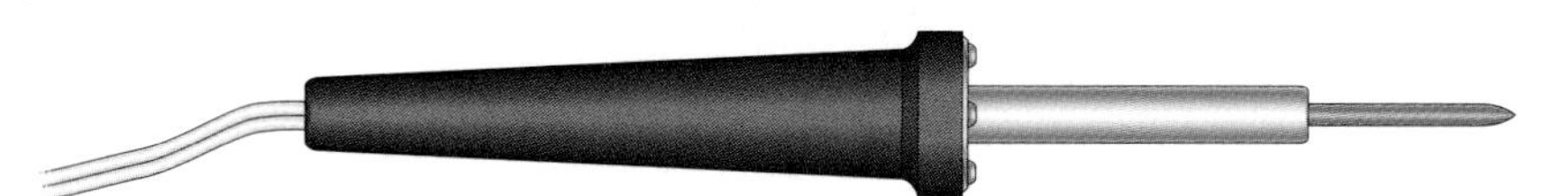

SOLDERING GUN
PISTOLA PARA SOLDAR
PISTOLET À SOUDER
LÖTPISTOLE

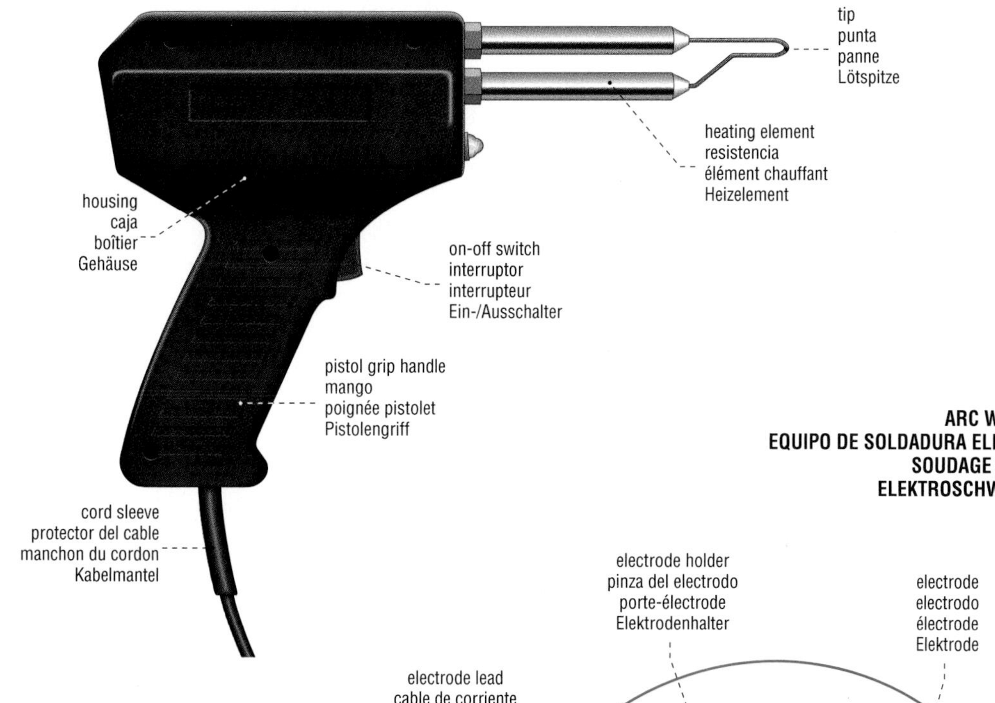
tip
punta
panne
Lötspitze
heating element
resistencia
élément chauffant
Heizelement
housing
caja
boîtier
Gehäuse
on-off switch
interruptor
interrupteur
Ein-/Ausschalter
pistol grip handle
mango
poignée pistolet
Pistolengriff
cord sleeve
protector del cable
manchon du cordon
Kabelmantel

ARC WELDING
EQUIPO DE SOLDADURA ELÉCTRICA
SOUDAGE À L'ARC
ELEKTROSCHWEISSEN

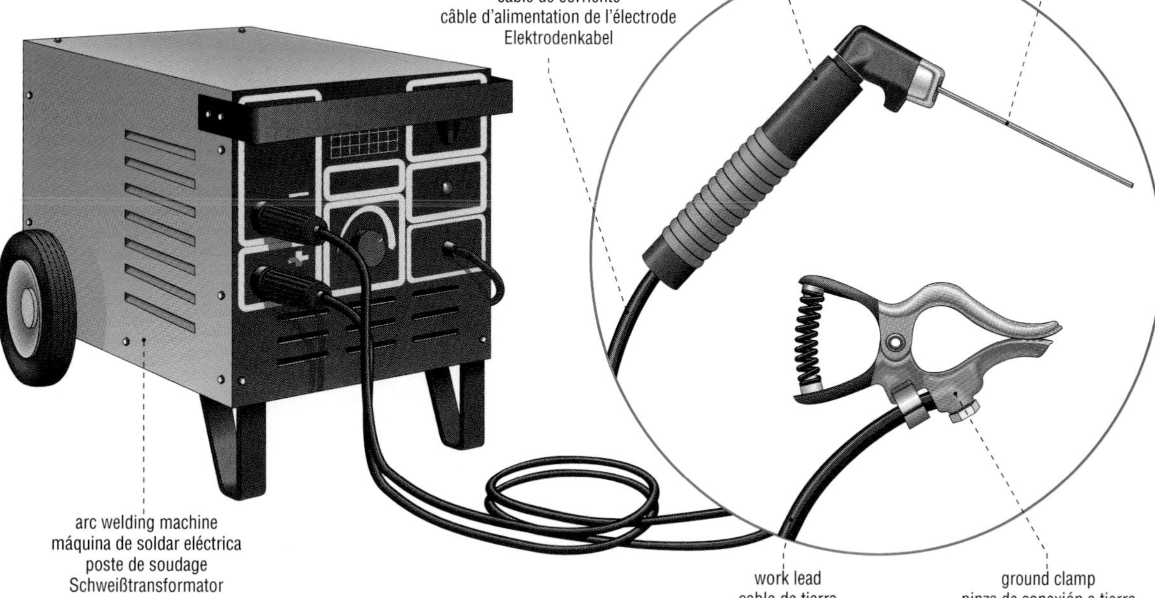
electrode holder
pinza del electrodo
porte-électrode
Elektrodenhalter
electrode
electrodo
électrode
Elektrode
electrode lead
cable de corriente
câble d'alimentation de l'électrode
Elektrodenkabel
arc welding machine
máquina de soldar eléctrica
poste de soudage
Schweißtransformator
work lead
cable de tierra
câble de masse
Massekabel
ground clamp
pinza de conexión a tierra
prise de masse
Polzwinge

SOLDERING AND WELDING
SOLDADURA
SOUDAGE
LÖTEN UND SCHWEISSEN

CUTTING TORCH
SOPLETE DE CORTE
CHALUMEAU COUPEUR
SCHWEISSBRENNER MIT SCHNEIDEEINSATZ

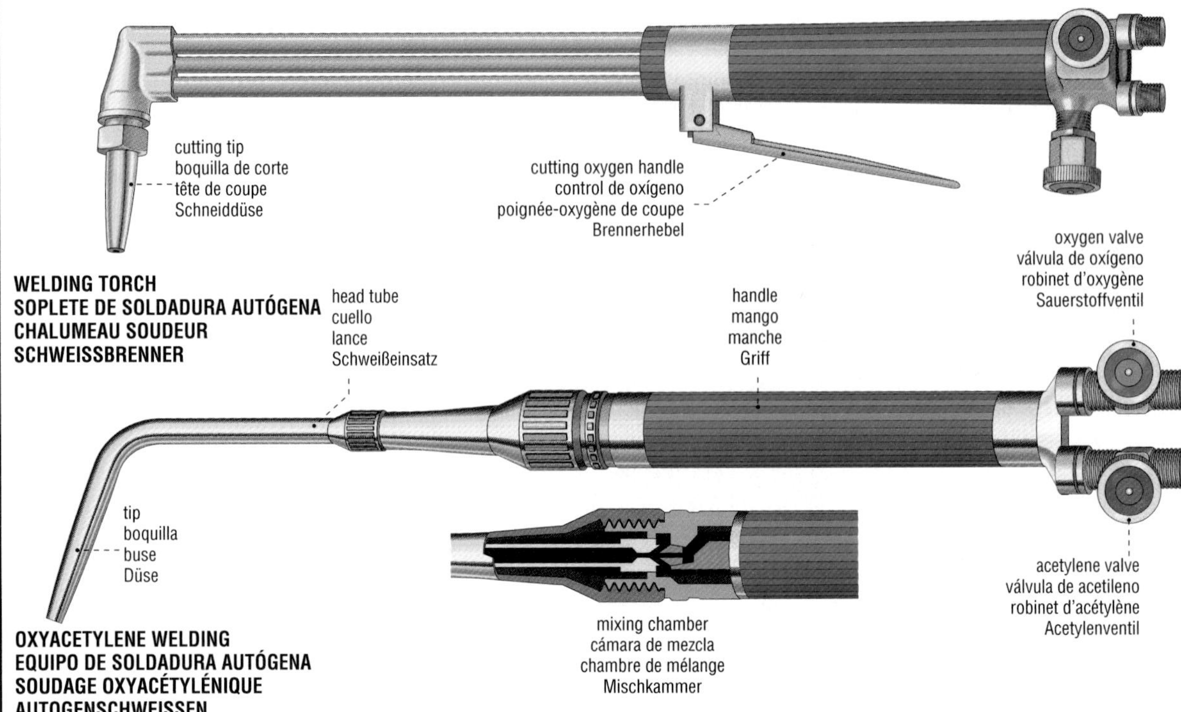
cutting tip
boquilla de corte
tête de coupe
Schneiddüse
cutting oxygen handle
control de oxígeno
poignée-oxygène de coupe
Brennerhebel
oxygen valve
válvula de oxígeno
robinet d'oxygène
Sauerstoffventil
WELDING TORCH
SOPLETE DE SOLDADURA AUTÓGENA
CHALUMEAU SOUDEUR
SCHWEISSBRENNER
head tube
cuello
lance
Schweißeinsatz
handle
mango
manche
Griff
tip
boquilla
buse
Düse
mixing chamber
cámara de mezcla
chambre de mélange
Mischkammer
acetylene valve
válvula de acetileno
robinet d'acétylène
Acetylenventil

OXYACETYLENE WELDING
EQUIPO DE SOLDADURA AUTÓGENA
SOUDAGE OXYACÉTYLÉNIQUE
AUTOGENSCHWEISSEN

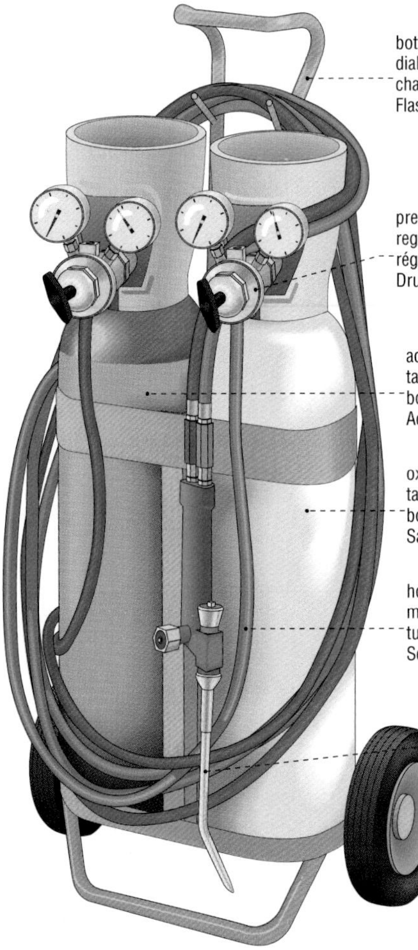

bottle cart
diablo
chariot
Flaschenwagen

pressure regulator
regulador de presión
régulateur de pression
Druckregler

acetylene cylinder
tanque de acetileno
bouteille d'acétylène
Acetylenflasche

oxygen cylinder
tanque de oxígeno
bouteille d'oxygène
Sauerstoffflasche

hose
manguera
tuyau
Schlauch

welding torch
soplete
chalumeau
Schweißbrenner

PRESSURE REGULATOR
REGULADOR DE PRESIÓN
RÉGULATEUR DE PRESSION
DRUCKREGLER

working pressure gauge
manómetro del soplete
manomètre de chalumeau
Arbeitsdruckmesser

cylinder pressure gauge
manómetro del tanque
manomètre de bouteille
Flaschendruckmesser

adjusting screw
tornillo de ajuste
vis de réglage
Stellschraube

check valve
válvula de freno
clapet de non-retour
Absperrventil

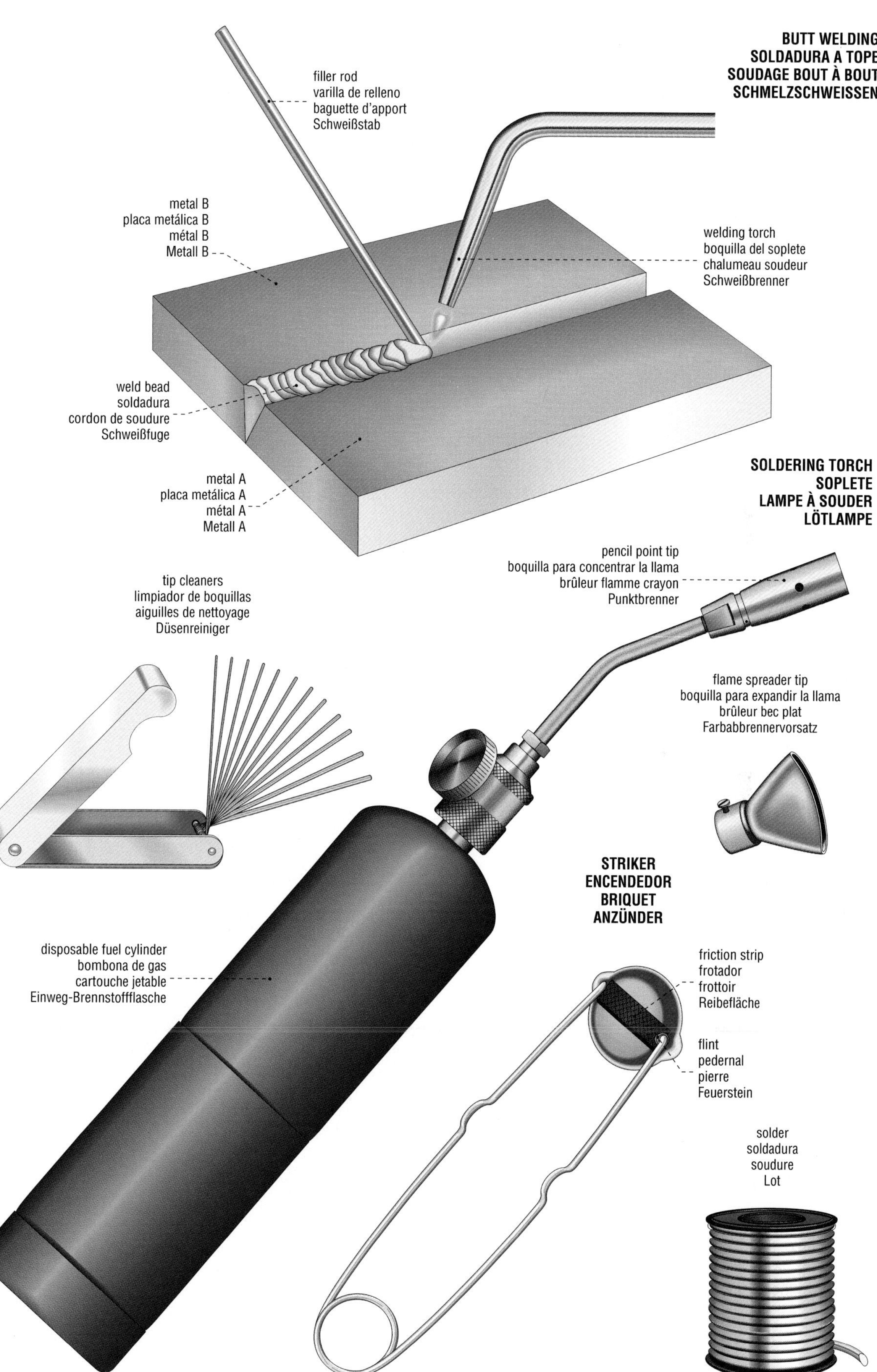
BUTT WELDING
SOLDADURA A TOPE
SOUDAGE BOUT À BOUT
SCHMELZSCHWEISSEN
filler rod
varilla de relleno
baguette d'apport
Schweißstab
metal B
placa metálica B
métal B
Metall B
welding torch
boquilla del soplete
chalumeau soudeur
Schweißbrenner
weld bead
soldadura
cordon de soudure
Schweißfuge
metal A
placa metálica A
métal A
Metall A
SOLDERING TORCH
SOPLETE
LAMPE À SOUDER
LÖTLAMPE
pencil point tip
boquilla para concentrar la llama
brûleur flamme crayon
Punktbrenner
tip cleaners
limpiador de boquillas
aiguilles de nettoyage
Düsenreiniger
flame spreader tip
boquilla para expandir la llama
brûleur bec plat
Farbabbrennervorsatz
STRIKER
ENCENDEDOR
BRIQUET
ANZÜNDER
disposable fuel cylinder
bombona de gas
cartouche jetable
Einweg-Brennstoffflasche
friction strip
frotador
frottoir
Reibefläche
flint
pedernal
pierre
Feuerstein
solder
soldadura
soudure
Lot

SOLDERING AND WELDING: PROTECTIVE CLOTHING
SOLDADURA: ACCESORIOS DE PROTECCIÓN
SOUDAGE: ÉQUIPEMENT DE PROTECTION
LÖTEN UND SCHWEISSEN: SCHUTZKLEIDUNG

goggles
anteojos protectores
lunettes
Schutzbrille

hand shield
careta de mano
écran à main
Handschild

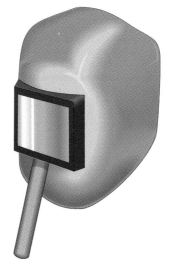

face shield
careta
casque
Gesichtsschutz

gauntlet
guantes
gant à crispin
fünffingriger Schweißerhandschuh

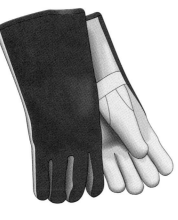

welding curtain
biombo para soldar
écran de soudeur
Schutzschirm

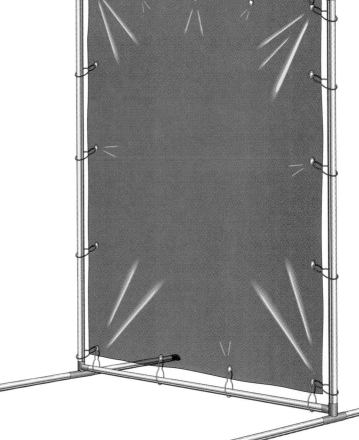

mitten
manoplas
moufle
Fausthandschuh

ELECTRICITY
ELECTRICIDAD
ÉLECTRICITÉ
ELEKTRIZITÄT

dimmer switch
conmutador de intensidad
rhéostat
Dimmerschalter

switch plate
placa del interruptor
plaque de commutateur
Schalterabdeckplatte

LAMP SOCKET
PORTALÁMPARAS
DOUILLE DE LAMPE
LAMPENFASSUNG

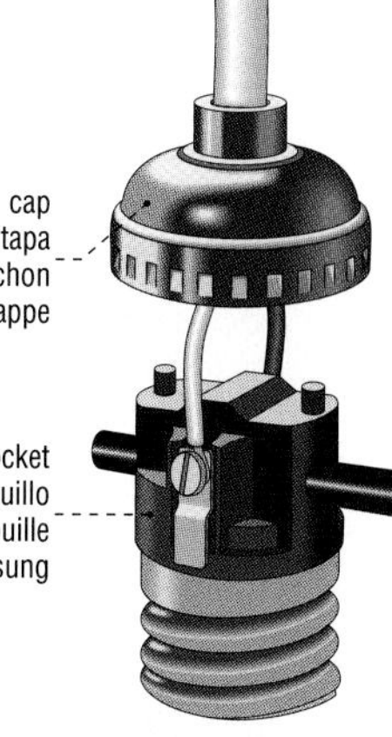

cap
tapa
capuchon
Kappe

socket
casquillo
douille
Fassung

electrical box
caja de conexiones
boîte électrique
Buchsenhalter

switch
interruptor
interrupteur
Schalter

insulating sleeve
manga de aislamiento
gaine isolante
Isolierhülse

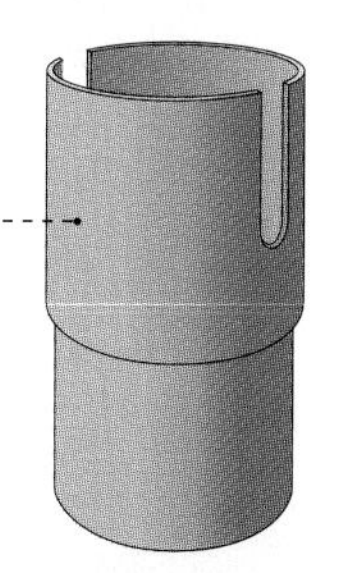

outlet
enchufe
prise de courant
dreipolige Steckdose

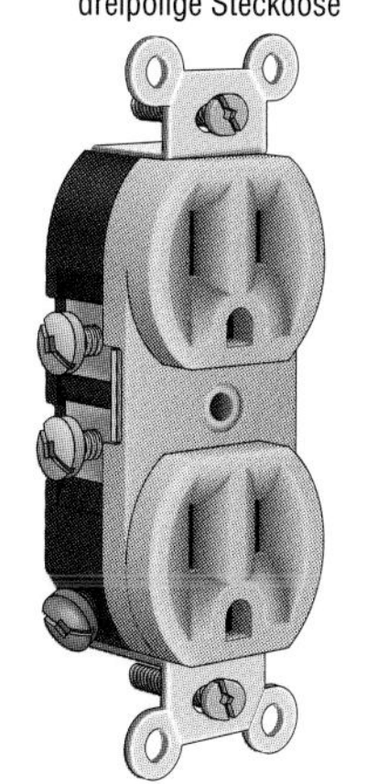

outer shell
cubierta
enveloppe
äußere Hülse

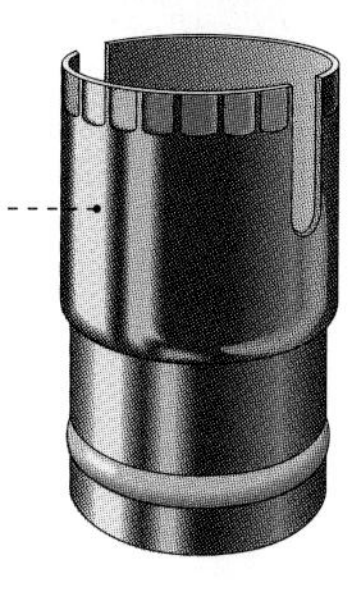

AMERICAN PLUG
ENCHUFE DE TIPO AMERICANO
FICHE AMÉRICAINE
AMERIKANISCHER DREIPOLIGER STECKER

blade
pata
lame
Spannungsstift

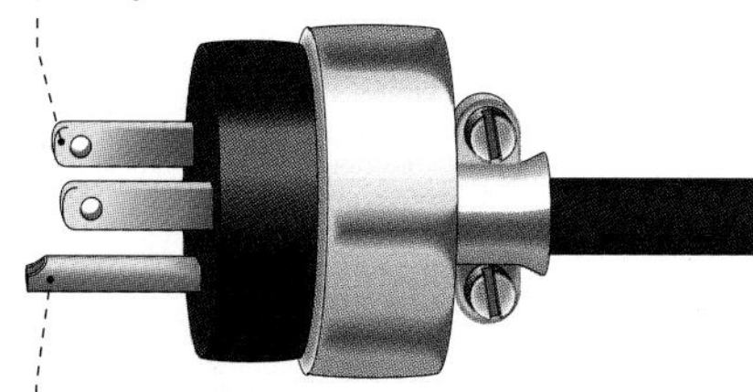

grounding prong
pata de conexión a tierra
prise de terre
Erdungsstift

EUROPEAN PLUG
ENCHUFE DE TIPO EUROPEO
FICHE EUROPÉENNE
STECKER

terminal
terminal
borne
Anschlußklemme

grounding prong
terminal de tierra
prise de terre
Erdungsklemme

clamp
abrazadera
étrier
Zugentlastungsklemme

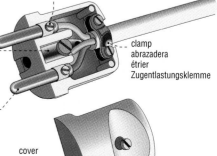

blade
pata
broche
Stift

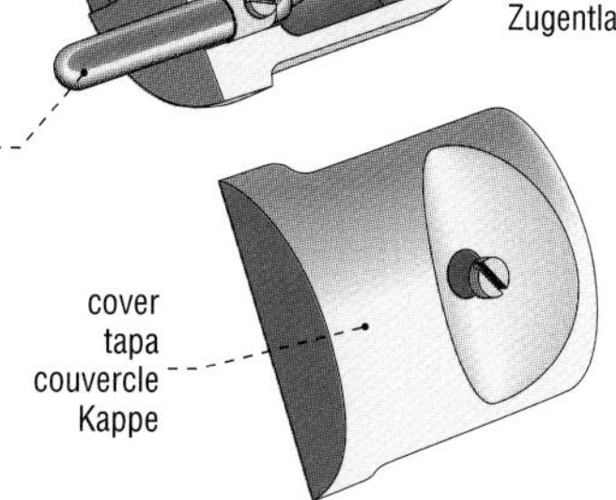

cover
tapa
couvercle
Kappe

ELECTRICITY
ELECTRICIDAD
ÉLECTRICITÉ
ELEKTRIZITÄT

ELECTRICIAN'S TOOLS
HERRAMIENTAS DE ELECTRICISTA
OUTILS D'ÉLECTRICIEN
ELEKTROINSTALLATEURWERKZEUGE

multimeter
voltímetro
multimètre
Multimeter

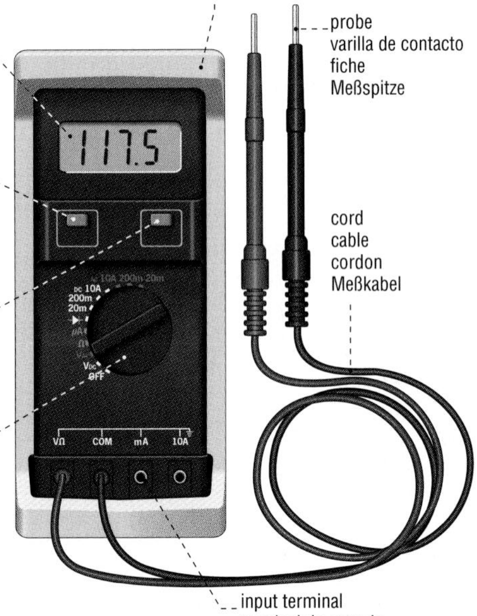

housing
caja
boîtier
Gehäuse

digital display
registro digital
afficheur numérique
Digitalanzeige

probe
varilla de contacto
fiche
Meßspitze

data hold
retención de datos
mémorisation des données
Meßspeicher

cord
cable
cordon
Meßkabel

auto/manual range
selección auto/manual
lecture automatique/manuelle
Auto-Manualumschalter

selector switch
selector
commutateur
Bereichsumschalter

input terminal
terminal de entrada
borne d'entrée
Eingangsbuchse

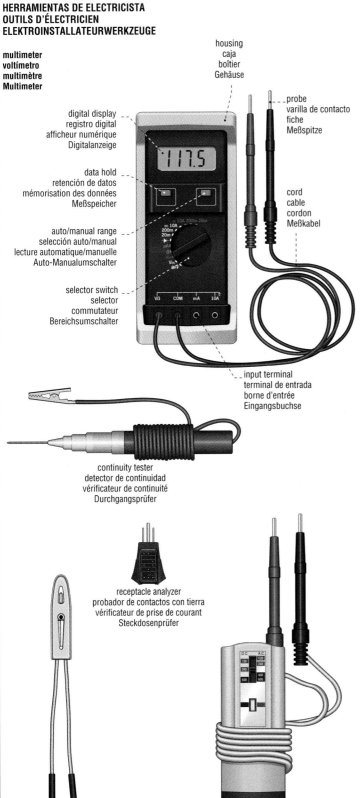

voltage tester
detector de tensión
vérificateur de tension
Spannungsprüfer

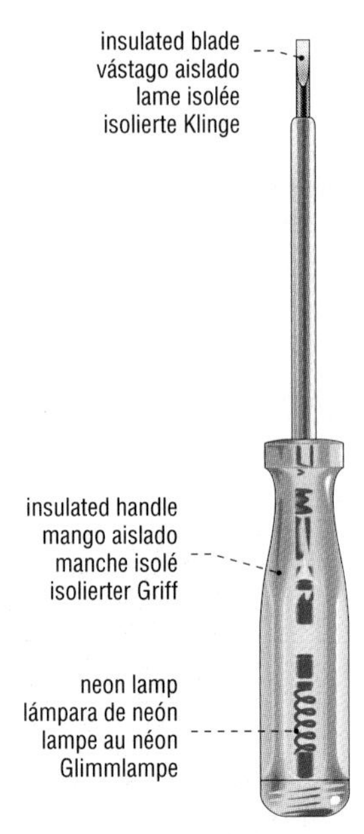

insulated blade
vástago aislado
lame isolée
isolierte Klinge

insulated handle
mango aislado
manche isolé
isolierter Griff

neon lamp
lámpara de neón
lampe au néon
Glimmlampe

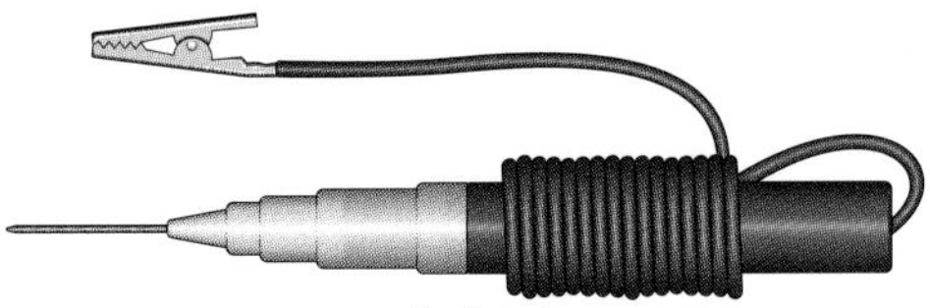

continuity tester
detector de continuidad
vérificateur de continuité
Durchgangsprüfer

receptacle analyzer
probador de contactos con tierra
vérificateur de prise de courant
Steckdosenprüfer

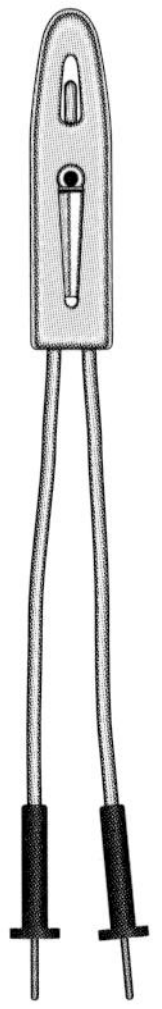

neon tester
lámpara de prueba de neón
vérificateur de circuit
Prüflampe

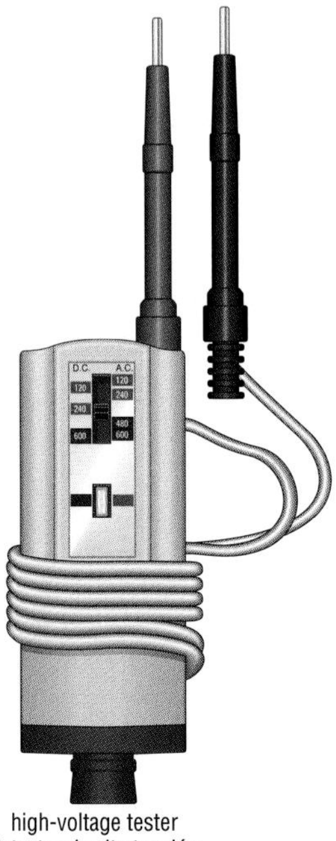

high-voltage tester
detector de alta tensión
vérificateur de haute tension
Hochspannungsprüfer

drop light
linterna movible
baladeuse
Handlampe

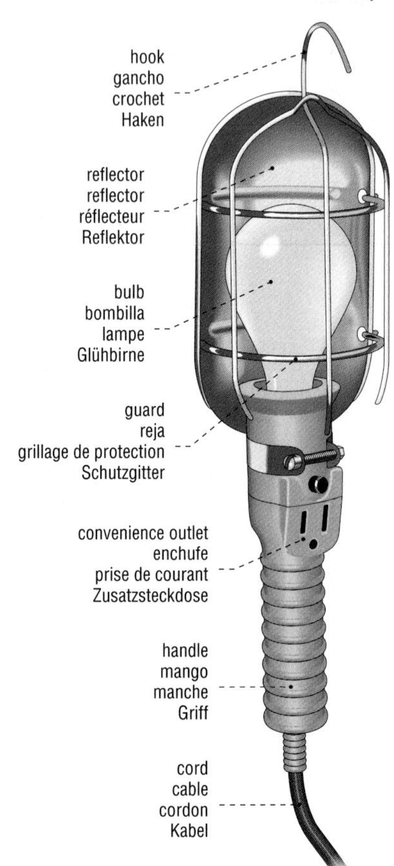

hook
gancho
crochet
Haken

reflector
reflector
réflecteur
Reflektor

bulb
bombilla
lampe
Glühbirne

guard
reja
grillage de protection
Schutzgitter

convenience outlet
enchufe
prise de courant
Zusatzsteckdose

handle
mango
manche
Griff

cord
cable
cordon
Kabel

ELECTRICIAN'S TOOLS
HERRAMIENTAS DE ELECTRICISTA
OUTILS D'ÉLECTRICIEN
ELEKTROINSTALLATEURWERKZEUGE

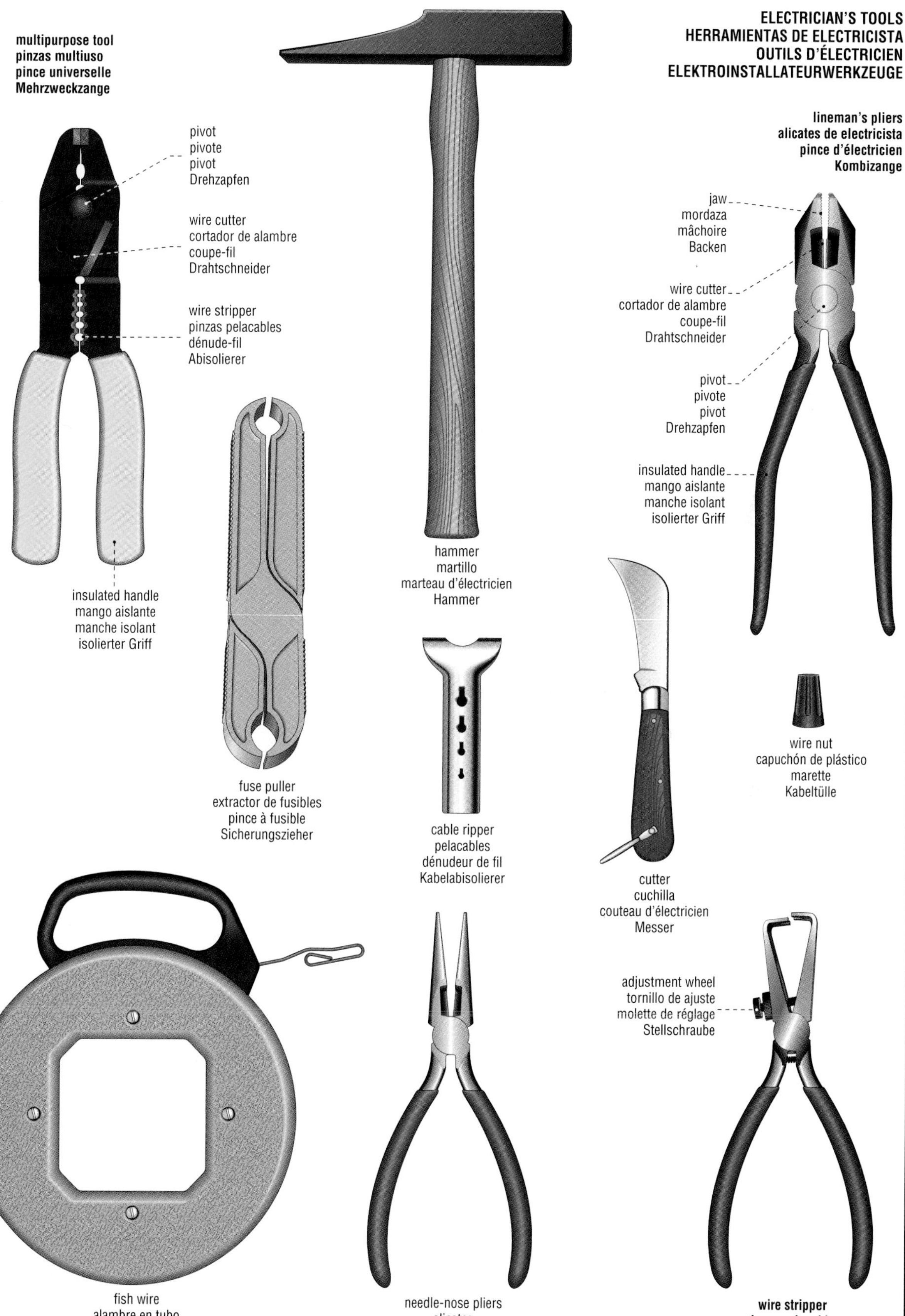
multipurpose tool
pinzas multiuso
pince universelle
Mehrzweckzange
pivot
pivote
pivot
Drehzapfen
wire cutter
cortador de alambre
coupe-fil
Drahtschneider
wire stripper
pinzas pelacables
dénude-fil
Abisolierer
insulated handle
mango aislante
manche isolant
isolierter Griff
lineman's pliers
alicates de electricista
pince d'électricien
Kombizange
jaw
mordaza
mâchoire
Backen
wire cutter
cortador de alambre
coupe-fil
Drahtschneider
pivot
pivote
pivot
Drehzapfen
insulated handle
mango aislante
manche isolant
isolierter Griff
hammer
martillo
marteau d'électricien
Hammer
fuse puller
extractor de fusibles
pince à fusible
Sicherungszieher
cable ripper
pelacables
dénudeur de fil
Kabelabisolierer
cutter
cuchilla
couteau d'électricien
Messer
wire nut
capuchón de plástico
marette
Kabeltülle
fish wire
alambre en tubo
câble de traction
Einziehdraht
needle-nose pliers
alicates
pince à long bec
Spitzzange
adjustment wheel
tornillo de ajuste
molette de réglage
Stellschraube
wire stripper
pinzas pelacables
pince à dénuder
Abisolierzange

ELECTRICITY
ELECTRICIDAD
ÉLECTRICITÉ
ELEKTRIZITÄT

FUSE BOX
CAJETÍN DE FUSIBLES
TABLEAU DE DISTRIBUTION
SICHERUNGSKASTEN

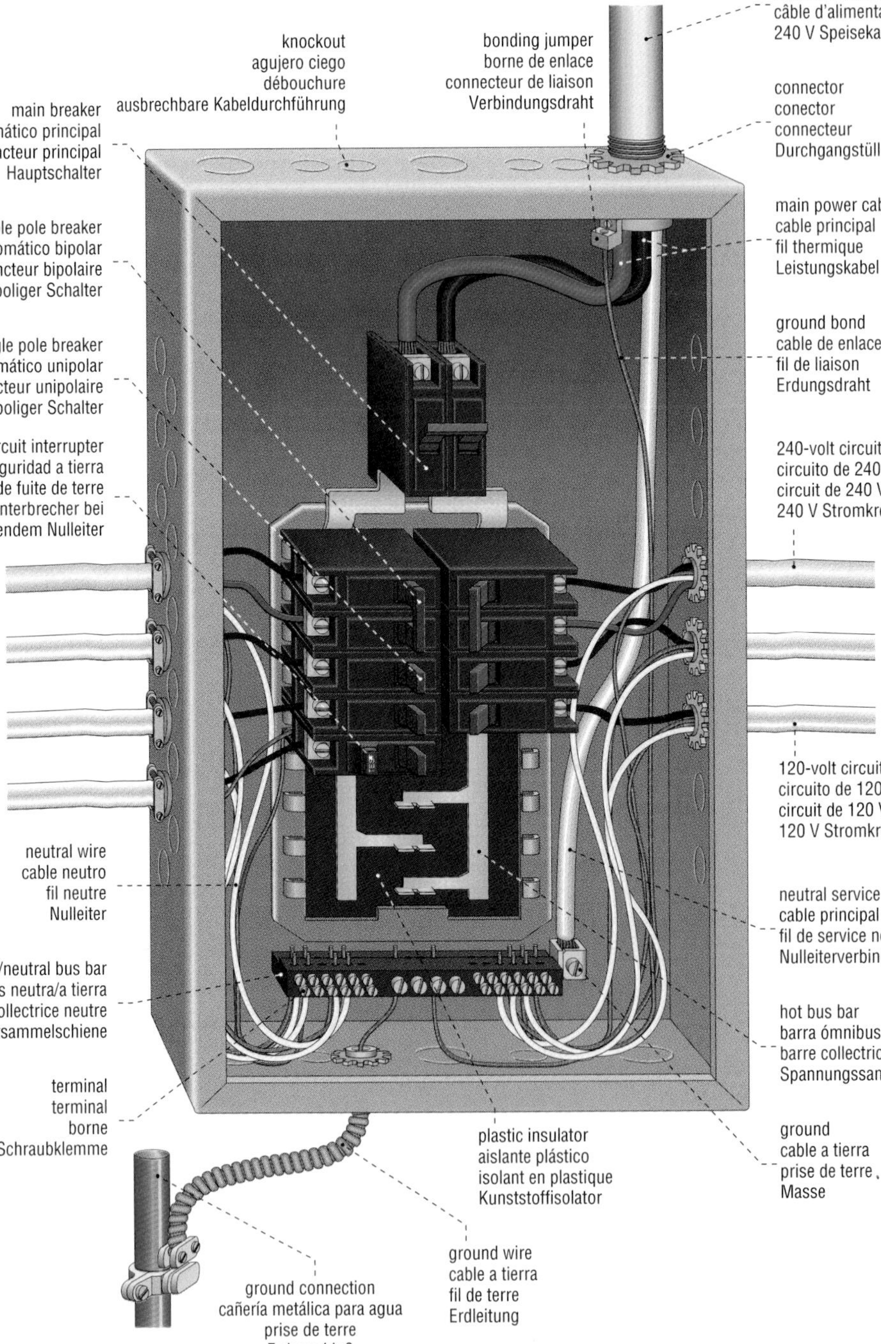

main breaker
interruptor automático principal
disjoncteur principal
Hauptschalter

knockout
agujero ciego
débouchure
ausbrechbare Kabeldurchführung

bonding jumper
borne de enlace
connecteur de liaison
Verbindungsdraht

240-volt feeder cable
cable de alimentación de 240 voltios
câble d'alimentation de 240 V
240 V Speisekabel

connector
conector
connecteur
Durchgangstülle

double pole breaker
interruptor automático bipolar
disjoncteur bipolaire
zweipoliger Schalter

main power cable
cable principal
fil thermique
Leistungskabel

single pole breaker
interruptor automático unipolar
disjoncteur unipolaire
einpoliger Schalter

ground bond
cable de enlace
fil de liaison
Erdungsdraht

ground fault circuit interrupter
fusible de seguridad a tierra
disjoncteur de fuite de terre
Stromunterbrecher bei
spannungsführendem Nulleiter

240-volt circuit
circuito de 240 voltios
circuit de 240 V
240 V Stromkreis

120-volt circuit
circuito de 120 voltios
circuit de 120 V
120 V Stromkreis

neutral wire
cable neutro
fil neutre
Nulleiter

neutral service wire
cable principal neutro
fil de service neutre
Nulleiterverbinder

ground/neutral bus bar
barra ómnibus neutra/a tierra
barre collectrice neutre
Nulleitersammelschiene

hot bus bar
barra ómnibus de carga
barre collectrice thermique
Spannungssammelschiene

terminal
terminal
borne
Schraubklemme

plastic insulator
aislante plástico
isolant en plastique
Kunststoffisolator

ground
cable a tierra
prise de terre,
Masse

ground wire
cable a tierra
fil de terre
Erdleitung

ground connection
cañería metálica para agua
prise de terre
Erdanschluß

FUSES
FUSIBLES
FUSIBLES
SICHERUNGEN

cartridge fuse
fusible de cartucho
fusible-cartouche
Patronensicherung

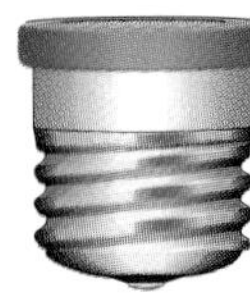

plug fuse
fusible de rosca
fusible à culot
Stöpselsicherung

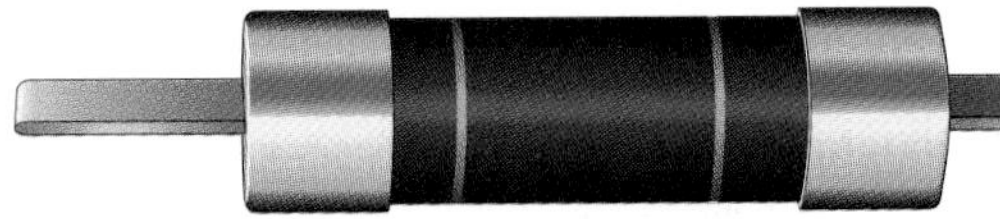

knife-blade cartridge fuse
fusible de bayoneta
fusible-cartouche à lames
Hauptsicherung

CLOTHING / VÊTEMENTS / VESTIDO / KLEIDUNG

CONTENTS

ELEMENTS OF ANCIENT COSTUME
VESTIDURAS ANTIGUAS
ÉLÉMENTS DU COSTUME ANCIEN
ELEMENTE HISTORISCHER KOSTÜME

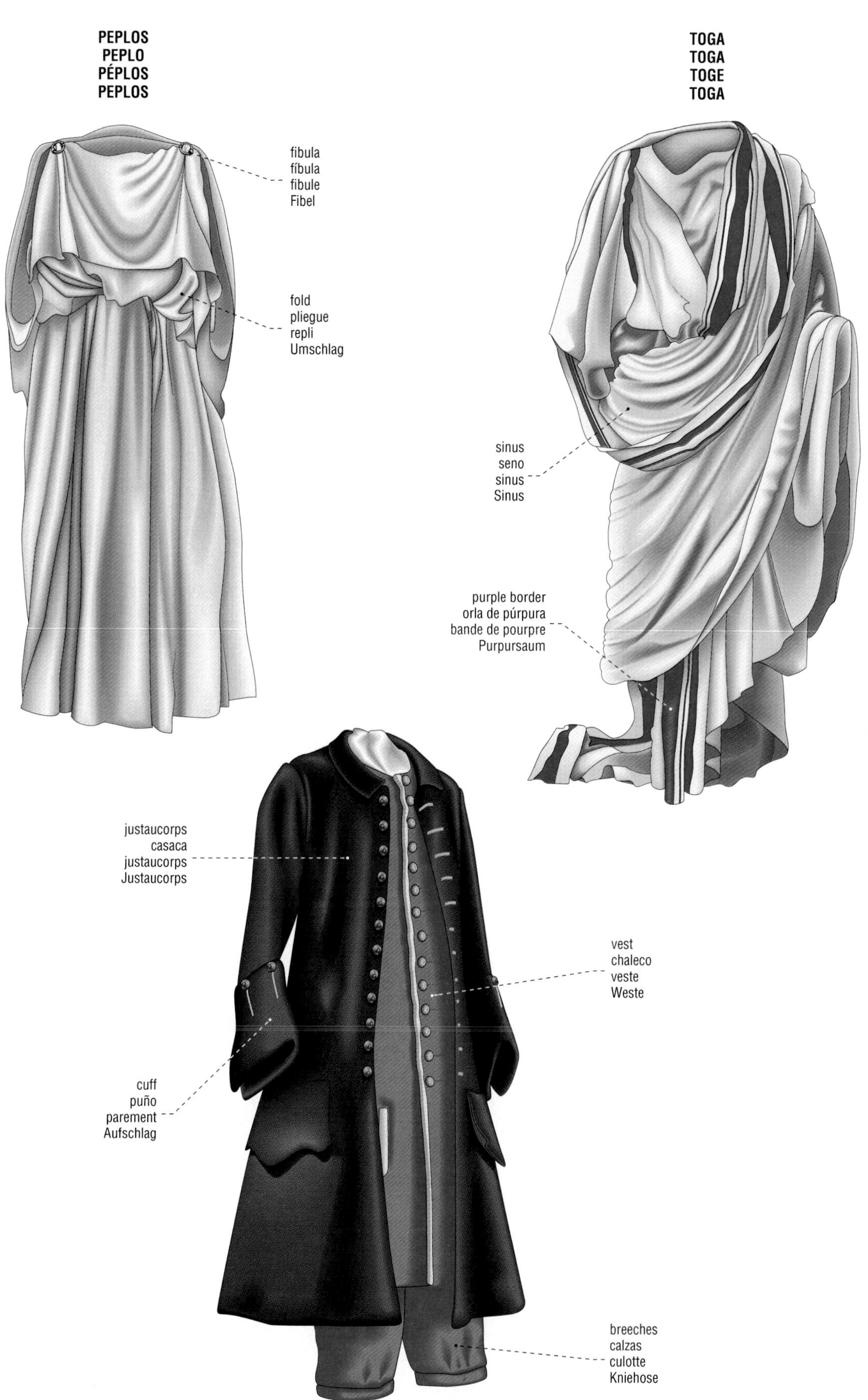

PEPLOS
PEPLO
PÉPLOS
PEPLOS
fibula
fíbula
fibule
Fibel
fold
pliegue
repli
Umschlag
TOGA
TOGA
TOGE
TOGA
sinus
seno
sinus
Sinus
purple border
orla de púrpura
bande de pourpre
Purpursaum
justaucorps
casaca
justaucorps
Justaucorps
vest
chaleco
veste
Weste
cuff
puño
parement
Aufschlag
breeches
calzas
culotte
Kniehose

ELEMENTS OF ANCIENT COSTUME
VESTIDURAS ANTIGUAS
ÉLÉMENTS DU COSTUME ANCIEN
ELEMENTE HISTORISCHER KOSTÜME

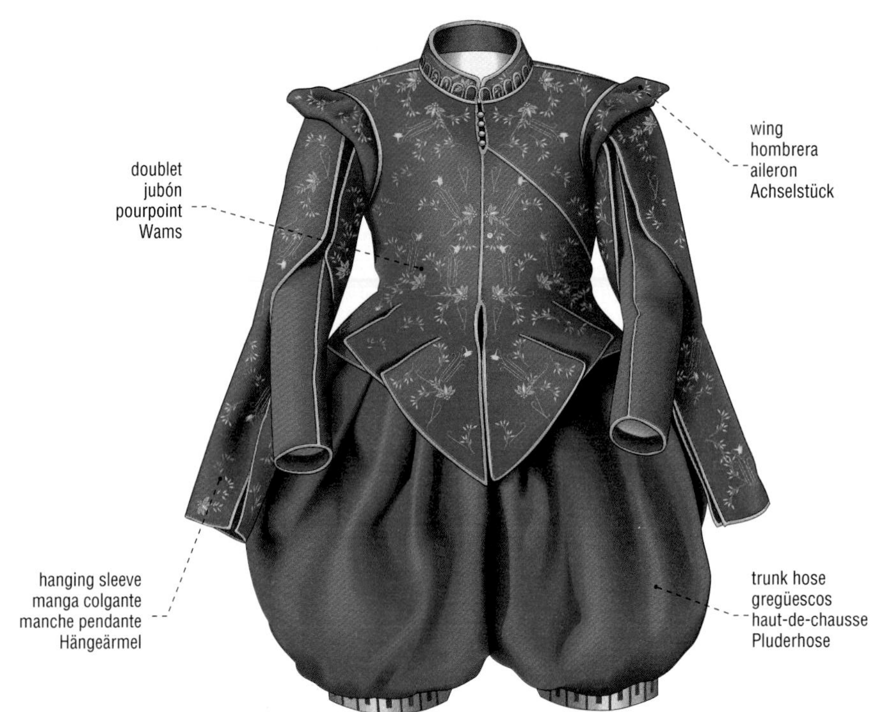
doublet
jubón
pourpoint
Wams
wing
hombrera
aileron
Achselstück
hanging sleeve
manga colgante
manche pendante
Hängeärmel
trunk hose
gregüescos
haut-de-chausse
Pluderhose

COTEHARDIE
TÚNICA DE MANGA LARGA
COTARDIE
COTARDIE

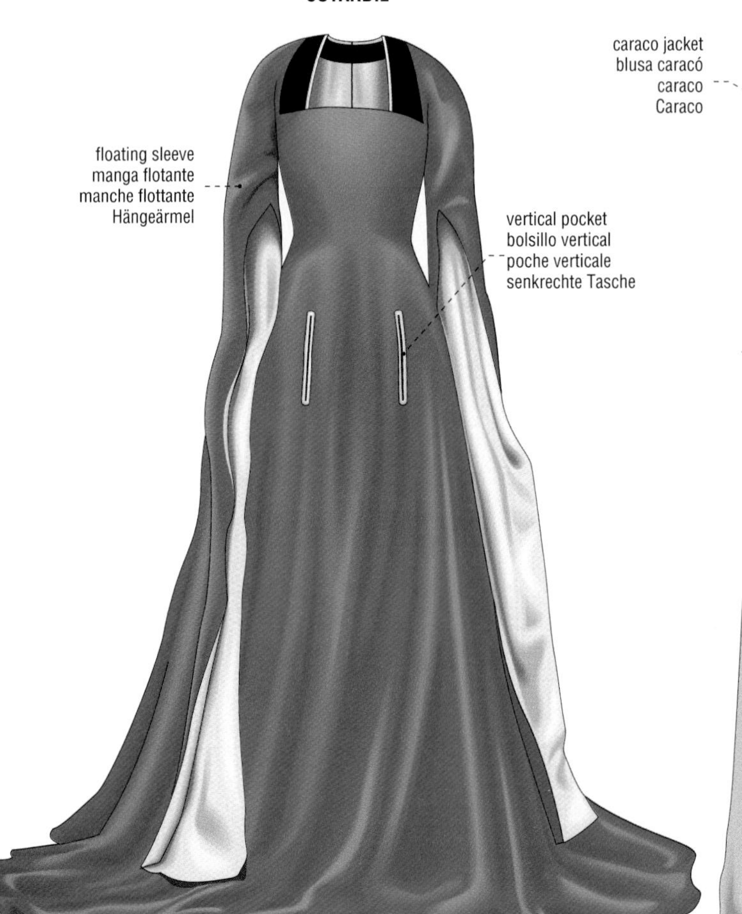
floating sleeve
manga flotante
manche flottante
Hängeärmel
vertical pocket
bolsillo vertical
poche verticale
senkrechte Tasche

DRESS WITH BUSTLE
VESTIDO CON POLISÓN
ROBE À TOURNURE
KLEID MIT TURNÜRE

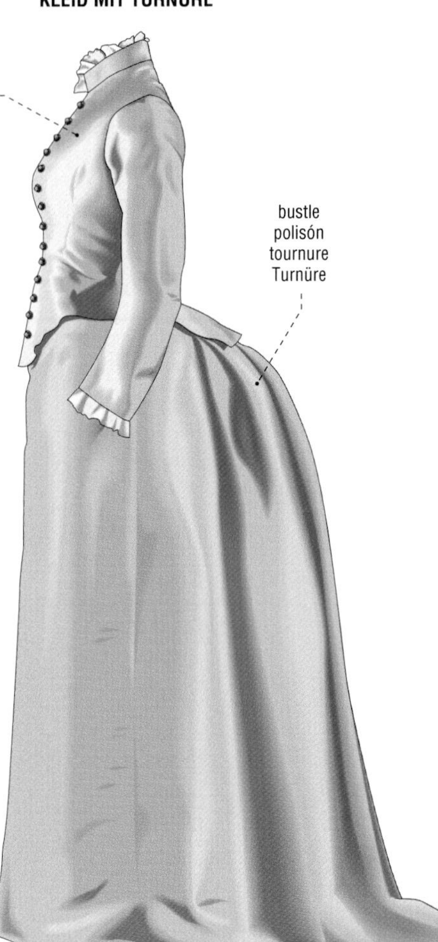
caraco jacket
blusa caracó
caraco
Caraco
bustle
polisón
tournure
Turnüre

frock coat
levita
frac
Schoßrock

waistcoat
chaleco
gilet
Weste

breeches
calzas
culotte
Kniehose

HOUPPELANDE
TOGA
HOUPPELANDE
HOUPPELANDE

DRESS WITH PANNIERS
GUARDAINFANTE
ROBE À PANIERS
KLEID MIT FLACHEM REIFROCK

ruffle
manga de volante
engageante
Spitzenvolant
stomacker
peto
pièce d'estomac
Mieder

ELEMENTS OF ANCIENT COSTUME
VESTIDURAS ANTIGUAS
ÉLÉMENTS DU COSTUME ANCIEN
ELEMENTE HISTORISCHER KOSTÜME

DRESS WITH CRINOLINE
MIRIÑAQUE
ROBE À CRINOLINE
KLEID MIT KRINOLINENROCK

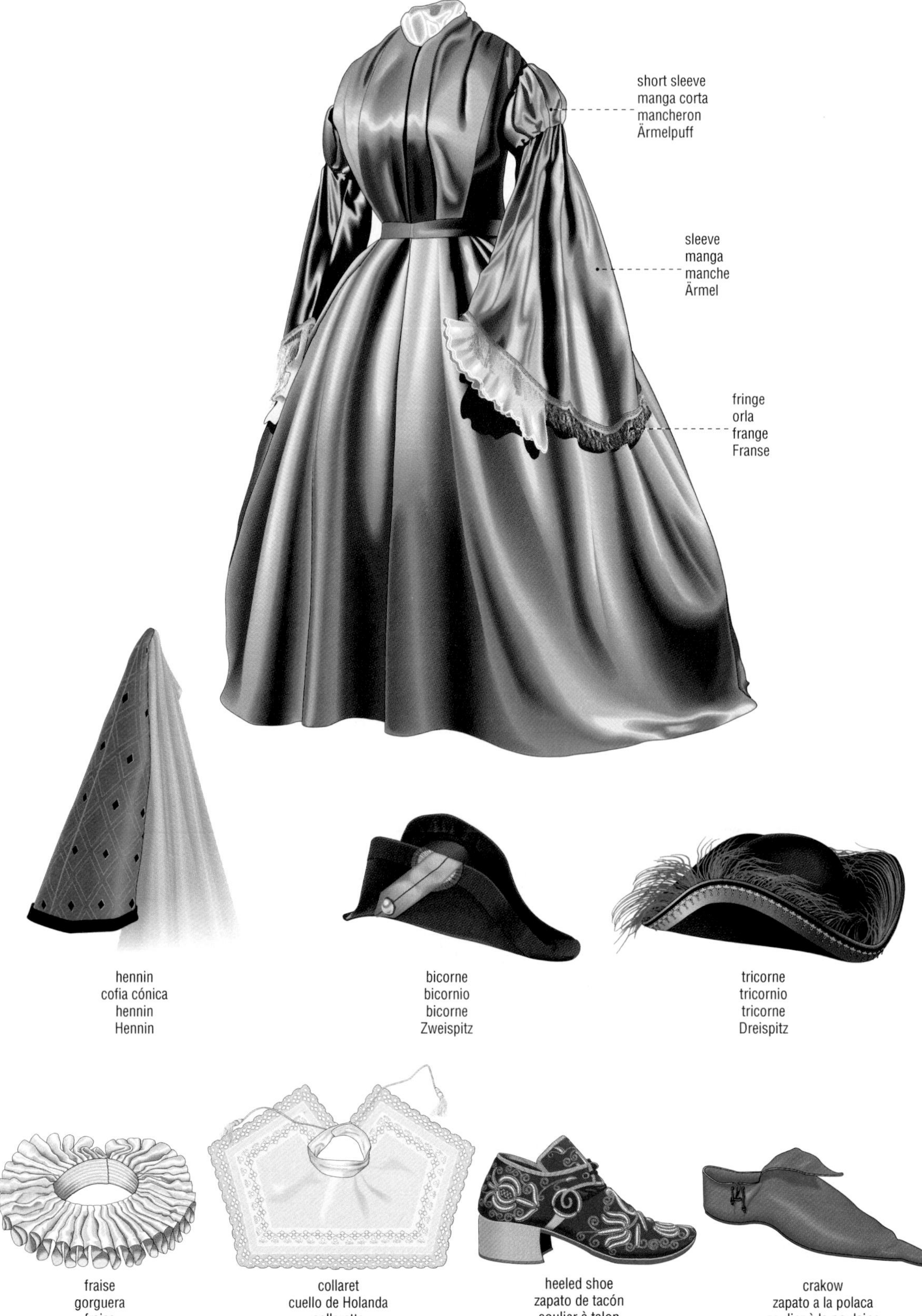
short sleeve
manga corta
mancheron
Ärmelpuff
sleeve
manga
manche
Ärmel
fringe
orla
frange
Franse
hennin
cofia cónica
hennin
Hennin
bicorne
bicornio
bicorne
Zweispitz
tricorne
tricornio
tricorne
Dreispitz
fraise
gorguera
fraise
Halskrause
collaret
cuello de Holanda
collerette
kleiner Kragen
heeled shoe
zapato de tacón
soulier à talon
Absatzschuh
crakow
zapato a la polaca
soulier à la poulaine
Schnabelschuh

RAINCOAT
IMPERMEABLE
IMPERMÉABLE
REGENMANTEL

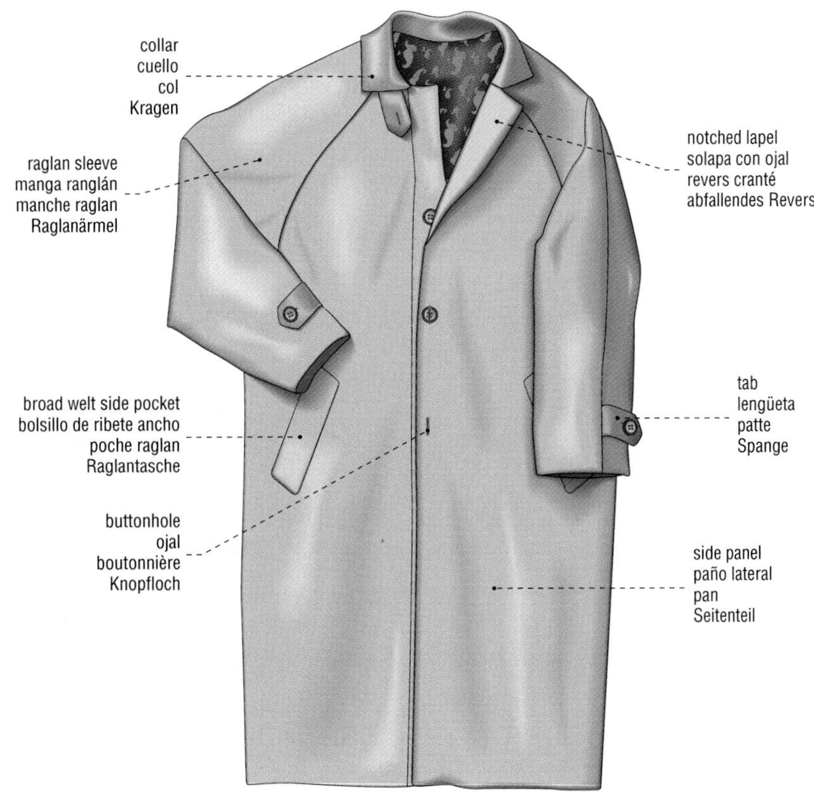
collar
cuello
col
Kragen
raglan sleeve
manga ranglán
manche raglan
Raglanärmel
notched lapel
solapa con ojal
revers cranté
abfallendes Revers
broad welt side pocket
bolsillo de ribete ancho
poche raglan
Raglantasche
tab
lengüeta
patte
Spange
buttonhole
ojal
boutonnière
Knopfloch
side panel
paño lateral
pan
Seitenteil

TRENCH COAT
TRINCHERA
TRENCH
TRENCHCOAT

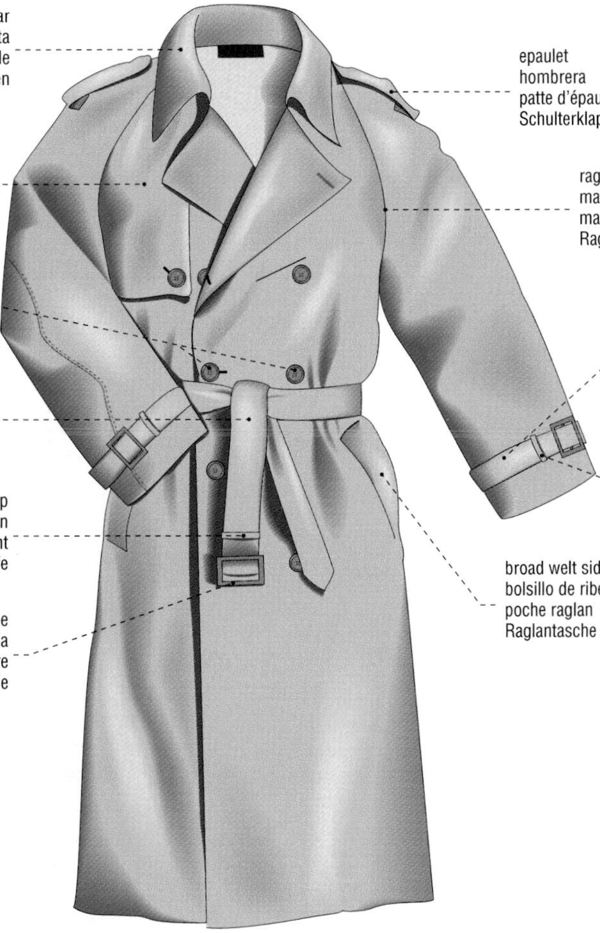

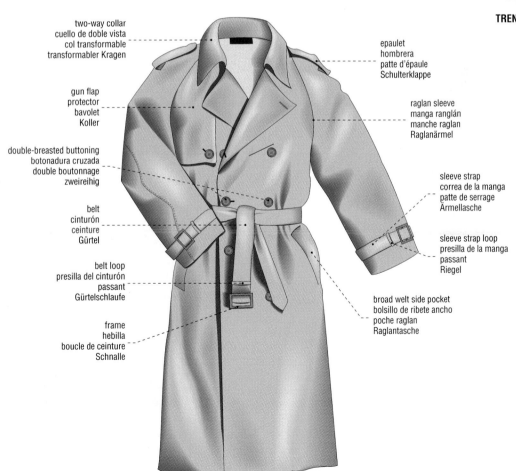

two-way collar
cuello de doble vista
col transformable
transformabler Kragen

epaulet
hombrera
patte d'épaule
Schulterklappe

gun flap
protector
bavolet
Koller

raglan sleeve
manga ranglán
manche raglan
Raglanärmel

double-breasted buttoning
botonadura cruzada
double boutonnage
zweireihig

sleeve strap
correa de la manga
patte de serrage
Ärmellasche

belt
cinturón
ceinture
Gürtel

sleeve strap loop
presilla de la manga
passant
Riegel

belt loop
presilla del cinturón
passant
Gürtelschlaufe

broad welt side pocket
bolsillo de ribete ancho
poche raglan
Raglantasche

frame
hebilla
boucle de ceinture
Schnalle

MEN'S CLOTHING
ROPA DE HOMBRE
VÊTEMENTS D'HOMME
HERRENKLEIDUNG

DUFFLE COAT
CAZADORA DE TRES CUARTOS
DUFFLE-COAT
DUFFLECOAT
hood
capucha
capuchon
Kapuze
yoke
hombrillo
empiècement
Sattel
frog
alamar
brandebourg
Lasche
patch pocket
bolsillo de parche
poche plaquée
aufgesetzte Tasche
toggle fastening
botón de madera
bûchette
Knebelverschluß
OVERCOAT
ABRIGO
PARDESSUS
MANTEL
notched lapel
solapa con ojal
revers cranté
abfallendes Revers
breast pocket
bolsillo superior
poche poitrine
Brusttasche
breast dart
pinza
pince de taille
Taillenabnäher
flap pocket
bolsillo con cartera
poche à rabat
Klappentasche
WINDBREAKER
CAZADORA
BLOUSON LONG
WINDJACKE
waistband
pretina
ceinture montée
Bund
drawstring
cordón
cordon coulissant
Durchziehschnur

three-quarter coat
abrigo de tres cuartos
paletot
dreiviertellanger Mantel

PARKA
PARKA
PARKA
PARKA

zipper
cremallera
fermeture à glissière
Reißverschluß

snap-fastening tab
corchete de presión
patte à boutons-pression
Druckknopfleiste

JACKET
CAZADORA
BLOUSON COURT
WINDJACKE

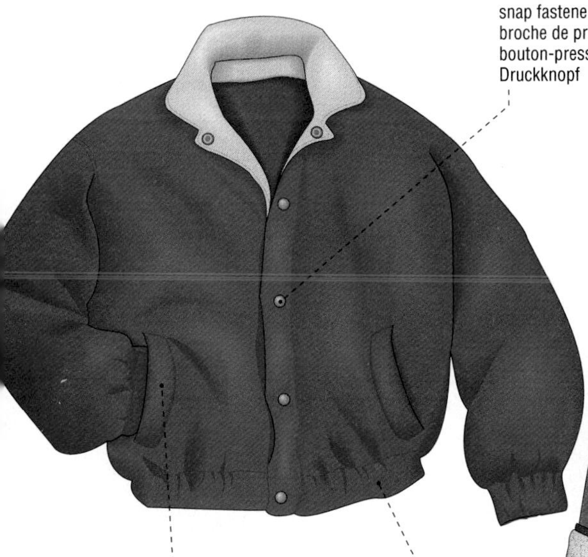

snap fastener
broche de presión
bouton-pression
Druckknopf

hand-warmer pocket
bolsillo de ojal
poche repose-bras
Mufftasche

elastic waistband
pretina elástica
ceinture élastique
elastischer Bund

sheepskin jacket
zamarra
canadienne
Lammfelljacke

MEN'S CLOTHING
ROPA DE HOMBRE
VÊTEMENTS D'HOMME
HERRENKLEIDUNG

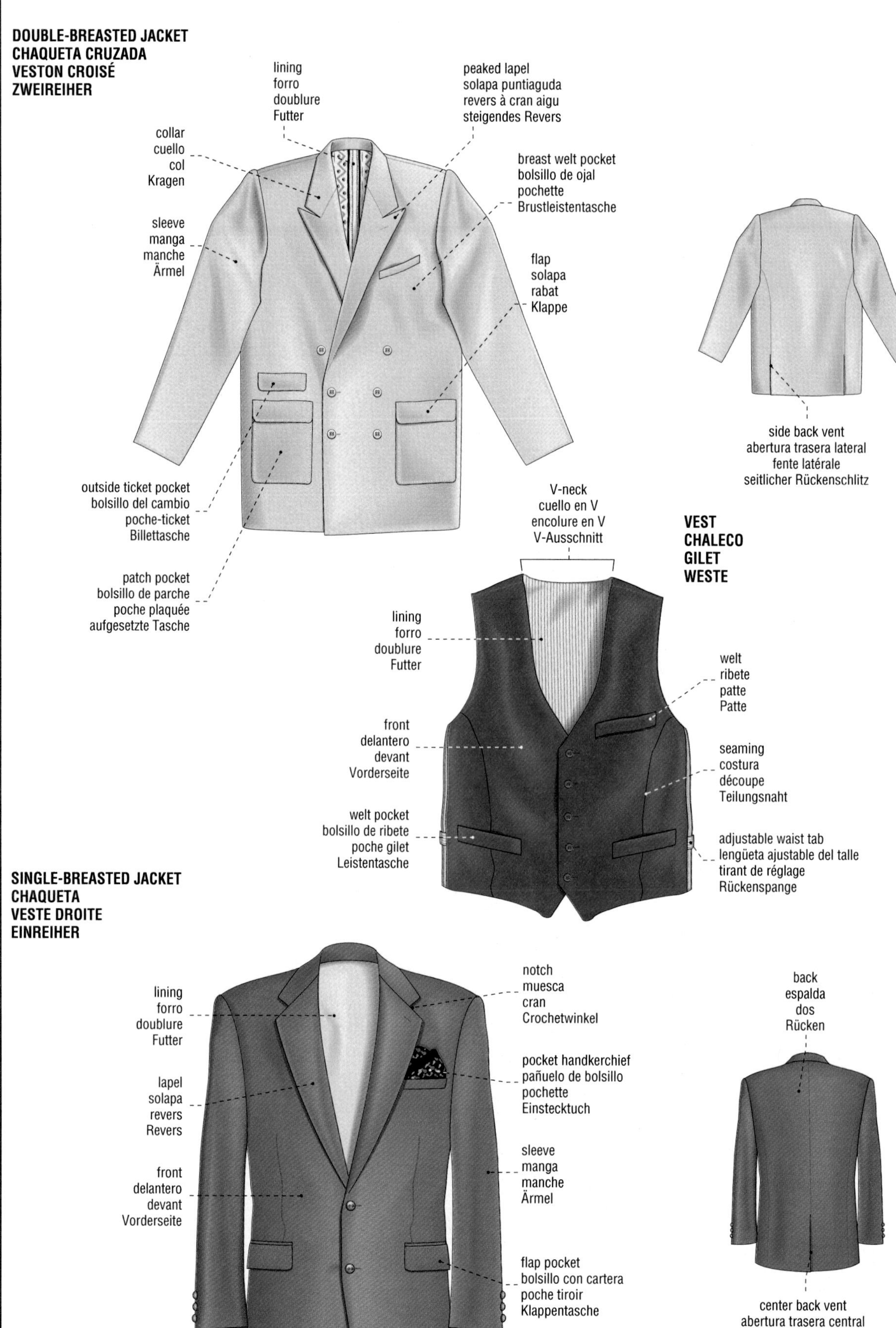
DOUBLE-BREASTED JACKET
CHAQUETA CRUZADA
VESTON CROISÉ
ZWEIREIHER
lining
forro
doublure
Futter
peaked lapel
solapa puntiaguda
revers à cran aigu
steigendes Revers
collar
cuello
col
Kragen
breast welt pocket
bolsillo de ojal
pochette
Brustleistentasche
sleeve
manga
manche
Ärmel
flap
solapa
rabat
Klappe
side back vent
abertura trasera lateral
fente latérale
seitlicher Rückenschlitz
outside ticket pocket
bolsillo del cambio
poche-ticket
Billettasche
patch pocket
bolsillo de parche
poche plaquée
aufgesetzte Tasche
V-neck
cuello en V
encolure en V
V-Ausschnitt
VEST
CHALECO
GILET
WESTE
lining
forro
doublure
Futter
welt
ribete
patte
Patte
front
delantero
devant
Vorderseite
seaming
costura
découpe
Teilungsnaht
welt pocket
bolsillo de ribete
poche gilet
Leistentasche
adjustable waist tab
lengüeta ajustable del talle
tirant de réglage
Rückenspange
SINGLE-BREASTED JACKET
CHAQUETA
VESTE DROITE
EINREIHER
notch
muesca
cran
Crochetwinkel
back
espalda
dos
Rücken
lining
forro
doublure
Futter
pocket handkerchief
pañuelo de bolsillo
pochette
Einstecktuch
lapel
solapa
revers
Revers
sleeve
manga
manche
Ärmel
front
delantero
devant
Vorderseite
flap pocket
bolsillo con cartera
poche tiroir
Klappentasche
center back vent
abertura trasera central
fente médiane
Rückenmittelschlitz

BELT
CINTURÓN
CEINTURE
GÜRTEL

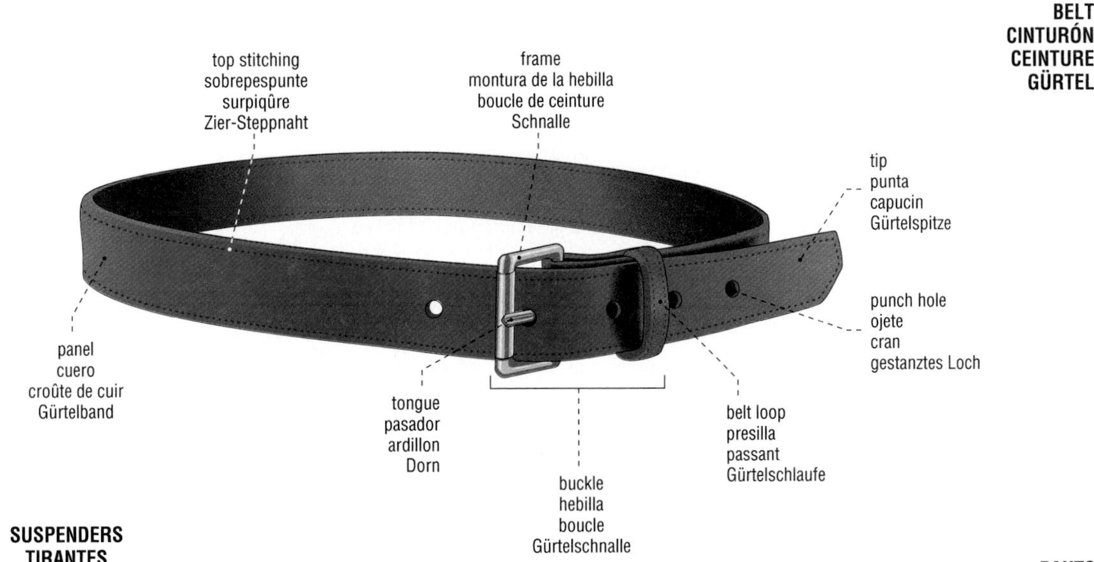
top stitching
sobrepespunte
surpiqûre
Zier-Steppnaht
frame
montura de la hebilla
boucle de ceinture
Schnalle
tip
punta
capucin
Gürtelspitze
punch hole
ojete
cran
gestanztes Loch
panel
cuero
croûte de cuir
Gürtelband
tongue
pasador
ardillon
Dorn
buckle
hebilla
boucle
Gürtelschnalle
belt loop
presilla
passant
Gürtelschlaufe

SUSPENDERS
TIRANTES
BRETELLES
HOSENTRÄGER

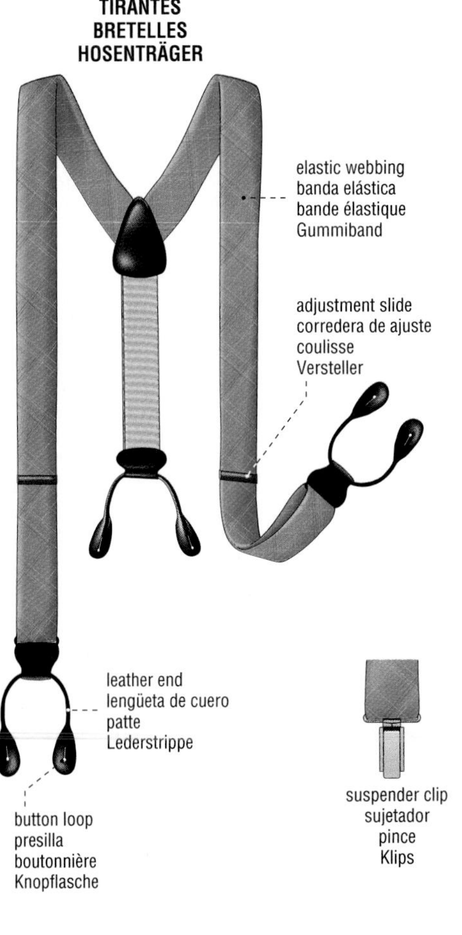
elastic webbing
banda elástica
bande élastique
Gummiband
adjustment slide
corredera de ajuste
coulisse
Versteller
leather end
lengüeta de cuero
patte
Lederstrippe
button loop
presilla
boutonnière
Knopflasche
suspender clip
sujetador
pince
Klips

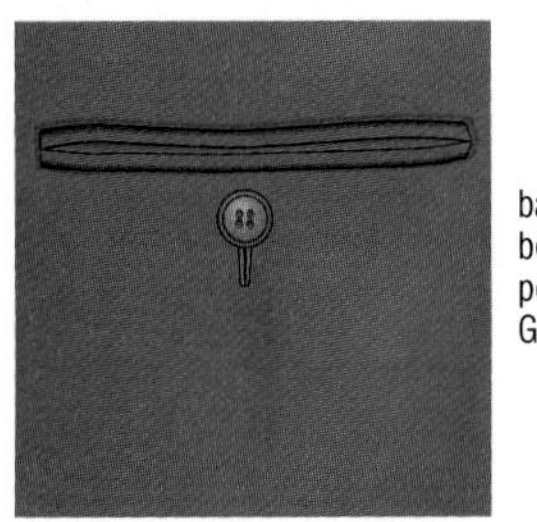
back pocket
bolsillo trasero
poche-revolver
Gesäßtasche

PANTS
PANTALONES
PANTALON
HOSE

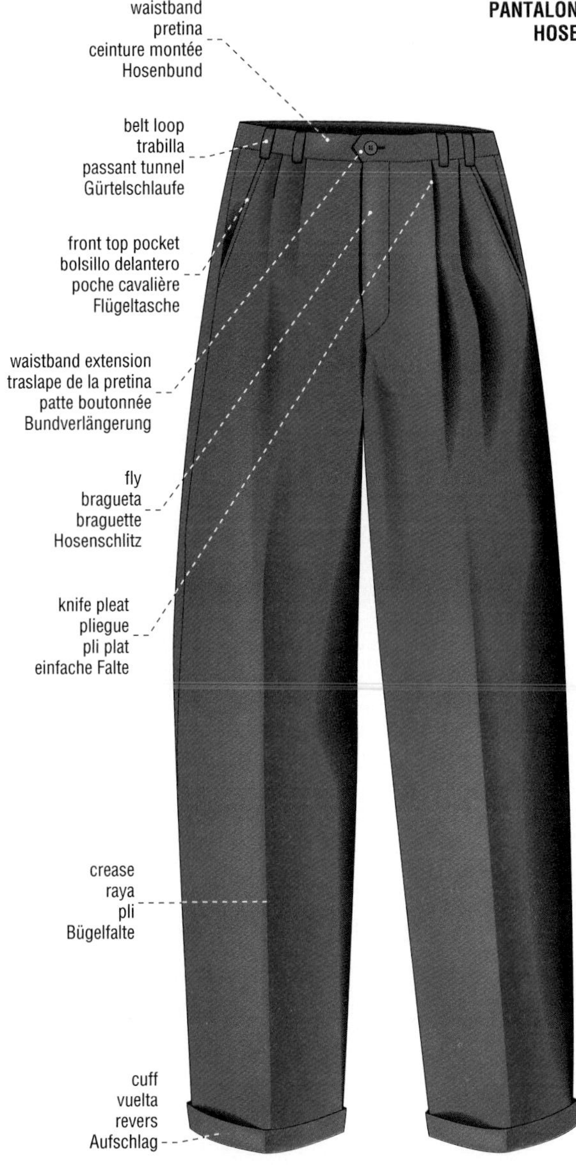
waistband
pretina
ceinture montée
Hosenbund
belt loop
trabilla
passant tunnel
Gürtelschlaufe
front top pocket
bolsillo delantero
poche cavalière
Flügeltasche
waistband extension
traslape de la pretina
patte boutonnée
Bundverlängerung
fly
bragueta
braguette
Hosenschlitz
knife pleat
pliegue
pli plat
einfache Falte
crease
raya
pli
Bügelfalte
cuff
vuelta
revers
Aufschlag

MEN'S CLOTHING
ROPA DE HOMBRE
VÊTEMENTS D'HOMME
HERRENKLEIDUNG

SHIRT
CAMISA
CHEMISE
HEMD
yoke
canesú
empiècement
Sattel
set-in sleeve
manga empotrada
manche montée
eingesetzter Ärmel
collar
cuello
col
Kragen
breast pocket
bolsillo superior
poche poitrine
Brusttasche
collar point
punta del cuello
pointe de col
Kragenspitze
buttoned placket
aletilla
patte de boutonnage
Knopfleiste
front
delantero
devant
Vorderseite
pointed tab end
abertura con aletilla
patte capucin
Ärmelschlitz
button
botón
bouton
Knopf
cuff
puño
poignet
Manschette
shirttail
faldón de la camisa
pan
Schoß
buttondown collar
cuello con botones
col pointes boutonnées
Button-down-Kragen
spread collar
cuello italiano
col italien
gespreizter Kragen
ascot tie
corbata inglesa
lavallière
Krawattenschal
collar stay
ballena
baleine de col
Kragenstäbchen
bow tie
pajarita
nœud papillon
Fliege
NECKTIE
CORBATA
CRAVATE
KRAWATTE
front apron
faldón delantero
pan avant
Vorderteil
neck end
contorno del cuello
tour de cou
Bindeteil
rear apron
faldón trasero
pan arrière
Endteil
lining
forro
doublure
Futter
loop
presilla
passant
Schlaufe
slip-stitched seam
costura invisible
couture médiane
Verziehnaht

UNDERWEAR
ROPA INTERIOR
SOUS-VÊTEMENTS
UNTERWÄSCHE

athletic shirt
camiseta
gilet athlétique
Trägerhemd

neckhole
cuello
encolure
Halsausschnitt

armhole
sisa
emmanchure
Armausschnitt

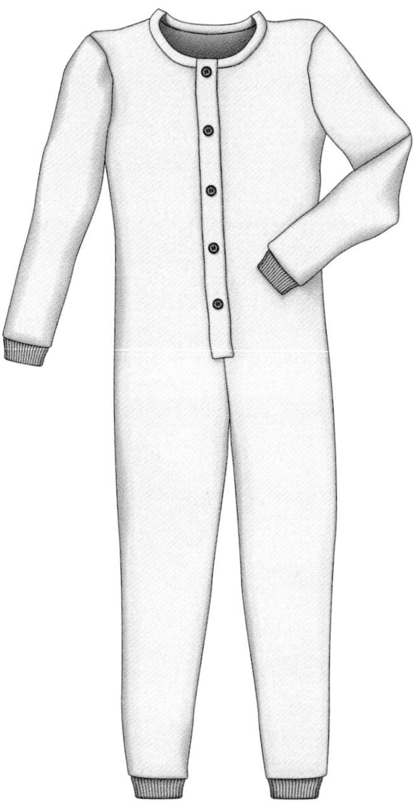

briefs
trusa
slip ouvert
Slip

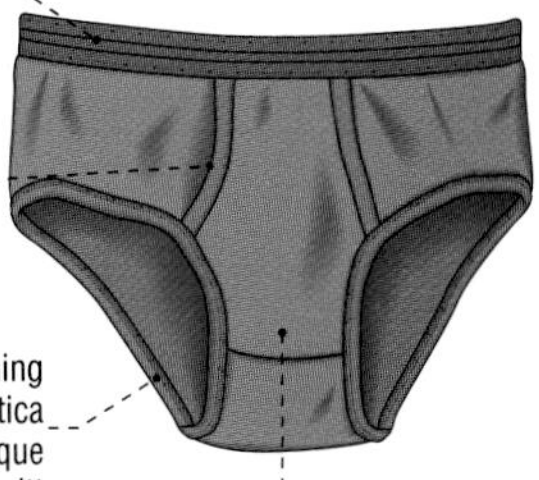

waistband
pretina elástica
ceinture élastique
Bündchen

fly
bragueta
braguette
Schlitz

elasticized leg opening
pierna elástica
jambe élastique
elastischer Beinausschnitt

crotch
entrepierna
enfourchure
Schritt

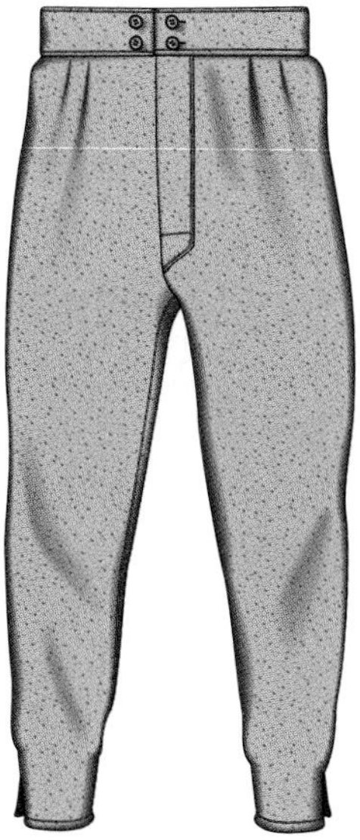

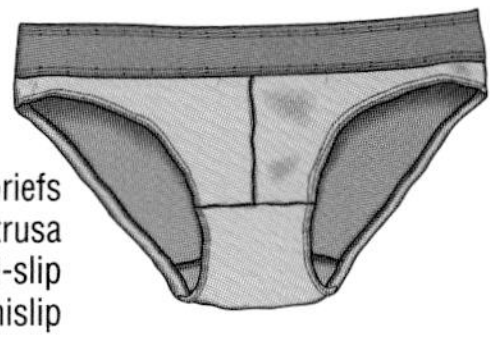

union suit
mameluco
combinaison
Hemdhose

drawers
calzoncillos largos
caleçon long
lange Unterhose

bikini briefs
minitrusa
mini-slip
Minislip

boxer shorts
calzoncillos
caleçon
Boxershorts

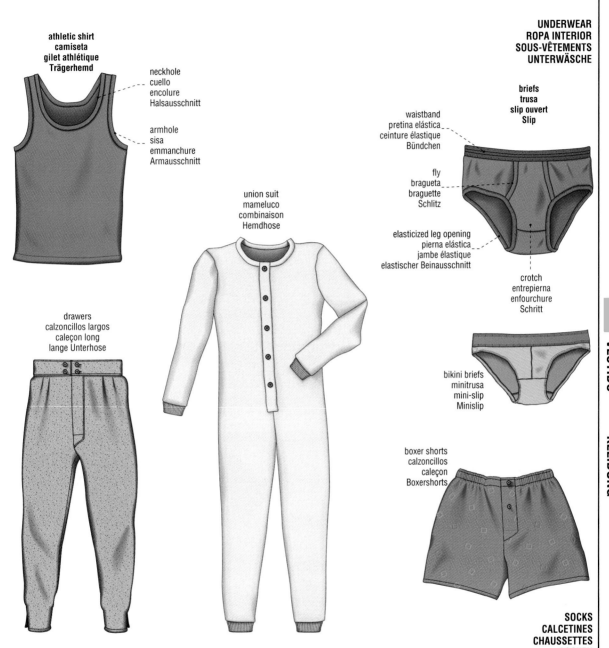

SOCKS
CALCETINES
CHAUSSETTES
SOCKEN

executive length
largo ejecutivo
mi-bas
Kniestrumpf

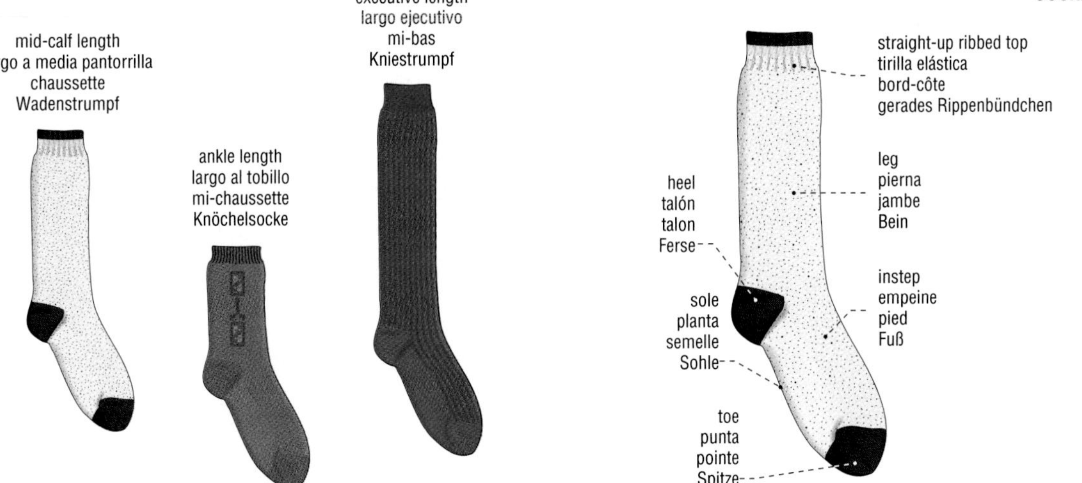
mid-calf length
largo a media pantorrilla
chaussette
Wadenstrumpf
ankle length
largo al tobillo
mi-chaussette
Knöchelsocke
straight-up ribbed top
tirilla elástica
bord-côte
gerades Rippenbündchen
leg
pierna
jambe
Bein
heel
talón
talon
Ferse
instep
empeine
pied
Fuß
sole
planta
semelle
Sohle
toe
punta
pointe
Spitze

SWEATERS
SUÉTERES
TRICOTS
PULLOVER

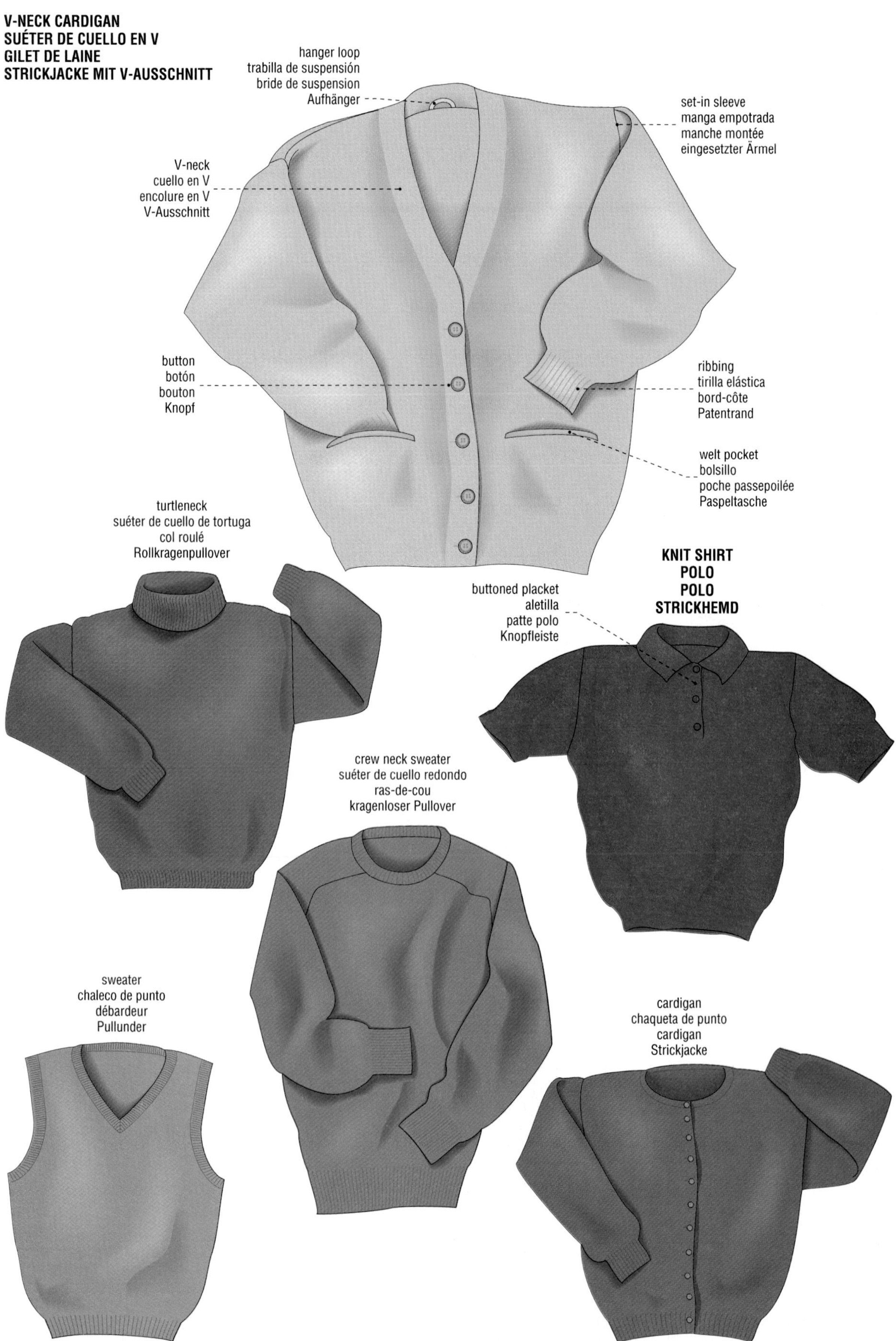
V-NECK CARDIGAN
SUÉTER DE CUELLO EN V
GILET DE LAINE
STRICKJACKE MIT V-AUSSCHNITT
hanger loop
trabilla de suspensión
bride de suspension
Aufhänger
set-in sleeve
manga empotrada
manche montée
eingesetzter Ärmel
V-neck
cuello en V
encolure en V
V-Ausschnitt
button
botón
bouton
Knopf
ribbing
tirilla elástica
bord-côte
Patentrand
welt pocket
bolsillo
poche passepoilée
Paspeltasche
turtleneck
suéter de cuello de tortuga
col roulé
Rollkragenpullover
KNIT SHIRT
POLO
POLO
STRICKHEMD
buttoned placket
aletilla
patte polo
Knopfleiste
crew neck sweater
suéter de cuello redondo
ras-de-cou
kragenloser Pullover
sweater
chaleco de punto
débardeur
Pullunder
cardigan
chaqueta de punto
cardigan
Strickjacke

GLOVES
GUANTES
GANTS
HANDSCHUHE

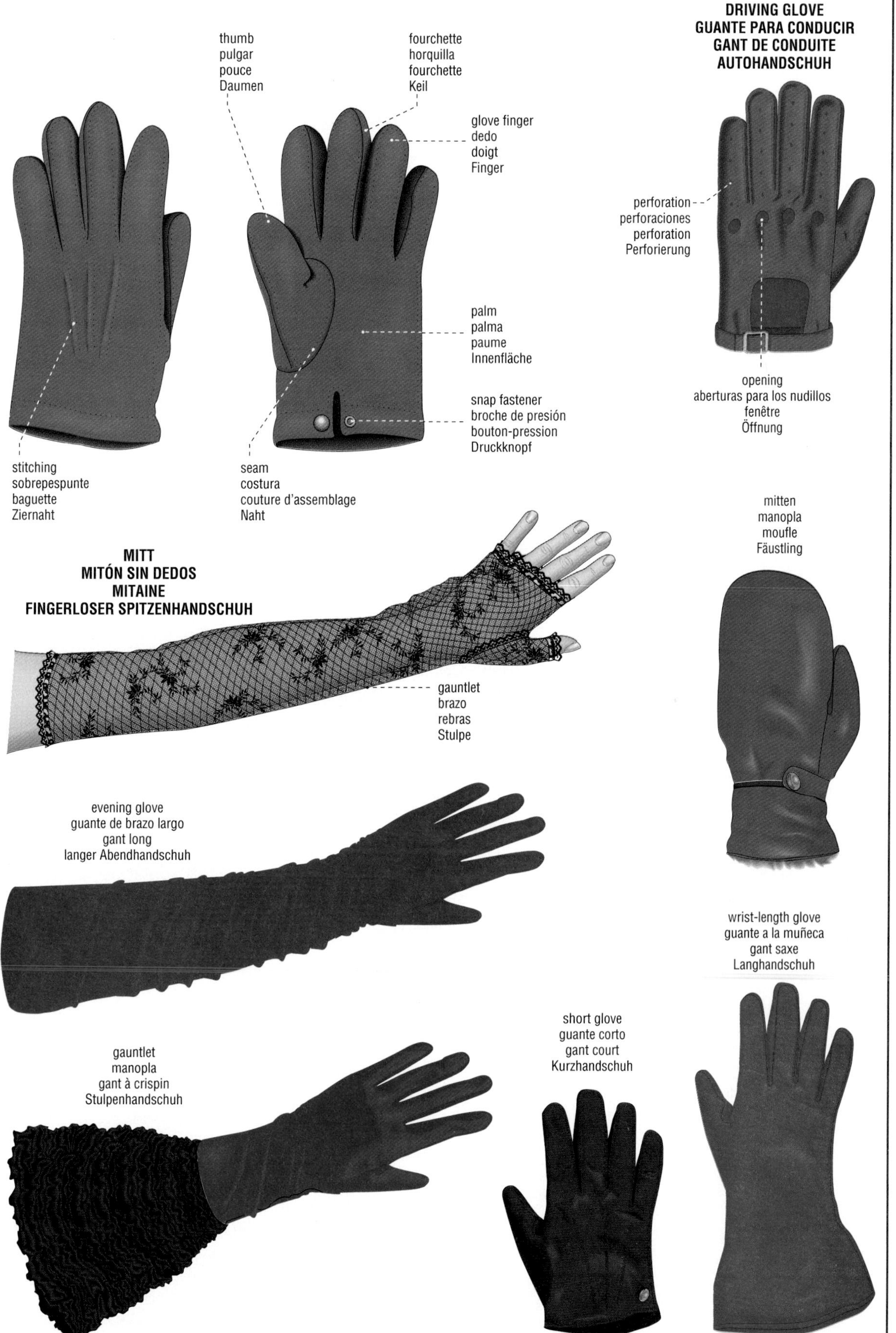

thumb
pulgar
pouce
Daumen
fourchette
horquilla
fourchette
Keil
glove finger
dedo
doigt
Finger
palm
palma
paume
Innenfläche
snap fastener
broche de presión
bouton-pression
Druckknopf
stitching
sobrepespunte
baguette
Ziernaht
seam
costura
couture d'assemblage
Naht
DRIVING GLOVE
GUANTE PARA CONDUCIR
GANT DE CONDUITE
AUTOHANDSCHUH
perforation
perforaciones
perforation
Perforierung
opening
aberturas para los nudillos
fenêtre
Öffnung
MITT
MITÓN SIN DEDOS
MITAINE
FINGERLOSER SPITZENHANDSCHUH
gauntlet
brazo
rebras
Stulpe
mitten
manopla
moufle
Fäustling
evening glove
guante de brazo largo
gant long
langer Abendhandschuh
wrist-length glove
guante a la muñeca
gant saxe
Langhandschuh
short glove
guante corto
gant court
Kurzhandschuh
gauntlet
manopla
gant à crispin
Stulpenhandschuh

HEADGEAR
SOMBREROS
COIFFURE
KOPFBEDECKUNGEN

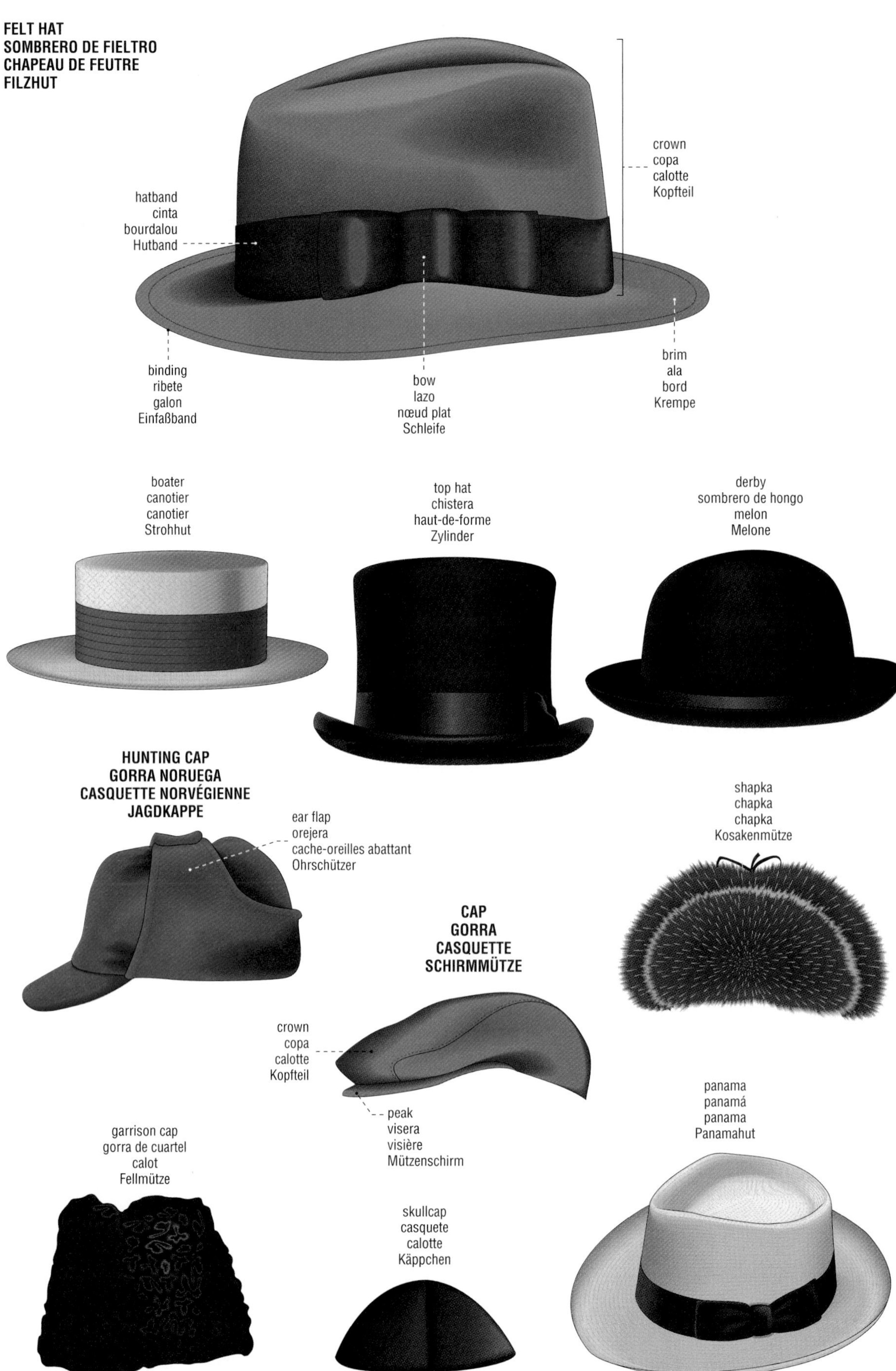

FELT HAT
SOMBRERO DE FIELTRO
CHAPEAU DE FEUTRE
FILZHUT
crown
copa
calotte
Kopfteil
hatband
cinta
bourdalou
Hutband
binding
ribete
galon
Einfaßband
bow
lazo
nœud plat
Schleife
brim
ala
bord
Krempe
boater
canotier
canotier
Strohhut
top hat
chistera
haut-de-forme
Zylinder
derby
sombrero de hongo
melon
Melone
HUNTING CAP
GORRA NORUEGA
CASQUETTE NORVÉGIENNE
JAGDKAPPE
ear flap
orejera
cache-oreilles abattant
Ohrschützer
shapka
chapka
chapka
Kosakenmütze
CAP
GORRA
CASQUETTE
SCHIRMMÜTZE
crown
copa
calotte
Kopfteil
peak
visera
visière
Mützenschirm
panama
panamá
panama
Panamahut
garrison cap
gorra de cuartel
calot
Fellmütze
skullcap
casquete
calotte
Käppchen

toque
toca
toque
Toque
pillbox hat
sombrero sin alas
tambourin
Pagenkäppi
beret
boina
béret
Baskenmütze
turban
turbante
turban
Turban
cloche
sombrero de campana
cloche
Topfhut
felt hat
sombrero de fieltro
feutre
Filzhut
BALACLAVA
BALACLAVA
CAGOULE
KAPUZENMÜTZE
peak
visera
visière
Mützenschirm
southwester
sueste
suroît
Südwester
stocking cap
gorro de punto
bonnet pompon
Pudelmütze
knit cap
gorro de punto
bonnet
Strickmütze
GOB HAT
SOMBRERO DE MARINERO
BOB
REGENHUT
crown
copa
calotte
Kopfteil
cartwheel hat
pamela
capeline
Wagenradhut
brim
ala
bord
Krempe

TYPES OF COATS
ABRIGOS Y CHAQUETAS
TYPES DE MANTEAUX
MANTELARTEN

pea jacket
chaquetón marinero
caban
Caban
tailored collar
cuello hechura sastre
col tailleur
Schneiderkragen
hand warmer pocket
bolsillo de ojal
poche repose-bras
Mufftasche
mock pocket
bolsillo simulado
fausse poche
falsche Tasche
car coat
chaquetón
paletot
Autocoat
back belt
cinturón trasero
martingale
Rückengürtel
raglan
abrigo corto
raglan
Raglanmantel
raglan sleeve
manga ranglán
manche raglan
Raglanärmel
fly front closing
pestaña
boutonnage sous patte
verdeckte Knopfleiste
broad welt side pocket
bolsillo de ribete ancho
poche raglan
schräge Pattentasche
pelerine
abrigo con esclavina
pèlerine
Pelerine
pelerine
esclavina
pèlerine
Pelerine
seam pocket
bolsillo disimulado
poche prise dans une couture
Nahttasche

cape
capa
cape
Cape
overcoat
abrigo
manteau
Mantel
top coat
abrigo cruzado
redingote
Redingote
arm slit
abertura para el brazo
passe-bras
Durchgrifftasche
poncho
poncho
poncho
Poncho
suit
traje
tailleur
Kostüm
jacket
chaqueta
veste
Jacke
jacket
chaquetón
veste
Blazer
skirt
falda
jupe
Rock

WOMEN'S CLOTHING
ROPA DE MUJER
VÊTEMENTS DE FEMME
DAMENKLEIDUNG

TYPES OF DRESSES
TIPOS DE VESTIDO
TYPES DE ROBES
KLEIDERARTEN

coat dress
vestido abrigo
robe-manteau
Mantelkleid

princess dress
corte princesa
robe princesse
Prinzeßkleid

sheath dress
recto entallado
robe fourreau
Schlauchkleid

drop waist dress
de talle largo
robe taille basse
Kleid mit angesetztem Schoß

trapeze dress
de campana
robe trapèze
Trapez-Form

sundress
de verano
robe bain-de-soleil
Trägerkleid

polo dress
de camiseta
robe-polo
Polokleid

house dress
casero
robe de maison
Hauskleid

shirtwaist dress
camisero
robe chemisier
Hemdblusenkleid

jumper
jumper
chasuble
Kleiderrock

wraparound dress
cruzado
robe enveloppe
Wickelkleid

tunic dress
túnica
robe tunique
Tunikakleid

WOMEN'S CLOTHING
ROPA DE MUJER
VÊTEMENTS DE FEMME
DAMENKLEIDUNG

TYPES OF SKIRTS
TIPOS DE FALDA
TYPES DE JUPES
ROCKARTEN

sheath skirt
recta con abertura al frente
jupe fourreau
Etuirock

yoke skirt
de campana
jupe à empiècement
Sattelrock

gored skirt
de piezas
jupe à lés
Bahnenrock

ruffled skirt
de volantes
jupe à volants étagés
Stufenrock

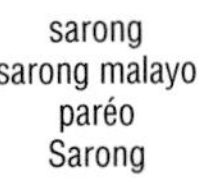

sarong
sarong malayo
paréo
Sarong

wraparound skirt
cruzada
jupe portefeuille
Wickelrock

straight skirt
recta
jupe droite
gerader Rock

culottes
falda pantalón
jupe-culotte
Hosenrock

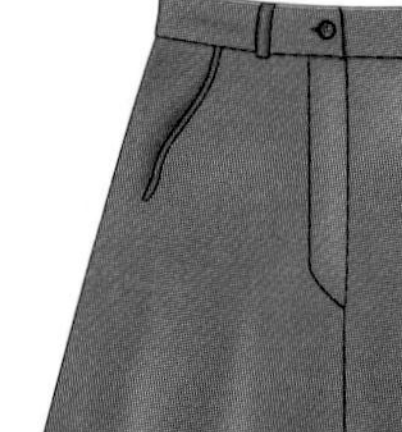

kilt
escocesa
kilt
Schottenrock

gather skirt
fruncida
jupe froncée
Kräuselrock

TYPES OF PLEATS
TIPOS DE PLIEGUE
TYPES DE PLIS
FALTENARTEN

inverted pleat
tablón delantero
pli creux
Kellerfalte

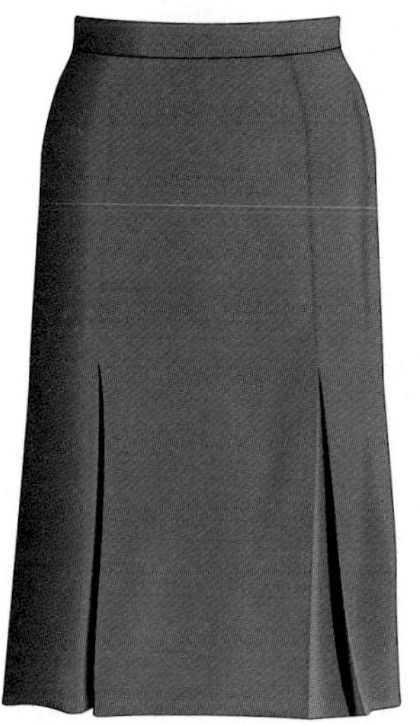

kick pleat
tabla abierta
pli d'aisance
Gehfalte

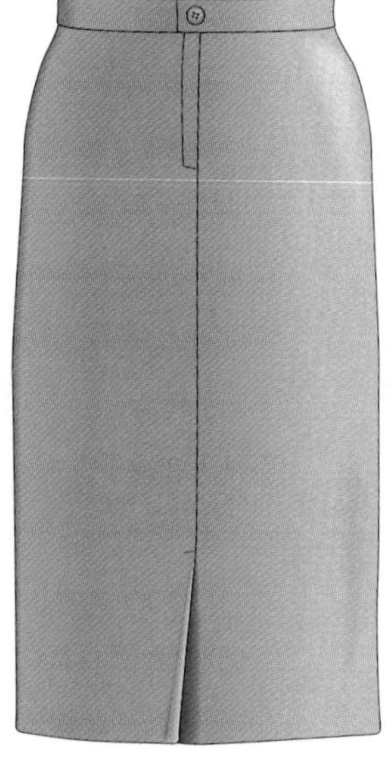

accordion pleat
plisada
plissé accordéon
Bahnenplissee

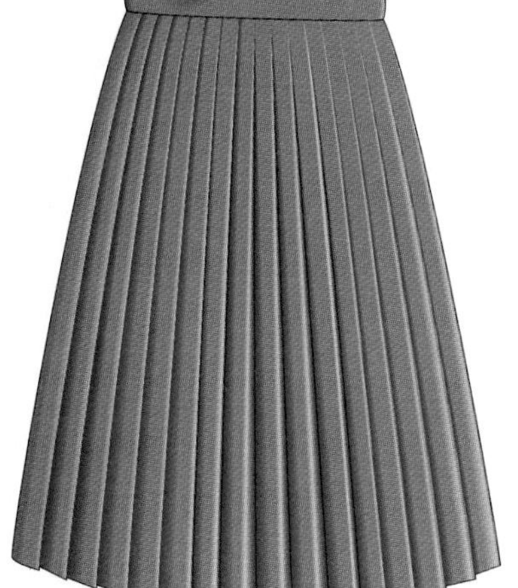

knife pleat
tablas
pli plat
einfache Falte

top stitched pleat
sobrepespunteada
pli surpiqué
abgesteppte Falte

WOMEN'S CLOTHING
ROPA DE MUJER
VÊTEMENTS DE FEMME
DAMENKLEIDUNG

TYPES OF PANTS
PANTALONES
TYPES DE PANTALONS
HOSENARTEN
jeans
vaqueros
jean
Jeans
Bermuda shorts
bermudas
bermuda
Bermudashorts
shorts
pantalón corto
short
Shorts
ski pants
pantalones de tubo
fuseau
Steghose
knickers
bombachos
knicker
Kniebundhose
pedal pushers
pescadores
corsaire
Caprihose
footstrap
trabilla
sous-pied
Steg
jumpsuit
traje pantalón
combinaison-pantalon
Overall
overalls
mono
salopette
Latzhose
bell bottoms
acampanado
pantalon pattes d'éléphant
Schlaghose

TYPES OF BLOUSES
BLUSAS
TYPES DE CHEMISIERS
BLUSENARTEN

classic blouse
camisera clásica
chemisier classique
klassische Bluse
middy
marinera
marinière
Matrosenbluse
polo shirt
camiseta
polo
Polohemd
smock
blusón
tablier-blouse
Kittelbluse
yoke
canesú
empiècement
Sattel
gather
fruncido
fronce
Kräuselfalte
tunic
blusón con aletilla
tunique
Arbeitskittel
wrap-over top
blusa cruzada
cache-cœur
Wickelbluse
mini shirtdress
camisa
liquette
Hosenbluse
body shirt
pantiblusa
corsage-culotte
Bodyshirt
over-blouse
túnica
casaque
Tunika
shirttail
faldón
pan
Schoß
crotch piece
entrepierna
patte d'entrejambe
Schritt

WOMEN'S CLOTHING
ROPA DE MUJER
VÊTEMENTS DE FEMME
DAMENKLEIDUNG

JACKETS, VEST AND SWEATERS
CHALECOS, SUÉTERES Y CHAQUETAS
VESTES ET PULLS
WESTEN UND JACKEN

safari jacket
cazadora
saharienne
Safarijacke
blazer
blazer
blazer
Blazer
gusset pocket
bolsillo de fuelle
poche soufflet
Blasebalgtasche
bolero
bolero
boléro
Bolero
spencer
bolero con botones
spencer
Spenzer
vest
chaleco
gilet
Weste
twin-set
suéteres combinados
tandem
Twinset
turtleneck
de tortuga
col roulé
Rollkragen
V-neck cardigan
suéter abierto de cuello en V
gilet de laine
Strickjacke mit V-Ausschnitt

TYPES OF POCKETS
TIPOS DE BOLSILLO
TYPES DE POCHES
TASCHENARTEN

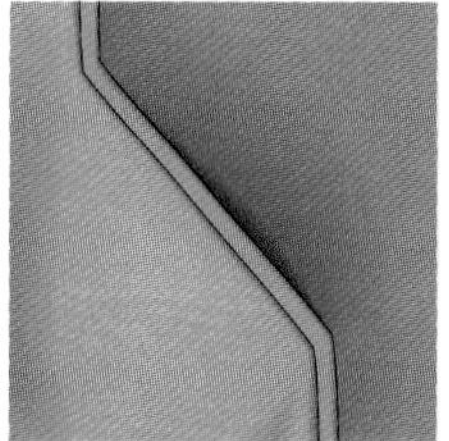
inset pocket
simulado
poche prise dans une découpe
eingesetzte Tasche

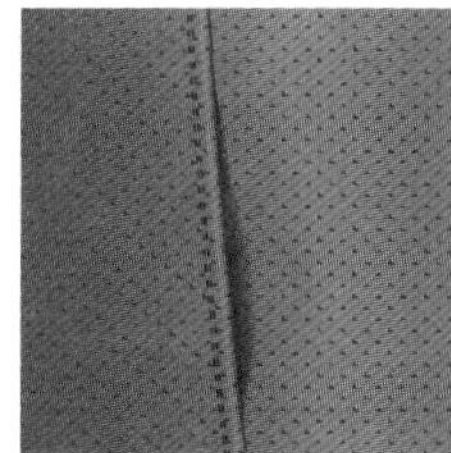
seam pocket
bolsillo disimulado
poche prise dans une couture
Nahttasche

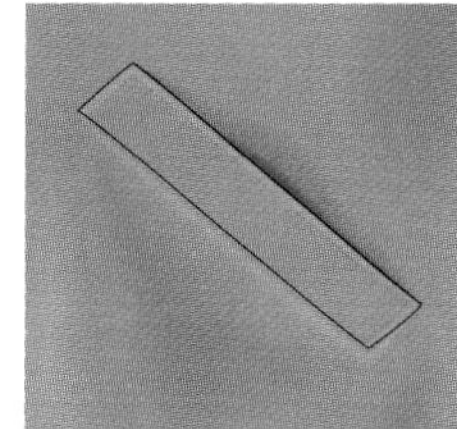
broad welt side pocket
de ojal con ribete
poche raglan
Raglantasche

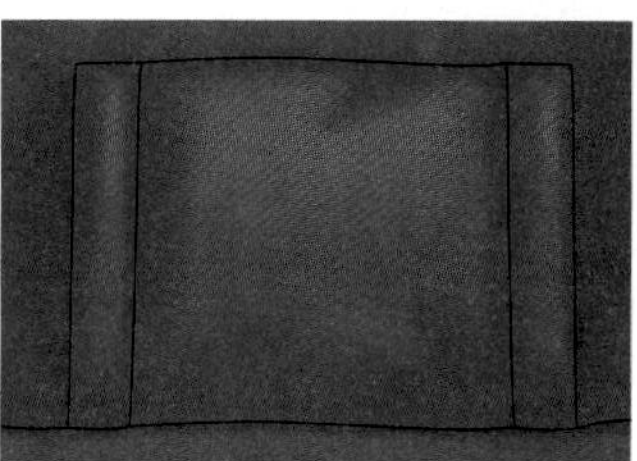
hand warmer pouch
de manguito
poche manchon
Mufftasche

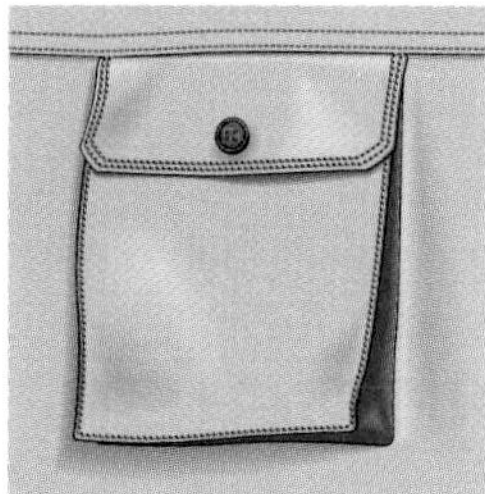
gusset pocket
de fuelle
poche soufflet
Blasebalgtasche

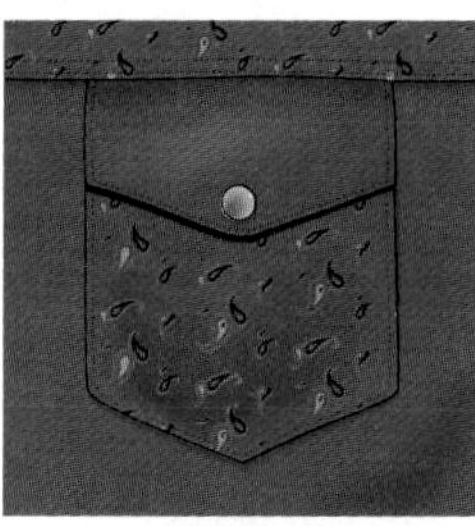
flap pocket
bolsa de parche con cartera
poche à rabat
Klappentasche

patch pocket
de parche
poche plaquée
aufgesetzte Tasche

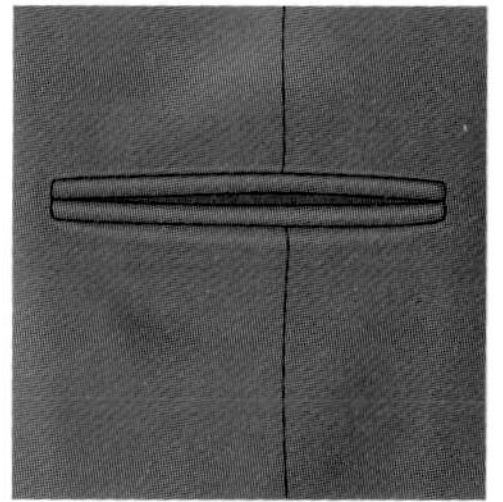
welt pocket
de ojal de sastre
poche passepoilée
Paspeltasche

TYPES OF SLEEVES
TIPOS DE MANGA
TYPES DE MANCHES
ÄRMELARTEN

French cuff
puño para gemelos
poignet mousquetaire
Doppelmanschette

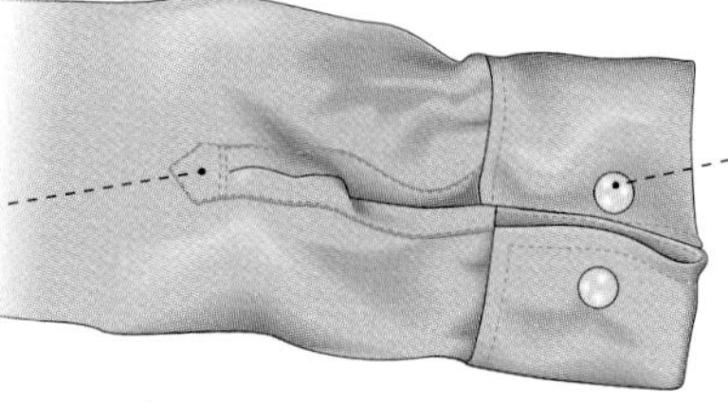
pointed tab end
aletilla
patte capucin
Ärmelschlitz
cuff link
gemelos
bouton de manchette
Manschettenknopf

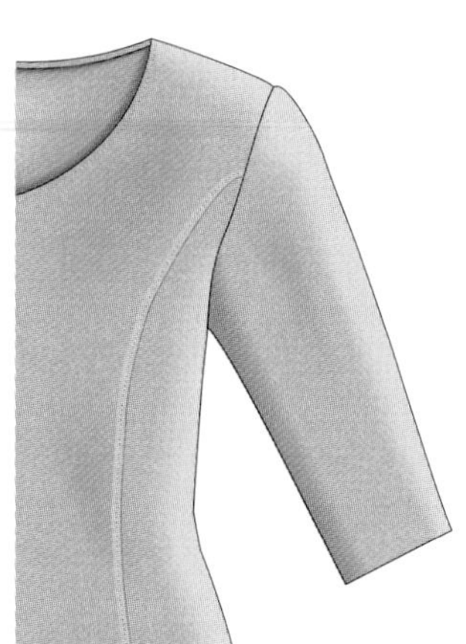
three-quarter sleeve
recta de tres cuartos
manche trois-quarts
Dreiviertelarm

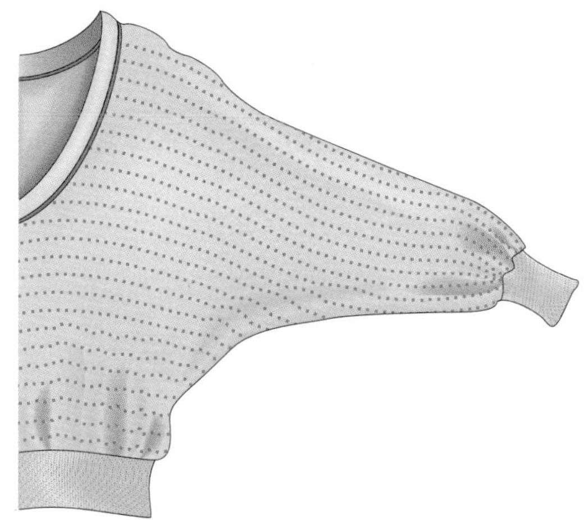
batwing sleeve
de murciélago
manche chauve-souris
Fledermausärmel

cap sleeve
corta sencilla
mancheron
angeschnittener Ärmel

TYPES OF SLEEVES
TIPOS DE MANGA
TYPES DE MANCHES
ÄRMELARTEN

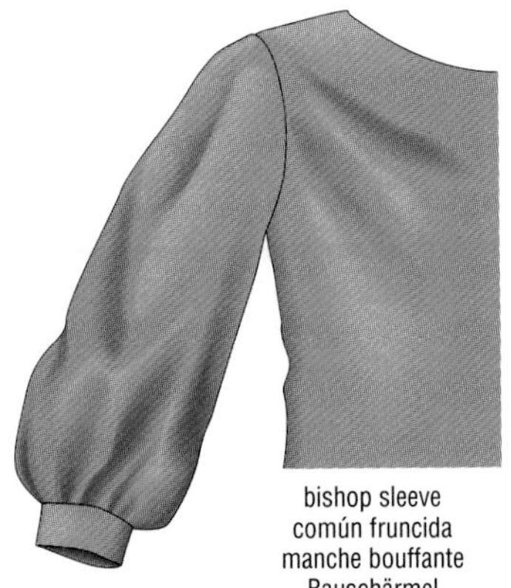

bishop sleeve
común fruncida
manche bouffante
Bauschärmel

leg-of-mutton sleeve
de jamón
manche gigot
Keulenärmel

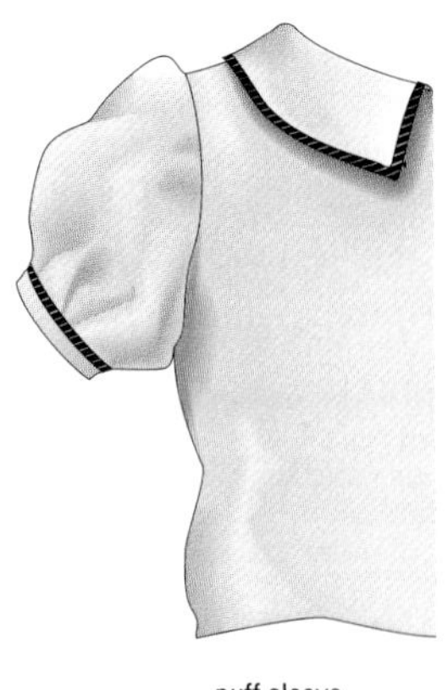

puff sleeve
de globo
manche ballon
Puffärmel

tailored sleeve
hechura sastre
manche tailleur
Schneiderärmel

epaulet sleeve
con hombrera
manche marteau
Zungenraglan

kimono sleeve
kimono
manche kimono
Kimonoärmel

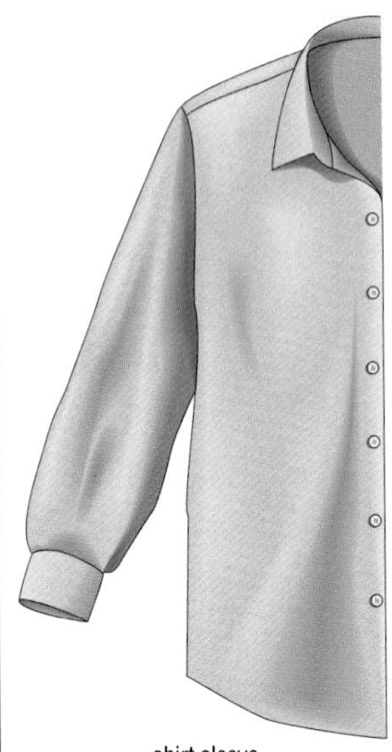

shirt sleeve
camisera
manche chemisier
Hemdblusenärmel

raglan sleeve
manga ranglán
manche raglan
Raglanärmel

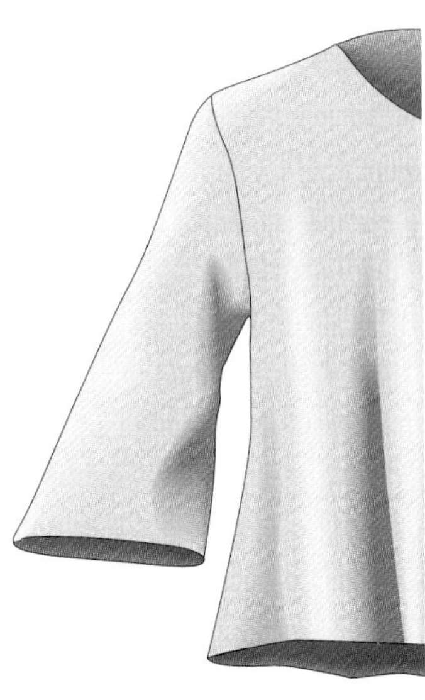

pagoda sleeve
de pagoda
manche pagode
Pagodenärmel

COLLAR
CUELLO
COL
KRAGEN

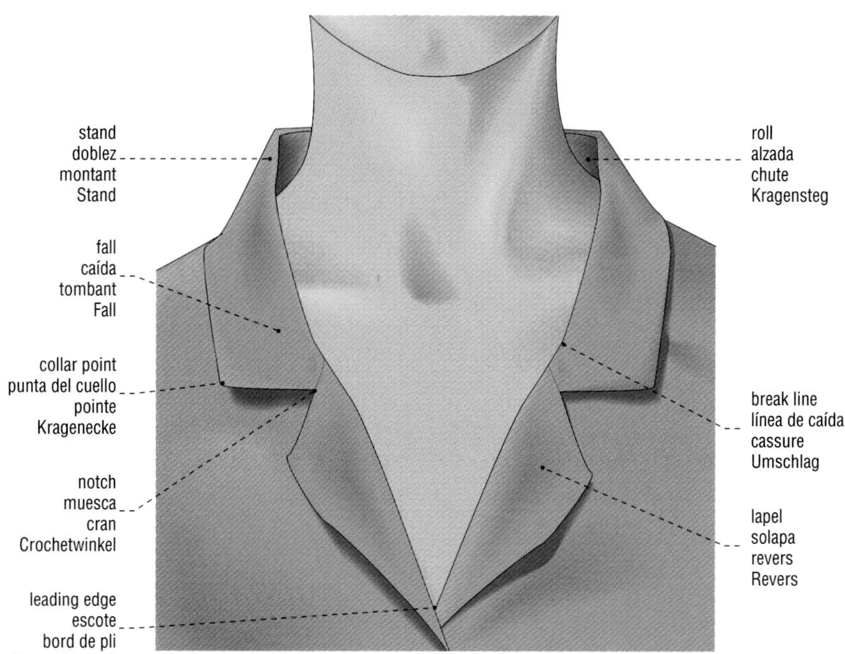
stand
doblez
montant
Stand
fall
caída
tombant
Fall
collar point
punta del cuello
pointe
Kragenecke
notch
muesca
cran
Crochetwinkel
leading edge
escote
bord de pli
Fassonübertritt
roll
alzada
chute
Kragensteg
break line
línea de caída
cassure
Umschlag
lapel
solapa
revers
Revers

TYPES OF COLLARS
CUELLOS
TYPES DE COLS
KRAGENARTEN

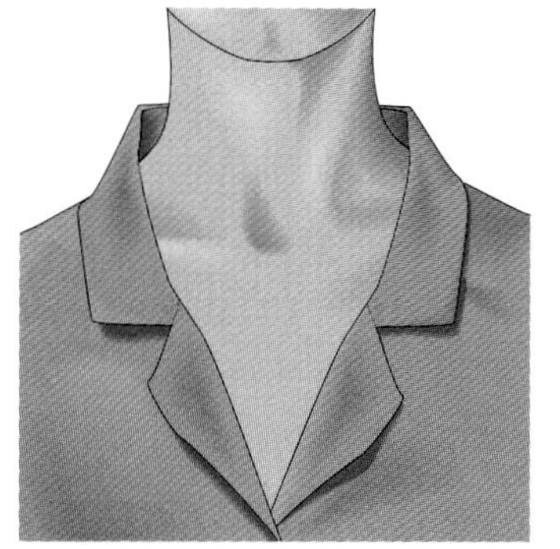
shirt collar
camisero
col chemisier
Hemdblusenkragen

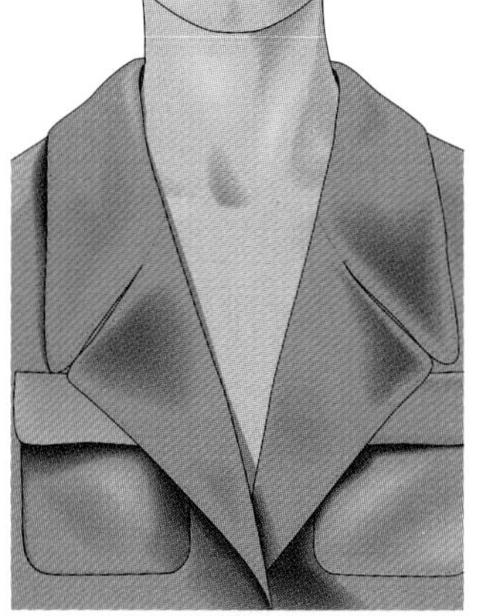
tailored collar
hechura de sastre
col tailleur
Schneiderkragen

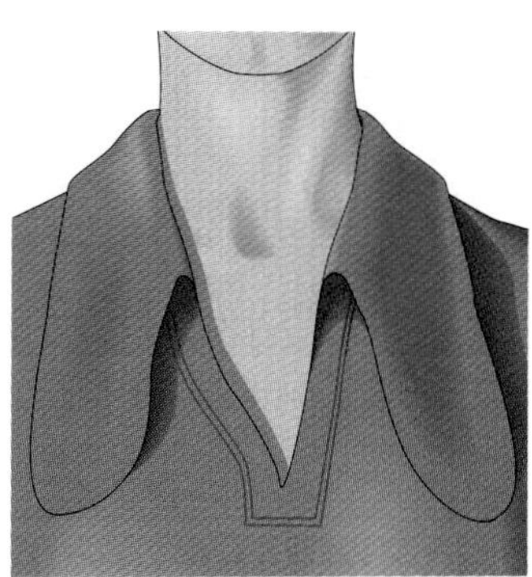
dog ear collar
plano con orejas
col banane
Dackelohrkragen

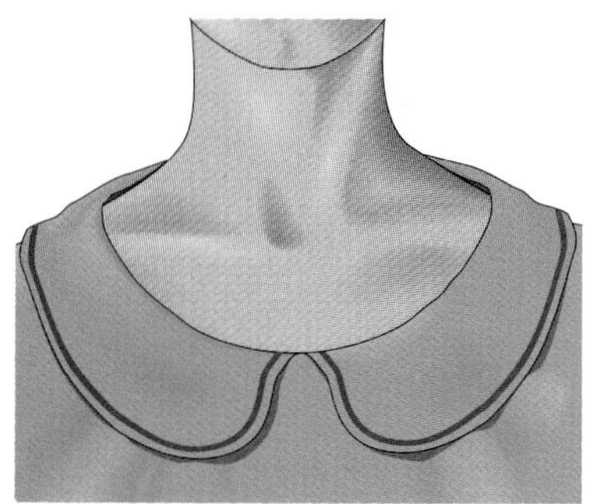
Peter Pan collar
plano tipo Peter Pan
col Claudine
Bubikragen

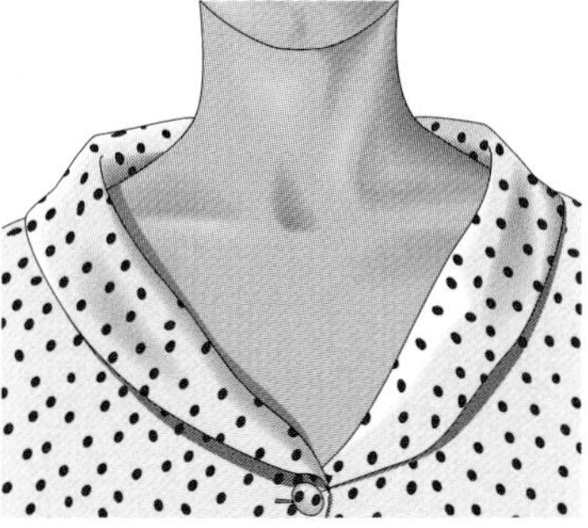
shawl collar
de chal
col châle
Schalkragen

collaret
de volantes
collerette
Halskrause

TYPES OF COLLARS
CUELLOS
TYPES DE COLS
KRAGENARTEN

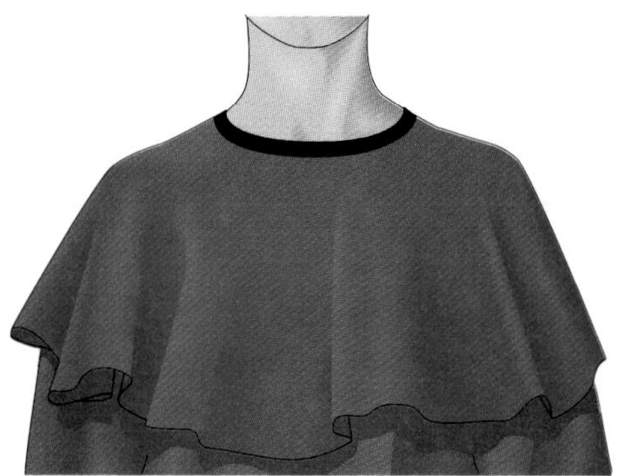

bertha collar
Berta
col berthe
Berthe

bow collar
de lazo
col cravate
Schleifenkragen

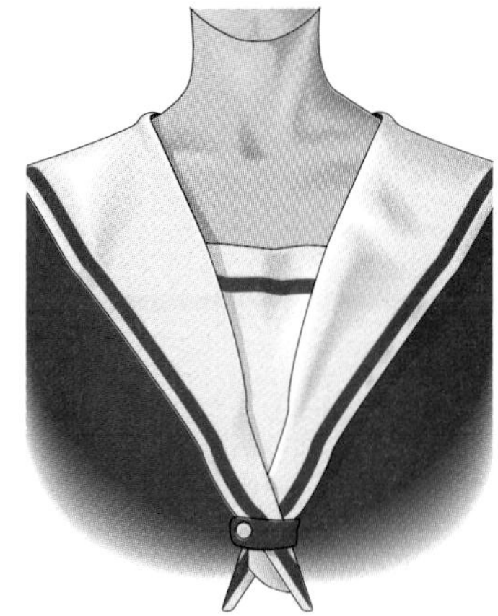

sailor collar
marinero
col marin
Matrosenkragen

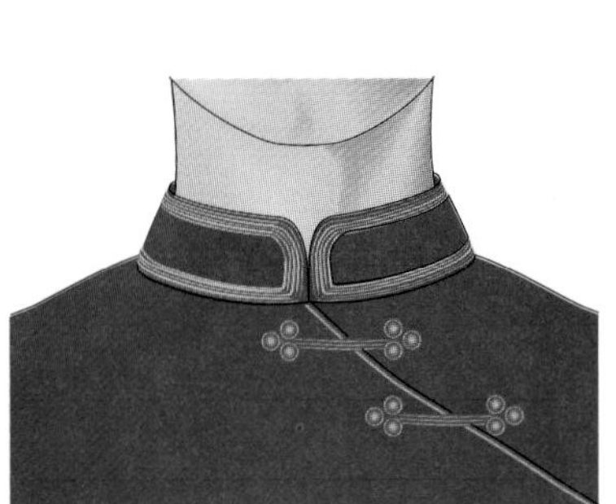

mandarin collar
chino
col chinois
Chinesenkragen

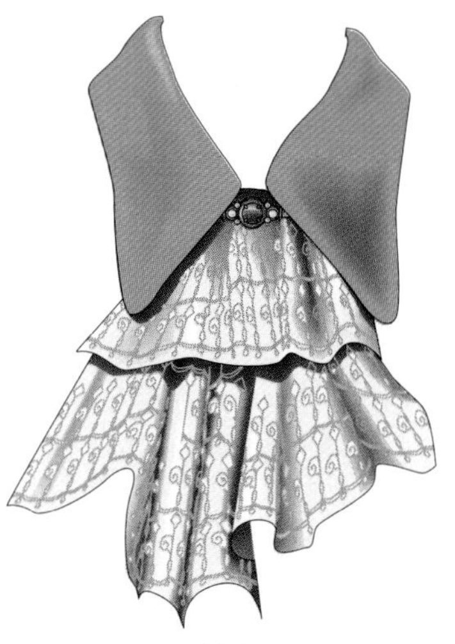

jabot
con chorrera
jabot
Jabot

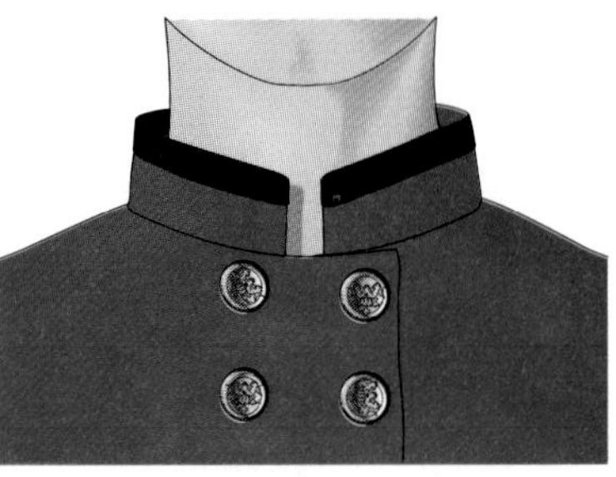

stand-up collar
Mao
col officier
Stehbordkragen

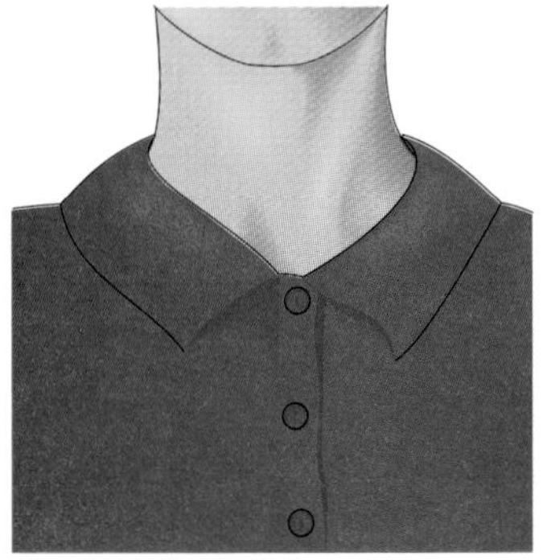

polo collar
con aletilla
col polo
Polokragen

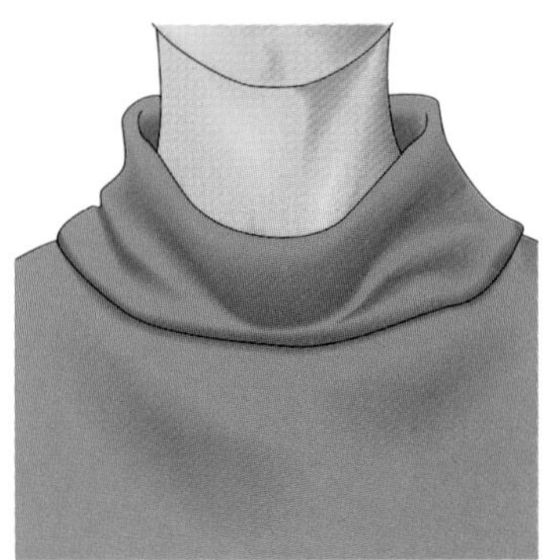

cowl neck
tipo cogulla
col cagoule
Kuttenkragen

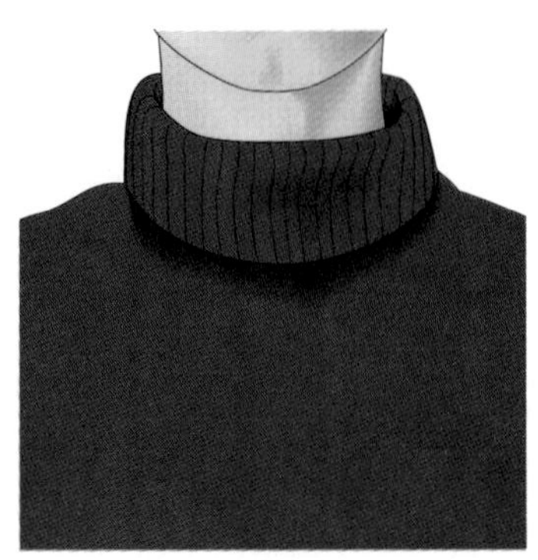

turtleneck
de tortuga
col roulé
Rollkragen

plunging neckline
bajo
décolleté plongeant
spitzes Dekolleté

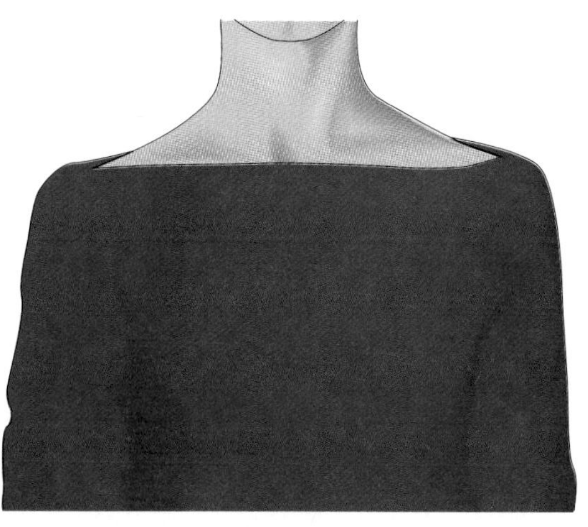

bateau neck
de ojal
encolure bateau
Bateau-Kragen

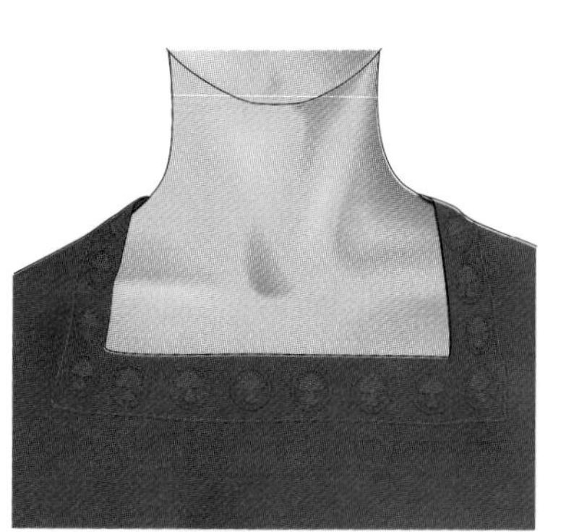

square neck
cuadrado
décolleté carré
viereckiger Ausschnitt

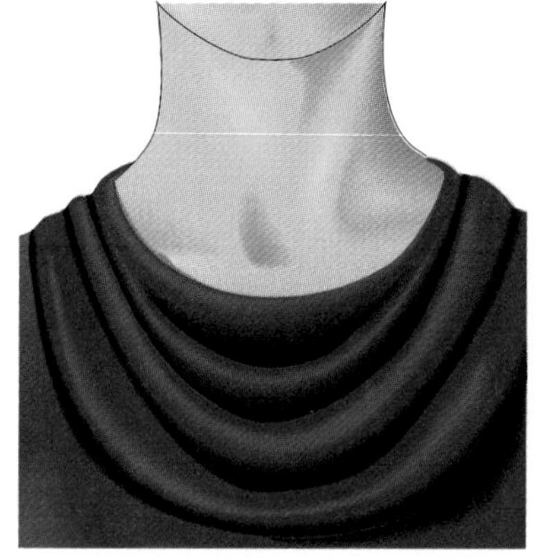

draped neck
drapeado
encolure drapée
drapierter Kragen

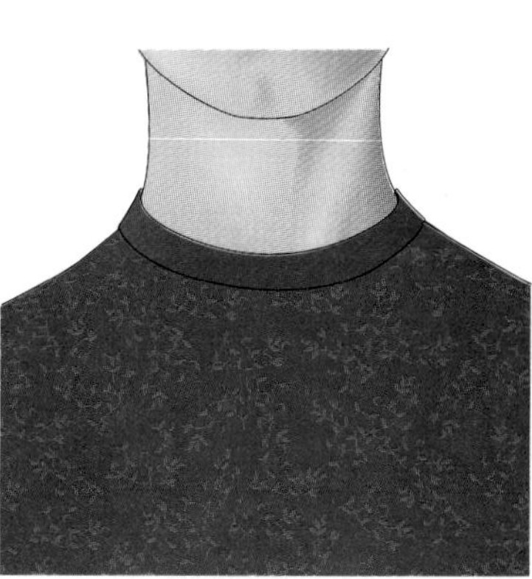

round neck
redondo
encolure ras-de-cou
runder Ausschnitt

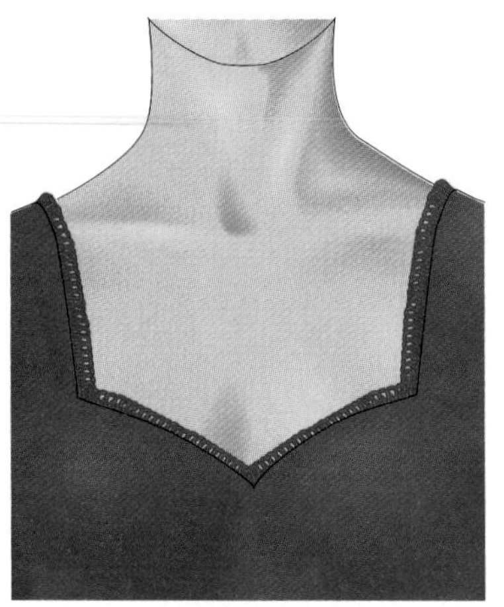

sweetheart neckline
de corazón
décolleté en cœur
Coeur-Dekolleté

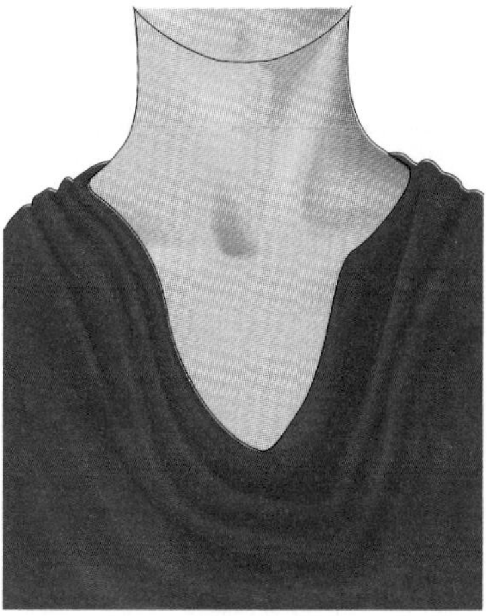

draped neckline
drapeado
décolleté drapé
drapierter Ausschnitt

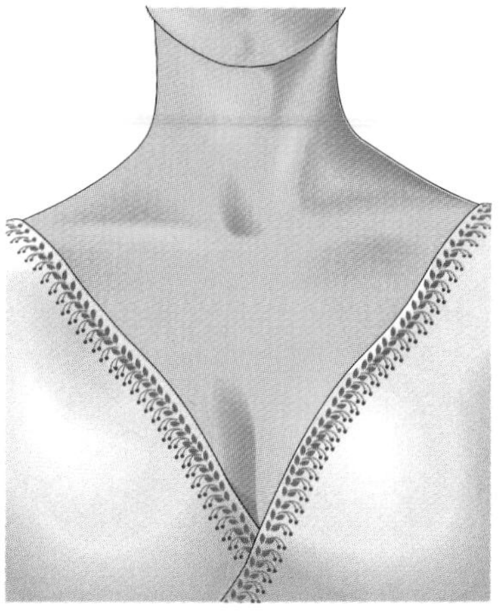

V-shaped neck
en V
décolleté en V
V-Ausschnitt

WOMEN'S CLOTHING
ROPA DE MUJER
VÊTEMENTS DE FEMME
DAMENKLEIDUNG

HOSE
MEDIAS
BAS
STRÜMPFE

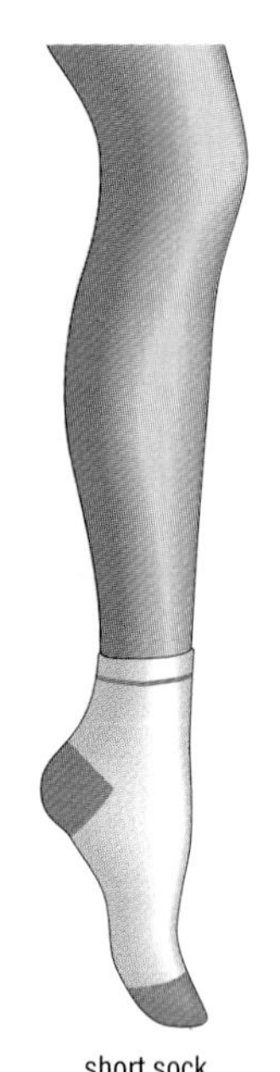

short sock
calcetín
socquette
Kurzsocke

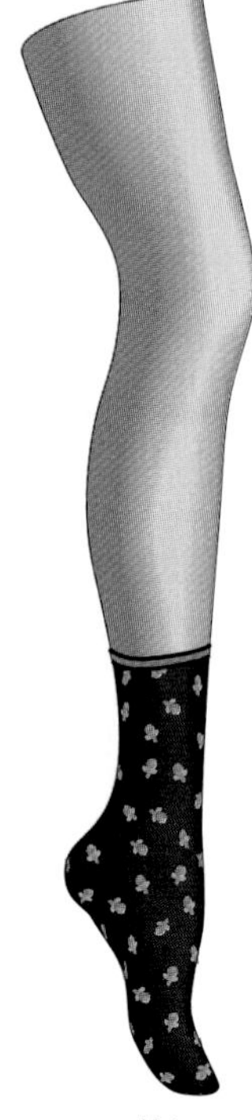

anklet
tobillera
mi-chaussette
Söckchen

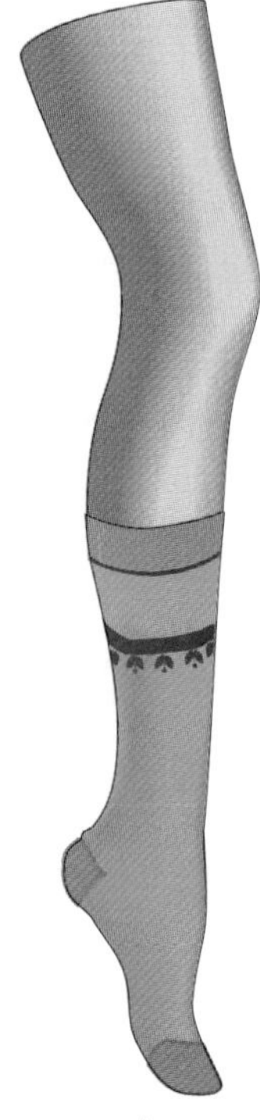

sock
calcetín largo
chaussette
Socke

knee-high sock
calceta
mi-bas
Kniestrumpf

panty hose
pantimedias
collant
Strumpfhose

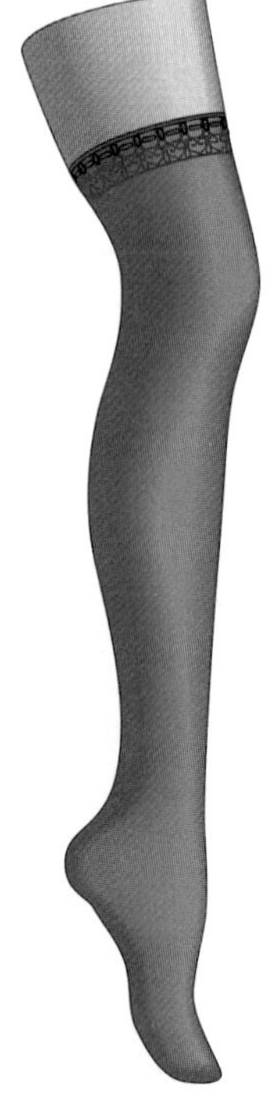

stocking
medias
bas
Strumpf

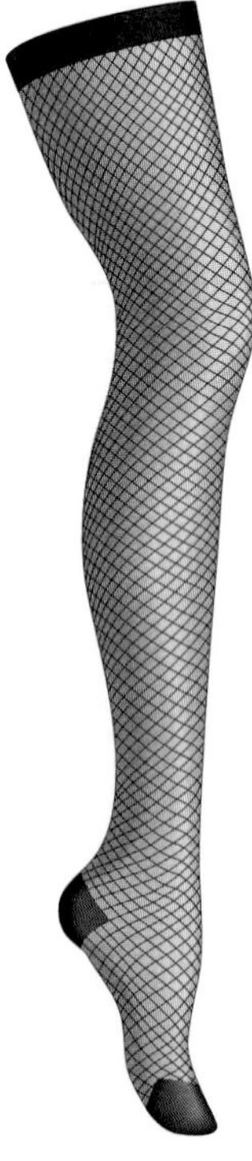

thigh-high stocking
media tres-cuartos
bas-cuissarde
Overknee-Strumpf

net stocking
medias de malla
bas résille
Netzstrumpf

body suit
corpiño
body
Bodysuit

teddy
canesú
teddy
Teddy

camisole
camisola
caraco
Camisol

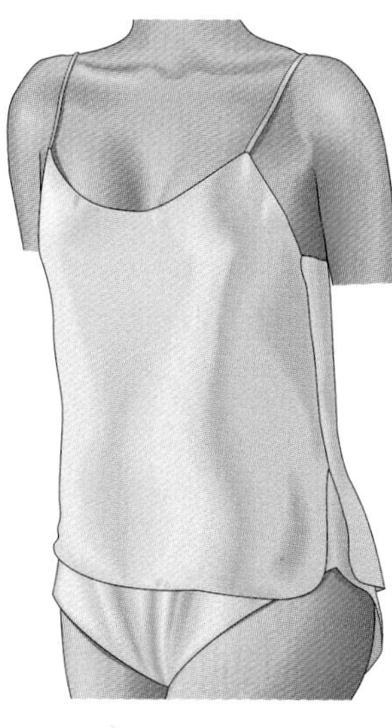

foundation slip
combinación
fond de robe
Vollachsel-Unterkleid

princess seaming
costura de corte princesa
découpe princesse
Prinzeßnaht

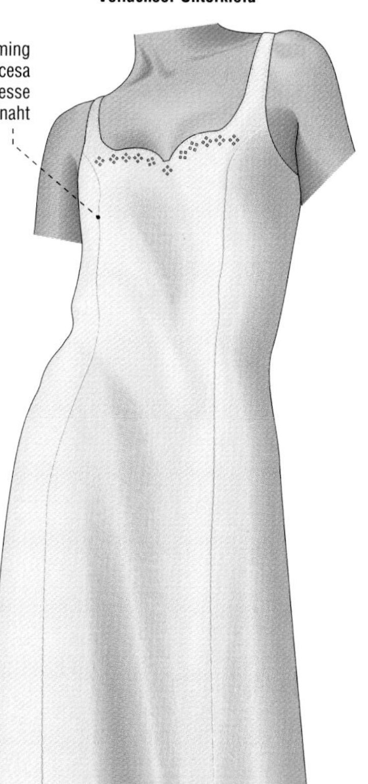

slip
combinación con sostén
combinaison-jupon
Unterkleid

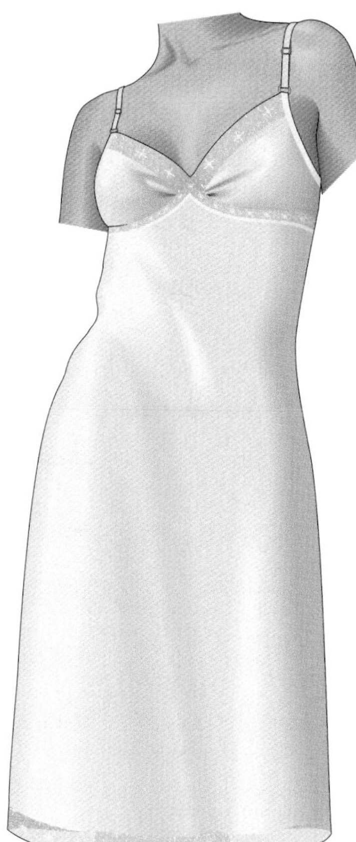

half-slip
media combinación
jupon
Unterrock

WOMEN'S CLOTHING
ROPA DE MUJER
VÊTEMENTS DE FEMME
DAMENKLEIDUNG

UNDERWEAR
ROPA INTERIOR
SOUS-VÊTEMENTS
UNTERWÄSCHE

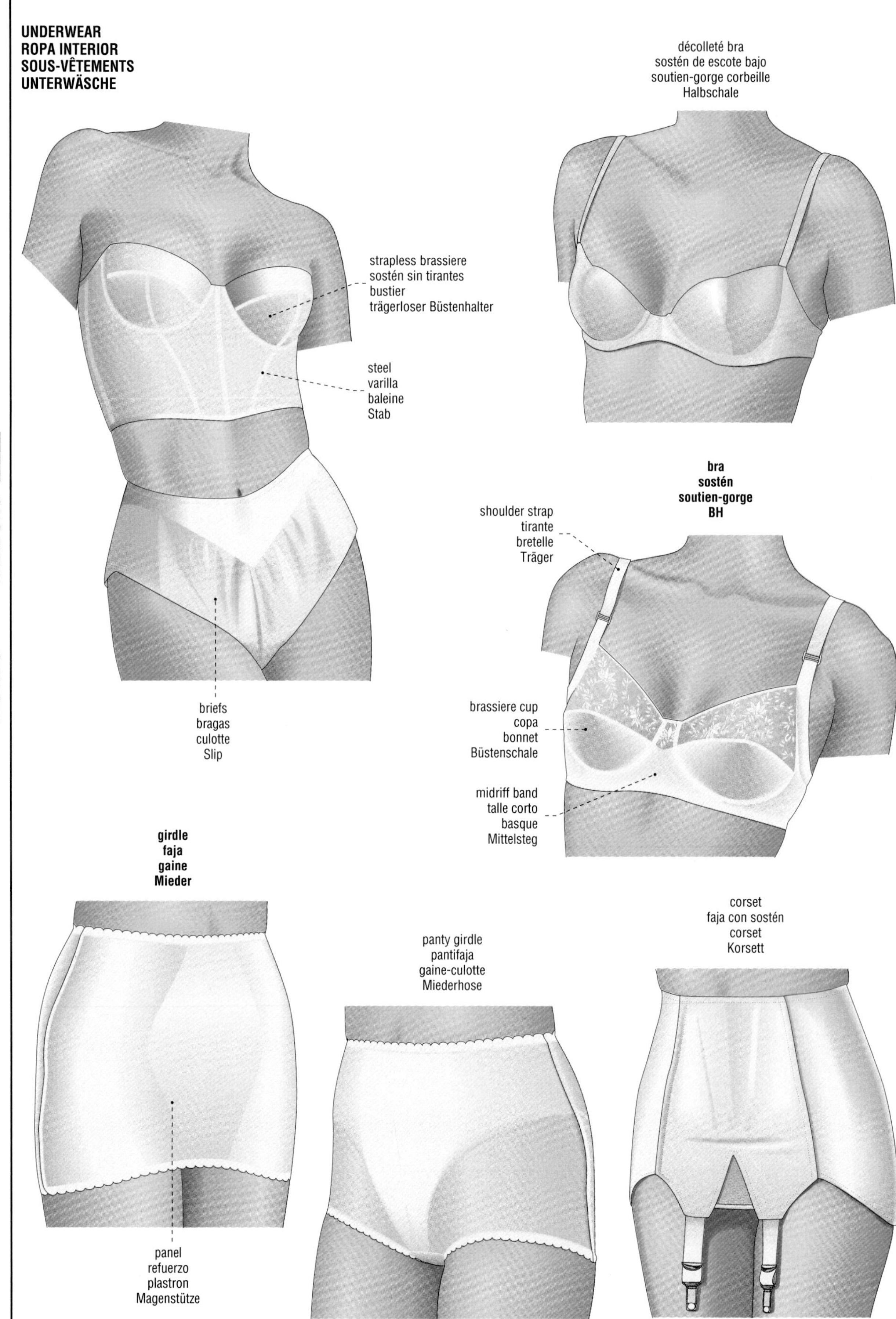

décolleté bra
sostén de escote bajo
soutien-gorge corbeille
Halbschale
strapless brassiere
sostén sin tirantes
bustier
trägerloser Büstenhalter
steel
varilla
baleine
Stab
briefs
bragas
culotte
Slip
bra
sostén
soutien-gorge
BH
shoulder strap
tirante
bretelle
Träger
brassiere cup
copa
bonnet
Büstenschale
midriff band
talle corto
basque
Mittelsteg
girdle
faja
gaine
Mieder
panty girdle
pantifaja
gaine-culotte
Miederhose
corset
faja con sostén
corset
Korsett
panel
refuerzo
plastron
Magenstütze

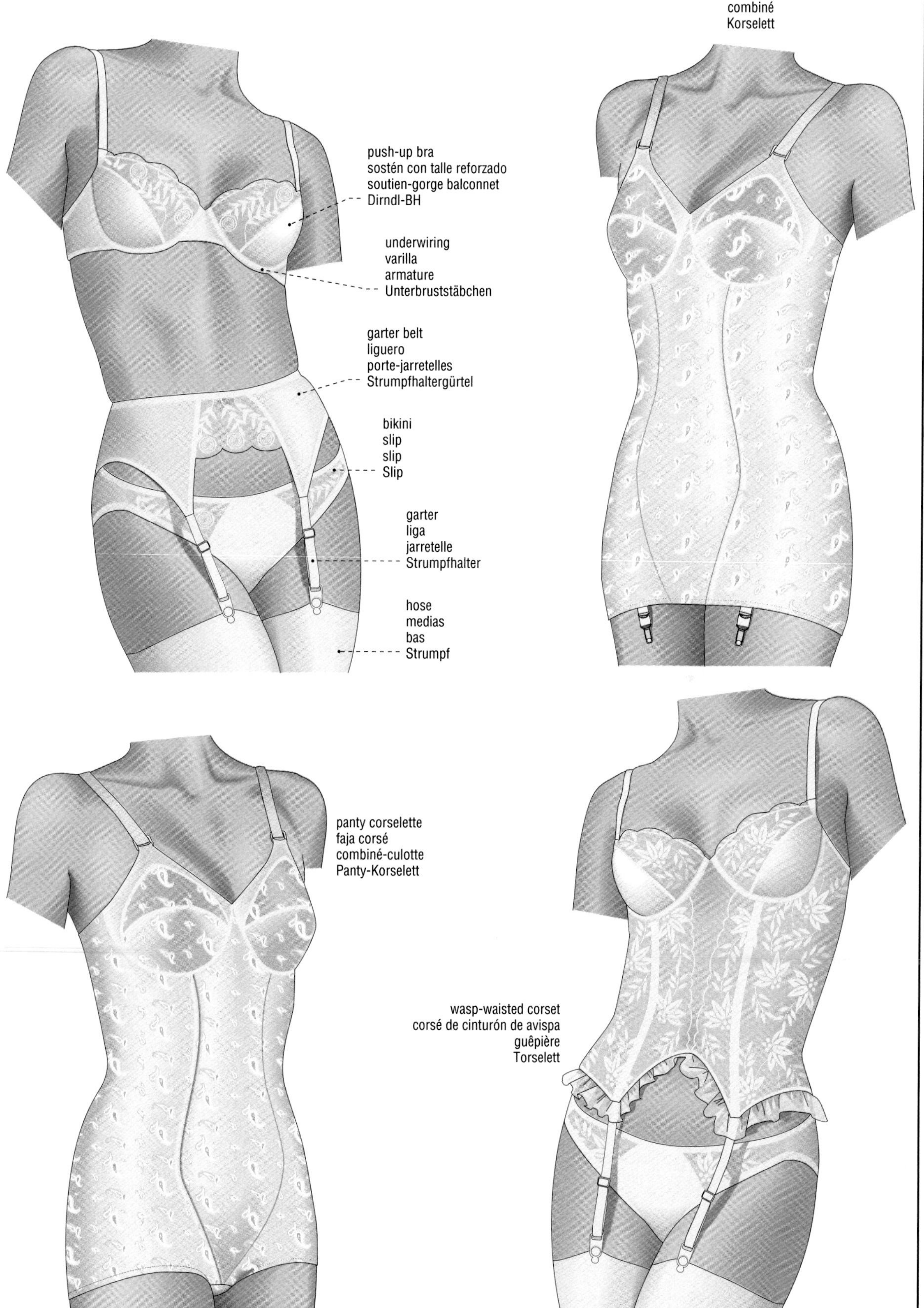
corselette
faja con sostén
combiné
Korselett
push-up bra
sostén con talle reforzado
soutien-gorge balconnet
Dirndl-BH
underwiring
varilla
armature
Unterbruststäbchen
garter belt
liguero
porte-jarretelles
Strumpfhaltergürtel
bikini
slip
slip
Slip
garter
liga
jarretelle
Strumpfhalter
hose
medias
bas
Strumpf
panty corselette
faja corsé
combiné-culotte
Panty-Korselett
wasp-waisted corset
corsé de cinturón de avispa
guêpière
Torselett

WOMEN'S CLOTHING
ROPA DE MUJER
VÊTEMENTS DE FEMME
DAMENKLEIDUNG

NIGHTWEAR
LENCERÍA
VÊTEMENTS DE NUIT
NACHTWÄSCHE

nightgown
camisón
chemise de nuit
Nachthemd
baby doll
camisón corto
nuisette
Baby-Doll
kimono
kimono
kimono
Kimono
pajamas
pijama
pyjama
Schlafanzug
negligee
salto de cama
déshabillé
Negligé
bathrobe
bata de baño
peignoir
Bademantel

CHILDREN'S CLOTHING
ROPA DE NIÑOS
VÊTEMENTS D'ENFANT
KINDERKLEIDUNG

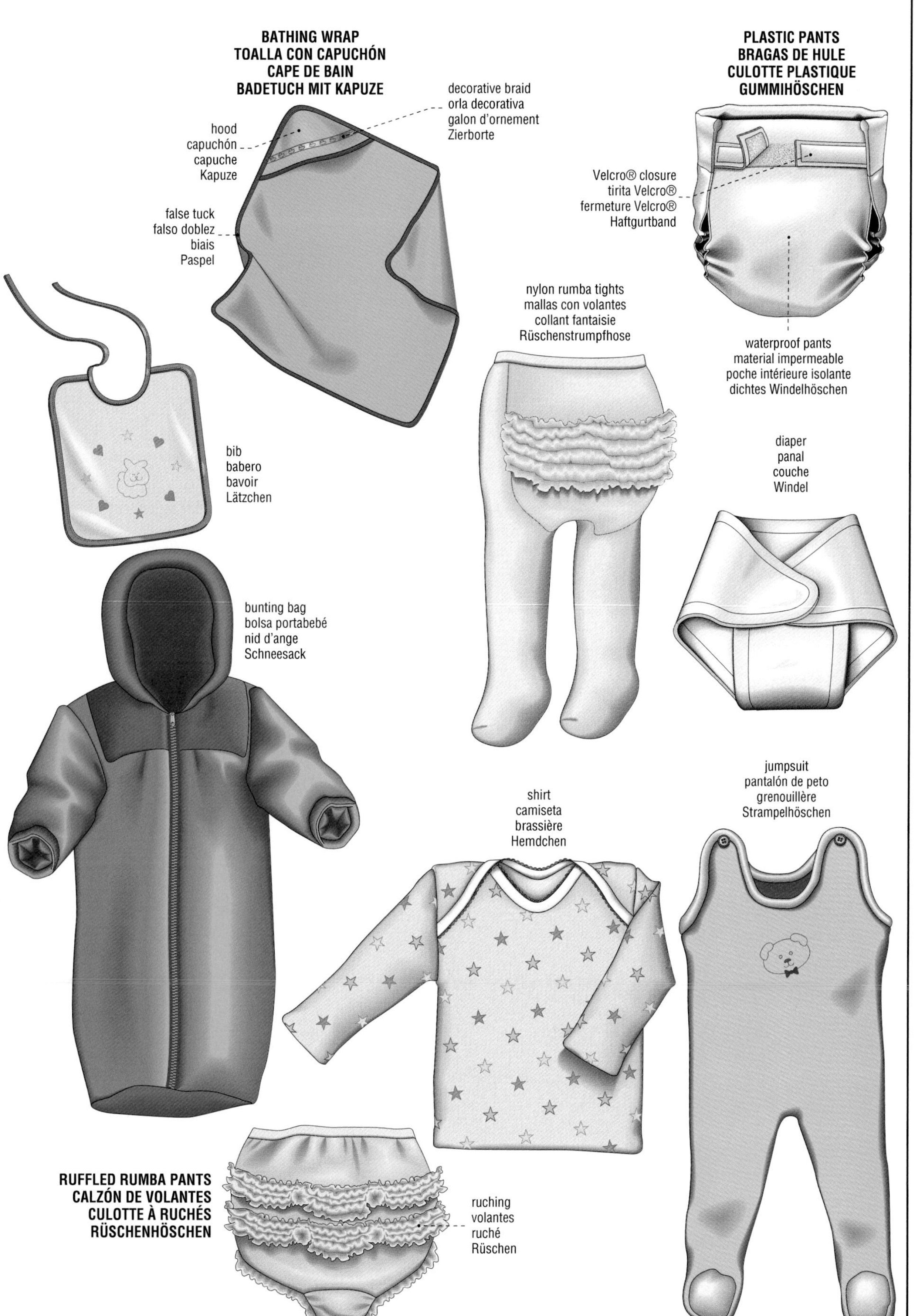
BATHING WRAP
TOALLA CON CAPUCHÓN
CAPE DE BAIN
BADETUCH MIT KAPUZE
hood
capuchón
capuche
Kapuze
decorative braid
orla decorativa
galon d'ornement
Zierborte
false tuck
falso doblez
biais
Paspel
PLASTIC PANTS
BRAGAS DE HULE
CULOTTE PLASTIQUE
GUMMIHÖSCHEN
Velcro® closure
tirita Velcro®
fermeture Velcro®
Haftgurtband
waterproof pants
material impermeable
poche intérieure isolante
dichtes Windelhöschen
nylon rumba tights
mallas con volantes
collant fantaisie
Rüschenstrumpfhose
bib
babero
bavoir
Lätzchen
diaper
panal
couche
Windel
bunting bag
bolsa portabebé
nid d'ange
Schneesack
jumpsuit
pantalón de peto
grenouillère
Strampelhöschen
shirt
camiseta
brassière
Hemdchen
RUFFLED RUMBA PANTS
CALZÓN DE VOLANTES
CULOTTE À RUCHÉS
RÜSCHENHÖSCHEN
ruching
volantes
ruché
Rüschen

CHILDREN'S CLOTHING
ROPA DE NIÑOS
VÊTEMENTS D'ENFANT
KINDERKLEIDUNG

BLANKET SLEEPERS
MAMELUCO
DORMEUSE-COUVERTURE
WAGENANZUG
ribbing
tirilla elástica
bord-côte
Rippenbündchen
zipper
cremallera
fermeture à glissière
Reißverschluß
vinyl grip sole
suela de hule
semelle antidérapante
Vinyl-Laufsohle
SLEEPERS
MAMELUCOS
COMBINAISON DE NUIT
SCHLAFANZUG
raglan sleeve
manga ranglán
manche raglan
Raglanärmel
ribbing
tirilla elástica
bord-côte
Rippenbündchen
screen print
dibujo
motif
Druckmotiv
snap-fastening front
broches delanteros
pression devant
vordere Druckknopfleiste
inside-leg snap-fastening
broches de la pierna
entrejambe pressionné
Druckknopfleiste an der Beininnenseite
HIGH-BACK OVERALLS
PANTALÓN CON TIRANTES
SALOPETTE À DOS MONTANT
LATZHOSE MIT HOHEM RÜCKENTEIL
adjustable strap
tirante ajustable
bretelle réglable
verstellbarer Träger
patch pocket
bolsillo de parche
poche plaquée
aufgesetzte Tasche
bib
peto
bavette
Lätzchen
top stitching
sobrepespunte
surpiqûre
Zier-Steppnaht
fly
bragueta
braguette
Schlitz
inside-leg snap-fastening
broches de presión
entrejambe pressionné
Druckknopfleiste an der Beininnenseite
GROW SLEEPERS
MAMELUCOS DE DOS PIEZAS
DORMEUSE DE CROISSANCE
ZWEITEILIGER SCHLAFANZUG
screen print
dibujo
motif
Aufdruck
crew neck
cuello redondo
encolure ras-de-cou
halsnaher Ausschnitt
snap-fastening waist
pretina con broches
pression à la taille
Bund mit Druckknöpfen
foot
pujamen
pied
Fuß

TRAINING SET
CONJUNTO DEPORTIVO
TENUE D'EXERCICE
SPORTSET
tank top
camiseta
débardeur
Trägerhemdchen
shorts
pantalón corto
short
kurze Hose
CROSSOVER BACK STRAPS OVERALLS
MONO DE TIRANTES CRUZADOS ATRÁS
SALOPETTE À BRETELLES CROISÉES
LATZHOSE MIT GEKREUZTEN RÜCKENTRÄGERN
button strap
tirante con botones
bretelle boutonnée
Träger mit Knopf
bib
peto
bavette
Lätzchen
polojama
pijama
polojama
Schlafanzug in Schlupfform
SNOWSUIT
TRAJE DE INVIERNO CON CAPUCHÓN
ESQUIMAU
SCHNEEANZUG
drawstring hood
capuchón con cordón
capuche coulissée
Kapuze mit Zugband
fly front closing
cremallera
fermeture sous patte
Verschluß mit verdeckter Knopfleiste
rompers
pelele
barboteuse
Spielanzug
jumpsuit
traje pantalón
combinaison
Overall
T-shirt dress
camiseta de cuerpo entero
robe tee-shirt
T-Shirt Kleid

SPORTSWEAR
ROPA DEPORTIVA
TENUE D'EXERCICE
SPORTKLEIDUNG

RUNNING SHOE
ZAPATO DEPORTIVO
CHAUSSURE DE SPORT
JOGGINGSCHUH

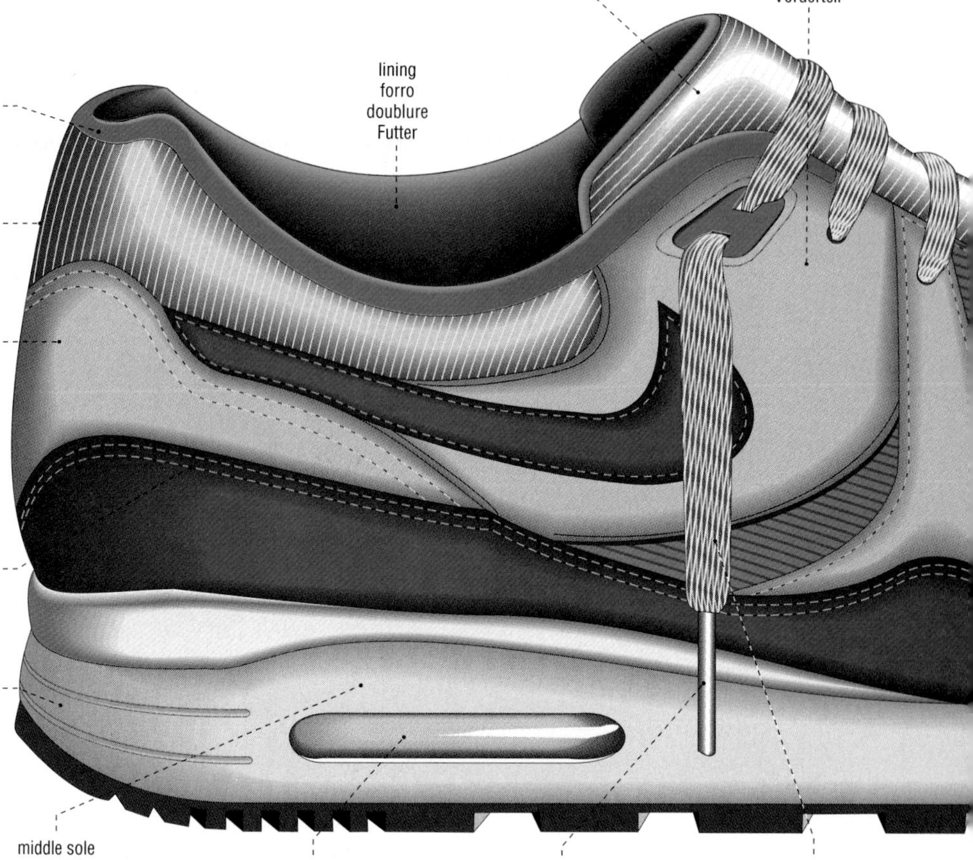

tongue
lengüeta
languette
Zunge

nose of the quarter
ala del cuarto
aile de quartier
Vorderteil

collar
ribete
col
Fersenrand

lining
forro
doublure
Futter

counter
contrafuerte
contrefort
Hinterkappe

quarter
cuarto
quartier
Quartier

stitch
pespunteado
surpiqûre
Naht

heel
talón
talon
Absatz

middle sole
cambrillón
semelle intercalaire
Zwischensohle

air unit
cámara de aire
coussin d'air
Luftpolster

aglet
herrete
ferret
Schnürsenkelende

shoelace
cordón
lacet
Schnürsenkel

TRAINING SUIT
TRAJE DE ENTRENAMIENTO
SURVÊTEMENT
TRAININGSANZUG

hooded sweat shirt
camisa de entrenamiento con capucha
pull à capuche
Sweatshirt mit Kapuze

sweat pants
pantalones de entrenamiento
pantalon molleton
Trainingshose

sweat shirt
camisa de entrenamiento
pull d'entraînement
Sweatshirt

EXERCISE WEAR
ROPA PARA EJERCICIO
VÊTEMENT D'EXERCICE
SPORTKLEIDUNG

swimming trunks
pantalón de baño
slip de bain
Badehose
swimsuit
traje de baño
maillot de bain
Badeanzug
leotard
leotardo
justaucorps
Trikot
eyelet
ojillo
œillet
Öse
vamp
empella
claque
Vorderblatt
punch hole
perforación
perforation
gestanztes Loch
footless tights
traje de malla
collant sans pied
Gymnastikhose ohne Fuß
stud
montante
crampon
Stollen
outsole
suela
semelle d'usure
Laufsohle
boxer shorts
pantalón de boxeo
short boxeur
Shorts
leg-warmer
calentador de pierna
jambière
Legwarmer
pants
pantalones
pantalon
Hose
anorak
anorak
anorak
Anorak
tank top
camiseta
débardeur
Trägerhemd

SHOES
ZAPATOS
CHAUSSURES
SCHUHE

PARTS OF A SHOE
PARTES DE UN ZAPATO
PARTIES D'UNE CHAUSSURE
TEILE DES SCHUHS

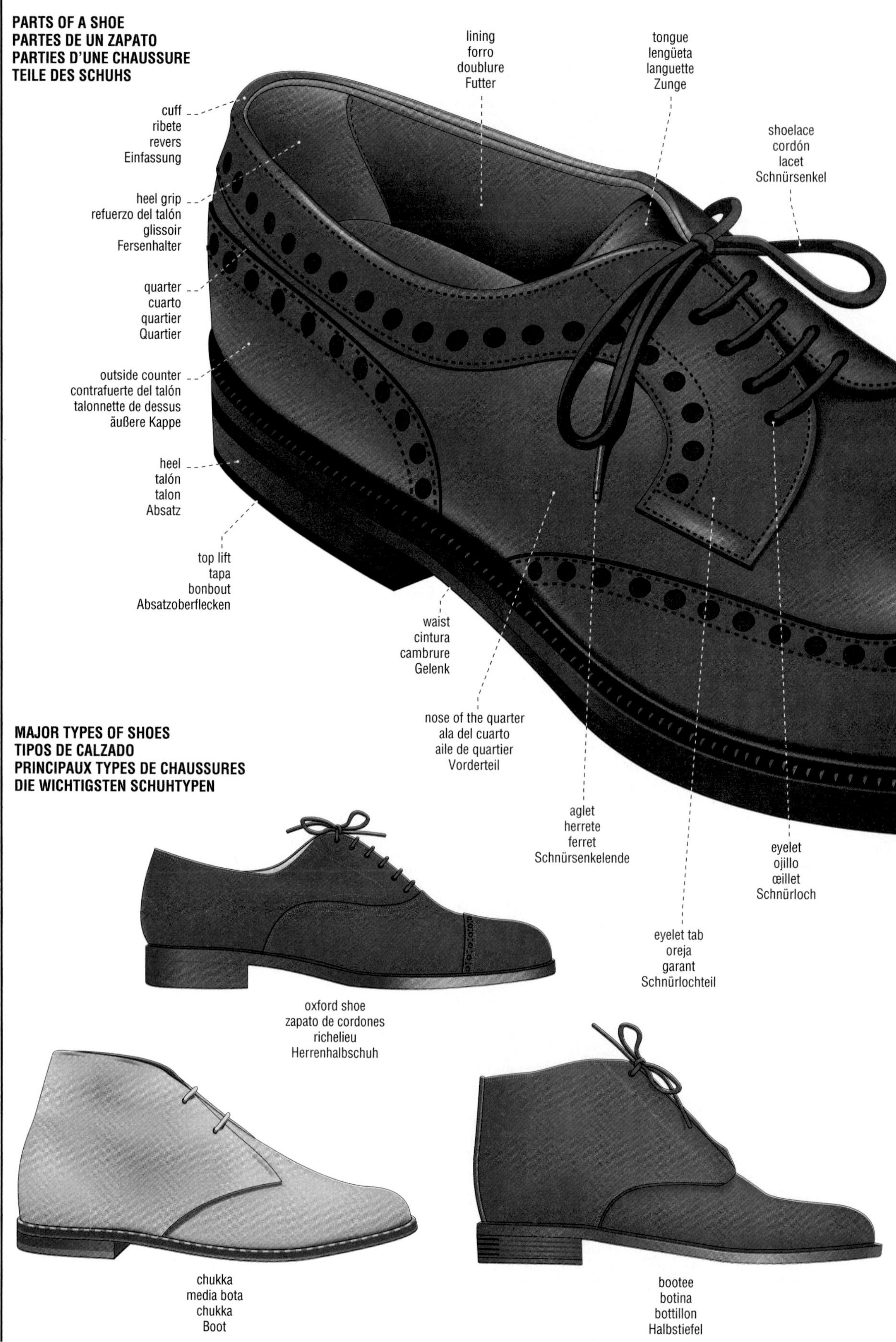

cuff
ribete
revers
Einfassung
heel grip
refuerzo del talón
glissoir
Fersenhalter
quarter
cuarto
quartier
Quartier
outside counter
contrafuerte del talón
talonnette de dessus
äußere Kappe
heel
talón
talon
Absatz
top lift
tapa
bonbout
Absatzoberflecken
lining
forro
doublure
Futter
tongue
lengüeta
languette
Zunge
shoelace
cordón
lacet
Schnürsenkel
waist
cintura
cambrure
Gelenk
nose of the quarter
ala del cuarto
aile de quartier
Vorderteil
aglet
herrete
ferret
Schnürsenkelende
eyelet
ojillo
œillet
Schnürloch
eyelet tab
oreja
garant
Schnürlochteil

MAJOR TYPES OF SHOES
TIPOS DE CALZADO
PRINCIPAUX TYPES DE CHAUSSURES
DIE WICHTIGSTEN SCHUHTYPEN

oxford shoe
zapato de cordones
richelieu
Herrenhalbschuh

chukka
media bota
chukka
Boot

bootee
botina
bottillon
Halbstiefel

CLOTHING VESTIDO
VÊTEMENTS KLEIDUNG

MAJOR TYPES OF SHOES
TIPOS DE CALZADO
PRINCIPAUX TYPES DE CHAUSSURES
DIE WICHTIGSTEN SCHUHTYPEN

tennis shoe
zapato de tenis
tennis
Tennisschuh
blucher oxford
zapato de vestir
derby
Schnürschuh
vamp
empella
claque
Vorderblatt
stitch
costura
surpiqûre
Naht
moccasin
mocasín
mocassin
Mokassin
punch hole
perforaciones
perforation
gestanztes Loch
perforated toe cap
puntera
bout fleuri
perforierte Vorderkappe
loafer
zapato de calle
loafer
Slipper
welt
vira
trépointe
Rahmen
outsole
suela
semelle d'usure
Laufsohle
mule
pantufla
mule
Pantoffel
heavy duty boot
bota de trabajo
brodequin
Arbeitsstiefel
rubber
chanclo de goma
claque
Überziehschuh

SHOES
CALZADO
CHAUSSURES
SCHUHE

MAJOR TYPES OF SHOES
TIPOS DE CALZADO
PRINCIPAUX TYPES DE CHAUSSURES
DIE WICHTIGSTEN SCHUHTYPEN

pump
zapato de tacón alto
escarpin
Pumps
sling back shoe
zapato de tacón alto con presillas
escarpin-sandale
Slingpumps
sandal
sandalia
sandale
Sandalette mit Fersenriemen
T-strap shoe
zapato de correa
salomé
Stegspangenschuh
one-bar shoe
escarpín con correa
Charles IX
Einspangenschuh
ballerina
zapatilla de ballet
ballerine
Ballerinaschuh
casual shoe
zapato de calle
trotteur
Straßenschuh
boot
bota
botte
Stiefel

sandal
sandalia
nu-pied
Sandale mit Zehenriemchen

thong
chancleta
tong
Römerpantolette

ankle boot
botín
bottine
knöchelhohe Stiefelette

clog
chanclo
socque
Pantolette

espadrille
alpargata
espadrille
Espadrille

thigh-boot
bota de medio muslo
cuissarde
Schaftstiefel

sandal
sandalia
sandalette
Sandale

SHOES
CALZADO
CHAUSSURES
SCHUHE

ACCESSORIES
ACCESORIOS
ACCESSOIRES
ZUBEHÖR

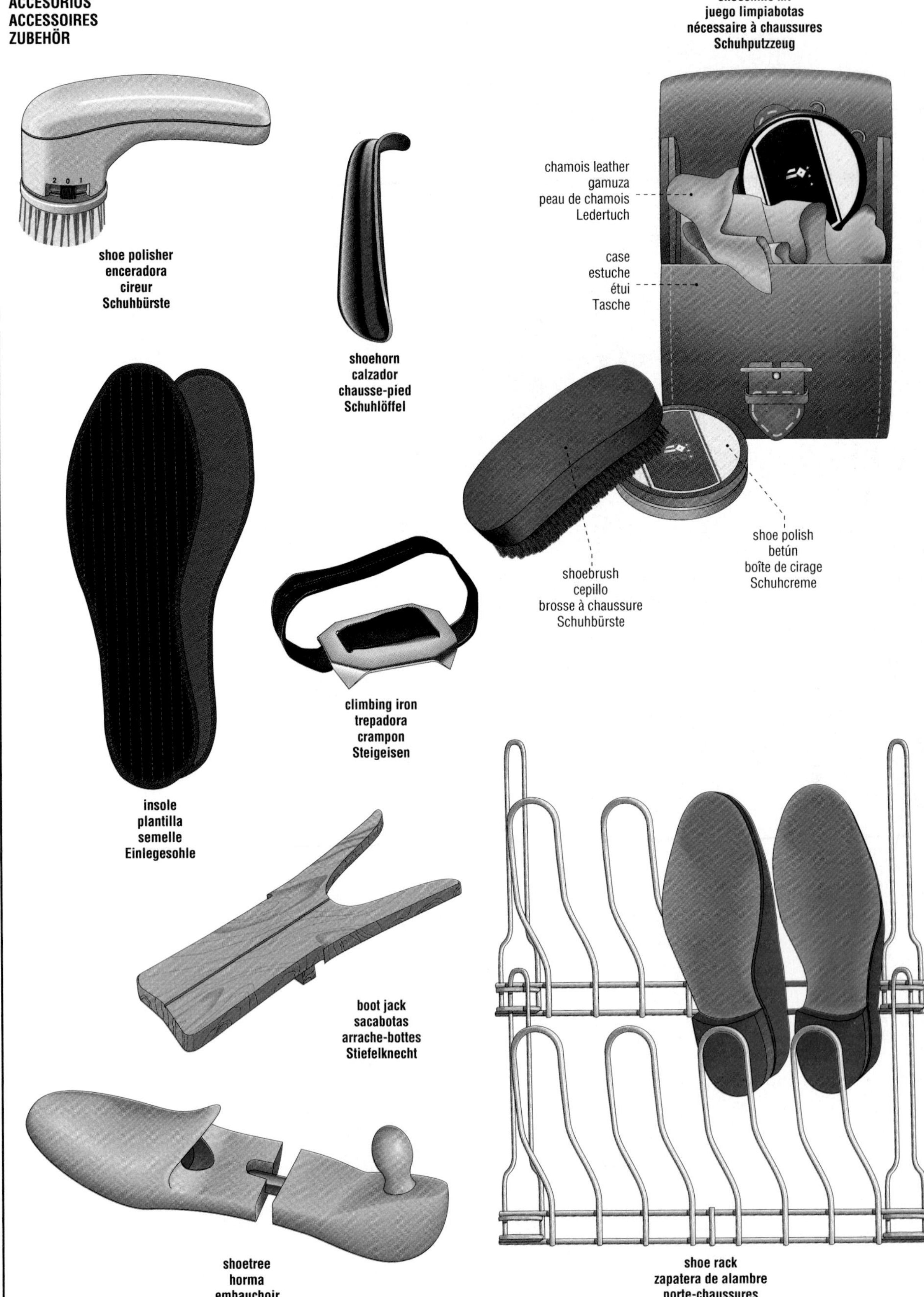

2 0 1
chamois leather
gamuza
peau de chamois
Ledertuch
case
estuche
étui
Tasche
shoebrush
cepillo
brosse à chaussure
Schuhbürste
shoe polish
betún
boîte de cirage
Schuhcreme

shoe polisher
enceradora
cireur
Schuhbürste

shoehorn
calzador
chausse-pied
Schuhlöffel

shoeshine kit
juego limpiabotas
nécessaire à chaussures
Schuhputzzeug

insole
plantilla
semelle
Einlegesohle

climbing iron
trepadora
crampon
Steigeisen

boot jack
sacabotas
arrache-bottes
Stiefelknecht

shoetree
horma
embauchoir
Schuhspanner

shoe rack
zapatera de alambre
porte-chaussures
Schuhständer

PERSONAL ADORNMENT
ADORNOS PERSONALES
PARURE
SCHMUCK UND SCHÖNHEITSPFLEGE

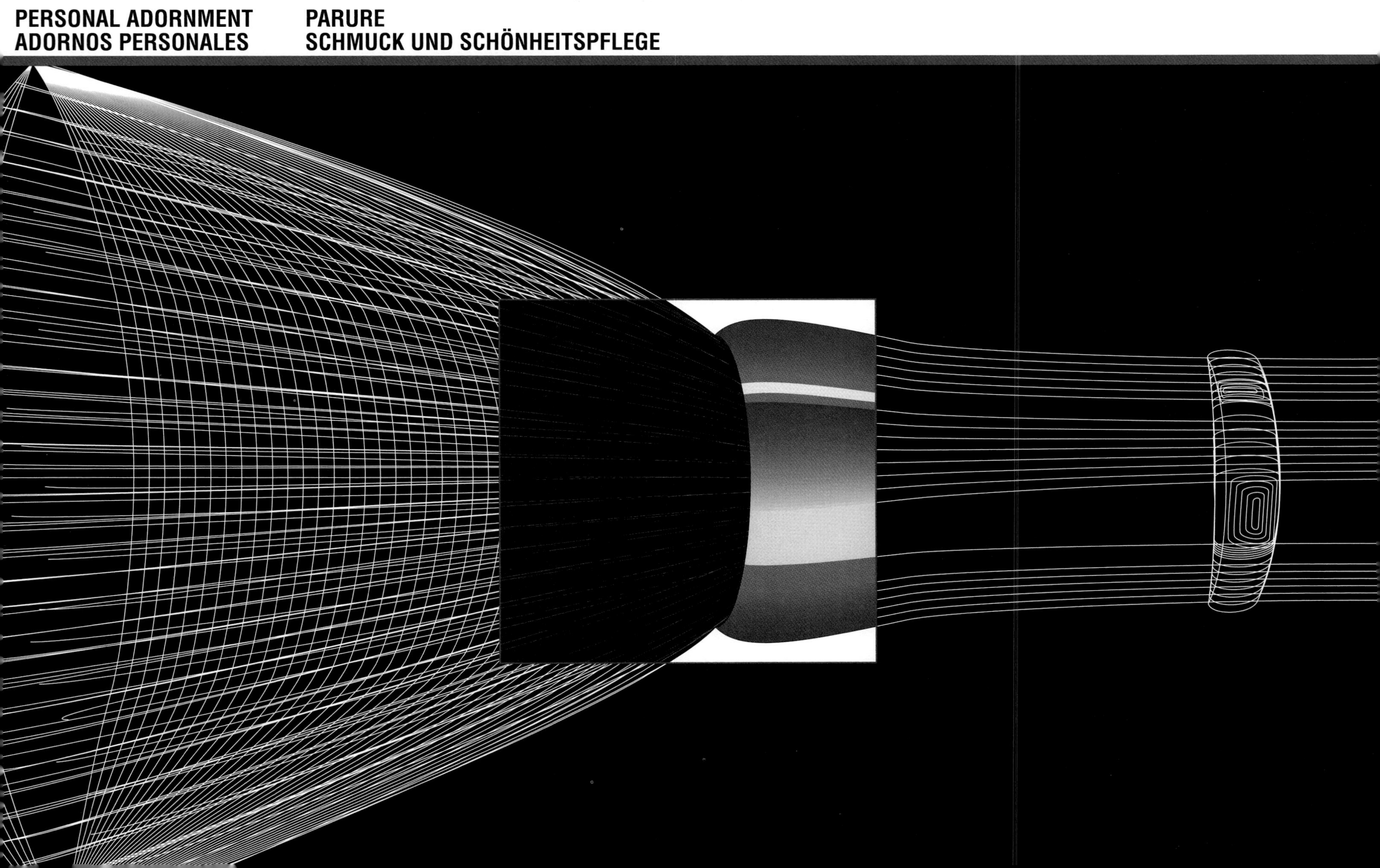

CONTENTS

JEWELRY
JOYERÍA
BIJOUTERIE
SCHMUCK

EARRINGS
PENDIENTES
BOUCLES D'OREILLE
OHRRINGE

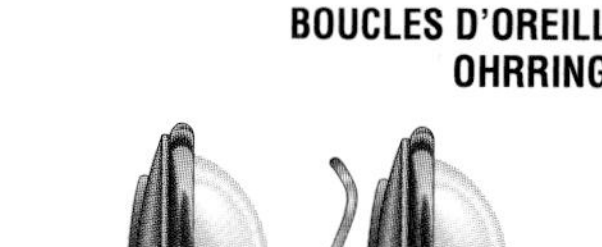

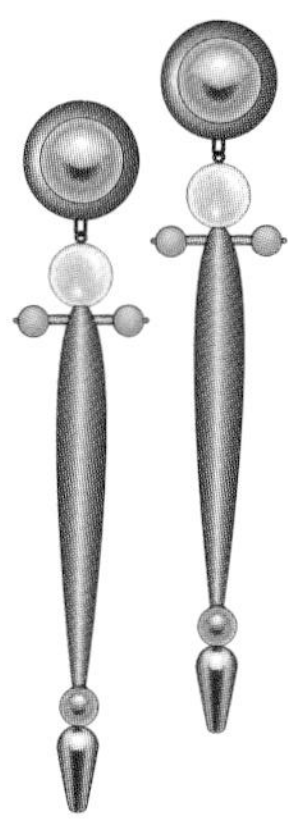

drop earrings
pendientes
pendants d'oreille
Ohrgehänge

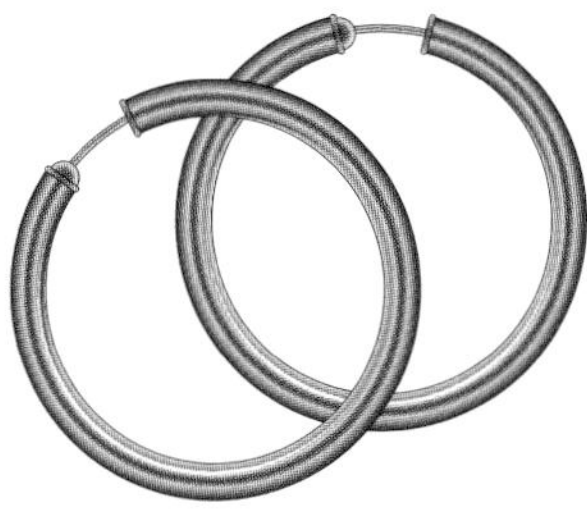

hoop earrings
zarcillos de aro
anneaux
Kreolen

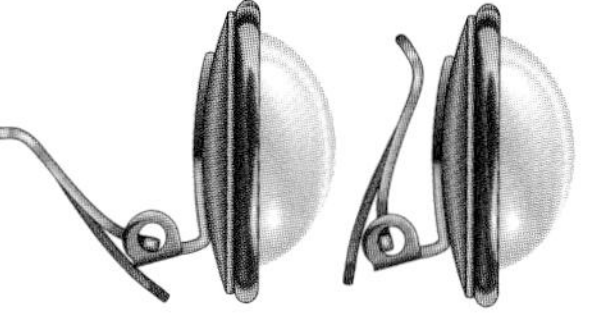

clip earrings
pendientes de clip
boucles d'oreille à pince
Klips

post earrings
pendientes de espiga
boucles d'oreille à tige
Ohrstecker

screw earrings
pendientes de tornillo
boucles d'oreille à vis
Ohrringe mit Schraubverschluß

NECKLACES
COLLARES
COLLIERS
HALSKETTEN

pendant
pendiente
pendentif
Anhänger

locket
relicario
médaillon
Medaillon

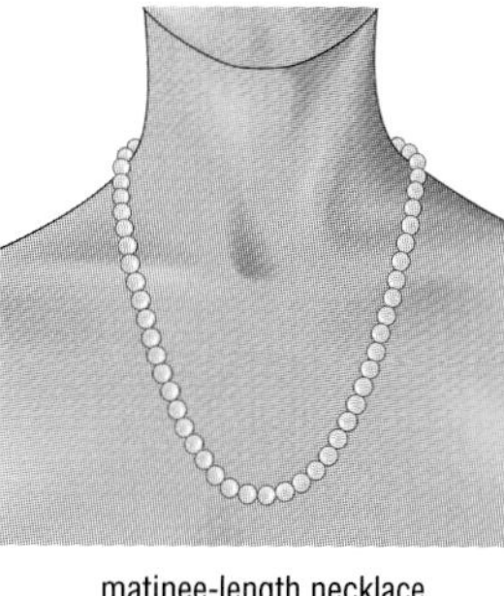

matinee-length necklace
collar de una vuelta
collier de perles, longueur matinée
Halskette in Matineelänge

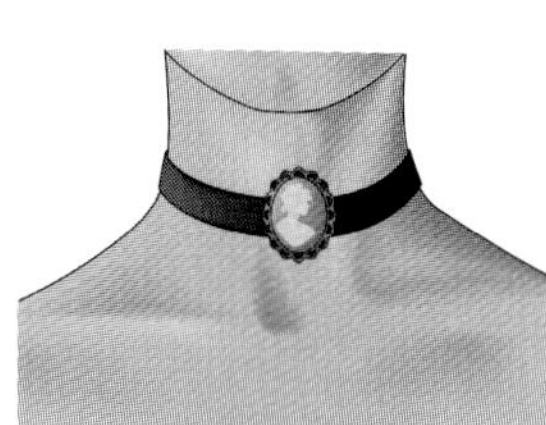

velvet-band choker
garagantilla de terciopelo
collier-de-chien
Samtkropfband

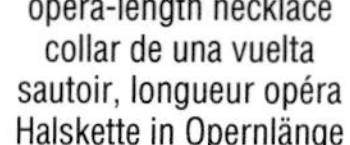

opera-length necklace
collar de una vuelta
sautoir, longueur opéra
Halskette in Opernlänge

rope
sarta
sautoir
Endlosperlenkette

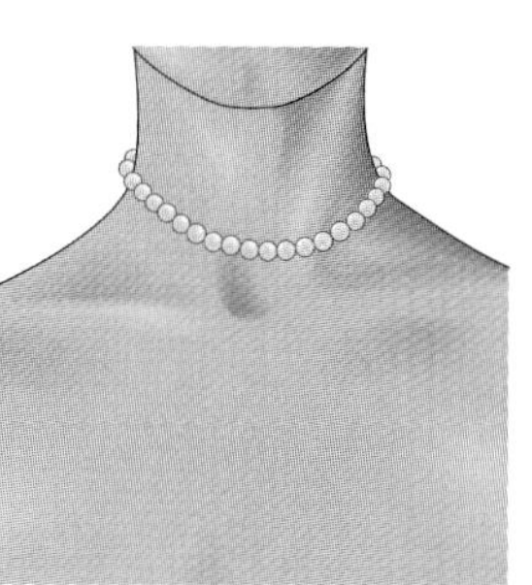

choker
gargantilla
ras-de-cou
Chokerkette

bib necklace
collar de 5 hilos
collier de soirée
mehrreihige Halskette

JEWELRY
JOYERÍA
BIJOUTERIE
SCHMUCK

CUT FOR GEMSTONES
TALLAS DE PIEDRAS PRECIOSAS
TAILLE DES PIERRES
SCHLIFFORMEN FÜR EDELSTEINE

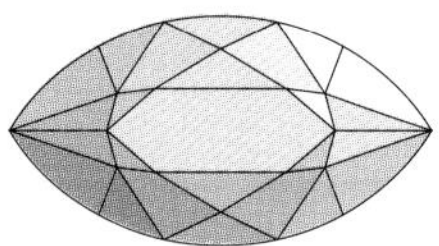

navette cut
marquesa
taille marquise
Navette

baguette cut
baguette
taille baguette
Baguetteform

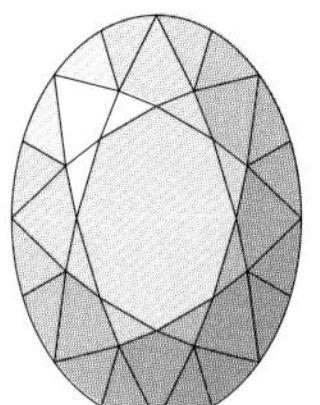

oval cut
oval
taille ovale
ovale Form

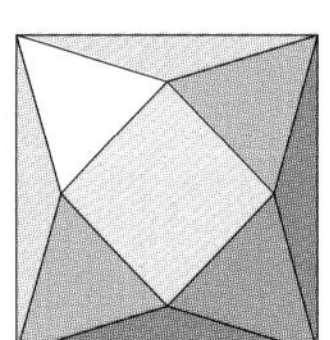

French cut
francés
taille française
French-cut

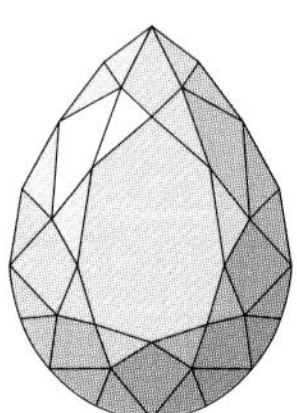

pear-shaped cut
pera
taille en poire
Birnkernform

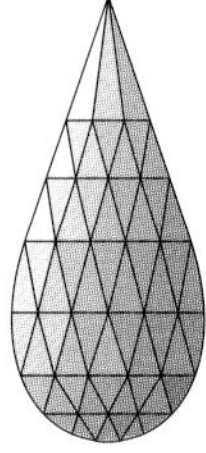

briolette cut
gota
taille en goutte
Briolettform

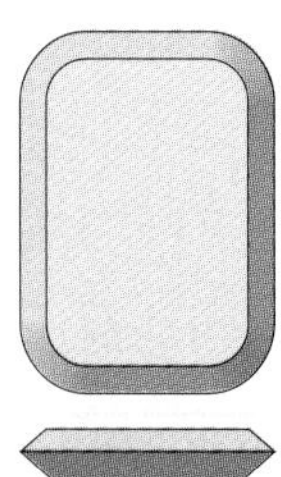

table cut
tabla
taille en table
Tafelschliff

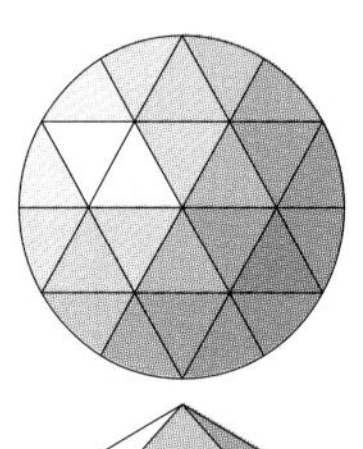

rose cut
rosa holandesa
taille en rose
Rosenschliff

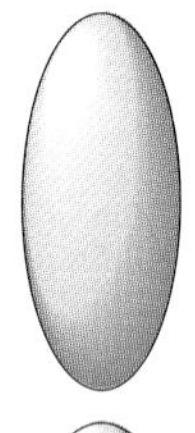

cabochon cut
cabujón
taille cabochon
Cabochonschliff

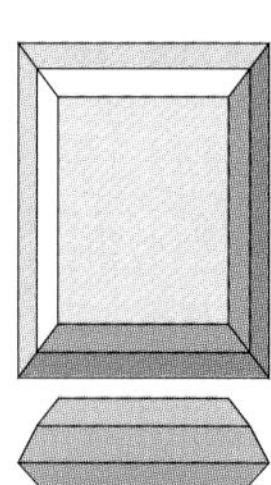

step cut
en escalera
taille en escalier
Treppenschliff

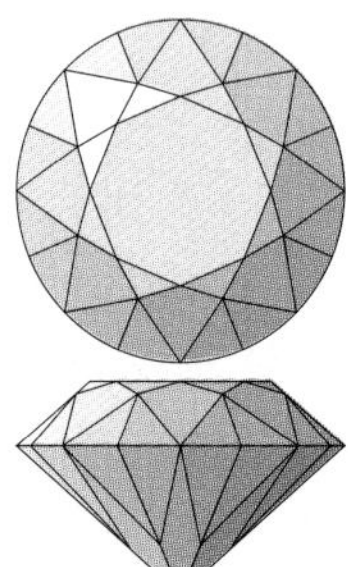

brilliant full cut
brillante
taille brillant
Vollbrillantschliff

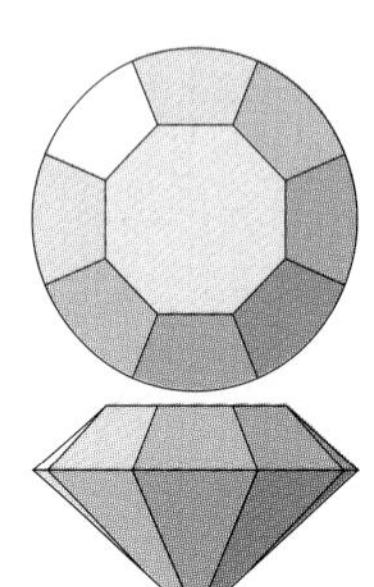

eight cut
ocho facetas
taille huit facettes
Achtkant

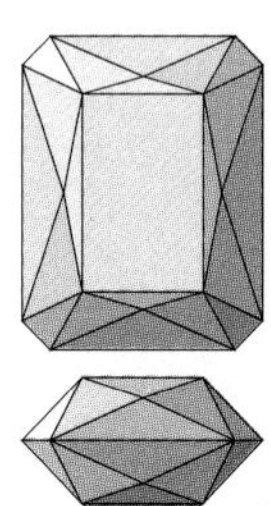

scissors cut
en tijera
taille en ciseaux
Scherenschliff

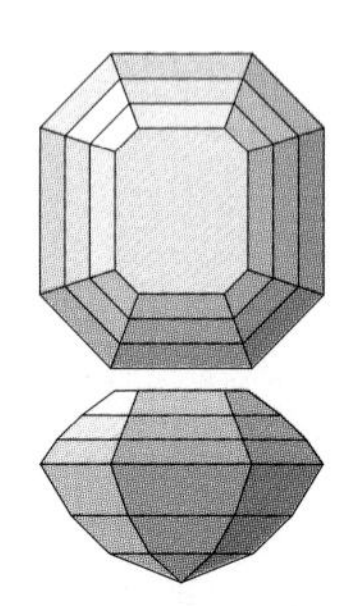

emerald cut
esmeralda
taille émeraude
Smaragdschliff

BRILLIANT CUT FACETS
CORTE DE UN DIAMANTE
TAILLE D'UN DIAMANT
FACETTEN DES BRILLANTSCHLIFFS

BOTTOM FACE
CARA INFERIOR
FACE INFÉRIEURE
RÜCKSEITE

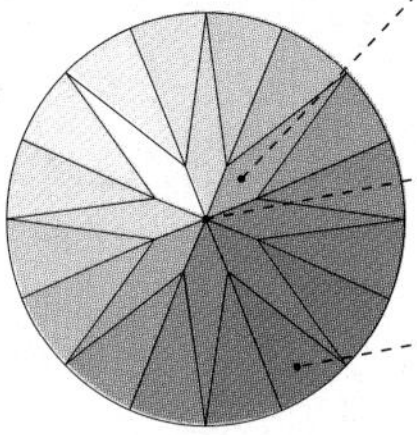

pavilion facet (8)
faceta de pabellón
pavillon (8)
Unterteilhauptfacette (8)

culet
culata
colette
Kulette

lower girdle facet (16)
faceta inferior del contorno
halefis de culasse (16)
untere Rondistenfacette (16)

TOP FACE
CARA SUPERIOR
FACE SUPÉRIEURE
VORDERSEITE

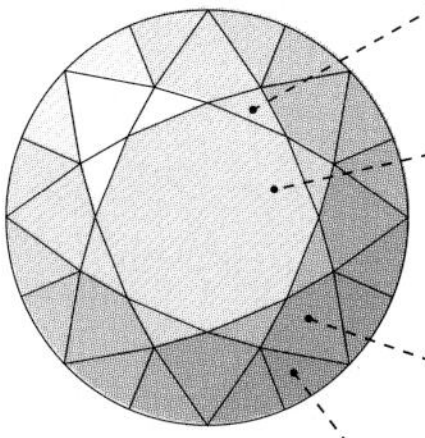

star facet (8)
faceta de estrella (8)
étoile (8)
Tafelfacette (8)

table
tabla
table
Tafel

bezel facet (8)
faceta bisel (8)
bezel (8)
Oberteilhauptfacette (8)

upper girdle facet (16)
faceta superior del contorno
halefis de table (16)
obere Rondistenfacette (16)

SIDE FACE
PERFIL
PROFIL
SEITENANSICHT

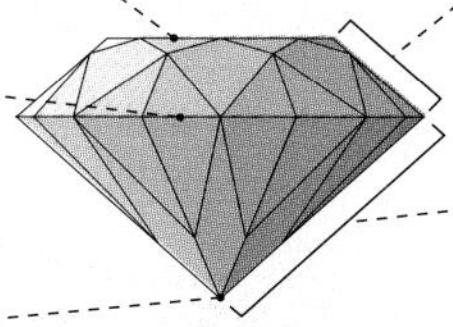

table
tabla
table
Tafel

girdle
cinturón
rondiste
Rondiste

culet
culata
colette
Kulette

crown
corona
couronne de table
Krone

pavilion
pabellón
culasse
Unterteil

PRECIOUS STONES
PIEDRAS PRECIOSAS
PIERRES PRÉCIEUSES
EDELSTEINE

emerald
esmeralda
émeraude
Smaragd

ruby
rubí
rubis
Rubin

sapphire
zafiro
saphir
Saphir

diamond
diamante
diamant
Diamant

SEMIPRECIOUS STONES
PIEDRAS SEMIPRECIOSAS
PIERRES FINES
HALBEDELSTEINE

amethyst
amatista
améthyste
Amethyst

garnet
granate
grenat
Granat

topaz
topacio
topaze
Topas

aquamarine
aguamarina
aigue-marine
Aquamarin

tourmaline
turmalina
tourmaline
Turmalin

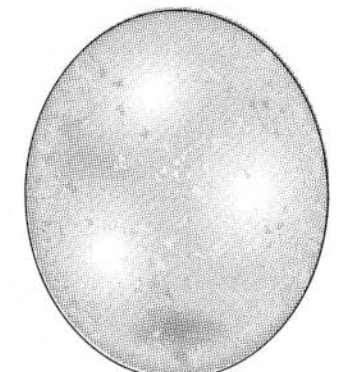
opal
ópalo
opale
Opal

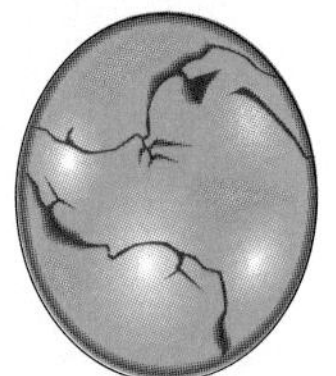
turquoise
turquesa
turquoise
Türkis

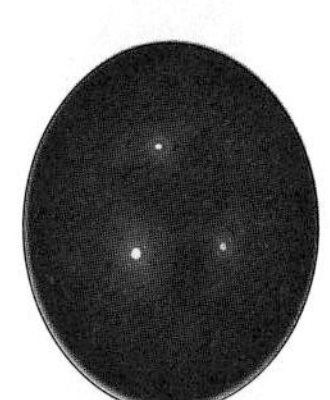
lapis lazuli
lapislázuli
lapis-lazuli
Lapislazuli

JEWELRY
JOYERÍA
BIJOUTERIE
SCHMUCK

RINGS
ANILLOS
BAGUES
RINGE

signet ring
sortija de sello
chevalière
Herrenring

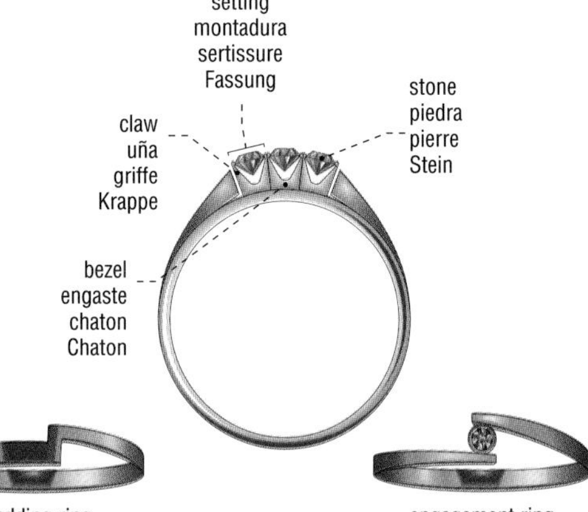

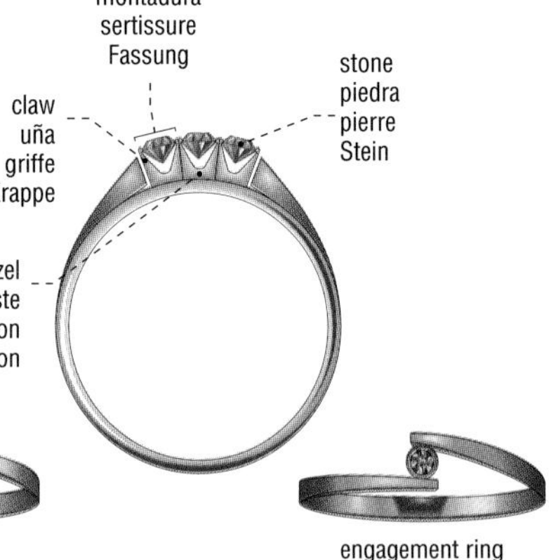
setting
montadura
sertissure
Fassung
claw
uña
griffe
Krappe
stone
piedra
pierre
Stein
bezel
engaste
chaton
Chaton

class ring
anillo de graduación
bague de finissant
Collegering

band ring
anillo de bodas
jonc
Bandring

wedding ring
anillo de bodas
alliance
Ehering

engagement ring
anillo de compromiso
bague de fiançailles
Verlobungsring

solitaire ring
solitario
bague solitaire
Solitärring

BRACELETS
BRAZALETES
BRACELETS
ARMBÄNDER

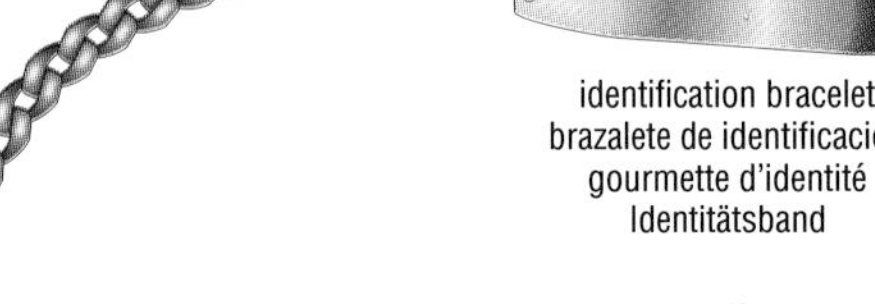

identification bracelet
brazalete de identificación
gourmette d'identité
Identitätsband

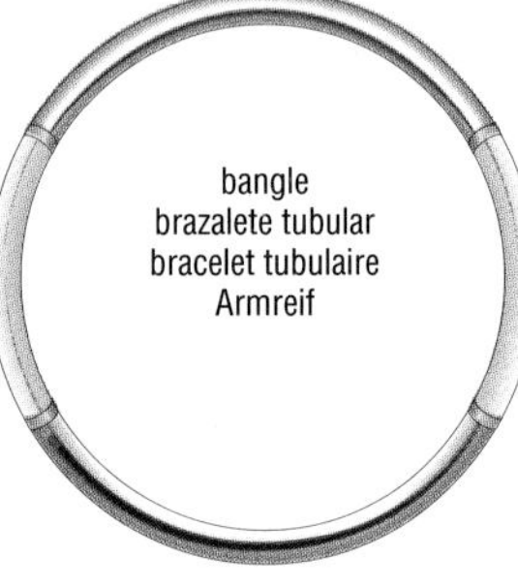

bangle
brazalete tubular
bracelet tubulaire
Armreif

charm bracelet
pulsera de dijes
gourmette
Armband

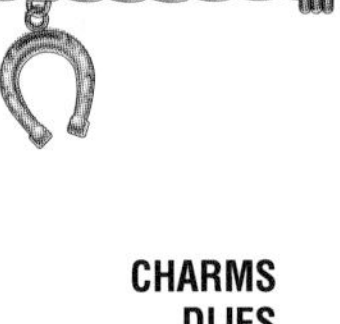

CHARMS
DIJES
BRELOQUES
ANHÄNGER

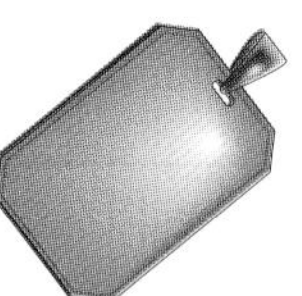

nameplate
placa de identificación
plaque d'identité
Gravurplatte

horseshoe
herradura
fer à cheval
Hufeisen

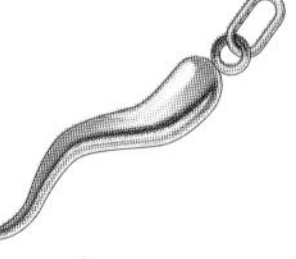

horn
cuerno
corne
Horn

PINS
ALFILERES
ÉPINGLES
ANSTECKNADELN

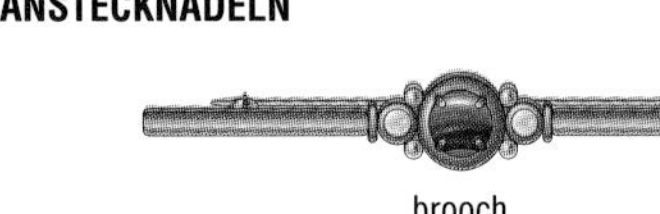

brooch
broche
broche
Brosche

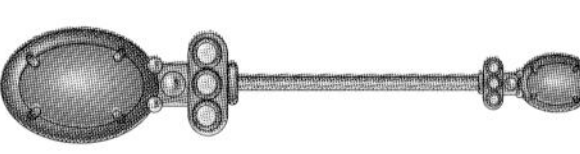

stickpin
alfiler de corbata
broche épingle
Sticker

tiepin
alfiler de corbata
épingle à cravate
Krawattennadel

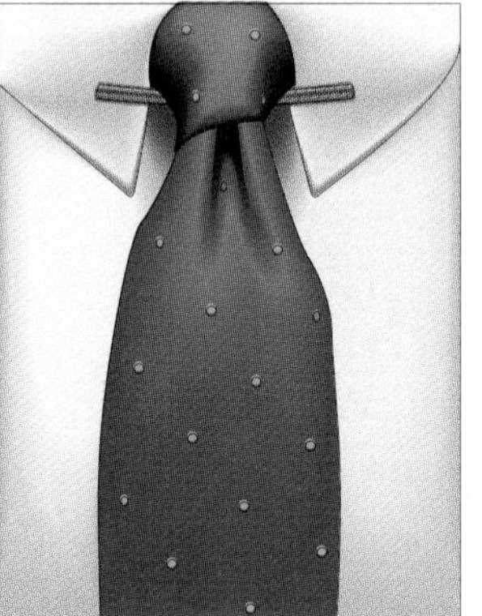

collar bar
yugo
tige pour col
Kragenklammer

tie bar
pisacorbatas
pince à cravate
Krawattenklemme

MANICURE
MANICURA
MANUCURE
MANIKÜRE

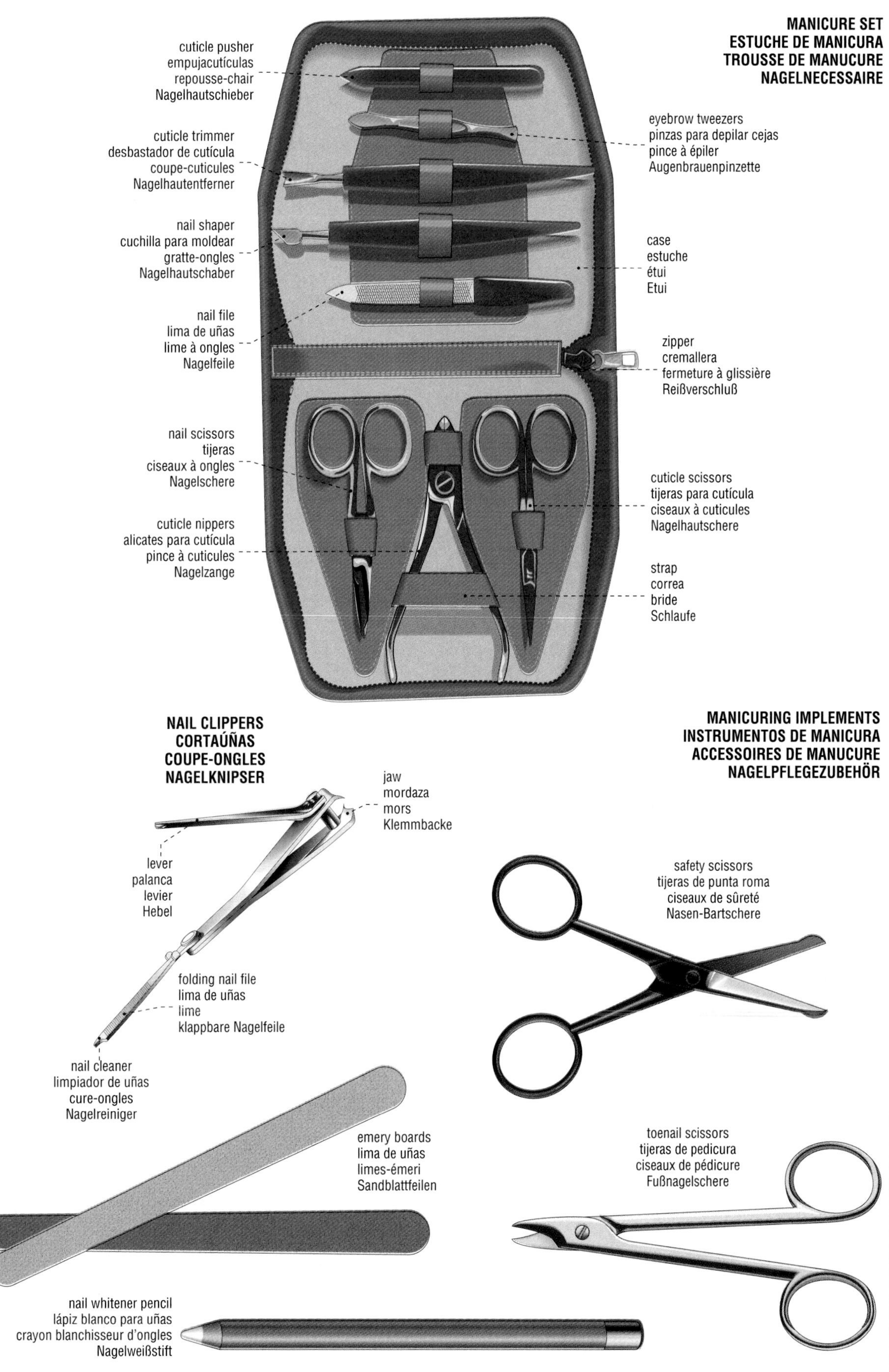
MANICURE SET
ESTUCHE DE MANICURA
TROUSSE DE MANUCURE
NAGELNECESSAIRE
cuticle pusher
empujacutículas
repousse-chair
Nagelhautschieber
cuticle trimmer
desbastador de cutícula
coupe-cuticules
Nagelhautentferner
nail shaper
cuchilla para moldear
gratte-ongles
Nagelhautschaber
nail file
lima de uñas
lime à ongles
Nagelfeile
nail scissors
tijeras
ciseaux à ongles
Nagelschere
cuticle nippers
alicates para cutícula
pince à cuticules
Nagelzange
eyebrow tweezers
pinzas para depilar cejas
pince à épiler
Augenbrauenpinzette
case
estuche
étui
Etui
zipper
cremallera
fermeture à glissière
Reißverschluß
cuticle scissors
tijeras para cutícula
ciseaux à cuticules
Nagelhautschere
strap
correa
bride
Schlaufe
NAIL CLIPPERS
CORTAÚÑAS
COUPE-ONGLES
NAGELKNIPSER
jaw
mordaza
mors
Klemmbacke
lever
palanca
levier
Hebel
folding nail file
lima de uñas
lime
klappbare Nagelfeile
nail cleaner
limpiador de uñas
cure-ongles
Nagelreiniger
MANICURING IMPLEMENTS
INSTRUMENTOS DE MANICURA
ACCESSOIRES DE MANUCURE
NAGELPFLEGEZUBEHÖR
safety scissors
tijeras de punta roma
ciseaux de sûreté
Nasen-Bartschere
emery boards
lima de uñas
limes-émeri
Sandblattfeilen
toenail scissors
tijeras de pedicura
ciseaux de pédicure
Fußnagelschere
nail whitener pencil
lápiz blanco para uñas
crayon blanchisseur d'ongles
Nagelweißstift

MAKEUP
MAQUILLAJE
MAQUILLAGE
MAKE-UP

FACIAL MAKEUP
MAQUILLAJE FACIAL
MAQUILLAGE
MAKE-UP
fan brush
brocha en forma de abanico
pinceau éventail
Fächerpinsel
loose powder
polvos sueltos
poudre libre
loser Puder
liquid foundation
base líquida
fond de teint liquide
flüssige Grundierung
loose powder brush
brocha
pinceau pour poudre libre
Puderpinsel
powder puff
borla
houpette
Puderkissen
blusher brush
brocha aplicadora de rubor
pinceau pour fard à joues
Rougepinsel
compact
polvera
poudrier
Puderdose
pressed powder
polvo compacto
poudre pressée
gepreßter Puder
powder blusher
rubor en polvo
fard à joues en poudre
Puderrouge
LIP MAKEUP
MAQUILLAJE LABIAL
MAQUILLAGE DES LÈVRES
LIPPEN-MAKE-UP
lipbrush
pincel para labios
pinceau à lèvres
Lippenpinsel
lipstick
lápiz labial
rouge à lèvres
Lippenstift
lipliner
delineador de labios
crayon contour des lèvres
Lippenkonturenstift

EYE MAKEUP
MAQUILLAJE PARA OJOS
MAQUILLAGE DES YEUX
AUGEN-MAKE-UP

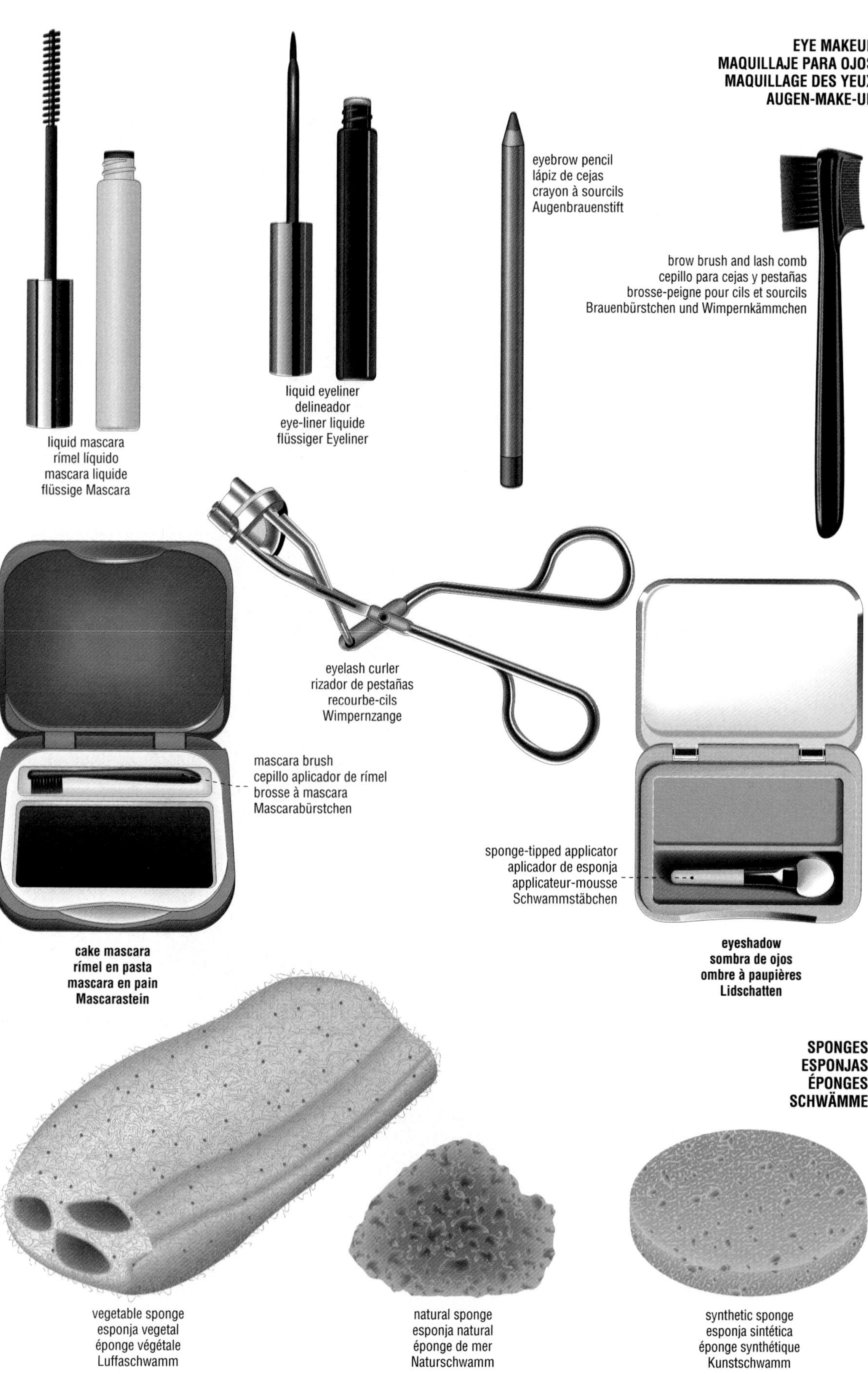
liquid mascara
rímel líquido
mascara liquide
flüssige Mascara
liquid eyeliner
delineador
eye-liner liquide
flüssiger Eyeliner
eyebrow pencil
lápiz de cejas
crayon à sourcils
Augenbrauenstift
brow brush and lash comb
cepillo para cejas y pestañas
brosse-peigne pour cils et sourcils
Brauenbürstchen und Wimpernkämmchen
eyelash curler
rizador de pestañas
recourbe-cils
Wimpernzange
mascara brush
cepillo aplicador de rímel
brosse à mascara
Mascarabürstchen
sponge-tipped applicator
aplicador de esponja
applicateur-mousse
Schwammstäbchen
cake mascara
rímel en pasta
mascara en pain
Mascarastein
eyeshadow
sombra de ojos
ombre à paupières
Lidschatten
SPONGES
ESPONJAS
ÉPONGES
SCHWÄMME
vegetable sponge
esponja vegetal
éponge végétale
Luffaschwamm
natural sponge
esponja natural
éponge de mer
Naturschwamm
synthetic sponge
esponja sintética
éponge synthétique
Kunstschwamm

HAIRDRESSING
PEINADO
COIFFURE
HAARPFLEGE

LIGHTED MIRROR
ESPEJO LUMINOSO
MIROIR LUMINEUX
BELEUCHTETER SPIEGEL

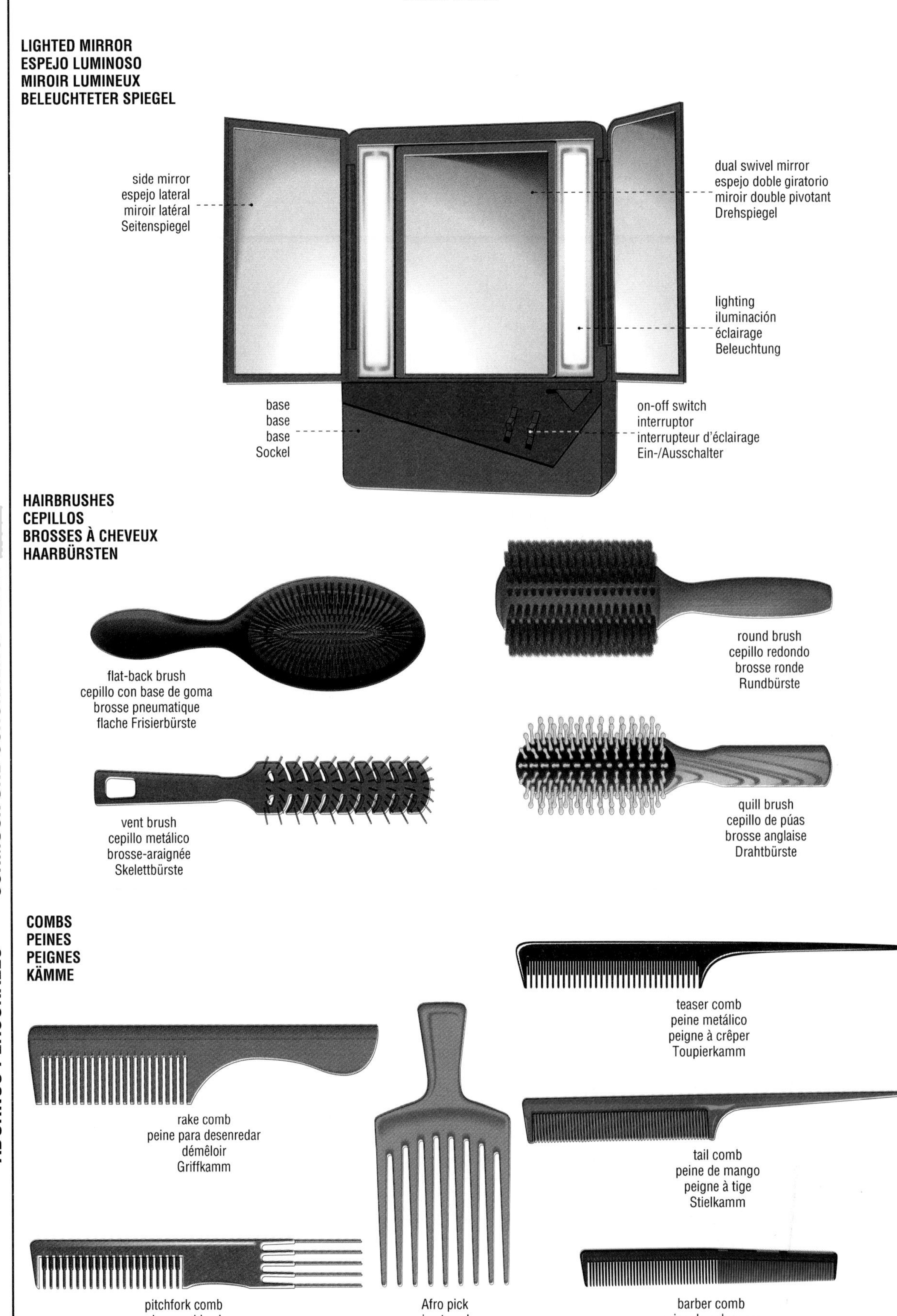
side mirror
espejo lateral
miroir latéral
Seitenspiegel
dual swivel mirror
espejo doble giratorio
miroir double pivotant
Drehspiegel
lighting
iluminación
éclairage
Beleuchtung
base
base
base
Sockel
on-off switch
interruptor
interrupteur d'éclairage
Ein-/Ausschalter
HAIRBRUSHES
CEPILLOS
BROSSES À CHEVEUX
HAARBÜRSTEN
flat-back brush
cepillo con base de goma
brosse pneumatique
flache Frisierbürste
round brush
cepillo redondo
brosse ronde
Rundbürste
vent brush
cepillo metálico
brosse-araignée
Skelettbürste
quill brush
cepillo de púas
brosse anglaise
Drahtbürste
COMBS
PEINES
PEIGNES
KÄMME
teaser comb
peine metálico
peigne à crêper
Toupierkamm
rake comb
peine para desenredar
démêloir
Griffkamm
tail comb
peine de mango
peigne à tige
Stielkamm
pitchfork comb
peine combinado
combiné 2 dans 1
Haarliftkamm
Afro pick
peine tenedor
peigne afro
Strähnenkamm
barber comb
peine de peluquero
peigne de coiffeur
Haarschneidekamm

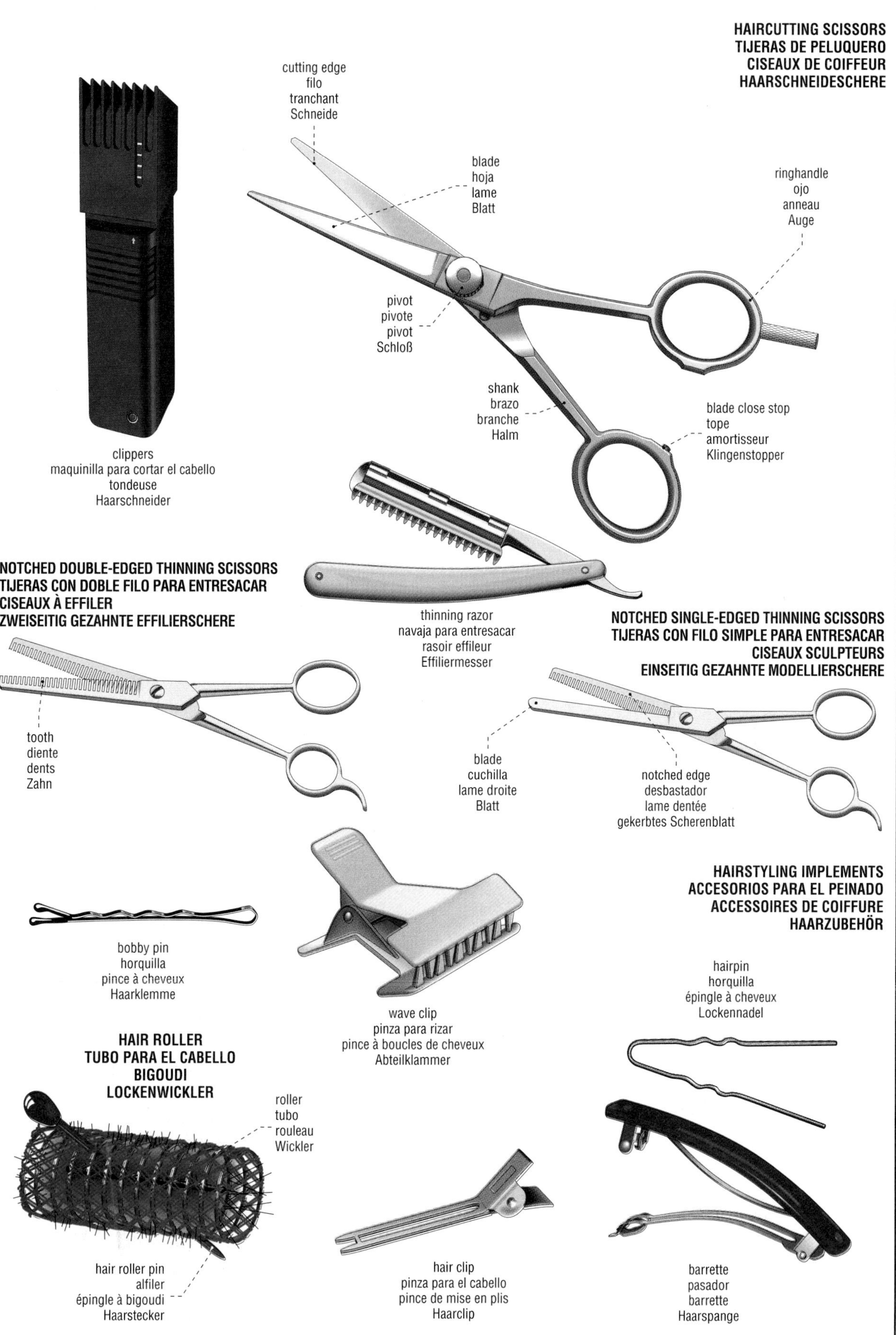
HAIRCUTTING SCISSORS
TIJERAS DE PELUQUERO
CISEAUX DE COIFFEUR
HAARSCHNEIDESCHERE
cutting edge
filo
tranchant
Schneide
blade
hoja
lame
Blatt
ringhandle
ojo
anneau
Auge
pivot
pivote
pivot
Schloß
shank
brazo
branche
Halm
blade close stop
tope
amortisseur
Klingenstopper
clippers
maquinilla para cortar el cabello
tondeuse
Haarschneider
thinning razor
navaja para entresacar
rasoir effileur
Effiliermesser
NOTCHED DOUBLE-EDGED THINNING SCISSORS
TIJERAS CON DOBLE FILO PARA ENTRESACAR
CISEAUX À EFFILER
ZWEISEITIG GEZAHNTE EFFILIERSCHERE
tooth
diente
dents
Zahn
NOTCHED SINGLE-EDGED THINNING SCISSORS
TIJERAS CON FILO SIMPLE PARA ENTRESACAR
CISEAUX SCULPTEURS
EINSEITIG GEZAHNTE MODELLIERSCHERE
blade
cuchilla
lame droite
Blatt
notched edge
desbastador
lame dentée
gekerbtes Scherenblatt
HAIRSTYLING IMPLEMENTS
ACCESORIOS PARA EL PEINADO
ACCESSOIRES DE COIFFURE
HAARZUBEHÖR
bobby pin
horquilla
pince à cheveux
Haarklemme
wave clip
pinza para rizar
pince à boucles de cheveux
Abteilklammer
hairpin
horquilla
épingle à cheveux
Lockennadel
HAIR ROLLER
TUBO PARA EL CABELLO
BIGOUDI
LOCKENWICKLER
roller
tubo
rouleau
Wickler
hair roller pin
alfiler
épingle à bigoudi
Haarstecker
hair clip
pinza para el cabello
pince de mise en plis
Haarclip
barrette
pasador
barrette
Haarspange

HAIRDRESSING
PEINADO
COIFFURE
HAARPFLEGE

CURLING IRON
PINZA RIZADORA
FER À FRISER
LOCKENSTAB
handle
mango
poignée profilée
Griff
clamp lever
palanca
levier
Hebel für den Klemmbügel
on-off indicator
luz piloto
voyant lumineux
Kontrollampe
swivel cord
cable giratorio
cordon d'alimentation pivotant
Drehanschlußleitung
heat ready indicator
indicador de temperatura
point indicateur de température
Bereitschaftsanzeige
clamp
pinza
pince
Klemmbügel
on-off switch
interruptor
interrupteur
Ein-/Ausschalter
STYLING BRUSH
CEPILLO ELÉCTRICO
BROSSE À COIFFER
LOCKENBÜRSTE
stand
soporte
support
Ständer
cool tip
punta de plástico
embout isolant
Cool tip
barrel
varilla rizadora
tube
Zylinder
HAIR DRYER
SECADOR MANUAL
SÈCHE-CHEVEUX
FÖN
curling brush
cepillo rizador
brosse à peignes
Lockenbürste
fan housing
caja del ventilador
boîtier du ventilateur
Föngehäuse
air-inlet grille
rejilla de entrada de aire
grille d'aspiration
Ansauggitter
barrel
tubo de aire
corps
Heizfläche
speed selector switch
botón seleccionador de velocidad
sélecteur de vitesse
Luftstromschalter
heat
air
on-off switch
interruptor
interrupteur
Ein-/Ausschalter
heat selector switch
botón seleccionador de temperatura
sélecteur de température
Temperaturschalter
hang-up ring
trabilla
anneau de suspension
Aufhängeöse
air-outlet grille
rejilla de salida de aire
grille de sortie d'air
Luftaustrittsöffnung
handle
mango
poignée
Griff
air concentrator
concentrador de aire
buse
Luftstromrichtdüse
power supply cord
cable de corriente
cordon d'alimentation
Netzkabel

PERSONAL ARTICLES
ARTÍCULOS PERSONALES

OBJETS PERSONNELS
PERSÖNLICHE ARTIKEL

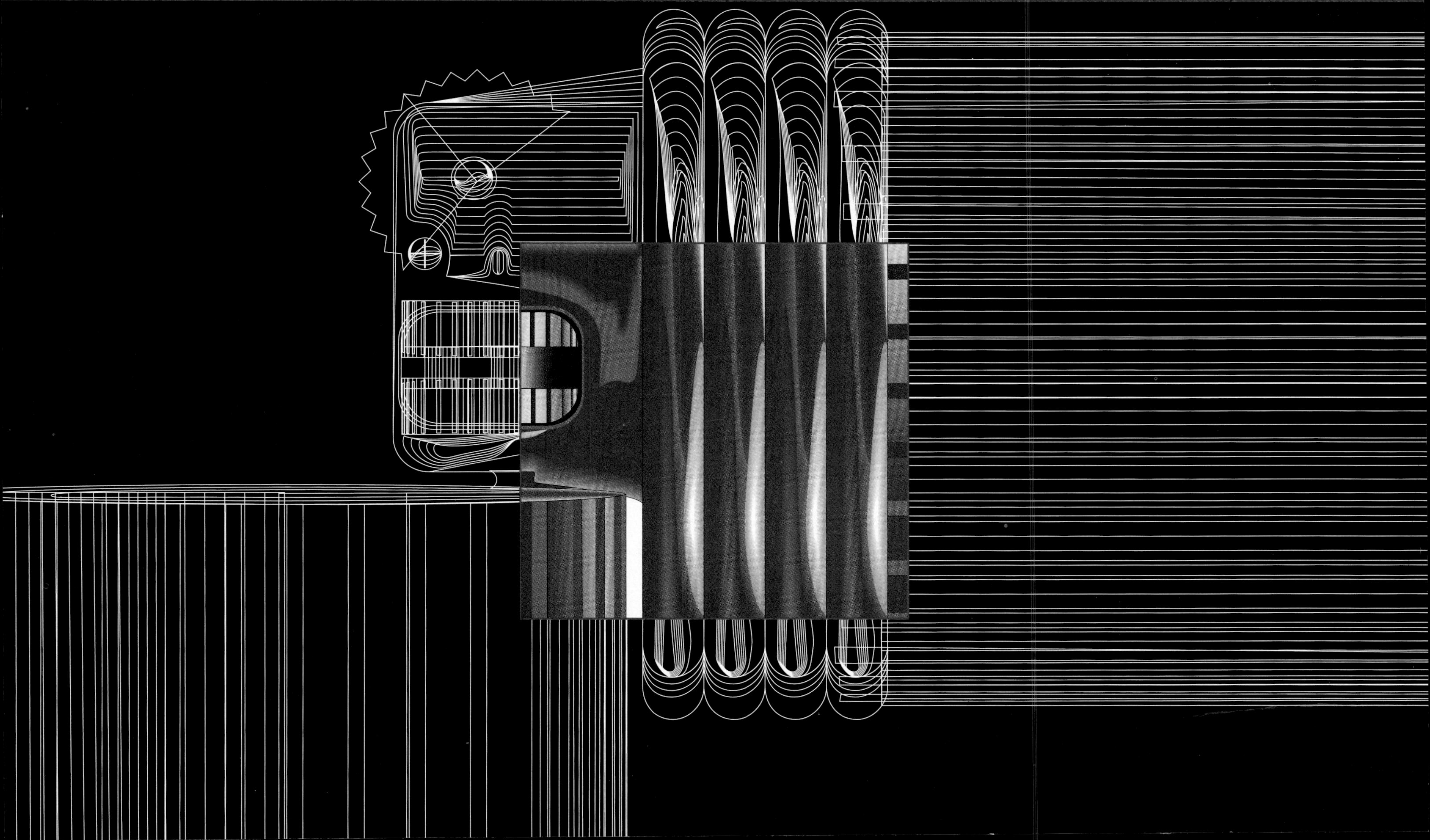

CONTENTS

DENTAL CARE
HIGIENE DENTAL
HYGIÈNE DENTAIRE
ZAHNPFLEGE

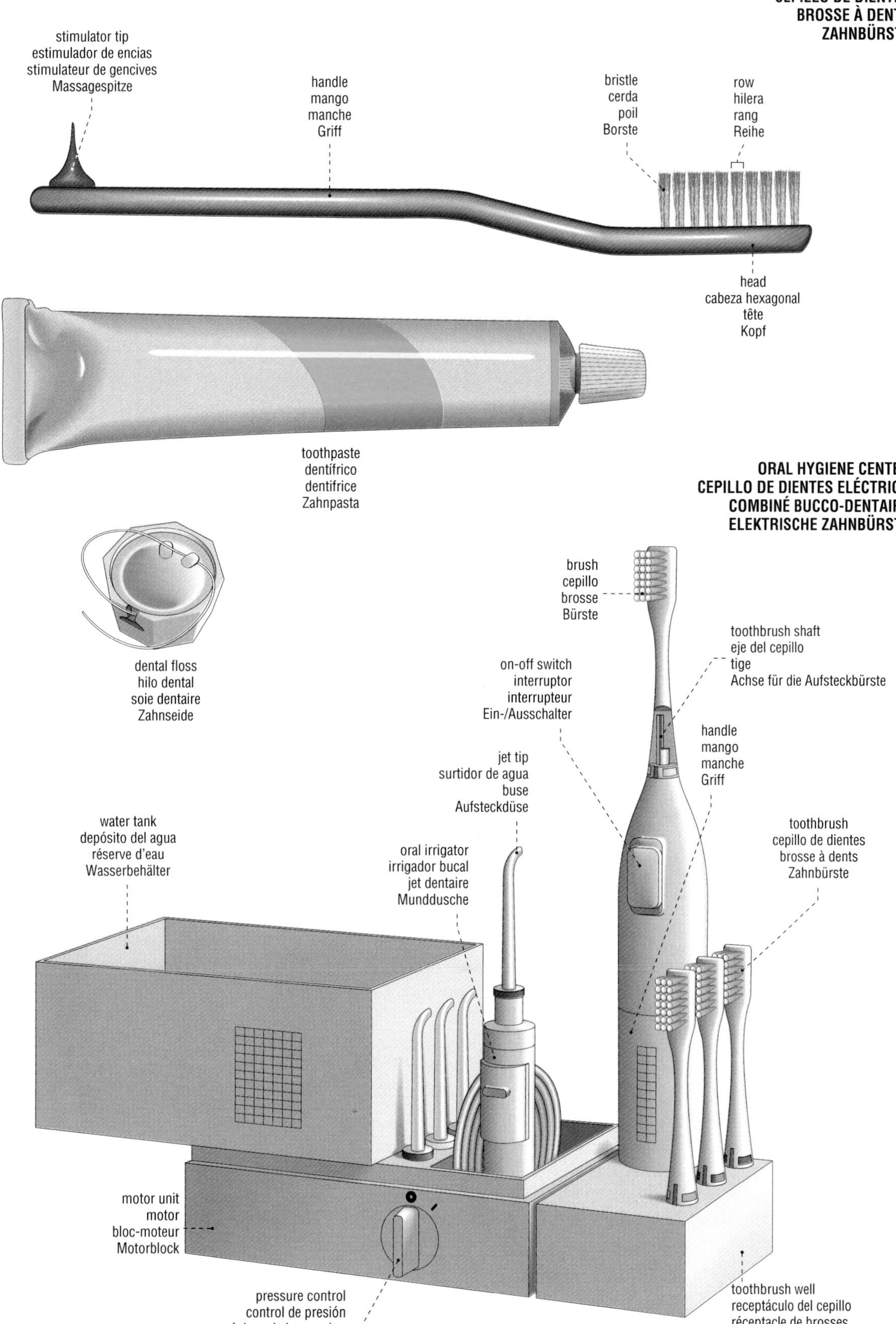
TOOTHBRUSH
CEPILLO DE DIENTES
BROSSE À DENTS
ZAHNBÜRSTE
stimulator tip
estimulador de encias
stimulateur de gencives
Massagespitze
handle
mango
manche
Griff
bristle
cerda
poil
Borste
row
hilera
rang
Reihe
head
cabeza hexagonal
tête
Kopf
toothpaste
dentífrico
dentifrice
Zahnpasta
ORAL HYGIENE CENTER
CEPILLO DE DIENTES ELÉCTRICO
COMBINÉ BUCCO-DENTAIRE
ELEKTRISCHE ZAHNBÜRSTE
dental floss
hilo dental
soie dentaire
Zahnseide
brush
cepillo
brosse
Bürste
toothbrush shaft
eje del cepillo
tige
Achse für die Aufsteckbürste
on-off switch
interruptor
interrupteur
Ein-/Ausschalter
handle
mango
manche
Griff
jet tip
surtidor de agua
buse
Aufsteckdüse
water tank
depósito del agua
réserve d'eau
Wasserbehälter
oral irrigator
irrigador bucal
jet dentaire
Mundddusche
toothbrush
cepillo de dientes
brosse à dents
Zahnbürste
motor unit
motor
bloc-moteur
Motorblock
pressure control
control de presión
réglage de la pression
Druckregler
toothbrush well
receptáculo del cepillo
réceptacle de brosses
Box für die Aufsteckbürsten

RAZORS
RASURADORAS
RASOIRS
RASIERER

ELECTRIC RAZOR
MAQUINILLA DE AFEITAR ELÉCTRICA
RASOIR ÉLECTRIQUE
ELEKTRORASIERER
floating head
cabeza flotante
tête flottante
Scherkopf
trimmer
recortador de patillas
tondeuse
Langhaarschneider
screen
peine y cuchilla
grille
Scherkopfhalter
closeness setting
selector de corte
sélecteur de coupe
Justierring
housing
caja
boîtier
Gehäuse
cleaning brush
escobilla limpiadora
brosse de nettoyage
Reinigungsbürste
charging light
luz de encendido
voyant de charge
Ladekontrollampe
100
80
60
40
20
on-off switch
interruptor
interrupteur
Ein-/Ausschalter
charge indicator
indicador de recarga
indicateur de charge
Kapazitätsanzeige
charging plug
enchufe de recarga
prise de charge
Geräteanschluß
power cord
cable de corriente
cordon d'alimentation
Netzkabel
plug adapter
adaptador de enchufes
adaptateur de fiche
Adapter
STRAIGHT RAZOR
NAVAJA DE BARBERO
RASOIR À MANCHE
RASIERMESSER
blade
hoja
lame
Klinge
pivot
eje
pivot
Schloß
handle
mango
manche
Griff
DOUBLE-EDGE RAZOR
MAQUINILLA DE AFEITAR
RASOIR À DOUBLE TRANCHANT
ZWEISCHNEIDIGER RASIERER
head
cabeza
tête
Kopf
collar
anillo
anneau
Ring
bristle
cerdas
soie
Borste
disposable razor
maquinilla desechable
rasoir jetable
Einwegrasierer
double-edge blade
hoja de afeitar
lame à double tranchant
zweischneidige Klinge
5
5
handle
mango
manche
Griff
SHAVING BRUSH
BROCHA DE AFEITAR
BLAIREAU
RASIERPINSEL
shaving mug
jabonera
bol à raser
Seifenbecher
blade injector
despachador de hojas de afeitar
distributeur de lames
Klingenkassette

UMBRELLA AND STICK
PARAGUAS Y BASTONES
PARAPLUIE ET CANNE
SCHIRM UND STOCK

UMBRELLA
PARAGUAS
PARAPLUIE
SCHIRM

TELESCOPIC UMBRELLA
PARAGUAS PLEGABLE
PARAPLUIE TÉLESCOPIQUE
TASCHENSCHIRM

STICK UMBRELLA
PARAGUAS DE BASTÓN
PARAPLUIE-CANNE
STOCKSCHIRM

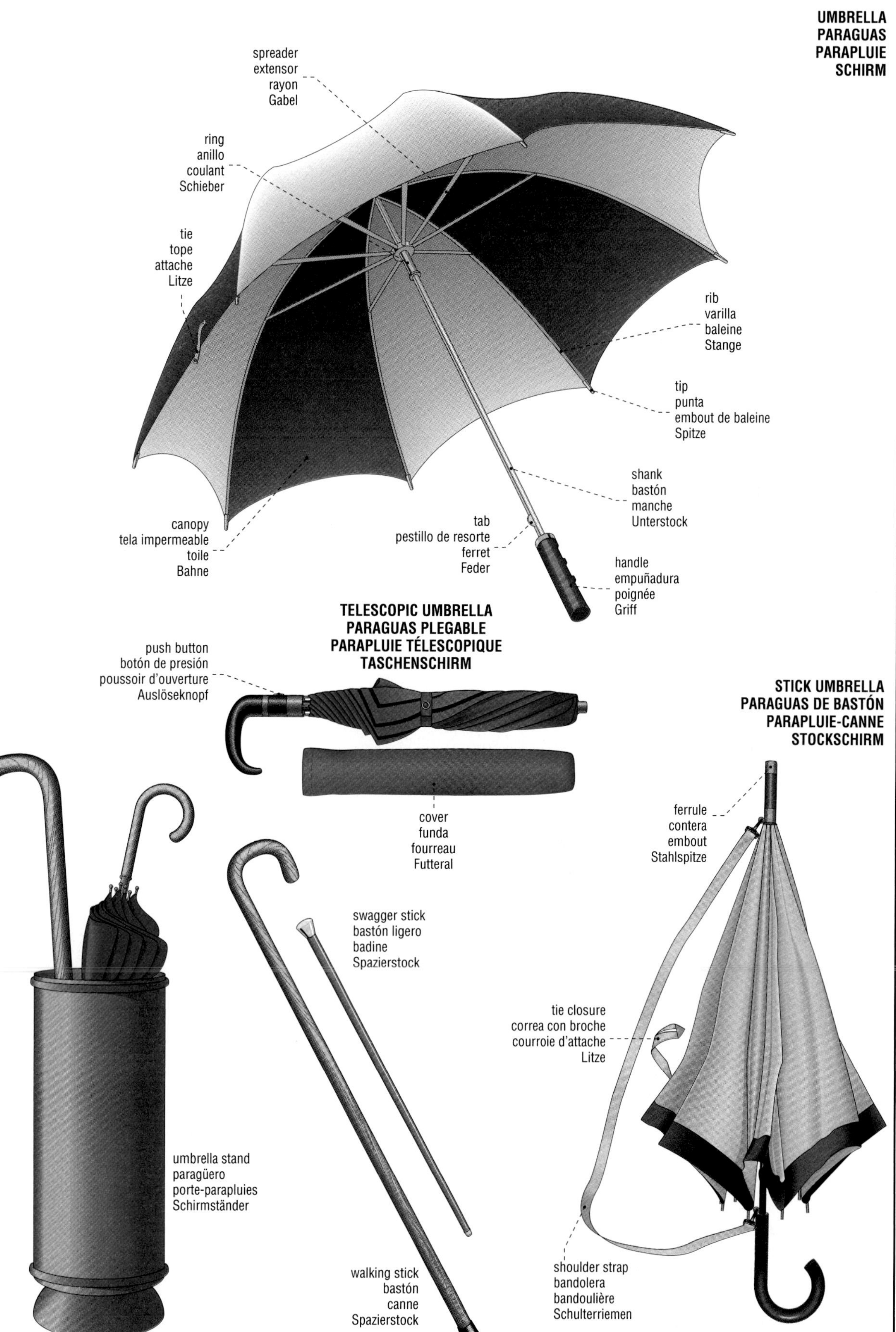
spreader
extensor
rayon
Gabel
ring
anillo
coulant
Schieber
tie
tope
attache
Litze
rib
varilla
baleine
Stange
tip
punta
embout de baleine
Spitze
shank
bastón
manche
Unterstock
canopy
tela impermeable
toile
Bahne
tab
pestillo de resorte
ferret
Feder
handle
empuñadura
poignée
Griff
push button
botón de presión
poussoir d'ouverture
Auslöseknopf
cover
funda
fourreau
Futteral
ferrule
contera
embout
Stahlspitze
swagger stick
bastón ligero
badine
Spazierstock
tie closure
correa con broche
courroie d'attache
Litze
umbrella stand
paragüero
porte-parapluies
Schirmständer
walking stick
bastón
canne
Spazierstock
shoulder strap
bandolera
bandoulière
Schulterriemen

EYEGLASSES
GAFAS
LUNETTES
BRILLE

EYEGLASSES PARTS
GAFAS: PARTES
PARTIES DES LUNETTES
TEILE DER BRILLE

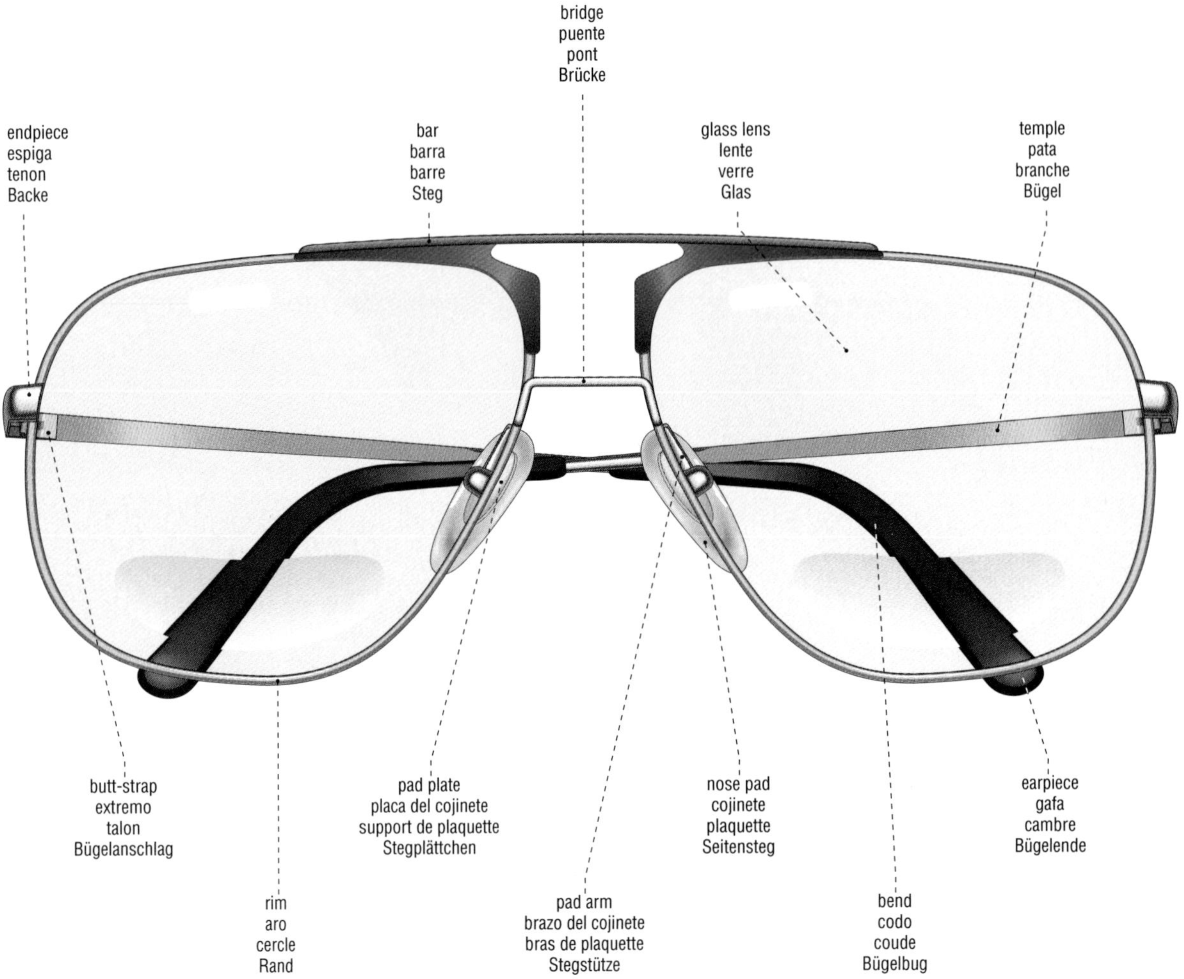

bridge
puente
pont
Brücke

endpiece
espiga
tenon
Backe

bar
barra
barre
Steg

glass lens
lente
verre
Glas

temple
pata
branche
Bügel

butt-strap
extremo
talon
Bügelanschlag

pad plate
placa del cojinete
support de plaquette
Stegplättchen

nose pad
cojinete
plaquette
Seitensteg

earpiece
gafa
cambre
Bügelende

rim
aro
cercle
Rand

pad arm
brazo del cojinete
bras de plaquette
Stegstütze

bend
codo
coude
Bügelbug

BIFOCAL LENS
LENTE BIFOCAL
VERRE BIFOCAL
BIFOKALGLAS

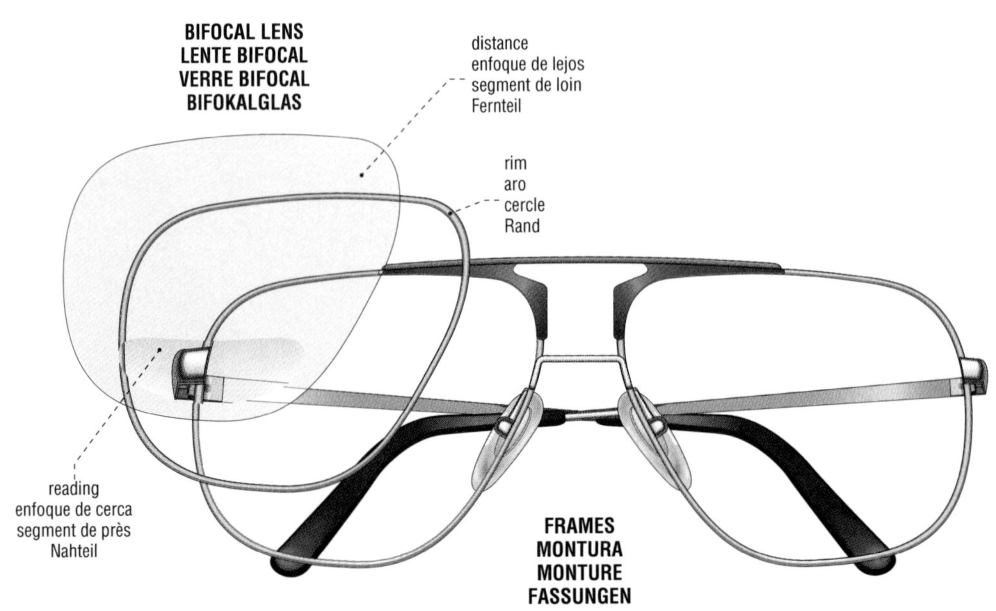
distance
enfoque de lejos
segment de loin
Fernteil
rim
aro
cercle
Rand
reading
enfoque de cerca
segment de près
Nahteil

FRAMES
MONTURA
MONTURE
FASSUNGEN

MAJOR TYPES OF EYEGLASSES
PRINCIPALES TIPOS DE LENTES
PRINCIPAUX TYPES DE LUNETTES
DIE WICHTIGSTEN BRILLENARTEN

scissors-glasses
binóculos de tijera
binocle
Scherenbrille
half-glasses
media luna
demi-lune
Halbbrille
sunglasses
gafas de sol
lunettes de soleil
Sonnenbrille
pince-nez
quevedos
bésicles à pont élastique
Kneifer
lorgnette
impertinentes
face-à-main
Lorgnette
monocle
monóculo
monocle
Monokel
opera glasses
gemelos de teatro
lorgnette
Opernglas

LEATHER GOODS
ARTÍCULOS DE PIEL
ARTICLES DE MAROQUINERIE
LEDERWAREN

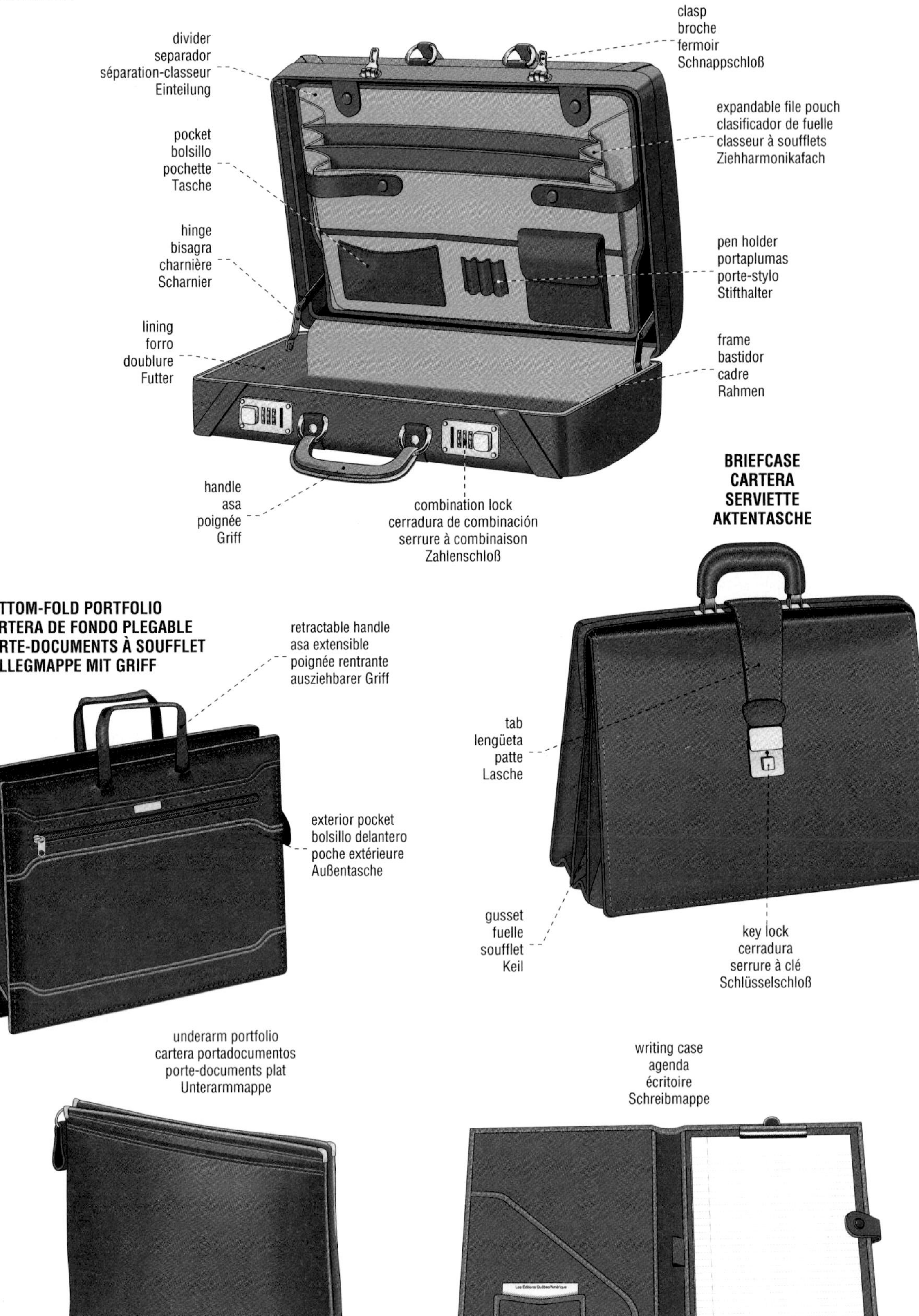

ATTACHÉ CASE
MALETÍN
MALLETTE PORTE-DOCUMENTS
AKTENKOFFER
divider
separador
séparation-classeur
Einteilung
clasp
broche
fermoir
Schnappschloß
expandable file pouch
clasificador de fuelle
classeur à soufflets
Ziehharmonikafach
pocket
bolsillo
pochette
Tasche
hinge
bisagra
charnière
Scharnier
pen holder
portaplumas
porte-stylo
Stifthalter
lining
forro
doublure
Futter
frame
bastidor
cadre
Rahmen
handle
asa
poignée
Griff
combination lock
cerradura de combinación
serrure à combinaison
Zahlenschloß
BRIEFCASE
CARTERA
SERVIETTE
AKTENTASCHE
BOTTOM-FOLD PORTFOLIO
CARTERA DE FONDO PLEGABLE
PORTE-DOCUMENTS À SOUFFLET
KOLLEGMAPPE MIT GRIFF
retractable handle
asa extensible
poignée rentrante
ausziehbarer Griff
tab
lengüeta
patte
Lasche
exterior pocket
bolsillo delantero
poche extérieure
Außentasche
gusset
fuelle
soufflet
Keil
key lock
cerradura
serrure à clé
Schlüsselschloß
underarm portfolio
cartera portadocumentos
porte-documents plat
Unterarmmappe
writing case
agenda
écritoire
Schreibmappe

eyeglasses case
funda para gafas
étui à lunettes
Brillenetui

CHECKBOOK/SECRETARY CLUTCH
PORTACHEQUERA CON CALCULADORA
PORTEFEUILLE CHÉQUIER
ETUI FÜR RECHNER UND SCHECKHEFT

trimming
filete
grébiche
Druckverschluß

card case
tarjetero
porte-cartes
Kreditkartenfach

calculator
calculadora
calculette
Taschenrechner

pen holder
portaplumas
porte-stylo
Stifthalter

hidden pocket
bolsillo secreto
poche secrète
Unterfach

checkbook
talonario de cheques
chéquier
Scheckheft

CARD CASE
TARJETERO
PORTE-CARTES
KREDITKARTENETUI

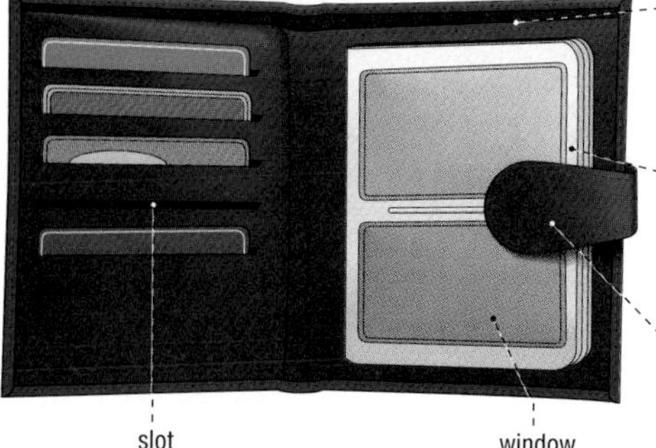

bill compartment
billetera
poche américaine
Scheinfach

windows
plásticos transparentes
feuillets
Klarsichtfenster

tab
lengüeta
patte
Lasche

slot
ranura
fente
Fach

window
plástico transparente
volet transparent
Klarsichtfenster

key case
llavero
porte-clés
Schlüsseletui

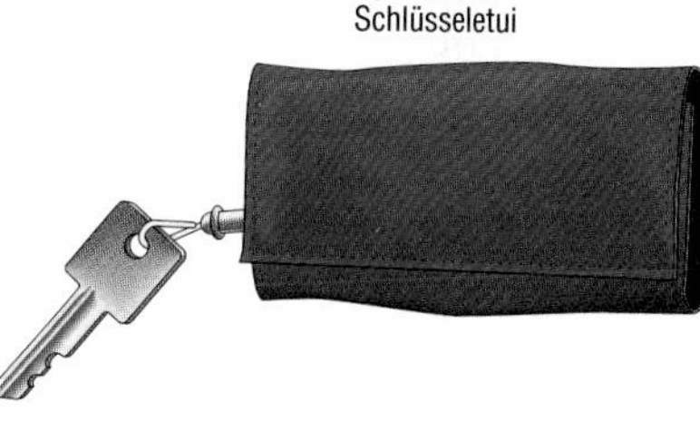

billfold
billetera
porte-coupures
Scheintasche

purse
monedero
bourse à monnaie
Knipsbörse

wallet
billetera
portefeuille
Scheintasche

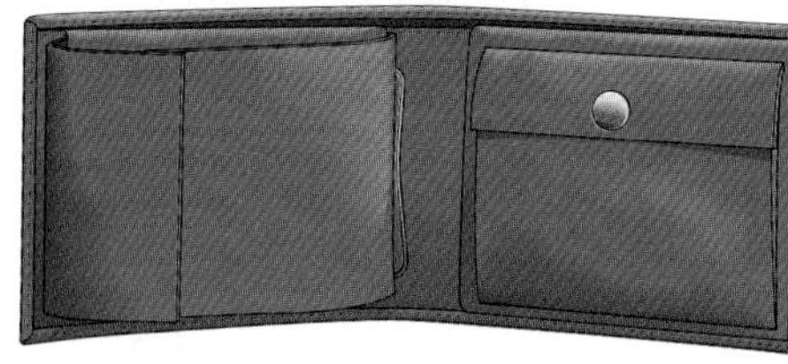

passport case
portapasaportes
porte-passeport
Brieftasche

checkbook
talonario de cheques
porte-chéquier
Scheckhülle

coin purse
portamonedas
porte-monnaie
Schüttelbörse

HANDBAGS
BOLSAS DE MANO
SACS À MAIN
HANDTASCHEN

men's bag
bolso de hombre
pochette d'homme
Herrentasche
SATCHEL BAG
BOLSO CLÁSICO
SAC CARTABLE
AKTENTASCHE
handle
mango
poignée
Griff
flap
ala
rabat
Überschlag
clasp
broche
fermoir
Schnappschloß
lock
cierre
serrure
Schloß
pouch
bolsita de cordones
aumonière
Beutel
SHOULDER BAG
BOLSO
SAC À BANDOULIÈRE
SCHULTERTASCHE
buckle
hebilla
boucle
Schnalle
shoulder strap
bandolera
bandoulière
Schulterriemen
ACCORDION BAG
BOLSA DE ACORDEÓN
SAC ACCORDÉON
UMHÄNGETASCHE MIT DEHNFALTE
gusset
fuelle
soufflet
Keil

tote bag
bolsa de paja
sac fourre-tout
Stadttasche

duffel bag
saco de viaje
balluchon
kleine Beuteltasche

hobo bag
morral
sac besace
Umhängetasche mit Reißverschluß

clutch bag
monedero
pochette
Klemmtasche
box bag
bolsa de vestir
sac boîte
Boxtasche
DRAWSTRING BAG
BOLSA DE CORDONES
SAC SEAU
BEUTELTASCHE
eyelet
ojal
œillet
Öse
drawstring
cordón
lacet de serrage
Zugschnur
front pocket
bolsillo exterior
poche frontale
Vortasche
sea bag
saco de marinero
sac marin
Matchbeutel
duffel bag
bolsa de viaje
sac polochon
Dreivierteltasche
muff
bolsa manguito
manchon
Mufftasche
shopping bag
cesto de la compra
cabas
Einkaufstasche
carrier bag
cesto
sac à provisions
Tragetasche

LUGGAGE
EQUIPAJE
BAGAGES
GEPÄCK

CARRY-ON BAG
BOLSA DE VIAJE
SAC DE VOL
REISETASCHE

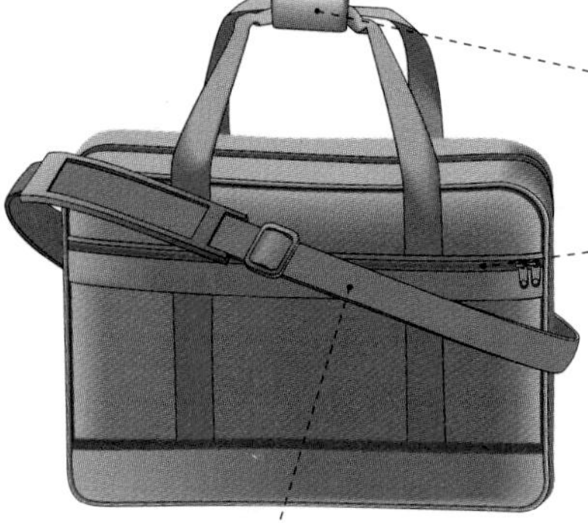
handle
asa
poignée
Griff
exterior pocket
bolsillo exterior
poche extérieure
Außentasche
shoulder strap
bandolera
bandoulière
Schulterriemen

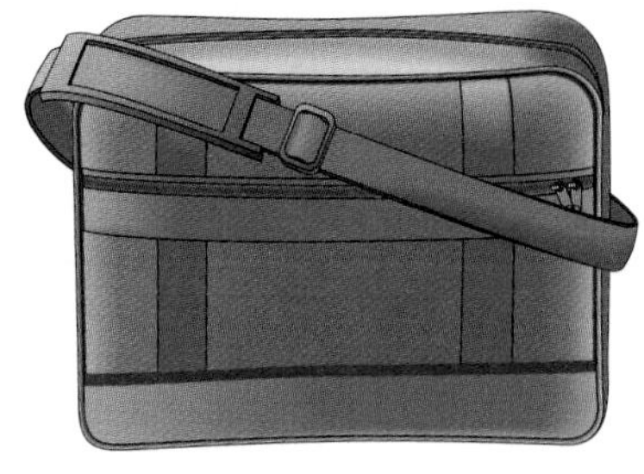
tote bag
maletín
sac fourre-tout
Flugtasche

VANITY CASE
NECESER
MALLETTE DE TOILETTE
KOSMETIKKOFFER

mirror
espejo
miroir
Spiegel
hinge
bisagra
charnière
Scharnier
cosmetic tray
bandeja para cosméticos
plateau
Einsatz

GARMENT BAG
BOLSA PARA TRAJES
HOUSSE À VÊTEMENTS
KLEIDERSACK

zipper
cremallera
fermeture à glissière
Reißverschluß

utility case
estuche de tocador
trousse de toilette
Kulturbeutel

LUGGAGE CARRIER
CARRITO PORTAMALETAS
PORTE-BAGAGES
GEPÄCKROLLER

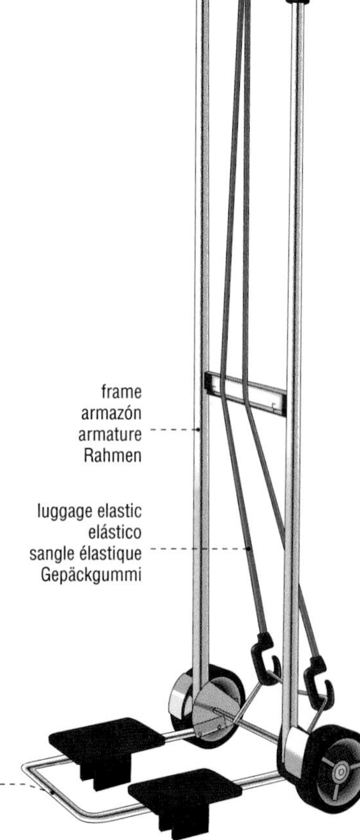
frame
armazón
armature
Rahmen
luggage elastic
elástico
sangle élastique
Gepäckgummi
stand
soporte
béquille
Ständer

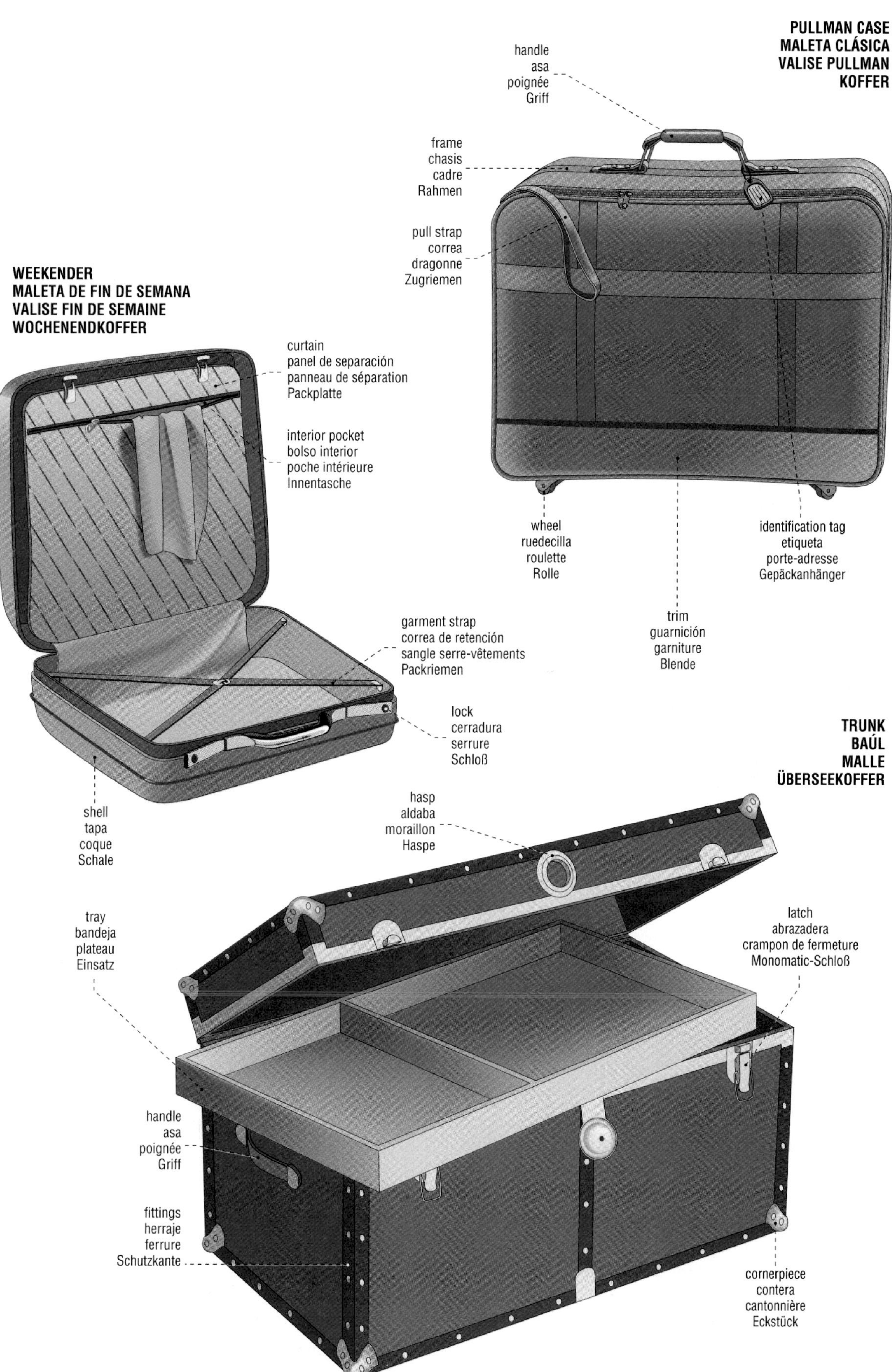
PULLMAN CASE
MALETA CLÁSICA
VALISE PULLMAN
KOFFER
handle
asa
poignée
Griff
frame
chasis
cadre
Rahmen
pull strap
correa
dragonne
Zugriemen
wheel
ruedecilla
roulette
Rolle
identification tag
etiqueta
porte-adresse
Gepäckanhänger
trim
guarnición
garniture
Blende
WEEKENDER
MALETA DE FIN DE SEMANA
VALISE FIN DE SEMAINE
WOCHENENDKOFFER
curtain
panel de separación
panneau de séparation
Packplatte
interior pocket
bolso interior
poche intérieure
Innentasche
garment strap
correa de retención
sangle serre-vêtements
Packriemen
lock
cerradura
serrure
Schloß
shell
tapa
coque
Schale
TRUNK
BAÚL
MALLE
ÜBERSEEKOFFER
hasp
aldaba
moraillon
Haspe
tray
bandeja
plateau
Einsatz
latch
abrazadera
crampon de fermeture
Monomatic-Schloß
handle
asa
poignée
Griff
fittings
herraje
ferrure
Schutzkante
cornerpiece
contera
cantonnière
Eckstück

SMOKING ACCESSORIES
ACCESORIOS PARA FUMAR
ARTICLES DE FUMEUR
RAUCHERBEDARF

CIGAR
PURO
CIGARE
ZIGARRE

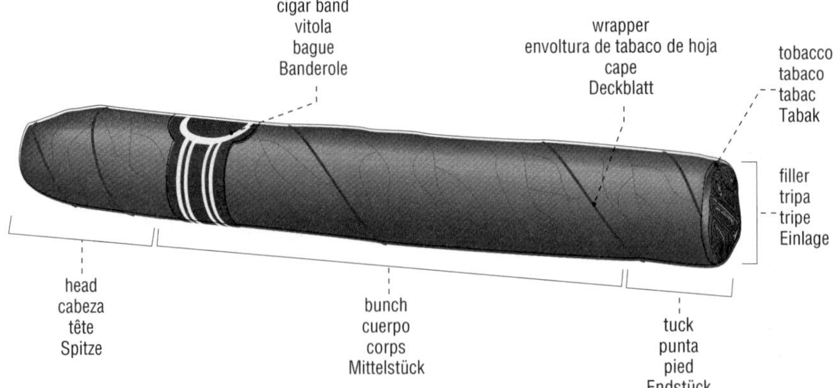
cigar band
vitola
bague
Banderole
wrapper
envoltura de tabaco de hoja
cape
Deckblatt
tobacco
tabaco
tabac
Tabak
filler
tripa
tripe
Einlage
head
cabeza
tête
Spitze
bunch
cuerpo
corps
Mittelstück
tuck
punta
pied
Endstück

CIGARETTE
CIGARRILLO
CIGARETTE
ZIGARETTE

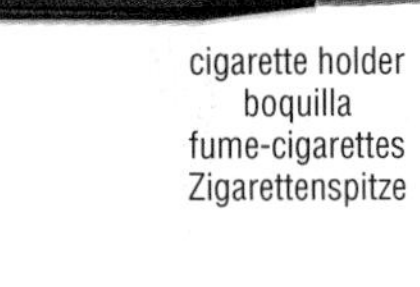
cigarette holder
boquilla
fume-cigarettes
Zigarettenspitze

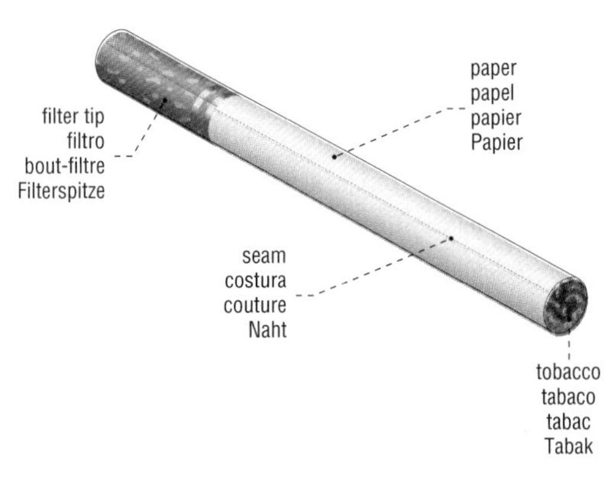
paper
papel
papier
Papier
filter tip
filtro
bout-filtre
Filterspitze
seam
costura
couture
Naht
tobacco
tabaco
tabac
Tabak

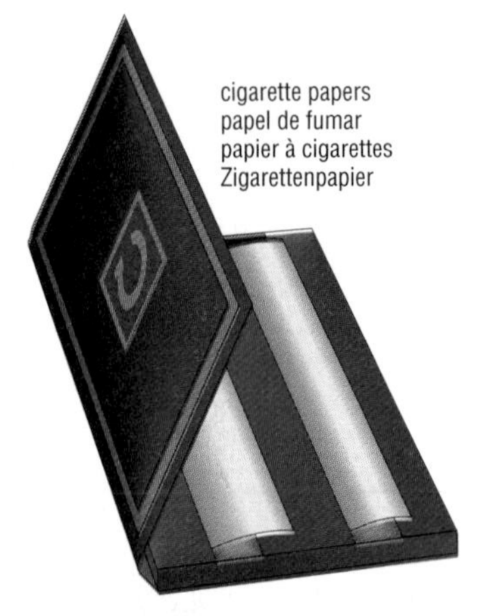
cigarette papers
papel de fumar
papier à cigarettes
Zigarettenpapier

CIGARETTE PACK
PAQUETE DE CIGARRILLOS
PAQUET DE CIGARETTES
ZIGARETTENPACKUNG

stamp
timbre
timbre
Steuermarke
tear tape
tira para rasgar la envoltura
bandelette d'arrachage
Aufreißband
trade name
marca registrada
marque déposée
Markenname

carton
cartón de cigarrillos
cartouche
Stange

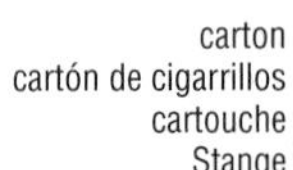

PIPE
PIPA
PIPE
PFEIFE

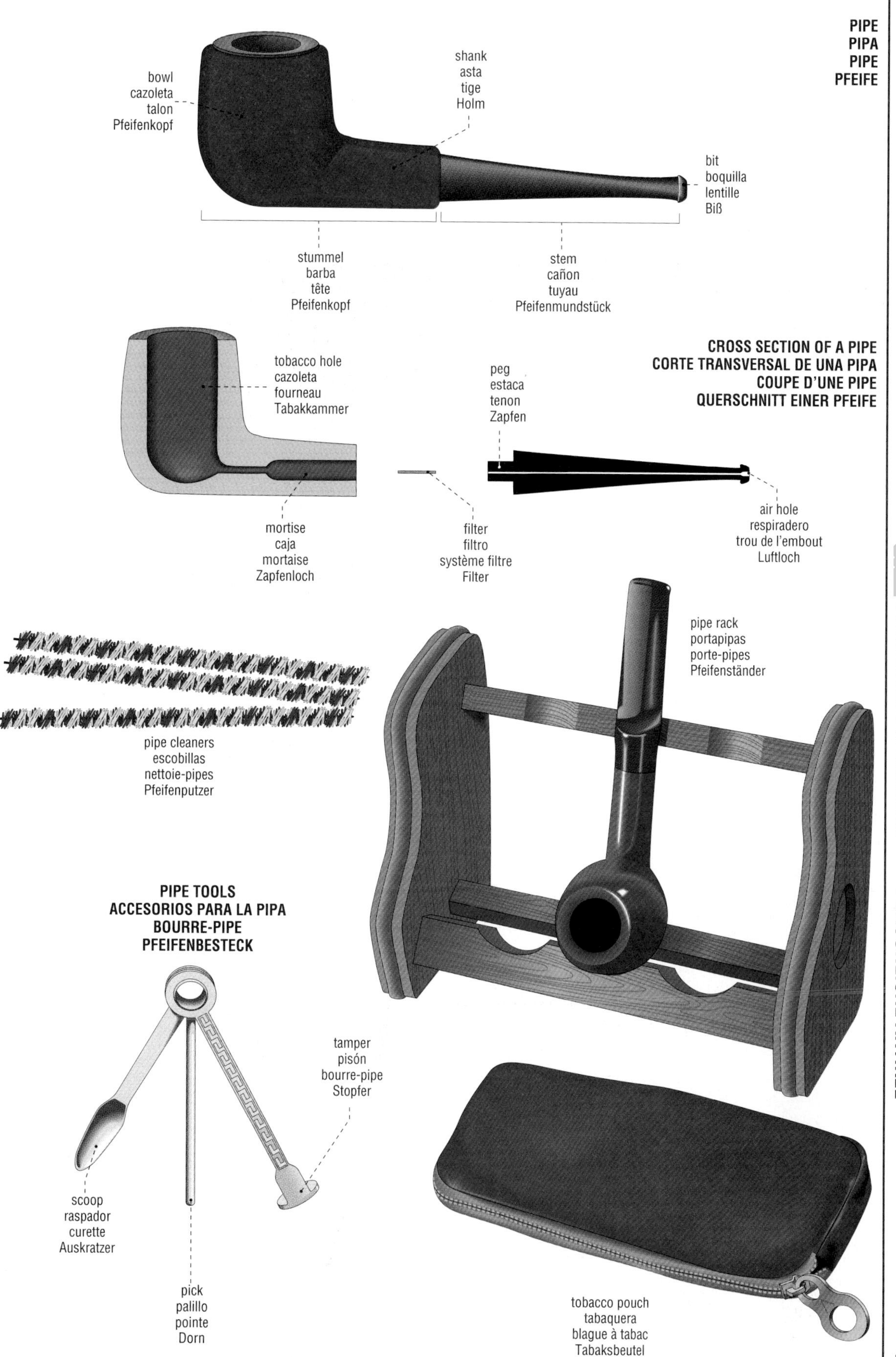
bowl
cazoleta
talon
Pfeifenkopf
shank
asta
tige
Holm
bit
boquilla
lentille
Biß
stummel
barba
tête
Pfeifenkopf
stem
cañon
tuyau
Pfeifenmundstück
CROSS SECTION OF A PIPE
CORTE TRANSVERSAL DE UNA PIPA
COUPE D'UNE PIPE
QUERSCHNITT EINER PFEIFE
tobacco hole
cazoleta
fourneau
Tabakkammer
peg
estaca
tenon
Zapfen
mortise
caja
mortaise
Zapfenloch
filter
filtro
système filtre
Filter
air hole
respiradero
trou de l'embout
Luftloch
pipe rack
portapipas
porte-pipes
Pfeifenständer
pipe cleaners
escobillas
nettoie-pipes
Pfeifenputzer
PIPE TOOLS
ACCESORIOS PARA LA PIPA
BOURRE-PIPE
PFEIFENBESTECK
tamper
pisón
bourre-pipe
Stopfer
scoop
raspador
curette
Auskratzer
pick
palillo
pointe
Dorn
tobacco pouch
tabaquera
blague à tabac
Tabaksbeutel

SMOKING ACCESSORIES
ACCESORIOS PARA FUMAR
ARTICLES DE FUMEUR
RAUCHERBEDARF

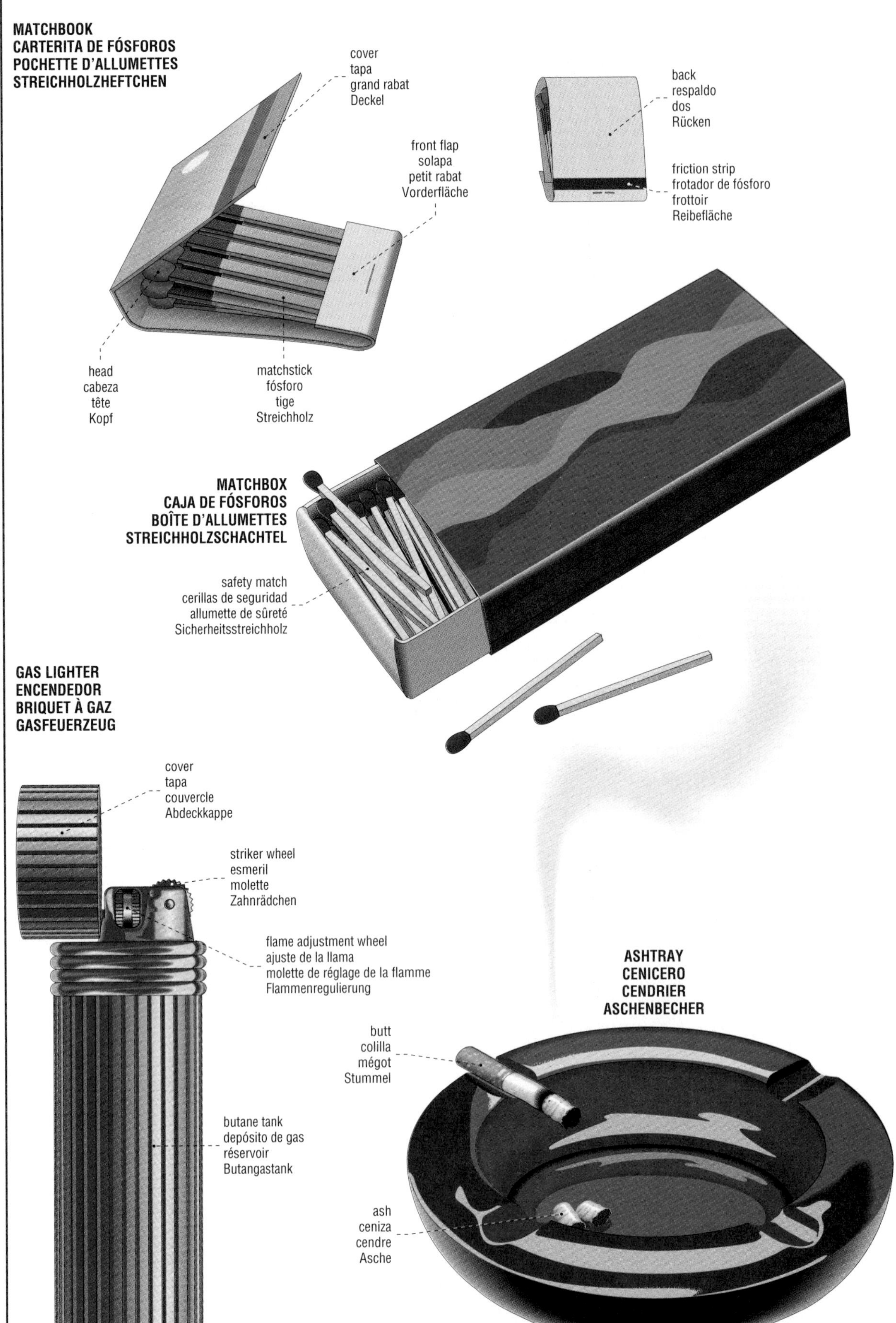
MATCHBOOK
CARTERITA DE FÓSFOROS
POCHETTE D'ALLUMETTES
STREICHHOLZHEFTCHEN
cover
tapa
grand rabat
Deckel
front flap
solapa
petit rabat
Vorderfläche
back
respaldo
dos
Rücken
friction strip
frotador de fósforo
frottoir
Reibefläche
head
cabeza
tête
Kopf
matchstick
fósforo
tige
Streichholz
MATCHBOX
CAJA DE FÓSFOROS
BOÎTE D'ALLUMETTES
STREICHHOLZSCHACHTEL
safety match
cerillas de seguridad
allumette de sûreté
Sicherheitsstreichholz
GAS LIGHTER
ENCENDEDOR
BRIQUET À GAZ
GASFEUERZEUG
cover
tapa
couvercle
Abdeckkappe
striker wheel
esmeril
molette
Zahnrädchen
flame adjustment wheel
ajuste de la llama
molette de réglage de la flamme
Flammenregulierung
butane tank
depósito de gas
réservoir
Butangastank
ASHTRAY
CENICERO
CENDRIER
ASCHENBECHER
butt
colilla
mégot
Stummel
ash
ceniza
cendre
Asche

COMMUNICATIONS
COMUNICACIONES
COMMUNICATIONS
KOMMUNIKATION

CONTENTS

WRITING INSTRUMENTS
INSTRUMENTOS PARA ESCRIBIR
INSTRUMENTS D'ÉCRITURE
SCHREIBGERÄTE

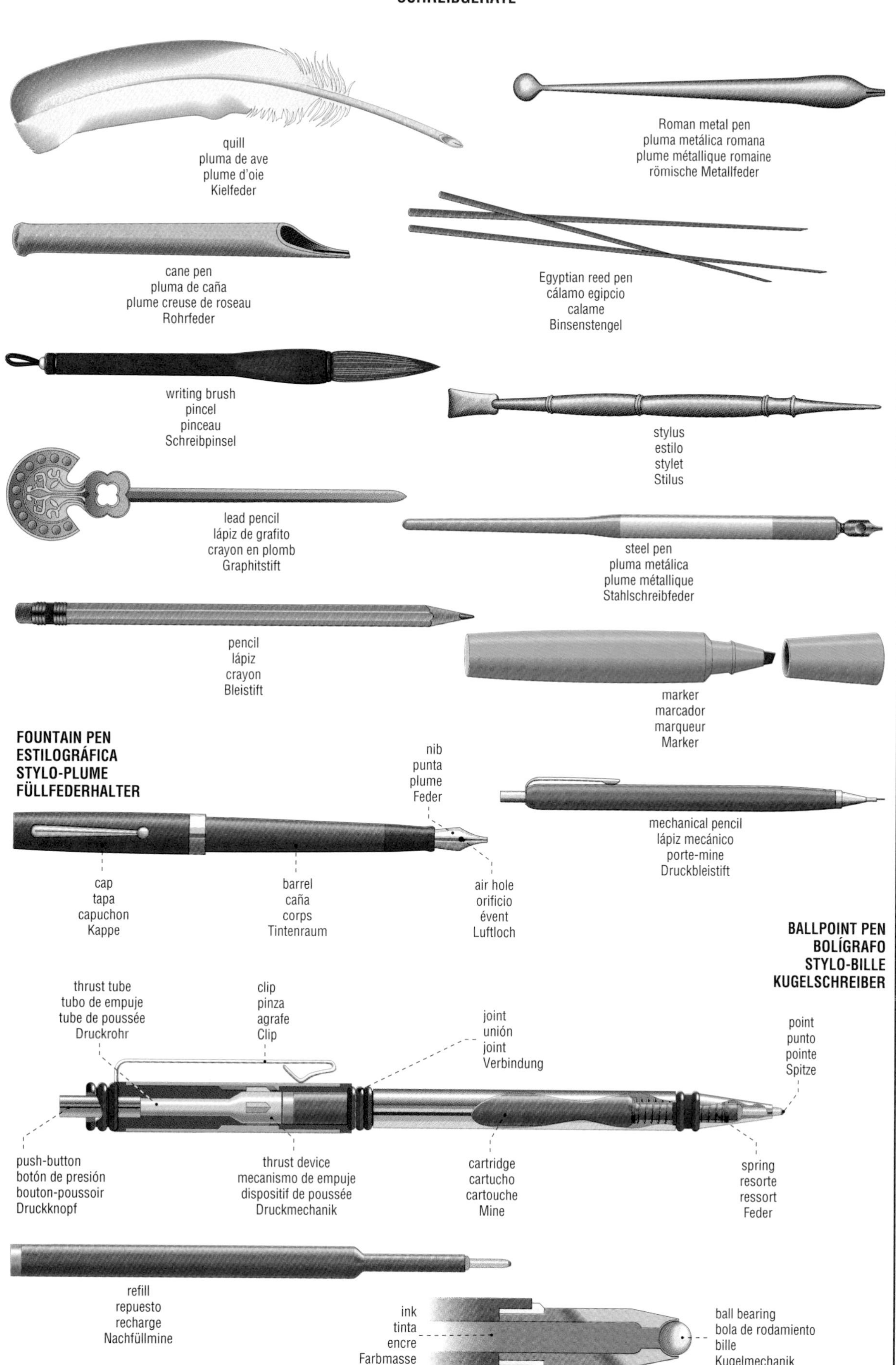

quill
pluma de ave
plume d'oie
Kielfeder
Roman metal pen
pluma metálica romana
plume métallique romaine
römische Metallfeder
cane pen
pluma de caña
plume creuse de roseau
Rohrfeder
Egyptian reed pen
cálamo egipcio
calame
Binsenstengel
writing brush
pincel
pinceau
Schreibpinsel
stylus
estilo
stylet
Stilus
lead pencil
lápiz de grafito
crayon en plomb
Graphitstift
steel pen
pluma metálica
plume métallique
Stahlschreibfeder
pencil
lápiz
crayon
Bleistift
marker
marcador
marqueur
Marker
FOUNTAIN PEN
ESTILOGRÁFICA
STYLO-PLUME
FÜLLFEDERHALTER
nib
punta
plume
Feder
mechanical pencil
lápiz mecánico
porte-mine
Druckbleistift
cap
tapa
capuchon
Kappe
barrel
caña
corps
Tintenraum
air hole
orificio
évent
Luftloch
BALLPOINT PEN
BOLÍGRAFO
STYLO-BILLE
KUGELSCHREIBER
thrust tube
tubo de empuje
tube de poussée
Druckrohr
clip
pinza
agrafe
Clip
joint
unión
joint
Verbindung
point
punto
pointe
Spitze
push-button
botón de presión
bouton-poussoir
Druckknopf
thrust device
mecanismo de empuje
dispositif de poussée
Druckmechanik
cartridge
cartucho
cartouche
Mine
spring
resorte
ressort
Feder
refill
repuesto
recharge
Nachfüllmine
ink
tinta
encre
Farbmasse
ball bearing
bola de rodamiento
bille
Kugelmechanik

PHOTOGRAPHY
FOTOGRAFÍA
PHOTOGRAPHIE
FOTOGRAFIE

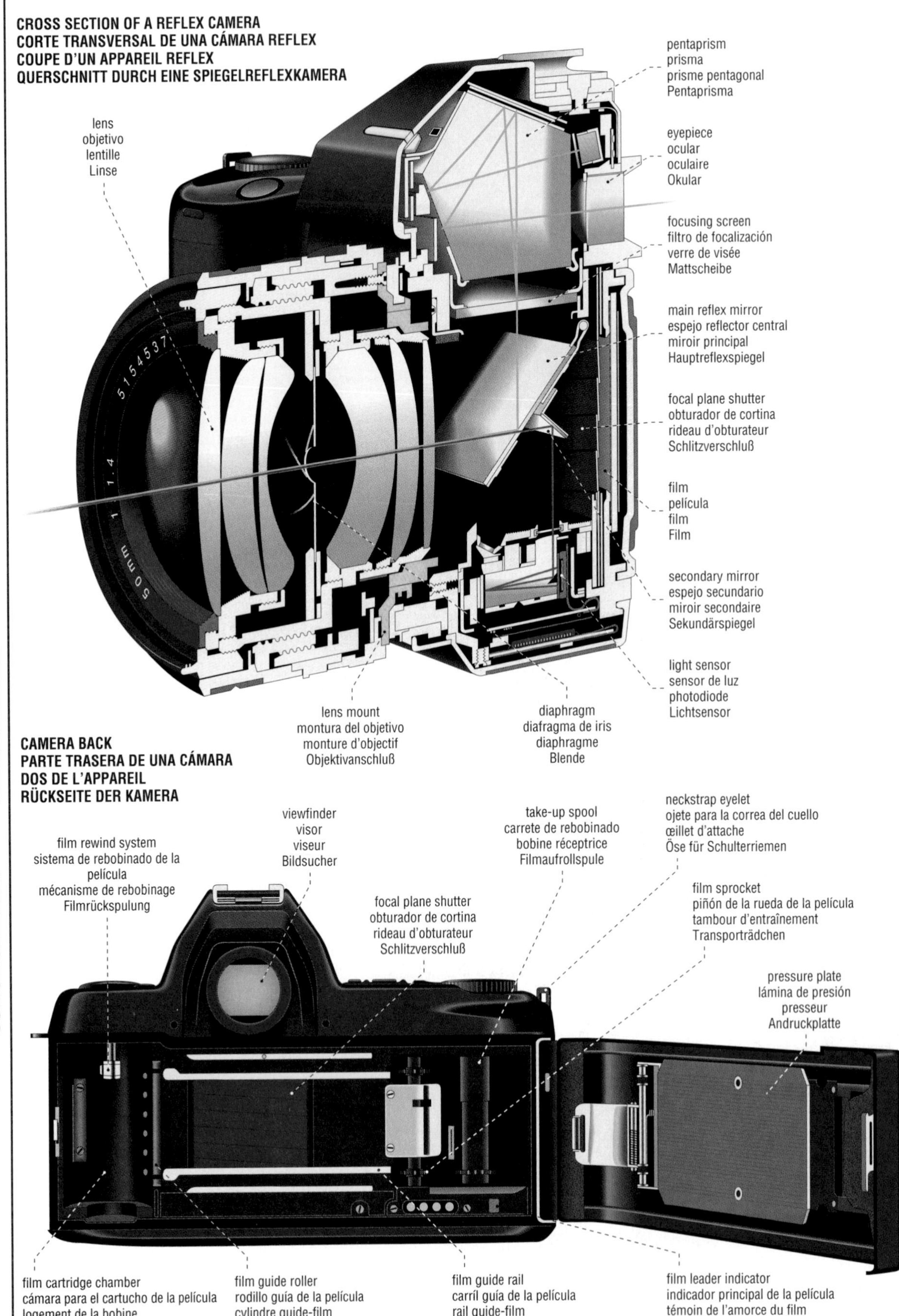

CROSS SECTION OF A REFLEX CAMERA
CORTE TRANSVERSAL DE UNA CÁMARA REFLEX
COUPE D'UN APPAREIL REFLEX
QUERSCHNITT DURCH EINE SPIEGELREFLEXKAMERA
lens
objetivo
lentille
Linse
pentaprism
prisma
prisme pentagonal
Pentaprisma
eyepiece
ocular
oculaire
Okular
focusing screen
filtro de focalización
verre de visée
Mattscheibe
main reflex mirror
espejo reflector central
miroir principal
Hauptreflexspiegel
focal plane shutter
obturador de cortina
rideau d'obturateur
Schlitzverschluß
film
película
film
Film
secondary mirror
espejo secundario
miroir secondaire
Sekundärspiegel
light sensor
sensor de luz
photodiode
Lichtsensor
lens mount
montura del objetivo
monture d'objectif
Objektivanschluß
diaphragm
diafragma de iris
diaphragme
Blende
CAMERA BACK
PARTE TRASERA DE UNA CÁMARA
DOS DE L'APPAREIL
RÜCKSEITE DER KAMERA
film rewind system
sistema de rebobinado de la película
mécanisme de rebobinage
Filmrückspulung
viewfinder
visor
viseur
Bildsucher
focal plane shutter
obturador de cortina
rideau d'obturateur
Schlitzverschluß
take-up spool
carrete de rebobinado
bobine réceptrice
Filmaufrollspule
neckstrap eyelet
ojete para la correa del cuello
œillet d'attache
Öse für Schulterriemen
film sprocket
piñón de la rueda de la película
tambour d'entraînement
Transporträdchen
pressure plate
lámina de presión
presseur
Andruckplatte
film cartridge chamber
cámara para el cartucho de la película
logement de la bobine
Patronenkammer
film guide roller
rodillo guía de la película
cylindre guide-film
Transportwalze
film guide rail
carríl guía de la película
rail guide-film
Transportschiene
film leader indicator
indicador principal de la película
témoin de l'amorce du film
Markierung für Filmanfang

SINGLE-LENS REFLEX (SLR) CAMERA
CÁMARA RÉFLEX DE UN OBJETIVO
APPAREIL À VISÉE REFLEX MONO-OBJECTIF
EINÄUGIGE SPIEGELREFLEXKAMERA

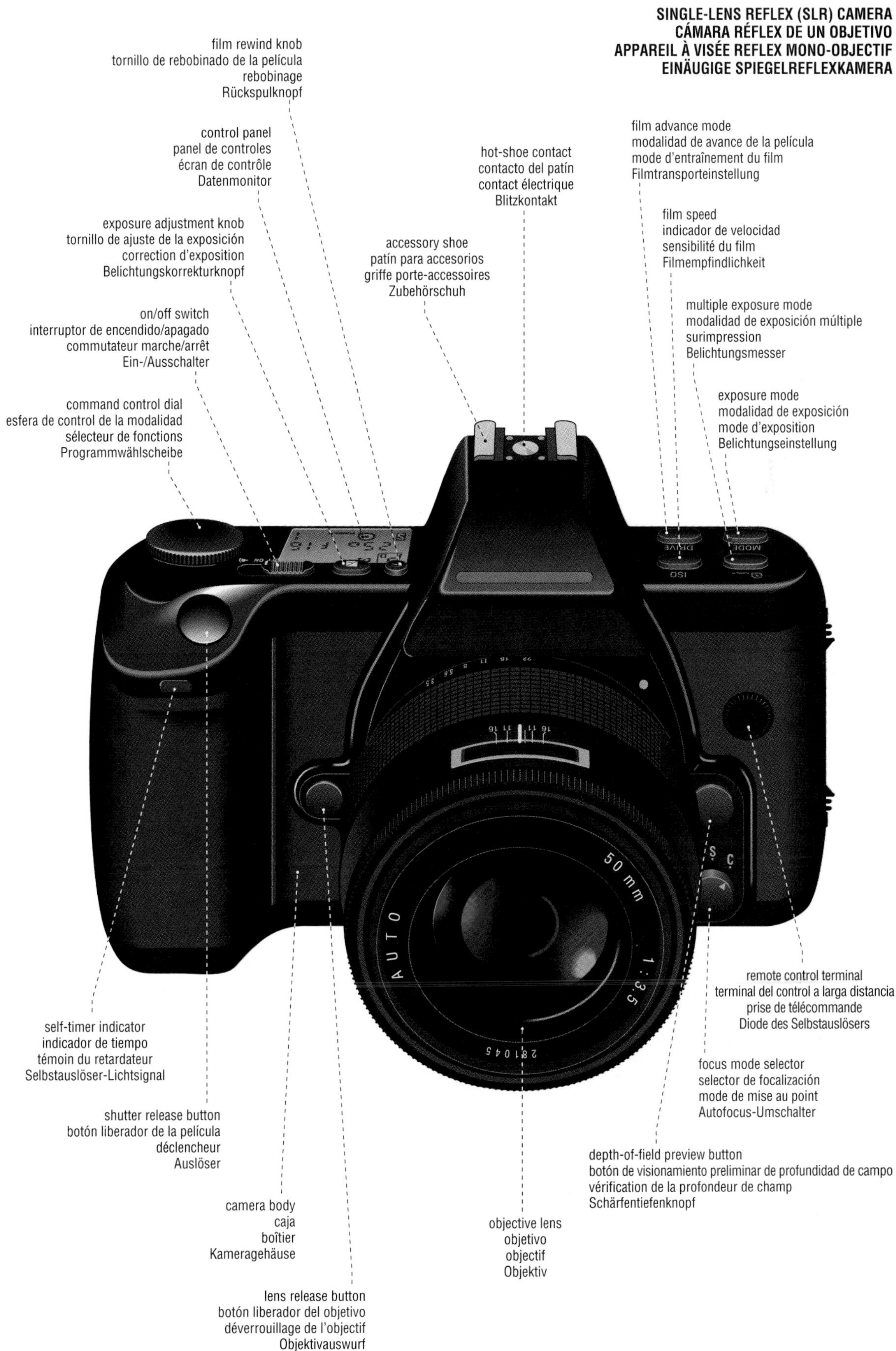

film rewind knob
tornillo de rebobinado de la película
rebobinage
Rückspulknopf
control panel
panel de controles
écran de contrôle
Datenmonitor
exposure adjustment knob
tornillo de ajuste de la exposición
correction d'exposition
Belichtungskorrekturknopf
on/off switch
interruptor de encendido/apagado
commutateur marche/arrêt
Ein-/Ausschalter
command control dial
esfera de control de la modalidad
sélecteur de fonctions
Programmwählscheibe
accessory shoe
patín para accesorios
griffe porte-accessoires
Zubehörschuh
hot-shoe contact
contacto del patín
contact électrique
Blitzkontakt
film advance mode
modalidad de avance de la película
mode d'entraînement du film
Filmtransporteinstellung
film speed
indicador de velocidad
sensibilité du film
Filmempfindlichkeit
multiple exposure mode
modalidad de exposición múltiple
surimpression
Belichtungsmesser
exposure mode
modalidad de exposición
mode d'exposition
Belichtungseinstellung
remote control terminal
terminal del control a larga distancia
prise de télécommande
Diode des Selbstauslösers
focus mode selector
selector de focalización
mode de mise au point
Autofocus-Umschalter
depth-of-field preview button
botón de visionamiento preliminar de profundidad de campo
vérification de la profondeur de champ
Schärfentiefenknopf
objective lens
objetivo
objectif
Objektiv
lens release button
botón liberador del objetivo
déverrouillage de l'objectif
Objektivauswurf
camera body
caja
boîtier
Kameragehäuse
shutter release button
botón liberador de la película
déclencheur
Auslöser
self-timer indicator
indicador de tiempo
témoin du retardateur
Selbstauslöser-Lichtsignal
DRIVE
MODE
ISO
50 mm
AUTO
1:3.5

PHOTOGRAPHY
FOTOGRAFÍA
PHOTOGRAPHIE
FOTOGRAFIE

LENSES
OBJETIVOS
OBJECTIFS
OBJEKTIVE

standard lens
objetivo normal
objectif normal
Standardobjektiv

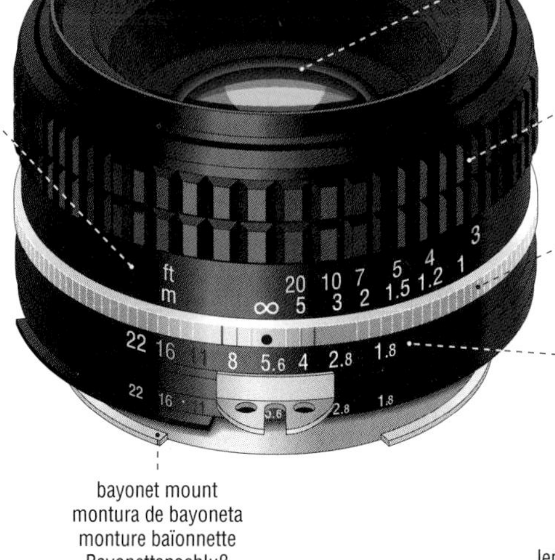
lens
objetivo
lentille
Linse
distance scale
escala de distancia
échelle des distances
Entfernungsskala
focus setting ring
anillo de ajuste del enfoque
bague de mise au point
Blendenring
depth-of-field scale
escala de profundidad de campo de visión
échelle de profondeur de champ
Schärfentiefenskala
lens aperture scale
escala de abertura del diafragma
échelle d'ouverture de diaphragme
Blendenskala
bayonet mount
montura de bayoneta
monture baïonnette
Bayonettanschluß
50 mm 1:1.8

wide-angle lens
gran angular
objectif grand-angulaire
Weitwinkelobjektiv

zoom lens
zoom
objectif zoom
Zoomobjektiv

semi-fisheye lens
ojo de pez
objectif super-grand-angle
Super-Weitwinkelobjektiv

telephoto lens
teleobjetivo
téléobjectif
Teleobjektiv

fisheye lens
lente de 180 grados
hypergone
Fischaugenobjektiv

LENS ACCESSORIES
OBJETIVOS Y ACCESORIOS
ACCESSOIRES DE L'OBJECTIF
OBJEKTIVZUBEHÖR

lens cap
tapa del objetivo
capuchon d'objectif
Objektivschutzdeckel

lens hood
capuchón
parasoleil
Gegenlichtblende

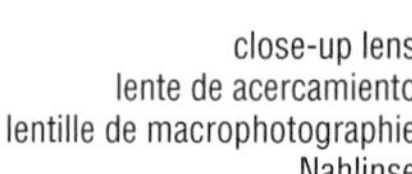

color filter
filtro de color
filtre de couleur
Farbfilter

close-up lens
lente de acercamiento
lentille de macrophotographie
Nahlinse

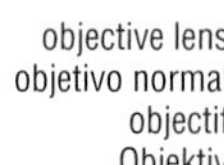

polarizing filter
filtro de polarización
filtre de polarisation
Polarisationsfilter

objective lens
objetivo normal
objectif
Objektiv

tele-converter
teleconvertidor
multiplicateur de focale
Telekonverter

PHOTOGRAPHIC ACCESSORIES
ACCESORIOS FOTOGRÁFICOS
ACCESSOIRES PHOTOGRAPHIQUES
FOTOGRAFISCHES ZUBEHÖR

electronic flash
flash electrónico
flash électronique
Elektronenblitz

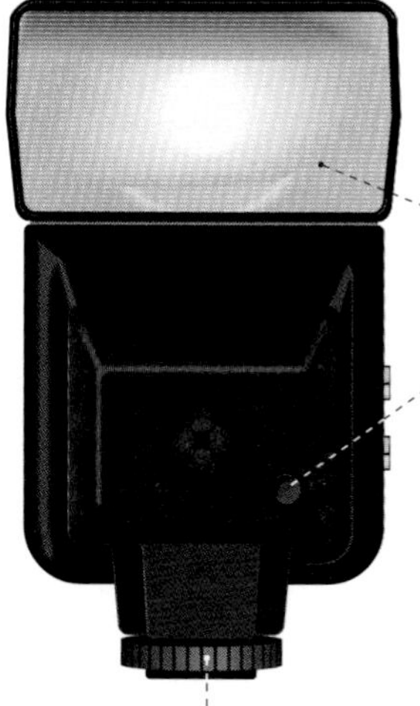

flashtube
tubo de flash
réflecteur
Blitzröhre

photoelectric cell
celda fotoeléctrica
cellule photoélectrique
Fotozelle

mounting foot
pie de montura
pied de fixation
Aufsteckschuh

air bulb shutter release
disparador neumático
déclencheur pneumatique
pneumatischer Auslöser

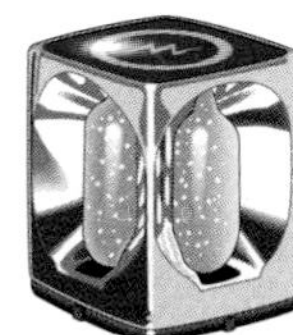

flashcube
cubo de flash
flash-cube
Blitzwürfel

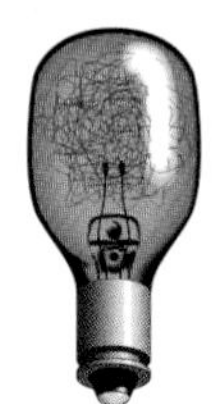

flash lamp
bombilla de flash
lampe-éclair
Blitzbirne

battery
pila
pile
Batterie

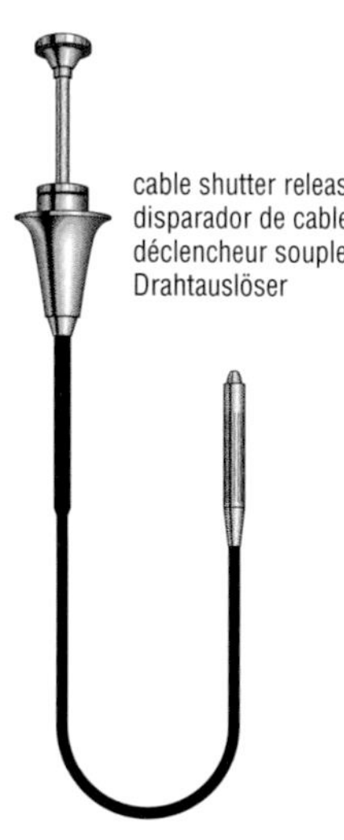

cable shutter release
disparador de cable
déclencheur souple
Drahtauslöser

TRIPOD
TRÍPODE
TRÉPIED
STATIV

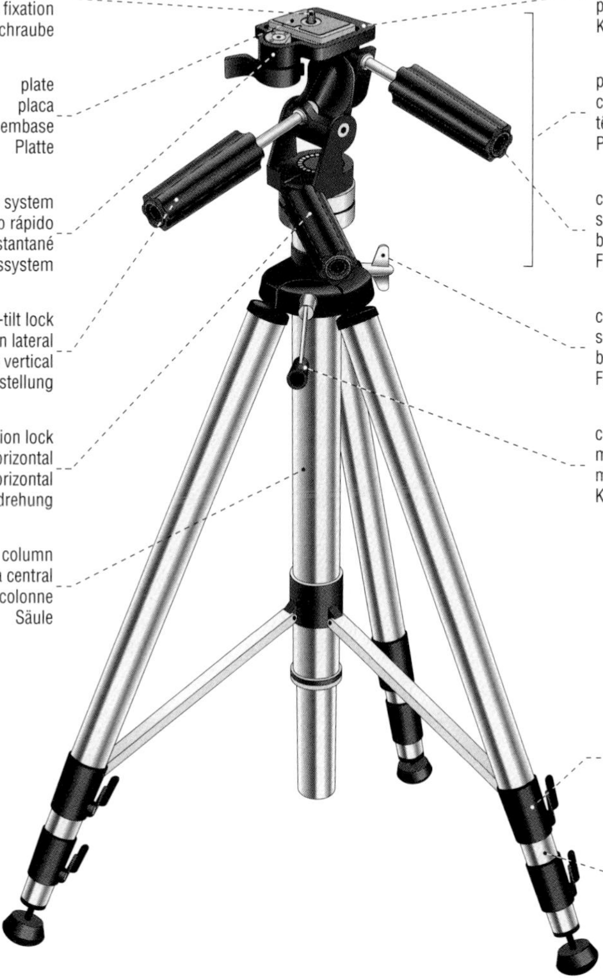

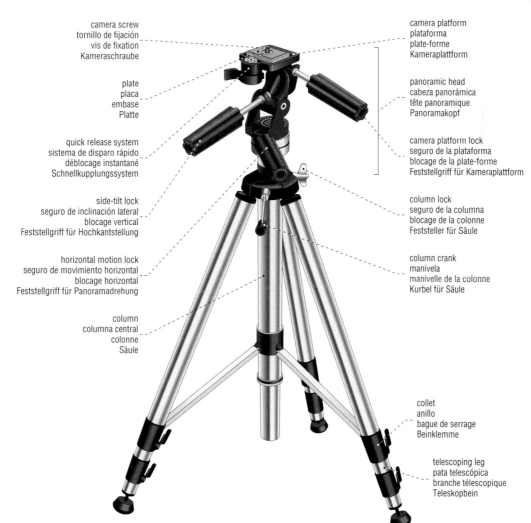

camera screw
tornillo de fijación
vis de fixation
Kameraschraube

camera platform
plataforma
plate-forme
Kameraplattform

plate
placa
embase
Platte

panoramic head
cabeza panorámica
tête panoramique
Panoramakopf

quick release system
sistema de disparo rápido
déblocage instantané
Schnellkupplungssystem

camera platform lock
seguro de la plataforma
blocage de la plate-forme
Feststellgriff für Kameraplattform

side-tilt lock
seguro de inclinación lateral
blocage vertical
Feststellgriff für Hochkantstellung

column lock
seguro de la columna
blocage de la colonne
Feststeller für Säule

horizontal motion lock
seguro de movimiento horizontal
blocage horizontal
Feststellgriff für Panoramadrehung

column crank
manivela
manivelle de la colonne
Kurbel für Säule

column
columna central
colonne
Säule

collet
anillo
bague de serrage
Beinklemme

telescoping leg
pata telescópica
branche télescopique
Teleskopbein

PHOTOGRAPHY
FOTOGRAFÍA
PHOTOGRAPHIE
FOTOGRAFIE

STILL CAMERAS
CÁMARAS FIJAS
APPAREILS PHOTOGRAPHIQUES
FOTOAPPARATE

rangefinder
telémetro
appareil à télémètre couplé
Sucherkamera

Polaroid® Land camera
cámara Polaroid Land
Polaroid®
Sofortbildkamera

underwater camera
cámara submarina
appareil de plongée
Unterwasserkamera

single-lens reflex camera
cámara reflex con objetivo simple
appareil à visée reflex mono-objectif
einäugige Spiegelreflexkamera

disposable camera
cámara desechable
appareil jetable
Einwegkamera

twin-lens reflex camera
cámara tipo réflex con dos objetivos
appareil reflex à deux objectifs
zweiäugige Spiegelreflexkamera

view camera
cámara de enfoque
chambre photographique
Großformatkamera

STILL CAMERAS
DIFERENTES TIPOS DE CÁMARAS FOTOGRÁFICAS
APPAREILS PHOTOGRAPHIQUES
FOTOAPPARATE

pocket camera
cámara de bolsillo
appareil petit-format
Pocket-Instamatic Kamera

medium format SLR (6 x 6)
formato mediano SLR (6x6)
appareil reflex 6 X 6 mono-objectif
Mittelformatkamera SLR(6 x 6)

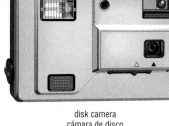

disk camera
cámara de disco
appareil pour photodisque
Disc-Kamera

stereo camera
cámara estereofotogramétrica
appareil stéréoscopique
Stereokamera

still video camera
cámara de video fijo
appareil de videophoto
Videokamera

FILMS
PELÍCULAS
PELLICULES
FILME

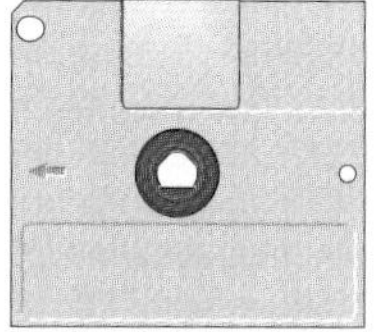

still video film disk
película de disco para video fijo
disque videophoto
Videofilmdiskette

film leader
principio de la película
amorce
Filmlasche

perforation
perforación
perforation
Perforierung

cassette film
cartucho de la película
cartouche de pellicule
Patronenfilm

film disk
película de disco
film-disque
Filmdiskette

cartridge film
cartucho de la película
cassette de pellicule
Kassettenfilm

sheet film
hoja de la película
pellicule en feuille
Planfilm

roll film
rollo de la película
rouleau de pellicule
Rollfilm

film pack
paquete de placas fotográficas
film-pack
Filmkassette

PHOTOGRAPHY
FOTOGRAFÍA
PHOTOGRAPHIE
FOTOGRAFIE

EXPOSURE METER
FOTÓMETRO
POSEMÈTRE PHOTO-ÉLECTRIQUE
BELICHTUNGSMESSER

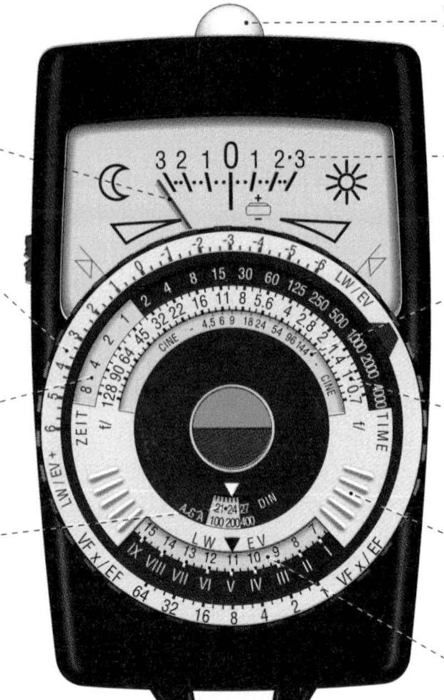
diffuser
difusor
tête diffusante
Diffusionskalotte
indicator needle
aguja indicadora
aiguille
Anzeigenadel
light-reading scale
escala de lectura
échelle de lecture de la luminosité
Lichtwertskala
exposure value
índices de exposición
indice d'exposition
Belichtungswert
cine scale
escala de imágenes por segundo
cadence images/seconde
Cine-Skala
exposure-time scale
escala de duración de la exposición
échelle des temps d'exposition
Belichtungszeitskala
aperture scale
escala de abertura
échelle d'ouverture
Blendenskala
film speed
velocidad de la película
sensibilité du film
Filmempfindlichkeit
calculator dial
cuadrante calculador
disque de réglage
Rechenscheibe
transfer scale
escala de transferencia
report de lecture
Umrechnungsskala

SPOTMETER
FOTÓMETRO ELECTRÓNICO
POSEMÈTRE À VISÉE REFLEX
SPOTMETER

average key
botón de luminosidad media
réglage sur demi-teinte
Taste für Mittelwerte

highlight key
botón de fuerte luminosidad
réglage sur haute lumière
Hi.-Taste

shadow key
botón de sombra
réglage sur ombre
Shadow-Taste

eyepiece
ocular
oculaire
Okular

lock switch
seguro
fixe-lecture
Ein-/Ausschalter

data display
visualización de la información
écran d'affichage
Display

objective lens
objetivo
objectif
Objektiv

memory cancel
botón para cancelar la memoria
effacement de mémoire
Speicherlöschtaste

shutter speed setting
ajuste de la velocidad del obturador
réglage de la vitesse d'obturation
Tasten für Erhöhen/Absenken

measuring button
botón de medición
bouton de mise en circuit
Meßtaste

aperture/exposure value display
visualización de valores de abertura y de exposición
affichage ouverture/temps d'exposition
Anzeige für Blende/Belichtungswert

film speed
sensibilidad de la película
sensibilité du film
Filmempfindlichkeit

memory recall key
botón de llamado de memoria
rappel de mémoire
Rückruftaste

data display illumination button
botón de iluminación de la pantalla
éclairage de l'écran d'affichage
Displaybeleuchtungstaste

memory key
botón de memoria
commande de mémoire
Speichertaste

SLIDE PROJECTOR
PROYECTOR DE DIAPOSITIVAS
PROJECTEUR DE DIAPOSITIVES
DIAPROJEKTOR

PROJECTION SCREEN
PANTALLA DE PROYECCIÓN
ÉCRAN DE PROJECTION
PROJEKTIONSWAND

TRANSPARENCY SLIDE
DIAPOSITIVA
DIAPOSITIVE
DIA

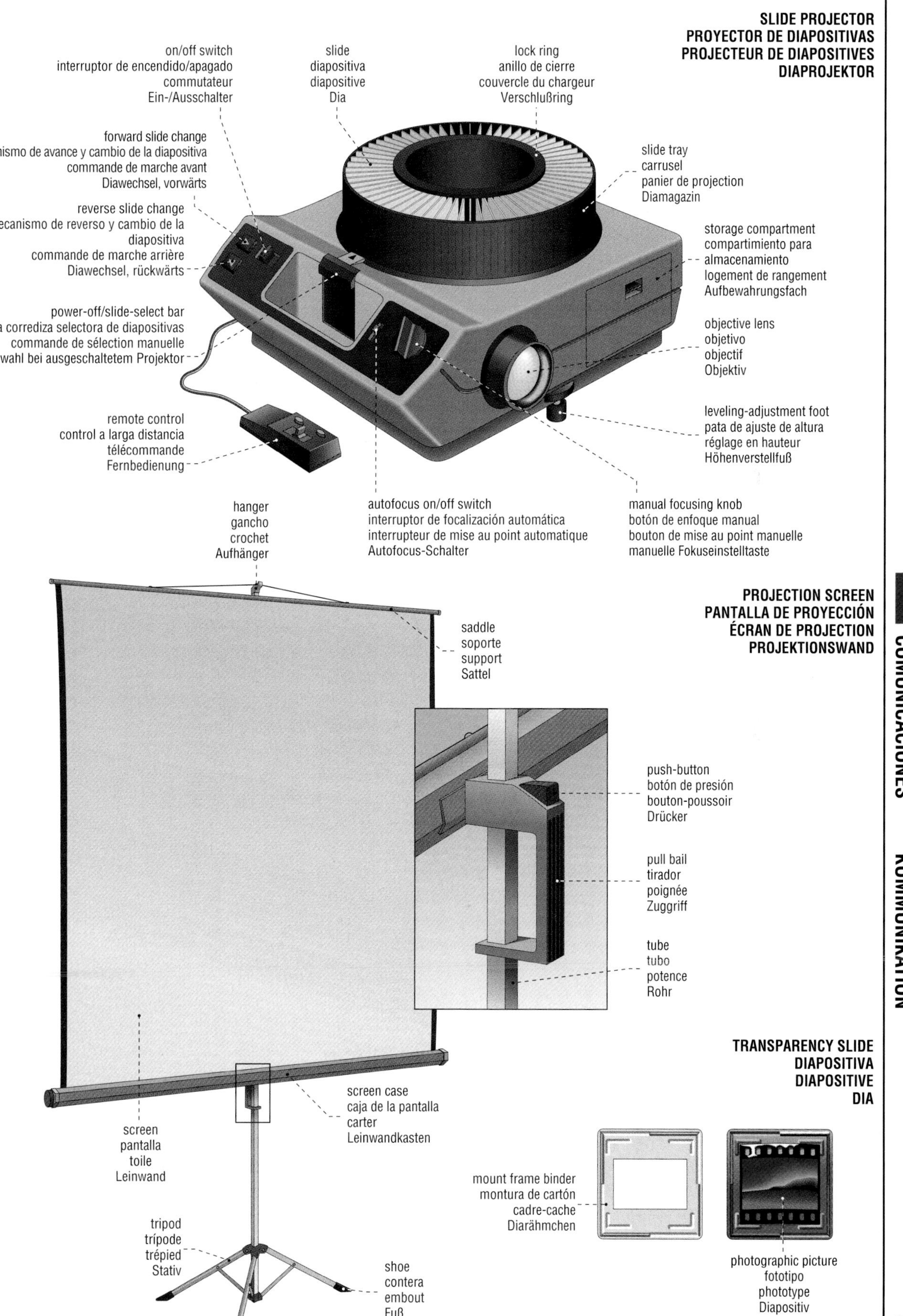

on/off switch
interruptor de encendido/apagado
commutateur
Ein-/Ausschalter
slide
diapositiva
diapositive
Dia
lock ring
anillo de cierre
couvercle du chargeur
Verschlußring
forward slide change
ecanismo de avance y cambio de la diapositiva
commande de marche avant
Diawechsel, vorwärts
slide tray
carrusel
panier de projection
Diamagazin
reverse slide change
mecanismo de reverso y cambio de la diapositiva
commande de marche arrière
Diawechsel, rückwärts
storage compartment
compartimiento para almacenamiento
logement de rangement
Aufbewahrungsfach
power-off/slide-select bar
anca corrediza selectora de diapositivas
commande de sélection manuelle
Diawahl bei ausgeschaltetem Projektor
objective lens
objetivo
objectif
Objektiv
remote control
control a larga distancia
télécommande
Fernbedienung
leveling-adjustment foot
pata de ajuste de altura
réglage en hauteur
Höhenverstellfuß
autofocus on/off switch
interruptor de focalización automática
interrupteur de mise au point automatique
Autofocus-Schalter
manual focusing knob
botón de enfoque manual
bouton de mise au point manuelle
manuelle Fokuseinstelltaste
hanger
gancho
crochet
Aufhänger
saddle
soporte
support
Sattel
push-button
botón de presión
bouton-poussoir
Drücker
pull bail
tirador
poignée
Zuggriff
tube
tubo
potence
Rohr
screen case
caja de la pantalla
carter
Leinwandkasten
screen
pantalla
toile
Leinwand
mount frame binder
montura de cartón
cadre-cache
Diarähmchen
tripod
trípode
trépied
Stativ
shoe
contera
embout
Fuß
photographic picture
fototipo
phototype
Diapositiv

PHOTOGRAPHY
FOTOGRAFÍA
PHOTOGRAPHIE
FOTOGRAFIE

DEVELOPING TANK
TANQUE DE REVELADO
CUVE DE DÉVELOPPEMENT
ENTWICKLUNGSTROMMEL
cap
capuchón
capuchon
Kappe
lid
tapa
couvercle
Deckel
reel
espiral
spirale
Spirale
tank
cubeta
cuve
Dose
lightbox
caja luminosa
négatoscope
Leuchtpult
timer
reloj
minuterie
Laboruhr
safelight
luz inactínica
éclairage inactinique
Laborleuchte
guillotine trimmer
guillotina
cisaille
Längsschneidemaschine
film drying cabinet
armario de secado de negativos
armoire de séchage
Trockenschrank
easel
marginadora
margeur
Vergrößerungsrahmen
contact printer
prensa de contactos
châssis-presse
Kontaktkopiergerät

NEGATIVE CARRIER
PORTANEGATIVOS
PORTE-NÉGATIF
NEGATIVHALTER

window
ventana
fenêtre
Sichtfenster

negative
negativo
négatif
Negativ

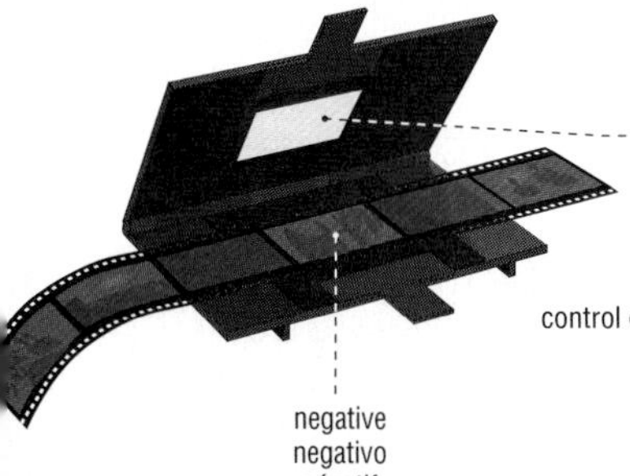

enlarger timer
reloj de la ampliadora
compte-pose
Belichtungs-Schaltuhr

ENLARGER
AMPLIADORA
AGRANDISSEUR
VERGRÖSSERER

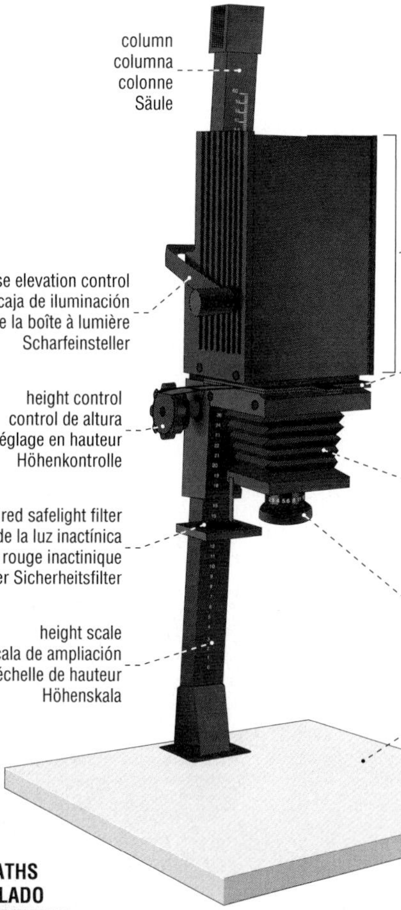

column
columna
colonne
Säule

lamphouse head
cabeza de la caja de iluminación
boîte à lumière
Beleuchtungskopf

lamphouse elevation control
control de elevación de la caja de iluminación
ouverture de la boîte à lumière
Scharfeinsteller

negative carrier
portanegativos
porte-négatif
Negativhalter

height control
control de altura
réglage en hauteur
Höhenkontrolle

bellows
fuelle
soufflet
Balgen

red safelight filter
filtro rojode la luz inactínica
filtre rouge inactinique
roter Sicherheitsfilter

enlarging lens
lente de ampliación
objectif d'agrandissement
Vergrößerungsobjektiv

height scale
escala de ampliación
échelle de hauteur
Höhenskala

baseboard
tablero de base
plateau
Grundplatte

DEVELOPING BATHS
BAÑOS DE REVELADO
BAINS DE DÉVELOPPEMENT
ENTWICKLUNGSBÄDER

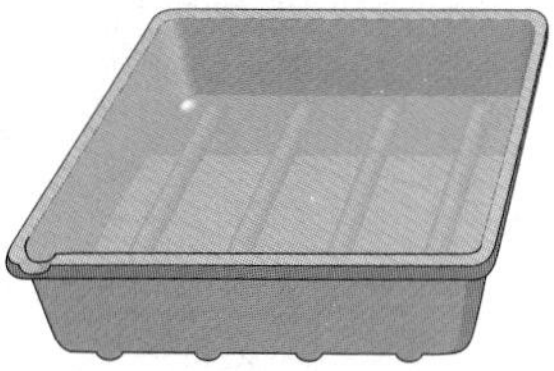

developer bath
baño de revelado
bain de révélateur
Entwickler

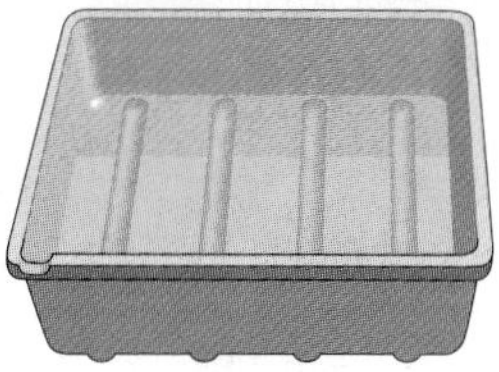

stop bath
baño de pare
bain d'arrêt
Stoppbad

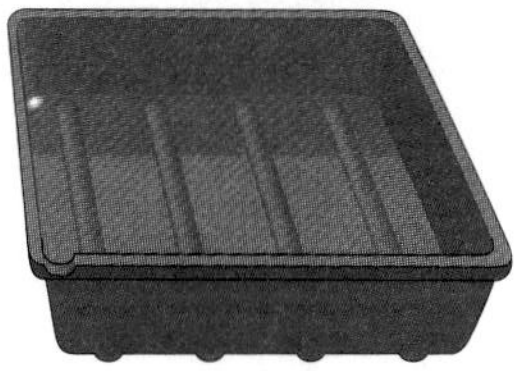

fixing bath
baño de fijación
bain de fixation
Fixierbad

focusing magnifier
lupade focalización
loupe de mise au point
Scharfsteller

PRINT WASHER
CUBETA PARA LAVAR IMPRESIONES
LAVEUSE POUR ÉPREUVES
BILDERWASCHER

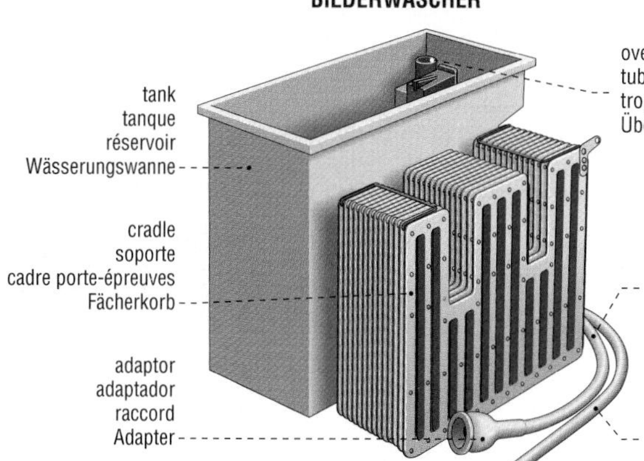

tank
tanque
réservoir
Wässerungswanne

overflow tube
tubo de drenaje
trop-plein
Überlaufstutzen

cradle
soporte
cadre porte-épreuves
Fächerkorb

inlet hose
manguera de llenado
flexible de branchement
Schlauch für Wasserzufluß

adaptor
adaptador
raccord
Adapter

outlet hose
manguera de vaciado
renvoi d'eau
Schlauch für Wasserablauf

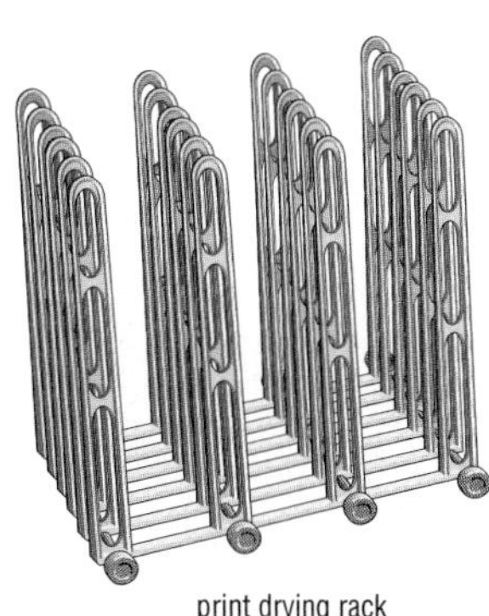

print drying rack
secadora de pruebas
séchoir d'épreuves
Trockenständer

SOUND REPRODUCING SYSTEM
EQUIPO ESTEREOFÓNICO
CHAÎNE STÉRÉO
TONWIEDERGABESYSTEM

SYSTEM COMPONENTS
COMPONENTES
COMPOSANTES D'UN SYSTÈME
SYSTEMBAUSTEINE

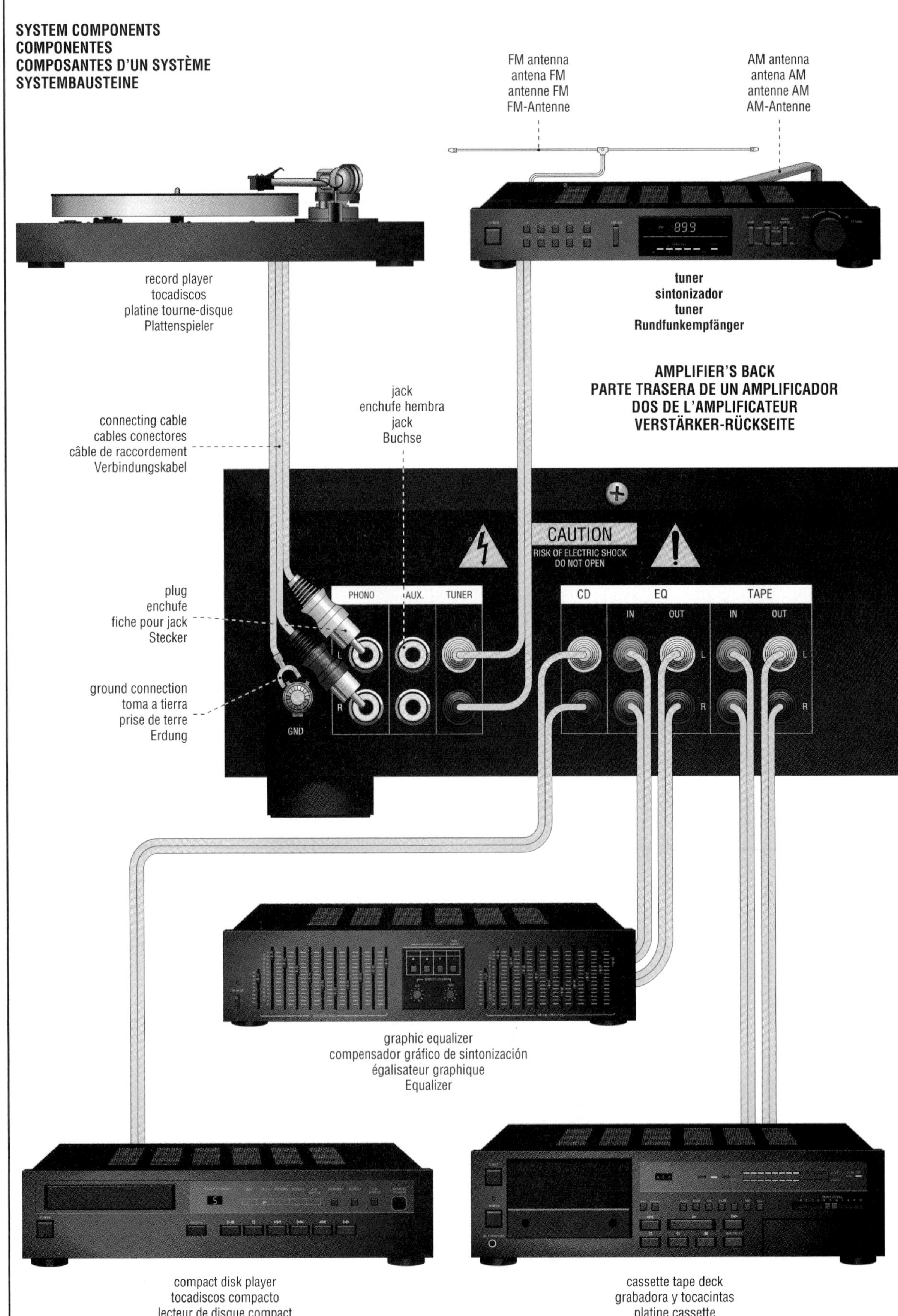

FM antenna
antena FM
antenne FM
FM-Antenne
AM antenna
antena AM
antenne AM
AM-Antenne
record player
tocadiscos
platine tourne-disque
Plattenspieler
tuner
sintonizador
tuner
Rundfunkempfänger
AMPLIFIER'S BACK
PARTE TRASERA DE UN AMPLIFICADOR
DOS DE L'AMPLIFICATEUR
VERSTÄRKER-RÜCKSEITE
jack
enchufe hembra
jack
Buchse
connecting cable
cables conectores
câble de raccordement
Verbindungskabel
CAUTION
RISK OF ELECTRIC SHOCK
DO NOT OPEN
PHONO
AUX.
TUNER
CD
EQ
TAPE
IN
OUT
IN
OUT
L
R
plug
enchufe
fiche pour jack
Stecker
ground connection
toma a tierra
prise de terre
Erdung
GND
graphic equalizer
compensador gráfico de sintonización
égalisateur graphique
Equalizer
compact disk player
tocadiscos compacto
lecteur de disque compact
CD-Spieler
cassette tape deck
grabadora y tocacintas
platine cassette
Kassettendeck

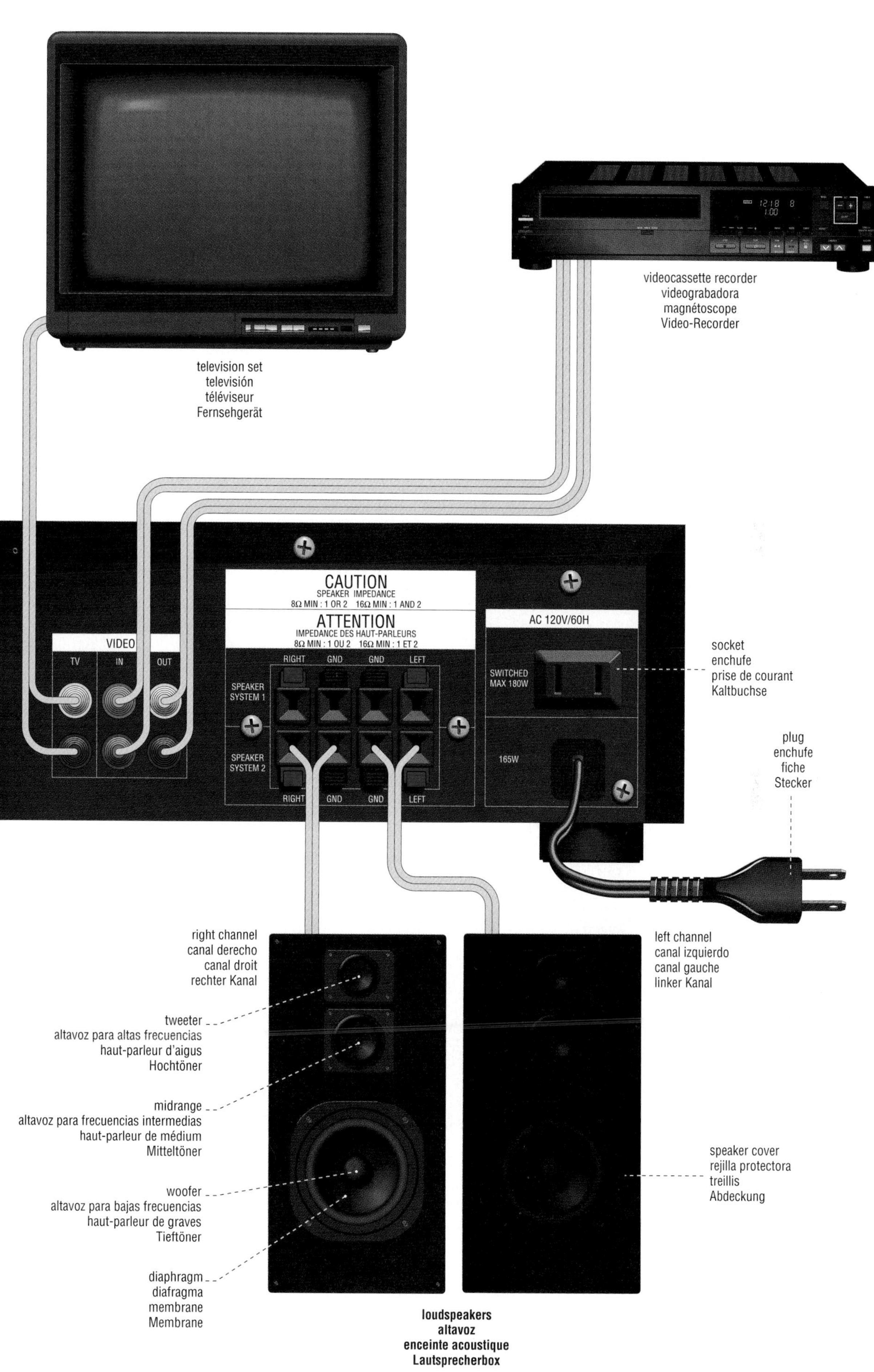
videocassette recorder
videograbadora
magnétoscope
Video-Recorder
television set
televisión
téléviseur
Fernsehgerät
VIDEO
TV
IN
OUT
CAUTION
SPEAKER IMPEDANCE
8Ω MIN : 1 OR 2 16Ω MIN : 1 AND 2
ATTENTION
IMPEDANCE DES HAUT-PARLEURS
8Ω MIN : 1 OU 2 16Ω MIN : 1 ET 2
RIGHT
GND
GND
LEFT
SPEAKER SYSTEM 1
SPEAKER SYSTEM 2
AC 120V/60H
SWITCHED MAX 180W
165W
socket
enchufe
prise de courant
Kaltbuchse
plug
enchufe
fiche
Stecker
right channel
canal derecho
canal droit
rechter Kanal
left channel
canal izquierdo
canal gauche
linker Kanal
tweeter
altavoz para altas frecuencias
haut-parleur d'aigus
Hochtöner
midrange
altavoz para frecuencias intermedias
haut-parleur de médium
Mitteltöner
woofer
altavoz para bajas frecuencias
haut-parleur de graves
Tieftöner
diaphragm
diafragma
membrane
Membrane
speaker cover
rejilla protectora
treillis
Abdeckung

loudspeakers
altavoz
enceinte acoustique
Lautsprecherbox

SOUND REPRODUCING SYSTEM
EQUIPO ESTEREOFÓNICO
CHAÎNE STÉRÉO
TONWIEDERGABESYSTEM

TUNER
SINTONIZADOR
TUNER
RUNDFUNKEMPFÄNGER

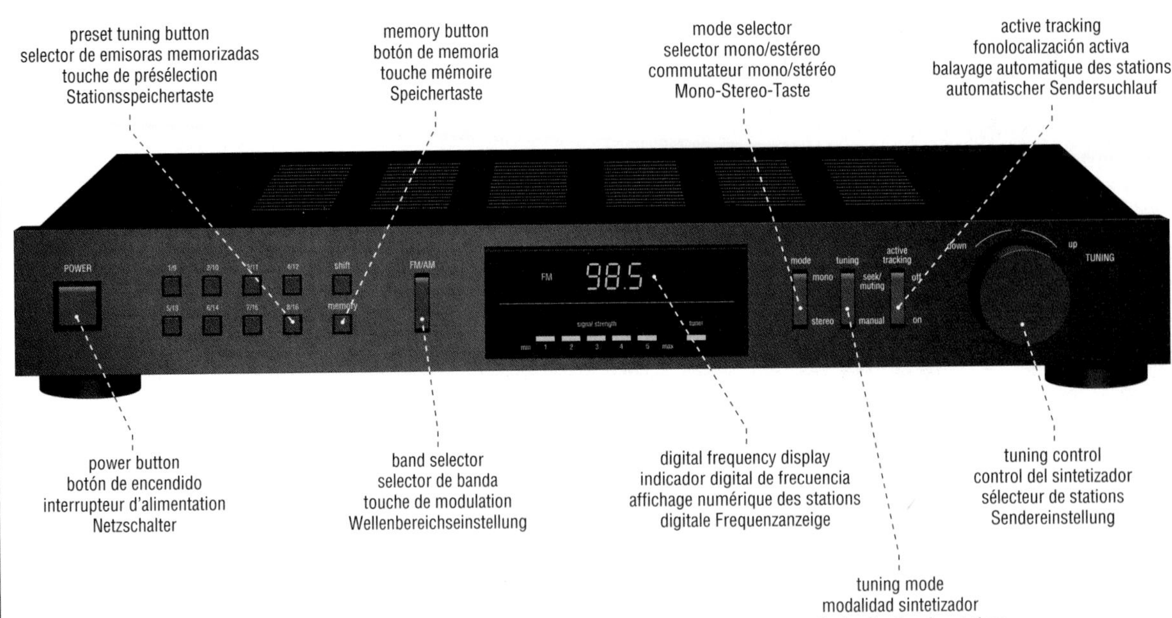

POWER
shift
memory
FM/AM
FM
98.5
signal strength
tuner
mode
tuning
active tracking
mono
stereo
seek/muting
manual
off
on
down
up
TUNING

preset tuning button
selector de emisoras memorizadas
touche de présélection
Stationsspeichertaste

memory button
botón de memoria
touche mémoire
Speichertaste

mode selector
selector mono/estéreo
commutateur mono/stéréo
Mono-Stereo-Taste

active tracking
fonolocalización activa
balayage automatique des stations
automatischer Sendersuchlauf

power button
botón de encendido
interrupteur d'alimentation
Netzschalter

band selector
selector de banda
touche de modulation
Wellenbereichseinstellung

digital frequency display
indicador digital de frecuencia
affichage numérique des stations
digitale Frequenzanzeige

tuning control
control del sintetizador
sélecteur de stations
Sendereinstellung

tuning mode
modalidad sintetizador
mode de sélection des stations
Modus-Taste

AMPLIFIER
AMPLIFICADOR
AMPLIFICATEUR
VERSTÄRKER

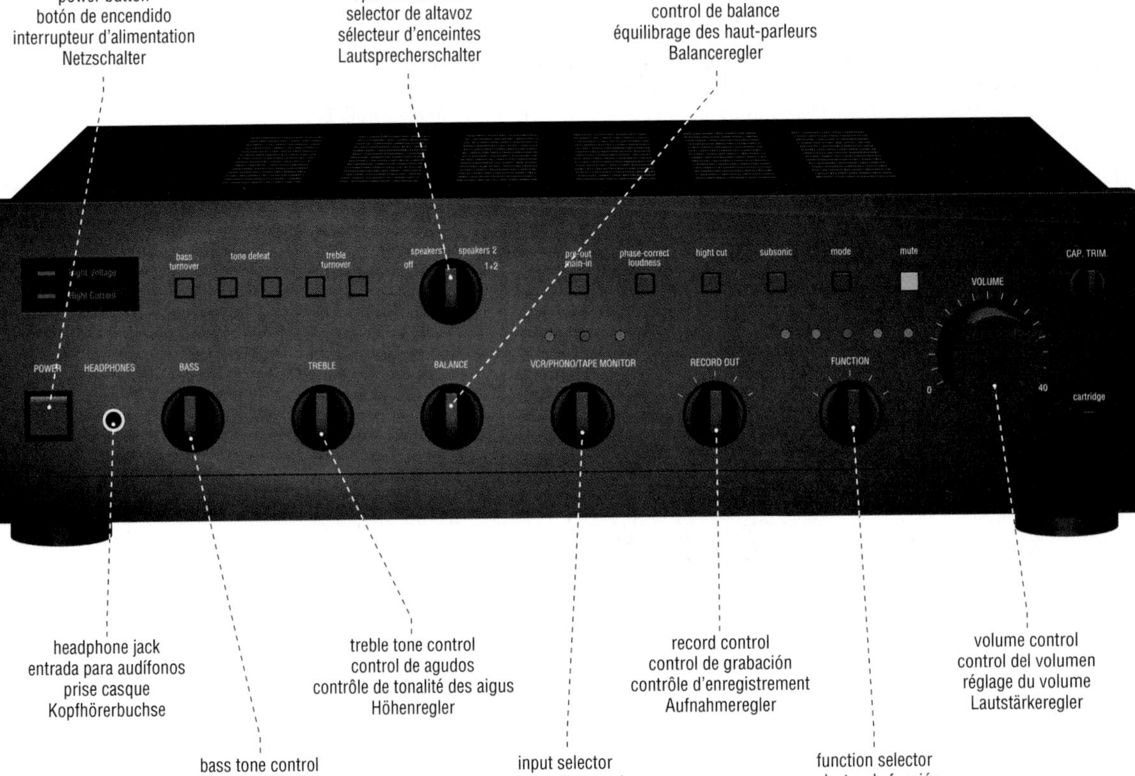

bass turnover
tone defeat
treble turnover
speakers 1
speakers 2
off
1+2
pre-out main-in
phase-correct loudness
high cut
subsonic
mode
mute
CAP. TRIM
VOLUME
POWER
HEADPHONES
BASS
TREBLE
BALANCE
VCR/PHONO/TAPE MONITOR
RECORD OUT
FUNCTION
0
40
cartridge

power button
botón de encendido
interrupteur d'alimentation
Netzschalter

speaker selector
selector de altavoz
sélecteur d'enceintes
Lautsprecherschalter

balance control
control de balance
équilibrage des haut-parleurs
Balanceregler

headphone jack
entrada para audífonos
prise casque
Kopfhörerbuchse

treble tone control
control de agudos
contrôle de tonalité des aigus
Höhenregler

record control
control de grabación
contrôle d'enregistrement
Aufnahmeregler

volume control
control del volumen
réglage du volume
Lautstärkeregler

bass tone control
control de graves
contrôle de tonalité des graves
Baßregler

input selector
selector de entrada
commutateur d'entrée
Eingangsschalter

function selector
selector de función
commutateur de fonctions
Funktionsschalter

CASSETTE
CASETE
CASSETTE
KASSETTE

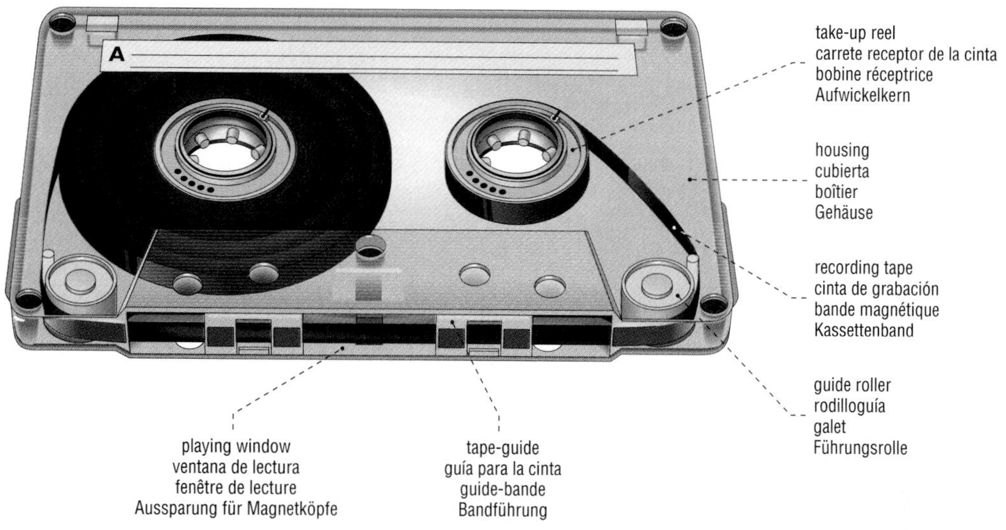
take-up reel
carrete receptor de la cinta
bobine réceptrice
Aufwickelkern
housing
cubierta
boîtier
Gehäuse
recording tape
cinta de grabación
bande magnétique
Kassettenband
guide roller
rodilloguía
galet
Führungsrolle
playing window
ventana de lectura
fenêtre de lecture
Aussparung für Magnetköpfe
tape-guide
guía para la cinta
guide-bande
Bandführung

CASSETTE TAPE DECK
GRABADORA Y TOCACINTAS
PLATINE CASSETTE
KASSETTENDECK

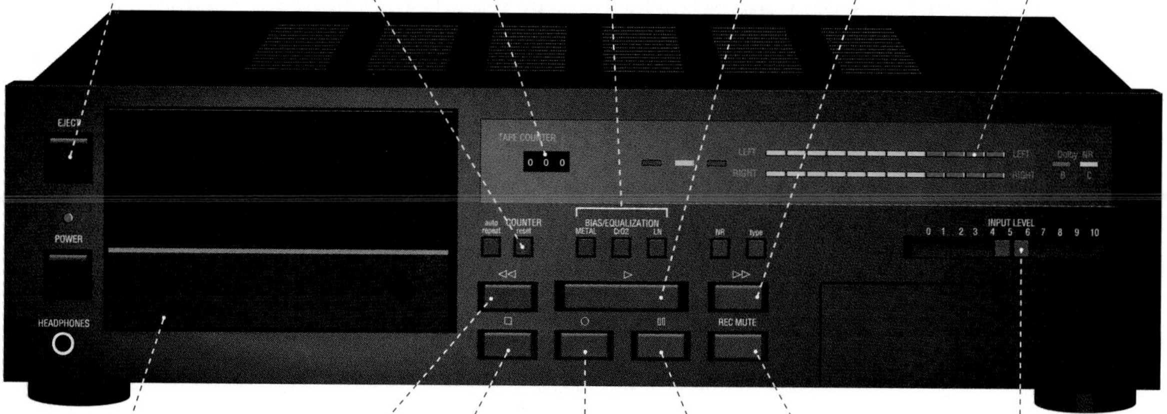

counter reset button
botón del contador a ceros
bouton de remise à zéro
Rückstelltaste

tape selector
selector de tipo de cinta
sélecteur de bandes
Bandsortenschalter

fast-forward button
botón de avance rápido
avance rapide
Schnellvorlauf-Taste

eject button
botón de expulsión
bouton d'éjection
Auswurf-Taste

tape counter
contador
compteur
Zählwerk

play button
botón de reproducción
lecture
Play-Taste

peak level meter
medidor de altos niveles de frecuencia
indicateur de niveau
LED-Pegelanzeige

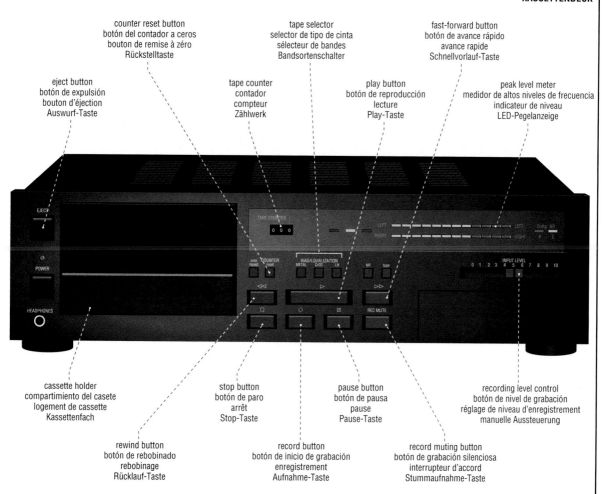

cassette holder
compartimiento del casete
logement de cassette
Kassettenfach

stop button
botón de paro
arrêt
Stop-Taste

pause button
botón de pausa
pause
Pause-Taste

recording level control
botón de nivel de grabación
réglage de niveau d'enregistrement
manuelle Aussteuerung

rewind button
botón de rebobinado
rebobinage
Rücklauf-Taste

record button
botón de inicio de grabación
enregistrement
Aufnahme-Taste

record muting button
botón de grabación silenciosa
interrupteur d'accord
Stummaufnahme-Taste

SOUND REPRODUCING SYSTEM
EQUIPO ESTEREOFÓNICO
CHAÎNE STÉRÉO
TONWIEDERGABESYSTEM

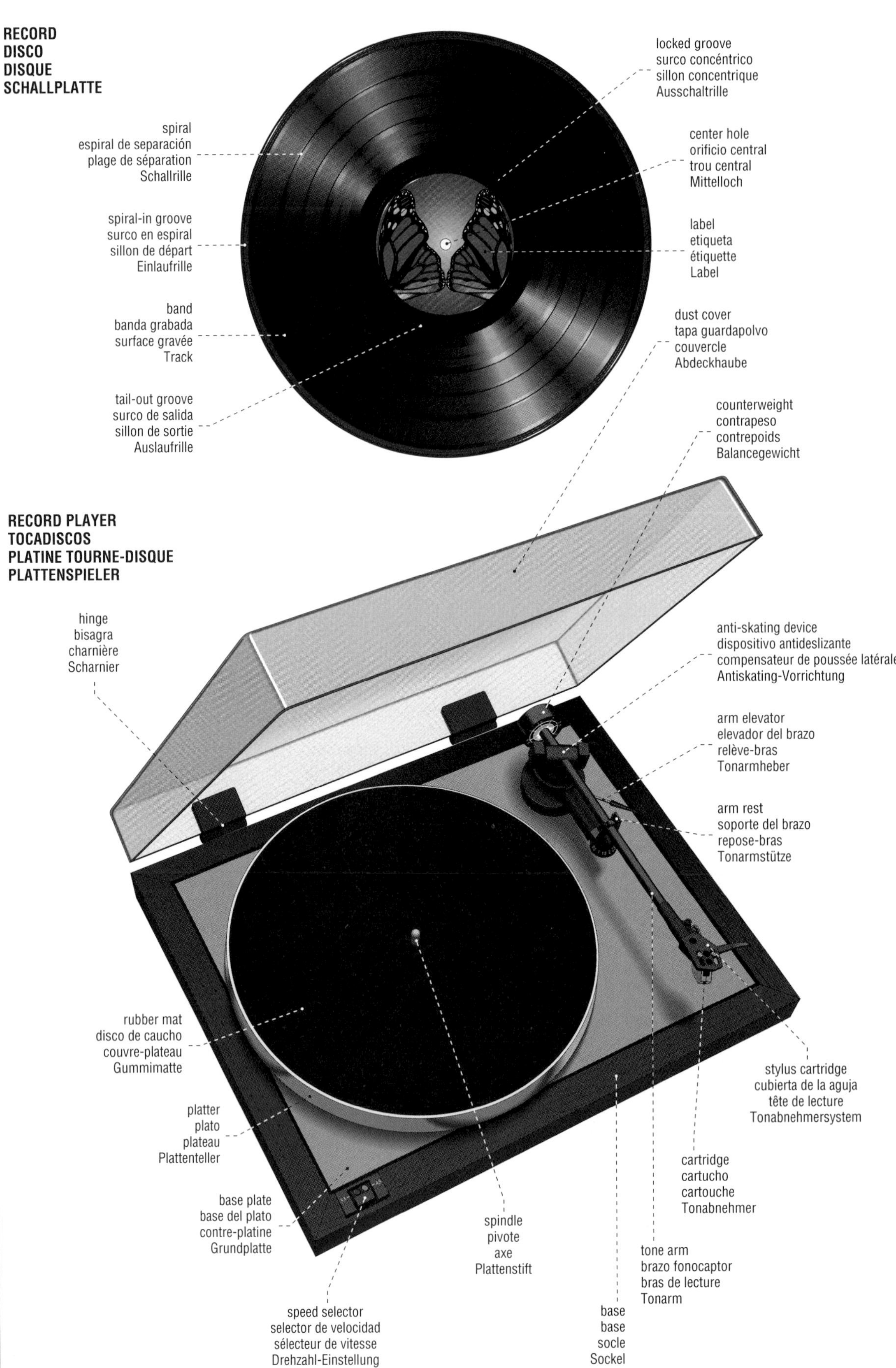
RECORD
DISCO
DISQUE
SCHALLPLATTE
spiral
espiral de separación
plage de séparation
Schallrille
spiral-in groove
surco en espiral
sillon de départ
Einlaufrille
band
banda grabada
surface gravée
Track
tail-out groove
surco de salida
sillon de sortie
Auslaufrille
locked groove
surco concéntrico
sillon concentrique
Ausschaltrille
center hole
orificio central
trou central
Mittelloch
label
etiqueta
étiquette
Label
dust cover
tapa guardapolvo
couvercle
Abdeckhaube
counterweight
contrapeso
contrepoids
Balancegewicht
RECORD PLAYER
TOCADISCOS
PLATINE TOURNE-DISQUE
PLATTENSPIELER
hinge
bisagra
charnière
Scharnier
anti-skating device
dispositivo antideslizante
compensateur de poussée latérale
Antiskating-Vorrichtung
arm elevator
elevador del brazo
relève-bras
Tonarmheber
arm rest
soporte del brazo
repose-bras
Tonarmstütze
rubber mat
disco de caucho
couvre-plateau
Gummimatte
platter
plato
plateau
Plattenteller
base plate
base del plato
contre-platine
Grundplatte
stylus cartridge
cubierta de la aguja
tête de lecture
Tonabnehmersystem
cartridge
cartucho
cartouche
Tonabnehmer
spindle
pivote
axe
Plattenstift
tone arm
brazo fonocaptor
bras de lecture
Tonarm
speed selector
selector de velocidad
sélecteur de vitesse
Drehzahl-Einstellung
base
base
socle
Sockel

COMPACT DISK
DISCO COMPACTO
DISQUE COMPACT
COMPACT DISC

COMPACT DISK PLAYER
LECTOR DE DISCO COMPACTO
LECTEUR DE DISQUE COMPACT
CD-SPIELER

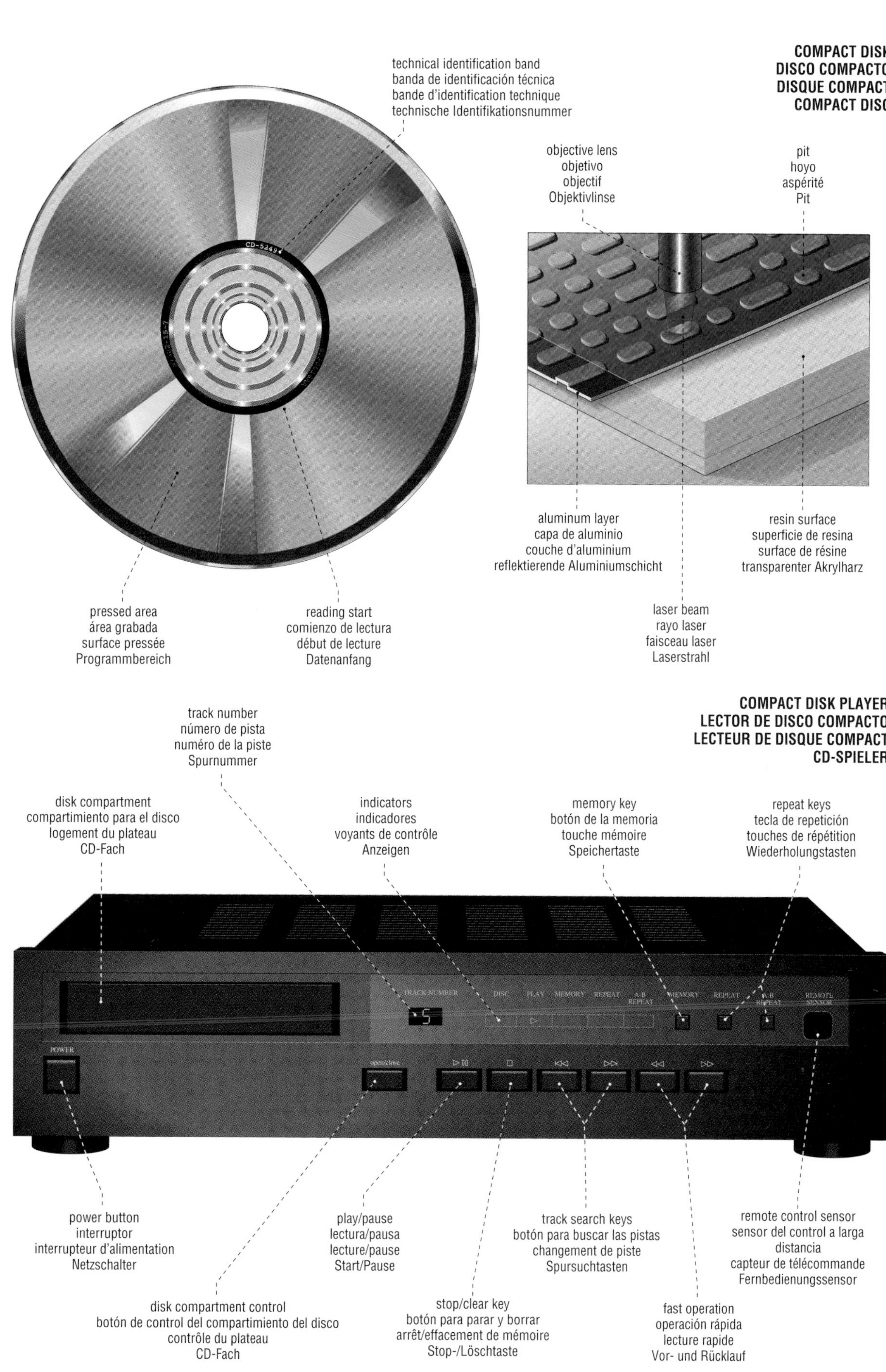

technical identification band
banda de identificación técnica
bande d'identification technique
technische Identifikationsnummer
CD-5249
objective lens
objetivo
objectif
Objektivlinse
pit
hoyo
aspérité
Pit
aluminum layer
capa de aluminio
couche d'aluminium
reflektierende Aluminiumschicht
resin surface
superficie de resina
surface de résine
transparenter Akrylharz
laser beam
rayo laser
faisceau laser
Laserstrahl
pressed area
área grabada
surface pressée
Programmbereich
reading start
comienzo de lectura
début de lecture
Datenanfang
track number
número de pista
numéro de la piste
Spurnummer
disk compartment
compartimiento para el disco
logement du plateau
CD-Fach
indicators
indicadores
voyants de contrôle
Anzeigen
memory key
botón de la memoria
touche mémoire
Speichertaste
repeat keys
tecla de repetición
touches de répétition
Wiederholungstasten
TRACK NUMBER
DISC
PLAY
MEMORY
REPEAT
A-B REPEAT
MEMORY
REPEAT
A-B REPEAT
REMOTE SENSOR
POWER
open/close
power button
interruptor
interrupteur d'alimentation
Netzschalter
play/pause
lectura/pausa
lecture/pause
Start/Pause
track search keys
botón para buscar las pistas
changement de piste
Spursuchtasten
remote control sensor
sensor del control a larga distancia
capteur de télécommande
Fernbedienungssensor
disk compartment control
botón de control del compartimiento del disco
contrôle du plateau
CD-Fach
stop/clear key
botón para parar y borrar
arrêt/effacement de mémoire
Stop-/Löschtaste
fast operation
operación rápida
lecture rapide
Vor- und Rücklauf

DYNAMIC MICROPHONE
MICRÓFONO ELECTRODINÁMICO
MICROPHONE DYNAMIQUE
ELEKTRODYNAMISCHES MIKROFON

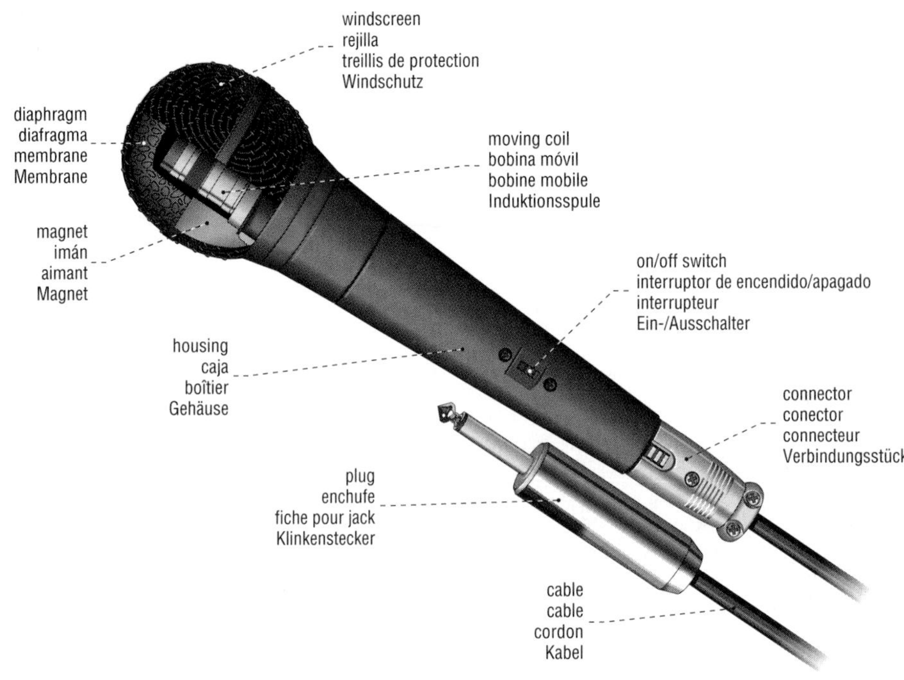

windscreen
rejilla
treillis de protection
Windschutz
diaphragm
diafragma
membrane
Membrane
moving coil
bobina móvil
bobine mobile
Induktionsspule
magnet
imán
aimant
Magnet
on/off switch
interruptor de encendido/apagado
interrupteur
Ein-/Ausschalter
housing
caja
boîtier
Gehäuse
connector
conector
connecteur
Verbindungsstück
plug
enchufe
fiche pour jack
Klinkenstecker
cable
cable
cordon
Kabel

HEADPHONES
AURICULARES
CASQUE D'ÉCOUTE
KOPFHÖRER

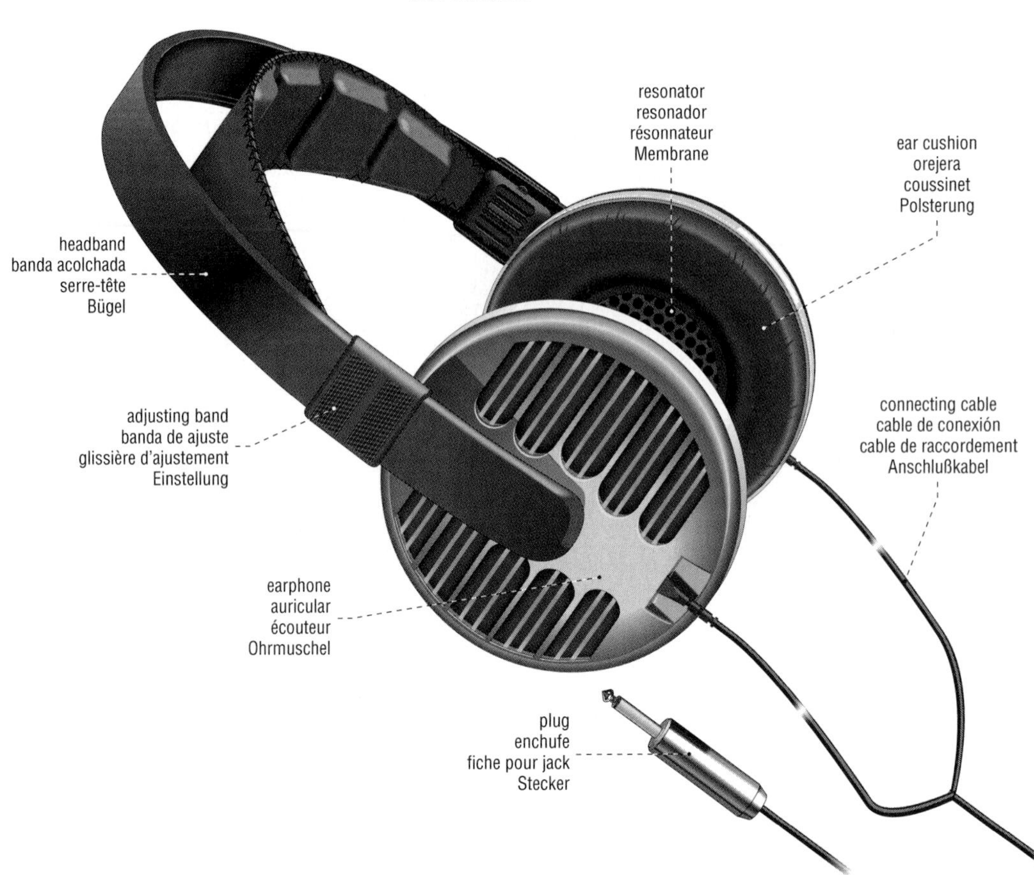

resonator
resonador
résonnateur
Membrane
ear cushion
orejera
coussinet
Polsterung
headband
banda acolchada
serre-tête
Bügel
adjusting band
banda de ajuste
glissière d'ajustement
Einstellung
connecting cable
cable de conexión
cable de raccordement
Anschlußkabel
earphone
auricular
écouteur
Ohrmuschel
plug
enchufe
fiche pour jack
Stecker

RADIO: STUDIO AND CONTROL ROOM
ESTUDIO DE RADIO Y SALA DE CONTROL
RADIO: STUDIO ET RÉGIE
RUNDFUNK: SPRECHERRAUM UND REGIERAUM

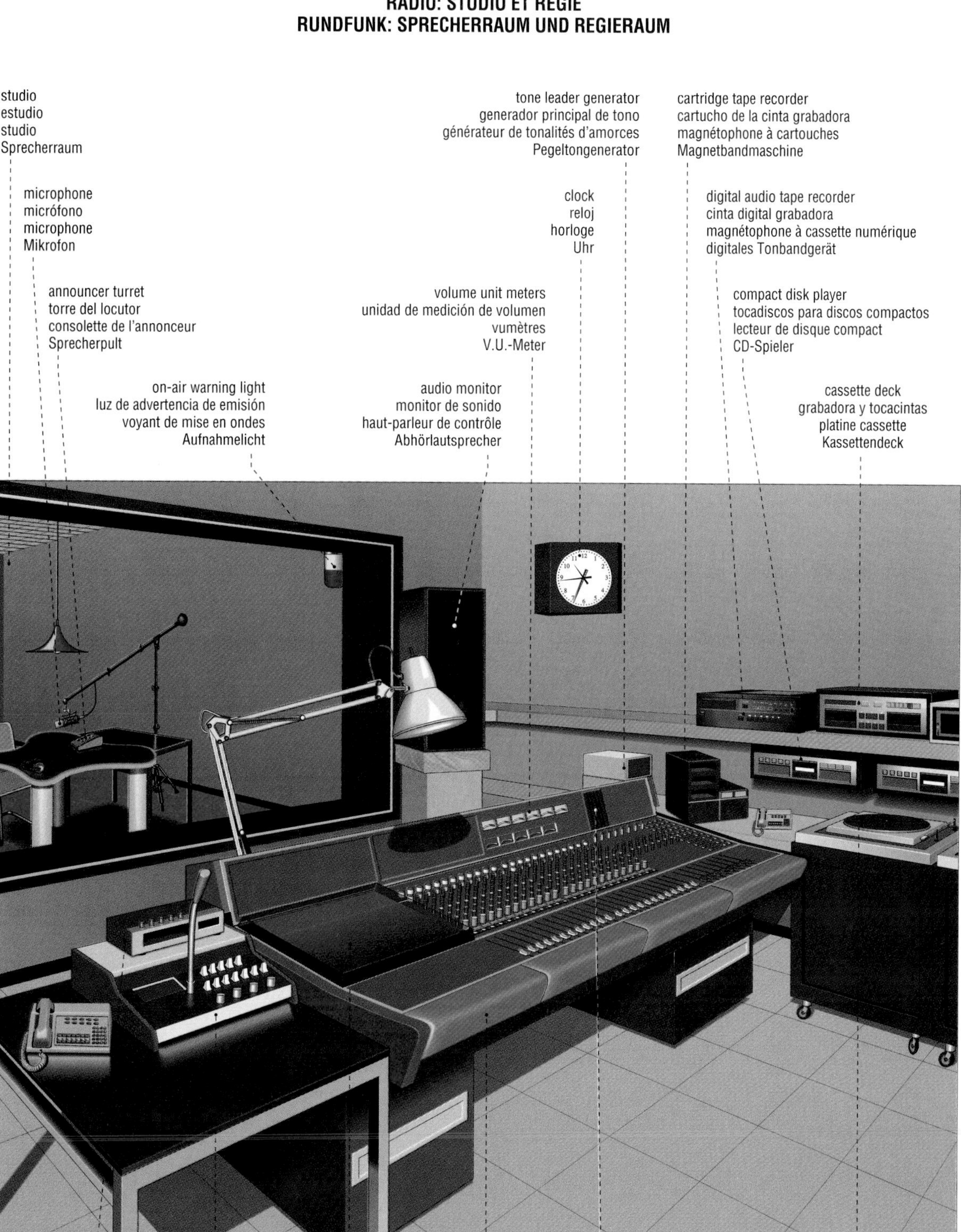

studio
estudio
studio
Sprecherraum
microphone
micrófono
microphone
Mikrofon
announcer turret
torre del locutor
consolette de l'annonceur
Sprecherpult
on-air warning light
luz de advertencia de emisión
voyant de mise en ondes
Aufnahmelicht
audio monitor
monitor de sonido
haut-parleur de contrôle
Abhörlautsprecher
volume unit meters
unidad de medición de volumen
vumètres
V.U.-Meter
clock
reloj
horloge
Uhr
tone leader generator
generador principal de tono
générateur de tonalités d'amorces
Pegeltongenerator
cartridge tape recorder
cartucho de la cinta grabadora
magnétophone à cartouches
Magnetbandmaschine
digital audio tape recorder
cinta digital grabadora
magnétophone à cassette numérique
digitales Tonbandgerät
compact disk player
tocadiscos para discos compactos
lecteur de disque compact
CD-Spieler
cassette deck
grabadora y tocacintas
platine cassette
Kassettendeck
stop watch
reloj de pare
chronomètre
Aufnahmezeitanzeige
producer turret
torre del productor
consolette du réalisateur
Regiepult
jack field
entrada de campo
baie de jacks
Anschlußtafel
audio console
consola de sonido
pupitre de son
Mischpult
bargraph type peak meter
gráfico de lineas
crêtemètre graphique
digitale Pegelanzeige
control room
sala de control
régie
Regieraum
turntable
tocadiscos
platine tourne-disque
Plattenspieler

PORTABLE SOUND SYSTEMS
SISTEMAS DE SONIDO PORTÁTILES
APPAREILS DE SON PORTATIFS
TRAGBARE TONWIEDERGABESYSTEME

PERSONAL RADIO CASSETTE PLAYER
RADIO AM \ FM Y LECTOR DE CASETES PERSONAL
BALADEUR
WALKMAN ® MIT RADIOTEIL

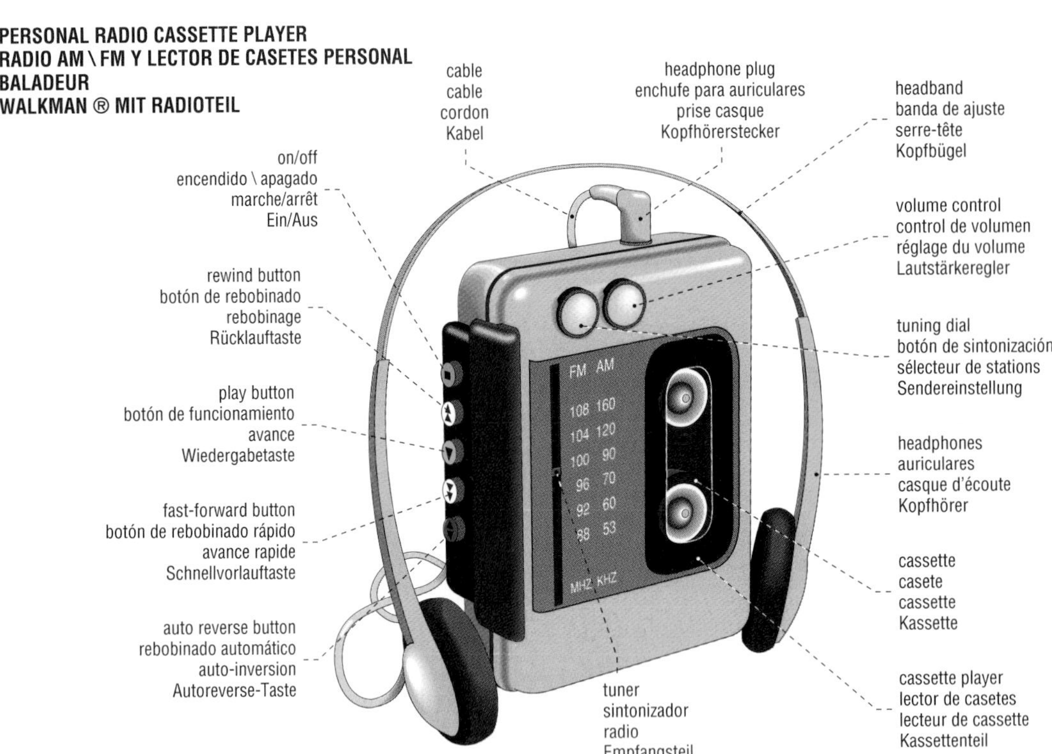

cable
cable
cordon
Kabel
headphone plug
enchufe para auriculares
prise casque
Kopfhörerstecker
headband
banda de ajuste
serre-tête
Kopfbügel
on/off
encendido \ apagado
marche/arrêt
Ein/Aus
volume control
control de volumen
réglage du volume
Lautstärkeregler
rewind button
botón de rebobinado
rebobinage
Rücklauftaste
tuning dial
botón de sintonización
sélecteur de stations
Sendereinstellung
play button
botón de funcionamiento
avance
Wiedergabetaste
headphones
auriculares
casque d'écoute
Kopfhörer
fast-forward button
botón de rebobinado rápido
avance rapide
Schnellvorlauftaste
cassette
casete
cassette
Kassette
auto reverse button
rebobinado automático
auto-inversion
Autoreverse-Taste
tuner
sintonizador
radio
Empfangsteil
cassette player
lector de casetes
lecteur de cassette
Kassettenteil
FM AM
108 160
104 120
100 90
96 70
92 60
88 53
MHZ KHZ

PORTABLE CD RADIO CASSETTE RECORDER
GRABADORA PORTÁTIL
RADIOCASSETTE
RADIORECORDER MIT CD-SPIELER

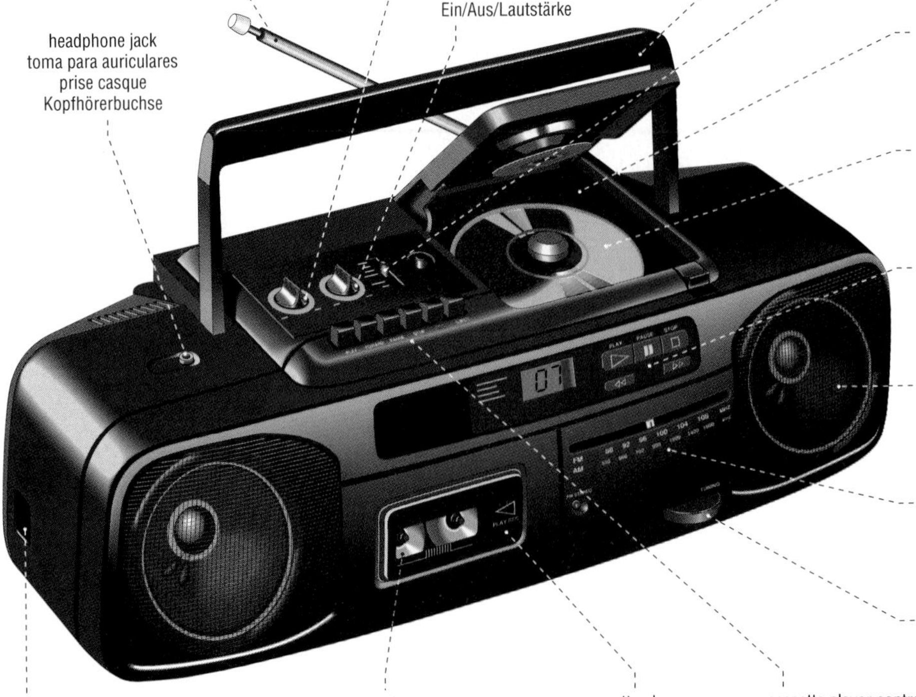

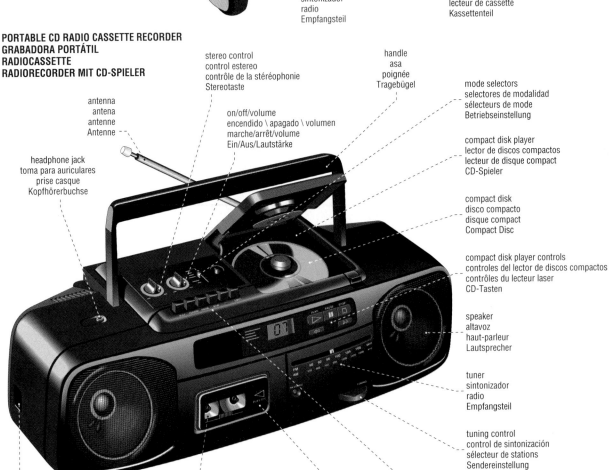

stereo control
control estereo
contrôle de la stéréophonie
Stereotaste

handle
asa
poignée
Tragebügel

mode selectors
selectores de modalidad
sélecteurs de mode
Betriebseinstellung

antenna
antena
antenne
Antenne

on/off/volume
encendido \ apagado \ volumen
marche/arrêt/volume
Ein/Aus/Lautstärke

compact disk player
lector de discos compactos
lecteur de disque compact
CD-Spieler

headphone jack
toma para auriculares
prise casque
Kopfhörerbuchse

compact disk
disco compacto
disque compact
Compact Disc

compact disk player controls
controles del lector de discos compactos
contrôles du lecteur laser
CD-Tasten

speaker
altavoz
haut-parleur
Lautsprecher

tuner
sintonizador
radio
Empfangsteil

tuning control
control de sintonización
sélecteur de stations
Sendereinstellung

power plug
enchufe
alimentation sur secteur
Netzanschluß

cassette
casete
cassette
Kassette

cassette player
lector de casetes
lecteur de cassette
Kassettenteil

cassette player controls
controles del lector de casetes
contrôles du lecteur de cassette
Kassettendecktasten

VIDEO CAMERA
CÁMARA DE VIDEO
CAMÉRA VIDÉO
VIDEOKAMERA

eyepiece
adaptador al ojo
oculaire
Okular
power zoom button
botón de funcionamiento del zoom
commande électrique du zoom
Telezoom-Taste
electronic viewfinder
visor electrónico
viseur électronique
elektronischer Bildsucher
white balance sensor
captor de luz
senseur d'équilibrage des blancs
Weißabgleichsensor
accessory shoe
patín para accesorios
griffe porte-accessoires
Zubehörschuh
cassette eject switch
botón de eyección del casete
commande d'éjection de la cassette
Kassettenauswurfschalter
videotape operation controls
controles del video casete
commandes de la bande vidéo
Videobedientasten
viewfinder adjustment keys
botones de ajuste del visor
réglage du viseur
Scharfeinstellung des Bildsuchers
built-in microphone
micrófono integrado
microphone incorporé
eingebautes Mikrofon
DATA SET
ZERO MEM.
ADJUST
RESET
SELECT
BATT
EDIT SEARCH
EXPOSURE
SPEED
FOCUS
WHITE BAL.
FADER
AUTO LOCK
macro set button
botón de acercamiento
commande de réglage macro
Makro-Einstelltaste
cassette compartment
compartimento para el casete
logement de la cassette
Kassettenlift
zoom lens
lente zoom
objectif zoom
Zoomobjektiv
data display
visualización de la información
affichage des données
Display
battery eject switch
botón para sacar la pila
commande d'éjection de la pile
Batterieauswurfschalter
lens hood
capuchón
pare-soleil
Gegenlichtblende
shooting adjustment keys
botones de ajuste del rodaje
commandes de prise de vue
Aufnahmeeinstellungstasten
battery
pila
pile
Batterie
edit/search buttons
botones de montaje y búsqueda
commandes de montage
Editsearch-Tasten

TELEVISION
TELEVISIÓN
TÉLÉVISION
FERNSEHEN

TELEVISION SET
TELEVISOR
TÉLÉVISEUR
FERNSEHAPPARAT

PICTURE TUBE
TUBO DE PANTALLA
TUBE-IMAGE
BILDRÖHRE

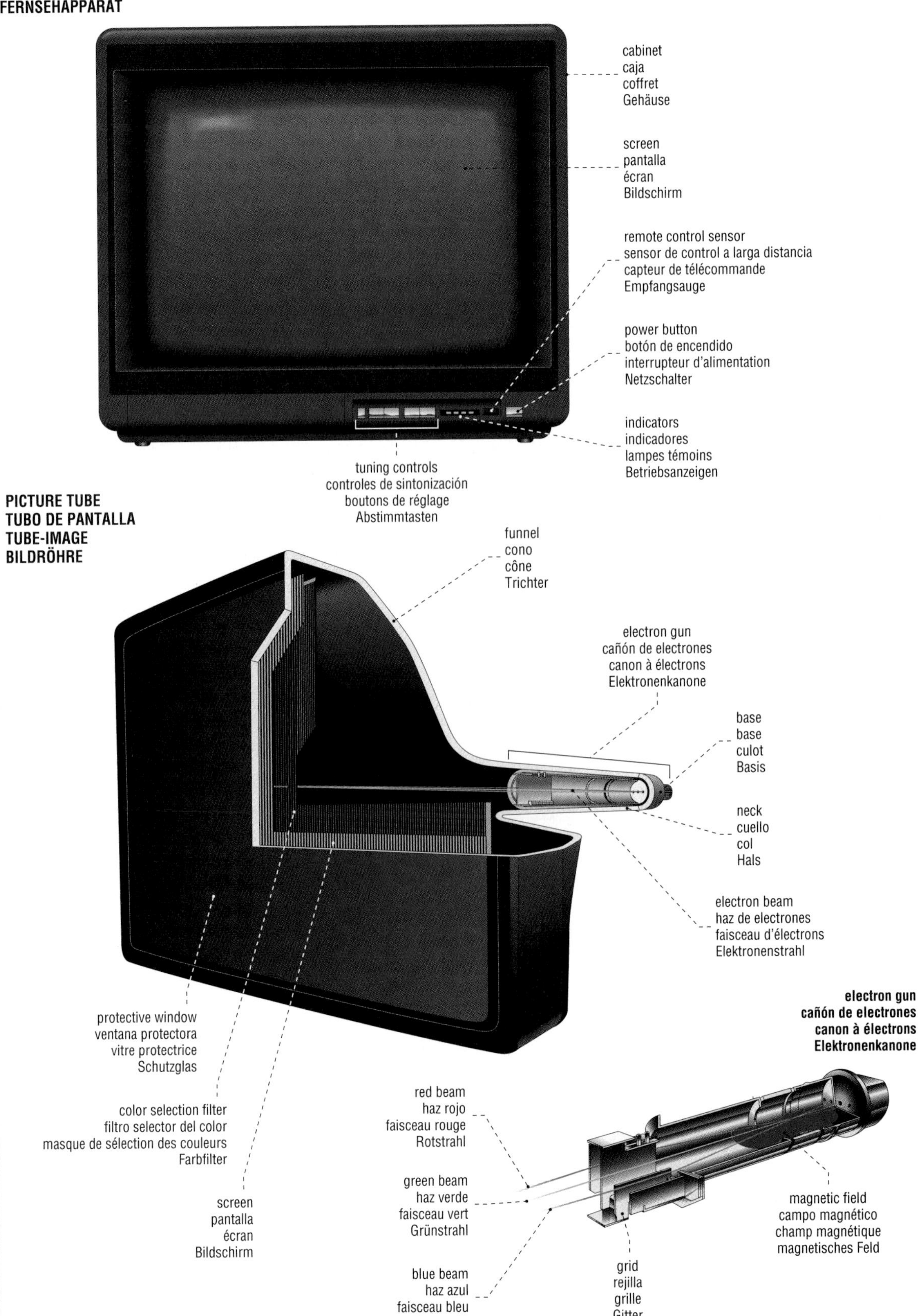
cabinet
caja
coffret
Gehäuse
screen
pantalla
écran
Bildschirm
remote control sensor
sensor de control a larga distancia
capteur de télécommande
Empfangsauge
power button
botón de encendido
interrupteur d'alimentation
Netzschalter
indicators
indicadores
lampes témoins
Betriebsanzeigen
tuning controls
controles de sintonización
boutons de réglage
Abstimmtasten
funnel
cono
cône
Trichter
electron gun
cañón de electrones
canon à électrons
Elektronenkanone
base
base
culot
Basis
neck
cuello
col
Hals
electron beam
haz de electrones
faisceau d'électrons
Elektronenstrahl
protective window
ventana protectora
vitre protectrice
Schutzglas
color selection filter
filtro selector del color
masque de sélection des couleurs
Farbfilter
screen
pantalla
écran
Bildschirm
electron gun
cañón de electrones
canon à électrons
Elektronenkanone
red beam
haz rojo
faisceau rouge
Rotstrahl
green beam
haz verde
faisceau vert
Grünstrahl
blue beam
haz azul
faisceau bleu
Blaustrahl
grid
rejilla
grille
Gitter
magnetic field
campo magnético
champ magnétique
magnetisches Feld

REMOTE CONTROL
CONTROL A LARGA DISTANCIA
TÉLÉCOMMANDE
FERNBEDIENUNG

VIDEOCASSETTE RECORDER
VIDEOGRABADORA
MAGNÉTOSCOPE
VIDEORECORDER

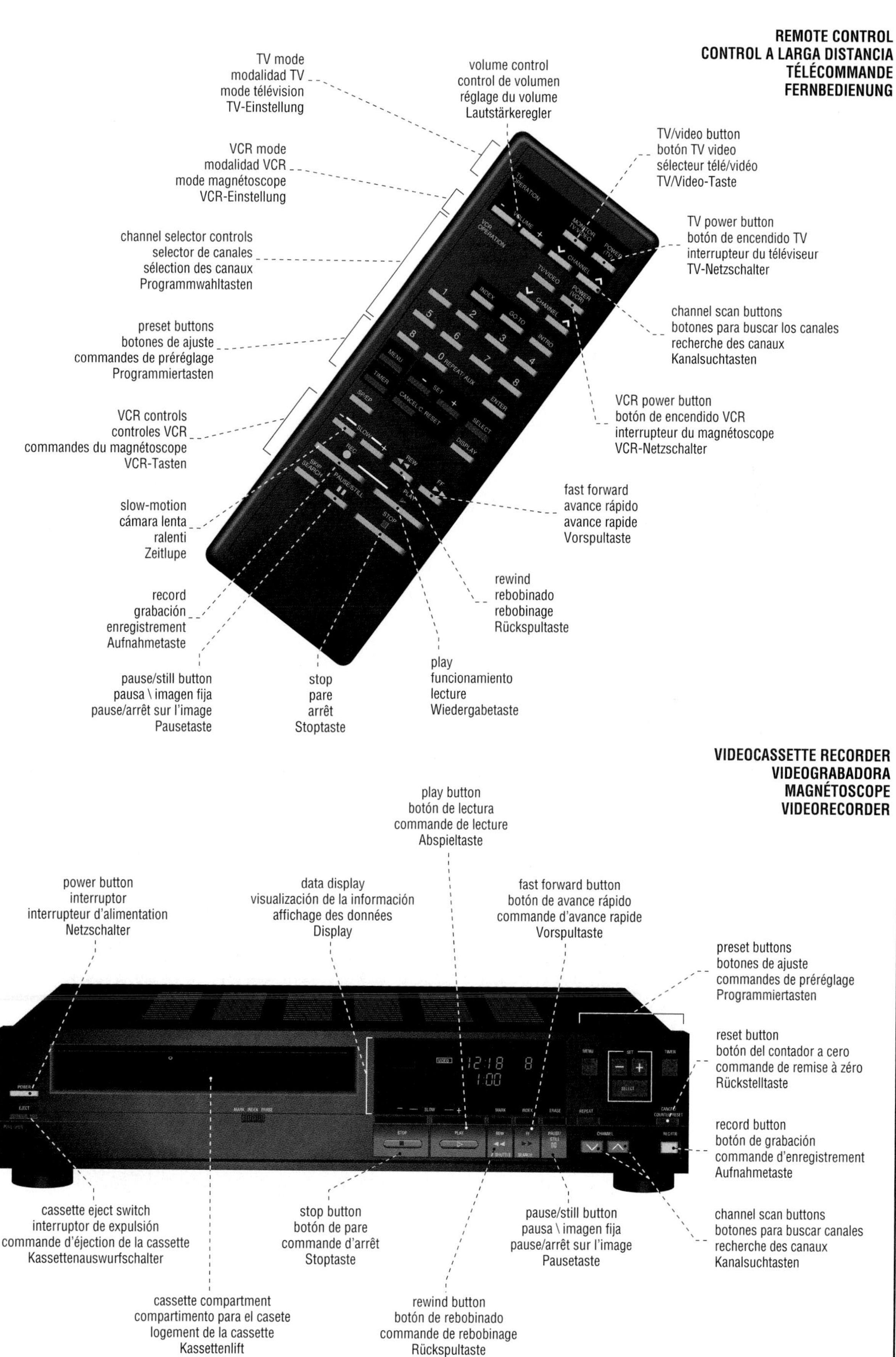

TV mode
modalidad TV
mode télévision
TV-Einstellung
volume control
control de volumen
réglage du volume
Lautstärkeregler
TV/video button
botón TV video
sélecteur télé/vidéo
TV/Video-Taste
VCR mode
modalidad VCR
mode magnétoscope
VCR-Einstellung
TV power button
botón de encendido TV
interrupteur du téléviseur
TV-Netzschalter
channel selector controls
selector de canales
sélection des canaux
Programmwahltasten
channel scan buttons
botones para buscar los canales
recherche des canaux
Kanalsuchtasten
preset buttons
botones de ajuste
commandes de préréglage
Programmiertasten
VCR power button
botón de encendido VCR
interrupteur du magnétoscope
VCR-Netzschalter
VCR controls
controles VCR
commandes du magnétoscope
VCR-Tasten
fast forward
avance rápido
avance rapide
Vorspultaste
slow-motion
cámara lenta
ralenti
Zeitlupe
rewind
rebobinado
rebobinage
Rückspultaste
record
grabación
enregistrement
Aufnahmetaste
pause/still button
pausa \ imagen fija
pause/arrêt sur l'image
Pausetaste
stop
pare
arrêt
Stoptaste
play
funcionamiento
lecture
Wiedergabetaste
play button
botón de lectura
commande de lecture
Abspieltaste
power button
interruptor
interrupteur d'alimentation
Netzschalter
data display
visualización de la información
affichage des données
Display
fast forward button
botón de avance rápido
commande d'avance rapide
Vorspultaste
preset buttons
botones de ajuste
commandes de préréglage
Programmiertasten
reset button
botón del contador a cero
commande de remise à zéro
Rückstelltaste
record button
botón de grabación
commande d'enregistrement
Aufnahmetaste
cassette eject switch
interruptor de expulsión
commande d'éjection de la cassette
Kassettenauswurfschalter
stop button
botón de pare
commande d'arrêt
Stoptaste
pause/still button
pausa \ imagen fija
pause/arrêt sur l'image
Pausetaste
channel scan buttons
botones para buscar canales
recherche des canaux
Kanalsuchtasten
cassette compartment
compartimento para el casete
logement de la cassette
Kassettenlift
rewind button
botón de rebobinado
commande de rebobinage
Rückspultaste

STUDIO AND CONTROL ROOMS
ESTUDIO DE TELEVISIÓN Y CABINAS DE CONTROL
PLATEAU ET RÉGIES
SPRECHER- UND REGIERÄUME

lighting grid access
puerta de acceso a la rejilla de las luces
accès à la grille d'éclairage
Zugang zur Beleuchtungsanlage

additional production personnel
personal suplementario de producción
personnel additionnel de production
zusätzliches Studiopersonal

auxiliary facilities room
sala de instalaciones auxiliares
salle polyvalente
allgemeiner Geräteraum

connection box
caja de conexiones
boîte de raccordement
Kamera-Steckfeld

lighting technician
técnico de luces
éclairagiste
Beleuchter(in)

camera control unit
unidad de control de cámaras
bloc de commande des caméras
Bildkontrolle

camera
cámara
caméra
Kamera

dimmer room
sala de regulación de luces
salle des gradateurs
abgedunkelter Raum

lighting board operator
tablero de operación de luces
opérateur de régie d'éclairage
Oberbeleuchter(in)

camera control technician
técnico de control de cámaras
contrôleur d'images
Bildtechniker(in)

microphone boom
jirafa del micrófono
perche
Mikrofonausleger

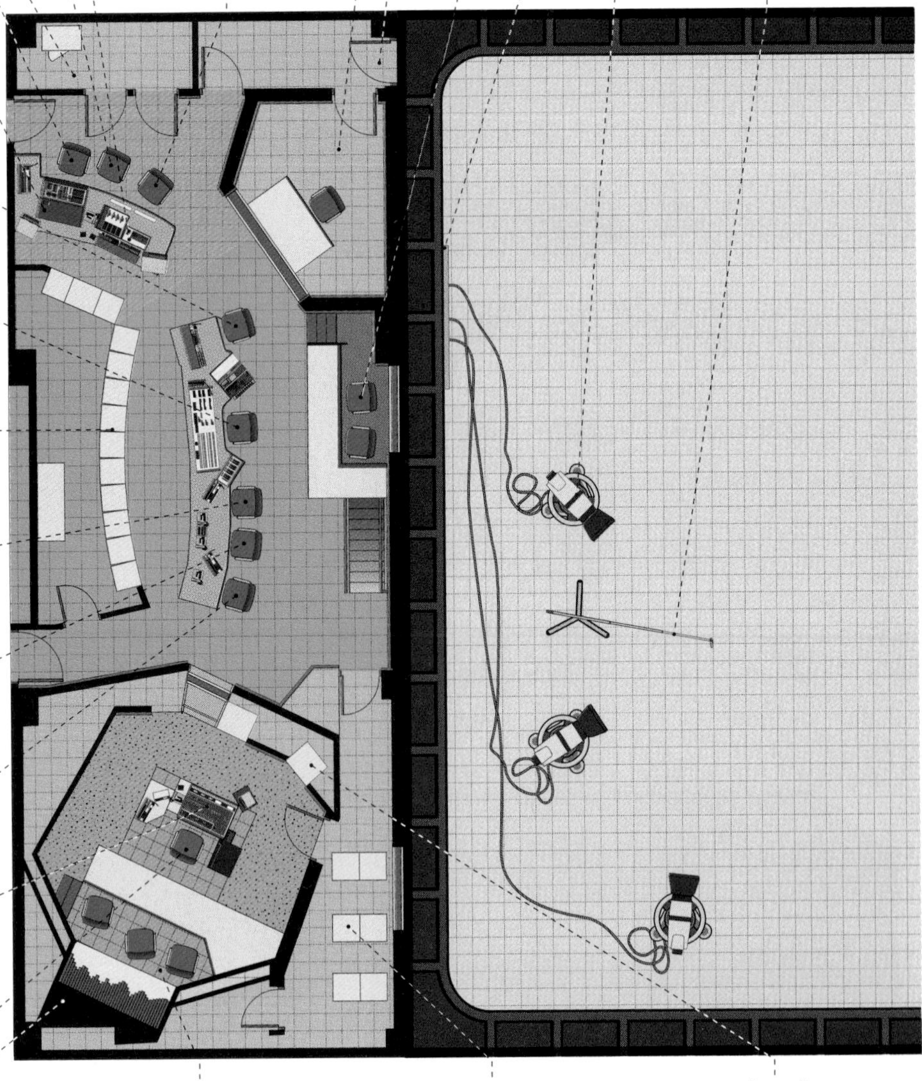

lighting board
tablero de luces
pupitre d'éclairage
Lichtregelanlage

technical producer
productor técnico
directeur technique
Aufsichtsingenieur(in)

video switcher technician
operador técnico de video
technicien aiguilleur
Video-Switcher

monitor wall
panel de monitores
baie de contrôle
Kontrollmonitore

producer
productor
réalisateur
Sendeleiter(in)

script assistant
asistente del guionista
assistant à la réalisation
Skript-Assistent(in)

production adviser
consejero de producción
conseiller de production
Regieassistent(in)

audio console
consola de sonido
pupitre de son
Tonregiepult

audio technician
técnico de sonido
preneur de son
Tontechniker(in)

bass trap
retenedor de frecuencias bajas
trappe acoustique
Baßfalle

musical advisers
consejeros musicales
conseillers musicaux
Musikregie

equipment rack
soporte para el equipo
bâti d'équipement
Ausrüstungsspind

audio monitor
monitor del sonido
haut-parleur de contrôle
Lautsprecher

studio floor
estudio
plateau
Studioebene

lighting/camera control area
sala de control de luces
régie image/éclairage
Beleuchtung/Bildregie

audio control room
control de sonido
régie du son
Tonregieraum

production control room
sala de producción y control
régie de production
Regieraum

PRODUCTION CONTROL ROOM
SALA DE CONTROL DE PRODUCCIÓN
RÉGIE DE PRODUCTION
REGIERAUM

audio/video preview unit
unidad de visualización de imagen \ sonido
poste de contrôle audio/vidéo
Ton-/Bild-Vorschaueinheit

stereo phase monitor
control del sonido estereofónico
oscilloscope de phase audio
Lautsprecher zum Prüfen von Zweikanalton

monitor wall
panel de monitores
baie de contrôle
Kontrollmonitore

preview monitors
monitores de visualización previa
écrans de précontrôle
Vorschaumonitore

vector/waveform monitor
control del vector de vibraciones
oscilloscope/vectoscope
Oszillograph-/Oszilloskopmonitor

input monitors
monitores de entrada
écrans d'entrée
Eingangsmonitore

digital video effects monitor
monitor de efectos video\digitales
écran du truqueur numérique
Trickmischer

technical producer monitor
monitor de la producción técnica
écran du directeur technique
Kontrollmonitor des Aufsichtsingenieurs

audio monitor
monitor de sonido
haut-parleur de contrôle
Lautsprecher

clock
reloj
horloge
Kontrolluhr

intercom microphone
micrófono de intercomunicación
microphone d'interphone
Mikrofon zum Studio

auxiliary video switcher
interruptor para el video auxiliar
sélecteur vidéo auxiliaire
zusätzlicher Video-Switcher

video monitoring selector
selector del control de video
sélecteur de contrôle vidéo
Video-Kreuzschiene

intercom station
estación de intercomunicación
interphone
Studio-Kommandoanlage

output monitor
monitor de salida
écran de sortie
Ausgangsmonitor

audio monitoring selector
selector del control de volumen
sélecteur de contrôle audio
Tonvormischung

telephone
teléfono
poste téléphonique
Telefon

main preview monitor
monitor principal de visualización previa
écran principal de précontrôle
Hauptvorschaumonitor

audio volume unit meters
compás del volumen
vumètres audio
Ton V.U.Meter

production desk
mesa de producción
table de production
Regiepult

production video switcher
interruptor para la producción video
aiguilleur vidéo de production
Video-Switcher

digital video special effects
efectos especiales video\digital
truqueur numérique
Trickmischer

TELEVISION
TELEVISIÓN
TÉLÉVISION
FERNSEHEN

STUDIO FLOOR
ESTUDIO
PLATEAU
STUDIOEBENE

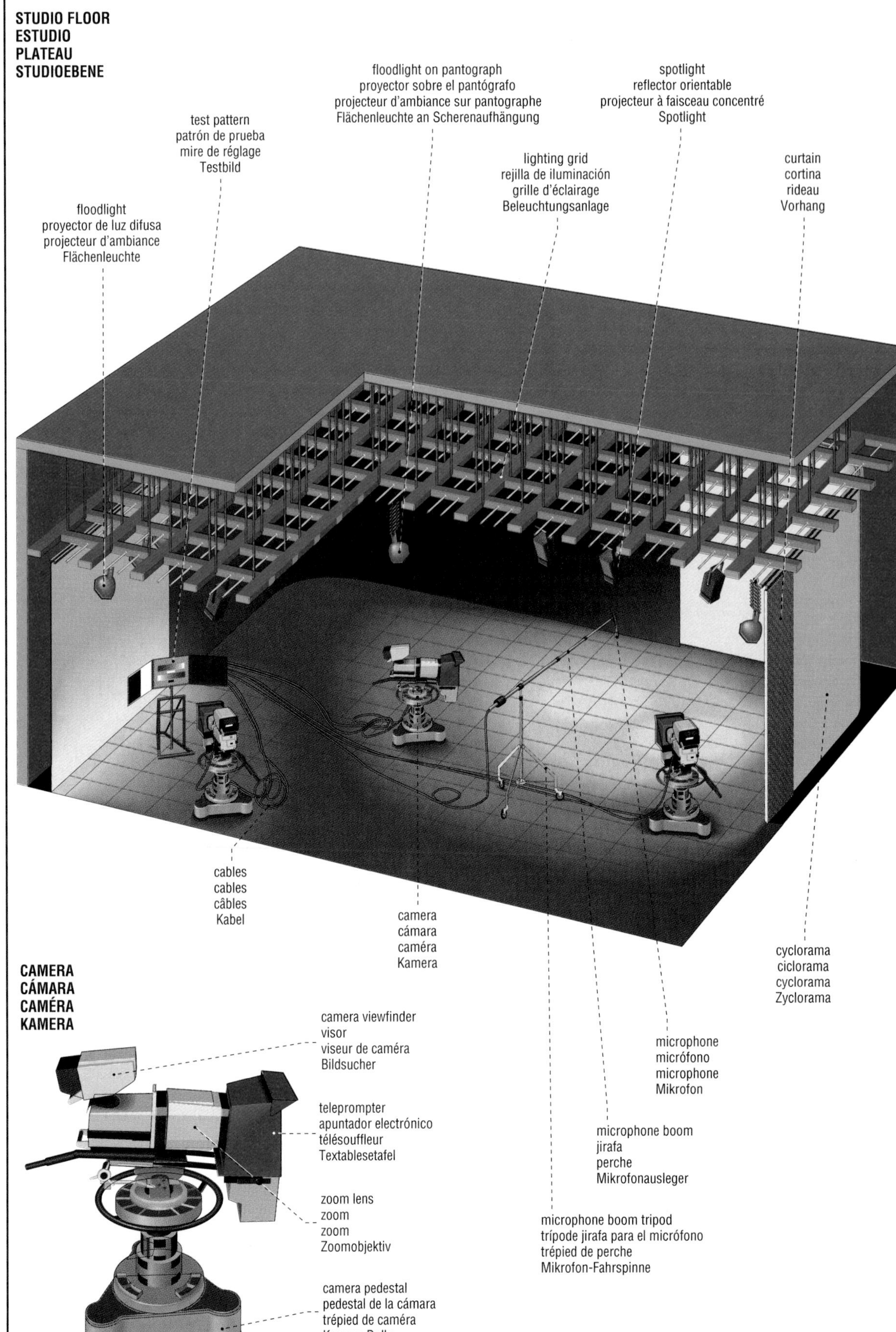

test pattern
patrón de prueba
mire de réglage
Testbild
floodlight on pantograph
proyector sobre el pantógrafo
projecteur d'ambiance sur pantographe
Flächenleuchte an Scherenaufhängung
spotlight
reflector orientable
projecteur à faisceau concentré
Spotlight
lighting grid
rejilla de iluminación
grille d'éclairage
Beleuchtungsanlage
curtain
cortina
rideau
Vorhang
floodlight
proyector de luz difusa
projecteur d'ambiance
Flächenleuchte
cables
cables
câbles
Kabel
camera
cámara
caméra
Kamera
cyclorama
ciclorama
cyclorama
Zyclorama
microphone
micrófono
microphone
Mikrofon
microphone boom
jirafa
perche
Mikrofonausleger
microphone boom tripod
trípode jirafa para el micrófono
trépied de perche
Mikrofon-Fahrspinne
CAMERA
CÁMARA
CAMÉRA
KAMERA
camera viewfinder
visor
viseur de caméra
Bildsucher
teleprompter
apuntador electrónico
télésouffleur
Textablesetafel
zoom lens
zoom
zoom
Zoomobjektiv
camera pedestal
pedestal de la cámara
trépied de caméra
Kamera-Dolly

MOBILE UNIT
UNIDAD MÓBIL
CAR DE REPORTAGE
ÜBERTRAGUNGSWAGEN

microwave transmitter
transmisor de microondas
émetteur micro-ondes
Mikrowellensender

wave guide
guía de la onda
guide d'ondes
Wellenleiter

parabolic antenna
antena parabólica
antenne parabolique
Parabolantenne

microwave dish
disco microondas
réflecteur parabolique
Mikrowellenschüssel

tripod
trípode
trépied
Stativ

equipment rack
equipo de soporte
bâti d'équipement
Ausrüstungsspind

equipment rack
equipo de soporte
bâti d'équipement
Ausrüstungsspind

audio control room
sala de control de sonido
régie du son
Tonregieraum

camera control area
área de control de la cámara
régie image
Bereich der Bildkontrolle

audio technician
técnico de sonido
preneur de son
Tontechniker(in)

production control room
sala de control de la producción
régie de production
Regieraum

camera control unit
unidad de control de la cámara
bloc de commande des caméras
Bildkontrolle

telephone set
teléfono
poste téléphonique
Telefonapparat

monitor wall
panel de control
baie de contrôle
Kontrollmonitore

camera control technician
técnico de control de la cámara
contrôleur d'images
Bildtechniker(in)

audio monitor
monitor de sonido
haut-parleur de contrôle
Abhörlautsprecher

audio monitor
monitor de sonido
haut-parleur de contrôle
Abhörlautsprecher

maintenance area
área de mantenimiento
secteur maintenance
Eingangsbereich

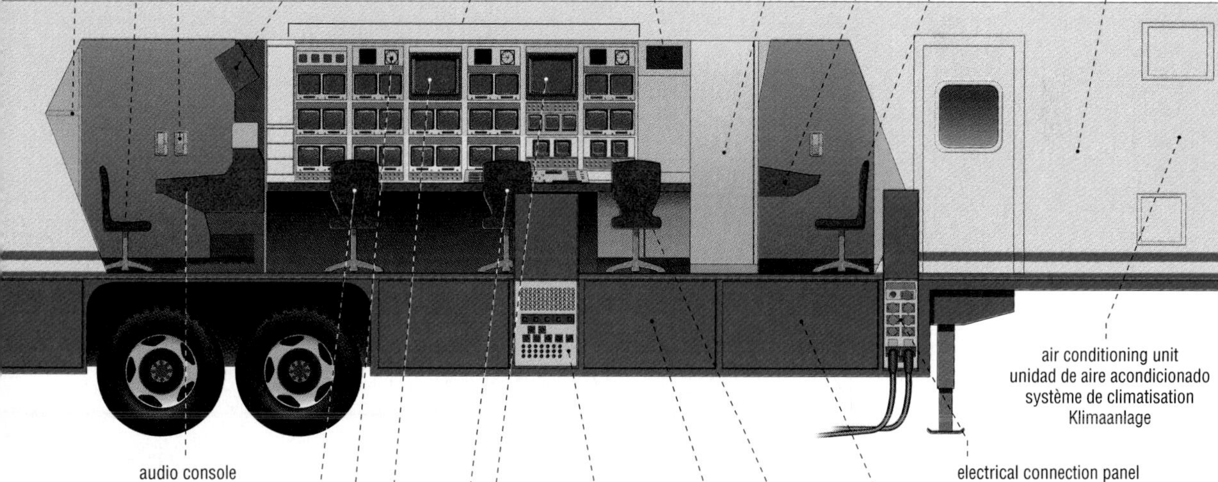

air conditioning unit
unidad de aire acondicionado
système de climatisation
Klimaanlage

audio console
consola de sonido
pupitre de son
Tonregiepult

electrical connection panel
panel de conexiones eléctricas
panneau de raccordement électrique
Stromverteiler

producer
productor
réalisateur
Sendeleiter(in)

video connection panel
panel de conexión del video
panneau de raccordement vidéo
Videoschalttafel

technical equipment compartment
compartimiento del equipo técnico
soute d'équipement technique
Fach für technische Ausrüstung

clock
reloj
horloge
Kontrolluhr

preview monitor
monitor de visualización previa
écran de précontrôle
Vorschaumonitor

technical producer
productor técnico
directeur technique
Aufsichtsingenieur(in)

output monitor
monitor de producción
écran de sortie
Ausgangsmonitor

video switcher technician
operador técnico de video
technicien aiguilleur
Video-Switcher

cable drum compartment
compartimiento del cable de la batería
soute des bobines de câbles
Fach für Kabeltrommel

BROADCAST SATELLITE COMMUNICATION
COMUNICACIÓN POR SATÉLITE DE TRANSMISIÓN
TÉLÉDIFFUSION PAR SATELLITE
ÜBERTRAGUNGSSATELLITENTECHNIK

satellite
satélite
satellite
Satellit

local station
estación local
station locale
Ortsstation

cable distributor
cable distribuidor
câblodistributeur
Kabelverteiler

private broadcasting network
red de transmisión privada
réseau privé
privates Rundfunknetz

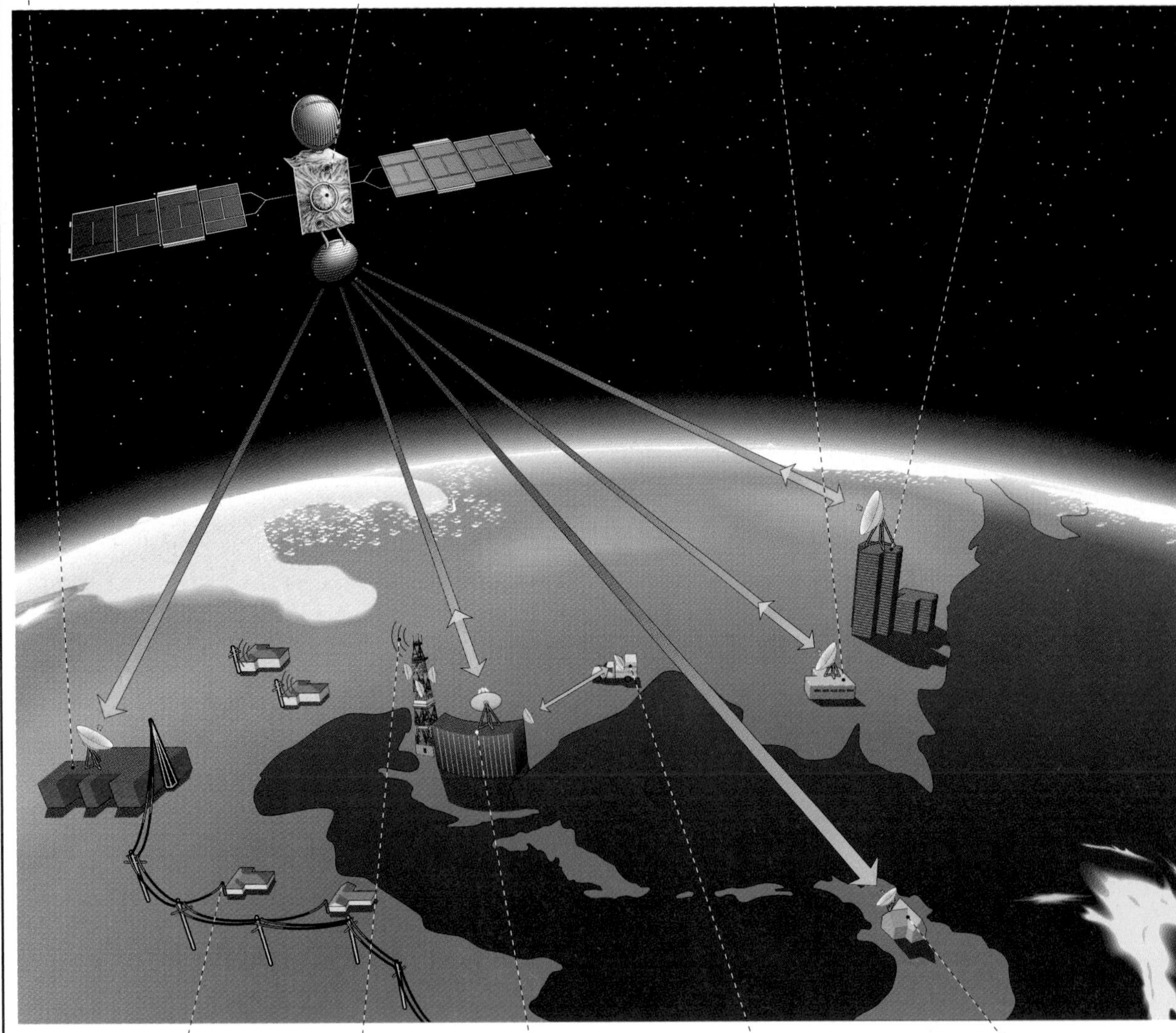

distribution by cable network
distribución por redes de cable
transmission par câble
Verteilung durch Kabelnetz

direct home reception
recepción directa en la casa
réception directe
Satelliten-Direktempfang

Hertzian wave transmission
transmisión de ondas Hertzianas
transmission hertzienne
Sendung auf Hertz-Wellen

mobile unit
unidad móvil
car de reportage
mobile Einheit

national broadcasting network
red nacional de transmisión
réseau national
öffentliches Übertragungsnetz

TELECOMMUNICATIONS BY SATELLITE
TELECOMUNICACIONES POR SATÉLITE
TÉLÉCOMMUNICATIONS PAR SATELLITE
TELEKOMMUNIKATION ÜBER NACHRICHTENSATELLIT

industrial communications
comunicaciones industriales
communications industrielles
industrielle Telekommunikation

teleport
teleporte
téléport
Teleport

air communications
comunicaciones aéreas
communications aériennes
Telekommunikation für die Luftfahrt

military communications
comunicaciones militares
communications militaires
militärische Telekommunikation

maritime communications
comunicaciones marítimas
communications maritimes
maritime Telekommunikation

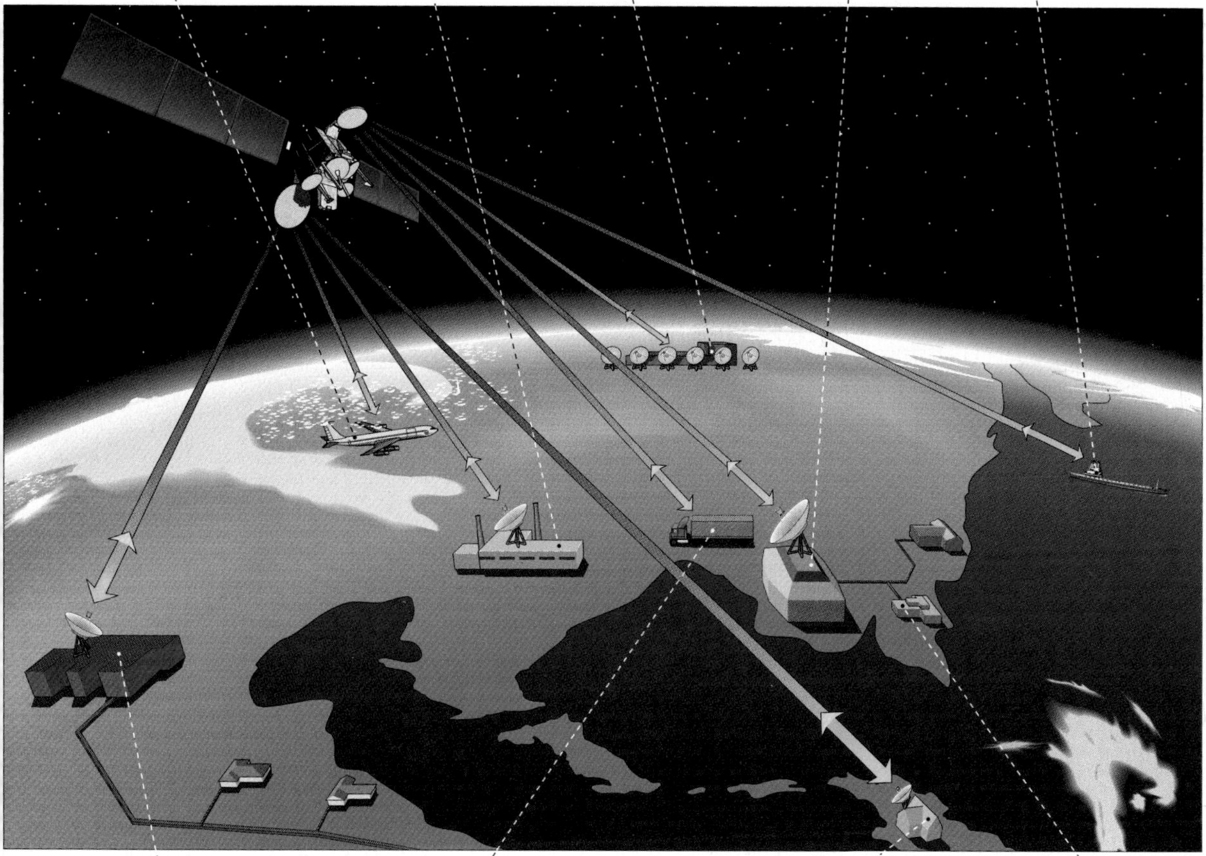

telephone network
red telefónica
réseau téléphonique
Telefonnetz

road communications
comunicaciones terrestres
communications routières
Telekommunikation für den Straßenverkehr

personal communications
comunicaciones personales
communications individuelles
persönliche Telekommunikation

consumer
consumidor
client
Konsument

TELECOMMUNICATIONS BY TELEPHONE NETWORK
TELECOMUNICACIONES POR RED TELEFÓNICA
TÉLÉCOMMUNICATIONS PAR LIGNE TÉLÉPHONIQUE
TELEKOMMUNIKATIONSTECHNIK ÜBER DAS TELEFONNETZ

computer communication
comunicación por computador
téléinformatique
Telekommunikation über Computer

facsimile machine
facsímil
télécopieur
Telefax-Gerät

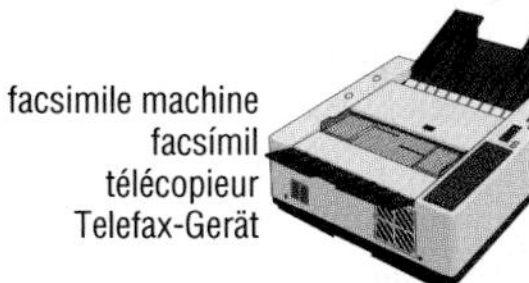

cellular telephone
teléfono celular
téléphone cellulaire
Zellfunktelefon

telex
télex
télex
Telex

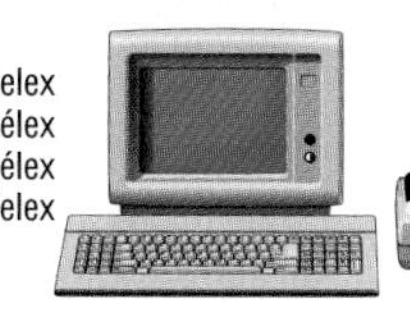

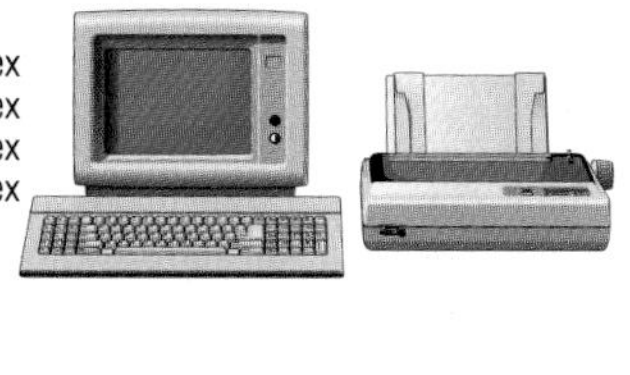

telephone set
teléfono
poste téléphonique
Telefonapparat

TELECOMMUNICATION SATELLITES
SATÉLITES DE TELECOMUNICACIONES
SATELLITES DE TÉLÉCOMMUNICATIONS
FERNMELDESATELLITEN

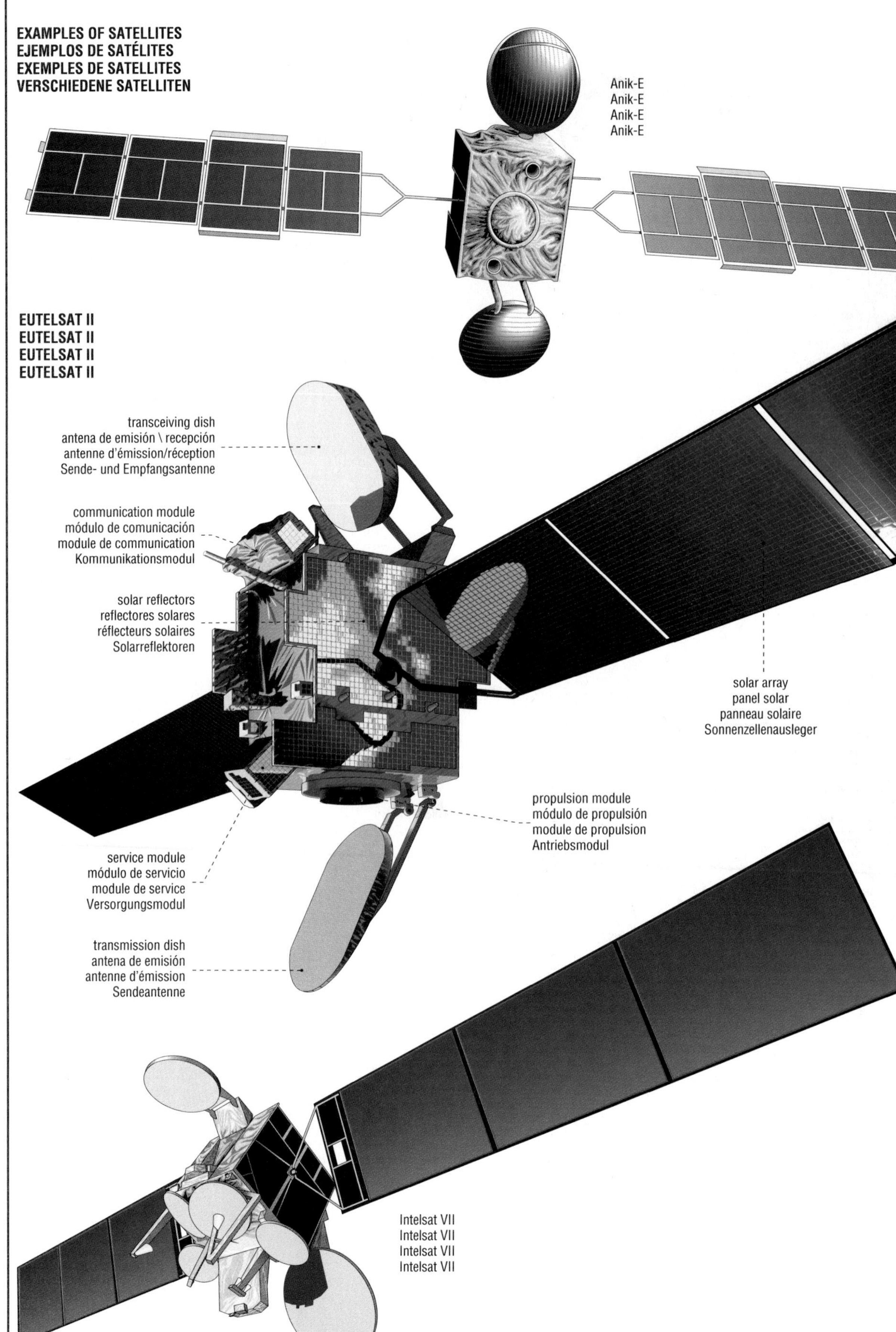

EXAMPLES OF SATELLITES
EJEMPLOS DE SATÉLITES
EXEMPLES DE SATELLITES
VERSCHIEDENE SATELLITEN
Anik-E
Anik-E
Anik-E
Anik-E
EUTELSAT II
EUTELSAT II
EUTELSAT II
EUTELSAT II
transceiving dish
antena de emisión \ recepción
antenne d'émission/réception
Sende- und Empfangsantenne
communication module
módulo de comunicación
module de communication
Kommunikationsmodul
solar reflectors
reflectores solares
réflecteurs solaires
Solarreflektoren
solar array
panel solar
panneau solaire
Sonnenzellenausleger
propulsion module
módulo de propulsión
module de propulsion
Antriebsmodul
service module
módulo de servicio
module de service
Versorgungsmodul
transmission dish
antena de emisión
antenne d'émission
Sendeantenne
Intelsat VII
Intelsat VII
Intelsat VII
Intelsat VII

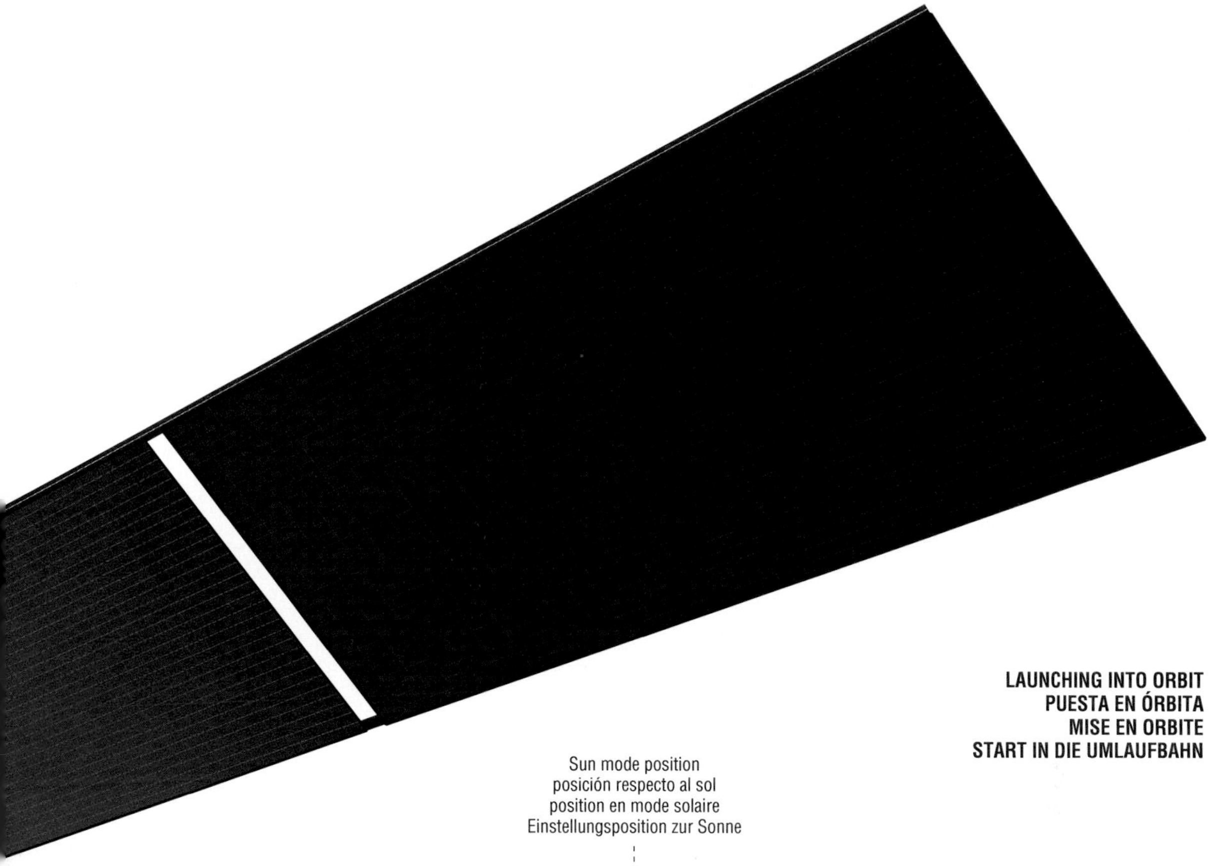

LAUNCHING INTO ORBIT
PUESTA EN ÓRBITA
MISE EN ORBITE
START IN DIE UMLAUFBAHN

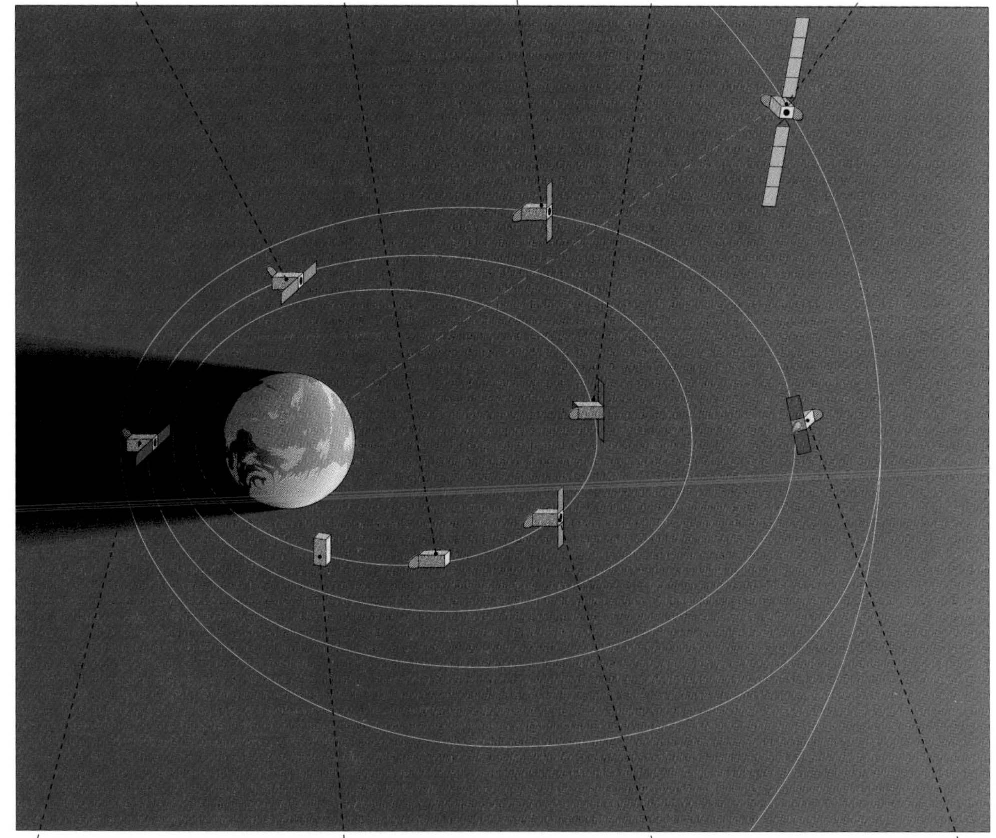

Sun mode position
posición respecto al sol
position en mode solaire
Einstellungsposition zur Sonne
eclipse preparation
preparación del eclipse
préparation avant éclipse
Vorbereitung auf die Ekliptik
East reflector deployment
despliegue del reflector del este
déploiement du réflecteur est
östlich gerichtete Entfaltung des Reflektors
apogee passage
apogeo de la trayectoria
passage en apogée
Bahn durch das Apogäum
full deployment
despliegue completo
stade final de déploiement
volle Entfaltung
eclipse crossing
cruce del eclipse
passage en éclipse
Bahn durch die Ekliptik
launcher/satellite separation
separación del lanzador de satélites
séparation lanceur/satellite
Abtrennung des Satelliten von der Trägerrakete
solar array deployment
despliegue del panel solar
déploiement du panneau solaire
Entfaltung der Sonnenzellenausleger
apogee motor firing
apogeo de encendido del motor
manœuvres d'apogée
Zündung des Apogäum-Motors

COMMUNICATION BY TELEPHONE
COMUNICACIONES POR TELÉFONO
COMMUNICATION PAR TÉLÉPHONE
TELEFONISCHE KOMMUNIKATION

TELEPHONE ANSWERING MACHINE
CONTESTADORA AUTOMÁTICA
RÉPONDEUR TÉLÉPHONIQUE
ANRUFBEANTWORTER

TELEPHONE SET
TELÉFONO
POSTE TÉLÉPHONIQUE
TELEFONAPPARAT

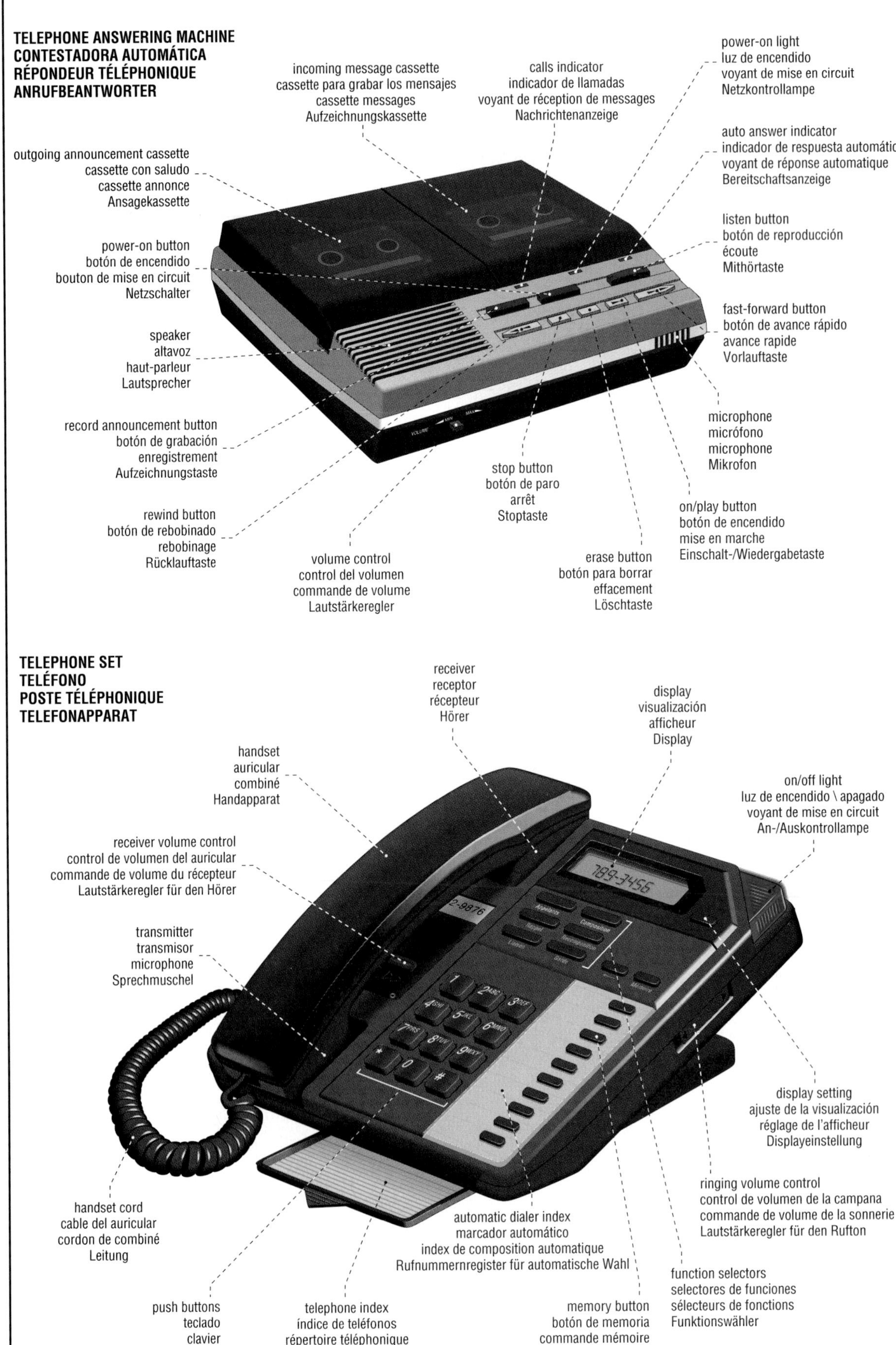
incoming message cassette
cassette para grabar los mensajes
cassette messages
Aufzeichnungskassette
calls indicator
indicador de llamadas
voyant de réception de messages
Nachrichtenanzeige
power-on light
luz de encendido
voyant de mise en circuit
Netzkontrollampe
auto answer indicator
indicador de respuesta automática
voyant de réponse automatique
Bereitschaftsanzeige
outgoing announcement cassette
cassette con saludo
cassette annonce
Ansagekassette
listen button
botón de reproducción
écoute
Mithörtaste
power-on button
botón de encendido
bouton de mise en circuit
Netzschalter
fast-forward button
botón de avance rápido
avance rapide
Vorlauftaste
speaker
altavoz
haut-parleur
Lautsprecher
microphone
micrófono
microphone
Mikrofon
record announcement button
botón de grabación
enregistrement
Aufzeichnungstaste
stop button
botón de paro
arrêt
Stoptaste
on/play button
botón de encendido
mise en marche
Einschalt-/Wiedergabetaste
rewind button
botón de rebobinado
rebobinage
Rücklauftaste
volume control
control del volumen
commande de volume
Lautstärkeregler
erase button
botón para borrar
effacement
Löschtaste
receiver
receptor
récepteur
Hörer
display
visualización
afficheur
Display
handset
auricular
combiné
Handapparat
on/off light
luz de encendido \ apagado
voyant de mise en circuit
An-/Auskontrollampe
receiver volume control
control de volumen del auricular
commande de volume du récepteur
Lautstärkeregler für den Hörer
transmitter
transmisor
microphone
Sprechmuschel
display setting
ajuste de la visualización
réglage de l'afficheur
Displayeinstellung
ringing volume control
control de volumen de la campana
commande de volume de la sonnerie
Lautstärkeregler für den Rufton
handset cord
cable del auricular
cordon de combiné
Leitung
automatic dialer index
marcador automático
index de composition automatique
Rufnummernregister für automatische Wahl
function selectors
selectores de funciones
sélecteurs de fonctions
Funktionswähler
push buttons
teclado
clavier
Tasten
telephone index
índice de teléfonos
répertoire téléphonique
Rufnummernregister
memory button
botón de memoria
commande mémoire
Speichertaste

TELEX
TÉLEX
TÉLEX
TELEX

terminal
terminal
terminal
Terminal

visual display unit
pantalla
écran d'affichage
Datensichtgerät

transmission/reception of messages
recepción y transmisión de mensajes
expédition/réception des messages
Senden/Empfangen von Nachrichten

printer
impresora
imprimante
Drucker

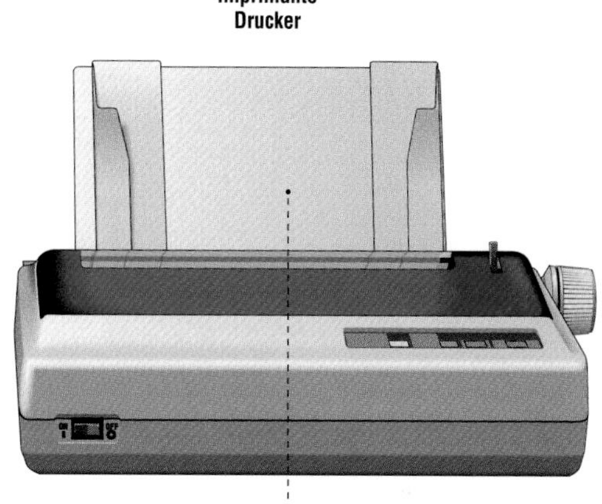

printing of messages
impresión de mensajes
impression des messages
Ausdrucken von Nachrichten

FACSIMILE MACHINE
FACSIMIL
TÉLÉCOPIEUR
TELEFAXGERÄT

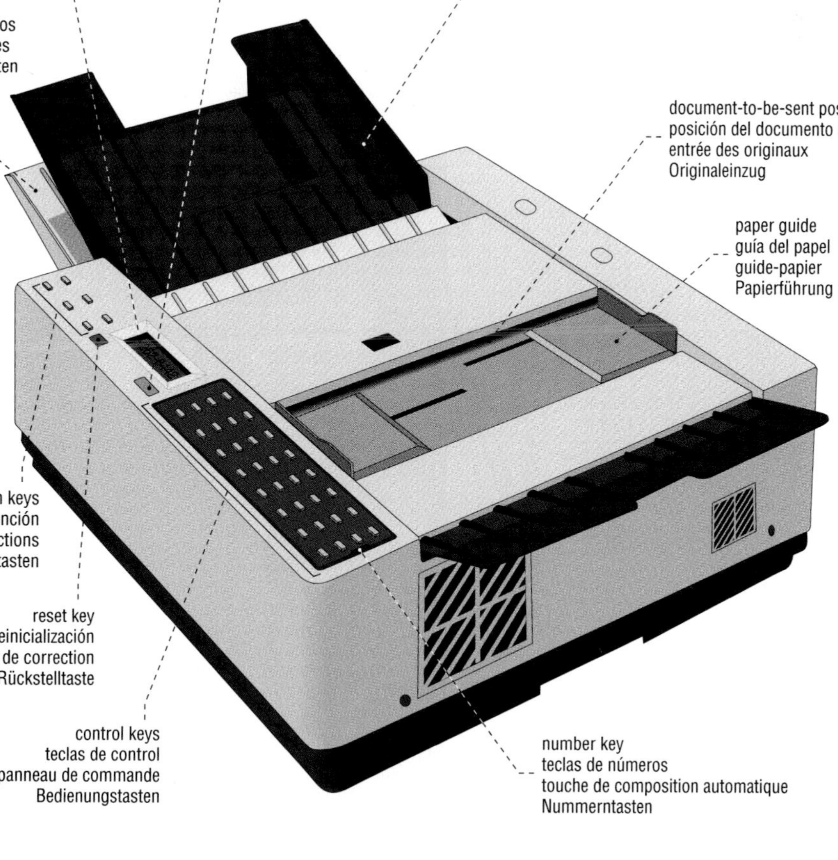

data display
visualización de datos
écran d'affichage
Datendisplay

start key
tecla de iniciación
mise en marche
Starttaste

sent document recovery
recuperación del documento enviado
sortie des originaux
Originalrückführung

document receiving
recepción de documentos
réception des messages
Empfang von Dokumenten

document-to-be-sent position
posición del documento para enviar
entrée des originaux
Originaleinzug

paper guide
guía del papel
guide-papier
Papierführung

function keys
teclas de función
panneau de fonctions
Funktionstasten

reset key
tecla de reinicialización
touche de correction
Rückstelltaste

control keys
teclas de control
panneau de commande
Bedienungstasten

number key
teclas de números
touche de composition automatique
Nummerntasten

COMMUNICATION BY TELEPHONE
COMUNICACIONES POR TELÉFONO
COMMUNICATION PAR TÉLÉPHONE
TELEFONISCHE KOMMUNIKATION

TYPES OF TELEPHONES
TELÉFONOS
TYPES DE POSTES TÉLÉPHONIQUES
TELEFONARTEN

TELECOMMUNICATION TERMINAL
TERMINAL DE COMUNICACIONES
TERMINAL DE TÉLÉCOMMUNICATION
FERNMELDETERMINAL

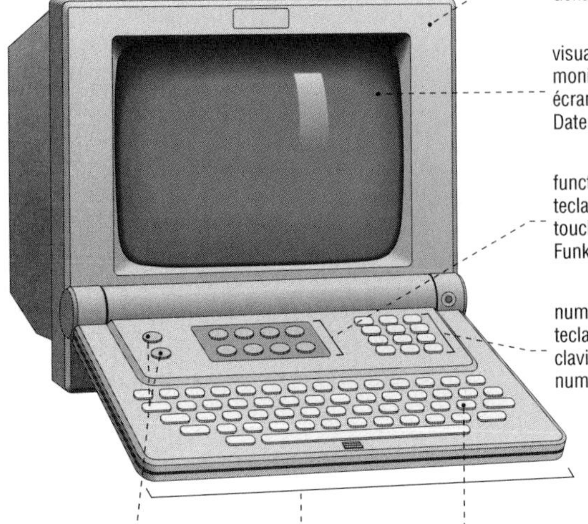

housing
caja
boîtier
Gehäuse

visual display unit
monitor
écran
Datensichtgerät

function keys
teclas de función
touches de fonctions
Funktionstasten

numeric keyboard
teclado numérico
clavier numérique
numerische Tastatur

operation keys
teclas de operación
touches de commande
Bedienungstasten

alphanumeric keyboard
teclado alfanumérico
clavier alphanumérique
alphanumerische Tastatur

keyboard
teclado
clavier
Tastatur

cordless telephone
teléfono inalámbrico
poste sans cordon
drahtloses Telefon

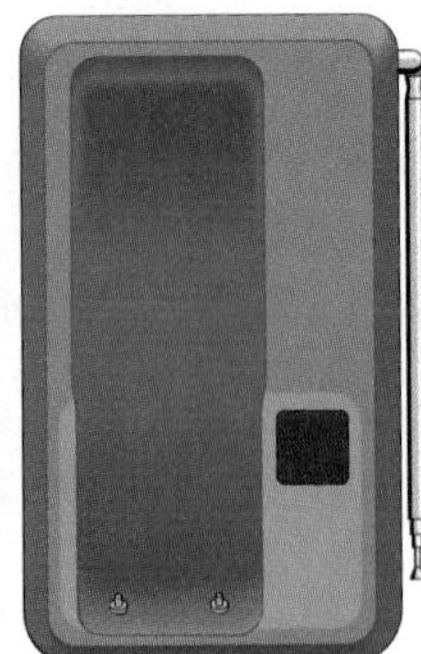

call director telephone
teléfono para ejecutivo
pupitre dirigeur
Abfrageapparat

514-393-1452

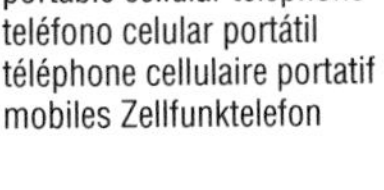

portable cellular telephone
teléfono celular portátil
téléphone cellulaire portatif
mobiles Zellfunktelefon

push-button telephone
teléfono de teclado
poste à clavier
Tastentelefon

PAY PHONE
TELÉFONO PÚBLICO
TÉLÉPHONE PUBLIC
ÖFFENTLICHER FERNSPRECHER

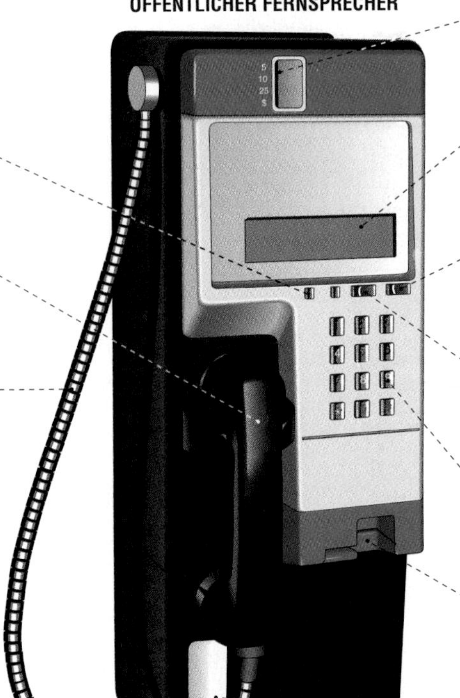

coin slot
ranura para monedas
fente à monnaie
Münzeinwurf

display
visualización
écran
Display

volume control
control de volumen
contrôle du volume
Lautstärkeregler

next call
próxima llamada
appel suivant
nächster Ruf

handset
auricular
combiné
Handapparat

language display button
botón de selección de lengua
choix de la langue d'affichage
Sprachanzeigetaste

armored cord
cable con funda metálica
cordon à gaine métallique
Panzerschnur

push buttons
teclas
clavier
Tasten

card reader
lector de tarjetas
lecteur de carte
Kartenschlitz

coin return bucket
devolución de monedas
sébile de remboursement
Geldrückgabe

TRANSPORT
TRANSPORTE

TRANSPORT
FORTBEWEGUNG

TRANSPORT TRANSPORTE

TRANSPORT FORTBEWEGUNG

CONTENTS

ROAD TRANSPORT

RAIL TRANSPORT

SUBWAY TRANSPORT

MARITIME TRANSPORT

AIR TRANSPORT

SPACE TRANSPORT

AUTOMOBILE
AUTOMÓVIL
AUTOMOBILE
AUTO

TYPES OF BODIES
TIPOS DE CARROCERÍAS
TYPES DE CARROSSERIES
WAGENTYPEN

sports car
deportivo
voiture sport
Sportwagen

two-door sedan
turismo de dos puertas
coach
Coupé

hatchback
turismo de tres puertas
trois-portes
Schrägheckmodell

station wagon
rubia
break
Kombiwagen

convertible
descapotable
cabriolet
Kabriolett

pickup truck
camioneta
camionnette
Pickup

four-door sedan
sedán de cuatro puertas
berline
viertürige Limousine

minivan
camioneta cubierta
fourgonnette
Minibus

multipurpose vehicle
vehículo todo terreno
véhicule tout-terrain
Geländewagen

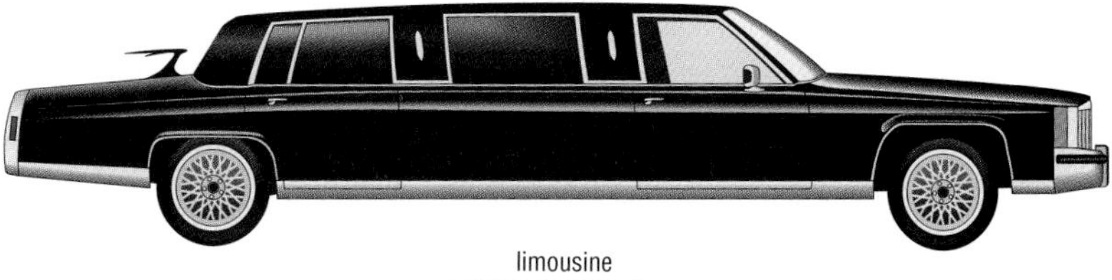

limousine
pullman de ocho plazas
limousine
Pullman-Limousine

AUTOMOBILE
AUTOMÓVIL
AUTOMOBILE
AUTO

BODY
CARROCERÍA
CARROSSERIE
KAROSSERIE

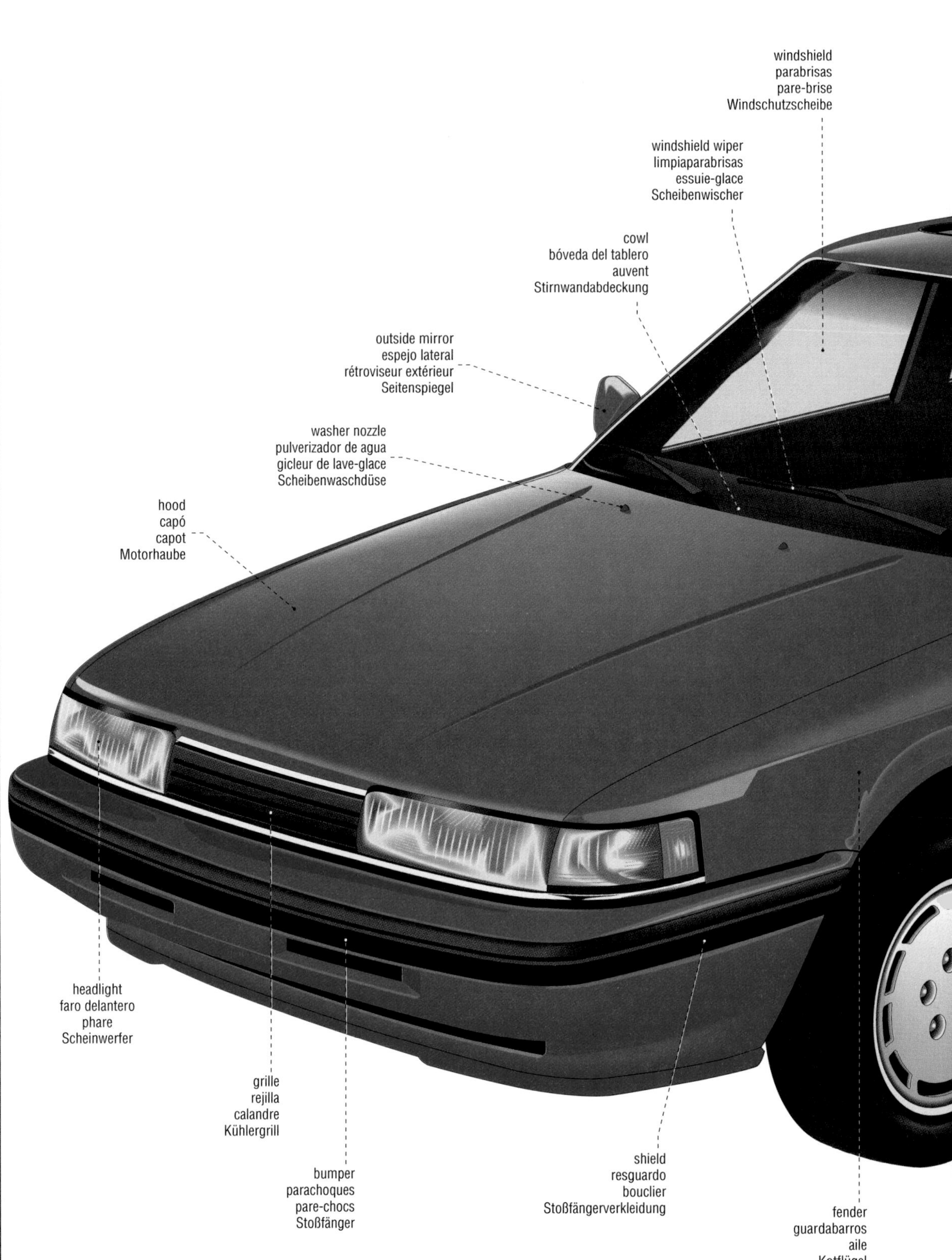
windshield
parabrisas
pare-brise
Windschutzscheibe
windshield wiper
limpiaparabrisas
essuie-glace
Scheibenwischer
cowl
bóveda del tablero
auvent
Stirnwandabdeckung
outside mirror
espejo lateral
rétroviseur extérieur
Seitenspiegel
washer nozzle
pulverizador de agua
gicleur de lave-glace
Scheibenwaschdüse
hood
capó
capot
Motorhaube
headlight
faro delantero
phare
Scheinwerfer
grille
rejilla
calandre
Kühlergrill
bumper
parachoques
pare-chocs
Stoßfänger
shield
resguardo
bouclier
Stoßfängerverkleidung
fender
guardabarros
aile
Kotflügel

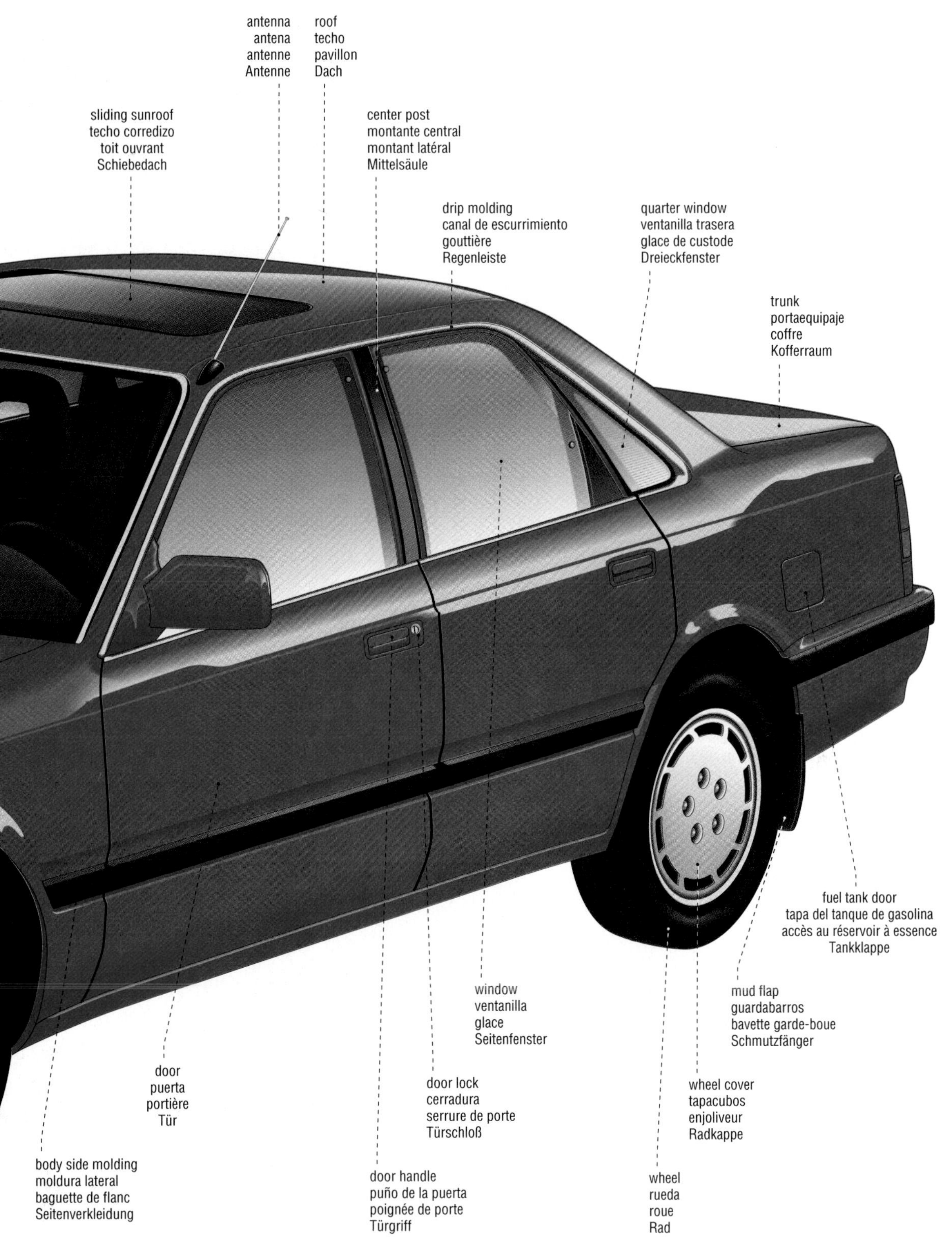
antenna
antena
antenne
Antenne
roof
techo
pavillon
Dach
sliding sunroof
techo corredizo
toit ouvrant
Schiebedach
center post
montante central
montant latéral
Mittelsäule
drip molding
canal de escurrimiento
gouttière
Regenleiste
quarter window
ventanilla trasera
glace de custode
Dreieckfenster
trunk
portaequipaje
coffre
Kofferraum
fuel tank door
tapa del tanque de gasolina
accès au réservoir à essence
Tankklappe
window
ventanilla
glace
Seitenfenster
mud flap
guardabarros
bavette garde-boue
Schmutzfänger
door
puerta
portière
Tür
door lock
cerradura
serrure de porte
Türschloß
wheel cover
tapacubos
enjoliveur
Radkappe
body side molding
moldura lateral
baguette de flanc
Seitenverkleidung
door handle
puño de la puerta
poignée de porte
Türgriff
wheel
rueda
roue
Rad

AUTOMOBILE
AUTOMÓVIL
AUTOMOBILE
AUTO

BUCKET SEAT
ASIENTO RECLINABLE
SIÈGE-BAQUET
SCHALENSITZ

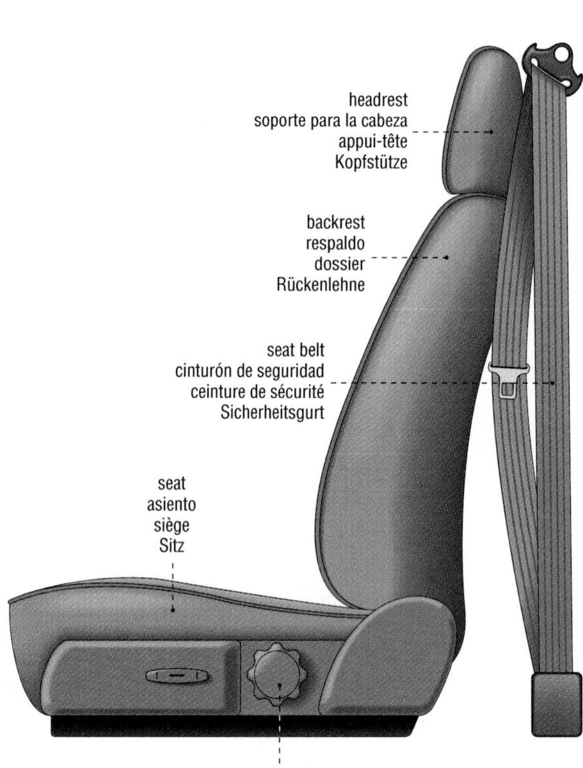
headrest
soporte para la cabeza
appui-tête
Kopfstütze
backrest
respaldo
dossier
Rückenlehne
seat belt
cinturón de seguridad
ceinture de sécurité
Sicherheitsgurt
seat
asiento
siège
Sitz
adjustment knob
palanca para graduar el respaldo
commande de dossier
Einstellrad

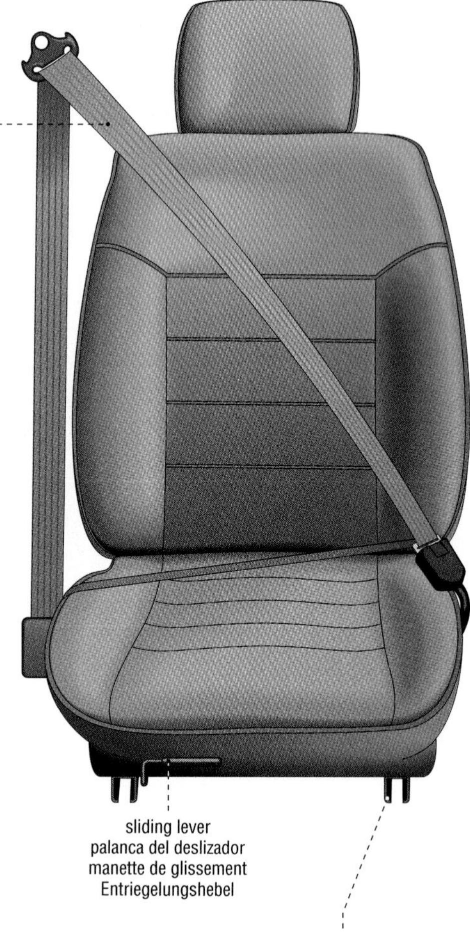
shoulder belt
cinturón de hombros
baudrier
Schultergurt
sliding lever
palanca del deslizador
manette de glissement
Entriegelungshebel
sliding rail
riel deslizador
rail de glissement
Führungsschiene

REAR SEAT
ASIENTO TRASERO
BANQUETTE ARRIÈRE
RÜCKSITZBANK

armrest
soporte para el brazo
appui-bras
Armstütze
webbing
correa
sangle
Beckengurt
buckle
hebilla
boucle
Gurtschließe
bench seat
asiento
banquette
Sitzbank

DOOR
PUERTA
PORTIÈRE
WAGENTÜR

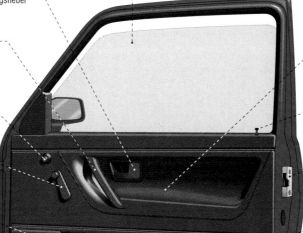

window
ventanilla
glace
Fenster
interior door handle
puño interior de la puerta
poignée intérieure
Türöffnungshebel
assist grip
asidera
poignée de maintien
Seitengriff
outside mirror control
control del espejo retrovisor exterior
commande du rétroviseur
Seitenspiegelverstellhebel
window regulator handle
manivela de la ventanilla
manivelle de lève-glace
Fensterhebel
accessory pocket
bolsillo lateral
vide-poches
Türtasche
hinge
bisagra
charnière
Scharnier
armrest
soporte para el brazo
appui-bras
Armstütze
interior door lock button
botón del seguro
bouton de verrouillage
Sicherungsknopf
lock
cerradura
serrure
Türschloß
trim panel
panel de la puerta
panneau de garnissage
Türverkleidung
inner door shell
revestimiento interior
caisson de porte
Türinnenschale

LIGHTS
FAROS
FEUX
FAHRZEUGBELEUCHTUNG

headlights
faros delanteros
feux avant
Bugleuchten

high beam
luz larga
feux de route
Fernlicht
low beam
luz de cruce
feux de croisement
Abblendlicht
fog light
luz antiniebla
feux de brouillard
Nebelleuchte
turn signal
intermitente
feux clignotants
Blinkleuchte
side-marker light
luz de posición
feux de gabarit
Begrenzungsleuchte

taillights
luces traseras
feux arrière
Heckleuchten

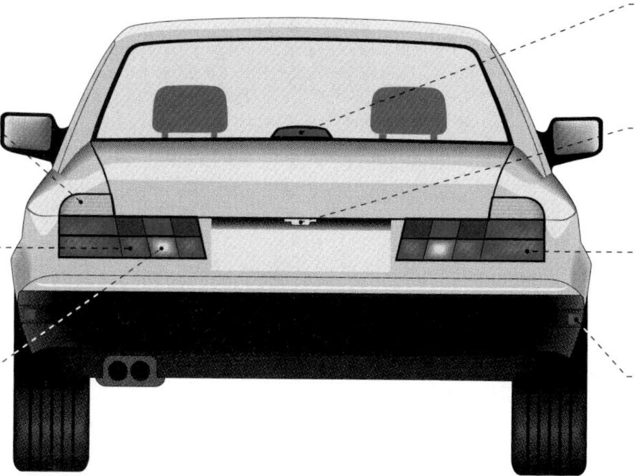
turn signal
intermitente
feux clignotants
Blinkleuchte
brakelight
luz de freno
feux stop
Bremsleuchte
backup light
luz de marcha atrás
feux de recul
Rückfahrscheinwerfer
brakelight
luz de freno
feu stop
Bremsleuchte
license plate light
iluminación de la placa de matrícula
feu de plaque
Nummernschildbeleuchtung
taillight
luz trasera
feux rouges arrière
Schlußleuchte
side-marker light
luz de posición
feux de gabarit
Begrenzungsleuchte

AUTOMOBILE
AUTOMÓVIL
AUTOMOBILE
AUTO

DASHBOARD
TABLERO
TABLEAU DE BORD
ARMATURENBRETT

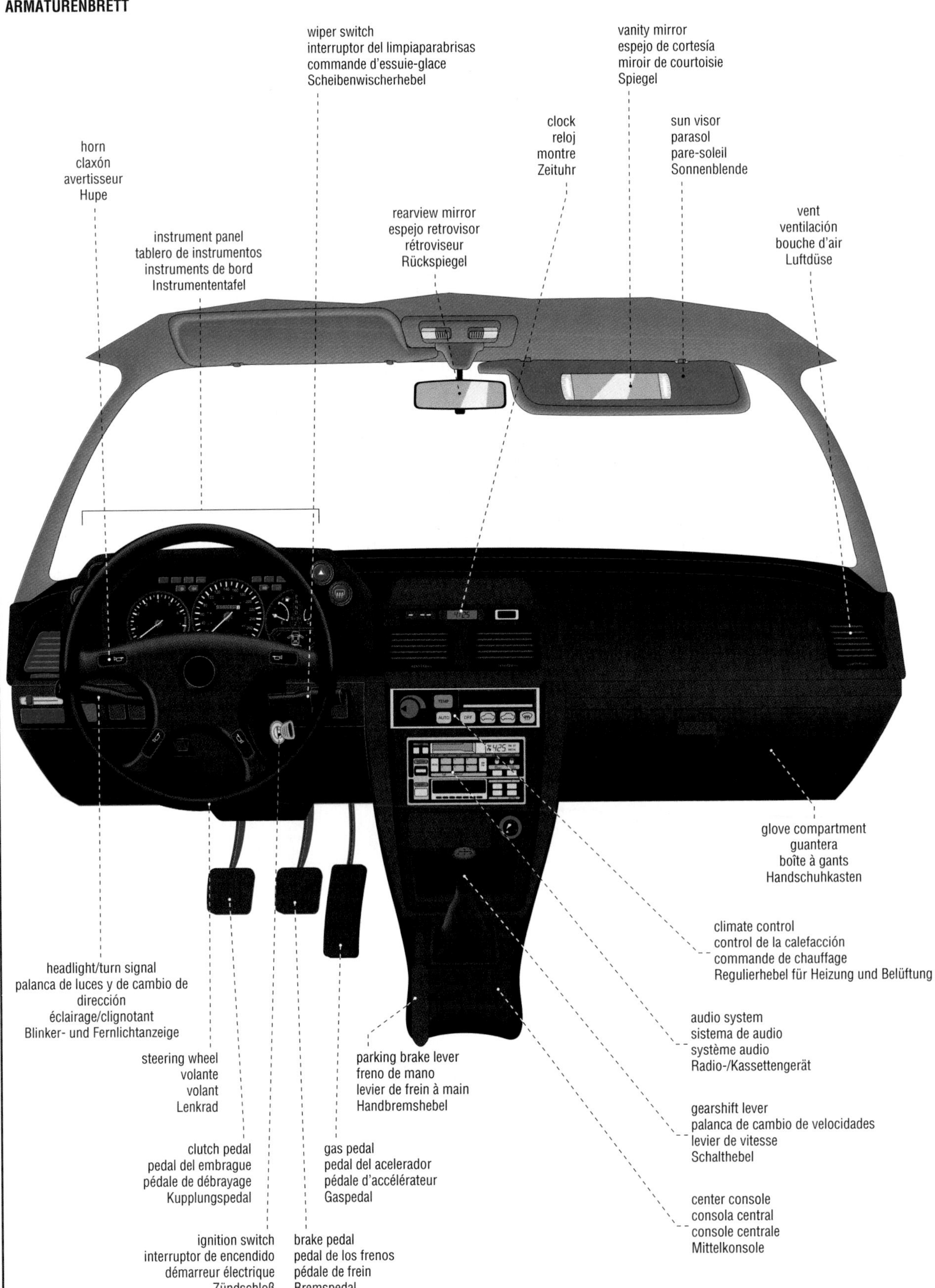
wiper switch
interruptor del limpiaparabrisas
commande d'essuie-glace
Scheibenwischerhebel
vanity mirror
espejo de cortesía
miroir de courtoisie
Spiegel
clock
reloj
montre
Zeituhr
sun visor
parasol
pare-soleil
Sonnenblende
horn
claxón
avertisseur
Hupe
rearview mirror
espejo retrovisor
rétroviseur
Rückspiegel
vent
ventilación
bouche d'air
Luftdüse
instrument panel
tablero de instrumentos
instruments de bord
Instrumententafel
glove compartment
guantera
boîte à gants
Handschuhkasten
climate control
control de la calefacción
commande de chauffage
Regulierhebel für Heizung und Belüftung
headlight/turn signal
palanca de luces y de cambio de dirección
éclairage/clignotant
Blinker- und Fernlichtanzeige
audio system
sistema de audio
système audio
Radio-/Kassettengerät
steering wheel
volante
volant
Lenkrad
parking brake lever
freno de mano
levier de frein à main
Handbremshebel
gearshift lever
palanca de cambio de velocidades
levier de vitesse
Schalthebel
clutch pedal
pedal del embrague
pédale de débrayage
Kupplungspedal
gas pedal
pedal del acelerador
pédale d'accélérateur
Gaspedal
center console
consola central
console centrale
Mittelkonsole
ignition switch
interruptor de encendido
démarreur électrique
Zündschloß
brake pedal
pedal de los frenos
pédale de frein
Bremspedal

INSTRUMENT PANEL
INSTRUMENTOS DEL TABLERO
INSTRUMENTS DE BORD
INSTRUMENTENTAFEL

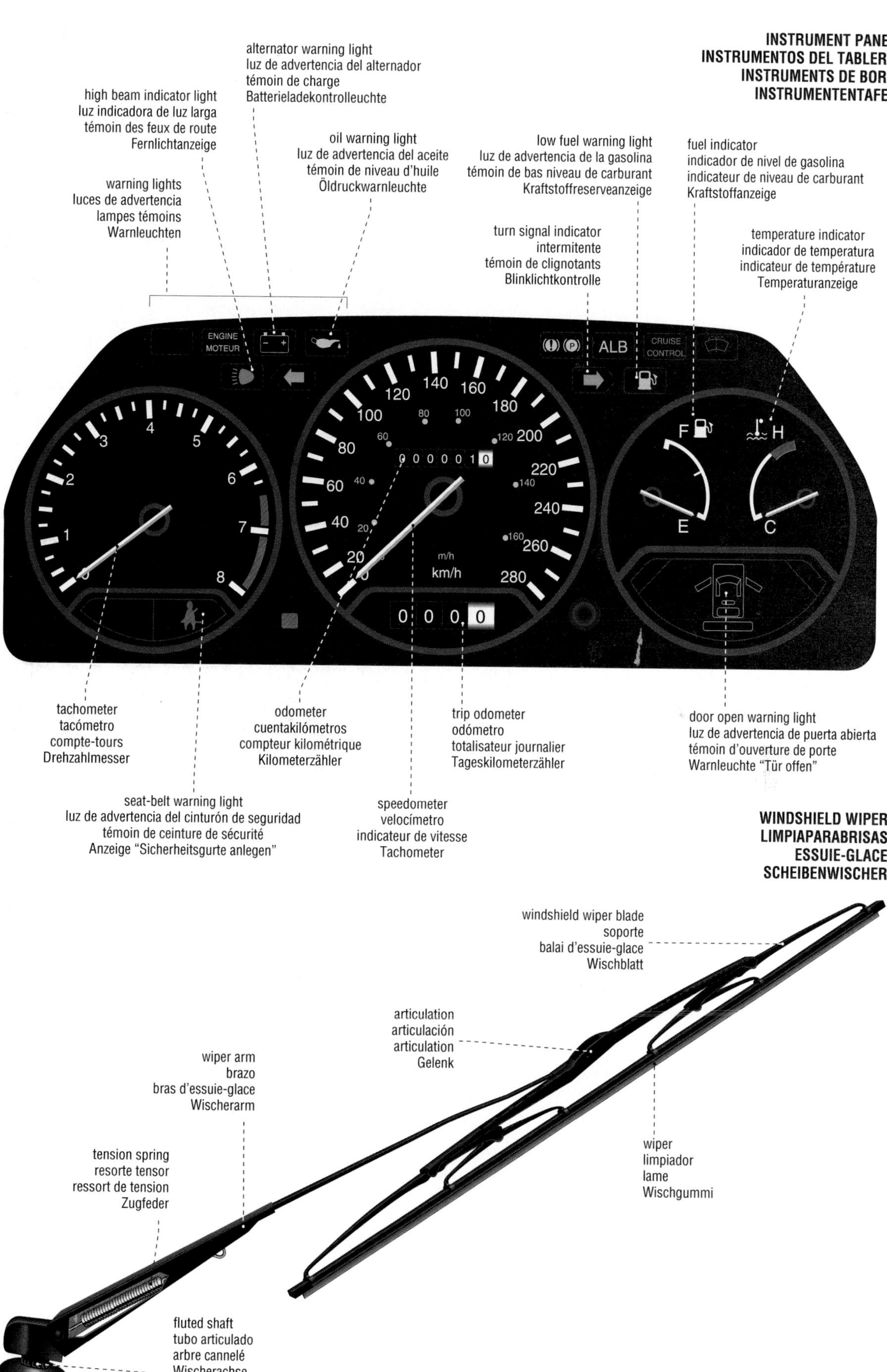
alternator warning light
luz de advertencia del alternador
témoin de charge
Batterieladekontrolleuchte
high beam indicator light
luz indicadora de luz larga
témoin des feux de route
Fernlichtanzeige
oil warning light
luz de advertencia del aceite
témoin de niveau d'huile
Öldruckwarnleuchte
low fuel warning light
luz de advertencia de la gasolina
témoin de bas niveau de carburant
Kraftstoffreserveanzeige
fuel indicator
indicador de nivel de gasolina
indicateur de niveau de carburant
Kraftstoffanzeige
warning lights
luces de advertencia
lampes témoins
Warnleuchten
turn signal indicator
intermitente
témoin de clignotants
Blinklichtkontrolle
temperature indicator
indicador de temperatura
indicateur de température
Temperaturanzeige
ENGINE
MOTEUR
ALB
CRUISE
CONTROL
F
H
E
C
km/h
m/h
tachometer
tacómetro
compte-tours
Drehzahlmesser
odometer
cuentakilómetros
compteur kilométrique
Kilometerzähler
trip odometer
odómetro
totalisateur journalier
Tageskilometerzähler
door open warning light
luz de advertencia de puerta abierta
témoin d'ouverture de porte
Warnleuchte "Tür offen"
seat-belt warning light
luz de advertencia del cinturón de seguridad
témoin de ceinture de sécurité
Anzeige "Sicherheitsgurte anlegen"
speedometer
velocímetro
indicateur de vitesse
Tachometer

WINDSHIELD WIPER
LIMPIAPARABRISAS
ESSUIE-GLACE
SCHEIBENWISCHER

windshield wiper blade
soporte
balai d'essuie-glace
Wischblatt
articulation
articulación
articulation
Gelenk
wiper arm
brazo
bras d'essuie-glace
Wischerarm
tension spring
resorte tensor
ressort de tension
Zugfeder
wiper
limpiador
lame
Wischgummi
fluted shaft
tubo articulado
arbre cannelé
Wischerachse

AUTOMOBILE
AUTOMÓVIL
AUTOMOBILE
AUTO

DISK BRAKE
FRENO DE DISCO
FREIN À DISQUE
SCHEIBENBREMSE

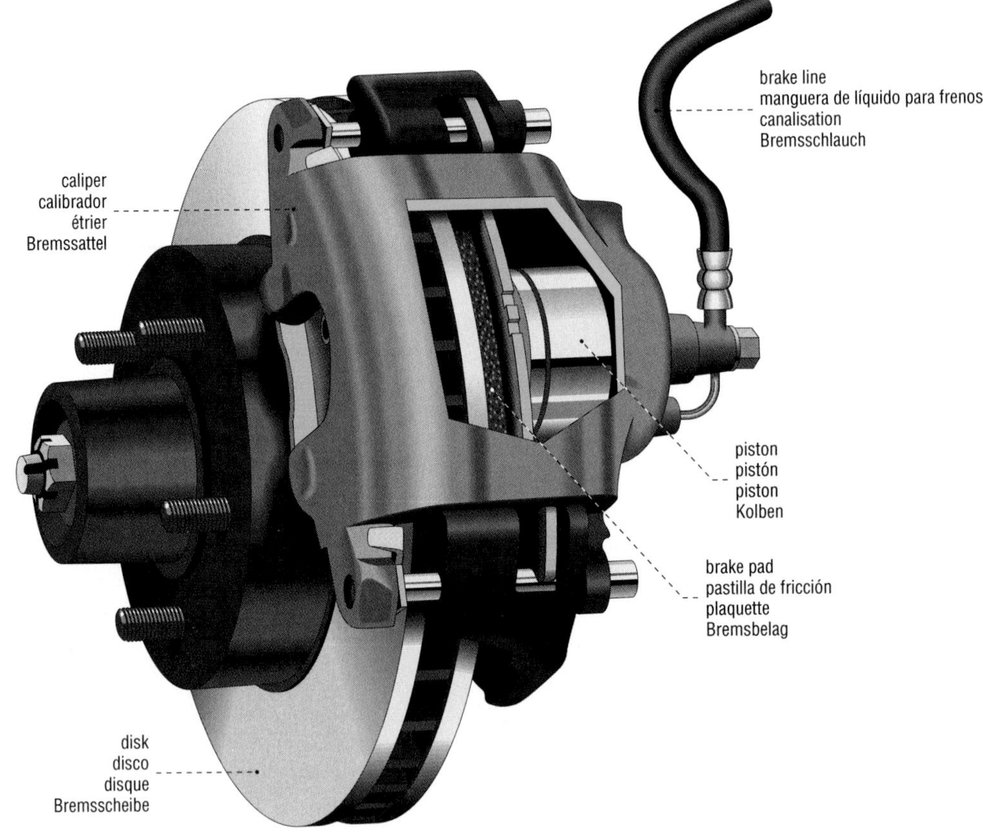
brake line
manguera de líquido para frenos
canalisation
Bremsschlauch
caliper
calibrador
étrier
Bremssattel
piston
pistón
piston
Kolben
brake pad
pastilla de fricción
plaquette
Bremsbelag
disk
disco
disque
Bremsscheibe

DRUM BRAKE
FRENO DE TAMBOR
FREIN À TAMBOUR
TROMMELBREMSE

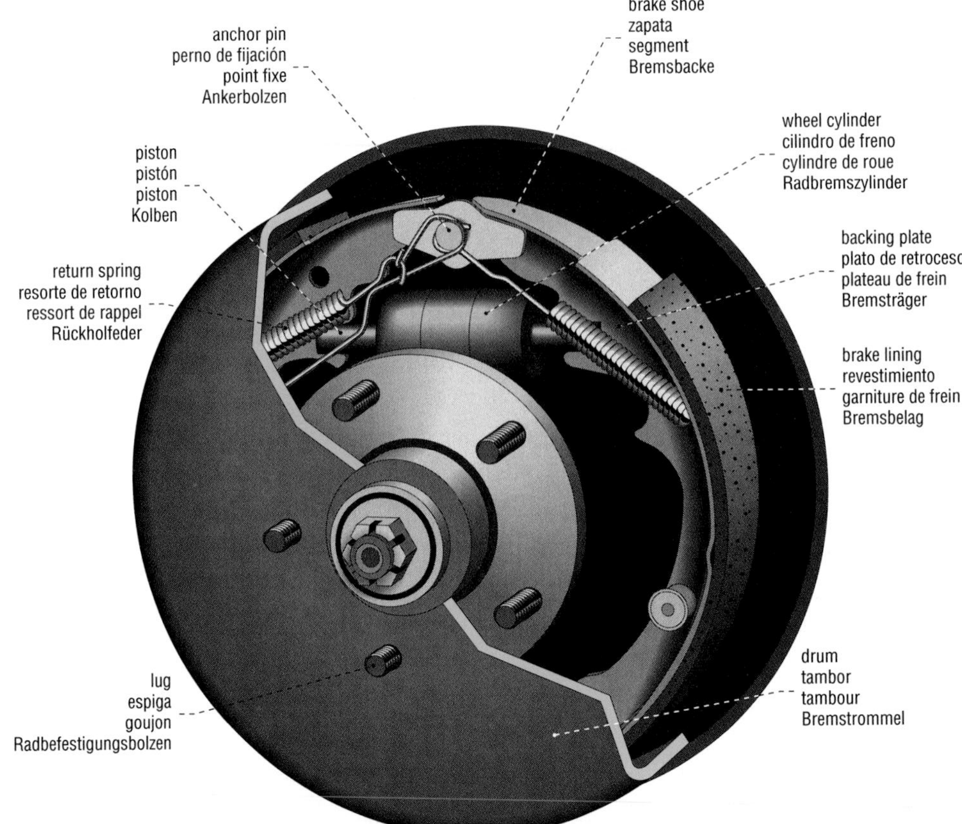
brake shoe
zapata
segment
Bremsbacke
anchor pin
perno de fijación
point fixe
Ankerbolzen
wheel cylinder
cilindro de freno
cylindre de roue
Radbremszylinder
piston
pistón
piston
Kolben
backing plate
plato de retroceso
plateau de frein
Bremsträger
return spring
resorte de retorno
ressort de rappel
Rückholfeder
brake lining
revestimiento
garniture de frein
Bremsbelag
drum
tambor
tambour
Bremstrommel
lug
espiga
goujon
Radbefestigungsbolzen

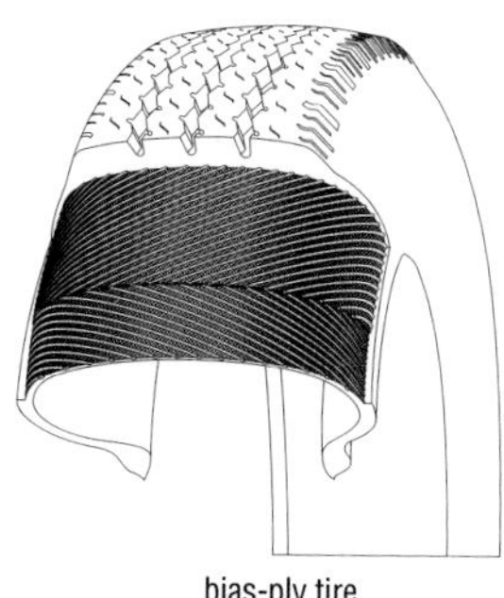

bias-ply tire
neumático de capas al sesgo
pneu à carcasse diagonale
Diagonalreifen

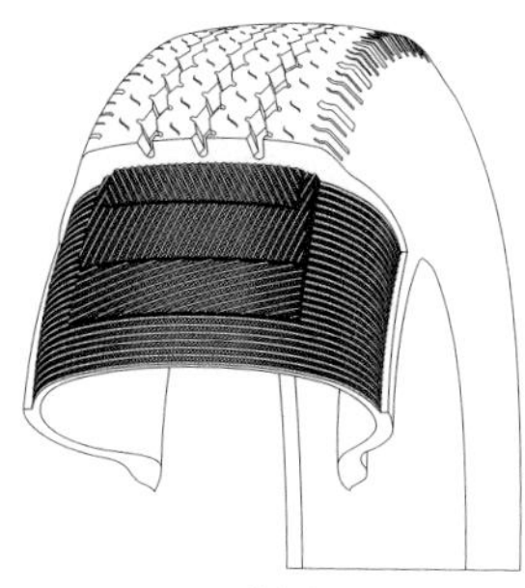

radial tire
neumático radial
pneu à carcasse radiale
Radialreifen

STEEL BELTED RADIAL TIRE
NEUMÁTICO RADIAL CON CINTURONES
PNEU À CARCASSE RADIALE CEINTURÉE
RADIALGÜRTELREIFEN

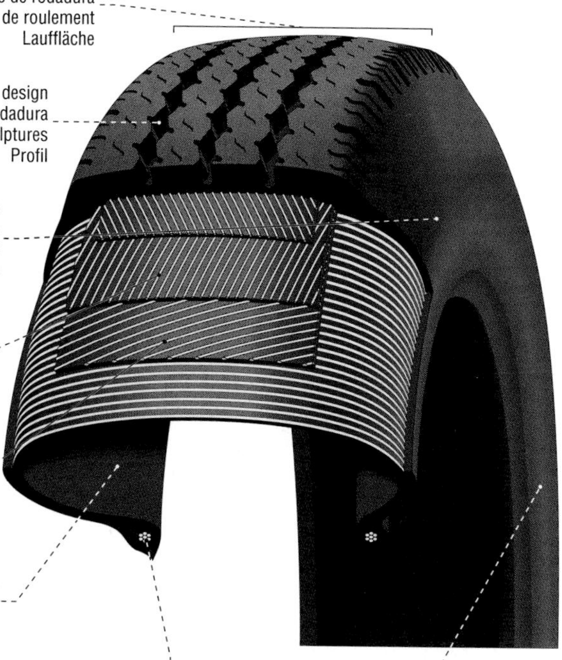

tread
superficie de rodadura
bande de roulement
Lauffläche

tread design
diseño de la superficie de rodadura
sculptures
Profil

rubbing strip
banda protectora
bourrelet
Scheuerleiste

belt
cinturón
ceinture
Gürtellage

radial ply
capa del casco
pli
Radialkarkasse

inner lining
revestimiento interior
revêtement intérieur
Innendichtschicht

bead wire
alambre del reborde
tringle
Wulstkern

rubber wall
costado
flanc
Reifenflanke

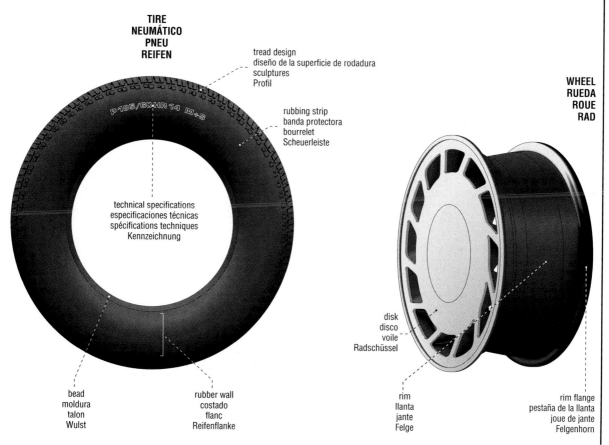

TIRE
NEUMÁTICO
PNEU
REIFEN

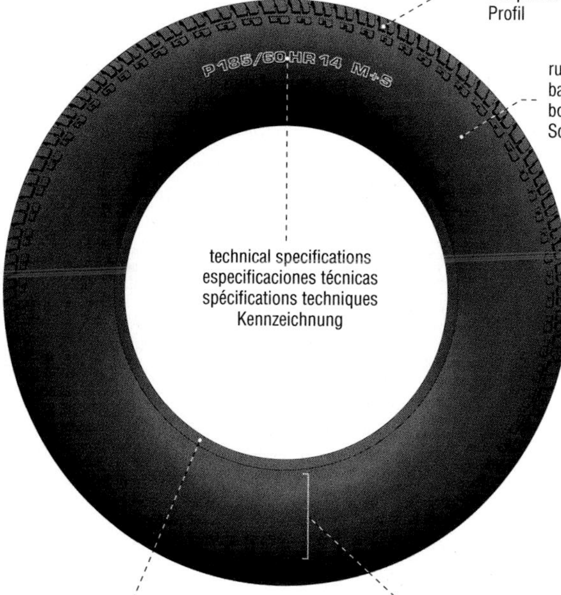

tread design
diseño de la superficie de rodadura
sculptures
Profil

rubbing strip
banda protectora
bourrelet
Scheuerleiste

P185/60HR14 M+S

technical specifications
especificaciones técnicas
spécifications techniques
Kennzeichnung

bead
moldura
talon
Wulst

rubber wall
costado
flanc
Reifenflanke

WHEEL
RUEDA
ROUE
RAD

disk
disco
voile
Radschüssel

rim
llanta
jante
Felge

rim flange
pestaña de la llanta
joue de jante
Felgenhorn

AUTOMOBILE
AUTOMÓVIL
AUTOMOBILE
AUTO

GASOLINE ENGINE
MOTOR DE GASOLINA
MOTEUR À ESSENCE
OTTOMOTOR

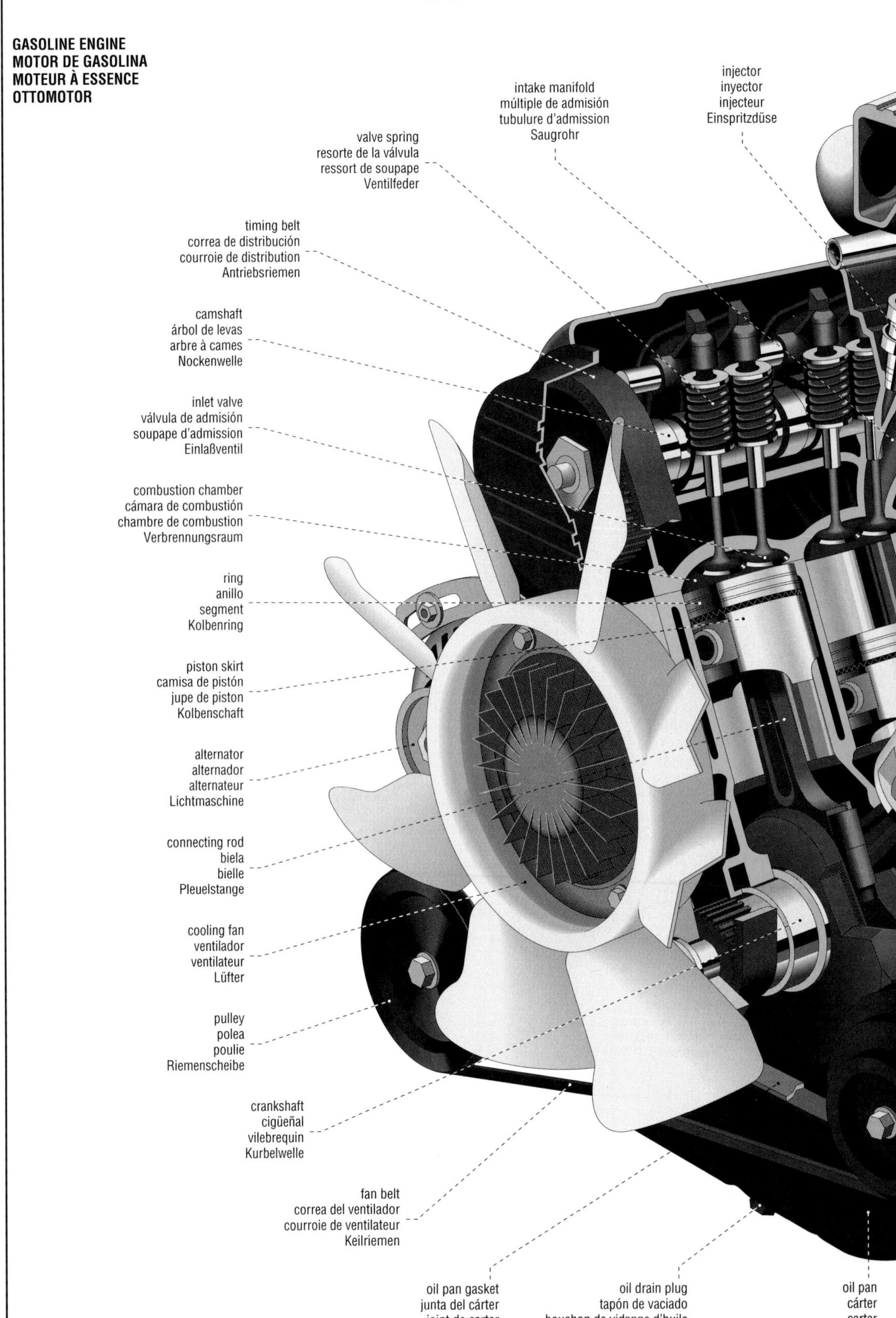
intake manifold
múltiple de admisión
tubulure d'admission
Saugrohr
injector
inyector
injecteur
Einspritzdüse
valve spring
resorte de la válvula
ressort de soupape
Ventilfeder
timing belt
correa de distribución
courroie de distribution
Antriebsriemen
camshaft
árbol de levas
arbre à cames
Nockenwelle
inlet valve
válvula de admisión
soupape d'admission
Einlaßventil
combustion chamber
cámara de combustión
chambre de combustion
Verbrennungsraum
ring
anillo
segment
Kolbenring
piston skirt
camisa de pistón
jupe de piston
Kolbenschaft
alternator
alternador
alternateur
Lichtmaschine
connecting rod
biela
bielle
Pleuelstange
cooling fan
ventilador
ventilateur
Lüfter
pulley
polea
poulie
Riemenscheibe
crankshaft
cigüeñal
vilebrequin
Kurbelwelle
fan belt
correa del ventilador
courroie de ventilateur
Keilriemen
oil pan gasket
junta del cárter
joint de carter
Ölwannendichtung
oil drain plug
tapón de vaciado
bouchon de vidange d'huile
Ölablaßschraube
oil pan
cárter
carter
Ölwanne

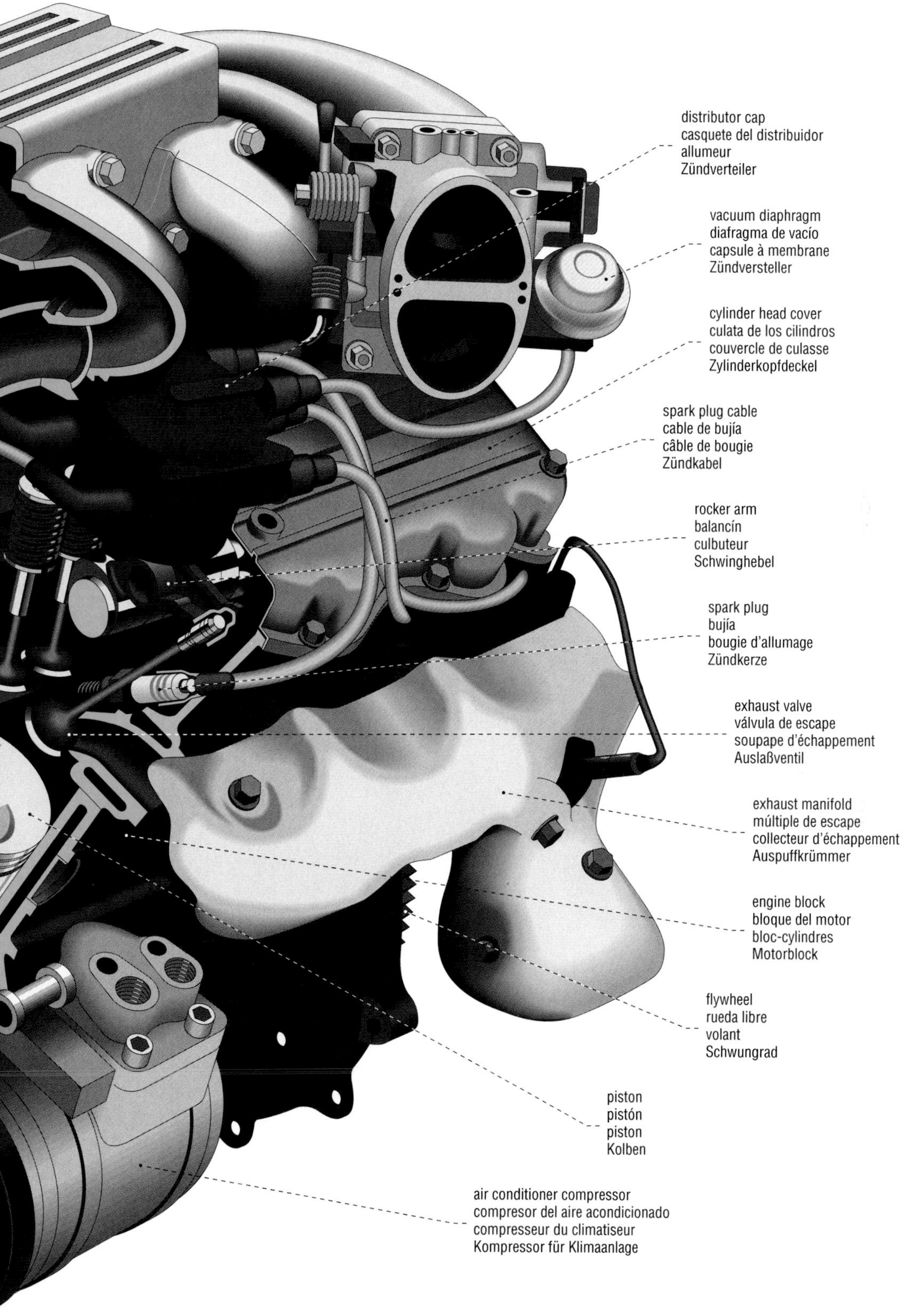
distributor cap
casquete del distribuidor
allumeur
Zündverteiler
vacuum diaphragm
diafragma de vacío
capsule à membrane
Zündversteller
cylinder head cover
culata de los cilindros
couvercle de culasse
Zylinderkopfdeckel
spark plug cable
cable de bujía
câble de bougie
Zündkabel
rocker arm
balancín
culbuteur
Schwinghebel
spark plug
bujía
bougie d'allumage
Zündkerze
exhaust valve
válvula de escape
soupape d'échappement
Auslaßventil
exhaust manifold
múltiple de escape
collecteur d'échappement
Auspuffkrümmer
engine block
bloque del motor
bloc-cylindres
Motorblock
flywheel
rueda libre
volant
Schwungrad
piston
pistón
piston
Kolben
air conditioner compressor
compresor del aire acondicionado
compresseur du climatiseur
Kompressor für Klimaanlage

TYPES OF ENGINES
TIPOS DE MOTORES
TYPES DE MOTEURS
MOTORTYPEN

FOUR-STROKE-CYCLE ENGINE
MOTOR DE CUATRO TIEMPOS
MOTEUR À QUATRE TEMPS
VIERTAKTMOTOR

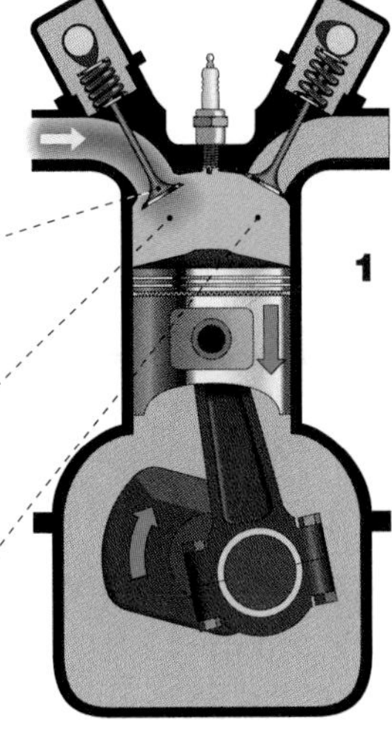
inlet valve
válvula de admisión
soupape d'admission
Einlaßventil
air/fuel mixture
mezcla de aire y combustible
mélange air/carburant
Kraftstoff-Luft-Gemisch
cylinder
cilindro
cylindre
Zylinder
1

intake
admisión
admission
Ansaugen

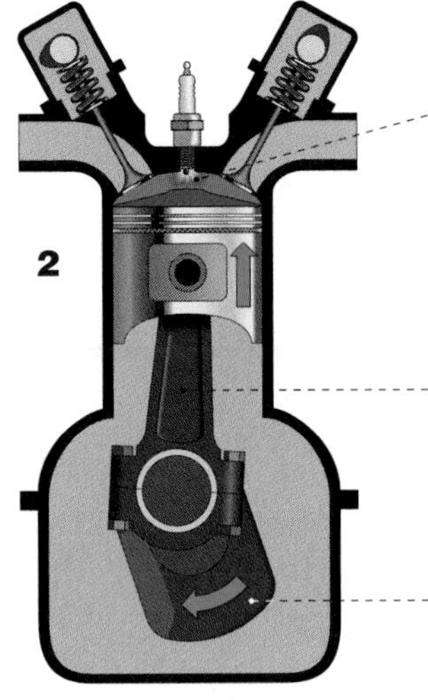
2
spark
chispa
étincelle
Funken
connecting rod
biela
bielle
Pleuelstange
crankshaft
cigüeñal
vilebrequin
Kurbelwelle

compression
compresión
compression
Verdichten

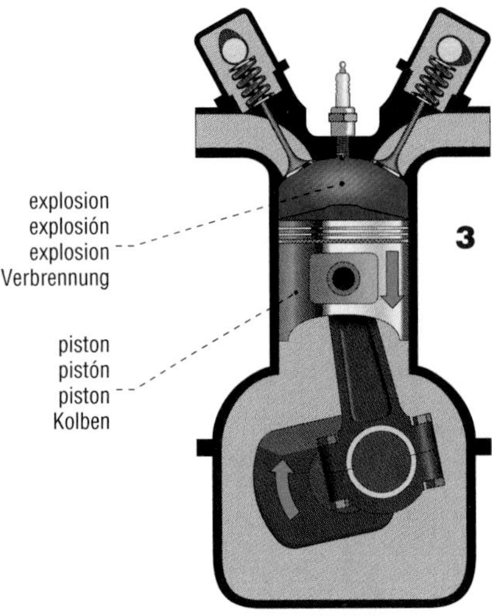
explosion
explosión
explosion
Verbrennung
piston
pistón
piston
Kolben
3

combustion
combustión
combustion
Zünden

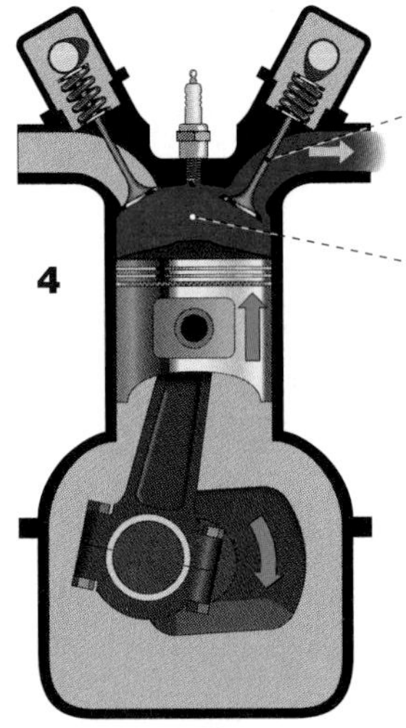
4
exhaust valve
válvula de escape
soupape d'échappement
Auslaßventil
burned gases
gases quemados
gaz brûlés
Abgase

exhaust
escape
échappement
Ausstoßen

TWO-STROKE-CYCLE ENGINE
MOTOR DE DOS TIEMPOS
MOTEUR À DEUX TEMPS
ZWEITAKTMOTOR

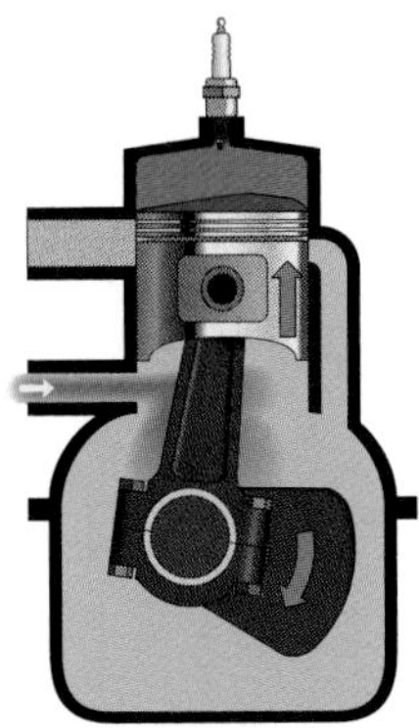

compression/admission
compresión/admisión
compression/admission
Verdichten/Ansaugen

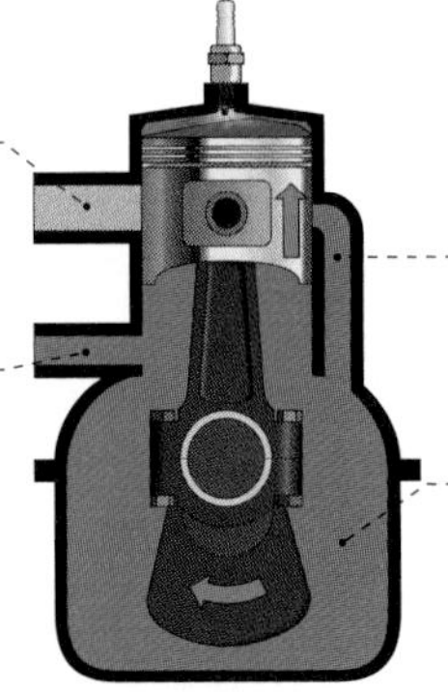
exhaust port
lumbrera de escape
canal d'échappement
Auspuffkanal
intake port
lumbrera de admisión
canal d'admission
Ansaugkanal
transfer port
lumbrera de transferencia
canal de transfert
Überströmschlitz
crankcase
cárter
carter
Kurbelgehäuse

combustion
combustión
combustion
Verbrennen

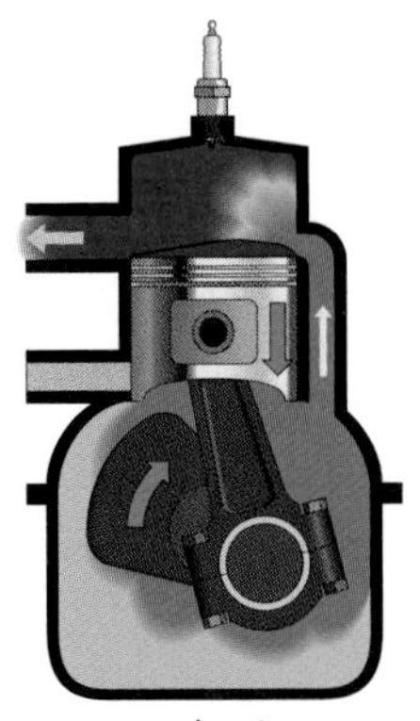

exhaust
escape
échappement
Ausstoßen

DIESEL ENGINE
MOTOR DIESEL
MOTEUR DIESEL
DIESELMOTOR

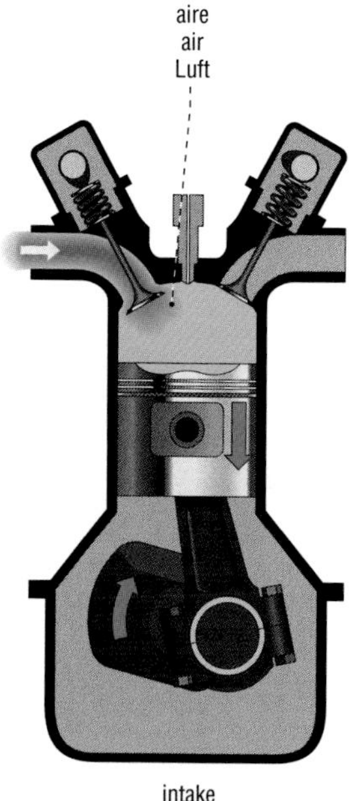
air
aire
air
Luft

intake
admisión
admission
Ansaugen

injection/explosion
injección/explosión
injection/explosion
Einspritzung/Verbrennung

compression
compresión
compression
Verdichten

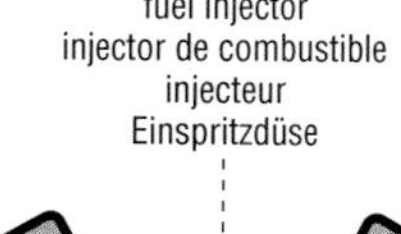
fuel injector
injector de combustible
injecteur
Einspritzdüse

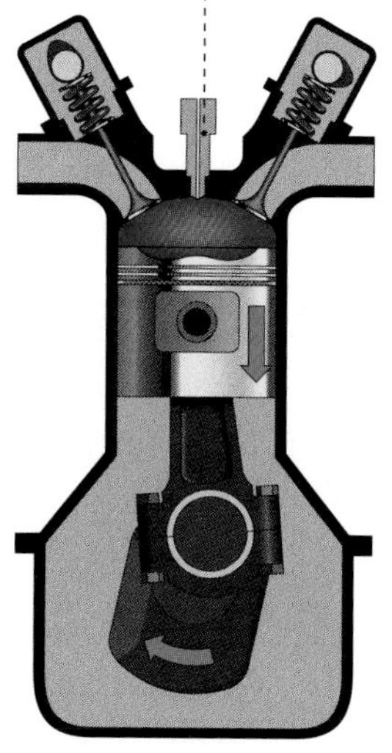

combustion
combustión
combustion
Zünden

exhaust
escape
échappement
Ausstoßen

ROTARY ENGINE
MOTOR ROTATORIO
MOTEUR ROTATIF
KREISKOLBENMOTOR

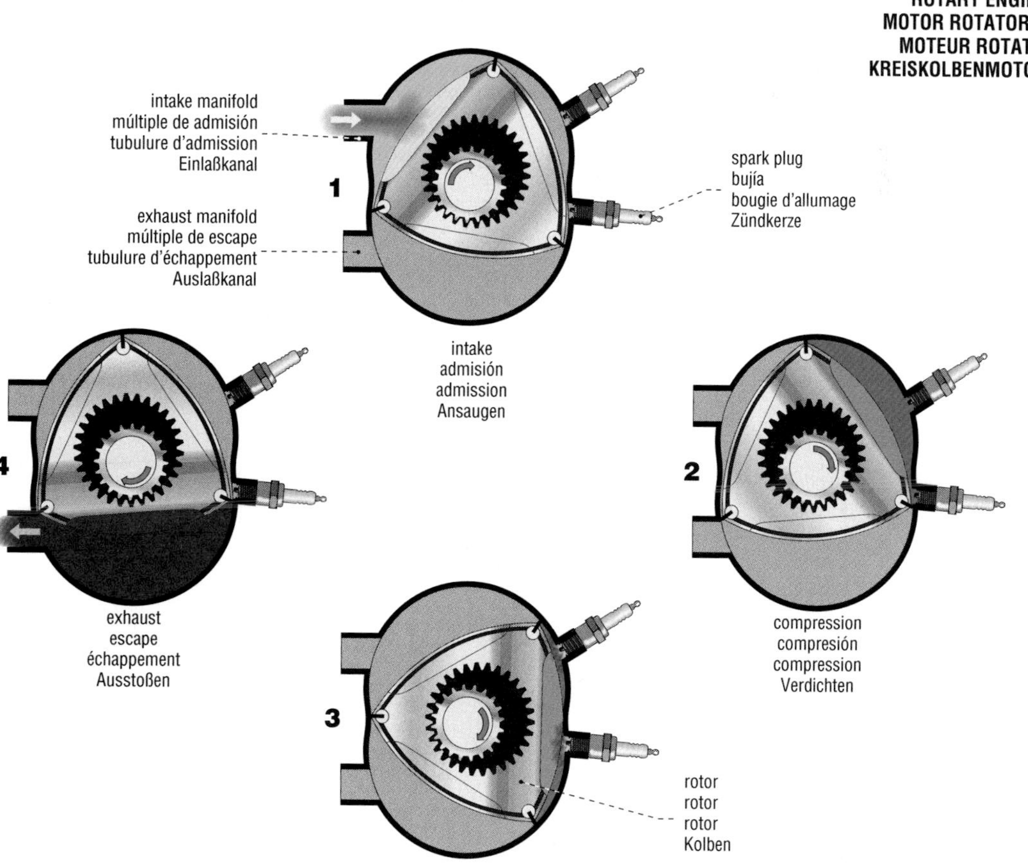
intake manifold
múltiple de admisión
tubulure d'admission
Einlaßkanal
exhaust manifold
múltiple de escape
tubulure d'échappement
Auslaßkanal
1
spark plug
bujía
bougie d'allumage
Zündkerze
4
2
3
rotor
rotor
rotor
Kolben

intake
admisión
admission
Ansaugen

exhaust
escape
échappement
Ausstoßen

compression
compresión
compression
Verdichten

combustion
combustión
combustion
Zünden

AUTOMOBILE
AUTOMÓVIL
AUTOMOBILE
AUTO

RADIATOR
RADIADOR
RADIATEUR
KÜHLER

filler cap
tapa
bouchon de remplissage
Kühlerverschlußdeckel
cooling fan
ventilador
ventilateur
Lüfter
fan thermostat
termostato del ventilador
thermocontact
Thermoschalter
radiator hose
manguera
durite de radiateur
Kühlwasserschlauch
grille
rejilla
grille
Kühlerblock
electric motor
motor eléctrico
moteur électrique
Elektromotor

TURBO-COMPRESSOR ENGINE
MOTOR TURBO COMPRESOR
MOTEUR À TURBOCOMPRESSION
MOTOR MIT ABGASTURBOLADER

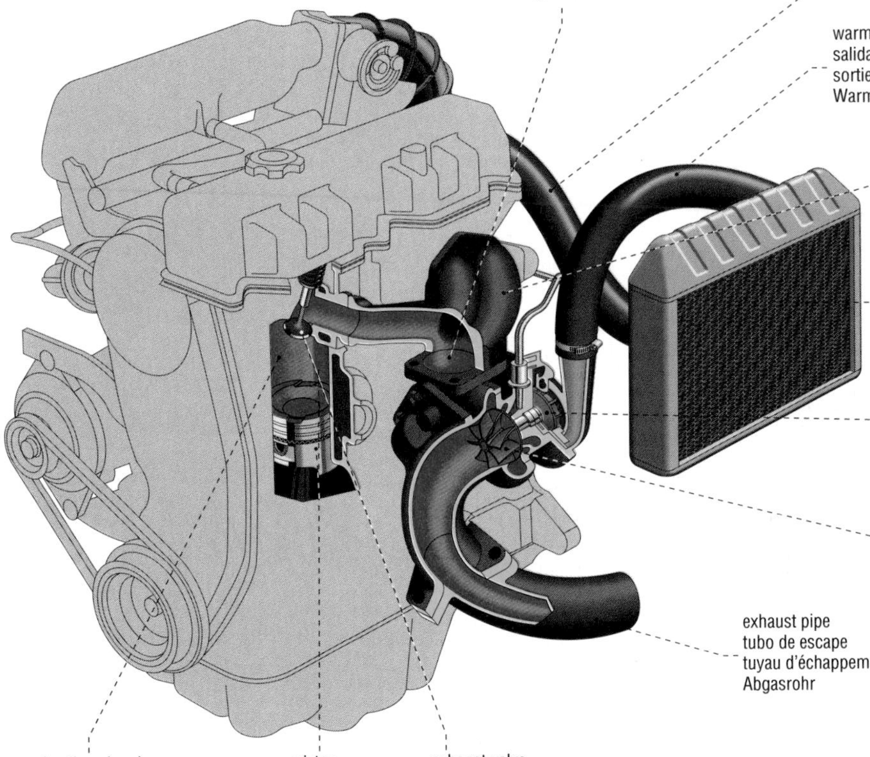

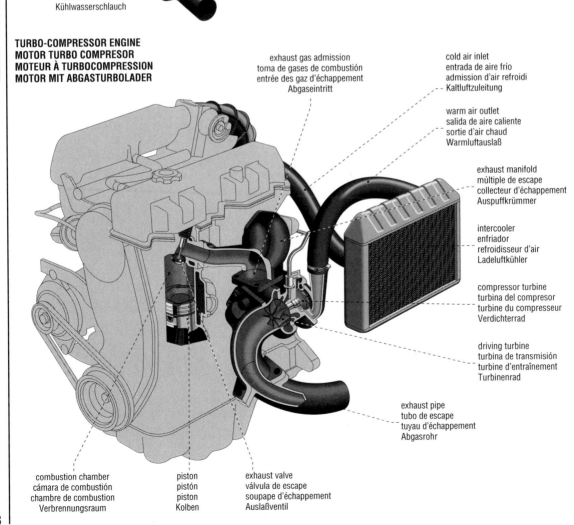

exhaust gas admission
toma de gases de combustión
entrée des gaz d'échappement
Abgaseintritt

cold air inlet
entrada de aire frío
admission d'air refroidi
Kaltluftzuleitung

warm air outlet
salida de aire caliente
sortie d'air chaud
Warmluftauslaß

exhaust manifold
múltiple de escape
collecteur d'échappement
Auspuffkrümmer

intercooler
enfriador
refroidisseur d'air
Ladeluftkühler

compressor turbine
turbina del compresor
turbine du compresseur
Verdichterrad

driving turbine
turbina de transmisión
turbine d'entraînement
Turbinenrad

exhaust pipe
tubo de escape
tuyau d'échappement
Abgasrohr

combustion chamber
cámara de combustión
chambre de combustion
Verbrennungsraum

piston
pistón
piston
Kolben

exhaust valve
válvula de escape
soupape d'échappement
Auslaßventil

SPARK PLUG
BUJÍA
BOUGIE D'ALLUMAGE
ZÜNDKERZE

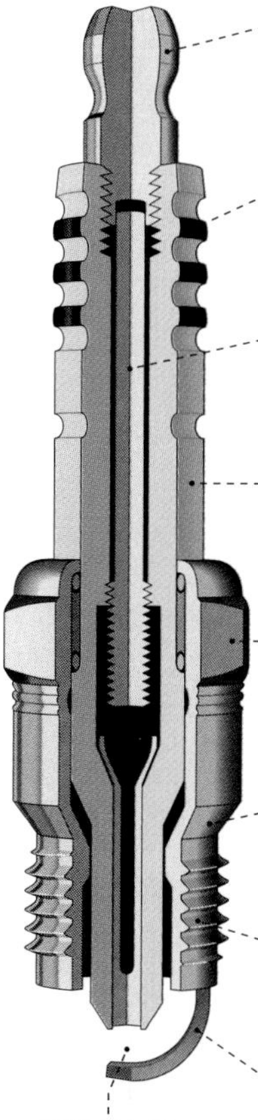

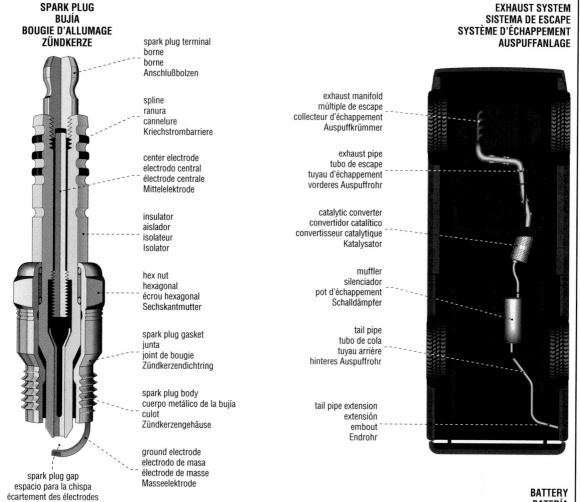

spark plug terminal
borne
borne
Anschlußbolzen

spline
ranura
cannelure
Kriechstrombarriere

center electrode
electrodo central
électrode centrale
Mittelelektrode

insulator
aislador
isolateur
Isolator

hex nut
hexagonal
écrou hexagonal
Sechskantmutter

spark plug gasket
junta
joint de bougie
Zündkerzendichtring

spark plug body
cuerpo metálico de la bujía
culot
Zündkerzengehäuse

ground electrode
electrodo de masa
électrode de masse
Masseelektrode

spark plug gap
espacio para la chispa
écartement des électrodes
Funkenstrecke

EXHAUST SYSTEM
SISTEMA DE ESCAPE
SYSTÈME D'ÉCHAPPEMENT
AUSPUFFANLAGE

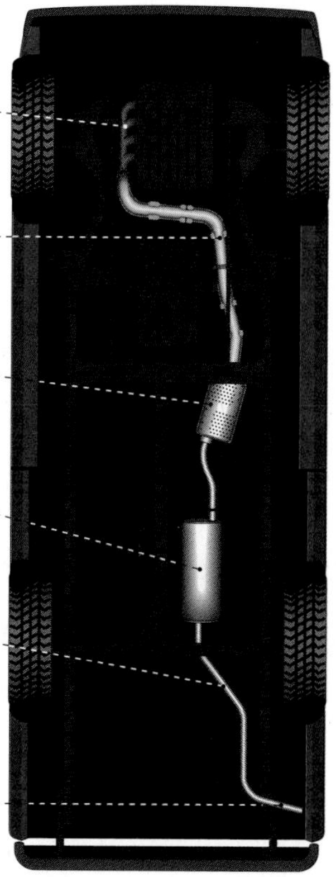

exhaust manifold
múltiple de escape
collecteur d'échappement
Auspuffkrümmer

exhaust pipe
tubo de escape
tuyau d'échappement
vorderes Auspuffrohr

catalytic converter
convertidor catalítico
convertisseur catalytique
Katalysator

muffler
silenciador
pot d'échappement
Schalldämpfer

tail pipe
tubo de cola
tuyau arrière
hinteres Auspuffrohr

tail pipe extension
extensión
embout
Endrohr

BATTERY
BATERÍA
BATTERIE D'ACCUMULATEURS
BATTERIE

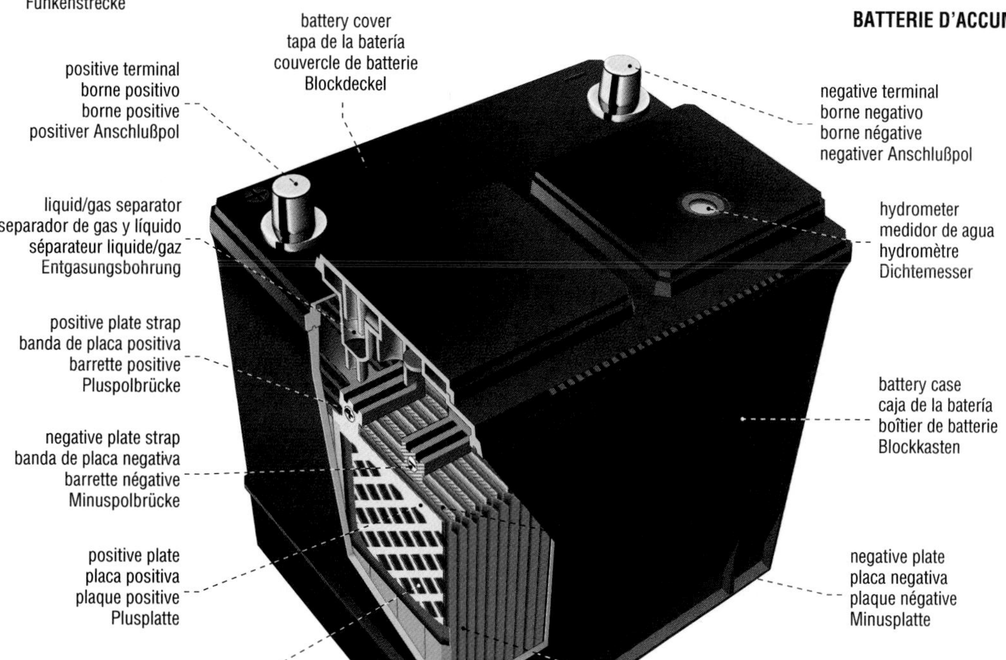
battery cover
tapa de la batería
couvercle de batterie
Blockdeckel
positive terminal
borne positivo
borne positive
positiver Anschlußpol
negative terminal
borne negativo
borne négative
negativer Anschlußpol
liquid/gas separator
separador de gas y líquido
séparateur liquide/gaz
Entgasungsbohrung
hydrometer
medidor de agua
hydromètre
Dichtemesser
positive plate strap
banda de placa positiva
barrette positive
Pluspolbrücke
battery case
caja de la batería
boîtier de batterie
Blockkasten
negative plate strap
banda de placa negativa
barrette négative
Minuspolbrücke
positive plate
placa positiva
plaque positive
Plusplatte
negative plate
placa negativa
plaque négative
Minusplatte
plate grid
rejilla
alvéole de plaque
Plattengitter
separator
separador de placas
séparateur
Plattenscheider

TRUCKING
CAMIONES
CAMIONNAGE
LASTKRAFTFAHRZEUGE

TRUCK TRACTOR
CAMIÓN TRACTOR
TRACTEUR ROUTIER
SATTELSCHLEPPER

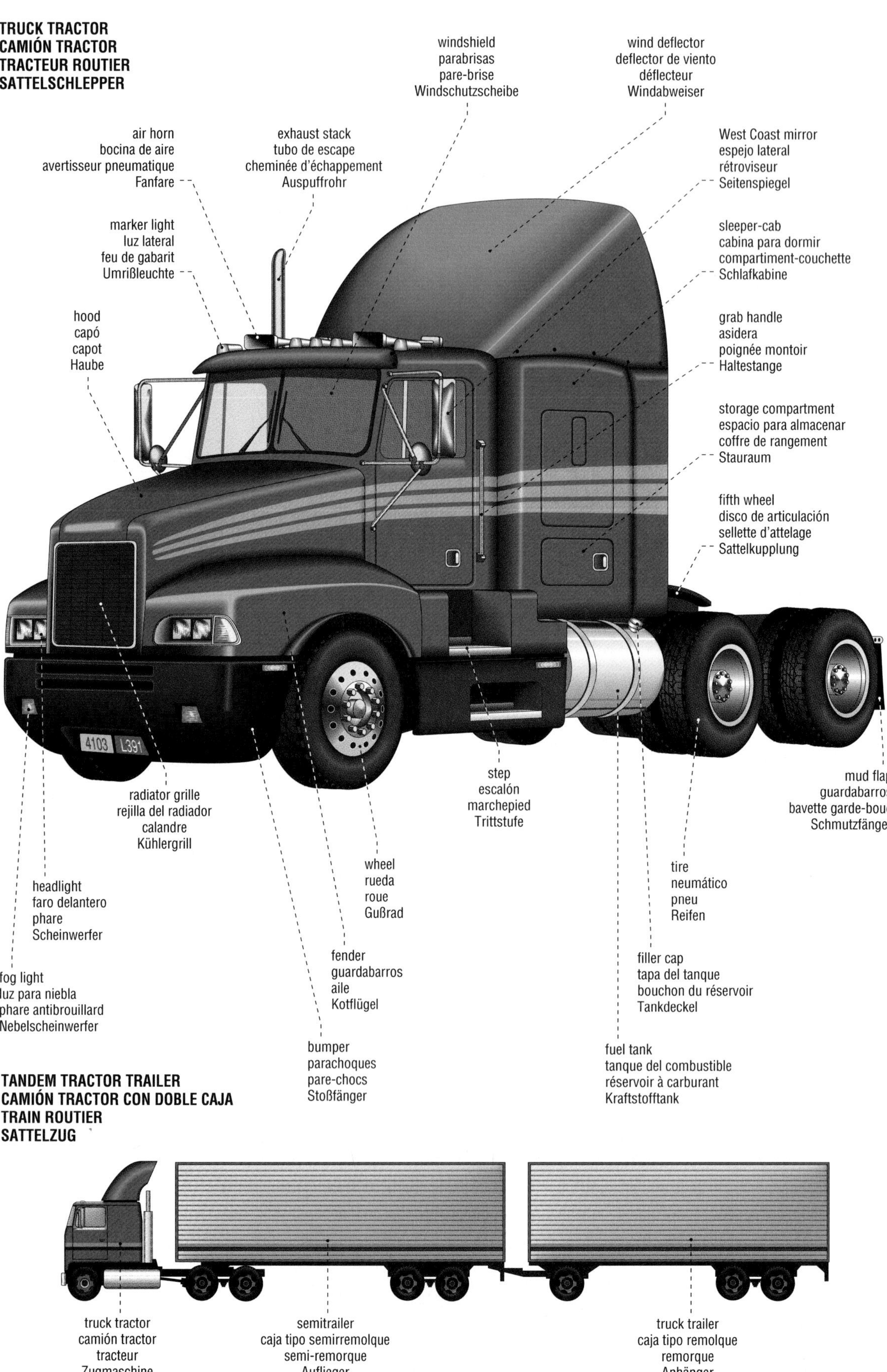
windshield
parabrisas
pare-brise
Windschutzscheibe
wind deflector
deflector de viento
déflecteur
Windabweiser
air horn
bocina de aire
avertisseur pneumatique
Fanfare
exhaust stack
tubo de escape
cheminée d'échappement
Auspuffrohr
West Coast mirror
espejo lateral
rétroviseur
Seitenspiegel
marker light
luz lateral
feu de gabarit
Umrißleuchte
sleeper-cab
cabina para dormir
compartiment-couchette
Schlafkabine
hood
capó
capot
Haube
grab handle
asidera
poignée montoir
Haltestange
storage compartment
espacio para almacenar
coffre de rangement
Stauraum
fifth wheel
disco de articulación
sellette d'attelage
Sattelkupplung
4103
L391
step
escalón
marchepied
Trittstufe
mud flap
guardabarros
bavette garde-boue
Schmutzfänger
radiator grille
rejilla del radiador
calandre
Kühlergrill
wheel
rueda
roue
Gußrad
tire
neumático
pneu
Reifen
headlight
faro delantero
phare
Scheinwerfer
fender
guardabarros
aile
Kotflügel
filler cap
tapa del tanque
bouchon du réservoir
Tankdeckel
fog light
luz para niebla
phare antibrouillard
Nebelscheinwerfer
bumper
parachoques
pare-chocs
Stoßfänger
fuel tank
tanque del combustible
réservoir à carburant
Kraftstofftank

TANDEM TRACTOR TRAILER
CAMIÓN TRACTOR CON DOBLE CAJA
TRAIN ROUTIER
SATTELZUG

truck tractor
camión tractor
tracteur
Zugmaschine
semitrailer
caja tipo semirremolque
semi-remorque
Auflieger
truck trailer
caja tipo remolque
remorque
Anhänger

SEMITRAILER
CAJA TIPO SEMIRREMOLQUE
SEMI-REMORQUE
AUFLIEGER

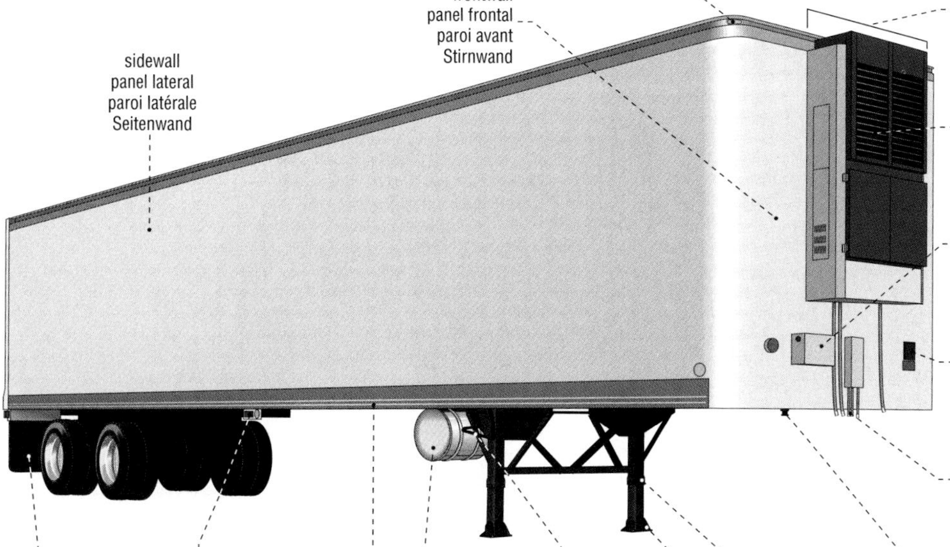

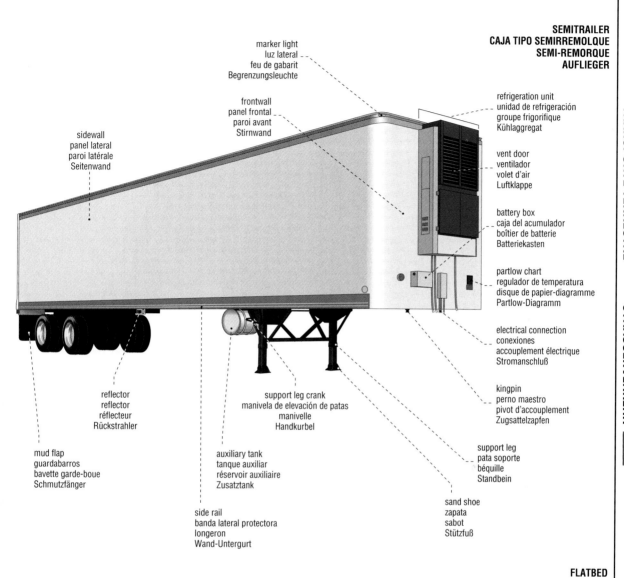

marker light
luz lateral
feu de gabarit
Begrenzungsleuchte

frontwall
panel frontal
paroi avant
Stirnwand

sidewall
panel lateral
paroi latérale
Seitenwand

refrigeration unit
unidad de refrigeración
groupe frigorifique
Kühlaggregat

vent door
ventilador
volet d'air
Luftklappe

battery box
caja del acumulador
boîtier de batterie
Batteriekasten

partlow chart
regulador de temperatura
disque de papier-diagramme
Partlow-Diagramm

electrical connection
conexiones
accouplement électrique
Stromanschluß

kingpin
perno maestro
pivot d'accouplement
Zugsattelzapfen

support leg crank
manivela de elevación de patas
manivelle
Handkurbel

reflector
reflector
réflecteur
Rückstrahler

support leg
pata soporte
béquille
Standbein

mud flap
guardabarros
bavette garde-boue
Schmutzfänger

auxiliary tank
tanque auxiliar
réservoir auxiliaire
Zusatztank

sand shoe
zapata
sabot
Stützfuß

side rail
banda lateral protectora
longeron
Wand-Untergurt

FLATBED
PLATAFORMA
SEMI-REMORQUE PLATE-FORME
KOFFER-SATTELANHÄNGER

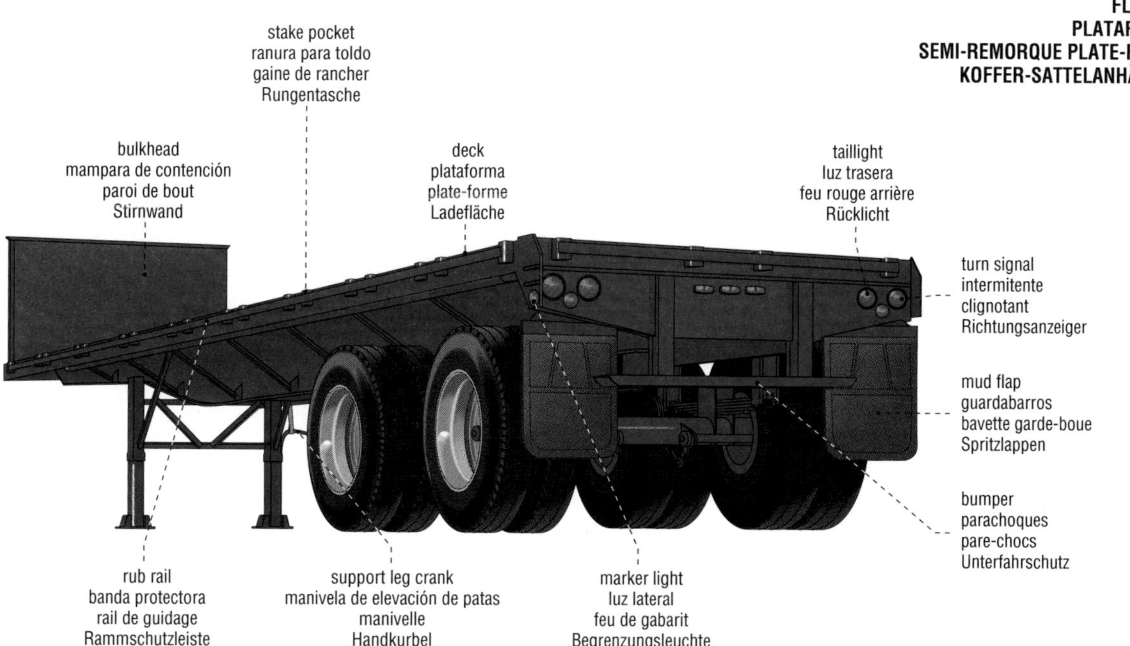
stake pocket
ranura para toldo
gaine de rancher
Rungentasche
bulkhead
mampara de contención
paroi de bout
Stirnwand
deck
plataforma
plate-forme
Ladefläche
taillight
luz trasera
feu rouge arrière
Rücklicht
turn signal
intermitente
clignotant
Richtungsanzeiger
mud flap
guardabarros
bavette garde-boue
Spritzlappen
bumper
parachoques
pare-chocs
Unterfahrschutz
rub rail
banda protectora
rail de guidage
Rammschutzleiste
support leg crank
manivela de elevación de patas
manivelle
Handkurbel
marker light
luz lateral
feu de gabarit
Begrenzungsleuchte

MOTORCYCLE
MOTOCICLETA
MOTO
MOTORRAD

SIDE VIEW
VISTA LATERAL
VUE LATÉRALE
SEITENANSICHT

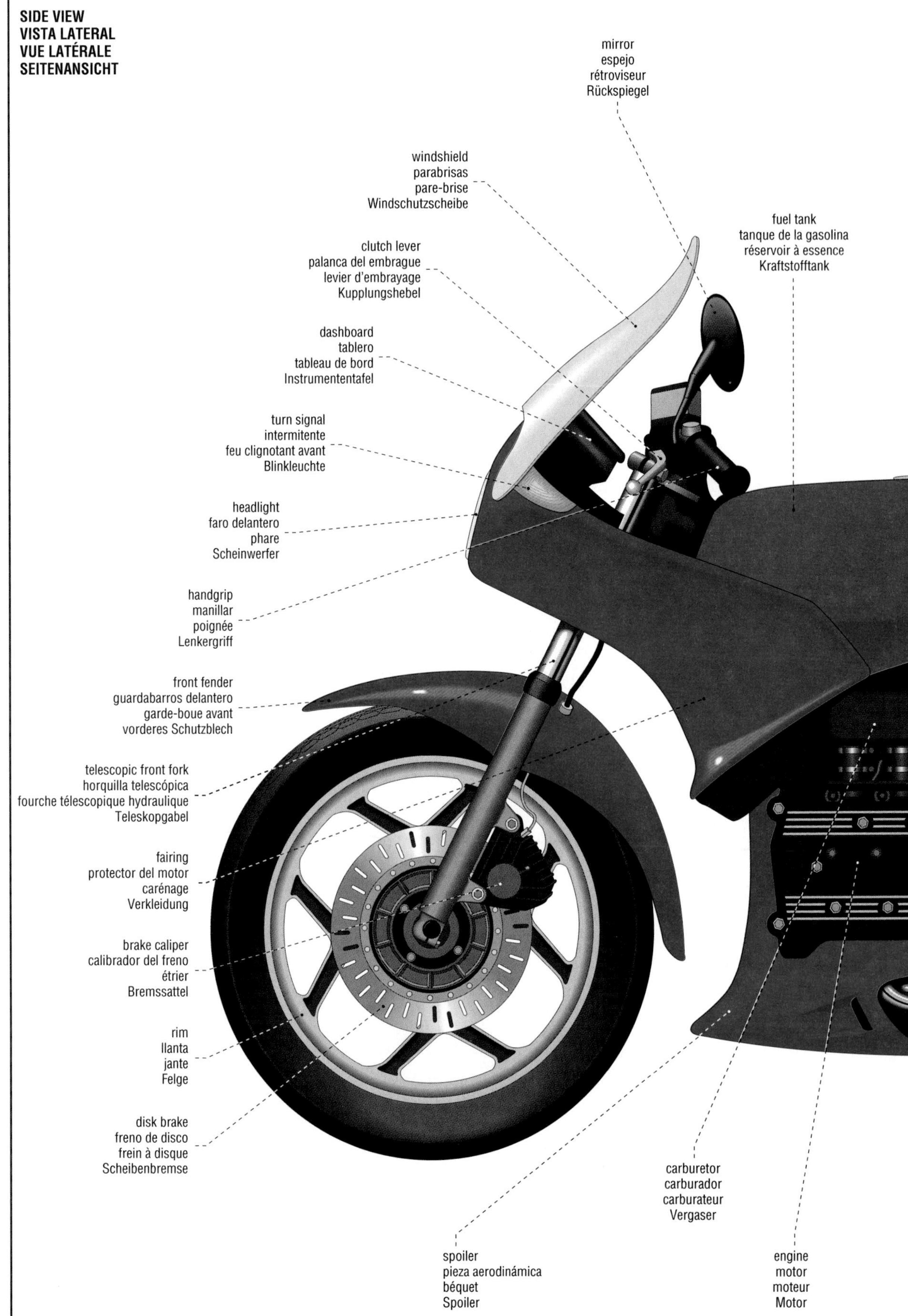
mirror
espejo
rétroviseur
Rückspiegel
windshield
parabrisas
pare-brise
Windschutzscheibe
fuel tank
tanque de la gasolina
réservoir à essence
Kraftstofftank
clutch lever
palanca del embrague
levier d'embrayage
Kupplungshebel
dashboard
tablero
tableau de bord
Instrumententafel
turn signal
intermitente
feu clignotant avant
Blinkleuchte
headlight
faro delantero
phare
Scheinwerfer
handgrip
manillar
poignée
Lenkergriff
front fender
guardabarros delantero
garde-boue avant
vorderes Schutzblech
telescopic front fork
horquilla telescópica
fourche télescopique hydraulique
Teleskopgabel
fairing
protector del motor
carénage
Verkleidung
brake caliper
calibrador del freno
étrier
Bremssattel
rim
llanta
jante
Felge
disk brake
freno de disco
frein à disque
Scheibenbremse
carburetor
carburador
carburateur
Vergaser
spoiler
pieza aerodinámica
béquet
Spoiler
engine
motor
moteur
Motor

PROTECTIVE HELMET
CASCO PROTECTOR
CASQUE DE PROTECTION
SCHUTZHELM

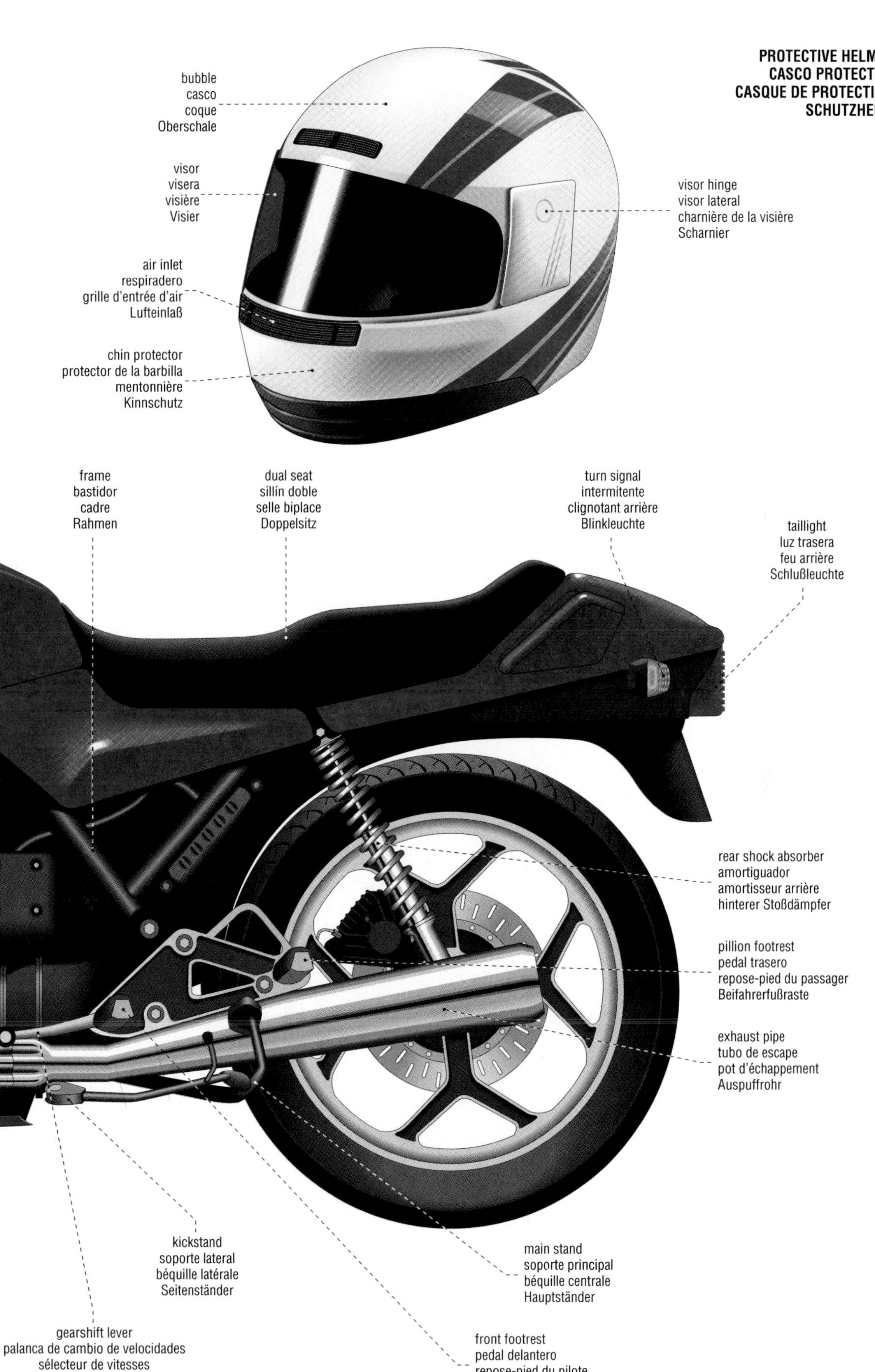
bubble
casco
coque
Oberschale
visor
visera
visière
Visier
air inlet
respiradero
grille d'entrée d'air
Lufteinlaß
chin protector
protector de la barbilla
mentonnière
Kinnschutz
visor hinge
visor lateral
charnière de la visière
Scharnier
frame
bastidor
cadre
Rahmen
dual seat
sillín doble
selle biplace
Doppelsitz
turn signal
intermitente
clignotant arrière
Blinkleuchte
taillight
luz trasera
feu arrière
Schlußleuchte
rear shock absorber
amortiguador
amortisseur arrière
hinterer Stoßdämpfer
pillion footrest
pedal trasero
repose-pied du passager
Beifahrerfußraste
exhaust pipe
tubo de escape
pot d'échappement
Auspuffrohr
kickstand
soporte lateral
béquille latérale
Seitenständer
main stand
soporte principal
béquille centrale
Hauptständer
gearshift lever
palanca de cambio de velocidades
sélecteur de vitesses
Schaltpedal
front footrest
pedal delantero
repose-pied du pilote
vordere Fußraste

MOTORCYCLE
MOTOCICLETA
MOTO
MOTORRAD

VIEW FROM ABOVE
VISTA POR ENCIMA
VUE EN PLONGÉE
DRAUFSICHT

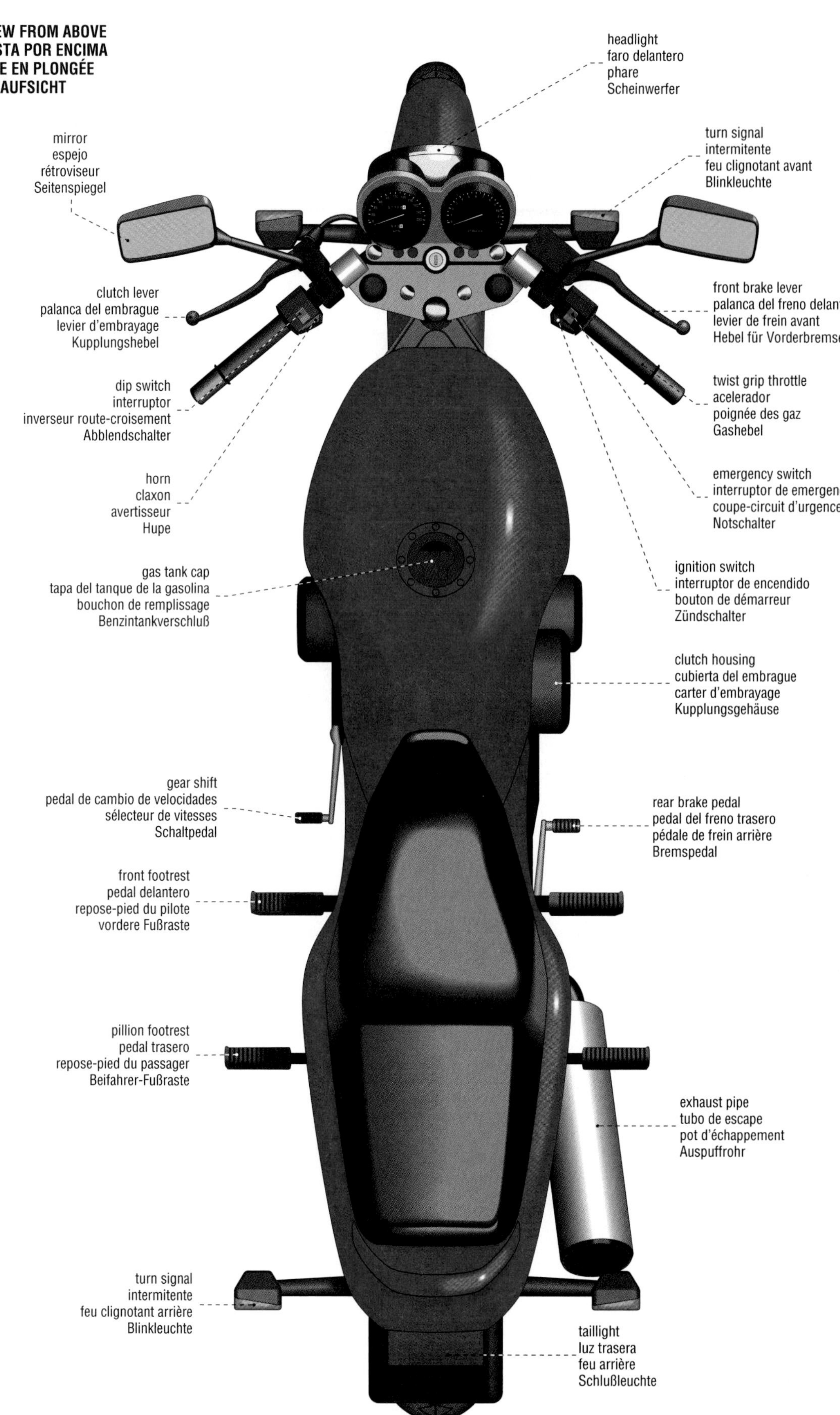
headlight
faro delantero
phare
Scheinwerfer
mirror
espejo
rétroviseur
Seitenspiegel
turn signal
intermitente
feu clignotant avant
Blinkleuchte
clutch lever
palanca del embrague
levier d'embrayage
Kupplungshebel
front brake lever
palanca del freno delantero
levier de frein avant
Hebel für Vorderbremse
dip switch
interruptor
inverseur route-croisement
Abblendschalter
twist grip throttle
acelerador
poignée des gaz
Gashebel
horn
claxon
avertisseur
Hupe
emergency switch
interruptor de emergencia
coupe-circuit d'urgence
Notschalter
gas tank cap
tapa del tanque de la gasolina
bouchon de remplissage
Benzintankverschluß
ignition switch
interruptor de encendido
bouton de démarreur
Zündschalter
clutch housing
cubierta del embrague
carter d'embrayage
Kupplungsgehäuse
gear shift
pedal de cambio de velocidades
sélecteur de vitesses
Schaltpedal
rear brake pedal
pedal del freno trasero
pédale de frein arrière
Bremspedal
front footrest
pedal delantero
repose-pied du pilote
vordere Fußraste
pillion footrest
pedal trasero
repose-pied du passager
Beifahrer-Fußraste
exhaust pipe
tubo de escape
pot d'échappement
Auspuffrohr
turn signal
intermitente
feu clignotant arrière
Blinkleuchte
taillight
luz trasera
feu arrière
Schlußleuchte

MOTORCYCLE DASHBOARD
TABLERO
TABLEAU DE BORD
INSTRUMENTENTAFEL

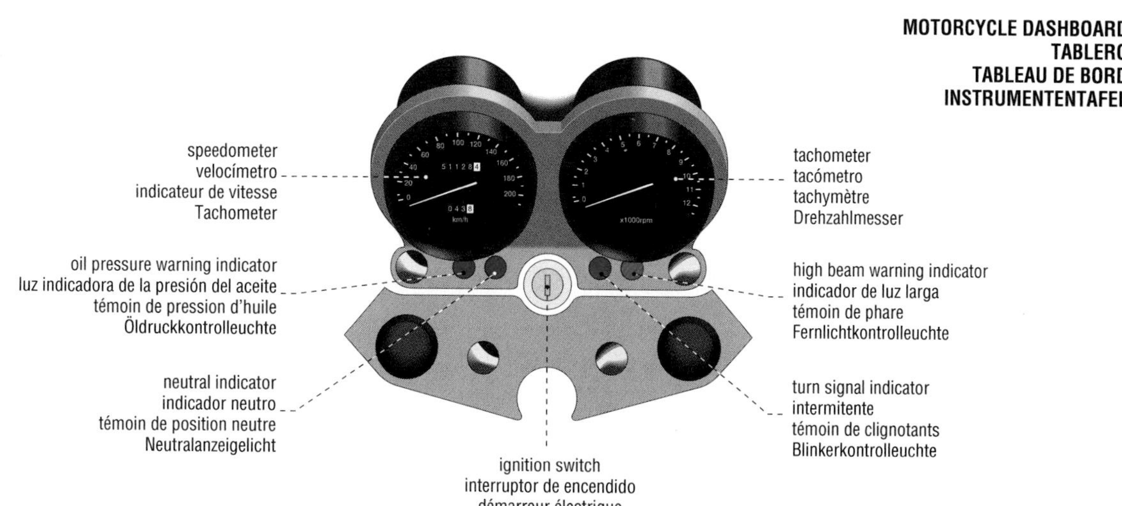
speedometer
velocímetro
indicateur de vitesse
Tachometer
tachometer
tacómetro
tachymètre
Drehzahlmesser
oil pressure warning indicator
luz indicadora de la presión del aceite
témoin de pression d'huile
Öldruckkontrolleuchte
high beam warning indicator
indicador de luz larga
témoin de phare
Fernlichtkontrolleuchte
neutral indicator
indicador neutro
témoin de position neutre
Neutralanzeigelicht
turn signal indicator
intermitente
témoin de clignotants
Blinkerkontrolleuchte
ignition switch
interruptor de encendido
démarreur électrique
Zündschalter

SNOWMOBILE
TRINEO MOTORIZADO
MOTONEIGE
SCHNEEMOBIL

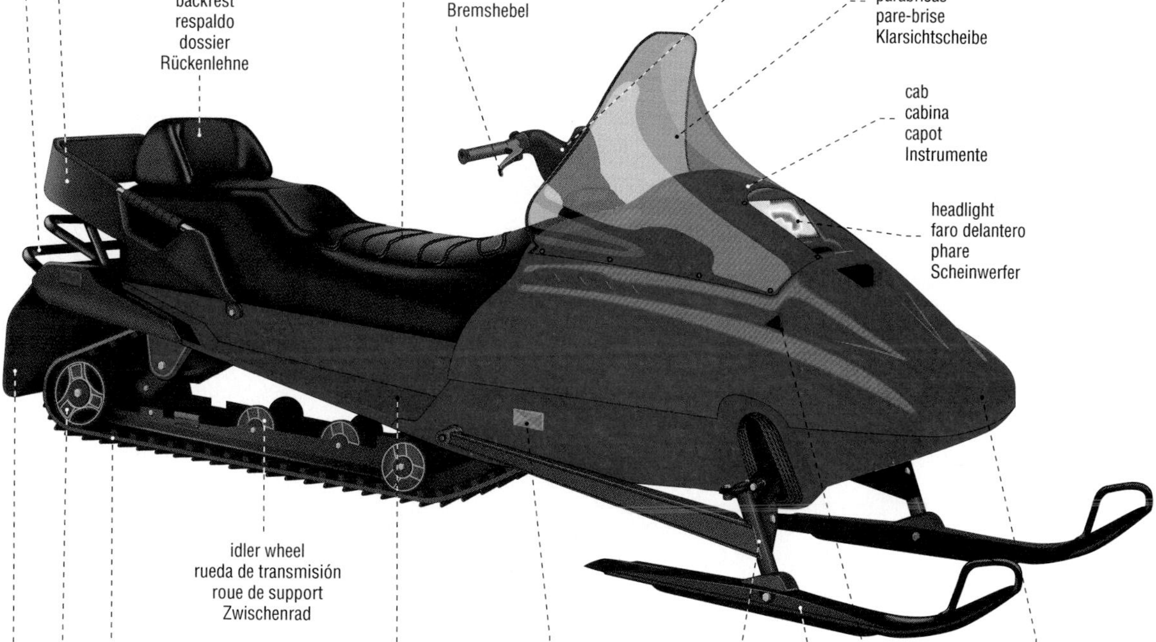

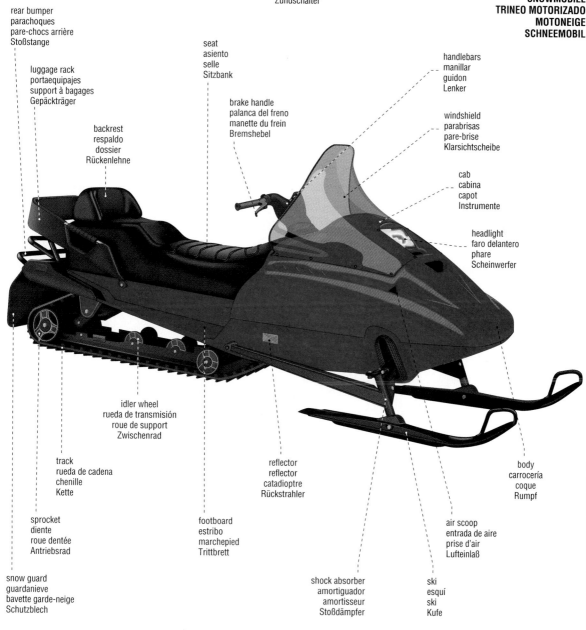

rear bumper
parachoques
pare-chocs arrière
Stoßstange

luggage rack
portaequipajes
support à bagages
Gepäckträger

backrest
respaldo
dossier
Rückenlehne

seat
asiento
selle
Sitzbank

brake handle
palanca del freno
manette du frein
Bremshebel

handlebars
manillar
guidon
Lenker

windshield
parabrisas
pare-brise
Klarsichtscheibe

cab
cabina
capot
Instrumente

headlight
faro delantero
phare
Scheinwerfer

idler wheel
rueda de transmisión
roue de support
Zwischenrad

track
rueda de cadena
chenille
Kette

reflector
reflector
catadioptre
Rückstrahler

body
carrocería
coque
Rumpf

sprocket
diente
roue dentée
Antriebsrad

footboard
estribo
marchepied
Trittbrett

air scoop
entrada de aire
prise d'air
Lufteinlaß

snow guard
guardanieve
bavette garde-neige
Schutzblech

shock absorber
amortiguador
amortisseur
Stoßdämpfer

ski
esquí
ski
Kufe

BICYCLE
BICICLETA
BICYCLETTE
FAHRRAD

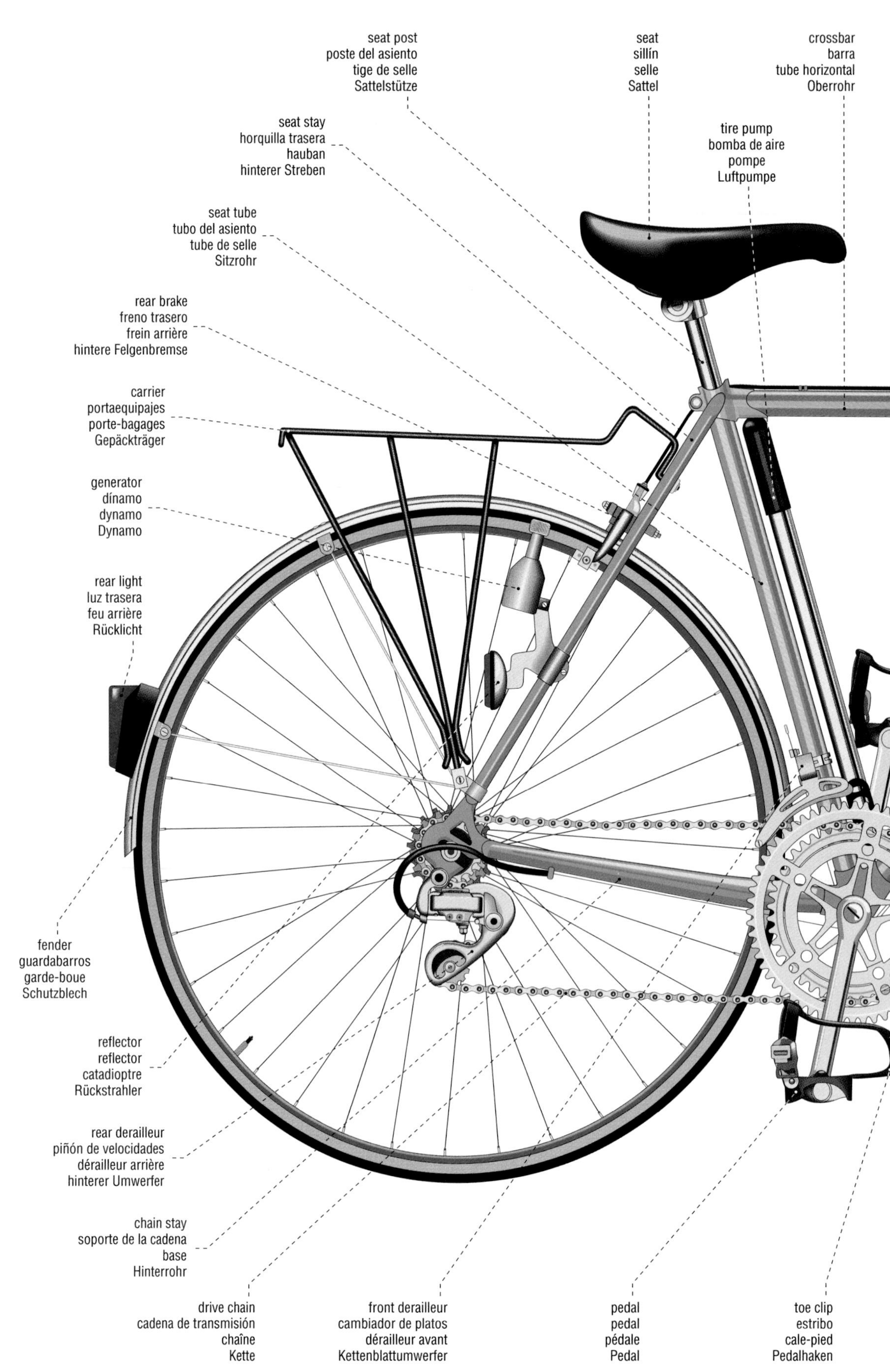
seat post
poste del asiento
tige de selle
Sattelstütze
seat
sillín
selle
Sattel
crossbar
barra
tube horizontal
Oberrohr
seat stay
horquilla trasera
hauban
hinterer Streben
tire pump
bomba de aire
pompe
Luftpumpe
seat tube
tubo del asiento
tube de selle
Sitzrohr
rear brake
freno trasero
frein arrière
hintere Felgenbremse
carrier
portaequipajes
porte-bagages
Gepäckträger
generator
dínamo
dynamo
Dynamo
rear light
luz trasera
feu arrière
Rücklicht
fender
guardabarros
garde-boue
Schutzblech
reflector
reflector
catadioptre
Rückstrahler
rear derailleur
piñón de velocidades
dérailleur arrière
hinterer Umwerfer
chain stay
soporte de la cadena
base
Hinterrohr
drive chain
cadena de transmisión
chaîne
Kette
front derailleur
cambiador de platos
dérailleur avant
Kettenblattumwerfer
pedal
pedal
pédale
Pedal
toe clip
estribo
cale-pied
Pedalhaken

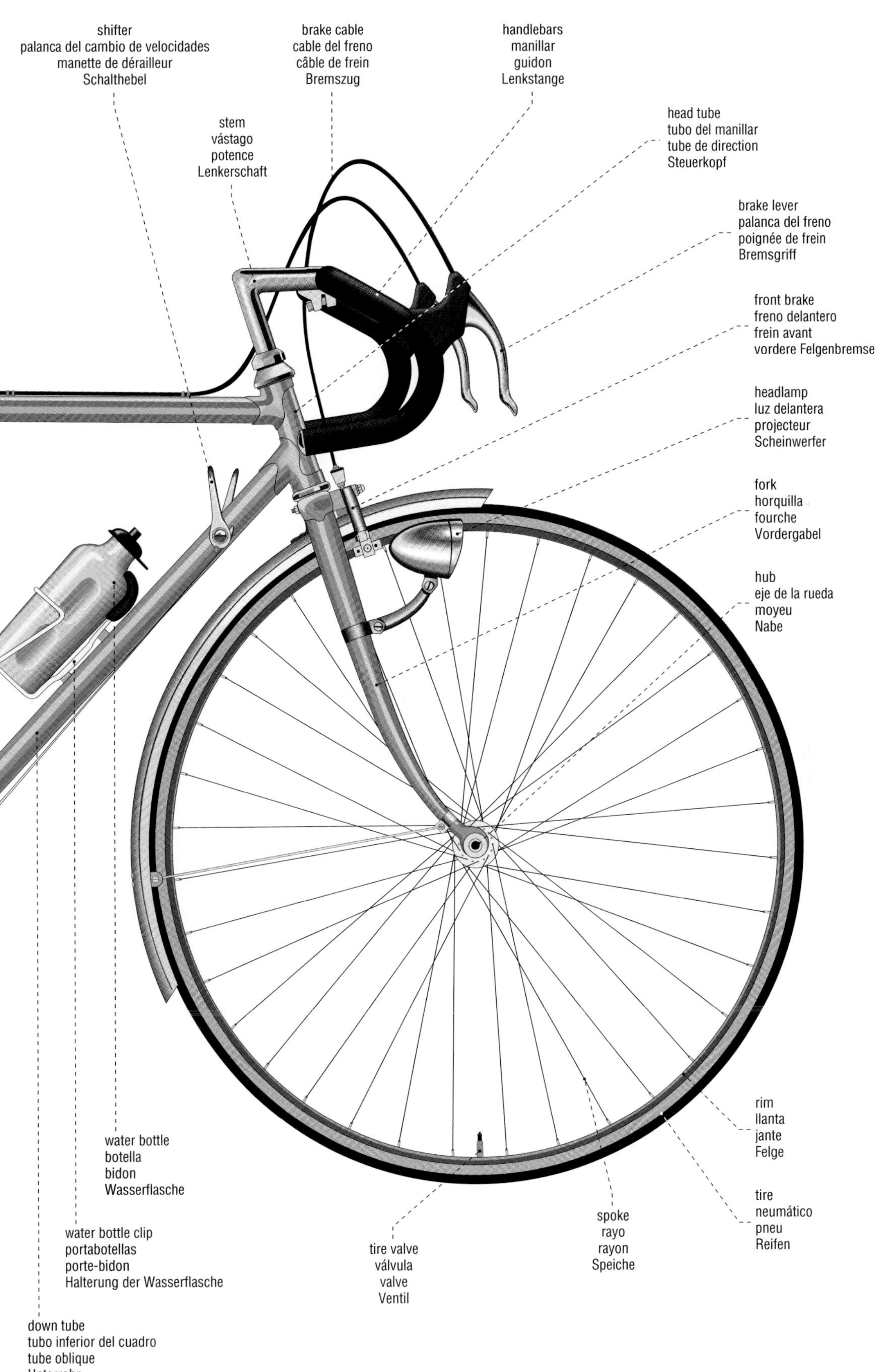
shifter
palanca del cambio de velocidades
manette de dérailleur
Schalthebel
brake cable
cable del freno
câble de frein
Bremszug
handlebars
manillar
guidon
Lenkstange
stem
vástago
potence
Lenkerschaft
head tube
tubo del manillar
tube de direction
Steuerkopf
brake lever
palanca del freno
poignée de frein
Bremsgriff
front brake
freno delantero
frein avant
vordere Felgenbremse
headlamp
luz delantera
projecteur
Scheinwerfer
fork
horquilla
fourche
Vordergabel
hub
eje de la rueda
moyeu
Nabe
rim
llanta
jante
Felge
tire
neumático
pneu
Reifen
spoke
rayo
rayon
Speiche
tire valve
válvula
valve
Ventil
water bottle
botella
bidon
Wasserflasche
water bottle clip
portabotellas
porte-bidon
Halterung der Wasserflasche
down tube
tubo inferior del cuadro
tube oblique
Unterrohr

BICYCLE
BICICLETA
BICYCLETTE
FAHRRAD

POWER TRAIN
TRANSMISIÓN DE CADENA
MÉCANISME DE PROPULSION
KRAFTÜBERTRAGUNG

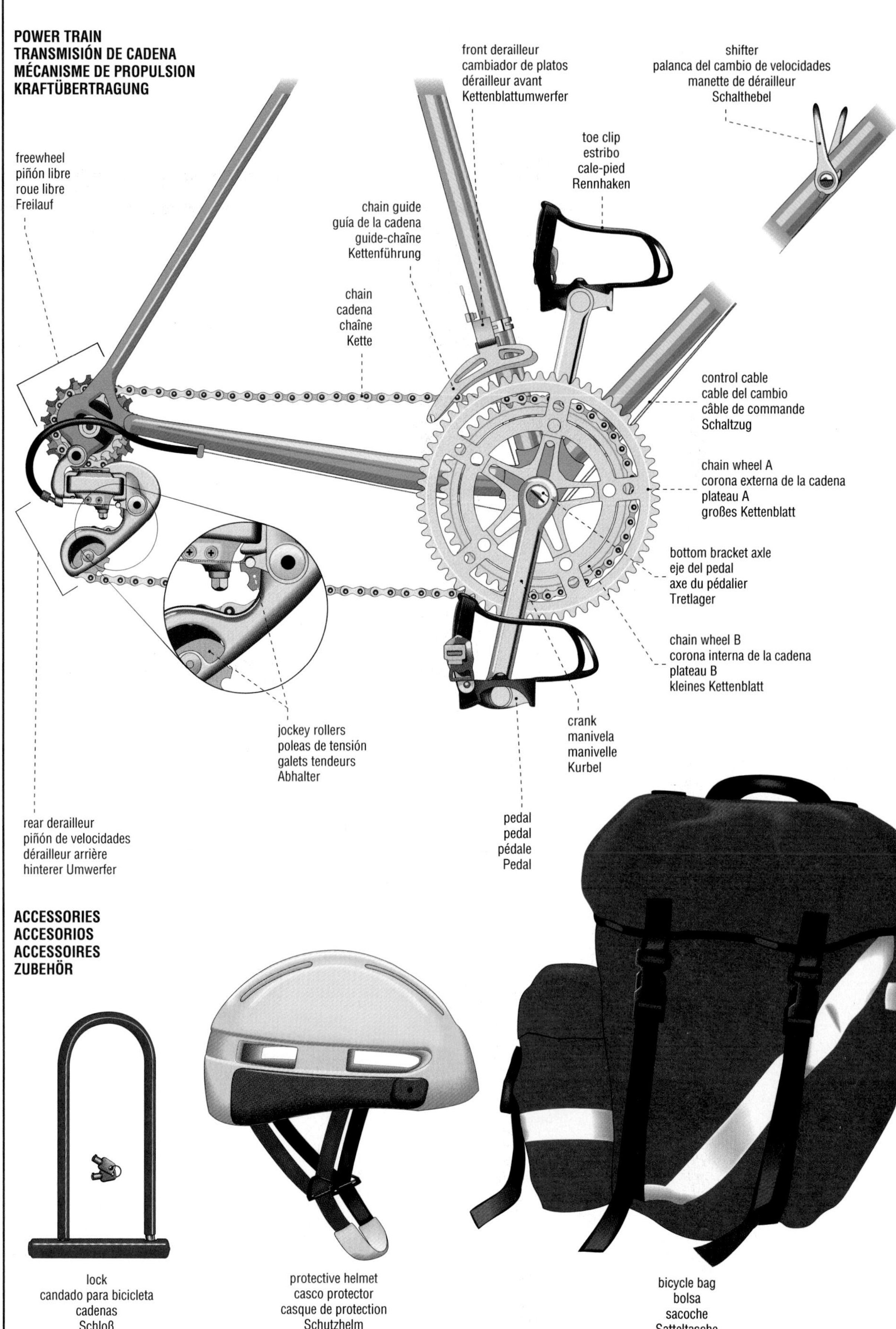
front derailleur
cambiador de platos
dérailleur avant
Kettenblattumwerfer
shifter
palanca del cambio de velocidades
manette de dérailleur
Schalthebel
toe clip
estribo
cale-pied
Rennhaken
freewheel
piñón libre
roue libre
Freilauf
chain guide
guía de la cadena
guide-chaîne
Kettenführung
chain
cadena
chaîne
Kette
control cable
cable del cambio
câble de commande
Schaltzug
chain wheel A
corona externa de la cadena
plateau A
großes Kettenblatt
bottom bracket axle
eje del pedal
axe du pédalier
Tretlager
chain wheel B
corona interna de la cadena
plateau B
kleines Kettenblatt
crank
manivela
manivelle
Kurbel
jockey rollers
poleas de tensión
galets tendeurs
Abhalter
pedal
pedal
pédale
Pedal
rear derailleur
piñón de velocidades
dérailleur arrière
hinterer Umwerfer
ACCESSORIES
ACCESORIOS
ACCESSOIRES
ZUBEHÖR
lock
candado para bicicleta
cadenas
Schloß
protective helmet
casco protector
casque de protection
Schutzhelm
bicycle bag
bolsa
sacoche
Satteltasche

CARAVAN
CARAVANA
CARAVANE
WOHNWAGEN

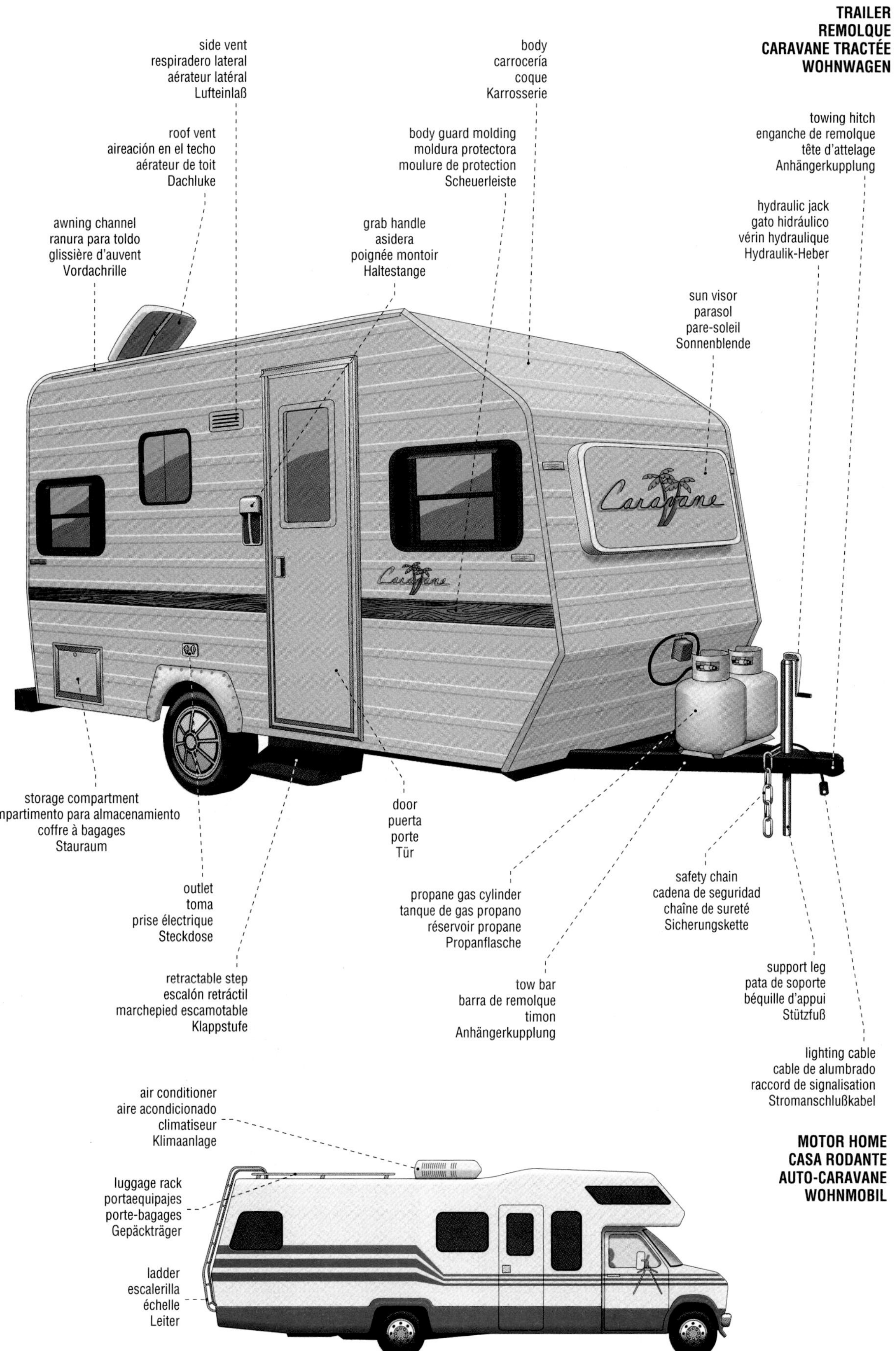

TRAILER
REMOLQUE
CARAVANE TRACTÉE
WOHNWAGEN
side vent
respiradero lateral
aérateur latéral
Lufteinlaß
body
carrocería
coque
Karrosserie
roof vent
aireación en el techo
aérateur de toit
Dachluke
body guard molding
moldura protectora
moulure de protection
Scheuerleiste
towing hitch
enganche de remolque
tête d'attelage
Anhängerkupplung
awning channel
ranura para toldo
glissière d'auvent
Vordachrille
grab handle
asidera
poignée montoir
Haltestange
hydraulic jack
gato hidráulico
vérin hydraulique
Hydraulik-Heber
sun visor
parasol
pare-soleil
Sonnenblende
Caravane
storage compartment
compartimento para almacenamiento
coffre à bagages
Stauraum
door
puerta
porte
Tür
safety chain
cadena de seguridad
chaîne de sureté
Sicherungskette
outlet
toma
prise électrique
Steckdose
propane gas cylinder
tanque de gas propano
réservoir propane
Propanflasche
support leg
pata de soporte
béquille d'appui
Stützfuß
retractable step
escalón retráctil
marchepied escamotable
Klappstufe
tow bar
barra de remolque
timon
Anhängerkupplung
lighting cable
cable de alumbrado
raccord de signalisation
Stromanschlußkabel
air conditioner
aire acondicionado
climatiseur
Klimaanlage
MOTOR HOME
CASA RODANTE
AUTO-CARAVANE
WOHNMOBIL
luggage rack
portaequipajes
porte-bagages
Gepäckträger
ladder
escalerilla
échelle
Leiter

ROAD SYSTEM
SISTEMA DE CARRETERAS
SYSTÈME ROUTIER
STRASSENBAU

CROSS SECTION OF A ROAD
VISTA TRANSVERSAL DE UNA CARRETERA
COUPE D'UNE ROUTE
QUERSCHNITT EINER STRASSE

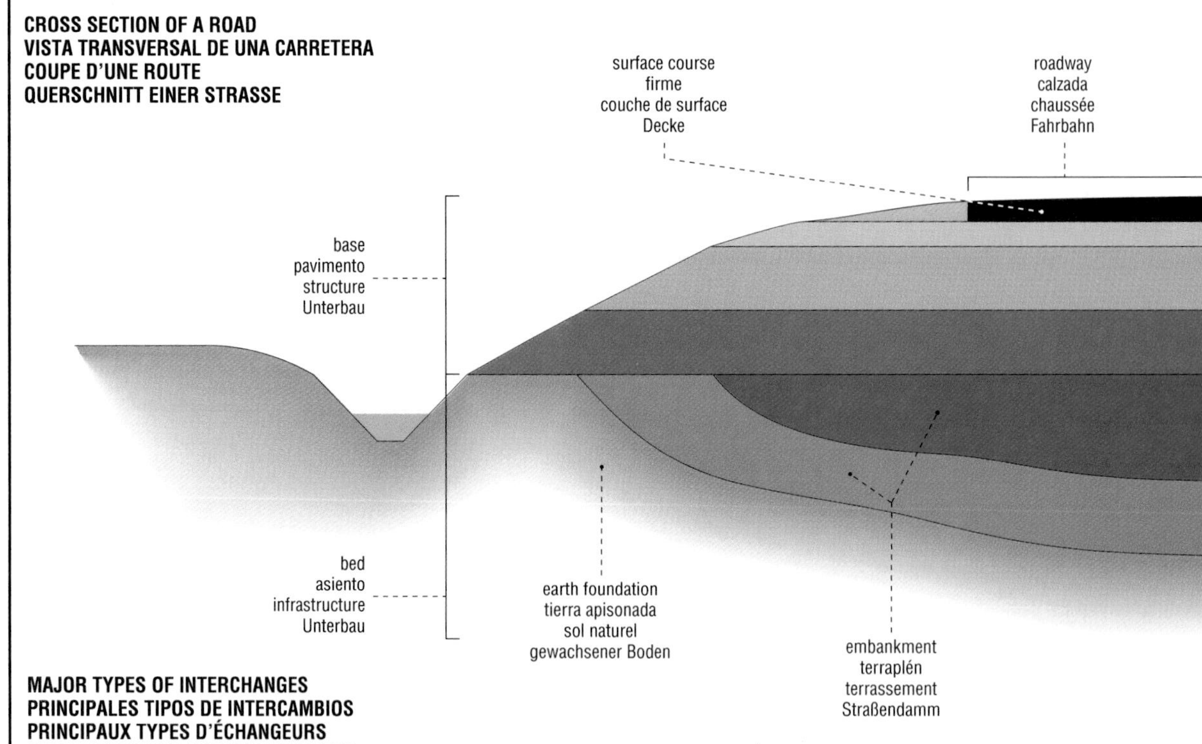
surface course
firme
couche de surface
Decke
roadway
calzada
chaussée
Fahrbahn
base
pavimento
structure
Unterbau
bed
asiento
infrastructure
Unterbau
earth foundation
tierra apisonada
sol naturel
gewachsener Boden
embankment
terraplén
terrassement
Straßendamm

MAJOR TYPES OF INTERCHANGES
PRINCIPALES TIPOS DE INTERCAMBIOS
PRINCIPAUX TYPES D'ÉCHANGEURS
HAUPTTYPEN VON AUTOBAHNKREUZEN

cloverleaf
trébol
échangeur en trèfle
Kleeblatt

traffic circle
glorieta
carrefour giratoire
Verteiler

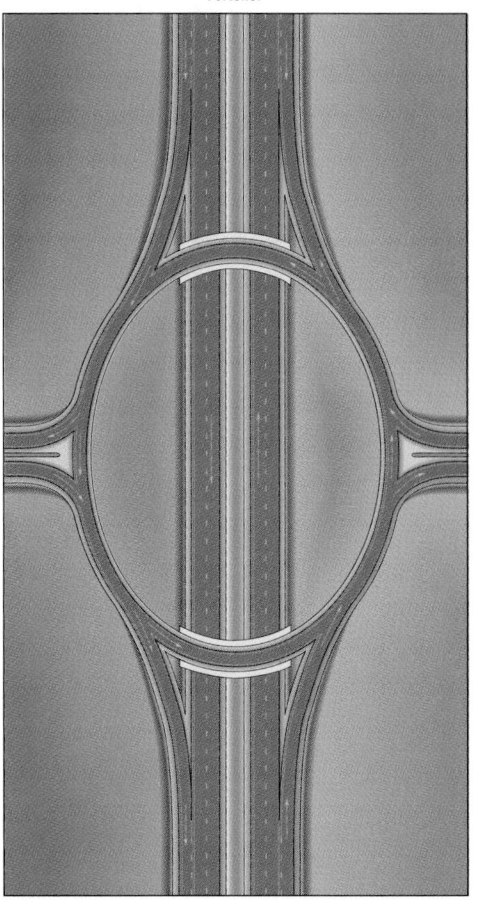

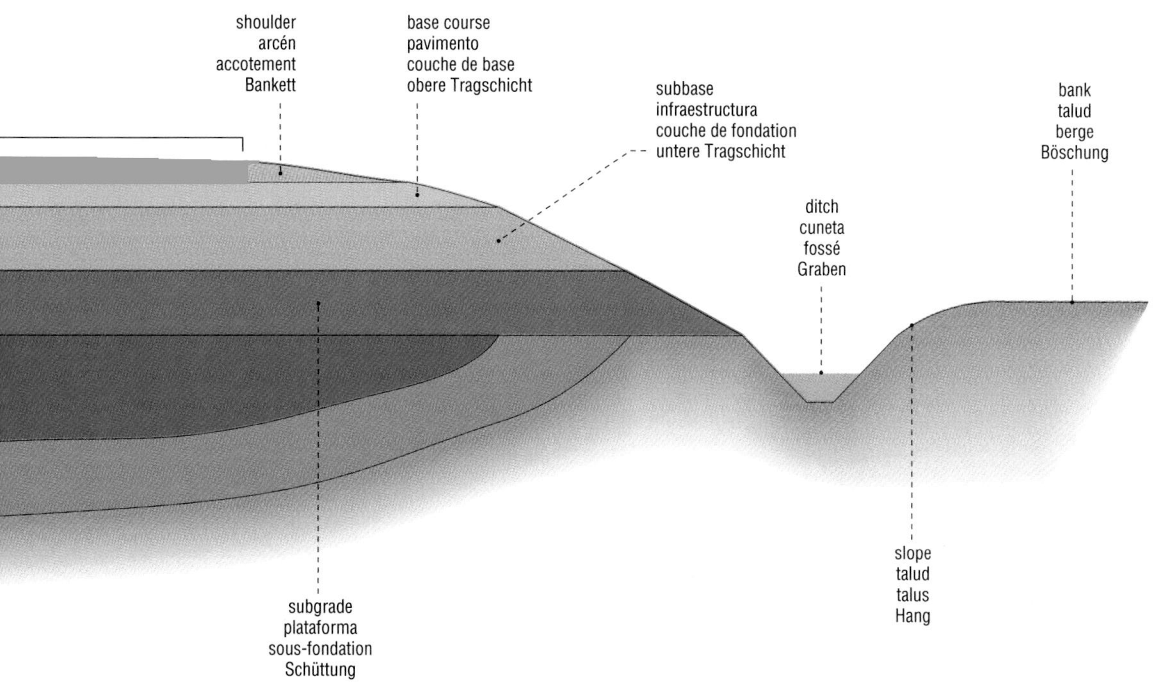
shoulder
arcén
accotement
Bankett
base course
pavimento
couche de base
obere Tragschicht
subbase
infraestructura
couche de fondation
untere Tragschicht
bank
talud
berge
Böschung
ditch
cuneta
fossé
Graben
subgrade
plataforma
sous-fondation
Schüttung
slope
talud
talus
Hang

diamond interchange
diamante
échangeur en losange
Raute

trumpet interchange
trompeta
échangeur en trompette
Trompete

ROAD SYSTEM
SISTEMA DE CARRETERAS
SYSTÈME ROUTIER
AUTOBAHNKREUZ

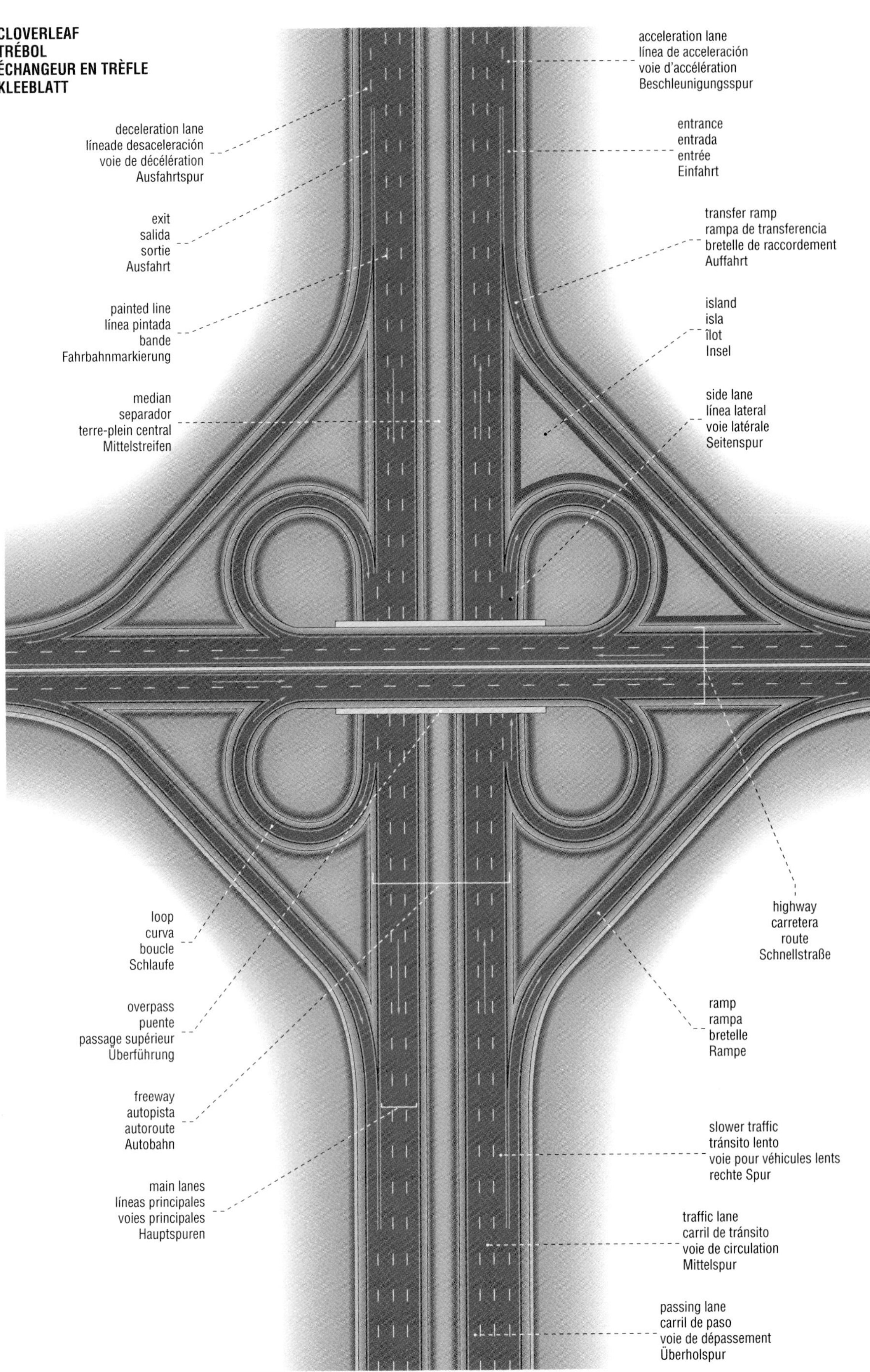
CLOVERLEAF
TRÉBOL
ÉCHANGEUR EN TRÈFLE
KLEEBLATT
deceleration lane
líneade desaceleración
voie de décélération
Ausfahrtspur
exit
salida
sortie
Ausfahrt
painted line
línea pintada
bande
Fahrbahnmarkierung
median
separador
terre-plein central
Mittelstreifen
acceleration lane
línea de acceleración
voie d'accélération
Beschleunigungsspur
entrance
entrada
entrée
Einfahrt
transfer ramp
rampa de transferencia
bretelle de raccordement
Auffahrt
island
isla
îlot
Insel
side lane
línea lateral
voie latérale
Seitenspur
loop
curva
boucle
Schlaufe
overpass
puente
passage supérieur
Überführung
freeway
autopista
autoroute
Autobahn
main lanes
líneas principales
voies principales
Hauptspuren
highway
carretera
route
Schnellstraße
ramp
rampa
bretelle
Rampe
slower traffic
tránsito lento
voie pour véhicules lents
rechte Spur
traffic lane
carril de tránsito
voie de circulation
Mittelspur
passing lane
carril de paso
voie de dépassement
Überholspur

SERVICE STATION
ESTACIÓN DE SERVICIO
STATION-SERVICE
TANKSTELLE

GASOLINE PUMP
SURTIDOR DE GASOLINA
DISTRIBUTEUR D'ESSENCE
ZAPFSÄULE

Super
Diesel
1
2

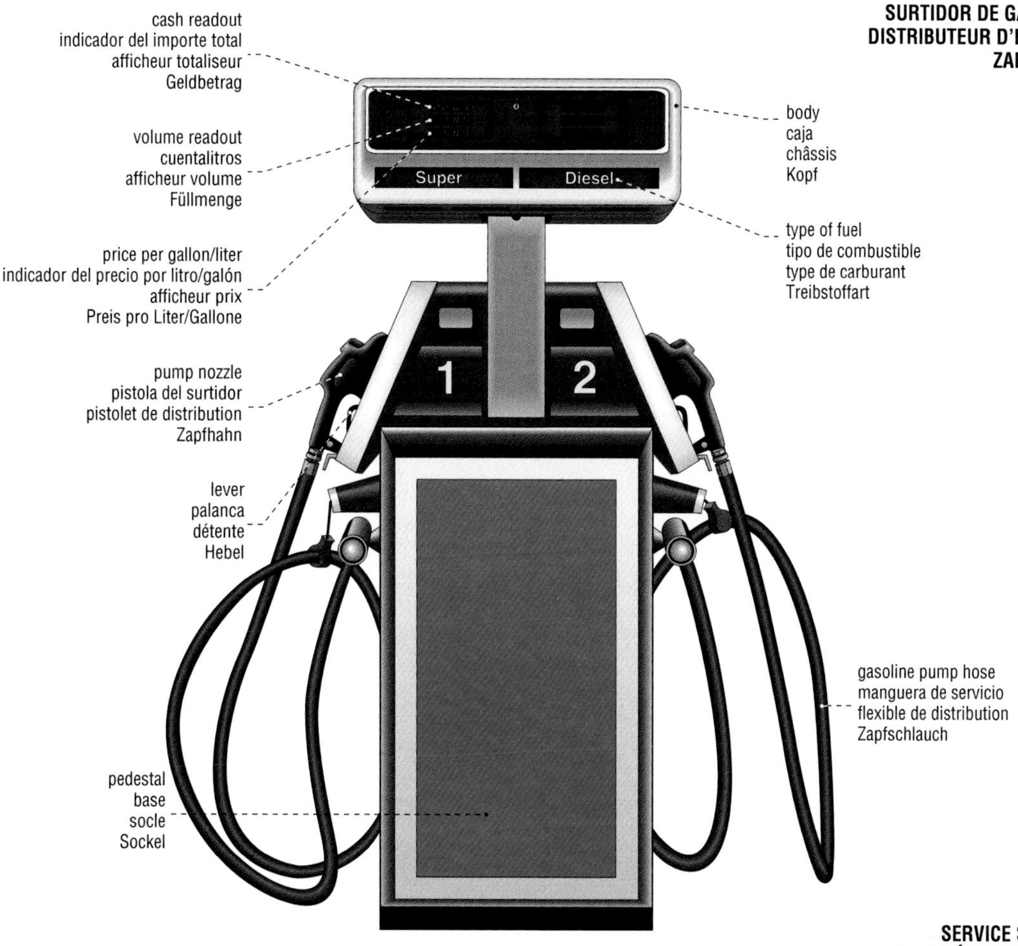

cash readout
indicador del importe total
afficheur totaliseur
Geldbetrag

volume readout
cuentalitros
afficheur volume
Füllmenge

price per gallon/liter
indicador del precio por litro/galón
afficheur prix
Preis pro Liter/Gallone

pump nozzle
pistola del surtidor
pistolet de distribution
Zapfhahn

lever
palanca
détente
Hebel

pedestal
base
socle
Sockel

body
caja
châssis
Kopf

type of fuel
tipo de combustible
type de carburant
Treibstoffart

gasoline pump hose
manguera de servicio
flexible de distribution
Zapfschlauch

SERVICE STATION
ESTACIÓN DE SERVICIO
STATION-SERVICE
TANKSTELLE

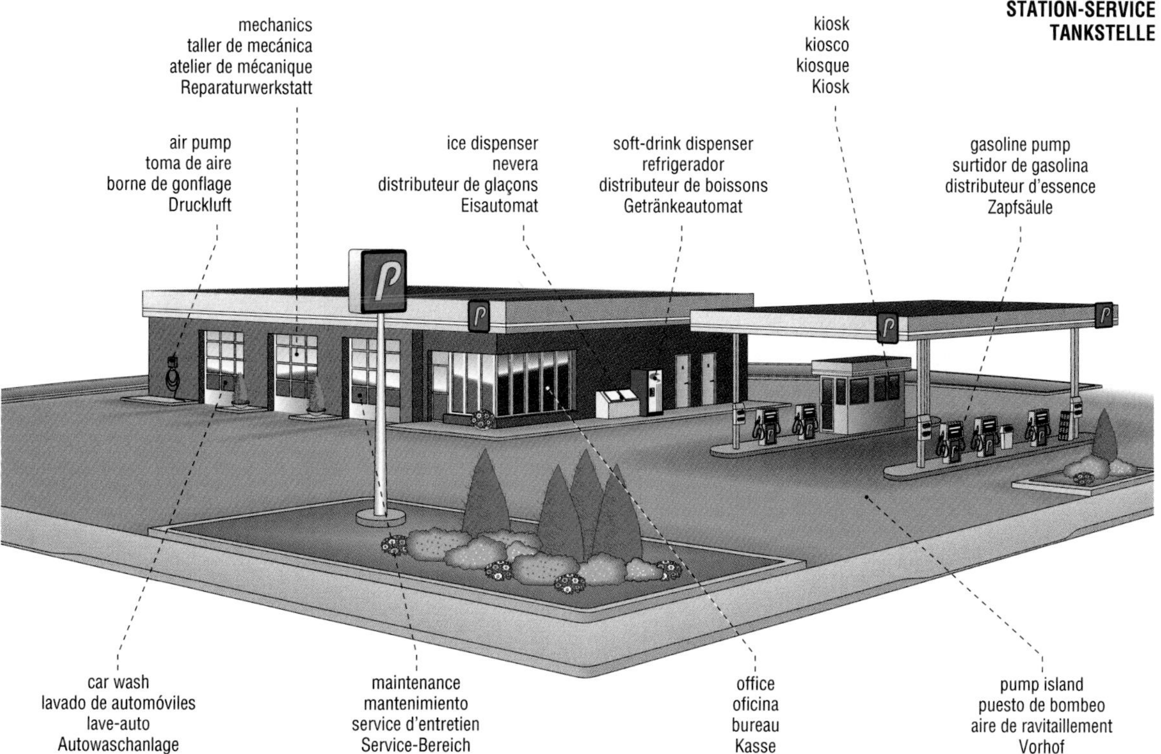
mechanics
taller de mecánica
atelier de mécanique
Reparaturwerkstatt
air pump
toma de aire
borne de gonflage
Druckluft
ice dispenser
nevera
distributeur de glaçons
Eisautomat
soft-drink dispenser
refrigerador
distributeur de boissons
Getränkeautomat
kiosk
kiosco
kiosque
Kiosk
gasoline pump
surtidor de gasolina
distributeur d'essence
Zapfsäule
car wash
lavado de automóviles
lave-auto
Autowaschanlage
maintenance
mantenimiento
service d'entretien
Service-Bereich
office
oficina
bureau
Kasse
pump island
puesto de bombeo
aire de ravitaillement
Vorhof

FIXED BRIDGES
PUENTES FIJOS
PONTS FIXES
STARRE BRÜCKEN

BEAM BRIDGE
PUENTE DE VIGA
PONT À POUTRE
BALKENBRÜCKE

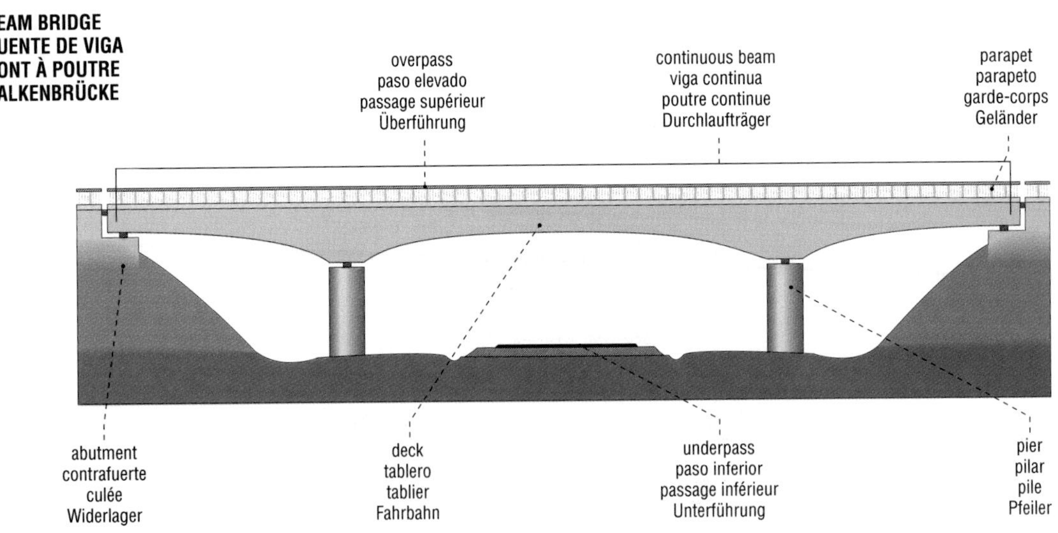
overpass
paso elevado
passage supérieur
Überführung
continuous beam
viga continua
poutre continue
Durchlaufträger
parapet
parapeto
garde-corps
Geländer
abutment
contrafuerte
culée
Widerlager
deck
tablero
tablier
Fahrbahn
underpass
paso inferior
passage inférieur
Unterführung
pier
pilar
pile
Pfeiler

TYPES OF BEAM BRIDGES
TIPOS DE PUENTES DE VIGA
TYPES DE PONTS À POUTRE
BALKENBRÜCKEN

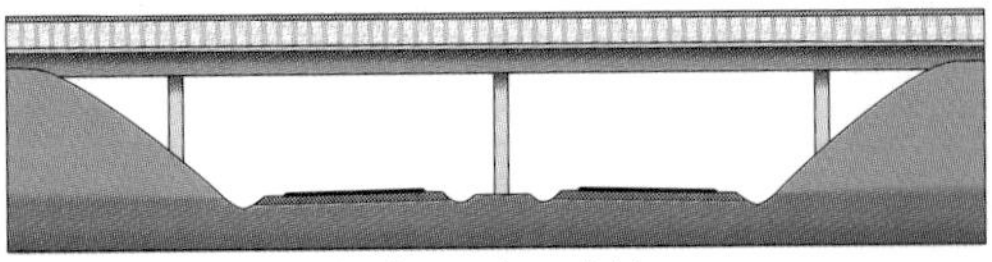

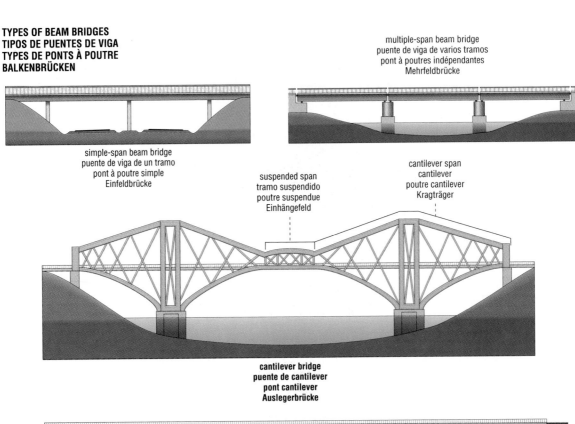

multiple-span beam bridge
puente de viga de varios tramos
pont à poutres indépendantes
Mehrfeldbrücke

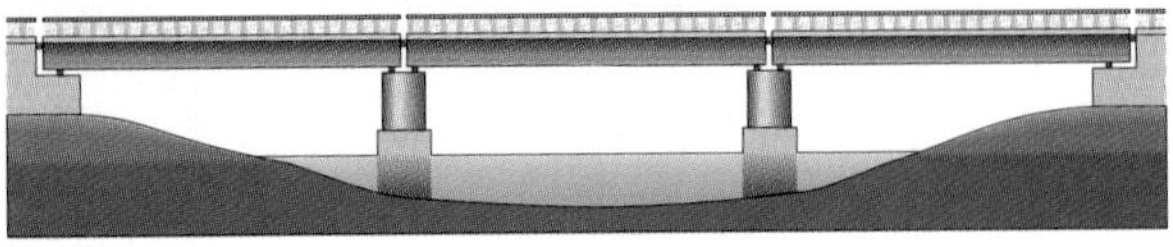

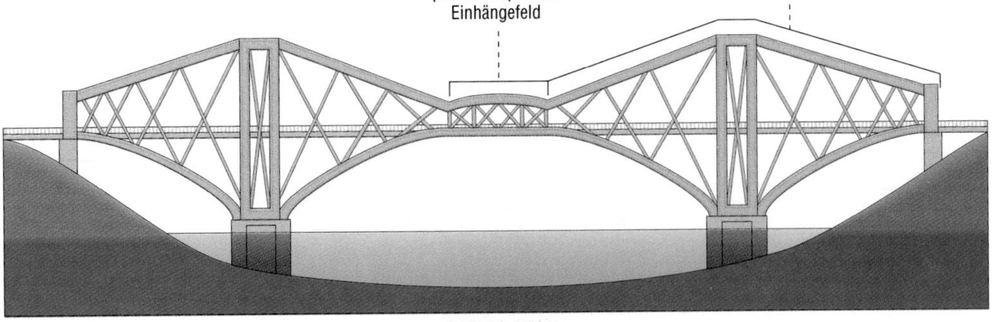

simple-span beam bridge
puente de viga de un tramo
pont à poutre simple
Einfeldbrücke

suspended span
tramo suspendido
poutre suspendue
Einhängefeld

cantilever span
cantilever
poutre cantilever
Kragträger

cantilever bridge
puente de cantilever
pont cantilever
Auslegerbrücke

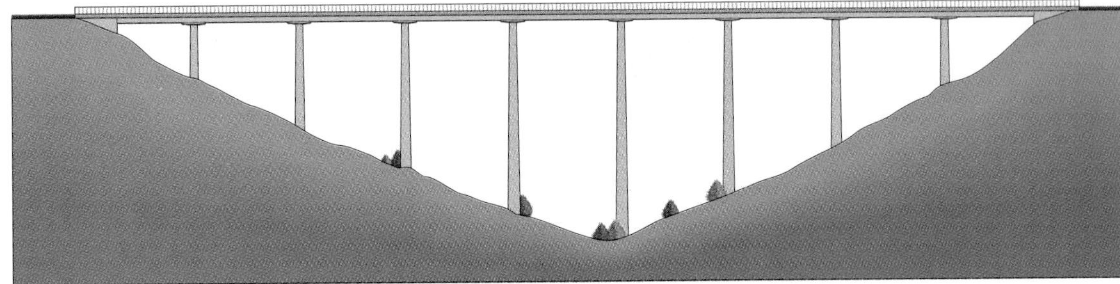

viaduct
viaducto
viaduc
Viadukt

ARCH BRIDGE
PUENTE DE ARCO
PONT EN ARC
BOGENBRÜCKE

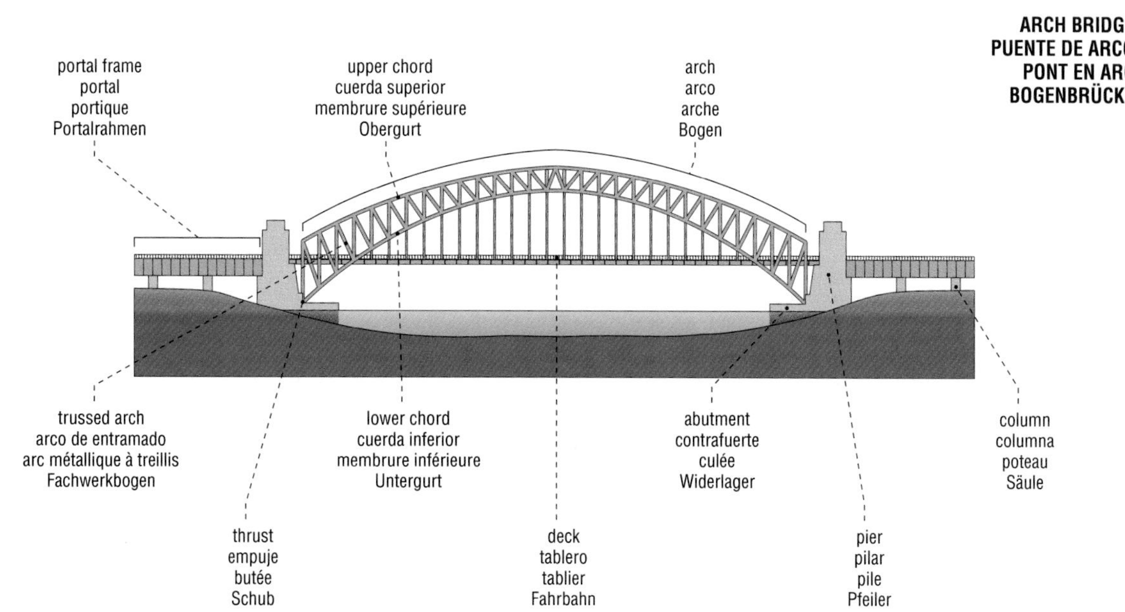
portal frame
portal
portique
Portalrahmen
upper chord
cuerda superior
membrure supérieure
Obergurt
arch
arco
arche
Bogen
trussed arch
arco de entramado
arc métallique à treillis
Fachwerkbogen
lower chord
cuerda inferior
membrure inférieure
Untergurt
abutment
contrafuerte
culée
Widerlager
column
columna
poteau
Säule
thrust
empuje
butée
Schub
deck
tablero
tablier
Fahrbahn
pier
pilar
pile
Pfeiler

TYPES OF ARCH BRIDGES
TIPOS DE PUENTES DE ARCO
TYPES DE PONTS EN ARC
BOGENBRÜCKEN

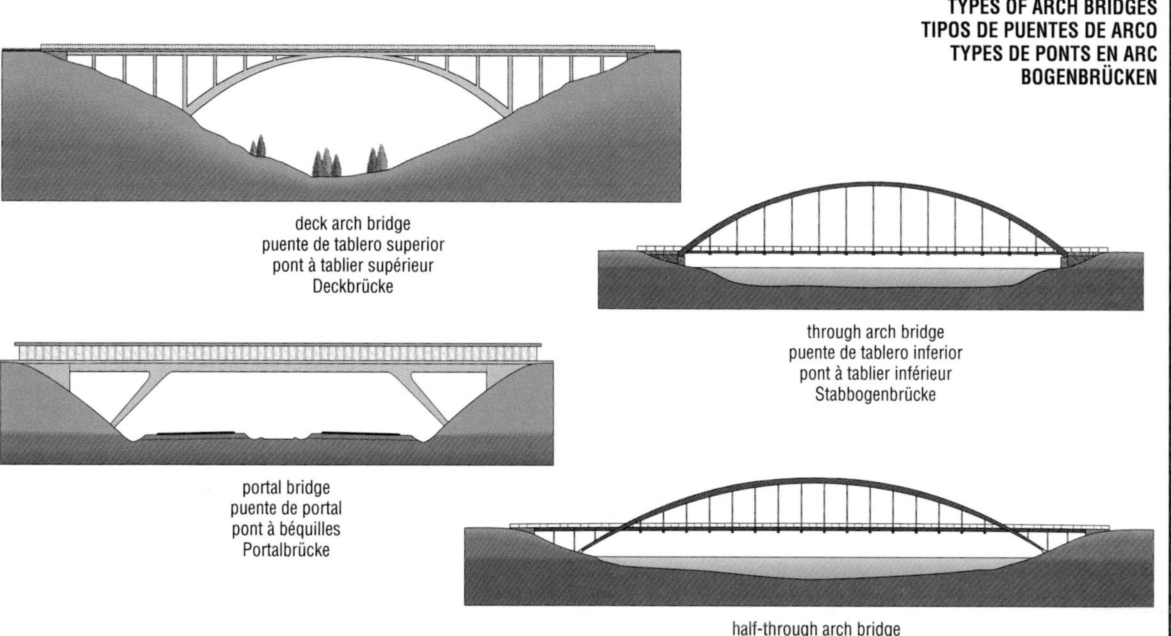

deck arch bridge
puente de tablero superior
pont à tablier supérieur
Deckbrücke

through arch bridge
puente de tablero inferior
pont à tablier inférieur
Stabbogenbrücke

portal bridge
puente de portal
pont à béquilles
Portalbrücke

half-through arch bridge
puente de tablero intermedio
pont à tablier intermédiaire
Hängesprengwerkbrücke

TYPES OF ARCHES
VARIEDADES DE ARCOS
TYPES D'ARCS
BOGENARTEN

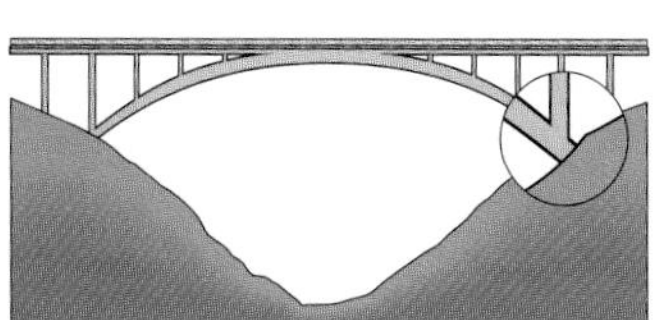

fixed arch
arco fijo
arc encastré
gelenkloser Bogen

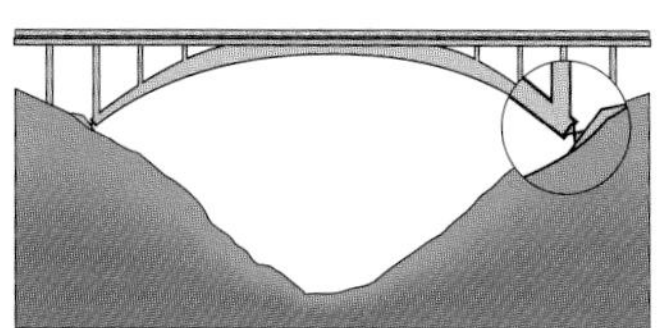

two-hinged arch
arco de dos articulaciones
arc à deux articulations
zweiteiliger Bogen

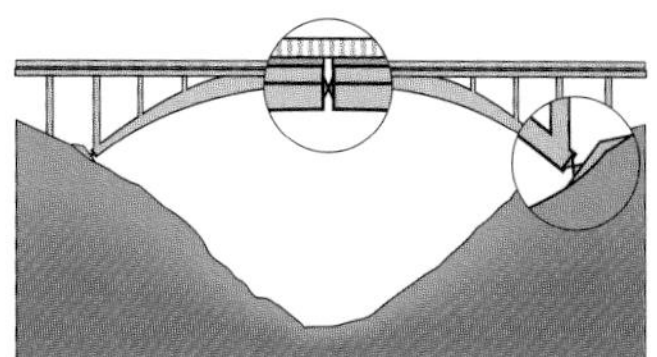

three-hinged arch
arco de tres articulaciones
arc à trois articulations
dreiteiliger Bogen

FIXED BRIDGES
PUENTES FIJOS
PONTS FIXES
STARRE BRÜCKEN

SUSPENSION BRIDGE
PUENTE COLGANTE
PONT SUSPENDU À CÂBLE PORTEUR
HÄNGEBRÜCKE

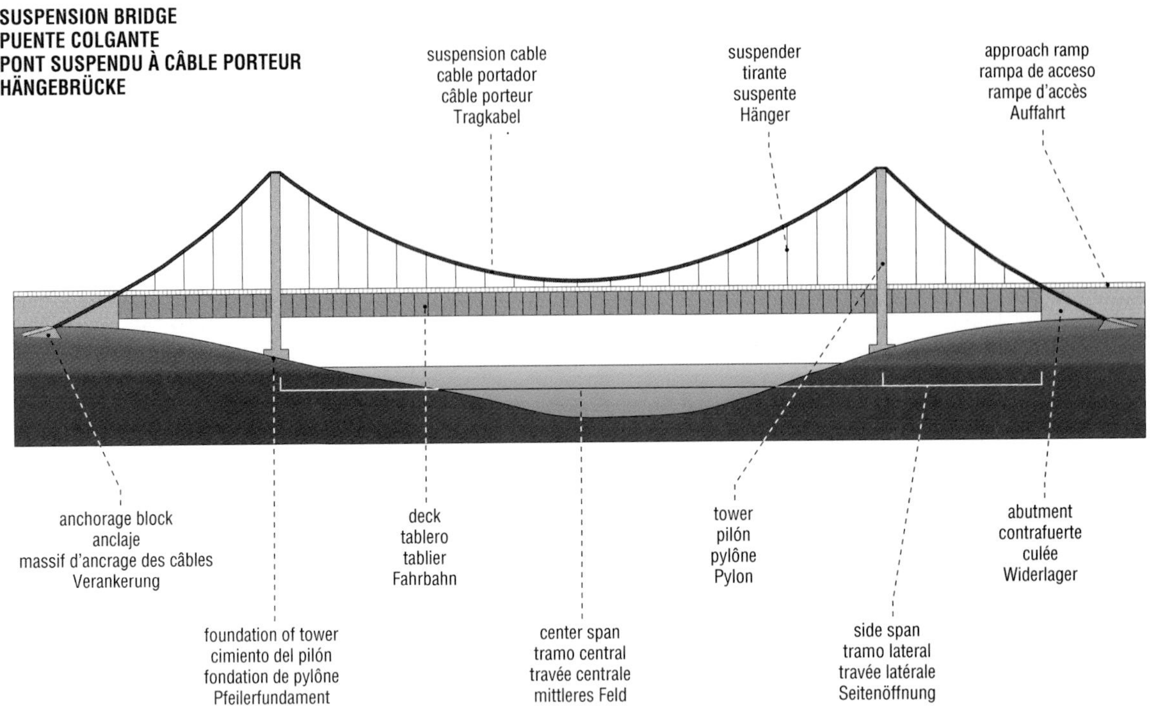
suspension cable
cable portador
câble porteur
Tragkabel
suspender
tirante
suspente
Hänger
approach ramp
rampa de acceso
rampe d'accès
Auffahrt
anchorage block
anclaje
massif d'ancrage des câbles
Verankerung
deck
tablero
tablier
Fahrbahn
tower
pilón
pylône
Pylon
abutment
contrafuerte
culée
Widerlager
foundation of tower
cimiento del pilón
fondation de pylône
Pfeilerfundament
center span
tramo central
travée centrale
mittleres Feld
side span
tramo lateral
travée latérale
Seitenöffnung

CABLE-STAYED BRIDGES
PUENTES DE TIRANTES
PONTS SUSPENDUS À HAUBANS
SCHRÄGSEILBRÜCKE

fan cable stays
tirantes en abanico
haubans en éventail
Fächerschrägseile

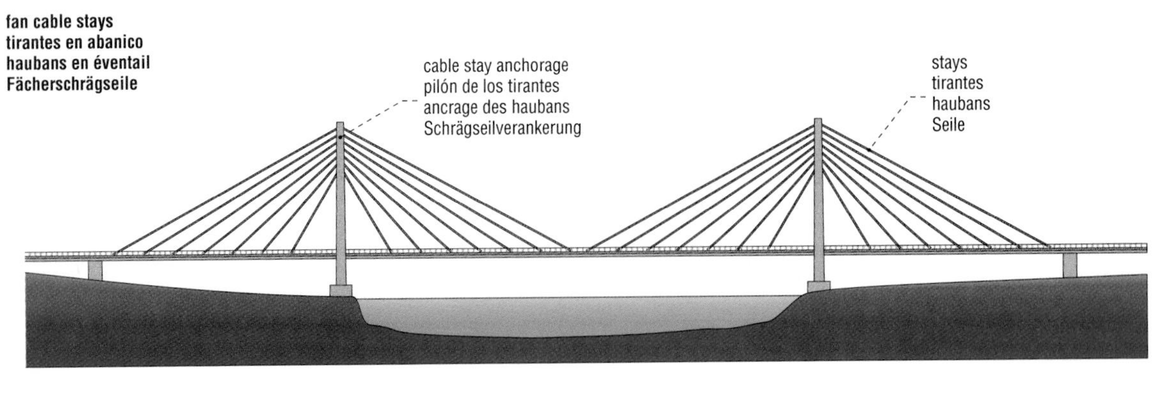
cable stay anchorage
pilón de los tirantes
ancrage des haubans
Schrägseilverankerung
stays
tirantes
haubans
Seile

harp cable stays
tirantes en forma de arpa
haubans en harpe
parallele Schrägseile

MOVABLE BRIDGES
PUENTES MOVIBLES
PONTS MOBILES
BEWEGLICHE BRÜCKEN

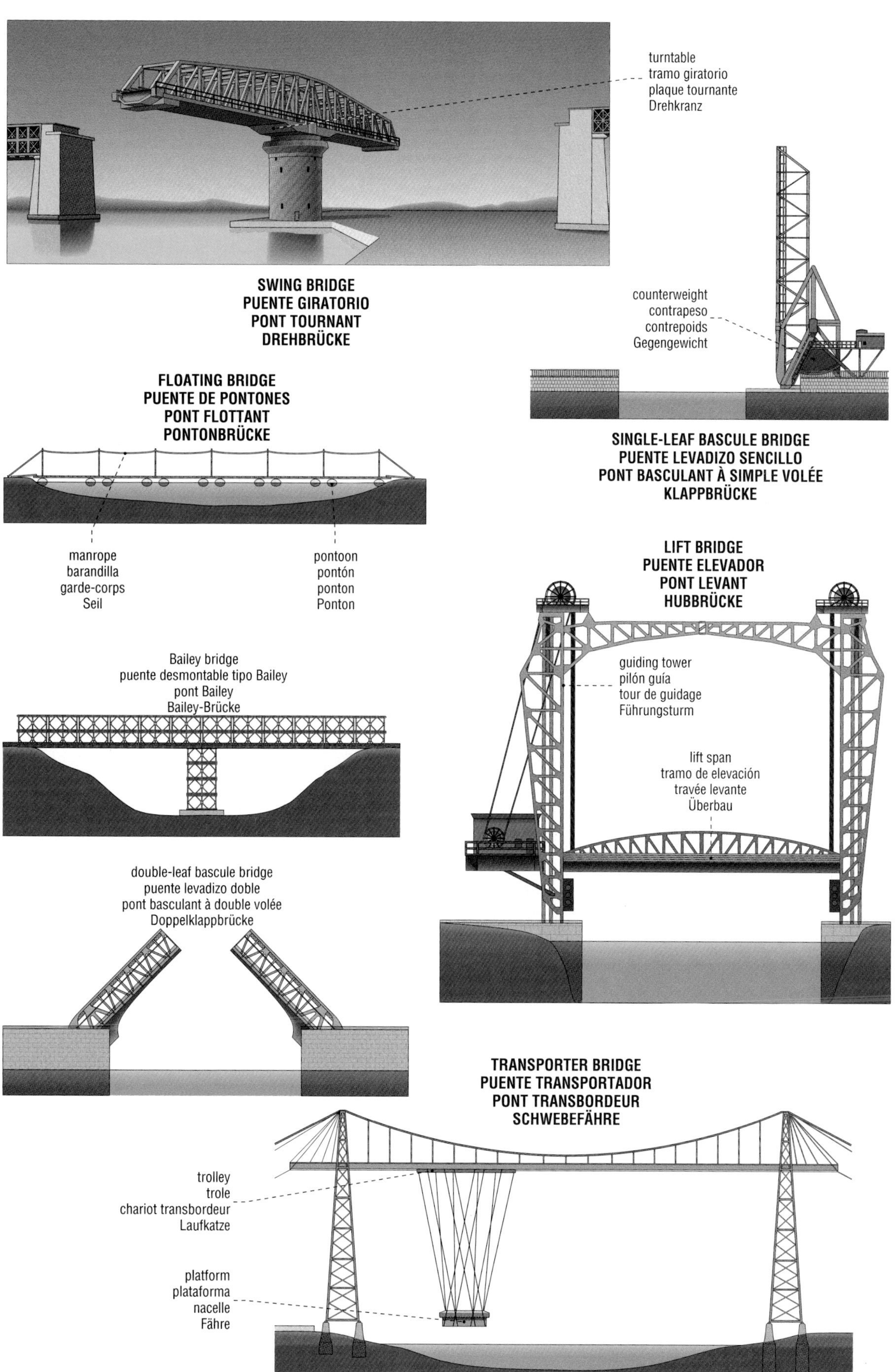

turntable
tramo giratorio
plaque tournante
Drehkranz
SWING BRIDGE
PUENTE GIRATORIO
PONT TOURNANT
DREHBRÜCKE
counterweight
contrapeso
contrepoids
Gegengewicht
FLOATING BRIDGE
PUENTE DE PONTONES
PONT FLOTTANT
PONTONBRÜCKE
SINGLE-LEAF BASCULE BRIDGE
PUENTE LEVADIZO SENCILLO
PONT BASCULANT À SIMPLE VOLÉE
KLAPPBRÜCKE
manrope
barandilla
garde-corps
Seil
pontoon
pontón
ponton
Ponton
LIFT BRIDGE
PUENTE ELEVADOR
PONT LEVANT
HUBBRÜCKE
Bailey bridge
puente desmontable tipo Bailey
pont Bailey
Bailey-Brücke
guiding tower
pilón guía
tour de guidage
Führungsturm
lift span
tramo de elevación
travée levante
Überbau
double-leaf bascule bridge
puente levadizo doble
pont basculant à double volée
Doppelklappbrücke
TRANSPORTER BRIDGE
PUENTE TRANSPORTADOR
PONT TRANSBORDEUR
SCHWEBEFÄHRE
trolley
trole
chariot transbordeur
Laufkatze
platform
plataforma
nacelle
Fähre

HIGH-SPEED TRAIN
TREN DE ALTA VELOCIDAD
TRAIN À GRANDE VITESSE (T.G.V.)
HOCHGESCHWINDIGKEITSZUG

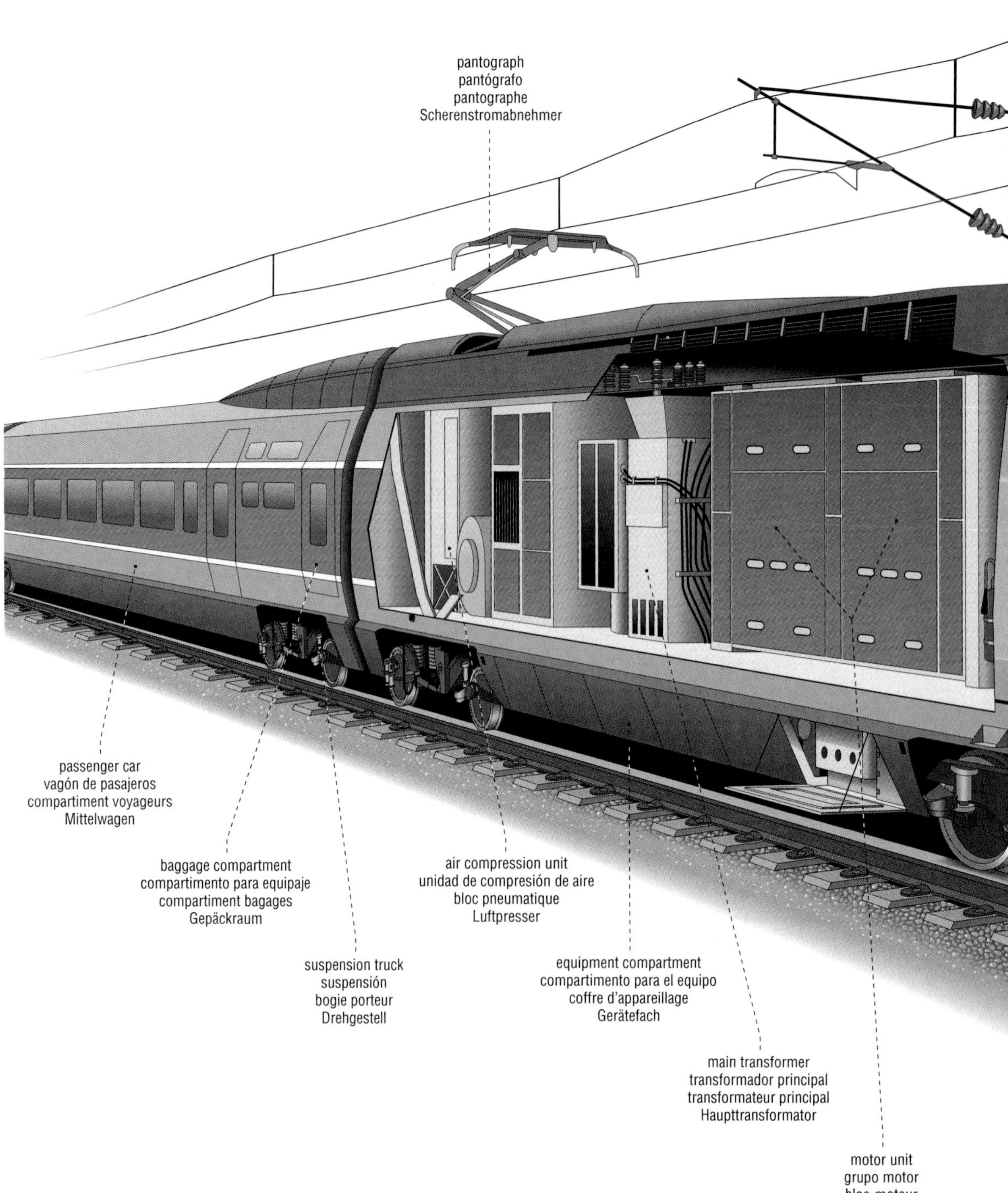
pantograph
pantógrafo
pantographe
Scherenstromabnehmer
passenger car
vagón de pasajeros
compartiment voyageurs
Mittelwagen
baggage compartment
compartimento para equipaje
compartiment bagages
Gepäckraum
air compression unit
unidad de compresión de aire
bloc pneumatique
Luftpresser
suspension truck
suspensión
bogie porteur
Drehgestell
equipment compartment
compartimento para el equipo
coffre d'appareillage
Gerätefach
main transformer
transformador principal
transformateur principal
Haupttransformator
motor unit
grupo motor
bloc-moteur
Fahrmotor

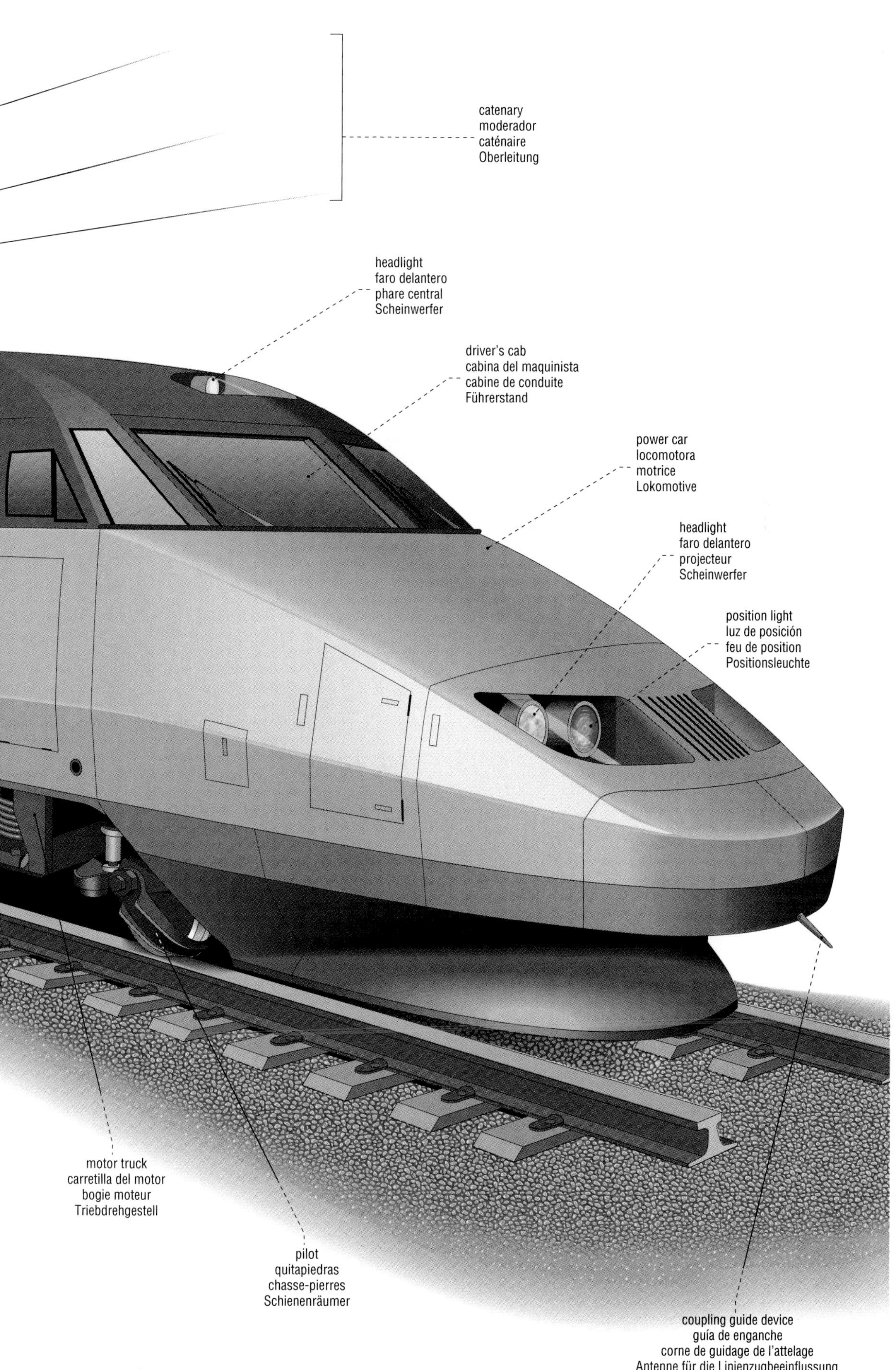
catenary
moderador
caténaire
Oberleitung
headlight
faro delantero
phare central
Scheinwerfer
driver's cab
cabina del maquinista
cabine de conduite
Führerstand
power car
locomotora
motrice
Lokomotive
headlight
faro delantero
projecteur
Scheinwerfer
position light
luz de posición
feu de position
Positionsleuchte
motor truck
carretilla del motor
bogie moteur
Triebdrehgestell
pilot
quitapiedras
chasse-pierres
Schienenräumer
coupling guide device
guía de enganche
corne de guidage de l'attelage
Antenne für die Linienzugbeeinflussung

TYPES OF PASSENGER CARS
VAGONES DE PASAJEROS
TYPES DE VOITURES
PERSONENZÜGE: WAGENTYPEN

COACH CAR
VAGÓN DE PASAJEROS
VOITURE-COACH
GROSSRAUMWAGEN

center aisle
pasillo central
couloir central
Mittelgang
adjustable seat
asiento ajustable
siège réglable
verstellbarer Sitz

SLEEPING CAR
COCHE CAMA
VOITURE-LIT
SCHLAFWAGEN

berth
litera
couchette
Schlafplatz
linen
lencería
lingerie
Bettwäsche
sleeping compartment
dormitorio
chambre
Schlafwagenabteil

DINING CAR
VAGÓN COMEDOR
VOITURE-RESTAURANT
SPEISEWAGEN

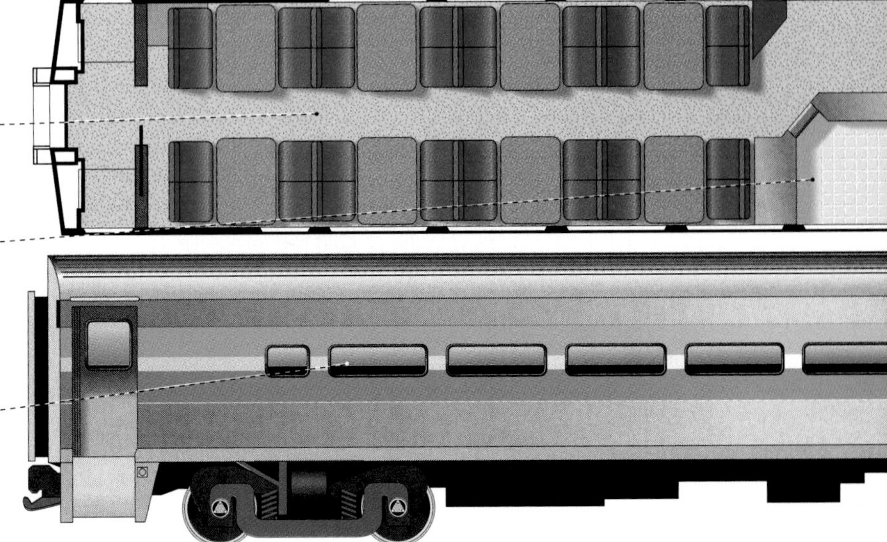
dining section
comedor
salle à manger
Speiseraum
kitchen
cocina
cuisine
Zugküche
panoramic window
ventanilla panorámica
fenêtre panoramique
Panoramafenster

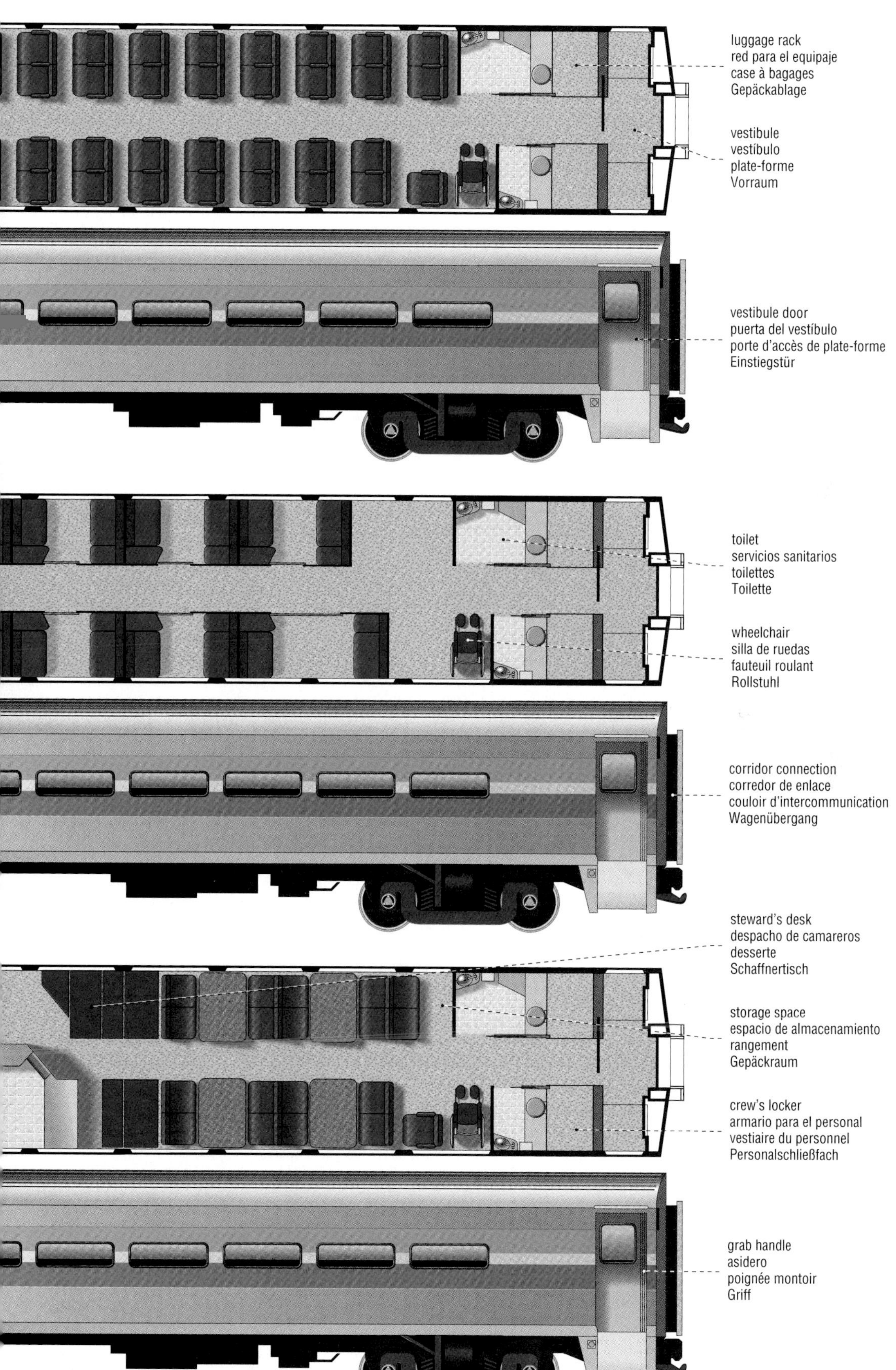

luggage rack
red para el equipaje
case à bagages
Gepäckablage
vestibule
vestíbulo
plate-forme
Vorraum
vestibule door
puerta del vestíbulo
porte d'accès de plate-forme
Einstiegstür
toilet
servicios sanitarios
toilettes
Toilette
wheelchair
silla de ruedas
fauteuil roulant
Rollstuhl
corridor connection
corredor de enlace
couloir d'intercommunication
Wagenübergang
steward's desk
despacho de camareros
desserte
Schaffnertisch
storage space
espacio de almacenamiento
rangement
Gepäckraum
crew's locker
armario para el personal
vestiaire du personnel
Personalschließfach
grab handle
asidero
poignée montoir
Griff

PASSENGER STATION
ESTACIÓN DE FERROCARRIL
GARE DE VOYAGEURS
BAHNHOF

office
oficina
locaux administratifs
Büro
glassed roof
techo de vidiro
verrière
Glasüberdachung
indicator board
pizarra de información
panneau indicateur
Fahrplan
passenger train
tren de pasajeros
train
Reisezug
booking hall
vestíbulo
salle des pas perdus
Bahnhofshalle
parcels office
consigna
service de colis
Paketannahme
platform edge
borde del andén
bordure de quai
Bahnsteigkante
platform number
indicador de número de andén
numéro de quai
Gleisnummer
baggage room
sala de equipajes
enregistrement des bagages
Gepäckaufbewahrung
passenger platform
andén de pasajeros
quai de gare
Bahnsteig
gate
barrera
barrière
Sperre

metal structure
estrucutra de metal
structure métallique
Eisenträger

baggage cart
carro portaequipaje
chariot à bagages
Förderwagen

departure time indicator
indicador de hora de salida
affichage de l'heure de départ
Abfahrtzeiten

ticket collector
colector de billetes
contrôleur
Fahrkartenkontrolleur

baggage lockers
casillas de consigna automática
consigne automatique
Gepäckschließfächer

destination
destinos
destination
Zielbahnhof

platform entrance
acceso a los andenes
accès aux quais
Zugang zum Gleis

track
vía
voie ferrée
Gleis

schedules
horarios
tableau horaire
Kursbuchtafeln

ticket control
control de billetes
contrôle des billets
Fahrkartenkontrolle

RAILROAD STATION
ESTACIÓN DE FERROCARRIL
GARE
BAHNHOF

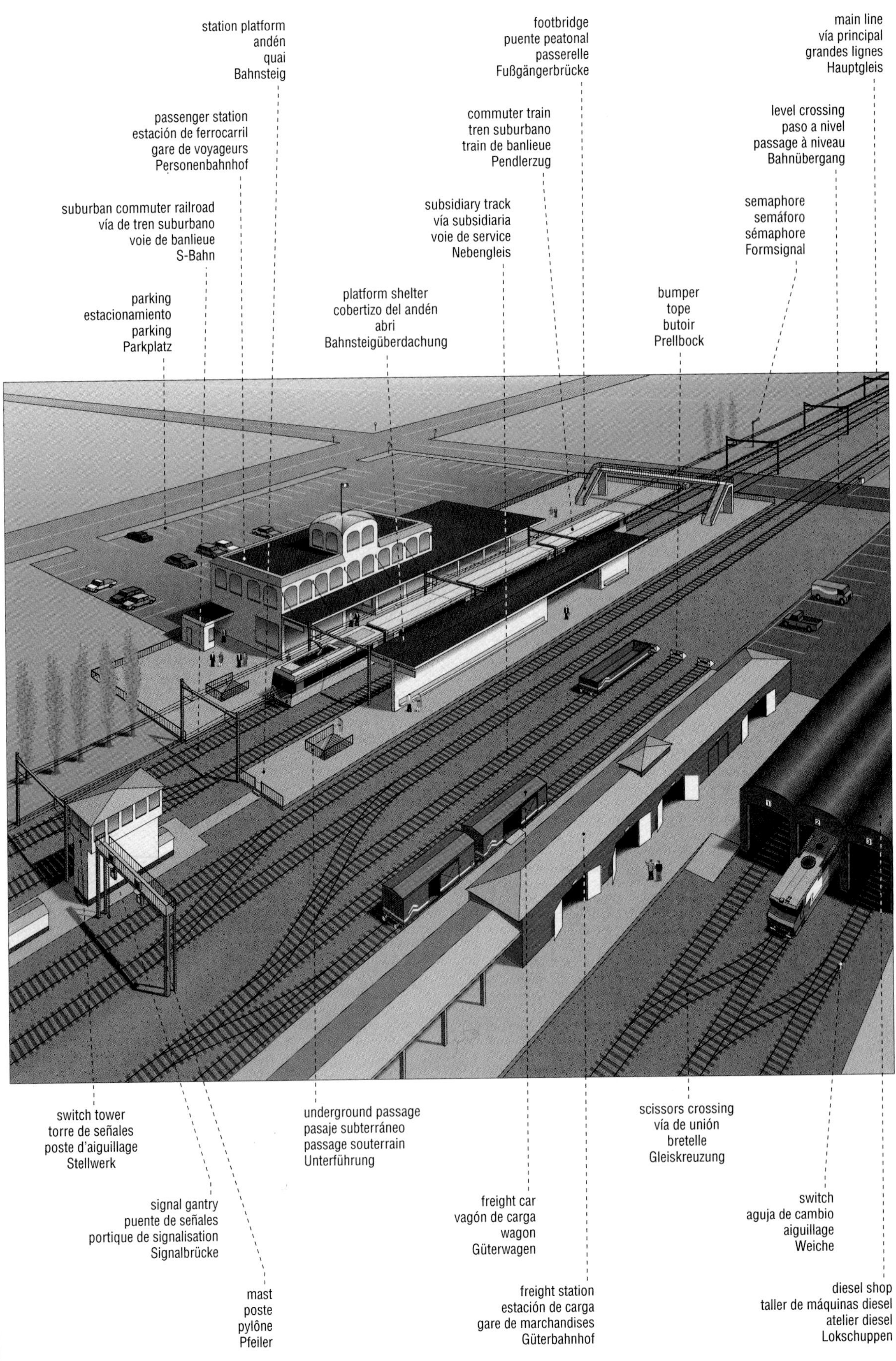
station platform
andén
quai
Bahnsteig
passenger station
estación de ferrocarril
gare de voyageurs
Personenbahnhof
suburban commuter railroad
vía de tren suburbano
voie de banlieue
S-Bahn
parking
estacionamiento
parking
Parkplatz
platform shelter
cobertizo del andén
abri
Bahnsteigüberdachung
subsidiary track
vía subsidiaria
voie de service
Nebengleis
commuter train
tren suburbano
train de banlieue
Pendlerzug
footbridge
puente peatonal
passerelle
Fußgängerbrücke
bumper
tope
butoir
Prellbock
semaphore
semáforo
sémaphore
Formsignal
level crossing
paso a nivel
passage à niveau
Bahnübergang
main line
vía principal
grandes lignes
Hauptgleis
switch tower
torre de señales
poste d'aiguillage
Stellwerk
signal gantry
puente de señales
portique de signalisation
Signalbrücke
mast
poste
pylône
Pfeiler
underground passage
pasaje subterráneo
passage souterrain
Unterführung
freight car
vagón de carga
wagon
Güterwagen
freight station
estación de carga
gare de marchandises
Güterbahnhof
scissors crossing
vía de unión
bretelle
Gleiskreuzung
switch
aguja de cambio
aiguillage
Weiche
diesel shop
taller de máquinas diesel
atelier diesel
Lokschuppen

YARD
TALLERES DE FERROCARRIL
GARE DE TRIAGE
RANGIERBAHNHOF

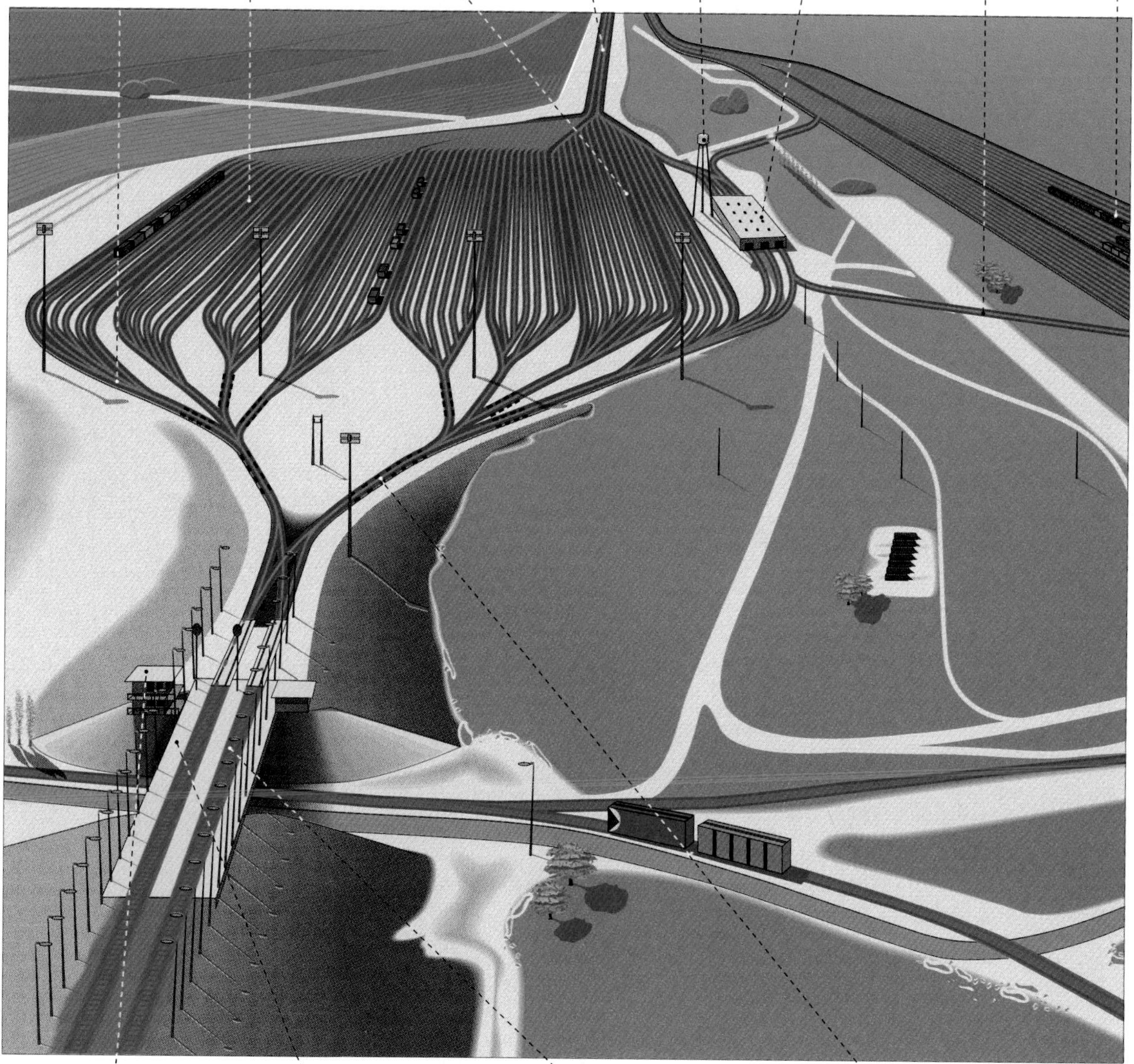
classification yard
patio de clasificación
zone de triage
Ordnungsgleise
outbound track
vía de salida
voie de sortie
Ausfahrgleis
car repair shop
taller de reparación de vagones
atelier de réparation des wagons
Wagenausbesserungshalle
receiving yard
patio de recepción
zone de réception
Empfangsgleise
second classification track
segunda vía de clasificación
voie de tri secondaire
Richtungsgleis
car cleaning yard
patio de lavado de vagones
zone de lavage des wagons
Waschplatte
water tower
tanque de agua
château d'eau
Wasserturm
locomotive track
vía locomotriz
voie de circulation des locomotives
Lokverkehrsgleis
hump office
oficina
poste de débranchement
Ablaufstellwerk
hump
lomo de maniobra
butte de débranchement
Ablaufberg
hump lead
dirección
voie de butte
Auffahrgleis
first classification track
primera vía de clasificación
voie de tri primaire
Einfahrgleis

RAILROAD TRACK
VÍA FÉRREA
VOIE FERRÉE
EISENBAHN-OBERBAU

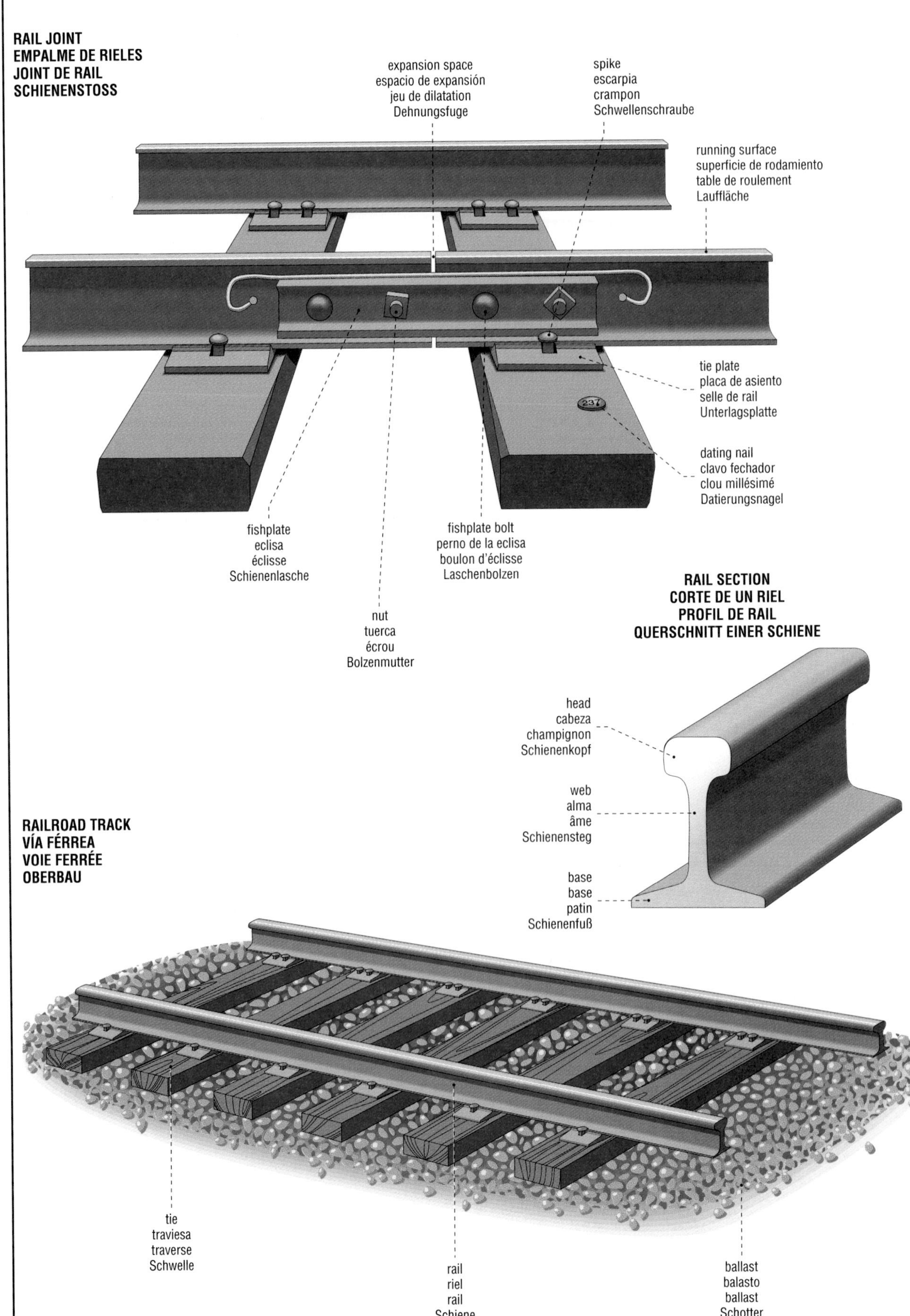
RAIL JOINT
EMPALME DE RIELES
JOINT DE RAIL
SCHIENENSTOSS
expansion space
espacio de expansión
jeu de dilatation
Dehnungsfuge
spike
escarpia
crampon
Schwellenschraube
running surface
superficie de rodamiento
table de roulement
Lauffläche
tie plate
placa de asiento
selle de rail
Unterlagsplatte
237
dating nail
clavo fechador
clou millésimé
Datierungsnagel
fishplate
eclisa
éclisse
Schienenlasche
fishplate bolt
perno de la eclisa
boulon d'éclisse
Laschenbolzen
nut
tuerca
écrou
Bolzenmutter
RAIL SECTION
CORTE DE UN RIEL
PROFIL DE RAIL
QUERSCHNITT EINER SCHIENE
head
cabeza
champignon
Schienenkopf
web
alma
âme
Schienensteg
base
base
patin
Schienenfuß
RAILROAD TRACK
VÍA FÉRREA
VOIE FERRÉE
OBERBAU
tie
traviesa
traverse
Schwelle
rail
riel
rail
Schiene
ballast
balasto
ballast
Schotter

REMOTE-CONTROLLED SWITCH
AGUJA DE CONTROL A LARGA DISTANCIA
AIGUILLAGE MANŒUVRÉ À DISTANCE
FERNBEDIENTE WEICHE

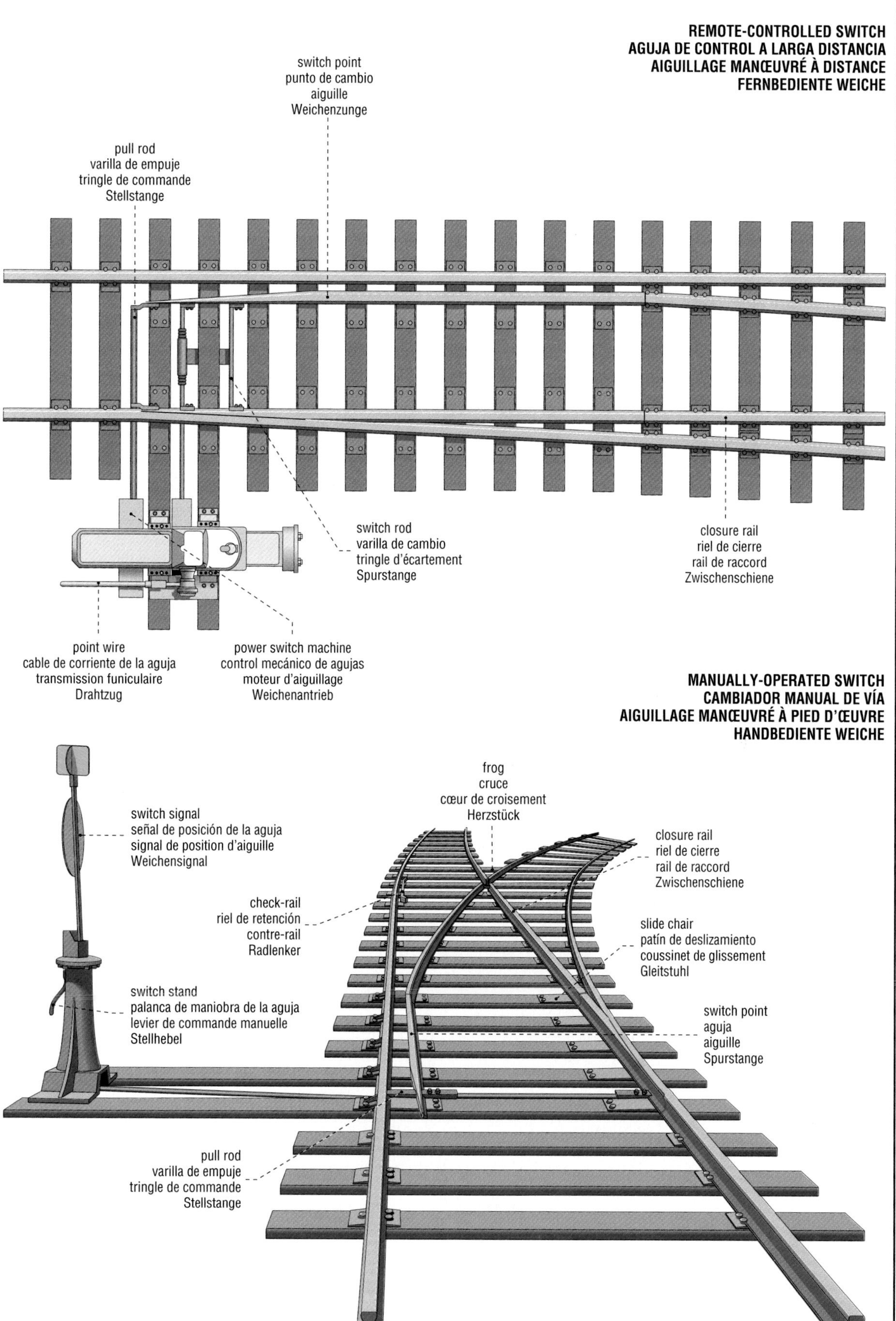
switch point
punto de cambio
aiguille
Weichenzunge
pull rod
varilla de empuje
tringle de commande
Stellstange
switch rod
varilla de cambio
tringle d'écartement
Spurstange
closure rail
riel de cierre
rail de raccord
Zwischenschiene
point wire
cable de corriente de la aguja
transmission funiculaire
Drahtzug
power switch machine
control mecánico de agujas
moteur d'aiguillage
Weichenantrieb
MANUALLY-OPERATED SWITCH
CAMBIADOR MANUAL DE VÍA
AIGUILLAGE MANŒUVRÉ À PIED D'ŒUVRE
HANDBEDIENTE WEICHE
frog
cruce
cœur de croisement
Herzstück
switch signal
señal de posición de la aguja
signal de position d'aiguille
Weichensignal
closure rail
riel de cierre
rail de raccord
Zwischenschiene
check-rail
riel de retención
contre-rail
Radlenker
slide chair
patín de deslizamiento
coussinet de glissement
Gleitstuhl
switch stand
palanca de maniobra de la aguja
levier de commande manuelle
Stellhebel
switch point
aguja
aiguille
Spurstange
pull rod
varilla de empuje
tringle de commande
Stellstange

DIESEL-ELECTRIC LOCOMOTIVE
LOCOMOTORA DIESEL ELÉCTRICA
LOCOMOTIVE DIESEL-ÉLECTRIQUE
DIESELELEKTRISCHE LOKOMOTIVE

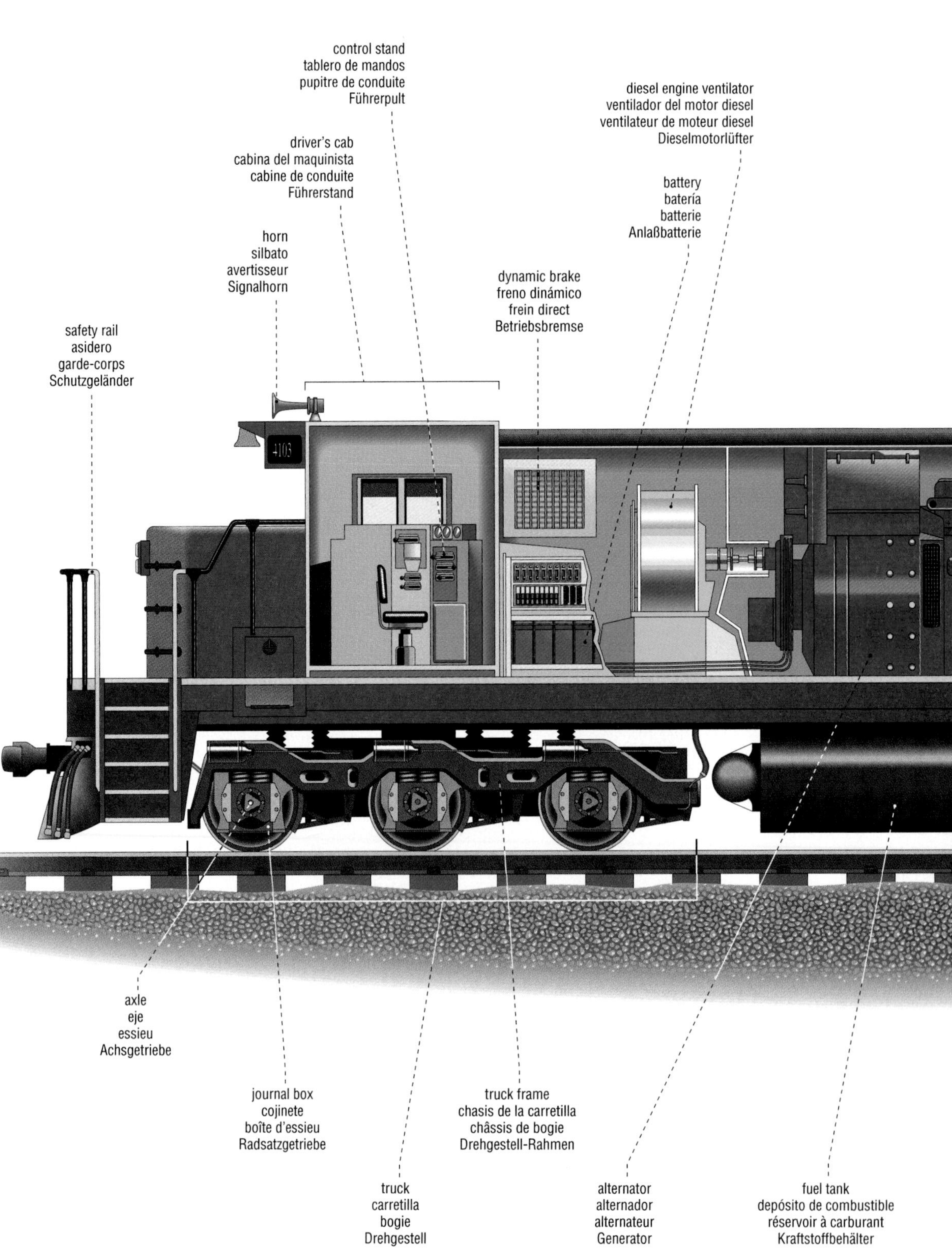
control stand
tablero de mandos
pupitre de conduite
Führerpult
driver's cab
cabina del maquinista
cabine de conduite
Führerstand
diesel engine ventilator
ventilador del motor diesel
ventilateur de moteur diesel
Dieselmotorlüfter
battery
batería
batterie
Anlaßbatterie
horn
silbato
avertisseur
Signalhorn
dynamic brake
freno dinámico
frein direct
Betriebsbremse
safety rail
asidero
garde-corps
Schutzgeländer
4103
axle
eje
essieu
Achsgetriebe
journal box
cojinete
boîte d'essieu
Radsatzgetriebe
truck frame
chasis de la carretilla
châssis de bogie
Drehgestell-Rahmen
truck
carretilla
bogie
Drehgestell
alternator
alternador
alternateur
Generator
fuel tank
depósito de combustible
réservoir à carburant
Kraftstoffbehälter

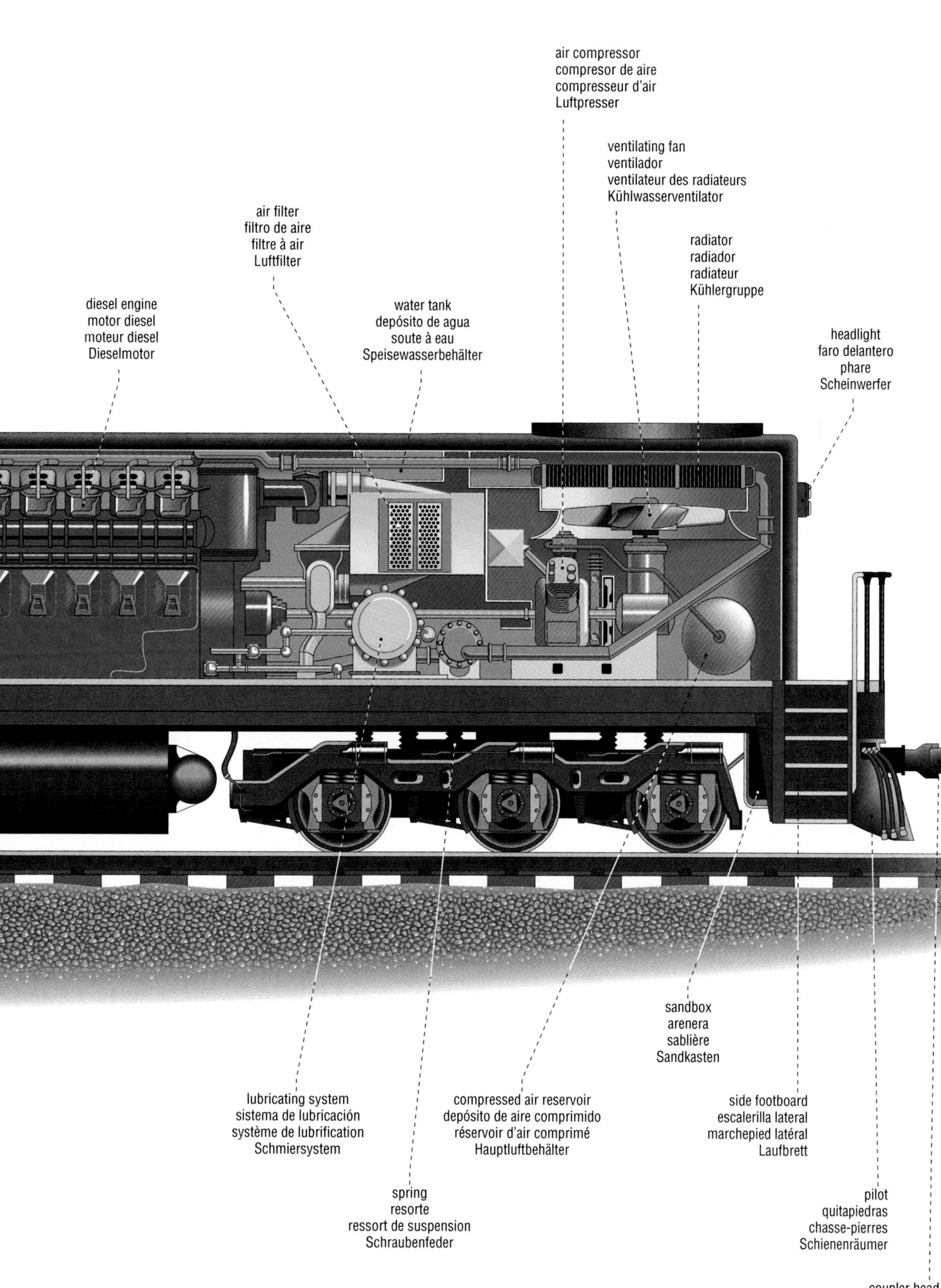
air compressor
compresor de aire
compresseur d'air
Luftpresser
ventilating fan
ventilador
ventilateur des radiateurs
Kühlwasserventilator
air filter
filtro de aire
filtre à air
Luftfilter
radiator
radiador
radiateur
Kühlergruppe
diesel engine
motor diesel
moteur diesel
Dieselmotor
water tank
depósito de agua
soute à eau
Speisewasserbehälter
headlight
faro delantero
phare
Scheinwerfer
sandbox
arenera
sablière
Sandkasten
lubricating system
sistema de lubricación
système de lubrification
Schmiersystem
compressed air reservoir
depósito de aire comprimido
réservoir d'air comprimé
Hauptluftbehälter
side footboard
escalerilla lateral
marchepied latéral
Laufbrett
spring
resorte
ressort de suspension
Schraubenfeder
pilot
quitapiedras
chasse-pierres
Schienenräumer
coupler head
cabeza de empalme
tête d'attelage
Kupplungsbügel

CAR
VAGÓN
WAGON
WAGEN

BOX CAR
FURGÓN
WAGON COUVERT
DREHGESTELLKASTENWAGEN

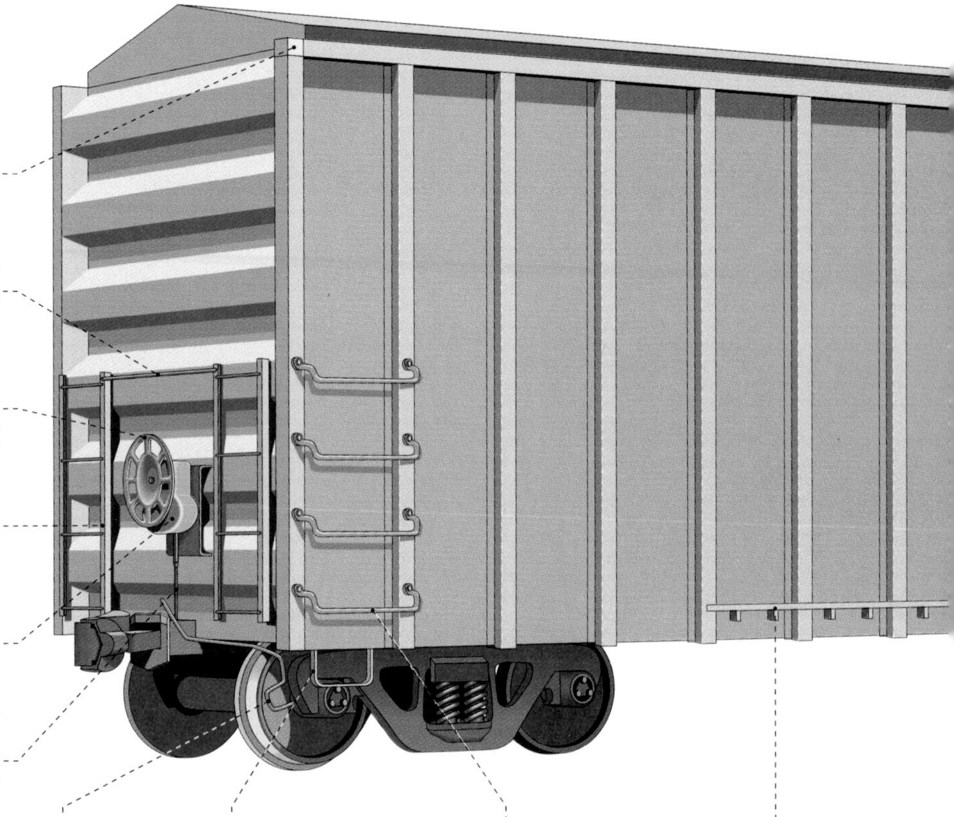

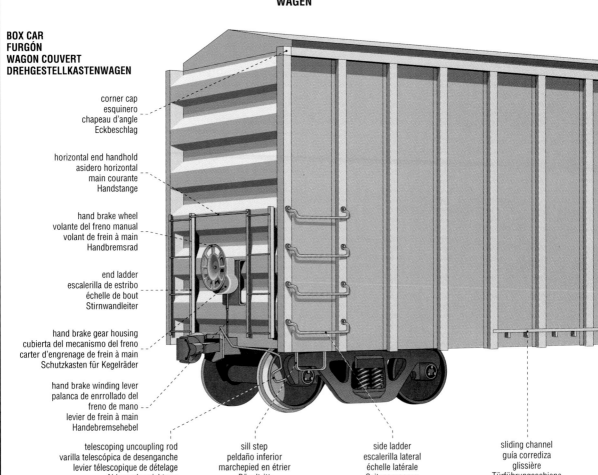

corner cap
esquinero
chapeau d'angle
Eckbeschlag

horizontal end handhold
asidero horizontal
main courante
Handstange

hand brake wheel
volante del freno manual
volant de frein à main
Handbremsrad

end ladder
escalerilla de estribo
échelle de bout
Stirnwandleiter

hand brake gear housing
cubierta del mecanismo del freno
carter d'engrenage de frein à main
Schutzkasten für Kegelräder

hand brake winding lever
palanca de enrollado del freno de mano
levier de frein à main
Handebremsehebel

telescoping uncoupling rod
varilla telescópica de desenganche
levier télescopique de dételage
Abkoppelvorrichtung

sill step
peldaño inferior
marchepied en étrier
Bügeltritt

side ladder
escalerilla lateral
échelle latérale
Seitensprossen

sliding channel
guía corrediza
glissière
Türführungsschiene

CONTAINER
CONTENEDOR
CONTENEUR
CONTAINER

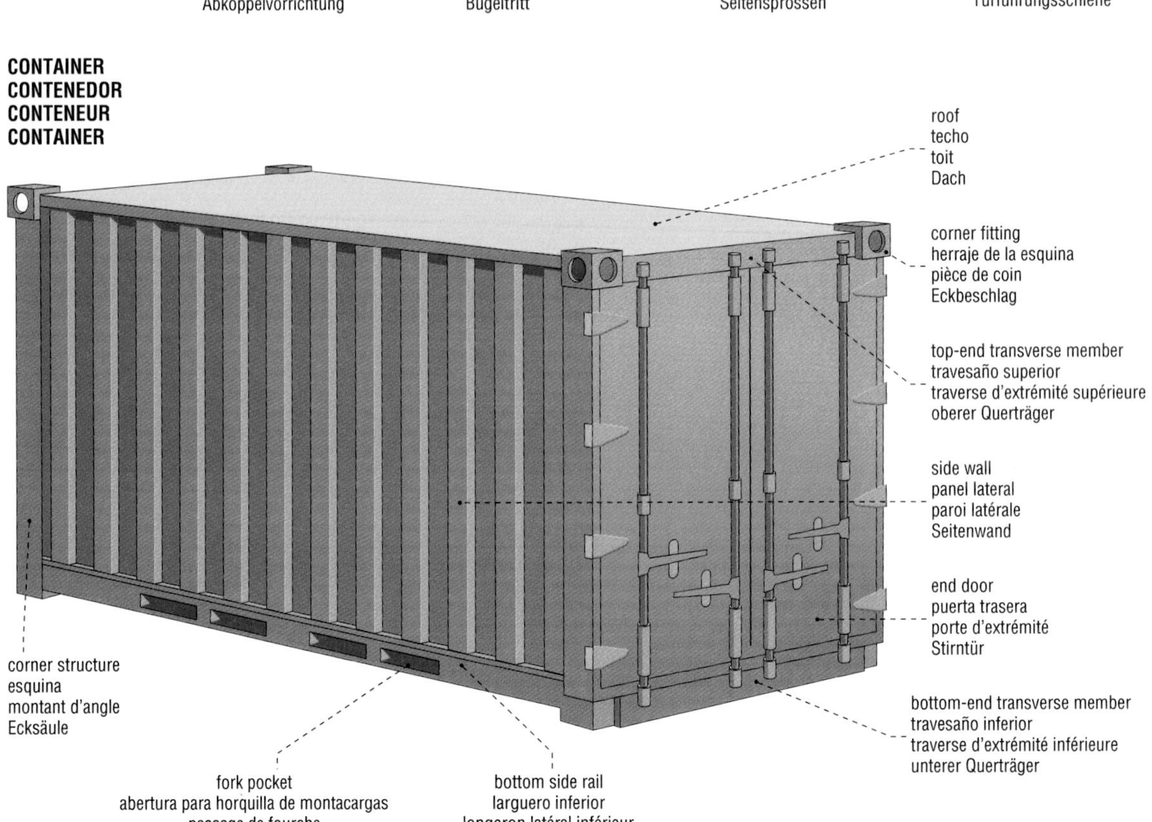
roof
techo
toit
Dach
corner fitting
herraje de la esquina
pièce de coin
Eckbeschlag
top-end transverse member
travesaño superior
traverse d'extrémité supérieure
oberer Querträger
side wall
panel lateral
paroi latérale
Seitenwand
end door
puerta trasera
porte d'extrémité
Stirntür
bottom-end transverse member
travesaño inferior
traverse d'extrémité inférieure
unterer Querträger
corner structure
esquina
montant d'angle
Ecksäule
fork pocket
abertura para horquilla de montacargas
passage de fourche
Gabelstaplertasche
bottom side rail
larguero inferior
longeron latéral inférieur
unterer Längsträger

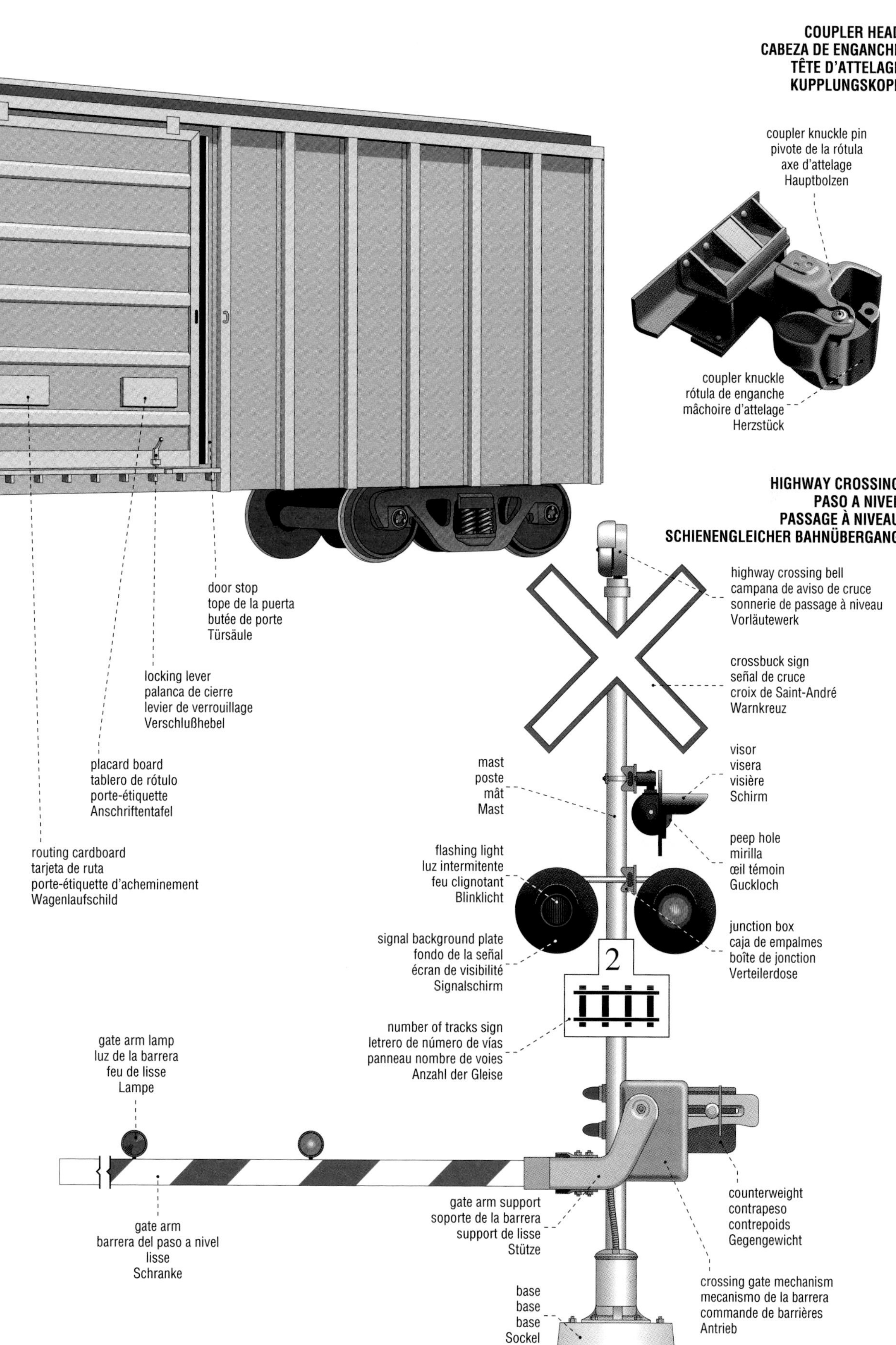
COUPLER HEAD
CABEZA DE ENGANCHE
TÊTE D'ATTELAGE
KUPPLUNGSKOPF
coupler knuckle pin
pivote de la rótula
axe d'attelage
Hauptbolzen
coupler knuckle
rótula de enganche
mâchoire d'attelage
Herzstück
door stop
tope de la puerta
butée de porte
Türsäule
locking lever
palanca de cierre
levier de verrouillage
Verschlußhebel
placard board
tablero de rótulo
porte-étiquette
Anschriftentafel
routing cardboard
tarjeta de ruta
porte-étiquette d'acheminement
Wagenlaufschild
HIGHWAY CROSSING
PASO A NIVEL
PASSAGE À NIVEAU
SCHIENENGLEICHER BAHNÜBERGANG
highway crossing bell
campana de aviso de cruce
sonnerie de passage à niveau
Vorläutewerk
crossbuck sign
señal de cruce
croix de Saint-André
Warnkreuz
visor
visera
visière
Schirm
mast
poste
mât
Mast
peep hole
mirilla
œil témoin
Guckloch
flashing light
luz intermitente
feu clignotant
Blinklicht
junction box
caja de empalmes
boîte de jonction
Verteilerdose
signal background plate
fondo de la señal
écran de visibilité
Signalschirm
2
number of tracks sign
letrero de número de vías
panneau nombre de voies
Anzahl der Gleise
gate arm lamp
luz de la barrera
feu de lisse
Lampe
gate arm
barrera del paso a nivel
lisse
Schranke
gate arm support
soporte de la barrera
support de lisse
Stütze
counterweight
contrapeso
contrepoids
Gegengewicht
crossing gate mechanism
mecanismo de la barrera
commande de barrières
Antrieb
base
base
base
Sockel

TYPES OF FREIGHT CARS
TIPOS DE VAGONES DE CARGA
TYPES DE WAGONS
GÜTERWAGEN

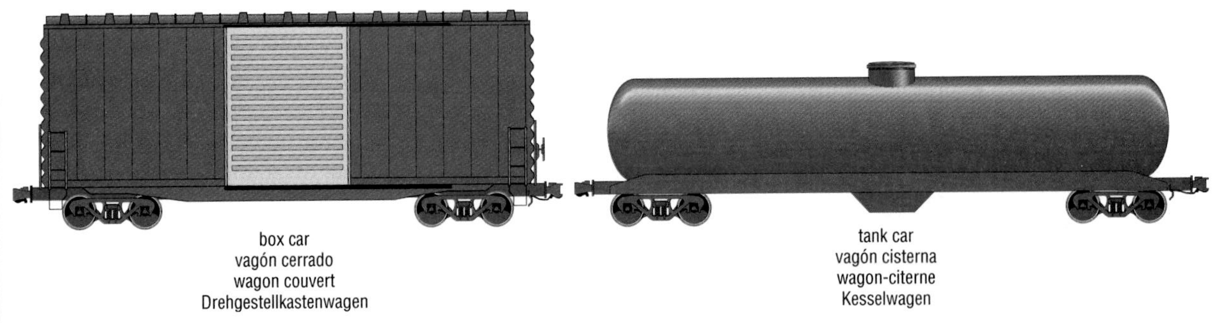

box car
vagón cerrado
wagon couvert
Drehgestellkastenwagen

tank car
vagón cisterna
wagon-citerne
Kesselwagen

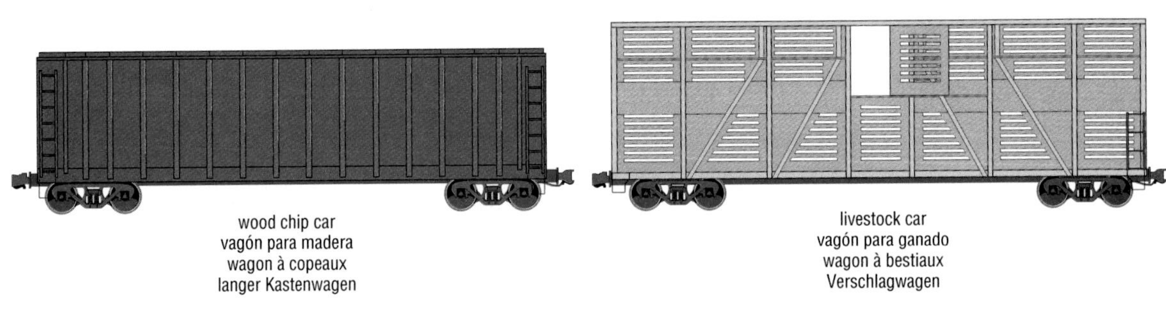

wood chip car
vagón para madera
wagon à copeaux
langer Kastenwagen

livestock car
vagón para ganado
wagon à bestiaux
Verschlagwagen

hopper car
vagón tolva
wagon-trémie
Selbstentladetankwagen

hard top gondola
vagón con cubierta alquitranada
wagon-tombereau couvert
Planenwagen

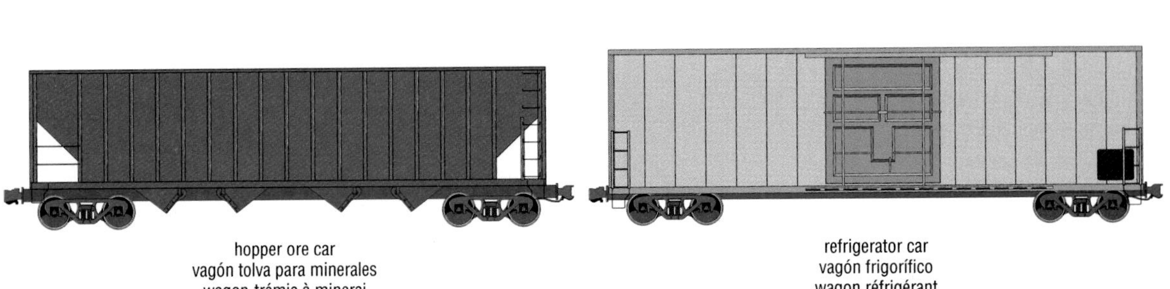

hopper ore car
vagón tolva para minerales
wagon-trémie à minerai
Schüttgutwagen

refrigerator car
vagón frigorífico
wagon réfrigérant
Kühlwagen

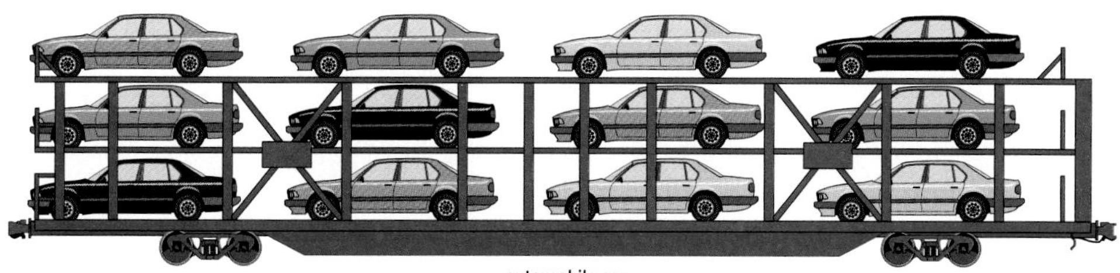

automobile car
vagón para automóviles
wagon porte-automobiles
Autotransportwagen

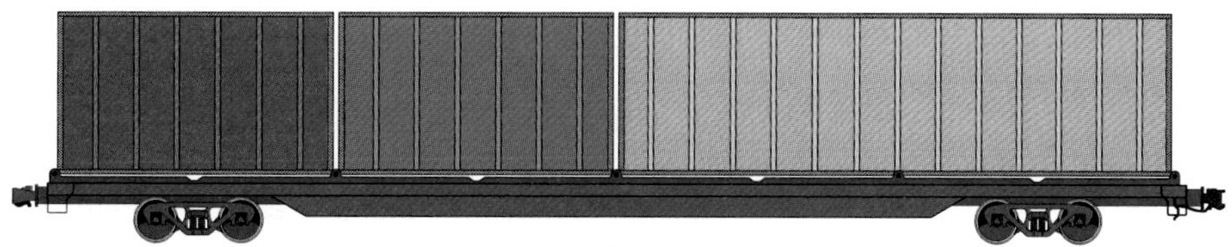

container car
vagón para contenedores
wagon porte-conteneurs
Containerflachwagen

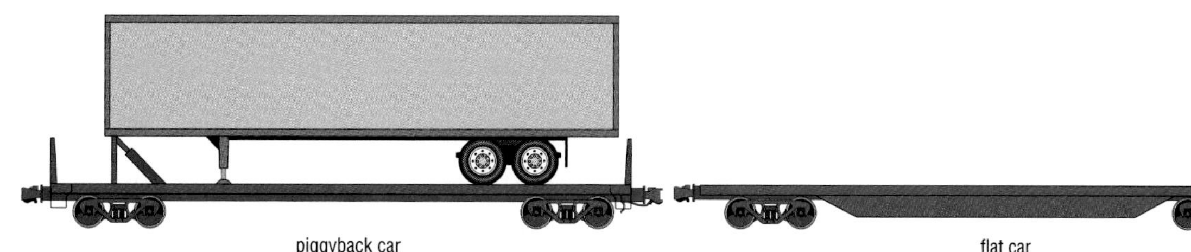

piggyback car
plataforma para transportar vagones
wagon rail-route
Spezialflachwagen für den Transport von Schwerfahrzeugen

flat car
plataforma
wagon plat
Drehgestellflachwagen

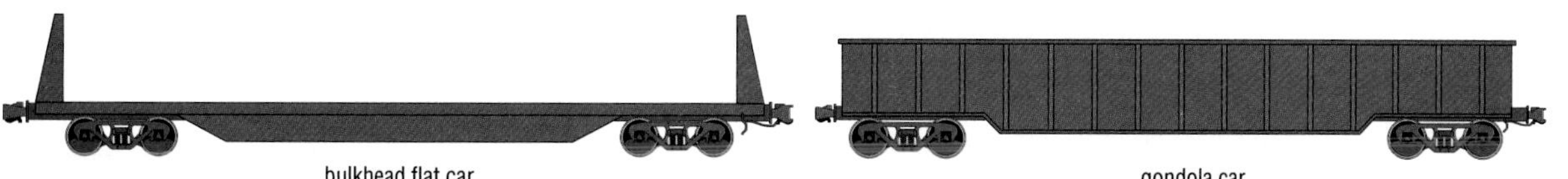

bulkhead flat car
vagón plano con retenedores
wagon plat à parois de bout
Stirnwandflachwagen

gondola car
vagón de mercancías
wagon-tombereau
offener Güterwagen

depressed-center flat car
plataforma de piso bajo
wagon plat surbaissé
Tiefladewagen

caboose
furgón de cola
wagon de queue
Bremswagen

SUBWAY
METRO
CHEMIN DE FER MÉTROPOLITAIN
U-BAHN

SUBWAY STATION
ESTACIÓN DE METRO
STATION DE MÉTRO
U-BAHN-STATION

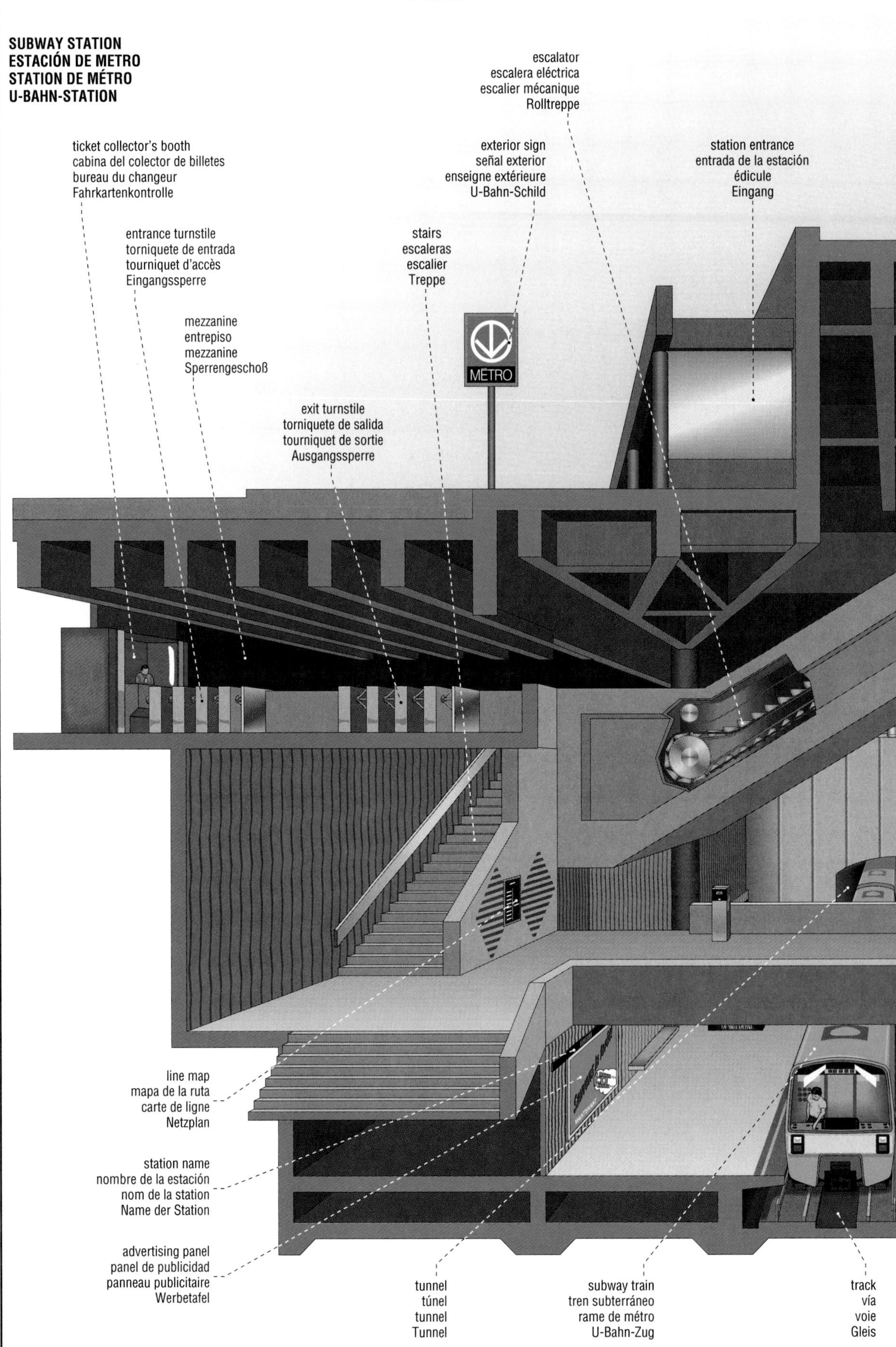
escalator
escalera eléctrica
escalier mécanique
Rolltreppe
ticket collector's booth
cabina del colector de billetes
bureau du changeur
Fahrkartenkontrolle
exterior sign
señal exterior
enseigne extérieure
U-Bahn-Schild
station entrance
entrada de la estación
édicule
Eingang
entrance turnstile
torniquete de entrada
tourniquet d'accès
Eingangssperre
stairs
escaleras
escalier
Treppe
mezzanine
entrepiso
mezzanine
Sperrengeschoß
MÉTRO
exit turnstile
torniquete de salida
tourniquet de sortie
Ausgangssperre
line map
mapa de la ruta
carte de ligne
Netzplan
station name
nombre de la estación
nom de la station
Name der Station
advertising panel
panel de publicidad
panneau publicitaire
Werbetafel
tunnel
túnel
tunnel
Tunnel
subway train
tren subterráneo
rame de métro
U-Bahn-Zug
track
vía
voie
Gleis

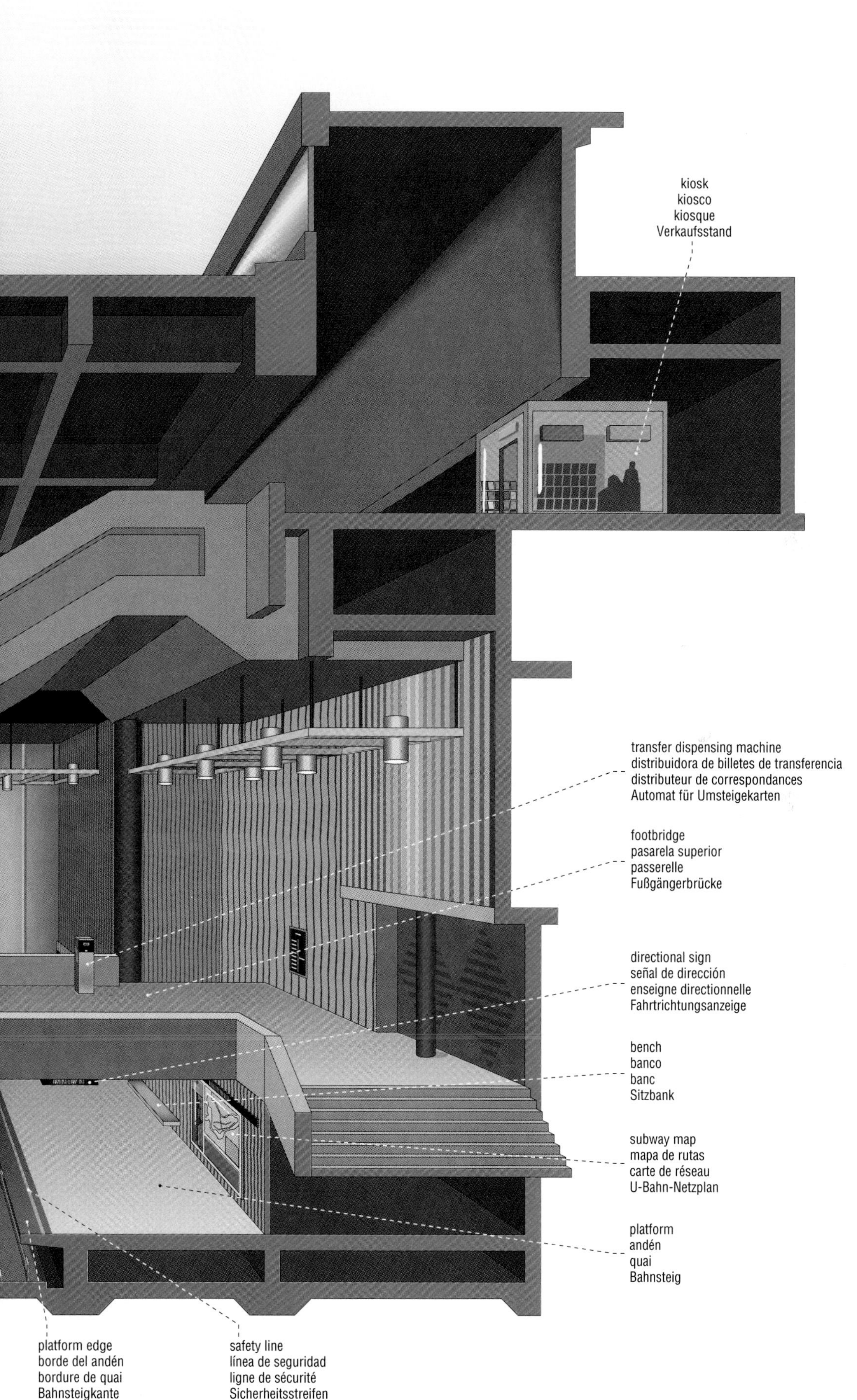
kiosk
kiosco
kiosque
Verkaufsstand
transfer dispensing machine
distribuidora de billetes de transferencia
distributeur de correspondances
Automat für Umsteigekarten
footbridge
pasarela superior
passerelle
Fußgängerbrücke
directional sign
señal de dirección
enseigne directionnelle
Fahrtrichtungsanzeige
bench
banco
banc
Sitzbank
subway map
mapa de rutas
carte de réseau
U-Bahn-Netzplan
platform
andén
quai
Bahnsteig
platform edge
borde del andén
bordure de quai
Bahnsteigkante
safety line
línea de seguridad
ligne de sécurité
Sicherheitsstreifen

SUBWAY
METRO
CHEMIN DE FER MÉTROPOLITAIN
U-BAHN

TRUCK AND TRACK
CARRETILLA Y VÍA
BOGIE ET VOIE
DREHGESTELL UND GLEIS

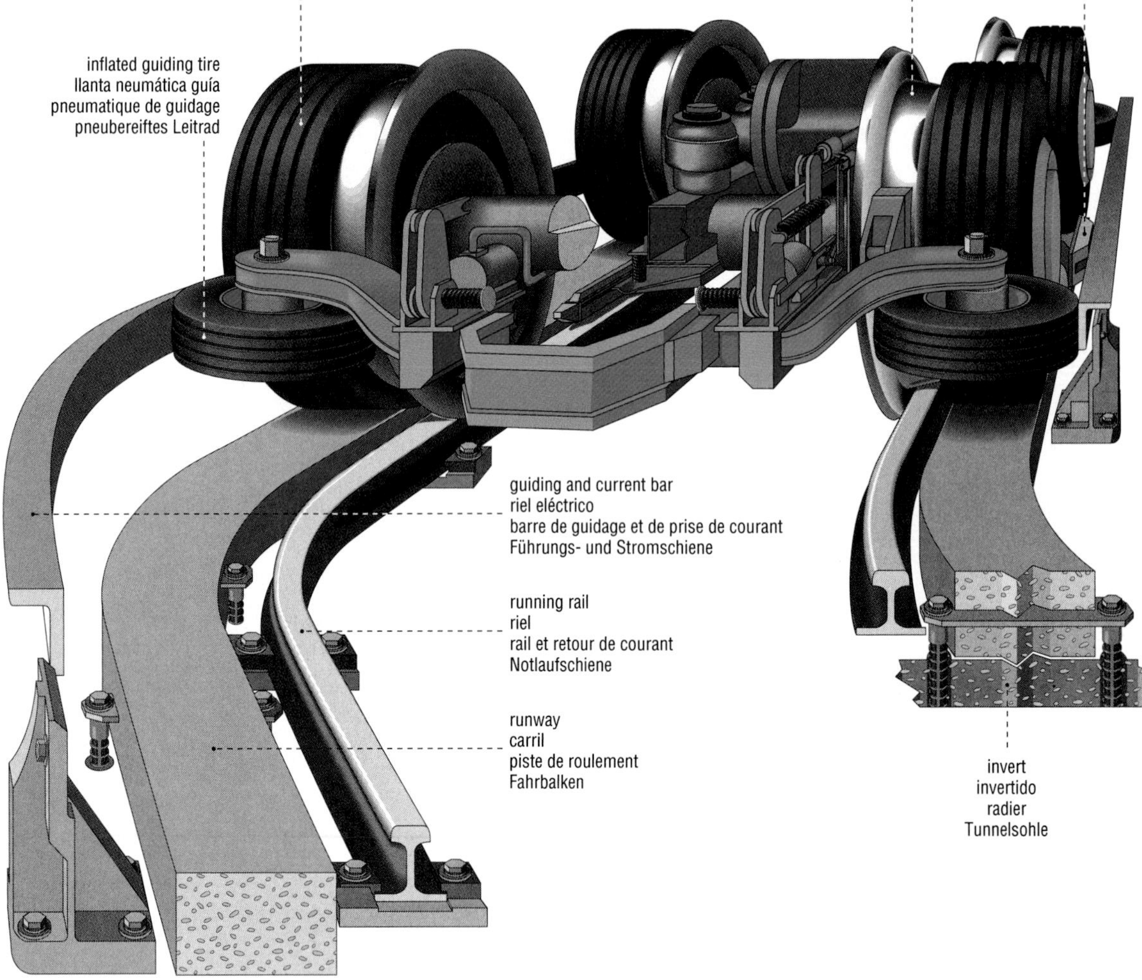

inflated carrying tire
llanta neumática de tracción
pneumatique porteur
pneubereiftes Laufrad

steel safety wheel
rueda metálica de seguridad
roue de sécurité
Spurkranzrad

sliding block
bloque corredizo
frotteur
Stromabnehmer

inflated guiding tire
llanta neumática guía
pneumatique de guidage
pneubereiftes Leitrad

guiding and current bar
riel eléctrico
barre de guidage et de prise de courant
Führungs- und Stromschiene

running rail
riel
rail et retour de courant
Notlaufschiene

runway
carril
piste de roulement
Fahrbalken

invert
invertido
radier
Tunnelsohle

SUBWAY TRAIN
TREN SUBTERRÁNEO
RAME DE MÉTRO
U-BAHN-ZUG

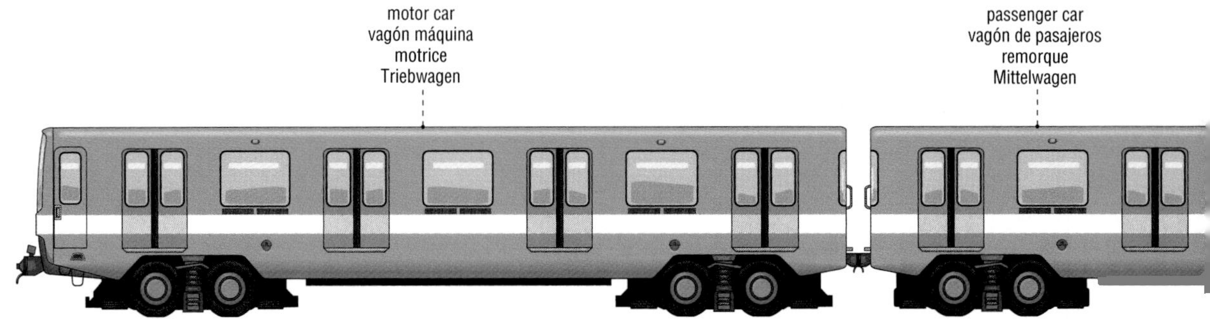
motor car
vagón máquina
motrice
Triebwagen
passenger car
vagón de pasajeros
remorque
Mittelwagen

PASSENGER CAR
VAGÓN DE PASAJEROS
VOITURE
MITTELWAGEN

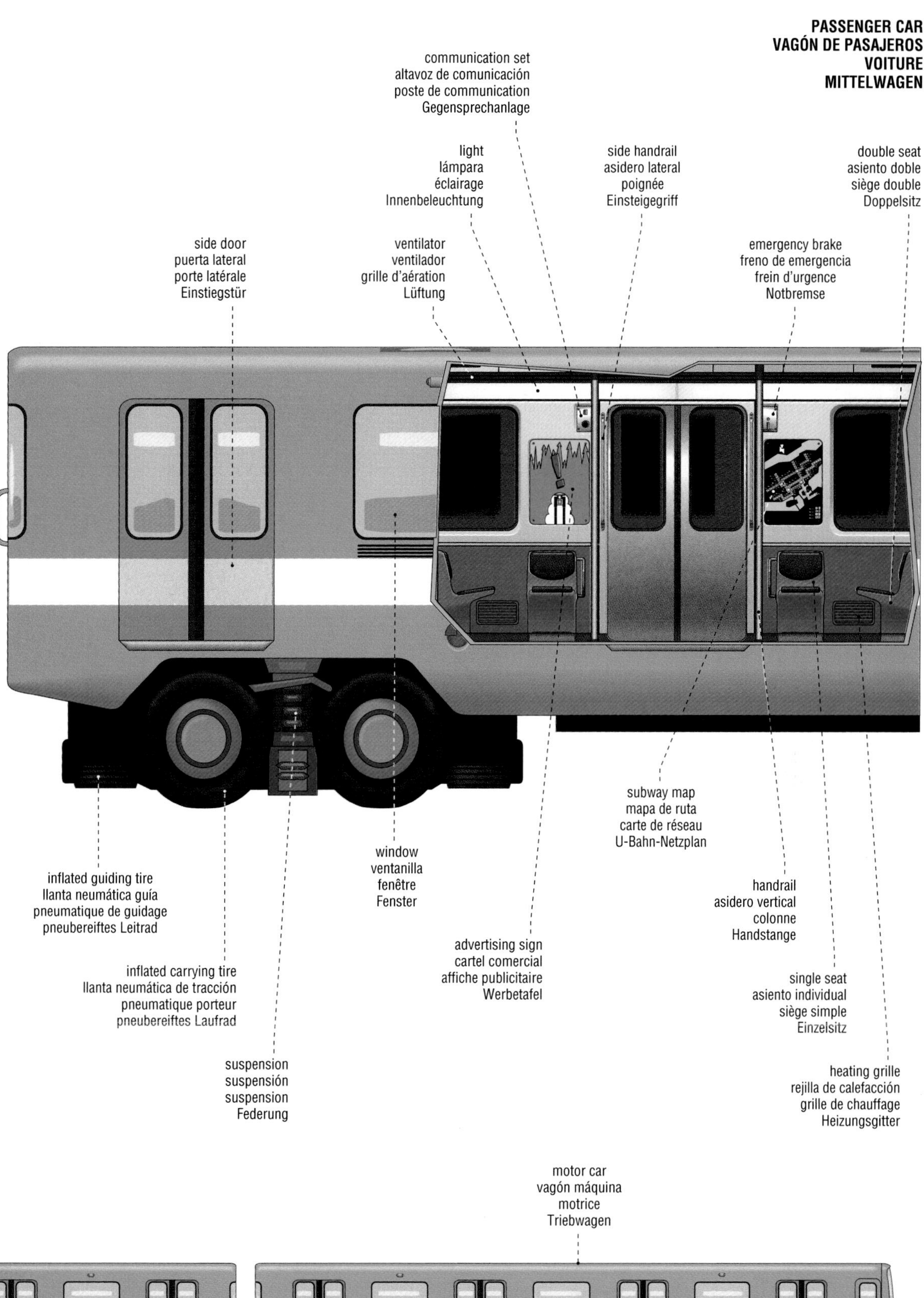
communication set
altavoz de comunicación
poste de communication
Gegensprechanlage
light
lámpara
éclairage
Innenbeleuchtung
side handrail
asidero lateral
poignée
Einsteigegriff
double seat
asiento doble
siège double
Doppelsitz
side door
puerta lateral
porte latérale
Einstiegstür
ventilator
ventilador
grille d'aération
Lüftung
emergency brake
freno de emergencia
frein d'urgence
Notbremse
subway map
mapa de ruta
carte de réseau
U-Bahn-Netzplan
window
ventanilla
fenêtre
Fenster
inflated guiding tire
llanta neumática guía
pneumatique de guidage
pneubereiftes Leitrad
handrail
asidero vertical
colonne
Handstange
advertising sign
cartel comercial
affiche publicitaire
Werbetafel
inflated carrying tire
llanta neumática de tracción
pneumatique porteur
pneubereiftes Laufrad
single seat
asiento individual
siège simple
Einzelsitz
suspension
suspensión
suspension
Federung
heating grille
rejilla de calefacción
grille de chauffage
Heizungsgitter
motor car
vagón máquina
motrice
Triebwagen

FOUR-MASTED BARK
BARCO DE VELA DE CUATRO PALOS
QUATRE-MÂTS BARQUE
VIERMASTBARK

MASTING AND RIGGING
ARBOLADURA Y APAREJOS
MÂTURE ET GRÉEMENT
TAKELAGE

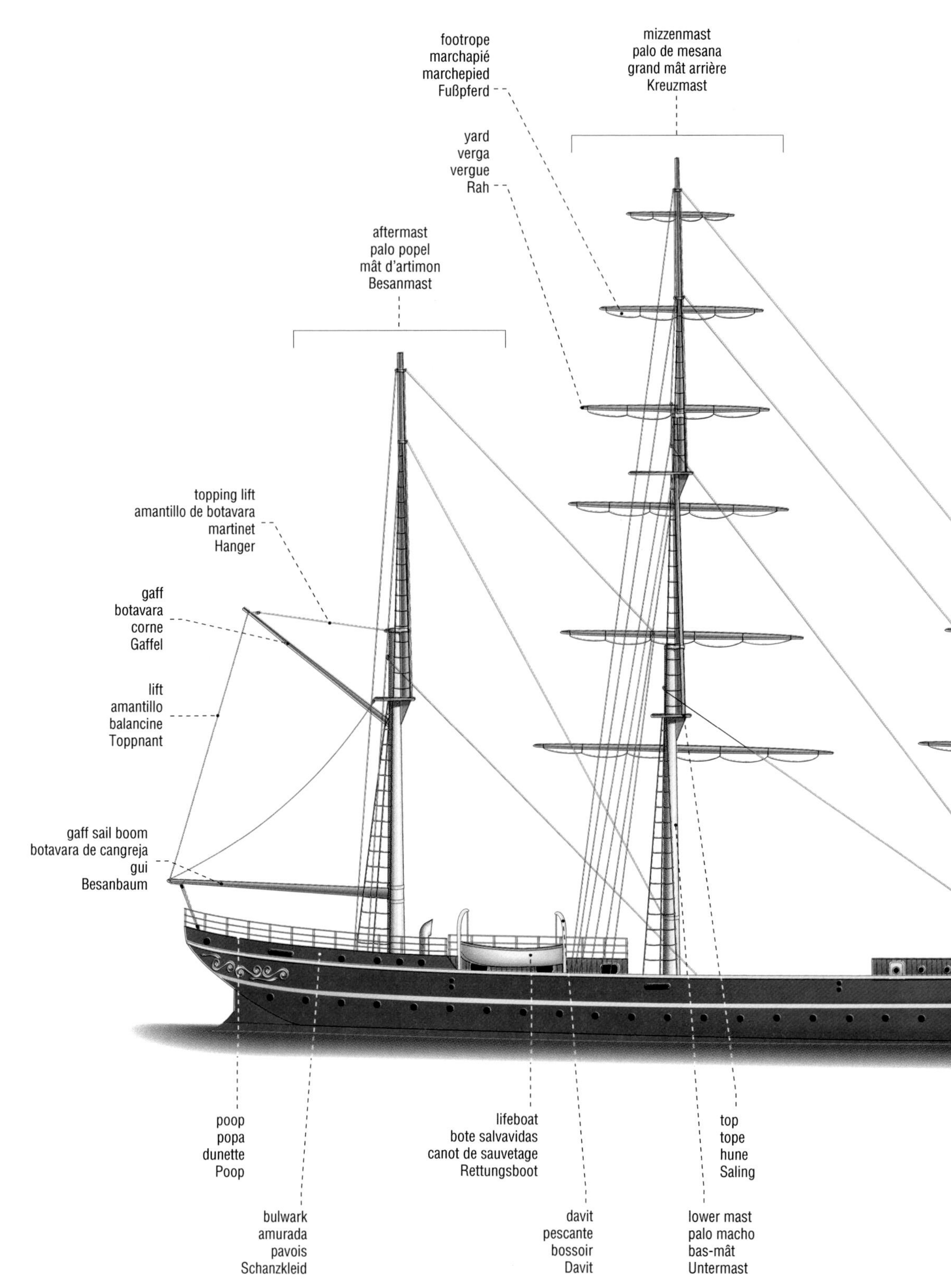
footrope
marchapié
marchepied
Fußpferd
mizzenmast
palo de mesana
grand mât arrière
Kreuzmast
yard
verga
vergue
Rah
aftermast
palo popel
mât d'artimon
Besanmast
topping lift
amantillo de botavara
martinet
Hanger
gaff
botavara
corne
Gaffel
lift
amantillo
balancine
Toppnant
gaff sail boom
botavara de cangreja
gui
Besanbaum
poop
popa
dunette
Poop
lifeboat
bote salvavidas
canot de sauvetage
Rettungsboot
top
tope
hune
Saling
bulwark
amurada
pavois
Schanzkleid
davit
pescante
bossoir
Davit
lower mast
palo macho
bas-mât
Untermast

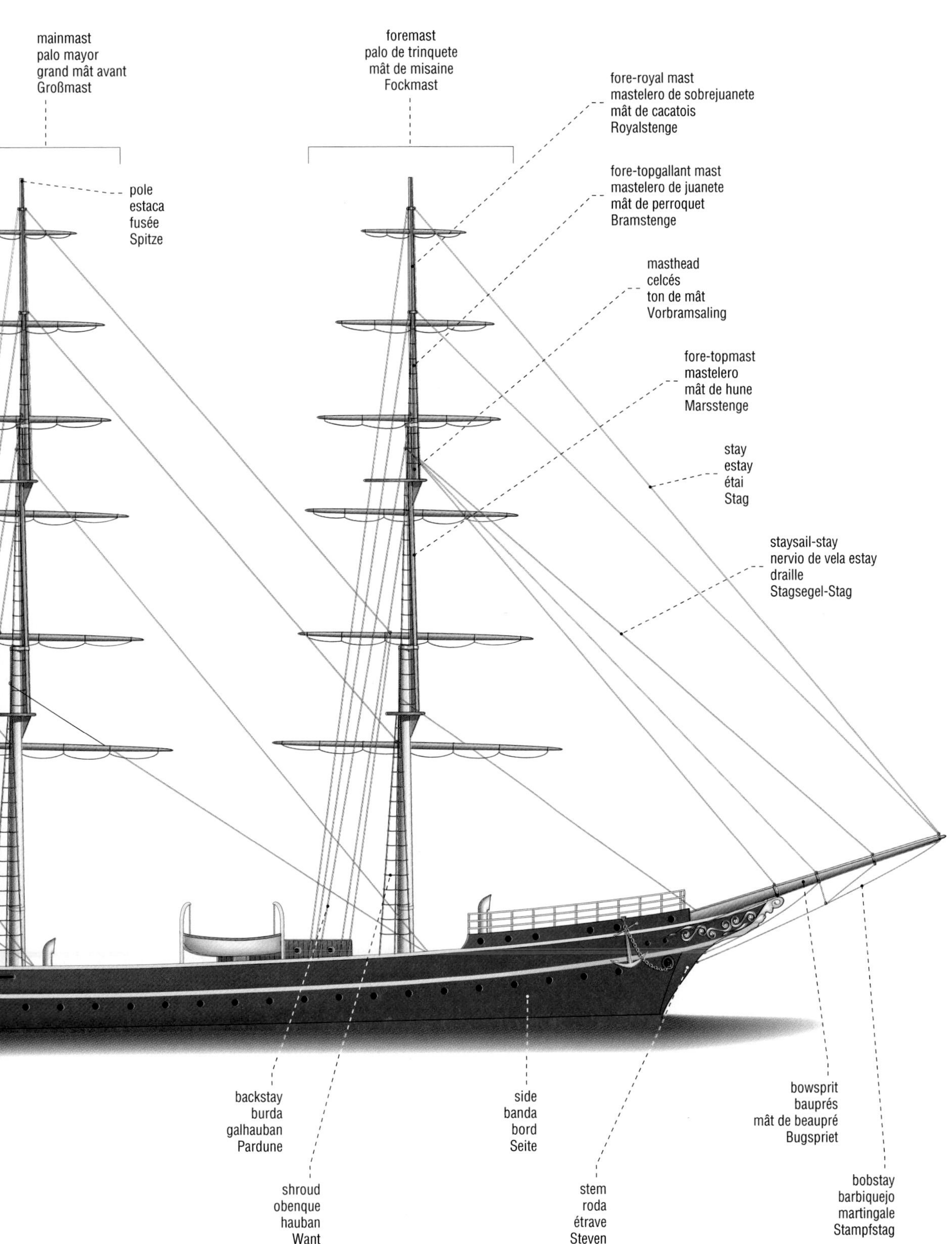
mainmast
palo mayor
grand mât avant
Großmast
foremast
palo de trinquete
mât de misaine
Fockmast
fore-royal mast
mastelero de sobrejuanete
mât de cacatois
Royalstenge
pole
estaca
fusée
Spitze
fore-topgallant mast
mastelero de juanete
mât de perroquet
Bramstenge
masthead
celcés
ton de mât
Vorbramsaling
fore-topmast
mastelero
mât de hune
Marsstenge
stay
estay
étai
Stag
staysail-stay
nervio de vela estay
draille
Stagsegel-Stag
backstay
burda
galhauban
Pardune
side
banda
bord
Seite
bowsprit
bauprés
mât de beaupré
Bugspriet
shroud
obenque
hauban
Want
stem
roda
étrave
Steven
bobstay
barbiquejo
martingale
Stampfstag

FOUR-MASTED BARK
BARCO DE VELA DE CUATRO PALOS
QUATRE-MÂTS BARQUE
VIERMASTBARK

SAILS
VELAMEN
VOILURE
SEGEL

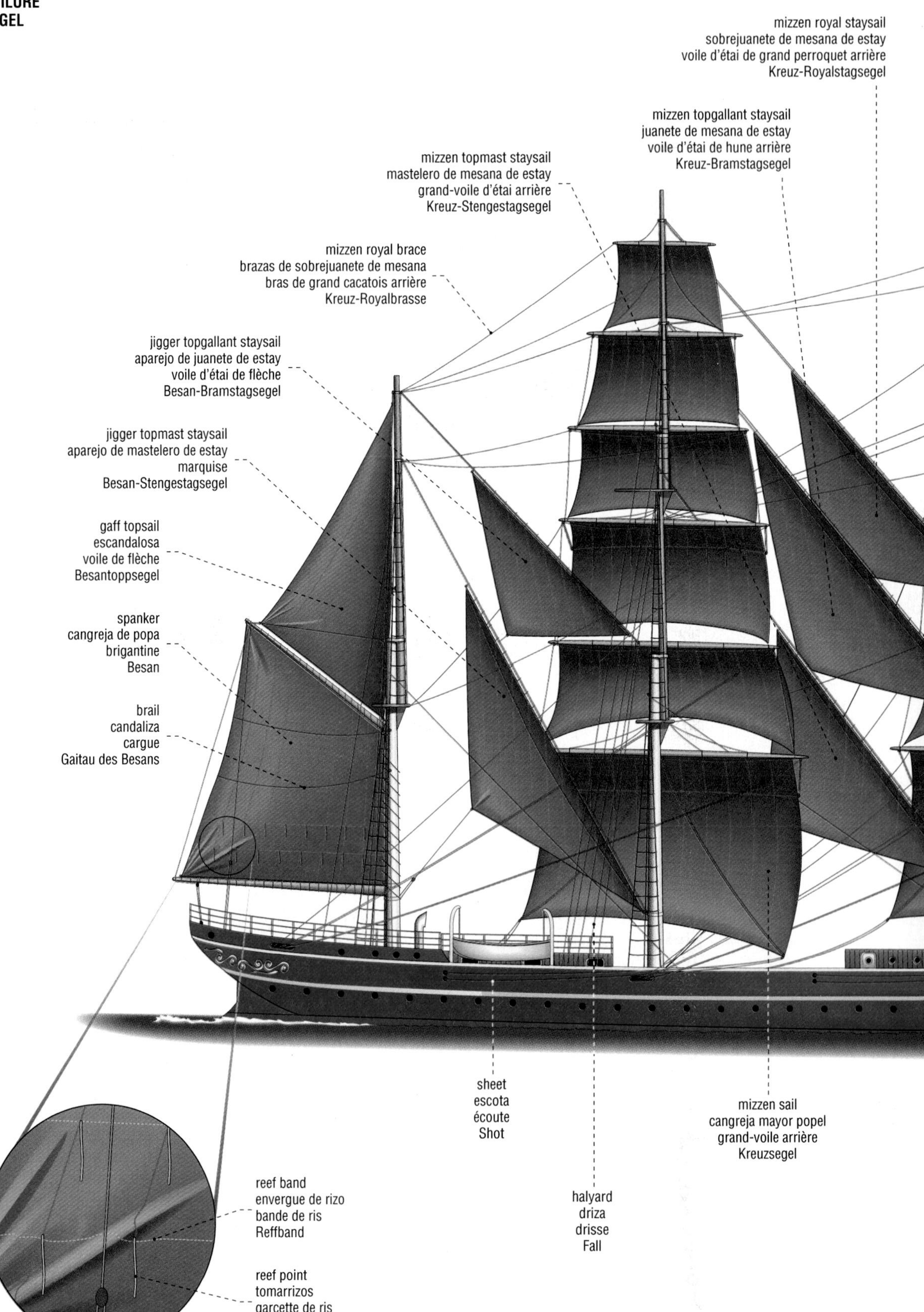
mizzen royal staysail
sobrejuanete de mesana de estay
voile d'étai de grand perroquet arrière
Kreuz-Royalstagsegel
mizzen topgallant staysail
juanete de mesana de estay
voile d'étai de hune arrière
Kreuz-Bramstagsegel
mizzen topmast staysail
mastelero de mesana de estay
grand-voile d'étai arrière
Kreuz-Stengestagsegel
mizzen royal brace
brazas de sobrejuanete de mesana
bras de grand cacatois arrière
Kreuz-Royalbrasse
jigger topgallant staysail
aparejo de juanete de estay
voile d'étai de flèche
Besan-Bramstagsegel
jigger topmast staysail
aparejo de mastelero de estay
marquise
Besan-Stengestagsegel
gaff topsail
escandalosa
voile de flèche
Besantoppsegel
spanker
cangreja de popa
brigantine
Besan
brail
candaliza
cargue
Gaitau des Besans
sheet
escota
écoute
Shot
mizzen sail
cangreja mayor popel
grand-voile arrière
Kreuzsegel
halyard
driza
drisse
Fall
reef band
envergue de rizo
bande de ris
Reffband
reef point
tomarrizos
garcette de ris
Reffbänsel

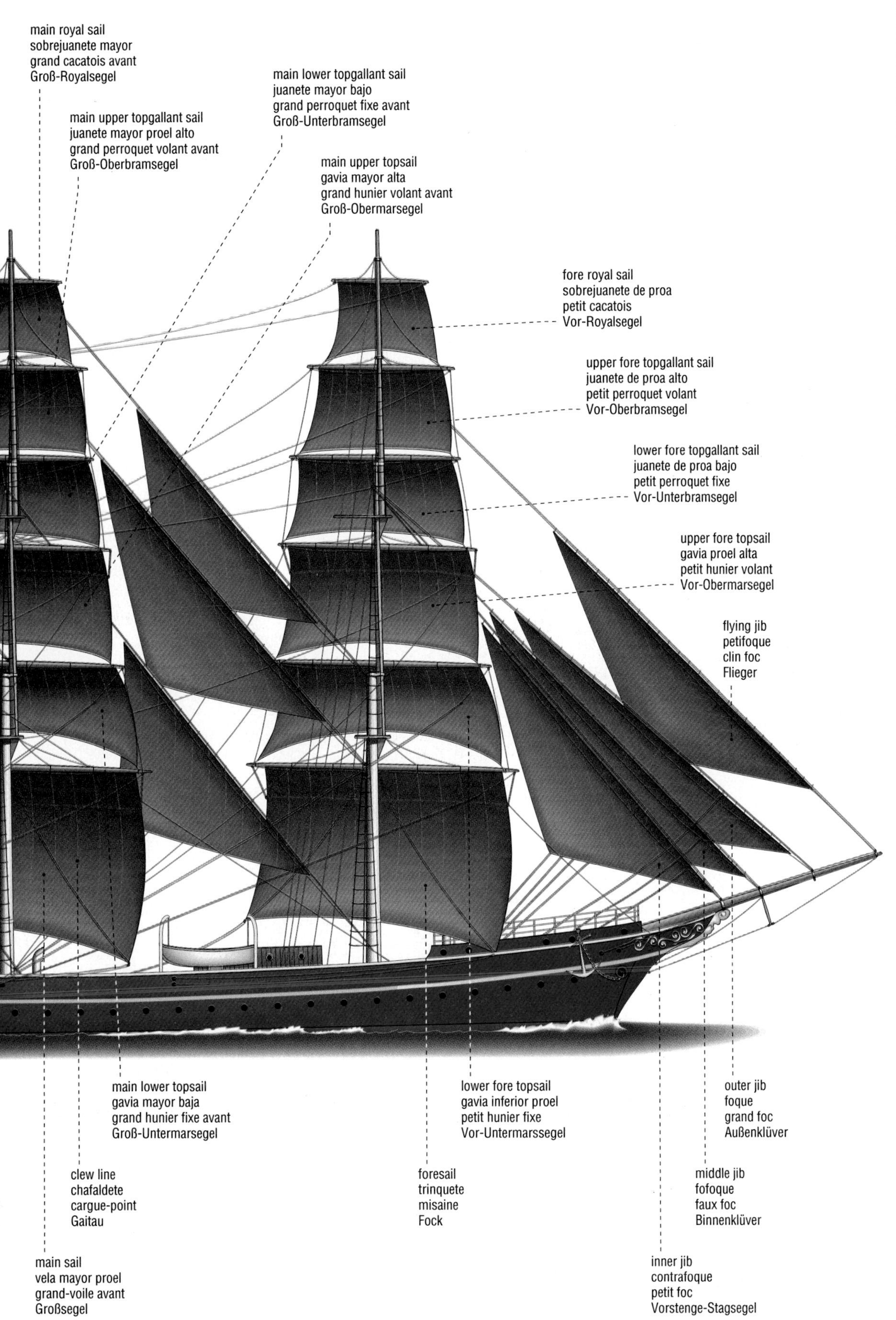
main royal sail
sobrejuanete mayor
grand cacatois avant
Groß-Royalsegel
main upper topgallant sail
juanete mayor proel alto
grand perroquet volant avant
Groß-Oberbramsegel
main lower topgallant sail
juanete mayor bajo
grand perroquet fixe avant
Groß-Unterbramsegel
main upper topsail
gavia mayor alta
grand hunier volant avant
Groß-Obermarsegel
fore royal sail
sobrejuanete de proa
petit cacatois
Vor-Royalsegel
upper fore topgallant sail
juanete de proa alto
petit perroquet volant
Vor-Oberbramsegel
lower fore topgallant sail
juanete de proa bajo
petit perroquet fixe
Vor-Unterbramsegel
upper fore topsail
gavia proel alta
petit hunier volant
Vor-Obermarsegel
flying jib
petifoque
clin foc
Flieger
main lower topsail
gavia mayor baja
grand hunier fixe avant
Groß-Untermarsegel
lower fore topsail
gavia inferior proel
petit hunier fixe
Vor-Untermarssegel
outer jib
foque
grand foc
Außenklüver
clew line
chafaldete
cargue-point
Gaitau
foresail
trinquete
misaine
Fock
middle jib
fofoque
faux foc
Binnenklüver
main sail
vela mayor proel
grand-voile avant
Großsegel
inner jib
contrafoque
petit foc
Vorstenge-Stagsegel

TYPES OF SAILS
TIPOS DE VELAS
TYPES DE VOILES
SEGELTYPEN

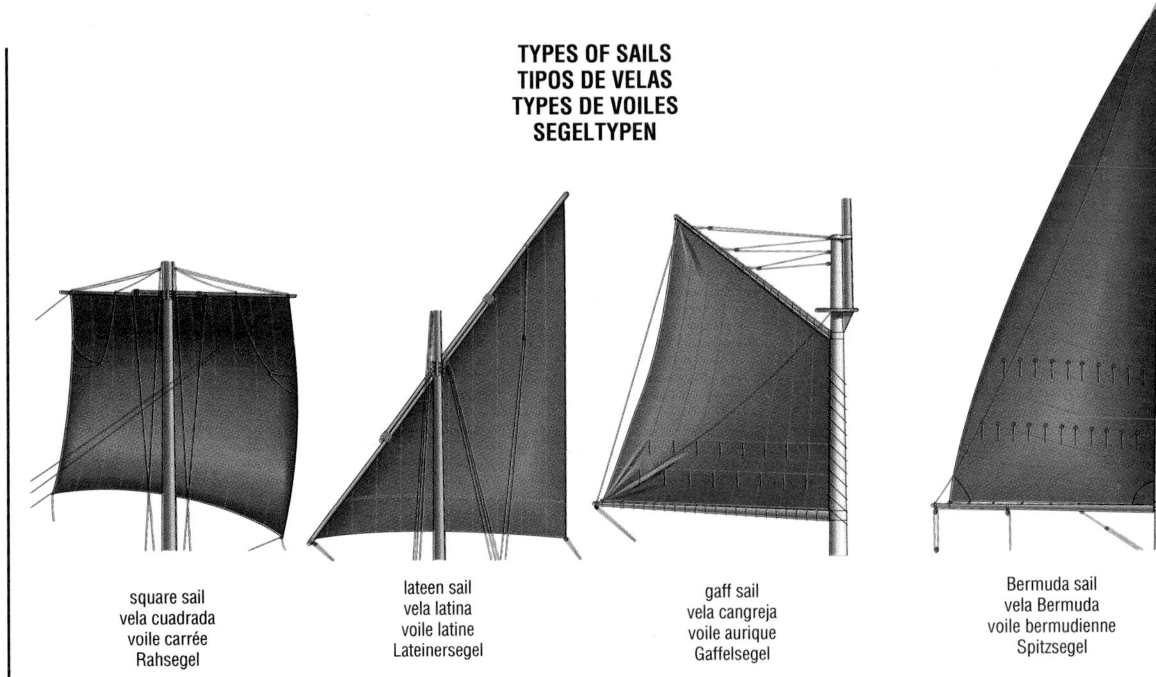

square sail
vela cuadrada
voile carrée
Rahsegel

lateen sail
vela latina
voile latine
Lateinersegel

gaff sail
vela cangreja
voile aurique
Gaffelsegel

Bermuda sail
vela Bermuda
voile bermudienne
Spitzsegel

TYPES OF RIGS
TIPOS DE APAREJOS
TYPES DE GRÉEMENTS
ARTEN DER TAKELUNG

whale boat
ballenera
baleinière
Walboot

brigantine
bergantín goleta
brigantin
Brigantine

ketch
queche
ketch
Ketsch

Marconi cutter
cúter Marconi
cotre Marconi
Marconikutter

brig
bergantín
brick
Brigg

schooner
goleta
goélette
Schoner

ANCHOR
ANCLA
ANCRE
ANKER

SHIP'S ANCHOR
ANCLA DE BUQUE
ANCRE DE MARINE
SCHIFFSANKER

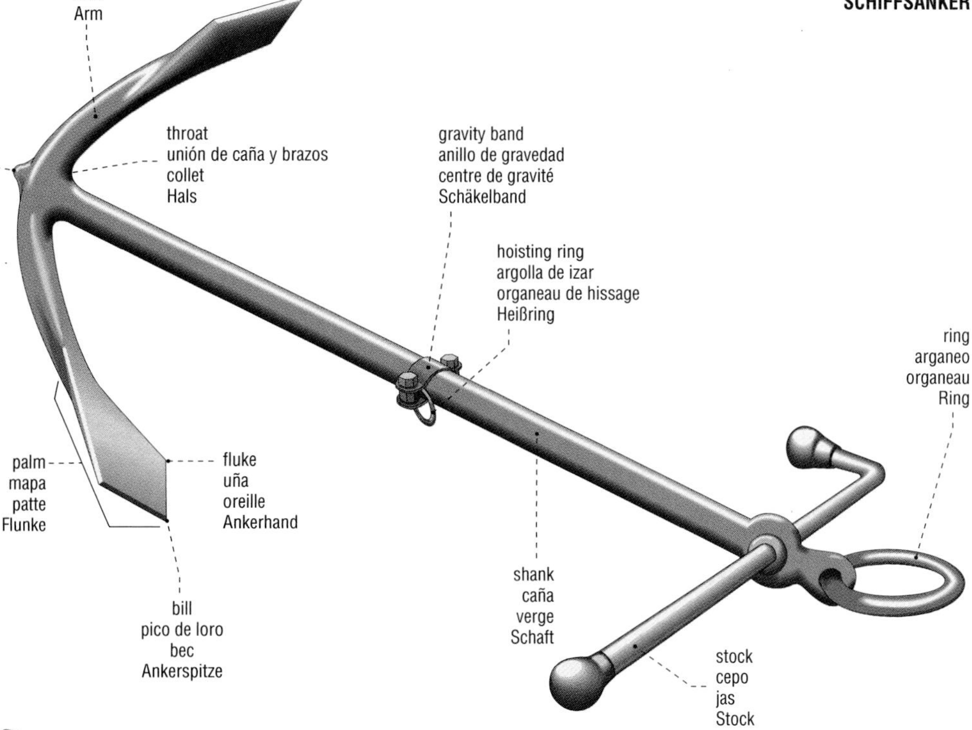

arm
brazo
bras
Arm

crown
cruz
diamant
Kreuz

throat
unión de caña y brazos
collet
Hals

gravity band
anillo de gravedad
centre de gravité
Schäkelband

hoisting ring
argolla de izar
organeau de hissage
Heißring

ring
arganeo
organeau
Ring

palm
mapa
patte
Flunke

fluke
uña
oreille
Ankerhand

bill
pico de loro
bec
Ankerspitze

shank
caña
verge
Schaft

stock
cepo
jas
Stock

TYPES OF ANCHORS
TIPOS DE ANCLAS
TYPES D'ANCRES
ANKERARTEN

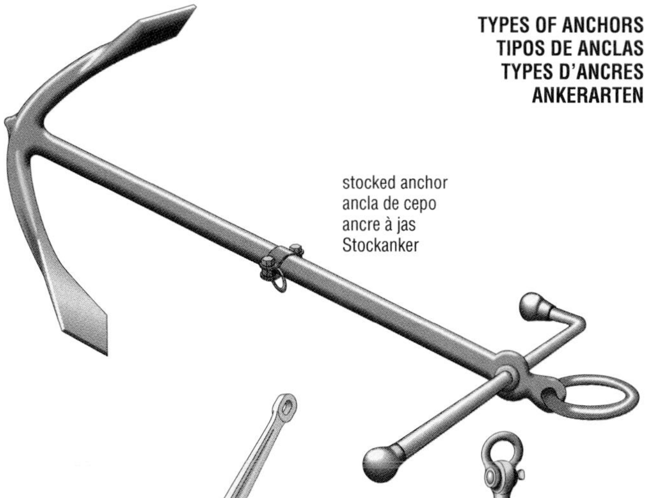

stocked anchor
ancla de cepo
ancre à jas
Stockanker

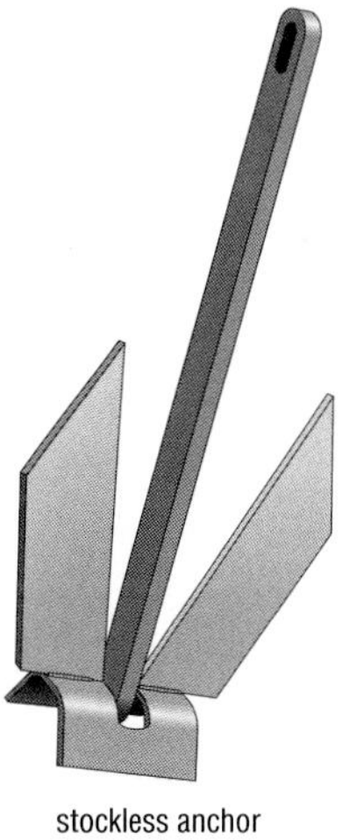

stockless anchor
ancla sin cepo
ancre sans jas
Patentanker

mushroom anchor
ancla de hongo
ancre à champignon
Pilzanker

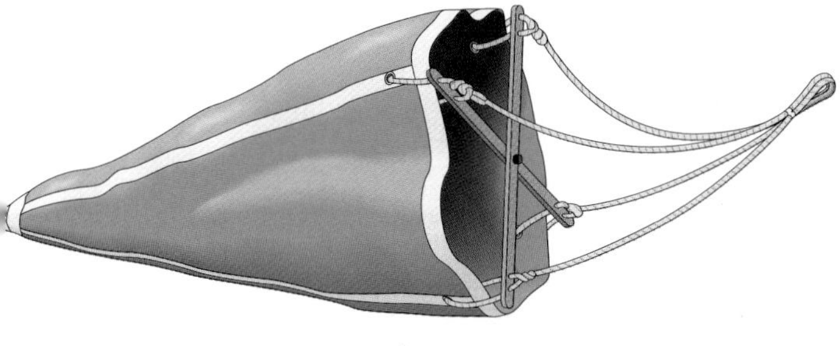

sea anchor
ancla flotante
ancre flottante
Treibanker

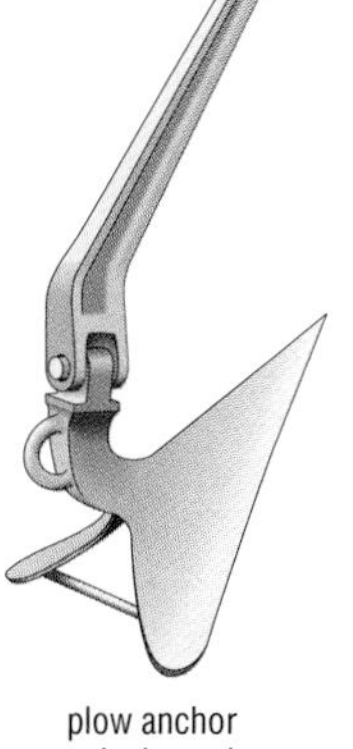

plow anchor
ancla de arado
ancre charrue
Pfluganker

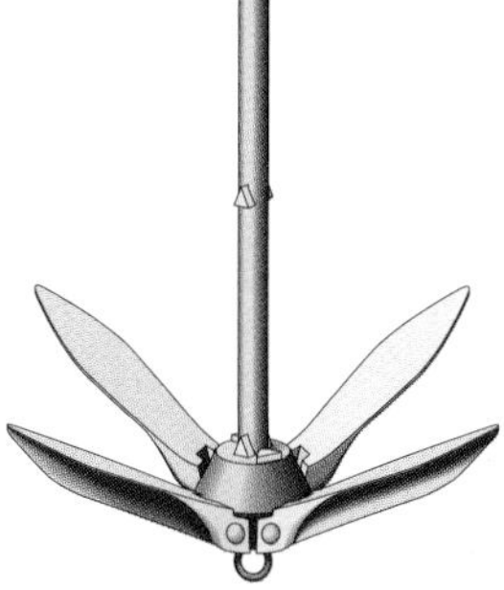

grapnel
anclote
grappin
Draggen

NAVIGATION DEVICES
APARATOS DE NAVEGACIÓN
APPAREILS DE NAVIGATION
NAVIGATIONSINSTRUMENTE

SEXTANT
SEXTANTE
SEXTANT
SEXTANT

LIQUID COMPASS
BRÚJULA LÍQUIDA
COMPAS MAGNÉTIQUE LIQUIDE
FLÜSSIGKEITSKOMPASS

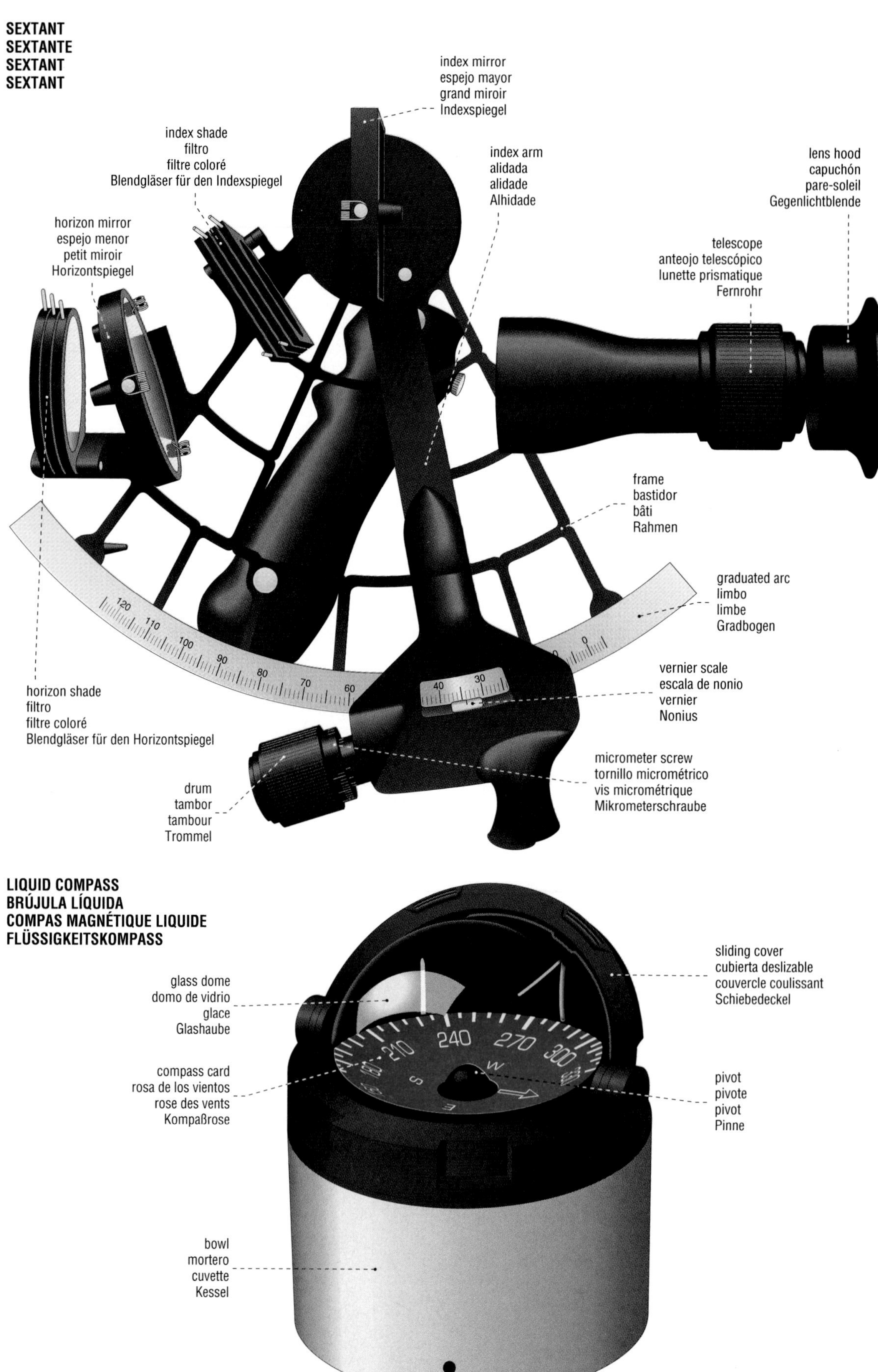
index mirror
espejo mayor
grand miroir
Indexspiegel
index shade
filtro
filtre coloré
Blendgläser für den Indexspiegel
index arm
alidada
alidade
Alhidade
lens hood
capuchón
pare-soleil
Gegenlichtblende
horizon mirror
espejo menor
petit miroir
Horizontspiegel
telescope
anteojo telescópico
lunette prismatique
Fernrohr
frame
bastidor
bâti
Rahmen
graduated arc
limbo
limbe
Gradbogen
horizon shade
filtro
filtre coloré
Blendgläser für den Horizontspiegel
vernier scale
escala de nonio
vernier
Nonius
micrometer screw
tornillo micrométrico
vis micrométrique
Mikrometerschraube
drum
tambor
tambour
Trommel
glass dome
domo de vidrio
glace
Glashaube
sliding cover
cubierta deslizable
couvercle coulissant
Schiebedeckel
compass card
rosa de los vientos
rose des vents
Kompaßrose
pivot
pivote
pivot
Pinne
bowl
mortero
cuvette
Kessel

ECHO SOUNDER
SONAR
SONDEUR À ÉCLATS
ECHOLOT

ECHO SOUNDER PROBE
SONDA
SONDE
SCHWINGER

CROSS SECTION OF A LIQUID COMPASS
CORTE TRANSVERSAL DE UNA BRÚJULA LÍQUIDA
COUPE D'UN COMPAS MAGNÉTIQUE LIQUIDE
QUERSCHNITT DURCH EINEN FLÜSSIGKEITSKOMPASS

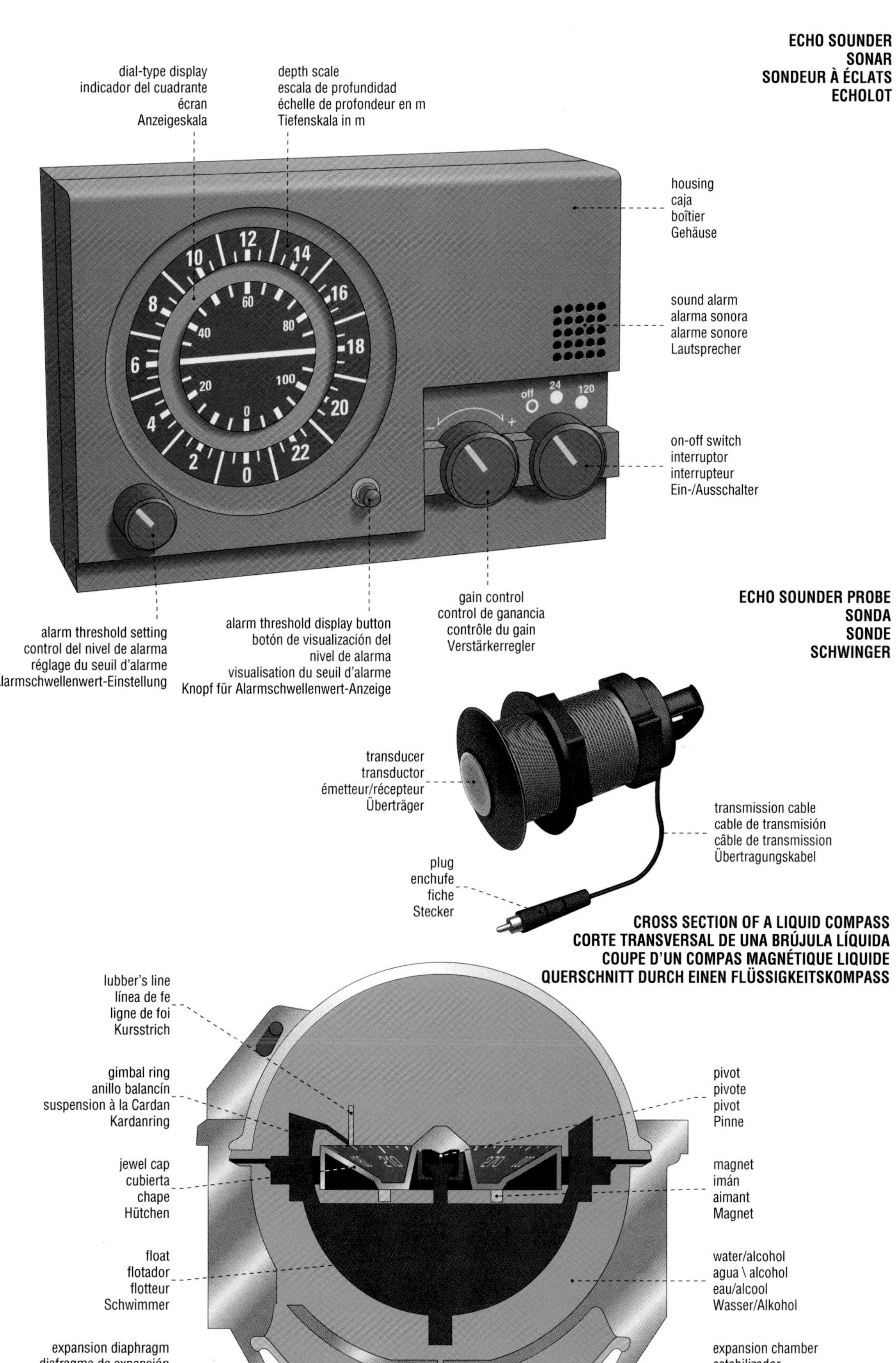
dial-type display
indicador del cuadrante
écran
Anzeigeskala
depth scale
escala de profundidad
échelle de profondeur en m
Tiefenskala in m
housing
caja
boîtier
Gehäuse
sound alarm
alarma sonora
alarme sonore
Lautsprecher
on-off switch
interruptor
interrupteur
Ein-/Ausschalter
gain control
control de ganancia
contrôle du gain
Verstärkerregler
alarm threshold setting
control del nivel de alarma
réglage du seuil d'alarme
Alarmschwellenwert-Einstellung
alarm threshold display button
botón de visualización del
nivel de alarma
visualisation du seuil d'alarme
Knopf für Alarmschwellenwert-Anzeige
transducer
transductor
émetteur/récepteur
Überträger
transmission cable
cable de transmisión
câble de transmission
Übertragungskabel
plug
enchufe
fiche
Stecker
lubber's line
línea de fe
ligne de foi
Kursstrich
gimbal ring
anillo balancín
suspension à la Cardan
Kardanring
jewel cap
cubierta
chape
Hütchen
float
flotador
flotteur
Schwimmer
expansion diaphragm
diafragma de expansión
diaphragme de dilatation
Ausdehnungsmembran
pivot
pivote
pivot
Pinne
magnet
imán
aimant
Magnet
water/alcohol
agua \ alcohol
eau/alcool
Wasser/Alkohol
expansion chamber
estabilizador
chambre de dilatation
Ausdehnungskammer

MARITIME SIGNALS
SEÑALES MARÍTIMAS
SIGNALISATION MARITIME
SEEZEICHEN

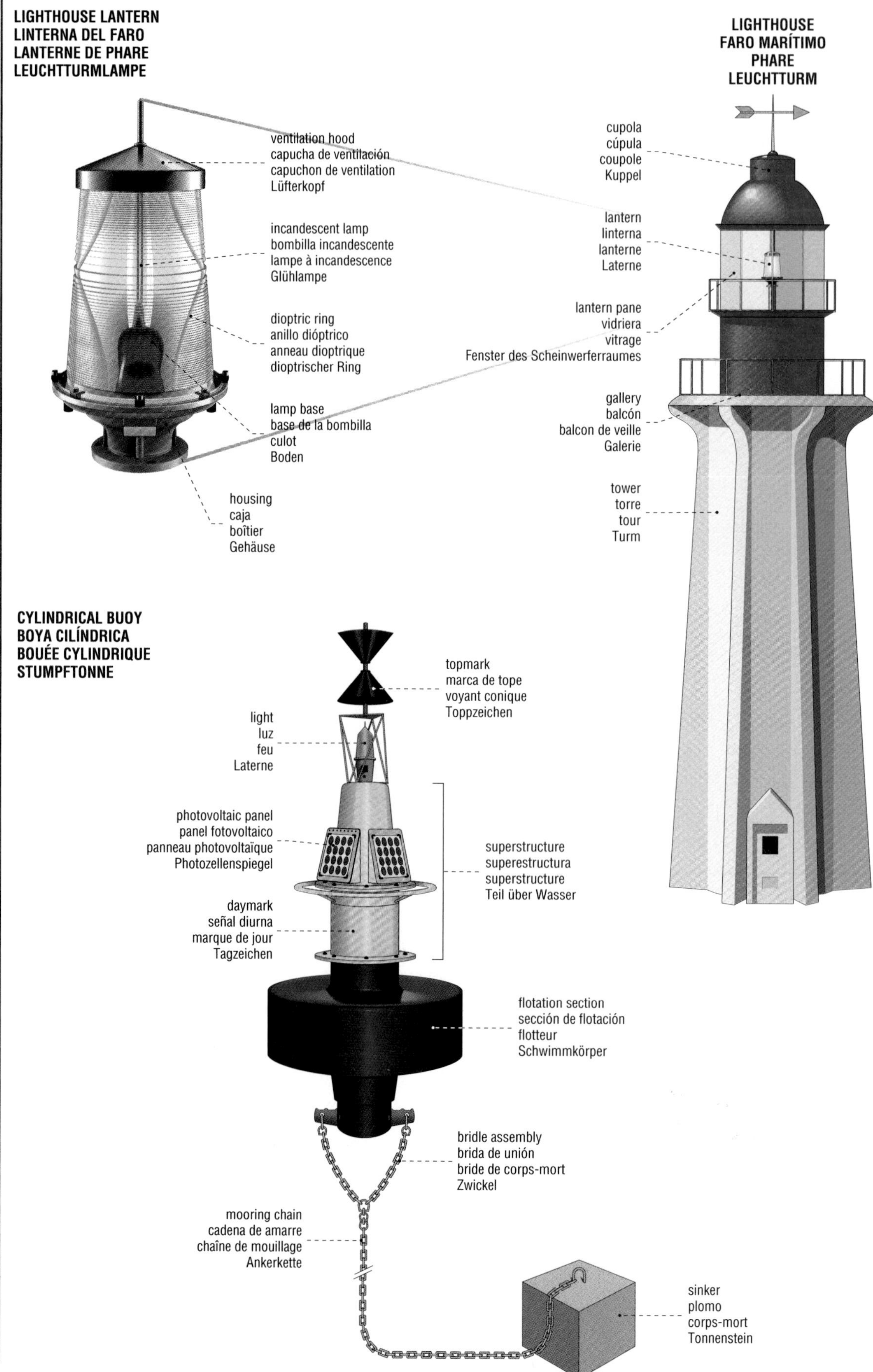
LIGHTHOUSE LANTERN
LINTERNA DEL FARO
LANTERNE DE PHARE
LEUCHTTURMLAMPE
ventilation hood
capucha de ventilación
capuchon de ventilation
Lüfterkopf
incandescent lamp
bombilla incandescente
lampe à incandescence
Glühlampe
dioptric ring
anillo dióptrico
anneau dioptrique
dioptrischer Ring
lamp base
base de la bombilla
culot
Boden
housing
caja
boîtier
Gehäuse
LIGHTHOUSE
FARO MARÍTIMO
PHARE
LEUCHTTURM
cupola
cúpula
coupole
Kuppel
lantern
linterna
lanterne
Laterne
lantern pane
vidriera
vitrage
Fenster des Scheinwerferraumes
gallery
balcón
balcon de veille
Galerie
tower
torre
tour
Turm
CYLINDRICAL BUOY
BOYA CILÍNDRICA
BOUÉE CYLINDRIQUE
STUMPFTONNE
topmark
marca de tope
voyant conique
Toppzeichen
light
luz
feu
Laterne
photovoltaic panel
panel fotovoltaico
panneau photovoltaïque
Photozellenspiegel
superstructure
superestructura
superstructure
Teil über Wasser
daymark
señal diurna
marque de jour
Tagzeichen
flotation section
sección de flotación
flotteur
Schwimmkörper
bridle assembly
brida de unión
bride de corps-mort
Zwickel
mooring chain
cadena de amarre
chaîne de mouillage
Ankerkette
sinker
plomo
corps-mort
Tonnenstein

HIGH FOCAL PLANE BUOY
BOYA DE PLANO FOCAL ELEVADO
BOUÉE À PLAN FOCAL ÉLEVÉ
GROSSTONNE

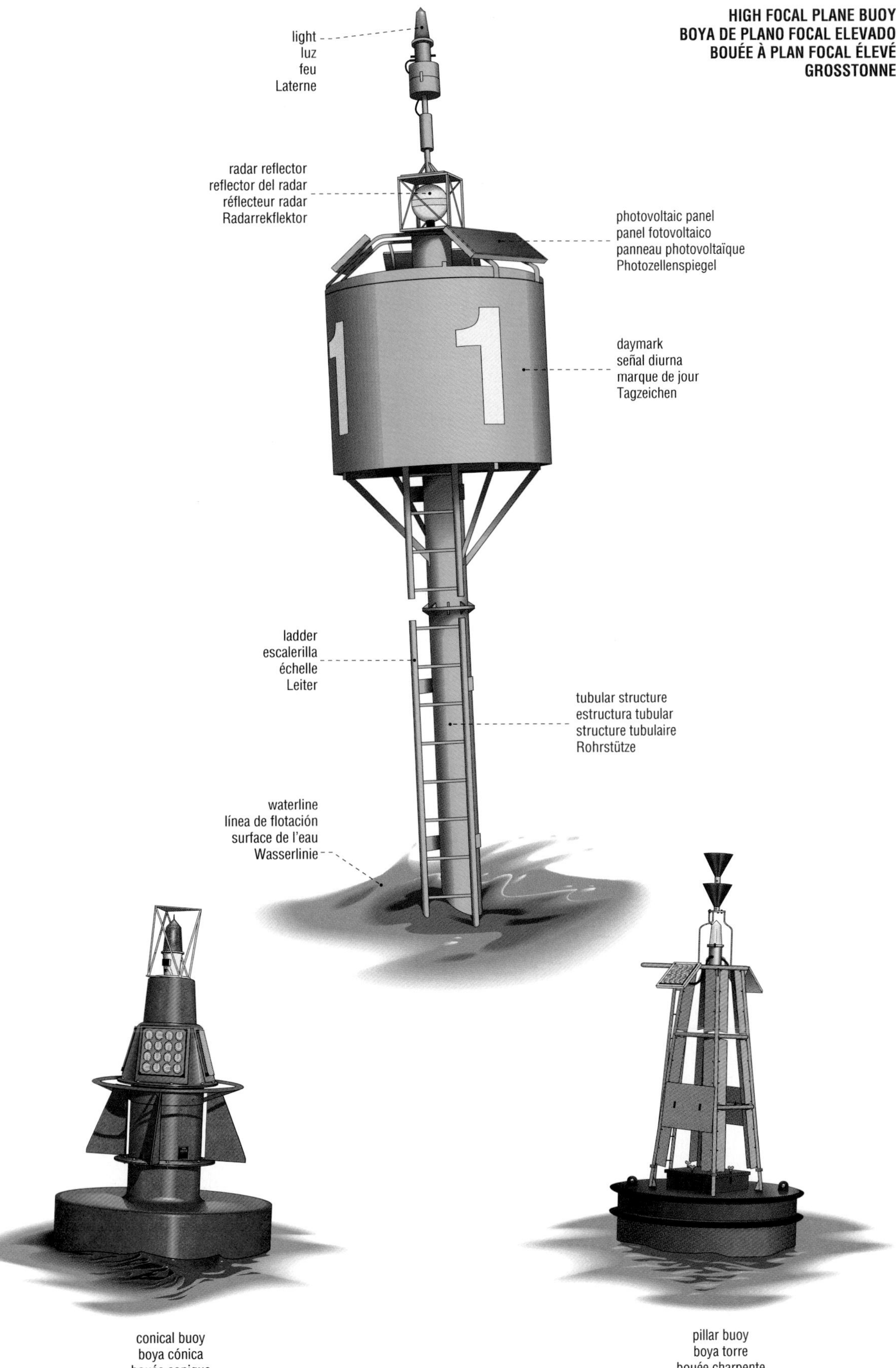
light
luz
feu
Laterne
radar reflector
reflector del radar
réflecteur radar
Radarrekflektor
photovoltaic panel
panel fotovoltaico
panneau photovoltaïque
Photozellenspiegel
daymark
señal diurna
marque de jour
Tagzeichen
ladder
escalerilla
échelle
Leiter
tubular structure
estructura tubular
structure tubulaire
Rohrstütze
waterline
línea de flotación
surface de l'eau
Wasserlinie

conical buoy
boya cónica
bouée conique
Spitztonne

pillar buoy
boya torre
bouée charpente
Spierentonne

MARITIME BUOYAGE SYSTEM
SISTEMA DE BOYAS MARITIMAS
SYSTÈME DE BALISAGE MARITIME
BETONNUNGSSYSTEM

CARDINAL MARKS
SEÑALES DE LOS PUNTOS CARDINALES
MARQUES CARDINALES
KARDINALSEEZEICHEN

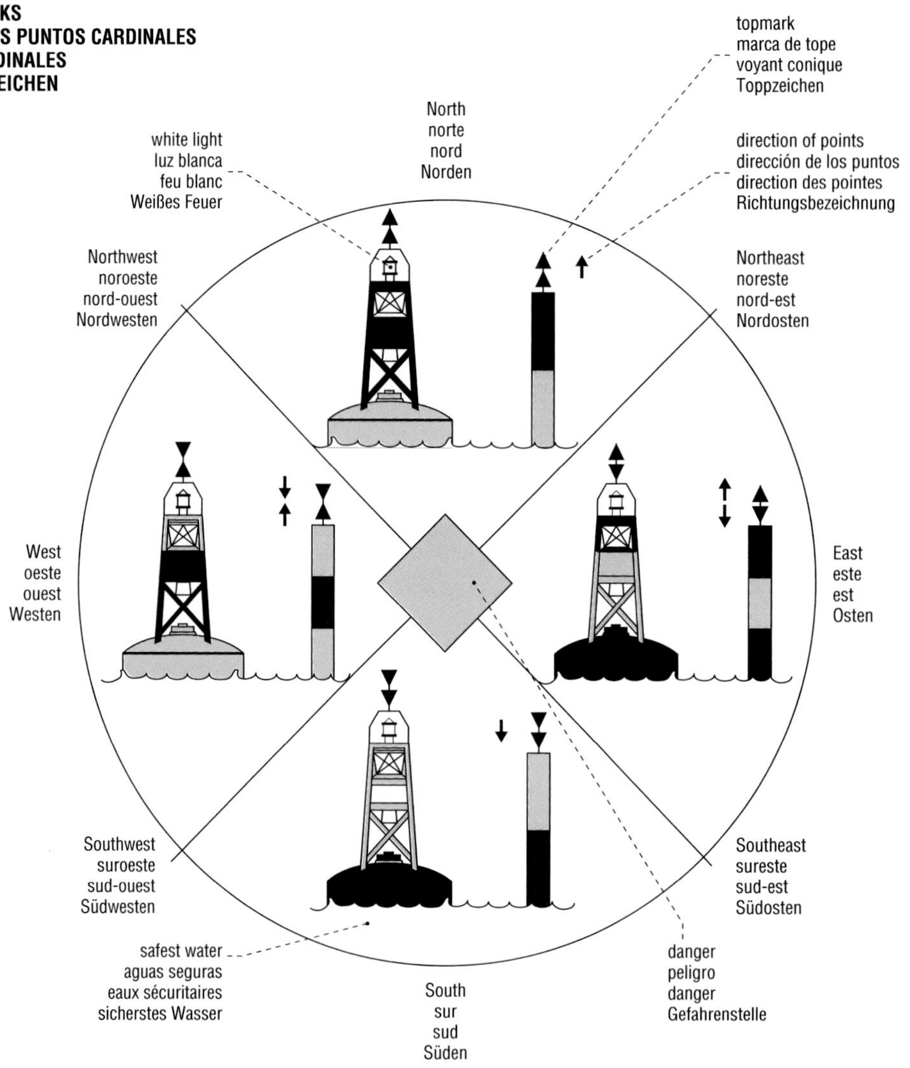

topmark
marca de tope
voyant conique
Toppzeichen

North
norte
nord
Norden

white light
luz blanca
feu blanc
Weißes Feuer

direction of points
dirección de los puntos
direction des pointes
Richtungsbezeichnung

Northwest
noroeste
nord-ouest
Nordwesten

Northeast
noreste
nord-est
Nordosten

West
oeste
ouest
Westen

East
este
est
Osten

Southwest
suroeste
sud-ouest
Südwesten

Southeast
sureste
sud-est
Südosten

safest water
aguas seguras
eaux sécuritaires
sicherstes Wasser

South
sur
sud
Süden

danger
peligro
danger
Gefahrenstelle

BUOYAGE REGIONS
REGIONES DE BOYAS
RÉGIONS DE BALISAGE
BETONNTE FAHRWASSER

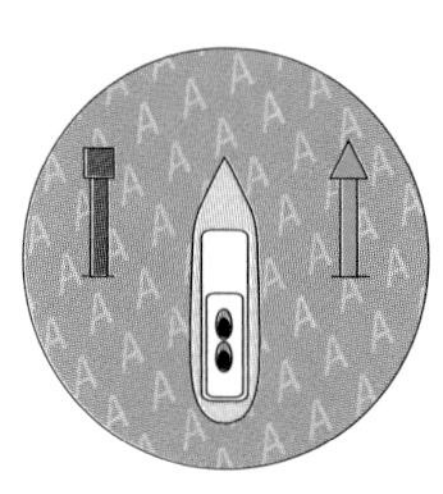

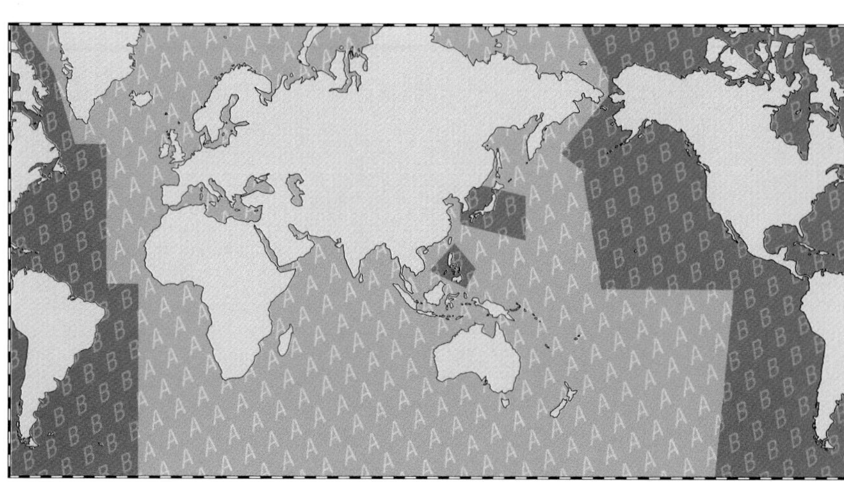

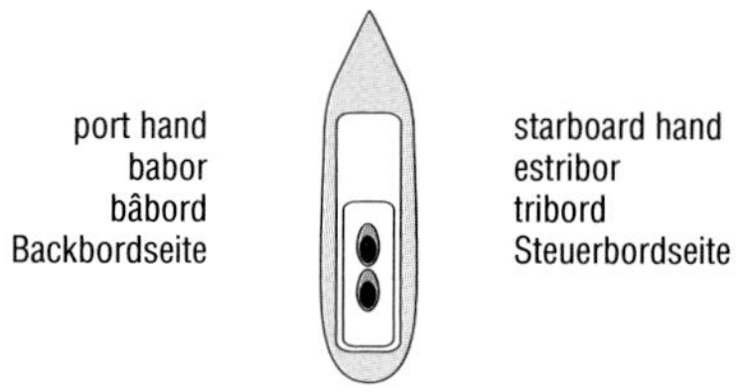

port hand
babor
bâbord
Backbordseite

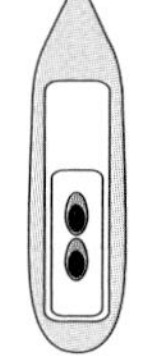

starboard hand
estribor
tribord
Steuerbordseite

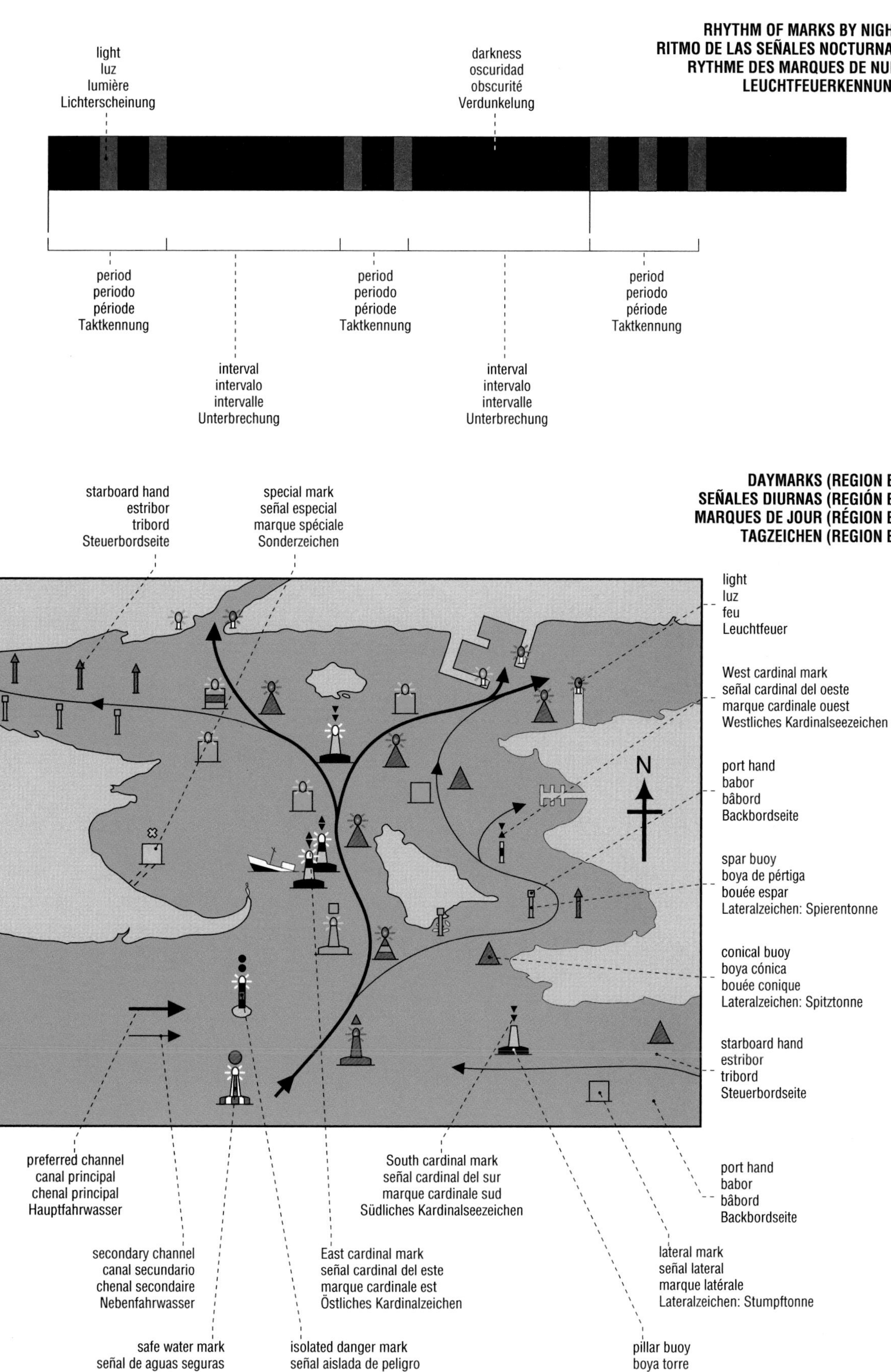
RHYTHM OF MARKS BY NIGHT
RITMO DE LAS SEÑALES NOCTURNAS
RYTHME DES MARQUES DE NUIT
LEUCHTFEUERKENNUNG
light
luz
lumière
Lichterscheinung
darkness
oscuridad
obscurité
Verdunkelung
period
periodo
période
Taktkennung
interval
intervalo
intervalle
Unterbrechung
period
periodo
période
Taktkennung
interval
intervalo
intervalle
Unterbrechung
period
periodo
période
Taktkennung
DAYMARKS (REGION B)
SEÑALES DIURNAS (REGIÓN B)
MARQUES DE JOUR (RÉGION B)
TAGZEICHEN (REGION B)
starboard hand
estribor
tribord
Steuerbordseite
special mark
señal especial
marque spéciale
Sonderzeichen
light
luz
feu
Leuchtfeuer
West cardinal mark
señal cardinal del oeste
marque cardinale ouest
Westliches Kardinalseezeichen
N
port hand
babor
bâbord
Backbordseite
spar buoy
boya de pértiga
bouée espar
Lateralzeichen: Spierentonne
conical buoy
boya cónica
bouée conique
Lateralzeichen: Spitztonne
starboard hand
estribor
tribord
Steuerbordseite
preferred channel
canal principal
chenal principal
Hauptfahrwasser
South cardinal mark
señal cardinal del sur
marque cardinale sud
Südliches Kardinalseezeichen
port hand
babor
bâbord
Backbordseite
secondary channel
canal secundario
chenal secondaire
Nebenfahrwasser
East cardinal mark
señal cardinal del este
marque cardinale est
Östliches Kardinalzeichen
lateral mark
señal lateral
marque latérale
Lateralzeichen: Stumpftonne
safe water mark
señal de aguas seguras
marque d'eaux sécuritaires
Fahrwassermitte
isolated danger mark
señal aislada de peligro
marque de danger isolé
Einzelgefahrenzeichen
pillar buoy
boya torre
bouée charpente
Lateralzeichen: Spierentonne

HARBOR
PUERTO
PORT MARITIME
HAFEN

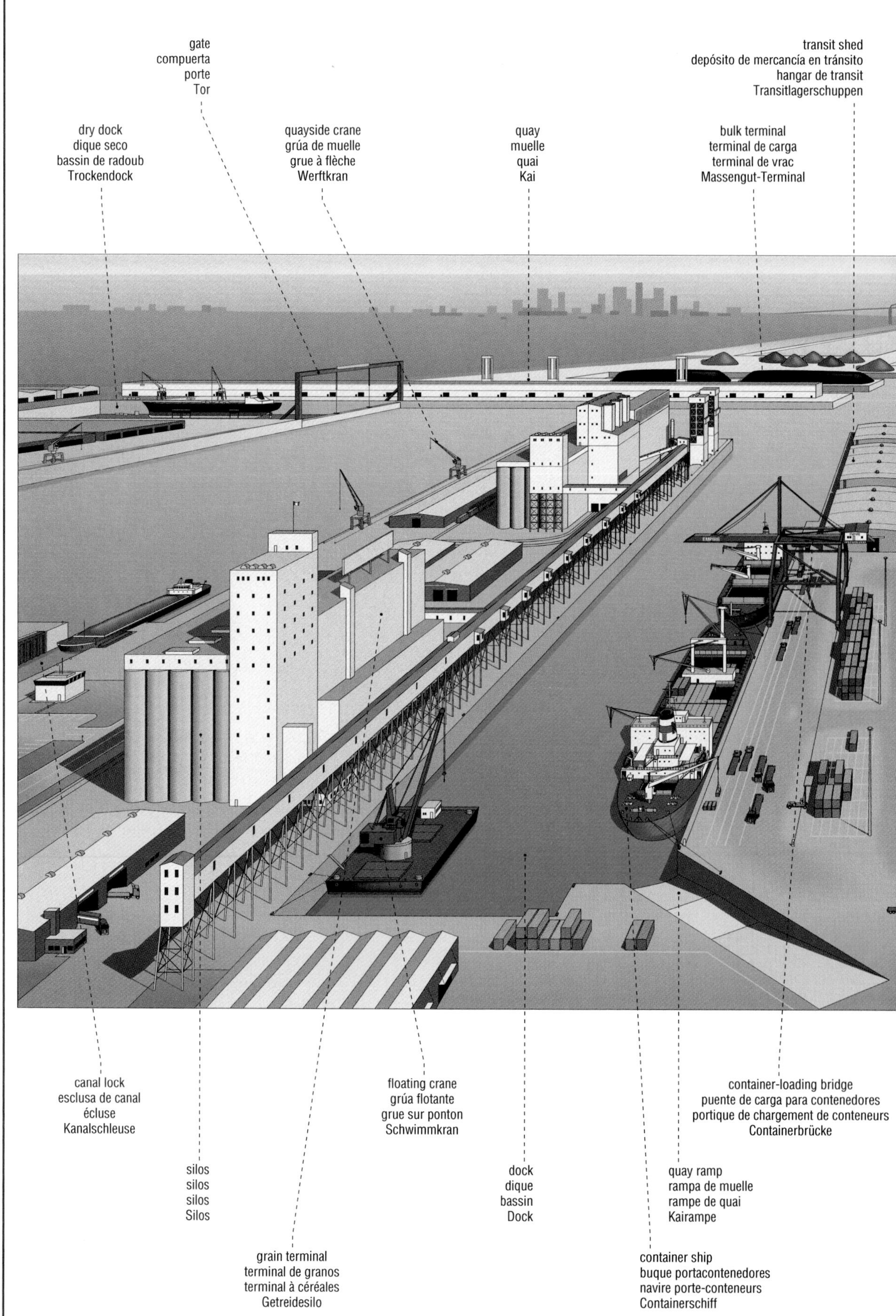

gate
compuerta
porte
Tor
transit shed
depósito de mercancía en tránsito
hangar de transit
Transitlagerschuppen
dry dock
dique seco
bassin de radoub
Trockendock
quayside crane
grúa de muelle
grue à flèche
Werftkran
quay
muelle
quai
Kai
bulk terminal
terminal de carga
terminal de vrac
Massengut-Terminal
EMPIRE
canal lock
esclusa de canal
écluse
Kanalschleuse
floating crane
grúa flotante
grue sur ponton
Schwimmkran
container-loading bridge
puente de carga para contenedores
portique de chargement de conteneurs
Containerbrücke
silos
silos
silos
Silos
dock
dique
bassin
Dock
quay ramp
rampa de muelle
rampe de quai
Kairampe
grain terminal
terminal de granos
terminal à céréales
Getreidesilo
container ship
buque portacontenedores
navire porte-conteneurs
Containerschiff

cold shed
cámara frigorífica
entrepôt frigorifique
Kühlhaus
ferryboat
transbordador
transbordeur
Hafenfähre
tanker
buque cisterna
pétrolier
Tanker
lighthouse
faro
phare
Leuchtturm
passenger terminal
terminal de pasajeros
gare maritime
Fahrgastanlage
oil terminal
terminal de petróleo
terminal pétrolier
Öllöschbrücke
quayside railway
ferrocarril de muelle
voie ferrée bord à quai
Hafenbahn
road transport
transporte terrestre
transport routier
Straßengüterverkehr
customs house
aduana
bureau des douanes
Hafenzollamt
bridge
puente
portique
Brücke
office building
oficina del puerto
bâtiment administratif
Bürogebäude
container terminal
depósito de contenedores
terminal à conteneurs
Containerterminal
parking lot
estacionamiento
parking
Parkplatz

CANAL LOCK
ESCLUSA DE CANAL
ÉCLUSE
KANALSCHLEUSE

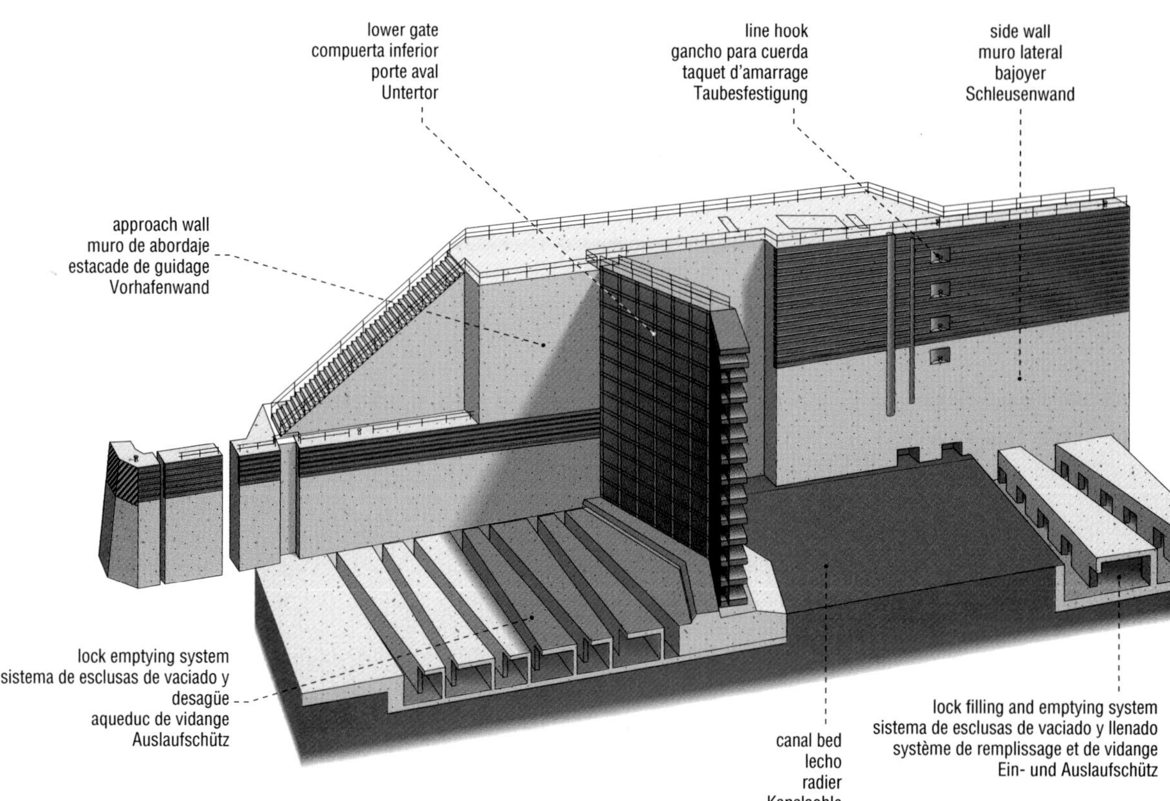

lower gate
compuerta inferior
porte aval
Untertor
line hook
gancho para cuerda
taquet d'amarrage
Taubesfestigung
side wall
muro lateral
bajoyer
Schleusenwand
approach wall
muro de abordaje
estacade de guidage
Vorhafenwand
lock emptying system
sistema de esclusas de vaciado y desagüe
aqueduc de vidange
Auslaufschütz
canal bed
lecho
radier
Kanalsohle
lock filling and emptying system
sistema de esclusas de vaciado y llenado
système de remplissage et de vidange
Ein- und Auslaufschütz

HOVERCRAFT
AERODESLIZADOR (HOVERCRAFT)
AÉROGLISSEUR
LUFTKISSENFAHRZEUG

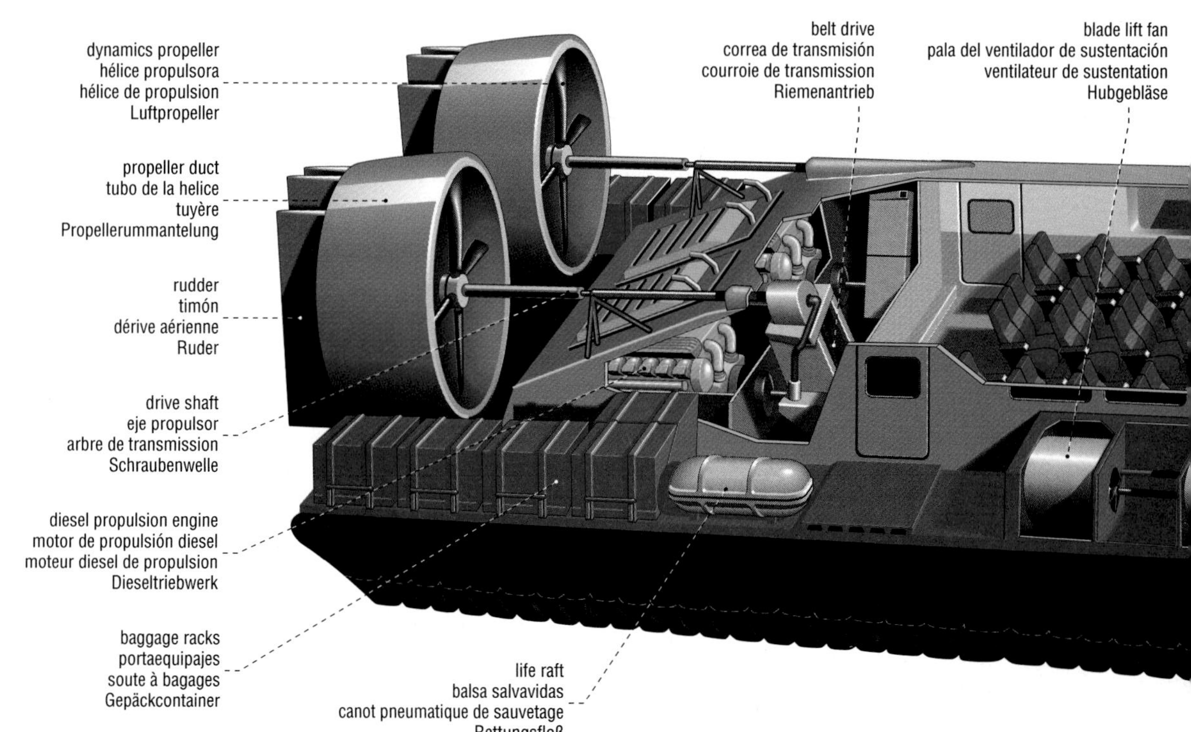

dynamics propeller
hélice propulsora
hélice de propulsion
Luftpropeller
belt drive
correa de transmisión
courroie de transmission
Riemenantrieb
blade lift fan
pala del ventilador de sustentación
ventilateur de sustentation
Hubgebläse
propeller duct
tubo de la helice
tuyère
Propellerummantelung
rudder
timón
dérive aérienne
Ruder
drive shaft
eje propulsor
arbre de transmission
Schraubenwelle
diesel propulsion engine
motor de propulsión diesel
moteur diesel de propulsion
Dieseltriebwerk
baggage racks
portaequipajes
soute à bagages
Gepäckcontainer
life raft
balsa salvavidas
canot pneumatique de sauvetage
Rettungsfloß

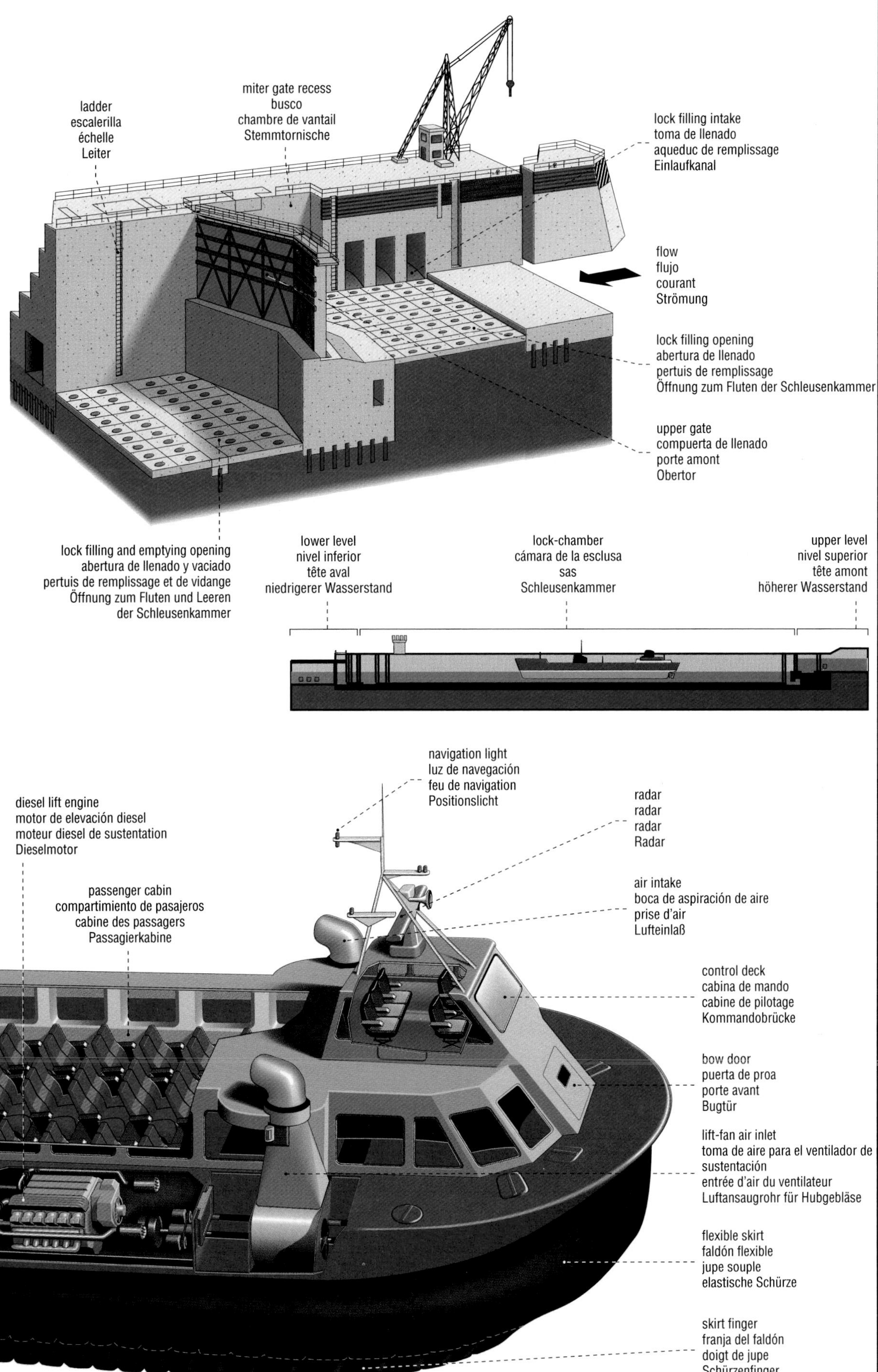
ladder
escalerilla
échelle
Leiter
miter gate recess
busco
chambre de vantail
Stemmtornische
lock filling intake
toma de llenado
aqueduc de remplissage
Einlaufkanal
flow
flujo
courant
Strömung
lock filling opening
abertura de llenado
pertuis de remplissage
Öffnung zum Fluten der Schleusenkammer
upper gate
compuerta de llenado
porte amont
Obertor
lock filling and emptying opening
abertura de llenado y vaciado
pertuis de remplissage et de vidange
Öffnung zum Fluten und Leeren
der Schleusenkammer
lower level
nivel inferior
tête aval
niedrigerer Wasserstand
lock-chamber
cámara de la esclusa
sas
Schleusenkammer
upper level
nivel superior
tête amont
höherer Wasserstand
navigation light
luz de navegación
feu de navigation
Positionslicht
diesel lift engine
motor de elevación diesel
moteur diesel de sustentation
Dieselmotor
radar
radar
radar
Radar
passenger cabin
compartimiento de pasajeros
cabine des passagers
Passagierkabine
air intake
boca de aspiración de aire
prise d'air
Lufteinlaß
control deck
cabina de mando
cabine de pilotage
Kommandobrücke
bow door
puerta de proa
porte avant
Bugtür
lift-fan air inlet
toma de aire para el ventilador de sustentación
entrée d'air du ventilateur
Luftansaugrohr für Hubgebläse
flexible skirt
faldón flexible
jupe souple
elastische Schürze
skirt finger
franja del faldón
doigt de jupe
Schürzenfinger

FERRY
TRANSBORDADOR
TRANSBORDEUR
FÄHRE

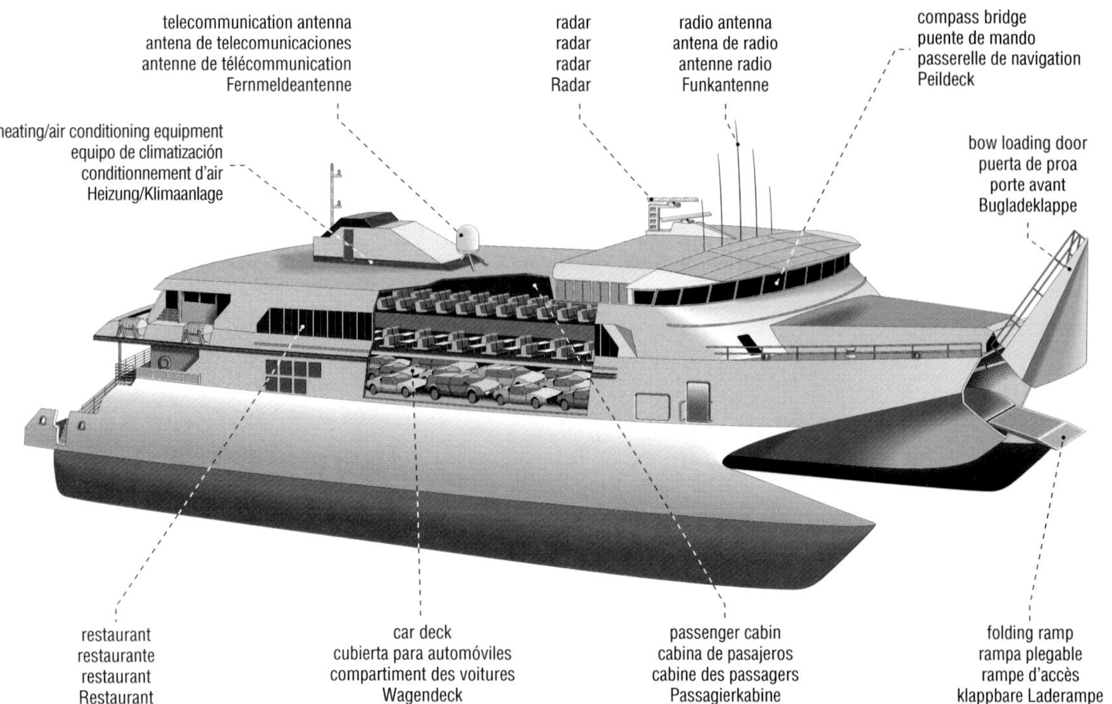
telecommunication antenna
antena de telecomunicaciones
antenne de télécommunication
Fernmeldeantenne
radar
radar
radar
Radar
radio antenna
antena de radio
antenne radio
Funkantenne
compass bridge
puente de mando
passerelle de navigation
Peildeck
heating/air conditioning equipment
equipo de climatización
conditionnement d'air
Heizung/Klimaanlage
bow loading door
puerta de proa
porte avant
Bugladeklappe
restaurant
restaurante
restaurant
Restaurant
car deck
cubierta para automóviles
compartiment des voitures
Wagendeck
passenger cabin
cabina de pasajeros
cabine des passagers
Passagierkabine
folding ramp
rampa plegable
rampe d'accès
klappbare Laderampe

CONTAINER SHIP
CARGUERO PORTACONTENEDORES
CARGO PORTE-CONTENEURS
CONTAINERSCHIFF

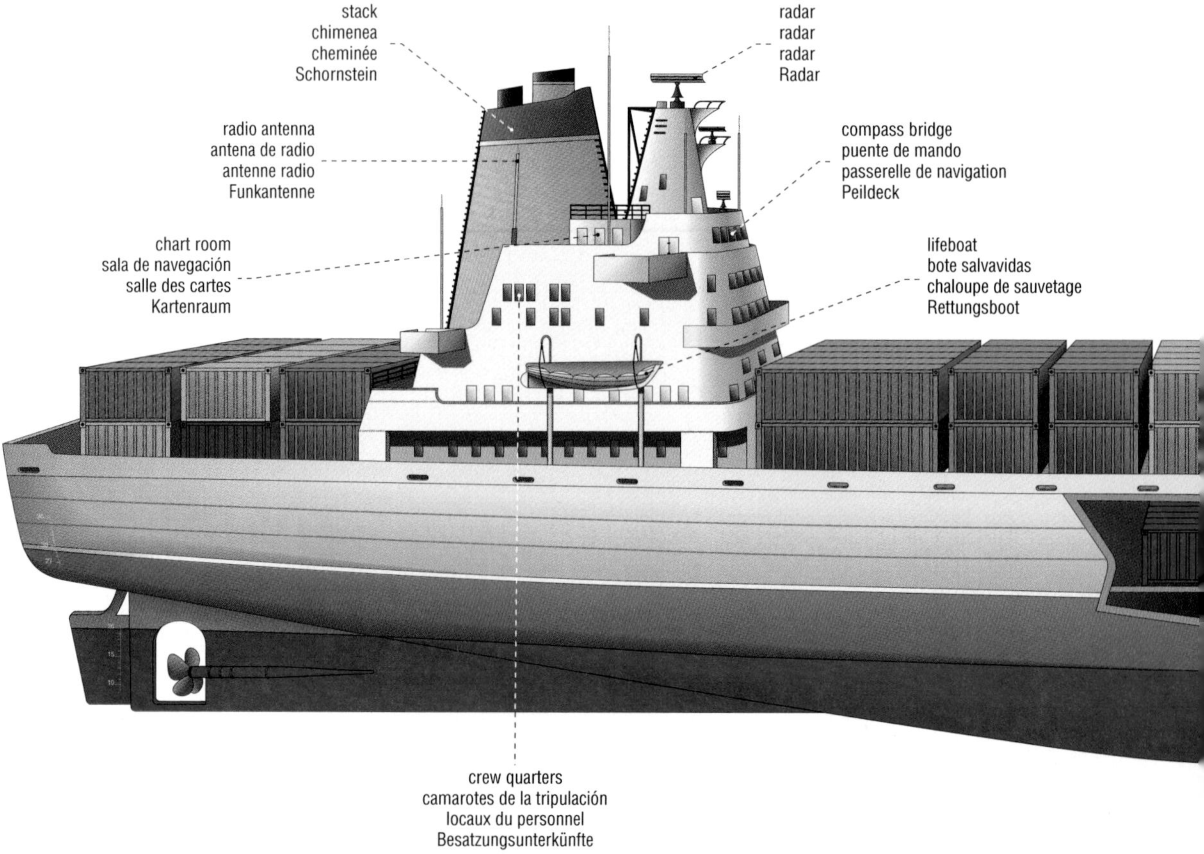

stack
chimenea
cheminée
Schornstein

radar
radar
radar
Radar

radio antenna
antena de radio
antenne radio
Funkantenne

compass bridge
puente de mando
passerelle de navigation
Peildeck

chart room
sala de navegación
salle des cartes
Kartenraum

lifeboat
bote salvavidas
chaloupe de sauvetage
Rettungsboot

crew quarters
camarotes de la tripulación
locaux du personnel
Besatzungsunterkünfte

HYDROFOIL BOAT
AERODESLIZADOR
HYDROPTÈRE
TRAGFLÜGELSCHIFF

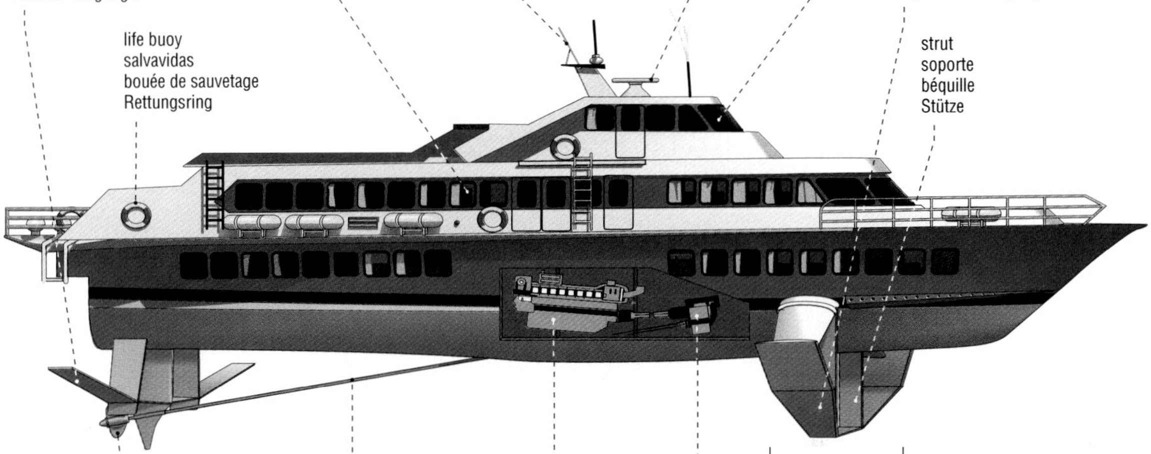

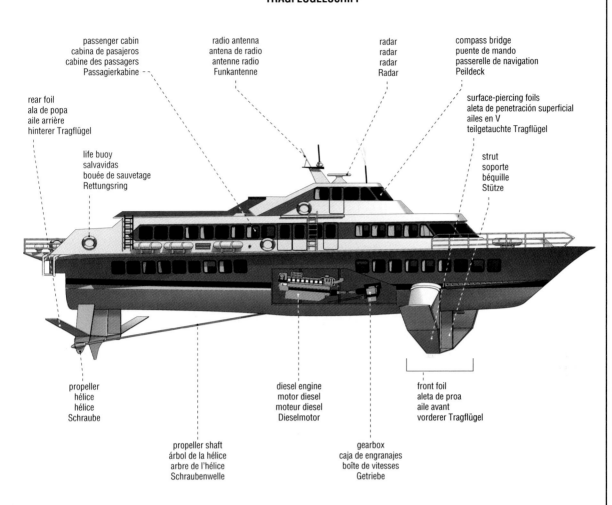

passenger cabin
cabina de pasajeros
cabine des passagers
Passagierkabine

radio antenna
antena de radio
antenne radio
Funkantenne

radar
radar
radar
Radar

compass bridge
puente de mando
passerelle de navigation
Peildeck

rear foil
ala de popa
aile arrière
hinterer Tragflügel

surface-piercing foils
aleta de penetración superficial
ailes en V
teilgetauchte Tragflügel

life buoy
salvavidas
bouée de sauvetage
Rettungsring

strut
soporte
béquille
Stütze

propeller
hélice
hélice
Schraube

diesel engine
motor diesel
moteur diesel
Dieselmotor

front foil
aleta de proa
aile avant
vorderer Tragflügel

propeller shaft
árbol de la hélice
arbre de l'hélice
Schraubenwelle

gearbox
caja de engranajes
boîte de vitesses
Getriebe

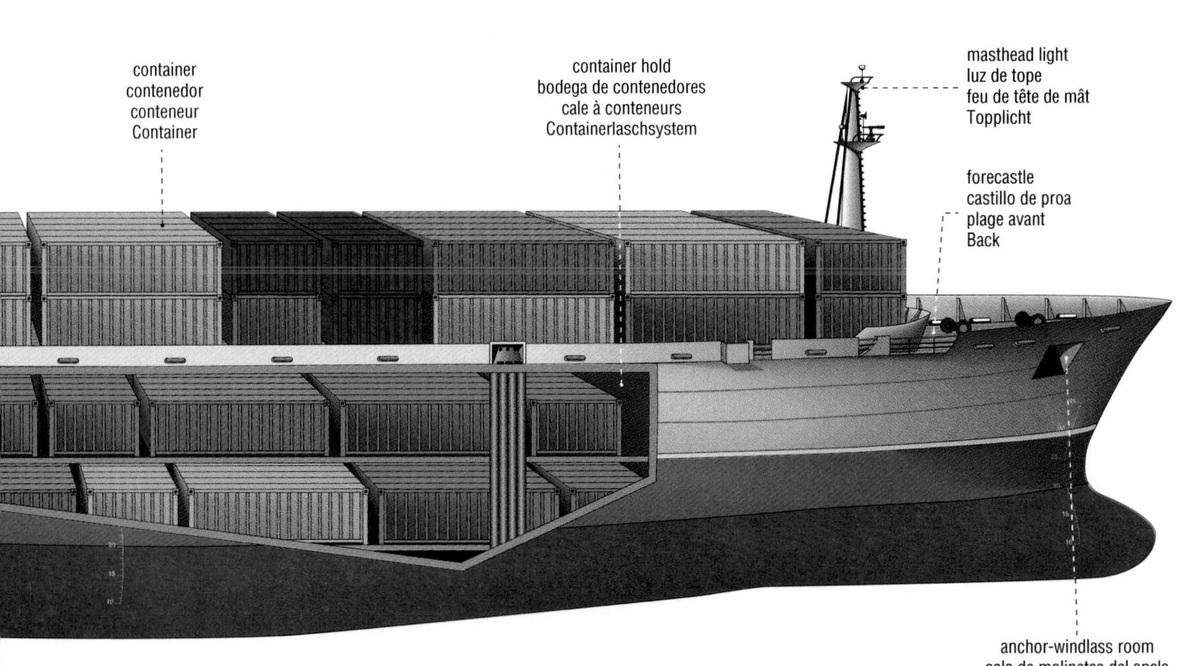
container
contenedor
conteneur
Container
container hold
bodega de contenedores
cale à conteneurs
Containerlaschsystem
masthead light
luz de tope
feu de tête de mât
Topplicht
forecastle
castillo de proa
plage avant
Back
anchor-windlass room
sala de molinetes del ancla
écubier
Ankerklüse

PASSENGER LINER
BUQUE TRASATLÁNTICO
PAQUEBOT
PASSAGIERDAMPFER

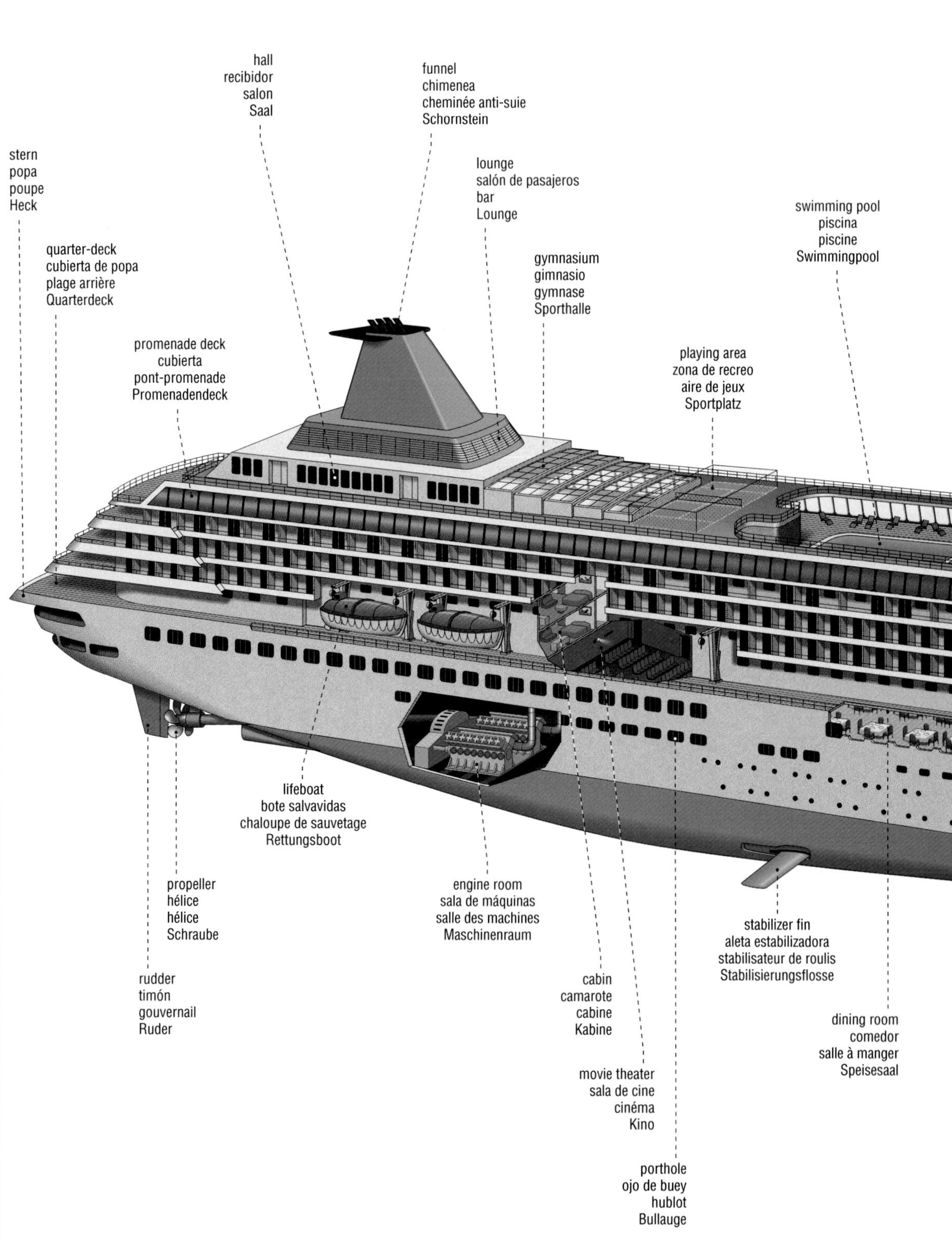
hall
recibidor
salon
Saal
funnel
chimenea
cheminée anti-suie
Schornstein
stern
popa
poupe
Heck
lounge
salón de pasajeros
bar
Lounge
swimming pool
piscina
piscine
Swimmingpool
quarter-deck
cubierta de popa
plage arrière
Quarterdeck
gymnasium
gimnasio
gymnase
Sporthalle
promenade deck
cubierta
pont-promenade
Promenadendeck
playing area
zona de recreo
aire de jeux
Sportplatz
lifeboat
bote salvavidas
chaloupe de sauvetage
Rettungsboot
propeller
hélice
hélice
Schraube
engine room
sala de máquinas
salle des machines
Maschinenraum
stabilizer fin
aleta estabilizadora
stabilisateur de roulis
Stabilisierungsflosse
rudder
timón
gouvernail
Ruder
cabin
camarote
cabine
Kabine
dining room
comedor
salle à manger
Speisesaal
movie theater
sala de cine
cinéma
Kino
porthole
ojo de buey
hublot
Bullauge

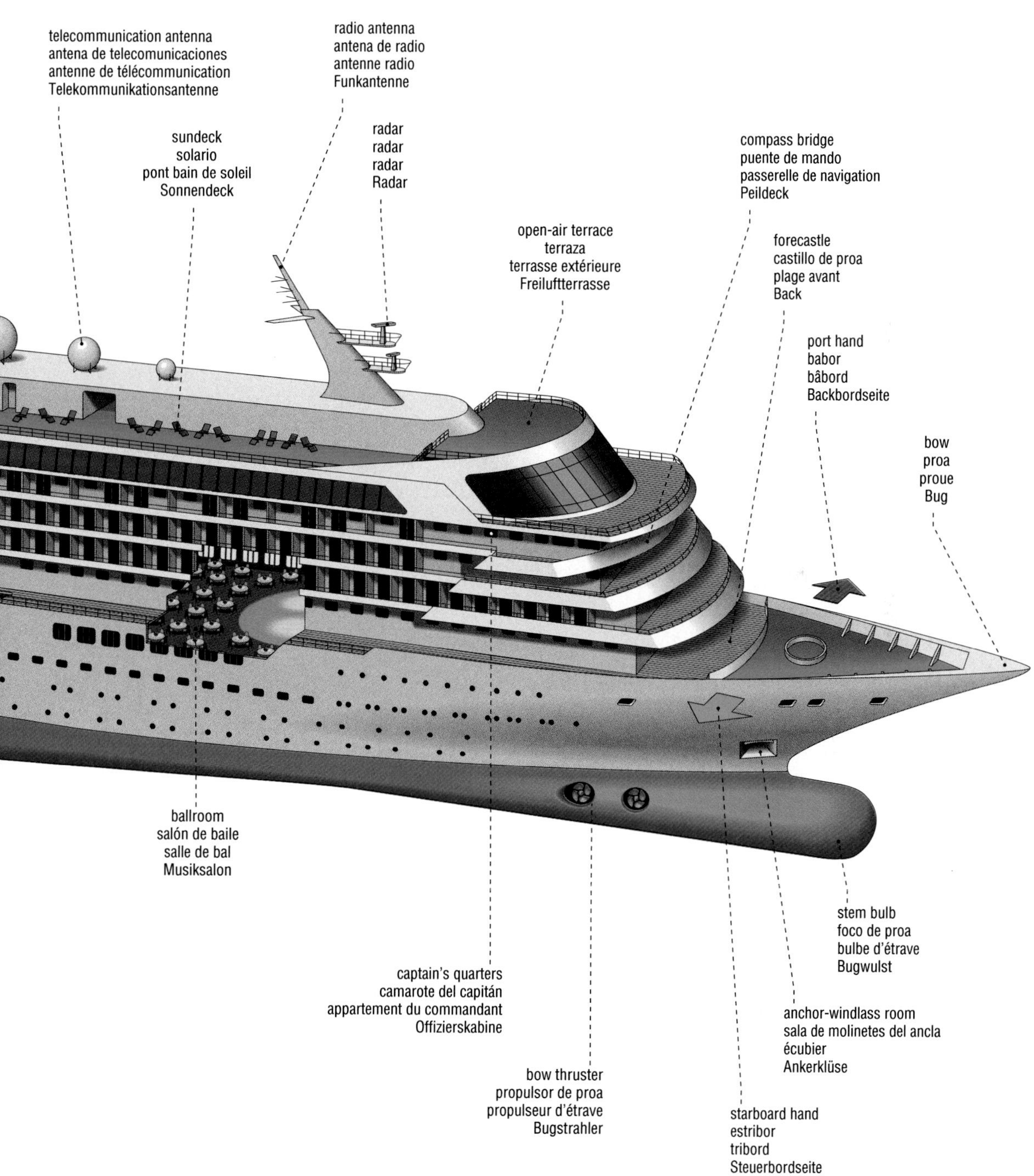
telecommunication antenna
antena de telecomunicaciones
antenne de télécommunication
Telekommunikationsantenne
radio antenna
antena de radio
antenne radio
Funkantenne
sundeck
solario
pont bain de soleil
Sonnendeck
radar
radar
radar
Radar
compass bridge
puente de mando
passerelle de navigation
Peildeck
open-air terrace
terraza
terrasse extérieure
Freiluftterrasse
forecastle
castillo de proa
plage avant
Back
port hand
babor
bâbord
Backbordseite
bow
proa
proue
Bug
ballroom
salón de baile
salle de bal
Musiksalon
stem bulb
foco de proa
bulbe d'étrave
Bugwulst
captain's quarters
camarote del capitán
appartement du commandant
Offizierskabine
anchor-windlass room
sala de molinetes del ancla
écubier
Ankerklüse
bow thruster
propulsor de proa
propulseur d'étrave
Bugstrahler
starboard hand
estribor
tribord
Steuerbordseite

LONG-RANGE JET
AVIÓN TURBORREACTOR DE PASAJEROS
AVION LONG-COURRIER
LANGSTRECKEN-DÜSENFLUGZEUG

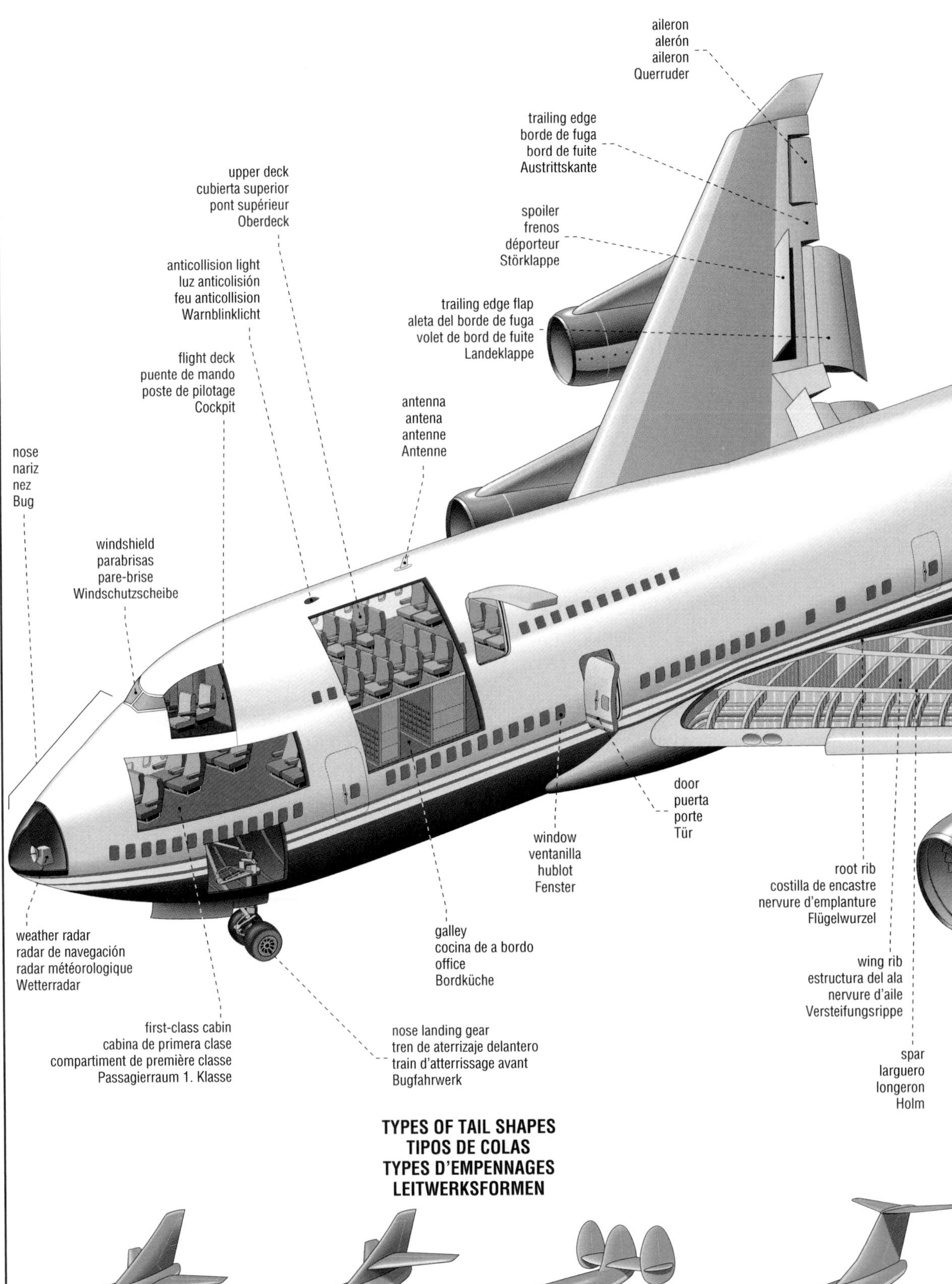
aileron
alerón
aileron
Querruder
trailing edge
borde de fuga
bord de fuite
Austrittskante
spoiler
frenos
déporteur
Störklappe
upper deck
cubierta superior
pont supérieur
Oberdeck
anticollision light
luz anticolisión
feu anticollision
Warnblinklicht
trailing edge flap
aleta del borde de fuga
volet de bord de fuite
Landeklappe
flight deck
puente de mando
poste de pilotage
Cockpit
antenna
antena
antenne
Antenne
nose
nariz
nez
Bug
windshield
parabrisas
pare-brise
Windschutzscheibe
door
puerta
porte
Tür
window
ventanilla
hublot
Fenster
root rib
costilla de encastre
nervure d'emplanture
Flügelwurzel
weather radar
radar de navegación
radar météorologique
Wetterradar
galley
cocina de a bordo
office
Bordküche
wing rib
estructura del ala
nervure d'aile
Versteifungsrippe
first-class cabin
cabina de primera clase
compartiment de première classe
Passagierraum 1. Klasse
nose landing gear
tren de aterrizaje delantero
train d'atterrissage avant
Bugfahrwerk
spar
larguero
longeron
Holm

TYPES OF TAIL SHAPES
TIPOS DE COLAS
TYPES D'EMPENNAGES
LEITWERKSFORMEN

fuselage mounted tail unit
guías normales
empennage bas
Rumpfleitwerk

fin-mounted tail unit
unidad cruciforme
empennage surélevé
Flossenleitwerk

triple tail unit
triple plano vertical
stabilisateur à triple plan vertical
Dreifachleitwerk

T-tail unit
guías en T
empennage en T
T-Leitwerk

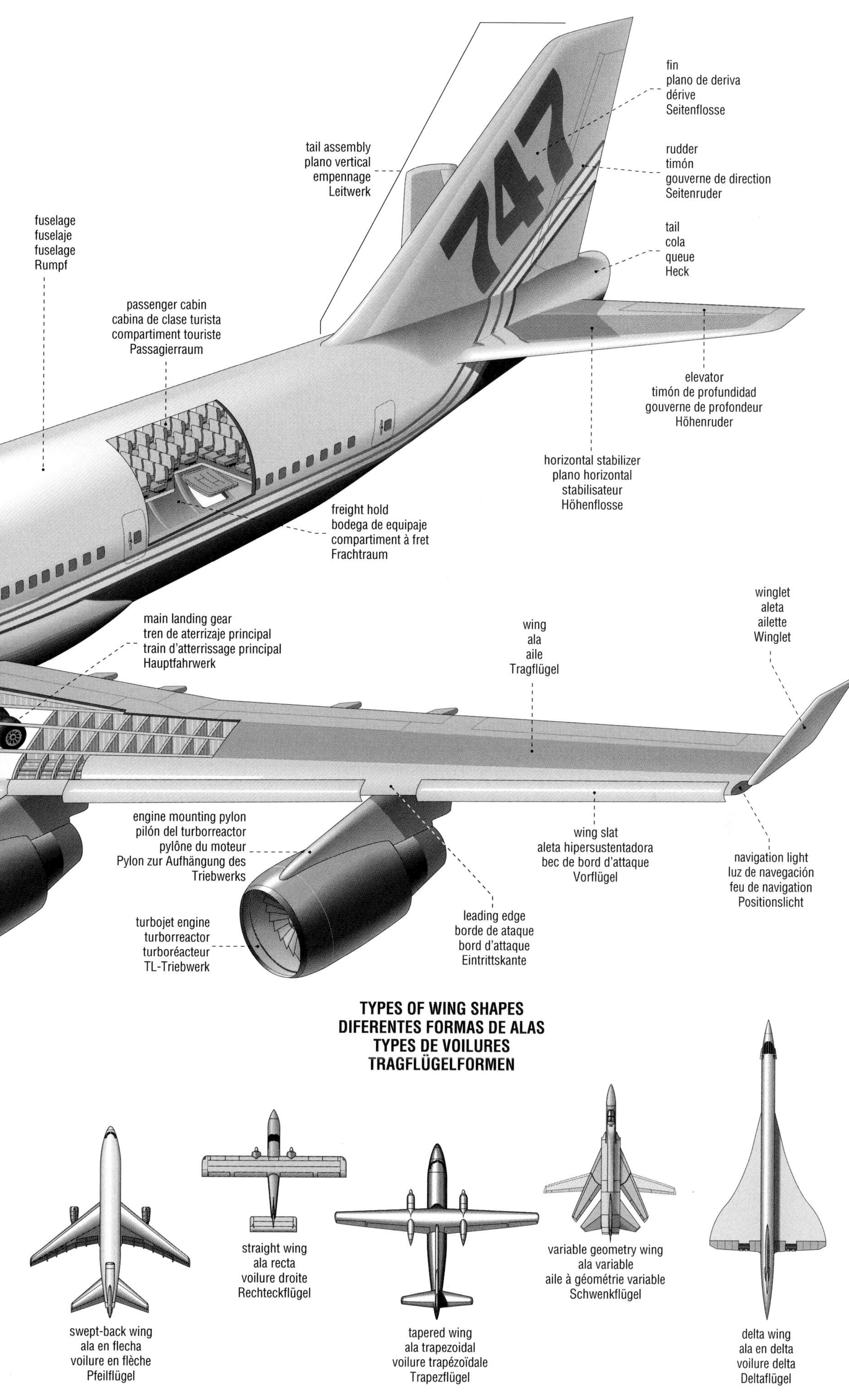
747
fin
plano de deriva
dérive
Seitenflosse
tail assembly
plano vertical
empennage
Leitwerk
rudder
timón
gouverne de direction
Seitenruder
fuselage
fuselaje
fuselage
Rumpf
tail
cola
queue
Heck
passenger cabin
cabina de clase turista
compartiment touriste
Passagierraum
elevator
timón de profundidad
gouverne de profondeur
Höhenruder
horizontal stabilizer
plano horizontal
stabilisateur
Höhenflosse
freight hold
bodega de equipaje
compartiment à fret
Frachtraum
winglet
aleta
ailette
Winglet
main landing gear
tren de aterrizaje principal
train d'atterrissage principal
Hauptfahrwerk
wing
ala
aile
Tragflügel
engine mounting pylon
pilón del turborreactor
pylône du moteur
Pylon zur Aufhängung des Triebwerks
wing slat
aleta hipersustentadora
bec de bord d'attaque
Vorflügel
navigation light
luz de navegación
feu de navigation
Positionslicht
turbojet engine
turborreactor
turboréacteur
TL-Triebwerk
leading edge
borde de ataque
bord d'attaque
Eintrittskante
TYPES OF WING SHAPES
DIFERENTES FORMAS DE ALAS
TYPES DE VOILURES
TRAGFLÜGELFORMEN
straight wing
ala recta
voilure droite
Rechteckflügel
variable geometry wing
ala variable
aile à géométrie variable
Schwenkflügel
swept-back wing
ala en flecha
voilure en flèche
Pfeilflügel
tapered wing
ala trapezoidal
voilure trapézoïdale
Trapezflügel
delta wing
ala en delta
voilure delta
Deltaflügel

FLIGHT DECK
PUENTE DE MANDO
POSTE DE PILOTAGE
COCKPIT

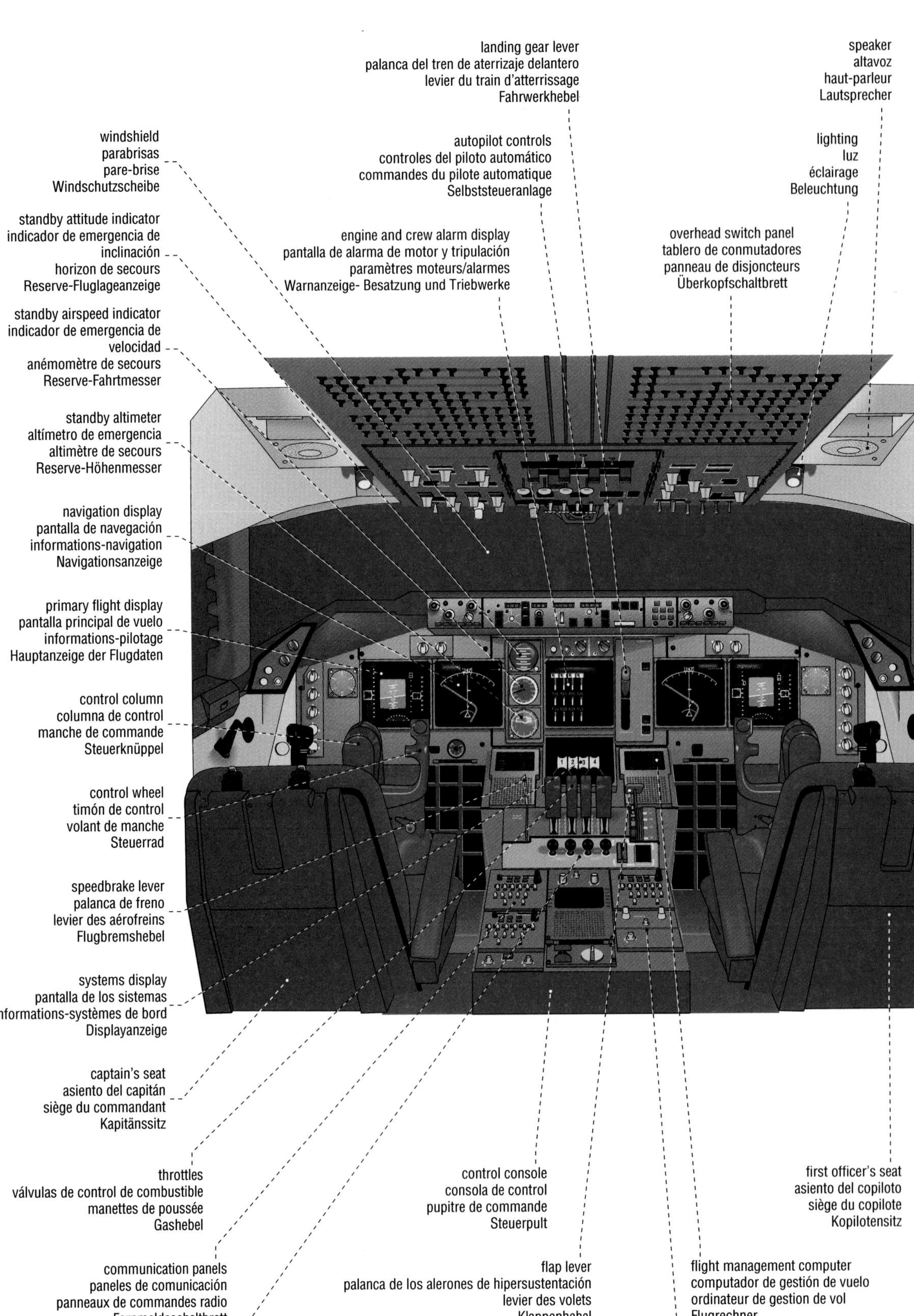
landing gear lever
palanca del tren de aterrizaje delantero
levier du train d'atterrissage
Fahrwerkhebel
speaker
altavoz
haut-parleur
Lautsprecher
windshield
parabrisas
pare-brise
Windschutzscheibe
autopilot controls
controles del piloto automático
commandes du pilote automatique
Selbststeueranlage
lighting
luz
éclairage
Beleuchtung
standby attitude indicator
indicador de emergencia de inclinación
horizon de secours
Reserve-Fluglageanzeige
engine and crew alarm display
pantalla de alarma de motor y tripulación
paramètres moteurs/alarmes
Warnanzeige- Besatzung und Triebwerke
overhead switch panel
tablero de conmutadores
panneau de disjoncteurs
Überkopfschaltbrett
standby airspeed indicator
indicador de emergencia de velocidad
anémomètre de secours
Reserve-Fahrtmesser
standby altimeter
altímetro de emergencia
altimètre de secours
Reserve-Höhenmesser
navigation display
pantalla de navegación
informations-navigation
Navigationsanzeige
primary flight display
pantalla principal de vuelo
informations-pilotage
Hauptanzeige der Flugdaten
control column
columna de control
manche de commande
Steuerknüppel
control wheel
timón de control
volant de manche
Steuerrad
speedbrake lever
palanca de freno
levier des aérofreins
Flugbremshebel
systems display
pantalla de los sistemas
informations-systèmes de bord
Displayanzeige
captain's seat
asiento del capitán
siège du commandant
Kapitänssitz
throttles
válvulas de control de combustible
manettes de poussée
Gashebel
control console
consola de control
pupitre de commande
Steuerpult
first officer's seat
asiento del copiloto
siège du copilote
Kopilotensitz
communication panels
paneles de comunicación
panneaux de commandes radio
Fernmeldeschaltbrett
flap lever
palanca de los alerones de hipersustentación
levier des volets
Klappenhebel
flight management computer
computador de gestión de vuelo
ordinateur de gestion de vol
Flugrechner
engine fuel valves
válvulas de combustible del motor
robinets de carburant
Brennstoffventile
air data computer
computador de vuelo
ordinateur des données aérodynamiques
Luftdatenrechner

TURBOFAN ENGINE
TURBOREACTOR
TURBORÉACTEUR À DOUBLE FLUX
ZWEISTROMTRIEBWERK

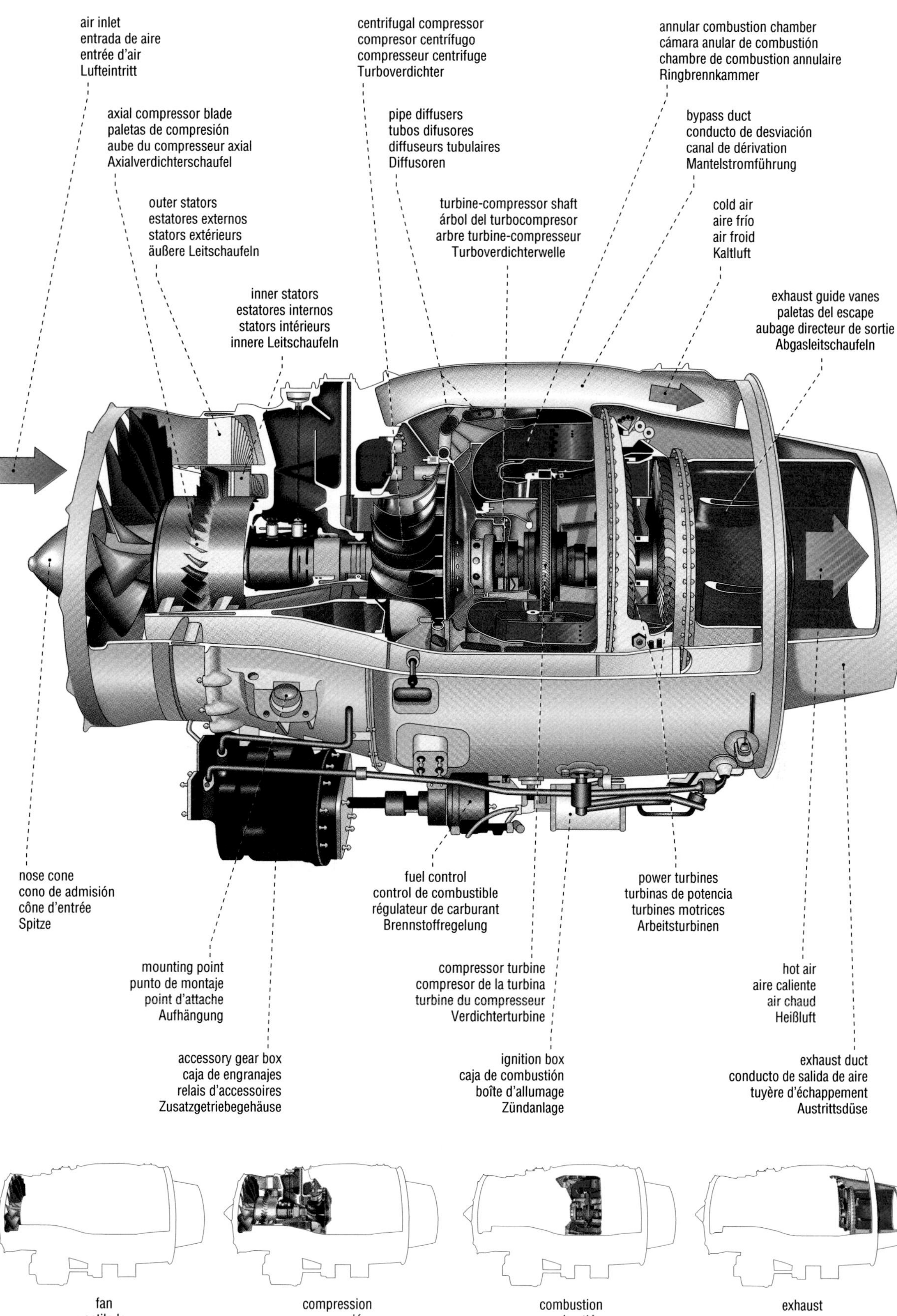
air inlet
entrada de aire
entrée d'air
Lufteintritt
axial compressor blade
paletas de compresión
aube du compresseur axial
Axialverdichterschaufel
outer stators
estatores externos
stators extérieurs
äußere Leitschaufeln
inner stators
estatores internos
stators intérieurs
innere Leitschaufeln
centrifugal compressor
compresor centrífugo
compresseur centrifuge
Turboverdichter
pipe diffusers
tubos difusores
diffuseurs tubulaires
Diffusoren
turbine-compressor shaft
árbol del turbocompresor
arbre turbine-compresseur
Turboverdichterwelle
annular combustion chamber
cámara anular de combustión
chambre de combustion annulaire
Ringbrennkammer
bypass duct
conducto de desviación
canal de dérivation
Mantelstromführung
cold air
aire frío
air froid
Kaltluft
exhaust guide vanes
paletas del escape
aubage directeur de sortie
Abgasleitschaufeln
nose cone
cono de admisión
cône d'entrée
Spitze
fuel control
control de combustible
régulateur de carburant
Brennstoffregelung
power turbines
turbinas de potencia
turbines motrices
Arbeitsturbinen
mounting point
punto de montaje
point d'attache
Aufhängung
compressor turbine
compresor de la turbina
turbine du compresseur
Verdichterturbine
hot air
aire caliente
air chaud
Heißluft
accessory gear box
caja de engranajes
relais d'accessoires
Zusatzgetriebegehäuse
ignition box
caja de combustión
boîte d'allumage
Zündanlage
exhaust duct
conducto de salida de aire
tuyère d'échappement
Austrittsdüse

fan
ventilador
soufflante
Niederdruckverdichtung

compression
compresión
compression
Verdichtung

combustion
combustión
combustion
Verbrennung

exhaust
escape
échappement
Abgas

AIRPORT
AEROPUERTO
AÉROPORT
FLUGHAFEN

control tower cab
cabina de la torre de control
vigie
Kontrollraum
access road
carretera de acceso
route d'accès
Zufahrtsstraße
high-speed exit taxiway
salida de la pista de alta velocidad
sortie de piste à grande vitesse
Schnellabrollbahn
control tower
torre de control
tour de contrôle
Kontrollturm
taxiway
pista de maniobras
voie de circulation
Rollbahn
by-pass taxiway
pista de enlace
bretelle
Überholrollbahn
apron
pista de estacionamiento
aire de trafic
Vorfeld
apron
zona de circulación
aire de manœuvre
Vorfeld
taxiway
pista de maniobras
voie de circulation
Rollbahn
service road
ruta de servicio
voie de service
Versorgungsstraße

maintenance hangar
hangar de mantenimiento
hangar
Flugzeugwartungshalle
passenger terminal
terminal de pasajeros
aérogare de passagers
Passagierterminal
parking area
zona de estacionamiento
aire de stationnement
Abstellplatz
telescopic corridor
corredor telescópico
passerelle télescopique
ausziehbare Fluggastbrücke
boarding walkway
túnel de embarque
quai d'embarquement
Fluggastbrücke
radial passenger loading area
terminal radial de pasajeros
aérogare satellite
radiale Einsteigestation
service area
zona de servicio
aire de service
Versorgungsbereich
taxiway line
línea de pista
marques de circulation
Rollbahnmarkierung

AIRPORT
AEROPUERTO
AÉROPORT
FLUGHAFEN

PASSENGER TERMINAL
TERMINAL DE PASAJEROS
AÉROGARE
PASSAGIERTERMINAL

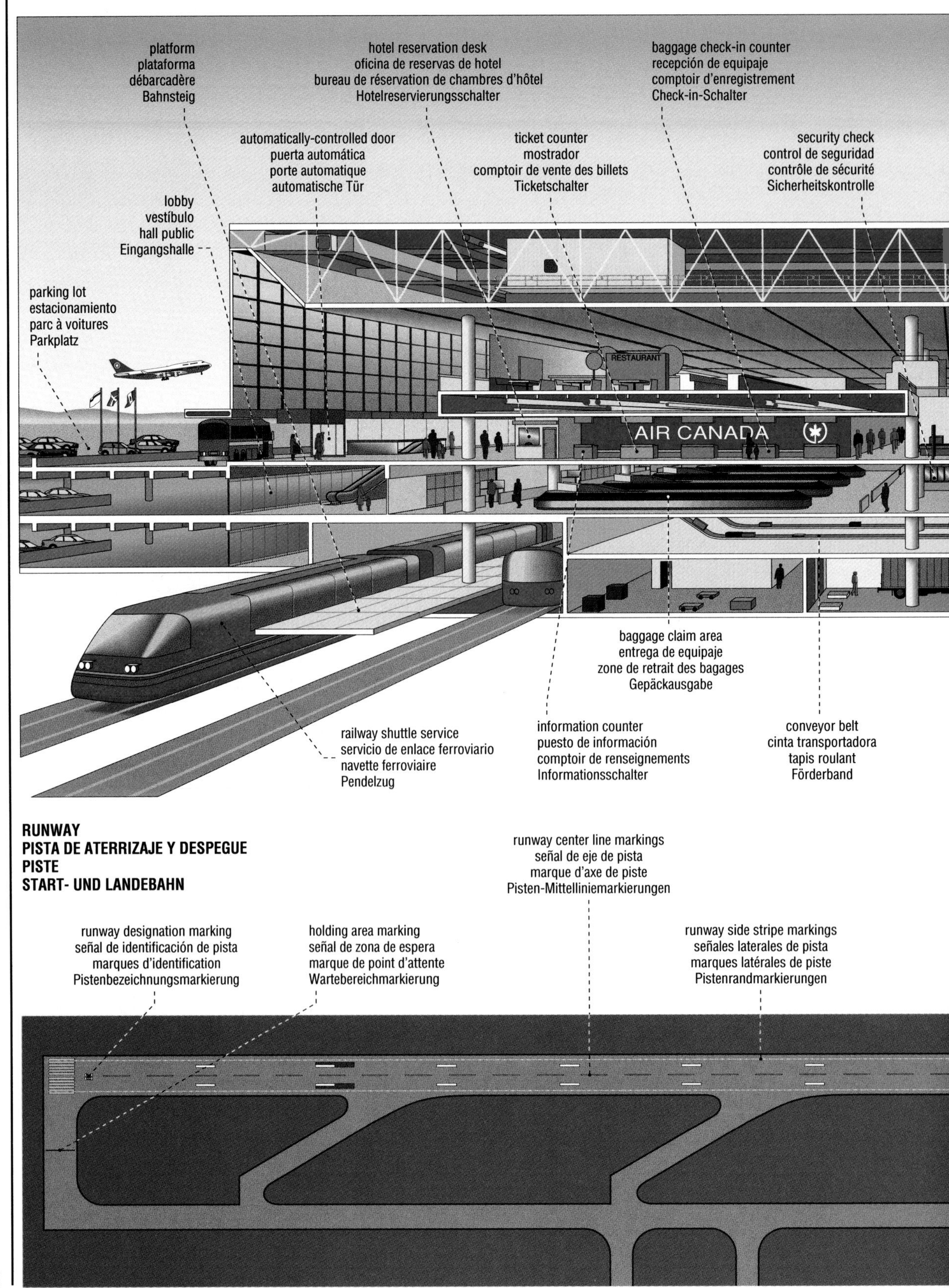
platform
plataforma
débarcadère
Bahnsteig
hotel reservation desk
oficina de reservas de hotel
bureau de réservation de chambres d'hôtel
Hotelreservierungsschalter
baggage check-in counter
recepción de equipaje
comptoir d'enregistrement
Check-in-Schalter
automatically-controlled door
puerta automática
porte automatique
automatische Tür
ticket counter
mostrador
comptoir de vente des billets
Ticketschalter
security check
control de seguridad
contrôle de sécurité
Sicherheitskontrolle
lobby
vestíbulo
hall public
Eingangshalle
parking lot
estacionamiento
parc à voitures
Parkplatz
RESTAURANT
AIR CANADA
baggage claim area
entrega de equipaje
zone de retrait des bagages
Gepäckausgabe
railway shuttle service
servicio de enlace ferroviario
navette ferroviaire
Pendelzug
information counter
puesto de información
comptoir de renseignements
Informationsschalter
conveyor belt
cinta transportadora
tapis roulant
Förderband
RUNWAY
PISTA DE ATERRIZAJE Y DESPEGUE
PISTE
START- UND LANDEBAHN
runway center line markings
señal de eje de pista
marque d'axe de piste
Pisten-Mittelliniemarkierungen
runway designation marking
señal de identificación de pista
marques d'identification
Pistenbezeichnungsmarkierung
holding area marking
señal de zona de espera
marque de point d'attente
Wartebereichmarkierung
runway side stripe markings
señales laterales de pista
marques latérales de piste
Pistenrandmarkierungen

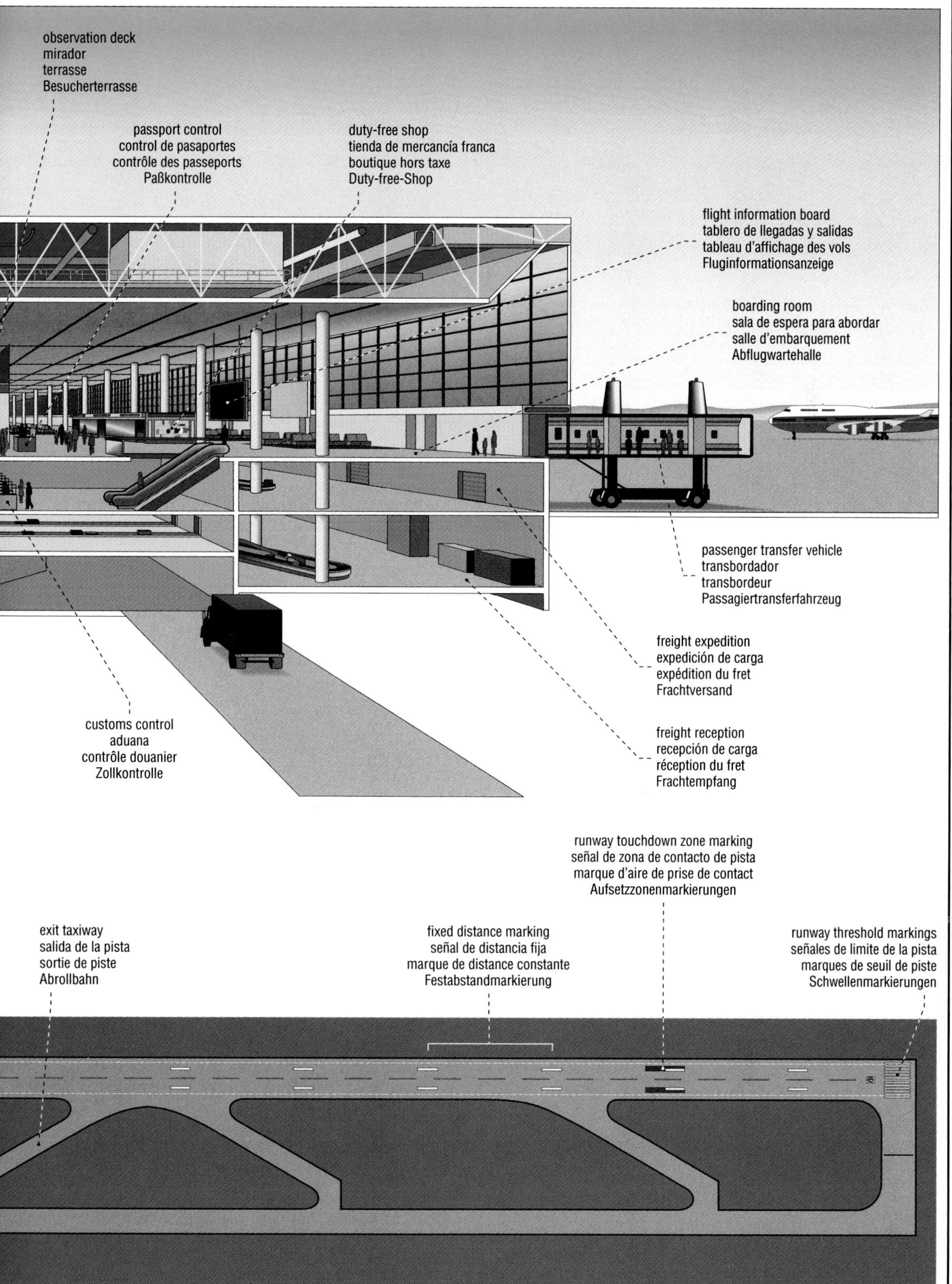
observation deck
mirador
terrasse
Besucherterrasse
passport control
control de pasaportes
contrôle des passeports
Paßkontrolle
duty-free shop
tienda de mercancía franca
boutique hors taxe
Duty-free-Shop
flight information board
tablero de llegadas y salidas
tableau d'affichage des vols
Fluginformationsanzeige
boarding room
sala de espera para abordar
salle d'embarquement
Abflugwartehalle
passenger transfer vehicle
transbordador
transbordeur
Passagiertransferfahrzeug
freight expedition
expedición de carga
expédition du fret
Frachtversand
freight reception
recepción de carga
réception du fret
Frachtempfang
customs control
aduana
contrôle douanier
Zollkontrolle
runway touchdown zone marking
señal de zona de contacto de pista
marque d'aire de prise de contact
Aufsetzzonenmarkierungen
exit taxiway
salida de la pista
sortie de piste
Abrollbahn
fixed distance marking
señal de distancia fija
marque de distance constante
Festabstandmarkierung
runway threshold markings
señales de limite de la pista
marques de seuil de piste
Schwellenmarkierungen

AIRPORT
AEROPUERTO
AÉROPORT
FLUGHAFEN

GROUND AIRPORT EQUIPMENT
EQUIPO DE TIERRA
ÉQUIPEMENTS AÉROPORTUAIRES
BODENAUSRÜSTUNG

tow bar
barra de remolque
barre de tractage
Abschleppstange

tow tractor
tractor remolque
tracteur de piste
Schlepper

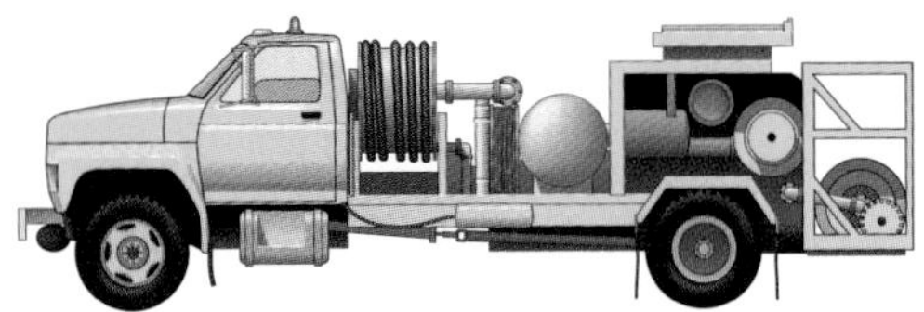

air start unit
unidad de aire
groupe de démarrage pneumatique
Bodenanlaßgerät

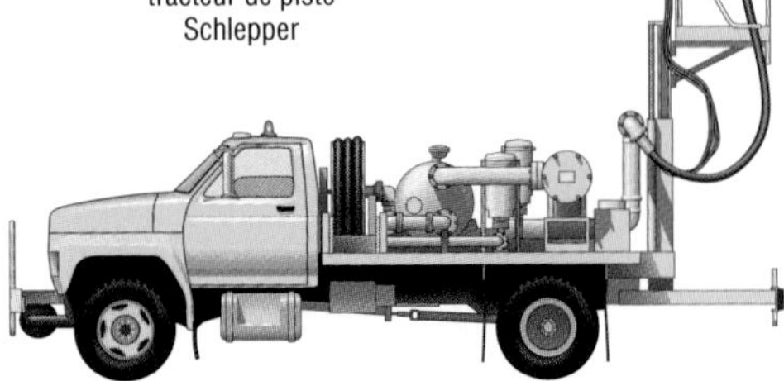

jet refueler
camión cisterna de combustible
camion avitailleur
Tankwagen

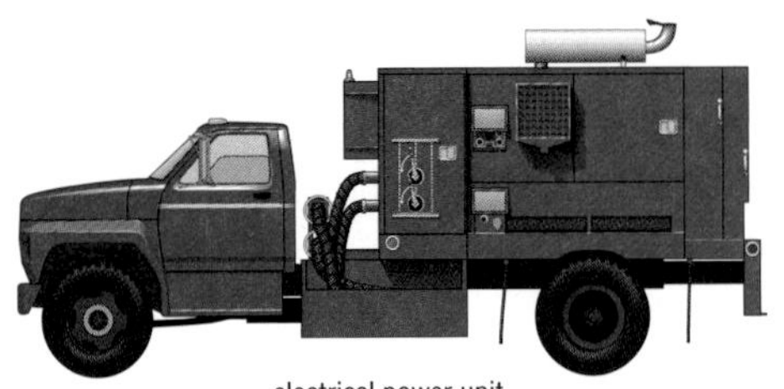

electrical power unit
grupo electrógeno
groupe électrogène
Bodenstromgerät

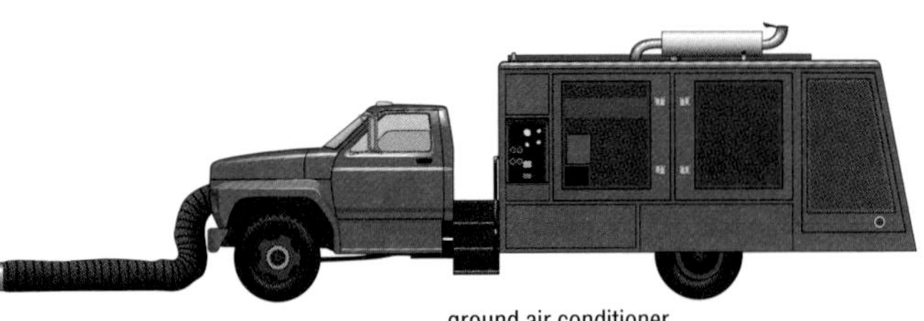

ground air conditioner
aire acondicionado de tierra
groupe de climatisation
Klimagerät

lavatory truck
camión sanitario
camion vide-toilette
Toilettenwagen

aircraft maintenance truck
camioneta de mantenimiento de aviones
véhicule de service technique
Wartungsfahrzeug

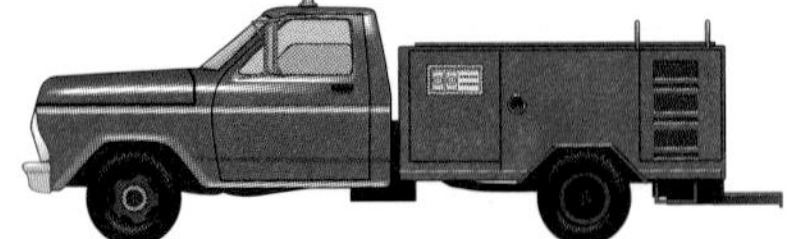

potable water truck
camión cisterna de agua potable
camion-citerne d'eau potable
Frischwasserwagen

127

wheel chock
calzo de la rueda
cale
Bremsklotz

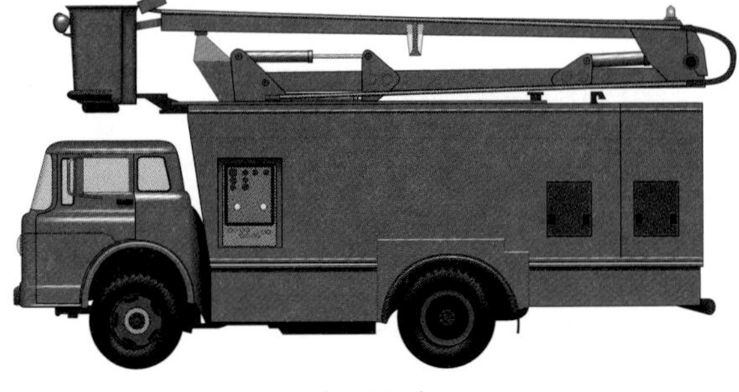

boom truck
camioneta con canastilla telescópica
nacelle élévatrice
Tankwagen mit beweglichem Ausleger

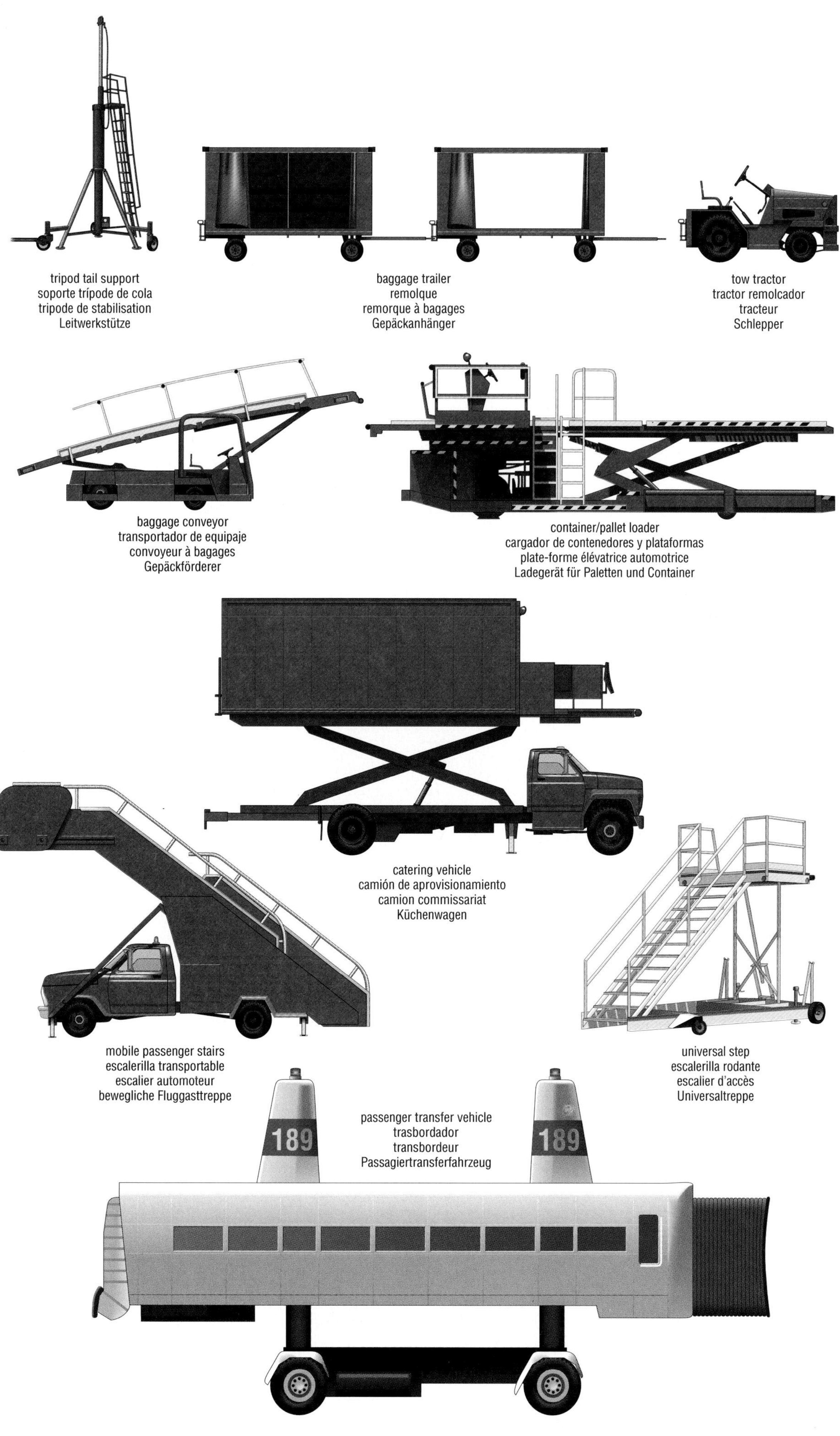
189
189

tripod tail support
soporte trípode de cola
tripode de stabilisation
Leitwerkstütze

baggage trailer
remolque
remorque à bagages
Gepäckanhänger

tow tractor
tractor remolcador
tracteur
Schlepper

baggage conveyor
transportador de equipaje
convoyeur à bagages
Gepäckförderer

container/pallet loader
cargador de contenedores y plataformas
plate-forme élévatrice automotrice
Ladegerät für Paletten und Container

catering vehicle
camión de aprovisionamiento
camion commissariat
Küchenwagen

mobile passenger stairs
escalerilla transportable
escalier automoteur
bewegliche Fluggasttreppe

universal step
escalerilla rodante
escalier d'accès
Universaltreppe

passenger transfer vehicle
trasbordador
transbordeur
Passagiertransferfahrzeug

HELICOPTER
HELICÓPTERO
HÉLICOPTÈRE
HUBSCHRAUBER

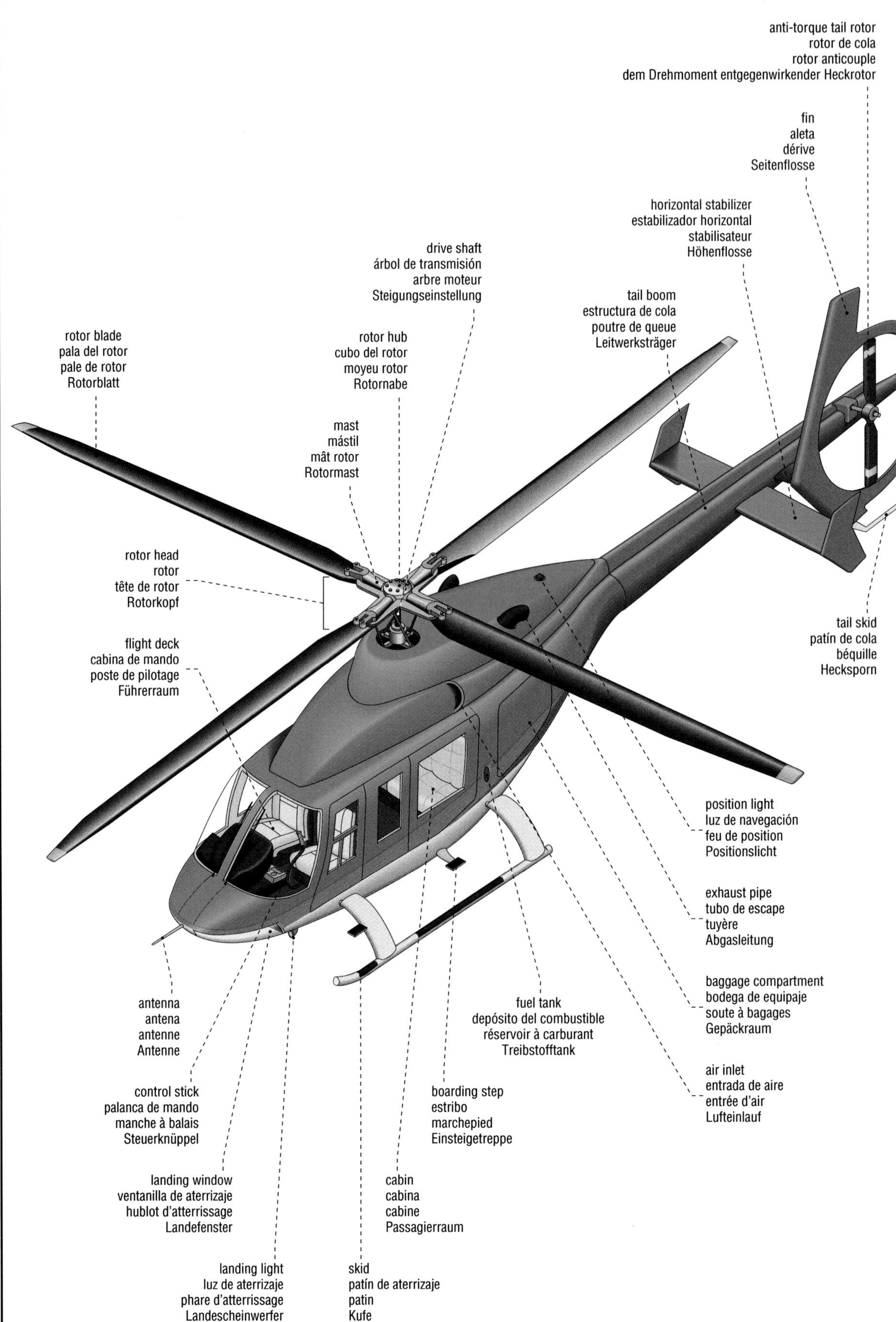
anti-torque tail rotor
rotor de cola
rotor anticouple
dem Drehmoment entgegenwirkender Heckrotor
fin
aleta
dérive
Seitenflosse
horizontal stabilizer
estabilizador horizontal
stabilisateur
Höhenflosse
drive shaft
árbol de transmisión
arbre moteur
Steigungseinstellung
tail boom
estructura de cola
poutre de queue
Leitwerksträger
rotor blade
pala del rotor
pale de rotor
Rotorblatt
rotor hub
cubo del rotor
moyeu rotor
Rotornabe
mast
mástil
mât rotor
Rotormast
rotor head
rotor
tête de rotor
Rotorkopf
tail skid
patín de cola
béquille
Hecksporn
flight deck
cabina de mando
poste de pilotage
Führerraum
position light
luz de navegación
feu de position
Positionslicht
exhaust pipe
tubo de escape
tuyère
Abgasleitung
baggage compartment
bodega de equipaje
soute à bagages
Gepäckraum
antenna
antena
antenne
Antenne
fuel tank
depósito del combustible
réservoir à carburant
Treibstofftank
air inlet
entrada de aire
entrée d'air
Lufteinlauf
control stick
palanca de mando
manche à balais
Steuerknüppel
boarding step
estribo
marchepied
Einsteigetreppe
landing window
ventanilla de aterrizaje
hublot d'atterrissage
Landefenster
cabin
cabina
cabine
Passagierraum
landing light
luz de aterrizaje
phare d'atterrissage
Landescheinwerfer
skid
patín de aterrizaje
patin
Kufe

ROCKET
COHETE
FUSÉE
RAKETE

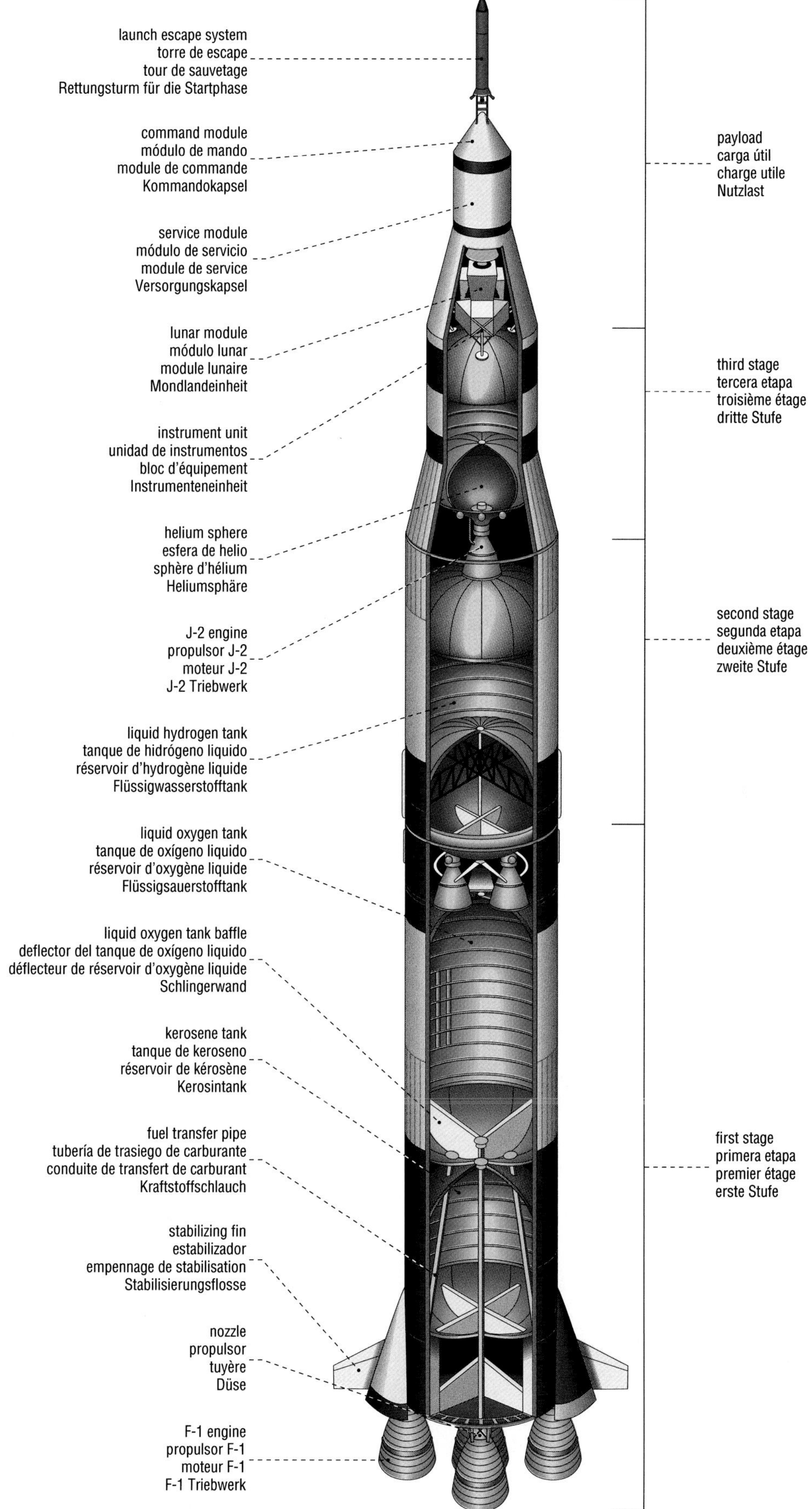
launch escape system
torre de escape
tour de sauvetage
Rettungsturm für die Startphase
command module
módulo de mando
module de commande
Kommandokapsel
service module
módulo de servicio
module de service
Versorgungskapsel
lunar module
módulo lunar
module lunaire
Mondlandeinheit
instrument unit
unidad de instrumentos
bloc d'équipement
Instrumenteneinheit
helium sphere
esfera de helio
sphère d'hélium
Heliumsphäre
J-2 engine
propulsor J-2
moteur J-2
J-2 Triebwerk
liquid hydrogen tank
tanque de hidrógeno liquido
réservoir d'hydrogène liquide
Flüssigwasserstofftank
liquid oxygen tank
tanque de oxígeno liquido
réservoir d'oxygène liquide
Flüssigsauerstofftank
liquid oxygen tank baffle
deflector del tanque de oxígeno liquido
déflecteur de réservoir d'oxygène liquide
Schlingerwand
kerosene tank
tanque de keroseno
réservoir de kérosène
Kerosintank
fuel transfer pipe
tubería de trasiego de carburante
conduite de transfert de carburant
Kraftstoffschlauch
stabilizing fin
estabilizador
empennage de stabilisation
Stabilisierungsflosse
nozzle
propulsor
tuyère
Düse
F-1 engine
propulsor F-1
moteur F-1
F-1 Triebwerk
payload
carga útil
charge utile
Nutzlast
third stage
tercera etapa
troisième étage
dritte Stufe
second stage
segunda etapa
deuxième étage
zweite Stufe
first stage
primera etapa
premier étage
erste Stufe

SPACE SHUTTLE
TRANSBORDADOR ESPACIAL
NAVETTE SPATIALE
RAUMFÄHRE

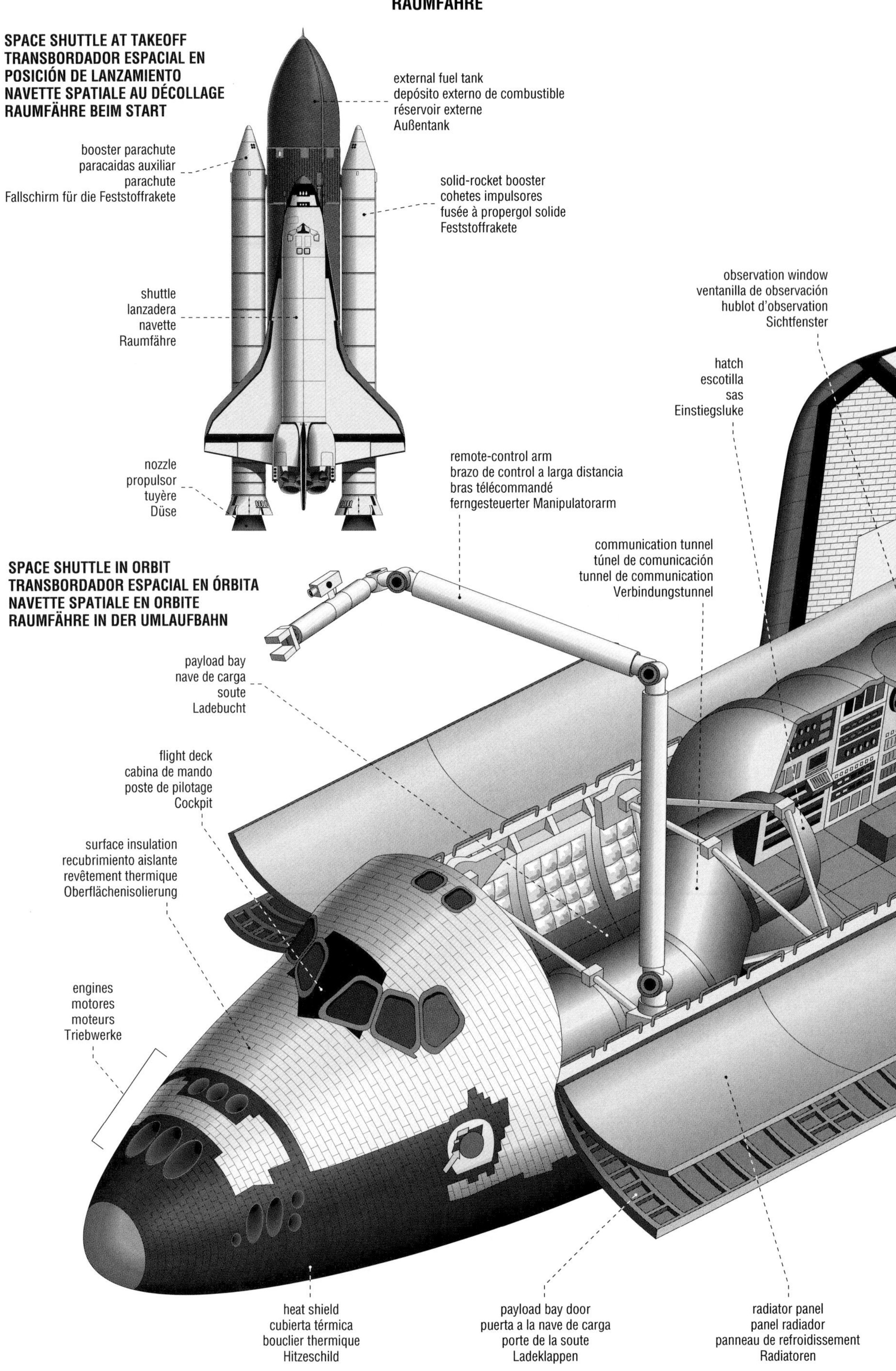
SPACE SHUTTLE AT TAKEOFF
TRANSBORDADOR ESPACIAL EN POSICIÓN DE LANZAMIENTO
NAVETTE SPATIALE AU DÉCOLLAGE
RAUMFÄHRE BEIM START
external fuel tank
depósito externo de combustible
réservoir externe
Außentank
booster parachute
paracaidas auxiliar
parachute
Fallschirm für die Feststoffrakete
solid-rocket booster
cohetes impulsores
fusée à propergol solide
Feststoffrakete
shuttle
lanzadera
navette
Raumfähre
nozzle
propulsor
tuyère
Düse
SPACE SHUTTLE IN ORBIT
TRANSBORDADOR ESPACIAL EN ÓRBITA
NAVETTE SPATIALE EN ORBITE
RAUMFÄHRE IN DER UMLAUFBAHN
observation window
ventanilla de observación
hublot d'observation
Sichtfenster
hatch
escotilla
sas
Einstiegsluke
remote-control arm
brazo de control a larga distancia
bras télécommandé
ferngesteuerter Manipulatorarm
communication tunnel
túnel de comunicación
tunnel de communication
Verbindungstunnel
payload bay
nave de carga
soute
Ladebucht
flight deck
cabina de mando
poste de pilotage
Cockpit
surface insulation
recubrimiento aislante
revêtement thermique
Oberflächenisolierung
engines
motores
moteurs
Triebwerke
heat shield
cubierta térmica
bouclier thermique
Hitzeschild
payload bay door
puerta a la nave de carga
porte de la soute
Ladeklappen
radiator panel
panel radiador
panneau de refroidissement
Radiatoren

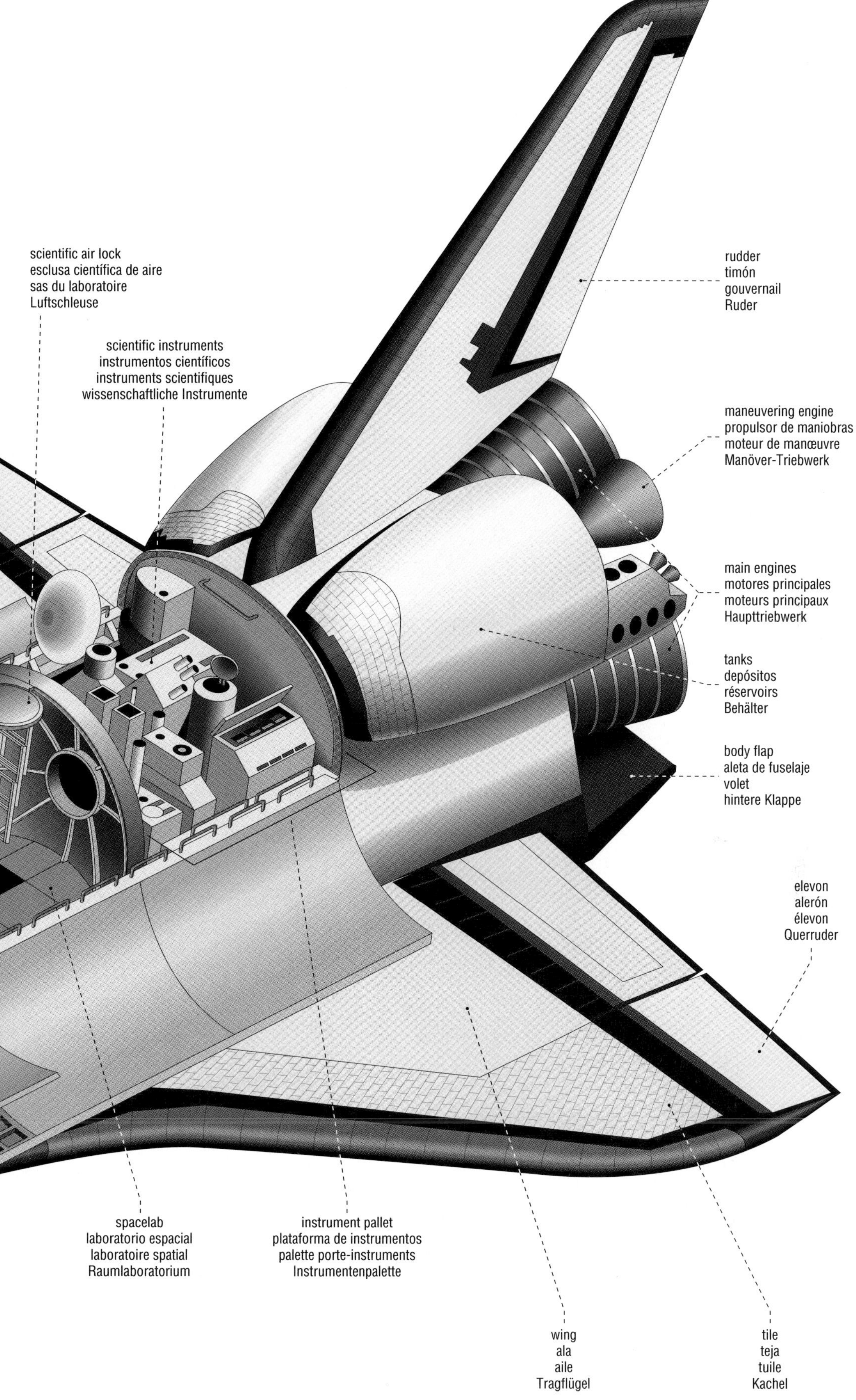
scientific air lock
esclusa científica de aire
sas du laboratoire
Luftschleuse
scientific instruments
instrumentos científicos
instruments scientifiques
wissenschaftliche Instrumente
rudder
timón
gouvernail
Ruder
maneuvering engine
propulsor de maniobras
moteur de manœuvre
Manöver-Triebwerk
main engines
motores principales
moteurs principaux
Haupttriebwerk
tanks
depósitos
réservoirs
Behälter
body flap
aleta de fuselaje
volet
hintere Klappe
elevon
alerón
élevon
Querruder
spacelab
laboratorio espacial
laboratoire spatial
Raumlaboratorium
instrument pallet
plataforma de instrumentos
palette porte-instruments
Instrumentenpalette
wing
ala
aile
Tragflügel
tile
teja
tuile
Kachel

SPACESUIT
TRAJE ESPACIAL
SCAPHANDRE SPATIAL
RAUMANZUG

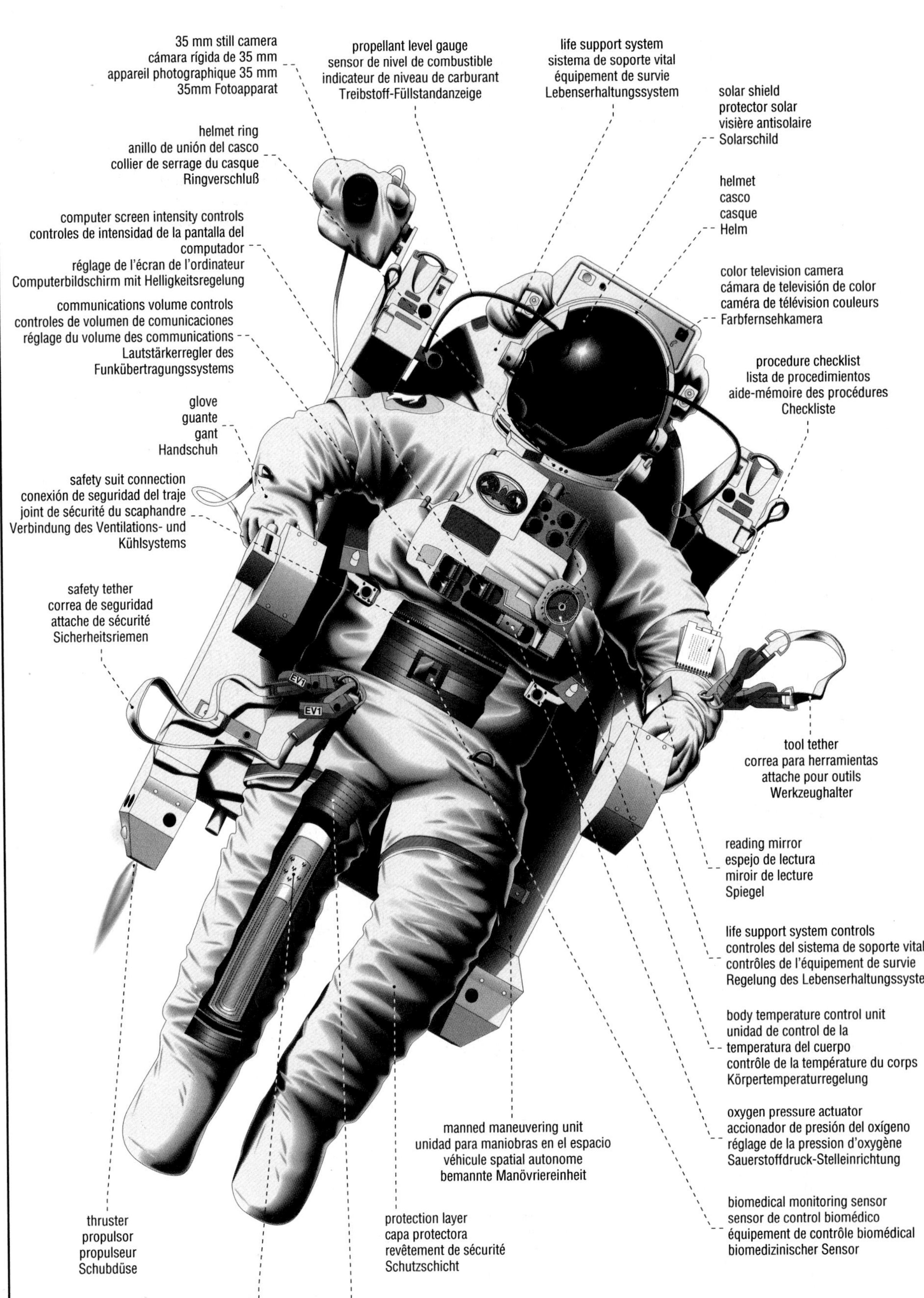
35 mm still camera
cámara rígida de 35 mm
appareil photographique 35 mm
35mm Fotoapparat
propellant level gauge
sensor de nivel de combustible
indicateur de niveau de carburant
Treibstoff-Füllstandanzeige
life support system
sistema de soporte vital
équipement de survie
Lebenserhaltungssystem
solar shield
protector solar
visière antisolaire
Solarschild
helmet ring
anillo de unión del casco
collier de serrage du casque
Ringverschluß
helmet
casco
casque
Helm
computer screen intensity controls
controles de intensidad de la pantalla del computador
réglage de l'écran de l'ordinateur
Computerbildschirm mit Helligkeitsregelung
color television camera
cámara de televisión de color
caméra de télévision couleurs
Farbfernsehkamera
communications volume controls
controles de volumen de comunicaciones
réglage du volume des communications
Lautstärkerregler des Funkübertragungssystems
procedure checklist
lista de procedimientos
aide-mémoire des procédures
Checkliste
glove
guante
gant
Handschuh
safety suit connection
conexión de seguridad del traje
joint de sécurité du scaphandre
Verbindung des Ventilations- und Kühlsystems
safety tether
correa de seguridad
attache de sécurité
Sicherheitsriemen
EV1
EV1
tool tether
correa para herramientas
attache pour outils
Werkzeughalter
reading mirror
espejo de lectura
miroir de lecture
Spiegel
life support system controls
controles del sistema de soporte vital
contrôles de l'équipement de survie
Regelung des Lebenserhaltungssystems
body temperature control unit
unidad de control de la temperatura del cuerpo
contrôle de la température du corps
Körpertemperaturregelung
oxygen pressure actuator
accionador de presión del oxígeno
réglage de la pression d'oxygène
Sauerstoffdruck-Stelleinrichtung
manned maneuvering unit
unidad para maniobras en el espacio
véhicule spatial autonome
bemannte Manövriereinheit
biomedical monitoring sensor
sensor de control biomédico
équipement de contrôle biomédical
biomedizinischer Sensor
thruster
propulsor
propulseur
Schubdüse
protection layer
capa protectora
revêtement de sécurité
Schutzschicht
liquid cooling and ventilation garment
liquido de enfriamiento y ventilación del traje
sous-vêtement de contrôle thermique
Unteranzug zur Kühlung und Ventilation
insulation layers
capas aislantes
sous-vêtement d'isolation
Isolierschichten

OFFICE SUPPLIES
EQUIPO DE OFICINA
FOURNITURES DE BUREAU
BÜROBEDARF

CONTENTS

STATIONERY
ARTÍCULOS DE ESCRITORIO
ARTICLES DE BUREAU
SCHREIBWAREN

mechanical pencil
lapicero
porte-mine
Druckbleistift
ballpoint pen
bolígrafo
stylo-bille
Kugelschreiber
pencil
lápiz
crayon
Bleistift
fountain pen
estilográfica
stylo-plume
Füllfederhalter
eraser holder
portaborrador
porte-gomme
Radiergummihalter
stick eraser
lápiz borrador
crayon gomme
Radierstift
marker
marcador
marqueur
Textmarker
eraser
borrador
gomme
Radiergummi
highlighter pen
destacador
surligneur
Leuchtstift
glue stick
lápiz adhesivo
bâtonnet de colle
Klebestift
correction fluid
corrector líquido
correcteur liquide
Korrekturflüssigkeit
clip
pinza
pince-notes
Papierclip
paper clips
presillas
trombones
Büroklammern
stapler
engrapadora
agrafeuse
Hefter
staples
grapas
agrafes
Heftklammern
paper fasteners
tachuelas para papel
attaches parisiennes
Beutelklammern
letter opener
abrecartas
coupe-papier
Brieföffner
thumb tacks
chinches
punaises
Reißnägel
pencil sharpener
sacapuntas
taille-crayon
Bleistiftspitzer
correction paper
papel corrector
ruban correcteur
Korrekturstreifen
staple remover
uñas
dégrafeuse
Entklammerer

STATIONERY
ARTÍCULOS DE ESCRITORIO
ARTICLES DE BUREAU
SCHREIBWAREN

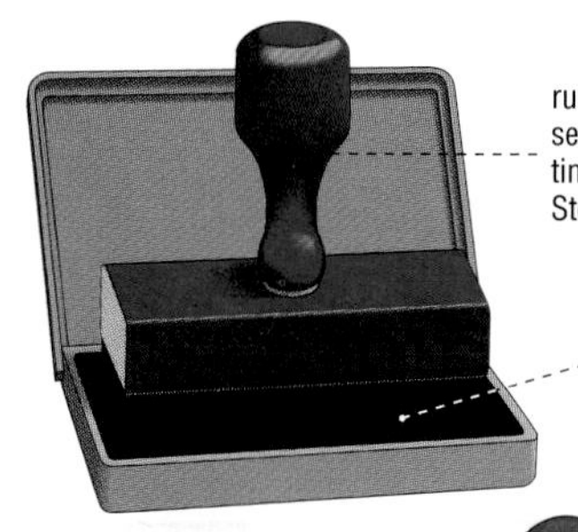

rubber stamp
sello de goma
timbre caoutchouc
Stempel

stamp pad
cojín para sellos
tampon encreur
Stempelkissen

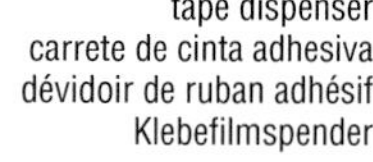

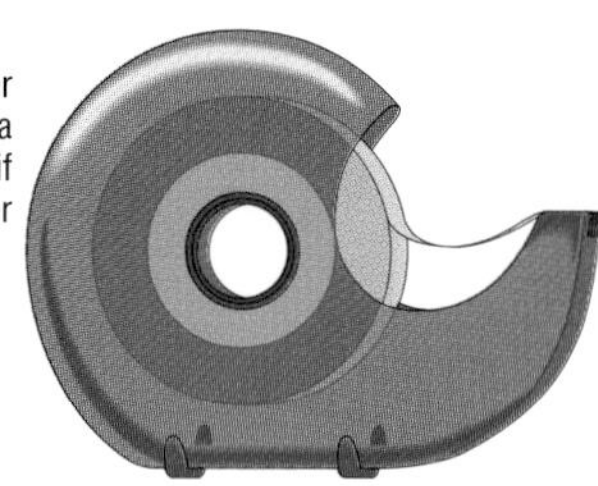

tape dispenser
carrete de cinta adhesiva
dévidoir de ruban adhésif
Klebefilmspender

numbering machine
foliador
numéroteur
Numerierstempel

dater
fechador
timbre dateur
Datumstempel

stamp rack
portasellos
porte-timbres
Stempelträger

bill-file
pinchador
pique-notes
Dornablage

paper punch
perforadora
perforatrice
Locher

label maker
rotulador
pince à étiqueter
Präger

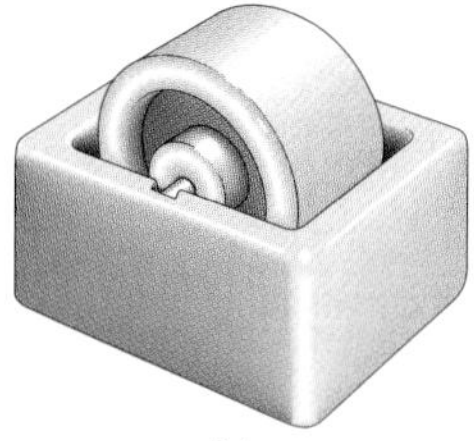

moistener
rueda humedecedora
mouilleur
Befeuchter

rotary file
fichero giratorio
fichier rotatif
Drehkartei

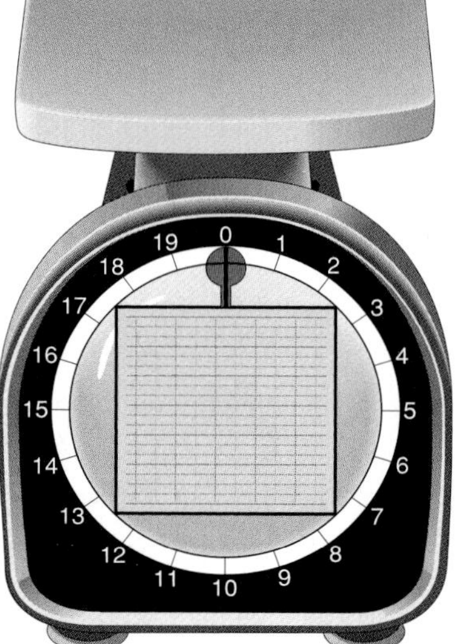

letter scale
balanza para cartas
pèse-lettres
Briefwaage

pencil sharpener
sacapuntas
taille-crayon
Bleistiftspitzer

telephone index
directorio telefónico
répertoire téléphonique
Telefonnummernverzeichnis

INDEX CARD DRAWER
GAVETA DE ARCHIVADOR
TIROIR DE FICHIER
KARTEISCHUBFACH

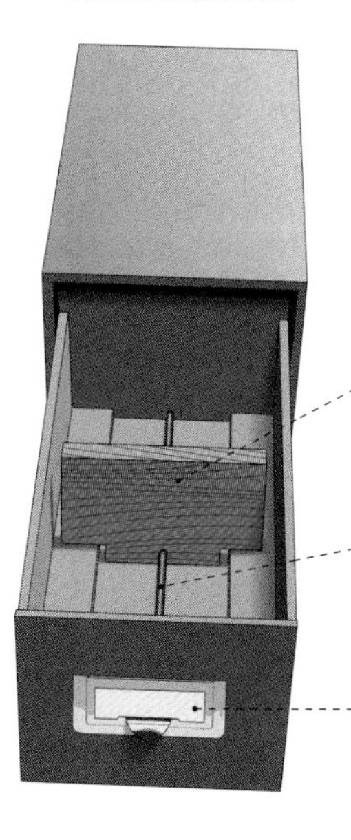

compressor
compresor
compresseur
Begrenzungseinsatz

metal rail
riel metálico
tringle métallique
Führungsschiene

label holder
soporte del rótulo
porte-étiquette
Etikettenfenster

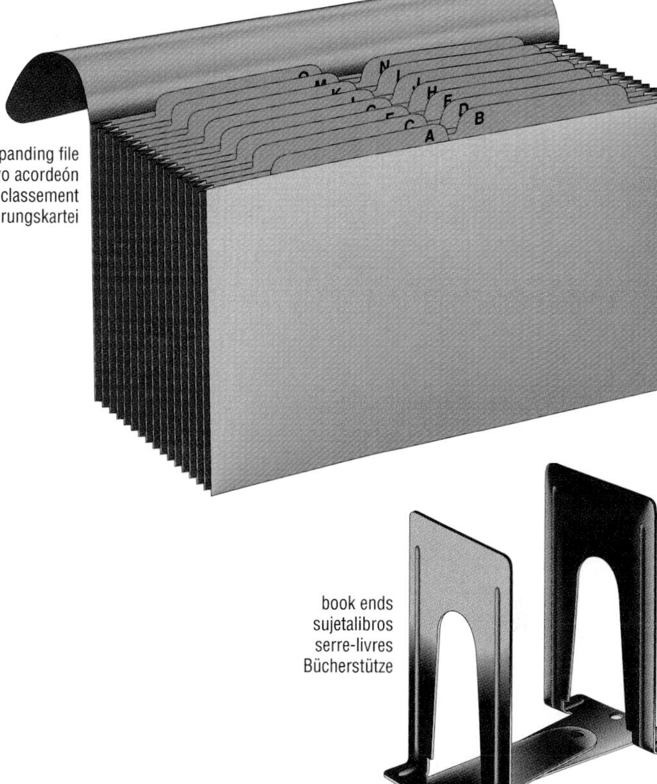

expanding file
archivo acordeón
pochette de classement
Erweiterungskartei

book ends
sujetalibros
serre-livres
Bücherstütze

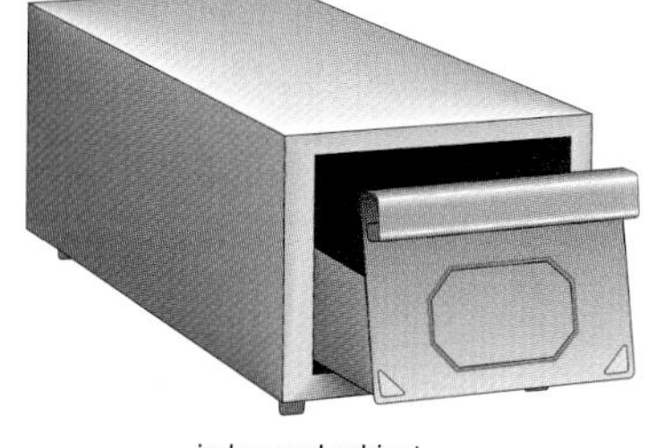

index card cabinet
archivador de fichas
fichier
Karteikasten

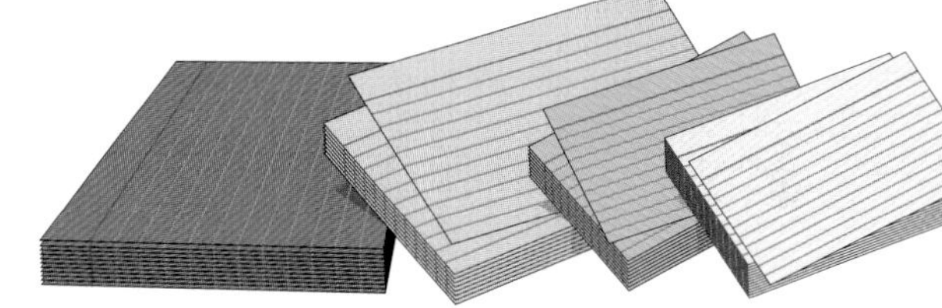

index cards
fichas
fiches
Karteikarten

filing box
caja archivo
boîte-classeur
Aktenbox

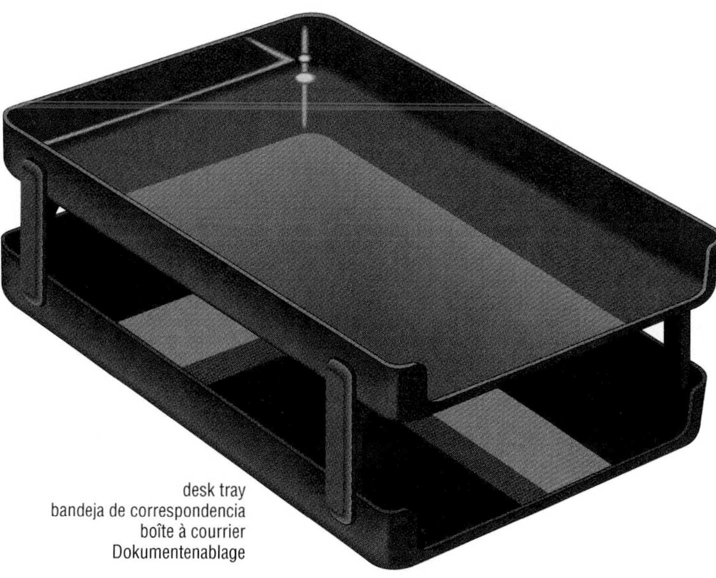

desk tray
bandeja de correspondencia
boîte à courrier
Dokumentenablage

STATIONERY
ARTÍCULOS DE ESCRITORIO
ARTICLES DE BUREAU
SCHREIBWAREN

MERCREDI
WEDNESDAY
24
JUIN
JUNE

tear-off calendar
calendario de pared
calendrier-mémorandum
Abreißkalender

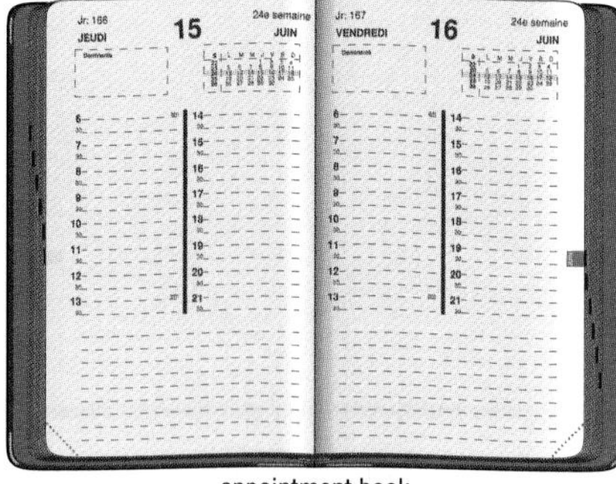
JEUDI
15
JUIN
24e semaine
VENDREDI
16
JUIN
24e semaine

appointment book
agenda
agenda
Terminkalender

MARDI
TUESDAY
23
JUIN
JUNE
MERCREDI
WEDNESDAY
24
JUIN
JUNE

calendar pad
calendario de escritorio
bloc-éphéméride
Ringbuchkalender

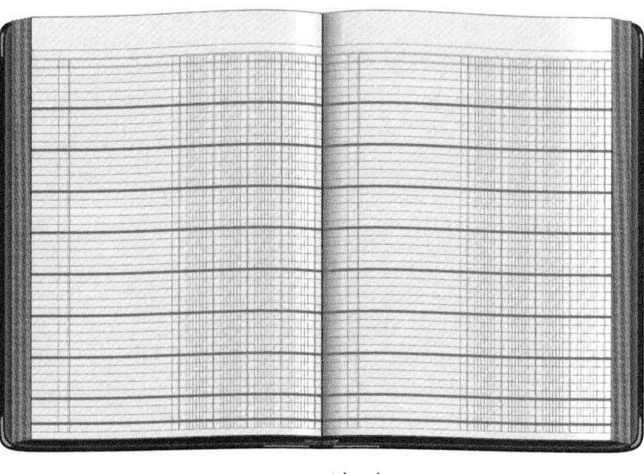

account book
agenda de caja
registre de comptabilité
Geschäftsbuch

memo pad
libreta
bloc-notes
Notizblock

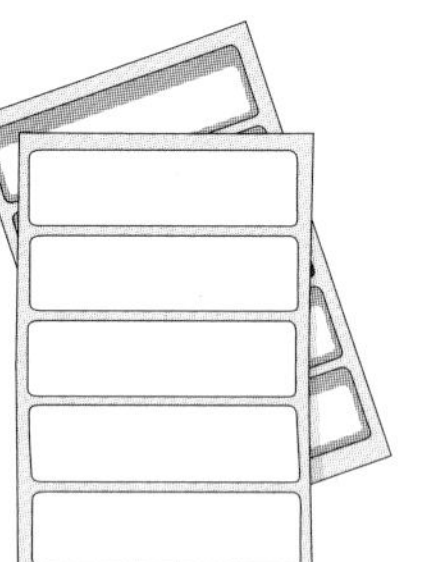

self-adhesive labels
etiquetas adhesivas
étiquettes autocollantes
Klebeetiketten

tab
indicador
onglet
Reiter

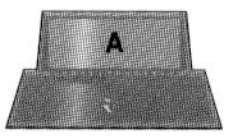
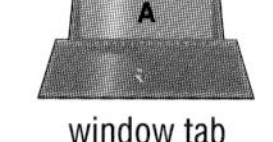
A

window tab
indicador transparente
onglet à fenêtre
durchsichtiger Reiter

archboard
tabla con argollas
planchette à arches
Ringablage

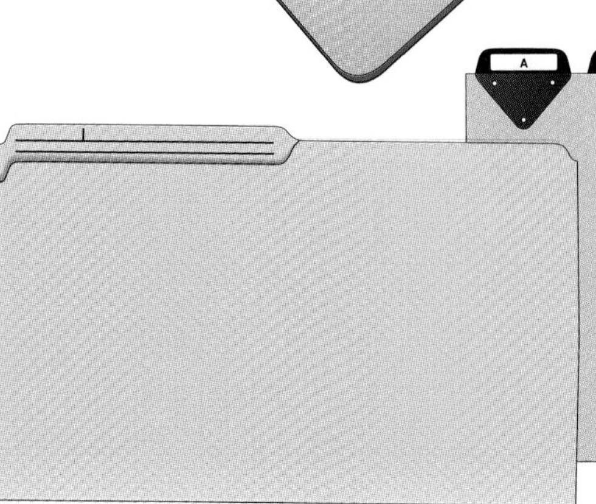

A
B
C
D
E

folder
carpeta de archivo
chemise
Aktenmappe

file guides
guías de archivo
guides de classement
Karteiregister

hanging file
archivador colgante
dossier suspendu
Hängemappe

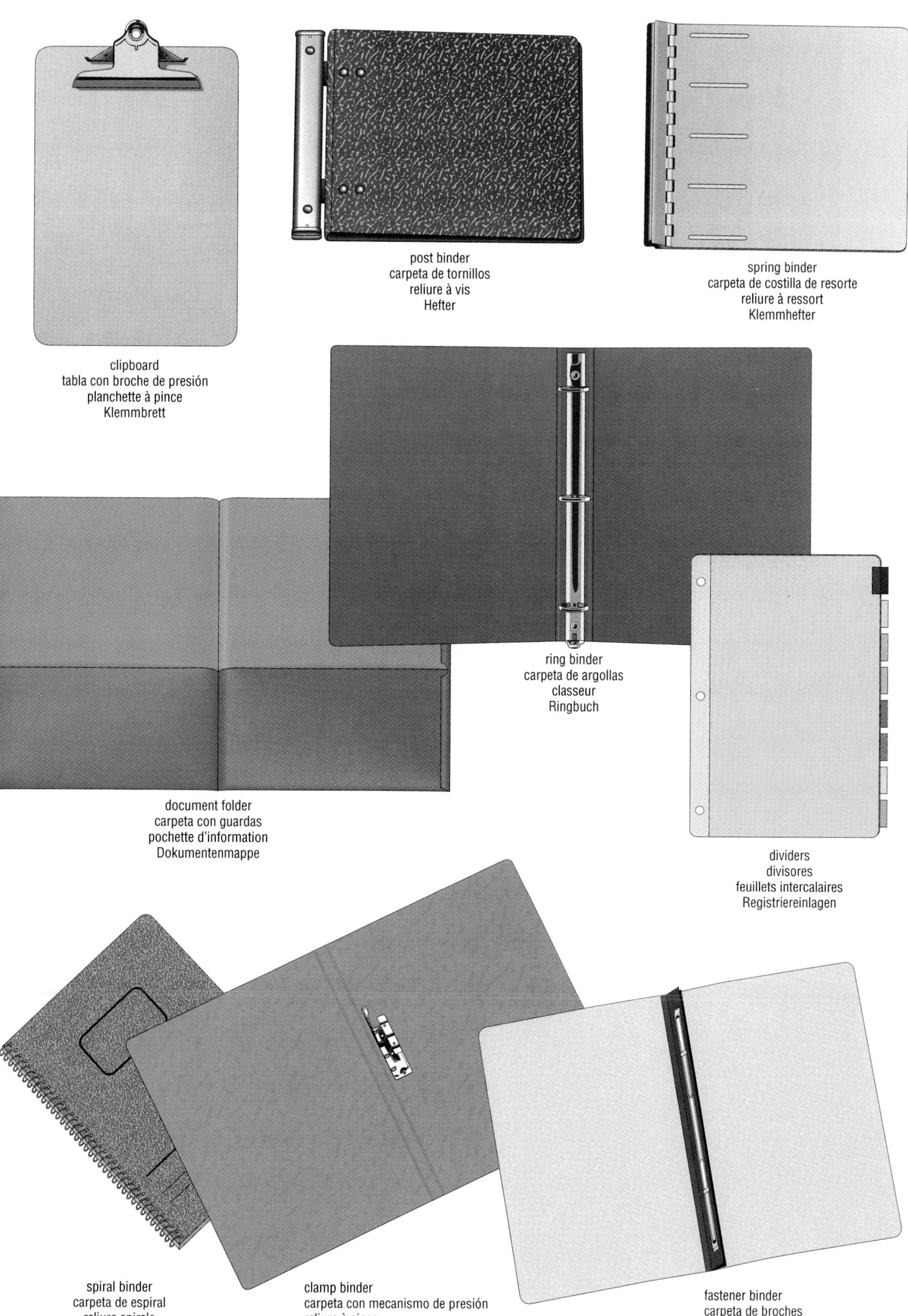

clipboard
tabla con broche de presión
planchette à pince
Klemmbrett

post binder
carpeta de tornillos
reliure à vis
Hefter

spring binder
carpeta de costilla de resorte
reliure à ressort
Klemmhefter

ring binder
carpeta de argollas
classeur
Ringbuch

document folder
carpeta con guardas
pochette d'information
Dokumentenmappe

dividers
divisores
feuillets intercalaires
Registriereinlagen

spiral binder
carpeta de espiral
reliure spirale
Spiralringbuch

clamp binder
carpeta con mecanismo de presión
reliure à pince
Aktenordner

fastener binder
carpeta de broches
reliure à glissière
Schnellhefter

OFFICE FURNITURE
MUEBLES DE OFICINA
MOBILIER DE BUREAU
BÜROMÖBEL

executive desk
escritorio de ejecutivo
bureau de direction
Chefschreibtisch
swivel-tilter armchair
sillón giratorio
fauteuil pivotant à bascule
Drehsessel
credenza
aparador
bahut
Aktenschrank
desk mat
carpeta
sous-main
Schreibunterlage
partition
biombo
cloison amovible
Trennwand
lateral filing cabinet
archivero lateral
classeur à clapets
Hängekartei

COMPUTER TABLE
MESA DEL COMPUTADOR
TABLE D'ORDINATEUR
COMPUTERTISCH
adjustable platen
plato ajustable
support ajustable
verstellbare Tastaturablage
modesty panel
panel
panneau de modestie
Abschlußtafel
PRINTER TABLE
MESA DE LA IMPRESORA
TABLE D'IMPRIMANTE
DRUCKERTISCH
paper catcher
bandeja para recoger el papel
panier de réception
Papierfänger
paper tray
bandeja para el papel
panier d'alimentation
Papierablage
paper feed channel
canal de arrastre del papel
fente d'alimentation
Öffnung für die Papierzufuhr
mobile filing unit
archivo movible
classeur mobile
fahrbare Aktenablage
mobile drawer unit
archivador movible con cajones
caisson
fahrbares Schubladenelement
typist's chair
silla de secretaria
chaise dactylo
Bürodrehstuhl
return
aparador de escritorio
retour
Winkeltisch
SECRETARIAL DESK
ESCRITORIO DE SECRETARIA
BUREAU SECRÉTAIRE
ARBEITSPLATZ

OFFICE FURNITURE
MUEBLES DE OFICINA
MOBILIER DE BUREAU
BÜROMÖBEL

display cabinet
estante para revistas
présentoir à revues
Ausstellungsregal

coat hook
perchero de pared
patère
Kleiderhaken

stationery cabinet
gabinete para papelería
armoire à papeterie
Schrank

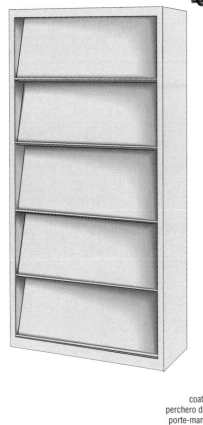

coat tree
perchero de pie
porte-manteau
Garderobenständer

locker
armario
armoire-vestiaire
Kleiderschrank

coat rack
perchero
vestiaire de bureau
Garderobe

CALCULATOR
CALCULADORAS
CALCULATRICE
RECHNER

POCKET CALCULATOR
CALCULADORA DE BOLSILLO
CALCULETTE
TASCHENRECHNER

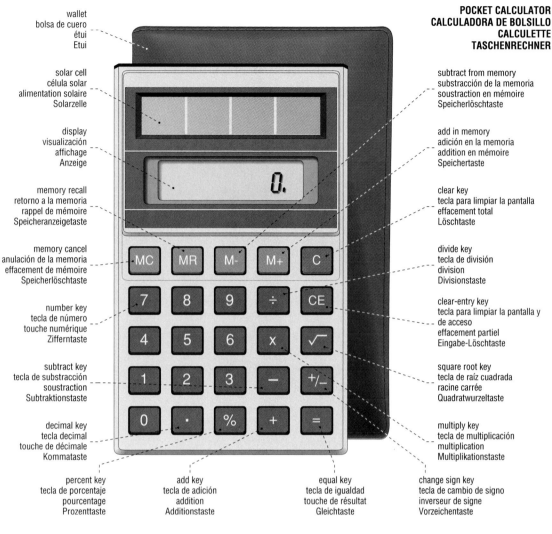

wallet
bolsa de cuero
étui
Etui

solar cell
célula solar
alimentation solaire
Solarzelle

display
visualización
affichage
Anzeige

memory recall
retorno a la memoria
rappel de mémoire
Speicheranzeigetaste

memory cancel
anulación de la memoria
effacement de mémoire
Speicherlöschtaste

number key
tecla de número
touche numérique
Zifferntaste

subtract key
tecla de substracción
soustraction
Subtraktionstaste

decimal key
tecla decimal
touche de décimale
Kommataste

subtract from memory
substracción de la memoria
soustraction en mémoire
Speicherlöschtaste

add in memory
adición en la memoria
addition en mémoire
Speichertaste

clear key
tecla para limpiar la pantalla
effacement total
Löschtaste

divide key
tecla de división
division
Divisionstaste

clear-entry key
tecla para limpiar la pantalla y de acceso
effacement partiel
Eingabe-Löschtaste

square root key
tecla de raíz cuadrada
racine carrée
Quadratwurzeltaste

multiply key
tecla de multiplicación
multiplication
Multiplikationstaste

percent key
tecla de porcentaje
pourcentage
Prozenttaste

add key
tecla de adición
addition
Additionstaste

equal key
tecla de igualdad
touche de résultat
Gleichtaste

change sign key
tecla de cambio de signo
inverseur de signe
Vorzeichentaste

MC MR M- M+ C
7 8 9 ÷ CE
4 5 6 x √
1 2 3 – +/–
0 · % + =

PRINTING CALCULATOR
CALCULADORA CON IMPRESORA
CALCULATRICE À IMPRIMANTE
TISCHRECHNER MIT DRUCKERTEIL

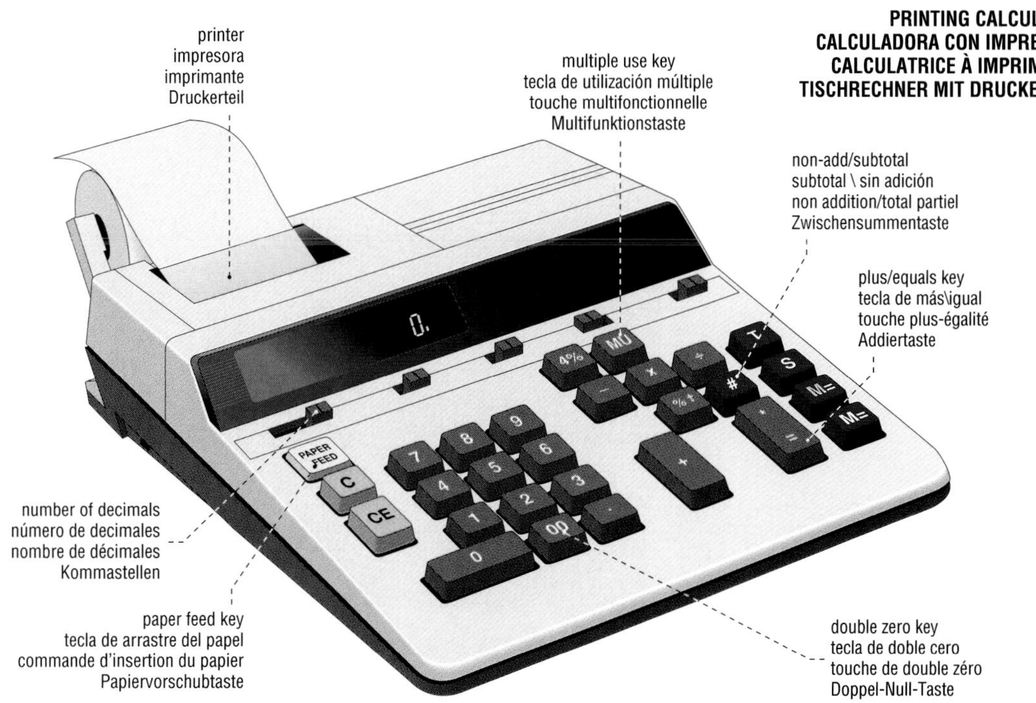
printer
impresora
imprimante
Druckerteil
multiple use key
tecla de utilización múltiple
touche multifonctionnelle
Multifunktionstaste
non-add/subtotal
subtotal \ sin adición
non addition/total partiel
Zwischensummentaste
plus/equals key
tecla de más\igual
touche plus-égalité
Addiertaste
number of decimals
número de decimales
nombre de décimales
Kommastellen
paper feed key
tecla de arrastre del papel
commande d'insertion du papier
Papiervorschubtaste
double zero key
tecla de doble cero
touche de double zéro
Doppel-Null-Taste
PAPER FEED
C
CE

ELECTRONIC TYPEWRITER
MÁQUINA DE ESCRIBIR ELECTRÓNICA
MACHINE À ÉCRIRE ÉLECTRONIQUE
ELEKTRISCHE SCHREIBMASCHINE

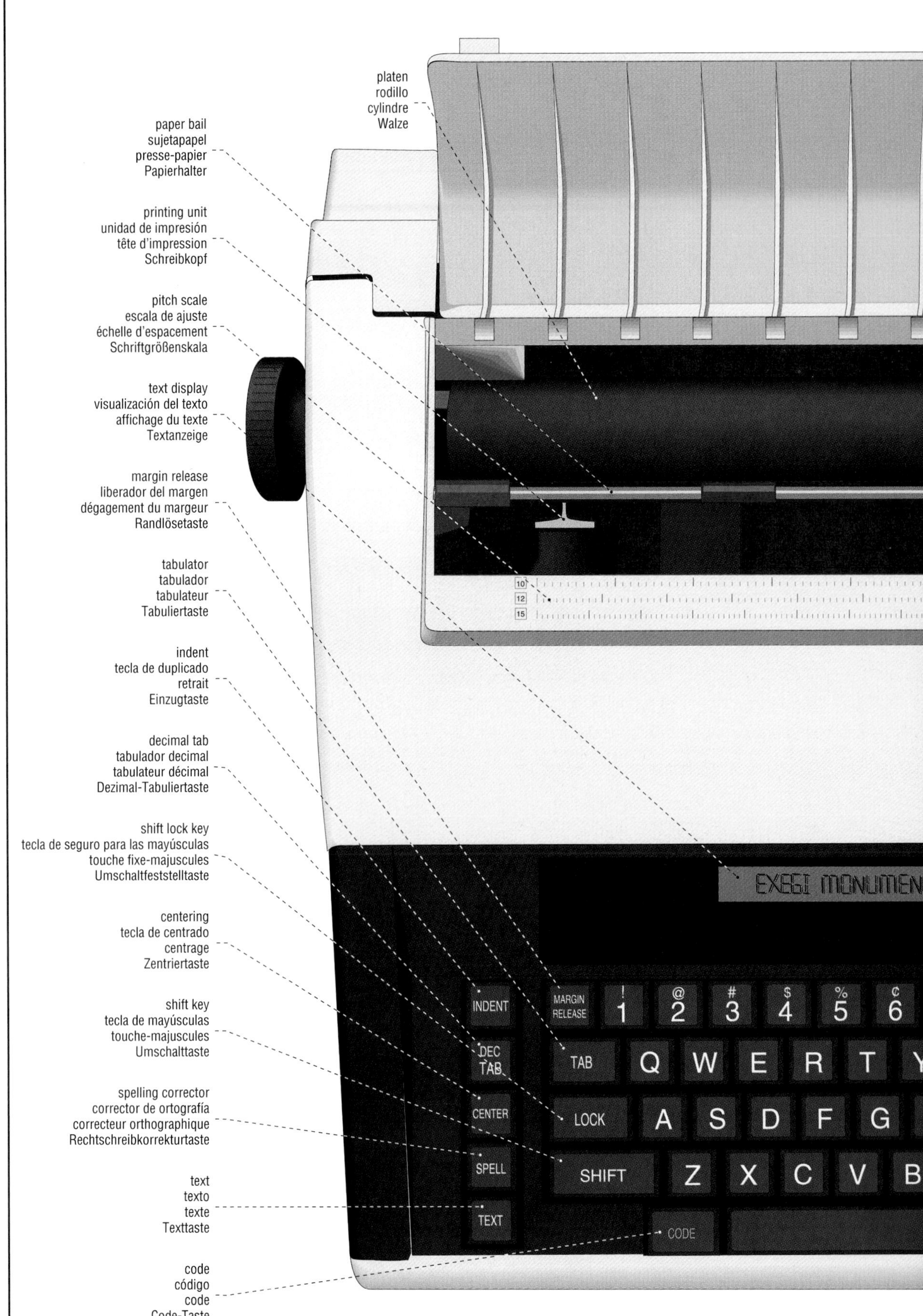
platen
rodillo
cylindre
Walze
paper bail
sujetapapel
presse-papier
Papierhalter
printing unit
unidad de impresión
tête d'impression
Schreibkopf
pitch scale
escala de ajuste
échelle d'espacement
Schriftgrößenskala
text display
visualización del texto
affichage du texte
Textanzeige
margin release
liberador del margen
dégagement du margeur
Randlösetaste
tabulator
tabulador
tabulateur
Tabuliertaste
indent
tecla de duplicado
retrait
Einzugtaste
decimal tab
tabulador decimal
tabulateur décimal
Dezimal-Tabuliertaste
shift lock key
tecla de seguro para las mayúsculas
touche fixe-majuscules
Umschaltfeststelltaste
centering
tecla de centrado
centrage
Zentriertaste
shift key
tecla de mayúsculas
touche-majuscules
Umschalttaste
spelling corrector
corrector de ortografía
correcteur orthographique
Rechtschreibkorrekturtaste
text
texto
texte
Texttaste
code
código
code
Code-Taste
EXEGI MONUMEN
INDENT
MARGIN RELEASE
DEC TAB
TAB
CENTER
LOCK
SPELL
SHIFT
TEXT
CODE

RE PERENNIUS
8
9
0
I
O
P
RELEASE
PHRASE
K
L
M
SHIFT
MODE
MAR
P MAR
RELOC
paper support
soporte del papel
support-papier
Papierstütze
paper release lever
palanca de aflojar el papel
levier de dégagement du papier
Papierlösehebel
paper bail release lever
palanca para liberar el sujetapapel
levier de dégagement du presse-papier
Papierfreigabehebel
variable spacer
embrague de espacios
bouton d'interligne variable
Walzendrehknopf
top plate
lámina superior
capot
Gehäuseabdeckung
word correction
corrección de palabras
correction de mots
Wortkorrekturtaste
character correction
corrección de caracteres
correction de caractères
Zeichenkorrekturtaste
half indexing
indicador de la mitad
positionnement du papier
Hoch-/Tiefstelltaste
carriage return
tecla de regreso del carro
retour de chariot
Wagenrücklauftaste
margin control
control del margen
commande de marge
Randkontrolltaste
tab setting
ajuste del tabulador
contrôle de tabulation
Tabulatoreinstelltaste
set
ajuste
validation
Tabulatorsetztaste
relocation
otra posición
repositionnement
Fixiertaste
mode
modalidad
mode
Mode-Taste
space bar
barra espaciadora
barre d'espacement
Leertaste

CONFIGURATION OF AN OFFICE AUTOMATION SYSTEM
CONFIGURACIÓN DEL SISTEMA DE UNA OFICINA AUTOMATIZADA
CONFIGURATION D'UN SYSTÈME BUREAUTIQUE
ZUSAMMENSTELLUNG EINES AUTOMATISIERTEN BÜROS

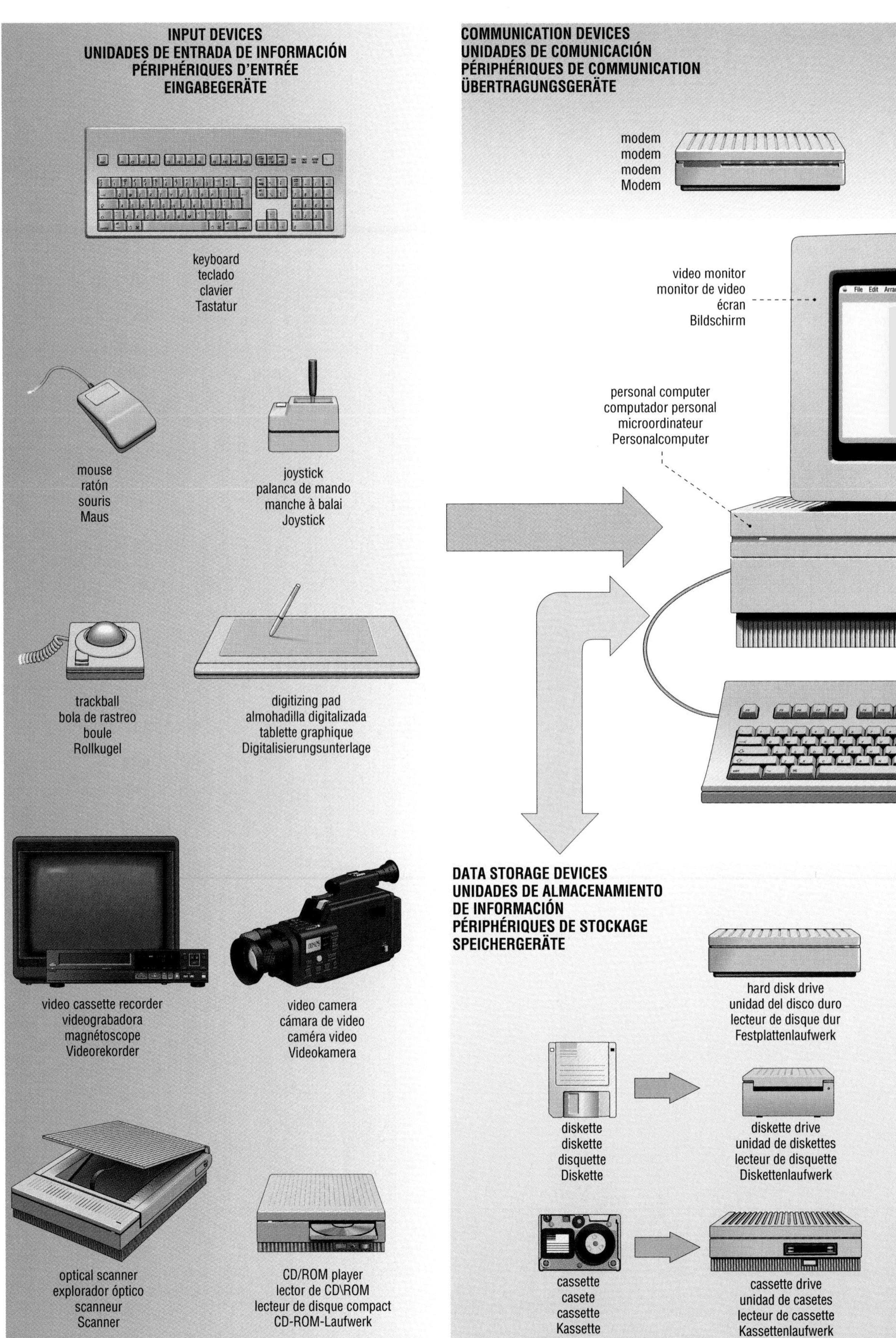
INPUT DEVICES
UNIDADES DE ENTRADA DE INFORMACIÓN
PÉRIPHÉRIQUES D'ENTRÉE
EINGABEGERÄTE
keyboard
teclado
clavier
Tastatur
mouse
ratón
souris
Maus
joystick
palanca de mando
manche à balai
Joystick
trackball
bola de rastreo
boule
Rollkugel
digitizing pad
almohadilla digitalizada
tablette graphique
Digitalisierungsunterlage
video cassette recorder
videograbadora
magnétoscope
Videorekorder
video camera
cámara de video
caméra video
Videokamera
optical scanner
explorador óptico
scanneur
Scanner
CD/ROM player
lector de CD\ROM
lecteur de disque compact
CD-ROM-Laufwerk
COMMUNICATION DEVICES
UNIDADES DE COMUNICACIÓN
PÉRIPHÉRIQUES DE COMMUNICATION
ÜBERTRAGUNGSGERÄTE
modem
modem
modem
Modem
video monitor
monitor de video
écran
Bildschirm
File Edit Arrange
personal computer
computador personal
microordinateur
Personalcomputer
DATA STORAGE DEVICES
UNIDADES DE ALMACENAMIENTO
DE INFORMACIÓN
PÉRIPHÉRIQUES DE STOCKAGE
SPEICHERGERÄTE
hard disk drive
unidad del disco duro
lecteur de disque dur
Festplattenlaufwerk
diskette
diskette
disquette
Diskette
diskette drive
unidad de diskettes
lecteur de disquette
Diskettenlaufwerk
cassette
casete
cassette
Kassette
cassette drive
unidad de casetes
lecteur de cassette
Kassettenlaufwerk

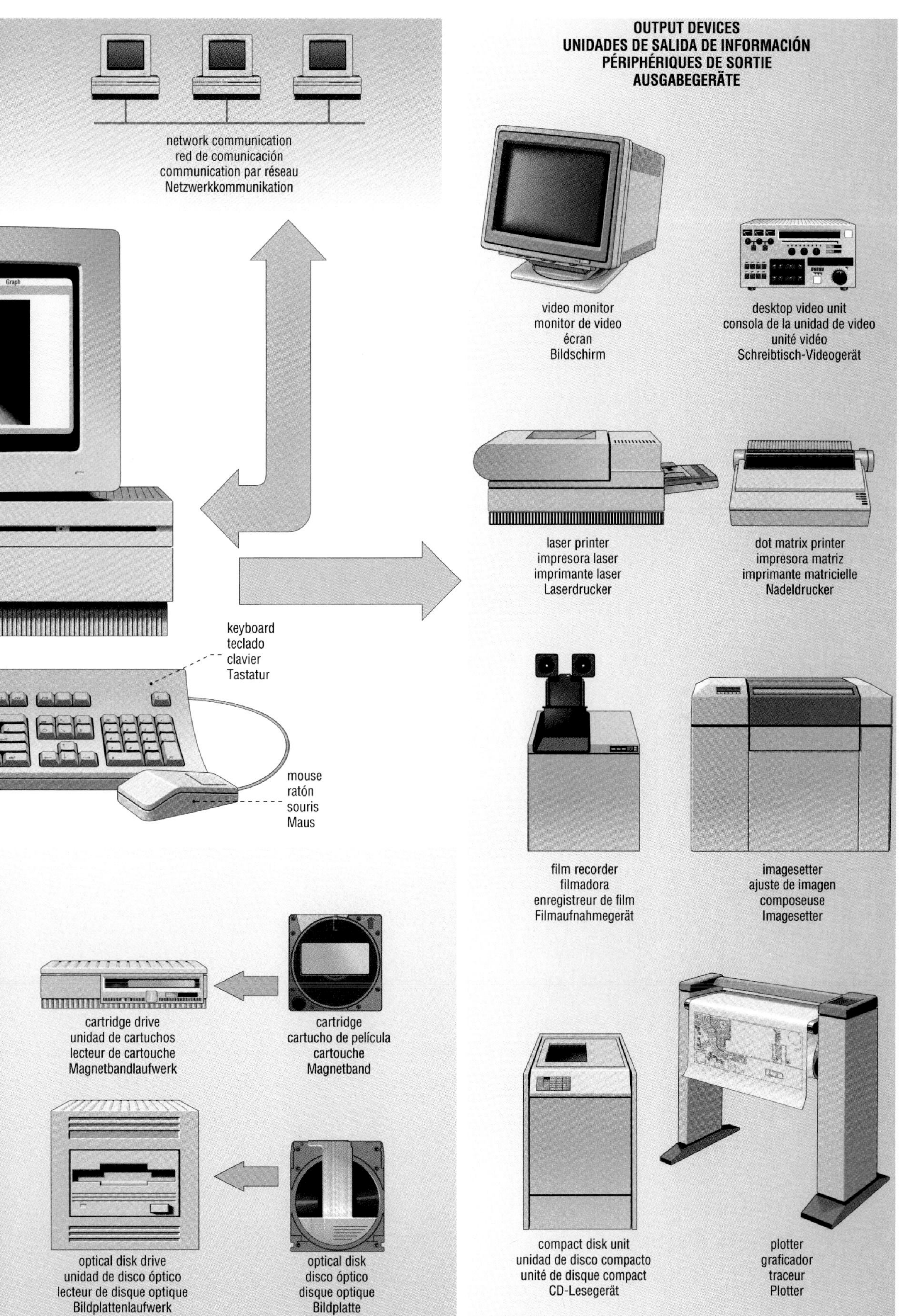
network communication
red de comunicación
communication par réseau
Netzwerkkommunikation
keyboard
teclado
clavier
Tastatur
mouse
ratón
souris
Maus
OUTPUT DEVICES
UNIDADES DE SALIDA DE INFORMACIÓN
PÉRIPHÉRIQUES DE SORTIE
AUSGABEGERÄTE
video monitor
monitor de video
écran
Bildschirm
desktop video unit
consola de la unidad de video
unité vidéo
Schreibtisch-Videogerät
laser printer
impresora laser
imprimante laser
Laserdrucker
dot matrix printer
impresora matriz
imprimante matricielle
Nadeldrucker
film recorder
filmadora
enregistreur de film
Filmaufnahmegerät
imagesetter
ajuste de imagen
composeuse
Imagesetter
cartridge drive
unidad de cartuchos
lecteur de cartouche
Magnetbandlaufwerk
cartridge
cartucho de película
cartouche
Magnetband
compact disk unit
unidad de disco compacto
unité de disque compact
CD-Lesegerät
plotter
graficador
traceur
Plotter
optical disk drive
unidad de disco óptico
lecteur de disque optique
Bildplattenlaufwerk
optical disk
disco óptico
disque optique
Bildplatte

BASIC COMPONENTS
COMPONENTES BÁSICOS
SYSTÈME DE BASE
GRUNDBAUTEILE

PERSONAL COMPUTER (VIEW FROM ABOVE)
VISTA POR ENCIMA DE UN COMPUTADOR PERSONAL
MICRO-ORDINATEUR (VUE EN PLONGÉE)
PERSONALCOMPUTER

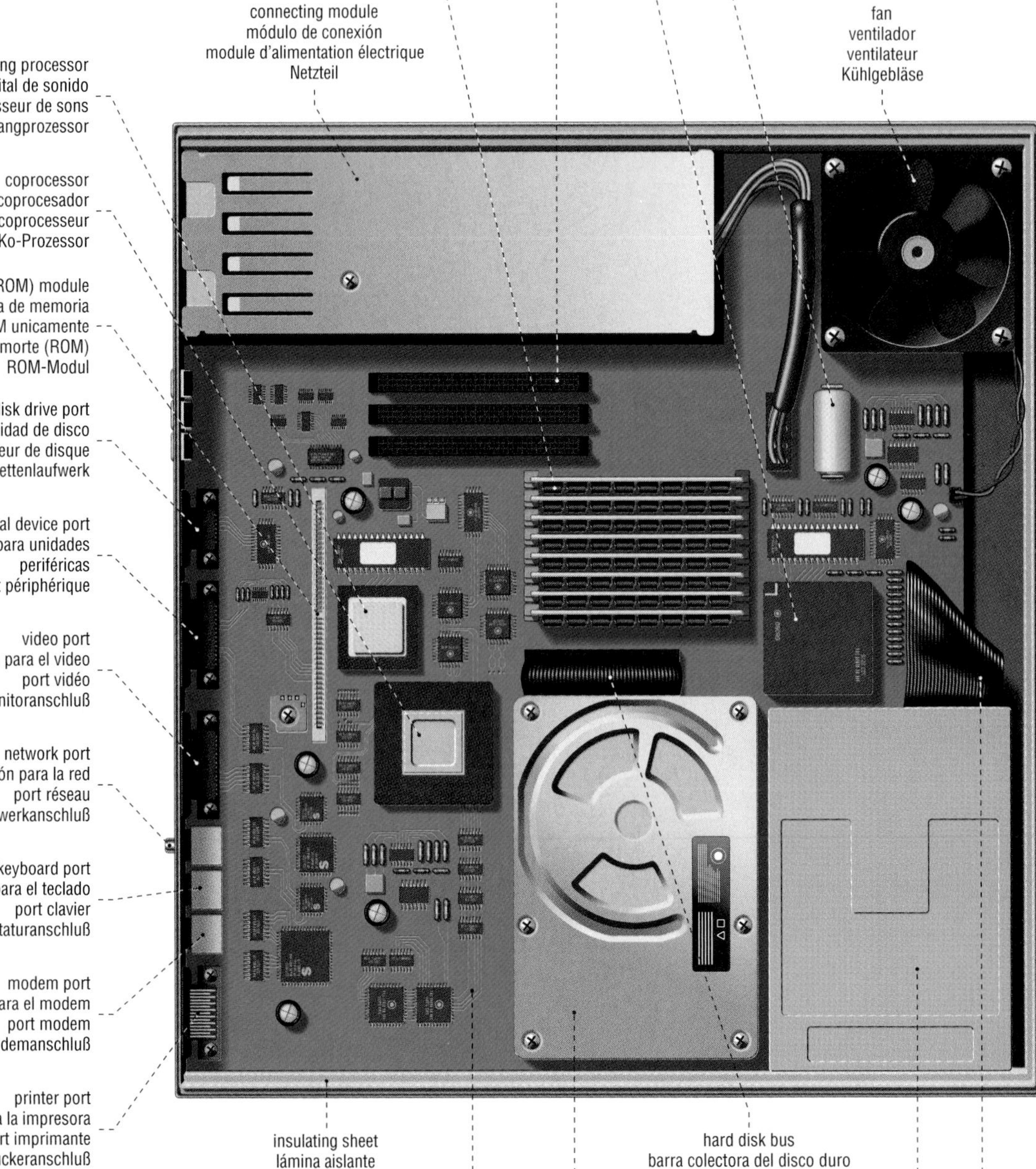

expansion connector
conector de expansión
connecteur d'extension
Speichererweiterungsanschluß

microprocessor
microprocesador
microprocesseur
Mikroprozessor

random access memory (RAM) module
módulo de acceso a la memoria RAM
module de mémoire vive (RAM)
Arbeitsspeicher(RAM)-Modul

battery
batería
pile
Batterie

connecting module
módulo de conexión
module d'alimentation électrique
Netzteil

fan
ventilador
ventilateur
Kühlgebläse

sound digitizing processor
procesador digital de sonido
processeur de sons
Klangprozessor

coprocessor
coprocesador
coprocesseur
Ko-Prozessor

read-only memory (ROM) module
módulo de lectura de memoria ROM unicamente
module de mémoire morte (ROM)
ROM-Modul

disk drive port
conexión para unidad de disco
port lecteur de disque
Anschluß für Diskettenlaufwerk

peripheral device port
conexión para unidades periféricas
port périphérique

video port
conexión para el video
port vidéo
Monitoranschluß

network port
conexión para la red
port réseau
Netzwerkanschluß

keyboard port
conexión para el teclado
port clavier
Tastaturanschluß

modem port
conexión para el modem
port modem
Modemanschluß

printer port
conexión para la impresora
port imprimante
Druckeranschluß

insulating sheet
lámina aislante
surface isolante
Isolierabdeckung

hard disk bus
barra colectora del disco duro
bus du disque dur
Festplattenbus

printed circuit
circuito impreso
circuit imprimé
Platine

floppy disk drive
unidad del disco flexible
lecteur de disquette
Diskettenlaufwerk

hard disk drive
unidad del disco duro
lecteur de disque dur
Festplattenlaufwerk

data bus
barra colectora de información
bus de données
Datenbus

VIDEO MONITOR
MONITOR DEL VIDEO
ÉCRAN
BILDSCHIRMEINHEIT

vertical control
control vertical
réglage vertical
vertikale Einstellung
horizontal control
control horizontal
réglage horizontal
horizontale Einstellung
centering control
control de centrado
réglage de centrage
Zentriereinstellung
contrast control
control de contraste
réglage du contraste
Kontrastregler
power indicator
indicador de encendido
témoin d'alimentation
Leuchtanzeige
power switch
interruptor
interrupteur
Netzschalter
brightness control
control de brillo
réglage de la luminosité
Helligkeitsregler

FLOPPY DISK
DISCO FLEXIBLE
DISQUETTE SOUPLE
FLOPPY-DISK

MINI-FLOPPY DISK
DISCO FLEXIBLE PEQUEÑO
DISQUETTE RIGIDE
MINI-DISKETTE

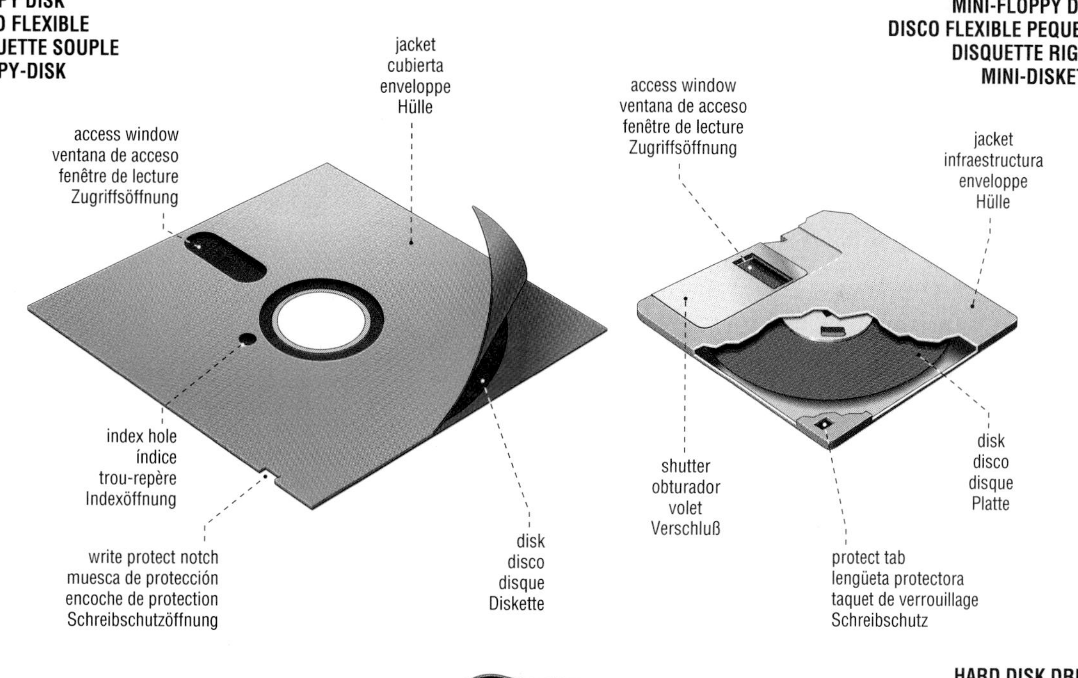
jacket
cubierta
enveloppe
Hülle
access window
ventana de acceso
fenêtre de lecture
Zugriffsöffnung
index hole
índice
trou-repère
Indexöffnung
write protect notch
muesca de protección
encoche de protection
Schreibschutzöffnung
disk
disco
disque
Diskette
access window
ventana de acceso
fenêtre de lecture
Zugriffsöffnung
jacket
infraestructura
enveloppe
Hülle
shutter
obturador
volet
Verschluß
disk
disco
disque
Platte
protect tab
lengüeta protectora
taquet de verrouillage
Schreibschutz

HARD DISK DRIVE
UNIDAD DEL DISCO DURO
LECTEUR DE DISQUE DUR
FESTPLATTENLAUFWERK

actuator arm
brazo actuador
guide
Sucharm
actuator arm motor
motor del brazo actuador
moteur de guides
Führungsschienenantrieb
disk
disco
disque
Platte
disk motor
motor del disco
moteur de disques
Plattenantrieb
read/write head
cabeza de lectura \ escritura
tête de lecture/écriture
Schreib-/Lesekopf

BASIC COMPONENTS
COMPONENTES BÁSICOS
SYSTÈME DE BASE
GRUNDBAUTEILE

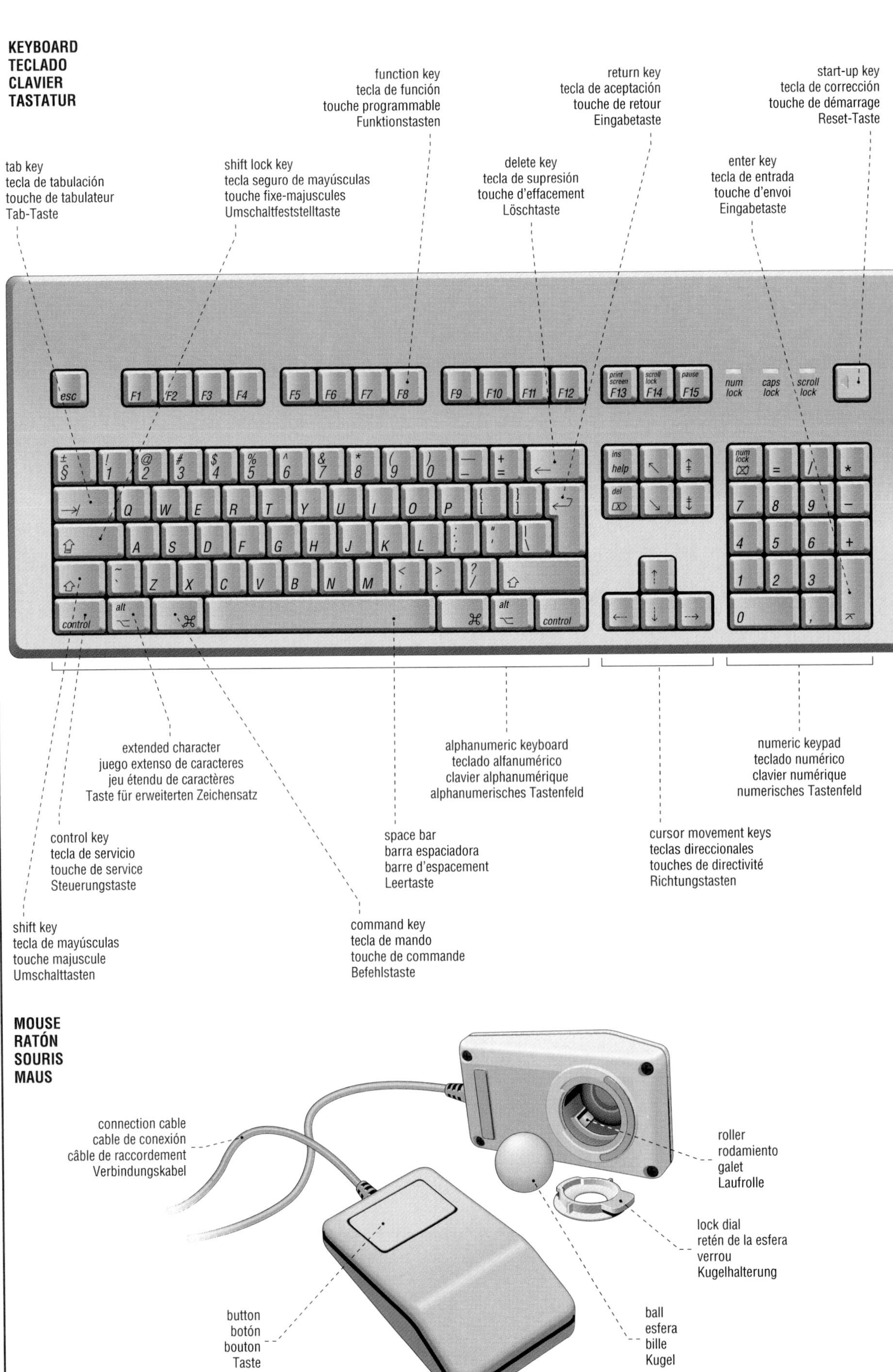
KEYBOARD
TECLADO
CLAVIER
TASTATUR
function key
tecla de función
touche programmable
Funktionstasten
return key
tecla de aceptación
touche de retour
Eingabetaste
start-up key
tecla de corrección
touche de démarrage
Reset-Taste
tab key
tecla de tabulación
touche de tabulateur
Tab-Taste
shift lock key
tecla seguro de mayúsculas
touche fixe-majuscules
Umschaltfeststelltaste
delete key
tecla de supresión
touche d'effacement
Löschtaste
enter key
tecla de entrada
touche d'envoi
Eingabetaste
extended character
juego extenso de caracteres
jeu étendu de caractères
Taste für erweiterten Zeichensatz
alphanumeric keyboard
teclado alfanumérico
clavier alphanumérique
alphanumerisches Tastenfeld
numeric keypad
teclado numérico
clavier numérique
numerisches Tastenfeld
control key
tecla de servicio
touche de service
Steuerungstaste
space bar
barra espaciadora
barre d'espacement
Leertaste
cursor movement keys
teclas direccionales
touches de directivité
Richtungstasten
shift key
tecla de mayúsculas
touche majuscule
Umschalttasten
command key
tecla de mando
touche de commande
Befehlstaste
MOUSE
RATÓN
SOURIS
MAUS
connection cable
cable de conexión
câble de raccordement
Verbindungskabel
roller
rodamiento
galet
Laufrolle
lock dial
retén de la esfera
verrou
Kugelhalterung
button
botón
bouton
Taste
ball
esfera
bille
Kugel

DOT MATRIX PRINTER
IMPRESORA MATRIZ
IMPRIMANTE MATRICIELLE
NADELDRUCKER

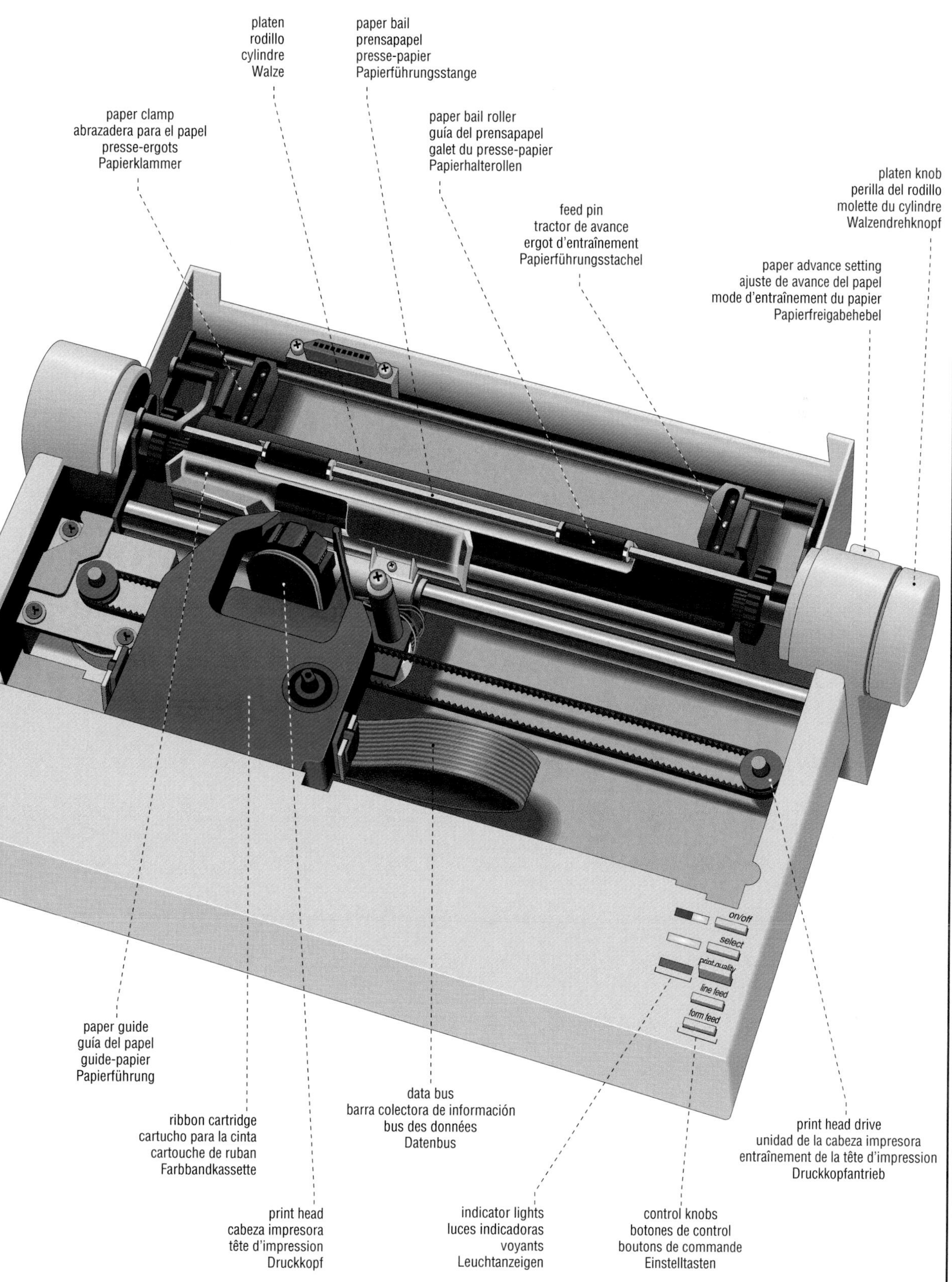
platen
rodillo
cylindre
Walze
paper bail
prensapapel
presse-papier
Papierführungsstange
paper clamp
abrazadera para el papel
presse-ergots
Papierklammer
paper bail roller
guía del prensapapel
galet du presse-papier
Papierhalterollen
feed pin
tractor de avance
ergot d'entraînement
Papierführungsstachel
platen knob
perilla del rodillo
molette du cylindre
Walzendrehknopf
paper advance setting
ajuste de avance del papel
mode d'entraînement du papier
Papierfreigabehebel
on/off
select
print quality
line feed
form feed
paper guide
guía del papel
guide-papier
Papierführung
data bus
barra colectora de información
bus des données
Datenbus
ribbon cartridge
cartucho para la cinta
cartouche de ruban
Farbbandkassette
print head drive
unidad de la cabeza impresora
entraînement de la tête d'impression
Druckkopfantrieb
print head
cabeza impresora
tête d'impression
Druckkopf
indicator lights
luces indicadoras
voyants
Leuchtanzeigen
control knobs
botones de control
boutons de commande
Einstelltasten

PHOTOCOPIER
FOTOCOPIADORA
PHOTOCOPIEUR
FOTOKOPIERER

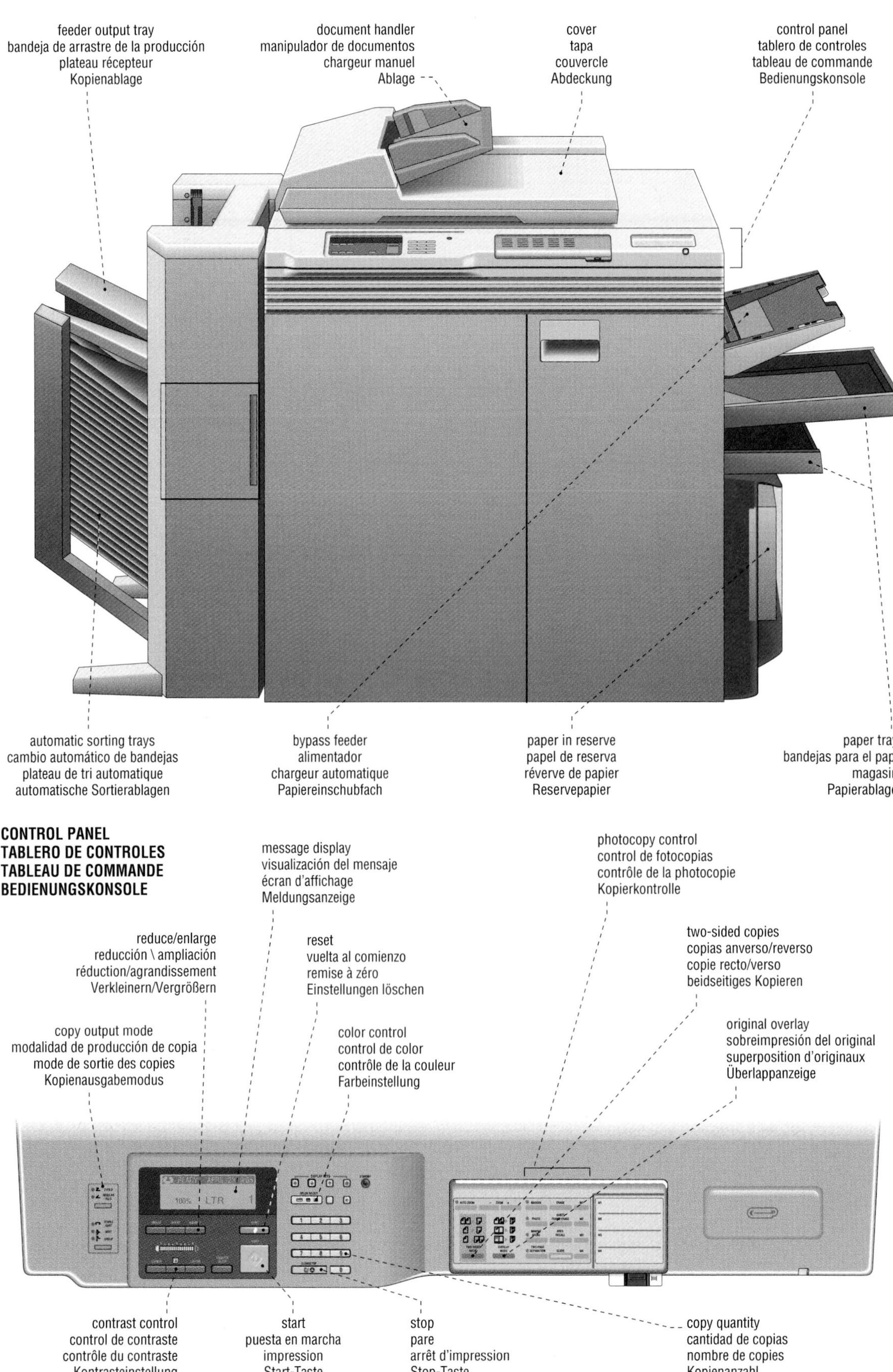
feeder output tray
bandeja de arrastre de la producción
plateau récepteur
Kopienablage
document handler
manipulador de documentos
chargeur manuel
Ablage
cover
tapa
couvercle
Abdeckung
control panel
tablero de controles
tableau de commande
Bedienungskonsole
automatic sorting trays
cambio automático de bandejas
plateau de tri automatique
automatische Sortierablagen
bypass feeder
alimentador
chargeur automatique
Papiereinschubfach
paper in reserve
papel de reserva
réverve de papier
Reservepapier
paper trays
bandejas para el papel
magasins
Papierablagen
CONTROL PANEL
TABLERO DE CONTROLES
TABLEAU DE COMMANDE
BEDIENUNGSKONSOLE
message display
visualización del mensaje
écran d'affichage
Meldungsanzeige
photocopy control
control de fotocopias
contrôle de la photocopie
Kopierkontrolle
reduce/enlarge
reducción \ ampliación
réduction/agrandissement
Verkleinern/Vergrößern
reset
vuelta al comienzo
remise à zéro
Einstellungen löschen
two-sided copies
copias anverso/reverso
copie recto/verso
beidseitiges Kopieren
copy output mode
modalidad de producción de copia
mode de sortie des copies
Kopienausgabemodus
color control
control de color
contrôle de la couleur
Farbeinstellung
original overlay
sobreimpresión del original
superposition d'originaux
Überlappanzeige
100% LTR 1
contrast control
control de contraste
contrôle du contraste
Kontrasteinstellung
start
puesta en marcha
impression
Start-Taste
stop
pare
arrêt d'impression
Stop-Taste
copy quantity
cantidad de copias
nombre de copies
Kopienanzahl

MUSIC MÚSICA MUSIQUE MUSIK

CONTENTS

TRADITIONAL MUSICAL INSTRUMENTS
INSTRUMENTOS MUSICALES TRADICIONALES
INSTRUMENTS TRADITIONNELS
TRADITIONELLE MUSIKINSTRUMENTE

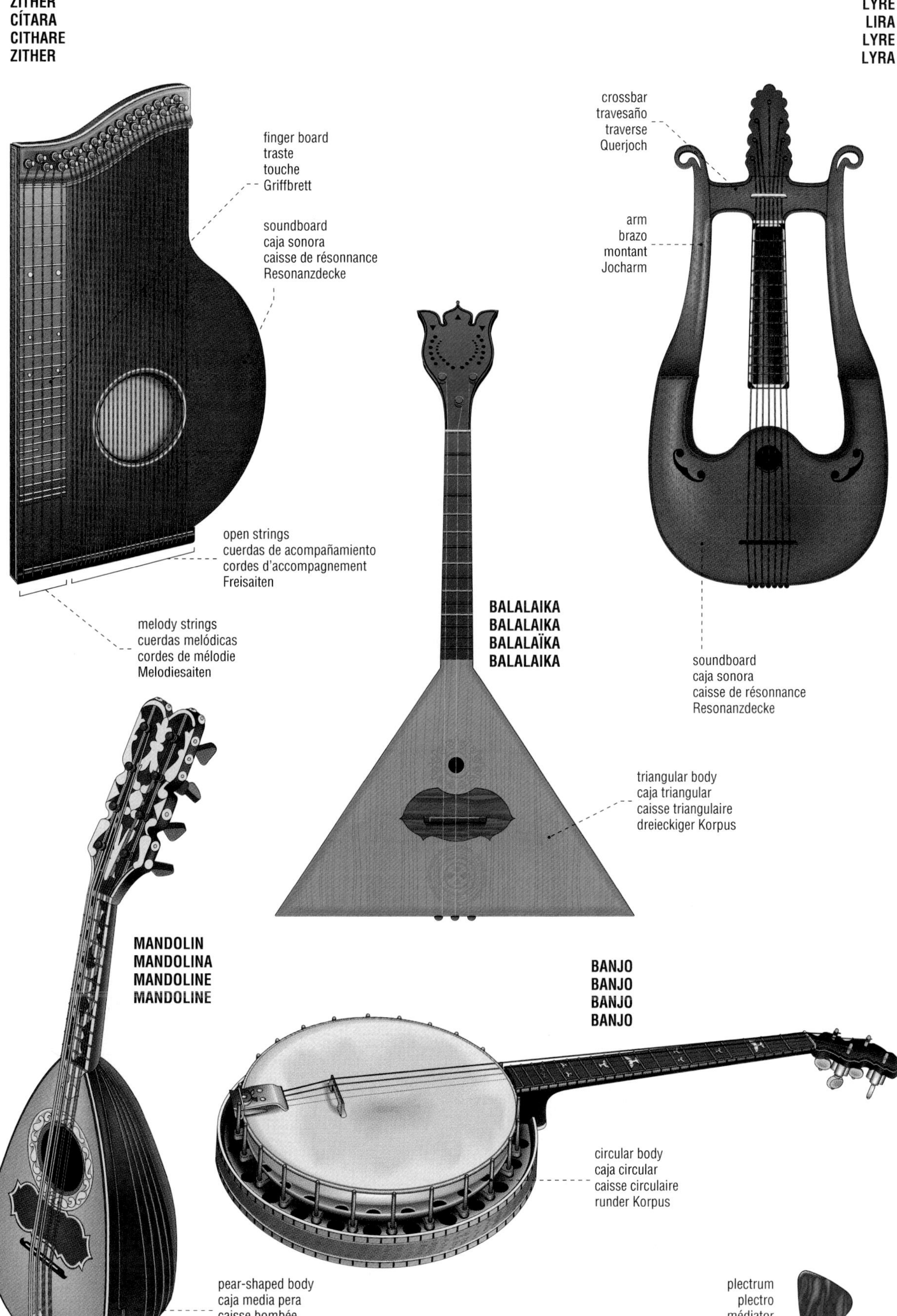

ZITHER
CÍTARA
CITHARE
ZITHER
finger board
traste
touche
Griffbrett
soundboard
caja sonora
caisse de résonnance
Resonanzdecke
open strings
cuerdas de acompañamiento
cordes d'accompagnement
Freisaiten
melody strings
cuerdas melódicas
cordes de mélodie
Melodiesaiten
LYRE
LIRA
LYRE
LYRA
crossbar
travesaño
traverse
Querjoch
arm
brazo
montant
Jocharm
soundboard
caja sonora
caisse de résonnance
Resonanzdecke
BALALAIKA
BALALAIKA
BALALAÏKA
BALALAIKA
triangular body
caja triangular
caisse triangulaire
dreieckiger Korpus
MANDOLIN
MANDOLINA
MANDOLINE
MANDOLINE
BANJO
BANJO
BANJO
BANJO
circular body
caja circular
caisse circulaire
runder Korpus
pear-shaped body
caja media pera
caisse bombée
birnenförmiger Korpus
plectrum
plectro
médiator
Plektron

TRADITIONAL MUSICAL INSTRUMENTS
INSTRUMENTOS MUSICALES TRADICIONALES
INSTRUMENTS TRADITIONNELS
TRADITIONELLE MUSIKINSTRUMENTE

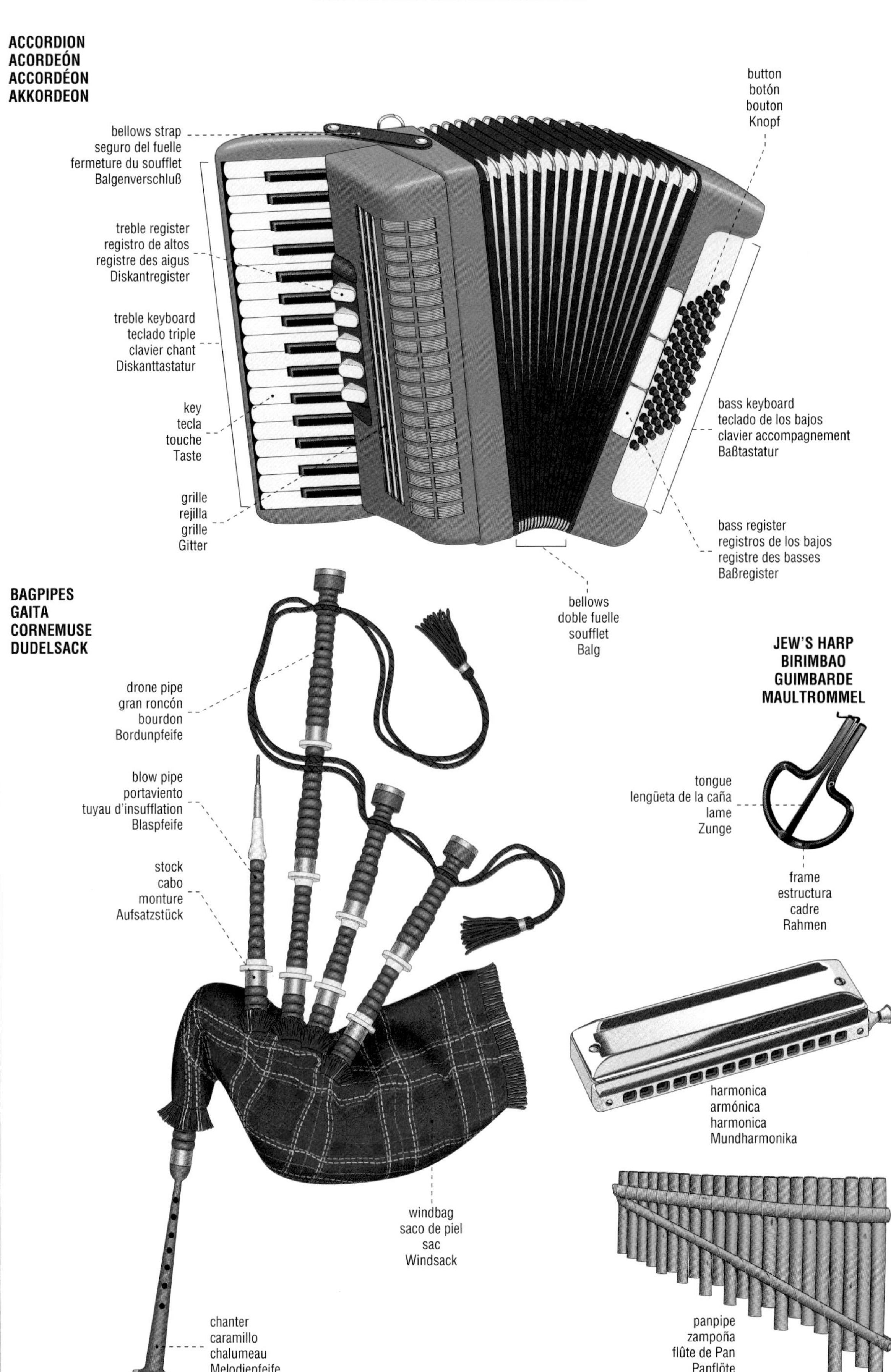

ACCORDION
ACORDEÓN
ACCORDÉON
AKKORDEON
bellows strap
seguro del fuelle
fermeture du soufflet
Balgenverschluß
treble register
registro de altos
registre des aigus
Diskantregister
treble keyboard
teclado triple
clavier chant
Diskanttastatur
key
tecla
touche
Taste
grille
rejilla
grille
Gitter
button
botón
bouton
Knopf
bass keyboard
teclado de los bajos
clavier accompagnement
Baßtastatur
bass register
registros de los bajos
registre des basses
Baßregister
bellows
doble fuelle
soufflet
Balg
BAGPIPES
GAITA
CORNEMUSE
DUDELSACK
drone pipe
gran roncón
bourdon
Bordunpfeife
blow pipe
portaviento
tuyau d'insufflation
Blaspfeife
stock
cabo
monture
Aufsatzstück
windbag
saco de piel
sac
Windsack
chanter
caramillo
chalumeau
Melodiepfeife
JEW'S HARP
BIRIMBAO
GUIMBARDE
MAULTROMMEL
tongue
lengüeta de la caña
lame
Zunge
frame
estructura
cadre
Rahmen
harmonica
armónica
harmonica
Mundharmonika
panpipe
zampoña
flûte de Pan
Panflöte

MUSICAL NOTATION
NOTACIÓN MUSICAL
NOTATION MUSICALE
MUSIKNOTATION

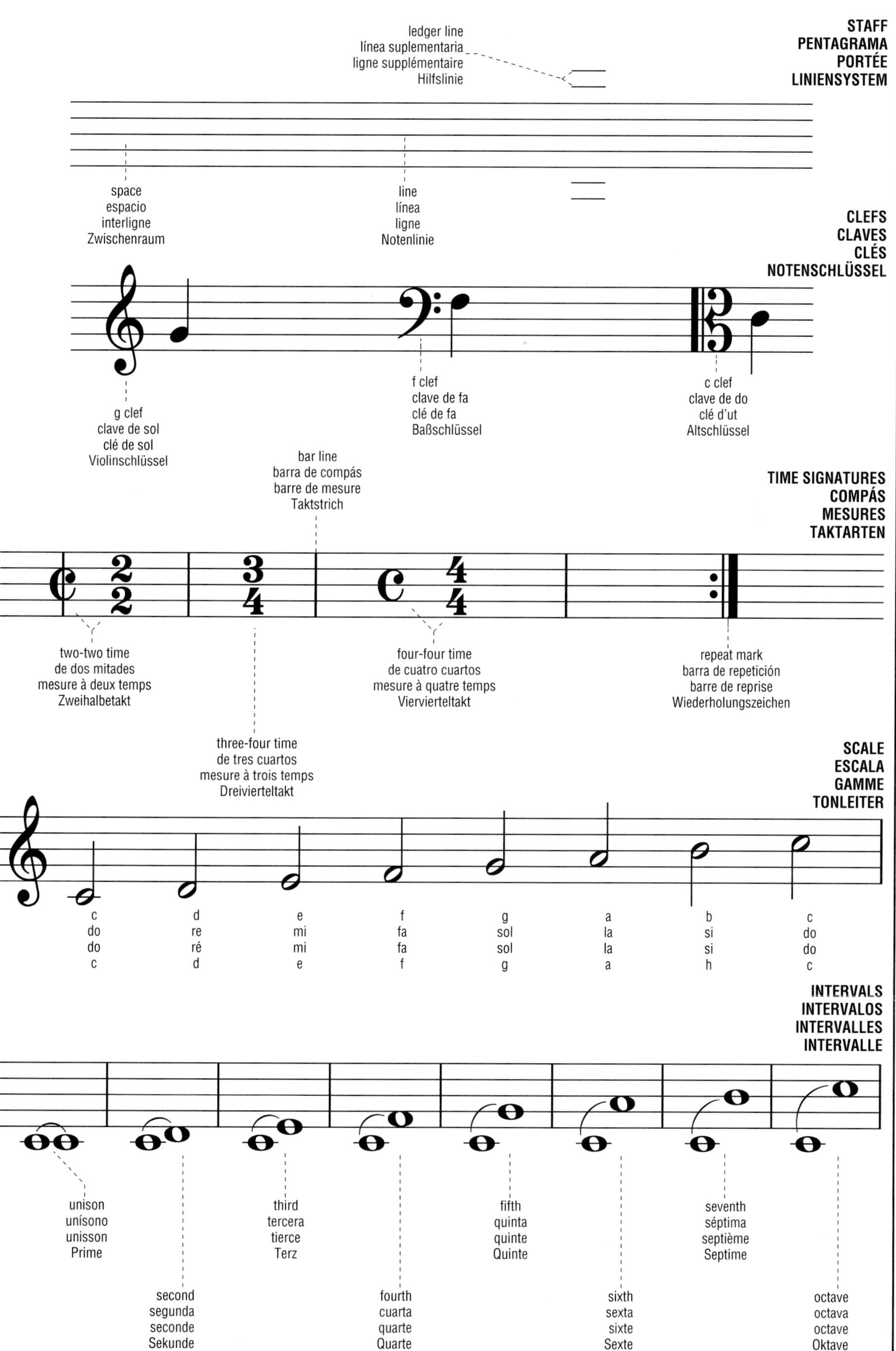

STAFF
PENTAGRAMA
PORTÉE
LINIENSYSTEM
ledger line
línea suplementaria
ligne supplémentaire
Hilfslinie
space
espacio
interligne
Zwischenraum
line
línea
ligne
Notenlinie
CLEFS
CLAVES
CLÉS
NOTENSCHLÜSSEL
g clef
clave de sol
clé de sol
Violinschlüssel
f clef
clave de fa
clé de fa
Baßschlüssel
c clef
clave de do
clé d'ut
Altschlüssel
TIME SIGNATURES
COMPÁS
MESURES
TAKTARTEN
bar line
barra de compás
barre de mesure
Taktstrich
2
2
3
4
4
4
two-two time
de dos mitades
mesure à deux temps
Zweihalbetakt
three-four time
de tres cuartos
mesure à trois temps
Dreivierteltakt
four-four time
de cuatro cuartos
mesure à quatre temps
Viervierteltakt
repeat mark
barra de repetición
barre de reprise
Wiederholungszeichen
SCALE
ESCALA
GAMME
TONLEITER
c do do c
d re ré d
e mi mi e
f fa fa f
g sol sol g
a la la a
b si si h
c do do c
INTERVALS
INTERVALOS
INTERVALLES
INTERVALLE
unison
unísono
unisson
Prime
second
segunda
seconde
Sekunde
third
tercera
tierce
Terz
fourth
cuarta
quarte
Quarte
fifth
quinta
quinte
Quinte
sixth
sexta
sixte
Sexte
seventh
séptima
septième
Septime
octave
octava
octave
Oktave

MUSICAL NOTATION
NOTACIÓN MUSICAL
NOTATION MUSICALE
MUSIKNOTATION

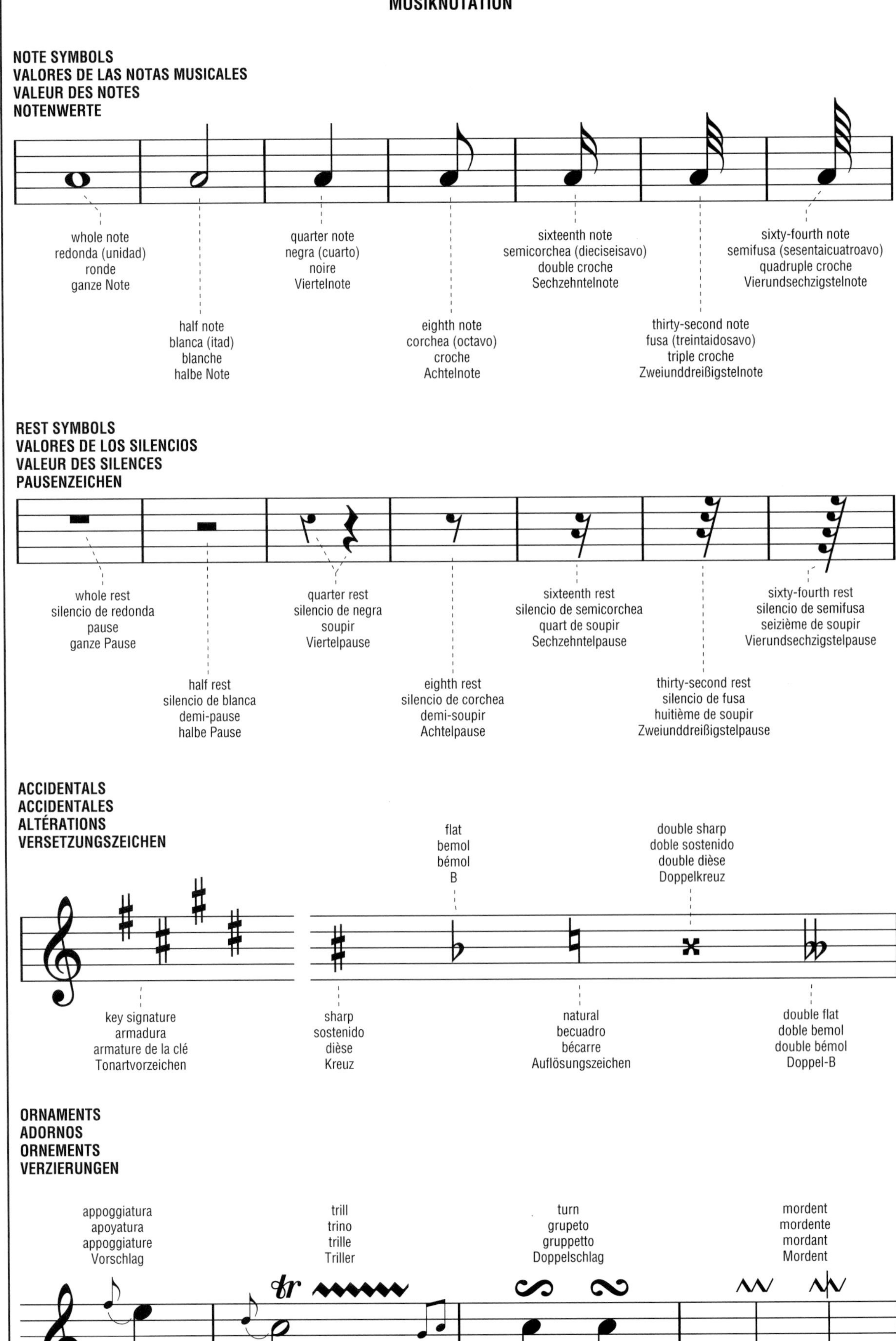
NOTE SYMBOLS
VALORES DE LAS NOTAS MUSICALES
VALEUR DES NOTES
NOTENWERTE
whole note
redonda (unidad)
ronde
ganze Note
half note
blanca (itad)
blanche
halbe Note
quarter note
negra (cuarto)
noire
Viertelnote
eighth note
corchea (octavo)
croche
Achtelnote
sixteenth note
semicorchea (dieciseisavo)
double croche
Sechzehntelnote
thirty-second note
fusa (treintaidosavo)
triple croche
Zweiunddreißigstelnote
sixty-fourth note
semifusa (sesentaicuatroavo)
quadruple croche
Vierundsechzigstelnote
REST SYMBOLS
VALORES DE LOS SILENCIOS
VALEUR DES SILENCES
PAUSENZEICHEN
whole rest
silencio de redonda
pause
ganze Pause
half rest
silencio de blanca
demi-pause
halbe Pause
quarter rest
silencio de negra
soupir
Viertelpause
eighth rest
silencio de corchea
demi-soupir
Achtelpause
sixteenth rest
silencio de semicorchea
quart de soupir
Sechzehntelpause
thirty-second rest
silencio de fusa
huitième de soupir
Zweiunddreißigstelpause
sixty-fourth rest
silencio de semifusa
seizième de soupir
Vierundsechzigstelpause
ACCIDENTALS
ACCIDENTALES
ALTÉRATIONS
VERSETZUNGSZEICHEN
flat
bemol
bémol
B
double sharp
doble sostenido
double dièse
Doppelkreuz
key signature
armadura
armature de la clé
Tonartvorzeichen
sharp
sostenido
dièse
Kreuz
natural
becuadro
bécarre
Auflösungszeichen
double flat
doble bemol
double bémol
Doppel-B
ORNAMENTS
ADORNOS
ORNEMENTS
VERZIERUNGEN
appoggiatura
apoyatura
appoggiature
Vorschlag
trill
trino
trille
Triller
tr
turn
grupeto
gruppetto
Doppelschlag
mordent
mordente
mordant
Mordent

CHORD
ACORDE
ACCORD
AKKORD

OTHER SIGNS
OTROS SIGNOS
AUTRES SIGNES
ANDERE ZEICHEN

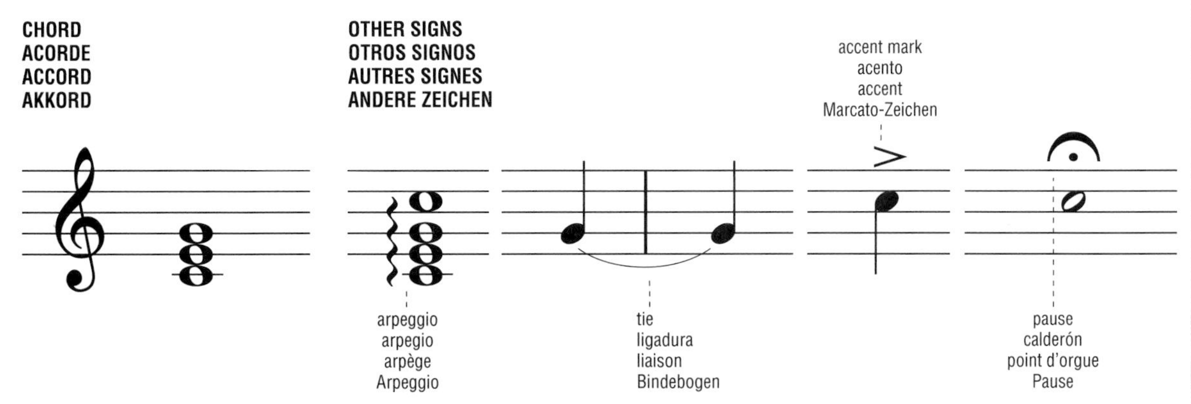
accent mark
acento
accent
Marcato-Zeichen
arpeggio
arpegio
arpège
Arpeggio
tie
ligadura
liaison
Bindebogen
pause
calderón
point d'orgue
Pause

MUSICAL ACCESSORIES
ACCESORIOS MUSICALES
ACCESSOIRES
MUSIKZUBEHÖR

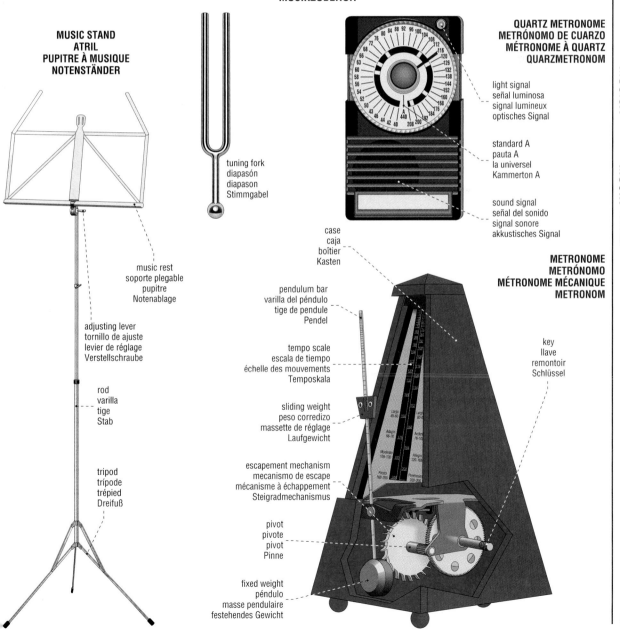

MUSIC STAND
ATRIL
PUPITRE À MUSIQUE
NOTENSTÄNDER

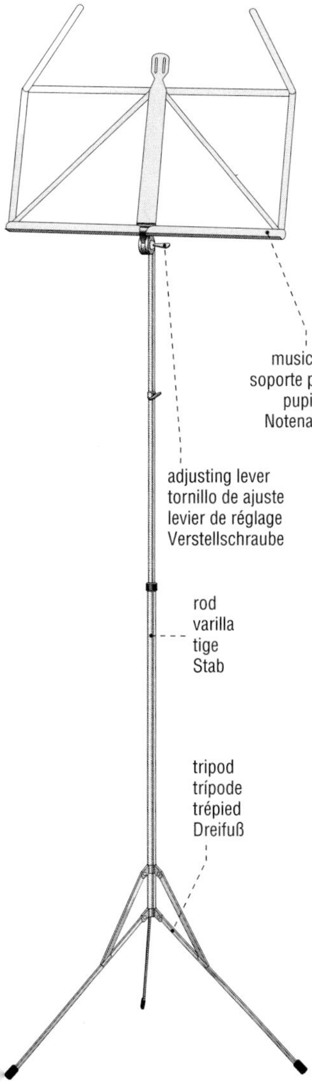

music rest
soporte plegable
pupitre
Notenablage

adjusting lever
tornillo de ajuste
levier de réglage
Verstellschraube

rod
varilla
tige
Stab

tripod
trípode
trépied
Dreifuß

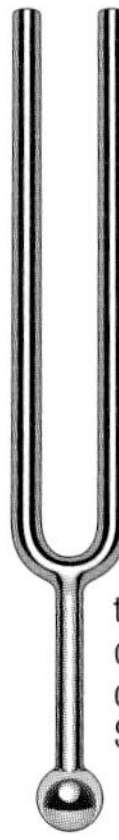

tuning fork
diapasón
diapason
Stimmgabel

QUARTZ METRONOME
METRÓNOMO DE CUARZO
MÉTRONOME À QUARTZ
QUARZMETRONOM

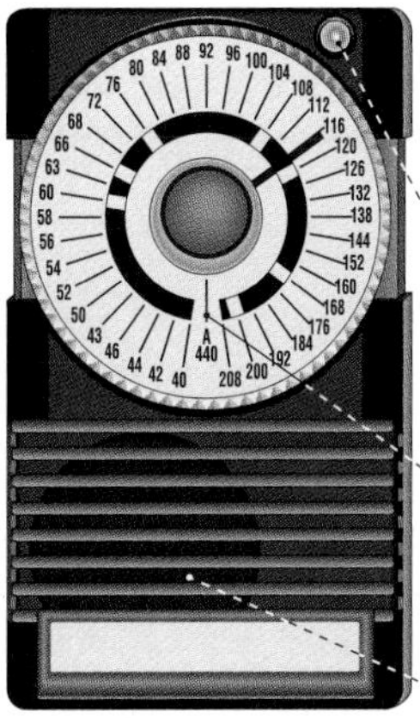

light signal
señal luminosa
signal lumineux
optisches Signal

standard A
pauta A
la universel
Kammerton A

sound signal
señal del sonido
signal sonore
akkustisches Signal

METRONOME
METRÓNOMO
MÉTRONOME MÉCANIQUE
METRONOM

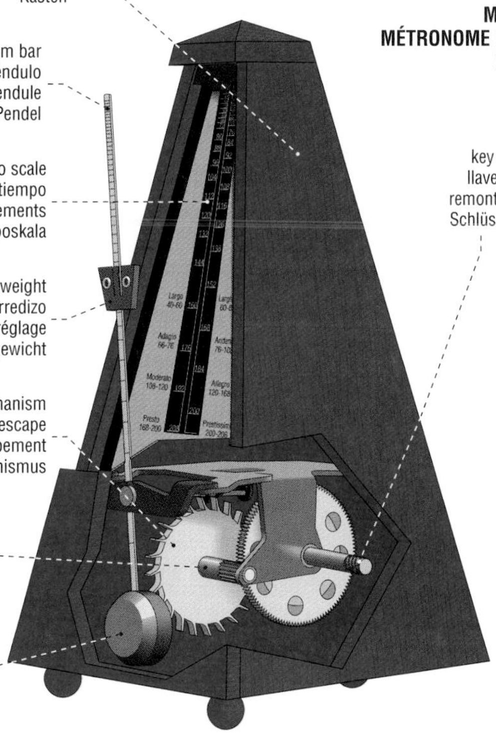

case
caja
boîtier
Kasten

pendulum bar
varilla del péndulo
tige de pendule
Pendel

tempo scale
escala de tiempo
échelle des mouvements
Temposkala

sliding weight
peso corredizo
massette de réglage
Laufgewicht

escapement mechanism
mecanismo de escape
mécanisme à échappement
Steigradmechanismus

pivot
pivote
pivot
Pinne

fixed weight
péndulo
masse pendulaire
festehendes Gewicht

key
llave
remontoir
Schlüssel

KEYBOARD INSTRUMENTS
INSTRUMENTOS DE TECLADO
INSTRUMENTS À CLAVIER
TASTENINSTRUMENTE

UPRIGHT PIANO
PIANO VERTICAL
PIANO DROIT
KLAVIER

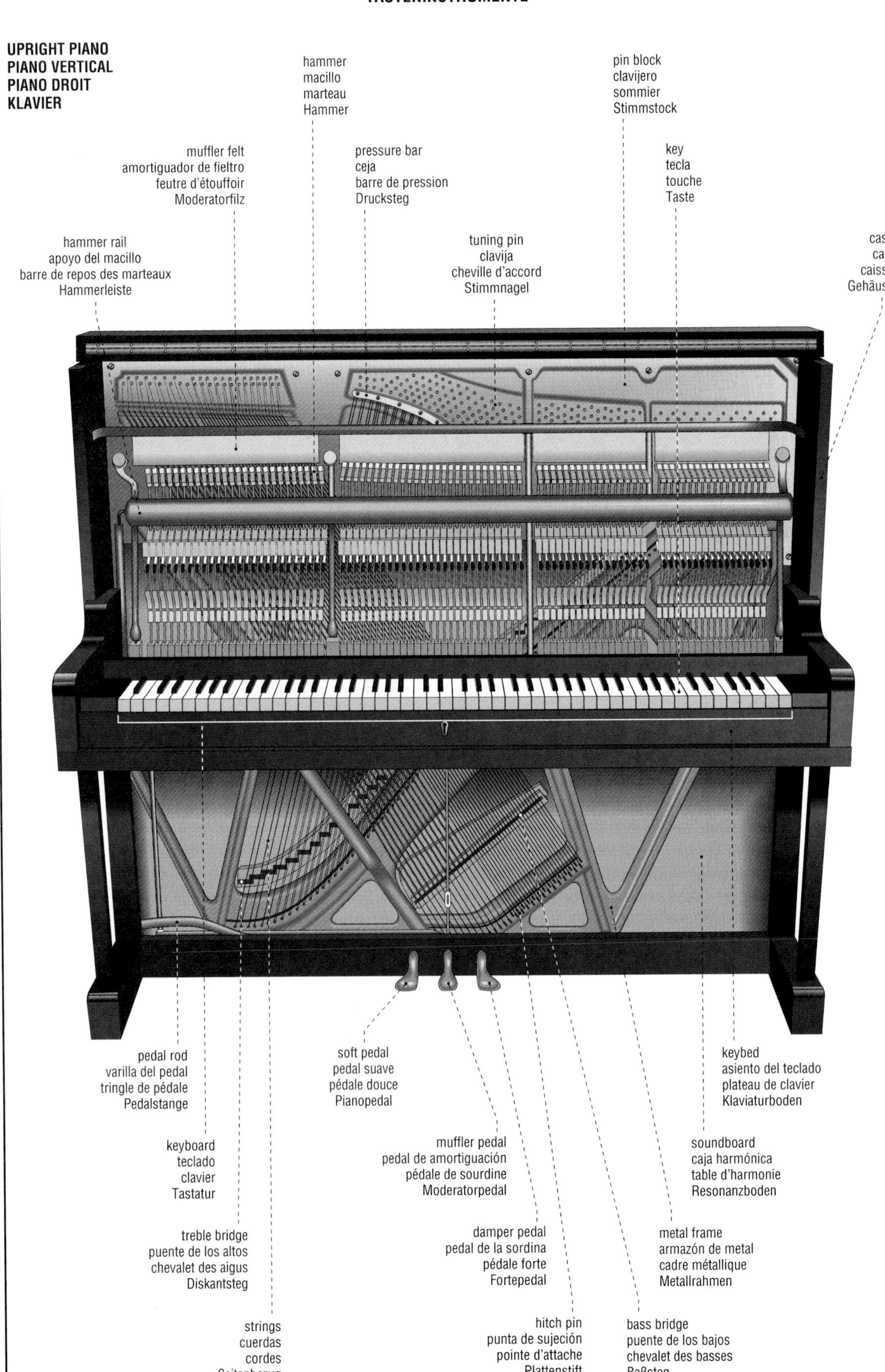

hammer
macillo
marteau
Hammer
pin block
clavijero
sommier
Stimmstock
muffler felt
amortiguador de fieltro
feutre d'étouffoir
Moderatorfilz
pressure bar
ceja
barre de pression
Drucksteg
key
tecla
touche
Taste
hammer rail
apoyo del macillo
barre de repos des marteaux
Hammerleiste
tuning pin
clavija
cheville d'accord
Stimmnagel
case
caja
caisse
Gehäuse
pedal rod
varilla del pedal
tringle de pédale
Pedalstange
soft pedal
pedal suave
pédale douce
Pianopedal
keybed
asiento del teclado
plateau de clavier
Klaviaturboden
keyboard
teclado
clavier
Tastatur
muffler pedal
pedal de amortiguación
pédale de sourdine
Moderatorpedal
soundboard
caja harmónica
table d'harmonie
Resonanzboden
treble bridge
puente de los altos
chevalet des aigus
Diskantsteg
damper pedal
pedal de la sordina
pédale forte
Fortepedal
metal frame
armazón de metal
cadre métallique
Metallrahmen
strings
cuerdas
cordes
Saitenbezug
hitch pin
punta de sujeción
pointe d'attache
Plattenstift
bass bridge
puente de los bajos
chevalet des basses
Baßsteg

UPRIGHT PIANO ACTION
MECANISMO DEL PIANO VERTICAL
MÉCANIQUE DU PIANO DROIT
KLAVIERMECHANIK

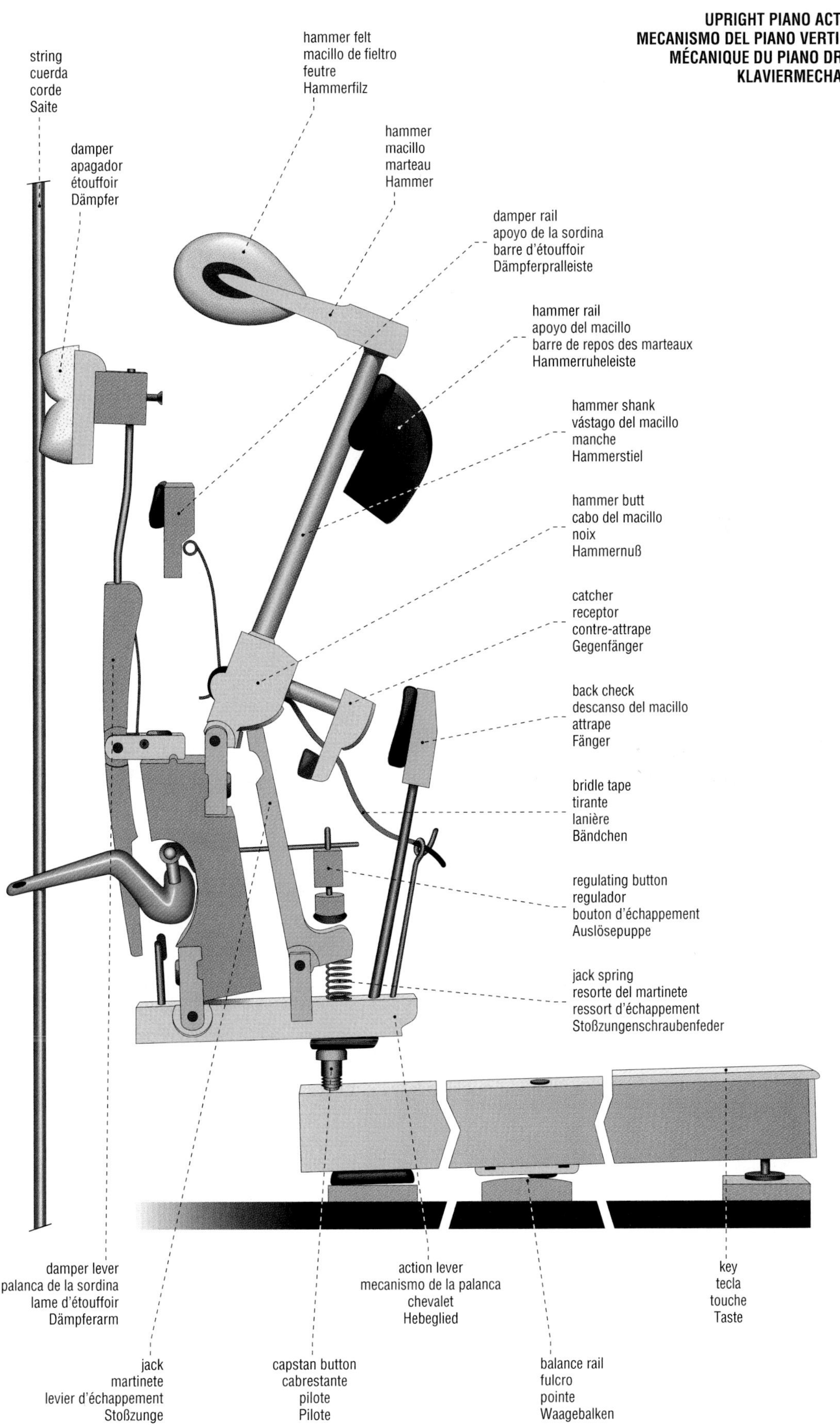

string
cuerda
corde
Saite
hammer felt
macillo de fieltro
feutre
Hammerfilz
damper
apagador
étouffoir
Dämpfer
hammer
macillo
marteau
Hammer
damper rail
apoyo de la sordina
barre d'étouffoir
Dämpferpralleiste
hammer rail
apoyo del macillo
barre de repos des marteaux
Hammerruheleiste
hammer shank
vástago del macillo
manche
Hammerstiel
hammer butt
cabo del macillo
noix
Hammernuß
catcher
receptor
contre-attrape
Gegenfänger
back check
descanso del macillo
attrape
Fänger
bridle tape
tirante
lanière
Bändchen
regulating button
regulador
bouton d'échappement
Auslösepuppe
jack spring
resorte del martinete
ressort d'échappement
Stoßzungenschraubenfeder
damper lever
palanca de la sordina
lame d'étouffoir
Dämpferarm
action lever
mecanismo de la palanca
chevalet
Hebeglied
key
tecla
touche
Taste
jack
martinete
levier d'échappement
Stoßzunge
capstan button
cabrestante
pilote
Pilote
balance rail
fulcro
pointe
Waagebalken

ORGAN
ÓRGANO ELECTRONEUMÁTICO
ORGUE
ORGEL

ORGAN CONSOLE
CONSOLA
CONSOLE D'ORGUE
ORGELSPIELTISCH

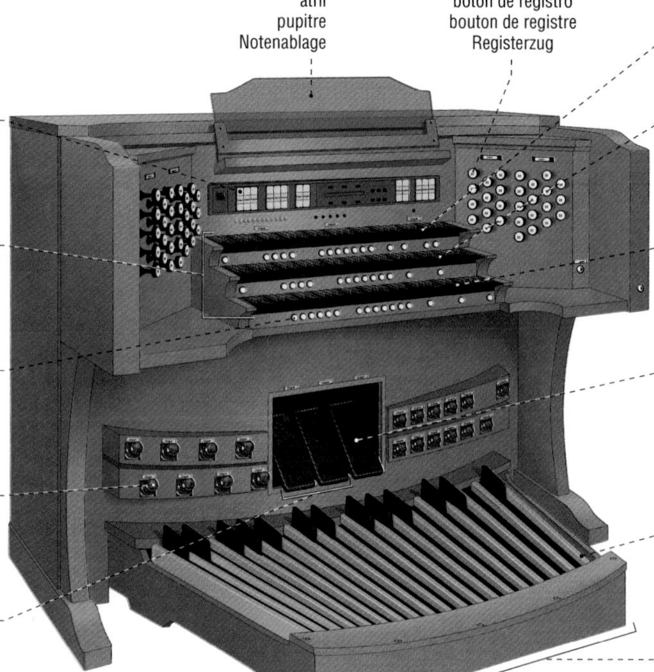
music stand
atril
pupitre
Notenablage
stop knob
botón de registro
bouton de registre
Registerzug
swell organ manual
teclado del órgano de expresión
clavier de récit
Manual für das Oberwerk
coupler-tilt tablet
tableta de resonancia
domino d'accouplement
Koppel-Kipptaste
choir organ manual
teclado del órgano positivo
clavier de positif
Manual für das Rückpositiv
manuals
teclados manuales
claviers manuels
Manuale
great organ manual
teclado del gran órgano
clavier de grand orgue
Manual für das Hauptwerk
thumb piston
botón de acoplamiento
bouton de combinaisons
Druckknopf
crescendo pedal
pedal crescendo
pédale crescendo
Rollschweller
toe piston
acoplamiento de pedal
pédale de combinaisons
Fußtritt
pedal key
tecla de pedal
touche de pédalier
Pedaltaste
swell pedals
pedal de expresión
pédales d'expression
Jalousieschweller
pedal keyboard
pedalero
clavier à pédales
Pedalklaviatur

FLUE PIPE
CAÑO DEL ÓRGANO
TUYAU À BOUCHE
LIPPENPFEIFE

REED PIPE
TUBO DE LENGÜETA
TUYAU À ANCHE
ZUNGENPFEIFE

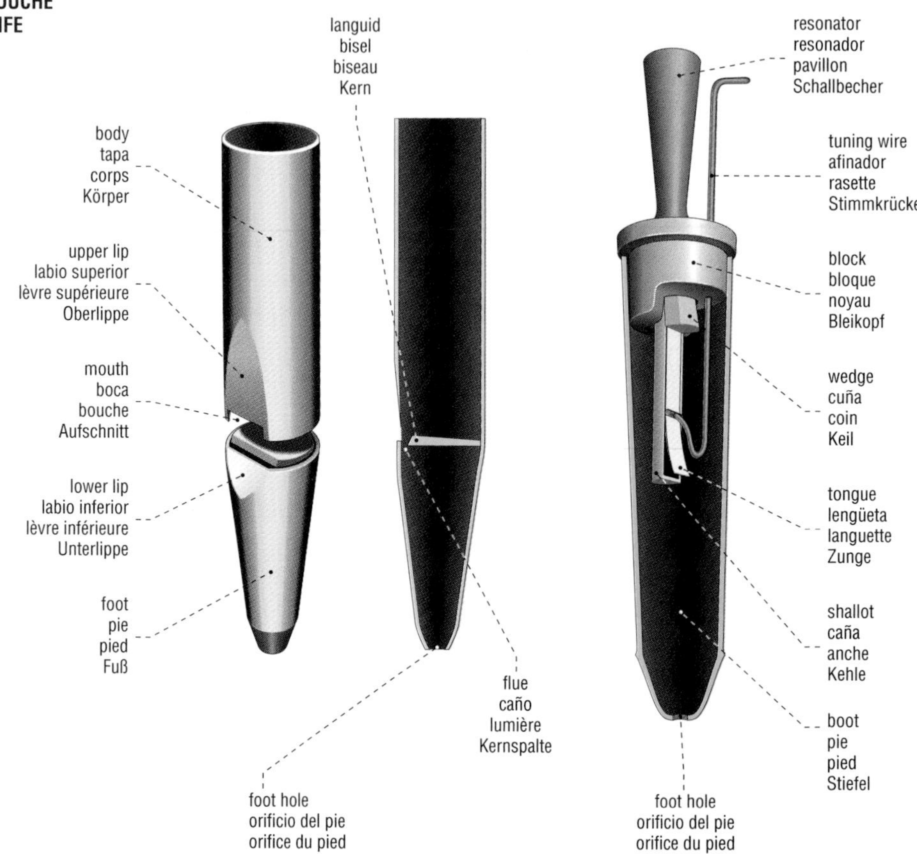
languid
bisel
biseau
Kern
body
tapa
corps
Körper
upper lip
labio superior
lèvre supérieure
Oberlippe
mouth
boca
bouche
Aufschnitt
lower lip
labio inferior
lèvre inférieure
Unterlippe
foot
pie
pied
Fuß
flue
caño
lumière
Kernspalte
foot hole
orificio del pie
orifice du pied
Fußbohrung
resonator
resonador
pavillon
Schallbecher
tuning wire
afinador
rasette
Stimmkrücke
block
bloque
noyau
Bleikopf
wedge
cuña
coin
Keil
tongue
lengüeta
languette
Zunge
shallot
caña
anche
Kehle
boot
pie
pied
Stiefel
foot hole
orificio del pie
orifice du pied
Fußbohrung

MECHANISM OF THE ORGAN
MECANISMO DEL ÓRGANO
MÉCANISME DE L'ORGUE
ORGELMECHANIK

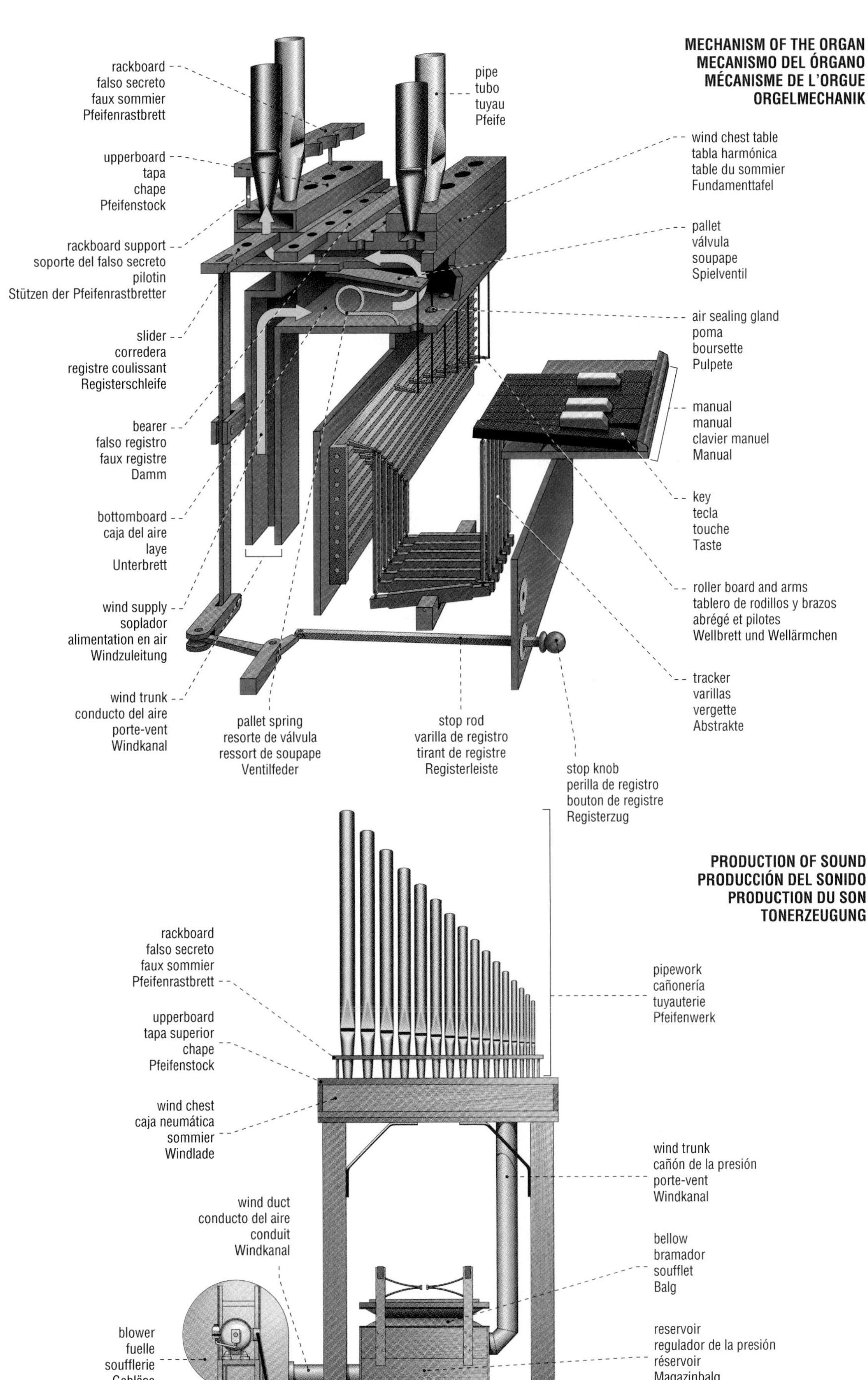
rackboard
falso secreto
faux sommier
Pfeifenrastbrett
pipe
tubo
tuyau
Pfeife
upperboard
tapa
chape
Pfeifenstock
wind chest table
tabla harmónica
table du sommier
Fundamenttafel
rackboard support
soporte del falso secreto
pilotin
Stützen der Pfeifenrastbretter
pallet
válvula
soupape
Spielventil
air sealing gland
poma
boursette
Pulpete
slider
corredera
registre coulissant
Registerschleife
manual
manual
clavier manuel
Manual
bearer
falso registro
faux registre
Damm
key
tecla
touche
Taste
bottomboard
caja del aire
laye
Unterbrett
roller board and arms
tablero de rodillos y brazos
abrégé et pilotes
Wellbrett und Wellärmchen
wind supply
soplador
alimentation en air
Windzuleitung
tracker
varillas
vergette
Abstrakte
wind trunk
conducto del aire
porte-vent
Windkanal
pallet spring
resorte de válvula
ressort de soupape
Ventilfeder
stop rod
varilla de registro
tirant de registre
Registerleiste
stop knob
perilla de registro
bouton de registre
Registerzug

PRODUCTION OF SOUND
PRODUCCIÓN DEL SONIDO
PRODUCTION DU SON
TONERZEUGUNG

rackboard
falso secreto
faux sommier
Pfeifenrastbrett
pipework
cañonería
tuyauterie
Pfeifenwerk
upperboard
tapa superior
chape
Pfeifenstock
wind chest
caja neumática
sommier
Windlade
wind trunk
cañón de la presión
porte-vent
Windkanal
wind duct
conducto del aire
conduit
Windkanal
bellow
bramador
soufflet
Balg
blower
fuelle
soufflerie
Gebläse
reservoir
regulador de la presión
réservoir
Magazinbalg

STRINGED INSTRUMENTS
INSTRUMENTOS DE CUERDA
INSTRUMENTS À CORDES
SAITENINSTRUMENTE

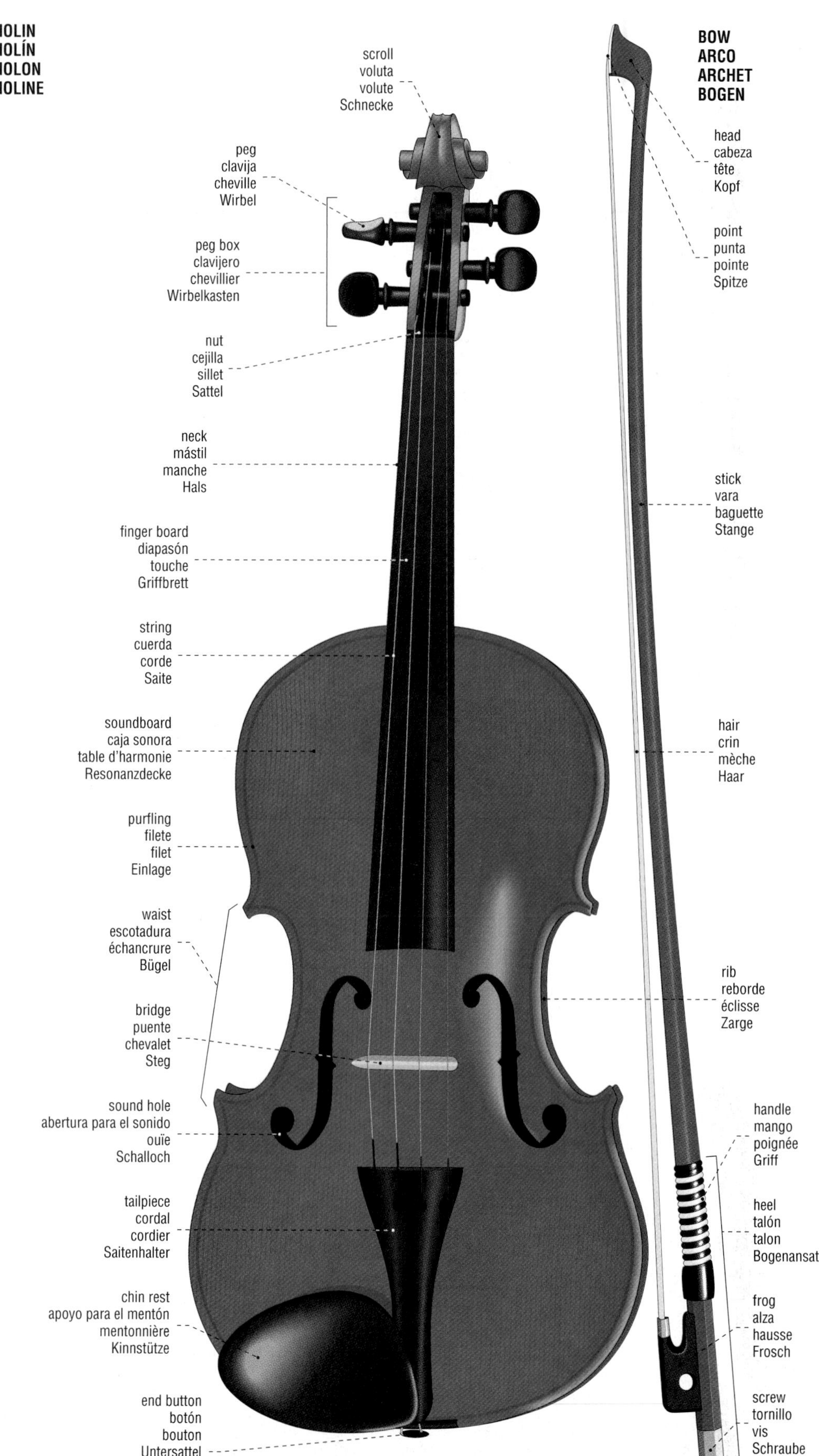

VIOLIN
VIOLÍN
VIOLON
VIOLINE
scroll
voluta
volute
Schnecke
peg
clavija
cheville
Wirbel
peg box
clavijero
chevillier
Wirbelkasten
nut
cejilla
sillet
Sattel
neck
mástil
manche
Hals
finger board
diapasón
touche
Griffbrett
string
cuerda
corde
Saite
soundboard
caja sonora
table d'harmonie
Resonanzdecke
purfling
filete
filet
Einlage
waist
escotadura
échancrure
Bügel
bridge
puente
chevalet
Steg
sound hole
abertura para el sonido
ouïe
Schalloch
tailpiece
cordal
cordier
Saitenhalter
chin rest
apoyo para el mentón
mentonnière
Kinnstütze
end button
botón
bouton
Untersattel
BOW
ARCO
ARCHET
BOGEN
head
cabeza
tête
Kopf
point
punta
pointe
Spitze
stick
vara
baguette
Stange
hair
crin
mèche
Haar
rib
reborde
éclisse
Zarge
handle
mango
poignée
Griff
heel
talón
talon
Bogenansatz
frog
alza
hausse
Frosch
screw
tornillo
vis
Schraube

VIOLIN FAMILY
FAMILIA DE LOS VIOLINES
FAMILLE DU VIOLON
GEIGENFAMILIE

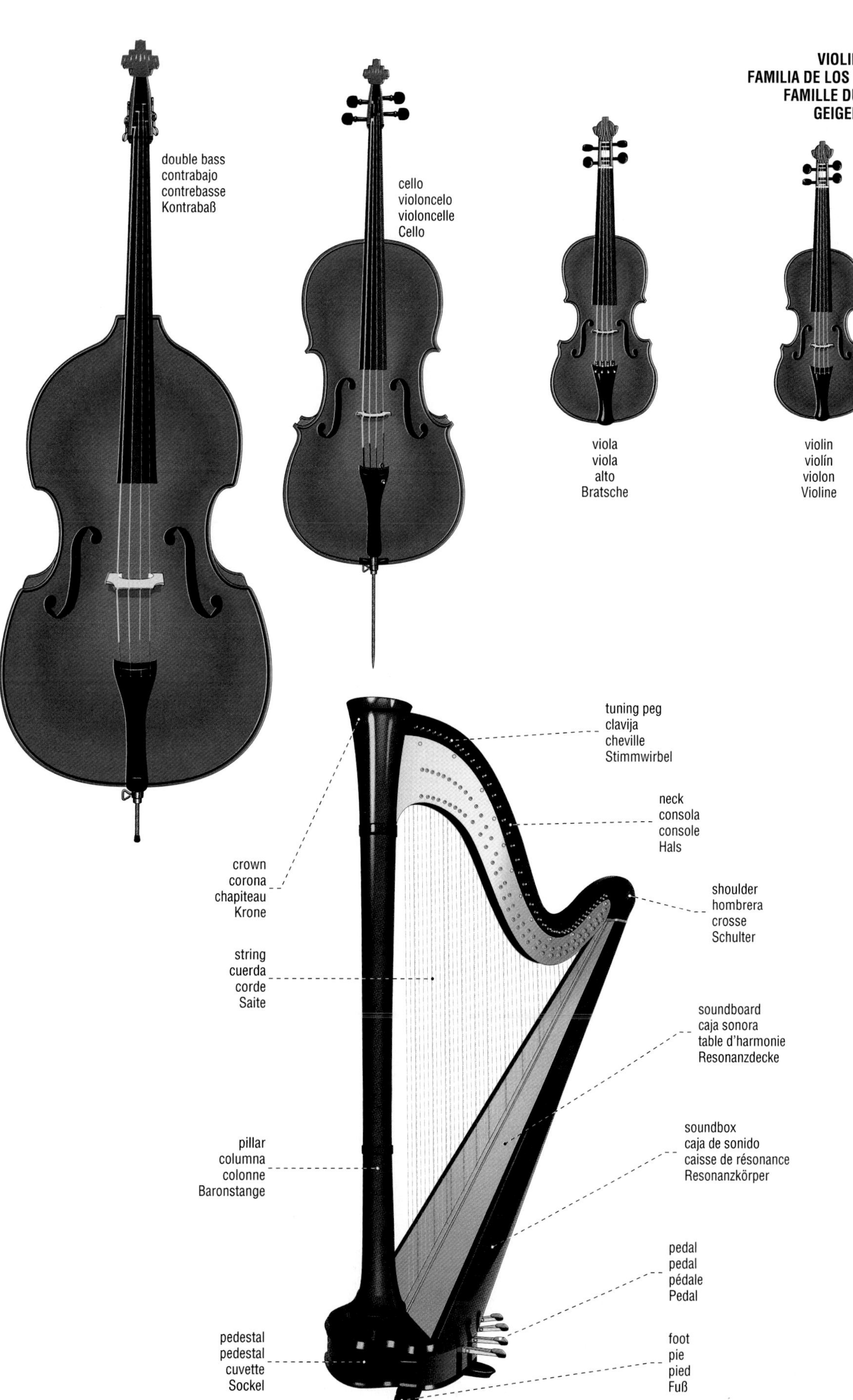
double bass
contrabajo
contrebasse
Kontrabaß
cello
violoncelo
violoncelle
Cello
viola
viola
alto
Bratsche
violin
violín
violon
Violine
tuning peg
clavija
cheville
Stimmwirbel
neck
consola
console
Hals
crown
corona
chapiteau
Krone
shoulder
hombrera
crosse
Schulter
string
cuerda
corde
Saite
soundboard
caja sonora
table d'harmonie
Resonanzdecke
soundbox
caja de sonido
caisse de résonance
Resonanzkörper
pillar
columna
colonne
Baronstange
pedal
pedal
pédale
Pedal
pedestal
pedestal
cuvette
Sockel
foot
pie
pied
Fuß

HARP
ARPA
HARPE
HARFE

STRINGED INSTRUMENTS
INSTRUMENTOS DE CUERDA
INSTRUMENTS À CORDES
SAITENINSTRUMENTE

ACOUSTIC GUITAR
GUITARRA CLÁSICA
GUITARE ACOUSTIQUE
AKUSTISCHE GITARRE

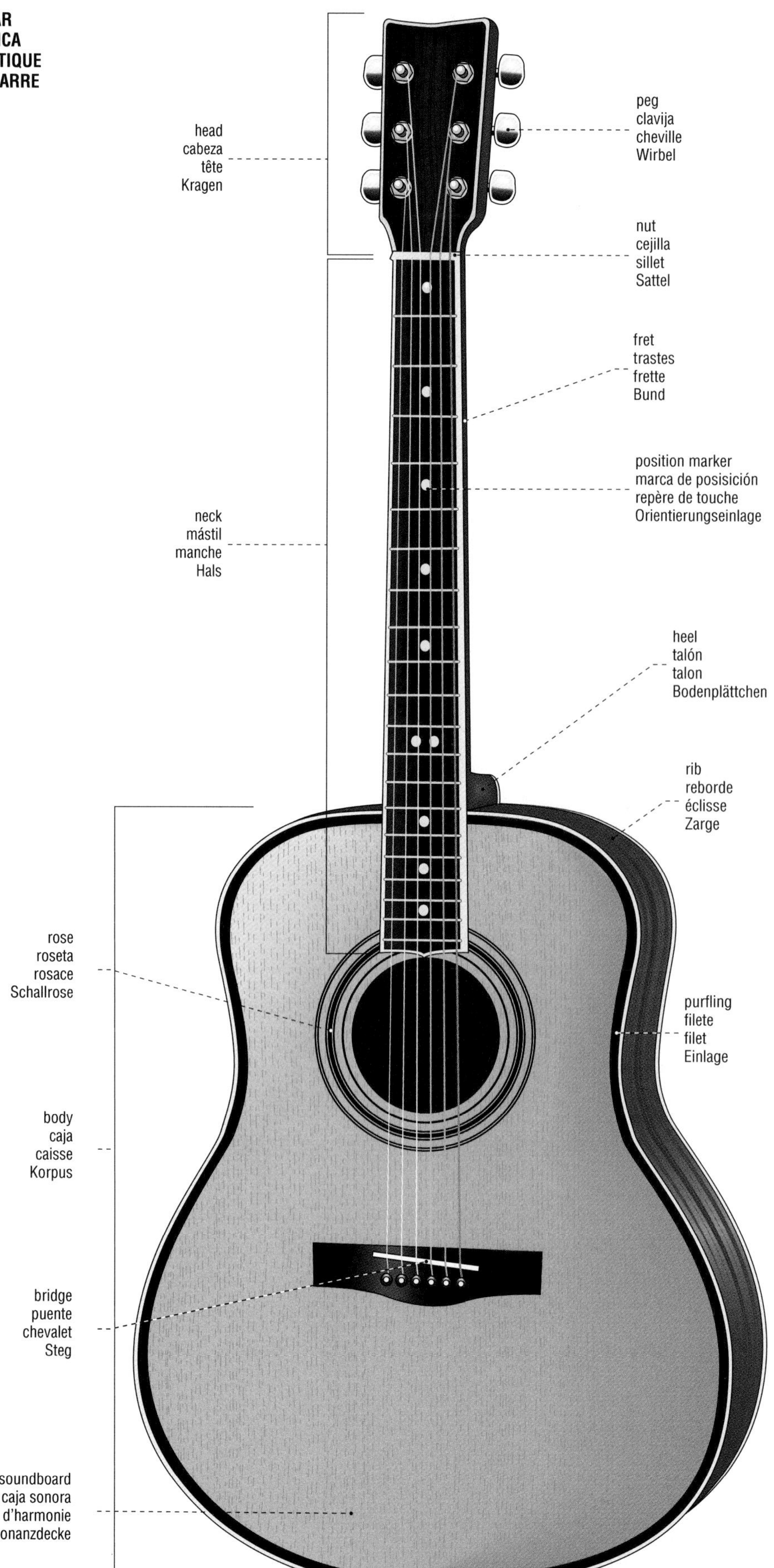
head
cabeza
tête
Kragen
peg
clavija
cheville
Wirbel
nut
cejilla
sillet
Sattel
fret
trastes
frette
Bund
position marker
marca de posisición
repère de touche
Orientierungseinlage
neck
mástil
manche
Hals
heel
talón
talon
Bodenplättchen
rib
reborde
éclisse
Zarge
rose
roseta
rosace
Schallrose
purfling
filete
filet
Einlage
body
caja
caisse
Korpus
bridge
puente
chevalet
Steg
soundboard
caja sonora
table d'harmonie
Resonanzdecke

ELECTRIC GUITAR
GUITARRA ELÉCTRICA
GUITARE ÉLECTRIQUE
ELEKTRISCHE GITARRE

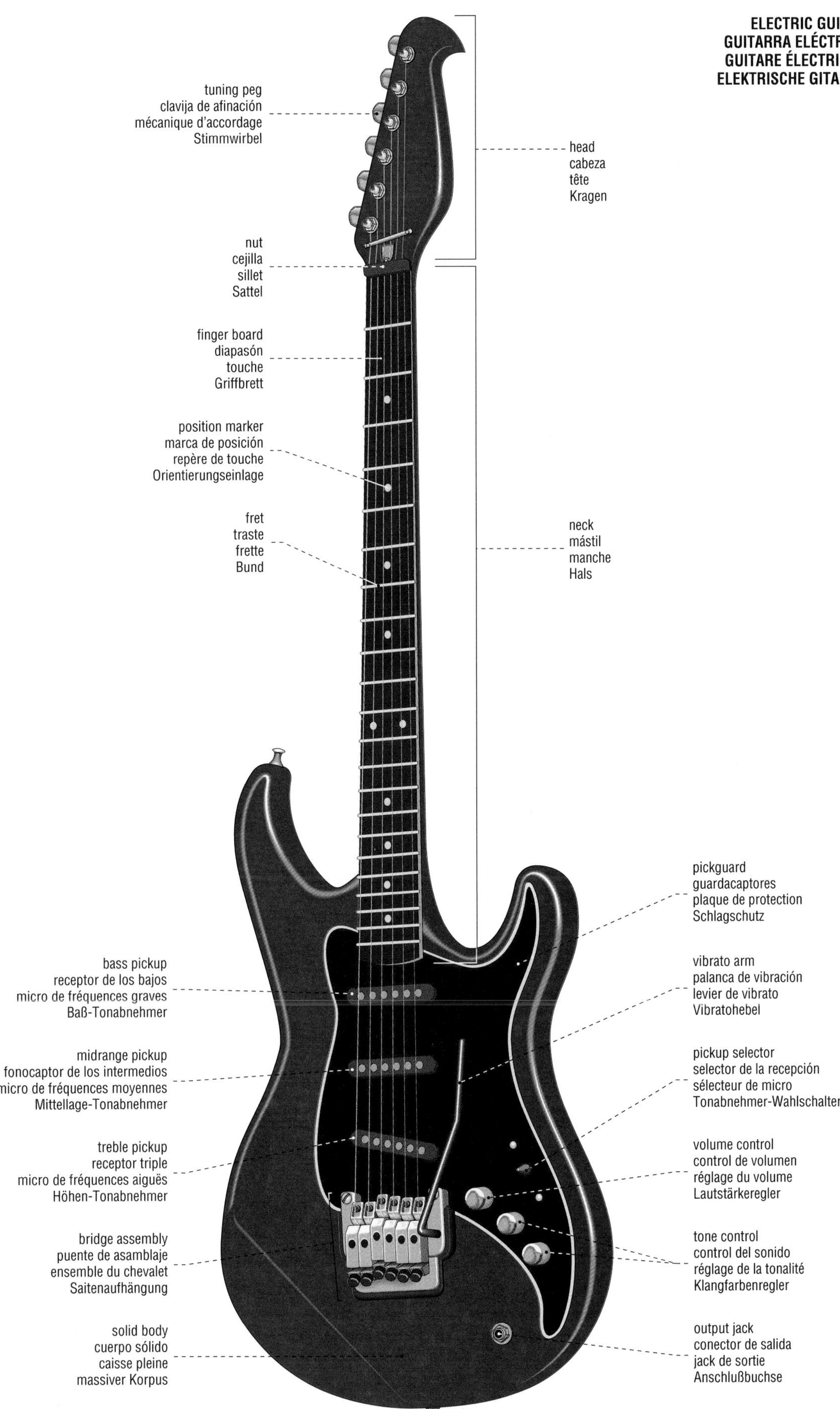

tuning peg
clavija de afinación
mécanique d'accordage
Stimmwirbel
head
cabeza
tête
Kragen
nut
cejilla
sillet
Sattel
finger board
diapasón
touche
Griffbrett
position marker
marca de posición
repère de touche
Orientierungseinlage
fret
traste
frette
Bund
neck
mástil
manche
Hals
pickguard
guardacaptores
plaque de protection
Schlagschutz
bass pickup
receptor de los bajos
micro de fréquences graves
Baß-Tonabnehmer
vibrato arm
palanca de vibración
levier de vibrato
Vibratohebel
midrange pickup
fonocaptor de los intermedios
micro de fréquences moyennes
Mittellage-Tonabnehmer
pickup selector
selector de la recepción
sélecteur de micro
Tonabnehmer-Wahlschalter
treble pickup
receptor triple
micro de fréquences aiguës
Höhen-Tonabnehmer
volume control
control de volumen
réglage du volume
Lautstärkeregler
bridge assembly
puente de asamblaje
ensemble du chevalet
Saitenaufhängung
tone control
control del sonido
réglage de la tonalité
Klangfarbenregler
solid body
cuerpo sólido
caisse pleine
massiver Korpus
output jack
conector de salida
jack de sortie
Anschlußbuchse

WIND INSTRUMENTS
INSTRUMENTOS DE VIENTO
INSTRUMENTS À VENT
BLASINSTRUMENTE

SAXOPHONE
SAXOFÓN
SAXOPHONE
SAXOPHON

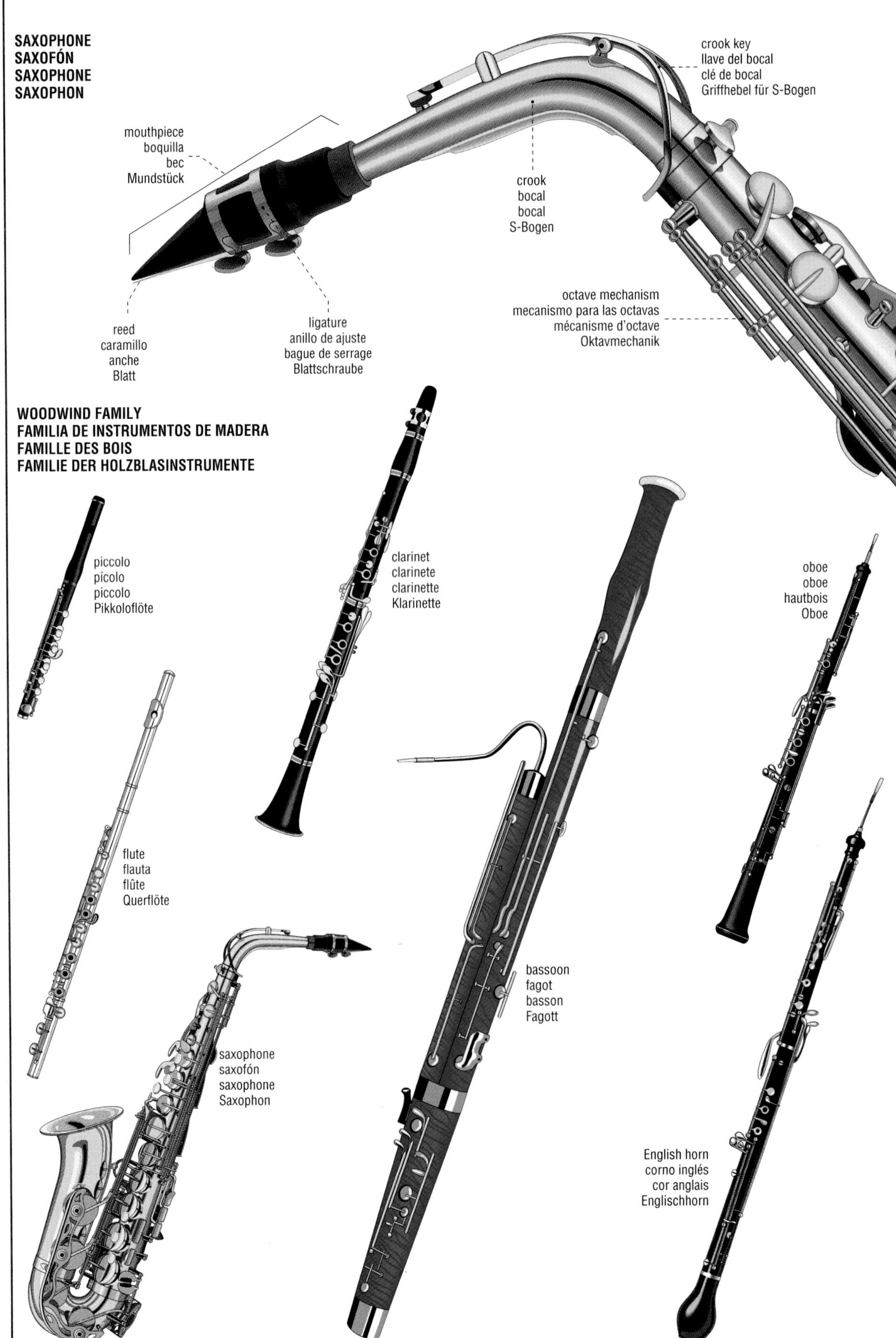

crook key
llave del bocal
clé de bocal
Griffhebel für S-Bogen
mouthpiece
boquilla
bec
Mundstück
crook
bocal
bocal
S-Bogen
octave mechanism
mecanismo para las octavas
mécanisme d'octave
Oktavmechanik
reed
caramillo
anche
Blatt
ligature
anillo de ajuste
bague de serrage
Blattschraube
WOODWIND FAMILY
FAMILIA DE INSTRUMENTOS DE MADERA
FAMILLE DES BOIS
FAMILIE DER HOLZBLASINSTRUMENTE
piccolo
pícolo
piccolo
Pikkoloflöte
clarinet
clarinete
clarinette
Klarinette
oboe
oboe
hautbois
Oboe
flute
flauta
flûte
Querflöte
bassoon
fagot
basson
Fagott
saxophone
saxofón
saxophone
Saxophon
English horn
corno inglés
cor anglais
Englischhorn

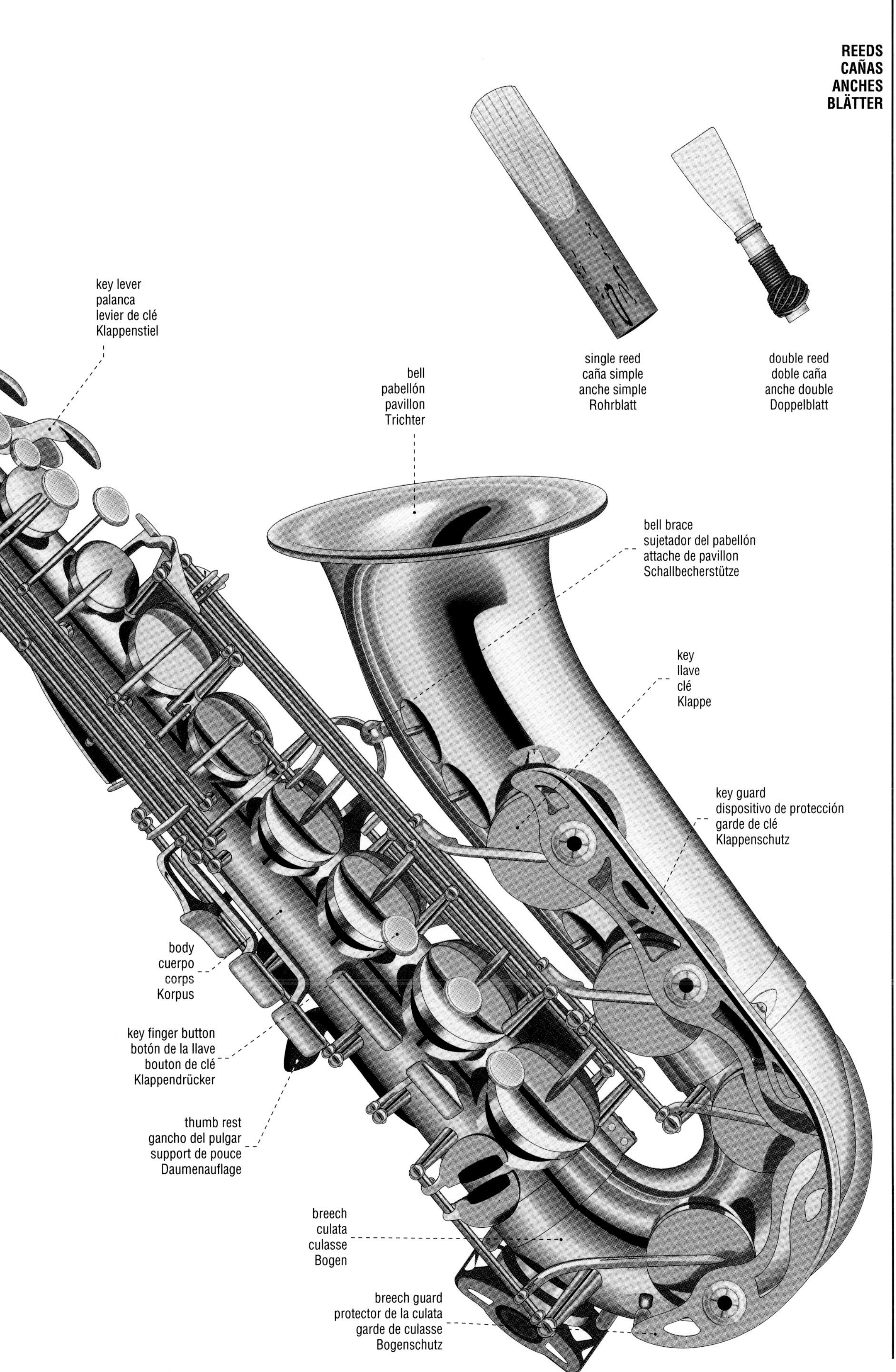
single reed
caña simple
anche simple
Rohrblatt
double reed
doble caña
anche double
Doppelblatt
key lever
palanca
levier de clé
Klappenstiel
bell
pabellón
pavillon
Trichter
bell brace
sujetador del pabellón
attache de pavillon
Schallbecherstütze
key
llave
clé
Klappe
key guard
dispositivo de protección
garde de clé
Klappenschutz
body
cuerpo
corps
Korpus
key finger button
botón de la llave
bouton de clé
Klappendrücker
thumb rest
gancho del pulgar
support de pouce
Daumenauflage
breech
culata
culasse
Bogen
breech guard
protector de la culata
garde de culasse
Bogenschutz

WIND INSTRUMENTS
INSTRUMENTOS DE VIENTO
INSTRUMENTS À VENT
BLASINSTRUMENTE

TRUMPET
TROMPETA
TROMPETTE
TROMPETE
mouthpiece
boquilla
embouchure
Mundstück
mouthpiece receiver
empate de la boquilla
boisseau d'embouchure
Mundstückaufnahme
mouthpipe
tubo
branche d'embouchure
Mundrohr
finger button
llave
bouton de piston
Drücker
thumb hook
gancho del pulgar
crochet de pouce
Daumenring
first valve slide
primer pistón móvil
coulisse du premier piston
erster Ventilzug
valve casing
tubo del pistón
corps de piston
Ventilbüchse
second valve slide
segundo pistón móvil
coulisse du deuxième piston
zweiter Ventilzug
valve
pistón
piston
Ventil
BRASS FAMILY
FAMILIA DE LOS METALES
FAMILLE DES CUIVRES
FAMILIE DER BLECHBLÄSER
cornet
cornetín
cornet à pistons
Kornett
trumpet
trompeta
trompette
Trompete
bugle
clarín
clairon
Bügelhorn
trombone
trombón
trombone
Posaune

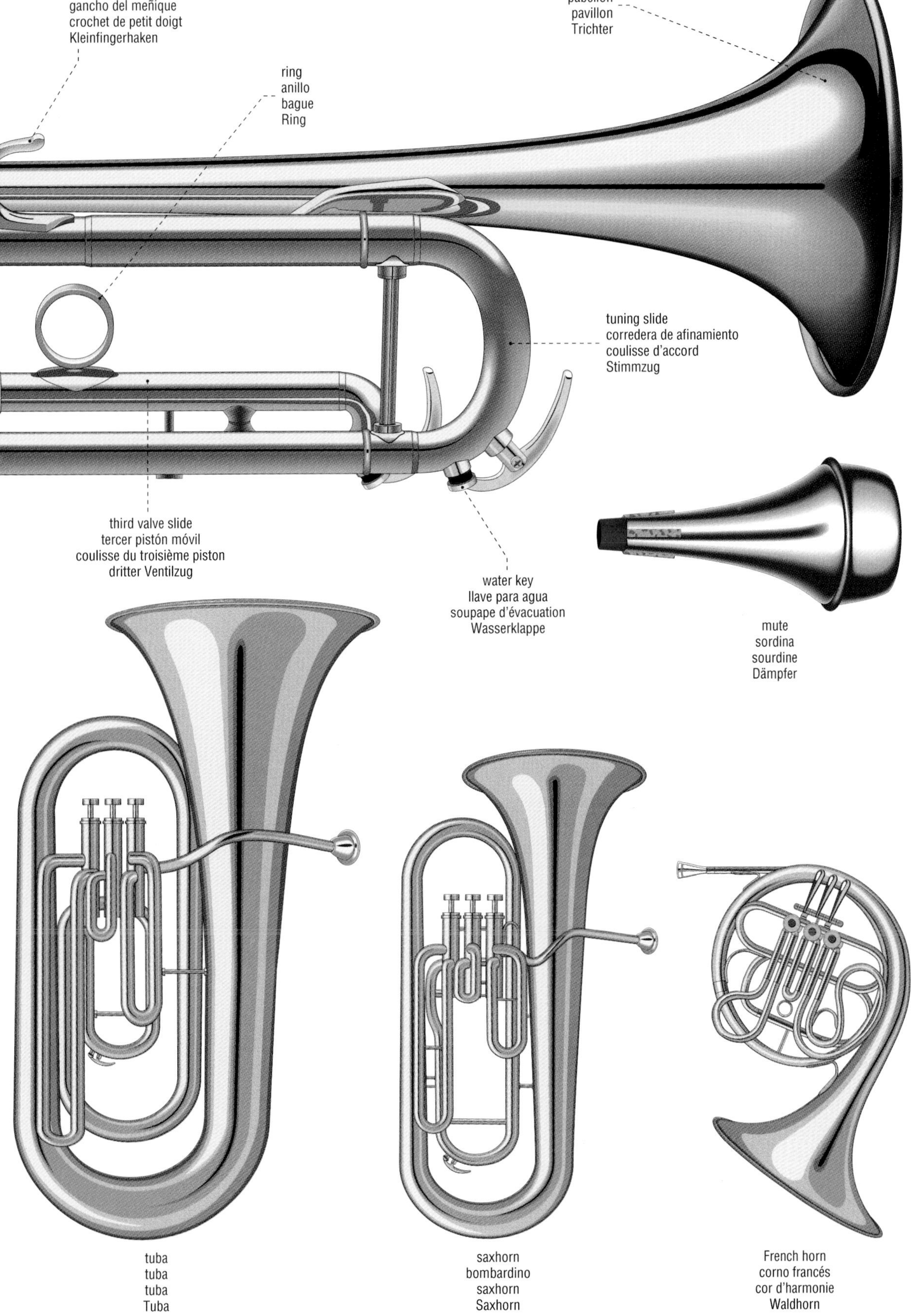
little finger hook
gancho del meñique
crochet de petit doigt
Kleinfingerhaken
ring
anillo
bague
Ring
bell
pabellón
pavillon
Trichter
tuning slide
corredera de afinamiento
coulisse d'accord
Stimmzug
third valve slide
tercer pistón móvil
coulisse du troisième piston
dritter Ventilzug
water key
llave para agua
soupape d'évacuation
Wasserklappe
mute
sordina
sourdine
Dämpfer
tuba
tuba
tuba
Tuba
saxhorn
bombardino
saxhorn
Saxhorn
French horn
corno francés
cor d'harmonie
Waldhorn

PERCUSSION INSTRUMENTS
INSTRUMENTOS DE PERCUSIÓN
INSTRUMENTS À PERCUSSION
SCHLAGINSTRUMENTE

DRUMS
TAMBORES
BATTERIE
TROMMELN

cymbal
platillo
cymbale suspendue
Becken
tom-tom
tam-tam
tam-tam
Tomtom
Charleston cymbal
platillo charleston
cymbale charleston
Charlestonmaschine
superior cymbal
platillo superior
cymbale supérieure
oberes Becken
inferior cymbal
platillo inferior
cymbale inférieure
unteres Becken
batter head
parche superior
peau de batterie
Schlagfell
snare drum
tambor
caisse claire
kleine Trommel
tripod stand
trípode
trépied
Dreifußständer
bass drum
bombo
grosse caisse
Baßtrommel
tension screw
clavija de tensión
vis de tension
Stellschraube
spur
espolón
éperon
Feststellspitze
pedal
pedal
pédale
Pedal
stand
soporte
support
Ständer
mallet
palillo
mailloche
Schlegel

SNARE DRUM
TAMBOR DE TIRANTES
CAISSE CLAIRE
KLEINE TROMMEL

lug
sujetador
attache
Böckchen
snare
cuerdas
cordes de timbre
Schnarrsaite
snare head
parche inferior
peau de timbre
Resonanzfell
tension rod
varilla de tensión
tringle de tension
Stimmeinrichtung
snare strainer
tensor de las cuerdas
tendeur de timbre
Schnarrsaitenspanner
sticks
palillos
baguettes
Stöcke
mallets
maza
mailloches
Schlegel
wire brush
escobilla metálica
balai métallique
Jazzbesen
tenor drum
tamboril
caisse roulante
Standtom
leg
pata
pied
Bein
batter head
parche superior
peau de batterie
Schlagfell
tie rod
barra sujetadora
tirant
Spannschraube
metal counterhoop
arco tensor
cercle de serrage
Metallspannreifen
tuning gauge
afinación
manomètre d'accord
Stimmanzeiger
shell
concha
fût
Kessel
strut
puntal
châssis
Strebe
tension rod
varilla de tensión
tringle de tension
Stimmeinrichtung
crown
corona
couronne
Aufhängung
caster
ruedecilla
roulette
Rolle
foot
pata
pied
Bodenplatte
pedal
pedal
pédale
Pedal

KETTLEDRUM
TIMBAL
TIMBALE
KESSELPAUKE

PERCUSSION INSTRUMENTS
INSTRUMENTOS DE PERCUSIÓN
INSTRUMENTS À PERCUSSION
SCHLAGINSTRUMENTE

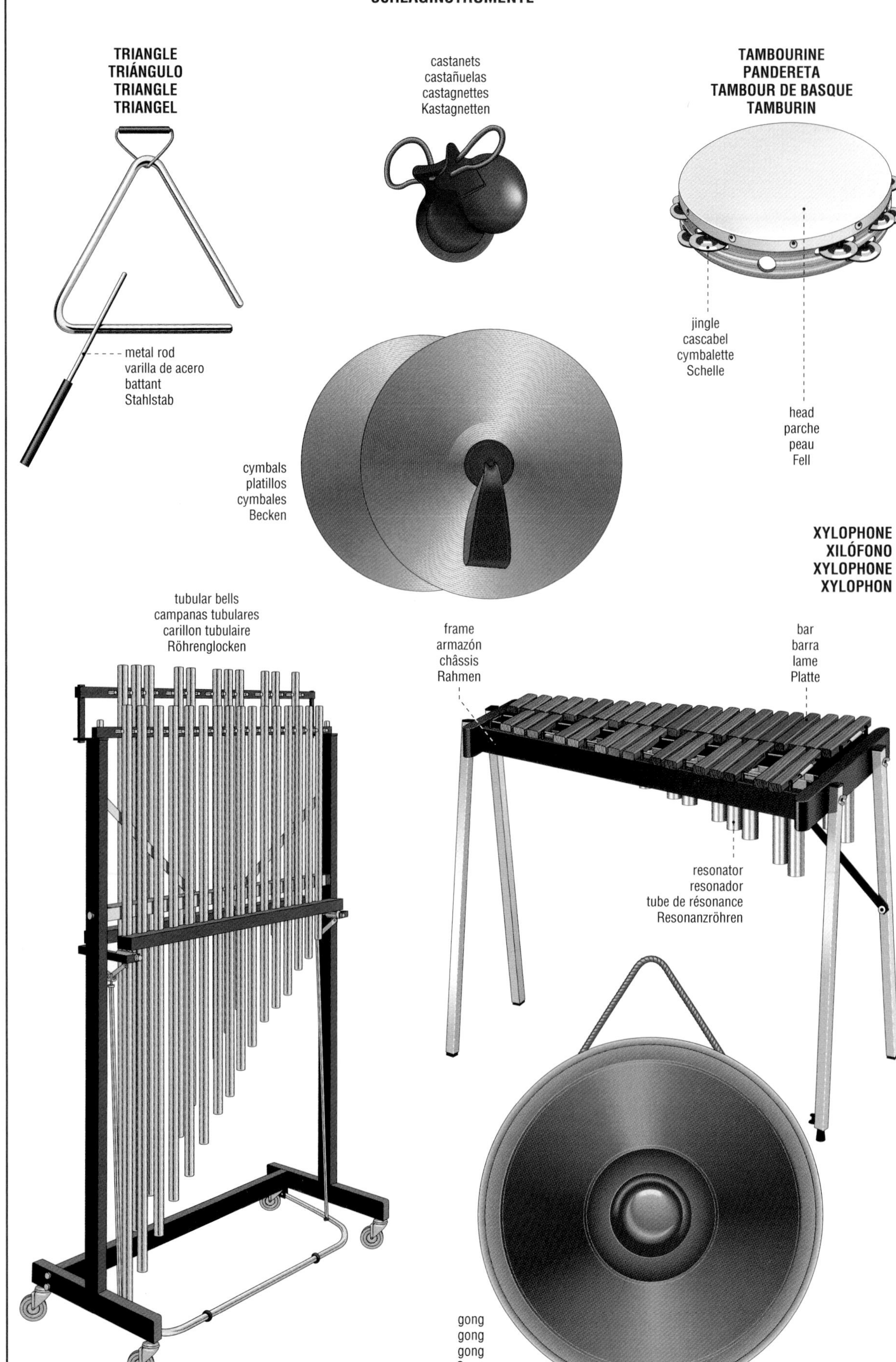

TRIANGLE
TRIÁNGULO
TRIANGLE
TRIANGEL
metal rod
varilla de acero
battant
Stahlstab
castanets
castañuelas
castagnettes
Kastagnetten
TAMBOURINE
PANDERETA
TAMBOUR DE BASQUE
TAMBURIN
jingle
cascabel
cymbalette
Schelle
head
parche
peau
Fell
cymbals
platillos
cymbales
Becken
XYLOPHONE
XILÓFONO
XYLOPHONE
XYLOPHON
tubular bells
campanas tubulares
carillon tubulaire
Röhrenglocken
frame
armazón
châssis
Rahmen
bar
barra
lame
Platte
resonator
resonador
tube de résonance
Resonanzröhren
gong
gong
gong
Gong

ELECTRONIC INSTRUMENTS
INSTRUMENTOS ELECTRÓNICOS
INSTRUMENTS ÉLECTRONIQUES
ELEKTRONISCHE INSTRUMENTE

SYNTHESIZER
SINTETIZADOR
SYNTHÉTISEUR
SYNTHESIZER

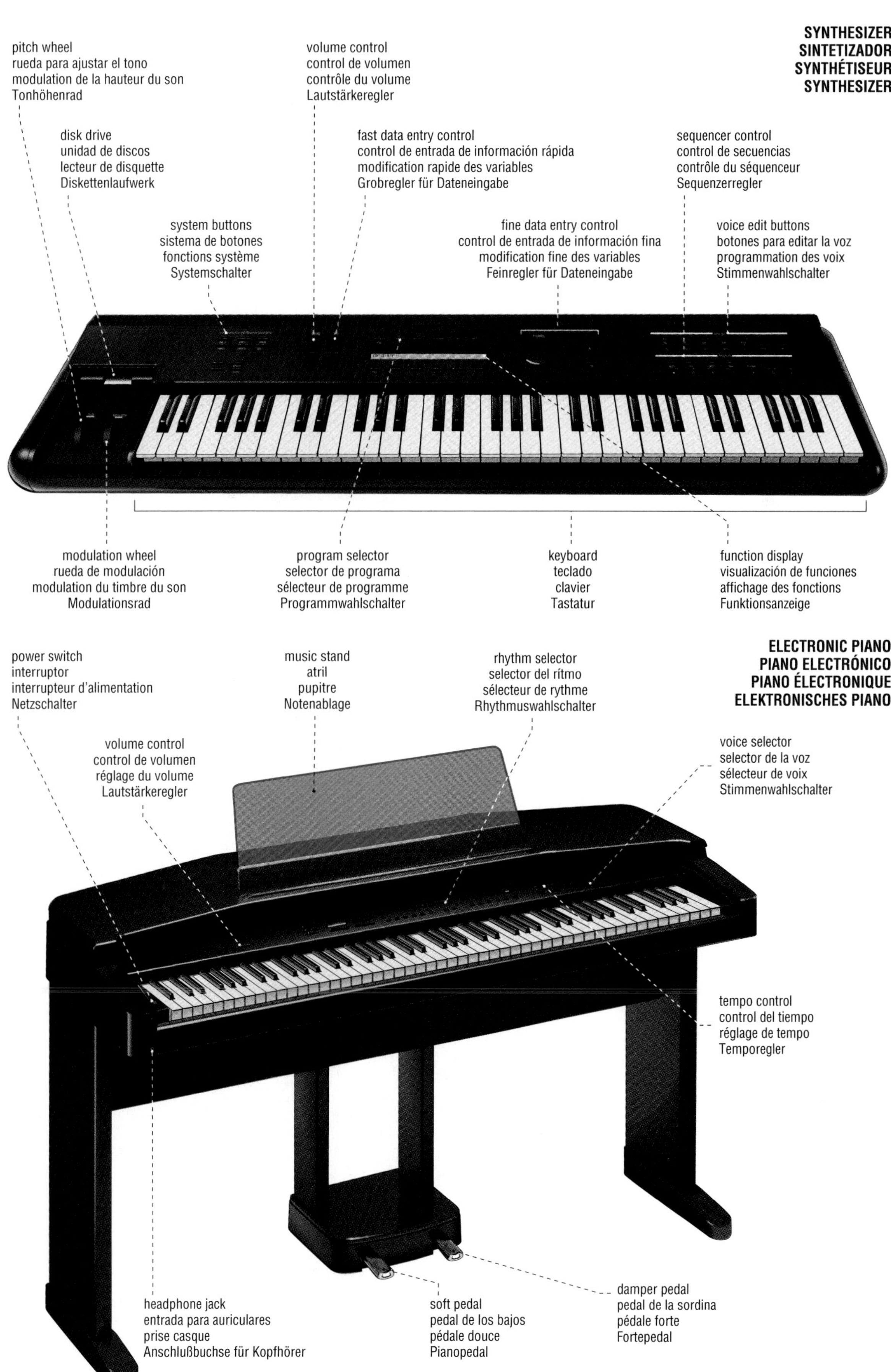

pitch wheel
rueda para ajustar el tono
modulation de la hauteur du son
Tonhöhenrad
volume control
control de volumen
contrôle du volume
Lautstärkeregler
disk drive
unidad de discos
lecteur de disquette
Diskettenlaufwerk
fast data entry control
control de entrada de información rápida
modification rapide des variables
Grobregler für Dateneingabe
sequencer control
control de secuencias
contrôle du séquenceur
Sequenzerregler
system buttons
sistema de botones
fonctions système
Systemschalter
fine data entry control
control de entrada de información fina
modification fine des variables
Feinregler für Dateneingabe
voice edit buttons
botones para editar la voz
programmation des voix
Stimmenwahlschalter
modulation wheel
rueda de modulación
modulation du timbre du son
Modulationsrad
program selector
selector de programa
sélecteur de programme
Programmwahlschalter
keyboard
teclado
clavier
Tastatur
function display
visualización de funciones
affichage des fonctions
Funktionsanzeige

ELECTRONIC PIANO
PIANO ELECTRÓNICO
PIANO ÉLECTRONIQUE
ELEKTRONISCHES PIANO

power switch
interruptor
interrupteur d'alimentation
Netzschalter
music stand
atril
pupitre
Notenablage
rhythm selector
selector del rítmo
sélecteur de rythme
Rhythmuswahlschalter
volume control
control de volumen
réglage du volume
Lautstärkeregler
voice selector
selector de la voz
sélecteur de voix
Stimmenwahlschalter
tempo control
control del tiempo
réglage de tempo
Temporegler
headphone jack
entrada para auriculares
prise casque
Anschlußbuchse für Kopfhörer
soft pedal
pedal de los bajos
pédale douce
Pianopedal
damper pedal
pedal de la sordina
pédale forte
Fortepedal

SYMPHONY ORCHESTRA
ORQUESTA SINFÓNICA
ORCHESTRE SYMPHONIQUE
SINFONIEORCHESTER

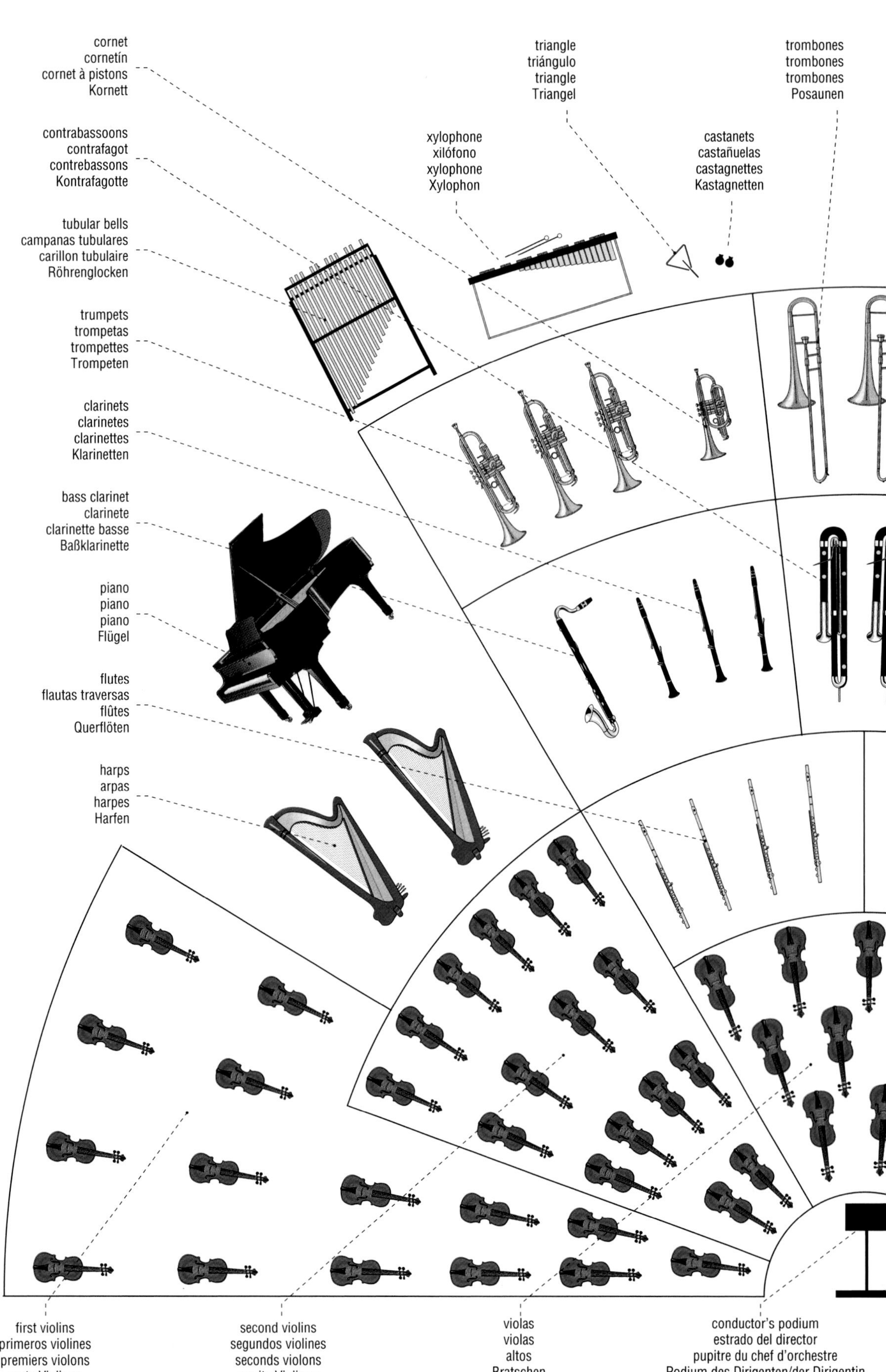
cornet
cornetín
cornet à pistons
Kornett
triangle
triángulo
triangle
Triangel
trombones
trombones
trombones
Posaunen
contrabassoons
contrafagot
contrebassons
Kontrafagotte
xylophone
xilófono
xylophone
Xylophon
castanets
castañuelas
castagnettes
Kastagnetten
tubular bells
campanas tubulares
carillon tubulaire
Röhrenglocken
trumpets
trompetas
trompettes
Trompeten
clarinets
clarinetes
clarinettes
Klarinetten
bass clarinet
clarinete
clarinette basse
Baßklarinette
piano
piano
piano
Flügel
flutes
flautas traversas
flûtes
Querflöten
harps
arpas
harpes
Harfen
first violins
primeros violines
premiers violons
erste Violinen
second violins
segundos violines
seconds violons
zweite Violinen
violas
violas
altos
Bratschen
conductor's podium
estrado del director
pupitre du chef d'orchestre
Podium des Dirigenten/der Dirigentin

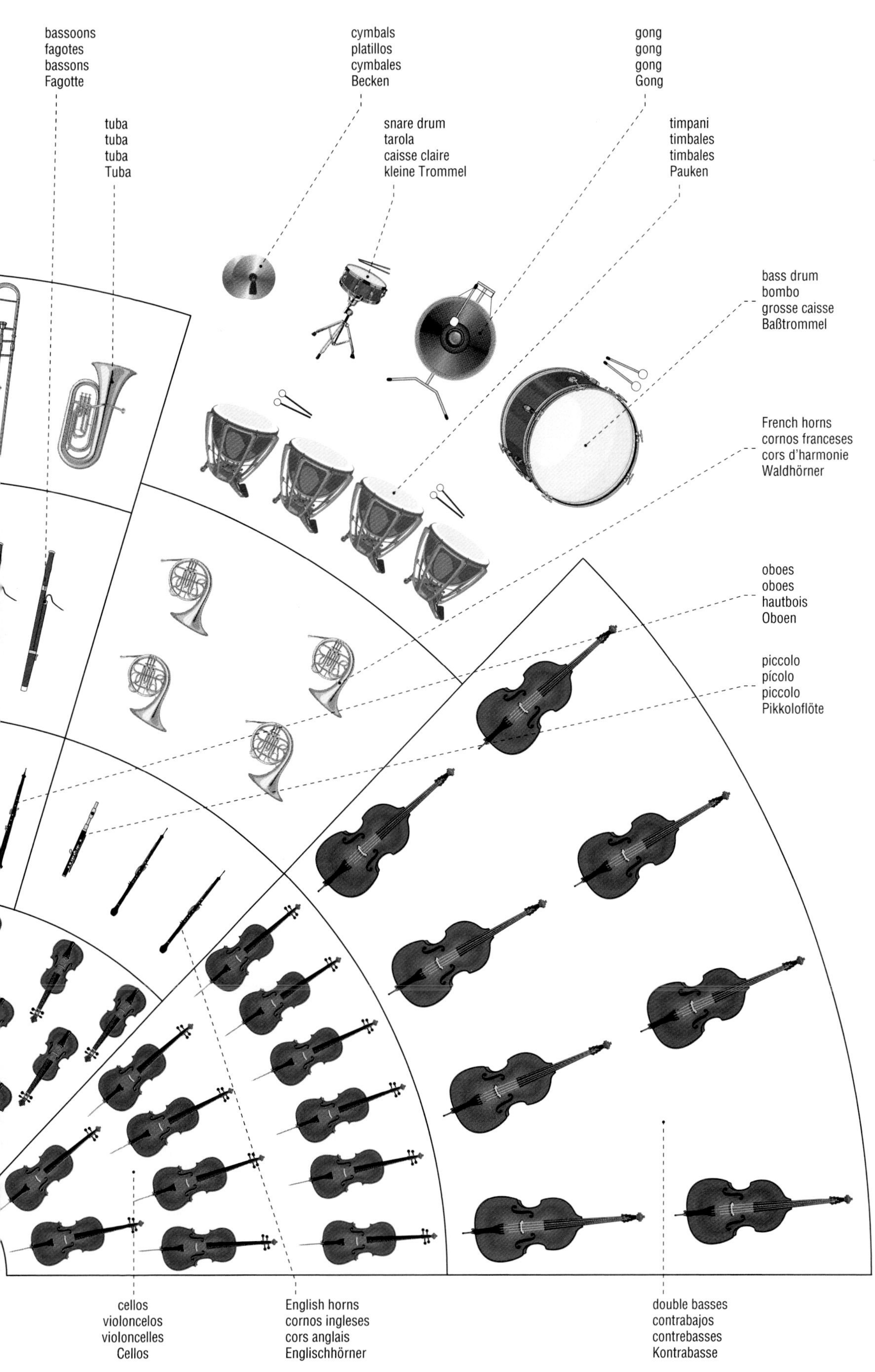
bassoons
fagotes
bassons
Fagotte
tuba
tuba
tuba
Tuba
cymbals
platillos
cymbales
Becken
snare drum
tarola
caisse claire
kleine Trommel
gong
gong
gong
Gong
timpani
timbales
timbales
Pauken
bass drum
bombo
grosse caisse
Baßtrommel
French horns
cornos franceses
cors d'harmonie
Waldhörner
oboes
oboes
hautbois
Oboen
piccolo
pícolo
piccolo
Pikkoloflöte
cellos
violoncelos
violoncelles
Cellos
English horns
cornos ingleses
cors anglais
Englischhörner
double basses
contrabajos
contrebasses
Kontrabasse

EXAMPLES OF INSTRUMENTAL GROUPS
EJEMPLOS DE CONJUNTOS INSTRUMENTALES
EXEMPLES DE GROUPES INSTRUMENTAUX
BEISPIELE FÜR INSTRUMENTALGRUPPIERUNGEN

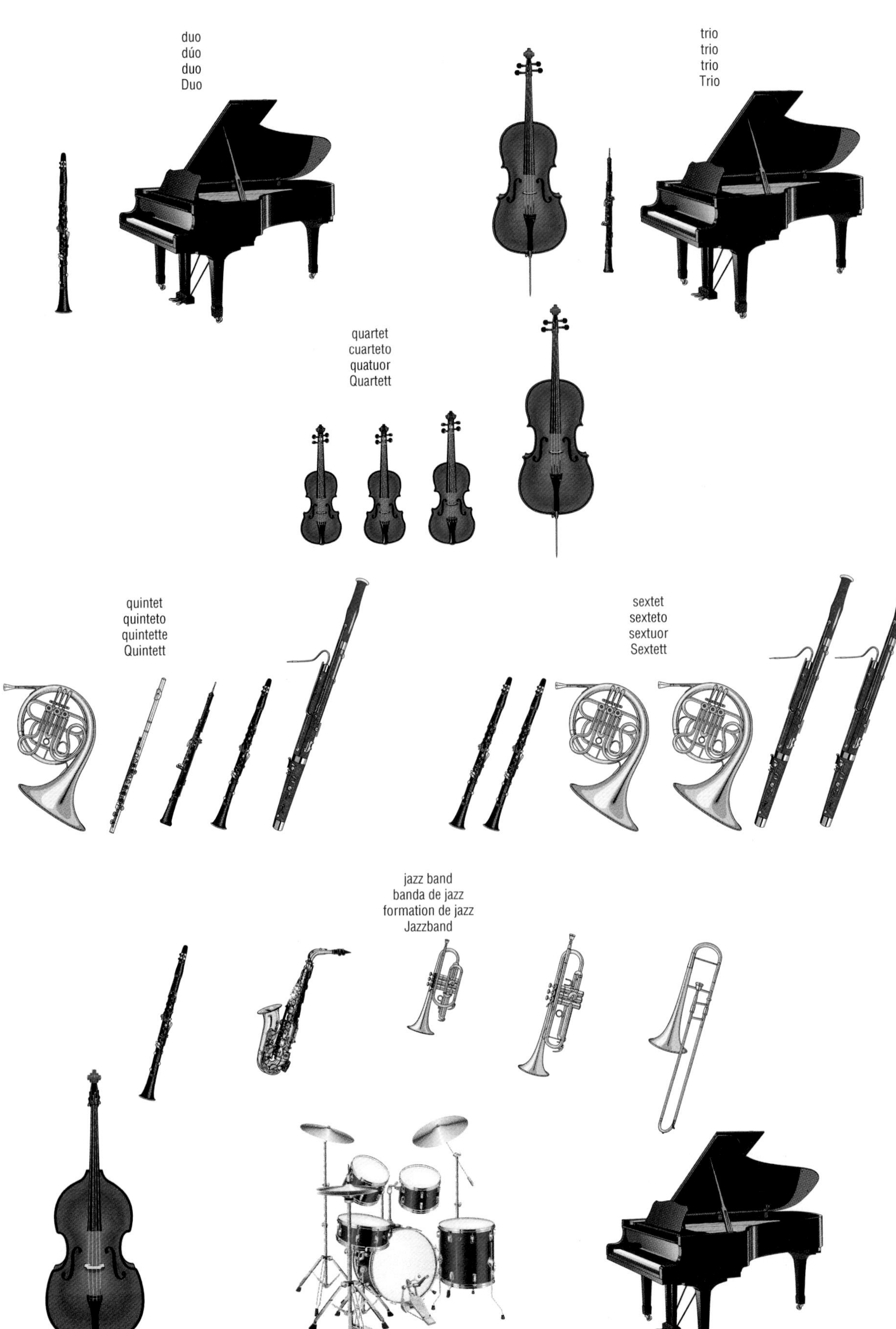
duo
dúo
duo
Duo
trio
trio
trio
Trio
quartet
cuarteto
quatuor
Quartett
quintet
quinteto
quintette
Quintett
sextet
sexteto
sextuor
Sextett
jazz band
banda de jazz
formation de jazz
Jazzband

CREATIVE LEISURE ACTIVITIES
TRABAJOS MANUALES

LOISIRS DE CRÉATION
KREATIVE FREIZEITAKTIVITÄTEN

CONTENTS

SEWING MACHINE
MÁQUINA DE COSER
MACHINE À COUDRE
NÄHMASCHINE

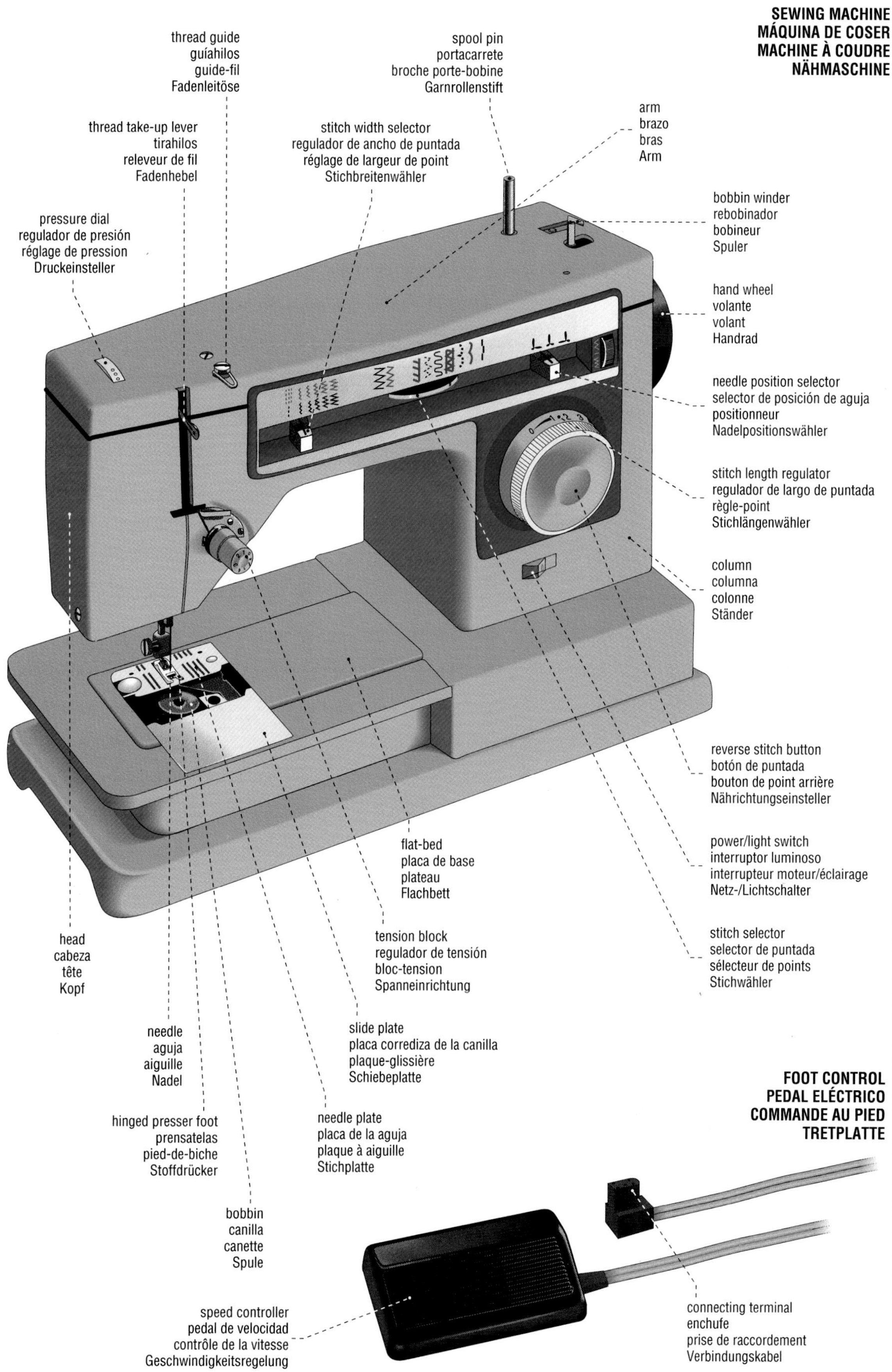
thread guide
guíahilos
guide-fil
Fadenleitöse
spool pin
portacarrete
broche porte-bobine
Garnrollenstift
arm
brazo
bras
Arm
thread take-up lever
tirahilos
releveur de fil
Fadenhebel
stitch width selector
regulador de ancho de puntada
réglage de largeur de point
Stichbreitenwähler
pressure dial
regulador de presión
réglage de pression
Druckeinsteller
bobbin winder
rebobinador
bobineur
Spuler
hand wheel
volante
volant
Handrad
needle position selector
selector de posición de aguja
positionneur
Nadelpositionswähler
stitch length regulator
regulador de largo de puntada
règle-point
Stichlängenwähler
column
columna
colonne
Ständer
reverse stitch button
botón de puntada
bouton de point arrière
Nährichtungseinsteller
flat-bed
placa de base
plateau
Flachbett
power/light switch
interruptor luminoso
interrupteur moteur/éclairage
Netz-/Lichtschalter
head
cabeza
tête
Kopf
tension block
regulador de tensión
bloc-tension
Spanneinrichtung
stitch selector
selector de puntada
sélecteur de points
Stichwähler
needle
aguja
aiguille
Nadel
slide plate
placa corrediza de la canilla
plaque-glissière
Schiebeplatte
hinged presser foot
prensatelas
pied-de-biche
Stoffdrücker
needle plate
placa de la aguja
plaque à aiguille
Stichplatte
FOOT CONTROL
PEDAL ELÉCTRICO
COMMANDE AU PIED
TRETPLATTE
bobbin
canilla
canette
Spule
speed controller
pedal de velocidad
contrôle de la vitesse
Geschwindigkeitsregelung
connecting terminal
enchufe
prise de raccordement
Verbindungskabel

SEWING
COSTURA
COUTURE
NÄHEN

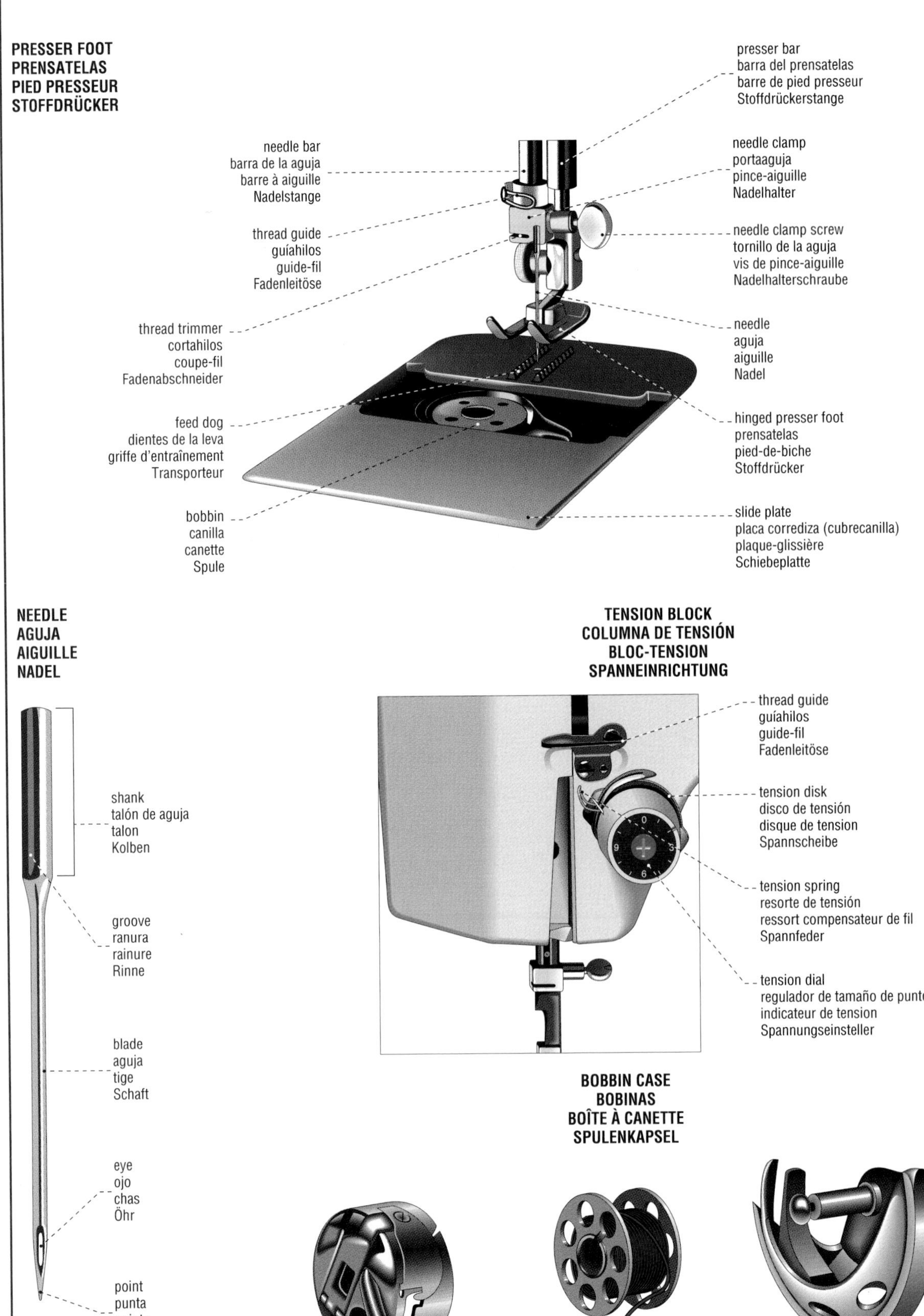
PRESSER FOOT
PRENSATELAS
PIED PRESSEUR
STOFFDRÜCKER
presser bar
barra del prensatelas
barre de pied presseur
Stoffdrückerstange
needle bar
barra de la aguja
barre à aiguille
Nadelstange
needle clamp
portaaguja
pince-aiguille
Nadelhalter
thread guide
guíahilos
guide-fil
Fadenleitöse
needle clamp screw
tornillo de la aguja
vis de pince-aiguille
Nadelhalterschraube
thread trimmer
cortahilos
coupe-fil
Fadenabschneider
needle
aguja
aiguille
Nadel
feed dog
dientes de la leva
griffe d'entraînement
Transporteur
hinged presser foot
prensatelas
pied-de-biche
Stoffdrücker
bobbin
canilla
canette
Spule
slide plate
placa corrediza (cubrecanilla)
plaque-glissière
Schiebeplatte
NEEDLE
AGUJA
AIGUILLE
NADEL
shank
talón de aguja
talon
Kolben
groove
ranura
rainure
Rinne
blade
aguja
tige
Schaft
eye
ojo
chas
Öhr
point
punta
pointe
Spitze
TENSION BLOCK
COLUMNA DE TENSIÓN
BLOC-TENSION
SPANNEINRICHTUNG
thread guide
guíahilos
guide-fil
Fadenleitöse
tension disk
disco de tensión
disque de tension
Spannscheibe
tension spring
resorte de tensión
ressort compensateur de fil
Spannfeder
tension dial
regulador de tamaño de punto
indicateur de tension
Spannungseinsteller
BOBBIN CASE
BOBINAS
BOÎTE À CANETTE
SPULENKAPSEL
latch lever
lengüeta
verrou
Kapselfinger
bobbin
canilla
canette
Spule
hook
portacanilla
crochet
Greifer

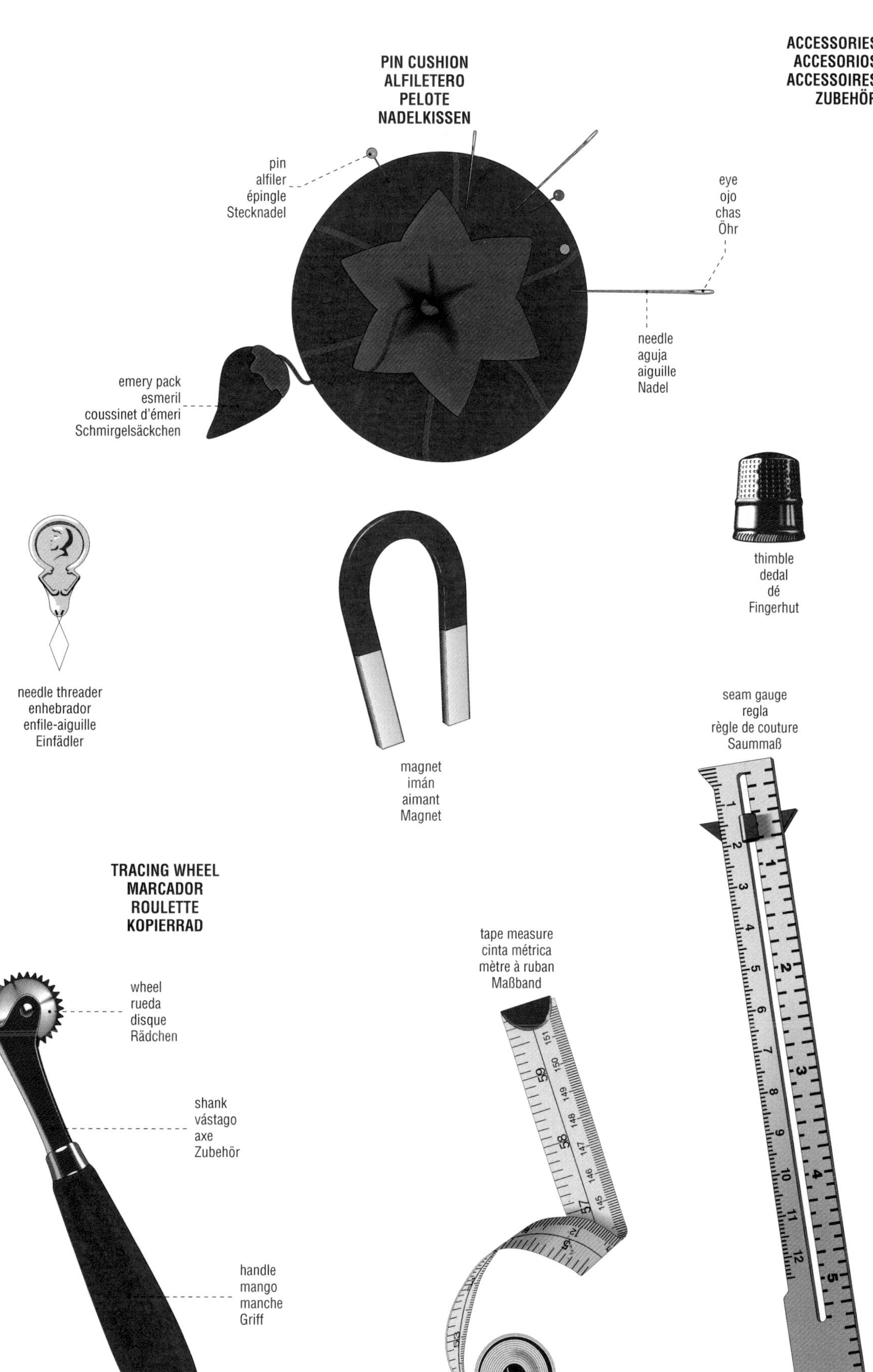
PIN CUSHION
ALFILETERO
PELOTE
NADELKISSEN
pin
alfiler
épingle
Stecknadel
eye
ojo
chas
Öhr
needle
aguja
aiguille
Nadel
emery pack
esmeril
coussinet d'émeri
Schmirgelsäckchen
thimble
dedal
dé
Fingerhut
needle threader
enhebrador
enfile-aiguille
Einfädler
magnet
imán
aimant
Magnet
seam gauge
regla
règle de couture
Saummaß
TRACING WHEEL
MARCADOR
ROULETTE
KOPIERRAD
wheel
rueda
disque
Rädchen
shank
vástago
axe
Zubehör
handle
mango
manche
Griff
tape measure
cinta métrica
mètre à ruban
Maßband

SEWING
COSTURA
COUTURE
NÄHEN

ACCESSORIES
ACCESORIOS DE COSTURA
ACCESSOIRES
ZUBEHÖR

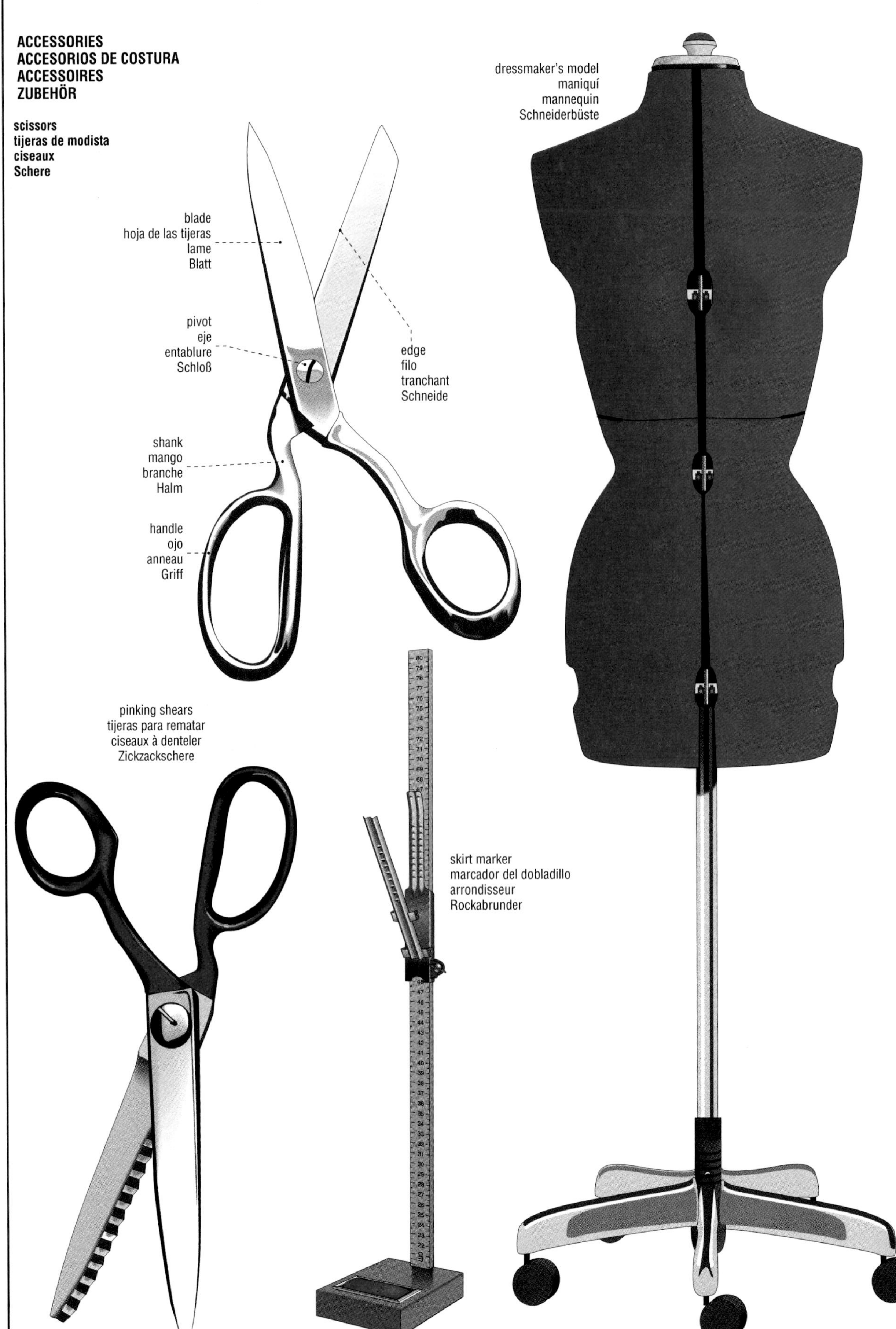
scissors
tijeras de modista
ciseaux
Schere
blade
hoja de las tijeras
lame
Blatt
pivot
eje
entablure
Schloß
edge
filo
tranchant
Schneide
shank
mango
branche
Halm
handle
ojo
anneau
Griff
dressmaker's model
maniquí
mannequin
Schneiderbüste
pinking shears
tijeras para rematar
ciseaux à denteler
Zickzackschere
skirt marker
marcador del dobladillo
arrondisseur
Rockabrunder

UNDERLYING FABRICS
FORRO Y ENTRETELAS
TISSUS DE SOUTIEN
FUTTERSTOFFE

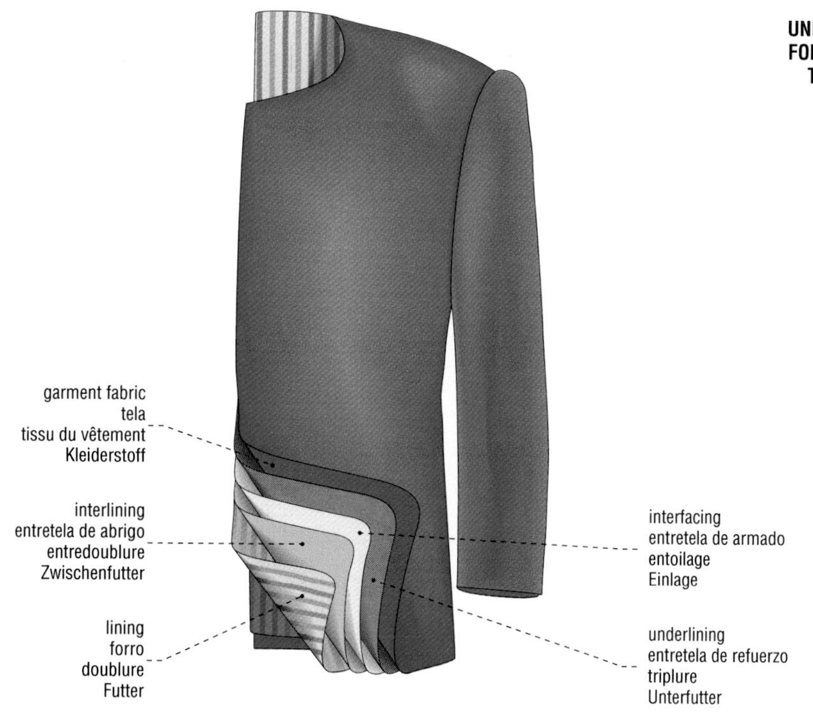
garment fabric
tela
tissu du vêtement
Kleiderstoff
interlining
entretela de abrigo
entredoublure
Zwischenfutter
lining
forro
doublure
Futter
interfacing
entretela de armado
entoilage
Einlage
underlining
entretela de refuerzo
triplure
Unterfutter

PATTERN
PATRÓN
PATRON
SCHNITTMUSTER

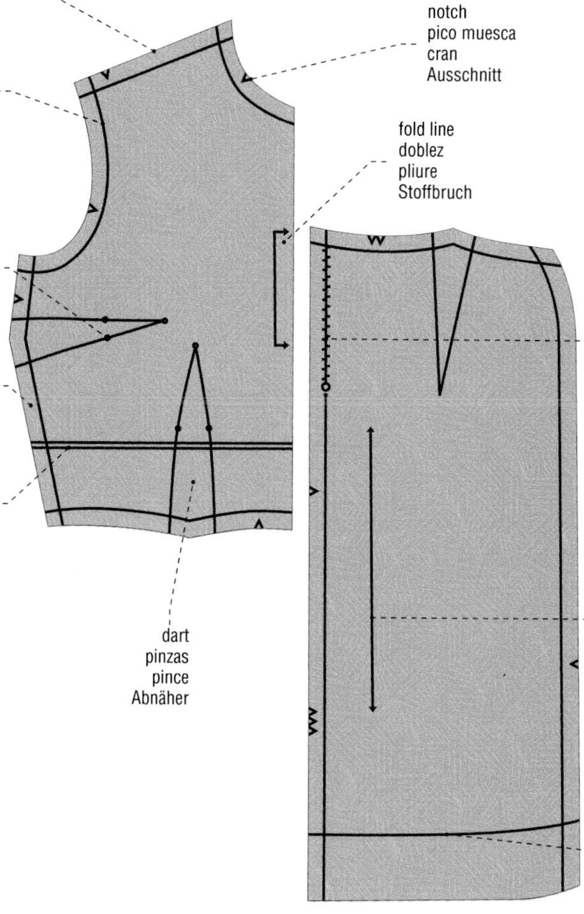

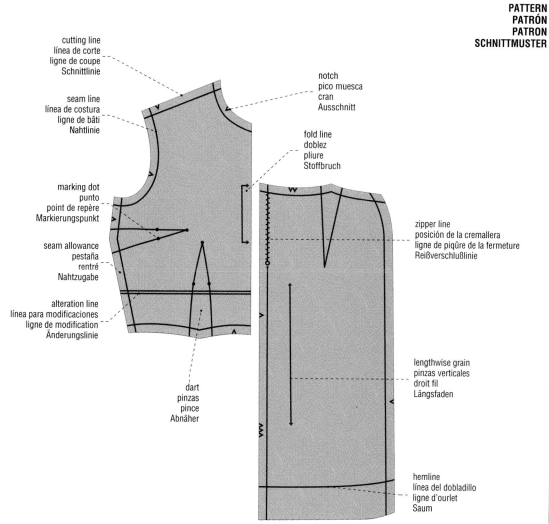

cutting line
línea de corte
ligne de coupe
Schnittlinie

seam line
línea de costura
ligne de bâti
Nahtlinie

marking dot
punto
point de repère
Markierungspunkt

seam allowance
pestaña
rentré
Nahtzugabe

alteration line
línea para modificaciones
ligne de modification
Änderungslinie

dart
pinzas
pince
Abnäher

notch
pico muesca
cran
Ausschnitt

fold line
doblez
pliure
Stoffbruch

zipper line
posición de la cremallera
ligne de piqûre de la fermeture
Reißverschlußlinie

lengthwise grain
pinzas verticales
droit fil
Längsfaden

hemline
línea del dobladillo
ligne d'ourlet
Saum

SEWING
COSTURA
COUTURE
NÄHEN

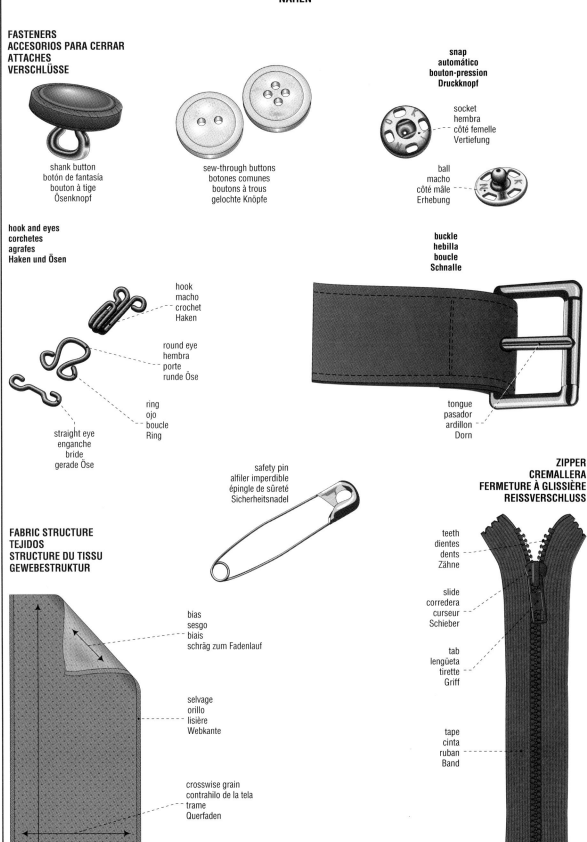

FASTENERS
ACCESORIOS PARA CERRAR
ATTACHES
VERSCHLÜSSE

shank button
botón de fantasía
bouton à tige
Ösenknopf

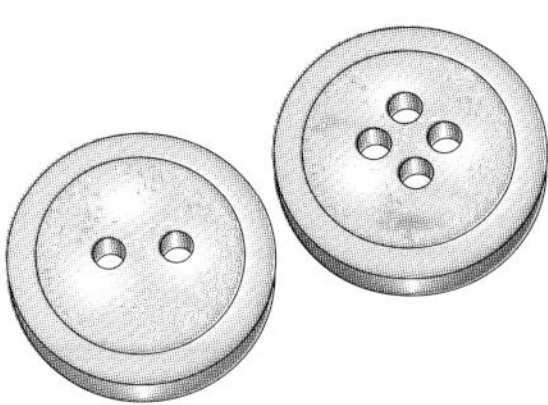

sew-through buttons
botones comunes
boutons à trous
gelochte Knöpfe

snap
automático
bouton-pression
Druckknopf

socket
hembra
côté femelle
Vertiefung

ball
macho
côté mâle
Erhebung

hook and eyes
corchetes
agrafes
Haken und Ösen

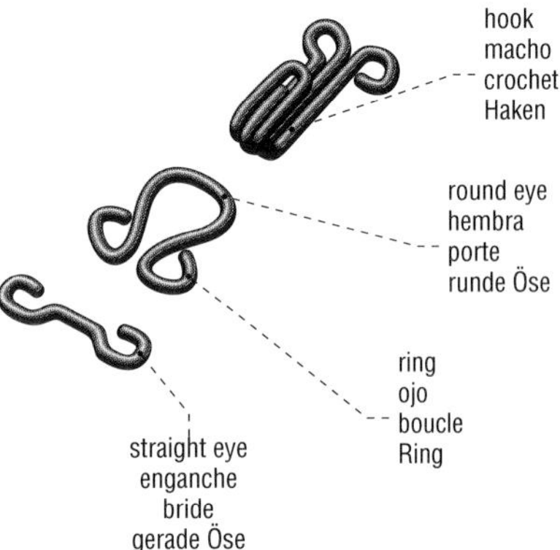
hook
macho
crochet
Haken
round eye
hembra
porte
runde Öse
ring
ojo
boucle
Ring
straight eye
enganche
bride
gerade Öse

buckle
hebilla
boucle
Schnalle

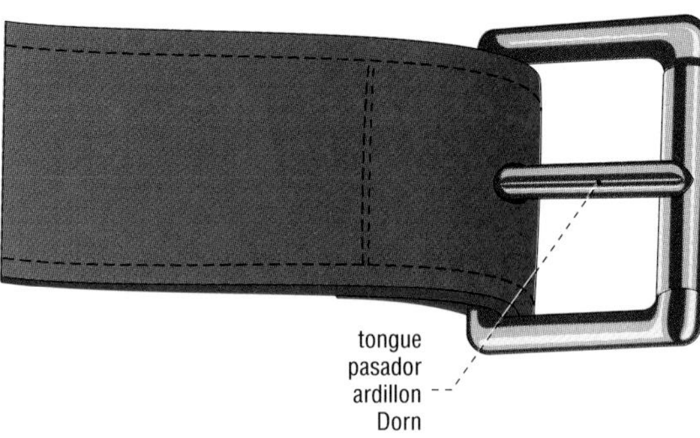
tongue
pasador
ardillon
Dorn

safety pin
alfiler imperdible
épingle de sûreté
Sicherheitsnadel

ZIPPER
CREMALLERA
FERMETURE À GLISSIÈRE
REISSVERSCHLUSS

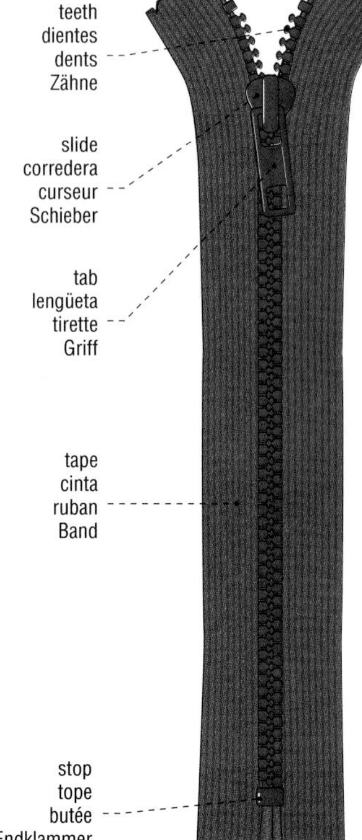
teeth
dientes
dents
Zähne
slide
corredera
curseur
Schieber
tab
lengüeta
tirette
Griff
tape
cinta
ruban
Band
stop
tope
butée
Endklammer

FABRIC STRUCTURE
TEJIDOS
STRUCTURE DU TISSU
GEWEBESTRUKTUR

bias
sesgo
biais
schräg zum Fadenlauf

selvage
orillo
lisière
Webkante

crosswise grain
contrahilo de la tela
trame
Querfaden

lengthwise grain
hilo de la tela
chaîne
Längsfaden

KNITTING
TEJIDO DE PUNTO
TRICOT
STRICKEN

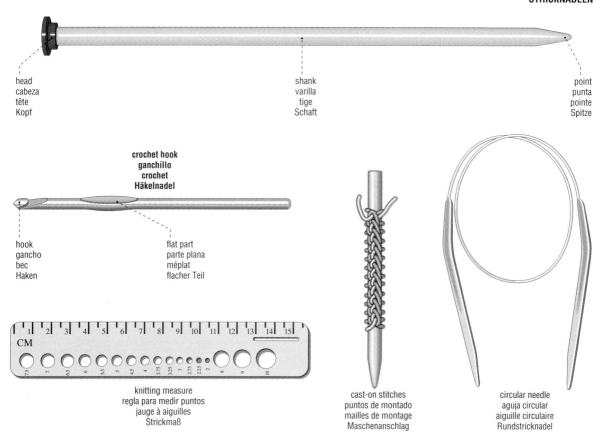

KNITTING NEEDLES
AGUJAS PARA TEJER
AIGUILLES À TRICOTER
STRICKNADELN

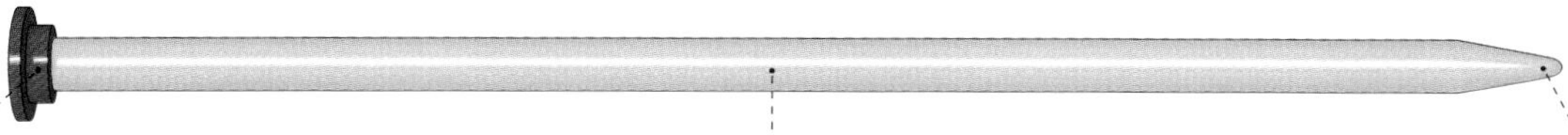

head
cabeza
tête
Kopf

shank
varilla
tige
Schaft

point
punta
pointe
Spitze

crochet hook
ganchillo
crochet
Häkelnadel

hook
gancho
bec
Haken

flat part
parte plana
méplat
flacher Teil

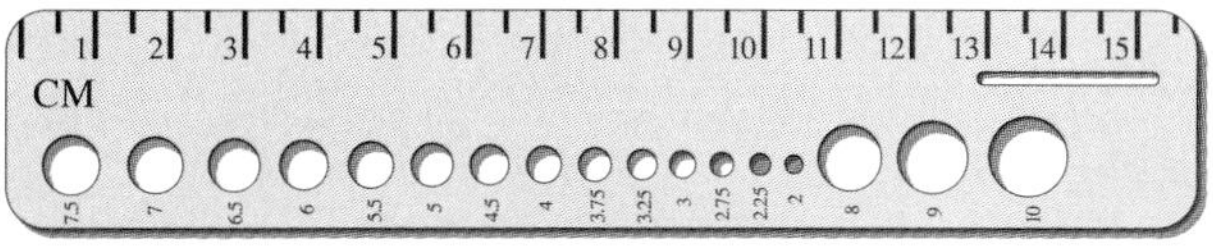

knitting measure
regla para medir puntos
jauge à aiguilles
Strickmaß

cast-on stitches
puntos de montado
mailles de montage
Maschenanschlag

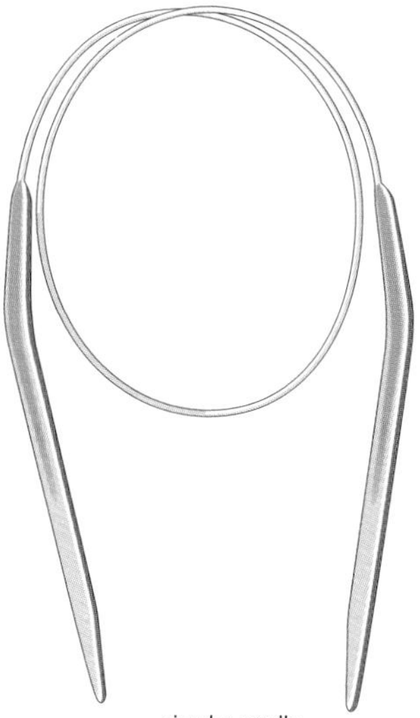

circular needle
aguja circular
aiguille circulaire
Rundstricknadel

STITCH PATTERNS
TIPOS DE PUNTO
POINTS DE TRICOT
STRICKMUSTER

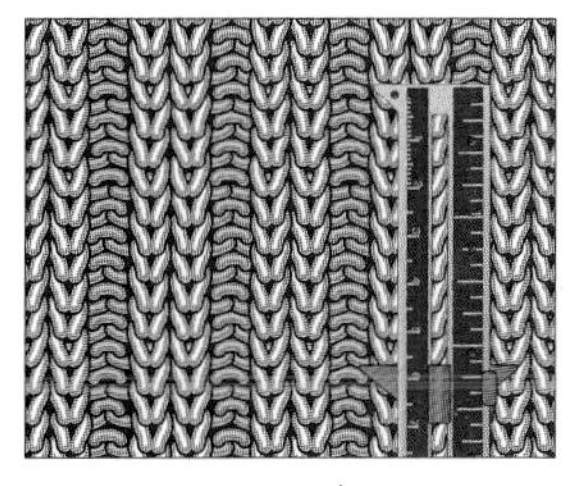

sample
muestra
échantillon
Maschenprobe

stocking stitch
derecho
point de jersey
Glattstrick

garter stitch
revés
point mousse
Krausstrick

moss stitch
punto de musgo
point de riz
Gerstenkornmuster

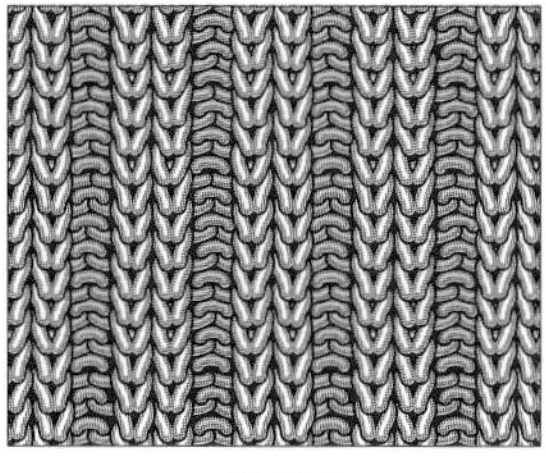

rib stitch
punto de respiguilla
point de côtes
Perlrippen

basket stitch
punto de malla
point de damier
Korbstich

cable stitch
punto de ochos
point de torsades
Zopfmuster

KNITTING MACHINE
MÁQUINA DE TRICOTAR
MACHINE À TRICOTER
STRICKMASCHINE

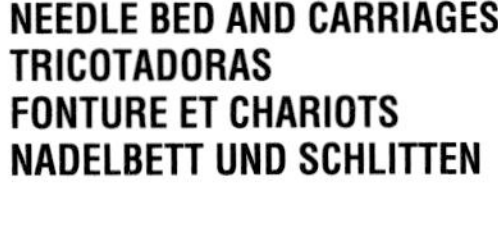

NEEDLE BED AND CARRIAGES
TRICOTADORAS
FONTURE ET CHARIOTS
NADELBETT UND SCHLITTEN

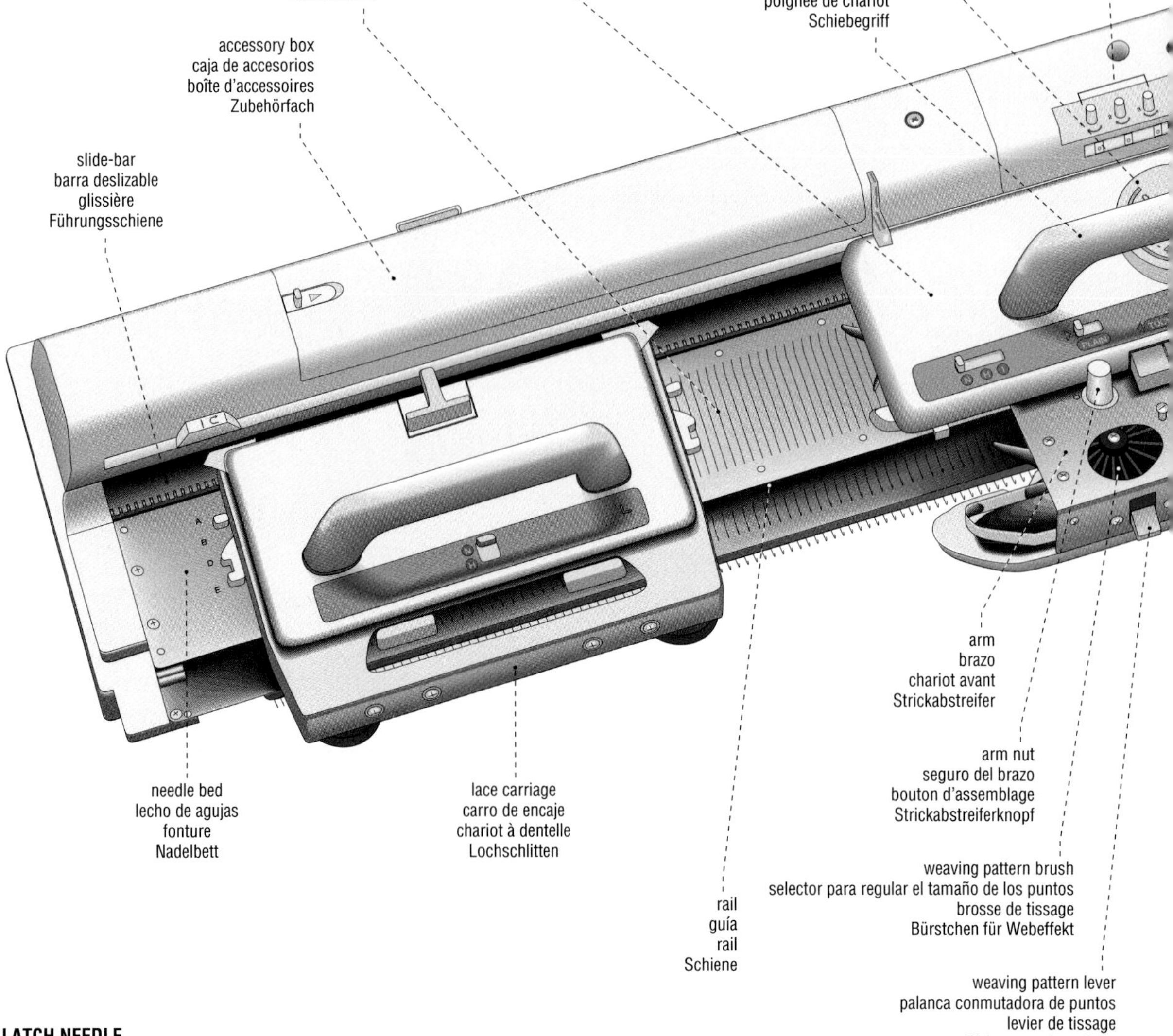

row counter
contador de pasadas
compte-rangs
Reihenzähler

main carriage
carro principal deslizante
chariot
Hauptschlitten

tension dial
regulador de tensión
cadran de tension
Spannungseinsteller

needle bed groove
placa de agujas
rainure
Nadelbettrille

carriage handle
empuñadura del carro
poignée de chariot
Schiebegriff

accessory box
caja de accesorios
boîte d'accessoires
Zubehörfach

slide-bar
barra deslizable
glissière
Führungsschiene

arm
brazo
chariot avant
Strickabstreifer

arm nut
seguro del brazo
bouton d'assemblage
Strickabstreiferknopf

needle bed
lecho de agujas
fonture
Nadelbett

lace carriage
carro de encaje
chariot à dentelle
Lochschlitten

weaving pattern brush
selector para regular el tamaño de los puntos
brosse de tissage
Bürstchen für Webeffekt

rail
guía
rail
Schiene

weaving pattern lever
palanca conmutadora de puntos
levier de tissage
Webmustereinstellung

LATCH NEEDLE
AGUJA CON LENGÜETA
AIGUILLE À CLAPET
ZUNGENNADEL

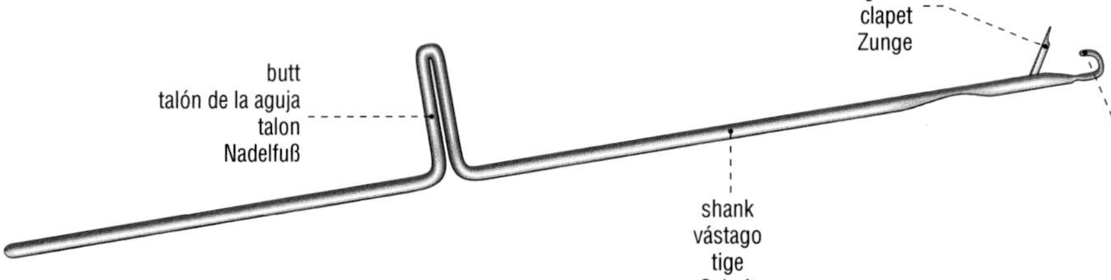

latch
lengüeta
clapet
Zunge

butt
talón de la aguja
talon
Nadelfuß

shank
vástago
tige
Schaft

hook
gancho
crochet
Haken

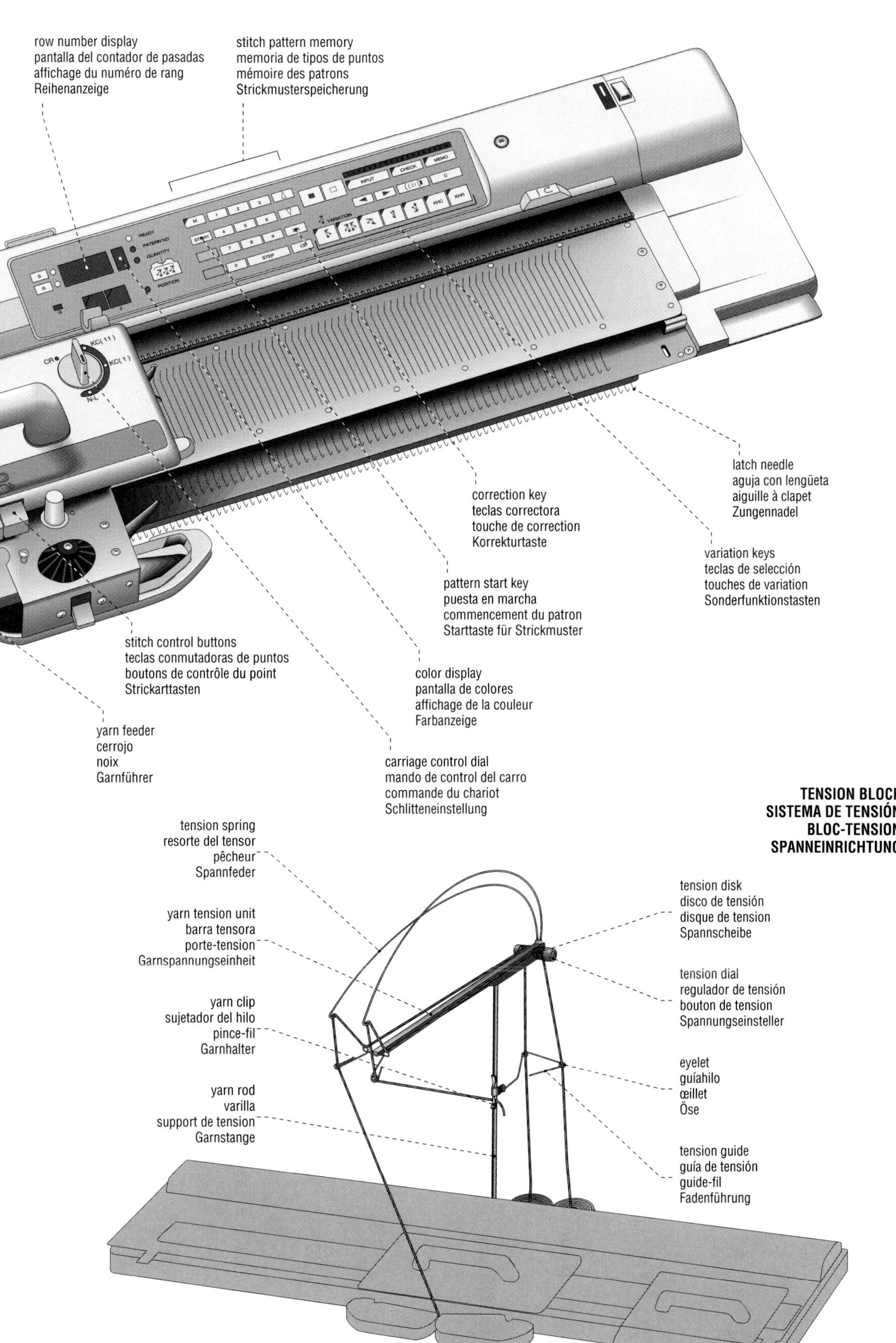
row number display
pantalla del contador de pasadas
affichage du numéro de rang
Reihenanzeige
stitch pattern memory
memoria de tipos de puntos
mémoire des patrons
Strickmusterspeicherung
latch needle
aguja con lengüeta
aiguille à clapet
Zungennadel
correction key
teclas correctora
touche de correction
Korrekturtaste
variation keys
teclas de selección
touches de variation
Sonderfunktionstasten
pattern start key
puesta en marcha
commencement du patron
Starttaste für Strickmuster
stitch control buttons
teclas conmutadoras de puntos
boutons de contrôle du point
Strickarttasten
color display
pantalla de colores
affichage de la couleur
Farbanzeige
yarn feeder
cerrojo
noix
Garnführer
carriage control dial
mando de control del carro
commande du chariot
Schlitteneinstellung
TENSION BLOCK
SISTEMA DE TENSIÓN
BLOC-TENSION
SPANNEINRICHTUNG
tension spring
resorte del tensor
pêcheur
Spannfeder
yarn tension unit
barra tensora
porte-tension
Garnspannungseinheit
yarn clip
sujetador del hilo
pince-fil
Garnhalter
yarn rod
varilla
support de tension
Garnstange
tension disk
disco de tensión
disque de tension
Spannscheibe
tension dial
regulador de tensión
bouton de tension
Spannungseinsteller
eyelet
guíahilo
œillet
Öse
tension guide
guía de tensión
guide-fil
Fadenführung

BOBBIN LACE
ENCAJE DE BOLILLOS
DENTELLE AUX FUSEAUX
KLÖPPELSPITZE

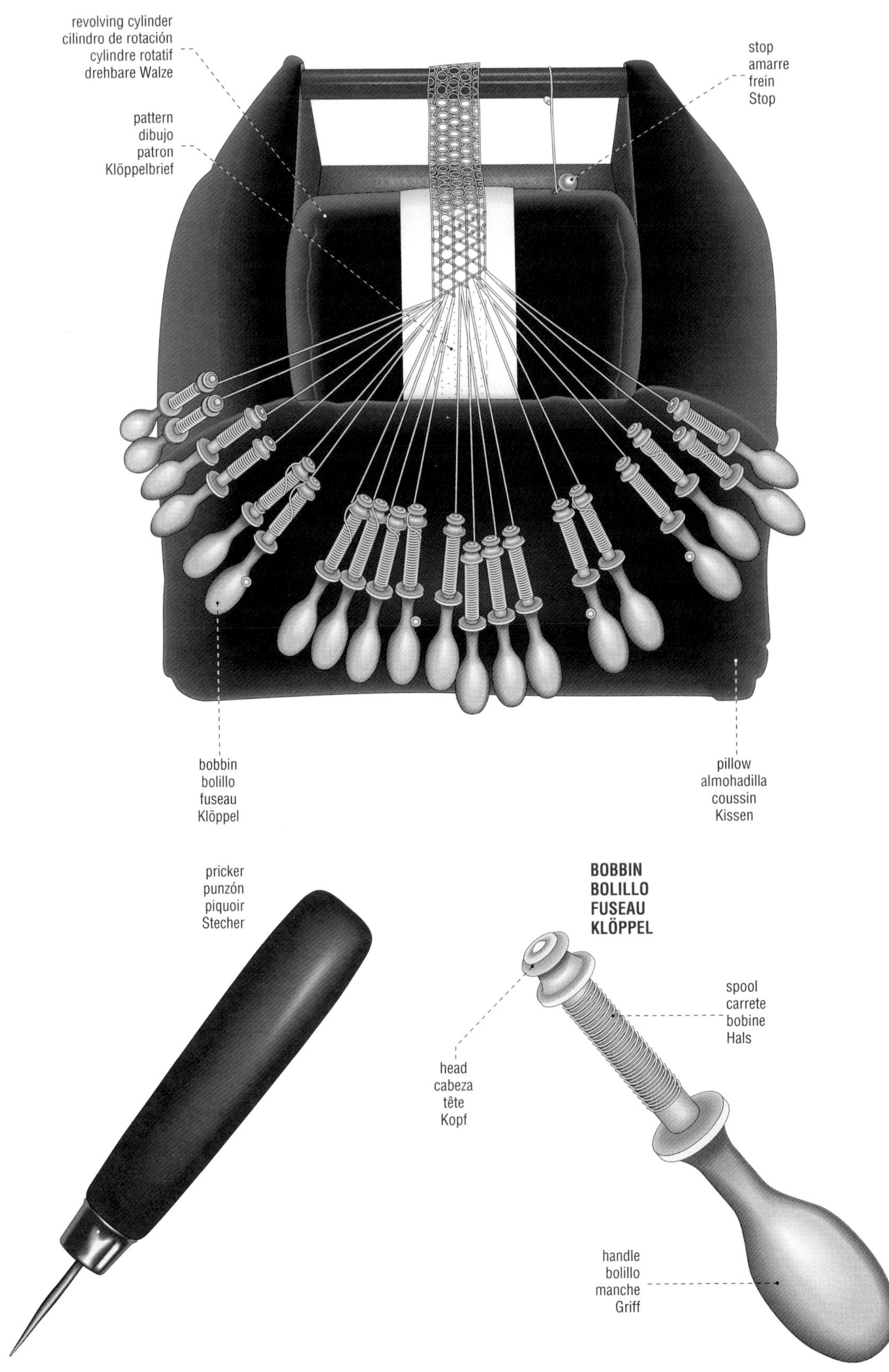
PILLOW
ALMOHADILLA
CARREAU
KLÖPPELKISSEN
revolving cylinder
cilindro de rotación
cylindre rotatif
drehbare Walze
pattern
dibujo
patron
Klöppelbrief
stop
amarre
frein
Stop
bobbin
bolillo
fuseau
Klöppel
pillow
almohadilla
coussin
Kissen
pricker
punzón
piquoir
Stecher
BOBBIN
BOLILLO
FUSEAU
KLÖPPEL
spool
carrete
bobine
Hals
head
cabeza
tête
Kopf
handle
bolillo
manche
Griff

EMBROIDERY
BORDADO
BRODERIE
STICKEREI

FRAME
BASTIDOR
MÉTIER À BRODER
RAHMEN

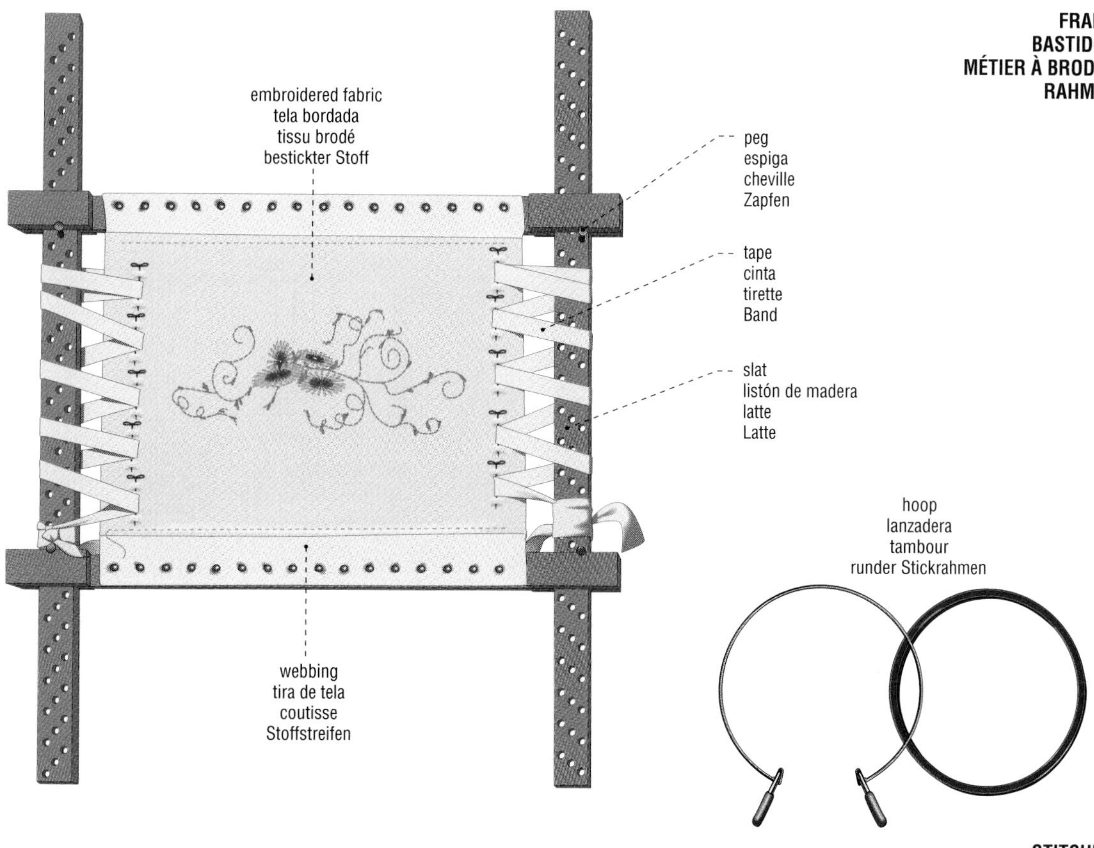
embroidered fabric
tela bordada
tissu brodé
bestickter Stoff
peg
espiga
cheville
Zapfen
tape
cinta
tirette
Band
slat
listón de madera
latte
Latte
webbing
tira de tela
coutisse
Stoffstreifen
hoop
lanzadera
tambour
runder Stickrahmen

STITCHES
TIPOS DE PUNTOS
CATÉGORIES DE POINTS
STICKSTICHE

cross stitches
puntos de cruz
points croisés
Kreuzstiche

herringbone stitch
punto de escapulario
point de chausson
Smokstich

chevron stitch
punto de cruz
point de chevron
Hexenstich

flat stitches
puntos de relleno
points plats
Plattstiche

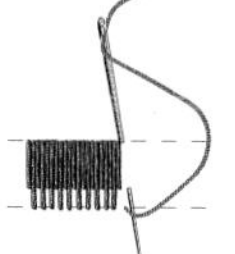

long and short stitch
lanzado desigual
point passé empiétant
langer und kurzer Spannstich

fishbone stitch
punto de espiga
point d'arête
Zopfstich

couched stitches
bordados planos
points couchés
Überfangstiche

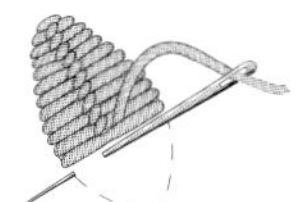

Romanian couching stitch
bordado plano
point roumain
rumänischer Überfangstich

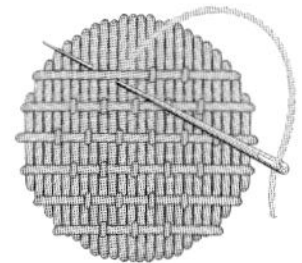

Oriental couching stitch
relleno alternado
point d'Orient
orientalischer Überfangstich

knot stitches
puntos de relleno sueltos
points noués
Knötchenstiche

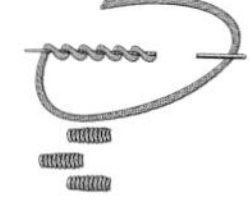

bullion stitch
pespunte
point de poste
Tressenstich

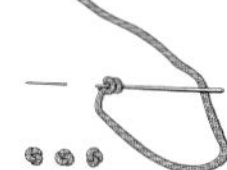

French knot stitch
punto de nudos
point de nœud
französischer Knötchenstich

loop stitches
puntos de malla
points bouclés
Schlingstiche

chain stitch
cadeneta
point de chaînette
Kettenstich

feather stitch
pata de gallo
point d'épine
Krähenfußstich

WEAVING
TELAR
TISSAGE
WEBEN

LOW WARP LOOM
TELAR DE CUATRO MARCOS
MÉTIER DE BASSE LISSE
FLACHWEBSTUHL

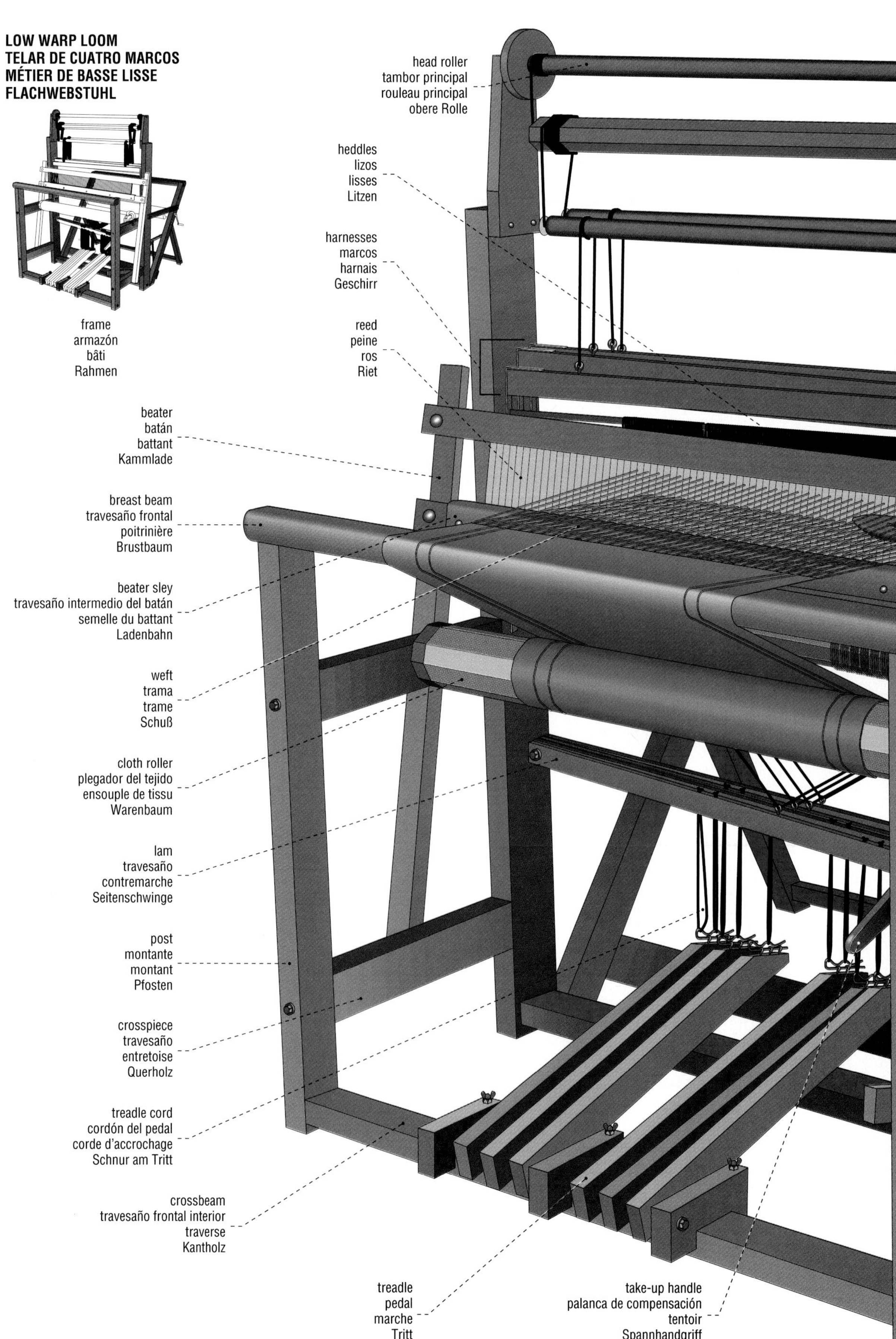
frame
armazón
bâti
Rahmen
head roller
tambor principal
rouleau principal
obere Rolle
heddles
lizos
lisses
Litzen
harnesses
marcos
harnais
Geschirr
reed
peine
ros
Riet
beater
batán
battant
Kammlade
breast beam
travesaño frontal
poitrinière
Brustbaum
beater sley
travesaño intermedio del batán
semelle du battant
Ladenbahn
weft
trama
trame
Schuß
cloth roller
plegador del tejido
ensouple de tissu
Warenbaum
lam
travesaño
contremarche
Seitenschwinge
post
montante
montant
Pfosten
crosspiece
travesaño
entretoise
Querholz
treadle cord
cordón del pedal
corde d'accrochage
Schnur am Tritt
crossbeam
travesaño frontal interior
traverse
Kantholz
treadle
pedal
marche
Tritt
take-up handle
palanca de compensación
tentoir
Spannhandgriff

ACCESSORIES
ACCESORIOS
ACCESSOIRES
ZUBEHÖR

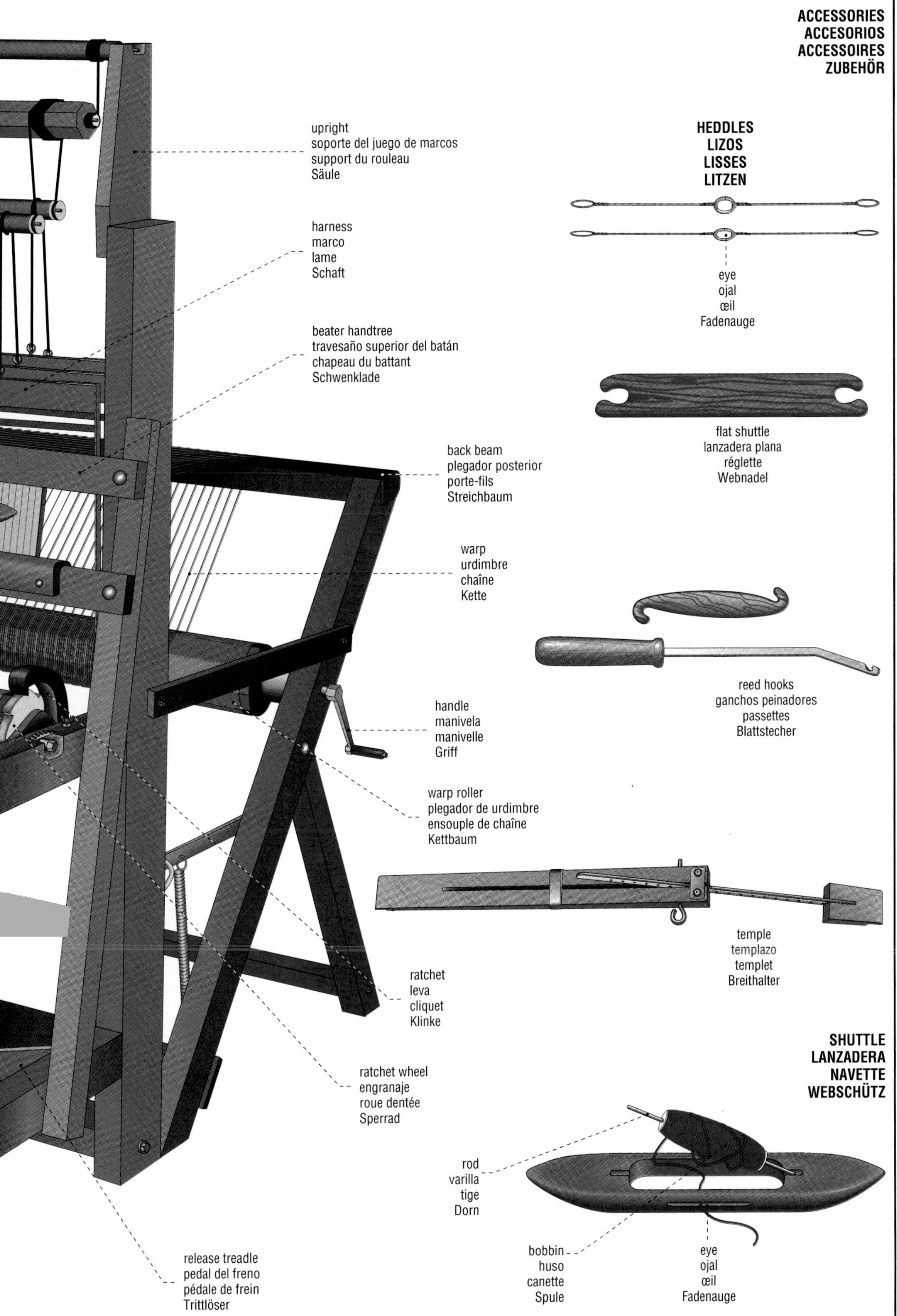
upright
soporte del juego de marcos
support du rouleau
Säule
harness
marco
lame
Schaft
beater handtree
travesaño superior del batán
chapeau du battant
Schwenklade
back beam
plegador posterior
porte-fils
Streichbaum
warp
urdimbre
chaîne
Kette
handle
manivela
manivelle
Griff
warp roller
plegador de urdimbre
ensouple de chaîne
Kettbaum
ratchet
leva
cliquet
Klinke
ratchet wheel
engranaje
roue dentée
Sperrad
release treadle
pedal del freno
pédale de frein
Trittlöser
HEDDLES
LIZOS
LISSES
LITZEN
eye
ojal
œil
Fadenauge
flat shuttle
lanzadera plana
réglette
Webnadel
reed hooks
ganchos peinadores
passettes
Blattstecher
temple
templazo
templet
Breithalter
SHUTTLE
LANZADERA
NAVETTE
WEBSCHÜTZ
rod
varilla
tige
Dorn
bobbin
huso
canette
Spule
eye
ojal
œil
Fadenauge

WEAVING
TEJIDO
TISSAGE
WEBEN

HIGH WARP LOOM
TELAR DE TAPICERÍA
MÉTIER DE HAUTE LISSE
HOCHWEBSTUHL

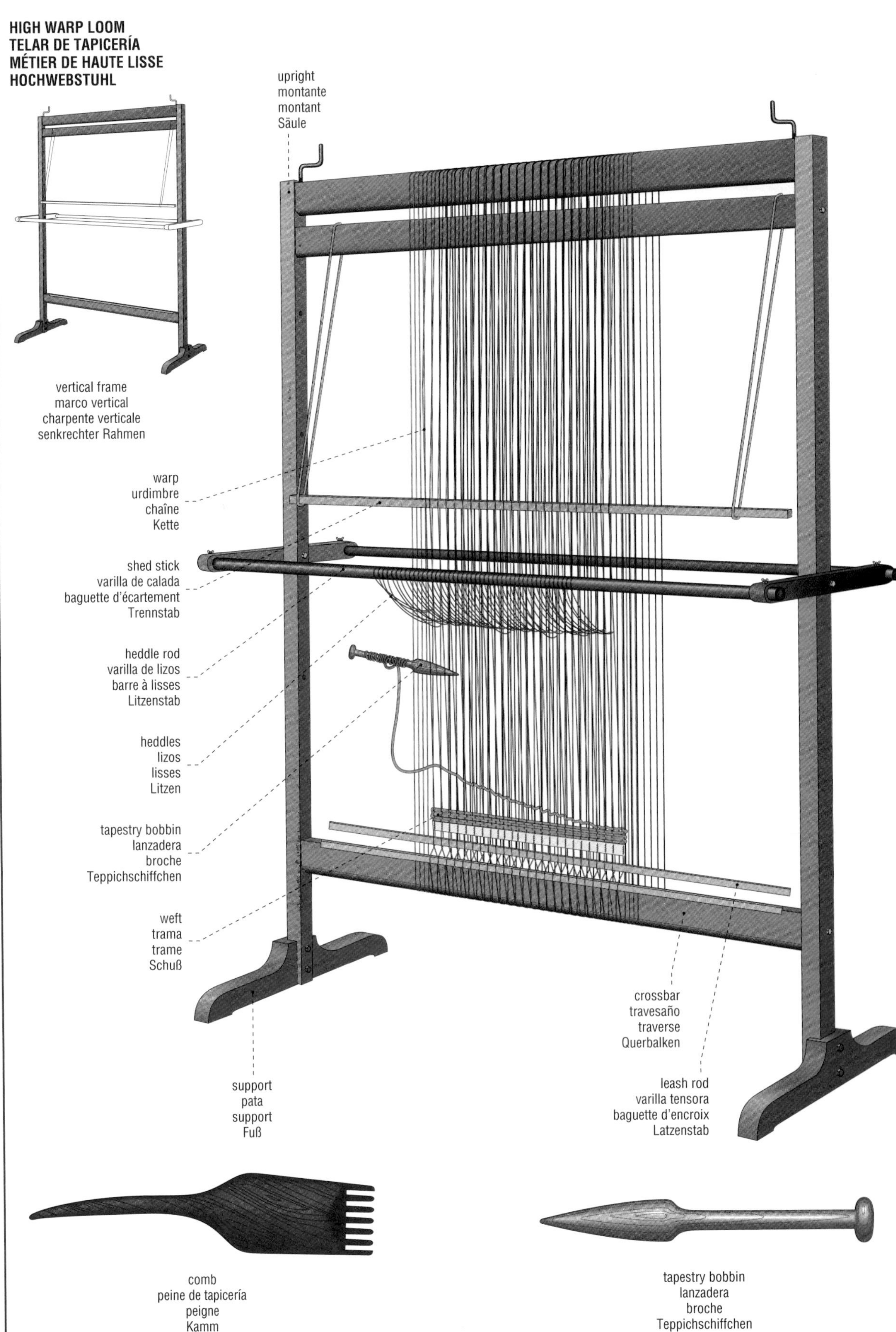
upright
montante
montant
Säule
vertical frame
marco vertical
charpente verticale
senkrechter Rahmen
warp
urdimbre
chaîne
Kette
shed stick
varilla de calada
baguette d'écartement
Trennstab
heddle rod
varilla de lizos
barre à lisses
Litzenstab
heddles
lizos
lisses
Litzen
tapestry bobbin
lanzadera
broche
Teppichschiffchen
weft
trama
trame
Schuß
crossbar
travesaño
traverse
Querbalken
support
pata
support
Fuß
leash rod
varilla tensora
baguette d'encroix
Latzenstab
comb
peine de tapicería
peigne
Kamm
tapestry bobbin
lanzadera
broche
Teppichschiffchen

ACCESSORIES
ACCESORIOS
ACCESSOIRES
ZUBEHÖR

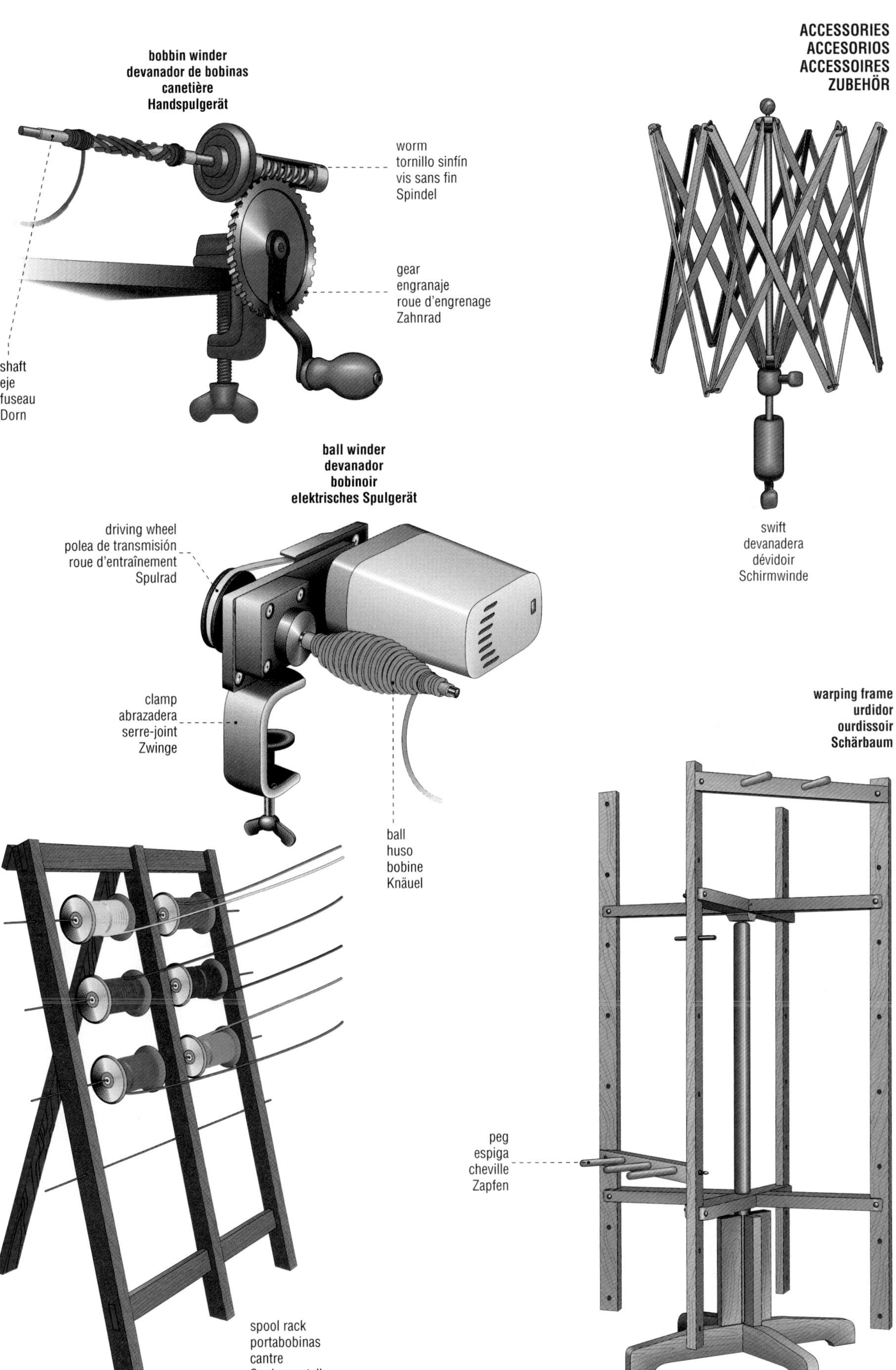
bobbin winder
devanador de bobinas
canetière
Handspulgerät
worm
tornillo sinfín
vis sans fin
Spindel
gear
engranaje
roue d'engrenage
Zahnrad
shaft
eje
fuseau
Dorn
swift
devanadera
dévidoir
Schirmwinde
ball winder
devanador
bobinoir
elektrisches Spulgerät
driving wheel
polea de transmisión
roue d'entraînement
Spulrad
clamp
abrazadera
serre-joint
Zwinge
ball
huso
bobine
Knäuel
warping frame
urdidor
ourdissoir
Schärbaum
peg
espiga
cheville
Zapfen
spool rack
portabobinas
cantre
Spulengestell

WEAVING
TEJIDOS
TISSAGE
WEBEN

DIAGRAM OF WEAVING PRINCIPLE
DIAGRAMAS DE TEJIDOS
SCHÉMA DE PRINCIPE DU TISSAGE
SCHAUBILD FÜR DAS WEBPRINZIP

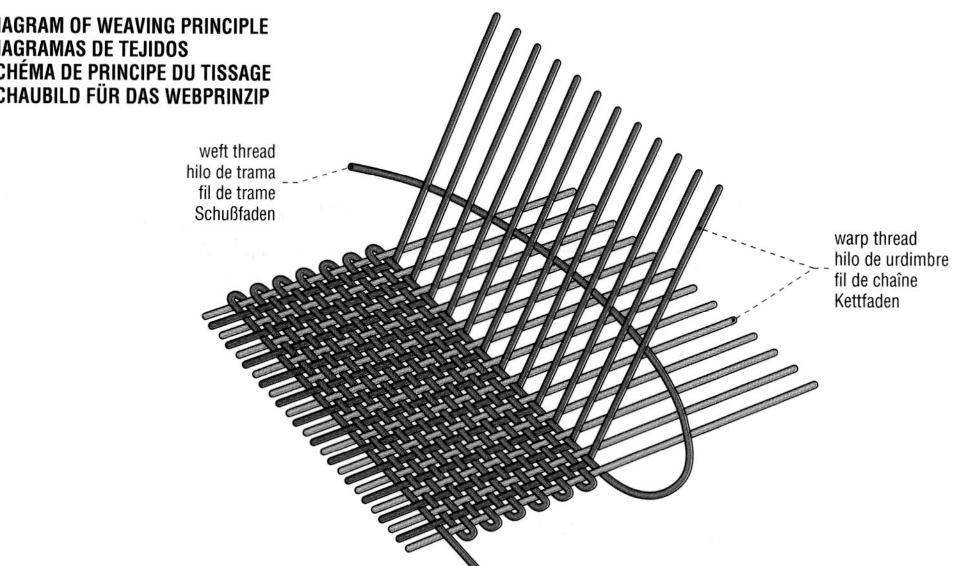
weft thread
hilo de trama
fil de trame
Schußfaden
warp thread
hilo de urdimbre
fil de chaîne
Kettfaden

BASIC WEAVES
LIGAMENTOS TEXTILES BÁSICOS
ARMURES DE BASE
GRUNDBINDUNGEN

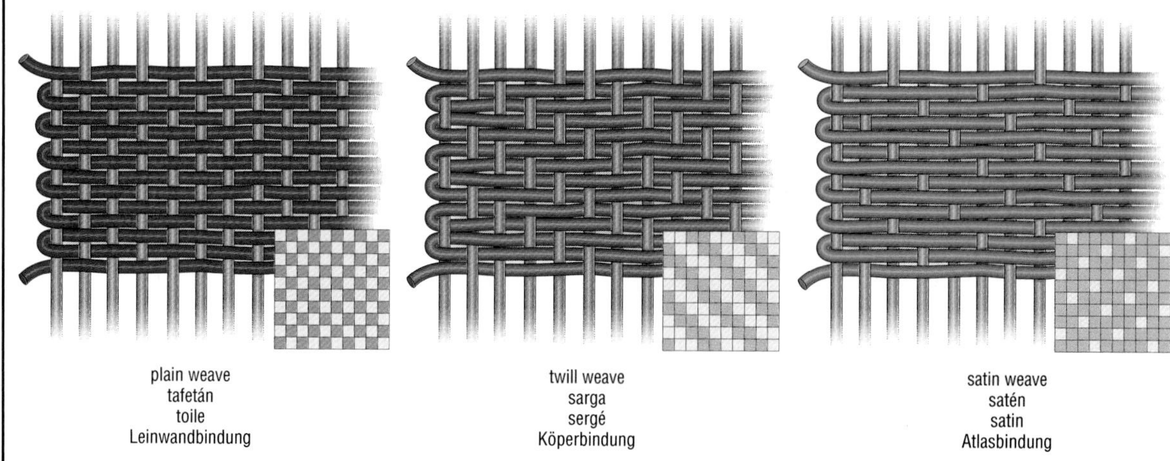
plain weave
tafetán
toile
Leinwandbindung
twill weave
sarga
sergé
Köperbindung
satin weave
satén
satin
Atlasbindung

OTHER TECHNIQUES
OTROS LIGAMENTOS TEXTILES
AUTRES TECHNIQUES
ANDERE TECHNIKEN

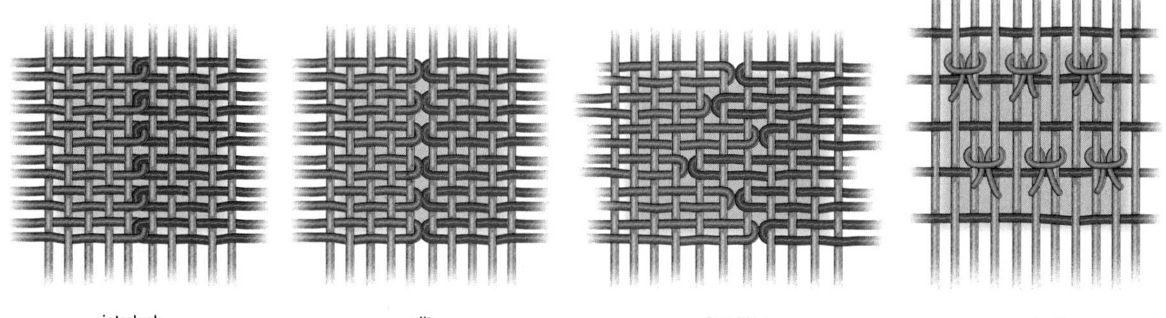
interlock
ligamento entrecruzado
croisement
Gobelinbindung
slit
ligamento vertical
fente
senkrechte Kelimbindung
hatching
ligamento de rayas
hachure
Kelimbindung mit wechselnden Wenden
knot
ligamento de nudos
nœud
Knoten

FINE BOOKBINDING
ENCUADERNACIÓN ARTÍSTICA
RELIURE D'ART
HANDBUCHBINDEREI

BOUND BOOK
LIBRO ENCUADERNADO
LIVRE RELIÉ
GEBUNDENES BUCH

GATHERING
COSIDO
PLAÇURE
ZUSAMMENTRAGEN

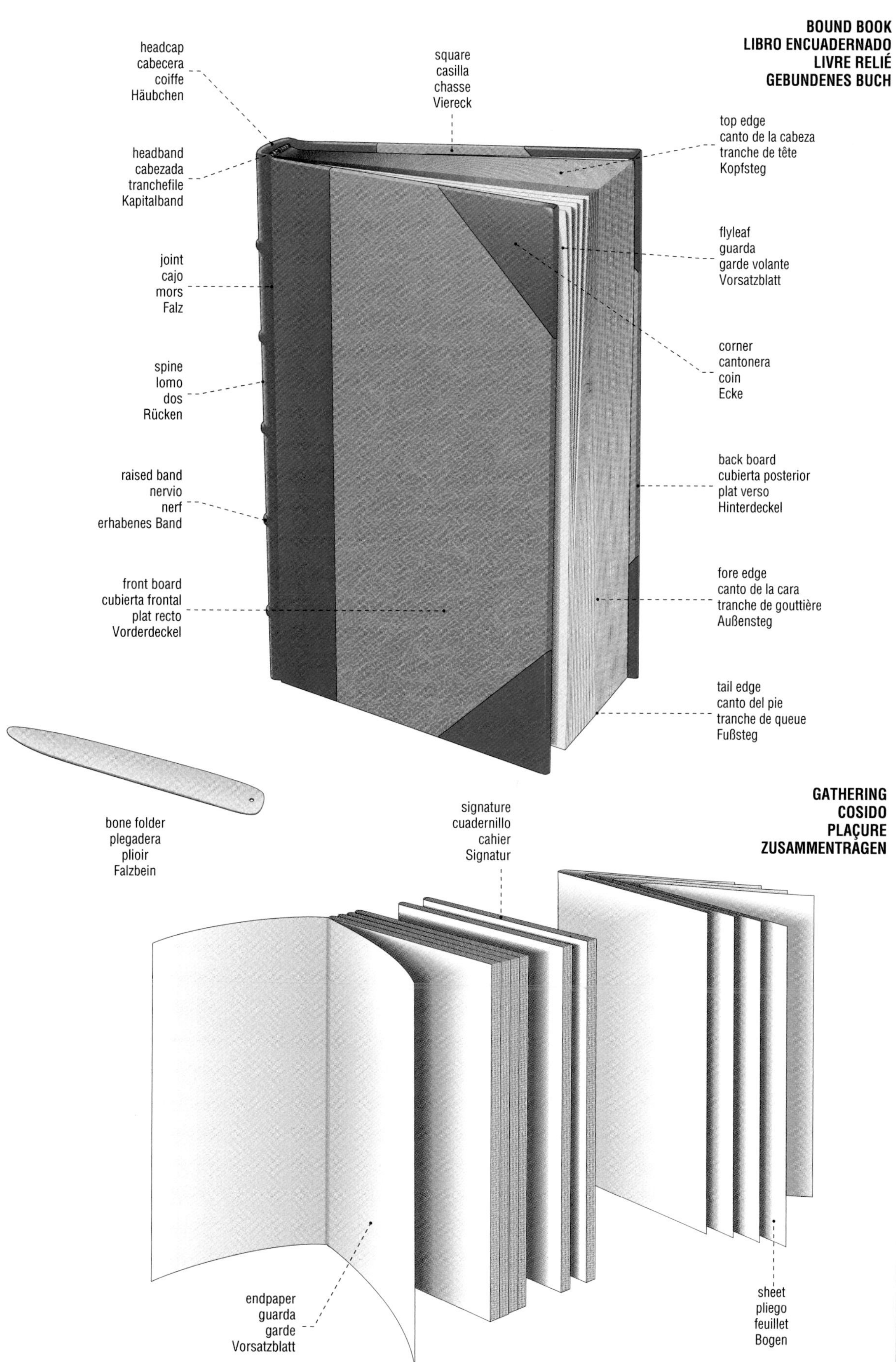
headcap
cabecera
coiffe
Häubchen
square
casilla
chasse
Viereck
top edge
canto de la cabeza
tranche de tête
Kopfsteg
headband
cabezada
tranchefile
Kapitalband
flyleaf
guarda
garde volante
Vorsatzblatt
joint
cajo
mors
Falz
corner
cantonera
coin
Ecke
spine
lomo
dos
Rücken
back board
cubierta posterior
plat verso
Hinterdeckel
raised band
nervio
nerf
erhabenes Band
fore edge
canto de la cara
tranche de gouttière
Außensteg
front board
cubierta frontal
plat recto
Vorderdeckel
tail edge
canto del pie
tranche de queue
Fußsteg
bone folder
plegadera
plioir
Falzbein
signature
cuadernillo
cahier
Signatur
endpaper
guarda
garde
Vorsatzblatt
sheet
pliego
feuillet
Bogen

FINE BOOKBINDING
ENCUADERNACIÓN ARTÍSTICA
RELIURE D'ART
HANDBUCHBINDEREI

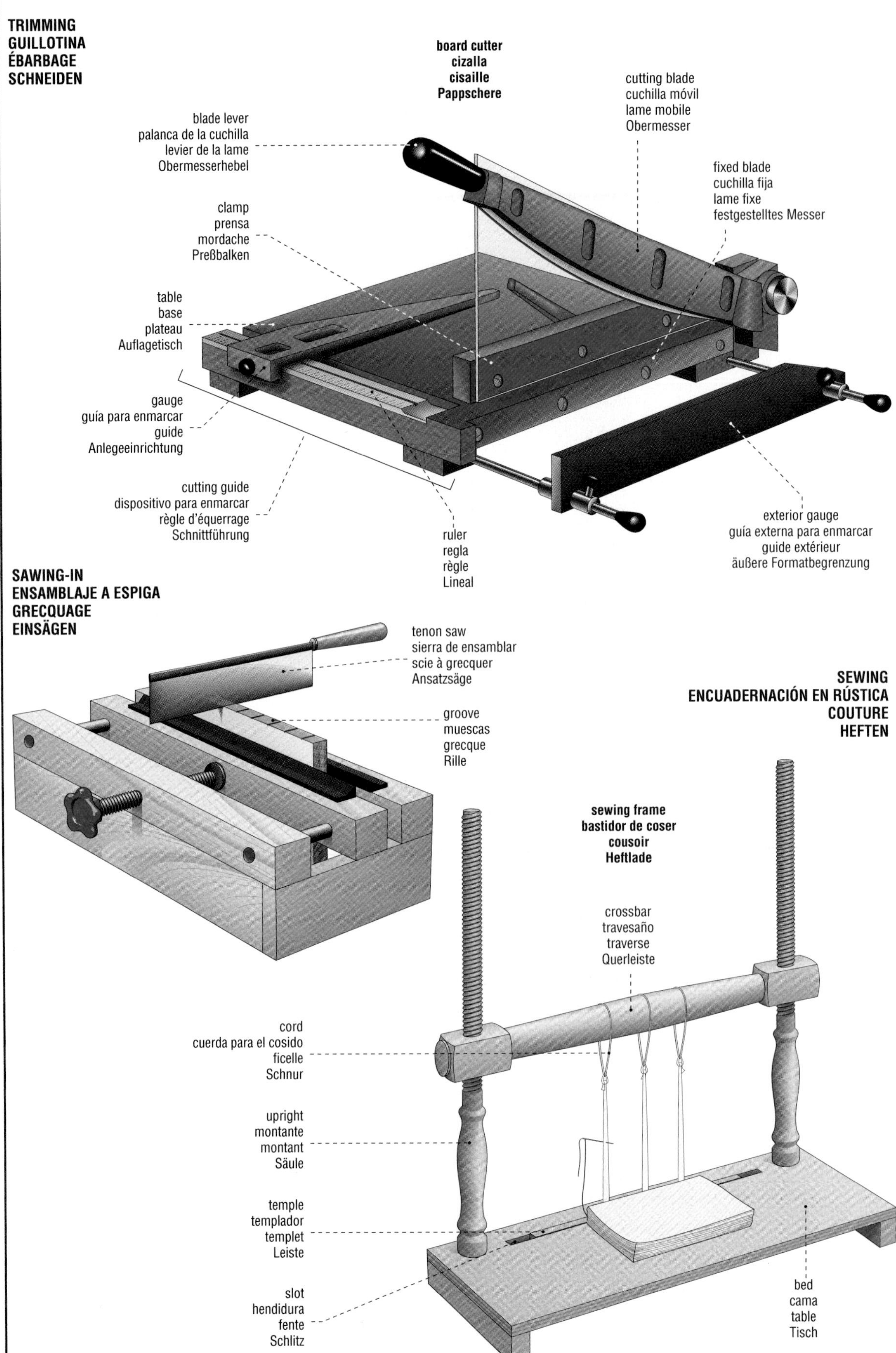
TRIMMING
GUILLOTINA
ÉBARBAGE
SCHNEIDEN
board cutter
cizalla
cisaille
Pappschere
blade lever
palanca de la cuchilla
levier de la lame
Obermesserhebel
cutting blade
cuchilla móvil
lame mobile
Obermesser
fixed blade
cuchilla fija
lame fixe
festgestelltes Messer
clamp
prensa
mordache
Preßbalken
table
base
plateau
Auflagetisch
gauge
guía para enmarcar
guide
Anlegeeinrichtung
cutting guide
dispositivo para enmarcar
règle d'équerrage
Schnittführung
ruler
regla
règle
Lineal
exterior gauge
guía externa para enmarcar
guide extérieur
äußere Formatbegrenzung
SAWING-IN
ENSAMBLAJE A ESPIGA
GRECQUAGE
EINSÄGEN
tenon saw
sierra de ensamblar
scie à grecquer
Ansatzsäge
groove
muescas
grecque
Rille
SEWING
ENCUADERNACIÓN EN RÚSTICA
COUTURE
HEFTEN
sewing frame
bastidor de coser
cousoir
Heftlade
crossbar
travesaño
traverse
Querleiste
cord
cuerda para el cosido
ficelle
Schnur
upright
montante
montant
Säule
temple
templador
templet
Leiste
slot
hendidura
fente
Schlitz
bed
cama
table
Tisch

BACKING
REDONDEO
ENDOSSURE
BUCHRÜCKENBEARBEITUNG

BACKING PRESS
PRENSA DE CAJOS
ÉTAU À ENDOSSER
BUCHRÜCKENPRESSE

PRESSING
PRENSA
MISE EN PRESSE
PRESSEN

standing press
prensa de tornillo
presse à percussion
Stockpresse

BACKING HAMMER
MARTILLO DE ENCUADERNADOR
MARTEAU À ENDOSSER
HAMMER ZUM RUNDKLOPFEN

COVERING
CUBIERTA
COUVRURE
EINBINDEN

bookbinding leather
piel para encuadernar
peau
Einbandleder

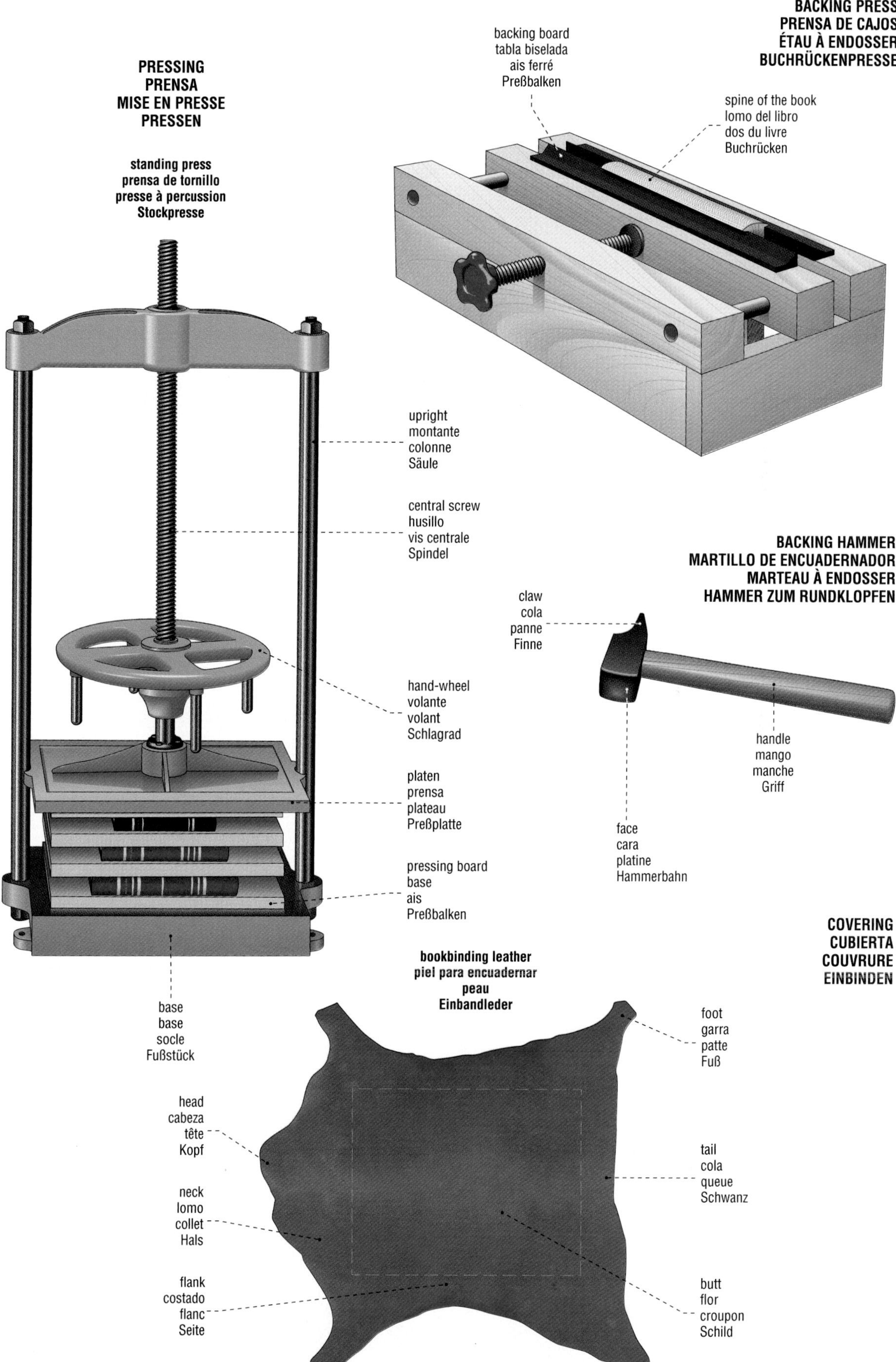
backing board
tabla biselada
ais ferré
Preßbalken
spine of the book
lomo del libro
dos du livre
Buchrücken
upright
montante
colonne
Säule
central screw
husillo
vis centrale
Spindel
hand-wheel
volante
volant
Schlagrad
platen
prensa
plateau
Preßplatte
pressing board
base
ais
Preßbalken
base
base
socle
Fußstück
claw
cola
panne
Finne
handle
mango
manche
Griff
face
cara
platine
Hammerbahn
foot
garra
patte
Fuß
head
cabeza
tête
Kopf
tail
cola
queue
Schwanz
neck
lomo
collet
Hals
flank
costado
flanc
Seite
butt
flor
croupon
Schild

PRINTING
IMPRESIÓN
IMPRESSION
DRUCKEN

RELIEF PRINTING
IMPRESIÓN EN RELIEVE
IMPRESSION EN RELIEF
HOCHDRUCK

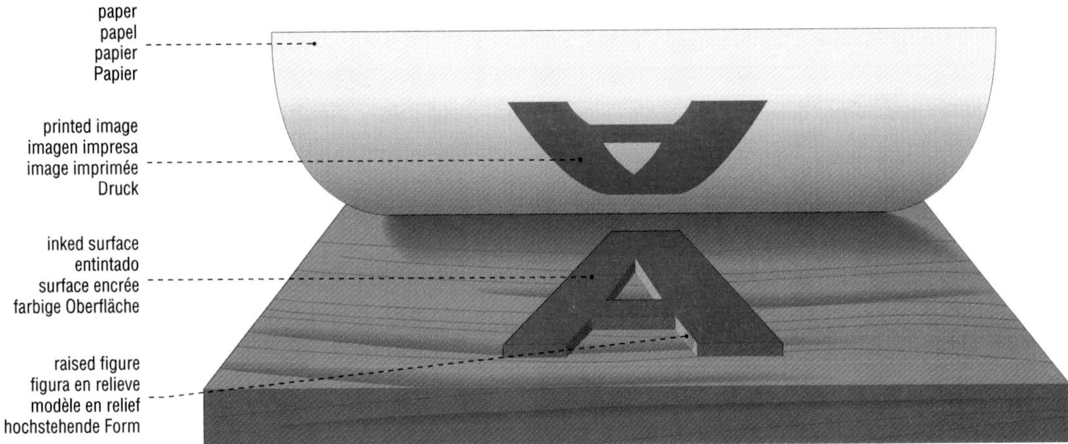
paper
papel
papier
Papier
printed image
imagen impresa
image imprimée
Druck
inked surface
entintado
surface encrée
farbige Oberfläche
raised figure
figura en relieve
modèle en relief
hochstehende Form

INTAGLIO PRINTING
HUECOGRABADO
IMPRESSION EN CREUX
TIEFDRUCK

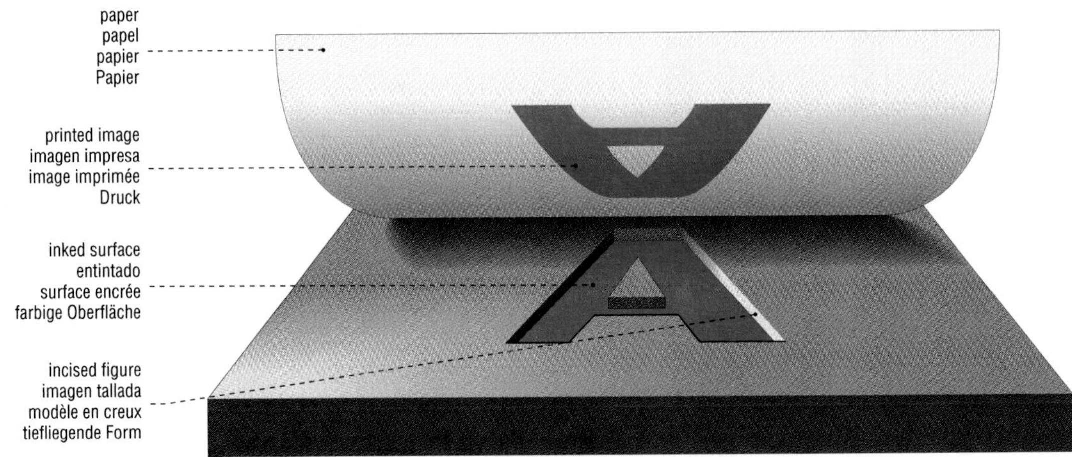
paper
papel
papier
Papier
printed image
imagen impresa
image imprimée
Druck
inked surface
entintado
surface encrée
farbige Oberfläche
incised figure
imagen tallada
modèle en creux
tiefliegende Form

LITHOGRAPHIC PRINTING
IMPRESIÓN LITOGRÁFICA
IMPRESSION À PLAT
LITHOGRAPHIE

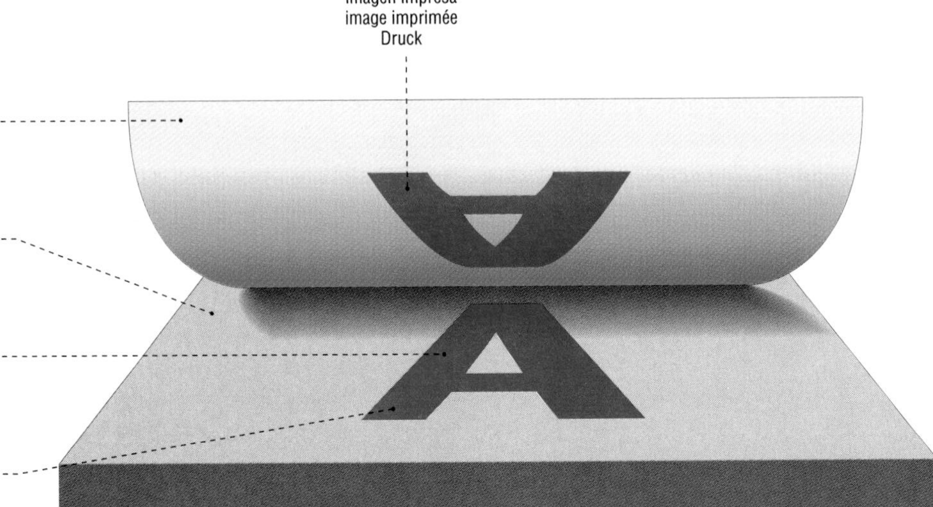
printed image
imagen impresa
image imprimée
Druck
paper
papel
papier
Papier
moist surface
superficie humedecida
surface mouillée
befeuchtete Oberfläche
inked surface
entintado
surface encrée
farbige Oberfläche
plane figure
figura plana
modèle à plat
Flachform

RELIEF PRINTING PROCESS
IMPRESIÓN EN RELIEVE
GRAVURE EN RELIEF
HOCHDRUCKVERFAHREN

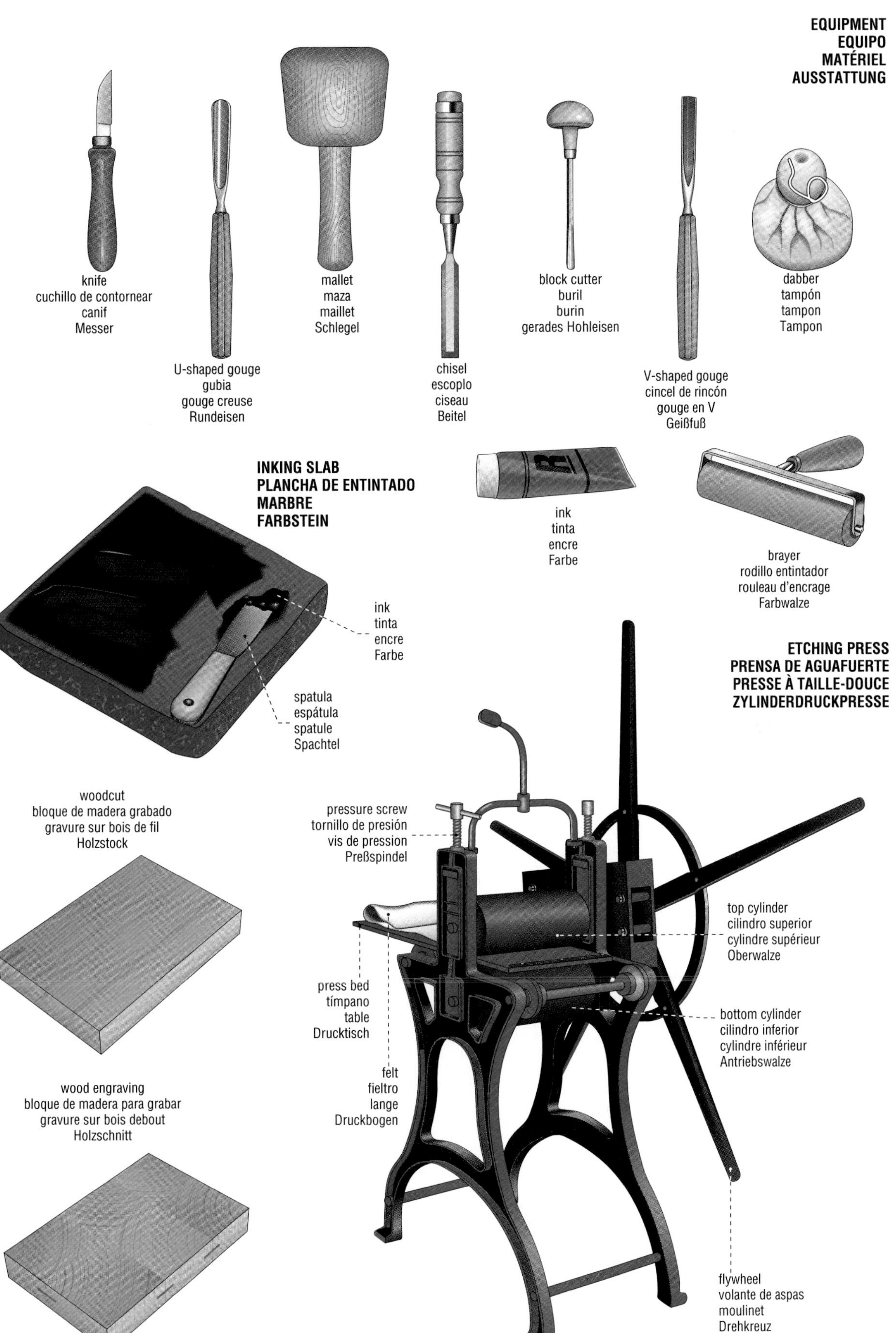
EQUIPMENT
EQUIPO
MATÉRIEL
AUSSTATTUNG
knife
cuchillo de contornear
canif
Messer
U-shaped gouge
gubia
gouge creuse
Rundeisen
mallet
maza
maillet
Schlegel
chisel
escoplo
ciseau
Beitel
block cutter
buril
burin
gerades Hohleisen
V-shaped gouge
cincel de rincón
gouge en V
Geißfuß
dabber
tampón
tampon
Tampon
INKING SLAB
PLANCHA DE ENTINTADO
MARBRE
FARBSTEIN
ink
tinta
encre
Farbe
spatula
espátula
spatule
Spachtel
ink
tinta
encre
Farbe
brayer
rodillo entintador
rouleau d'encrage
Farbwalze
ETCHING PRESS
PRENSA DE AGUAFUERTE
PRESSE À TAILLE-DOUCE
ZYLINDERDRUCKPRESSE
woodcut
bloque de madera grabado
gravure sur bois de fil
Holzstock
pressure screw
tornillo de presión
vis de pression
Preßspindel
top cylinder
cilindro superior
cylindre supérieur
Oberwalze
press bed
tímpano
table
Drucktisch
bottom cylinder
cilindro inferior
cylindre inférieur
Antriebswalze
felt
fieltro
lange
Druckbogen
wood engraving
bloque de madera para grabar
gravure sur bois debout
Holzschnitt
flywheel
volante de aspas
moulinet
Drehkreuz

INTAGLIO PRINTING PROCESS
IMPRESIÓN EN HUECOGRABADO
GRAVURE EN CREUX
TIEFDRUCKVERFAHREN

EQUIPMENT
EQUIPO
MATÉRIEL
AUSSTATTUNG

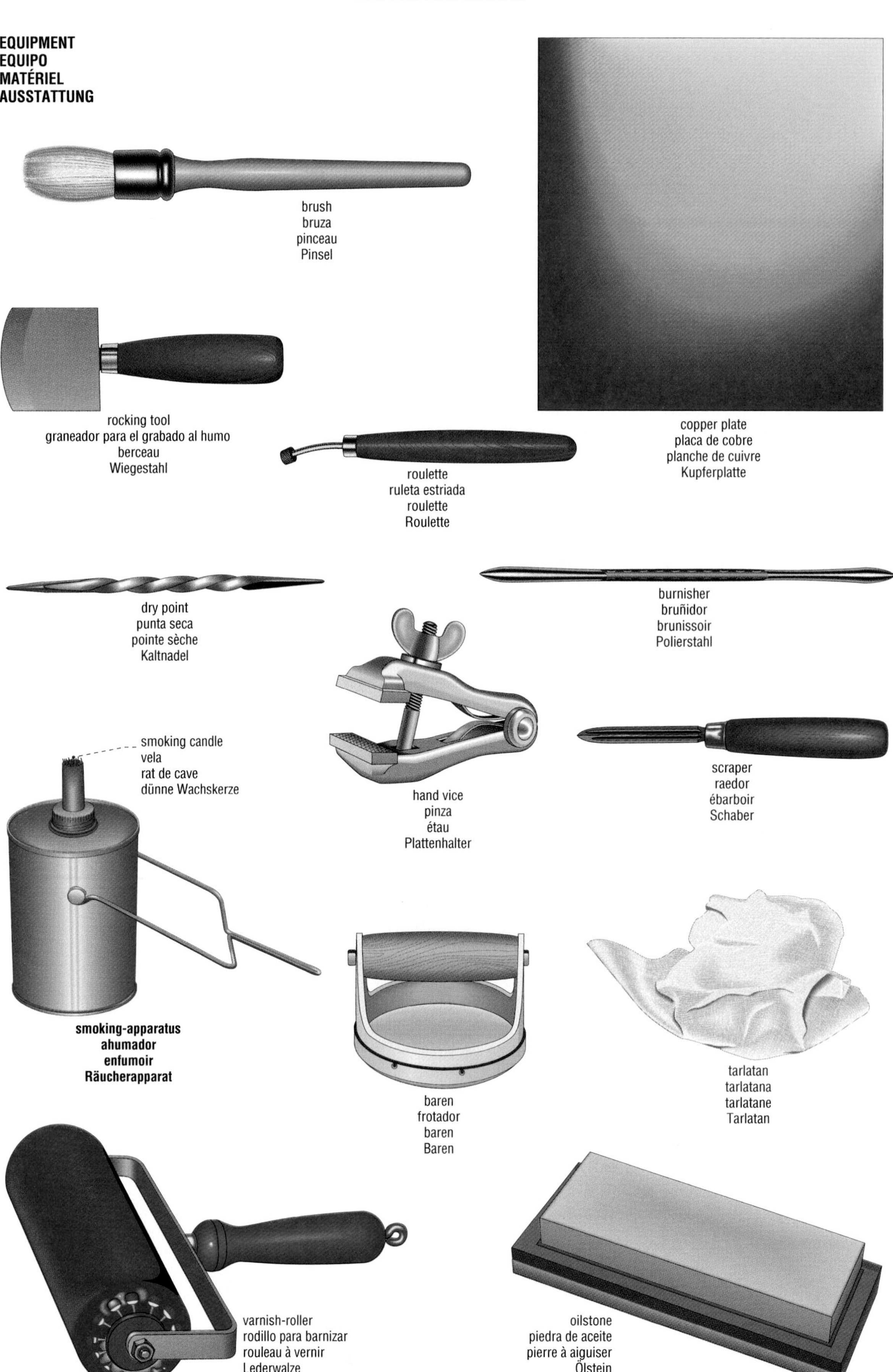
brush
bruza
pinceau
Pinsel
rocking tool
graneador para el grabado al humo
berceau
Wiegestahl
roulette
ruleta estriada
roulette
Roulette
copper plate
placa de cobre
planche de cuivre
Kupferplatte
dry point
punta seca
pointe sèche
Kaltnadel
burnisher
bruñidor
brunissoir
Polierstahl
hand vice
pinza
étau
Plattenhalter
scraper
raedor
ébarboir
Schaber
smoking candle
vela
rat de cave
dünne Wachskerze
smoking-apparatus
ahumador
enfumoir
Räucherapparat
baren
frotador
baren
Baren
tarlatan
tarlatana
tarlatane
Tarlatan
varnish-roller
rodillo para barnizar
rouleau à vernir
Lederwalze
oilstone
piedra de aceite
pierre à aiguiser
Ölstein

LITHOGRAPHY
LITOGRAFÍA
LITHOGRAPHIE
LITHOGRAPHIE

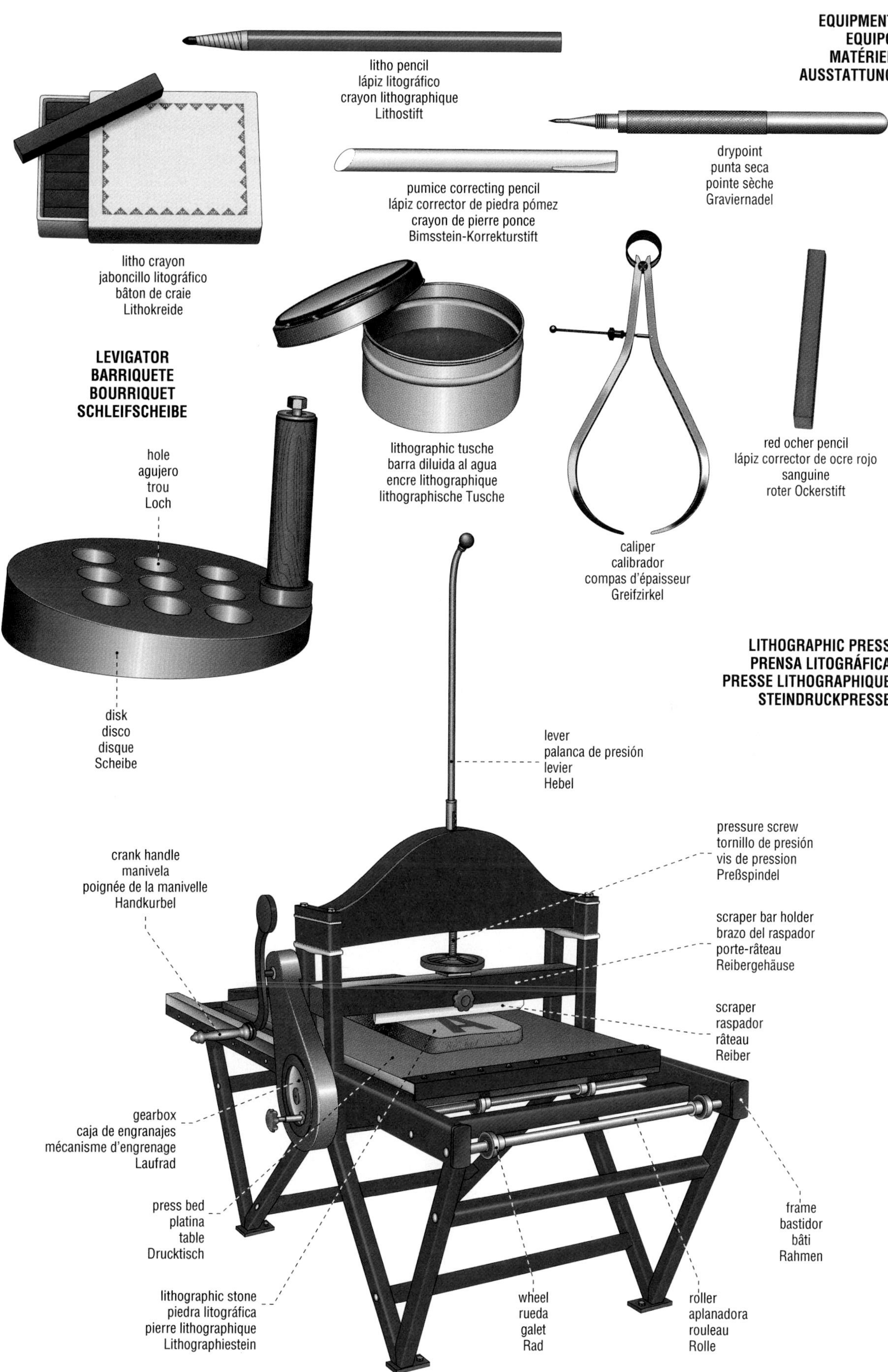
EQUIPMENT
EQUIPO
MATÉRIEL
AUSSTATTUNG
litho pencil
lápiz litográfico
crayon lithographique
Lithostift
drypoint
punta seca
pointe sèche
Graviernadel
pumice correcting pencil
lápiz corrector de piedra pómez
crayon de pierre ponce
Bimsstein-Korrekturstift
litho crayon
jaboncillo litográfico
bâton de craie
Lithokreide
LEVIGATOR
BARRIQUETE
BOURRIQUET
SCHLEIFSCHEIBE
hole
agujero
trou
Loch
disk
disco
disque
Scheibe
lithographic tusche
barra diluida al agua
encre lithographique
lithographische Tusche
caliper
calibrador
compas d'épaisseur
Greifzirkel
red ocher pencil
lápiz corrector de ocre rojo
sanguine
roter Ockerstift
LITHOGRAPHIC PRESS
PRENSA LITOGRÁFICA
PRESSE LITHOGRAPHIQUE
STEINDRUCKPRESSE
lever
palanca de presión
levier
Hebel
pressure screw
tornillo de presión
vis de pression
Preßspindel
crank handle
manivela
poignée de la manivelle
Handkurbel
scraper bar holder
brazo del raspador
porte-râteau
Reibergehäuse
scraper
raspador
râteau
Reiber
gearbox
caja de engranajes
mécanisme d'engrenage
Laufrad
press bed
platina
table
Drucktisch
frame
bastidor
bâti
Rahmen
lithographic stone
piedra litográfica
pierre lithographique
Lithographiestein
wheel
rueda
galet
Rad
roller
aplanadora
rouleau
Rolle

POTTERY
CERÁMICA
POTERIE
TÖPFEREI

TURNING
TORNO
TOURNAGE
DREHEN

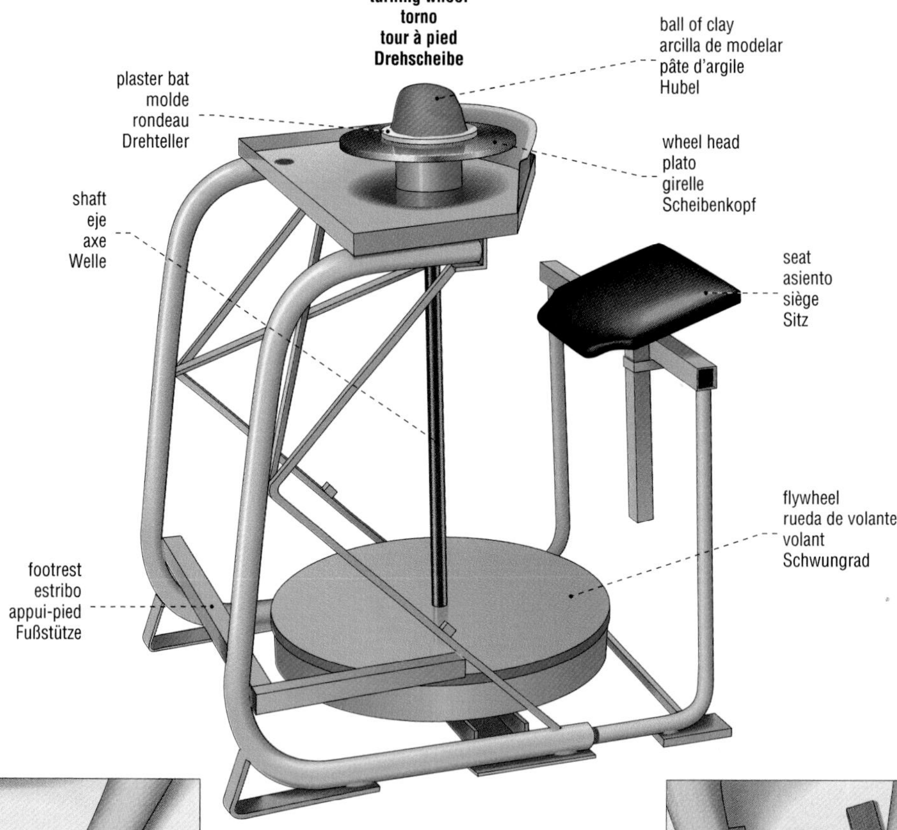
turning wheel
torno
tour à pied
Drehscheibe
ball of clay
arcilla de modelar
pâte d'argile
Hubel
plaster bat
molde
rondeau
Drehteller
wheel head
plato
girelle
Scheibenkopf
shaft
eje
axe
Welle
seat
asiento
siège
Sitz
flywheel
rueda de volante
volant
Schwungrad
footrest
estribo
appui-pied
Fußstütze

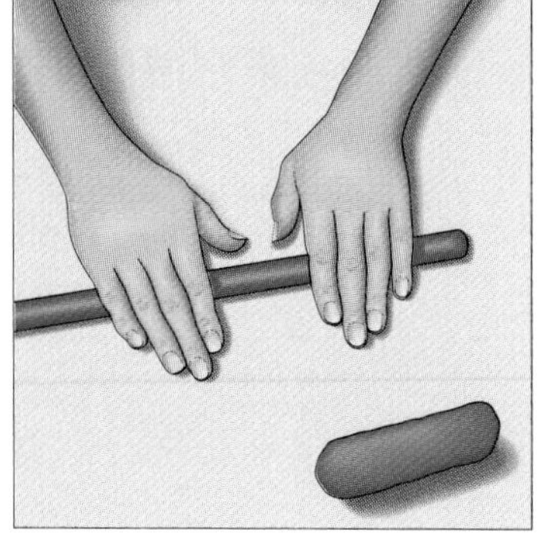

COILING
CORDÓN PARA ESPIRALES
COLOMBIN
SPIRALWÜLSTE ROLLEN

SLAB BUILDING
RODILLO
GALETTAGE
PLATTEN AUSROLLEN

TOOLS
HERRAMIENTAS
OUTILS
WERKZEUG

ribs
costillar
esthèques
Drehschiene

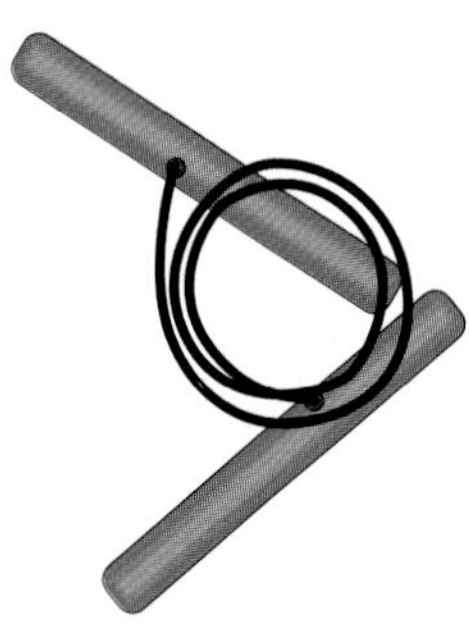

cutting wire
alambre para cortar
fil à couper la pâte
Schneidedraht

banding wheel
torneta
tournette
Modellierscheibe

TOOLS
HERRAMIENTAS
OUTILS
WERKZEUG

FIRING
COCCIÓN
CUISSON
BRENNEN

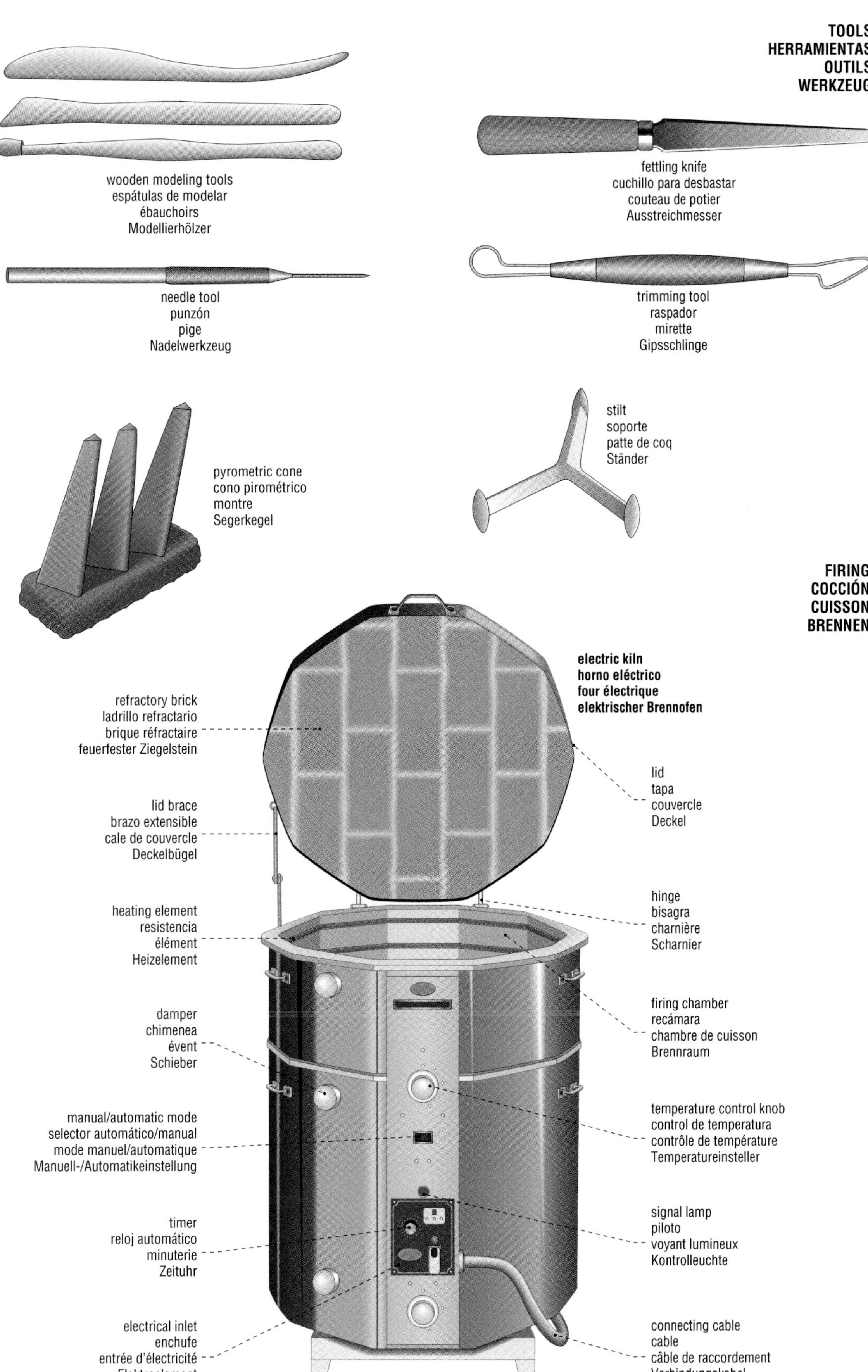
wooden modeling tools
espátulas de modelar
ébauchoirs
Modellierhölzer
fettling knife
cuchillo para desbastar
couteau de potier
Ausstreichmesser
needle tool
punzón
pige
Nadelwerkzeug
trimming tool
raspador
mirette
Gipsschlinge
stilt
soporte
patte de coq
Ständer
pyrometric cone
cono pirométrico
montre
Segerkegel
electric kiln
horno eléctrico
four électrique
elektrischer Brennofen
refractory brick
ladrillo refractario
brique réfractaire
feuerfester Ziegelstein
lid
tapa
couvercle
Deckel
lid brace
brazo extensible
cale de couvercle
Deckelbügel
hinge
bisagra
charnière
Scharnier
heating element
resistencia
élément
Heizelement
firing chamber
recámara
chambre de cuisson
Brennraum
damper
chimenea
évent
Schieber
temperature control knob
control de temperatura
contrôle de température
Temperatureinsteller
manual/automatic mode
selector automático/manual
mode manuel/automatique
Manuell-/Automatikeinstellung
signal lamp
piloto
voyant lumineux
Kontrolleuchte
timer
reloj automático
minuterie
Zeituhr
electrical inlet
enchufe
entrée d'électricité
Elektroelement
connecting cable
cable
câble de raccordement
Verbindungskabel

WOOD CARVING
TALLA EN MADERA
SCULPTURE SUR BOIS
HOLZSCHNITZEREI

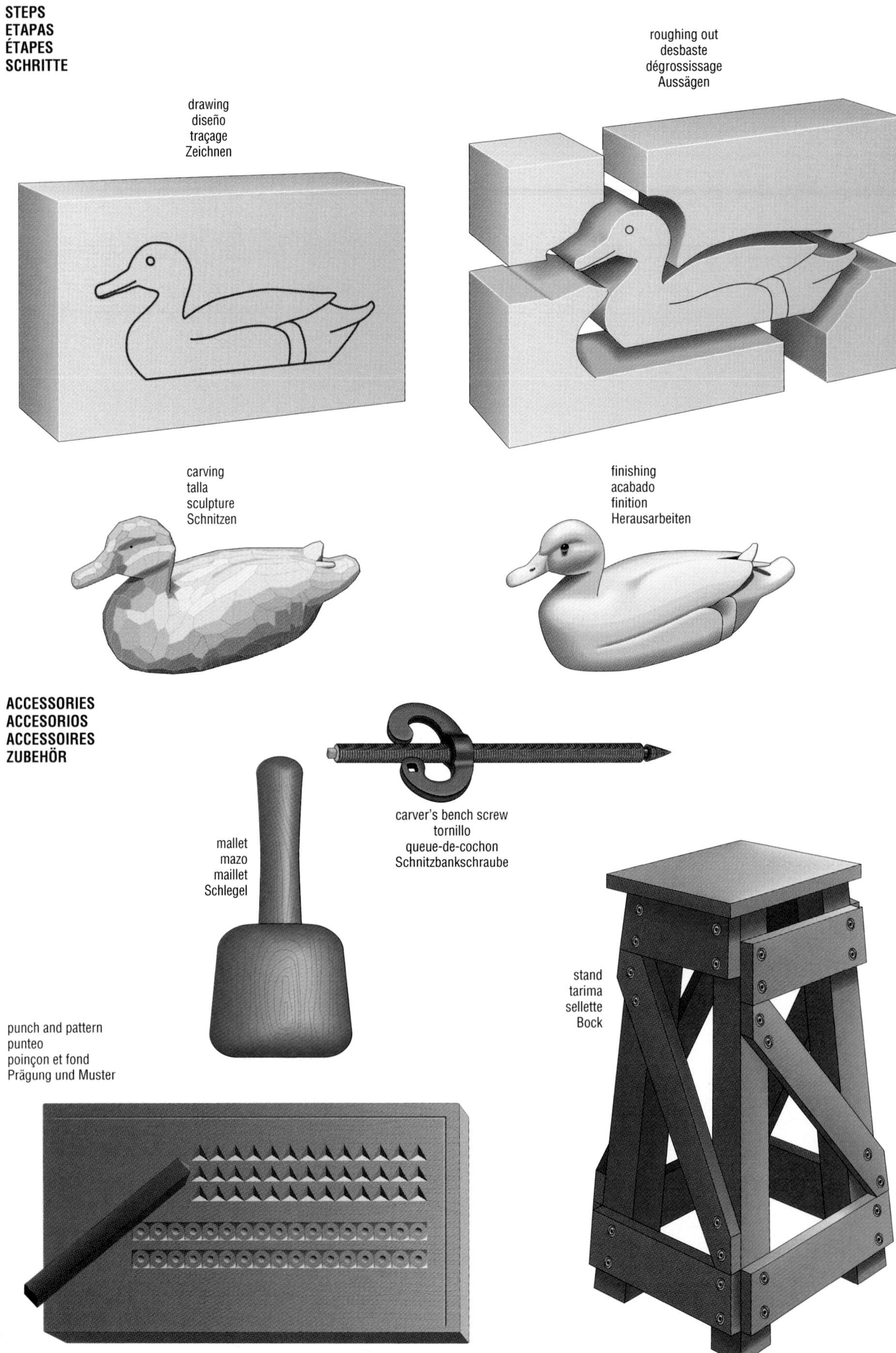
STEPS
ETAPAS
ÉTAPES
SCHRITTE
drawing
diseño
traçage
Zeichnen
roughing out
desbaste
dégrossissage
Aussägen
carving
talla
sculpture
Schnitzen
finishing
acabado
finition
Herausarbeiten
ACCESSORIES
ACCESORIOS
ACCESSOIRES
ZUBEHÖR
carver's bench screw
tornillo
queue-de-cochon
Schnitzbankschraube
mallet
mazo
maillet
Schlegel
stand
tarima
sellette
Bock
punch and pattern
punteo
poinçon et fond
Prägung und Muster

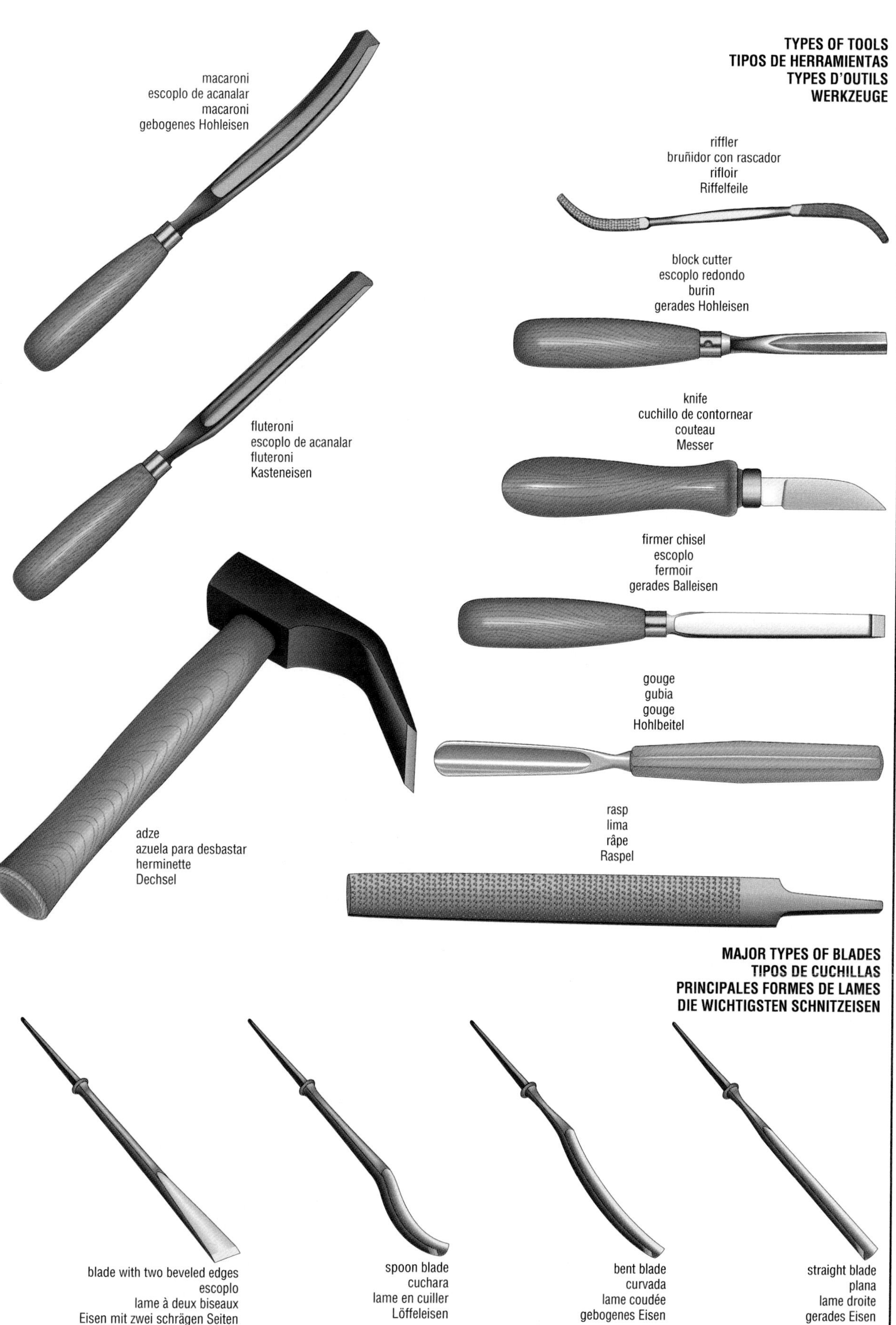
TYPES OF TOOLS
TIPOS DE HERRAMIENTAS
TYPES D'OUTILS
WERKZEUGE
macaroni
escoplo de acanalar
macaroni
gebogenes Hohleisen
riffler
bruñidor con rascador
rifloir
Riffelfeile
block cutter
escoplo redondo
burin
gerades Hohleisen
knife
cuchillo de contornear
couteau
Messer
fluteroni
escoplo de acanalar
fluteroni
Kasteneisen
firmer chisel
escoplo
fermoir
gerades Balleisen
gouge
gubia
gouge
Hohlbeitel
rasp
lima
râpe
Raspel
adze
azuela para desbastar
herminette
Dechsel
MAJOR TYPES OF BLADES
TIPOS DE CUCHILLAS
PRINCIPALES FORMES DE LAMES
DIE WICHTIGSTEN SCHNITZEISEN
blade with two beveled edges
escoplo
lame à deux biseaux
Eisen mit zwei schrägen Seiten
spoon blade
cuchara
lame en cuiller
Löffeleisen
bent blade
curvada
lame coudée
gebogenes Eisen
straight blade
plana
lame droite
gerades Eisen

PAINTING AND DRAWING
PINTURA Y DIBUJO
PEINTURE ET DESSIN
MALEN UND ZEICHNEN

MAJOR TECHNIQUES
TÉCNICAS PRINCIPALES
PRINCIPALES TECHNIQUES
DIE WICHTIGSTEN TECHNIKEN

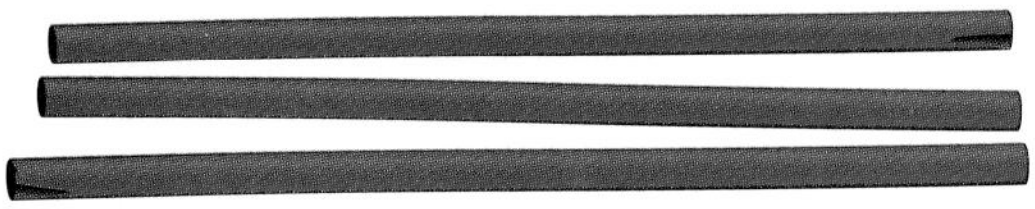

charcoal
carboncillo
fusain
Kohle

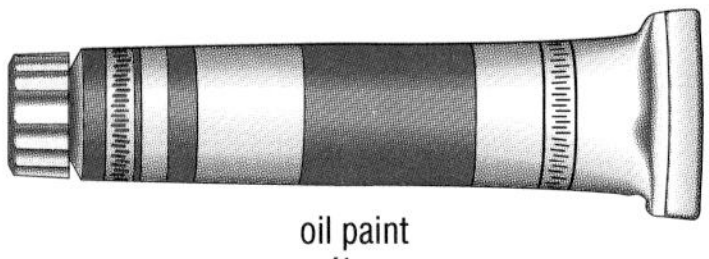

oil paint
óleo
couleur à l'huile
Ölfarbe

ink
tinta china
encre
Tinte

watercolor and gouache
acuarela y aguazo
aquarelle et gouache
Aquarellfarbe und Gouache

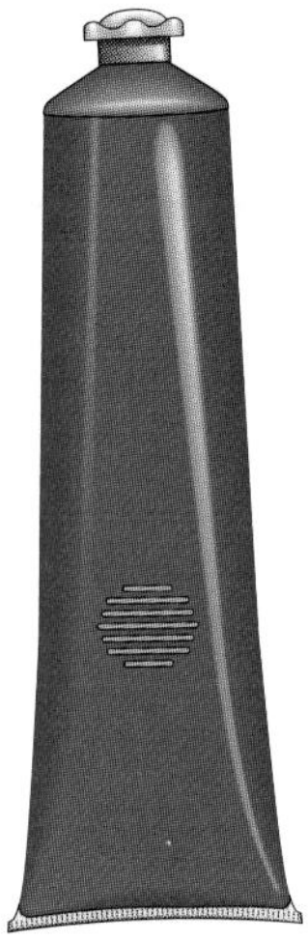

tube
tubo
tube
Tube

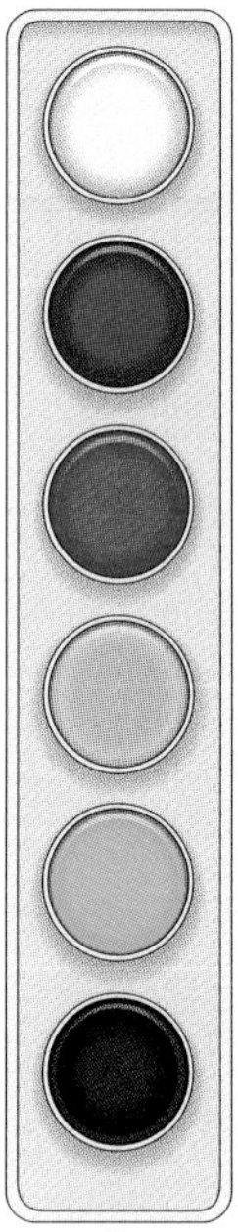

cakes
cajade acuarelas
pastilles
Kissen

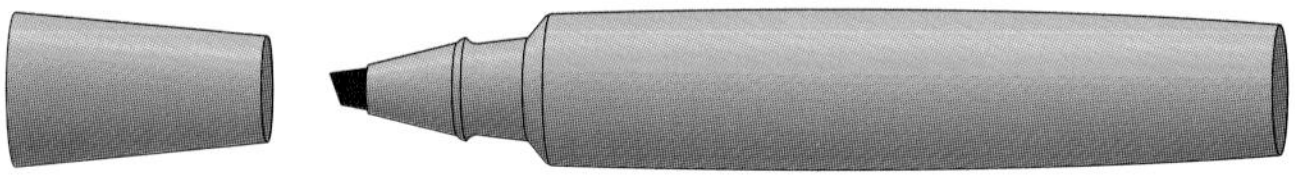

marker pen
rotulador
marqueur
Marker

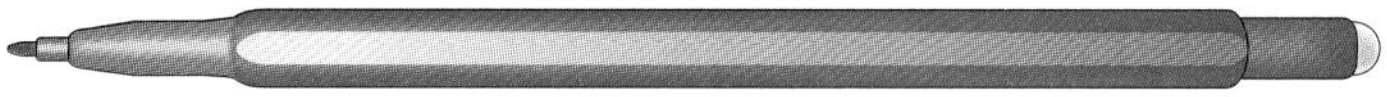

felt tip pen
rotulador
feutre
Filzstift

soft pastel
pastel
pastel sec
Pastell

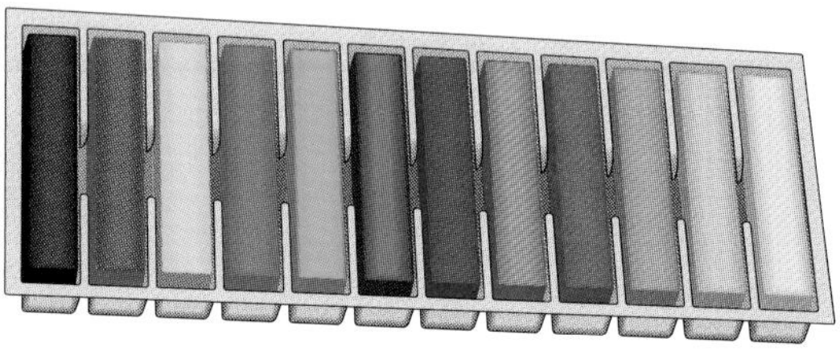

oil pastel
pastel de óleo
pastel gras
Ölpastell

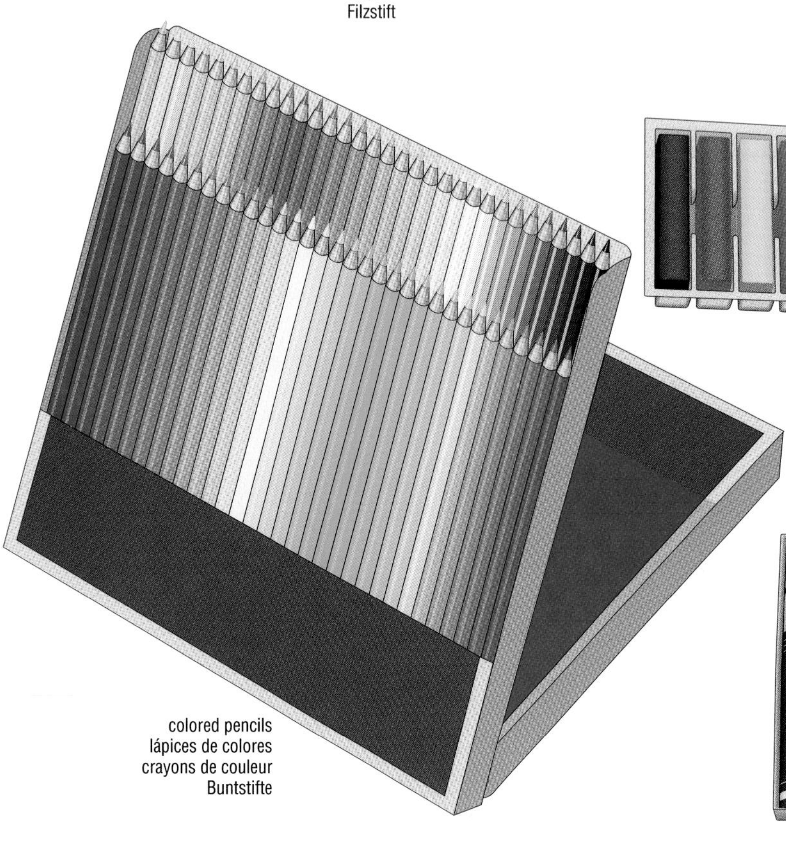

colored pencils
lápices de colores
crayons de couleur
Buntstifte

EQUIPMENT
EQUIPO
MATÉRIEL
AUSSTATTUNG

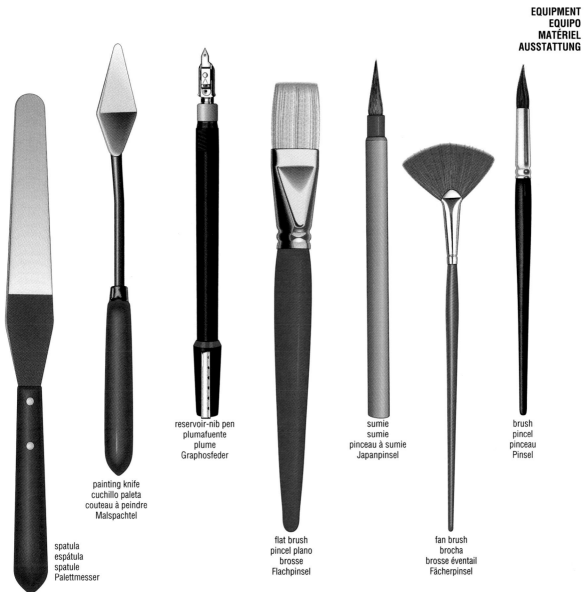

spatula
espátula
spatule
Palettmesser

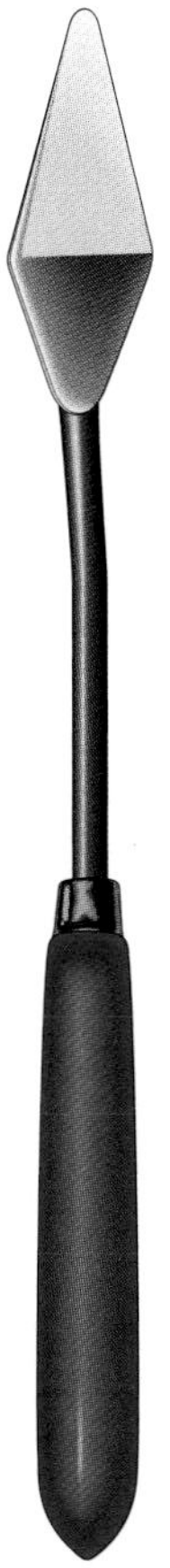

painting knife
cuchillo paleta
couteau à peindre
Malspachtel

reservoir-nib pen
plumafuente
plume
Graphosfeder

flat brush
pincel plano
brosse
Flachpinsel

sumie
sumie
pinceau à sumie
Japanpinsel

fan brush
brocha
brosse éventail
Fächerpinsel

brush
pincel
pinceau
Pinsel

SUPPORTS
LIENZOS
SUPPORTS
BILDTRÄGER

paper
papel
papier
Papier

cardboard
cartón
carton
Malpappe

canvas
lienzo
toile
Leinwand

panel
tabla
panneau
Platte

PAINTING AND DRAWING
PINTURA Y DIBUJO
PEINTURE ET DESSIN
MALEN UND ZEICHNEN

AIRBRUSH
PISTOLA DE PINTAR
AÉROGRAPHE
SPRITZPISTOLE

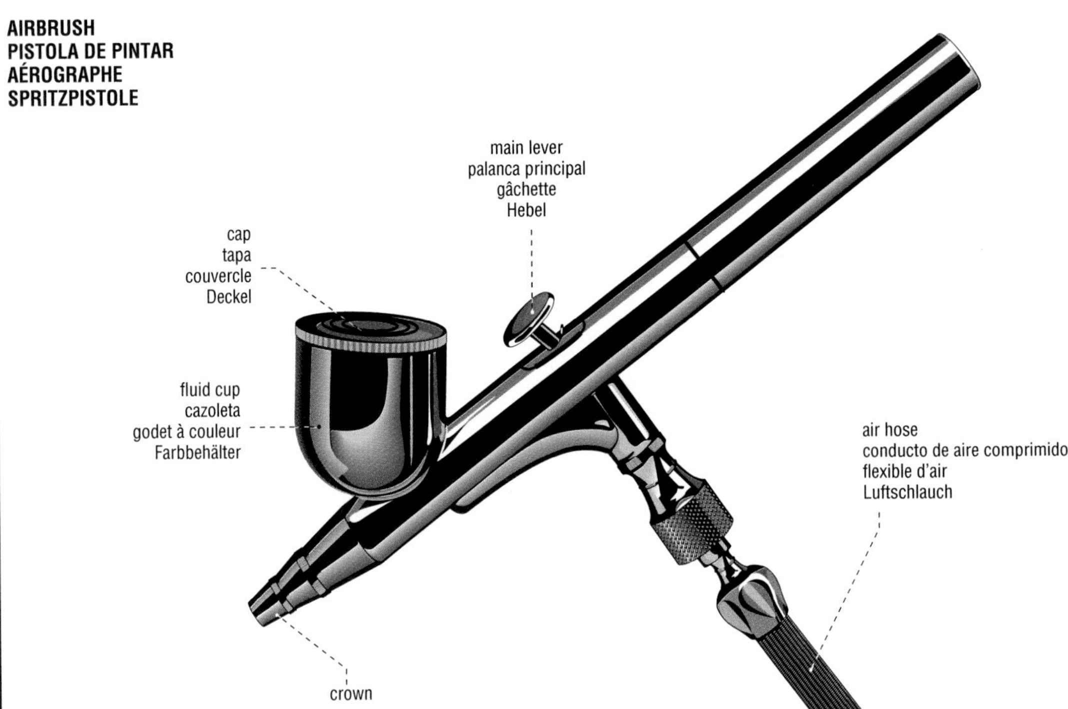
main lever
palanca principal
gâchette
Hebel
cap
tapa
couvercle
Deckel
fluid cup
cazoleta
godet à couleur
Farbbehälter
air hose
conducto de aire comprimido
flexible d'air
Luftschlauch
crown
corona
couronne
Düsenkappe

CROSS SECTION OF AN AIRBRUSH
CORTE TRANSVERSAL DE UNA PISTOLA DE PINTAR
COUPE D'UN AÉROGRAPHE
QUERSCHNITT DURCH EINE SPRITZPISTOLE

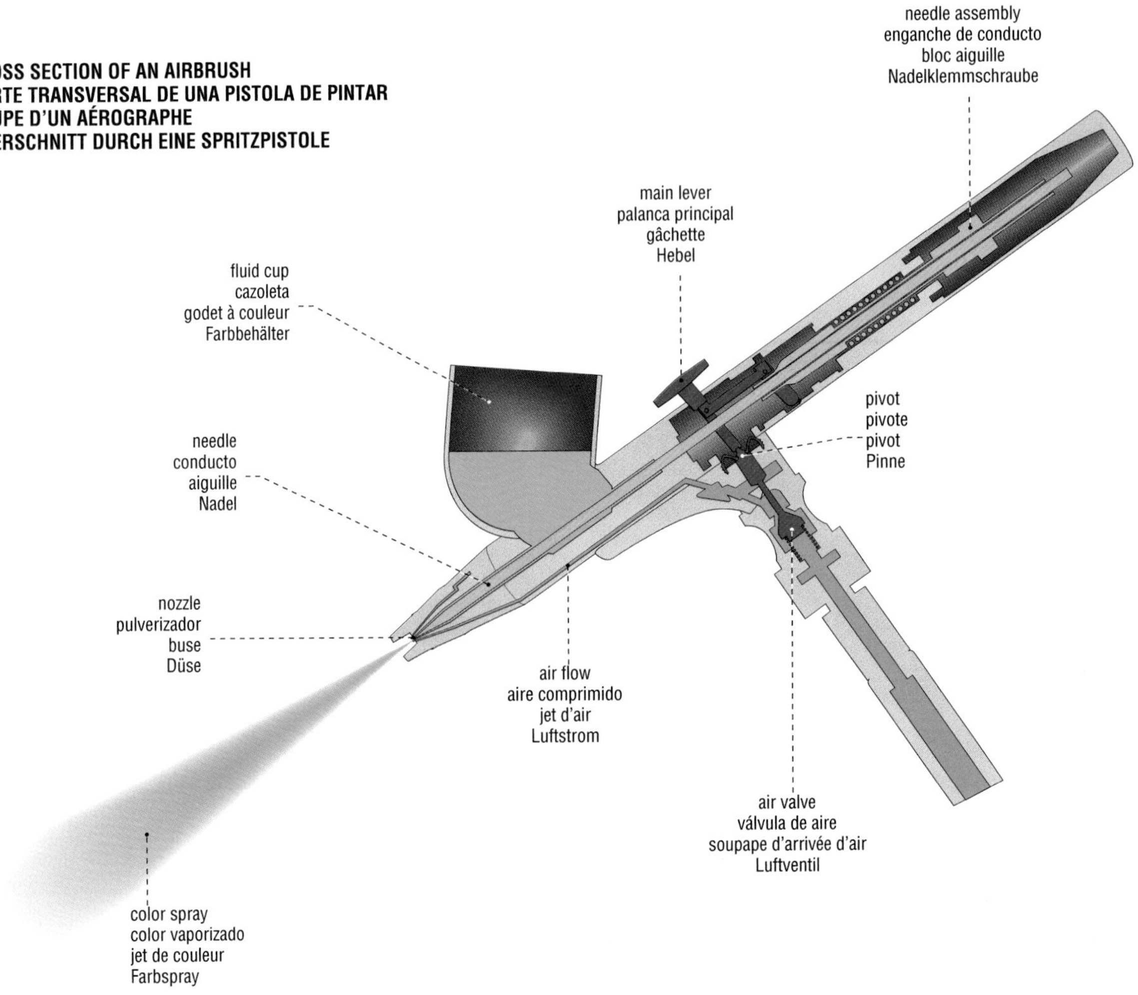

needle assembly
enganche de conducto
bloc aiguille
Nadelklemmschraube

main lever
palanca principal
gâchette
Hebel

fluid cup
cazoleta
godet à couleur
Farbbehälter

pivot
pivote
pivot
Pinne

needle
conducto
aiguille
Nadel

nozzle
pulverizador
buse
Düse

air flow
aire comprimido
jet d'air
Luftstrom

air valve
válvula de aire
soupape d'arrivée d'air
Luftventil

color spray
color vaporizado
jet de couleur
Farbspray

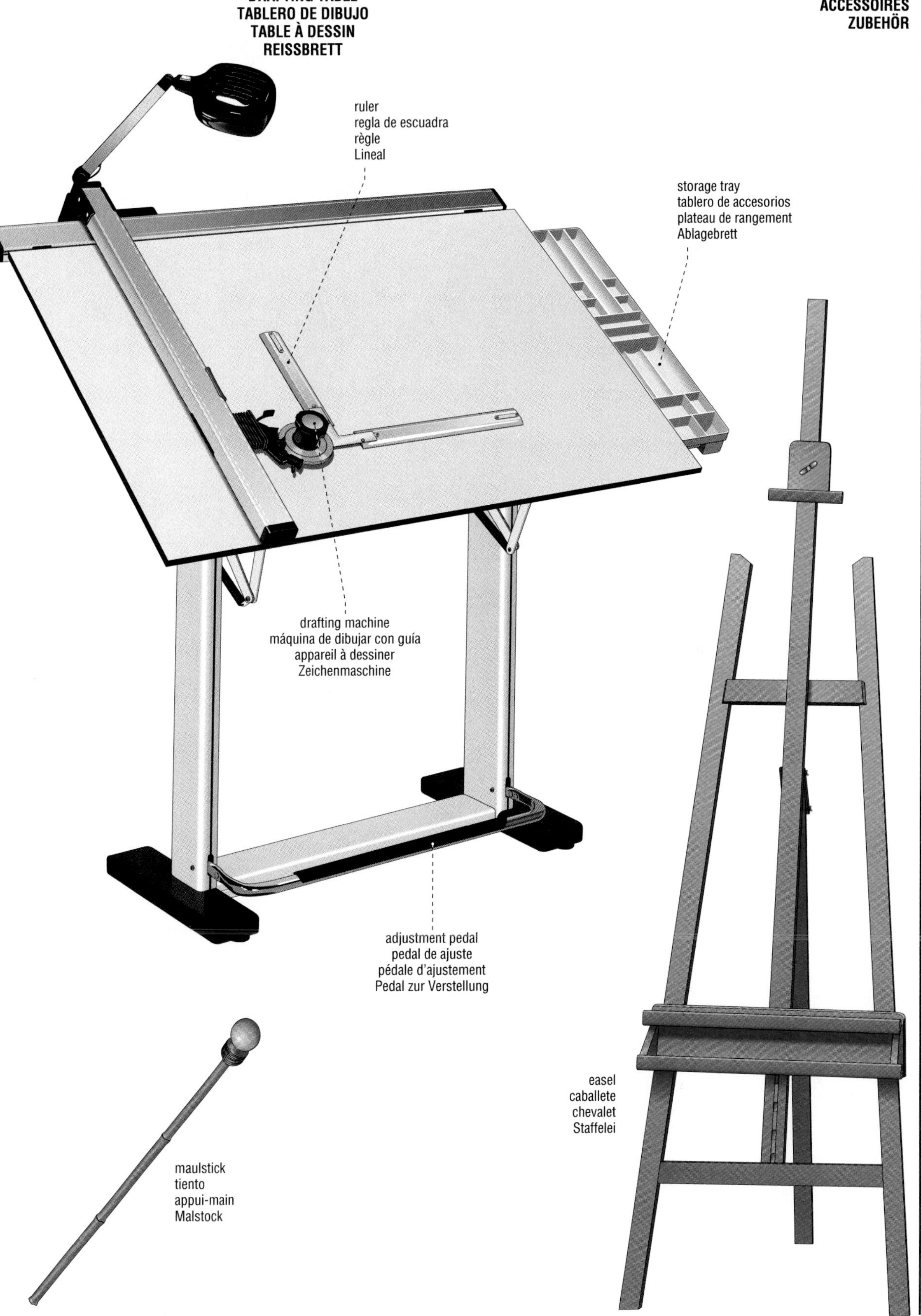
DRAFTING TABLE
TABLERO DE DIBUJO
TABLE À DESSIN
REISSBRETT
ruler
regla de escuadra
règle
Lineal
storage tray
tablero de accesorios
plateau de rangement
Ablagebrett
drafting machine
máquina de dibujar con guía
appareil à dessiner
Zeichenmaschine
adjustment pedal
pedal de ajuste
pédale d'ajustement
Pedal zur Verstellung
easel
caballete
chevalet
Staffelei
maulstick
tiento
appui-main
Malstock

PAINTING AND DRAWING
PINTURA Y DIBUJO
PEINTURE ET DESSIN
MALEN UND ZEICHNEN

ACCESSORIES
ACCESORIOS
ACCESSOIRES
ZUBEHÖR

color chart
gama de colores
nuancier
Farbtafel

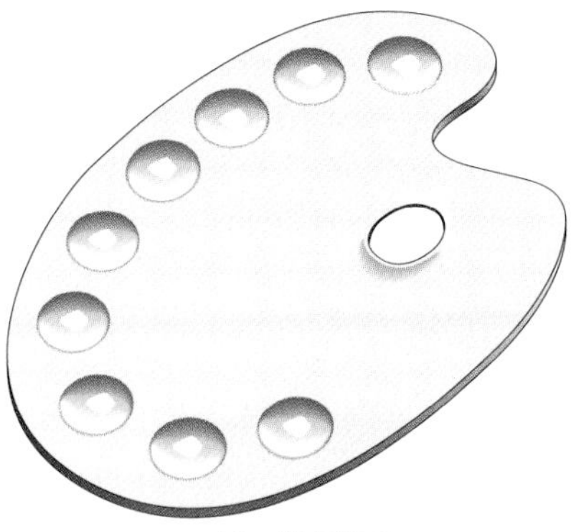
palette with hollows
paleta con huecos para pintura
palette à alvéoles
Palette mit Vertiefungen

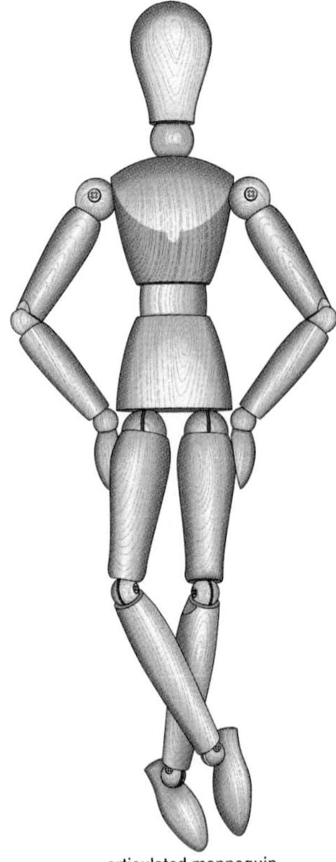
articulated mannequin
maniquí
mannequin articulé
Gliederpuppe

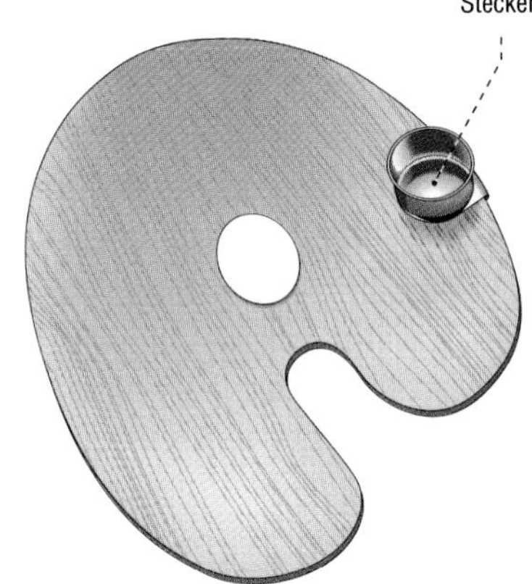
dipper
tarrito para pincel
godet
Stecker
palette with dipper
paleta con tarrito
palette avec godet
Palette mit Stecker

UTILITY LIQUIDS
LÍQUIDOS ACCESORIOS
LIQUIDES D'APPOINT
HILFSMITTEL

varnish
barniz
vernis
Firnis

linseed oil
aceite de linaza
huile de lin
Leinöl

turpentine
aguarrás
térébenthine
Terpentin

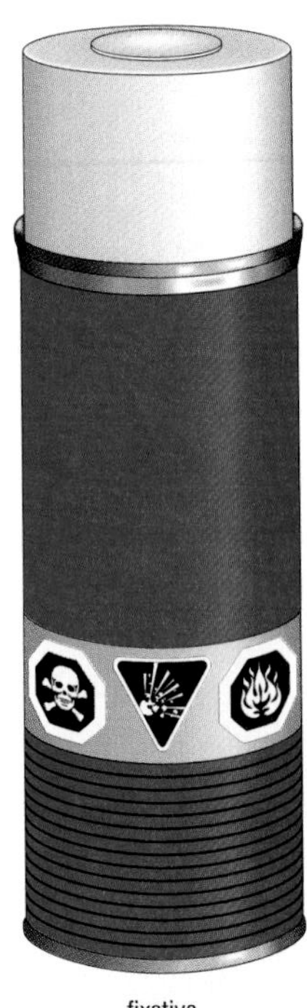
fixative
fijador
fixatif
Fixativ

SPORTS
DEPORTES
SPORTS
SPORTARTEN

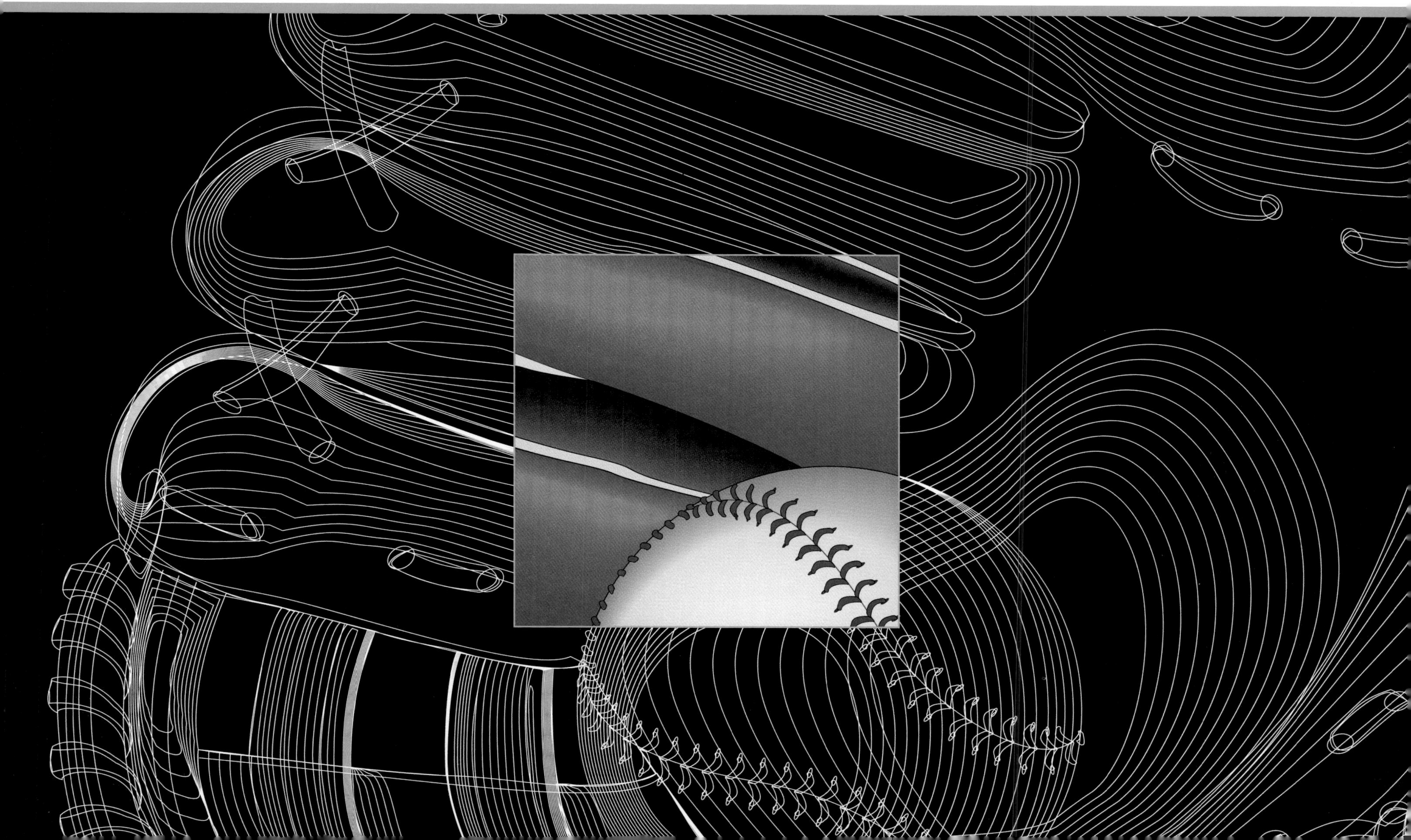

CONTENTS

BASEBALL
BÉISBOL
BASEBALL
BASEBALL

CATCHER
RECEPTOR
RECEVEUR
FÄNGER
frame
armazón de la máscara
grille
Visiergestell
mask
máscara
masque
Maske
throat protector
protector de la garganta
protège-gorge
Halsschutz
catcher's glove
guante del receptor
gant de receveur
Fanghandschuh
shin guard
espinillera
protège-tibia
Schienbeinschützer
toe guard
protector del pie
protège-orteils
Zehenschützer
chest protector
peto
protecteur de poitrine
Brustschutz
knee pad
rodillera
genouillère
Knieschützer
BATTER
BATEADOR
FRAPPEUR
SCHLAGMANN
batter's helmet
casco del bateador
casque de frappeur
Schlagmannshelm
team shirt
camiseta
chandail d'équipe
Mannschaftstrikot
bat
bate
bâton
Schläger
batting glove
guante de bateo
gant de frappeur
Schlaghandschuh
undershirt
camiseta interior
chandail de dessous
Unterhemd
stirrup sock
calcetín con tirante
chaussette-étrier
Stutzen
pants
pantalón
pantalon
Hose
spiked shoe
zapatilla con tacos
chaussure à crampons
Stollenschuh

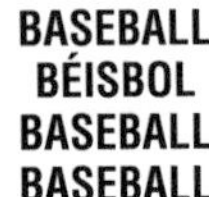

BASEBALL
BÉISBOL
BASEBALL
BASEBALL

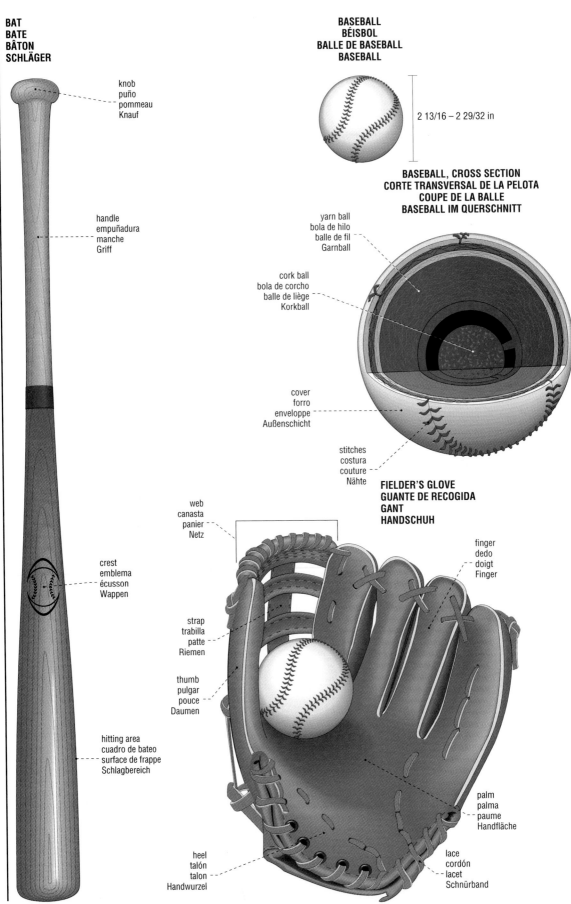

BAT
BATE
BÂTON
SCHLÄGER

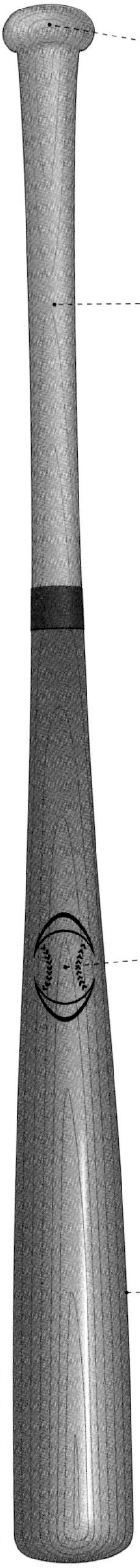

knob
puño
pommeau
Knauf

handle
empuñadura
manche
Griff

crest
emblema
écusson
Wappen

hitting area
cuadro de bateo
surface de frappe
Schlagbereich

BASEBALL
BÉISBOL
BALLE DE BASEBALL
BASEBALL

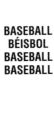

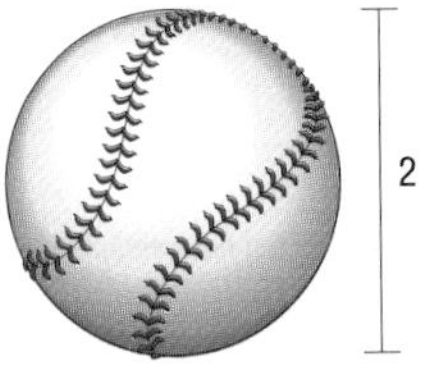

2 13/16 – 2 29/32 in

BASEBALL, CROSS SECTION
CORTE TRANSVERSAL DE LA PELOTA
COUPE DE LA BALLE
BASEBALL IM QUERSCHNITT

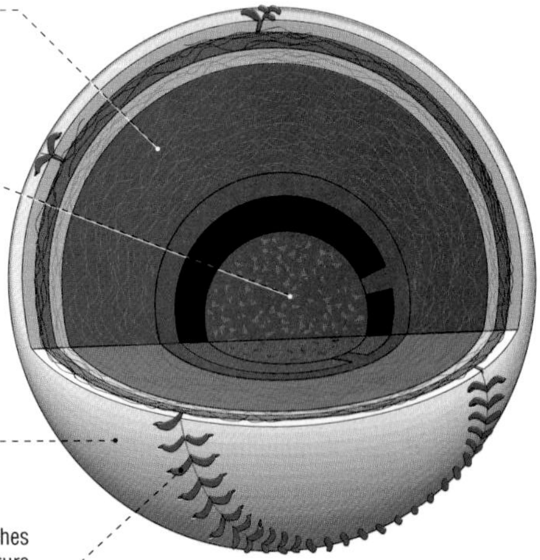

yarn ball
bola de hilo
balle de fil
Garnball

cork ball
bola de corcho
balle de liège
Korkball

cover
forro
enveloppe
Außenschicht

stitches
costura
couture
Nähte

FIELDER'S GLOVE
GUANTE DE RECOGIDA
GANT
HANDSCHUH

web
canasta
panier
Netz

finger
dedo
doigt
Finger

strap
trabilla
patte
Riemen

thumb
pulgar
pouce
Daumen

palm
palma
paume
Handfläche

heel
talón
talon
Handwurzel

lace
cordón
lacet
Schnürband

FIELD
TERRENO
TERRAIN
SPIELFELD

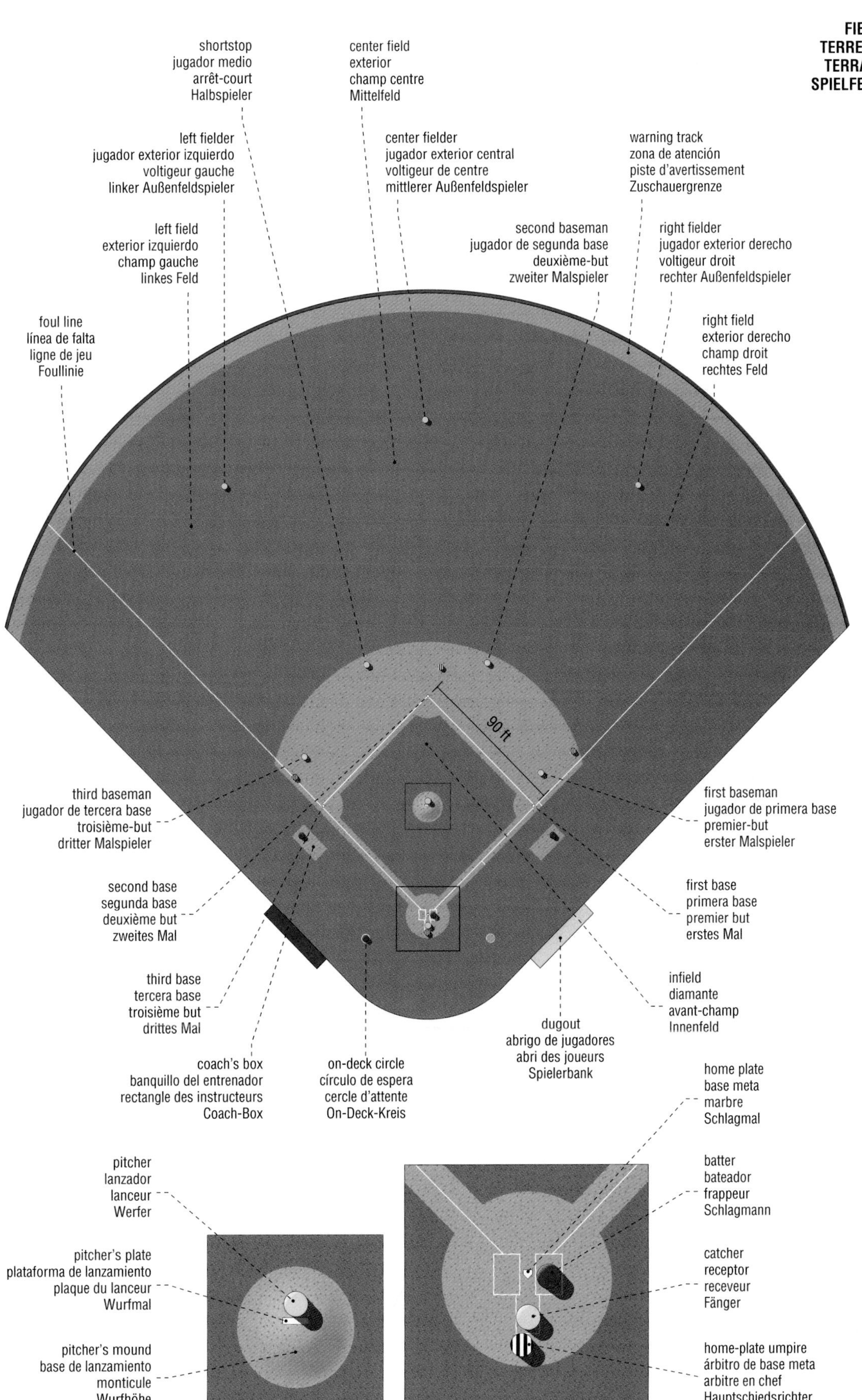
shortstop
jugador medio
arrêt-court
Halbspieler
center field
exterior
champ centre
Mittelfeld
left fielder
jugador exterior izquierdo
voltigeur gauche
linker Außenfeldspieler
center fielder
jugador exterior central
voltigeur de centre
mittlerer Außenfeldspieler
warning track
zona de atención
piste d'avertissement
Zuschauergrenze
left field
exterior izquierdo
champ gauche
linkes Feld
second baseman
jugador de segunda base
deuxième-but
zweiter Malspieler
right fielder
jugador exterior derecho
voltigeur droit
rechter Außenfeldspieler
foul line
línea de falta
ligne de jeu
Foullinie
right field
exterior derecho
champ droit
rechtes Feld
90 ft
third baseman
jugador de tercera base
troisième-but
dritter Malspieler
first baseman
jugador de primera base
premier-but
erster Malspieler
second base
segunda base
deuxième but
zweites Mal
first base
primera base
premier but
erstes Mal
third base
tercera base
troisième but
drittes Mal
infield
diamante
avant-champ
Innenfeld
dugout
abrigo de jugadores
abri des joueurs
Spielerbank
coach's box
banquillo del entrenador
rectangle des instructeurs
Coach-Box
on-deck circle
círculo de espera
cercle d'attente
On-Deck-Kreis
home plate
base meta
marbre
Schlagmal
pitcher
lanzador
lanceur
Werfer
batter
bateador
frappeur
Schlagmann
pitcher's plate
plataforma de lanzamiento
plaque du lanceur
Wurfmal
catcher
receptor
receveur
Fänger
pitcher's mound
base de lanzamiento
monticule
Wurfhöhe
home-plate umpire
árbitro de base meta
arbitre en chef
Hauptschiedsrichter

CRICKET
CRICKET
CRICKET
CRICKET

CRICKET PLAYER
JUGADOR DE CRICKET
JOUEUR DE CRICKET
CRICKETSPIELER

bat
pala
batte
Schlagholz

glove
guante
gant
Handschuh

stump
rastrillo con los travesaños
piquet
Stab

pad
protector
jambière
Polster

cricket shoe
zapatilla
chaussure
Cricketschuh

studs
tacos
crampons
Stollen

BAT
PALA
BATTE
SCHLAGHOLZ

handle
mango
manche
Griff

ball
pelota
balle
Ball

willow
pala
plat
Weidenholz

groove
ranura guía
rainure
Rille

CRICKET BALL
PELOTA DE CRICKET
BALLE DE CRICKET
CRICKETBALL

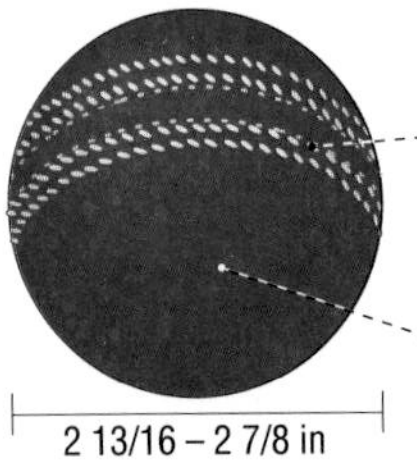

seam
costura
couture
Saum

leather skin
forro de cuero
enveloppe
Lederhaut

2 13/16 – 2 7/8 in

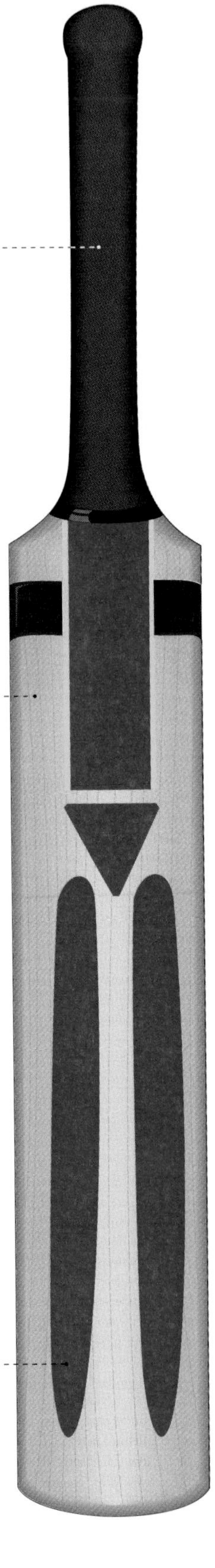

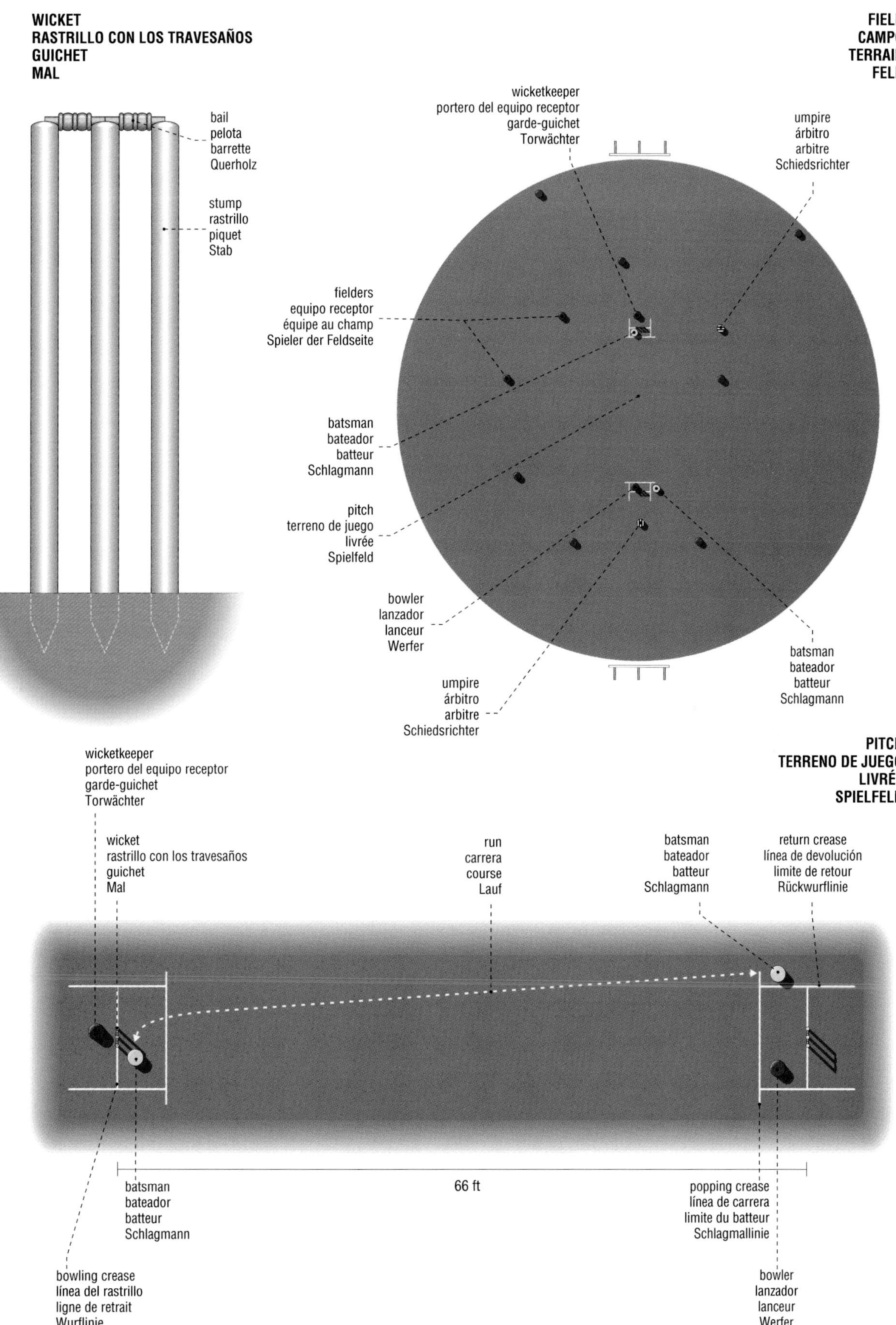
WICKET
RASTRILLO CON LOS TRAVESAÑOS
GUICHET
MAL
bail
pelota
barrette
Querholz
stump
rastrillo
piquet
Stab
FIELD
CAMPO
TERRAIN
FELD
wicketkeeper
portero del equipo receptor
garde-guichet
Torwächter
umpire
árbitro
arbitre
Schiedsrichter
fielders
equipo receptor
équipe au champ
Spieler der Feldseite
batsman
bateador
batteur
Schlagmann
pitch
terreno de juego
livrée
Spielfeld
bowler
lanzador
lanceur
Werfer
umpire
árbitro
arbitre
Schiedsrichter
batsman
bateador
batteur
Schlagmann
PITCH
TERRENO DE JUEGO
LIVRÉE
SPIELFELD
wicketkeeper
portero del equipo receptor
garde-guichet
Torwächter
wicket
rastrillo con los travesaños
guichet
Mal
run
carrera
course
Lauf
batsman
bateador
batteur
Schlagmann
return crease
línea de devolución
limite de retour
Rückwurflinie
66 ft
batsman
bateador
batteur
Schlagmann
popping crease
línea de carrera
limite du batteur
Schlagmallinie
bowling crease
línea del rastrillo
ligne de retrait
Wurflinie
bowler
lanzador
lanceur
Werfer

SOCCER
FÚTBOL
FOOTBALL
FUSSBALL

SOCCER PLAYER
FUTBOLISTA
FOOTBALLEUR
FUSSBALLSPIELER

SOCCER BALL
BALÓN
BALLON DE FOOTBALL
FUSSBALL

8 1/2 in
team shirt
camiseta de equipo
chandail d'équipe
Trikot
shorts
pantalones
short
Hose
shin guard
espinillera
protège-tibia
Schienbeinschützer
soccer shoe
bota
chaussure de football
Fußballschuh
interchangeable studs
tacos de rosca
crampons interchangeables
Schraubstollen

PLAYING FIELD
CAMPO
TERRAIN
SPIELFELD

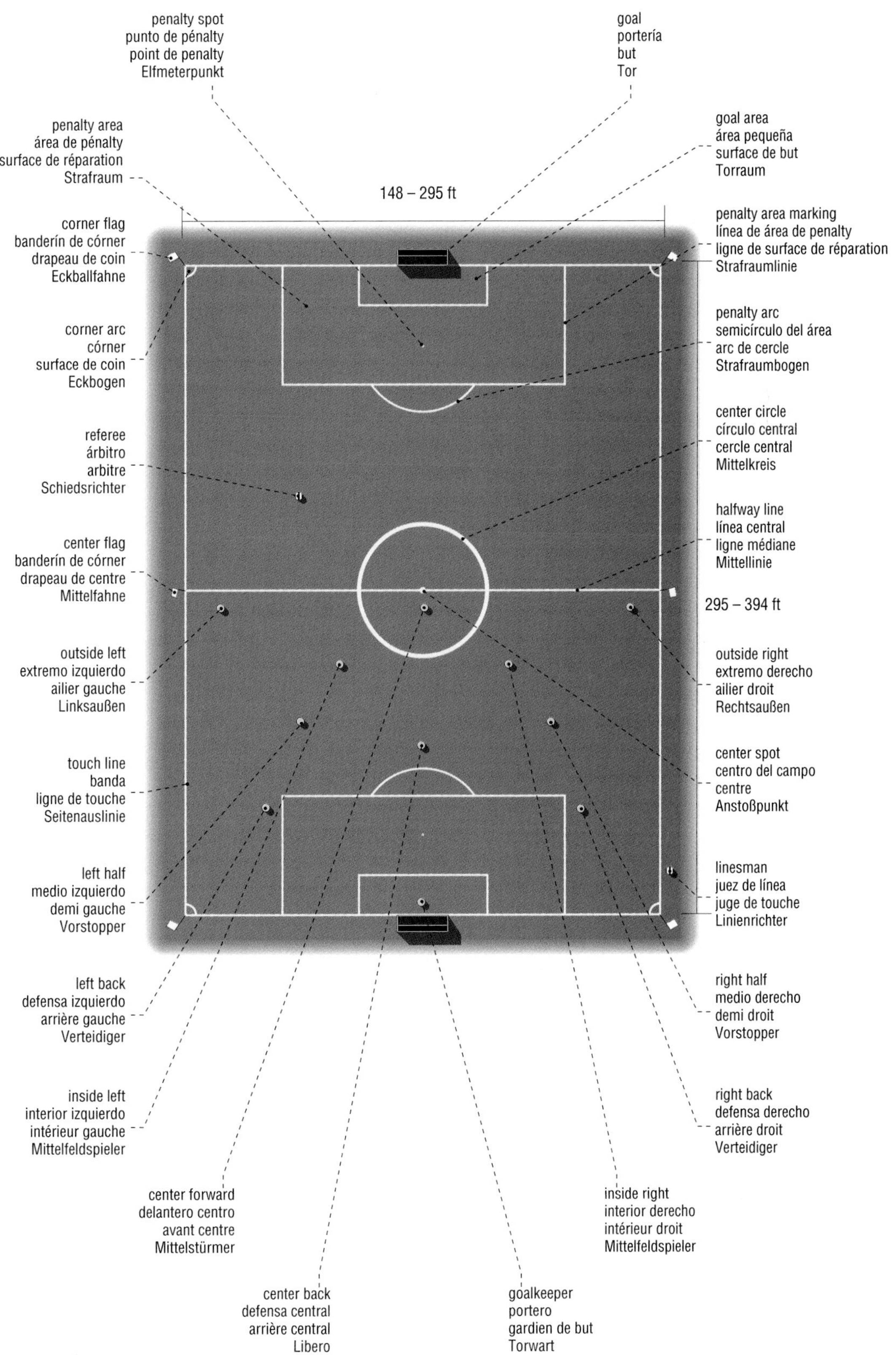
penalty spot
punto de pénalty
point de penalty
Elfmeterpunkt
goal
portería
but
Tor
penalty area
área de pénalty
surface de réparation
Strafraum
goal area
área pequeña
surface de but
Torraum
148 – 295 ft
corner flag
banderín de córner
drapeau de coin
Eckballfahne
penalty area marking
línea de área de penalty
ligne de surface de réparation
Strafraumlinie
corner arc
córner
surface de coin
Eckbogen
penalty arc
semicírculo del área
arc de cercle
Strafraumbogen
referee
árbitro
arbitre
Schiedsrichter
center circle
círculo central
cercle central
Mittelkreis
center flag
banderín de córner
drapeau de centre
Mittelfahne
halfway line
línea central
ligne médiane
Mittellinie
295 – 394 ft
outside left
extremo izquierdo
ailier gauche
Linksaußen
outside right
extremo derecho
ailier droit
Rechtsaußen
touch line
banda
ligne de touche
Seitenauslinie
center spot
centro del campo
centre
Anstoßpunkt
left half
medio izquierdo
demi gauche
Vorstopper
linesman
juez de línea
juge de touche
Linienrichter
left back
defensa izquierdo
arrière gauche
Verteidiger
right half
medio derecho
demi droit
Vorstopper
inside left
interior izquierdo
intérieur gauche
Mittelfeldspieler
right back
defensa derecho
arrière droit
Verteidiger
center forward
delantero centro
avant centre
Mittelstürmer
inside right
interior derecho
intérieur droit
Mittelfeldspieler
center back
defensa central
arrière central
Libero
goalkeeper
portero
gardien de but
Torwart

FOOTBALL
FÚTBOL AMERICANO
FOOTBALL AMÉRICAIN
FOOTBALL

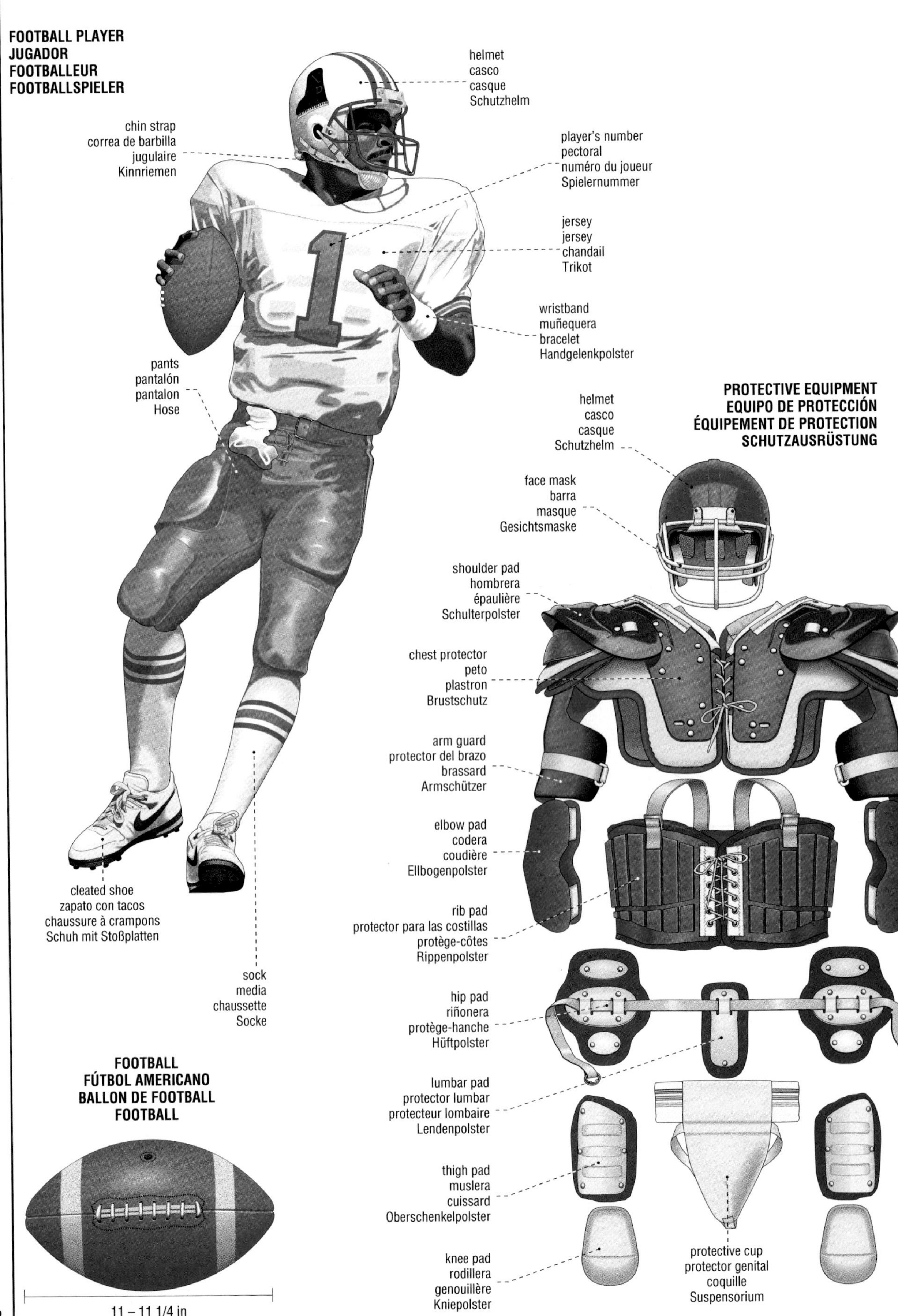

FOOTBALL PLAYER
JUGADOR
FOOTBALLEUR
FOOTBALLSPIELER
helmet
casco
casque
Schutzhelm
chin strap
correa de barbilla
jugulaire
Kinnriemen
player's number
pectoral
numéro du joueur
Spielernummer
jersey
jersey
chandail
Trikot
wristband
muñequera
bracelet
Handgelenkpolster
pants
pantalón
pantalon
Hose
cleated shoe
zapato con tacos
chaussure à crampons
Schuh mit Stoßplatten
sock
media
chaussette
Socke
PROTECTIVE EQUIPMENT
EQUIPO DE PROTECCIÓN
ÉQUIPEMENT DE PROTECTION
SCHUTZAUSRÜSTUNG
helmet
casco
casque
Schutzhelm
face mask
barra
masque
Gesichtsmaske
shoulder pad
hombrera
épaulière
Schulterpolster
chest protector
peto
plastron
Brustschutz
arm guard
protector del brazo
brassard
Armschützer
elbow pad
codera
coudière
Ellbogenpolster
rib pad
protector para las costillas
protège-côtes
Rippenpolster
hip pad
riñonera
protège-hanche
Hüftpolster
lumbar pad
protector lumbar
protecteur lombaire
Lendenpolster
thigh pad
muslera
cuissard
Oberschenkelpolster
knee pad
rodillera
genouillère
Kniepolster
protective cup
protector genital
coquille
Suspensorium
FOOTBALL
FÚTBOL AMERICANO
BALLON DE FOOTBALL
FOOTBALL
11 – 11 1/4 in

SCRIMMAGE
MELÉ
MÊLÉE
SCRIMMAGE

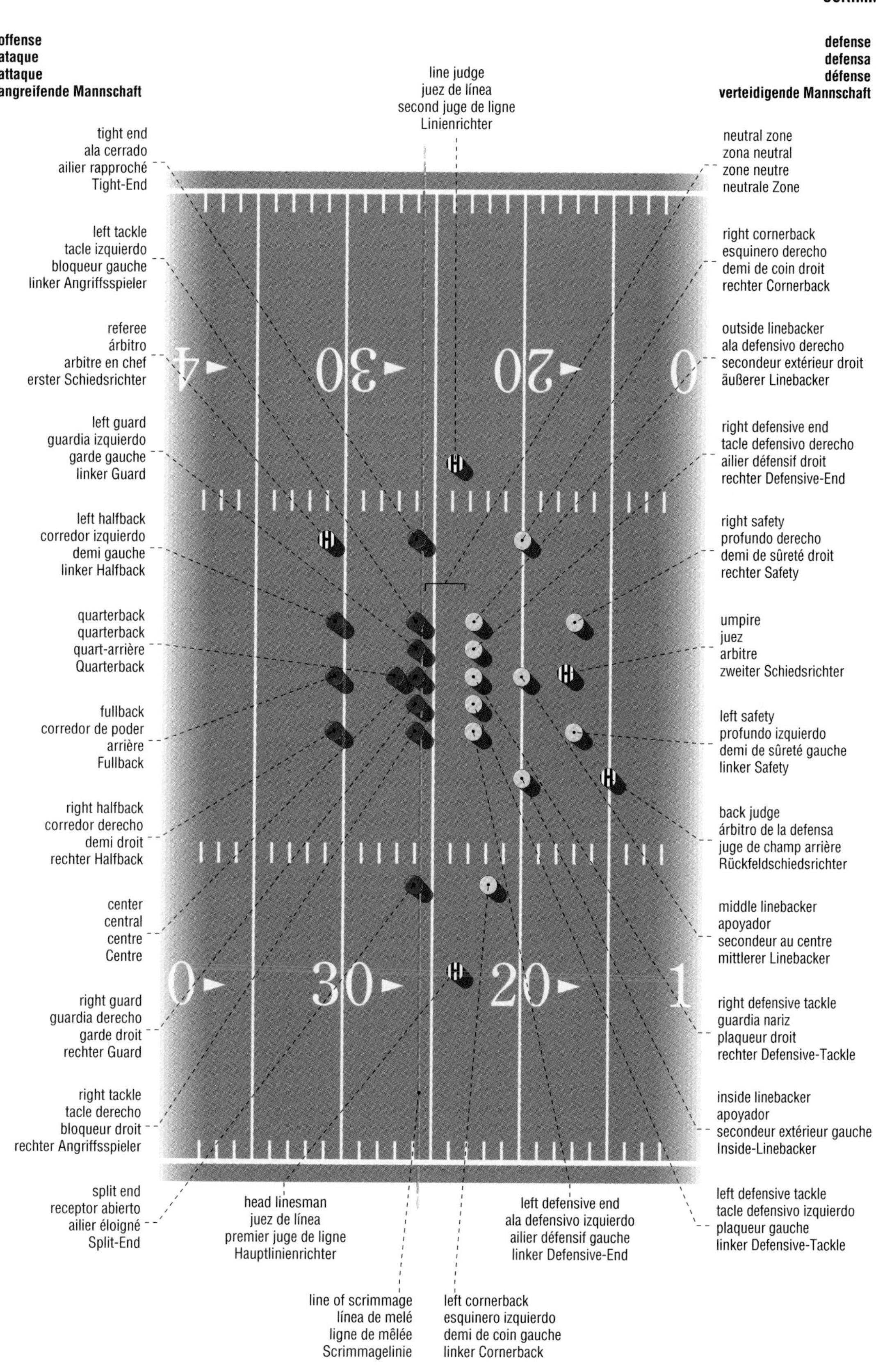

offense
ataque
attaque
angreifende Mannschaft
defense
defensa
défense
verteidigende Mannschaft
line judge
juez de línea
second juge de ligne
Linienrichter
tight end
ala cerrado
ailier rapproché
Tight-End
neutral zone
zona neutral
zone neutre
neutrale Zone
left tackle
tacle izquierdo
bloqueur gauche
linker Angriffsspieler
right cornerback
esquinero derecho
demi de coin droit
rechter Cornerback
referee
árbitro
arbitre en chef
erster Schiedsrichter
outside linebacker
ala defensivo derecho
secondeur extérieur droit
äußerer Linebacker
left guard
guardia izquierdo
garde gauche
linker Guard
right defensive end
tacle defensivo derecho
ailier défensif droit
rechter Defensive-End
left halfback
corredor izquierdo
demi gauche
linker Halfback
right safety
profundo derecho
demi de sûreté droit
rechter Safety
quarterback
quarterback
quart-arrière
Quarterback
umpire
juez
arbitre
zweiter Schiedsrichter
fullback
corredor de poder
arrière
Fullback
left safety
profundo izquierdo
demi de sûreté gauche
linker Safety
right halfback
corredor derecho
demi droit
rechter Halfback
back judge
árbitro de la defensa
juge de champ arrière
Rückfeldschiedsrichter
center
central
centre
Centre
middle linebacker
apoyador
secondeur au centre
mittlerer Linebacker
right guard
guardia derecho
garde droit
rechter Guard
right defensive tackle
guardia nariz
plaqueur droit
rechter Defensive-Tackle
right tackle
tacle derecho
bloqueur droit
rechter Angriffsspieler
inside linebacker
apoyador
secondeur extérieur gauche
Inside-Linebacker
split end
receptor abierto
ailier éloigné
Split-End
head linesman
juez de línea
premier juge de ligne
Hauptlinienrichter
left defensive end
ala defensivo izquierdo
ailier défensif gauche
linker Defensive-End
left defensive tackle
tacle defensivo izquierdo
plaqueur gauche
linker Defensive-Tackle
line of scrimmage
línea de melé
ligne de mêlée
Scrimmagelinie
left cornerback
esquinero izquierdo
demi de coin gauche
linker Cornerback

FOOTBALL
FÚTBOL AMERICANO
FOOTBALL
FOOTBALL

PLAYING FIELD FOR AMERICAN FOOTBALL
CAMPO DE JUEGO PARA FÚTBOL AMERICANO
TERRAIN DE FOOTBALL AMÉRICAIN
SPIELFELD FÜR AMERIKANISCHES FOOTBALL

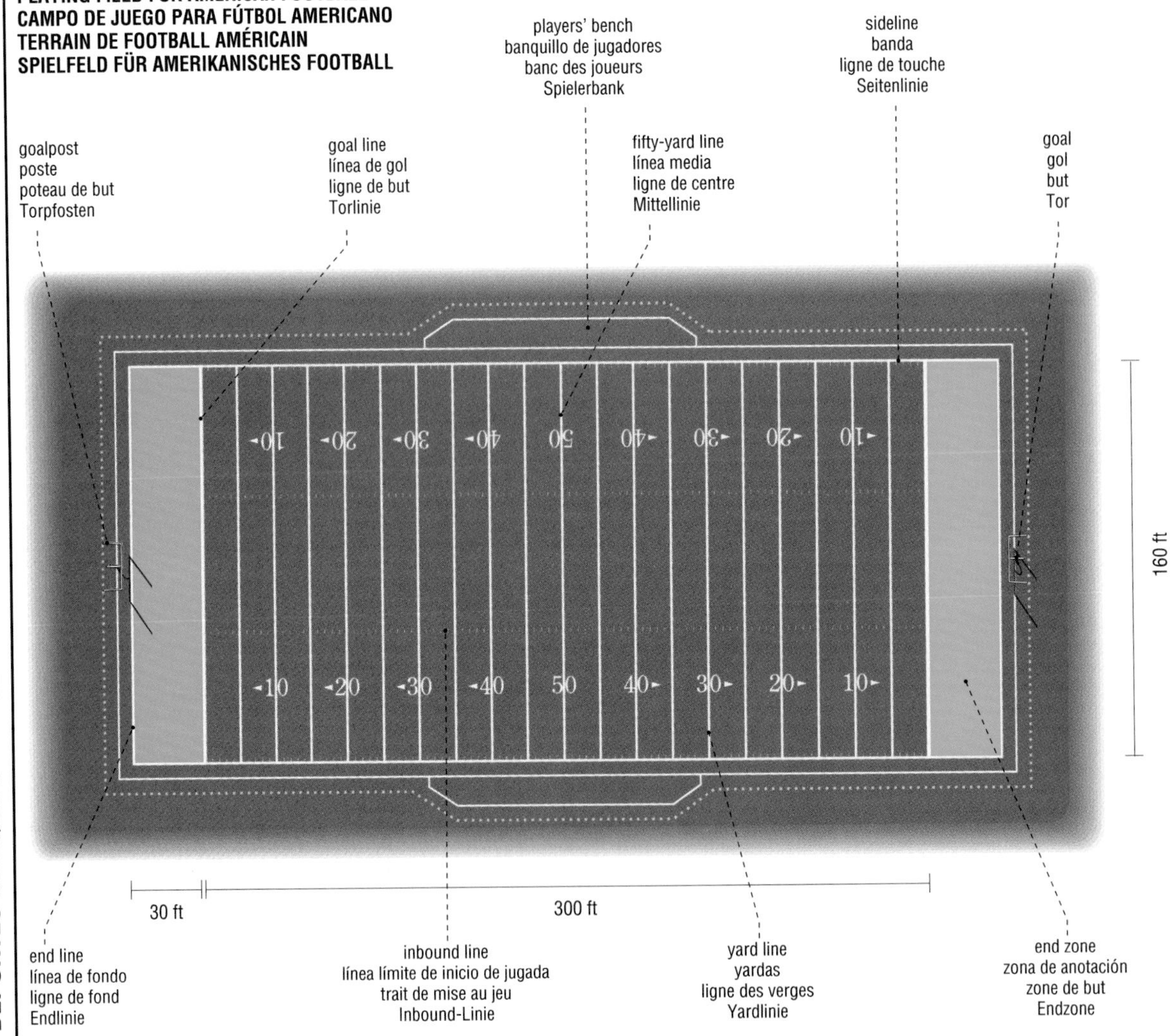

players' bench
banquillo de jugadores
banc des joueurs
Spielerbank

sideline
banda
ligne de touche
Seitenlinie

goalpost
poste
poteau de but
Torpfosten

goal line
línea de gol
ligne de but
Torlinie

fifty-yard line
línea media
ligne de centre
Mittellinie

goal
gol
but
Tor

160 ft

30 ft

300 ft

end line
línea de fondo
ligne de fond
Endlinie

inbound line
línea límite de inicio de jugada
trait de mise au jeu
Inbound-Linie

yard line
yardas
ligne des verges
Yardlinie

end zone
zona de anotación
zone de but
Endzone

PLAYING FIELD FOR CANADIAN FOOTBALL
CAMPO DE JUEGO PARA FÚTBOL CANADIENSE
TERRAIN DE FOOTBALL CANADIEN
SPIELFELD FÜR KANADISCHES FOOTBALL

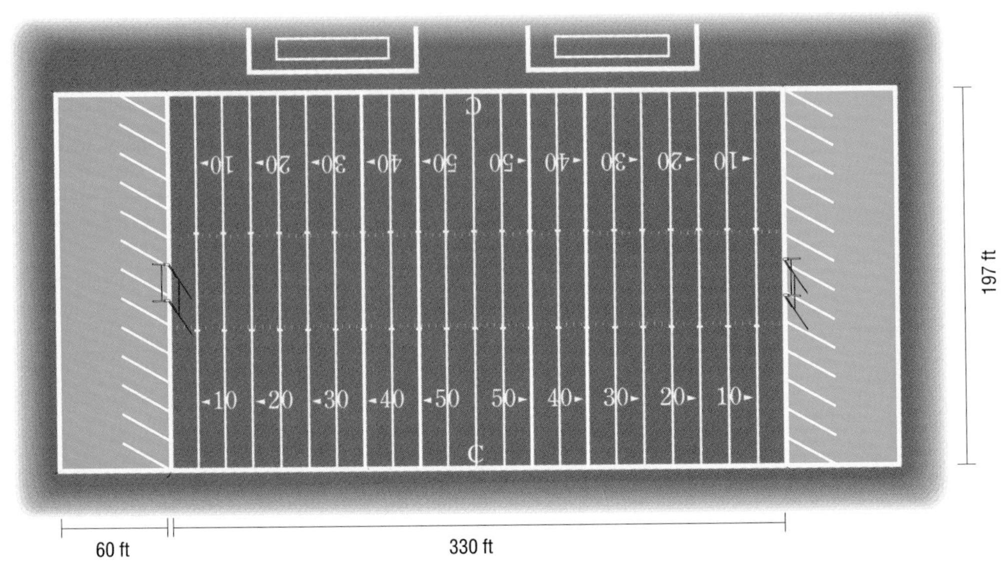
197 ft
60 ft
330 ft

SCRIMMAGE IN CANADIAN FOOTBALL
MELÉ EN EL FÚTBOL CANADIENSE
MÊLÉE AU FOOTBALL CANADIEN
SCRIMMAGE IM KANADISCHEN FOOTBALL

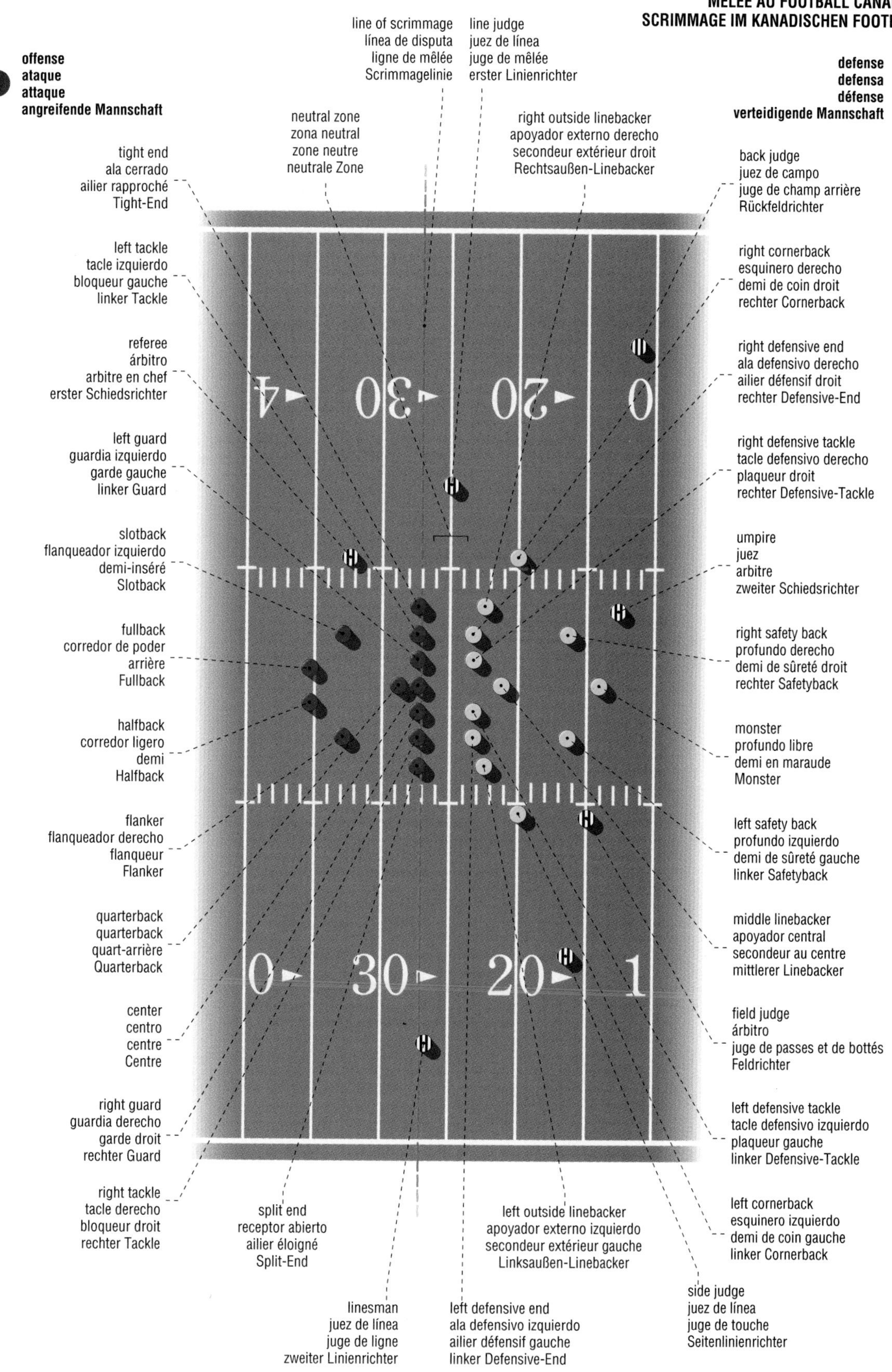

offense
ataque
attaque
angreifende Mannschaft
defense
defensa
défense
verteidigende Mannschaft
line of scrimmage
línea de disputa
ligne de mêlée
Scrimmagelinie
line judge
juez de línea
juge de mêlée
erster Linienrichter
neutral zone
zona neutral
zone neutre
neutrale Zone
right outside linebacker
apoyador externo derecho
secondeur extérieur droit
Rechtsaußen-Linebacker
tight end
ala cerrado
ailier rapproché
Tight-End
back judge
juez de campo
juge de champ arrière
Rückfeldrichter
left tackle
tacle izquierdo
bloqueur gauche
linker Tackle
right cornerback
esquinero derecho
demi de coin droit
rechter Cornerback
referee
árbitro
arbitre en chef
erster Schiedsrichter
right defensive end
ala defensivo derecho
ailier défensif droit
rechter Defensive-End
left guard
guardia izquierdo
garde gauche
linker Guard
right defensive tackle
tacle defensivo derecho
plaqueur droit
rechter Defensive-Tackle
slotback
flanqueador izquierdo
demi-inséré
Slotback
umpire
juez
arbitre
zweiter Schiedsrichter
fullback
corredor de poder
arrière
Fullback
right safety back
profundo derecho
demi de sûreté droit
rechter Safetyback
halfback
corredor ligero
demi
Halfback
monster
profundo libre
demi en maraude
Monster
flanker
flanqueador derecho
flanqueur
Flanker
left safety back
profundo izquierdo
demi de sûreté gauche
linker Safetyback
quarterback
quarterback
quart-arrière
Quarterback
middle linebacker
apoyador central
secondeur au centre
mittlerer Linebacker
center
centro
centre
Centre
field judge
árbitro
juge de passes et de bottés
Feldrichter
right guard
guardia derecho
garde droit
rechter Guard
left defensive tackle
tacle defensivo izquierdo
plaqueur gauche
linker Defensive-Tackle
right tackle
tacle derecho
bloqueur droit
rechter Tackle
split end
receptor abierto
ailier éloigné
Split-End
left outside linebacker
apoyador externo izquierdo
secondeur extérieur gauche
Linksaußen-Linebacker
left cornerback
esquinero izquierdo
demi de coin gauche
linker Cornerback
linesman
juez de línea
juge de ligne
zweiter Linienrichter
left defensive end
ala defensivo izquierdo
ailier défensif gauche
linker Defensive-End
side judge
juez de línea
juge de touche
Seitenlinienrichter

RUGBY
RUGBY
RUGBY
RUGBY

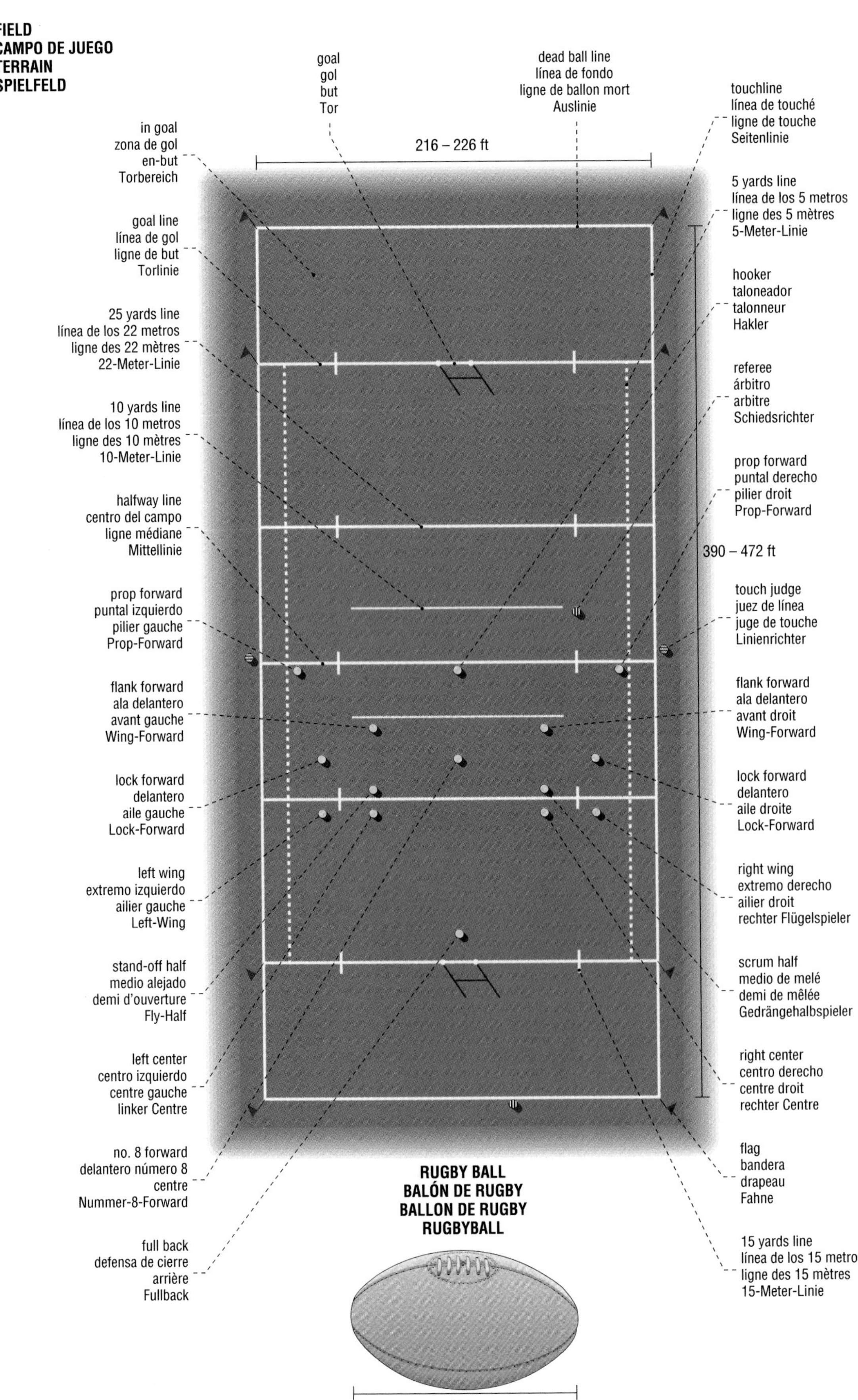
FIELD
CAMPO DE JUEGO
TERRAIN
SPIELFELD
goal
gol
but
Tor
dead ball line
línea de fondo
ligne de ballon mort
Auslinie
touchline
línea de touché
ligne de touche
Seitenlinie
216 – 226 ft
in goal
zona de gol
en-but
Torbereich
5 yards line
línea de los 5 metros
ligne des 5 mètres
5-Meter-Linie
goal line
línea de gol
ligne de but
Torlinie
hooker
taloneador
talonneur
Hakler
25 yards line
línea de los 22 metros
ligne des 22 mètres
22-Meter-Linie
referee
árbitro
arbitre
Schiedsrichter
10 yards line
línea de los 10 metros
ligne des 10 mètres
10-Meter-Linie
prop forward
puntal derecho
pilier droit
Prop-Forward
halfway line
centro del campo
ligne médiane
Mittellinie
390 – 472 ft
prop forward
puntal izquierdo
pilier gauche
Prop-Forward
touch judge
juez de línea
juge de touche
Linienrichter
flank forward
ala delantero
avant gauche
Wing-Forward
flank forward
ala delantero
avant droit
Wing-Forward
lock forward
delantero
aile gauche
Lock-Forward
lock forward
delantero
aile droite
Lock-Forward
left wing
extremo izquierdo
ailier gauche
Left-Wing
right wing
extremo derecho
ailier droit
rechter Flügelspieler
stand-off half
medio alejado
demi d'ouverture
Fly-Half
scrum half
medio de melé
demi de mêlée
Gedrängehalbspieler
left center
centro izquierdo
centre gauche
linker Centre
right center
centro derecho
centre droit
rechter Centre
no. 8 forward
delantero número 8
centre
Nummer-8-Forward
flag
bandera
drapeau
Fahne
RUGBY BALL
BALÓN DE RUGBY
BALLON DE RUGBY
RUGBYBALL
full back
defensa de cierre
arrière
Fullback
15 yards line
línea de los 15 metros
ligne des 15 mètres
15-Meter-Linie
11 in

FIELD HOCKEY
HOCKEY SOBRE HIERBA
HOCKEY SUR GAZON
HOCKEY

PLAYING FIELD
CAMPO DE JUEGO
TERRAIN
SPIELFELD

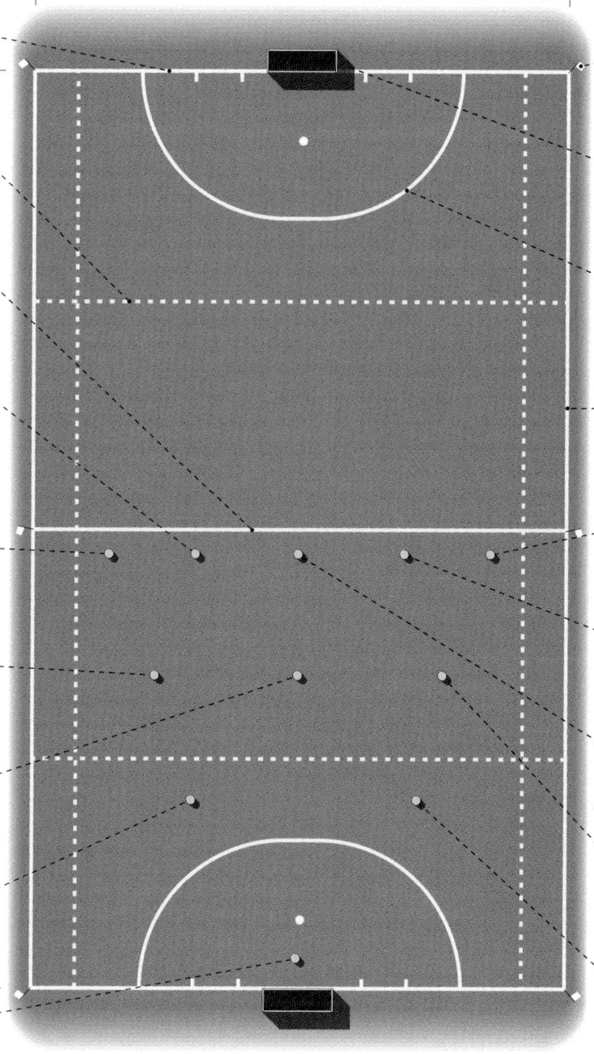

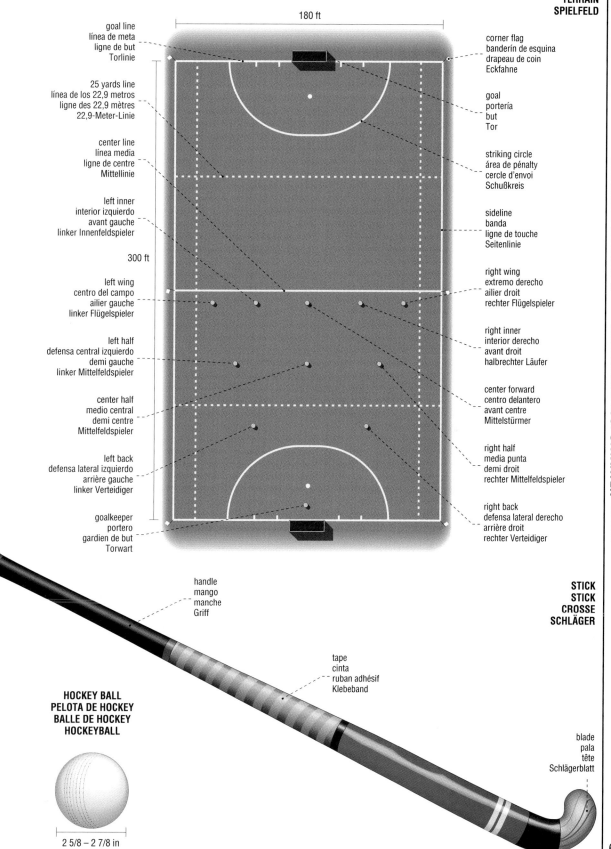

180 ft

300 ft

goal line
línea de meta
ligne de but
Torlinie

25 yards line
línea de los 22,9 metros
ligne des 22,9 mètres
22,9-Meter-Linie

center line
línea media
ligne de centre
Mittellinie

left inner
interior izquierdo
avant gauche
linker Innenfeldspieler

left wing
centro del campo
ailier gauche
linker Flügelspieler

left half
defensa central izquierdo
demi gauche
linker Mittelfeldspieler

center half
medio central
demi centre
Mittelfeldspieler

left back
defensa lateral izquierdo
arrière gauche
linker Verteidiger

goalkeeper
portero
gardien de but
Torwart

corner flag
banderín de esquina
drapeau de coin
Eckfahne

goal
portería
but
Tor

striking circle
área de pénalty
cercle d'envoi
Schußkreis

sideline
banda
ligne de touche
Seitenlinie

right wing
extremo derecho
ailier droit
rechter Flügelspieler

right inner
interior derecho
avant droit
halbrechter Läufer

center forward
centro delantero
avant centre
Mittelstürmer

right half
media punta
demi droit
rechter Mittelfeldspieler

right back
defensa lateral derecho
arrière droit
rechter Verteidiger

STICK
STICK
CROSSE
SCHLÄGER

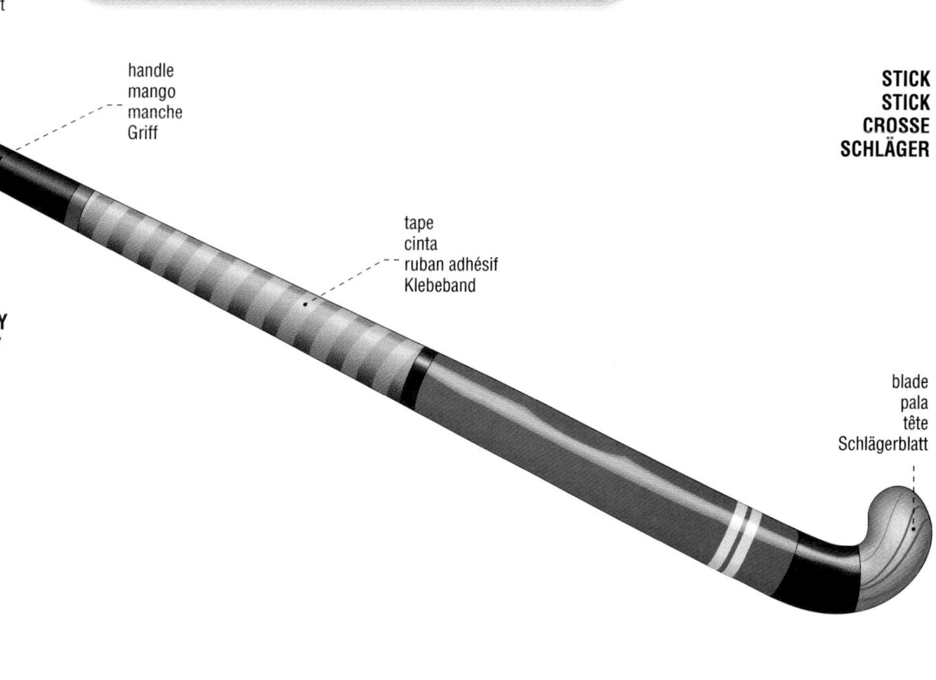

handle
mango
manche
Griff

tape
cinta
ruban adhésif
Klebeband

blade
pala
tête
Schlägerblatt

HOCKEY BALL
PELOTA DE HOCKEY
BALLE DE HOCKEY
HOCKEYBALL

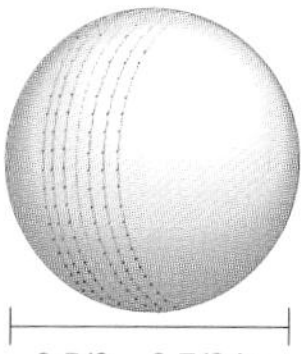

2 5/8 – 2 7/8 in

ICE HOCKEY
HOCKEY SOBRE HIELO
HOCKEY SUR GLACE
EISHOCKEY

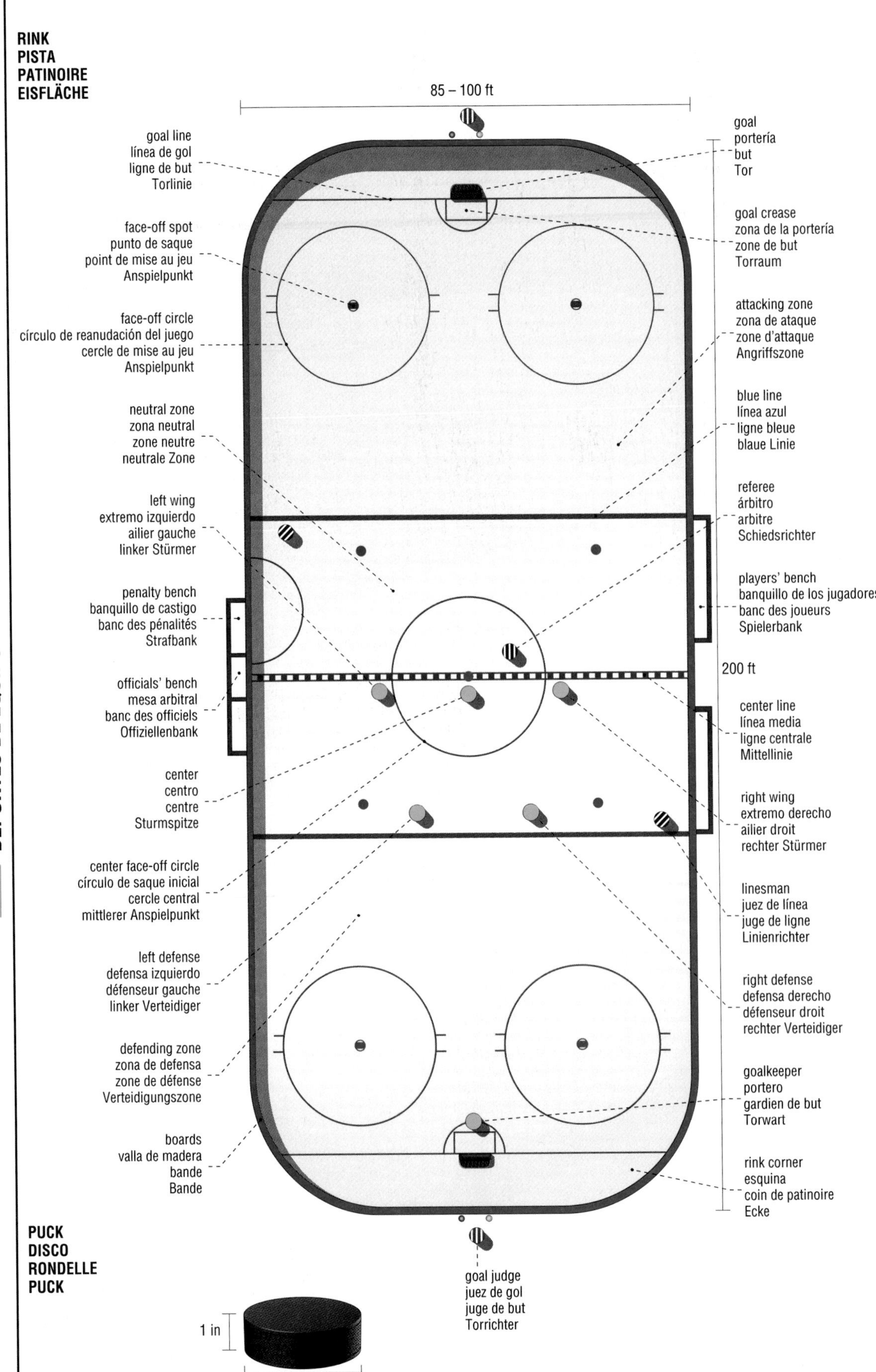

RINK
PISTA
PATINOIRE
EISFLÄCHE
85 – 100 ft
goal line
línea de gol
ligne de but
Torlinie
goal
portería
but
Tor
face-off spot
punto de saque
point de mise au jeu
Anspielpunkt
goal crease
zona de la portería
zone de but
Torraum
face-off circle
círculo de reanudación del juego
cercle de mise au jeu
Anspielpunkt
attacking zone
zona de ataque
zone d'attaque
Angriffszone
neutral zone
zona neutral
zone neutre
neutrale Zone
blue line
línea azul
ligne bleue
blaue Linie
left wing
extremo izquierdo
ailier gauche
linker Stürmer
referee
árbitro
arbitre
Schiedsrichter
penalty bench
banquillo de castigo
banc des pénalités
Strafbank
players' bench
banquillo de los jugadores
banc des joueurs
Spielerbank
200 ft
officials' bench
mesa arbitral
banc des officiels
Offiziellenbank
center line
línea media
ligne centrale
Mittellinie
center
centro
centre
Sturmspitze
right wing
extremo derecho
ailier droit
rechter Stürmer
center face-off circle
círculo de saque inicial
cercle central
mittlerer Anspielpunkt
linesman
juez de línea
juge de ligne
Linienrichter
left defense
defensa izquierdo
défenseur gauche
linker Verteidiger
right defense
defensa derecho
défenseur droit
rechter Verteidiger
defending zone
zona de defensa
zone de défense
Verteidigungszone
goalkeeper
portero
gardien de but
Torwart
boards
valla de madera
bande
Bande
rink corner
esquina
coin de patinoire
Ecke
PUCK
DISCO
RONDELLE
PUCK
goal judge
juez de gol
juge de but
Torrichter
1 in
3 in

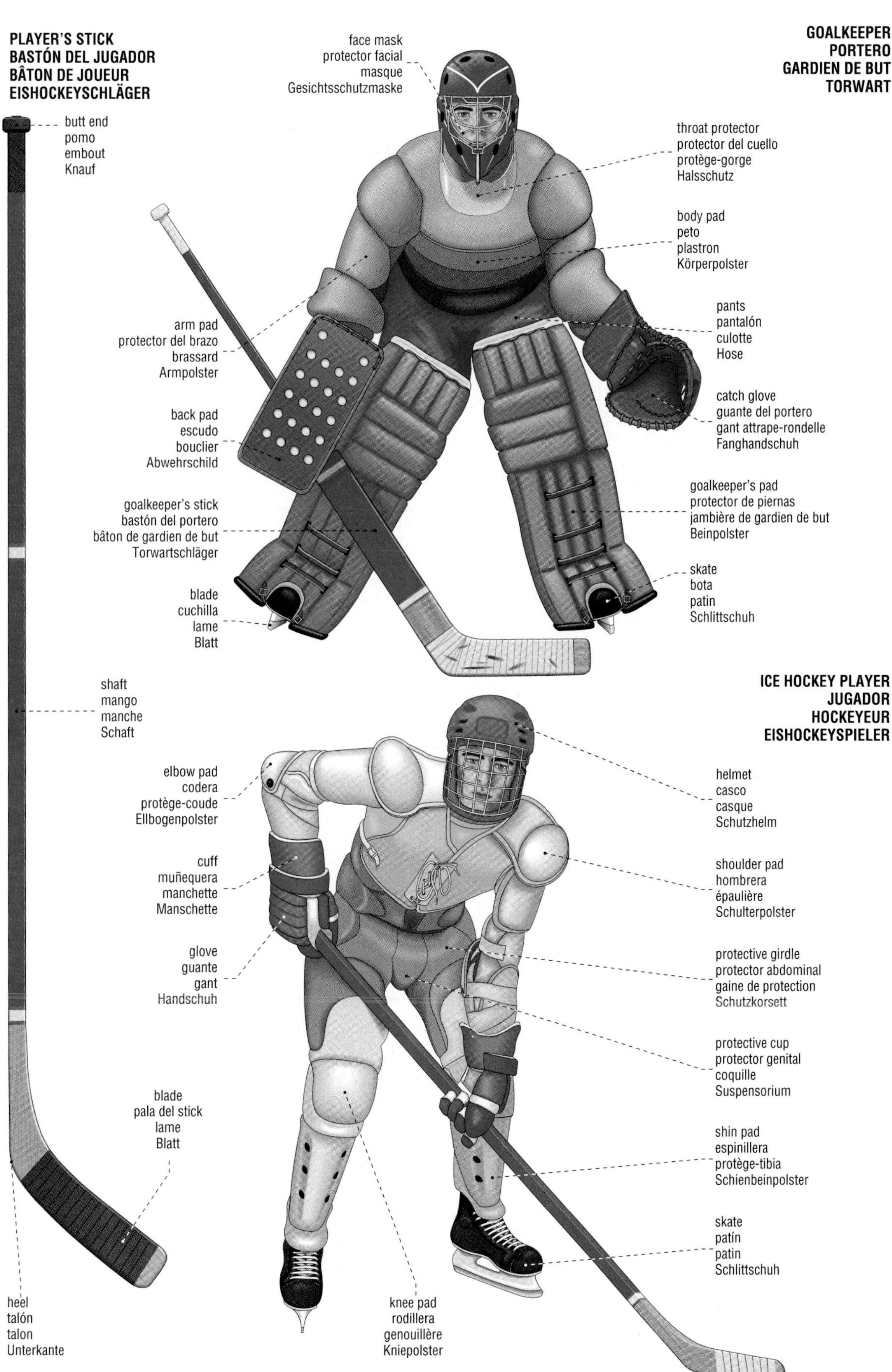
PLAYER'S STICK
BASTÓN DEL JUGADOR
BÂTON DE JOUEUR
EISHOCKEYSCHLÄGER
butt end
pomo
embout
Knauf
shaft
mango
manche
Schaft
blade
pala del stick
lame
Blatt
heel
talón
talon
Unterkante
face mask
protector facial
masque
Gesichtsschutzmaske
GOALKEEPER
PORTERO
GARDIEN DE BUT
TORWART
throat protector
protector del cuello
protège-gorge
Halsschutz
body pad
peto
plastron
Körperpolster
arm pad
protector del brazo
brassard
Armpolster
pants
pantalón
culotte
Hose
catch glove
guante del portero
gant attrape-rondelle
Fanghandschuh
back pad
escudo
bouclier
Abwehrschild
goalkeeper's stick
bastón del portero
bâton de gardien de but
Torwartschläger
goalkeeper's pad
protector de piernas
jambière de gardien de but
Beinpolster
skate
bota
patin
Schlittschuh
blade
cuchilla
lame
Blatt
ICE HOCKEY PLAYER
JUGADOR
HOCKEYEUR
EISHOCKEYSPIELER
elbow pad
codera
protège-coude
Ellbogenpolster
helmet
casco
casque
Schutzhelm
cuff
muñequera
manchette
Manschette
shoulder pad
hombrera
épaulière
Schulterpolster
glove
guante
gant
Handschuh
protective girdle
protector abdominal
gaine de protection
Schutzkorsett
protective cup
protector genital
coquille
Suspensorium
shin pad
espinillera
protège-tibia
Schienbeinpolster
skate
patín
patin
Schlittschuh
knee pad
rodillera
genouillère
Kniepolster

BASKETBALL
BALONCESTO
BASKETBALL
BASKETBALLSPIEL

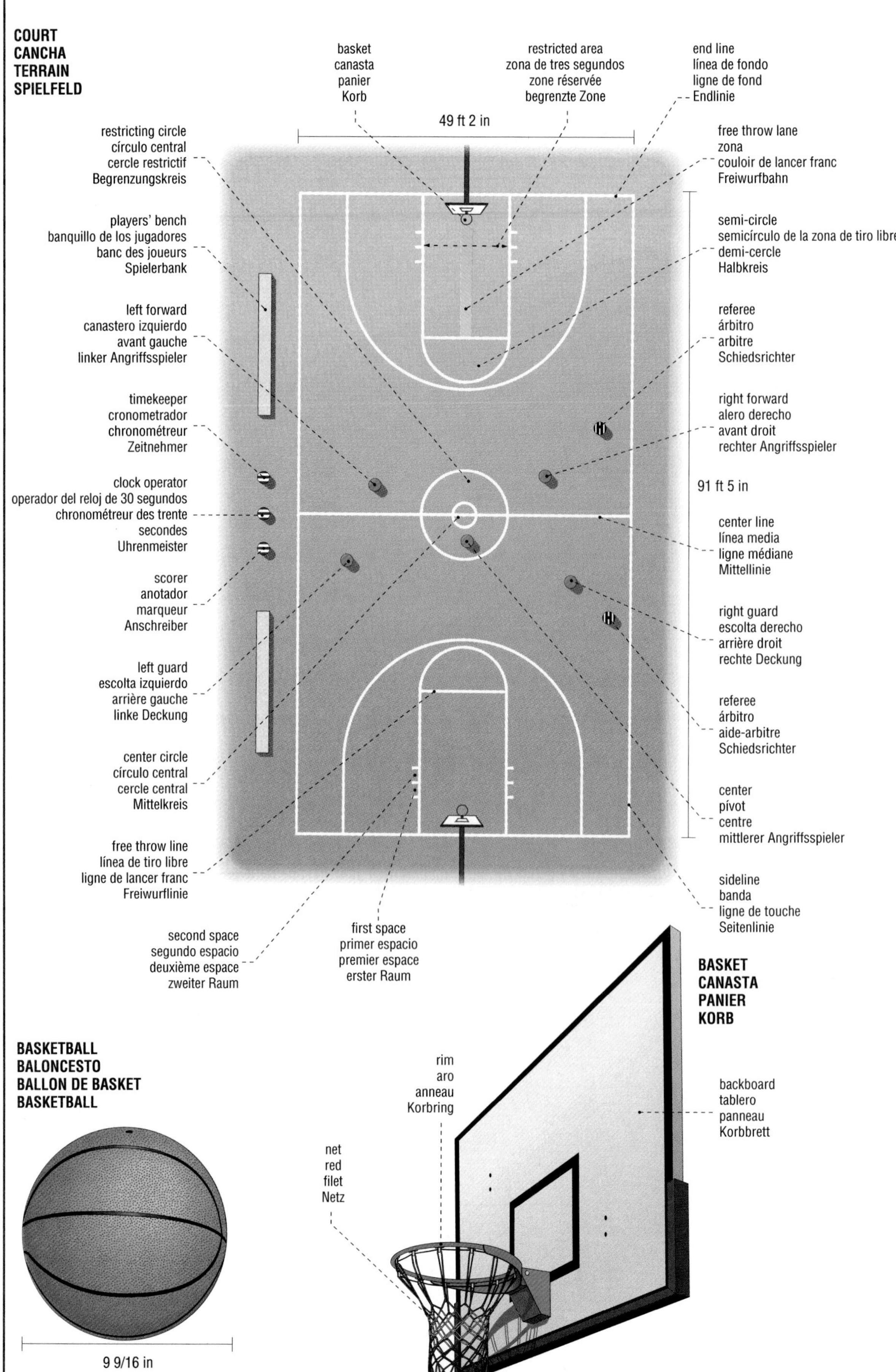
COURT
CANCHA
TERRAIN
SPIELFELD
basket
canasta
panier
Korb
restricted area
zona de tres segundos
zone réservée
begrenzte Zone
end line
línea de fondo
ligne de fond
Endlinie
49 ft 2 in
restricting circle
círculo central
cercle restrictif
Begrenzungskreis
free throw lane
zona
couloir de lancer franc
Freiwurfbahn
players' bench
banquillo de los jugadores
banc des joueurs
Spielerbank
semi-circle
semicírculo de la zona de tiro libre
demi-cercle
Halbkreis
left forward
canastero izquierdo
avant gauche
linker Angriffsspieler
referee
árbitro
arbitre
Schiedsrichter
timekeeper
cronometrador
chronométreur
Zeitnehmer
right forward
alero derecho
avant droit
rechter Angriffsspieler
clock operator
operador del reloj de 30 segundos
chronométreur des trente secondes
Uhrenmeister
91 ft 5 in
center line
línea media
ligne médiane
Mittellinie
scorer
anotador
marqueur
Anschreiber
right guard
escolta derecho
arrière droit
rechte Deckung
left guard
escolta izquierdo
arrière gauche
linke Deckung
referee
árbitro
aide-arbitre
Schiedsrichter
center circle
círculo central
cercle central
Mittelkreis
center
pívot
centre
mittlerer Angriffsspieler
free throw line
línea de tiro libre
ligne de lancer franc
Freiwurflinie
sideline
banda
ligne de touche
Seitenlinie
second space
segundo espacio
deuxième espace
zweiter Raum
first space
primer espacio
premier espace
erster Raum
BASKET
CANASTA
PANIER
KORB
BASKETBALL
BALONCESTO
BALLON DE BASKET
BASKETBALL
rim
aro
anneau
Korbring
backboard
tablero
panneau
Korbbrett
net
red
filet
Netz
9 9/16 in

NETBALL
BALONCESTO DE MUJERES
NETBALL
NETZBALLSPIEL

COURT
CANCHA
TERRAIN
SPIELFELD

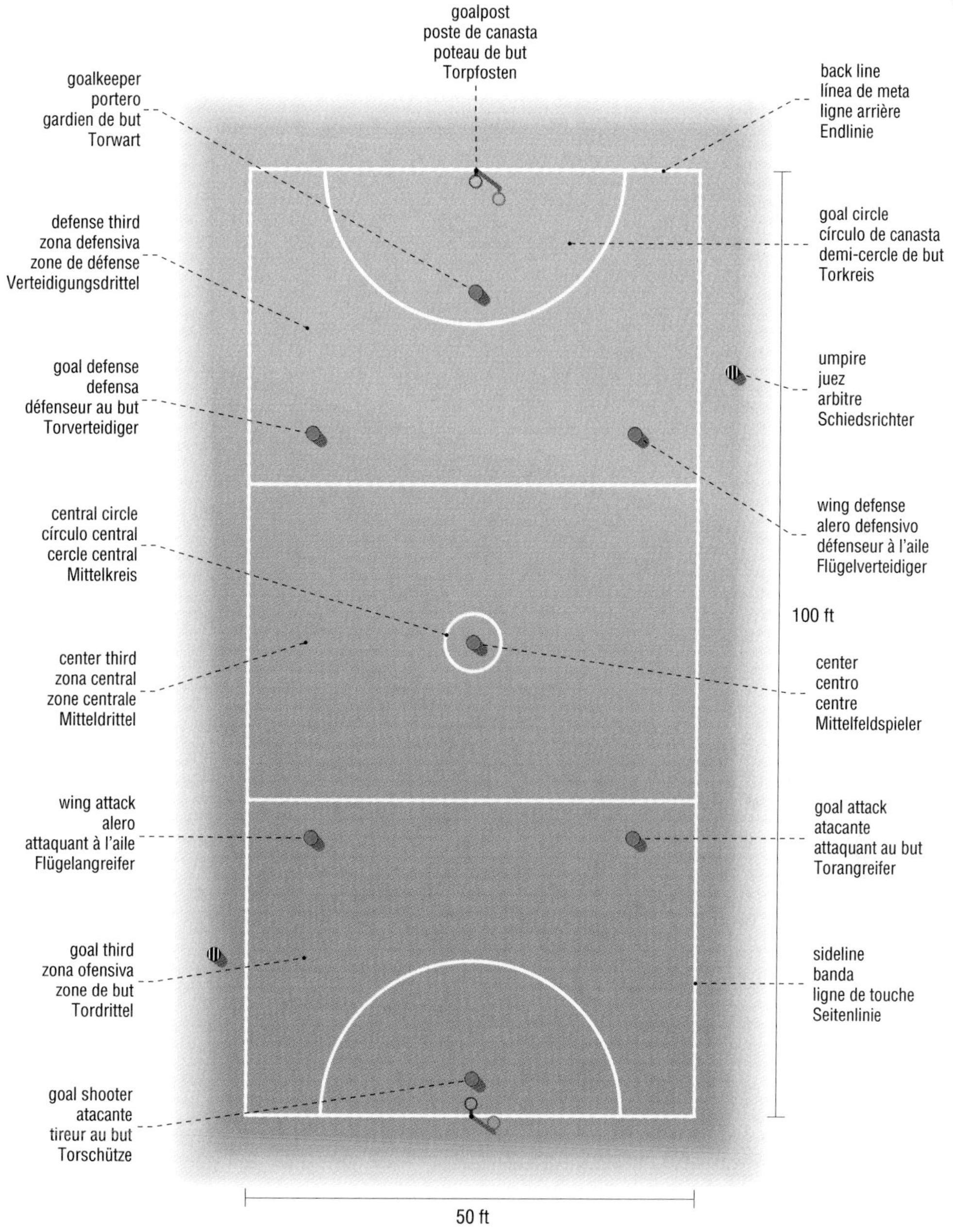

goalpost
poste de canasta
poteau de but
Torpfosten

goalkeeper
portero
gardien de but
Torwart

back line
línea de meta
ligne arrière
Endlinie

defense third
zona defensiva
zone de défense
Verteidigungsdrittel

goal circle
círculo de canasta
demi-cercle de but
Torkreis

goal defense
defensa
défenseur au but
Torverteidiger

umpire
juez
arbitre
Schiedsrichter

central circle
círculo central
cercle central
Mittelkreis

wing defense
alero defensivo
défenseur à l'aile
Flügelverteidiger

100 ft

center third
zona central
zone centrale
Mitteldrittel

center
centro
centre
Mittelfeldspieler

wing attack
alero
attaquant à l'aile
Flügelangreifer

goal attack
atacante
attaquant au but
Torangreifer

goal third
zona ofensiva
zone de but
Tordrittel

sideline
banda
ligne de touche
Seitenlinie

goal shooter
atacante
tireur au but
Torschütze

50 ft

NETBALL
BALÓN
BALLON DE NETBALL
NETZBALLSPIEL

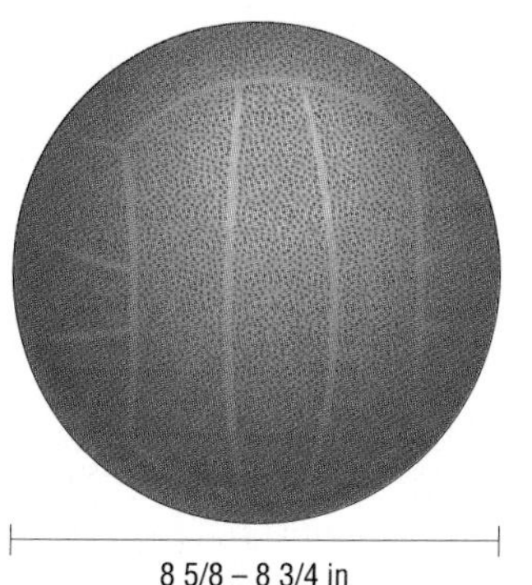

8 5/8 – 8 3/4 in

HANDBALL
BALÓN
HANDBALL
HANDBALL

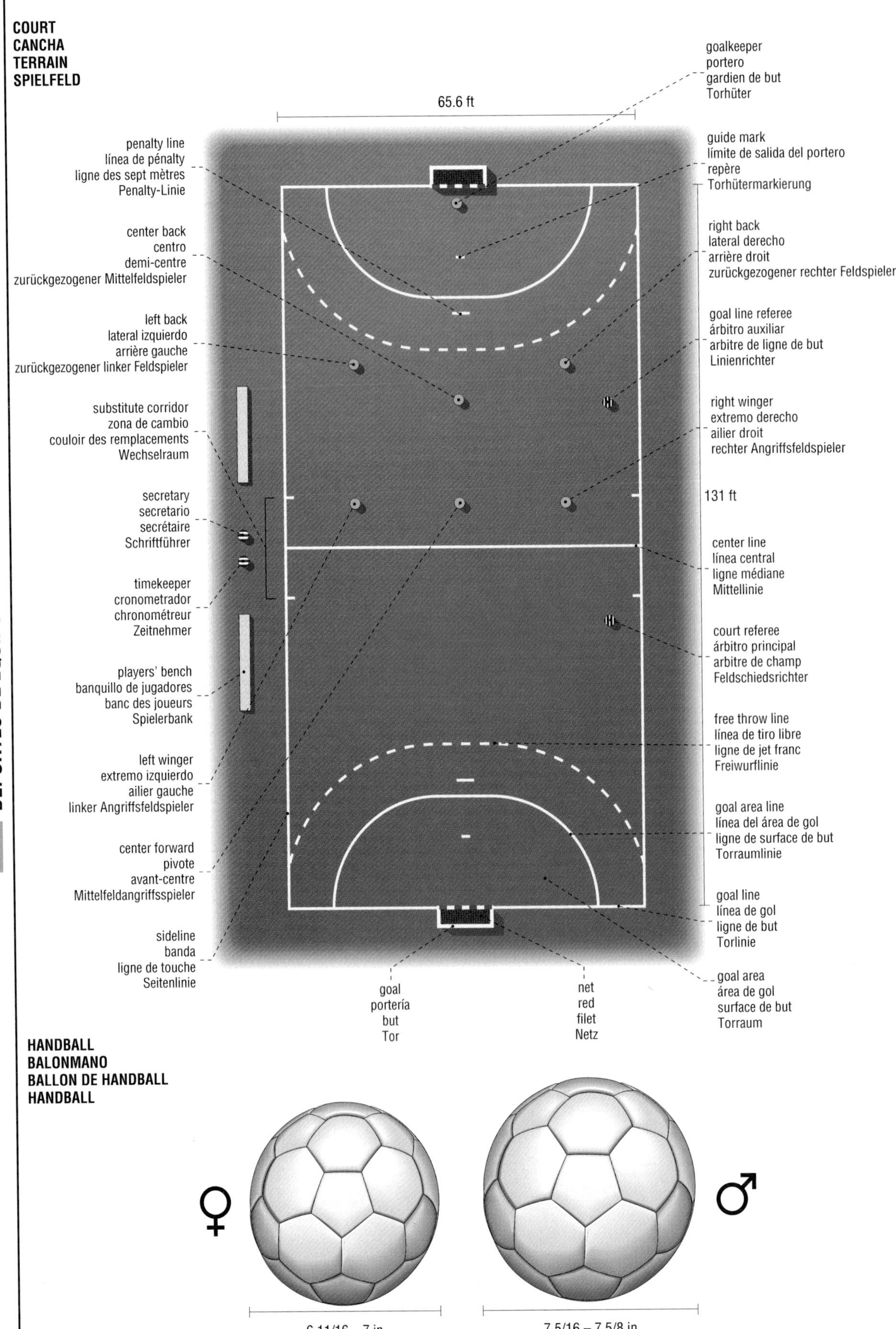
COURT
CANCHA
TERRAIN
SPIELFELD
65.6 ft
goalkeeper
portero
gardien de but
Torhüter
penalty line
línea de pénalty
ligne des sept mètres
Penalty-Linie
guide mark
límite de salida del portero
repère
Torhütermarkierung
center back
centro
demi-centre
zurückgezogener Mittelfeldspieler
right back
lateral derecho
arrière droit
zurückgezogener rechter Feldspieler
left back
lateral izquierdo
arrière gauche
zurückgezogener linker Feldspieler
goal line referee
árbitro auxiliar
arbitre de ligne de but
Linienrichter
substitute corridor
zona de cambio
couloir des remplacements
Wechselraum
right winger
extremo derecho
ailier droit
rechter Angriffsfeldspieler
secretary
secretario
secrétaire
Schriftführer
131 ft
center line
línea central
ligne médiane
Mittellinie
timekeeper
cronometrador
chronométreur
Zeitnehmer
court referee
árbitro principal
arbitre de champ
Feldschiedsrichter
players' bench
banquillo de jugadores
banc des joueurs
Spielerbank
free throw line
línea de tiro libre
ligne de jet franc
Freiwurflinie
left winger
extremo izquierdo
ailier gauche
linker Angriffsfeldspieler
goal area line
línea del área de gol
ligne de surface de but
Torraumlinie
center forward
pivote
avant-centre
Mittelfeldangriffsspieler
goal line
línea de gol
ligne de but
Torlinie
sideline
banda
ligne de touche
Seitenlinie
goal
portería
but
Tor
net
red
filet
Netz
goal area
área de gol
surface de but
Torraum
HANDBALL
BALONMANO
BALLON DE HANDBALL
HANDBALL
♀
♂
6 11/16 – 7 in
7 5/16 – 7 5/8 in

VOLLEYBALL
BALÓN VOLEA
VOLLEYBALL
VOLLEYBALLSPIEL

COURT
CANCHA
TERRAIN
SPIELFELD

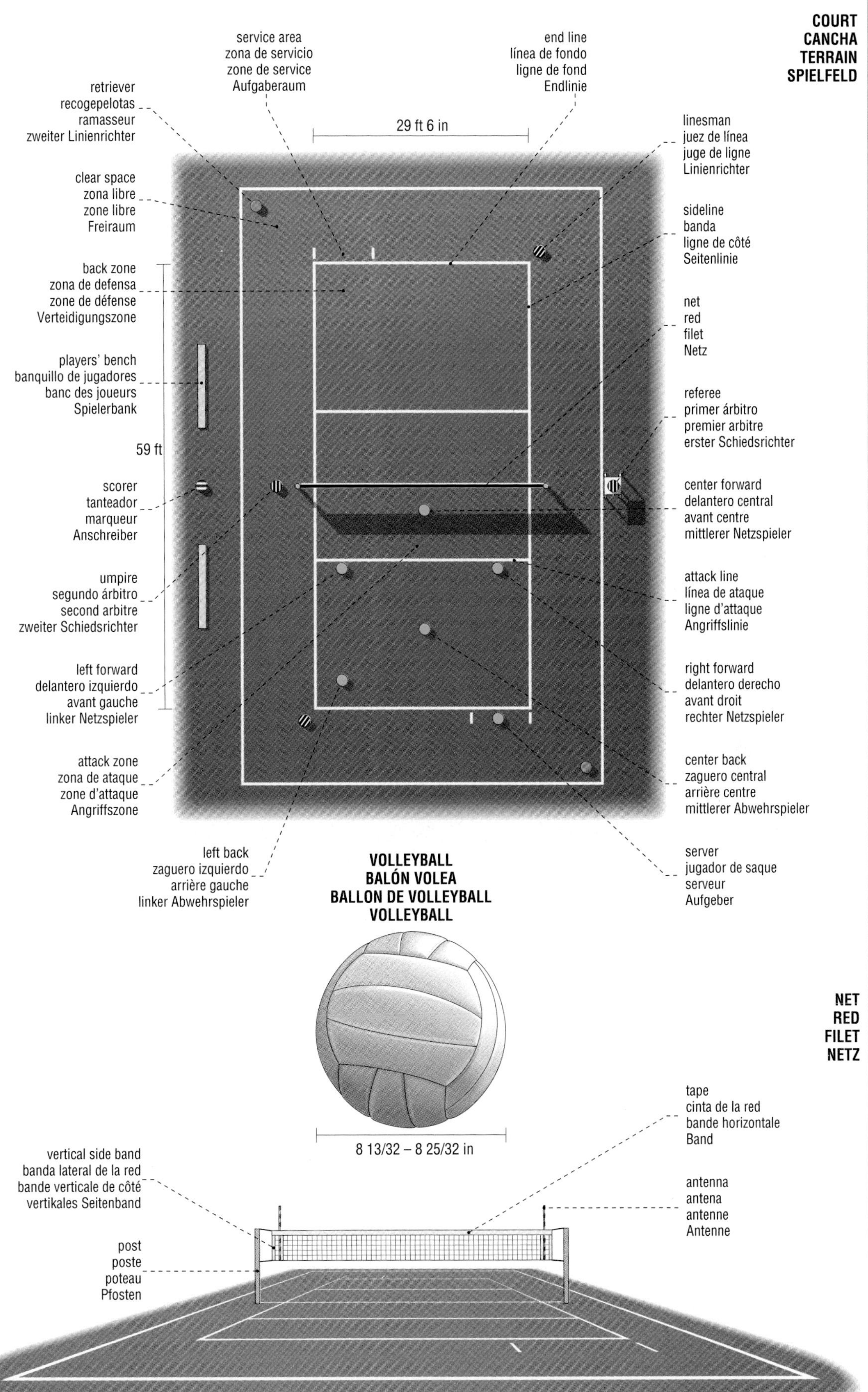

service area
zona de servicio
zone de service
Aufgaberaum
end line
línea de fondo
ligne de fond
Endlinie
retriever
recogepelotas
ramasseur
zweiter Linienrichter
29 ft 6 in
linesman
juez de línea
juge de ligne
Linienrichter
clear space
zona libre
zone libre
Freiraum
sideline
banda
ligne de côté
Seitenlinie
back zone
zona de defensa
zone de défense
Verteidigungszone
net
red
filet
Netz
players' bench
banquillo de jugadores
banc des joueurs
Spielerbank
referee
primer árbitro
premier arbitre
erster Schiedsrichter
59 ft
scorer
tanteador
marqueur
Anschreiber
center forward
delantero central
avant centre
mittlerer Netzspieler
umpire
segundo árbitro
second arbitre
zweiter Schiedsrichter
attack line
línea de ataque
ligne d'attaque
Angriffslinie
left forward
delantero izquierdo
avant gauche
linker Netzspieler
right forward
delantero derecho
avant droit
rechter Netzspieler
attack zone
zona de ataque
zone d'attaque
Angriffszone
center back
zaguero central
arrière centre
mittlerer Abwehrspieler
left back
zaguero izquierdo
arrière gauche
linker Abwehrspieler
server
jugador de saque
serveur
Aufgeber
VOLLEYBALL
BALÓN VOLEA
BALLON DE VOLLEYBALL
VOLLEYBALL
8 13/32 – 8 25/32 in
NET
RED
FILET
NETZ
tape
cinta de la red
bande horizontale
Band
vertical side band
banda lateral de la red
bande verticale de côté
vertikales Seitenband
antenna
antena
antenne
Antenne
post
poste
poteau
Pfosten

TENNIS
TENIS
TENNIS
TENNIS

COURT
CANCHA
TERRAIN
TENNISPLATZ

27 ft

78 ft

36 ft

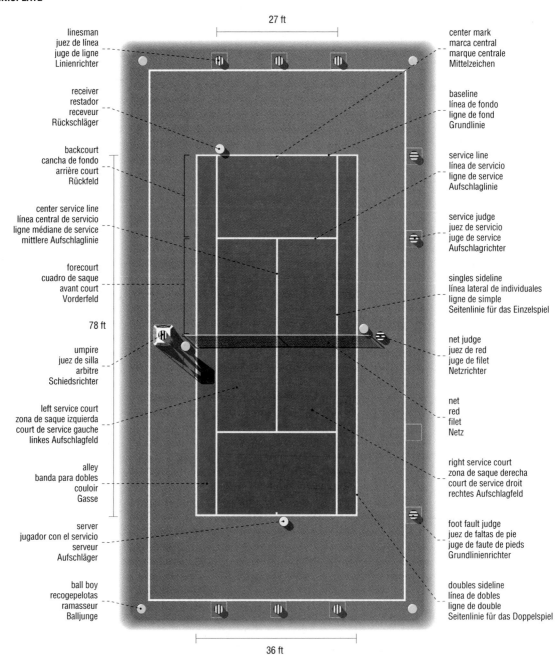

linesman
juez de línea
juge de ligne
Linienrichter

receiver
restador
receveur
Rückschläger

backcourt
cancha de fondo
arrière court
Rückfeld

center service line
línea central de servicio
ligne médiane de service
mittlere Aufschlaglinie

forecourt
cuadro de saque
avant court
Vorderfeld

umpire
juez de silla
arbitre
Schiedsrichter

left service court
zona de saque izquierda
court de service gauche
linkes Aufschlagfeld

alley
banda para dobles
couloir
Gasse

server
jugador con el servicio
serveur
Aufschläger

ball boy
recogepelotas
ramasseur
Balljunge

center mark
marca central
marque centrale
Mittelzeichen

baseline
línea de fondo
ligne de fond
Grundlinie

service line
línea de servicio
ligne de service
Aufschlaglinie

service judge
juez de servicio
juge de service
Aufschlagrichter

singles sideline
línea lateral de individuales
ligne de simple
Seitenlinie für das Einzelspiel

net judge
juez de red
juge de filet
Netzrichter

net
red
filet
Netz

right service court
zona de saque derecha
court de service droit
rechtes Aufschlagfeld

foot fault judge
juez de faltas de pie
juge de faute de pieds
Grundlinienrichter

doubles sideline
línea de dobles
ligne de double
Seitenlinie für das Doppelspiel

NET
RED
FILET
NETZ

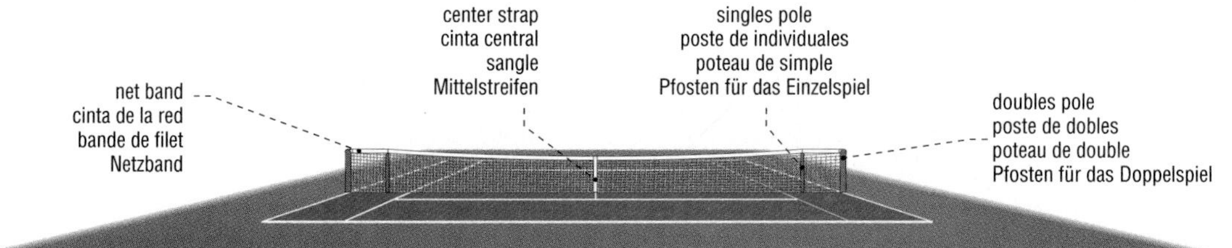
center strap
cinta central
sangle
Mittelstreifen
singles pole
poste de individuales
poteau de simple
Pfosten für das Einzelspiel
net band
cinta de la red
bande de filet
Netzband
doubles pole
poste de dobles
poteau de double
Pfosten für das Doppelspiel

TENNIS PLAYER
TENISTA
JOUEUSE DE TENNIS
TENNISSPIELERIN
headband
cinta para el sudor
serre-tête
Stirnband
polo shirt
polo
polo
Polohemd
wristband
muñequera
serre-poignet
Schweißband
skirt
falda
jupette
Rock
sock
calcetin
chaussette
Socke
tennis shoe
zapato de tenis
chaussure de tennis
Tennisschuh
TENNIS BALL
PELOTA DE TENIS
BALLE DE TENNIS
TENNISBALL
2 1/2 – 2 5/8 in
TENNIS RACKET
RAQUETA DE TENIS
RAQUETTE DE TENNIS
TENNISSCHLÄGER
frame
marco
cadre
Rahmen
head
cabeza
tête
Kopf
stringing
cordaje
tamis
Bespannung
shoulder
hombro
épaule
Herz
throat
garganta
cœur
Hals
shaft
mango
manche
Schaft
handle
empuñadura
poignée
Griff
butt
puño
talon
Knauf

SQUASH
SQUASH
SQUASH
SQUASH

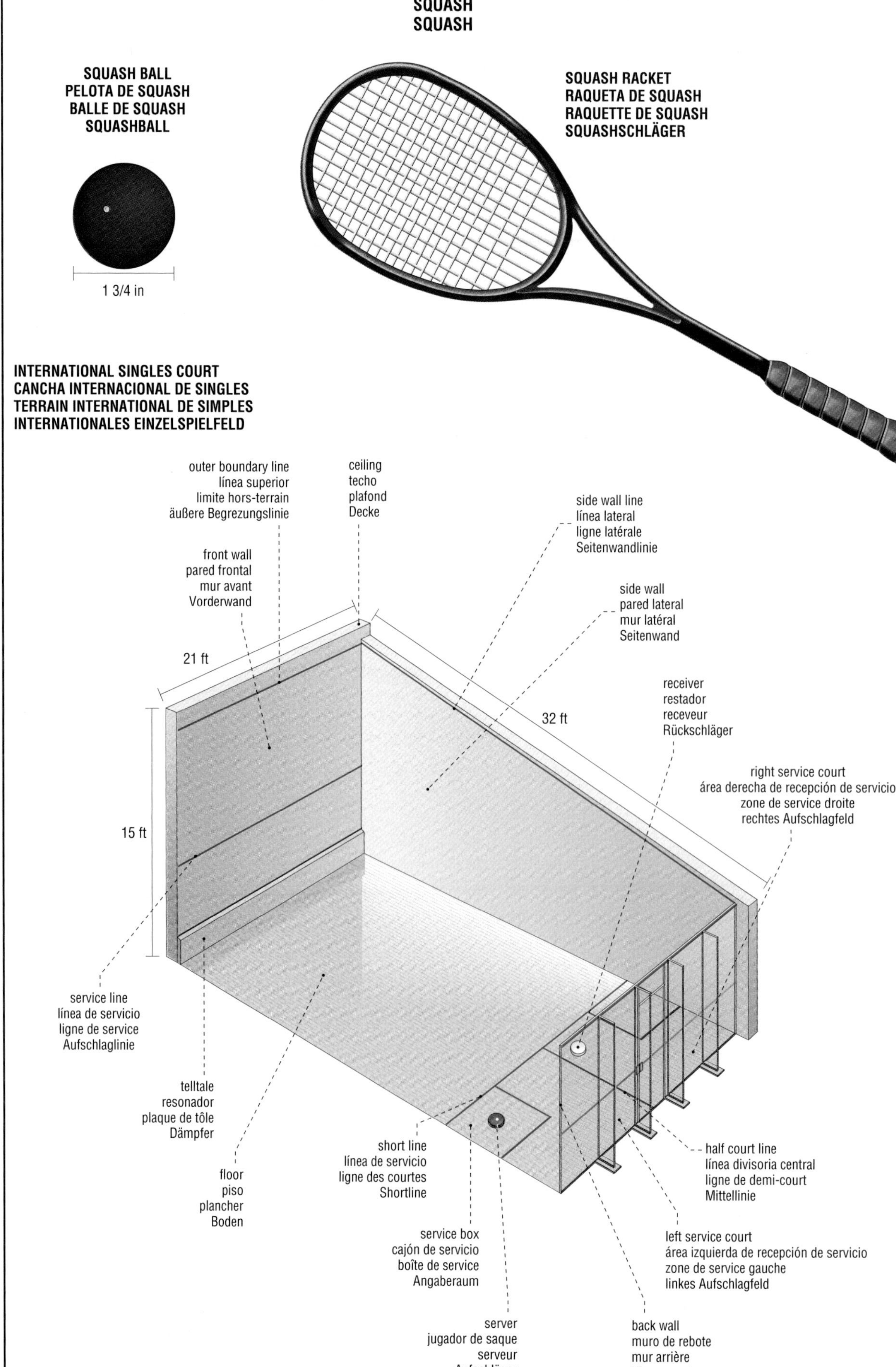
SQUASH BALL
PELOTA DE SQUASH
BALLE DE SQUASH
SQUASHBALL
1 3/4 in
SQUASH RACKET
RAQUETA DE SQUASH
RAQUETTE DE SQUASH
SQUASHSCHLÄGER
INTERNATIONAL SINGLES COURT
CANCHA INTERNACIONAL DE SINGLES
TERRAIN INTERNATIONAL DE SIMPLES
INTERNATIONALES EINZELSPIELFELD
outer boundary line
línea superior
limite hors-terrain
äußere Begrezungslinie
ceiling
techo
plafond
Decke
side wall line
línea lateral
ligne latérale
Seitenwandlinie
front wall
pared frontal
mur avant
Vorderwand
side wall
pared lateral
mur latéral
Seitenwand
21 ft
32 ft
receiver
restador
receveur
Rückschläger
15 ft
right service court
área derecha de recepción de servicio
zone de service droite
rechtes Aufschlagfeld
service line
línea de servicio
ligne de service
Aufschlaglinie
telltale
resonador
plaque de tôle
Dämpfer
floor
piso
plancher
Boden
short line
línea de servicio
ligne des courtes
Shortline
half court line
línea divisoria central
ligne de demi-court
Mittellinie
service box
cajón de servicio
boîte de service
Angaberaum
left service court
área izquierda de recepción de servicio
zone de service gauche
linkes Aufschlagfeld
server
jugador de saque
serveur
Aufschläger
back wall
muro de rebote
mur arrière
Hinterwand

RACQUETBALL
RAQUETBOL
RACQUETBALL
RACQUETBALLSPIEL

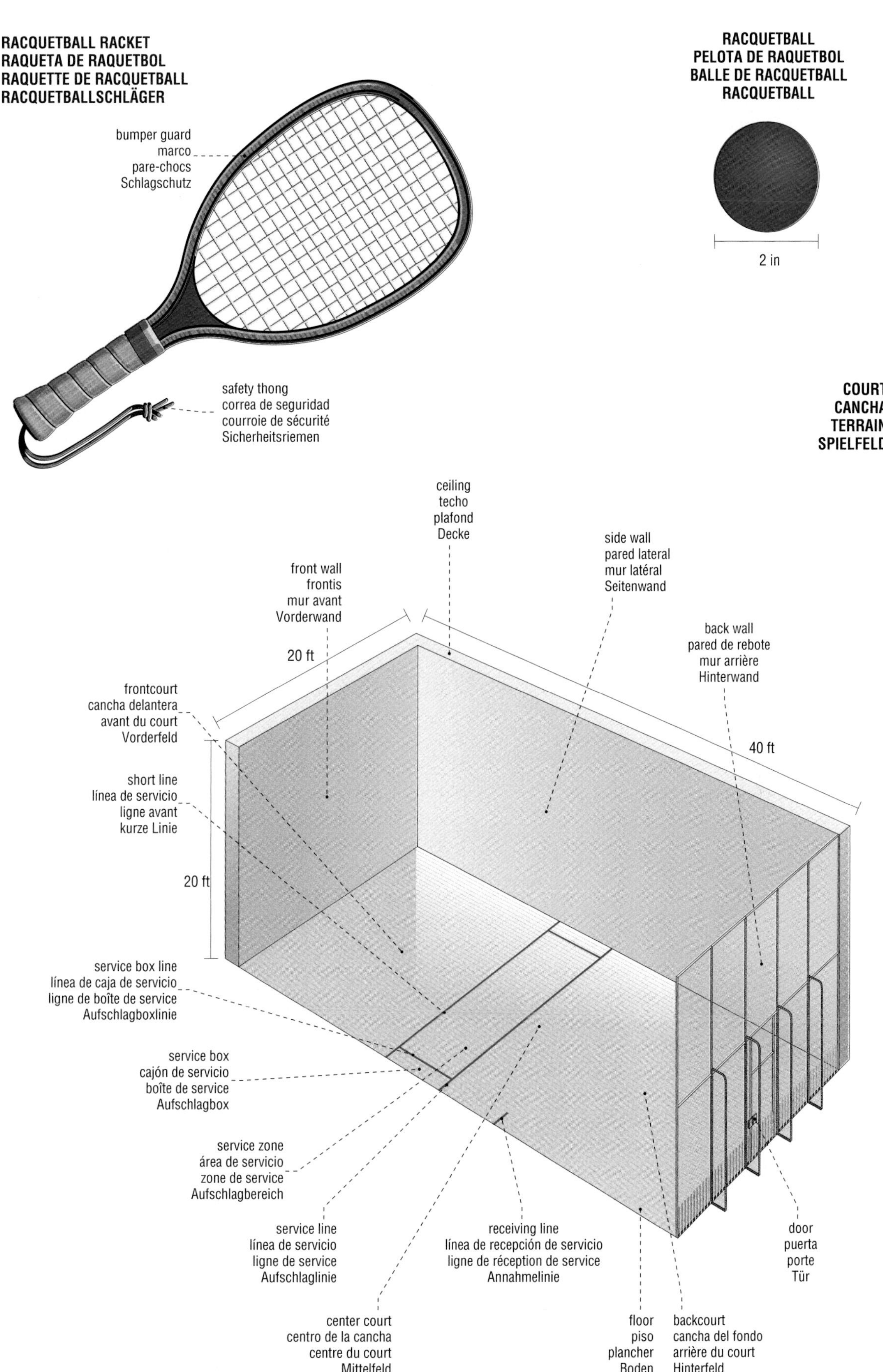

RACQUETBALL RACKET
RAQUETA DE RAQUETBOL
RAQUETTE DE RACQUETBALL
RACQUETBALLSCHLÄGER
bumper guard
marco
pare-chocs
Schlagschutz
safety thong
correa de seguridad
courroie de sécurité
Sicherheitsriemen
RACQUETBALL
PELOTA DE RAQUETBOL
BALLE DE RACQUETBALL
RACQUETBALL
2 in
COURT
CANCHA
TERRAIN
SPIELFELD
ceiling
techo
plafond
Decke
front wall
frontis
mur avant
Vorderwand
side wall
pared lateral
mur latéral
Seitenwand
back wall
pared de rebote
mur arrière
Hinterwand
20 ft
40 ft
20 ft
frontcourt
cancha delantera
avant du court
Vorderfeld
short line
línea de servicio
ligne avant
kurze Linie
service box line
línea de caja de servicio
ligne de boîte de service
Aufschlagboxlinie
service box
cajón de servicio
boîte de service
Aufschlagbox
service zone
área de servicio
zone de service
Aufschlagbereich
service line
línea de servicio
ligne de service
Aufschlaglinie
receiving line
línea de recepción de servicio
ligne de réception de service
Annahmelinie
door
puerta
porte
Tür
center court
centro de la cancha
centre du court
Mittelfeld
floor
piso
plancher
Boden
backcourt
cancha del fondo
arrière du court
Hinterfeld

BADMINTON
BÁDMINTON
BADMINTON
BADMINTON

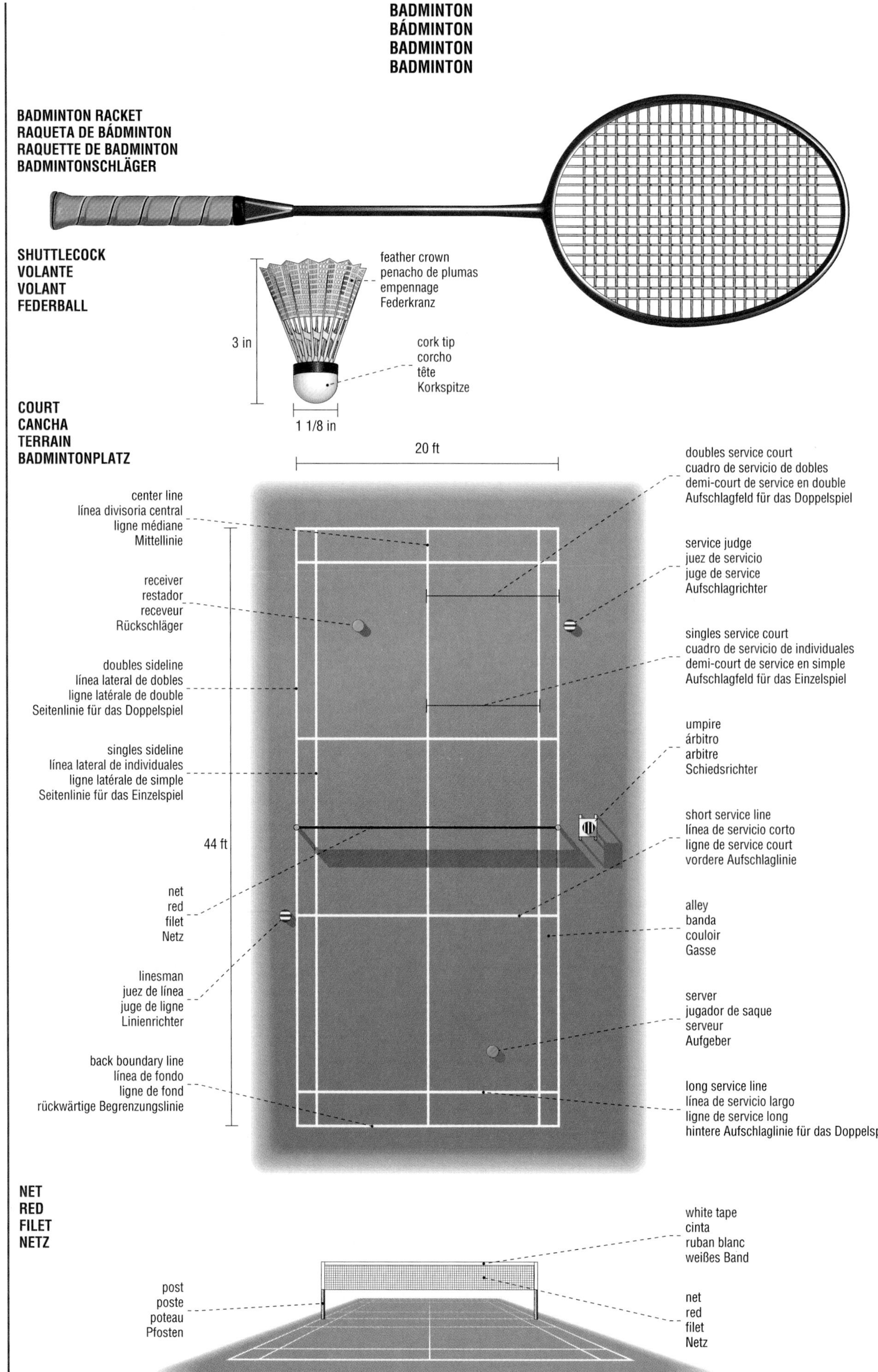
BADMINTON RACKET
RAQUETA DE BÁDMINTON
RAQUETTE DE BADMINTON
BADMINTONSCHLÄGER
SHUTTLECOCK
VOLANTE
VOLANT
FEDERBALL
feather crown
penacho de plumas
empennage
Federkranz
3 in
cork tip
corcho
tête
Korkspitze
1 1/8 in
COURT
CANCHA
TERRAIN
BADMINTONPLATZ
20 ft
center line
línea divisoria central
ligne médiane
Mittellinie
receiver
restador
receveur
Rückschläger
doubles sideline
línea lateral de dobles
ligne latérale de double
Seitenlinie für das Doppelspiel
singles sideline
línea lateral de individuales
ligne latérale de simple
Seitenlinie für das Einzelspiel
44 ft
net
red
filet
Netz
linesman
juez de línea
juge de ligne
Linienrichter
back boundary line
línea de fondo
ligne de fond
rückwärtige Begrenzungslinie
doubles service court
cuadro de servicio de dobles
demi-court de service en double
Aufschlagfeld für das Doppelspiel
service judge
juez de servicio
juge de service
Aufschlagrichter
singles service court
cuadro de servicio de individuales
demi-court de service en simple
Aufschlagfeld für das Einzelspiel
umpire
árbitro
arbitre
Schiedsrichter
short service line
línea de servicio corto
ligne de service court
vordere Aufschlaglinie
alley
banda
couloir
Gasse
server
jugador de saque
serveur
Aufgeber
long service line
línea de servicio largo
ligne de service long
hintere Aufschlaglinie für das Doppelspi
NET
RED
FILET
NETZ
white tape
cinta
ruban blanc
weißes Band
post
poste
poteau
Pfosten
net
red
filet
Netz

TABLE TENNIS
PING PONG
TENNIS DE TABLE
TISCHTENNIS

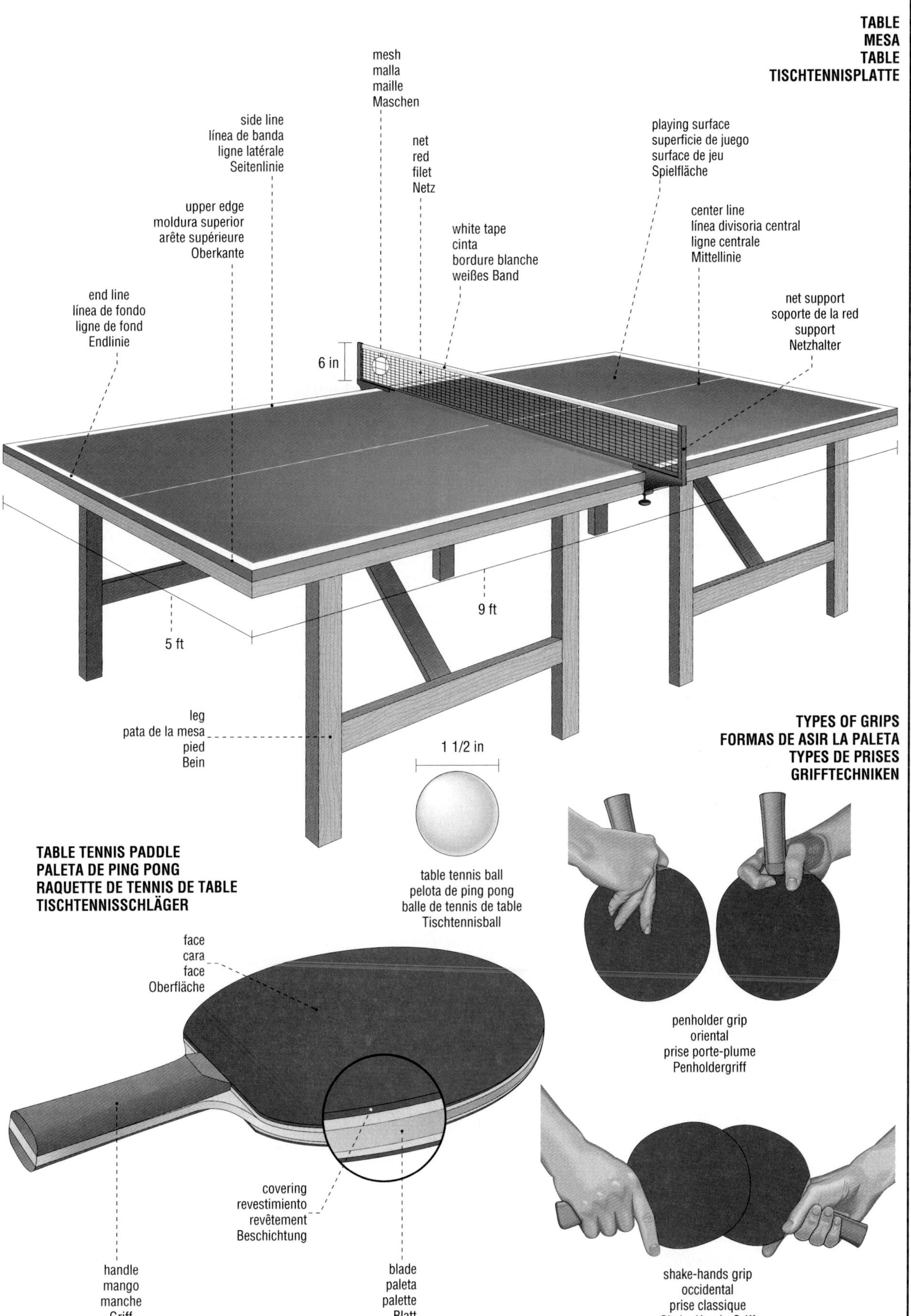
TABLE
MESA
TABLE
TISCHTENNISPLATTE
mesh
malla
maille
Maschen
side line
línea de banda
ligne latérale
Seitenlinie
net
red
filet
Netz
playing surface
superficie de juego
surface de jeu
Spielfläche
upper edge
moldura superior
arête supérieure
Oberkante
white tape
cinta
bordure blanche
weißes Band
center line
línea divisoria central
ligne centrale
Mittellinie
end line
línea de fondo
ligne de fond
Endlinie
net support
soporte de la red
support
Netzhalter
6 in
9 ft
5 ft
leg
pata de la mesa
pied
Bein
1 1/2 in
TYPES OF GRIPS
FORMAS DE ASIR LA PALETA
TYPES DE PRISES
GRIFFTECHNIKEN
TABLE TENNIS PADDLE
PALETA DE PING PONG
RAQUETTE DE TENNIS DE TABLE
TISCHTENNISSCHLÄGER
table tennis ball
pelota de ping pong
balle de tennis de table
Tischtennisball
face
cara
face
Oberfläche
penholder grip
oriental
prise porte-plume
Penholdergriff
covering
revestimiento
revêtement
Beschichtung
handle
mango
manche
Griff
blade
paleta
palette
Blatt
shake-hands grip
occidental
prise classique
Shake-Hands-Griff

CURLING
CURLING
CURLING
CURLING

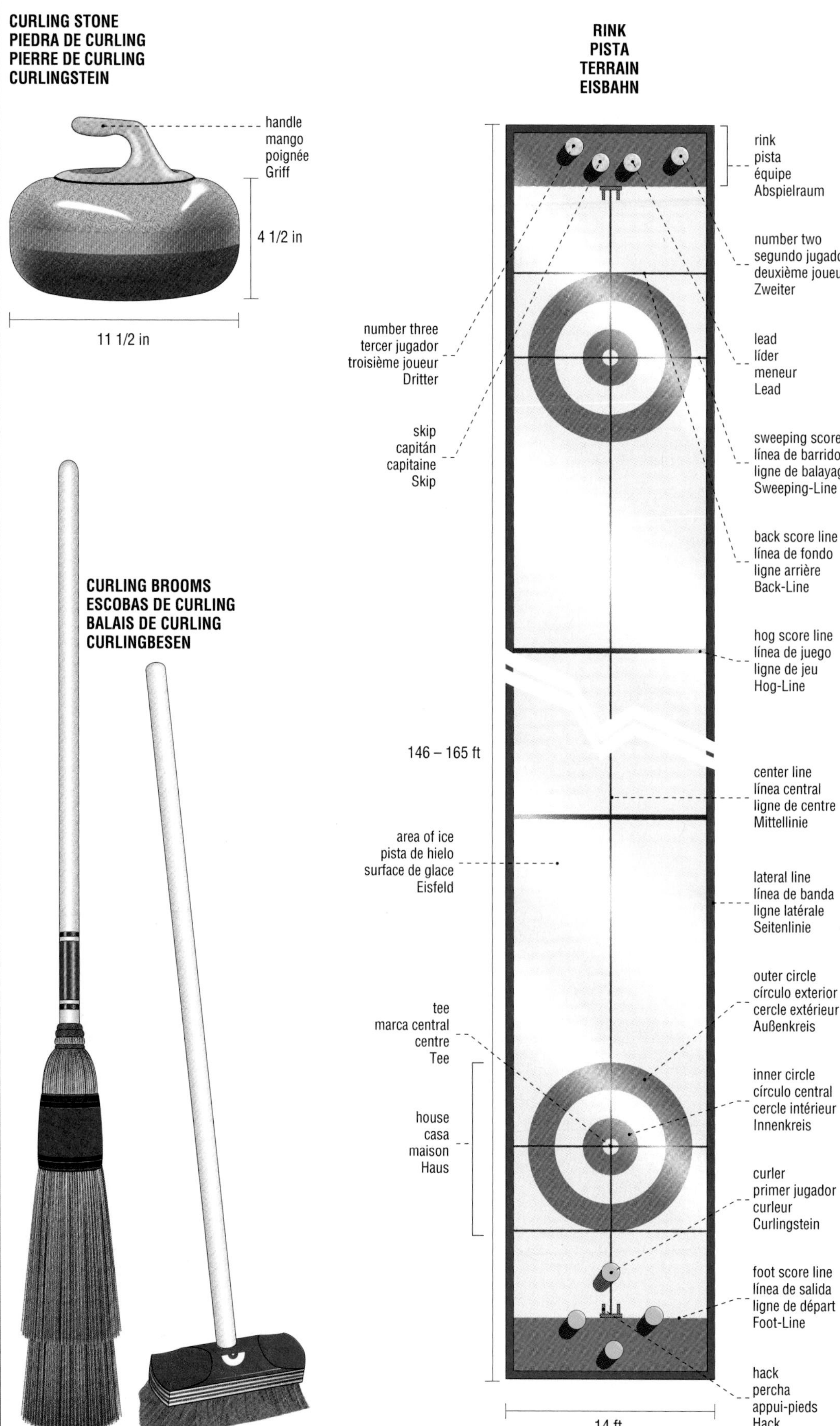
CURLING STONE
PIEDRA DE CURLING
PIERRE DE CURLING
CURLINGSTEIN
handle
mango
poignée
Griff
4 1/2 in
11 1/2 in
CURLING BROOMS
ESCOBAS DE CURLING
BALAIS DE CURLING
CURLINGBESEN
RINK
PISTA
TERRAIN
EISBAHN
rink
pista
équipe
Abspielraum
number two
segundo jugador
deuxième joueur
Zweiter
number three
tercer jugador
troisième joueur
Dritter
lead
líder
meneur
Lead
skip
capitán
capitaine
Skip
sweeping score line
línea de barrido
ligne de balayage
Sweeping-Line
back score line
línea de fondo
ligne arrière
Back-Line
hog score line
línea de juego
ligne de jeu
Hog-Line
146 – 165 ft
center line
línea central
ligne de centre
Mittellinie
area of ice
pista de hielo
surface de glace
Eisfeld
lateral line
línea de banda
ligne latérale
Seitenlinie
outer circle
círculo exterior
cercle extérieur
Außenkreis
tee
marca central
centre
Tee
inner circle
círculo central
cercle intérieur
Innenkreis
house
casa
maison
Haus
curler
primer jugador
curleur
Curlingstein
foot score line
línea de salida
ligne de départ
Foot-Line
hack
percha
appui-pieds
Hack
14 ft

SWIMMING
NATACIÓN
NATATION
SCHWIMMEN

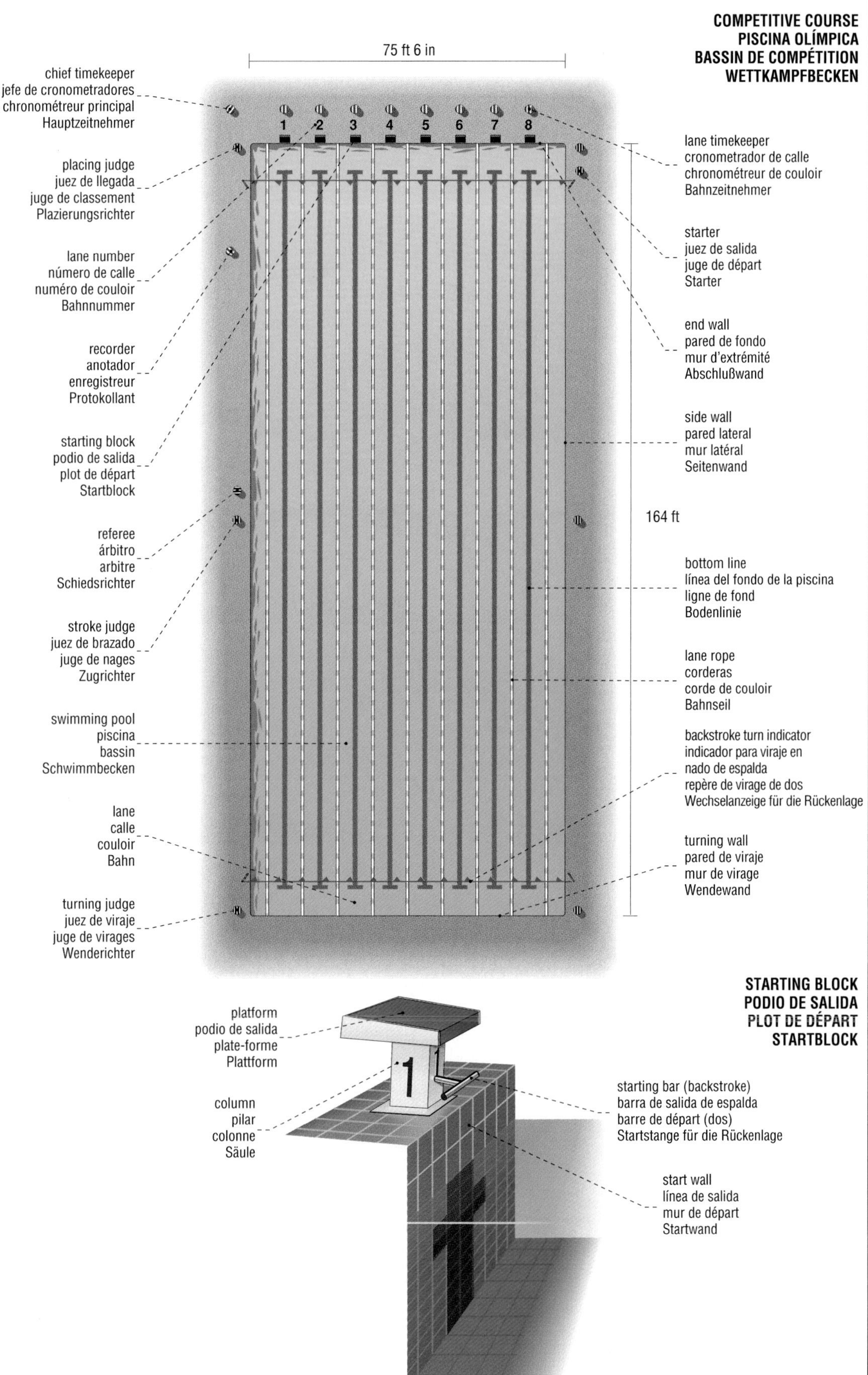
COMPETITIVE COURSE
PISCINA OLÍMPICA
BASSIN DE COMPÉTITION
WETTKAMPFBECKEN
75 ft 6 in
164 ft
1 2 3 4 5 6 7 8
chief timekeeper
jefe de cronometradores
chronométreur principal
Hauptzeitnehmer
placing judge
juez de llegada
juge de classement
Plazierungsrichter
lane number
número de calle
numéro de couloir
Bahnnummer
recorder
anotador
enregistreur
Protokollant
starting block
podio de salida
plot de départ
Startblock
referee
árbitro
arbitre
Schiedsrichter
stroke judge
juez de brazado
juge de nages
Zugrichter
swimming pool
piscina
bassin
Schwimmbecken
lane
calle
couloir
Bahn
turning judge
juez de viraje
juge de virages
Wenderichter
lane timekeeper
cronometrador de calle
chronométreur de couloir
Bahnzeitnehmer
starter
juez de salida
juge de départ
Starter
end wall
pared de fondo
mur d'extrémité
Abschlußwand
side wall
pared lateral
mur latéral
Seitenwand
bottom line
línea del fondo de la piscina
ligne de fond
Bodenlinie
lane rope
corderas
corde de couloir
Bahnseil
backstroke turn indicator
indicador para viraje en
nado de espalda
repère de virage de dos
Wechselanzeige für die Rückenlage
turning wall
pared de viraje
mur de virage
Wendewand
STARTING BLOCK
PODIO DE SALIDA
PLOT DE DÉPART
STARTBLOCK
platform
podio de salida
plate-forme
Plattform
column
pilar
colonne
Säule
1
starting bar (backstroke)
barra de salida de espalda
barre de départ (dos)
Startstange für die Rückenlage
start wall
línea de salida
mur de départ
Startwand

SWIMMING
NATACIÓN
NATATION
SCHWIMMEN

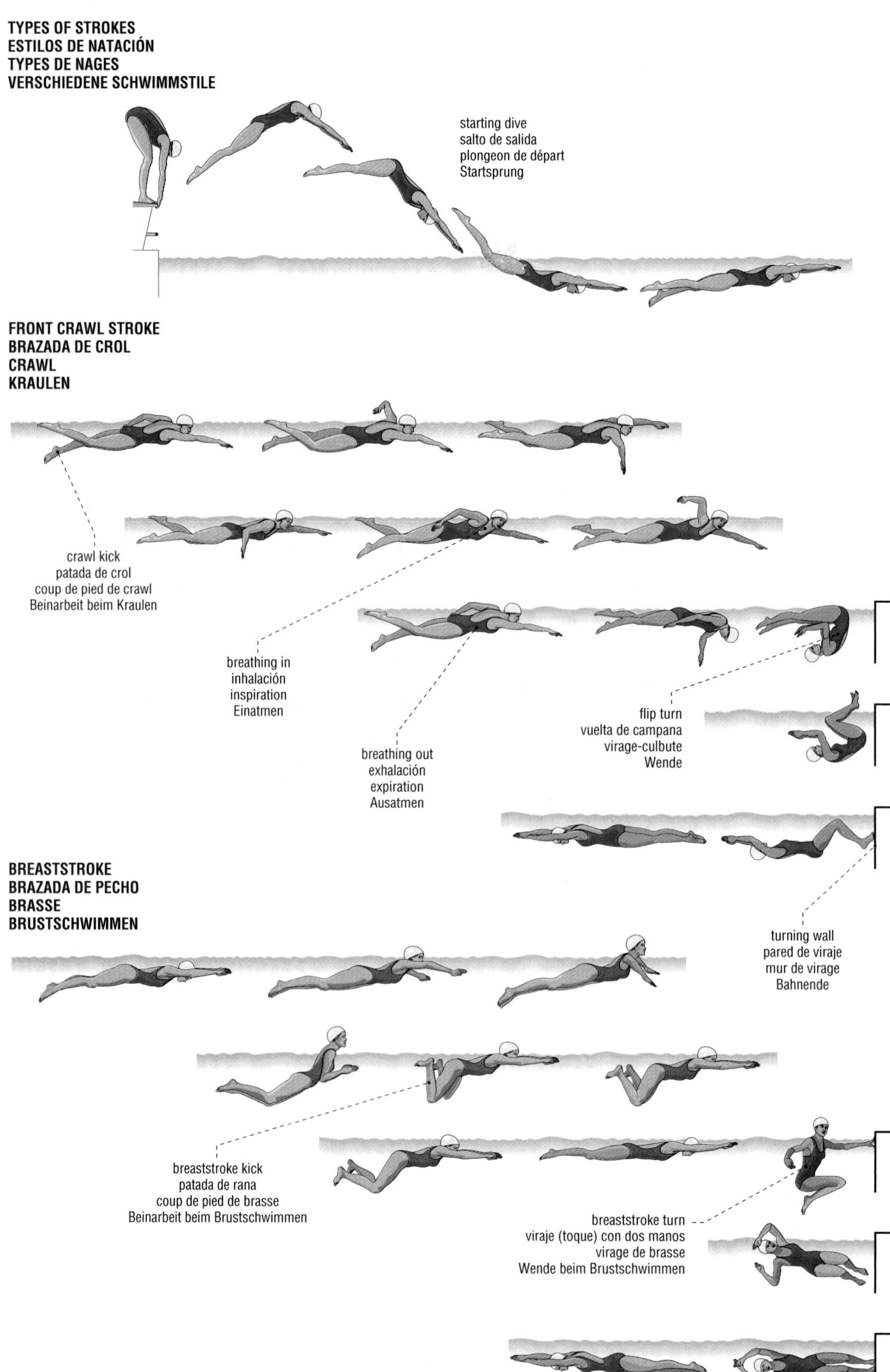
TYPES OF STROKES
ESTILOS DE NATACIÓN
TYPES DE NAGES
VERSCHIEDENE SCHWIMMSTILE
starting dive
salto de salida
plongeon de départ
Startsprung
FRONT CRAWL STROKE
BRAZADA DE CROL
CRAWL
KRAULEN
crawl kick
patada de crol
coup de pied de crawl
Beinarbeit beim Kraulen
breathing in
inhalación
inspiration
Einatmen
breathing out
exhalación
expiration
Ausatmen
flip turn
vuelta de campana
virage-culbute
Wende
BREASTSTROKE
BRAZADA DE PECHO
BRASSE
BRUSTSCHWIMMEN
turning wall
pared de viraje
mur de virage
Bahnende
breaststroke kick
patada de rana
coup de pied de brasse
Beinarbeit beim Brustschwimmen
breaststroke turn
viraje (toque) con dos manos
virage de brasse
Wende beim Brustschwimmen

BUTTERFLY STROKE
BRAZADA DE MARIPOSA
PAPILLON
BUTTERFLYSCHWIMMSTIL

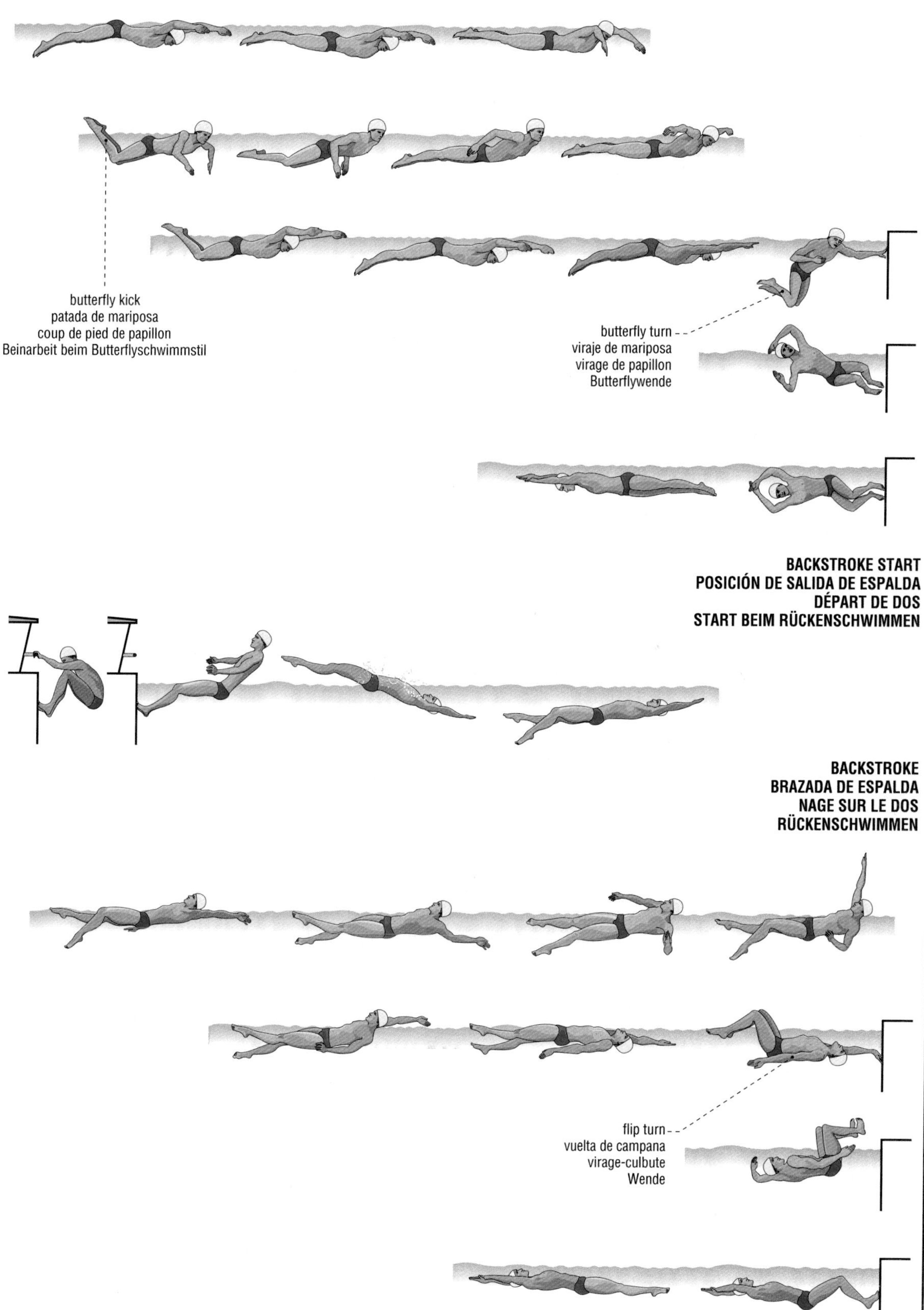
butterfly kick
patada de mariposa
coup de pied de papillon
Beinarbeit beim Butterflyschwimmstil
butterfly turn
viraje de mariposa
virage de papillon
Butterflywende
flip turn
vuelta de campana
virage-culbute
Wende

BACKSTROKE START
POSICIÓN DE SALIDA DE ESPALDA
DÉPART DE DOS
START BEIM RÜCKENSCHWIMMEN

BACKSTROKE
BRAZADA DE ESPALDA
NAGE SUR LE DOS
RÜCKENSCHWIMMEN

DIVING
SALTO
PLONGEON
KUNSTSPRINGEN

DIVING INSTALLATIONS
TORRE DE SALTOS
PLONGEOIR
SPRINGEINRICHTUNGEN

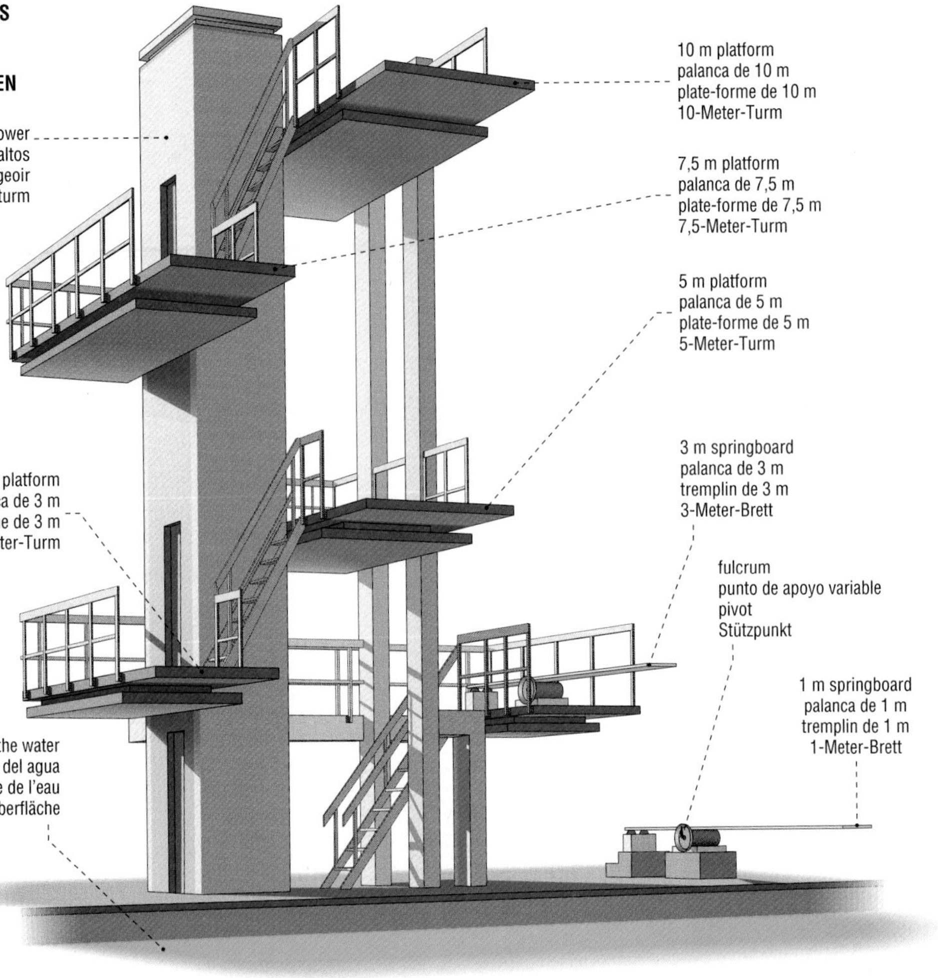

diving tower
torre de saltos
tour du plongeoir
Sprungturm

10 m platform
palanca de 10 m
plate-forme de 10 m
10-Meter-Turm

7,5 m platform
palanca de 7,5 m
plate-forme de 7,5 m
7,5-Meter-Turm

5 m platform
palanca de 5 m
plate-forme de 5 m
5-Meter-Turm

3 m platform
palanca de 3 m
plate-forme de 3 m
3-Meter-Turm

3 m springboard
palanca de 3 m
tremplin de 3 m
3-Meter-Brett

fulcrum
punto de apoyo variable
pivot
Stützpunkt

1 m springboard
palanca de 1 m
tremplin de 1 m
1-Meter-Brett

surface of the water
superficie del agua
surface de l'eau
Wasseroberfläche

STARTING POSITIONS
POSICIONES DE SALTO
POSITIONS DE DÉPART
STARTPOSITIONEN

forward
salto al frente
avant
vorwärts

backward
salto atrás
arrière
rückwärts

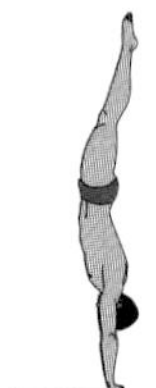

armstand
equilibrio
en équilibre
Handstand

FLIGHTS
SALTOS
VOLS
SPRUNGFIGUREN

pike position
posición B - hacer la carpa
position carpée
Hechtsprungstellung

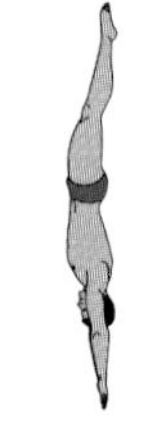

straight position
posición A - derecho
position droite
Bohrerstellung

tuck position
posición C - cuerpo encogido
position groupée
Saltostellung

ENTRIES
ENTRADAS AL AGUA
ENTRÉES DANS L'EAU
EINTAUCHSTELLUNGEN

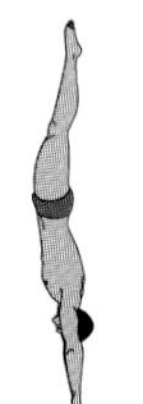

head-first entry
entrada de cabeza
entrée tête première
Kopf voraus

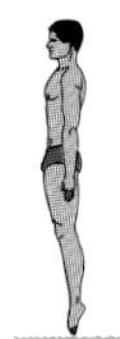

feet-first entry
entrada de pie
entrée pieds premiers
Füße voraus

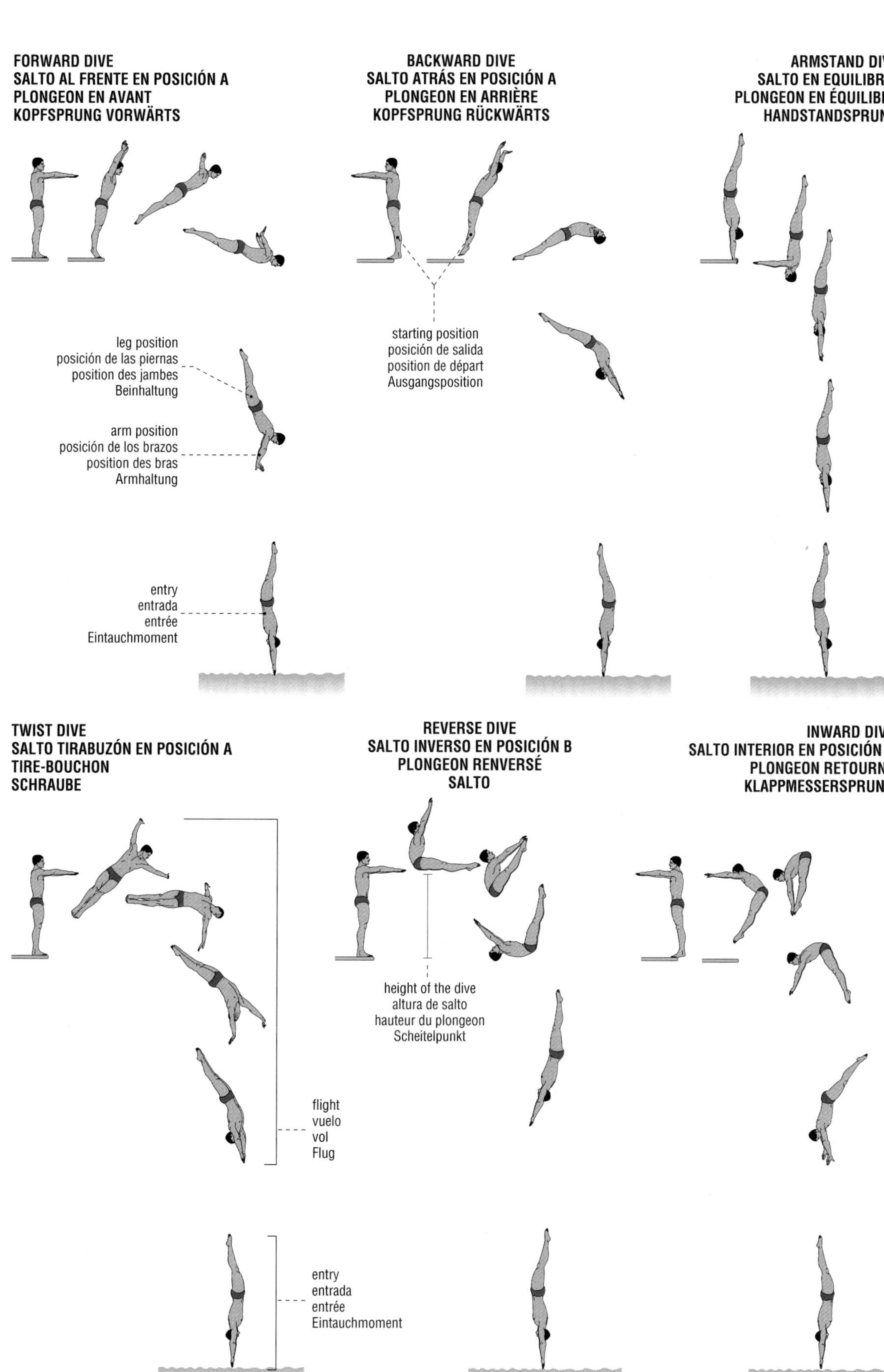
FORWARD DIVE
SALTO AL FRENTE EN POSICIÓN A
PLONGEON EN AVANT
KOPFSPRUNG VORWÄRTS
BACKWARD DIVE
SALTO ATRÁS EN POSICIÓN A
PLONGEON EN ARRIÈRE
KOPFSPRUNG RÜCKWÄRTS
ARMSTAND DIVE
SALTO EN EQUILIBRIO
PLONGEON EN ÉQUILIBRE
HANDSTANDSPRUNG
leg position
posición de las piernas
position des jambes
Beinhaltung
arm position
posición de los brazos
position des bras
Armhaltung
starting position
posición de salida
position de départ
Ausgangsposition
entry
entrada
entrée
Eintauchmoment
TWIST DIVE
SALTO TIRABUZÓN EN POSICIÓN A
TIRE-BOUCHON
SCHRAUBE
REVERSE DIVE
SALTO INVERSO EN POSICIÓN B
PLONGEON RENVERSÉ
SALTO
INWARD DIVE
SALTO INTERIOR EN POSICIÓN B
PLONGEON RETOURNÉ
KLAPPMESSERSPRUNG
height of the dive
altura de salto
hauteur du plongeon
Scheitelpunkt
flight
vuelo
vol
Flug
entry
entrada
entrée
Eintauchmoment

WATER POLO
WATERPOLO
WATER-POLO
WASSERBALLSPIEL

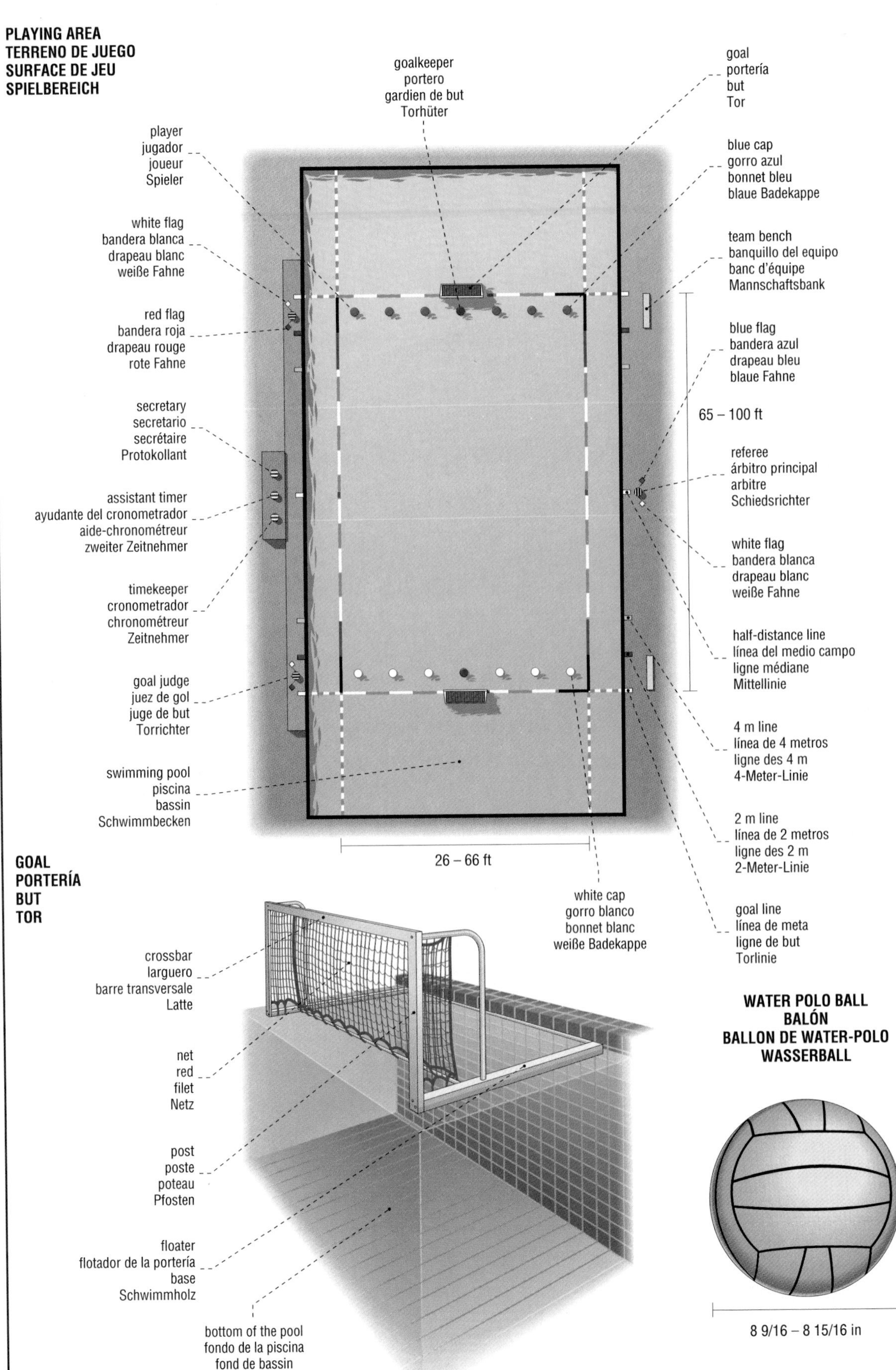
PLAYING AREA
TERRENO DE JUEGO
SURFACE DE JEU
SPIELBEREICH
goalkeeper
portero
gardien de but
Torhüter
goal
portería
but
Tor
player
jugador
joueur
Spieler
blue cap
gorro azul
bonnet bleu
blaue Badekappe
white flag
bandera blanca
drapeau blanc
weiße Fahne
team bench
banquillo del equipo
banc d'équipe
Mannschaftsbank
red flag
bandera roja
drapeau rouge
rote Fahne
blue flag
bandera azul
drapeau bleu
blaue Fahne
secretary
secretario
secrétaire
Protokollant
65 – 100 ft
referee
árbitro principal
arbitre
Schiedsrichter
assistant timer
ayudante del cronometrador
aide-chronométreur
zweiter Zeitnehmer
white flag
bandera blanca
drapeau blanc
weiße Fahne
timekeeper
cronometrador
chronométreur
Zeitnehmer
half-distance line
línea del medio campo
ligne médiane
Mittellinie
goal judge
juez de gol
juge de but
Torrichter
4 m line
línea de 4 metros
ligne des 4 m
4-Meter-Linie
swimming pool
piscina
bassin
Schwimmbecken
2 m line
línea de 2 metros
ligne des 2 m
2-Meter-Linie
26 – 66 ft
GOAL
PORTERÍA
BUT
TOR
white cap
gorro blanco
bonnet blanc
weiße Badekappe
goal line
línea de meta
ligne de but
Torlinie
crossbar
larguero
barre transversale
Latte
WATER POLO BALL
BALÓN
BALLON DE WATER-POLO
WASSERBALL
net
red
filet
Netz
post
poste
poteau
Pfosten
floater
flotador de la portería
base
Schwimmholz
bottom of the pool
fondo de la piscina
fond de bassin
Beckengrund
8 9/16 – 8 15/16 in

SCUBA DIVING
BUCEO
PLONGÉE SOUS-MARINE
TAUCHEN

SCUBA DIVER
BUCEADOR
PLONGEUR
TAUCHER

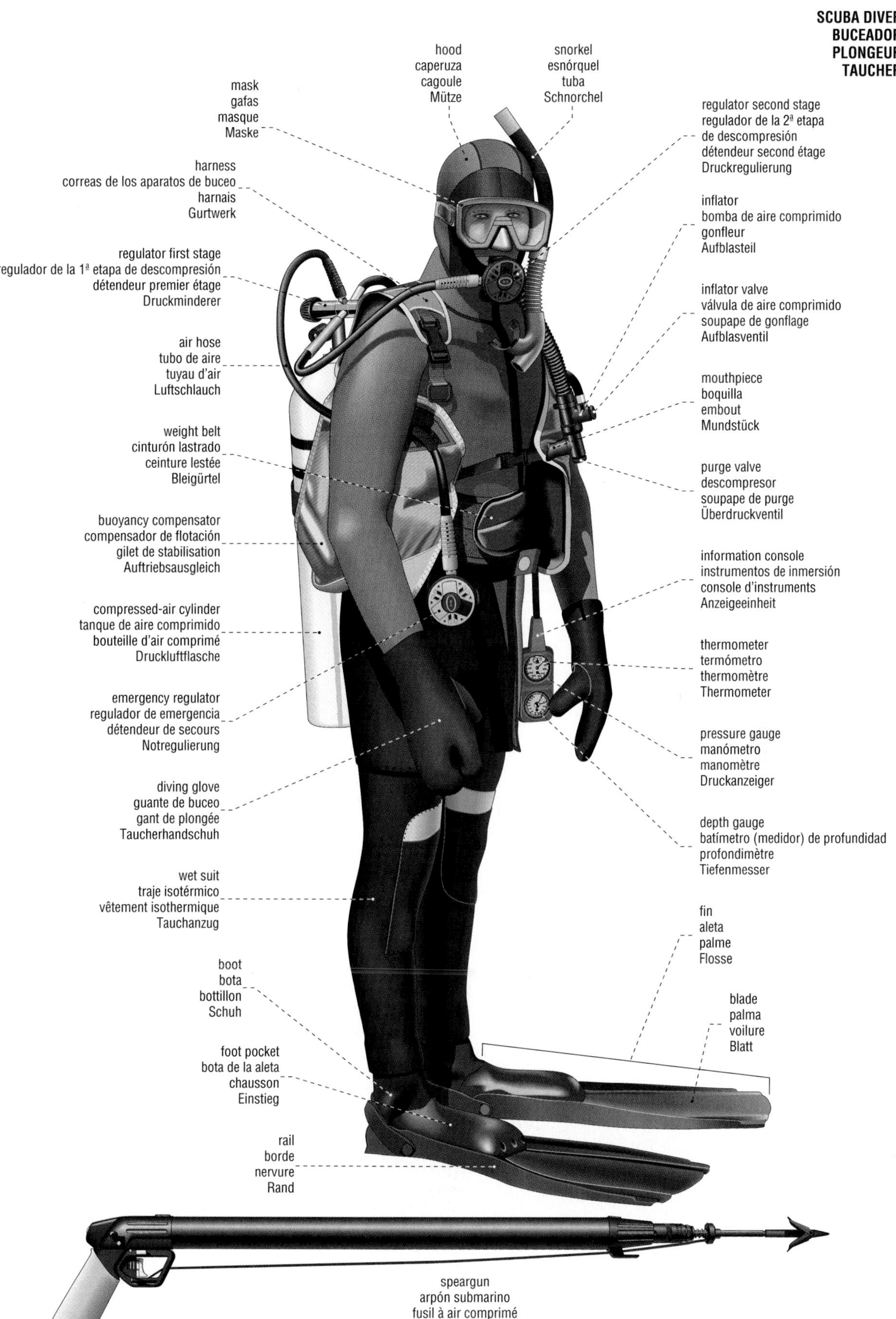
hood
caperuza
cagoule
Mütze
snorkel
esnórquel
tuba
Schnorchel
mask
gafas
masque
Maske
harness
correas de los aparatos de buceo
harnais
Gurtwerk
regulator first stage
regulador de la 1ª etapa de descompresión
détendeur premier étage
Druckminderer
air hose
tubo de aire
tuyau d'air
Luftschlauch
weight belt
cinturón lastrado
ceinture lestée
Bleigürtel
buoyancy compensator
compensador de flotación
gilet de stabilisation
Auftriebsausgleich
compressed-air cylinder
tanque de aire comprimido
bouteille d'air comprimé
Druckluftflasche
emergency regulator
regulador de emergencia
détendeur de secours
Notregulierung
diving glove
guante de buceo
gant de plongée
Taucherhandschuh
wet suit
traje isotérmico
vêtement isothermique
Tauchanzug
boot
bota
bottillon
Schuh
foot pocket
bota de la aleta
chausson
Einstieg
rail
borde
nervure
Rand
regulator second stage
regulador de la 2ª etapa
de descompresión
détendeur second étage
Druckregulierung
inflator
bomba de aire comprimido
gonfleur
Aufblasteil
inflator valve
válvula de aire comprimido
soupape de gonflage
Aufblasventil
mouthpiece
boquilla
embout
Mundstück
purge valve
descompresor
soupape de purge
Überdruckventil
information console
instrumentos de inmersión
console d'instruments
Anzeigeeinheit
thermometer
termómetro
thermomètre
Thermometer
pressure gauge
manómetro
manomètre
Druckanzeiger
depth gauge
batímetro (medidor) de profundidad
profondimètre
Tiefenmesser
fin
aleta
palme
Flosse
blade
palma
voilure
Blatt
speargun
arpón submarino
fusil à air comprimé
Harpune

SAILING
VELA
VOILE
SEGELSPORT

SAILBOAT
VELERO
DÉRIVEUR
SEGELBOOT

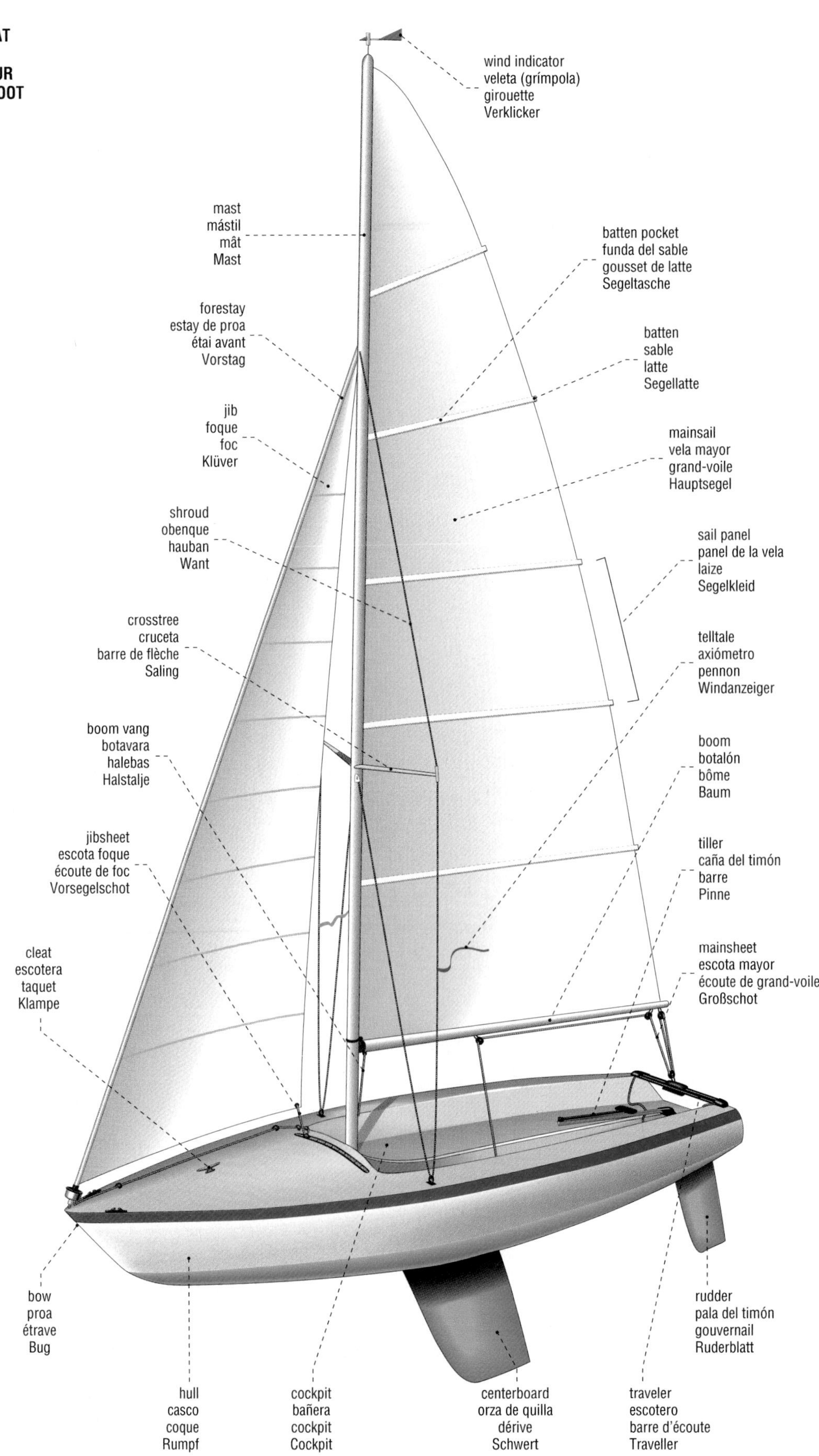

wind indicator
veleta (grímpola)
girouette
Verklicker
mast
mástil
mât
Mast
batten pocket
funda del sable
gousset de latte
Segeltasche
forestay
estay de proa
étai avant
Vorstag
batten
sable
latte
Segellatte
jib
foque
foc
Klüver
mainsail
vela mayor
grand-voile
Hauptsegel
shroud
obenque
hauban
Want
sail panel
panel de la vela
laize
Segelkleid
crosstree
cruceta
barre de flèche
Saling
telltale
axiómetro
pennon
Windanzeiger
boom vang
botavara
halebas
Halstalje
boom
botalón
bôme
Baum
jibsheet
escota foque
écoute de foc
Vorsegelschot
tiller
caña del timón
barre
Pinne
cleat
escotera
taquet
Klampe
mainsheet
escota mayor
écoute de grand-voile
Großschot
bow
proa
étrave
Bug
rudder
pala del timón
gouvernail
Ruderblatt
hull
casco
coque
Rumpf
cockpit
bañera
cockpit
Cockpit
centerboard
orza de quilla
dérive
Schwert
traveler
escotero
barre d'écoute
Traveller

POINTS OF SAILING
DISPOSICIONES DE LAS VELAS
ALLURES
KURSE

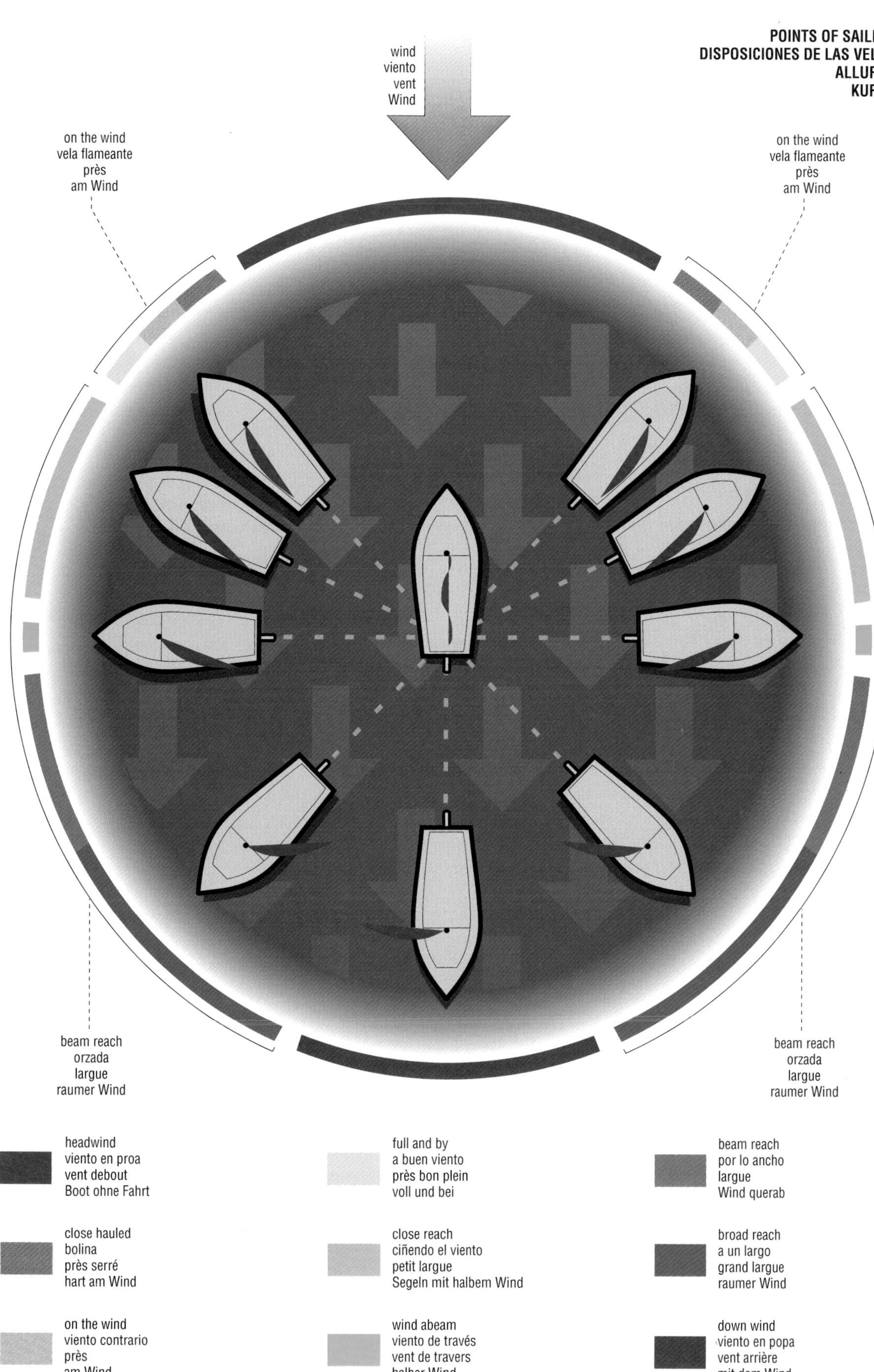
wind
viento
vent
Wind
on the wind
vela flameante
près
am Wind
on the wind
vela flameante
près
am Wind
beam reach
orzada
largue
raumer Wind
beam reach
orzada
largue
raumer Wind
headwind
viento en proa
vent debout
Boot ohne Fahrt
full and by
a buen viento
près bon plein
voll und bei
beam reach
por lo ancho
largue
Wind querab
close hauled
bolina
près serré
hart am Wind
close reach
ciñendo el viento
petit largue
Segeln mit halbem Wind
broad reach
a un largo
grand largue
raumer Wind
on the wind
viento contrario
près
am Wind
wind abeam
viento de través
vent de travers
halber Wind
down wind
viento en popa
vent arrière
mit dem Wind

SAILING
VELA
VOILE
SEGELSPORT

UPPERWORKS
OBRA MUERTA
ACCASTILLAGE
BESCHLÄGE

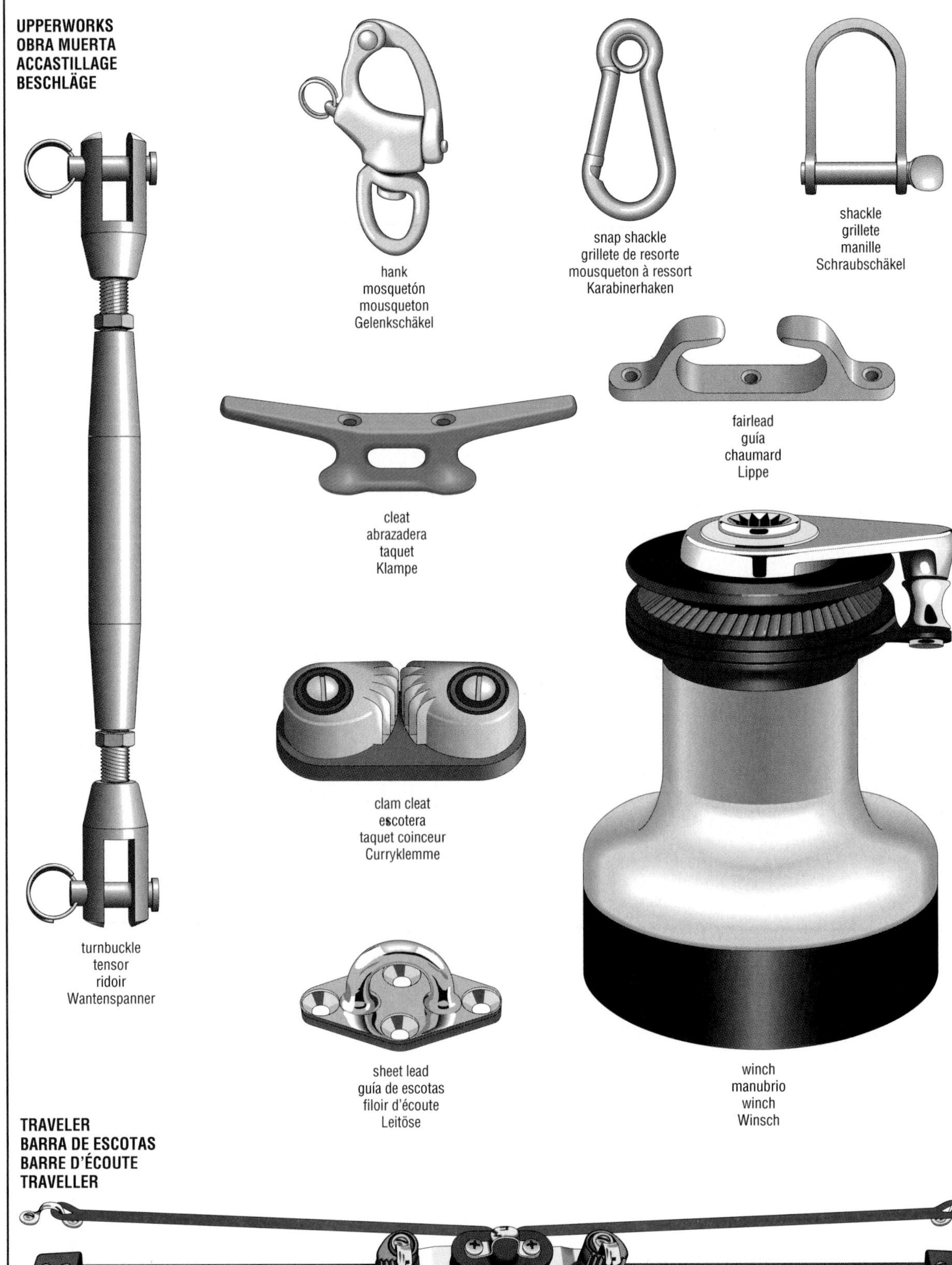
turnbuckle
tensor
ridoir
Wantenspanner
hank
mosquetón
mousqueton
Gelenkschäkel
snap shackle
grillete de resorte
mousqueton à ressort
Karabinerhaken
shackle
grillete
manille
Schraubschäkel
fairlead
guía
chaumard
Lippe
cleat
abrazadera
taquet
Klampe
clam cleat
escotera
taquet coinceur
Curryklemme
sheet lead
guía de escotas
filoir d'écoute
Leitöse
winch
manubrio
winch
Winsch
TRAVELER
BARRA DE ESCOTAS
BARRE D'ÉCOUTE
TRAVELLER
sliding rail
riel corredizo
rail de glissement
Schlitten
car
carro
chariot
Wagen
clam cleat
abrazadera
taquet coinceur
Curryklemme
end stop
amarre
butée
Anschlag

SAILBOARD
PLANCHA DE WINDSURF
PLANCHE À VOILE
SURFBRETT

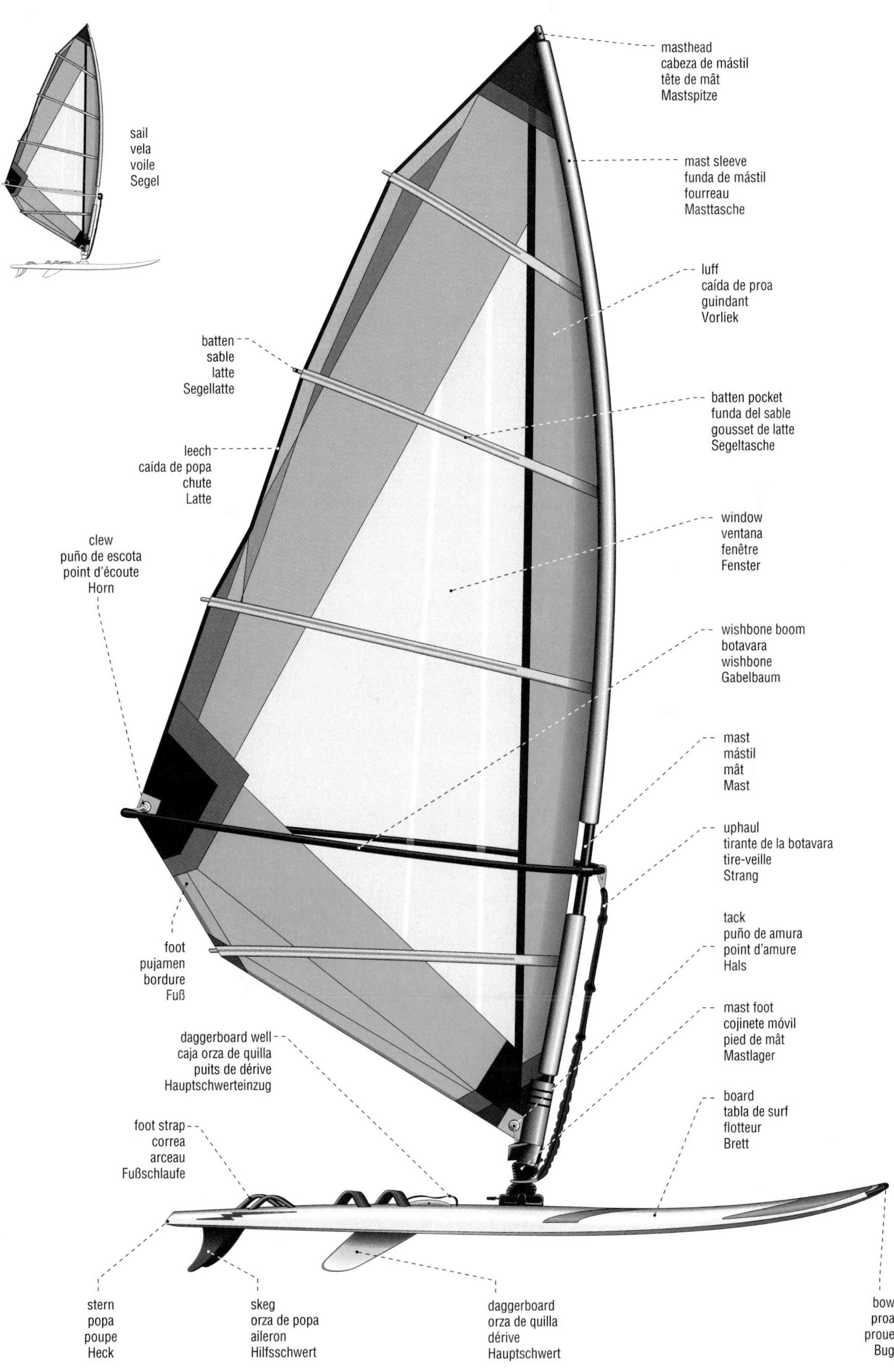
sail
vela
voile
Segel
masthead
cabeza de mástil
tête de mât
Mastspitze
mast sleeve
funda de mástil
fourreau
Masttasche
luff
caída de proa
guindant
Vorliek
batten
sable
latte
Segellatte
batten pocket
funda del sable
gousset de latte
Segeltasche
leech
caída de popa
chute
Latte
window
ventana
fenêtre
Fenster
clew
puño de escota
point d'écoute
Horn
wishbone boom
botavara
wishbone
Gabelbaum
mast
mástil
mât
Mast
uphaul
tirante de la botavara
tire-veille
Strang
foot
pujamen
bordure
Fuß
tack
puño de amura
point d'amure
Hals
daggerboard well
caja orza de quilla
puits de dérive
Hauptschwerteinzug
mast foot
cojinete móvil
pied de mât
Mastlager
foot strap
correa
arceau
Fußschlaufe
board
tabla de surf
flotteur
Brett
stern
popa
poupe
Heck
skeg
orza de popa
aileron
Hilfsschwert
daggerboard
orza de quilla
dérive
Hauptschwert
bow
proa
proue
Bug

ROWING AND SCULLING
REMO
AVIRON
RUDERN UND SKULLEN

SCULLING (TWO OARS)
SKIF
AVIRONS À COUPLE
SKULLEN (ZWEI SKULLS)
grip
guión
poignée
Griff
shaft
cuello del remo
manche
Schaft
oarlock
chumalera giratoria
dame de nage
Dolle
stop
tope
bourrelet
Anschlag
outrigger
arbotante
portant
Ausleger
leather sheath
luchadero
manchon
Belederung
ROWING (ONE OAR)
REMO
AVIRON EN POINTE
RUDERN (EIN RIEMEN)
TYPES OF OARS
TIPOS DE REMOS
TYPES D'AVIRONS
RIEMENARTEN
needle
cuello del remo
aviron de pointe
Nadelriemen
blade
pala
pelle
Blatt
SCULLING BOATS
SKIF
BATEAUX DE COUPLE
SKULLBOOTE
spade
timón
aviron de couple
Spatenriemen
single scull
skif unipersonal
skiff
Einer
double scull
skif doble
double-scull
Zweier
blade
pala
pelle
Blatt
ROWING BOATS
OUTRIGGERS
BATEAUX DE POINTE
RUDERBOOTE
coxless pair
el dos
deux sans barreur
Zweier ohne Steuermann
coxed pair
el dos con timonel
deux avec barreur
Zweier mit Steuermann
coxless four
el cuatro
quatre sans barreur
Vierer ohne Steuermann
coxed four
el cuatro con timonel
quatre avec barreur
Vierer mit Steuermann
eight
bote de a ocho (con timonel)
huit
Achter

WATER SKIING
ESQUÍ ACUÁTICO
SKI NAUTIQUE
WASSERSKI

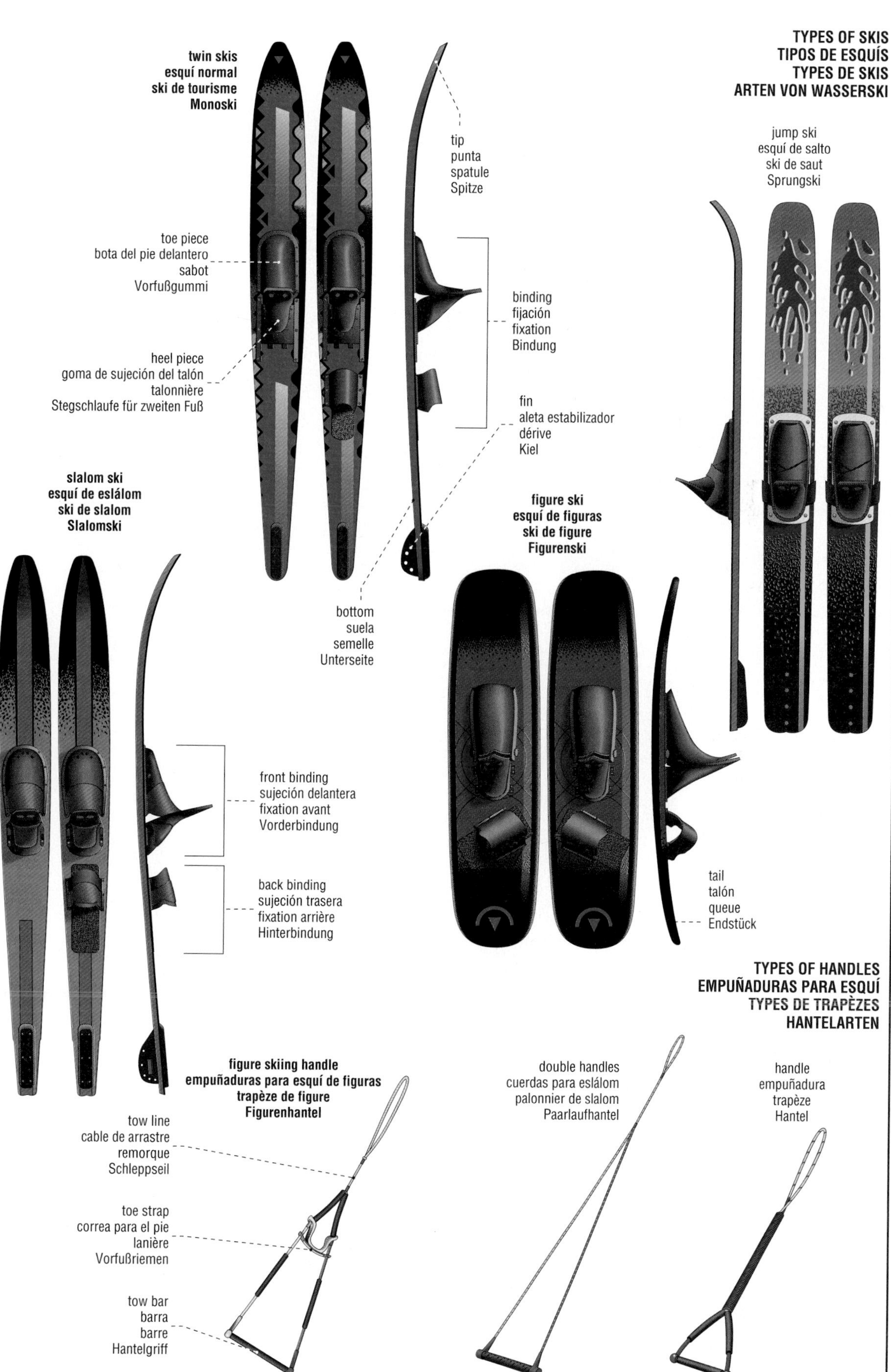

twin skis
esquí normal
ski de tourisme
Monoski
tip
punta
spatule
Spitze
toe piece
bota del pie delantero
sabot
Vorfußgummi
binding
fijación
fixation
Bindung
heel piece
goma de sujeción del talón
talonnière
Stegschlaufe für zweiten Fuß
fin
aleta estabilizador
dérive
Kiel
slalom ski
esquí de eslálom
ski de slalom
Slalomski
bottom
suela
semelle
Unterseite
figure ski
esquí de figuras
ski de figure
Figurenski
front binding
sujeción delantera
fixation avant
Vorderbindung
back binding
sujeción trasera
fixation arrière
Hinterbindung
tail
talón
queue
Endstück
TYPES OF SKIS
TIPOS DE ESQUÍS
TYPES DE SKIS
ARTEN VON WASSERSKI
jump ski
esquí de salto
ski de saut
Sprungski
TYPES OF HANDLES
EMPUÑADURAS PARA ESQUÍ
TYPES DE TRAPÈZES
HANTELARTEN
figure skiing handle
empuñaduras para esquí de figuras
trapèze de figure
Figurenhantel
tow line
cable de arrastre
remorque
Schleppseil
toe strap
correa para el pie
lanière
Vorfußriemen
tow bar
barra
barre
Hantelgriff
double handles
cuerdas para eslálom
palonnier de slalom
Paarlaufhantel
handle
empuñadura
trapèze
Hantel

BALLOONING
VUELO EN GLOBO
MONTGOLFIÈRE
FREIBALLONSPORT

BALLOON
GLOBO AEROSTÁTICO
BALLON
FREIBALLON

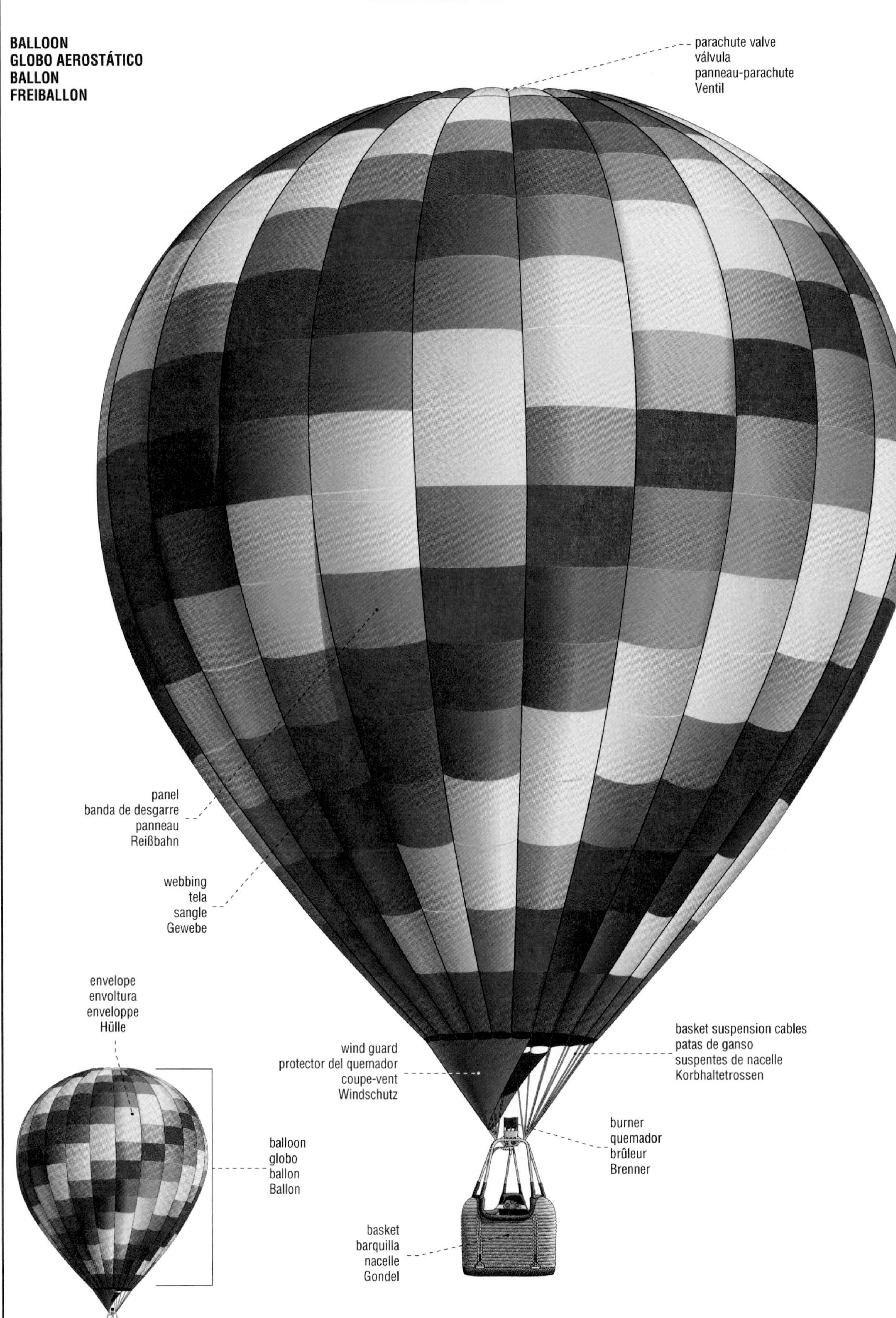
parachute valve
válvula
panneau-parachute
Ventil
panel
banda de desgarre
panneau
Reißbahn
webbing
tela
sangle
Gewebe
envelope
envoltura
enveloppe
Hülle
basket suspension cables
patas de ganso
suspentes de nacelle
Korbhaltetrossen
wind guard
protector del quemador
coupe-vent
Windschutz
burner
quemador
brûleur
Brenner
balloon
globo
ballon
Ballon
basket
barquilla
nacelle
Gondel

BASKET
BARQUILLA
NACELLE
GONDEL

burner
quemador
brûleur
Brenner
fuel lines
cañerías
flexibles d'alimentation
Treibstoffzufuhrleitungen
load support
armazón
cadre de charge
Korbtragerohr
variometer
varіómetro
variomètre
Variometer
altimeter
altímetro
altimètre
Höhenmesser
wicker basket
barquilla de mimbre
nacelle d'osier
Weidenkorb
hardwood base
suelo de madera
base en bois
Holzboden
heating coil
calentador
serpentin
Heizspirale
blast valve
válvula del quemador
soupape d'admission
Heizventil
flight instruments
instrumentos
instruments de vol
Bordinstrumente
thermometer
termómetro
thermomètre
Thermometer
padding
revestimiento
rembourrage
Polsterung
basket handle
asa de la barquilla
poignée de nacelle
Gondelhaltegriff

SKY DIVING
PARACAIDISMO
CHUTE LIBRE
FALLSCHIRMSPRINGEN

SKY DIVER
PARACAIDISTA
SAUTEUR
FALLSCHIRMSPRINGER

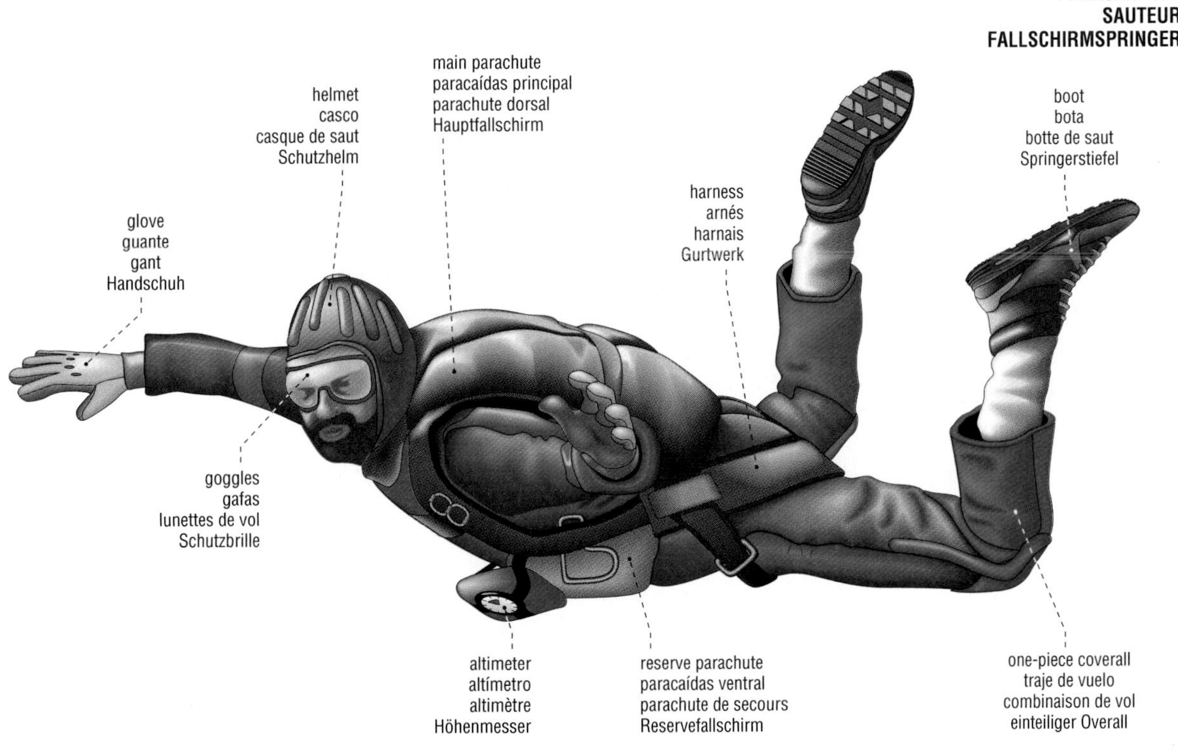
main parachute
paracaídas principal
parachute dorsal
Hauptfallschirm
helmet
casco
casque de saut
Schutzhelm
glove
guante
gant
Handschuh
harness
arnés
harnais
Gurtwerk
boot
bota
botte de saut
Springerstiefel
goggles
gafas
lunettes de vol
Schutzbrille
altimeter
altímetro
altimètre
Höhenmesser
reserve parachute
paracaídas ventral
parachute de secours
Reservefallschirm
one-piece coverall
traje de vuelo
combinaison de vol
einteiliger Overall

PARAGLIDING
PLANEADOR
PARAPENTE
GLEITSCHIRMFLIEGEN

CANOPY
CASQUETE
AILE
GLEITSCHIRM

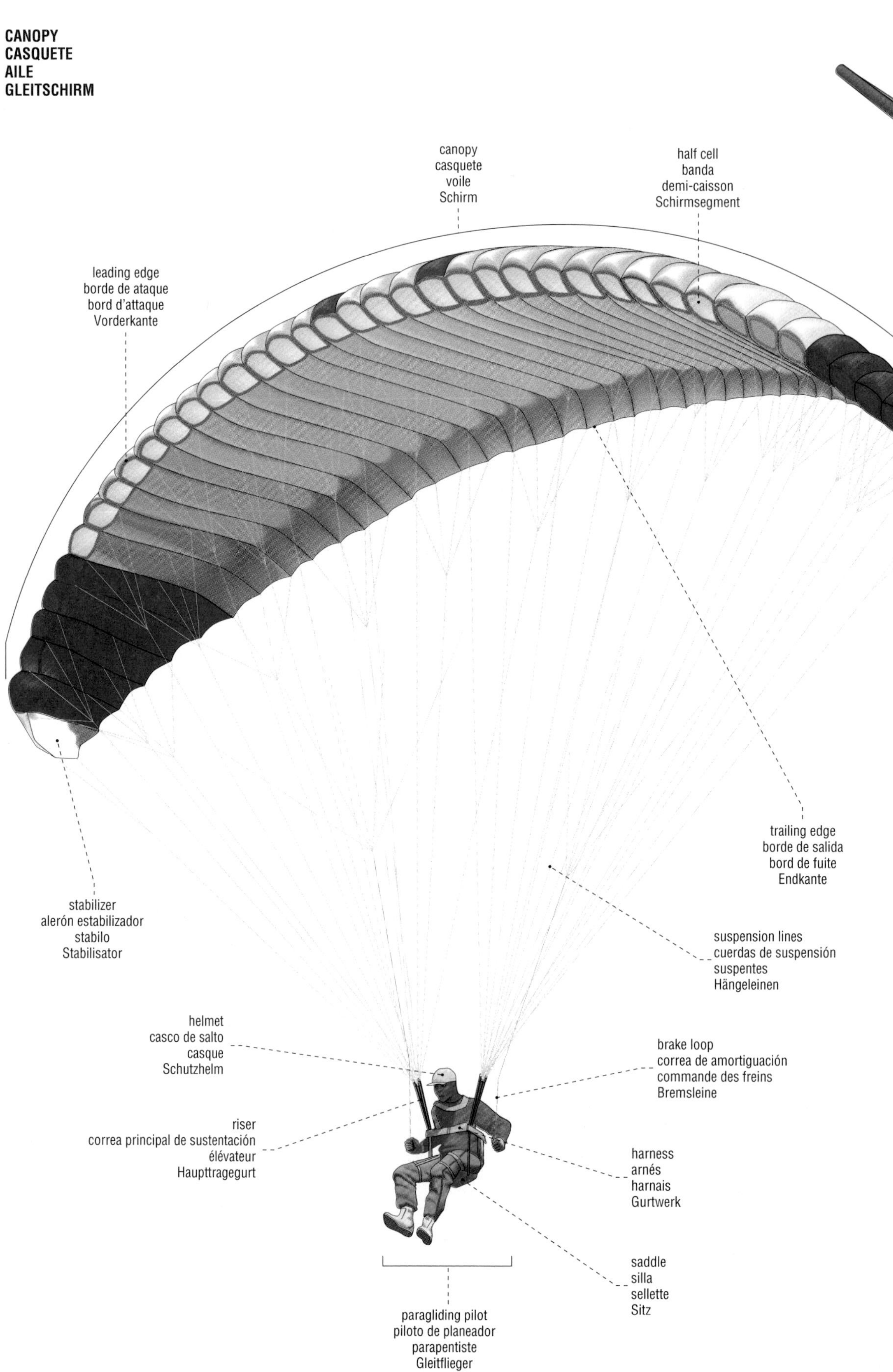
canopy
casquete
voile
Schirm
half cell
banda
demi-caisson
Schirmsegment
leading edge
borde de ataque
bord d'attaque
Vorderkante
trailing edge
borde de salida
bord de fuite
Endkante
stabilizer
alerón estabilizador
stabilo
Stabilisator
suspension lines
cuerdas de suspensión
suspentes
Hängeleinen
helmet
casco de salto
casque
Schutzhelm
brake loop
correa de amortiguación
commande des freins
Bremsleine
riser
correa principal de sustentación
élévateur
Haupttragegurt
harness
arnés
harnais
Gurtwerk
saddle
silla
sellette
Sitz
paragliding pilot
piloto de planeador
parapentiste
Gleitflieger

HANG GLIDING
VUELO LIBRE
VOL LIBRE
DRACHENFLIEGEN

HANG GLIDER
AERODESLIZADOR
AILE LIBRE
FLUGDRACHEN

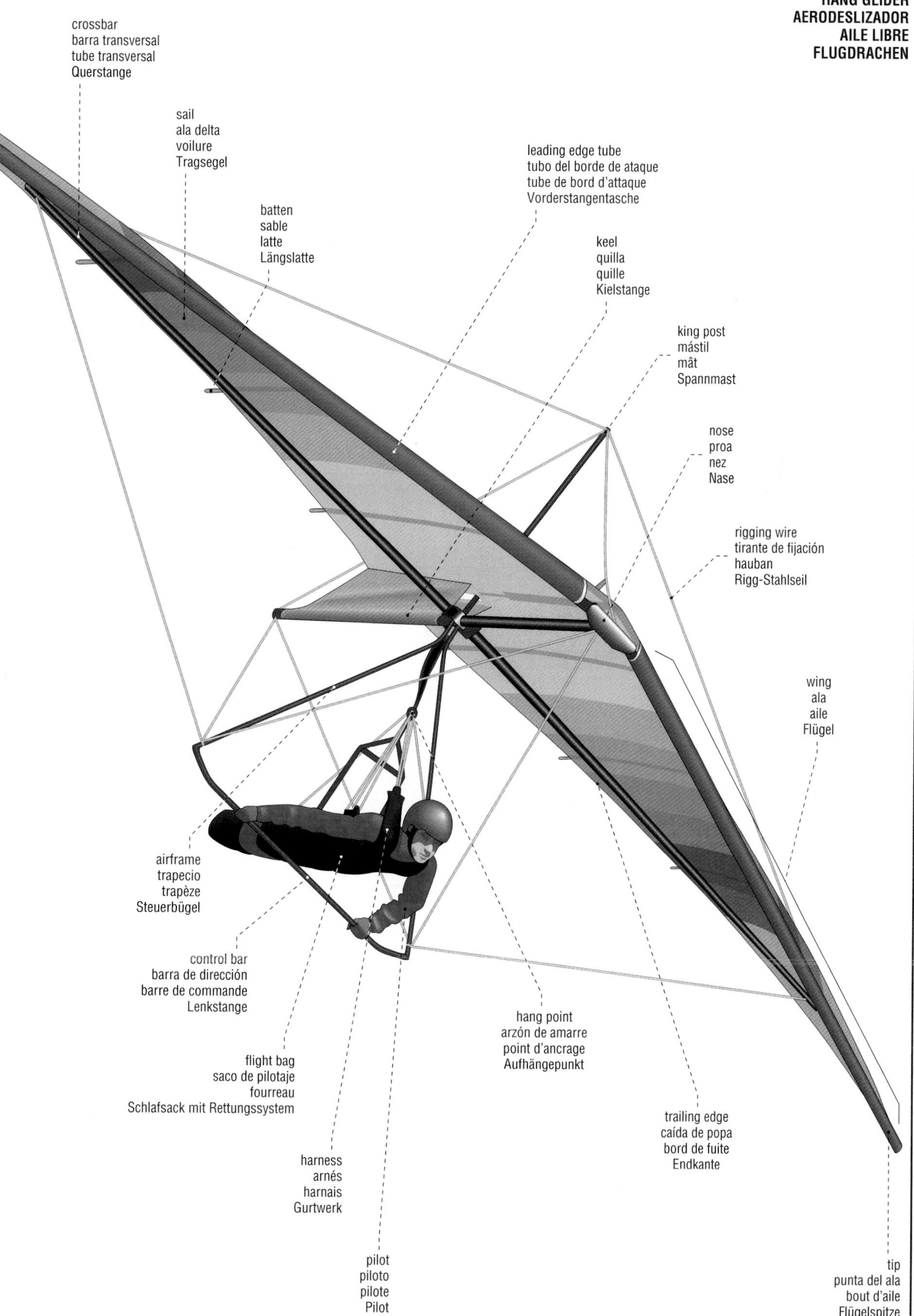

crossbar
barra transversal
tube transversal
Querstange
sail
ala delta
voilure
Tragsegel
batten
sable
latte
Längslatte
leading edge tube
tubo del borde de ataque
tube de bord d'attaque
Vorderstangentasche
keel
quilla
quille
Kielstange
king post
mástil
mât
Spannmast
nose
proa
nez
Nase
rigging wire
tirante de fijación
hauban
Rigg-Stahlseil
wing
ala
aile
Flügel
airframe
trapecio
trapèze
Steuerbügel
control bar
barra de dirección
barre de commande
Lenkstange
hang point
arzón de amarre
point d'ancrage
Aufhängepunkt
flight bag
saco de pilotaje
fourreau
Schlafsack mit Rettungssystem
trailing edge
caída de popa
bord de fuite
Endkante
harness
arnés
harnais
Gurtwerk
pilot
piloto
pilote
Pilot
tip
punta del ala
bout d'aile
Flügelspitze

GLIDING
VUELO SIN MOTOR
VOL À VOILE
SEGELFLIEGEN

GLIDER
PLANEADOR
PLANEUR
SEGELFLUGZEUG

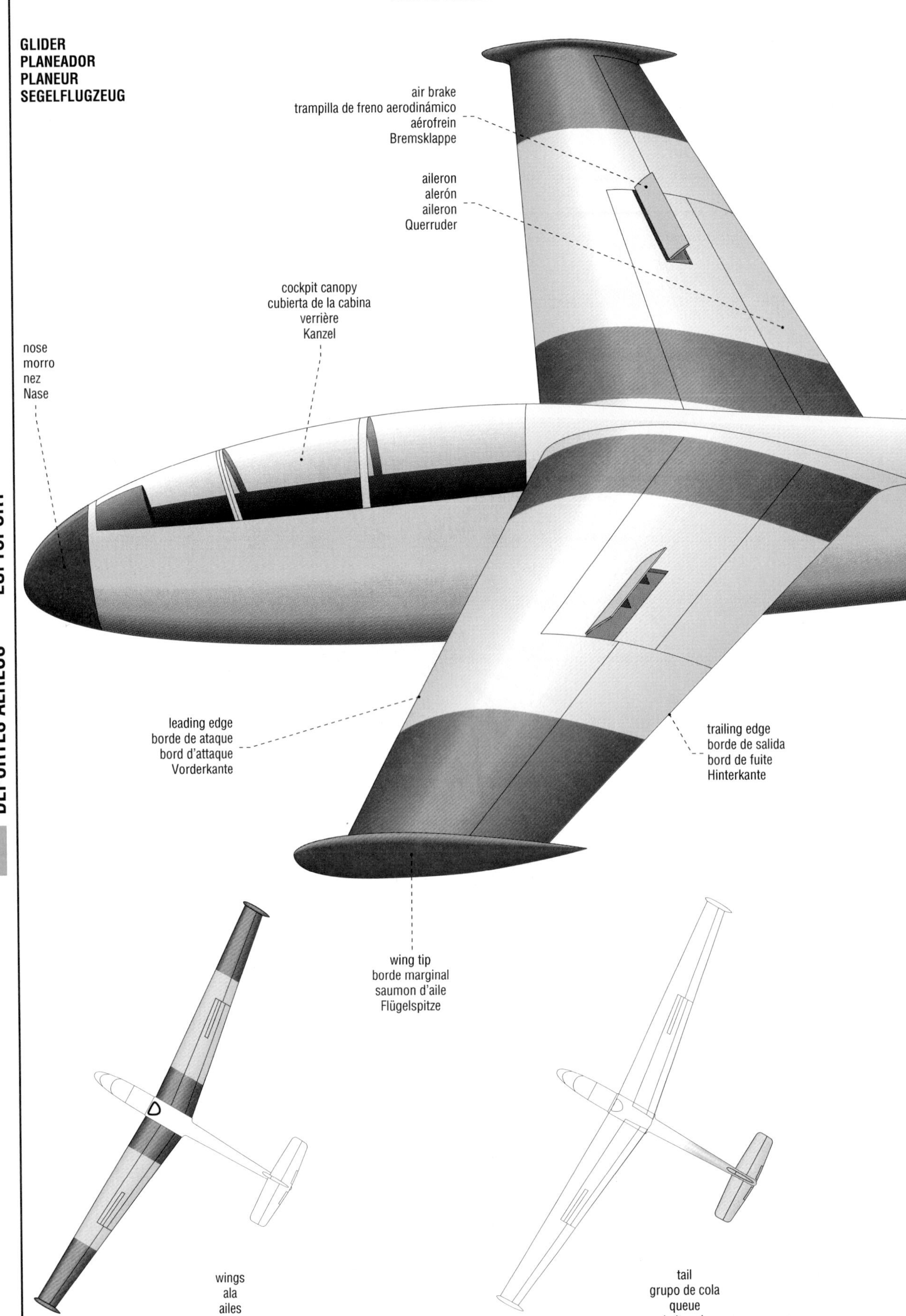
air brake
trampilla de freno aerodinámico
aérofrein
Bremsklappe
aileron
alerón
aileron
Querruder
cockpit canopy
cubierta de la cabina
verrière
Kanzel
nose
morro
nez
Nase
leading edge
borde de ataque
bord d'attaque
Vorderkante
trailing edge
borde de salida
bord de fuite
Hinterkante
wing tip
borde marginal
saumon d'aile
Flügelspitze
wings
ala
ailes
Flügel
tail
grupo de cola
queue
Leitwerk

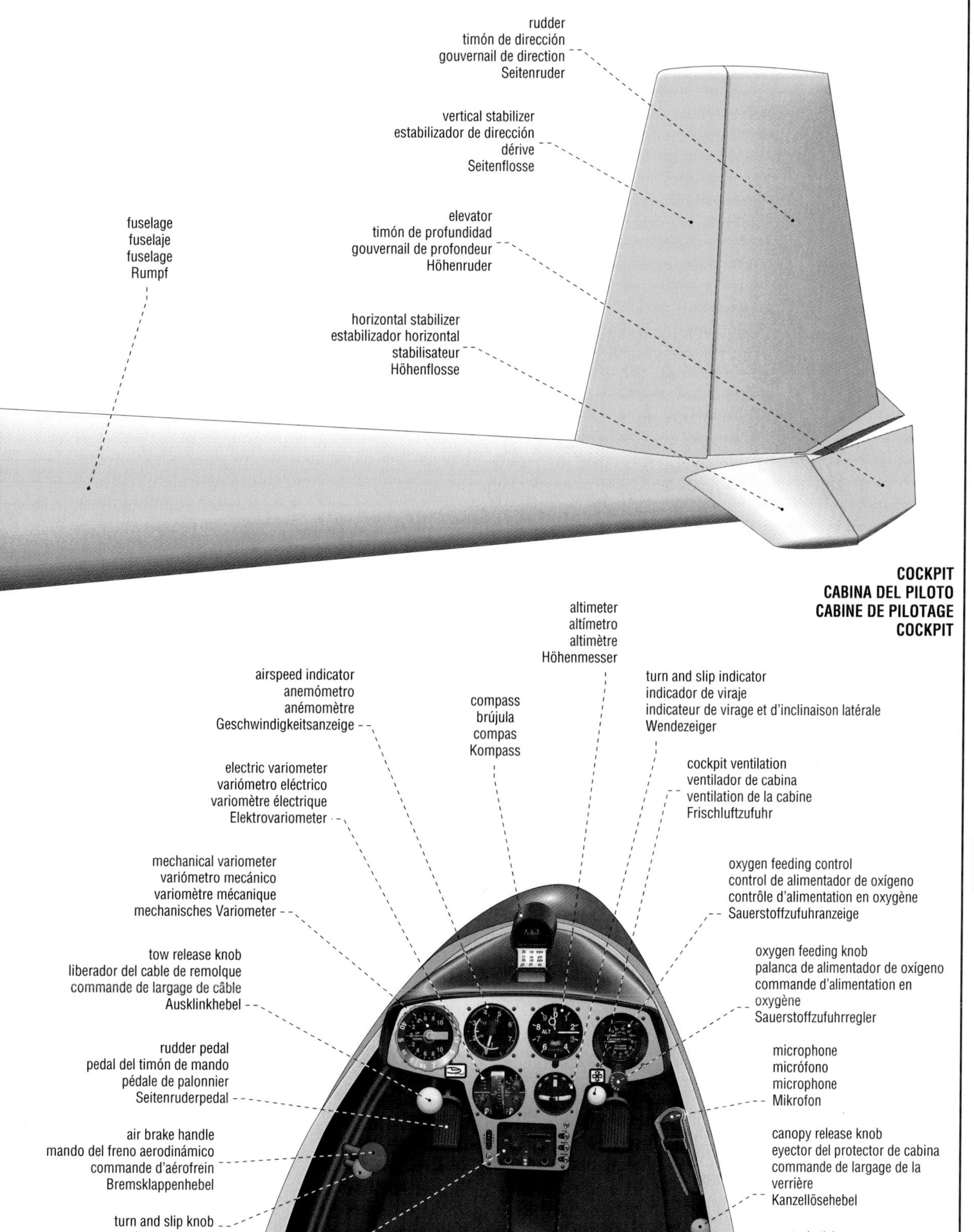
rudder
timón de dirección
gouvernail de direction
Seitenruder
vertical stabilizer
estabilizador de dirección
dérive
Seitenflosse
fuselage
fuselaje
fuselage
Rumpf
elevator
timón de profundidad
gouvernail de profondeur
Höhenruder
horizontal stabilizer
estabilizador horizontal
stabilisateur
Höhenflosse
altimeter
altímetro
altimètre
Höhenmesser
airspeed indicator
anemómetro
anémomètre
Geschwindigkeitsanzeige
compass
brújula
compas
Kompass
turn and slip indicator
indicador de viraje
indicateur de virage et d'inclinaison latérale
Wendezeiger
cockpit ventilation
ventilador de cabina
ventilation de la cabine
Frischluftzufuhr
electric variometer
variómetro eléctrico
variomètre électrique
Elektrovariometer
mechanical variometer
variómetro mecánico
variomètre mécanique
mechanisches Variometer
oxygen feeding control
control de alimentador de oxígeno
contrôle d'alimentation en oxygène
Sauerstoffzufuhranzeige
tow release knob
liberador del cable de remolque
commande de largage de câble
Ausklinkhebel
oxygen feeding knob
palanca de alimentador de oxígeno
commande d'alimentation en
oxygène
Sauerstoffzufuhrregler
rudder pedal
pedal del timón de mando
pédale de palonnier
Seitenruderpedal
microphone
micrófono
microphone
Mikrofon
air brake handle
mando del freno aerodinámico
commande d'aérofrein
Bremsklappenhebel
canopy release knob
eyector del protector de cabina
commande de largage de la
verrière
Kanzellösehebel
turn and slip knob
palanca de viraje
commande de virage et
d'inclinaison latérale
Wendehebel
control stick
palanca de mando
manche à balai
Steuerknüppel
radio
radio
radio
Fungerät
seat
asiento
siège
Sitz

COCKPIT
CABINA DEL PILOTO
CABINE DE PILOTAGE
COCKPIT

ALPINE SKIING
ESQUÍ ALPINO
SKI ALPIN
ALPINES SKILAUFEN

ALPINE SKIER
ESQUIADOR ALPINO
SKIEUR ALPIN
ALPINER SKILÄUFER

ski hat
gorro de esquí
bonnet
Skimütze
ski goggles
gafas de esquí
lunettes de ski
Skibrille
ski suit
trajepara esquiar
combinaison de ski
Skianzug
ski glove
guante de esquí
gant de ski
Skihandschuhe
handle
puño
poignée
Griff
wrist strap
correa para la mano
dragonne
Handschlaufe
ski pole
bastón de esquí
bâton de ski
Skistock
bottom
superficie de deslizamiento
semelle
Laufsohle
ski stop
freno del esquí
frein
Skibremse
shovel
pala
spatule
Schaufel
edge
canto
carre
Stahlkante
heel piece
pieza automática del talón
talonnière
Fersenstütze
ski boot
bota
chaussure de ski
Skistiefel
tip
punta
pointe
Spitze
toe piece
pieza de sujeción de la punta del pie
butée
Kopfautomatik

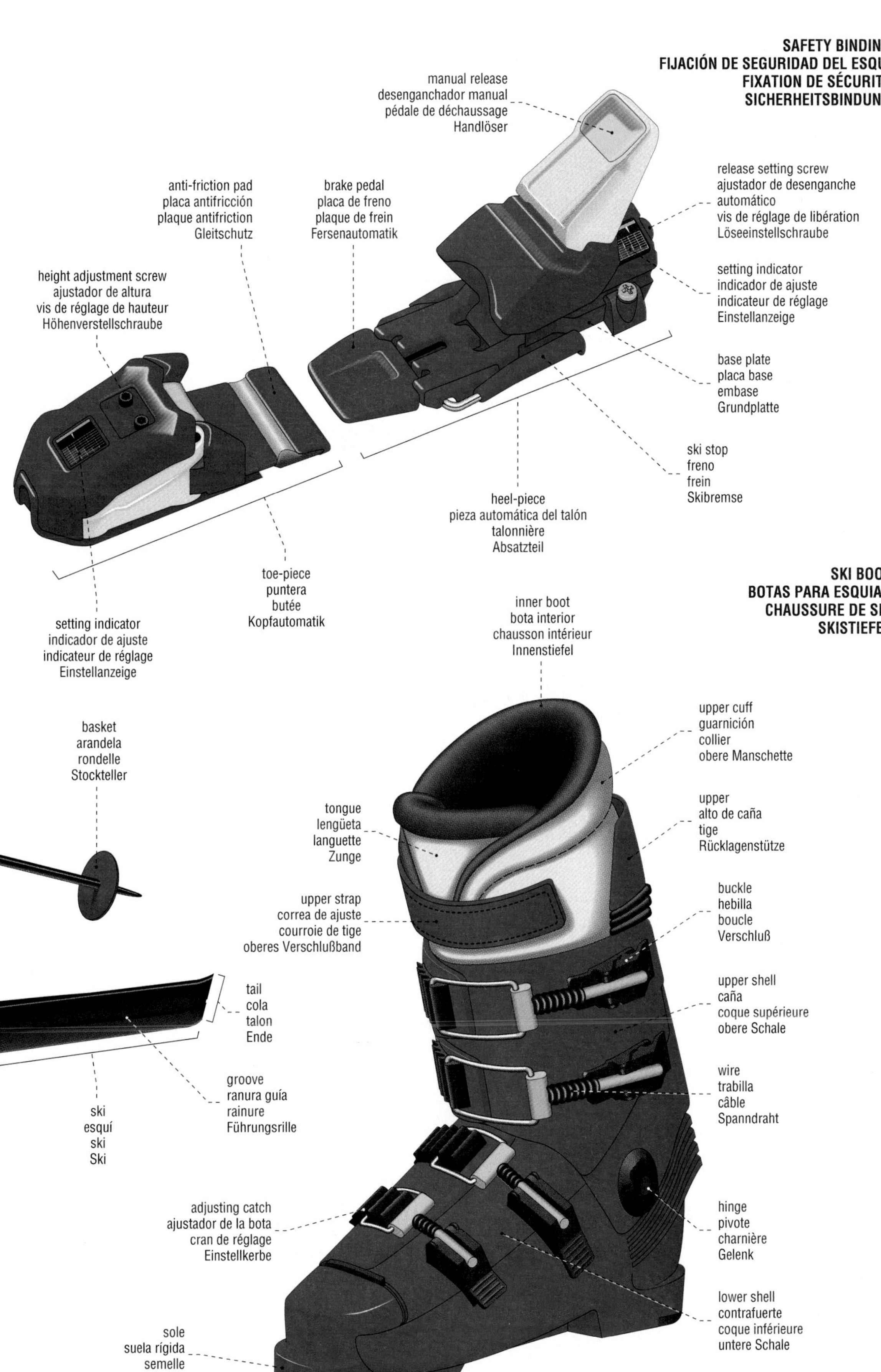
SAFETY BINDING
FIJACIÓN DE SEGURIDAD DEL ESQUÍ
FIXATION DE SÉCURITÉ
SICHERHEITSBINDUNG
manual release
desenganchador manual
pédale de déchaussage
Handlöser
release setting screw
ajustador de desenganche automático
vis de réglage de libération
Löseeinstellschraube
anti-friction pad
placa antifricción
plaque antifriction
Gleitschutz
brake pedal
placa de freno
plaque de frein
Fersenautomatik
height adjustment screw
ajustador de altura
vis de réglage de hauteur
Höhenverstellschraube
setting indicator
indicador de ajuste
indicateur de réglage
Einstellanzeige
base plate
placa base
embase
Grundplatte
ski stop
freno
frein
Skibremse
heel-piece
pieza automática del talón
talonnière
Absatzteil
toe-piece
puntera
butée
Kopfautomatik
setting indicator
indicador de ajuste
indicateur de réglage
Einstellanzeige
SKI BOOT
BOTAS PARA ESQUIAR
CHAUSSURE DE SKI
SKISTIEFEL
inner boot
bota interior
chausson intérieur
Innenstiefel
upper cuff
guarnición
collier
obere Manschette
basket
arandela
rondelle
Stockteller
tongue
lengüeta
languette
Zunge
upper
alto de caña
tige
Rücklagenstütze
upper strap
correa de ajuste
courroie de tige
oberes Verschlußband
buckle
hebilla
boucle
Verschluß
tail
cola
talon
Ende
upper shell
caña
coque supérieure
obere Schale
groove
ranura guía
rainure
Führungsrille
wire
trabilla
câble
Spanndraht
ski
esquí
ski
Ski
adjusting catch
ajustador de la bota
cran de réglage
Einstellkerbe
hinge
pivote
charnière
Gelenk
lower shell
contrafuerte
coque inférieure
untere Schale
sole
suela rígida
semelle
Sohle

CROSS-COUNTRY SKIING
ESQUÍ DE FONDO
SKI DE FOND
SKILANGLAUF

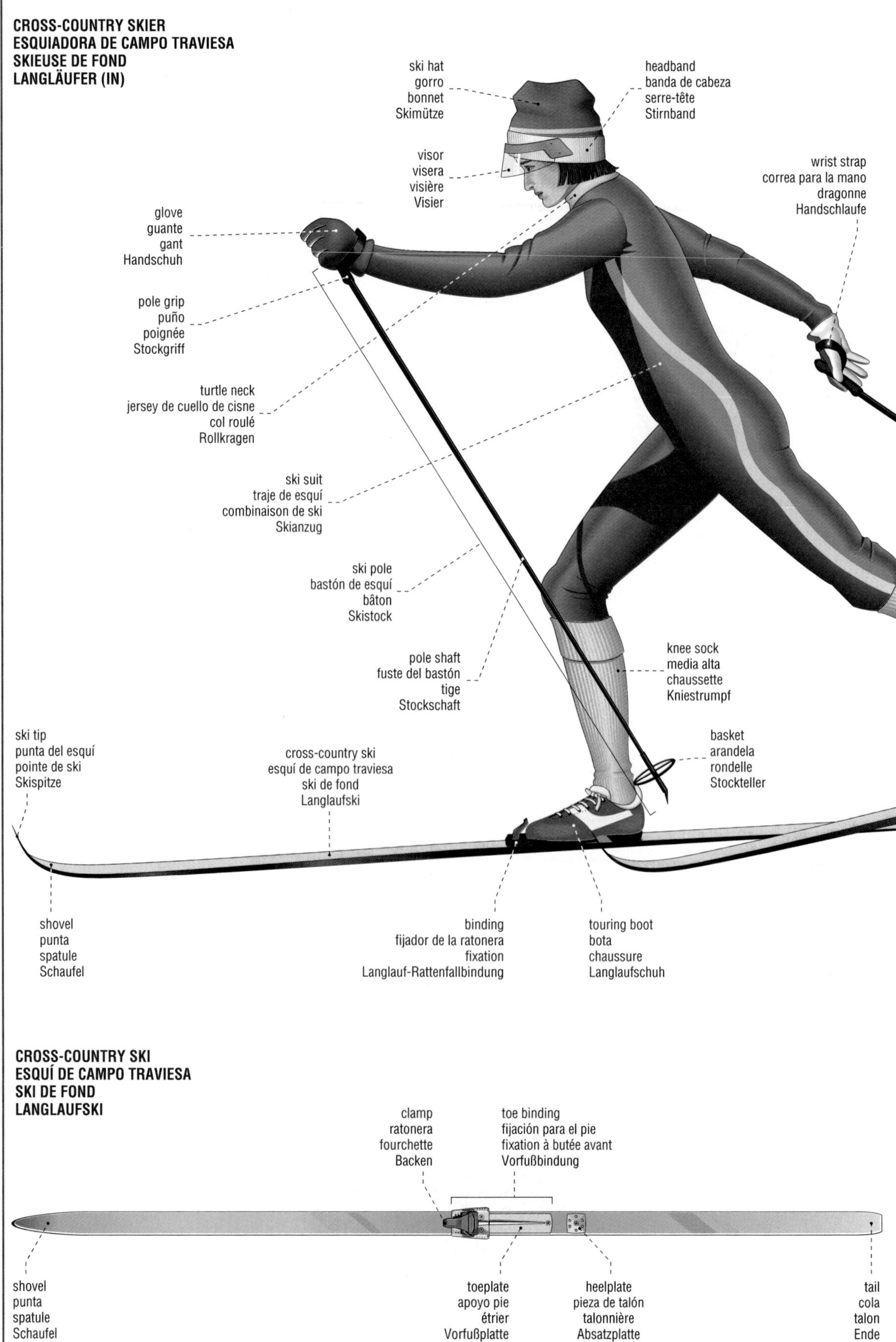
CROSS-COUNTRY SKIER
ESQUIADORA DE CAMPO TRAVIESA
SKIEUSE DE FOND
LANGLÄUFER (IN)
ski hat
gorro
bonnet
Skimütze
headband
banda de cabeza
serre-tête
Stirnband
visor
visera
visière
Visier
wrist strap
correa para la mano
dragonne
Handschlaufe
glove
guante
gant
Handschuh
pole grip
puño
poignée
Stockgriff
turtle neck
jersey de cuello de cisne
col roulé
Rollkragen
ski suit
traje de esquí
combinaison de ski
Skianzug
ski pole
bastón de esquí
bâton
Skistock
pole shaft
fuste del bastón
tige
Stockschaft
knee sock
media alta
chaussette
Kniestrumpf
basket
arandela
rondelle
Stockteller
ski tip
punta del esquí
pointe de ski
Skispitze
cross-country ski
esquí de campo traviesa
ski de fond
Langlaufski
shovel
punta
spatule
Schaufel
binding
fijador de la ratonera
fixation
Langlauf-Rattenfallbindung
touring boot
bota
chaussure
Langlaufschuh
CROSS-COUNTRY SKI
ESQUÍ DE CAMPO TRAVIESA
SKI DE FOND
LANGLAUFSKI
clamp
ratonera
fourchette
Backen
toe binding
fijación para el pie
fixation à butée avant
Vorfußbindung
shovel
punta
spatule
Schaufel
toeplate
apoyo pie
étrier
Vorfußplatte
heelplate
pieza de talón
talonnière
Absatzplatte
tail
cola
talon
Ende

LUGE
LUGE
LUGE
RENNRODEL

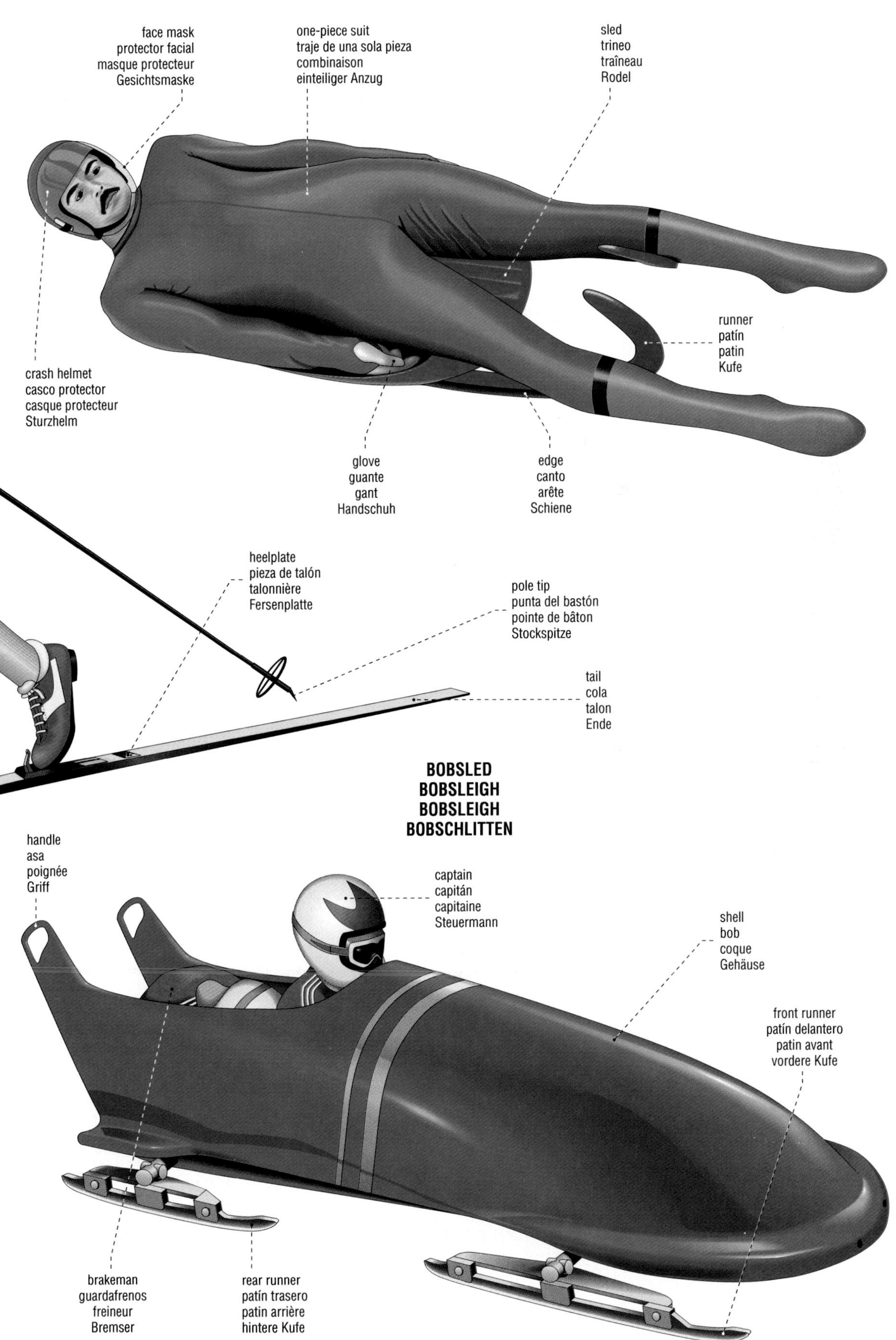
face mask
protector facial
masque protecteur
Gesichtsmaske
one-piece suit
traje de una sola pieza
combinaison
einteiliger Anzug
sled
trineo
traîneau
Rodel
runner
patín
patin
Kufe
crash helmet
casco protector
casque protecteur
Sturzhelm
glove
guante
gant
Handschuh
edge
canto
arête
Schiene
heelplate
pieza de talón
talonnière
Fersenplatte
pole tip
punta del bastón
pointe de bâton
Stockspitze
tail
cola
talon
Ende
BOBSLED
BOBSLEIGH
BOBSLEIGH
BOBSCHLITTEN
handle
asa
poignée
Griff
captain
capitán
capitaine
Steuermann
shell
bob
coque
Gehäuse
front runner
patín delantero
patin avant
vordere Kufe
brakeman
guardafrenos
freineur
Bremser
rear runner
patín trasero
patin arrière
hintere Kufe

SKATING
PATINAJE
PATINAGE
EISLAUFEN

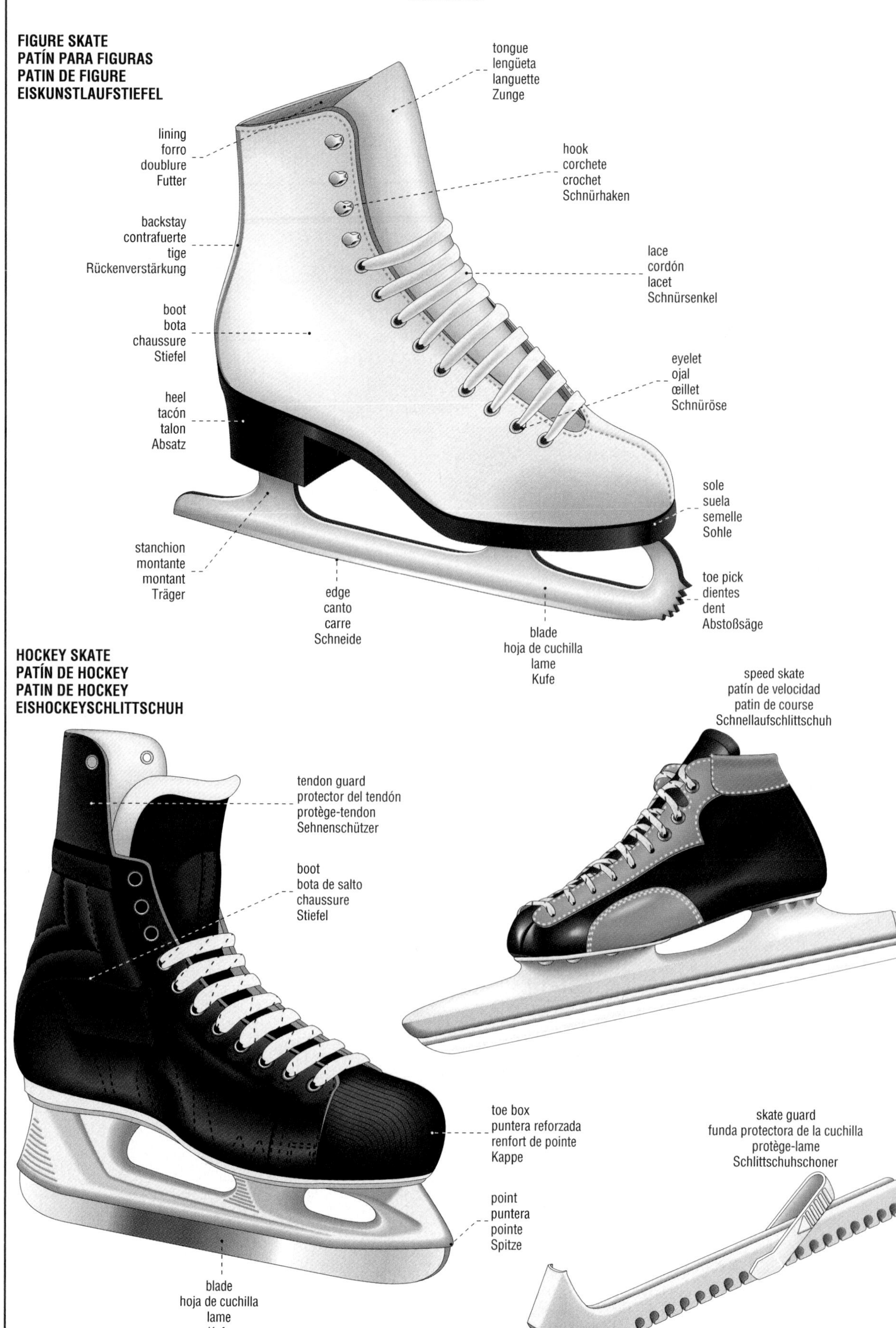
FIGURE SKATE
PATÍN PARA FIGURAS
PATIN DE FIGURE
EISKUNSTLAUFSTIEFEL
tongue
lengüeta
languette
Zunge
lining
forro
doublure
Futter
hook
corchete
crochet
Schnürhaken
backstay
contrafuerte
tige
Rückenverstärkung
lace
cordón
lacet
Schnürsenkel
boot
bota
chaussure
Stiefel
eyelet
ojal
œillet
Schnüröse
heel
tacón
talon
Absatz
sole
suela
semelle
Sohle
stanchion
montante
montant
Träger
toe pick
dientes
dent
Abstoßsäge
edge
canto
carre
Schneide
blade
hoja de cuchilla
lame
Kufe
HOCKEY SKATE
PATÍN DE HOCKEY
PATIN DE HOCKEY
EISHOCKEYSCHLITTSCHUH
speed skate
patín de velocidad
patin de course
Schnellaufschlittschuh
tendon guard
protector del tendón
protège-tendon
Sehnenschützer
boot
bota de salto
chaussure
Stiefel
toe box
puntera reforzada
renfort de pointe
Kappe
skate guard
funda protectora de la cuchilla
protège-lame
Schlittschuhschoner
point
puntera
pointe
Spitze
blade
hoja de cuchilla
lame
Kufe

SNOWSHOE
RAQUETA
RAQUETTE
SCHNEESCHUH

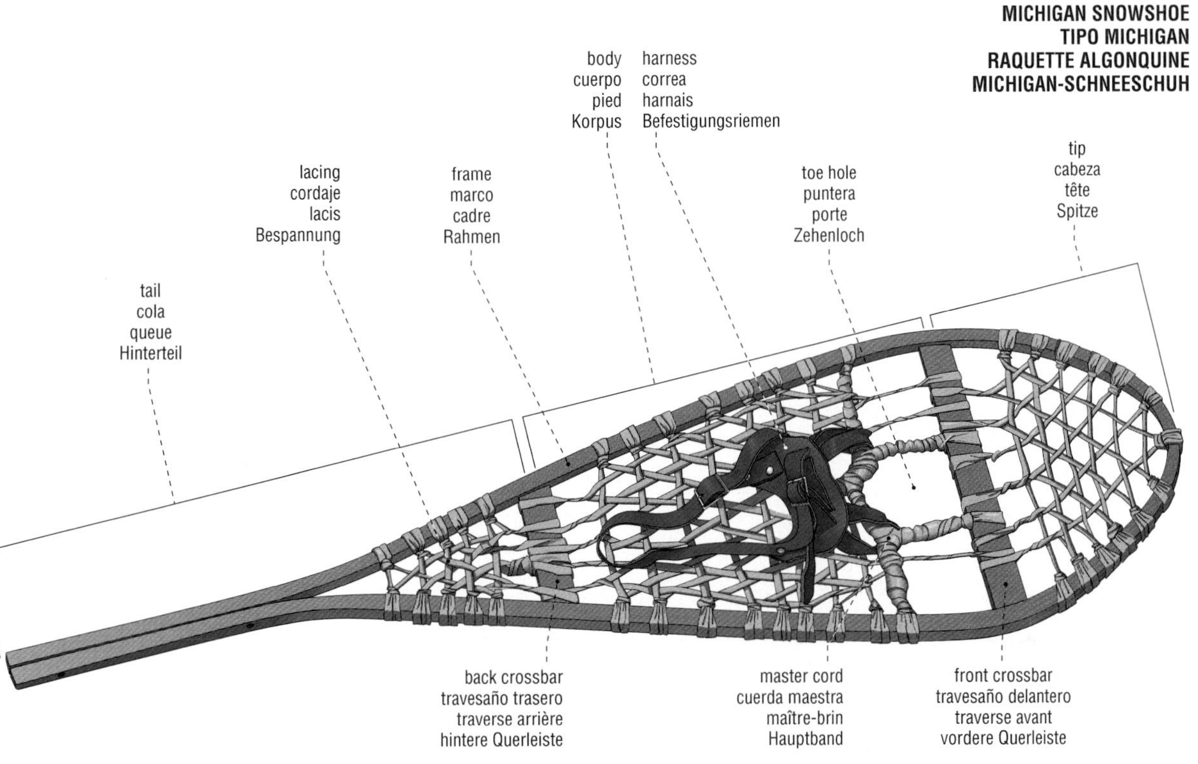

MICHIGAN SNOWSHOE
TIPO MICHIGAN
RAQUETTE ALGONQUINE
MICHIGAN-SCHNEESCHUH
body
cuerpo
pied
Korpus
harness
correa
harnais
Befestigungsriemen
lacing
cordaje
lacis
Bespannung
frame
marco
cadre
Rahmen
toe hole
puntera
porte
Zehenloch
tip
cabeza
tête
Spitze
tail
cola
queue
Hinterteil
back crossbar
travesaño trasero
traverse arrière
hintere Querleiste
master cord
cuerda maestra
maître-brin
Hauptband
front crossbar
travesaño delantero
traverse avant
vordere Querleiste

ROLLER SKATE
PATÍN DE RUEDAS
PATIN À ROULETTES
ROLLSCHUH

inner boot
bota interior
chausson intérieur
Innenstiefel
upper shell
caña
coque supérieure
Oberschale
adjusting buckle
hebilla de ajuste
boucle de réglage
Einstellspanner
boot
bota
chaussure
Stiefel
heel stop
freno trasero
frein de talon
Absatzstopper
wheel
rueda
roulette
Rolle
truck
bogie
bloc-essieu
Wagen
axle
eje
essieu
Achse

RIDING
EQUITACIÓN: CONCURSO DE SALTOS
ÉQUITATION
REITEN

COMPETITION RING
PISTA PARA PRUEBA DE OBSTÁCULOS
PARCOURS D'OBSTACLES
WETTKAMPFPARCOURS

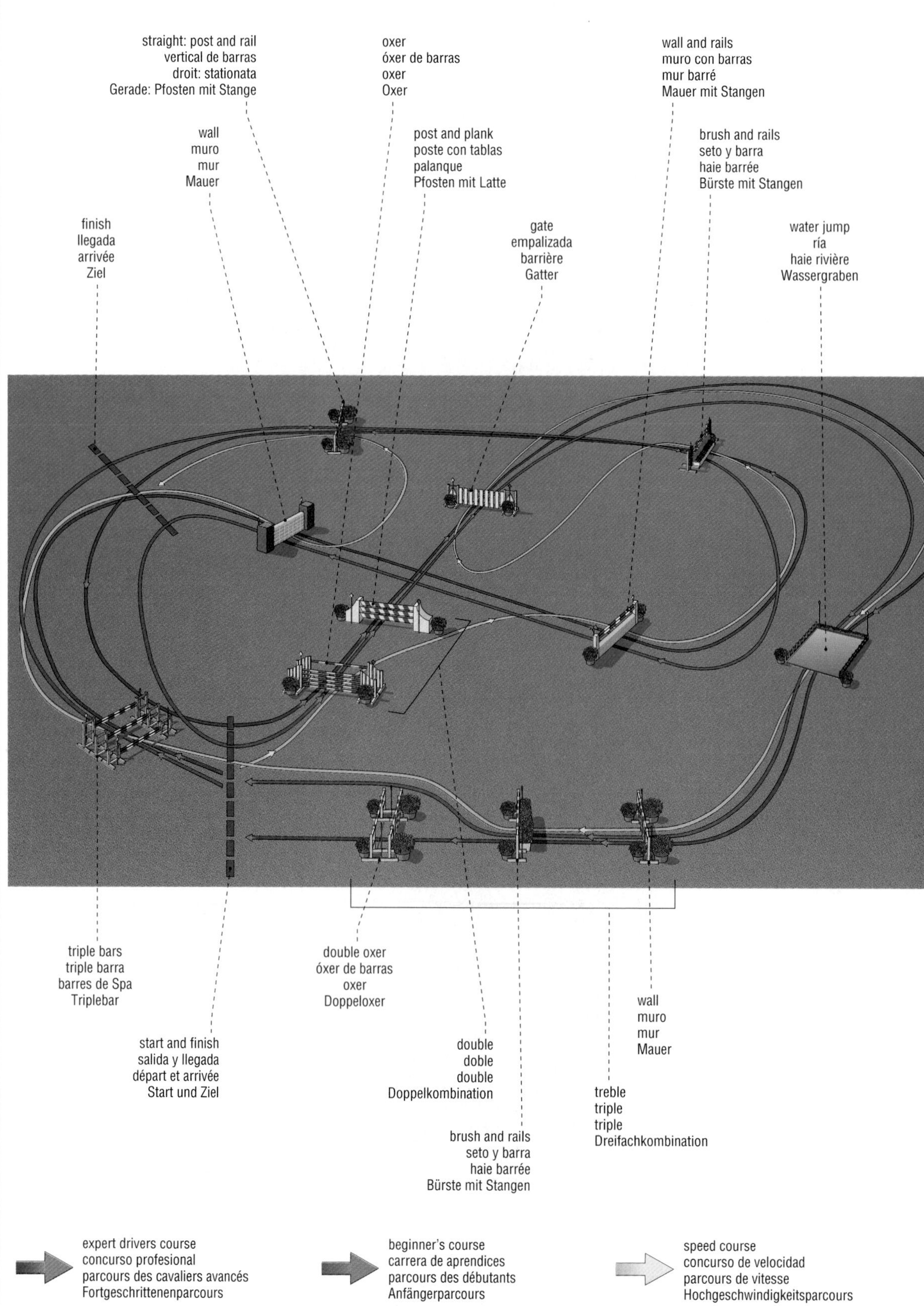
straight: post and rail
vertical de barras
droit: stationata
Gerade: Pfosten mit Stange
oxer
óxer de barras
oxer
Oxer
wall and rails
muro con barras
mur barré
Mauer mit Stangen
wall
muro
mur
Mauer
post and plank
poste con tablas
palanque
Pfosten mit Latte
brush and rails
seto y barra
haie barrée
Bürste mit Stangen
finish
llegada
arrivée
Ziel
gate
empalizada
barrière
Gatter
water jump
ría
haie rivière
Wassergraben
triple bars
triple barra
barres de Spa
Triplebar
double oxer
óxer de barras
oxer
Doppeloxer
wall
muro
mur
Mauer
start and finish
salida y llegada
départ et arrivée
Start und Ziel
double
doble
double
Doppelkombination
treble
triple
triple
Dreifachkombination
brush and rails
seto y barra
haie barrée
Bürste mit Stangen
expert drivers course
concurso profesional
parcours des cavaliers avancés
Fortgeschrittenenparcours
beginner's course
carrera de aprendices
parcours des débutants
Anfängerparcours
speed course
concurso de velocidad
parcours de vitesse
Hochgeschwindigkeitsparcours

OBSTACLES
OBSTÁCULOS
OBSTACLES
HÜRDEN

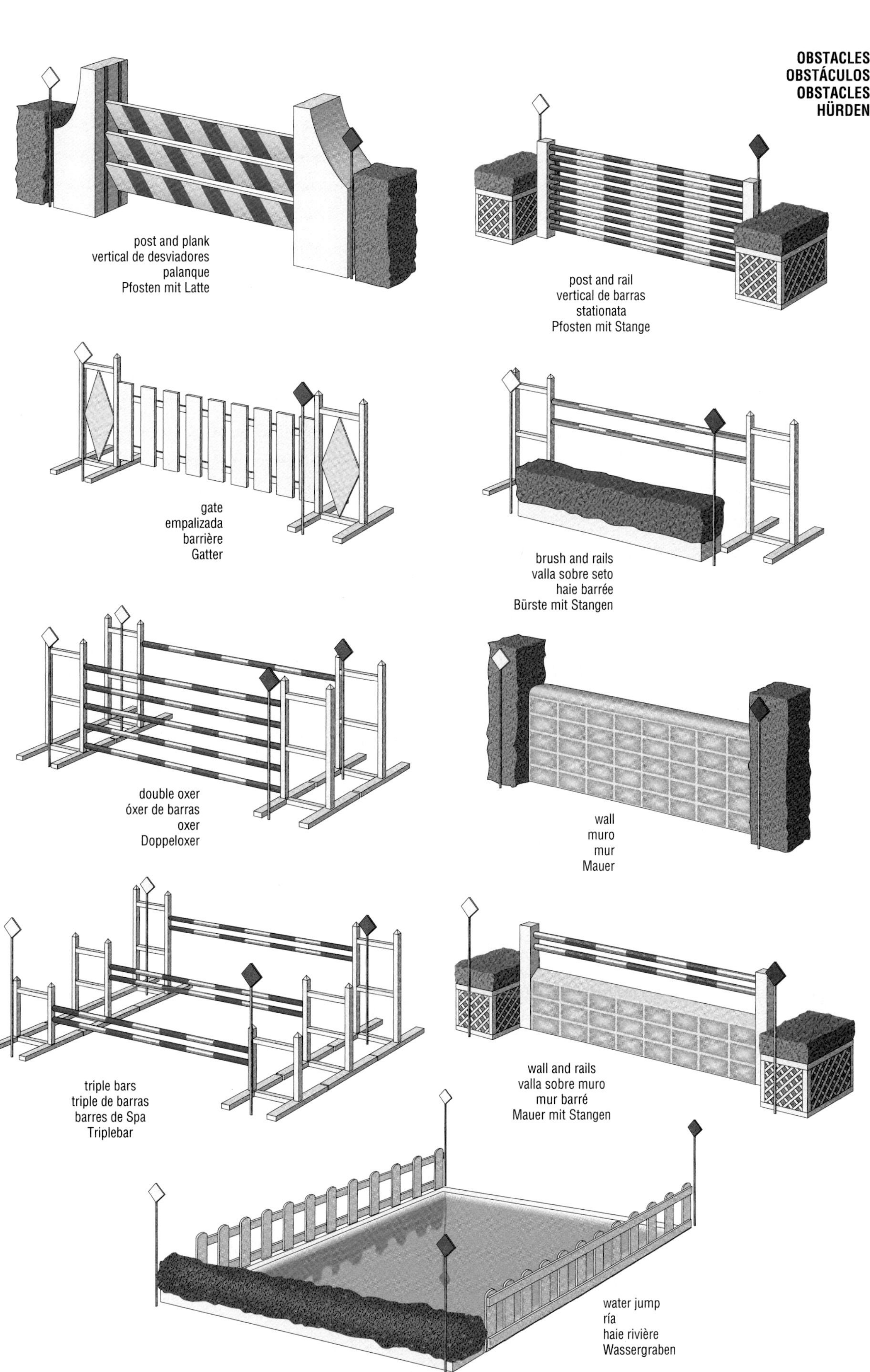
post and plank
vertical de desviadores
palanque
Pfosten mit Latte
post and rail
vertical de barras
stationata
Pfosten mit Stange
gate
empalizada
barrière
Gatter
brush and rails
valla sobre seto
haie barrée
Bürste mit Stangen
double oxer
óxer de barras
oxer
Doppeloxer
wall
muro
mur
Mauer
triple bars
triple de barras
barres de Spa
Triplebar
wall and rails
valla sobre muro
mur barré
Mauer mit Stangen
water jump
ría
haie rivière
Wassergraben

RIDING
EQUITACIÓN
ÉQUITATION
REITEN

RIDER
JINETE
CAVALIER
REITER

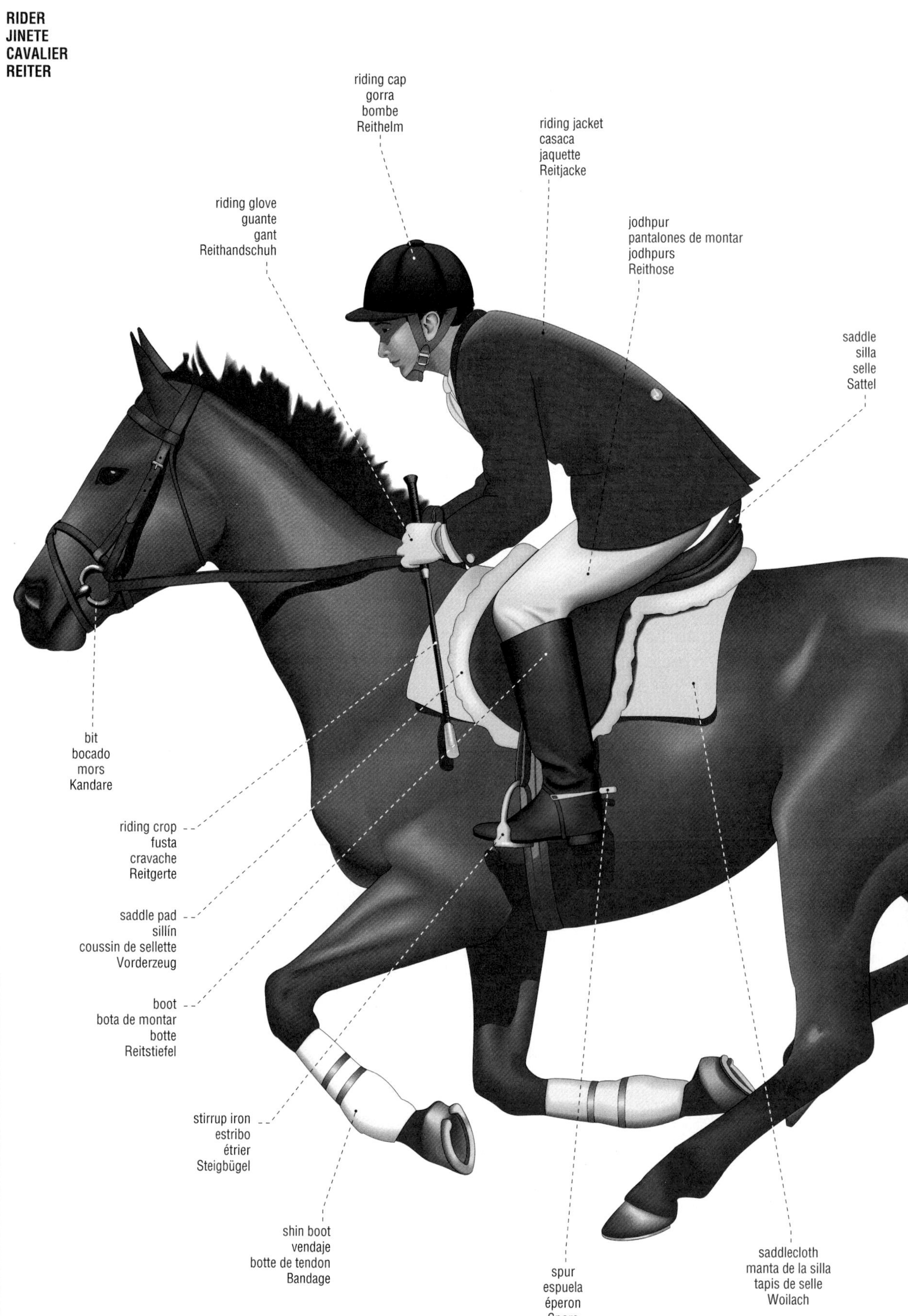
riding cap
gorra
bombe
Reithelm
riding jacket
casaca
jaquette
Reitjacke
riding glove
guante
gant
Reithandschuh
jodhpur
pantalones de montar
jodhpurs
Reithose
saddle
silla
selle
Sattel
bit
bocado
mors
Kandare
riding crop
fusta
cravache
Reitgerte
saddle pad
sillín
coussin de sellette
Vorderzeug
boot
bota de montar
botte
Reitstiefel
stirrup iron
estribo
étrier
Steigbügel
shin boot
vendaje
botte de tendon
Bandage
spur
espuela
éperon
Spore
saddlecloth
manta de la silla
tapis de selle
Woilach

SADDLE
SILLA DE MONTAR
SELLE
SATTEL

BRIDLE
BRIDA
BRIDE
ZAUMZEUG

pommel
borrén
pommeau
Vorderzwiesel
tree
arzón
arcade
Baum
seat
sillín
siège
Sitz
skirt
faldoncillo
petit quartier
Schnallenabdeckung
knee roll
rodillera
faux quartier
Schweißblatt
tab
latiguillo
contre-sanglon
Gurtstrippe
girth
cincha
sangle
Sattelgurt
girth strap
correa de la cincha
sanglon
Gurtschnalle
tread
hondón
plancher
Trittfläche
cantle
borrén trasero
troussequin
Hinterzwiesel
panel
forro
matelassure
Sattelpolster
flap
hoja del faldón lateral
quartier
Pausche
stirrup leather
correa
étrivière
Bügelriemen
eye
ojo
œil
Auge
branch
aro
branche
Bügel
browband
frontalera
frontal
Stirnriemen
cheek strap
trabilla
montant de bride
Backenriemen
snaffle strap
quijera
montant de filet
Gebißriemen
noseband
muserola
muserolle
Nasenriemen
curb bit
cambocadura
mors de bride
Kandare
curb chain
freno
gourmette
Kandarenkette
crownpiece
cabezada
têtière
Genickstück
throat latch
ahogadero
sous-gorge
Kehlriemen
snaffle rein
rienda del freno
rêne de filet
Trensenzügel
curb rein
rienda del bocado
rêne de bride
Kandarenzügel
snaffle bit
barbada
mors de filet
Trense

TYPES OF BITS
BOCADOS
TYPES DE MORS
GEBISSTÜCKARTEN

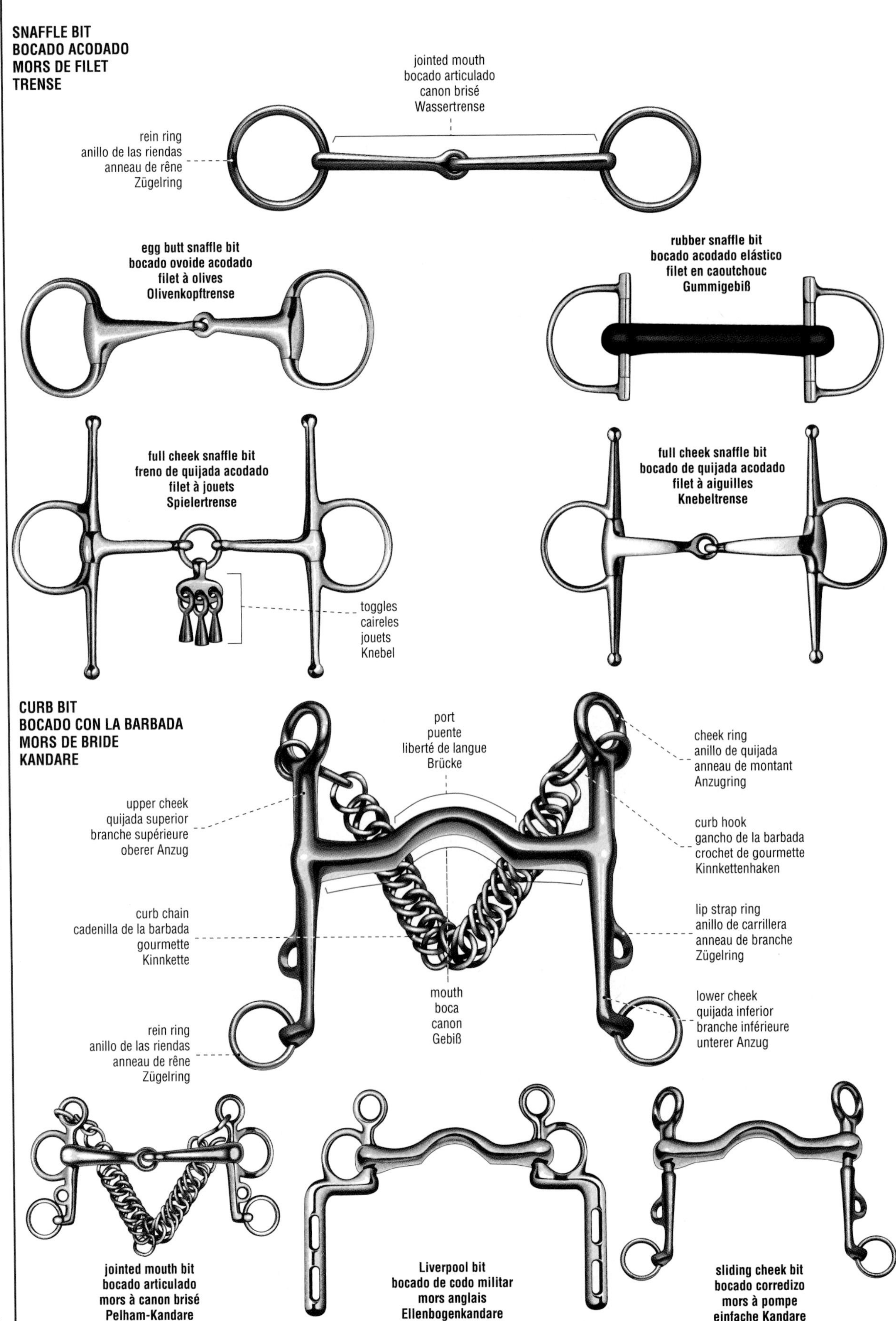
SNAFFLE BIT
BOCADO ACODADO
MORS DE FILET
TRENSE
jointed mouth
bocado articulado
canon brisé
Wassertrense
rein ring
anillo de las riendas
anneau de rêne
Zügelring
egg butt snaffle bit
bocado ovoide acodado
filet à olives
Olivenkopftrense
rubber snaffle bit
bocado acodado elástico
filet en caoutchouc
Gummigebiß
full cheek snaffle bit
freno de quijada acodado
filet à jouets
Spielertrense
full cheek snaffle bit
bocado de quijada acodado
filet à aiguilles
Knebeltrense
toggles
caireles
jouets
Knebel
CURB BIT
BOCADO CON LA BARBADA
MORS DE BRIDE
KANDARE
port
puente
liberté de langue
Brücke
cheek ring
anillo de quijada
anneau de montant
Anzugring
upper cheek
quijada superior
branche supérieure
oberer Anzug
curb hook
gancho de la barbada
crochet de gourmette
Kinnkettenhaken
curb chain
cadenilla de la barbada
gourmette
Kinnkette
lip strap ring
anillo de carrillera
anneau de branche
Zügelring
mouth
boca
canon
Gebiß
lower cheek
quijada inferior
branche inférieure
unterer Anzug
rein ring
anillo de las riendas
anneau de rêne
Zügelring
jointed mouth bit
bocado articulado
mors à canon brisé
Pelham-Kandare
Liverpool bit
bocado de codo militar
mors anglais
Ellenbogenkandare
sliding cheek bit
bocado corredizo
mors à pompe
einfache Kandare

HORSE RACING
CARRERA DE CABALLOS
COURSE DE CHEVAUX
GALOPPRENNEN

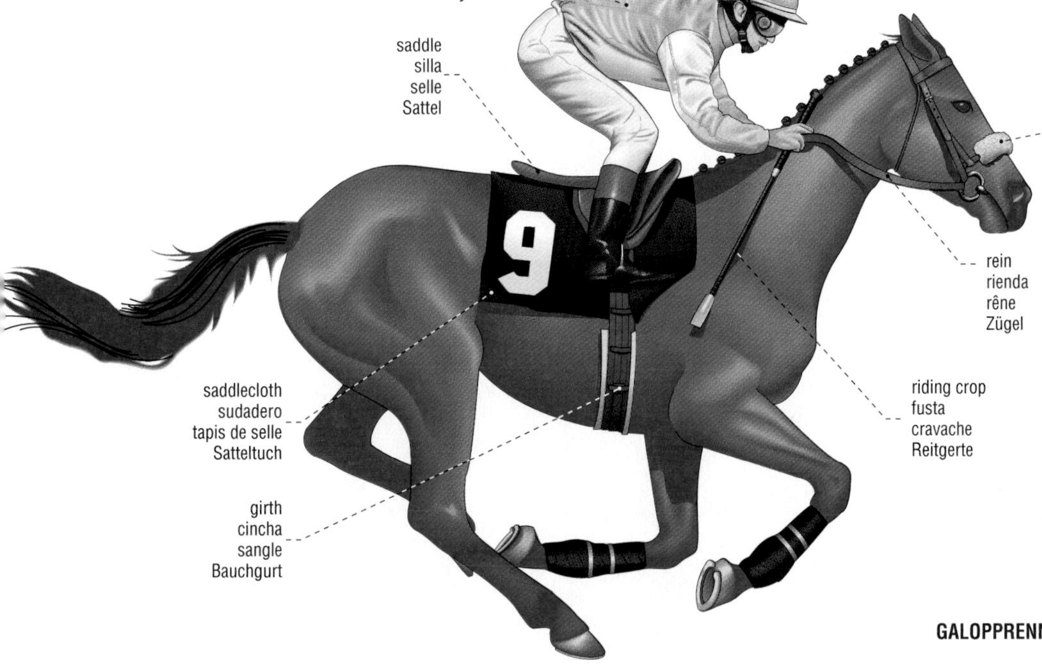

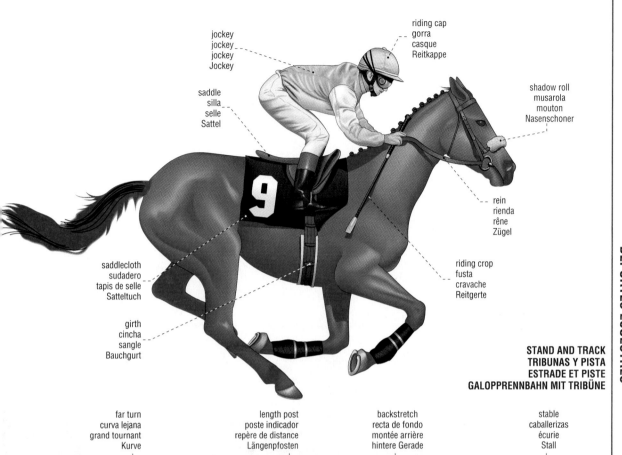

riding cap
gorra
casque
Reitkappe

jockey
jockey
jockey
Jockey

shadow roll
musarola
mouton
Nasenschoner

saddle
silla
selle
Sattel

rein
rienda
rêne
Zügel

saddlecloth
sudadero
tapis de selle
Satteltuch

riding crop
fusta
cravache
Reitgerte

girth
cincha
sangle
Bauchgurt

STAND AND TRACK
TRIBUNAS Y PISTA
ESTRADE ET PISTE
GALOPPRENNBAHN MIT TRIBÜNE

far turn
curva lejana
grand tournant
Kurve

length post
poste indicador
repère de distance
Längenpfosten

backstretch
recta de fondo
montée arrière
hintere Gerade

stable
caballerizas
écurie
Stall

clubhouse
jockey club
club-house
Klubhaus

clubhouse turn
curva del club
tournant de club-house
Klubhauskurve

tote board
tablero indicador
tableau indicateur
Totalisator

judge's stand
tribuna de los jueces
tribune des juges
Kampfrichtertribüne

finishing line
linea de llegada
fil d'arrivée
Ziellinie

paddock
cercado para entrenar los caballos
paddock
Sattelplatz

grandstand
tribuna para el público
tribune populaire
Haupttribüne

homestretch
última recta
dernier droit
Zielgerade

furlong chute
salida de la pista
chute de départ
Achtelmeileneinlauf

HARNESS RACING
CARRERAS DE TROTONES
COURSE SOUS HARNAIS
TRABRENNSPORT

STANDARDBRED PACER
ARNESES PARA TROTONES
AMBLEUR SOUS HARNAIS
SULKY

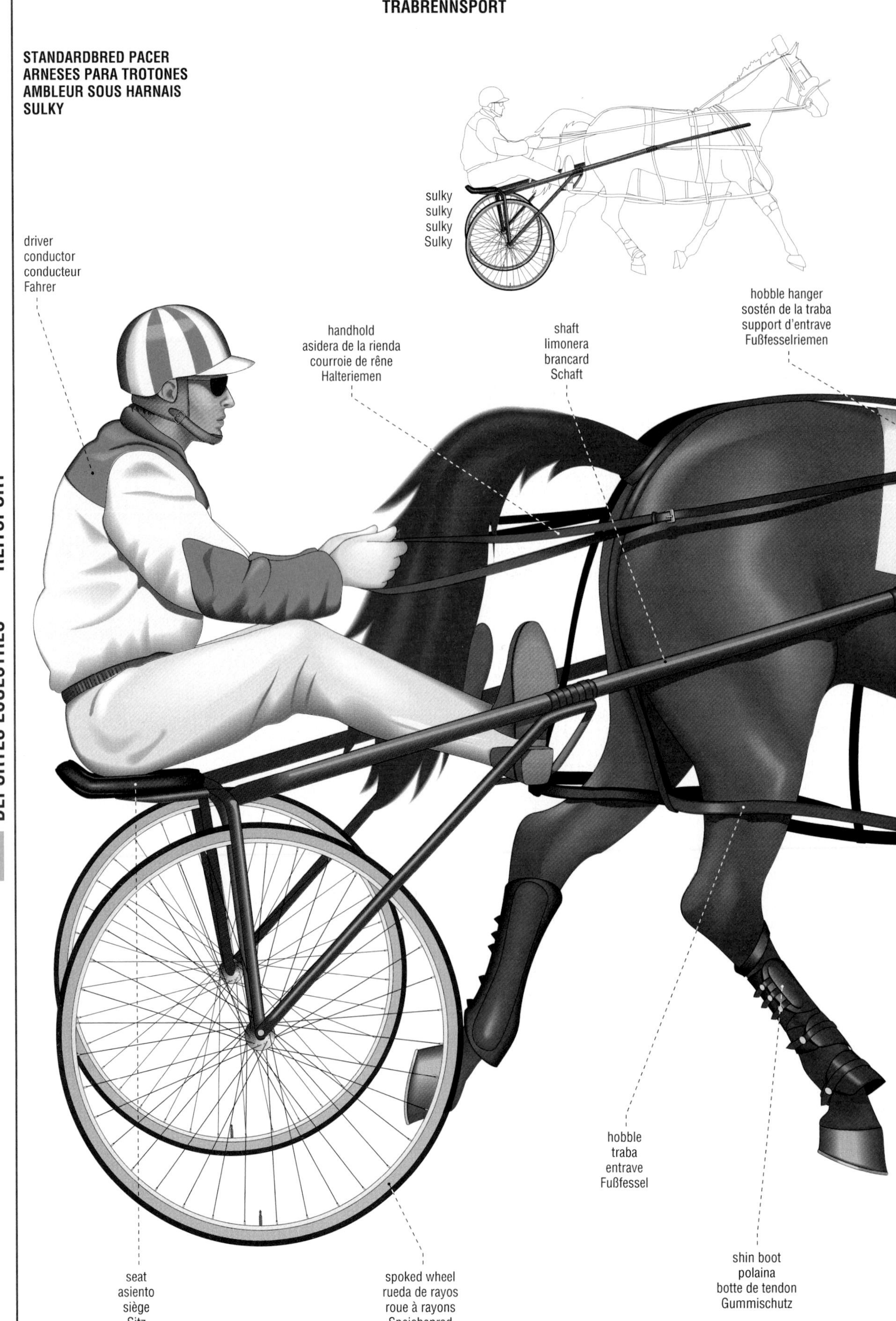
sulky
sulky
sulky
Sulky
driver
conductor
conducteur
Fahrer
handhold
asidera de la rienda
courroie de rêne
Halteriemen
shaft
limonera
brancard
Schaft
hobble hanger
sostén de la traba
support d'entrave
Fußfesselriemen
hobble
traba
entrave
Fußfessel
seat
asiento
siège
Sitz
spoked wheel
rueda de rayos
roue à rayons
Speichenrad
shin boot
polaina
botte de tendon
Gummischutz

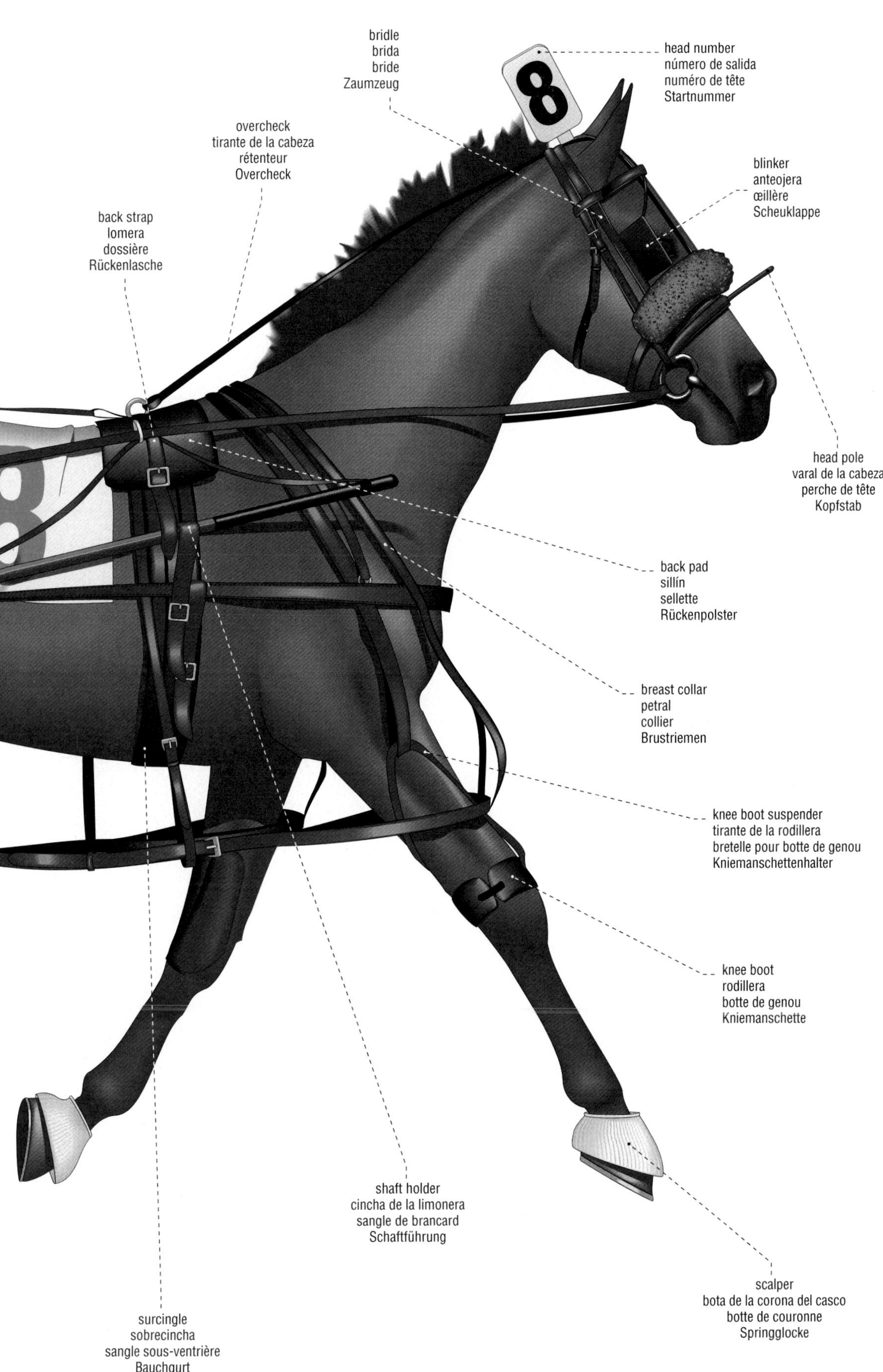
bridle
brida
bride
Zaumzeug
head number
número de salida
numéro de tête
Startnummer
overcheck
tirante de la cabeza
rétenteur
Overcheck
blinker
anteojera
œillère
Scheuklappe
back strap
lomera
dossière
Rückenlasche
head pole
varal de la cabeza
perche de tête
Kopfstab
back pad
sillín
sellette
Rückenpolster
breast collar
petral
collier
Brustriemen
knee boot suspender
tirante de la rodillera
bretelle pour botte de genou
Kniemanschettenhalter
knee boot
rodillera
botte de genou
Kniemanschette
shaft holder
cincha de la limonera
sangle de brancard
Schaftführung
scalper
bota de la corona del casco
botte de couronne
Springglocke
surcingle
sobrecincha
sangle sous-ventrière
Bauchgurt

TRACK AND FIELD ATHLETICS
ATLETISMO DE CAMPO Y PISTA
ATHLÉTISME
LEICHTATHLETIK

ARENA
ESTADIO
STADE
STADION

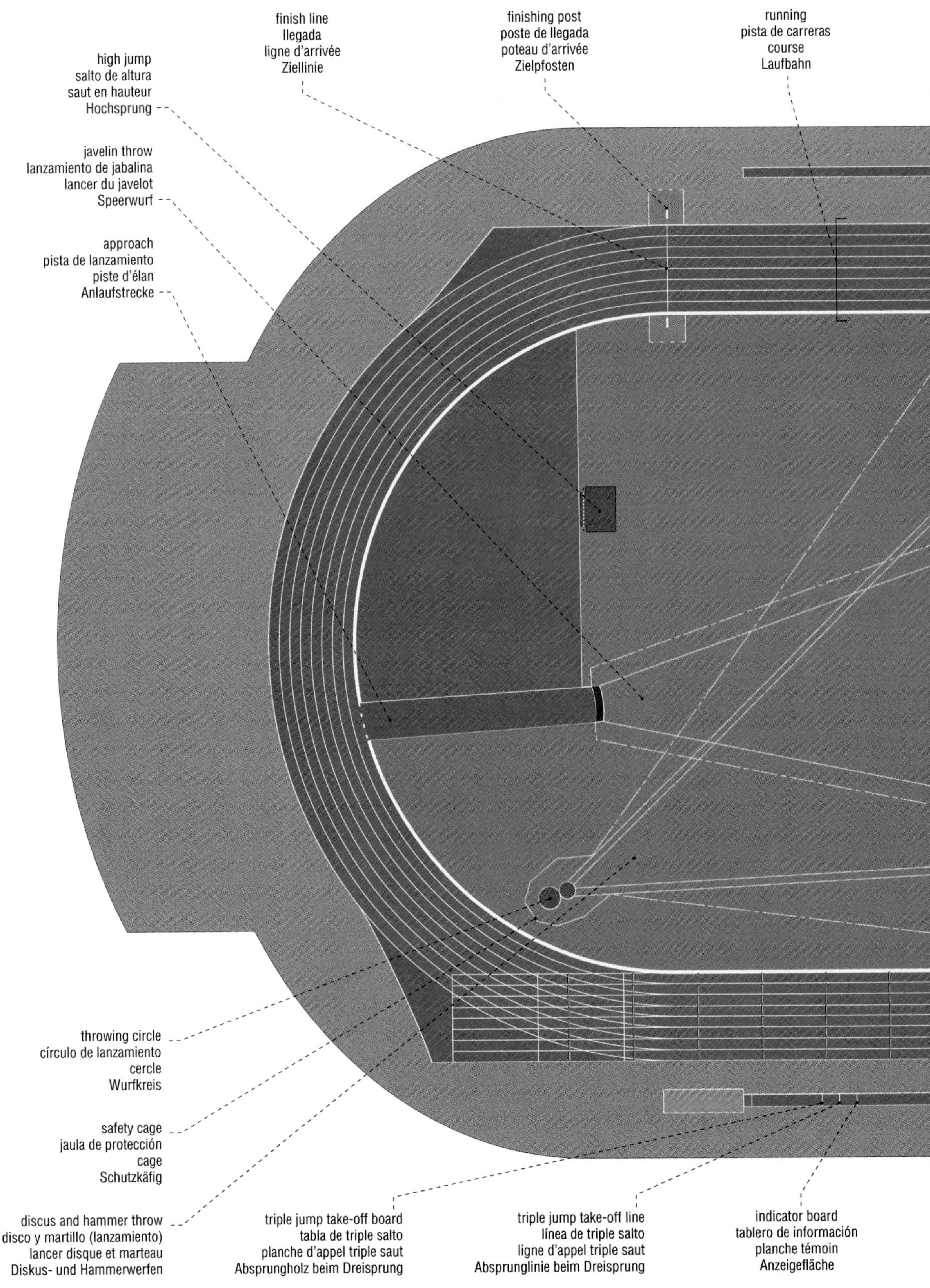
high jump
salto de altura
saut en hauteur
Hochsprung
finish line
llegada
ligne d'arrivée
Ziellinie
finishing post
poste de llegada
poteau d'arrivée
Zielpfosten
running
pista de carreras
course
Laufbahn
javelin throw
lanzamiento de jabalina
lancer du javelot
Speerwurf
approach
pista de lanzamiento
piste d'élan
Anlaufstrecke
throwing circle
círculo de lanzamiento
cercle
Wurfkreis
safety cage
jaula de protección
cage
Schutzkäfig
discus and hammer throw
disco y martillo (lanzamiento)
lancer disque et marteau
Diskus- und Hammerwerfen
triple jump take-off board
tabla de triple salto
planche d'appel triple saut
Absprungholz beim Dreisprung
triple jump take-off line
línea de triple salto
ligne d'appel triple saut
Absprunglinie beim Dreisprung
indicator board
tablero de información
planche témoin
Anzeigefläche

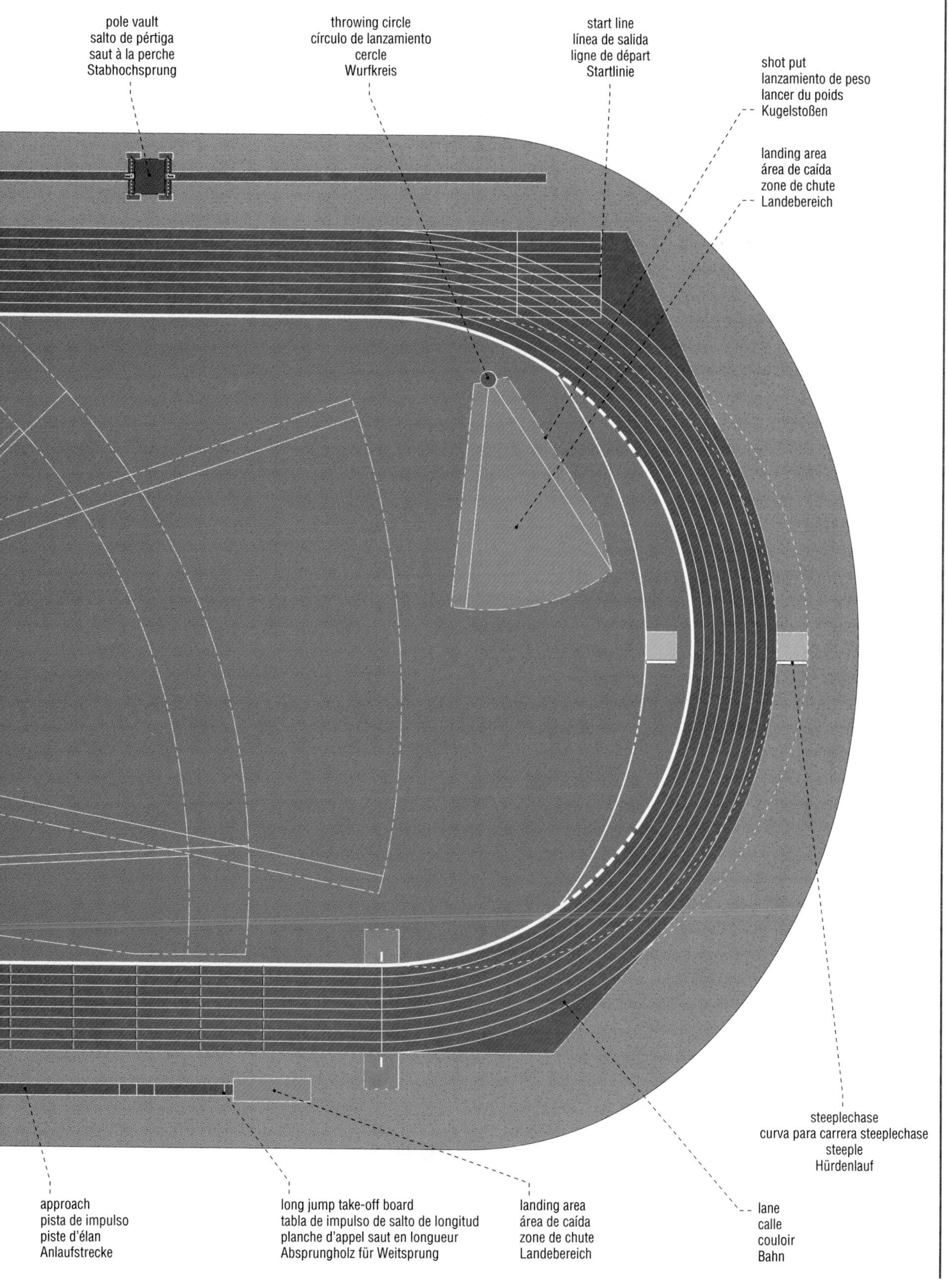
pole vault
salto de pértiga
saut à la perche
Stabhochsprung
throwing circle
círculo de lanzamiento
cercle
Wurfkreis
start line
línea de salida
ligne de départ
Startlinie
shot put
lanzamiento de peso
lancer du poids
Kugelstoßen
landing area
área de caída
zone de chute
Landebereich
steeplechase
curva para carrera steeplechase
steeple
Hürdenlauf
approach
pista de impulso
piste d'élan
Anlaufstrecke
long jump take-off board
tabla de impulso de salto de longitud
planche d'appel saut en longueur
Absprungholz für Weitsprung
landing area
área de caída
zone de chute
Landebereich
lane
calle
couloir
Bahn

TRACK AND FIELD ATHLETICS
ATLETISMO DE CAMPO Y PISTA
ATHLÉTISME
LEICHTATHLETIK

STARTING BLOCK
TACO DE SALIDA
BLOC DE DÉPART
STARTBLOCK

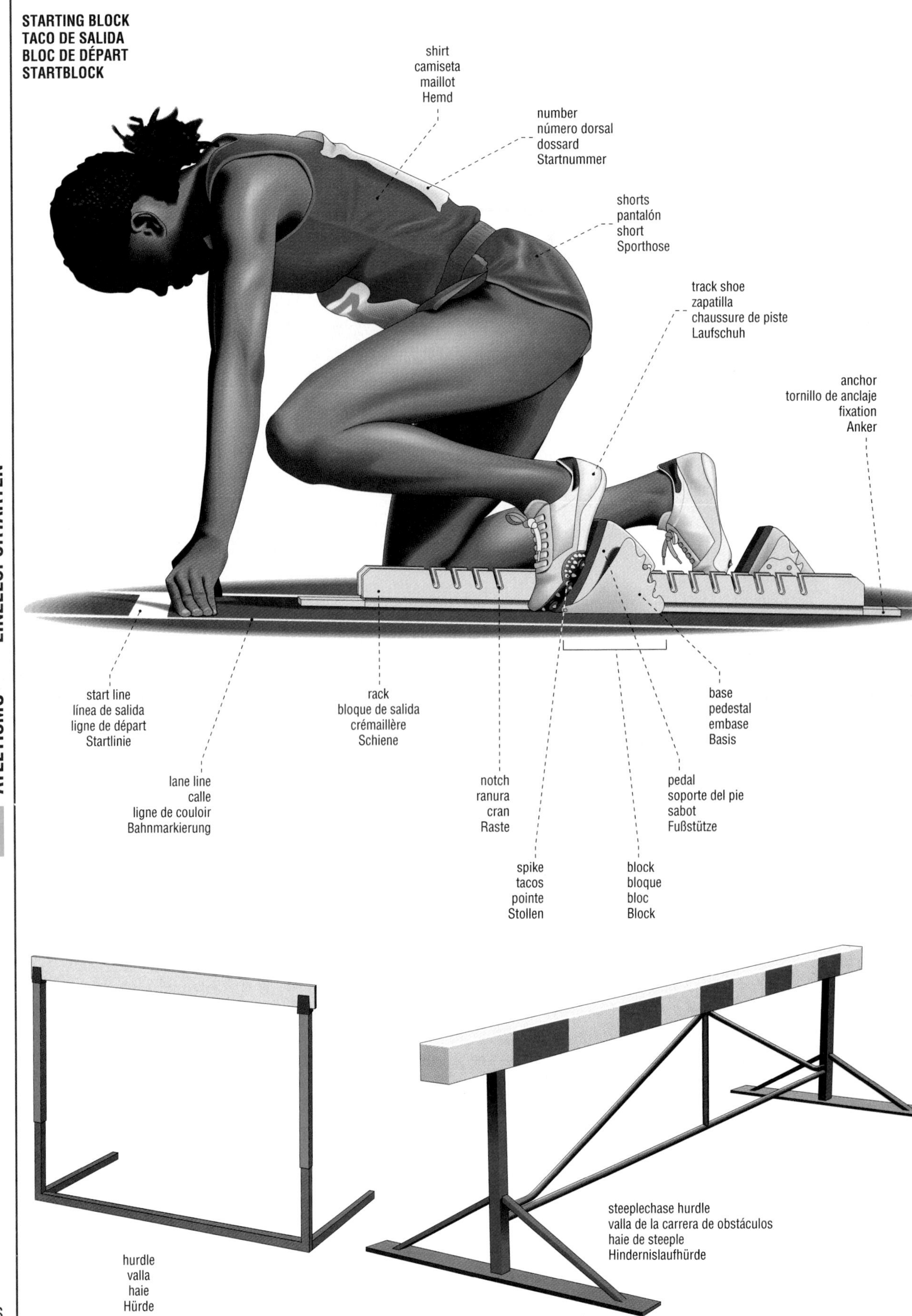
shirt
camiseta
maillot
Hemd
number
número dorsal
dossard
Startnummer
shorts
pantalón
short
Sporthose
track shoe
zapatilla
chaussure de piste
Laufschuh
anchor
tornillo de anclaje
fixation
Anker
start line
línea de salida
ligne de départ
Startlinie
rack
bloque de salida
crémaillère
Schiene
base
pedestal
embase
Basis
lane line
calle
ligne de couloir
Bahnmarkierung
notch
ranura
cran
Raste
pedal
soporte del pie
sabot
Fußstütze
spike
tacos
pointe
Stollen
block
bloque
bloc
Block
steeplechase hurdle
valla de la carrera de obstáculos
haie de steeple
Hindernislaufhürde
hurdle
valla
haie
Hürde

pole
pértiga
perche
Stab

HIGH JUMP
SALTO DE ALTURA
SAUT EN HAUTEUR
HOCHSPRUNG

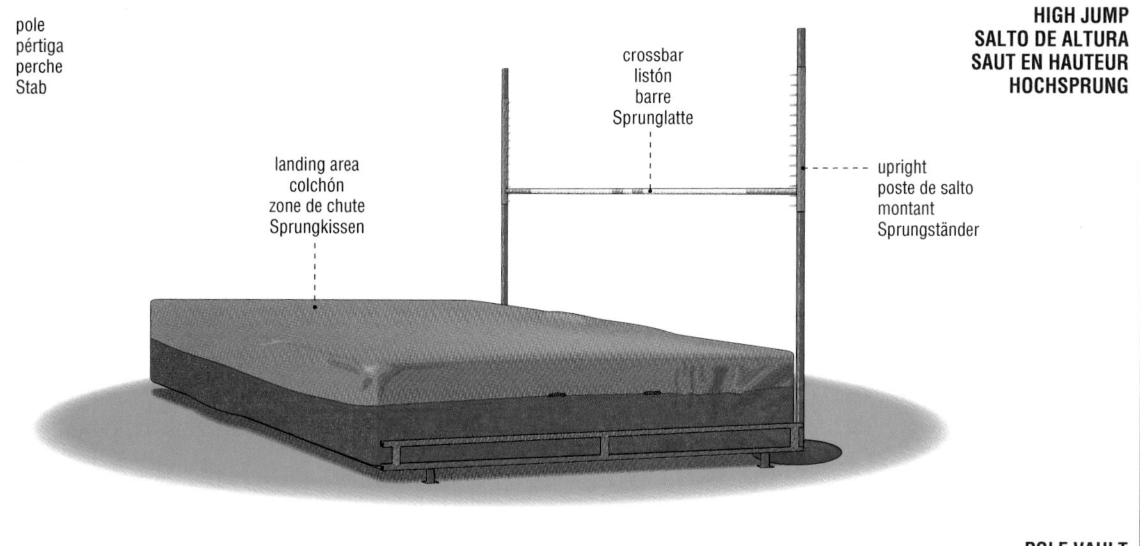
crossbar
listón
barre
Sprunglatte
landing area
colchón
zone de chute
Sprungkissen
upright
poste de salto
montant
Sprungständer

POLE VAULT
SALTO DE PÉRTIGA
SAUT À LA PERCHE
STABHOCHSPRUNG

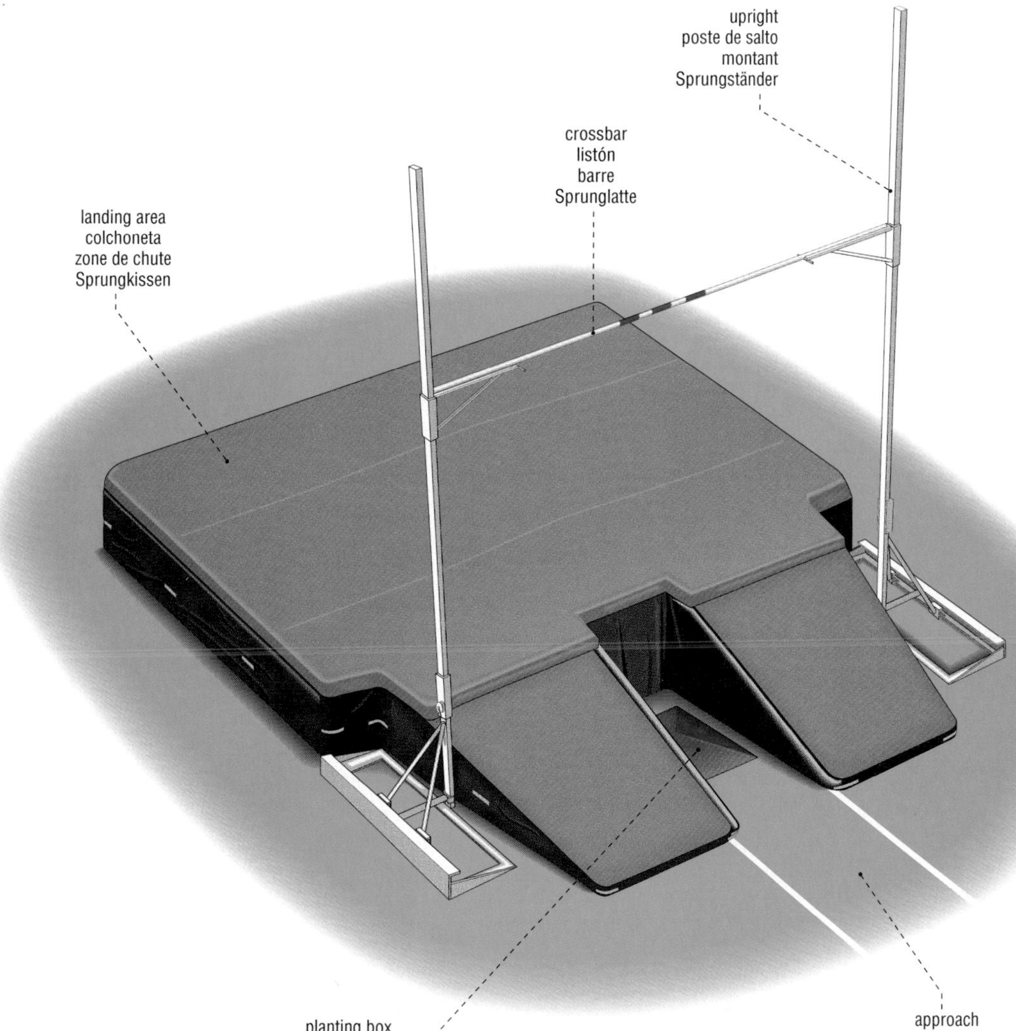

upright
poste de salto
montant
Sprungständer

crossbar
listón
barre
Sprunglatte

landing area
colchoneta
zone de chute
Sprungkissen

planting box
cajón de batir
butoir de saut
Einstichkasten

approach
pista de impulso
piste d'élan
Anlaufstrecke

TRACK AND FIELD ATHLETICS
ATHLETISMO DE CAMPO Y PISTA
ATHLÉTISME
LEICHTATHLETIK

THROWINGS
LANZAMIENTOS
LANCERS
WURFGERÄTE

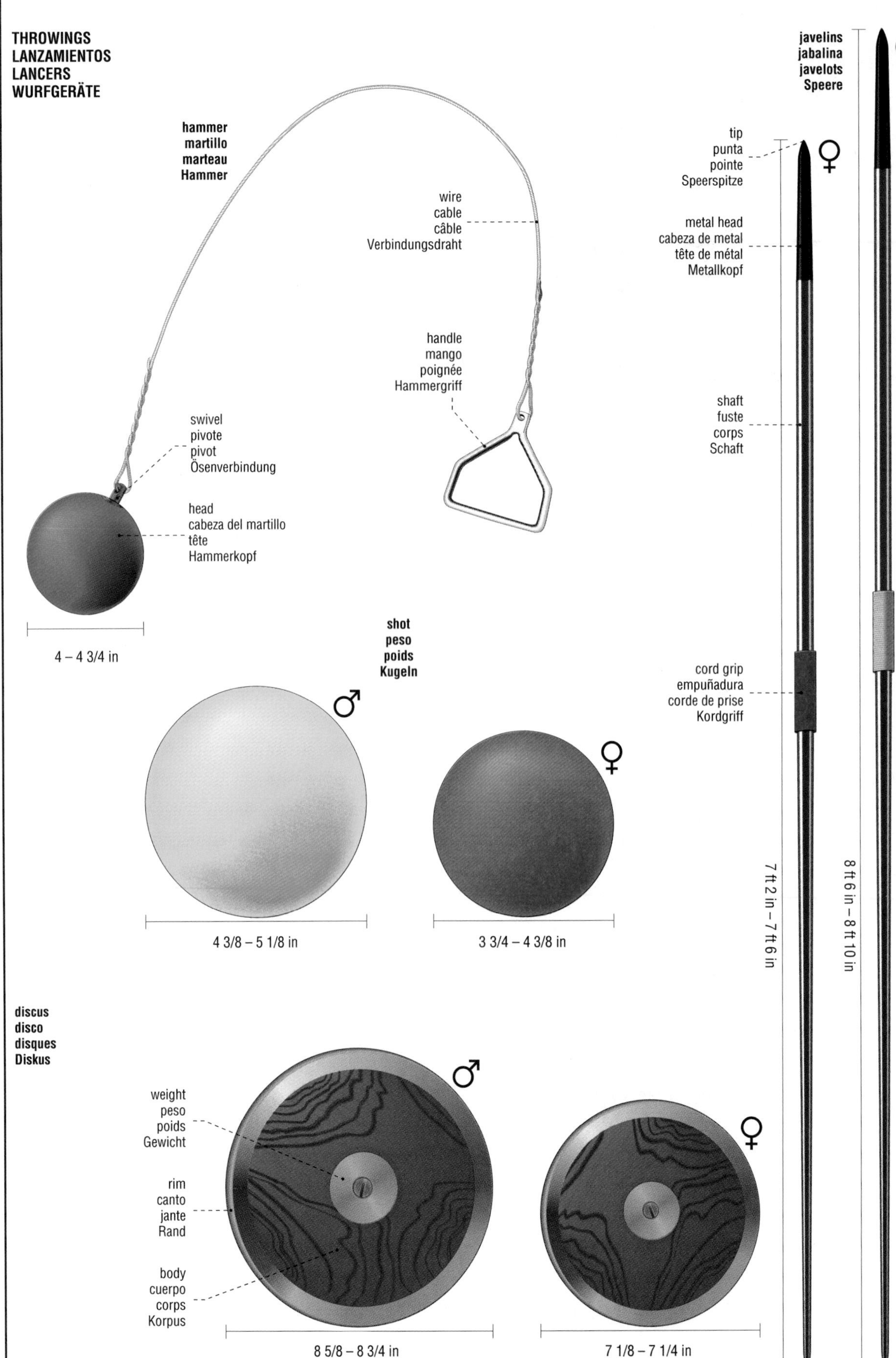
hammer
martillo
marteau
Hammer
wire
cable
câble
Verbindungsdraht
handle
mango
poignée
Hammergriff
swivel
pivote
pivot
Ösenverbindung
head
cabeza del martillo
tête
Hammerkopf
4 – 4 3/4 in
shot
peso
poids
Kugeln
4 3/8 – 5 1/8 in
3 3/4 – 4 3/8 in
discus
disco
disques
Diskus
weight
peso
poids
Gewicht
rim
canto
jante
Rand
body
cuerpo
corps
Korpus
8 5/8 – 8 3/4 in
7 1/8 – 7 1/4 in
javelins
jabalina
javelots
Speere
tip
punta
pointe
Speerspitze
metal head
cabeza de metal
tête de métal
Metallkopf
shaft
fuste
corps
Schaft
cord grip
empuñadura
corde de prise
Kordgriff
7 ft 2 in – 7 ft 6 in
8 ft 6 in – 8 ft 10 in

GYMNASTICS
GIMNASIA
GYMNASTIQUE
GERÄTETURNEN

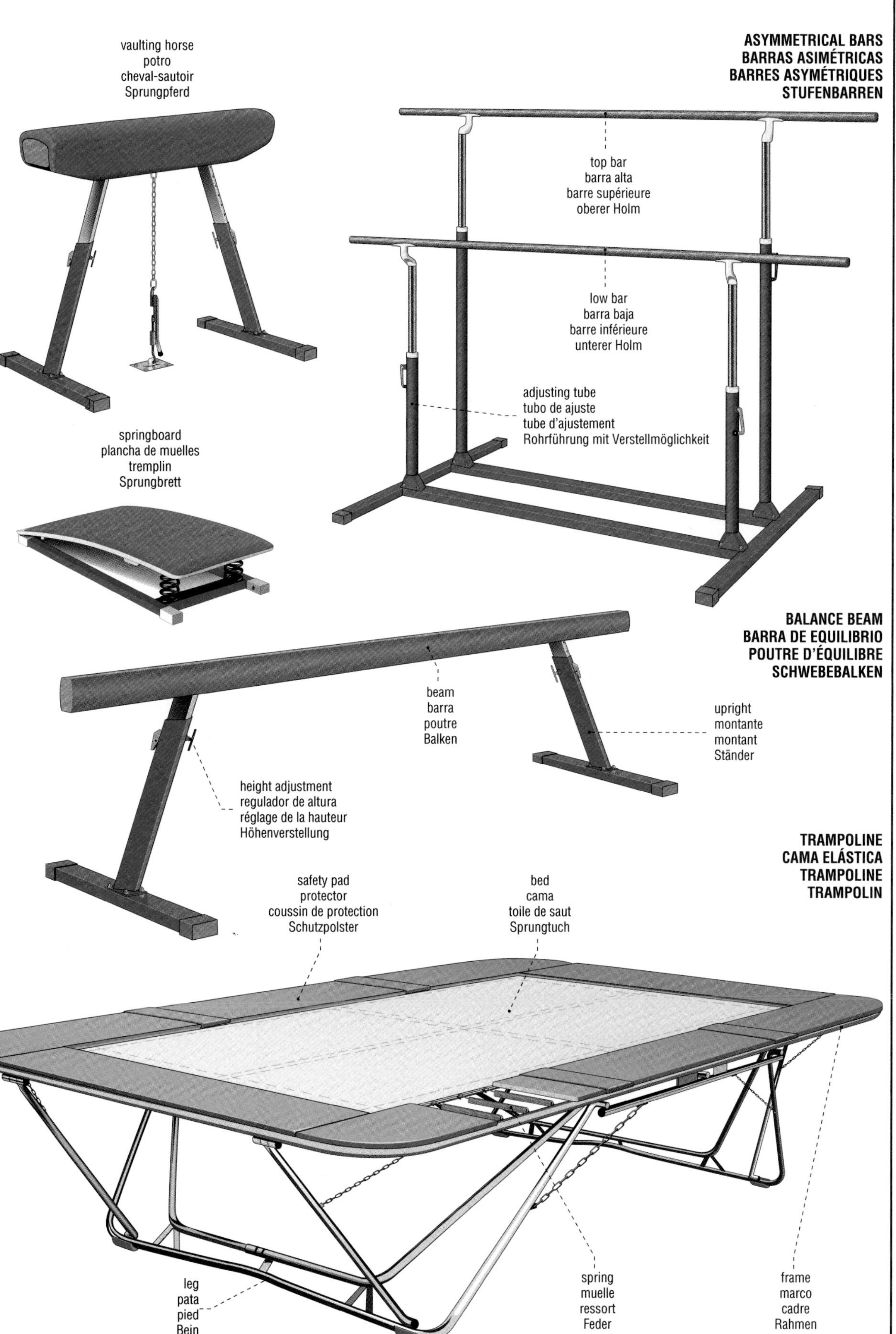
vaulting horse
potro
cheval-sautoir
Sprungpferd
ASYMMETRICAL BARS
BARRAS ASIMÉTRICAS
BARRES ASYMÉTRIQUES
STUFENBARREN
top bar
barra alta
barre supérieure
oberer Holm
low bar
barra baja
barre inférieure
unterer Holm
adjusting tube
tubo de ajuste
tube d'ajustement
Rohrführung mit Verstellmöglichkeit
springboard
plancha de muelles
tremplin
Sprungbrett
BALANCE BEAM
BARRA DE EQUILIBRIO
POUTRE D'ÉQUILIBRE
SCHWEBEBALKEN
beam
barra
poutre
Balken
upright
montante
montant
Ständer
height adjustment
regulador de altura
réglage de la hauteur
Höhenverstellung
TRAMPOLINE
CAMA ELÁSTICA
TRAMPOLINE
TRAMPOLIN
safety pad
protector
coussin de protection
Schutzpolster
bed
cama
toile de saut
Sprungtuch
leg
pata
pied
Bein
spring
muelle
ressort
Feder
frame
marco
cadre
Rahmen

GYMNASTICS
GIMNASIA
GYMNASTIQUE
GERÄTETURNEN

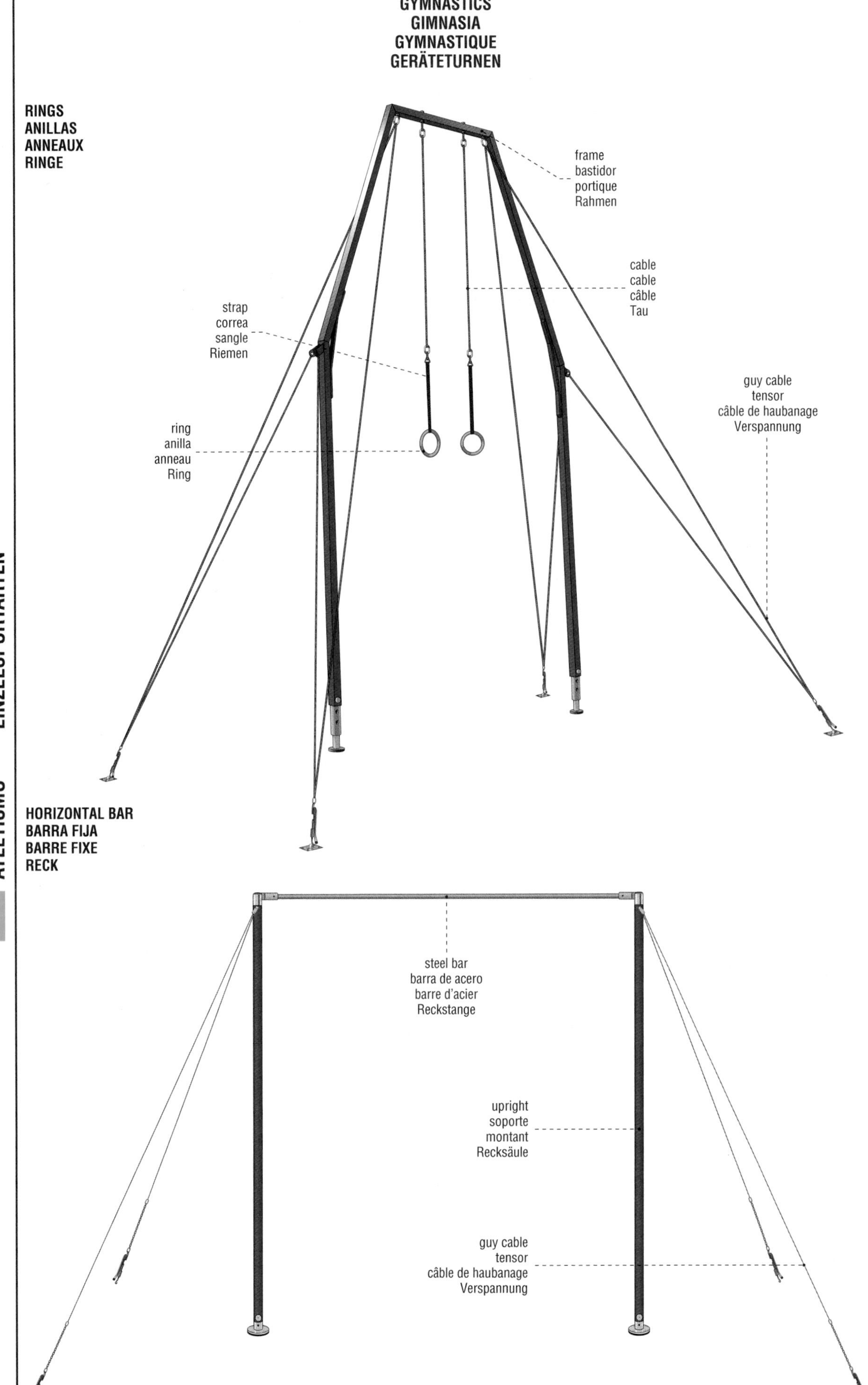
RINGS
ANILLAS
ANNEAUX
RINGE
frame
bastidor
portique
Rahmen
cable
cable
câble
Tau
strap
correa
sangle
Riemen
guy cable
tensor
câble de haubanage
Verspannung
ring
anilla
anneau
Ring
HORIZONTAL BAR
BARRA FIJA
BARRE FIXE
RECK
steel bar
barra de acero
barre d'acier
Reckstange
upright
soporte
montant
Recksäule
guy cable
tensor
câble de haubanage
Verspannung

POMMEL HORSE
CABALLO DE ARZÓN
CHEVAL D'ARÇONS
PAUSCHENPFERD

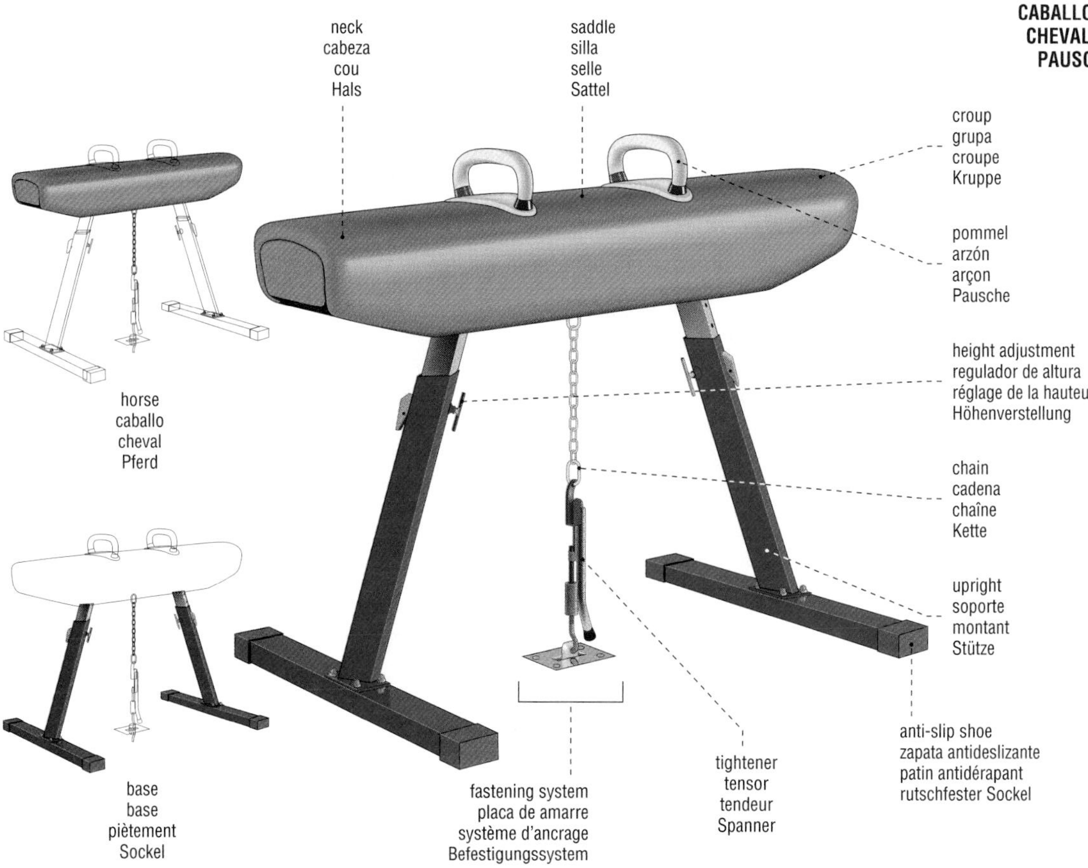

neck
cabeza
cou
Hals

saddle
silla
selle
Sattel

croup
grupa
croupe
Kruppe

pommel
arzón
arçon
Pausche

horse
caballo
cheval
Pferd

height adjustment
regulador de altura
réglage de la hauteur
Höhenverstellung

chain
cadena
chaîne
Kette

upright
soporte
montant
Stütze

base
base
piètement
Sockel

fastening system
placa de amarre
système d'ancrage
Befestigungssystem

tightener
tensor
tendeur
Spanner

anti-slip shoe
zapata antideslizante
patin antidérapant
rutschfester Sockel

PARALLEL BARS
BARRAS PARALELAS
BARRES PARALLÈLES
PARALLELBARREN

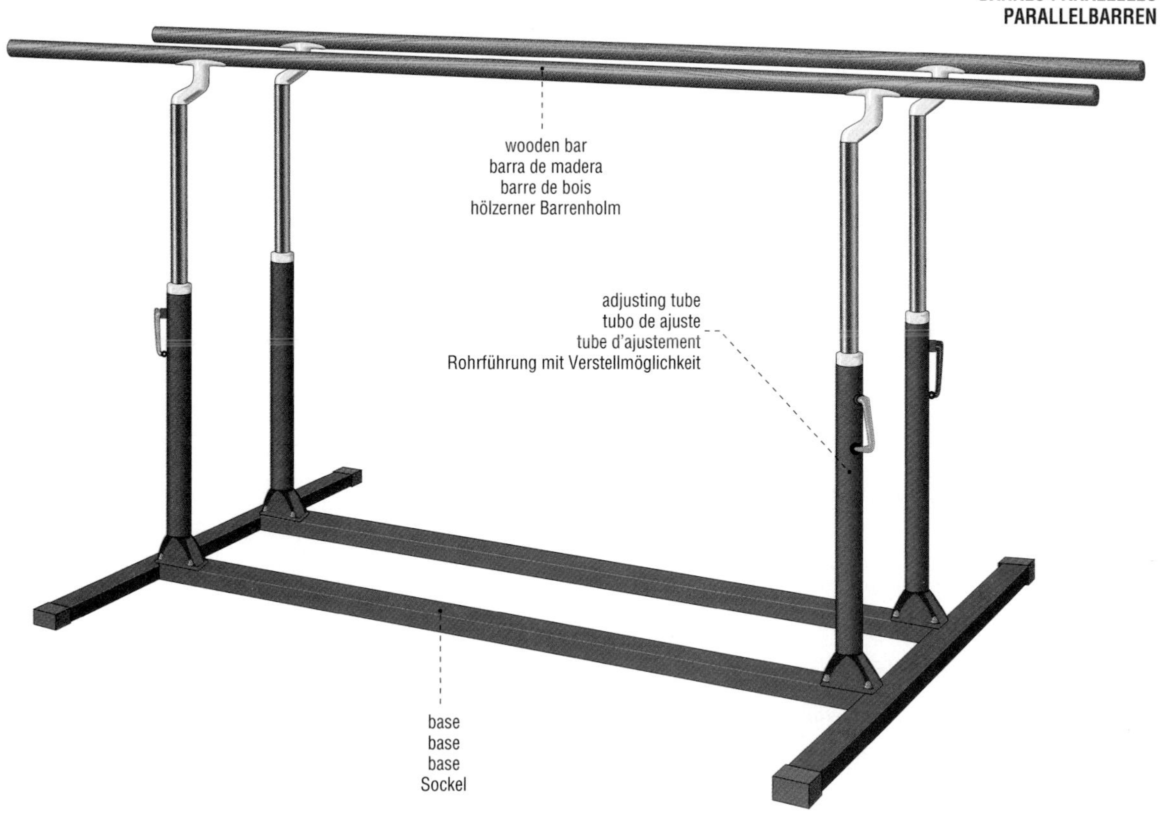
wooden bar
barra de madera
barre de bois
hölzerner Barrenholm
adjusting tube
tubo de ajuste
tube d'ajustement
Rohrführung mit Verstellmöglichkeit
base
base
base
Sockel

WEIGHTLIFTING
HALTEROFILIA
HALTÉROPHILIE
GEWICHTHEBEN

WEIGHTLIFTER
LEVANTADOR DE PESAS
HALTÉROPHILE
GEWICHTHEBER
bar
barra
manchon
Hantelstange
gauze bandage
muñequera
bandage de gaze
Bandage
sleeveless jersey
camiseta sin mangas
maillot de corps
ärmelloses Sporthemd
weightlifting belt
cinturón
ceinture d'haltérophilie
Gewichthebergürtel
trunks
pantalón
culotte
Hose
weightlifting shoe
zapatilla
chaussure d'haltérophilie
Gewichtheberschuh
strap
correa
lanière
Riemen
TWO-HAND SNATCH
MODALIDAD ARRANQUE
ARRACHÉ À DEUX BRAS
ZWEIARMIGES REISSEN
TWO-HAND CLEAN AND JERK
MODALIDAD CON IMPULSO EN DOS TIEMPOS
ÉPAULÉ-JETÉ À DEUX BRAS
ZWEIARMIGES STOSSEN MIT AUSFALLSCHRITT

FITNESS EQUIPMENT
APARATOS DE EJERCICIOS
APPAREILS DE CONDITIONNEMENT PHYSIQUE
FITNESSGERÄTE

WEIGHT STACK EXERCISE UNIT
UNIDAD DE PESAS
BANC DE MUSCULATION
MULTITRAINER

cable
cable
câble
Draht
pectoral deck
pectoral
presse à pectoraux
Butterfly
lateral bar
barra lateral
barre à dorsaux
Latissimuszug
press bar
presión
barre à pectoraux
Drückstange
bench
banco
planche
Bank
leg curl bar
barra de flexión de piernas
balancier de traction
Beincurler
leg extension bar
barra de extensión de piernas
balancier d'extension
Beinstreckerzug
triceps bar
barra de triceps
barre à triceps
Trizepszug
weights
pesas
poids
Gewichte

BARBELL
HALTERA
HALTÈRE LONG
HANTEL

bar
barra
barre
Stange
disk
disco
disque
Scheibe
collar
collarín
collier de serrage
Manschette
sleeve
manguito
manchon
Hantelstange

FITNESS EQUIPMENT
APARATOS DE EJERCICIOS
APPAREILS DE CONDITIONNEMENT PHYSIQUE
FITNESSGERÄTE

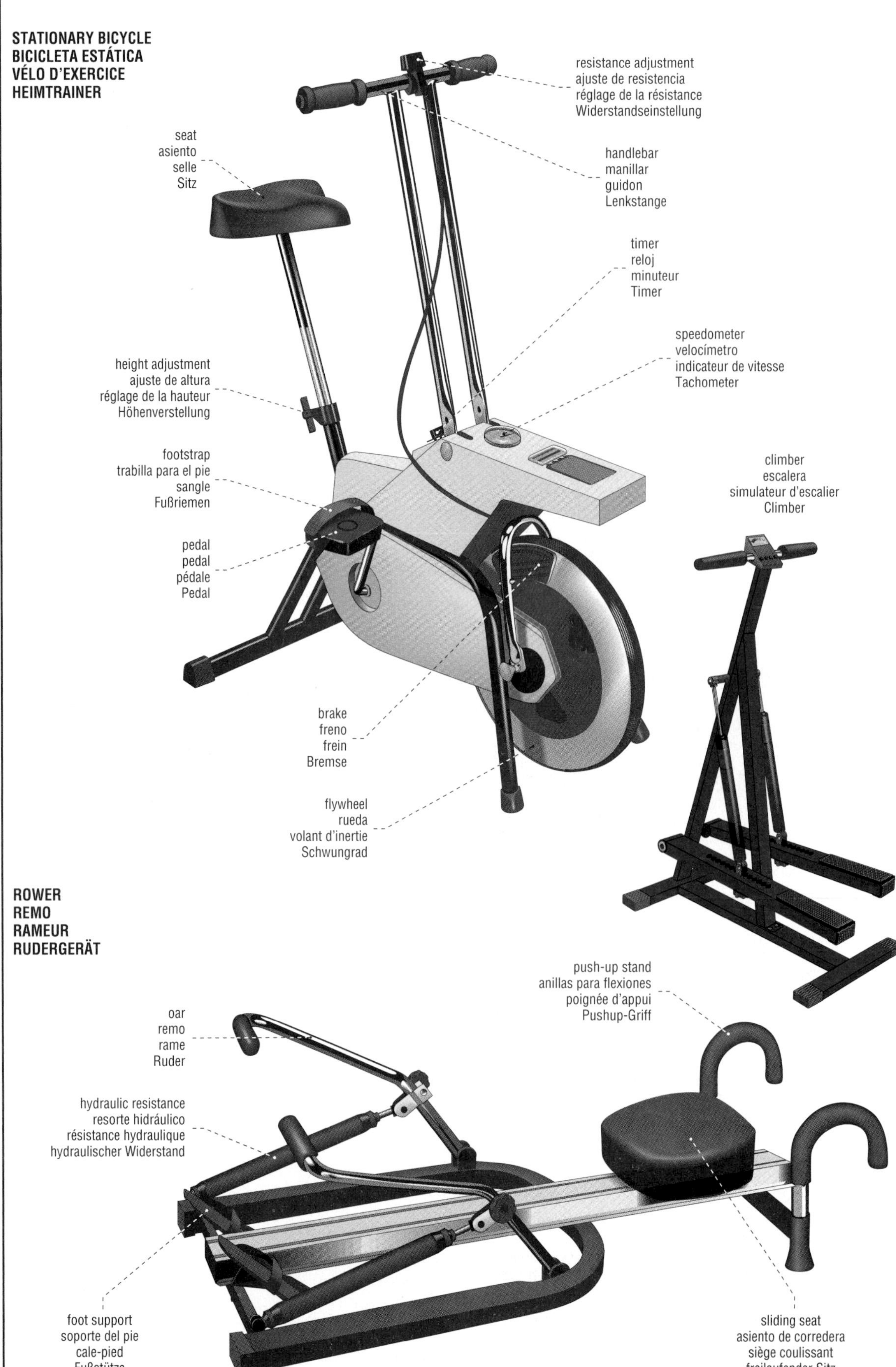

STATIONARY BICYCLE
BICICLETA ESTÁTICA
VÉLO D'EXERCICE
HEIMTRAINER
resistance adjustment
ajuste de resistencia
réglage de la résistance
Widerstandseinstellung
seat
asiento
selle
Sitz
handlebar
manillar
guidon
Lenkstange
timer
reloj
minuteur
Timer
speedometer
velocímetro
indicateur de vitesse
Tachometer
height adjustment
ajuste de altura
réglage de la hauteur
Höhenverstellung
footstrap
trabilla para el pie
sangle
Fußriemen
climber
escalera
simulateur d'escalier
Climber
pedal
pedal
pédale
Pedal
brake
freno
frein
Bremse
flywheel
rueda
volant d'inertie
Schwungrad
ROWER
REMO
RAMEUR
RUDERGERÄT
push-up stand
anillas para flexiones
poignée d'appui
Pushup-Griff
oar
remo
rame
Ruder
hydraulic resistance
resorte hidráulico
résistance hydraulique
hydraulischer Widerstand
foot support
soporte del pie
cale-pied
Fußstütze
sliding seat
asiento de corredera
siège coulissant
freilaufender Sitz

DUMBBELL
PESAS
HALTÈRE COURT
HANTEL

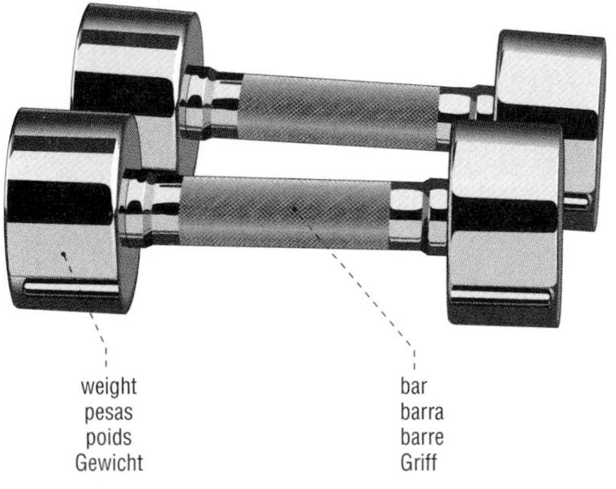

weight
pesas
poids
Gewicht

bar
barra
barre
Griff

handgrips
empuñaderas
poignée à ressort
Handmuskeltrainer

ankle/wrist weight
pesas para muñecas y tobillos
bracelet lesté
Fuß-/Handgelenksgewicht

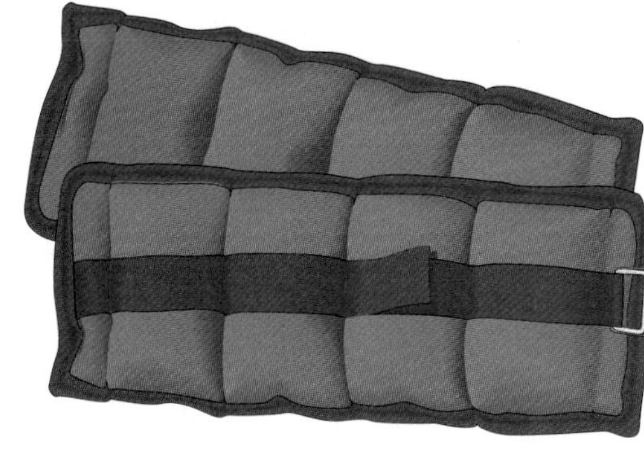

jump rope
cuerda
corde à sauter
Springseil

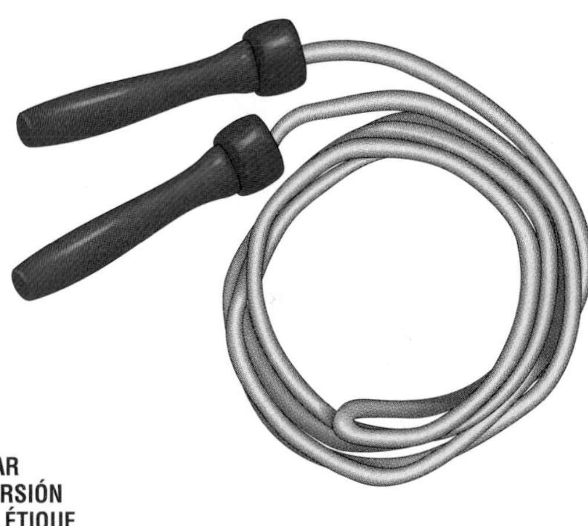

TWIST BAR
BARRA DE TORSIÓN
RESSORT ATHLÉTIQUE
FEDERSTANGE

grip
empuñadura
poignée
Griff

tension spring
resorte de tensión
ressort de tension
Spannfeder

chest expander
tensores pectorales
extenseur
Expander

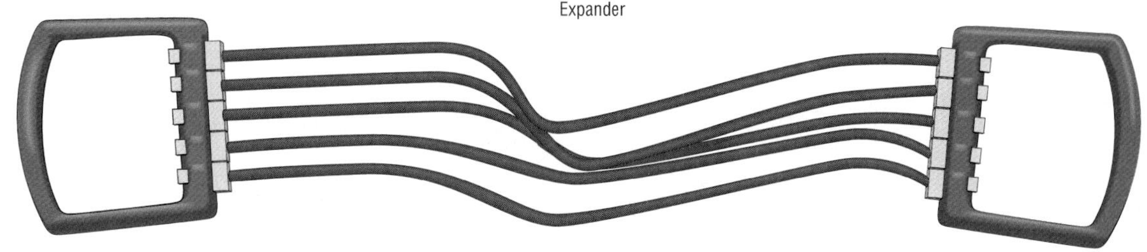

FENCING
ESGRIMA
ESCRIME
FECHTSPORT

PARTS OF THE WEAPON
PARTES DEL ARMA
PARTIES DE L'ARME
TEILE DER WAFFE

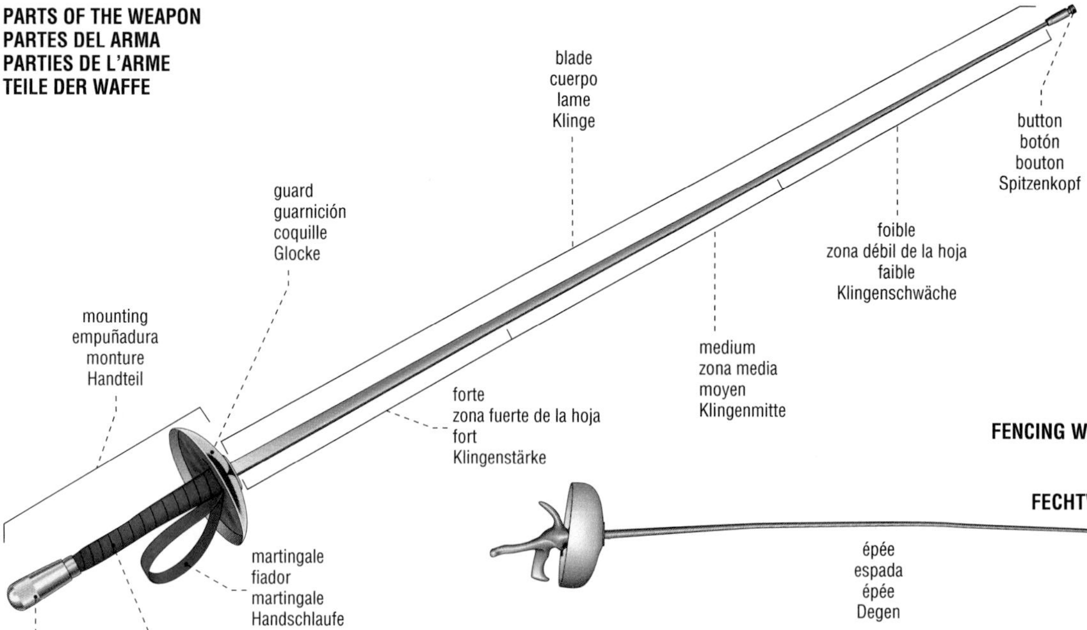

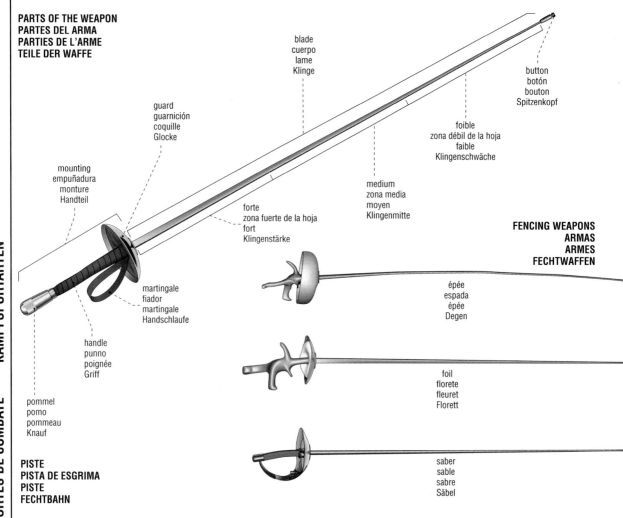

blade
cuerpo
lame
Klinge

button
botón
bouton
Spitzenkopf

guard
guarnición
coquille
Glocke

foible
zona débil de la hoja
faible
Klingenschwäche

mounting
empuñadura
monture
Handteil

medium
zona media
moyen
Klingenmitte

forte
zona fuerte de la hoja
fort
Klingenstärke

martingale
fiador
martingale
Handschlaufe

handle
punno
poignée
Griff

pommel
pomo
pommeau
Knauf

FENCING WEAPONS
ARMAS
ARMES
FECHTWAFFEN

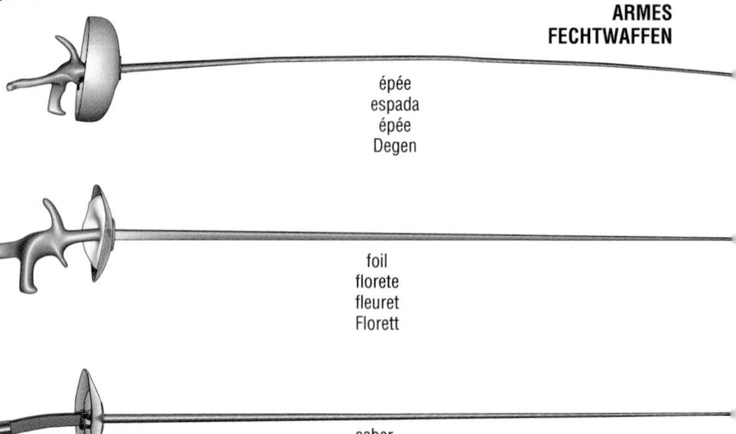

épée
espada
épée
Degen

foil
florete
fleuret
Florett

saber
sable
sabre
Säbel

PISTE
PISTA DE ESGRIMA
PISTE
FECHTBAHN

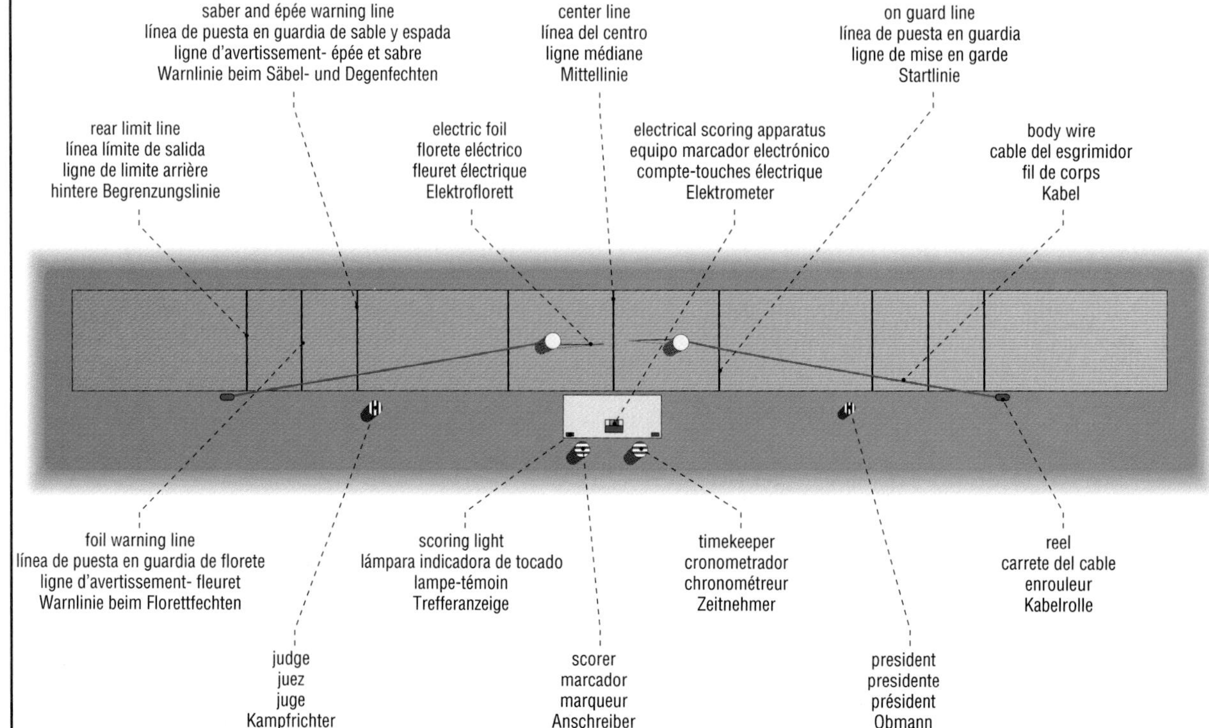
saber and épée warning line
línea de puesta en guardia de sable y espada
ligne d'avertissement- épée et sabre
Warnlinie beim Säbel- und Degenfechten
center line
línea del centro
ligne médiane
Mittellinie
on guard line
línea de puesta en guardia
ligne de mise en garde
Startlinie
rear limit line
línea límite de salida
ligne de limite arrière
hintere Begrenzungslinie
electric foil
florete eléctrico
fleuret électrique
Elektroflorett
electrical scoring apparatus
equipo marcador electrónico
compte-touches électrique
Elektrometer
body wire
cable del esgrimidor
fil de corps
Kabel
foil warning line
línea de puesta en guardia de florete
ligne d'avertissement- fleuret
Warnlinie beim Florettfechten
scoring light
lámpara indicadora de tocado
lampe-témoin
Trefferanzeige
timekeeper
cronometrador
chronométreur
Zeitnehmer
reel
carrete del cable
enrouleur
Kabelrolle
judge
juez
juge
Kampfrichter
scorer
marcador
marqueur
Anschreiber
president
presidente
président
Obmann

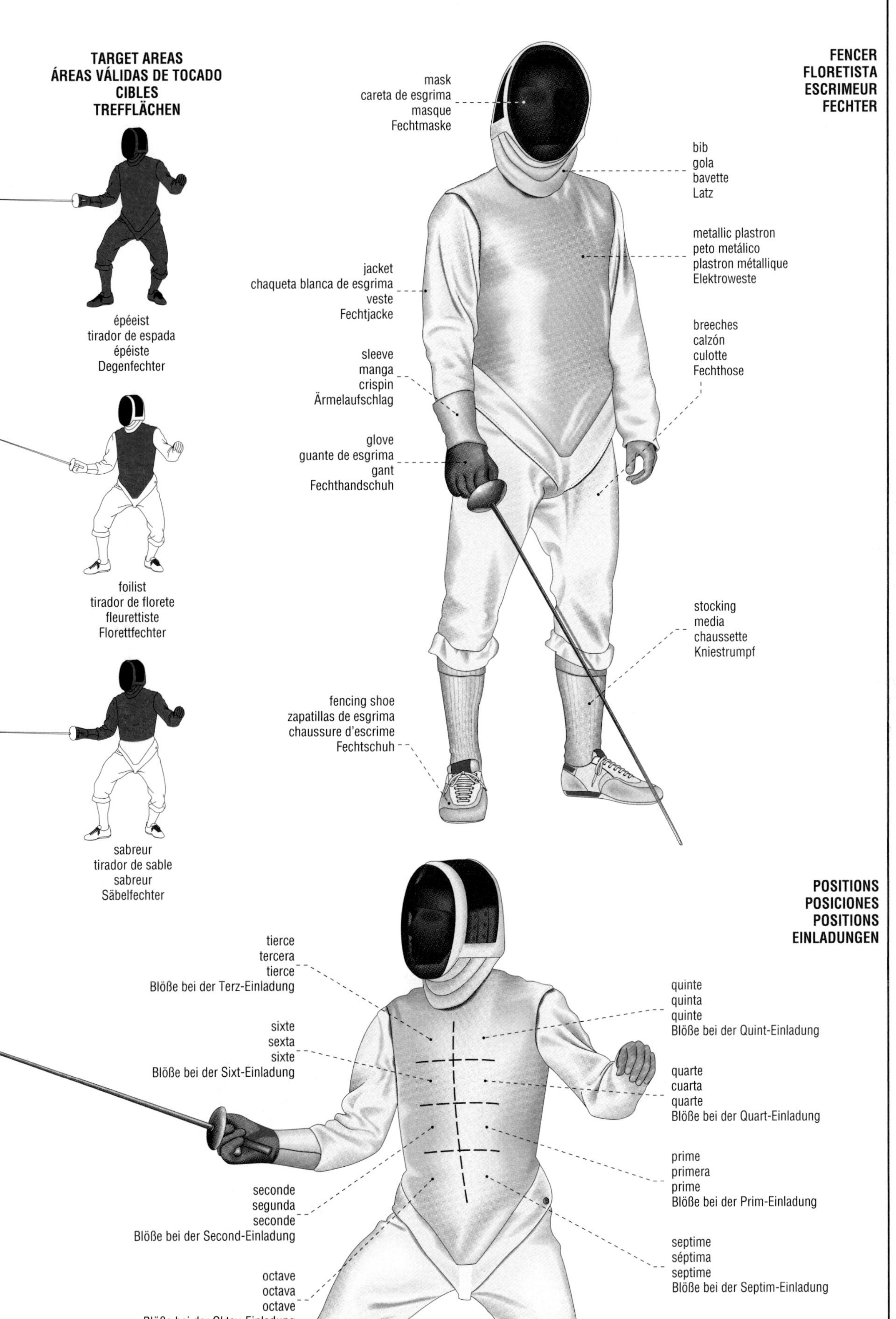
TARGET AREAS
ÁREAS VÁLIDAS DE TOCADO
CIBLES
TREFFLÄCHEN
épéeist
tirador de espada
épéiste
Degenfechter
foilist
tirador de florete
fleurettiste
Florettfechter
sabreur
tirador de sable
sabreur
Säbelfechter
FENCER
FLORETISTA
ESCRIMEUR
FECHTER
mask
careta de esgrima
masque
Fechtmaske
bib
gola
bavette
Latz
metallic plastron
peto metálico
plastron métallique
Elektroweste
jacket
chaqueta blanca de esgrima
veste
Fechtjacke
breeches
calzón
culotte
Fechthose
sleeve
manga
crispin
Ärmelaufschlag
glove
guante de esgrima
gant
Fechthandschuh
stocking
media
chaussette
Kniestrumpf
fencing shoe
zapatillas de esgrima
chaussure d'escrime
Fechtschuh
POSITIONS
POSICIONES
POSITIONS
EINLADUNGEN
tierce
tercera
tierce
Blöße bei der Terz-Einladung
quinte
quinta
quinte
Blöße bei der Quint-Einladung
sixte
sexta
sixte
Blöße bei der Sixt-Einladung
quarte
cuarta
quarte
Blöße bei der Quart-Einladung
prime
primera
prime
Blöße bei der Prim-Einladung
seconde
segunda
seconde
Blöße bei der Second-Einladung
septime
séptima
septime
Blöße bei der Septim-Einladung
octave
octava
octave
Blöße bei der Oktav-Einladung

JUDO
JUDO
JUDO
JUDO

JUDO SUIT
JUDOKA
COSTUME DE JUDO
JUDOANZUG

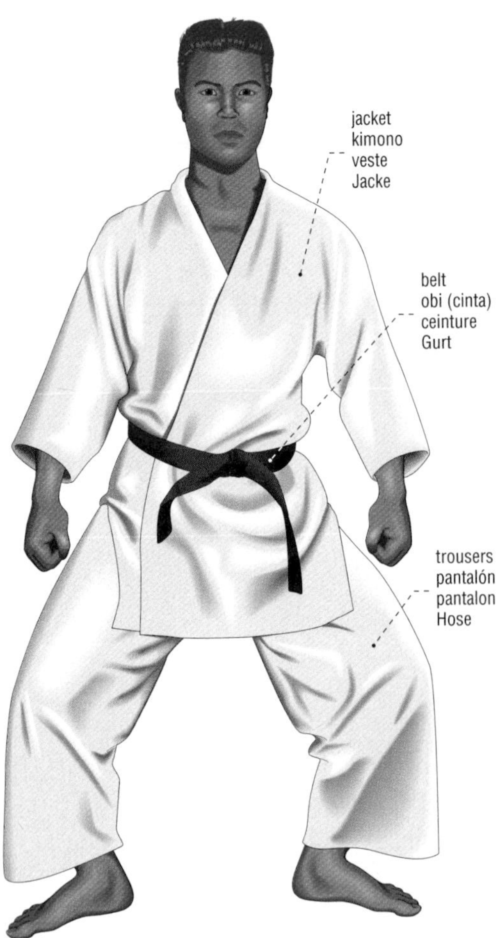
jacket
kimono
veste
Jacke
belt
obi (cinta)
ceinture
Gurt
trousers
pantalón
pantalon
Hose

EXAMPLES OF HOLDS
EJEMPLOS DE LLAVES
EXEMPLES DE PRISES
GRIFF- UND WURFBEISPIELE

arm lock
presa de brazo
clé de bras
Armhebel

holding
presa
immobilisation
Haltegriffe

major outer reaping throw
osoto-gari (gran siega) exterior
grand fauchage extérieur
Große Außensichel

one-arm shoulder throw
ippon-seoi-nage (proyección) por encima del hombro con una mano
projection d'épaule par un côté
einarmiger Schulterwurf

major inner reaping throw
o-uchi-gari (gran siega) interior
grand fauchage intérieur
Große Innensichel

naked strangle
estrangulación
étranglement
Halsumklammerung

stomach throw
proyección en círculo
projection en cercle
Kopfwurf

sweeping hip throw
proyección primera de cadera
hanche ailée
Hüftwurf

MAT
TATAMI
TAPIS
MATTE

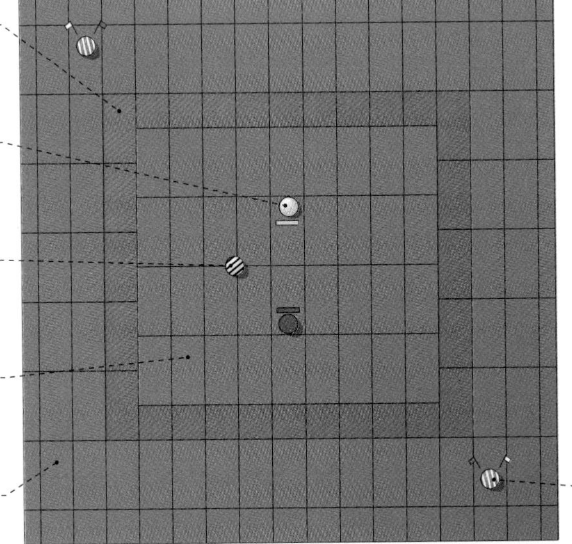
danger area
área de peligro
zone de danger
Gefahrenbereich
contestant
uke (defensor)
combattant
Judokämpfer
referee
judoka neutral
arbitre
Schiedsrichter
contest area
área de combate
surface de combat
Kampfbereich
safety area
área de seguridad
surface de sécurité
Sicherheitsbereich
red flag
bandera roja
drapeau rouge
rote Fahne
timekeeper
cronometrador
chronométreur
Zeitnehmer
holding timekeeper
cronometrador de presas
chronométreur des immobilisations
Griffzeitnehmer
scorer
anotador
marqueur
Punktezähler
judge
juez
juge
Kampfrichter

BOXING
BOXEO
BOXE
BOXEN

RING
RING DE BOXEO
RING
RING

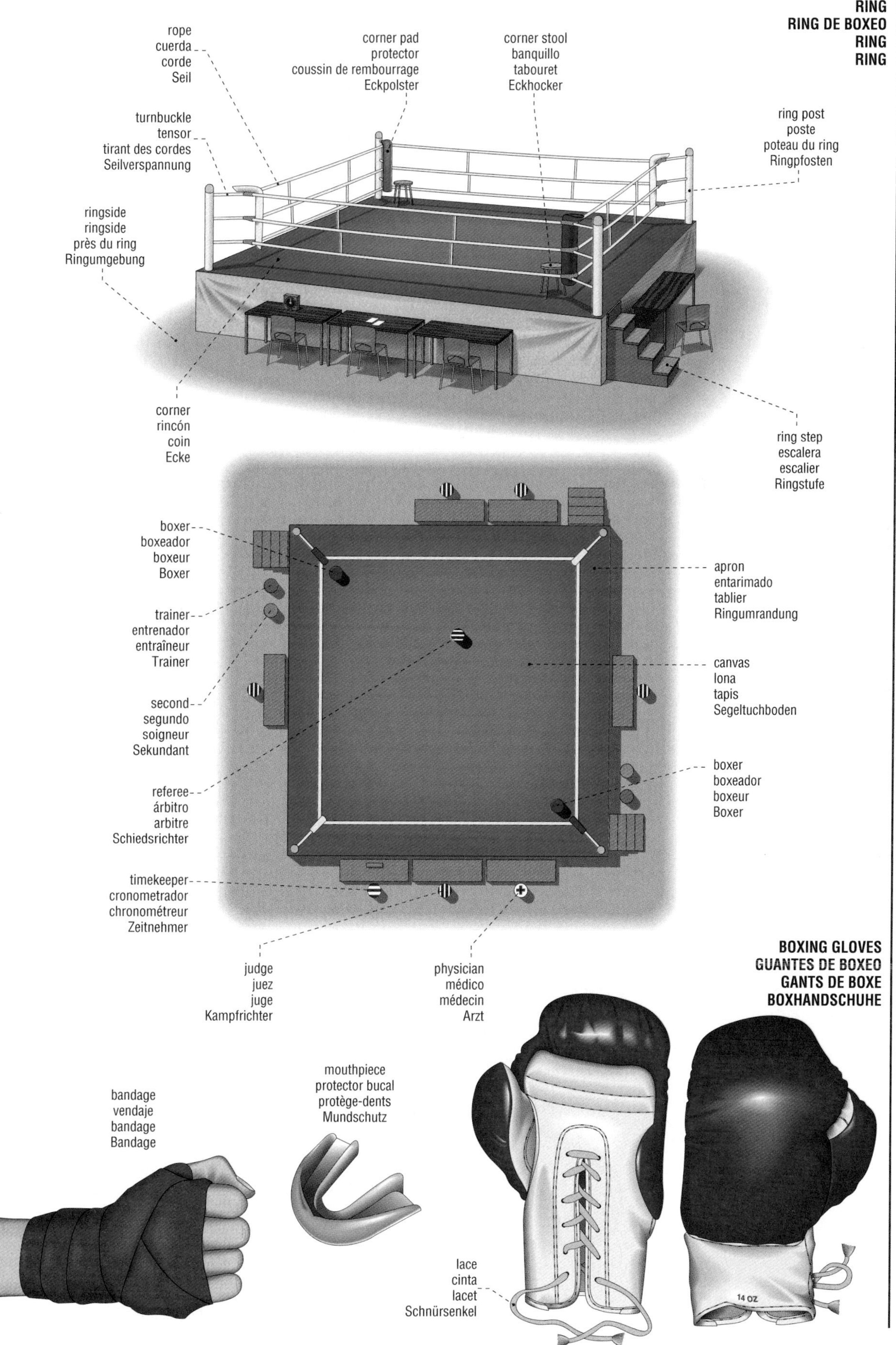
rope
cuerda
corde
Seil
corner pad
protector
coussin de rembourrage
Eckpolster
corner stool
banquillo
tabouret
Eckhocker
turnbuckle
tensor
tirant des cordes
Seilverspannung
ring post
poste
poteau du ring
Ringpfosten
ringside
ringside
près du ring
Ringumgebung
corner
rincón
coin
Ecke
ring step
escalera
escalier
Ringstufe
boxer
boxeador
boxeur
Boxer
apron
entarimado
tablier
Ringumrandung
trainer
entrenador
entraîneur
Trainer
canvas
lona
tapis
Segeltuchboden
second
segundo
soigneur
Sekundant
boxer
boxeador
boxeur
Boxer
referee
árbitro
arbitre
Schiedsrichter
timekeeper
cronometrador
chronométreur
Zeitnehmer
judge
juez
juge
Kampfrichter
physician
médico
médecin
Arzt
BOXING GLOVES
GUANTES DE BOXEO
GANTS DE BOXE
BOXHANDSCHUHE
bandage
vendaje
bandage
Bandage
mouthpiece
protector bucal
protège-dents
Mundschutz
lace
cinta
lacet
Schnürsenkel
14 OZ

FISHING
PESCA
PÊCHE
SPORTFISCHEREI

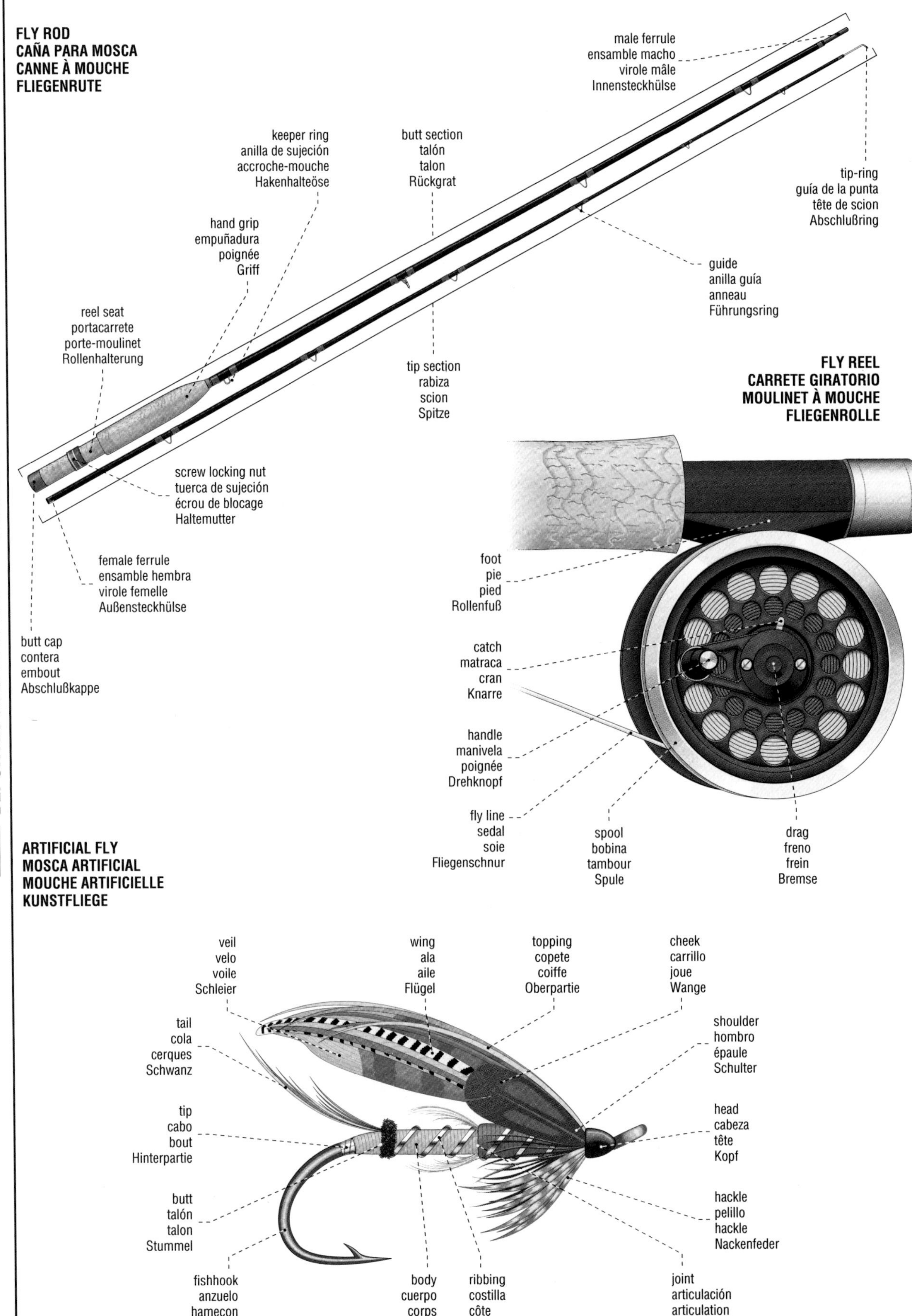

FLY ROD
CAÑA PARA MOSCA
CANNE À MOUCHE
FLIEGENRUTE
male ferrule
ensamble macho
virole mâle
Innensteckhülse
keeper ring
anilla de sujeción
accroche-mouche
Hakenhalteöse
butt section
talón
talon
Rückgrat
tip-ring
guía de la punta
tête de scion
Abschlußring
hand grip
empuñadura
poignée
Griff
guide
anilla guía
anneau
Führungsring
reel seat
portacarrete
porte-moulinet
Rollenhalterung
tip section
rabiza
scion
Spitze
FLY REEL
CARRETE GIRATORIO
MOULINET À MOUCHE
FLIEGENROLLE
screw locking nut
tuerca de sujeción
écrou de blocage
Haltemutter
female ferrule
ensamble hembra
virole femelle
Außensteckhülse
foot
pie
pied
Rollenfuß
butt cap
contera
embout
Abschlußkappe
catch
matraca
cran
Knarre
handle
manivela
poignée
Drehknopf
fly line
sedal
soie
Fliegenschnur
spool
bobina
tambour
Spule
drag
freno
frein
Bremse
ARTIFICIAL FLY
MOSCA ARTIFICIAL
MOUCHE ARTIFICIELLE
KUNSTFLIEGE
veil
velo
voile
Schleier
wing
ala
aile
Flügel
topping
copete
coiffe
Oberpartie
cheek
carrillo
joue
Wange
tail
cola
cerques
Schwanz
shoulder
hombro
épaule
Schulter
tip
cabo
bout
Hinterpartie
head
cabeza
tête
Kopf
butt
talón
talon
Stummel
hackle
pelillo
hackle
Nackenfeder
fishhook
anzuelo
hameçon
Angelhaken
body
cuerpo
corps
Körper
ribbing
costilla
côte
Wicklung
joint
articulación
articulation
Spiralbindung

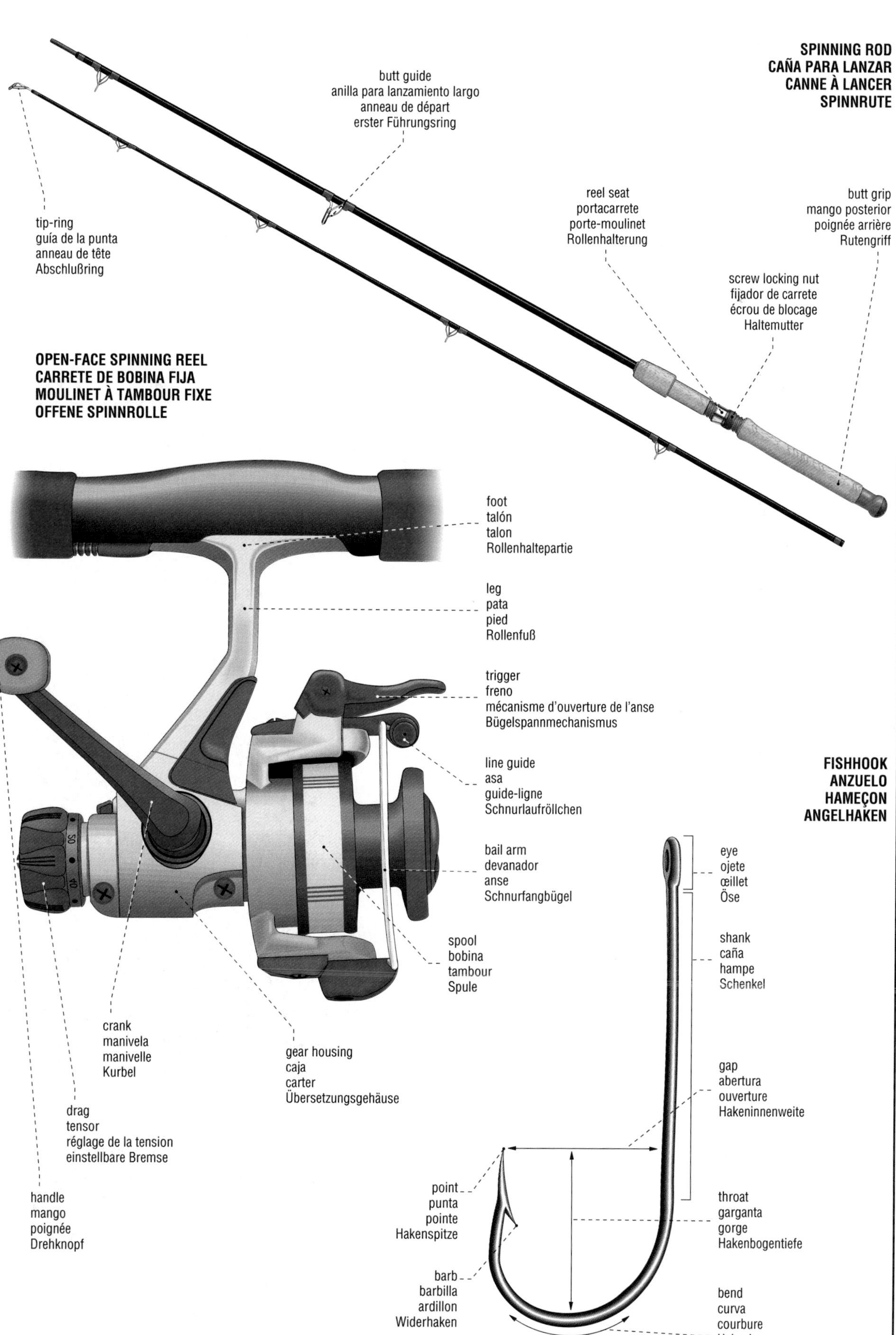
SPINNING ROD
CAÑA PARA LANZAR
CANNE À LANCER
SPINNRUTE
butt guide
anilla para lanzamiento largo
anneau de départ
erster Führungsring
tip-ring
guía de la punta
anneau de tête
Abschlußring
reel seat
portacarrete
porte-moulinet
Rollenhalterung
butt grip
mango posterior
poignée arrière
Rutengriff
screw locking nut
fijador de carrete
écrou de blocage
Haltemutter
OPEN-FACE SPINNING REEL
CARRETE DE BOBINA FIJA
MOULINET À TAMBOUR FIXE
OFFENE SPINNROLLE
foot
talón
talon
Rollenhaltepartie
leg
pata
pied
Rollenfuß
trigger
freno
mécanisme d'ouverture de l'anse
Bügelspannmechanismus
line guide
asa
guide-ligne
Schnurlaufröllchen
bail arm
devanador
anse
Schnurfangbügel
spool
bobina
tambour
Spule
crank
manivela
manivelle
Kurbel
gear housing
caja
carter
Übersetzungsgehäuse
drag
tensor
réglage de la tension
einstellbare Bremse
handle
mango
poignée
Drehknopf
FISHHOOK
ANZUELO
HAMEÇON
ANGELHAKEN
eye
ojete
œillet
Öse
shank
caña
hampe
Schenkel
gap
abertura
ouverture
Hakeninnenweite
point
punta
pointe
Hakenspitze
throat
garganta
gorge
Hakenbogentiefe
barb
barbilla
ardillon
Widerhaken
bend
curva
courbure
Hakenbogen

FISHING
PESCA
PÊCHE
SPORTFISCHEREI

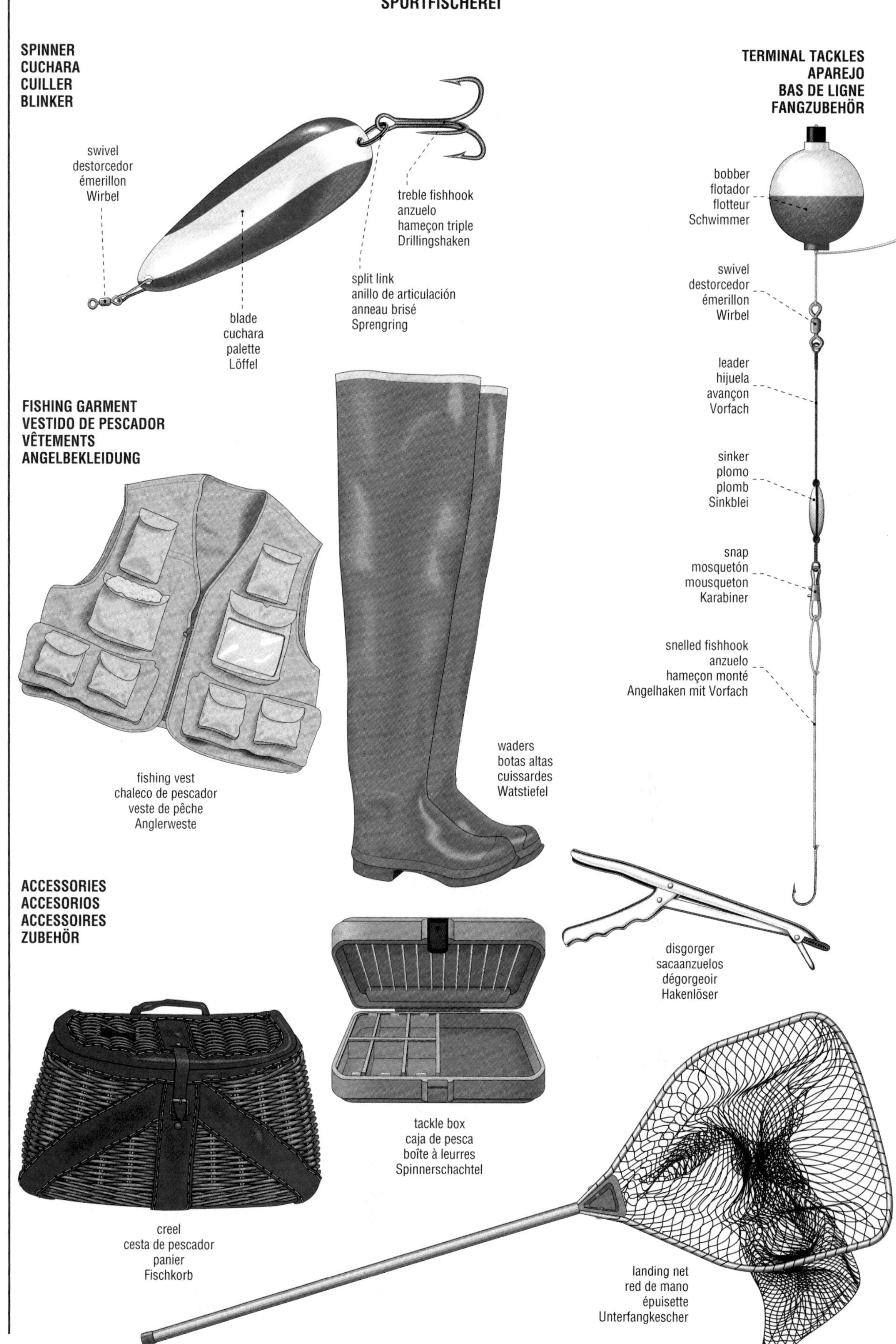
SPINNER
CUCHARA
CUILLER
BLINKER
swivel
destorcedor
émerillon
Wirbel
treble fishhook
anzuelo
hameçon triple
Drillingshaken
split link
anillo de articulación
anneau brisé
Sprengring
blade
cuchara
palette
Löffel
TERMINAL TACKLES
APAREJO
BAS DE LIGNE
FANGZUBEHÖR
bobber
flotador
flotteur
Schwimmer
swivel
destorcedor
émerillon
Wirbel
leader
hijuela
avançon
Vorfach
sinker
plomo
plomb
Sinkblei
snap
mosquetón
mousqueton
Karabiner
snelled fishhook
anzuelo
hameçon monté
Angelhaken mit Vorfach
FISHING GARMENT
VESTIDO DE PESCADOR
VÊTEMENTS
ANGELBEKLEIDUNG
fishing vest
chaleco de pescador
veste de pêche
Anglerweste
waders
botas altas
cuissardes
Watstiefel
ACCESSORIES
ACCESORIOS
ACCESSOIRES
ZUBEHÖR
disgorger
sacaanzuelos
dégorgeoir
Hakenlöser
tackle box
caja de pesca
boîte à leurres
Spinnerschachtel
creel
cesta de pescador
panier
Fischkorb
landing net
red de mano
épuisette
Unterfangkescher

BILLIARDS
BILLAR
BILLARD
BILLIARD

CAROM BILLIARDS
CARAMBOLA
BILLARD FRANÇAIS
KARAMBOLAGEBILLARD

POOL
POOL
BILLARD POOL
POOL

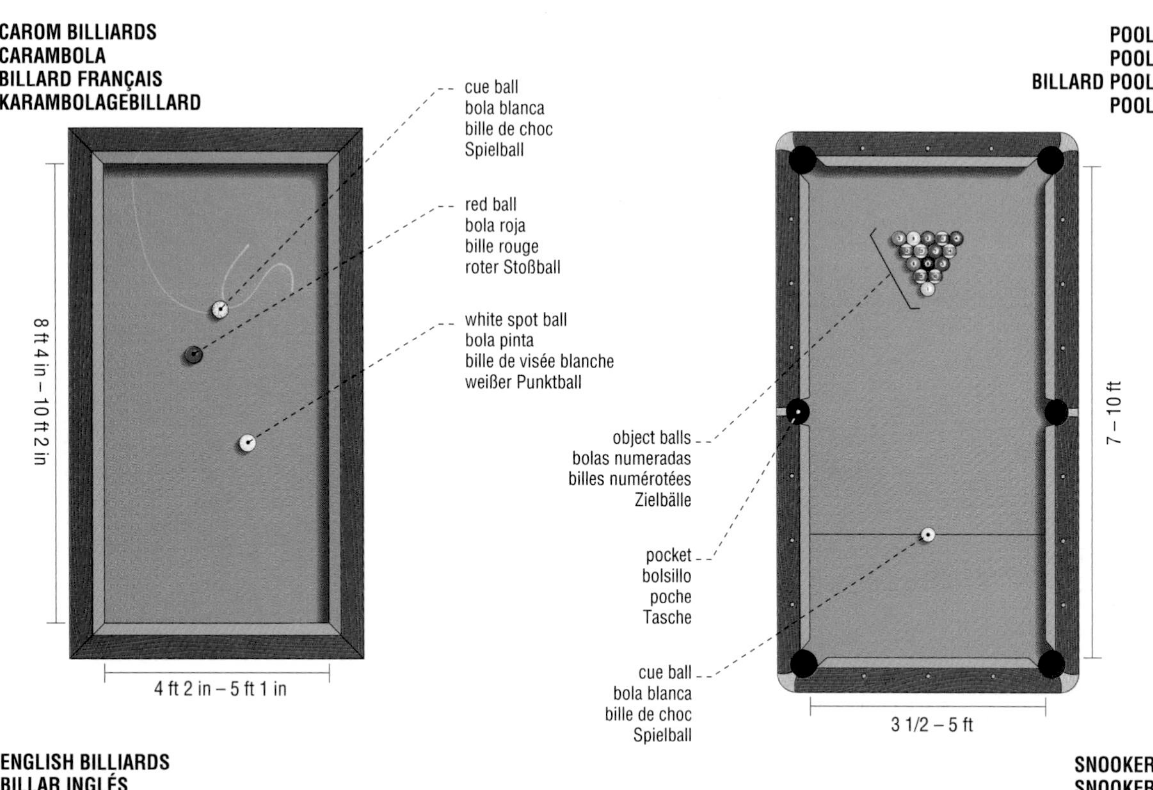

cue ball
bola blanca
bille de choc
Spielball
red ball
bola roja
bille rouge
roter Stoßball
white spot ball
bola pinta
bille de visée blanche
weißer Punktball
8 ft 4 in – 10 ft 2 in
4 ft 2 in – 5 ft 1 in
object balls
bolas numeradas
billes numérotées
Zielbälle
pocket
bolsillo
poche
Tasche
cue ball
bola blanca
bille de choc
Spielball
7 – 10 ft
3 1/2 – 5 ft

ENGLISH BILLIARDS
BILLAR INGLÉS
BILLARD ANGLAIS
LOCHBILLARD

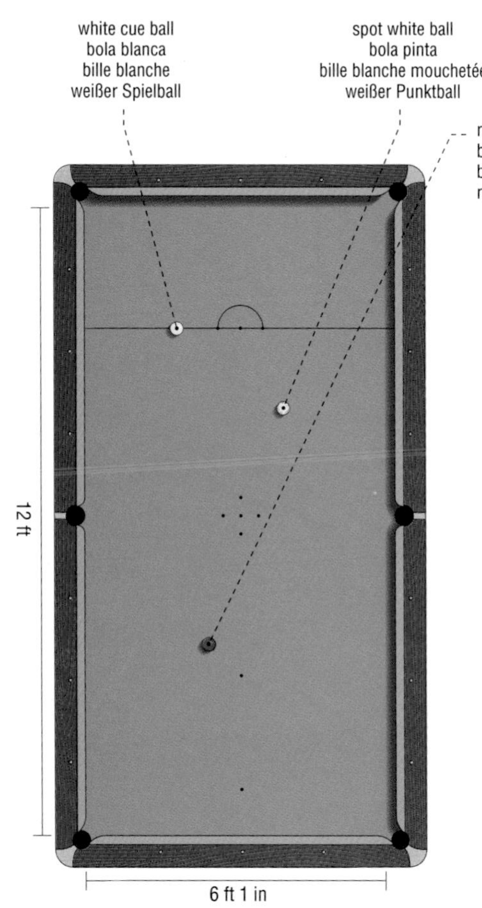

white cue ball
bola blanca
bille blanche
weißer Spielball
spot white ball
bola pinta
bille blanche mouchetée
weißer Punktball
red ball
bola roja
bille rouge
roter Ball
12 ft
6 ft 1 in

SNOOKER
SNOOKER
SNOOKER
SNOOKER

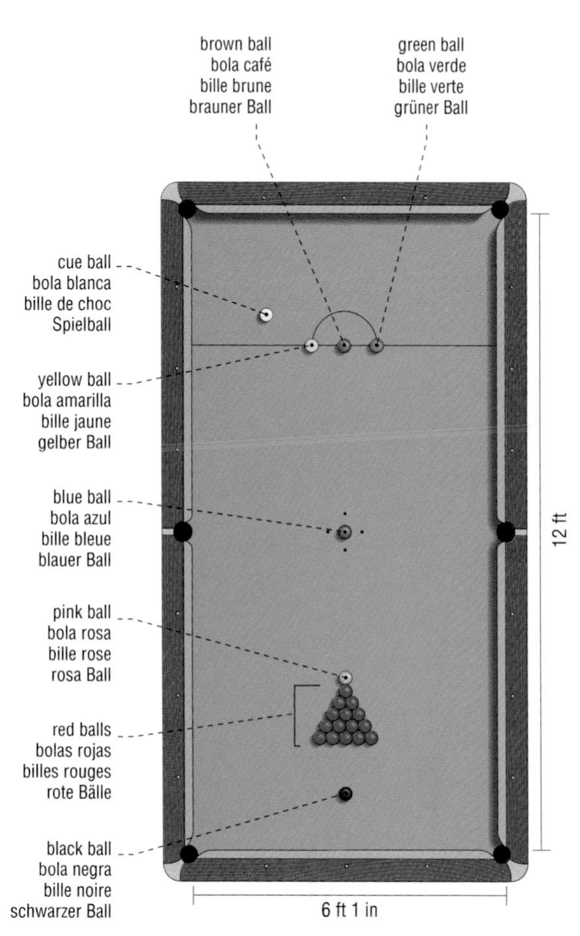

brown ball
bola café
bille brune
brauner Ball
green ball
bola verde
bille verte
grüner Ball
cue ball
bola blanca
bille de choc
Spielball
yellow ball
bola amarilla
bille jaune
gelber Ball
blue ball
bola azul
bille bleue
blauer Ball
pink ball
bola rosa
bille rose
rosa Ball
red balls
bolas rojas
billes rouges
rote Bälle
black ball
bola negra
bille noire
schwarzer Ball
12 ft
6 ft 1 in

ENGLISH BILLIARDS AND SNOOKER
BILLAR INGLÉS Y SNOOKER
BILLARD ANGLAIS ET SNOOKER
LOCHBILLARD UND SNOOKER

TABLE
MESA
TABLE
BILLARDTISCH
balk line spot
mosca de la línea de cuadro
mouche de ligne de cadre
Anstoßpunkt
center spot
mosca central
mouche centrale
Mittelpunkt
balk area
cuadro
cadre
Anstoßraum
«D»
semicírculo
«D»
«D»
bottom pocket
bolsillo
poche inférieure
untere Tasche
head cushion
banda de goma
coussin de tête
Endbande
balk line
línea de cuadro
ligne de cadre
Anstoßlinie
hook
vástago
crochet
Haken
center pocket
bolsillo
poche centrale
Mitteltasche
BRIDGE
BURRA
RÂTEAU
STEG
shaft
mango
manche
Stiel
notch
muesca
dent
Kerbe
end-piece
cabeza
tête
Endstück
rack
triángulo
triangle
Dreieck

baize
tapete
tapis
Bespannung
pyramid spot
mosca superior
mouche supérieure
Aufstellpunkt
billiard spot
mosca
mouche
Aufstellpunkt
foot cushion
banda de la cabecera
coussin arrière
Stirnbande
top pocket
bolsillo
poche supérieure
obere Tasche
rail
baranda
bande
Rahmen
chalk
tiza
craie
Kreide
BILLIARD CUE
TACO DE BILLAR
QUEUE DE BILLARD
BILLARDQUEUE
tip
suela
procédé
Kuppe
ferrule
casquillo
virole
Kuppenring
shaft
mango
flèche
Schaft
joint
articulación
tourillon
Gewinde
butt
maza
talon
Griffteil

COURSE
CAMPO DE GOLF
PARCOURS
GOLFPLATZ

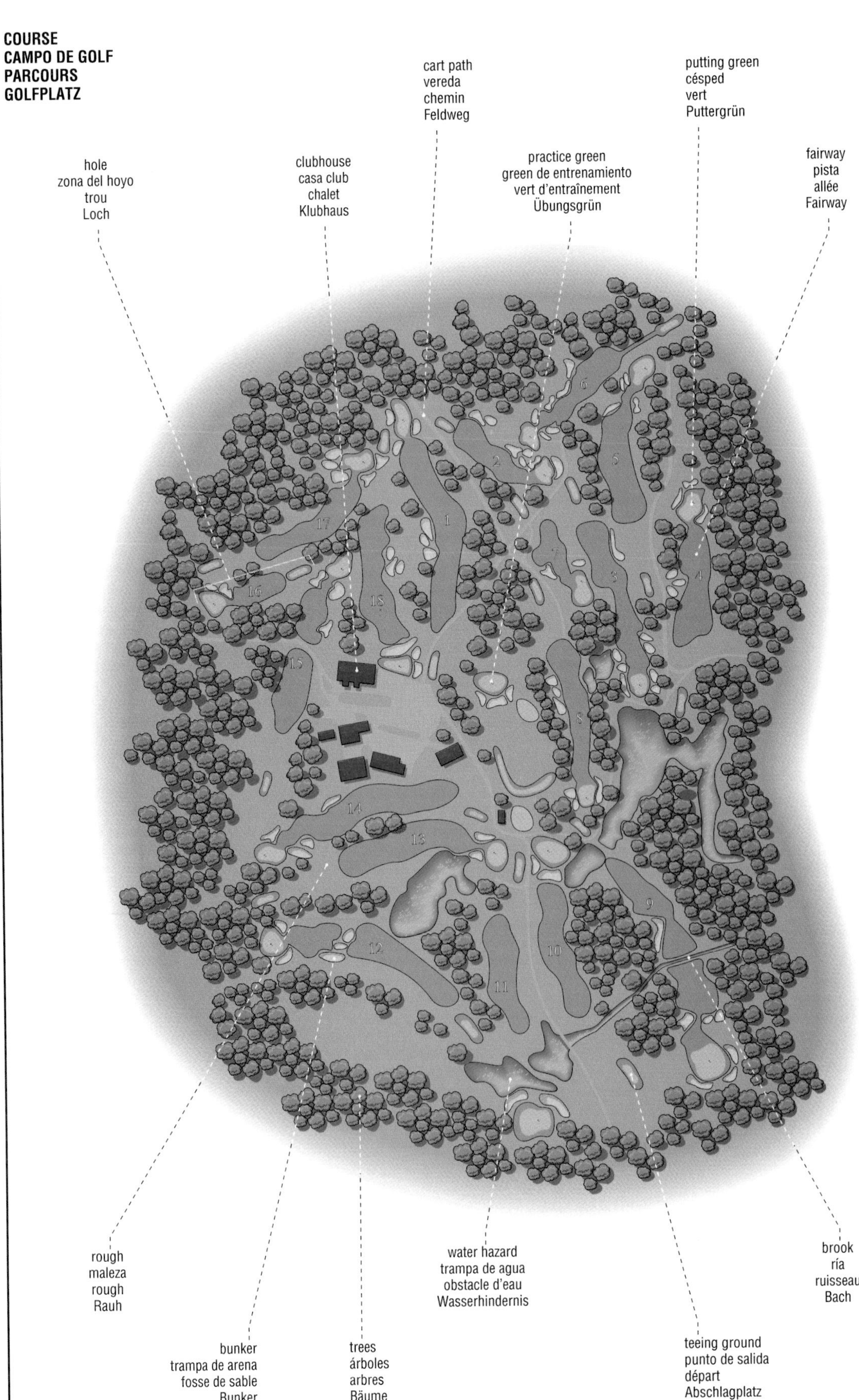
hole
zona del hoyo
trou
Loch
clubhouse
casa club
chalet
Klubhaus
cart path
vereda
chemin
Feldweg
practice green
green de entrenamiento
vert d'entraînement
Übungsgrün
putting green
césped
vert
Puttergrün
fairway
pista
allée
Fairway
rough
maleza
rough
Rauh
bunker
trampa de arena
fosse de sable
Bunker
trees
árboles
arbres
Bäume
water hazard
trampa de agua
obstacle d'eau
Wasserhindernis
teeing ground
punto de salida
départ
Abschlagplatz
brook
ría
ruisseau
Bach

CROSS SECTION OF A GOLF BALL
CORTE TRANSVERSAL DE UNA PELOTA DE GOLF
COUPE D'UNE BALLE DE GOLF
GOLFBALL IM QUERSCHNITT

GOLF BALL
PELOTA DE GOLF
BALLE DE GOLF
GOLFBALL

TYPES OF GOLF CLUBS
BASTONES
TYPES DE BÂTONS DE GOLF
ARTEN VON GOLFSCHLÄGER

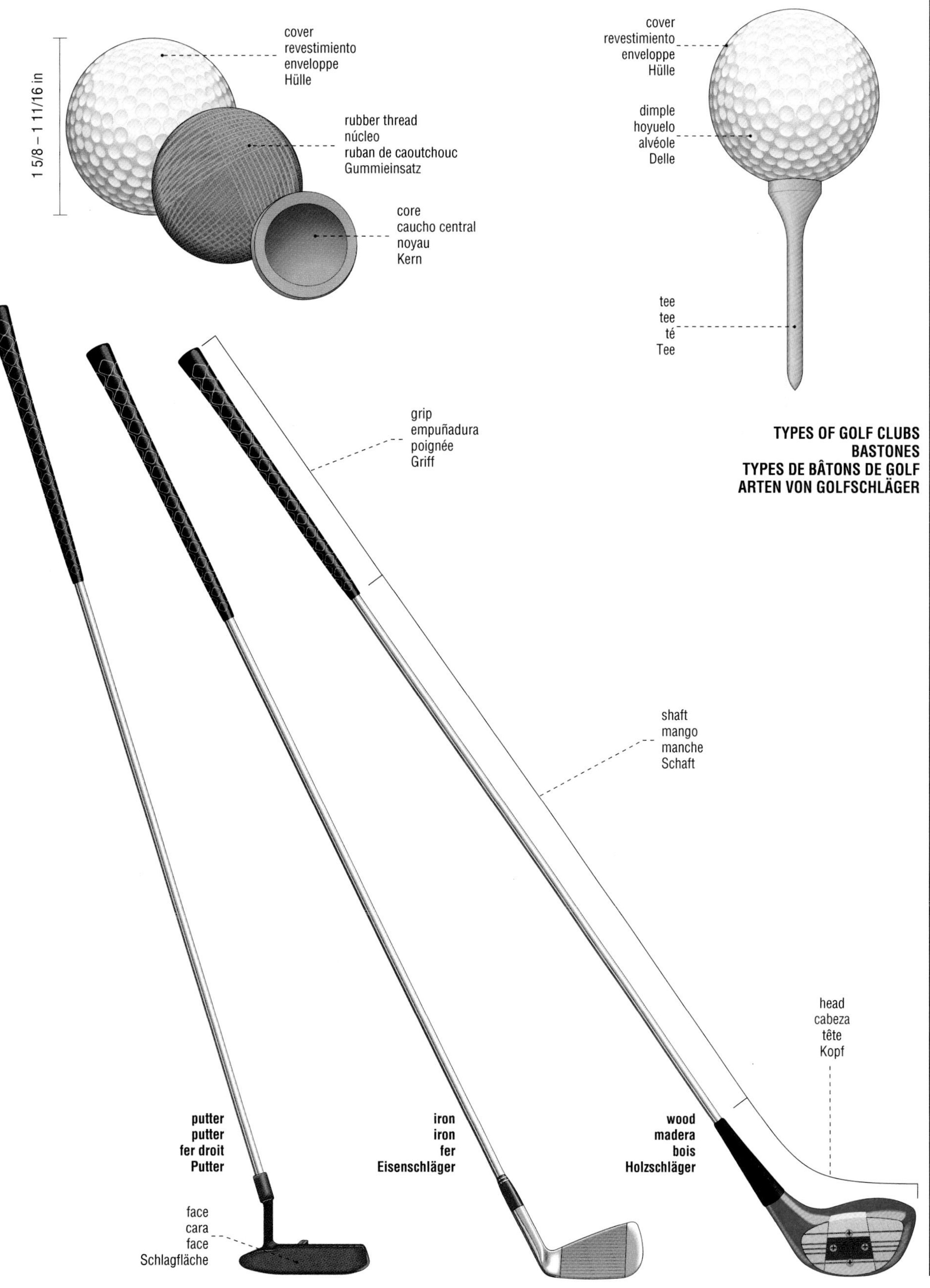
1 5/8 – 1 11/16 in
cover
revestimiento
enveloppe
Hülle
rubber thread
núcleo
ruban de caoutchouc
Gummieinsatz
core
caucho central
noyau
Kern
cover
revestimiento
enveloppe
Hülle
dimple
hoyuelo
alvéole
Delle
tee
tee
té
Tee
grip
empuñadura
poignée
Griff
shaft
mango
manche
Schaft
head
cabeza
tête
Kopf
putter
putter
fer droit
Putter
iron
iron
fer
Eisenschläger
wood
madera
bois
Holzschläger
face
cara
face
Schlagfläche

GOLF
GOLF
GOLF
GOLFSPIEL

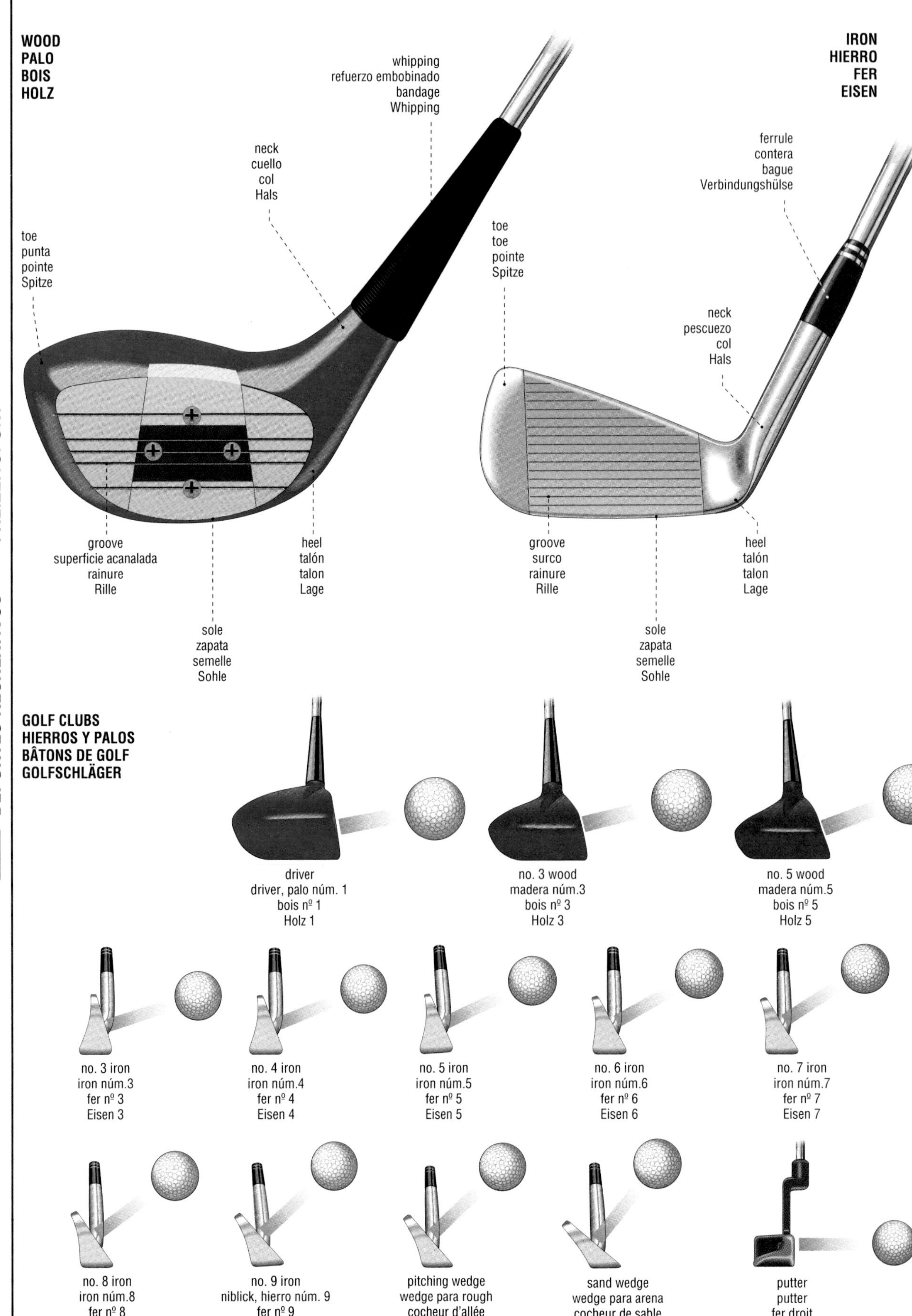
WOOD
PALO
BOIS
HOLZ
IRON
HIERRO
FER
EISEN
whipping
refuerzo embobinado
bandage
Whipping
neck
cuello
col
Hals
toe
punta
pointe
Spitze
groove
superficie acanalada
rainure
Rille
heel
talón
talon
Lage
sole
zapata
semelle
Sohle
ferrule
contera
bague
Verbindungshülse
toe
toe
pointe
Spitze
neck
pescuezo
col
Hals
groove
surco
rainure
Rille
heel
talón
talon
Lage
sole
zapata
semelle
Sohle
GOLF CLUBS
HIERROS Y PALOS
BÂTONS DE GOLF
GOLFSCHLÄGER
driver
driver, palo núm. 1
bois nº 1
Holz 1
no. 3 wood
madera núm.3
bois nº 3
Holz 3
no. 5 wood
madera núm.5
bois nº 5
Holz 5
no. 3 iron
iron núm.3
fer nº 3
Eisen 3
no. 4 iron
iron núm.4
fer nº 4
Eisen 4
no. 5 iron
iron núm.5
fer nº 5
Eisen 5
no. 6 iron
iron núm.6
fer nº 6
Eisen 6
no. 7 iron
iron núm.7
fer nº 7
Eisen 7
no. 8 iron
iron núm.8
fer nº 8
Eisen 8
no. 9 iron
niblick, hierro núm. 9
fer nº 9
Eisen 9
pitching wedge
wedge para rough
cocheur d'allée
Pitching-Wedge
sand wedge
wedge para arena
cocheur de sable
Sand-Wedge
putter
putter
fer droit
Putter

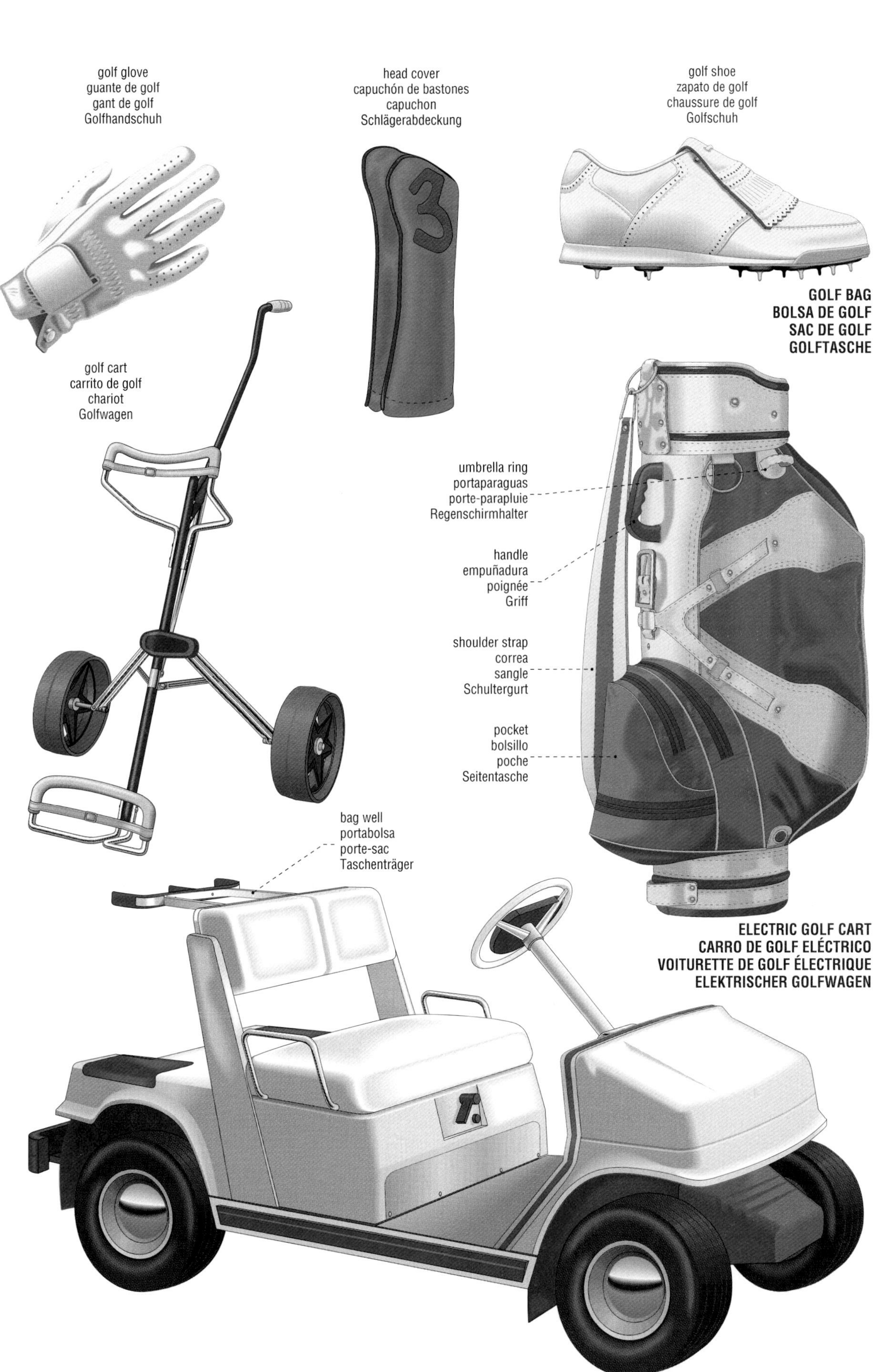
golf glove
guante de golf
gant de golf
Golfhandschuh
head cover
capuchón de bastones
capuchon
Schlägerabdeckung
golf shoe
zapato de golf
chaussure de golf
Golfschuh
GOLF BAG
BOLSA DE GOLF
SAC DE GOLF
GOLFTASCHE
golf cart
carrito de golf
chariot
Golfwagen
umbrella ring
portaparaguas
porte-parapluie
Regenschirmhalter
handle
empuñadura
poignée
Griff
shoulder strap
correa
sangle
Schultergurt
pocket
bolsillo
poche
Seitentasche
bag well
portabolsa
porte-sac
Taschenträger
ELECTRIC GOLF CART
CARRO DE GOLF ELÉCTRICO
VOITURETTE DE GOLF ÉLECTRIQUE
ELEKTRISCHER GOLFWAGEN

MOUNTAINEERING
ALPINISMO
ALPINISME
BERGSTEIGEN

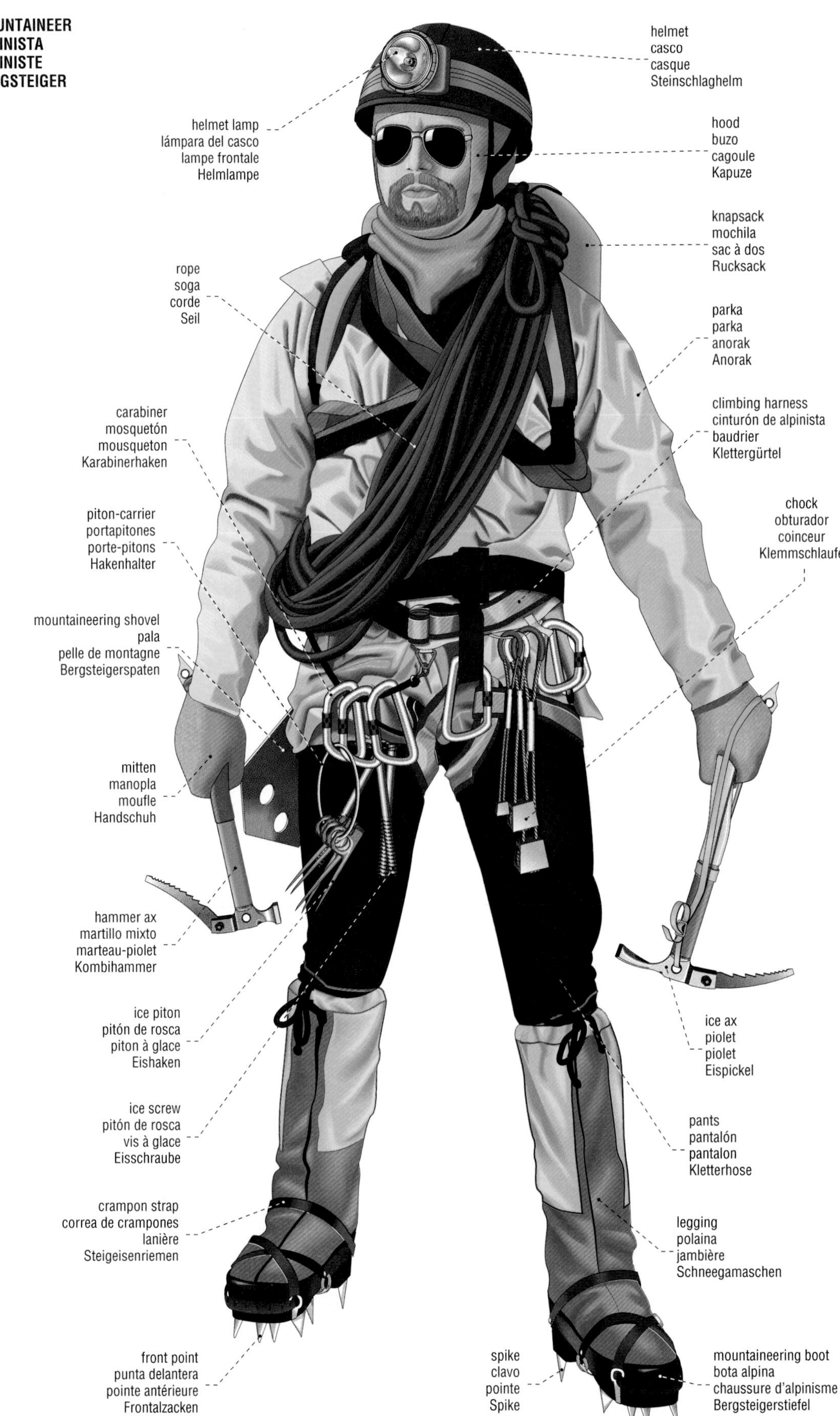
MOUNTAINEER
ALPINISTA
ALPINISTE
BERGSTEIGER
helmet
casco
casque
Steinschlaghelm
helmet lamp
lámpara del casco
lampe frontale
Helmlampe
hood
buzo
cagoule
Kapuze
knapsack
mochila
sac à dos
Rucksack
rope
soga
corde
Seil
parka
parka
anorak
Anorak
carabiner
mosquetón
mousqueton
Karabinerhaken
climbing harness
cinturón de alpinista
baudrier
Klettergürtel
piton-carrier
portapitones
porte-pitons
Hakenhalter
chock
obturador
coinceur
Klemmschlaufe
mountaineering shovel
pala
pelle de montagne
Bergsteigerspaten
mitten
manopla
moufle
Handschuh
hammer ax
martillo mixto
marteau-piolet
Kombihammer
ice ax
piolet
piolet
Eispickel
ice piton
pitón de rosca
piton à glace
Eishaken
ice screw
pitón de rosca
vis à glace
Eisschraube
pants
pantalón
pantalon
Kletterhose
crampon strap
correa de crampones
lanière
Steigeisenriemen
legging
polaina
jambière
Schneegamaschen
front point
punta delantera
pointe antérieure
Frontalzacken
spike
clavo
pointe
Spike
mountaineering boot
bota alpina
chaussure d'alpinisme
Bergsteigerstiefel

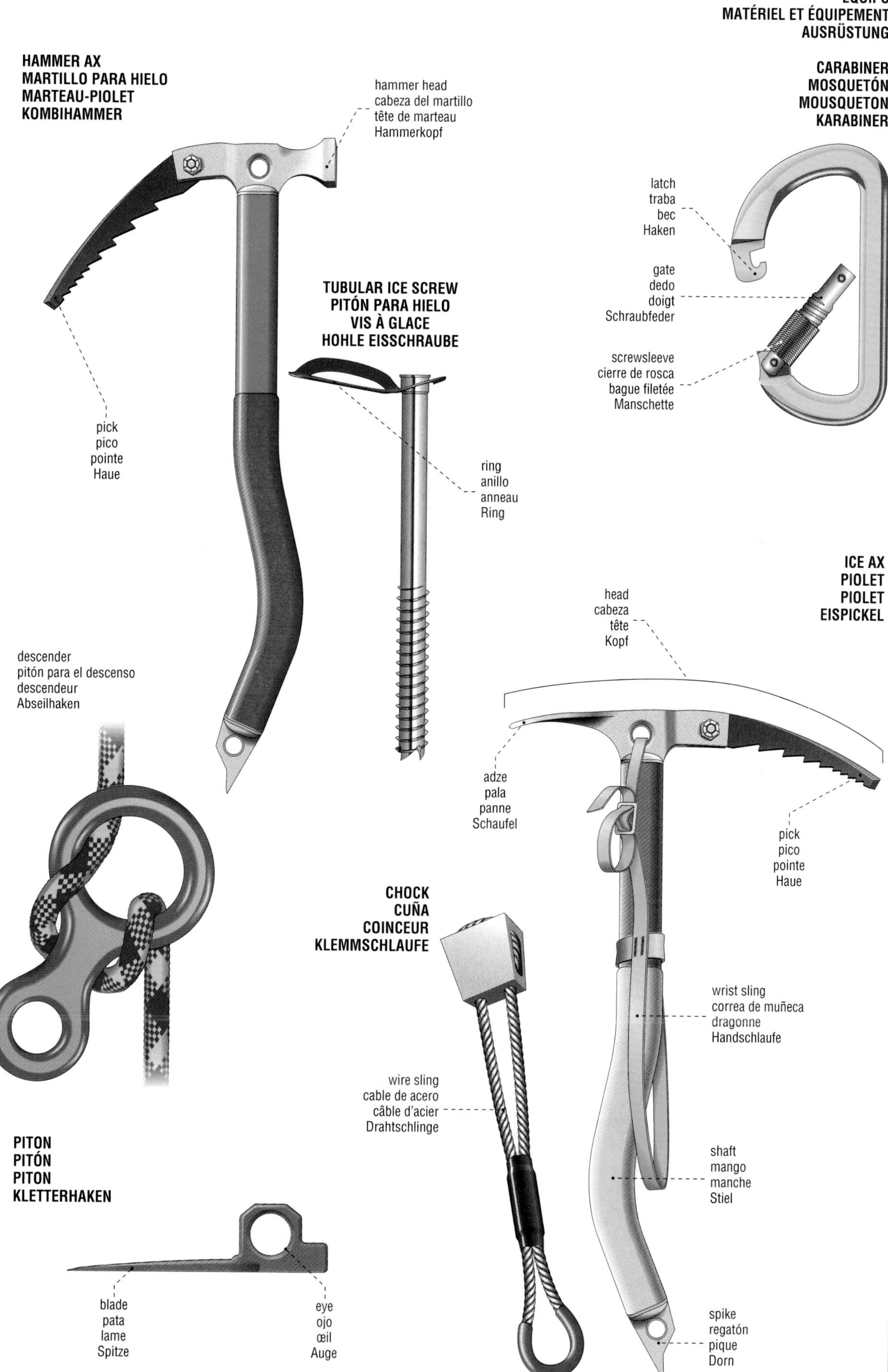
HAMMER AX
MARTILLO PARA HIELO
MARTEAU-PIOLET
KOMBIHAMMER
hammer head
cabeza del martillo
tête de marteau
Hammerkopf
pick
pico
pointe
Haue
TUBULAR ICE SCREW
PITÓN PARA HIELO
VIS À GLACE
HOHLE EISSCHRAUBE
ring
anillo
anneau
Ring
CARABINER
MOSQUETÓN
MOUSQUETON
KARABINER
latch
traba
bec
Haken
gate
dedo
doigt
Schraubfeder
screwsleeve
cierre de rosca
bague filetée
Manschette
ICE AX
PIOLET
PIOLET
EISPICKEL
head
cabeza
tête
Kopf
adze
pala
panne
Schaufel
pick
pico
pointe
Haue
descender
pitón para el descenso
descendeur
Abseilhaken
CHOCK
CUÑA
COINCEUR
KLEMMSCHLAUFE
wrist sling
correa de muñeca
dragonne
Handschlaufe
wire sling
cable de acero
câble d'acier
Drahtschlinge
shaft
mango
manche
Stiel
PITON
PITÓN
PITON
KLETTERHAKEN
blade
pata
lame
Spitze
eye
ojo
œil
Auge
spike
regatón
pique
Dorn

BOWLS AND PETANQUE
BOLOS Y PETANCA
BOULES ANGLAISES ET PÉTANQUE
BOULE UND PETANQUE

GREEN
BOLERA EN EL CÉSPED
PELOUSE
GRÜN

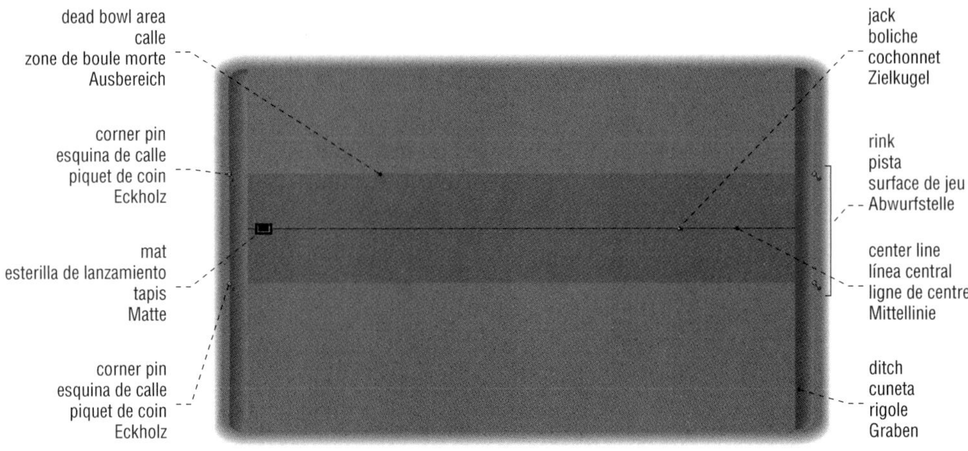
dead bowl area
calle
zone de boule morte
Ausbereich
corner pin
esquina de calle
piquet de coin
Eckholz
mat
esterilla de lanzamiento
tapis
Matte
corner pin
esquina de calle
piquet de coin
Eckholz
jack
boliche
cochonnet
Zielkugel
rink
pista
surface de jeu
Abwurfstelle
center line
línea central
ligne de centre
Mittellinie
ditch
cuneta
rigole
Graben

DELIVERY
LANZAMIENTO
LANCEMENT DE LA BOULE
ABWURF

forward swing
impulso de lanzamiento
élan
Schwungholen

delivery
lanzamiento
lancer
Aufsetzen

follow-through
seguimiento de la bola
accompagnement
Abwurf

bowl
bola
boule anglaise
Boulekugel

petanque bowl
bocha
boule de pétanque
Petanquekugel

jack
boliche
cochonnet
Zielkugel

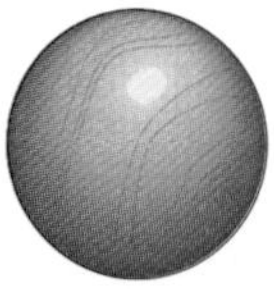

BOWLING
JUEGO DE BOLOS
JEU DE QUILLES
BOWLING

BOWLING BALL
BOLA
BOULE DE QUILLES
BOWLINGKUGEL

TYPES OF PINS
TIPOS DE BOLOS
TYPES DE QUILLES
VERSCHIEDENE PINS

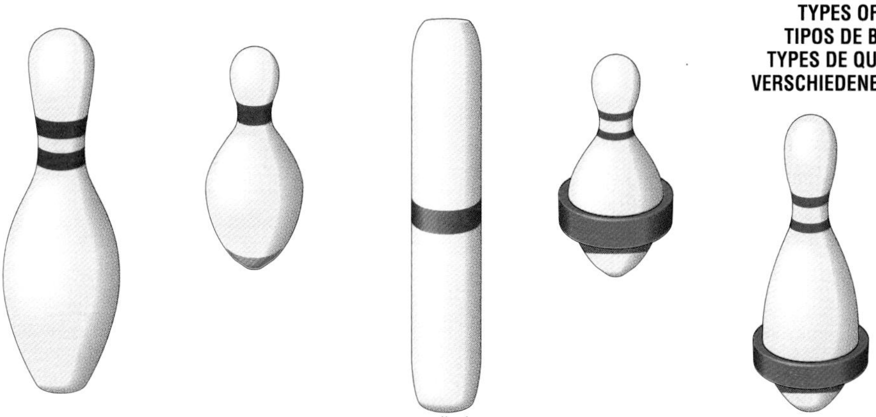

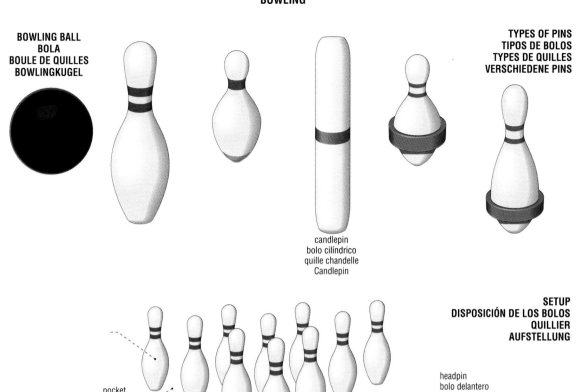

candlepin
bolo cilíndrico
quille chandelle
Candlepin

SETUP
DISPOSICIÓN DE LOS BOLOS
QUILLIER
AUFSTELLUNG

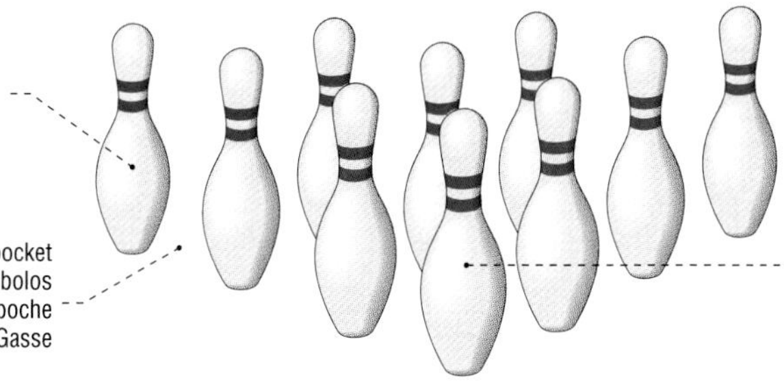

pocket
separación entre bolos
poche
Gasse

headpin
bolo delantero
quille-reine
Vordereckpin

LANE
PISTA
PISTE
BAHN

score-console
marcador
tableau marqueur
Punktekonsole

ball return
devolvedor
monte-boules
Kugelrücklaufkasten

keyboard
teclado
clavier
Kontrollkonsole

ball stand
stand de bolos
boulier
Kugelträger

setup
disposición de los bolos
quillier
Aufstellmaschine

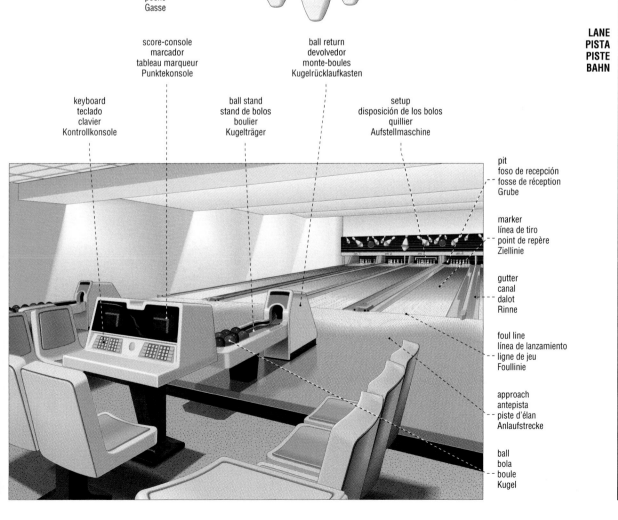

pit
foso de recepción
fosse de réception
Grube

marker
línea de tiro
point de repère
Ziellinie

gutter
canal
dalot
Rinne

foul line
línea de lanzamiento
ligne de jeu
Foullinie

approach
antepista
piste d'élan
Anlaufstrecke

ball
bola
boule
Kugel

ARCHERY
TIRO AL ARCO
TIR À L'ARC
BOGENSCHIESSEN

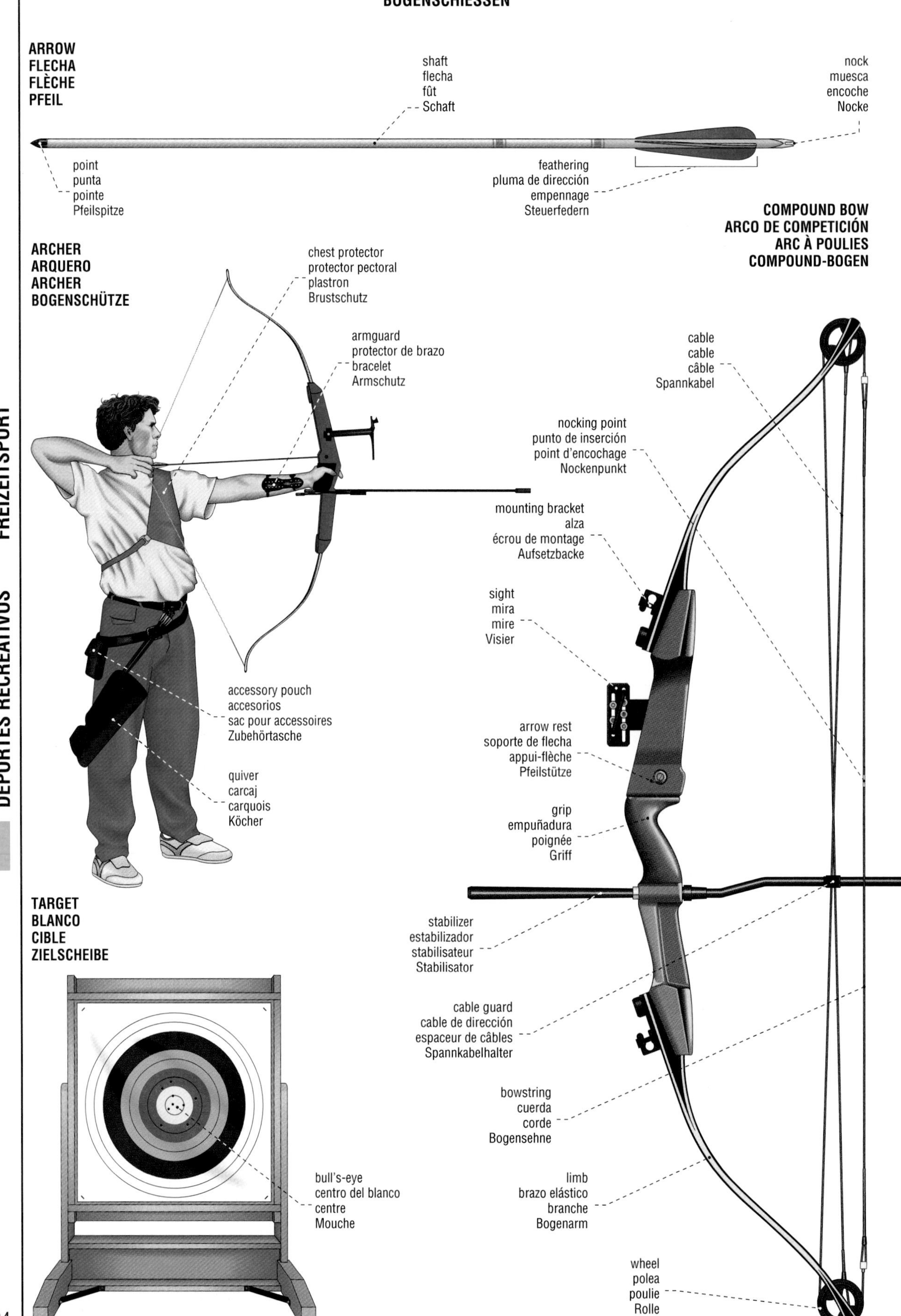
ARROW
FLECHA
FLÈCHE
PFEIL
shaft
flecha
fût
Schaft
nock
muesca
encoche
Nocke
point
punta
pointe
Pfeilspitze
feathering
pluma de dirección
empennage
Steuerfedern
COMPOUND BOW
ARCO DE COMPETICIÓN
ARC À POULIES
COMPOUND-BOGEN
ARCHER
ARQUERO
ARCHER
BOGENSCHÜTZE
chest protector
protector pectoral
plastron
Brustschutz
armguard
protector de brazo
bracelet
Armschutz
cable
cable
câble
Spannkabel
nocking point
punto de inserción
point d'encochage
Nockenpunkt
mounting bracket
alza
écrou de montage
Aufsetzbacke
sight
mira
mire
Visier
accessory pouch
accesorios
sac pour accessoires
Zubehörtasche
arrow rest
soporte de flecha
appui-flèche
Pfeilstütze
quiver
carcaj
carquois
Köcher
grip
empuñadura
poignée
Griff
TARGET
BLANCO
CIBLE
ZIELSCHEIBE
stabilizer
estabilizador
stabilisateur
Stabilisator
cable guard
cable de dirección
espaceur de câbles
Spannkabelhalter
bowstring
cuerda
corde
Bogensehne
bull's-eye
centro del blanco
centre
Mouche
limb
brazo elástico
branche
Bogenarm
wheel
polea
poulie
Rolle

CAMPING
CAMPING
CAMPING
CAMPING

TWO-PERSON TENT
TIENDA PARA DOS
TENTE DEUX PLACES
ZWEIPERSONENZELT

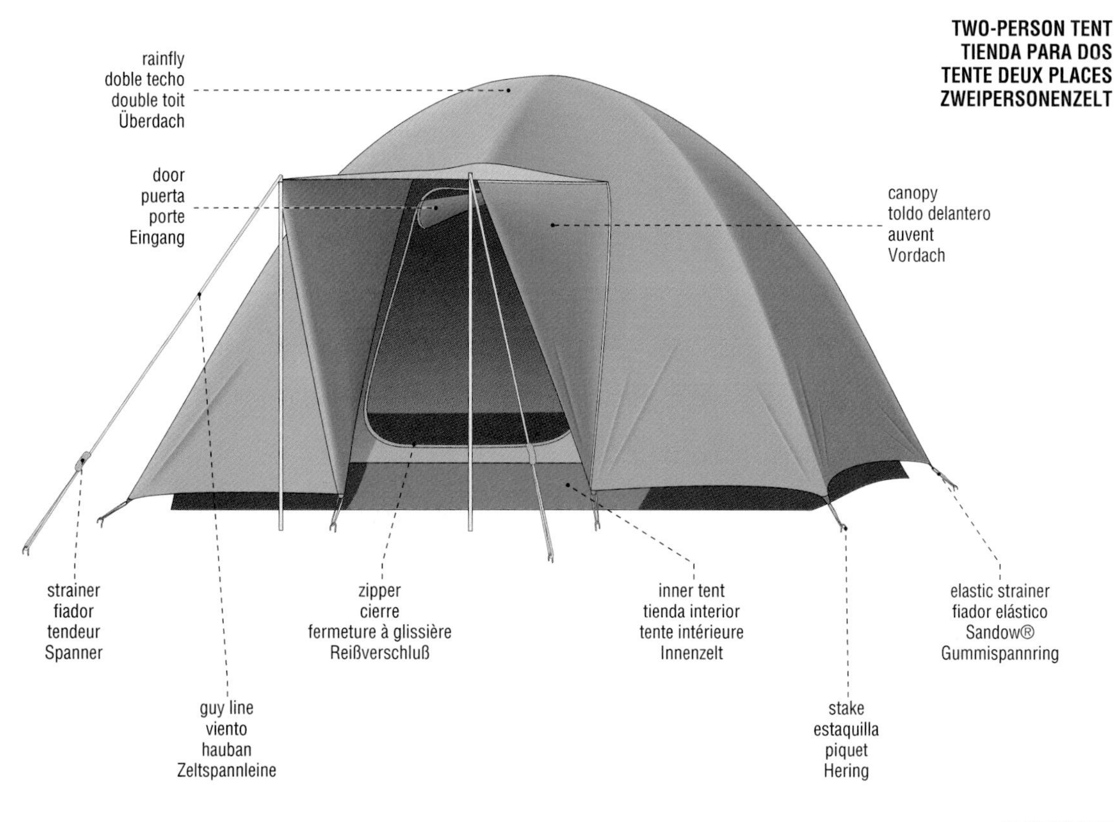
rainfly
doble techo
double toit
Überdach
door
puerta
porte
Eingang
canopy
toldo delantero
auvent
Vordach
strainer
fiador
tendeur
Spanner
zipper
cierre
fermeture à glissière
Reißverschluß
inner tent
tienda interior
tente intérieure
Innenzelt
elastic strainer
fiador elástico
Sandow®
Gummispannring
guy line
viento
hauban
Zeltspannleine
stake
estaquilla
piquet
Hering

FAMILY TENT
TIENDA DE CAMPAÑA TAMAÑO FAMILIAR
TENTE FAMILIALE
FAMILIENZELT

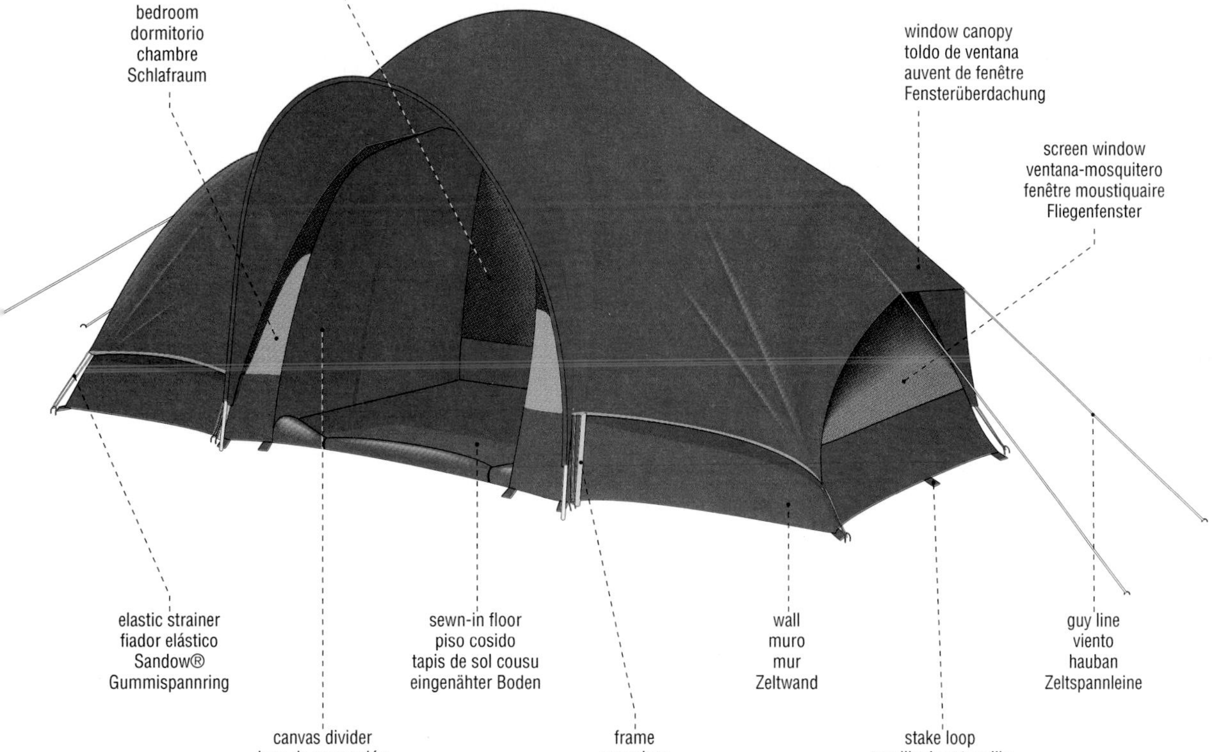

living room
cuarto de estar
séjour
Wohnraum

bedroom
dormitorio
chambre
Schlafraum

window canopy
toldo de ventana
auvent de fenêtre
Fensterüberdachung

screen window
ventana-mosquitero
fenêtre moustiquaire
Fliegenfenster

elastic strainer
fiador elástico
Sandow®
Gummispannring

sewn-in floor
piso cosido
tapis de sol cousu
eingenähter Boden

wall
muro
mur
Zeltwand

guy line
viento
hauban
Zeltspannleine

canvas divider
lona de separación
cloison
Raumteiler

frame
armadura
armature
Gestänge

stake loop
presilla de estaquilla
boucle de piquet
Heringsschlaufe

PUP TENT
TIENDA DE CAMPAÑA CLÁSICA
TENTE CANADIENNE
HAUSZELT

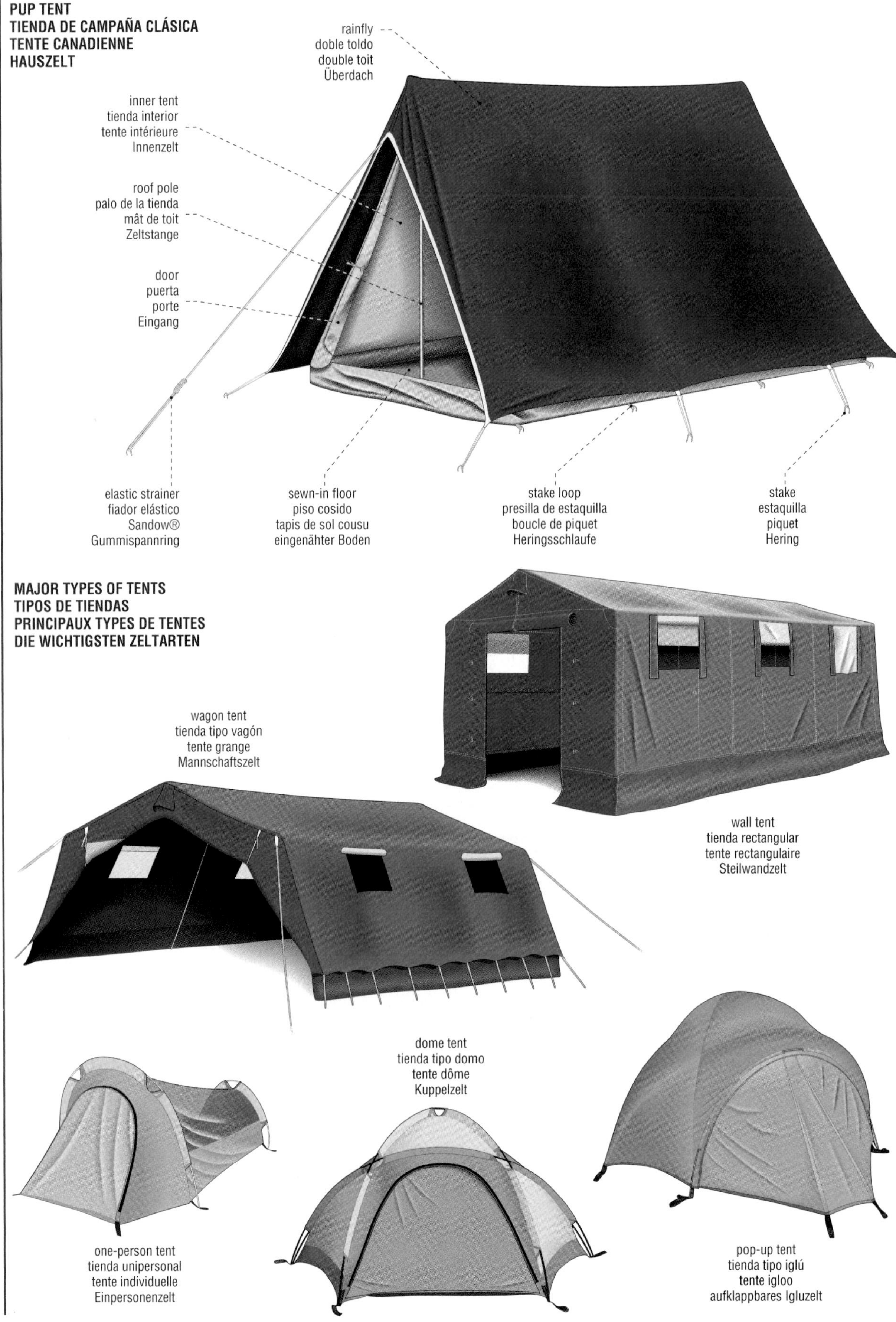
rainfly
doble toldo
double toit
Überdach
inner tent
tienda interior
tente intérieure
Innenzelt
roof pole
palo de la tienda
mât de toit
Zeltstange
door
puerta
porte
Eingang
elastic strainer
fiador elástico
Sandow®
Gummispannring
sewn-in floor
piso cosido
tapis de sol cousu
eingenähter Boden
stake loop
presilla de estaquilla
boucle de piquet
Heringsschlaufe
stake
estaquilla
piquet
Hering
MAJOR TYPES OF TENTS
TIPOS DE TIENDAS
PRINCIPAUX TYPES DE TENTES
DIE WICHTIGSTEN ZELTARTEN
wagon tent
tienda tipo vagón
tente grange
Mannschaftszelt
wall tent
tienda rectangular
tente rectangulaire
Steilwandzelt
dome tent
tienda tipo domo
tente dôme
Kuppelzelt
one-person tent
tienda unipersonal
tente individuelle
Einpersonenzelt
pop-up tent
tienda tipo iglú
tente igloo
aufklappbares Igluzelt

BED AND MATTRESS
CAMAS Y COLCHONETAS
LIT ET MATELAS
BETT MIT MATRATZE

foam pad
colchón de espuma
matelas mousse
Schaumgummimatratze
self-inflating mattress
colchón aislante
matelas autogonflant
Luftmatratze
air mattress
colchón de aire
matelas pneumatique
Luftmatratze
inflator
inflador
gonfleur
Blasebalg
inflator-deflator
muelle para inflar y desinflar
gonfleur-dégonfleur
Kombipumpe
folding cot
catre desmontable
lit de camp pliant
Faltfeldbett
SLEEPING BAGS
SACOS DE DORMIR
SACS DE COUCHAGE
SCHLAFSÄCKE
mummy
montañero
à cagoule
Mumienschlafsack
semi-mummy
saco semirrectangular
semi-rectangulaire
Halbmumienschlafsack
rectangular
saco rectangular
rectangulaire
Rechteckschlafsack

CAMPING EQUIPMENT
EQUIPO PARA ACAMPAR
MATÉRIEL DE CAMPING
CAMPINGAUSRÜSTUNG

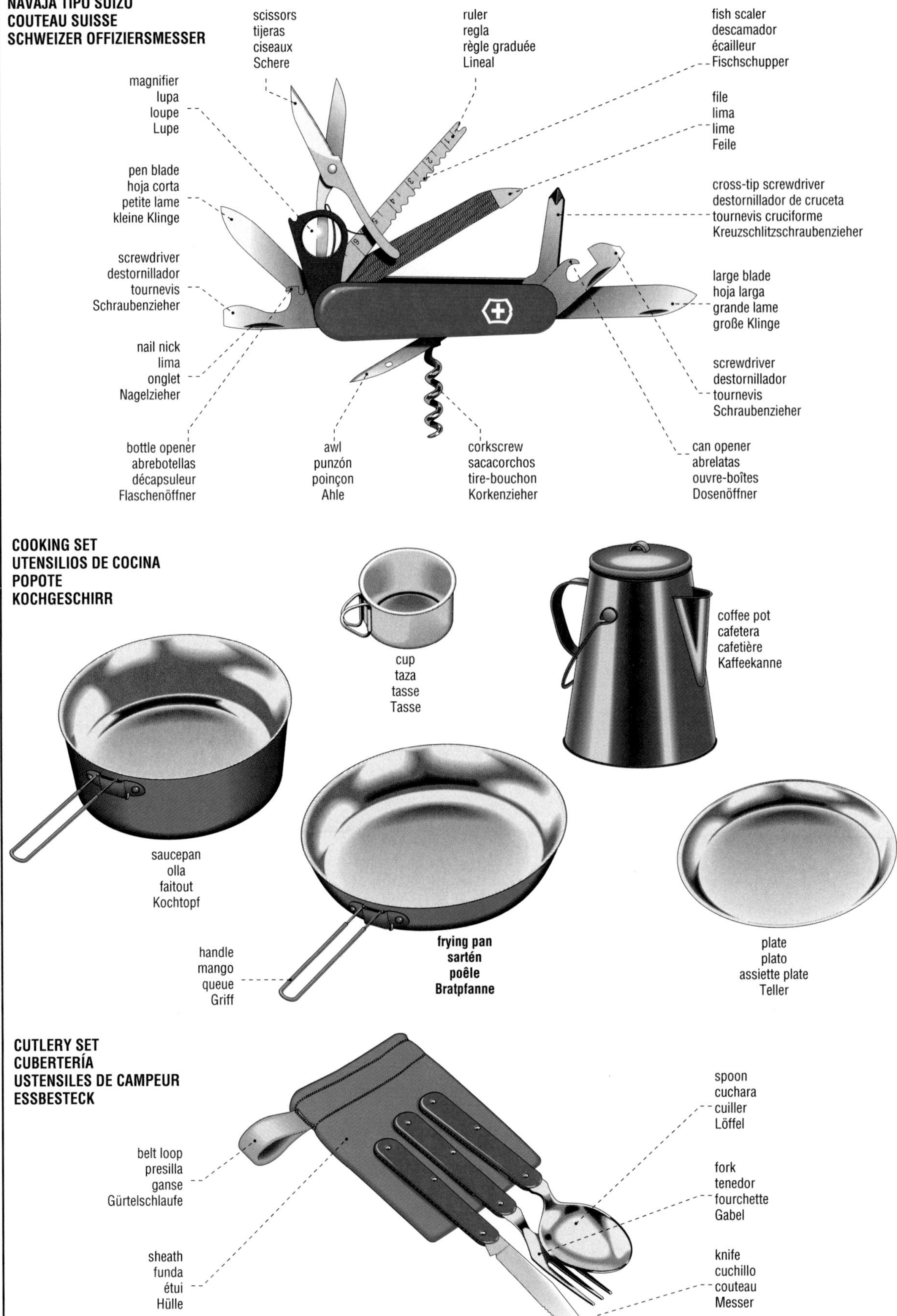

SWISS ARMY KNIFE
NAVAJA TIPO SUIZO
COUTEAU SUISSE
SCHWEIZER OFFIZIERSMESSER
scissors
tijeras
ciseaux
Schere
ruler
regla
règle graduée
Lineal
fish scaler
descamador
écailleur
Fischschupper
magnifier
lupa
loupe
Lupe
file
lima
lime
Feile
pen blade
hoja corta
petite lame
kleine Klinge
cross-tip screwdriver
destornillador de cruceta
tournevis cruciforme
Kreuzschlitzschraubenzieher
screwdriver
destornillador
tournevis
Schraubenzieher
large blade
hoja larga
grande lame
große Klinge
nail nick
lima
onglet
Nagelzieher
screwdriver
destornillador
tournevis
Schraubenzieher
bottle opener
abrebotellas
décapsuleur
Flaschenöffner
awl
punzón
poinçon
Ahle
corkscrew
sacacorchos
tire-bouchon
Korkenzieher
can opener
abrelatas
ouvre-boîtes
Dosenöffner
COOKING SET
UTENSILIOS DE COCINA
POPOTE
KOCHGESCHIRR
cup
taza
tasse
Tasse
coffee pot
cafetera
cafetière
Kaffeekanne
saucepan
olla
faitout
Kochtopf
handle
mango
queue
Griff
frying pan
sartén
poêle
Bratpfanne
plate
plato
assiette plate
Teller
CUTLERY SET
CUBERTERÍA
USTENSILES DE CAMPEUR
ESSBESTECK
spoon
cuchara
cuiller
Löffel
belt loop
presilla
ganse
Gürtelschlaufe
fork
tenedor
fourchette
Gabel
sheath
funda
étui
Hülle
knife
cuchillo
couteau
Messer

PROPANE OR BUTANE ACCESSORIES
EQUIPO DE GAS
ACCESSOIRES AU PROPANE OU AU BUTANE
PROPAN-/BUTANGASBETRIEBENE GERÄTE

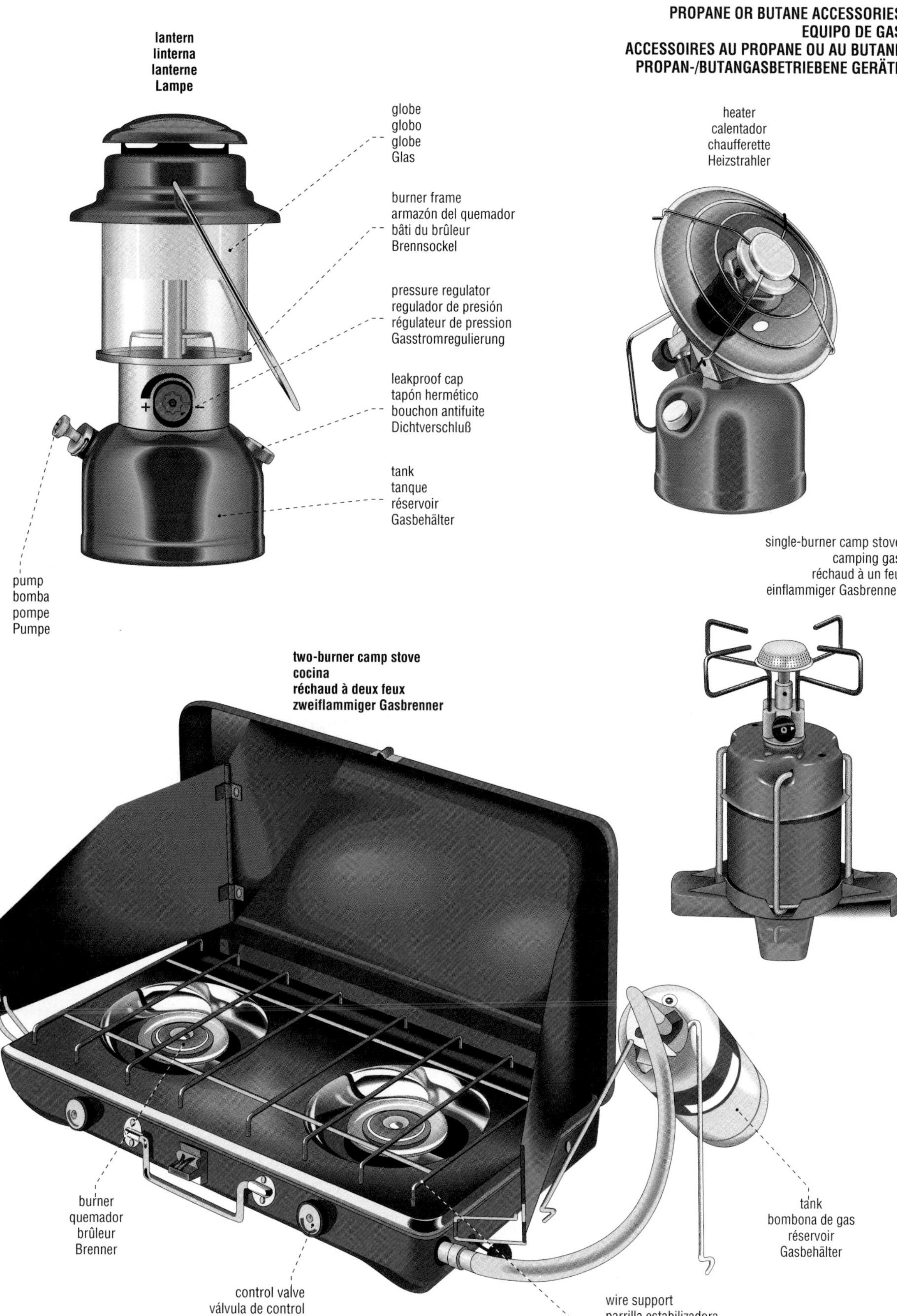
lantern
linterna
lanterne
Lampe
globe
globo
globe
Glas
burner frame
armazón del quemador
bâti du brûleur
Brennsockel
pressure regulator
regulador de presión
régulateur de pression
Gasstromregulierung
leakproof cap
tapón hermético
bouchon antifuite
Dichtverschluß
tank
tanque
réservoir
Gasbehälter
pump
bomba
pompe
Pumpe
heater
calentador
chaufferette
Heizstrahler
single-burner camp stove
camping gas
réchaud à un feu
einflammiger Gasbrenner
two-burner camp stove
cocina
réchaud à deux feux
zweiflammiger Gasbrenner
burner
quemador
brûleur
Brenner
control valve
válvula de control
robinet relais
Reglerventil
wire support
parrilla estabilizadora
grille stabilisatrice
Metallaufsatz
tank
bombona de gas
réservoir
Gasbehälter

CAMPING EQUIPMENT
EQUIPO PARA ACAMPAR
MATÉRIEL DE CAMPING
CAMPINGAUSRÜSTUNG

thermos
termos
bouteille isolante
Thermosflasche
water carrier
termos con llave de servicio
cruche
Wasserkanister
canteen
cantimplora
gourde
Feldflasche
hurricane lamp
lámpara de petróleo
lampe-tempête
Sturmlampe
cooler
nevera
glacière
Kühlbox
folding grill
parrilla plegable
gril pliant
Faltgrill
TOOLS
HERRAMIENTAS
OUTILS
WERKZEUG
hatchet
hacha
hachette
Beil
leather sheath
funda de cuero
étui de cuir
Lederschutz
sheath
funda
gaine
Scheide
knife
cuchillo
couteau
Messer
folding shovel
pala plegable
pelle-pioche pliante
Klappspaten
bow saw
sierra de campo
scie de camping
Bogensäge

KNOTS
NUDOS
NŒUDS
KNOTEN

square knot
nudo de rizo
nœud plat
Kreuzknoten

overhand knot
nudo llano
nœud simple
Hausfrauenknoten

granny knot
nudo de tejedor
nœud de vache
Altweiberknoten

running bowline
balso
nœud coulant
laufender Pahlstek

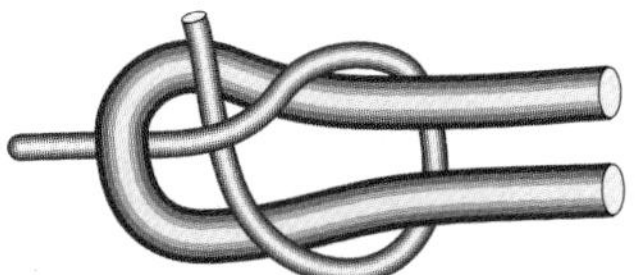

sheet bend
vuelta de escota
noeud d'écoute simple
einfacher Schotstek

double sheet bend
vuelta de escota doble
noeud d'écoute double
doppelter Schotstek

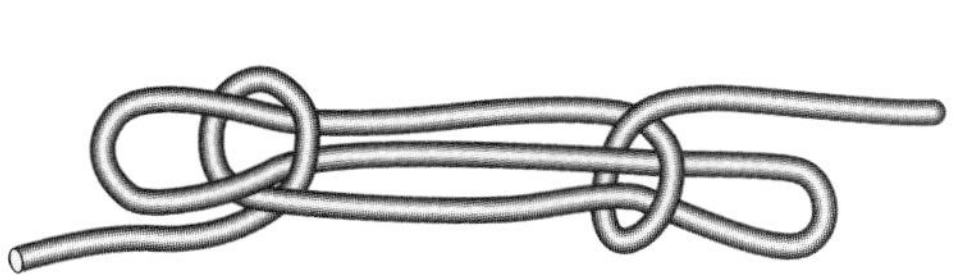

sheepshank
margarita
nœud de jambe de chien
Verkürzungsstek

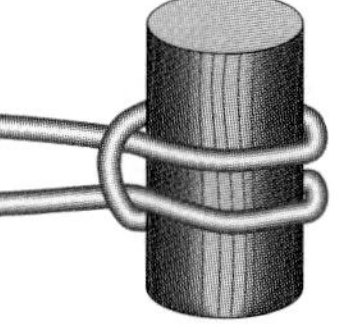

cow hitch
vuelta de cabo
demi-clé renversée
Kuhstek

heaving line knot
nudo de guía
noeud de Franciscain
Wurflinienknoten

fisherman's knot
nudo de pescador
nœud de pêcheur
Fischerknoten

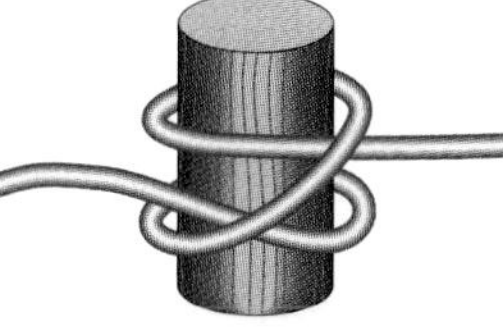

clove hitch
nudo de dos cotes
nœud de cabestan
Slipstek

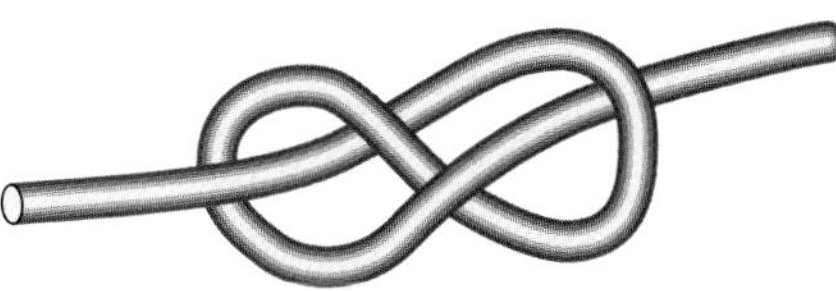

figure-eight knot
lasca doble
nœud d'arrêt
Achtknoten

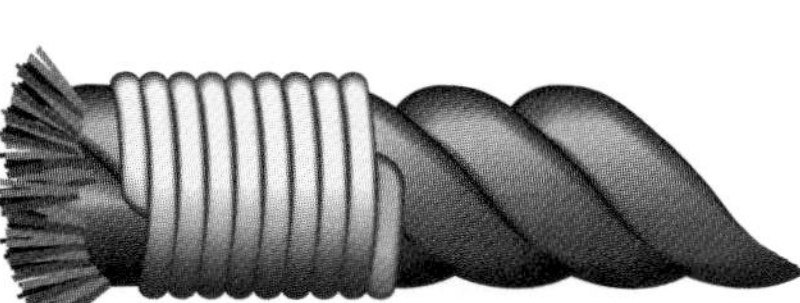

common whipping
sobrenudo
surliure
einfacher Takling

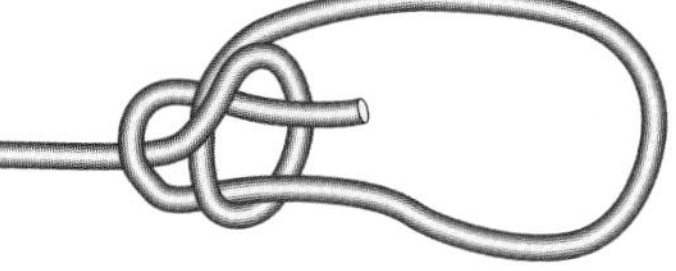

bowline
as de guía
nœud de chaise simple
Pahlstek

bowline on a bight
as de guía de eslinga doble
nœud de chaise double
doppelter Pahlstek

KNOTS
NUDOS NÁUTICOS
NŒUDS
KNOTEN

SHORT SPLICE
EMPALMADURA
ÉPISSURE COURTE
SPLEISS

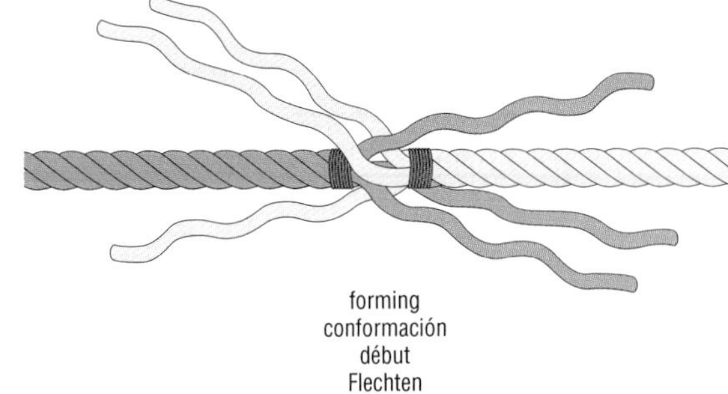

forming
conformación
début
Flechten

completion
acabado
fin
fertige Verbindung

CABLE
CABLE
CÂBLE
TAUWERK

TWISTED ROPE
CABLE TORCIDO
CORDAGE COMMIS
GEDREHTES SEIL

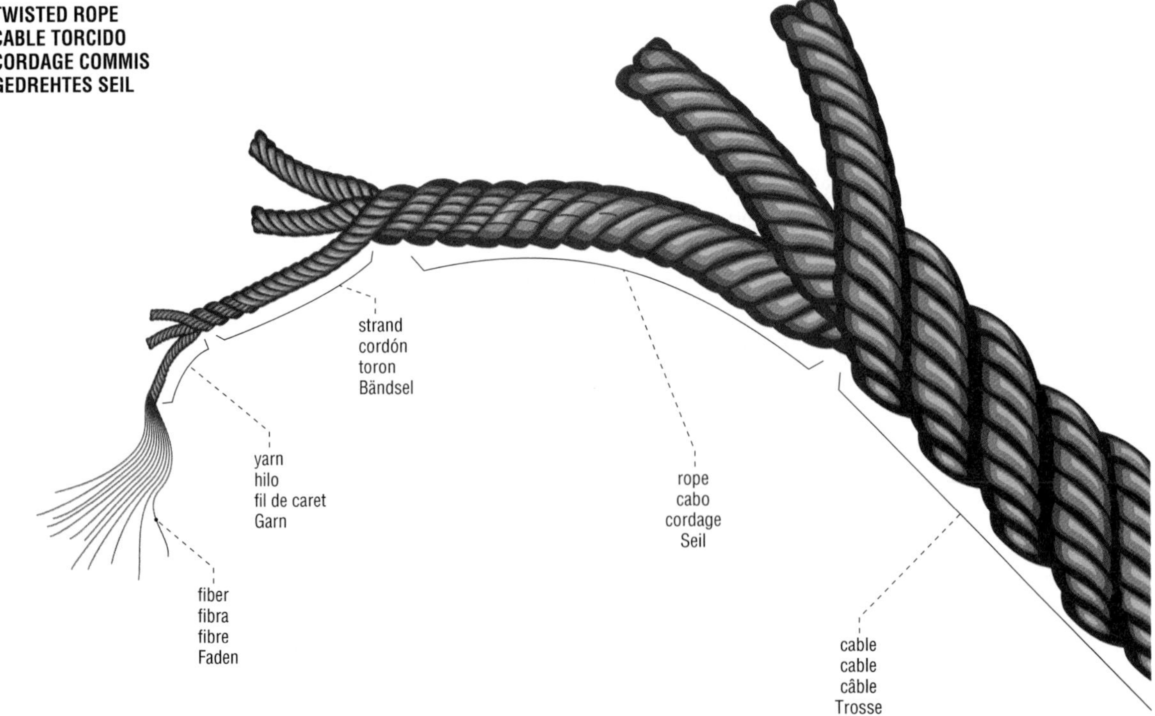
strand
cordón
toron
Bändsel
yarn
hilo
fil de caret
Garn
rope
cabo
cordage
Seil
fiber
fibra
fibre
Faden
cable
cable
câble
Trosse

BRAIDED ROPE
CABLE TRENZADO
CORDAGE TRESSÉ
GEFLOCHTENES SEIL

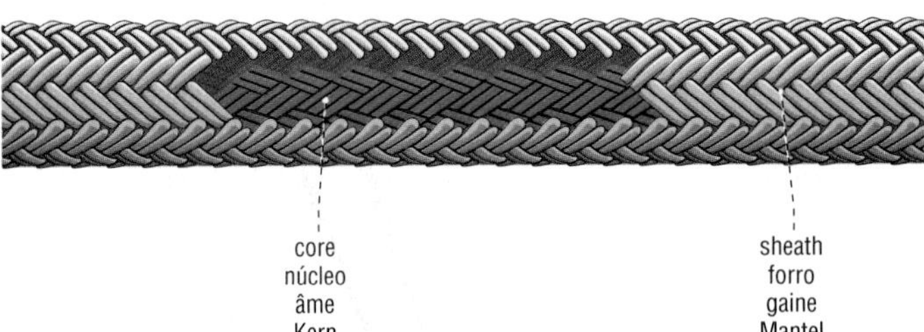
core
núcleo
âme
Kern
sheath
forro
gaine
Mantel

INDOOR GAMES
JUEGOS DE INTERIOR
JEUX DE SOCIÉTÉ
SPIELE

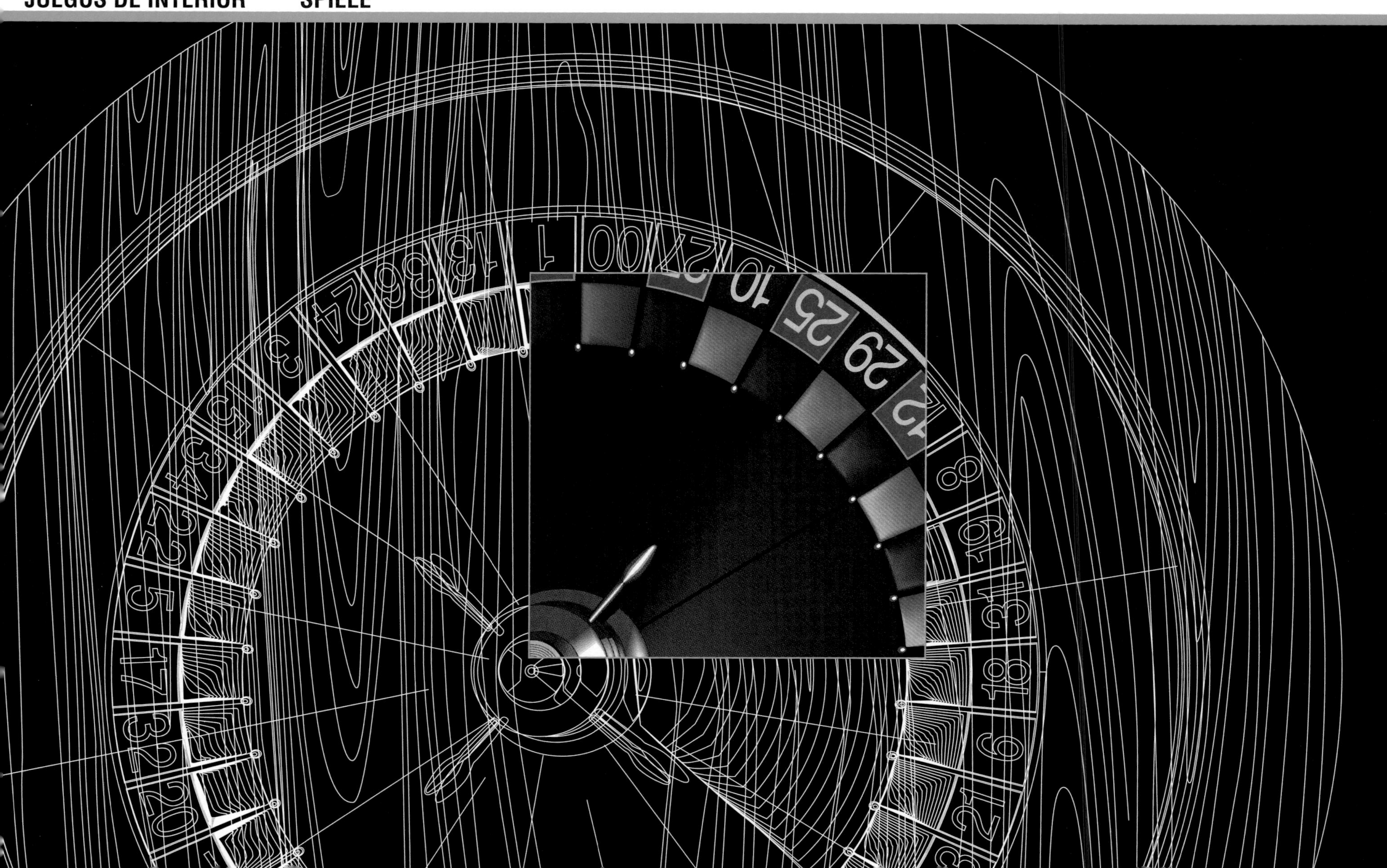

CONTENTS

CARD GAMES
BARAJA
CARTES
KARTENSPIELE

SYMBOLS
SÍMBOLOS
SYMBOLES
FARBEN

heart
corazón
cœur
Herz

diamond
diamante
carreau
Karo

club
trébol
trèfle
Kreuz

spade
espada
pique
Pik

Joker
comodín
Joker
Joker

Ace
as
As
Ass

King
rey
Roi
König

Queen
reina
Dame
Dame

Jack
jota
Valet
Bube

STANDARD POKER HANDS
MANOS DE PÓQUER
COMBINAISONS AU POKER
NORMALE POKERBLÄTTER

royal flush
escalera real
quinte royale
Royal Flush

straight flush
escalera de color
quinte
Straight Flush

four-of-a-kind
póquer
carré
Vierling

full house
full
main pleine
Full House

flush
color
couleur
Flush

straight
escalera
séquence
Straße

three-of-a-kind
trío
brelan
Drilling

two pairs
dos pares
double paire
zwei Pärchen

one pair
un par
paire
ein Pärchen

high card
cartas altas
carte isolée
höchste Karte

DOMINOES
DOMINÓ
DOMINOS
DOMINO

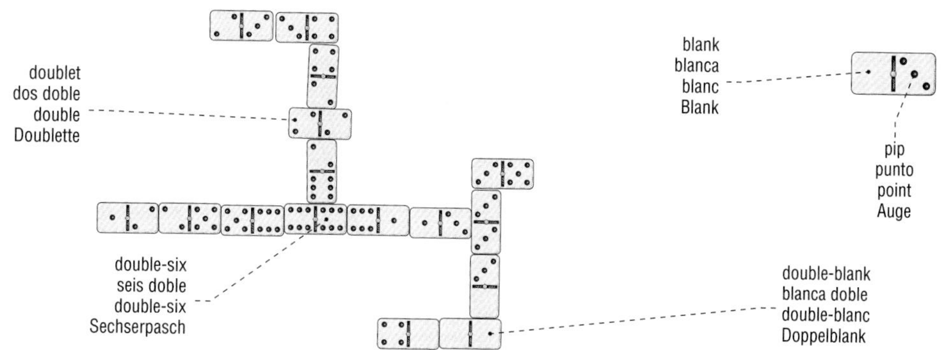
doublet
dos doble
double
Doublette
blank
blanca
blanc
Blank
pip
punto
point
Auge
double-six
seis doble
double-six
Sechserpasch
double-blank
blanca doble
double-blanc
Doppelblank

CHESS
AJEDREZ
ÉCHECS
SCHACH

CHESSBOARD
TABLERO DE AJEDREZ
ÉCHIQUIER
SCHACHBRETT

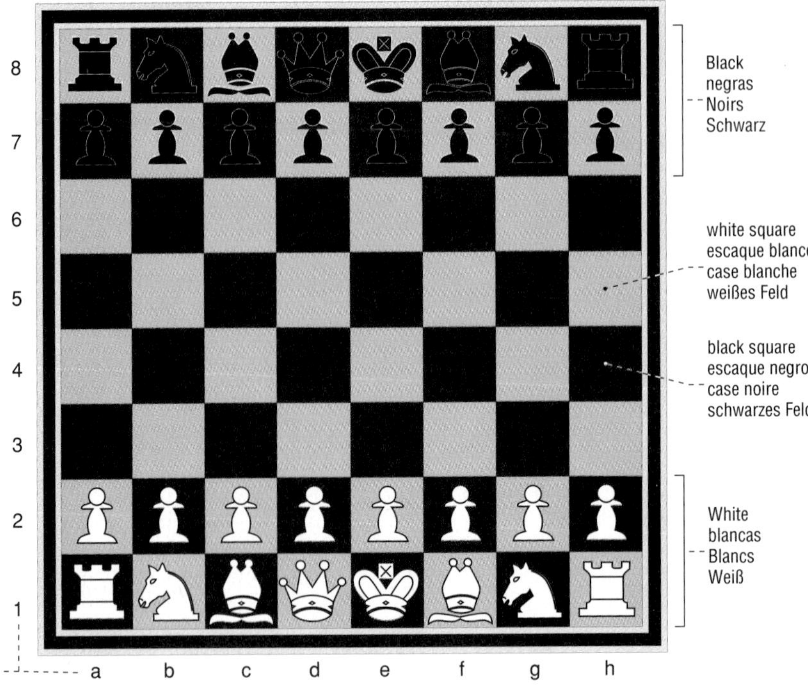
Queen's side
lado de la dama
aile Dame
Damenflanke
King's side
lado del rey
aile Roi
Königsflanke
8
7
6
5
4
3
2
1
a
b
c
d
e
f
g
h
Black
negras
Noirs
Schwarz
white square
escaque blanco
case blanche
weißes Feld
black square
escaque negro
case noire
schwarzes Feld
White
blancas
Blancs
Weiß
chess notation
notación del ajedrez
notation algébrique
Notation

TYPES OF MOVEMENTS
TIPOS DE MOVIMIENTOS
TYPES DE DÉPLACEMENTS
GANGARTEN

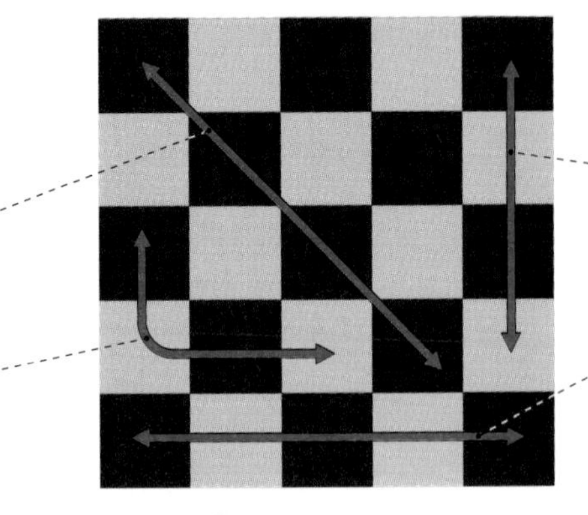
diagonal movement
movimiento diagonal
déplacement diagonal
diagonaler Zug
square movement
movimiento en ángulo
déplacement en équerre
Rösselsprung
vertical movement
movimiento vertical
déplacement vertical
vertikaler Zug
horizontal movement
movimiento horizontal
déplacement horizontal
horizontaler Zug

MEN
PIEZAS
PIÈCES
FIGUREN

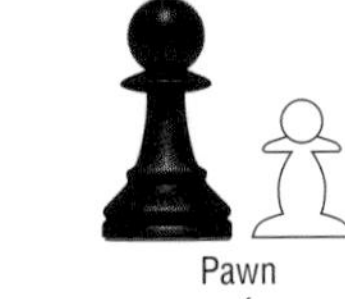

Pawn
peón
Pion
Bauer

Rook
torre
Tour
Turm

King
rey
Roi
König

Queen
reina
Dame
Dame

Bishop
alfil
Fou
Läufer

Knight
caballo
Cavalier
Pferd

BACKGAMMON
BACKGAMMON
JACQUET
BACKGAMMON

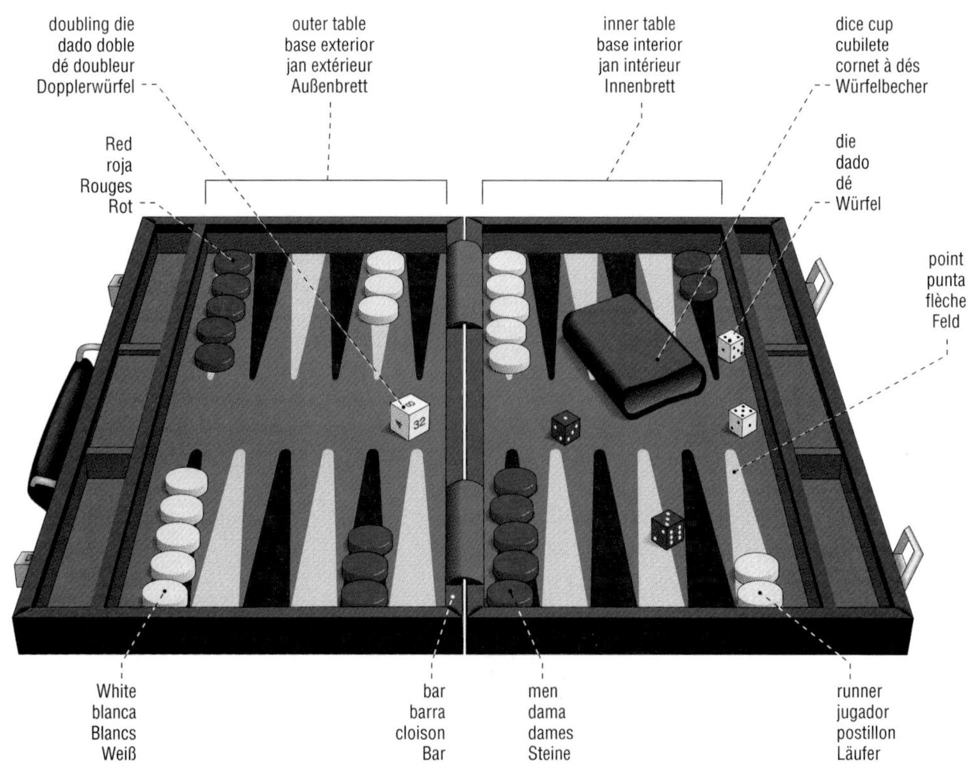

doubling die
dado doble
dé doubleur
Dopplerwürfel
outer table
base exterior
jan extérieur
Außenbrett
inner table
base interior
jan intérieur
Innenbrett
dice cup
cubilete
cornet à dés
Würfelbecher
Red
roja
Rouges
Rot
die
dado
dé
Würfel
point
punta
flèche
Feld
White
blanca
Blancs
Weiß
bar
barra
cloison
Bar
men
dama
dames
Steine
runner
jugador
postillon
Läufer

GO
GO(SUN-TSE)
GO
GO

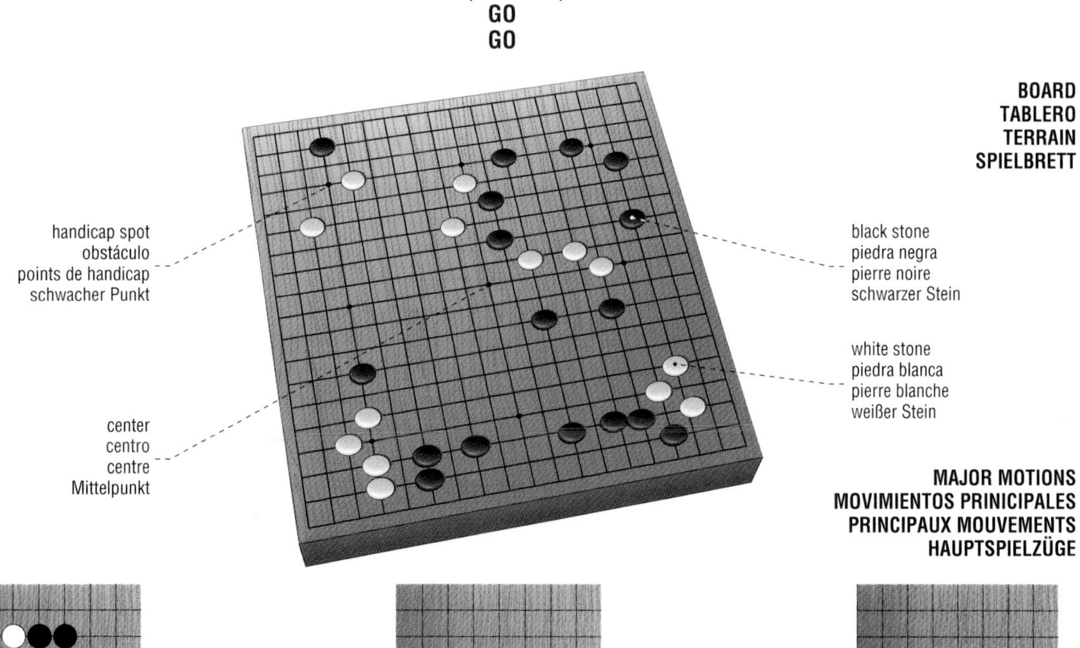

BOARD
TABLERO
TERRAIN
SPIELBRETT
handicap spot
obstáculo
points de handicap
schwacher Punkt
black stone
piedra negra
pierre noire
schwarzer Stein
white stone
piedra blanca
pierre blanche
weißer Stein
center
centro
centre
Mittelpunkt

MAJOR MOTIONS
MOVIMIENTOS PRINCIPALES
PRINCIPAUX MOUVEMENTS
HAUPTSPIELZÜGE

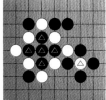

capture
captura
capture
Fangen

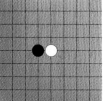

contact
contacto
contact
Berührung

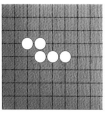

connection
conexión
connexion
Verbindung

SLOT MACHINE
TRAGAMONEDAS
MACHINE À SOUS
EINARMIGER BANDIT

casing
caja
boîtier
Gehäuse
coin slot
ranura para monedas
fente à monnaie
Münzeinwurf
symbol
símbolo
symbole
Symbol
lever
palanca
bras
Hebel
coin reject slot
devolución de monedas rechazadas
réceptacle pour les pièces refusées
Münzrückgabe
winning line
combinación ganadora
combinaison gagnante
Gewinnkombination
payout tray
bandeja de pago
plateau réceptacle de paiement
Auszahlungsschale
KING CASINO
1$
100
50
25
10

CROSS SECTION
CORTE TRANSVERSAL
COUPE
QUERSCHNITT

reel plate
engranaje
plaque de rouleau
Drehkranz
payout trigger
disparador de pago
déclencheur de paiement
Auszahlungshebel
reel
tambor
rouleau
Glücksrad
spring linkage
resorte del sistema articulado
levier à ressort
Federverbindung
coin chute
conducto de monedas
conduite des pièces
Münzleitung
jackpot feed
selector del premio
alimentation jackpot
Jackpot-Leitung
strongbox
caja fuerte
caisse blindée
Gehäuseverstärkung
jackpot box
casilla del dinero
boîte jackpot
Jackpot-Kasten
electrical payout linkage
control eléctrico de pago
commande électrique de paiement
elektrisches Auszahlungselement
KING CASINO
1$
100
50
25
10

BACKGAMMON
BACKGAMMON
JACQUET
BACKGAMMON

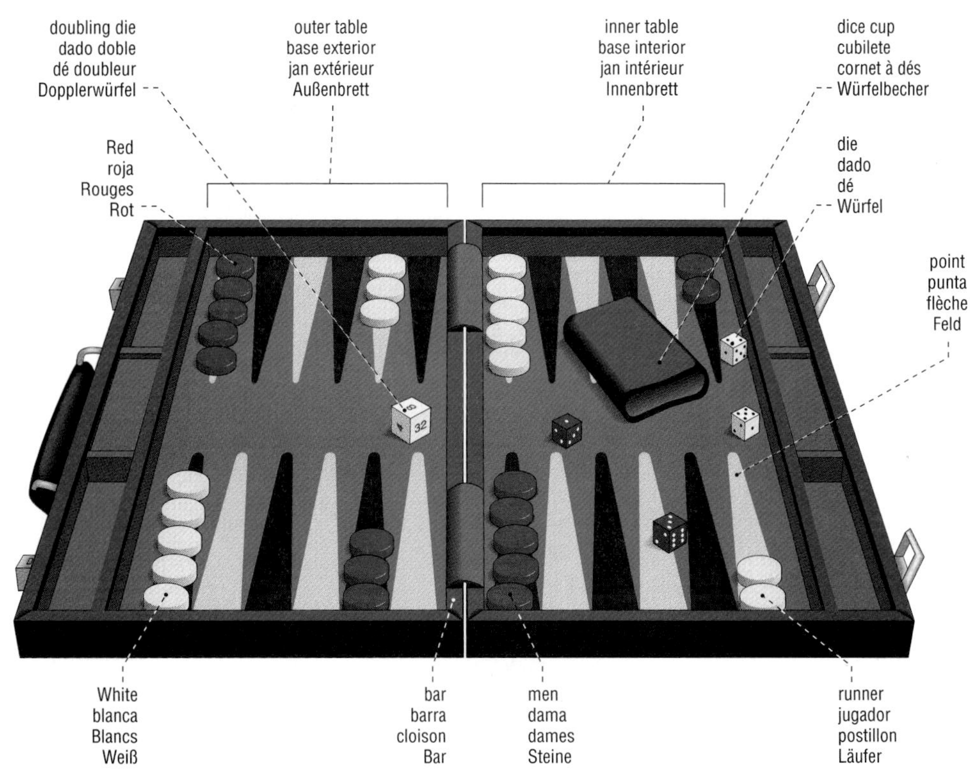
doubling die
dado doble
dé doubleur
Dopplerwürfel
outer table
base exterior
jan extérieur
Außenbrett
inner table
base interior
jan intérieur
Innenbrett
dice cup
cubilete
cornet à dés
Würfelbecher
Red
roja
Rouges
Rot
die
dado
dé
Würfel
point
punta
flèche
Feld
White
blanca
Blancs
Weiß
bar
barra
cloison
Bar
men
dama
dames
Steine
runner
jugador
postillon
Läufer

GO
GO(SUN-TSE)
GO
GO

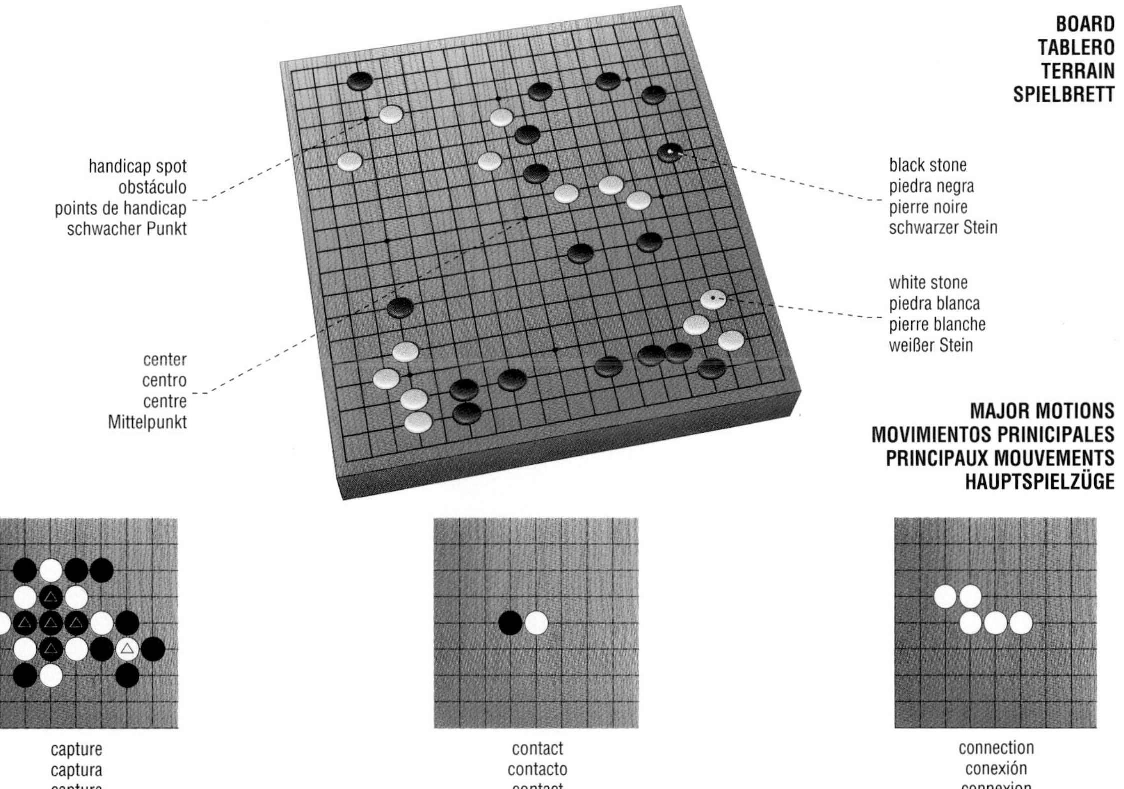
BOARD
TABLERO
TERRAIN
SPIELBRETT
handicap spot
obstáculo
points de handicap
schwacher Punkt
black stone
piedra negra
pierre noire
schwarzer Stein
white stone
piedra blanca
pierre blanche
weißer Stein
center
centro
centre
Mittelpunkt
MAJOR MOTIONS
MOVIMIENTOS PRINCIPALES
PRINCIPAUX MOUVEMENTS
HAUPTSPIELZÜGE
capture
captura
capture
Fangen
contact
contacto
contact
Berührung
connection
conexión
connexion
Verbindung

GAME OF DARTS
JUEGO DE DARDOS
JEU DE FLÉCHETTES
DARTSPIEL

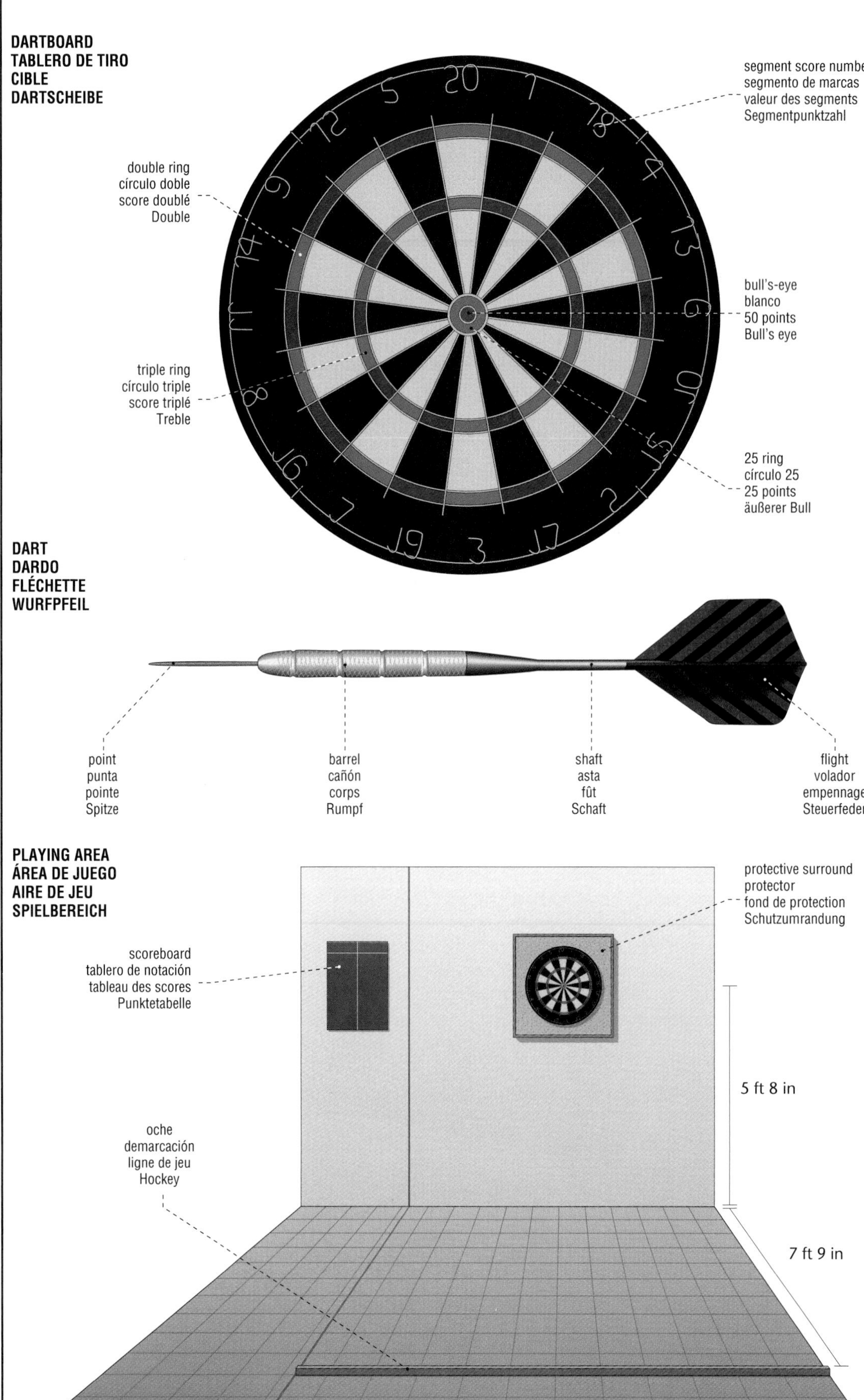

DARTBOARD
TABLERO DE TIRO
CIBLE
DARTSCHEIBE
segment score number
segmento de marcas
valeur des segments
Segmentpunktzahl
double ring
círculo doble
score doublé
Double
bull's-eye
blanco
50 points
Bull's eye
triple ring
círculo triple
score triplé
Treble
25 ring
círculo 25
25 points
äußerer Bull
20
1
18
4
13
6
10
15
2
17
3
19
7
16
8
11
14
9
12
5
DART
DARDO
FLÉCHETTE
WURFPFEIL
point
punta
pointe
Spitze
barrel
cañón
corps
Rumpf
shaft
asta
fût
Schaft
flight
volador
empennage
Steuerfeder
PLAYING AREA
ÁREA DE JUEGO
AIRE DE JEU
SPIELBEREICH
protective surround
protector
fond de protection
Schutzumrandung
scoreboard
tablero de notación
tableau des scores
Punktetabelle
5 ft 8 in
oche
demarcación
ligne de jeu
Hockey
7 ft 9 in

VIDEO ENTERTAINMENT SYSTEM
SISTEMA DE VIDEO DE JUEGOS
SYSTÈME DE JEUX VIDÉO
VIDEOSPIELSYSTEM

visual display
pantalla
écran
Monitor

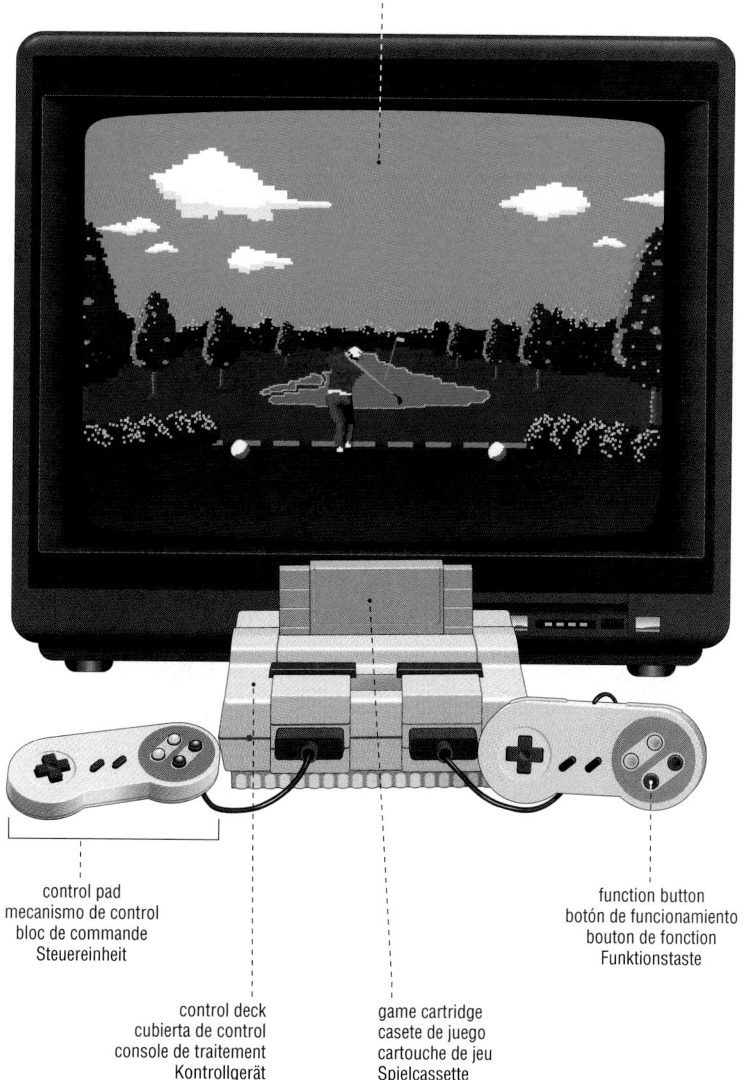

control pad
mecanismo de control
bloc de commande
Steuereinheit

function button
botón de funcionamiento
bouton de fonction
Funktionstaste

control deck
cubierta de control
console de traitement
Kontrollgerät

game cartridge
casete de juego
cartouche de jeu
Spielcassette

DICE
DADOS
DÉS
WÜRFEL

poker die
dado de póquer
dé à poker
Pokerwürfel

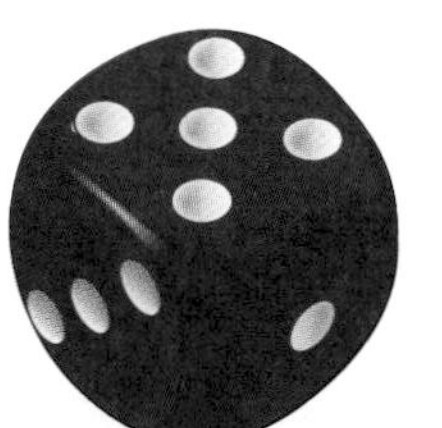

ordinary die
dado común
dé régulier
gewöhnlicher Würfel

ROULETTE TABLE
MESA DE LA RULETA
TABLE DE ROULETTE
ROULETTESPIELTISCH

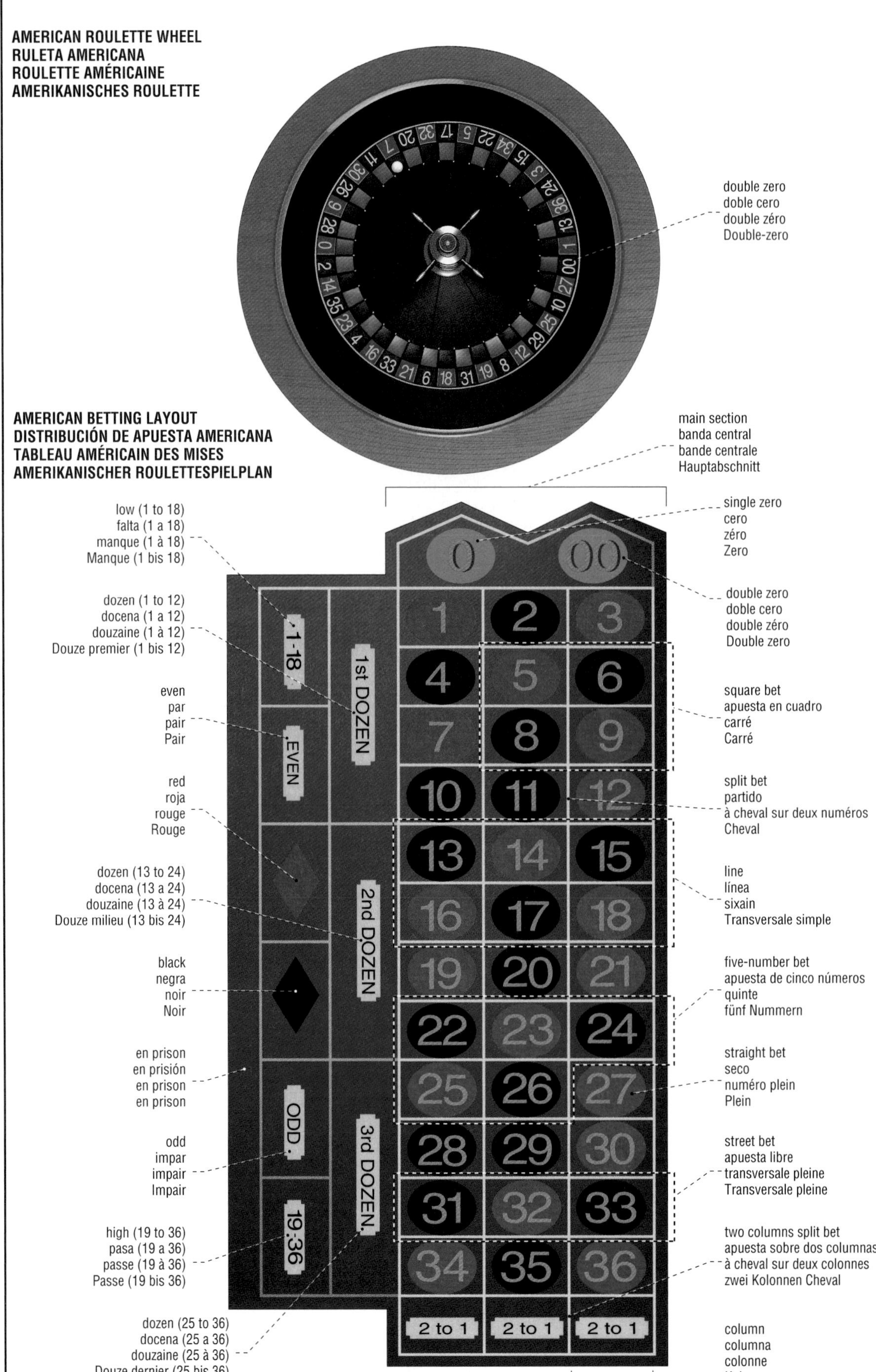
AMERICAN ROULETTE WHEEL
RULETA AMERICANA
ROULETTE AMÉRICAINE
AMERIKANISCHES ROULETTE
double zero
doble cero
double zéro
Double-zero
AMERICAN BETTING LAYOUT
DISTRIBUCIÓN DE APUESTA AMERICANA
TABLEAU AMÉRICAIN DES MISES
AMERIKANISCHER ROULETTESPIELPLAN
main section
banda central
bande centrale
Hauptabschnitt
low (1 to 18)
falta (1 a 18)
manque (1 à 18)
Manque (1 bis 18)
single zero
cero
zéro
Zero
double zero
doble cero
double zéro
Double zero
dozen (1 to 12)
docena (1 a 12)
douzaine (1 à 12)
Douze premier (1 bis 12)
square bet
apuesta en cuadro
carré
Carré
even
par
pair
Pair
split bet
partido
à cheval sur deux numéros
Cheval
red
roja
rouge
Rouge
line
línea
sixain
Transversale simple
dozen (13 to 24)
docena (13 a 24)
douzaine (13 à 24)
Douze milieu (13 bis 24)
five-number bet
apuesta de cinco números
quinte
fünf Nummern
black
negra
noir
Noir
straight bet
seco
numéro plein
Plein
en prison
en prisión
en prison
en prison
odd
impar
impair
Impair
street bet
apuesta libre
transversale pleine
Transversale pleine
high (19 to 36)
pasa (19 a 36)
passe (19 à 36)
Passe (19 bis 36)
two columns split bet
apuesta sobre dos columnas
à cheval sur deux colonnes
zwei Kolonnen Cheval
dozen (25 to 36)
docena (25 a 36)
douzaine (25 à 36)
Douze dernier (25 bis 36)
column
columna
colonne
Kolonne
1-18
EVEN
ODD
19-36
1st DOZEN
2nd DOZEN
3rd DOZEN
2 to 1
2 to 1
2 to 1

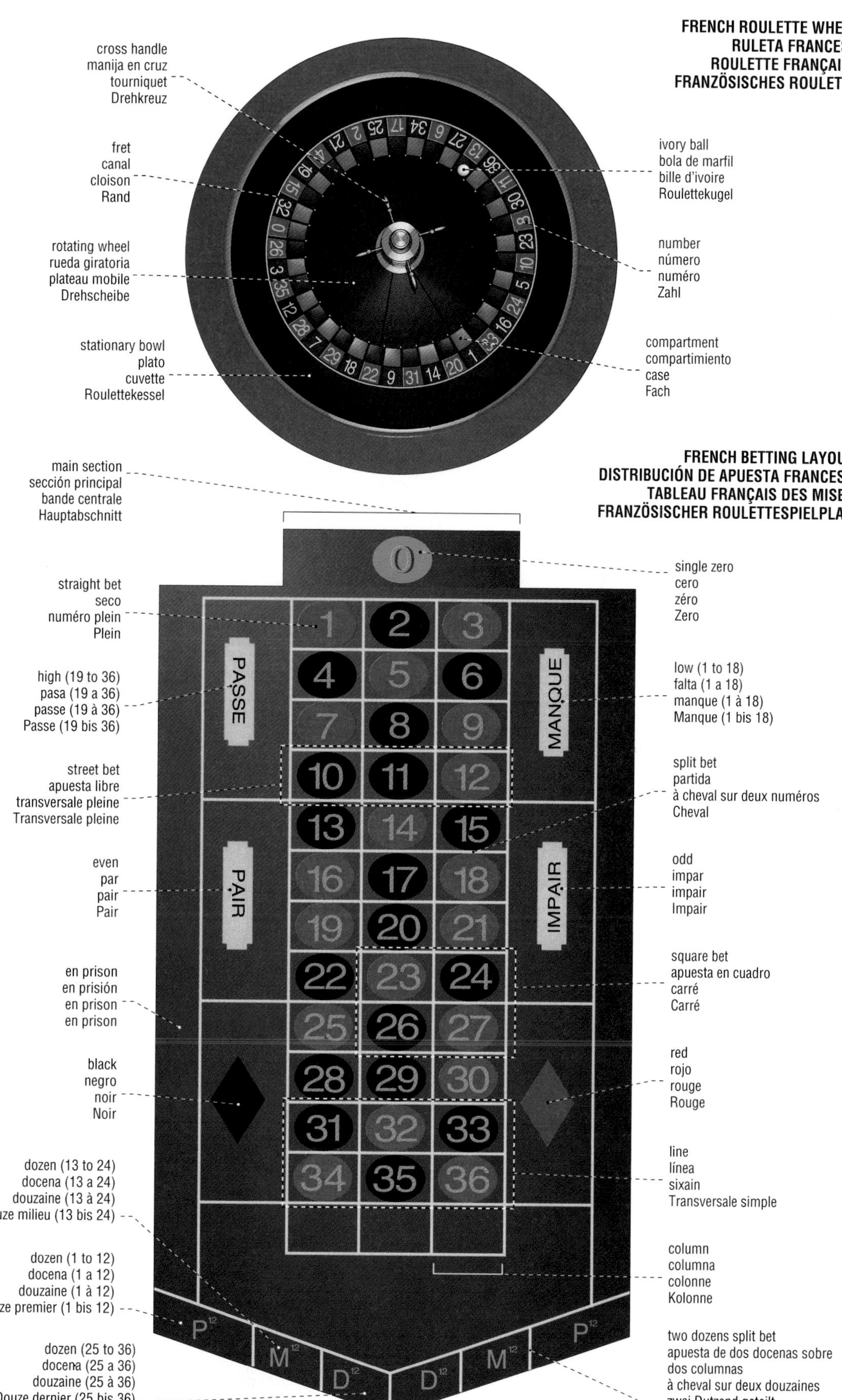
FRENCH ROULETTE WHEEL
RULETA FRANCESA
ROULETTE FRANÇAISE
FRANZÖSISCHES ROULETTE
cross handle
manija en cruz
tourniquet
Drehkreuz
fret
canal
cloison
Rand
rotating wheel
rueda giratoria
plateau mobile
Drehscheibe
stationary bowl
plato
cuvette
Roulettekessel
ivory ball
bola de marfil
bille d'ivoire
Roulettekugel
number
número
numéro
Zahl
compartment
compartimiento
case
Fach
FRENCH BETTING LAYOUT
DISTRIBUCIÓN DE APUESTA FRANCESA
TABLEAU FRANÇAIS DES MISES
FRANZÖSISCHER ROULETTESPIELPLAN
main section
sección principal
bande centrale
Hauptabschnitt
single zero
cero
zéro
Zero
straight bet
seco
numéro plein
Plein
high (19 to 36)
pasa (19 a 36)
passe (19 à 36)
Passe (19 bis 36)
low (1 to 18)
falta (1 a 18)
manque (1 à 18)
Manque (1 bis 18)
PASSE
MANQUE
street bet
apuesta libre
transversale pleine
Transversale pleine
split bet
partida
à cheval sur deux numéros
Cheval
even
par
pair
Pair
odd
impar
impair
Impair
PAIR
IMPAIR
square bet
apuesta en cuadro
carré
Carré
en prison
en prisión
en prison
en prison
black
negro
noir
Noir
red
rojo
rouge
Rouge
line
línea
sixain
Transversale simple
dozen (13 to 24)
docena (13 a 24)
douzaine (13 à 24)
Douze milieu (13 bis 24)
column
columna
colonne
Kolonne
dozen (1 to 12)
docena (1 a 12)
douzaine (1 à 12)
Douze premier (1 bis 12)
two dozens split bet
apuesta de dos docenas sobre
dos columnas
à cheval sur deux douzaines
zwei Dutzend geteilt
dozen (25 to 36)
docena (25 a 36)
douzaine (25 à 36)
Douze dernier (25 bis 36)

SLOT MACHINE
TRAGAMONEDAS
MACHINE À SOUS
EINARMIGER BANDIT

casing
caja
boîtier
Gehäuse
KING CASINO
1$
coin slot
ranura para monedas
fente à monnaie
Münzeinwurf
symbol
símbolo
symbole
Symbol
lever
palanca
bras
Hebel
coin reject slot
devolución de monedas rechazadas
réceptacle pour les pièces refusées
Münzrückgabe
100
50
25
10
winning line
combinación ganadora
combinaison gagnante
Gewinnkombination
payout tray
bandeja de pago
plateau réceptacle de paiement
Auszahlungsschale

CROSS SECTION
CORTE TRANSVERSAL
COUPE
QUERSCHNITT

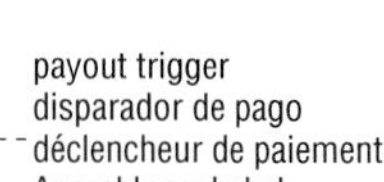

reel plate
engranaje
plaque de rouleau
Drehkranz

payout trigger
disparador de pago
déclencheur de paiement
Auszahlungshebel

reel
tambor
rouleau
Glücksrad

spring linkage
resorte del sistema articulado
levier à ressort
Federverbindung

coin chute
conducto de monedas
conduite des pièces
Münzleitung

jackpot feed
selector del premio
alimentation jackpot
Jackpot-Leitung

strongbox
caja fuerte
caisse blindée
Gehäuseverstärkung

jackpot box
casilla del dinero
boîte jackpot
Jackpot-Kasten

electrical payout linkage
control eléctrico de pago
commande électrique de paiement
elektrisches Auszahlungselement

MEASURING DEVICES
APARATOS DE MEDICIÓN
APPAREILS DE MESURE
MESSINSTRUMENTE

CONTENTS

MEASURE OF TEMPERATURE
MEDICIÓN DE LA TEMPERATURA
MESURE DE LA TEMPÉRATURE
TEMPERATURMESSUNG

THERMOMETER
TERMÓMETRO
THERMOMÈTRE
THERMOMETER

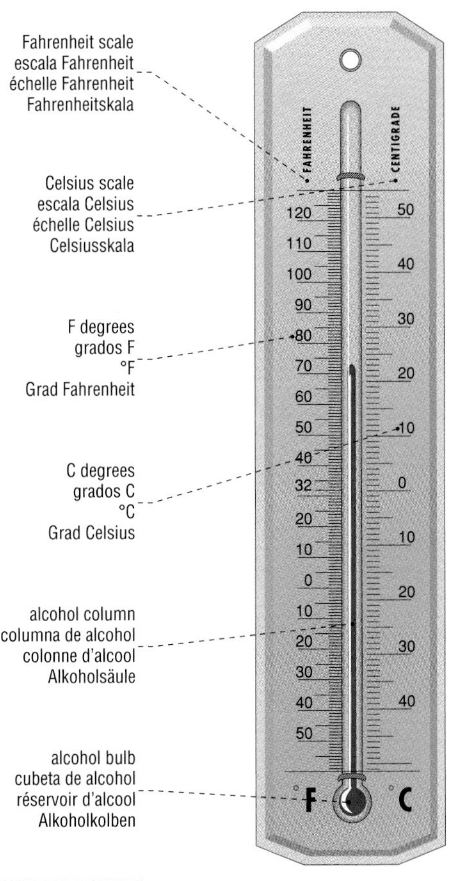
Fahrenheit scale
escala Fahrenheit
échelle Fahrenheit
Fahrenheitskala
Celsius scale
escala Celsius
échelle Celsius
Celsiusskala
F degrees
grados F
°F
Grad Fahrenheit
C degrees
grados C
°C
Grad Celsius
alcohol column
columna de alcohol
colonne d'alcool
Alkoholsäule
alcohol bulb
cubeta de alcohol
réservoir d'alcool
Alkoholkolben
FAHRENHEIT
CENTIGRADE
°F
°C

CLINICAL THERMOMETER
TERMÓMETRO CLÍNICO
THERMOMÈTRE MÉDICAL
FIEBERTHERMOMETER

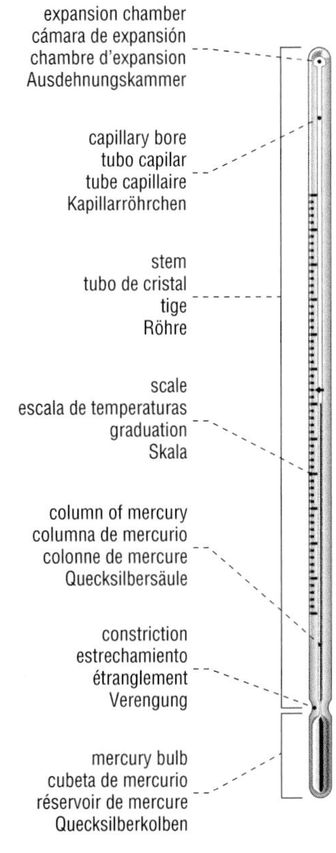
expansion chamber
cámara de expansión
chambre d'expansion
Ausdehnungskammer
capillary bore
tubo capilar
tube capillaire
Kapillarröhrchen
stem
tubo de cristal
tige
Röhre
scale
escala de temperaturas
graduation
Skala
column of mercury
columna de mercurio
colonne de mercure
Quecksilbersäule
constriction
estrechamiento
étranglement
Verengung
mercury bulb
cubeta de mercurio
réservoir de mercure
Quecksilberkolben

BIMETALLIC THERMOMETER
TERMÓMETRO BIMETÁLICO
THERMOMÈTRE BIMÉTALLIQUE
BIMETALL-THERMOMETER

pointer
aguja
aiguille
Zeiger

case
caja
boîtier
Gehäuse

dial
cuadrante
cadran
Anzeigeskala

shaft
barra
arbre
Welle

bimetallic helix
hélice bimetálica
élément bimétallique hélicoïdal
Bimetallfeder

ROOM THERMOSTAT
TERMOSTATO AMBIENTAL
THERMOSTAT D'AMBIANCE
RAUMTHERMOSTAT

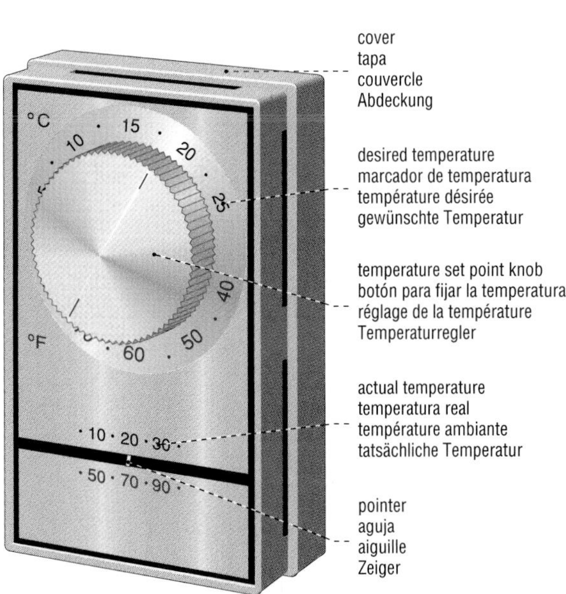
cover
tapa
couvercle
Abdeckung
desired temperature
marcador de temperatura
température désirée
gewünschte Temperatur
temperature set point knob
botón para fijar la temperatura
réglage de la température
Temperaturregler
actual temperature
temperatura real
température ambiante
tatsächliche Temperatur
pointer
aguja
aiguille
Zeiger

MEASURE OF TIME
MEDICIÓN DEL TIEMPO
MESURE DU TEMPS
ZEITMESSUNG

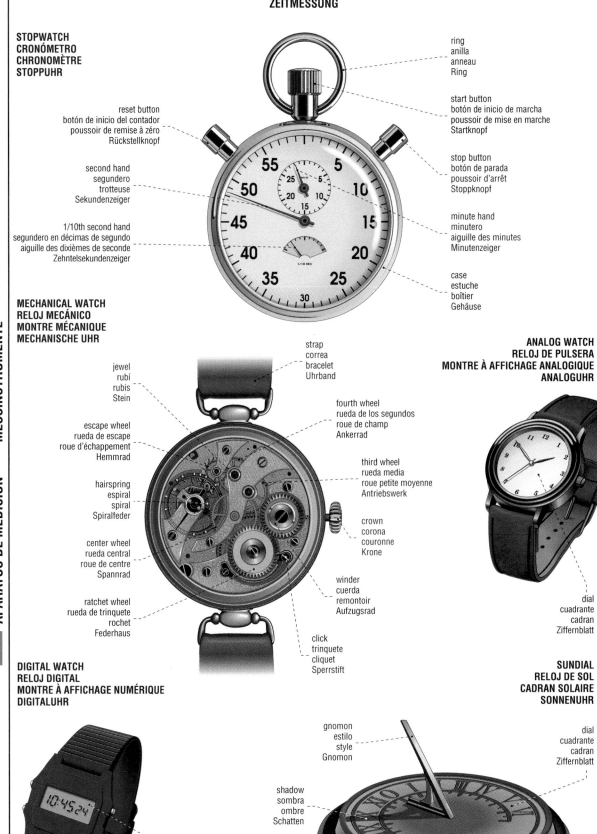

STOPWATCH
CRONÓMETRO
CHRONOMÈTRE
STOPPUHR

ring
anilla
anneau
Ring

start button
botón de inicio de marcha
poussoir de mise en marche
Startknopf

reset button
botón de inicio del contador
poussoir de remise à zéro
Rückstellknopf

stop button
botón de parada
poussoir d'arrêt
Stoppknopf

second hand
segundero
trotteuse
Sekundenzeiger

minute hand
minutero
aiguille des minutes
Minutenzeiger

1/10th second hand
segundero en décimas de segundo
aiguille des dixièmes de seconde
Zehntelsekundenzeiger

case
estuche
boîtier
Gehäuse

MECHANICAL WATCH
RELOJ MECÁNICO
MONTRE MÉCANIQUE
MECHANISCHE UHR

strap
correa
bracelet
Uhrband

jewel
rubí
rubis
Stein

fourth wheel
rueda de los segundos
roue de champ
Ankerrad

escape wheel
rueda de escape
roue d'échappement
Hemmrad

third wheel
rueda media
roue petite moyenne
Antriebswerk

hairspring
espiral
spiral
Spiralfeder

crown
corona
couronne
Krone

center wheel
rueda central
roue de centre
Spannrad

winder
cuerda
remontoir
Aufzugsrad

ratchet wheel
rueda de trinquete
rochet
Federhaus

click
trinquete
cliquet
Sperrstift

ANALOG WATCH
RELOJ DE PULSERA
MONTRE À AFFICHAGE ANALOGIQUE
ANALOGUHR

dial
cuadrante
cadran
Ziffernblatt

DIGITAL WATCH
RELOJ DIGITAL
MONTRE À AFFICHAGE NUMÉRIQUE
DIGITALUHR

SUNDIAL
RELOJ DE SOL
CADRAN SOLAIRE
SONNENUHR

liquid-crystal display
registro de cristal líquido
cristaux liquides
LCD-Anzeige
gnomon
estilo
style
Gnomon
dial
cuadrante
cadran
Ziffernblatt
shadow
sombra
ombre
Schatten

GRANDFATHER CLOCK
RELOJ DE PÉNDULO
HORLOGE DE PARQUET
STANDUHR

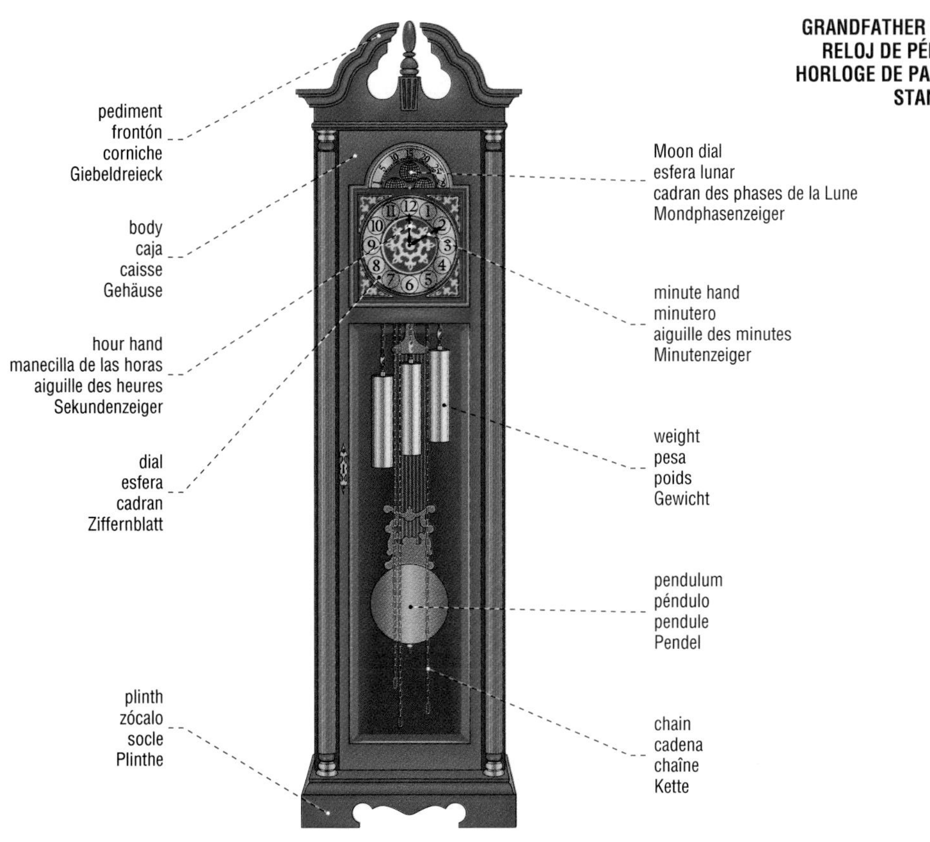
pediment
frontón
corniche
Giebeldreieck
body
caja
caisse
Gehäuse
hour hand
manecilla de las horas
aiguille des heures
Sekundenzeiger
dial
esfera
cadran
Ziffernblatt
plinth
zócalo
socle
Plinthe
Moon dial
esfera lunar
cadran des phases de la Lune
Mondphasenzeiger
minute hand
minutero
aiguille des minutes
Minutenzeiger
weight
pesa
poids
Gewicht
pendulum
péndulo
pendule
Pendel
chain
cadena
chaîne
Kette

WEIGHT-DRIVEN CLOCK MECHANISM
MECANISMO DEL RELOJ DE PESAS
MÉCANISME DE L'HORLOGE À POIDS
ZUGGETRIEBENES UHRWERK

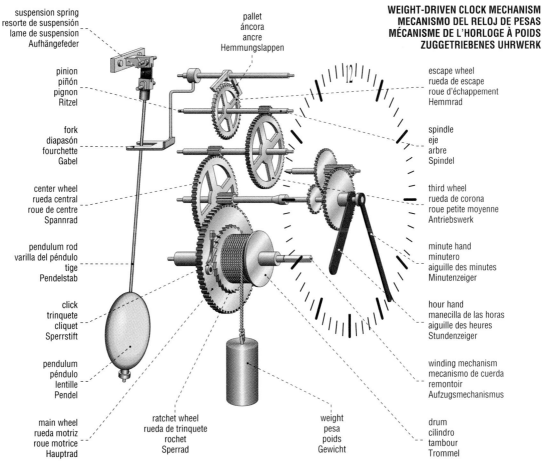

suspension spring
resorte de suspensión
lame de suspension
Aufhängefeder

pinion
piñón
pignon
Ritzel

fork
diapasón
fourchette
Gabel

center wheel
rueda central
roue de centre
Spannrad

pendulum rod
varilla del péndulo
tige
Pendelstab

click
trinquete
cliquet
Sperrstift

pendulum
péndulo
lentille
Pendel

main wheel
rueda motriz
roue motrice
Hauptrad

pallet
áncora
ancre
Hemmungslappen

ratchet wheel
rueda de trinquete
rochet
Sperrad

weight
pesa
poids
Gewicht

escape wheel
rueda de escape
roue d'échappement
Hemmrad

spindle
eje
arbre
Spindel

third wheel
rueda de corona
roue petite moyenne
Antriebswerk

minute hand
minutero
aiguille des minutes
Minutenzeiger

hour hand
manecilla de las horas
aiguille des heures
Stundenzeiger

winding mechanism
mecanismo de cuerda
remontoir
Aufzugsmechanismus

drum
cilindro
tambour
Trommel

MEASURE OF WEIGHT
MEDICIÓN DEL PESO
MESURE DE LA MASSE
WIEGEN

BEAM BALANCE
BALANZA DE ASTIL
BALANCE À FLÉAU
BALKENWAAGE

STEELYARD
BÁSCULA ROMANA
BALANCE ROMAINE
HANDWAAGE

ROBERVAL'S BALANCE
BALANZA DE ROBERVAL
BALANCE DE ROBERVAL
ROBERVAL-WAAGE

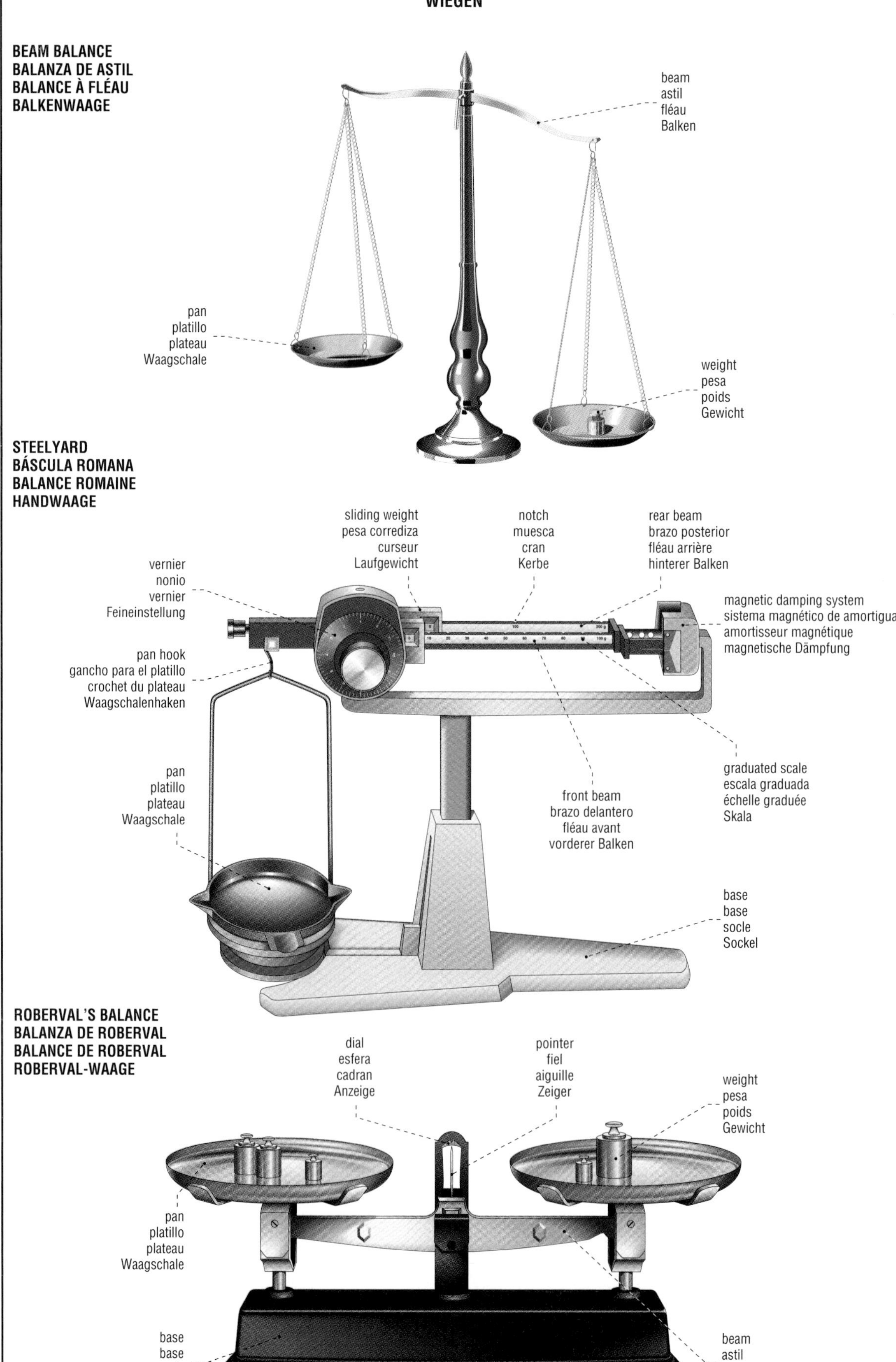
beam
astil
fléau
Balken
pan
platillo
plateau
Waagschale
weight
pesa
poids
Gewicht
sliding weight
pesa corrediza
curseur
Laufgewicht
notch
muesca
cran
Kerbe
rear beam
brazo posterior
fléau arrière
hinterer Balken
vernier
nonio
vernier
Feineinstellung
magnetic damping system
sistema magnético de amortiguación
amortisseur magnétique
magnetische Dämpfung
pan hook
gancho para el platillo
crochet du plateau
Waagschalenhaken
graduated scale
escala graduada
échelle graduée
Skala
pan
platillo
plateau
Waagschale
front beam
brazo delantero
fléau avant
vorderer Balken
base
base
socle
Sockel
dial
esfera
cadran
Anzeige
pointer
fiel
aiguille
Zeiger
weight
pesa
poids
Gewicht
pan
platillo
plateau
Waagschale
base
base
socle
Sockel
beam
astil
fléau
Balken

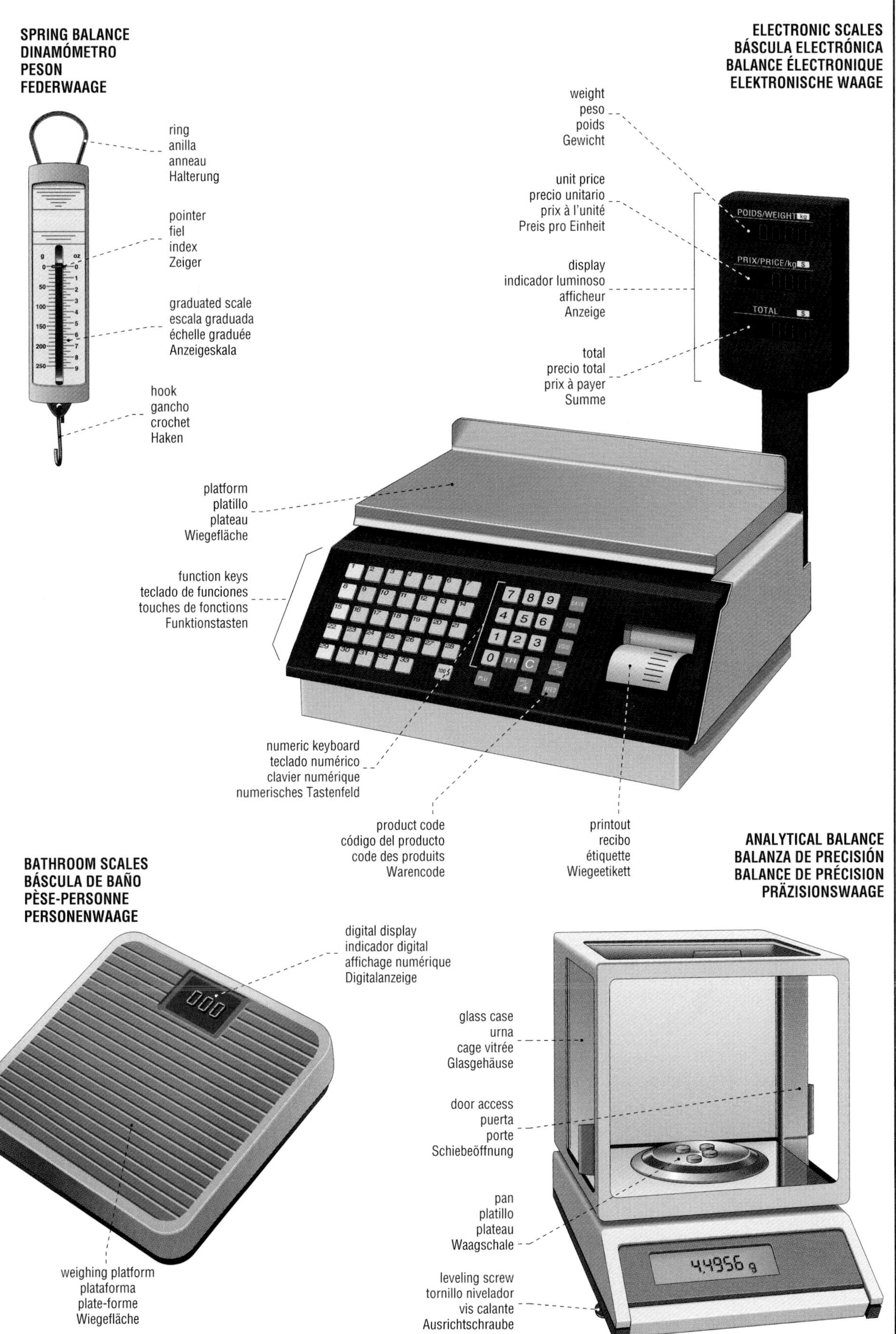
SPRING BALANCE
DINAMÓMETRO
PESON
FEDERWAAGE
ring
anilla
anneau
Halterung
pointer
fiel
index
Zeiger
graduated scale
escala graduada
échelle graduée
Anzeigeskala
hook
gancho
crochet
Haken
ELECTRONIC SCALES
BÁSCULA ELECTRÓNICA
BALANCE ÉLECTRONIQUE
ELEKTRONISCHE WAAGE
weight
peso
poids
Gewicht
unit price
precio unitario
prix à l'unité
Preis pro Einheit
display
indicador luminoso
afficheur
Anzeige
total
precio total
prix à payer
Summe
POIDS/WEIGHT kg
PRIX/PRICE/kg $
TOTAL $
platform
platillo
plateau
Wiegefläche
function keys
teclado de funciones
touches de fonctions
Funktionstasten
numeric keyboard
teclado numérico
clavier numérique
numerisches Tastenfeld
product code
código del producto
code des produits
Warencode
printout
recibo
étiquette
Wiegeetikett
BATHROOM SCALES
BÁSCULA DE BAÑO
PÈSE-PERSONNE
PERSONENWAAGE
digital display
indicador digital
affichage numérique
Digitalanzeige
weighing platform
plataforma
plate-forme
Wiegefläche
ANALYTICAL BALANCE
BALANZA DE PRECISIÓN
BALANCE DE PRÉCISION
PRÄZISIONSWAAGE
glass case
urna
cage vitrée
Glasgehäuse
door access
puerta
porte
Schiebeöffnung
pan
platillo
plateau
Waagschale
leveling screw
tornillo nivelador
vis calante
Ausrichtschraube
4.4956 g

MEASURE OF PRESSURE
MEDICIÓN DE LA PRESIÓN
MESURE DE LA PRESSION
DRUCKMESSUNG

BAROMETER/THERMOMETER
BARÓMETRO/TERMÓMETRO
BAROMÈTRE/THERMOMÈTRE
BAROMETER/THERMOMETER

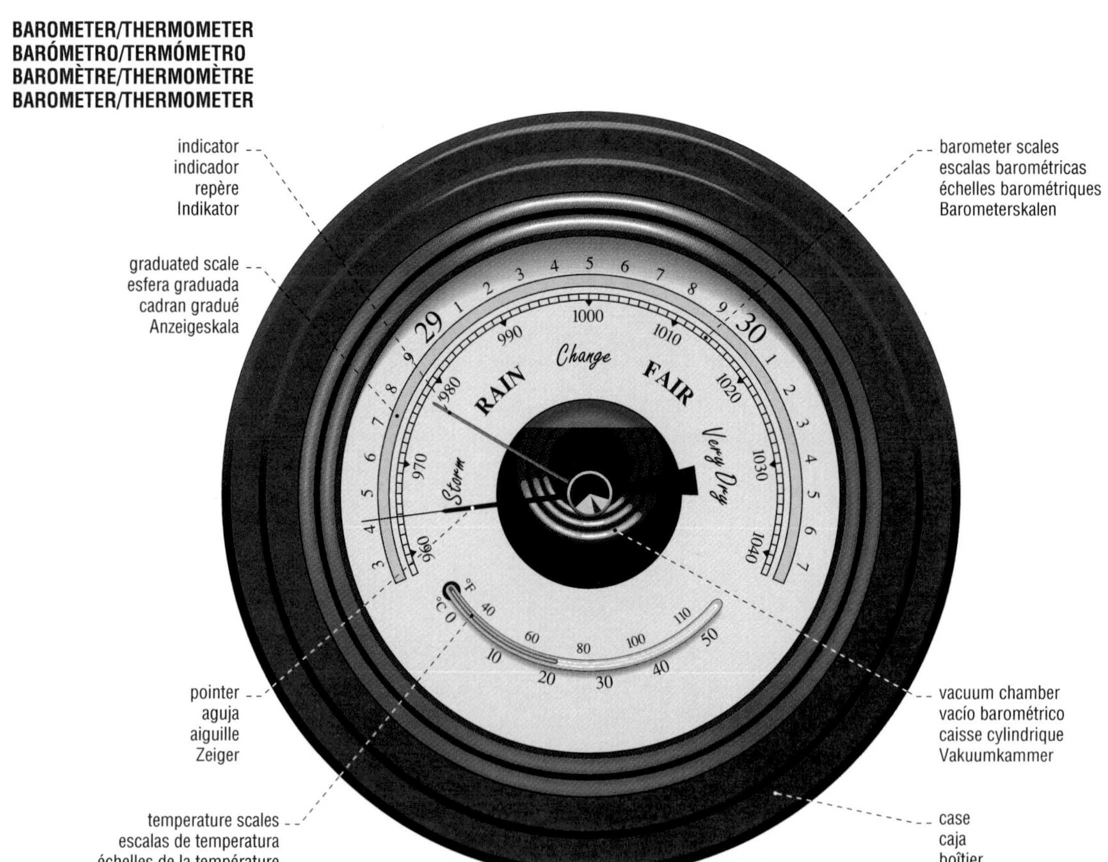
indicator
indicador
repère
Indikator
barometer scales
escalas barométricas
échelles barométriques
Barometerskalen
graduated scale
esfera graduada
cadran gradué
Anzeigeskala
pointer
aguja
aiguille
Zeiger
vacuum chamber
vacío barométrico
caisse cylindrique
Vakuumkammer
temperature scales
escalas de temperatura
échelles de la température
Temperaturskalen
case
caja
boîtier
Gehäuse
RAIN
Change
FAIR
Storm
Very Dry
29
30
°F
°C

TENSIOMETER
TENSIÓMETRO
TENSIOMÈTRE
BLUTDRUCKMESSGERÄT

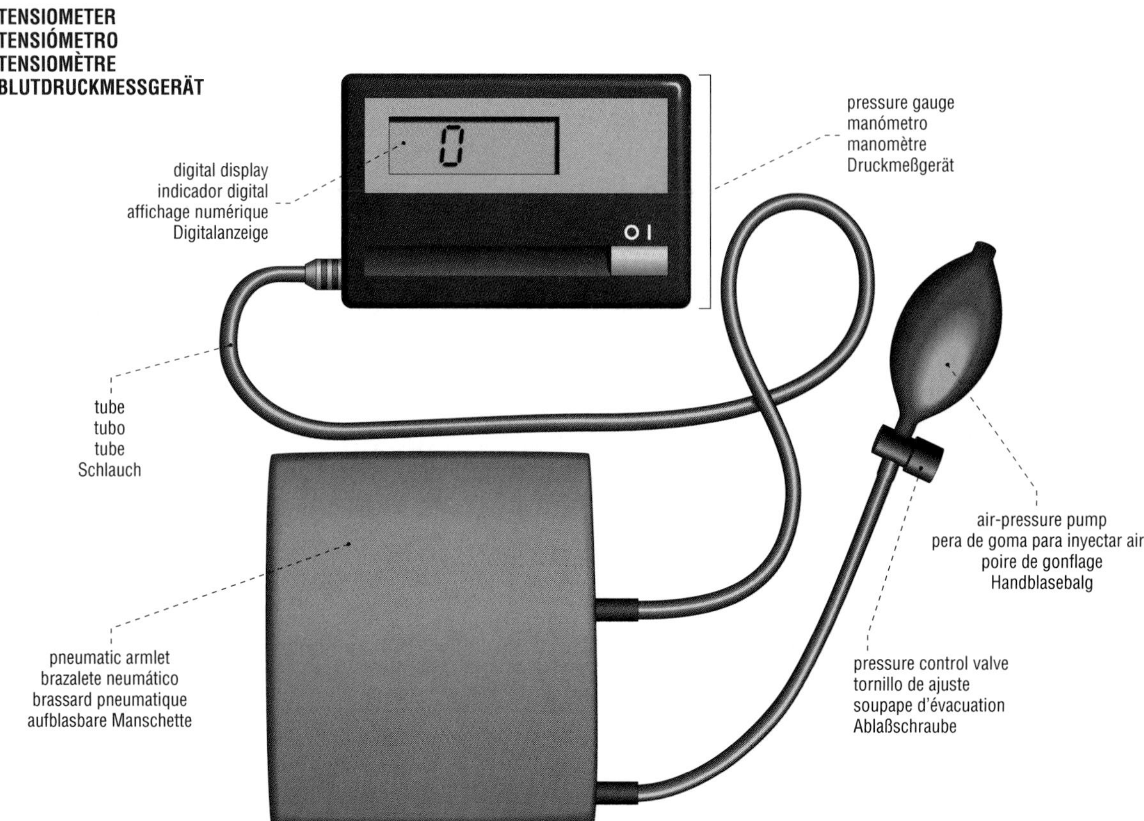
pressure gauge
manómetro
manomètre
Druckmeßgerät
digital display
indicador digital
affichage numérique
Digitalanzeige
tube
tubo
tube
Schlauch
air-pressure pump
pera de goma para inyectar aire
poire de gonflage
Handblasebalg
pneumatic armlet
brazalete neumático
brassard pneumatique
aufblasbare Manschette
pressure control valve
tornillo de ajuste
soupape d'évacuation
Ablaßschraube

MEASURE OF LENGTH
MEDICIÓN DE LA LONGITUD
MESURE DE LA LONGUEUR
LÄNGENMESSUNG

TAPE MEASURE
CINTA MÉTRICA
MÈTRE À RUBAN
MESSBAND

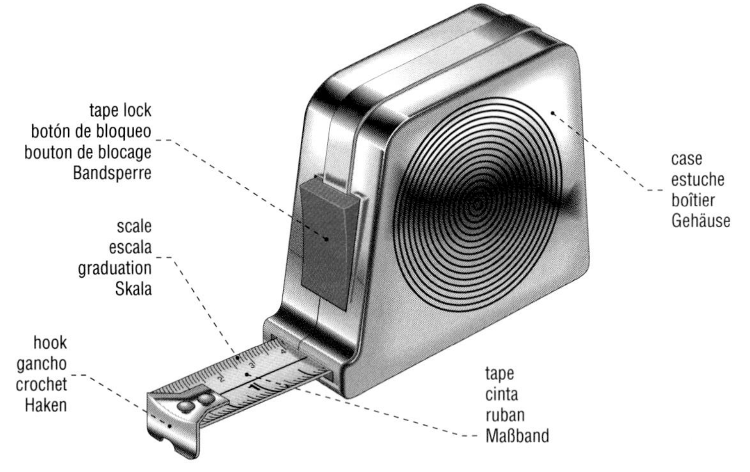
tape lock
botón de bloqueo
bouton de blocage
Bandsperre
scale
escala
graduation
Skala
hook
gancho
crochet
Haken
case
estuche
boîtier
Gehäuse
tape
cinta
ruban
Maßband

MEASURE OF DISTANCE
MEDICIÓN DE LA DISTANCIA
MESURE DE LA DISTANCE
ENTFERNUNGSMESSUNG

PEDOMETER
ODÓMETRO
PODOMÈTRE
PEDOMETER

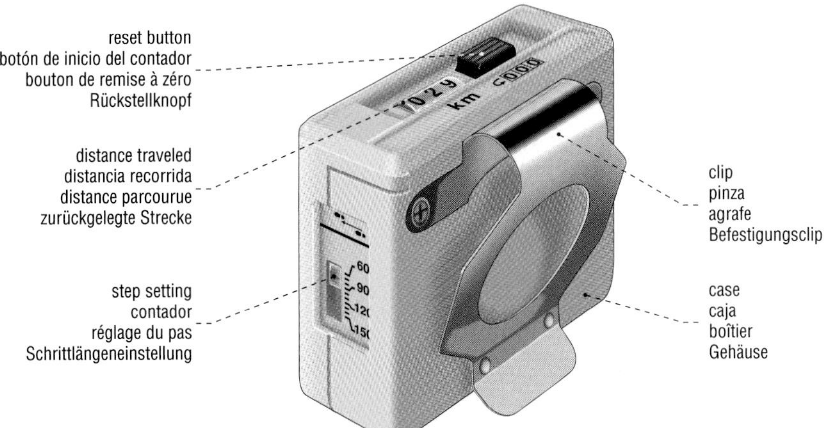
reset button
botón de inicio del contador
bouton de remise à zéro
Rückstellknopf
distance traveled
distancia recorrida
distance parcourue
zurückgelegte Strecke
step setting
contador
réglage du pas
Schrittlängeneinstellung
clip
pinza
agrafe
Befestigungsclip
case
caja
boîtier
Gehäuse

MEASURE OF THICKNESS
MEDICIÓN DEL ESPESOR
MESURE DE L'ÉPAISSEUR
DICKEMESSUNG

MICROMETER CALIPER
MICRÓMETRO
MICROMÈTRE PALMER
MIKROMETERSCHRAUBE

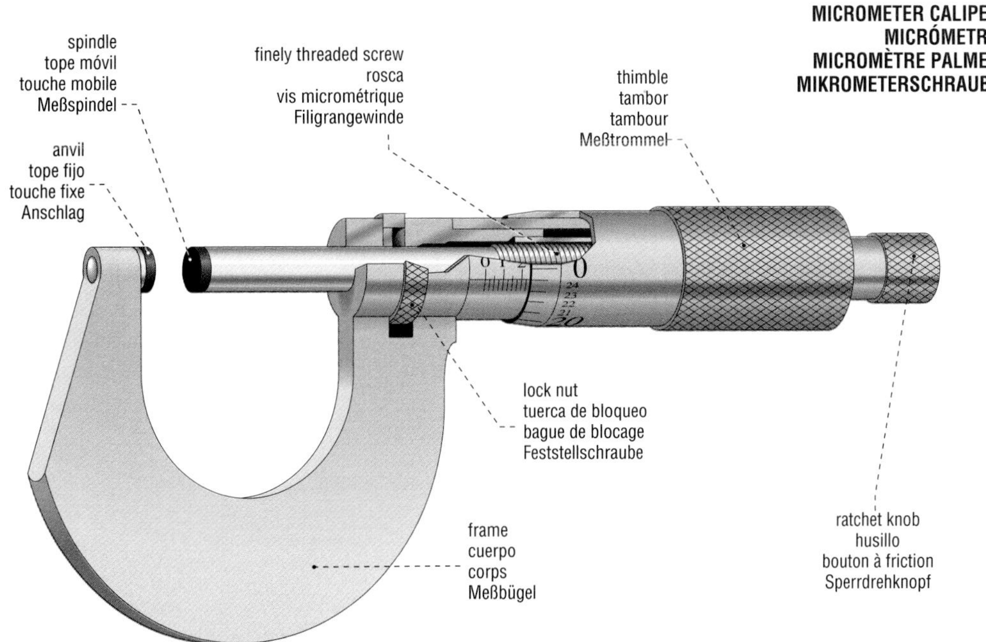
spindle
tope móvil
touche mobile
Meßspindel
anvil
tope fijo
touche fixe
Anschlag
finely threaded screw
rosca
vis micrométrique
Filigrangewinde
thimble
tambor
tambour
Meßtrommel
lock nut
tuerca de bloqueo
bague de blocage
Feststellschraube
frame
cuerpo
corps
Meßbügel
ratchet knob
husillo
bouton à friction
Sperrdrehknopf

WATT-HOUR METER
VATÍMETRO
WATTHEUREMÈTRE
STROMZÄHLER

EXTERIOR VIEW
VISTA EXTERIOR
VUE EXTÉRIEURE
AUSSENANSICHT

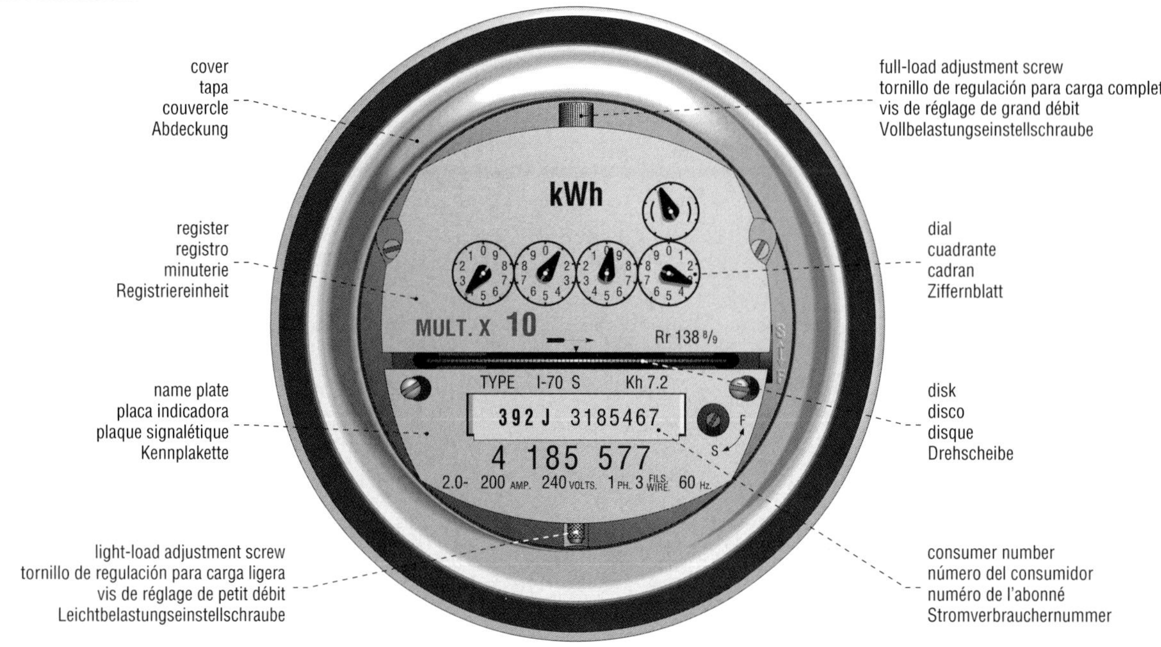
cover
tapa
couvercle
Abdeckung
full-load adjustment screw
tornillo de regulación para carga completa
vis de réglage de grand débit
Vollbelastungseinstellschraube
register
registro
minuterie
Registriereinheit
dial
cuadrante
cadran
Ziffernblatt
name plate
placa indicadora
plaque signalétique
Kennplakette
disk
disco
disque
Drehscheibe
light-load adjustment screw
tornillo de regulación para carga ligera
vis de réglage de petit débit
Leichtbelastungseinstellschraube
consumer number
número del consumidor
numéro de l'abonné
Stromverbrauchernummer
kWh
MULT. X 10
Rr 138 8/9
TYPE I-70 S
Kh 7.2
392 J 3185467
4 185 577
2.0- 200 AMP. 240 VOLTS. 1 PH. 3 FILS WIRE. 60 Hz.

MECHANISM
MECANISMO
MÉCANISME
MECHANISMUS

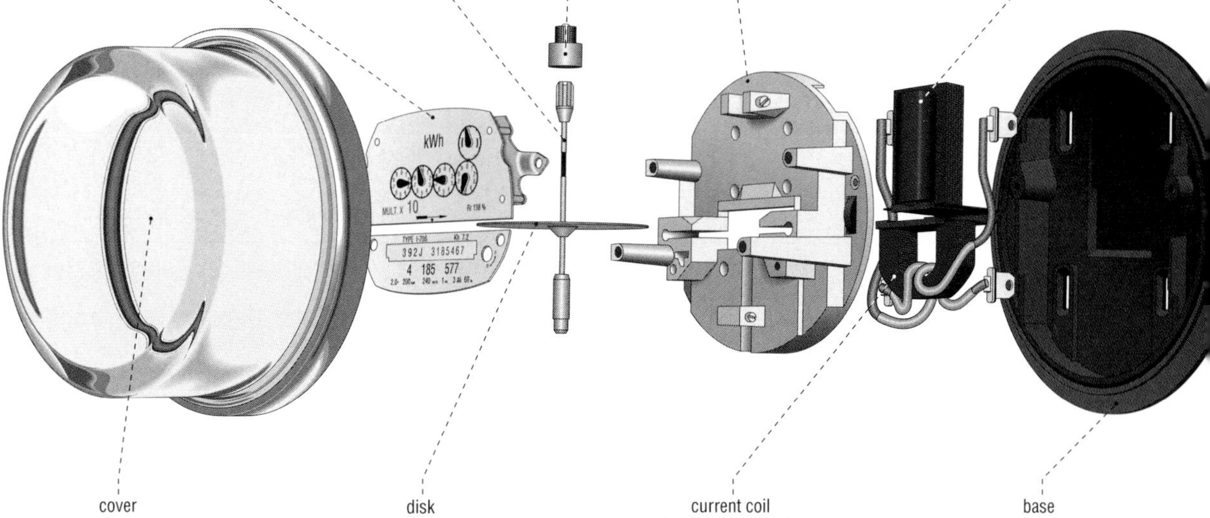

magnetic suspension
suspensión magnética
palier magnétique
Magnetaufhängung

register
registro
minuterie
Registriereinheit

spindle
árbol
arbre
Spindel

retarding magnet
imán frenador
aimant-frein
Retardiermagnet

potential coil
bobina de tensión
bobine de tension
Potentialspule

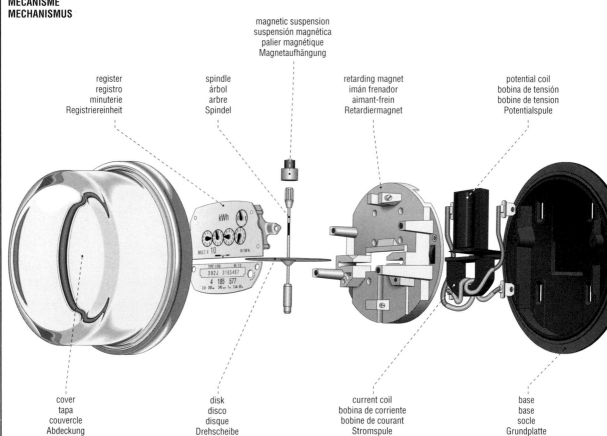

cover
tapa
couvercle
Abdeckung

disk
disco
disque
Drehscheibe

current coil
bobina de corriente
bobine de courant
Stromspule

base
base
socle
Grundplatte

MEASURE OF ANGLES
MEDICIÓN DE ÁNGULOS
MESURE DES ANGLES
WINKELMESSUNG

THEODOLITE
TEODOLITO
THÉODOLITE
THEODOLIT

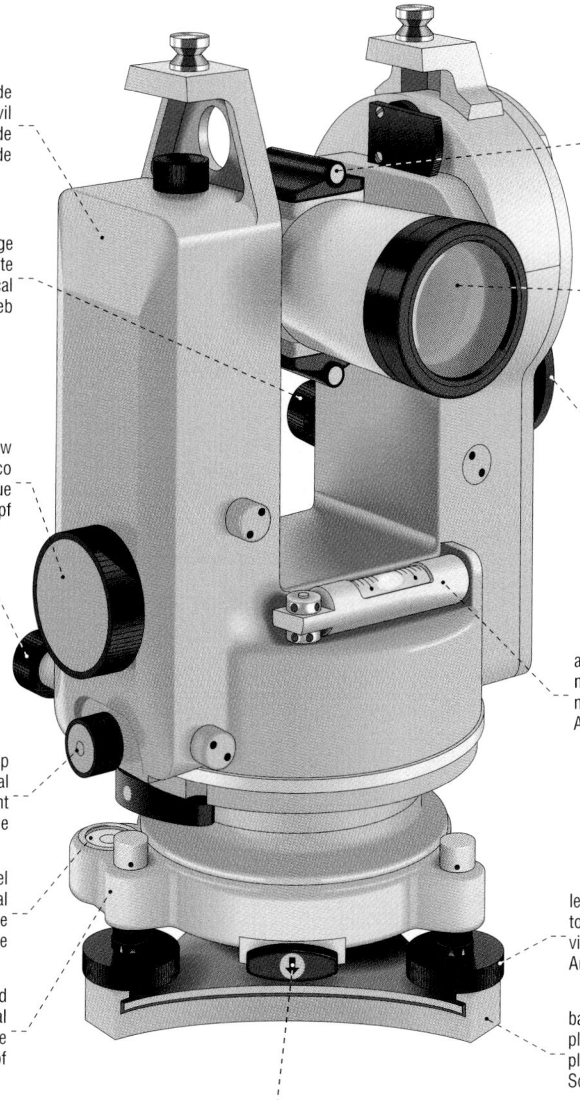

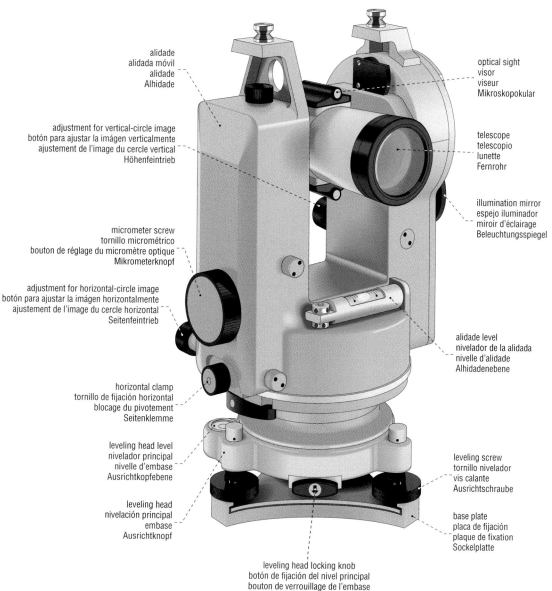

alidade
alidada móvil
alidade
Alhidade

optical sight
visor
viseur
Mikroskopokular

adjustment for vertical-circle image
botón para ajustar la imágen verticalmente
ajustement de l'image du cercle vertical
Höhenfeintrieb

telescope
telescopio
lunette
Fernrohr

illumination mirror
espejo iluminador
miroir d'éclairage
Beleuchtungsspiegel

micrometer screw
tornillo micrométrico
bouton de réglage du micromètre optique
Mikrometerknopf

adjustment for horizontal-circle image
botón para ajustar la imágen horizontalmente
ajustement de l'image du cercle horizontal
Seitenfeintrieb

alidade level
nivelador de la alidada
nivelle d'alidade
Alhidadenebene

horizontal clamp
tornillo de fijación horizontal
blocage du pivotement
Seitenklemme

leveling head level
nivelador principal
nivelle d'embase
Ausrichtkopfebene

leveling screw
tornillo nivelador
vis calante
Ausrichtschraube

leveling head
nivelación principal
embase
Ausrichtknopf

base plate
placa de fijación
plaque de fixation
Sockelplatte

leveling head locking knob
botón de fijación del nivel principal
bouton de verrouillage de l'embase
Ausrichtkopfblockierung

bevel square
falsa escuadra
fausse-équerre
Schrägmaß

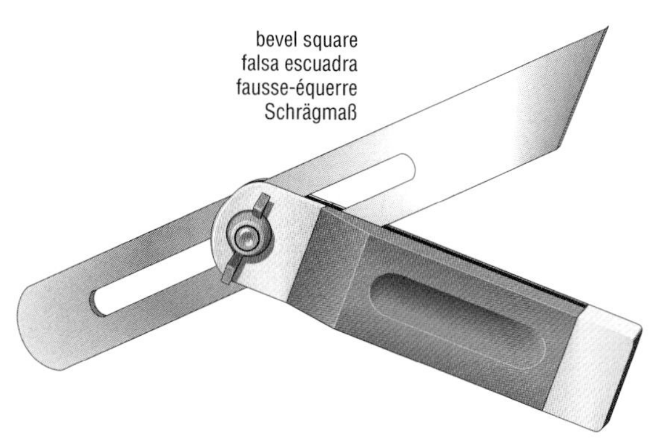

protractor
transportador
rapporteur d'angle
Winkelmesser

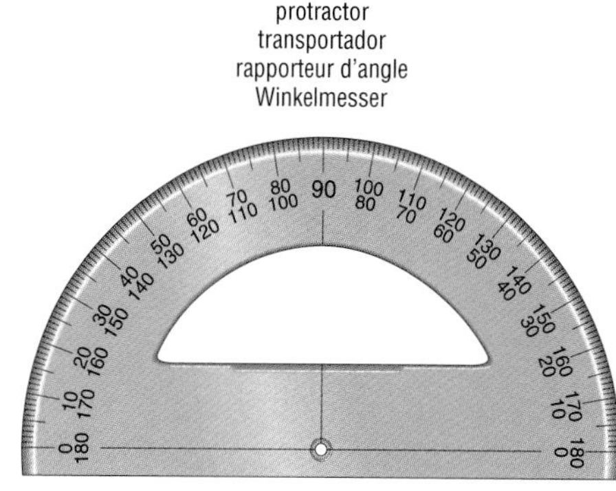

MEASURE OF SEISMIC WAVES
MEDICIÓN DE ONDAS SÍSMICAS
MESURE DES ONDES SISMIQUES
MESSUNG SEISMISCHER WELLEN

DETECTION OF SEISMIC WAVES
DETECCIÓN DE ONDAS SÍSMICAS
DÉTECTION DES ONDES SISMIQUES
REGISTRIERUNG SEISMISCHER WELLEN

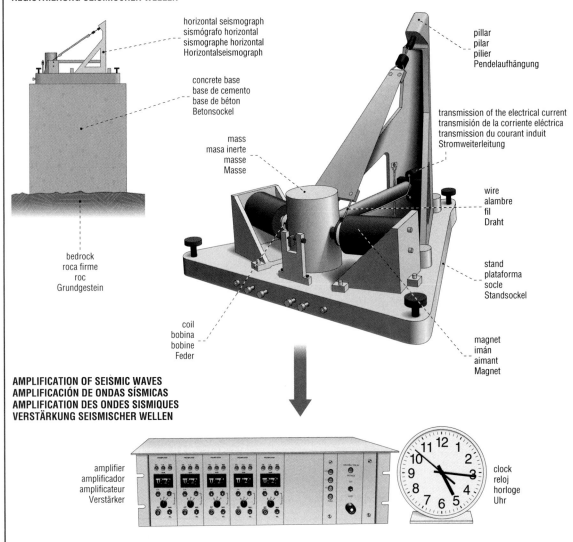

horizontal seismograph
sismógrafo horizontal
sismographe horizontal
Horizontalseismograph

concrete base
base de cemento
base de béton
Betonsockel

bedrock
roca firme
roc
Grundgestein

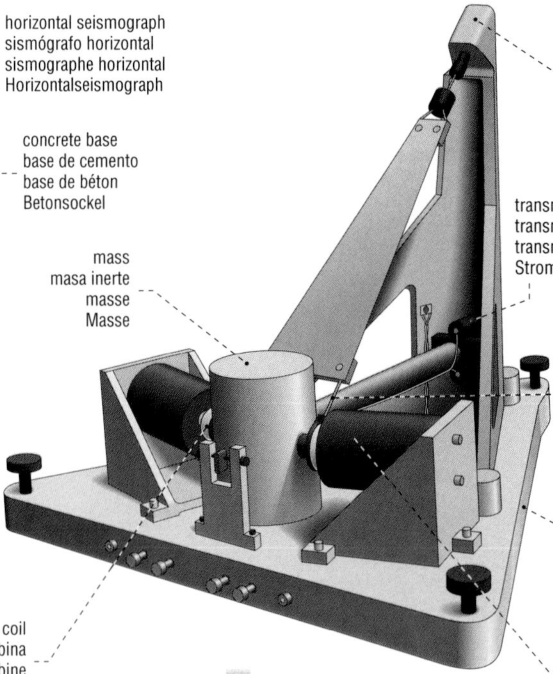

pillar
pilar
pilier
Pendelaufhängung

mass
masa inerte
masse
Masse

transmission of the electrical current
transmisión de la corriente eléctrica
transmission du courant induit
Stromweiterleitung

wire
alambre
fil
Draht

stand
plataforma
socle
Standsockel

coil
bobina
bobine
Feder

magnet
imán
aimant
Magnet

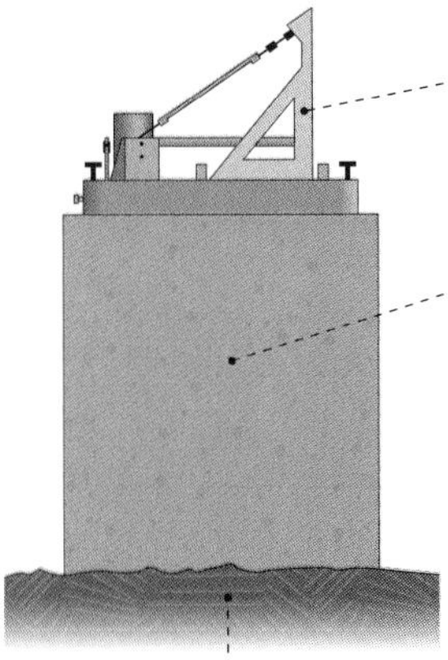

AMPLIFICATION OF SEISMIC WAVES
AMPLIFICACIÓN DE ONDAS SÍSMICAS
AMPLIFICATION DES ONDES SISMIQUES
VERSTÄRKUNG SEISMISCHER WELLEN

amplifier
amplificador
amplificateur
Verstärker

clock
reloj
horloge
Uhr

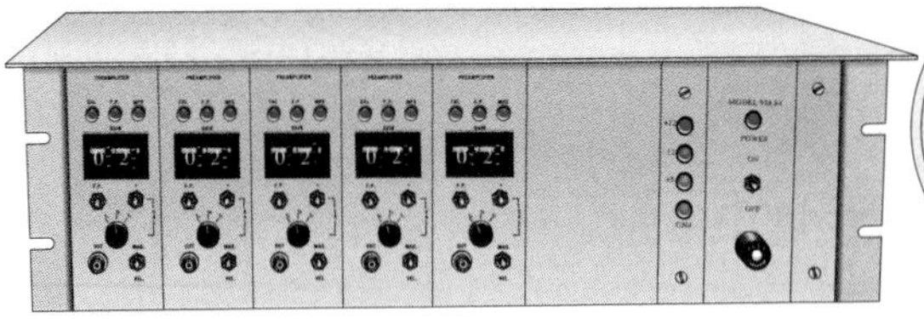

TRANSCRIPTION OF SEISMIC WAVES
TRANSCRIPCIÓN DE ONDAS SÍSMICAS
TRANSCRIPTION DES ONDES SISMIQUES
AUFZEICHNUNG SEISMISCHER WELLEN

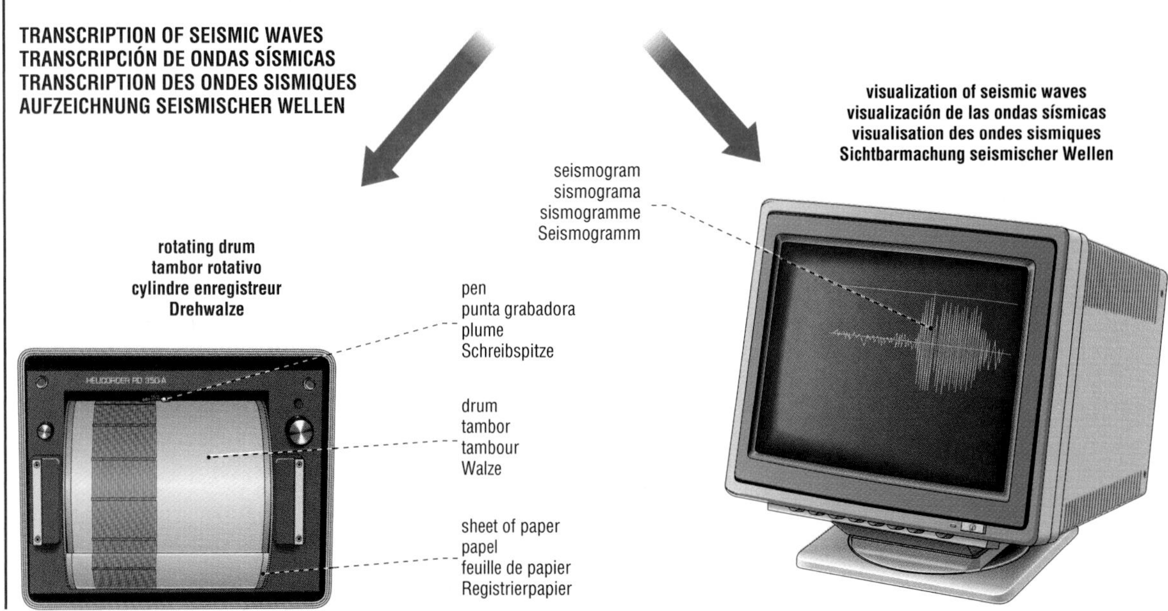
rotating drum
tambor rotativo
cylindre enregistreur
Drehwalze
pen
punta grabadora
plume
Schreibspitze
drum
tambor
tambour
Walze
sheet of paper
papel
feuille de papier
Registrierpapier
visualization of seismic waves
visualización de las ondas sísmicas
visualisation des ondes sismiques
Sichtbarmachung seismischer Wellen
seismogram
sismograma
sismogramme
Seismogramm

OPTICAL INSTRUMENTS | APPAREILS DE VISION
INSTRUMENTOS ÓPTICOS | OPTISCHE INSTRUMENTE

CONTENTS

ELECTRON MICROSCOPE
MICROSCOPIO DE ELECTRONES
MICROSCOPE ÉLECTRONIQUE
ELEKTRONENMIKROSKOP

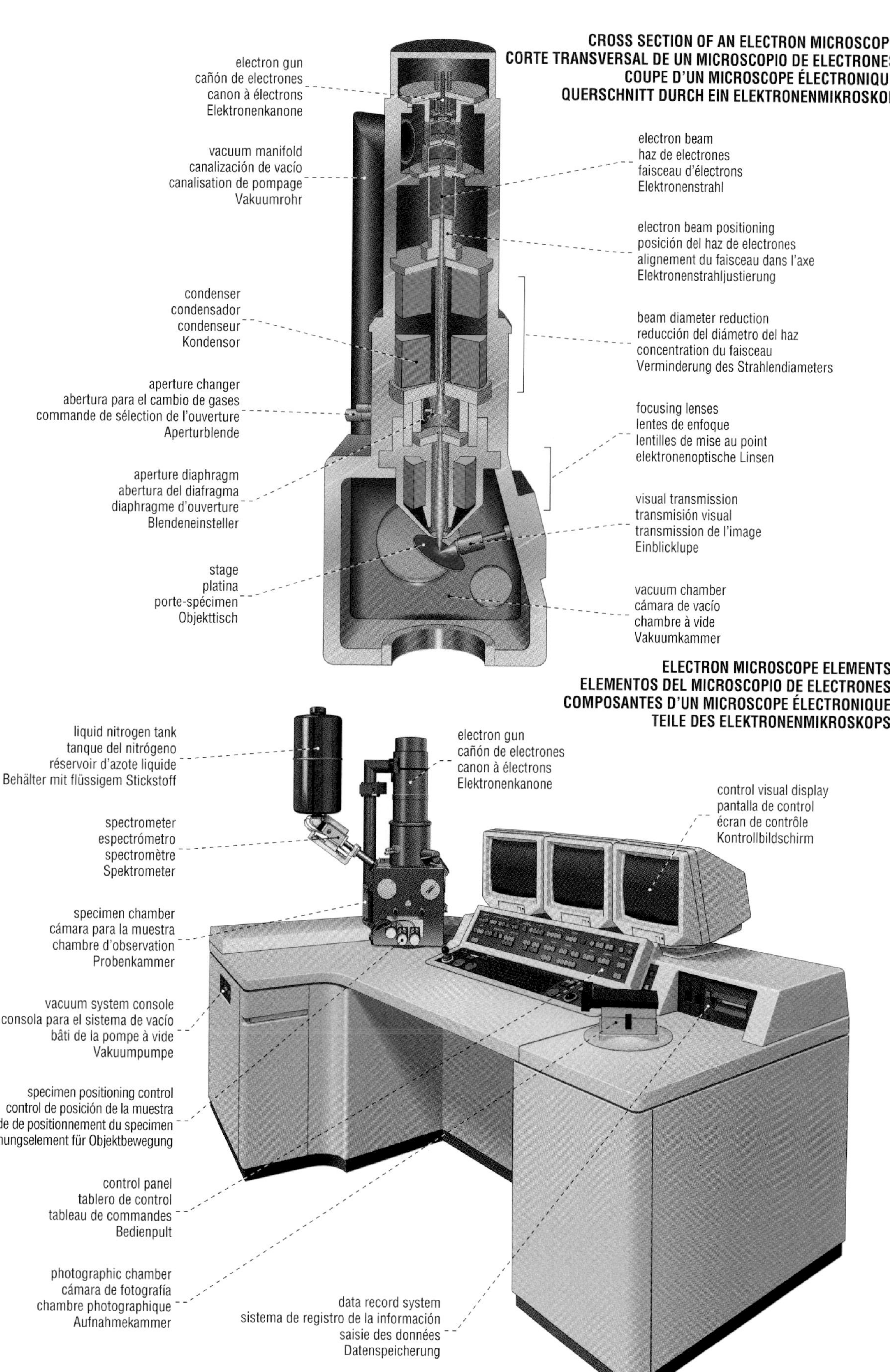
CROSS SECTION OF AN ELECTRON MICROSCOPE
CORTE TRANSVERSAL DE UN MICROSCOPIO DE ELECTRONES
COUPE D'UN MICROSCOPE ÉLECTRONIQUE
QUERSCHNITT DURCH EIN ELEKTRONENMIKROSKOP
electron gun
cañón de electrones
canon à électrons
Elektronenkanone
vacuum manifold
canalización de vacío
canalisation de pompage
Vakuumrohr
condenser
condensador
condenseur
Kondensor
aperture changer
abertura para el cambio de gases
commande de sélection de l'ouverture
Aperturblende
aperture diaphragm
abertura del diafragma
diaphragme d'ouverture
Blendeneinsteller
stage
platina
porte-spécimen
Objekttisch
electron beam
haz de electrones
faisceau d'électrons
Elektronenstrahl
electron beam positioning
posición del haz de electrones
alignement du faisceau dans l'axe
Elektronenstrahljustierung
beam diameter reduction
reducción del diámetro del haz
concentration du faisceau
Verminderung des Strahlendiameters
focusing lenses
lentes de enfoque
lentilles de mise au point
elektronenoptische Linsen
visual transmission
transmisión visual
transmission de l'image
Einblicklupe
vacuum chamber
cámara de vacío
chambre à vide
Vakuumkammer
ELECTRON MICROSCOPE ELEMENTS
ELEMENTOS DEL MICROSCOPIO DE ELECTRONES
COMPOSANTES D'UN MICROSCOPE ÉLECTRONIQUE
TEILE DES ELEKTRONENMIKROSKOPS
liquid nitrogen tank
tanque del nitrógeno
réservoir d'azote liquide
Behälter mit flüssigem Stickstoff
spectrometer
espectrómetro
spectromètre
Spektrometer
specimen chamber
cámara para la muestra
chambre d'observation
Probenkammer
vacuum system console
consola para el sistema de vacío
bâti de la pompe à vide
Vakuumpumpe
specimen positioning control
control de posición de la muestra
ommande de positionnement du specimen
Bedienungselement für Objektbewegung
control panel
tablero de control
tableau de commandes
Bedienpult
photographic chamber
cámara de fotografía
chambre photographique
Aufnahmekammer
electron gun
cañón de electrones
canon à électrons
Elektronenkanone
control visual display
pantalla de control
écran de contrôle
Kontrollbildschirm
data record system
sistema de registro de la información
saisie des données
Datenspeicherung

BINOCULAR MICROSCOPE
MICROSCOPIO BINOCULAR
MICROSCOPE BINOCULAIRE
BINOKULARMIKROSKOP

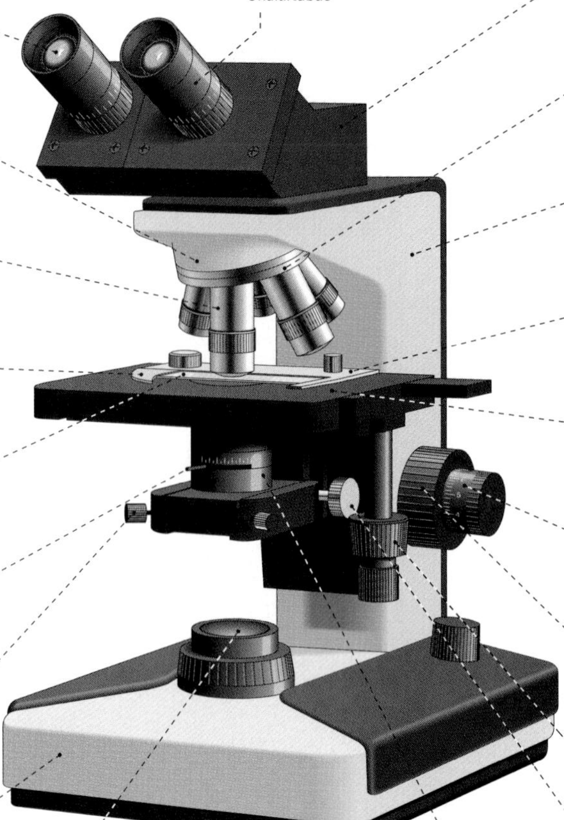

eyepiece
ocular
oculaire
Okular

limb top
portatubo
porte-tube
Tubusträger

objective
objetivo
objectif
Objektiv

stage clip
sujetador
valet
Objektklammer

glass slide
portaobjetos
lame porte-objet
Glasscheibe

field lens adjustment
ajuste de la lente de campo
réglage du diaphragme
Feldlinseneinstellung

condenser adjustment knob
tornillo de ajuste del condensador
vis de réglage du condenseur
Kondensoreinstellung

base
pie
pied
Fuß

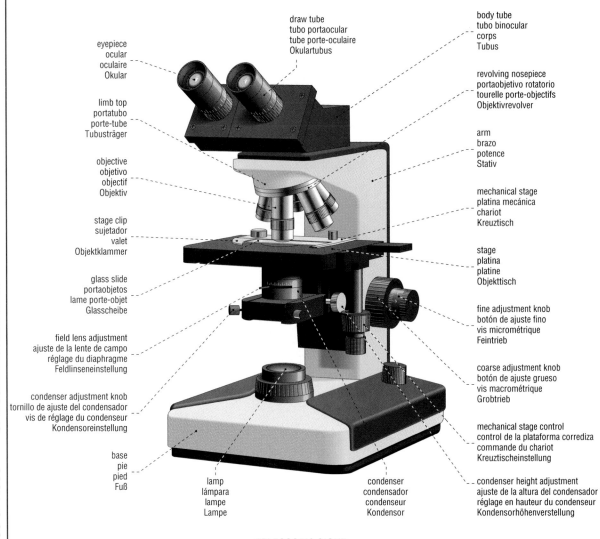

draw tube
tubo portaocular
tube porte-oculaire
Okulartubus

lamp
lámpara
lampe
Lampe

condenser
condensador
condenseur
Kondensor

body tube
tubo binocular
corps
Tubus

revolving nosepiece
portaobjetivo rotatorio
tourelle porte-objectifs
Objektivrevolver

arm
brazo
potence
Stativ

mechanical stage
platina mecánica
chariot
Kreuztisch

stage
platina
platine
Objekttisch

fine adjustment knob
botón de ajuste fino
vis micrométrique
Feintrieb

coarse adjustment knob
botón de ajuste grueso
vis macrométrique
Grobtrieb

mechanical stage control
control de la plataforma corrediza
commande du chariot
Kreuztischeinstellung

condenser height adjustment
ajuste de la altura del condensador
réglage en hauteur du condenseur
Kondensorhöhenverstellung

TELESCOPIC SIGHT
VISOR TELESCÓPICO
LUNETTE DE VISÉE
ZIELFERNROHR

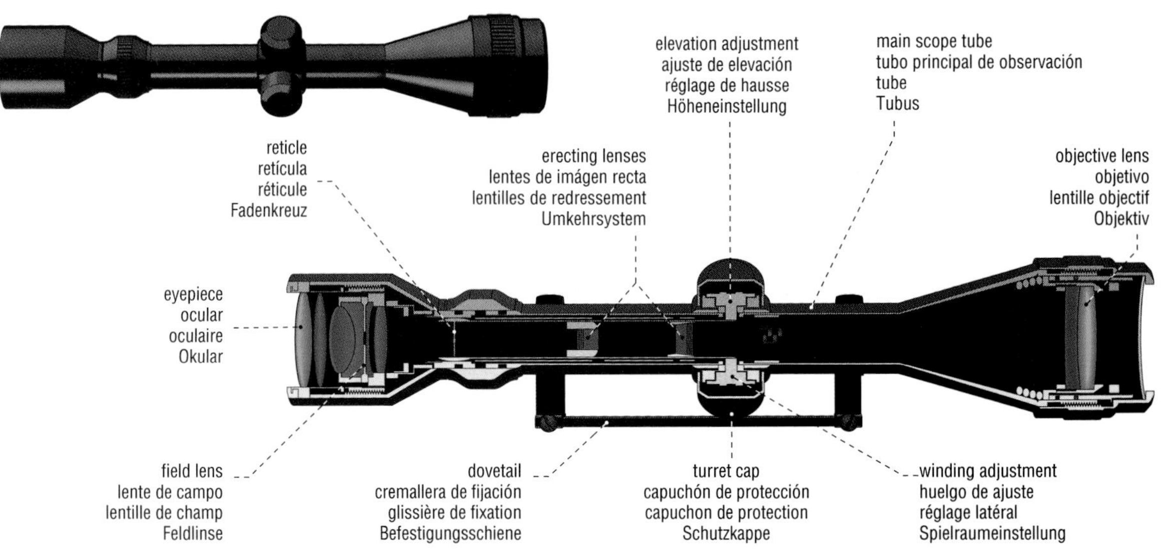
elevation adjustment
ajuste de elevación
réglage de hausse
Höheneinstellung
main scope tube
tubo principal de observación
tube
Tubus
reticle
retícula
réticule
Fadenkreuz
erecting lenses
lentes de imágen recta
lentilles de redressement
Umkehrsystem
objective lens
objetivo
lentille objectif
Objektiv
eyepiece
ocular
oculaire
Okular
field lens
lente de campo
lentille de champ
Feldlinse
dovetail
cremallera de fijación
glissière de fixation
Befestigungsschiene
turret cap
capuchón de protección
capuchon de protection
Schutzkappe
winding adjustment
huelgo de ajuste
réglage latéral
Spielraumeinstellung

PRISM BINOCULARS
PRISMÁTICOS BINOCULARES
JUMELLES À PRISMES
PRISMENFERNGLAS

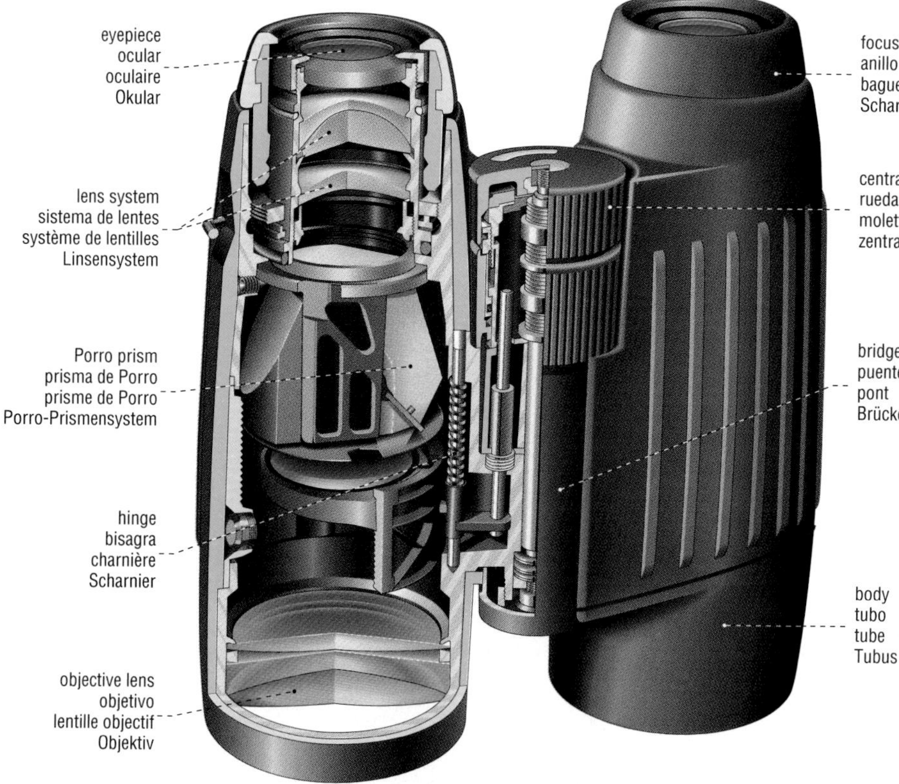
eyepiece
ocular
oculaire
Okular
lens system
sistema de lentes
système de lentilles
Linsensystem
Porro prism
prisma de Porro
prisme de Porro
Porro-Prismensystem
hinge
bisagra
charnière
Scharnier
objective lens
objetivo
lentille objectif
Objektiv
focusing ring
anillo de enfoque
bague de correction dioptrique
Scharfstellring
central focusing wheel
rueda central de enfoque
molette de mise au point
zentrales Scharfstellrad
bridge
puente
pont
Brücke
body
tubo
tube
Tubus

MAGNETIC COMPASS
BRÚJULA MAGNÉTICA
BOUSSOLE MAGNÉTIQUE
MAGNETKOMPASS

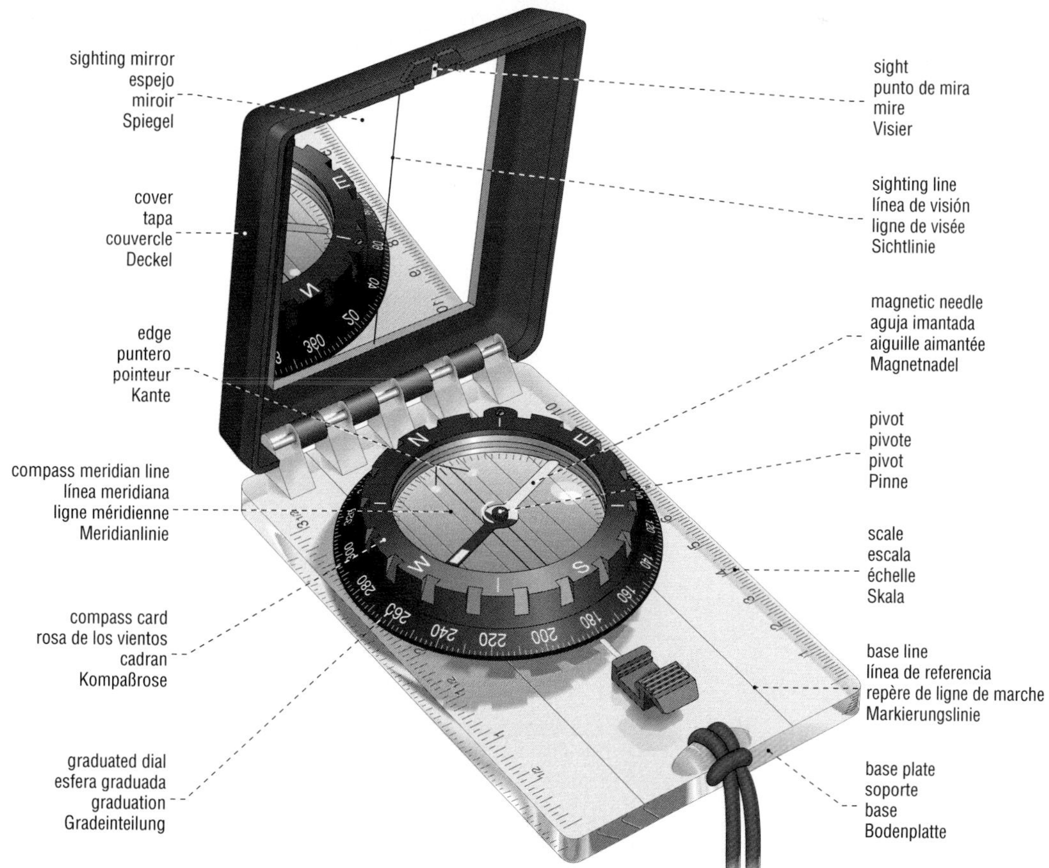
sighting mirror
espejo
miroir
Spiegel
cover
tapa
couvercle
Deckel
edge
puntero
pointeur
Kante
compass meridian line
línea meridiana
ligne méridienne
Meridianlinie
compass card
rosa de los vientos
cadran
Kompaßrose
graduated dial
esfera graduada
graduation
Gradeinteilung
sight
punto de mira
mire
Visier
sighting line
línea de visión
ligne de visée
Sichtlinie
magnetic needle
aguja imantada
aiguille aimantée
Magnetnadel
pivot
pivote
pivot
Pinne
scale
escala
échelle
Skala
base line
línea de referencia
repère de ligne de marche
Markierungslinie
base plate
soporte
base
Bodenplatte

REFLECTING TELESCOPE
TELESCOPIO REFLECTOR
TÉLESCOPE
SPIEGELTELESKOP

support
soporte
support de fixation
Stütze

finderscope
anteojo buscador
chercheur
Sucher

eyepiece
ocular
oculaire
Okular

cradle
abrazadera
bride de fixation
Wiege

main tube
tubo principal
tube
Tubus

focusing knob
botón de enfoque
bouton de mise au point
Scharfeinstellung

declination setting scale
disco de ajuste de declinación
cercle de déclinaison
Einstellung der Deklinationsachse

right ascension setting scale
disco de ajuste de ascención recta
cercle d'ascension droite
Einstellung der Rektaszensionsachse

azimuth clamp
bloqueo del ajuste del acimut
vis de blocage (azimut)
Azimutfeststeller

azimuth fine adjustment
ajuste fino del acimut
réglage micrométrique (azimut)
Azimutfeineinstellung

altitude clamp
bloqueo del ajuste de la altura
vis de blocage (latitude)
Höhenfeststeller

altitude fine adjustment
ajuste fino de la altura
réglage micrométrique (latitude)
Höhenfeineinstellung

CROSS SECTION OF A REFLECTING TELESCOPE
CORTE TRANSVERSAL DE UN TELECOPIO REFLECTOR
COUPE D'UN TÉLESCOPE
QUERSCHNITT DURCH EIN SPIEGELTELESKOP

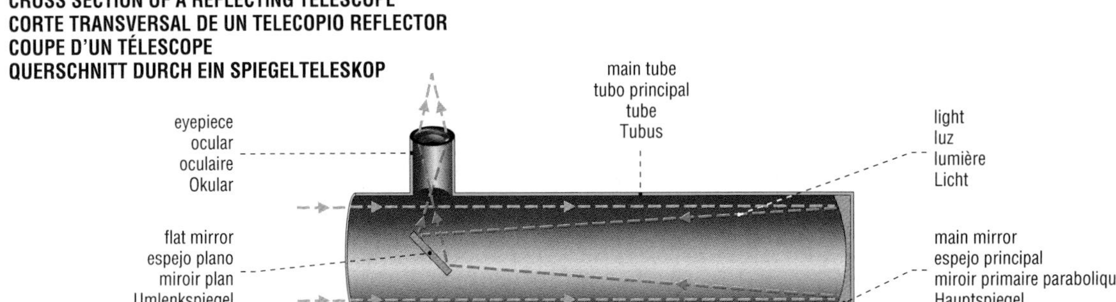
main tube
tubo principal
tube
Tubus
eyepiece
ocular
oculaire
Okular
light
luz
lumière
Licht
flat mirror
espejo plano
miroir plan
Umlenkspiegel
main mirror
espejo principal
miroir primaire parabolique
Hauptspiegel

REFRACTING TELESCOPE
TELESCOPIO REFRACTOR
LUNETTE ASTRONOMIQUE
LINSENFERNROHR

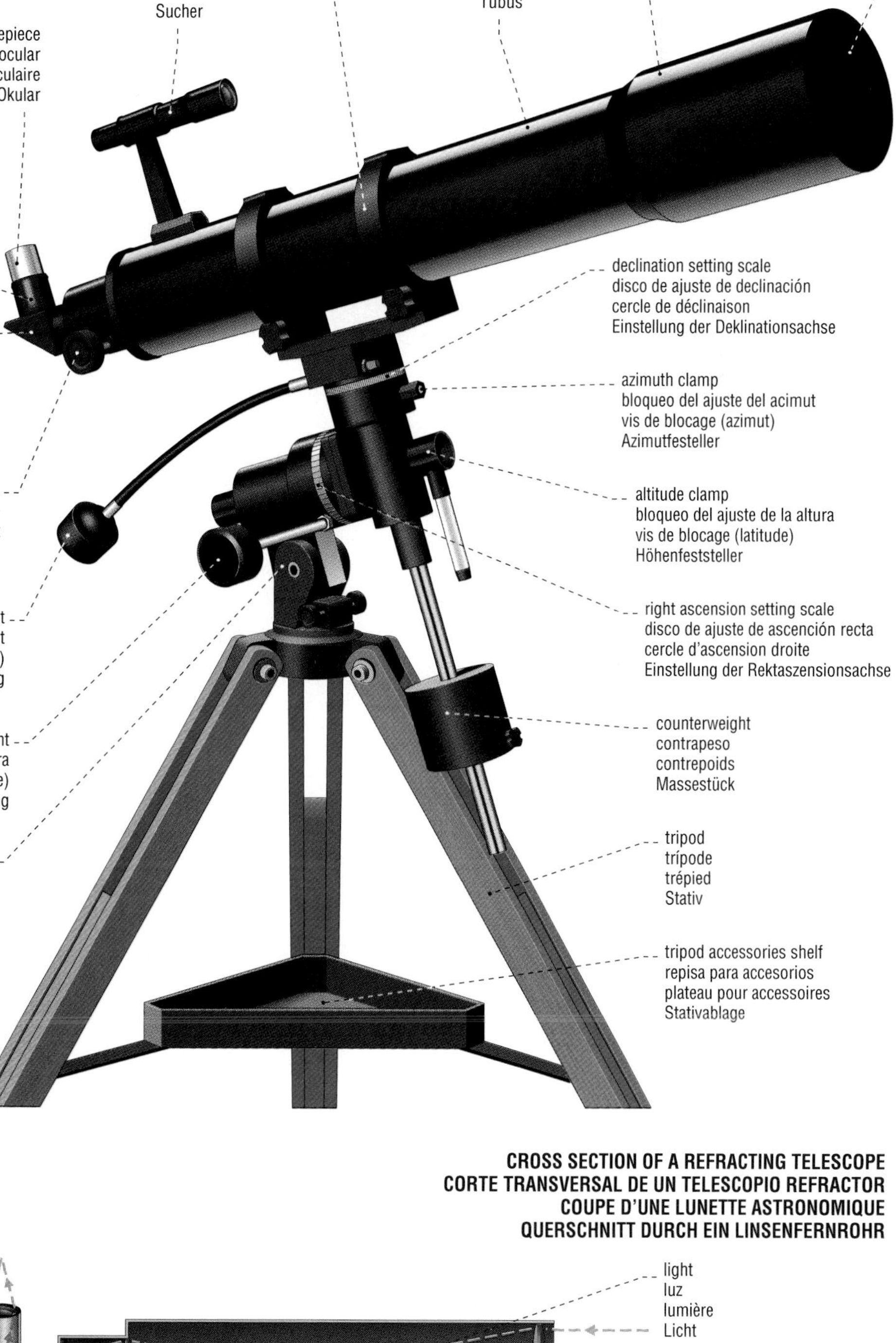

dew shield
protección contra el vaho
pare-soleil
Sonnenblende

cradle
abrazadera
bride de fixation
Wiege

objective lens
objetivo
lentille objectif
Objektiv

main tube
tubo principal
tube
Tubus

finderscope
anteojo buscador
chercheur
Sucher

eyepiece
ocular
oculaire
Okular

eyepiece holder
portaocular
tube porte-oculaire
Okularträger

declination setting scale
disco de ajuste de declinación
cercle de déclinaison
Einstellung der Deklinationsachse

star diagonal
ocular acodado
oculaire coudé
Coudé-Okular

azimuth clamp
bloqueo del ajuste del acimut
vis de blocage (azimut)
Azimutfesteller

focusing knob
botón de enfoque
bouton de mise au point
Scharfeinstellung

altitude clamp
bloqueo del ajuste de la altura
vis de blocage (latitude)
Höhenfeststeller

azimuth fine adjustment
ajuste fino del acimut
réglage micrométrique (azimut)
Azimutfeineinstellung

right ascension setting scale
disco de ajuste de ascención recta
cercle d'ascension droite
Einstellung der Rektaszensionsachse

altitude fine adjustment
ajuste fino de la altura
réglage micrométrique (latitude)
Höhenfeineinstellung

counterweight
contrapeso
contrepoids
Massestück

fork
horquilla
fourche
Gabel

tripod
trípode
trépied
Stativ

tripod accessories shelf
repisa para accesorios
plateau pour accessoires
Stativablage

CROSS SECTION OF A REFRACTING TELESCOPE
CORTE TRANSVERSAL DE UN TELESCOPIO REFRACTOR
COUPE D'UNE LUNETTE ASTRONOMIQUE
QUERSCHNITT DURCH EIN LINSENFERNROHR

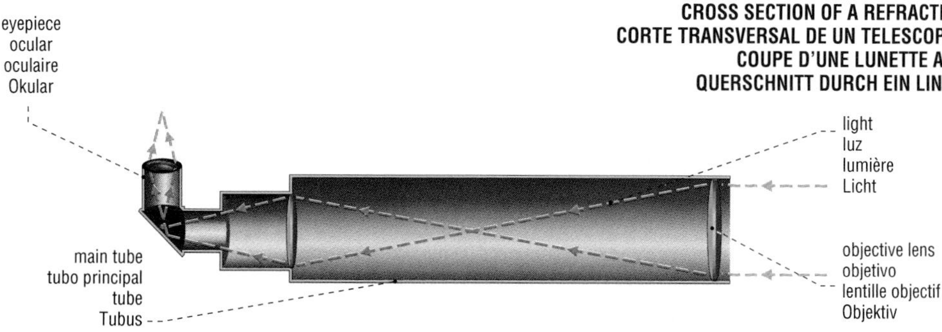
eyepiece
ocular
oculaire
Okular
light
luz
lumière
Licht
main tube
tubo principal
tube
Tubus
objective lens
objetivo
lentille objectif
Objektiv

LENSES
LENTES
LENTILLES
LINSEN

CONVERGING LENSES
LENTES CONVERGENTES
LENTILLES CONVERGENTES
SAMMELLINSEN

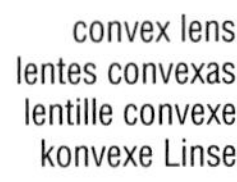

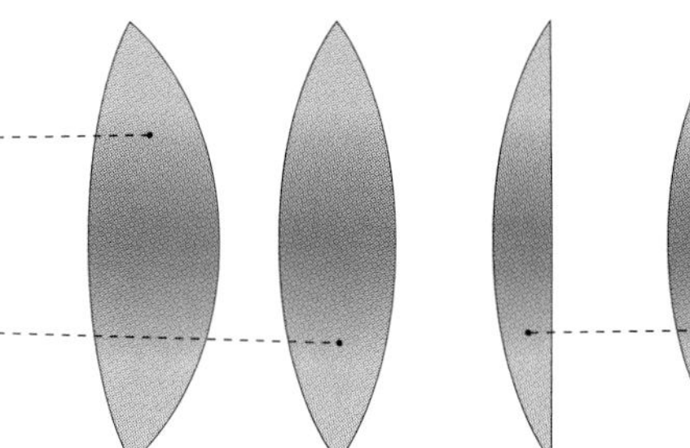

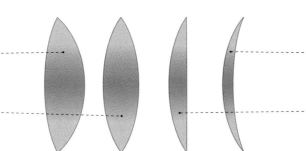

convex lens
lentes convexas
lentille convexe
konvexe Linse

biconvex lens
lentes biconvexas
lentille biconvexe
bikonvexe Linse

positive meniscus
menisco convergente
ménisque convergent
konkavkonvexe Linse

plano-convex lens
lente convexo-plana
lentille plan-convexe
plankonvexe Linse

DIVERGING LENSES
LENTES DIVERGENTES
LENTILLES DIVERGENTES
ZERSTREUUNGSLINSEN

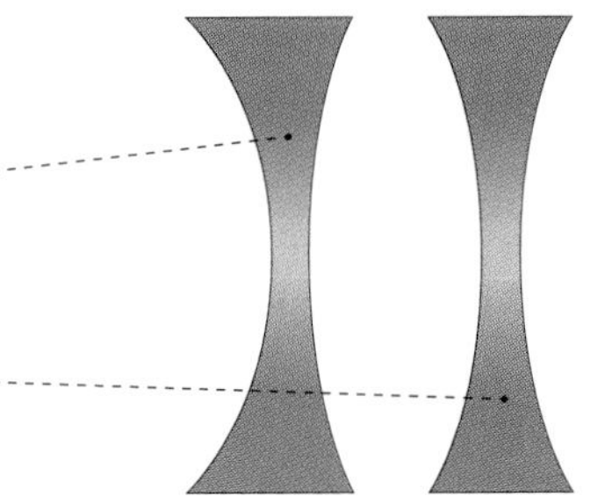

concave lens
lentes cóncavas
lentille concave
konkave Linse

biconcave lens
lentes bicóncavas
lentille biconcave
bikonkave Linse

negative meniscus
menisco divergente
ménisque divergent
konvexkonkave Linse

plano-concave lens
lentes cóncavo-planas
lentille plan-concave
plankonkave Linse

RADAR
RADAR
RADAR
RADAR

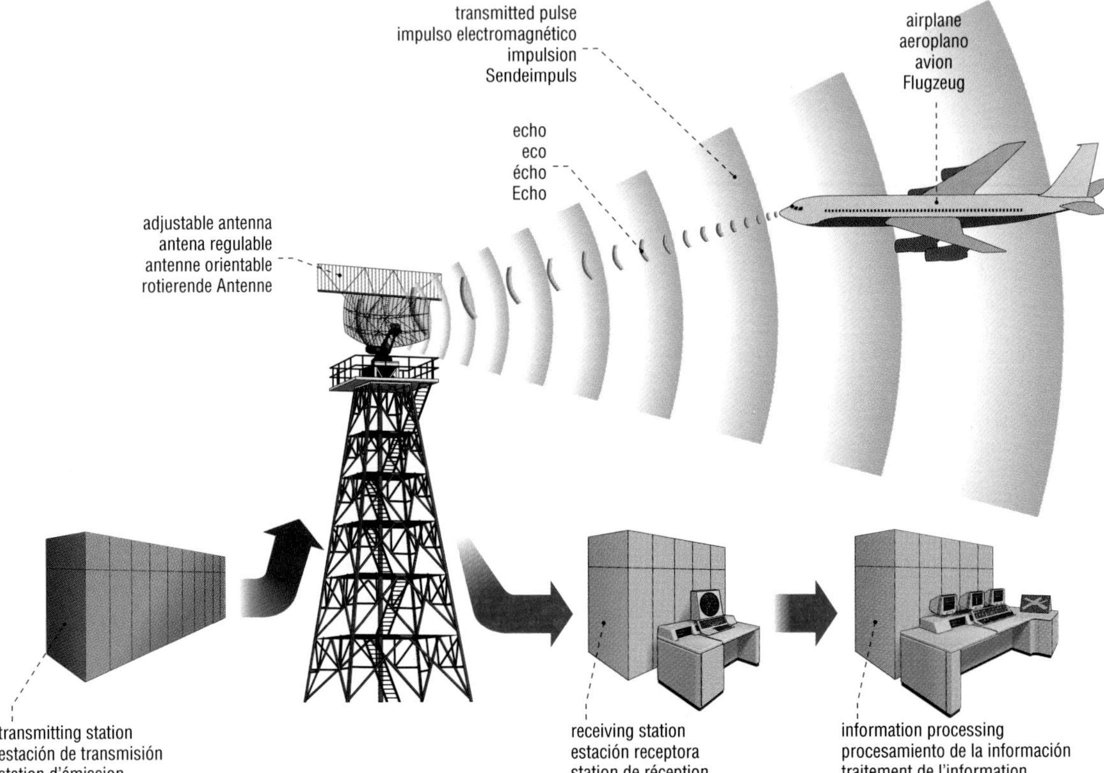
transmitted pulse
impulso electromagnético
impulsion
Sendeimpuls
airplane
aeroplano
avion
Flugzeug
echo
eco
écho
Echo
adjustable antenna
antena regulable
antenne orientable
rotierende Antenne
transmitting station
estación de transmisión
station d'émission
Übertragungsstation
receiving station
estación receptora
station de réception
Empfängerstation
information processing
procesamiento de la información
traitement de l'information
Datenverarbeitung

HEALTH AND SAFETY
SALUD Y SEGURIDAD
SANTÉ ET SÉCURITÉ
GESUNDHEIT UND UNFALLSCHUTZ

CONTENTS

FIRST AID KIT
BOTIQUÍN DE PRIMEROS AUXILIOS
TROUSSE DE SECOURS
ERSTE-HILFE-KASTEN

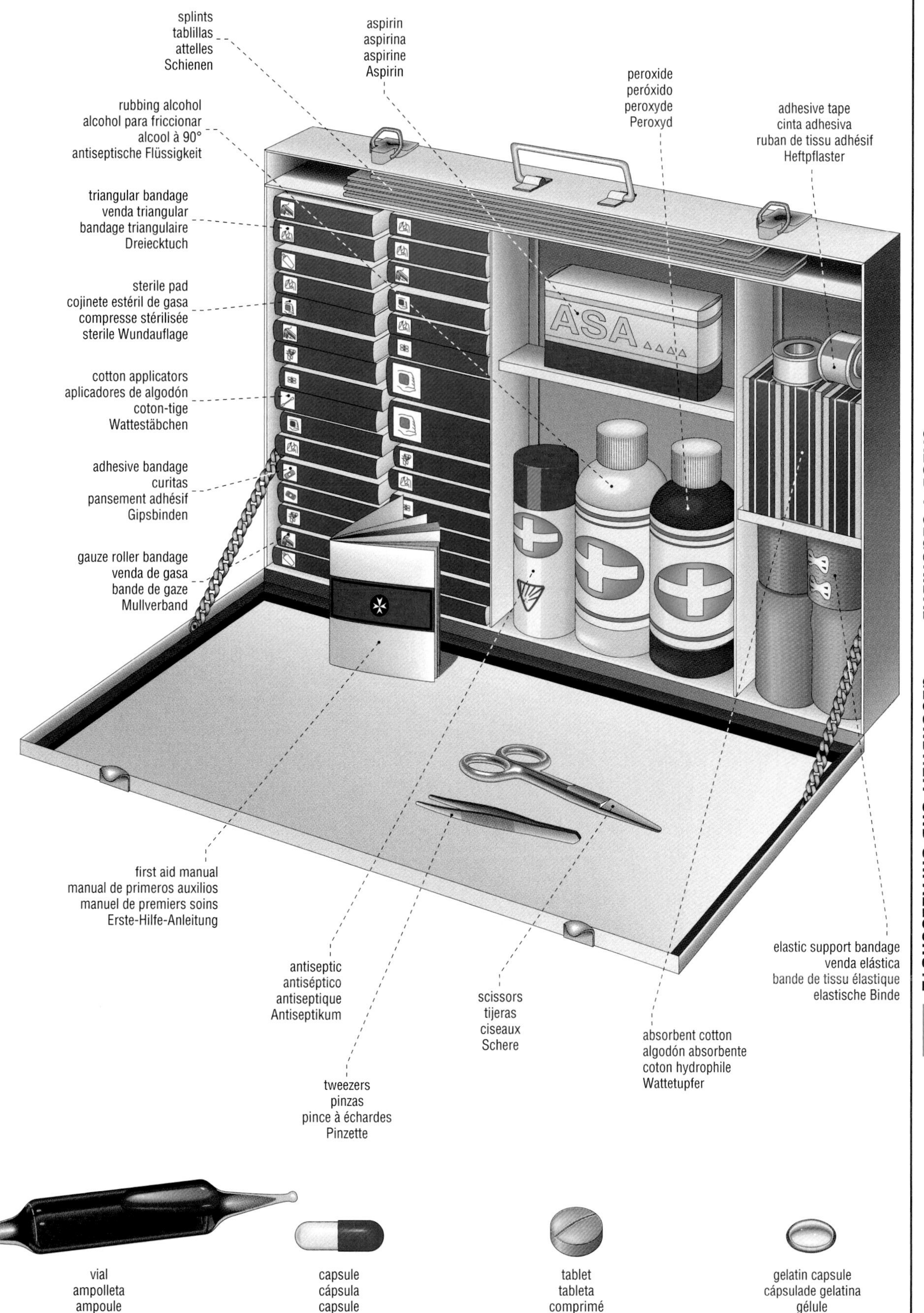

splints
tablillas
attelles
Schienen
aspirin
aspirina
aspirine
Aspirin
peroxide
peróxido
peroxyde
Peroxyd
adhesive tape
cinta adhesiva
ruban de tissu adhésif
Heftpflaster
rubbing alcohol
alcohol para friccionar
alcool à 90°
antiseptische Flüssigkeit
triangular bandage
venda triangular
bandage triangulaire
Dreiecktuch
sterile pad
cojinete estéril de gasa
compresse stérilisée
sterile Wundauflage
cotton applicators
aplicadores de algodón
coton-tige
Wattestäbchen
adhesive bandage
curitas
pansement adhésif
Gipsbinden
gauze roller bandage
venda de gasa
bande de gaze
Mullverband
ASA
first aid manual
manual de primeros auxilios
manuel de premiers soins
Erste-Hilfe-Anleitung
antiseptic
antiséptico
antiseptique
Antiseptikum
scissors
tijeras
ciseaux
Schere
tweezers
pinzas
pince à échardes
Pinzette
absorbent cotton
algodón absorbente
coton hydrophile
Wattetupfer
elastic support bandage
venda elástica
bande de tissu élastique
elastische Binde
vial
ampolleta
ampoule
Ampulle
capsule
cápsula
capsule
Kapsel
tablet
tableta
comprimé
Tablette
gelatin capsule
cápsulade gelatina
gélule
Gelatinekapsel

FIRST AID EQUIPMENT
EQUIPO DE PRIMEROS AUXILIOS
MATÉRIEL DE SECOURS
NOTFALLAUSRÜSTUNG

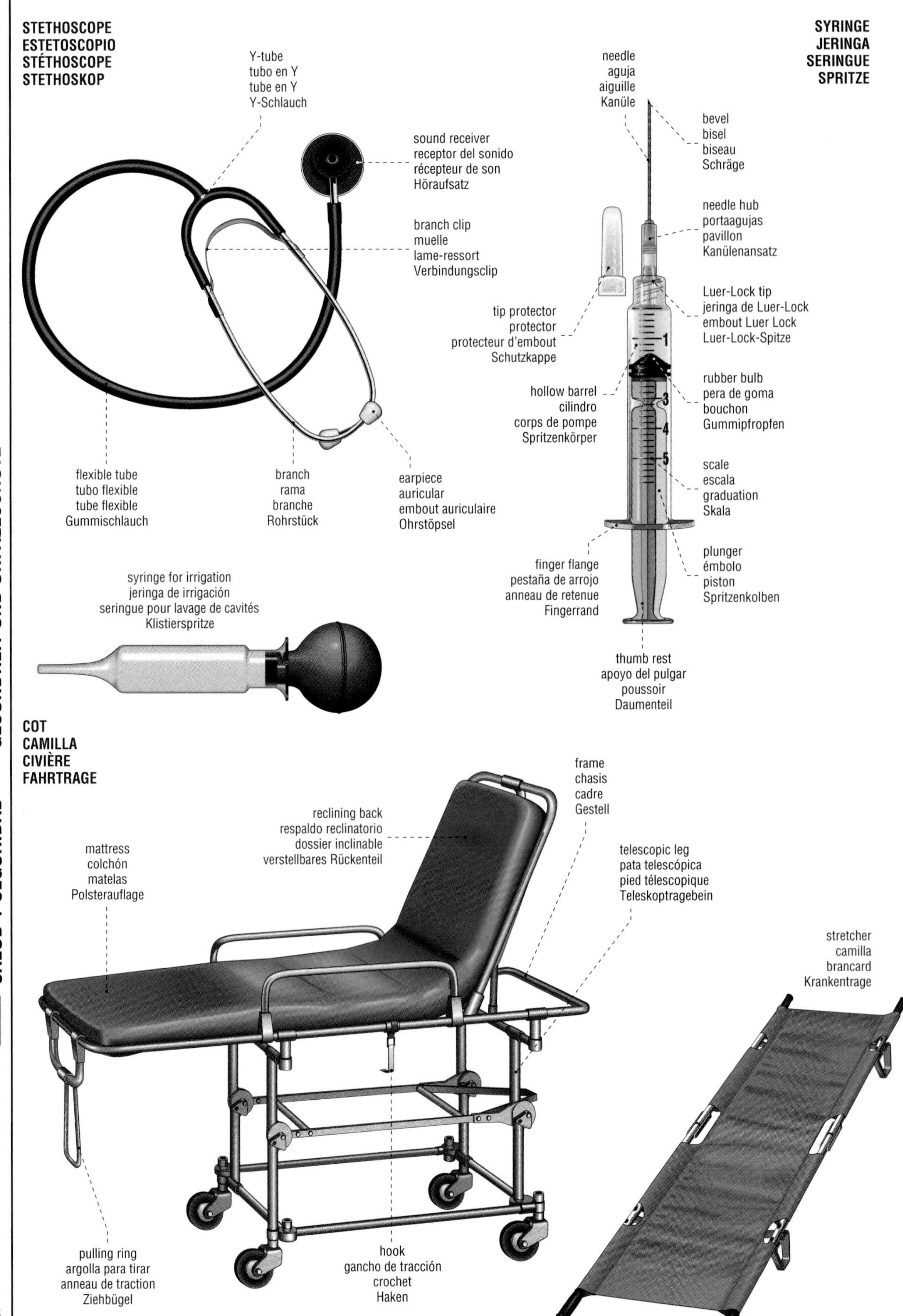

STETHOSCOPE
ESTETOSCOPIO
STÉTHOSCOPE
STETHOSKOP
Y-tube
tubo en Y
tube en Y
Y-Schlauch
sound receiver
receptor del sonido
récepteur de son
Höraufsatz
branch clip
muelle
lame-ressort
Verbindungsclip
flexible tube
tubo flexible
tube flexible
Gummischlauch
branch
rama
branche
Rohrstück
earpiece
auricular
embout auriculaire
Ohrstöpsel
SYRINGE
JERINGA
SERINGUE
SPRITZE
needle
aguja
aiguille
Kanüle
bevel
bisel
biseau
Schräge
needle hub
portaagujas
pavillon
Kanülenansatz
Luer-Lock tip
jeringa de Luer-Lock
embout Luer Lock
Luer-Lock-Spitze
tip protector
protector
protecteur d'embout
Schutzkappe
hollow barrel
cilindro
corps de pompe
Spritzenkörper
rubber bulb
pera de goma
bouchon
Gummipfropfen
scale
escala
graduation
Skala
plunger
émbolo
piston
Spritzenkolben
finger flange
pestaña de arrojo
anneau de retenue
Fingerrand
thumb rest
apoyo del pulgar
poussoir
Daumenteil
syringe for irrigation
jeringa de irrigación
seringue pour lavage de cavités
Klistierspritze
COT
CAMILLA
CIVIÈRE
FAHRTRAGE
frame
chasis
cadre
Gestell
reclining back
respaldo reclinatorio
dossier inclinable
verstellbares Rückenteil
mattress
colchón
matelas
Polsterauflage
telescopic leg
pata telescópica
pied télescopique
Teleskoptragebein
stretcher
camilla
brancard
Krankentrage
pulling ring
argolla para tirar
anneau de traction
Ziehbügel
hook
gancho de tracción
crochet
Haken

WHEELCHAIR
SILLA DE RUEDAS
FAUTEUIL ROULANT
ROLLSTUHL

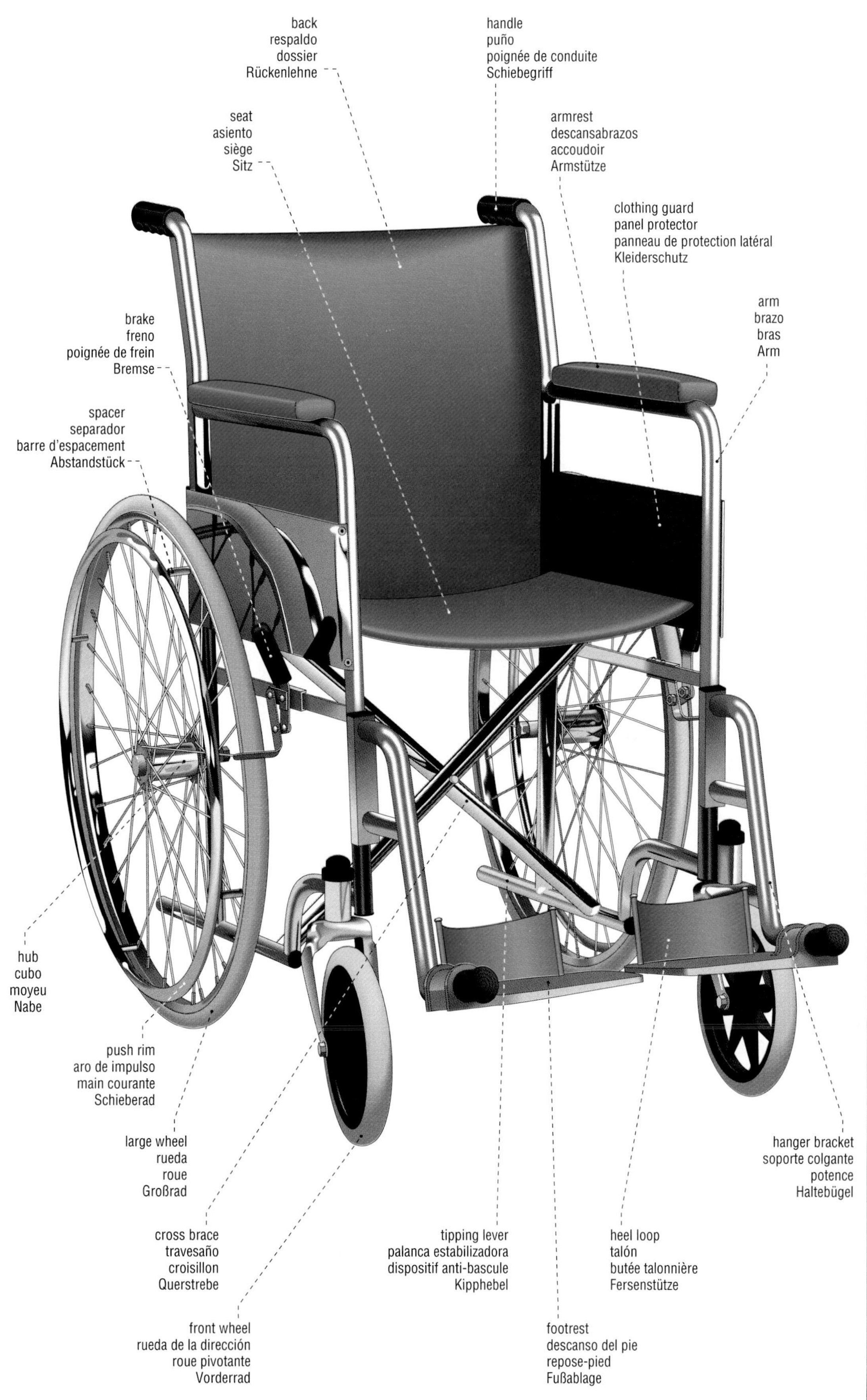
back
respaldo
dossier
Rückenlehne
handle
puño
poignée de conduite
Schiebegriff
seat
asiento
siège
Sitz
armrest
descansabrazos
accoudoir
Armstütze
clothing guard
panel protector
panneau de protection latéral
Kleiderschutz
arm
brazo
bras
Arm
brake
freno
poignée de frein
Bremse
spacer
separador
barre d'espacement
Abstandstück
hub
cubo
moyeu
Nabe
push rim
aro de impulso
main courante
Schieberad
large wheel
rueda
roue
Großrad
hanger bracket
soporte colgante
potence
Haltebügel
cross brace
travesaño
croisillon
Querstrebe
tipping lever
palanca estabilizadora
dispositif anti-bascule
Kipphebel
heel loop
talón
butée talonnière
Fersenstütze
front wheel
rueda de la dirección
roue pivotante
Vorderrad
footrest
descanso del pie
repose-pied
Fußablage

WALKING AIDS
AUXILIARES ORTOPÉDICOS PARA CAMINAR
AIDES À LA MARCHE
GEHHILFEN

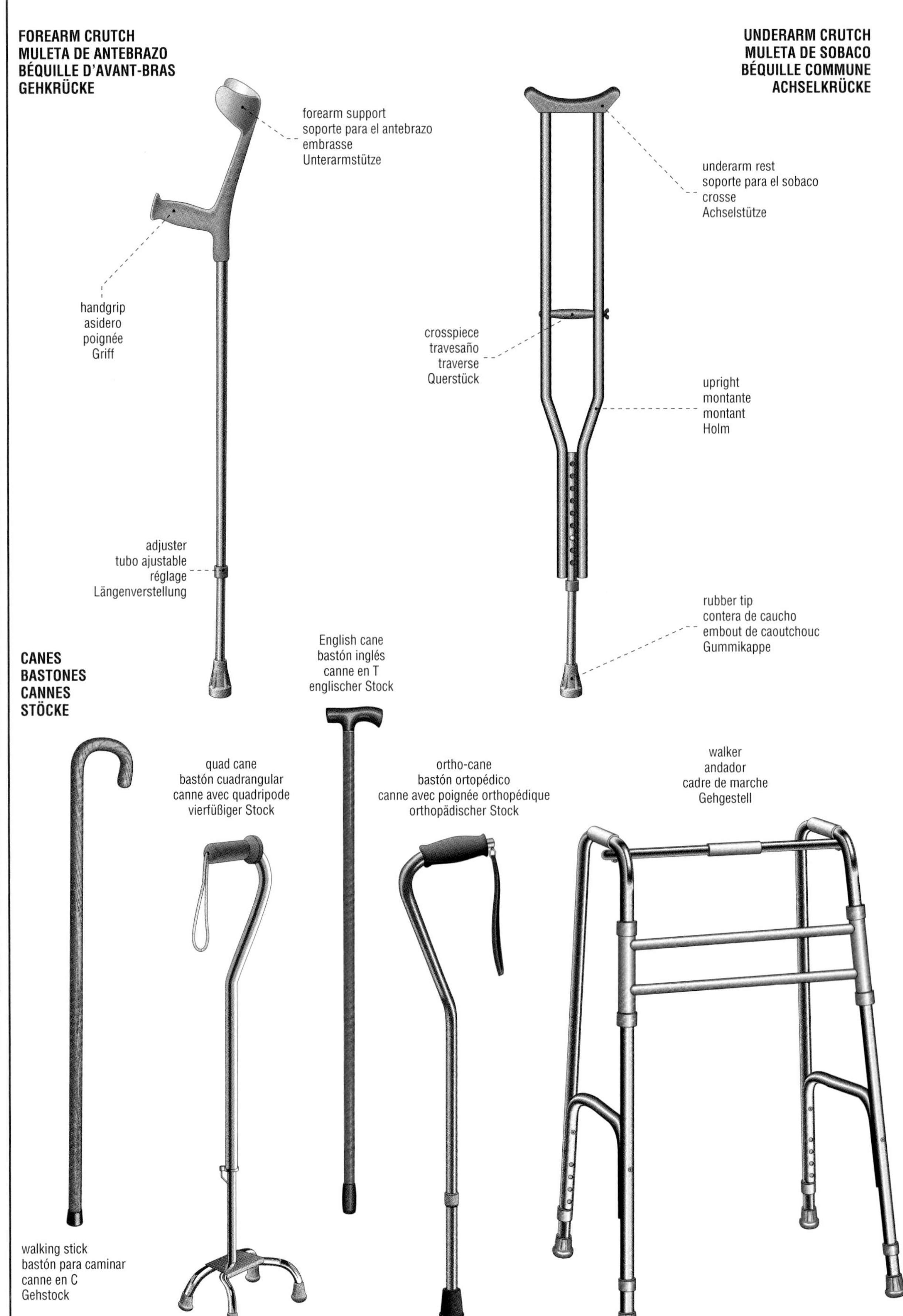
FOREARM CRUTCH
MULETA DE ANTEBRAZO
BÉQUILLE D'AVANT-BRAS
GEHKRÜCKE
forearm support
soporte para el antebrazo
embrasse
Unterarmstütze
handgrip
asidero
poignée
Griff
adjuster
tubo ajustable
réglage
Längenverstellung
UNDERARM CRUTCH
MULETA DE SOBACO
BÉQUILLE COMMUNE
ACHSELKRÜCKE
underarm rest
soporte para el sobaco
crosse
Achselstütze
crosspiece
travesaño
traverse
Querstück
upright
montante
montant
Holm
rubber tip
contera de caucho
embout de caoutchouc
Gummikappe
CANES
BASTONES
CANNES
STÖCKE
English cane
bastón inglés
canne en T
englischer Stock
quad cane
bastón cuadrangular
canne avec quadripode
vierfüßiger Stock
ortho-cane
bastón ortopédico
canne avec poignée orthopédique
orthopädischer Stock
walker
andador
cadre de marche
Gehgestell
walking stick
bastón para caminar
canne en C
Gehstock

EAR PROTECTION
PROTECCIÓN PARA LOS OÍDOS
PROTECTION DE L'OUÏE
GEHÖRSCHUTZ

SAFETY EARMUFF
OREJERA DE SEGURIDAD
SERRE-TÊTE ANTIBRUIT
SICHERHEITSOHRENSCHÜTZER
ear plugs
protector de oídos
protège-tympan
Ohrschützer
headband
diadema
serre-tête
Kopfband
foam cushion
resguardo de espuma
coussinet en mousse
Schaumgummipolsterung

EYE PROTECTION
PROTECCIÓN PARA LOS OJOS
PROTECTION DES YEUX
AUGENSCHUTZ

safety glasses
anteojos de seguridad
lunettes de sécurité
Schutzbrille
safety goggles
anteojos protectores
lunettes de protection
Schutzmaske

HEAD PROTECTION
PROTECCIÓN PARA LA CABEZA
PROTECTION DE LA TÊTE
KOPFSCHUTZ

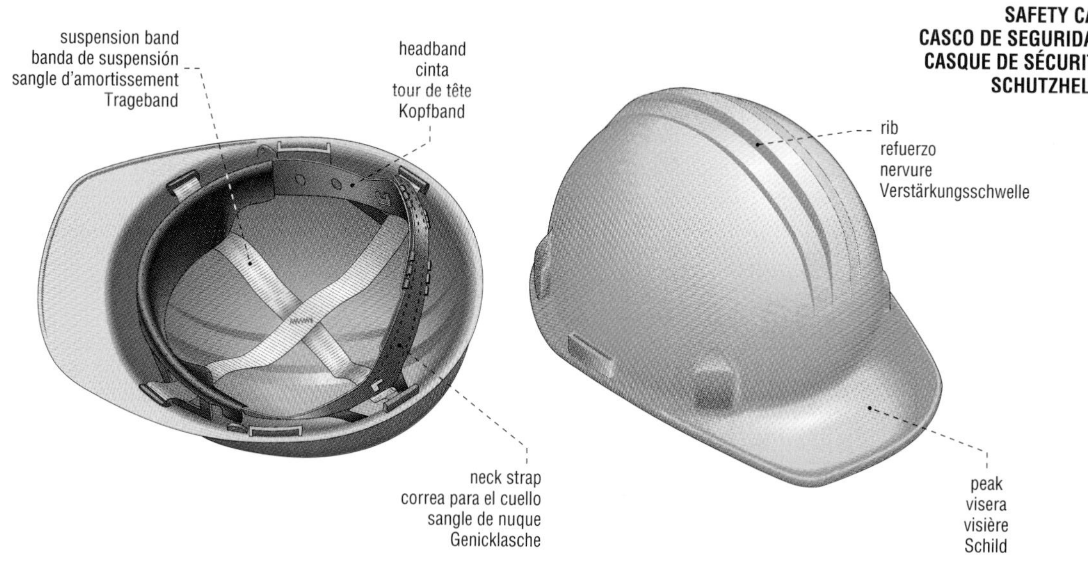
SAFETY CAP
CASCO DE SEGURIDAD
CASQUE DE SÉCURITÉ
SCHUTZHELM
suspension band
banda de suspensión
sangle d'amortissement
Trageband
headband
cinta
tour de tête
Kopfband
rib
refuerzo
nervure
Verstärkungsschwelle
neck strap
correa para el cuello
sangle de nuque
Genicklasche
peak
visera
visière
Schild

RESPIRATORY SYSTEM PROTECTION
PROTECCIÓN PARA EL SISTEMA RESPIRATORIO
PROTECTION DES VOIES RESPIRATOIRES
ATEMSCHUTZ

RESPIRATOR
MÁSCARA DE GAS
MASQUE RESPIRATOIRE
GASMASKE

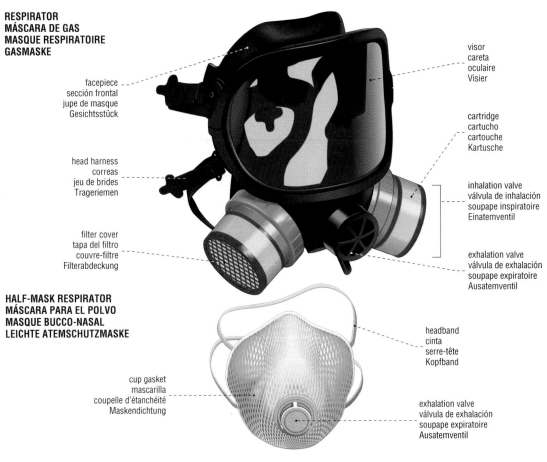

facepiece
sección frontal
jupe de masque
Gesichtsstück

visor
careta
oculaire
Visier

cartridge
cartucho
cartouche
Kartusche

head harness
correas
jeu de brides
Trageriemen

inhalation valve
válvula de inhalación
soupape inspiratoire
Einatemventil

filter cover
tapa del filtro
couvre-filtre
Filterabdeckung

exhalation valve
válvula de exhalación
soupape expiratoire
Ausatemventil

HALF-MASK RESPIRATOR
MÁSCARA PARA EL POLVO
MASQUE BUCCO-NASAL
LEICHTE ATEMSCHUTZMASKE

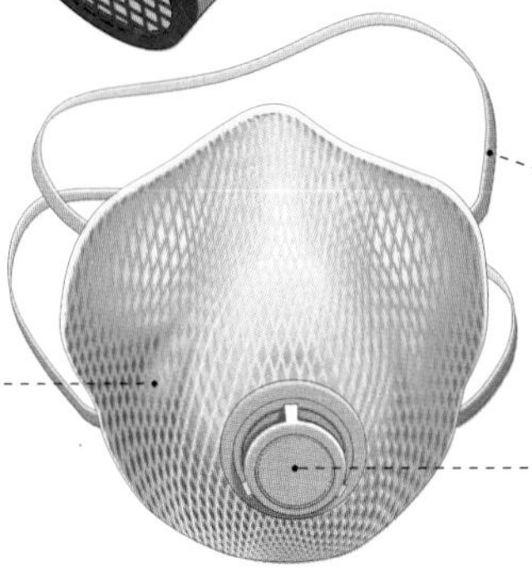

headband
cinta
serre-tête
Kopfband

cup gasket
mascarilla
coupelle d'étanchéité
Maskendichtung

exhalation valve
válvula de exhalación
soupape expiratoire
Ausatemventil

SAFETY VEST
CHALECO DE SEGURIDAD
GILET DE SÉCURITÉ
SICHERHEITSWESTE

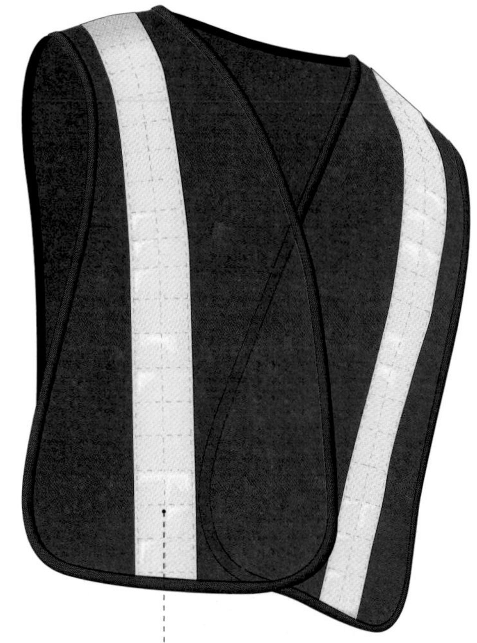

reflective stripe
banda reflectora
bande réfléchissante
Leuchtstreifen

FEET PROTECTION
PROTECCIÓN PARA LOS PIES
PROTECTION DES PIEDS
FUSSCHUTZ

toe guard
puntera protectora
protège-orteils
Zehenschützer

SAFETY BOOT
BOTA DE SEGURIDAD
BRODEQUIN DE SÉCURITÉ
SICHERHEITSSCHUH

reinforced toe
tope
embout de protection
Stahlkappe

ENERGY ÉNERGIES
ENERGÍA ENERGIE

CONTENTS

COAL MINE
MINAS DE CARBÓN
MINE DE CHARBON
KOHLEBERGWERK

OPEN-PIT MINE
MINA A CIELO ABIERTO
CARRIÈRE EN ENTONNOIR
OFFENE GRUBE

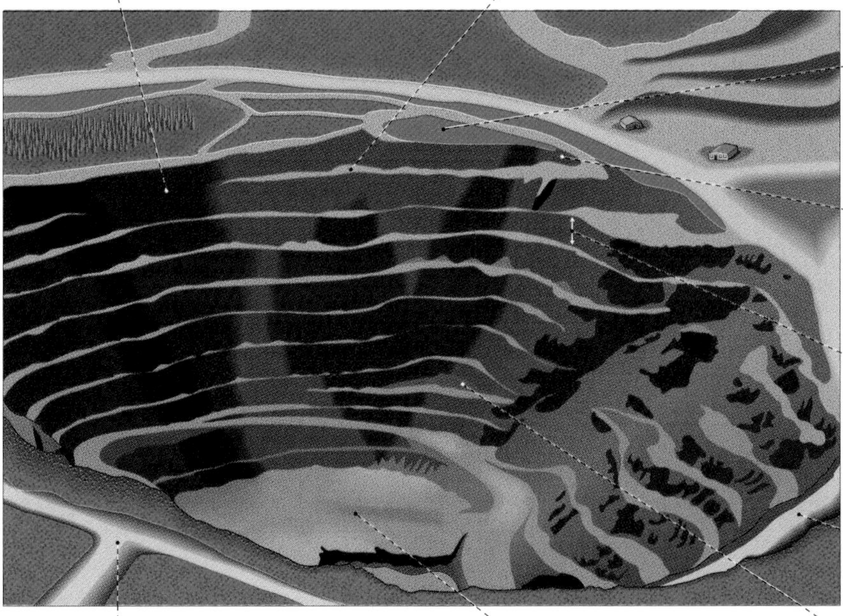

face
frente de corte
front de taille
Streb

bench
antepecho
gradin
Bank

ground surface
superficie del terreno
terrain naturel
Erdoberfläche

overburden
relleno exterior
morts-terrains
Obergestein

bench height
altura del antepecho
hauteur du gradin
Bankhöhe

ramp
talud
rampe
Rampe

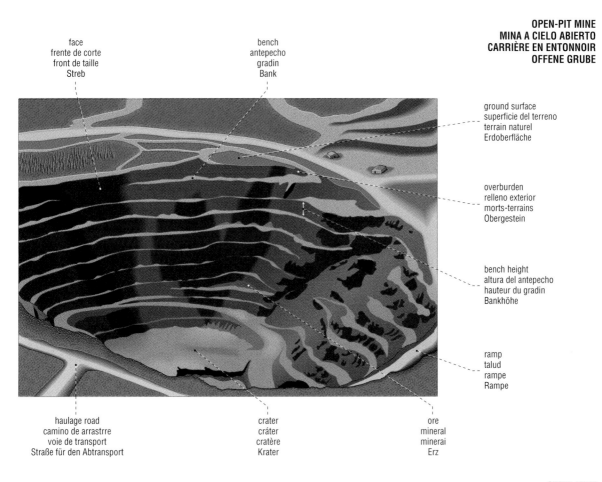

haulage road
camino de arrastrre
voie de transport
Straße für den Abtransport

crater
cráter
cratère
Krater

ore
mineral
minerai
Erz

STRIP MINE
EXCAVACIÓN A CIELO ABIERTO
CARRIÈRE EXPLOITÉE EN CHASSANT
ÜBERTAGEABBAU

dump
basurero
terril
Bergehalde

conveyor
banda transportadora
convoyeur
Förderband

mechanical shovel
pala mecánica
pelle mécanique
Standbagger

bucket wheel excavator
excavadora de rueda de cangilones
excavatrice à roue
Schaufelradbagger

belt loader
banda de carga
sauterelle
Ladeband

overburden
relleno exterior
morts-terrains
Obergestein

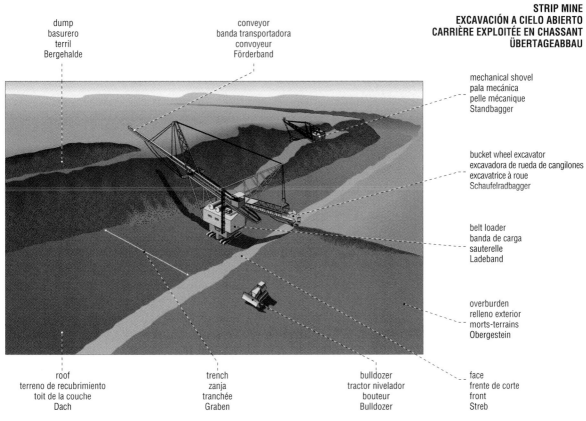

roof
terreno de recubrimiento
toit de la couche
Dach

trench
zanja
tranchée
Graben

bulldozer
tractor nivelador
bouteur
Bulldozer

face
frente de corte
front
Streb

COAL MINE
MINA DE CARBÓN SUBTERRÁNEA
MINE DE CHARBON
KOHLEBERGWERK

JACKLEG DRILL
TALADRO DE POSTE EXTENSIBLE
MARTEAU PERFORATEUR À POUSSOIR PNEUMATIQUE
BOHRHAMMER

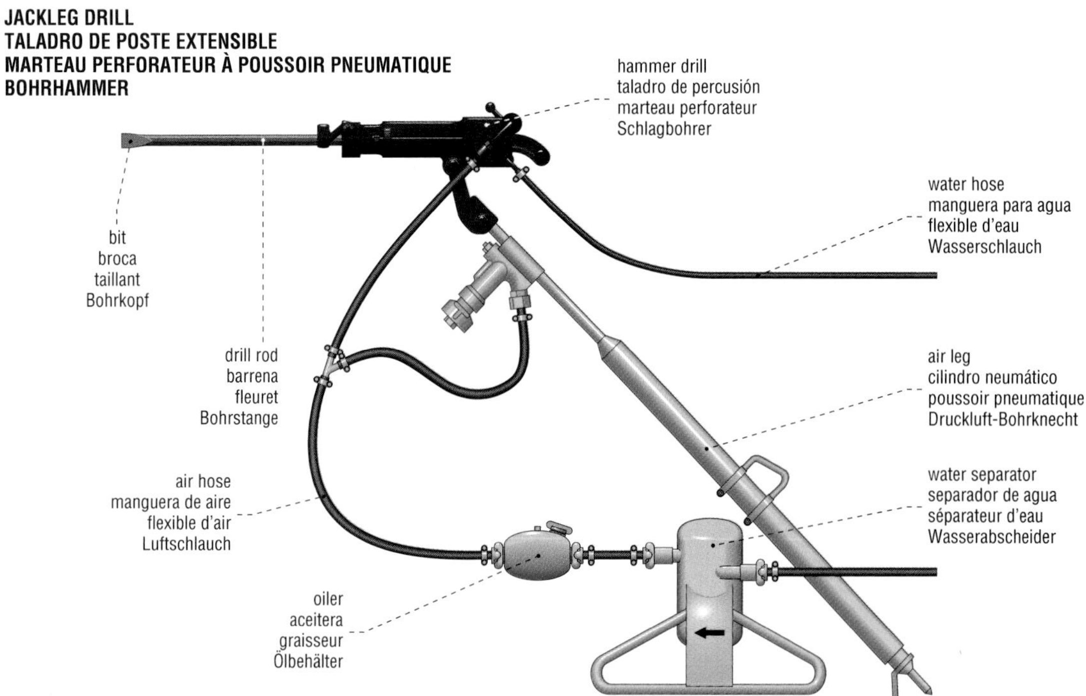
hammer drill
taladro de percusión
marteau perforateur
Schlagbohrer
water hose
manguera para agua
flexible d'eau
Wasserschlauch
bit
broca
taillant
Bohrkopf
drill rod
barrena
fleuret
Bohrstange
air leg
cilindro neumático
poussoir pneumatique
Druckluft-Bohrknecht
air hose
manguera de aire
flexible d'air
Luftschlauch
water separator
separador de agua
séparateur d'eau
Wasserabscheider
oiler
aceitera
graisseur
Ölbehälter

PITHEAD
PLANTA EXTERIOR
CARREAU DE MINE
ÜBERTAGEANLAGEN

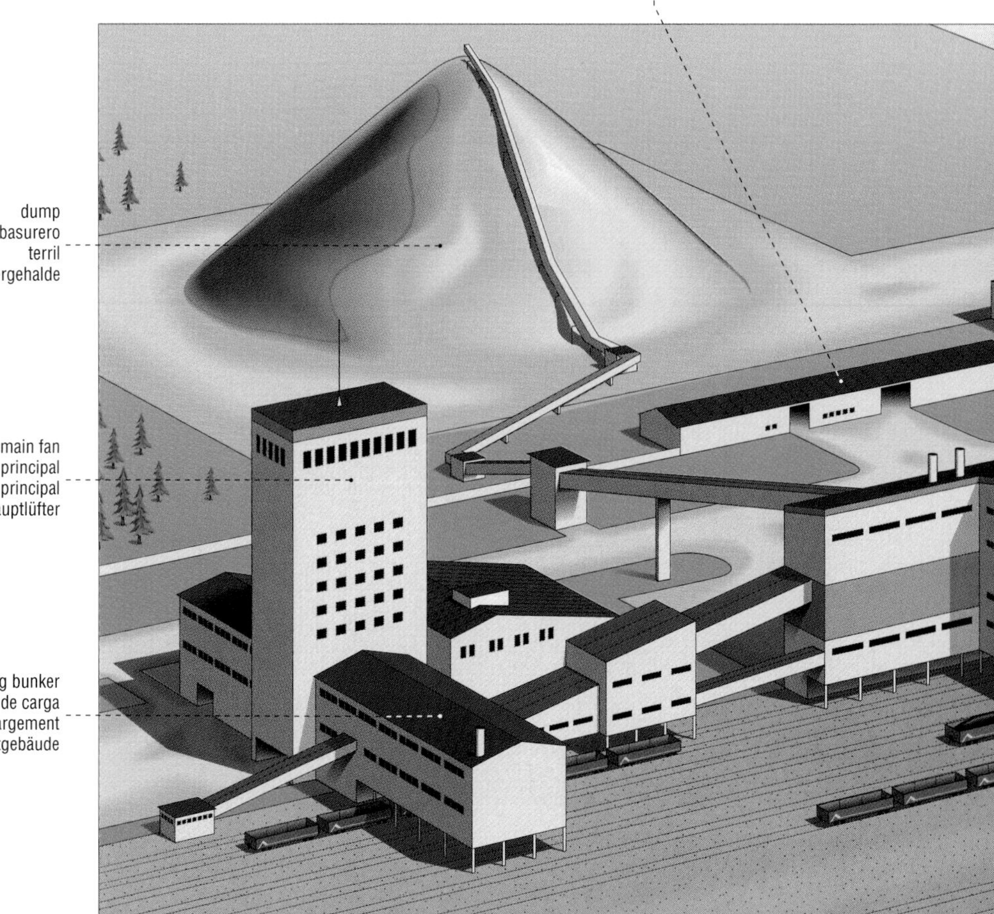
maintenance shop
taller de mantenimiento
atelier d'entretien
Maschinenhaus
dump
basurero
terril
Bergehalde
main fan
ventilador principal
ventilateur principal
Hauptlüfter
loading bunker
carbonera de carga
silo de chargement
Schachtgebäude

PNEUMATIC HAMMER
MARTILLO NEUMÁTICO
MARTEAU PNEUMATIQUE
PRESSLUFTBOHRER

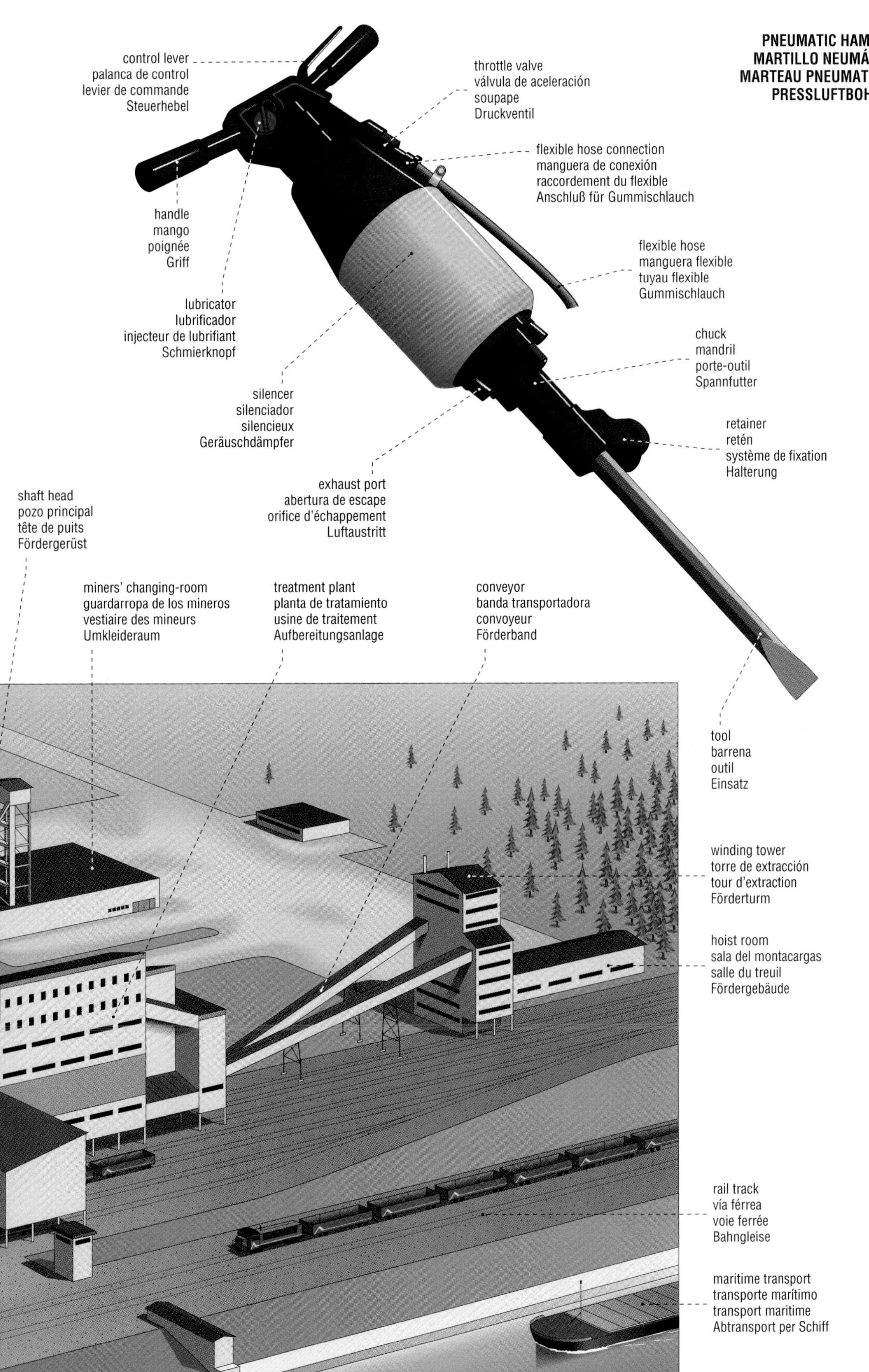

control lever
palanca de control
levier de commande
Steuerhebel
throttle valve
válvula de aceleración
soupape
Druckventil
flexible hose connection
manguera de conexión
raccordement du flexible
Anschluß für Gummischlauch
handle
mango
poignée
Griff
flexible hose
manguera flexible
tuyau flexible
Gummischlauch
lubricator
lubrificador
injecteur de lubrifiant
Schmierknopf
chuck
mandril
porte-outil
Spannfutter
silencer
silenciador
silencieux
Geräuschdämpfer
retainer
retén
système de fixation
Halterung
exhaust port
abertura de escape
orifice d'échappement
Luftaustritt
shaft head
pozo principal
tête de puits
Fördergerüst
miners' changing-room
guardarropa de los mineros
vestiaire des mineurs
Umkleideraum
treatment plant
planta de tratamiento
usine de traitement
Aufbereitungsanlage
conveyor
banda transportadora
convoyeur
Förderband
tool
barrena
outil
Einsatz
winding tower
torre de extracción
tour d'extraction
Förderturm
hoist room
sala del montacargas
salle du treuil
Fördergebäude
rail track
vía férrea
voie ferrée
Bahngleise
maritime transport
transporte marítimo
transport maritime
Abtransport per Schiff

COAL MINE
MINA DE CARBÓN
MINE DE CHARBON
KOHLEBERGWERK

UNDERGROUND MINE
MINA SUBTERRÁNEA
MINE SOUTERRAINE
GRUBE

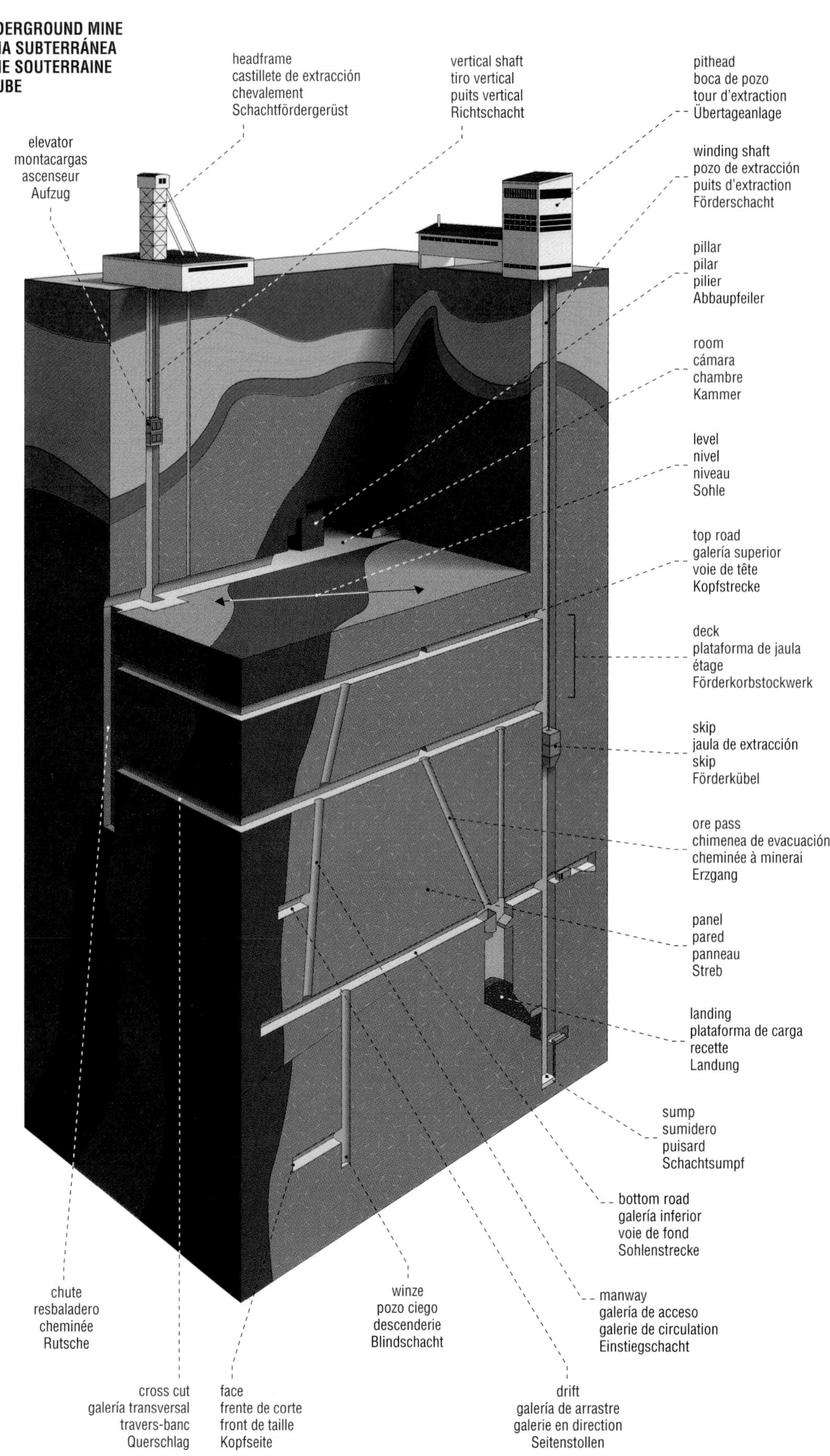
headframe
castillete de extracción
chevalement
Schachtfördergerüst
vertical shaft
tiro vertical
puits vertical
Richtschacht
pithead
boca de pozo
tour d'extraction
Übertageanlage
elevator
montacargas
ascenseur
Aufzug
winding shaft
pozo de extracción
puits d'extraction
Förderschacht
pillar
pilar
pilier
Abbaupfeiler
room
cámara
chambre
Kammer
level
nivel
niveau
Sohle
top road
galería superior
voie de tête
Kopfstrecke
deck
plataforma de jaula
étage
Förderkorbstockwerk
skip
jaula de extracción
skip
Förderkübel
ore pass
chimenea de evacuación
cheminée à minerai
Erzgang
panel
pared
panneau
Streb
landing
plataforma de carga
recette
Landung
sump
sumidero
puisard
Schachtsumpf
bottom road
galería inferior
voie de fond
Sohlenstrecke
chute
resbaladero
cheminée
Rutsche
winze
pozo ciego
descenderie
Blindschacht
manway
galería de acceso
galerie de circulation
Einstiegschacht
cross cut
galería transversal
travers-banc
Querschlag
face
frente de corte
front de taille
Kopfseite
drift
galería de arrastre
galerie en direction
Seitenstollen

OIL
PETRÓLEO
PÉTROLE
ERDÖL

DRILLING RIG
TORRE DE PERFORACIÓN
APPAREIL DE FORAGE
BOHRANLAGE

ROTARY SYSTEM
SISTEMA ROTATIVO
SYSTÈME ROTARY
DREHBOHRVERFAHREN

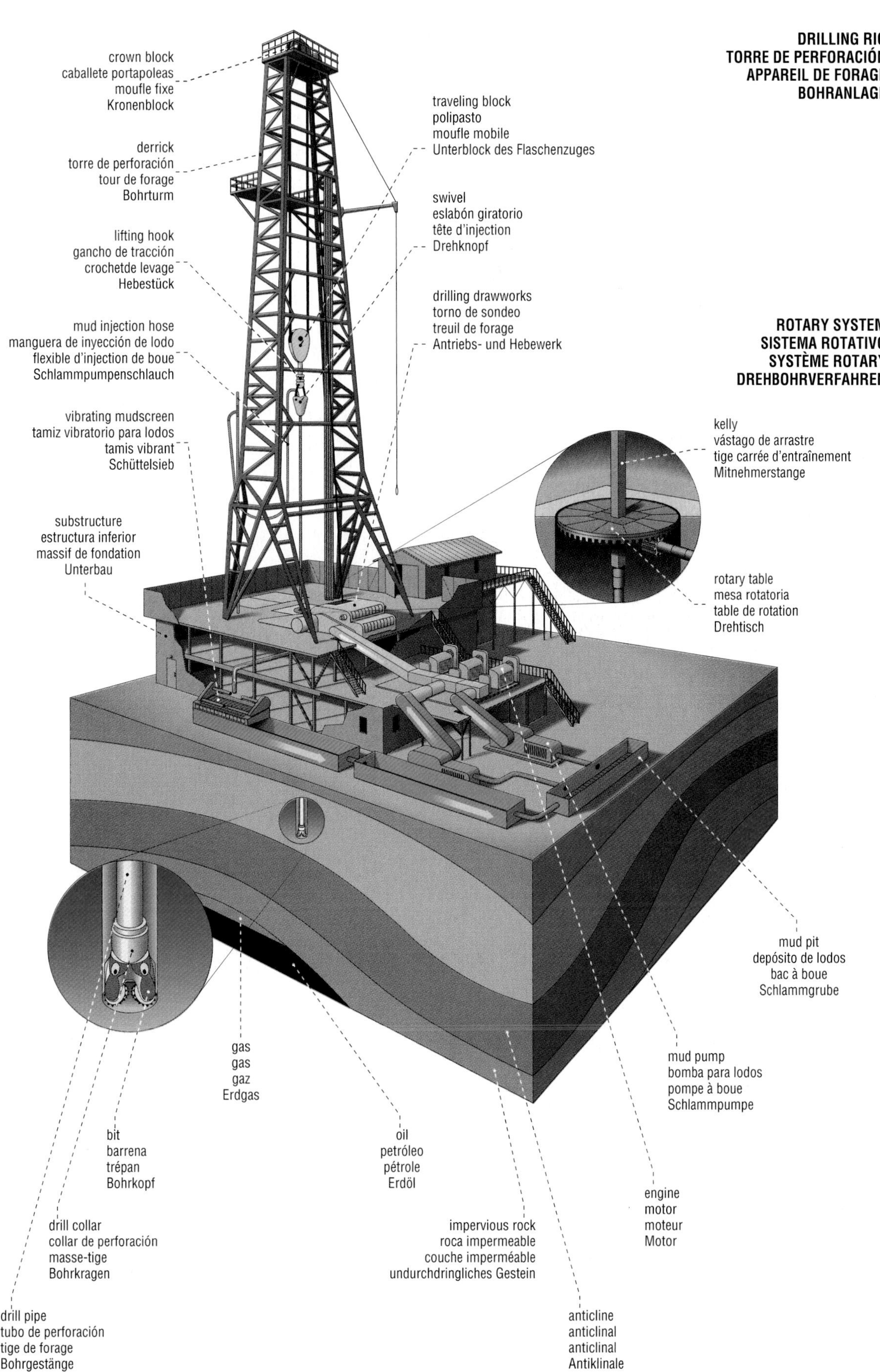

crown block
caballete portapoleas
moufle fixe
Kronenblock
derrick
torre de perforación
tour de forage
Bohrturm
lifting hook
gancho de tracción
crochetde levage
Hebestück
mud injection hose
manguera de inyección de lodo
flexible d'injection de boue
Schlammpumpenschlauch
vibrating mudscreen
tamiz vibratorio para lodos
tamis vibrant
Schüttelsieb
substructure
estructura inferior
massif de fondation
Unterbau
traveling block
polipasto
moufle mobile
Unterblock des Flaschenzuges
swivel
eslabón giratorio
tête d'injection
Drehknopf
drilling drawworks
torno de sondeo
treuil de forage
Antriebs- und Hebewerk
kelly
vástago de arrastre
tige carrée d'entraînement
Mitnehmerstange
rotary table
mesa rotatoria
table de rotation
Drehtisch
mud pit
depósito de lodos
bac à boue
Schlammgrube
mud pump
bomba para lodos
pompe à boue
Schlammpumpe
gas
gas
gaz
Erdgas
bit
barrena
trépan
Bohrkopf
oil
petróleo
pétrole
Erdöl
engine
motor
moteur
Motor
drill collar
collar de perforación
masse-tige
Bohrkragen
impervious rock
roca impermeable
couche imperméable
undurchdringliches Gestein
drill pipe
tubo de perforación
tige de forage
Bohrgestänge
anticline
anticlinal
anticlinal
Antiklinale

OIL
PETRÓLEO
PÉTROLE
ERDÖL

PRODUCTION PLATFORM
PLATAFORMA DE PRODUCCIÓN
PLATE-FORME DE PRODUCTION
BOHRINSEL

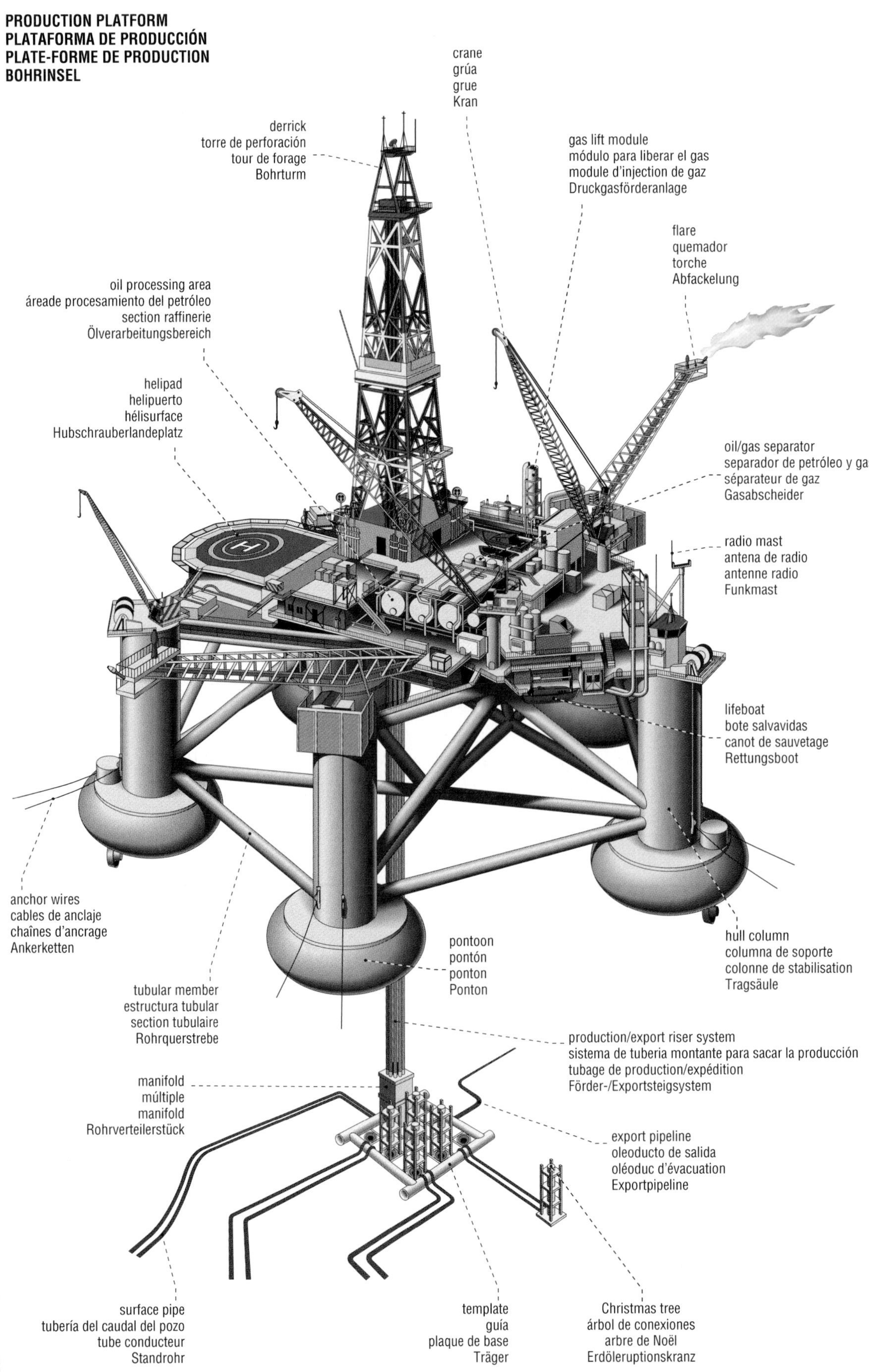
crane
grúa
grue
Kran
derrick
torre de perforación
tour de forage
Bohrturm
gas lift module
módulo para liberar el gas
module d'injection de gaz
Druckgasförderanlage
flare
quemador
torche
Abfackelung
oil processing area
áreade procesamiento del petróleo
section raffinerie
Ölverarbeitungsbereich
helipad
helipuerto
hélisurface
Hubschrauberlandeplatz
oil/gas separator
separador de petróleo y gas
séparateur de gaz
Gasabscheider
radio mast
antena de radio
antenne radio
Funkmast
lifeboat
bote salvavidas
canot de sauvetage
Rettungsboot
anchor wires
cables de anclaje
chaînes d'ancrage
Ankerketten
hull column
columna de soporte
colonne de stabilisation
Tragsäule
pontoon
pontón
ponton
Ponton
tubular member
estructura tubular
section tubulaire
Rohrquerstrebe
production/export riser system
sistema de tuberia montante para sacar la producción
tubage de production/expédition
Förder-/Exportsteigsystem
manifold
múltiple
manifold
Rohrverteilerstück
export pipeline
oleoducto de salida
oléoduc d'évacuation
Exportpipeline
surface pipe
tubería del caudal del pozo
tube conducteur
Standrohr
template
guía
plaque de base
Träger
Christmas tree
árbol de conexiones
arbre de Noël
Erdöleruptionskranz

pier
muelle saliente
jetée
Pier
emergency support vessel
embarcación de emergencia
barge de service d'urgence
Hilfs- und Rettungsschiff
jack-up platform
plataforma montada en gatos mecánicos
plate-forme auto-élévatrice
Hubplattform
fixed platform
plataforma fija
plate-forme fixe
Festplattform
semi-submersible platform
plataforma semisumergida
plate-forme semi-submersible
Halbtaucher
drill ship
barco perforador
navire de forage
Bohrschiff

OIL
PETRÓLEO
PÉTROLE
ERDÖL

CHRISTMAS TREE
ÁRBOL DE CONEXIONES
ARBRE DE NOËL
ERDÖLERUPTIONSKRANZ

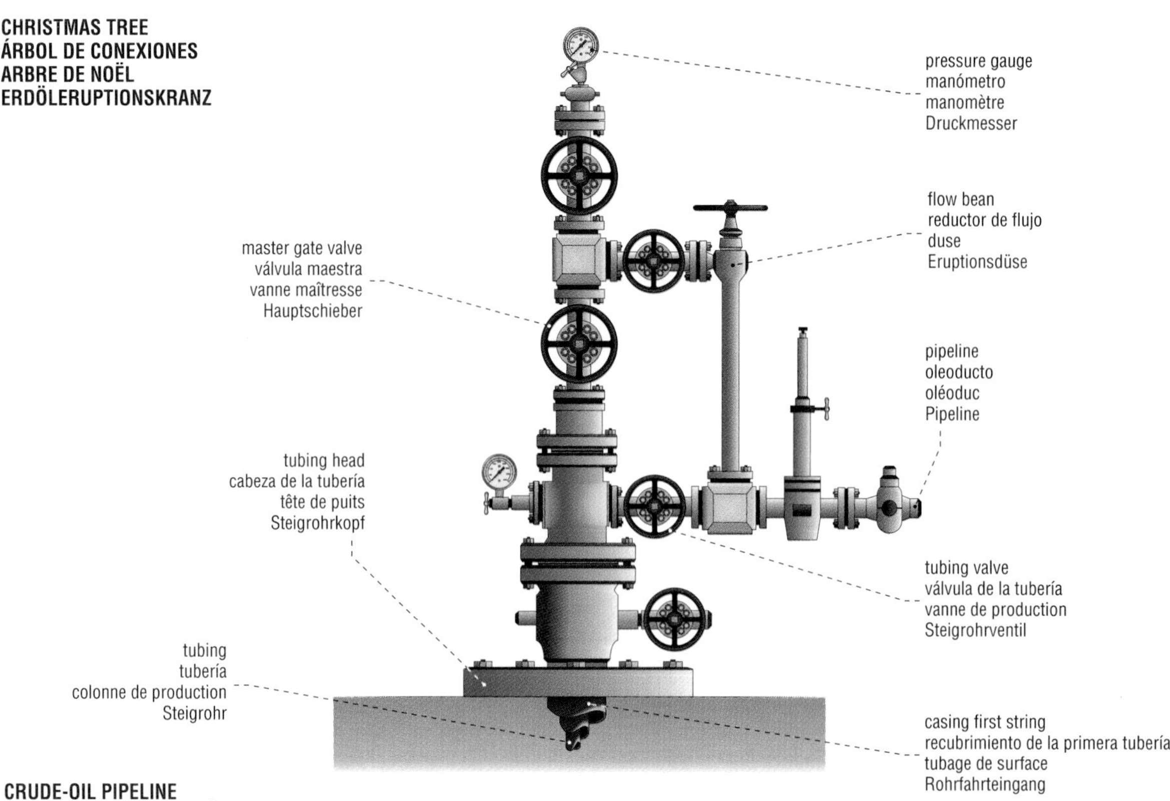
pressure gauge
manómetro
manomètre
Druckmesser
flow bean
reductor de flujo
duse
Eruptionsdüse
master gate valve
válvula maestra
vanne maîtresse
Hauptschieber
pipeline
oleoducto
oléoduc
Pipeline
tubing head
cabeza de la tubería
tête de puits
Steigrohrkopf
tubing valve
válvula de la tubería
vanne de production
Steigrohrventil
tubing
tubería
colonne de production
Steigrohr
casing first string
recubrimiento de la primera tubería
tubage de surface
Rohrfahrteingang

CRUDE-OIL PIPELINE
OLEODUCTO PARA PETRÓLEO CRUDO
RÉSEAU D'OLÉODUCS
ROHÖLPIPELINE

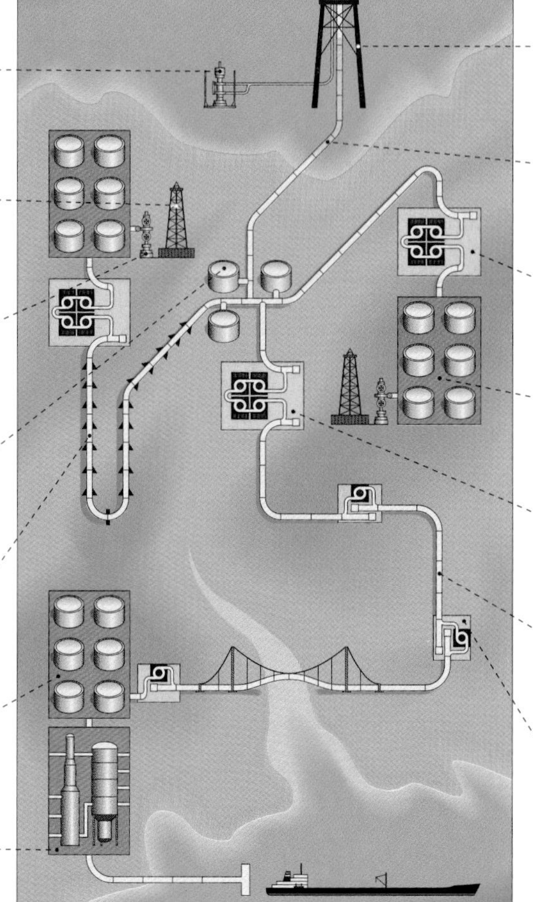
offshore well
pozo marino
puits sous-marin
Bohranlage vor der Meeresküste
production platform
plataforma de producción
plate-forme de production
Förderplattform
submarine pipeline
oleoducto submarino
oléoduc sous-marin
Unterwasserpipeline
derrick
torre de perforación
tour de forage
Bohrturm
pumping station
planta de bombeo
station de pompage
Pumpstation
Christmas tree
árbol de conexiones
arbre de Noël
Erdöleruptionskranz
tank farm
patio de tanques
parc de stockage
Tankanlage
buffer tank
tanque de regulación de presión
réservoir tampon
Puffertank
central pumping station
estación central de bombeo
station de pompage principale
zentrale Pumpstation
aboveground pipeline
oleoducto de superficie
oléoduc surélevé
überirdische Pipeline
pipeline
oleoducto
oléoduc
Pipeline
terminal
terminal
parc de stockage terminal
Erdölterminal
intermediate booster station
planta intermedia de refuerzo
station de pompage intermédiaire
Druckverstärkerpumpanlage
refinery
refinería
raffinerie
Raffinerie

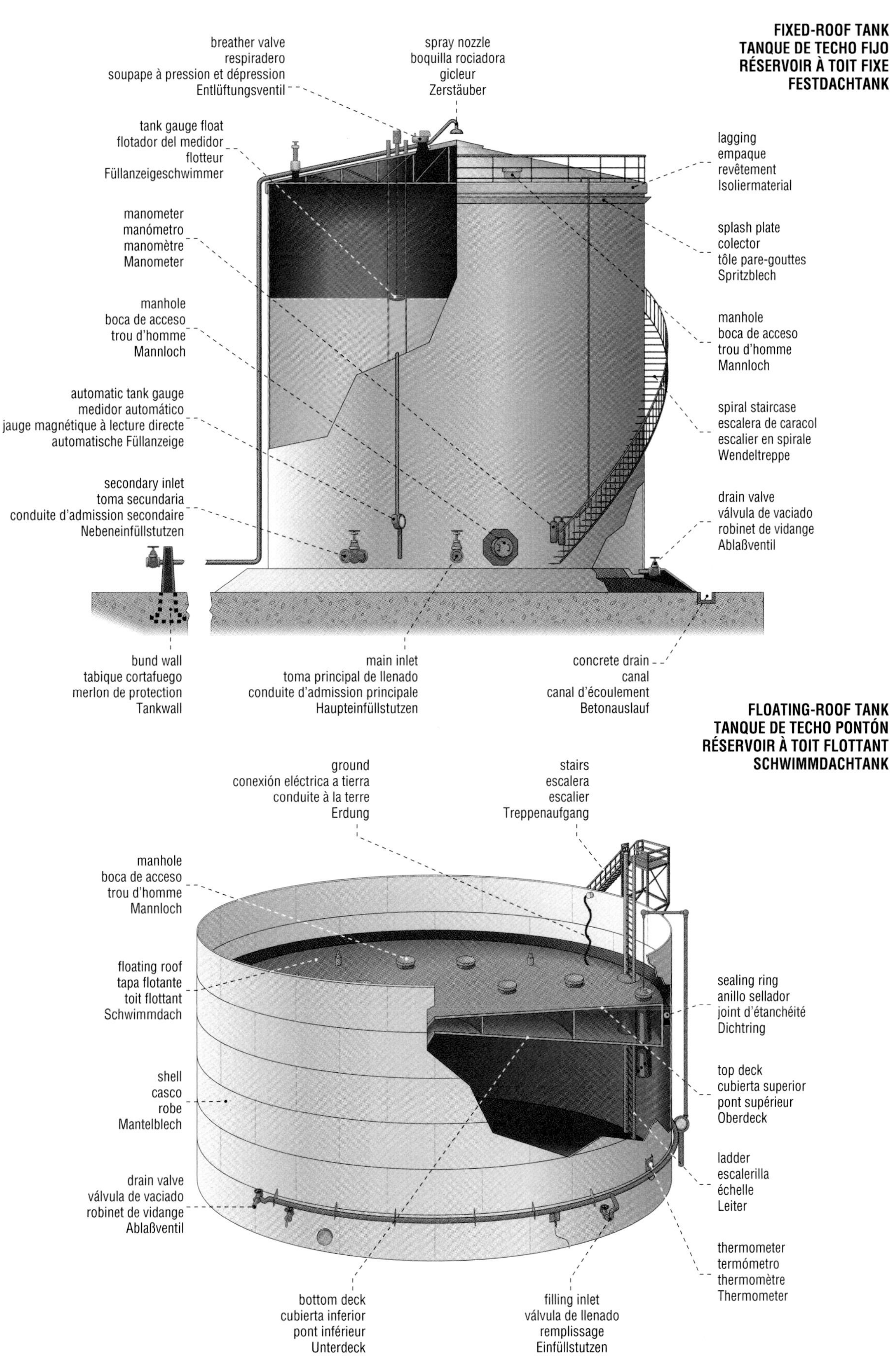
FIXED-ROOF TANK
TANQUE DE TECHO FIJO
RÉSERVOIR À TOIT FIXE
FESTDACHTANK
breather valve
respiradero
soupape à pression et dépression
Entlüftungsventil
spray nozzle
boquilla rociadora
gicleur
Zerstäuber
tank gauge float
flotador del medidor
flotteur
Füllanzeigeschwimmer
lagging
empaque
revêtement
Isoliermaterial
manometer
manómetro
manomètre
Manometer
splash plate
colector
tôle pare-gouttes
Spritzblech
manhole
boca de acceso
trou d'homme
Mannloch
manhole
boca de acceso
trou d'homme
Mannloch
automatic tank gauge
medidor automático
jauge magnétique à lecture directe
automatische Füllanzeige
spiral staircase
escalera de caracol
escalier en spirale
Wendeltreppe
secondary inlet
toma secundaria
conduite d'admission secondaire
Nebeneinfüllstutzen
drain valve
válvula de vaciado
robinet de vidange
Ablaßventil
bund wall
tabique cortafuego
merlon de protection
Tankwall
main inlet
toma principal de llenado
conduite d'admission principale
Haupteinfüllstutzen
concrete drain
canal
canal d'écoulement
Betonauslauf
FLOATING-ROOF TANK
TANQUE DE TECHO PONTÓN
RÉSERVOIR À TOIT FLOTTANT
SCHWIMMDACHTANK
ground
conexión eléctrica a tierra
conduite à la terre
Erdung
stairs
escalera
escalier
Treppenaufgang
manhole
boca de acceso
trou d'homme
Mannloch
floating roof
tapa flotante
toit flottant
Schwimmdach
sealing ring
anillo sellador
joint d'étanchéité
Dichtring
shell
casco
robe
Mantelblech
top deck
cubierta superior
pont supérieur
Oberdeck
ladder
escalerilla
échelle
Leiter
drain valve
válvula de vaciado
robinet de vidange
Ablaßventil
thermometer
termómetro
thermomètre
Thermometer
bottom deck
cubierta inferior
pont inférieur
Unterdeck
filling inlet
válvula de llenado
remplissage
Einfüllstutzen

OIL
PETRÓLEO
PÉTROLE
ERDÖL

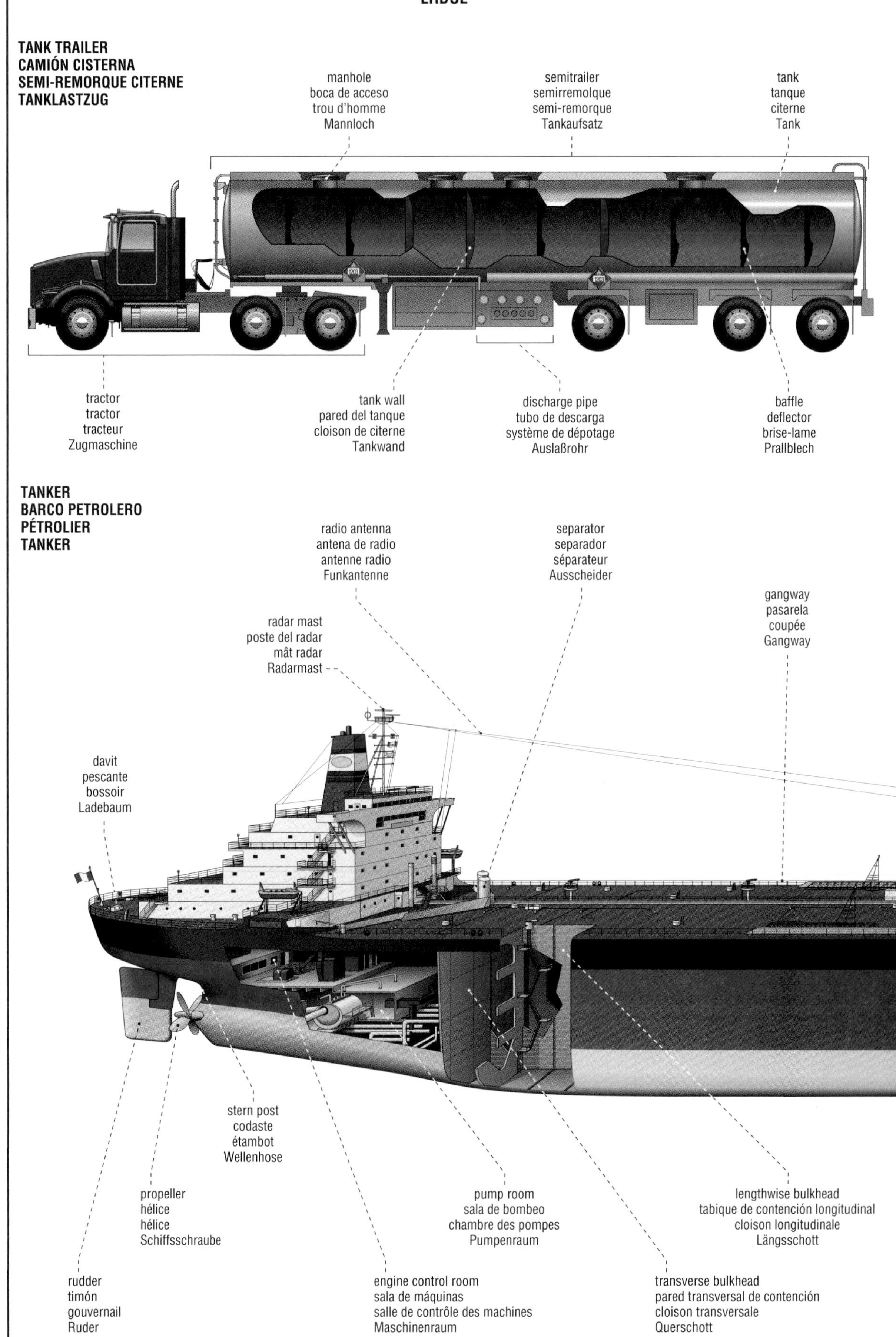

TANK TRAILER
CAMIÓN CISTERNA
SEMI-REMORQUE CITERNE
TANKLASTZUG
manhole
boca de acceso
trou d'homme
Mannloch
semitrailer
semirremolque
semi-remorque
Tankaufsatz
tank
tanque
citerne
Tank
tractor
tractor
tracteur
Zugmaschine
tank wall
pared del tanque
cloison de citerne
Tankwand
discharge pipe
tubo de descarga
système de dépotage
Auslaßrohr
baffle
deflector
brise-lame
Prallblech
TANKER
BARCO PETROLERO
PÉTROLIER
TANKER
radio antenna
antena de radio
antenne radio
Funkantenne
separator
separador
séparateur
Ausscheider
gangway
pasarela
coupée
Gangway
radar mast
poste del radar
mât radar
Radarmast
davit
pescante
bossoir
Ladebaum
stern post
codaste
étambot
Wellenhose
propeller
hélice
hélice
Schiffsschraube
pump room
sala de bombeo
chambre des pompes
Pumpenraum
lengthwise bulkhead
tabique de contención longitudinal
cloison longitudinale
Längsschott
rudder
timón
gouvernail
Ruder
engine control room
sala de máquinas
salle de contrôle des machines
Maschinenraum
transverse bulkhead
pared transversal de contención
cloison transversale
Querschott

TANK CAR
VAGÓN CISTERNA
WAGON-CITERNE
TANKANHÄNGER

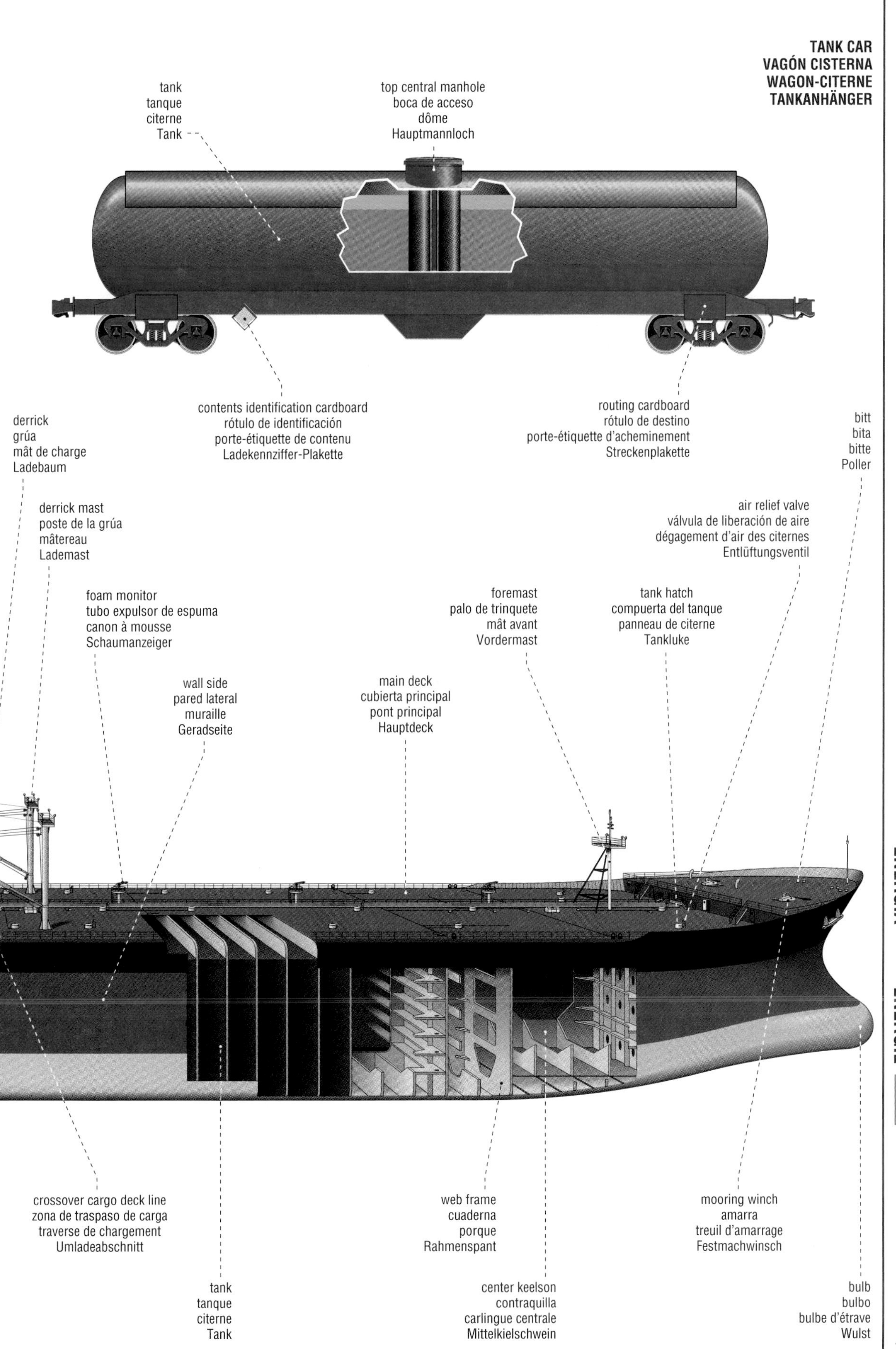

tank
tanque
citerne
Tank
top central manhole
boca de acceso
dôme
Hauptmannloch
contents identification cardboard
rótulo de identificación
porte-étiquette de contenu
Ladekennziffer-Plakette
routing cardboard
rótulo de destino
porte-étiquette d'acheminement
Streckenplakette
derrick
grúa
mât de charge
Ladebaum
derrick mast
poste de la grúa
mâtereau
Lademast
foam monitor
tubo expulsor de espuma
canon à mousse
Schaumanzeiger
wall side
pared lateral
muraille
Geradseite
main deck
cubierta principal
pont principal
Hauptdeck
foremast
palo de trinquete
mât avant
Vordermast
tank hatch
compuerta del tanque
panneau de citerne
Tankluke
air relief valve
válvula de liberación de aire
dégagement d'air des citernes
Entlüftungsventil
bitt
bita
bitte
Poller
crossover cargo deck line
zona de traspaso de carga
traverse de chargement
Umladeabschnitt
tank
tanque
citerne
Tank
web frame
cuaderna
porque
Rahmenspant
center keelson
contraquilla
carlingue centrale
Mittelkielschwein
mooring winch
amarra
treuil d'amarrage
Festmachwinsch
bulb
bulbo
bulbe d'étrave
Wulst

OIL
PETRÓLEO
PÉTROLE
ERDÖL

REFINERY PRODUCTS
PRODUCTOS DEL REFINADO
PRODUITS DE LA RAFFINERIE
RAFFINERIEERZEUGNISSE

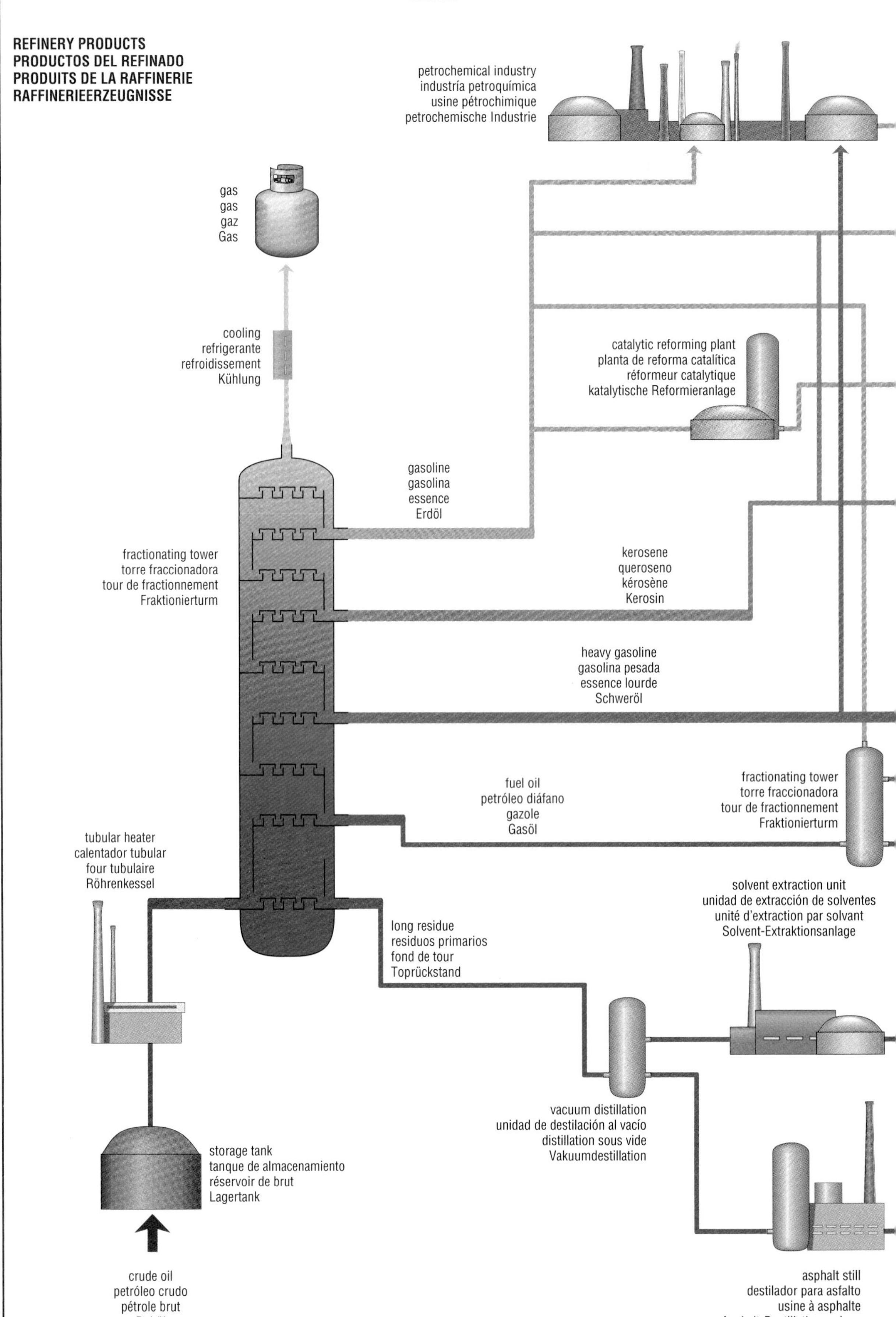

petrochemical industry
industría petroquímica
usine pétrochimique
petrochemische Industrie
gas
gas
gaz
Gas
cooling
refrigerante
refroidissement
Kühlung
catalytic reforming plant
planta de reforma catalítica
réformeur catalytique
katalytische Reformieranlage
gasoline
gasolina
essence
Erdöl
fractionating tower
torre fraccionadora
tour de fractionnement
Fraktionierturm
kerosene
queroseno
kérosène
Kerosin
heavy gasoline
gasolina pesada
essence lourde
Schweröl
fuel oil
petróleo diáfano
gazole
Gasöl
fractionating tower
torre fraccionadora
tour de fractionnement
Fraktionierturm
tubular heater
calentador tubular
four tubulaire
Röhrenkessel
solvent extraction unit
unidad de extracción de solventes
unité d'extraction par solvant
Solvent-Extraktionsanlage
long residue
residuos primarios
fond de tour
Toprückstand
vacuum distillation
unidad de destilación al vacío
distillation sous vide
Vakuumdestillation
storage tank
tanque de almacenamiento
réservoir de brut
Lagertank
crude oil
petróleo crudo
pétrole brut
Rohöl
asphalt still
destilador para asfalto
usine à asphalte
Asphalt-Destillationsanlage

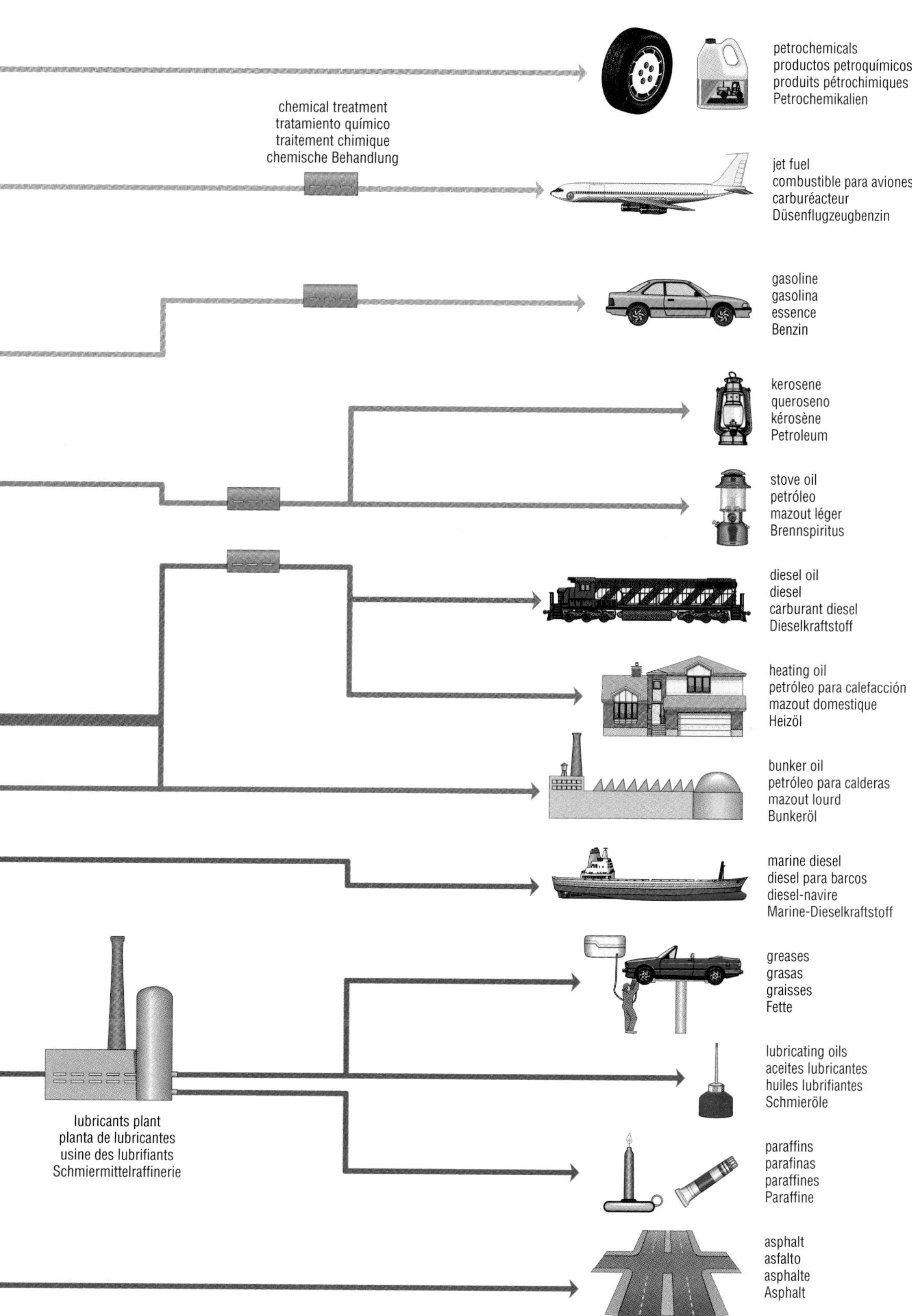
petrochemicals
productos petroquímicos
produits pétrochimiques
Petrochemikalien
chemical treatment
tratamiento químico
traitement chimique
chemische Behandlung
jet fuel
combustible para aviones
carburéacteur
Düsenflugzeugbenzin
gasoline
gasolina
essence
Benzin
kerosene
queroseno
kérosène
Petroleum
stove oil
petróleo
mazout léger
Brennspiritus
diesel oil
diesel
carburant diesel
Dieselkraftstoff
heating oil
petróleo para calefacción
mazout domestique
Heizöl
bunker oil
petróleo para calderas
mazout lourd
Bunkeröl
marine diesel
diesel para barcos
diesel-navire
Marine-Dieselkraftstoff
greases
grasas
graisses
Fette
lubricating oils
aceites lubricantes
huiles lubrifiantes
Schmieröle
lubricants plant
planta de lubricantes
usine des lubrifiants
Schmiermittelraffinerie
paraffins
parafinas
paraffines
Paraffine
asphalt
asfalto
asphalte
Asphalt

HYDROELECTRIC COMPLEX
COMPLEJO HIDROELÉCTRICO
COMPLEXE HYDROÉLECTRIQUE
WASSERKRAFTWERK

crest of spillway
cresta del aliviadero
seuil de déversoir
Überlaufkrone
spillway
aliviadero
déversoir
Überlaufwehr
spillway gate
compuerta del aliviadero
vanne
Überlauftor
top of dam
cresta de la presa
crête
Dammkrone
reservoir
embalse
réservoir
Stausee
penstock
tubería de carga
conduite forcée
Falleitung
headbay
embalse
bief d'amont
Oberwasser
gantry crane
grúa de caballete
portique
Bockkran
log chute
rebosadero
passe à billes
Trift
control room
sala de control
salle de commande
Steuerzentrale
diversion canal
canal de derivación
canal de dérivation
Ablenkkanal
dam
presa
barrage
Damm
afterbay
cámara de salida
bief d'aval
Unterwasser
spillway chute
canal del aliviadero
coursier d'évacuateur
Überfallrinne
bushing
boquilla reducidora
traversée de transformateur
Stromführung
training wall
muro de encauzamiento
mur bajoyer
Leitwerk
powerhouse
central hidroeléctrica
centrale
Kraftwerk
machine hall
sala de máquinas
salle des machines
Maschinenhalle

CROSS SECTION OF HYDROELECTRIC POWER STATION
CORTE TRANSVERSAL DE UNA CENTRAL HIDROELÉCTRICA
COUPE D'UNE CENTRALE HYDROÉLECTRIQUE
WASSERKRAFTWERK IM QUERSCHNITT

gate
compuerta
vanne
Schieber

circuit breaker
interruptor automático
disjoncteur
Abschalter

gantry crane
grúa de caballete
portique
Bockkran

bushing
boquilla reducidora
traversée de transformateur
Stromführung

transformer
transformador
transformateur
Transformator

lightning arrester
pararrayos
parafoudre
Blitzableiter

traveling crane
grúa de puente
pont roulant
Laufkran

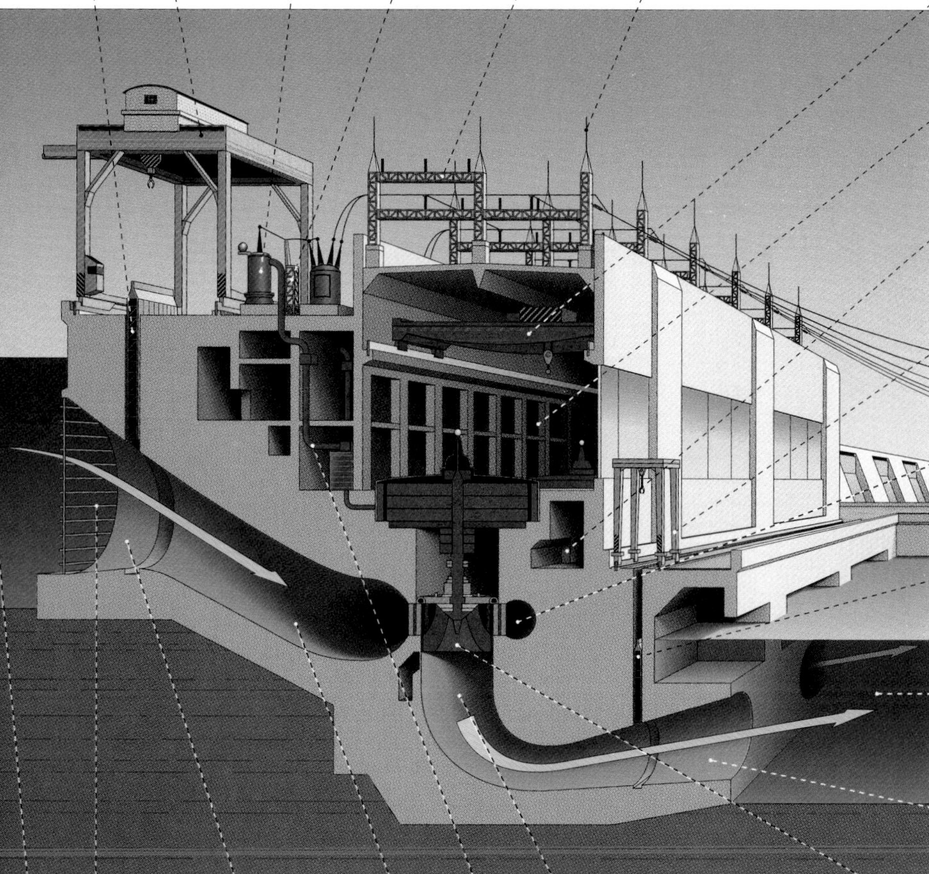

machine hall
sala de máquinas
salle des machines
Maschinenhalle

access gallery
galería de acceso
galerie de visite
Zugang

gantry crane
grúa de caballete
portique
Bockkran

scroll case
caja de caracol
bâche spirale
Umlaufgehäuse

gate
compuerta
vanne
Rechen

afterbay
cámara de salida
bief d'aval
Unterwasser

tailrace
canal de descarga
canal de fuite
Auslaufrohr

generator unit
turbinas
groupe turbo-alternateur
Generatoreinheit

water intake
entrada de agua
prise d'eau
Wassereinlaß

draft tube
tubo de aspiración
aspirateur
Saugrohr

screen
enrejado
grille
Rechen

busbar
barra colectora
barre blindée
Sammelschiene

reservoir
embalse de la presa
réservoir
Stausee

penstock
tubería de carga
conduite forcée
Falleitung

EMBANKMENT DAM
DIQUE DE TERRAPLÉN
BARRAGE EN REMBLAI
UFERDAMM

CROSS SECTION OF AN EMBANKMENT DAM
CORTE TRANSVERSAL DE UN DIQUE DE TERRAPLÉN
COUPE D'UN BARRAGE EN REMBLAI
UFERDAMM IM QUERSCHNITT

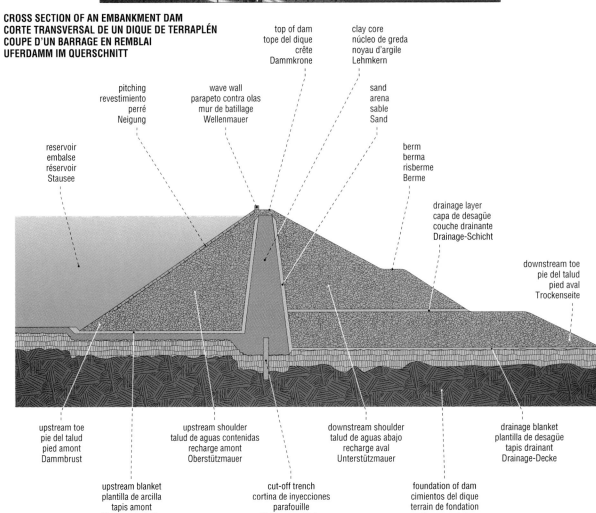

top of dam
tope del dique
crête
Dammkrone

clay core
núcleo de greda
noyau d'argile
Lehmkern

pitching
revestimiento
perré
Neigung

wave wall
parapeto contra olas
mur de batillage
Wellenmauer

sand
arena
sable
Sand

reservoir
embalse
réservoir
Stausee

berm
berma
risberme
Berme

drainage layer
capa de desagüe
couche drainante
Drainage-Schicht

downstream toe
pie del talud
pied aval
Trockenseite

upstream toe
pie del talud
pied amont
Dammbrust

upstream shoulder
talud de aguas contenidas
recharge amont
Oberstützmauer

downstream shoulder
talud de aguas abajo
recharge aval
Unterstützmauer

drainage blanket
plantilla de desagüe
tapis drainant
Drainage-Decke

upstream blanket
plantilla de arcilla
tapis amont
Oberwasserdecke

cut-off trench
cortina de inyecciones
parafouille
Dichtungsschleier

foundation of dam
cimientos del dique
terrain de fondation
Dammsockel

GRAVITY DAM
PRESA
BARRAGE-POIDS
GEWICHTSSTAUDAMM

CROSS SECTION OF A GRAVITY DAM
CORTE TRANSVERSAL DE UNA PRESA
COUPE D'UN BARRAGE-POIDS
GEWICHTSSTAUDAMM IM QUERSCHNITT

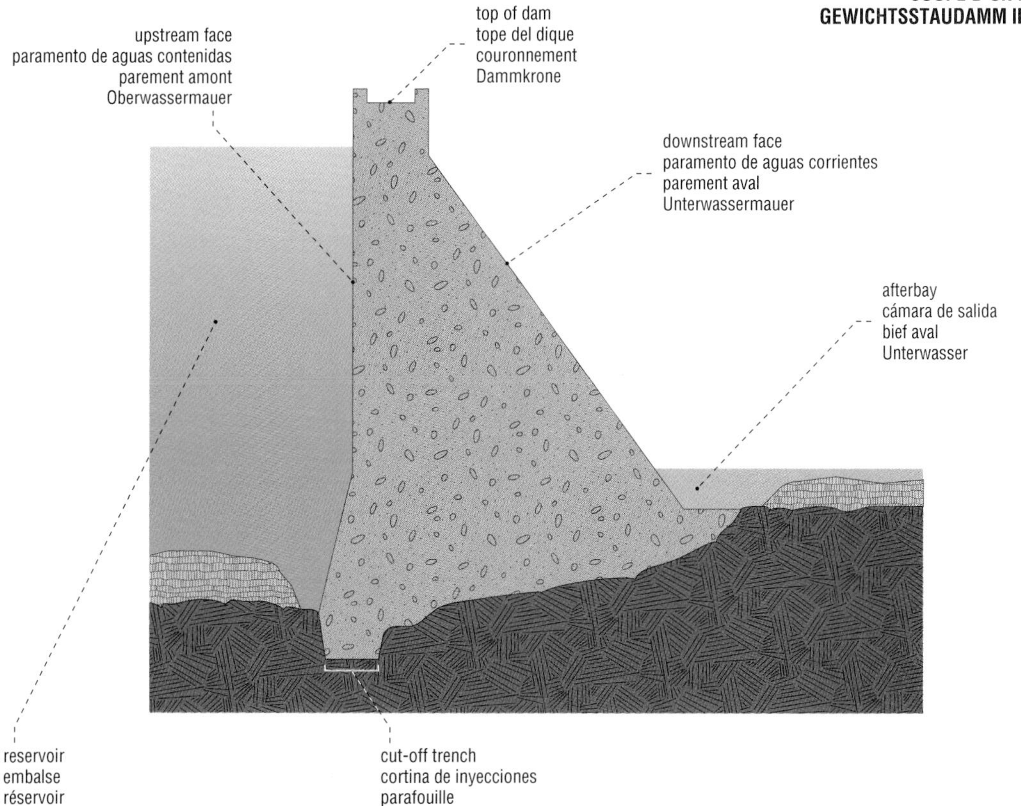
upstream face
paramento de aguas contenidas
parement amont
Oberwassermauer
top of dam
tope del dique
couronnement
Dammkrone
downstream face
paramento de aguas corrientes
parement aval
Unterwassermauer
afterbay
cámara de salida
bief aval
Unterwasser
reservoir
embalse
réservoir
Stausee
cut-off trench
cortina de inyecciones
parafouille
Dichtungsschleier

ARCH DAM
PRESA DE ARCO
BARRAGE-VOÛTE
BOGENSTAUDAMM

CROSS SECTION OF AN ARCH DAM
CORTE TRANSVERSAL DE UNA PRESA DE ARCO
COUPE D'UN BARRAGE-VOÛTE
BOGENSTAUDAMM IM QUERSCHNITT

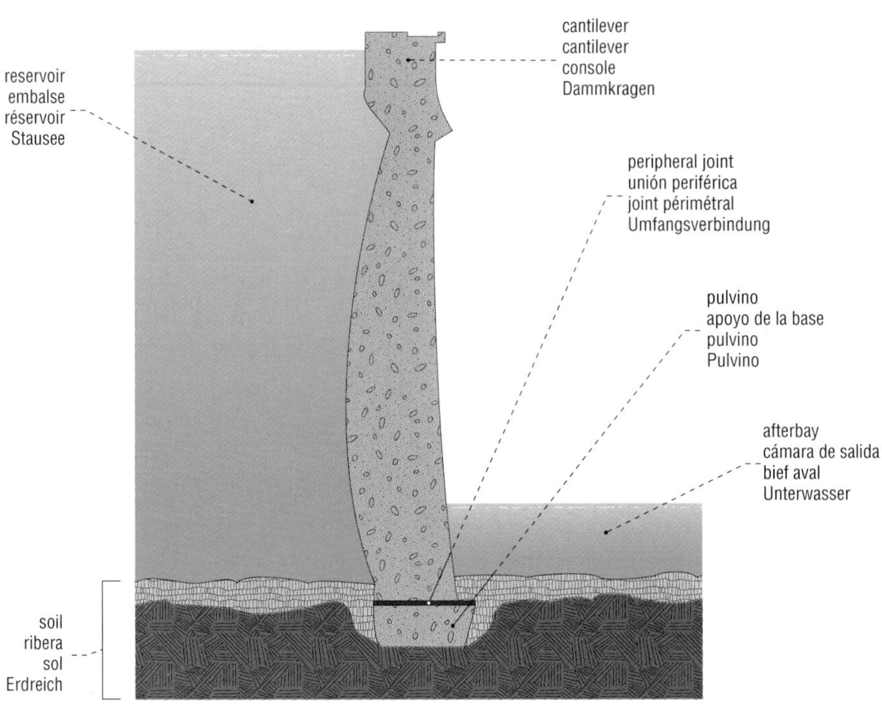
cantilever
cantilever
console
Dammkragen
reservoir
embalse
réservoir
Stausee
peripheral joint
unión periférica
joint périmétral
Umfangsverbindung
pulvino
apoyo de la base
pulvino
Pulvino
afterbay
cámara de salida
bief aval
Unterwasser
soil
ribera
sol
Erdreich

BUTTRESS DAM
DIQUE DE MACHONES
BARRAGE À CONTREFORTS
STÜTZPFEILERSTAUDAMM

CROSS SECTION OF A BUTTRESS DAM
CORTE TRANSVERSAL DE UN DIQUE DE MACHONES
COUPE D'UN BARRAGE À CONTREFORTS
STÜTZPFEILERSTAUDAMM IM QUERSCHNITT

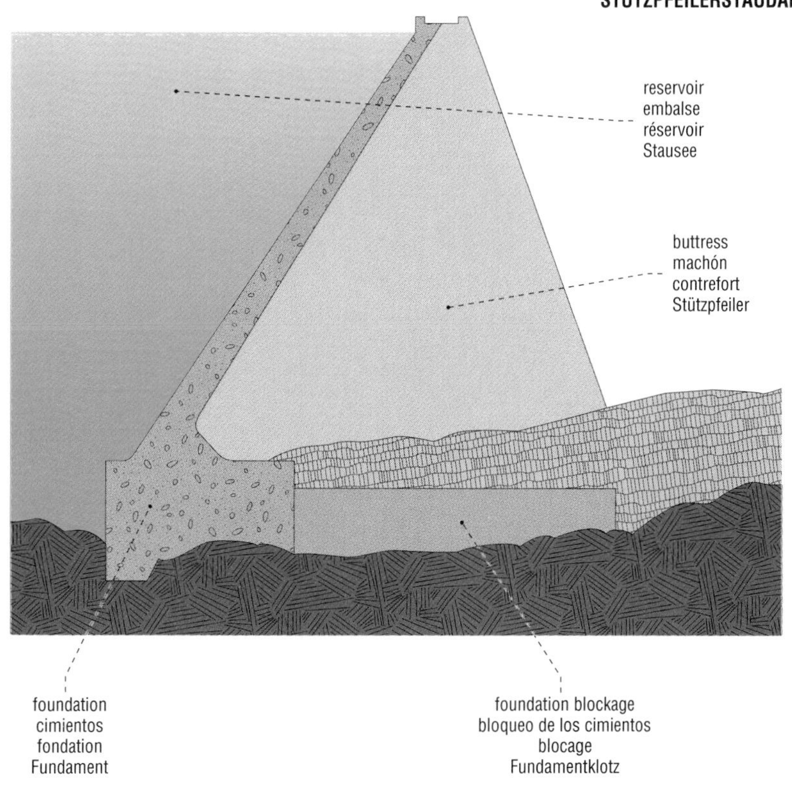
reservoir
embalse
réservoir
Stausee
buttress
machón
contrefort
Stützpfeiler
foundation
cimientos
fondation
Fundament
foundation blockage
bloqueo de los cimientos
blocage
Fundamentklotz

ELECTRICITY
ELECTRICIDAD
ÉLECTRICITÉ
ELEKTRIZITÄT

TIDAL POWER PLANT
CENTRAL MAREMOTRIZ
USINE MARÉMOTRICE
GEZEITENKRAFTWERK

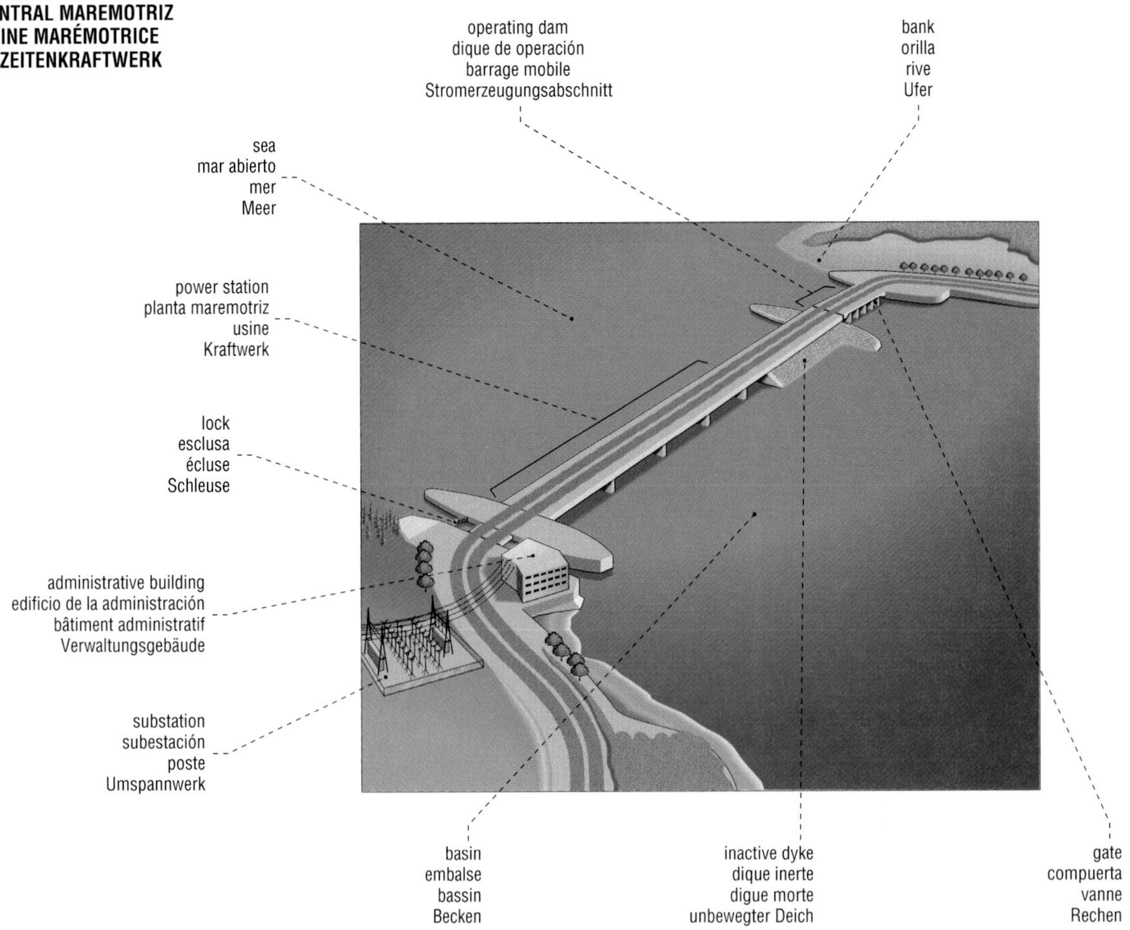

operating dam
dique de operación
barrage mobile
Stromerzeugungsabschnitt

bank
orilla
rive
Ufer

sea
mar abierto
mer
Meer

power station
planta maremotriz
usine
Kraftwerk

lock
esclusa
écluse
Schleuse

administrative building
edificio de la administración
bâtiment administratif
Verwaltungsgebäude

substation
subestación
poste
Umspannwerk

basin
embalse
bassin
Becken

inactive dyke
dique inerte
digue morte
unbewegter Deich

gate
compuerta
vanne
Rechen

CROSS SECTION OF POWER PLANT
CORTE TRANSVERSAL DE UNA PLANTA MAREMOTRIZ
COUPE DE L'USINE
KRAFTWERK IM QUERSCHNITT

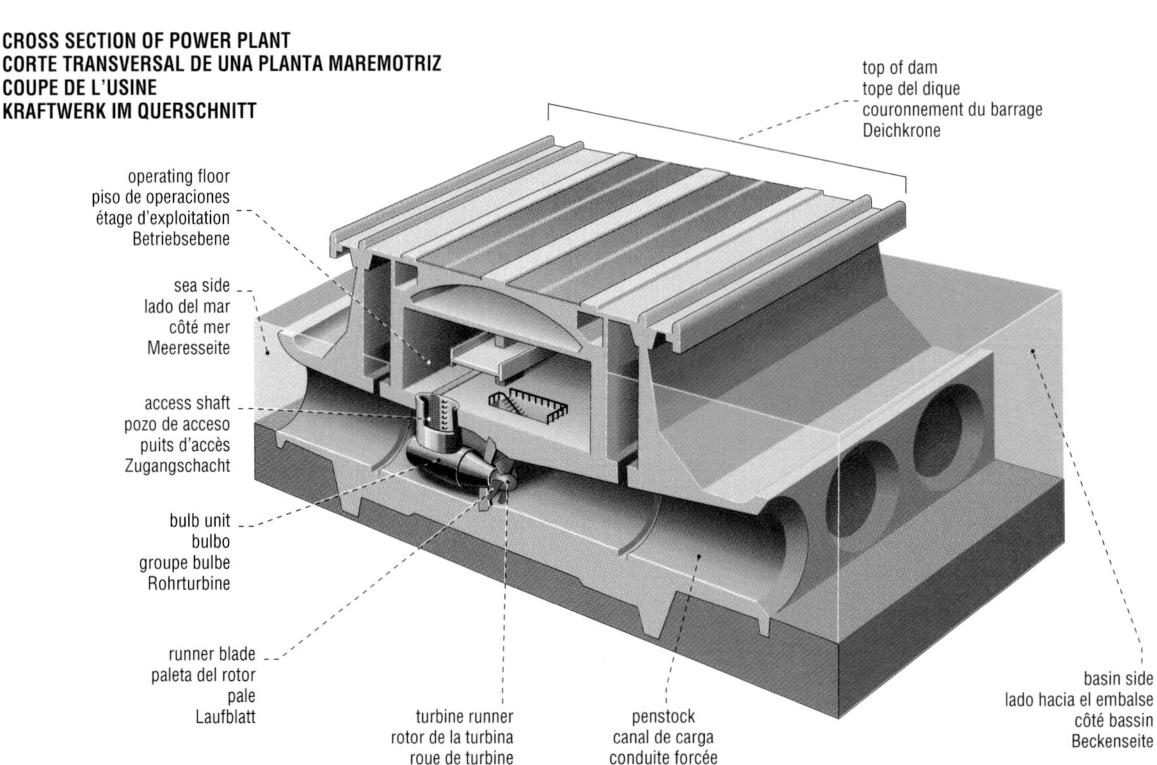
top of dam
tope del dique
couronnement du barrage
Deichkrone
operating floor
piso de operaciones
étage d'exploitation
Betriebsebene
sea side
lado del mar
côté mer
Meeresseite
access shaft
pozo de acceso
puits d'accès
Zugangschacht
bulb unit
bulbo
groupe bulbe
Rohrturbine
runner blade
paleta del rotor
pale
Laufblatt
turbine runner
rotor de la turbina
roue de turbine
Turbinenläufer
penstock
canal de carga
conduite forcée
Falleitung
basin side
lado hacia el embalse
côté bassin
Beckenseite

GENERATOR UNIT
UNIDAD GENERADORA
GROUPE TURBO-ALTERNATEUR
STROMGENERATOR

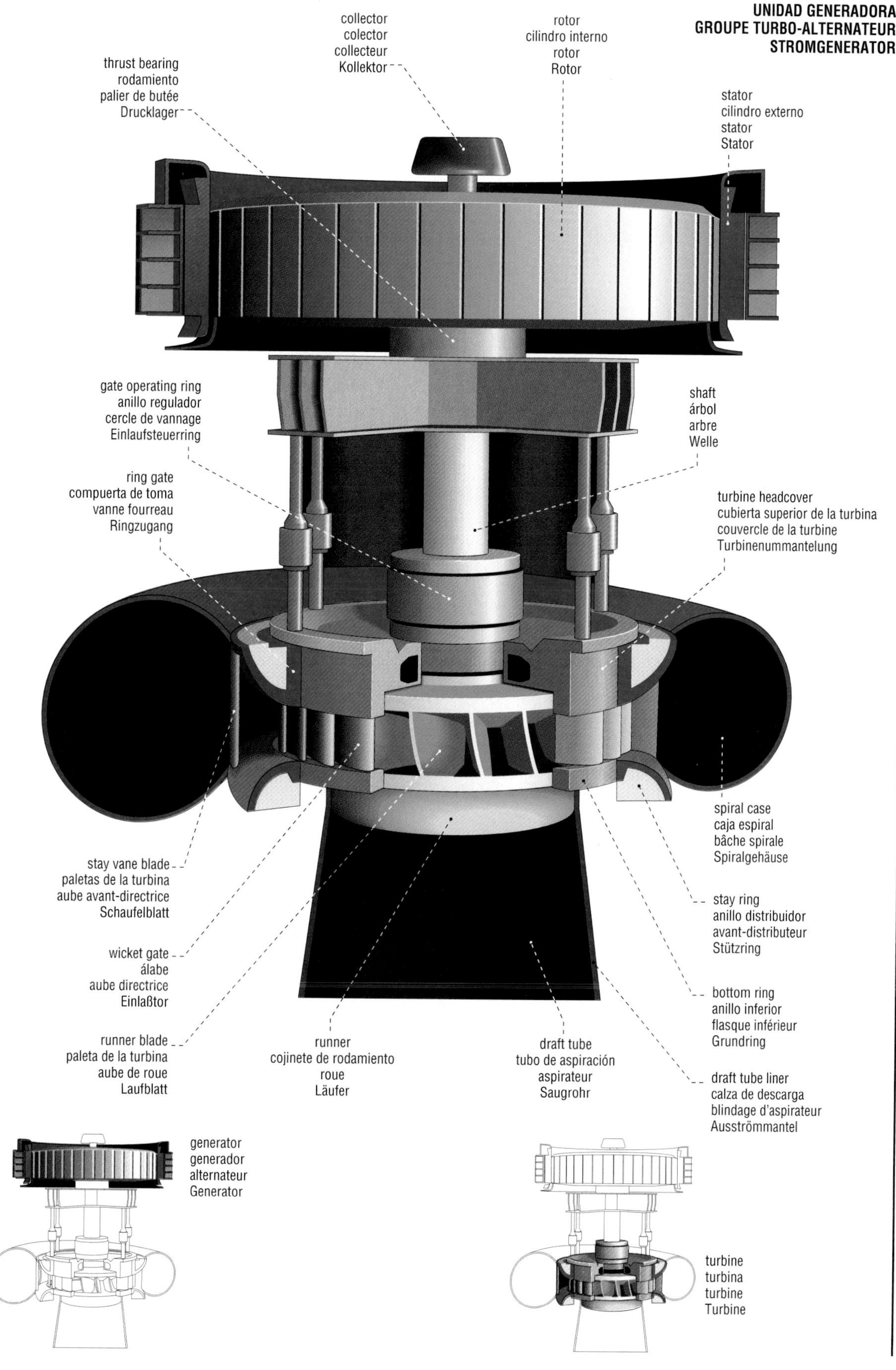
collector
colector
collecteur
Kollektor
rotor
cilindro interno
rotor
Rotor
thrust bearing
rodamiento
palier de butée
Drucklager
stator
cilindro externo
stator
Stator
gate operating ring
anillo regulador
cercle de vannage
Einlaufsteuerring
shaft
árbol
arbre
Welle
ring gate
compuerta de toma
vanne fourreau
Ringzugang
turbine headcover
cubierta superior de la turbina
couvercle de la turbine
Turbinenummantelung
spiral case
caja espiral
bâche spirale
Spiralgehäuse
stay vane blade
paletas de la turbina
aube avant-directrice
Schaufelblatt
stay ring
anillo distribuidor
avant-distributeur
Stützring
wicket gate
álabe
aube directrice
Einlaßtor
bottom ring
anillo inferior
flasque inférieur
Grundring
runner blade
paleta de la turbina
aube de roue
Laufblatt
runner
cojinete de rodamiento
roue
Läufer
draft tube
tubo de aspiración
aspirateur
Saugrohr
draft tube liner
calza de descarga
blindage d'aspirateur
Ausströmmantel
generator
generador
alternateur
Generator
turbine
turbina
turbine
Turbine

ELECTRICITY
ELECTRICIDAD
ÉLECTRICITÉ
ELEKTRIZITÄT

FRANCIS RUNNER
TURBINA FRANCIS
ROUE FRANCIS
FRANCISTURBINE

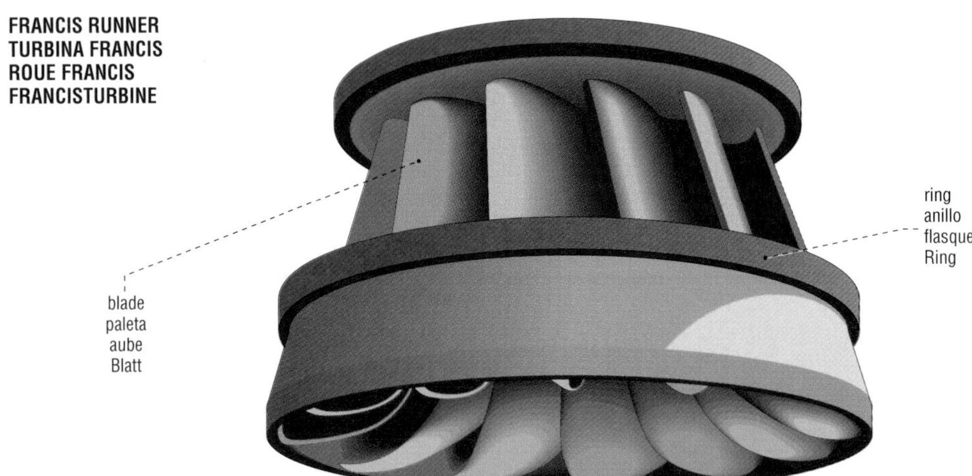
ring
anillo
flasque
Ring
blade
paleta
aube
Blatt

KAPLAN RUNNER
TURBINA KAPLAN
ROUE KAPLAN
KAPLANTURBINE

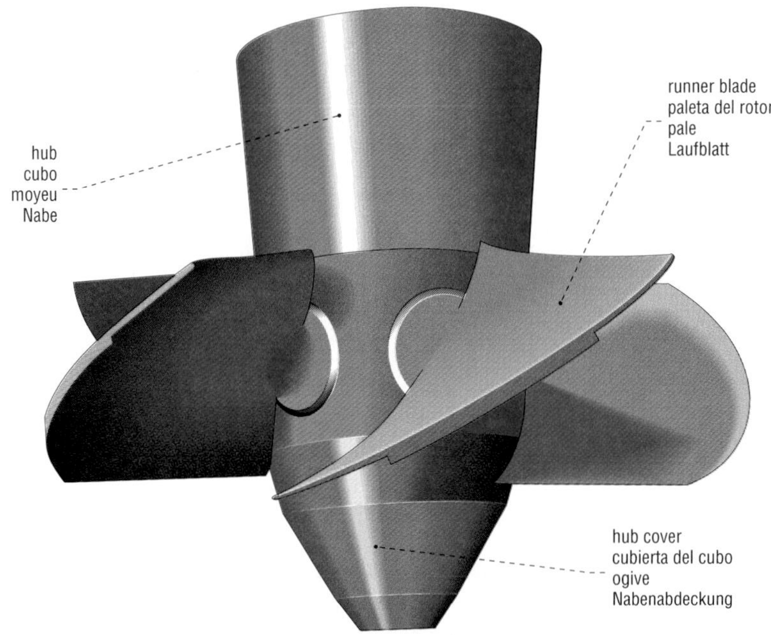
runner blade
paleta del rotor
pale
Laufblatt
hub
cubo
moyeu
Nabe
hub cover
cubierta del cubo
ogive
Nabenabdeckung

PELTON RUNNER
TURBINA PELTON
ROUE PELTON
PELTONTURBINE

bucket ring
rueda de cangilones
couronne d'aubage
Zellenring

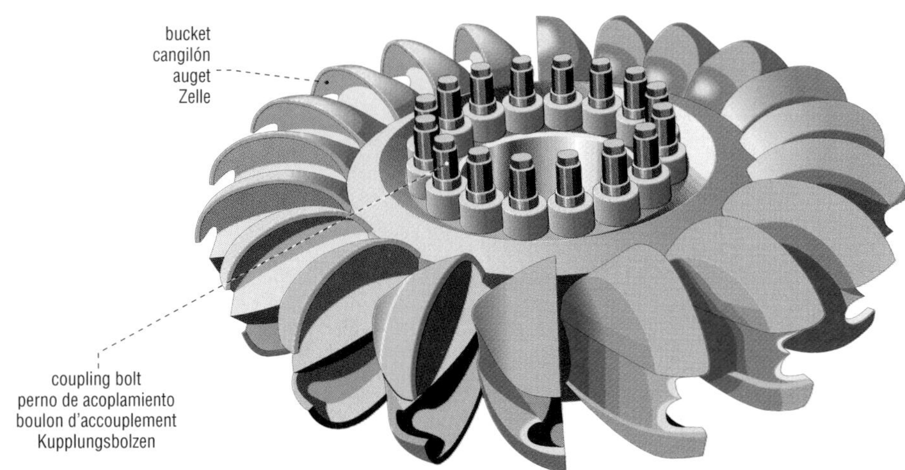
bucket
cangilón
auget
Zelle
coupling bolt
perno de acoplamiento
boulon d'accouplement
Kupplungsbolzen

STEPS IN PRODUCTION OF ELECTRICITY
ETAPAS DE LA PRODUCCIÓN DE ELECTRICIDAD
ÉTAPES DE PRODUCTION DE L'ÉLECTRICITÉ
EINZELSCHRITTE BEI DER STROMERZEUGUNG

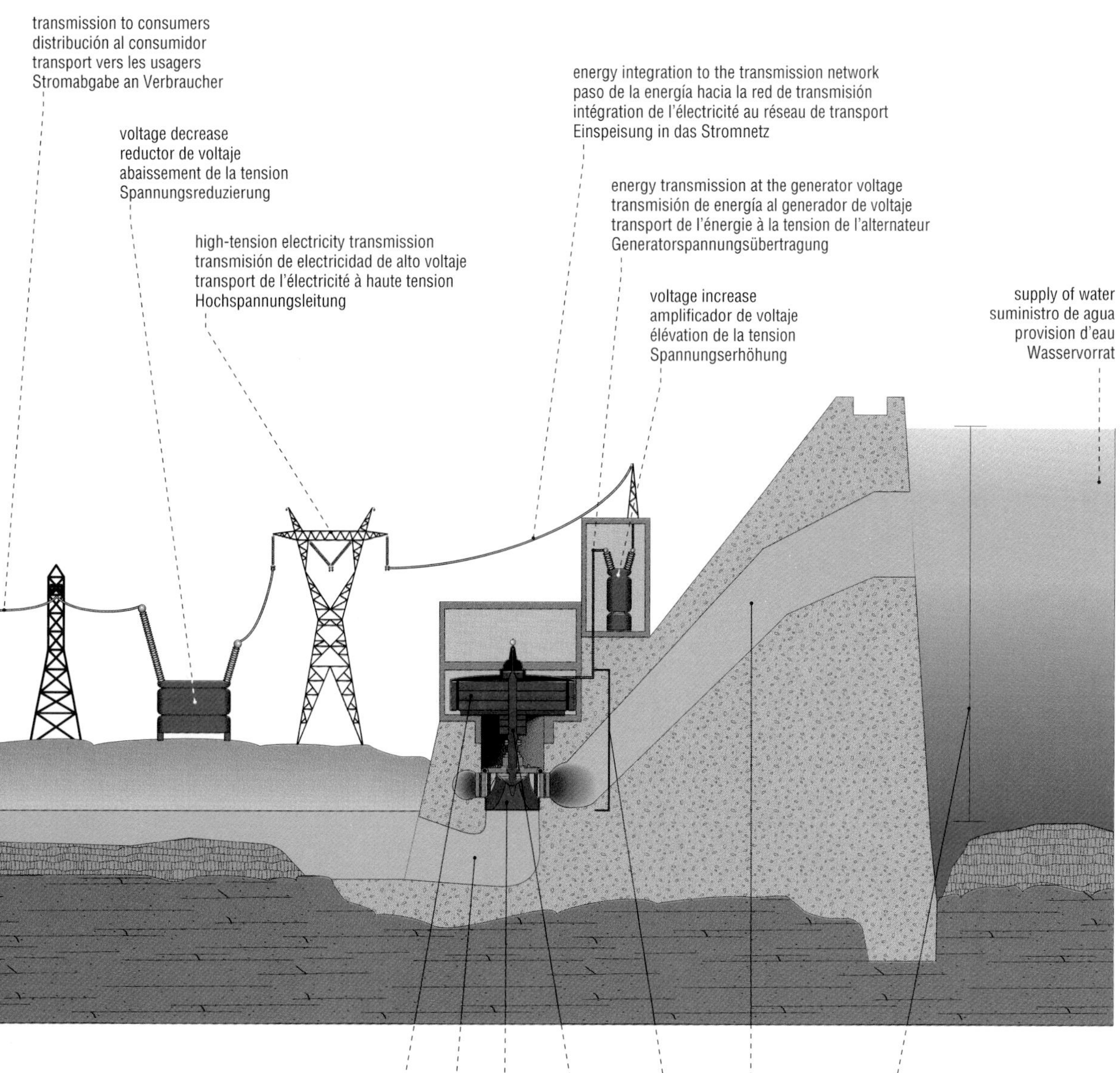

transmission to consumers
distribución al consumidor
transport vers les usagers
Stromabgabe an Verbraucher
voltage decrease
reductor de voltaje
abaissement de la tension
Spannungsreduzierung
high-tension electricity transmission
transmisión de electricidad de alto voltaje
transport de l'électricité à haute tension
Hochspannungsleitung
energy integration to the transmission network
paso de la energía hacia la red de transmisión
intégration de l'électricité au réseau de transport
Einspeisung in das Stromnetz
energy transmission at the generator voltage
transmisión de energía al generador de voltaje
transport de l'énergie à la tension de l'alternateur
Generatorspannungsübertragung
voltage increase
amplificador de voltaje
élévation de la tension
Spannungserhöhung
supply of water
suministro de agua
provision d'eau
Wasservorrat
head of water
volumen de agua
hauteur de chute
Wasserstand
production of electricity by the generator
producción de electricidad por generador
production d'électricité par l'alternateur
Stromerzeugung durch den Generator
water under pressure
agua a presión
eau sous pression
Druckwasser
turbined water draining
desagüe de la turbina
évacuation de l'eau turbinée
Turbinenwasserabfluß
transformation of mechanical work into electricity
transformación del trabajo mecánico en electricidad
conversion du travail mécanique en électricité
Umwandlung von Bewegungsenergie in Elektrizität
rotation of the turbine
rotación de la turbina
mouvement rotatif de la turbine
Turbinendrehung
transmission of the rotative movement to the rotor
transmisión del movimiento hacia el rotor
transmission du mouvement au rotor
Übertragung der Drehbewegung auf den Rotor

ELECTRICITY
ELECTRICIDAD
ÉLECTRICITÉ
ELEKTRIZITÄT

PYLON
TORRE DE ALTA TENSIÓN
PYLÔNE
HOCHSPANNUNGSMAST

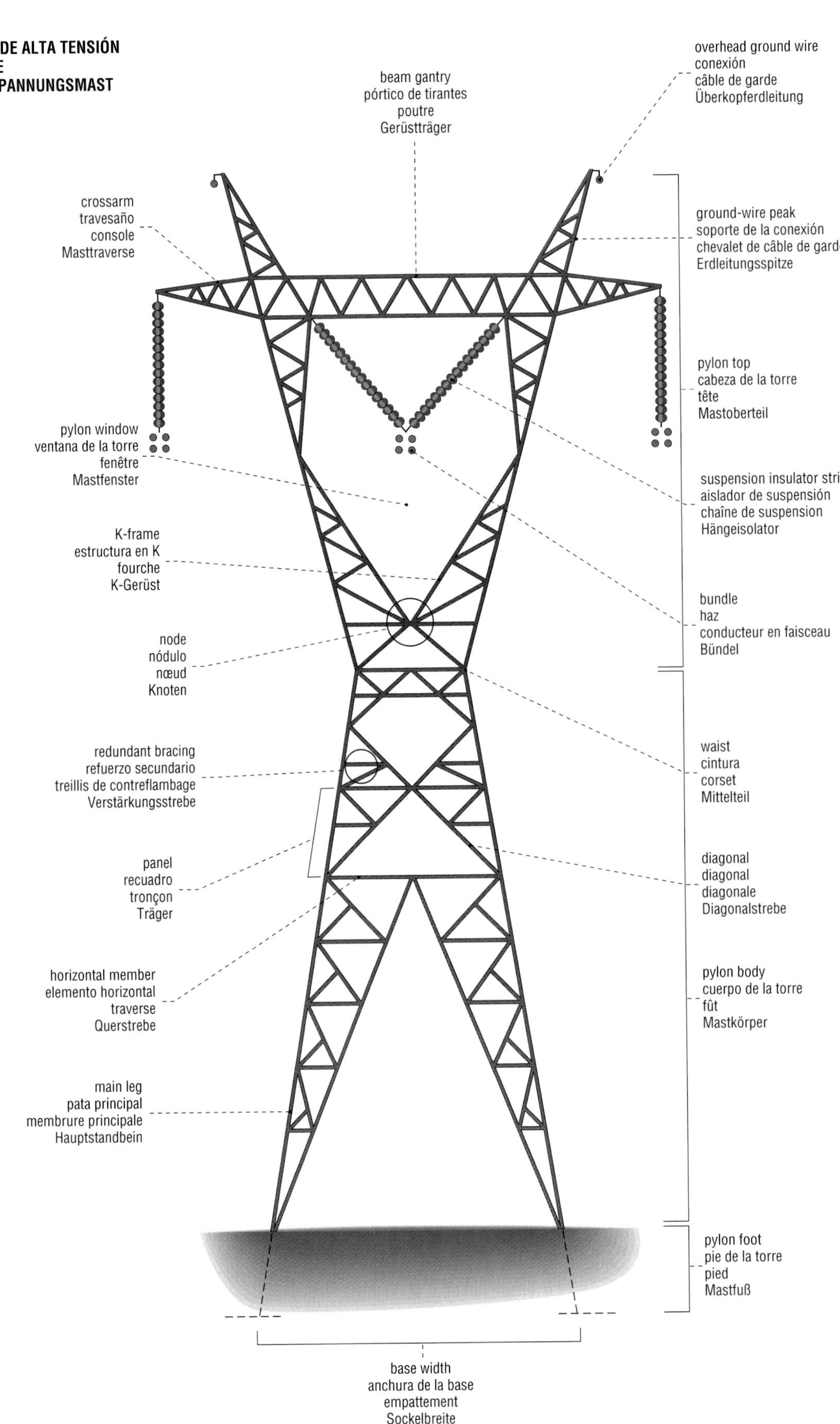

beam gantry
pórtico de tirantes
poutre
Gerüstträger
overhead ground wire
conexión
câble de garde
Überkopferdleitung
crossarm
travesaño
console
Masttraverse
ground-wire peak
soporte de la conexión
chevalet de câble de garde
Erdleitungsspitze
pylon top
cabeza de la torre
tête
Mastoberteil
pylon window
ventana de la torre
fenêtre
Mastfenster
suspension insulator string
aislador de suspensión
chaîne de suspension
Hängeisolator
K-frame
estructura en K
fourche
K-Gerüst
bundle
haz
conducteur en faisceau
Bündel
node
nódulo
nœud
Knoten
redundant bracing
refuerzo secundario
treillis de contreflambage
Verstärkungsstrebe
waist
cintura
corset
Mittelteil
panel
recuadro
tronçon
Träger
diagonal
diagonal
diagonale
Diagonalstrebe
horizontal member
elemento horizontal
traverse
Querstrebe
pylon body
cuerpo de la torre
fût
Mastkörper
main leg
pata principal
membrure principale
Hauptstandbein
pylon foot
pie de la torre
pied
Mastfuß
base width
anchura de la base
empattement
Sockelbreite

ELECTRICITY TRANSMISSION
TRANSMISIÓN DE ELECTRICIDAD
TRANSPORT DE L'ÉLECTRICITÉ
STROMTRANSPORT

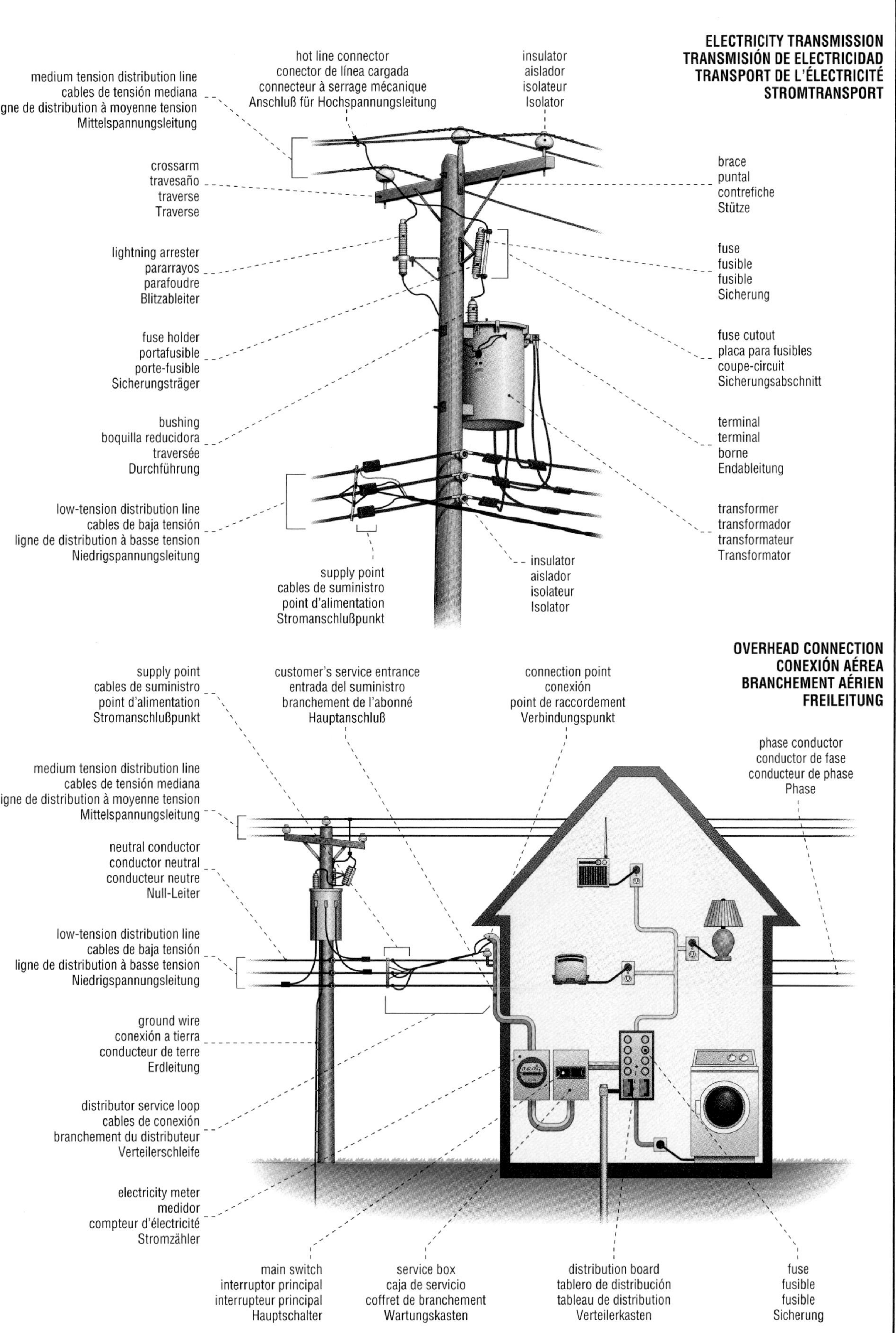
medium tension distribution line
cables de tensión mediana
ligne de distribution à moyenne tension
Mittelspannungsleitung
hot line connector
conector de línea cargada
connecteur à serrage mécanique
Anschluß für Hochspannungsleitung
insulator
aislador
isolateur
Isolator
crossarm
travesaño
traverse
Traverse
brace
puntal
contrefiche
Stütze
lightning arrester
pararrayos
parafoudre
Blitzableiter
fuse
fusible
fusible
Sicherung
fuse holder
portafusible
porte-fusible
Sicherungsträger
fuse cutout
placa para fusibles
coupe-circuit
Sicherungsabschnitt
bushing
boquilla reducidora
traversée
Durchführung
terminal
terminal
borne
Endableitung
low-tension distribution line
cables de baja tensión
ligne de distribution à basse tension
Niedrigspannungsleitung
transformer
transformador
transformateur
Transformator
supply point
cables de suministro
point d'alimentation
Stromanschlußpunkt
insulator
aislador
isolateur
Isolator
OVERHEAD CONNECTION
CONEXIÓN AÉREA
BRANCHEMENT AÉRIEN
FREILEITUNG
supply point
cables de suministro
point d'alimentation
Stromanschlußpunkt
customer's service entrance
entrada del suministro
branchement de l'abonné
Hauptanschluß
connection point
conexión
point de raccordement
Verbindungspunkt
phase conductor
conductor de fase
conducteur de phase
Phase
medium tension distribution line
cables de tensión mediana
ligne de distribution à moyenne tension
Mittelspannungsleitung
neutral conductor
conductor neutral
conducteur neutre
Null-Leiter
low-tension distribution line
cables de baja tensión
ligne de distribution à basse tension
Niedrigspannungsleitung
ground wire
conexión a tierra
conducteur de terre
Erdleitung
distributor service loop
cables de conexión
branchement du distributeur
Verteilerschleife
electricity meter
medidor
compteur d'électricité
Stromzähler
main switch
interruptor principal
interrupteur principal
Hauptschalter
service box
caja de servicio
coffret de branchement
Wartungskasten
distribution board
tablero de distribución
tableau de distribution
Verteilerkasten
fuse
fusible
fusible
Sicherung

NUCLEAR ENERGY
ENERGÍA NUCLEAR
ÉNERGIE NUCLÉAIRE
KERNENERGIE

NUCLEAR GENERATING STATION
CENTRAL NUCLEAR
CENTRALE NUCLÉAIRE
KERNKRAFTWERK

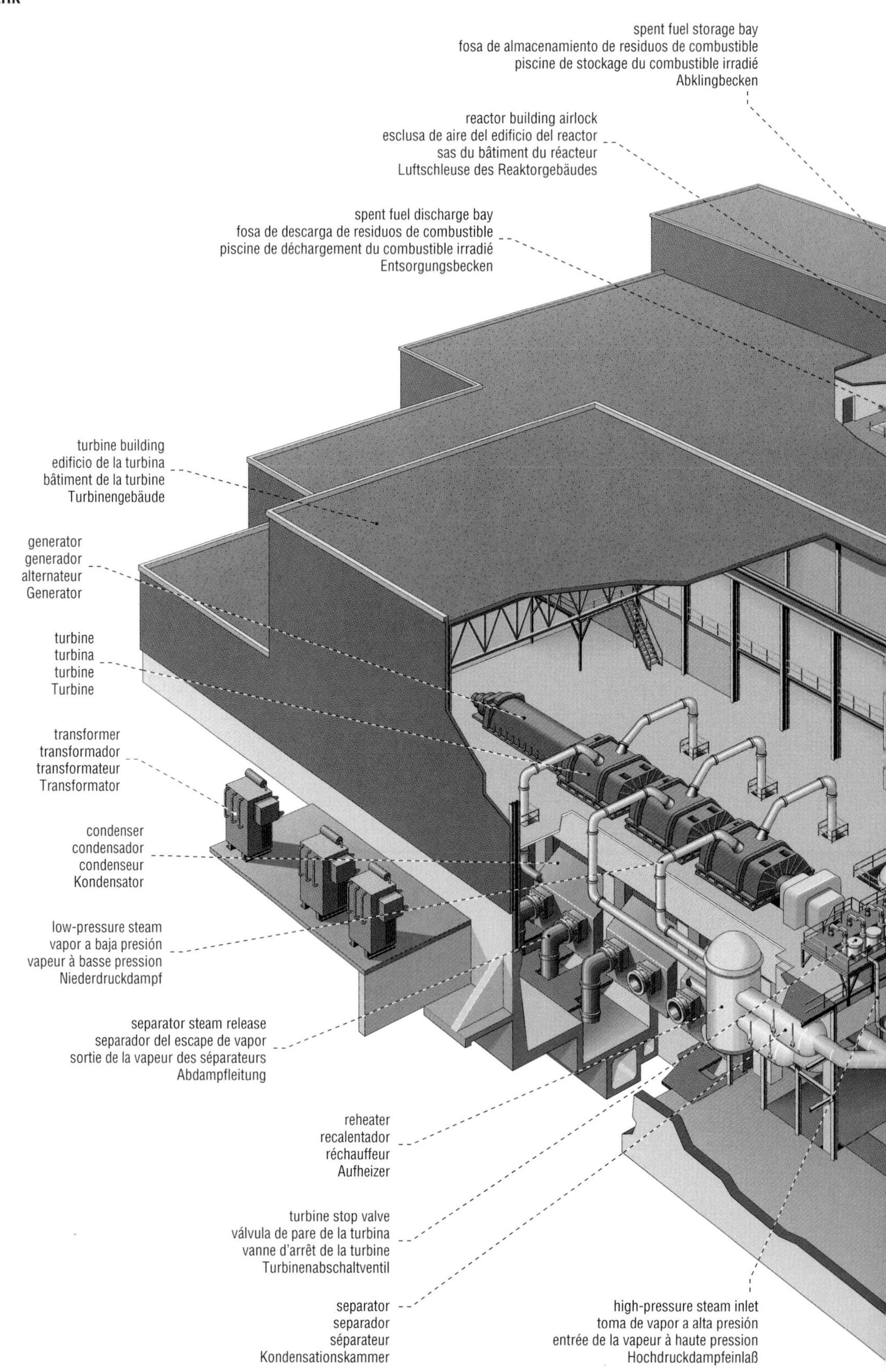

spent fuel storage bay
fosa de almacenamiento de residuos de combustible
piscine de stockage du combustible irradié
Abklingbecken
reactor building airlock
esclusa de aire del edificio del reactor
sas du bâtiment du réacteur
Luftschleuse des Reaktorgebäudes
spent fuel discharge bay
fosa de descarga de residuos de combustible
piscine de déchargement du combustible irradié
Entsorgungsbecken
turbine building
edificio de la turbina
bâtiment de la turbine
Turbinengebäude
generator
generador
alternateur
Generator
turbine
turbina
turbine
Turbine
transformer
transformador
transformateur
Transformator
condenser
condensador
condenseur
Kondensator
low-pressure steam
vapor a baja presión
vapeur à basse pression
Niederdruckdampf
separator steam release
separador del escape de vapor
sortie de la vapeur des séparateurs
Abdampfleitung
reheater
recalentador
réchauffeur
Aufheizer
turbine stop valve
válvula de pare de la turbina
vanne d'arrêt de la turbine
Turbinenabschaltventil
separator
separador
séparateur
Kondensationskammer
high-pressure steam inlet
toma de vapor a alta presión
entrée de la vapeur à haute pression
Hochdruckdampfeinlaß

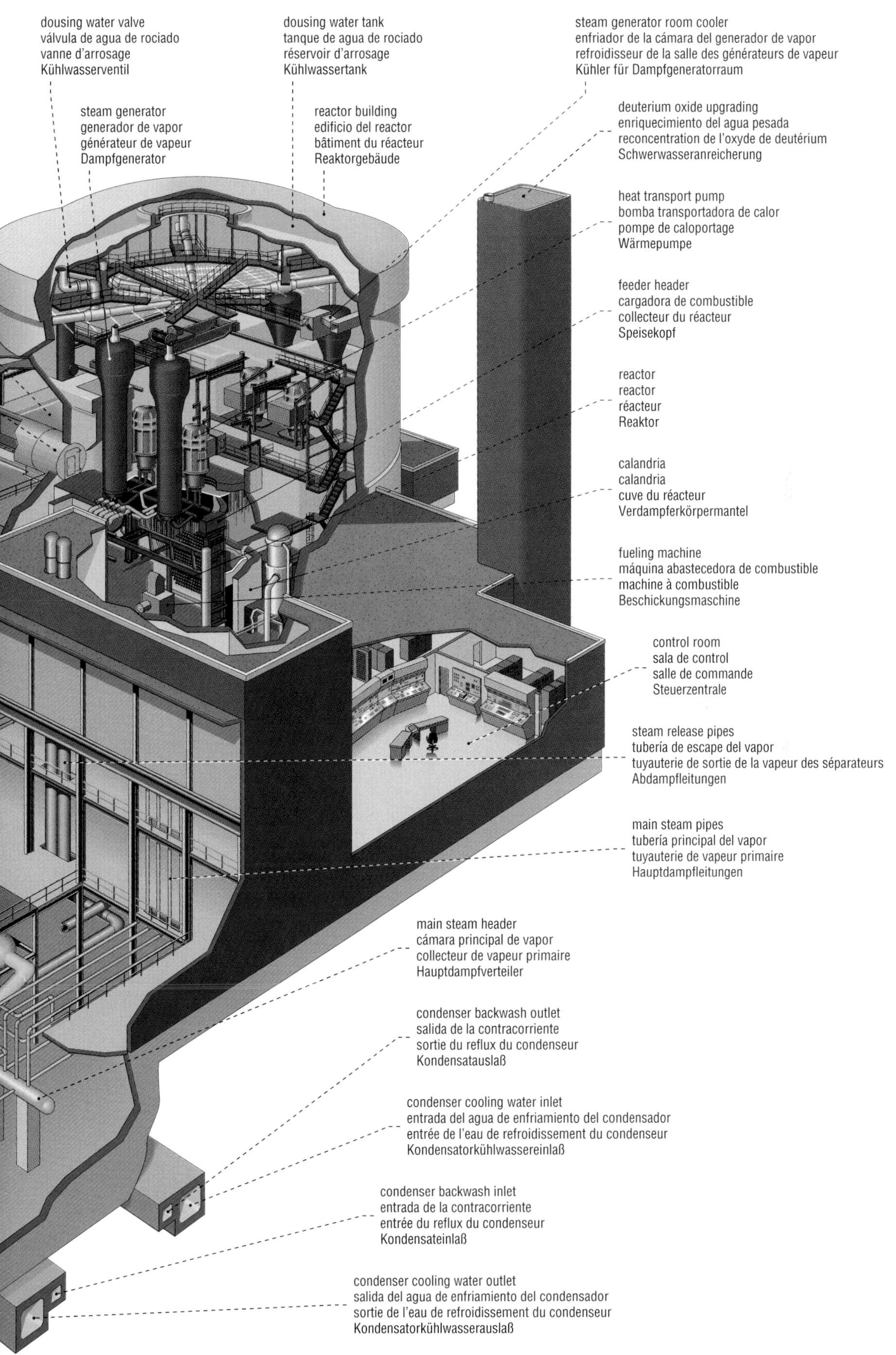
dousing water valve
válvula de agua de rociado
vanne d'arrosage
Kühlwasserventil
steam generator
generador de vapor
générateur de vapeur
Dampfgenerator
dousing water tank
tanque de agua de rociado
réservoir d'arrosage
Kühlwassertank
reactor building
edificio del reactor
bâtiment du réacteur
Reaktorgebäude
steam generator room cooler
enfriador de la cámara del generador de vapor
refroidisseur de la salle des générateurs de vapeur
Kühler für Dampfgeneratorraum
deuterium oxide upgrading
enriquecimiento del agua pesada
reconcentration de l'oxyde de deutérium
Schwerwasseranreicherung
heat transport pump
bomba transportadora de calor
pompe de caloportage
Wärmepumpe
feeder header
cargadora de combustible
collecteur du réacteur
Speisekopf
reactor
reactor
réacteur
Reaktor
calandria
calandria
cuve du réacteur
Verdampferkörpermantel
fueling machine
máquina abastecedora de combustible
machine à combustible
Beschickungsmaschine
control room
sala de control
salle de commande
Steuerzentrale
steam release pipes
tubería de escape del vapor
tuyauterie de sortie de la vapeur des séparateurs
Abdampfleitungen
main steam pipes
tubería principal del vapor
tuyauterie de vapeur primaire
Hauptdampfleitungen
main steam header
cámara principal de vapor
collecteur de vapeur primaire
Hauptdampfverteiler
condenser backwash outlet
salida de la contracorriente
sortie du reflux du condenseur
Kondensatauslaß
condenser cooling water inlet
entrada del agua de enfriamiento del condensador
entrée de l'eau de refroidissement du condenseur
Kondensatorkühlwassereinlaß
condenser backwash inlet
entrada de la contracorriente
entrée du reflux du condenseur
Kondensateinlaß
condenser cooling water outlet
salida del agua de enfriamiento del condensador
sortie de l'eau de refroidissement du condenseur
Kondensatorkühlwasserauslaß

NUCLEAR ENERGY
ENERGÍA NUCLEAR
ÉNERGIE NUCLÉAIRE
KERNENERGIE

CARBON DIOXIDE REACTOR
REACTOR DE BIÓXIDO DE CARBONO
RÉACTEUR AU GAZ CARBONIQUE
KOHLENDIOXIDREAKTOR

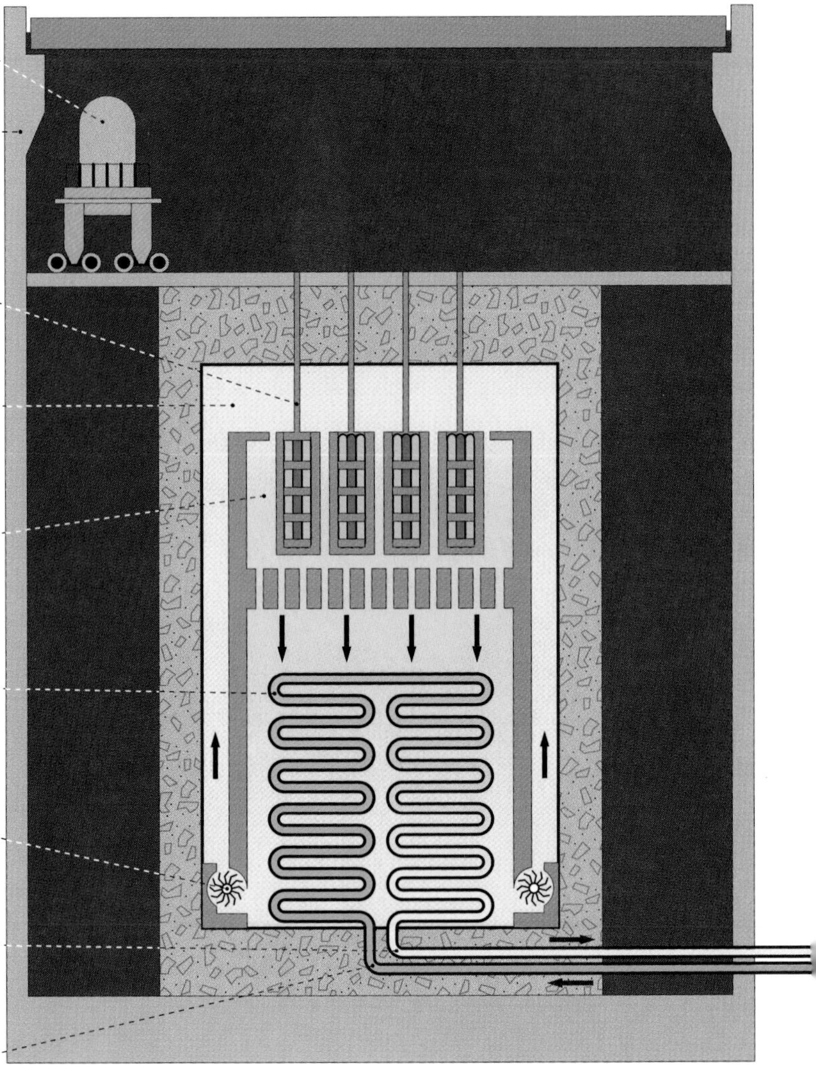

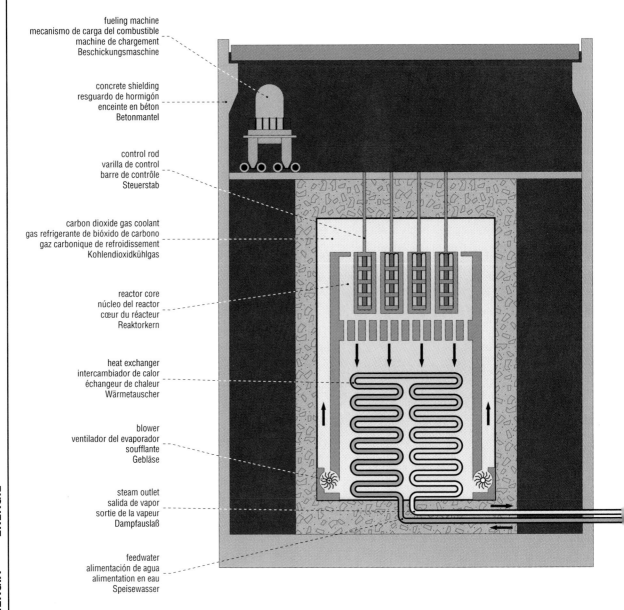

fueling machine
mecanismo de carga del combustible
machine de chargement
Beschickungsmaschine

concrete shielding
resguardo de hormigón
enceinte en béton
Betonmantel

control rod
varilla de control
barre de contrôle
Steuerstab

carbon dioxide gas coolant
gas refrigerante de bióxido de carbono
gaz carbonique de refroidissement
Kohlendioxidkühlgas

reactor core
núcleo del reactor
cœur du réacteur
Reaktorkern

heat exchanger
intercambiador de calor
échangeur de chaleur
Wärmetauscher

blower
ventilador del evaporador
soufflante
Gebläse

steam outlet
salida de vapor
sortie de la vapeur
Dampfauslaß

feedwater
alimentación de agua
alimentation en eau
Speisewasser

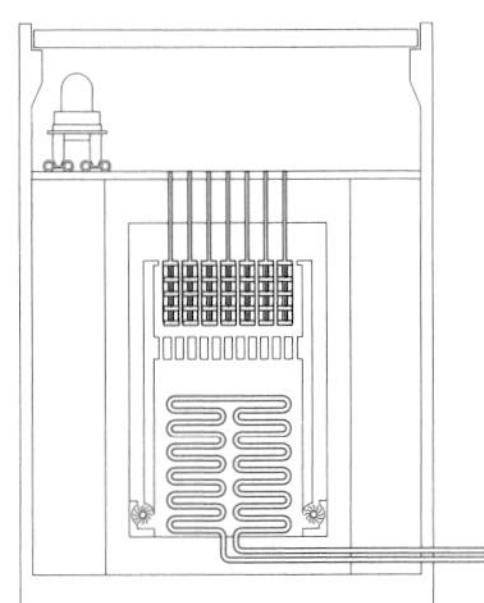

fuel: natural uranium
combustible: uranio natural
combustible: uranium naturel
Brennstoff: nichtangereichertes Uran

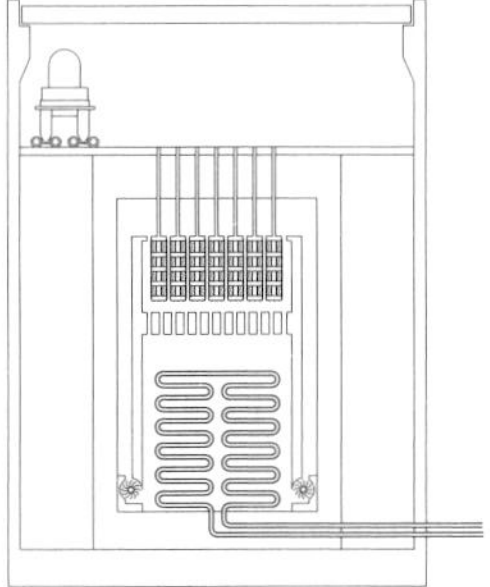

moderator: graphite
moderador: grafito
modérateur: graphite
Moderator: Graphit

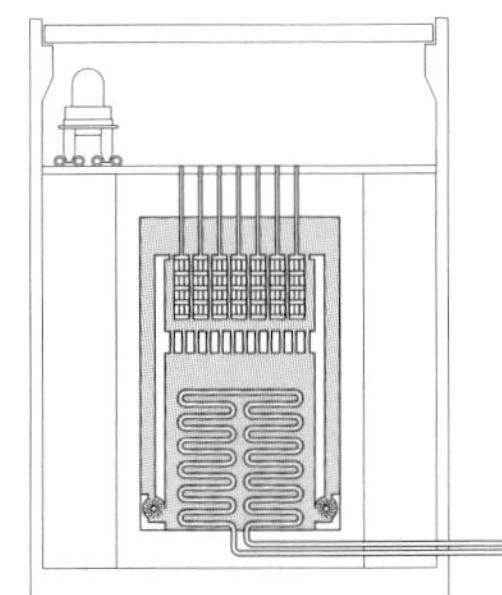

coolant: carbon dioxide
refrigerante: bióxido de carbono
caloporteur: gaz carbonique
Kühlmittel: Kohlendioxid

HEAVY-WATER REACTOR
REACTOR DE AGUA PESADA
RÉACTEUR À EAU LOURDE
SCHWERWASSERREAKTOR

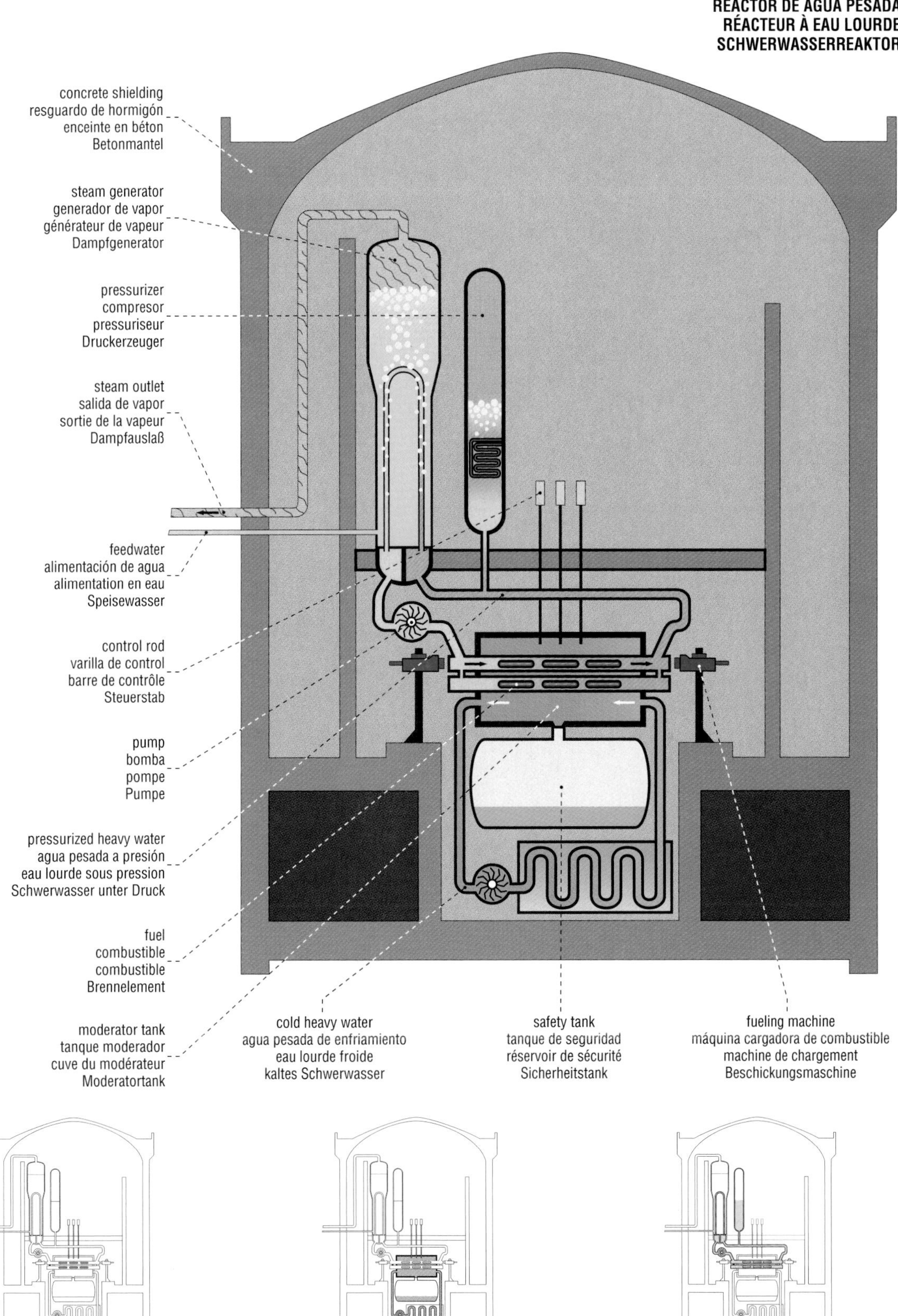

concrete shielding
resguardo de hormigón
enceinte en béton
Betonmantel
steam generator
generador de vapor
générateur de vapeur
Dampfgenerator
pressurizer
compresor
pressuriseur
Druckerzeuger
steam outlet
salida de vapor
sortie de la vapeur
Dampfauslaß
feedwater
alimentación de agua
alimentation en eau
Speisewasser
control rod
varilla de control
barre de contrôle
Steuerstab
pump
bomba
pompe
Pumpe
pressurized heavy water
agua pesada a presión
eau lourde sous pression
Schwerwasser unter Druck
fuel
combustible
combustible
Brennelement
moderator tank
tanque moderador
cuve du modérateur
Moderatortank
cold heavy water
agua pesada de enfriamiento
eau lourde froide
kaltes Schwerwasser
safety tank
tanque de seguridad
réservoir de sécurité
Sicherheitstank
fueling machine
máquina cargadora de combustible
machine de chargement
Beschickungsmaschine

fuel: natural uranium
combustible: uranio natural
combustible: uranium naturel
Brennstoff: nichtangereichertes Uran

moderator: heavy water
moderador: agua pesada
modérateur: eau lourde
Moderator: schweres Wasser

coolant: pressurized heavy water
refrigerante: agua pesada a presión
caloporteur: eau lourde sous pression
Kühlmittel: Druckwasser

NUCLEAR ENERGY
ENERGÍA NUCLEAR
ÉNERGIE NUCLÉAIRE
KERNENERGIE

PRESSURIZED-WATER REACTOR
REACTOR DE AGUA A PRESIÓN
RÉACTEUR À EAU SOUS PRESSION
DRUCKWASSERREAKTOR

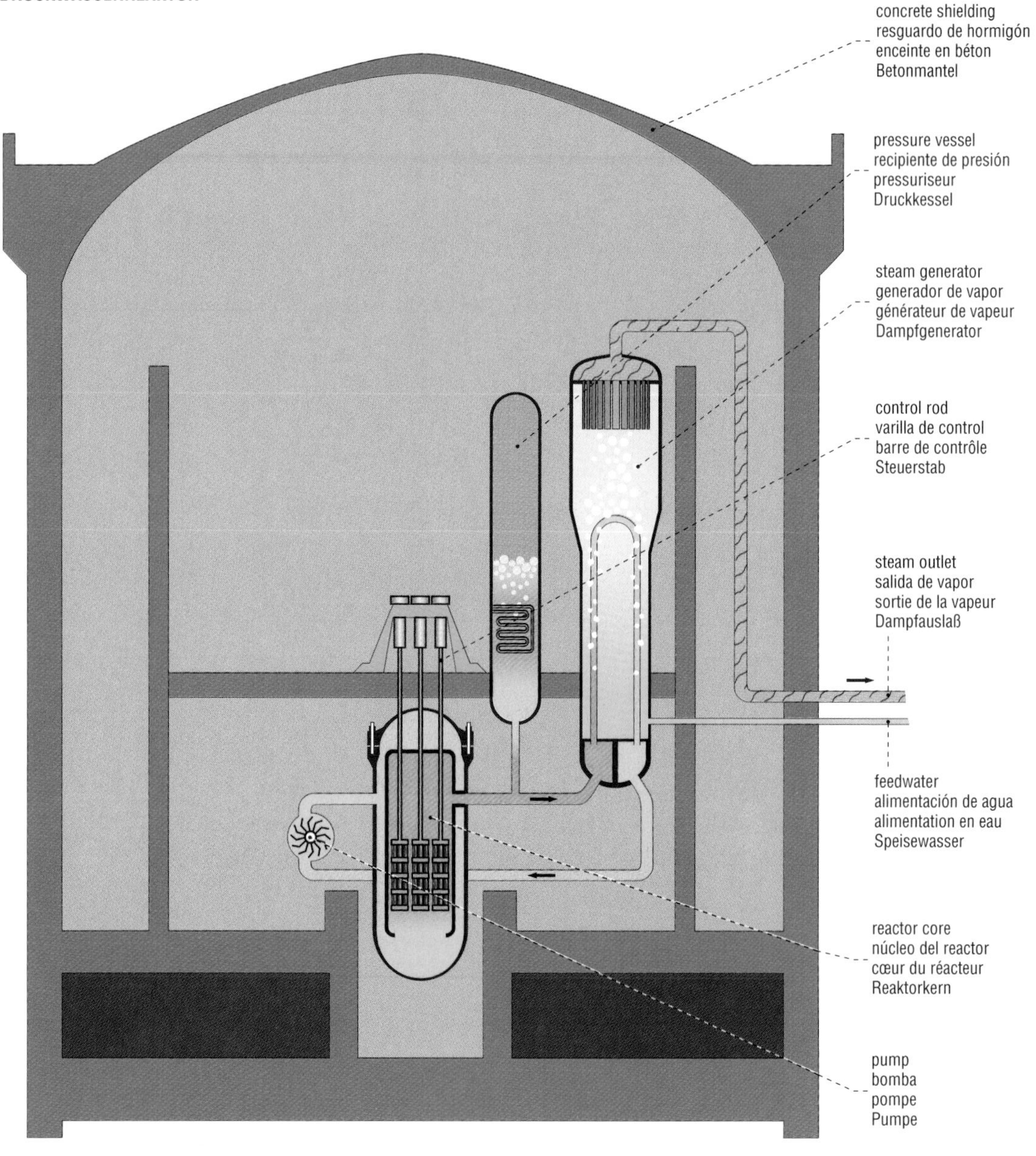

concrete shielding
resguardo de hormigón
enceinte en béton
Betonmantel

pressure vessel
recipiente de presión
pressuriseur
Druckkessel

steam generator
generador de vapor
générateur de vapeur
Dampfgenerator

control rod
varilla de control
barre de contrôle
Steuerstab

steam outlet
salida de vapor
sortie de la vapeur
Dampfauslaß

feedwater
alimentación de agua
alimentation en eau
Speisewasser

reactor core
núcleo del reactor
cœur du réacteur
Reaktorkern

pump
bomba
pompe
Pumpe

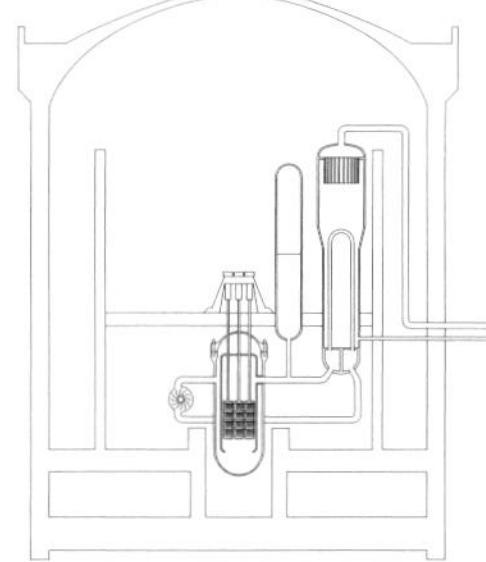

fuel: enriched uranium
combustible: uranio enriquecido
combustible: uranium enrichi
Brennstoff: angereichertes Uran

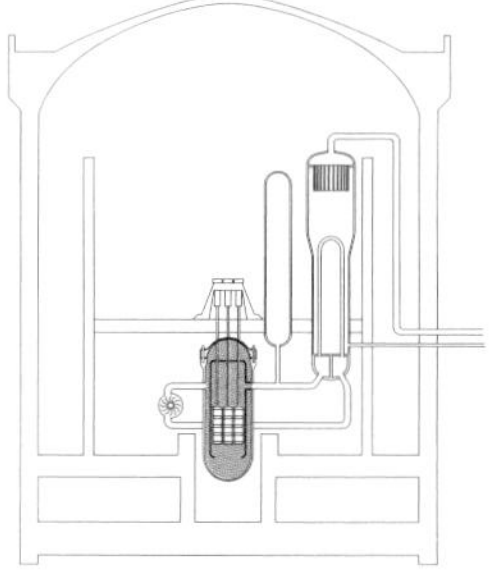

moderator: natural water
moderador: agua natural
modérateur: eau naturelle
Moderator: Wasser

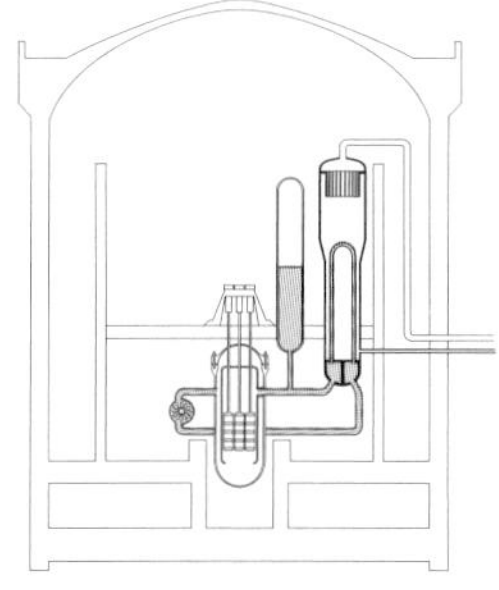

coolant: pressurized water
refrigerante: agua a presión
caloporteur: eau sous pression
Kühlmittel: Druckwasser

BOILING-WATER REACTOR
REACTOR DE AGUA HIRVIENTE
RÉACTEUR À EAU BOUILLANTE
SIEDEWASSERREAKTOR

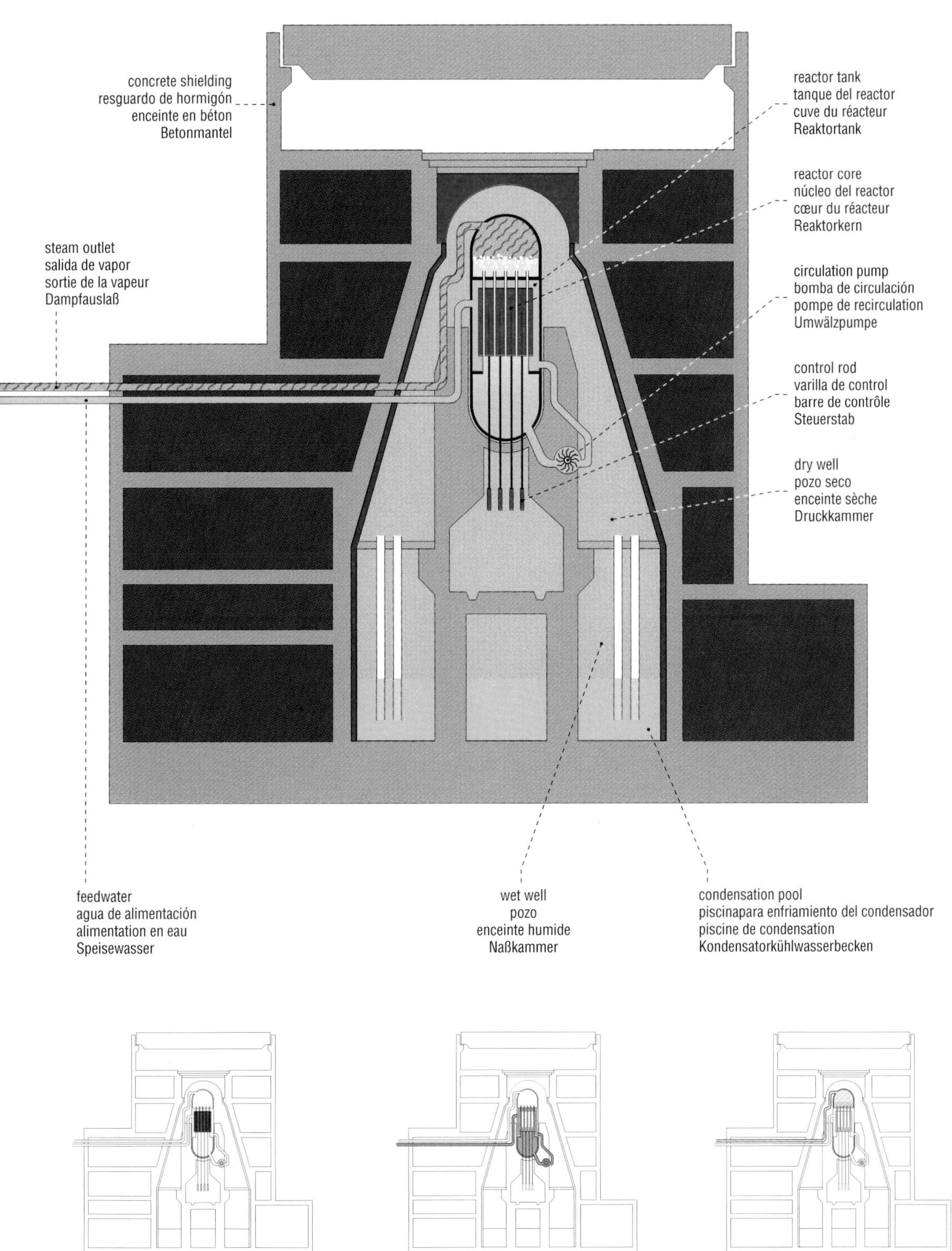

concrete shielding
resguardo de hormigón
enceinte en béton
Betonmantel
reactor tank
tanque del reactor
cuve du réacteur
Reaktortank
reactor core
núcleo del reactor
cœur du réacteur
Reaktorkern
steam outlet
salida de vapor
sortie de la vapeur
Dampfauslaß
circulation pump
bomba de circulación
pompe de recirculation
Umwälzpumpe
control rod
varilla de control
barre de contrôle
Steuerstab
dry well
pozo seco
enceinte sèche
Druckkammer
feedwater
agua de alimentación
alimentation en eau
Speisewasser
wet well
pozo
enceinte humide
Naßkammer
condensation pool
piscinapara enfriamiento del condensador
piscine de condensation
Kondensatorkühlwasserbecken

fuel: enriched uranium
combustible: uranio enriquecido
combustible: uranium enrichi
Brennstoff: angereichertes Uran

moderator: natural water
moderador: agua natural
modérateur: eau naturelle
Moderator: Wasser

coolant: boiling water
refrigerante: agua hirviente
caloporteur: eau bouillante
Kühlmittel: Siedewasser

FUEL HANDLING SEQUENCE
SECUENCIA EN EL MANEJO DE COMBUSTIBLE
SÉQUENCE DE MANIPULATION DU COMBUSTIBLE
BRENNELEMENTEBESCHICKUNG

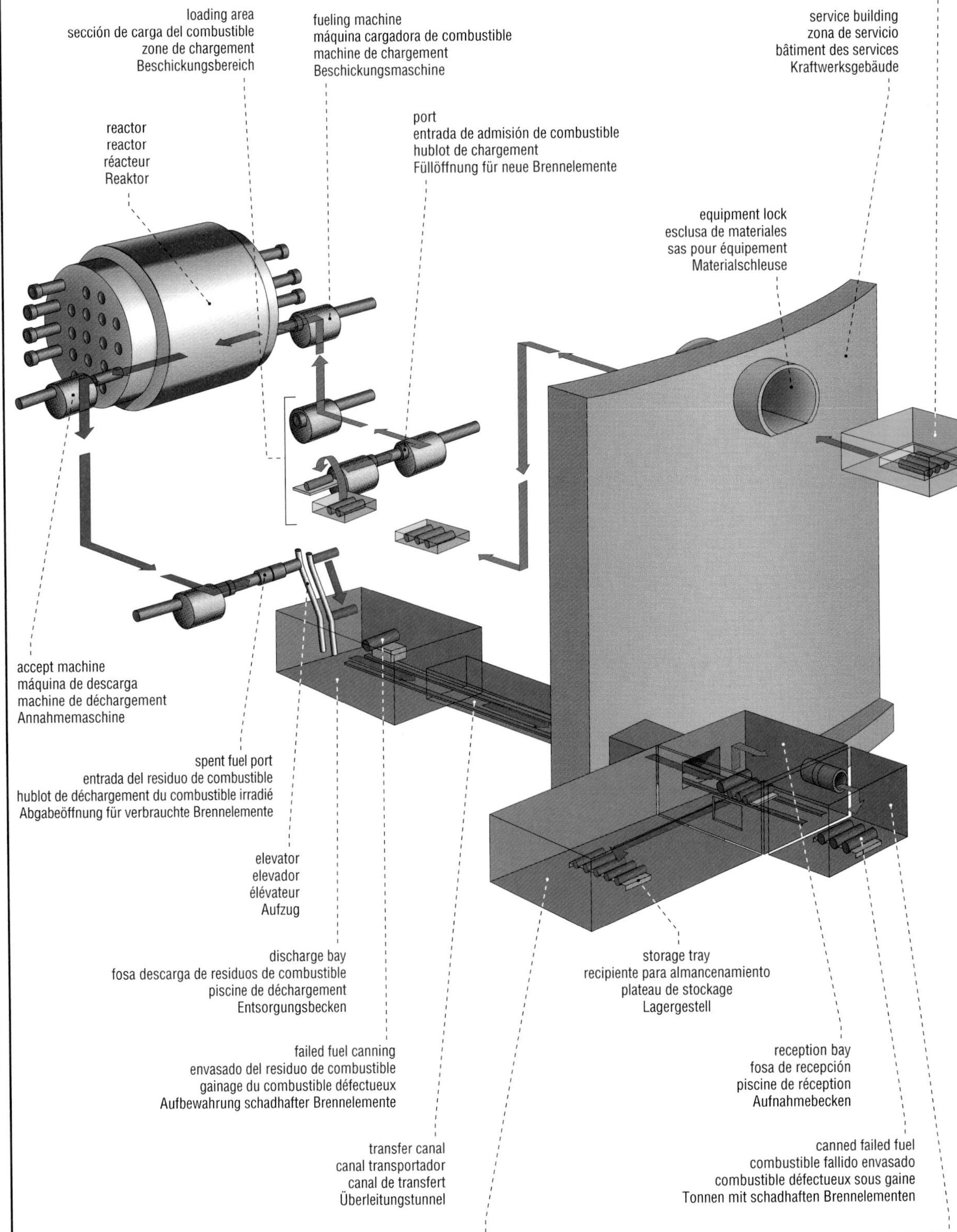
new fuel storage room
almacén de combustible nuevo
salle de stockage du combustible neuf
Lagerraum für neue Brennelemente
loading area
sección de carga del combustible
zone de chargement
Beschickungsbereich
fueling machine
máquina cargadora de combustible
machine de chargement
Beschickungsmaschine
service building
zona de servicio
bâtiment des services
Kraftwerksgebäude
reactor
reactor
réacteur
Reaktor
port
entrada de admisión de combustible
hublot de chargement
Füllöffnung für neue Brennelemente
equipment lock
esclusa de materiales
sas pour équipement
Materialschleuse
accept machine
máquina de descarga
machine de déchargement
Annahmemaschine
spent fuel port
entrada del residuo de combustible
hublot de déchargement du combustible irradié
Abgabeöffnung für verbrauchte Brennelemente
elevator
elevador
élévateur
Aufzug
discharge bay
fosa descarga de residuos de combustible
piscine de déchargement
Entsorgungsbecken
storage tray
recipiente para almancenamiento
plateau de stockage
Lagergestell
failed fuel canning
envasado del residuo de combustible
gainage du combustible défectueux
Aufbewahrung schadhafter Brennelemente
reception bay
fosa de recepción
piscine de réception
Aufnahmebecken
transfer canal
canal transportador
canal de transfert
Überleitungstunnel
canned failed fuel
combustible fallido envasado
combustible défectueux sous gaine
Tonnen mit schadhaften Brennelementen
spent fuel storage bay
fosa de desechos de combustible
piscine de stockage du combustible irradié
Abklingbecken
failed fuel bay
fosa de combustible fallido
piscine du combustible défectueux
Becken für schadhafte Brennelement

FUEL BUNDLE
ELEMENTO CARGADOR DE COMBUSTIBLE
GRAPPE DE COMBUSTIBLE
BRENNELEMENT

spacer
separador
patin d'espacement
Distanzstück

pressure tube
inyector de píldoras
tube de force
druckfestes Außenrohr

end plate
placa terminal
grille d'extrémité
Abschlußplatte

pencil
inyector unitario de alimentación
crayon
Brennstab

bearing pad
soporte
patin d'appui
Lagerraster

pencil
inyector unitario de alimentación
crayon
Brennstab

fuel pellet
píldora de combustible
pastille de combustible
Brennstofftablette

end plate
placa terminal
grille d'extrémité
Abschlußplatte

end cap
tapa
bouchon
Endstück

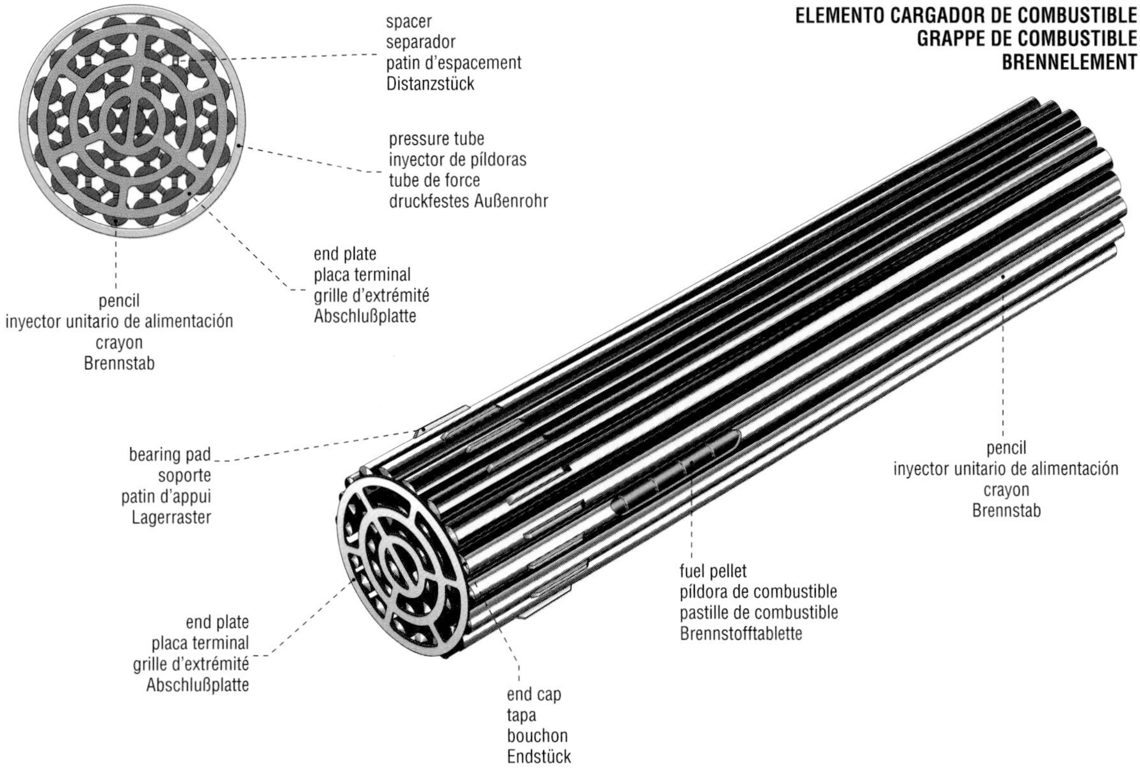

NUCLEAR REACTOR
CARGA DEL REACTOR NUCLEAR
RÉACTEUR NUCLÉAIRE
KERNREAKTOR

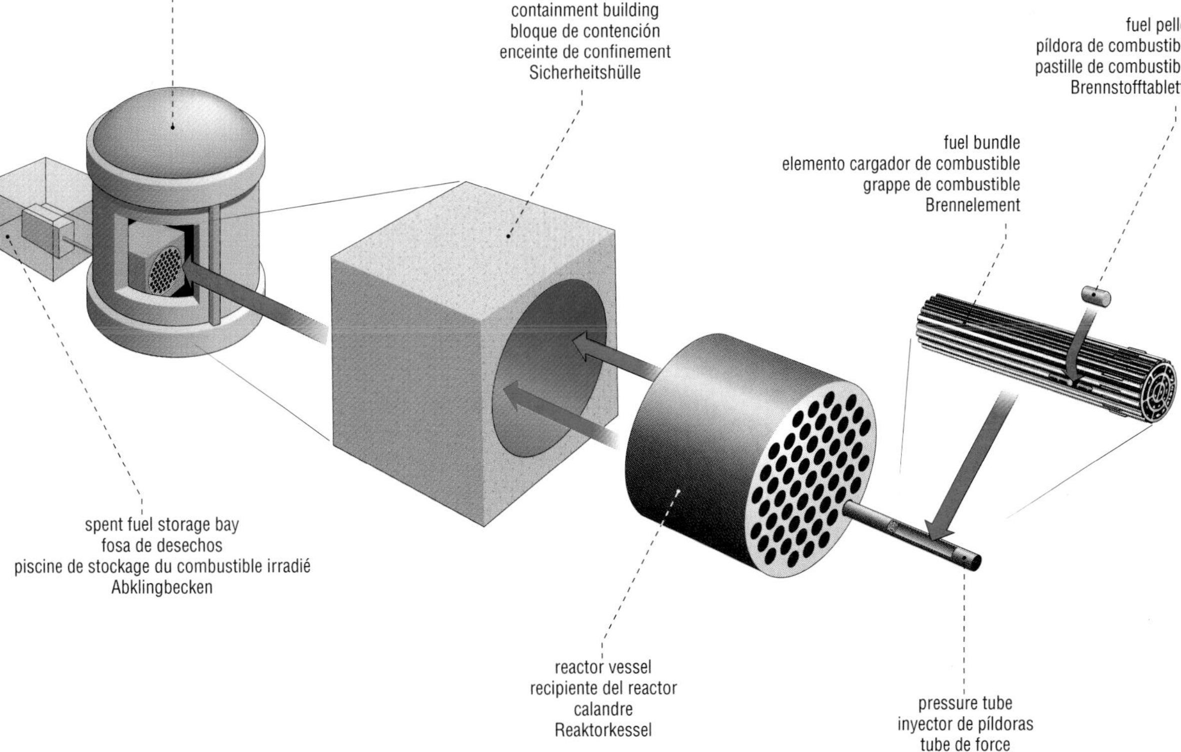
reactor building
edificio del reactor
bâtiment du réacteur
Reaktorgebäude
containment building
bloque de contención
enceinte de confinement
Sicherheitshülle
fuel pellet
píldora de combustible
pastille de combustible
Brennstofftablette
fuel bundle
elemento cargador de combustible
grappe de combustible
Brennelement
spent fuel storage bay
fosa de desechos
piscine de stockage du combustible irradié
Abklingbecken
reactor vessel
recipiente del reactor
calandre
Reaktorkessel
pressure tube
inyector de píldoras
tube de force
druckfestes Außenrohr

NUCLEAR ENERGY
ENERGÍA NUCLEAR
ÉNERGIE NUCLÉAIRE
KERNENERGIE

PRODUCTION OF ELECTRICITY FROM NUCLEAR ENERGY
PRODUCCIÓN DE ELECTRICIDAD POR MEDIO DE ENERGÍA NUCLEAR
PRODUCTION D'ÉLECTRICITÉ PAR ÉNERGIE NUCLÉAIRE
STROMERZEUGUNG AUS KERNENERGIE

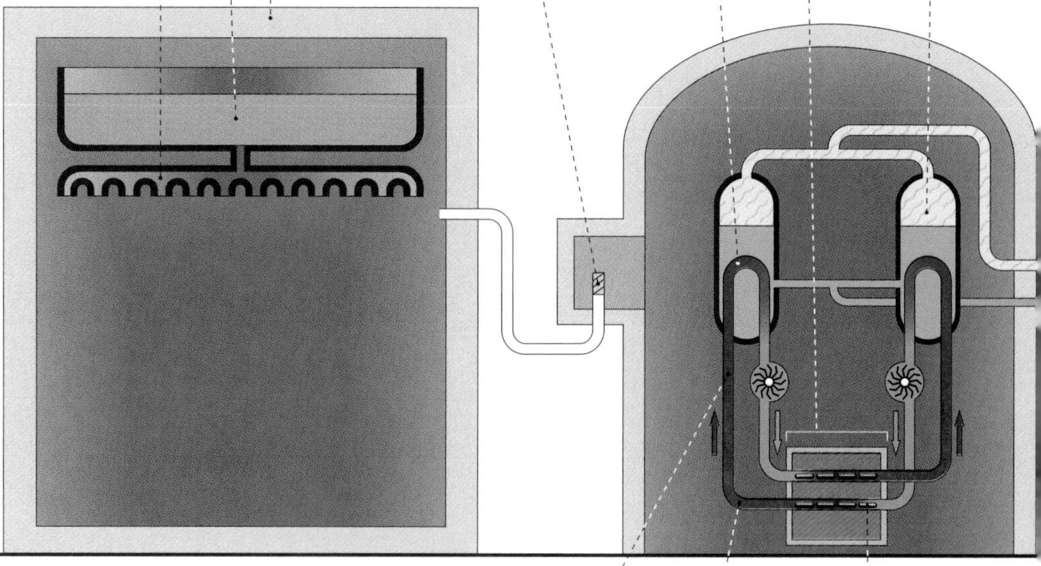

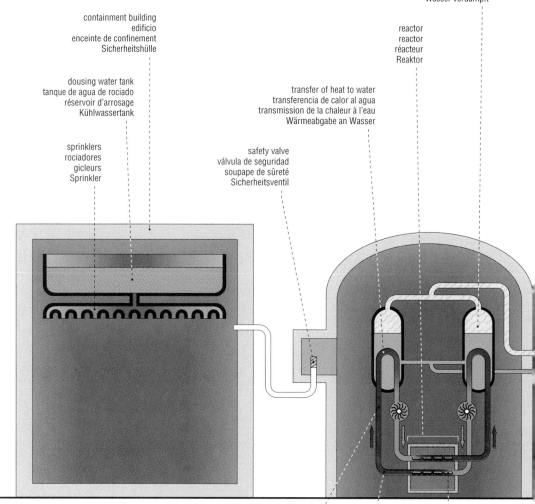

water turns into steam
conversión del agua en vapor
transformation de l'eau en vapeur
Wasser verdampft

containment building
edificio
enceinte de confinement
Sicherheitshülle

reactor
reactor
réacteur
Reaktor

dousing water tank
tanque de agua de rociado
réservoir d'arrosage
Kühlwassertank

transfer of heat to water
transferencia de calor al agua
transmission de la chaleur à l'eau
Wärmeabgabe an Wasser

sprinklers
rociadores
gicleurs
Sprinkler

safety valve
válvula de seguridad
soupape de sûreté
Sicherheitsventil

coolant transfers the heat to the steam generator
el refrigerante transfiere el calor al generador de vapor
acheminement de la chaleur au générateur de vapeur par le caloporteur
Kühlmittel überträgt Wärme an Dampfgenerator

heat production
producción de calor
production de chaleur
Wärmeerzeugung

fission of uranium fuel
uranio en fisión
fission de l'uranium
Spaltung des Uranbrennstoffs

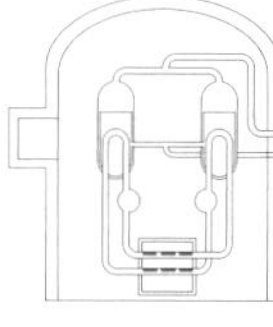

fuel
combustible
combustible
Brennstoff

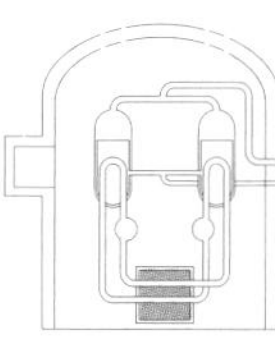

moderator
moderador
modérateur
Moderator

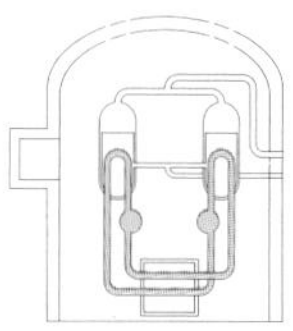

coolant
refrigerante
caloporteur
Kühlmittel

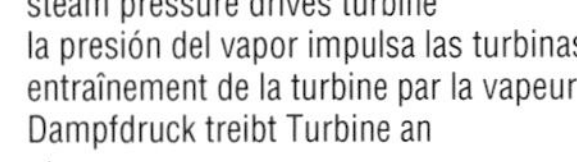

steam pressure drives turbine
la presión del vapor impulsa las turbinas
entraînement de la turbine par la vapeur
Dampfdruck treibt Turbine an

electricity transmission
transmisión de electricidad
transport de l'électricité
Stromfortleitung

voltage increase
ampliación del voltaje
élévation de la tension
Spannungserhöhung

turbine shaft turns generator
la flecha de la turbina hace girar el generador
entraînement du rotor de l'alternateur
Turbinenwelle treibt Generator an

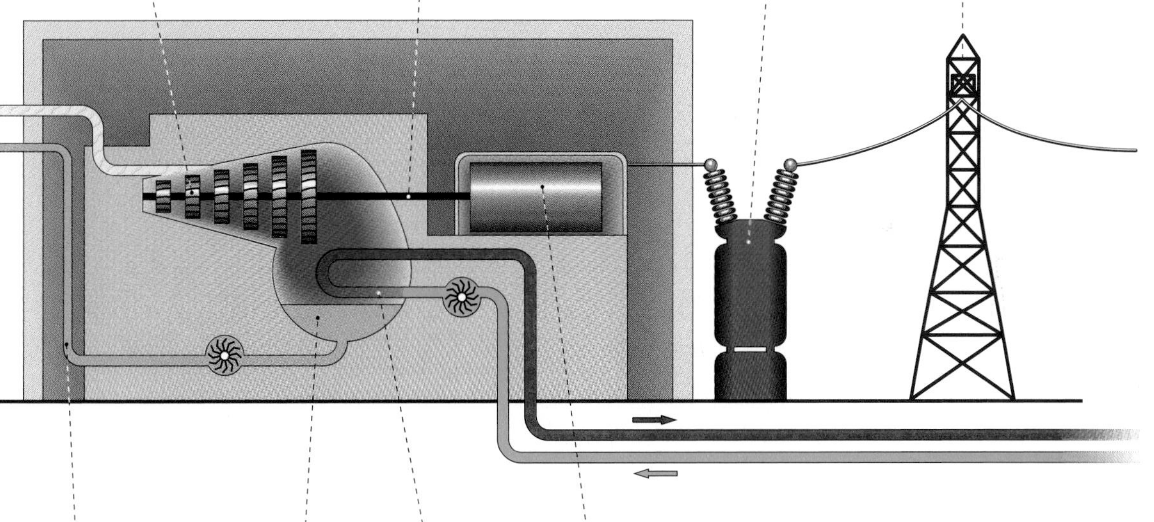

electricity production
producción de electricidad
production d'électricité
Stromerzeugung

water cools the used steam
el agua de un lago o de un río enfría el vapor utilizado
refroidissement de la vapeur par l'eau
Wasser kühlt Brauchdampf ab

condensation of steam into water
el vapor se condensa en agua
condensation de la vapeur
Dampf kondensiert zu Wasser

water is pumped back into the steam generator
el agua regresa al generador de vapor
retour de l'eau au générateur de vapeur
Wasser wird zum Dampfgenerator zurückgepumpt

SOLAR ENERGY
ENERGÍA SOLAR
ÉNERGIE SOLAIRE
SONNENENERGIE

SOLAR CELL
CELDA SOLAR
PHOTOPILE
SOLARZELLE

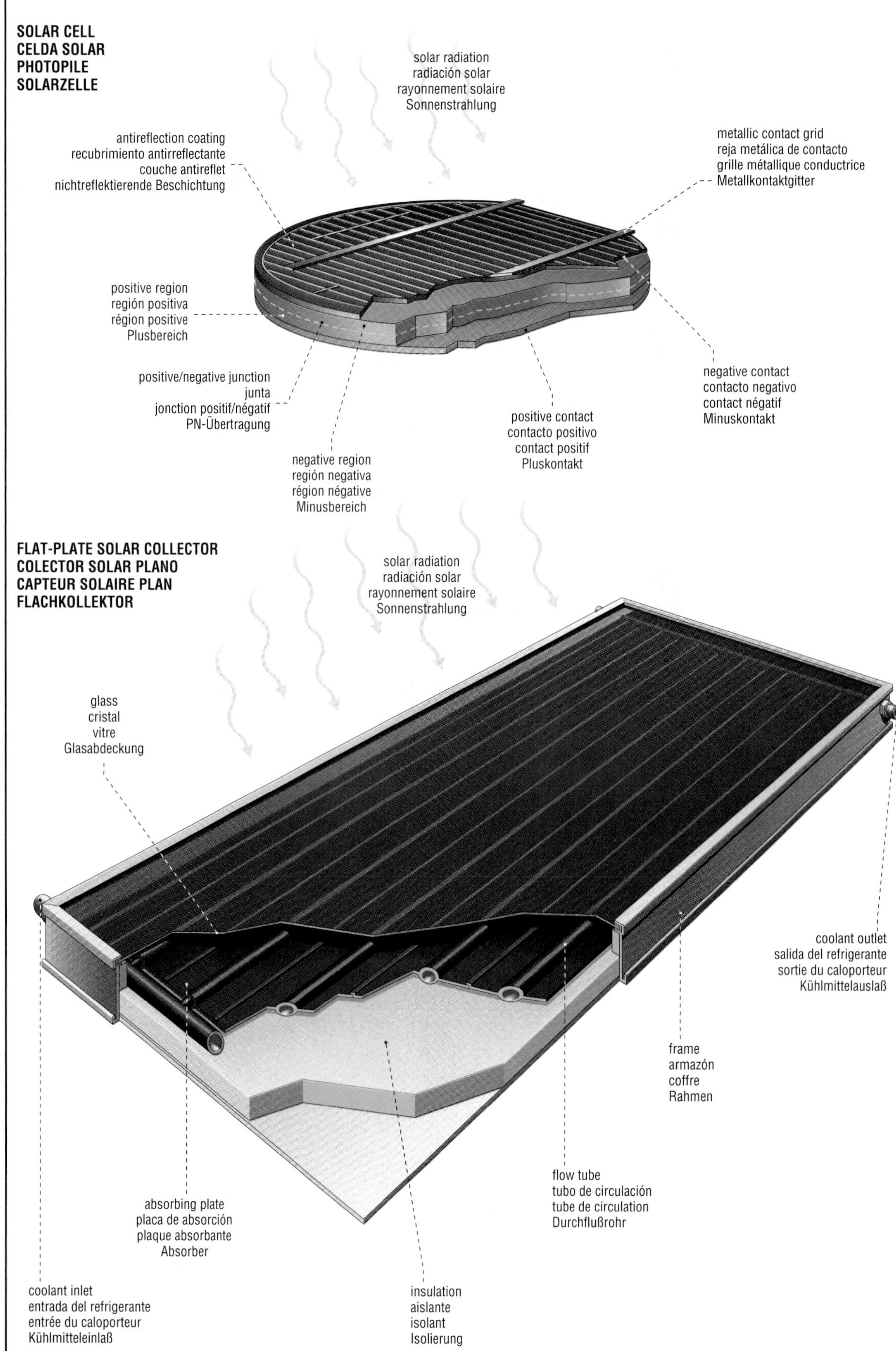
solar radiation
radiación solar
rayonnement solaire
Sonnenstrahlung
antireflection coating
recubrimiento antirreflectante
couche antireflet
nichtreflektierende Beschichtung
metallic contact grid
reja metálica de contacto
grille métallique conductrice
Metallkontaktgitter
positive region
región positiva
région positive
Plusbereich
positive/negative junction
junta
jonction positif/négatif
PN-Übertragung
negative contact
contacto negativo
contact négatif
Minuskontakt
positive contact
contacto positivo
contact positif
Pluskontakt
negative region
región negativa
région négative
Minusbereich
FLAT-PLATE SOLAR COLLECTOR
COLECTOR SOLAR PLANO
CAPTEUR SOLAIRE PLAN
FLACHKOLLEKTOR
solar radiation
radiación solar
rayonnement solaire
Sonnenstrahlung
glass
cristal
vitre
Glasabdeckung
coolant outlet
salida del refrigerante
sortie du caloporteur
Kühlmittelauslaß
frame
armazón
coffre
Rahmen
flow tube
tubo de circulación
tube de circulation
Durchflußrohr
absorbing plate
placa de absorción
plaque absorbante
Absorber
coolant inlet
entrada del refrigerante
entrée du caloporteur
Kühlmitteleinlaß
insulation
aislante
isolant
Isolierung

SOLAR-CELL SYSTEM
SISTEMA DE CELDAS SOLARES
CIRCUIT DE PHOTOPILES
SOLARZELLENSYSTEM

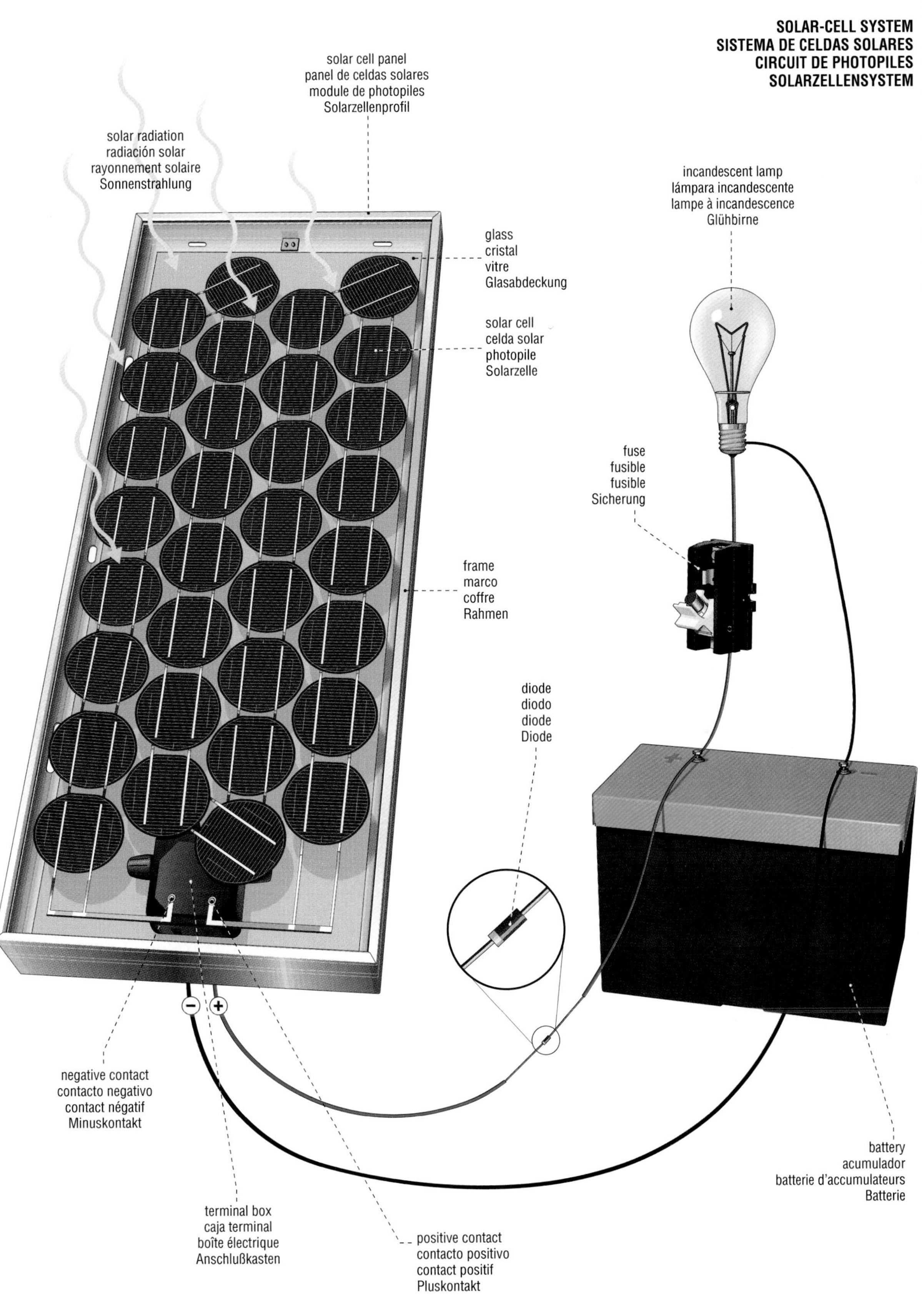
solar cell panel
panel de celdas solares
module de photopiles
Solarzellenprofil
solar radiation
radiación solar
rayonnement solaire
Sonnenstrahlung
glass
cristal
vitre
Glasabdeckung
solar cell
celda solar
photopile
Solarzelle
frame
marco
coffre
Rahmen
incandescent lamp
lámpara incandescente
lampe à incandescence
Glühbirne
fuse
fusible
fusible
Sicherung
diode
diodo
diode
Diode
negative contact
contacto negativo
contact négatif
Minuskontakt
terminal box
caja terminal
boîte électrique
Anschlußkasten
positive contact
contacto positivo
contact positif
Pluskontakt
battery
acumulador
batterie d'accumulateurs
Batterie

SOLAR ENERGY
ENERGÍA SOLAR
ÉNERGIE SOLAIRE
SONNENENERGIE

SOLAR FURNACE
HORNO SOLAR
FOUR SOLAIRE
SONNENOFEN

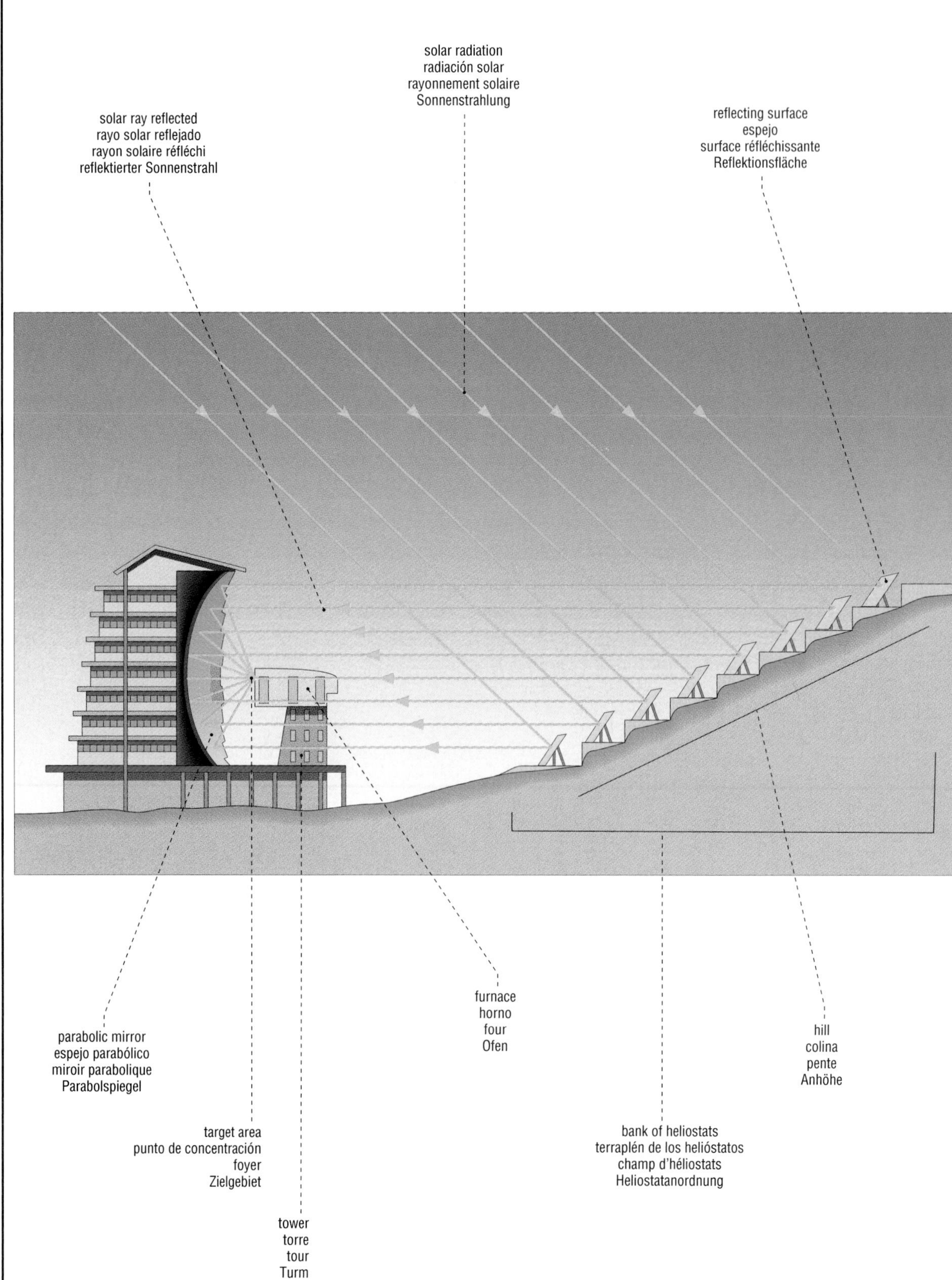

solar radiation
radiación solar
rayonnement solaire
Sonnenstrahlung
solar ray reflected
rayo solar reflejado
rayon solaire réfléchi
reflektierter Sonnenstrahl
reflecting surface
espejo
surface réfléchissante
Reflektionsfläche
parabolic mirror
espejo parabólico
miroir parabolique
Parabolspiegel
furnace
horno
four
Ofen
hill
colina
pente
Anhöhe
target area
punto de concentración
foyer
Zielgebiet
bank of heliostats
terraplén de los helióstatos
champ d'héliostats
Heliostatanordnung
tower
torre
tour
Turm

PRODUCTION OF ELECTRICITY FROM SOLAR ENERGY
PRODUCCIÓN DE ELECTRICIDAD POR ENERGÍA SOLAR
PRODUCTION D'ÉLECTRICITÉ PAR ÉNERGIE SOLAIRE
STROMERZEUGUNG AUS SONNENENERGIE

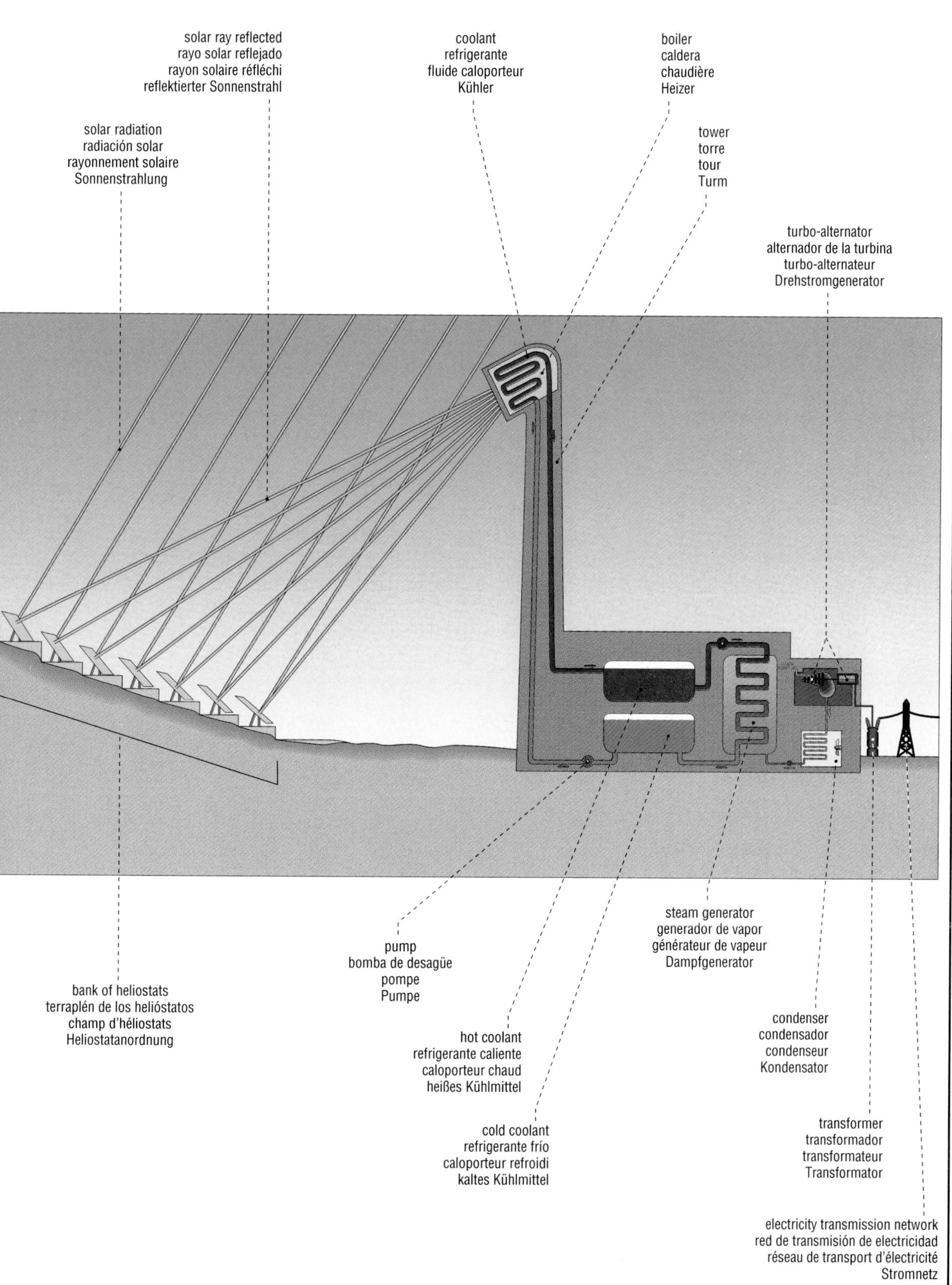

solar ray reflected
rayo solar reflejado
rayon solaire réfléchi
reflektierter Sonnenstrahl
coolant
refrigerante
fluide caloporteur
Kühler
boiler
caldera
chaudière
Heizer
solar radiation
radiación solar
rayonnement solaire
Sonnenstrahlung
tower
torre
tour
Turm
turbo-alternator
alternador de la turbina
turbo-alternateur
Drehstromgenerator
steam generator
generador de vapor
générateur de vapeur
Dampfgenerator
pump
bomba de desagüe
pompe
Pumpe
bank of heliostats
terraplén de los helióstatos
champ d'héliostats
Heliostatanordnung
hot coolant
refrigerante caliente
caloporteur chaud
heißes Kühlmittel
condenser
condensador
condenseur
Kondensator
cold coolant
refrigerante frío
caloporteur refroidi
kaltes Kühlmittel
transformer
transformador
transformateur
Transformator
electricity transmission network
red de transmisión de electricidad
réseau de transport d'électricité
Stromnetz

SOLAR ENERGY
ENERGÍA SOLAR
ÉNERGIE SOLAIRE
SONNENENERGIE

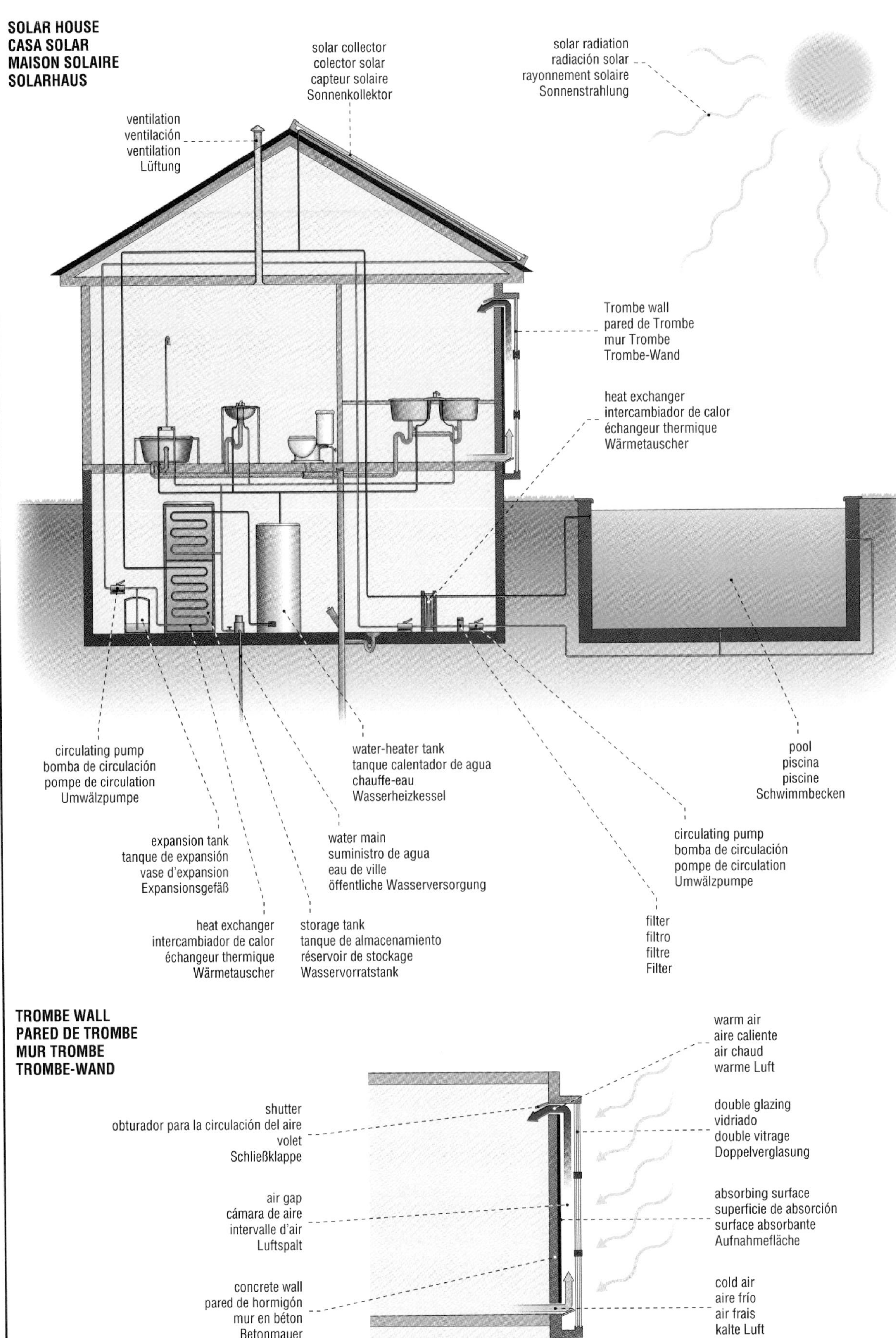

SOLAR HOUSE
CASA SOLAR
MAISON SOLAIRE
SOLARHAUS
solar collector
colector solar
capteur solaire
Sonnenkollektor
solar radiation
radiación solar
rayonnement solaire
Sonnenstrahlung
ventilation
ventilación
ventilation
Lüftung
Trombe wall
pared de Trombe
mur Trombe
Trombe-Wand
heat exchanger
intercambiador de calor
échangeur thermique
Wärmetauscher
circulating pump
bomba de circulación
pompe de circulation
Umwälzpumpe
water-heater tank
tanque calentador de agua
chauffe-eau
Wasserheizkessel
pool
piscina
piscine
Schwimmbecken
expansion tank
tanque de expansión
vase d'expansion
Expansionsgefäß
water main
suministro de agua
eau de ville
öffentliche Wasserversorgung
circulating pump
bomba de circulación
pompe de circulation
Umwälzpumpe
heat exchanger
intercambiador de calor
échangeur thermique
Wärmetauscher
storage tank
tanque de almacenamiento
réservoir de stockage
Wasservorratstank
filter
filtro
filtre
Filter
TROMBE WALL
PARED DE TROMBE
MUR TROMBE
TROMBE-WAND
warm air
aire caliente
air chaud
warme Luft
shutter
obturador para la circulación del aire
volet
Schließklappe
double glazing
vidriado
double vitrage
Doppelverglasung
absorbing surface
superficie de absorción
surface absorbante
Aufnahmefläche
air gap
cámara de aire
intervalle d'air
Luftspalt
concrete wall
pared de hormigón
mur en béton
Betonmauer
cold air
aire frío
air frais
kalte Luft

WIND ENERGY
ENERGÍA EÓLICA
ÉNERGIE ÉOLIENNE
WINDENERGIE

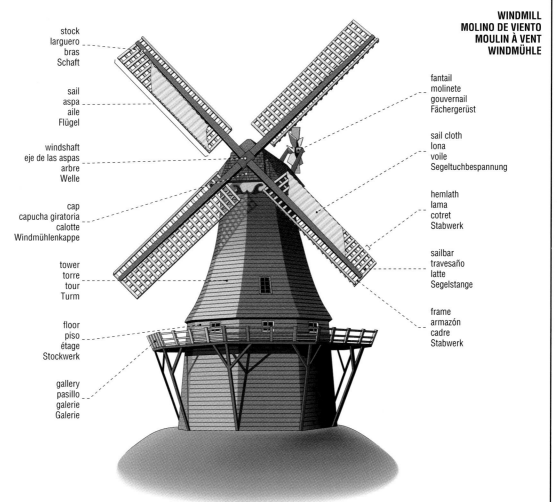

WINDMILL
MOLINO DE VIENTO
MOULIN À VENT
WINDMÜHLE

stock
larguero
bras
Schaft

sail
aspa
aile
Flügel

windshaft
eje de las aspas
arbre
Welle

cap
capucha giratoria
calotte
Windmühlenkappe

tower
torre
tour
Turm

floor
piso
étage
Stockwerk

gallery
pasillo
galerie
Galerie

fantail
molinete
gouvernail
Fächergerüst

sail cloth
lona
voile
Segeltuchbespannung

hemlath
lama
cotret
Stabwerk

sailbar
travesaño
latte
Segelstange

frame
armazón
cadre
Stabwerk

POST MILL
MOLINO DE PLATAFORMA GIRATORIA
MOULIN PIVOT
BOCKMÜHLE

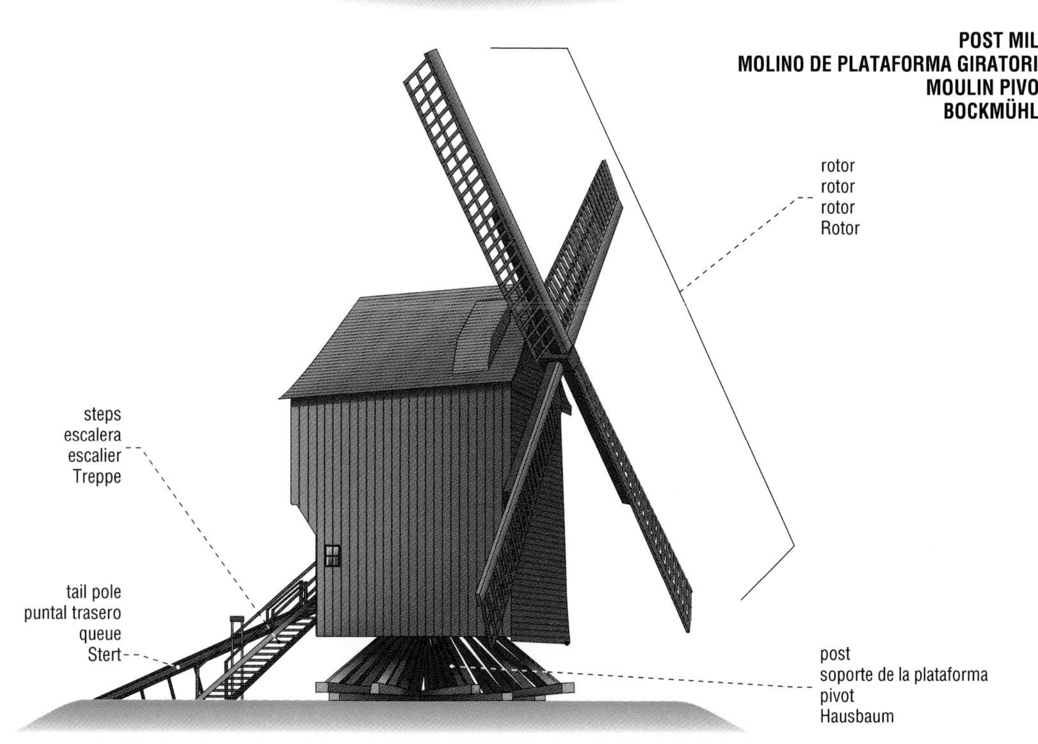
rotor
rotor
rotor
Rotor
steps
escalera
escalier
Treppe
tail pole
puntal trasero
queue
Stert
post
soporte de la plataforma
pivot
Hausbaum

WIND ENERGY
ENERGÍA EÓLICA
ÉNERGIE ÉOLIENNE
WINDENERGIE

HORIZONTAL-AXIS WIND TURBINE
TURBINA DE VIENTO DE EJE HORIZONTAL
ÉOLIENNE À AXE HORIZONTAL
LÄNGSACHSENWINDTURBINE

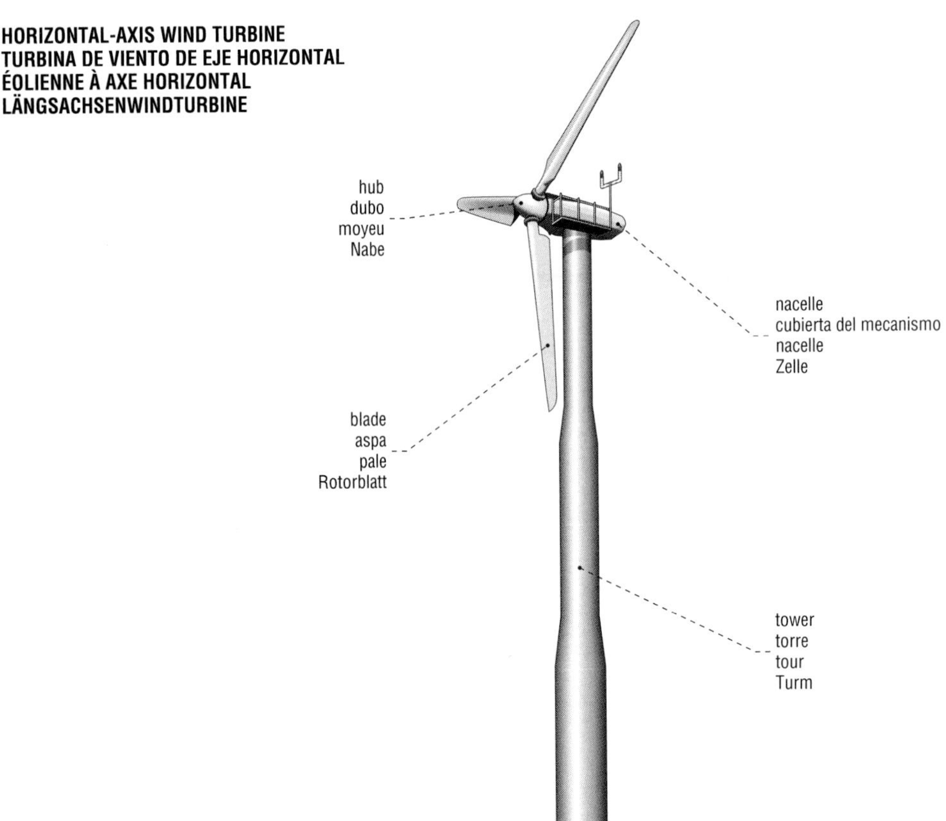
hub
dubo
moyeu
Nabe
nacelle
cubierta del mecanismo
nacelle
Zelle
blade
aspa
pale
Rotorblatt
tower
torre
tour
Turm

VERTICAL-AXIS WIND TURBINE
TURBINA DE VIENTO DE EJE VERTICAL
ÉOLIENNE À AXE VERTICAL
VERTIKALACHSENWINDTURBINE

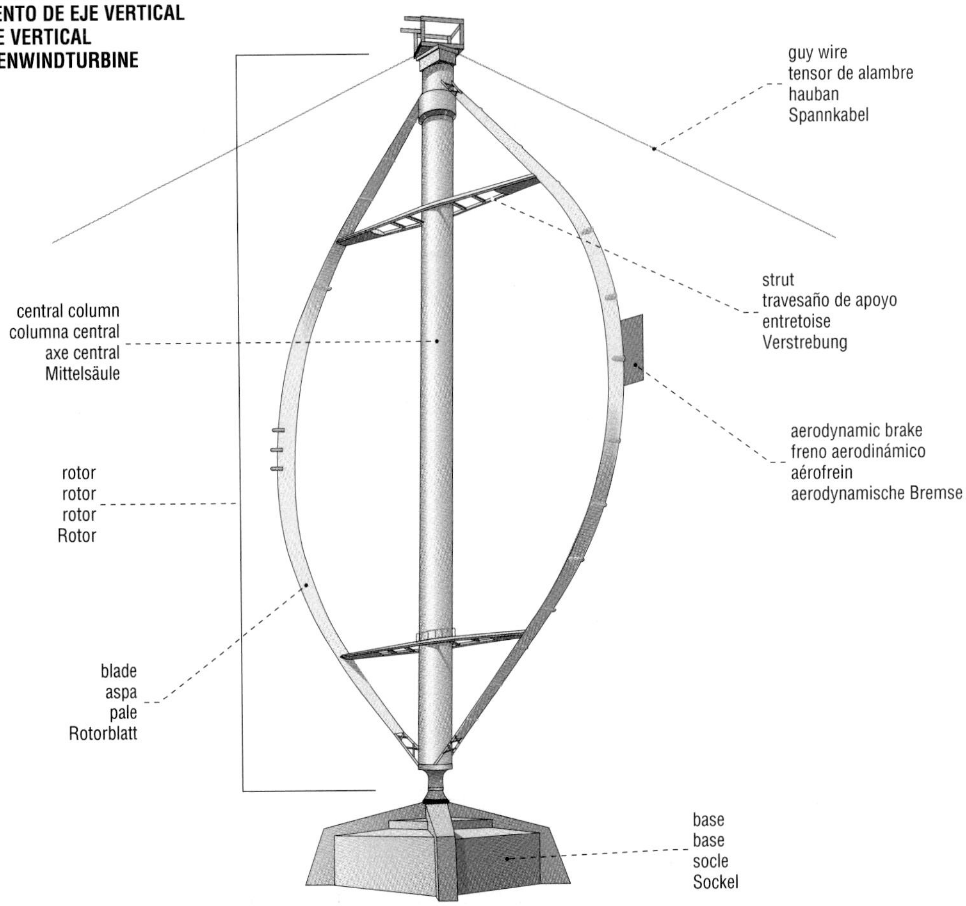

guy wire
tensor de alambre
hauban
Spannkabel

strut
travesaño de apoyo
entretoise
Verstrebung

central column
columna central
axe central
Mittelsäule

aerodynamic brake
freno aerodinámico
aérofrein
aerodynamische Bremse

rotor
rotor
rotor
Rotor

blade
aspa
pale
Rotorblatt

base
base
socle
Sockel

HEAVY MACHINERY
MAQUINARIA PESADA
ENGINS ET MACHINES
SCHWERMASCHINEN

CONTENTS

FIRE PREVENTION
PREVENCIÓN DE INCENDIOS
PRÉVENTION DES INCENDIES
BRANDBEKÄMPFUNG

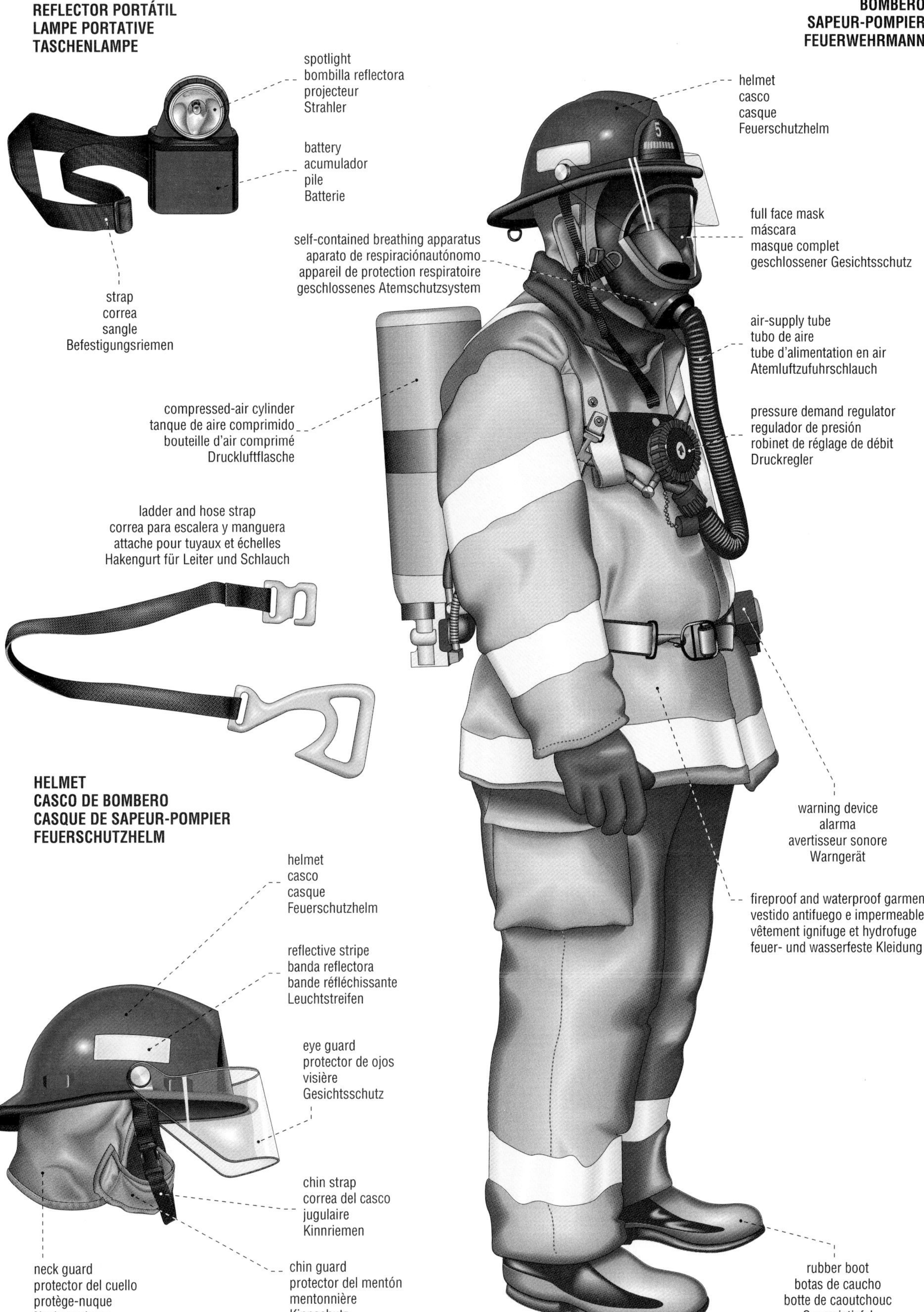
HAND LAMP
REFLECTOR PORTÁTIL
LAMPE PORTATIVE
TASCHENLAMPE
spotlight
bombilla reflectora
projecteur
Strahler
battery
acumulador
pile
Batterie
strap
correa
sangle
Befestigungsriemen
FIREMAN
BOMBERO
SAPEUR-POMPIER
FEUERWEHRMANN
helmet
casco
casque
Feuerschutzhelm
full face mask
máscara
masque complet
geschlossener Gesichtsschutz
self-contained breathing apparatus
aparato de respiraciónautónomo
appareil de protection respiratoire
geschlossenes Atemschutzsystem
air-supply tube
tubo de aire
tube d'alimentation en air
Atemluftzufuhrschlauch
compressed-air cylinder
tanque de aire comprimido
bouteille d'air comprimé
Druckluftflasche
pressure demand regulator
regulador de presión
robinet de réglage de débit
Druckregler
ladder and hose strap
correa para escalera y manguera
attache pour tuyaux et échelles
Hakengurt für Leiter und Schlauch
HELMET
CASCO DE BOMBERO
CASQUE DE SAPEUR-POMPIER
FEUERSCHUTZHELM
warning device
alarma
avertisseur sonore
Warngerät
helmet
casco
casque
Feuerschutzhelm
fireproof and waterproof garment
vestido antifuego e impermeable
vêtement ignifuge et hydrofuge
feuer- und wasserfeste Kleidung
reflective stripe
banda reflectora
bande réfléchissante
Leuchtstreifen
eye guard
protector de ojos
visière
Gesichtsschutz
chin strap
correa del casco
jugulaire
Kinnriemen
neck guard
protector del cuello
protège-nuque
Nackenschutz
chin guard
protector del mentón
mentonnière
Kinnschutz
rubber boot
botas de caucho
botte de caoutchouc
Gummistiefel

FIRE ENGINE
COCHE DE BOMBEROS
VÉHICULES D'INCENDIE
FEUERWEHRAUTO

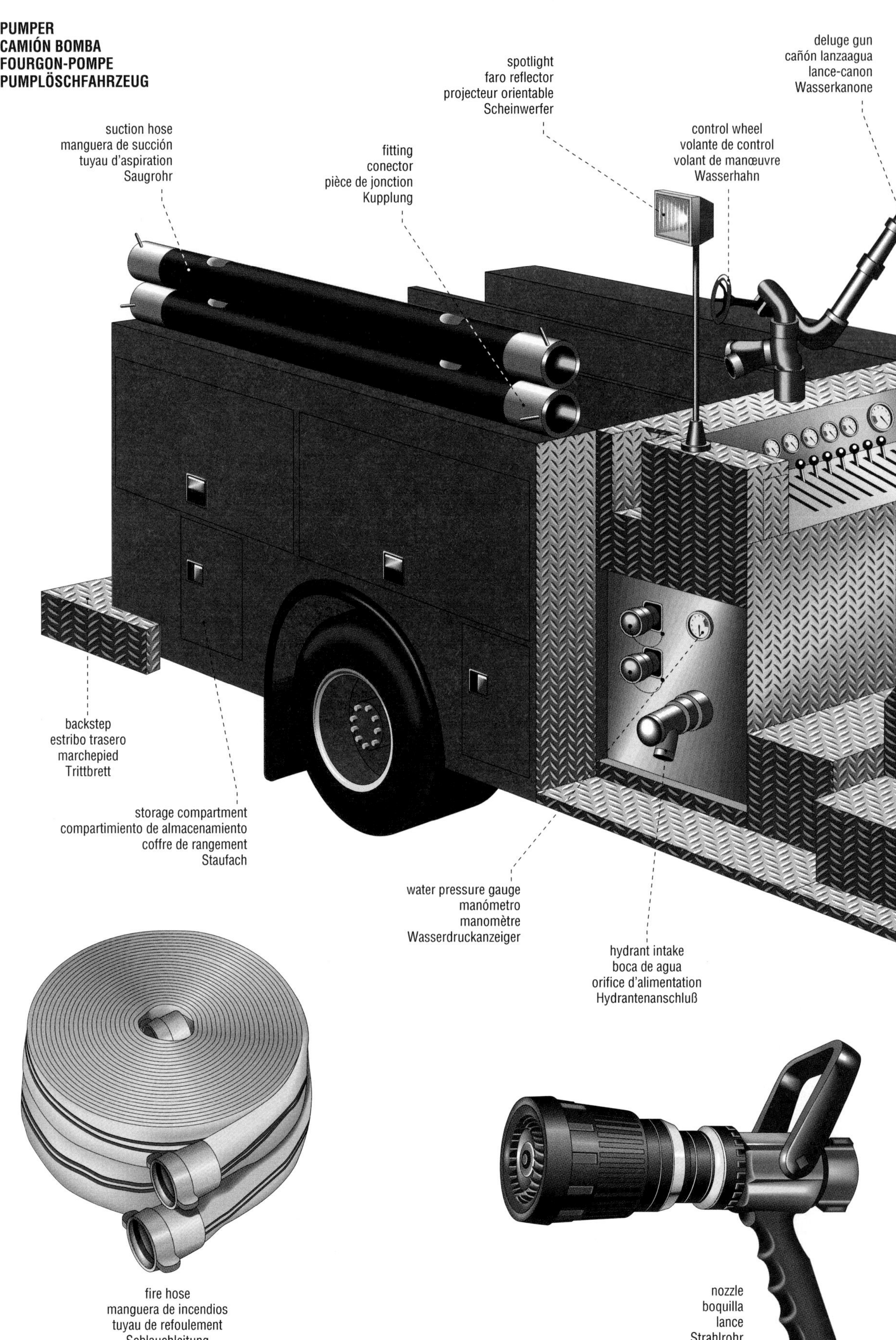
PUMPER
CAMIÓN BOMBA
FOURGON-POMPE
PUMPLÖSCHFAHRZEUG
suction hose
manguera de succión
tuyau d'aspiration
Saugrohr
fitting
conector
pièce de jonction
Kupplung
spotlight
faro reflector
projecteur orientable
Scheinwerfer
control wheel
volante de control
volant de manœuvre
Wasserhahn
deluge gun
cañón lanzaagua
lance-canon
Wasserkanone
backstep
estribo trasero
marchepied
Trittbrett
storage compartment
compartimiento de almacenamiento
coffre de rangement
Staufach
water pressure gauge
manómetro
manomètre
Wasserdruckanzeiger
hydrant intake
boca de agua
orifice d'alimentation
Hydrantenanschluß
fire hose
manguera de incendios
tuyau de refoulement
Schlauchleitung
nozzle
boquilla
lance
Strahlrohr

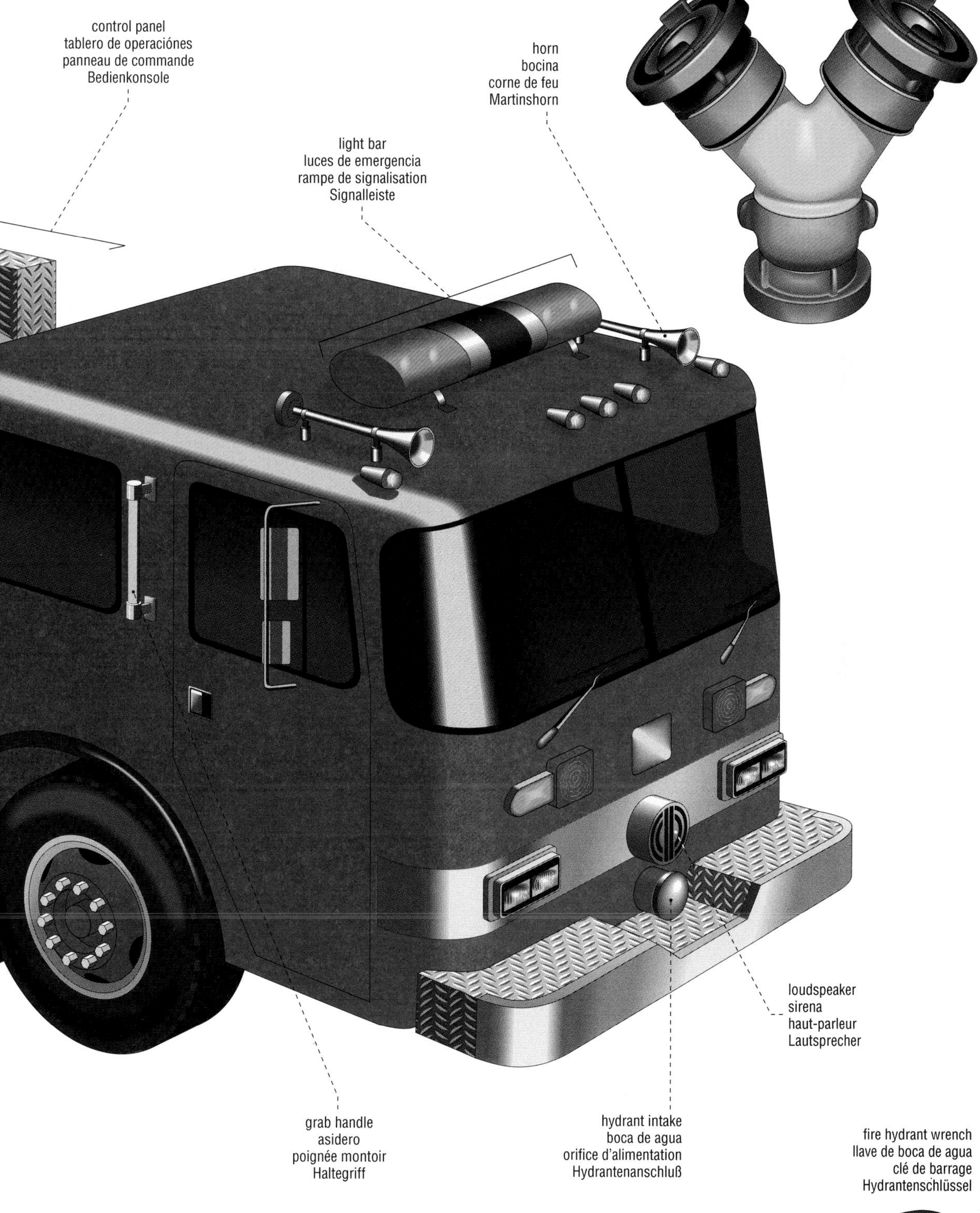
dividing breeching
separador de boca de agua
pièce d'embranchement
Y-Verbindungsstück
control panel
tablero de operaciónes
panneau de commande
Bedienkonsole
horn
bocina
corne de feu
Martinshorn
light bar
luces de emergencia
rampe de signalisation
Signalleiste
loudspeaker
sirena
haut-parleur
Lautsprecher
grab handle
asidero
poignée montoir
Haltegriff
hydrant intake
boca de agua
orifice d'alimentation
Hydrantenanschluß
fire hydrant wrench
llave de boca de agua
clé de barrage
Hydrantenschlüssel

FIRE ENGINE
COCHE DE BOMBEROS
VÉHICULES D'INCENDIE
FEUERWEHRAUTO

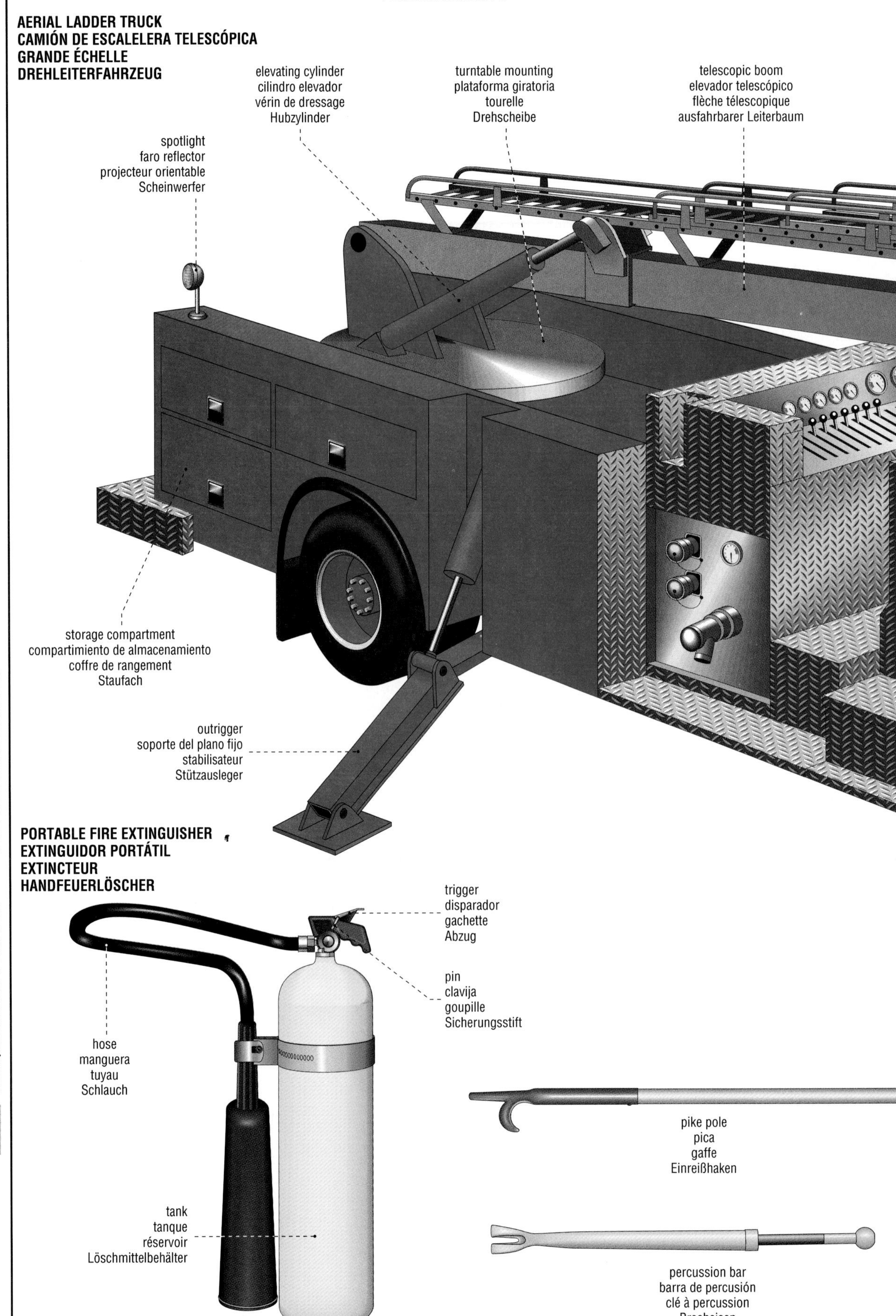
AERIAL LADDER TRUCK
CAMIÓN DE ESCALELERA TELESCÓPICA
GRANDE ÉCHELLE
DREHLEITERFAHRZEUG
elevating cylinder
cilindro elevador
vérin de dressage
Hubzylinder
turntable mounting
plataforma giratoria
tourelle
Drehscheibe
telescopic boom
elevador telescópico
flèche télescopique
ausfahrbarer Leiterbaum
spotlight
faro reflector
projecteur orientable
Scheinwerfer
storage compartment
compartimiento de almacenamiento
coffre de rangement
Staufach
outrigger
soporte del plano fijo
stabilisateur
Stützausleger
PORTABLE FIRE EXTINGUISHER
EXTINGUIDOR PORTÁTIL
EXTINCTEUR
HANDFEUERLÖSCHER
trigger
disparador
gachette
Abzug
pin
clavija
goupille
Sicherungsstift
hose
manguera
tuyau
Schlauch
tank
tanque
réservoir
Löschmittelbehälter
pike pole
pica
gaffe
Einreißhaken
percussion bar
barra de percusión
clé à percussion
Brecheisen

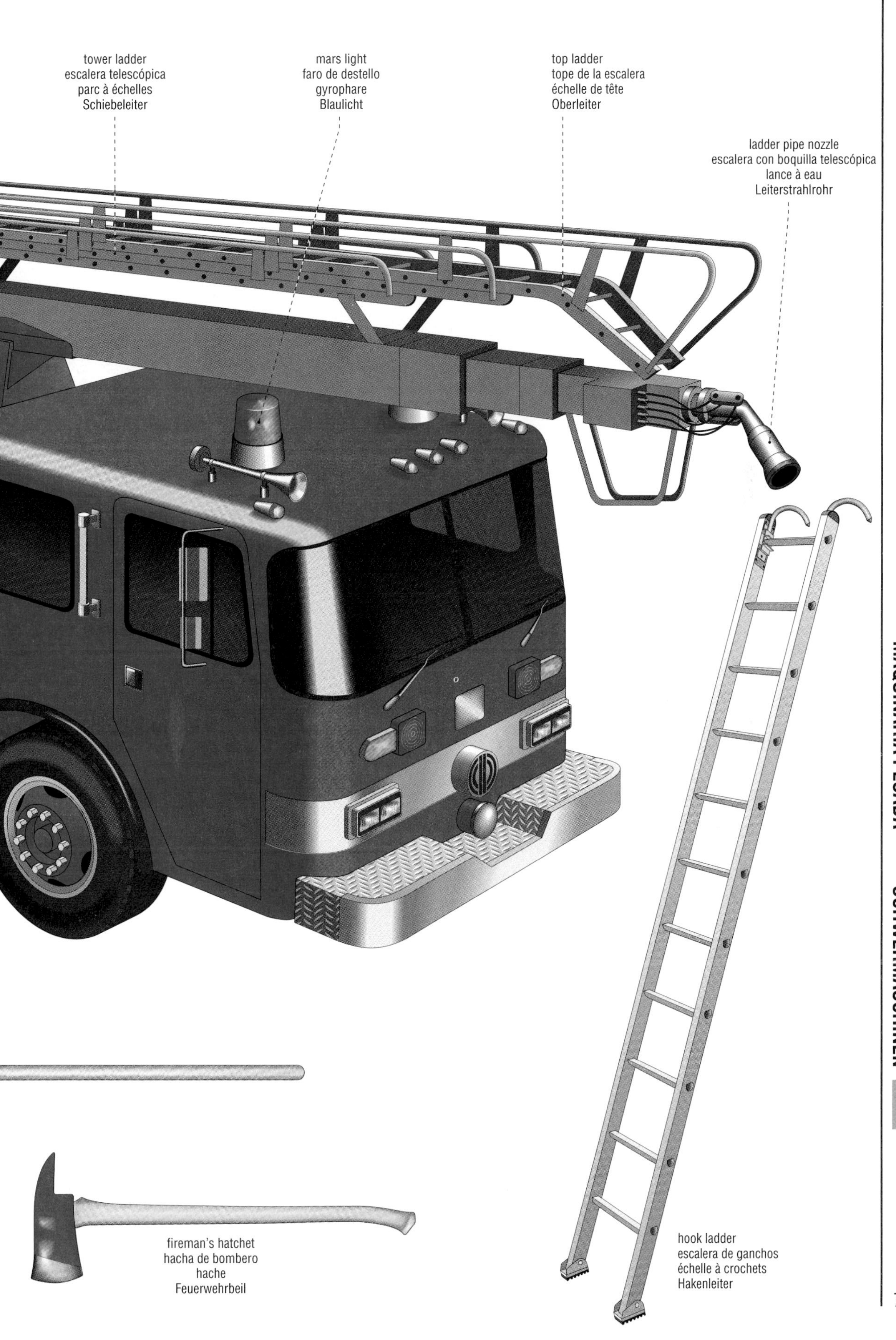
tower ladder
escalera telescópica
parc à échelles
Schiebeleiter
mars light
faro de destello
gyrophare
Blaulicht
top ladder
tope de la escalera
échelle de tête
Oberleiter
ladder pipe nozzle
escalera con boquilla telescópica
lance à eau
Leiterstrahlrohr
fireman's hatchet
hacha de bombero
hache
Feuerwehrbeil
hook ladder
escalera de ganchos
échelle à crochets
Hakenleiter

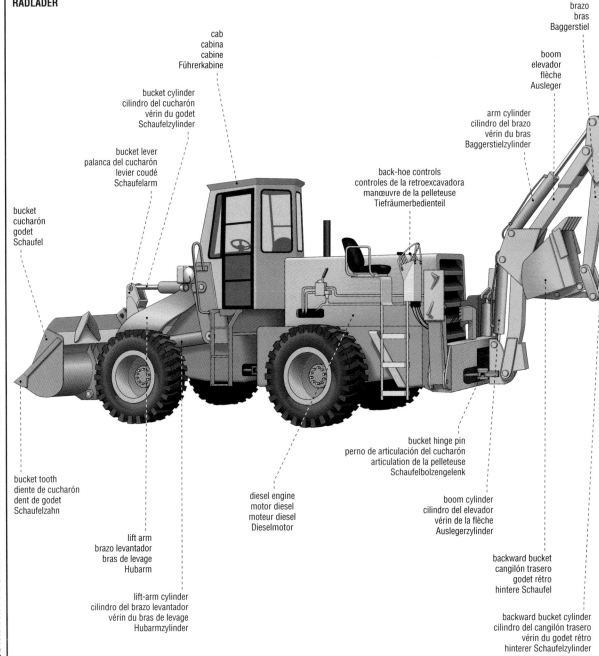

HEAVY VEHICLES
VEHÍCULOS PESADOS
MACHINERIE LOURDE
SCHWERFAHRZEUGE

WHEEL LOADER
RETROEXCAVADORA CARGADORA
CHARGEUSE-PELLETEUSE
RADLADER

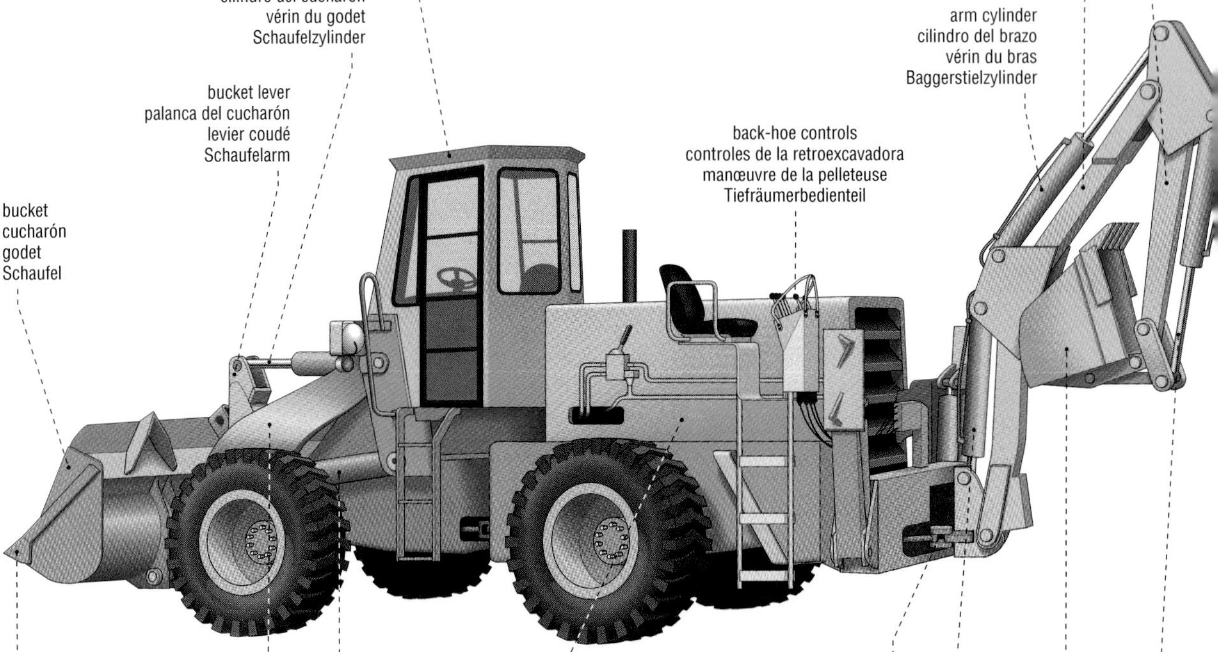

arm
brazo
bras
Baggerstiel

cab
cabina
cabine
Führerkabine

boom
elevador
flèche
Ausleger

bucket cylinder
cilindro del cucharón
vérin du godet
Schaufelzylinder

arm cylinder
cilindro del brazo
vérin du bras
Baggerstielzylinder

bucket lever
palanca del cucharón
levier coudé
Schaufelarm

back-hoe controls
controles de la retroexcavadora
manœuvre de la pelleteuse
Tiefräumerbedienteil

bucket
cucharón
godet
Schaufel

bucket hinge pin
perno de articulación del cucharón
articulation de la pelleteuse
Schaufelbolzengelenk

bucket tooth
diente de cucharón
dent de godet
Schaufelzahn

diesel engine
motor diesel
moteur diesel
Dieselmotor

boom cylinder
cilindro del elevador
vérin de la flèche
Auslegerzylinder

lift arm
brazo levantador
bras de levage
Hubarm

backward bucket
cangilón trasero
godet rétro
hintere Schaufel

lift-arm cylinder
cilindro del brazo levantador
vérin du bras de levage
Hubarmzylinder

backward bucket cylinder
cilindro del cangilón trasero
vérin du godet rétro
hinterer Schaufelzylinder

front-end loader
cargador delantero
chargeuse frontale
Schaufellader

wheel tractor
tractor de ruedas
tracteur
Radtraktor

back-hoe
retroexcavadora
pelleteuse
Tiefräumer

BULLDOZER
BULLDOZER
BOUTEUR
PLANIERRAUPE

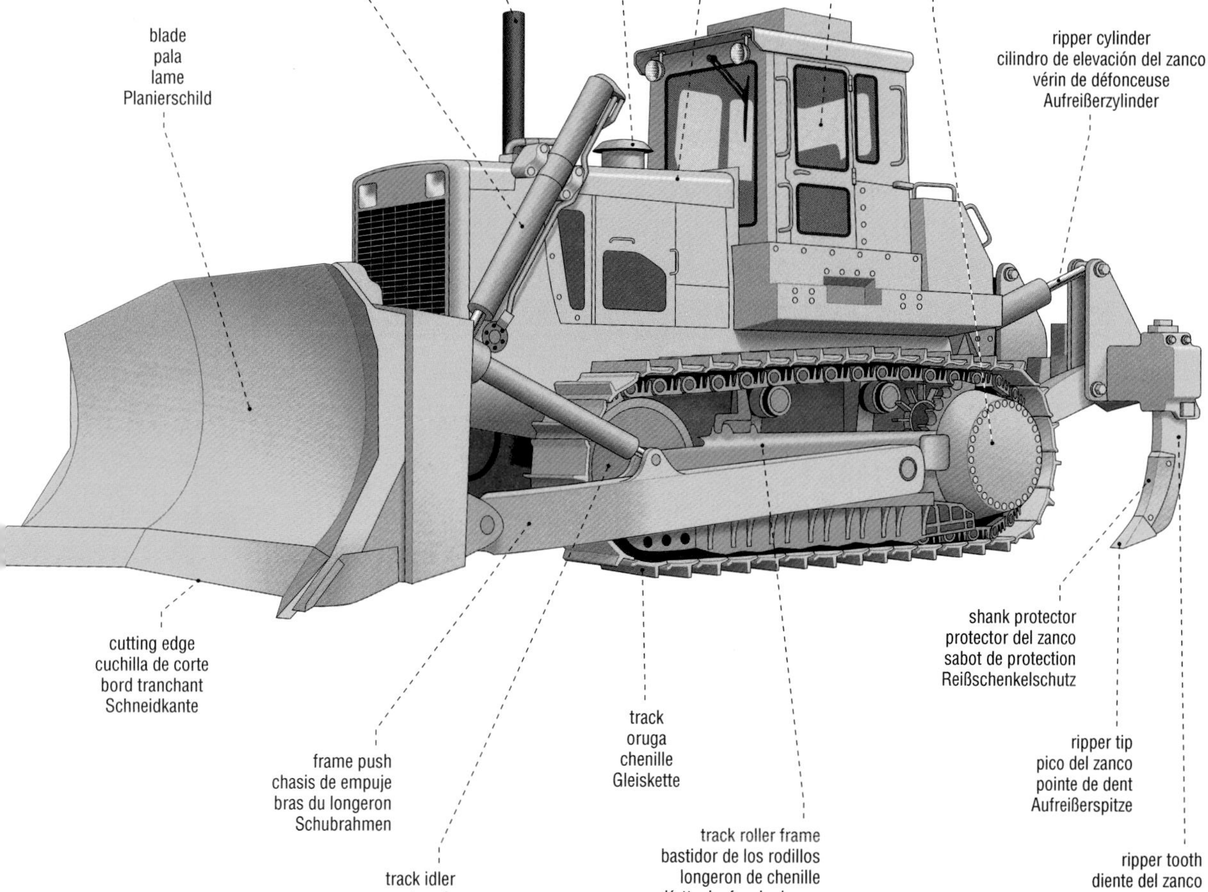

air-cleaner filter
filtro de aire
filtre à air
Luftfilter

diesel motor
motor diesel
moteur diesel
Dieselmotor

exhaust pipe
tubo de escape
tuyau d'échappement
Auspuffrohr

cab
cabina
cabine
Führerkabine

blade lift cylinder
cilindro del elevador de la pala
vérin de levage de la lame
Schildhubzylinder

sprocket wheel
rueda catalina
barbotin
Antriebsrad

blade
pala
lame
Planierschild

ripper cylinder
cilindro de elevación del zanco
vérin de défonceuse
Aufreißerzylinder

cutting edge
cuchilla de corte
bord tranchant
Schneidkante

shank protector
protector del zanco
sabot de protection
Reißschenkelschutz

track
oruga
chenille
Gleiskette

frame push
chasis de empuje
bras du longeron
Schubrahmen

ripper tip
pico del zanco
pointe de dent
Aufreißerspitze

track roller frame
bastidor de los rodillos
longeron de chenille
Kettenlaufwerkrahmen

ripper tooth
diente del zanco
dent de défonceuse
Aufreißerzahn

track idler
rueda guía
roue folle
Spannrad

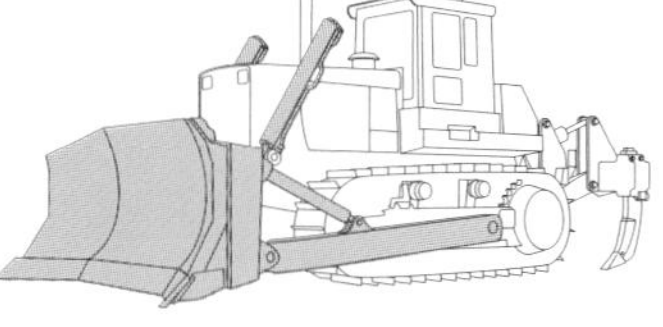

blade
pala
lame
Planierschaufel

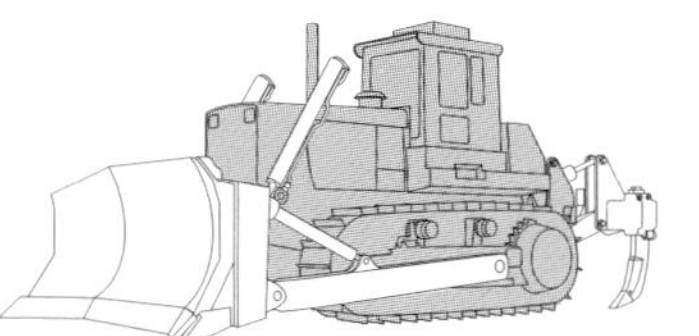

crawler tractor
tractor de orugas
tracteur à chenilles
Gleiskettenschlepper

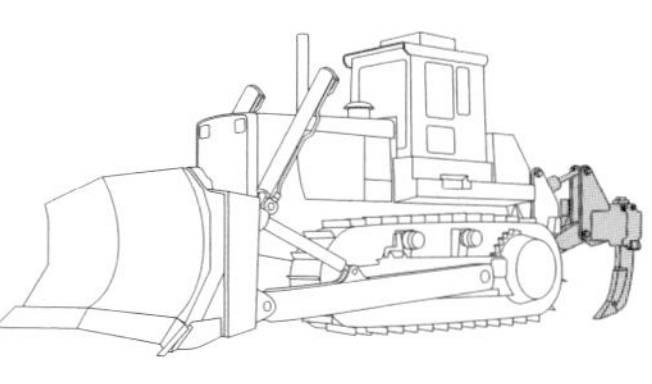

ripper
zanco
défonceuse
Aufreißer

HEAVY VEHICLES
VEHÍCULOS PESADOS
MACHINERIE LOURDE
SCHWERFAHRZEUGE

SCRAPER
RASPADOR
DÉCAPEUSE
SCHRAPPER

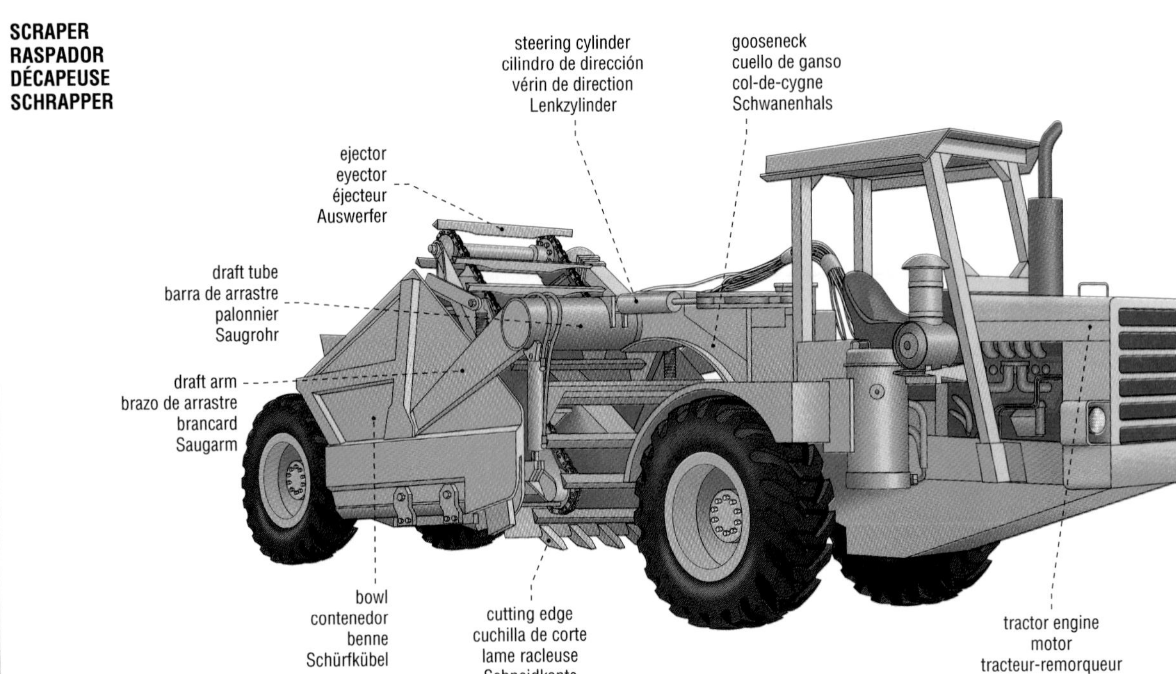
steering cylinder
cilindro de dirección
vérin de direction
Lenkzylinder
gooseneck
cuello de ganso
col-de-cygne
Schwanenhals
ejector
eyector
éjecteur
Auswerfer
draft tube
barra de arrastre
palonnier
Saugrohr
draft arm
brazo de arrastre
brancard
Saugarm
bowl
contenedor
benne
Schürfkübel
cutting edge
cuchilla de corte
lame racleuse
Schneidkante
tractor engine
motor
tracteur-remorqueur
Traktormotor

GRADER
NIVELADORA
NIVELEUSE
STRASSENHOBEL

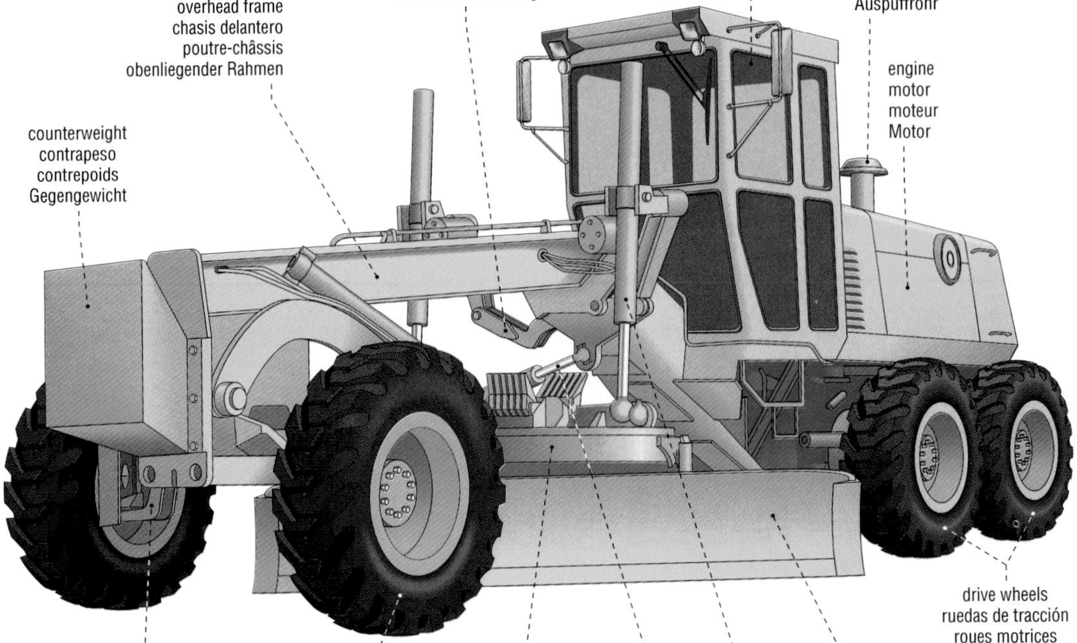

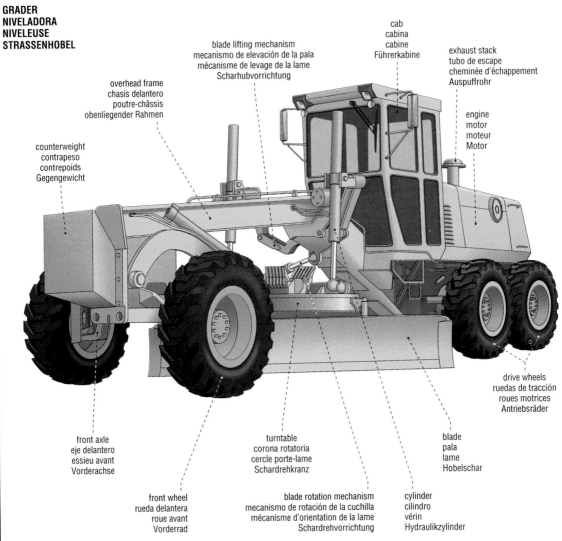

cab
cabina
cabine
Führerkabine

blade lifting mechanism
mecanismo de elevación de la pala
mécanisme de levage de la lame
Scharhubvorrichtung

exhaust stack
tubo de escape
cheminée d'échappement
Auspuffrohr

overhead frame
chasis delantero
poutre-châssis
obenliegender Rahmen

engine
motor
moteur
Motor

counterweight
contrapeso
contrepoids
Gegengewicht

drive wheels
ruedas de tracción
roues motrices
Antriebsräder

front axle
eje delantero
essieu avant
Vorderachse

turntable
corona rotatoria
cercle porte-lame
Schardrehkranz

blade
pala
lame
Hobelschar

front wheel
rueda delantera
roue avant
Vorderrad

blade rotation mechanism
mecanismo de rotación de la cuchilla
mécanisme d'orientation de la lame
Schardrehvorrichtung

cylinder
cilindro
vérin
Hydraulikzylinder

HEAVY MACHINERY
MAQUINARIA PESADA
MACHINERIE LOURDE
SCHWERMASCHINEN

DUMP TRUCK
CAMIÓN BASCULANTE
CAMION-BENNE
HINTERKIPPER

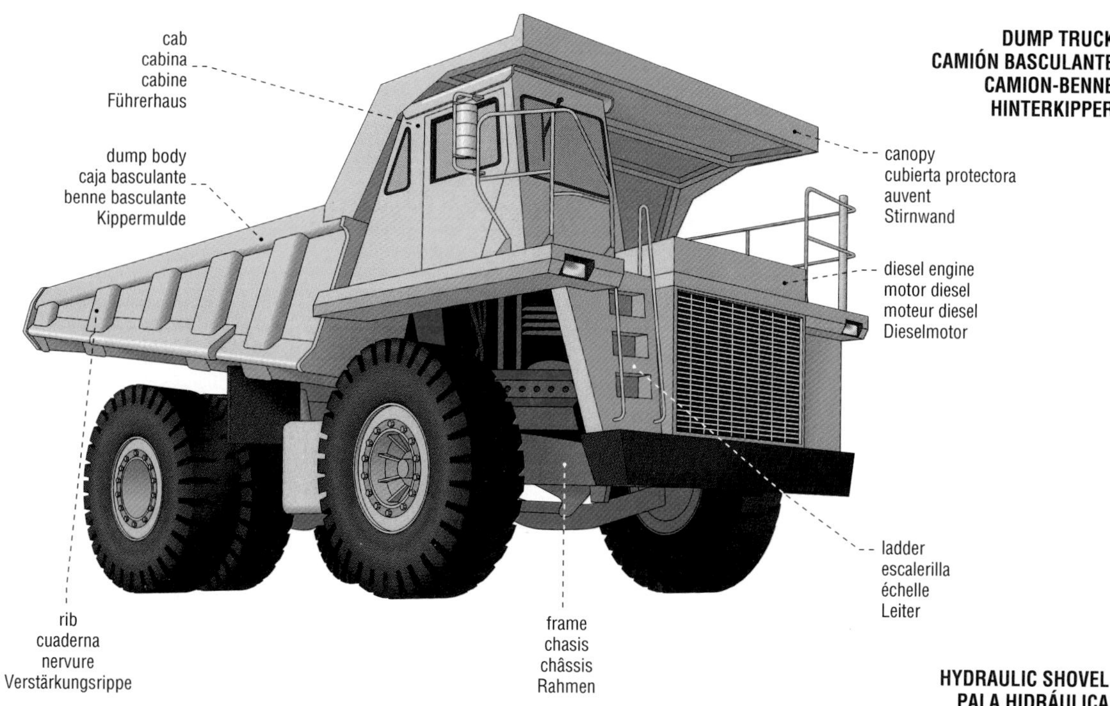
cab
cabina
cabine
Führerhaus
dump body
caja basculante
benne basculante
Kippermulde
canopy
cubierta protectora
auvent
Stirnwand
diesel engine
motor diesel
moteur diesel
Dieselmotor
ladder
escalerilla
échelle
Leiter
rib
cuaderna
nervure
Verstärkungsrippe
frame
chasis
châssis
Rahmen

HYDRAULIC SHOVEL
PALA HIDRÁULICA
PELLE HYDRAULIQUE
HYDRAULIK-HOCHLÖFFELBAGGER

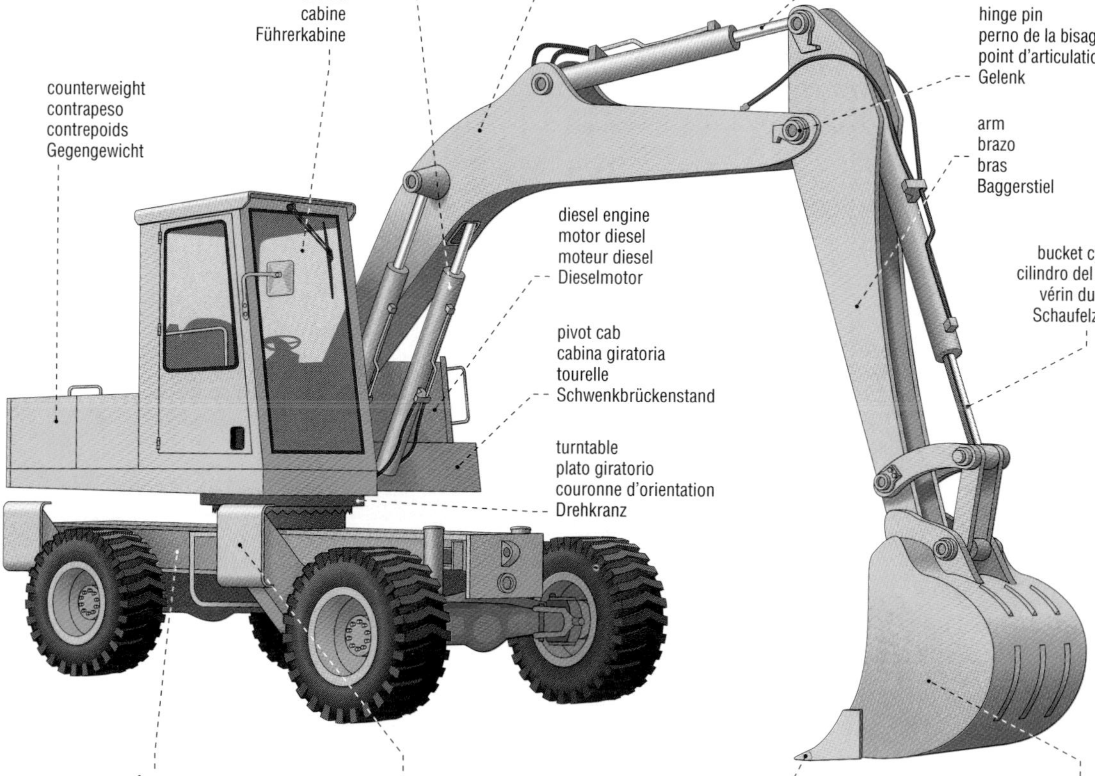

boom cylinder
cilindro del elevador
vérin de la flèche
Auslegerzylinder

boom
pluma
flèche
Ausleger

arm cylinder
cilindro del brazo
vérin du bras
Baggerstielzylinder

cab
cabina
cabine
Führerkabine

hinge pin
perno de la bisagra
point d'articulation
Gelenk

counterweight
contrapeso
contrepoids
Gegengewicht

arm
brazo
bras
Baggerstiel

diesel engine
motor diesel
moteur diesel
Dieselmotor

bucket cylinder
cilindro del cucharón
vérin du godet
Schaufelzylinder

pivot cab
cabina giratoria
tourelle
Schwenkbrückenstand

turntable
plato giratorio
couronne d'orientation
Drehkranz

frame
chasis
châssis
Rahmen

outrigger
soporte del plano fijo
stabilisateur
Heber

tooth
diente
dent
Schaufelzahn

dipper bucket
cucharón excavador
godet chargeur
Baggerlöffel

MATERIAL HANDLING
MANEJO DE MATERIALES
MANUTENTION
LASTENFORTBEWEGUNG

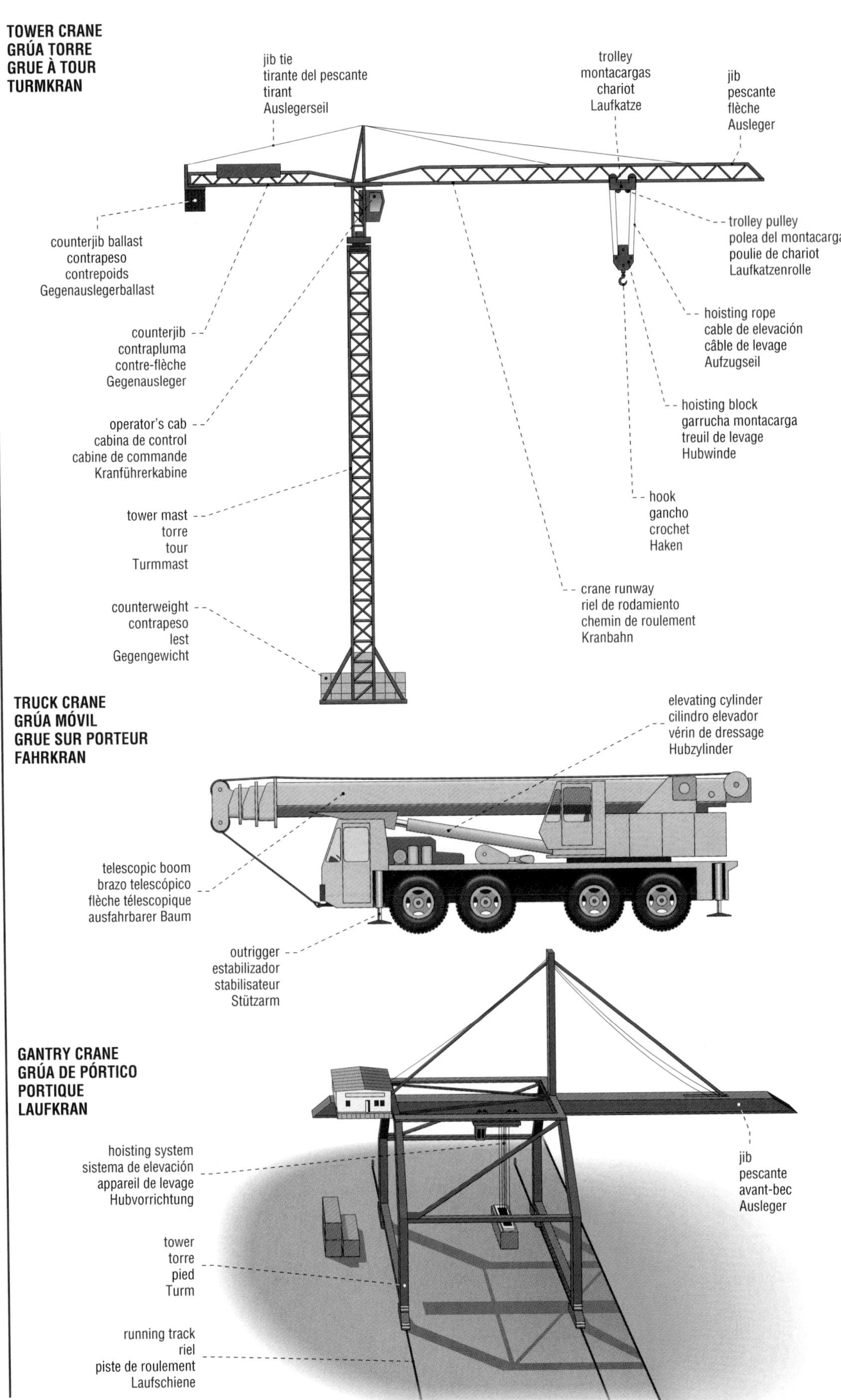

TOWER CRANE
GRÚA TORRE
GRUE À TOUR
TURMKRAN
jib tie
tirante del pescante
tirant
Auslegerseil
trolley
montacargas
chariot
Laufkatze
jib
pescante
flèche
Ausleger
counterjib ballast
contrapeso
contrepoids
Gegenauslegerballast
trolley pulley
polea del montacargas
poulie de chariot
Laufkatzenrolle
counterjib
contrapluma
contre-flèche
Gegenausleger
hoisting rope
cable de elevación
câble de levage
Aufzugseil
operator's cab
cabina de control
cabine de commande
Kranführerkabine
hoisting block
garrucha montacarga
treuil de levage
Hubwinde
hook
gancho
crochet
Haken
tower mast
torre
tour
Turmmast
crane runway
riel de rodamiento
chemin de roulement
Kranbahn
counterweight
contrapeso
lest
Gegengewicht
TRUCK CRANE
GRÚA MÓVIL
GRUE SUR PORTEUR
FAHRKRAN
elevating cylinder
cilindro elevador
vérin de dressage
Hubzylinder
telescopic boom
brazo telescópico
flèche télescopique
ausfahrbarer Baum
outrigger
estabilizador
stabilisateur
Stützarm
GANTRY CRANE
GRÚA DE PÓRTICO
PORTIQUE
LAUFKRAN
hoisting system
sistema de elevación
appareil de levage
Hubvorrichtung
jib
pescante
avant-bec
Ausleger
tower
torre
pied
Turm
running track
riel
piste de roulement
Laufschiene

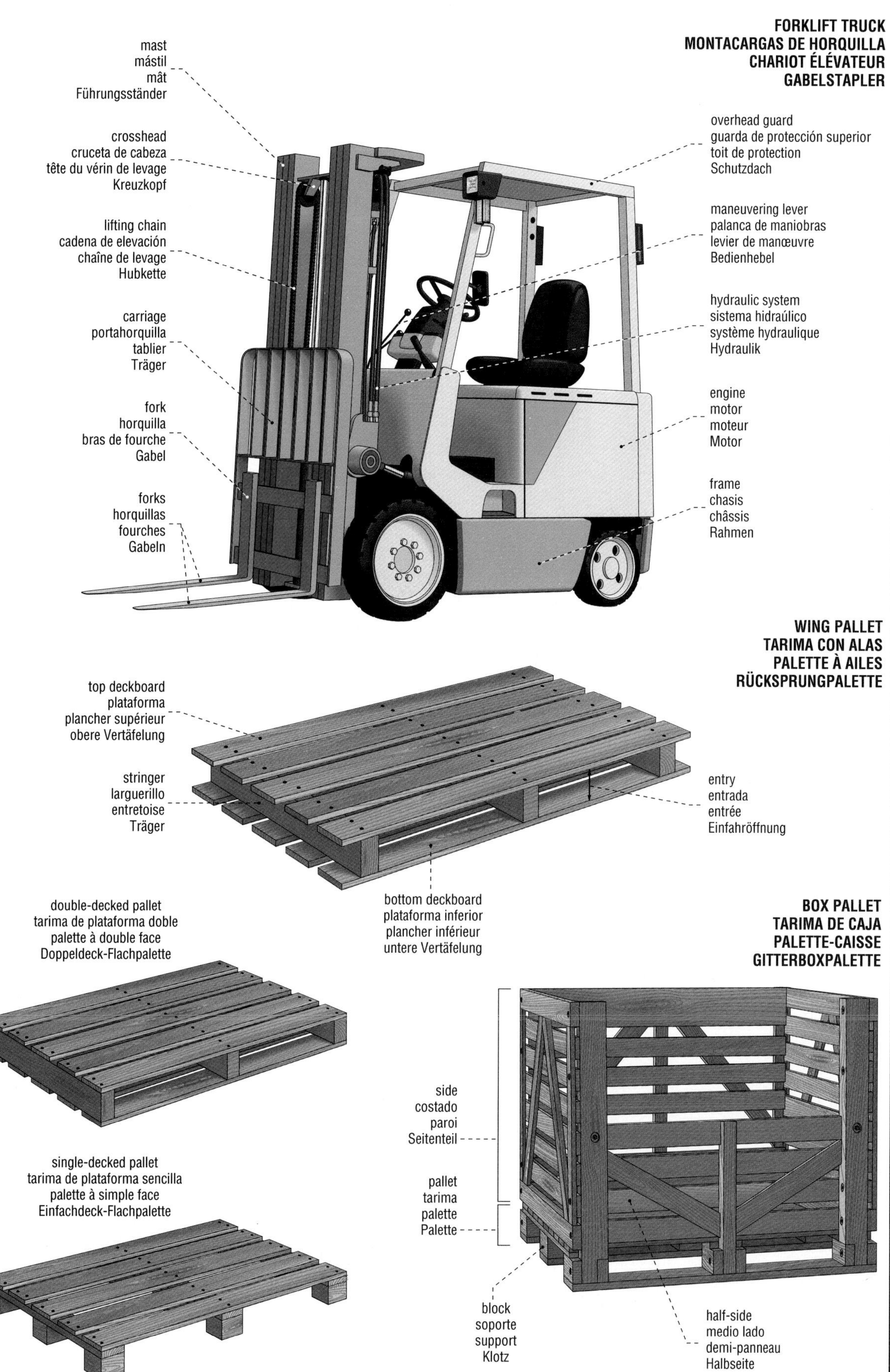
FORKLIFT TRUCK
MONTACARGAS DE HORQUILLA
CHARIOT ÉLÉVATEUR
GABELSTAPLER
mast
mástil
mât
Führungsständer
crosshead
cruceta de cabeza
tête du vérin de levage
Kreuzkopf
lifting chain
cadena de elevación
chaîne de levage
Hubkette
carriage
portahorquilla
tablier
Träger
fork
horquilla
bras de fourche
Gabel
forks
horquillas
fourches
Gabeln
overhead guard
guarda de protección superior
toit de protection
Schutzdach
maneuvering lever
palanca de maniobras
levier de manœuvre
Bedienhebel
hydraulic system
sistema hidraúlico
système hydraulique
Hydraulik
engine
motor
moteur
Motor
frame
chasis
châssis
Rahmen
WING PALLET
TARIMA CON ALAS
PALETTE À AILES
RÜCKSPRUNGPALETTE
top deckboard
plataforma
plancher supérieur
obere Vertäfelung
stringer
larguerillo
entretoise
Träger
entry
entrada
entrée
Einfahröffnung
bottom deckboard
plataforma inferior
plancher inférieur
untere Vertäfelung
double-decked pallet
tarima de plataforma doble
palette à double face
Doppeldeck-Flachpalette
single-decked pallet
tarima de plataforma sencilla
palette à simple face
Einfachdeck-Flachpalette
BOX PALLET
TARIMA DE CAJA
PALETTE-CAISSE
GITTERBOXPALETTE
side
costado
paroi
Seitenteil
pallet
tarima
palette
Palette
block
soporte
support
Klotz
half-side
medio lado
demi-panneau
Halbseite

MATERIAL HANDLING
MANEJO DE MATERIALES
MANUTENTION
LASTENFORTBEWEGUNG

HYDRAULIC PALLET TRUCK
MONTACARGAS HIDRÁULICO DE TARIMA
GERBEUR
HYDRAULISCHER PALETTENHUBWAGEN

pallet truck
carretilla hidráulica
transpalette manuel
Palettenhubwagen
maneuvering lever
palanca de maniobras
levier de manœuvre
Bedienhebel
mast
mástil
mât
Führungsständer
steering lever
palanca de dirección
levier de conduite
Lenkhebel
hydraulic cylinder
cilindro hidráulico
vérin hydraulique
Hydraulikzylinder
hand truck
carretilla
diable
Sackkarren
forks
horquillas
fourches
Gabeln
solid rubber tire
llanta maciza
bandage de roue caoutchoutée
Vollgummirad
stabilizing shaft
barra estabilizadora
longeron stabilisateur
Stabilisator
steering axle
eje de dirección
essieu directeur
Lenkachse
frame
chasis
châssis
Rahmen
roller
rueda
roulette
Rolle
platform pallet truck
plataforma hidráulica
chariot à palette
Flachpalettenwagen
flatbed pushcart
plataforma móvil
chariot à plateau
Handwagen

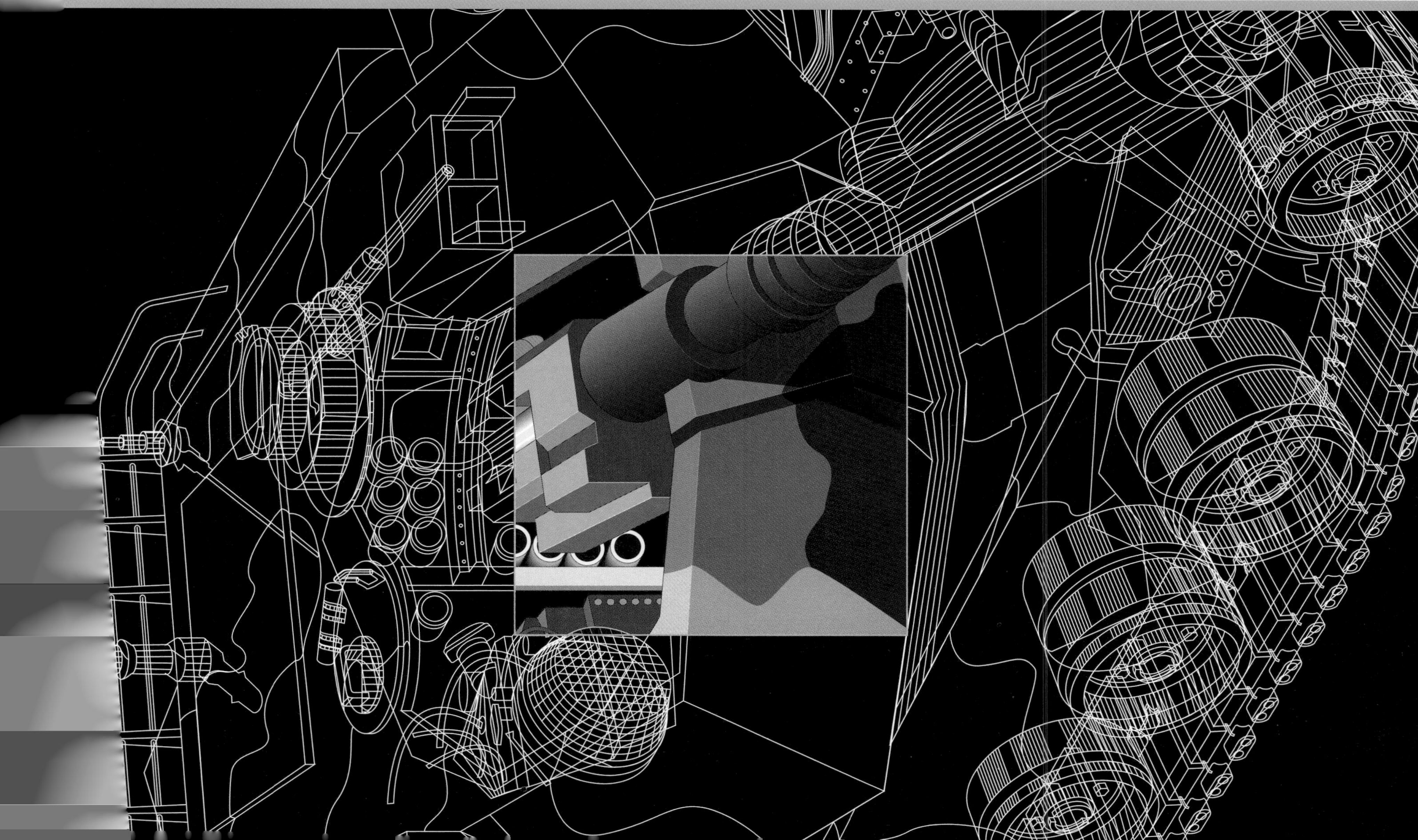

CONTENTS

STONE AGE WEAPONS
ARMAS DE LA EDAD DE PIEDRA
ARMES DE L'ÂGE DE PIERRE
WAFFEN IN DER STEINZEIT

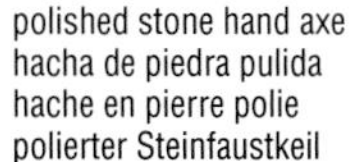

polished stone hand axe
hacha de piedra pulida
hache en pierre polie
polierter Steinfaustkeil

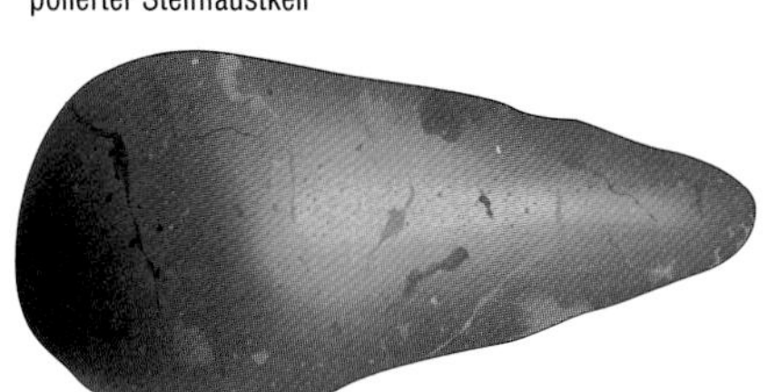

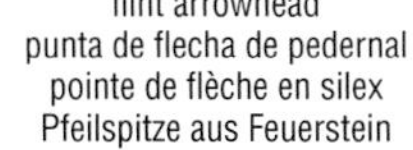

flint arrowhead
punta de flecha de pedernal
pointe de flèche en silex
Pfeilspitze aus Feuerstein

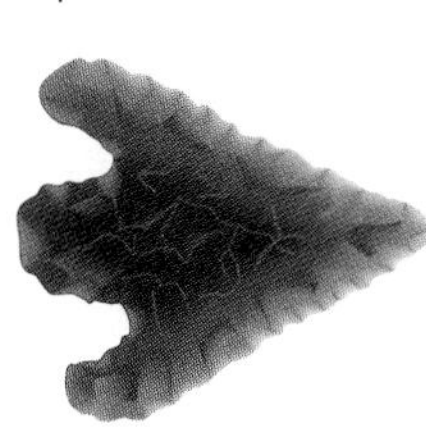

flint knife
cuchillo de pedernal
couteau en silex
Messer aus Feuerstein

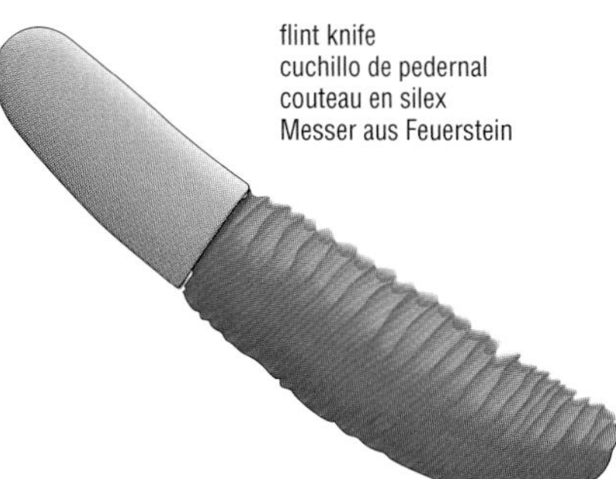

WEAPONS IN THE AGE OF THE ROMANS
ARMAS DEL IMPERIO ROMANO
ARMES DE L'ÉPOQUE ROMAINE
WAFFEN IN DER RÖMERZEIT

GALLIC WARRIOR
GUERRERO GALO
GUERRIER GAULOIS
GALLISCHER KRIEGER

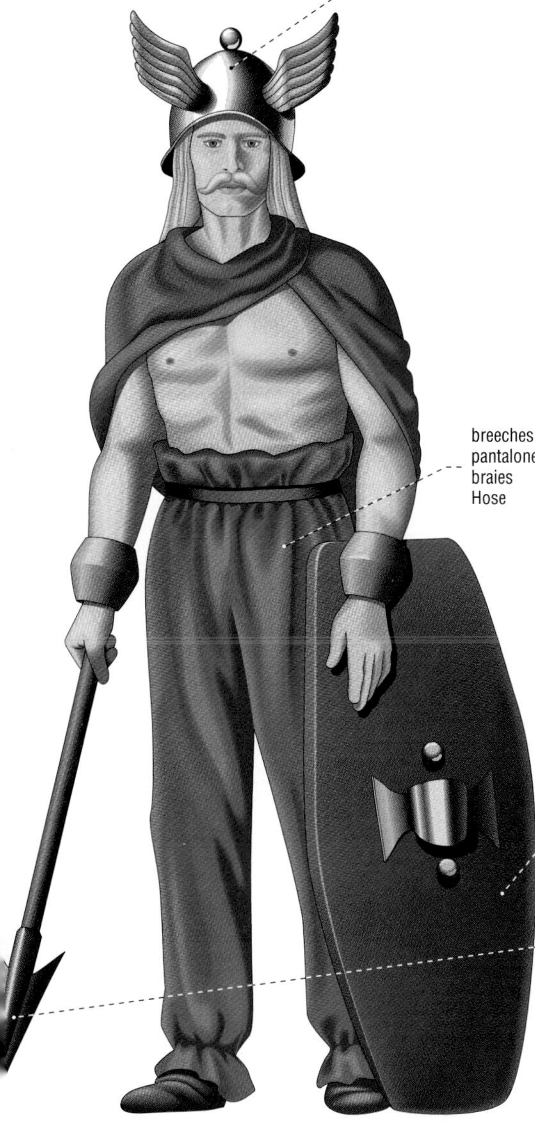

helmet
casco
casque
Helm

breeches
pantalones
braies
Hose

shield
escudo
bouclier
Schild

spear
lanza
lance
Speer

ROMAN LEGIONARY
LEGIONARIO ROMANO
LÉGIONNAIRE ROMAIN
RÖMISCHER LEGIONÄR

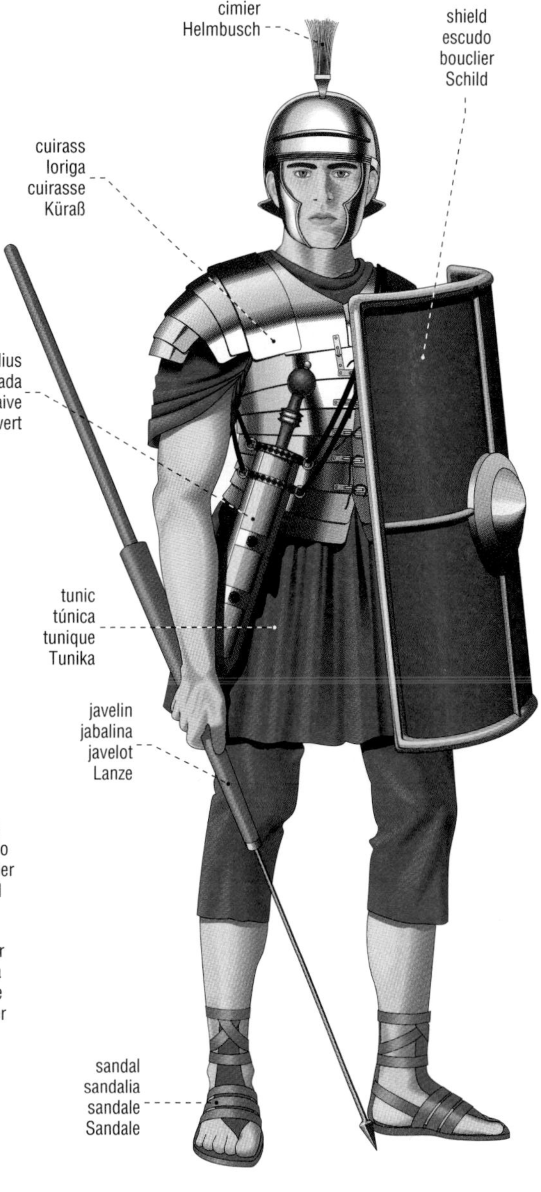

crest
penacho
cimier
Helmbusch

shield
escudo
bouclier
Schild

cuirass
loriga
cuirasse
Küraß

gladius
espada
glaive
Kurzschwert

tunic
túnica
tunique
Tunika

javelin
jabalina
javelot
Lanze

sandal
sandalia
sandale
Sandale

ARMOR
ARMADURA
ARMURE
RÜSTUNG

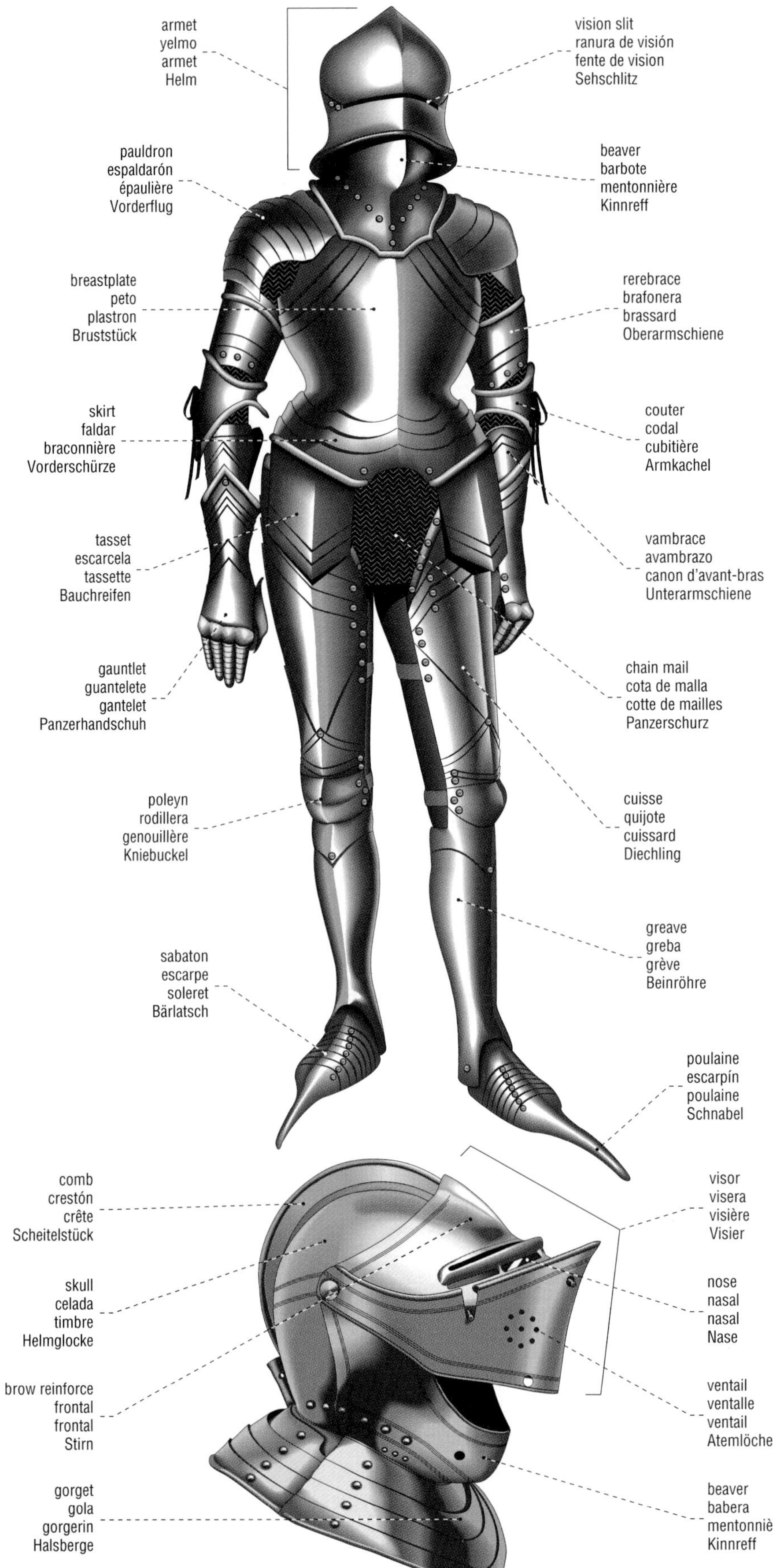
armet
yelmo
armet
Helm
vision slit
ranura de visión
fente de vision
Sehschlitz
pauldron
espaldarón
épaulière
Vorderflug
beaver
barbote
mentonnière
Kinnreff
breastplate
peto
plastron
Bruststück
rerebrace
brafonera
brassard
Oberarmschiene
skirt
faldar
braconnière
Vorderschürze
couter
codal
cubitière
Armkachel
tasset
escarcela
tassette
Bauchreifen
vambrace
avambrazo
canon d'avant-bras
Unterarmschiene
gauntlet
guantelete
gantelet
Panzerhandschuh
chain mail
cota de malla
cotte de mailles
Panzerschurz
poleyn
rodillera
genouillère
Kniebuckel
cuisse
quijote
cuissard
Diechling
greave
greba
grève
Beinröhre
sabaton
escarpe
soleret
Bärlatsch
poulaine
escarpín
poulaine
Schnabel
comb
crestón
crête
Scheitelstück
visor
visera
visière
Visier
skull
celada
timbre
Helmglocke
nose
nasal
nasal
Nase
brow reinforce
frontal
frontal
Stirn
ventail
ventalle
ventail
Atemlöcher
gorget
gola
gorgerin
Halsberge
beaver
babera
mentonnière
Kinnreff

ARMET
YELMO
ARMET
HELM

BOWS AND CROSSBOW
ARCOS Y BALLESTA
ARCS ET ARBALÈTE
BOGEN UND ARMBRUST

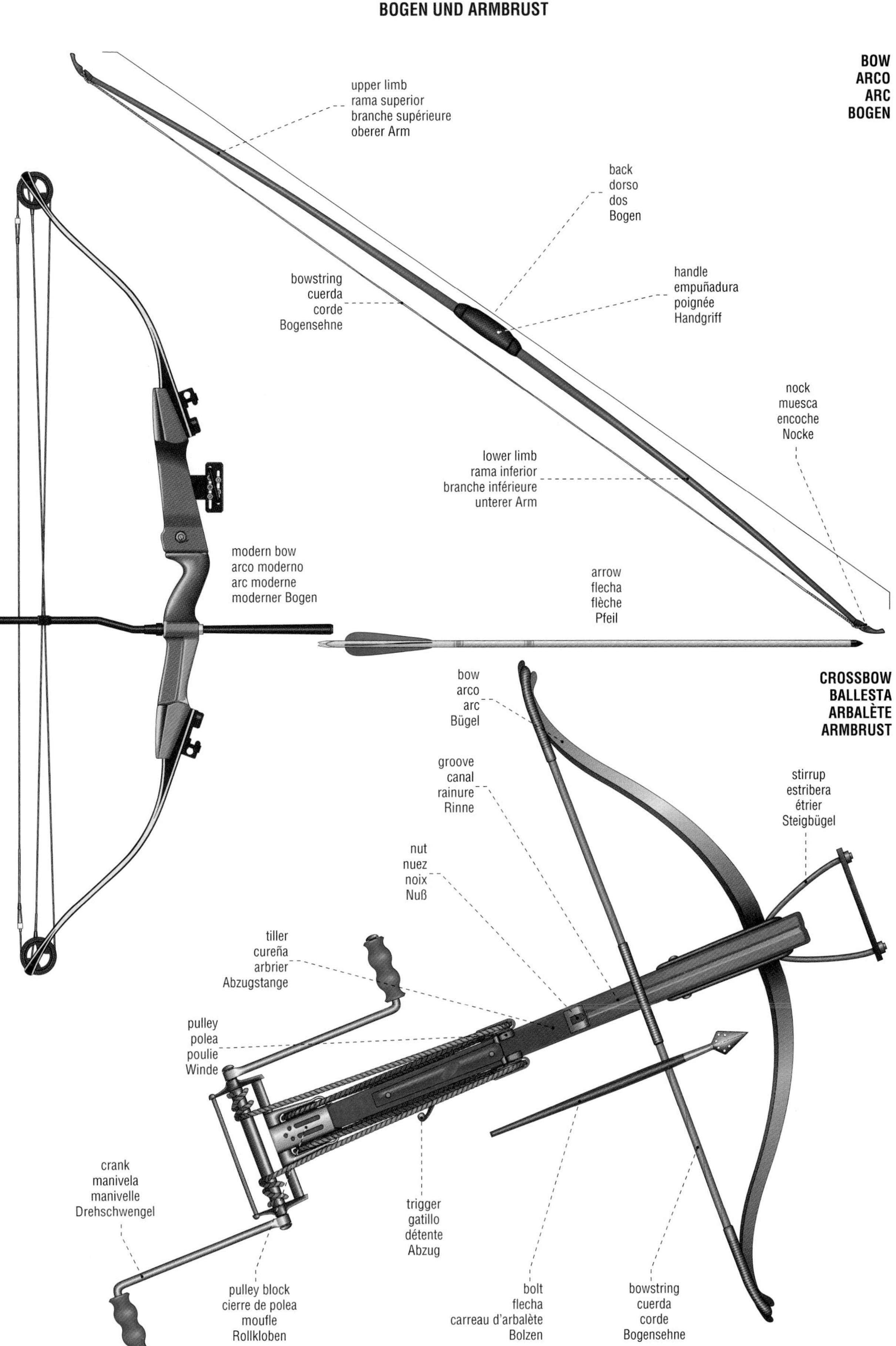
BOW
ARCO
ARC
BOGEN
upper limb
rama superior
branche supérieure
oberer Arm
back
dorso
dos
Bogen
bowstring
cuerda
corde
Bogensehne
handle
empuñadura
poignée
Handgriff
nock
muesca
encoche
Nocke
lower limb
rama inferior
branche inférieure
unterer Arm
modern bow
arco moderno
arc moderne
moderner Bogen
arrow
flecha
flèche
Pfeil
CROSSBOW
BALLESTA
ARBALÈTE
ARMBRUST
bow
arco
arc
Bügel
groove
canal
rainure
Rinne
stirrup
estribera
étrier
Steigbügel
nut
nuez
noix
Nuß
tiller
cureña
arbrier
Abzugstange
pulley
polea
poulie
Winde
crank
manivela
manivelle
Drehschwengel
trigger
gatillo
détente
Abzug
pulley block
cierre de polea
moufle
Rollkloben
bolt
flecha
carreau d'arbalète
Bolzen
bowstring
cuerda
corde
Bogensehne

THRUSTING AND CUTTING WEAPONS
ARMAS CORTANTES Y DE ESTOCADA
ARMES BLANCHES
HIEB- UND STICHWAFFEN

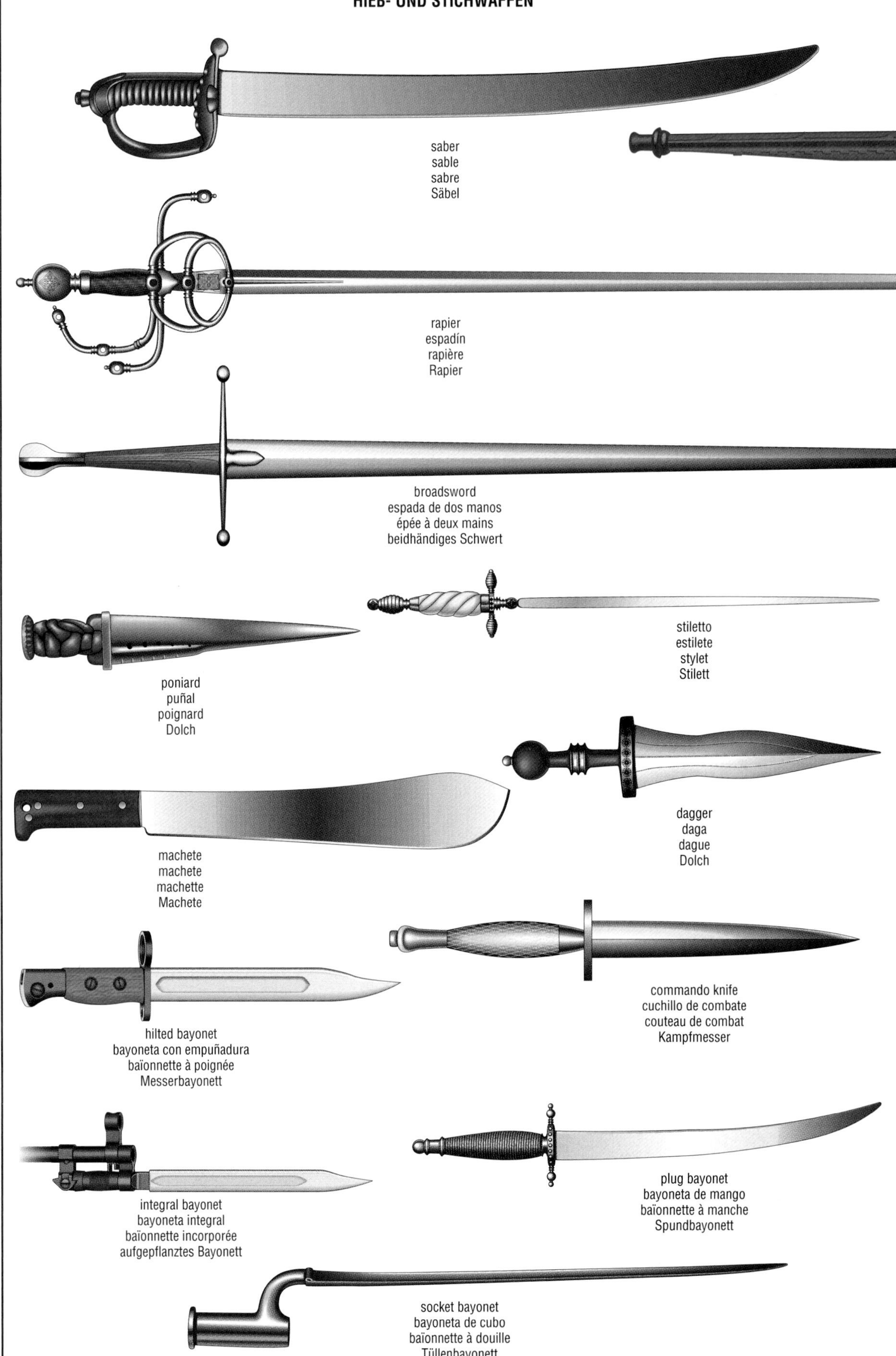

saber
sable
sabre
Säbel
rapier
espadín
rapière
Rapier
broadsword
espada de dos manos
épée à deux mains
beidhändiges Schwert
stiletto
estilete
stylet
Stilett
poniard
puñal
poignard
Dolch
dagger
daga
dague
Dolch
machete
machete
machette
Machete
commando knife
cuchillo de combate
couteau de combat
Kampfmesser
hilted bayonet
bayoneta con empuñadura
baïonnette à poignée
Messerbayonett
plug bayonet
bayoneta de mango
baïonnette à manche
Spundbayonett
integral bayonet
bayoneta integral
baïonnette incorporée
aufgepflanztes Bayonett
socket bayonet
bayoneta de cubo
baïonnette à douille
Tüllenbayonett

HARQUEBUS
ARCABUZ
ARQUEBUSE
ARKEBUSE

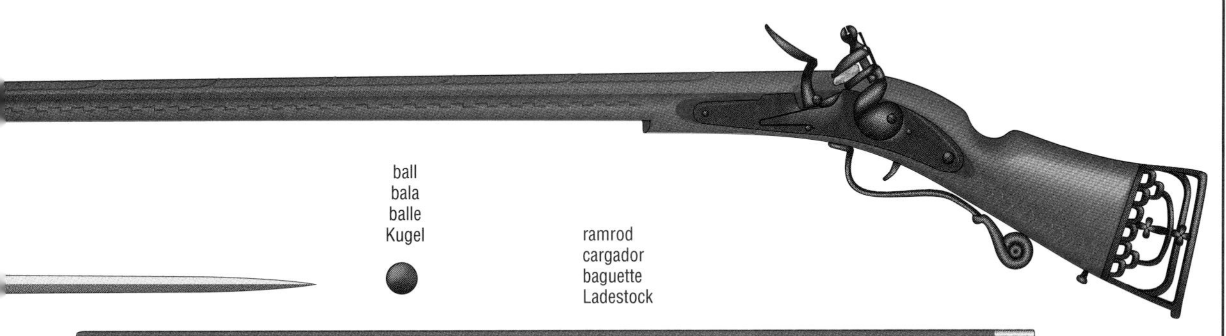
ball
bala
balle
Kugel
ramrod
cargador
baguette
Ladestock

FLINTLOCK
PEDERNAL
PLATINE À SILEX
STEINSCHLOSS

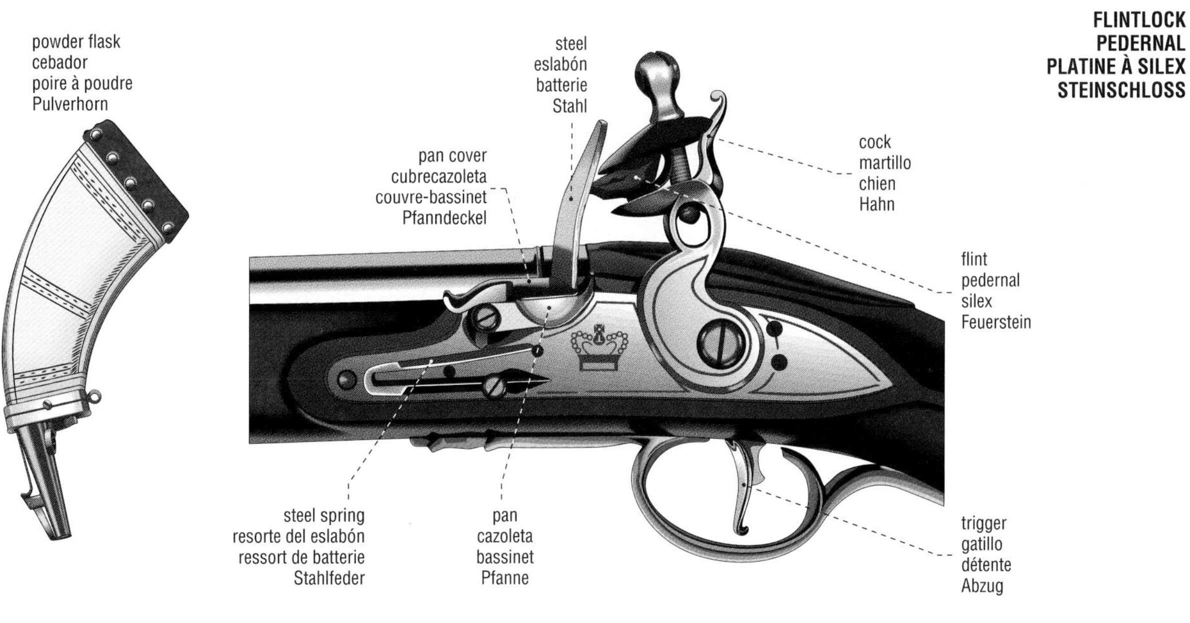
powder flask
cebador
poire à poudre
Pulverhorn
steel
eslabón
batterie
Stahl
pan cover
cubrecazoleta
couvre-bassinet
Pfanndeckel
cock
martillo
chien
Hahn
flint
pedernal
silex
Feuerstein
steel spring
resorte del eslabón
ressort de batterie
Stahlfeder
pan
cazoleta
bassinet
Pfanne
trigger
gatillo
détente
Abzug

SUBMACHINE GUN
METRALLETA
PISTOLET MITRAILLEUR
MASCHINENPISTOLE

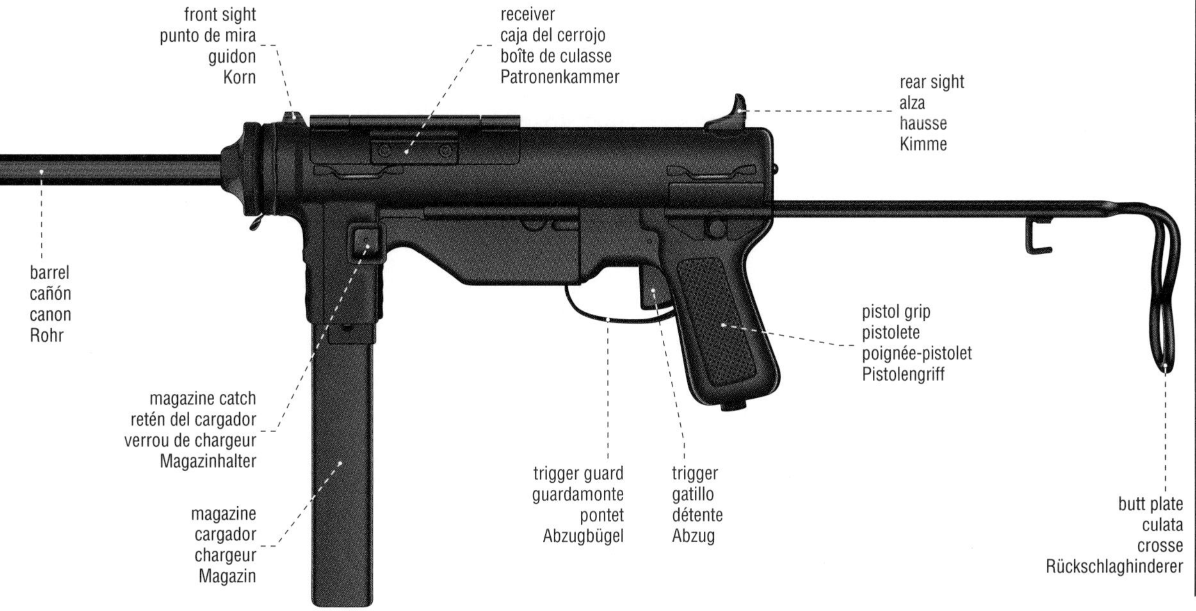
front sight
punto de mira
guidon
Korn
receiver
caja del cerrojo
boîte de culasse
Patronenkammer
rear sight
alza
hausse
Kimme
barrel
cañón
canon
Rohr
pistol grip
pistolete
poignée-pistolet
Pistolengriff
magazine catch
retén del cargador
verrou de chargeur
Magazinhalter
magazine
cargador
chargeur
Magazin
trigger guard
guardamonte
pontet
Abzugbügel
trigger
gatillo
détente
Abzug
butt plate
culata
crosse
Rückschlaghinderer

AUTOMATIC RIFLE
FUSIL AUTOMÁTICO
FUSIL AUTOMATIQUE
AUTOMATISCHES GEWEHR

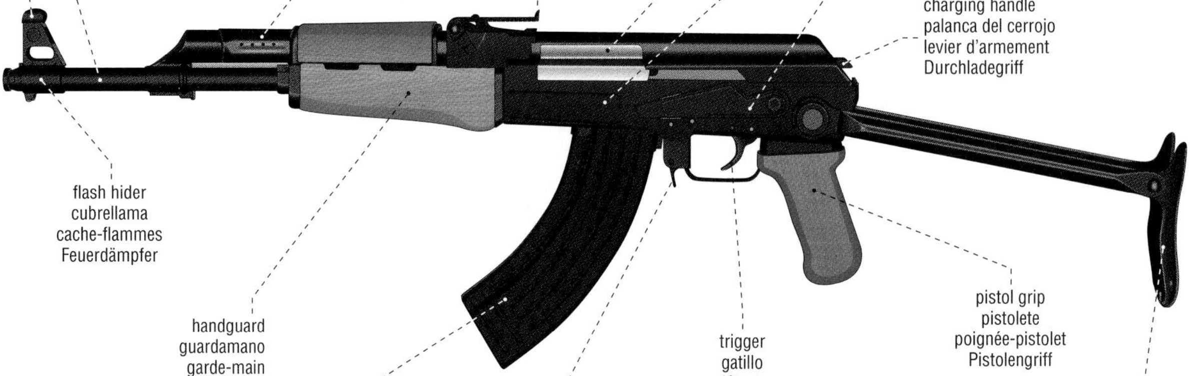

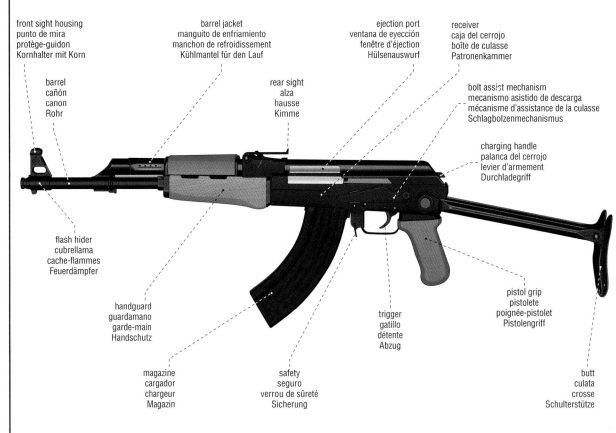

front sight housing
punto de mira
protège-guidon
Kornhalter mit Korn

barrel jacket
manguito de enfriamiento
manchon de refroidissement
Kühlmantel für den Lauf

ejection port
ventana de eyección
fenêtre d'éjection
Hülsenauswurf

receiver
caja del cerrojo
boîte de culasse
Patronenkammer

barrel
cañón
canon
Rohr

rear sight
alza
hausse
Kimme

bolt assist mechanism
mecanismo asistido de descarga
mécanisme d'assistance de la culasse
Schlagbolzenmechanismus

charging handle
palanca del cerrojo
levier d'armement
Durchladegriff

flash hider
cubrellama
cache-flammes
Feuerdämpfer

handguard
guardamano
garde-main
Handschutz

trigger
gatillo
détente
Abzug

pistol grip
pistolete
poignée-pistolet
Pistolengriff

magazine
cargador
chargeur
Magazin

safety
seguro
verrou de sûreté
Sicherung

butt
culata
crosse
Schulterstütze

LIGHT MACHINE GUN
FUSIL AMETRALLADOR
FUSIL MITRAILLEUR
LEICHTES MASCHINENGEWEHR

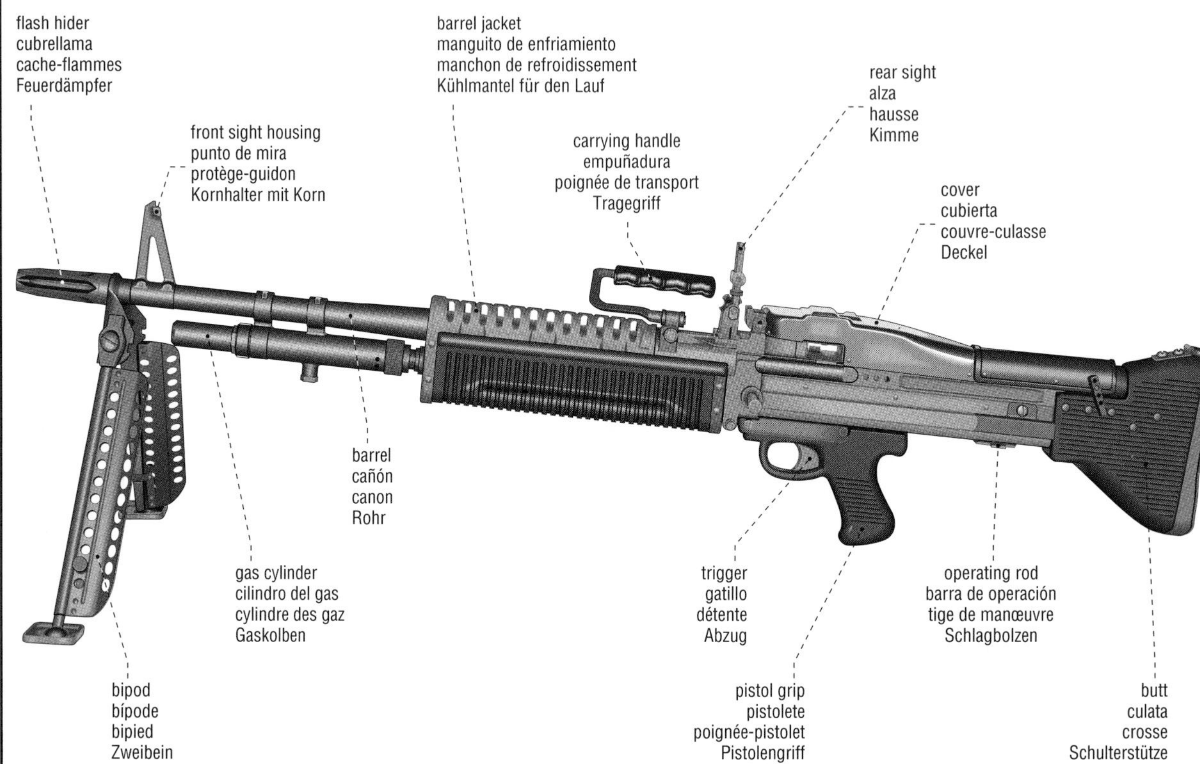
flash hider
cubrellama
cache-flammes
Feuerdämpfer
barrel jacket
manguito de enfriamiento
manchon de refroidissement
Kühlmantel für den Lauf
rear sight
alza
hausse
Kimme
front sight housing
punto de mira
protège-guidon
Kornhalter mit Korn
carrying handle
empuñadura
poignée de transport
Tragegriff
cover
cubierta
couvre-culasse
Deckel
barrel
cañón
canon
Rohr
gas cylinder
cilindro del gas
cylindre des gaz
Gaskolben
trigger
gatillo
détente
Abzug
operating rod
barra de operación
tige de manœuvre
Schlagbolzen
bipod
bípode
bipied
Zweibein
pistol grip
pistolete
poignée-pistolet
Pistolengriff
butt
culata
crosse
Schulterstütze

REVOLVER
REVÓLVER
REVOLVER
REVOLVER

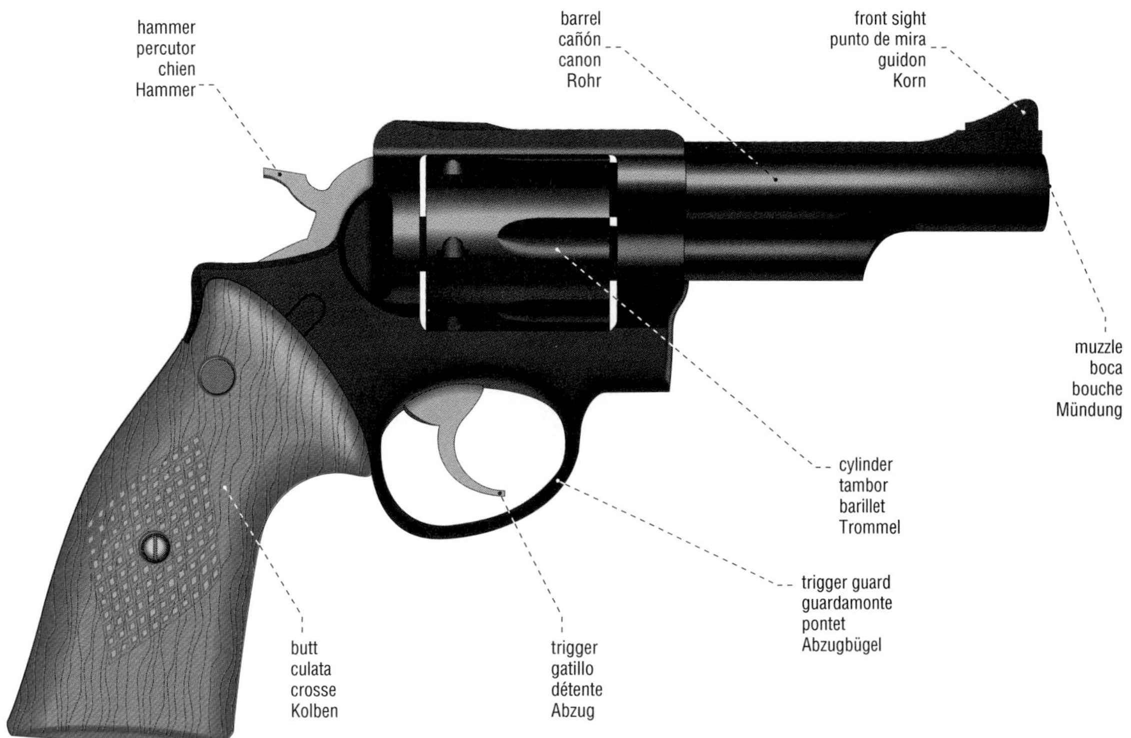
hammer
percutor
chien
Hammer
barrel
cañón
canon
Rohr
front sight
punto de mira
guidon
Korn
muzzle
boca
bouche
Mündung
cylinder
tambor
barillet
Trommel
trigger guard
guardamonte
pontet
Abzugbügel
butt
culata
crosse
Kolben
trigger
gatillo
détente
Abzug

PISTOL
PISTOLA
PISTOLET
PISTOLE

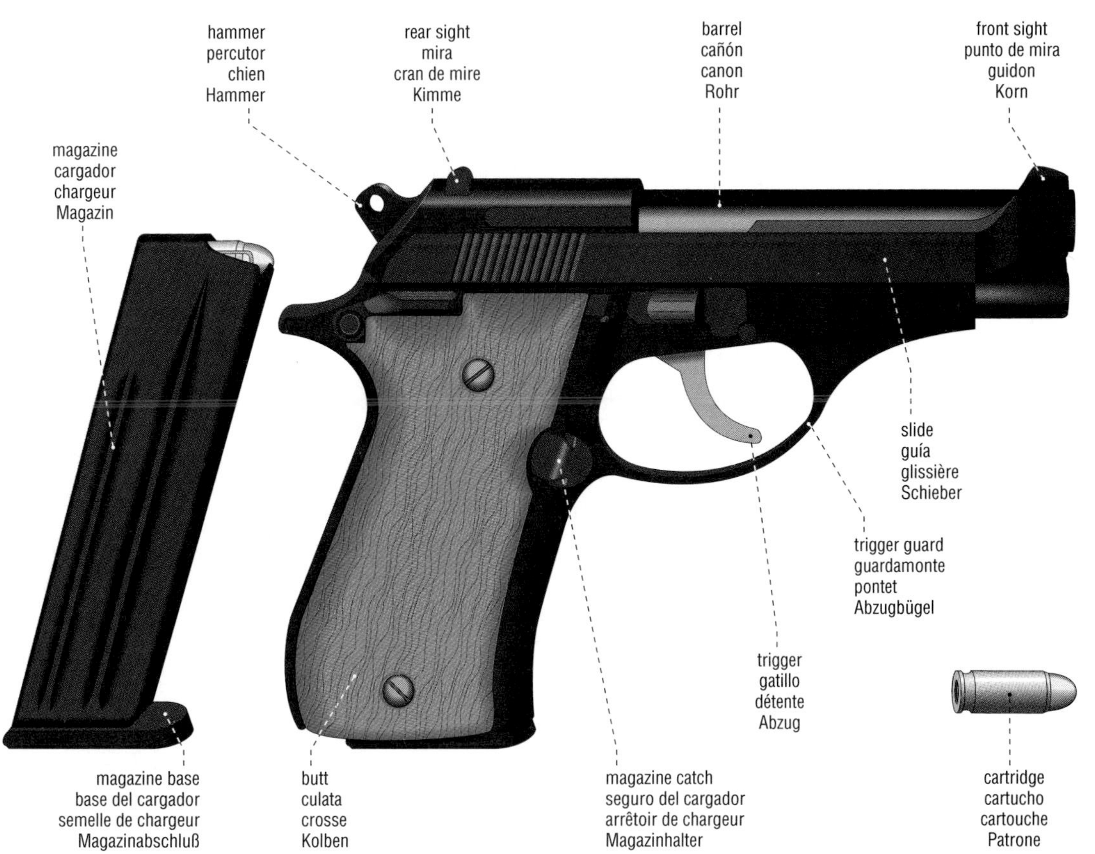
hammer
percutor
chien
Hammer
rear sight
mira
cran de mire
Kimme
barrel
cañón
canon
Rohr
front sight
punto de mira
guidon
Korn
magazine
cargador
chargeur
Magazin
slide
guía
glissière
Schieber
trigger guard
guardamonte
pontet
Abzugbügel
trigger
gatillo
détente
Abzug
magazine base
base del cargador
semelle de chargeur
Magazinabschluß
butt
culata
crosse
Kolben
magazine catch
seguro del cargador
arrêtoir de chargeur
Magazinhalter
cartridge
cartucho
cartouche
Patrone

HUNTING WEAPONS
ARMAS DE CAZA
ARMES DE CHASSE
JAGDWAFFEN

CARTRIDGE (RIFLE)
CARTUCHO DE RIFLE
CARTOUCHE (CARABINE)
PATRONE (GEWEHR)

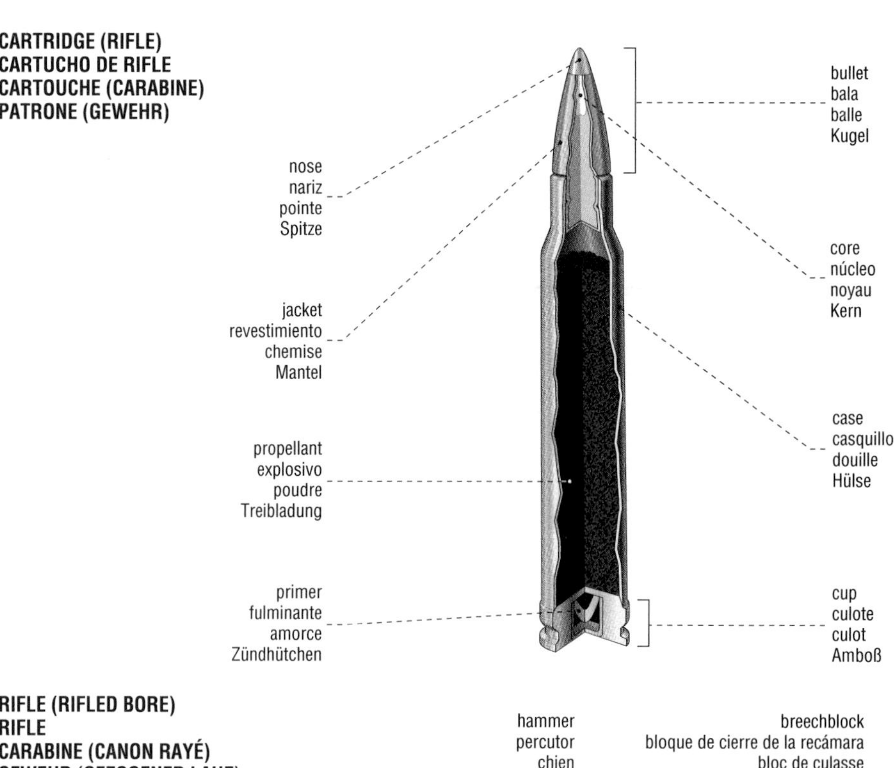

bullet
bala
balle
Kugel
nose
nariz
pointe
Spitze
core
núcleo
noyau
Kern
jacket
revestimiento
chemise
Mantel
case
casquillo
douille
Hülse
propellant
explosivo
poudre
Treibladung
primer
fulminante
amorce
Zündhütchen
cup
culote
culot
Amboß

RIFLE (RIFLED BORE)
RIFLE
CARABINE (CANON RAYÉ)
GEWEHR (GEZOGENER LAUF)

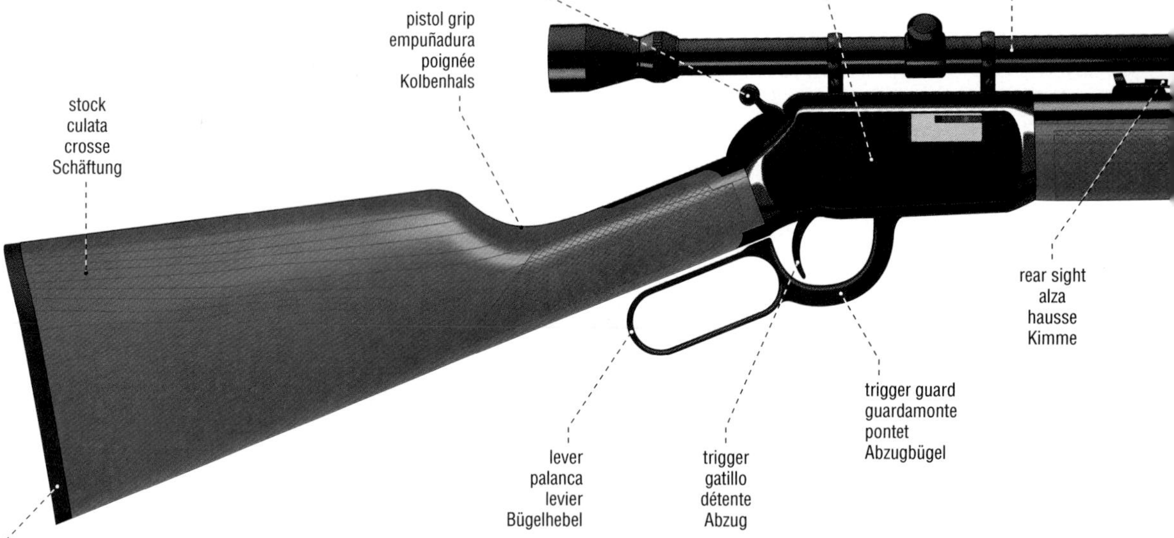

hammer
percutor
chien
Hammer

breechblock
bloque de cierre de la recámara
bloc de culasse
Verschlußstück

telescopic sight
mira telescópica
lunette de visée
Zielfernrohr

pistol grip
empuñadura
poignée
Kolbenhals

stock
culata
crosse
Schäftung

rear sight
alza
hausse
Kimme

trigger guard
guardamonte
pontet
Abzugbügel

lever
palanca
levier
Bügelhebel

trigger
gatillo
détente
Abzug

butt plate
cantonera
plaque de couche
Rückschlaghinderer

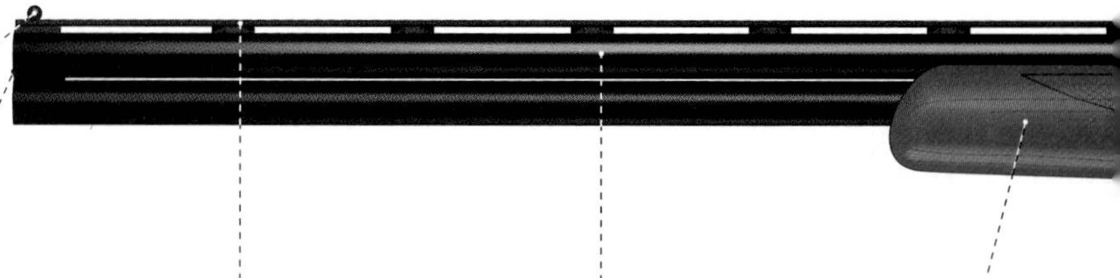

front sight
punto de mira
guidon
Korn

muzzle
boca
bouche
Mündung

ventilated rib
banda de ventilación
bande ventilée
Laufschiene

barrel
cañón
canon
Rohr

forearm
caña
fût
Vorderschaft

CARTRIDGE (SHOTGUN)
CARTUCHO DE ESCOPETA
CARTOUCHE (FUSIL)
PATRONE (SCHROTFLINTE)

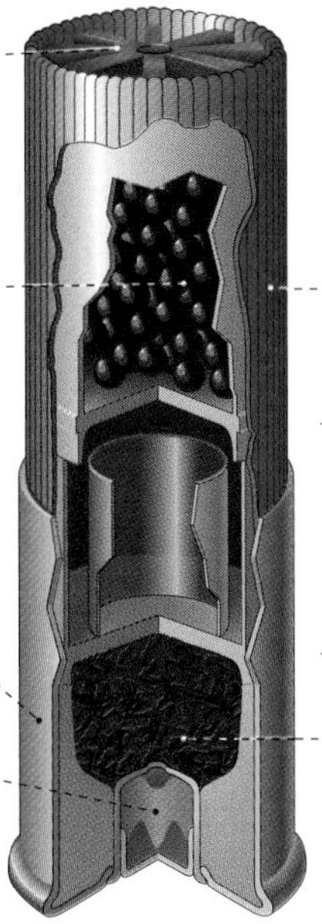

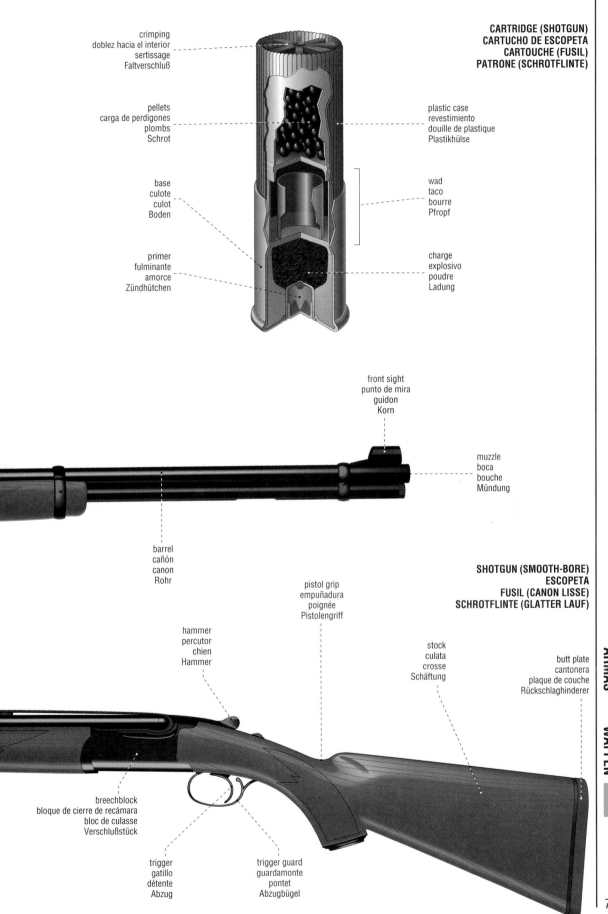

crimping
doblez hacia el interior
sertissage
Faltverschluß

pellets
carga de perdigones
plombs
Schrot

plastic case
revestimiento
douille de plastique
Plastikhülse

base
culote
culot
Boden

wad
taco
bourre
Pfropf

primer
fulminante
amorce
Zündhütchen

charge
explosivo
poudre
Ladung

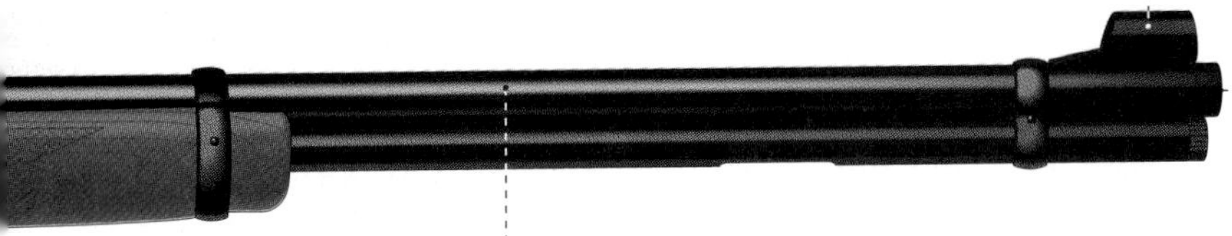

front sight
punto de mira
guidon
Korn

muzzle
boca
bouche
Mündung

barrel
cañón
canon
Rohr

SHOTGUN (SMOOTH-BORE)
ESCOPETA
FUSIL (CANON LISSE)
SCHROTFLINTE (GLATTER LAUF)

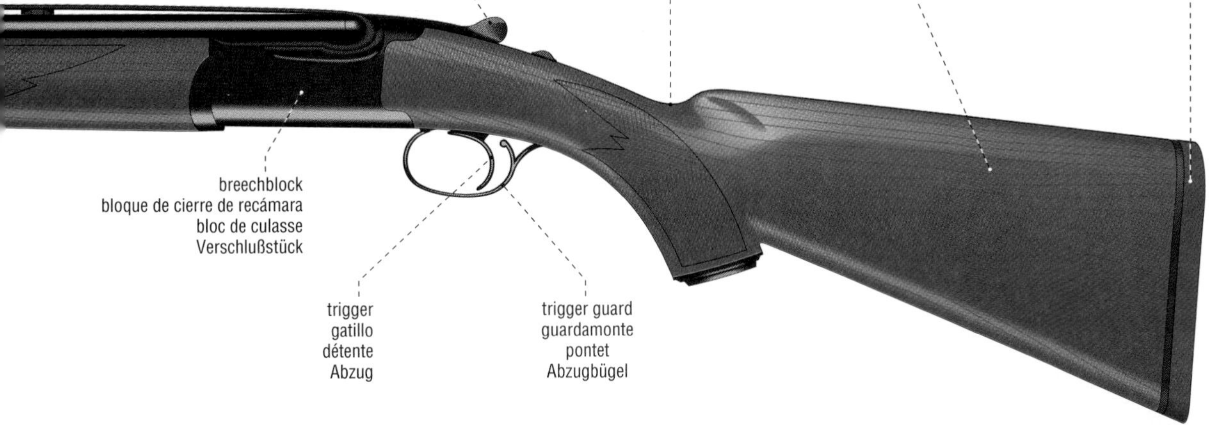

pistol grip
empuñadura
poignée
Pistolengriff

hammer
percutor
chien
Hammer

stock
culata
crosse
Schäftung

butt plate
cantonera
plaque de couche
Rückschlaghinderer

breechblock
bloque de cierre de recámara
bloc de culasse
Verschlußstück

trigger
gatillo
détente
Abzug

trigger guard
guardamonte
pontet
Abzugbügel

SEVENTEENTH CENTURY CANNON
CAÑÓN DEL SIGLO XVII
CANON DU XVIIᴱ SIÈCLE
KANONE AUS DEM 17. JAHRHUNDERT

MUZZLE LOADING
CAÑÓN DE AVANCARGA
BOUCHE À FEU
VORDERLADE-GESCHÜTZ

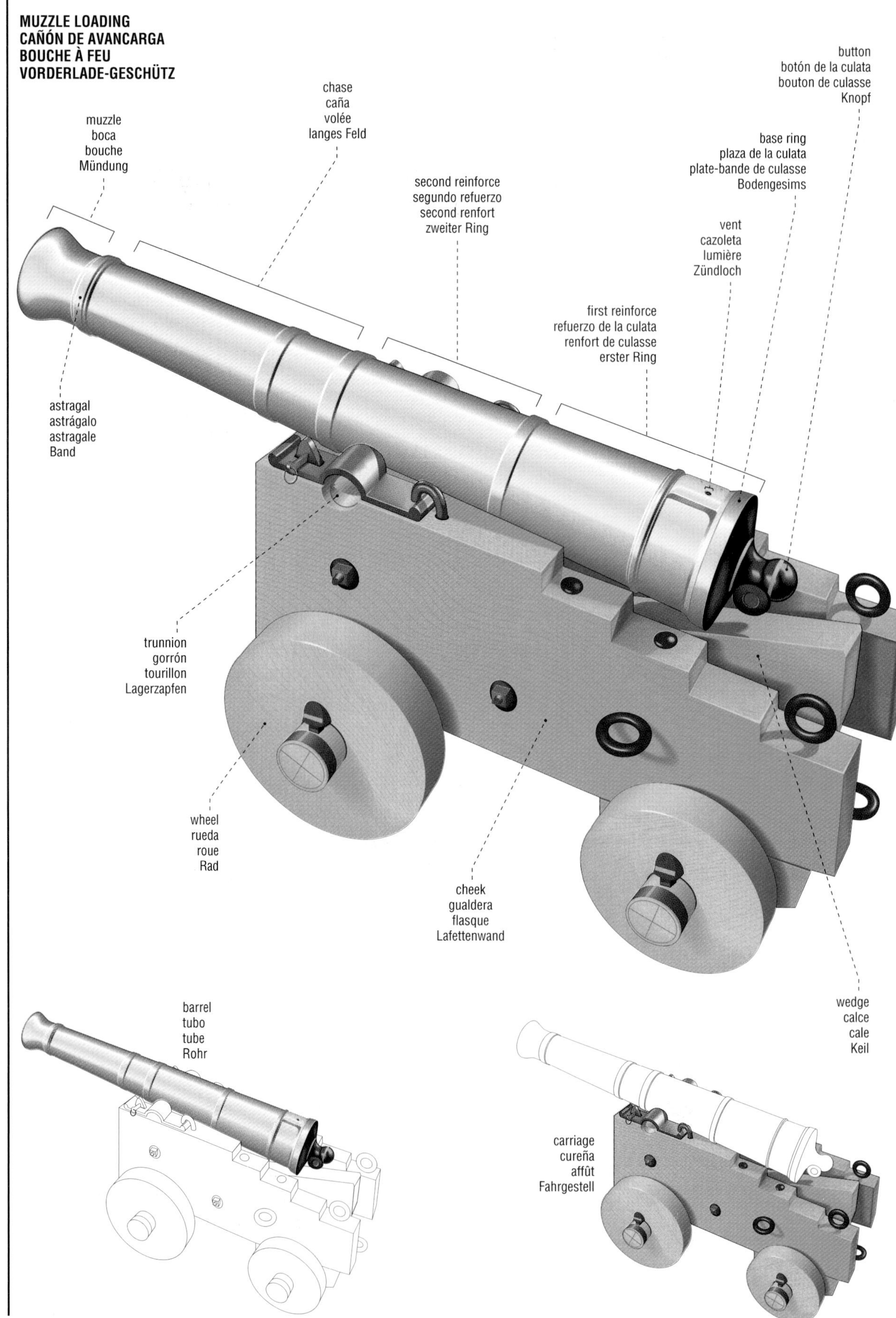

button
botón de la culata
bouton de culasse
Knopf
chase
caña
volée
langes Feld
muzzle
boca
bouche
Mündung
base ring
plaza de la culata
plate-bande de culasse
Bodengesims
second reinforce
segundo refuerzo
second renfort
zweiter Ring
vent
cazoleta
lumière
Zündloch
first reinforce
refuerzo de la culata
renfort de culasse
erster Ring
astragal
astrágalo
astragale
Band
trunnion
gorrón
tourillon
Lagerzapfen
wheel
rueda
roue
Rad
cheek
gualdera
flasque
Lafettenwand
wedge
calce
cale
Keil
barrel
tubo
tube
Rohr
carriage
cureña
affût
Fahrgestell

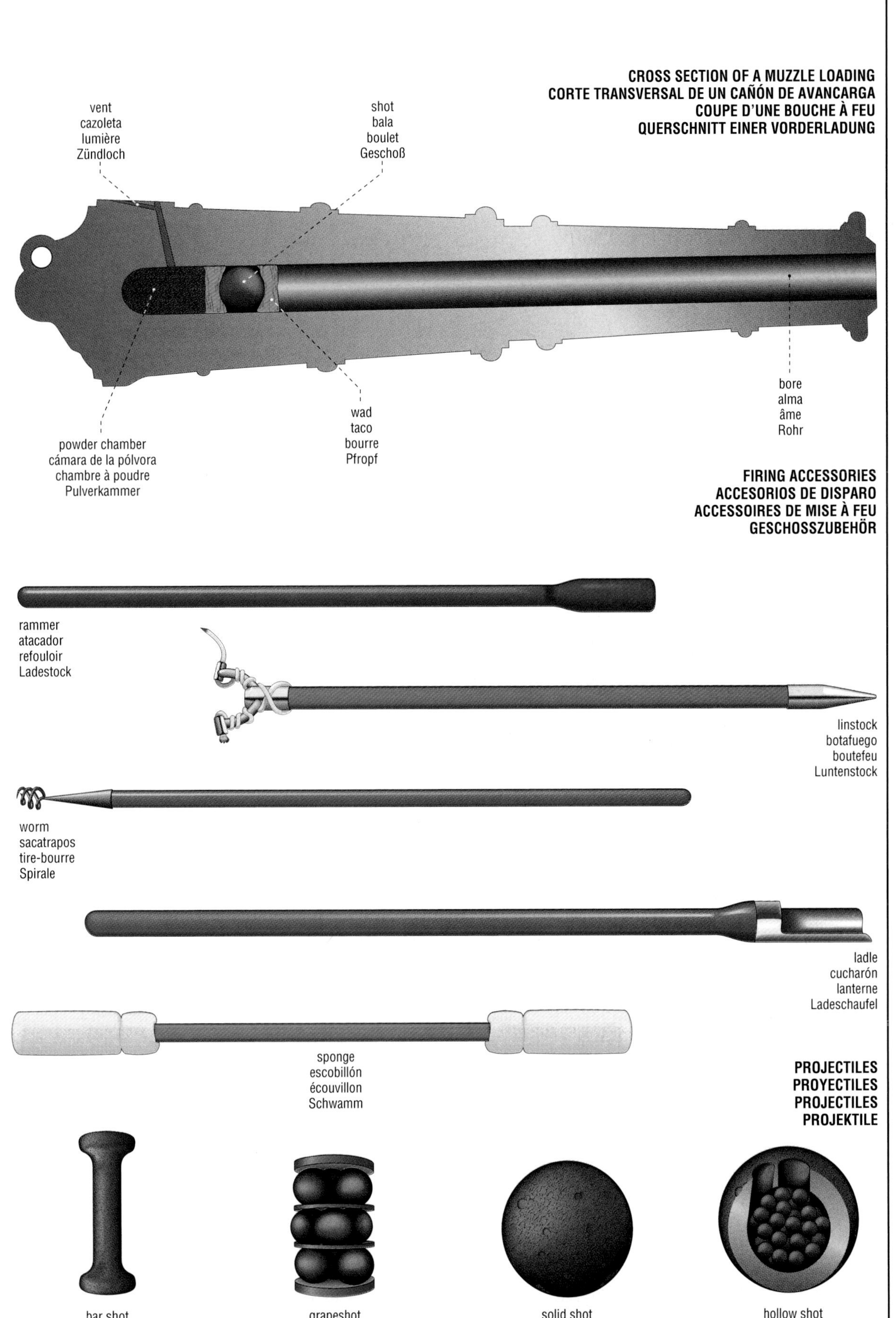
CROSS SECTION OF A MUZZLE LOADING
CORTE TRANSVERSAL DE UN CAÑÓN DE AVANCARGA
COUPE D'UNE BOUCHE À FEU
QUERSCHNITT EINER VORDERLADUNG
vent
cazoleta
lumière
Zündloch
shot
bala
boulet
Geschoß
bore
alma
âme
Rohr
powder chamber
cámara de la pólvora
chambre à poudre
Pulverkammer
wad
taco
bourre
Pfropf
FIRING ACCESSORIES
ACCESORIOS DE DISPARO
ACCESSOIRES DE MISE À FEU
GESCHOSSZUBEHÖR
rammer
atacador
refouloir
Ladestock
linstock
botafuego
boutefeu
Luntenstock
worm
sacatrapos
tire-bourre
Spirale
ladle
cucharón
lanterne
Ladeschaufel
sponge
escobillón
écouvillon
Schwamm
PROJECTILES
PROYECTILES
PROJECTILES
PROJEKTILE
bar shot
bala de barra
boulet ramé
Stangenkugel
grapeshot
metralla
grappe de raisin
Kartätsche
solid shot
bala sólida
boulet
Vollgeschoß
hollow shot
bala con perdigones
boulet creux
Hohlladungsgeschoß

MODERN HOWITZER
OBÚS MODERNO
OBUSIER MODERNE
MODERNE HAUBITZE

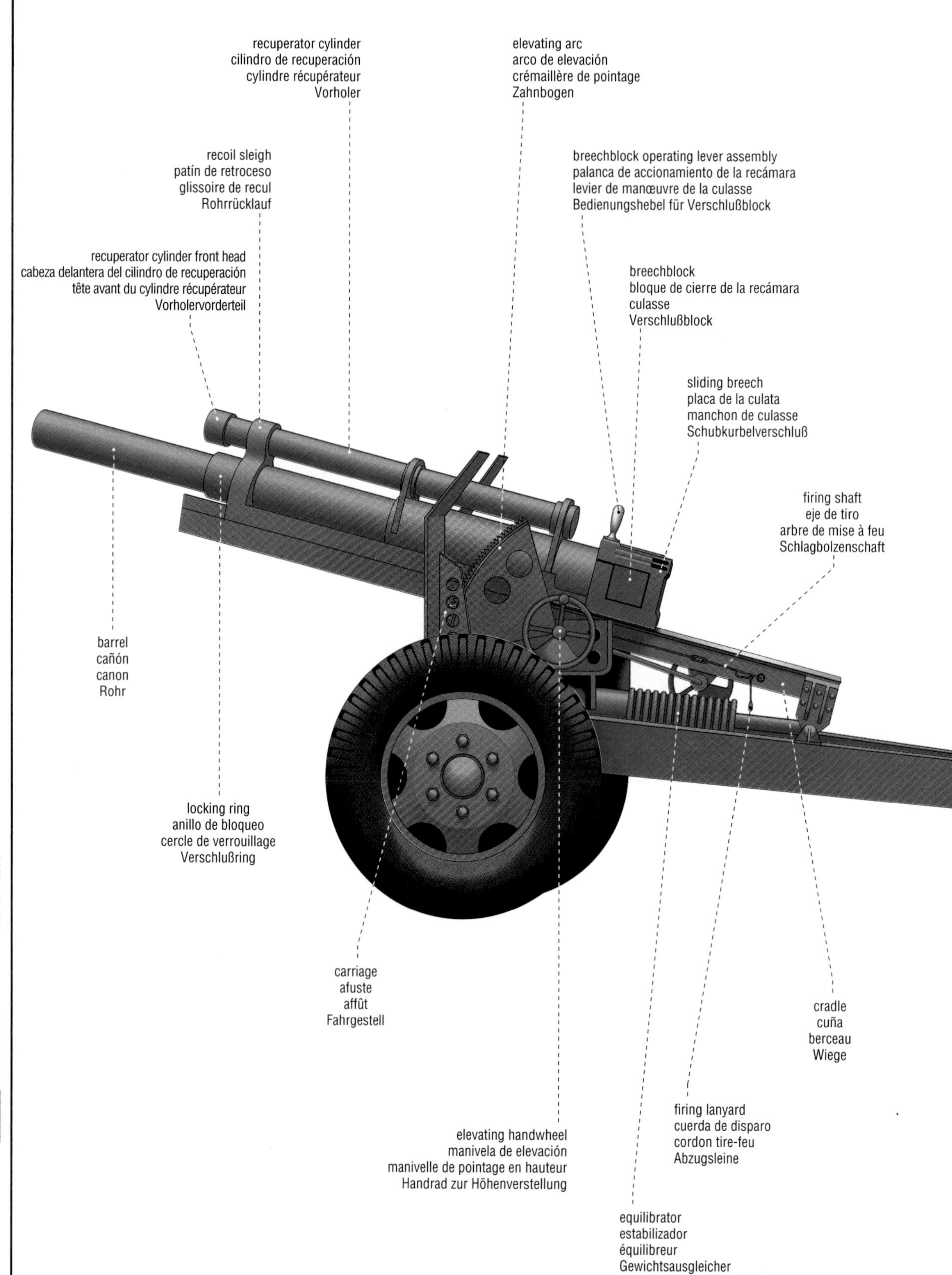

recuperator cylinder
cilindro de recuperación
cylindre récupérateur
Vorholer
elevating arc
arco de elevación
crémaillère de pointage
Zahnbogen
recoil sleigh
patín de retroceso
glissoire de recul
Rohrrücklauf
breechblock operating lever assembly
palanca de accionamiento de la recámara
levier de manœuvre de la culasse
Bedienungshebel für Verschlußblock
recuperator cylinder front head
cabeza delantera del cilindro de recuperación
tête avant du cylindre récupérateur
Vorholervorderteil
breechblock
bloque de cierre de la recámara
culasse
Verschlußblock
sliding breech
placa de la culata
manchon de culasse
Schubkurbelverschluß
firing shaft
eje de tiro
arbre de mise à feu
Schlagbolzenschaft
barrel
cañón
canon
Rohr
locking ring
anillo de bloqueo
cercle de verrouillage
Verschlußring
carriage
afuste
affût
Fahrgestell
cradle
cuña
berceau
Wiege
firing lanyard
cuerda de disparo
cordon tire-feu
Abzugsleine
elevating handwheel
manivela de elevación
manivelle de pointage en hauteur
Handrad zur Höhenverstellung
equilibrator
estabilizador
équilibreur
Gewichtsausgleicher

MORTAR
MORTEROS
MORTIER
MÖRSER

MODERN MORTAR
MORTERO MODERNO
MORTIER MODERNE
MODERNER MÖRSER

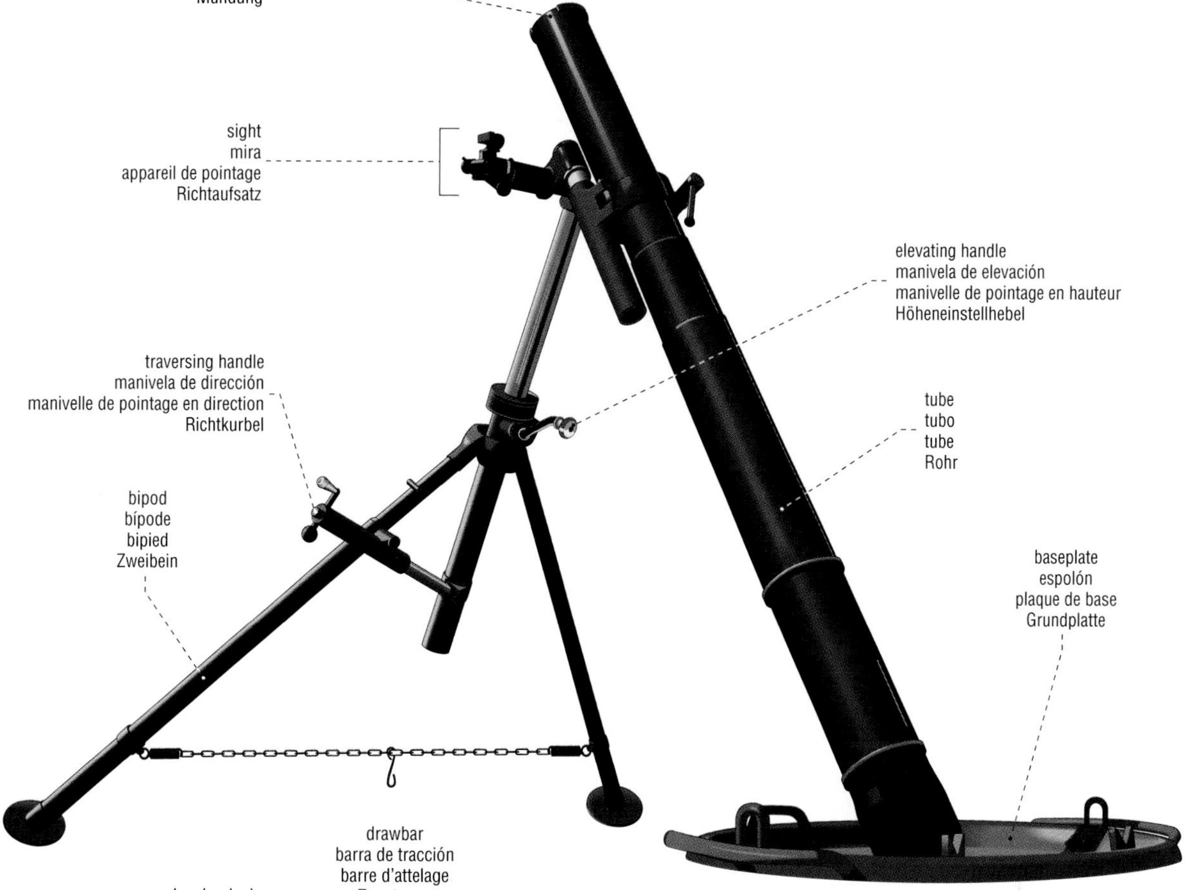

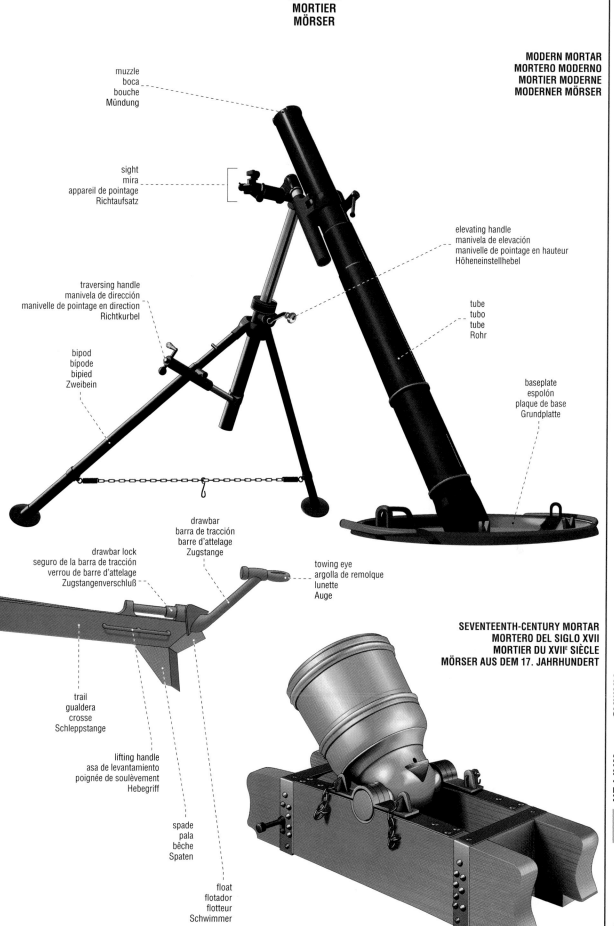

muzzle
boca
bouche
Mündung

sight
mira
appareil de pointage
Richtaufsatz

elevating handle
manivela de elevación
manivelle de pointage en hauteur
Höheneinstellhebel

traversing handle
manivela de dirección
manivelle de pointage en direction
Richtkurbel

tube
tubo
tube
Rohr

bipod
bípode
bipied
Zweibein

baseplate
espolón
plaque de base
Grundplatte

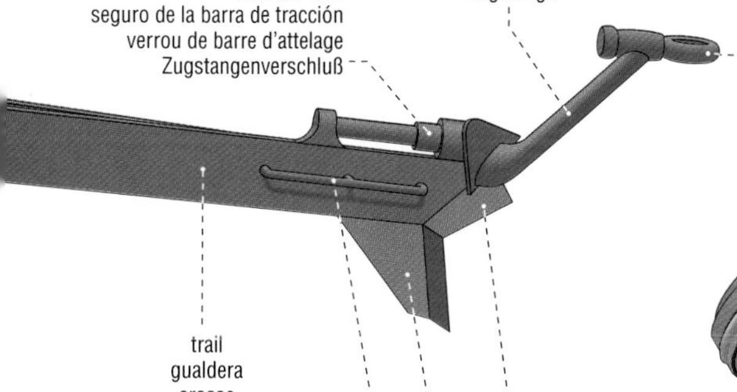

drawbar
barra de tracción
barre d'attelage
Zugstange

drawbar lock
seguro de la barra de tracción
verrou de barre d'attelage
Zugstangenverschluß

towing eye
argolla de remolque
lunette
Auge

SEVENTEENTH-CENTURY MORTAR
MORTERO DEL SIGLO XVII
MORTIER DU XVIIE SIÈCLE
MÖRSER AUS DEM 17. JAHRHUNDERT

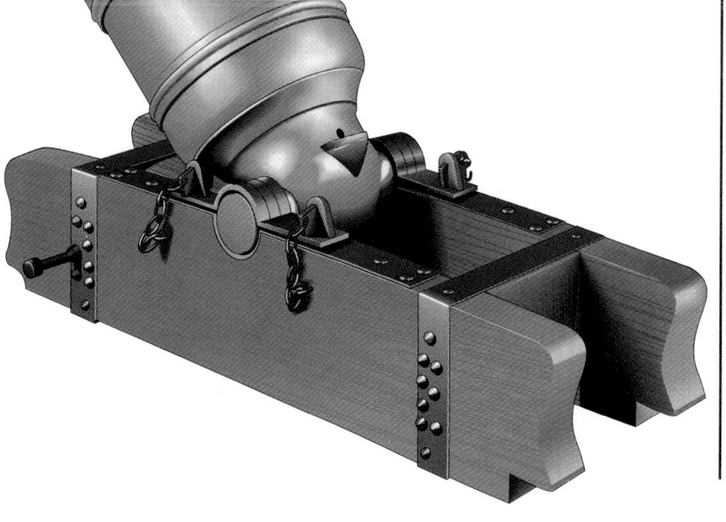

trail
gualdera
crosse
Schleppstange

lifting handle
asa de levantamiento
poignée de soulèvement
Hebegriff

spade
pala
bêche
Spaten

float
flotador
flotteur
Schwimmer

HAND GRENADE
GRANADA DE MANO
GRENADE À MAIN
HANDGRANATE

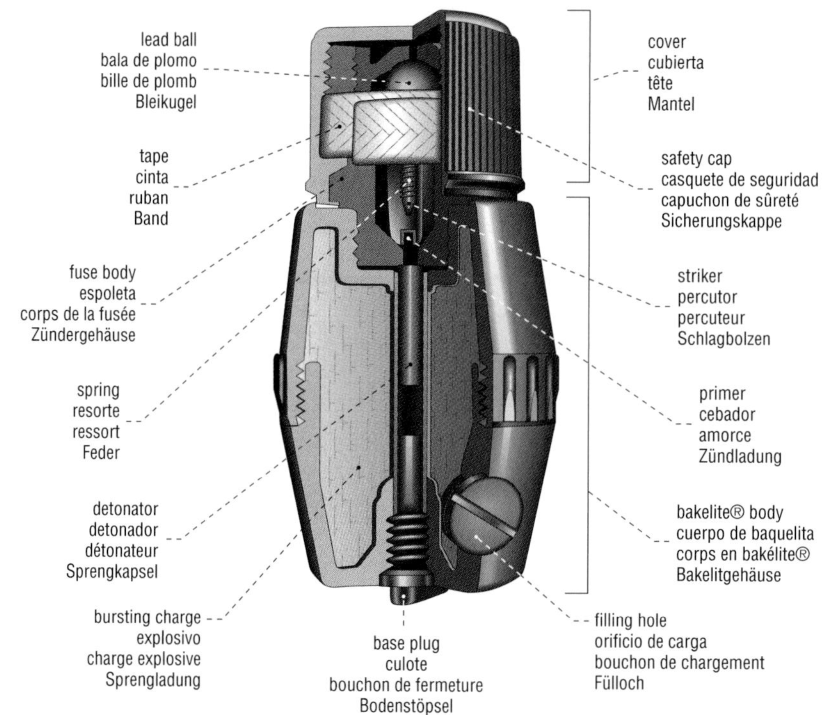
lead ball
bala de plomo
bille de plomb
Bleikugel
tape
cinta
ruban
Band
fuse body
espoleta
corps de la fusée
Zündergehäuse
spring
resorte
ressort
Feder
detonator
detonador
détonateur
Sprengkapsel
bursting charge
explosivo
charge explosive
Sprengladung
base plug
culote
bouchon de fermeture
Bodenstöpsel
cover
cubierta
tête
Mantel
safety cap
casquete de seguridad
capuchon de sûreté
Sicherungskappe
striker
percutor
percuteur
Schlagbolzen
primer
cebador
amorce
Zündladung
bakelite® body
cuerpo de baquelita
corps en bakélite®
Bakelitgehäuse
filling hole
orificio de carga
bouchon de chargement
Fülloch

BAZOOKA
BAZUCA
BAZOOKA
PANZERFAUST

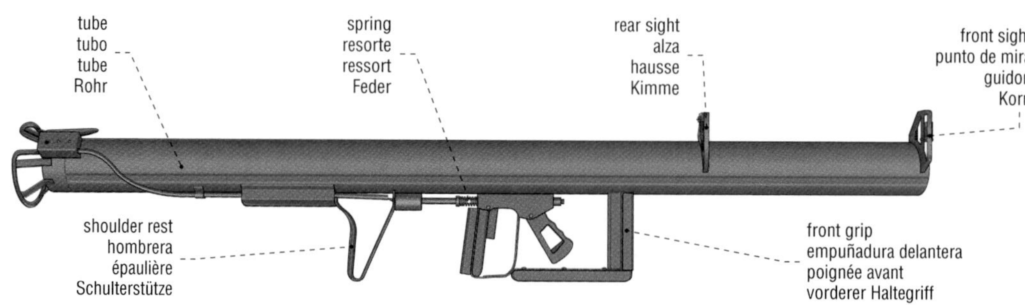
tube
tubo
tube
Rohr
spring
resorte
ressort
Feder
rear sight
alza
hausse
Kimme
front sight
punto de mira
guidon
Korn
shoulder rest
hombrera
épaulière
Schulterstütze
front grip
empuñadura delantera
poignée avant
vorderer Haltegriff

RECOILLESS RIFLE
FUSIL SIN RETROCESO
CANON SANS RECUL
RÜCKSTOSSFREIES GESCHÜTZ

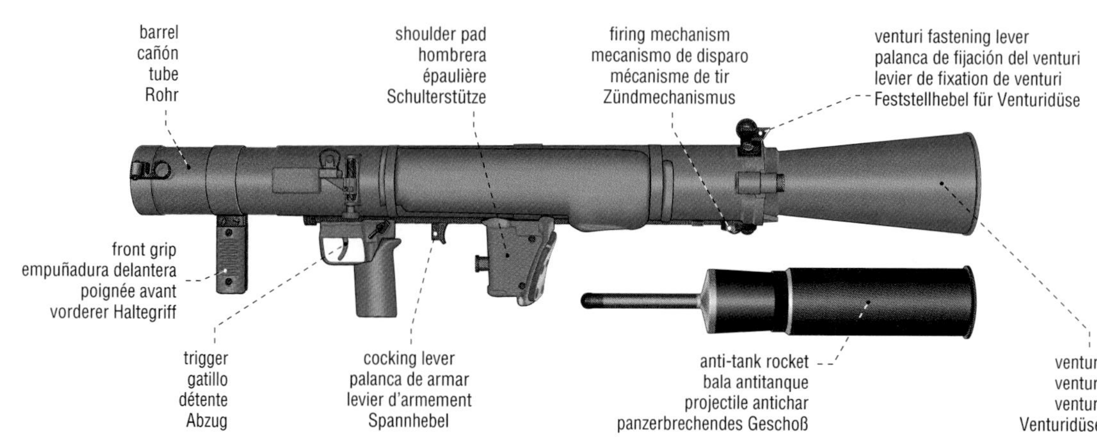
barrel
cañón
tube
Rohr
shoulder pad
hombrera
épaulière
Schulterstütze
firing mechanism
mecanismo de disparo
mécanisme de tir
Zündmechanismus
venturi fastening lever
palanca de fijación del venturi
levier de fixation de venturi
Feststellhebel für Venturidüse
front grip
empuñadura delantera
poignée avant
vorderer Haltegriff
trigger
gatillo
détente
Abzug
cocking lever
palanca de armar
levier d'armement
Spannhebel
anti-tank rocket
bala antitanque
projectile antichar
panzerbrechendes Geschoß
venturi
venturi
venturi
Venturidüse

TANK
TANQUE
CHAR D'ASSAUT
PANZER

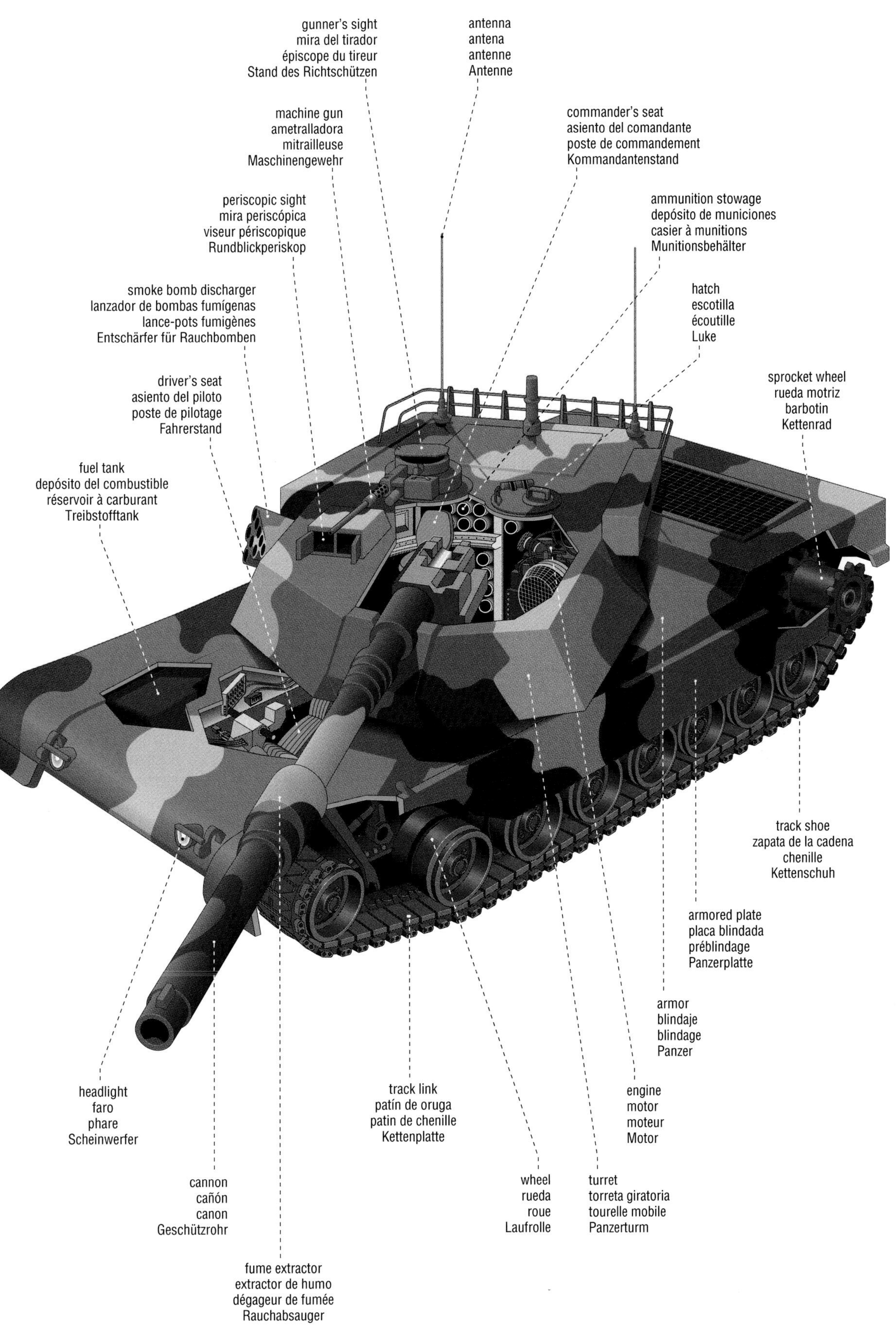

gunner's sight
mira del tirador
épiscope du tireur
Stand des Richtschützen
antenna
antena
antenne
Antenne
machine gun
ametralladora
mitrailleuse
Maschinengewehr
commander's seat
asiento del comandante
poste de commandement
Kommandantenstand
periscopic sight
mira periscópica
viseur périscopique
Rundblickperiskop
ammunition stowage
depósito de municiones
casier à munitions
Munitionsbehälter
smoke bomb discharger
lanzador de bombas fumígenas
lance-pots fumigènes
Entschärfer für Rauchbomben
hatch
escotilla
écoutille
Luke
driver's seat
asiento del piloto
poste de pilotage
Fahrerstand
sprocket wheel
rueda motriz
barbotin
Kettenrad
fuel tank
depósito del combustible
réservoir à carburant
Treibstofftank
track shoe
zapata de la cadena
chenille
Kettenschuh
armored plate
placa blindada
préblindage
Panzerplatte
armor
blindaje
blindage
Panzer
headlight
faro
phare
Scheinwerfer
track link
patín de oruga
patin de chenille
Kettenplatte
engine
motor
moteur
Motor
cannon
cañón
canon
Geschützrohr
wheel
rueda
roue
Laufrolle
turret
torreta giratoria
tourelle mobile
Panzerturm
fume extractor
extractor de humo
dégageur de fumée
Rauchabsauger

SUBMARINE
SUBMARINO
SOUS-MARIN
UNTERSEEBOOT

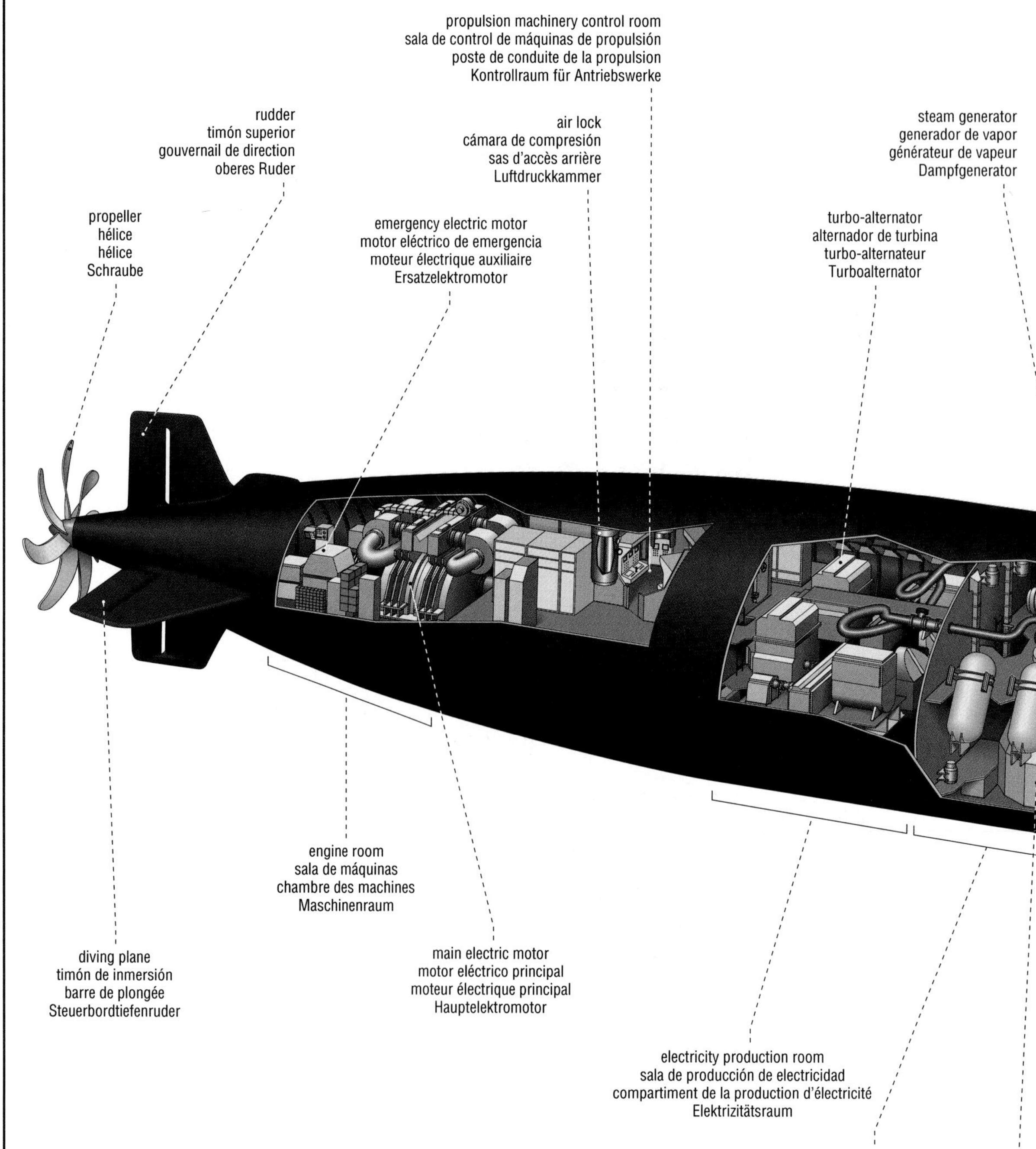

propulsion machinery control room
sala de control de máquinas de propulsión
poste de conduite de la propulsion
Kontrollraum für Antriebswerke
rudder
timón superior
gouvernail de direction
oberes Ruder
air lock
cámara de compresión
sas d'accès arrière
Luftdruckkammer
steam generator
generador de vapor
générateur de vapeur
Dampfgenerator
propeller
hélice
hélice
Schraube
emergency electric motor
motor eléctrico de emergencia
moteur électrique auxiliaire
Ersatzelektromotor
turbo-alternator
alternador de turbina
turbo-alternateur
Turboalternator
engine room
sala de máquinas
chambre des machines
Maschinenraum
diving plane
timón de inmersión
barre de plongée
Steuerbordtiefenruder
main electric motor
motor eléctrico principal
moteur électrique principal
Hauptelektromotor
electricity production room
sala de producción de electricidad
compartiment de la production d'électricité
Elektrizitätsraum
nuclear boiler room
sala de la caldera nuclear
compartiment du réacteur
Kernreaktorraum
reactor
reactor
réacteur
Reaktor

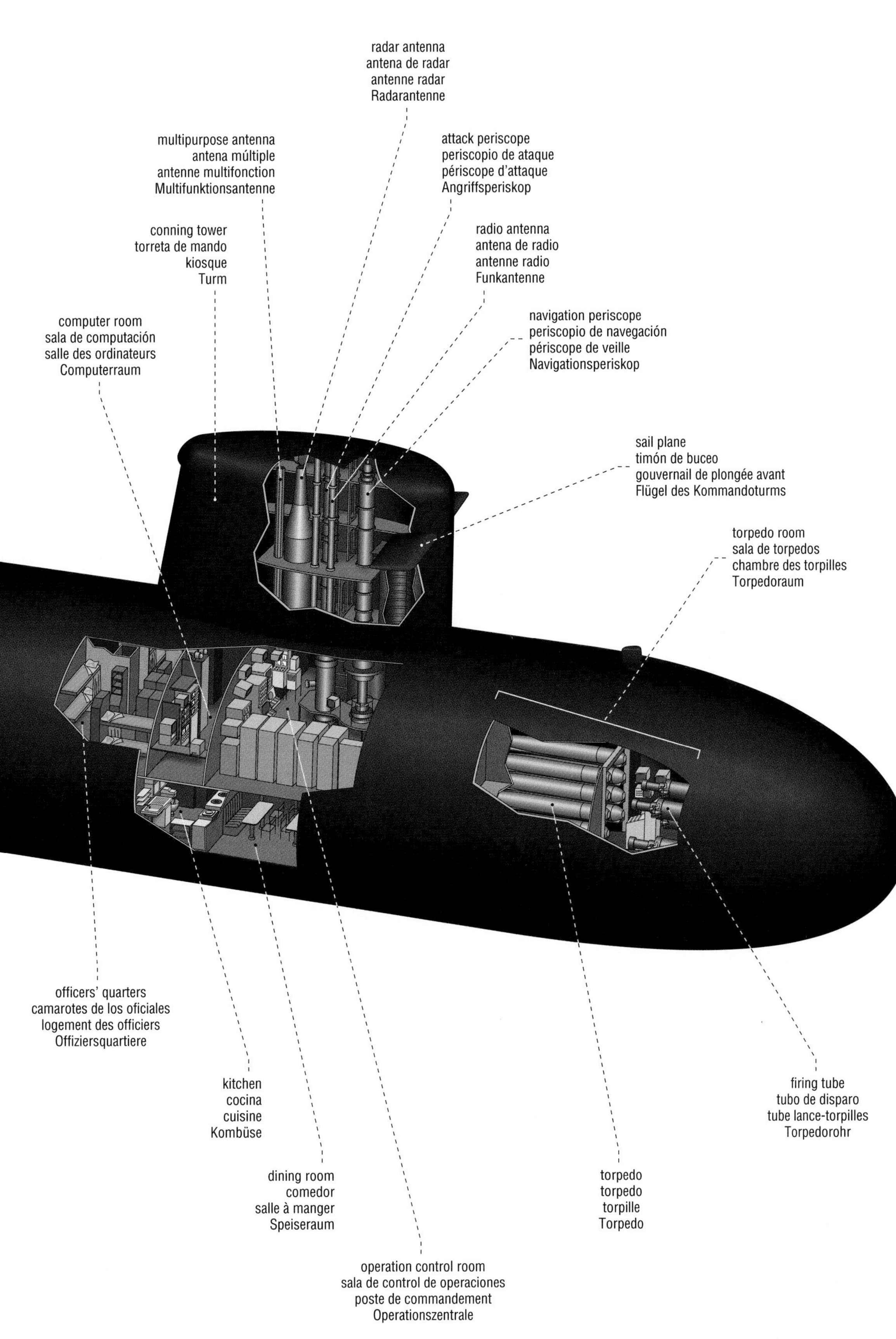
radar antenna
antena de radar
antenne radar
Radarantenne
multipurpose antenna
antena múltiple
antenne multifonction
Multifunktionsantenne
attack periscope
periscopio de ataque
périscope d'attaque
Angriffsperiskop
conning tower
torreta de mando
kiosque
Turm
radio antenna
antena de radio
antenne radio
Funkantenne
computer room
sala de computación
salle des ordinateurs
Computerraum
navigation periscope
periscopio de navegación
périscope de veille
Navigationsperiskop
sail plane
timón de buceo
gouvernail de plongée avant
Flügel des Kommandoturms
torpedo room
sala de torpedos
chambre des torpilles
Torpedoraum
officers' quarters
camarotes de los oficiales
logement des officiers
Offiziersquartiere
kitchen
cocina
cuisine
Kombüse
firing tube
tubo de disparo
tube lance-torpilles
Torpedorohr
dining room
comedor
salle à manger
Speiseraum
torpedo
torpedo
torpille
Torpedo
operation control room
sala de control de operaciones
poste de commandement
Operationszentrale

FRIGATE
FRAGATA
FRÉGATE
FREGATTE

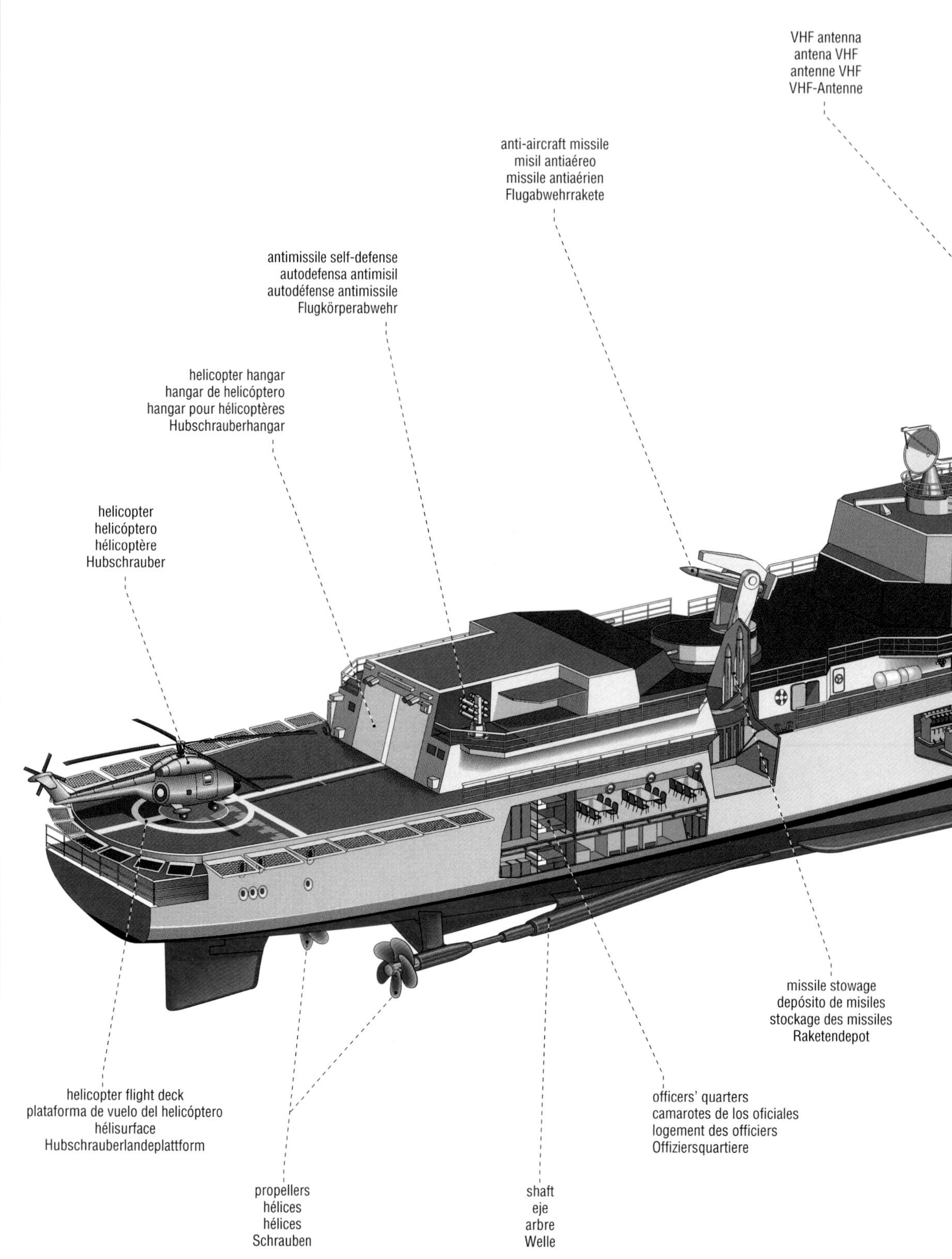

VHF antenna
antena VHF
antenne VHF
VHF-Antenne
anti-aircraft missile
misil antiaéreo
missile antiaérien
Flugabwehrrakete
antimissile self-defense
autodefensa antimisil
autodéfense antimissile
Flugkörperabwehr
helicopter hangar
hangar de helicóptero
hangar pour hélicoptères
Hubschrauberhangar
helicopter
helicóptero
hélicoptère
Hubschrauber
missile stowage
depósito de misiles
stockage des missiles
Raketendepot
helicopter flight deck
plataforma de vuelo del helicóptero
hélisurface
Hubschrauberlandeplattform
officers' quarters
camarotes de los oficiales
logement des officiers
Offiziersquartiere
propellers
hélices
hélices
Schrauben
shaft
eje
arbre
Welle

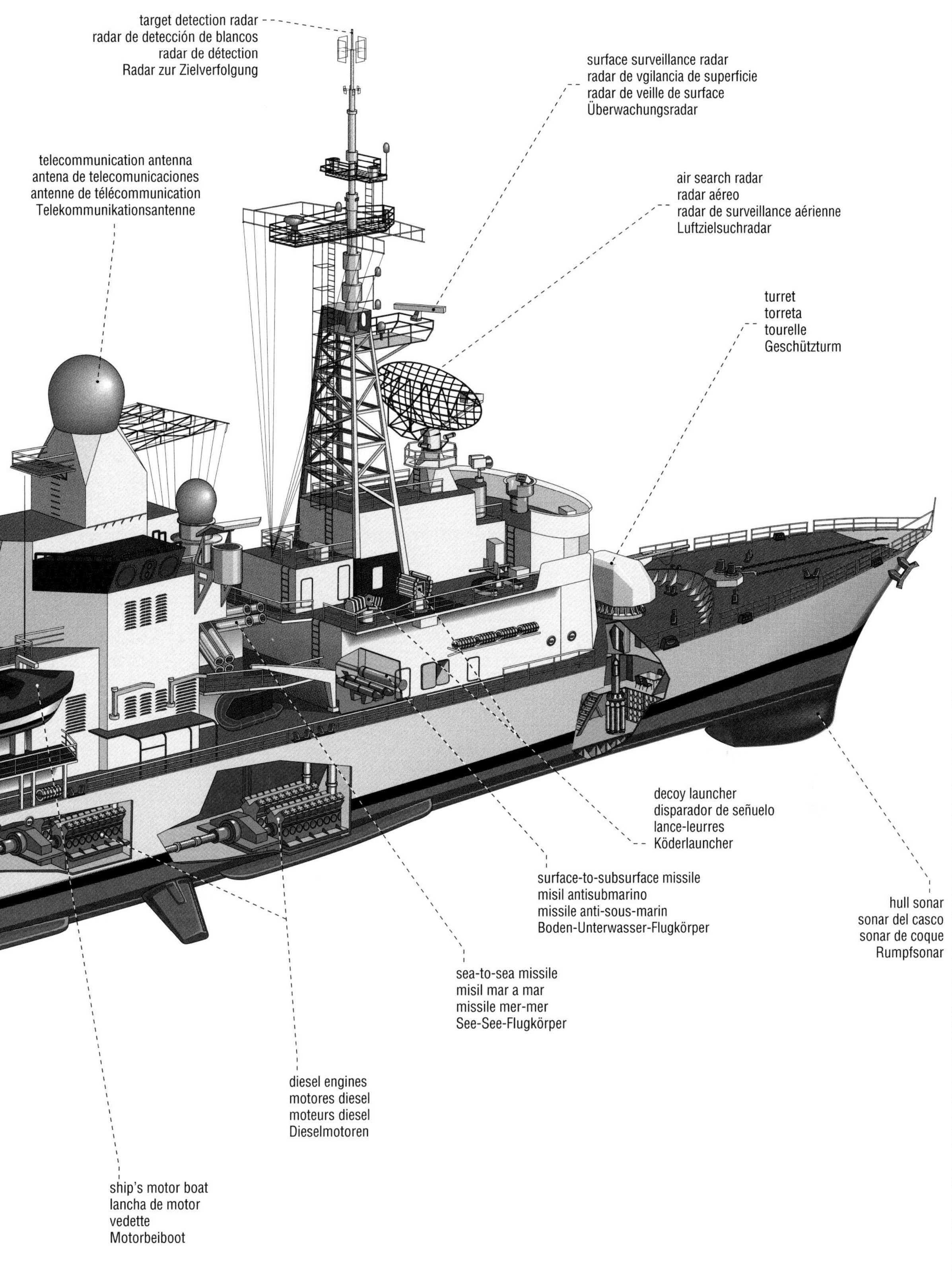
target detection radar
radar de detección de blancos
radar de détection
Radar zur Zielverfolgung
surface surveillance radar
radar de vgilancia de superficie
radar de veille de surface
Überwachungsradar
telecommunication antenna
antena de telecomunicaciones
antenne de télécommunication
Telekommunikationsantenne
air search radar
radar aéreo
radar de surveillance aérienne
Luftzielsuchradar
turret
torreta
tourelle
Geschützturm
decoy launcher
disparador de señuelo
lance-leurres
Köderlauncher
surface-to-subsurface missile
misil antisubmarino
missile anti-sous-marin
Boden-Unterwasser-Flugkörper
hull sonar
sonar del casco
sonar de coque
Rumpfsonar
sea-to-sea missile
misil mar a mar
missile mer-mer
See-See-Flugkörper
diesel engines
motores diesel
moteurs diesel
Dieselmotoren
ship's motor boat
lancha de motor
vedette
Motorbeiboot

AIRCRAFT CARRIER
PORTAAVIONES
PORTE-AVIONS
FLUGZEUGTRÄGER

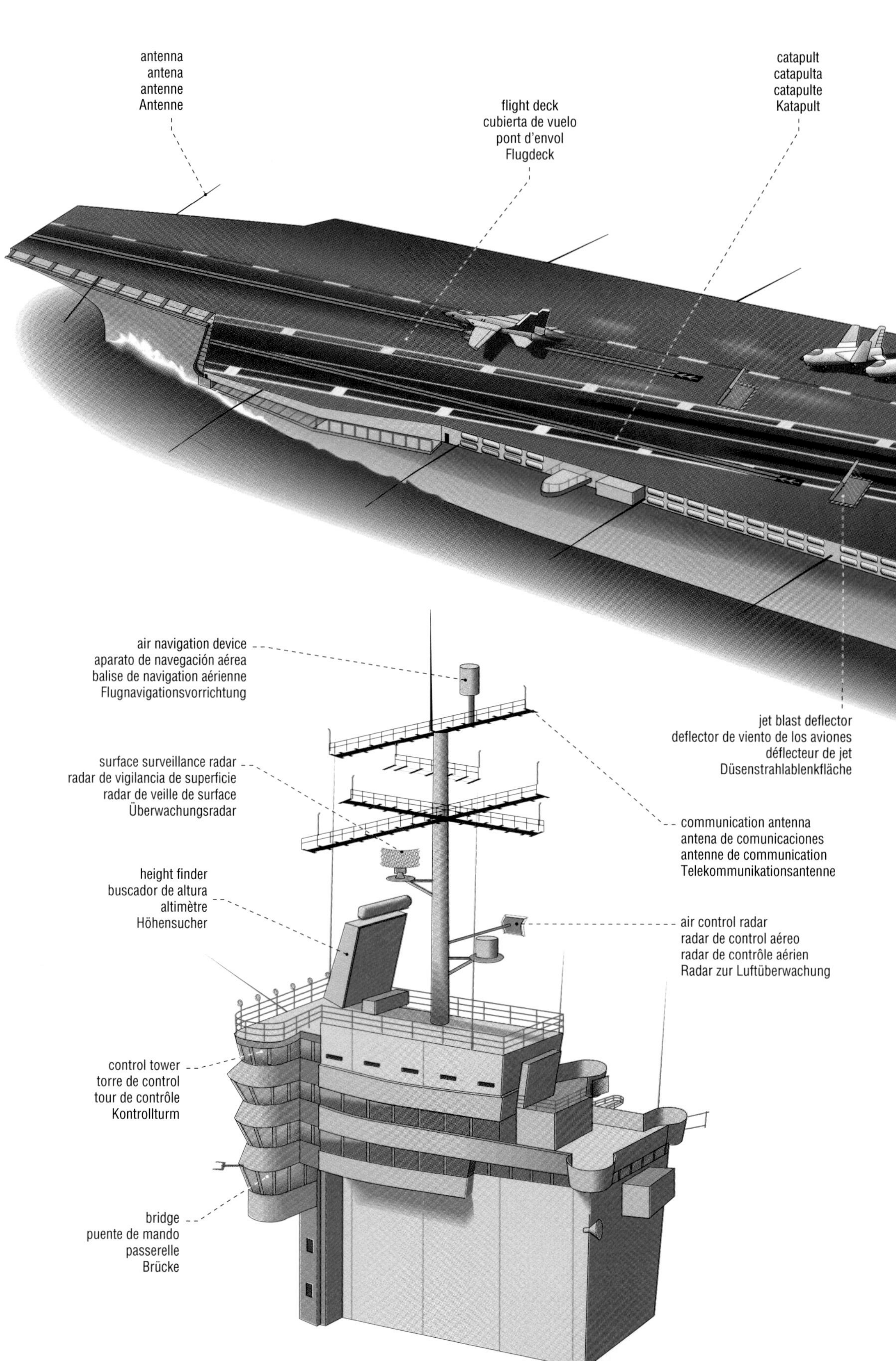

antenna
antena
antenne
Antenne
flight deck
cubierta de vuelo
pont d'envol
Flugdeck
catapult
catapulta
catapulte
Katapult
air navigation device
aparato de navegación aérea
balise de navigation aérienne
Flugnavigationsvorrichtung
jet blast deflector
deflector de viento de los aviones
déflecteur de jet
Düsenstrahlablenkfläche
surface surveillance radar
radar de vigilancia de superficie
radar de veille de surface
Überwachungsradar
communication antenna
antena de comunicaciones
antenne de communication
Telekommunikationsantenne
height finder
buscador de altura
altimètre
Höhensucher
air control radar
radar de control aéreo
radar de contrôle aérien
Radar zur Luftüberwachung
control tower
torre de control
tour de contrôle
Kontrollturm
bridge
puente de mando
passerelle
Brücke

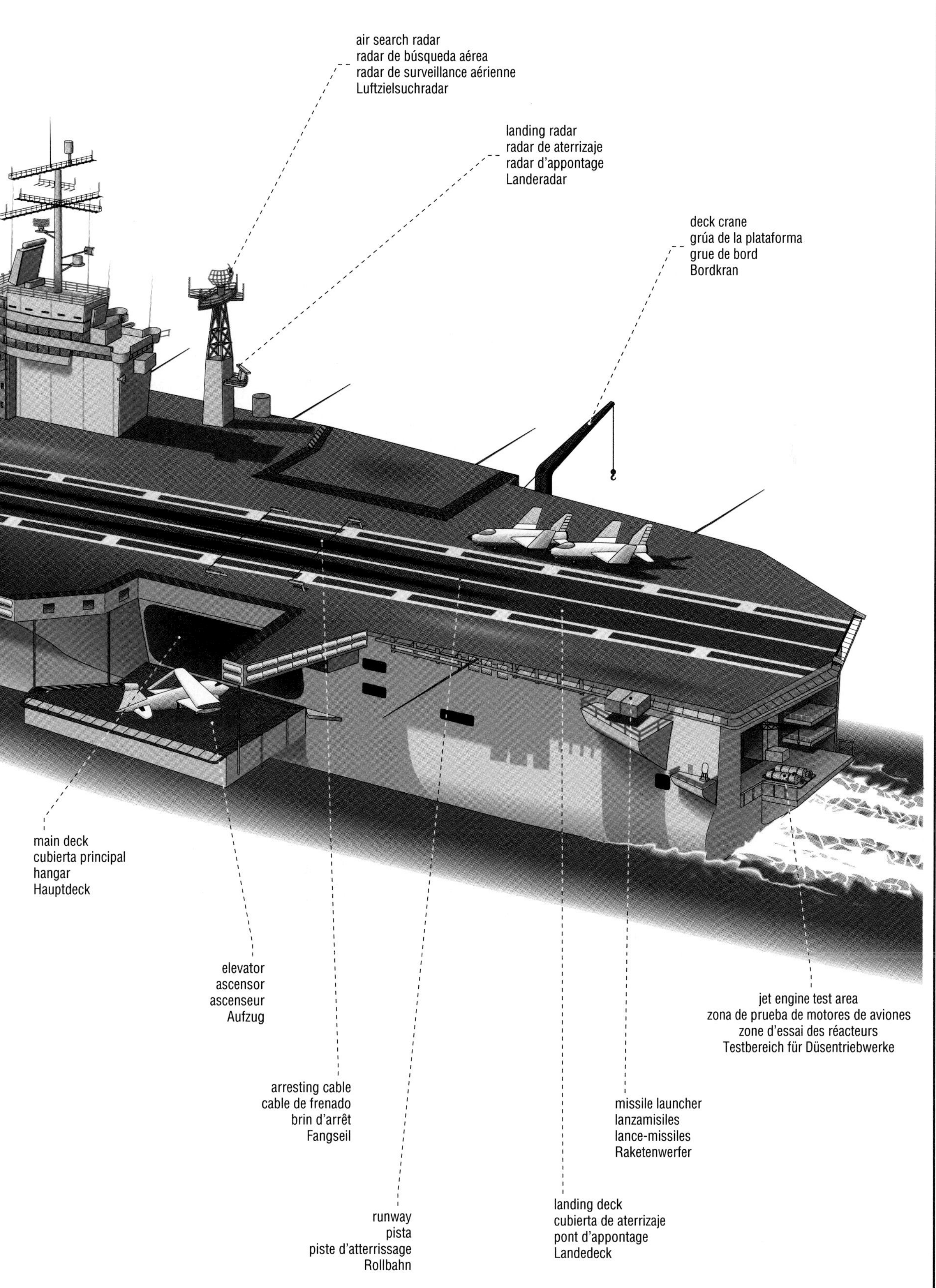
air search radar
radar de búsqueda aérea
radar de surveillance aérienne
Luftzielsuchradar
landing radar
radar de aterrizaje
radar d'appontage
Landeradar
deck crane
grúa de la plataforma
grue de bord
Bordkran
main deck
cubierta principal
hangar
Hauptdeck
elevator
ascensor
ascenseur
Aufzug
jet engine test area
zona de prueba de motores de aviones
zone d'essai des réacteurs
Testbereich für Düsentriebwerke
arresting cable
cable de frenado
brin d'arrêt
Fangseil
missile launcher
lanzamisiles
lance-missiles
Raketenwerfer
runway
pista
piste d'atterrissage
Rollbahn
landing deck
cubierta de aterrizaje
pont d'appontage
Landedeck

COMBAT AIRCRAFT
AVIÓN DE COMBATE
AVION DE COMBAT
KAMPFFLUGZEUG

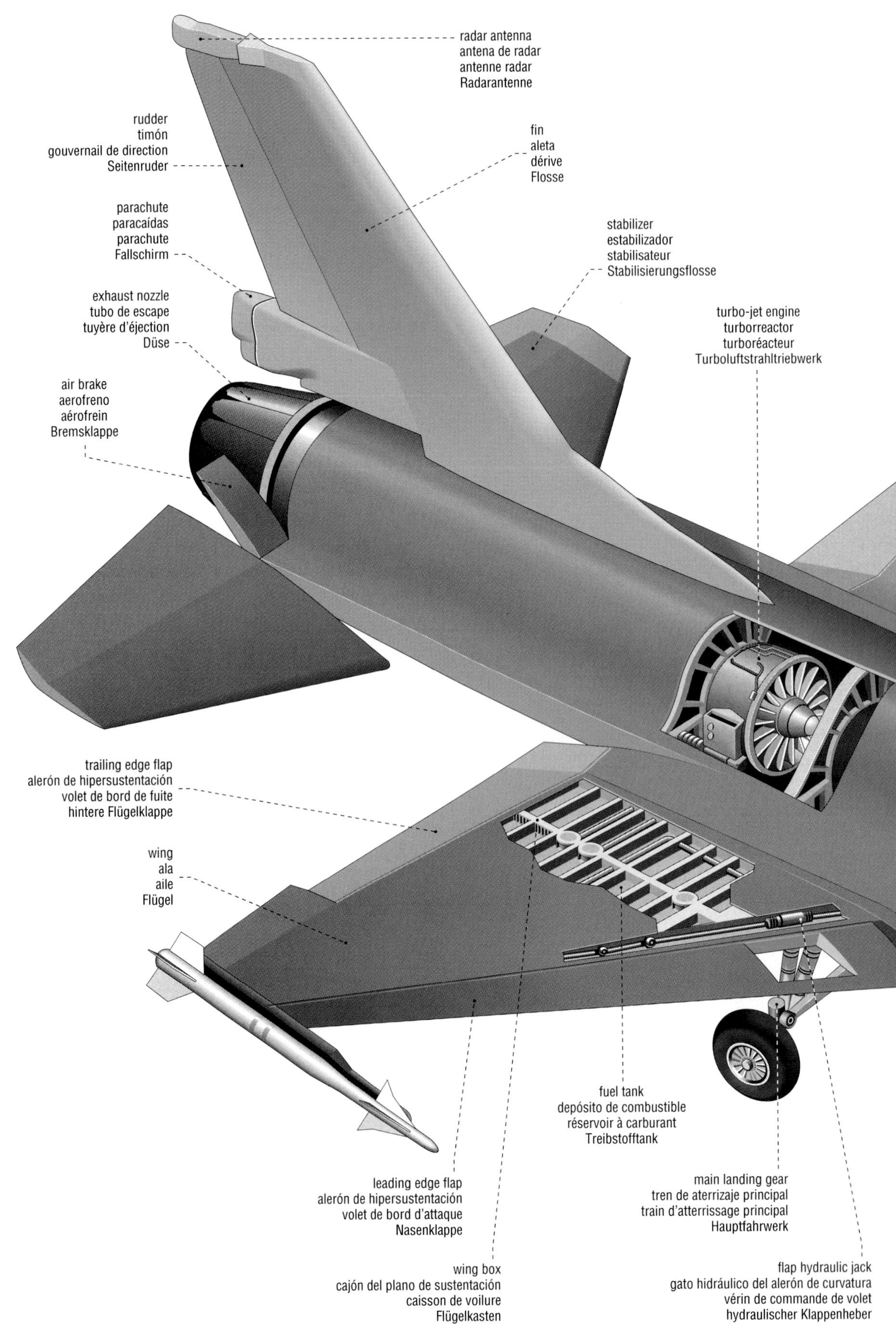
radar antenna
antena de radar
antenne radar
Radarantenne
rudder
timón
gouvernail de direction
Seitenruder
fin
aleta
dérive
Flosse
parachute
paracaídas
parachute
Fallschirm
stabilizer
estabilizador
stabilisateur
Stabilisierungsflosse
exhaust nozzle
tubo de escape
tuyère d'éjection
Düse
turbo-jet engine
turborreactor
turboréacteur
Turboluftstrahltriebwerk
air brake
aerofreno
aérofrein
Bremsklappe
trailing edge flap
alerón de hipersustentación
volet de bord de fuite
hintere Flügelklappe
wing
ala
aile
Flügel
fuel tank
depósito de combustible
réservoir à carburant
Treibstofftank
leading edge flap
alerón de hipersustentación
volet de bord d'attaque
Nasenklappe
main landing gear
tren de aterrizaje principal
train d'atterrissage principal
Hauptfahrwerk
wing box
cajón del plano de sustentación
caisson de voilure
Flügelkasten
flap hydraulic jack
gato hidráulico del alerón de curvatura
vérin de commande de volet
hydraulischer Klappenheber

IN-FLIGHT REFUELING
REAPROVISIONAMIENTO DE COMBUSTIBLE EN VUELO
RAVITAILLEMENT EN VOL
LUFTBETANKUNG

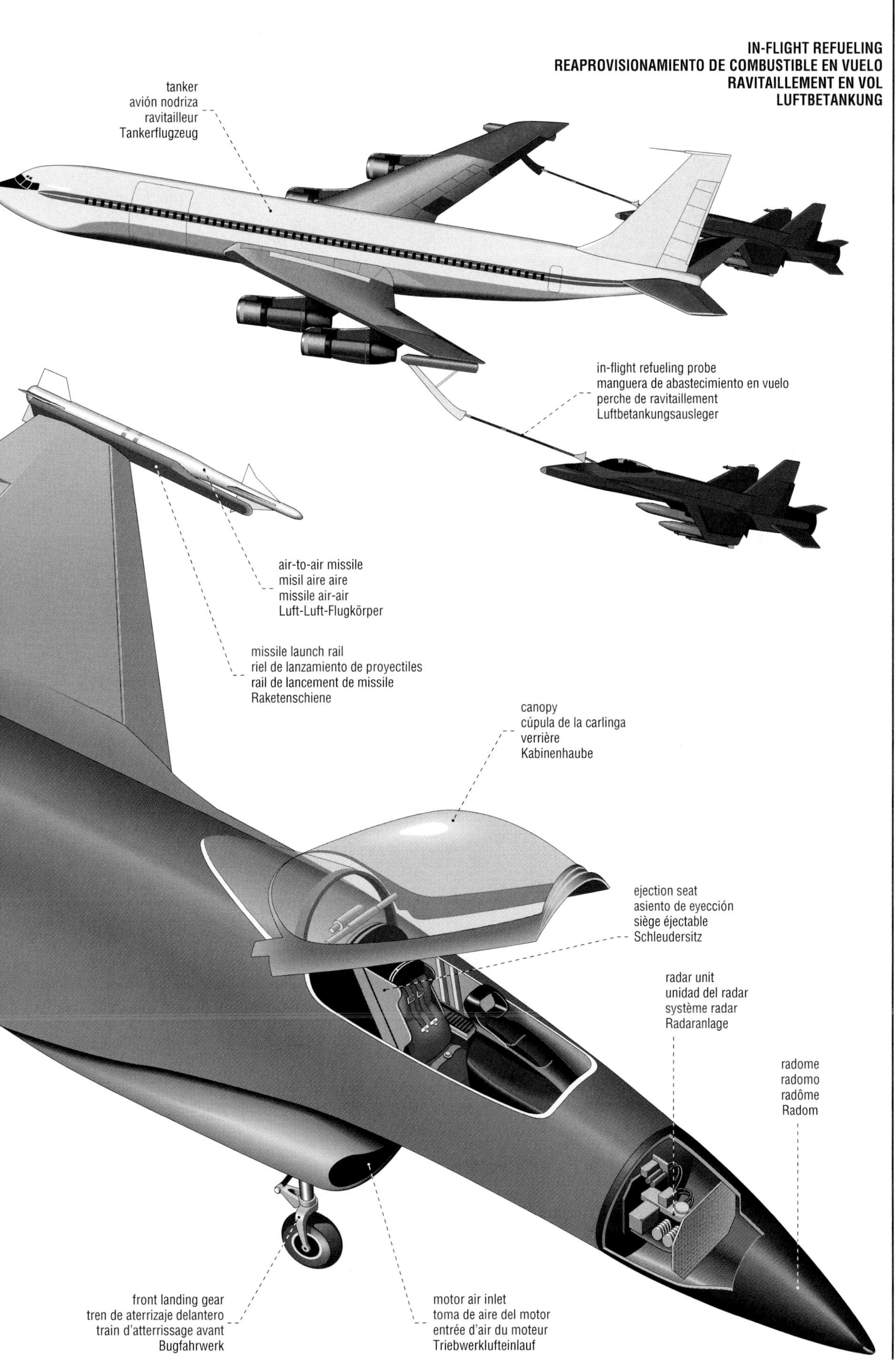

tanker
avión nodriza
ravitailleur
Tankerflugzeug
in-flight refueling probe
manguera de abastecimiento en vuelo
perche de ravitaillement
Luftbetankungsausleger
air-to-air missile
misil aire aire
missile air-air
Luft-Luft-Flugkörper
missile launch rail
riel de lanzamiento de proyectiles
rail de lancement de missile
Raketenschiene
canopy
cúpula de la carlinga
verrière
Kabinenhaube
ejection seat
asiento de eyección
siège éjectable
Schleudersitz
radar unit
unidad del radar
système radar
Radaranlage
radome
radomo
radôme
Radom
front landing gear
tren de aterrizaje delantero
train d'atterrissage avant
Bugfahrwerk
motor air inlet
toma de aire del motor
entrée d'air du moteur
Triebwerklufteinlauf

STRUCTURE OF A MISSILE
ESTRUCTURA DE UN MISIL
STRUCTURE D'UN MISSILE
AUFBAU EINES FLUGKÖRPERS

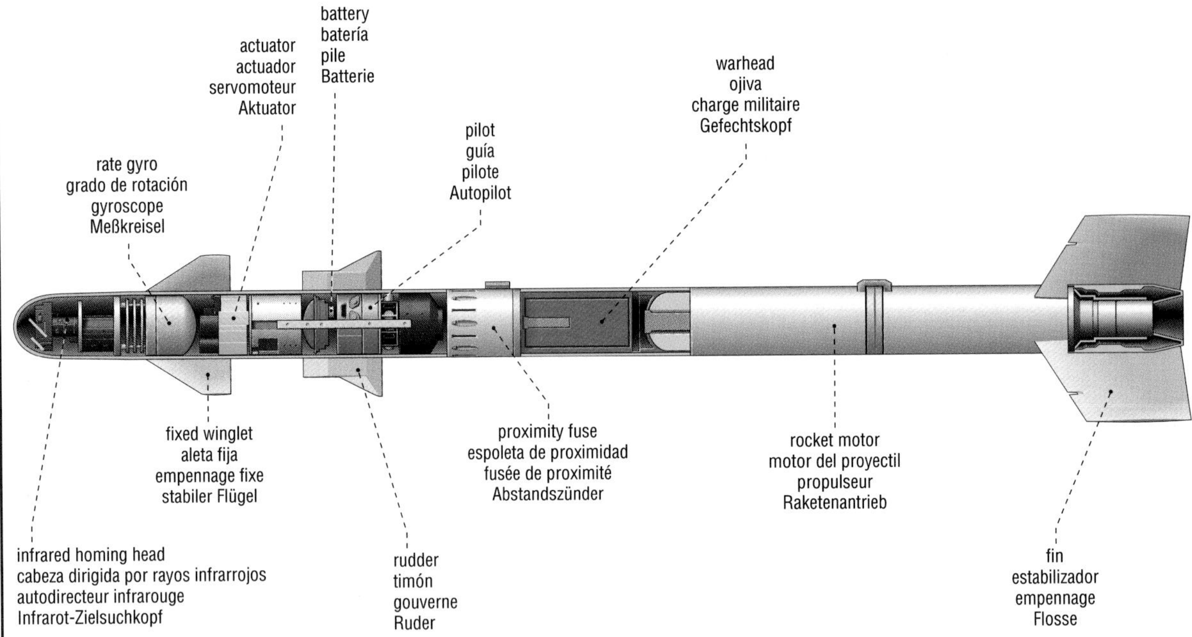

battery
batería
pile
Batterie
actuator
actuador
servomoteur
Aktuator
warhead
ojiva
charge militaire
Gefechtskopf
pilot
guía
pilote
Autopilot
rate gyro
grado de rotación
gyroscope
Meßkreisel
fixed winglet
aleta fija
empennage fixe
stabiler Flügel
proximity fuse
espoleta de proximidad
fusée de proximité
Abstandszünder
rocket motor
motor del proyectil
propulseur
Raketenantrieb
infrared homing head
cabeza dirigida por rayos infrarrojos
autodirecteur infrarouge
Infrarot-Zielsuchkopf
rudder
timón
gouverne
Ruder
fin
estabilizador
empennage
Flosse

MAJOR TYPES OF MISSILES
PRINCIPALES TIPOS DE MISILES
PRINCIPAUX TYPES DE MISSILES
DIE WICHTIGSTEN FLUGKÖRPER

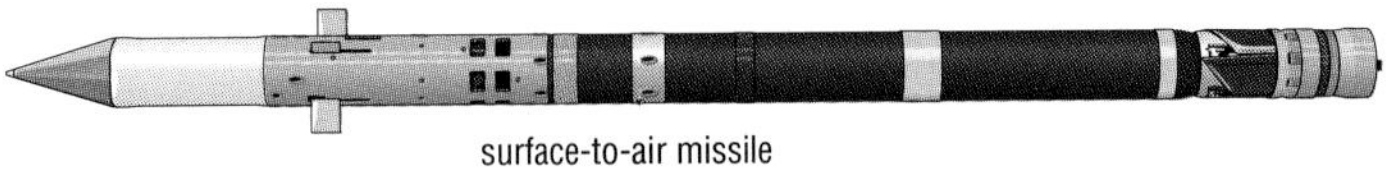

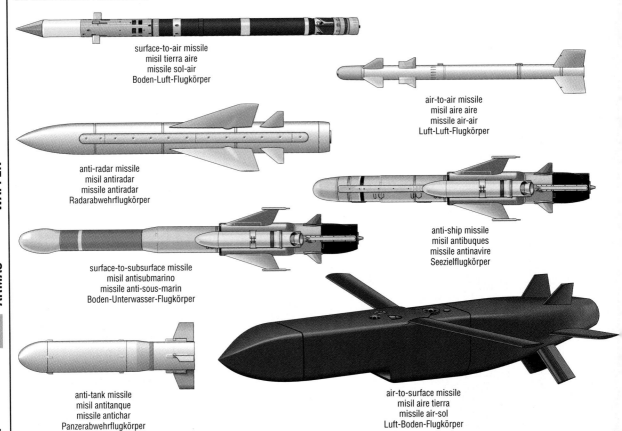

surface-to-air missile
misil tierra aire
missile sol-air
Boden-Luft-Flugkörper

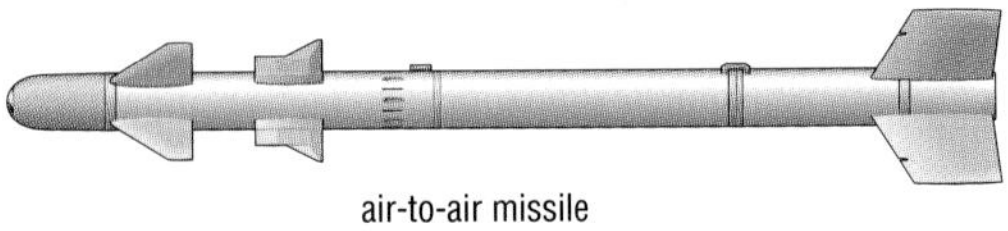

air-to-air missile
misil aire aire
missile air-air
Luft-Luft-Flugkörper

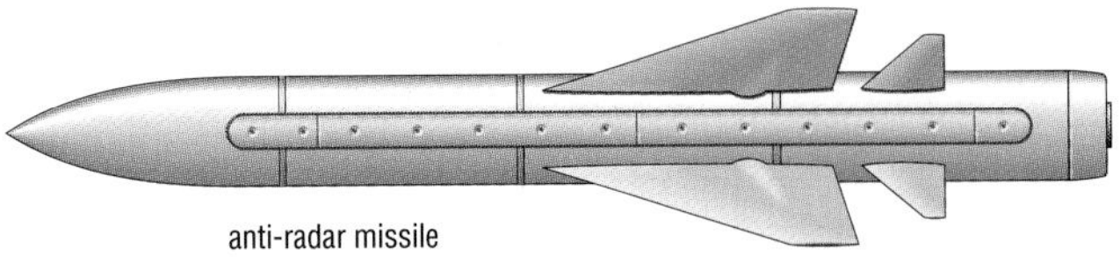

anti-radar missile
misil antiradar
missile antiradar
Radarabwehrflugkörper

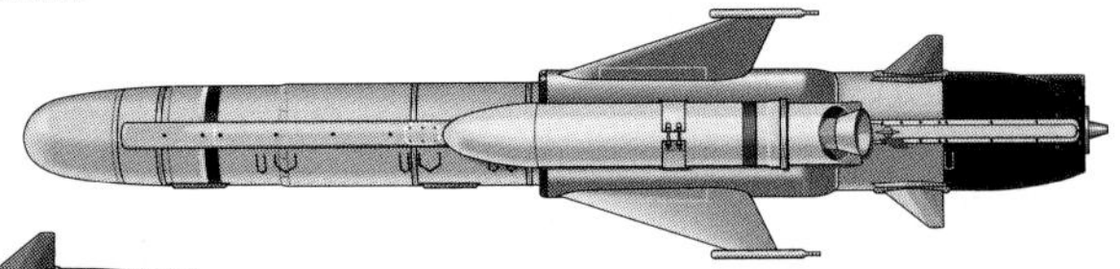

anti-ship missile
misil antibuques
missile antinavire
Seezielflugkörper

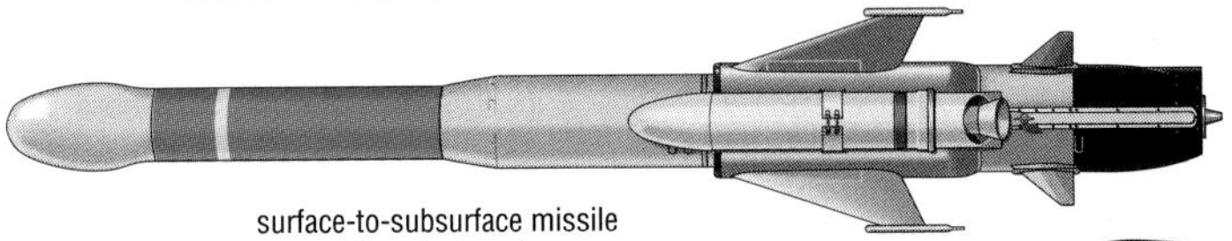

surface-to-subsurface missile
misil antisubmarino
missile anti-sous-marin
Boden-Unterwasser-Flugkörper

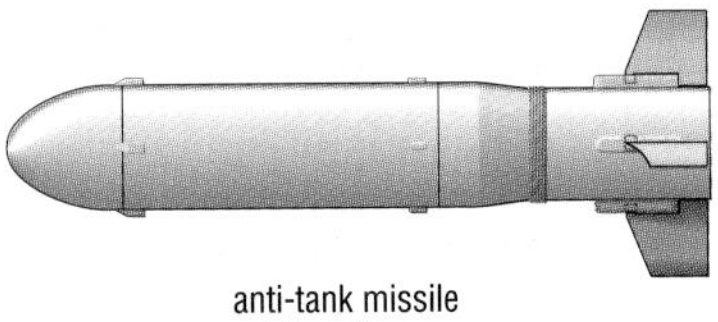

anti-tank missile
misil antitanque
missile antichar
Panzerabwehrflugkörper

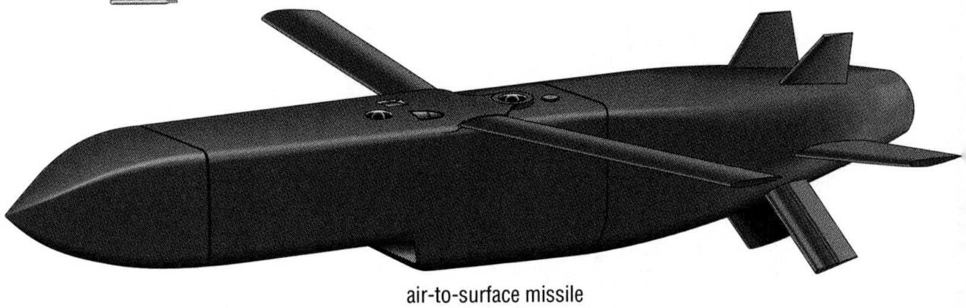

air-to-surface missile
misil aire tierra
missile air-sol
Luft-Boden-Flugkörper

CONTENTS

HERALDRY
HERÁLDICA
HÉRALDIQUE
HERALDIK

PARTS OF A FLAG
PARTES DE UNA BANDERA
ÉLÉMENTS D'UN DRAPEAU
TEILE DER FAHNE

FLAG SHAPES
FORMAS DE BANDERAS
FORMES DE DRAPEAUX
FAHNENFORMEN

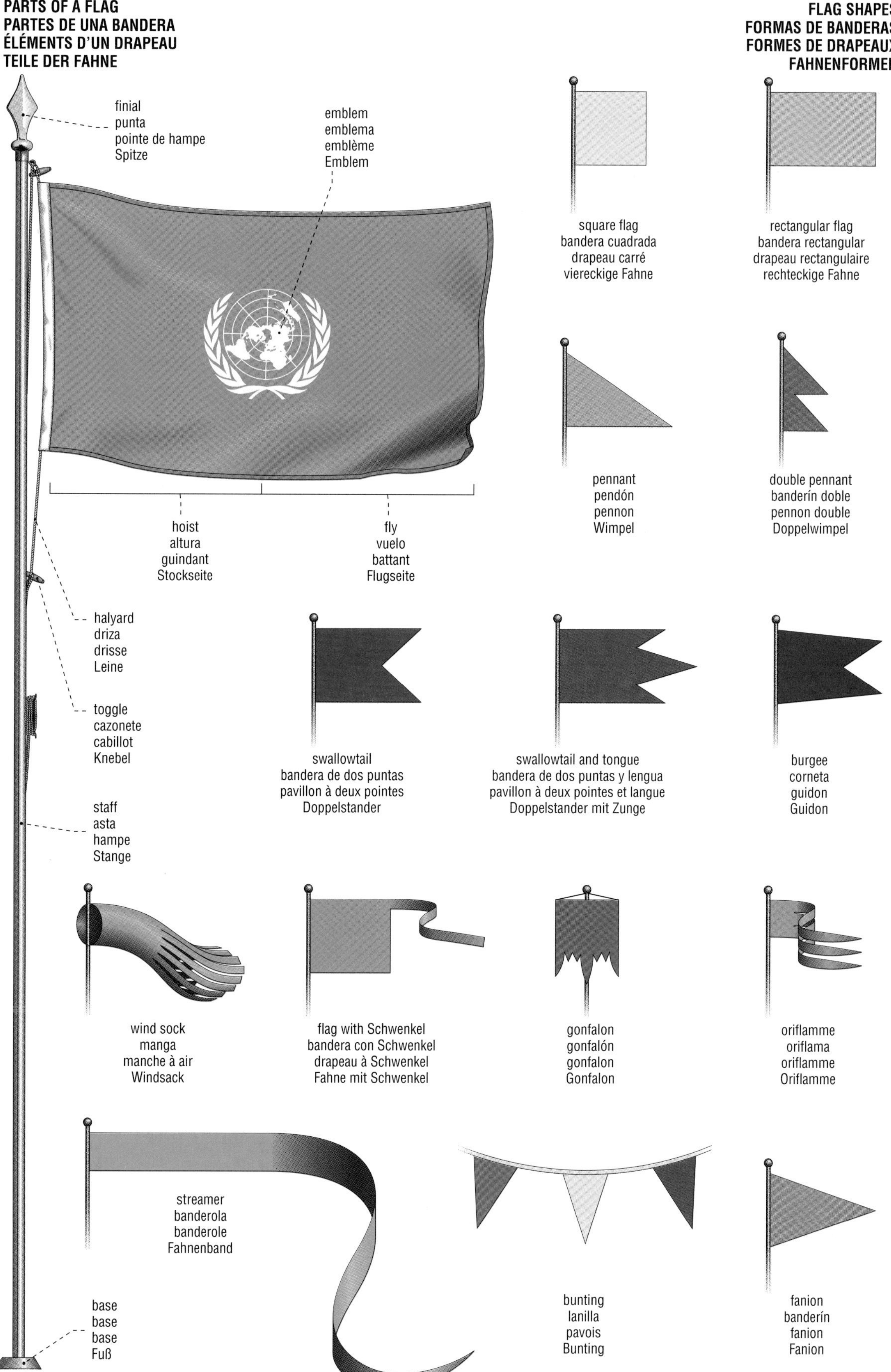

finial
punta
pointe de hampe
Spitze
emblem
emblema
emblème
Emblem
hoist
altura
guindant
Stockseite
fly
vuelo
battant
Flugseite
halyard
driza
drisse
Leine
toggle
cazonete
cabillot
Knebel
staff
asta
hampe
Stange
base
base
base
Fuß
square flag
bandera cuadrada
drapeau carré
viereckige Fahne
rectangular flag
bandera rectangular
drapeau rectangulaire
rechteckige Fahne
pennant
pendón
pennon
Wimpel
double pennant
banderín doble
pennon double
Doppelwimpel
swallowtail
bandera de dos puntas
pavillon à deux pointes
Doppelstander
swallowtail and tongue
bandera de dos puntas y lengua
pavillon à deux pointes et langue
Doppelstander mit Zunge
burgee
corneta
guidon
Guidon
wind sock
manga
manche à air
Windsack
flag with Schwenkel
bandera con Schwenkel
drapeau à Schwenkel
Fahne mit Schwenkel
gonfalon
gonfalón
gonfalon
Gonfalon
oriflamme
oriflama
oriflamme
Oriflamme
streamer
banderola
banderole
Fahnenband
bunting
lanilla
pavois
Bunting
fanion
banderín
fanion
Fanion

HERALDRY
HERÁLDICA
HÉRALDIQUE
HERALDIK

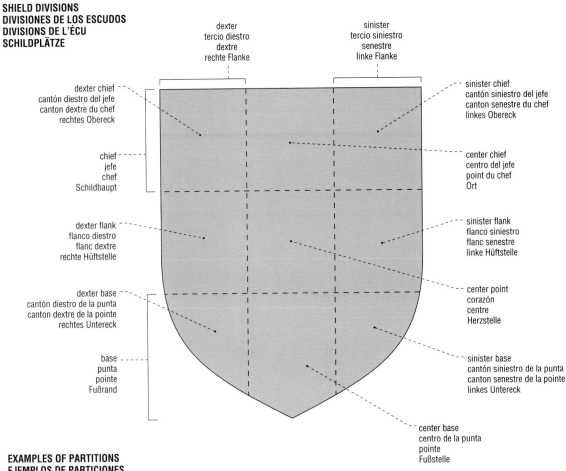

SHIELD DIVISIONS
DIVISIONES DE LOS ESCUDOS
DIVISIONS DE L'ÉCU
SCHILDPLÄTZE

dexter
tercio diestro
dextre
rechte Flanke

sinister
tercio siniestro
senestre
linke Flanke

dexter chief
cantón diestro del jefe
canton dextre du chef
rechtes Obereck

sinister chief
cantón siniestro del jefe
canton senestre du chef
linkes Obereck

chief
jefe
chef
Schildhaupt

center chief
centro del jefe
point du chef
Ort

dexter flank
flanco diestro
flanc dextre
rechte Hüftstelle

sinister flank
flanco siniestro
flanc senestre
linke Hüftstelle

center point
corazón
centre
Herzstelle

dexter base
cantón diestro de la punta
canton dextre de la pointe
rechtes Untereck

base
punta
pointe
Fußrand

sinister base
cantón siniestro de la punta
canton senestre de la pointe
linkes Untereck

center base
centro de la punta
pointe
Fußstelle

EXAMPLES OF PARTITIONS
EJEMPLOS DE PARTICIONES
EXEMPLES DE PARTITIONS
TEILUNGSBEISPIELE

per fess
escudo cortado
coupé
geteilt

party
escudo partido
parti
gespalten

per bend
escudo tronchado
tranché
schrägrechts geteilt

quarterly
escudo acuartelado
écartelé
geviert

EXAMPLES OF ORDINARIES
EJEMPLOS DE PIEZAS HONORABLES
EXEMPLES DE PIÈCES HONORABLES
BEISPIELE FÜR HEROLDSBILDER

chief
jefe
chef
Hauptrand

chevron
cheurón
chevron
Sparren

pale
palo
pal
Pfahl

cross
cruz
croix
Kreuz

EXAMPLES OF CHARGES
EJEMPLOS DE CARGAS
EXEMPLES DE MEUBLES
BEISPIELE FÜR WAPPENZEICHEN

fleur-de-lis
flor de lis
fleur de lis
Lilie

crescent
creciente
croissant
Mond

lion passant
león rampante
lion passant
schreitender Löwe

eagle
aguila
aigle
Adler

mullet
estrella
étoile
Stern

EXAMPLES OF METALS
EJEMPLOS DE METALES
EXEMPLES DE MÉTAUX
BEISPIELE FÜR METALL

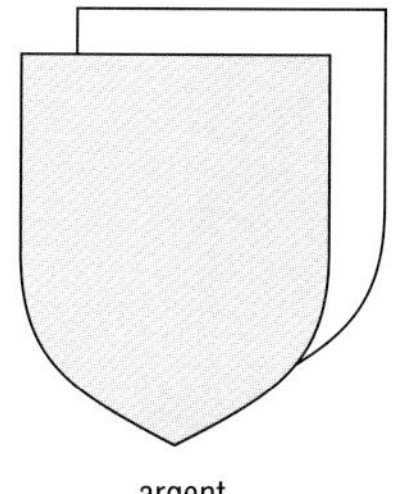

argent
plata
argent
Silber

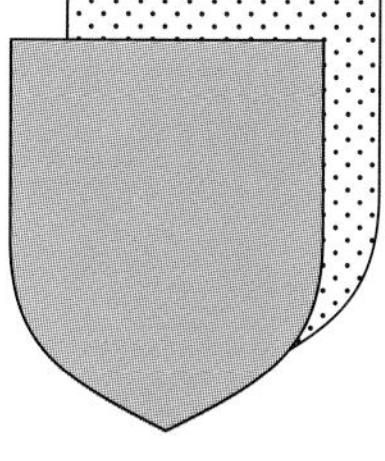

or
oro
or
Gold

EXAMPLES OF FURS
EJEMPLOS DE FORROS
EXEMPLES DE FOURRURES
BEISPIELE FÜR PELZWERK

ermine
armiño
hermine
Hermelin

vair
cerros
vair
Eishutfeh

EXAMPLES OF COLORS
EJEMPLOS DE COLORES
EXEMPLES DE COULEURS
FARBBEISPIELE

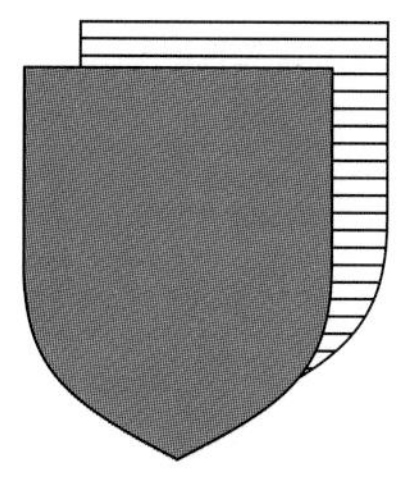

azure
azur
azur
blau

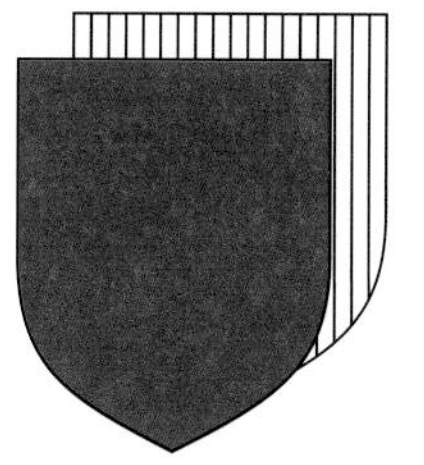

gules
gules
gueules
rot

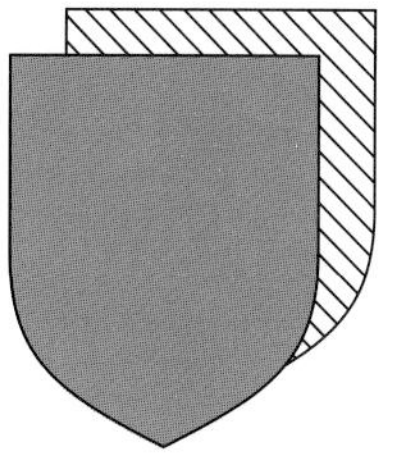

vert
sinople
sinople
grün

purpure
púrpura
pourpre
purpur

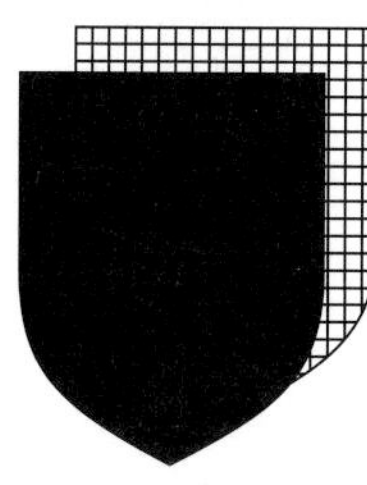

sable
sable
sable
schwarz

SIGNS OF THE ZODIAC
SIGNOS DEL ZODÍACO
SIGNES DU ZODIAQUE
TIERKREISZEICHEN

FIRE SIGNS
SIGNOS DE FUEGO
SIGNES DE FEU
FEUERZEICHEN

Aries the Ram (March 21)
Aries, el Carnero (21 de marzo)
Bélier (21 mars)
Widder, Aries (21. März)

Leo the Lion (July 23)
Leo, el León (23 de julio)
Lion (23 juillet)
Löwe, Leo (23. Juli)

Sagittarius the Archer (November 22)
Sagitario, el Arquero (22 de noviembre)
Sagittaire (22 novembre)
Schütze, Sagittarius (22. November)

EARTH SIGNS
SIGNOS DE TIERRA
SIGNES DE TERRE
ERDZEICHEN

Taurus the Bull (April 20)
Tauro, el Toro (20 de abril)
Taureau (20 avril)
Stier, Taurus (20. April)

Virgo the Virgin (August 23)
Virgo, la Virgen (23 de agosto)
Vierge (23 août)
Jungfrau, Virgo (23. August)

Capricorn the Goat (December 22)
Capricornio, la Cabra (22 de diciembre)
Capricorne (22 décembre)
Steinbock, Capricornus (22. Dezember)

AIR SIGNS
SIGNOS DE AIRE
SIGNES D'AIR
LUFTZEICHEN

Libra the Balance (September 23)
Libra, la Balanza (23 de septiembre)
Balance (23 septembre)
Waage, Libra (23. September)

Aquarius the Water Bearer (January 20)
Acuario, el Aguador (20 de enero)
Verseau (20 janvier)
Wassermann, Aquarius (20. Januar)

Gemini the Twins (May 21)
Géminis, los Gemelos (21 de mayo)
Gémeaux (21 mai)
Zwillinge, Gemini (21. Mai)

WATER SIGNS
SIGNOS DE AGUA
SIGNES D'EAU
WASSERZEICHEN

Cancer the Crab (June 22)
Cáncer, el Cangrejo (22 de junio)
Cancer (22 juin)
Krebs, Cancer (22. Juni)

Scorpio the Scorpion (October 24)
Escorpio, el Escorpión (24 de octubre)
Scorpion (24 octobre)
Skorpion, Scorpius (24. Oktober)

Pisces the Fishes (February 19)
Piscis, los peces (19 de febrero)
Poissons (19 février)
Fische, Pisces (19. Februar)

SAFETY SYMBOLS
SÍMBOLOS DE SEGURIDAD
SYMBOLES DE SÉCURITÉ
WARN- UND GEBOTSZEICHEN

DANGEROUS MATERIALS
MATERIALES PELIGROSOS
MATIÈRES DANGEREUSES
GEFÄHRLICHE SUBSTANZEN

corrosive
corrosivo
matières corrosives
ätzend

electrical hazard
alto voltaje
danger électrique
elektrische Spannung

explosive
explosivo
matières explosives
explosionsgefährlich

flammable
inflamable
matières inflammables
leicht entzündlich

radioactive
radioactivo
matières radioactives
radioaktiv

poison
veneno
matières toxiques
Gift

PROTECTION
PROTECCIÓN
PROTECTION
SCHUTZMASSNAHMEN

eye protection
protección de los ojos
protection obligatoire de la vue
Augenschutz tragen

ear protection
protección de los oidos
protection obligatoire de l'ouïe
Gehörschutz tragen

head protection
protección de la cabeza
protection obligatoire de la tête
Schutzhelm tragen

hand protection
protección de las manos
protection obligatoire des mains
Schutzhandschuhe tragen

feet protection
protección de los pies
protection obligatoire des pieds
Schutzschuhe tragen

respiratory system protection
protección del sistema respiratorio
protection obligatoire des voies respiratoires
Atemschutz tragen

COMMON SYMBOLS
SÍMBOLOS DE USO COMÚN
SYMBOLES D'USAGE COURANT
ALLGEMEINE ZEICHEN

coffee shop
cafetería
casse-croûte
Cafeteria

telephone
teléfono
téléphone
Telefon

restaurant
restaurante
restaurant
Restaurant

men's rest room
Servicios (Caballeros)
toilettes pour hommes
Toiletten (Herren)

women's rest room
Servicios (Señoras)
toilettes pour dames
Toiletten (Damen)

access for physically handicapped
acceso para minusválidos
accès pour handicapés physiques
für Schwerbehinderte

pharmacy
farmacia
pharmacie
Apotheke

no access for wheelchairs
prohibido usar silla de ruedas
ne pas utiliser avec une chaise roulante
nicht für Rollstuhlfahrer

first aid
puesto de socorro
premiers soins
Erste Hilfe

H

hospital
hospital
hôpital
Krankenhaus

POLICE

police
policía
police
Polizei

TAXI

taxi transportation
servicio de taxis
transport par taxi
Taxi

camping (tent)
zona para acampar
camping
Zeltplatz

camping prohibited
prohibido acampar
camping interdit
Zelten verboten

camping (trailer)
zona para casas rodantes
caravaning
Platz für Wohnwagen

camping (trailer and tent)
zona para acampar y para casas rodantes
camping et caravaning
Platz für Zelte und Wohnwagen

picnics prohibited
prohibido hacer comidas campestres
pique-nique interdit
Picknick verboten

picnic area
zona de comidas campestres
pique-nique
Rastplatz

service station
gasolinera
poste de carburant
Tankstelle

information
información
renseignements
Information

information
información
renseignements
Information

currency exchange
casa de cambio
change
Geldwechsel

lost and found articles
oficina de objetos perdidos
articles perdus et retrouvés
Fundbüro

fire extinguisher
extintor de incendios
extincteur d'incendie
Feuerlöscher

ROAD SIGNS
SEÑALES DE TRANSITO
SIGNALISATION ROUTIÈRE
VERKEHRSZEICHEN

MAJOR NORTH AMERICAN ROAD SIGNS
PRINCIPALES SEÑALES DE TRANSITO NORTEAMERICANAS
PRINCIPAUX PANNEAUX NORD-AMÉRICAINS
DIE WICHTIGSTEN NORDAMERIKANISCHEN VERKEHRSZEICHEN

STOP

stop at intersection
alto
arrêt à l'intersection
Halt! Vorfahrt gewähren

no entry
prohibido el paso
accès interdit
Verbot der Einfahrt

yield
ceda el paso
cédez le passage
Vorfahrt gewähren

one-way traffic
una vía
voie à sens unique
Einbahnstraße

direction to be followed
dirección obligatoria
direction obligatoire
vorgeschriebene Fahrtrichtung

direction to be followed
dirección obligatoria
direction obligatoire
vorgeschriebene Fahrtrichtung

direction to be followed
dirección obligatoria
direction obligatoire
vorgeschriebene Fahrtrichtung

direction to be followed
dirección obligatoria
direction obligatoire
vorgeschriebene Fahrtrichtung

no U-turn
prohibido dar vuelta en U
interdiction de faire demi-tour
Wenden verboten

passing prohibited
prohibido adelantar
interdiction de dépasser
Überholverbot

two-way traffic
doble vía
circulation dans les deux sens
Gegenverkehr

merging traffic
señal de unión
intersection avec priorité
Vorfahrt an nächster Einmündung

MAJOR INTERNATIONAL ROAD SIGNS
PRINCIPALES SEÑALES DE TRÁNSITO INTERNACIONALES
PRINCIPAUX PANNEAUX INTERNATIONAUX
DIE WICHTIGSTEN INTERNATIONALEN VERKEHRSZEICHEN

STOP

stop at intersection
alto
arrêt à l'intersection
Halt! Vorfahrt gewähren

no entry
prohibido el paso
accès interdit
Verbot der Einfahrt

yield
ceda el paso
cédez le passage
Vorfahrt gewähren

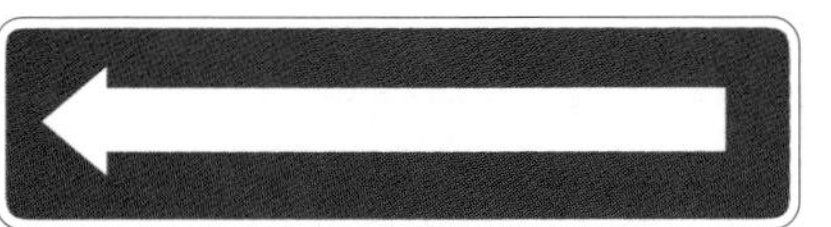

one-way traffic
una vía
voie à sens unique
Einbahnstraße

direction to be followed
dirección obligatoria
direction obligatoire
vorgeschriebene Fahrtrichtung

direction to be followed
dirección obligatoria
direction obligatoire
vorgeschriebene Fahrtrichtung

direction to be followed
dirección obligatoria
direction obligatoire
vorgeschriebene Fahrtrichtung

direction to be followed
dirección obligatoria
direction obligatoire
vorgeschriebene Fahrtrichtung

no U-turn
prohibido dar vuelta en U
interdiction de faire demi-tour
Wenden verboten

passing prohibited
prohibido adelantar
interdiction de dépasser
Überholen verboten

two-way traffic
doble vía
circulation dans les deux sens
Gegenverkehr

priority intersection
cruce con preferencia
intersection avec priorité
Vorfahrt an nächster Einmündung

ROAD SIGNS
SEÃLES DE TRÁNSITO
SIGNALISATION ROUTIÈRE
VERKEHRSZEICHEN

MAJOR NORTH AMERICAN ROAD SIGNS
PRINCIPALES SEÑALES DE TRÁNSITO NORTEAMERICANAS
PRINCIPAUX PANNEAUX NORD-AMÉRICAINS
DIE WICHTIGSTEN NORDAMERIKANISCHEN VERKEHRSZEICHEN

right bend
curva a la derecha
virage à droite
Rechtskurve

double bend
curva doble
double virage
Doppelkurve

roadway narrows
estrechamiento del camino
chaussée rétrécie
verengte Fahrbahn

slippery road
camino resbaladizo
chaussée glissante
Schleudergefahr

bumps
superficie irregular
chaussée cahoteuse
unebene Fahrbahn

8%

steep hill
bajada pronunciada
descente dangereuse
Gefälle

falling rocks
zona de derrumbes
chutes de pierres
Steinschlag

3.5 m

overhead clearance
altura máxima
limitation de hauteur
Verbot für Fahrzeuge über angegebene Höhe

signal ahead
semáforo
signalisation lumineuse
Lichtzeichenanlage

school zone
zona escolar
zone scolaire
Schule

pedestrian crossing
paso de peatones
passage pour piétons
Fußgängerüberweg

road work ahead
obras
travaux
Baustelle

MAJOR INTERNATIONAL ROAD SIGNS
PRINCIPALES SEÑALES DE TRÁNSITO INTERNACIONALES
PRINCIPAUX PANNEAUX INTERNATIONAUX
DIE WICHTIGSTEN INTERNATIONALEN VERKEHRSZEICHEN

right bend
curva a la derecha
virage à droite
Rechtskurve

double bend
curva doble
double virage
Doppelkurve

roadway narrows
estrechamiento del camino
chaussée rétrécie
verengte Fahrbahn

slippery road
camino resbaladizo
chaussée glissante
Schleudergefahr

bumps
badén
chaussée cahoteuse
unebene Fahrbahn

8%

steep hill
bajada pronunciada
descente dangereuse
Gefälle

falling rocks
zona de derrumbes
chutes de pierres
Steinschlag

3.5 m

overhead clearance
altura máxima
limitation de hauteur
Verbot für Fahrzeuge über angegebene Höhe

signal ahead
semáforo
signalisation lumineuse
Lichtzeichenanlage

school zone
zona escolar
zone scolaire
Schule

pedestrian crossing
paso de peatones
passage pour piétons
Fußgängerüberweg

road work ahead
obras
travaux
Baustelle

ROAD SIGNS
SEÑALES DE TRÁNSITO
SIGNALISATION ROUTIÈRE
VERKEHRSZEICHEN

MAJOR NORTH AMERICAN ROAD SIGNS
PRINCIPALES SEÑALES DE TRÁNSITO NORTEAMERICANAS
PRINCIPAUX PANNEAUX NORD-AMÉRICAINS
DIE WICHTIGSTEN NORDAMERIKANISCHEN VERKEHRSZEICHEN

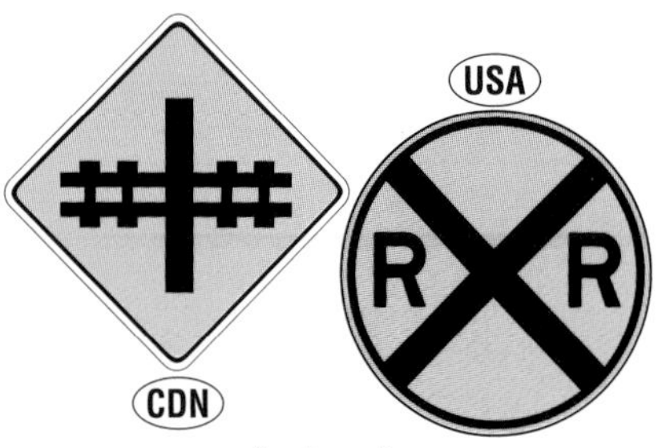
USA
R
R
CDN

railroad crossing
paso a nivel
passage à niveau
Bahnübergang

deer crossing
cruce de animales salvajes
passage d'animaux sauvages
Wildwechsel

closed to pedestrians
prohibido el paso de peatones
accès interdit aux piétons
gesperrt für Fußgänger

closed to bicycles
prohibido el paso de bicicletas
accès interdit aux bicyclettes
gesperrt für Radfahrer

closed to motorcycles
prohibido el paso de motocicletas
accès interdit aux motocycles
gesperrt für Krafträder

closed to trucks
prohibido el paso de camiones
accès interdit aux camions
gesperrt für Kfz über 2,8t

MAJOR INTERNATIONAL ROAD SIGNS
PRINCIPALES SEÑALES DE TRÁNSITO INTERNACIONALES
PRINCIPAUX PANNEAUX INTERNATIONAUX
DIE WICHTIGSTEN INTERNATIONALEN VERKEHRSZEICHEN

railroad crossing
paso a nivel
passage à niveau
Bahnübergang

deer crossing
cruce de animales salvajes
passage d'animaux sauvages
Wildwechsel

closed to pedestrians
prohibido el paso de peatones
accès interdit aux piétons
gesperrt für Fußgänger

closed to bicycles
prohibido el paso de bicicletas
accès interdit aux bicyclettes
gesperrt für Radfahrer

closed to motorcycles
prohibido el paso de motocicletas
accès interdit aux motocycles
gesperrt für Krafträder

closed to trucks
prohibido el paso de camiones
accès interdit aux camions
gesperrt für Kfz über 2,8t

FABRIC CARE
CUIDADO DE TELAS
ENTRETIEN DES TISSUS
TEXTILPFLEGE

WASHING
LAVADO
LAVAGE
WASCHEN

do not wash
no se lave
ne pas laver
nicht waschen

hand wash in lukewarm water
lávese a mano con agua tibia
laver à la main à l'eau tiède
Handwäsche in handwarmem Wasser

40°C
100°F

machine wash in lukewarm water at a gentle setting/reduced agitation
lávese en lavadora con agua tibia en el ciclo para ropa delicada
laver à la machine à l'eau tiède avec agitation réduite
Hand- und Maschinenwäsche, Schonwaschgang

50°C
120°F

machine wash in warm water at a gentle setting/reduced agitation
lávese en lavadora con agua caliente en el ciclo para ropa delicada
laver à la machine à l'eau chaude avec agitation réduite
Hand- und Maschinenwäsche, Schonwaschgang

50°C
120°F

machine wash in warm water at a normal setting
lávese en lavadora con agua caliente, en el ciclo normal
laver à la machine à l'eau chaude avec agitation normale
Hand- und Maschinenwäsche, Normalwaschgang

70°C
160°F

machine wash in hot water at a normal setting
lávese en lavadora con agua muy caliente, en el ciclo normal
laver à la machine à l'eau très chaude avec agitation normale
Hand- und Maschinenwäsche, Normalwaschgang

Cl

do not use chlorine bleach
no use blanqueador de cloro
ne pas utiliser de chlorure décolorant
nicht chloren

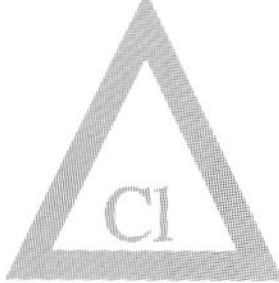
Cl

use chlorine bleach as directed
use blanqueador de cloro siguiendo las indicaciones
utiliser un chlorure décolorant suivant les indications
chloren möglich

DRYING
SECADO
SÉCHAGE
TROCKNEN

hang to dry
cuelgue al aire libre después de escurrir
suspendre pour sécher
zum Trocknen hängen

dry flat
seque extendido sobre una toalla después de escurrir
sécher à plat
zum Trocknen legen

tumble dry at medium to high temperature
seque en secadora a temperatura de mediana a alta
sécher par culbutage à moyenne ou haute température
Wäschetrockner mit mittlerer bis hoher Temperatur

tumble dry at low temperature
seque en secadora a temperatura baja
sécher par culbutage à basse température
Wäschetrockner mit niedriger Temperatur

drip dry
cuelgue sin exprimir, dando forma a mano
suspendre pour sécher sans essorer
tropfnaß hängen

IRONING
PLANCHADO
REPASSAGE
BÜGELN

do not iron
no use plancha
ne pas repasser
nicht bügeln

110°C 225°F

iron at low setting
use plancha tibia
repasser à basse température
bügeln bei niedriger Einstellung

150°C 300°F

iron at medium setting
use plancha caliente
repasser à moyenne température
bügeln bei mittlerer Einstellung

200°C 400°F

iron at high setting
use plancha muy caliente
repasser à haute température
bügeln bei hoher Einstellung

COMMON SCIENTIFIC SYMBOLS
SÍMBOLOS CIENTÍFICOS COMUNES
SYMBOLES SCIENTIFIQUES USUELS
ALLGEMEINE SYMBOLE IN DEN WISSENSCHAFTEN

MATHEMATICS
MATEMÁTICAS
MATHÉMATIQUES
MATHEMATIK

−

subtraction
menos
soustraction
Subtraktion

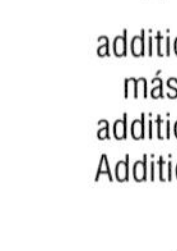

addition
más
addition
Addition

multiplication
por
multiplication
Multiplikation

division
entre
division
Division

is equal to
igual a
égale
ist gleich

is not equal to
desigual a
n'égale pas
ist ungleich

is approximately equal to
casi igual a
égale à peu près
ist annähernd gleich

is equivalent to
equivalente a
équivaut à
ist äquivalent mit

is identical with
idéntico a
est identique à
ist identisch mit

is not identical with
no es idéntico a
n'est pas identique à
ist nicht identisch mit

plus or minus
más o menos
plus ou moins
plus oder minus

empty set
conjunto vacío
ensemble vide
Leermenge

is greater than
mayor que
plus grand que
ist größer als

is equal to or greater than
igual o mayor que
égal ou plus grand que
ist gleich oder größer als

is less than
menor que
plus petit que
ist kleiner als

is equal to or less than
igual o menor que
égal ou plus petit que
ist gleich oder kleiner als

union
unión
réunion
Vereinigung

intersection
intersección
intersection
Durchschnitt

is contained in
contenido en
inclusion
echte Teilmenge von

percent
porcentaje
pourcentage
Prozent

belongs to
pertenece a
appartenance
Element von

does not belong to
no pertenece a
non-appartenance
nicht Element von

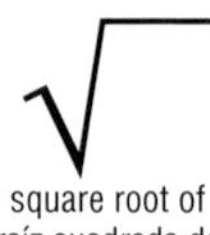

square root of
raíz cuadrada de
racine carrée de
Quadratwurzel aus

sum
suma
sommation
Summe

infinity
infinito
infini
unendlich

integral
integral
intégrale
Integral

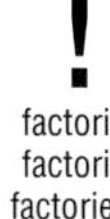

factorial
factorial
factorielle
Fakultät

GEOMETRY
GEOMETRÍA
GÉOMÉTRIE
GEOMETRIE

degree
grado
degré
Grad

minute
minuto
minute
Minute

second
segundo
seconde
Sekunde

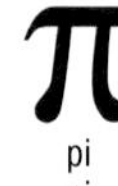

pi
pi
pi
Pi

perpendicular
perpendicular
perpendiculaire
Senkrechte

acute angle
ángulo agudo
angle aigu
spitzer Winkel

right angle
ángulo recto
angle droit
rechter Winkel

obtuse angle
ángulo obtuso
angle obtu
stumpfer Winkel

is parallel to
es paralelo a
parallèle
ist parallel zu

is not parallel to
no es paralelo a
non-parallèle
ist nicht parallel zu

BIOLOGY
BIOLOGÍA
BIOLOGIE
BIOLOGIE

♂

male
masculino
mâle
männlich

female
femenino
femelle
weiblich

birth
nacimiento
naissance
geboren

Rh+

blood factor positive
factorRH positivo
facteur Rhésus positif
Rhesusfaktor positiv

Rh-

blood factor negative
factorRH negativo
facteur Rhésus négatif
Rhesusfaktor negativ

death
muerte
mort
gestorben

CHEMISTRY
QUÍMICA
CHIMIE
CHEMIE

—

negative charge
elemento negativo
négatif
negativ geladen

+

positive charge
elemento positivo
positif
positiv geladen

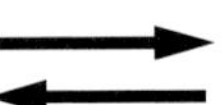

reversible reaction
reacción
réaction réversible
reversible Reaktion

reaction direction
dirección
direction d'une réaction
Reaktionsrichtung

MISCELLANEOUS
VARIOS
SYMBOLES DIVERS
WEITERE SYMBOLE

recycled
recuperado
recyclé
wiederverwertet

recyclable
recuperable
recyclable
wiederverwertbar

ampersand
y
esperluette
Et-Zeichen

registered trademark
marca registrada
marque déposée
eingetragenes Warenzeichen

copyright
copyright (derechos de autor)
copyright
Copyright

prescription
receta médica
ordonnance
verschreibungspflichtig

pause/still
pausa
pause/arrêt sur l'image
Pause

stop
paro
arrêt
Stop

rewind
rebobinado
rebobinage
Rücklauf

play
reproducción
lecture
Spiel

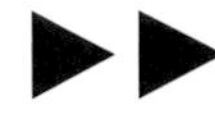

fast forward
avance rápido
avance rapide
Vorlauf

DIACRITIC SYMBOLS
SIGNOS DIACRÍTICOS
SIGNES DIACRITIQUES
DIAKRITISCHE ZEICHEN

acute accent
acento agudo
accent aigu
Accent aigu

umlaut
diéresis
tréma
Umlaut

grave accent
acento grave
accent grave
Accent grave

circumflex accent
acento circunflejo
accent circonflexe
Accent circonflexe

cedilla
cedilla
cédille
Cedille

tilde
tilde
tilde
Tilde

PUNCTUATION MARKS
SIGNOS DE PUNTUACIÓN
SIGNES DE PONCTUATION
SATZZEICHEN

;

semicolon
punto y coma
point-virgule
Semikolon

.

period
punto
point
Punkt

comma
coma
virgule
Komma

ellipses
puntos suspensivos
points de suspension
Fortführungspunkte

:

colon
dos puntos
deux-points
Doppelpunkt

asterisk
asterisco
astérisque
Sternchen

quotation marks (French)
comillas
guillemets
Anführungszeichenn (französische)

‘ ’

single quotation marks
comillas sencillas
guillemets
halbe Anführungszeichen

quotation marks
comillas
guillemets
Anführungszeichen

—

dash
guión largo
tiret
Gedankenstrich

( )

parentheses
paréntesis
parenthèses
runde Klammern

virgule
diagonal
barre oblique
Querstrich

exclamation point
admiración
point d'exclamation
Ausrufezeichen

question mark
interrogación
point d'interrogation
Fragezeichen

square brackets
corchetes
crochets
eckige Klammern

EXAMPLES OF CURRENCY ABBREVIATIONS
EJEMPLOS DE ABREVIACIONES DE MONEDAS
EXEMPLES D'UNITÉS MONÉTAIRES
BEISPIELE FÜR WÄHRUNGSABKÜRZUNGEN

dollar
dólar
dollar
Dollar

cent
centavo
cent
Cent

pound
libras
livre
Pfund

yen
yen
yen
Yen

franc
franco
franc
Franc

deutsche mark
marco
mark
Deutsche Mark

Dr

drachma
dracma
drachme
Drachme

L

lira
lira
lire
Lira

Kr

krone
corona
couronne
Krone

IS

shekel
shekel
shekel
Schekel

ECU

European Currency Unit
monedas de la Comunidad Europea
écu
Europäische Verrechnungseinheit

escudo
escudo
escudo
Escudo

Pta

peseta
peseta
peseta
Peseta

florin
florín
florin
Florin

ENGLISH INDEX

A

The terms in **bold type** indicate the title of an illustration.

B

The terms in **bold type** indicate the title of an illustration.

The terms in **bold type** indicate the title of an illustration.

C

The terms in **bold type** indicate the title of an illustration.

The terms in **bold type** indicate the title of an illustration.

The terms in **bold type** indicate the title of an illustration.

D

The terms in **bold type** indicate the title of an illustration.

E

The terms in **bold type** indicate the title of an illustration.

The terms in **bold type** indicate the title of an illustration.

G

The terms in **bold type** indicate the title of an illustration.

The terms in **bold type** indicate the title of an illustration.

I

J

K

The terms in **bold type** indicate the title of an illustration.

L

The terms in **bold type** indicate the title of an illustration.

M

The terms in **bold type** indicate the title of an illustration.

N

The terms in **bold type** indicate the title of an illustration.

The terms in **bold type** indicate the title of an illustration.

ENGLISH INDEX

The terms in **bold type** indicate the title of an illustration.

Q

R

The terms in **bold type** indicate the title of an illustration.

The terms in **bold type** indicate the title of an illustration.

The terms in **bold type** indicate the title of an illustration.

The terms in **bold type** indicate the title of an illustration.

The terms in **bold type** indicate the title of an illustration.

T

The terms in **bold type** indicate the title of an illustration.

The terms in **bold type** indicate the title of an illustration.

U

The terms in **bold type** indicate the title of an illustration.

The terms in **bold type** indicate the title of an illustration.

X

Y

Z

The terms in **bold type** indicate the title of an illustration.

INDICE ESPAÑOL

A

Las entradas en **negritas** corresponden a los títulos de página.

Las entradas en **negritas** corresponden a los títulos de página.

B

Las entradas en **negritas** corresponden a los títulos de página.

Las entradas en **negritas** corresponden a los títulos de página.

C

Las entradas en **negritas** corresponden a los titulos de página.

Las entradas en **negritas** corresponden a los títulos de página.

Las entradas en **negritas** corresponden a los títulos de página.

Las entradas en **negritas** corresponden a los títulos de página.

E

Las entradas en **negritas** corresponden a los titulos de página.

Las entradas en **negritas** corresponden a los titulos de página.

F

Las entradas en **negritas** corresponden a los titulos de página.

G

Las entradas en **negritas** corresponden a los títulos de página.

Las entradas en **negritas** corresponden a los títulos de página.

J

K

L

Las entradas en **negritas** corresponden a los titulos de página.

M

Las entradas en **negritas** corresponden a los titulos de página.

Las entradas en **negritas** corresponden a los titulos de página.

Las entradas en **negritas** corresponden a los títulos de página.

P

Las entradas en **negritas** corresponden a los titulos de página.

Las entradas en **negritas** corresponden a los titulos de página.

Las entradas en **negritas** corresponden a los titulos de página.

Las entradas en **negritas** corresponden a los títulos de página.

Las entradas en **negritas** corresponden a los títulos de página.

S

Las entradas en **negritas** corresponden a los titulos de página.

Las entradas en **negritas** corresponden a los titulos de página.

Las entradas en **negritas** corresponden a los titulos de página.

Las entradas en **negritas** corresponden a los titulos de página.

U

V

Las entradas en **negritas** corresponden a los títulos de página.

Las entradas en **negritas** corresponden a los títulos de página.

INDEX FRANÇAIS

A

Les termes en **caractères gras** renvoient à une illustration.

B

Les termes en **caractères gras** renvoient à une illustration.

Les termes en **caractères gras** renvoient à une illustration.

Les termes en **caractères gras** renvoient à une illustration.

Les termes en **caractères gras** renvoient à une illustration.

Les termes en **caractères gras** renvoient à une illustration.

Les termes en **caractères gras** renvoient à une illustration.

Les termes en **caractères gras** renvoient à une illustration.

Les termes en **caractères gras** renvoient à une illustration.

Les termes en **caractères gras** renvoient à une illustration.

Les termes en **caractères gras** renvoient à une illustration.

G

Les termes en **caractères gras** renvoient à une illustration.

H

I

J

Les termes en **caractères gras** renvoient à une illustration.

Les termes en **caractères gras** renvoient à une illustration.

M

Les termes en **caractères gras** renvoient à une illustration.

Les termes en **caractères gras** renvoient à une illustration.

N

O

Les termes en **caractères gras** renvoient à une illustration.

P

Les termes en **caractères gras** renvoient à une illustration.

Les termes en **caractères gras** renvoient à une illustration.

Les termes en **caractères gras** renvoient à une illustration.

Les termes en **caractères gras** renvoient à une illustration.

Les termes en **caractères gras** renvoient à une illustration.

Les termes en **caractères gras** renvoient à une illustration.

Les termes en **caractères gras** renvoient à une illustration.

Les termes en **caractères gras** renvoient à une illustration.

Les termes en **caractères gras** renvoient à une illustration.

Les termes en **caractères gras** renvoient à une illustration.

Les termes en **caractères gras** renvoient à une illustration.

DEUTSCHES REGISTER

A

Die Bezeichnungen der Illustrationen sind **fettgedruckt**.

B

Die Bezeichnungen der Illustrationen sind **fettgedruckt**.

Die Bezeichnungen der Illustrationen sind **fettgedruckt**.

C

Die Bezeichnungen der Illustrationen sind **fettgedruckt**.

D

Die Bezeichnungen der Illustrationen sind **fettgedruckt**.

E

Die Bezeichnungen der Illustrationen sind **fettgedruckt**.

Die Bezeichnungen der Illustrationen sind **fettgedruckt**.

Die Bezeichnungen der Illustrationen sind **fettgedruckt**.

H

Die Bezeichnungen der Illustrationen sind **fettgedruckt**.

Die Bezeichnungen der Illustrationen sind **fettgedruckt**.

K

Die Bezeichnungen der Illustrationen sind **fettgedruckt**.

Die Bezeichnungen der Illustrationen sind **fettgedruckt**.

L

Die Bezeichnungen der Illustrationen sind **fettgedruckt**.

M

N

Die Bezeichnungen der Illustrationen sind **fettgedruckt**.

O

P

Die Bezeichnungen der Illustrationen sind **fettgedruckt**.

Q

Die Bezeichnungen der Illustrationen sind **fettgedruckt**.

R

Die Bezeichnungen der Illustrationen sind **fettgedruckt**.

S

Die Bezeichnungen der Illustrationen sind **fettgedruckt**.

Die Bezeichnungen der Illustrationen sind **fettgedruckt**.

Die Bezeichnungen der Illustrationen sind **fettgedruckt**.

Die Bezeichnungen der Illustrationen sind **fettgedruckt**.

Die Bezeichnungen der Illustrationen sind **fettgedruckt**.

Die Bezeichnungen der Illustrationen sind **fettgedruckt**.

U

V

Die Bezeichnungen der Illustrationen sind **fettgedruckt**.

W

Die Bezeichnungen der Illustrationen sind **fettgedruckt**.